EPONYMS DICTIONARIES INDEX

OTHER GALE PUBLICATIONS

TRADE NAMES DICTIONARY—First Edition. 2 volumes. Contains 106,000 alphabetically arranged entries for consumer products and their manufacturers. Product entries give: trade name, brief description, name of manufacturer, and a code identifying the source of the information. Includes entries providing company names and addresses. **NEW TRADE NAMES.** 1976 and 1977 Supplements.

ENCYCLOPEDIA OF ASSOCIATIONS— Tenth Edition. Volume 1, **NATIONAL ORGANIZATIONS OF THE U.S.,** contains 13,583 entries in 17 categories. With index to organization names and keywords. Volume 2, **GEOGRAPHIC AND EXECUTIVE INDEX.** Volume 3, **NEW ASSOCIATIONS AND PROJECTS,** quarterly supplements to Volume 1. With cumulative alphabetical and keyword indexes. (Eleventh Edition ready March 1977)

DIRECTORY OF SPECIAL LIBRARIES AND INFORMATION CENTERS— Third Edition. Volume 1 contains information on 13,078 special libraries, information centers, and documentation centers in the U.S. and Canada. With 35,000-reference subject index. Volume 2, **GEOGRAPHIC—PERSONNEL INDEX.** Volume 3, **NEW SPECIAL LIBRARIES,** a periodical supplement to Volume 1. Cumulatively indexed. (Fourth Edition ready April 1977)

SUBJECT DIRECTORY OF SPECIAL LIBRARIES AND INFORMATION CENTERS—First Edition. A subject arrangement of all 13,078 entries in the *Directory of Special Libraries.* Five volumes covering these major fields: Business and Law, Education and Information Science, Health Sciences, Social Sciences and Humanities, and Science and Technology.

RESEARCH CENTERS DIRECTORY—Fifth Edition. A guide to 5,491 university-related and other nonprofit research organizations in the U.S. and Canada. With indexes of subjects, institutions, and research centers. **NEW RESEARCH CENTERS,** periodical supplements to RCD. Cumulatively indexed.

STATISTICS SOURCES—Fourth Edition. A subject guide to data on industrial, business, social, educational, financial, and other topics for the U.S. and selected foreign countries. Contains 21,000 references on about 11,800 subjects. (Fifth Edition ready May 1977)

ENCYCLOPEDIA OF GOVERNMENTAL ADVISORY ORGANIZATIONS—Second Edition. A reference guide to about 2,500 presidential advisory committees, public advisory committees, interagency committees, and other government-related boards, panels, task forces, commissions, conferences, and other similar bodies serving in a consultative, coordinating, advisory, research, or investigative capacity. With index to organization names and keywords. **NEW GOVERNMENTAL ADVISORY ORGANIZATIONS,** periodical supplements to the *Encyclopedia.* Cumulatively indexed.

NATIONAL FACULTY DIRECTORY—1977. Seventh Edition. 2 volumes. An alphabetical list, with departments and full institutional addresses, of about 450,000 members of teaching faculties at junior colleges, colleges, and universities in the U.S. and at selected Canadian institutions. With list of institutions covered.

CONSULTANTS AND CONSULTING ORGANIZATIONS DIRECTORY— Third Edition. A reference guide to 5,314 concerns and individuals engaged in consultation for business, industry, and government. With subject index of U.S. firms by location and index of individuals. **NEW CONSULTANTS,** a periodical supplement to the *Directory.* Cumulatively indexed. **WHO'S WHO IN CONSULTING**—Second Edition, a reference guide to 7,600 individuals engaged in consultation. With subject index of consultants by location.

MANAGEMENT INFORMATION GUIDE SERIES. Authoritative, comprehensive, carefully indexed guides to the literature of such major business and governmental areas as Accounting, Commercial Law, Computers, Insurance, Communications, Transportation, Public Relations, and Economic and Business History.

WORLD GUIDE TO ABBREVIATIONS OF ORGANIZATIONS— Fifth Edition. 18,000 entries giving the full names behind abbreviations currently used to identify companies, institutions, international agencies, and government departments throughout the world.

Eponyms Dictionaries Index

A reference guide to persons, both real and imaginary, and the terms derived from their names, providing basic biographical identification and citing dictionaries, encyclopedias, word books, journal articles, and other sources for additional information: includes acts, analyses, awards, axioms, bills, cases, circles, codes, coefficients, collections, commissions, complexes, costumes, diseases, dynasties, effects, equations, expeditions, experiments, forces, formulas, functions, laws, maneuvers, medals, methods, mixtures, organs, paradoxes, phenomena, presses, prizes, processes, ratios, reactions, rebellions, rules, schemes, societies, solutions, styles, syndromes, systems, techniques, tests, theories, trophies, units, and wars.

Covers: *Agriculture, Anthropology, Applied Arts, Architecture, Astronomy, Botany, Business, Chemistry, Earth Sciences, Economics, Education, Engineering and Industry, Exploration, Fashion, Fine Arts, Food and Drink, Generic Words, History, Law, Library Science, Linguistics, Literature, Mathematics, Medicine, Music, Mythology and Folklore, Numismatics, Philosophy, Photography, Physics, Politics, Printing, Psychology, Recreation and Sports, Religion, Sociology, Statistics, Weaponry, Zoology, and Other Fields.*

Edited by
JAMES A. RUFFNER

Associate Editors:
JENNIFER BERGER
GEORGIA SCHOENUNG

GALE RESEARCH COMPANY • BOOK TOWER • DETROIT, MICHIGAN 48226

Editorial Staff

Editor: James A. Ruffner
Associate Editors: Jennifer Berger, Georgia Schoenung
Editorial Coordinator: Ellen Crowley
Editorial Staff: Christopher Crocker, Trenna Ruffner, Donna Wood

Production Staff

Production Supervisor: Laura Bryant
Production Manager: Michaeline Nowinski
Production Staff: David Carey, William Davis, Eutropia Henderson, Marian Sood
Typists: Alice Stachowiak, Katie Watanabe
Cover Design: Arthur Chartow

CONTENTS

PREFACE

There is more to someone's name than first glance reveals, especially when the person is an eponym. Derived in the middle of the nineteenth century from the Greek words *epi* and *onyma,* the literal meaning of this strange term is "upon a name." The term "eponym" was coined to denote "the person for whom something is or is believed to be named." Thus, Albert Einstein is an eponym because of the many concepts, theories, and laws named after him, such as "Einstein universe."

As a quick survey of colleagues and friends will likely reveal, however, there is a strong tendency today to associate "eponym" with the named law, object, phenomenon, etc., rather than with the name giver. In this usage, it is the *thing* which is built "upon a name," rather than the person so honored, and this usage has been given as a second meaning of "eponym" in both *Webster's Third New International Dictionary* (1966) and its derivative, *Webster's New Collegiate Dictionary* (1973). According to these usages, "Albert Einstein" and "Einstein universe" are equally eponyms, being two sides of the same coin, so to speak.

A single word for two concepts, however, can lead to problems in communication. Various phrases or circumlocutions are required to distinguish between eponym-as-person and eponym-as-thing. Older usages, which included *nouns* such as "eponymus" and "eponymy," as well as "eponym," have become equally confused.

The editors of *Eponyms Dictionaries Index* have found it convenient to use "eponym" in the new, second sense, i.e., as the main term for the laws, objects, phenomena, and other things under consideration. Thus, for the purposes of this book, which lists the persons and the eponymic terms in a single straight alphabet, the listings are distinguished as "biography entry" and "eponym entry."

Guide to a Vast Literature

As the title indicates, *Eponyms Dictionaries Index* is a guide or index to a vast literature of dictionaries and word books and to more complete biographical sources.

In the eponym entry, *EDI* classifies the eponymic "things" according to some 60 different subject areas (some of which are listed on the title page) and leads the investigator and reference librarian into some 100 sources where these eponyms are defined or more completely explained. By means of the biography entry, *EDI* provides brief biographical facts (such as dates, nationality, and profession) and then cites hundreds of different sources for further biographical information.

All told, Gale researchers uncovered more than 500 biographical sources (some of them exceedingly obscure) while attempting to find biographical information about not only the famous but also many nearly forgotten people whose only marks on history are the things to which their names are attached. Some sources, of course, include information about the person as well as the thing defined. Yet, because of an apparent publishing tradition (or because publishers haven't wanted to track down obscure names in hundreds of sources), the majority of eponymic publications do not contain biographical information, especially if the person concerned is otherwise unknown. Herein lies another major contribution of *EDI,* the reuniting of certain biographical details with the information about the eponymic terms.

Scope of EDI

Compiling an eponyms text tends to be exhausting rather than exhaustive, as indicated by the fact that more than two years were required to assemble the 33,000 entries of the present work. These entries include approximately 13,000 persons and 20,000 "things" (relationships, etc.), of over 200 kinds: angles, compromises, effects, groups, laws, rebellions, and zones, to list only a few.

The subject areas particularly well represented include chemical tests and reagents (Hartman's solution, LeRoy Hartman); foods and fashions (Graham crackers, Sylvester Graham); literary and other types of movements (Muggletonians, Lodowicke Muggleton); mathematics (Gaussian distribution, Karl Frederick Gauss); medical syndromes and diseases (Parkinson's disease, Thomas Parkinson); mechanical inventions (Ferris wheel, George Ferris); physical laws and units of measurement (Avogadro's law, Count Amadeo Avogadro); plants and minerals (Poinsettia, Joel Poinsett); and legislative enactments (Taft-Hartley Act, Robert A. Taft and Fred Hartley, Jr.). The natural sciences, particularly chemistry and medicine, contain unusually large numbers of eponyms, while the humanities and social sciences contain relatively few.

A very large number of eponyms are found in the language of everyday words, usually in lowercase form. They may or may not have originated in a technical field. The plethora of eponyms such as boycott (Captain Boycott), nicotine (Jean Nicot), masochism (Leopold von Sacher-Masoch), and silhouette (Etienne de Silhouette) might in each instance be assigned to subject fields such as Economics, Chemistry, Psychology, and Applied Arts, respectively. In some instances such an assignment might be useful; in others, pedantic or misleading. Hence, in many cases, the subject category of common language words is designated simply "Generic Word."

In order to bring the project within acceptable time limits, several large categories of eponyms were excluded from *EDI:* trade names (Edsel), legal cases (Brown vs. Board of Education), and the names of geographical features, streets, airports, buildings, and other places (Kennedy Airport, Boulevard, Center, etc.). By extension of the principle of geographical exclusion, astronomical bodies such as stars, planets, and comets, and astronomical features such as craters of the moon or regions of Mars, were also excluded.

Eponyms, the Greats, and the Fates

Some persons are eponyms many times over. *EDI* lists 42 eponyms for Isaac Newton; 50 for Mary, the Virgin Mother; 41 for Jesus; and 38 for Albert Einstein. These examples are not particularly surprising. The leader, however, is the somewhat obscure French chemist Georges Deniges, with a list of 78. Equally surprising—or shocking—is the solitary one for Deniges's very great compatriot and the father of modern chemistry, Antoine Lavoisier, who had his enormously productive life cut short under the eponymic blade of another countryman, Joseph

Guillotin. Lavoisier, who frequently used Occam's Razor in slashing his way through the over-grown weeds of unreformed eighteenth-century chemistry, must be content with an all but forgotten honorific association with a genus of showy Brazilian shrubs, *Lavoisiera*. Thus, eponym is not synonymous with great. Such is the fickle finger of fate. (The Fates—three goddesses of classical mythology who directed the course of human events, but who alas did not make *EDI* because their collective name apparently derived from a common verb rather than the other way around.)

Research Problems

The major difficulty to be overcome in preparing such a work as *EDI* is the publishing practice that has tended to separate biographic and eponymic information, especially in the cases of lesser-known persons. In the 100-odd basic sources of eponyms that were used, biographical connection is usually not given in any form. Even where brief vital information is given with a term, the task of finding a fuller biographical source for reference may be very great. Biographical information for lesser known people is inherently very scattered. Some potentially useful foreign sources, which would have been unavailable to most users of *EDI* in any case, were not accessible. Because the search for a definitive association and fuller biographical sources was an enormously time-consuming operation, it was not practical to continue searching in the most obscure cases. Where sources were not found, or where uncertainty remains, this fact is indicated.

The source literature is full of inconsistencies and mistaken associations. The editors of *EDI* have tried to follow what we believe to be the best authority and to include variants when they might be useful.

The editors feel that *EDI* will be the most complete listing for some time to come, although their experience in compiling the book demonstrates that no list can be wholly complete or wholly accurate even within self-imposed limits. *EDI* editors, for example, noted to their chagrin during the final stages of work that "degauss," a term in electronics named for Karl Frederick Gauss, German mathematician and physicist (1777-1855), had nearly slipped through the net. How many we may have actually missed only time, further research, and our specially informed readers will tell. Suggestions are welcome.

GUIDE TO USE

Eponyms Dictionaries Index is arranged in a straight alphabetical sequence. It consists of two types of entries: the biography entry and the eponym entry:

Biography Entry

Ⓐ → BELLINI, LORENZO. 1643-1704. Italian anatomist. ← Ⓓ
See: Dict. Sci. Biog. Bellini's duct, Bellini's
ligament, Bellini's tube.

(Ⓑ and Ⓒ point to "1643-1704." and "Italian anatomist." respectively; Ⓔ points to "Dict. Sci. Biog."; Ⓕ points to "Bellini's tube.")

Ⓐ **Name** (in capital letters)—with spelling as given in the biography source. Appropriate cross references are made from variant spellings, pseudonyms, nicknames, etc.

Ⓑ **Dates**—if known. Birth or death date is given alone if that is only information available. Flourishing dates ("fl. 5th c. B.C.") are used if more exact dates are not known.   If dates are unknown, entry appears as "No dates."

Ⓒ **Nationality**—If a person was born in one country, but did most of his work in another, both places are given: "English-born American."

Ⓓ **Occupation**—chemist, physician, etc.

Ⓔ **Biography source**—given in abbreviated form. Refers the user to source for additional information about the person. If several sources have been located, selection is made on the basis of (1) comprehensiveness of coverage, (2) availability in libraries, and (3) language (English being preferred over a foreign language source). Full citation to the biography source is given in the *Bibliography of Sources Cited* (pp. xiii-xxviii).

When no biographical source has been located, an attempt is made to show how the connection between the person and the term was made: "Cited in: Chem. Abstr., vol. 6, p. 1209." When this is not possible, the entry appears as "Biography source unavailable."

Ⓕ **Eponyms**—an alphabetical listing of all terms derived from a person's name. If the connection between person and term is uncertain, this is indicated by a question mark following the term.

Eponym Entry

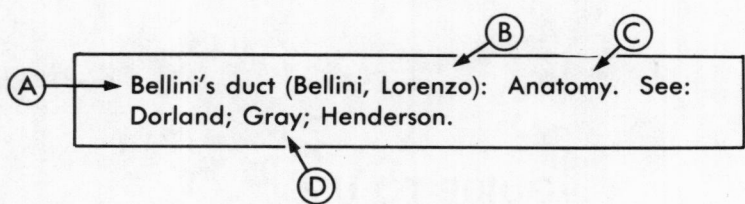

(A) **Eponym** (in lowercase letters)—with spelling as given in source(s) cited. If there are variant forms or spellings, all are included:

> Lutembacher's syndrome (complex or disease)
> Poggendor<u>ff</u> (Poggendor<u>f</u>) cell.

If one source gives the term in a possessive form and another does not, this is indicated by enclosing the "'s" in parentheses:

> Dominici('s) tube

Occasionally, an additional word will be added in parentheses in order to clarify the term:

> Lyman's long summer (apple)

If a term is believed to be derived from a name, but no appropriate person has been located, entry will appear as:

> Feist reagent (Derivation undetermined): Chemistry. See:
> Van Nostrand Chem. Dict.

(B) **Name**—Person whose name is associated with the term is given as it appears in the biography entry. If there are differences in the spelling of a name between sources, both spellings are given:

> Nei<u>l</u>'s parabola (Nei<u>le</u>, William)
> Nee<u>f</u>'s hammer (Nee<u>ff</u>, Christopher)
> Polue<u>t</u>kov test for germanium (Polue<u>k</u>tov, N. S.)

If there are several possible derivations for a term, effort is taken to include them all:

> real McCoy (McCoy, Elijah? McCoy, Kid? or McKay, A. M.?)

When the connection between person and term is uncertain, this is indicated by a question mark following the person's name:

> Tod's muscle (Tod, Hunter Finlay?)
> Bushnell's wasp (Bushnell, John Horace, Jr.?)

(C) **Subject**—The term is assigned one of 60 broad subject categories, some of which are listed on the title page.

(D) **Source(s)**—Refers the user to additional information about the term. Complete bibliographic information for location of these sources can be found in the *Bibliography of Sources Cited* (pp. xiii-xxviii).

BIBLIOGRAPHY OF SOURCES CITED

A.M.A. Arch. Derm. Syph.   See: **Arch. of Derm.**

Acta Chir. Scand.   *Acta Chirurgia Scandinavica.* Stockholm, vol. 52, 1919-   . (Continues *Nordiskt Medicinskt Arkiv,* 51 vols.)

Acta Paed.   *Acta Paediatrica.* Uppsala, vol. 1, 1921-   . (Continued as *Acta Paediatrica Scandinavica.)*

Acta Path. Microbiol.   *Acta Pathologica et Microbiologica Scandinavica.* Copenhagen: Nordisk Patologforening, vol. 1, 1924-

Afro-Amer. Encyc.   Rywell, Martin, ed. *Afro-American Encyclopedia.* North Miami, Fla.: Educational Book Publishers, Inc., 1974.

Albany Med. Ann.   *Albany Medical Annals.* Albany, N.Y.: Medical Society of the County of Albany, vols. 1-58, 1880-1939.

Album Amer. Gynec. Soc., Phila.   American Gynecological Society. *Album of the Fellows of the American Gynecological Society, 1876-1930.* Ed. by Floyd E. Keene. Philadelphia: W. J. Dornan, 1930.

Allg. Deut. Biog.   *Allgemeine Deutsche Biographie;* hrsg. durch die Historische Commission bei der K. Akademie der Wissenschaften. 56 vols. Leipzig: Duncker, 1875-1912.

Allg. Z. Psychiatr.   *Allgemeine Zeitschrift fuer Psychiatrie und Ihre Grenzgebiete.* Berlin, vols. 1-125, no. 1/3, 1844-1949.

Alman. Sofijsk. Univers.   *Almanakh Sofia Universitet.* Sofia, 1888/1928.

Amer. Acad. Ped.   *American Academy of Pediatrics.*

Amer. Chem. J.   *American Chemical Journal.* Baltimore, vols. 1-50, no. 6, Apr. 1879-Dec. 1913.

Amer. Doc.   *American Documentation.* Washington, D.C.: American Documentation Institute, vols. 1-20, 1950-1967. (Society name changed in 1967 to American Society for Information Science [ASIS].)

Amer. Geol.   *American Geologist.* Minneapolis, Minn., vols. 1-36, Jan. 1888-Dec. 1905.

Amer. J. Dis. Child.   *American Journal of Diseases of Children.* Chicago: American Medical Association, vol. 1, 1911-   .

Amer. J. Ment. Def.   *American Journal of Mental Deficiency.* Albany: American Association on Mental Deficiency, vol. 45, July 1940-   . (Supersedes association's *Proceedings.)*

Amer. J. Ophth.   *American Journal of Ophthalmology.* St. Louis and Chicago, vols. 1-34, 1884-1917; s. 3, vol. 1, 1918-   .

Amer. J. Pharm.   *American Journal of Pharmacy.* Philadelphia, vol. 1, April 1829-   .

Amer. J. Psych.   *American Journal of Psychology.* Ithaca, N.Y., vol. 1, 1887-   .

Amer. J. Roentg.   *American Journal of Roentgenology.* New York, vol. 1, July 1913-   . (Continued as *Radium Therapy and Medicine.)*

Amer. J. Sci.   *American Journal of Science.* New Haven, Conn., vol. 1, July 1818-   .

Amer. J. Surg.   *American Journal of Surgery.* Kansas City, St. Louis, and New York: American Association of Anesthetics, vols. 1-40, Oct. 1890-June 1926; n.s., vol. 1, July 1926-   .

Amer. Libr. Assoc. Membership Direct.   American Library Association. *Membership Directory 1965.* Chicago: American Library Association, 1965.

Amer. Med. Direct.   *American Medical Directory; ...a Register of Physicians...of the United States...and Canada.* Chicago: American Medical Association, 1st ed., 1906-   .

Amer. Men and Women Sci.   *American Men and Women of Science.* New York: Bowker, 12th ed., 1971-   . (Continues *American Men of Science.)*

Amer. Men Sci.   *American Men of Science; a Biographical Directory.* Lancaster, Pa.: Science Press, 1st ed., 1906-   .

Amer. Min.   *American Mineralogist.* Lancaster, Pa.: Mineralogical Society of America, vol. 1, July 1916-   .

Amer. Neurol. Assoc. Anniv. Vol.   American Neurological Association. *Semi-Centennial Anniversary Volume: 1875-1924.* New York: American Neurological Association, 1924.

Amer. Psych. Assoc. Direct.   American Psychological Association. *Directory.* Washington, D.C.: The Association, 1948-1967. (Continued as *Biographical Directory of the American Psychological Association,* 1970-   .)

Amer. Psychiat. Assoc. Biog. Direct.   American Psychiatric Association. *Biographical Directory of Fellows and Members.* New York: Bowker, 1st ed., 1941-   .

Amer. Women   *American Women; the Official Who's Who Among the Women of the Nation.* Los Angeles: American Publications, vol. 1, 1935/1936-   .

Analyst   *Analyst.* London: Society of Public Analysts and Other Analytical Chemists, vol. 1, April 1877-   .

Anat. Anz.   *Anatomischer Anzeiger.* Jena: Anatomische Gesellschaft, vol. 1, June 1886-   .

Ann. Bot.   *Annals of Botany.* London: Balfour, Vines and Farlow, vols. 1-50, Aug. 1887-1936; n.s., vol. 1, 1937-   .

Ann. de Derm. Syph.   *Annales de Dermatologie et de Syphilologie.* Paris, vol. 78, 1951-   . (Began in 1868.)

Ann. de Geophys.   *Annales de Geophysique.* Paris: Centre National de la Recherche Scientifique, vol. 1, August 1, 1944-

BIBLIOGRAPHY OF SOURCES CITED

Ann. Entom. Soc. Amer. *Entomological Society of America. Annals.* Columbus, Ohio, vol. 1, March 1908- .

Ann. Eugen. *Annals of Human Eugenics.* London, vol. 1, 1925 . (Oct. 1925-March 1954 as *Annals of Eugenics.*)

Ann. Int. Med. *Annals of Internal Medicine.* Ann Arbor: American College of Physicians, vol. 1, July 1927- .

Ann. Math. Stat. *Annals of Mathematical Statistics.* Baltimore and Ann Arbor: Institute of Mathematical Statistics, vol. 1, Feb. 1930- .

Ann. Nestle *Annales Nestle.* (English Edition) Sydney, Australia: Nestle Company, Inc., vol. 1, 1956?- .

Ann. Otol.-Laryngol. *Annales d'Oto-Laryngologie.* Paris: Societe de Laryngologie des Hopitaux de Paris, vol. 1, 1931- .

Ann. Otol. Rhinol. Laryngol. *Annals of Otology, Rhinology and Laryngology.* St. Louis, vol. 6, no. 1, Feb. 1897- .

Ann. Register *Annual Register.* London, vols. 1-104, 1758-1862; n.s., 1863-1919; vol. 162, 1920- .

Ann. Surg. *Annals of Surgery.* St. Louis and Philadelphia, vol. 1, 1885- .

Ann. Univers. Roma *Annuario di Universita di Roma.* Roma, 18____.

Annales Univers. *Annales de l'Universite de Paris, publiees par la Societe des Amis de l'Universite.* Annee. Vol. 1, March 1926- .

Annuaire Geolog. Mineralog., Russie *Ezhegodnik po Geologii i Mineralogii Rossii.* (French title: *Annuaire Geologique et Mineralogique de la Russie*) Warsaw and Novo Alexandria, vols. 1-17, no. 8, 1895-1917?

Apel Apel, Willi, and Daniel, Ralph T. *The Harvard Brief Dictionary of Music.* Cambridge, Mass.: Harvard University Press, 1960.

Arch. d'Ophth. *Archives d'Ophthalmologie.* Paris, vols. 1-53, 1880-1936.

Arch. Exper. Path. *Naunyn-Schmiedeberg's Archiv fuer Experimentelle Pathologie und Pharmakologie.* Leipzig, vol. 1, 1873- . (Vols. 1-109, 1873-Nov. 1925 as *Archiv fuer Experimentelle Pathologie und Pharmakologie.*)

Arch. f. Ges. Phonetik *Archiv fuer Vergleichende Phonetik.* Berlin: Deutsches Spracharchiv; Gesellschaft fuer Phonetik, vols. 1-7, Jan. 1937-1943/44. (At head of title: *Archiv fuer die Gesamte Phonetik.*)

Arch. f. Klin. Chir., Berlin *Langenbecks Archiv fuer Klinische Chirurgie. Vereinigt mit Deutsche Zeitschrift fuer Chirurgie.* Berlin: Deutsches Gesellschaft fuer Chirurgie, vol. 1, 1860- . (1860-1944 as *Archiv fuer Klinische Chirurgie.*)

Arch. f. Naturgeschichte *Archiv fuer Naturgeschichte.* Berlin, vols. 1-77, 1835-1911. (Continued in two sections, 1912-1926.)

Arch. Gesch. Naturw. Tech. *Archiv fuer Geschichte der Mathematik, der Naturwissenschaften und der Technik.* Leipzig: Berliner fuer Geschichte der Naturwissenschaften und Medizin, vols. 1-13, no. 3/4, Nov. 1908-Feb. 1931. (Vols. 1-9, no. 2, 1908-Aug. 1922 as *Archiv fuer die Geschichte der Naturwissenschaften und der Technik.*)

Arch. Neurocir. Buenos Aires *Archivos de Neurocirurgia.* Buenos Aires, vol. 1, Jan./Mar. 1944- .

Arch. Neurol. Psychiatr., Chicago *A.M.A. Archives of Neurology and Psychiatry.* Chicago: American Medical Association, vols. 1-81, Jan. 1919-June 1959. (Jan. 1919-Sept. 1950 as *Archives of Neurology and Psychiatry.*)

Arch. of Derm. *Archives of Dermatology.* Chicago: American Medical Association, vol. 1, Jan. 1920- . (Oct. 1950-Dec. 1954 as *A.M.A. Archives of Dermatology and Syphilology.*)

Archiv. Ital. di Otolog. *Archivio Italiano di Otologia, Rinologia e Laringologia.* Turin, vol. 1, 1893- .

Archo. Stor. Sci. *Archivo di Storia della Scienzia.* Roma, vols. 1-8, no. 2, Mar. 1919-May/July 1927.

Arlott Arlott, John, ed. *The Oxford Companion to World Sports and Games.* London: Oxford University Press, 1975.

Arnim Arnim, Max. *Internationale Personalbibliographie, 1880-1959.* 3 vols. Leipzig: K. W. Hiersemann, 1944-1963.

Ascherson and Graebner Ascherson, Paul F. A., and Graebner, Paul. *Synopsis der Mitteleuropaischen Flora.* Leipzig: W. Engelmann, 1896-1938.

Asimov Asimov, Isaac. *Asimov's Biographical Encyclopedia of Science and Technology.* 1st ed. Garden City, N.Y.: Doubleday, 1964.

Athena *Athena.*

Atlanta J. *Atlanta Journal.* Daily newspaper. Atlanta, Ga., vol. 1, 1883- .

Atti Pontif. Accad. Sci. Nuovo Lincei *Pontificia Accademia delle Scienze, Roma. Atti.* Vols. 1-88, 1847-1934/1935. (1932-35 as *Pontificia Accademia delle Scienzia, Nuovi Lincei.*)

Atti Soc. Med. Chir. Padova *Societa Medico-Chirurgica di Padova. Atti.* Padova, vol. 1, Mar. 1923- .

Attwater Attwater, Donald, ed. *A Catholic Dictionary.* 3d ed. New York: Macmillan, 1958.

Auger Auger, Charles P. *Engineering Eponyms.* London: Library Association, 1965.

Australian Biog. Dict. *An Australian Biographical Dictionary.* Ed. by Fred Johns. Melbourne and London: Macmillan, 1934.

Australian Dict. Biog. *Australian Dictionary of Biography.* Ed. by Douglas Pike. London: Cambridge University Press and Melbourne: Melbourne University Press, 1966- .

Australian Encyc. *The Australian Encyclopedia.* Ed. by Alec H. Chisholm. 10 vols. East Lansing, Mich.: Michigan State University Press, 1958.

Avis Avis, Frederick Compton. *The Bookman's Concise Dictionary.* 1st ed. London: F. C. Avis, 1956.

Bailey Bailey, Dorothy, and Bailey, Kenneth C. *An Etymological Dictionary of Chemistry and Mineralogy.* London: Edward Arnold, 1929.

Bailey, L.H. Bailey, Liberty Hyde. *Cyclopedia of American Horticulture.* 4 vols. New York: Doubleday-Page, 1906.

Baker Baker, Theodore. *Baker's Biographical Dictionary of Musicians.* 5th ed. completely revised by Nicolas Slonimsky. New York: G. Schirmer, 1958.

Ballentyne Ballentyne, Denis W. G., and Lovett, D. R. *A Dictionary of Named Effects and Laws in Chemistry, Physics and Mathematics.* 3d ed. London: Chapman and Hall, 1970.

Baring-Gould and Fisher Baring-Gould, Sabine, and Fisher, John. *The Lives of the British Saints.* 4 vols. London: for the Honourable Society of Cymmrodarion by C. J. Clark, 1907-1913.

Barnet Barnet, Sylvan; Berman, Morton; and Burto, William. *A Dictionary of Literary, Dramatic and Cinematic Terms.* 2d ed. Boston: Little Brown, 1971.

Barnhart (Cycl. Names) *New Century Cyclopedia of Names.* Ed. by Clarence L. Barnhart. New York: Appleton-Century-Crofts, 1954.

Barnhart (Eng. Lit.) *New Century Handbook of English Literature.* Ed. by Clarence L. Barnhart. Revised ed. New York: Appleton-Century-Crofts, 1967.

Barnhart (New Eng.) *The Barnhart Dictionary of New English Since 1963.* Ed. by Clarence L. Barnhart, Sol Steinmetz and Robert K. Barnhart. 1st ed. Bronsville, N.Y.: Barnhart/Harper & Row, 1973.

Benet Benet, William Rose, ed. *The Reader's Encyclopedia; an Encyclopedia of World Literature and the Arts, with Supplement.* New York: Thomas Y. Crowell, 1948.

Ber. Deut. Bot. Ges. *Deutsche Botanische Gesellschaft, Berlin. Berichte.* Vol. 1, Sept. 17, 1883- .

Ber. Deut. Chem. Ges. See: **Chem. Ber.**

Ber. Naturw.-Medizin. Ver. Innsbruck *Naturwissenschaftlich-Medizinischer Verein, Innsbruck. Berichte.* Vol. 1, 1870- .

Ber. Senckenberg. Naturf. *Senckenbergische Naturforschende Gesellschaft, Frankfurt a. M. Bericht.* 1829-1868/1869. (Continued as the association's *Bericht,* 1869-1921.)

Bibliog. Med. *Bibliographia Medica. Recueil Mensuel. Classement Methodique de la Bibliographie Internationale des Sciences Medicales.* Paris: Institut de Bibliographie, vols. 1-3, Jan. 1900-Dec. 1902. (Supersedes and is superseded by *Index Medicus.*)

Bibliographie Academique Louvain *Universite Catholique de Louvain. Bibliographie Academique.* Louvain: C. Peeters, 1880-1954.

Bio-Chem. J. See: **Biochem. J.**

Biochem. J. *The Biochemical Journal.* Liverpool and Cambridge, Eng.: Biochemical Society, vol. 1, 1906- .

Biochim. Terap. Sper. *Biochimica e Terapia Sperimentale.* Milan: Societa Italiana di Biochimica, vol. 1, 1909- .

Biog. Direct Amer. Congress *Biographical Directory of the American Congress, 1774-1971.* Comp. by Lawrence F. Kennedy. Washington, D.C.: Government Printing Office, 1971.

Biog. Direct. Amer. Psych. Assoc. *Biographical Directory of the American Psychological Association.* Ed. by John A. Lazo. Washington, D.C.: American Psychological Association, 1970- . (Continuation of the association's *Directory,* 1948-1967.)

Biog. Index *Biography Index; a Cumulative Index to Biographical Material in Books and Magazines.* New York: H. W. Wilson, vol. 1, Jan. 1946/July 1949- .

Biog. Jahrb. Deut. Nekr. *Biographisches Jahrbuch und Deutscher Nekrolog, 1896-1913.* A. Bettelheim. 18 vols. Berlin: G. Reimer, 1897-1917.

Biog. Lex. hervorr. Aerzte *Biographisches Lexikon der Hervorragenden Aerzte Aller Zeiten und Voelker, unter Mitwirkung der Herren E. Albert, et al. Herausgegeben von August Hirsch.* 2d ed. 5 vols. Berlin: Urban & Schwarzenberg, 1929-1934.

Biog. Lex. hervorr. Aerzte, 1880-1930 *Biographisches Lexikon der Hervorragenden Aerzte der Letzen Fuenfzig Jahre. Zugleich Fortsetzung des Biographischen Lexikon der Hervorragen den*

Aerzte Aller Zeiten und Voelker. Ed. by Isidor Fischer. 2 vols. Berlin: Urban & Schwarzenberg, 1932-1933.

Biog. Nat. de Belgique *Academie Royal des Sciences, des Lettres et des Beaux-Arts de Belgique. Biographie Nationale.* 28 vols. Bruxelles: H. Thiry-Van Buggenhoudt, 1866-1944. (Vols. 29- are supplementary.)

Biog. Notes Upon Botanists *Biographical Notes Upon Botanists,* maintained in the New York Botanical Garden Library. Comp. by John Hendley Barnhart. 3 vols. Boston: G. K. Hall, 1966.

Biog. Woordenb. der Nederl. (Aa) *Biographisches Woordenboek der Nederlanden.* Ed. by Abraham Jacob van der Aa. 21 vols. in 17. Haarlem: J. J. Van Brederode, 1852-1878.

Biolog. Abstr. *Biological Abstracts.* Menasha, Wis., and Philadelphia: Union of American Biological Societies, vol. 1, Dec. 1926- .

Black Black, Henry Campbell. *Black's Law Dictionary.* 4th ed. revised by the publisher's editorial staff. St. Paul, Minn.: West Publishing Co., 1968.

Blakiston's Gould *Blakiston's Gould Medical Dictionary.* Ed. by Arthur Osol. 3d ed. New York: McGraw-Hill, 1972.

Blumberg Blumberg, Dorothy Rose. *Whose What? Aaron's Beard to Zorn's Lemma.* 1st ed. New York: Holt, Rinehart and Winston, 1969.

Blunt Blunt, John Henry, ed. *Dictionary of Sects, Heresies, Ecclesiastical Parties and Schools of Religious Thought.* London: Longmans, Green & Co., 1892.

Blut *Blut; Zeitschrift fuer die Gesamte Blutforschung.* Munich: Deutschen Gesellschaft fuer Haemotologie und Deutschen Gesellschaft fuer Bluttransfusion, vol. 1, Mar. 1955- .

Boase Boase, Frederick. *Modern English Biography.* 6 vols. Reprint of 1st ed., 1892-1921. London: F. Cass, 1965.

Boatner Boatner, Mark Mayo III. *The Civil War Dictionary.* New York: David McKay, 1959.

Boger Boger, Louise A., and Boger, H. Batterson, eds. *The Dictionary of Antiques and the Decorative Arts.* New York: Scribner, 1957.

Bowman Bowman, Walter Parker, and Ball, Robert Hamilton. *Theatre Language.* New York: Theatre Arts Books, 1961.

Brasil Med. *Brasil-Medico.* Rio de Janeiro: Policlinica Geral do Rio de Janeiro, vol. 1, Jan. 1887- .

Brelsford Brelsford, William V., ed. *Handbook to the Federation of Rhodesia and Nyasaland.* London: Cassell, 1960.

Brewer Brewer, Ebenezer Cobham. *Brewer's Dictionary of Phrase and Fable.* Centenary edition. Revised by Ivor H. Evans. New York: Harper & Row, 1970.

Briggs Briggs, Martin S. *Everyman's Concise Encyclopedia of Architecture.* New York: Dutton, 1959.

Brit. Chem. Abstr. *British Abstracts.* London: Bureau of Abstracts, secs. A + B, Jan. 1926-Dec. 1953. (1936-1937 as *British Chemical Abstracts.*)

Brit. Heart J. *British Heart Journal.* London: British Medical Association and Cardiac Society of Great Britain and Ireland, vol. 1, Jan. 1939- .

Brit. J. Ophthal. *British Journal of Ophthalmology.* London, vol. 1, 1917- .

Brit. Med. J. *British Medical Journal.* London: British Medical Association, vol. 1, 1857- .

Britten and Boulger Britten, James, and Boulger, George S., comps. *A Biographical Index of Deceased British and Irish Botanists.* 2d ed. revised and completed by A. B. Rendle. London: Taylor and Francis, 1931.

Brockhaus *Brockhaus Enzyklopaedie in Zwanzig Baenden. Siebzehnte voellig neu Bearb. Aufl. des Grossen Brockhaus.* Wiesbaden: F. A. Brockhaus, 1966.

Bruxelles-med. *Bruxelles-medical.* Brussels, vol. 1, 1921- .

Bryan Bryan, Michael. *Bryan's Dictionary of Painters and Engravers.* 4th ed. revised by G. C. Williamson. 5 vols. London: G. Bell, 1903-1905.

Bull. Acad. Med. Paris *Academie Nationale de Medecine, Paris. Bulletin.* Vols. 1-36, 1836-1871; n.s., vols. 1-18, 1872-1887; s. 3, vol. 19, 1888- . (Jan.? 1820-Jan. 1947 as *Academie de Medecin. Bulletin.*)

Bull. Acad. vet. Fr. *Academie Veterinaire de France, Paris. Bulletin.* Vol. 1, 1844- . (Vol. 81, 1928- ; also as n.s. (s. 4?), vol. 1, 1928- .)

Bull. Almanac *The Bulletin Almanac and Yearbook.* Philadelphia: The Evening Bulletin, vol. 1, 1924- .

Bull. Chem. Soc. Japan *Chemical Society of Japan. Bulletin.* Tokyo, vol. 1?, 1926?- .

Bull. Cleveland Med. Libr. *Bulletin of the Cleveland Medical Library.* Cleveland: Cleveland Medical Library Association, vol. 1, Jan. 1954- .

Bull. de l'Acad. Royale de Med. de Belgique *Academie Royale de Medecine de Belgique, Brussels. Bulletin.* S. 5, vols. 1-15, 1921-1935; s. 6, vol. 1, 1936- .

Bull. et Mem. Soc. Franc. Opht. *Societe Francaise d'Ophthalmologie. Bulletin et Memoires.* Vol. 1, 1883- .

Bull. Hist. Med. *Bulletin of the History of Medicine.* (American Association of the History of Medicine; Johns Hopkins University. Institute of the History of Medicine) Baltimore, vol. 1, 1933- .

Bull. Johns Hopkins Hosp. *Johns Hopkins Hospital, Baltimore. Bulletin.* Vol. 1, Dec. 1889- .

Bull. Mem. Soc. Med. Hop. Paris *Societe Medicale des Hopitaux de Paris. Bulletin et Memoires.* Vol. 1, 1849- . (Annee 1945, 1929- .)

Bull. Sciences Pharmacol. *Bulletin des Sciences Pharmacologiques.* Paris, vols. 1-49, 1899-1942.

Bull. Soc. Belge Geolog. *Societe Belge de Geologie, de Paleontologie et d'Hydrologie, Brussels. Bulletin.* Vols. 1-28, 1877-1914; vol. 29, 1919- .

Bull. Soc. Bot. Fr. *Societe Botanique de France, Paris. Bulletin.* Vol. 1, 1854- .

Bull. Soc. Chim. France *Societe Chimique de France. Bulletin.* Paris, vol. 1, 1858- ; s. 4, vols. 1-54, 1907-1933.

Bull. Soc. Fr. Derm. Syph. *Societe Francaise de Dermatologie et Syphiligraphie, Paris. Bulletin.* Vol. 1, 1890- .

Bull. Soc. Franc. Hist. Med. *Societe Francaise d'Histoire de la Medecine. Bulletin.* Paris, vols. 1-36, 1902-1940.

Bull. Soc. Geogr. Anvers *Societe Royale de Geographie d'Anvers. Bulletin.* Antwerp, vol. 1, 1876- . (Society formerly known as Societe Belge de Geographie, Anvers.)

Bull. Soc. Geolog. France *Societe Geologique de France, Paris. Bulletin.* Vols. 1-14, 1830-1843; n.s. (s. 5), vol. 1, 1931- .

Bull. Soc. Lepidopt. Geneve *Societe Lepidopterologique de Geneve. Bulletin.* Vols. 1-6, 1905-1931.

Bull. Soc. Nat. Chir., Paris *Academie de Chirurgie, Paris. Bulletin et Memoires.* Vols. 1-7, 1847-1874; n.s., vol. 1, 1875- . (1924-1935 as *Societe Nationale de Chirurgie. Bulletin et Memoires.*)

Bull. Soc. Roman. Geolog. *Societatea Romana de Geologie, Bucharest. Buletinul.* Vol. 1, 1932- .

Bull. Soc. Sci. Pau *Societe des Sciences, Lettres et Arts de Pau. Bulletin trimestrial.* Vols. 1-4, 1841-1844; s. 2, vols. 1-57, 1871-1937; s. 3, vol. 1, 1938- .

Bull. U.S. Geol. Survey *U.S. Geological Survey. Bulletin.* Washington, D.C., vol. 1, 1883- .

Bullen Bullen, Keith Edward. *An Introduction to the Theory of Seismology.* 3d ed. Cambridge, Eng.: University Press, 1963.

Bulloch Bulloch, William. *The History of Bacteriology.* London: Oxford University Press, 1938.

Burrage Burrage, Walter Lincoln. *A History of the Massachusetts Medical Society with Brief Biographies of the Founders and Chief Officers, 1781-1922.* Norwood, Mass.: By the author, 1923.

Butler's Lives of the Saints Butler, Alban. *Lives of the Saints.* Edited, revised, and supplemented by Herbert Thurston and Donald Attwater. 4 vols. New York: P. J. Kenedy, 1956.

Buttrick Buttrick, George A., ed. *The Interpreter's Dictionary of the Bible.* 4 vols. New York: Abingdon Press, 1962.

Canadian Med. Direct. *Canadian Medical Directory.* Toronto: Current Publications, 1st ed., 1955- .

Canadian Who's Who *The Canadian Who's Who.* Toronto: Trans-Canada Press, vol. 1, 1910?- .

Canney Canney, Maurice A. *An Encyclopedia of Religions.* Reprint of the 1921 ed. Detroit: Gale Research Co., 1970.

Carter Carter, Ernest F. *Dictionary of Inventions and Discoveries.* London: Muller, 1966.

Casopis Ceska Spolecnost Entomol. *Ceskoslovenska Spolecnost Entomologicka, Prague. Casopis. Acta.* Prague, vol. 1, 1904- . (1904-1919; 1939-1944? as *Ceska Spolecnost Entomologicka.*)

Castiglioni Castiglioni, Arturo. *A History of Medicine.* 2d revised ed. Trans. and ed. by E. B. Krumbhaar. New York: Knopf, 1947.

Chambers' Biog. Dict. *Chambers's Biographical Dictionary.* Ed. by J. O. Thorne. New ed. Edinburgh: W. & R. Chambers, 1961.

Chambers's Dict. Sci. *Chambers's Dictionary of Scientists.* By Arthur V. Howard. New York: Dutton, 1958.

Chaplin Chaplin, James P. *Dictionary of Psychology.* New York: Dell Publishing Co., 1968.

Charnock Charnock, Richard S. *Verba Nominalia; or Words Derived from Proper Names.* Facsimile reprint of the 1866 ed. Ann Arbor: Gryphon Books, 1971.

Chem. Abstr. *Chemical Abstracts.* Easton, Pa.: American Chemical Society, vol. 1, 1907- .

Chem-Analyst *Chemist-Analyst.* Phillipsburg, N.J.: J. T. Baker Chemical Co., no. 1, 1911- .

Chem. Ber. *Chemische Berichte.* Heidelberg, vol. 1, 1868- . (Vols. 1-77, no. 11/12, 1868-Feb. 21, 1945, as *Berichte der Deutschen Chemischen Gesellschaft* (Ber. Deut. Chem. Ges. and Chem. Ges. Ber.)

Chem. Ges. Ber. See: **Chem. Ber.**

Chem. Weekblad *Chemisch Weekblad.* Amsterdam: Nederlandsch Chemische Vereeniging, vol. 1, Oct. 3, 1903- .

Chem. Who's Who *Chemical Who's Who.* New York: Lewis Historical Publishing Co., 1st ed., 1928- .

Chem. Zentralblatt *Chemisches Zentralblatt.* Vollstaendiges Repertorium fuer Alle Zweige der Reinen und Angewandten Chemie. Leipzig and Berlin: Deutsche Chemische Gesellschaft, vol. 1, 1830- .

Chem. Ztg. *Chemiker-Zeitung-Chemische Apparatur.* Heidelberg, vol. 1, 1877- .

Chemicke Listy *Chemicke Listy.* Prague, vol. 1, 1906- .

Chi e? *Chi e? Dizionario Biografico degli Italiani d'Oggi.* Roma: Filippo Scarano, 1st ed., 1928- .

Chicago Med. Recorder *Chicago Medical Recorder.* Chicago: Chicago Medical Society, vols. 1-49, no. 4, 1891-April 1927.

Chir. Torac. *Chirurgia Toracica.* Roma: Societa Italiana di Chirurgia Toracica, vol. 1, Feb. 1948- .

Chironis Chironis, Nicholas P., ed. *Gear Design and Application.* New York: McGraw-Hill, 1967.

Chirurgen-Verzeichnis See: **Deut. Chirurgen Verzeichnis**

Chirurgenverz. See: **Deut. Chirurgen Verzeichnis**

Chron. Bot. Leiden *Chronica Botanica.* Leiden, Netherlands, and Waltham, Mass., vol. 1, 1935- .

Chujoy Chujoy, Anatole, and Manchester, Phyllis W., eds. *The Dance Encyclopedia.* Revised ed. New York: Simon and Schuster, 1967.

Ciba Symposium *Ciba Symposium.* Basel: Gesellschaft fuer Chemische Industrie, vol. 1, April 1953- .

Cincin. Lancet and Clinic *Lancet-Clinic: a Weekly Journal of Medicine and Surgery.* Cincinnati, vols. 1-116, May 1842-Nov. 1916. (Vols. 40-55 as *Cincinnati Lancet and Clinic.*)

Clapin Clapin, Sylva. *A New Dictionary of Americanisms.* Reprint of the 1902? ed. Detroit: Gale Research Co., 1968.

Clark Clark, Donald T., and Gottfried, Bert A. *University Dictionary of Business and Finance.* New York: Crowell, 1967.

Columbia Encyc. *The Columbia Encyclopedia.* Ed. by William Bridgwater and Seymour Kurtz. 3d ed. New York: Columbia University Press, 1963.

Columbia-Viking Desk Encyc. *The Columbia-Viking Desk Encyclopedia.* Ed. by William Bridgwater. 2d ed. New York: Dell Publishing Co., 1964.

Compend. Meteorol. *Compendium of Meteorology.* Ed. by Thomas F. Malone for the American Meteorological Society. Boston: The Society, 1951.

Congres Internat. Med. *The 16th Congres International de Medecin, Budapest, Aout-Septembre, 1909. Compte-Rendu.* Volume General, publie par Emile von Grosz. Budapest, 1910.

Contemp. Authors *Contemporary Authors; the International Bio-Bibliographical Guide to Current Authors and their Works.* Detroit: Gale Research Co., vol. 1, 1962- .

Crone Crone, John Smyth. *A Concise Dictionary of Irish Biography.* Revised ed. Dublin: The Talbot Press, 1937.

Cum. Auth. Index to Psych. Index, 1894-1935, and Psych. Abstr., 1927-1958 *Cumulative Author Index to Psychological Index, 1894-1935, and Psychological Abstracts, 1927-1958.* Compiled by the Columbia University Psychology Library. 4 vols. Boston: G. K. Hall, 1960. (3 suppl. issued to 1971.)

Cur. Biog. *Current Biography and Current Biography Yearbook.* New York: H. W. Wilson, vol. 1, 1940- .

Cutolo Cutolo, Vicente Osvaldo. *Nuevo Diccionario Biografico Argentino.* Buenos Aires: Editorial Elche, 1968.

Dakin Dakin, Susanna Bryant. *The Perennial Adventure.* San Francisco: California Academy of Sciences, 1954.

Dana Dana, James Dwight, and Bush, George Jarvis. *A System of Mineralogy.* 9th ed. New York: Wiley.

Danmarks Hist. Bla Bog *Danmarks Historiens Bla Bog.* Ed. by Palle Birkelund, et al. Kobenhavn, 1970.

Dansk Biog. Lek. *Dansk Biografisk Leksikon,* Tillage Omfattende Norge for Tidsrummet, 1537-1814. Ed. by Carl F. Bricka. 19 vols. Copenhagen: Gyldenhal, 1887-1905.

Davison Davison, Charles. *Founders of Seismology.* Cambridge, Eng.: The University Press, 1927.

Derm. Verzeich. *Deutsches Dermatologen-Verzeichnis.* Ed. by E. Riecke. 2d ed. 1939.

De Sola De Sola, Ralph, and De Sola, Dorothy. *A Dictionary of Cooking.* London: Constable, 1971.

Det. Free Press *Detroit Free Press.* Daily newspaper. Detroit, Mich., vol. 1, 1831- .

Deut. Biog. Jahrb. *Deutsches Biographisches Jahrbuch.* Hrsg. von Verbande der Deutschen Akademien. Stuttgart: Deutsche Verlags-Anstalt, 1925-1932.

Deut. Chirurgen Verzeichnis *Deutsches Chirurgen Verzeichnis.* Leipzig: Barth, 1st ed., 1920- . (1st and 2d ed. issued under title: *Deutscher Chirurgen-Kalender.*)

Deut. Chirurgenkal. See: **Deut. Chirurgen Verzeichnis**

Deut. Dermatologenkal. *Deutscher Dermatologenkalender.* Biographisch-Bibliographisches Dermatologen-Verzeichnis. Ed. by E. Riecke. Leipzig: L. Voss, 1929.

Deut. Med. Wchnschr. *Deutsche Medizinische Wochenschrift.* Leipzig and Stuttgart, vol. 1, Sept. 1875- .

Deut. Z. f. Chir. *Deutsche Zeitschrift fuer Chirurgie.* Leipzig, vols. 1-259, 1872-1944.

Dicc. Biog. Cubano Peruza Sarausa, Fermin, ed. *Diccionario Biografico Cubano.* Habana: Ediciones Anuario Bibliografico Cubano, 1951- .

Dicc. Biog. de Chile *Diccionario Biografico de Chile.* Santiago: Empresa Periodistica "Chile," 1st ed., 1936- .

Dicc. Biog. General de Chile Figueroa, Pedro P., ed. *Diccionario Biografico General de Chile, 1550-1887.* 2d ed. Santiago: H. Izquierdo, 1888.

Dicc. Biog. Mexico Peral, Miguel Angel, ed. *Diccionario Biografico Mexicano.* 2 vols. Mexico: Editorial P.A.C. 1944.

Dicc. Biog. Venezuela *Diccionario Biografico de Venezuela.* Ed. by Garrido Mezquita y Compania and Julio Cardenas Ramirez. 1st ed. Madrid: Blass, 1953.

Dicc. Biog. y Bibliog. Colombia *Diccionario Biografico y Bibliografico de Colombia por Joaquin Ospina.* 3 vols. Bogota: Editorial Aguila, 1927-1939.

Dicc. Hist. Espana *Diccionario de Historia de Espana.* Ed. by German Bleiberg. 2d ed. 3 vols. Madrid: Ediciones de la Revista de Occidente, 1968-1969.

Dicc. Porrua de Hist. Biog. y Geog. de Mexico *Diccionario Porrua de Historia, Biografia y Geographia de Mexico.* Mexico: Editorial Porrua, S.A., 1st ed., 1964- .

Dict. Amer. Biog. *Dictionary of American Biography,* under the Auspices of the American Council of Learned Societies. New York: C. Scribner's Sons, 1928- .

Dict. Amer. Hist. *Dictionary of American History.* Ed. by James Truslow Adams. 5 vols. and supplement and index vol. 2d ed., revised. New York: Scribner, 1942-61.

Dict. Amer. Med. Biog. Kelly, Howard Atwood, and Burrage, Walter L. *Dictionary of American Medical Biography.* New York: Appleton, 1928.

Dict. Australian Biog. Serle, Percival. *Dictionary of Australian Biography.* 2 vols. Sydney: Angus and Robertson, 1949.

Dict. Biog. Fran. *Dictionnaire de Biographie Francaise.* Ed. by J. Balteau, et al. Paris: Letouzey et Ane, 1933- .

Dict. Canadian Biog. *The Dictionary of Canadian Biography (Dictionnaire Biographique du Canada).* Ed. by George W. Brown. Toronto: University of Toronto Press, 1966- .

Dict. Cat. Hist. Print. *Dictionary Catalogue of the History of Printing.* From the John M. Wing Foundation in the Newberry Library, Chicago. 6 vols. 1st supplement in 3 vols. Boston: G. K. Hall, 1961.

Dict. Christian Biog. Smith, Sir William, and Wace, Henry. *A Dictionary of Christian Biography.* Reprint. 4 vols. New York: Kraus Reprint Corp., 1967.

Dict. Grk. Rom. Antiq. Smith, Sir William; Wayte, William; and Marindin, G. E. *A Dictionary of Greek and Roman Antiquities.* 2 vols. 3d ed. London: John Murray, 1914.

Dict. Grk. Rom. Biog. Myth. Smith, Sir William. *A Dictionary of Greek and Roman Biography and Mythology.* Reprint. 3 vols. New York: A.M.S. Press, 1967.

Dict. Hist. Biog. Suisse *Dictionnaire Historique et Biographique de la Suisse.* Sous la direction de Marcel Godet, Henri Tuerler, et al. Neuchatel: Administration du Dictionnaire Historique et Biographique de la Suisse, 1920-1933. Supplement. Neuchatel: V. Attinger, 1934.

Dict. Nat. Biog. *Dictionary of National Biography.* Ed. by Leslie Stephen and Sidney Lee. 63 vols. and 7 suppl. to 1960. London: Smith, Elder & Co., 1885-1901.

Dict. Nat. Contemp. *Dictionnaire National des Contemporains.* Ed. by Nath Imbert. 3 vols. Paris: Editions Lajeunesse, 1938-1939.

Dict. Scandinavian Biog. *Dictionary of Scandinavian Biography.* Ed. by Ernest Kay. London: Melrose Press, 1972.

Dict. Sci. Biog. *Dictionary of Scientific Biography.* Ed. by Charles Coulston Gillespie. New York: Scribner, 1970- .

Die Med. Welt. *Die Medizinische Welt.* Berlin and Stuttgart, vol. 1, Feb. 5, 1937- .

Direct. Brit. Sci. *Directory of British Scientists.* London: E. Benn, 1st ed., 1963- .

Direct. Med. Specialists *Directory of Medical Specialists Holding Certification by American Specialty Boards.* Chicago: Marquis-Who's Who, vol. 1, 1939- .

Diz. Biog. Ital. *Dizionario Biografico degli Italiani.* Ed. by Alberto M. Ghisalberti. Roma: Istituto della Enciclopedia Italiana, 1960- .

Diz. Encic. Ital. *Dizionario Enciclopedia Italiano.* Ed. by Bosco Umberto. Roma: Istituto della Enciclopedia Italiana, 1955-1961.

Dobson Dobson, Jesse. *Anatomical Eponyms.* 2d ed. Edinburgh: Livingstone, 1962.

Dobutsugaku Zasshi *Dobutsugaku Zasshi.* Tokyo: Zoological Society of Japan, vol. 1, 1889- .

Doc. p. servir a l'histoire de l'Univ. de Geneve *Documents pour Servir a l'Histoire de l'Universite de Geneve.* Geneve: Librairie de l'Universite, 1878?- .

Docum. Ophthal. *Documenta Ophthalmologica; Recent Advances in Ophthalmology.* Zurich and Paris, vol. 1, 1938- .

Donath Donath, Tibor. *Anatomical Dictionary.* 1st English ed. revised by G. N. C. Crawford. Oxford: Pergamon Press, 1968.

Dorland *Dorland's Illustrated Medical Dictionary.* 23rd ed., 1957; 24th ed., 1965; 25th ed., 1974. Philadelphia: W. B. Saunders.

Dossin Great Lakes Museum *Dossin Great Lakes Museum,* Belle Isle, Detroit, Mich.

Dresner Dresner, Stephen. *Units of Measurement.* New York: Hastings House, 1971

Drever Drever, James. *A Dictionary of Psychology.* 2d ed. Baltimore: Penguin Books, 1964.

Duffy Duffy, Charles, and Pettit, Henry. *A Dictionary of Literary Terms.* Revised ed. New York: Brown Book Co., 1952.

Dugdale Dugdale, Robert Louis. *The Jukes; a Study in Crime, Pauperism, Disease, and Heredity.* 4th ed. New York: Putnam, 1910.

Dupuy Dupuy, Richard Ernest, and Dupuy, Trevor Nevitt. *The Encyclopedia of Military History from 3500 B.C. to the Present.* New York: Harper & Row, 1970.

Dutton Dutton, W. S. *The Rockefeller Foundation Story.*

Edinburgh J. of Sci. *Edinburgh Journal of Science.* Edinburgh, vols. 1-10, July 1824-April 1829; n.s., vols. 1-6, July 1829-April 1832.

Edinburgh Med. J. *Edinburgh Medical Journal.* Edinburgh, 1855-1954.

Edinburgh Med. Surg. J. *Edinburgh Medical and Surgical Journal.* Edinburgh and London, vols. 1-82, no. 2, Jan. 1805-April 1855.

Edinburgh Royal Soc. Proc. *Royal Society of Edinburgh. Proceedings.* Vol. 1, Dec. 1832- . With vol. 61, 1941- , in 2 sections: s. A (Mathematical and Physical Sciences) and s. B (Biology).

Edwards Edwards, Paul, ed. *The Encyclopedia of Philosophy.* 8 vols. New York: Macmillan and Free Press, 1967.

Electrician *The Electrical Journal.* London, vol. 1, May 25, 1878- . (May 25, 1878-Oct. 10, 1952 as *Electrician.*)

Electronics *Electronics.* New York, vol. 1, 1930- .

Encic. Cattolica *Enciclopedia Cattolica.* Ed. by G. C. Sansoni. 12 vols. Firenze: Casa Editrice, 1972.

Encic. Ital. *Enciclopedia Italiana di Scienze, Lettere et Arti.* 36 vols. Roma: Istituto della Enciclopedia Italiana, 1930-1950.

Encic. Univ. Ilus. *Enciclopedia Universal Ilustrada.* Barcelona: J. Espasa, 1907?-1930.

Encyc. Amer. *The Encyclopedia Americana.* New York: Americana Corp., 1959.

Encyc. Brit., 9th ed. *The Encyclopaedia Britannica; a Dictionary of Arts, Sciences and General Literature.* 9th ed. 25 vols. New York: Scribner, 1878-1879.

Encyc. Brit., 1911 *The Encyclopaedia Britannica; a Dictionary of Arts, Sciences, Literature and General Information.* 11th ed. 29 vols. New York: The Encyclopaedia Britannica Co., 1910-1911.

Encyc. Brit., 1973 *Encyclopaedia Britannica.* 24 vols. Chicago: Encyclopaedia Britannica, Inc., 1973.

Encyc. Brit. Bk. Yr. *Encyclopaedia Britannica Book of the Year.* Chicago: Encyclopaedia Britannica, Inc., 1938-

Encyc. Judaica *Encyclopedia Judaica.* Ed. by Cecil Roth. 16 vols. Jerusalem: Macmillan, 1972.

Encyc. S. Africa Rosenthal, Eric, ed. *Encyclopaedia of Southern Africa.* 1st ed. London: F. Warne, 1961. 2d ed. London, F. Warne, 1965.

Encyc. Soc. Sci. *Encyclopaedia of the Social Sciences.* Ed. by Edwin R. A. Seligman. 15 vols. New York: Macmillan, 1937.

Encyc. Southern Africa See: **Encyc. S. Africa**

Encyc. World Art *Encyclopedia of World Art.* 15 vols. New York: McGraw-Hill, 1959-1968.

English English, Horace B., and English, Ava C. *A Comprehensive Dictionary of Psychological and Psychoanalytical Terms.* New York: Van Nostrand Reinhold, 1970 (c. 1958).

Environ. Terms United States. Army Natick Laboratories. Natick, Mass. *Military Standard Glossary of Environmental Terms (Terrestrial).* Reprint of 1968 ed. Detroit: Gale Research Co., 1973.

Ergebn d. Physiol. *Ergebnisse der Physiologie.* (Asher-Spiro) Wiesbaden and Munich, vol. 1, 1902- .

Ewart Ewart, Andrew. *Great Lovers.* New York: Hart, 1968.

Fairbridge Fairbridge, Rhodes W. *Encyclopedia of Geomorphology.* New York: Reinhold, 1968.

Fairchild Fairchild, Henry Pratt. *Dictionary of Sociology.* Totowa, N.J.: Littlefield Adams, 1970.

Family Circle *Family Circle.* Newark, N.J., and Mount Morris, Ill., vol. 1, 1932- .

Farm. Vestnik Mosk. *Farmatsevticheskii Viestnik.* Moscow, vols. 1-6, 1897-1902?

Fielding Fielding, Mantle. *Dictionary of American Painters, Sculptors and Engravers.* Philadelphia: Printed for the Subscribers, 1927.

Finsk Biog. Handb. *Finsk Biografisk Handbok.* Ed. by Tor Carpelan. Helsingfors: G. W. Edlunds Forlag, 1903.

Focal Encyc. Film *The Focal Encyclopedia of Film and Television Techniques.* 1st Amer. ed. New York: Hastings House, 1969.

Focal Encyc. Photog. *The Focal Encyclopedia of Photography.* Revised desk ed. New York: McGraw-Hill, 1969.

Folia Neuropath. Eston. *Folia Neuropathologica Estoniana.* Tartu, vol. 1, 1923- .

Forhandlinger Kgl. Norske Vidensk. Selskab. *K. Norske Videnskabers Selskab, Trondhjem. Forhandlinger.* Vol. 1, 1926/1928- .

Frankf. Zool. Garten *Frankfurt am Main. Zoologischer Garten.* (Zoologische Gesellschaft, Neue Zoologisches Gesellschaft) Vols. 1-17, 1859-1876.

Frey Frey, Albert Romer. *Sobriquets and Nicknames.* Reprint of the 1888 ed. Detroit: Gale Research Co., 1966.

Funk Funk, Wilfred. *Word Origins and Their Romantic Stories.* New York: Funk & Wagnalls, 1950.

Funk & Wagnalls *Funk & Wagnalls Standard Dictionary of Folklore, Mythology and Legend.* Ed. by Maria Leach. New York: Funk & Wagnalls, 1949-1950.

Funk & Wagnalls New Std. Dict. Eng. Language *Funk & Wagnalls New Standard Dictionary of the English Language.* Ed. by Isaac K. Funk. New York: Funk & Wagnalls, 1963.

Garrison and Morton Garrison, Fielding Hudson, and Morton, Leslie T. *A Medical Bibliography (Garrison and Morton); an Annotated Check-List of Texts Illustrating the History of Medicine.* 3d ed. revised by Leslie T. Morton. London: Andre Deutsch, 1970.

Gazeta Medica Portugesa *Gazeta Medica Portugesa.* Lisbon, vol. 1, Jan./March 1948- .

Gazz. Internaz. Med. Chir. *Gazzetta Internazionale di Medicina e Chirurgia.* Naples: Scuola Medica Oespedaliera, vol. 1, 1899- . (Vols. 11-27, no. 24, Jan. 1908-Dec. 31, 1919, as *Gazzetta Internazionale Medico-Chirurgica e di Interessi Professionali.*)

Geistige Wien *Das Geistige Wien.* By Ludwig Eisenberg and Richard Groner. Wien: Brockhausen, 1889-1893.

Genie Civil *Genie Civil.* Paris, vol. 1, Nov. 1880- .

Geol. Soc. Amer. Proc. *Geological Society of America. Proceedings.* New York, vol. 46, 1933- . (Vols. 1-45 included in the society's *Bulletin.*)

Geolog. Bavarica *Geologica Bavarica.* Munich: Geologisches Landesamt, no. 1, 1949- .

Geolog. Foren. Forhandlingar *Geologiska Foreningen i Stockholm. Forhandlingar.* Stockholm, vol. 1, 1872 .

Gerwig Gerwig, Henrietta, ed. *University Handbook for Readers and Writers.* New York: Crowell, 1965.

Gibb and Kramers Gibb, H. A. R. and Kramers, J. H. *Shorter Encyclopedia of Islam.* Ithaca, N.Y.: Cornell University Press, 1953.

Glaister Glaister, Geoffrey Ashall. *Glossary of the Book.* London: Geo. Allen and Unwin, 1960.

Goddard Goddard, Henry Herbert. *The Kallikak Family; a Study in the Heredity of Feeblemindedness.* New York: Macmillan, 1912.

Good Good, Carter V., ed. *Dictionary of Education.* 3d ed. New York: McGraw-Hill, 1973.

Gran Encic. Argentina *Gran Enciclopedia Argentina; Todo Lo Argentino Ordenado Alfabeticamente.* Ed. by Diego Abad de Santillan. 8 vols. Buenos Aires: Ediar, 1956-1964.

Grand Larousse Encyc. *Grand Larousse Encyclopedique en dix volumes.* Paris: Librairie Larousse, 1960-1964.

Gray Gray, Peter. *The Dictionary of the Biological Sciences.* New York: Reinhold Publishing Corp., 1967.

Greenwald Greenwald, Douglas. *The McGraw-Hill Dictionary of Modern Economics.* New York: McGraw-Hill, 1965.

Grinstein Grinstein, Alexander. *The Index of Psychoanalytic Writings*. 5 vols. New York: International Press, 1956-1959.

Grove Grove, Sir George. *Dictionary of Music and Musicians*. 5th ed. Ed. by Eric Blom. 9 vols. New York: St. Martin's Press, 1955. Suppl. vol. Ed. by Eric Blom. New York: St. Martin's Press, 1961.

Gynaekol.-Verzeich. *Deutsches Gynaekologen-Verzeichnis*. Leipzig: Barth, 1st ed., 1928- . (1st ed. issued under title: *Deutsche Gynaekologenkalender*.)

Gynecologie *Gynecologie; Revue Periodique Mensuelle*. Paris, vols. 1-39, Feb. 15, 1896-1939.

Hackh Hackh, Ingo Waldemar Dagobert. *Hackh's Chemical Dictionary*. 4th ed. revised by Julius Grant. New York: McGraw-Hill, 1969.

Hagerups Illus. Kon. Lek. *Hagerups Illustrerede Konversations Leksikon*. Ed. by Povl Engelstoft. 10 vols. Kobenhavn: Hagerup, 1948-1953.

Hamberger Hamberger, Georg Christoph. *Das Gelerte Teutschland*. Lemgo: Im Verlag der Meyerschen Buchhandlung, 1776.

Hamilton Hamilton, Milton Wheaton. *Adam Ramage and His Presses*. Portland, Me.: Southworth-Anthoensen Press, 1942.

Handb. der Deut. Wissensch. *Handbuch der Deutschen Wissenschaft*. Berlin: F. K. Keotschau, vol. 1, 1949- .

Harbottle Harbottle, Thomas Benfield. *Dictionary of Historical Allusions*. Reprint of the 1904 ed. Detroit: Gale Research Co., 1968.

Hargrave Hargrave, Basil. *Origins and Meanings of Popular Phrases and Names*. Reprint of the 1925 ed. Detroit: Gale Research Co., 1968.

Harper Peck, Harry Thurston, ed. *Harper's Dictionary of Classical Literature and Antiquities*. New York: Cooper Square Publishers, 1962.

Harrod Harrod, Leonard Montague. *Librarians' Glossary*. 3d ed. London: Andre Deutsch, 1971.

Hart Hart, James David, ed. *The Oxford Companion to American Literature*. 4th ed. New York: Oxford University Press, 1965.

Hartmann Hartmann, R. R. K. and Stork, F. C. *Dictionary of Language and Linguistics*. New York: Wiley, 1971.

Hartnoll Hartnoll, Phyllis, ed. *The Oxford Companion to the Theatre*. 3d ed. London: Oxford University Press, 1967.

Hartshorn Hartshorn, Winifred Morgan. *History of the New York Polyclinic Medical School and Hospital*. New York; Camden, N.J.: The Haddon Craftsmen, Inc., 1942.

Harvey Harvey, Paul, ed. *The Oxford Companion to English Literature*. 4th ed. revised by Dorothy Eagle. New York Oxford University Press, 1967.

Harvey and Heseltine Harvey, Sir Paul, and Heseltine, Janet E., eds. *The Oxford Companion to French Literature*. Oxford: Clarendon Press, 1959.

Hastings (Dict. Bible) Hastings, James, ed. *Dictionary of the Bible*. 2d ed. revised by Frederick C. Grant and Harold H. Rowley. New York: Scribner, 1963.

Hastings (Encyc. Rel. Ethics) Hastings, James, ed. *Encyclopaedia of Religion and Ethics*. 12 vols. New York: Scribner, 1959-1961.

Hautarzt *Hautarzt; Zeitschrift fuer Dermatologie, Venerologie und Verwandte Gebiete*. Berlin, vol. 1, 1950- .

Hazlitt Hazlitt, William Carew. *Faiths and Folklore: A Dictionary*. London: Reeves and Turner, 1905.

Heart Bull. *Heart Bulletin*. Houston: Medical Arts Publishing Foundation, vol. 1, Mar./Apr. 1952- .

Helvetica Chim. Acta *Helvetica Chimica Acta*. Basel and Geneva: Schweizerische Chemische Gesellschaft, vol. 1, 1918- .

Henderson Henderson, Isabella Ferguson, and Henderson, William Dawson. *A Dictionary of Biological Terms*. 8th ed. revised by John Henry Kenneth. New York: Van Nostrand, 1963.

Hendrickson Hendrickson, Robert. *Human Words*. Philadelphia: Chilton, 1972.

Hinsie Hinsie, Leland E., and Campbell, Robert Jean. *Psychiatric Dictionary*. 4th ed. New York: Oxford University Press, 1970.

Hintze Hintze, Carl. *Handbuch der Mineralogie*. 2 vols. in 7. Leipzig: Veit & Co., 1897-1933. Ergaenzungsband. Berlin: Der Gruyter, 1938- .

Hirsch Hirsch, Gottwalt Christian. *Index Biologorum: Investigatores, Laboratoria, Periodica*. 1st ed. Berlin: J. Springer, 1928.

Hist. Boston City Hosp. *A History of the Boston City Hospital from its Foundation until 1904*. Ed. by David W. Cheever, et al. Boston: Municipal Printing Office, 1906.

Hist. Dict. Panama Hedrick, Basil C., and Hedrick, Anne K. *Historical Dictionary of Panama*. Latin American Historical Dictionaries #2. Metuchen, N.J.: Scarecrow Press, 1970.

Holweck Holweck, Frederick G. *Biographical Dictionary of the Saints*. Reprint of the 1924 edition. Detroit: Gale Research Co., 1969.

Hospitalstidende *Hospitalstidende*. Copenhagen, vols. 1-81, no. 52, 1858-Dec. 27, 1938.

Hoult Hoult, Thomas Ford. *Dictionary of Modern Sociology*. Totowa, N.J.: Littlefield Adams, 1969.

Hughes Hughes, Leslie E. C.; Stephens, Raymond W. B.; and Brown, L. Denis. *Dictionary of Electronics and Nucleonics*. Edinburgh: W. & R. Chambers, 1969.

Hunt Hunt, Cecil. *A Dictionary of Word Makers; Pen Pictures of the People Behind Our Language*. New York: Philosophical Library, 1949.

Huschke Huschke, Ralph E., ed. *Glossary of Meteorology*. Boston: American Meteorological Society, 1959.

Hvem er Hvem? *Hvem er Hvem?* (Who's Who in Norway.) Oslo: H. Aschehoug, vol. 1, 1912- .

Hygiea, Stockh. *Hygiea; Medicinsk och Pharmaceutisk Manadskrift*. Stockholm: Svenska Lakare-Sallskapet. 1839-1938.

Index-Cat. Libr. Surg.-Gen. Off. U.S. National Library of Medicine. *Index-Catalogue of the Library of the Surgeon-General's Office, United States Army*. 1st-5th Series, 1880-1959. Washington, D.C.: Government Printing Office, 1880-1961.

Index-Cat. Med. Veter. Zool. U.S. Bureau of Animal Industry: Zoological Division. *Index-Catalogue of Medical and Veterinary Zoology, Authors, Aall-Zyukov*. 12 vols. Washington, D.C.: Government Printing Office, 1932-1952. Supplement. Vol. 1, 1953- .

Index Medicus *Index Medicus*. Washington, D.C.: National Library of Medicine, vol. 1, Jan. 1960- .

Int. Who's Who *The International Who's Who*. London: Europa Publications and Allen & Unwin, vol. 1, 1935- .

BIBLIOGRAPHY OF SOURCES CITED

Internat. Chem. Direct. *International Chemistry Directory.* New York: Benjamin, vol. 1, 1969/1970- .

Internat. Dict. Ap. Math *The International Dictionary of Applied Mathematics.* Ed. by W. F. Freiberger. Princeton, N.J.: Van Nostrand, 1960.

Internat. Dict. Phys. Elec. *The International Dictionary of Physics and Electronics.* Ed. by Walter C. Michels. 2d ed. Princeton, N.J.: Van Nostrand, 1961.

Internat. Direct. Psych. *International Directory of Psychologists, Exclusive of the U.S.A.* 2d ed. Assen, Netherlands: Royal Van Gorcum, 1966. (Prepared by the Committee on Publication and Communication of the International Union of Psychological Science.)

Internat. Encyc. Soc. Sci. *International Encyclopedia of the Social Sciences.* Ed. by David L. Sills. 17 vols. New York: Macmillan and Free Press, 1968.

Internat. J. Neurol. *International Journal of Neurology.* Montevideo, vol. 1, Dec. 1959- .

Internat. Physics Astr. Direct. *International Physics & Astronomy Directory.* New York: W. A. Benjamin, 1st ed., 1969/1970- .

J.A.M.A. *American Medical Association. Journal.* Chicago: American Medical Association, vol. 1, 1883- .

J. Amer. Chem. Soc. *American Chemical Society. Journal.* Vol. 1, 1879- .

J. Bone Joint Surg. *Journal of Bone and Joint Surgery.* Boston, vol. 1, 1922- .

J. Chir. *Journal de Chirurgie.* Paris, vol. 1, Apr. 1908- .

J. de Pharm. Antwerp *Journal de Pharmacie.* Antwerp and Brussels, vols. 1-70, no. 16, 1845-Aug. 31, 1914.

J. Ind. Chem. Eng. *I/EC. Industrial and Engineering Chemistry.* Washington, D.C.: American Chemical Society, vol. 1, Jan. 1909- . (1909-1922 as *Journal of Industrial and Engineering Chemistry.*)

J. Internat. Coll. Surg. *International College of Surgeons, Chicago. Journal.* Vol. 1, July 1938- .

J. Lar. Otol. *Journal of Laryngology and Otology.* London, vol. 1, 1887- .

J. Libr. Automation *Journal of Library Automation.* Chicago: American Library Association, vol. 1, March 1968- .

J. Med. Lyon *Journal de Medecine de Lyon.* Societe de Medecine de Lyon, vols. 1-11, 1841-1846; s. 2, vols. 1-3, 1847-June 1848?

J. Mount Sinai Hosp. *Mount Sinai Hospital. Journal.* New York, vol. 1, May/June 1934- .

J. Nerv. Ment. Dis. *Journal of Nervous and Mental Diseases.* Chicago: American Neurological Association, vol. 1, 1874- .

J. Path. Bact. *Journal of Pathology and Bacteriology.* Cambridge, Eng.: Pathological Society of Great Britain and Ireland, vol. 1, 1892- .

J. Pharm. *Journal de Pharmacie et de Chimie.* Paris: Societe de Pharmacie de Paris, 1809-1942 in 9 separately numbered series.

J. Pharm. Belg. *Journal de Pharmacie de Belgique.* Brussels: Federations des Unions et des Oeuvres Pharmaceutiques Belges, vol. 1, 1919- .

Jablonski Jablonski, Stanley. *Illustrated Dictionary of Eponymic Syndromes and Diseases, and Their Synonyms.* Philadelphia: Saunders, 1969.

Jahresbericht der Chemie *Jahresbericht Ueber die Fortschritte der Chemie und Verwandter Theile Anderer Wissenschaften.* Giessen and Brunswick, 1847/1848-1910.

James James, Glenn, and James, Robert Clarke, eds. *James and James Mathematical Dictionary.* 3d ed. New York: Van Nostrand, 1968.

Jameson Jameson, J. Franklin. *Dictionary of United States History.* Revised by Albert E. McKinley. Reprint of the 1931 edition. Detroit, Gale Research Co., 1971.

Japanese Biog. Encyc. and Who's Who *The Japan Biographical Encyclopedia and Who's Who.* Tokyo: Japan Biographical Research Department (Rengo Press), 1st ed., 1958- .

Jasznigi Jasznigi, Alexander. *Das Geistige Ungarn; Biographisches Lexikon.* Hrsg. von Oskar Kruecken (pseud) and Imre Parlagi. 2 vols. Wien: W. Braumueller, 1918.

Jber. Deutsch. Math. Verein. *Deutsche Mathematiker-Vereinigung, Bielefeld. Jahresbericht.* Vol. 1, 1890- .

Jewish Encyc. *The Jewish Encyclopedia.* Prepared under the direction of Cyrus Adler, et al. New York: Funk & Wagnalls, 1925.

Jobes Jobes, Gertrude. *Dictionary of Mythology, Folklore and Symbols.* New York: Scarecrow Press, 1961.

Kelly Kelly, Emerson Crosby. *Encyclopedia of Medical Sources.* Baltimore: Williams and Wilkins, 1948.

Kendall Kendall, Maurice, and Buckland, William R. *A Dictionary of Statistical Terms.* 3d ed. New York: Hafner, 1971.

Kendall and Doig Kendall, Maurice G., and Doig, Alison G. *Bibliography of Statistical Literature.* 3 vols. New York: Hafner, 1962-1968.

King King, Henry C. *The History of the Telescope.* Cambridge, Mass.: Sky, 1955.

Kingzett Kingzett, Charles T. *Chemical Encyclopedia,* 5th ed. London: Bailliere, Tindall and Cox, 1932.

Kosminski: Slownik lekarzow polskich Kosminski, Stanislaw Lubicz. *Slownik Lekarzow Polskich.* Warzawa: Naklad Autora, 1883-1888.

Kraks Blaa Bog *Kraks Blaa Bog; Fire Tusinde Nulevende Danske Maend og Kvinders Levnedslob.* Kobenhavn: Krak, vol. 1, 1910- .

Krauch and Kunz Krauch, Helmut, and Kunz, Werner. *Organic Name Reactions.* Translated from the 2d revised German ed. by John M. Harkin. New York: Wiley, 1964.

Krok Krok, Thorgny. *Bibliotheca Botanica Suecana ab Antiquis simis Temporibus as Finem Anni MCMXVII.* Uppsala and Stockholm: Almqvist and Wiksells, 1925.

Kuerschner's Deut. Gel. Kal. *Kuerschner's Deutscher Gelehrten-Kalender.* Berlin: William De Gruyter, vol. 1, 1925- .

Kukula Kukula, Richard. *Bibliographisches Jahrbuch der Deutschen Hochschulen.* Innsbruck: Wagner, 1892. Supplement. Innsbruck: Wagner, 1893.

Kunitz Kunitz, Stanley J., and Haycraft, Howard, eds. *Twentieth Century Authors: A Biographical Dictionary of Modern Literature.* New York: Wilson, 1942.

L.A. County Med. Assoc. Bull *Los Angeles County Medical Association. Bulletin.* Vol. 40, 1910- .

Lancet *Lancet.* London, vol. 1, Oct. 5, 1823- .

Latham Latham, Edward. *Dictionary of Names, Nicknames and Surnames of Persons, Places and Things.* Reprint of the 1904 edition. Detroit: Gale Research Co., 1966.

Laughlin Laughlin, William. *Laughlin's Fact Finder; People, Places, Things and Events.* West Nyack, N.Y.: Parker, 1969.

Lead. Amer Sci. *Leaders in American Science.* Nashville: Who's Who in American Education, vol. 1, 1953/1954- .

Lead. Educ. *Leaders in Education: A Biographical Directory.* Ed. by Jacques Cattell. Lancaster, Pa.: Science Press, 1st ed. 1932- .

Leaders in Educ. See: **Lead. Educ.**

Legit. Laekare *Legitimarade Laekare.* Stockholm: Svenska Socialstyrelsen, 1st ed., 1968- .

Lek. Listy *Lekarske Listy.* Brno: Spolek Ceskych Lekaru v Brno a Olomouci, vols. 1-9, 1946-1954.

Leon Leon, Nicolas. *Bibliotheca Botanico-Mexicana.* Mexico: Oficina Tip de la Secretaria de Fomento, 1895.

Leonardo Leonardo, Richard. *Lives of Master Surgeons.* New York: Froben, 1948.

Leopoldina *Leopoldina.* Jena and Leipzig: Deutsche Akademie der Naturforscher zu Halle, s. 1, 1859-Aug. 1923; s. 2, 1926-1930; s. 3, vol. 1, Jan/June 1955- .

Lib. Assoc. Rec. *Library Association Record.* London: Library Association, vol. 1, 1899- , s. 4, vol. 1, 1934- .

Liber Mem. Gand Ghent. Rijksuniversiteit. *Liber Memorialis; Notices Biographiques.* Gand: I. Vanderpoorten, 1913.

Libr. Congress Cat. Printed Cards U.S. Library of Congress. *A Catalog of Books Represented by Library of Congress Printed Cards Issued to July 31, 1942.* 167 vols. Ann Arbor: Edwards, 1942-1946. Supplement: cards issued Aug. 1, 1942-Dec. 31, 1947. Ann Arbor: Edwards, 1948.

Libr. Lit. *Library Literature; An Annotated Index to Current Books, Pamphlets and Periodical Literature Relating to the Library Profession.* New York: H. W. Wilson, 1933/1935- .

Lieber and Olbrich Lieber, Bernfried, and Olbrich, Gertrud. *Die Klinischen Syndrome.* 2 vols. Muenchen: Urban and Schwarzenburg, 1972.

Lijst geschr. ver. Kath. Nederl. *Lijst Geschriften Vereeniging Katholieken Nederland.* 1922.

Lilley Liley, Samuel. *Men, Machines and History.* New York: International Publishers, 1965.

Liverpool Lit. Phil. Soc. Proc. *Literary and Philosophical Society of Liverpool. Proceedings.* London and Liverpool, vol. 1, 1844/1845- .

Loc. Rail. Carr. Review *Locomotive, Railway Carriage and Wagon Review.* London, vol. 1, 1896- .

Lockwood *American Dictionary of Printing and Bookmaking.* Reprint of the Howard Lockwood & Co. 1894 edition. Detroit: Gale Research Co., 1967.

Lodzkie Towarzystwo Naukowe. Sprawozdania z czynnosci i Posiedzen *Lodzkie Towarzystwo Naukowe. Sprawozdania z Czynnosci i Posiedzen.* Lodz, vol. 1, June 1946- .

Lomas Lomas, Sophia Crawford, ed. *Letters and Speeches of Oliver Cromwell.* 3 vols. London: Methuen, 1904.

London Hosp. Gaz. *London Hospital Gazette.* London: London Hospital, Medical School, vol. 1, 1894- .

London Times *The Times.* Daily newspaper. London, vol. 1, 1785- .

Lotta contra la tuberculosi *Lotta Contra la Tuberculosi.* Roma, vol. 1, May 1930- .

Lutte Contre Tuberculose *La Lutte Contre la Tuberculose en Pologne.* Varsovie: Imp. Scientifique, 1934.

Lyon Med. *Lyon Medical.* Lyon: Societe de Medecine de Lyon, vol. 1, 1869- .

McGraw-Hill Encyc. Sci. Tech. *McGraw-Hill Encyclopedia of Science and Technology: An International Reference Work.* 3d ed. 15 vols. New York: McGraw-Hill, 1971.

McGraw-Hill Mod. Men Sci. *McGraw-Hill Modern Men of Science.* Ed. by Jay E. Greene. New York: McGraw-Hill, 1966.

McKenzie McKenzie, John L. *Dictionary of the Bible.* Milwaukee: Bruce, 1965.

Macmillan Dict. Canadian Biog. *The Macmillan Dictionary of Canadian Biography.* Ed. by W. Stewart Wallace. 3d ed. revised and enlarged. London: Macmillan, 1963. (Previous editions under title: *Dictionary of Canadian Biography.*)

Magill Magill, Frank N. *Cyclopedia of Literary Characters.* New York: Harper & Row, 1963.

Magyar Eletr. Lex. *Magyar Eletrajzi Lexikon.* Foszerkeszto Kenyeres Agnes. Ed. by Bortnyik Sandor, et al. Budapest: Akademiai Kiado, 1967.

Major Major, Ralph Hermon. *A History of Medicine.* 2 vols. Springfield, Ill.: Thomas, 1954.

Mansch Mansch, Anton. *Medical World; A Gallery of Contemporaries in the Field of Medical Science.* Berlin: A. Eckstein, 191?

Mansell *The National Union Catalog Pre-1956 Imprints.* By the American Library Association and the Library of Congress. London: Balding and Mansell Ltd., 1968- .

Marcellia *Marcellia; Revista Internazionale di Cecidologia.* Avellino, vol. 1, 1902- .

Markus Markus, John. *Electronics and Nucleonics Dictionary.* 3d ed. New York: McGraw-Hill, 1966.

Martin Martin, Thomas J., Jr. *Malice in Blunderland.* New York: McGraw-Hill, 1973.

Matematika v. SSSR. *Matematika v. SSSR. za sorok let, 1917-1957.* Ed. by A. G. Kurosh. Moskva, 1959. (Vol. 2: Biobibliografi.)

Materialy Biograf. Slovar Imp. Akad. Nauk I Akademiia Nauk SSSR. *Materialy dlia Biograficheskago Slovaria Dieistvitelnykh Chlenov Imperatorskoi Akademii Nauk.* 2 vols. Petrograd: Tip. Rossiskoi Akademii Nauk, 1915-1917 (Its Imperatorskaia Akademiia Nauk, 1899-1914.)

Materialy k Biobibliografii ucenych SSSR. *Materialy k Biobibliografii ucenych SSSR.*

Math. Rev. *Mathematical Reviews.* Lancaster, Pa. and Providence, R.I.: American Mathematical Society, vol. 1, Jan. 1940- .

Mathews, M. M. Mathews, Mitford McLeod, ed. *A Dictionary of Americanisms on Historical Principles.* Chicago: University of Chicago Press, 1951.

Mathews, S. Mathews, Shailer, and Smith, Gerald Birney. *Dictionary of Religion and Ethics.* Reprint of the 1921 edition. Detroit: Gale Research Co., 1973.

Med.-Chir. Trans., London Royal Medical and Chirurgical Society of London. *Medico-Chirurgical Transactions.* London, vols. 1-90, 1809-1907.

Med. Direct. *The Medical Directory.* London: Churchill, vol. 1, 1845- .

Med. Direct. Australia *Medical Directory for Australia.* Sydney: Australasian Publishing Co., Ltd., 1st ed., 19___- . Cover title: *Knox's Medical Directory for Australia.*

Med. J. Australia *Medical Journal of Australia.* Sydney: British Medical Association, Australian Branch, vol. 1, 1914- .

Med. Libr. Assn. Bull. *Medical Library Association. Bulletin.* Baltimore, vol. 1, no. 4, Jan-Oct. 1902; n.s., vol. 1, 1911- .

Med. Rec., N.Y. *International Record of Medicine.* New York, vol. 1, April 1865- . (1934-1950 as *Medical Record.*)

Med. Register *The Medical Register.* London, 1859- .

Med. Soc. Rep., Scranton Lackawanna County Medical Society. *Medical Society Reporter.* Vol. 1, 1910- .

Meddelelser Dansk Foren. *Dansk Geologisk Forening, Copenhagen. Meddelelser.* Vol. 1, 1894- .

Mellor Mellor, Joseph William. *A Comprehensive Treatise on Inorganic and Theoretical Chemistry.* 16 vols. London: Longmans and Green, 1922-1937. Supplement, 1956- .

Mem. Acad. de Chir. *Academie de Chirurgie, Paris. Memoires.* Vols. 1-7, 1847-1874; n.s., vol. 1, 1875- .

Menke Menke, Frank Grant. *The Encyclopedia of Sports.* 4th ed. revised by Roger Treat. South Brunswick, N.J.: A. S. Barnes, 1969.

Merrill and Walker Merrill, Elmer Drew, and Walker, Egbert H. *A Bibliography of Eastern Asiatic Botany.* Jamaica Plains, Mass.: Arnold Arboretum of Harvard University, 1938.

Meteorolog. and Geoastrophys. Abstr., Cum. Index *Meteorological and Geoastrophysical Abstracts. Cumulative Index.* Boston: American Meteorological Society, vols. 1-10, 1950-1959.

Michaud Michaud, Louis Gabriel. *Biographie Universelle (Michaud) Ancienne et Moderne.* Nouvelle edition. 45 vols. Paris: Chez Madame C. Desplaces, 1854-1865.

Milani, Ist Lomb. Rendiconti *R. Istituto Lombardo di Scienze e Lettere, Milan. Rendiconti. Classe di Scienze Mathematiche et Naturali.* Vols. 1-4, 1864-1867; s. 2, vol. 1, 1868- . (s. 2, vol. 70, 1937- ; also as s. 3, vol. 1)

Milchwirtschaftliche *Milchwirtschaftliche Forschungen.* Berlin, vol. 1, 1923- .

Min. Abstr. *Mineralogical Abstracts.* London, vol. 1, 1920- .

Min. Mag. *Mineralogical Magazine and Journal of the Mineralogical Society.* London, vol. 1, Aug. 1876- .

Minerva Med. *Minerva Medica; Rivista delle Riviste di Scienze Mediche.* Rome and Turin, vol. 1, 1909- .

Miss. Doct. *Mississippi Doctor.* Booneville, vol. 1, 1922- .

Monatschr. f. Ohrenheilk. Laryngo-Rhinol. *Monatschrift fuer Ohrenheilkunde und Laryngo-Rhinologie.* Vienna and Berlin: Gesellschaft der Wiener Hals-,Nasen-und Ohrenaerzte, vol. 1, Oct. 1, 1867- .

Monitore Zool. Ital. *Monitore Zoologico Italiano.* Sienna: Unione Zoologica Italiana, vol. 1, 1890- .

Monkhouse Monkhouse, Francis J. *A Dictionary of Geography.* 2d ed. Chicago: Aldine, 1970.

Montgomery Montgomery, Hugh, and Cambray, Philip G. *A Dictionary of Political Phrases and Allusions.* Reprint of the 1906 edition. Detroit: Gale Research Co., 1968.

Montpellier Med. *Montpellier Medical; Journal Mensuel de Medecine.* Montpellier, France, vols. 1-50, 1858-1883; s. 2, vols. 1-17, 1883-1891; n.s. (s. 2a) vols. 1-53, 1892-1931; s. 3, vol. 1, 1932- .

Moore Moore, Wilfred George. *A Dictionary of Geography.* 4th ed. Hammondsworth, Eng.: Penguin, 1968.

Morris Morris, Richard Brandon, ed. *Encyclopedia of American History.* New York: Harper, 1961.

Morris and Irwin Morris, Richard Brandon, and Irwin, Graham W., eds. *Harper Encyclopedia of the Modern World.* New York: Harper & Row, 1970.

Munchen. Med. Wchnschr. *Muenchener Medizinische Wochenschrift.* Munich, vol. 1, 1854- .

N.W. Med. *Northwest Medicine.* Seattle, vol. 1, 1903- .

N.Y. Med. J. *International Record of Medicine.* New York, vol. 1, April, 1865- . (1865-June 1881; 1883-1923 as *New York Medical Journal.*)

Nat. Acad. Sci. Biog. Mem. *National Academy of Sciences. Biographical Memoirs.* New York: Columbia University Press, 1877- .

Nat. Cyc. Amer. Biog. *The National Cyclopedia of American Biography.* New York: J. T. White & Co., 1893- .

Nat. Faculty Direct. *The National Faculty Directory.* Detroit: Gale Research Co., vol. 1, 1970- .

Nat. Soc. Stud. Educ. Yearbook *National Society for the Study of Education. Yearbook.* Chicago, nos. 1-5, 1895-1899; n.s., no. 1, 1902- .

Nat. Union Cat. *The National Union Catalog.* Compiled by the Library of Congress and the American Library Association. Ann Arbor: Edwards, 1953- .

Nature *Nature.* London, vol. 1, Nov. 4, 1869- .

Natuurwetensch. Tijdschr. *Natuurwetenschappelijk Tijdschrift.* Antwerp, vol. 1, 1914- .

Nederl. Tijdschr. v. geneesk. *Nederlandsch Tijdschrift voor Geneeskunde.* Amsterdam: Nederlandsche Maatschappij Tot Bevordering der Geneeskunst, vol. 1, 1857- .

Neue Deut. Biog. *Neue Deutsche Biographie.* Hrsg. von der Historischen Kommission bei der Bayerischen Akademie der Wissenschaften. Berlin: Duncker & Humblot, 1953- .

Neue Oesterr. Biog. *Neue Oesterreichische Biographie, 1815-1918.* Wien: Amalthea-Verlag, 1923- .

Neue Schweiz. Biog. *Neue Schweizer Biographie.* Ed. by Albert T. Bruckner. Basel: Buchdruckerei zum Basler Berichthaus Ag, 1938.

Neurology *Neurology.* Minneapolis: American Academy of Neurology, vol. 1, Jan./Feb. 1951- .

New Catholic Encyc. *The New Catholic Encyclopedia.* 15 vols. New York: McGraw-Hill, 1967.

New Cent. Clas. Handb. *The New Century Classical Handbook.* Ed. by Catherine B. Avery. New York: Appleton-Century-Crofts, 1962.

New Encyc. Brit. *The New Encyclopaedia Britannica.* 15th ed. 30 vols. Cover title: *Encyclopaedia Britannica.* Chicago: Encyclopaedia Britannica, 1974. (Divided into Micropedia and Macropedia.)

New Schaff-Herzog Encyc. Rel. Know. *New Schaff-Herzog Encyclopedia of Religious Knowledge.* Ed. by Samuel Macauley Jackson. Grand Rapids, Mich.: Baker Book House, 1950.

New York Acad. Med. Portrait Cat. *New York Academy of Medicine, Library. Portrait Catalog.* 5 vols. Boston: G. K. Hall, 1960.

New York J. Dent. *New York Journal of Dentistry.* New York: Society of the State of New York, vol. 1, 1931- .

New York Times *The New York Times.* Daily newspaper. New York, vol. 1, Sept. 18, 1851- .

New York Times Index *The New York Times Index.* New York, vol. 1, Jan./March 1913- .

New Yorker *New Yorker.* New York, vol. 1, Feb. 21, 1925- .

Newhall Newhall, Beaumont. *Photography: A Short Critical History.* 2d revised ed. New York: The Museum of Modern Art, 1938.

Newsweek *Newsweek.* Dayton, Ohio and New York, vol. 1, Feb. 17, 1933- .

Nieuw Nederl. Biog. Woordenb. *Nieuw Nederlandsch Biografisch Woordenboeck.* Ed. by Philip Christiaan Molhuysen. 10 vols. Leiden: A. W. Sijhoff, 1911-1937.

Nord. Med. *Nordisk Medicin.* Helsingfors, vol. 1, Jan. 7, 1939- .

Norges Laeger *Norges Laeger, 1800-1908.* Ed. by Isak Kobro. 3. udg. af F. C. Kiaer: Norges Laeger i det Nittende Aarhundrede (1800-1886) 2 vols. Kristiana: A Cammermeyer, 1915.

Norsk Allkunnebok *Norsk Allkunnebok.* Ed. by Arnalv Sudman. Oslo: Fonna Forlag, 1948.

Norsk Biog. Lek. *Norsk Biografisk Leksikon.* Ed. by Edvard Bull. Kristiana: H. Aschehoug, 1923.

Nos Docteurs *Nos Docteurs.* Paris, 2d s., 1897?

Nouv. Biog. Univ. *Nouvelle Biographie Generale depuis les Temps les Plus Recules jusqu'a nos Jours.* Ed. by Jean Hoefer. 46 vols. Paris: Didot Freres, 1852-1856.

Nu Sigma Nu Bull. *Nu Sigma Nu Bulletin.* Madison, Wis., 1910?- .

Odiorne Odiorne, George S. *Management Decisions by Objectives.* Englewood Cliffs, N.J.: Prentice-Hall, 1969.

Oesterr. Biog. Lex., 1815-1950 *Oesterreichisches Biographisches Lexikon, 1815-1950.* Graz: H. Boehlaus Nachf., 1957 (i.e. 1954). (Issued by Oesterreichischen Akademie der Wissenschaften.)

Osborne Osborne, Harold, ed. *The Oxford Companion to Art.* Oxford: Clarendon Press, 1970.

Otorinolar. Ital. *Oto-Rino-Laringologia Italiana.* Bologna, vol. 1, Aug. 1930- .

Oursel Oursel, Noemi Noire. *Nouvelle Biographie Normande.* 2 vols. in 1. Paris: A. Picard, 1886-1888. Supplement. Paris: A. Picard, 1888.

Oxford Clas. Dict. *The Oxford Classical Dictionary.* Ed. by N. G. L. Hammond and H. H. Scullard. 2d ed. Oxford: Clarendon Press, 1970.

Oxford Eng. Dict. *Oxford English Dictionary.* Ed. by James A. H. Murray. 12 vols. and supplement. Oxford: Clarendon Press, 1933.

Pagel Pagel, Julius Leopold. *Biographisches Lexikon Hervorragender Aerzte des Neunzehnten Jahrundeerts.* Berlin: Urban & Schwarzenburg, 1901.

Paris, Soc. Biol. Mem. Societe de Biologie, Paris. *Comptes Rendus Hebdomadaires des Seances et Memoires.* Paris, vol. 1, 1849- .

Partington Partington, James Riddick. *A History of Chemistry.* 3 vols. in 4. London: Macmillan, 1961-1970.

Partridge Partridge, Eric. *Name into Word.* 2d ed. Freeport, N.J.: Books for Libraries, 1970 (c. 1950).

Pennak Pennak, Robert W. *Collegiate Dictionary of Zoology.* New York: Ronald Press, 1964.

People *People Weekly.* Chicago: Time, Inc., vol. 1, Mar. 4, 1974- .

Pharmaceut. (Pharmazeut.) Rundschau *Pharmaceutische Rundschau.* Prague and Vienna, vols. 1-28, 1873-1902?

Phi Beta Pi Q. *Phi Beta Pi Medical Fraternity. Quarterly.* St. Paul, vols. 1-56, 1904?-1959. (1904?-1928 as the *Phi Beta Pi Quarterly.*)

Phyfe Phyfe, William Henry. *5,000 Facts and Fancies.* Reprint of the 1901 ed. Detroit: Gale Research Co., 1966.

Phys. Surg. Amer. *Physicians and Surgeons of America.* Ed. by Irving A. Watson. Concord, N. H.: Republican Press Association, 1896.

Physicians Mayo Clinic Mayo Clinic, Rochester, Minn. *Physicians of the Mayo Clinic and Mayo Foundation.* St. Paul, Minn.: Bruce, 1923.

Picken Picken, Mary Brooks. *The Fashion Dictionary.* New York: Funk & Wagnalls, 1973.

Pogg. Poggendorff, Johann Christian, ed. *Biographisch-Literarisches Handwoerterbuch fuer Mathematik, Astronomie, Physik, mit Geophysik, Chemie, Kristallographie und Verwandte Wissensgebiete.* Leipzig: J. A. Barth, 1863-1904.

Polk's Med. Reg. *Polk's Medical Register and Directory of North America.* Detroit, 1886- .

Polska Gaz. lek. *Polska Gazeta Lekarska.* Krakow, vols. 1-18, no. 34/35, 1922-Aug. 1939.

Poorman Poorman, Alfred Peter. *Strength of Materials.* 4th ed. New York: McGraw-Hill, 1945.

Postgrad. Med. *Postgraduate Medicine.* Minneapolis: Interstate Postgraduate Medical Association of North America, vol. 1, Jan. 1947- .

Preminger Preminger, Alexander, ed. *Encyclopedia of Poetry and Poetics.* Princeton, N.J.: Princeton University Press, 1965.

Presse Med. *Presse Medicale.* Paris, vol. 1, Dec. 23, 1893- .

Pritzel Pritzel, Georg August, ed. *Thesaurus Literaturae Botanicae Omnium Gentium.* Leipzig: F. A. Brockhaus, 1872-1887.

Proc. Amer. Phil. Soc., Phila. *American Philosophical Society. Proceedings.* Philadelphia, vol. 1, 1838- .

Proc. Inst. Med. Chicago *Institute of Medicine of Chicago. Proceedings.* Vol. 1, 1916- .

Proc. Vol. of Geol. Soc. Amer. *Geological Society of America. Proceedings.* New York, vol. 46, 1933- . (vols. 1-45, 1888-1932 in the Society's *Bulletin*)

Prom. Pers. USSR *Prominent Personalities in the USSR.* Ed. by Edward L. Crowley, et al. Metuchen, N.J.: Scarecrow, 1968.

Psych. Abstr. *Psychological Abstracts.* Lancaster, Pa.: American Psychological Abstracts, vol. 1, Jan. 1927- .

Psych. Reg. *Psychological Register.* Ed. by Carl Murchison, et al. 3 vols. Worcester, Mass.: Clark University Press, 1929-1932.

Psych. Rev. *Psychological Review.* Lancaster, Pa., vol. 1, 1894- .

Psychiatr-Neurolog. Wochenschr. *Psychiatrisch-Neurologische Wochenschrift.* Halle, vols. 1-47, nos. 9-13, May 1, 1889-1945.

Psycho Sources *Psycho Sources.*

Quarterly Cum. Ind. Med. *Quarterly Cumulative Index Medicus.* Chicago: American Medical Association, vols. 1-60, Jan. 1927-Dec. 1956.

Quick Quick, John *Dictionary of Weapons and Military Terms.* New York: McGraw-Hill, 1973.

Ranz Ranz, Jim. *The Printed Book Catalogue in American Libraries: 1723-1900.* Chicago: American Library Association, 1964.

Rass. Ital. d'Ottalm. *Rassegna Italiana d'Ottalmologia.* Torino, vol. 1, 1932- .

Rees' Cycl. Rees, Abraham. *Cyclopaedia; or Universal Dictionary of Arts, Sciences and Literature.* 41 vols. and 6 vols. plates. Philadelphia: Bradford, n.d.

Repert. Anal. Chem. *Repertorium der Analytischen Chemie fuer Handel Gewerbe, und Offentliche Gesundheitspflege.* Leipzig and Hamburg: Verein Analytischer Chemiker, vols. 1-7, 1881-1887.

Rev. Colombiana *Revista Colombiana de Pediatria y Puericultura.* Bogota, vol. 1, Oct. 1941- .

Rev. cubana de oftal., Habana *Revista Cubana de Oftalmologia.* Habana, vols. 1-4, no. 2, 1919-June 1922.

Rev. Gen. Bot. *Revue Generale de Botanique.* Paris, vol. 1, 1889- .

Rev. Gen. Sci. *Revue Generale des Sciences Pures et Appliques.* Paris, vol. 1, 1890- .

Rev. hebd. Lar. Otol. Rhinol., Paris *Revue de Laryngologie, d'Otologie et de Rhinologie.* Paris, vol. 1, Aug. 1880- . (vols. 16-35, 1896-1915 as *Revue Hebdomadaire de Laryngologie, d'Otologie et de Rhinologie.*)

Rev. Med. de Nancy *Revue Medicale de Nancy.* Paris and Nancy, vol. 1, 1874- .

Rev. Metal. *Revue de Metallurgie.* Paris: Societe d'Encouragement pour l'Industrie Nationale; Comite des Forges de France, vols. 1-56, 1904-May 1959.

Rev. Stiint. Med. *Revista Stiintelor Medicale.* Bucharest: Societatea Stiintelor Medicale Din Republica Populara Romana, vols. 1-37, no. 11/12, 1905-Nov./Dec. 1948; n.s., vol. 1, Aug. 1949- .

Revista de Biologia *Revista de Biologia.* Buenos Aires: Association Medica Argentina, vol. 1, 1925- .

Revue Medic. Suisse Rom. *Revue Medicale de la Suisse Romande.* Lausanne and Geneva: Societe Medicale de la Suisse Romande, vol. 1, 1881- .

Richter Richter, Charles F. *Elementary Seismology.* San Francisco: Freeman, 1955.

Riemann *Riemann Musik Lexikon.* Ed. by Wilibald Gurlitt. 3 vols. Mainz: B. Schott's Soehne, 1959-1961.

Riv. Sci. Ind. *Rivista Scientifico-Industriale delle Principali Scoperte ed Invenzioni Fatte Nelle Scienze e Nelle Industrie.* Florence, vols. 1-41, 1869-1909.

Rosenthal Rosenthal, Eric, ed. *Southern African Dictionary of National Biography.* London: Warne, 1966.

Royal Soc. Biog. Mem. of Fellows *Royal Society of London. Biographical Memoirs of Fellows.* London: Royal Society, vol. 1, 1955- . (Supersedes the Society's *Obituary Notices of Fellows.*)

Royal Soc. Cat. Sci. Pap. *Royal Society of London. Catalogue of Scientific Papers, 1800-1900.* 19 vols. London: The Society, 1867-1925.

Royal Soc. Obit. Not. of Fellows *Royal Society of London. Obituary Notices of Fellows.* London: Royal Society, vols. 1-9, Dec. 1932-Nov. 1954. (Superseded by the Society's *Biographical Memoirs of Fellows.*)

Royal Soc. of Canada. Proc. and Trans. *Royal Society of Canada. Proceedings and Transactions.* Ottawa and Montreal, vols. 1-12, 1882-1894; s. 2, vols. 1-12, 1895-1906; s. 3, vol. 1, 1907- .

Royal Soc. Proc. *Royal Society of London. Proceedings.* London: Royal Society, vols. 1-75, 1800-1905; vol. 76, 1905- , in 2 sections: A (Math./Physics) + B (Biol.).

Sadoul Sadoul, Georges. *Dictionary of Film Makers.* Translated by Peter Morris. Berkeley: University of California Press, 1972.

Sang, Paris *Sang: Biologie et Pathologie.* Paris, vol. 1, 1927- .

Satterthwaite Satterthwaite, Gilbert E. *Encyclopedia of Astronomy.* New York: St. Martin's Press, 1971.

Schles. Gesellsch. f. vaterl. Kultur, Breslau. Jahresb. *Schlesische Gesellschaft fuer Vaterlaendische Kultur, Breslau. Jahresbericht.* 1824-1849; vols. 28-108, 1850-1935. (Continued in 3 sections.)

Scholes Scholes, Percy. *The Oxford Companion to Music.* 10th ed. revised by John Owen Ward. London: Oxford University Press, 1970.

Schweiz. Med. Wchnschr. *Schweizerische Medizinische Wochenschrift.* Basel, vol. 1, 1870- .

Sci. *Science.* Lancaster, Pa., vols. 1-23, Feb. 9, 1883-Mar. 23, 1894; n.s., vol. 1, Jan. 4, 1895- .

Sci. Abstr. (Elec. Engin.) *Science Abstracts.* London and New York: American Physical Society, Section B. Electrical Engineering Abstracts, vol. 6, 1903- .

Scott Scott, Arthur Finley. *Current Literary Terms.* London: Macmillan, 1965.

Sebeok Sebeok, Thomas Albert, ed. *Portraits of Linguists; A Biographical Source Book for the History of Western Linguistics, 1746-1963.* 2 vols. Bloomington, Ind.: Indiana University Press, 1966.

Seldon Seldon, Arthur, and Pennance, F. G., comps. *Everyman's Dictionary of Economics.* London: J. M. Dent, 1965.

Sem. Hop. Inform. *Semaine des Hopitaux Informations.* Paris: Association d'Enseignemenet Medical des Hopitaux de Paris, vol. 1, Jan. 1961- .

Serrao Serrao, Joel, ed. *Dicionario de Historia de Portugal.* 4 vols. Lisboa: Iniciativas Editoriais, 1971.

Seyn   Seyn, Eugene de, ed. *Dictionnaire Biographique des Sciences, des Lettres et des Arts en Belgique.* 2 vols. Brussels: Editions L'Avenir, 1935.

Shockley   Shockley, Ann Allen, and Chandler, Sue P. *Living Black American Authors.* New York: Bowker, 1973.

Siecle Med.   *Siecle Medical.* Paris, vols. 1-2, no. 31, May 1, 1880-1881.

Singer   Singer, Charles J., ed. *A History of Technology.* 5 vols. New York: Oxford University Press, 1954-1958.

Smith   Smith, Edward Conrad, and Zurcher, Arnold John. *A Dictionary of American Politics.* Revised ed. New York: Barnes & Noble, 1946.

Smith, E. F.   Smith, Edgar Fahs. *Chemistry in America.* New York: Appleton, 1929.

Sobel   Sobel, Robert, ed. *Biographical Directory of the United States Executive Branch, 1774-1971.* Westport, Conn.: Greenwood Publishing Co., 1971.

Southall   Southall, James P. C. *Introduction to Physiological Optics.* New York: Oxford University Press, 1937.

Speert   Speert, Harold. *Obstetric and Gynecologic Milestones; Essays in Eponymy.* New York: Macmillan, 1958.

Sport Brockhaus   *Der Sport Brockhaus.* Wiesbaden: F. A. Brockhaus, 1971.

Sprawozd. Towarzystowo Nauk. Lwowie.   *Towarzystowo Naukowe We Lwowie. Sprawozdania.* vol. 1, 1921- .

Std. Encyc. So. Afr.   *Standard Encyclopedia of South Africa.* Capetown: Nason, Ltd., 1st ed., 1972- .

Stedman   *Stedman's Medical Dictionary.* 22d ed. Baltimore: William & Wilkins, 1972.

Steinberg   Steinberg, Sigfrid Henry, and Evans, Ivor H., eds. *Steinberg's Dictionary of British History.* 2d ed. New York: St. Martin's Press, 1971.

Stenhouse   Stenhouse, Thomas. *Lives Enshrined in Language.* Reprint of the 1928 ed. Ann Arbor: Gryphon, 1971.

Stenton   Stenton, Frank Merry. *Anglo-Saxon England.* 3d ed. Oxford: Clarendon Press, 1971. (The Oxford History of England # 2)

Stevenson   Stevenson, Burton Egbert, comp. *The Home Book of Modern Verse.* 2d ed. New York: Henry Holt & Co., 1953.

Strahlen.   *Strahlentherapie.* Berlin, vol. 1, 1912- .

Surrey   Surrey, Alexander R. *Name Reactions in Organic Chemistry.* 2d ed. New York: Academic Press, 1961.

Svensk Laekarmatrikel   *Svensk Laekarmatrikel, 1970.* Stockholm: Bokfoerlaget Vem Ar Vem ab/ Haegers, 1970.

Svensk Uppslagsbok   *Svensk Uppslagsbok.* ed. by Gunnar Carlquist and Josef Carlsson. Malmo, Sweden: Forlagschuset Norden, 1947-1948.

Svenska Maen Och Kvinnor   *Svenska Maen Och Kvinnor; Biografisk Uppslagsbok.* Ed. by Nils Bohman. 8 vols. Stockholm: Albert Bonniers Forlag, 1942-1955.

Svenska Vetensk. Akad. Arsbok   *Svenska Vetenskapsakademien, Stockholm. Arsbok.* 1903- .

Svenskt Biog. Handlex.   *Svenskt Biografiskt Handlexikon.* Ed. by Hermann Hofberg. 2 pt. in 1 vol. Stockholm: A Bonnier, 1873-1876.

Taylor, I.   Taylor, Isaac. *Names and Their Histories; A Handbook of Historical Geography and Topographical Nomenclature.* Reprint of the 1898 (2d) ed. Detroit: Gale Research Co., 1969.

Taylor, N.   Taylor, Norman. *Taylor's Encyclopedia of Gardening.* 4th ed. Boston: Houghton Mifflin, 1961.

Temple Dent. Rev.   *Temple Dental Review and Garretsonian.* Philadelphia: Temple University, Dental School, vol. 1, Nov. 1930- .

Thewlis   Thewlis, James. *Concise Dictionary of Physics and Related Subjects.* Oxford: Pergamon, 1973.

Thewlis, unabridged   Thewlis, James, ed. *Encyclopaedic Dictionary of Physics.* 8 vols. New York: Pergamon Press, 1961-1963.

Thompson   Thompson, Elizabeth, comp. *A.L.A. Glossary of Library Terms.* Chicago: American Library Association, 1943.

Thompson, O.   Thompson, Oscar. *The International Cyclopedia of Music and Musicians.* 9th ed. Ed. by Robert Sabin. New York: Dodd Mead, 1964.

Thompson, S.P.   Thompson, Silvanus P. *The Life of William Thompson, Baron Kelvin of Largs.* 2 vols. London: Macmillan, 1910.

Thrush   Thrush, Paul, ed. *A Dictionary of Mining, Mineral and Related Terms.* Washington, D.C.: U.S. Bureau of Mines, 1968.

Time   *Time; the Weekly News-Magazine.* New York, vol. 1, March 3, 1923- .

Toulouse Soc. Sci. Bull.   *Societe des Sciences Physiques et Naturelles de Toulouse. Bulletin.* Toulouse, France, vols. 1-8, 1872-1889.

Transact. Norfolk Norwich Naturalists' Soc.   *Norfolk and Norwich Naturalists' Society. Transactions.* Norwich, Eng., vol. 1, 1869/1974- .

Treadwell   Treadwell, Frederick Pearson. *Analytical Chemistry.* 8th ed. 2 vols. New York: Wiley, 1935.

Turkevich   Turkevich, John. *Soviet Men of Science; Academicians and Corresponding Members of the Academy of Sciences of the USSR.* Princeton, N.J.: Van Nostrand, 1963.

Turkevich and Turkevich   Turkevich, John, and Turkevich, Ludmilla B. *Prominent Scientists of Continental Europe.* New York: American Elsevier, 1968.

Ugeskr. Laeg.   *Ugeskrift for Laeger.* Copenhagen: Almanna Danske Laegeforening. vol. 1, May 4, 1839- .

Ule   Ule, Willi. *Geschichte de Kaiserlichen Leopoldinisch-Carolinischen Deutschen Akademie der Naturforscher.* Halle: E. Blochmann und Sohn in Dresden, 1889.

Univ. Liege   L'Universite de Liege. *Liber Memorialis de l'Universite de Liege de 1867 a 1935.* Notices Biographiques publiees par les soins de Leon Halkin. Liege: Rectorat de l'Universite (Gembloux: J. Duculot), 1936.

Univ. Poznanski   *Uniwersytet Poznanski w Pierwszych Latach Swego Istnienia (1919-1923).* Ed. by Adam Wrzosek. Poznan: Odbito w Drukarni Uniwersytetu Poznanskiego, 1924.

Upjohn   Upjohn, Everard M.; Wingert, Paul; and Mahler, Jane Gaston. *History of World Art.* New York: Oxford University Press, 1949.

Urmson   Urmson, J. O., ed. *The Concise Encyclopedia of Western Philosophy and Philosophers.* 1st ed. New York: Hawthorn Books, 1960.

Valentine   Valentine, Alan. *The British Establishment, 1760-1784; An Eighteenth Century Biographical Dictionary.* 2 vols. Norman: University of Oklahoma Press, 1970.

Van Nostrand Chem. Dict.   *The Van Nostrand Chemist's Dictionary.* Ed. by Jurgen M. Honig, et al. Princeton, N.J.: Van Nostrand, 1953.

Van Nostrand Sci. Encyc.   *Van Nostrand Scientific Encyclopedia.* 4th ed. Princeton, N.J.: Van Nostrand, 1968.

Vem Ar Det?   *Vem Ar Det? Svensk Biografisk Handbok.* Stockholm: Norstedt, vol. 1, 1912-   .

Verh. Deut. Pathol. Ges.   *Deutsche Gesellschaft fuer Pathologie.* Jena and Stuttgart: vol. 1, 1898-   . (Supersedes Deutsche Pathologische Gesellschaft. Verhandlungen.)

Vestnik statniho geolog. ustavu   *Vestnik Statniho Geologickeho Ustavu Ceskoslovenske Republiky.* Praha, 1925-1950.

Vopr. Neurokhir.   *Voprosy Neurokhirurgii.* Moskva, vol. 1, 1936-   .

Voyenno-Med. J.   *Voyenno-Meditsinskii Journal.* St. Petersburg, vols. 1-181, 1823-1894.

W. Va. Med. J.   *West Virginia Medical Journal.* Charleston: West Virginia State Medical Association, vol. 1, Aug. 1, 1906-   .

Wagner (More Names)   Wagner, Leopold. *More About Names.* Reprint of the 1898 ed. Detroit: Gale Research Co., 1968.

Wagner (Names)   Wagner, Leopold. *Names and Their Meaning.* Reprint of the 1893 ed. Detroit: Gale Research Co., 1968.

Warsz. Czas. lek.   *Warszawskie Czasopismo Lekarskie.* Warszawa, vol. 1, 1924-   .

Watford Building Research Station Bibliog.   *Watford Building Research Station. Bibliography.* No. 158. Watford, Eng., 1954.

Wayne County Med. Soc. Bull.   *Detroit Medical News.* Chicago: Wayne County Medical Society, vol. 1, Oct. 1909-   . (Vols. 13-24 as *Wayne County Medical Society. Bulletin.*)

Webster, H. T.   Webster, Harold Tucker. *The Timid Soul; a Pictorial Account of the Life and Times of Casper Milquetoast.* New York: Simon and Schuster, 1931.

Webster's Biog. Dict.   *Webster's Biographical Dictionary.* 1st ed. Springfield, Mass.: G. & C. Merriam Co., 1972 (c. 1967?).

Webster's 2d   *Webster's New International Dictionary of the English Language.* 2d ed. Unabridged. Ed. by William Allan Nielson. Springfield, Mass.: G. & C. Merriam Co., 1935.

Webster's 3d   *Webster's Third New International Dictionary of the English Language.* Unabridged. Ed. by Philip Babcock Gove, et al. Springfield, Mass.: G. & C. Merriam Co., 1971.

Weekley   Weekley, Ernest. *An Etymological Dictionary of Modern English.* 2 vols. New York: Dover, 1967.

Wer Ist Wer?   *Wer Ist Wer? Das Deutsche Who's Who.* Berlin: Arani, vol. 1, 1905-   . (Vols. 1-9 as *Wer Ist's?*)

"Wer Ist Wer" Lex. Oesterr. Zeitgen.   *"Wer Ist Wer"; Lexikon Oesterreichischer Zeitgenossen.* Ed. by Robert Teichl and Paul Emodi. Wien: Selbstverlag des Biographischen Lexikons "Wer Ist Wer."

Wer Ist's?   See: **Wer Ist Wer?**

Westermann Lex. der Geog.   *Westermann Lexikon der Geographie.* Ed. by Wolf Tietze. 4 vols. Braunschweig: Georg Westermann Verlag, 1970.

Who Was Who   *Who Was Who; A Companion to Who's Who, Containing the Biographies of Those Who Died. . .* London: Adam & Charles Black, vol. 1, 1897/1916-   .

Who Was Who Amer.   *Who Was Who in America.* Chicago: A.N. Marquis Co., vol. 1, 1897/1942-   .

Who Was Who USSR   *Who Was Who in the USSR.* Compiled by the Institute for the Study of the USSR. Ed. by Heinrich E. Schulz, et al. Metuchen, N.J.: The Scarecrow Press, 1972.

Who's Imp. Med.   *American Men of Medicine.* New York: Institute for Research in Biography, 1st ed., 1945-   . (1st and 2d eds., 1945, 1952 as *Who's Important in Medicine.*)

Who's Who   *Who's Who; An Annual Biographical Dictionary.* London: Adam & Charles Black, 1st ed., 1849-   .

Who's Who Amer.   *Who's Who in America.* Chicago: A. N. Marquis Co., vol. 1, 1899/1900-   .

Who's Who Amer. Educ.   *Who's Who in American Education; A Biographical Dictionary of Eminent Living Educators of the United States.* New York: Who's Who in American Education, vol. 1, 1928-   .

Who's Who Amer. Med.   *Who's Who in American Medicine.* New York: Who's Who Publications, vol. 1, 1925-   .

Who's Who Amer. Women   *Who's Who of American Women; A Biographical Dictionary of Notable Living American Women.* Chicago: Marquis-Who's Who, vol. 1, 1958/1959-   .

Who's Who Among Physicians and Surg.   *Who's Who Among Physicians and Surgeons.* Ed. by J. C. Schwarz. New York: n.p., 1938.

Who's Who Australia   *Who's Who in Australia.* 1st ed. Melbourne: Herald and Weekly Times Ltd., 1922-   .

Who's Who Belg.   *Who's Who in Belgium and the Grand Duchy of Luxembourg.* Brussels: Intercontinental Book and Publishing Co., 1st ed., 1957/1958-   .

Who's Who Brit. Engin.   *Who's Who of British Engineers.* London: Macmillan, vol. 1, 1966-   .

Who's Who Brit. Sci.   *Who's Who in British Science.* London: L. Hill, 1953-   . (Superseded by *Directory of British Scientists.*)

Who's Who Brit. Scientists   *Who's Who of British Scientists.* London: Longman, 1969/1970-   . (Supersedes *Directory of British Scientists.*)

Who's Who Central East Europe   *Who's Who in Central and East Europe.* Zurich: Central European Times Publishing Co., 1st ed., 1933/1934-   .

Who's Who East   *Who's Who in the East and Eastern Canada.* Chicago: Marquis Who's Who, 1st ed., 1942/1943-   .

Who's Who Engin.   *Who's Who in Engineering; A Biographical Directory of the Engineering Profession.* New York: Lewis Historical Publishing Co., vol. 1, 1922/1923-   .

Who's Who Fin. Ind.   *Who's Who in Finance and Industry.* Chicago: Marquis Who's Who, 17th ed., 1972/1973-   .

Who's Who France   *Who's Who in France.* Paris: J. Lafitte, 1st ed., 1953/1954-   .

Who's Who Ger.   *Who's Who in Germany.* Munich: Intercontinental Book and Publishing Co., Inc., vol. 1, 1956-   .

Who's Who Israel   *Who's Who Israel.* Tel Aviv: Who's Who in the State of Israel Publishing House, 1st ed., 1945/1946-   . (1st ed., 1945/1946 as *The Near and Middle East Who's Who.*)

Who's Who Italy *Who's Who in Italy.* Milano: Intercontinental Book and Publishing Co., vol. 1, 1957/1958- .

Who's Who Latin Amer. *Who's Who in Latin America.* Stanford, Calif.: Stanford University Press, 1st ed., 1935- .

Who's Who Libr. Service *Who's Who in Library Service.* New York: H. W. Wilson, 1st ed., 1933- .

Who's Who Librarianship *Who's Who in Librarianship.* Ed. by Thomas Landau. Cambridge, Eng.: Bowes & Bowes, 1954.

Who's Who Librarianship Info. Sci. *Who's Who in Librarianship and Information Science.* Ed. by Thomas Landau. 2d ed. London: Abelard-Schuman, 1972.

Who's Who Methodist Church *Who's Who in the Methodist Church.* Compiled by the editors of Who's Who in America and the A.N. Marquis Co., Inc. Nashville, Tenn.: Abingdon Press, 1966.

Who's Who Netherl. *Who's Who in the Netherlands.* Ed. by Stephen S. Taylor and Martinus Spruytenburg. New York: Intercontinental Book and Publishing Co., Ltd., 1st ed., 1962- .

Who's Who New Zealand *Who's Who in New Zealand.* Wellington: A. H. & A. W. Reed, vol. 1, 1908- .

Who's Who Pro. Baseball *Who's Who in Professional Baseball.* Ed. by Gene Karst and Martin J. Mones. New Rochelle, N.Y.: Arlington House, 1973.

Who's Who S. Africa *Who's Who of Southern Africa.* Johannesburg: Combined Publishers, Ltd., vol. 1, 1905?- .

Who's Who Sci. Europe *Who's Who in Science in Europe; A New Reference Guide to West European Scientists.* Guernsey, Channel Islands: F. Hodgson, 1st ed., 1967- .

Who's Who South Southwest *Who's Who in the South and Southwest.* Chicago: A. N. Marquis Co., vol. 1, 1950- .

Who's Who Spain *Who's Who in Spain.* Montreal: Intercontinental Book and Publishing Co., Ltd., 1st ed., 1963- .

Who's Who Switz. *Who's Who in Switzerland, Including the Principality of Lichtenstein.* Zurich: Central European Times Publishing Co., vol. 1, 1950/1951- .

Who's Who USSR *Who's Who in the USSR.* Compiled by the Institute for the Study of the USSR, Munich. Montreal: Intercontinental Book and Publishing Co., vol. 1, 1961/1962- .

Wiadomosci Lekarskie *Wiadomosci Lekarskie.* Warsaw: Zakblad Ubezpieczen Spolecznych; Rada Naukowa Lekarska, vol. 1, 1948- .

Wickwire Wickwire, Franklin, and Wickwire, Mary. *Cornwallis: The American Adventure.* Boston: Houghton-Mifflin, 1970.

Wie is dat? *Wie is dat? Biografische Gegevens van Nederlanders.* s'-Gravenhage, Netherlands: Martinus Wijhoff, vol. 1, 1931- .

Wien. Klin. Wchnschr. *Wiener Klinische Wochenschrift.* Vienna and Leipzig: Gesellschaft der Aerzte zu Wien, vol. 1, April 5, 1888- . (Vol. 58 also called n.s. vol. 1.)

Wien Med. Wchnschr. *Wien Medizinische Wochenschrift.* Vienna, vol. 1, April 5, 1851- .

Winburne Winburne, John N. *A Dictionary of Agriculture and Allied Terminology.* East Lansing, Mich.: Michigan State University Press, 1962.

Winick Winick, Charles. *Dictionary of Anthropology.* Totowa, N.J.: Littlefield Adams, 1970 (c. 1956?).

Wisconsin Med. J. *Wisconsin Medical Journal.* Milwaukee: State Medical Society of Wisconsin, vol. 1, 1903- .

Wolman Wolman, Benjamin B., ed. *Dictionary of Behavioral Science.* New York: Van Nostrand, 1973.

Wood Wood, William Wallace. *The Walschaert Locomotive Valve Gear.* New York: Norman W. Henley, 1908.

World Authors *World Authors.* Ed. by John Wakeman. New York: H. W. Wilson, 1975.

World Direct. Math. *World Directory of Mathematicians.* Bombay: Tata Institute of Fundamental Research, 1st ed., 1958- . (Published under the Auspices of the International Mathematical Union.)

World Who's Who Sci. *World Who's Who in Science; a Biographical Dictionary of Notable Scientists from Antiquity to the Present.* Ed. by Allen G. Debus. Chicago: Marquis-Who's Who, Inc., 1968.

Wurzbach Wurzbach, Constantin, ed. *Biographisches Lexikon des Kaiserthums Oesterreich.* Wien: L. C. Zamarski, 1856-1891.

Z. Anorg. Allgem. Chem. *Zeitschrift fuer Anorganische und Allgemeine Chemie.* Hamburg and Leipzig, vol. 1, Feb. 27, 1892- .

Z. f. Morphologie u. Anthropologie *Zeitschrift fuer Morphologie und Anthropologie.* Stuttgart, vol. 1, 1899- .

Z. Kristallogr. *Zeitschrift fuer Kristallographie, Kristallogeometrie, Kristallphysik, Kristallchemie.* Leipzig and Frankfort a. Main, vol. 1, 1877- .

Z. Larngo. Rhino. Oto. und Ihre Grenzgebiete *Zeitschrift fuer Laryngologie, Rhinologie, Otologie und Ihre Grenzbebiete.* Stuttgart vol. 1, April 27/May, 1948- .

Z. Orthop. Chir. *Zeitschrift fuer Orthopaedie und Ihre Grenzgebiete.* Stuttgart and Berlin: Deutsche Orthopaedische Gesellschaft, vol. 1, 1891- . (Vols. 1-63, 1891-1935, as Zeitschrift fuer Orthopaedische Chirurgie, Einschliesslich der Heilgymnastik und Massage.)

Zadrozny Zadrozny, John T. *Dictionary of Social Science.* Washington: Public Affairs Press, 1959.

Zentralb. Allg. Path. Path. Anat. *Zentralblatt fuer Allgemeine Pathologie und Pathologische Anatomie.* Jena and Wurzburg: Deutsche Pathologische Gesellschaft, vol. 1, 1890- .

Zentralb. f. Mineralogie *Zentralblatt fuer Mineralogie, Geologie und Paleontologie.* Stuttgart, 1830-1949. (Continued as Neues Jahrbuch fuer Mineralogie, Geologie und Paleontologie. Monatshefte. Stuttgart. 1950- .)

EPONYMS DICTIONARIES INDEX

A

a la Beauharnais (Beauharnais family): Food and Drink. See: De Sola.

a la Croissy (Croissy, Charles Colbert, Marquis de): Food and Drink. See: De Sola.

a la Houmy (style) (Houmy, Comtesse de): Food and Drink. See: De Sola.

a la Maintenon (Maintenon, Francoise D'Aubigne, Marquise de): Food and Drink. See: Charnock; De Sola.

a la Massena (Rivoli, Andre Massena Duc de): Food and Drink. See: De Sola.

a la Mazarine (Mazarin, Jules): Food and Drink. See: Charnock.

a la Meyerbeer (Meyerbeer, Giacomo): Food and Drink. See: De Sola.

a la Parmentier (Parmentier, Antoine-August). See: Parmentier(e).

a la Pompadour (Pompadour, Jeanne Antoinette Poisson, Marquise de): Food and Drink. See: De Sola.

a la Richelieu (Richelieu, Armand Jean du Plessis, Cardinal and Duc de): Food and Drink. See: De Sola.

a la Rossini (Rossini, Gioachinno Antonio): Food and Drink. See: De Sola.

A. B. Taylor cylinder press (Taylor, Alva B.): Printing. See: Lockwood under "Press."

A. J. Mundella's Act (Mundella, Anthony John): Education. See: Steinberg under "Education Acts."

AARON. fl. 1200 B.C. Jewish patriarch. See: Encyc. Brit., 1973. Aaron lily, Aaronical, Aaronite, Aaron's beard, Aaron's rod, Aaron's serpent.

AARON, CHARLES DETTIE. 1866-1951. American physician. See: Who's Who Amer. Med. Aaron's sign.

Aaron lily (Aaron): Botany. See: Hendrickson.

Aaronical (Aaron): Generic Word. See: Hendrickson.

Aaronite (Aaron): Religion. See: Webster's 3d.

Aaron's beard (Aaron): Botany. See: Brewer; Gray; Winburne.

Aaron's rod (Aaron): Botany. See: Brewer; Gray; Partridge.

Aaron's serpent (Aaron): Generic Word. See: Brewer; Hendrickson.

Aaron's sign (Aaron, Charles Dettie): Medicine. See: Dorland; Stedman.

ABADIE, CHARLES (In full: JEAN MARIE CHARLES). 1842-1932. French ophthalmologist. See: Biog. Lex. hervorr. Aerzte. Abadie's sign.

ABADIE, JOSEPH LOUIS IRENEE JEAN. 1873-1946. French neurosurgeon. See: Biog. Lex. hervorr. Aerzte. Abadie's sign of tabes dorsalis.

Abadie's sign (Abadie, Charles): Medicine. See: Dorland; Hinsie; Jablonski.

Abadie's sign of tabes dorsalis (Abadie, Joseph Louis Irenee Jean): Medicine. See: Dorland; Stedman.

ABAILARD, PIERRE. 1079-1142. French philosopher and theologian. See: Dict. Sci. Biog. Eloisa and Abailard.

ABAS II. 1629-1666. Shah of Persia. See: Nouv. Biog. Univ. Abassi.

Abassi (Abas II): Numismatics. See: Hendrickson.

ABAZA, ALPHONSE. 1909- . French physician. Who's Who France. Hoet-Abaza syndrome?

ABBAD I. d. 1042. Moorish King of Seville. See: Nouv. Biog. Univ. Abbadides.

Abbadides (Abbad I): History. See: Hendrickson.

ABBAS (In full: ABBAS BEN ABDAL MOTALLEB). 566-652. Merchant of Mecca and uncle of Mohammed. See: Nouv. Biog. Univ. Abbassides.

Abbassides (Abbas): History. See: Brewer; Phyfe; Weekley.

ABBE, CLEVELAND. 1838-1916. American meteorologist and mathematician. See: Pogg., vols. 3, 4, 5. Abbe-Helmert criterion?

Abbe condenser (Abbe, Ernst Karl): Physics. See: Dorland; Pennak; Van Nostrand Sci. Encyc.

ABBE, ERNST KARL. 1840-1905. German physicist and industrialist. See: Dict. Sci. Biog. Abbe condenser, Abbe-Maxwell theorem, Abbe number, Abbe refractometer, Abbe sine condition, Abbe theory, Abbe-Zeiss apparatus.

Abbe-Estlander operation (Abbe and Estlander, Jakob August): Medicine. See: Stedman.

Abbe-Helmert criterion (Abbe, Cleveland? and Helmert, Friedrich Robert): Statistics. See: Kendall. Also known as: Helmert criterion.

Abbe jar (Abbe, Paul O): Earth Sciences. See: Thrush.

Abbe-Maxwell theorem (Abbe, Ernst Karl and Maxwell, James Clerk): Physics. See: Internat. Dict. Ap. Math.

Abbe number (Abbe, Ernst Karl): Physics. See: Focal Encyc. Photog.; Internat. Dict. Ap. Math.; Van Nostrand Sci. Encyc.

ABBE, PAUL O. fl. 1938. American inventor. Cited in: Chem. Abstr., vol. 32, p. 6513. Abbe jar, Abbe tube mill.

Abbe refractometer (Abbe, Ernst Karl): Physics. See: Thewlis; Van Nostrand Sci. Encyc.; Winburne.

ABBE, ROBERT. 1851-1928. American surgeon. See: World Who's Who Sci. Abbe's operation, Abbe's rings, Abbe's string method.

Abbe sine condition (Abbe, Ernst Karl): Physics. See: Ballentyne; Internat. Dict. Ap. Math.; Van Nostrand Sci. Encyc.

Abbe theory (Abbe, Ernst Karl): Physics. See: Ballentyne; Thrush; Van Nostrand Chem. Dict.

Abbe tube mill (Abbe, Paul O.): Earth Sciences. See: Thrush.

Abbe-Zeiss apparatus (Abbe, Ernst Karl and Zeiss, Carl): Medicine. See: Stedman.

Abbe's operation (Abbe, Robert): Medicine. See: Dorland.

Abbe's rings (Abbe, Robert): Medicine. See: Dorland.

Abbe's string method (Abbe, Robert): Medicine. See: Dorland.

Abbots' paste (Abbots, William A.): Medicine. See: Dorland.

ABBOTS, WILLIAM A. b. 1831. English physician. See: Biog. Lex. hervorr. Aerzte. Abbots' paste.

ABBOTT, ALEXANDER CREVER. 1860-1935. American bacteriologist. See: Who's Who Amer. Med. Abbott's stain.

ABBOTT, CHARLES (1ST BARON TENTERDEN). 1762-1832. English Lord Chief Justice. See: Dict. Nat. Biog. Tenterden's Act.

ABBOTT, EDVILLE GERHARDT. 1870-1938. American surgeon. See: Who's Who Amer. Med. Abbott's method.

ABBOTT, ERNEST JAMES. 1900- . American physicist. See: Who's Who Engin. Abbott profilometer.

Abbott-Miller tube (Abbott, William Osler and Miller, Thomas Grier). See: Miller-Abbott tube.

Abbott profilometer (Abbott, Ernest James): Engineering and Industry. See: Auger.

Abbott-Rawson tube (Abbott, William Osler and Rawson, Arthur Joy): Medicine. See: Dorland.

ABBOTT, WILLIAM OSLER. 1902-1943. American physician. See: World Who's Who Sci. Abbott-Rawson tube, Miller-Abbott tube.

Abbott's method (Abbott, Edville Gerhardt): Medicine. See: Dorland; Stedman.

Abbott's stain (Abbott, Alexander Crever): Medicine. See: Stedman.

Abbott's tube (Abbott, William Osler). See: Miller-Abbott tube.

ABD AL-QADIR AL JILANI. d. 1165. Islamic religious leader. (Biography source unavailable.) Qadiriyeh.

ABDERHALDEN, EMIL. 1877-1950. Swiss chemist and physiologist. See: World Who's Who Sci. Abderhalden-Fanconi syndrome, Abderhalden-Kautzsch test reaction, Abderhalden reaction or test, Abderhalden-Schmidt reagent, Abderhalden test reaction for cystine, Abderhalden-Weil test reaction.

Abderhalden-Fanconi syndrome (Abderhalden, Emil and Fanconi, Guido): Medicine. See: Jablonski. Also known as: Abderhalden-Kaufmann-Lignac syndrome, De Toni-Fanconi syndrome, Fanconi-De Toni-Debre syndrome, Fanconi's syndrome, Lignac-Fanconi syndrome, Lignac's disease.

Abderhalden-Kaufmann-Lignac syndrome (Abderhalden, Emil; Kaufmann; and Lignac, Georges Otto Emile). See: Abderhalden-Fanconi syndrome.

Abderhalden-Kautzsch test reaction (Abderhalden, Emil and Kautzsch, Karl Friedrich): Chemistry. See: Van Nostrand Chem. Dict.

Abderhalden reaction or test (Abderhalden, Emil): Medicine. See: Ballentyne; Dorland; Van Nostrand Chem. Dict.

Abderhalden-Schmidt reagent (Abderhalden, Emil and Schmidt, Hubert): Chemistry. See: Van Nostrand Chem. Dict.

Abderhalden test reaction for cystine (Abderhalden, Emil): Chemistry. See: Van Nostrand Chem. Dict.

Abderhalden-Weil test reaction (Abderhalden, Emil and Weil, Arthur): Chemistry. See: Van Nostrand Chem. Dict.

Abdim's stork (Derivation undetermined): Zoology. See: Gray.

ABDUL-MEDJID. 1823-1861. Turkish sultan. See: Encyc. Brit., 1973. Medjidie (order), Medjidite.

ABDUL-WAHHAB. 1691-1787. Mohammedan reformer. See: Webster's Biog. Dict. Wahabis.

Abe Lincoln bug (Lincoln, Abraham): Zoology. See: Gray.

ABEE, ERNST. 1843-1913. German physician. (Biography source unavailable.) Abee's support.

Abee's support (Abee, Ernst): Medicine. See: Dorland.

ABEGG, META VON. fl. 1830. German friend of Robert Schumann. (Biography source unavailable.) Abegg variations.

ABEGG, RICHARD. 1869-1910. Danish chemist. See: World Who's Who Sci. Abegg's rule.

Abegg variations (Abegg, Meta von): Music. See: Apel.

Abegg's rule (Abegg, Richard): Chemistry. See: Ballentyne; Dorland; Stedman.

ABEL. Biblical son of Adam and Eve. See: Encyc. Brit., 1973. Abelites.

ABEL, CLARKE. 1780-1826. English botanist. See: Dict. Nat. Biog. Abelia.

Abel equation (Abel, Niels Henrik): Mathematics. See: Internat. Dict. Ap. Math; Internat. Dict. Phys. Elec.

Abel flashpoint apparatus or tester (Abel, Sir Frederick Augustus): Chemistry. See: Thrush. Also known as: Abel-Pensky apparatus.

ABEL, SIR FREDERICK AUGUSTUS. 1827-1902. English chemist. See: Dict. Nat. Biog., 2nd suppl. Abel flashpoint apparatus or tester, Abel heat test, Abel reagent, Abel test reactions for ethyl sulfide, Abelite.

Abel heat test (Abel, Sir Frederick Augustus): Chemistry. See: Hackh; Thrush.

Abel identity (Abel, Niels Henrik): Mathematics. See: Ballentyne; Internat. Dict. Ap. Math.; James.

Abel inequality (Abel, Niels Henrik): Mathematics. See: Ballentyne; Internat. Dict. Ap. Math.

ABEL, JOHN JACOB. 1857-1938. American physiologist. See: Dict. Sci. Biog. Abel's vividiffusion apparatus.

ABEL, KARL FRIEDRICH. 1725-1787. German musician. See: Encyc. Brit., 1973. Bach-Abel concerts.

ABEL, NIELS HENRIK. 1802-1829. Norwegian mathematician. See: Dict. Sci. Biog. Abel equation, Abel identity, Abel inequality, Abel-Ruffini theorem, Abel test for convergence, Abel theorem on power series, Abelian group, Abel's test for infinite integrals, Abel's theorem on multiplication of series.

Abel-Pensky apparatus (Abel, Sir Frederick Augustus and Pensky, B. ?). See: Abel flashpoint apparatus.

Abel reagent (Abel, Sir Frederick Augustus): Chemistry. See: Hackh; Thrush; Van Nostrand Chem. Dict.

ABEL, RUDOLF. 1868-1942. German bacteriologist. See: Wer Ist's. Abel's bacillus.

Abel-Ruffini theorem (Abel, Niels Henrik and Ruffini, Paolo): Mathematics. Cited in: Dict. Sci. Biog.

Abel test for convergence (Abel, Niels Henrik): Mathematics. See: Ballentyne; Internat. Dict. Ap. Math.

Abel test reactions for ethyl sulfide (Abel, Sir Frederick Augustus): Chemistry. See: Van Nostrand Chem. Dict.

Abel theorem on power series (Abel, Niels Henrik): Mathematics. See: Internat. Dict. Ap. Math.

Abelard, Peter. See: Abailard, Pierre.

Abelia (Abel, Clarke): Botany. See: Taylor, N.

Abelian group (Abel, Niels Henrik): Mathematics. See: Ballentyne; Internat. Dict. Ap. Math.; Internat. Dict. Phys. Elec.

ABELIN, ISAAK. 1883- . Swiss physiologist. See: Who's Who Switz. Abelin's reaction (or test) for arsphenamine.

Abelin's reaction (or test) for arsphenamine (Abelin, Isaak): Chemistry. See: Dorland; Van Nostrand Chem. Dict.

Abelite (Abel, Sir Frederick Augustus): Chemistry. See: Thrush.

Abelites (Abel): Religion. See: Brewer; Canney.

Abel's bacillus (Abel, Rudolf): Medicine. See: Dorland; Stedman.

Abel's test for infinite integrals (Abel, Niels Henrik): Mathematics. See: Ballentyne.

Abel's theorem on multiplication of series (Abel, Niels Henrik): Mathematics. See: Ballentyne.

Abel's vividiffusion apparatus (Abel, John Jacob): Medicine. See: Stedman.

ABENSOUR, J. fl. 1907. French chemist. Cited in: Chem. Abstr. vol. 1, p. 2624. Abensour tests for quinine.

Abensour tests for quinine (Abensour, J.): Chemistry. See: Van Nostrand Chem. Dict.

ABERCROMBIE, JOHN. 1780-1844. Scottish physician. See: Dict. Nat. Biog. Abercrombie's degeneration, Abercrombie's tumor.

Abercrombie's degeneration (Abercrombie, John): Medicine. See: Dorland; Stedman.

Abercrombie's tumor (Abercrombie, John). See: Hutchinson's disease.

ABERNATHY, JESS. No dates. American mineralogist. Cited in: Min. Mag., vol. 31 (1958) p. 952.

Abernathyite (Abernathy, Jess): Earth Sciences. See: Thrush.

Abernethy biscuit (Abernethy, John): Food and Drink. See: Charnock; Partridge; Phyfe.

ABERNETHY, JOHN. 1764-1831. English surgeon. See: Dict. Nat. Biog. Abernethy biscuit, Abernethy's fascia, Abernethy's operation, Abernethy's sarcoma.

Abernethy's fascia (Abernethy, John): Medicine. See: Dorland; Stedman.

Abernethy's operation (Abernethy, John): Medicine. See: Dorland.

Abernethy's sarcoma (Abernethy, John): Medicine. See: Dorland; Jablonski; Stedman.

ABERSON, JOHANNES HENDRIKUS. 1857-1935. Dutch engineer. Cited in: Chem. Abstr. Aberson machine?

Aberson machine (Aberson, Johannes Hendrikus?): Earth Sciences. See: Thrush.

ABERT, JAMES WILLIAM. 1820-1897. American soldier and scientist. See: Nat. Cyc. Amer. Biog. Abert's finch, Abert's pipilo, Abert's squirrel, Abert's towhee.

Abert's finch (Abert, James William): Zoology. Cited in: Mathews, M. M.

Abert's pipilo (Abert, James William): Zoology. Cited in: Mathews, M. M.

Abert's squirrel (Abert, James William): Zoology. Cited in: Mathews, M. M.

Abert's towhee (Abert, James William): Zoology. Cited in: Gray; Mathews, M. M.

Abich, Otto Wilhelm Hermann von. See: Von Abich, Otto Wilhelm Hermann.

Abichite (Von Abich, Otto Wilhelm Hermann): Earth Sciences. Cited in: World Who's Who Sci.

Abigail (Abigail the Maid): Generic Word (servant). See: Hendrickson; Partridge; Wagner (Names).

ABIGAIL THE MAID. Fictional character from Beaumont and Fletcher's "The Scornful Lady." See: Benet.

Abington cap (Abington, Francis): Fashion. Cited in: Encyc. Brit., 1973.

ABINGTON, FRANCIS. 1737-1815. English actress. See: Encyc. Brit., 1973. Abington cap.

Abney effect (Abney, Sir William de Wiveleslie): Physics. See: Van Nostrand Sci. Encyc.

Abney law (Abney, Sir William de Wiveleslie): Physics. See: Ballentyne; Chaplin; Thewlis.

Abney level (or clinometer) (Abney, Sir William de Wiveleslie): Physics. See: Monkhouse; Thrush.

Abney mounting (Abney, Sir William de Wiveleslie): Physics. See: Internat. Dict. Phys. Elec.; Thewlis.

ABNEY, SIR WILLIAM DE WIVELESLIE. 1843-1920. English chemist and physicist. See: Dict. Sci. Biog. Abney effect; Abney law, Abney level (or clinometer), Abney mounting.

Abohm (Ohm, Georg Simon): Physics. See: Dresner, Markus; Thewlis; Van Nostrand Sci. Encyc.

abortus Bang ring test (Bang, Bernhard Laurits Frederik): Medicine. See: Stedman.

ABRAHAM. Hebrew patriarch. See: Encyc. Brit., 1973. Abraham man, Abrahamic covenant, Abraham's bosom.

ABRAHAM, HENRI. 1868-1943. French physicist and inventor. See: World Who's Who Sci. Abraham's voltmeter.

Abraham man (Abraham): Generic Word (beggar). See: Hendrickson.

ABRAHAM, MAX. 1857-1922. German physicist. See: Dict. Sci. Biog. Abraham theory.

Abraham Newland(s) (Newland, Abraham): Generic Word (bank-notes). See: Harvey; Latham.

ABRAHAM OF ANTIOCH. fl. 9th c. Syrian religious leader. See: Webster's Biog. Dict. Abrahamites.

Abraham theory (Abraham, Max): Chemistry. See: Van Nostrand Chem. Dict.

Abrahamic covenant (Abraham): Religion. See: Brewer.

Abrahamites (Abraham of Antioch): Religion. See: Canney.

Abraham's bosom (Abraham): Generic Word. See: Brewer; Hendrickson.

ABRAHAMS, ROBERT. 1861-1935. American physician. See: New York Acad. of Med. Portrait Cat. Abrahams' sign.

Abrahams sign (Abrahams, Robert): Medicine. See: Dorland; Stedman.

Abraham's tree (Derivation undetermined): Earth Sciences. See: Huschke; Van Nostrand Sci. Encyc.

Abraham's voltmeter (Abraham, Henri): Physics. Cited in: World Who's Who Sci.

ABRAHAMSON, EMANUEL M. 1897-1956. American physician. See: Amer. Men Sci., 9th ed. Abrahamson reagent.

Abrahamson reagent (Abrahamson, Emanuel M.): Chemistry. See: Van Nostrand Chem. Dict.

ABRAHAMSZ, GALENUS. 1622-1706. Dutch physician and Baptist minister. Cited in: Mansell. Galenists.

ABRAMI, PIERRE. 1879-1943. French physician. See: Biog. Lex. hervorr. Aerzte. Abrami's disease.

Abrami's disease (Abrami, Pierre). See: Hayem-Widal syndrome.

Abramov-Fiedler myocarditis (Abramov, S. S. and Fiedler, Carl Ludwig Alfred). See: Fiedler's myrocarditis.

ABRAMS, ALBERT. 1863-1924. American physician. See: Dict. Amer. Biog. Abrams' heart reflex, Abrams' lung reflex, electronic reactions of Abrams.

ABRAMS, DUFF ANDREW. 1880-   . American civil engineer. See: Amer. Men Sci., 3d. ed. Abrams' law.

Abrams' heart reflex (Abrams, Albert): Medicine. See: Stedman.

Abrams' law (Abrams, Duff Andrew): Earth Sciences. See: Thrush.

Abrams' lung reflex (Abrams, Albert): Medicine. See: Stedman.

ABRIKOSSOV, ALEKSEI IVANOVICH. b. 1875. Russian pathologist. See: World Who's Who Sci. Abrikossov's tumor.

Abrikossov's tumor (Abrikossov, Aleksei Ivanovich): Medicine. See: Dorland.

ABRUZZI, DUKE OF THE (In full: LUIGI ALOISIUS AMEDEO GUISEPPE MARIA FERDINANDO FRANCESCO). 1873-1933. Italian naval officer and explorer. See: Webster's Biog. Dict. Aloisiite.

ABT, ARTHUR FREDERIC. 1867-1955. American pediatrician. See: Who's Imp. Med., 2nd ed. Abt-Letterer-Siwe syndrome.

Abt-Letterer-Siwe syndrome (Abt, Arthur Frederic; Letterer, Erich; and Siwe, Sture August): Medicine. See: Jablonski. Also known as: Letterer-Siwe disease; Letterer's reticulosis.

ABT, ROMAN. 1850-1933. Swiss railroad engineer. See: Dict. Hist. Biog. Suisse. Abt system.

Abt system (Abt, Roman): Engineering and Industry. See: Webster's 3d.

ABU-HANIFAH (AL-NUMAN IBN-THABIT). 699-767. Mohammedan jurist. See: Encyc. Brit., 1911. Hanafites.

abwatt (Watt, James): Physics. See: Markus.

Acacian schisms (Acacius): Religion. See: Attwater.

Acacians (Acacius): Religion. See: Canney.

ACACIUS. d. 366. Bishop of Caesarea. See: Nouv. Biog. Univ. Acacian schisms, Acacians.

ACADEMUS. Greek mythological hero. See: Jobes. Academy.

Academy (Academus): Generic Word (school). See: Charnock.

according to Cocker (Cocker, Edward): Generic Word (very accurate). See: Brewer; Hendrickson; Partridge.

according to Fowler (Fowler, Henry Watson): Generic Word. See: Hendrickson.

according to Guinness (Guiness family): Generic Word (correct world record information). See: Hendrickson.

according to Gunter (Gunter, Edmund): Generic Word (correct). See: Brewer; Clapin; Hendrickson; Mathews, M. M.; Phyfe.

according to Hoyle (or Hoyle) (Hoyle, Edmond): Generic Word (correct). See: Brewer; Hendrickson; Partridge; Weekley.

ACHAEMENES. fl. 7th c. B.C. Persian ruler. See: Webster's Biog. Dict. Achaemenidae.

Achaemenidae (Achaemenes): History. See: Encyc. Brit., 1973.

ACHALME, PIERRE JEAN. b. 1866. French physician. See: Pogg., vol. 6. Achalme's bacillus.

Achalme's bacillus (Achalme, Pierre Jean): Medicine. See: Dorland.

Achard-Castaigne method (Achard, Emile Charles and Castaigne, Joseph): Medicine. See: Dorland; Stedman.

ACHARD, EMILE CHARLES. 1860-1944. French physician. See: World Who's Who Sci. Achard-Castaigne method, Achard syndrome, Achard-Thiers syndrome, Marfan-Achard syndrome.

Achard syndrome (Achard, Emile Charles): Medicine. See: Stedman.

Achard-Thiers syndrome (Achard, Emile Charles and Thiers, Joseph): Medicine. See: Dorland; Jablonski; Stedman.

Achariaceae (Acharius, Erik): Botany. See: Webster's 3d.

ACHARIUS, ERIK. 1757-1819. Swedish botanist and physician. See: Dict. Sci. Biog. Achariaceae.

ACHATES. Fictional character in Virgil's "Aeneid." See: Benet. fidas Achates.

ACHENBACH, WALTER. fl. 1957. Italian? physician. (Biography source unavailable.) Achenbach's syndrome.

Achenbach's syndrome (Achenbach, Walter): Medicine. See: Jablonski.

Acheson biennial prize (Acheson, Edward Goodrich): Engineering and Industry. Cited in: World Who's Who Sci.

ACHESON, EDWARD GOODRICH. 1856-1931. American inventor. See: Dict. Amer. Biog. vol. 1. Acheson biennial prize, Acheson furnace, Acheson graphite, Acheson medal, Acheson process.

Acheson furnace (Acheson, Edward Goodrich): Engineering and Industry. See: Thrush.

Acheson graphite (Acheson, Edward Goodrich): Engineering and Industry. See: Thrush.

Acheson medal (Acheson, Edward Goodrich): Engineering and Industry. Cited in: World Who's Who Sci.

Acheson process (Acheson, Edward Goodrich): Engineering and Industry. See: Thrush.

Achiardite (d'Achiardi, Antonio). See: Dachiardite.

ACHILLES. Greek mythological warrior. See: Encyc. Brit., 1973. Achilles bursa, Achilles heel, Achilles jerk (or reflex), Achilles tendon.

Achilles bursa (Achilles): Medicine. See: Dorland; Stedman.

Achilles heel (Achilles): Generic Word (vulnerable point). See: Webster's 3d.

Achilles jerk (or reflex) (Achilles): Medicine. See: English; Hinsie; Wolman.

Achilles tendon (Achilles): Medicine. See: Brewer; Donath; Phyfe. Also known as: Hippocrates cord.

ACHILLI, GIOVANNI. fl. 1852. Dominican apostate. (Biography source unavailable.) Achilli trial.

Achilli trial (Achilli, Giovanni): Religion. See: Attwater.

ACHOR, RICHARD W. P. 1922- . American physician. See: Direct. Med. Specialists., vol. 8. Achor-Smith syndrome.

Achor-Smith syndrome (Achor, Richard W.P. and Smith, Lucian A.): Medicine. See: Jablonski.

ACHUCARRO, NOCOLAS. 1851-1918. Spanish histologist. See: World Who's Who Sci. Achucarro's stain.

Achucarro's stain (Achucarro, Nicolas): Medicine. See: Dorland.

ACKER, CHARLES ERNEST. 1868-1920. American inventor and manufacturer. See: Dict. Amer. Biog. Acker process.

Acker process (Acker, Charles Ernest): Chemistry. See: Hackh; Van Nostrand Chem. Dict.

ACKERET, JACOB. 1898- . Swiss aeronautical engineer. See: Collier's Encyc. under "Aviation, history." Ackeret-Keller gas turbine, Ackeret theory.

Ackeret-Keller gas turbine (Ackeret, Jacob and Keller, Curt): Engineering and Industry. See: Auger.

Ackeret theory (Ackeret, Jacob): Physics. See: Internat. Dict. Ap. Math.; Thewlis.

Ackermann automatic reckoner (Ackermann, Edwin): Chemistry. See: Hackh.

ACKERMANN, CONRAD THEODOR. 1825-1896. German physician. See: World Who's Who Sci. Ackermann's angles.

ACKERMANN, DANKWART. b. 1878. German physiologist and chemist. See: World Who's Who Sci. Ackermann test for guanidine, Ackermann test for thio-para-tolyl-beta-naphthylamine?

ACKERMANN, EDWIN. fl. 1890-1907. Swiss chemist. Cited in: Chem. Abstr. Ackermann automatic reckoner.

ACKERMANN, RUDOLPH. 1764-1834. German-born English inventor and art publisher. See: Dict. Nat. Biog. Ackermann steering.

Ackermann steering (Ackermann, Rudolph): Engineering and Industry. See: Auger.

Ackermann test for guanidine (Ackermann, Dankwart): Chemistry. See: Van Nostrand Chem. Dict.

Ackermann test for thio-para-tolyl-beta-naphthylamine (Ackermann, Dankwart?): Chemistry. See: Van Nostrand Chem. Dict.

Ackermann's angles (Ackermann, Conrad Theodor): Medicine. See: Stedman.

ACOSTA, JOSE DE. 1539-1600. Spanish missionary and geographer. See: Dict. Sci. Biog. Acosta's disease.

Acosta's disease (Acosta, Jose de): Medicine. See: Dorland; Stedman.

acoustic(al) Ohm (Ohm, Georg Simon): Physics. See: Dresner; Internat. Dict. Phys. Elec.; Thewlis.

Acree-Rosenheim test (or reaction) (Acree, Solomon Farley and Rosenheim, Sigmund Otto): Chemistry. See: Hackh; Stedman; Van Nostrand Chem. Dict. Also known as: Acree's reaction.

ACREE, SOLOMON FARLEY. 1875-1957. American physician and chemist. See: World Who's Who Sci. Acree-Rosenheim test (or reaction).

Acree's reaction (Acree, Solomon Farley). See: Acree-Rosenheim test (or reaction).

ACREL, OLOF. 1717-1806. Swedish surgeon. See: Nouv. Biog. Univ. Acrel's ganglion.

Acrel's ganglion (Acrel, Olof): Medicine. See: Dorland; Stedman.

ACRES, BIRT. 1854-1918. English photographer and manufacturer. (Biography source unavailable.) Birtac camera.

ACRES, BOB. Fictional character in Sheridan's "The Rivals." See: Benet. Bob Acres.

ACTON, JOHN EMERICK EDWARD DALBERG. 1834-1902. English historian. See: Dict. Nat. Biog. 2nd suppl. Lord Acton's Law.

ACUAN. No dates. Mesopotamian religious leader. (Biography source unavailable.) Acuanites.

Acuanites (Acuan): Religion. See: Canney.

ADA. fl. 8th c. Sister of Charlemagne. (Biographical source unavailable.) Ada school.

Ada school (Ada): Art. See: Osborne.

Adair Dighton's syndrome (Dighton, Adair). See: Van der Hoeve's syndrome.

ADAM. Biblical name given to first man. See: Encyc. Brit., 1973. Adam and Eve (orchid), Adamic, Adamites, Adam's ale (or wine), Adam's apple, Adam's apple tree, Adam's cup, Adam's fig, Adam's leather, Adam's needle (and thread), Adam's profession, old Adam.

Adam and Eve (orchid) (Adam and Eve): Botany. See: Clapin; Partridge.

Adam, Francis. See: Waldstein, Franz Adam Graf von.

Adam galactometer (Adam, Rauf Cemil?): Chemistry. See: Hackh.

ADAM, M. d. 1881. French mineralogist. Cited in: Dana, vol. 2, p. 866. Adamite.

ADAM, RAUF CEMIL. fl. 1950. Turkish chemist. Cited in: Chem. Abstr. Adam galactometer?, Adam's method?

ADAM, ROBERT. 1728-1792. Scottish architect. Dict. Nat. Biog. Adam style.

Adam style (Adam, Robert): Architecture. See: Brewer; Partridge.

ADAM, W. 1823-1904. English engineer? (Biography source unavailable.) Adam's bogie.

ADAMANTIADES, B. fl. 1931. French physician? (Biography source unavailable.) Adamantiades-Behcet syndrome.

Adamantiades-Behcet syndrome (Adamantiades, B. and Behcet, Halushi). See: Behcet's syndrome.

ADAMI, JOHN GEORGE. 1861-1926. Canadian pathologist. See: Dict. Nat. Biog., vol. 4. Adami's theory.

Adamic (Adam): Generic Word. See: Hendrickson.

Adami's theory (Adami, John George): Medicine. See: Dorland

Adamite (Adam, M.): Earth Science. See: Thrush.

Adamite (Adams, John Quincy): History. See: Clapin, Mathews, M.M.

Adamites (Adam): Religion. Attwater; Canney; Latham.

ADAMKIEWICZ, ALBERT. 1850-1921. Polish-born Austrian pathologist. See: World Who's Who Sci. Adamkiewicz's demilunes, Adamkiewicz's protein reaction (or test).

Adamkiewicz's demilunes (Adamkiewicz, Albert): Medicine. See: Dorland.

Adamkiewicz's protein reaction (or test) (Adamkiewicz, Albert): Chemistry. See: Hackh; Stedman; Van Nostrand Chem. Dict.

Adamowski string quartet (Adamowski, Timothee): Music. Cited in: Webster's Biog. Dict.

ADAMOWSKI, TIMOTHEE. 1858-1943. Polish-born American violinist. See: Webster's Biog. Dict. Adamowski string quartet, Adamowski trio.

Adamowski trio (Adamowski, Timothee): Music. Cited in: Webster's Biog. Dict.

Adam's ale (or wine) (Adam): Generic Word (water). See: Brewer; Harvey.

Adams and Clay Republicans (Adams, John Quincy and Clay, Henry): History. See: Smith.

Adam's apple (Adam): Anatomy. See: Hartmann; Hendrickson; Pennak.

Adam's apple tree (Adam): Botany. See: Hendrickson. Also known as: Nero's crown.

Adams-Bashforth process (or method) (Adams, John Couch and Bashforth, Francis): Mathematics. See: Ballentyne, Internat. Dict. Ap. Math.

Adam's bogie (Adam, W.): Engineering and Industry. See: Auger.

ADAMS, CHARLES FRANCIS. 1866-1954. American lawyer and financier. See: Webster's Biog. Dict. Charles F. Adams (destroyers).

ADAMS, ELEANOR G. fl. 1935. American chemist. Cited in: Chem. Abstr., vol. 30, p. 1322. Scott-Adams reagent and test.

Adams chromatic value system (Derivation undetermined): Earth Sciences. See: Thrush.

Adam's cup (Adam): Botany. Cited in: Mathews, M.M.

ADAMS, ELLIOT QUINCY. b. 1888. American chemist. See: Pogg., vol. 6. Lewis-Adams formula.

ADAMS, FANNY. d. ca. 1812 or 1867. English murder victim. (Biography source unavailable.) Fanny Adams.

Adam's fig (Adam): Botany. See: Gray.

Adams-Hall-Bailey reagent (Adams, Jane; Hall, Martha and Bailey, William Fleming?): Chemistry. See: Van Nostrand Chem. Dict.

ADAMS, ISAAC. 1802-1883. American inventor. See: Dict. Amer. Biog. Adams press.

ADAMS, JAMES ALEXANDER. 1857-1930. Scottish gynecologist. See: World Who's Who Sci. Alexander-Adams operation.

ADAMS, JANE. fl. 1935. American? chemist. Cited in: Chem. Abstr., vol. 29. Adams-Hall-Bailey reagent.

ADAMS, JOHN. 1735-1826. American president. See: Dict. Amer. Biog. Washington and Adams federalist.

ADAMS, JOHN COUCH. 1819-1892. English astronomer and mathematician. See: Dict. Sci. Biog. Adams-Bashforth process (or method)?

ADAMS, JOHN QUINCY. 1767-1848. American president. See: Dict. Amer. Biog. Adamite, Adams and Clay Republicans, Adams-Onis treaty, Adamsism.

ADAMS, LEASON HEBERLING. 1887- . American physical chemist. See: World Who's Who Sci. Adams process? Adams-Williamson annealing schedule.

Adam's leather (Adam): Generic Word (skin). Cited in: Mathews, M.M.

Adam's method (Adam, Rauf Cemil?): Chemistry. See: Winburne.

Adam's needle (and thread) (Adam): Botany. See: Brewer; Gray; Winburne.

Adams-Onis treaty (Adams, John Quincy and Onis, Luis de): History. See: Morris and Irwin.

Adams operation (Adams, William): Medicine. See: Dorland.

Adams' operation for ectropion (Adams, Sir William): Medicine. See: Dorland; Stedman.

Adams press (Adams, Isaac): Printing. See: Lockwood, Mathews, M.M.

Adams process (Adams, Leason Heberling?): Earth Science. See: Thrush.

Adam's profession (Adam): Generic Word (gardening). See: Brewer; Phyfe.

ADAMS, ROBERT. 1791-1875. Irish physician. See: Dict. Nat. Biog. Morgagni-Adams-Stokes syndrome.

ADAMS, ROGER. b. 1889. American chemist. See: World Who's Who Sci. Adamsite.

Adams' saw (Adams, William): Medicine. See: Dorland.

Adam's snuffboxes (Derivation undetermined): Earth Sciences. See: Thrush.

Adams-Stokes syndrome (Adams, Robert and Stokes, William). See: Morgagni-Adams-Stokes syndrome.

ADAMS, SIR WILLIAM. 1783-1827. English ophthalmologist. See: Dict. Nat. Biog. Adams' operation for ectropion.

ADAMS, WILLIAM. 1820-1900. English surgeon. See: Boase. Adams' operation, Adams' saw.

ADAMS, WILLIAM BRIDGES. 1797-1872. English inventor. See: World Who's Who Sci.; Dict. Nat. Biog. Webley and Adams revolver?

ADAMS, WILLIAM ELIAS. 1902- . American surgeon and educator. See: World Who's Who Sci. Kershner-Adams syndrome.

Adams-Williamson annealing schedule (Adams, Leason Heberling and Williamson, Erskine Douglas): Earth Science. See: Thrush.

Adamsism (Adams, John Quincy): History. Cited in: Mathews, M.M.

Adamsite (Adams, Roger): Chemistry. See: Quick; Thrush.

Adamson Act (or Law) (Adamson, William Charles): History. See: Jameson; Morris; Smith.

ADAMSON, ARTHUR WILSON. 1919- . Chinese-born American chemist. See: Amer. Men Sci., 8th ed. Boyd, Schubert, and Adamson equation.

ADAMSON, DANIEL. 1818-1890. English engineer. See: Nature vol. 41 (1890). Adamson's seam.

ADAMSON, WILLIAM CHARLES. 1854-1929. American legislator. See: Biog. Direct. Amer. Congress. Adamson Act (or Law).

Adamson's seam (Adamson, Daniel): Engineering and Industry. See: Auger.

ADANSON, MICHEL. 1727-1806. French botanist. See: Dict. Sci. Biog. Adansonia.

Adansonia (Adanson, Michel): Botany. See: Charnock; Dorland; Taylor, N.

Adcock antenna (Adcock, Willis Alfred?): Electronics. See: Hughes; Internat. Dict. Phys. Elec.; Markus.

Adcock direction finder (Adcock, Willis Alfred?): Electronics. See: Hughes; Markus.

Adcock radio range (Adcock, Willis Alfred?): Electronics. See: Markus.

ADCOCK, WILLIS ALFRED. 1922- . American chemist. See: Amer. Men and Women Sci. Adcock antenna?, Adcock direction finder?, Adcock radio range?

ADDAMS, JANE. 1860-1935. American sociologist. See: Dict. Amer. Biog., 1st suppl. Jane Addams Award.

Addis count (Addis, Thomas): Medicine. See: Dorland.

ADDIS, THOMAS. 1881-1949. American physician. See: Who's Who Amer. Med. Addis count.

Addisin (Addison, Thomas): Medicine. See: Stedman.

Addison-Biermer anemia (Addison, Thomas and Biermer, Anton): Medicine. See: Jablonski. Also known as: Addison's anemia, Biermer's anemia, Biermer-Ehrlich anemia.

ADDISON, CHRISTOPHER. 1869-1951. English anatomist. See: World Who's Who Sci. Addison's clinical planes.

Addison-Gull disease (Addison, Thomas and Gull, William Whitley): Medicine. See: Jablonski. Also known as: Rayer's disease.

ADDISON, JOSEPH. 1672-1719. English essayist, poet and statesman. See: Dict. Nat. Biog. Addisonian termination.

ADDISON, THOMAS. 1793-1860. English physician. See: Dict. Sci. Biog. Addisin, Addison-Biermer anemia, Addison-Gull disease, Addisonism, Addison's disease (or melanoderma), Addison's keloid.

Addisonian termination (Addison, Joseph): Literature. See: Brewer.

Addisonism (Addison, Thomas): Medicine. See: Stedman.

Addison's anemia (Addison, Thomas). See: Addison-Biermer anemia.

Addison's clinical planes (Addison, Christopher): Medicine. See: Dorland; Stedman.

Addison's disease (or melanoderma) (Addison, Thomas): Medicine. See: Chaplin; Pennak; Van Nostrand Sci. Encyc.

Addison's keloid (Addison, Thomas): Medicine. See: Dorland; Jablonski; Stedman.

ADELAIDE (In full: ADELAIDE EUGENIE LOUISE). 1777-1847. Princess of Orleans. See: Webster's Biog. Dict.; Nouv. Biog. Univ. Adelaide concerto?

Adelaide concerto (Adelaide, Princess?): Music. See: Apel.

Adelaide ruby (Derivation undetermined): Earth Sciences. See: Thrush.

Adelaide's warbler (Derivation undetermined): Zoology. See: Gray.

ADELINE, PIERRE G. fl. 1935. French metallurgist. Cited in: Chem. Abstr. Adeline steelmaking process?

Adeline steelmaking process (Adeline, Pierre G.?): Engineering and Industry. See: Thrush.

ADELMANN, GEORG FRANZ BLASIUS. 1811-1888. German physician and surgeon. See: Allg. Deut. Biog. Adelmann's maneuver (or method), Adelmann's operation.

Adelmann's maneuver (or method) (Adelmann, Georg Franz Blasius): Medicine. See: Dorland; Stedman.

Adelmann's operation (Adelmann, Georg Franz Blasius): Medicine. See: Dorland.

Adelphians (Adelphius): Religion. See: Canney.

ADELPHIUS. No dates. Mesopotomian religious leader. (Biography source unavailable.) Adelphians.

ADENDORFF. fl. 1891. Leader of the Transvaal Boers. (Biography source unavailable.) Adendorff trek.

Adendorff trek (Adendorff): History. See: Harbottle.

Adie-Holmes syndrome (Adie, William John and Holmes, Gordon). See: Adie's syndrome.

ADIE, WILLIAM JOHN. 1886-1935. English neurologist. See: Who Was Who, 1929-1940. Adie's syndrome, Cole and Adie's method.

Adie's syndrome (Adie, William John): Medicine. See: Dorland; Hinsie; Jablonski. Also known as: Adie-Holmes syndrome, Kehrer-Adie syndrome, Markus-Adie syndrome, Markus' syndrome, Saenger's syndrome, Weill-Reys-Adie syndrome, Weill-Reys syndrome, Weill's syndrome.

ADLER, ALFRED. 1870-1937. Austrian psychiatrist. See: Internat. Encyc. Soc. Sci. Adlerian psychology (or psychotherapy), Adler's theory.

ADLER, ERICH. 1905- . German-born chemist. See: World Who's Who Sci. Adler test reaction for pentoses?, Adler test reaction for wood.

ADLER, OSCAR. 1879-1932. German physician. See: Wer Ist's. Adler's benzidine test (or reaction).

ADLER, ROBERT. 1913- . Austrian-born physicist. See: World Who's Who Sci. Adler tube.

Adler test reaction for pentoses (Adler, Erich?): Chemistry. See: Van Nostrand Chem. Dict.

Adler test reaction for wood (Adler, Erich): Chemistry. See: Van Nostrand Chem. Dict.

Adler tube (Adler, Robert): Electronics. See: Hughes.

Adlerian psychology (or psychotherapy) (Adler, Alfred): Psychology. See: English; Stedman; Wolman.

Adler's benzidine test (or reaction) (Adler, Oscar): Medicine. See: Dorland; Hackh; Stedman.

Adler's theory (Adler, Alfred): Psychology. See: Dorland.

ADLUM, JOHN. 1759-1836. American gardener. See: Dict. Amer. Biog. Adlumia.

Adlumia (Adlum, John): Botany. See: Mathews, M.M.; Taylor, N.

Admirable Crichton (Crichton, James): Generic Word. See: Hendrickson; Partridge; Stenhouse.

Adonia (Adonis, the Youth): Generic Word (festival). See: Brewer; Charnock.

Adonic verse (Adonis, the Youth): Literature. See: Charnock; Preminger.

Adonis (Adonis, the Youth): Generic Word (handsome man). See: Charnock; Partridge; Stenhouse.

Adonis flower (Adonis, the Youth): Botany. See: Brewer; Taylor N.; Wagner (Names).

Adonis garden (Adonis, the Youth): Generic Word (worthless toy). See: Brewer.

ADONIS, THE YOUTH. Mythological figure. See: Encyc. Brit., 1973. Adonia, Adonic verse, Adonis, Adonis flower, Adonis garden, Adonis wig, Adonize.

Adonis wig (Adonis, the Youth): Fashion. See: Picken.

Adonize (Adonis, the Youth): Generic Word (dandify). See: Partridge; Picken.

ADRIAN IV. 1100-1159. Pope. See: Dict. Nat. Biog. Adrian's Bull (or Donation).

Adrian test for nitrite (Derivation undetermined): Chemistry. See: Van Nostrand Chem. Dict.

Adrian test for oil of wine (Derivation undetermined): Chemistry. See: Van Nostrand Chem. Dict.

Adrian test reaction for aldehydes (Derivation undetermined): Chemistry. See: Van Nostrand Chem. Dict.

Adrianists (Hamsted, Adrian): Religion. See: Canney.

Adrian's Bull (or Donation) (Adrian IV): History. See: Attwater; Harbottle.

ADSON, ALFRED WASHINGTON. 1887-1951. American surgeon. See: World Who's Who Sci. Adson's syndrome, Adson's test?

Adson's syndrome (Adson, Alfred Washington). See: Naffiziger's syndrome.

Adson's test (Adson, Alfred Washington?): Medicine. See: Stedman.

AEBY, CHRISTOPH THEODOR. 1835-1885. Swiss anatomist. See: World Who's Who Sci. Aeby's plane.

Aeby's plane (Aeby, Christoph Theodor): Medicine. See: Stedman.

AEGIR. Norse sea god. See: Encyc. Amer., 1959. Aegirite.

Aegirite (Aegir): Earth Sciences. See: Van Nostrand Sci. Encyc.

AELFRIC. fl. ca. 955-ca. 1022. English writer and abbot. See: Encyc. Brit., 1973. Aelfric Society.

Aelfric Society (Aelfric): Literature. Cited in: Chamber's Biog. Dict.

Aelfrid. See: Alfred.

Aeliopyle (Aeolus): Engineering and Industry. See: Partridge.

Aemilian Law (Mamercus, Aemilius): History. See: Brewer.

Aeolian deposits (Aeolus): Earth Sciences. See: Monkhouse; Moore; Van Nostrand Sci. Encyc.

Aeolian flute (Aeolus): Music. See: Winick.

Aeolian harp (Aeolus): Music. See: Apel; Good; Scholes.

Aeolian tones (or sounds) (Aeolus): Physics. See: Hughes; Huschke; Internat. Dict. Phys. Elec.

AEOLUS. Mythological god of the winds. See: Encyc. Brit., 1973. Aeliopyle, Aeolian deposits, Aeolian flute, Aeolian harp, Aeolian tones (or sounds).

AEPPLI. fl. early 20th c. European mathematician. (Biography source unavailable.) Polya-Aeppli distribution.

Aerians (Aerius): Religion. See: Canney.

AERIUS. fl. 360. Armenian monk. See: Nouv. Biog. Univ. Aerians.

AERTS, M. No dates. Belgian engineer? (Biography source unavailable.) Aerts's water axle box.

Aerts's water axle box (Aerts, M.): Engineering and Industry. See: Auger.

AESCHINES. 389-314 B.C. Greek orator. See: Encyc. Brit., 1973. Aeschynite.

Aeschynite (Aeschines): Earth Sciences. See: Charnock.

Aesculapian (Aesculapius): Generic Word (medical). See: Charnock; Partridge; Stedman.

AESCULAPIUS. Greek god of medicine. See: Jobes. Aesculapian.

AETHELWOLD, SAINT. 908?-984. English ecclesiastical leader. See: Dict. Nat. Biog. Benedictional of St. Aethelwold.

Aetians (Aetius of Antioch): Religion. See: Canney.

AETIUS OF ANTIOCH. d. 367. Syrian theologian. See: Encyc. Brit., 1911. Aetians.

AFANASIEV, MIKHAIL IVANOVICH. 1850-1910. Russian bacteriologist. (Biography source unavailable.) Afanasiev test?

Afanasiev test (Afanasiev, Mikhail Ivanovich?): Chemistry. See: Van Nostrand Chem. Dict.

Afwillite (Williams, Alpheus Fuller): Earth Sciences. See: Thrush; Webster's 3d.

AFZELIUS, ARVID. fl. 1921. Swedish physician. (Biography source unavailable.) Afzelius' erythema.

Afzelius' erythema (Afzelius, Arvid). See: Lipschuetz's erythema.

AGAG. Biblical King of Amalekites. See: Webster's Biog. Dict. walk like Agag.

AGASSIZ, ALEXANDER. 1835-1910. American zoologist. See: Dict. Sci. Biog. Agassiz trawl, Agassizocrinus.

Agassiz trawl (Agassiz, Alexander): Zoology. See: Webster's 3d.

Agassizocrinus (Agassiz, Alexander): Zoology. See: Webster's 3d.

AGATHA, SAINT. fl. 3d. c. Christian martyr. See: Encyc. Brit., 1973. Saint Agatha's disease.

AGAVE. Greek legendary daughter of Cadmus. See: Jobes. Agave cactus.

Agave cactus (Agave): Botany. See: Partridge.

Agecroft device (Derivation undetermined): Engineering and Industry. See: Thrush.

AGGAZZOTTI, ALBERTO. b. 1877. Italian aviator. See: Diz. Encic. Ital. Aggazzotti's mixture.

Aggazzotti's mixture (Aggazzotti, Alberto): Medicine. See: Dorland; Stedman.

Aghlabids (or Aghlabite) (dynasty) (Ibrahim ibn-al-Aghlab): History. See: Encyc. Brit., 1973; Webster's 3d.

AGLIPAY, GREGORIO. fl. ca. 1864-1940. Philippine religious leader. See: Encyc. Amer., 1959. Aglipayans.

Aglipayans (Aglipay, Gregorio): Religion. See: Attwater; Webster's 3d.

AGNES, SAINT. fl. 4th c. Roman martyr. See: Encyc. Brit., 1973. Saint Agnes's eve, St. Agnes' flower.

AGNESI, MARIA GAETANA. 1718-1799. Italian mathematician. See: Dict. Sci. Biog. witch of Agnesi.

AGNEW, CORNELIUS REA. 1830-1888. American ophthalmologist. See: Dict. Amer. Biog. Agnew-Verhoeff incision.

AGNEW, DAVID HAYES. 1818-1892. American surgeon. See: Dict. Amer. Biog. Agnew's splint.

AGNEW, SPIRO THEODORE. 1918- . American politician. See: Encyc. Brit., 1973. Agnewism.

Agnew-Verhoeff incision (Agnew, Cornelius Rea and Verhoeff, Frederick Herman): Medicine. See: Stedman.

Agnewism (Agnew, Spiro Theodore): Political Science. See: Barnhart, (New Eng.).

Agnew's splint (Agnew, David Hayes): Medicine. See: Dorland.

AGOSTINI, CESARE. 1864-1942. Italian physician. See: Diz. Biog. Ital. Agostini's reaction (or test) for glucose in urine.

AGOSTINI, PAOLO. fl. 1928-1952. Italian chemist. Cited in: Chem. Abstr. Agostini's test for magnesium.

Agostini's reaction (or test) for glucose in urine (Agostini, Cesare): Medicine. See: Dorland; Stedman.

Agostini's test for magnesium (Agostini, Paolo): Chemistry. See: Van Nostrand Chem. Dict.

AGRAZ, JUAN SALVADOR. fl. 1914. Mexican chemist. Cited in: Chem. Abstr., vol. 8, p. 308. Agraz test reaction.

Agraz test reaction (Agraz, Juan Salvador): Chemistry. See: Van Nostrand Chem. Dict.

AGRESTINI, A. fl. 1890-1918. Italian chemist. Cited in: Chem. Abstr., vol. 13, p. 821. Agrestini test.

Agrestini test (Agrestini, A.): Chemistry. See: Van Nostrand Chem. Dict.

AGRICOLA, GEORGIUS (GEORG BAUER). 1494-1555. German mineralogist. See: World Who's Who Sci. Agricolite.

Agricolite (Agricola, Georgius): Earth Sciences. See: Encyc. Amer., 1959.

AGUILAR, P. fl. 1892. Mexican mine superintendent. Cited in: Dana, vol. 1, p. 179. Aguilarite.

Aguilarite (Aguilar, P.): Earth Sciences. See: Thrush.

AGULHON, HENRI. fl. 1910. French physician and chemist. Cited in: Chem. Abstr. Agulhon's reagent, Agulhon's solution.

Agulhon's reagent (Agulhon, Henri): Chemistry. See: Hackh.

Agulhon's solution (Agulhon, Henri): Chemistry. See: Van Nostrand Chem. Dict.

AHAZ. d. 720? B.C. Biblical King of Judah. See: Encyc. Brit., 1973. dial of Ahaz.

Ahlfeld breathing movements (or sign) (Ahlfeld, Johann Friedrich): Medicine. See: Dorland; English. Also known as: Braxton Hicks' sign.

AHLFELD, FRIEDRICH. 1892- . German mineralogist. Cited in: Chem. Abstr. Ahlfeldite.

AHLFELD, JOHANN FRIEDRICH. 1843-1929. German obstetrician. See: World Who's Who Sci. Ahlfeld breathing movements (or sign), Ahlfeld's method.

Ahlfeldite (Ahlfeld, Friedrich): Earth Sciences. See: Thrush.

Ahlfeld's method (Ahlfeld, Johann Friedrich): Medicine. See: Stedman.

AHMAD B. MUHAMMAD B. HANBAL (IBN HANBAL). 780-855. Arab jurist. See: Gibb and Kramers. Hanbali.

AHMAD SHAH DURRANI. 1724-1773. Amir of Afghanistan. See: Encyc. Brit., 1973. Durrani.

Ahmadiyyah (Ahmadiya) (Ghulam Ahmad, Mirza): Religion. See: Canney; Mathews, S.

AHMED EL-BEDAWI. 1200?-1276. Saint of Egyptian Mohammedans. See: Webster's Biog. Dict. Bedawiyeh.

AHMED ER-REFA'I. d. 1182. Religious leader. (Biography source unavailable.) Refa'iyeh.

AHMED IBN-TULUN. 835-884. Egyptian sectary. See: Nouv. Biog. Univ. Tulunids.

AHMED, PRINCE. Character in the "Arabian Nights." See: Benet. Prince Ahmed's apple.

AHNFELT, NILS OTTO. 1801-1837. Swedish botanist. See: Biog. Notes Upon Botanists. Ahnfeltia, Ahnfelt's seaweed.

Ahnfeltia (Ahnfelt, Nils Otto): Botany. See: Webster's 3d.

Ahnfelt's seaweed (Ahnfelt, Nils Otto): Botany. See: Hendrickson.

Ahumada-Del Castillo syndrome (Ahumada, Juan Carlos and Del Castillo, E.B.): Medicine. See: Jablonski.

AHUMADA, JUAN CARLOS. fl. 1932-1939. Argentinian? physician. See: New York Acad. of Med. Portrait Cat. Ahumada-Del Castillo syndrome.

AHURA MAZDA. Zoroastrian supreme god. See: Jobes. Mazdaism (Mazdeism).

AICH, J. No dates. Patented the alloy. Cited in: Bailey. Aich's metal.

Aich's metal (Aich, J.): Chemistry. See: Hackh.

AIGNAN, SAINT. d. 453. Bishop of Orleans. See: Holweck. Saint Aignan's disease.

AIKIN, ARTHUR. 1773-1854. English chemist and mineralogist. See: Dict. Nat. Biog. Aikinite.

Aikinite (Aikin, Arthur): Earth Sciences. See: Thrush.

AINSWORTH, GEORGE C. 1852-1948. American dentist. See: New York Times. Ainsworth's punch.

Ainsworth's punch (Ainsworth, George C.): Medicine. See: Dorland.

Airy disc (Airy, George Biddel): Physics. See: Ballentyne; Internat. Dict. Ap. Math.; Satterthwaite.

Airy experiment (Airy, George Biddel): Physics. See: Internat. Dict. Phys. Elec.; Van Nostrand Sci. Encyc.

Airy eyepiece (Airy, George Biddel): Astronomy. See: Satterthwaite.

Airy functions (Airy, George Biddel): Mathematics. See: Internat. Dict. Ap. Math.

AIRY, GEORGE BIDDEL. 1801-1892. English astronomer and mathematician. See: Dict. Sci. Biog. Airy disc, Airy experiment, Airy eyepiece, Airy functions, Airy isostasy, Airy points, Airy spirals, Airy transit circle, Airy's equation, Airy's integral.

Airy isostasy (Airy, George Biddel): Earth Sciences. See: Thrush.

Airy points (Airy, George Biddel): Physics. See: Ballentyne; Thewlis.

Airy spirals (Airy, George Biddel): Earth Sciences. See: Thewlis; Thrush.

Airy transit circle (Airy, George Biddel): Astronomy. See: Satterthwaite.

Airy's equation (Airy, George Biddel): Mathematics. See: Ballentyne.

Airy's integral (Airy, George Biddel): Mathematics. See: Ballentyne.

Aitch piece (Derivation undetermined): Engineering and Industry. See: Thrush.

AITKEN, ALEXANDER CRAIG. 1895- . New Zealand mathematician. See: Direct. Brit. Sci. Aitken delta-square process?, Aitken estimator?, Aitken method of interpolation?, Aitken's formula?

Aitken delta-square process (Aitken, Alexander Craig?): Mathematics. See: Internat. Dict. Ap. Math.

Aitken dust-counter (Aitken, John): Earth Sciences. See: Huschke.

Aitken estimator (Aitken, Alexander Craig?): Mathematics. See: Kendall.

AITKEN, JOHN. 1839-1919. Scottish physicist. See: World Who's Who Sci. Aitken dust-counter, Aitken nuclei.

Aitken method of interpolation (Aitken, Alexander Craig?): Mathematics. See: Internat. Dict. Ap. Math.; Van Nostrand Sci. Encyc.

Aitken nuclei (Aitken, John): Earth Sciences. See: Huschke; Internat. Dict. Ap. Math.;Van Nostrand Sci. Encyc.

AITKEN, ROBERT. 1800-1873. English clergyman. See: Dict. Nat. Biog. Aitkenites.

AITKEN, WILLIAM. 1825-1892. Scottish physician. See: World Who's Who Sci. Aitken's pill.

Aitkenites (Aitken, Robert): Religion. See: Canney; Latham.

Aitken's formula (Aitken, Alexander Craig?): Mathematics. See: Ballentyne.

Aitken's pill (Aitken, William): Medicine. Cited in: World Who's Who Sci.

AITOFF, DAVID. d. 1933. Russian geographer. (Biography source unavailable.) Aitoff-Hammer projection, Aitoff's projection.

Aitoff-Hammer projection (Aitoff, David and Von Hammer, Ernst Hermann Heinrich). See: Hammer projection.

Aitoff's projection (Aitoff, David): Geography. See: Monkhouse; Moore; Webster's 3d.

AITON, WILLIAM. 1731-1793. Scottish horticulturist. See: Dict. Sci. Biog. Aitonia.

Aitonia (Aiton, William): Botany. Cited in: Dict. Sci. Biog.

AJAX. Greek legendary figure, described in Homer's "Iliad." See: Encyc. Brit., 1973. Ajax powder, Jakes.

Ajax-Northrup furnace (Ajax and Northrup, Edwin Fitch): Engineering and Industry. See: Thrush.

Ajax powder (Ajax): Engineering and Industry. See: Webster's 3d.

Ajax-Wyatt furnace (Derivation undetermined): Engineering and Industry. See: Thrush.

AJTAI, MIKLOS. fl. 1937. Hungarian chemist. Cited in: Chem. Abstr. vol. 32, p. 1610. Szebelledy-Ajtai test.

AKERLUND, AKE. fl. 20th c. Swedish roentgenologist. (Biography source unavailable.) Akerlund deformity.

Akerlund deformity (Akerlund, Ake): Medicine. See: Dorland; Stedman.

AKERMAN, RICHARD. fl. 19th c. Swedish mineralogist. Cited in: Bailey. Akermanite.

Akermanite (Akerman, Richard): Earth Sciences. See: Thrush.

AKIMOFF, NICHOLAS WLADIMIR. b. 1877- . American engineer. See: Amer. Men Sci., 3d. ed. Akimoff's balancing machine.

Akimoff's balancing machine (Akimoff, Nicholas Wladimir): Engineering and Industry. See: Auger.

Akins' classifier (Derivation undetermined): Engineering and Industry. See: Thrush.

Akroyd Stuart engine (Akroyd Stuart, H.): Engineering and Industry. See: Auger.

AKROYD STUART, H. 1864-1927. English engineer? (Biography source unavailable.) Akroyd Stuart engine, Hornesby-Akroyd engine.

ALADDIN. Fictional character in the "Arabian Nights." See: Benet. Aladdin's lamp, Aladdin's window.

Aladdin's lamp (Aladdin): Generic Word. See: Brewer; Partridge.

Aladdin's window (Aladdin): Generic Word. See: Barnhart, (Eng. Lit.)

ALAJOUANINE, THEOPHILE. 1890- . French neurologist. See: Grand Larousse Encyc. Alajouanine's syndrome, Foix-Alajouanine syndrome.

Alajouanine's syndrome (Alajouanine, Theophile): Medicine. See: Jablonski.

ALANSON, EDWARD. 1747-1823. English surgeon. See: World Who's Who Sci. Alanson's amputation.

Alanson's amputation (Alanson, Edward): Medicine. See: Dorland; Stedman.

ALARIC II. d. 507 A.D. King of Visigoths. See: Encyc. Brit., 1973. Breviary of Alaric.

Alascans (Laski, Jan, the younger): Religion. See: Harbottle.

Alba Bible (Alba, Fernando Alvarez de Toledo, Duke): Art. See: Osborne.

ALBA, FERNANDO ALVAREZ DE TOLEDO, DUKE. 1508-1582. Spanish general. See: Encyc. Brit., 1973. Alba Bible, Dolphins.

Albada finder (Albada, L.E.W. von): Photography. See: Focal Encyc. Photog.

ALBADA, L. E. W. VON. fl. 1924. Inventor. (Biography source unavailable.) Albada finder.

Alban engine (Alban, Ernst): Engineering and Industry. See: Auger.

ALBAN, ERNST. 1791-1846. German inventor. See: World Who's Who Sci. Alban engine.

ALBARRAN Y DOMINGUEZ, JOAQUIN. 1860-1912. Cuban-born surgeon. See: World Who's Who Sci. Albarran's disease, Albarran's gland (or tubule), Albarran's test.

Albarran's disease (Albarran y Dominguez, Joaquin): Medicine. See: Dorland.

Albarran's gland (or tubule) (Albarran y Dominguez, Joaquin): Medicine. See: Dorland; Stedman.

Albarran's test (Albarran y Dominguez, Joaquin): Medicine. See: Dorland; Stedman.

ALBEE, FRED HOUDLETT. 1876-1945. American orthopedic surgeon. See: World Who's Who Sci. Albee's operation, Albee's saw.

Albee's operation (Albee, Fred Houdlett): Medicine. See: Dorland; Stedman.

Albee's saw (Albee, Fred Houdlett): Medicine. Cited in: World Who's Who Sci.

ALBEMARLE, DIANA CICELY, COUNTESS OF. 1909- . English noblewoman. See: Who's Who, 1958. Albemarle Report.

Albemarle Report (Albemarle, Diana Cicely, Countess of): Education. See: Harrod

Alber starch test (Derivation undetermined): Chemistry. See: Van Nostrand Chem. Dict.

Alberger process (Derivation undetermined): Chemistry. See: Van Nostrand Chem. Dict.

ALBERS, F. H. fl. 1952. American physician? (Biography source unavailable.) Taussig-Snellen-Albers syndrome.

ALBERS, HEINRICH C. 1773-1833. German cartographer. See: World Who's Who Sci. Albers' projection.

Albers' projection (Albers, Heinrich C.): Geography. See: Monkhouse.

Albers-Schoenberg disease (or syndrome) (Albers-Schoenberg, Heinrich Ernst): Medicine. See: Dorland; Jablonski; Stedman.

ALBERS-SCHOENBERG, HEINRICH ERNST. 1865-1921. German roentgenologist. See: World Who's Who Sci. Albers-Schoenberg disease (or syndrome).

ALBERT (In full: ALBERT FRANCIS CHARLES AUGUSTUS EMMANUEL OF SAXECOBURG-GOTHA). 1819-1861. Prince Consort of England. See: Dict. Nat. Biog. Albert crepe, Albert envelopes, Albert watch-chain, Prince Albert frock coat, Prince Albert slipper, Prince Albert's lyrebird.

ALBERT III. 1443-1500. Duke of Saxony. See: Encyc. Brit., 1973. Albertine line.

Albert coal (Derivation undetermined): Earth Sciences. See: Thrush.

Albert crepe (Albert): Fashion. See: Picken.

ALBERT, EDUARD. 1841-1900. Austrian surgeon. See: World Who's Who Sci. Albert's disease, Albert's operation, Albert's suture, Albert's syndrome.

Albert effect (Albert, E.): Photography. See: Focal Encyc. Photog.; Van Nostrand Sci. Encyc.

Albert envelopes (Albert): Printing. See: Lockwood.

ALBERT, HENRY. 1878-1930. American physician. See: Who's Who Amer. Med. Albert's stain.

ALBERT, JOSEPH. 1825-1886. German photographer. See: Webster's Biog. Dict. Albertype.

Albert Mouchet's syndrome (Mouchet, Albert). See: Mouchet's syndrome.

Albert watch-chain (Albert): Fashion. See: Brewer; Partridge.

ALBERT, WILHELM AUGUST JULIUS. 1787-1846. German mining official. See: Brockhaus. Albert's lay.

ALBERTI, B. fl. 1932. German pharmaceutical chemist. Cited in: Chem. Abstr., vol. 27, p. 2758. Alberti test.

Alberti bass (Alberti, Domenico): Music. See: Apel; Partridge; Scholes.

ALBERTI, DOMENICO. ca. 1710-1740. Italian composer. See: Grove. Alberti bass.

ALBERTI, FRIEDRICH AUGUST VON. 1795-1878. German geologist and mining engineer. See: Dict. Sci. Biog. Alberti furnace?

Alberti furnace (Alberti, Friedrich August von?): Engineering and Industry. See: Thrush.

Alberti test (Alberti, B.): Chemistry. See: Van Nostrand Chem. Dict.

Albertine line (Albert III): History. Cited in: Webster's Biog. Dict.

ALBERTINI, AMBROSIUS VON. 1894- . Swiss physician. See: Biog. Lex. hervorr. Aerzte. Fanconi-Albertini-Zellweger syndrome.

Albert's disease (Albert, Eduard): Medicine. See: Dorland. Also known as: Swediauer's disease.

Albert's lay (Albert, Wilhelm August Julius): Engineering and Industry. See: Auger. Also known as: Lang's lay (or lay rope).

Albert's operation (Albert, Eduard): Medicine. See: Dorland; Stedman.

Albert's stain (Albert, Henry): Medicine. See: Stedman.

Albert's suture (Albert, Eduard): Medicine. See: Dorland; Stedman.

Albert's syndrome (Albert, Eduard): Medicine. See: Jablonski.

Albertype (Albert, Joseph): Printing. Cited in: Focal Encyc. Photog.; See: Lockwood.

ALBINI, GIUSEPPE. 1830-1911. Italian physiologist. See: World Who's Who Sci. Albini's nodules.

Albini's nodules (Albini, Giuseppe): Medicine. See: Dorland; Stedman.

ALBINUS, BERNHARD SIEGFRIED. 1697-1770. German anatomist and surgeon. See: Encyc. Brit., 1973. Albinus's muscle.

Albinus's muscle (Albinus, Berhard Siegfried): Medicine. See: Dorland; Stedman.

ALBIZZI, FILIPPO DEGLI. fl. 1749. Italian naturalist. (Biography source unavailable.) Albizzia.

Albizzia (Albizzi, Filippo degli): Botany. See: Webster's 3d.

Albl's ring (Derivation undetermined): Medicine. See: Stedman.

Albrecht condenser (Albrecht, Max): Engineering and Industry. See: Thrush.

Albrecht, Jacob. See: Albright, Jacob.

ALBRECHT, KARL MARTIN PAUL. 1851-1894. German anatomist. See: Allg. Deut. Biog. Albrecht's bone.

ALBRECHT, MAX. 1851-1925. German petroleum engineer. See: World Who's Who Sci. Albrecht condenser.

Albrecht's bone (Albrecht, Karl Martin Paul): Medicine. See: Dorland; Stedman.

Albright-Butler-Bloomberg syndrome (Albright, Fuller; Butler, Allan Macy and Bloomberg, Esther): Medicine. See: Jablonski.

ALBRIGHT, FULLER. 1900- . American physician. See: World Who's Who Sci. Albright-Butler-Bloomberg syndrome, Albright-Hadorn syndrome, Albright's syndrome (1), Albright's syndrome (2), Lightwood-Albright syndrome, Martin-Albright syndrome.

Albright–Hadorn syndrome (Albright, Fuller and Hadorn, Walter): Medicine. See: Jablonski.

ALBRIGHT, JACOB. 1759-1808. American clergyman. See: Dict. Amer. Biog. Albright's children (or brethren).

Albright–McCune–Sternberg syndrome (Albright, Fuller; McCune, Donovan James and Sternberg, Carl von). See: Albright's syndrome (2).

Albright's children (or brethren) (Albright, Jacob): Religion. Cited in: Mathews, M. M.

Albright's syndrome(1) (Albright, Fuller): Medicine. See: Jablonski.

Albright's syndrome (2) (Albright, Fuller): Medicine. See: Jablonski. Also known as: Albright–McCune–Sternberg syndrome, Fuller Albright's syndrome, McCune–Albright syndrome.

Albright's syndrome (3) (Albright, Fuller). See: Lightwood–Albright syndrome.

Albright's syndrome (4) (Albright, Fuller). See: Martin–Albright syndrome.

ALCAEUS. fl. 606-589 B.C. Greek lyric poet. See: Encyc. Brit., 1973. Alcaic verse (or Alcaics).

Alcaic verse (or Alcaics) (Alcaeus): Literature. See: Partridge; Preminger; Scott.

Alcantarines (Peter of Alcantara, Saint): Religion. See: Attwater.

ALCHORNE, STANESBY. 1727-1799. English botanist. See: Biog. Notes Upon Botanists. Alchornea.

Alchornea (Alchorne, Stanesby): Botany. See: Charnock.

ALCMAN. fl. 672-631 B.C. Greek lyric poet. See: Encyc. Brit., 1973. Alcmanic verse.

Alcmanic verse (Alcman): Literature. See: Preminger.

ALCOCK, BENJAMIN. b. 1801. Irish anatomist. See: Dobson. Alcock's canal.

Alcock reaction for chromium (Derivation undetermined): Chemistry. See: Van Nostrand Chem. Dict.

ALCOCK, RUTHERFORD. 1809-1897. English diplomat. See: Dict. Nat. Biog., 1st suppl. Alcock spruce.

Alcock spruce (Alcock, Rutherford): Botany. See: Winburne.

Alcock–Wilkin test reaction (Derivation undetermined): Chemistry. See: Van Nostrand Chem. Dict.

Alcock's canal (Alcock, Benjamin): Medicine. See: Donath; Dorland; Stedman.

Alcorn Club (Alcorn, James L.): History. See: Mathew, M. M.

ALCORN, JAMES L. 1816-1894. American legislator. See: Dict. Amer. Biog. Alcorn Club.

ALDEN, GEORGE IRA. b. 1843. American mechanical engineer. See: Who's Who Engin., 2nd. ed. Alden power brake.

Alden power brake (Alden, George Ira): Engineering and Industry. See: Auger.

ALDER, ALBERT VON. b. 1888. German physician. See: New York Acad. of Med. Portrait Cat. Alder bodies, Alder's anomaly.

Alder bodies (Alder, Albert von): Medicine. See: Stedman.

ALDER, KURT. 1902-1958. German chemist. See: Dict. Sci. Biog. Aldrin, Diels–Alder reaction.

Alder–Reilly anomaly (Alder, Albert and Reilly, William Anthony). See: Alder's anomaly.

Alder's anomaly (Alder, Albert von): Medicine. See: Jablonski; Stedman. Also known as: Alder–Reilly anomaly.

Aldine Club (Manutius, Aldus): Printing. See: Lockwood.

Aldine (editions) (Manutius, Aldus): Printing. See: Brewer; Charnock; Phyfe.

Aldine leaves (Manutius, Aldus): Printing. See: Harrod.

Aldine press (Manutius, Aldus): Printing. See: Harrod; Osborne.

Aldine style (Manutius, Aldus): Printing. See: Harrod.

Aldine type (Manutius, Aldus): Printing. See: Lockwood.

Aldis lamp (Derivation undetermined): Engineering and Industry. See: Partridge.

Aldobrandini, Ippolito. See: Clement VIII.

Aldrich Act (Aldrich, Nelson Wilmarth): History. See: Smith.

ALDRICH, MARTHA. 1897- . American biochemist. Cited in: Kelly. Hench–Aldrich test (or index).

Aldrich mixture (Aldrich, Robert Henry): Medicine. See: Dorland.

ALDRICH, NELSON WILMARTH. 1841-1915. American financier and statesman. See: Dict. Amer. Biog. Aldrich Act, Aldrich–Vreeland Act, Payne–Aldrich Tarriff Act.

ALDRICH, ROBERT ANDERSON. 1917- . American pediatrician. See: Amer. Men Sci., 10th ed. Wiskott–Aldrich syndrome.

ALDRICH, ROBERT HENRY. 1902- . American surgeon. Cited in: Amer. Med. Direct., 1950. Aldrich mixture.

Aldrich–Vreeland Act (Aldrich, Nelson Wilmarth and Vreeland, Edward Butterfield): History. See: Jameson; Morris; Smith.

Aldrich's syndrome (Aldrich, Robert Anderson). See: Wiskott–Aldrich syndrome.

Aldrin (Alder, Kurt): Chemistry. See: Webster's 3d.

Aldrovanda (Adrovandi, Ulisse): Botany. See: Charnock.

ALDROVANDI, ULISSE. 1522-1605. Italian naturalist. See: Dict. Sci. Biog. Aldrovanda.

Aldus Manutius. See: Manutius, Aldus.

Aleichem, Shalom. See: Rabinowitz, Solomon.

ALEKSEEV, VLADIMIR FEODOROVICH. 1852-1919. Russian chemist. See: World Who's Who Sci. Alekseevkii test?

Alekseevkii test (Alekseev, Vladimir Feodorovich?): Chemistry. See: Van Nostrand Chem. Dict.

ALEMBERT, JEAN LE ROND D'. 1717-1783. French mathematician and physicist. See: Dict. Sci. Biog. D'Alembert equation, D'Alembert('s) paradox, D'Alembert('s) principle, D'Alembert('s) test (for convergence), D'Alembertian.

Alexander (Alexander, Sir Jerome): Generic Word (hanging). See: Hendrickson.

ALEXANDER II. 1818-1881. Russian czar. See: Encyc. Brit., 1973. Alexandrite.

ALEXANDER III (ALEXANDER THE GREAT). 356-323 B.C. King of Macedonia. See: Encyc. Brit., 1973. Alexander mosaic, Alexander sarcophagus, Alexanderism, Alexanders, Alexander's beard, Alexandrine.

Alexander–Adams operation (Alexander, William and Adams, James Alexander): Medicine. See: Dorland; Stedman. Also known as: Alexander's operation.

ALEXANDER, BENJAMIN. 1909- . American physician. See: Direct. Med. Specialists, vol. 14. Alexander's syndrome.

ALEXANDER, CHARLES LEE. 1861-1933. American dentist. See: New York Acad. of Med. Portrait Cat. Alexander's crown, Alexander's gold.

ALEXANDER, JAMES WADDELL. 1888- . American mathematician. See: World Who's Who Sci. Alexander's subbase theorem.

ALEXANDER, SIR JEROME. 1660-1674. Irish judge. (Biography source unavailable.) Alexander.

ALEXANDER, JEROME. 1876-1959. American chemist. See: World Who's Who Sci. Alexander tester.

Alexander mosaic (Alexander III): Art. See: Osborne.

ALEXANDER, O. A. fl. 1870. American horticulturist. (Biography source unavailable.) Alexander (peach).

Alexander (peach) (Alexander, O. A.): Botany. See: Mathews, M. M.

ALEXANDER, W. STEWART. fl. 1949. English pathologist. (Biography source unavailable.) Alexander's disease.

Alexander sarcophagus (Alexander III): Art. See: Osborne.

Alexander tester (Alexander, Jerome): Chemistry. See: Hackh.

ALEXANDER, WILLIAM. 1844-1919. English surgeon. See: New York Acad. of Med. Portrait Cat. Alexander–Adams operation.

Alexanderism (Alexander III): Psychology. See: Hinsie; Wolman.

Alexanderite (Alexander II). See: Alexandrite.

Alexanders (Alexander III): Botany. See: Partridge; Winburne.

Alexander's beard (Alexander III): Generic Word. See: Hendrickson.

Alexander's crown (Alexander, Charles Lee): Dentistry. See: Dorland.

Alexander's disease (Alexander, W. Stewart): Medicine. See: Jablonski; Stedman.

Alexander's gold (Alexander, Charles Lee): Dentistry. See: Dorland.

Alexander's operation (Alexander, William). See: Alexander-Adams operation.

Alexander's subbase theorem (Alexander, James Waddell): Mathematics. See: James.

Alexander's syndrome (Alexander, Benjamin): Medicine. See: Jablonski.

Alexanderson alternator (Alexanderson, Ernst Frederik Werner): Engineering and Industry. See: Internat. Dict. Phys. Elec.; Markus.

ALEXANDERSON, ERNST FREDERIK WERNER. b. 1878. Swedish-born electrical and radio engineer. See: Webster's Biog. Dict. Alexanderson alternator.

ALEXANDRA. 1844-1925. Queen consort of England. See: Dict. Nat. Biog., vol. 4. Alexandra Day; Alexandra limp; Alexandra palm.

Alexandra Day (Alexandra): Generic Word. See: Brewer.

Alexandra limp (Alexandra): Fashion. See: Webster's 3d.

Alexandra palm (Alexandra): Botany. See: Webster's 3d.

Alexandrine (Alexander III): Literature. See: Harvey; Preminger; Scott.

Alexandrite (Alexander II): Earth Sciences. See: Partridge; Thrush; Van Nostrand Sci. Encyc.

Alexian Brothers (or Alexians) (Alexius, Saint): Religion. See: Attwater; Canney; Mathews, S.

ALEXIUS, SAINT. fl. 5th c. Roman religious leader. See: Holweck. Alexian Brothers (or Alexians).

ALEXJEJEV. No dates. Russian investigator. Cited in: Bailey. Alexjejevite (or Alexeyevite).

Alexjejevite (or Alexeyevite) (Alexjejev): Earth Sciences. See: Thrush.

Alfonso X. See: Alphonso X.

Alford antenna (or slotted tubular antenna) (Derivation undetermined): Electronics. See: Hughes; Internat. Dict. Phys. Elec.; Markus.

Alford loop (antenna) (Derivation undetermined): Electronics. See: Internat. Dict. Phys. Elec.; Markus.

ALFRED THE GREAT. 849-899. King of the West Saxons in England. See: Dict. Nat. Biog. Alfredian, King Alfred's candle.

Alfredian (Alfred the Great): History. See: Webster's 3d.

ALFVEN, HANNES. 1908- . Swedish physicist. See: Webster's Biog. Dict. Alvfen speed, Alfven waves.

Alfven speed (Alfven, Hannes): Physics. See: Markus.

Alfven waves (Alfven, Hannes): Physics. See: Ballentyne; Hushke; Internat. Dict. Ap. Math.

Algaroth powder (Algarotto, Vittorio): Chemistry. See: Charnock; Thrush; Webster's 3d.

ALGAROTTO, VITTORIO. d. 1604. Italian physician. See: Diz. Encic. Ital. Algaroth powder.

ALGER, HORATIO, JR. 1832-1899. American author. See: Dict. Amer. Biog. Horatio Alger story.

algorism (Khwarizmi, al): Mathematics. See: Asimov; Hendrickson; Partridge; Webster's 3d.

ALHAZEN. fl. 10-11th c. Arabian mathematician and physicist. See: World Who's Who Sci. Alhazen's problem.

Alhazen's problem (Alhazen): Mathematics. Cited in: World Who's Who Sci.

ALI BABA. Fictional character from the "Arabian Nights." See: Benet. Ali Baba jar?

Ali Baba jar (Ali Baba?): Chemistry. See: Thrush.

ALI MOHAMMED OF SHIRAZ ("BAB"). 1819-1850. Persian religious leader. See: Webster's Biog. Dict. Babism (or Babists).

Aliamet test (Derivation undetermined): Chemistry. See: Van Nostrand Chem. Dict.

Alibert-Bazin syndrome (Alibert, Jean Louis and Bazin, Antoine Pierre Ernest): Medicine. See: Jablonski. Also knows as: Auspitz's dermatosis, Auspitz's disease.

ALIBERT, JEAN LOUIS. 1768-1837. French physician. See: Nouv. Biog. Univ. Alibert-Bazin syndrome, Alibert's disease (1) (or keloid), Alibert's disease (2), Alibert's mentagra.

Alibert's disease (1) (or keloid) (Alibert, Jean Louis): Medicine. See: Dorland; Jablonski; Stedman. Also known as: Hawkins' keloid.

Alibert's disease (2) (Alibert, Jean Louis): Medicine. See: Jablonski. Also known as: Borovskii's disease.

Alibert's mentagra (Alibert, Jean Louis): Medicine. See: Jablonski.

Alice blue (Longworth, Alice Roosevelt): Fashion. See: Mathews, M. M.; Picken; Webster's 3d.

ALICE IN WONDERLAND. Character from Lewis Carroll's "Alice's Adventures in Wonderland." See: Benet. Alice-in-Wonderland, Alice in Wonderland syndrome.

Alice-in-Wonderland (Alice in Wonderland): Generic Word (unreal). See: Barnhart, (New Eng.); Hendrickson; Partridge.

Alice in Wonderland syndrome (Alice in Wonderland): Medicine. See: Stedman.

Alimarin-Frid reagent (Alimarin, Ivan Pavlovich and Frid, B. I.): Chemistry. See: Van Nostrand Chem. Dict.

ALIMARIN, IVAN PAVLOVICH. 1903- . Russian chemist. See: World Who's Who Sci. Alimarin-Frid reagent.

Alisonite (Alison, Robert Edward): Earth Sciences. See: Internat. Dict. Phys. Elec.; Partridge; Thrush.

ALISON, ROBERT EDWARD. fl. 1856. Chilean mineral developer. Cited in: Bailey. Alisonite.

Aliva concrete sprayer (Derivation undetermined): Engineering and Industry. See: Thrush.

Al-Khwarizmi. See: Khwarizmi, Al.

all my eye and Betty Martin (Martin of Tours, Saint?): Generic Word (nonsense). See: Hendrickson.

all Sir Garnet (Wolseley, Garnet Joseph): Generic Words (all well). See: Partridge. Also known as: all sigarneo (or sigarney).

ALLAMAND, JEAN NICOLAS SEBASTIEN. 1713-1787. Swiss-born Dutch naturalist and physicist. See: Nouv. Biog. Univ. Allamanda.

Allamanda (Allamand, Jean Nicolas Sebastien): Botany. See: Taylor, N.

ALLAN, ALEXANDER. fl. 1855-56. English? engineer. (Biography source unavailable.) Allan link motion, Allan valve.

ALLAN, ETHAN. 1738-1789. American soldier. See: Dict. Amer. Biog. Ethan Allen (submarine).

Allan link motion (Allan, Alexander): Engineering and Industry. See: Auger.

Allan (red) metal (Derivation undetermined): Chemistry. See: Thrush.

ALLAN, THOMAS. 1777-1833. Scottish mineralogist. See: Dict. Nat. Biog. Allanite.

Allan valve (Allan, Alexander): Engineering and Industry. See: Auger.

Allanite (Allan, Thomas): Earth Sciences. See: Charnock; Thrush; Van Nostrand Sci. Encyc.

Allard's law (Derivation undetermined): Earth Sciences. See: Huschke.

ALLEE, WARDER CLYDE. 1885-1955. American ecologist and zoologist. See: World Who's Who Sci. Allee's law (or principle).

Allee's law (or principle) (Allee, Warder Clyde): Zoology. See: Gray; Pennak.

ALLEMANN, RICHARD. 1893-1958. German physician. (Biography source unavailable.) Allemann's syndrome.

Allemann's syndrome (Allemann, Richard): Medicine. See: Jablonski.

ALLEN, ALBERT BROMLEY. 1862-1943. American dentist. (Biography source unavailable.) Allen's root pliers.

ALLEN, ALFRED HENRY. 1847-1904. English chemist. See: Sci., new ser., vol. 20 (1904) p. 189. Allen test for phenol, Allen test for phenol in creosote, Allen's test (for sugar in urine).

Allen and Scott-Smith test reaction (Allen, Charles Francis Hitchcock? and Scott-Smith, George Egerton): Chemistry. See: Van Nostrand Chem. Dict.

ALLEN, C. fl. 1915. American metallurgist. Cited in: Chem. Abstr., vol. 9, p. 2376. Allen cone?

Allen charge (Derivation undetermined): Law. See: Black.

ALLEN, CHARLES FRANCIS HITCHCOCK. b. 1895. American chemist. See: Pogg., vol. 7a. Allen and Scott-Smith test reaction?, Allen test of vinegar?, Allen test reaction for strychnine?

ALLEN, CHARLES WARREN. 1854-1906. American dermatologist. Who Was Who Amer., vol. 1. Allen's test.

Allen cone (Allen, C.?): Earth Sciences. See: Thrush.

Allen-Doisy test (Allen, Edgar V. and Doisy, Edward Adelbert): Medicine. See: Dorland; Stedman.

Allen-Doisy unit (Allen, Edgar V. and Doisy, Edward Adelbert): Medicine. See: Dorland; Stedman.

ALLEN, DORIS TWITCHELL. 1901- . American psychologist. See: World Who's Who Sci. Twitchell-Allen three dimensional personality test.

ALLEN, E. A. fl. 1922. American chemist. Cited in: Chem. Abstr., vol. 16, p. 1541. Allen-Moore cell.

ALLEN, EDGAR V. 1892-1943. American anatomist. See: Dict. Sci. Biog. Allen-Doisy test, Allen-Doisy unit.

ALLEN, EDWIN. 1812-1891. American inventor. (Biography source unavailable.) Allen press.

ALLEN, EUGENE THOMAS. b. 1864. American chemist. Cited in: Min. Mag., vol. 29 (1952), p. 974. Allenite.

ALLEN, FREDERICK MADISON. 1879-1964. American physician. See: Who's Who Amer. Med. Allen's law, Allen's test (for glucose), Allen's test (for phenol), Allen's test (for strychnine), Allen's treatment, radial compression test of Allen.

ALLEN, HARRISON. 1841-1897. American anatomist. See: Dict. Amer. Biog. Allen's fossa.

Allen, James Alfred Van. See: Van Allen, James Alfred.

ALLEN, JOEL ASAPH. 1838-1921. American zoologist and author. See: Dict. Amer. Biog. Allen's hummingbird, Allen's law (or rule).

ALLEN, JOHN. 1810-1892. American dentist. See: Dict. Amer. Biog. Allen's cement.

ALLEN, JOHN T. F. 1829-1900. English-born American engineer. See: Dict. Amer. Biog. Allen steam engine.

Allen-Masters syndrome (Allen, William M. and Masters, William Howell): Medicine. See: Jablonski.

Allen-Moore cell (Allen, E. A. and Moore, Hugh Kelsea): Chemistry. See: Van Nostrand Chem. Dict.

Allen-O'Hara furnace (Derivation undetermined): Engineering and Industry. See: Thrush.

Allen press (Allen, Edwin): Printing. See: Lockwood.

Allen steam engine (Allen, John T. F.): Engineering and Industry. See: Auger.

Allen test for phenol (Allen, Alfred Henry): Chemistry. See: Van Nostrand Chem. Dict.

Allen test for phenol in creosote (Allen, Alfred Henry): Chemistry. See: Van Nostrand Chem. Dict.

Allen test of vinegar (Allen, Charles Francis Hitchcock?): Chemistry. See: Van Nostrand Chem. Dict.

Allen test reaction for strychnine (Allen, Charles Francis Hitchcock?): Chemistry. See: Van Nostrand Chem. Dict.

ALLEN, WILLARD MYRON. 1904- . American gynecologist. See: World Who's Who Sci. Corner-Allen test, Corner-Allen unit.

ALLEN, WILLIAM M. fl. 1955. American obstetrician. (Biography source unavailable.) Allen-Masters syndrome.

Allenite (Allen, Eugene Thomas): Earth Sciences. See: Thrush.

Allen's cement (Allen, John): Dentistry. See: Dorland.

Allen's fossa (Allen, Harrison): Medicine. See: Stedman.

Allen's hummingbird (Allen, Joel Asaph): Zoology. Cited in: Gray.

Allen's law (Allen, Frederick Madison): Medicine. See: Dorland; Stedman.

Allen's law (or rule) (Allen, Joel Asaph): Zoology. See: Gray; Pennak; Winick.

Allen's pepper box (or revolver) (Derivation undetermined): Weapons. See: Mathews, M. M.

Allen's root pliers (Allen, Albert Bromley): Dentistry. See: Dorland.

Allen's swamp monkey (Derivation undetermined): Zoology. See: Pennak.

Allen's test (Allen, Charles Warren): Medicine. See: Dorland; Stedman.

Allen's test (for glucose) (Allen, Frederick Madison): Medicine. See: Stedman.

Allen's test (for phenol) (Allen, Frederick Madison): Medicine. See: Stedman.

Allen's test (for strychnine) (Allen, Frederick Madison): Medicine. See: Stedman.

Allen's test (for sugar in urine) (Allen, Alfred Henry): Chemistry. See: Hackh.

Allen's treatment (Allen, Frederick Madison): Medicine. See: Dorland; Stedman.

Allihn condenser (Derivation undetermined): Chemistry. See: Hackh; Van Nostrand Chem. Dict.

ALLINGHAM, HERBERT WILLIAM. 1862-1904. English surgeon. See: Who Was Who, 1897-1916. Allingham's operation.

ALLINGHAM, WILLIAM A. 1830-1908. English surgeon. See: Biog. Lex. hervorr. Aerzte. Allingham's operation, Allingham's ulcer.

Allingham's operation (Allingham, Herbert William): Medicine. See: Dorland.

Allingham's operation (Allingham, William A.): Medicine. See: Dorland.

Allingham's ulcer (Allingham, William A.): Medicine. See: Dorland; Jablonski.

ALLIONI, CARLO. 1725-1804. Italian physician and botanist. See: Nouv. Biog. Univ. Allionia.

Allionia (Allioni, Carlo): Botany. See: Webster's 3d.

ALLIS, EDWARD PHELPS. 1824-1889. American manufacturer. See: Dict. Amer. Biog. Allis steam engine.

Allis' inhaler (Allis, Oscar Huntington): Medicine. See: Dorland.

ALLIS, OSCAR HUNTINGTON. 1833-1921. American surgeon. See: Who Was Who Amer., vol. 1. Allis' inhaler, Allis' sign.

Allis steam engine (Allis, Edward Phelps): Engineering and Industry. See: Auger.

Allis' sign (Allis, Oscar Huntington): Medicine. See: Dorland; Stedman.

ALLISON, JAMES A. fl. 1920 American ichthyologist. (Biography source unavailable.) Allison tuna.

ALLISON, NATHANIEL. 1876-1932. American orthopaedic surgeon. See: Dict. Amer. Biog., 1st suppl. Allison's atrophy.

Allison tuna (Allison, James A.): Zoology. See: Webster's 3d.

ALLISON, WILLIAM BOYD. 1829-1908. American lawyer and legislator. See: Biog. Direct. Amer. Congress. Bland-Allison Act.

Allison's atrophy (Allison, Nathaniel): Medicine. See: Jablonski.

Allport A-S reaction study (Allport, Gordon Willard): Psychology. See: Chaplin; English; Wolman.

ALLPORT, GORDON WILLARD. 1897-1967. American psychologist. Encyc. Brit., 1973. Allport A-S reaction study, Allport-Vernon-Lindzey study of values, Allport's psychology (of individuality).

Allport-Vernon-Lindzey study of values (Allport, Gordon Willard; Vernon, Philip Ewart; and Lindzey, Gardner Edmond): Psychology. See: Chaplin; Wolman.

Allport's psychology (of individuality) (Allport, Gordon Willard): Psychology. See: Chaplin.

Allstroem relay (Derivation undetermined): Electronics. See: Hughes.

ALLUAUD, FRANCOIS. 1778-1865. French mineralogist. See: Dict. Biog. Fran. Alluaudite.

Alluaudite (Alluaud, Francois): Earth Sciences. See: Thrush.

Ally Sloper's cavalry (Derivation undetermined): History. See: Hargrave.

ALMEIDA, FLORIANO PAULO DE. fl. 1928. Brazilian physician. (Biography source unavailable.) Lutz-Splendore-De Almeida syndrome.

ALMEN, AUGUST THEODOR ANDERSSON. 1833-1903. Swedish physiologist. See: Pogg., vol. 3. Almen-Nylander test, Almen test (for carbohydrates), Almen test reaction for cyanide, Almen's (solution or test) for albumin, Almen's (solution or test) for blood, Almen's (solution or test) for glucose.

Almen-Nylander test (Almen, August Theodor Andersson and Nylander, Claes Wilhelm G.): Chemistry. See: Ballentyne.

Almen-Schoenbein solution (Almen, August Theodor and Schoenbein, Christian Friedrich). See: Almen's (solution or test) for blood.

Almen test (for carbohydrates) (Almen, August Theodor Andersson): Chemistry. See: Hackh.

Almen test reaction for cyanide (Almen, August Theodor Andersson): Chemistry. See: Van Nostrand Chem. Dict.

Almen's (solution or test) for albumin (Almen, August Theodor Andersson): Chemistry. See: Dorland; Stedman; Van Nostrand Chem. Dict.

Almen's (solution or test) for blood (Almen, August Theodor Andersson): Chemistry. See: Dorland; Stedman. Also known as: Almen-Schoenbein solution, Schoenbein's test, Van Deen test reaction.

Almen's (solution or test) for glucose (Almen, August Theodor Andersson): Chemistry. See: Stedman; Van Nostrand Chem. Dict.

ALMOND. fl. 1890. American engineer. (Biography source unavailable.) Almond coupling.

Almond coupling (Almond): Engineering and Industry. See: Auger.

ALNASCHAR. Character in the "Arabian Nights." See: Benet. Alnaschar dreams.

Alnaschar dreams (Alnaschar): Generic Word. See: Brewer; Partridge; Weekley.

Aloisiite (Abruzzi, Duke of the): Earth Sciences. See: Webster's 3d.

Alonsoa (Zanoni, Alonzo): Botany. See: Taylor, N.

alopecia Celsi (Celsus, Aulus Cornelius). See: Celsus' vitiligo.

Alouette's amputation (Derivation undetermined): Medicine. See: Stedman.

ALOY, JULES FRANCOIS. fl. 1903. French physician. See: Pogg., vol. 5. Aloy-Laprade reagent, Aloy-Rabaut test, Aloy reagent for alkaloids, Aloy test reaction for morphine, Aloy tests for uranium and hydrogen peroxide, Aloy-Valdiguie morphine reagent, Aloy-Valdiguie strychnine reagent, Aloy-Valdiguie test for copper and hydroquinone, Aloy-Valdiguie test reaction for formaldehyde, trioxymethylene and methenamine.

Aloy-Laprade reagent (Aloy, Jules Francois and Laprade, F.): Chemistry. See: Van Nostrand Chem. Dict.

Aloy-Rabaut test (Aloy, Jules Francois and Rabaut, Charles): Chemistry. See: Van Nostrand Chem. Dict.

Aloy reagent for alkaloids (Aloy, Jules Francois): Chemistry. See: Van Nostrand Chem. Dict.

Aloy test reaction for morphine (Aloy, Jules Francois): Chemistry. See: Van Notrand Chem. Dict.

Aloy tests for uranium and hydrogen peroxide (Aloy, Jules Francois): Chemistry. See: Van Nostrand Chem. Dict.

Aloy-Valdiguie morphine reagent (Aloy, Jules Francois and Valdiguie, A.): Chemistry. See: Van Nostrand Chem. Dict.

Aloy-Valdiguie strychnine reagent (Aloy, Jules Francois and Valdiguie, A.): Chemistry. See: Van Nostrand Chem. Dict.

Aloy-Valdiguie test for copper and hydroquinone (Aloy, Jules Francois and Valdiguie, A.): Chemistry. See: Van Nostrand Chem. Dict.

Aloy-Valdiguie test reaction for formaldehyde, trioxymethylene and methenamine (Aloy, Jules Francois and Valdiguie, A.): Chemistry. See: Van Nostrand Chem. Dict.

Aloysia (Maria Luisa Teresa): Botany. See: Webster's 3d.

ALPERS, BERNARD JACOB. 1900- . American neurologist. See: Who's Imp. Med., 2d. ed. Alpers' disease.

Alpers' disease (Alpers, Bernard Jacob): Medicine. See: Jablonski; Wolman. Also known as: Christensen-Krabbe disease.

ALPERT, DANIEL. 1917- . American physicist. See: World Who's Who. Sci. Bayard and Alpert gauge.

Alphen, Pieter Martinus van. See: Van Alphen, Pieter Martinus.

ALPHONSE. Character from comic strip by Frederick B. Opper. (Biography source unavailable.) Alphonse and Gaston.

Alphonse and Gaston (Alphonse and Gaston, the comic strip characters): Generic Word. See: Webster's 3d.

Alphonsin (surgical instrument) (Ferri, Alphonso): Medicine. See: Brewer; Charnock; Partridge.

Alphonsine tables (Alphonso X): Astronomy. See: Brewer; Harvey; Phyfe.

ALPHONSO X. 1226-1284. King of Castile and Leon. Encyc. Brit., 1973. Alphonsine tables.

ALPINI, PROSPERO. 1553-1617. Italian botanist. See: Dict. Sci. Biog. Alpinia.

Alpinia (Alpini, Prospero): Botany. See: Dorland; Taylor, N.

ALPORT, ARTHUR CECIL. fl. 1927. English physician. (Biography source unavailable.) Alport's syndrome.

Alport's syndrome (Alport, Arthur Cecil): Medicine. See: Jablonski; Stedman. Also known as: Dickinson's syndrome.

ALSBERG, ALBERT A. b. 1856. German physician. See: Biog. Lex. hervorr. Aerzte. Alsberg's triangle?

Alsberg's triangle (Alsberg, Albert A.?): Medicine. See: Stedman.

Alsing cylinder (Derivation undetermined): Engineering and Industry. See: Thrush.

ALSTON, CHARLES. 1683-1760. Scottish physician. See: Dict. Nat. Biog. Alstonia.

Alstonia (Alston, Charles): Botany. See: Dorland; Stedman; Webster's 3d.

ALSTROEM, CARL HENRY. fl. 1957. Swedish physician. (Biography source unavailable.) Alstroem-Hallgren syndrome, Alstroem-Olsen syndrome.

Alstroem-Hallgren syndrome (Alstroem, Carl Henry and Hallgren, Bertil): Medicine. See: Jablonski.

Alstroem-Olsen syndrome (Alstroem, Carl Henry and Olsen, Olaf): Medicine. See: Jablonski.

ALSTROEMER, KLAS VON. 1736-1794. Swedish botanist. See: Nouv. Biog. Univ. Alstroemeria.

Alstroemeria (Alstroemer, Klas von): Botany. See: Webster's 3d.

ALT, A. fl. 1926. German chemist. (Biography source unavailable.) Tillmans-Alt test reaction for tryptophane.

Alteneck, Friedrich von Hefner-. See: Von Hefner-Alteneck, Friedrich.

ALTER, J. CECIL. fl. 1902- . American meteorologist. See: Amer. Men Sci., 10th ed. Alter shield.

Alter shield (Alter, J. Cecil): Earth Sciences. See: Huschke.

ALTHAEA. Greek mythical figure. See: Jobes. Althaea's brand.

Althaea's brand (Althaea): Generic Word (fatal contingency). See: Brewer.

Althausen test (Althausen, Theodore L.): Medicine. See: Dorland.

ALTHAUSEN, THEODORE L. 1897- . American physician. See: Who's Imp. Med., 2d. ed. Althausen test.

ALTHERR, FRANZ. fl. 1936. German physician. (Biography source unavailable.) Mayenburg-Altherr-Uehlinger syndrome.

Althorp, Viscount. See: Spencer, John Charles (Viscount Althorp).

Althorp's Irish Church Act (Spencer, John Charles, Viscount Althorp): History. See: Harbottle.

Altman solution (Derivation undetermined): Chemistry. See: Van Nostrand Chem. Dict.

Altmann-Gersh method (Altmann, Richard and Gersh, Isidore): Medicine. See: Dorland; Stedman.

ALTMANN, RICHARD. 1852-1900. German histologist. See: World Who's Who Sci. Altmann-Gersh method, Altmann solution, Altmann's fluid, Altmann's granule, Altmann's theory.

Altmann solution (Altmann, Richard): Chemistry. See: Van Nostrand Chem. Dict.

Altmann's fluid (Altmann, Richard): Medicine. See: Dorland; Stedman.

Altmann's granule (Altmann, Richard): Medicine. See: Dorland; Henderson; Stedman.

Altmann's theory (Altmann, Richard): Medicine. See: Dorland; Stedman.

Alvarez cholic acid reagent (Pinerua y Alvarez, Eugenio): Chemistry. See: Van Nostrand Chem. Dict.

Alvarez, Eugenio y Pinerua. See: Pinerua y Alvarez, Eugenio.

Alvarez, Fernando. See: Alba, Fernando Alvarez de Toledo.

Alvarez nitrate reagent (Pinerua y Alvarez, Eugenio): Chemistry. See: Van Nostrand Chem. Dict.

Alvarez reaction for aconitine (Pinerua y Alvarez, Eugenio): Chemistry. See: Van Nostrand Chem. Dict.

Alvarez reagent for cobalt, nickel, and zinc (Pinerua y Alvarez, Eugenio): Chemistry. See: Van Nostrand Chem. Dict.

Alvarez reagent for nickel (Pinerua y Alvarez, Eugenio): Chemistry. See: Van Nostrand Chem. Dict.

Alvarez reagent for organic acids (Pinerua y Alvarez, Eugenio): Chemistry. See: Van Nostrand Chem. Dict.

Alvarez reagent for organic compounds (Pinerua y Alvarez, Eugenio): Chemistry. See: Van Nostrand Chem. Dict.

Alvarez reagent for osmic acid (Pinerua y Alvarez, Eugenio): Chemistry. See: Van Nostrand Chem. Dict.

Alvarez reagent for potassium (Pinerua y Alvarez, Eugenio): Chemistry. See: Van Nostrand Chem. Dict.

Alvarez test for pyruvic acid (Pinerua y Alvarez, Eugenio): Chemistry. See: Van Nostrand Chem. Dict.

Alvegniat's pump (Derivation undetermined): Medicine. See: Stedman.

Alven, Hannes. See: Alfven, Hannes.

ALZHEIMER, ALOIS. 1864-1915. German neurologist. See: World Who's Who Sci. Alzheimer's baskets, Alzheimer's cells, Alzheimer's disease (dementia, sclerosis or syndrome), Alzheimer's stain.

Alzheimer's baskets (Alzheimer, Alois): Medicine. See: Dorland.

Alzheimer's cells (Alzheimer, Alois): Medicine. See: Dorland.

Alzheimer's disease (dementia, sclerosis or syndrome) (Alzheimer, Alois): Medicine. See: Hinsie; Jablonski; Wolman.

Alzheimer's stain (Alzheimer, Alois): Medicine. See: Dorland.

Amadis (Amadis of Gaul): Generic Word (hero). See: Weekley.

AMADIS OF GAUL. Fictional hero of the Spanish romance "Amadis of Gaul." See: Benet. Amadis.

Amadori arrangement (Amadori, Mario): Chemistry. See: Van Nostrand Chem. Dict.

AMADORI, MARIO. b. 1886. Italian chemist. See: Pogg., vol. 5. Amadori arrangement.

Amadot (pear) (Oudet, Dame): Botany. See: Charnock.

Amagat coordinates (Amagat, Emile Hilaire): Physics. See: Internat. Dict. Ap. Math.

AMAGAT, EMILE HILAIRE. 1841-1915. French physicist. See: Dict. Sci. Biog. Amagat coordinates, Amagat-Leduc rule, Amagat unit.

Amagat law (Amagat, Emile Hilaire). See: Amagat-Leduc rule.

Amagat-Leduc rule (Amagat, Emile Hilaire and Leduc, Anatole): Physics. See: Ballentyne; Internat. Dict. Phys. Elec. Also known as: Amagat law; Leduc law.

Amagat unit (Amagat, Emile Hilaire): Physics. See: Ballentyne; Internat. Dict. Ap. Math.; Internat. Dict. Phys. Elec.

AMALRIC OF BENA. d. 1209. French theologian and mystical philosopher. See: Encyc. Brit., 1911. Amalricians.

Amalricians (Amalric of Bena): Religion. See: Canney.

Amalric's syndrome (Amalric, P.): Medicine. See: Jablonski.

AMALTHEA. Greek mythological foster mother of Zeus. See: Encyc. Brit., 1973. Amalthea's horn.

Amalthea's horn (Amalthea): Mythology (cornucopia). See: Brewer.

Aman. See: Haman.

AMANN, JULES. fl. 1896. French pharmacist. (Biography source unavailable.) Amann solution.

Amann solution (Amann, Jules): Chemistry. See: Van Nostrand Chem. Dict.

AMATI. Celebrated 16th and 17th c. Italian family of violin-makers. See: Grove. Amati (violin).

Amati (violin) (Amati): Music. See: Brewer; Latham; Partridge.

amaurosis congenita of Leber (Leber, Theodor). See: Leber's amaurosis.

AMBARD, LEON. 1876-1962. French physiologist. Cited in: New York Acad. Med. Portrait Cat. Ambard's constant (or coefficient), Ambard's laws.

Ambard's constant (or coefficient) (Ambard, Leon): Medicine. See: Dorland; Stedman.

Ambard's laws (Ambard, Leon): Medicine. See: Stedman.

AMBERG, EMIL. 1868-1948. American otologist. See: Who's Who Among Physicians and Surg. Amberg's line.

Amberg's line (Amberg, Emil): Medicine. See: Dorland; Stedman.

AMBOISE, GEORGES D'. 1460-1510. Archbishop of Rouen. See: Encyc. Brit., 1973. Let George do it.

Amboy clay (Derivation undetermined): Earth Sciences. See: Thrush.

Ambrogal printing (Galetzka, Ambrosius): Printing. See: Harrod.

AMBROSE. fl. 16th c. French Anabaptist. (Biography source unavailable.) Ambrosians.

AMBROSE, SAINT. 333-397. Bishop of Milan. Encyc. Brit., 1973. Ambrosian chant, Ambrosian hymns, Ambrosian modes, Ambrosian rite (or liturgy), Ambrosians, Ambrosiaster, Ambrosin.

Ambrosian chant (Ambrose, Saint): Music. See: Apel; Attwater; Phyfe.

Ambrosian hymns (Ambrose, Saint): Music. See: Apel.

Ambrosian modes (Ambrose, Saint): Music. See: Apel.

Ambrosian rite (or liturgy) (Ambrose, Saint): Religion. See: Attwater; Canney.

Ambrosians (Ambrose): Religion. See: Canney.

Ambrosians (Ambrose, Saint): Religion. See: Mathews, S.

Ambrosiaster (Ambrose, Saint): Religion. See: Mathews, S.

Ambrosin (Ambrose, Saint): Numismatics. See: Charnock.

Ambu bag (Derivation undetermined): Medicine. See: Stedman.

Amedeo, Luigi Aloisius. See: Abruzzi, Duke of the.

AMES, ADELBERT JR. 1880-1955. American educator. Who Was Who Amer. Ames demonstrations.

AMES, BRUCE NATHAN. 1928- . American biochemist and geneticist. See: World Who's Who Sci. Ames waltzer?

Ames demonstrations (Ames, Adelbert Jr.): Psychology. See: Chaplin; English; Wolman.

AMES, JAMES. fl. 1876. American mine owner. Cited in: Bailey. Amesite.

AMES, JOHN W. fl. 1910-1921. American chemist. Cited in: Chem. Abstr., vol. 13, p. 986. Ames limestone.

Ames limestone (Ames, John W.): Earth Sciences. See: Thrush.

Ames moisture tester (Derivation undetermined): Chemistry. See: Hackh.

Ames' waltzer (Ames, Bruce Nathan?): Genetics. See: Gray.

Amesite (Ames, James): Earth Sciences. See: Thrush.

AMHERST, SARAH ELIZABETH. d. 1876. English amateur naturalist. See: Biog. Notes Upon Botanist. Lady Amherst's pheasant.

AMICI, GIOVANNI BATTISTA. 1786-1868. Italian astronomer and physicist. See: Dict. Sci. Biog. Amici prism, Amici's disk.

Amici prism (Amici, Giovanni Battista): Physics. See: Internat. Dict. Phys. Elec.; Van Nostrand Chem. Dict.; Van Nostrand Sci. Encyc.

Amici's disk (Amici, Giovanni Battista): Medicine. See: Dorland.

Amish (Amman, Jakob): Religion. See: Hendrickson.

AMMAN, JAKOB. fl. 17th c. Swiss Mennonite bishop. See: Webster's Biog. Dict. Amish.

AMMER, G. fl. 1934. German chemist. Cited in: Chem. Abstr., vol. 29, p. 4285. Ammer-Schmitz test reaction.

Ammer-Schmitz test reaction (Ammer, G. and Schmitz, H.): Chemistry. See: Van Nostrand Chem. Dict.

Ammon, Friedrich August von. See: Von Ammon, Friedrich August.

AMMON, JUPITER. Greek and Roman name for the Egyptian god Amen. See: Jobes. Ammonia, Ammonite, Ammon's horn.

AMMON, OTTO GEORG. 1842-1916. German anthropologist. See: World Who's Who Sci. Ammon's law.

Ammonia (Ammon, Jupiter): Chemistry. See: Charnock; Dorland.

Ammonians (Ammonius Saccas): Philosophy. See: Canney.

Ammonite (Ammon, Jupiter): Earth Sciences. See: Charnock.

AMMONIUS SACCAS. fl. 2d c. Alexandrian philosopher. See: Dict. Christian Biog. Ammonians.

Ammon's fissure (Von Ammon, Friedrich August): Medicine. See: Dorland.

Ammon's horn (Ammon, Jupiter): Anatomy. See: Gray; Stedman.

Ammon's law (Ammon, Otto Georg): Anthropology. See: Winick; Zadrozny.

Ammon's operation (Von Ammon, Friedrich August): Medicine. See: Dorland; Stedman.

AMONTONS, GUILLAUME. 1663-1705. French physicist. See: Dict. Sci. Biog. Amontons' law.

Amontons' law (Amontons, Guillaume): Chemistry. See: Ballentyne.

AMOS. fl. 8th c. B.C. Hebrew prophet. See: Webster's Biog. Dict. Amosites?

Amosites (Amos?): Religion. See: Canney.

AMOSS, HAROLD LINDSAY. 1886-1956. American physician. See: World Who's Who Sci. Amoss' sign.

Amoss' sign (Amoss, Harold Lindsay): Medicine. See: Dorland; Stedman.

AMPERE, ANDRE MARIE. 1775-1836. French mathematician and physicist. See: Dict. Sci. Biog. Ampere hour, Ampere law, Ampere rule, Ampere theorem, Ampere theory (of magnetism), Ampere turn, Ampere (unit), Amperian currents, Amperometric titration.

Ampere hour (Ampere, Andre Marie): Physics. See: Internat. Dict. Phys. Elec.; Markus; Van Nostrand Sci. Encyc.

Ampere law (Ampere, Andre Marie): Physics. See: Ballentyne; Internat. Dict. Phys. Elec.; Thewlis.

Ampere rule (Ampere, Andre Marie): Physics. See: Internat. Dict. Ap. Math.; Markus; Thewlis.

Ampere theorem (Ampere, Andre Marie): Physics. See: Internat. Dict. Phys. Elec.

Ampere theory (of magnetism) (Ampere, Andre Marie): Physics. See: Internat. Dict. Phys. Elec.

Ampere turn (Ampere, Andre Marie): Physics. See: Ballentyne; Dresner; Internat. Dict. Ap. Math.

Ampere (unit) (Ampere, Andre Marie): Physics. See: Ballentyne; Dresner; Van Nostrand Sci. Encyc.

Amperian currents (Ampere, Andre Marie): Physics. See: Internat. Dict. Phys. Elec.

Amperometric titration (Ampere, Andre Marie): Physics. See: Van Nostrand Sci. Encyc.

AMPHITRITE. Greek mythological sea goddess. See: Jobes. Amphitrite.

Amphitrite (Amphitrite): Zoology. See: Charnock.

AMPHITRYON. Mythological son of Alcaeus. See: Oxford Clas. Dict. Amphitryon.

Amphitryon (Amphitryon, the hero): Generic Word (host). See: Barnhart, (Eng. Lit.); De Sola; Partridge.

ampulla of Vater (Vater, Abraham). See: Vater's ampulla.

ampullae of Lorenzini (Lorenzini, Stefano). See: Lorenzini's ampulla(-ae).

AMSDORF, NIKOLAUS VON. 1483-1565. German Protestant theologian. See: Encyc. Brit., 1973. Amsdorfians.

Amsdorfians (Amsdorf, Nikolaus von): Religion. See: Canney.

AMSLER-LAFFON, JAKOB. 1823-1912. Swiss mathematician. See: Dict. Sci. Biog. Amsler testing machines, Amsler's planimeter.

AMSLER, MARC. b. 1891. Swiss ophthalmologist. See: Who's Who Switz., 1950. Amsler's chart, Amsler's marker.

Amsler testing machines (Amsler-Laffon, Jakob): Engineering and Industry. See: Auger.

Amsler's chart (Amsler, Marc): Medicine. See: Stedman.

Amsler's marker (Amsler, Marc): Medicine. See: Dorland; Stedman.

Amsler's planimeter (Amsler-Laffon, Jakob): Engineering and Industry. See: Encyc. Brit., 1973 under "Mathematical Instruments."

AMSON, CHARLES. fl. 18th c. American physician. (Biography source unavailable.) Amsonia.

Amsonia (Amson, Charles): Botany. See: Taylor, N.

Amundsen-Ellsworth-Nobile expedition (Amundsen, Roald; Ellsworth, Lincoln; and Nobile, Umberto): History. See: Jameson.

Amundsen-Ellsworth North Pole expedition (Amundsen, Roald and Ellsworth, Lincoln): History. See: Jameson.

AMUNDSEN, ROALD. 1872-1928. Norwegian polar explorer. See: Ann. Register. Amundsen-Ellsworth North Pole expedition, Amundsen-Ellsworth-Nobile expedition.

AMUSSAT, JEAN ZULEMA. 1796-1856. French surgeon. See: Nouv. Biog. Univ. Amussat's operation, Amussat's probe, Amussat's valve (or valvula).

Amussat's operation (Amussat, Jean Zulema): Medicine. See: Dorland.

Amussat's probe (Amussat, Jean Zulema): Medicine. See: Dorland.

Amussat's valve (or valvala) (Amussat, Jean Zulema): Anatomy. See: Donath; Dorland; Stedman.

Amyraldists (Amyraut, Moise): Religion. See: Canney.

AMYRAUT, MOISE. 1596-1664. French Protestant theologian. See: Encyc. Brit., 1973. Amyraldists.

Amy's case (Dardin, Amy): Generic Word (procrastination). See: Mathews, M. M.

ANACREON. 560-475 B.C. Greek lyric poet. See: Encyc. Brit., 1973. Anacreontic poetry.

Anacreontic poetry (Anacreon): Literature. See: Barnet; Preminger; Scott.

ANAGNOSTAKIS, ANDREAS. 1826-1897. Cretan ophthalmologist. See: World Who's Who Sci. Hotz-Anagnostakis operation.

ANAN BEN DAVID. fl. 8th c. Jewish religious leader in Persia. See: Encyc. Brit., 1911. Ananism.

Anandatirtha. See: Madhva.

Ananias (Ananias the Christian): Generic Word (liar). See: Hendrickson; Mathews, M. M.; Partridge.

Ananias Club (Ananias the Christian): History. See: Hendrickson; Mathews, M.M.

ANANIAS THE CHRISTIAN. Biblical member of the church at Jerusalem. See: Webster's Biog. Dict. Ananias, Ananias Club.

Ananism (Anan ben David): Religion. See: Webster's 3d.

ANAXAGORAS. 500?-428 B.C. Greek philosopher. See: Dict. Sci. Biog. Anaxagorean.

Anaxagorean (Anaxogoras): Philosophy. See: Webster's 3d.

ANAXIMANDER. 611-547 B.C. Greek astronomer and philosopher. See: Encyc. Brit., 1973. Anaximandrian.

Anaximandrian (Anaximander): Philosophy. See: Webster's 3d.

ANCELL, HENRY A. b. 1802. English physician. See: Biog. Lex. hervorr. Aerzte. Ancell-Spiegler cylindroma.

Ancell-Spiegler cylindroma (Ancell, Henry A. and Spiegler, Eduard). See: Spiegler's tumor.

ANCHIETA, JOSE DE. 1533-1597. Portuguese Jesuit missionary in Brazil. See: Nouv. Biog. Univ. Anchietea.

Anchietea (Anchieta, Jose de): Botany. See: Webster's 3d.

ANDERNACH, JOHANN WINTHER VON. 1487-1574. German physician. See: Dict. Sci. Biog. Andernach's ossicles.

Andernach's ossicles (Andernach, Johann Winther von): Medicine. See: Dorland.

Anders' disease (Anders, James Meschter): Medicine. See: Dorland.

ANDERS, JAMES MESCHTER. 1854-1936. American physician. Who's Who Amer., 1936-37. Anders' disease, Anders' syndrome.

Anders' syndrome (Anders, James Meschter). See: Dercum's syndrome.

ANDERSCH, CARL SAMUEL. 1732-1777. German anatomist. See: Webster's Biog. Dict. Andersch's ganglion, Andersch's nerve.

Andersch's ganglion (Andersch, Carl Samuel): Anatomy. See: Donath; Dorland; Stedman.

Andersch's nerve (Andersch, Carl Samuel): Anatomy. See: Dorland; Stedman. Also known as: Jacobson's nerve.

Andersen Award (Andersen, Hans Christian): Literature. See: Harrod.

ANDERSEN, DOROTHY HANSINE. 1901- . American pediatrician. Who's Who Amer. Women, 1961/62. Andersen's disease, Andersen's syndrome (or triad).

ANDERSEN, HANS CHRISTIAN. 1805-1875. Danish author. See: Encyc. Brit., 1973. Andersen Award.

Andersen's disease (Andersen, Dorothy Hansine): Medicine. See: Jablonski; Stedman.

Andersen's syndrome (or triad) (Andersen, Dorothy Hansine): Medicine. See: Dorland; Jablonski. Also known as: Clarke-Hadfield syndrome; Fanconi's syndrome; Glanzmann's dysporia.

Anderson bridge (Derivation undetermined): Electronics. See: Hughes; Internat. Dict. Phys. Elec.; Markus.

ANDERSON, CHARLES ALFRED. 1902- . American geologist. See: World Who's Who Sci. Andersonite.

ANDERSON, CLINTON PRESBA. 1895- . American legislator. See: Biog. Direct. Amer. Congress. Price-Anderson Act.

Anderson-Collip test (Anderson, Evelyn and Collip, James Bertram): Medicine. See: Stedman.

Anderson-Darling statistic (Anderson, Theodore Wilbur and Darling, Donald Allan): Statistics. See: Kendall.

ANDERSON, E. W. fl. 1922. English? engineer. (Biography source unavailable.) Anderson ram.

ANDERSON, ELIZABETH MILBANK. 1850-1921. American philanthropist. See: Dict. Amer. Biog. Milbank Memorial Fund.

ANDERSON, EVELYN. 1899- . American physician. Who's Imp. Med., 2d. ed. Anderson-Collip test.

ANDERSON, SIR JOHN. 1882-1958. English civil servant. See: Dict. Nat. Biog., 1951-60. suppl. Anderson shelter.

ANDERSON, JOHN AUGUST. 1876-1959. American physicist. See: Pogg., vol. 7b. Wood-Anderson seismograph.

Anderson larkspur (Derivation undetermined): Botany. See: Winburne.

ANDERSON, OSKAR JOHANN VIKTOR. 1887-1960. Russian-born mathematician. See: Dict. Sci. Biog. Anderson-Darling statistic?

Anderson ram (Anderson, E. W.): Engineering and Industry. See: Auger.

ANDERSON, ROGER. 1891- . American orthopedic surgeon. See: Direct. Med. Specialists, 1968/69. Anderson splint.

ANDERSON, ROSE GUSTAVA. 1893- . American psychologist. See: World Who's Who Sci. Kuhlmann-Anderson tests of academic potential.

Anderson shelter (Anderson, Sir John): Engineering and Industry. See: Partridge.

Anderson splint (Anderson, Roger): Medicine. See: Dorland; Stedman.

Anderson test reaction for papaverine (Anderson, Thomas?): Chemistry. See: Van Nostrand Chem. Dict.

Anderson test reaction for pyridine bases (Anderson, Thomas): Chemistry. See: Van Nostrand Chem. Dict.

ANDERSON, THEODORE WILBUR. 1918- . American statistician. See: Amer. Men Sci., 11th ed. Anderson-Darling statistic.

ANDERSON, THOMAS. 1819-1874. Scottish organic chemist. See: Dict. Sci. Biog. Anderson test reaction for papaverine?, Anderson test reaction for pyridine bases.

ANDERSON, VIRGINIA. Friend of American naturalist, Spencer Fullerton Baird. (Biography source unavailable.) Virginia's warbler.

ANDERSON, WILLIAM. d. 1778. English surgeon, naturalist and explorer. See: Dict. Nat. Biog. Andersonia.

ANDERSON, WILLIAM A. b. 1842. English dermatologist. See: Biog. Lex. hervorr. Aerzte. Fabry-Anderson syndrome.

Andersonia (Anderson, William): Botany. See: Charnock.

Andersonite (Anderson, Charles Alfred): Earth Sciences. See: Thrush; Webster's 3d.

ANDERTON, BENJAMIN ALBERT. b. 1889. American scientist. Cited in: Chem. Abstr. Anderton shearer loader?

Anderton shearer loader (Anderton, Benjamin Albert?): Engineering and Industry. See: Thrush.

ANDOGSKY, N. fl. 1914. German physician. (Biography source unavailable.) Andogsky's syndrome.

Andogsky's syndrome (Andogsky, N.): Medicine. See: Jablonski.

Andorite (Semsey, Andor von): Earth Sciences. See: Thrush; Webster's 3d.

ANDRADA E SILVA, JOSE BONIFACIO DE. 1763?-1838. Brazilian statesman and geologist. See: Encyc. Brit., 1973. Andradite.

ANDRADE, CORINO M. fl. 1952. English physician. (Biography source unavailable.) Andrade's syndrome.

ANDRADE, EDUARDO PENNY. 1872-1906. American bacteriologist. (Biography source unavailable.) Andrade solution.

ANDRADE, EDWARD NEVILLE DA COSTA. 1887-1971. English physicist. See: Webster's Biog. Dict. Andrade's creep law.

Andrade solution (Andrade, Eduardo Penny): Chemistry. See: Van Nostrand Chem. Dict.

Andrade's creep law (Andrade, Edward Neville da Costa): Physics. See: Ballentyne.

Andrade's syndrome (Andrade, Corino M.): Medicine. See: Jablonski. Also known as: Corino de Andrade's paramyloidosis; Wohlwill-Corino Andrade syndrome.

Andradite (Andrada e Silva, Jose Bonifacio de): Earth Sciences. See: Thrush; Van Nostrand Sci. Encyc.; Webster's 3d.

ANDRAL, GABRIEL. 1797-1876. French physician. See: Nouv. Biog. Univ. Andral's decubitus.

Andral's decubitus (Andral, Gabriel): Medicine. See: Dorland.

ANDRASSY, GYULA. 1823-1890. Hungarian statesman. See: Encyc. Brit., 1973. Andrassy note.

Andrassy note (Andrassy, Gyula): History. See: Harbottle; Latham; Montgomery.

ANDRE, EMILE. b. 1877. French chemist. See: Pogg., vol. 7b. Andre reagent for alkaloids? Andre test reaction for quinine?

Andre reagent for alkaloids (Andre, Emile?): Chemistry. See: Van Nostrand Chem. Dict.

Andre test reaction for quinine (Andre, Emile?): Chemistry. See: Van Nostrand Chem. Dict.

Andre-Venner accumulator (Derivation undetermined): Engineering and Industry. See: Hughes.

Andrea Ferrara (sword) (Ferrara, Andrea): Weapons. See: Brewer; Hendrickson; Partridge.

ANDREASCH, RUDOLPH. 1857-1928. Austrian chemist. See: Pogg., vol. 4. Andreasch test reaction.

Andreasch test reaction (Andreasch, Rudolph): Chemistry. See: Van Nostrand Chem. Dict.

ANDREASEN, ALFRED HERMAN MUNCH. b. 1896. Danish chemist. See: Pogg., vol. 6. Andreasen pipette.

Andreasen pipette (Andreasen, Alfred Herman Munch): Engineering and Industry. See: Thrush.

Andreau engine (Derivation undetermined): Engineering and Industry. See: Auger.

Andree gauge (Andree, Louis): Engineering and Industry. See: Auger.

ANDREE, LOUIS. fl. 1849. German engineer. (Biography source unavailable.) Andree gauge.

Andrew (Millar, Andrew): Generic Word (British Royal Navy). See: Hendrickson.

ANDREW, SAINT. d. 60 A.D. Patron saint of Scotland and Russia. See: Encyc. Brit., 1973. Brotherhood of St. Andrew, Order of St. Andrew, Religious of St. Andrew, Saint Andrew, Saint Andrew's cross, Saint Andrew's Day.

ANDREWES, CHRISTOPHER HOWARD. 1896- . English physician. See: World Who's Who Sci. Andrewes' test.

Andrewes' test (Andrewes, Christopher Howard): Medicine. See: Dorland.

Andrews' disease (or bacterid) (Andrews, George Clinton): Medicine. See: Dorland; Jablonski.

ANDREWS, EDWARD WYLLYS. 1856-1927. American surgeon. See: Who Was Who Amer., vol. 1. Andrews' operation.

Andrews' elutriator (Andrews, Leonard): Engineering and Industry. See: Thrush.

Andrews gentian (Derivation undetermined): Botany. See: Winburne.

ANDREWS, GEORGE CLINTON. 1891- . American dermatologist. See: Who's Imp. Med., 2d. ed. Andrews' disease (or bacterid).

ANDREWS, LEONARD. fl. 1928. English metallurgist. Cited in: Chem. Abstr. Andrews' elutriator.

Andrews' operation (Andrews, Edward Wyllys): Medicine. See: Dorland.

Andrews' pump (Andrews, William Draper): Engineering and Industry. See: Auger.

ANDREWS, THOMAS. 1813-1885. Irish physicist and chemist. See: Dict. Sci. Biog. Andrewsite.

ANDREWS, WILLIAM DRAPER. 1818-1896. American inventor. See: Webster' Biog. Dict. Andrews' pump.

Andrewsite (Andrews, Thomas): Earth Sciences. See: Partridge; Thrush; Webster's 3d.

ANDROMEDA. Mythical Ethiopian princess. See: Oxford Clas. Dict. Andromeda (shrub).

Andromeda (shrub) (Andromeda): Botany. See: Webster's 3d.; Cited in: Weekley.

ANDRUS, CHARLES FREDERICK. 1906- . American plant breeder. See: World Who's Who Sci. Andrus' green stem.

Andrus' green stem (Andrus, Charles Frederick): Botany. See: Gray.

ANEL, DOMINIQUE. 1679-1725. French surgeon. See: Encyc. Brit., 1911. Anel's method, Anel's operation, Anel's probe.

Anel's method (Anel, Dominique): Medicine. See: Stedman.

Anel's operation (Anel, Dominique): Medicine. See: Dorland.

Anel's probe (Anel, Dominique): Medicine. See: Dorland; Stedman.

aneurysm of Charcot (Charcot, Jean-Martin): Medicine. See: Stedman. Also known as: aneurysm of Charcot and Bouchard.

aneurysm of Charcot and Bouchard (Charcot, Jean-Martin and Bouchard, Charles Jacques). See: aneurysm of Charcot.

ANGELESCO, CONSTANTIN. 1869-1948. Roumanian surgeon. See: Who's Who Central East Europe. Angelesco's sign.

Angelesco's sign (Angelesco, Constantin): Medicine. See: Stedman.

ANGELI, ANGELO. b. 1864. Italian chemist. See: Pogg., vol. 4. Angeli-Rimini reaction, Angeli test reaction for indole, Angeli test reaction for hydroxylamine.

Angeli-Rimini reaction (Angeli, Angelo and Rimini, Enrico): Chemistry. See: Van Nostrand Chem. Dict.

Angeli test reaction for hydroxylamine (Angeli, Angelo): Chemistry. See: Van Nostrand Chem. Dict.

Angeli test reaction for indole (Angeli, Angelo): Chemistry. See: Van Nostrand Chem. Dict.

Angelici (Isaac II?): Religion. See: Canney.

ANGELICO, FRANCISCO. fl. 1904-1926. Italian chemist. See: Pogg., vol. 6. Angelico test reaction for aromatic hydroxyaldehydes.

Angelico test reaction for aromatic hydroxyaldehydes (Angelico, Francisco): Chemistry. See: Van Nostrand Chem. Dict.

ANGELUCCI, ARNALDO. 1854-1934. Italian ophthalmologist. See: Diz. Biog. Ital. Angelucci's syndrome.

Angelucci's syndrome (Angelucci, Arnaldo): Medicine. See: Jablonski; Stedman.

ANGELUS CLARENUS. d. 1337. Italian writer and religious leader. See: New Catholic Encyc. Clareni.

Angelus, Isaac. See: Isaac II.

ANGER, V. fl. 1934-1938. German chemist. Cited in: Chem. Abstr., vol. 32, p. 3295. and vol. 28, p. 2334. Anger-Wang test, Feigl-Anger test.

Anger-Wang test (Anger, V. and Wang, S.): Chemistry. See: Van Nostrand Chem. Dict.

Angevin empire (Henry II, Count of Anjou): History. See: Steinberg.

ANGIOLANI, A. fl. 1915. Italian chemist. Cited in: Chem. Abstr. vol. 9, p. 2388. Toschi-Angiolani reagent.

ANGLE, EDWARD, HARTLEY. 1855-1930. American dentist. See: Who Was Who Amer., vol. 1. Angle's classification, Angle's splint.

angle of Louis (Louis, Pierre-Charles-Alexandre). See: Louis' angle.

Angle's classification (Angle, Edward Hartley): Medicine. See: Stedman.

Angle's splint (Angle, Edward Hartley): Medicine. See: Stedman.

anglesea Morris (Morris, William): Zoology. See: Wagner (More Names).

ANGSTROM, ANDERS JONAS. 1814-1874. Swedish astronomer and physicist. See: Dict. Sci. Biog. Angstrom coefficient, Angstrom line, Angstrom unit, Angstrom's formula, Angstrom's law, Angstrom's scale.

Angstrom coefficient (Angstrom, Anders Jonas): Physics. See: Internat. Dict. Ap. Math.

Angstrom compensation pyrheliometer (Angstrom, Knut Johan): Earth Sciences. See: Huschke.

ANGSTROM, KNUT JOHAN. 1857-1910. Swedish physicist. See: World Who's Who. Sci. Angstrom compensation pyrheliometer, Angstrom pyrgeometer.

Angstrom line (Angstrom, Anders Jonas): Astronomy. See: Hendrickson.

Angstrom pyrgeometer (Angstrom, Knut Johan): Earth Sciences. See: Huschke.

Angstrom unit (Angstrom, Anders Jonas): Physics. See: Satterthwaite; Thewlis; Thrush.

Angstrom's formula (Angstrom, Anders Jonas): Physics. See: Ballentyne.

Angstrom's law (Angstrom, Anders Jonas): Physics. See: Dorland; Stedman.

Angstrom's scale (Angstrom, Anders Jonas): Physics. See: Stedman.

Angus-Smith compound (Smith, Robert Angus): Chemistry. See: Thrush.

Angus-Smith process (Smith, Robert Angus): Chemistry. See: Ballentyne.

Angus Smith, Robert. See: Smith, Robert Angus.

anhalonium Lewinii (Lewin, Louis): Botany. See: Stedman.

Anichkov, Nikolay Nikolaevich. See: Anitschkov, Nikolay Nikolaevich.

Aniello, Tommaso. See: Masaniello.

Anima Christi (Jesus Christ): Religion. See: Attwater.

ANITSCHKOV, NIKOLAY NIKOLAEVICH. b. 1885. Russian pathologist. See: Who's Who USSR, 1960/61. Anitschkov's cell (or myocyte).

Anitschkov's cell (or myocyte) (Anitschkov, Nikolay Nikolaevich): Medicine. See: Dorland; Stedman.

Anjou, Count of. See: Henry II of England.

Anjou, Geoffrey Plantagenet, Count of. See: Geoffrey IV.

ANKARSTROEM, JOHAN JAKOB. 1762-1792. Swedish army officer. See: Nouv. Biog. Univ. Ankarstroem's conspiracy.

Ankarstroem's conspiracy (Ankarstroem, Johan Jakob): History. See: Harbottle.

ANKER, MATHIAS JOSEF. 1771-1843. Austrian mineralogist. See: World Who's Who Sci. Ankerite.

Ankerite (Anker, Mathias Josef): Earth Sciences. See: Van Nostrand Sci. Encyc.; Webster's 3d.

ANNA OF RIVOLI. fl. 1829. Italian duchess. (Biography source unavailable.) Anna's hummingbird.

ANNA PAULOWNA. 1795-1865. Russian princess and queen of Willem II of the Netherlands. See: Nieuw Nederl. Biog. Woordenb. Paulownia.

ANNA, SAINT. Mother of the Virgin Mary. See: Holweck. Saint Anne marble?, Saint Ann's bark.

ANNANDALE, THOMAS. 1838-1907. Scottish surgeon. See: Dict. Nat. Biog., 2d. suppl. Annandale's operation.

Annandale's operation (Annandale, Thomas): Medicine. See: Dorland; Stedman.

Anna's hummingbird (Anna of Rivoli): Zoology. See: Gray; Mathews, M. M.; Pennak.

ANNE. 1665-1714. Queen of Britain and Ireland. See: Dict. Nat. Biog. Queen Anne style, Queen Anne's bounty, Queen Anne's dead, Queen Anne's fan, Queen Anne's farthings, Queen Anne's men, Queen Anne's War.

Anne Boleyn costume (Boleyn, Anne): Fashion. See: Picken.

ANNE OF BOHEMIA. 1366-1394. Queen of England. See: Dict. Nat. Biog. Queen Anne's lace.

Annie Oakley(s) (Oakley, Annie): Generic Word (complimentary ticket). See: Brewer; Hendrickson; Webster's 3d.

Annie Oakley (costume) (Oakley, Annie): Fashion. See: Picken.

Anno Domini (Jesus Christ): Generic Word. See: Webster's 3d.

another Richmond in the field (Henry VII, Earl of Richmond): Generic Word (unexpected opponent). See: Hendrickson.

ANSELM OF CANTERBURY, SAINT. 1033-1109. English scholastic philosopher. See: Dict. Nat. Biog. Anselmian.

ANSELMI, GIORGIO. 1723-1797. Italian painter. See: Diz. Biog. Ital. Anselmo (yellow).

Anselmian (Anselm of Canterbury, Saint): Philosophy. See: Webster's 3d.

Anselmier test (Derivation undetermined): Chemistry. See: Van Nostrand Chem. Dict.

Anselmo (yellow) (Anselmi, Giorgio): Fine Art. See: Hendrickson; Partridge.

Anson by-law (Anson, William): Education. See: Montgomery.

ANSON, GEORGE. 1697-1762. English admiral. See: Webster's Biog. Dict. Lord Anson's pea?

ANSON, WILLIAM. 1843-1914. English politician and professor of law. See: Dict. Nat. Biog., 3d. suppl. Anson by-law.

ANSTIE, FRANCIS EDMUND. 1833-1874. English physician. See: Dict. Nat. Biog. Anstie's limit (or rule), Anstie's reagent, Anstie's test.

Anstie's limit (or rule) (Anstie, Francis Edmund): Medicine. See: Dorland.

Anstie's reagent (Anstie, Francis Edmund): Medicine. See: Dorland.

Anstie's test (Anstie, Francis Edmund): Medicine. See: Dorland; Stedman.

Antaean (Antaeus): (strength) Generic Word. See: Partridge; Webster's 3d.

ANTAEUS. Greek mythical giant. See: Jobes. Antaean.

Anthony Eden (hat) (Eden, Robert Anthony): Fashion. See: Brewer; Hendrickson; Partridge.

ANTHONY, HENRY BOWEN. 1859-1894. American legislator. See: Dict. Amer. Biog. Anthony rule.

Anthony pig. See: Tantony pig.

Anthony rule (Anthony, Henry Bowen): Political Science. See: Mathews, M. M.; Smith.

ANTHONY, SAINT. 251-356. Egyptian monk. See: Encyc. Brit., 1973. Antonians, Orders of Saint Anthony, Rule of Saint Anthony, Saint Anthony, Saint Anthony variations, Saint Anthony's cross, Saint Anthony's dance, Saint Anthony's fire, Tantony bell, Tantony (pig).

Anthony stain (Derivation undetermined): Chemistry. See: Van Nostrand Chem. Dict.

ANTIGONE. Greek mythical daughter of Oedipus. See: Jobes. Antigone complex.

Antigone complex (Antigone): Psychology. See: Wolman.

ANTINOUS. d. 130 A.D. Greek-born favorite of Emperor Hadrian. See: Encyc. Brit., 1973. Antinous.

Antinous (Antinous): (handsome) Generic Word. See: Partridge; Weekley.

Antipoys apparatus (Derivation undetermined): Engineering and Industry. See: Thrush.

Antoine equation (Antoine, Louis Charles): Chemistry. See: Ballentyne.

ANTOINE, LOUIS CHARLES. b. 1825. French marine engineer. See: Pogg., vol. 3. Antoine equation.

Anton-Babinski syndrome (Anton, Gabriel and Babinski, Joseph Francois Felix): Medicine. See: Jablonski. Also known as: Anton's symptom (or syndrome).

ANTON, GABRIEL. 1858-1933. German neuropsychiatrist. See: Wer Ist's, 1906. Anton-Babinski syndrome.

ANTONI, NILS RAGNER EUGEN. 1887- . Danish neurologist. Cited in: New York Acad. Med. Portrait Cat. Antoni type neurilemoma?

Antoni type neurilemoma (Antoni, Nils Ragner Eugen?): Medicine. See: Stedman.

ANTONIADI, EUGENE M. 1870-1944. Turkish-born French astronomer. See: Dict. Sci. Biog. Antoniadi scale.

Antoniadi scale (Antoniadi, Eugene M.): Astronomy. See: Satterthwaite.

Antonians (Anthony, Saint): Religion. See: Attwater.

Antonianus (Antoninus Caracalla, Marcus Aurelius): Numismatics. See: Stenhouse; Webster's 3d.

Antonine (Antoninus Pius): History. See: Webster's 3d.

ANTONINUS CARACALLA, MARCUS AURELIUS. 186-217. Roman emperor. See: Encyc. Brit., 1973. Antonianus.

ANTONINUS PIUS. d. 161 A.D. Roman emperor. See: Webster's Biog. Dict. Antonine.

ANTONOFF, GEORGE. 1880-1959. Russian chemist. See: Pogg., vol. 5. Antonoff's rule.

Antonoff's rule (Antonoff, George): Chemistry. See: Ballentyne; Internat. Dict. Phys. Elec.; Thewlis.

Anton's symptom (or syndrome) (Anton, Gabriel). See: Anton-Babinski syndrome.

antrum of Highmore (or Highmore's antrum) (Highmore, Nathaniel): Anatomy. See: Donath; Dorland; Stedman; Webster's 3d.

ANTYLLUS. fl. 2nd c. A.D. Greek physician and surgeon. See: Webster's Biog. Dict. Antyllus method (or operation).

Antyllus' method (or operation) (Antyllus): Medicine. See: Dorland; Stedman.

ANUBIS. Egyptian jackal god of the underworld. See: Jobes. Anubis baboon.

Anubis baboon (Anubis): Zoology. See: Webster's 3d.

Aoki-Kimberley Treaty (Aoki, Shuzo and Wodehouse, John, 1st Earl of Kimberley): History. Cited in: Webster's Biog. Dict.

AOKI, SHUZO. 1844-1914. Japanese diplomat. See: Webster's Biog. Dict. Aoki-Kimberley Treaty.

AOYAMA, FUNIO. fl. 20th c. Japanese anatomist. (Biography source unavailable.) Aoyama's fluid.

Aoyama's fluid (Aoyama, Fumio): Medicine. See: Webster's 3d.

APELLES. fl. 150 A.D. Religious leader. See: Nouv. Biog. Univ. Apellianists.

Apellianists (Apelles): Religion. See: Canney.

APELT, FRIEDRICH. 1877-1911. German physician. Cited in: Kelly. Nonne-Apelt reaction.

APERT, EUGENE. 1868-1940. French pediatrician. Cited in: New York Acad. Med. Portrait Cat. Apert's disease (or syndrome), Apert's hirsutism, Cook-Apert-Gallais syndrome.

Apert-Gallais syndrome (Apert, Eugene and Gallais, Alfred). See: Cooke-Apert-Gallais syndrome.

Apert's disease (or syndrome) (Apert, Eugene): Medicine. See: Dorland; Jablonski; Stedman.

Apert's hirsutism (Apert, Eugene): Medicine. See: Stedman.

Apfelbaum, Hirsch. See: Grigori E. Zinoviev.

Apgar score (Apgar, Virginia): Medicine. See: Stedman.

APGAR, VIRGINIA. 1909- . American anesthesiologist. See: Who's Who Amer., 1966-67. Apgar score.

aphorisms of Hippocrates (Hippocrates of Cos): Medicine. See: Dorland; Stedman.

Aphrodisiac (Aphrodite): Generic Word. See: Partridge; Stenhouse.

APHRODITE. Greek goddess of love, beauty and fertility. See: Oxford Clas. Dict. Aphrodisiac. See also: Venus.

Api (apple) (Apicius, Marcus Gabius): Botany. See: Hendrickson.

Apicia (cakes) (Apicius, Marcus Gabius): Food and Drink. See: Stenhouse.

Apicium (wine) (Apicius, Marcus Gabius): Food and Drink. See: Stenhouse.

Apicius (or Apician) (1) (Apicius, Marcus Gabius): (gourmand) Generic Word. See: Brewer; Hendrickson.

Apicius (or Apician) (2) (Apicius, Marcus Gabius): (gluttony) Generic Word. See: Partridge; Stenhouse.

APICIUS, MARCUS GABIUS. fl. 1st c. A.D. Roman nobleman. See: Encyc. Brit., 1911. Api (apple), Apicia (cakes), Apicium (wine), Apicius (or Apician) (1), Apicius (or Apician) (2).

APJOHN, JAMES. 1796-1875. Irish chemist. See: Royal Soc. Proc., vol. 41 (1887). Apjohnite; Apjohn's formula?

Apjohnite (Apjohn, James): Earth Sciences. See: Thrush; Webster's 3d.

Apjohn's formula (Apjohn, James?): Chemistry. See: Ballentyne.

APOLD, ANTON. fl. 1926. German chemist. Cited in: Chem. Abstr., vol. 20, p. 1677. Apold-Fleissner process.

Apold-Fleissner process (Apold, Anton and Fleissner, Hans): Engineering and Industry. See: Thrush.

Apollinarianism (or Apollinarians) (Apollinaris of Laodicea): Religion. See: Attwater; Canney; Mathews, S.

APOLLINARIS OF LAODICEA. 310-390. Syrian teacher and theologian. See: Encyc. Brit., 1973. Apollinarianism (or Apollinarians).

Apolline (Apollo): Religion. See: Webster's 3d.

Apollino (Apollo): Music. See: Mathews, M. M.

APOLLO. Graeco-Roman god of manly beauty, poetry, music, and wisdom. See: Oxford Clas. Dict. Apolline, Apollino, Apollo, Apollonian, Apollonian (culture pattern), Apollonicon, Apollo's knots, Mount of Apollo, Paean, Paeon (metrical unit), Phoebad, Phoebus (or Phoebean).

Apollo (Apollo, the god): Generic Word (handsome). See: Partridge; Webster's 3d.

Apollonian (Apollo): Literature (classicism). See: Barnet; Preminger; Scott.

Apollonian (Apollonius of Perga): Mathematics. See: Webster's 3d.

Apollonian (culture pattern) (Apollo): Anthropology. See: Hoult; Winick; Zadrozny.

Apollonicon (Apollo): Music (harmonium). See: Partridge.

Apollonius' circle (Apollonius of Perga): Mathematics. See: Ballentyne.

APOLLONIUS OF PERGA. 255-170 B.C. Greek mathematician. See: Dict. Sci. Biog. Apollonian, Apollonius' circle, Apollonius' theorem, problem of Apollonius.

Apollonius' theorem (Apollonius of Perga): Mathematics. See: Ballentyne.

Apollo's knots (Apollo): Fashion. See: Picken.

Apollyon (Apollyon the Angel): Generic Word (destructive fiend). See: Partridge; Webster's 3d.

APOLLYON THE ANGEL. Biblical angel of the bottomless pit. See: Encyc. Amer., 1959. Apollyon.

Apologie of William of Orange (William I of Orange): History. See: Harbottle.

APOSTOLI, GEORGE. 1847-1900. French physician. Cited in: New York Acad. Med. Portrait Cat. Apostoli's method.

Apostoli's method (Apostoli, George): Medicine. See: Stedman.

APOSTOOL, SAMUEL. 1638-1699. Flemish Anabaptist. See: Nouv. Biog. Univ. Apostoolians.

Apostoolians (Apostool, Samuel): Religion. See: Canney.

apparatus of Rezzonico (Rezzonico, Giulio). See: Rezzonico-Golgi threads (or spirals).

appeal from Philip drunk to Philip sober (Philip II of Macedon): Generic Word (appeal to one's better nature). See: Hendrickson; Partridge.

APPELBAUM, L. fl. 1902. German internist. Cited in: Bibliog. Med., vol. 3, 1902. Recklinghausen-Appelbaum disease?

Appelius-Schmidt reagent (Appelius, Wilhelm and Schmidt, R.): Chemistry. See: Van Nostrand Chem. Dict.

APPELIUS, WILHELM. b. 1869. German chemist. Cited in: Chem. Abstr., vol. 9, p. 251. Appelius-Schmidt reagent.

Appianum (apple) (Appius Claudius): Botany. See: Stenhouse.

APPIUS CLAUDIUS. Roman emperor. (Biography source unavailable.) Appianum (apple).

apple Charlotte (Charlotte Augusta): Food and Drink. See: Hendrickson.

APPLEBY, JOHN FRANCIS. 1840-1917. American inventor. See: World Who's Who Sci. Appleby knotter.

Appleby knotter (Appleby, John Francis): Engineering and Industry. Cited in: World Who's Who Sci.

Applegate diagram (Derivation undetermined): Electronics. See: Hughes; Internat. Dict. Phys. Elec.; Markus.

APPLETON, EDWARD VICTOR. 1892-1965. English physicist. See: Dict. Sci. Biog. Appleton layer.

Appleton layer (Appleton, Edward Victor): Physics. See: Hughes; Markus; Thewlis.

APPOLD, JOHN GEORGE. 1800-1865. English inventor. See: Dict. Nat. Biog. Appold pump.

Appold pump (Appold, John George): Engineering and Industry. See: Auger.

Appolt oven (Derivation undetermined): Engineering and Industry. See: Thrush.

APPUNN, ANTON. 1839-1900. French instrument maker. See: Pogg., vol. 4. Appunn's lamella.

Appunn's lamella (Appunn, Anton): Psychology. See: Chaplin; Drever.

aqua Tofana (Tofana): History. See: Brewer; Harvey; Hendrickson.

aqueduct of Sylvius (Sylvius, Franciscus). See: Sylvian aqueduct.

AQUINAS, SAINT THOMAS. 1225-1274. Italian scholastic theologian. See: Internat. Encyc. Soc. Sci. cord of St. Thomas, Thomism (or Thomists).

ARA, KIYOSHI. No dates. Japanese pathologist. (Biography source unavailable.) Takata-Ara reaction.

ARABI PASHA (AHMED ARABI). 1841?-1911. Egyptian army officer. See: Encyc. Brit., 1911. Arabi's rebellion.

Arabi's rebellion (Arabi Pasha): History. See: Harbottle.

ARACHNE. Lydian woman in Ovid's "Metamorphosis." See: Oxford Clas. Dict. Arachne's labours, Arachnid, Arakne.

Arachne's labours (Arachne): Generic Word (weaving). See: Brewer.

Arachnid (Arachne): Zoology. See: Brewer; Partridge.

Arago distance (Arago, Dominique Francois Jean): Physics. See: Huschke.

ARAGO, DOMINIQUE FRANCOIS JEAN. 1786-1853. French physicist and astronomer. See: Dict. Sci. Biog. Arago distance, Arago point, Arago spot, law(s) of Fresnel-Arago.

Arago point (Arago, Dominique Francois Jean): Physics. See: Huschke; Thewlis; Van Nostrand Sci. Encyc.

Arago spot (Arago, Dominique Francois Jean): Physics. See: Internat. Dict. Ap. Math.; Internat. Dict. Phys. Elec.

Arakawa-Higashi syndrome (Arakawa, Tsuneo and Higashi, Ototaka): Medcine. See: Jablonski.

ARAKAWA, TSUNEO. fl. 1965. Japanese physician. (Biography source unavailable.) Arakawa-Higashi syndrome.

Arakne (Arachne): Psychology (death instinct). See: Zadrozny.

ARAMAYO, FELIX AVELINO. fl. 20th c. Mine director in Bolivia. Cited in: Bailey. Aramayoite.

Aramayoite (Aramayo, Felix Avelino): Earth Sciences. See: Thrush; Webster's 3d.

Aran-Duchenne disease (or atrophy) (Aran, Francois Amilcar and Duchenne, Guillaume Benjamin Amand): Medicine. See: Dorland; Jablonski.

ARAN, FRANCOIS AMILCAR. 1817-1861. French physician. See: Dict. Biog. Fran. Aran-Duchenne disease (or atrophy), Aran's cancer, Aran's law.

Aran's cancer (Aran, Francois Amilcar): Medicine. See: Dorland; Stedman.

Aran's law (Aran, Francois Amilcar): Medicine. See: Dorland; Stedman.

Arantius, Julius Caesar. See: Aranzio, Giulio Caesar.

ARANZIO, GIULIO CAESAR. 1530-1589. Italian anatomist and physician. See: Dict. Sci. Biog. Aranzio's band, Aranzio's bodies, Aranzio's duct.

Aranzio's band (Aranzio, Giulio Caesar): Anatomy. See: Donath; Stedman.

Aranzio's bodies (Aranzio, Giulio Caesar): Anatomy. See: Donath; Dorland; Stedman.

Aranzio's duct (Aranzio, Giulio Caesar): Anatomy. See: Donath; Stedman.

Araujia (Araujo de Azevedo, Antonio de): Botany. See: Webster's 3d.

ARAUJO DE AZEVEDO, ANTONIO DE. 1754-1817. Portuguese statesman and diplomat. See: Nouv. Biog. Univ. Araujia.

ARBACES. d. ca. 848. King of Media. See: Nouv. Biog. Univ. Arbacia.

Arbacia (Arbaces): Zoology. See: Webster's 3d.

ARBER, AGNES ROBERTSON. 1879-1960. English botanist. See: Dict. Sci. Biog. Arber's law.

Arber's law (Arber, Agnes Robertson): Botany. See: Gray.

ARBUSOV, ALEKSANDR ERMININGELDOVICH. 1877-1968. Russian organic chemist. See: World Who's Who Sci. Arbusov reaction (or rearrangement).

Arbusov reaction (or rearrangement) (Arbusov, Aleksandr Erminingeldovich): Chemistry. See: Ballentyne; Van Nostrand Chem. Dict.

arc(s) of Lowitz (or Lowitz arcs) (Lovits, Johann Tobias): Earth Sciences. See: Huschke; Van Nostrand Sci. Encyc.; Webster's 3d.

arch of Corti (Corti, Alfonso Giacomo Gaspare). See: Corti's arch.

Archaouloff pump (Archaouloff, Vadim P.): Engineering and Industry. See: Auger.

ARCHAOULOFF, VADIM P. fl. 1918-21. English? engineer. (Biography source unavailable.) Archaouloff pump.

Archduke trio (Rudolph of Hapsburg): Music. See: Scholes.

ARCHER, JAMES. fl. 1902. English engineer. (Biography source unavailable.) Sturmey-Archer gear.

Archetti test (Derivation undetermined): Chemistry. See: Van Nostrand Chem. Dict.

ARCHIBALD. Hero of song by George Robey. Archies.

ARCHIBALD, ROBERT GEORGE. 1880-1953. Indian-born physician. See: World Who's Who Sci. Archibald's fever.

Archibald's fever (Archibald, Robert George): Medicine. See: Stedman.

Archies (Archibald): Weapons. See: Brewer.

Archilochian bitterness (Archilochus of Paros): Literature. See: Brewer.

Archilochian (verse) (Archilochus of Paros): Literature. See: Preminger; Webster's 3d.

ARCHILOCHUS OF PAROS. fl. 714-676 B.C. Greek lyric poet and lampoonist. See: Encyc. Brit., 1973. Archilochian bitterness, Archilochian (verse).

Archimedean (Archimedes): Mathematics. See: Webster's 3d.; Weekley.

Archimedean buoyant force (Archimedes): Physics. See: Huschke.

Archimedean property (Archimedes): Mathematics. See: James.

Archimedean solid (Archimedes): Mathematics. See: Webster's 3d.

ARCHIMEDES. 287-212 B.C. Greek mathematician and engineer. See: Dict. Sci. Biog. Archimedean, Archimedean buoyant force, Archimedean property, Archimedean solid, Archimedes' axiom, Archimedes (bryozoans), Archimedes' drill, Archimedes' principle, Archimedes problem, Archimedes' pulley, Archimedes' screw, Archimedes' spiral, Archimedes' windlass.

Archimedes' axiom (Archimedes): Mathematics. See: Ballentyne.

Archimedes (bryozoans) (Archimedes): Zoology. See: Webster's 3d.

Archimedes' drill (Archimedes): Engineering and Industry. See: Hendrickson; Partridge.

Archimedes' principle (Archimedes): Physics. See: Internat. Dict. Phys. Elec.; Thewlis; Van Nostrand Chem. Dict.

Archimedes problem (Archimedes): Mathematics. See: Webster's 3d.

Archimedes' pulley (Archimedes): Engineering and Industry. See: Hendrickson; Partridge.

Archimedes' screw (Archimedes): Engineering and Industry. See: Auger; Phyfe; Thrush.

Archimedes' spiral (Archimedes): Mathematics. See: Ballentyne; Van Nostrand Sci. Encyc.; Webster's 3d.

Archimedes' windlass (Archimedes): Engineering and Industry. See: Partridge.

ARCHON. Religious leader. (Biography source unavailable.) Archontics.

Archontics (Archon): Religion. See: Canney.

Ardeer double cartridge test (Derivation undetermined): Engineering and Industry. See: Thrush.

ARDEN, ENOCH. Hero of Tennyson's poem, "Enoch Arden". See: Benet. Enoch Arden, Enoch Arden law.

ARDREY, ROBERT. 1908- . American writer. See: Contemp. Authors. Ardrey's pecking order postulate, Ardrey's laws of the noyau, Ardrey's laws.

Ardrey's laws (Ardrey, Robert): Sociology. See: Martin.

Ardrey's laws of the noyau (Ardrey, Robert): Sociology. See: Martin.

Ardrey's pecking order postulate (Ardrey, Robert): Sociology. See: Martin.

Ard's rover (Derivation undetermined): Botany. See: Winburne.

Arduinite (Arduino, Giovanni): Earth Sciences. See: Webster's 3d.

ARDUINO, GIOVANNI. 1714-1795. Italian geologist. See: Dict. Sci. Biog. Arduinite.

area Celsi (Celsus, Aulus Cornelius). See: Celsus' vitiligo.

ARENTS, ALBERT. 1840-1914. German-born American metallurgist. See: Dict. Amer. Biog. Arents' lead well (or tap).

Arents' lead well (or tap) (Arents, Albert): Engineering and Industry. See: Thrush.

Aretinian syllables (Guido of Arezzo (or Aretino)). See: Guidonian syllable (or scale).

AREY, LESLIE BRAINERD. b. 1891. American anatomist. See: World Who's Who Sci. Arey's rule.

Arey's rule (Arey, Leslie Brainerd): Medicine. See: Dorland.

Arezzo, Guittone d'. See: Guittone d' Arezzo.

ARFVEDSON, JOHAN AUGUST. 1792-1841. Swedish chemist. See: World Who's Who Sci. Arfvedsonite.

Arfwedson distribution (Derivation undetermined): Statistics. See: Kendall.

Argall furnace (Argall, Phillip): Engineering and Industry. See: Thrush.

ARGALL, PHILLIP. 1854-1922. Irish-born American engineer and metallurgist. See: Dict. Amer. Biog. Argall furnace.

ARGAND, AIME. 1755-1803. Swiss physicist. See: Nouv. Biog. Univ. Argand burner, Argand lamp.

Argand burner (Argand, Aime): Engineering and Industry. See: Dorland; Hackh; Webster's 3d.

Argand diagram (Argand, Jean Robert): Mathematics. See: Ballentyne; James; Van Nostrand Sci. Encyc.

ARGAND, JEAN ROBERT. 1768-1825. French mathematician. See: Dict. Sci. Biog. Argand diagram, Argand plane.

Argand lamp (Argand, Aime): Engineering and Industry. See: Carter; Charnock; Webster's 3d.

Argand plane (Argand, Jean Robert): Mathematics. See: Internat. Dict. Ap. Math.

ARGELANDER, FRIEDRICH WILHELM AUGUST. 1799-1875. German astronomer. See: Dict. Sci. Biog. Argelander's method.

Argelander's method (Argelander, Friedrich Wilhelm August): Astronomy. See: Webster's 3d.

Argonz-Del Castillo syndrome (Argonz, J. and Del Castillo, E.B.): Medicine. See: Jablonski. Also known as: Forbes-Albright syndrome.

ARGONZ, J. fl 1953. English? physician. (Biography source unavailable.) Argonz-Del Castillo syndrome.

Arguesian transformation (Desargues, Girard): Mathematics. Cited in: Webster's Biog. Dict.

ARGUS. Greek mythical herdsman. See: Jobes. Argus-eyed.

Argus-eyed (Argus): Generic Word (watchful). See: Brewer; Partridge; Weekley.

ARGYLE. Branch of the Scottish clan of Campbell. See: Webster's Biog. Dict. Argyle plaid.

Argyle plaid (Argyle): Fashion. See: Picken.

Argyll, 3rd Duke and 9th Earl. See: Campbell, Archibald.

ARGYLL-ROBERTSON, DOUGLAS MORAY COOPER LAMB. 1837-1909. Scottish ophthalmologist. See: Dict. Nat. Biog. 2d. suppl. Argyll-Robertson pupil (sign, or syndrome).

Argyll-Robertson pupil (sign, or syndrome) (Argyll-Robertson, Douglas Moray Cooper Lamb): Psychology. See: Chaplin; Hinsie; Wolman. Also known as: Robertson's syndrome.

Argyllia (Campbell, Archibald): Botany. See: Charnock.

Argyll's rebellion (Campbell, Archibald, 9th Earl of Argyll): History. See: Steinberg.

Arianism (Arius): Religion. See: Attwater; Canney; Mathews, S.

ARIAS, IRWIN MONROE. 1926- . American physician. See: Amer. Men Sci., 10th ed. Arias' syndrome.

Arias-Stella effect (or phenomenon) (Arias-Stella, Javier): Medicine. See: Jablonski; Stedman.

ARIAS-STELLA, JAVIER. fl. 1920. Peruvian pathologist. See: Direct. Med. Specialists, 1970-71. Arias-Stella effect (or phenomenon).

Arias' syndrome (Arias, Irwin Monroe): Medicine. See: Jablonski.

ARIEL. "Ayrie spirit" in Shakespeare's "The Tempest". See: Benet. Ariel, Ariel petrel, Ariel phalanger, Ariel toucan .

Ariel (Ariel): (B.B.C.) Mass Media. See: Partridge.

Ariel petrel (Ariel): Zoology. See: Partridge.

Ariel phalanger (Ariel): Zoology. See: Partridge.

Ariel toucan (Ariel): Zoology. See: Partridge.

ARION. fl. 7th c. B.C. Semi-legendary Greek poet. See: Encyc. Brit., 1973. Orpharion.

ARISAKA, NARIAKA. fl. 1896. Japanese army officer and superintendent of Tokyo arsenal. (Biography source unavailable.) Arisaka rifle.

Arisaka rifle (Arisaka, Nariaka): Weapons. See: Webster's 3d.

Aristarchus (Aristarchus of Samothrace): Generic Word (critic). See: Charnock; Partridge; Weekley.

ARISTARCHUS OF SAMOTHRACE. 220-143 B.C. Greek grammarian and critic. See: Encyc. Brit. 1973. Aristarchus.

ARISTEIDES (ARISTIDES) OF MILETUS. fl. 2d c. B.C. Asia Minor? romance writer. See: Dict. Grk. Rom. Biog. Myth. Milesian tales (or fables).

ARISTIPPUS OF CYRENE. 435?-356? B.C. Greek philosopher. See: Encyc. Brit., 1973. Cyrenaic.

Aristophanic (Aristophanes): Literature. See: Webster's 3d.

ARISTOPHANES. 448?-380 B.C. Athenian dramatist. See: Encyc. Brit., 1973. Aristophaic.

Aristotelia (Aristotle): Botany. See: Charnock; Taylor N.

Aristotelian (Aristotle): Philosophy. See: Partridge; Webster's 3d; Weekley.

Aristotelian categories (Aristotle): Philosophy. See: Phyfe.

Aristotelian causes (Aristotle): Philosophy. See: Brewer.

Aristotelian classification (Aristotle): Philosophy. See: English.

Aristotelian logic (Aristotle): Philosophy. See: Webster's 3d.

Aristotelian method (Aristotle): Philosophy. See: English; Good; Stedman.

Aristotelianism (Aristotle): Philosophy. See: Attwater; Hendrickson; Mathews, S.

Aristotelize (Aristotle): Philosophy. See: Partridge.

ARISTOTLE. 384-322 B.C. Greek philosopher. See: Internat. Encyc. Soc. Sci. Aristotelia, Aristotelian, Aristotelian categories, Aristotelian causes, Aristotelian classification, Aristotelian logic, Aristotelian method, Aristotelianism, Aristotelize, Aristotle's anomaly (or illusion), Aristotle's golden mean, Aristotle's lantern.

Aristotle's anomaly (or illusion) (Aristotle): Psychology. See: Chaplin; Dorland; Stedman.

Aristotle's golden mean (Aristotle): Generic Word. See: Good.

Aristotle's lantern (Aristotle): Zoology. See: Gray; Henderson; Pennak.

ARIUS. 256-326. Deacon of Alexandria. See: Encyc. Brit., 1973. Arianism.

Arkel, Anton Eduard van. See: Van Arkel, Anton Eduard.

ARKIN, AARON. 1888-1966. Latvian-born American physician. See: World Who's Who Sci. Arkin's disease.

Arkin's disease (Arkin, Aaron). See: Bayford-Autenrieth dysphagia.

ARKOEVY, JOSEF VON. 1851-1922. Hungarian dentist. (Biography source unavailable.) Arkoevy's mixture.

Arkoevy's mixture (Arkoevy, Josef von): Dentistry. See: Dorland.

ARKWRIGHT, RICHARD. 1732-1792. English inventor. See: Dict. Nat. Biog. Arkwright water frame.

Arkwright water frame (Arkwright, Richard): Engineering and Industry. See: Morris and Irwin.

Arloing-Courmont test (Arloing, Saturnin and Courmont, Jules): Medicine. See: Dorland.

ARLOING, SATURNIN. 1846-1911. French pathologist. See: Dict. Biog. Fran. Arloing-Courmont test.

ARLT, CARL FERDINAND RITTER VON. 1812-1887. Austrian oculist. Allg. Deut. Biog. Arlt's disease, Arlt's line, Arlt's operation, Arlt's sinus, Arlt's trachoma.

Arlt's disease (Arlt, Carl Ferdinand Ritter von): Medicine. See: Jablonski.

Arlt's line (Arlt, Carl Ferdinand Ritter von): Anatomy. See: Donath.

Arlt's operation (Arlt, Carl Ferdinand Ritter von): Medicine. See: Dorland; Stedman.

Arlt's sinus (Arlt, Carl Ferdinand Ritter von): Medicine. See: Dorland; Stedman.

Arlt's trachoma (Arlt, Carl Ferdinand Ritter von): Medicine. See: Dorland; Stedman.

ARMAGNAC, BERNARD. 1364-1418. French nobleman. See: Nouv. Biog. Univ. Armagnacs.

Armagnacs (Armagnac, Bernard): History. See: Latham.

Armand clematis (Armand, L.?): Botany. See: Winburne.

ARMAND, L. No dates. French botanist. See: Biog. Notes Upon Botanists. Armand clematis?

Armani-Barboni reaction for gold and silver (Armani, G. and Barboni, J.): Chemistry. See: Van Nostrand Chem. Dict.

Armani-Barboni test for caffeine (Armani, G. and Barboni, J.): Chemistry. See: Van Nostrand Chem. Dict.

ARMANI, G. fl. 1910. Italian chemist. Cited in: Chem. Abstr., vol. 4, p. 2428; vol. 5, p. 1132. Armani-Barboni reaction for gold and silver, Armani-Barboni test for caffeine, Armani-Rodano test.

Armanni-Ebstein cells (Armanni, Luciano and Ebstein, Wilhelm): Medicine. See: Dorland.

Armanni-Ebstein change (or kidney) (Armanni, Luciano and Ebstein, Wilhelm): Medicine. See: Stedman.

Armanni-Ebstein lesion (Armanni, Luciano and Ebstein, Wilhelm): Medicine. See: Jablonski.

ARMANNI, LUCIANO. 1839-1903. Italian pathologist. See: Diz. Encic. Ital. Armanni-Ebstein cells, Armanni-Ebstein change (or kidney), Armanni-Ebstein lesion.

Armengaud and Lemale gas turbine (Armengaud, Rene and Lemale, Charles): Engineering and Industry. See: Auger.

ARMENGAUD, RENE. fl. 1894. French engineer. Cited in: Encyc. Amer. under "Internal Combustion Engine." Armengaud and Lemale gas turbine.

Arminians (or Arminianism) (Arminius, Jacobus): Religion. See: Attwater; Canney; Mathews, S.

ARMINIUS, JACOBUS. 1560-1608. Dutch theologian. Encyc. Brit., 1973. Arminians (or Arminianism).

ARMITAGE, PETER. 1934- . English statistician. See: World Who's Who Sci. Armitage's restricted procedure.

Armitage's restricted procedure (Armitage, Peter): Statistics. See: Kendall.

Armsby feeding standard (Armsby, Henry Prentiss): Agriculture. See: Winburne.

ARMSBY, HENRY PRENTISS. 1853-1921. American agricultural chemist. See: Dict. Amer. Biog. Armsby feeding standard.

Armstrong acid (Armstrong, Henry Edward): Chemistry. See: Hackh.

ARMSTRONG, ALFRED RINGGOLD. 1911- . American chemist. See: Amer. Men Sci., 10th ed. King-Armstrong unit?

ARMSTRONG, EDWIN HOWARD. 1890-1954. American engineer. See: Dict. Sci. Biog. Armstrong circuit, Armstrong frequency-modulation system (or method), Armstrong oscillator.

Armstrong circuit (Armstrong, Edwin Howard): Engineering and Industry. See: Hughes.

ARMSTRONG, EDWIN JAMES. b. 1861. American engineer. See: Who's Who Engin., 1925. Armstrong governor.

Armstrong freesia (Armstrong, W.): Botany. See: Winburne.

Armstrong frequency-modulation system (or method) (Armstrong, Edwin Howard): Engineering and Industry. See: Internat. Dict. Phys. Elec.; Markus.

Armstrong governor (Armstrong, Edwin James): Engineering and Industry. See: Auger.

Armstrong gun (Armstrong, William George): Weapons. See: Phyfe; Quick; Stenhouse.

ARMSTRONG, HENRY EDWARD. 1848-1937. English organic chemist. See: Dict. Sci. Biog. Armstrong acid, Armstrong metal.

Armstrong joint (Derivation undetermined): Engineering and Industry. See: Thrush.

ARMSTRONG, LOUIS. 1900-1971. American musician. See: Cur. Biog. Armstrong (note).

Armstrong metal (Armstrong, Henry Edward): Chemistry. See: Hackh.

Armstrong (note) (Armstrong, Louis): Music. See: Hendrickson.

Armstrong oscillator (Armstrong, Edwin Howard): Engineering and Industry. See: Hughes; Internat. Dict. Phys. Elec.; Markus.

ARMSTRONG, W. No dates. South African botanist. (Biography source unavailable.) Armstrong freesia.

ARMSTRONG, WILLIAM GEORGE. 1810-1900. English inventor. See: Dict. Nat. Biog., 1st suppl. Armstrong gun.

ARNAUD, ALBERT LEON. 1853-1915. French organic chemist. See: Pogg., vol. 4. Arnaud-Pade reagent.

Arnaud-Pade reagent (Arnaud, Albert Leon and Pade, Leon): Chemistry. See: Van Nostrand Chem. Dict.

Arnaudon's green (Derivation undetermined): Chemistry. See: Hackh.

Arndt alloy (Derivation undetermined): Chemistry. See: Hackh.

Arndt-Eistert synthesis (Arndt, Fritz and Eistert, Bernd): Chemistry. See: Ballentyne; Van Nostrand Chem. Dict.

ARNDT, FRITZ. b. 1885. German chemist. See: Pogg., vol. 6. Arndt-Eistert synthesis.

ARNDT, GEORG. 1875-1929. German dermatologist. See: New York Acad. of Med. Portrait Cat. Arndt-Gottron disease.

Arndt-Gottron disease (Arndt, Georg and Gottron, Heinrich Adolf): Medicine. See: Jablonski.

ARNDT, RUDOLF GOTTFRIED. 1835-1900. German psychiatrist. See: World Who's Who Sci. Arndt's law (or rule).

Arndt-Schulz law (Arndt, Rudolf Gottfried and Schulz, Hugo). See: Arndt's law (or rule).

Arndt tube (Derivation undetermined): Chemistry. See: Van Nostrand Chem. Dict.

Arndt's law (or rule) (Arndt, Rudolf Gottfried): Psychiatry. See: Dorland; Hackh; Stedman. Also known as: Arndt-Schulz law.

Arneth count (Arneth, Joseph): Medicine. See: Dorland; Stedman.

Arneth formula (Arneth, Joseph): Medicine. See: Pennak; Stedman.

Arneth index (Arneth, Joseph): Medicine. See: Stedman; Webster's 3d.

ARNETH, JOSEPH. 1873-1955. German physician. See: World Who's Who Sci. Arneth count, Arneth formula, Arneth index, Arneth stages, Arneth's classification.

Arneth stages (Arneth, Joseph): Medicine. See: Stedman.

Arneth's classification (Arneth, Joseph): Medicine. See: Dorland; Stedman.

Arneth's syndrome (Derivation undetermined): Medicine. See: Jablonski.

Arnimite (Von Arnim): Earth Sciences. See: Thrush; Webster's 3d.

ARNING, EDUARD. b. 1855. German physician. See: Wer Ist's?, 1906. Arning's carcinoid.

Arning's carcinoid (Arning, Eduard): Medicine. See: Jablonski.

ARNOLD, BENEDICT. 1741-1801. American army officer. See: Dict. Amer. Biog. Benedict Arnold.

Arnold-Chiari syndrome (malformation or deformity) (Arnold, Julius and Chiari, Hans): Medicine. See: Dorland; Hinsie, Jablonski.

ARNOLD, FRIEDRICH. 1803-1890. German anatomist. See: World Who's Who Sci. Arnold's area, Arnold's canal, Arnold's ganglion, Arnold's nerve, Arnold's substance, Arnold's tract.

ARNOLD, JOSEPH. 1782-1818. English botanist. See: Dict. Nat. Biog. rafflesia Arnoldi.

ARNOLD, JULIUS. 1835-1915. German pathologist. See: Sci., vol.41, p. 422. Arnold-Chiari syndrome (malformation or deformity), Arnold sterilizer, Arnold's bodies, Arnold's neuralgia, Friedrich-Erb-Arnold syndrome.

ARNOLD, KARL. 1853-1929. German chemist. See: Pogg., vol 6; Wer Ist's?, 1906. Arnold-Mentzel reagent for hydrogen peroxide, Arnold-Mentzel reagent for ozone, Arnold-Mentzel reagent for ozone in water, Arnold-Mentzel reagents for milk, Arnold-Mentzel test for formaldehyde.

ARNOLD, KENNETH JAMES. 1914- . American mathematical statistician. See: Amer. Men Sci., 9th ed. WAGR test.

Arnold-Mentzel reagent for hydrogen peroxide (Arnold, Karl and Mentzel, C.): Chemistry. See: Van Nostrand Chem. Dict.

Arnold-Mentzel reagent for ozone (Arnold, Karl and Mentzel, C.): Chemistry. See: Van Nostrand Chem. Dict.

Arnold-Mentzel reagent for ozone in water (Arnold, Karl and Mentzel, C.): Chemistry. See: Van Nostrand Chem. Dict.

Arnold-Mentzel reagents for milk (Arnold, Karl and Mentzel, C.): Chemistry. See: Van Nostrand Chem. Dict.

Arnold-Mentzel test for formaldehyde (Arnold, Karl and Mentzel, C.): Chemistry. See: Van Nostrand Chem. Dict.

ARNOLD OF BRESCIA. 1079-1164. Italian priest and monk. See: Encyc. Brit., 1973. Arnoldists.

Arnold Pick. See: Pick, Arnold.

Arnold reactions for alkaloids (Arnold, Vincenz): Chemistry. See: Van Nostrand Chem. Dict.

Arnold solution (Arnold, Vincenz): Chemistry. See: Van Nostrand Chem. Dict.

Arnold sterilizer (Arnold, Julius): Medicine. See: Webster's 3d.

Arnold test reaction for proteins (Arnold, Vincenz): Chemistry. See: Van Nostrand Chem. Dict.

ARNOLD, VINCENZ. b. 1864. Austrian physician. Cited in: Chem. Abstr. Cum. Author Index. Arnold reactions for alkaloids, Arnold solution, Arnold test reaction for proteins, Arnold's test (for diacetic acid).

Arnoldists (Arnold of Brescia): Religion. See: Canney; Webster's 3d.

Arnold's area (Arnold, Friedrich): Anatomy. See: Donath.

Arnold's bodies (Arnold, Julius): Medicine. See: Dorland; Stedman.

Arnold's canal (Arnold, Friedrich): Anatomy. See: Dorland; Stedman.

Arnold's ganglion (Arnold, Friedrich): Anatomy. See: Dorland; Stedman; Webster's 3d.

Arnold's nerve (Arnold, Friedrich): Anatomy. See: Stedman.

Arnold's neuralgia (Arnold, Julius): Medicine. See: Jablonski.

Arnold's substance (Arnold, Friedrich): Anatomy. See: Donath; Stedman.

Arnold's test (for diacetic acid) (Arnold, Vincenz): Medicine. See: Ballentyne; Dorland; Stedman.

Arnold's tract (Arnold, Friedrich): Anatomy. Cited in: Donath.

ARNOTT, NEIL. 1788-1874. Scottish physician. See: Dict. Nat. Biog. Arnott's bed.

Arnott's bed (Arnott, Neil): Medicine. See: Dorland.

ARNU, CHARLES. fl. 1935. Belgian chemist. Cited in: Chem. Abstr., vol. 30, p. 5759. Audibert-Arnu dilatometer.

Arny-Dimler test (Arny, Henry Vinecome and Dimler, Marguerite C.): Chemistry. See: Van Nostrand Chem. Dict.

ARNY, HENRY VINECOME. 1868-1943. American pharmacist. See: World Who's Who Sci. Arny-Dimler test, Arny solutions.

Arny solutions (Arny, Henry Vinecome): Chemistry. See: Van Nostrand Chem. Dict.

ARONHOLD, SIEGFRIED HEINRICH. 1819-1884. German mathematician. See: Dict. Sci. Biog. Aronhold's differential equations, Aronhold's process, Clebsch-Aronhold symbolic notation.

Aronhold's differential equations (Aronhold, Siegfried Heinrich): Mathematics. Cited in: Dict. Sci. Biog.

Aronhold's process (Aronhold, Siegfried Heinrich): Mathematics. Cited in: Dict. Sci. Biog.

Aroult, Francois Marie. See: Voltaire.

ARRAGON, C. fl. 1909. German chemist. Cited in: Chem. Abstr., vol. 3, p. 1683. Arragon test reaction.

Arragon test reaction (Arragon, C.): Chemistry. See: Van Nostrand Chem. Dict.

Arreguine test reaction for citric acid (Arreguine, Victor): Chemistry. See: Van Nostrand Chem. Dict.

Arreguine test reaction for glycerol (Arreguine, Victor): Chemistry. See: Van Nostrand Chem. Dict.

ARREGUINE, VICTOR. b. 1863. Argentinian physician. See: Cutolo. Arreguine test reaction for citric acid, Arreguine test reaction for glycerol.

Arrhenite (Arrhenius, Carl Axel): Earth Sciences. See: Webster's 3d.

ARRHENIUS, CARL AXEL. 1757-1824. Swedish army officer. See: Pogg., vol. 1. Arrhenite.

Arrhenius' equation (Arrhenius, Svante August): Chemistry. See: Ballentyne; Thewlis; Van Nostrand Chem. Dict.

Arrhenius-Guzman equation (Arrhenius, Svante August and Guzman, J.?): Chemistry. See: Internat. Dict. Phys. Elec.; Thewlis; Van Nostrand Sci. Encyc.

Arrhenius' law (Arrhenius, Svante August): Chemistry. See: Hackh; Pennak; Stedman.

Arrhenius-Madsen theory (Arrhenius, Svante August and Madsen, Thorvald J.M.): Chemistry. See: Stedman.

ARRHENIUS, SVANTE AUGUST. 1859-1927. Swedish physicist and chemist. See: Dict. Sci. Biog. Arrhenius' equation, Arrhenius-Guzman equation, Arrhenius law, Arrhenius-Madsen theory, Arrhenius theory (of activation), Arrhenius' theory (of electrolytic dissociation), Arrhenius viscosity equations (or formulae).

Arrhenius theory (of activation) (Arrhenius, Svante August): Chemistry. See: Van Nostrand Chem. Dict.

Arrhenius' theory (of electrolytic dissociation) (Arrhenius, Svante August): Chemistry. See: Ballentyne; Internat. Dict. Phys. Elec.; Van Nostrand Sci. Encyc.

Arrhenius viscosity equations (or formulae) (Arrhenius, Svante August): Chemistry. See: Van Nostrand Sci. Encyc.

Arrojadite (Arrojado Lisboa, Miguel): Earth Sciences. See: Thrush; Webster's 3d.

ARROJADO LISBOA, MIGUEL. fl. 20th c. Brazilian geologist. Cited in: Bailey. Arrojadite.

ARROYO, CARLOS F. 1892-1928. American physician. See: Amer. Med. Direct., 1927. Arroyo's sign.

Arroyo's sign (Arroyo, Carlos F.): Medicine. See: Dorland; Stedman.

Arsem furnace (Arsem, William Collins): Engineering and Industry. See: Webster's 3d.

ARSEM, WILLIAM COLLINS. 1880- . American chemical engineer. See: Amer. Men Sci., 10th ed. Arsem furnace.

ARSINOE II. 316-271 B.C. Queen of Egypt. See: Encyc. Brit., 1973. Arsinoitherium.

Arsinoitherium (Arsinoe II): Zoology. See: Webster's 3d.

Arsonval, Jacques Arsene. See: d'Arsonval.

Art Ross Trophy (Ross, Art): Recreation and Sports. See: Encyc. Brit., 1973, under "Ice Hockey," p. 1033.

ARTEDI, PETER. 1705-1735. Swedish naturalist. See: Dict. Sci. Biog. Artedia.

Artedia (Artedi, Peter): Botany. See: Charnock.

Artemesina (Artemis the goddess?): Zoology. See: Pennak.

ARTEMIA (Artemis): Zoology. See: Pennak; Webster's 3d.

Artemis (surveillance system) (Artemis the goddess?): Weapons. See: Markus.

Artemisia (Artemis): Botany. See: Charnock; Harvey; Partridge.

ARTEMON. fl. 3rd c. Religious leader. See: Nouv. Biog. Univ. Artemonites.

Artemonites (Artemon): Religion. See: Canney.

Arthaud-Butte reagent (Arthaud, G. and Butte, Lucien): Chemistry. See: Van Nostrand Chem. Dict.

ARTHAUD, G. No dates. French biologist. (Biography source unavailable.) Arthaud-Butte reagent.

ARTHUR. fl. 6th c. Semilegendary king of the Britons. See: Dict. Nat. Biog. Arthurian cycle of romances, Arthuriana.

ARTHUR, MARY GRACE. 1883- . American psychologist. See: Amer. Psych. Assoc. Direct., 1960. Arthur scale, Grace-Arthur performance scale.

Arthur scale (Arthur, Mary Grace): Psychology. See: Chaplin; English; Hinsie.

Arthurian cycle of romances (Arthur): Literature. See: Barnhart, (Eng. Lit.); Brewer.

Arthuriana (Arthur): Literature. See: Webster's 3d.

Arthurite (Russell, Arthur Edward Ian Montagu and Kingsbury, Arthur W. G.): Earth Sciences. See: Thrush.

ARTHUS, NICOLAS MAURICE. 1862-1945. French bacteriologist. See: World Who's Who Sci. Arthus' phenomenon (or reaction).

Arthus' phenomenon (or reaction) (Arthus, Nicolas Maurice): Medicine. See: Dorland; Stedman; Webster's 3d.

Articles of Henry (Henry III): History. See: Harbottle.

ARTIGUE, M. No dates. French inventor. (Biography source unavailable.) Artigue process.

Artigue process (Artigue, M.): Photography. See: Focal Encyc. Photog.

ARTIN, EMIL. 1898-1962. Austrian mathematician. See: Dict. Sci. Biog. Artin rings.

Artin rings (Artin, Emil): Mathematics. Cited in: Dict. Sci. Biog.

ARTINI, ETTORE. 1866-1928. Italian mineralogist. See: Pogg., vol. 4. Artinite.

Artinite (Artini, Ettore): Earth Sciences. See: Thrush; Webster's 3d.

Arundel, 14th Earl of. See: Howard, Thomas (14th Earl of Arundel).

Arundel prints (Howard, Thomas, 14th Earl of Arundel): Fine Arts. See: Osborne.

Arundel Society (and Club) (Howard, Thomas, 14th Earl of Arundel): Fine Arts. See: Latham; Osborne under "Arundel Prints"; Phyfe.

Arundelian (or Arundel) marbles (Howard, Thomas, 14th Earl of Arundel): Fine Arts. See: Brewer; Harvey; Phyfe.

ARZBERGER, FRIEDRICH. 1833-1905. Austrian physicist. See: Pogg., vol. 4. Arzberger's pear.

Arzberger test for oil of peppermint (Derivation undetermined): Chemistry. See: Van Nostrand Chem. Dict.

Arzberger tests for curcuma in rhubarb (Derivation undetermined): Chemistry. See: Van Nostrand Chem. Dict.

Arzberger's pear (Arzberger, Friedrich): Medicine. See: Dorland.

ARZRUNI, ANDREAS. 1847-1898. Russian mineralogist. See: Sci., vol. 8 (1898) p. 591. Arzrunite.

Arzrunite (Arzruni, Andreas): Earth Science. See: Webster's 3d.

ASAPH. fl. 10th c. B.C. Biblical musician. See: Encyc. Amer., 1959. Asaphic, Asaphite.

Asaphic (Asaph): Religion. See: Webster's 3d.

Asaphite (Asaph): Religion. See: Webster's 3d.

ASBOE-HANSEN, GUSTAV. 1917- . Danish physician. See: World Who's Who Sci. Asboe-Hansen's disease (or incontinentia pigmenti), Asboe-Hansen's sign.

Asboe-Hansen's disease (or incontinentia pigmenti) (Asboe-Hansen, Gustav): Medicine. See: Jablonski.

Asboe-Hansen's sign (Asboe-Hansen, Gustav): Medicine. Cited in: World Who's Who Sci.

ASCH, MORRIS JOSEPH. 1833-1902. American laryngologist. See: Dict. Amer. Biog. Asch's operation, Asch's splint.

ASCHE, OSCAR. 1872-1936. Australian actor. See: Dict. Nat. Biog., 5th suppl. Oscar.

ASCHER, KARL WOLFGANG. b. 1887. Czech-born American ophthalmologist. See: Amer. Men Sci., 11th ed. Ascher's phenomenon, Ascher's syndrome.

Ascher's phenomenon (Ascher, Karl Wolfgang): Medicine. See: Dorland; Stedman.

Ascher's syndrome (Ascher, Karl Wolfgang): Medicine. See: Jablonski. Also known as: Laffer-Ascher syndrome.

ASCHERSON, FERDINAND MORITZ. 1798-1879. German physician. See: Biog. Lex. hervorr. Aerzte. Ascherson's membrane, Ascherson's vesicle.

ASCHERSON, PAUL FRIEDRICH AUGUST. 1834-1913. German botanist. See: World Who's Who Sci. Aschersonia.

Aschersonia (Ascherson, Paul Friedrich August): Botany. See: Webster's 3d.

Ascherson's membrane (Ascherson, Ferdinand Moritz): Medicine. See: Dorland.

Ascherson's vesicle (Ascherson, Ferdinand Moritz): Medicine. See: Dorland.

ASCHHEIM, SELMAR. b. 1878. German obstetrician and gynecologist. See: World Who's Who Sci. Aschheim-Zondek test.

Aschheim-Zondek test (Aschheim, Selmar and Zondek, Bernhardt): Medicine. See: Dorland; Pennak; Stedman.

ASCHNER, BERNHARD. 1883-1960. Austrian physician. See: Who's Imp. Med. Aschner's phenomenon (or reflex), Aschner's treatment (of schizophrenia).

Aschner-Dagnini reflex (Aschner, Bernhardt and Dagnini, Giuseppe). See: Aschner's phenomenon (or reflex).

Aschner's phenomenon (or reflex) (Aschner, Bernhardt): Medicine. See: Dorland; Hinsie; Stedman. Also known as: Aschner-Dagnini reflex.

Aschner's treatment (of schizophrenia) (Aschner, Bernhardt): Psychiatry. See: Hinsie.

Aschoff bodies (or nodules) (Aschoff, Ludwig): Medicine. See: Dorland; Stedman, Webster's 3d.

ASCHOFF, LUDWIG. 1866-1942. German pathologist. See: Wer Ist's?, 1906. Aschoff bodies (or nodules), Aschoff-Tawara's node, Aschoff's ducts, Rokitansky-Aschoff sinuses.

Aschoff-Tawara's node (Aschoff, Ludwig and Tawara, K. Sunao): Anatomy. See: Donath; Dorland; Stedman. Also known as: Tawara's node.

Aschoff's ducts (Aschoff, Ludwig): Anatomy. Cited in: Donath.

Asch's operation (Asch, Morris Joseph): Medicine. See: Dorland; Stedman.

Asch's splint (Asch, Morris Joseph): Medicine. See: Dorland.

ASCLEPIADES OF SAMOS. fl. 3rd c. B.C. Greek poet. See: Encyc. Brit., 1911. Asclepiadic metre (or verse).

Asclepiadic metre (or verse) (Asclepiades of Samos): Literature. See: Brewer; Partridge; Preminger.

Asclepias (Asclepios): Botany. See: Webster's 3d.

Asclepiodotians (Asclepiodotus): Religion. See: Canney.

ASCLEPIODOTUS. No dates. Religious leader and disciple of Theodotus of Byzantium. (Biography source unavailable.) Asclepiodotians.

ASCLEPIOS. Greek mythological god of healing. See: Jobes. Asclepias.

ASCLEPIUS. See: Aesculapius.

ASCOLI, ALBERTO. 1877-1957. Italian serologist. See: New York Acad. Med. Portrait Cat. Ascoli's reaction (or test), Ascoli's treatment.

ASCOLI, GIULIO. 1843-1896. Italian mathematician. See: Pogg., vol. 3. Ascoli theorem.

ASCOLI, MAURIZIO. 1876-1958? Italian pathologist. See: New York Acad. Med. Portrait Cat. Ascoli's reaction (or test).

Ascoli theorem (Ascoli, Giulio): Mathematics. See: Internat. Dict. Ap. Math.; James.

Ascoli's reaction (or test) (Ascoli, Alberto): Medicine. See: Dorland; Stedman.

Ascoli's reaction (or test) (Ascoli, Maurizio): Medicine. See: Dorland.

Ascoli's treatment (Ascoli, Alberto): Medicine. See: Dorland.

ASELLI, GASPARO. 1581-1626. Italian physician and anatomist. See: Encyc. Brit., 1973. Aselli's glands (or pancreas), Aselli's vessels.

Aselli's glands (or pancreas) (Aselli, Gasparo): Anatomy. See: Dorland; Stedman.

Aselli's vessels (Aselli, Gasparo): Anatomy. Cited in: Donath.

Ashbourne, Lord. See: Gibson, Edward (Lord Ashbourne).

Ashburton, 1st Baron. See: Dunning, John.

Ashburton, Lord. See: Baring, Alexander (Lord Ashburton).

Ashburton Treaty (Baring, Alexander, Lord Ashburton): History. See: Harbottle; Jameson; Phyfe.

Ashby's law of requisite variety (Derivation undetermined): Psychology. See: Wolman.

Ashcroft paper tester (Derivation undetermined): Chemistry. See: Hackh.

ASHER. Biblical son of Jacob. See: Webster's Biog. Dict. Asherite.

Asherite (Asher): Religion. See: Webster's 3d.

ASHERMAN, JOSEPH G. fl. 1948. English ? gynecologist. (Biography source unavailable.) Asherman's syndrome, Fritsch-Asherman syndrome.

Asherman's syndrome (Asherman, Joseph G.): Medicine. See: Jablonski.

ASHHURST, JOHN. 1839-1900. American surgeon. See: Dict. Amer. Biog. Ashhurst's splint.

Ashhurst's splint (Ashhurst, John): Medicine. See: Dorland.

ASHLEY, H. fl. 1898. English engineer? (Biography source unavailable.) Ashley pump.

Ashley pump (Ashley, H.): Engineering and Industry. See: Auger.

Ashley's phenomenon (Derivation undetermined): Medicine. See: Stedman.

ASHMAN, RICHARD. 1890- . American physiologist. See: Amer. Men Sci., 10th ed. Ashman's phenomenon?

Ashman's phenomenon (Ashman, Richard?): Medicine. See: Stedman.

Ash's furnace (Derivation undetermined): Engineering and Industry. See: Thrush.

ASHURST, HENRY FOUNTAIN. 1874-1962. American legislator. See: Biog. Direct. Amer. Congress. Ashurst-Sumners Act.

Ashurst-Sumners Act (Ashurst, Henry Fountain and Sumners, John William): Politics. See: Smith.

Askanazy cell (Askanazy, Max?). See: Huerthle cell.

ASKANAZY, MAX. 1865-1940. German pathologist. See: World Who's Who Sci. Askanazy cell?

ASMACHER, FR. fl. 1936. German pharmacologist. (Biography source unavailable.) Asmacher test reaction.

Asmacher test reaction (Asmacher, Fr.): Chemistry. See: Van Nostrand Chem. Dict.

Asmonaean (Hasmon). See: Hasmonaean.

ASPASIA. fl. 432 B.C. Mistress of Pericles, the Greek orator and statesman. See: Nouv. Biog. Univ. Aspasia.

Aspasia (Aspasia, the mistress of Pericles): Generic Word (influential woman). See: Partridge; Weekley.

ASPERGER, HANS. fl. 1844-1954. Austrian physician. (Biography source unavailable.) Asperger's psychopathy.

Asperger's psychopathy (Asperger, Hans). See: Kanner's syndrome.

Aspin engine (Derivation undetermined): Engineering and Industry. See: Auger.

As-Sanusi, Muhammed ibn Ali. See: Sanusi, Muhammed ibn Ali as-.

assassin (Ehissisin, Cheik): Generic Word. See: Charnock.

ASSEZAT, JULES. 1832-1876. French anthropologist. See: Dobson. Assezat's triangle.

Assezat's triangle (Assezat, Jules): Medicine. See: Dorland; Stedman.

ASSMANN, HERBERT. 1882-1950. German internist. See: World Who's Who Sci. Assmann's focus, Assmann's tuberculous infiltrate.

Assmann psychrometer (Assmann, Richard): Earth Sciences. See: Huschke; Thrush.

ASSMANN, RICHARD. 1845-1918. German meteorologist. See: World Who's Who Sci. Assmann psychrometer.

Assmann's focus (Assmann, Herbert): Medicine. See: Dorland.

Assmann's tuberculous infiltrate (Assmann, Herbert): Medicine. See: Dorland; Stedman.

associated Laguerre functions (Laguerre, Edmond Nicolas): Mathematics. See: James.

associated Laguerre polynomials (Laguerre, Edmond Nicolas): Mathematics. See: James.

associated Legendre functions (or equation) (Legendre, Adrien Marie): Mathematics. See: Encyc. Brit., 1973 under "Spherical Harmonics, vol. 21, p. 15a; James; Thewlis.

ASTARTE. Principal deity of Tyre and Sidon. See: Encyc. Brit., 1973. Astarte (mollusk).

Astarte (mollusk) (Astarte): Zoology. See: Pennak; Webster's 3d.

Aston dark space (Aston, Francis William): Physics. See: Ballentyne; Hughes; Internat. Dict. Phys. Elec.

ASTON, FRANCIS WILLIAM. 1877-1945. English physicist and experimental chemist. See: Dict. Sci. Biog. Aston dark space, Aston mass spectrograph, Aston rule, Aston spectrum, Aston whole number rule.

Aston mass spectrograph (Aston, Francis William): Physics. See: Internat. Dict. Phys. Elec.; Markus.

Aston rule (Aston, Francis William): Chemistry. See: Hackh.

Aston spectrum (Aston, Francis William): Chemistry. See: Hackh.

Aston whole number rule (Aston, Francis William): Chemistry. See: Ballentyne; Hughes; Internat. Dict. Phys. Elec.

ASTOR, NANCY LANGHORNE. 1879-1964. American-born English parliamentarian. See: Webster's Biog. Dict. Lady Astor.

ASTRAEA. Greek goddess of justice. See: Harper. Astraea.

Astraea (Astraea, the goddess): Generic Word (justice). See: Brewer.

ASTRUP, TAGE. 1908- . Danish-born biochemist. See: World Who's Who Sci. micro-Astrup method?.

ASTWOOD, EDWIN BENNETT. 1909- . American endocrinologist. See: Lead. Amer. Sci., 8th ed. Astwood's test.

Astwood's test (Astwood, Edwin Bennett): Medicine. See: Stedman.

asymptotic Bayes procedure (Bayes, Thomas): Statistics. See: Kendall.

asynergia of Babinski (Babinski, Joseph Francois Felix): Psychology. See: Hinsie.

Athanasian creed (Athanasius, Saint): Religion. See: Attwater; Canney; Mathews, S.

ATHANASIUS, SAINT. 293-373. Bishop of Alexandria. See: Encyc. Brit., 1911. Athanasian creed.

ATHENA (PASSAS ATHENE). Greek goddess of wisdom. See: Jobes. Palladian, Palladium.

ATHERTON, CHARLES GORDON. 1804-1853. American legislator. See: Dict. Amer. Biog. Atherton gag.

Atherton gag (Atherton, Charles Gordon): History. See: Latham; Mathews, M.M.

ATKINS, TOMMY. Fictitious name for an English private soldier. See: Benet. Tommy, Tommy Atkins.

Atkinson coin (Atkinson, Thomas): Numismatics. See: Partridge.

Atkinson cycle (Atkinson, J.): Engineering and Industry. See: Auger; Ballentyne.

Atkinson formula (Derivation undetermined): Engineering and Industry. See: Thrush.

Atkinson hemin test (Derivation undetermined): Chemistry. See: Hackh.

ATKINSON, J. fl. 1885. English engineer. (Biography source unavailable.) Atkinson cycle.

Atkinson, Louisa. See: Calvert, Caroline Louisa Waring.

ATKINSON, THOMAS. fl. 1581-1611. Scottish mint-master. (Biography source unavailable.) Atkinson coin.

Atkinsonia (Calvert, Caroline Louisa Waring): Botany. Cited in: Webster's Biog. Dict.

Atkinson's friction coefficient (Derivation undetermined): Engineering and Industry. See: Thrush.

Atlantean shoulders (Atlas): Generic Word. See: Brewer.

Atlantes (Atlas): Architecture. See: Brewer; Charnock; Osborne.

ATLAS. Greek mythical giant. See: Oxford Clas. Dict. Atlantean shoulders, Atlantes, Atlas, Atlas beetle, Atlas (computer), Atlas (drawing paper), Atlas (missile), Atlas moth, Atlas (vertebra).

Atlas (Atlas, the mythical giant): Geography. See: Funk; Moore; Partridge.

Atlas beetle (Atlas): Zoology. See: Pennak.

Atlas (computer) (Atlas): Engineering and Industry. See: Hughes.

Atlas (drawing paper) (Atlas): Printing. See: Brewer.

Atlas (missile) (Atlas): Engineering and Industry. See: Markus.

Atlas moth (Atlas): Zoology. See: Pennak; Picken.

Atlas (vertebra) (Atlas): Zoology. See: Charnock; Pennak.

Atropine (Atropos): Chemistry. See: Partridge.

ATROPOS. One of the three Fates in Greek mythology. See: Jobes. Atropine.

Atta, Lester Clare Van. See: Van Atta, Lester Clare.

ATTERBERG, ALBERT. b. 1846. Swedish chemist. See: Pogg., vol. 3. Atterberg limits?

Atterberg limits (Atterberg, Albert?): Earth Sciences. See: Environ. Terms; Thrush.

Atterberg scale (Derivation undetermined): Engineering and Industry. See: Thrush.

Atterberg test (Atterberg, Albert): Earth Sciences. See: Thrush.

ATTERBURY, FRANCIS. 1662-1732. English ecclesiastic. See: Dict. Nat. Biog. Atterbury's plot.

Atterbury's plot (Atterbury, Francis): History. See: Harbottle; Steinberg.

Attila (Attila the Hun): Generic Word (invader). See: Partridge; Weekley.

ATTILA THE HUN. 406?-453. European tribal king. See: Encyc. Brit., 1973. Attila.

ATWOOD, GEORGE. 1745-1807. English mathematician. See: Dict. Nat. Biog. Atwood machine.

Atwood machine (Atwood, George): Physics. See: Auger; Internat. Dict. Phys. Elec.; Van Nostrand Sci. Encyc.

Aub-Dubois table (Aub, Joseph Charles and Du Bois, Eugene F.): Medicine. See: Dorland; Stedman.

AUB, JOSEPH CHARLES. b. 1890. American physician. See: Who's Imp. Med., 2d ed. Aub-Dubois table.

Auberger blood group (Auberger, Madame): Medicine. See: Stedman.

AUBERGER, MADAME. No dates. Female patient who had received many blood transfusions. (Biography source unavailable.) Auberger blood group.

Aubert diaphragm (Aubert, Hermann): Psychology. See: Drever; Wolman.

Aubert-Foerster phenomenon (Aubert, Hermann and Foerster, Carl Friedrich Richard): Psychology. See: Chaplin; Drever; Wolman.

AUBERT, HERMANN. 1826-1892. German physiologist and psychologist. See: Allg. Deut. Biog. Aubert diaphragm, Aubert-Foerster phenomenon, Aubert phenomenon.

Aubert phenomenon (Aubert, Hermann): Psychology. See: Chaplin; English; Wolman.

AUBINEAU, ERNEST RENE EMILE. b. 1871. French physician. (Biography source unavailable.) Lenoble-Aubineau syndrome.

AUBRIET, CLAUDE. 1665-1743. French painter. See: Nouv. Biog. Univ. Aubrietia.

Aubrietia (Aubriet, Claude): Botany. See: Partridge; Webster's 3d.

AUBRY, PIERRE ERNST MARIE. fl. 1922. French chemist. Cited in: Chem. Abstr., vol. 16, p. 2343. Aubry reagent.

Aubry reagent (Aubry, Pierre Ernst Marie): Chemistry. See: Van Nostrand Chem. Dict.

AUCHE, AUGUST. fl. 1908. French chemist. Cited in: Chem. Abstr., vol. 2, p. 1572. Auche-Deniges reagent.

Auche-Deniges reagent (Auche, August and Deniges, Georges): Chemistry. See: Van Nostrand Chem. Dict.

Audeanism (Audeus): Religion. See: Charnock.

AUDEN, WYSTAN HUGH. 1907- . English-born poet and critic. See: Webster's Biog. Dict. Audenesque.

Audenesque (Auden, Wystan Hugh): Literature. See: Oxford Eng. Dict., 2nd. suppl.

AUDEUS. d. 372. Syrian bishop. See: Encyc. Brit., 1911. Audeanism, Audiani.

Audiani (Audeus): Religion. See: Canney.

Audibert-Arnu dilatometer (Audibert, Etienne? and Arnu, Charles): Engineering and Industry. See: Thrush.

AUDIBERT, ETIENNE. b. 1888. French engineer. See: Who's Who France. Audibert-Arnu dilatometer?

AUDIBERT, URBAIN. 1789-1846. French botanist. See: Nouv. Biog. Univ. Audibertia.

Audibertia (Audibert, Urbain): Botany. See: Taylor, N.; Webster's 3d. Also known as: Ramona.

AUDIFFREN. fl. 1934. French chemist. Cited in: Chem. Abstr., vol. 28, p. 7287. Audiffren test reaction.

Audiffren test reaction (Audiffren): Chemistry. See: Van Nostrand Chem. Dict.

AUDOUIN, JEAN VICTOR. 1797-1838. French physician. See: Dict. Sci. Biog. Audouin's microsporon.

Audouin's microsporon (Audouin, Jean Victor): Medicine. See: Dorland.

AUDREY, SAINT. d. 679. English abbess. See: Holweck. Tawdry, Tawdry lace.

AUDRY, CHARLES. 1865-1934. French physician. See: New York Acad. Med. Portrait Cat. Audry's syndrome.

Audry's syndrome (Audry, Charles). See: Uehlinger's syndrome.

Audubon Association (Audubon, John James): Zoology. Cited in: Mathews, M.M.

Audubon bird (Audubon, John James): Fine Art. Cited in: Mathews, M.M.

AUDUBON, JOHN JAMES. 1785-1851. American ornithologist. See: Dict. Sci. Biog. Audubon Association, Audubon bird, Audubon Law, Audubon print, Audubon Society, Audubon's bighorn, Audubon's caracara, Audubon's oriole, Audubon's shearwater, Audubon's warbler, Audubon's woodpecker.

Audubon Law (Audubon, John James): Law. Cited in: Mathews, M.M.

Audubon print (Audubon, John James): Fine Art. See: Mathews, M.M.

Audubon Society (Audubon, John James): Zoology. Cited in: Mathews, M. M.

Audubon's bighorn (Audubon, John James): Zoology (sheep). See: Mathews, M. M.

Audubon's caracara (Audubon, John James): Zoology (hawk). Cited in: Gray. See: Mathews, M.M.; Webster's 3d.

Audubon's oriole (Audubon, John James): Zoology. Cited in: Mathews, M. M.

Audubon's shearwater (Audubon, John James): Zoology. See: Gray; Webster's 3d.

Audubon's warbler (Audubon, John James): Zoology. See: Gray; Mathews, M. M.; Webster's 3d.

Audubon's woodpecker (Audubon, John James): Zoology. See: Mathews, M.M.

AUENBRUGGER, LEOPOLD JOSEPH. 1722-1809. Austrian physician. See: Dict. Sci. Biog. Auenbrugger's sign.

Auenbrugger's sign (Auenbrugger, Leopold Joseph): Medicine. See: Dorland; Stedman.

AUER, JOHN. 1875-1948. American physician. See: World Who's Who Sci. Auer's bodies, Meltzer-Auer test.

AUER, KARL. 1858-1929. Austrian-born chemist. See: World Who's Who Sci. Auer metal.

Auer metal (Auer, Karl): Chemistry. See: Hackh.

AUER VON WELSBACH, BARON KARL. 1858-1929. Austrian chemist and physicist. See: Pogg., vols. 5, 6. Welsbach mantle.

AUERBACH, FRIEDRICH. 1870-1925. German chemist. See: World Who's Who Sci. Auerbach method?

AUERBACH, LEOPOLD. 1828-1897. German anatomist. See: Allg. Deut. Biog. Auerbach's ganglion, Auerbach's plexus.

Auerbach method (Auerbach, Friedrich?): Chemistry. See: Van Nostrand Chem. Dict.

Auerbach's ganglion (Auerbach, Leopold): Anatomy. See: Dorland; Stedman.

Auerbach's plexus (Auerbach, Leopold): Anatomy. See: Donath; Gray; Jennak.

Auer's bodies (Auer, John): Medicine. See: Dorland; Stedman.

AUFRECHT, EMANUEL. 1844-1933. German physician. See: Biog. Lex. hervorr. Aerzte. Aufrecht's sign.

Aufrecht test (Derivation undetermined): Chemistry. See: Van Nostrand Chem. Dict.

Aufrecht's sign (Aufrecht, Emanuel): Medicine. See: Dorland; Stedman.

Augean stables (Augeas): Generic Word (corruption). See: Brewer; Partridge; Phyfe.

AUGEAS. Legendary King of Elis. See: Harper. Augean stables.

Auger coefficient (Auger, Pierre Victor): Physics. See: Internat. Dict. Ap. Math.; Internat. Dict. Phys. Elec.; Markus.

Auger effect (Auger, Pierre Victor): Physics. See: Ballentyne; Hughes; Thewlis.

Auger electron (Auger, Pierre Victor): Physics. See: Internat. Dict. Phys. Elec.; Markus; Van Nostrand Sci. Encyc.

Auger emission spectroscopy (Auger, Pierre Victor): Physics. See: Thewlis.

AUGER, PIERRE VICTOR. 1899- . French physicist. See: World Who's Who Sci. Auger coefficient, Auger effect, Auger electron, Auger emission spectroscopy, Auger shower, Auger yield.

Auger shower (Auger, Pierre Victor): Physics. See: Internat. Dict. Phys. Elec.; Webster's 3d.

Auger yield (Auger, Pierre Victor): Physics. See: Hughes; Internat. Dict. Ap. Math.; Internat. Dict. Phys. Elec.

Aughey spark chamber (Aughey, William Henry): Physics. See: Internat. Dict. Phys. Elec.

AUGHEY, WILLIAM HENRY. 1906- . American physicist. See: Amer. Men Sci., 10th ed. Aughey spark chamber.

August (Augustus Caesar): Generic Word. See: Brewer; Funk; Hendrickson.

August d'or (Augustus I): Numismatics. See: Charnock.

Augustal (coin) (Frederick II Augustus of Hohenstaufen): Numismatics. See: Webster's 3d.

Augustan age (Augustus Caesar): Literature. See: Barnet; Harvey; Scott.

Augusti microtest for mercurous ion (Augusti, S.): Chemistry. See: Van Nostrand Chem. Dict.

Augusti microtest for the manganous ion (Augusti, S.): Chemistry. See: Van Nostrand Chem. Dict.

Augusti solution for copper and iron (Augusti, S.): Chemistry. See: Van Nostrand Chem. Dict.

Augustin process (Derivation undetermined): Engineering and Industry. See: Thrush.

Augustine of Canterbury. See: Austin, Saint.

AUGUSTINE OF HIPPO, SAINT. 354-430. Church Father, philosopher and writer. See: Encyc. Brit., Augustines, Augustinians, Augustinians of the Assumption, Augustinism (or Augustinianism), St. Augustine grass.

Augustines (Augustine of Hippo, Saint): Religion. See: Canney.

Augustinian Hermits (Austin, Saint). See: Austin (or Augustinian) Friars.

Augustinians (Augustine of Hippo, Saint): Religion. See: Canney.

Augustinians of the Assumption (Augustine of Hippo, Saint): Religion. See: Attwater; Canney.

Augustinism (or Augustinianism) (Augustine of Hippo, Saint): Philosophy. See: Attwater; Good; Webster's 3d.

AUGUSTUS I. 1526-1586. Elector of Saxony. See: Encyc. Brit., 1973. August D'or.

AUGUSTUS CAESAR. 27 B.C.-14 A.D. Roman Emperor. See: Encyc. Brit., 1973. August, Augustan age, Caesarism (Caesarist or Caesarize).

AUJESZKY, ALADAR. 1869-1933. Hungarian physician. See: New York Acad. Med. Portrait Cat. Aujeszky's disease.

Aujeszky's disease (Aujeszky, Aladar): Medicine. See: Dorland; Jablonski; Stedman.

Auld-Hantzsch test (Auld, Samuel James Manson and Hantzsch, Arthur): Chemistry. See: Van Nostrand Chem. Dict.

AULD, SAMUEL JAMES MANSON. b. 1884. English chemist. See: Pogg., vol. 5. Auld-Hantzsch test.

Aunt May (Hanrahan, May): Generic Word (person generous to sailors). See: Hendrickson.

Aurantia solution (Derivation undetermined): Chemistry. See: Van Nostrand Chem. Dict.

Aurelj test reaction (Derivation undetermined): Chemistry. See: Van Nostrand Chem. Dict.

Aurora (Aurora the Goddess): Generic Word (morning). See: Brewer; Partridge.

Aurora borealis (Aurora the Goddess): Astronomy. See: Partridge.

AURORA THE GODDESS. Greek deity of morning. See: Harper. Aurora, Aurora borealis, Aurora's tears.

Aurora's tears (Aurora the Goddess): Generic Word (dew). See: Brewer.

AUSONIUS, DECIMUS MAGNUS. 310-395. Roman poet and rhetorician. See: Encyc. Brit., 1973. Chateau Ausone (claret).

AUSPITZ, HEINRICH. 1835-1886. Austrian dermatologist. See: Allg. Deut. Biog. Auspitz's dermatosis (or disease).

Auspitz's dermatosis (or disease) (Auspitz, Heinrich). See: Alibert-Bazin syndrome.

Austemper (or Austempering) (Roberts-Austen, William Chandler): Engineering and Industry. See: Thrush; Webster's 3d.

AUSTEN, JANE. 1775-1817. English novelist. See: Dict. Nat. Biog. Janeite.

Austenite (Roberts-Austen, William Chandler): Engineering and Industry. See: Thewlis; Thrush; Van Nostrand Sci. Encyc.; Webster's 3d.

Austenitic (stainless steels) (Roberts-Austen, William Chandler): Engineering and Industry. See: Stedman; Thrush; Webster's 3d.

Austenitizing (Roberts-Austen, William Chandler): Engineering and Industry. See: Thrush; Webster's 3d.

AUSTER. Greek god of the south-west wind. See: Harper. Austral.

Austin (or Augustinian) Canons (Austin, Saint): Religion. See: Attwater; Brewer; Harvey.

Austin-Cohen formula (Austin, Louis Winslow and Cohen, Louis): Physics. See: Hughes.

Austin-Cohen law (Austin, Louis Winslow and Cohen, Louis): Physics. See: Ballentyne:

Austin Flint. See: Flint, Austin.

Austin Flint's murmur (Flint, Austin). See: Flint's murmur.

Austin (or Augustinian) Friars (Austin, Saint): Religion. See: Attwater; Brewer; Webster's 3d. Also known as: Augustinian Hermits.

AUSTIN, JOHN. 1790-1859. English jurist and legal writer. See: Internat. Encyc. Soc. Sci. Austinian theory.

AUSTIN, LOUIS WINSLOW. 1867-1932. American physicist. See: Dict. Sci. Biog. Austin-Cohen formula, Austin-Cohen law.

AUSTIN, SAINT. d. 604. Archbishop of Canterbury. See: Dict. Nat. Biog. Austin (or Augustinian) Canons, Austin (or Augustinian) Friars, Saint Austin pear, Saint Austin's summer.

Austinian theory (Austin, John): Law. See: Smith; Webster's 3d.

Austinite (Rogers, Austin Flint): Earth Sciences. See: Thrush; Webster's 3d.

Austral (Auster): Generic Word (southern). See: Partridge.

Autenrieth-Hinsberg test reaction (Autenrieth, Wilhelm Ludwig and Hinsberg, Oscar Heinrich Daniel): Chemistry. See: Van Nostrand Chem. Dict.

AUTENRIETH, JOHANN HERRMANN FERDINAND VON. 1772-1835. German physician. See: Pogg., vol. 1. Autenrieth's salve, Bayford-Autenrieth dysphagia.

Autenrieth test for colchicine (Autenrieth, Wilhelm Ludwig?): Chemistry. See: Van Nostrand Chem. Dict.

Autenrieth test for methanol (Autenrieth, Wilhelm Ludwig): Chemistry. See: Van Nostrand Chem. Dict.

AUTENRIETH, WILHELM LUDWIG. b. 1863. German chemist. See: Pogg., vol. 4. Autenrieth-Hinsberg test reaction, Autenrieth test for colchicine?, Autenrieth test for methanol.

Autenrieth's salve (Autenrieth, Johann Herrmann Ferdinand von): Medicine. See: Dorland.

Autolycus (Autolycus the Rogue): Generic Word. See: Partridge.

AUTOLYCUS THE ROGUE. Greek mythological son of Hermes. See: Oxford Clas. Dict. Autolycus.

Automedon (Automedon the charioteer): Generic Word. See: Partridge; Weekley.

AUTOMEDON THE CHARIOTEER. Legendary friend of Achilles. See: Oxford Clas. Dict. Automedon.

AUWERS, KARL FRIEDRICH VON. 1863-1939. German chemist. See: Dict. Sci. Biog. Auwers-Skita rule, Auwers synthesis.

Auwers-Skita rule (Auwers, Karl Friedrich von and Skita, Aladar): Chemistry. See: Van Nostrand Chem. Dict.

Auwers synthesis (Auwers, Karl Friedrich von): Chemistry. See: Von Nostrand Chem. Dict.

AUZINGER, AUGUST. fl. 1910. German chemist. Cited in: Chem. Abstr., vol. 4, p. 1201. Auzinger tests for honey.

Auzinger tests for honey (Auzinger, August): Chemistry. See: Van Nostrand Chem. Dict.

Ave Maria (or Hail Mary) (Mary, Virgin-Mother): Religion. See: Apel; Attwater; Mathews, S.

Ave Maria lace (Mary, Virgin-Mother): Applied Arts. See: Picken.

Aveling gearing (Aveling, Thomas): Engineering and Industry. See: Auger.

AVELING, JAMES HOBSON. 1825-1892. English obstetrician. See: Biog. Lex. hervorr. Aerzte. Aveling's repositor.

AVELING, THOMAS. 1824-1882. English inventor. See: Boase. Aveling gearing.

Aveling's repositor (Aveling, James Hobson): Medicine. See: Dorland.

AVELLAR DE LOUREIRO, J. fl. 1927-1935. Portuguese chemist. Cited in: Chem. Abstr., vol. 21, p. 2484. Avellar de Loureiro reagent.

Avellar de Loureiro reagent (Avellar de Loureiro, J): Chemistry. See: Van Nostrand Chem. Dict.

AVELLIS, GEORG. 1864-1916. German laryngologist. See: Neue Deut. Biog. Avellis' paralysis (or syndrome).

Avellis-Longhi syndrome (Avellis, Georg and Longhi, Giovanni?). See: Avellis' paralysis (or syndrome).

Avellis' paralysis (or syndrome) (Avellis, Georg): Medicine. See: Dorland; Hinsie; Jablonski. Also known as: Avellis-Longhi syndrome.

Averrhoa (Averroes): Botany. See: Charnock; Taylor, N.; Webster's 3d.

AVERROES (MOHAMMED IBN ROSHD). 1126-1198. Arabic philosopher. See: Encyc. Brit., 1973. Averrhoa, Averroism.

Averroism (Averroes): Philosophy. See: Attwater; Canney; Partridge.

AVERTIN, SAINT. ca. 1120-1180. English deacon. See: Holweck. Saint Avertin's disease.

AVICENNA (IBN SINA). 980-1037. Persian physician and philosopher. See: Encyc. Brit., 1973. Avicenna's gland, Avicenna's sand viper?, Avicennia, Avicennism.

Avicenna's gland (Avicenna): Medicine. See: Stedman.

Avicenna's sand viper (Avicenna?): Zoology. See: Stedman.

Avicennia (Avicenna): Botany. See: Charnock; Webster's 3d.

Avicennism (Avicenna): Philosophy. See: Webster's 3d.

Avogadrite (Avogadro, Amadeo): Earth Sciences. See: Thrush; Webster's 3d.

AVOGADRO, AMADEO. 1776-1856. Italian chemist. See: Dict. Sci. Biog. Avogadrite, Avogadro constant (or number), Avogadro hypothesis (or law), Avogram.

Avogadro constant (or number) (Avogadro, Amadeo): Chemistry. See: Internat. Dict. Phys. Elec.; Van Nostrand Chem. Dict.; Van Nostrand Sci. Encyc. Also known as: Loschmidt number.

Avogadro hypothesis (or law) (Avogadro, Amadeo): Chemistry. See: Internat. Dict. Ap. Math.; Internat. Dict. Phys. Elec.; Van Nostrand Sci. Encyc.

Avogram (Avogadro, Amadeo): Chemistry. See: Webster's 3d.

Avon, Sir Robert Anthony Eden, Earl of. See: Eden, Sir Robert Anthony.

Awakening of Hercules (Hercules): Mythology. See: Canney.

Awberg and Griffiths method for latent heat of vaporization (Derivation undetermined): Physics. See: Internat. Dict. Phys. Elec.

AWENG, E. fl. 1912. German chemist. Cited in: Chem. Abstr. Aweng microtest for methanol?, Aweng test reaction for papaverine?

Aweng microtest for methanol (Aweng, E.?): Chemistry. See: Van Nostrand Chem. Dict.

Aweng test reaction for papaverine (Aweng, E.?): Chemistry. See: Van Nostrand Chem. Dict.

Axel (skating jump) (Paulsen, Axel): Recreation and Sports. See: Webster's 3d.

AXELROD, GEORGE. 1922- . American playwright. See: Who's Who Amer., 1972-73. Axelrodding.

Axelrodding (Axelrod, George): Generic Word. See: Det. Free Press, Dec. 2, 1974.

AXENFELD, DAVID. 1848-1912. German physiologist. See: Sci., vol. 36 (1912) p. 823. Axenfeld reaction for propeptone?, Axenfeld reagent for albumin, Axenfeld's test.

AXENFELD, KARL THEODOR PAUL POLYKARPUS. 1867-1930. German ophthalmologist. See: World Who's Who Sci. Axenfeld-Krukenberg spindle, Axenfeld-Schuerenberg syndrome, Axenfeld's anomaly, Axenfeld's calcareous degeneration, Morax-Axenfeld conjunctivitis, Morax-Axenfeld diplobacillus.

Axenfeld-Krukenberg spindle (Axenfeld, Karl Theodor Paul Polykarpus and Krukenberg, Friedrich Ernst). See: Krukenberg's spindle.

Axenfeld reaction for propeptone (Axenfeld, David?): Chemistry. See: Van Nostrand Chem. Dict.

Axenfeld reagent for albumin (Axenfeld, David): Chemistry. See: Van Nostrand Chem. Dict.

Axenfeld-Schuerenberg syndrome (Axenfeld, Karl Theodor Paul Polykarpus and Schuerenberg): Medicine. See: Jablonski.

Axenfeld's anomaly (Axenfeld, Karl Theodor Paul Polykarpus): Medicine. See: Jablonski.

Axenfeld's calcareous degeneration (Axenfeld, Karl Theodor Paul Polykarpus): Medicine. See: Jablonski.

Axenfeld's conjunctivitis (Axenfeld, Karl Theodor Paul Polykarpus). See: Morax-Axenfeld conjunctivitis.

Axenfeld's test (Axenfeld, David): Medicine. See: Dorland; Stedman.

AYALA, A.G. No dates. Italian neurologist. (Biography source unavailable.) Ayala's equation (index, or quotient).

Ayala's equation (index, or quotient) (Ayala, A.G.): Medicine. See: Dorland; Stedman.

AYER, JAMES BOURNE. b. 1882. American neurologist. See: Who's Who Amer. Med. Ayer's test, Tobey-Ayer test.

Ayer's test (Ayer, James Bourne): Medicine. See: Dorland.

AYERZA, ABEL. 1861-1918. Argentinian physician. See: New York Acad. Med. Portrait cat. Ayerza's disease, Ayerza's syndrome.

Ayerza's disease (Ayerza, Abel): Medicine. See: Dorland; Stedman; Webster's 3d.

Ayerza's syndrome (Ayerza, Abel): Medicine. See: Dorland; Jablonski.

AYMEN, JEAN BAPTISTE. 1729-1784. French physician. See: World Who's Who Sci. Aymenea.

Aymenea (Aymen, Jean Baptiste): Botany. Cited in: World Who's Who Sci.

Aymonier solution (Derivation undetermined): Chemistry. See: Van Nostrand Chem. Dict.

Ayre brush (Ayre, James Ernest): Medicine. See: Stedman.

AYRE, JAMES ERNEST. 1910- . American gynecologist. See: Amer. Men Sci., 10th ed. Ayre brush.

Ayres handwriting scale (Derivation undetermined): Education. See: English.

Ayres spelling scale (Derivation undetermined): Education. See: English.

Ayrton antigas fan (Ayrton, Hertha Marks): Engineering and Industry. Cited in: Encyc. Brit., 1973.

Ayrton equation (Ayrton, William Edward): Engineering and Industry. See: Thewlis.

AYRTON, HERTHA MARKS. 1854-1923. English physicist. See: Encyc. Brit., 1973. Ayrton antigas fan.

Ayrton-Jones current balance (Ayrton, William Edward and Jones, John Viriamu): Engineering and Industry. See: Dresner.

Ayrton-Mather shunt (Ayrton, William Edward and Mather, Thomas): Engineering and Industry. See: Hughes.

Ayrton shunt (Ayrton, William Edward): Engineering and Industry. See: Internat. Dict. Phys. Elec.; Markus; Webster's 3d.,

AYRTON, WILLIAM EDWARD. 1847-1908. English electrical engineer. See: Dict. Nat. Biog., 2d. suppl. Ayrton equation, Ayrton-Jones current balance, Ayrton-Mather shunt, Ayrton shunt.

AYYUB IBN-SHADHI. d. 1173. Kurd general. See: Webster's Biog. Dict. Ayyubid.

Ayyubid (Ayyub ibn-Shadhi): History. See: Webster's 3d.

Azara (Azara, Jose Nicolas): Botany. See: Taylor, N.

AZARA, FELIX DE. 1746-1811. Spanish soldier, naturalist and traveler. See: Dict. Sci. Biog. Azara's dog.

AZARA, JOSE NICOLAS. 1731-1804. Spanish diplomat. See: Encyc. Brit., 1911. Azara.

Azara's dog (Azara, Felix de): Zoology (jackal). Cited in: Gray; Webster's 3d.

Azbell-Kaner resonance (Azbell, William and Kaner, E. A.): Physics. See: Ballentyne.

AZBELL, WILLIAM. 1906- . American physicist. See: Amer. Men Sci., 10th ed. Azbell-Kaner resonance.

Azua's pseudoepithelioma (De Azua y Suarez, Juan). See: De Azua's pseudo-epithelioma.

AZZARELLO, E. fl. 1907. Italian chemist. Cited in: Chem. Abstr. Azzarello test for alcohol in ether, chloroform and volatile oils?

Azzarello test for alcohol in ether, chloroform and volatile oils (Azzarello, E.?): Chemistry. See: Van Nostrand Chem. Dict.

AZZOLINI, B. fl. 1931. Italian chemist. Cited in: Chem. Abstr., vol. 26, p. 252. Azzolini test.

Azzolini test (Azzolini, B.): Chemistry. See: Van Nostrand Chem. Dict.

B

B lines of Kerley (Kerley, Peter James): Medicine. See: Stedman.

BET adsorption equation (or method). See: Brunauer, Emmett and Teller adsorption equation (method or theory).

BAADER, ERNST W. b. 1892. German physician. See: Wer Ist Wer?, 8th ed. Baader's dermatostomatitis.

Baader's dermatostomatitis (Baader, Ernst W.). See: Stevens-Johnson syndrome.

BAAL. Ancient Near Eastern weather god. See: Encyc. Brit., 1973. Baalism.

Baalism (Baal): Religion. See: Winick.

BAANES. fl. 810. Religious leader and disciple of Josephus Epaphrodites. (Biography source unavailable.) Baanites.

Baanites (Baanes): Religion. See: Canney; Latham.

BAASTRUP, CHRISTIAN INGERSLEV. 1885-1950. Scandanavian physician. See: New York Acad. Med. Portrait Cat. Baastrups syndrome.

Baastrup's syndrome (Baastrup, Christian Ingerslev): Medicine. See: Jablonski. Also known as: Michotte's syndrome.

BABA, NOBUHIDE. fl. 1935. Japanese chemist. Cited in: Chem. Abstr., vol. 31, p. 8827. Baba test reaction.

Baba test reaction (Baba, Nobuhide): Chemistry. See: Van Nostrand Chem. Dict.

Babakiyah (Babek): Religion. See: Canney.

BABBAGE, CHARLES. 1792-1871. English mathematician. See: Internat. Encyc. Soc. Sci. Babbage engine.

Babbage engine (Babbage, Charles): Engineering and Industry. See: Auger.

Babbitt (or Babbitry) (Babbitt, George Folansbee): Generic Word (conformity). See: Hoult; Partridge; Zadrozny.

BABBITT, GEORGE FOLANSBEE. Leading character in Sinclair Lewis' novel of this name. See: Benet. Babbitt (or Babbitry).

BABBITT, ISAAC. 1799-1862. American inventor. See: Encyc. Brit., 1973. Babbitt metal, Babbitt soap.

Babbitt metal (Babbitt, Isaac): Engineering and Industry. See: Mathews, M. M.; Partridge; Thrush.

Babbitt soap (Babbitt, Isaac): Engineering and Industry. See: Hendrickson.

Babcock and Wilcox boiler (Babcock, George Herman and Wilcox, Stephen). Engineering and Industry. See: Auger; Thrush.

Babcock and Wilcox mill (Babcock, George Herman and Wilcox, Stephen): Engineering and Industry. See: Thrush.

Babcock bottle (Babcock, Stephen Moulton): Chemistry. See: Hackh.

Babcock fire extinguisher (Babcock, James Francis): Engineering and Industry. Cited in: Webster's Biog. Dict.

BABCOCK, GEORGE HERMAN. 1832-1893. American inventor. See: Dict. Amer. Biog. Babcock and Wilcox boiler, Babcock and Wilcox mill.

BABCOCK, JAMES FRANCIS. 1844-1897. American chemist. See: Dict. Amer. Biog. Babcock fire extinguisher.

Babcock milk tester (Babcock, Stephen Moulton): Chemistry. See: Hackh.

BABCOCK, NATHAN. b. 1824. American manufacturer. (Biography source unavailable.) Babcock printing presses.

Babcock pipette (Babcock, Stephen Moulton): Chemistry. See: Van Nostrand Chem. Dict.

Babcock printing presses (Babcock, Nathan): Printing. See: Lockwood.

BABCOCK, STEPHEN MOULTON. 1843-1931. American agricultural chemist. See: Dict. Sci. Biog. Babcock bottle, Babcock milk tester, Babcock pipette Babcock test, Babcock tube.

Babcock test (Babcock, Stephen Moulton): Chemistry. See: Dorland; Hendrickson; Winburne.

Babcock tube (Babcock, Stephen Moulton): Chemistry. See: Stedman.

BABCOCK, WILLIAM WAYNE. 1872-1963. American surgeon. Who's Imp. Med., 2d. ed. Babcock's operation.

Babcock's operation (Babcock, William Wayne): Medicine. See: Dorland; Stedman.

BABE. fl. 1880. American inventor. (Biography source unavailable.) Baby (sifting machine).

Babe Ruth (Ruth, George Herman): Generic Word (baseball player). See: Hendrickson; Partridge.

BABEK. No dates. Religious leader. (Biography source unavailable.) Babakiyah.

BABER, MARGARET DOREEN. fl. 1934-1956. English pediatrician. See: Med. Direct., 1956. Baber's syndrome.

Baber's syndrome (Baber, Margaret Doreen): Medicine. See: Jablonski.

Babes-Ernst bodies (Babes, Victor and Ernst, Paul): Medicine. See: Dorland; Henderson; Stedman.

Babes nodes (Babes, Victor): Medicine. See: Stedman.

Babes stain (Babes, Victor): Medicine. See: Stedman.

Babes treatment (Babes, Victor): Medicine. See: Dorland.

Babes tubercle (Babes, Victor): Medicine. See: Dorland.

Babes vaccine (Babes, Victor): Medicine. See: Stedman.

BABES, VICTOR. 1854-1926. Romanian bacteriologist. See: Webster's Biog. Dict. Babes-Ernst bodies, Babes nodes, Babes stain, Babes treatment, Babes tubercle, Babes vaccine, Babesia.

Babesia (Babes, Victor): Zoology. See: Dorland; Pennak; Stedman. Also known as: Nuttallia.

BABEUF, FRANCOIS EMILE. 1760-1797. French revolutionary. Encyc. Brit., 1973. Babouvism.

Babinet absorption rule (Babinet, Jacques): Physics. See: Internat. Dict. Phys. Elec.

Babinet compensator (Babinet, Jacques): Physics. See: Thewlis.

BABINET, JACQUES. 1794-1872. French physicist. See: Dict. Sci. Biog. Babinet absorption rule, Babinet compensator, Babinet point, Babinet principle.

Babinet point (Babinet, Jacques): Physics. See: Huschke; Van Nostrand Sci. Encyc.

Babinet principle (Babinet, Jacques): Physics. See: Ballentyne; Hughes; Internat. Dict. Ap. Math.

BABINGTON, ANTHONY. 1561-1586. English Roman Catholic conspirator. See: Dict. Nat. Biog. Babington conspiracy (or plot).

BABINGTON, BENJAMIN GUY. 1794-1866. English physician. See: World Who's Who Sci. Babington's disease.

Babington conspiracy (or plot) (Babington, Anthony): History. See: Attwater; Harbottle; Steinberg.

BABINGTON, WILLIAM. 1756-1833. English mineralogist. See: Dict. Sci. Biog. Babintonite.

Babingtonite (Babington, William): Earth Sciences. See: Thrush; Van Nostrand Sci. Encyc.; Webster's 3d.

Babington's disease (Babington, Benjamin Guy). See: Osler's syndrome (2).

Babinski-Froehlich syndrome (Babinski, Joseph Francois Felix and Froelich, Alfred). See: Froehlich's syndrome.

BABINSKI, JOSEPH FRANCOIS FELIX. 1857-1932. French neurologist. See: Chambers' Biog. Dict. Anton-Babinski syndrome, asynergia of Babinski, Babinski-Froehlich syndrome, Babinski-Nageotte's syndrome, Babinski reflex (or sign), Babinski's law, Babinski's syndrome.

Babinski-Nageotte's syndrome (Babinski, Joseph Francois Felix and Nageotte, Jean): Psychology. See: Hinsie; Jablonski.

Babinski reflex (or sign) (Babinski, Joseph Francois Felix): Pyschology. See: Chaplin; Hinsie; Wolman.

Babinski-Vaquez syndrome (Babinski, Joseph Francois Felix and Vaquez, Louis Henri). See: Babinski's syndrome.

Babinski's law (Babinski, Joseph Francois Felix): Medicine. See: Dorland.

Babinski's syndrome (Babinski, Joseph Francois Felix): Medicine. See: Dorland; Jablonski. Also known as: Babinski-Vaquez syndrome.

Babism (or Babists) (Ali Mohammed of Shiraz): Religion. See: Barnhart, (Eng. Lit.); Harvey; Latham.

BABKIN, M. P. fl. 1934. Russian chemist. Cited in: Chem. Abstr. vol. 28, p. 5004. Babkin test.

Babkin test (Babkin, M. P.): Chemistry. See: Van Nostrand Chem. Dict.

Babo absorption tube (Babo, Clement Heinrich Lambert Freiherr von): Chemistry. See: Hackh.

BABO, CLEMENT HEINRICH LAMBERT FREIHERR VON. 1818-1899. German chemist. See: Allg. Deut. Biog. Babo absorption tube, Babo's law.

Babo's law (Babo, Clement Heinrich Lambert Freiherr von): Chemistry. See: Ballentyne; Internat. Dict. Phys. Elec.

Babouvism (Babeuf, Francois Emile): Sociology. See: Webster's 3d.

BABY, EDWARD CHARLES CYRIL. 1871-1948. English physicist. See: World Who's Who Sci. Baby tube (or cell).

Baby (sifting machine) (Babe): Engineering and Industry. See: Hendrickson.

Baby Stuart cap (James I): Fashion. See: Picken.

Baby tube (or cell) (Baby, Edward Charles Cyril): Physics. See: Hackh; Internat. Dict. Phys. Elec.; Van Nostrand Chem. Dict.

Baccanari, Niccolo. See: Paccanari, Niccolo.

Baccanarists (Paccanari, Niccolo): Religion. See: Canney; New Catholic Encyc. Also known as: Paccanarists.

BACCAREDDA, ALDO. 1902- . Italian physician. See: Who's Who Sci. Europe. Sezary-Baccaredda syndrome?

BACCELLI, GUIDO. 1832-1916. Italian physician. See: Dict. Sci. Biog. Baccelli's method, Baccelli's sign.

Baccelli's method (Baccelli, Guido): Medicine. See: Dorland; Stedman.

Baccelli's sign (Baccelli, Guido): Medicine. See: Dorland; Stedman.

Bacchanal (or Bacchanalian) (Bacchus): Generic Word (drunkard). See: Charnock; Partridge; Webster's 3d.

Bacchanalia (Bacchus): Generic Word (festival). See: Barnhart, (Eng. Lit.); Harvey; Winnick.

Bacchanalians (Bacchus): Religion. See: Charnock.

Baccharis (Bacchus): Botany. See: Charnock; Taylor, N.

Bacchius (verse) (Bacchus): Literature. See: Charnock; .Preminger, Webster's 3d.

BACCHUS. God of Wine. See: Oxford Clas. Dict. Bacchanal (or Bacchanalian), Bacchanalia, Bacchanalians, Baccharis, Bacchius (verse).

Bach-Abel concerts (Bach, Johann Christian and Abel, Karl Friedrich): Music. Cited in: Webster's Biog. Dict.

BACH, ALEKSEI NIKOLAEVICH. 1857-1946. Russian chemist. See: Dict. Sci. Biog. Bach-Engler peroxide theory of oxidation, Bach readings, Bach reagent for copper and nickel?, Bach, solution for hydrogen peroxide?, Bach test reaction for solanine?

BACH, ALEXANDER VON. 1813-1893. Austrian statesman. See: Allg. Deut. Biog. Bach system.

Bach-Engler peroxide theory of oxidation (Bach, Aleksei Nikolaevich and Engler, Carl Oswald Viktor): Chemistry. Cited in: Dict. Sci. Biog.

BACH, JOHANN CHRISTIAN. 1735-1782. English organist and composer. See: Webster's Biog. Dict. Bach-Abel concerts.

BACH, JOHANN SEBASTIAN. 1685-1750. German organist, composer and master contrapuntist. See: Encyc. Brit., 1973. Bach trumpet.

BACH, JULIUS CARL VON. 1847-1931. German engineer. See: Pogg., vol. 7a. Winkler-Bach formula.

Bach readings (Bach, Aleksei Nikolaevich): Chemistry. Cited in: Dict. Sci. Biog.

Bach reagent for copper and nickel (Bach, Aleksei Nikolaevich?): Chemistry. See: Van Nostrand Chem. Dict.

Bach solution for hydrogen peroxide (Bach, Aleksei Nikolaevich?): Chemistry. See: Van Nostrand Chem. Dict.

Bach system (Bach, Alexander von): History. See: Morris and Irwin.

Bach test reaction for solanine (Bach, Aleksei Nikolaevich?): Chemistry. See: Van Nostrand Chem. Dict.

Bach trumpet (Bach, Johann Sebastian): Music. See: Apel; Scholes; Webster's 3d.

BACHMAN, GEORGE WILLIAM. b. 1890. American pathologist. See: Who's Who Among Physicians and Surg. Bachman-Pettit test, Bachman reaction (or test).

BACHMAN, JOHN. 1790-1874. American clergyman and naturalist. See: Dict. Amer. Biog. Bachman's sparrow, Bachman's warbler.

Bachman-Pettit test (Bachman, George William and Pettit, Auguste): Medicine. See: Stedman.

Bachman reaction (or test) (Bachman, George William): Medicine. See: Dorland.

Bachmann, August. See: Rivinus, August Quirinus.

BACHMANN, JEAN GEORGE. b. 1877. American physiologist. See: Who's Who Amer. Med. Bachmann's bundle.

BACHMANN, WERNER EMMANUEL. 1901- . American chemist. See: World Who's Who Sci. Gomberg-Bachmann-Hey reaction.

Bachmann's bundle (Bachmann, Jean George): Medicine. See: Dorland.

Bachman's sparrow (Bachman, John): Zoology. See: Gray; Webster's 3d.

Bachman's warbler (Bachman, John): Zoology. See: Gray.

Bachmeyer test reaction (Derivation undetermined): Chemistry. See: Van Nostrand Chem. Dict.

BACHOULKOVA-BRUN, R. fl. 1934. Swiss? chemist. Cited in: Chem. Abstr., vol. 28, p. 3332. Gutzeit-Monnier-Bachoulkova-Brun reagent for magnesium.

Bachstez-Cavallini test reaction (Bachstez, Marcell and Cavallini, Guido): Chemistry. See: Van Nostrand Chem. Dict.

BACHSTEZ, MARCELL. b. 1888. German chemist. See: Pogg., vol. 6. Bachstez-Cavallini test reaction.

bacillus Calmette-Guerin (Calmette, Albert and Guerin, Camille). See: Calmette-Guerin bacillus.

BACK, ERNST E. A. 1881-1959. German physicist. See: Dict. Sci. Biog. Back-Goudsmit effect, Paschen-Back effect.

Back-Goudsmit effect (Back, Ernst E. A. and Goudsmit, Samuel): Physics. See: Thewlis; Van Nostrand Sci. Encyc.

BACKSTROM, CHARLES. fl. ca. 1902. American? engineer. (Biography source unavailable.) Backstrom turbine.

Backstrom turbine (Backstrom, Charles): Engineering and Industry. See: Auger.

Bacon-Davis Act (Bacon, Robert Low and Davis, James John): Law. See: Clark.

BACON, HARRY ELLICOTT. 1900- . American proctologist. See: Who's Imp. Med., 2d. ed. Bacon's anoscope.

BACON, NATHANIEL. 1647-1676. American colonial leader. See: Dict. Amer. Biog. Baconists (or Baconian), Bacon's rebellion.

BACON, ROBERT LOW. 1884-1938. American legislator. See: Biog. Direct. Amer. Congress. Bacon-Davis Act.

Baconian classification (Bacon, Francis): Philosophy. See: Harrod.

Baconian method (or philosophy) (Bacon, Francis): Philosophy. See: Brewer; Good; Phyfe.

Baconian theory (Bacon, Francis): Literature. See: Barnhart, (Eng. Lit.); Brewer; Harvey.

Baconists (or Baconian) (Bacon, Nathaniel): History. See: Harbottle; Mathews, M. M.

Bacon's anoscope (Bacon, Harry Ellicott): Medicine. See: Dorland; Stedman.

Bacon's rebellion (Bacon, Nathaniel): History. See: Jameson; Morris; Smith.

BACOVESCU, A. fl. 1909. Roumanian chemist. Cited in: Chem. Abstr. Bacovescu reagent?

Bacovescu reagent (Bacovescu, A.?): Chemistry. See: Van Nostrand Chem. Dict.

BADAL, ANTOINE JULES. 1840-1929. French ophthalmologist. See: New York Acad. Med. Portrait Cat. Badal's operation.

Badal's operation (Badal, Antoine Jules): Medicine. See: Dorland; Stedman.

Baddeley cake (Baddeley, Robert): Food and Drink. See: Hendrickson; Latham; Partridge.

BADDELEY, JOSEPH. fl. 1892. English traveler. Cited in: Min. Mag., vol. 10 (1892) p. 148. Baddeleyite.

BADDELEY, ROBERT. 1733-1794. English actor. See: Dict. Nat. Biog. Baddeley cake.

Baddeleyite (Baddeley, Joseph): Earth Sciences. See: Thrush; Webster's 3d.

BADEN. No dates. American horticulturist. (Biography source unavailable.) Baden corn.

Baden corn (Baden): Botany. See: Mathews, M. M.

BADGER, RICHARD McLEAN. 1896- . American physical chemist and physicist. See: Amer. Men Sci., 10th ed. Badger rule?

Badger rule (Badger, Richard McLean?): Physics. See: Ballentyne; Hughes; Internat. Dict. Phys. Elec.

Badminton, 1st Duke of. See: Somerset, Henry, 1st Duke of Beaufort or Badminton.

Badminton (cup) (Somerset, Henry, 1st Duke of Beaufort or Badminton): Food and Drink. See: Latham.

BAECCHI, BRUNETTO. fl. 1913. Italian physician. Cited in: Chem. Abstr. Cum. Author Index. Baecchi reagent for blood.

Baecchi reagent for blood (Baecchi, Brunetto): Chemistry. See: Van Nostrand Chem. Dict.

BAECK, ABRAHAM. 1713-1795. Swedish naturalist and physician. See: Nouv. Biog. Univ. Baeckia.

Baeckia (Baeck, Abraham): Botany. See: Charnock.

Baedeker (Baedeker, Karl): Generic Word (guide book). See: Hendrickson; Latham; Webster's 3d.

BAEDEKER, KARL. 1801-1859. German publisher. See: Encyc. Brit., 1973. Baedeker, Baedeker public, Baedeker raids.

Baedeker public (Baedeker, Karl): Generic Word. See: Partridge.

Baedeker raids (Baedeker, Karl): History. See: Partridge.

BAEFVERSTEDT, BO ERIK. 1905- . Swedish physician. (Biography source unavailable.) Baefverstedt's syndrome.

Baefverstedt's syndrome (Baefverstedt, Bo Erik): Medicine. See: Jablonski. Also known as: Kaposi-Spiegler sarcomatosis, Spiegler-Fendt sarcoid (or sarcomatosis).

BAEHR, GEORGE. 1887- . American physician. See: World Who's Who Sci. Baehr-Schiffrin disease, Brill-Baehr-Rosenthal disease, Loehlein-Baehr lesion.

Baehr-Schiffrin disease (Baehr, George and Schiffrin, Arthur). See: Moschcowitz's syndrome (or disease).

Baekeland-Lederer-Manasse phenol-formaldehyde polycondensation (Baekeland, Leo Hendrik; Lederer, Leonhard; and Manasse, Otto). See: Lederer-Manasse reaction.

BAEKELAND, LEO HENDRIK. 1863-1944. Flemish-born chemist. See: Dict. Sci. Biog. Baekeland-Lederer-Manasse phenol-formaldehyde polycondensation, Baekeland process, Bakelite.

Baekeland process (Baekeland, Leo Hendrik): Chemistry. See: Van Nostrand Chem. Dict.

BAELZ, ERWIN VON. 1845-1913. German physician. See: World Who's Who Sci. Baelz's disease (or syndrome).

Baelz's disease (or syndrome) (Baelz, Erwin von): Medicine. See: Dorland; Stedman. Also known as: Volkmann's cheilitis.

Baemes solution (Derivation undetermined): Chemistry. See: Van Nostrand Chem. Dict.

Baer, G. See: Ursinus, Johann Heinrich.

BAER, KARL ERNST VON. 1792-1876. Estonian naturalist. See: Encyc. Brit., 1973. Baeria, Baer's cavity, Baer's vesicle, Von Baer's law.

BAER, WILLIAM STEVENSON. 1872-1931. American orthopedic surgeon. Dict. Amer. Biog., 1st suppl. Baer's method.

BAERENSPRUNG, FRIEDRICH WILHELM FELIX VON. 1822-1864. German physician. See: Biog. Lex. hervorr. Aerzte. Baerensprung's erythrasma.

Baerensprung's erythrasma (Baerensprung, Friedrich Wilhelm Felix von): Medicine. See: Dorland; Jablonski.

Baeria (Baer, Karl Ernst von): Botany. See: Taylor, N.; Webster's 3d.

Baermann apparatus (Derivation undetermined): Zoology. See: Pennak.

Baer's cavity (Baer, Karl Ernst von): Medicine. See: Dorland; Gray.

Baer's method (Baer, William Stevenson): Medicine. See: Dorland; Stedman.

Baer's nystagmus (Derivation undetermined): Medicine. See: Jablonski.

Baer's vesicle (Baer, Karl Ernst von): Medicine. See: Dorland.

BAERTS, F. fl. 1933. Belgian chemist. Cited in: Chem. Abstr., vol. 27, p. 4117. Baerts test.

Baerts test (Baerts, F.): Chemistry. See: Van Nostrand Chem. Dict.

BAERTSCHI-ROCHAIX, WERNER. b. 1911. Swiss physician. See: Who's Who Switz., 1950-51. Baertschi-Rochaix's syndrome.

Baertschi-Rochaix's syndrome (Baertschi-Rochaix, Werner): Medicine. See: Jablonski.

BAES, CARLO. fl. 1908. Italian sculptor. (Biography source unavailable.) Baes' method.

Baes' method (Baes, Carlo): Photography. See: Focal Encyc. Photog.

Baeyer acid (Baeyer, Adolf Johann Friedrich Wilhelm von): Chemistry. See: Hackh.

BAEYER, ADOLF JOHANN FRIEDRICH WILHELM VON. 1835-1917. German chemist. See: Dict. Sci. Biog. Baeyer acid, Baeyer-Drewson indigo synthesis, Baeyer-Drewson test for acetone, Baeyer reaction?, Baeyer strain theory, Baeyer test reaction for eosine?, Baeyer test reaction for glucose, Baeyer test reaction for phenol?, Baeyer test reaction for thiophene?, Baeyer test reactions for indoxyl, Baeyer test reactions for resorcinol?, Baeyer tests for indole, Baeyer-Villiger reaction, Baeyer-Villiger test reaction for acetone.

Baeyer-Drewsen indigo synthesis (Baeyer, Adolf Johann Friedrich Wilhelm von and Drewsen, Viggo): Chemistry. See: Van Nostrand Chem. Dict.

Baeyer-Drewsen test for acetone (Baeyer, Adolf Johann Friedrich Wilhelm von and Drewsen, Viggo): Chemistry. See: Van Nostrand Chem. Dict.

Baeyer reaction (Baeyer, Adolf Johann Friedrich Wilhelm von?): Chemistry. See: Van Nostrand Chem. Dict.

Baeyer strain theory (Baeyer, Adolf Johann Friedrich Wilhelm von): Chemistry. See: Ballentyne; Stedman; Van Nostrand Chem. Dict.

Baeyer test reaction for eosine (Baeyer, Adolf Johann Friedrich Wilhelm von?): Chemistry. See: Van Nostrand Chem. Dict.

Baeyer test reaction for glucose (Baeyer, Adolf Johann Friedrich Wilhelm von): Chemistry. See: Van Nostrand Chem. Dict.

Baeyer test reaction for phenol (Baeyer, Adolf Johann Friedrich Wilhelm von?): Chemistry. See: Van Nostrand Chem. Dict.

Baeyer test reaction for thiophene (Baeyer, Adolf Johann Friedrich Wilhelm von?): Chemistry. See: Van Nostrand Chem. Dict.

Baeyer test reactions for indoxyl (Baeyer, Adolf Johann Friedrich Wilhelm von?): Chemistry. See: Van Nostrand Chem. Dict.

Baeyer test reactions for resorcinol (Baeyer, Adolf Johann Friedrich Wilhelm von?): Chemistry. See: Van Nostrand Chem. Dict.

Baeyer tests for indole (Baeyer, Adolf Johann Friedrich Wilhelm von): Chemistry. See: Dorland; Van Nostrand Chem. Dict.

Baeyer-Villiger reaction (Baeyer, Adolf Johann Friedrich Wilhelm von and Villiger, V.): Chemistry. See: Ballentyne.

Baeyer-Villiger test reaction for acetone (Baeyer, Adolf Johann Friedrich Wilhelm von and Villiger, V.): Chemistry. See: Van Nostrand Chem. Dict.

BAGAI, O. P. fl. 1962. Indian mathematician. Cited in: World Direct. Math. Bagai's Y_1 statistic.

Bagai's Y_1 statistic (Bagai, O. P.): Mathematics. See: Kendall.

Bagford ballads (Bagford, John): Music. See: Harvey.

BAGFORD, JOHN. 1550-1716. English antiquarian and book collector. See: Dict. Nat. Biog. Bagford ballads.

BAGGENSTOSS, ARCHIE H. 1908- . American physician. See: World Who's Who Sci. Baggenstoss change.

Baggenstoss change (Baggenstoss, Archie H.): Medicine. See: Stedman.

BAGIMONT. fl. 1274. Italian churchman. See: Chambers' Biog. Dict. Bagimont's roll.

Bagimont's roll (Bagimont): History. See: Harbottle; Latham.

Baginski solution (Baginski, Stefan): Chemistry. See: Van Nostrand Chem. Dict.

BAGINSKI, STEFAN. fl. 1928-1952. Polish chemist. Cited in: Chem. Abstr., vol. 23, p. 1920. Baginski solution.

Bagley & Sewall presses (Derivation undetermined): Printing. See: Lockwood.

BAGOT, SIR CHARLES. 1781-1843. English diplomat and administrator. See: Dict. Nat. Biog. Rush-Bagot agreement.

BAGRATION, PETR IVANOVICH. 1765-1812. Russian army officer. See: Encyc. Brit., 1973. Bagrationite.

Bagrationite (Bagration, Petr Ivanovich): Earth Sciences. See: Charnock.

BAGULEY, E. E. No dates. English engineer. See: Who's Who Sci. Europe. Baguley valve gear.

Baguley valve gear (Baguley, E. E.): Engineering and Industry. See: Auger.

Bahadur efficiency (Bahadur, Raghu Raj): Statistics. See: Kendall.

BAHADUR, RAGHU RAJ. 1924- . Indian-born American mathematician. See: Amer. Men and Women Sci. Bahadur efficiency.

Baianism (or Bajanism) (Baius, Michael): Religion. See: Webster's 3d.

BAIER, JOHANN JACOB. 1677-1735. German naturalist. See: Dict. Sci. Biog. Baiera.

Baiera (Baier, Johann Jacob): Earth Sciences. See: Webster's 3d.

BAIL, OSCAR. 1869-1927. German bacteriologist. See: Biog. Lex. hervorr. Aerzte, 1880-1930. Bail's hypothesis.

Bailey bridge (Bailey, Donald Coleman): Engineering and Industry. See: Brewer; Hendrickson; Partridge.

BAILEY, DONALD COLEMAN. 1901- . English engineer. See: Chambers' Biog. Dict. Bailey bridge.

BAILEY, JAMES. fl. 1898. English? chemist. (Biography source unavailable.) Thiele-Bailey test reaction.

Bailey test for camphor (Derivation undetermined): Chemistry. See: Van Nostrand Chem. Dict.

Bailey test reaction for sulfur (Derivation undetermined): Chemistry. See: Van Nostrand Chem. Dict.

BAILEY, WILLIAM FLEMING. 1901- . American chemist. See: Amer. Men Sci., 6th ed. Adams-Hall-Bailey reagent?

Bailey's flask (Derivation undetermined): Medicine. See: Dorland.

BAILLARGER, JULES GABRIEL FRANCOIS. 1809-1890. French neurologist. See: Webster's Biog. Dict. Baillarger's line (or band), Baillarger's sign, Baillarger's syndrome.

Baillarger's line (or band) (Baillarger, Jules Gabriel Francois): Medicine. See: Gray; Henderson; Stedman.

Baillarger's sign (Baillarger, Jules Gabriel Francois): Medicine. See: Dorland; Stedman.

Baillarger's syndrome (Baillarger, Jules Gabriel Francois). See: Frey's syndrome.

Bail's hypothesis (Bail, Oscar): Medicine. See: Stedman.

BAILY, FRANCIS. 1774-1844. English astronomer. See: Dict. Sci. Biog. Baily's beads.

Baily's beads (Baily, Francis): Astronomy. See: Ballentyne; Satterthwaite; Thewlis.

BAIN, EDGAR COLLINS. 1891- . American physicist and metallurgist. See: World Who's Who Sci. Bainite.

bain-Marie (Mary, Virgin-Mother? or Miriam, sister of Moses?): Generic Word (double saucepan). See: Brewer; Partridge; Webster's 3d.

BAINBRIDGE, FRANCIS ARTHUR. 1874-1921. English physiologist. See: Dict. Nat. Biog., 3rd suppl. Bainbridge reflex.

Bainbridge-Jordan mass spectrograph (Bainbridge, Kenneth Tompkins and Jordan, Edward Brent, Jr.): Physics. See: Internat. Dict. Phys. Elec.

BAINBRIDGE, KENNETH TOMPKINS. 1904- . American physicist. See: World Who's Who Sci. Bainbridge-Jordan mass spectrograph.

Bainbridge reflex (Bainbridge, Francis Arthur): Medicine. See: Pennak; Stedman; Webster's 3d.

BAINE, JAMES OGDEN. 1909- . American chemist. See: Amer. Men Sci., 10th ed. Baine reagent?

Baine reagent (Baine, James Ogden?): Chemistry. See: Van Nostrand Chem. Dict.

Bainite (Bain, Edgar Collins): Earth Sciences. See: Thrush; Van Nostrand Sci. Encyc.; Webster's 3d.

Baird beaked whale (Baird, Spencer Fullerton): Zoology. See: Pennak.

BAIRD, JAMES. 1802-1876. Scottish ironmaster. See: Dict. Nat. Biog. Baird lectures.

Baird lectures (Baird, James): Religion. See: Wagner, (More Names).

BAIRD, SPENCER FULLERTON. 1823-1887. American zoologist. See: Dict. Amer. Biog. Baird beaked whale, Baird's sandpiper, Baird's sparrow, Baird's wren.

Baird's sandpiper (Baird, Spencer Fullerton): Zoology. Cited in: Mathews, M. M.; Webster's 3d.

Baird's sparrow (Baird, Spencer Fullerton): Zoology. Cited in: Gray.

Baird's wren (Baird, Spencer Fullerton): Zoology. Cited in: Mathews, M. M.

Baire class (Baire, Rene Louis): Mathematics. See: James.

Baire function (Baire, Rene Louis): Mathematics. See: James. Also known as: Borel measurable function.

BAIRE, RENE LOUIS. 1874-1932. French mathematician. See: Dict. Sci. Biog. Baire class, Baire function, Baire's category theorem, property of Baire.

Baire's category theorem (Baire, Rene Louis): Mathematics. See: James.

Bairstow method (Derivation undetermined): Mathematics. See: Internat. Dict. Ap. Math.; Van Nostrand Sci. Encyc.

baiser de Lamourette (Lamourette, Adrien). See: Lamourette's kiss.

BAIUS, MICHAEL. 1513-1589. Belgian theologian. See: Encyc. Brit., 1973. Baianism (or Bajanism).

Bajus, Michael. See: Baius, Michael.

Bakelite (Baekeland, Leo Hendrik): Chemistry. See: Hendrickson; Partridge; Thrush.

BAKER, ARTHUR D. b. 1853. American engineer. See: Pogg., vol. 4. Baker valve gear?

Baker bell dolphin (Derivation undetermined): Engineering and Industry. See: Thrush.

BAKER, CHARLES FULLER. 1872-1927. American entomologist. See: World Who's Who Sci. Baker cicadella circellata, ignotus Baker.

Baker cicadella circellata (Baker, Charles Fuller): Zoology. Cited in: World Who's Who Sci.

BAKER, E. B. H. fl. 1961-62. English librarian? (Biography source unavailable.) Baker report.

BAKER, EZEKIEL. fl. before 1800. English gunsmith. (Biography source unavailable.) Baker rifle.

BAKER, HENRY. 1698-1774. English naturalist. See: Dict. Sci. Biog. Bakerian Lecture.

BAKER, J. G. fl. 1873. English engineer. (Biography source unavailable.) Baker's blower.

BAKER, JAMES GILBERT. American inventor. 1914- . See: Who's Who Amer., 1956-57. Baker-Nunn camera, Baker-Schmidt telescope.

BAKER, JAMES PORTER. 1902- . American physician. See: Who's Imp. Med., 2nd ed. Charcot-Weiss-Baker syndrome.

BAKER, JOHN WILLIAM. fl. 1935. English chemist. Cited in: Chem. Abstr. Baker-Nathan effect.

Baker-Nathan effect (Baker, John William and Nathan, W.S.): Chemistry. See: Ballentyne.

Baker-Nunn camera (Baker, James Gilbert and Nunn, Joseph): Astronomy. See: Barnhart, (New Eng.).

Baker-Pilloid gear (Baker, Arthur D.? and Pilloid, Charles J.). See: Baker valve gear.

BAKER, R. C. fl. 20th c. English discoverer. Cited in: Min. Mag., vol. 13, p. 364. Bakerite.

Baker report (Baker, E. B. H.): Library Science. See: Harrod.

Baker rifle (Baker, Ezekiel): Weapons. See: Quick.

BAKER, RUSSELL WAYNE. 1925- . American newspaperman. See: Who's Who Amer., 1974-75. Baker's law.

Baker-Schmidt telescope (Baker, James Gilbert and Schmidt, Gernhard): Astronomy. See: Satterthwaite.

Baker valve gear (Baker, Arthur D.?): Engineering and Industry. See: Auger. Also known as: Baker-Pilloid gear.

Baker-Venkataraman transformation (Derivation undetermined); Chemistry. See: Van Nostrand Chem. Dict.

BAKER, WILLIAM MORRANT. 1839-1896. English surgeon. See: World Who's Who Sci. Baker's cyst.

Bakerian Lecture (Baker, Henry): Science. Cited in: Dict. Sci. Biog.

Bakerite (Baker, R. C.): Earth Sciences. See: Thrush; Webster's 3d.

Baker's blower (Baker, J. G.): Engineering and Industry. See: Auger.

Baker's cyst (Baker, William Morrant): Medicine. See: Dorland; Jablonski; Stedman.

Baker's law (Baker, Russell Wayne): Sociology. See: Martin.

BAKHTASH, HAJI. d. 1357. Turkish religious leader. Cited in: Encyc. Brit., 1973 under "Balkan Peninsula." Bakhtashiyeh.

Bakhtashiyeh (Bakhtash, Haji): Religion. See: Canney.

BAKR, ABU MOHAMED. fl. 1926. American chemist. Cited in: Chem. Abstr., Decenn. Index, 1917-1926. McBain-Baker (Bakr) balance.

BAKUNIN, MIKHAIL ALEKSANDROVICH. 1814-1876. Russian anarchist and writer. See: Internat. Encyc. Soc. Sci. Bakuninism.

Bakuninism (Bakunin, Mikhail Aleksandrovich): Political Science. See: Webster's 3d.

Bakwin-Eiger syndrome (Bakwin, Harry and Eiger, Marvin S.): Medicine. See: Jablonski.

BAKWIN, HARRY. 1894- . American physician. See: World Who's Who Sci. Bakwin-Eiger syndrome, Bakwin-Krida syndrome.

Bakwin-Krida syndrome (Bakwin, Harry and Krida, Arthur). See: Pyle's disease.

Balaam (Balaam, the Prophet): Generic Word (disappointing prophet). See: Lockwood, Partridge; Weekley.

BALAAM, THE PROPHET. Biblical prophet. See: Encyc. Brit., 1973. Balaam.

BALAREFF, DIMITUR. b. 1885. Bulgarian chemist. See: Pogg., vol. 4. Balareff test for metals, Balareff tests for pyrophosphates.

Balareff test for metals (Balareff, Dimitur): Chemistry. See: Van Nostrand Chem. Dict.

Balareff tests for pyrophosphates (Balareff, Dimitur): Chemistry. See: Van Nostrand Chem. Dict.

BALAVIONE, PIERRE. fl. 1909. Swiss chemist. Cited in: Chem. Abstr. Decenn. Index. Balavione test.

Balavione test (Balavione, Pierre): Chemistry. See: Van Nostrand Chem. Dict.

Balb (Balbo, Italo): Aviation. See: Partridge.

BALBACH, EDWARD. 1839-1910. German-born American metallurgist. See: Dict. Amer. Biog. Balbach process, Thum-Balbach process.

Balbach process (Balbach, Edward): Engineering and Industry. See: Thrush; Van Nostrand Chem. Dict.

BALBIANI, EDOUARD-GERARD. 1823-1899. French biologist. See: Dict. Sci. Biog. Balbiani's body (or nucleus).

Balbiani's body (or nucleus) (Balbiani, Edouard-Gerard): Medicine. See: Dorland; Henderson.

Balbo (Balbo, Italo): Aviation. See: Partridge.

BALBO, ITALO. 1896-1940. Italian aviator and statesman. See: Encyc. Brit., Bk. Yr., vol. 4. Balb, Balbo.

Balboa (Balboa, Vasco Nunez de): Numismatics. See: Hendrickson; Partridge.

BALBOA, VASCO NUNEZ DE. 1475-1519. Spanish explorer. See: Encyc. Brit., 1973. Balboa.

Baldie (Garibaldi, Giuseppe): Generic Word (fishing boat). See: Webster's 3d.

BALDRY, J.D. fl. before 1871. English? engineer. (Biography source unavailable.) Baldry's rule.

Baldry's rule (Baldry, J. D.): Engineering and Industry. See: Auger.

Balduzzi's reflex (Derivation undetermined): Medicine. See: Stedman.

Baldwin (apple) (Baldwin, Loammi): Food and Drink. See: De Sola; Partridge; Winburne.

BALDWIN, CHRISTIAN ADOLPHUS. 1632-1682. German alchemist. See: World Who's Who Sci. Baldwin's phosphorus.

BALDWIN, EVELYN BRIGGS. 1862-1933. American meteorologist and Arctic explorer. See: Dict. Amer. Biog., 1st suppl. Baldwin-Ziegler polar expedition.

BALDWIN, HENRY IVES. 1896- . American research forester. See: Amer. Men Sci., 10th ed. Baldwin hoe.

Baldwin hoe (Baldwin, Henry Ives): Forestry. See: Webster's 3d.

Baldwin hoptree (Derivation undetermined): Botany. See: Winburne.

BALDWIN, LOAMMI. 1740-1807. American engineer and army officer. See: Dict. Amer. Biog. Baldwin (apple).

BALDWIN, RUTH WORKMAN. 1915- . American pediatrician. See: Direct. Med. Specialists, vol. 14. Bessman-Baldwin syndrome.

Baldwin-Ziegler polar expedition (Baldwin, Evelyn Briggs and Ziegler, William): Exploration: Cited in: World Who's Who Sci.

Baldwin's phosphorus (Baldwin, Christian Adolphus): Chemistry. Cited in: World Who's Who Sci.

BALDY, JOHN MONTGOMERY. 1860-1934. American gynecologist. See: World Who's Who Sci. Baldy's operation, Webster-Baldy operation.

Baldy's operation (Baldy, John Montgomery): Medicine. See: Dorland; Stedman.

BALESTRA, G. fl. 1951. Italian physician. (Biography source unavailable.) De Martini-Balestra syndrome.

BALFOUR, ANDREW. 1873-1931. Scottish surgeon. See: Dict. Nat. Biog., 5th suppl. Balfour's granule.

BALFOUR, ARTHUR JAMES. 1848-1930. English philosopher and statesman. See: Dict. Nat. Biog., 4th suppl. Balfour Declaration, Balfour's poodle.

Balfour Declaration (Balfour, Arthur James): History. See: Morris and Irwin; Steinberg.

BALFOUR, GEORGE WILLIAM. 1822-1903. English physician. See: Dict. Nat. Biog., 2nd suppl. Balfour's disease.

BALFOUR, JOHN HUTTON. 1808-1884. Scottish botanist and physician. See: Dict. Sci. Biog. Balfour pine.

Balfour pine (Balfour, John Hutton): Botany. See: Webster's 3d.

Balfour's disease (Balfour, George William): Medicine. See: Dorland; Jablonski; Stedman.

Balfour's granule (Balfour, Andrew): Medicine. See: Dorland; Stedman.

Balfour's poodle (Balfour, Arthur James): History. See: Brewer.

BALINT, REZSOE. b. 1874. Hungarian physician. See: Biog. Lex. hervorr. Aerzte, 1880-1930. Balint's syndrome.

Balint's syndrome (Balint, Rezsoe): Medicine. See: Jablonski; Stedman.

BALJET, HENK. fl. 1918. Swiss chemist. Cited in: Chem. Abstr., vol. 12, p. 1336. Baljet reagent.

Baljet reagent (Baljet, Henk): Chemistry. See: Van Nostrand Chem. Dict.

Ball and Wingham process (Derivation undetermined): Chemistry. See: Van Nostrand Chem. Dict.

BALL, SIR CHARLES BENT. 1851-1916. Irish surgeon. See: World Who's Who Sci. Ball's operation, Ball's valve.

BALL, LIONEL CLIVE. b. 1878. Australian geologist. Cited in: Chem. Abstr. Ball-Norton magnetic separator?

Ball-Norton magnetic separator (Ball, Lionel Clive? and Norton goldfield, Australia): Engineering and Industry. See: Thrush.

Ball reagents (Ball, W. C.): Chemistry. See: Van Nostrand Chem. Dict.

Ball test reaction for hydroxylamine (Derivation undetermined): Chemistry. See: Van Nostrand Chem. Dict.

BALL, W. C. fl. 1910. English chemist. Cited in: Chem. Abstr., vol. 4, p. 883. Ball reagents.

BALLANCE, CHARLES ALFRED. 1857-1936. English surgeon. See: Dict. Nat. Biog., 5th suppl. Ballance's sign, Koerte-Ballance operation.

Ballance's sign (Ballance, Charles Alfred): Medicine. See: Dorland; Stedman.

Ballantine hardness test (Derivation undetermined): Engineering and Industry. See: Thrush.

BALLANTYNE, JOHN WILLIAM. 1861-1923. Scottish pathologist. See: World Who's Who Sci. Ballantyne-Runge syndrome.

Ballantyne-Runge syndrome (Ballantyne, John William and Runge, Hans): Medicine. See: Jablonski. Also known as: Ballantyne's syndrome.

Ballantyne's syndrome (Ballantyne, John William): See: Ballantyne-Runge syndrome.

BALLARD, C. H. fl. 1851. American rifle manufacturer. (Biography source unavailable.) Ballard rifle.

Ballard rifle (Ballard, C. H.): Weapons. See: Mathews, M. M.

BALLET, GILBERT. (In full: LOUIS GILBERT). 1853-1916. French neurologist. See: World Who's Who Sci. Ballet's disease, Ballet's sign.

Ballet's disease (Ballet, Gilbert): Medicine. See: Dorland; Jablonski; Stedman.

Ballet's sign (Ballet, Gilbert): Medicine. See: Dorland; Stedman.

Balling degree (Balling, Karl Josef Napoleon): Chemistry. See: Hackh.

BALLING, KARL JOSEF NAPOLEON. 1805-1868. Austrian chemist. See: World Who's Who Sci. Balling degree, Balling scale.

Balling scale (Balling, Karl Josef Napoleon): Chemistry. See: Webster's 3d.

BALLINGALL, GEORGE. 1780-1855. English surgeon. See: Nouv. Biog. Univ. Ballingall's disease.

Ballingall's disease (Ballingall, George): Medicine. See: Dorland; Jablonski.

Ballinger-Pinchot controversy (Ballinger, Richard Achilles and Pinchot, Gifford): History. See: James; Smith.

BALLINGER, RICHARD ACHILLES. 1858-1922. American lawyer and politician. See: Webster's Biog. Dict. Ballinger-Pinchot controversy.

BALLONI, ANTONIO. fl. 1935. Italian pathologist. Cited in: Chem. Abstr., vol 29, p. 2989. Balloni reagent.

Balloni reagent (Balloni, Antonio): Chemistry. See: Van Nostrand Chem. Dict.

Ballot, Christoph Buys. See: Buys Ballot, Christoph.

Ball's operation (Ball, Sir Charles Bent): Medicine. See: Dorland; Stedman.

Ball's valve (Ball, Sir Charles Bent) See: Morgagni's valves.

BALME, PAUL JEAN. b. 1857. French physician. (Biography source unavailable.) Balme's cough, Balme's disease.

BALMER, JOHANN JAKOB. 1825-1898. Swiss mathematician and physicist. See: Dict. Sci. Biog. Balmer lines, Balmer series, Balmer spectrum, Balmer terms, Balmer (unit), Balmer's constant, Balmer's law.

Balmer lines (Balmer, Johann Jakob): Physics. Cited in: Internat. Dict. Ap. Math. under "Balmer series".

Balmer series (Balmer, Johann Jakob): Physics. See: Ballentyne; Internat. Dict. Ap. Math.; Internat. Dict. Phys. Elec.

Balmer spectrum (Balmer, Johann Jakob): Physics. See: Satterthwaite.

Balmer terms (Balmer, Johann Jakob): Physics. See: Internat. Dict. Ap. Math.

Balmer (unit) (Balmer, Johann Jakob): Physics. See: Ballentyne; Dresner.

Balmer's constant (Balmer, Johann Jakob): Physics. See: Partridge.

Balmer's law (Balmer, Johann Jakob): Physics. See: Partridge.

Balme's cough (Balme, Paul Jean): Medicine. See: Dorland; Jablonski.

Balme's disease (Balme, Paul Jean): Medicine. See: Stedman.

BALO, JOZSEF MATTHIAS. 1895- . Hungarian neurologist. See: World Who's Who Sci. Balo's disease (or syndrome).

BALOGH, JOSEF. fl. 19th c. Hungarian botanist. See: Biog. Notes Upon Botanists. Baloghia.

Baloghia (Balogh, Josef): Botany. See: Webster's 3d.

Balo's disease (or syndrome) (Balo, Jozsef Matthias): Medicine. See: Jablonski; Stedman.

BALSER, WILHELM AUGUST. fl. 1882-1892. German physician. (Biography source unavailable.) Balser's necrosis (or disease).

Balser's necrosis (or disease) (Balser, Wilhelm August): Medicine. See: Dorland; Jablonski; Stedman.

BALTHAZAR. fl. 6th c. B.C. King of Babylon. See: Encyc. Brit., 1973. Balthazar (wine bottle).

Balthazar (wine bottle) (Balthazar): Food and Drink. See: Webster's 3d.

Baltimore (butterfly) (Calvert, George, 1st Lord Baltimore): Zoology. See: Webster's 3d.

Baltimore, Lady. See: Calvert, Mrs. George (Lady Baltimore).

Baltimore, Lord. See: Calvert, George (1st Lord Baltimore).

Baltimore oriole (Calvert, George, 1st Lord Baltimore): Zoology. See: Hendrickson; Mathews, M. M.; Partridge.

Baltimore starling (Calvert, George, 1st Lord Baltimore): Zoology. See: Weekley.

BALZ, GUENTHER. fl. 1927. German chemist. Cited in: Chem. Abstr., vol. 21, p. 2668. Balz-Schiemann reaction.

Balz-Schiemann reaction (Balz, Guenther and Schiemann, Guenther): Chemistry. See: Ballentyne. Also known as: Schiemann reaction.

BALZAC, HONORE DE. 1799-1850. French novelist. See: Encyc. Brit., 1973. Balzacian.

Balzacian (Balzac, Honore de): Literature. See: Webster's 3d.

BAMATTER, FRED. fl. 1950. Swiss physician. (Biography source unavailable.) Bamatter's syndrome.

Bamatter's syndrome (Bamatter, Fred): Medicine. See: Jablonski.

BAMBERGER, EUGEN. 1857-1932. German chemist. See: Dict. Sci. Biog. Bamberger quinoline test reaction, Bamberger reagent for aldehydes and ketones?, Bamberger-Seeberger test reaction?, Bamberger test reaction for ortho-diketones?, Bamberger's formula.

BAMBERGER, EUGEN. 1858-1921. Austrian physician. (Biography source unavailable.) Bamberger's disease (1), Marie-Bamberger syndrome.

BAMBERGER, HEINRICH VON. 1822-1888. Austrian physician. See: Allg. Deut. Biog. Bamberger's albuminuria, Bamberger's disease (3), Bamberger's fluid, Bamberger's pulse, Bamberger's sign.

Bamberger-Marie disease (Bamberger, Eugen and Marie, Pierre). See: Marie-Bamberger syndrome.

Bamberger quinoline test reaction (Bamberger, Eugen): Chemistry. See: Van Nostrand Chem. Dict.

Bamberger reagent for aldehydes and ketones (Bamberger, Eugen?): Chemistry. See: Van Nostrand Chem. Dict.

Bamberger-Seeberger test reaction (Bamberger, Eugen and Seeberger, Ludwig): Chemistry. See: Van Nostrand Chem. Dict.

Bamberger test reaction for ortho-diketones (Bamberger, Eugen?): Chemistry. See: Van Nostrand Chem. Dict.

Bamberger's albuminuria (Bamberger, Heinrich von): Medicine. See: Dorland; Jablonski; Stedman.

Bamberger's disease (1) (Bamberger, Eugen): Medicine. See: Jablonski. Also known as: Concato's disease.

Bamberger's disease (2) (Bamberger, Eugen). See: Marie-Bamberger syndrome.

Bamberger's disease (3) (Bamberger, Heinrich von): Medicine. See: Dorland; Jablonski.

Bamberger's fluid (Bamberger, Heinrich von): Medicine. See: Dorland.

Bamberger's formula (Bamberger, Eugen): Chemistry. See: Ballentyne.

Bamberger's pulse (Bamberger, Heinrich von): Medicine. See: Dorland.

Bamberger's sign (Bamberger, Heinrich von): Medicine. See: Dorland; Stedman.

bambocciades (bambocciate or bambochades) (Laar, Pieter van): Fine Arts. See: Hendrickson; Osborne.

bamboche (Laar, Pieter van): Generic Word. See: Webster's 3d.

BAMPTON, JOHN. 1690?-1751. English clergyman. See: Dict. Nat. Biog. Bampton lectures.

Bampton lectures (Bampton, John): Religion. See: Brewer; Canney; Harvey.

Banach algebra (Banach, Stefan): Mathematics. See: James.

Banach space (Banach, Stefan): Mathematics. See: Internat. Dict. Ap. Math.; James; Van Nostrand Sci. Encyc.

BANACH, STEFAN. 1892-1945. Polish-born Russian mathematician. See: Dict. Sci. Biog. Banach algebra, Banach space, Banach-Steinhaus theorem, Banach-Tarski paradox, Hahn-Banach theorem, Mazur-Banach game.

Banach-Steinhaus theorem (Banach, Stefan and Steinhaus, H.): Mathematics. See: James.

Banach-Tarski paradox (Banach, Stefan and Tarski, Alfred): Mathematics. See: James.

BANCROFT, EDITH SUSAN WHITAKER. b. 1893. American botanist. See: Amer. Men Sci., 9th ed. Bancroft's law.

BANCROFT, JOSEPH. 1836-1894. English physician. See: World Who's Who Sci. Bancroft's filariasis.

Bancroft's filariasis (Bancroft, Joseph): Medicine. See: Dorland; Jablonski; Webster's 3d.

Bancroft's law (Bancroft, Edith Susan Whitaker): Botany. See: Pennak; Webster's 3d.

BANDI, IVO. 1867-1926. Italian physician. See: Biog. Lex. hervorr. Aerzte, 1880-1930. Bandi's method.

Bandi's method (Bandi, Ivo): Medicine. See: Stedman.

BANDL, LUDWIG. 1842-1892. German obstetrician. See: World Who's Who Sci. Bandl's ring.

Bandl's ring (Bandl, Ludwig): Medicine. See: Stedman. Also known as: Scanzoni's second os.

BANDONI, ALFREDO JOSE. fl. 1933-1944. Argentinian chemist. Cited in: Chem. Abstr., vol 27, p. 3033. Bandoni test reaction.

Bandoni test reaction (Bandoni, Alfredo Jose): Chemistry. See: Van Nostrand Chem. Dict.

Bandrowski's base (Von Bandrowsky, Ernst Titus): Chemistry. See: Hackh.

Bandrowsky, Ernst Titus von. See: Von Bandrowsky, Ernst Titus.

BANDY, MARK CHANCE. 1900-1963. American mining engineer. World Who's Who Sci. Bandylite.

Bandylite (Bandy, Mark Chance): Earth Sciences. See: Webster's 3d.

BANFI, CARLO. No dates. Italian chemist. See: Who's Who Sci. Europe. Banfi test reaction?

Banfi test reaction (Banfi, Carlo?): Chemistry. See: Van Nostrand Chem. Dict.

BANG, BERNHARD LAURITS FREDERIK. 1848-1932. Danish veterinarian. See: Webster's Biog. Dict. abortus Bang ring test, Bang's bacillus, Bang's disease, Bang's method (1).

BANG, HOFFMAN. fl. 19th. c. Danish botanist. (Biography source unavailable.) Bangiaceae.

BANG, IVAR CHRISTIAN. 1869-1918. Swedish physiological chemist. See: Biog. Lex. hervorr. Aerzte, 1880-1930. Bang's method (2).

BANGERTER, ALFRED P.D. 1909- . Swiss ophthalmologist. See: World Who's Who Sci. Bangerter's method.

Bangerter's method (Bangerter, Alfred P. D.): Medicine. See: Stedman.

Bangiaceae (Bang, Hoffman): Botany. See: Webster's 3d.

Bangor, Bishop of. See: Hoadley, Benjamin (Bishop of Bangor).

Bangorian controversy (Hoadley, Benjamin, Bishop of Bangor): Religion. See: Barnhart (Eng. Lit.); Canney; Harvey.

Bang's bacillus (Bang, Bernhard Laurits Frederik): Medicine. See: Dorland; Stedman.

Bang's disease (Bang, Bernhard Laurits Frederik): Medicine. See: Hendrickson; Jablonski; Stedman. Also known as: Bruce's septicemia.

Bang's method (1) (Bang, Bernhard Laurits Frederik): Medicine. See: Stedman.

Bang's method (2) (Bang, Ivar Christian): Medicine. See: Dorland; Hackh; Stedman.

BANISTER, JOHN. 1650-1692. English-born American botanist. See: Dict. Sci. Biog. Banisteria.

Banisteria (Banister, John): Botany. See: Charnock.

Banka drill (Derivation undetermined): Engineering and Industry. See: Thrush.

Banka method (Derivation undetermined): Engineering and Industry. See: Thrush.

Bankhead Cotton Control Act (Bankhead, William Brockman): Politics. See: Morris.

Bankhead-Jones Farm Tenant Act (Bankhead, William Brockman and Jones, Marvin): Politics. See: Morris; Morris and Irwin; Smith.

BANKHEAD, WILLIAM BROCKMAN. 1874-1940. American legislator. See: Biog. Direct. Amer. Congress. Bankhead Cotton Control Act, Bankhead-Jones Farm Tenant Act.

BANKI, DONAT. fl. ca. 1915. Hungarian professor. (Biography source unavailable.) Banki turbine.

Banki turbine (Banki, Donat): Engineering and Industry. See: Auger.

Bankia (Banks, Joseph): Zoology. See: Pennak; Webster's 3d.

Banks' air pine. See: Banksian pine.

BANKS, JOSEPH. 1743-1820. English naturalist. See: Dict. Sci. Biog. Bankia, Banksia, Banksia-rose, Banksian pine.

Banks rose (Banks, Joseph). See: Banksia rose.

Banksia (Banks, Joseph): Botany. See: Charnock; Partridge; Taylor, N.

Banksia-rose (Banks, Joseph): Botany. See: Hargrave; Webster's 3d.

Banksian pine (Banks, Joseph): Botany. See: Webster's 3d.

Bannatyne Club (Bannatyne, George): Literature. See: Barnhart, (Eng. Lit.); Harvey; Latham.

BANNATYNE, GEORGE. 1545-1608. Scottish antiquarian. See: Dict. Nat. Biog. Bannatyne Club.

BANNISTER, HENRY MARTYN. 1844-1920. American physician. See: Who Was Who Amer., vol. 4. Bannister's disease.

Bannister's disease (Bannister, Henry Martyn): See: Quincke's edema (or disease).

BANNWARTH, ALFRED. fl. 1941. German physician. See: Wer Ist Wer?, 8th ed. Bannwarth's syndrome.

Bannwarth's syndrome (Bannwarth, Alfred): Medicine. See: Jablonski.

BANTI, GUIDO. 1852-1925. Italian pathologist. See: Dict. Sci. Biog. Banti's disease (or syndrome).

Banting (or Bantingism) (Banting, William): Medicine. See: Brewer; Dorland; Stedman.

BANTING, WILLIAM. 1797-1878. English undertaker and writer. See: Dict. Nat. Biog. Banting (or Bantingism).

Banti's disease (or syndrome) (Banti, Guido): Medicine. See: Dorland; Jablonski; Stedman.

BAPTISTE, JEAN. fl. 13th c. French linen weaver. (Biography source unavailable.) Batiste fabric.

bar of Michelangelo (Michelangelo): Fine Arts. See: Webster's 3d.

bar of Sanio (Sanio, Karl Gustav): Botany. See: Henderson; Webster's 3d.

BAR, PAUL. 1853-1945. French obstetrician. See: World Who's Who Sci. Bar's incision.

BARAC, G. fl. 1935. `French? chemist. Cited in: Chem. Abstr. vol. 32, p. 204. Barac test reaction.

Barac test reaction (Barac, G.): Chemistry. See: Van Nostrand Chem. Dict.

BARACH, ALVAN LEROY. 1895- . American physician. See: World Who's Who Sci. Barach's index.

Barach's index (Barach, Alvan Leroy): Medicine. See: Dorland.

Baradaeus, Jacobus. See: Jacob of Edessa.

Baradai, Jacob. See: Jacob of Edessa.

Barany chair (Barany, Robert): Medicine. See: Webster's 3d.

BARANY, ROBERT. 1876-1936. Austrian physician. See: Dict. Sci. Biog. Barany chair; Barany test; Barany's caloric test; Barany's sign; Barany's syndrome.

Barany test (Barany, Robert): Medicine. See: Chaplin; English; Wolman.

Barany's caloric test (Barany, Robert): Medicine. See: Stedman.

Barany's sign (Barany, Robert): Medicine. See: Stedman.

Barany's syndrome (Barany, Robert): Medicine. See: Jablonski.

BARBA, ALVARO ALONSO. 1569-1640. Spanish priest and metallurgist. See: Dict. Sci. Biog. Barba law.

Barba law (Barba, Alvaro Alonso): Earth Sciences. See: Internat. Dict. Ap. Math.

Barbache reagent (Derivation undetermined): Chemistry. See: Van Nostrand Chem. Dict.

BARBARA, SAINT. fl. 3rd. c. Virgin martyr. See: Encyc. Brit., 1973. Barbarea.

Barbarea (Barbara, Saint): Botany. See: Taylor, N. Also known as: herb of St. Barbara.

BARBER, C. GLENN. 1895- . American orthopedic surgeon. See: Direct. Med. Specialists, vol. 8. Blount-Barber syndrome.

Barber gas turbine (Barber, John): Engineering and Industry. See: Auger.

BARBER, HAROLD WORDSWORTH. b. 1886. English dermatologist. See: Who's Who, 1936. Barber's dermatosis (or disease).

BARBER, HARRY JAMES. b. 1904. English chemist. See: Who's Who Sci. Europe. Barber reagent.

BARBER, JOHN. d. 1801. English inventor. (Biography source unavailable.) Barber gas turbine.

Barber reagent (Barber, Harry James): Chemistry. See: Van Nostrand Chem. Dict.

BARBERINI. fl. 16-17th c. Tuscan family. See: Webster's Biog. Dict. Barberini faun.

Barberini faun (Barberini): Fine Arts. See: Osborne.

BARBERIO, MICHELE. b. 1862. Italian pathologist. Cited in: Chem. Abstr., vol 6, p. 2089. Barberio reagent for indican, Barberio's test.

Barberio reagent for indican (Barberio, Michele): Chemistry. See: Van Nostrand Chem. Dict.

Barberio's test (Barberio, Michele): Medicine. See: Dorland; Stedman.

Barber's dermatosis (or disease) (Barber, Harold Wordsworth): Medicine. See: Jablonski.

Barbet-Jandrier reagent for formaldehyde (Barbet and Jandrier, Edmond): Chemistry. See: Van Nostrand Chem. Dict.

Barbet-Jandrier test (Barbet and Jandrier, Edmond): Chemistry. See: Van Nostrand Chem. Dict.

BARBIER, PHILIPPE ANTOINE. 1848-1922. French chemist. See: Surrey. Barbier test?, Barbier-Wieland degradation, Barbierite.

Barbier test (Barbier, Phillippe Antoine?): Chemistry. See: Van Nostrand Chem. Dict.

Barbier-Wieland degradation (Barbier, Phillippe Antoine and Wieland, Heinrich): Chemistry. See: Van Nostrand Chem. Dict.

BARBIERI. fl. 18th c. Italian instrument manufacturer. (Biography source unavailable.) orgue de Barbarie.

Barbierite (Barbier Phillippe Antoine): Earth Sciences. See: Thrush, Webster's 3d.

BARBONI, J. fl. 1910. Italian chemist. Cited in: Chem. Abstr., vol. 4, p. 2428. Armani-Barboni reaction for gold and silver, Armani-Barboni test for caffeine.

BARCLAY, ALFRED ERNEST. 1876-1949. English radiologist. See: Who's Who 1948. Barclay-Baron disease.

Barclay-Baron disease (Barclay, Alfred Ernest and Baron): Medicine. See: Stedman.

BARCLAY, JOHN. 1734-1798. Scottish clergyman. See: Dict. Nat. Biog. Barclayites.

Barclay press (Derivation undetermined): Printing. See: Lockwood.

Barclayites (Barclay, John): Religion. Cited in: Webster's Biog. Dict.

BARCROFT, SIR JOSEPH F. 1872-1947. English physiologist. See: Dict. Sci. Biog. Barcroft-Warburg apparatus (or technique), Barcroft's apparatus.

Barcroft-Warburg apparatus (or technique) (Barcroft, Sir Joseph F. and Warburg, Otto). See: Warburg's apparatus.

Barcroft's apparatus (Barcroft, Sir Joseph F.): Medicine. See: Dorland; Pennak.

BARD, LOUIS. 1857-1930. French physician. See: World Who's Who Sci. Bard-Pic's syndrome, Bard's sign.

Bard-Pic's syndrome (Bard, Louis and Pic, Adrian): Medicine. See: Dorland; Jablonski. Also known as: Pic's syndrome.

BARDACH, BRUNO. fl. 1901-1908. Austrian chemist. (Biography source unavailable.) Bardach reaction (or test).

Bardach reaction (or test) (Bardach, Bruno): Chemistry. See: Hackh; Van Nostrand Chem. Dict.

Bardeen-Cooper-Schrieffer theory of superconductivity (Bardeen, John; Cooper, Leon N.; and Schrieffer, John Robert): Physics. See: Ballentyne; Internat. Dict. Ap. Math.

BARDEEN, JOHN. 1908- . American physicist. See: Encyc. Brit., 1973. Bardeen-Cooper-Schrieffer theory of superconductivity, Frohlich-Bardeen theory.

Bardeleben, Heinrich Adolf von. See: Von Bardeleben, Heinrich Adolf.

Bardeleben's bandage (Von Bardeleben, Heinrich Adolf): Medicine. See: Dorland.

BARDEN, GRAHAM ARTHUR. 1896-1967. American legislator. See: Biog. Direct. Amer. Congress. George-Barden Act.

BARDENHEUER, BERNHARD (In full: FRANZ BERNHARD HUBERT). 1839-1913. German surgeon. See: World Who's Who Sci. Bardenheuer's extension.

Bardenheuer's extension (Bardenheuer, Bernhard): Medicine. See: Dorland.

BARDESANES. 154-222. Syrian poet and theologian. See: Nouv. Biog. Univ. Bardesanists.

Bardesanists (Bardesanes): Religion. See: Canney.

BARDET, GEORGES. b. 1885. French physician. (Biography source unavailable.) Laurence-Moon-Biedl-Bardet syndrome.

BARDHAN, JOGENDRA C. fl. 1933. Indian? chemist in England. Cited in: Chem. Abstr., vol. 27, p. 84. Bardhan-Sengupta synthesis.

Bardhan-Sengupta synthesis (Bardhan, Jogendra C. and Sengupta, Suresh C.): Chemistry. See: Van Nostrand Chem. Dict.

Bardine process (Derivation undetermined): Engineering and Industry. See: Thrush.

BARDINET, BARTHOLEMY ALPHONSE. 1809-1874. French physician. See: Dobson. Bardinet's ligament.

Bardinet's ligament (Bardinet, Bartholemy Alphonse): Medicine. See: Dorland; Stedman.

Bard's sign (Bard, Louis): Medicine. See: Dorland; Stedman.

Bard's syndrome (Derivation undetermined): Medicine. See: Jablonski.

BAREACRES, COUNTESS OF. Character in William Makepeace Thackeray's novel, "Vanity Fair." (1847-48) See: Benet. Lady Bareacres.

BAREBONE, PRAISE-GOD. 1596?-1679. English Anabaptist and leather merchant. See: Dict. Nat. Biog. Barebone's parliament.

Barebone's parliament (Barebone, Praise-God): History. See: Harbottle; Hendrickson; Steinberg.

BAREGGI, CARLO. fl. 19th c. Italian physician. (Biography source unavailable.) Bareggi's test.

Bareggi's test (Bareggi, Carlo): Medicine. See: Stedman.

BARETY, JEAN PAUL. 1887-1912. French surgeon. (Biography source unavailable.) Barety's method.

Barety's method (Barety, Jean Paul): Medicine. See: Dorland; Stedman.

Barff borogylcerin (Barff, F. S.?): Chemistry. See: Hackh.

BARFF, F. S. fl. 19th c. American engineer. (Biography source unavailable.) Barff borogylcerin?, Barff process, Bower-Barff process.

Barff process (Barff, F. S.): Chemistry. See: Van Nostrand Chem. Dict.

BARFOED, CHRISTEN THOMSEN. 1815-1889. Swedish physician. See: Pogg., vol. 3. Barfoed's test.

BARFOED, CHRISTIAN THEODOR. 1816-1889. Danish chemist. (Biography source unavailable.) Barfoed solution, Barfoed test.

Barfoed solution (Barfoed, Christian Theodor): Chemistry. See: Hackh.

Barfoed test (Barfoed, Christian Theodor): Chemistry. See: Hackh.

Barfoed's test (Barfoed, Christen Thomsen): Chemistry. See: Ballentyne; Dorland; Stedman.

BARFURTH, DIETRICH. 1849-1927. German anatomist. See: World Who's Who Sci. Barfurth's law.

Barfurth's law (Barfurth, Dietrich): Zoology. See: Gray.

Bargeboer atomizer (Derivation undetermined): Engineering and Industry. See: Auger.

BARGEN, JACOB ARNOLD. 1894- . American physician. See: World Who's Who Sci. Bargen's serum, Bargen's streptococcus, Bargen's treatment.

Bargen's serum (Bargen, Jacob Arnold): Medicine. See: Dorland; Stedman.

Bargen's streptococcus (Bargen, Jacob Arnold): Medicine. See: Dorland.

Bargen's treatment (Bargen, Jacob Arnold): Medicine. Dorland.

Barger-Bergel-Todd test reaction (Barger, George; Bergel, Franz; and Todd, Alexander Robertus): Chemistry. See: Van Nostrand Chem. Dict.

BARGER, GEORGE. 1878-1939. English chemist. See: Dict. Nat. Biog., 5th suppl. Barger-Bergel-Todd test reaction.

BARING, ALEXANDER, LORD ASHBURTON. 1774-1848. English financier and statesman. See: Dict. Nat. Biog. Ashburton Treaty.

Barisol process (Derivation undetermined): Chemistry. See: Van Nostrand Chem. Dict.

Barker brake (Barker, E. D.): Engineering and Industry. See: Auger.

BARKER, E. D. fl. 1871. English engineer. (Biography source unavailable.) Barker brake.

BARKER, ELLIOTT R. fl. 1899. American chemist. Cited in: Royal Soc. Cat. Sci. Pap., 1884-1900. Mullikan-Barker test reaction.

BARKER, FREDERICK. 1808-1882. Australian bishop. See: Dict. Nat. Biog. Bishop Barker (beer).

BARKER, GEORGE JOHN. b. 1888. American metallurgical engineer. See: Who's Who Engin., 1937. Barker-Truog process.

Barker index (Barker, Thomas Vapond?): Chemistry. See: Hackh.

BARKER, ROBERT. d. 1789. English inventor. See: Pogg., vol. 1. Barker's mill.

BARKER, THOMAS VAPOND. 1881-1931. Mineralogist. See: World Who's Who Sci. Barker index?

Barker-Truog process (Barker, George John and Truog, Emil): Engineering and Industry. See: Thrush.

Barker's mill (Barker, Robert): Engineering and Industry. See: Auger; Carter.

Barkhausen criterion (for oscillators) (Barkhausen, Heinrich): Engineering and Industry. See: Hughes; Internat. Dict. Phys. Elec.; Van Nostrand Sci. Encyc.

Barkhausen effect (Barkhausen, Heinrich): Physics. See: Ballentyne; Hackh; Internat. Dict. Phys. Elec.

BARKHAUSEN, HEINRICH. 1881-1956. German physicist and electrical engineer. See: Dict. Sci. Biog. Barkhausen criterion (for oscillators), Barkausen effect, Barkhausen-Kurz oscillator (or oscillations), Barkhausen magnet.

Barkhausen-Kurz oscillator (or oscillations) (Barkhausen, Heinrich and Kurz, Karl): Engineering and Industry. See: Ballentyne; Hughes; Internat. Dict. Phys. Elec.

Barkhausen magnet (Barkhausen, Heinrich): Physics. See: Markus.

Barkhausen oscillator (or oscillation) (Barkhausen, Heinrich). See: Barkhausen-Kurz oscillator (or oscillation).

BARKLY, SIR HENRY. 1815-1898. English colonial administrator. See: Dict. Nat. Biog., 1st suppl. Barklyite.

Barklyite (Barkly, Sir Henry): Earth Sciences. See: Webster's 3d.

Barkman's reflex (Derivation undetermined): Medicine. See: Stedman.

BARKOW, HANS KARL LEOPOLD. 1798-1873. German anatomist. See: Biog. Lex. hervorr. Aerzte. Barkow's ligament.

Barkow's ligament (Barkow, Hans Karl Leopold): Medicine. See: Dorland; Stedman.

Barkston distributor (Derivation undetermined): Engineering and Industry. See: Thrush.

BARLAAM, BERNARD. 1300-1348. Calabrian abbot. See: Nouv. Biog. Univ. Barlaamites.

Barlaamites (Barlaam, Bernard): Religion. See: Canney.

Barleria (Barrelier, Jacques): Botany. See: Taylor, N.

Barletta (Barletta, Gabriel): Generic Word (preaching). See: Stenhouse.

BARLETTA, GABRIEL. b. 1400. Italian monk. See: Nouv. Biog. Univ. Barletta.

BARLOW, ALAN (In full: SIR JAMES ALAN NOEL). fl. 1900-1947. English parliamentarian. See: Who's Who, 1947. Barlow report.

Barlow and Pope theory (Barlow, William and Pope, William Jackson): Chemistry. See: Van Nostrand Chem. Dict.

BARLOW, BILLY. fl. 19th c. English retardate. (Biography source unavailable.) Billy Barlow.

BARLOW, HENRY CLARK. 1806-1876. English writer. See: Dict. Nat. Biog. Barlow lectures.

Barlow knife (Barlow, Russell): Weapons. See: Hendrickson; Mathews, M. M.; Partridge.

Barlow lectures (Barlow, Henry Clark): Literature. See: Wagner, (More Names).

Barlow lens (Barlow, Peter): Physics. See: Satterthwaite.

BARLOW, PETER. 1776-1862. English mathematician and physicist. See: Dict. Sci. Biog. Barlow lens, Barlow's plate.

Barlow report (Barlow, Alan): Education. See: Good.

Barlow rule (Barlow, William): Chemistry. See: Ballentyne; Internat. Dict. Phys. Elec.

BARLOW, RUSSELL. fl. 18th c. English inventor. (Biography source unavailable.) Barlow knife.

BARLOW, THOMAS. 1845-1945. English physician. See: Ann. Register. Moeller-Barlow disease.

BARLOW, WILLIAM. 1845-1934. English crystallographer. See: Dict. Sci. Biog. Barlow and Pope theory, Barlow rule.

Barlow's disease (Barlow, Thomas). See: Moeller-Barlow disease.

Barlow's plate (Barlow, Peter): Physics. See: Webster's 3d.

BARMECIDE. Family of Baghdad princes described in the "Arabian Nights." fl. 752-803. See: Webster's Biog. Dict. Barmecide (or Barmecidal), Barmecide's feast.

Barmecide (or Barmedical) (Barmecide family): Generic Word (Illusory). See: Harvey; Hendrickson; Webster's 3d.

Barmecide's feast (Barmecide family): Generic Word (disappointment). See: Brewer; Latham; Phyfe.

BARNABAS, SAINT. In Bible, Cyprian Levite converted to Christianity. See: Webster's Biog. Dict. Barnaby bright (or day), Saint Barnaby's thistle.

Barnaby bright (or day) (Barnabas, Saint): Generic Word. See: Barnhart, (Eng. Lit.); Brewer; Webster's 3d.

BARNACLE, TITE. Fictional character from Charles Dickens' novel, "Little Dorrit." (1857-58) See: Benet. Title Barnacle.

BARNARD, EDWARD. 1786-1861. English botanist. See: Biog. Notes Upon Botanists. Barnardia?

BARNARD, HARRY EVERETT. 1874-1946. American chemist. See: World Who's Who Sci. Barnard reagent?

Barnard reagent (Barnard, Harry Everett?): Chemistry. See: Van Nostrand Chem. Dict.

BARNARD, WILLIAM GEORGE. b. 1892. English physician. See: Who's Who, 1936. Barnard's carcinoma.

Barnardia (Barnard, Edward?): Botany. See: Charnock.

Barnard's carcinoma (Barnard, William George): Medicine. See: Jablonski.

BARNEBEY, OSCAR LEONARD. b. 1886. American chemical engineer. See: Amer. Men. Sci., 3d. ed. Barnebey test.

Barnebey test (Barnebey, Oscar Leonard): Chemistry. See: Van Nostrand Chem. Dict.

BARNES, ALFRED ATKINSON. fl. 1916. American? chemist. Cited in: Chem. Abstr., vol. 10, p. 3026. Barnes' formula?

Barnes' bag (or dilator) (Barnes, Robert): Medicine. See: Dorland; Stedman.

Barnes' curve (Barnes, Robert): Medicine. See: Dorland; Stedman.

Barnes' dystrophy (Barnes, Richard Henry?): Medicine. See: Stedman.

BARNES, ERNEST W. b. 1874. English mathematician. See: Pogg., vol. 5. Pochhammer-Barnes equation.

Barnes' formula (Barnes, Alfred Atkinson?): Engineering and Industry. See: Thrush.

BARNES, HOWARD TURNER. 1873-1950. American-born physicist. See: World Who's Who Sci. Callendar and Barnes method for mechanical equivalent of heat.

BARNES, RICHARD HENRY. 1911- . American nutritionist. See: World Who's Who Sci. Barnes' dystrophy?

BARNES, ROBERT. 1817-1907. English obstetrician. See: Dict. Nat. Biog. 2d. suppl. Barnes' bag (or dilator), Barnes' curve, Barnes' speculum, Barnes' zone.

Barnes' speculum (Barnes, Robert): Medicine. See: Stedman.

BARNES, W. H. No dates. Mineralogist. Cited in: Min. Mag., vol. 32 (1961) p. 945. Barnesite.

Barnes' zone (Barnes, Robert): Medicine. See: Stedman.

Barnesite (Barnes, W.H.): Earth Sciences. See: Thrush.

Barnett effect (Barnett, Samuel Jackson): Physics. See: Ballentyne; Hughes; Internat. Dict. Phys. Elec.

Barnett gas engine (Barnett, William): Engineering and Industry. See: Auger.

BARNETT, SAMUEL JACKSON. b. 1873. American physicist. See: World Who's Who Sci. Barnett effect.

BARNETT, WILLIAM. fl. 1838. English inventor. (Biography source unavailable.) Barnett gas engine.

BARNHARDT, DAN. No dates. American landowner. (Biography source unavailable.) Barnehardtite.

Barnhardtite (Barnhardt, Dan): Earth Sciences. See: Charnock.

BARNUM, PHINEAS TAYLOR. 1810-1891. American showman. See: Dict. Amer. Biog. Barnumize (or Barnumism).

Barnumize (or Barnumism) (Barnum, Phineas Taylor): Generic Word (bombastic). See: Clapin; Hendrickson; Partridge.

BAROT, J. fl. 1928. French physicist. Cited in: Chem. Abstr. vol. 24, p. 4602. Fabry and Barot method.

Barr body (Barr, Murray Llewellyn): Medicine. See: Stedman; Wolman.

BARR, GUY. b. 1885. English chemist. See: Pogg., vol. 6. Fenton-Barr test reactions.

BARR, MURRAY LLEWELLYN. 1908- . Canadian microanatomist. See: World Who's Who Sci. Barr body.

Barr, Y. M. fl. 1964. English virologist. (Biography source unavailable.) Epstein-Barr virus.

BARRAL, ETIENNE VICTOR. 1860-1938. French pharmacist. See: Pogg., vol. 6. Barral solution?, Barral test for acetanilid?, Barral tests for acetophenetidin?, Barral tests for aminopyrine?, Barral tests for cryogenine?, Barral tests for hermophenyl?, Barral tests for pilocarpine?, Barral tests for sulfosalicylic acid.

Barral solution (Barral, Etienne Victor?): Chemistry. See: Van Nostrand Chem. Dict.

Barral test for acetanilid (Barral, Etienne Victor?): Chemistry. See: Van Nostrand Chem. Dict.

Barral tests for acetophenetidin (Barral, Etienne Victor?): Chemistry. See: Van Nostrand Chem. Dict.

Barral tests for aminopyrine (Barral, Etienne Victor?): Chemistry. See: Van Nostrand Chem. Dict.

Barral tests for cryogenine (Barral, Etienne Victor?): Chemistry. See: Van Nostrand Chem. Dict.

Barral tests for hermophenyl (Barral, Etienne Victor?): Chemistry. See: Van Nostrand Chem. Dict.

Barral tests for pilocarpine (Barral, Etienne Victor?): Chemistry. See: Van Nostrand Chem. Dict.

Barral tests for sulfosalicylic acid (Barral, Etienne Victor): Chemistry. See: Van Nostrand Chem. Dict.

BARRANDE, JOACHIM. 1799-1883. French geologist. See: Dict. Sci. Biog. Barrandite.

Barrandite (Barrande, Joachim): Earth Sciences. See: Webster's 3d.

BARRAQUER, IGNACIO. 1884-1965. Spanish ophthalmologist. See: Who's Who Spain. Barraquer's method (or operation).

BARRAQUER, JOSE ANTONIO. b. 1852. Spanish physician. See: Encic. Univ. Ilus. Barraquer's syndrome.

Barraquer-Simons syndrome (Barraquer, Jose Antonio and Simons, Arthur). See: Simons' disease (or syndrome).

Barraquer's method (or operation) (Barraquer, Ignacio): Medicine. See: Dorland; Stedman.

Barraquer's syndrome (Barraquer, Jose Antonio). See: Simons' disease (or syndrome).

Barratt method (Derivation undetermined): Physics. See: Internat. Dict. Phys. Elec.

Barre-Guillain syndrome (Barre, Jean Alexandre and Guillain, Georges). See: Guillain-Barre syndrome.

BARRE, JEAN ALEXANDRE. b. 1880. French neurologist. See: New York Acad. Med. Portrait Cat. Barre-Lieou syndrome, Barre-Masson syndrome, Barre's sign, Guillain-Barre reflex, Guillain-Barre syndrome.

Barre-Lieou syndrome (Barre, Jean Alexandre and Lieou, Young Choen): Medicine. See: Jablonski. Also known as: Neri-Barre syndrome.

Barre-Masson syndrome (Barre, Jean Alexandre and Masson, Pierre): Medicine. See: Jablonski.

BARRELIER, JACQUES. 1606-1673. French botanist. See: Nouv. Biog. Univ. Barleria.

BARRERE, PIERRE. ca. 1690-1755. French naturalist. See: Nouv. Biog. Univ. Barreria.

Barreria (Barrere, Pierre): Botany. See: Charnock.

Barre's sign (Barre, Jean Alexandre): Medicine. See: Stedman.

BARRESWIL, CHARLES-LOUIS. 1817-1870. French chemist. See: Dict. Sci. Biog. Barreswil test reaction for chromate, Barreswil test reaction for vanadium.

Barreswil test reaction for chromate (Barreswil, Charles-Louis): Chemistry. See: Van Nostrand Chem. Dict.

Barreswil test reaction for vanadium (Barreswil, Charles-Louis): Chemistry. See: Van Nostrand Chem. Dict.

BARRETT, LUCAS. 1837-1862. English naturalist and geologist. See: World Who's Who Sci. Barrettia.

BARRETT, NORMAN RUPERT. 1903- . English surgeon. See: Who's Who, 1958. Barrett's syndrome (or ulcer).

BARRETT, SIR WILLIAM FLETCHER. 1844-1925. English physicist. See: Ann. Register. Barretter?

Barretter (Barrett, Sir William Fletcher?): Physics. See: Internat. Dict. Phys. Elec.

Barrettia (Barrett, Lucas): Earth Sciences. Cited in: World Who's Who Sci.

Barrett's syndrome (or ulcer) (Barrett, Norman Rupert): Medicine. See: Jablonski; Stedman.

BARRIER, FRANCOIS MARGUERITE. 1813-1870. French physician. See: Biog. Lex. hervorr. Aerzte. Barrier's vacuoles.

BARRIERE, HENRI. fl. 1957. French physician. (Biography source unavailable.) Bureau-Barriere disease.

Barrier's vacuoles (Barrier, Francois Marguerite): Medicine. See: Dorland; Stedman.

BARRINGTON, DAINES. 1727-1800. English lawyer, antiquarian and naturalist. See: Dict. Nat. Biog. Barringtonia.

Barringtonia (Barrington, Daines): Botany. See: Charnock; Webster's 3d.

BARROW, HENRY. d. 1593. English church reformer. See: Dict. Nat. Biog. Barrowists.

BARROW, SIR JOHN. 1764-1848. English traveler and admiralty official. See: Dict. Nat. Biog. Barrow's goldeneye.

Barrow, Joseph Louis. See: Louis, Joe.

Barrowists (Barrow, Henry): Religion. See: Brewer; Jameson; Steinberg.

Barrow's goldeneye (Barrow, Sir John): Zoology. See: Webster's 3d.

Barry, Comtesse du. See: Du Barry, Marie Jeanne Becu, Comtesse.

BARRY, MARTIN. 1802-1855. English embryologist. See: Dict. Sci. Biog. Barry's retinacula.

Barry mining (Derivation undetermined): Engineering and Industry. See: Thrush.

Barrymore collar (Barrymore, John Blythe): Fashion. See: Picken.

BARRYMORE, JOHN BLYTHE. 1882-1942. American actor. See: Encyc. Brit., Bk. Yr., vol. 6. Barrymore collar.

Barry's retinacula (Barry, Martin): Medicine. See: Dorland.

Bar's incision (Bar, Paul): Medicine. See: Dorland; Jablonski; Stedman.

BARSANOV, G. P. fl. 1937. Russian mineralogist. Cited in: Min. Mag. vol. 33 (1964) p. 1128. Barsanovite.

Barsanovite (Barsanov, G. P.): Earth Sciences. See: Thrush.

BARSANTI, EUGENIO. 1821-1864. Italian inventor. See: Diz. Encic. Ital. Barsanti-Matteucci gas engine.

Barsanti-Matteucci gas engine (Barsanti, Eugenio and Matteucci, Felice): Engineering and Industry. See: Auger.

Barsony-Polgar syndrome (Barsony, Theodor and Polgar, Franz): Medicine. See: Jablonski. Also known as: Barsony-Teschendorf syndrome.

Barsony-Teschendorf syndrome (Barsony, Theodor and Teschendorf, Werner). See: Barsony-Polgar syndrome.

BARSONY, THEODOR. 1887-1942. German physician. See: New York Acad. Med. Portrait Cat. Barsony-Polgar syndrome.

BART, HEINRICH. fl. 1909-1922. German chemist. See: Surrey. Bart reaction.

Bart-Pumphrey syndrome (Bart, Robert S. and Pumphrey, Robert E.): Medicine. See: Jablonski.

Bart reaction (Bart, Heinrich): Chemistry. See: Ballentyne; Van Nostrand Chem. Dict.

BART, ROBERT S. 1933- . American dermatologist. See: Direct. Med. Specialists, 14th ed. Bart-Pumphrey syndrome.

BARTENWERFER, KURT. 1892-1946. German physician. (Biography source unavailable.) Bartenwerfer's syndrome.

Bartenwerfer's syndrome (Bartenwerfer, Kurt): Medicine. See: Jablonski.

Barter (Barter, Robert Speccott): Recreation and Sports. See: Hendrickson.

BARTER, ROBERT SPECCOTT. 1790-1861. English educator. See: Boase. Barter.

BARTFAY, M. fl. 1936. Hungarian chemist. Cited in: Chem. Abstr. vol. 31, p. 66. Szebelledy-Bartfay test.

BARTH. fl. 20th c. Mining engineer in Southwest Africa. Cited in: Min. Mag., vol. 17 (1916) p. 345. Barthite.

BARTH, CARL GEORGE LANGE. 1860-1939. Norwegian-born management scientist and mechanical engineer. See: World Who's Who Sci. Barth key?

BARTH, JEAN BAPTISTE. 1806-1877. German physician. See: World Who's Who Sci. Barth's hernia.

BARTH, KARL. 1886-1968. Swiss theologian. See: Webster's Biog. Dict. Barthian (or Barthianism).

Barth key (Barth, Carl George Lange?): Engineering and Industry. See: Auger.

BARTHELEMY, P. TOUSSAINT. 1850-1906. French dermatologist. See: World Who's Who Sci. Barthelemy's disease.

Barthelemy's disease (Barthelemy, P. Toussaint): Medicine. See: Dorland; Jablonski.

Barthian (or Barthianism) (Barth, Karl): Religion. See: Webster's 3d.

Barthite (Barth): Earth Sciences. See: Webster's 3d.

BARTHOLIN, CASPAR II. 1655-1738. Danish anatomist. See: Dict. Sci. Biog. Bartholinitis, Bartholin's duct, Bartholin's glands.

Bartholin-Patau syndrome (Bartholin and Patau, Klaus). See: Patau's syndrome.

BARTHOLIN, THOMAS. 1616-1680. Danish anatomist. See: Dict. Sci. Biog. Bartholin's anus.

Bartholinitis (Bartholin, Caspar II): Medicine. See: Stedman; Webster's 3d.

Bartholin's anus (Bartholin, Thomas): Anatomy. See: Dorland; Stedman.

Bartholin's duct (Bartholin, Caspar II): Anatomy. See: Dorland; Henderson; Stedman.

Bartholin's glands (Bartholin, Caspar II): Anatomy. See: Gray; Henderson; Stedman.

BARTHOLOMAE, CHRISTIAN. 1855-1925. German philologist. See: Webster's Biog. Dict. Bartholomae's law.

Bartholomae's law (Bartholomae, Christian): Linguistics. See: Winick.

BARTHOLOMEW, DAVID JOHN. fl. 1953-1970. English mathematician. See: Direct. Brit. Sci., 1963. Bartholomew's problem.

BARTHOLOMEW, SAINT. Biblical apostle. See: Encyc. Brit., 1973. Balmy, St. Bartholomew's Day.

Bartholomew's problem (Bartholomew, David John): Statistics. See: Kendall.

Barth's hernia (Barth, Jean Baptiste): Medicine. See: Dorland; Jablonski; Stedman.

Bartlett and Diananda test (Bartlett, Maurice Stevenson and Diananda, P. H.): Statistics. See: Kendall.

BARTLETT, ENOCH. 1779-1860. American merchant. See: Webster's Biog. Dict. Bartlett pear.

Bartlett force (Bartlett, James Holly): Physics. See: Ballentyne; Hughes; Internat. Dict. Ap. Math.

BARTLETT, JAMES HOLLY. 1904- . American physicist. See: World Who's Who Sci. Bartlett force.

BARTLETT, JOHN. 1820-1905. American publisher. See: Dict. Amer. Biog. Bartlett's quotations.

BARTLETT, MAURICE STEVENSON. 1910- . English statistician. See: World Who's Who Sci. Bartlett and Diananda test, Bartlett relation, Bartlett's collinearity test, Bartlett's decomposition, Bartlett's test, Bartlett's test of second-order interaction.

Bartlett pear (Bartlett, Enoch): Food and Drink. See: De Sola; Hendrickson; Winburne.

Bartlett relation (Bartlett, Maurice Stevenson): Statistics. See: Kendall.

Bartlett table (Derivation undetermined): Engineering and Industry. See: Thrush.

Bartlett's collinearity test (Bartlett, Maurice Stevenson): Statistics. See: Kendall.

Bartlett's decomposition (Bartlett, Maurice Stevenson): Statistics. See: Kendall.

Bartlett's quotations (Bartlett, John): Literature. See: Hendrickson.

Bartlett's test (Bartlett, Maurice Stevenson): Statistics. See: Good; Kendall.

Bartlett's test of second-order interaction (Bartlett, Maurice Stevenson): Statistics. See: Kendall.

Bartolist (Bartolus): Law. See: Brewer; Harvey.

BARTOLUS. 1314-1357. Italian jurist. See: Encyc. Brit., 1911. Bartolist.

BARTON, ALBERTO. L. 1871-1950. Peruvian physician. (Biography source unavailable.) Bartonella, Bartonellosis.

BARTON, BENJAMIN SMITH. 1766-1815. American botanist and physician. See: Dict. Sci. Biog. Bartonia.

BARTON, JOHN. 1771-1834. English inventor. See: Pogg., vol. I. Barton's packing, Barton's ruling engine.

BARTON, JOHN RHEA. 1794-1871. American surgeon. See: Dict. Amer. Biog. Barton's bandage, Barton's forcep, Barton's fracture.

Bartonella (Barton, Alberto L.): Medicine. See: Dorland; Stedman; Webster's 3d.

Bartonellosis (Barton, Alberto L.): Medicine. See: Stedman; Webster's 3d.

Bartonia (Barton, Benjamin Smith): Botany. See: Webster's 3d. Also known as: Mentzelia.

Barton's bandage (Barton, John Rhea): Medicine. See: Dorland; Stedman.

Barton's forcep (Barton, John Rhea): Medicine. See: Stedman.

Barton's fracture (Barton, John Rhea): Medicine. See: Dorland; Jablonski; Stedman.

Barton's packing (Barton, John): Engineering and Industry. See: Auger.

Barton's ruling engine (Barton, John): Engineering and Industry. See: Auger.

BARTRAM, JOHN. 1699-1777. American botanist. See: Dict. Sci. Biog. Bartram oak?

Bartram oak (Bartram, John or William): Botany. See: Mathews, M. M.; Partridge; Webster's 3d.

BARTRAM, WILLIAM. 1739-1823. American naturalist. See: Dict. Amer. Biog. Bartramia, Bartram's oak?, Bartram's sandpiper (tattler or plover).

Bartramia (Bartram, William): Botany. See: Webster's 3d.

Bartram's sandpiper (tattler or plover) (Bartram, William): Zoology. See: Mathews, M. M.; Partridge; Pennak.

BARTSCH, JOHANN. 1709-1738. German physician in Surinam. See: Biog. Notes Upon Botanists. Bartsia.

Bartsia (Bartsch, Johann): Botany. See: Charnock; Webster's 3d.

BARTTER, FREDERIC CROSBY. 1914- . American physiologist. See: World Who's Who Sci. Bartter's syndrome, Schwartz-Bartter syndrome.

Bartter's syndrome (Bartter, Frederic Crosby): Medicine. See: Jablonski; Stedman.

BARUCH, SIMON. 1840-1921. American physician. See: Dict. Amer. Biog. Baruch's law, Baruch's sign.

Baruch's law (Baruch, Simon): Medicine. See: Dorland; Stedman.

Baruch's sign (Baruch, Simon): Medicine. See: Dorland.

Barvoys process (Vooys, Gerard Jan de). See: Vooys process.

BARWELL, RICHARD. 1826-1916. English surgeon. See: Encyc. Amer. Barwell's operation.

Barwell's operation (Barwell, Richard): Medicine. See: Stedman.

BARZUN, JACQUES. 1907- . American historian. See: Webster's Biog. Dict. Barzun's bywords for committee pussyfooting, Barzun's lament, Barzun's law, Barzun's laws of learning.

Barzun's bywords for committee pussyfooting (Barzun, Jacques): Sociology. See: Martin.

Barzun's lament (Barzun, Jacques): Sociology. See: Martin.

Barzun's law (Barzun, Jacques): Sociology. See: Martin.

Barzun's laws of learning (Barzun, Jacques): Psychology. See: Martin.

Bascom folder (Derivation undetermined): Engineering and Industry. See: Lockwood.

BASEDOW, KARL ADOLPH VON. 1799-1854. German physician. See: Allg. Deut. Biog. Basedow type, Basedowian insanity, Basedow's disease, Basedow's pseudoparaplegia.

Basedow type (Basedow, Karl Adolph von): Psychiatry. See: Drever.

Basedowian insanity (Basedow, Karl Adolph von): Psychiatry. See: Stedman.

Basedow's disease (Basedow, Karl Adolph von): Medicine. See: Dorland; Hinsie; Jablonski. Also known as: Begbie's disease; Flajani–Basedow syndrome; Flajani's disease; Graves' disease; Marsh's disease; Parry's syndrome (or disease); Parson's disease.

Basedow's pseudoparaplegia (Basedow, Karl Adolph von): Medicine. See: Stedman.

BASHAM, WILLIAM RICHARD. 1804–1877. English physician. See: Dict. Nat. Biog. Basham's mixture.

Basham's mixture (Basham, William Richard): Medicine. See: Webster's 3d.

Bashford carcinoma 63 (Bashford, Ernest Francis): Medicine. See: Jablonski.

BASHFORD, ERNEST FRANCIS. 1873–1923. English physician. See: Ann. Register. Bashford carcinoma 63.

Bashforth chronograph (Bashforth, Francis): Engineering and Industry. Cited in: World Who's Who Sci.

BASHFORTH, FRANCIS. 1819–1912. English ballistician. See: Dict. Nat. Biog., 1912–1921. Adams–Bashforth process, Bashforth chronograph.

BASIL, SAINT. 330?–379? Bishop of Caesarea. See: Encyc. Brit., 1973. Basilian liturgy, Basilian monks (or Basilians), Basilian rule.

Basil Valentine. See: Valentine, Basil.

Basile, Mathieu. See: Guesde, Jules.

BASILEIOS, A. fl. 1935. Greek chemist. Cited in: Chem. Abst., vol. 29, p. 1360. Basileios test for iodate, Basileios test for iodide in the presence of bromate, chlorate, and iodate.

Basileios test for iodate (Basileios, A.): Chemistry. See: Van Nostrand Chem. Dict.

Basileios test for iodide in the presence of bromate, chlorate, and iodate (Basileios, A.): Chemistry. See: Van Nostrand Chem. Dict.

Basilian liturgy (Basil, Saint): Religion. See: Attwater; Weekley.

Basilian monks (or Basilians) (Basil, Saint.): Religion. See: Attwater; Brewer; Wagner, (Names).

Basilian rule (Basil, Saint): Religion. See: Attwater; Webster's 3d.

BASILIDES. ca. 140. Alexandrian Gnostic. See: Nouv. Biog. Univ. Basilidians.

Basilidians (Basilides): Religion. See: Canney; Latham; Webster's 3d.

Basilisco (Basilisco, the knight): Generic Word (braggart). See: Brewer.

BASILISCO, THE KNIGHT. Character in Kyd's tragedy. "Solyman and Perseda." (?1588) See: Benet. Basilisco.

Baskakov, Boris. See: Volkov, Boris.

BASKERVILLE, JOHN. 1706–1775. English printer and type-founder. See: Dict. Nat. Biog. Baskerville (typeface).

Baskerville (typeface) (Baskerville, John): Printing. See: Harrod; Hendrickson; Partridge.

Baskett's reducer (Derivation undetermined): Photography. See: Focal Encyc. Photog.

Bass (beer) (Bass, Michael Thomas): Food and Drink. See: Partridge.

BASS, MICHAEL THOMAS. 1799–1884. English brewer. See: Dict. Nat. Biog. Bass (beer).

BASSANI, FRANCESCO. 1853–1916. Italian geologist. See: Dict. Sci. Biog. Bassanite.

Bassanite (Bassani, Francesco): Earth Sciences. See: Webster's 3d.

BASSEN, FRANK ALBERT. 1903– . American physician. See: Amer. Med. Direct., 18th ed. Bassen–Kornzweig syndrome.

Bassen–Kornzweig syndrome (Bassen, Frank Albert and Kornzweig, Abraham Leon): Medicine. See: Jablonski; Stedman; Wolman.

BASSET, ANTOINE. 1882–1951. French surgeon. See: Biog. Lex hervorr. Aerzte, 1880–1930. Basset's operation.

Basset's operation (Basset, Antoine): Medicine. See: Dorland.

Bassett–Snyder reagent (Bassett, William Hastings and Snyder, C.J.): Chemistry. See: Van Nostrand Chem. Dict.

BASSETT, WILLIAM HASTINGS. b. 1868. American metallurgist. See: Amer. Men Sci., 5th ed. Bassett–Snyder reagent.

BASSI, FERDINANDO. 1710–1774. Italian naturalist. See: Biog. Notes Upon Botanists. Bassia

Bassia (Bassi, Ferdinando): Botany. See: Charnock; Webster's 3d.

BASSINI, EDOARDO. 1846–1924. Italian surgeon. See: World Who's Who Sci. Bassini's operation.

Bassini's operation (Bassini, Edoardo): Medicine. See: Dorland; Stedman.

BASSLER, ANTHONY. 1874–1959. American physician. See: Who's Who Amer. Med. Bassler's sign.

Bassler's sign (Bassler, Anthony): Medicine. See: Dorland; Stedman.

BASTEDO, WALTER ARTHUR. 1873–1952. American physician. See: Who's Who Amer. Med. Bastedo's sign.

Bastedo's sign (Bastedo, Walter Arthur): Medicine. See: Dorland; Stedman.

Bastian–Bruns law (Bastian, Henry Charlton and Bruns, Ludwig): Medicine. See: Dorland

BASTIAN, HENRY CHARLTON. 1837–1915. English neurologist. See: Dict. Sci. Biog. Bastian–Bruns law; Bastiania; Bastian's aphasia; Bastian's law.

BASTIANELLI, RAFFAELE. b. 1863. Italian surgeon. See: Biog. Lex. hervorr. Aerzte, 1880–1930. Bastianelli's method.

Bastianelli's method (Bastianelli, Raffaele): Medicine. See: Dorland.

Bastiania (Bastian, Henry Charlton): Zoology. See: Pennak.

Bastian's aphasia (Bastian, Henry Charlton). See: Wernicke's aphasia.

Bastian's law (Bastian, Henry Charlton): Medicine. See: Hinsie.

Batchelder Award (Batchelder, Mildred L.): Library Science. See: Harrod.

BATCHELDER, MILDRED L. b. 1901. American librarian. See: Who's Who Lib. Service, 4th ed. Batchelder Award.

Batchelor rope (Batchelor, T.C.): Engineering and Industry. See: Auger.

BATCHELOR, T. C. 1857–1947. English? inventor. (Biography source unavailable.) Batchelor rope.

Batchinski relation (Derivation undetermined): Physics. See: Internat. Dict. Phys. Elec.

BATE, CHARLES SPENCE. 1819–1889. English naturalist and dentist. See: World Who's Who Sci. Batea.

Bate equation (Derivation undetermined): Physics. See: Internat. Dict. Phys. Elec.

BATE, JOHN. fl. 1606. English merchant. See: Encyc. Brit., 1973. Bate's case.

Batea (Bate, Charles Spence): Zoology. See: Pennak.

Batelli's gland (Derivation undetermined): Zoology. See: Gray.

Bateman equations (Bateman, Harry): Mathematics. See: Ballentyne.

Bateman expansion (Bateman, Harry): Mathematics. Cited in: Dict. Sci. Biog.

BATEMAN, HARRY. 1882–1946. English-born American mathematician. See: Dict. Sci. Biog. Bateman equations, Bateman's expansion, Bateman's function.

BATEMAN, THOMAS. 1778–1821. English physician. See: World Who's Who Sci. Bateman's disease (1), Bateman's disease (2) (or purpura).

Bateman's disease (1) (Bateman, Thomas): Medicine. See: Dorland; Jablonski.

Bateman's disease (2) (or purpura) (Bateman, Thomas): Medicine. See: Jablonski.

Bateman's function (Bateman, Harry): Mathematics. Cited in: Dict. Sci. Biog.

Bates cadmium vapor arc lamp (Bates, Frederick John): Chemistry. Cited in: World Who's Who Sci.

Bate's case (Bate, John): Law. See: Harbottle.

BATES, FREDERICK JOHN. 1877–1958. American physical chemist. See: World Who's Who Sci. Bates cadmium vapor arc lamp, Bates polariscope, Bates sugar balance.

BATES, GRACE ELIZABETH. 1914- . American mathematician. See: World Who's Who Sci. Bates–Neyman model.

BATES, HENRY WALTER. 1825-1892. English naturalist. See:. Dict. Sci. Biog. Batesian mimicry.

Bates–Neyman model (Bates, Grace Elizabeth and Neyman, Jerzy): Statistics. See: Kendall.

Bates polariscope (Bates, Frederick John): Chemistry. See: Hackh.

Bates sugar balance (Bates, Frederick John): Chemistry. Cited in: World Who's Who Sci.

Batesian mimicry (Bates, Henry Walter): Zoology. See: Gray; Pennak; Webster's 3d.

Bath Oliver (biscuit) (Oliver, William): Food and Drink. See: Brewer; Webster's 3d.

BATHER, ROY. 1928- . English-born Canadian virologist. See: Amer. Men and Women Sci., 12th ed. Bather's leukemia.

Bather's leukemia (Bather, Roy): Medicine. See: Jablonski.

Batho formula (Batho, Harold Francis?): Physics. See: Internat. Dict. Ap. Math.

BATHO, HAROLD FRANCIS. 1905- . Canadian physicist. See: Amer. Men Sci., 9th ed. Batho formula?

bathypitotmeter (Pitot, Henri): Engineering and Industry. See: Webster's 3d.

Batiste fabric (Baptiste, Jean): Fashion. See: Hendrickson; Partridge; Picken.

BATTANDIER, JULES AIME. 1848-1922. French botanist and pharmacist. See: World Who's Who Sci. Battandier test reaction for chelidonine and narceine? Battandier test reaction for glaucine? Battandier test reaction for quinine and quinidine?

Battandier test reaction for chelidonine and narceine (Battandier, Jules Aime?): Chemistry. See: Van Nostrand Chem. Dict.

Battandier test reaction for glaucine (Battandier, Jules Aime?): Chemistry. See: Van Nostrand Chem. Dict.

Battandier test reaction for quinine and quinidine (Battandier, Jules Aime?): Chemistry. See: Van Nostrand Chem. Dict.

BATTELLI, FREDERIC. fl. 1909. Swiss? chemist. cited in: Chem. Abstr., vol. 3, p. 1415. Battelli–Stern solution.

Battelli–Stern solution (Battelli, Frederic and Stern, Lina): Chemistry. See: Van Nostrand Chem. Dict.

Batten cards (Batten, W.E.): Library Science. See: Harrod.

BATTEN, FREDERIC EUSTACE. 1865-1918. English ophthalmologist. See: Who Was Who, 1916-1928. Batten–Mayou syndrome, Curschmann–Batten–Steinert syndrome.

Batten–Mayou syndrome (Batten, Frederic Eustace and Mayou, Marmedukes). See: Stock–Spielmeyer–Vogt syndrome.

Batten–Steinert syndrome (Batten, Frederic Eustace and Steinert, Hans). See: Curschmann–Batten–Steinert syndrome.

Batten system (Batten, W.E.): Library Science. See: Harrod.

BATTEN, W. E. No dates. Inventor of indexing method. (Biography source unavailable.) Batten cards, Batten system.

Batten's disease (Batten, Frederic Eustace). See: Curschmann–Batten–Steinert syndrome.

Battey bacillus (Derivation undetermined): Medicine. See: Stedman.

BATTEY, ROBERT. 1828-1895. American surgeon. See: Dict. Amer. Biog. Battey's operation.

Battey's operation (Battey, Robert): Medicine. See: Stedman.

Battle–Jalaguier–Kammerer incision (Battle, William Henry; Jalaguier, Adolphe; and Kammerer, Frederic). See: Battle's incision.

BATTLE, WILLIAM HENRY. 1855-1936. English surgeon. See: World Who's Who Sci. Battle's incision, Battle's sign .

Battle's incision (Battle, William Henry): Medicine. See: Stedman. Also known as: Battle–Jalaguier–Kammerer incision.

Battle's sign (Battle, William Henry): Medicine. See: Hinsie; Stedman.

BATTLEY, RICHARD. 1770-1856. English chemist. See: Dict. Nat. Biog. Battley's sedative.

Battley's sedative (Battley, Richard): Medicine. See: Dorland.

Battology (or Battologist) (Battus): Generic Word (excessive repetition). See: Hendrickson.

BATTUS (Real name: ARISTOTELES). fl. 631 B.C. Lacedaemonian who helped to build the town of Cyrene. See: Harper. Battology (or Battologist).

BAUBIGNY, HENRY. b. 1842. French chemist. See: Pogg., vol. 4. Baubigny test.

Baubigny test (Baubigny, Henry): Chemistry. See: Van Nostrand Chem. Dict.

Baud (unit) (Baudot, Jean M. Emile): Engineering and Industry. See: Internat. Dict. Phys. Elec.; Markus; Partridge.

BAUDELOCQUE, JEAN LOUIS. 1746-1810. French surgeon and obstetrician. See: Nouv. Biog. Univ. Baudelocque's diameter (or line); Baudelocque's uterine circle.

BAUDELOCQUE, LOUIS AUGUSTE, JR. 1800-1864. French obstetrician. See: Biog. Lex. hervorr. Aerzte. Baudelocque's operation.

Baudelocque's diameter (or line) (Baudelocque, Jean Louis): Medicine. See: Donath; Dorland; Stedman.

Baudelocque's operation (Baudelocque, Louis Auguste, Jr.): Medicine. See: Stedman.

Baudelocque's uterine circle (Baudelocque, Jean Louis): Medicine. See: Stedman.

Baudelot cooler (Derivation undetermined): Engineering and Industry. See: Thrush.

BAUDISCH, OSKAR. b. 1881. Austrian-born American chemist. See: Amer. Men Sci., 6th ed. Baudisch reaction; Baudisch reagent.

Baudisch reaction (Baudisch, Oskar): Chemistry. See: Ballentyne.

Baudisch reagent (Baudisch, Oskar): Chemistry. See: Van Nostrand Chem. Dict.

Baudot code (Baudot, Jean M. Emile): Engineering and Industry. See: Hughes; Markus.

BAUDOT, JEAN M. EMILE. 1845-1903. French engineer. See: World Who's Who Sci. Baud (unit); Baudot code.

Baudouin('s) test (for sesame oil) (Derivation undetermined): Chemistry. See: Hackh; Van Nostrand Chem. Dict.; Winburne.

BAUER, EDOUARD. fl. 1924. French chemist. Cited in: Pogg., vol. 6 under "Haller, Albin." Haller–Bauer reaction.

BAUER, FERDINAND LUCAS. 1760-1826. Austrian illustrator. See: Dict. Sci. Biog. Bauera.

BAUER, FRANZ ANDREAS. 1758-1840. Austrian-born illustrator. See: Dict. Sci. Biog. Bauera.

BAUER, GUSTAV. fl. 1920's. German engineer. See: Wer Ist's, 1935. Bauer–Wach turbine?

BAUER, JULIUS. b. 1887. German physician. See: Biog. Lex. hervorr. Aerzte, 1880-1930. Bauer test for milk.

BAUER, OSWALD. 1876-1936. German metallurgist. See: Pogg., vol. 6. Heyn–Bauer reagent.

Bauer test for milk (Bauer, Julius): Chemistry. See: Van Nostrand Chem. Dict.

Bauer test reaction for solanine (Derivation undetermined): Chemistry. See: Van Nostrand Chem. Dict.

Bauer–Wach turbine (Bauer, Gustav? and Wach, Hugo?): Engineering and Industry. See: Auger; Internat. Dict. Ap. Math.

Bauera (Bauer, Franz Andreas and Bauer, Ferdinand Lucas): Botany. See: Taylor, N.; Webster's 3d.

BAUHIN, GASPARD. 1560-1624. Swiss botanist and anatomist. See: Dict. Sci. Biog. Bauhinia, Bauhin's gland, Bauhin's valve.

BAUHIN, JEAN. 1541-1613. Swiss physician and botanist. See: Dict. Sci. Biog. Bauhinia.

Bauhinia (Bauhin, Gaspard and Jean): Botany. See: Charnock; Taylor, N.; Webster's 3d.

Bauhin's gland (Bauhin, Gaspard): See: Blandin's gland.

Bauhin's valve (Bauhin, Gaspard): Anatomy. See: Donath; Stedman; Webster's 3d.

Baum jig (Derivation undetermined): Engineering and Industry. See: Thrush.

BAUMAN, LOUIS. 1880- . American physician. See: Who's Who Among Physicians and Surg. Bauman's diet.

Baumann benzoyl chloride reaction (Derivation undetermined): Chemistry. See: Van Nostrand Chem. Dict.

BAUMANN, EUGEN. 1846-1896. German physician and chemist. See: World Who's Who Sci. Schotten-Baumann reaction, Wolkow-Baumann test reaction.

BAUMANN, K. fl. 1921. English? engineer. (Biography source unavailable.) Baumann turbine.

Baumann print (Baumann, Richard Wilhelm?): Engineering and Industry. See: Thrush.

BAUMANN, RICHARD WILHELM. 1879-1928. German metallographer. See: World Who's Who Sci. Baumann print?

Baumann test for corn starch in wheat flour (Derivation undetermined): Chemistry. See: Van Nostrand Chem. Dict.

Baumann test reaction for agar-agar (Derivation undetermined): Chemistry. See: Van Nostrand Chem. Dict.

Baumann test reaction for iodide (Derivation undetermined): Chemistry. See: Van Nostrand Chem. Dict.

Baumann turbine (Baumann, K.): Engineering and Industry. See: Auger.

Bauman's diet (Bauman, Louis): Medicine. See: Dorland.

BAUME, ANTOINE. 1728-1804. French chemist. See: Dict. Sci. Biog. Baume gravity, Baume hydrometer, Baume scale (or hydrometer scale), degree Baume.

Baume gravity (Baume, Antoine): Chemistry. See: Thrush.

Baume hydrometer (Baume, Antoine): Chemistry. See: Hackh; Partridge.

Baume scale (or hydrometer scale) (Baume, Antoine): Chemistry. See: Ballentyne; Van Nostrand Chem. Dict.; Van Nostrand Sci. Encyc.

BAUMES, CALEB HOWARD. 1863-1937. American lawyer and politician. See: Webster's Biog. Dict. Baumes laws.

BAUMES, JEAN BAPTISTE TIMOTHY. 1777-1828. French physician. See: Nouv. Biog. Univ. Baumes' sign (or symptom).

Baumes' law (Baumes, Pierre Prosper Francois). See: Colles' law.

Baumes laws (Baumes, Caleb Howard): Law. See: Fairchild; Smith; Zadrozny.

BAUMES, PIERRE PROSPER FRANCOIS. 1791-1871. French physician. See: World Who's Who Sci. Baumes' law.

Baumes' sign (or symptom) (Baumes, Jean Baptiste Timothy): Medicine. See: Dorland; Stedman.

BAUMGARTEN, PAUL CLEMENS VON. 1848-1928. German pathologist. See: Wer Ist's. Baumgarten's stain, Cruveilhier-Baumgarten murmer, Cruveilhier-Baumgarten syndrome (or cirrhosis).

Baumgarten's stain (Baumgarten, Paul Clemens von): Medicine. See: Stedman.

BAUMHAUER, HEINRICH ADOLF. 1848-1926. Swiss mineralogist and chemist. See: Dict. Sci. Biog. Baumhauerite.

Baumhauerite (Baumhauer, Heinrich Adolf): Earth Sciences. See: Thrush; Webster's 3d.

BAUNSCHEIDT, KARL. 1809-1860. German mechanic. (Biography source unavailable.) Baunscheidtism.

Baunscheidtism (Baunscheidt, Karl): Medicine. See: Dorland; Stedman.

Bausch and Lomb dust counter (Bausch, John Jacob and Lomb, Henry): Engineering and Industry. See: Thrush.

BAUSCH, JOHN JACOB. 1830-1926. German-born American optician. See: Webster's Biog. Dict. Bausch and Lomb dust counter.

Bauschinger effect (Bauschinger, Johann): Engineering and Industry. See: Ballentyne; Internat. Dict. Ap. Math.; Van Nostrand Sci. Encyc.

BAUSCHINGER, JOHANN. 1834-1893. German technologist. See: World Who's Who Sci. Bauschinger effect.

Baveno law (Derivation undetermined): Engineering and Industry. See: Thrush.

Baveno twin (Derivation undetermined): Engineering and Industry. See: Thrush.

Bawbee (Sillabawby, Alexander Orrok, Laird of): Numismatics. See: Partridge; Webster's 3d; Weekley.

BAXTER, GEORGE. 1804-1867. English printer. See: Bryan. Baxter print.

BAXTER, JOHN. 1781-1858. English bookseller and printer. See: Dict. Nat. Biog. Baxter's Bible.

Baxter print (Baxter, George): Printing. Cited in: Webster's Biog. Dict.

BAXTER, RICHARD. 1615-1691. English Puritan scholar and writer. See: Dict. Nat. Biog. Baxterians.

Baxterians (Baxter, Richard): Religion. See: Brewer; Canney; Webster's 3d.

Baxter's Bible (Baxter, John): Printing. Cited in: Webster's Biog. Dict.

Bayard (Bayard, Pierre Terrail, Seigneur de): Generic Word (chivalrous person). See: Hendrickson; Partridge; Weekley.

Bayard and Alpert gauge (Derivation undetermined): Physics. See: Hughes; Internat. Dict. Phys. Elec.

Bayard-Chamberlain Treaty (Bayard, Thomas Francis and Chamberlain, Joseph): History. See: Morris.

BAYARD, HENRI LOUIS. 1812-1852. French physician. See: Biog. Lex. hervorr. Aerzte. Bayard's ecchymoses.

BAYARD, PIERRE TERRAIL, SEIGNEUR DE. 1476-1524. French soldier. See: Encyc. Brit., 1973. Bayard.

BAYARD, THOMAS FRANCIS. 1828-1898. American diplomat, senator, and lawyer. See: Dict. Amer. Biog. Bayard-Chamberlain Treaty.

Bayard's ecchymoses (Bayard, Henri Louis): Medicine. See: Stedman.

Bayer acid (Bayer, Friedrich): Chemistry. See: Hackh; Webster's 3d.

BAYER, FRIEDRICH. 1825-1880. German industrialist. See: Webster's Biog. Dict. Bayer acid.

BAYER, GUSTAV. 1879-1938. Austrian physiologist. See: Pogg., vol. 7a. Bayer test reaction for adrenaline.

BAYER, ISTVAN. 1923- . Hungarian pharmacist. See: World Who's Who Sci. Bayerite?

BAYER, KARL J. d. 1904. German metallurgist and chemist. (Biography source unavailable.) Bayer process.

Bayer process (Bayer, Karl J.): Engineering and Industry. See: Thrush; Van Nostrand Chem. Dict.; Webster's 3d.

Bayer test reaction for adrenaline (Bayer, Gustav): Chemistry. See: Van Nostrand Chem. Dict.

Bayer test reaction for gold (Derivation undetermined): Chemistry. See: Van Nostrand Chem. Dict.

Bayerite (Bayer, Istvan?): Earth Sciences. See: Thrush.

Bayes' estimation (Bayes, Thomas): Statistics. See: Kendall.

Bayes' postulate (Bayes, Thomas): Statistics. See: Kendall.

Bayes' risk (Bayes, Thomas): Statistics. See: Kendall.

Bayes' solution (Bayes, Thomas): Statistics. See: Internat. Dict. Ap. Math.; Kendall.

Bayes' strategy (Bayes, Thomas): Statistics. See: Kendall.

Bayes' theorem (Bayes, Thomas): Statistics. See: James; Kendall; Van Nostrand Sci. Encyc.

BAYES, THOMAS. 1702-1761. English mathematician. See: Internat. Encyc. Soc. Sci. asymptotic Bayes procedure, Bayes' estimation, Bayes' postulate, Bayes' risk, Bayes' solution, Bayes' strategy, Bayes' theorem, Bayesian inference, Bayesian probability point, Bayesian statistics, empirical Bayes' estimator, empirical Bayes' procedure.

Bayesian inference (Bayes, Thomas): Statistics. See: Kendall.

Bayesian probability point (Bayes, Thomas): Statistics. See: Kendall.

Bayesian statistics (Bayes, Thomas): Statistics. See: Greenwald.

Bayford–Autenrieth dysphagia (Bayford, David and Autenrieth, Johann Herrmann): Medicine. See: Jablonski.

BAYFORD, DAVID. fl. 1789. fl. 1789. English physician. (Biography source unavailable.) Bayford–Autenrieth dysphagia.

BAYHURST, BARBARA P. 1926–   . American chemist. See: Amer. Men and Women Sci., 12th ed. Bayhurst curve?

Bayhurst curve (Bayhurst, Barbara P.?): Electronics. See: Hughes.

BAYLDON, JOHN. fl. 19th c. Englishman. Cited in: Dana, vol. 2, p. 930. Bayldonite.

Bayldonite (Bayldon, John): Earth Sciences. See: Thrush.

BAYLE, ANTOINE LAURENT JESSE. 1799-1858. French physician. See: World Who's Who Sci. Bayle's disease.

BAYLE, GASPARD LAURENT. 1774-1861. French physician. See: Nouv. Biog. Univ. Bayle's granulations.

Bayle's disease (Bayle, Antoine Laurent Jesse): Medicine. See: Dorland; Hinsie; Jablonski.

Bayle's granulations (Bayle, Gaspard Laurent): Medicine. See: Dorland.

BAYLEY, NANCY. b. 1899. American psychologist. See: Amer. Men Sci., 9th ed., vol. 3. Bayley scale of infant development.

Bayley scale of infant development (Bayley, Nancy): Psychology. See: Wolman.

BAYLEY, WILLIAM SHIRLEY. 1861-1943. American geologist. See: World Who's Who Sci. Bayleyite.

Bayleyite (Bayley, William Shirley): Earth Sciences. See: Thrush; Webster's 3d.

BAYNTON, THOMAS. 1761-1820. English surgeon. See: Dict. Nat. Biog. Baynton's bandage.

Baynton's bandage (Baynton, Thomas): Medicine. See: Dorland; Stedman.

Bazeries cylinder (Bazeries, Etienne): Cryptography. See: Webster's 3d.

BAZERIES, ETIENNE. 1846-1931. French cryptographer. See: Dict. Biog. Fran. Bazeries cylinder.

BAZETT, HENRY CUTHBERT. 1885-1950. English physician and physiologist. See: World Who's Who Sci. Bazett's formula?

Bazett's formula (Bazett, Henry Cuthbert?): Medicine. See: Stedman.

BAZIN, ANTOINE PIERRE ERNEST. 1807-1877. French dermatologist. See: World Who's Who Sci. Alibert–Bazin syndrome, Bazin's disease (1) Bazin's disease (2) (or malady).

BAZIN, HENRI-EMILE. 1829-1917. French hydraulic engineer. See: World Who's Who Sci. Bazin's formula.

Bazin's disease (1) (Bazin, Antoine Pierre Ernest): Medicine. See: Jablonski.

Bazin's disease (2) (or malady) (Bazin, Antoine Pierre Ernst): Medicine. See: Jablonski.

Bazin's formula (Bazin, Henri-Emile): Engineering and Industry. See: Thrush.

BAZZI, ALESSANDRO E. d. 1929. Italian engineer. Cited in: Min. Mag., vol. 17 (1916) p. 345. Bazzite.

Bazzite (Bazzi, Alessandro E.): Earth Sciences. See: Webster's 3d.

Beacham pump (Derivation undetermined): Engineering and Industry. See: Auger.

Beacon reading method (Derivation undetermined): Education. See: Good.

BEAL, RAYMOND. fl. 1907. French ophthalmologist. (Biography source unavailable.) Beal's conjunctivitis (or syndrome).

BEALE, LIONEL SMITH. 1828-1906. English physician. See: Dict. Sci. Biog. Beale's cells, Beale's stain (or reagent).

Beale's cells (Beale, Lionel Smith): Medicine. See: Dorland; Stedman.

Beale's exhauster (Derivation undetermined): Engineering and Industry. See: Auger.

Beale's stain (or reagent) (Beale, Lionel Smith): Chemistry. See: Hackh; Stedman; Van Nostrand Chem. Dict.

BEALL, GEOFFREY. b. 1908. South African-born American statistician. See: Amer. Men Sci., 9th ed. Beall–Rescias generalization.

Beall–Rescias generalisation of Neyman's distribution (Beall, Geoffrey and Rescia, Richard R.): Statistics. See: Kendall.

Beal's conjunctivitis (or syndrome) (Beal, Raymond): Medicine. See: Jablonski.

Beaman arc (or stadia arc) (Derivation undetermined): Engineering and Industry. See: Thrush.

BEAMISH, FRED EARL. 1901–   . Canadian chemist. See: Amer. Men Sci., 6th ed. Thompson–Beamish–Scott test reactions for platinum, Thompson–Beamish–Scott tests for osmium.

BEAN, WILLIAM BENNETT. 1909–   . American physician. See: World Who's Who Sci. Bean's syndrome.

Bean's syndrome (Bean, William Bennett): Medicine. See: Jablonski.

BEARD, GEORGE MILLER. 1839-1883. American physician. See: Dict. Amer. Biog. Beard's disease (or syndrome).

Beard's disease (or syndrome) (Beard, George Miller): Psychiatry. See: Hinsie; Jablonski; Wolman.

BEARN, ALEXANDER GORDON. b. 1923. English-born American physician. See: Amer. Men Sci., 10th ed. Bearn–Kunkel syndrome.

Bearn–Kunkel–Slater syndrome (Bearn, Alexander Gordon; Kunkel, Henry George; and Slater, Robert James). See: Bearn–Kunkel syndrome.

Bearn–Kunkel syndrome (Bearn, Alexander Gordon and Kunkel, Henry George): Medicine. See: Jablonski. Also known as: Bearn–Kunkel–Slater syndrome.

Beatrice (Beatrice Portinari): Generic Word (beautiful, inspiring woman). See: Partridge.

BEATRICE PORTINARI. 1266-1290. Italian noblewoman. See: New Encyc. Brit., 1974, Microp. Beatrice.

Beattie–Bridgeman equation of state (Beattie, James Alexander and Bridgeman, Oscar Cleon): Chemistry. See: Ballentyne; Internat. Dict. Ap. Math.

BEATTIE, JAMES ALEXANDER. 1895–   . American chemist. See: World Who's Who Sci. Beattie–Bridgeman equation of state.

BEATTY, WALLACE APPLETON. fl. 1903. American chemist. Cited in: Mansell. Levene–Beatty reagent for amino acids?

BEATUS. 730-789. Spanish theologian and geographer. See: Nouv. Biog. Univ. Beatus manuscripts.

Beatus manuscripts (Beatus): Fine Arts. See: Osborne.

Beau Brummel(l) (or Brummelism) (Brummell, George Bryan): Generic Word. See: Hendrickson; Partridge; Picken.

BEAU DE ROCHAS, ADOLPHE-EUGENE. 1815-1893. French inventor. See: World Who's Who Sci. Beau de Rochas cycle.

Beau de Rochas cycle (Beau de Rochas, Adolphe-Eugene): Engineering and Industry. See: Auger; Thrush. Also known as: De Rochas cycle.

BEAU, JOSEPH HONORE SIMON. 1806-1865. French physician. See: World Who's Who Sci. Beau's disease (or syndrome), Beau's lines.

Beaufort, 1st Duke of. See: Somerset, Henry (1st Duke of Beaufort or Badminton).

Beaufort cipher (Beaufort, Francis): Earth Sciences. See: Webster's 3d.

Beaufort force (or number) (Beaufort, Francis): Earth Sciences. See Huschke.

BEAUFORT, FRANCIS. 1774-1857. English naval officer. See: Dict. Nat. Biog. Beaufort cipher, Beaufort force (or number), Beaufort notation, Beaufort scale (or wind scale).

BEAUFORT, MARGARET. 1443-1509. English noblewoman. See: Dict. Nat. Biog. Lady Margaret foundations.

Beaufort notation (Beaufort, Francis): Earth Sciences. See: Monkhouse; Thewlis.

Beaufort scale (or wind scale) (Beaufort, Francis): Earth Sciences. See: Hendrickson; Monkhouse; Moore.

BEAUHARNAIS. French family of Orleanais. See: Webster's Biog. Dict. a la Beauharnais.

Beauharnais, Josephine Tascher de La Pagerie de. See: Josephine.

BEAULIEU. fl. 1850. English hatter. (Biography source unavailable.) Bowler hat?

BEAUMONT. fl. 1870. Dutch engineer. (Biography source unavailable.) Beaumont (rifle).

BEAUMONT, LADY. fl. 19th c. English noblewoman. (Biography source unavailable.) Beaumontia.

Beaumont (rifle) (Beaumont): Weapons. See: Quick.

Beaumontage (or Beaumontague) (Elie de Beaumont, Jean-Baptiste-Armand-Louis-Leonce): Generic Word. See: Partridge.

Beaumontia (Beaumont, Lady): Botany. See: Taylor, N.; Webster's 3d.

Beaune, Florimond de. See: Debeaune, Florimond.

Beaune's problem (Debeaune, Florimond): Mathematics. Cited in: World Who's Who Sci.

BEAUPERTHUY, LOUIS DANIEL. 1803-1871. West Indian physian. See: World Who's Who Sci. Beauperthuy's treatment.

Beauperthuy's treatment (Beauperthuy, Louis Daniel): Medicine. See: Dorland; Stedman.

Beau's disease (or syndrome) (Beau, Joseph Honore Simon): Medicine. See: Dorland; Jablonski.

Beau's lines (Beau, Joseph Honore Simon): Medicine. See: Dorland; Stedman.

BEBB, MICHAEL SCHUCK. 1833-1895. American botanist. See: Biog. Notes Upon Botanists. Bebb willow.

Bebb willow (Bebb, Michael Schuck): Botany. See: Webster's 3d.

BECCARI, C. No dates. Brought mineral from Ceylon. Cited in: Bailey. Beccarite.

BECCARI, GUISEPPE. No dates. Italian physician. (Biography source unavailable.) Beccari process.

BECCARI, NELLO. b. 1883. Italian anatomist. See: Diz. Biog. Ital. Beccari's membrane (or stratum).

Beccari process (Beccari, Guiseppe): Medicine. See: Dorland.

BECCARIA, AUGUSTO. fl. 20th c. Italian physician. (Biography source unavailable.) Beccaria's sign.

Beccaria's sign (Beccaria, Augusto): Medicine. See: Stedman.

Beccari's membrane (or stratum) (Beccari, Nello): Anatomy. See: Dobson.

Beccarite (Beccari, C.): Earth Sciences. See: Thrush.

BECHAMEL, LOUIS DE. d. 1703. French financier and gastronome. See: Nouv. Biog. Univ. Bechamel (sauce).

Bechamel (sauce) (Bechamel, Louis de): Food and Drink. See: Charnock; De Sola; Hendrickson.

BECHAMP, PIERRE JACQUES ANTOINE. 1816-1908. French physician, surgeon and chemist. See: World Who's Who Sci. Bechamp process (or reduction), Bechamp reaction, Bechamp test for alkali sulfides, Bechamp test for nitrobenzene in oil of bitter almond.

Bechamp process (or reduction) (Bechamp, Pierre Jacques Antoine): Chemistry. See: Van Nostrand Chem. Dict.; Webster's 3d.

Bechamp reaction (Bechamp, Pierre Jacques Antoine): Chemistry. See: Van Nostrand Chem. Dict.

Bechamp test for alkali sulfides (Bechamp, Pierre Jacques Antoine): Chemistry. See: Van Nostrand Chem. Dict.

Bechamp test for nitrobenzene in oil of bitter almond (Bechamp, Pierre Jacques Antoine): Chemistry. See: Van Nostrand Chem. Dict.

Becher test reaction for apomorphine (Derivation undetermined): Chemistry. See: Van Nostrand Chem. Dict.

BECHERER, FRITZ. fl. 1925. Swiss chemist. Cited in: Chem. Abstr., vol. 17, p. 1923. Rupe-Becherer reagent.

Bechhold filter (Bechhold, Heinrich Jakob): Chemistry. See: Hackh.

BECHHOLD, HEINRICH JAKOB. 1866-1937. German chemist. See: World Who's Who Sci. Bechhold filter.

BECHI, EMILIO. fl. 1854-1879. Italian chemist and mineralogist. See: Pogg., vol. 3. Bechilite.

Bechi-Hehner solution (Bechi and Hehner, Otto?): Chemistry. See: Van Nostrand Chem. Dict.

Bechi solution (Derivation undetermined): Chemistry. See: Van Nostrand Chem. Dict.

Bechilite (Bechi, Emilio): Earth Sciences. See: Thrush.

BECHSTEIN, FRIEDRICH WILHELM CARL. 1826-1900. German piano maker. See: Grove.

Bechstein (piano) (Bechstein, Friedrich Wilhelm Carl): Music. See: Partridge.

Bechtel crabapple (tree) (Bechtel, Ernst A.): Botany. See: Webster's 3d; Winburne.

BECHTEL, ERNST A. fl. 19th c. American nurseryman. (Biography source unavailable.) Bechtel crabapple (tree).

Bechtereff, Bechterev, or Bechterew. See: Bekhterev, Vladimir Mikhailovich.

BECK, CARL. 1856-1911. German-born American surgeon. See: Dict. Amer. Biog. Beck's gastrostomy.

BECK, CLAUDE SCHAEFFER. 1894- . American surgeon. See: World Who's Who Sci. Beck operation (1), Beck operation (2), Beck's triad.

Beck effect (Derivation undetermined): Photography. See: Focal Encyc. Photog.

BECK, EMIL G. 1866-1932. American surgeon. See: World Who's Who Sci. Beck's method, Beck's paste.

Beck hydrometer (Derivation undetermined): Chemistry. See: Van Nostrand Chem. Dict.

Beck-Ibrahim's disease (Beck, Soma Cornelius and Ibrahim, Murad Jussuf Bey): Medicine. See: Jablonski. Also known as: Beck's disease, Ibrahim's disease.

BECK, KARL MARIA OTTO HANS. b. 1880. German neurologist. See: Wer Ist's, 10th ed. Beck's syndrome.

Beck operation (1) (Beck, Claude Schaeffer): Medicine. See: Stedman.

Beck operation (2) (Beck, Claude Schaeffer): Medicine. See: Stedman.

BECK, SAMUEL JACOB. 1896- . Rumanian-born American psychologist. See: World Who's Who Sci. Beck system.

BECK, SOMA CORNELIUS. b. 1872. Hungarian physician. See: Biog. Lex. hervorr. Aerzte, 1880-1930. Beck-Ibrahim's disease.

Beck system (Beck, Samuel Jacob): Psychology. See: Wolman.

BECKE, FRIEDRICH JOHANN KARL. 1855-1931. Czech-born Austrian mineralogist. See: Dict. Sci. Biog. Becke line, Becke method (or test), Beckelite.

Becke line (Becke, Friedrich Johann Karl): Earth Sciences. See: Ballentyne; Thewlis.

Becke method (or test) (Becke, Friedrich Johann Karl): Earth Sciences. See: Thrush; Van Nostrand Sci. Encyc.; Webster's 3d.

Beckelite (Becke, Friedrich Johann Karl): Earth Sciences. See: Thrush; Webster's 3d.

Becker brake (Becker, Eduard): Engineering and Industry. See: Auger.

BECKER, EDUARD. 1832-1913. German engineer. See: Neue Deut. Biog. Becker brake.

BECKER, GEORGE FERDINAND. 1847-1919. American geologist. See: Dict. Sci. Biog. Beckerite?

BECKER, HOWARD PAUL. 1899-1960. American sociologist. See: Internat. Encyc. Soc. Sci. Becker-Von Wiese personality types.

BECKER, JOSEPH. b. 1887. American engineer. Cited in: Chem. Abstr. Becker oven, Koppers-Becker oven.

BECKER, OTTO HEINRICH ENOCH. 1828-1890. German oculist. See: Allg. Deut. Biog. Becker's phenomenon, Becker's test.

Becker oven (Becker, Joseph): Engineering and Industry. See: Van Nostrand Chem. Dict.

BECKER, SAMUEL WILLIAM. b. 1894. American physician. See: Amer. Men Sci., 10th ed. Becker's nevus.

Becker-Von Wiese personality types (Becker, Howard Paul and Von Wiese, Leopold): Sociology. See: Zadrozny.

Beckerite (Becker, George Ferdinand?): Earth Sciences. See: Thrush.

Becker's disease (Derivation undetermined): Medicine. See: Stedman.

Becker's nevus (Becker, Samuel William): Medicine. See: Jablonski.

Becker's phenomenon (Becker, Otto Heinrich Enoch): Medicine. See: Dorland; Stedman.

Becker's test (Becker, Otto Heinrich Enoch): Medicine. See: Dorland; Stedman.

BECKET, FREDERICK MARK. 1875-1942. American chemist and metallurgist. See: World Who's Who Sci. Becket loop?

Becket loop (Becket, Frederick Mark?): Engineering and Industry. See: Thrush.

BECKETT, SIR EDMUND, 1ST BARON GRIMTHORPE. 1816-1905. English architect, lawyer and mechanician. See: Dict. Nat. Biog., 2d suppl. Grimthorpe.

BECKMAN, DORA. d. 1883. American religious leader. (Biography source unavailable.) Beckmanites.

Beckman spectrophotometer (Derivation undetermined): Physics. See: Internat. Dict. Phys. Elec.

Beckman test for amylodextrin in honey (Derivation undetermined): Chemistry. See: Van Nostrand Chem. Dict.

Beckman test reaction for veratrine (Derivation undetermined): Chemistry. See: Van Nostrand Chem. Dict.

Beckmanites (Beckman, Dora): Religion. See: Canney.

Beckmann apparatus (Beckmann, Ernst Otto): Chemistry. See: Dorland; Stedman; Van Nostrand Chem. Dict.

Beckmann burner (Beckmann, Ernst Otto): Chemistry. See: Hackh.

BECKMANN, ERNST OTTO. 1853-1923. German chemist. See: Dict. Sci. Biog. Beckmann apparatus, Beckmann burner, Beckmann method, Beckmann reaction, Beckmann rearrangement (or transformation), Beckmann thermometer.

Beckmann method (Beckmann, Ernst Otto): Chemistry. See: Internat. Dict. Phys. Elec.; Van Nostrand Sci. Encyc.

Beckmann mixture (Derivation undetermined): Chemistry. See: Van Nostrand Chem. Dict.; Van Nostrand Sci. Encyc.

Beckmann reaction (Beckmann, Ernst Otto): Chemistry. Cited in: Hackh.

Beckmann rearrangement (or transformation) (Beckmann, Ernst Otto): Chemistry. See: Ballentyne; Van Nostrand Chem. Dict.; Webster's 3d.

Beckmann thermometer (Beckmann, Ernst Otto): Chemistry. See: Thewlis; Van Nostrand Sci. Encyc.; Webster's 3d.

Beckmesser (Beckmesser, Sixtus): Generic Word (pedant). See: Webster's 3d.

BECKMESSER, SIXTUS. Character in Richard Wagner's opera, "Die Meistersinger". See: Benet. Beckmesser.

Beck's disease (Beck, Soma Cornelius). See: Beck-Ibrahim's disease.

Beck's gastrostomy (Beck, Carl): Medicine. See: Dorland.

Beck's method (Beck, Emil G.): Medicine. See: Stedman.

Beck's paste (Beck, Emil G.): Medicine. Cited in: World Who's Who Sci.

Beck's syndrome (Beck, Karl Maria Otto Hans): Medicine. See: Jablonski.

Beck's triad (Beck, Claude Schaeffer): Medicine. See: Dorland; Stedman.

BECKURTS, HEINRICH AUGUST. b. 1855. German chemist. See: Pogg., vol. 3. Beckurts reagent?

Beckurts reagent (Beckurts, Heinrich August?): Chemistry. See: Van Nostrand Chem. Dict.

BECKWITH, JOHN BRUCE. 1933- . American physician. See: Direct. Med. Specialists, vol. 14. Beckwith's syndrome.

BECKWITH, N. G. fl. 1919. English engineer. (Biography source unavailable.) Beckwith pump.

Beckwith pump (Beckwith, N. G.): Engineering and Industry. See: Auger.

Beckwith's syndrome (Beckwith, John Bruce): Medicine. See: Jablonski.

Becky Sharp (Sharp, Becky): Generic Word (scheming woman). See: Brewer.

BECLARD, PIERRE AUGUSTIN. 1785-1825. French anatomist. See: Nouv. Biog. Univ. Beclard's anastomosis, Beclard's hernia, Beclard's triangle.

Beclard's anastomosis (Beclard, Pierre Augustin): Medicine. See: Donath.

Beclard's hernia (Beclard, Pierre Augustin): Medicine. See: Dorland; Jablonski; Stedman.

Beclard's triangle (Beclard, Pierre Augustin): Medicine. See: Donath; Dorland; Stedman.

Becorit system (Derivation undetermined): Engineering and Industry. See: Thrush.

BECQUEREL, ALEXANDRE-EDMOND. 1820-1891. French physicist. See: Dict. Sci. Biog. Becquerel effect.

BECQUEREL, ANTOINE HENRI. 1852-1908. French physicist. See: Dict. Sci. Biog. Becquerel rays, Becquerelite.

Becquerel cell (Derivation undetermined): Electronics. See: Hughes.

Becquerel effect (Becquerel, Alexandre-Edmond): Physics. See: Ballentyne; Focal Encyc. Photog.; Hughes.

Becquerel rays (Becquerel, Antoine Henri): Physics. See: Dorland; Hackh; Hughes.

Becquerelite (Becquerel, Antoine Henri): Earth Sciences. See: Hackh; Thrush; Webster's 3d.

bed of Procrustes (Procrustes). See: Procrustean bed.

BEDAUX, CHARLES EUGENE. 1887-1944. French-born American industrialist. See: Webster's Biog. Dict. Bedaux system.

Bedaux system (Bedaux, Charles Eugene): Business. See: Clark; Webster's 3d.

Bedawiyeh (Ahmed el-Bedawi): Religion. See: Canney.

BEDELL, WILLIAM. 1571-1642. Anglican divine. See: Dict. Nat. Biog. Bedell's Bible.

Bedell's Bible (Bedell, William): Religion. See: Brewer.

Bedford, 4th Duke of. See: Russell, John (4th Duke of Bedford).

Bedford, 4th Earl of. See: Russell, Francis (4th Earl of Bedford).

Bedford bindings (Bedford, Francis): Fine Arts. See: Harrod.

BEDFORD, FRANCIS. 1799-1883. English bookbinder. See: Dict. Nat. Biog., 1st suppl. Bedford bindings.

Bedford level (Russell, Francis, 4th Earl of Bedford): Geography. See: Weekley.

Bedford protest (Russell, John, 4th Duke of Bedford): History. See: Harbottle.

BEDNAR, ALOIS. 1816-1888. Austrian physician. See: Biog. Lex. hervorr. Aerzte. Bednar-Parrot disease, Bednar's aphthae.

Bednar-Parrot disease (Bednar, Alois and Parrot, Jules Marie). See: Parrot's disease (I).

Bednar's aphthae (Bednar, Alois): Medicine. See: Dorland; Jablonski; Stedman.

Beecham Symphony concert orchestra (Beecham, Thomas): Music. Cited in: Webster's Biog. Dict.

BEECHAM, THOMAS. 1820-1907. English manufacturer. See: Dict. Nat. Biog., 2d. suppl. Beecham's pills.

BEECHAM, THOMAS. 1879–1961. English conductor. See: Webster's Biog. Dict. Beecham Symphony concert orchestra.

Beecham's pills (Beecham, Thomas): Medicine. Cited in: Stenhouse.

BEECHER, HENRY WARD. 1813–1887. American clergyman. See: Dict. Amer. Biog. Beecher's bibles.

Beecher's bibles (Beecher, Henry Ward): Weapons. See: Hendrickson; Partridge; Phyfe.

beef Stroganoff (Stroganoff, Count Paul): Food and Drink. See: De Sola; Hendrickson; Webster's 3d.

beef Wellington (Wellington, Arthur Wellesley): Food and Drink. See: Hendrickson.

BEEGER, HERMANN. fl. 19th c. American mineralogist. Cited in: Dana vol. 1, p. 393. Beegerite.

Beegerite (Beeger, Hermann): Earth Sciences. See: Thrush; Webster's 3d.

BEEKE, HENRY. 1751–1837. Dean of Bristol. See: Dict. Nat. Biog. Beekite.

Beekite (Beeke, Henry): Earth Sciences. See: Thrush; Webster's 3d.

Beelzebub (Beelzebub, the Prince): Religion (devil incarnate). See: Partridge.

Beelzebub (monkey) (Beelzebub, the Prince): Zoology. See: Webster's 3d.

BEELZEBUB, THE PRINCE. Biblical prince of the devils. See: Encyc. Amer. Beelzebub, Beelzebub (monkey).

BEER, AUGUST. 1825–1863. German physicist. See: World Who's Who Sci. Beer's law, Bouger–Beer law.

BEER, GEORG JOSEPH. 1763–1821. German ophthalmologist. See: Nouv. Biog. Univ. Beer's collyrium, Beer's knife, Beer's operation.

Beer's collyrium (Beer, Georg Joseph): Medicine. See: Dorland.

Beers' crown (Beers, William George): Dentistry. See: Stedman.

Beer's knife (Beer, Georg Joseph): Medicine. See: Dorland; Stedman.

Beer's law (Beer, August): Physics. See: Ballentyne; Internat. Dict. Phys. Elec.; Thewlis.

Beer's operation (Beer, Georg Joseph): Medicine. See: Dorland; Stedman.

BEERS, WILLIAM GEORGE. 1843–1900. Canadian dentist. See: New York Acad. Med. Portrait Cat. Beers' crown.

Beethoven (Beethoven, Ludwig van): Generic Word (musical genius). See: Partridge.

Beethoven exploder (Beethoven, Ludwig van?): Engineering and Industry. See: Thrush.

BEETHOVEN, LUDWIG VAN. 1770–1827. German composer. See: Encyc. Brit., 1973. Beethoven, Beethoven exploder? Beethovenian.

Beethovenian (Beethoven, Ludwig van): Music. See: Webster's 3d.

BEEVERS, CECIL ARNOLD. fl. 1930–1942. English physicist. See: Direct. Brit. Sci., 1966–1967. Beevers–Lipson strips.

Beevers–Lipson strips (Beevers, Cecil Arnold and Lipson, Henry Solomon): Physics. See: Thewlis.

BEEVOR, CHARLES EDWARD. 1854–1908. English neurologist. See: Dict. Sci. Biog. Beevor's sign.

Beevor's sign (Beevor, Charles Edward): Medicine. See: Dorland; Hinsie; Stedman.

before you can say Jack Robinson (Robinson, Jack): Generic Word (quick visit). See: Weekley.

BEGBIE, JAMES. 1798–1869. Scottish physician. See: Dict. Nat. Biog. Begbie's disease.

Begbie's disease (Begbie, James). See: Basedow's disease.

Beggar (Begue, Lambert le): Generic Word. See: Hendrickson.

BEGGIATO, FRANCESCO SECONDO. 1806–1883. Italian botanist. See: Biog. Notes Upon Botanists. Beggiatoa.

Beggiatoa (Beggiato, Francesco Secondo): Botany. See: Dorland; Webster's 3d.

Beghards (Begue, Lambert le): Religion. See: Attwater; Harvey; Mathews, S.

BEGON, MICHEL. 1638–1710. French administrator. See: Nouv. Biog. Univ. Begonia.

Begonia (Begon, Michel): Botany. See: Funk; Hendrickson; Taylor, N.

BEGUE, LAMBERT LE. d. 1177. Belgian priest. See: Nouv. Biog. Univ. Beggar, Beghards, Beguines.

BEGUEZ CESAR, ANTONIO. fl. 1943. Cuban ? physician. (Biography source unavailable.) Beguez Cesar–Steinbrinck–Chediak–Higashi syndrome.

Beguez Cesar–Steinbrinck–Chediak–Higashi syndrome (Beguez Cesar, Antonio; Steinbrinck, W.; Chediak, Moises; and Higashi, Ototaka): Medicine. See: Jablonski.

Beguines (Begue, Lambert le): Religion. See: Attwater; Brewer; Canney.

BEHAL, AUGUSTE. 1859–1941. French chemist. See: World Who's Who Sci. Behal reagent for acetylene hydrocarbons, Behal test reaction for alcohols.

Behal reagent for acetylene hydrocarbons (Behal, Auguste): Chemistry. See: Van Nostrand Chem. Dict.

Behal test reaction for alcohols (Behal, Auguste): Chemistry. See: Van Nostrand Chem. Dict.

BEHCET, HALUSHI. 1889–1948. Turkish dermatologist. See: New York Acad. Med. Portrait Cat. Behcet's syndrome (aphthae, or disease).

Behcet's syndrome (aphthae, or disease) (Behcet, Halushi): Medicine. See: Dorland; Jablonski; Stedman. Also known as: Adamantiades–Behcet syndrome, Behcet's triple symptom complex, Gilbert–Behcet syndrome.

Behcet's triple symptom complex (Behcet, Halushi). See: Behcet's syndrome (aphthae or disease).

Behier–Hardy symptom (Behier, Louis Jules and Hardy, Louis Phillipe Alfred): Medicine. See: Dorland.

BEHIER, LOUIS JULES. 1813–1875. French physician. See: World Who's Who Sci. Behier–Hardy symptom.

BEHLA, ROBERT FRANZ. b. 1850. German physician. See: Wer Ist's. Behla's bodies.

Behla's bodies (Behla, Robert Franz): Medicine. See: Dorland.

Behmen, Jacob. See: Boehme, Jakob.

Behmenists (or Boehmenism) (Boehme, Jakob): Religion. See: Brewer; Canney; Webster's 3d.

BEHN–ESCHENBURG, H. fl. 1927–35. Psychologist. Cited in: Cum. Auth. Index Psych. Abstr. Behn–Rorschach test.

Behn–Rorschach test (Behn–Eschenburg, H. and Rorschach, Hermann): Psychology. See: English; Hinsie; Wolman.

BEHR, CARL. b. 1876. German physician. See: Biog. Lex. hervorr. Aerzte, 1880–1930. Behr's disease, Behr's sign, Behr's syndrome.

BEHRE, JEANETTE ALLEN. b. 1891. American biochemist. See: Amer. Men Sci., 9th ed. Benedict–Behre test reaction for creatinine.

Behrens–Fisher problem (Behrens, W. V. and Fisher, Sir Ronald Alymer): Mathematics. See: James.

Behrens–Fisher test (Behrens, W. V. and Fisher, Sir Ronald Alymer): Statistics. See: Good; Internat. Dict. Ap. Math.; Kendall.

BEHRENS, MARTIN. 1899– . German physiological chemist. See: Pogg., vol. 7a. Neuberg–Behren reagent for isolating sugars.

Behrens' method (Behrens, W. V.): Statistics. See: Kendall. Also known as: Dragstedt–Behrens method.

Behren's pump (Derivation undetermined): Engineering and Industry. See: Auger.

Behrens reagent for aldehydes and ketones (Derivation undetermined): Chemistry. See: Van Nostrand Chem. Dict.

Behrens solution for cellulose (Derivation undetermined): Chemistry. See: Van Nostrand Chem. Dict.

BEHRENS, W. V. fl. 1929. Mathematician. (Biography source unavailable.) Behrens-Fisher problem, Behrens-Fisher test, Behrens' method.

BEHRING, EMIL ADOLF VON. 1854-1917. German bacteriologist. See: Dict. Sci. Biog. Behring's law.

Behring's law (Behring, Emil Adolf von): Medicine. See: Dorland; Stedman; Van Nostrand Chem. Dict.

Behr's disease (Behr, Carl): Medicine. See: Jablonski; Stedman.

Behr's sign (Behr, Carl): Medicine. See: Jablonski.

Behr's syndrome (Behr, Carl): Medicine. See: Jablonski.

BEIEN, A. fl. 1912. German inventor. Cited in: Chem. Abstr. Beien kep gear? Beien machine?

Beien kep gear (Beien, A.?): Engineering and Industry. See: Thrush.

Beien machine (Beien, A.?): Engineering and Industry. See: Thrush.

Beier gear (Derivation undetermined): Engineering and Industry. See: Auger.

BEIGEL, HERMANN. 1830-1879. Austrian-born physician. See: Biog. Lex. hervorr. Aerzte. Beigel's disease.

Beigel's disease (Beigel, Hermann): Medicine. See: Dorland; Jablonski; Stedman. Also known as: Chignon's disease, Paxton's disease.

BEIJERINCK, MARTINUS WILLEM. 1851-1931. Dutch botanist and physician. See: World Who's Who Sci. Beijerinck reaction, Beijerinck reagent.

Beijerinck reaction (Beijerinck, Martinus Willem): Medicine. See: Dorland; Stedman.

Beijerinck reagent (Beijerinck, Martinus Willem): Chemistry. See: Van Nostrand Chem. Dict. Also known as Poehl's test.

BEILBY, GEORGE THOMAS. 1850-1924. Scottish industrial chemist. See: Dict. Nat. Biog., 4th suppl. Beilby layer.

Beilby layer (Beilby, George Thomas): Chemistry. See: Ballentyne; Hackh; Thewlis.

BEILSTEIN, FRIEDRICH KONRAD. 1838-1906. German chemist. See: Dict. Sci. Biog. Beilstein's test.

Beilstein's test (Beilstein, Friedrich Konrad): Chemistry. See: Ballentyne; Van Nostrand Chem. Dict.

Beissenhirtz test reaction (Derivation undetermined): Chemistry. See: Van Nostrand Chem. Dict.

BEK, E. V. fl. 1906. Russian? physician. (Biography source unavailable.) Kashin-Bek disease.

Bekesy audiometry (Bekesy, Georg von): Medicine. See: Stedman.

BEKESY, GEORG VON. 1899- . Hungarian-born American biophysicist. See: World Who's Who Sci. Bekesy audiometry.

Bekhterev-Mendel reflex (Bekhterev, Vladimir Mikhailovich and Mendel, Kurt): Medicine. See: Hinsie; Stedman; Wolman.

Bekhterev-Struempell-Marie syndrome (Bekhterev, Vladimir Mikhailovich; Struempell, Ernst Adolph Gustav Gottfried von; and Marie, Pierre): Medicine. See: Jablonski. Also known as: Bekhterev's disease, Marie-Struempell disease, Marie's disease, Pierre Marie's disease.

Bekhterev technique (Bekhterev, Vladimir Mikhailovich): Medicine. See: Drever.

BEKHTEREV, VLADIMIR MIKHAILOVICH. 1857-1927. Russian neurologist. See: Dict. Sci. Biog. Bekhterev-Mendel reflex, Bekhterev-Struempell-Marie syndrome, Bekhterev technique, Bekhterev's band (or layer), Bekhterev's bundle, Bekhterev's nucleus, Bekhterev's nystagmus, Bekhterev's sign.

Bekhterev's band (or layer) (Bekhterev, Vladimir Mikhailovich): Medicine. See: Stedman. Also known as: Kaes' layer.

Bekhterev's bundle (Bekhterev, Vladimir Mikhailovich): Medicine. See: Donath.

Bekhterev's disease (Bekhterev, Vladimir Mikhailovich). See: Bekhterev-Struempell-Marie syndrome.

Bekhterev's nucleus (Bekhterev, Vladimir Mikhailovich): Medicine. See: Dorland; Stedman; Webster's 3d.

Bekhterev's nystagmus (Bekhterev, Vladimir Mikhailovich): Medicine. See: Jablonski.

Bekhterev's sign (Bekhterev, Vladimir Mikhailovich): Medicine. See: Dorland; Stedman.

Bel (Bell, Alexander Graham): Physics. See: Apel; Dresner; Internat. Dict. Phys. Elec.

Belcher gastrectomy (Derivation undetermined): Medicine. See: Stedman.

Belcher (handkerchief) (Belcher, James): Fashion. See: Brewer; Charnock; Harvey.

BELCHER, JAMES. 1781-1811. English pugilist. See: Dict. Nat. Biog. Belcher (handkerchief), Belcher ring.

Belcher ring (Belcher, James): Fashion. See: Hendrickson.

Belcher's chorus (Derivation undetermined): Zoology. See: Gray.

Belding's yellowthroat (Derivation undetermined): Zoology. See: Gray.

BELFIELD, WILLIAM THOMAS. 1856-1929. American surgeon. See: Who's Who Amer. Med. Belfield's operation.

Belfield's operation (Belfield, William Thomas): Medicine. See: Dorland; Stedman.

Belisha beacon (or Hore-Belisha) (Hore-Belisha, Leslie): Generic Word. See: Brewer; Hendrickson; Partridge; Webster's 3d.

Belitski's reducer (Derivation undetermined): Photography. See: Focal Encyc. Photog.

Belknap chloride washer (Derivation undetermined): Engineering and Industry. See: Thrush.

Belknap process (Derivation undetermined): Engineering and Industry. See: Thrush.

Belknap scandal (Belknap, William Worth): History. See: Smith.

BELKNAP, WILLIAM WORTH. 1829-1890. American army officer and politician. See: Dict. Amer. Biog. Belknap scandal.

BELL. No dates. Army officer. (Biography source unavailable.) Bell harp.

Bell adjustment inventory (Bell, Hugh McKee): Psychology. See: Chaplin; Wolman.

BELL, ALEXANDER GRAHAM. 1847-1922. Scottish-born American inventor. See: Dict. Sci. Biog. Bel, decibel.

BELL, ANDREW. 1753-1832. Scottish clergyman and educator. See: Dict. Nat. Biog. Bell system.

BELL, CHARLES. 1774-1842. Scottish anatomist. See: Internat. Encyc. Soc. Sci. Bell-Magendie law, Bell's nerve, Bell's palsy, Bell's phenomenon, Bell's spasm.

Bell dresser (Derivation undetermined): Engineering and Industry. See: Thrush.

Bell harp (Bell): Music. See: Scholes.

BELL, HUGH MCKEE. 1902- . American psychologist. See: Amer. Men Sci., 9th ed., vol. 3. Bell adjustment inventory.

BELL, ISAAC LOWTHIAN. 1816-1904. English metallurgical chemist. See: World Who's Who Sci. Bell-Krupp process, Bell's dephosphorizing process.

BELL, J. G. 1812-1889. American physician and ornithologist. (Biography source unavailable.) Bell's greenlet, Bell's sparrow, Bell's vireo.

BELL, JOHN. 1763-1820. Scottish surgeon and anatomist. See: Dict. Nat. Biog. Bell's muscle.

Bell-Krupp process (Bell, Isaac Lowthian and Krupp family). See: Krupp process.

BELL, LUTHER VOSE. 1806-1862. American physician. See: Dict. Amer. Biog. Bell's disease (or mania).

Bell-Magendie law (Bell, Charles and Magendie, Francois): Medicine. See: Chaplin; Webster's 3d.; Wolman. Also known as: Bell's law.

Bell reagent for alum in flour (Derivation undetermined): Chemistry. See: Van Nostrand Chem. Dict.

Bell reagent for curcuma (Derivation undetermined): Chemistry. See: Van Nostrand Chem. Dict.

Bell system (Bell, Andrew): Education. Cited in: Webster's Biog. Dict.

BELL, W. R. No dates. Prospector in Tasmania. Cited in: Min. Mag., vol. 14 (1907) p. 395. Bellite.

BELL, WILLIAM BLAIR. 1871-1936. English gynecologist. See: Who's Who, 1936 under "Blair-Bell, William." Bell's calcimeter; Bell's treatment.

Bell-Young helicopter (Derivation undetermined): Engineering and Industry. Cited in: Van Nostrand Sci. Encyc. under "Helicopter," p. 826.

Bellarmine (beer jug) (Ballarmine, Roberto Francesco Romolo): Generic Word. See: Brewer; Harvey; Hendrickson.

BELLARMINE, ROBERTO FRANCESCO ROMOLO. 1542-1621. Italian prelate. See: Encyc. Brit., 1973. Ballarmine (beer jug).

BELLEROPHON. Greek sun hero. See: Jobes. Bellerophon (mollusks).

Bellerophon (mollusks) (Bellerophon): Zoology. See: Webster's 3d.

Belleville boiler (Belleville, Julien): Engineering and Industry. See: Auger.

BELLEVILLE, J. F. fl. 1866. English? engineer. (Biography source unavailable.) Belleville spring (or washer).

BELLEVILLE, JULIEN. fl. 1855. French engineer. (Biography source unavailable.) Belleville boiler.

Belleville spring (or washer) (Belleville, J. F.): Engineering and Industry. See: Auger; Internat. Dict. Ap. Math.

BELLIER, JEAN. fl. 1886. French chemist. Cited in: Royal Soc. Cat. Sci. Pap., 4th ser. Bellier number?, Bellier reagent for coconut oil?, Bellier reagents for wheat flour?, Bellier test for peanut oil?, Bellier test reaction for dulcin?, Bellier's test (for arachis oil)?, Evers-Bellier test?

Bellier number (Bellier, Jean?): Chemistry. See: Van Nostrand Chem. Dict.

Bellier reagent for coconut oil (Bellier, Jean?): Chemistry. See: Van Nostrand Chem. Dict.

Bellier reagents for wheat flour (Bellier, Jean?): Chemistry. See: Van Nostrand Chem. Dict.

Bellier test for peanut oil (Bellier, Jean?): Chemistry. See: Van Nostrand Chem. Dict.

Bellier test reaction for dulcin (Bellier, Jean?): Chemistry. See: Van Nostrand Chem. Dict.

Bellier's test (for arachis oil) (Bellier, Jean?): Chemistry. See: Hackh.

BELLINGER, HERMAN CARL. d. 1940. Metallurgist. Cited in: Min. Mag., vol. 26 (1943) p. 334. Bellingerite.

Bellingerite (Bellinger, Herman Carl): Earth Sciences. See: Thrush; Webster's 3d.

BELLINI, LORENZO. 1643-1704. Italian physician and anatomist. See: Dict. Sci. Biog. Bellini's duct, Bellini's ligament, Bellini's tube (or tubule).

Bellini-Tosi antenna (Derivation undetermined): Electronics. See: Hughes.

Bellini's duct (Bellini, Lorenzo): Anatomy. See: Dorland; Gray; Henderson.

Bellini's ligament (Bellini, Lorenzo): Anatomy. See: Dorland; Stedman.

Bellini's tube (or tubule) (Bellini, Lorenzo): Anatomy. See: Donath; Webster's 3d.

Bellis engine (Bellis, G.E.): Engineering and Industry. See: Auger.

BELLIS, G. E. 1838-1909. English? engineer. (Biography source unavailable.) Bellis engine.

Bellite (Bell, W. R.): Chemistry. See: Thrush.

BELLOC, JEAN JACQUES. 1732-1807. French surgeon. See: Nouv. Biog. Univ. Belloc's cannula (or sound).

Belloc's cannula (or sound) (Belloc, Jean Jacques): Medicine. See: Dorland; Stedman.

Bellona (Bellona, the goddess): Generic Word. See: Partridge; Weekley.

BELLONA, THE GODDESS. Roman goddess of war. See: Oxford Clas. Dict. Bellona.

Bell's calcimeter (Bell, William Blair): Medicine. See: Stedman.

Bell's dephosphorizing process (Bell, Isaac Lowthian): Chemistry. See: Thrush; Van Nostrand Chem. Dict.

Bell's disease (or mania) (Bell, Luther Vose): Medicine. See: Dorland; Hinsie; Jablonski.

Bell's greenlet (Bell, J. G.): Zoology. See: Mathews, M. M.

Bell's law (Bell, Charles). See: Bell-Magendie law.

Bell's muscle (Bell, John): Medicine. See: Dorland; Stedman.

Bell's nerve (Bell, Charles): Medicine. See: Dorland; Stedman.

Bell's palsy (Bell, Charles): Medicine. See: Dorland; Jablonski; Stedman.

Bell's phenomenon (Bell, Charles): Medicine. See: Dorland; Stedman.

Bell's sparrow (Bell, J. G.): Zoology. See: Mathews, M. M.; Pennak; Webster's 3d.

Bell's spasm (Bell, Charles): Medicine. See: Stedman.

Bell's treatment (Bell, William Blair): Medicine. See: Dorland.

Bell's vireo (Bell, J. G.): Zoology. See: Gray; Mathews, M. M.; Webster's 3d.

BELLUCCI, ITALO. b. 1878. Italian chemist. See: Pogg., vol. 5. Bellucci reagent?

Bellucci reagent (Bellucci, Italo?): Chemistry. See: Van Nostrand Chem. Dict.

Beloe report (Beloe, Robert): Education. See: Good.

BELOE, ROBERT. 1905-   . English educator. See: Who's Who, 1960. Beloe report.

BELOKON, A. N. fl. 1938. Russian chemist. Cited in: Chem. Abstr., vol. 32, p. 4467. Shemyakin-Belokon micro-reactions.

BELON, PIERRE. 1517-1564. French naturalist. See: Dict. Sci. Biog. Belonidae, Beloniformes, Belonorhynchii.

Belonidae (Belon, Pierre): Zoology. See: Pennak.

Beloniformes (Belon, Pierre): Zoology. See: Pennak.

Belonorhynchii (Belon, Pierre): Zoology. See: Pennak.

BELOV, NIKOLAI VASILEVICH. 1891-   . Russian crystallographer. See: World Who's Who Sci. Belovite.

Belovite (Belov, Nikolai Vasilevich): Earth Sciences. See: Thrush.

BELPAIRE, A. 1820-1893. Belgian? engineer. See: Loc. Rail. Carr. Review, vol. 38 (1932) pp. 313-16. Belpaire firebox.

Belpaire firebox (Belpaire, A.): Engineering and Industry. See: Auger.

Belshazzar. See: Balthazar.

Beltrami differential parameters (Beltrami, Eugenio): Mathematics. See: Internat. Dict. Ap. Math.

Beltrami-Enneper theorem (Betrami, Eugenio and Enneper, Alfred?): Mathematics. See: Internat. Dict. Ap. Math.

BELTRAMI, EUGENIO. 1835-1900. Italian mathematician and physicist. See: Dict. Sci. Biog. Beltrami differential parameters, Beltrami-Enneper theorem, Beltrami flow, Beltrami-Michell compatibility equations.

Beltrami flow (Beltrami, Eugenio): Physics. See: Huschke; Internat. Dict. Ap. Math.

Beltrami-Michell compatibility equations (Beltrami, Eugenio and Michell, John Henry): Physics. See: Internat. Dict. Ap. Math.

Belt's corpuscle (Derivation undetermined): Biology. See: Gray.

BELTZER, FRANCIS J. G. 1866-1912. French chemist. See: Pogg., vol. 5. Beltzer reagent?

Beltzer reagent (Beltzer, Francis J.G.?): Chemistry. See: Van Nostrand Chem. Dict.

Belugou imperfection coefficient (Derivation undetermined): Engineering and Industry. See: Thrush.

BELYNSKI, S.V. fl. 1908. Russian metallurgist. Cited in: Chem. Abstr., Decenn. Index. Belynski's reagent?

Belynski's reagent (Belynski, S.V.?): Chemistry. See: Thrush.

BEMBO, PIETRO. 1470-1547. Italian writer and ecclesiastic. See: Encyc. Brit., 1973. Bembo (type face).

Bembo (type face) (Bembo, Pietro): Printing. See: Harrod.

BEMENT, CLARENCE SWEET. 1843-1923. American manufacturer and mineral collector. See: Dict. Amer. Biog. Bementite.

Bementite (Bement, Clarence Sweet): Earth Sciences. See: Thrush; Webster's 3d.

BEMPORAD, AZEGLIO. 1875-1945. Italian mathematician. See: Pogg., vol. 5. Bemporad's formula?

Bemporad's formula (Bemporad, Azeglio?): Earth Sciences. See: Huschke.

Ben Day (process) (or Ben Dayed) (Day, Benjamin): Printing. See: Harrod; Hendrickson; Mathews, M. M.

Benard cell (Benard, Henri): Physics. See: Huschke; Internat. Dict. Ap. Math.; Internat. Dict. Phys. Elec.

BENARD, HENRI. fl. 1911. French physicist. See: Pogg., vol. 5. Benard cell.

Bence Jones albumin (Bence Jones, Henry): Medicine. See: Dorland.

Bence Jones' albuminosuria (Bence Jones, Henry): Medicine. See: Dorland; Jablonski. Also known as: Bradshaw's albumosuria.

Bence Jones bodies (Bence Jones, Henry): Medicine. See: Dorland.

Bence Jones cylinders (Bence Jones, Henry): Medicine. See: Dorland; Stedman.

BENCE JONES, HENRY. 1814-1873. English physician. See: Encyc. Brit., 1911. Bence Jones albumin, Bence Jones' albuminosuria, Bence Jones bodies, Bence Jones cylinders, Bence-Jones protein, Bence Jones reaction.

Bence-Jones protein (Bence Jones, Henry): Medicine. See: Dorland; Hackh; Stedman.

Bence Jones reaction (Bence Jones, Henry): Medicine. See: Dorland; Stedman.

BENDA, CARL. 1857-1933. German physician. See: Biog. Lex. hervorr. Aerzte, 1880-1930. Benda solution, Benda stain.

Benda masks (Benda, Wladyslaw Theodor): Applied Arts. Cited in: Webster's Biog. Dict.

Benda solution (Benda, Carl): Chemistry. See: Van Nostrand Chem. Dict.

Benda stain (Benda, Carl): Chemistry. See: Van Nostrand Chem. Dict.

BENDA, WLADYSLAW THEODOR. 1873-1943. Polish-born American painter and illustrator. See: Webster's Biog. Dict. Benda masks.

Bendelari jig (Derivation undetermined): Engineering and Industry. See: Thrush.

Bender-Gestalt test (Bender, Lauretta): Psychology. See: Chaplin; English; Hinsie.

BENDER, LAURETTA. 1897- . American psychiatrist. See: World Who's Who Sci. Bender-Gestalt test.

Bendideia (Bendis): Generic Word (festival). See: Canney.

BENDIEN, SALOMO GERHARD TEKLA. b. 1873. Dutch physician. (Biography source unavailable.) Bendien's test.

Bendien's test (Bendien, Salomo Gerhard Tekla): Medicine. See: Dorland.

Bendigo (fur cap) (Thompson, William "Bendigo"): Fashion. See: Hendrickson; Partridge.

BENDIRE, CHARLES EMIL. 1836-1897? German ornithologist. See: Sci., vol. 5 (1897) pp. 261-62, 304. Bendire's thrasher.

Bendire's thrasher (Bendire, Charles Emil): Zoology. See: Gray.

BENDIS. Thracian moon goddess. See: Oxford Clas. Dict. Bendideia.

Bendix electric self-starter (Bendix, Vincent): Engineering and Industry. Cited in: Webster's Biog. Dict.

BENDIX, MAX. 1866-1945. American orchestra conductor. See: Webster's Biog. Dict. Bendix Music Bureau, Max Bendix String Quartet.

Bendix Music Bureau (Bendix, Max): Music. Cited in: Webster's Biog. Dict.

BENDIX, VINCENT. 1882-1945. American inventor and industrialist. See: Encyc. Brit., Bk. Yr., vol. 9. Bendix electric self-starter.

Benedek's reflex (Derivation undetermined): Medicine. See: Stedman.

Benedick (Benedick of Padua): Generic Word (married man): See: Charnock; Hendrickson; Partridge.

BENEDICK OF PADUA. Character in William Shakespeare's play, "Much Ado About Nothing." See: Benet. Benedick.

BENEDICT, A. L. 1865-1936. American gastro-enterologist. See: Who's Who Amer. Med. Benedict's test (1).

Benedict acetate reagent (Benedict, Stanley Rossiter): Chemistry. See: Van Nostrand Chem. Dict.

Benedict Arnold (Arnold, Benedict): Generic Word (traitor). See: Hendrickson; Mathews, M.M.

Benedict-Behre test reaction for creatinine (Benedict, Stanley Rossiter and Behre, Jeannette Allen): Chemistry. See: Van Nostrand Chem. Dict.

Benedict-Denis sulfur reagent (Benedict, Stanley Rossiter and Denis, Willey Glover?): Chemistry. See: Van Nostrand Chem. Dict.

BENEDICT, FRANCIS GANO. 1870-1957. American chemist and physiologist. See: Dict. Sci. Biog. Benedict-Roth apparatus (or calorimeter).

Benedict-Hopkins-Cole reagent (Benedict, Stanley Rossiter; Hopkins, Sir Frederick Gowland; and Cole, Sydney William): Chemistry. See: Stedman, Van Nostrand Chem. Dict.

BENEDICT, MANSON. 1907- . American chemical engineer. See: World Who's Who Sci. Benedict-Webb-Rubin equation.

BENEDICT OF NURSIA, SAINT. 480-543. Monastic founder. See: Encyc. Brit., 1973. Benedictines, Medal of St. Benedict, Oblate of St. Benedict, Rule of St. Benedict, Sanbenito (or Sanbenite).

Benedict reagent for barium, strontium and calcium (Benedict, Stanley Rossiter): Chemistry. See: Van Nostrand Chem. Dict.

Benedict-Roth apparatus (or calorimeter) (Benedict, Francis Gano and Roth, Paul?): Medicine. See: Stedman.

BENEDICT, RUTH FULTON. 1887-1948. American anthropologist. See: Internat. Encyc. Soc. Sci. Benedict's culture patterns.

BENEDICT, SAMUEL. fl. 1894. American socialite. (Biography source unavailable.) eggs Benedict.

Benedict solution (Benedict, Stanley Rossiter): Chemistry. See: Ballentyne, Hackh, Van Nostrand Chem. Dict.

BENEDICT, STANLEY ROSSITER. 1884-1936. American chemist. See: World Who's Who Sci. Benedict acetate reagent, Benedict-Behre test reaction for creatinine, Benedict-Denis sulfur reagent, Benedict-Hopkins-Cole reagent, Benedict reagent for barium, strontium, and calcium, Benedict solution, Benedict sulfur reagent, Benedict uric acid reagent, Benedict's test for glucose.

Benedict sulfur reagent (Benedict, Stanley Rossiter): Chemistry. See: Van Nostrand Chem. Dict.

Benedict the Moor. See: Benoit, Saint.

Benedict uric acid reagent (Benedict, Stanley Rossiter): Chemistry. See: Van Nostrand Chem. Dict.

Benedict-Webb-Rubin equation (Benedict, Manson; Webb, George Barlow; and Rubin, Louis Carl): Engineering and Industry. See: Internat. Dict. Ap. Math.

Benedictines (Benedict of Nursia, Saint): Religion. See: Attwater; Canney; Mathews, S.

Benedictional of St. Aethelwold (Aethelwold, Saint): Art. See: Osborne under "Illuminated Manuscripts."

Benedict's culture patterns (Benedict, Ruth Fulton): Anthropology. See: Zadrozny.

Benedict's test (1) (Benedict, A. L.): Medicine. See: Dorland;

Benedict's test for glucose (Benedict, Stanley Rossiter): Chemistry. See: Stedman; Webster's 3d.

BENEDIKT, MORITZ. 1835-1920. Austrian physician. See: Wer Ist's, 1906. Benedikt's syndrome.

Benedikt's syndrome (Benedikt, Mortiz): Medicine. See: Dorland; Hinsie; Jablonski.

Benfield process (Derivation undetermined): Engineering and Industry. See: Thrush.

Benger's food (Derivation undetermined): Medicine. See: Dorland.

Benham top (Derivation undetermined): Physics. See: Internat. Dict. Phys. Elec.

Benian's stain (Derivation undetermined): Medicine. See: Stedman.

BENINCASA, GIUSEPPE (Orig.: JOSEPH GOEDENHUYSE). ca. 1500-1596. Belgian-born Italian botanist. See: Biog. Notes Upon Botanists. Benincasa (vine).

Benincasa (vine) (Benincasa, Giuseppe): Botany. See: Taylor, N.

BENIOFF, HUGO. 1899-1968. American geophysicist. See: World Who's Who Sci. Banioff seismograph.

Benioff seismograph (Benioff, Hugo): Earth Sciences. Cited in: Van Nostrand Sci. Encyc. under "Earthquake."

BENIQUE, PIERRE JULES. 1806-1851. French urologist. See: World Who's Who Sci. Benique's sound.

Benique's sound (Benique, Pierre Jules): Medicine. See: Dorland; Stedman.

BENJAMIN. Biblical son of Jacob. See: Webster's Biog. Dict. Benjamin (overcoat), Benjamin's mess, Benjamite (or Benjaminite).

BENJAMIN, ERICH. b. 1880. German physician. See: Biog. Lex. hervorr. Aerzte, 1880-1930. Benjamin's syndrome (or anemia).

BENJAMIN, MARCUS. 1837-1932. American museum official and editor. See: Who Was Who Amer., vol. 1. Benjaminite.

Benjamin (overcoat) (Benjamin): Fashion. See: Hendrickson; Partridge; Picken.

Benjaminite (Benjamin, Marcus): Earth Sciences. See: Thrush; Webster's 3d.

Benjamin's mess (Benjamin): Generic Word (largest share). See: Brewer.

Benjamin's syndrome (or anemia) (Benjamin, Erich): Medicine. See: Jablonski.

Benjamite (or Benjaminite) (Benjamin): Religion. See: Webster's 3d.

BENNDORF, HANS. 1870-1953. Swiss physicist. See: World Who's Who Sci. Benndorf law.

Benndorf law (Benndorf, Hans): Physics. Cited in: World Who's Who Sci.

BENNET, JAMES HENRY. 1816-1891. English obstetrician. See: Boase. Bennet's corpuscles.

Bennet's corpuscles (Bennet, James Henry): Medicine. See: Dorland; Stedman.

Bennet's syndrome (Derivation undetermined): Medicine. See: Jablonski.

Bennett angle (Bennett, Norman Godfrey): Medicine. See: Stedman.

Bennett differential aptitude test (Bennett, George Kettner): Psychology. See: Chaplin; Wolman.

BENNETT, EDWARD HALLARAN. 1837-1907. Irish surgeon. See: World Who's Who Sci. Bennett's fracture, Bennett's operation.

Bennett filing plan (Derivation undetermined): Education. See: Good.

BENNETT, GEORGE KETTNER. 1904-   . American psychologist. See: Amer. Men Sci., 9th ed., vol. 3. Bennett differential aptitude test, Bennett test of mechanical comprehension.

BENNETT, JAMES GORDON. 1841-1918. American editor. See: Webster's Biog. Dict. Gordon Bennett international trophies, Gordon Bennett race.

BENNETT, JOHN HUGHES. 1812-1876. English physician. See: Dict. Nat. Biog. Bennett's disease.

BENNETT, JOHN JOSEPH. 1801-1876. English botanist. See: Dict. Nat. Biog. Bennettitales, Bennettites.

Bennett movement (Bennett, Norman Godfrey): Medicine. See: Stedman.

BENNETT, NORMAN GODFREY. 1870-1947. English dental surgeon. See: Who Was Who, 1941-1950. Bennett angle, Bennett movement.

Bennett test of mechanical comprehension (Bennett, George Kettner): Psychology. See: Chaplin; Wolman.

BENNETT, WILLIAM CROMPTON. No dates. American clergyman. (Biography source unavailable.) Bennett's beatitudes.

Bennettitales (Bennett, John Joseph): Botany. See: Van Nostrand Sci. Encyc. under "Paleobotany."

Bennettites (Bennett, John Joseph): Botany. See: Webster's 3d.

Bennett's beatitudes (Bennett, William Crompton): Sociology. See: Martin.

Bennett's disease (Bennett, John Hughes): Medicine. See: Dorland; Jablonski; Stedman.

Bennett's fracture (Bennett, Edward Hallaran): Medicine. See: Dorland; Jablonski; Stedman.

Bennett's operation (Bennett, Edward Hallaran): Medicine. See: Dorland.

BENNINGHOFF, ALFRED. b. 1890. German physician. See: Biog. Lex. hervorr. Aerzte, 1880-1930. Benninghoff's lines?

Benninghoff's lines (Benninghoff, Alfred?): Anthropology. See: Winick.

BENOIST, LOUIS. b. 1856. French physicist. See: Pogg., vol. 4. Benoist test, Benoist's scale.

Benoist test (Benoist, Louis): Chemistry. See: Van Nostrand Chem. Dict.

Benoist's scale (Benoist, Louis): Medicine. See: Dorland; Stedman.

BENOIT, SAINT. 1526-1589. Sicilian monk. See: Holweck under "Benedict the Moor." Saint Benoit.

BENSAUDE, RAOUL. 1866-1938. French physician. See: World Who's Who Sci. Launois-Bensaude syndrome?

Bensch's rail (Derivation undetermined): Zoology. See: Gray.

BENSLEY, ROBERT RUSSELL. 1867-1956. Canadian-born American anatomist. See: Dict. Sci. Biog. Bensley's specific granules.

Bensley's specific granules (Bensley, Robert Russell): Medicine. See: Stedman.

BENSON, ARTHUR H. 1860-1912. English ophthalmologist. See: World Who's Who Sci. Benson's disease.

Benson boiler (1) (Benson, Martin): Engineering and Industry. See: Auger; Internat. Dict. Ap. Math.

Benson boiler (2) (Benson, Mark): Engineering and Industry. See: Auger.

BENSON, FRANCIS COLGATE, JR. 1872-1941. American physician. See: World Who's Who Sci. Craig-Benson operation.

BENSON, MARK. fl. 1923. English engineer. (Biography source unavailable.) Benson boiler (2).

BENSON, MARTIN. fl. 1858. English? engineer. (Biography source unavailable.) Benson boiler (1).

Benson's disease (Benson, Arthur H.): Medicine. See: Dorland; Jablonski; Stedman.

BENSTON, O. J. No dates. Mineralogist. Cited in: Min. Mag., vol. 32 (1961), p. 989. Benstonite.

Benstonite (Benston, O. J.): Earth Sciences. See: Thrush.

BENTHAM, JEREMY. 1748-1832. English jurist and philosopher. See: Intenat. Encyc. Soc. Sci. Benthamism (or Benthamist).

BENTHAM, SIR SAMUEL. 1757-1831. English naval architect and engineer. See: Dict. Nat. Biog. Bentham's woodworking machinery.

Benthamism (or Benthamist) (Bentham, Jeremy): Philosophy. See: Partridge; Webster's 3d, Weekley.

Bentham's woodworking machinery (Bentham, Sir Samuel): Engineering and Industry. See: Auger.

Bentinck boom (Bentinck, John Albert): Engineering and Industry. See: Webster's 3d.

BENTINCK, JOHN ALBERT. 1737-1775. English naval officer. See: Dict. Nat. Biog. Bentinck boom, Bentinck (sail) .

Bentinck reforms (Bentinck, William Cavendish): History. See: Morris and Irwin.

Bentinck (sail) (Bentinck, John Albert): Engineering and Industry. See: Webster's 3d.

BENTINCK, WILLIAM CAVENDISH. 1774-1839. Governor-general of India. See: Dict. Nat. Biog. Bentinck reforms.

BENTINCK, WILLIAM HENRY CAVENDISH, 3D DUKE OF PORTLAND. 1738-1809. English statesman. See: Dict. Nat. Biog. Portland vase.

BENTLEY, EDMUND CLERIHEW. 1875-1956. English writer. See: Webster's Biog. Dict. Clerihew (verse).

BENTON, ARTHUR LESTER. 1909- . American psychologist. See: Amer. Men Sci., 9th ed., vol. 3. Benton visual retention tests.

BENTON, THOMAS HART. 1782-1858. American political leader. See: Dict. Amer. Biog. Bentonian delegation, Bentonite.

Benton visual retention tests (Benton, Arthur Lester): Psychology. See: Wolman.

Bentonian delegation (Benton, Thomas Hart): History. See: Mathews, M. M.

Bentonite (Benton, Thomas Hart): History. See: Mathews, M. M.

Bentzen test (Bentzen, Th.?): Chemistry. See: Van Nostrand Chem. Dict.

BENTZEN, TH. fl. 1925. American? chemist. Cited in: Chem. Abstr. Decenn. Index. Bentzen test?

Benz engine (Benz, Karl Friedrich): Engineering and Industry. See: Auger.

BENZ, KARL FRIEDRICH. 1844-1929. German engineer. See: World Who's Who Sci. Benz engine.

BEOC, SAINT. fl. 5th or 6th c. Irish abbot. See: Holweck. Daboecia (or Saint Daboec's heath).

BERANECK, EDMOND. 1859-1920. Swiss bacteriologist. See: Biog. Lex. hervorr. Aerzte, 1880-1930. Beraneck's tuberculin.

Beraneck's tuberculin (Beraneck, Edmond): Medicine. See: Dorland; Stedman.

BERARD, AUGUSTE. 1802-1846. French surgeon. See: World Who's Who Sci. Berard's aneurysm, Berard's ligament.

BERARD, JACQUES ETIENNE. 1779-1869. French physicist and chemist. See: Dict. Sci. Biog. law of Delaroche and Berard.

BERARDINELLI, WALDEMAR. 1903-1956. Argentinian physician. See: New York Acad. Med. Portrait Cat. Berardinelli's syndrome.

Berardinelli's syndrome (Berardinelli, Waldemar): Medicine. See: Jablonski. Also known as: Seip-Berardinelli syndrome, Seip's syndrome.

Berard's aneurysm (Berard, Auguste): Medicine. See: Dorland; Stedman.

Berard's ligament (Berard, Auguste): Medicine. See: Dorland.

BERAUD, BRUNO JEAN JACQUES. 1823-1865. French surgeon. Cited in: Royal Soc. Cat. Sci. Pap. Beraud's valve.

Beraud's valve (Beraud, Bruno Jean Jacques): Medicine. See: Dorland; Stedman. Also known as: Krause's valve.

BERCHEM, M. No dates. French botanist. (Biography source unavailable.) Berchemia (vines).

Berchemia (vines) (Berchem, M.): Botany. See: Taylor, N.

BERENBERG, WILLIAM. 1915- . American physician. See: Amer. Men Sci., 10th ed. Neuhauser-Berenberg syndrome.

BERENGAR OF TOURS (BERENGARIUS). 998-1088. French scholastic theologian. See: Encyc. Brit., 1973. heresy of Berengarius.

BERENGER, RENE. 1830-1915. French jurist and legislator. See: Webster's Biog. Dict. Loi Berenger.

Berenice (Berenice II): Chemistry (amber). See: Charnock; Hendrickson.

BERENICE II. d. 216 B.C. Egyptian queen. See: Nouv. Biog. Univ. Berenice.

Berenice, Saint. See: Veronica, Saint.

BERG, A. fl. 1904. French chemist. See: Pogg., vol. 5. Berg reaction for aldehyde sugars, Berg reagent.

Berg method (Derivation undetermined): Engineering and Industry. See: Thrush.

Berg reaction for aldehyde sugars (Berg, A.): Chemistry. See: Van Nostrand Chem. Dict.

Berg reagent (Berg, A.): Chemistry. See: Van Nostrand Chem. Dict.

Berg reagent for bismuth (Berg, Richard Hermann): Chemistry. See: Van Nostrand Chem. Dict.

Berg reagent for separating metals (Berg, Richard Hermann): Chemistry. See: Van Nostrand Chem. Dict.

BERG, RICHARD HERMANN. b. 1889. German chemist. See: Pogg., vol. 6. Berg reagent for bismuth, Berg reagent for separating metals, Berg-Teitelbaum test reaction for selenite.

Berg-Teitelbaum test reaction for selenite (Berg, Richard Hermann and Teitelbaum, M.): Chemistry. See: Van Nostrand Chem. Dict.

BERGE, HENRI. d. 1911. Belgian? chemist. See: Sci., vol. 33 (1911), p. 723. Berge reagent for wood fiber in paper?

BERGE, PER O. 1903- . Swedish actuary. See: Vem Ar Det, 1975. Berge's inequality.

Berge reagent for wood fiber in paper (Berge, Henri?): Chemistry. See: Van Nostrand Chem. Dict.

BERGEL, FRANZ. 1900- . Austrian chemist. See: World Who's Who Sci. Barger-Bergel-Todd test reaction.

BERGELL, PETER GEORG F. b. 1875. German chemist. Cited in: Chem. Abstr., vol. 8, p. 2404. Bergell reagent for proteins.

Bergell reagent for proteins (Bergell, Peter Georg F.): Chemistry. See: Van Nostrand Chem. Dict.

Bergen, Karl August von. See: Von Bergen, Karl August.

BERGENHEM, BENGT. 1898- . Swedish surgeon. (Biography source unavailable.) Bergenhem's operation.

Bergenhem's operation (Bergenhem, Bengt): Medicine. See: Dorland; Stedman.

Bergenia (herbs) (Von Bergen, Karl August): Botany. See: Taylor, N.; Webster's 3d.

BERGER. fl. 1928. German chemist. Cited in: Chem. Abstr., vol. 23, p. 4909. Berger reagent for differentiating benzene from benzine.

BERGER, ALWIN. 1871-1931. German horticulturist and botanist. See: Biog. Notes Upon Botanists. Bergerocactus.

Berger cells (Derivation undetermined): Medicine. See: Stedman.

BERGER, EMIL. 1855-1926. Austrian ophthalmologist. See: World Who's Who Sci. Berger's sign (or symptom).

BERGER, HANS. 1873-1941. German neurologist. See: Dict. Sci. Biog. Berger rhythm.

BERGER, JOHANN ERICH VON. 1772-1832. German professor. See: Pogg., vol. 1, Bergera?

BERGER, OSKAR. 1845-1908. German physician. See: Allg. Deut. Biog. Berger's paresthesia.

BERGER, PAUL. 1845-1908. French surgeon. See: World Who's Who Sci. Berger amputation, Berger's method, Berger's operation.

BERGER, RAOUL. fl. 1938. French chemist. Cited in: Chem. Abstr., vol. 32, p. 4908. Paget-Berger test.

Berger reagent for differentiating benzene from benzine (Berger): Chemistry. See: Van Nostrand Chem. Dict.

Berger rhythm (Berger, Hans): Medicine. See: Chaplin; Dorland; English.

Bergera (Berger, Johann Erich von?): Botany. See: Charnock.

BERGERAC, CYRANO DE. 1619-1655. French soldier, author, and hero of play by Edmond Rostand. See: Benet. Cyrano de Bergerac.

Bergerocactus (Berger, Alwin): Botany. See: Taylor, N.

Bergeron classification (Bergeron, Tor Harold Percival): Earth Sciences. See: Huschke, Van Nostrand Sci. Encyc. under "Air Mass."

BERGERON, ETIENNE JULES. 1817-1900. French physician. See: Biog. Lex. hervorr. Aerzte. Bergeron's disease (or chorea).

Bergeron-Findeisen theory (Bergeron, Tor Harold Percival and Findeisen, Walter): Earth Sciences. See: Huschke; Van Nostrand Sci. Encyc. Also known as: Wegener-Bergeron process.

BERGERON, TOR HAROLD PERCIVAL. 1891- . English-born Norwegian meteorologist. See: Pogg., vol. 7b. Bergeron classification, Bergeron-Findeisen theory.

Bergeron's disease (or chorea) (Bergeron, Etienne Jules): Medicine. See: Dorland; Jablonski; Stedman. Also known as: Begbie's disease.

Berger's amputation (Berger, Paul): Medicine. Cited in: World Who's Who Sci.

Berger's method (Berger, Paul): Medicine. See: Dorland.

Berger's operation (Berger, Paul): Medicine. See: Dorland.

Berger's paresthesia (Berger, Oskar): Medicine. See: Jablonski; Stedman.

Berger's sign (or symptom) (Berger, Emil): Medicine. See: Dorland.

Berge's inequality (Berge, Per O.): Statistics. See: Kendall.

BERGH, A. A. HYMANS VAN DEN. 1869-1943. Dutch physician. (Biography source unavailable.) Van den Bergh's disease, Van den Bergh's test.

BERGH, LUDVIG RUDOLPH SOPHUS. b. 1824. Danish physician. See: Biog. Lex. hervorr. Aerzte. Bergh's theory?

BERGHOEFFER, CHRISTIAN W. b. 1859. German librarian. See: Wer Ist's, 1906. Berghoeffer system.

Berghoeffer system (Berghoeffer, Christian W.): Library Science. See: Harrod.

Bergh's theory (Bergh, Ludvig Rudolph Sophus?): Biology. See: Gray.

Bergia (Bergius, Peter-Jonas): Botany. See: Charnock.

BERGIUS, FRIEDRICH KARL RUDOLPH. 1884-1949. German industrial chemist. See: Dict. Sci. Biog. Bergius process (or Berginization), Bergius-Willstatter saccharification process.

BERGIUS, PETER-JONAS. 1730-1790. Swedish botanist. See: World Who's Who Sci. Bergia.

Bergius process (or Berginization) (Bergius, Friedrich Karl Rudolph): Chemistry. See: Hackh; Thrush; Van Nostrand Chem. Dict.

Bergius-Willstaetter saccharification process (Bergius, Friedrich Karl Rudolph and Willstaetter, Richard): Chemistry. See: Van Nostrand Chem. Dict.

BERGLOEF. fl. 1914. Swedish chemist. Cited in: Chem. Abstr. vol. 10, p. 1501. Bergloef process?

Bergloef process (Bergloef): Engineering and Industry. See: Thrush.

BERGMAN, TORBERN OLOF. 1735-1784. Swedish analytical chemist and physicist. See: Dict. Sci. Biog. Bergmanite? Torbernite.

Bergmanite (Bergman, Torbern Olof?): Earth Sciences. See: Charnock.

Bergmann azlactone peptide synthesis (Bergmann, Max): Chemistry. See: Van Nostrand Chem. Dict.

Bergmann Bayard 9mm automatic pistol (Bergmann, Theodore): Weapons. See: Quick.

BERGMANN, CARL GEORG LUCAS CHRISTIAN. 1814-1865. German biologist. See: Pogg., vol. 7a. Bergmann's law (principle or rule).

Bergmann degradation (Bergmann, Max): Chemistry. See: Van Nostrand Chem. Dict.

BERGMANN, ERNST VON. 1836-1907. German surgeon. See: Encyc. Brit., 1973. Bergmann's incision.

BERGMANN, GOTTLIEB HEINRICH. 1781-1860. German neurologist and anatomist. See: Biog. Lex. hervorr. Aerzte. Bergmann's cords, Bergmann's fibers.

BERGMANN, GUSTAV VON. 1878-1955. German physician. See: Webster's Biog. Dict. Bergmann's syndrome.

BERGMANN, MAX. 1886-1945. German chemist. See: Pogg., vol. 6. Bergmann azlactone peptide synthesis, Bergmann degradation, Bergmann method (of polypeptide synthesis), Bergmann-Zervas carbobenzoxy method.

Bergmann method (of polypeptide synthesis) (Bergmann, Max): Chemistry. See: Ballentyne.

Bergmann series (Derivation undetermined): Physics. See: Internat. Dict. Ap. Math.

BERGMANN, THEODORE. fl. 1903. Dutch? inventor. (Biography source unavailable.) Bergmann Bayard 9mm automatic pistol.

Bergmann-Zervas carbobenzoxy method (Bergmann, Max and Zervas, Leonidas): Chemistry. See: Van Nostrand Chem. Dict.

Bergmann's cords (Bergmann, Gottlieb Heinrich): Medicine. See: Dorland; Stedman.

Bergmann's fibers (Bergmann, Gottlieb Heinrich): Medicine. See: Dorland; Stedman.

Bergmann's incision (Bergmann, Ernst von): Medicine. See: Dorland; Stedman.

Bergmann's law (principle or rule) (Bergmann, Carl Georg Lucas Christian): Biology. See: Gray; Pennak; Winick.

Bergmann's syndrome (Bergmann, Gustav von): Medicine. See: Jablonski.

BERGMEISTER, OTTO. 1845-1918. Austrian physician. See: Biog. Lex. hervorr. Aerzte., 1880-1930. Bergmeister's papilla?

Bergmeister's papilla (Bergmeister, Otto?): Medicine. See: Jablonski; Stedman.

BERGONIE, JEAN-ALBAN. 1857-1925. French physician. See: Biog. Lex. hervorr. Aerzte, 1880-1930. Bergonie method (or treatment).

Bergonie method (or treatment) (Bergonie, Jean-Alban): Medicine. See: Dorland; Stedman.

BERGSMAN, ENAR BOERJE. 1913- . Swedish metallurgist. See: Who's Who Sci. Europe. Bergsman tester.

Bergsman tester (Bergsman, Enar Boerje): Engineering and Industry. See: Auger.

BERGSON, HENRI LOUIS. 1859-1941. French philosopher. See: Dict. Sci. Biog. Bergsonian (or Bergsonism).

Bergsonian (or Bergsonism) (Bergson, Henri Louis): Philosophy. See: Partridge; Webster's 3d.

BERGSTRAND, HILDING. b. 1886. Swedish physician. See: Biog. Lex. hervorr. Aerzte, 1880-1930. Bergstrand's disease.

Bergstrand's disease (Bergstrand, Hilding). Medicine. See: Jablonski.

Beringer test for acetanilid in acetophenetidin (Derivation undetermined): Chemistry. See: Van Nostrand Chem. Dict.

Beringer test reaction for salophen (Derivation undetermined): Chemistry. See: Van Nostrand Chem. Dict.

Beringer test reactions for antipyrine (Derivation undetermined): Chemistry. See: Van Nostrand Chem. Dict.

Berkefeld filter (Berkefeld, Wilhelm). Chemistry. See: Dorland; Hackh; Stedman.

BERKEFELD, WILHELM. 1836-1897. German manufacturer. See: Webster's Biog. Dict. Berkefeld filter.

Berkeley and Hartley method (Berkeley, Randal Thomas Mowbray Rawdon, 8th Earl of and Hartley, Ernald George Justinian): Physics. See: Internat. Dict. Phys. Elec.

Berkeley clay (Derivation undetermined): Earth Sciences. See: Thrush.

BERKELEY, EDMUND C. fl. 1969. American researcher. (Biography source unavailable.) Berkeley's laws of mistakes.

BERKELEY, GEORGE. 1685-1753. Irish philosopher. See: Internat. Encyc. Soc. Sci. Berkeleyism (or Berkeleian).

BERKELEY, MILES JOSEPH. 1803-1889. English botanist. See: Dict. Sci. Biog. Berkeleya (sea-weeds).

BERKELEY, RANDAL THOMAS MOWBRAY RAWDON, 8TH EARL OF. 1865-1942. English physicist. See: Pogg., vol. 5. Berkeley and Hartley method.

Berkeleya (sea-weeds) (Berkeley, Miles Joseph): Botany. See: Charnock.

Berkeleyism (or Berkeleian) (Berkeley, George): Philosophy. See: Canney; Partridge; Weekley.

Berkeley's laws of mistakes (Berkeley, Edmund C.): Sociology. See: Martin.

BERKEY, CHARLES PETER. 1867-1955. American geologist. See: World Who's Who Sci. Berkeyite.

Berkeyite (Berkey, Charles Peter): Earth Sciences. See: Thrush.

BERKSON, JOSEPH. 1899- . American biometrician. See: Amer. Men Sci., 11th ed. Berksonian line.

Berksonian line (Berkson, Joseph): Statistics. See: Kendall.

BERL, ERNST. 1877-1946. Austrian chemist. See: World Who's Who Sci. Berl process.

Berl process (Berl, Ernst): Chemistry. See: Van Nostrand Chem. Dict.

BERLESE, ANTONIO. 1863-1927. Italian entomologist. See: New York Acad. Med. Portrait Cat. Berlese funnel, Berlese's organ, Berlese's theory.

Berlese funnel (Berlese, Antonio): Zoology. See: Pennak; Webster's 3d.

Berlese's organ (Berlese, Antonio): Zoology. See: Henderson; Pennak.

Berlese's theory (Berlese, Antonio): Zoology. See: Pennak.

BERLIN, CHAIM. fl. 1961. Swiss? physician. (Biography source unavailable.) Berlin's syndrome.

BERLIN, NILS JOHANNES. b. 1812. Swedish chemist and mineralogist. See: Pogg., vol. 1. Berlinite.

BERLIN, RUDOLF. 1833-1897. German oculist. See: Allg. Deut. Biog. Berlin's disease (or edema).

BERLINER, EMILE. 1851-1929. German-born American inventor. See: Dict. Amer. Biog., 1st. suppl. Berliner loose-contact telephone transmitter.

Berliner loose-contact telephone transmitter (Berliner, Emile): Engineering and Industry. Cited in: Webster's Biog. Dict.

Berlinite (Berlin, Nils Johannes). Earth Sciences. See: Webster's 3d.

Berlin's disease (or edema) (Berlin, Rudolf). Medicine. See: Dorland; Jablonski; Stedman.

Berlin's syndrome (Berlin, Chaim): Medicine. See: Jablonski.

BERMAN, HARRY. 1902-1944. American mineralogist. See: Amer. Men Sci., 7th ed. Bermanite.

Berman-Moorhead locator (Berman and Moorhead, John Joseph): Medicine. See: Stedman. Also known as: Moorhead foreign body locator.

Bermanite (Berman, Harry): Earth Sciences. See: Thrush; Webster's 3d.

Bernal chart (Bernal, John Desmond): Physics. See: Thewlis.

BERNAL, JOHN DESMOND. 1901- . Irish-born physicist. See: World Who's Who Sci. Bernal chart.

BERNARD, CLAUDE. 1813-1878. French physiologist. See: Dict. Sci. Biog. Bernard-Horner syndrome, Bernard-Sergent syndrome, Bernard's canal (or duct), Bernard's layer, Bernard's puncture.

Bernard-Horner syndrome (Bernard, Claude and Horner, Johann Friedrich): Medicine. See: Jablonski. Also known as: Bernard's syndrome, Claude Bernard's syndrome, Claude Bernard-Horner syndrome, Horner's symptom complex, Horner's syndrome, Mitchell's syndrome.

BERNARD, JEAN. 1907- . French hematologist. See: Who's Who Sci. Europe. Bernard-Soulier syndrome, Bernard's syndrome.

BERNARD OF CLAIRVAUX, SAINT. 1091-1153. French ecclesiastic. See: Encyc. Brit., 1973. Bernardines, rhythm of St. Bernard, St. Bernard (dog), St. Bernard's lily.

BERNARD OF TIRON, SAINT. d. 1117. French abbot. See: Holweck. Order of Tiron.

Bernard-Sergent syndrome (Bernard, Claude and Sergent, Emile): Medicine. See: Stedman.

Bernard-Soulier syndrome (Bernard, Jean and Soulier, Jean Pierre). See: Glanzmann's syndrome.

BERNARDI, ALESSANDRO GIOVANNI TITO MARIO. 1886-1953. Italian chemist. See: Pogg., vol. 6. Bernardi-Tartarini test for vanillin and piperonal in sugar solutions.

Bernardi-Tartarini test for vanillin and piperonal in sugar solutions (Bernardi, Alessandro Giovanni Tito Mario and Tartarini, M.): Chemistry. See: Van Nostrand Chem. Dict.

Bernardines (Bernard of Clairvaux, Saint): Religion. See: Attwater; Canney; Mathews, S.

Bernardo's process (Derivation undetermined): Engineering and Industry. See: Thrush.

Bernard's canal (or duct) (Bernard, Claude): Medicine. See: Donath; Dorland; Stedman. Also known as: Santorini's duct (or canal).

Bernard's layer (Bernard, Claude): Medicine. See: Dorland.

Bernard's puncture (Bernard, Claude): Medicine. See: Dorland; Stedman.

Bernard's syndrome (Bernard, Claude). See: Bernard-Horner syndrome.

Bernard's syndrome (Bernard, Jean): Medicine. See: Jablonski.

BERNAY, AUGUSTUS CHARLES. 1854-1907. American surgeon. See: Dict. Amer. Biog. Bernay's sponge.

BERNAYS, PAUL (In full: ISAAK PAUL). b. 1888. German mathematician. See: Pogg., vols. 5, 6, 7a. Neumann-Bernays-Goedel axioms.

Bernay's sponge (Bernay, Augustus Charles): Medicine. See: Dorland; Stedman.

Bernbeck test (Derivation undetermined): Chemistry. See: Van Nostrand Chem. Dict.

Bernede reagent (Derivation undetermined): Chemistry. See: Van Nostrand Chem. Dict.

Bernesque poetry (Berni, Francesco): Literature. See: Brewer; Stenhouse; Wagner (More Names).

BERNHARD, J. fl. 1931. Geologist. (Biography source unavailable.) Bernhard's index of concentration.

Bernhard's index of concentration (Bernhard, J.): Earth Sciences. See: Monkhouse.

BERNHARDT, MARTIN. 1844-1915. German neurologist. See: Wer Ist's., 1906. Rot-Bernhardt disease.

BERNHARDT, SARAH ("SALLY BEE"). 1844-1923. French actress. See: Encyc. Brit., 1973. Sally Bee, Sarah Bernhardt.

Bernhardt sleeve (Derivation undetermined): Fashion. See: Picken.

Bernhardt's disease (Bernhardt, Martin). See: Rot-Bernhardt disease.

Bernhardt's formula (Derivation undetermined): Medicine. See: Stedman.

BERNHEIM, HIPPOLYTE. 1840-1919. French psychologist. See: Dict. Sci. Biog. Bernheim's syndrome.

BERNHEIMER, STEFAN. 1861-1918. Austrian ophthalmologist. See: Biog. Lex. hervorr. Aerzte, 1880-1930. Bernheimer's fibers.

Bernheimer's fibers (Bernheimer, Stefan): Medicine. See: Dorland; Stedman.

Bernheim's syndrome (Bernheim, Hippolyte). Medicine. See: Jablonski; Stedman.

BERNI, FRANCESCO. 1497-1536. Italian satirist and burlesque poet. See: Encyc. Brit., 1973. Bernesque poetry.

Berninesque style (Bernini, Giovanni Lorenzo): Fine Arts. Cited in: Webster's Biog. Dict.

BERNINI, GIOVANNI LORENZO. 1598-1680. Italian sculptor, architect, and painter. See: Encyc. Brit., 1973. Berninesque style.

BERNOULLI, DANIEL. 1700-1782. Dutch-born mathematician and physicist. See: Dict. Sci. Biog. Bernoulli-Euler law? Bernoulli polynomials. Bernoulli's assumption? Bernoulli's theorem (equation, law, or principle).

Bernoulli differential equation (Bernoulli, Jakob): Mathematics. See: Ballentyne; Internat. Dict. Ap. Math.; James.

Bernoulli distribution (or probability function) (Bernoulli, Jakob): Mathematics. See: Kendall; Van Nostrand Sci. Encyc.; Webster's 3d.

Bernoulli-Euler law (Bernoulli, Daniel? and Euler, Leonhard): Physics. See: Ballentyne; Thewlis.

BERNOULLI, JAKOB. 1654-1705. Swiss mathematician. See: Dict. Sci. Biog. Bernoulli differential equation, Bernoulli distribution (or probability function), Bernoulli numbers, Bernoulli sample?, Bernoulli trials, Bernoulli variation?, Bernoulli's inequality, Bernoulli's theorem (or law), lemniscate of Bernoulli.

BERNOULLI, JOHANN (OR JEAN). 1667-1748. Swiss mathematician. See: Dict. Sci. Biog. Bernoulli series.

Bernoulli method (Derivation undetermined): Mathematics. See: Internat. Dict. Ap. Math.

Bernoulli numbers (Bernoulli, Jakob): Mathematics. See: Internat. Dict. Ap. Math.; Internat. Dict. Phys. Elec.; James.

Bernoulli polynomials (Bernoulli, Daniel): Mathematics. See: Ballentyne; Internat. Dict. Ap. Math.; Internat. Dict. Phys. Elec.

Bernoulli sample (Bernoulli, Jakob?): Statistics. See: Zadrozny.

Bernoulli series (Bernoulli, Johann (or Jean): Mathematics. Cited in: Dict. Sci. Biog.

Bernoulli trials (Bernoulli, Jakob): Statistics. See: Kendall; Wolman.

Bernoulli variation (Bernoulli, Jakob?): Statistics. See: Kendall.

Bernoulli's assumption (Bernoulli, Daniel?): Physics. See: Thrush.

Bernoulli's inequality (Bernoulli, Jakob): Mathematics. See: Ballentyne.

Bernoulli's theorem (equation, law, or principle) (Bernoulli, Daniel): Physics. See: Hughes; Huschke; Internat. Dict. Ap. Math.

Bernoulli's theorem (or law) (Bernoulli, Jakob): Mathematics. See: Ballentyne; Good; Internat. Dict. Ap. Math.

Bernreuter personal adjustment inventory (Bernreuter, Robert Gibbon): Psychology. See: Chaplin; Wolman.

BERNREUTER, ROBERT GIBBON. 1901- . American psychologist. See: Amer. Men Sci., 9th ed., vol. 3. Bernreuter personal adjustment inventory.

BERNSTEIN, ALEXANDER. fl. 1897-1904. German chemist. Cited in: Chem. Abstr., Decenn. Index. Bernstein test?

Bernstein polynomial (Bernstein, Serge): Mathematics. See: Internat. Dict. Ap. Math.

BERNSTEIN, SERGE. b. 1880. Russian-born French mathematician. See: Pogg., vol. 5. Bernstein polynomial, Bernstein's inequality.

Bernstein test (Bernstein, Alexander?): Chemistry. See: Van Nostrand Chem. Dict.

Bernstein's inequality (Bernstein, Serge): Statistics. See: Kendall.

Bernstein's theorem (Bernstein, Serge): Statistics. See: Kendall.

Bernthsen acridine synthesis (Bernthsen, Heinrich August): Chemistry. See: Van Nostrand Chem. Dict.

BERNTHSEN, HEINRICH AUGUST. 1855-1931. German biochemist. See: Dict. Sci. Biog. Bernthsen acridine synthesis.

BERNUTH, FRITZ VON. fl. 1926. German physician. (Biography source unavailable.) Bernuth's syndrome.

Bernuth's syndrome (Bernuth, Fritz von): Medicine. See: Jablonski.

BERRY, ANDREW CAMPBELL. 1906- . American statistician. See: Amer. Men Sci., 11th ed. Berry's inequality.

BERRY, SIR GEORGE ANDREAS. 1853-1929. English ophthalmologist. See: Who Was Who, 1929-1940. Berry's syndrome.

BERRY, SIR JAMES. 1860-1946. Canadian surgeon. See: Biog. Lex. hervorr. Aerzte, 1880-1930. Berry's ligaments.

Berry machine (Derivation undetermined): Engineering and Industry. See: Thrush.

BERRY, MARTHA McCHESNEY. 1866-1942. American educator. See: Webster's Biog. Dict. Berry schools.

Berry pump (Derivation undetermined): Engineering and Industry. See: Auger.

Berry schools (Berry, Martha McChesney): Education. Cited in: Webster's Biog. Dict.

Berry's inequality (Berry, Andrew Campbell): Statistics. See: Kendall.

Berry's ligaments (Berry, Sir James): Medicine. See: Dorland; Stedman.

Berry's syndrome (Berry, Sir George Andreas). See: Franceschetti's syndrome (2).

Berserk (Berserk, the Warrior): Generic Word (savage fighter). See: Brewer; Harbottle; Harvey.

BERSERK, THE WARRIOR. Scandanavian warrior. See: Jobes. Berserk.

BERT, PAUL. 1833-1886. French physiologist and politician. See: Dict. Sci. Biog. Bertiella.

BERTAGNINI, CESARE PIETRO T. 1827-1857. Italian chemist. See: Pogg., vol. 3. Bertagnini test reaction?

Bertagnini test reaction (Bertagnini, Cesare Pietro T.?): Chemistry. See: Van Nostrand Chem. Dict.

BERTERO, CARLO GIUSEPPE. 1789-1831. Italian botanist. See: Biog. Notes Upon Botanists. Berteroa (herbs).

Berteroa (herbs) (Bertero, Carlo Giuseppe): Botany. See: Webster's 3d.

Bertha (cape or collar) (Bertha, Queen): Fashion. See: Hendrickson; Partridge; Picken.

BERTHA, QUEEN. d. 783. Frankish queen. See: Nouv. Biog. Univ. Bertha (cape or collar).

BERTHEIM, ALFRED. 1879-1914. German chemist. See: Sci., vol. 40 (1914) p. 479. Ehrlich-Berteim test reaction.

Berthelot('s) equation (of state) (Berthelot, Pierre Eugene Marcellin): Chemistry. See: Ballentyne; Internat. Dict. Ap. Math.

Berthelot method (or condensation method) (Berthelot, Pierre Eugene Marcellin): Chemistry. See: Internat. Dict. Phys. Elec.; Thewlis.

Berthelot-Michel test reaction for alpha and beta naphthol (Berthelot, Pierre Eugene Marcellin and Michel, M.): Chemistry. See: Van Nostrand Chem. Dict.

Berthelot-Michel test reaction for dihydroxybenzene (Berthelot, Pierre Eugene Marcellin and Michel, M.): Chemistry. See: Van Nostrand Chem. Dict.

BERTHELOT, PIERRE EUGENE MARCELLIN. 1827-1907. French chemist. See: Dict. Sci. Biog. Berthelot('s) equation (of state), Berthelot method (or condensation method), Berthelot-Michel test reaction for alpha and beta naphthol, Berthelot-Michel test reaction for dihydroxybenzene, Berthelot reagent for peroxide in ether, Berthelot test for alcohol, Berthelot test for carbon monoxide, Berthelot test for ethyl alcohol in methanol, Berthelot-Thomsen principle, law of Berthelot-Nernst, Martin-Berthelot principle.

Berthelot principle (Berthelot, Pierre Eugene Marcellin). See: Berthelot-Thomsen principle.

Berthelot reagent for peroxide in ether (Berthelot, Pierre Eugene Marcellin): Chemistry. See: Van Nostrand Chem. Dict.

Berthelot test for alcohol (Berthelot, Pierre Eugene Marcellin): Chemistry. See: Van Nostrand Chem. Dict.

Berthelot test for carbon monoxide (Berthelot, Pierre Eugene Marcellin): Chemistry. See: Van Nostrand Chem. Dict.

Berthelot test for ethyl alcohol in methanol (Berthelot, Pierre Eugene Marcellin): Chemistry. See: Van Nostrand Chem. Dict.

Berthelot-Thomsen principle (Berthelot, Pierre Eugene Marcellin and Thomsen, Julius): Chemistry. See: Ballentyne. Also known as: Berthelot principle, Thomsen-Berthelot principle.

BERTHIER, PIERRE. 1782-1861. French mineralogist. See: Dict. Sci. Biog. Berthiera (shrub?), Berthierite.

Berthiera (shrub) (Berthier, Pierre?): Botany. See: Charnock.

Berthierite (Berthier, Pierre): Earth Sciences. See: Charnock; Thrush; Webster's 3d.

BERTHOLLET, CLAUDE LOUIS. 1748-1822. French chemist. See: Dict. Sci. Biog. Berthollet rule, Bertholletia, Berthollet's fluid, Berthollet's law, Berthollide compound.

Berthollet rule (Berthollet, Claude Louis): Chemistry. See: Van Nostrand Chem. Dict.

Bertholletia (Berthollet, Claude Louis): Botany. See: Charnock; Taylor, N., Webster's 3d.

Berthollet's fluid (Berthollet, Claude Louis): Chemistry. See: Dorland; Stedman.

Berthollet's law (Berthollet, Claude Louis): Chemistry. See: Dorland; Stedman.

Berthollide compound (Berthollet, Claude Louis): Chemistry. See: Van Nostrand Sci. Encyc.; Webster's 3d.

Berthon boat (Berthon, Edward Lyon): Engineering and Industry. See: Webster's 3d.

Berthon dynamometer (Derivation undetermined): Astronomy. See: Satterthwaite.

BERTHON, EDWARD LYON. 1813-1899. English ecclesiastic and physician. See: Dict. Nat. Biog., 1st suppl. Berthon boat, Berthon's log.

BERTHON, L. No dates. Engineer in Tunis. Cited in: Bailey. Berthonite.

BERTHON, RODOLPHE. fl. 19th c. French engineer and optical scientist. (Biography source unavailable.) K. D. B. process.

Berthonite (Berthon, L.): Earth Sciences. See: Thrush.

Berthon's log (Berthon, Edward Lyon): Engineering and Industry. Cited in: Dict. Nat. Biog., 1st suppl.

Bertiella (Bert, Paul): Zoology. See: Pennak; Webster's 3d.

BERTILLON, ALPHONSE. 1853-1914. French anthropologist and criminologist. See: Encyc. Brit., 1973. Bertillon system (or Bertillonage).

Bertillon classification (Bertillon, Jacques): Statistics. Cited in: New Encyc. Brit., Microp. under "Bertillon, Jacques."

BERTILLON, JACQUES. 1851-1922. French statistician and demographer. See: New Encyc. Brit., Microp. Bertillon classification.

Bertillon system (or Bertillonage) (Bertillon, Alphonse): Sociology. See: Fairchild; Hendrickson; Zadrozny.

BERTIN, EXUPERE JOSEPH. 1712-1781. French anatomist. See: Nouv. Biog. Univ. Bertin's bones (or ossicle), Bertin's columns, Bertin's ligament.

BERTIN, GABRIEL. No dates. French engineer. (Biography source unavailable.) Bertin gas turbine.

Bertin gas turbine (Bertin, Gabriel): Engineering and Industry. See: Auger.

Bertin's bones (or ossicle) (Bertin, Exupere Joseph): Anatomy. See: Dorland; Stedman.

Bertin's columns (Bertin, Exupere Joseph): Anatomy. See: Donath; Gray; Henderson.

Bertin's ligament (Bertin, Exupere Joseph): Anatomy. See: Dorland; Stedman. Also known as: Bigelow's ligament.

BERTOLONI, ANTONIO. 1775-1869. Italian botanist. See: Biog. Notes Upon Botanists. Bertolonia (herb).

Bertolonia (herb) (Bertoloni, Antonio): Botany. See: Taylor, N., Webster's 3d.

Bertolotti-Garcin syndrome (Bertolotti, Mario? and Garcin, Raymond). See: Garcin's syndrome.

BERTOLOTTI, MARIO. b. 1876. Italian physician. See: Biog. Lex. hervorr. Aerzte, 1880-1930. Bertolotti-Garcin syndrome?

Bertrand blood reagent (Bertrand, Gabriel Emile): Chemistry. See: Van Nostrand Chem. Dict.

Bertrand curves (Bertrand, Joseph Louis Francois): Mathematics. See: Internat. Dict. Ap. Math.; James; Webster's 3d.

Bertrand-Desaint-Rat reagent for copper (Bertrand, Gabriel Emile and De Saint-Rat, Louis): Chemistry. See: Van Nostrand Chem. Dict.

BERTRAND, EMILE. fl. 1872. French mineralogist. Cited in: Royal Soc. Cat. Sci. Pap. Bertrandite.

BERTRAND, ERNEST. fl. 1931. French chemist. Cited in: Chem. Abstr., vol. 25, p. 3268. Bertrand molybdenum reagent.

BERTRAND, GABRIEL EMILE. 1867-1962. French biochemist. See: Dict. Sci. Biog. Bertrand blood reagent, Bertrand-Desaint-Rat reagent for copper, Bertrand-Javillier test reaction for zinc, Bertrand reagent for alkaloids, Bertrand's test for dextrose.

BERTRAND, IVAN GEORGES. 1863-1965. French neurologist. See: Presse Med. vol. 74 (April, 1966) p. 1093. Van Bogaert-Bertrand syndrome.

Bertrand-Javillier test reaction for zinc (Bertrand, Gabriel Emile and Javillier, Jean-Maurice): Chemistry. See: Van Nostrand Chem. Dict.

BERTRAND, JOSEPH LOUIS FRANCOIS. 1822-1900. French mathematician. See: Dict. Sci. Biog. Bertrand curves, Bertrand lens, Bertrand's paradox, Bertrand's postulate, Bertrand's test.

Bertrand lens (Bertrand, Joseph Louis Francois): Engineering and Industry. See: Thewlis; Thrush; Van Nostrand Sci. Encyc.

Bertrand molybdenum reagent (Bertrand, Ernest): Chemistry. See: Van Nostrand Chem. Dict.

Bertrand process (Derivation undetermined): Engineering and Industry. See: Thrush.

Bertrand reagent for alkaloids (Bertrand, Gabriel Emile): Chemistry. See: Van Nostrand Chem. Dict.

Bertrandite (Bertrand, Emile): Earth Sciences. See: Thrush; Webster's 3d.

Bertrand's paradox (Bertrand, Joseph Louis Francois): Mathematics. Cited in: Dict. Sci. Biog.

Bertrand's postulate (Bertrand, Joseph Louis Francois): Mathematics. See: James.

Bertrand's test (for convergence) (Bertrand, Joseph Louis Francois): Mathematics. See: Ballentyne.

Bertrand's test for dextrose (Bertrand, Gabriel Emile): Chemistry. See: Dorland.

BERTSCH, HEINRICH. b. 1897. German chemist. See: Pogg., vol. 7a. Bertsch test?

Bertsch test (Bertsch, Heinrich?): Chemistry. See: Van Nostrand Chem. Dict.

Berzelian formula (Berzelius, Jons Jakob): Chemistry. See: Webster's 3d.

Berzelianite (Berzelius, Jons Jakob): Earth Sciences. See: Thrush; Webster's 3d.

Berzelite (Berzelius, Jons Jakob): Earth Sciences. See: Thrush; Webster's 3d.

BERZELIUS, JONS JAKOB. 1779-1848. Swedish chemist. See: Dict. Sci. Biog. Berzelian formula, Berzelianite, Berzelite, Berzelius' test.

Berzelius' test (Berzelius, Jons Jakob): Chemistry. See: Dorland; Stedman.

BESEMANN. fl. 1929. German chemist. Cited in: Chem. Abstr., vol. 23, p. 792. Besemann test.

Besemann test (Besemann): Chemistry. See: Van Nostrand Chem. Dict.

BESLER, BASILE. 1561-1629. German naturalist. See: Nouv. Biog. Univ. Besleria.

Besleria (Besler, Basile): Botany. See: Charnock.

Besnier-Boeck sarcoid (Besnier, Ernest and Boeck, Caesar). See: Besnier-Boeck-Schaumann syndrome.

Besnier-Boeck-Schaumann syndrome (Besnier, Ernest; Boeck, Caesar Peter Moeller; and Schaumann, Joergen): Medicine. See: Jablonski; Stedman. Also known as: Besnier-Boeck sarcoid, Besnier-Tenneson syndrome, Boeck's lupoid (or sarcoid), Hutchinson-Boeck granulomatosis, Jungling's disease, Moeller Boeck's disease, Schaumann's disease.

BESNIER, ERNEST. 1831-1909. French dermatologist. See: Biog. Lex. hervorr. Aerzte. Besnier-Boeck-Schaumann syndrome, Besnier's prurigo, Kaposi-Besnier-Libman-Sacks syndrome, Tarral-Besnier disease.

Besnier–Tenneson syndrome (Besnier, Ernest and Tenneson, Henri). See: Besnier–Boeck–Schaumann syndrome.

Besnier's prurigo (Besnier, Ernest): Medicine. See: Jablonski; Stedman.

BESREDKA, ALEXANDRE. 1870–1940. Russian pathologist. See: World Who's Who Sci. Besredka's antivirus, Besredka's method, Besredka's reaction.

Besredka's antivirus (Besredka, Alexandre): Medicine. See: Dorland.

Besredka's method (Besredka, Alexandre): Medicine. See: Stedman.

Bessel–Clifford differential equation (Bessel, Friedrich Wilhelm and Clifford, William Kingdon?): Mathematics. See: Ballentyne.

Bessel('s) equation (or differential equation) (Bessel, Friedrich Wilhelm): Mathematics. See: Internat. Dict. Phys. Elec.; James; Thewlis.

BESSEL, FRIEDRICH WILHELM. 1784–1846. German astronomer and mathematician. See: Dict. Sci. Biog. Bessel–Clifford differential equation, Bessel('s) equation (or differential equation), Bessel function(s), Bessel('s) inequality, Bessel interpolation formula (or formula for interpolation), Bessel–zero method, Besselian elements, Besselian year, Bessel's day numbers (or star numbers), Bessel's integral equation, Fourier–Bessel integral, Fourier–Bessel transform, Riccati–Bessel functions.

Bessel function(s) (Bessel, Friedrich Wilhelm): Mathematics. See: Ballentyne; Internat. Dict. Ap. Math.; James.

Bessel functions of Weber (Weber, Hienrich): Mathematics. See: Thewlis.

Bessel('s) inequality (Bessel, Friedrich Wilhelm): Mathematics. See: Internat. Dict. Ap. Math.; Internat. Dict. Phys. Elec.; James.

Bessel interpolation formula (or formula for interpolation) (Bessel, Friedrich Wilhelm): Mathematics. See: Internat. Dict. Ap. Math.; Internat. Dict. Phys. Elec.; Van Nostrand Sci. Encyc.

Bessel–zero method (Bessel, Friedrich Wilhelm): Physics. See: Internat. Dict. Phys. Elec.; Van Nostrand Sci. Encyc.

Besselian elements (Bessel, Friedrich Wilhelm): Astronomy. See: Satterthwaite; Webster's 3d.

Besselian year (Bessel, Friedrich Wilhelm): Astronomy. See: Thewlis.

Bessel's day numbers (or star numbers) (Bessel, Friedrich Wilhelm): Astronomy. See: Webster's 3d.

Bessel's integral equation (Bessel, Friedrich Wilhelm): Mathematics. See: Ballentyne.

Bessemer afterblow (Bessemer, Sir Henry): Engineering and Industry. See: Thrush.

Bessemer blow (Bessemer, Sir Henry): Engineering and Industry. See: Thrush.

Bessemer converter (Bessemer, Sir Henry): Engineering and Industry. See: Hackh; Hendrickson; Thrush.

BESSEMER, SIR HENRY. 1813–1893. English engineer and inventor. See: Dict. Nat. Biog., 1st suppl. Bessemer afterblow, Bessemer blow, Bessemer converter, Bessemer iron (or pig iron), Bessemer matte, Bessemer ore, Bessemer process, Bessemer steel.

Bessemer iron (or pig iron) (Bessemer, Sir Henry): Engineering and Industry. See: Hackh; Thrush; Webster's 3d.

Bessemer matte (Bessemer, Sir Henry): Engineering and Industry. See: Thrush.

Bessemer ore (Bessemer, Sir Henry): Engineering and Industry. See: Thrush.

Bessemer process (Bessemer, Sir Henry): Engineering and Industry. See: Ballentyne; Monkhouse; Partridge.

Bessemer steel (Bessemer, Sir Henry): Engineering and Industry. See: Charnock; Thrush; Webster's 3d.

BESSER, WILIBALD SWIBERT JOSEPH GOTTLIEB VON. 1784–1842. Austrian-born Polish botanist. See: Biog. Notes Upon Botanists. Bessera (herbs).

Bessera (herbs) (Besser, Wilibald Swibert Joseph Gottlieb von): Botany. See: Taylor, N.

BESSEY, CHARLES EDWIN. 1845–1915. American botanist. See: Dict. Sci. Biog. Bessey cherry, Bessey's cactus.

Bessey cherry (Bessey, Charles Edwin): Botany. See: Winburne.

BESSEY, OTTO ARTHUR. 1904– . American biochemist. See: Amer. Men Sci., 10th ed. Lowry–Lopez–Bessey method.

Bessey's cactus (Bessey, Charles Edwin): Botany. Cited in: Dict. Sci. Biog.

BESSIERE. No dates. French engineer. (Biography source unavailable.) V.B. rifle grenade.

Bessman–Baldwin syndrome (Bessman, Samuel Paul and Baldwin, Ruth): Medicine. See: Jablonski.

BESSMAN, SAMUEL PAUL. 1921– . American biochemist. See: World Who's Who Sci. Bessman–Baldwin syndrome.

BEST, FRANZ. 1878–1920. German pathologist. Cited in: Kelly. Best's carmine stain, Best's macular degeneration.

BEST, VAN. 1836–1875. Scottish surgeon. (Biography source unavailable.) Best's operation.

Best's carmine stain (Best, Franz): Medicine. See: Stedman; Van Nostrand Chem. Dict.

Best's macular degeneration (Best, Franz): Medicine. See: Jablonski; Stedman.

Best's operation (Best, Van): Medicine. See: Dorland.

BESTUSCHEFF, GRAF ALEXEI PETROWITSCH. b. 1693. Russian fieldmarshall. See: Biog. Lex. hervorr. Aerzte. Bestuscheff's tincture.

Bestuscheff's tincture (Bestuscheff, Graf Alexei Petrowitsch): Chemistry. See: Hackh.

Bethe–Bloch formula (Bethe, Hans Albrecht and Bloch, Felix): Physics. See: Thewlis.

BETHE, HANS ALBRECHT. 1906– . French-born American physicist. See: World Who's Who Sci. Bethe–Bloch formula, Bethe–Heitler theory, Bethe hole (directional coupler), Bethe method, Bethe–Salpeter equation, Bethe–Slater curve, Bethe–Weizsaecker cycle.

Bethe–Heitler theory (Bethe, Hans Albrecht and Heitler, Walter Heinrich): Physics. See: Thewlis.

Bethe hole (directional coupler) (Bethe, Hans Albrecht): Physics. See: Hughes; Internat. Dict. Phys. Elec.; Markus.

Bethe method (Bethe, Hans Albrecht): Physics. See: Internat. Dict. Ap. Math.

Bethe–Salpeter equation (Bethe, Hans Albrecht and Salpeter, Edwin Ernest): Physics. See: Internat. Dict. Ap. Math; Internat. Dict. Phys. Elec.; Thewlis.

Bethe–Slater curve (Bethe, Hans Albrecht and Slater, John Clarke): Physics. See: Thewlis.

Bethe–Weizsaecker cycle (Bethe, Hans Albrecht and Weizsaecker, Carl Friedrich Freiherr von): Physics. Cited in: World Who's Who Sci.

BETHEA, OSCAR WALTER. b. 1878. American physician. See: Amer. Men Sci., 10th ed. Bethea's method (or sign).

Bethea's method (or sign) (Bethea, Oscar Walter): Medicine. See: Dorland; Stedman.

BETHELL, JOHN. fl. 19th c. American inventor. See: Webster's Biog. Dict. Bethell's process.

Bethell's process (Bethell, John): Engineering and Industry. See: Thrush; Webster's 3d.

BETHENOD, JOSEPH. 1883–1944. French electrical engineer. See: World Who's Who Sci. Bethenod–Latour alternator.

Bethenod–Latour alternator (Bethenod, Joseph and Latour, Marius): Engineering and Industry. See: Hughes.

Betsies (Elizabeth I): Fashion. See: Picken.

Bett test (Derivation undetermined): Chemistry. See: Van Nostrand Chem. Dict.

Bettel test reaction (Bettel, W.): Chemistry. See: Van Nostrand Chem. Dict.

BETTEL, W. fl. 1908. English chemist. Cited in: Chem. Abstr., vol. 2, p. 1248. Bettel test reaction.

Bettelli test (Derivation undetermined): Chemistry. See: Van Nostrand Chem. Dict.

BETTENDORFF, ANTON JOSEPH HUBERT MARIA. 1839-1902. German chemist. See: World Who's Who Sci. Bettendorff-Winkler reagent, Bettendorff's test.

Bettendorff-Winkler reagent (Bettendorff, Anton Joseph Hubert Maria and Winkler, Clemens): Chemistry. See: Van Nostrand Chem. Dict.

Bettendorff's test (Bettendorff, Anton Joseph Hubert Maria): Chemistry. See: Dorland; Hackh.

BETTERTON, JESSE OATMAN. b. 1884. American metallurgist. Cited in: Chem. Abstr., Decenn. Index. Betterton-Kroll process?

Betterton-Kroll process (Betterton, Jesse Oatman? and Kroll, Wilhelm): Engineering and Industry. See: Thrush.

BETTI, ENRICO. 1823-1892. Italian mathematician. See: Dict. Sci. Biog. Betti number, Betti's reciprocal theorem.

BETTI, MARIO. b. 1875. Italian chemist. See: Pogg., vol. 4. Betti reagent.

Betti number (Betti, Enrico): Mathematics. See: James.

Betti reagent (Betti, Mario): Chemistry. See: Van Nostrand Chem. Dict.

Bettink test reaction for mannitol (Derivation undetermined): Chemistry. See: Van Nostrand Chem. Dict.

Bettink test reaction for sulfonal (Derivation undetermined): Chemistry. See: Van Nostrand Chem. Dict.

Betti's reciprocal theorem (Betti, Enrico): Mathematics. See: Ballentyne; Thewlis. Also known as: reciprocity theorem of Maxwell and Betti.

BETTS, ANSON GARDNER. b. 1876. American metallurgist. See: Amer. Men Sci., 10th ed. Betts' process.

Betts' process (Betts, Anson Gardner): Chemistry. See: Ballentyne; Hackh; Thrush.

between Scylla and Charybdis (Scylla): Generic Word. See: Partridge.

Betz cell (Betz, Vladimir Aleksandrovich): Anatomy. See: Chaplin; Donath; Dorland.

BETZ, VLADIMIR ALEKSANDROVICH. 1834-1894. Russian anatomist. See: World Who's Who Sci. Betz cell.

BEUDANT, FRANCOIS SULPICE. 1787-1850. French mineralogist. See: Dict. Sci. Biog. Beaudantite.

Beudantite (Beudant, Francois Sulpice): Earth Sciences. See: Thrush; Webster's 3d.

BEUKEL, WILLIAM. fl. 14th c. Dutch inventor. (Biography source unavailable.) Pickle.

Beukelzoon, William. See: Beukel, William.

BEUNDIA, ROGELIO. fl. 1916. Spanish chemist. Cited in: Chem. Abstr., vol. 11, p. 2018. Peset-Beundia reagent.

BEUREN, ALOIS JOSEPH. 1919- . German physician and cardiologist. See: World Who Who Sci. Beuren's syndrome.

Beuren's syndrome (Beuren, Alois Joseph): Medicine. See: Jablonski.

Beurmann, Charles Lucien de. See: De Beurmann, Charles Lucien.

Beurmann-Gougerot disease (De Beurmann, Charles Lucien and Gougerot, Henri). See: Schenck's disease.

Beurmann's disease (De Beurmann, Charles Lucien). See: Schenck's disease.

Beutel buret float (Beutel, Ernst Emanuel?): Chemistry. See: Hackh.

BEUTEL, ERNST EMANUEL. b. 1877. Austrian chemist. See: Pogg., vol. 6. Beutel buret float?

BEUTTNER, OSKAR. 1866-1929. Swiss gynecologist. See: Biog. Lex. hervorr. Aerzte, 1880-1930. Beuttner's method.

Beuttner's method (Beuttner, Oskar): Medicine. See: Stedman.

BEVAN, ANEURIN. 1897-1960. English politician. See: Encyc. Brit., 1973. Bevanism.

BEVAN, ARTHUR DEAN. 1861-1943. American surgeon. See: World Who's Who Sci. Bevan's incision.

BEVAN, EDWARD JOHN. 1856-1921. English chemist. See: World Who's Who Sci. Cross-Bevan process, Cross-Bevan reagent for cellulose, Cross-Bevan solution, Cross-Bevan test for jute.

Bevan-Lewis cells (Lewis, William Bevan): Medicine. See: Dorland; Stedman.

Bevan-Lewis, William. See: Lewis, William Bevan.

Bevanism (Bevan, Aneurin): History. Cited in: Chambers' Biog. Dict.

Bevan's incision (Bevan, Arthur Dean): Medicine. See: Dorland; Stedman.

Beverage antenna (Beverage, Harold Henry): Electronics. See: Hughes; Internat. Dict. Phys. Elec.; Markus.

BEVERAGE, HAROLD HENRY. b. 1893. American radio engineer. See: Amer. Men Sci., 10th ed. Beverage antenna.

Beveridge plan (Beveridge, Sir William Henry): Economics. See: Greenwald.

Beveridge report (Beveridge, Sir William Henry): Economics. See: Steinberg.

BEVERIDGE, SIR WILLIAM HENRY. 1876-1963. English economist. See: Internat. Encyc. Soc. Sci. Beveridge plan, Beveridge report.

Bevin boys (Bevin, Ernest): History. See: Brewer.

BEVIN, ERNEST. 1884-1951. English labor leader. See: Encyc. Brit., 1973. Bevin boys.

BEWICK, THOMAS. 1753-1828. English wood engraver, and naturalist. See: Dict. Nat. Biog. Bewick's swan, Bewick's wren.

Bewick's swan (Bewick, Thomas): Zoology. Cited in: Gray; Webster's 3d.

Bewick's wren (Bewick, Thomas): Zoology. See: Gray; Mathews, M.M.; Partridge.

BEY, LIGOR. fl. 1931. French chemist. Cited in: Chem. Abstr., vol. 25, p. 1761. Bey reagent.

Bey reagent (Bey, Ligor): Chemistry. See: Van Nostrand Chem. Dict.

BEYER, ADOLPH. 1743-1805. German mining engineer and mineralogist. See: Pogg., vol. 1. Beyerite.

Beyerinck, Martinus Willem. See: Beijerinck, Martinus Willem.

Beyerite (Beyer, Adolph): Earth Sciences. See: Thrush; Webster's 3d.

BEZOLD, ALBERT VON. 1838-1868. German physiologist. See: Dict. Sci. Biog. Bezold-Jarisch reflex, Bezold's ganglion.

Bezold-Bruecke phenomenon (Derivation undetermined): Psychology. See: Chaplin; Drever; English.

BEZOLD, FRIEDRICH. 1842-1908. German otologist. See: World Who's Who Sci. Bezold's abscess, Bezold's disease (or mastoiditis), Bezold's perforation, Bezold's sign (or symptom), Bezold's triad.

Bezold-Jarisch reflex (Bezold, Albert von and Jarisch, Adolf): Medicine. See: Stedman.

Bezold's abscess (Bezold, Friedrich): Medicine. See: Dorland; Stedman.

Bezold's disease (or mastoiditis) (Bezold, Friedrich): Medicine. See: Dorland; Jablonski; Stedman.

Bezold's ganglion (Bezold, Albert von): Medicine. See: Dorland; Stedman.

Bezold's perforation (Bezold, Friedrich): Medicine. See: Dorland; Stedman.

Bezold's sign (or symptom) (Bezold, Friedrich): Medicine. See: Dorland; Stedman.

Bezold's triad (Bezold, Friedrich): Medicine. See: Dorland; Stedman.

BEZOUT, ETIENNE. 1730-1783. French mathematician. See: Dict. Sci. Biog. Bezout's theorem.

Bezout's theorem (Bezout, Etienne): Mathematics. See: James.

BEZSSONOV, NICOLAI. b. 1885. Russian-born French chemist. See: Pogg., vol. 6. Bezssonov reagent.

Bezssonov reagent (Bezssonov, Nicolai): Chemistry. See: Van Nostrand Chem. Dict.

BHABHA, HOMI JEHANGIR. 1909-1966. Indian physicist. See: Cur. Biog., 1956. Bhabba scattering?

Bhabha scattering (Bhabha, Homi Jehangir?): Physics. See: Ballentyne.

Bharata (Bharata, the King): Generic Word. See: Webster's 3d.

Bharata natya (Bharata, the sage): Dance. See: Webster's 3d.

BHARATA, THE KING. Indian legendary monarch. See: Jobes. Bharata.

BHARATA, THE SAGE. fl. 3d. c. Indian sage. Cited in: Encyc. Brit., 1973, under "Theatre, the East." Bharata natya.

BHATTACHARYYA, A. fl. 1943-1946. Indian mathematician. Cited in: Kendall and Doig. Bhattacharyya bounds, Bhattacharyya's distance.

Bhattacharyya bounds (Bhattacharyya, A.): Statistics. See: Kendall.

Bhattacharyya's distance (Bhattacharyya, A.): Statistics. See: Kendall.

BIAL, MANFRED. 1870-1908. German physician. See: Biog. Lex. hervorr. Aerzte, 1880-1930. Bial's reagent, Bial's test.

Bial's reagent (Bial, Manfred): Chemistry. See: Hackh; Van Nostrand Chem. Dict.

Bial's test (Bial, Manfred): Chemistry. See: Ballentyne; Dorland; Stedman.

BIANCHI, ANGELO. b. 1892. Italian mineralogist. See: Who's Who Sci. Europe. Bianchi-Nola test?, Bianchite.

BIANCHI, GIOVANNI BATTISTA. 1681-1761. Italian anatomist. See: World Who's Who Sci. Bianchi's nodules (or node), Bianchi's valve.

Bianchi identity (Bianchi, Luigi?): Mathematics. See: Internat. Dict. Ap. Math.; Internat. Dict. Phys. Elec.

BIANCHI, LEONARDO. 1848-1927. Italian psychiatrist. See: World Who's Who Sci. Bianchi's syndrome.

BIANCHI, LUIGI. 1856-1928. Italian mathematician. See: Dict. Sci. Biog. Bianchi identity?

Bianchi-Nola test (Bianchi, Angelo? and Di Nola, Ettore): Chemistry. See: Van Nostrand Chem. Dict.

Bianchi's nodules (or node) (Bianchi, Giovanni Battista): Medicine. See: Dorland; Stedman.

Bianchi's syndrome (Bianchi, Leonardo): Medicine. See: Dorland; Jablonski.

Bianchi's valve (Bianchi, Giovanni Battista): Medicine. See: Dorland; Stedman.

Bianchite (Bianchi, Angelo): Earth Sciences. See: Webster's 3d.

BIANCO, I. fl. 1948. Italian physician. (Biography source unavailable.) Silvestroni-Bianco syndrome.

BIASOTTI, ALFREDO. 1903- . Argentinian physician. See: Gran Encic. Argentina. Houssay-Biasotti syndrome.

BIBB, JOHN B. fl. 1850. American gardner. (Biography source unavailable.) Bibb lettuce.

Bibb lettuce (Bibb, John B.): Agriculture. See: Hendrickson.

Biber-Haab-Dimmer degeneration (Biber, Hugo; Haab, Otto; and Dimmer, Friedrich): Medicine. See: Jablonski. Also known as: Haab-Dimmer syndrome.

BIBER, HUGO. 1864-1918. Swiss? physician. (Biography source unavailable.) Biber-Haab-Dimmer degeneration.

BIBIKOVA, V. fl. 1933. Russian chemist. Cited in: Chem. Abstr., vol. 27, p. 681. Kronman-Bibikova micro-chemical reaction for rhenium.

BIBRON, GABRIEL. 1806-1848. French naturalist. See: Nouv. Biog. Univ. Bibron's antidote.

Bibron's antidote (Bibron, Gabriel): Medicine. See: Dorland.

BICHAT, MARIE FRANCOIS XAVIER. 1771-1802. French anatomist and physiologist. See: Dict. Sci. Biog. Bichat's canal, Bichat's fat-pad, Bichat's fissure, Bichat's foramen, Bichat's fossa, Bichat's ligament, Bichat's membrane, Bichat's protuberance, Bichat's tunic, law of Bichat.

Bichat's canal (Bichat, Marie Francois Xavier): Anatomy. See: Dorland; Stedman.

Bichat's fat-pad (Bichat, Marie Francois Xavier): Anatomy. See: Donath; Stedman.

Bichat's fissure (Bichat, Marie Francois Xavier): Anatomy. See: Dorland; Stedman.

Bichat's foramen (Bichat, Marie Francois Xavier): Anatomy. See: Donath; Dorland.

Bichat's fossa (Bichat, Marie Francois Xavier): Anatomy. See: Stedman.

Bichat's ligament (Bichat, Marie Francois Xavier): Anatomy. See: Stedman.

Bichat's membrane (Bichat, Marie Francois Xavier): Anatomy. See: Stedman.

Bichat's protuberance (Bichat, Marie Francois Xavier): Anatomy. See: Stedman.

Bichat's tunic (Bichat, Marie Francois Xavier): Anatomy. See: Stedman.

BICHEROUX, MAX. fl. 1918. German glass-maker. Cited in: Chem. Abstr., vol. 6, p. 1827; and vol. 8, p. 2931. Bicheroux process.

Bicheroux process (Bicheroux, Max): Chemistry. See: Thrush; Van Nostrand Chem. Dict.

Bickel-French test reaction (Bickel, Verne Tillman and French, Herbert E.): Chemistry. See: Van Nostrand Chem. Dict.

BICKEL, GUSTAV. fl. 1884. German physician. (Biography source unavailable.) Bickel's ring.

BICKEL, VERNE TILLMAN. 1902- . American surgeon. Cited in: Chem. Abstr., vol. 20, p. 1232. Bickel-French test reaction.

Bickel's ring (Bickel, Gustav): Medicine. See: Stedman.

BICKERSTAFF, EDWIN ROBERT. fl. 1951. English physician. See: Med. Register, 1952. Bickerstaff's encephalitis.

Bickerstaff's encephalitis (Bickerstaff, Edwin Robert): Medicine. See: Jablonski.

BICKERSTETH, HENRY, LORD LANGDALE. 1783-1851. English Master of the Rolls. See: Dict. Nat. Biog. Lord Langdale's Act.

BICKERTON, WILLIAM. fl. 19th c. American religious leader. (Biography source unavailable.) Bickertonite.

Bickertonite (Bickerton, William): Earth Sciences. See: Webster's 3d.

Bickford fuse (Bickford, William): Engineering and Industry. See: Webster's 3d.

BICKFORD, WILLIAM. 1794-1834. English leather merchant. See: New Encyc. Brit., Microp. Bickford fuse.

BICKNELL, EUGENE PINTARD. 1859-1925. American botanist, ornithologist, and banker. See: Biog. Notes Upon Botanists. Bicknell's thrush.

Bicknell's thrush (Bicknell, Eugene Pintard): Zoology. See: Webster's 3d.

Biddelians (Biddle, John): Religion. See: Canney.

BIDDER, FRIEDRICH HEINRICH. 1810-1894. Russian anatomist. See: Dict. Sci. Biog. Bidder's canal, Bidder's ganglion, Bidder's organ.

Bidder's canal (Bidder, Friedrich Heinrich): Anatomy. See: Gray.

Bidder's ganglion (Bidder, Friedrich Heinrich): Anatomy. See: Dorland; Henderson; Webster's 3d.

Bidder's organ (Bidder, Friedrich Heinrich): Anatomy. See: Gray; Henderson; Pennak.

Biddle expedition (Biddle, James): History. See: Morris and Irwin.

BIDDLE, JAMES. 1783-1848. American naval officer. See: Dict. Amer. Biog. Biddle expedition.

BIDDLE, JOHN. 1615-1662. English religious leader. See: Dict. Nat. Biog. Biddelians.

BIDDULPH, G. fl. 1843. English botanist. Cited in: Royal Soc. Cat. Sci. Pap., 1800-63. Biddulphia.

Biddulphia (Biddulph, G.): Botany. See: Webster's 3d.

BIDLACK, BENJAMIN ALDEN. 1804-1849. American diplomat. See: Dict. Amer. Biog. Bidlack Treaty.

Bidlack Treaty (Bidlack, Benjamin Alden): History. See: New Encyc. Brit., Microp.

BIDOT, EMILE. fl. 1885-1909. French biological chemist. Cited in: Royal Soc. Cat. Sci. Pap., 1884-1900. Richaud-Bidot solution?

BIDWELL, SHELFORD. 1848-1909. English physicist. See: Dict. Nat. Biog., 2d. suppl. Bidwell's ghost.

Bidwell's ghost (Bidwell, Shelford): Psychology. See: Chaplin; Drever; English. Also known as: Purkinje afterimage.

Bieber test (Derivation undetermined): Chemistry. See: Van Nostrand Chem. Dict.

Biebl loop (Derivation undetermined): Medicine. See: Stedman.

Biebrich scale (Derivation undetermined): Medicine. See: Stedman.

Biedenharn identity (Biedenharn, Lawrence Christian, Jr.?): Physics. See: Internat. Dict. Ap. Math.

BIEDENHARN, LAWRENCE CHRISTIAN, JR. 1922- . American physicist. See: World Who's Who Sci. Biedenharn identity?

BIEDERMAN, J. B. 1907- . American physician. (Biography source unavailable.) Biederman's sign.

BIEDERMANN, KARL. b. 1873. German chemist. Cited in: Royal Soc. Cat. Sci. Pap., 1884-1900. Jannasch-Biedermann reagent.

Biederman's sign (Biederman, J. B.): Medicine. See: Stedman.

Biedermeier (Biedermeier, Gottlieb): Generic Word (conventional). See: Webster's 3d.

Biedermeier cabinet (Biedermeier, Gottlieb): Applied Arts. See: Hendrickson.

Biedermeier (furniture style) (Biedermeier, Gottlieb): Applied Arts. See: Partridge; Picken; Webster's 3d.

BIEDERMEIER, GOTTLIEB. Imaginary German writer. See: Benet. Biedermeier, Biedermeier cabinet, Biedermeier (furniture style).

BIEDERT, PHILIPP. 1847-1916. German physician. See: Wer Ist's?, 1906. Biedert's cream mixture.

Biedert's cream mixture (Biedert, Philipp): Medicine. See: Dorland.

BIEDL, ARTHUR. 1869-1933. Austrian physician. See: Biog. Lex. hervorr. Aerzte, 1880-1930. Laurence-Moon-Biedl syndrome.

Biehringer-Busch test reaction (Biehringer, Joachim and Busch, A.): Chemistry. See: Van Nostrand Chem. Dict.

BIEHRINGER, JOACHIM (In full: FRIEDRICH AUGUST JOACHIM). 1858-1920. German chemist. See: Pogg., vol. 5. Biehringer-Busch test reaction.

Biel test for picric acid in iodoform (Derivation undetermined): Chemistry. See: Van Nostrand Chem. Dict.

Biel test reaction for cocaine (Derivation undetermined): Chemistry. See: Van Nostrand Chem. Dict.

BIELA, WILHELM VON. 1782-1856. German astronomer. See: Dict. Sci. Biog. Bielids.

Bielids (Biela, Wilhelm von): Astronomy. See: Van Nostrand Sci. Encyc.

Bieling reagent (Bieling, Richard Franz Ludwig): Chemistry. See: Van Nostrand Chem. Dict.

BIELING, RICHARD FRANZ LUDWIG. 1888-1967. German physician. See: World Who's Who Sci. Bieling reagent.

BIELSCHOWSKY, ALFRED. 1871-1940. German ophthalmologist. See: World Who's Who Sci. Bielschowsky-Lutz-Cogan syndrome, Bielschowsky's disease, Bielschowsky's sign, Rot-Bielschowsky syndrome.

Bielschowsky-Lutz-Cogan syndrome (Bielschowsky, Alfred; Lutz, Adolfo; and Cogan, David Glendenning): Medicine. See: Jablonski.

BIELSCHOWSKY, MAX. 1869-1940. German neurologist. See: World Who's Who Sci. Bielschowsky's disease, Bielschowsky's method, Dollinger-Bielschowsky syndrome, Scholz-Bielschowsky-Henneberg syndrome.

Bielschowsky's disease (Bielschowsky, Alfred): Medicine. See: Jablonski.

Bielschowsky's disease (Bielschowsky, Max): Medicine. See: Hinsie; Stedman; Wolman.

Bielschowsky's method (Bielschowsky, Max): Medicine. See: Dorland; Stedman.

Bielschowsky's sign (Bielschowsky, Alfred): Medicine. See: Stedman.

BIELZ, EDUARD ALBERT. 1827-1898. German mineralogist. Cited in: Royal Soc. Cat. Sci. Papers, 1864-73. Bielzite.

Bielzite (Bielz, Eduard Albert): Earth Sciences. See: Thrush.

BIEMOND, A. fl. 1954. French physician. See: Who's Who Sci. Europe. Biemond's ataxia, Biemond's syndrome.

Biemond's ataxia (Biemond, A.): Medicine. See: Jablonski.

Biemond's syndrome (Biemond, A.): Medicine. See: Jablonski.

BIEN, GEORGE E. fl. 1933-1934. American biochemist. Cited in: Chem. Abstr., vol. 28, pp. 5843, 5781; vol. 30, p. 3456. Levine-Bien reagents for differentiating carotene and oils rich in vitamin A, Levine-Bien tests for carotene.

Bienayme-Chebyshev inequality (Bienayme, Irenee Jules and Chebyshev, Pafnuti Lvovich): Mathematics. See: Ballentyne; Internat. Dict. Ap. Math.; James.

BIENAYME, IRENEE JULES. 1796-1878. French mathematician. See: Internat. Encyc. Soc. Sci. Bienayme-Chebyshev inequality.

BIER, AUGUST KARL GUSTAV. 1861-1949. German physician. See: World Who's Who Sci. Bier's amputation, Bier's anesthesia, Bier's hyperemia, Bier's method, Bier's spots.

BIERBAUM, CHRISTOPHER HENRY. 1864-1947. American engineer. See: World Who's Who Sci. Bierbaum hardness test, Bierbaum microcharacter.

Bierbaum hardness test (Bierbaum, Christopher Henry): Engineering and Industry. See: Auger; Internat. Dict. Phys. Elec.; Van Nostrand Chem. Dict.

Bierbaum microcharacter (Bierbaum, Christopher Henry): Engineering and Industry. Cited in: Internat. Dict. Phys. Elec. under "Hardness, Bierbaum."

BIERMER, ANTON (In full: MICHAEL ANTON). 1827-1892. German physician. See: World Who's Who Sci. Addison-Biermer anemia, Biermer's sign.

Biermer-Ehrlich anemia (Biermer, Anton and Ehrlich, Paul). See: Addison-Biermer anemia.

Biermer's anemia (Biermer, Anton). See: Addison-Biermer anemia.

Biermer's sign (Biermer, Anton): Medicine. See: Dorland; Stedman. Also known as: Gerhardt's sign.

BIERNACKI, EDMUND ADOLFOVICH. 1866-1912. Polish pathologist. See: Biog. Lex. hervorr. Aerzte, 1880-1930. Biernacki's sign.

Biernacki's sign (Biernacki, Edmund Adolfovich): Medicine. See: Dorland; Stedman.

Bier's amputation (Bier, August Karl Gustav): Medicine. See: Stedman.

Bier's anesthesia (Bier, August Karl Gustav): Medicine. See: Dorland.

Bier's hyperemia (Bier, August Karl Gustav): Medicine. See: Dorland; Stedman.

Bier's method (Bier, August Karl Gustav): Medicine. See: Stedman.

Bier's spots (Bier, August Karl Gustav). See: Marshall-White syndrome.

BIESIADECKI, ALFRED VON. 1839-1888. Polish physician. See: Biog. Lex. hervorr. Aerzte, 1880-1930. Biesiadecki's fossa.

Biesiadecki's fossa (Biesiadecki, Alfred von): Medicine. See: Dorland; Stedman.

BIETT, LAURENT THEODORE. 1781-1840. French dermatologist. See: Nouv. Biog. Univ. Biett's disease, Biett's solution.

BIETTI, GIAMBATTISTA. 1907- . Italian oculist. See: World Who's Who Sci. Bietti's dystrophy, Bietti's syndrome.

Bietti's dystrophy (Bietti, Giambattista): Medicine. See: Jablonski.

Bietti's syndrome (Bietti, Giambattista): Medicine. See: Jablonski.

Biett's disease (Biett, Laurent Theodore): Medicine. See: Dorland; Stedman.

Biett's solution (Biett, Laurent Theodore): Medicine. See: Dorland.

Big Bertha (1) (or Bertha) (gun) (Krupp von Bohlen und Halbach): Weapons. See: Barnhart (Eng. Lit.): Hendrickson; Jameson; Quick; Webster's 3d.

Big Bertha (2) (Krupp von Bohlen und Halbach): Generic Word (large or cumbersome). See: Webster's 3d.

Big Bertha (3) (Krupp von Bohlen und Halbach): Generic Word (fat woman). See: Brewer.

Big Bertha (4) (Krupp von Bohlen und Halbach): Photography. See: Webster's 3d.

BIGELOW; HENRY JACOB. 1818-1890. American surgeon. See: World Who's Who Sci. Bigelow's ligament, Bigelow's litholapaxy, Bigelow's septum.

BIGELOW, JACOB. 1789-1879. American physician and botanist. See: Dict. Amer. Biog. Bigelowia.

Bigelowia (Bigelow, Jacob): Botany. See: Dorland; Webster's 3d.

Bigelow's ligament (Bigelow, Henry Jacob): Medicine. See: Donath; Dorland; Stedman.

Bigelow's litholapaxy (Bigelow, Henry Jacob): Medicine. See: Dorland.

Bigelow's septum (Bigelow, Henry Jacob): Medicine. See: Dorland; Stedman.

BIGGE, JOHN THOMAS. fl. 1819-1821. English barrister. Cited in: Encyc. Amer. under "Australia, History." Bigge report.

Bigge report (Bigge, John Thomas): History. See: Morris and Irwin.

BIGGIN. fl. 1800. English? inventor. (Biography source unavailable.) Biggin (coffee percolator).

Biggin (coffee percolator) (Biggin): Generic Word. See: Partridge; Webster's 3d.

Biglow, Hosea. See: Lowell, James Russell.

Biglow papers (Lowell, James Russell): Literature. See: Jameson.

BIGNAMI, AMICO. 1862-1929. Italian physician. See: Biog. Lex. hervorr. Aerzte, 1880-1930. Marchiafava-Bignami syndrome.

BIGNON, JOHN PAUL. 1662-1743. French royal librarian. See: Biog. Notes Upon Botanists. Bignonia.

Bignonia (Bignon, John Paul): Botany. See: Charnock; Hendrickson; Partridge.

BIGOT. No dates. French inventor. (Biography source unavailable.) Bigotphone.

Bigotphone (Bigot): Music. See: Partridge.

BIILMANN, EINAR CHRISTIAN SAXTORPH. 1873-1946. Danish chemist. See: Pogg., vol. 5. Biilmann reagent for potassium?

Biilmann reagent for potassium (Biilmann, Einar Christian Saxtorph?): Chemistry. See: Van Nostrand Chem. Dict.

BILGRAM, HUGO. b. 1847. German-born American machinist. See: Who's Who Engin., 1925. Bilgram valve diagram.

Bilgram valve diagram (Bilgram, Hugo): Engineering and Industry. See: Auger.

Bilharz table (Derivation undetermined): Engineering and Industry. See: Thrush.

BILHARZ, THEODOR MAXIMILIAN. 1825-1862. German helminthologist. See: Dict. Sci. Biog. Bilharzia, Bilharziasis.

Bilharzia (Bilharz, Theodor Maximilian): Zoology. See: Dorland; Pennak; Stedman.

Bilharziasis (Bilharz, Theodor Maximilian): Medicine. See: Partridge; Thrush; Van Nostrand Sci. Encyc.

BILL, ARTHUR HOLBROOK. b. 1877. American gynecologist. See: New York Acad. Med. Portrait Cat. Bill's maneuver.

BILL, J.W. fl. 1858. American chemist. Cited in: Royal Soc. Cat. Sci. Pap., 1800-63. Bill test reaction.

Bill Sikes (Sikes, Bill): Generic Word (burglar). See: Brewer; Partridge.

Bill test reaction (Bill, J.W.): Chemistry. See: Van Nostrand Chem. Dict.

BILLBERG, GUSTAF JOHANNES. 1772-1844. Swedish botanist. See: Biog. Notes Upon Botanists. Billbergia.

Billbergia (Billberg, Gustaf Johannes): Botany. See: Taylor, N.; Webster's 3d.

BILLET, FELIX. 1808-1882. French physicist. See: World Who's Who Sci. Billet's bi-lentil.

Billet's bi-lentil (Billet, Felix): Physics. Cited in: World Who's Who Sci.

Billie Sol Estes scandal (Estes, Billie Sol): History. See: Smith.

Billies and Charlies (Smith, William and Eaton, Charles): Fine Arts. See: Brewer; Hendrickson.

BILLIET, VALERE LOUIS. 1880-1945. Belgian mineralogist. Cited in: Arnim. Billietite.

Billietite (Billiet, Valere Louis): Earth Sciences. See: Thrush; Webster's 3d.

BILLINGS, FRANK SEAVER. 1845-1912. American physician. See: Who Was Who Amer., vol. 4. Billings' plague.

Billings, Josh, pseud. See: Shaw, Henry Wheeler.

Billings' plague (Billings, Frank Seaver): Medicine. See: Jablonski.

BILLIO, JOSEPH. fl. 1696. English rector. (Biography source unavailable.) like Billio.

Billon test reaction (Derivation undetermined): Chemistry. See: Van Nostrand Chem. Dict.

BILLROTH, CHRISTIAN ALBERT THEODOR. 1829-1894. German surgeon. See: Dict. Sci. Biog. Billroth's anesthetic, Billroth's cords, Billroth's disease (1), Billroth's disease (2), Billroth's mixture, Billroth's operations, Billroth's strands, Billroth's suture, Billroth's venae cavernosae.

Billroth's anesthetic (Billroth, Christian Albert Theodor): Medicine. See: Stedman.

Billroth's cords (Billroth, Christian Albert Theodor): Medicine. See: Stedman.

Billroth's disease (1) (Billroth, Christian Albert Theodor): Medicine. See: Jablonski.

Billroth's disease (2) (Billroth, Christian Albert Theodor): Medicine. See: Jablonski.

Billroth's mixture (Billroth, Christian Albert Theodor): Medicine. See: Dorland; Hackh.

Billroth's operations (Billroth, Christian Albert Theodor): Medicine. See: Dorland; Stedman.

Billroth's strands (Billroth, Christian Albert Theodor): Medicine. See: Dorland.

Billroth's suture (Billroth, Christian Albert Theodor): Medicine. See: Dorland.

Billroth's venae cavernosae (Billroth, Christian Albert Theodor): Medicine. See: Stedman.

Bill's axis traction handle (Derivation undetermined): Medicine. See: Stedman.

Bill's maneuver (Bill, Arthur Holbrook): Medicine. See: Stedman.

Billy Barlow (Barlow, Billy): Generic Word (street droll). See: Brewer.

Billy cups (Speers, Billy): Engineering and Industry. See: Thrush.

Billy Wells (gun or shell) (Wells, Billy): Weapons. See: Hendrickson under "Jack Johnson..."

Billycock hat (Coke, Thomas William): Fashion. See: Brewer; Hendrickson under "Bowler, Billycock."

BILTZ, EUGEN WILHELM. 1877-1943. German chemist. See: Pogg., vol. 4. Biltz-Mecklenburg test reaction.

Biltz-Mecklenburg test reaction (Biltz, Eugen Wilhelm and Mecklenburg, Werner): Chemistry. See: Van Nostrand Chem. Dict.

Biltz reagent for carbonate (Derivation undetermined): Chemistry. See: Van Nostrand Chem. Dict.

Biltz reagent for water (Derivation undetermined): Chemistry. See: Van Nostrand Chem. Dict.

BIMELER, JOSEPH MICHAEL. ca. 1778-1853. German-born American religious reformer. See: Dict. Amer. Biog. Bimelerite.

Bimelerite (Bimeler, Joseph Michael): Earth Sciences. See: Webster's 3d.

BINDER, F. fl. 1925. German chemist. Cited in: Chem. Abstr. vol. 20, p. 1040. Vortmann-Binder solution.

BINDER, KARL. fl. 1913. German chemist. Cited in: Chem. Abstr., vol. 6, p. 998. Binder-Weinland reagent.

Binder test (Derivation undetermined): Chemistry. See: Van Nostrand Chem. Dict.

Binder-Weinland reagent (Binder, Karl and Weinland, Rudolf F.): Chemistry. See: Van Nostrand Chem. Dict.

BINDHEIM, JOHANN JACOB. 1750-1825. German chemist. See: Pogg., vol. 1. Bindheimite.

Bindheimite (Bindheim, Johann Jacob): Earth Sciences. See: Thrush; Webster's 3d.

BINDSCHEDLER, E. fl. 1921. American chemist. Cited in: Chem. Abstr. Decenn. Index, 1917-26. Bindschedler test reaction?

Bindschedler test reaction (Bindschedler, E.?): Chemistry. See: Van Nostrand Chem. Dict.

Binet age (Binet, Alfred): Psychology. See: Stedman.

BINET, ALFRED. 1857-1911. French psychologist. See: Internat. Encyc. Soc. Sci. Binet age, Binet class, Binet school, Binet-Simon scale, Binet-Simon tests, Hayes-Binet scale, Herring-Binet test, Kuhlmann-Binet test, Stanford-Binet test (or scale).

Binet class (Binet, Alfred): Education. See: Good.

Binet scale (Binet, Alfred). See: Binet-Simon scale.

Binet school (Binet, Alfred): Education. See: Good.

Binet-Simon scale (Binet, Alfred and Simon, Theodore): Psychology. See: Drever; English; Good. Also known as: Binet scale.

Binet-Simon tests (Binet, Alfred and Simon, Theodore): Psychology. See: Hendrickson; Hinsie; Wolman. Also known as: Binet test.

Binet test (Binet, Alfred). See: Binet-Simon tests.

BING. fl. 1875. Chinese-American agriculturalist. (Biography source unavailable.) Bing cherry.

BING, ALBERT. 1844-1922. German otologist. See: Biog. Lex. hervorr. Aerzte. Bing's entotic test.

Bing Boys (Byng, Julian Hedworth George, Viscount): History. See: Brewer.

Bing cherry (Bing): Botany. See: Hendrickson. Also known as: Napoleon cherry.

Bing-Horton syndrome (Bing, Richard J. and Horton, Bayard Taylor). See: Horton's neuralgia.

BING, JENS. 1906- . Danish physician. See: Who's Who Sci. Europe. Bing-Neel syndrome.

Bing-Neel syndrome (Bing, Jens and Neel, Axel V.): Medicine. See: Jablonski.

BING, RICHARD JOHN. 1909- . American physician. See: Amer. Men Sci., 9th ed. Bing-Horton syndrome, Bing's erythroprosopalgia, Taussig-Bing syndrome.

BINGHAM, EUGENE COOK. b. 1878. American physical chemist. See: Amer. Men Sci., 4th ed. Bingham fluid, Bingham material, Bingham plastometer.

Bingham fluid (Bingham, Eugene Cook): Physics. See: Ballentyne.

BINGHAM, GEORGE CHARLES. 1800-1888. English soldier. See: Dict. Nat. Biog., 1st suppl. Bingham's dandies.

Bingham material (Bingham, Eugene Cook): Physics. See: Internat. Dict. Ap. Math.

Bingham plastometer (Bingham, Eugene Cook): Engineering and Industry. See: Thrush.

Bingham's dandies (Bingham, George Charles): History. See: Brewer; Wagner (More Names).

Bing's entotic test (Bing, Albert): Medicine. See: Dorland.

Bing's erythroprosopalgia (or syndrome) (Bing, Richard J.). See: Horton's neuralgia.

Bing's reflex (Derivation undetermined): Medicine. See: Stedman.

Binn's bacterium (Derivation undetermined): Medicine. See: Stedman.

binomial law of Quetelet-Gauss (Quetelet, Lambert Adolph Jacques and Gauss, Carl Friedrich): Statistics. See: Hinsie.

BINSWANGER, OTTO. 1852-1929. German psychiatrist. See: World Who's Who Sci. Binswanger's disease (or dementia).

Binswanger's disease (or dementia) (Binswanger, Otto): Medicine. See: Hinsie; Jablonski.

BINZ, KARL. 1832-1913. German pharmacologist. See: World Who's Who Sci. Binz' test.

Binz' test (Binz, Karl): Medicine. See: Dorland; Stedman.

BIOERCK, GUNNAR CARL WILHELM. 1916- . Swedish physician. See: World Who's Who Sci. Bioerck-Thorson syndrome, Bioerck's syndrome.

Bioerck-Thorson syndrome (Bioerck, Gunnar Carl Wilhelm and Thorson, Ake). See: Cassidy's syndrome.

Bioerck's syndrome (Bioerck, Gunnar Carl Wilhelm). See: Cassidy's syndrome.

BIONDI, DOMENICO. d. 1914. Italian chemist. Cited in: Arnim. Biondi-Heidenhain mixture (or stain), Ehrlich-Biondi triacid stain.

Biondi-Heidenhain mixture (or stain) (Biondi, Domenico and Heidenhain, Rudolf Peter Heinrich): Chemistry. See: Stedman; Van Nostrand Chem. Dict.

BIOT, CAMILLE. fl. 1878. French physician. (Biography source unavailable.) Biot's breathing (or respiration).

Biot-Fourier equation (Biot, Jean-Baptiste and Fourier, Jean Baptiste Joseph): Physics. See: Ballentyne.

BIOT, JEAN-BAPTISTE. 1774-1862. French physicist. See: Dict. Sci. Biog. Biot-Fourier equation, Biot number, Biot-Savart law, Biot (unit), Biotite, Biot's law.

Biot number (Biot, Jean-Baptiste): Physics. See: Internat. Dict. Ap. Math.

Biot-Savart law (Biot, Jean-Baptiste and Savart, Felix): Physics. See: Internat. Dict. Ap. Math.; Markus; Thewlis.

Biot (unit) (Biot, Jean-Baptiste): Physics. See: Dresner; Thewlis.

Biotite (Biot, Jean-Baptiste): Earth Sciences. See: Thrush; Van Nostrand Sci. Encyc.; Webster's 3d.

Biot's breathing (or respiration) (Biot, Camille): Medicine. See: Dorland; Stedman.

Biot's law (Biot, Jean-Baptiste): Physics. See: Ballentyne; Thewlis.

BIRCH, ARTHUR JOHN. 1915- . Australian-born English chemist. See: World Who's Who Sci. Birch reduction.

BIRCH-HIRSCHFELD, FELIX VICTOR. 1842-1899. German pathologist. See: World Who's Who Sci. Birch-Hirschfeld stain, Birch-Hirschfeld's tumor.

Birch-Hirschfeld stain (Birch-Hirschfeld, Felix Victor): Medicine. See: Stedman.

Birch-Hirschfeld's tumor (Birch-Hirschfeld, Felix Victor). See: Wilms' tumor.

BIRCH, JOHN MORRISON. 1918-1945. American missionary. See: Biog. Index, 1952-1955. Bircher (or Birchite).

Birch reduction (Birch, Arthur John): Chemistry. See: Ballentyne; Van Nostrand Chem. Dict.

Bircher (or Birchite) (Birch, John Morrison): Politics. See: Barnhart, (New Eng.); Hendrickson; Smith.

BIRCHER, HEINRICH. 1850-1923. Swiss surgeon. See: Biog. Lex. hervorr. Aerzte, 1880-1930. Bircher's operation.

Bircher's operation (Bircher, Heinrich): Medicine. See: Dorland.

BIRD, BYRON MATTHEW. b. 1892. American engineer. See: Amer. Men Sci., 10th ed. Bird centrifuge (or coal filter)?

Bird centrifuge (or coal filter) (Bird, Byron Matthew?): Engineering and Industry. See: Thrush.

BIRD, GOLDING. 1814-1854. English physician. See: Dict. Nat. Biog. Bird's formula, Bird's treatment.

BIRD, SAMUEL DOUGAN. 1832-1904. Australian physician. See: Australian Dict. Biog., 1851-90. Bird's sign.

BIRD, T. fl. 1893. English chemist. Cited in: Royal Soc. Cat. Sci. Pap., 1884-1900. Hargreaves-Bird cell.

Bird's formula (Bird, Golding): Medicine. See: Dorland; Stedman.

Bird's sign (Bird, Samuel Dougan): Medicine. See: Dorland; Stedman.

Bird's treatment (Bird, Golding): Medicine. See: Dorland.

Birfield joint (Derivation undetermined): Engineering and Industry. See: Auger. Also known as: Rzeppa joint.

Birge-Mecke rule (Birge, Raymond Thayer? and Mecke, Reinhard): Physics. See: Thewlis.

BIRGE, RAYMOND THAYER. b. 1887. American physicist. See: World Who's Who Sci. Birge-Mecke rule?, Birge-Sponer extrapolation.

Birge-Sponer extrapolation (Birge, Raymond Thayer and Sponer, Hertha Dorothea Elizabeth): Physics. See: Thewlis.

Birkeland-Eyde method (or process) (Birkeland, Olaf Kristian and Eyde, Samuel): Physics. See: Ballentyne; Thrush; Van Nostrand Chem. Dict.

BIRKELAND, OLAF KRISTIAN. 1867-1917. Norwegian physicist. See: World Who's Who Sci. Birkeland-Eyde method (or process).

BIRKETT, JOHN. 1815-1904. English surgeon. Cited in: Kelly. Birkett's hernia.

Birkett's hernia (Birkett, John): Medicine. See: Dorland; Jablonski.

BIRKHAUG, KONRAD ELIAS. 1892- . Norwegian-born American bacteriologist. See: World Who's Who Sci. Birkhaug's test, Birkhaug's toxin.

Birkhaug's test (Birkhaug, Konrad Elias): Medicine. See: Dorland; Stedman.

Birkhaug's toxin (Birkhaug, Konrad Elias): Medicine. See: Dorland.

BIRKHOFF, GEORGE DAVID. 1884-1944. American mathematician. See: Dict. Sci. Biog. Poincare-Birkhoff fixed point theorem.

Birnbaum-Raymond-Zuckerman inequality (Birnbaum, Zygmunt William; Raymond, John H. and Zuckerman, Herbert Samuel): Statistics. See: Kendall.

BIRNBAUM, ZYGMUNT WILLIAM. 1903- . Polish-born American mathematician. See: Amer. Men Sci., 9th ed. Birnbaum-Raymond-Zuckerman inequality.

BIRON, CHARLES DE GONTAUT. 1562-1602. French ambassador. See: Nouv. Biog. Univ. Biron's plot.

Biron's plot (Biron, Charles de Gontaut): History. See: Harbottle.

BIRRELL, AUGUSTINE. 1850-1933. English barrister. See: Dict. Nat. Biog., 5th suppl. Birrellism.

Birrellism (Birrell, Augustine): Generic Word (cursory comment). See: Brewer; Hendrickson; Partridge.

Birtac camera (Acres, Birt): Photography. See: Focal Encyc. Photog.

BISCHLER, AUGUSTUS. 1865-1957. Russian-born Swiss chemist. See: Surrey. Bischler-Napieralski reaction.

Bischler-Napieralski reaction (Bischler, Augustus and Napieralski, Bernard): Chemistry. See: Van Nostrand Chem. Dict.

BISCHOF, CARL GUSTAV CHRISTOPH. 1792-1870. German geologist and chemist. See: Dict. Sci. Biog. Bischofite.

BISCHOF, W. No dates. German neurosurgeon. (Biography source unavailable.) Bischof's myelotomy.

BISCHOFF, CARL ADAM. 1855-1908. German chemist. See: World Who's Who Sci. Bischoff's test.

BISCHOFF, JOHANN JACQUES. 1841-1892. German gynecologist. See: Allg. Deut. Biog. Bischoff's operation.

BISCHOFF, THEODOR LUDWIG WILHELM. 1807-1882. German anatomist and physiologist. See: Dict. Sci. Biog. Bischoff's corona (or crown).

Bischoff's corona (or crown) (Bischoff, Theodor Ludwig Wilhelm): Anatomy. See: Dorland.

Bischoff's operation (Bischoff, Johann Jacques): Medicine. See: Stedman.

Bischoff's test (Bischoff, Carl Adam): Medicine. See: Dorland; Stedman.

Bischofite (Bischof, Carl Gustav Christoph): Earth Sciences. See: Thrush; Webster's 3d.

Bischof's myelotomy (Bischof, W.): Medicine. See: Stedman.

Biscoe time numbers (or date table) (Biscoe, Walter Stanley): Library Science. See: Harrod.

BISCOE, WALTER STANLEY. b. 1853. American librarian. See: Who's Who Libr. Service. Biscoe time numbers (or date table).

BISHOP. No dates. Horse-dealer. (Biography source unavailable.) Bishoping.

BISHOP. fl. 1831. English murderer. (Biography source unavailable.) to Bishop.

Bishop Barker (beer) (Barker, Frederick): Food and Drink. See: Brewer.

BISHOP, EDNA BRYTE. fl. 1953. American educator. (Biography source unavailable.) Bishop method of clothing construction.

BISHOP, GLADDEN. No dates. American religous leader. (Biography source unavailable.) Gladdenite.

Bishop-Kreis test reaction (Derivation undetermined): Chemistry. See: Van Nostrand Chem. Dict.

BISHOP, LOUIS FAUGERES. 1864-1941. American physician. See: World Who's Who Sci. Bishop's sphygmoscope.

Bishop method of clothing construction (Bishop, Edna Bryte): Education. See: Good.

BISHOP, SERENO EDWARDS. 1827-1909. Hawaiian minister. (Biography source unavailable.) Bishop's ring.

Bishop test reaction (Derivation undetermined): Chemistry. See: Van Nostrand Chem. Dict.

Bishop Usher's model (Ussher, James): History. See: Harbottle.

Bishoping (Bishop): Generic Word. See: Charnock; Stedman.

Bishop's ring (Bishop, Sereno Edwards): Earth Sciences. See: Huschke.

Bishop's sphygmoscope (Bishop, Louis Faugeres): Medicine. See: Dorland; Stedman.

Bismarck brown (Bismarck-Schoenhausen, Prince Otto Edward Leopold von): Chemistry. See: Pennak; Webster's 3d.

Bismarck (doughnut) (Bismarck-Schoenhausen, Prince Otto Edward Leopold von): Food and Drink. See: Webster's 3d.

Bismarck herring (Bismarck-Schoenhausen, Prince Otto Edward Leopold von): Food and Drink. See: De Sola; Webster's 3d.

BISMARCK-SCHOENHAUSEN, PRINCE OTTO EDWARD LEOPOLD VON. 1815-1898. German statesman. See: Encyc. Brit., 1973. Bismarck brown, Bismarck (doughnut), Bismarck herring, Bismarckian.

Bismarckian (Bismarck-Schoenhausen, Prince Otto Edward Leopold von): Politics. See: Hendrickson; Webster's 3d.

BISSCHOP, ALEXIS DE. fl. 1871. Engineer. (Biography source unavailable.) Bisschop engine.

Bisschop engine (Bisschop, Alexis de): Engineering and Industry. See: Auger.

ISSELL, LEVI. fl. 1857. American inventor. (Biography source unavailable.)
issell truck.

issell truck (Bissell, Levi): Engineering and Industry. See: Auger.

ISTON. Mythical son of Mars. (Biography source unavailable.) Bistonians.

istonians (Biston): History. See: Brewer.

TOT, PIERRE A. 1822-1888. French physician. See: Biog. Lex. hervorr.
erzte. Bitot's patches (or spots).

itot's patches (or spots) (Bitot, Pierre A.): Medicine. See: Dorland;
ablonski; Stedman. Also known as: Hubbenet's spots.

itter figures (or patterns) (Bitter, Francis): Physics. See: Ballentyne;
ughes; Internat. Dict. Phys. Elec.

ITTER, FRANCIS. 1902-1967. American physicist. See: World Who's Who
ci. Bitter figures (or patterns).

ittner agent (or milk factor) (Bittner, John Joseph): Medicine. See: Stedman.

ITTNER, JOHN JOSEPH. 1904-1961. American biologist. See: World
ho's Who Sci. Bittner agent (or milk factor).

itto, Bela von. See: Von Bitto, Bela.

ITTORF, ALEXANDER. 1876-1949. German physician. See: Biog. Lex.
ervorr. Aerzte, 1880-1930. Bittorf's reaction.

ittorf's reaction (Bittorf, Alexander): Medicine. See: Dorland; Stedman.

IVONA-BERNARDI, ANTONIO. 1778-1837. Italian botanist. See: Diz.
iog. Ital. Bivonaea.

ivonaea (Bivona-Bernardi, Antonio): Botany. See: Charnock.

xbite (Derivation undetermined): Earth Sciences. See: Thrush.

XBY, MAYNARD. fl. 1902. American mineralogist. Cited in: Bailey.
ixbyite.

ixbyite (Bixby, Maynard): Earth Sciences. See: Thrush.

zardite (Derivation undetermined): Earth Sciences. See: Thrush.

IZZOZERO, GUILIO CESAR. 1846-1901. Italian physician. See: Dict.
ci. Biog. Bizzozero picrocarmine solution, Bizzozero's cells (corpuscles, or
latelets).

izzozero picrocarmine solution (Bizzozero, Guilio Cesar): Chemistry. See:
an Nostrand Chem. Dict.

izzozero's cells (corpuscles, or platelets) (Bizzozero, Guilio Cesar): Medicine.
ee: Dorland; Stedman.

erknes' circulation theorem (Bjerknes, Vilhelm Frimann Koren): Physics.
ee: Huschke; Internat. Dict. Ap. Math.

JERKNES, VILHELM FRIMANN KOREN. 1862-1951. Norwegian physicist.
ee: Dict. Sci. Biog. Bjerknes' circulation theorem.

errum double band (Bjerrum, Niels Janniksen): Physics. See: Internat. Dict.
hys. Elec.

JERRUM, J. 1827-1892. Danish ophthalmologist. (Biography source
navailable.) Bjerrum's screen.

JERRUM, JANNIK PETERSEN. 1851-1920. Danish ophthalmologist. See:
og. Lex. hervorr. Aerzte, 1880-1930. Bjerrum's sign (or scotoma).

JERRUM, NIELS JANNIKSEN. 1879-1958. Danish chemist and physicist.
ee: Dict. Sci. Biog. Bjerrum double band, Bjerrum theory, Bjerrum theory of
olecular spectra, Bjerrum's treatment of ion association.

errum theory (Bjerrum, Niels Janniksen): Physics. See: Internat. Dict.
ys. Elec.

errum theory of molecular spectra (Bjerrum, Niels Janniksen): Physics. See:
llentyne.

errum's screen (Bjerrum, J.): Medicine. See: Dorland.

errum's sign (or scotoma) (Bjerrum, Jannik Petersen): Medicine. See:
orland; Jablonski.

Bjerrum's treatment of ion association (Bjerrum, Niels Janniksen): Physics.
See: Ballentyne.

BJORNSTAD, R. fl. 1965. Danish physician. (Biography source unavailable.)
Bjornstad's syndrome.

Bjornstad's syndrome (Bjornstad, R.): Medicine. See: Jablonski.

BLACHER, CARL JOHANN. b. 1867. German chemist. See: Pogg., vol.
4. Blacher reagent for hardness in water.

Blacher reagent for hardness in water (Blacher, Carl Johann): Chemistry.
See: Van Nostrand Chem. Dict.

Black amplifier (Black, Harold Stephen): Electronics. See: Hughes.

Black Brunswickers (Brunswick, Friedrich Wilhelm, Duke of): History. See:
Barnhart (Eng. Lit.); Brewer; Harbottle.

Black-Connery-Perkins Wages and Hours Bill (Black, Hugo La Fayette; Connery,
William Patrick, Jr.; and Perkins, Randolph): Politics. See: Morris.

Black feedback (Black, Harold Stephen): Electronics. See: Hughes.

BLACK, GREENE VARDIMAN. 1836-1915. American dentist. See: Dict.
Amer. Biog. Black's crown.

BLACK, HAROLD STEPHEN. 1898- . American research engineer. See:
World Who's Who Sci. Black amplifier, Black feedback.

BLACK HAWK. 1767-1838. American Indian chieftain. See: Encyc. Brit.,
1973. Black Hawk War.

Black Hawk War (Black Hawk): History. See: Morris; Phyfe.

BLACK, HUGO LA FAYETTE. 1886-1971. American legislator and jurist.
See: Biog. Direct. Amer. Congress. Black-Connery-Perkins Wages and Hours
Bill.

BLACK, J. A. No dates. English army surgeon. (Biography source unavailable.) Black's formula.

black Maria (police van) (Lee, Maria): Generic Word. See: Brewer;
Hendrickson; Weekley.

BLACK, OTIS FISHER. 1867-1933. American chemist. See: Amer. Men Sci.,
5th ed. Black's test (or reagent) for beta-hydroxybutyric acid.

Black spring brake (Derivation undetermined): Engineering and Industry. See:
Thrush.

Blackberg and Wanger's test (Blackberg, Solon Nathaniel and Wanger, J. O.):
Medicine. See: Dorland.

BLACKBERG, SOLON NATHANIEL. b. 1897. American physician. See:
Who's Imp. Med., 2d ed. Blackberg and Wanger's test.

Blackbird black burning clay (Derivation undetermined): Earth Sciences. See:
Thrush.

BLACKBURN, JANE. fl. 1862. English birdwatcher. (Biography source
unavailable.) Blackburnian warbler.

Blackburn palmetto (Derivation undetermined): Botany. See: Winburne.

Blackburnian warbler (Blackburn, Jane): Zoology. See: Hendrickson;
Mathews, M. M.; Webster's 3d.

Blackett and Rideal method for specific heat at constant pressure (Blackett,
Patrick Maynard Stuart and Rideal, Sir Eric Keightley): Physics. See: Internat.
Dict. Phys. Elec.

Blackett barrel washer (Blackett, William Cuthbert?): Engineering and Industry.
See: Thrush.

Blackett conveyor (Blackett, William Cuthbert?): Engineering and Industry.
See: Thrush.

BLACKETT, PATRICK MAYNARD STUART. 1897- . English physicist. See:
World Who's Who Sci. Blackett and Rideal method for specific heat at constant
pressure, Blackett relation.

Blackett relation (Blackett, Patrick Maynard Stuart): Physics. See: Internat.
Dict. Phys. Elec.

BLACKETT, WILLIAM CUTHBERT. 1859-1935. English mining engineer. See:
Encyc. Brit., 1973. Blackett barrel washer?, Blackett conveyor?

BLACKFAN, KENNETH D. 1883-1941. American physician. See: Who Was Who Amer., vol. 1 Diamond-Blackfan syndrome.

Black's crown (Black, Greene Vardiman): Dentistry. See: Dorland.

Black's formula (Black, J. A.): Medicine. See: Dorland; Stedman.

Black's test (or reagent) for beta-hydroxybutyric acid (Black, Otis Fisher): Chemistry. See: Ballentyne; Stedman; Van Nostrand Chem. Dict.

BLACKWELL, DAVID. 1919-   . American mathematician and statistician. See: World Who's Who Sci. Blackwell's theorem.

Blackwell's theorem (Blackwell, David): Statistics. See: Kendall.

Blackwood convention (Blackwood, Easley F.): Recreation and Sports. See: Webster's 3d.

BLACKWOOD, EASLEY F. 1903-   . American bridge expert. Cited in: Encyc. Brit., 1973, under "Bridge." Blackwood convention.

Blaeu press (Blaeu, Willem Janszoon): Printing. See: Lockwood.

BLAEU, WILLEM JANSZOON. 1571-1638. Dutch mathematician, geographer and astronomer. See: Dict. Sci. Biog. Blaeu press.

BLAGDEN, CHARLES. 1748-1820. Scottish physician. See: Dict. Sci. Biog. Blagden's law.

Blagden's law (Blagden, Charles): Chemistry. See: Ballentyne; Carter; Dorland.

BLAINE, JAMES GILLESPIE. 1830-1893. American statesman. See: Dict. Amer. Biog. Blaineism, Bond-Blaine convention.

BLAINE, RAYMOND LEONARD. 1905-   . American engineer. See: Amer. Men Sci., 9th ed. Blaine test.

Blaine test (Blaine, Raymond Leonard): Engineering and Industry. See: Thrush.

Blaineism (Blaine, James Gillespie): Politics. See: Mathews, M.M.

BLAINVILLE, HENRI MARIE DUCROTAY. 1778-1850. French zoologist and anthropologist. See: Dict. Sci. Biog. Blainville's ear.

Blainville's ear (Blainville, Henri Marie Ducrotay): Zoology. See: Dorland; Stedman.

BLAIR, ANDREW ALEXANDER. 1848-1932. American chemist. See: Encyc. Amer. Blair process?

Blair-Bell, William. See: Bell, William Blair.

Blair bill (Blair, Henry William): Politics. See: Jameson.

Blair-Brown graft (Blair, Vilray Papin and Brown, James Barrett): Medicine. See: Stedman.

Blair, Eric Arthur. See: Orwell, George.

BLAIR, HENRY WILLIAM. 1834-1920. American legislator. See: Encyc. Amer. Blair bill.

Blair process (Blair, Andrew Alexander?): Engineering and Industry. See: Thrush.

BLAIR, VILRAY PAPIN. 1871-1955. American surgeon. See: World Who's Who Sci. Blair-Brown graft.

Blaisdell excavator (Derivation undetermined): Engineering and Industry. See: Thrush.

Blaisdell loading machinery (Derivation undetermined): Engineering and Industry. See: Thrush.

Blaisdell sand distributor (Derivation undetermined): Engineering and Industry. See: Thrush.

BLAISE, EDMOND EMILE. 1872-1939. French chemist. See: Pogg., vol. 4. Blaise ketone synthesis, Blaise-Maire reaction, Blaise reaction.

Blaise ketone synthesis (Blaise, Edmond Emile): Chemistry. See: Van Nostrand Chem. Dict.

Blaise-Maire reaction (Blaise, Edmond Emile and Maire, Maurice): Chemistry. See: Van Nostrand Chem. Dict.

Blaise reaction (Blaise, Edmond Emile): Chemistry. See: Van Nostrand Chem. Dict.

BLAISE, SAINT. d. 316. Christian bishop and martyr. See: Nouv. Biog. Univ. blessing of St. Blaise, Saint Blaise's disease.

Blake breaker (or jaw crusher) (Blake, Eli Whitney): Engineering and Industry. See: Thrush.

BLAKE, CLARENCE JOHN. 1843-1919. American otologist. See: Who Was Who Amer., vol. 1. Blake's disk.

BLAKE, ELI WHITNEY. 1795-1886. American inventor. See: World Who's Who Sci. Blake breaker (or jaw crusher).

BLAKE, FRANCIS. 1850-1913. American inventor. See: World Who's Who Sci. Blake transmitter.

Blake furnace (Derivation undetermined): Engineering and Industry. See: Thrush.

BLAKE, LYMAN REED. 1835-1883. American inventor. See: Dict. Amer. Biog. Blake (shoe).

BLAKE, MAURICE ADIN. b. 1882. American botanist. See: Amer. Men Sci., 2-4 eds. Blakea?

Blake Morscher separator (Derivation undetermined): Engineering and Industry. See: Thrush.

Blake Prize (Blake, William): Fine Arts. See: Osborne under "Australian art."

BLAKE, R. No dates. Inventor. (Biography source unavailable.) Blakerage grid.

BLAKE, SEXTON. Fictional detective. (Biography source unavailable.) Sexton Blake.

Blake (shoe) (Blake, Lyman Reed): Fashion. See: Picken. Also known as: McKay (shoe or process).

Blake transmitter (Blake, Francis): Engineering and Industry. Cited in: World Who's Who Sci.

BLAKE, WILLIAM. 1757-1827. English poet, painter, and printer. See: Dict. Nat. Biog. Blake Prize.

BLAKE, WILLIAM PHIPPS. 1825-1910. American geologist and mineralogist. See: Dict. Amer. Biog. Blakeite.

Blakea (Blake, Maurice Adin?): Botany. See: Charnock.

Blakeite (Blake, William Phipps): Earth Sciences. See: Thrush.

Blakely test (Derivation undetermined): Engineering and Industry. See: Thrush.

BLAKEMAN, JOHN. fl. 1906. English statistician. Cited in: Kendall and Doig. Blakeman's criterion, Blakeman's test.

Blakeman's criterion (Blakeman, John): Statistics. See: Kendall.

Blakeman's test (Blakeman, John): Statistics. See: English.

BLAKEMORE, WILLIAM STEPHEN. 1920-   . American surgeon. See: World Who's Who Sci. Sengstaken-Blakemore tube.

Blakerage grid (Blake, R.): Engineering and Industry. See: Monkhouse.

Blake's disk (Blake, Clarence John): Medicine. See: Dorland.

Blake's pump (Derivation undetermined): Engineering and Industry. See: Auger.

Blakey engine (Blakey, William): Engineering and Industry. See: Auger.

BLAKEY, WILLIAM. 1712? - 1792?. English? inventor. Cited in: Encyc. Brit., 1973, under "Boiler." Blakey engine.

BLALOCK, ALFRED. 1899-1965. American surgeon. See: World Who's Who Sci. Blalock-Hanlon operation, Blalock-Taussig operation.

Blalock-Hanlon operation (Blalock, Alfred and Hanlon, C. Rollins): Medicine. See: Stedman.

Blalock-Taussig operation (Blalock, Alfred and Taussig, Helen Brooke): Medicine. See: Dorland; Stedman.

BLAMOUTIER, PIERRE. b. 1891. French physician. See: Who's Who France, 1953-54. Vallery-Radot and Blamoutier lipomatosis.

Blanc chloromethylation reaction (Blanc, Gustave Louis): Chemistry. See: Van Nostrand Chem. Dict.

BLANC, EMILE. 1901-1952. French physician. See: New York Acad. Med. Portrait Cat. Bonnet-Dechaume-Blanc syndrome.

BLANC, GUSTAVE LOUIS. 1872-1927. French chemist. See: Pogg., vol. 4. Blanc chloromethylation reaction, Blanc reaction?, Blanc rule?, Bouveault-Blanc reduction.

Blanc reaction (Blanc, Gustave Louis?): Chemistry. See: Van Nostrand Chem. Dict.

Blanc rule (Blanc, Gustave Louis?): Chemistry. See: Ballentyne; Van Nostrand Chem. Dict.

Blanchard brush (Derivation undetermined): Photography. See: Focal Encyc. Photog.

BLANCHARD, WALLACE. 1849-1922. American surgeon. See: Amer. Med. Direct., 1921. Blanchard's method.

Blanchard's method (Blanchard, Wallace): Medicine. See: Dorland; Stedman.

BLANCHETIERE, A. 1875-1934. French chemist. See: Pogg., vol. 6. Blanchetiere reagent?

Blanchetiere reagent (Blanchetiere, A.?): Chemistry. See: Van Nostrand Chem. Dict.

BLANCPAIN, CLAUDE-PAUL. fl. 1938. Swiss chemist. Cited in: Chem. Abstr., vol. 32, p. 1205. Wenger-Duckert-Blancpain reagent.

Bland Act (Bland, Richard Parks): Politics. See: Harbottle.

Bland-Allison Act (Bland, Richard Parks and Allison, William Boyd): Politics. See: Clark; Jameson; Morris.

Bland dollar (Bland, Richard Parks): History. See: Jameson; Webster's 3d.

BLAND, EDWARD FRANKLIN. 1901- . American physician. See: Direct. Med. Specialists, vol. 8. Bland-White-Garland syndrome.

BLAND, RICHARD PARKS. 1835-1899. American legislator. See: Dict. Amer. Biog. Bland Act, Bland-Allison Act, Bland dollar, Bland Silver Bill.

Bland Silver Bill (Bland, Richard Parks): Politics. See: Latham.

Bland-White-Garland syndrome (Bland, Edward Franklin; White, Paul Dudley; and Garland, Joseph): Medicine. See: Jablonski.

BLANDFORD, GEORGE, MARQUIS OF. fl. 19th c. English botanist. See: Biog. Notes Upon Botanists. Blandfordia.

Blandfordia (Blandford, George, Marquis of): Botany. See: Webster's 3d.

BLANDIN, PHILIPPE FREDERIC. 1798-1849. French surgeon. See: World Who's Who Sci. Blandin's gland.

BLANDING, WILLIAM. fl. 19th c. American herpetologist. (Biography source unavailable.) Blanding's turtle.

Blanding's turtle (Blanding, William): Zoology. See: Pennak; Webster's 3d.

Blandin's gland (Blandin, Philippe Frederic): Medicine. See: Dorland; Henderson; Stedman. Also known as: Bauhin's gland, Nuhn's gland.

Blanket (Blanket, Thomas): Generic Word. See: Charnock; Hendrickson; Wagner, (Names).

BLANKET, THOMAS. fl. 1340. English manufacturer. (Biography source unavailable.) Blanket.

BLANKSMA, JAN JOHANNES. b. 1875. Dutch chemist. See: Pogg., vol. 6. Van Ekenstein-Blanksma test reaction.

BLANQUI, LOUIS-AUGUSTE. 1805-1881. French socialist. See: Encyc. Brit., 1973. Blanquism.

Blanquism (Blanqui, Louis-Auguste): Politics. See: Webster's 3d.

BLAREZ, CHARLES (In full: PIERRE MARIE CHARLES). b. 1852. French chemist. See: Pogg., vol. 4. Blarez peanut oil test, Blarez wine test.

Blarez peanut oil test (Blarez, Charles): Chemistry. See: Van Nostrand Chem. Dict.

Blarez wine test (Blarez, Charles): Chemistry. See: Van Nostrand Chem. Dict.

Blaschka glass (Blaschka, Leopold): Zoology. See: New Encyc. Brit., Microp.

BLASCHKA, LEOPOLD. d. 1895. Czech-born German designer. Cited in: New Encyc. Brit., Microp. Blaschka glass.

Blasius' duct (Blasius, Gerhard): Anatomy. See: Dorland; Stedman. Also known as: Stensen's duct.

Blasius equation (Derivation undetermined): Physics. See: Internat. Dict. Ap. Math.

BLASIUS, GERHARD. fl. 17th c. Dutch anatomist. See: World Who's Who Sci. Blasius's duct.

Blasius solution (Derivation undetermined): Physics. See: Thrush.

BLASKOVICS, LASZLO DE. 1869-1938. Hungarian ophthalmologist. See: New York Acad. Med. Portrait Cat. Blaskovics' operation.

Blaskovics' operation (Blaskovics, Laszlo de): Medicine. See: Stedman.

BLATIN, MARC. b. 1878. French physician. (Biography source unavailable.) Blatin's syndrome.

Blatin's syndrome (Blatin, Marc): Medicine. See: Jablonski; Stedman.

Blaton's formula (Derivation undetermined): Physics. See: Huschke.

BLATTNER, DAVID GEORGE. b. 1892. American engineer. See: Amer. Men Sci., 9th ed. Blattnerphone.

Blattnerphone (Blattner, David George): Electronics. See: Hughes; Internat. Dict. Phys. Elec.

Blau gas (Blau, Hermann): Chemistry. See: Hackh.

BLAU, HERMANN. fl. 1906. German chemist. Cited in: Chem. Abstr., vol. 1, p. 1349. Blau gas.

Blau test for ferrous ion (Derivation undetermined): Chemistry. See: Van Nostrand Chem. Dict.

Blau test for p-phenylenediamine (Derivation undetermined): Chemistry. See: Van Nostrand Chem. Dict.

BLAUD, PIERRE. 1774-1858. French physician. See: Biog. Lex. hervorr. Aerzte. Blaud's pill.

Blaud's pill (Blaud, Pierre): Medicine. See: Dorland; Stedman; Webster's 3d.

BLAVATSKY, HELENA PETROVNA. 1831-1891. Russian traveler and theosophist. See: Dict. Amer. Biog. Blavatsky Institute.

Blavatsky Institute (Blavatsky, Helena Petrovna): Religion. See: Canney.

BLAVIER, EDOUARD ERNEST. 1802-1887. French mine inspector. See: Pogg., vol. 1. Blavierite?

Blavierite (Blavier, Edouard Ernest?): Earth Sciences. See: Thrush.

BLAXLAND, G. No dates. Engineer. (Biography source unavailable.) Blaxland propeller.

Blaxland propeller (Blaxland, G.): Engineering and Industry. See: Auger.

BLAYNEY, ANDREW THOMAS. 1770-1834. Irish soldier. See: Dict. Nat. Biog. Blayney's bloodhounds.

Blayney's bloodhounds (Blayney, Andrew Thomas): History. See: Brewer.

Bleakney mass spectrograph (Bleakney, Walker): Physics. See: Internat. Dict. Phys. Elec.

BLEAKNEY, WALKER. 1901- . American physicist. See: World Who's Who Sci. Bleakney mass spectrograph.

Bleeker method (Bleeker, Warren F.?): Chemistry. See: Hackh.

BLEEKER, WARREN F. fl. 1912. American chemist. Cited in: Chem. Abstr. Decenn. Index, 1906-17. Bleeker method?

Blegvad-Haxthausen syndrome (Blegvad, Olaf and Haxthausen, Holger): Medicine. See: Jablonski.

BLEGVAD, OLAF. 1888-1961. Danish physician. (Biography source unavailable.) Blegvad-Haxthausen syndrome.

BLENCKE, AUGUST. 1868-1937. German physician. See: Biog. Lex. hervorr. Aerzte, 1880-1930. Blencke's disease?

Blencke's disease (Blencke, August?): Medicine. See: Jablonski.

BLERIOT, LOUIS. 1872-1936. French engineer and pioneer aviator. See: Encyc. Brit., 1973. Bleriot monoplane.

Bleriot monoplane (Bleriot, Louis): Aviation. See: Van Nostrand Sci. Encyc. under "Flight, Artificial."

Blessig-Iwanoff cyst (Blessig, Robert and Iwanoff, Wladimir P.): Medicine. See: Jablonski. Also known as: Blessig's cysts, Iwanoff's cysts.

BLESSIG, ROBERT. 1830-1878. German physician. See: Biog. Lex. hervorr. Aerzte. Blessig-Iwanoff cyst, Blessig's groove (or lacuna).

Blessig's cysts (Blessig, Robert). See: Blessig-Iwanoff cyst.

Blessig's groove (or lacuna) (Blessig, Robert): Medicine. See: Dorland; Stedman.

blessing of St. Blaise (Blaise, Saint): Religion. See: Attwater.

BLET, LUIS. fl. 18th c. Spanish pharmacist and botanist. (Biography source unavailable.) Bletia, Bletilla.

Bletia (Blet, Luis): Botany. See: Webster's 3d.

Bletilla (Blet, Luis): Botany. See: Taylor, N.; Webster's 3d.

BLETON, BARTHELEMY. b. 1738. French water diviner. See: Dict. Biog. Fran. Bletonism.

Bletonism (Bleton, Barthelemy): Generic Word. See: Charnock.

BLIGH, WILLIAM. 1754-1817. English naval officer. See: Dict. Nat. Biog. Blighia, Captain Bligh.

Blighia (Bligh, William): Botany. See: Hendrickson; Taylor, N.

Blimp (Blimp, Colonel): Generic Word (unprogressive). See: Brewer.

BLIMP, COLONEL. Imaginary English officer, created by the cartoonist, David Low. See: Benet. Blimp.

Bliss, Reginald. See: Wells, Herbert George.

Bliss sandstone (Derivation undetermined): Earth Sciences. See: Thrush.

BLIX, MAGNUS GUSTAV. 1849-1904. Swedish physiologist. See: Sci., vol. 19 (1904) p. 478. Blix's temperature experiment.

Blix's temperature experiment (Blix, Magnus Gustav): Psychology. See: Drever.

BLOCH, B. No dates. Physician. (Biography source unavailable.) Bloch-Stauffer dyschormonal dermatosis.

Bloch band (Bloch, Felix?): Electronics. See: Markus.

BLOCH, BRUNO. 1878-1933. Swiss dermatologist. See: World Who's Who Sci. Bloch-Sulzberger syndrome (incontinentia pigmenti or melanoblastosis), Bloch's reaction.

Bloch equations (Bloch, Felix): Physics. See: Internat. Dict. Phys. Elec.

BLOCH, FELIX. 1905- . Swiss-born American physicist. See: Cur. Biog., 1954. Bethe-Bloch formula, Bloch band?, Bloch equations, Bloch functions, Bloch-Nordsieck method, Bloch wall, Bloch theorem (of superconductivity), Bloch theorem (of wave functions), Bloch theory, Bloch's $T^{3/2}$ law for magnetization.

Bloch functions (Bloch, Felix): Physics. See: Ballentyne; Internat. Dict. Ap. Math.; Thewlis.

Bloch-Grueneisen relationship (Bloch, Felix and Grueneisen, Eduard). See: Bloch theorem (of wave functions).

BLOCH, MARCEL. 1885-1925. French pathologist. See: Biog. Lex. hervorr. Aerzte, 1880-1930. Bloch's reaction, Bloch's scale.

Bloch-Nordsieck method (Bloch, Felix and Nordsieck, Arnold Theodore): Physics. See: Thewlis.

BLOCH, OLAF F. 1872-1944. English chemist. See: Who Was Who, 1941-1950. Olaf Bloch Memorial Award.

Bloch-Siemens syndrome (Bloch, Hugo and Siemens, Hermann Werner). See: Bloch-Sulzberger syndrome (incontinentia pigmenti or melanoblastosis).

Bloch-Stauffer dyschormonal dermatosis (Bloch, B. and Stauffer, H.). See: Rothmund's syndrome.

Bloch-Sulzberger syndrome (incontinentia pigmenti or melanoblastosis) (Bloch, Bruno and Sulzberger, Marion Baldur): Medicine. See: Jablonski. Also known as: Bloch-Siemens syndrome, Siemens-Bloch pigmented dermatosis.

Bloch theorem (of superconductivity) (Bloch, Felix): Physics. See: Ballentyne; Internat. Dict. Phys. Elec.

Bloch theorem (of wave functions) (Bloch, Felix): Physics. See: Internat. Dict. Phys. Elec. Also known as: Bloch-Grueneisen relationship.

Bloch theory (Bloch, Felix): Physics. See: Thewlis.

Bloch wall (Bloch, Felix): Physics. See: Ballentyne; Hughes; Internat. Dict. Phys. Elec.

BLOCHMANN, FRIEDRICH JOHANN WILHELM. 1858-1931. German zoologist. See: World Who's Who Sci. Blochmann's body.

Blochmann's body (Blochmann, Friedrich Johann Wilhelm): Zoology. See: Gray.

Bloch's reaction (Bloch, Bruno): Medicine. See: Dorland.

Bloch's reaction (Bloch, Marcel): Medicine. See: Stedman.

Bloch's scale (Bloch, Marcel): Medicine. See: Dorland; Stedman.

Bloch's $T^{3/2}$ law for magnetization (Bloch, Felix): Physics. See: Ballentyne.

BLOCKER, JOHN. No dates. American cattle roper. (Biography source unavailable.) Blocker loop.

Blocker loop (Blocker, John): Generic Word. See: Mathews, M. M.

Block's alloy (Derivation undetermined): Chemistry. See: Thrush.

BLOCQ, PAUL OSCAR. 1860-1896. French physician. See: Biog. Lex. hervorr. Aerzte, 1880-1930. Blocq's disease (or syndrome).

Blocq's disease (or syndrome) (Blocq, Paul Oscar): Medicine. See: Dorland; Jablonski; Stedman.

BLODGETT, KATHERINE BURR. 1898- . American physicist. See: World Who's Who Sci. Langmuir-Blodgett film.

BLODI, FREDERICK CHRISTOPHER. 1917- . Austrian-born American ophthalmologist. See: Amer. Men Sci., 10th ed. Reese-Blodi syndrome.

BLOEDE, CARL AUGUST. 1773-1820. German chemist and mineralogist. See: Pogg., vol. 1. Bloedite.

Bloedite (Bloede, Carl August): Earth Sciences. See: Thrush; Webster's 3d. Also known as: Simonyite.

BLOM, AXEL VIGGO. b. 1884. Swiss chemist. See: Pogg., vol. 6. Blom carbazole test.

Blom carbazole test (Blom, Axel Viggo): Chemistry. See: Van Nostrand Chem. Dict.

BLOM, JAKOB. fl. 1926. German chemist. Cited in: Chem. Abstr. Decenn. Index, 1917-26. Blom solutions for hydroxylamine?

Blom solutions for hydroxylamine (Blom, Jakob?): Chemistry. See: Van Nostrand Chem. Dict.

Bloman tube breathing apparatus (Derivation undetermined): Engineering and Industry. See: Thrush.

Blomberg test (Derivation undetermined): Chemistry. See: Van Nostrand Chem. Dict.

BLOMSTRAND, CHRISTIAN WILHELM. 1826-1897. Swedish chemist and mineralogist. See: Dict. Sci. Biog. Blomstrand test?, Blomstrandine.

Blomstrand test (Blomstrand, Christian Wilhelm?): Chemistry. See: Van Nostrand Chem. Dict.

Blomstrandine (Blomstrand, Christian Wilhelm): Earth Sciences. See: Webster's 3d.

Blon test (Derivation undetermined): Medicine. See: Stedman.

BLONDEL, ANDRE EUGENE. 1863–1938. French physicist. See: Dict. Sci. Biog. Blondel-Rey law, Blondel unit.

Blondel-Rey law (Blondel, Andre Eugene and Rey, Jean Alexandre): Physics. See: Ballentyne; Thewlis.

Blondel unit (Blondel, Andre Eugene): Physics. See: Dresner.

Blondin (Blondin, Charles): Generic Word (star acrobat). See: Hendrickson.

BLONDIN, CHARLES (Real Name: JEAN FRANCOIS GRAVELET). 1824–1897. French tightrope walker. See: Encyc. Brit., 1911. Blondin.

Blondlot rays (Blondlot, Rene-Prosper): Physics. See: Dorland.

BLONDLOT, RENE-PROSPER. 1849–1930. French physicist. See: Dict. Sci. Biog. Blondlot rays.

BLOODGOOD. fl. ca. 1825. American sanitation worker. (Biography source unavailable.) Bloodgood pies.

BLOODGOOD, JAMES. fl. before 1847. American who popularized the pear. (Biography source unavailable.) Bloodgood (pear).

BLOODGOOD, JOSEPH COLT. 1866–1935. American surgeon. See: Dict. Amer. Biog., 1st suppl. Bloodgood's disease.

Bloodgood (pear) (Bloodgood, James): Food and Drink. See: Mathews, M. M.

Bloodgood pies (Bloodgood): Generic Word (garbage). See: Mathews, M.M.

Bloodgood's disease (Bloodgood, Joseph Colt). See: Cheatle's disease.

Bloody Mary (cocktail) (Mary I): Food and Drink. See: De Sola; Webster's 3d.

BLOOM, DAVID. b. 1892. American dermatologist. See: Amer. Men Sci., 10th ed. Bloom's syndrome.

Bloom-Torre-Machacek syndrome (Bloom, David; Torre, Douglas P.; and Machacek, G. F.). See: Bloom's syndrome.

BLOOMBERG, ESTHER. fl. 1937. American physician. (Biography source unavailable.) Albright-Butler-Bloomberg syndrome.

BLOOMER, AMELIA JENKS. 1818–1894. American social reformer. See: Dict. Amer. Biog. Bloomers.

BLOOMER, HIRAM G. 1821–1874. American botanist. See: Biog. Notes Upon Botanists. Bloomeria.

Bloomeria (Bloomer, Hiram G.): Botany. See: Taylor, N.

Bloomers (Bloomer, Amelia Jenks): Fashion. See: Brewer; Hendrickson; Picken.

BLOOMFIELD, LEONARD. 1887–1949. American philologist and educator. See: Internat. Encyc. Soc. Sci. Bloomfieldianism.

Bloomfieldianism (Bloomfield, Leonard): Linguistics. See: Hartmann.

Bloom's syndrome (Bloom, David): Medicine. See: Jablonski; Stedman. Also known as: Bloom-Torre-Machacek syndrome.

BLOOR, WALTER RAY. b. 1877. American biochemist. See: Amer. Men Sci., 10th ed. Bloor's test.

Bloor's test (Bloor, Walter Ray): Chemistry. See: Dorland.

BLOSER, ELMER W. fl. 1906. American educator. (Biography source unavailable.) Zaner-Bloser handwriting system.

BLOT, CLAUDE PHILIBERT HIPPOLYTE. 1822–1888. French obstetrician. See: World Who's Who Sci. Blot's perforator, Blot's scissors.

Blot's perforator (Blot, Claude Philibert Hippolyte): Medicine. See: Dorland.

Blot's scissors (Blot, Claude Philibert Hippolyte): Medicine. See: Stedman.

Blount-Barber syndrome (Blount, Walter Putnam and Barber, C. Glenn). See: Erlacher-Blount syndrome.

BLOUNT, WALTER PUTNAM. 1900– . American orthopaedist. See: Direct. Med. Specialists, vol. 8. Erlacher-Blount syndrome.

Blount's syndrome (Blount, Walter Putnam). See: Erlacher-Blount syndrome.

BLOXAM, CHARLES LOUDON. 1832–1887. English chemist. Cited in: Royal Soc. Cat. Sci. Pap., 1800–63. Bloxam reagents for alkaloids?, Bloxam test for strychnine.

Bloxam reagents for alkaloids (Bloxam, Charles Loudon?): Chemistry. See: Van Nostrand Chem. Dict.

Bloxam test for strychnine (Bloxam, Charles Loudon): Chemistry. See: Van Nostrand Chem. Dict.

Bluebeard (Bluebeard, The Murderer): Generic Word. See: Hendrickson; Partridge.

BLUEBEARD, THE MURDERER. Character from Charles Perrault's story, "Barbe Bleue" (1697). See: Benet. Bluebeard, Bluebeard's key.

Bluebeard's key (Bluebeard, The Murderer): Generic Word. See: Brewer.

Bluecher boots (Bluecher, Gebhard Leberecht von): Fashion. See: Hendrickson; Partridge; Picken.

Bluecher (cab) (Bluecher, Gebhard Leberecht von): Generic Word. See: Hendrickson.

BLUECHER, GEBHARD LEBERECHT VON. 1742–1819. Prussian field marshall. See: Encyc. Brit., 1973. Bluecher boots, Bluecher (cab).

Blum approximation (Blum, Julius Rubin): Statistics. See: Kendall.

BLUM, JULIUS RUBIN. 1922– . German-born American mathematician. See: Amer. Men Sci., 10th ed. Blum approximation.

BLUM, LEON. 1878–1930. German physician. See: Biog. Lex. hervorr. Aerzte, 1880–1930. Blum's reaction, Blum's reagent test.

BLUM, PAUL. 1878–1933. French physician. Cited in: New York Acad. Med. Portrait Cat. Blum's syndrome, Gougerot-Blum syndrome.

Blum test for ferrous ion (Derivation undetermined): Chemistry. See: Van Nostrand Chem. Dict.

Blum-Van Caulaert syndrome (Blum, Paul and Van Caulaert, Camille). See: Blum's syndrome.

BLUMBERG, MORITZ. b. 1873. German surgeon. Cited in: Arnim, vol. 3. Blumberg's sign.

Blumberg's sign (Blumberg, Moritz): Medicine. See: Dorland.

BLUME, GUSTAV. b. 1880. German chemist. Cited in: Chem. Abstr., vol. 2, p. 1540. Busch-Blume test.

BLUME, KARL LUDWIG. 1796–1862. German botanist. See: World Who's Who Sci. Blumea.

Blumea (Blume, Karl Ludwig): Botany. See: Webster's 3d.

BLUMENAU, LEONID WASSILJEWITSCH. 1862–1932. Russian neurologist. Cited in: Arnim. Blumenau's nucleus.

Blumenau's nucleus (Blumenau, Leonid Wassiljewitsch): Medicine. See: Dorland; Stedman.

BLUMENBACH, JOHANN FRIEDRICH. 1752–1840. German zoologist and anthropologist. See: Dict. Sci. Biog. Blumenbach's clivus, Blumenbach's process, Blumenbach's racial classification.

Blumenbach's clivus (Blumenbach, Johann Friedrich): Medicine. See: Donath; Dorland; Stedman.

Blumenbach's process (Blumenbach, Johann Friedrich): Medicine. See: Dorland; Stedman.

Blumenbach's racial classification (Blumenbach, Johann Friedrich): Anthropology. See: Zadrozny.

BLUMENTHAL, FERDINAND. b. 1870. German physician. See: Pogg., vol. 4. Blumenthal's disease.

Blumenthal's disease (Blumenthal, Ferdinand): Medicine. See: Dorland.

BLUMER, GEORGE. 1858–1940. American physician. (Biography source unavailable.) Blumer's shelf.

Blumer's shelf (Blumer, George): Medicine. See: Jablonski; Stedman.

Blum's reaction (Blum, Leon): Chemistry. See: Stedman.

Blum's reagent test (Blum, Leon): Chemistry. See: Dorland; Van Nostrand Chem. Dict.

Blum's syndrome (Blum, Paul): Medicine. See: Jablonski. Also known as: Blum-Van Caulaert syndrome.

BLUNCK, G. fl. 1915. German chemist. Cited in: Chem. Abstr., vol. 9, p. 1809. Blunck test for potato starch.

Blunck test for potato starch (Blunck, G.): Chemistry. See: Van Nostrand Chem. Dict.

Bly, Nelly. See: Seaman, Elizabeth Cochrane.

BLYTH, ALEXANDER WYNTER. 1846–1921. English physician. See: Who Was Who, 1916–28. Blyth's test.

BLYTH, EDWARD. 1810–1873. English zoologist. See: Dict. Sci. Biog. Blyth's reed–warbler.

Blyth elutriator (Derivation undetermined): Engineering and Industry. See: Thrush.

Blyth's reed–warbler (Blyth, Edward): Zoology. See: Gray.

Blyth's test (Blyth, Alexander Wynter): Medicine. See: Dorland.

Blythswood, 1st Baron. See: Campbell, Sir Archibald (Lord Blythswood).

Blythswood engine (Campbell, Sir Archibald Campbell): Engineering and Industry. See: Auger.

BLYTT, AXEL. 1843–1898. Swedish geologist. See: New Encyc. Brit., Microp. Blytt–Sernander system.

Blytt–Sernander system (Blytt, Axel and Sernander, Johan Rutger): Earth Sciences. See: New Encyc. Brit., Microp.

Bo Peep costume (Bo Peep, Little): Fashion. See: Picken.

BO PEEP, LITTLE. Character in popular nursery rhyme. See: Barnhart (Cycl. Names). Bo Peep costume.

Boardman feeder (Derivation undetermined): Engineering and Industry. See: Winburne.

BOAS, ISMAR ISIDOR. 1858–1938. German physician. See: Wer Ist's, 1906. Boas–Oppler bacillus, Boas' point, Boas reagent for blood, Boas' sign, Boas' test (for atony of the bowels), Boas' test (for free hydrochloric acid), Boas test (for glucosamine), Boas' test (for lactic acid).

BOAS, KURT WALTER FERDINAND. b. 1890. German medical student. Cited in: Chem. Abstr., vol. 3, p. 1637. Boas test for adrenaline.

Boas–Oppler bacillus (Boas, Ismar Isidor and Oppler, Bruno): Medicine. See: Dorland.

Boas' point (Boas, Ismar Isidor): Medicine. See: Dorland.

Boas reagent for blood (Boas, Ismar Isidor): Chemistry. See: Van Nostrand Chem. Dict.

Boas' sign (Boas, Ismar Isidor): Medicine. See: Dorland.

Boas test for adrenaline (Boas, Kurt Walter Ferdinand): Chemistry. See: Van Nostrand Chem. Dict.

Boas' test (for atony of the bowels) (Boas, Ismar Isidor): Medicine. See: Dorland.

Boas' test (for free hydrochloric acid) (Boas, Ismar Isidor): Medicine. See: Ballentyne; Dorland; Van Nostrand Chem. Dict.

Boas test (for glucosamine) (Boas, Ismar Isidor): Medicine. See: Stedman.

Boas' test (for lactic acid) (Boas, Ismar Isidor): Medicine. See: Dorland.

Bob (Walpole, Sir Robert, 1st Earl of Orford): Generic Word (shilling). See: Hargrave; Hendrickson.

Bob Acres (Acres, Bob): Generic Word (coward). See: Brewer.

Bob Cook stroke (Cook, Robert Johnson): Recreation and Sports. Cited in: Webster's Biog. Dict.

Bobadil (Bobadil, Captain): Generic Word (braggart). See: Hendrickson; Partridge; Phyfe.

BOBADIL, CAPTAIN. Character from Ben Jonson's "Every Man in his Humor" (1598). See: Benet. Bobadil.

BOBBS, JOHN STOUGH. 1809–1870. American surgeon. See: Leonardo. Bobbs' operation.

Bobbs' operation (Bobbs, John Stough): Medicine. See: Dorland.

Bobby (Peel, Sir Robert): Generic Word (policeman). See: Hendrickson; Partridge; Webster's 3d. Also known as: Robert.

BOBIERRE, PIERRE ADOLPHE. 1823–1881. French chemist. See: Pogg., vol. 3. Bobierre test?, Bobierrite.

Bobierre test (Bobierre, Pierre Adolphe?): Chemistry. See: Van Nostrand Chem. Dict.

Bobierrite (Bobierre, Pierre Adolphe): Earth Sciences. See: Webster's 3d.

BOBROFF, V.F. b. 1858. Russian surgeon. (Biography source unavailable.) Bobroff's method, Bobroff's operation.

Bobroff's method (Bobroff, V. F.): Medicine. See: Stedman.

Bobroff's operation (Bobroff, V. F.): Medicine. See: Dorland.

Bobrowka garnet (Derivation undetermined): Earth Sciences. See: Thrush.

Bob's own (or Bobs) (Roberts, Frederick Sleigh): History. See: Brewer.

BOCA, A. D. DEL. fl. 1937. Spanish chemist. Cited in: Chem. Abstr., vol. 31, p. 4449. Del Boca–Remazzano test.

Bocaccio (Boccaccio, Giovanni): Zoology. See: Webster's 3d.

BOCCACCIO, GIOVANNI. 1313–1375. Italian writer. See: Encyc. Brit., 1973. Bocaccio.

BOCCONE, PAOLO SYLVIO. 1633–1704. Sicilian botanist, monk, and physician. See: Nouv. Biog. Univ. Bocconia.

Bocconia (Boccone, Paolo Sylvio): Botany. See: Charnock; Webster's 3d.

BOCHDALEK, VINCENZ ALEXANDER. 1801–1883. Czech anatomist. See: Biog. Lex. hervorr. Aerzte. Bochdalek's bouquet, Bochdalek's ganglion, Bochdalek's gap, Bochdalek's gland–tubules, Bochdalek's hernia, Bochdalek's muscle, Bochdalek's triangle, Bochdalek's valve.

Bochdalek's bouquet (Bochdalek, Vincenz Alexander): Anatomy. See: Donath.

Bochdalek's ganglion (Bochdalek, Vincenz Alexander): Anatomy. See: Donath; Dorland; Stedman.

Bochdalek's gap (Bochdalek, Vincenz Alexander): Anatomy. See: Stedman.

Bochdalek's gland–tubules (Bochdalek, Vincenz Alexander): Anatomy. See: Donath.

Bochdalek's hernia (Bochdalek, Vincenz Alexander): Anatomy. See: Jablonski. Also known as: foramen of Bochdalek, Rivinius' foramen.

Bochdalek's muscle (Bochdalek, Vincenz Alexander): Anatomy. See: Stedman.

Bochdalek's triangle (Bochdalek, Vincenz Alexander): Anatomy. See: Donath.

Bochdalek's valve (Bochdalek, Vincenz Alexander): Anatomy. See: Dorland; Stedman.

BOCHICCHIO, A. fl. 1902. Italian physician. Cited in: Kelly. Bochicchio test.

Bochicchio test (Bochicchio, A.): Chemistry. See: Van Nostrand Chem. Dict.

BOCK, AUGUST CARL. 1782–1833. German anatomist. See: World Who's Who Sci. Bock's ganglion, Bock's nerve.

BOCK, RICHARD DARRELL. 1927– . American statistician. See: Amer. Men Sci., 11th ed. Bock's three component model.

BOCKHART, MAX. fl. 1887. German dermatologist. Cited in: Arnim. Bockhart's impetigo.

Bockhart's impetigo (Bockhart, Max): Medicine. See: Dorland; Jablonski; Stedman.

Bock's ganglion (Bock, August Carl): Anatomy. See: Dorland; Stedman.

Bock's nerve (Bock, August Carl): Anatomy. See: Dorland; Stedman.

Bock's three component model (Bock, Richard Darrell): Statistics. See: Kendall.

Bodal's test (Derivation undetermined): Medicine. See: Stedman.

BODANSKY, AARON. b. 1887. Russian–born American biochemist. See: Amer. Men Sci., 10th ed. Bodansky unit.

Bodansky unit (Bodansky, Aaron): Medicine. See: Dorland; Stedman.

BODDE, JOHANN BERNHARD. 1760-1833. German chemist. See: Pogg., vol. 1. Bodde test?

Bodde test (Bodde, Johann Bernhard?): Chemistry. See: Van Nostrand Chem. Dict.

Bode diagram (or plot) (Bode, Hendrik Wade?): Electronics. See: Hughes; Markus; Van Nostrand Sci. Encyc.

Bode equalizer (Bode, Hendrik Wade?): Electronics. See: Hughes.

BODE, HENDRIK WADE. 1905- . American engineer. See: World Who's Who Sci. Bode diagram (or plot)?, Bode equalizer?

BODE, JOHANN ELERT. 1747-1826. German astronomer. See: Dict. Sci. Biog. Bode's law (or relation).

BODECHTEL, GUSTAV. b. 1899. German physician. See: Wer Ist Wer, 8th ed. Bodechtel-Guttmann encephalitis.

Bodechtel-Guttmann encephalitis (Bodechtel, Gustav and Guttmann, E.). See: Van Bogaert's encephalitis.

BODECKER, CHARLES FRANCIS. b. 1880. American dentist. See: Amer. Men Sci., 11th ed. Bodecker index.

Bodecker index (Bodecker, Charles Francis): Dentistry. See: Stedman.

BODEN, JOSEPH. d. 1811. English soldier. See: Dict. Nat. Biog. Boden Professor.

Boden Professor (Boden, Joseph): Linguistics. See: Wagner, (More Names).

BODENDORF, KURT. 1898- . German chemist. See: Pogg., vol. 6. Boehm-Bodendorf test.

BODER, ELENA. 1909- . American physician. See: Amer. Med. Direct., 1950. Boder-Sedgwick syndrome.

Boder-Sedgwick syndrome (Boder, Elena and Sedgwick, Robert Post). See: Louis-Bar's syndrome.

Bode's law (or relation) (Bode, Johann Elert): Astronomy. See: Ballentyne; Internat. Dict. Ap. Math.; Phyfe. Also known as: Titius-Bode law (or series).

Bodle (coin) (Bothwell): Numismatics. See: Harvey; Partridge.

Bodleian (Bodley, Sir Thomas): Library Science. See: Charnock.

BODLEY, SIR THOMAS. 1545-1613. English diplomat. See: Dict. Nat. Biog. Bodleian.

BODMER, JOHANN GEORG. 1786-1864. Swiss-born inventor. See: World Who's Who Sci. Bodmer screw thread, Bodmer stoker.

Bodmer screw thread (Bodmer, Johann Georg): Engineering and Industry. See: Auger.

Bodmer stoker (Bodmer, Johann Georg): Engineering and Industry. See: Auger.

BODONI, GIAMBATTISTA. 1740-1813. Italian printer and type designer. See: Encyc. Brit., 1973. Bodoni (type).

Bodoni (type) (Bodoni, Giambattista): Printing. See: Harrod; Lockwood; Partridge.

Bodroux-Chichibabin reaction (or aldehyde synthesis) (Bodroux, Fernand and Chichibabin, Alexei Yevgenievich): Chemistry. See: Ballentyne; Van Nostrand Chem. Dict.

BODROUX, FERNAND. fl. 1903-1930. French chemist. See: Pogg., vols. 5, 6. Bodroux-Chichibabin reaction (or aldehyde synthesis).

Body of Luys (Luys, Jules Bernard). See: Luys' nucleus (or body of Luys).

Boe, Franz de la. See: Sylvius, Franciscus.

BOEBER, JOHANNES VON. 1746-1820. German botanist. See: Biog. Notes Upon Botanists. Boebera.

Boebera (Boeber, Johannes von): Botany. See: Charnock; Webster's 3d.

BOECK, CAESAR PETER MOELLER. 1845-1917. Norwegian dermatologist. See: Biog. Lex. hervorr. Aerzte, 1880-1930. Besnier-Boeck-Schaumann syndrome.

BOECK, KARL WILHELM. 1808-1875. Norwegian dermatologist. See: Biog. Lex. hervorr. Aerzte. Boeck's itch (or scabies), Danielssen-Boeck disease.

Boeck's itch (or scabies) (Boeck, Karl Wilhelm): Medicine. See: Dorland; Jablonski.

Boeck's lupoid (Boeck, Caesar Peter Moeller). See: Besnier-Boeck-Schaumann syndrome.

Boeck's sarcoid (Boeck, Caesar Peter Moeller). See: Besnier-Boeck-Schaumann syndrome.

BOEDEKER, CARL HEINRICH DETLEV. 1815-1895. German chemist. See: Sci., vol. 1 (1895) p. 364. Boedeker's test.

Boedeker's test (Boedeker, Carl Heinrich Detlev): Chemistry. See: Dorland; Stedman; Van Nostrand Chem. Dict.

Boedromia (Boedromion): Generic Word (festival). See: Canney.

BOEDROMION. Mythical Greek god. See: Harper. Boedromia.

BOEHLER, LORENZ. 1885- . Austrian surgeon. See: World Who's Who Sci. Boehler splint.

Boehler splint (Boehler, Lorenz): Medicine. See: Dorland.

Boehm-Bodendorf test (Boehm, Theodor Andreas and Bodendorf, Kurt): Chemistry. See: Van Nostrand Chem. Dict.

Boehm system (Boehm, Theobold): Music. See: Apel; Scholes; Webster's 3d.

BOEHM, THEOBOLD. 1794-1881. German flutist and composer. See: Grove. Boehm system.

BOEHM, THEODOR ANDREAS. b. 1892. German chemist. See: Pogg., vols. 6, 7a. Boehm-Bodendorf test.

Boehme hammer (Derivation undetermined): Engineering and Industry. See: Thrush.

BOEHME, JAKOB. 1575-1624. German theosophist and mystic. See: Dict. Sci. Biog. Behmenists (or Boehmenism).

Boehme solutions (Derivation undetermined): Chemistry. See: Van Nostrand Chem. Dict.

BOEHMER, GEORGE RUDOLF. 1723-1803. German physician and botanist. See: Nouv. Biog. Univ. Boehmeria.

Boehmer('s) hematoxylin (Derivation undetermined): Medicine. See: Stedman; Webster's 3d.

Boehmeria (Boehmer, George Rudolf): Botany. See: Charnock; Taylor, N.; Webster's 3d.

BOELTER, LLEWELLYN MICHAEL KRAUS. b. 1898. American mechanical engineer. See: Who's Who Engin., 1959. Dittus-Boelter equation.

Boemer reagent for albumoses (Derivation undetermined): Chemistry. See: Van Nostrand Chem. Dict.

BOERHAAVE, HERMANN. 1668-1738. Dutch physician. See: Dict. Sci. Biog. Boerhaave's glands; Boerhaave's syndrome, Boerhaavia.

Boerhaave's glands (Boerhaave, Hermann): Medicine. See: Dorland; Stedman.

Boerhaave's syndrome (Boerhaave, Hermann): Medicine. See: Jablonski.

Boerhaavia (Boerhaave, Hermann): Botany. See: Charnock; Webster's 3d.

Boerjeson-Forssman-Lehmann syndrome (Boerjeson, Mats Gunnar; Forssman, Hans A.; and Lehmann, Orla J.O.L.): Medicine. See: Jablonski.

BOERJESON, MATS GUNNAR. 1922- . Swedish physician. See: Legit. Laekare, 1974. Boerjeson-Forssman-Lehmann syndrome.

BOERNSTEIN, ERNST. 1854-1932. German chemist. See: World Who's Who Sci. Boernstein test.

Boernstein test (Boernstein, Ernst): Chemistry. See: Van Nostrand Chem. Dict.

BOESEKEN, JACOB. b. 1868. Dutch chemist. See: Pogg., vol. 1. Boeseken reagent?

Boeseken reagent (Boeseken, Jacob?): Chemistry. See: Van Nostrand Chem. Dict.

BOETERS, OSKAR. fl. 1907. German chemist. Cited in: Chem. Abstr. Decenn. Index, 1907-16. Woelffenstein-Boeters reaction.

BOETHUS. fl. 1st. c. B.C. Jewish high priest. Cited in: Encyc. Brit., 1973, under "Jewish Sects." Boethusians.

Boethusians (Boethus): Religion. See: Mathews, S.; Webster's 3d.

Boetius furnace (Derivation undetermined): Engineering and Industry. See: Thrush.

BOETTCHER, ARTHUR. 1831-1889. German anatomist. See: World Who's Who Sci. Boettcher-Cotugno's duct (or pouch), Boettcher's canal, Boettcher's cells, Boettcher's crystals, Boettcher's ganglion, Boettcher's space, Charcot-Boettcher crystalloids.

Boettcher chamber (Derivation undetermined): Chemistry. See: Hackh.

Boettcher-Cotugno's duct (or pouch) (Boettcher, Arthur and Cotugno, Domenico Felice Antonio): Anatomy. See: Donath. Also known as: Cotugno-Boettcher's duct (or pouch).

Boettcher test (Derivation undetermined): Chemistry. See: Van Nostrand Chem. Dict.

Boettcher's canal (Boettcher, Arthur): Anatomy. See: Stedman.

Boettcher's cells (Boettcher, Arthur): Anatomy. See: Dorland; Henderson; Stedman.

Boettcher's crystals (Boettcher, Arthur): Anatomy. See: Dorland; Stedman.

Boettcher's ganglion (Boettcher, Arthur): Anatomy. See: Stedman.

Boettcher's space (Boettcher, Arthur). See: Cotunnius' space.

BOETTGER, JOHANN FRIEDRICH. 1682-1719. German chemist. See: World Who's Who Sci. Boettger ware.

BOETTGER, RUDOLPH CHRISTIAN VON. 1806-1881. German physicist and chemist. See: Dict. Sci. Biog. Boettger solution for nitrite, Boettger test for chlorate, Boettger test (for dextrose in urine).

Boettger solution for nitrite (Boettger, Rudolph Christian von): Chemistry. See: Van Nostrand Chem. Dict.

Boettger test for alcohol in volatile oils (Derivation undetermined): Chemistry. See: Van Nostrand Chem. Dict.

Boettger test for chlorate (Boettger, Rudolph Christian von): Chemistry. See: Van Nostrand Chem. Dict.

Boettger test (for dextrose in urine) (Boettger, Rudolph Christian von): Chemistry. See: Dorland.

Boettger test for ergot in flour (Derivation undetermined): Chemistry. See: Van Nostrand Chem. Dict.

Boettger test for hydrogen peroxide (Derivation undetermined): Chemistry. See: Van Nostrand Chem. Dict.

Boettger test for nickel (Derivation undetermined): Chemistry. See: Van Nostrand Chem. Dict.

Boettger test for ozone (Derivation undetermined): Chemistry. See: Van Nostrand Chem. Dict.

Boettger ware (Boettger, Johann Friedrich): Earth Sciences. See: Thrush; Webster's 3d.

BOETTGER, WILHELM CARL. 1871-1949. German chemist. See: World Who's Who Sci. Boettger's test for carbon monoxide, Boettger's test (for glucose), Boettger's test (for saccharoses).

Boettger's test for carbon monoxide (Boettger, Wilhelm Carl): Chemistry. See: Stedman; Van Nostrand Chem. Dict.

Boettger's test (for glucose) (Boettger, Wilhelm Carl): Chemistry. See: Hackh; Stedman.

Boettger's test (for saccharoses) (Boettger, Wilhelm Carl): Chemistry. See: Ballentyne.

BOETTINGER, CARL CONRAD. 1851-1901. German chemist. See: Pogg., vol. 1. Boettinger test for glyoxalic acid?, Boettinger test for pyrocatechol?, Boettinger test for tannin and gallic acid?

Boettinger test for glyoxalic acid (Boettinger, Carl Conrad?): Chemistry. See: Van Nostrand Chem. Dict.

Boettinger test for pyrocatechol (Boettinger, Carl Conrad?): Chemistry. See: Van Nostrand Chem. Dict.

Boettinger test for tannin and gallic acid (Boettinger, Carl Conrad?): Chemistry. See: Van Nostrand Chem. Dict.

Bogaert, Ludo van. See: Van Bogaert, Ludo.

BOGARDUS, EMORY STEPHEN. b. 1882. American sociologist and educator. See: Amer. Men Sci., 9th ed. Bogardus' law of social tension, Bogardus social distance scale.

Bogardus' law of social tension (Bogardus, Emory Stephen): Sociology. See: Zadrozny.

Bogardus social distance scale (Bogardus, Emory Stephen): Sociology. See: English; Wolman.

BOGDAEN, ALADAER. fl. 1916. German physician. (Biography source unavailable.) Bogdaen-Buday disease.

Bogdaen-Buday disease (Bogdaen, Aladaer and Buday, Kalman): Medicine. See: Jablonski.

Bogen cage (Derivation undetermined): Psychology. See: Chaplin; Drever; English.

Bogert-Cook synthesis (Bogert, Marston Taylor and Cook, Ellen Parmelee): Chemistry. See: Van Nostrand Chem. Dict.

BOGERT, MARSTON TAYLOR. 1868-1954. American chemist. See: World Who's Who Sci. Bogert-Cook synthesis.

Boggs law (Derivation undetermined): Politics. See: Zadrozny.

BOGOMIL. fl. 10th c. Bulgarian priest. Cited in: New Encyc. Brit., Microp. under "Bogomils." Bogomili.

Bogomili (Bogomil): Religion. See: Attwater; Mathews, S.; Webster's 3d.

BOGOMOLETS, ALEKSANDR ALEXSANDROVICH. 1881-1946. Russian endocrinologist and physiologist. See: Barnhart (Cycl. Names). Bogomolets' serum.

Bogomolets' serum (Bogomolets, Aleksandr Alexsandrovich): Medicine. See: Dorland.

BOGORAD, F. A. fl. 1928. Russian physician. (Biography source unavailable.) Bogorad's syndrome.

Bogorad's syndrome (Bogorad, F. A.): Medicine. See: Jablonski; Stedman.

Bogoslovski-Krasnova test (Bogoslovskii, B. M. and Krasnova, V. S.): Chemistry. See: Van Nostrand Chem. Dict.

BOGOSLOVSKII, B. M. fl. 1936. Russian chemist. Cited in: Chem. Abstr., vol. 30, p. 7492. Bogoslovski-Krasnova test.

BOGROS, ANNET JEAN. 1786-1823. French anatomist. See: Nouv. Biog. Univ. Bogros' space.

BOGROS, JACQUES ANTOINE. 1786?-1825. French anatomist. See: Dict. Biog. Fran. Bogros' serous membrane.

Bogros' serous membrane (Bogros, Jacques-Antoine): Medicine. See: Stedman.

Bogros' space (Bogros, Annet Jean): Anatomy. See: Donath; Dorland; Stedman.

BOGUE, EDWARD AUGUSTUS. 1838-1921. American dentist. See: J. A. M. A. (1908) p. 1797. Bogue's symptom.

Bogue's symptom (Bogue, Edward Augustus): Medicine. See: Dorland.

Bogus (Borghese): Generic Word (fraudulent). See: Clapin; Hendrickson.

Bohlig reagent (Derivation undetermined): Chemistry. See: Van Nostrand Chem. Dict.

Bohm and Pines method (Bohm, David Joseph and Pines, David): Physics. See: Internat. Dict. Phys. Elec.; Van Nostrand Sci. Encyc.

BOHM, DAVID JOSEPH. 1917- . American physicist. See: World Who's Who Sci. Bohm and Pines method, Bohm diffusion formula?

Bohm diffusion formula (Bohm, David Joseph?): Physics. See: Hughes.

Bohn (Bohn, Henry George): Generic Word (translation). See: Clapin; Partridge.

BOHN, HENRY GEORGE. 1796-1884. English publisher and translator. See: Dict. Nat. Biog. Bohn.

Bohn-Schmidt reaction (Derivation undetermined): Chemistry. See: Van Nostrand Chem. Dict.

Bohnenberger eyepiece (Bohnenberger, Johann Gottlieb Friedrich von): Astronomy. See: Satterthwaite; Thewlis.

BOHNENBERGER, JOHANN GOTTLIEB FRIEDRICH VON. 1765-1831. German astronomer. See: Allg. Deut. Biog. Bohnenberger eyepiece.

BOHR, CHRISTIAN. 1855-1911. Danish physiologist. See: World Who's Who Sci. Bohr effect, Bohr's equation.

Bohr effect (Bohr, Christian): Medicine. See: Pennak; Stedman.

BOHR, HARALD AUGUST. 1887-1951. Danish mathematician. See: New Encyc. Brit., Microp. Bohr-Landau theorem.

Bohr-Landau theorem (Bohr, Harald August and Landau, Edmund): Mathematics. Cited in: New Encyc. Brit., Microp. under "Bohr, Harald August."

BOHRISCH, PAUL. b. 1871. German chemist. Cited in: Chem. Abstr., vol. 1, p. 2622. Bohrisch tests for camphor.

Bohrisch tests for camphor (Bohrisch, Paul): Chemistry. See: Van Nostrand Chem. Dict.

Bohr's equation (Bohr, Christian): Medicine. See: Stedman.

BOISBAUDRAN, PAUL EMILE LECOQ DE. 1838-1912. French chemist. See: Dict. Sci. Biog. Gallium, Lecocq reaction for molybdenum?

BOJANUS, LUDWIG HEINRICH. 1776-1827. German anatomist. See: Biog. Lex. hervorr. Aerzte. Bojanus' organ.

Bojanus' organ (Bojanus, Ludwig Heinrich): Anatomy. See: Gray; Henderson; Pennak.

BOKORNY, THOMAS. 1856-1929. German chemist. See: Pogg., vol. 4. Loew-Bokorny reagent.

BOLANDER, HENRY NICHOLAS. 1831-1897. German-born American botanist. See: Biog. Notes Upon Botanists. Bolander waterhemlock?

Bolander waterhemlock (Bolander, Henry Nicholas?): Botany. See: Winburne.

BOLDO, BALTASAR MANUEL. d. 1799. Spanish botanist. See: Biog. Notes Upon Botanists. Boldoa.

Boldoa (Boldo, Baltasar Manuel): Botany. See: Charnock.

Boley gauge (gage) (Derivation undetermined): Dentistry. See: Stedman; Thrush.

BOLEYN, ANNE. 1507-1536. Queen of England. See: Dict. Nat. Biog. Anne Boleyn costume.

Bolgar-Fisher world test (Bolgar, Hedda and Fisher, Liselotte K.): Psychology. See: English; Wolman.

BOLGAR, HEDDA. 1909- . Swiss-born American psychologist. See: Amer. Men Sci., 9th ed. Bolgar-Fisher world test.

Bolivar (coin) (Bolivar, Simon): Numismatics. See: Hendrickson; Partridge; Webster's 3d.

Bolivar frock-coat (Bolivar, Simon): Fashion. See: Mathews, M. M.

Bolivar (gingercake) (Bolivar, Simon): Food and Drink. See: Mathews, M.M.

Bolivar hat (Bolivar, Simon): Fashion. See: Mathews, M. M.

BOLIVAR, SIMON. 1783-1830. Venezuelan soldier and statesman. See: Encyc. Brit., 1973. Bolivar (coin), Bolivar frock-coat, Bolivar (gingercake), Bolivar hat, Bolivarian, Bolivarian Society of the United States, Boliviano (coin).

Bolivarian (Bolivar, Simon): Politics. See: Webster's 3d.

Bolivarian Society of the United States (Bolivar, Simon): History. See: Encyc. Assoc.

Boliviano (coin) (Bolivar, Simon): Numismatics. See: Hendrickson; Partridge.

BOLK, LODEWIJK. 1866-1930. Dutch anatomist. See: Dict. Sci. Biog. Bolk's retardation theory.

Bolk's retardation theory (Bolk, Lodewijk): Medicine. See: Dorland.

BOLL, FRANZ CHRISTIAN. 1849-1879. German histologist and physiologist. See: Biog. Lex. hervorr. Aerzte. Boll's cells.

BOLLAND, JEAN DE. 1596-1665. Flemish Jesuit hagiologist. See: Nouv. Biog. Univ. Bollandists.

Bollandists (Bolland, Jean de): Religion. See: Attwater; Brewer; Canney.

Bollandus, Jan. See: Bolland, Jean de.

Bollenback reagent (Derivation undetermined): Chemistry. See: Van Nostrand Chem. Dict.

BOLLEY, ALEXANDER POMPEJUS. 1812-1870. Swiss chemist. See: Pogg., vols. 3, 4. Bolley's gold purple.

Bolley's gold purple (Bolley, Alexander Pompejus): Chemistry. See: Thrush.

BOLLIGER, ADOLPH. 1897-1962. Swiss-born Australian biologist. See: World Who's Who Sci. Bolliger tests for creatinine.

Bolliger tests for creatinine (Bolliger, Adolph): Chemistry. See: Van Nostrand Chem. Dict.

Bollinger granules (Bollinger, Otto von): Medicine. See: Dorland; Stedman.

BOLLINGER, OTTO VON. 1843-1909. German pathologist. See: World Who's Who Sci. Bollinger bodies, Bollinger granules.

Bollinger's bodies (Bollinger, Otto von): Medicine. See: Dorland; Stedman; Webster's 3d.

BOLLMAN, JESSE LOUIS. 1896- . American physiologist. See: World Who's Who Sci. Mann-Bollman fistula.

Boll's cells (Boll, Franz Christian): Medicine. See: Donath; Stedman.

Bolo (or Boloism) (Bolo, Paul): Generic Word (traitor). See: Hendrickson; Partridge; Weekley.

BOLO, PAUL ("BOLO PASHA"). d. 1918. French adventurer. See: Ann. Register. Bolo (or Boloism).

BOLOGNINI, ANGELO. fl. 15th - 16th c. Italian physician. See: Biog. Lex. hervorr. Aerzte. Bolognini's symptom?

Bolognini's symptom (Bolognini, Angelo?): Medicine. See: Stedman.

BOLTEN, JOHANNES. d. 1796. German naturalist and physician. (Biography source unavailable.) Boltenia.

Boltenia (Bolten, Johannes): Botany. See: Pennak; Webster's 3d.

Bolton-Broadbent plane (Bolton and Broadbent, Sir William Henry). See: Bolton plane.

BOLTON, JAMES. d. 1799. English naturalist. See: Dict. Nat. Biog. Boltonia.

BOLTON, JOHN WARD. 1897- . American metallurgist. See: Amer. Men Sci., 9th ed. Bolton's reagent.

Bolton plane (Derivation undetermined): Medicine. See: Stedman. Also known as: Bolton-Broadbent plane.

Bolton point (Derivation undetermined): Medicine. See: Stedman.

Boltonia (Bolton, James): Botany. See: Charnock; Taylor, N.; Webster's 3d.

Bolton's reagent (Bolton, John Ward): Earth Sciences. See: Thrush.

Boltwax (Boltwood, Bertram Borden): Chemistry. Cited in: Dict. Sci. Biog.

BOLTWOOD, BERTRAM BORDEN. 1870-1927. American chemist and physicist. See: Dict. Sci. Biog. Boltwax, Boltwoodite.

Boltwoodite (Boltwood, Bertram Borden): Chemistry. See: Thrush.

BOLTZ, OSWALD HERMAN. 1895- . American neurologist. See: Amer. Med. Direct., 1950. Boltz reaction (or test).

Boltz reaction (or test) (Boltz, Oswald Herman): Medicine. See: Dorland.

Boltzmann constant (or universal conversion factor) (Boltzmann, Ludwig Eduard): Physics. See: Ballentyne; Huschke; Internat. Dict. Ap. Math.

Boltzmann distribution law (Boltzmann, Ludwig Eduard). See: Maxwell-Boltzmann distribution law.

Boltzmann equation (Boltzmann, Ludwig Eduard): Physics. See: Ballentyne; Hughes; Internat. Dict. Ap. Math.

Boltzmann factor (Boltzmann, Ludwig Eduard). See: Stefan-Boltzmann constant.

Boltzmann formula (Boltzmann, Ludwig Eduard): Physics. See: Internat. Dict. Ap. Math.

Boltzmann H theorem (or minimum theorem) (Boltzmann, Ludwig Eduard): Physics. See: Ballentyne; Internat. Dict. Ap. Math.

Boltzmann law of radiation (Boltzmann, Ludwig Eduard). See: Stefan-Boltzmann law.

BOLTZMANN, LUDWIG EDUARD. 1844-1906. Austrian physicist. See: Dict. Sci. Biog. Boltzmann constant (or universal conversion factor), Boltzmann equation, Boltzmann formula, Boltzmann H theorem (or minimum theorem), Boltzmann-Planck equation, Boltzmann principle, Boltzmann ratio, Boltzmann transport equation, Boltzmann-Vlasov equations, H-theorem of Boltzmann and Lorentz, law of Boltzmann, Maxwell-Boltzmann distribution law, Maxwell-Boltzmann statistics, Stefan-Boltzmann constant, Stefan-Boltzmann equation, Stefan-Boltzmann law.

Boltzmann-Planck equation (Boltzmann, Ludwig Eduard and Planck, Max Karl Ernst Ludwig): Physics. See: Internat. Dict. Ap. Math.

Boltzmann principle (Boltzmann, Ludwig Eduard): Physics. See: Hughes; Internat. Dict. Ap. Math.; Thewlis.

Boltzmann ratio (Boltzmann, Ludwig Eduard): Physics. See: Ballentyne; Thewlis.

Boltzmann statistics (Boltzmann, Ludwig Eduard): Physics. See: Internat. Dict. Ap. Math.; Thewlis.

Boltzmann transport equation (Boltzmann, Ludwig Eduard): Physics. See: Ballentyne; Internat. Dict. Ap. Math.; Internat. Dict. Phys. Elec. Also known as: Maxwell-Boltzmann transport equation.

Boltzmann-Vlasov equations (Boltzmann, Ludwig Eduard and Vlasov, Aleksej Konstantinovic): Physics. See: Internat. Dict. Ap. Math.

BOLZA, OSKAR. 1857-1942. German mathematician. See: Dict. Sci. Biog. problem of Bolza.

BOLZANO, BERNHARD. 1781-1848. Czech mathematician and philosopher. See: Dict. Sci. Biog. Bolzano-Weierstrass theorem, Bolzano's theorem.

Bolzano-Weierstrass theorem (Bolzano, Bernhard and Weierstrass, Karl Theodor Wilhelm): Mathematics. See: Ballentyne; Internat. Dict. Ap. Math.; James.

Bolzano's theorem (Bolzano, Bernhard): Mathematics. See: James.

Bomare, Jacques Christophe Valmont de. See: Valmont de Bomare, Jacques Christophe.

Bomarea (Valmont de Bomare, Jacques Christophe): Botany. See: Webster's 3d.

BOMBICCI-PORTA, LUIGI. b. 1833. Italian geologist. See: Pogg., vols. 1, 4, 5. Bombiccite.

Bombiccite (Bombicci-Porta, Luigi): Earth Sciences. See: Thrush.

Bomford-Rhoads anemia (Bomford, Richard Raymond and Rhoads, Cornelius Packard). See: Davidson's anemia.

BOMFORD, RICHARD RAYMOND. fl. 1941. English physician. See: Med. Direct., 1937. Bomford-Rhoads anemia.

BONAPARTE, CHARLES LUCIEN (In full: LUCIEN JULES LAURENT). 1803-1857. American ornithologist. See: Dict. Sci. Biog. Bonaparte's flycatcher, Bonaparte's gull, Bonaparte's sandpiper, Bonaparte's weasel.

Bonaparte, Josephine. See: Josephine.

Bonaparte, Napoleon. See: Napoleon I.

Bonapartea (Napoleon I): Botany. See: Charnock.

Bonaparte's flycatcher (Bonaparte, Charles Lucien): Zoology. See: Mathews, M. M.

Bonaparte's gull (Bonaparte, Charles Lucien): Zoology. See: Gray; Hendrickson; Webster's 3d.

Bonaparte's sandpiper (Bonaparte, Charles Lucien): Zoology. See: Mathews, M. M.; Webster's 3d.

Bonaparte's weasel (Bonaparte, Charles Lucien): Zoology. See: Webster's 3d.

Bonapartism (or Bonapartist) (Napoleon I): History. See: Charnock; Webster's 3d.

Bonapartism (Napoleon III): History. See: Webster's 3d.

BONASTRE, J. F. fl. 1829. French chemist. Cited in: Royal Soc. Cat. Sci. Pap., 1800-63. Bonastre test.

Bonastre test (Bonastre, J. F.): Chemistry. See: Van Nostrand Chem. Dict.

Bonatea (Derivation undetermined): Botany. See: Charnock.

BONATTI, STEFANO. fl. 1938. Italian mineralogist. See: Who's Who Sci. Europe. Bonattite.

Bonattite (Bonatti, Stefano): Earth Sciences. See: Thrush.

Bond albedo (Bond, George Phillips): Physics. See: Thewlis.

Bond-Blaine Convention (Bond, Robert and Blaine, James Gillespie): History. See: Harbottle.

BOND, FRED C. 1899- . American mining engineer. Cited in: Chem. Abstr. Decenn. Index, 1937-46. Bond's third theory?

BOND, GEORGE M. fl. 1881. American physicist. Cited in: Royal Soc. Cat. Sci. Pap., 1884-1900. Rogers-Bond comparator.

BOND, GEORGE PHILLIPS. 1825-1865. American astronomer. See: Dict. Sci. Biog. Bond albedo.

Bond notation (Bond, Walter Lysander): Physics. See: Hughes.

BOND, ROBERT. 1857-1927. Canadian statesman. See: Dict. Nat. Biog., 4th suppl. Bond-Blaine Convention.

BOND, THOMAS. 1712-1784. American physician. See: Dict. Amer. Biog. Bond's splint.

BOND, WALTER LYSANDER. 1903- . American physicist. See: Amer. Men Sci., 10th ed. Bond notation.

Bond's splint (Bond, Thomas): Medicine. See: Dorland.

Bond's third theory (Bond, Fred C. ?): Engineering and Industry. See: Thrush.

BONELLI, FRANCESCO ANDREA. 1784-1830. Italian naturalist. See: Nouv. Biog. Univ. Bonellia.

Bonellia (Bonelli, Francesco Andrea): Zoology. See: Pennak; Webster's 3d.

Bonelli's eagle (Derivation undetermined): Zoology. See: Gray.

Bonelli's warbler (Derivation undetermined): Zoology. See: Gray.

Bonfils' disease (Bonfils, Emile Adolphe). See: Hodgkin's disease.

BONFILS, EMILE ADOLPHE. fl. 1857. French physician. Cited in: Royal Soc. Cat. Sci. Pap., 1800-63. Bonfils' disease.

BONGIOVANNI, ALFRED MARIUS. 1921- . American physician. See: World Who's Who Sci. Bongiovanni-Eisenmenger syndrome.

BONGIOVANNI, C. fl. 1909. Italian chemist. Cited in: Chem. Abstr. Decenn. Index, 1907-16. Bongiovanni test?

Bongiovanni-Eisenmenger syndrome (Bongiovanni, Alfred Marius and Eisenmenger, William J.): Medicine. See: Jablonski.

Bongiovanni test (Bongiovanni, C.?): Chemistry. See: Van Nostrand Chem. Dict.

BONHOEFFER, KARL. 1868-1948. German psychiatrist. See: Biog. Lex. hervorr. Aerzte., 1880-1930. Bonhoeffer's sign (or symptom).

Bonhoeffer's sign (or symptom) (Bonhoeffer, Karl): Medicine. See: Dorland; Jablonski; Stedman.

Bonhomme, Jacques. See: Cale, Guillaume.

Boniface (Boniface, Will): Generic Word (innkeeper). See: Latham; Partridge; Stenhouse.

BONIFACE VI. d. 896. Pope. See: Encyc. Brit., 1911. St. Boniface's cup.

BONIFACE, WILL. Character in George Farquhar's comedy, "The Beaux' Stratagem" (1707). See: Benet. Boniface.

BONNAIRE, ERASME. 1858-1918. French obstetrician. See: Biog. Lex. hervorr. Aerzte, 1880-1930. Bonnaire's method.

Bonnaire's method (Bonnaire, Erasme): Medicine. See: Dorland.

Bonnange card catalogue tray (Bonnange, M. F.): Library Science. See: Harrod.

Bonnaz (embroidery) (Bonnaz, J.): Applied Arts. See: Webster's 3d.

BONNAZ, J. fl. 19th c. French inventor. (Biography source unavailable.) Bonnaz (embroidery).

BONNE, RIGOBERT. 1727-1795. French cartographer. See: Pogg., vol. 3. Bonne's projection.

BONNEMAISON. No dates. French cryptogamist. (Biography source unavailable.) Bonnemaisonea.

Bonnemaisonea (Bonnemaison): Botany. See: Charnock.

Bonner's position (Derivation undetermined): Medicine. See: Stedman.

BONNES, LEO. fl. 1913. French chemist. Cited in: Chem. Abstr., vol. 7, p. 1468. Bonnes test.

Bonne's projection (Bonne, Rigobert): Geography. See: Monkhouse; Moore; Webster's 3d.

Bonnes test (Bonnes, Leo): Chemistry. See: Van Nostrand Chem. Dict.

BONNET, AMEDEE. 1802-1858. French surgeon. See: World Who's Who Sci. Bonnet's capsule, Bonnet's operation, Bonnet's sign.

BONNET, CHARLES. 1720-1793. Swiss naturalist. See: Dict. Sci. Biog. Bonnetia, Bonnet's syndrome.

Bonnet-Dechaume-Blanc syndrome (Bonnet, Paul; Dechaume, Jean; and Blanc, Emile): Medicine. See: Jablonski. Also known as: Bonnet's syndrome (1).

BONNET, FREDERIC JR. b. 1878. American chemist. See: Amer. Men Sci., 10th ed. Bonnet test for formaldehyde.

BONNET, PAUL. 1884-1959. French physician. See: Lyon Med., vol. 203 (1960) p. 143. Bonnet-Dechaume-Blanc syndrome, Bonnet's syndrome (2).

BONNET, PIERRE-OSSIAN. 1819-1892. French mathematician. See: Dict. Sci. Biog. Bonnet's form, Bonnet's mean value theorem.

Bonnet test for formaldehyde (Bonnet, Frederic Jr.): Chemistry. See: Van Nostrand Chem. Dict.

Bonnetia (Bonnet, Charles): Botany. See: Charnock.

Bonnet's capsule (Bonnet, Amedee): Medicine. See: Donath; Dorland; Stedman.

Bonnet's form (Bonnet, Pierre-Ossian): Mathematics. See: Ballentyne.

Bonnet's mean value theorem (Bonnet, Pierre-Ossian): Mathematics. See: James.

Bonnet's operation (Bonnet, Amedee): Medicine. See: Stedman.

Bonnet's sign (Bonnet, Amedee): Medicine. See: Stedman.

Bonnet's syndrome (Bonnet, Charles): Medicine. See: Jablonski. Also known as: Charles Bonnet's syndrome.

Bonnet's syndrome (1) (Bonnet, Paul). See: Bonnet-Dechaume-Blanc syndrome.

Bonnet's syndrome (2) (Bonnet, Paul): Medicine. See: Jablonski.

BONNEVIE, KRISTINE ELISABETH HEUCH. 1872-1950. Norwegian biologist. (Biography source unavailable.) Bennevie-Ullrich syndrome.

Bonnevie-Ullrich syndrome (Bonnevie, Kristine Elisabeth Heuch and Ullrich, Otto): Medicine. See: Jablonski.

Bonney's blue paint (Derivation undetermined): Chemistry. See: Hackh.

BONNIER, PIERRE. 1861-1918. French physician. See: Biog. Lex. hervorr. Aerzte, 1880-1930. Bonnier's syndrome.

Bonnier's syndrome (Bonnier, Pierre): Medicine. See: Dorland; Hinsie; Jablonski. Also known as: Deiters' nucleus syndrome.

Bonnot de-airing machine (Derivation undetermined): Engineering and Industry. See: Thrush.

BONONCINI, GIOVANNI BATTISTA. 1670-1755. Italian opera composer. See: Encyc. Brit., 1973. Tweedledum and Tweedledee.

BONPLAND, AIME JACQUES ALEXANDER. 1773-1858. French naturalist. See: Encyc. Brit., 1911. Bonplandia.

Bonplandia (Bonpland, Aime Jacques Alexander): Botany. See: Charnock.

BONSDORFF, PEHR ADOLPH VON. 1791-1839. Finnish mineralogist. See: Pogg., vol. 3. Bonsdorfite.

Bonsdorfite (Bonsdorff, Pehr Adolph von): Earth Sciences. See: Charnock.

BONSHTEDT (KUPLETSKAYA), ELZA MAKSIMOVA. fl. 1934-1951. Russian mineralogist. Cited in: Mansell. Kupletskite (or Koupletskite).

Bontia (Bontius, Jacobus): Botany. See: Charnock.

BONTIUS, JACOBUS. 1592-1631. Dutch physician. See: Nieuw Nederl. Biog. Woordenb. Bontia.

Bonwill crown (Bonwill, William Gibson Arlington): Dentistry. See: Dorland.

Bonwill triangle (Bonwill, William Gibson Arlington): Dentistry. See: Dorland; Stedman.

BONWILL, WILLIAM GIBSON ARLINGTON. 1833-1899. American dentist. See: Dict. Amer. Biog. Bonwill crown, Bonwill triangle.

Bonz test for tellurium in bismuth (Derivation undetermined): Chemistry. See: Van Nostrand Chem. Dict.

BOOEK, JAN ARVID. 1915- . Swedish geneticist. See: World Who's Who Sci. Booek's syndrome.

Booek's syndrome (Booek, Jan Arvid): Medicine. See: Jablonski.

Book of Mormon (Moroni): Religion. See: Latham; New Encyc. Brit., 1974, Microp.

BOOLE, GEORGE. 1815-1864. English mathematician. See: Dict. Sci. Biog. Boolean algebra, Boolean calculus, Boolean function, Boole's inequality, Boole's theorem.

Boolean algebra (Boole, George): Mathematics. See: Ballentyne; Internat. Dict. Ap. Math.; James.

Boolean calculus (Boole, George): Mathematics. See: Hughes; Markus.

Boolean function (Boole, George): Mathematics. See: Markus.

Boole's inequality (Boole, George): Statistics. See: Kendall.

Boole's theorem (Boole, George): Mathematics. See: Ballentyne.

BOONE, DANIEL. 1734-1820. American pioneer. See: Dict. Amer. Biog. Daniel Boone.

BOORD, CECIL ERNEST. b. 1884. American chemist. See: Amer. Men Sci., 10th ed. Boord synthesis?

Boord synthesis (Boord, Cecil Ernest?): Chemistry. See: Van Nostrand Chem. Dict.

Boot density bottle (Boot, Henry Albert Howard?): Chemistry. See: Hackh.

BOOT, HENRY ALBERT HOWARD. 1914- . English physicist. See: World Who's Who Sci. Boot density bottle?

BOOTH, EDWIN. d. 1917. American chemist. Cited in: Min. Mag., vol. 13 (1903) p. 365. Boothite.

BOOTH, GEORGE. 1622-1684. English political and military leader. See: Dict. Nat. Biog. Booth's rising.

BOOTH, JOHN WILKES. 1838-1865. American actor and assassin. See: Dict. Amer. Biog. Booth's conspiracy.

Boothby, Lovelace, and Bulbulian mask (Boothby, Walter Meredith; Lovelace, William Randolph II; and Bulbulian, Arthur H.): Medicine. See: Stedman.

BOOTHBY, WALTER MEREDITH. 1880-1953. American medical researcher. See: World Who's Who Sci. Boothby, Lovelace, and Bulbulian mask.

Boothite (Booth, Edwin): Earth Sciences. See: Thrush; Webster's 3d.

Boothroyd–Creamer system (Derivation undetermined): Physics. See: Hughes; Internat. Dict. Phys. Elec.

Booth's conspiracy (Booth, John Wilkes): History. See: Harbottle; Phyfe.

Booth's rising (Booth, George): History. See: Steinberg.

Booze (Booze, E.): Generic Word (whiskey). See: Hendrickson.

BOOZE, E. fl. 1840. American distiller. (Biography source unavailable.) Booze.

Borchardt automatic pistol (Borchardt, Hugo): Weapons. See: Quick.

BORCHARDT, HUGO. fl. 19th c. American inventor. (Biography source unavailable.) Borchardt automatic pistol.

BORCHARDT, LEO. b. 1879. German chemist. See: Biog. Lex. hervorr. Aerzte, 1880–1930. Borchardt's test.

Borchardt's test (Borchardt, Leo): Chemistry. See: Dorland.

Borcher('s) process (Derivation undetermined): Chemistry. See: Thrush; Van Nostrand Chem. Dict.

Borchers furnace (Borchers, Johannes Albert Wilhelm?): Chemistry. See: Van Nostrand Chem. Dict.

BORCHERS, JOHANNES ALBERT WILHELM. 1856–1925. German metallurgist. See: World Who's Who Sci. Borchers furnace?

BORDA, JEAN CHARLES. 1733–1799. French physicist and mathematician. See: Dict. Sci. Biog. Borda's mouthpiece (or nozzle).

Borda's mouthpiece (or nozzle) (Borda, Jean Charles): Physics. See: Auger; Internat. Dict. Phys. Elec.

BORDE, ANDREW. ca. 1490–1549. English physician. See: Dict. Nat. Biog. Merry–Andrew.

Borde reagents (Derivation undetermined): Chemistry. See: Van Nostrand Chem. Dict.

Bordet and Gengou's potato blood agar (Bordet, Jules Jean Baptiste Vincent and Gengou, Octave): Medicine. See: Stedman.

Bordet–Gengou bacillus (Bordet, Jules Jean Baptiste Vincent and Gengou, Octave): Medicine. See: Stedman.

Bordet–Gengou phenomenon (Bordet, Jules Jean Baptiste Vincent and Gengou, Octave): Medicine. See: Stedman.

Bordet–Gengou test (Bordet, Jules Jean Baptiste Vincent and Gengou, Octave): Medicine. See: Stedman; Webster's 3d.

BORDET, JULES JEAN BAPTISTE VINCENT. 1870–1961. Belgian bacteriologist. See: Dict. Sci. Biog. Bordet and Gengou's potato blood agar, Bordet–Gengou bacillus, Bordet–Gengou phenomenon, Bordet–Gengou test, Bordet test, Bordetella, Bordet's phenomenon, Bordet's precipitin test.

Bordet test (Bordet, Jules Jean Baptiste Vincent): Medicine. See: Hackh; Stedman; Van Nostrand Chem. Dict.

Bordetella (Bordet, Jules Jean Baptiste Vincent): Medicine. See: Stedman.

Bordet's phenomenon (Bordet, Jules Jean Baptiste Vincent): Medicine. See: Dorland; Stedman.

Bordet's precipitin test (Bordet, Jules Jean Baptiste Vincent): Medicine. See: Stedman.

BORDEU, THEOPHILE DE. 1722–1776. French physician. See: Dict. Sci. Biog. De Bordeu theory.

Bordeu theory (Bordeu, Theophile de). See: De Bordeu theory.

Bordoni effect (or peak) (Bordoni, Ugo?): Physics. See: Ballentyne; Thewlis; Van Nostrand Sci. Encyc.

BORDONI, UGO. 1884–1952. Italian physicist. See: Pogg., vols. 6, 7b. Bordoni effect (or peak)?

Boreal (Boreas): Generic Word (northern). See: Partridge.

BOREAS. Greek mythical God of the North Wind. See: Oxford Clas. Dict. Boreal.

Borel–Cantelli lemmas (Borel, Emile and Cantelli, Francesco Paolo): Statistics. See: Kendall.

Borel covering theorem (Borel, Emile). See: Heine–Borel theorem.

BOREL, EMILE (In full: FELIX EDOUARD EMILE). 1871–1956. French mathematician. See: Dict. Sci. Biog. Borel–Cantelli lemmas, Borel measurable function, Borel set (or measurable set), Borel–Tanner distribution, Heine–Borel theorem.

Borel measurable function (Borel, Emile). See: Baire function.

Borel set (or measurable set) (Borel, Emile): Mathematics. See: James.

Borel–Tanner distribution (Borel, Emile and Tanner, J. C.): Mathematics. See: James.

BOREN, JAMES. fl. 1970. American writer. (Biography source unavailable.) Boren's laws.

Boren's laws (Boren, James): Sociology. See: Martin.

Borgenet furnace (Derivation undetermined): Engineering and Industry. See: Thrush.

BORGHESE. fl. 1837. American counterfeiter. (Biography source unavailable.) Bogus.

BORGHESIO, G. fl. 1910. Italian chemist. Cited in: Chem. Abstr., vol. 5, p. 738. Borghesio test.

Borghesio test (Borghesio, G.): Chemistry. See: Van Nostrand Chem. Dict.

Borgia (Borgia family): Generic Word (poisoner). See: Hendrickson.

BORGIA FAMILY. fl. 15–16th c. Influential Italian family. See: Webster's Biog. Dict. Borgia, Borgia ring.

Borgia ring (Borgia family): Fashion. See: Picken.

Borgmann test for beta-naphthol (Derivation undetermined): Chemistry. See: Van Nostrand Chem. Dict.

Borgmann test for organic halogens (Derivation undetermined): Chemistry. See: Van Nostrand Chem. Dict.

BORINSKI, PAUL. b. 1881. German chemist. Cited in: Chem. Abstr., vol. 20, p. 3752. Borinski reagent.

Borinski reagent (Borinski, Paul): Chemistry. See: Van Nostrand Chem. Dict.

Born (and) Von Karman theory (of specific heat) (Born, Max and Von Karman, Theordore): Physics. See: Internat. Dict. Ap. Math.; Internat. Dict. Phys. Elec.; Van Nostrand Sci. Encyc.

Born approximation (Born, Max): Physics. See: Ballentyne; Internat. Dict. Ap. Math.; Markus.

Born equation (Born, Max): Physics. See: Ballentyne; Thrush.

BORN, GUSTAV JACOB. 1851–1900. German anatomist. See: Sci., vol. 12 (1900) p. 237. Born method of wax plate reconstruction.

Born–Haber cycle (Born, Max and Haber, Fritz): Physics. See: Ballentyne; Hackh; Internat. Dict. Ap. Math.

Born–Heisenberg representation (Born, Max and Heisenberg, Werner Karl): Physics. See: Internat. Dict. Phys. Elec. Also known as: Heisenberg representation.

BORN, IGNAZ VON. 1742–1791. Austrian mineralogist. See: Dict. Sci. Biog. Bornite.

Born–Infeld theory (Born, Max and Infeld, Leopold): Physics. See: Internat. Dict. Ap. Math.; Internat. Dict. Phys. Elec.

BORN, MAX. 1882–1970. German physicist. See: World Who's Who Sci. Born approximation, Born equation, Born–Haber cycle, Born–Heisenberg representation, Born–Infeld theory, Born–Mayer equation, Born–Oppenheimer approximation, Born–Oppenheimer method, Born repulsion, Born (and) Von Karman theory (of specific heat), Born–Von Karman boundary conditions.

Born–Mayer equation (Born, Max and Mayer, Joseph Edward): Physics. See: Internat. Dict. Ap. Math.; Internat. Dict. Phys. Elec.; Thewlis.

Born method of wax plate reconstruction (Born, Gustav Jacob): Medicine. See: Stedman.

Born–Oppenheimer approximation (Born, Max and Oppenheimer, J. Robert): Physics. See: Thewlis.

Born-Oppenheimer method (Born, Max and Oppenheimer, J. Robert): Physics. See: Internat. Dict. Ap. Math.; Thewlis; Van Nostrand Sci. Encyc.

Born repulsion (Born, Max): Physics. See: Internat. Dict. Ap. Math.

Born-Von Karman boundary conditions (Born, Max and Von Karman, Theodore): Physics. See: Thewlis.

Bornemann reaction (Derivation undetermined): Chemistry. See: Van Nostrand Chem. Dict.

BORNET, L. fl. 1924. French chemist. Cited in: Chem. Abstr., vol. 19, p. 1388. Bornet reagent.

Bornet reagent (Bornet, L.): Chemistry. See: Van Nostrand Chem. Dict.

Bornhardt (residual hill) (Bornhardt, B. W.): Earth Sciences. See: Monkhouse.

BORNHARDT, WILHELM. b. 1864. German geologist. Cited in: Min. Mag. vol. 31 (1958), p. 955. Bornhardtite.

Bornhardtite (Bornhardt, Wilhelm): Earth Sciences. See: Thrush.

Bornite (Born, Ignaz von): Earth Sciences. See: Thrush; Van Nostrand Sci. Encyc.; Webster's 3d.

BORNTRAEGER, HUGO. fl. 1879. German chemist. Cited in: Royal Soc. Cat. Sci. Pap., 1874-83. Borntraeger test for aloes?, Borntraeger test for amyl alcohol?, Borntraeger test for ferrous ion?, Borntraeger test for resorcinol and thymol?, Borntraeger test for senna?

Borntraeger test for aloes (Borntraeger, Hugo?): Chemistry. See: Van Nostrand Chem. Dict.

Borntraeger test for amyl alcohol (Borntraeger, Hugo?): Chemistry. See: Van Nostrand Chem. Dict.

Borntraeger test for ferrous ion (Borntraeger, Hugo?): Chemistry. See: Van Nostrand Chem. Dict.

Borntraeger test for resorcinol and thymol (Borntraeger, Hugo?): Chemistry. See: Van Nostrand Chem. Dict.

Borntraeger test for senna (Borntraeger, Hugo?): Chemistry. See: Van Nostrand Chem. Dict.

BOROSCHEK, L. fl. 1902. American chemist. Cited in: Kelly. Rudisch-Boroschek reagent.

BOROVSKII, PETER FOKITSCH. 1863-1932. Russian physician. See: Biog. Lex. hervorr. Aerzte, 1880-1930. Borovskii's disease.

Borovskii's disease (Borovskii, Peter Fokitsch). See: Alibert's disease (2).

Borovsky, Peter Fokich. See: Borovskii, Peter Fokitsch.

Borowsky, Peter Fokich. See: Borovskii, Peter Fokitsch.

BORREL, ADAM. fl. 1650. Religious leader. (Biography source unavailable.) Borrelists.

BORREL, AMEDEE. 1867-1936. French bacteriologist. See: World Who's Who Sci. Borrel bodies, Borrelia, Borrelomycetaceae, Borrel's blue stain.

Borrel bodies (Borrel, Amedee): Medicine. See: Stedman; Webster's 3d.

Borrel grinder (Derivation undetermined): Chemistry. See: Hackh.

Borrelia (Borrel, Amedee): Medicine. See: Dorland; Pennak; Stedman.

Borrelists (Borrel, Adam): Religion. See: Canney.

Borrelomycetaceae (Borrel, Amedee): Medicine. See: Webster's 3d.

Borrel's blue stain (Borrel, Amedee): Medicine. See: Stedman; Webster's 3d.

BORRER, WILLIAM. 1781-1862. English botanist. See: Dict. Nat. Biog. Borreria.

Borreria (Borrer, William): Botany. See: Webster's 3d.

Borrichia (Borrichius, Olaus): Botany. See: Webster's 3d.

BORRICHIUS, OLAUS. 1626-1690. Danish medical writer. See: Dict. Sci. Biog. Borrichia.

BORRIES, GUSTAV VALDEMAR THEODOR. fl. 1921. German? physician. Cited in: New York Acad. Med. Portrait Cat. Borries' syndrome.

Borries' syndrome (Borries, Gustav Valdemar Theodor): Medicine. See: Jablonski.

Borrmann effect (Borrmann, Gerhard Heinrich): Physics. See: Ballentyne; Thewlis.

BORRMANN, GERHARD HEINRICH. 1908- . German physicist. See: Who's Who Sci. Europe. Borrmann effect.

Borsche-Drechsel synthesis (Borsche, Walther Georg Rudolf and Drechsel, Ferdinand Heinrich Edmund): Chemistry. See: Van Nostrand Chem. Dict.

BORSCHE, WALTHER GEORG RUDOLF. 1877-1950. German chemist. See: World Who's Who Sci. Borsche-Drechsel synthesis.

BORSIERI DE KANIFELD, GIOVANNI BATTISTA. 1725-1785. Italian physician and medical writer. See: Nouv. Biog. Univ. Borsieri's line.

Borsieri's line (Borsieri de Kanifeld, Giovanni Battista): Medicine. See: Dorland.

Borst-Jadassohn epithelioma (Borst, Maximilian and Jadassohn, Josef): Medicine. See: Jablonski; Stedman.

BORST, MAXIMILIAN. 1869-1946. German pathologist. See: World Who's Who Sci. Borst-Jadassohn epithelioma.

BORTHEN, JOHAN. No dates. Norwegian oculist. (Biography source unavailable.) Borthen's operation.

Borthen's operation (Borthen, Johan): Medicine. See: Dorland; Stedman.

BORY DE SAINT VINCENT, JEAN BAPTISTE GEORGES MARIE. 1778-1846. French geographer and naturalist. See: Dict. Sci. Biog. Borya.

Borya (Bory de Saint Vincent, Jean Baptiste Georges Marie): Botany. See: Charnock.

BORZI, ANTONINO. 1852-1921. Italian botanist. See: Biog. Noes Upon Botanists. Borzicactus.

Borzicactus (Borzi, Antonino): Botany. See: Webster's 3d.

BOSANQUET, B. J. T. fl. 1900-1910. English bowler. (Biography source unavailable.) Bosey.

BOSANQUET, ROBERT HOLFORD MACDOWELL. 1841-1912. English physicist. See: Sci., vol. 36 (1912) p. 273. Bosanquet's law?

Bosanquet's law (Bosanquet, Robert Holford Macdowell?): Physics. See: Ballentyne; Internat. Dict. Ap. Math.

BOSCH HERNANDEZ, JUAN. fl. 1963. Spanish physician. (Biography source unavailable.) Gardner-Bosch syndrome.

BOSCH, KARL. 1874-1940. German chemist. See: Dict. Sci. Biog. Bosch-Meiser urea process, Bosch reactor, Haber-Bosch process.

Bosch lamp (Bosch, Robert August): Engineering and Industry. Cited in: Encyc. Brit., 1973 under "Bosch, Robert August."

Bosch magneto (Bosch, Robert August): Engineering and Industry. Cited in: Encyc. Brit., 1973 under "Bosch, Robert August."

Bosch-Meiser urea process (Bosch, Karl and Meiser, Wilhelm Ottmar): Chemistry. See: Van Nostrand Chem. Dict.

BOSCH MILLARES, JUAN. fl. 1963. Spanish physician. (Biography source unavailable.) Gardner-Bosch syndrome.

Bosch process (Bosch, Karl). See: Haber-Bosch process.

Bosch reactor (Bosch, Karl): Chemistry. See: New Encyc. Brit., 1974, Microp.

BOSCH, ROBERT AUGUST. 1861-1942. German engineer and industrialist. See: Encyc. Brit., 1973. Bosch lamp, Bosch magneto, Bosch spark plug.

Bosch spark plug (Bosch, Robert August): Engineering and Industry. Cited in: Encyc. Brit., 1973 under "Bosch, Robert August."

Boscia (Bose, L.): Botany. See: Charnock.

Bose distribution (Bose, Raj Chandra): Statistics. See: Kendall.

Bose-Einstein condensation (Bose, Satyendra Nath and Einstein, Albert): Physics. See: Ballentyne; Internat. Dict. Phys. Elec.; Thewlis.

Bose–Einstein distribution (Bose, Satyendra Nath and Einstein, Albert): Physics. See: Internat. Dict. Ap. Math.

Bose–Einstein gas (Bose, Satyendra Nath and Einstein, Albert): Physics. See: Internat. Dict. Ap. Math.; Internat. Dict. Phys. Elec.

Bose–Einstein liquid (Bose, Satyendra Nath and Einstein, Albert): Physics. See: Internat. Dict. Ap. Math.; Thewlis.

Bose–Einstein particles (Bose, Satyendra Nath and Einstein, Albert). See: Boson.

Bose–Einstein statistics (Bose, Satyendra Nath and Einstein, Albert): Physics. See: Ballentyne; Internat. Dict. Ap. Math.; Kendall.

BOSE, ERNST GOTTLOB. 1723-1788. German botanist. See: Biog. Notes Upon Botanists. Bosea.

BOSE, HEINRICH. 1840-1900. German surgeon. See: Biog. Lex. hervorr. Aerzte. Bose's hooks.

BOSE, L. No dates. French naturalist. (Biography source unavailable.) Boscia.

Bose–Nicholson test (Derivation undetermined): Chemistry. See: Van Nostrand Chem. Dict.

BOSE, PRAFULLA KUMAR. fl. 1924-1958. Indian chemist. See: Pogg., vols. 6, 7b. Bose test for nitro-group in organic compounds, Bose test for polyhydroxy phenols, Bose test for reducing sugars.

BOSE, RAJ CHANDRA. 1901- . Indian statistician and mathematician. See: World Who's Who Sci. Bose distribution.

BOSE, SATYENDRA NATH. 1894-1974. Indian physicist. See: Who's Who, 1974. Bose–Einstein condensation, Bose–Einstein distribution, Bose–Einstein gas, Bose–Einstein liquid, Bose–Einstein statistics, Boson.

Bose test for nitro-group in organic compounds (Bose, Prafulla Kumar): Chemistry. See: Van Nostrand Chem. Dict.

Bose test for polyhydroxy phenols (Bose, Prafulla Kumar): Chemistry. See: Van Nostrand Chem. Dict.

Bose test for reducing sugars (Bose, Prafulla Kumar): Chemistry. See: Van Nostrand Chem. Dict.

Bosea (Bose, Ernst Gottlob): Botany. See: Charnock.

BOSELEY, LEONARD KIDGELL. fl. 1893-1909. American chemist. Cited in: Royal Soc. Cat. Sci. Pap., 1884-1900. Richmond–Boseley test for formaldehyde in milk, Richmond–Boseley test reaction for formaldehyde.

Bose's hooks (Bose, Heinrich): Medicine. See: Dorland.

Bosey (Bosanquet, B. J. T.): Recreation and Sports. See: Brewer; Hendrickson; Partridge.

Boson (Bose, Satyendra Nath): Physics. See: Internat. Dict. Phys. Elec.; Markus; Van Nostrand Sci. Encyc. Also known as: Bose–Einstein particles.

BOSS, MARTIN P. fl. 1910. American metallurgist. Cited in: Chem. Abstr., Decenn. Index, 1907-16. Boss process?

Boss process (Boss, Martin P.?): Engineering and Industry. See: Thrush.

Bossi dilator (Bossi, Luigi Maria): Medicine. See: Dorland; Stedman.

BOSSI, LUIGI MARIA. 1859-1919. Italian gynecologist. See: Biog. Lex. hervorr. Aerzte, 1880-1930. Bossi dilator.

Bossioea (Martiniere, Antoine-Augustin-Bruzen de la?): Botany. See: Charnock.

BOSTOCK, JOHN. 1773-1846. English physician. See: Dict. Sci. Biog. Bostock's catarrh.

Bostock's catarrh (Bostock, John): Medicine. See: Dorland; Jablonski; Stedman.

BOSTON, LEONARD NAPOLEON. 1871-1931. American physician. See: World Who's Who Sci. Boston's sign.

Boston's sign (Boston, Leonard Napoleon): Medicine. See: Dorland; Stedman.

BOSTROEM, EUGEN WALDEMAR. 1850-1928. German pathologist and bacteriologist. See: Bulloch. Bostroem's stain.

Bostroem's stain (Bostroem, Eugen Waldemar): Medicine. See: Stedman.

BOSVIEL, J. fl. 1911. French physician. (Biography source unavailable.) Bosviel's syndrome.

Bosviel–Martin syndrome (Bosviel, J. and Martin, A.). See: Bosviel's syndrome.

Bosviel's syndrome (Bosviel, J.): Medicine. See: Jablonski. Also known as: Bosviel–Martin syndrome.

Boswell fluorescein reaction (Boswell, Maitland Crease?): Chemistry. See: Van Nostrand Chem. Dict.

BOSWELL, JAMES. 1740-1795. Scottish lawyer and biographer. See: Dict. Nat. Biog. Boswellia, Boswellism, Boswellize.

BOSWELL, MAITLAND CREASE. 1879-1952. American chemist. See: Pogg., vols. 6, 7b. Boswell fluorescein reaction?

Boswellia (Boswell, James): Botany. See: Charnock; Webster's 3d.

Boswellism (Boswell, James): Literature. See: Charnock.

Boswellize (Boswell, James): Generic Word. See: Hendrickson; Partridge; Webster's 3d.

BOTALLO, LEONARDO. 1530- ca. 1587. Italian physician. See: Dict. Sci. Biog. Botallo's bundle, Botallo's duct, Botallo's foramen, Botallo's ligament.

Botallo's bundle (Botallo, Leonardo): Medicine. See: Donath.

Botallo's duct (Botallo, Leonardo): Medicine. See: Dorland; Gray; Henderson.

Botallo's foramen (Botallo, Leonardo): Medicine. See: Dorland; Stedman.

Botallo's ligament (Botallo, Leonardo): Medicine. See: Stedman.

Botallus, Leonardus. See: Botallo, Leonardo.

BOTELHO. No dates. Physician in Paris. (Biography source unavailable.) Botelho's test.

Botelho's test (Botelho): Medicine. See: Dorland; Stedman.

BOTHWELL. No dates. Scottish mint-master. (Biography source unavailable.) Bodle (coin).

BOTKIN, SERGEI PETROVICH. 1832-1889. Russian physician. See: Biog. Lex. hervorr. Aerzte. Botkin's disease.

Botkin's disease (Botkin, Sergei Petrovich): Medicine. See: Jablonski; Stedman.

Botteri's sparrow (Derivation undetermined): Zoology. See: Gray.

Bottin (Bottin, Sebastien): Business. See: Partridge.

BOTTIN, SEBASTIEN. 1764-1853. French government administrator and statistician. See: Nouv. Biog. Univ. Bottin.

BOUCHARD, CHARLES JACQUES. 1837-1915. French physician. See: World Who's Who Sci. aneurysm of Charcot and Bouchard, Bouchard's coefficient, Bouchard's disease, Bouchard's nodes, Bouchard's sign.

BOUCHARDAT, APOLLINAIRE. 1806-1886. French chemist. See: World Who's Who Sci. Bouchardat reagent, Bouchardat's test.

Bouchardat reagent (Bouchardat, Apollinaire): Chemistry. See: Hackh; Van Nostrand Chem. Dict.

Bouchardat's test (Bouchardat, Apollinaire): Chemistry. See: Dorland; Stedman.

Bouchard's coefficient (Bouchard, Charles Jacques): Medicine. See: Dorland.

Bouchard's disease (Bouchard, Charles Jacques): Medicine. See: Dorland; Jablonski; Stedman.

Bouchard's nodes (Bouchard, Charles Jacques): Medicine. See: Dorland.

Bouchard's sign (Bouchard, Charles Jacques): Medicine. See: Dorland.

Boucher (Boucher de Crevecoeur de Perthes, Jacques): Anthropology. See: Partridge; Winick.

BOUCHER DE CREVECOEUR DE PERTHES, JACQUES. 1788-1868. French archaeologist. See: Dict. Sci. Biog. Boucher.

BOUCHERIE, AUGUSTE. 1801-1871. French chemist. Cited in: Royal Soc. Cat. Sci. Pap., 1800-63. Boucherie process (or Boucherize).

Boucherie process (or Boucherize) (Boucherie, Auguste): Chemistry. See: Partridge; Webster's 3d.; Weekley.

Boucheron speculum (Derivation undetermined): Medicine. See: Stedman.

Boucherot circuit (Boucherot, Paul Marie Joachim?): Electronics. See: Hughes.

BOUCHEROT, PAUL MARIE JOACHIM. 1869-1943. French electrical engineer. See: World Who's Who Sci. Boucherot circuit?

BOUCHUT, JEAN ANTOINE EUGENE. 1818-1891. French physician. See: World Who's Who Sci. Bouchut's method, Bouchut's respiration, Bouchut's tube.

Bouchut's method (Bouchut, Jean Antoine Eugene): Medicine. See: Stedman.

Bouchut's respiration (Bouchut, Jean Antoine Eugene): Medicine. See: Dorland; Stedman.

Bouchut's tube (Bouchut, Jean Antoine Eugene): Medicine. See: Dorland; Stedman.

BOUDIN, JEAN CHRISTIAN MARC FRANCOIS JOSEPH. 1806-1867. French physician. See: Biog. Lex. hervorr. Aerzte. Boudin's law, Boudin's method.

Boudin's law (Boudin, Jean Christian Marc Francois Joseph): Medicine. See: Dorland.

Boudin's method (Boudin, Jean Christian Marc Francois Joseph): Medicine. See: Stedman.

Bouffardi's black mycetoma (Derivation undetermined): Medicine. See: Stedman.

Bougainvillaea (Bougainville, Louis Antoine de): Botany. See: Hendrickson; Partridge; Taylor, N.

BOUGAINVILLE, LOUIS ANTOINE DE. 1729-1811. French navigator. See: Dict. Sci. Biog. Bougainvillaea, Bougainvillia.

Bougainvillia (Bougainville, Louis Antoine de): Zoology. See: Pennak; Webster's 3d.

BOUGARD, JEAN JOSEPH. 1815-1884. Belgian physician. See: Biog. Lex. hervorr. Aerzte. Bougard's paste.

Bougard's paste (Bougard, Jean Joseph): Medicine. See: Dorland.

Bougault arsenic reagent (Bougault, Joseph?): Chemistry. See: Van Nostrand Chem. Dict.

BOUGAULT, JOSEPH. 1870-1955. French chemist. See: Pogg., vols. 5, 6, 7b. Bougault arsenic reagent?, Bougault sodium reagent?

Bougault sodium reagent (Bougault, Joseph?): Chemistry. See: Van Nostrand Chem. Dict.

BOUGE, H. fl. 1913. French chemist. Cited in: Chem. Abstr., vol. 7, p. 679. Bouge test for chlorine in iodine.

Bouge test for chlorine in iodine (Bouge, H.): Chemistry. See: Van Nostrand Chem. Dict.

Bouguer anomaly (Bouguer, Pierre): Earth Sciences. See: Monkhouse; Thrush.

Bouguer-Beer law (Bouguer, Pierre and Beer, August). See: Bouguer's law.

Bouguer correction (or reduction) (Bouguer, Pierre): Earth Sciences. See: Thrush.

Bouguer gravity (Bouguer, Pierre): Earth Sciences. See: Thrush.

Bouguer-Lambert law of absorption (Bouguer, Pierre and Lambert, Johann Heinrich). See: Bouguer's law.

Bouguer photometer (Bouguer, Pierre): Physics. See: Thewlis.

BOUGUER, PIERRE. 1698-1758. French hydrographer and mathematician. See: Dict. Sci. Biog. Bouguer anomaly, Bouguer correction (or reduction), Bouguer gravity, Bouguer photometer, Bouguer's halo, Bouguer's law.

Bouguer's halo (Bouguer, Pierre). See: Ulloa's ring (bow, or circle).

Bouguer's law (Bouguer, Pierre): Physics. See: Huschke; Internat. Dict. Ap. Math.; Van Nostrand Sci. Encyc. Also known as: Bouguer-Beer law, Bouguer-Lambert law of absorption, Lambert-Bouguer law of absorption, Lambert's law (2) (law of absorption or law of Lambert).

BOUILLAUD, JEAN BAPTISTE. 1796-1881. French physician. See: Nouv. Biog. Univ. Bouillaud's disease, Bouillaud's tinkle.

Bouillaud's disease (Bouillaud, Jean Baptiste): Medicine. See: Dorland; Jablonski, Stedman. Also known as: Sokolskii-Bouillaud disease.

Bouillaud's tinkle (Bouillaud, Jean Baptiste): Medicine. See: Dorland.

BOUILLY, VINCENT GEORGES. 1848-1903. French gynecologist. See: World Who's Who Sci. Bouilly's operation.

Bouilly's operation (Bouilly, Vincent Georges): Medicine. See: Stedman.

BOUIN, POL ANDRE. 1870-1962. French histologist. See: Dict. Sci. Biog. Bouin's fluid (or solution).

Bouin's fluid (or solution) (Bouin, Pol Andre): Medicine. See: Hackh; Pennak; Stedman.

BOULANGER, CHARLES LOUIS. 1810-1849. French mining engineer. See: Pogg., vol. 3. Boulangerite.

BOULANGER, GEORGES ERNEST JEAN MARIE. 1837-1891. French general. See: Encyc. Brit., 1973. Boulangism (Boulangists or Boulangerite).

Boulangerite (Boulanger, Charles Louis): Earth Sciences. See: Charnock; Thrush; Van Nostrand Sci. Encyc.

Boulangism (Boulangists or Boulangerite) (Boulanger, Georges Ernest Jean Marie): History. See: Brewer; Harbottle; Hendrickson.

Boulle (Boulle, Andre Charles): Applied Arts. See: Brewer; Briggs; Partridge.

BOULLE, ANDRE CHARLES. 1642-1732. French cabinet-maker. See: Encyc. Brit., 1973. Boulle.

Boulton process (Derivation undetermined): Engineering and Industry. See: Thrush.

Boulvin diagram (Derivation undetermined): Physics. See: Internat. Dict. Ap. Math.

BOULWARE, LEMUEL RICKETTS. 1895- . American industrial executive. See: Who's Who Amer., 1950-51. Boulwarism.

Boulwarism (Boulware, Lemuel Ricketts): Sociology. See: Barnhart (New Eng.)

BOUMA, JAC. fl. 1901. Dutch physiologist. Cited in: Kelly. Bouma reagent.

Bouma reagent (Bouma, Jac): Chemistry. See: Van Nostrand Chem. Dict.

BOUNTIFUL, LADY. Character in George Farquhar's comedy, "The Beaux' Stratagem" (1707). See: Benet. Lady Bountiful.

Bourbon (or Bourbonism) (Bourbon family): Generic Word (ultra-conservatism). See: Partridge; Webster's 3d.

BOURBON FAMILY. fl. 16-19th c. French royal family. See: Encyc. Brit., 1973. Bourbon (or Bourbonism), Bourbon (whiskey).

Bourbon (whiskey) (Bourbon family): Food and Drink. See: Hendrickson; Partridge.

BOURCEAU. fl. 1897. French physician. Cited in: Kelly. Bourceau reagent.

Bourceau reagent (Bourceau): Chemistry. See: Van Nostrand Chem. Dict.

Bourcet test (Derivation undetermined): Chemistry. See: Van Nostrand Chem. Dict.

BOURDIER, LEON. fl. 1908. French chemist. Cited in: Chem. Abstr., vol. 2, p. 1595. Bourdier tests for verbenalin.

Bourdier tests for verbenalin (Bourdier, Leon): Chemistry. See: Van Nostrand Chem. Dict.

BOURDILLON, HENRY TOWNSEND. 1913- . English statesman. See: Who's Who, 1961. Bourdillon report.

Bourdillon report (Bourdillon, Henry Townsend): Library Science. See: Harrod.

BOURDON, EUGENE. 1808-1884. French instrument maker. See: Dict. Sci. Biog. Bourdon gauge, Bourdon spring, Bourdon thermometer, Bourdon tube.

Bourdon gauge (Bourdon, Eugene): Physics. See: Auger; Internat. Dict. Phys. Elec.; Thewlis.

Bourdon spring (Bourdon, Eugene): Physics. See: Webster's 3d.

Bourdon thermometer (Bourdon, Eugene): Physics. See: Van Nostrand Sci. Encyc.

Bourdon tube (Bourdon, Eugene): Physics. See: Huschke; Thewlis; Thrush.

BOURGEOIS. No dates. French type-founder and printer. (Biography source unavailable.) Bourgeois (type)?

Bourgeois (type) (Bourgeois?): Printing. See: Partridge.

BOURGERY, MARC-JEAN. 1797-1849. French anatomist and surgeon. See: Nouv. Biog. Univ. Bourgery's ligament.

Bourgery's ligament (Bourgery, Marc-Jean): Medicine. See: Dorland; Stedman.

BOURGET, LOUIS. 1856-1913. Swiss pathologist and chemist. See: Biog. Lex. hervorr. Aerzte, 1880-1930. Bourget's test.

Bourget's test (Bourget, Louis): Medicine. See: Dorland; Stedman.

Bourguignon, Louis Dominique. See: Cartouche.

BOURIGNON, ANTOINETTE. 1616-1680. Flemish mystic and visionary. See: Encyc. Brit., 1973. Bourignonists.

Bourignonists (Bourignon, Antoinette): Religion. See: Canney; Latham; Mathews, S.

BOURNE. No dates. English preacher. (Biography source unavailable.) Bourneans.

Bourneans (Bourne): Religion. See: Canney.

Bourneville-Brissaud disease (Bourneville, Desire-Magloire and Brissaud, Edouard). See: Bourneville's disease (or syndrome).

BOURNEVILLE, DESIRE-MAGLOIRE. 1840-1909. French neurologist. See: World Who's Who Sci. Bourneville's disease (or syndrome).

Bourneville-Pringle syndrome (Bourneville, Desire-Magloire and Pringle, John James). See: Bourneville's disease (or syndrome).

Bourneville's disease (or syndrome) (Bourneville, Desire-Magloire): Medicine. See: Dorland; Hinsie; Stedman. Also known as: Bourneville-Brissaud disease, Bourneville-Pringle syndrome, Pringle's disease (or adenoma).

BOURNON, JACQUES LOUIS, COMTE DE. 1751-1825. French mineralogist. See: Dict. Sci. Biog. Bournonite.

Bournonite (Bournon, Jacques Louis, Comte de): Earth Sciences. See: Charnock; Thrush; Van Nostrand Sci. Encyc.

BOURQUIN, ANN. 1897- . American chemist. See: Amer. Men Sci., 10th ed. Sherman-Bourquin unit.

Bourreria (Derivation undetermined): Botany. See: Charnock.

Boussinesq approximation (Boussinesq, Joseph Valentin): Physics. See: Huschke; Van Nostrand Sci. Encyc.

Boussinesq equation (Boussinesq, Joseph Valentin): Physics. See: Thrush.

BOUSSINESQ, JOSEPH VALENTIN. 1842-1929. French physicist. See: Dict. Sci. Biog. Boussinesq approximation, Boussinesq equation, Boussinesq number, problem of Boussinesq and Cerruti.

Boussinesq number (Boussinesq, Joseph Valentin): Physics. See: Huschke.

BOUSSINGAULT, JEAN BAPTISTE JOSEPH DIEUDONNE. 1802-1887. French chemist. See: Dict. Sci. Biog. Boussingault test, Boussingaultia, Boussingaultite.

Boussingault test (Boussingault, Jean Baptiste Joseph Dieudonne): Chemistry. See: Van Nostrand Chem. Dict.

Boussingaultia (Boussingault, Jean Baptiste Joseph Dieudonne): Botany. See: Taylor, N.; Webster's 3d.

Boussingaultite (Boussingault, Jean Baptiste Joseph Dieudonne): Earth Sciences. See: Webster's 3d.

BOUTELOU, CLAUDIO. 1774-1842. Spanish botanist. See: Biog. Notes Upon Botanists. Bouteloua.

Bouteloua (Boutelou, Claudio): Botany. See: Webster's 3d.

BOUVARD, CHARLES. 1572-1658. French physician. See: Nouv. Biog. Univ. Bouvardia.

Bouvardia (Bouvard, Charles): Botany. See: Charnock; Taylor, N.; Webster's 3d.

Bouveault aldehyde synthesis (Bouveault, Louis): Chemistry. See: Van Nostrand Chem. Dict.

Bouveault-Blanc reduction (Bouveault, Louis and Blanc, Gustave Louis): Chemistry. See: Ballentyne; Van Nostrand Chem. Dict.; Webster's 3d.

BOUVEAULT, LOUIS. 1864-1909. French chemist. See: World Who's Who Sci. Bouveault aldehyde synthesis, Bouveault-Blanc reduction, Bouveault reagent for fatty acids.

Bouveault reagent for fatty acids (Bouveault, Louis): Chemistry. See: Van Nostrand Chem. Dict.

Bouveret-Hoffmann syndrome (Bouveret, Leon and Hoffmann, August). See: Bouveret's syndrome.

BOUVERET, LEON. 1850-1929. French physician. See: World Who's Who Sci. Bouveret's disease, Bouveret's sign, Bouveret's syndrome, Bouveret's ulceration.

Bouveret's disease (Bouveret, Leon): Medicine. See: Dorland.

Bouveret's sign (Bouveret, Leon): Medicine. See: Dorland; Stedman.

Bouveret's syndrome (Bouveret, Leon): Medicine. See: Jablonski. Also known as: Bouveret-Hoffmann syndrome.

Bouveret's ulceration (Bouveret, Leon): Medicine. See: Dorland.

BOUVRAIN, YVES ROBERT. 1910- . French physician. (Biography source unavailable.) Sezary-Bouvrain disease.

BOUWERS, ALBERT. b. 1893. Dutch physicist. See: Pogg., vols. 6, 7b. Maksutov-Bouwers telescope.

Bovarism (or Bovarize) (Bovary, Emma): Generic Word. See: Hendrickson; Hinsie; Webster's 3d.

BOVARY, EMMA. Character in Gustav Flaubert's novel "Madame Bovary" (1856). See: Benet. Bovarism (or Bovarize), Madame Bovary.

BOVERI, PIERO. 1879-1932. Italian neurologist. (Biography source unavailable.) Boveri's test.

BOVERI, THEODOR. 1862-1915. German zoologist. See: Dict. Sci. Biog. Boveria?

Boveria (Boveri, Theodor?): Zoology. See: Pennak.

Boveri's test (Boveri, Piero): Medicine. See: Dorland; Stedman.

Bovero's muscle (Derivation undetermined): Medicine. See: Stedman. Also known as: Klein's muscle, Krause's muscle.

BOW, ROBERT HENRY. 1827-1909. Scottish engineer. See: Pogg., vols. 4, 6. Bow's notation.

Bowden cable (or wire) (Bowden, E. M.): Engineering and Industry. See: Webster's 3d.

BOWDEN, E.M. fl. 19th c. English inventor. (Biography source unavailable.) Bowden cable (or wire).

BOWDITCH, HENRY PICKERING. 1840-1911. American physiologist. See: Dict. Sci. Biog. Bowditch's law.

BOWDITCH, NATHANIEL. 1773-1838. American mathematician and astronomer. See: Dict. Sci. Biog. Bowditch (navigation manual).

Bowditch (navigation manual) (Bowditch, Nathaniel): Navigation. See: Webster's 3d.

BOWDITCH, THOMAS EDWARD. 1791-1824. English traveler. See: Dict. Nat. Biog. Bowditchia.

Bowditchia (Bowditch, Thomas Edward): Botany. See: Webster's 3d.

Bowditch's law (Bowditch, Henry Pickering): Medicine. See: Dorland; Henderson; Stedman.

Bowditch's rule (Derivation undetermined): See: Engineering and Industry. See: Thrush.

BOWDLER, THOMAS. 1754-1825. English editor. See: Dict. Nat. Biog. Bowdlerize.

Bowdlerize (Bowdler, Thomas): Generic Word (expurgate). See: Barnet; Brewer; Funk.

BOWEN, EZRA. 1891-1945. American economist. See: Who Was Who Amer., vol. 2. Bowen's law of population.

BOWEN, GEORGE T. 1803-1828. American mineralogist. See: Smith, E.F. Bowenite.

BOWEN, IRA SPRAGUE. 1898- . American physicist and astronomer. See: World Who's Who Sci. Bowen ratio, Bowen's device.

BOWEN, JOHN TEMPLETON. 1857-1941. American dermatologist. See: Who Was Who Amer., vol. 1. Bowen's disease (dermatosis or epithelioma).

BOWEN, NORMAN LEVI. 1887-1956. Canadian-born American petrologist. See: Dict. Sci. Biog. Bowen's reaction series.

Bowen ratio (Bowen, Ira Sprague): Physics. See: Huschke.

Bowen tube (Derivation undetermined): Chemistry. See: Hackh.

Bowenite (Bowen, George T.): Earth Sciences. See: Charnock; Thrush; Webster's 3d.

Bowen's device (Bowen, Ira Sprague): Astronomy. Cited in: World Who's Who Sci.

Bowen's disease (dermatosis or epithelioma) (Bowen, John Templeton): Medicine. See: Dorland; Jablonski; Stedman.

Bowen's law of population (Bowen, Ezra): Economics. See: Zadrozny.

Bowen's reaction series (Bowen, Norman Levi): Earth Sciences. See: Thrush.

BOWER, A.S. fl. 1883. American mining engineer. Cited in: Royal Soc. Cat. Sci. Pap., 1884-1900. Bower-Barff process.

Bower-Barff process (Bower, A.S.; Bower, George; and Barff, F.S.): Engineering and Industry. See: Ballentyne; Van Nostrand Chem. Dict.; Webster's 3d.

BOWER, GEORGE. fl. 1883. American engineer. Cited in: Royal Soc. Cat. Sci. Pap., 1874-1883. Bower-Barff process.

BOWIE, JAMES. 1799-1836. American soldier. See: Dict. Amer. Biog. Bowie knife?

Bowie knife (Bowie, James?): Weapons. See: Brewer; Hendrickson; Phyfe.

BOWIE, ROBERT McNEIL. 1906- . American physicist. See: Amer. Men Sci., 7th ed. Morse and Bowie gauge.

BOWKER, ALBERT HOSMER. 1919- . American educator. See: Who's Who Amer., 1974-75. Bowker's corollary.

Bowker's corollary (Bowker, Albert Hosmer): Education. See: Martin.

Bowler hat (Beaulieu? or Bowler, William?): Fashion. See: Brewer; Hendrickson; Picken.

BOWLER, WILLIAM. fl. 1861. English hatmaker. (Biography source unavailable.) Bowler hat?

Bowles type stethoscope (Derivation undetermined): Medicine. See: Stedman.

BOWLES, WILLIAM. 1705-1780. Irish-born botanist. See: Biog. Notes Upon Botanists. Bowlesia?

Bowlesia (Bowles, William?): Botany. See: Charnock.

BOWLEY, ARTHUR LYON. 1869-1957. English statistician. See: Internat. Encyc. Soc. Sci. Marshall-Edgeworth-Bowley index.

Bowley index (Bowley, Arthur Lyon). See: Marshall-Edgeworth-Bowley index.

BOWLING, TOM. Character from Tobias Smollett's novel, "Roderick Random" (1748). See: Benet. Tom Bowling.

BOWMAKER, E.J.C. fl. 1929. English scientist. Cited in: Chem. Abstr., vol. 23, p. 5288. Bowmaker test.

Bowmaker test (Bowmaker, E.J.C.): Engineering and Industry. See: Thrush.

BOWMAN, SIR WILLIAM. 1816-1892. English surgeon and anatomist. See: Dict. Sci. Biog. Bowman's capsule, Bowman's disks, Bowman's glands, Bowman's membrane, Bowman's muscle, Bowman's operation, Bowman's probe, Bowman's theory.

Bowman's capsule (Bowman, Sir William): Anatomy. See: Donath; Dorland; Gray. Also known as: Malpighian capsule, Mueller's capsule.

Bowman's disks (Bowman, Sir William): Anatomy. See: Stedman.

Bowman's glands (Bowman, Sir William): Anatomy. See: Donath; Gray; Henderson; Stedman. Also known as: Koelliker's gland.

Bowman's membrane (Bowman, Sir William): Anatomy. See: Donath; Dorland; Gray.

Bowman's muscle (Bowman, Sir William): Anatomy. See: Stedman. Also known as: Riolan's muscle.

Bowman's operation (Bowman, Sir William): Medicine. See: Stedman.

Bowman's probe (Bowman, Sir William): Medicine. See: Stedman.

Bowman's root (Derivation undetermined): Botany. See: Winburne.

Bowman's theory (Bowman, Sir William): Medicine. See: Dorland; Stedman.

BOWRING, SIR JOHN. 1792-1872. English author and diplomat. See: New Encyc. Brit., 1974, Microp. Bowring treaty.

Bowring treaty (Bowring, Sir John): History. See: New Encyc. Brit., 1974, Microp.

Bow's notation (Bow, Robert Henry): Engineering and Industry. See: Ballentyne; Internat. Dict. Ap. Math.; Van Nostrand Sci. Encyc.

BOX. Character in John M. Morton's farce, "Box and Cox" (1847). See: Benet. Box and Cox (arrangement).

Box and Cox (arrangement) (Box and Cox): Generic Word (alternating). See: Webster's 3d.

Box (calfskin) (Box, Joseph): Generic Word. See: Partridge.

BOX, GEORGE EDWARD PELHAM. 1919- . English statistician. See: World Who's Who Sci. Box-Jenkins model.

Box-Jenkins model (Box, George Edward Pelham and Jenkins, Gwilym Meirion): Statistics. See: Kendall.

BOX, JOSEPH. fl. before 1890. English bootmaker. (Biography source unavailable.) Box (calfskin).

Boxer cartridge (Boxer, Edward Mourrier): Weapons. See: Quick.

BOXER, EDWARD MOURRIER. 1822-1898. English army officer and inventor. See: Boase, vol. 4. Boxer cartridge.

Box's formula (Derivation undetermined): Engineering and Industry. See: Thrush.

Boyce burner (Derivation undetermined): Chemistry. See: Hackh; Van Nostrand Chem. Dict.

Boycott (Boycott, Charles Cunningham): Generic Word. See: Brewer; Funk; Harbottle.

BOYCOTT, CHARLES CUNNINGHAM. 1832-1897. English army officer. See: Dict. Nat. Biog., 1st suppl. Boycott.

BOYD, GEORGE EDWARD. 1912- . American chemist. See: Amer. Men Sci., 8th ed. Boyd, Schubert and Adamson equation.

BOYD, JULIAN DEIGH. b. 1894. American pediatrician. See: Amer. Men Sci., 10th ed. Boyd-Stearns syndrome.

Boyd, Schubert and Adamson equation (Boyd, George Edward; Schubert, Jack; and Adamson, Arthur Wilson): Chemistry. See: Van Nostrand Chem. Dict.

Boyd-Stearns syndrome (Boyd, Julian Deigh and Stearns, Genevieve): Medicine. See: Jablonski.

BOYDEN, EDWARD ALLEN. b. 1886. American anatomist. See: World Who's Who Sci. Boyden meal, Boyden's sphincter.

Boyden meal (Boyden, Edward Allen): Medicine. See: Stedman.

BOYDEN, URIAH ATHERTON. 1804-1879. American inventor. See: Dict. Amer. Biog. Boyden's diffuser.

Boyden's diffuser (Boyden, Uriah Atherton): Engineering and Industry. See: Auger.

Boyden's sphincter (Boyden, Edward Allen): Anatomy. See: Gray; Stedman.

Boydite (Derivation undetermined): Earth Sciences. See: Thrush.

Boyelle–Morin apparatus (Derivation undetermined): Engineering and Industry. See: Auger.

BOYER, ALEXIS DE. 1757-1833. French surgeon. See: Encyc. Brit., 1911. Boyer's bursa, Boyer's cyst.

Boyer's bursa (Boyer, Alexis de): Medicine. See: Dorland; Stedman.

Boyer's cyst (Boyer, Alexis de): Medicine. See: Dorland; Jablonski; Stedman.

BOYET, LUC ANTOINE. d. 1733. French book-binder. See: Dict. Biog. Fran. Boyet style.

Boyet style (Boyet, Luc Antoine): Fine Arts. See: Harrod.

BOYKIN, SAMUEL. 1786-1848. American planter, physician, banker, and naturalist. See: Biog. Notes Upon Botanists. Boykinia.

Boykinia (Boykin, Samuel): Botany. See: Taylor, N.

BOYLE, CHARLES, 4TH EARL OF ORRERY. 1676-1731. English nobleman. See: Dict. Nat. Biog. Boyle controversy, Orrery.

Boyle–Charles law (Boyle, Robert and Charles, Jacques Alexandre Cesar): Chemistry. See: Internat. Dict. Ap. Math.; Van Nostrand Sci. Encyc.

Boyle controversy (Boyle, Charles, 4th Earl of Orrery): History. See: Brewer; Weekley.

Boyle lectures (Boyle, Robert): Religion. See: Brewer; Canney; Harvey.

Boyle–Mariotte law (Boyle, Robert and Mariotte, Edme). See: Boyle's law.

BOYLE, ROBERT. 1627-1691. English physicist and chemist. See: Dict. Sci. Biog. Boyle-Charles law, Boyle lectures, Boyle temperature, Boyle's law.

Boyle temperature (Boyle, Robert): Physics. See: Ballentyne; Internat. Dict. Ap. Math.; Internat. Dict. Phys. Elec.

Boyle's law (Boyle, Robert): Chemistry. See: Ballentyne; Black; Blumberg. Also known as: Boyle-Mariotte law, Mariotte's law.

BOYLSTON, HERBERT MELVILLE. b. 1881. American metallurgist. See: Who's Who Engin., 1925. Boylston's reagent?

Boylston's reagent (Boylston, Herbert Melville?): Engineering and Industry. See: Thrush.

BOYNTON, WILLIAM HUTCHINS. b. 1881. American veterinarian. See: Amer. Men Sci., 10th ed. Boynton's tissue vaccine.

Boynton's tissue vaccine (Boynton, William Hutchins): Medicine. See: Winburne.

Boys camera (Boys, Sir Charles Vernon): Physics. See: Huschke.

BOYS, SIR CHARLES VERNON. 1855-1944. English physicist. See: World Who's Who Sci. Boys camera.

Boys type resonator (Derivation undetermined): Physics. See: Internat. Dict. Phys. Elec.

BOYSEN, RUDOLF. fl. early 1900's. American botanist. (Biography source unavailable.) Boysenberry.

Boysenberry (Boysen, Rudolf): Botany. See: De Sola; Hendrickson; Taylor, N.

Bozeman–Fritsch catheter (Bozeman, Nathan and Fritsch, Heinrich): Medicine. See: Dorland; Stedman.

BOZEMAN, NATHAN. 1825-1905. American surgeon. See: Dict. Amer. Biog. Bozeman-Fritsch catheter, Bozeman's catheter, Bozeman's operation, Bozeman's position, Bozeman's speculum.

Bozeman's catheter (Bozeman, Nathan): Medicine. See: Dorland.

Bozeman's operation (Bozeman, Nathan): Medicine. See: Stedman.

Bozeman's position (Bozeman, Nathan): Medicine. See: Dorland; Stedman.

Bozeman's speculum (Bozeman, Nathan): Medicine. See: Stedman.

Bozsin box (Bozsin, Michael): Engineering and Industry. See: Thrush.

BOZSIN, MICHAEL. 1910- . American chemist. See: Amer. Men Sci., 9th ed. Bozsin box.

Bozzi's foramen (Derivation undetermined): Medicine. See: Stedman. Also known as: Soemmering's spot.

BOZZOLO, CAMILLO. 1845-1920. Italian physician. See: Biog. Lex. hervorr. Aerzte, 1880-1930. Bozzolo's sign, Kahler-Bozzolo disease.

Bozzolo's sign (Bozzolo, Camillo): Medicine. See: Dorland; Stedman.

BRABENDER, C.W. fl. 1933. American chemist. Cited in: Chem. Abstr., vol. 27, p. 346. Brabender farinograph.

Brabender farinograph (Brabender, C.W.): Chemistry. See: Van Nostrand Chem. Dict.

Bracciolini, Gian Francesco Poggio-. See: Poggio-Bracciolini, Gian Francesco.

BRACE, DE WITT BRISTOL. 1859-1905. American physicist. See: Dict. Sci. Biog. Brace-Lemon spectrophotometer, Brace prism.

BRACE, DONALD K. fl. 1967. American educator. (Biography source unavailable.) Brace test.

Brace–Lemon spectrophotometer (Brace, De Witt Bistol and Lemon, Harvey Brace): Physics. See: Internat. Dict. Phys. Elec.

Brace prism (Brace, De Witt Bristol): Physics. See: Internat. Dict. Phys. Elec.

Brace test (Brace, Donald K.): Psychology. See: English.

Brachman–De Lange syndrome (Brachmann and De Lange, Cornelia Catharina). See: De Lange's syndrome (1).

BRACHT, ERICH. b. 1882. German physician. See: Biog. Lex. hervorr. Aerzte. Bracht-Waechter lesion.

Bracht–Waechter lesion (Bracht, Erich and Waechter, Hermann Julius Gustav): Medicine. See: Stedman.

BRACKEBUSCH, LUIS. 1849?-1906. German geologist. See: Amer. J. Sci., vol. 172 (1906) p. 194. Brackebuschite.

Brackebuschite (Brackebusch, Luis): Earth Sciences. See: Thrush.

BRACKELSBERG, CARL. fl. 1930. Inventor. Cited in: Chem. Abstr. Decenn. Index, 1927-36. Brackelsberg furnace.

Brackelsberg furnace (Brackelsberg, Carl): Engineering and Industry. See: Van Nostrand Sci. Encyc.

Brackelsberg process (Derivation undetermined): Engineering and Industry. See: Thrush.

BRACKETT, FREDERICK SUMNER. 1896- . American physicist. See: Amer. Men Sci., 9th ed. Brackett series.

Brackett series (Brackett, Frederick Sumner): Physics. See: Hughes; Internat. Dict. Ap. Math.; Internat. Dict. Phys. Elec.

Brada–Svejda tumor (Brada, Zbynek and Svejda, Jaroslav): Medicine. See: Jablonski.

BRADA, ZBYNEK. 1926- . Czechoslovakian biochemist. See: World Who's Who Sci. Brada-Svejda tumor.

BRADBURY, SIR JOHN SWANWICK. 1872-1950. English treasury official. See: Webster's Biog. Dict. Bradbury (treasury note).

Bradbury (treasury note) (Bradbury, Sir John Swanwick): Generic Word. See: Brewer; Partridge; Weekley.

BRADDOCK, EDWARD. 1695-1755. English army officer. See: Dict. Nat. Biog. Braddockian.

Braddockian (Braddock, Edward): Military Science. See: Mathews, M.M.

BRADEL. fl. 17th and 18th c. French family of book-binders. See: Dict. Biog. Fran. Bradel binding.

Bradel binding (Bradel family): Library Science. See: Harrod.

BRADEN, GLENN T. d. 1923. American oilman and inventor. (Biography source unavailable.) Bradenhead.

Bradenhead (Braden, Glenn T.): Engineering and Industry. See: Webster's 3d.

Bradford breaker (Derivation undetermined): Engineering and Industry. See: Thrush.

BRADFORD, EDWARD HICKLING. 1848-1926. American orthopedist. See: Dict. Amer. Biog. Bradford frame.

Bradford frame (Bradford, Edward Hickling): Medicine. See: Stedman; Webster's 3d.

BRADFORD, L. fl. 1916. American metallurgist. Cited in: Chem. Abstr., vol. 10, p.1841. Bradford preferential separation process.

Bradford preferential separation process (Bradford, L.): Engineering and Industry. See: Thrush.

Bradford press (Bradford, William): Printing. See: Lockwood.

BRADFORD, WILLIAM. 1663-1752. American printer. See: Dict. Nat. Biog. Bradford press.

BRADLAUGH, CHARLES. 1833-1891. English secularist, social and political reformer. See: Dict. Nat. Biog., 1st suppl. Bradlaugh's case (or incident).

Bradlaugh's case (or incident) (Bradlaugh, Charles): History. See: Montgomery; Morris and Irwin; Steinberg.

Bradley aberration method (Bradley, James): Astronomy. See: Internat. Dict. Phys. Elec.; Van Nostrand Sci. Encyc.

Bradley aberration of light (Bradley, James): Astronomy. See: Internat. Dict. Phys. Elec.

Bradley arc process (Bradley, Charles Schenck): Chemistry. See: Van Nostrand Chem. Dict.

BRADLEY, CHARLES SCHENCK. 1853-1929. American inventor. See: Webster's Biog. Dict. Bradley arc process.

BRADLEY, FRANCIS HERBERT. 1846-1924. English philosopher. See: Dict. Nat. Biog., 4th suppl. Bradleyan.

BRADLEY, JAMES. 1693-1762. English astronomer. See: Dict. Nat. Biog. Bradley aberration method, Bradley aberration of light.

BRADLEY, RICHARD. d. 1732. English botanist. See: Dict. Sci. Biog. Bradleya.

Bradley test (Derivation undetermined): Chemistry. See: Van Nostrand Chem. Dict.

BRADLEY, W. H. fl. 1943. English physician. (Biography source unavailable.) Bradley's disease.

BRADLEY, WILMOT HYDE. 1899- . American geologist. See: Amer. Men Sci., 9th ed. Bradleyite.

Bradleya (Bradley, Richard): Botany. See: Charnock.

Bradleyan (Bradley, Francis Herbert): Philosophy. See: Webster's 3d.

Bradleyite (Bradley, Wilmot Hyde): Earth Sciences. See: Thrush; Webster's 3d.

Bradley's disease (Bradley, W. H.): See: Spencer's disease.

Bradshaw gas generator (Bradshaw, G.): Engineering and Industry. See: Auger.

BRADSHAW, GEORGE. 1801-1853. English printer. See: Dict. Nat. Biog. Bradshaw (railway guide).

Bradshaw (railway guide) (Bradshaw, George): Transportation. See: Hendrickson; Partridge; Webster's 3d.

BRADSHAW, THOMAS ROBERT. 1857-1927. English physician. See: Who Was Who, 1916-28. Bradshaw's albumosuria.

Bradshaw's albumosuria (Bradshaw, Thomas Robert): See: Bence Jones' albuminosuria.

BRADY, MATHEW B. 1823-1896. American photographer. See: Dict. Amer. Biog. Mathew Brady Award.

BRAEUNER, J.J. fl. 18th c. German botanist. (Biography source unavailable.) Brauneria.

Brag (Bragi): Generic Word (boast). See: Charnock.

BRAG, JACK. Character in Theodore Hook's novel of the same name. See: Benet. Jack Brag.

Bragard's test (Derivation undetermined): Stedman. See: Medicine.

Bragg angle (Bragg, Sir William Henry and Bragg, Sir William Lawrence): Physics. See: Hughes; Partridge; Thrush.

Bragg crystal model (Bragg, Sir William Henry): Physics. See: Hackh.

Bragg crystallogram (Bragg, Sir William Henry): Physics. See: Hackh.

Bragg curve (Bragg, Sir William Henry and/or Bragg, Sir William Lawrence): Physics. See: Hughes; Internat. Dict. Phys. Elec.; Thewlis.

Bragg cut-off wavelength (Bragg, Sir William Henry and/or Bragg, Sir William Lawrence): Physics. See: Thewlis.

Bragg-Gray cavity (Derivation undetermined): Physics. See: Hughes.

Bragg-Kleeman rule (Bragg, Sir William Henry and Kleeman, Richard Daniel). See: Bragg rule.

Bragg law (or equation) (Bragg, Sir William Lawrence): Physics. See: Ballentyne; Hughes; Internat. Dict. Ap. Math.

Bragg loop (Bragg, Sir William Henry and Bragg, Sir William Lawrence): Military Science. See: Partridge.

Bragg method of crystal analysis (Bragg, Sir William Henry and/or Bragg, Sir William Lawrence): Physics. See: Internat. Dict. Phys. Elec.

Bragg-Paul pulsator (Bragg, Sir William Lawrence? and Paul, R. W.): Medicine. See: Dorland; Stedman.

BRAGG, PHILIP. d. 1759. English army officer. See: Dict. Nat. Biog. "Old Braggs" (or "The Braggs").

Bragg-Pierce law (Bragg, Sir William Henry and Peirce, S. E.): Physics. See: Ballentyne.

Bragg reflection (Bragg, Sir William Henry and Bragg, Sir William Lawrence): Physics. See: Thewlis; Webster's 3d.

Bragg rule (Bragg, Sir William Henry): Physics. See: Hughes; Internat. Dict. Ap. Math. Also known as: Bragg-Kleeman rule.

Bragg scattering (Bragg, Sir William Henry and/or Bragg, Sir William Lawrence): Physics. See: Markus.

Bragg spectrometer (Bragg, Sir William Henry and/or Bragg, Sir William Lawrence): Physics. See: Internat. Dict. Phys. Elec.; Markus; Thewlis.

Bragg treatment (Bragg, Sir William Henry and/or Bragg, Sir William Lawrence): Physics. See: Internat. Dict. Phys. Elec.

BRAGG, SIR WILLIAM HENRY. 1862-1942. English physicist. See: Dict. Sci. Biog. Bragg angle, Bragg crystal model, Bragg crystallogram, Bragg curve?, Bragg cut-off wavelength?, Bragg loop, Bragg method of crystal analysis?, Bragg-Pierce law, Bragg reflection, Bragg rule, Bragg scattering?, Bragg spectrometer?, Bragg treatment?, Braggite.

BRAGG, SIR WILLIAM LAWRENCE. 1890-1971. English physicist. See: Encyc. Brit., 1973. Bragg angle, Bragg curve?, Bragg cut-off wavelength?, Bragg law (or equation), Bragg loop, Bragg method of crystal analysis?, Bragg-Paul pulsator?, Bragg reflection, Bragg scattering?, Bragg spectrometer?, Bragg treatment?

BRAGGADOCIO. Character in Spenser's "Faerie Queen." See: Benet. Braggadocio.

Braggadocio (Braggadocio, the boaster): Generic Word (braggart). See: Brewer; Partridge.

Braggite (Bragg, Sir William Henry and Bragg, Sir William Lawrence): Earth Sciences. See: Thrush; Webster's 3d.

"The Braggs" (Bragg, Philip). See: "Old Braggs."

BRAGI. Scandinavian god of poetry. See: Benet. Brag.

BRAHE, TYCHO. 1546-1601. Danish astronomer. See: Dict. Sci. Biog. Brahea, Tychonic system.

Brahea (Brahe, Tycho): Botany. See: Taylor, N.

BRAHMA. Hindu creator god. See: Encyc. Brit., 1973. Brahmamaha, Brahmin (or Brahmanism).

BRAHMACHARI, UPENDRA NATH. 1875-1946. Indian physician. See: Pogg., vols. 6, 7b. Brahmachari's leishmanoid, Brahmachari's test.

Brahmachari's leishmanoid (Brahmachari, Upendra Nath.): Medicine. See: Jablonski.

Brahmachari's test (Brahmachari, Upendra Nath.): Medicine. See: Dorland; Stedman.

Brahmamaha (Brahma): Generic Word. See: Canney.

Brahmin (or Brahmanism) (Brahma): Religion. See: Brewer; Canney; Wagner, (Names).

BRAHMS, JOHANNES. 1833-1897. German composer. See: Encyc. Brit., 1973. Brahmsian.

Brahmsian (Brahms, Johannes): Music. See: Webster's 3d.

Brahn reaction (Derivation undetermined): Medicine. See: Stedman.

BRAID, GARRICK (SOKARI). d. 1918. Nigerian religious leader. Cited in: New Encyc. Brit., 1974, Microp. under "Braid movement." Braid movement.

BRAID, JAMES. 1795-1860. English surgeon. See: Dict. Nat. Biog. Braidism, Braid's strabismus.

Braid movement (Braid, Garrick): Religion. See: New Encyc. Brit., 1974, Microp.

Braidism (Braid, James): Psychology. See: Canney; Chaplin; Dorland.

Braid's strabismus (Braid, James): Medicine. See: Jablonski.

Braikenridge-Maclaurin theorem (Braikenridge, William and Maclaurin, Colin): Mathematics. Cited in: Dict. Sci. Biog.

BRAIKENRIDGE, WILLIAM. ca. 1700-1762. English mathematician. See: Dict. Sci. Biog. Braikenridge-Maclaurin theorem.

BRAILEY, WILLIAM ARTHUR. 1845-1915. English ophthalmologist. See: Who Was Who, 1897-1916. Brailey's operation.

Brailey's operation (Brailey, William Arthur): Medicine. See: Dorland; Stedman.

Braille (Braille, Louis): Printing. See: Funk; Harrod; Scott.

BRAILLE, LOUIS. 1809-1852. French teacher of the blind. See: Encyc. Brit., 1973. Braille.

BRAILSFORD, JAMES FREDERICK. b. 1888. English radiologist. See: J. Internat. Coll. Surg., vol. 7 (1944) p. 418. Brailsford-Morquio syndrome (or disease).

Brailsford-Morquio syndrome (or disease) (Brailsford, James Frederick and Morquio, Louis). See: Morquio's syndrome (or disease).

BRAIN, WALTER RUSSELL. 1895-1966. English physician. See: Direct. Brit. Sci., 1966-67. Brain's reflex.

Brain's reflex (Brain, Walter Russell): Medicine. See: Dorland; Stedman.

Braley-Hobart test (Braley, Silas Alonzo and Hobart, Floyd, B.): Chemistry. See: Van Nostrand Chem. Dict.

BRALEY, SILAS ALONZO. b. 1889. American chemist. See: Amer. Men Sci., 9th ed. Braley-Hobart test.

BRALY, KENNETH WALTER. 1906- . American psychologist. See: Amer. Men Sci., 8th ed. Katz and Braly questionnaire.

BRAMAH, JOSEPH. 1749-1814. English engineer. See: Dict. Nat. Biog. Bramah lock, Bramah press, Bramah pump.

Bramah lock (Bramah, Joseph): Engineering and Industry. See: Auger; Partridge; Webster's 3d.

Bramah press (Bramah, Joseph): Engineering and Industry. See: Auger; Partridge; Webster's 3d.

Bramah pump (Bramah, Joseph): Engineering and Industry. See: Auger.

BRAMANTE, DONATO D'AGNOLO. 1444-1514. Italian architect. See: Encyc. Brit., 1973. Bramantesque.

Bramantesque (Bramante, Donato d'Agnolo): Applied Arts. See: Webster's 3d.

BRAMLEY. No dates. English butcher. (Biography source unavailable.) Bramley's seedling.

Bramley's seedling (Bramley): Botany. See: Hendrickson; Partridge.

BRAMMALL, ALFRED. b. 1879. English mineralogist. Cited in: Min. Mag., vol. 26 (1943) p. 335. Brammallite.

Brammallite (Brammall, Alfred): Earth Sciences. See: Thrush.

BRANCA, GIOVANNI. 1571-1640. Italian architect. See: Nouv. Biog. Univ. Branca turbine.

Branca turbine (Branca, Giovanni): Engineering and Industry. See: Auger.

Brand bath (Brand, Ernst): Medicine. See: Dorland.

BRAND, ERNST. 1827-1897. German physician. See: Allg. Deut. Biog. Brand bath.

Brande, Pierre Van den. See: Van den Brande, Pierre.

BRANDE, WILLIAM THOMAS. 1788-1866. English chemist. See: Dict. Sci. Biog. Brande's test.

BRANDENBURG, CHRISTIAN LUDWIG, MARGRAVE OF. fl. 1721. German aristocrat. (Biography source unavailable.) Brandenburg concertos.

Brandenburg concertos (Brandenburg, Christian Ludwig, Margrave of): Music. See: Apel; Scholes.

Branderhorst test (Derivation undetermined): Chemistry. See: Van Nostrand Chem. Dict.

Brande's test (Brande, William Thomas): Medicine. See: Dorland.

Brandes test (Derivation undetermined): Chemistry. See: Van Nostrand Chem. Dict.

BRANDON, GREGORY. No dates. English hangman. See: Webster's Biog. Dict. Gregorian tree.

BRANDON, RICHARD, "YOUNG GREGORY." d. 1649. English executioner. See: Dict. Nat. Biog. Gregorian tree.

BRANDT, ALVA ESMOND. b. 1892. American statistician. See: Amer. Men Sci., 11th ed. Brandt-Snedecor method.

BRANDT, GEORG. 1694-1768. Swedish chemist and mineralogist. See: Dict. Sci. Biog. Brandtite.

BRANDT, JOHANN FRIEDRICH. 1802-1879. German zoologist. See: Dict. Sci. Biog. Brandt's cormorant.

Brandt-Snedecor method (Brandt, Alva Esmond and Snedecor, George Waddel): Statistics. See: Kendall.

BRANDT, THORE EDVARD. fl. 1936. Finnish? physician. (Biography source unavailable.) Brandt's syndrome.

BRANDT, THURE. 1819-1895. Swedish gynecologist. See: Biog. Lex. hervorr. Aerzte. Brandt's method.

Brandtite (Brandt, Georg): Earth Sciences. See: Webster's 3d.

Brandt's cormorant (Brandt, Johann Friedrich): Zoology. See: Gray; Webster's 3d.

Brandt's method (Brandt, Thure): Medicine. See: Dorland.

Brandt's syndrome (Brandt, Thore Edvard): Medicine. See: Jablonski. Also known as: Danbolt-Closs syndrome, Danbolt's syndrome.

BRANHAM, H. H. fl. 1890. American surgeon. Cited in: Kelly. Branham's sign.

BRANHAM, SARA ELIZABETH. b. 1888. American bacteriologist. See: Who Was Who Amer., vol. 4. Branhamella.

Branhamella (Branham, Sara Elizabeth): Medicine. See: Stedman.

Branham's sign (Branham, H. H.): Medicine. See: Dorland; Stedman.

Branly coherer (Branly, Edouard): Physics. See: Hughes.

BRANLY, EDOUARD. 1844-1940. French physicist. See: Webster's Biog. Dict. Branly coherer.

BRANNAN, CHARLES FRANKLIN. 1903- . American politician. See: Sobel. Brannan plan.

Brannan plan (Brannan, Charles Franklin): Agriculture. See: Smith.

BRANNER, JOHN CASPAR. 1850-1922. American geologist. See: Dict. Amer. Biog. Brannerite.

Brannerite (Branner, John Caspar): Earth Sciences. See: Thrush; Webster's 3d.

BRANS, CARL HENRY. 1935- . American physicist. See: Amer. Men Sci., 11th ed. Brans-Dicke theory.

Brans-Dicke theory (Brans, Carl Henry and Dicke, Robert Henry): Physics. See: Barnhart (New Eng.).

Brant reagent (Derivation undetermined): Chemistry. See: Van Nostrand Chem. Dict.

BRAQUEHAYE, JULES PIE LOUIS. 1865-1922. French gynecologist. See: Med. Med. Tunisie, p. 221. Braquehaye's method.

Braquehaye's method (Braquehaye, Jules Pie Louis): Medicine. See: Stedman.

BRARD, CYPRIAN PROSPER. 1788-1838. French mineralogist. See: Nouv. Biog. Univ. Brard's process.

Brard's process (Brard, Cyprian Prosper): Engineering and Industry. See: Thrush.

BRAS, GERRIT. fl. 1957. Indonesian pathologist. (Biography source unavailable.) Stuart-Bras disease?

BRASAVOLA, ANTONIO MUSA. 1500-1555. Italian botanist. See: Biog. Notes Upon Botanists. Brassavola.

BRASDOR, PIERRE. 1721-1798. French surgeon. See: Encyc. Brit., 1911. Brasdor's method, Brasdor's operation.

Brasdor's method (Brasdor, Pierre): Medicine. See: Stedman.

Brasdor's operation (Brasdor, Pierre): Medicine. See: Dorland.

Brashear-Hastings prism (Brashear, John Alfred and Hastings, Charles Sheldon): Physics. See: Internat. Dict. Phys. Elec.

BRASHEAR, JOHN ALFRED. 1840-1920. American astronomer and engineer. See: Dict. Sci. Biog. Brashear-Hastings prism.

Brasher doubloon (Brasher, Ephraim): Numismatics. See: Hendrickson; Partridge.

BRASHER, EPHRAIM. fl. 1787. American goldsmith. (Biography source unavailable.) Brasher doubloon.

BRASS, WILLIAM. d. 1783. English botanist. See: Biog. Notes Upon Botanists. Brassia.

Brassavola (Brasavola, Antonio Musa): Botany. See: Taylor, N.; Webster's 3d.

Brassia (Brass, William): Botany. See: Taylor, N.; Webster's 3d.

BRAU, EDUARDO F. fl. 1935. Argentinian chemist. Cited in: Chem. Abstr., vol. 30, p. 7059. Brau reagent for copper.

Brau reagent for copper (Brau, Eduardo F.): Chemistry. See: Van Nostrand Chem. Dict.

BRAUER, AUGUST. b. 1883. German physician. See: Wer Ist's, 1906. Brauer's syndrome.

BRAUER, KURT. 1888-1950. German chemist. See: Pogg., vols. 6, 7a. Brauer test for phenols, Brauer test reaction for organic acids, Brauer test reactions for resins.

BRAUER, LUDOLF. 1865-1951. German physician. See: World Who's Who Sci. Brauer's method, Brauer's operation.

Brauer test for phenols (Brauer, Kurt): Chemistry. See: Van Nostrand Chem. Dict.

Brauer test reaction for organic acids (Brauer, Kurt): Chemistry. See: Van Nostrand Chem. Dict.

Brauer test reactions for resins (Brauer, Kurt): Chemistry. See: Van Nostrand Chem. Dict.

Brauer's method (Brauer, Ludolf): Medicine. See: Dorland.

Brauer's operation (Brauer, Ludolf): Medicine. See: Stedman.

Brauer's syndrome (Brauer, August). See: Unna-Thost syndrome.

Brauetigam-Edelman test (Derivation undetermined): Chemistry. See: Van Nostrand Chem. Dict.

BRAUN, ALEXANDER CARL HEINRICH. 1805-1877. German botanist. See: Dict. Sci. Biog. Braun's holly fern, Schimper-Braun theory.

BRAUN, CARL DANIEL. fl. 1865. German chemist. Cited in: Royal Soc. Cat. Sci. Pap., 1800-63, 1864-73. Braun test for picric acid.

BRAUN, CARL RITTER VON FERNWALD. 1822-1891. Austrian obstetrician. See: Allg. Deut. Biog. Braun's canal.

BRAUN, CHRISTOPHER HEINRICH. b. 1847. German physician. See: Wer Ist's, 1906. Braun's test.

BRAUN, FERDINAND KARL. 1850-1918. German physicist. See: Wer Ist's?, 1906. Le Chatelier-Braun principle?

BRAUN-FERNWALD, RICHARD. b. 1866. Austrian obstetrician. See: Biog. Lex. hervorr. Aerzte, 1880-1930. Braun-Fernwald's sign.

Braun-Fernwald's sign (Braun-Fernwald, Richard): Medicine. See: Dorland; Stedman.

BRAUN, GEZA. fl. 1943. American chemist. Cited in: Chem. Abstr., vol. 37, p. 2391. Braun test for tartaric acid.

Braun graft (Braun, Wilhelm): Medicine. See: Stedman.

BRAUN, GUSTAV AUGUST. 1829-1911. Austrian gynecologist. See: Biog. Lex. hervorr. Aerzte. Braun's hook.

BRAUN, HEINRICH. 1847-1911. German surgeon. See: Biog. Lex. hervorr. Aerzte, 1880-1930. Braun's anastomosis, Roser-Braun sign?

Braun-Husler reaction (or test) (Braun, Ludwig and Husler, Josef): Medicine. See: Dorland.

Braun, Julius von. See: Von Braun, Julius.

BRAUN, KAMMERATH. fl. 19th c. German treasury official. Cited in: Dana, vol. 1, p. 553. Braunite.

BRAUN, KARL. fl. 1909. German chemist. Cited in: Chem. Abstr., vol. 3, p. 1100. Braun test for naphthenic acids.

BRAUN, KARL FERDINAND. 1850-1918. German physicist. See: Dict. Sci. Biog. Braun tube, Le Chatelier-Braun principle.

BRAUN, LUDWIG. b. 1881. German physician. Cited in: New York Acad. Med. Portrait Cat. Braun-Husler reaction (or test).

Braun test for cyanide (Derivation undetermined): Chemistry. See: Van Nostrand Chem. Dict.

Braun test for manganese (Derivation undetermined): Chemistry. See: Van Nostrand Chem. Dict.

Braun test for naphthenic acids (Braun, Karl): Chemistry. See: Van Nostrand Chem. Dict.

Braun test for nickel (Derivation undetermined): Chemistry. See: Van Nostrand Chem. Dict.

Braun test for picric acid (Braun, Carl Daniel): Chemistry. See: Van Nostrand Chem. Dict.

Braun test for pyrophosphate (Derivation undetermined): Chemistry. See: Van Nostrand Chem. Dict.

Braun test for tartaric acid (Braun, Geza): Chemistry. See: Van Nostrand Chem. Dict.

Braun test reactions for molybdic acid (Derivation undetermined): Chemistry. See: Van Nostrand Chem. Dict.

Braun tube (Braun, Karl Ferdinand): Physics. See: Hackh; Hughes; Markus.

Braun-Wangensteen graft (Braun, Wilhelm and Wangensteen, Owen Harding): Medicine. See: Stedman.

BRAUN, WILHELM. fl. 1921. German surgeon. See: Deut. Chirurgen Kal., (1926) S 34. Braun graft, Braun-Wangensteen graft.

BRAUNE, CHRISTIAN WILHELM. 1831-1892. German anatomist. See: Allg. Deut. Biog. Braune's canal, Braune's muscle, Braune's valve.

Brauneria (Braeuner, J.J.): Botany. See: Webster's 3d.

Braune's canal (Braune, Christian Wilhelm): Medicine. See: Dorland; Stedman.

Braune's muscle (Braune, Christian Wilhelm): Medicine. See: Stedman.

Braune's valve (Braune, Christian Wilhelm): Medicine. See: Stedman.

Braunite (Braun, Kammerath): Earth Sciences. See: Thrush; Webster's 3d.

Braun's anastomosis (Braun, Heinrich): Medicine. See: Dorland; Stedman.

Braun's canal (Braun, Carl Ritter von Fernwald): Medicine. See: Dorland.

Braun's holly fern (Braun, Alexander Carl Heinrich): Botany. See: Webster's 3d.

Braun's hook (Braun, Gustav August): Medicine. See: Dorland; Stedman.

Braun's test (Braun, Christopher Heinrich): Medicine. See: Dorland; Stedman.

BRAVAIS, AUGUSTE. 1811-1863. French physicist. See: Dict. Sci. Biog. Bravais biplate, Bravais correlation coefficient?, Bravais lattice, Bravais' law (or rule), Bravais-Miller indices, Bravais points, Bravaisite.

Bravais biplate (Bravais, Auguste): Physics. See: Thewlis.

Bravais correlation coefficient (Bravais, Auguste?): Statistics. See: Kendall.

Bravais-Jackson epilepsy (Bravais, Louis F. and Jackson, John Hughlings). See: Jacksonian epilepsy (or Jackson's epilepsy).

Bravais lattice (Bravais, Auguste): Physics. See: Ballentyne; Hughes; Thewlis.

Bravais' law (or rule) (Bravais, Auguste): Physics. See: Ballentyne; Thrush.

BRAVAIS, LOUIS F. fl. 1827. French physician. Cited in: Kelly. Bravais-Jackson epilepsy.

Bravais-Miller indices (Bravais, Auguste and Miller, William Hallowes): Physics. See: Internat. Dict. Ap. Math. Also known as: Miller-Bravais indices.

Bravais points (Bravais, Auguste): Physics. See: Internat. Dict. Ap. Math.

Bravaisite (Bravais, Auguste): Earth Sciences. See: Thrush.

BRAVO, JOSE J. d. 1928. Peruvian mineralogist. Cited in: Min. Mag., vol. 15 (1910) p. 418. Bravoite.

Bravoite (Bravo, Jose J.): Earth Sciences. See: Thrush; Webster's 3d.

Braxton Hicks, John. See: Hicks, Braxton.

Braxton Hicks' sign (Hicks, Braxton): Medicine. See: Dorland; Stedman. Also known as: Ahlfeld's sign, Hicks sign.

Braxton Hicks' version (Hicks, Braxton). See: Hicks' version.

BRAY, CHARLES WILLIAM. 1904- . American otologist. See: Amer. Men Sci., 9th ed., vol. 3. Wever-Bray phenomenon (or effect).

BRAY, HUBERT EVELYN. b. 1889. American mathematician. See: Pogg., vols. 6, 7b. Helly-Bray theorem?

BRAY, VICAR OF. Semilegendary 16th c. English vicar. See: Jobes, under "Vicar of Bray." Vicar of Bray.

BRAYER, A. fl. 1822. French physician. Cited in: Royal Soc. Cat. Sci. Pap., 1800-63. Brayera.

Brayera (Brayer, A.): Botany. See: Stedman; Webster's 3d.

Brayton cycle (Brayton, George B.): Engineering and Industry. See: Auger; Markus; Van Nostrand Sci. Encyc. Also known as: Joule's cycle.

BRAYTON, GEORGE B. 1830-1873. American engineer. See: World Who's Who Sci. Brayton cycle.

BRECKENRIDGE, JOHN CABELL. 1821-1875. American lawyer and statesman. See: Dict. Amer. Biog. Breckite.

Breckite (Breckenridge, John Cabell): History. See: Mathews, M.M.

BREDA, ACHILLE. 1850-1933. Italian dermatologist. See: Biog. Lex. hervorr. Aerzte, 1880-1930. Breda's disease.

Breda's disease (Breda, Achille). See: Charlouis disease.

BREDBERG, BENGT GUSTAF. 1797-1873. Swedish metallurgist. See: Pogg., vols. 1, 3. Bredbergite.

Bredbergite (Bredberg, Bengt Gustaf): Earth Sciences. See: Thrush.

BREDIG, GEORG. 1868-1944. German chemist. See: World Who's Who Sci. Bredig method.

BREDIG, MAX ALBERT. 1902- . German-born American chemist. See: Pogg., vol. 7b. Bredigite.

Bredig method (Bredig, Georg): Chemistry. Cited in: World Who's Who Sci.

Bredigite (Bredig, Max. Albert): Earth Sciences. See: Thrush.

Bredt formulas (Derivation undetermined): Physics. See: Internat. Dict. Ap. Math.

BREDT, KONRAD JULIUS. 1855-1937. German chemist. See: World Who's Who Sci. Bredt rule.

Bredt rule (Bredt, Konrad Julius): Chemistry. See: Ballentyne; Van Nostrand Chem. Dict.

BREGUET, ABRAHAM LOUIS. 1747-1823. Swiss watchmaker. See: Nouv. Biog. Univ. Breguet (watches).

BREGUET, LOUIS CHARLES. 1880-1955. French aviator. See: New Encyc. Brit., 1974, Microp. Breguet's equation.

Breguet (watches) (Breguet, Abraham Louis): Horology. See: Charnock; Webster's 3d.

Breguet's equation (Breguet, Louis Charles): Aeronautics. See: New Encyc. Brit., 1974, Microp.

BREH, F. fl. 1930. American biochemist. Cited in: Kelly. Breh-Gaebler reagent.

Breh-Gaebler reagent (Breh, F. and Gaebler, Oliver Henry): Chemistry. See: Van Nostrand Chem. Dict.

BREHMER, HERMAN. 1826-1889. German physician. See: Allg. Deut. Biog. Brehmer's method (or treatment).

Brehmer's method (or treatment) (Brehmer, Herman): Medicine. See: Dorland.

BREHN, JOHANN PHILIP. 1690-1764. German physician and botanist. See: Nouv. Biog. Univ. Breynia.

BREISKY, AUGUST. 1832-1889. German gynecologist. See: World Who's Who Sci. Breisky's disease.

Breisky's disease (Breisky, August): Medicine. See: Dorland; Jablonski; Stedman.

BREISLAK, SCIPIONE. 1750-1826. Italian geologist. See: Dict. Sci. Biog. Breislakite.

Breislakite (Breislak, Scipione): Earth Sciences. See: Charnock.

BREIT, GREGORY. 1899- . Russian-born American physicist. See: World Who's Who Sci. Bohr-Breit-Wigner theory, Breit-Wigner cross section, Breit-Wigner formula.

Breit-Wigner cross section (Breit, Gregory and Wigner, Eugene Paul): Physics. See: Internat. Dict. Ap. Math.

Breit-Wigner formula (Breit, Gregory and Wigner, Eugene Paul): Physics. See: Ballentyne; Hughes; Internat. Dict. Ap. Math.

BREITHAUPT, JOHANN FRIEDRICH AUGUST. 1791-1873. German mineralogist. See: Dict. Sci. Biog. Breithauptite.

Breithauptite (Breithaupt, Johann Friedrich August): Earth Sciences. See: Charnock; Thrush; Webster's 3d.

BREMER, LUDWIG. 1844-1914. American physician. See: Amer. Med. Direct., vol. 1. Bremer's test.

BREMERMANN, HANS JOACHIM. 1926- . German-born American mathematician and biophysicist. See: World Who's Who Sci. Bremermann's (Bremerman's) limit.

Bremermann's (Bremerman's) limit (Bremermann, Hans Joachim): Mathematics. See: Wolman.

Bremer's test (Bremer, Ludwig): Medicine. See: Dorland; Stedman.

BREMI-WOLF, JOHANN JAKOB. 1791-1857. Swiss naturalist. See: Biog. Notes Upon Botanists. Bremia.

Bremia (Bremi-Wolf, Johann Jakob): Botany. See: Webster's 3d.

BREMME, C.A. fl. 1879. English engineer. (Biography source unavailable.) Bremme valve gear.

Bremme valve gear (Bremme, C. A.): Engineering and Industry. See: Auger.

BRENNEMANN, JOSEPH. 1872-1944. American pediatrician. See: World Who's Who Sci. Brennemann's (Brenneman's) syndrome.

Brennemann's (Brenneman's) syndrome (Brennemann, Joseph): Medicine. See: Dorland; Jablonski.

BRENNER, ABNER. 1908- . American electrochemist. See: Amer. Men Sci., 11th ed. Brenner gage.

BRENNER, ALEXANDER. 1859-1936. Austrian surgeon. See: World Who's Who Sci. Brenner('s) operation.

BRENNER, FRITZ. b. 1877. German pathologist. See: Cancer, vol. 9, no. 2, (1956), p. 216. Brenner('s) tumor.

Brenner gage (Brenner, Abner): Engineering and Industry. See: Thrush.

Brenner('s) operation (Brenner, Alexander): Medicine. See: Dorland; Stedman.

BRENNER, RUDOLF. 1821-1884. German physician. See: Biog. Lex. hervorr. Aerzte. Brenner's formula (or test).

Brenner('s) tumor (Brenner, Fritz): Medicine. See: Dorland; Jablonski; Stedman. Also known as: Brenneroma, Orthmann's tumor.

Brenneroma (Brenner, Fritz). See: Brenner('s) tumor.

Brenner's formula (or test) (Brenner, Rudolf): Medicine. See: Dorland.

Brentano's syndrome (Derivation undetermined): Medicine. See: Jablonski.

BRESCHET, GILBERT. 1784-1845. French anatomist. See: World Who's Who Sci. Breschet's bones, Breschet's canals, Breschet's hiatus, Breschet's sinus, Breschet's veins.

Breschet's bones (Breschet, Gilbert): Anatomy. See: Stedman.

Breschet's canals (Breschet, Gilbert): Anatomy. See: Donath; Dorland; Stedman.

Breschet's hiatus (Breschet, Gilbert): Anatomy. See: Stedman.

Breschet's sinus (Breschet, Gilbert): Anatomy. See: Stedman.

Breschet's veins (Breschet, Gilbert): Anatomy. See: Donath; Dorland; Stedman.

BRET, J. fl. 1956. French physician. (Biography source unavailable.) Bret's syndrome.

Brethren of Chelcic (Peter of Chelcic): Religion. See: Canney.

BRETONNEAU, PIERRE FIDELE. 1778-1862. French physician. See: Dict. Sci. Biog. Bretonneau's disease (or angina).

Bretonneau's disease (or angina) (Bretonneau, Pierre Fidele): Medicine. See: Dorland; Jablonski.

Bret's syndrome (Bret, J.): Medicine. See: Jablonski. Also known as: Janus syndrome.

BRETT, REGINALD BALIOL, 2D. VISCOUNT ESHER. 1852-1930. English government official. See: Dict. Nat. Biog., 4th suppl. Esher Committee.

BREUER, JOSEF. 1842-1925. Austrian physician. See: Dict. Sci. Biog. Hering-Breuer reflex.

BREUNNER, COUNT. fl. 19th c. Austrian nobleman. Cited in: Bailey. Breunnerite.

Breunnerite (Breunner, Count): Earth Sciences. See: Thrush; Webster's 3d.

BREUS, KARL. 1852-1914. Austrian obstetrician. See: Biog. Lex. hervorr. Aerzte, 1880-1930. Breus'(s) mole.

Breus'(s) mole (Breus, Karl): Medicine. See: Dorland; Jablonski; Stedman.

Breviary of Alaric (Alaric II): Law. Cited in: Encyc. Brit., 1973.

BREVOORT, JAMES CARSON. 1818-1887. American civil engineer and naturalist. See: Who Was Who Amer., 1607-1896. Brevoortia.

Brevoortia (Brevoort, James): Botany. See: Hendrickson; Taylor, N.; Webster's 3d.

BREWER, GEORGE EMERSON. 1861-1939. American surgeon. See: World Who's Who Sci. Brewer's infarcts, Brewer's operation, Brewer's point.

BREWER, THOMAS MAYO. 1814-1880. American ornithologist. See: Dict. Amer. Biog. Brewer's blackbird, Brewer's sparrow.

Brewer's blackbird (Brewer, Thomas Mayo): Zoology. See: Mathews, M.M.; Partridge; Webster's 3d.

Brewer's infarcts (Brewer, George Emerson): Medicine. See: Dorland.

Brewer's operation (Brewer, George Emerson): Medicine. See: Dorland.

Brewer's point (Brewer, George Emerson): Medicine. See: Dorland.

Brewer's sparrow (Brewer, Thomas Mayo): Zoology. See: Gray; Mathews, M.M.; Webster's 3d.

BREWSTER. fl. 1830's-1840's. American hatmaker. (Biography source unavailable.) Brewster (hat).

Brewster angle (Brewster, Sir David): Physics. See: Hughes; Internat. Dict. Ap. Math.; Van Nostrand Chem. Dict.

Brewster (carriage) (Brewster, James B.): Engineering and Industry. See: Mathews, M.M.

Brewster chair (Brewster, William): Applied Arts. See: Mathews, M.M.; Webster's 3d.

BREWSTER, SIR DAVID. 1781-1868. Scottish physicist. See: Dict. Sci. Biog. Brewster angle, Brewster('s) fringes (or bands), Brewster green, Brewster('s) law, Brewster point, Brewster stereoscope, Brewster (unit), Brewster window(s), Brewsterite, Brewsterlinite.

Brewster('s) fringes (or bands) (Brewster, Sir David): Physics. See: Ballentyne; Internat. Dict. Phys. Elec.; Thewlis.

Brewster green (Brewster, Sir David): Fine Arts. See: Webster's 3d.

Brewster (hat) (Brewster): Fashion. See: Mathews, M. M.; Partridge.

BREWSTER, JAMES B. 1788-1866. American manufacturer. See: Dict. Amer. Biog. Brewster (carriage).

BREWSTER, JAMES COLLINS. b. 1826. American religious leader. (Biography source unavailable.) Brewsterite.

Brewster('s) law (Brewster, Sir David); Physics. See: Ballentyne; Hughes; Internat. Dict. Ap. Math.

Brewster point (Brewster, Sir David): Physics. See: Huschke; Van Nostrand Sci. Encyc.

Brewster process (Brewster, T.J.): Chemistry. See: Van Nostrand Chem. Dict.

Brewster stereoscope (Brewster, Sir David): Physics. See: Thewlis.

BREWSTER, T. J. fl. 1925. Canadian? chemist. Cited in: Chem. Abstr., vol. 19, p. 2345. Brewster process.

Brewster (unit) (Brewster, Sir David): Physics. See: Ballentyne; Dresner.

BREWSTER, WILLIAM. 1567-1644. American pioneer. See: Dict. Amer. Biog. Brewster chair.

BREWSTER, WILLIAM. 1851-1919. American ornithologist. See: Dict. Amer. Biog. Brewster's booby, Brewster's warbler.

Brewster window(s) (Brewster, Sir David): Physics. See: Hughes; Markus.

Brewsterite (Brewster, Sir David): Earth Sciences. See: Charnock; Webster's 3d.

Brewsterite (Brewster, James Collins): Religion. See: Mathews, M. M.

Brewsterlinite (Brewster, Sir David): Earth Sciences. See: Charnock; Thrush.

Brewster's booby (Brewster, William): Zoology. See: Webster's 3d.

Brewster's warbler (Brewster, William): Zoology. See: Gray.

BREYER, ALBRECHT. 1812-1876. German-born Belgian physician. (Biography source unavailable.) Breyertypes.

Breyertypes (Breyer, Albrecht): Photography. See: Focal Encyc. Photog. under "Breyer."

Breyn, Johann Philip. See: Brehn, Johann Philip.

Breynia (Brehn, Johann Philip): Botany. See: Charnock; Taylor, N.

Breynius, Johann Philip. See: Brehn, Johann Philip.

Brezhnev Doctrine (Brezhnev, Leonid Ilyich): Politics. See: Barnhart (New Eng.).

BREZHNEV, LEONID ILYICH. 1906- . Russian political leader. See: Encyc. Brit., 1973. Brezhnev Doctrine.

BRIANCHON, CHARLES JULIEN. 1785-1864. French mathematician. See: Dict. Sci. Biog. Brianchon's theorem.

Brianchon's theorem (Brianchon, Charles Julien): Mathematics. See: Ballentyne.

BRIAND, ARISTIDE. 1862-1932. French statesman. See: Encyc. Brit., 1973. Kellogg-Briand Pact.

Briarean (Briareus): Generic Word (hundred-handed). See: Charnock; Partridge; Weekley.

BRIAREUS. Greek hurricane deity. See: Jobes. Briarean, Briareus of languages.

Briareus of languages (Briareus): Generic Word (accomplished linguist). See: Hendrickson.

Bricker operation (Derivation undetermined): Medicine. See: Stedman.

Brickner's position (Derivation undetermined): Medicine. See: Stedman.

BRIDGEMAN, OSCAR CLEON. 1897- . Canadian-born American physical chemist. See: Amer. Men Sci., 10th ed. Beattie-Bridgeman equation of state.

BRIDGES, JAMES WINFRED. b. 1885. Canadian psychologist. See: Biog. Direct. Amer. Psych. Assoc., 1973. Yerkes-Bridges point scale.

BRIDGET, SAINT. 1303-1373. Swedish nun and mystic. See: Encyc. Brit., 1973. Bridgettines (Brigittines).

Bridgettines (Brigittines) (Bridget, Saint): Religion. See: Attwater; Canney; Mathews, S.

Bridgewater, 8th Earl of. See: Egerton, Francis Henry (8th Earl of Bridgewater).

Bridgewater prize (Egerton, Francis Henry, 8th Earl of Bridgewater): Religion. See: Weekley.

Bridgewater treatises (Egerton, Francis Henry, 8th Earl of Bridgewater): Religion. See: Barnhart (Eng. Lit.); Brewer; Canney.

Bridgman effect (Bridgman, Percy Williams): Physics. See: Ballentyne.

BRIDGMAN, GRENVILLE TEMPLE. b. 1881. American mining engineer. See: Who's Who Engin., 2nd ed. Bridgman sampler?

BRIDGMAN, PERCY WILLIAMS. 1882-1961. American physicist. See: Dict. Sci. Biog. Bridgman effect, Bridgman relation, Bridgman-Stockbarger method.

Bridgman relation (Bridgman, Percy Williams): Physics. See: Ballentyne.

Bridgman sampler (Bridgman, Grenville Temple?): Engineering and Industry. See: Thrush.

Bridgman-Stockbarger method (Bridgman, Percy Williams and Stockbarger, Donald Charles): Physics. See: Ballentyne.

BRIEGER, LUDWIG. 1849-1919. German physician. See: World Who's Who Sci. Brieger's reaction, Brieger's test (for pyrocatechin), Brieger's test (for strychnine).

Brieger test reaction (Derivation undetermined): Medicine. See: Van Nostrand Chem. Dict.

Brieger's reaction (Brieger, Ludwig): Medicine. See: Stedman.

Brieger's test (for pyrocatechin) (Brieger, Ludwig): Medicine. See: Dorland.

Brieger's test (for strychnine) (Brieger, Ludwig): Medicine. See: Dorland.

BRIEGLEB, GUENTHER. 1905- . German physicist. See: Wer Ist Wer, 8th ed. Stuart-Briegleb molecular models.

BRIEN, RICHARD HERMAN. 1939- . American marketing analyst. See: Amer. Men Women Sci., 12th ed. Brien's first law.

Brien's first law (Brien, Richard Herman): Sociology. See: Martin.

Brig (unit) (Briggs, Henry): Mathematics. See: Ballentyne; Dresner.

Briggs case (Briggs, Charles Augustus): Religion. See: Jameson.

BRIGGS, CHARLES AUGUSTUS. 1841-1913. American clergyman and Biblical scholar. See: Dict. Amer. Biog. Briggs case.

Briggs clinophone (Briggs, Henry?): Engineering and Industry. See: Thrush.

Briggs equalizer (Briggs, Henry?): Engineering and Industry. See: Thrush.

BRIGGS, HENRY. 1561-1630. English mathematician. See: Dict. Sci. Biog. Brig (unit), Briggs (or Briggsian) logarithm(s).

BRIGGS, HENRY. 1883-1935. English mining engineer. See: Pogg., vols. 6, 7b. Briggs clinophone?, Briggs equalizer?, Briggs stretcher carriage?

Briggs' law (Briggs, Lloyd Vernon): Psychiatry. See: Hinsie; Wolman.

BRIGGS, LLOYD VERNON. 1863-1941. American psychiatrist. See: Who Was Who Amer., vol. 1. Briggs' law.

Briggs (or Briggsian) logarithm(s) (Briggs, Henry): Mathematics. See: Ballentyne; James; Webster's 3d.

BRIGGS, ROBERT. 1822-1882. American engineer. See: Amer. Soc. Civ. Engin. Trans., vol. 36 (1896), pp. 542-45. Briggs screw thread?

Briggs screw thread (Briggs, Robert?): Engineering and Industry. See: Auger.

Briggs stretcher carriage (Briggs, Henry?): Engineering and Industry. See: Thrush.

Brigham tea (Young, Brigham): Botany. See: Hendrickson; Partridge; Webster's 3d.

Brighamite (Young, Brigham): Religion. See: Mathews, M.M.; Webster's 3d.

Bright clauses (Bright, John): History. See: Harbottle; Montgomery.

BRIGHT, JOHN. 1811-1889. English orator and statesman. See: Dict. Nat. Biog., 1st suppl. Bright clauses.

BRIGHT, RICHARD. 1789-1858. English physician. See: Dict. Sci. Biog. Bright's disease.

Bright's disease (Bright, Richard): Medicine. See: Dorland; Jablonski; Stedman.

Brill-Baehr-Rosenthal disease (Brill, Nathan Edwin; Baehr, George; and Rosenthal, Nathan). See: Brill-Symmers disease (or syndrome).

BRILL, NATHAN EDWIN. 1860-1925. American physician. See: Dict. Amer. Biog. Brill-Symmers disease (or syndrome), Brill's disease, Lederer-Brill syndrome.

Brill-Symmers disease (or syndrome) (Brill, Nathan Edwin and Symmers, Douglas): Medicine. See: Dorland; Jablonski; Stedman. Also known as: Brill-Baehr-Rosenthal disease.

Brill-Zinsser disease (Brill, Nathan Edwin and Zinsser, Hans). See: Brill's disease.

Brillat-Savarin (Brillat-Savarin, Jean Anthelme): Generic Word (gastronome). See: Hendrickson; Partridge.

BRILLAT-SAVARIN, JEAN ANTHELME. 1755-1826. French politician and writer. See: Encyc. Brit., 1973. Brillat-Savarin, Savarin (egg bread).

Brillouin balance (Brillouin, Louis Marcel): Physics. Cited in: Dict. Sci. Biog.

Brillouin effect (Brillouin, Louis Marcel or Leon Nicolas): Physics. See: Internat. Dict. Ap. Math.

Brillouin formula (Brillouin, Louis Marcel or Leon Nicolas): Physics. See: Hughes.

Brillouin function (Brillouin, Louis Marcel or Leon Nicolas): Physics. See: Ballentyne; Internat. Dict. Ap. Math.; Markus.

BRILLOUIN, L. fl. 1964. Scientist. (Biography source unavailable.) Brillouin scale.

BRILLOUIN, LEON NICOLAS. b. 1889. French-born American physicist. See: Amer. Men Sci., 9th ed. Brillouin effect?, Brillouin formula?, Brillouin function?, Wentzel-Kramers-Brillouin-Jeffreys approximation (or method)?

BRILLOUIN, LOUIS MARCEL. 1854-1948. French mathematician and physicist. See: Dict. Sci. Biog. Brillouin balance, Brillouin effect?, Brillouin formula?, Brillouin function?, Brillouin scattering, Brillouin zone.

Brillouin scale (Brillouin, L.): Earth Sciences. See: Monkhouse.

Brillouin scattering (Brillouin, Louis Marcel): Physics. See: Ballentyne; Hughes.

Brillouin zone (Brillouin, Louis Marcel): Physics. See: Ballentyne; Hughes; Internat. Dict. Ap. Math.

Brill's disease (Brill, Nathan Edwin): Medicine. See: Dorland; Jablonski; Webster's 3d. Also known as: Brill-Zinsser disease.

Brin('s) process (Derivation undetermined): Chemistry. See: Ballentyne; Hackh; Van Nostrand Chem. Dict.

Brinell hardness (Brinell, Johann August): Engineering and Industry. See: Clark; Hackh; Webster's 3d.

Brinell (hardness) number (Brinell, Johann August): Engineering and Industry. See: Hendrickson; Stedman; Webster's 3d.

Brinell('s) hardness test (Brinell, Johann August): Engineering and Industry. See: Auger; Ballentyne; Thrush.

Brinell (hardness) tester (or machine) (Brinell, Johann August): Engineering and Industry. See: Hackh; Hendrickson; Thrush.

BRINELL, JOHANN AUGUST. 1849-1925. Swedish engineer. See: Dict. Sci. Biog. Brinell hardness, Brinell (hardness) number, Brinell('s) hardness test, Brinell (hardness) tester (or machine), Brinell scale.

Brinell scale (Brinell, Johann August): Engineering and Industry. See: Hendrickson.

Bringhetti test (Derivation undetermined): Chemistry. See: Van Nostrand Chem. Dict.

BRINKERHOFF, WILLIAM CAREY. b. 1861. American physician. See: Amer. Med. Direct., 1909. Brinkerhoff's speculum.

Brinkerhoff's speculum (Brinkerhoff, William Carey): Medicine. See: Stedman.

Brinser (Brinser, Matthias): Religion. See: Webster's 3d.

BRINSER, MATTHIAS. fl. 1855. American theologist. (Biography source unavailable.) Brinser.

Brinton Reishauer bottle (Derivation undetermined): Chemistry. See: Hackh.

BRINTON, WILLIAM. 1823-1867. English physician. See: Dict. Nat. Biog. Brinton's disease.

Brinton's disease (Brinton, William): Medicine. See: Dorland; Jablonski; Stedman.

BRION, ALBERT. b. 1874. German physician. See: Biog. Lex. hervorr. Aerzte, 1880-1930. Brion-Kayser disease.

Brion-Kayser disease (Brion, Albert and Kayser, Heinrich). See: Schottmueller's disease.

BRIQUET, PIERRE. 1796-1881. French physician. See: World Who's Who Sci. Briquet's ataxia, Briquet's gangrene, Briquet's syndrome.

Briquet's ataxia (Briquet, Pierre): Medicine. See: Dorland; Jablonski; Stedman.

Briquet's gangrene (Briquet, Pierre): Medicine. See: Jablonski.

Briquet's syndrome (Briquet, Pierre): Medicine. See: Dorland; Jablonski; Stedman.

Briska detonator (Derivation undetermined): Engineering and Industry. See: Thrush.

BRISSAUD, EDOUARD. 1852-1909. French neurologist. See: World Who's Who Sci. Bourneville-Brissaud disease, Brissaud-Marie syndrome, Brissaud-Sicard syndrome, Brissaud's disease (1), Brissaud's disease (2), Brissaud's infantilism, Brissaud's reflex, Brissaud's scoliosis.

Brissaud-Marie syndrome (Brissaud, Edouard and Marie, Pierre): Medicine. See: Stedman.

Brissaud-Meige syndrome (Brissaud, Edouard and Meige, Henry). See: Brissaud's infantilism.

Brissaud-Sicard syndrome (Brissaud, Edouard and Sicard, Jean Athanase): Medicine. See: Jablonski. Also known as: Brissaud's syndrome.

Brissaud's disease (1) (Brissaud, Edouard): Medicine. See: Dorland; Jablonski; Stedman.

Brissaud's disease (2) (Brissaud, Edouard). See: Gilles de la Tourette's syndrome.

Brissaud's infantilism (Brissaud, Edouard): Medicine. See: Dorland; Jablonski; Stedman. Also known as: Brissaud-Meige syndrome.

Brissaud's reflex (Brissaud, Edouard): Medicine. See: Dorland; Stedman.

Brissaud's scoliosis (Brissaud, Edouard): Medicine. See: Dorland.

Brissaud's syndrome (Brissaud, Edouard). See: Brissaud-Sicard syndrome.

BRISSOT, JACQUES PIERRE. 1754-1793. French journalist. See: Encyc. Brit., 1973. Brissotins.

Brissotins (Brissot, Jacques Pierre): History. See: Brewer; Harbottle.

BRISTOWE, JOHN SYER. 1827-1895. English medical writer and physician. See: Dict. Nat. Biog. Bristowe's syndrome.

Bristowe's syndrome (Bristowe, John Syer): Medicine. See: Jablonski.

BRITTAIN, ROBERT SUNDERLIN. 1929- . American physician. See: Direct. Med. Specialists, vol. 14. Brittain's sign.

Brittain's sign (Brittain, Robert Sunderlin): Medicine. See: Dorland.

BRITTON, ELIZABETH GERTRUDE KNIGHT. 1858-1934. American botanist. See: Who Was Who Amer., vol. 1. Bryobrittonia.

BRITTON, NATHANIEL LORD. 1859-1934. American botanist. See: Dict. Sci. Biog. Brittonamra, Brittonastrom, Brittonella.

Brittonamra (Britton, Nathaniel Lord): Botany. Cited in: Dict. Sci. Biog.

Brittonastrom (Britton, Nathaniel Lord): Botany. Cited in: Dict. Sci. Biog.

Brittonella (Britton, Nathaniel Lord): Botany. Cited in: Dict. Sci. Biog.

Brix hydrometer (or scale) (Derivation undetermined): Chemistry. See: Hackh; Van Nostrand Chem. Dict.

BROADBENT, SIR WILLIAM HENRY. 1835-1907. English physician. See: Dict. Nat. Biog., 2nd suppl. Bolton-Broadbent plane, Broadbent's apoplexy (or syndrome), Broadbent's law, Broadbent's sign.

Broadbent's apoplexy (or syndrome) (Broadbent, Sir William Henry): Medicine. See: Dorland; Jablonski.

Broadbent's law (Broadbent, Sir William Henry): Medicine. See: Stedman.

Broadbent's sign (Broadbent, Sir William Henry): Medicine. See: Dorland; Stedman.

BROBBEL, L. M. fl. 1937. Dutch chemist. Cited in: Chem. Abstr., vol. 31, p. 4230. Nieuwenberg-Brobbel micro-test for malic acid.

BROBERGER, O. fl. 1959. Physician. (Biography source unavailable.) Broberger-Zetterstroem syndrome.

Broberger-Zetterstroem syndrome (Broberger, O. and Zetterstroem, R.): Medicine. See: Jablonski.

BROCA, ANDRE ELIE. 1863-1925. French physicist. See: Pogg., vols. 4, 5, 6. Pellin-Broca prism.

BROCA, PIERRE PAUL. 1824-1880. French surgeon, neurologist, and anthropologist. See: Dict. Sci. Biog. Broca's angles, Broca's aphasia, Broca's area (or convolution), Broca's cap, Broca's diagonal band, Broca's fissure, Broca's formula, Broca's point, Broca's pouch, Broca's space, Broca's visual plane.

Broca tube (Derivation undetermined): Physics. See: Hughes; Internat. Dict. Phys. Elec.

Brocard (Burchard): Generic Word (brief maxim). See: Hendrickson; Partridge; Webster's 3d.

Brocard, Bishop. See: Burchard.

BROCARD, HENRI. 1845-1922. French mathematician. See: Dict. Sci. Biog. Brocard's circle, Brocard's ellipse.

Brocard's circle (Brocard, Henri): Mathematics. See: Hendrickson; Partridge.

Brocard's ellipse (Brocard, Henri): Mathematics. Cited in: Hendrickson; Partridge.

Broca's angles (Broca, Pierre Paul): Medicine. See: Stedman.

Broca's aphasia (Broca, Pierre Paul): Medicine. See: Dorland; Jablonski; Stedman.

Broca's area (or convolution) (Broca, Pierre Paul): Medicine. See: Blumberg; Chaplin; English.

Broca's cap (Broca, Pierre Paul): Medicine. See: Stedman.

Broca's diagonal band (Broca, Pierre Paul): Medicine. See: Stedman.

Broca's fissure (Broca, Pierre Paul): Medicine. See: Dorland; Stedman.

Broca's formula (Broca, Pierre Paul): Medicine. See: Dorland; Stedman.

Broca's point (Broca, Pierre Paul): Medicine. See: Webster's 3d.

Broca's pouch (Broca, Pierre Paul): Medicine. See: Dorland; Stedman.

Broca's space (Broca, Pierre Paul): Medicine. See: Dorland; Stedman.

Broca's visual plane (Broca, Pierre Paul): Medicine. See: Dorland; Stedman.

BROCHANT DE VILLIERS, ANDRE JEAN FRANCOIS MARIE. 1772-1840. French mineralogist and geologist. See: Dict. Sci. Biog. Brochantite.

Brochantite (Brochant de Villiers, Andre Jean Francois Marie): Earth Sciences. See: Charnock; Thrush; Van Nostrand Sci. Encyc.

BROCK, DONALD R. 1926- . American pathologist. See: Direct. Med. Specialists, vol. 14. Brock-Suckow polyposis.

BROCK, M. No dates. American geologist. Cited in: Min. Mag., vol. 33 (1964) p. 1129. Brockite.

Brock operation (Derivation undetermined): Medicine. See: Stedman.

BROCK, SIR RUSSELL CLAUDE. 1903- . English surgeon. See: Med. Direct., 1937. Brock's syndrome.

Brock-Suckow polyposis (Brock, Donald R. and Suckow, Earl E.): Medicine. See: Jablonski.

Brockite (Brock, M.): Earth Sciences. See: Thrush.

Brockmann-Chen reagent (Brockmann, Hans and Chen, Yun Hwang): Chemistry. See: Van Nostrand Chem. Dict.

BROCKMANN, HANS HEINRICH. 1903- . German chemist. See: Pogg., vol. 7a. Brockmann-Chen reagent.

Brock's knife (Derivation undetermined): Medicine. See: Stedman.

Brock's syndrome (Brock, Sir Russell Claude): Medicine. See: Jablonski; Stedman.

BROCOT, ACHILLE. d. 1878. French horologist. (Biography source unavailable.) Brocot suspension.

Brocot suspension (Brocot, Achille): Horology. See: Webster's 3d.

Brocq-Duhring disease (Brocq, Louis Anne Jean and Duhring, Louis Adolphus). See: Duhring's disease.

BROCQ, LOUIS ANNE JEAN. 1856-1928. French dermatologist. See: World Who's Who Sci. Brocq-Duhring disease, Brocq-Pautrier glossitis (or syndrome), Brocq's disease (1), Brocq's disease (2), Brocq's disease (3), Brocq's pseudopelade.

Brocq-Pautrier glossitis (or syndrome) (Brocq, Louis Anne Jean and Pautrier, Lucien M.): Medicine. See: Jablonski.

Brocq's disease (1) (Brocq, Louis Anne Jean): Medicine. See: Jablonski. Also known as: Vidal's disease.

Brocq's disease (2) (Brocq, Louis Anne Jean): Medicine. See: Dorland; Jablonski; Stedman.

Brocq's disease (3) (Brocq, Louis Anne Jean): Medicine. See: Jablonski.

Brocq's pseudopelade (Brocq, Louis Anne Jean): Medicine. See: Jablonski.

Broderick (Broderick, Johnny): Generic Word (clobber). See: Hendrickson.

BRODERICK, JOHNNY. 1894-1966. American policeman. (Biography source unavailable.) Broderick.

BRODERS, ALBERT COMPTON. 1885- . American pathologist. See: World Who's Who Sci. Broders' classification (or index).

Broders' classification (or index) (Broders, Albert Compton): Medicine. See: Dorland.

BRODHUN, EUGEN. b. 1860. German physicist. See: Webster's Biog. Dict. Lummer-Brodhun cube (or photometer).

Brodiaea (Brodie, James J.): Botany. See: Mathews, M. M.; Taylor, N.; Webster's 3d.

Brodie (Brodie, Steve): Generic Word. See: Hendrickson; Partridge; Webster's 3d.

BRODIE, SIR BENJAMIN COLLINS. 1783-1862. English surgeon. See: Dict. Sci. Biog. Brodie's abscess, Brodie's bursa, Brodie's disease (1), Brodie's knee (or disease (2), Brodie's pile, Brodie's serocystic disease (or tumor).

BRODIE, CHARLES GORDON. 1786-1818. Scottish anatomist. Cited in: Kelly. Brodie's ligament.

Brodie coagulometer (Brodie, Thomas Gregor): Chemistry. See: Hackh.

BRODIE, JAMES J. 1744-1824. Scottish botanist. See: Britten and Boulger. Brodiaea.

Brodie kymograph (Brodie, Thomas Gregor?): Chemistry. See: Hackh.

Brodie solution (or fluid) (Brodie, Thomas Gregor): Chemistry. See: Hackh; Stedman.

BRODIE, STEVE. fl. 1886. American newsboy. (Biography source unavailable.) Brodie.

BRODIE, THOMAS GREGOR. 1866-1916. English physiologist. See: Sci., vol. 44 (1916) p. 349. Brodie coagulometer, Brodie kymograph, Brodie solution (or fluid).

Brodie's abscess (Brodie, Sir Benjamin Collins): Medicine. See: Dorland; Jablonski; Stedman.

Brodie's bursa (Brodie, Sir Benjamin Collins): Medicine. See: Stedman.

Brodie's disease (1) (Brodie, Sir Benjamin Collins): Medicine. See: Jablonski.

Brodie's knee (or disease (2)) (Brodie, Sir Benjamin Collins): Medicine. See: Dorland; Jablonski.

Brodie's ligament (Brodie, Charles Gordon): Medicine. See: Dorland; Stedman.

Brodie's pile (Brodie, Sir Benjamin Collins): Medicine. See: Jablonski.

Brodie's serocystic disease (or tumor) (Brodie, Sir Benjamin Collins): Medicine. See: Jablonski.

BRODIN, M. fl. 1941. French physician. (Biography source unavailable.) Brodin's syndrome.

Brodin's syndrome (Brodin, M.): Medicine. See: Jablonski.

BRODMANN, KORBINIAN. 1868-1918. German neurologist. See: Biog. Lex. hervorr. Aerzte., 1880-1930. Brodmann's (Broadmann's) area.

Brodmann's (Broadmann's) area (Brodmann, Korbinian): Medicine. See: Chaplin; Dorland; English.

Brodrick army scheme (Brodrick, William St. John Fremantle): History. See: Montgomery.

Brodrick (peaked cap) (Brodrick, William St. John Fremantle): Fashion. See: Partridge; Weekley.

BRODRICK, WILLIAM ST. JOHN FREMANTLE. 1856-1942. English political leader. See: Encyc. Brit., 1911. Brodrick army scheme, Brodrick (peaked cap), little Brodricks.

BROEDEL, MAX. 1870-1941. German-born American educator. See: Who Was Who Amer., vol. 1. Broedel's bloodless line.

Broedel's bloodless line (Broedel, Max): Medicine. See: Stedman.

BROEGGER, WALDEMAR CHRISTOPHER. 1851-1940. Norwegian mineralogist. See: Dict. Sci. Biog. Broeggerite (Broggerite).

Broeggerite (Broggerite) (Broegger, Waldemar Christopher): Earth Sciences. See: Thrush; Webster's 3d.

Broensted and Lewis treatment of acids (Broensted, Johannes Nicolaus and Lewis, Gilbert Newton): Chemistry. See: Van Nostrand Sci. Encyc.

Broensted base (Broensted, Johannes Nicolaus): Chemistry. See: Stedman.

BROENSTED, JOHANNES NICOLAUS. 1879-1947. Danish physical chemist. See: Dict. Sci. Biog. Broensted and Lewis treatment of acids, Broensted base, Broensted-Lowry definition (or theory), Broensted relationship, Broensted test?

Broensted-Lowry definition (or theory) (Broensted, Johannes Nicolaus and Lowry, Thomas Martin): Chemistry. See: Ballentyne; Van Nostrand Chem. Dict. Also known as: Broensted theory.

Broensted relationship (Broensted, Johannes Nicolaus): Chemistry. See: Van Nostrand Chem. Dict.

Broensted test (Broensted, Johannes Nicolaus?): Chemistry. See: Van Nostrand Chem. Dict.

Broensted theory (Broensted, Johannes Nicolaus). See: Broensted-Lowry definition (or theory).

BROESIKE, GUSTAV. b. 1853. German anatomist. See: Wer Ist's? 1906. Broesike's fossa, Treitz-Broesicke hernia.

Broesike's fossa (Broesike, Gustav): Anatomy. See: Dorland; Stedman.

BROGLIE, LOUIS VICTOR PIERRE RAYMOND, DUC DE. 1892- . French physicist. See: World Who's Who Sci. De Broglie atom, De Broglie (Broglie) equation (or formula), De Broglie('s) theory (or hypothesis), De Broglie wavelength.

BROMBERG, Y. M. No dates. Physician. (Biography source unavailable.) Zondek-Bromberg-Rozin syndrome.

BROMEL, OLAF. 1639-1705. Swedish botanist. See: Webster's Biog. Dict. Bromelain, Bromelia.

Bromelain (Bromel, Olaf): Medicine. See: Stedman.

Bromelia (Bromel, Olaf): Botany. See: Charnock; Taylor, N.; Webster's 3d.

BROMELL, MAGNUS VON. 1679-1731. Swedish mineralogist. See: Dict. Sci. Biog. Bromellite.

Bromellite (Bromell, Magnus von): Earth Sciences. See: Webster's 3d.

Bromwell apparatus (Bromwell, William?): Chemistry. See: Hackh.

BROMWELL, WILLIAM. fl. 1897. American chemist. Cited in: Royal Soc. Cat. Sci. Pap., 1884-1900. Bromwell apparatus?

Bromwich contour (Bromwich, Thomas John l'Anson): Mathematics. See: Internat. Dict. Phys. Elec.

BROMWICH, THOMAS JOHN l'ANSON. 1875-1929. English mathematician. See: Dict. Sci. Biog. Bromwich contour, Bromwich's expansion theorem.

Bromwich's expansion theorem (Bromwich, Thomas John l'Anson): Mathematics. See: Ballentyne.

Brongniardite (Brongniart, Alexandre): Earth Sciences. See: Thrush.

BRONGNIART, ALEXANDRE. 1770-1847. French geologist. See: Dict. Sci. Biog. Brongniardite, Brongniart's formula.

Brongniart's formula (Brongniart, Alexandre): Earth Sciences. See: Thrush.

Brons engine (Brons, J.): Engineering and Industry. See: Auger.

BRONS, J. fl. 1904. Dutch engineer. (Biography source unavailable.) Brons engine.

BRONSON, HOWARD LOGAN. b. 1878. American-born Canadian physicist. See: Amer. Men Sci., 9th ed. Bronson resistance.

Bronson resistance (Bronson, Howard Logan): Physics. See: Hughes; Internat. Dict. Phys. Elec.; Van Nostrand Sci. Encyc.

BRONSTRUP, FREDERICK. No dates. American printer. (Biography source unavailable.) Bronstrup press.

Bronstrup press (Bronstrup, Frederick): Printing. See: Lockwood.

Brooke-Fordyce disease (Brooke, Henry Ambrose Grundy and Fordyce, John Addison). See: Brooke's epithelioma (disease, syndrome, or tumor).

Brooke gun (Brooke, John Mercer): Weapons. Cited in: World Who's Who Sci.

BROOKE, HENRY AMBROSE GRUNDY. 1854-1919. English dermatologist. See: Biog. Lex. hervorr. Aerzte, 1880-1930. Brooke's epithelioma (disease, syndrome, or tumor), Morrow-Brooke syndrome.

BROOKE, HENRY JAMES. 1771-1857. English mineralogist. See: Dict. Nat. Biog. Brookite.

BROOKE, JOHN MERCER. 1826-1906. American physicist. See: World Who's Who Sci. Brooke gun.

Brooke press (Derivation undetermined): Printing. See: Lockwood.

Brooke's epithelioma (disease, syndrome, or tumor) (Brooke, Henry Ambrose Grundy): Medicine. See: Jablonski. Also known as: Brooke-Fordyce disease.

BROOKFIELD, DONALD W. fl. 1954. American chemist. Cited in: Chem. Abstr., vol. 48, p. 9766. Brookfield viscometer.

Brookfield viscometer (Brookfield, Donald W.): Chemistry. See: Thrush.

Brookite (Brooke, Henry James): Earth Sciences. See: Charnock; Thrush; Van Nostrand Sci. Encyc.

Brookland's experiment (Derivation undetermined): Psychology. See: Wolman.

BROOKS, ALFRED HULSE. 1871-1924. American geologist. See: Dict. Sci. Biog. Hulsite.

Brooks deflection potentiometer (Brooks, Herbert Barton): Physics. See: Internat. Dict. Phys. Elec.

BROOKS, HERBERT BARTON. b. 1869. American physicist. See: Pogg., vols. 6, 7b. Brooks deflection potentiometer, Brooks standard-cell comparator potentiometer.

Brooks standard-cell comparator potentiometer (Brooks, Herbert Barton): Physics. See: Internat. Dict. Phys. Elec.

BROPHY, TRUMAN WILLIAM. 1848-1928. American oral surgeon. See: Dict. Amer. Biog. Brophy's operation.

Brophy's operation (Brophy, Truman William): Medicine. See: Dorland.

Bross Foundation (Bross, William): Religion. See: Canney.

BROSS, WILLIAM. 1813-1890. American journalist. See: Dict. Amer. Biog. Bross Foundation.

Brother Jonathan (Trumbull, Jonathan): Generic Word (American). See: Hendrickson; Mathews, M. M.; Phyfe.

Brotherhood of As-Sanusi (Sanusi, Muhammad ibn Ali as-). See: Sanusi.

Brotherhood of St. Andrew (Andrew, Saint): Religion. See: Canney.

Brothers of Christ (Jesus Christ). See: Christadelphians.

Brothers of St. Patrick (Patrick, Saint): Religion. See: Attwater.

Brougham (carriage) (Brougham, Henry Peter): Engineering and Industry. See: Brewer; Charnock; Hendrickson.

BROUGHAM, HENRY PETER. 1778-1868. Scottish jurist and political leader. See: Dict. Nat. Biog. Brougham (carriage).

Broughton (de Gyfford), Baron. See: Hobhouse, John Cam, Baron Broughton.

BROUHA, ADELE. fl. 20th c. French physician. (Biography source unavailable.) Brouha test.

BROUHA, LUCIEN. 1899- . French physician. (Biography source unavailable.) Brouha test.

Brouha test (Brouha, Adele and Lucien): Medicine. See: Dorland; Stedman.

BROUSSAIS, FRANCOIS JOSEPH VICTOR. 1772-1838. French physician. See: Dict. Sci. Biog. Broussaisism.

Broussaisism (Broussais, Francois Joseph Victor): Medicine. See: Dorland; Stedman.

BROUSSONET, PIERRE AUGUSTE MARIE. 1761-1807. French naturalist. See: Dict. Sci. Biog. Broussonetia.

Broussonetia (Broussonet, Pierre Auguste Marie): Botany. See: Taylor, N.; Webster's 3d.

Brouwer('s) fixed point theorem (Brouwer, Luitzen Egbertus Jan): Mathematics. See: Internat. Dict. Ap. Math.; James.

BROUWER, LUITZEN EGBERTUS JAN. 1882-1966. Dutch mathematician. See: Dict. Sci. Biog. Brouwer('s) fixed point theorem.

Browall, John. See: Browallius, Johann.

Browallia (Browallius, Johann): Botany. See: Charnock; Taylor, N.; Webster's 3d.

BROWALLIUS, JOHANN. 1707-1755. Swedish theologian and naturalist. See: Nouv. Biog. Univ. Browallia.

BROWDER, EARL RUSSELL. 1891-1973. American political theorist. See: New Encyc. Brit., 1974, Microp. Browderism.

Browderism (Browder, Earl Russell): Politics. Cited in: New Encyc. Brit., 1974, Microp.

BROWN. Character in story by Richard Doyle (1870's). See: Benet. Brown, Jones, and Robinson.

BROWN, A. B. fl. 1890. English naval architect. (Biography source unavailable.) Brown steering gear.

Brown alcohol test (Derivation undetermined): Chemistry. See: Van Nostrand Chem. Dict.

BROWN, ALEXANDER CRUM. 1838-1922. Scottish chemist. See: Dict. Sci. Biog. Crum-Brown and Gibson rule, Crum-Brown and Walker synthesis (or reaction).

BROWN, C. L. M. fl. 1933. English chemist. Cited in: Chem. Abstr., vol. 27, p. 5681. Brown-Lum test reaction.

BROWN, CHARLES LEONARD. 1899- . American physician. See: Who's Who Among Physicians and Surg. Brown-Symmers disease.

Brown classification (Brown, James Duff): Library Science. See: Harrod.

Brown decree (Derivation undetermined): Law. See: Black.

BROWN, DENIS. fl. 1934. English surgeon. Cited in: Kelly. Denis-Browne splint.

Brown engine (Brown, Samuel): Engineering and Industry. See: Auger.

BROWN, GEORGE ELGIE. 1885-1935. American physician. See: Who's Who Amer. Med. Horton-Magath-Brown disease, Nygaard-Brown syndrome.

BROWN, GEORGE WILLIAM. 1917- . American mathematician. See: Amer. Men and Women Sci., 12th ed. Mood-Brown estimation (of a line), Mood-Brown median test.

BROWN, GLENN VINTON. b. 1875. American chemist. See: Amer. Men Sci., 1st ed. Brown-MacAdam colorimeter?

BROWN, HAROLD WHALEY. 1898- . American ophthalmologist. See: Direct. Med. Specialist, 14th ed. Brown's syndrome.

Brown horseshoe furnace (Derivation undetermined): Engineering and Industry. See: Thrush.

BROWN, JAMES BARRETT. 1899- . American physician. See: World Who's Who Sci. Blair-Brown graft.

BROWN, JAMES DUFF. 1862-1914. Scottish librarian. See: Grove. Brown classification.

BROWN, JAMES HOWARD. b. 1884. American pathologist. See: Amer. Men Sci., 9th ed., Biol. Sci. Kimpton-Brown tube.

BROWN, JASON W. fl. 1966. American physician. (Biography source unavailable.) Brown's syndrome.

BROWN, JOHN. 1735-1788. Scottish physician. See: Dict. Nat. Biog. Brunonianism (or Brownism).

BROWN, JOHN. 1800-1859. American abolitionist. See: Dict. Amer. Biog. Brown's insurrection.

Brown, Jones, and Robinson (Brown; Jones; and Robinson, the Englishmen): Generic Word (Victorian snobbery). See: Brewer; Latham.

BROWN, JOSEPH EMERSON. 1821-1894. American statesman. See: Dict. Amer. Biog. Joe Brown's pets.

Brown Kelly. See: Kelly, Adam Brown.

Brown loudspeaker (Derivation undetermined): Electronics. See: Hughes.

Brown-Lum test reaction (Brown, C. L. M. and Lum, E. A.): Chemistry. See: Van Nostrand Chem. Dict.

Brown-MacAdam colorimeter (Brown, Glenn Vinton? and MacAdam, David Lewis): Physics. See: Internat. Dict. Phys. Elec.

Brown muffle furnace (Derivation undetermined): Engineering and Industry. See: Thrush.

BROWN, NATHAN L. No dates. American clergyman. (Biography source unavailable.) Parson Brown orange.

BROWN, O. S. fl. 1870. American inventor. (Biography source unavailable.) Brown's typesetting machine.

Brown-O'Hara furnace (Derivation undetermined): Engineering and Industry. See: Thrush.

Brown panel system (Derivation undetermined): Engineering and Industry. See: Thrush.

Brown-Pearce tumor (carcinoma or epithelioma) (Brown, Wade Hampton and Pearce, Louise): Medicine. See: Jablonski; Stedman.

BROWN, ROBERT. 1773-1858. English botanist. See: Dict. Sci. Biog. Brownian movement (or motion), Brunonia.

BROWN, ROBERT GOODELL. 1923- . American operations researcher. See: Amer. Men and Women Sci., 12th ed. Brown's method.

Brown rule (Brown, Alexander Crum). See: Crum-Brown and Gibson rule.

BROWN, SAMUEL. fl. 1823. English engineer. (Biography source unavailable.) Brown engine.

BROWN, SANGER. 1852-1928. American neuropsychiatrist. See: Who Was Who Amer., vol. 1. Sanger-Brown ataxia.

BROWN-SEQUARD, CHARLES EDOUARD. 1818-1894. French physiologist. See: Dict. Sci. Biog. Brown-Sequard injections, Brown-Sequard('s) syndrome, Brown-Sequard's disease, Brown-Sequard's epilepsy, Brown-Sequard's paralysis.

Brown-Sequard injections (Brown-Sequard, Charles Edouard): Medicine. See: Stedman.

Brown-Sequard('s) syndrome (Brown-Sequard, Charles Edouard): Medicine. See: Chaplin; Drever; Hinsie.

Brown-Sequard's disease (Brown-Sequard, Charles Edouard): Medicine. See: Dorland.

Brown-Sequard's epilepsy (Brown-Sequard, Charles Edouard): Medicine. See: Jablonski.

Brown-Sequard's paralysis (Brown-Sequard, Charles Edouard): Medicine. See: Stedman.

Brown-Spearman prophesy (or formula) (Brown, W. and Spearman, Charles Edward). See: Spearman-Brown formula.

Brown steering gear (Brown, A. B.): Engineering and Industry. See: Auger.

Brown-Symmers disease (Brown, Charles Leonard and Symmers, Douglas): Medicine. See: Jablonski.

Brown tank (or agitator) (Derivation undetermined): Engineering and Industry. See: Thrush.

BROWN, THOMAS KENNETH. 1898-1951. American gynecologist. See: Who's Who Among Physicians and Surg. Brown's reaction (or test for pregnancy).

BROWN, W. fl. 1910. English scientist. Cited in: Kendall and Doig. Spearman-Brown formula.

BROWN, WADE HAMPTON. 1878-1942. American pathologist. See: World Who's Who Sci. Brown-Pearce tumor (carcinoma or epithelioma).

BROWNE. No dates. Jamaican historian. (Biography source unavailable.) Brownea.

Browne air-lift mine pump (Browne, Ralph Cowan): Engineering and Industry. Cited in: World Who's Who Sci.

BROWNE, ARTHUR WESLEY. b. 1877. American chemist. See: Amer. Men Sci., 1st ed. Dennis-Browne test reaction.

Browne book charging system (Browne, Nina Elizabeth): Library Science. See: Harrod.

BROWNE, JOHN SYMONDS LYON. 1904- . English-born Canadian endocrinologist. See: Amer. Men Sci., 9th ed. Browne-Venning test.

BROWNE, NINA ELIZABETH. b. 1860. American librarian. See: Who Was Who Amer., vol. 4. Browne book charging system.

Browne portable x-ray apparatus (Browne, Ralph Cowan): Engineering and Industry. Cited in: World Who's Who Sci.

BROWNE, RALPH COWAN. 1880-1960. American roentgenologist and inventor. See: World Who's Who Sci. Browne air-lift mine pump, Browne portable x-ray apparatus.

BROWNE, ROBERT. 1550-1633. English clergyman. See: Dict. Nat. Biog. Brownism, Brownists.

BROWNE, SIR SAMUEL JAMES. 1824-1901. English army officer. See: Dict. Nat. Biog., 2nd suppl. Sam Browne belt.

Browne-Venning test (Browne, John Symonds Lyon and Venning, Eleanor Hill): Medicine. See: Stedman.

Brownea (Browne): Botany. See: Charnock.

Brownian movement (or motion) (Brown, Robert): Physics. See: Ballentyne; Huschke; Thewlis. Also known as: Brownian-Zsigmondy movement, Zsigmondy's movements.

Brownian-Zsigmondy movement (Brown, Robert and Zsigmondy, Richard). See: Brownian movement (or motion).

Browning automatic machine rifle (or light machine rifle) (Browning, John Moses): Weapons. See: Mathews, M. M.; Webster's 3d.

Browning automatic rifle (Browning, John Moses): Weapons. See: Hendrickson; Partridge; Webster's 3d.

BROWNING, CARL HAMILTON. b. 1881. Scottish bacteriologist. See: Biog. Lex. hervorr. Aerzte., 1880-1930. Browning's phenomenon?

BROWNING, JOHN MOSES. 1855-1926. American inventor. See: Dict. Amer. Biog. Browning automatic machine rifle (or light machine rifle), Browning automatic rifle, Browning machine gun(s), Browning revolver (pistol or 7.65 mm automatic pistol).

Browning machine gun(s) (Browning, John Moses): Weapons. See: Hendrickson; Partridge; Webster's 3d.

Browning-Palmer test (Browning, Philip Embury and Palmer, Howard E.): Chemistry. See: Van Nostrand Chem. Dict.

BROWNING, PHILIP EMBURY. 1866-1937. American chemist. See: Amer. Men Sci., 5th ed. Browning-Palmer test.

Browning revolver (pistol or 7.65 mm automatic pistol) (Browning, John Moses): Weapons. See: Partridge; Quick; Weekley.

BROWNING, WILLIAM. 1855-1941. American anatomist. See: Who Was Who Amer., vol. 1. Browning's vein.

Browning's phenomenon (Browning, Carl Hamilton?): Medicine. See: Stedman.

Browning's vein (Browning, William): Medicine. See: Dorland; Stedman.

Brownism (Browne, Robert): Religion. See: Charnock; Mathews, S.; Webster's 3d.

Brownists (Browne, Robert): Religion. See: Brewer; Canney; Harbottle.

BROWNMILLER, LORRIN THOMAS. 1902- . American chemist. See: Amer. Men Sci., 9th ed. Brownmillerite.

Brownmillerite (Brownmiller, Lorrin Thomas): Earth Sciences. See: Thrush; Webster's 3d.

Brown's formula (Brown, W.). See: Spearman-Brown formula.

Brown's insurrection (Brown, John): History. See: Phyfe.

Brown's method (Brown, Robert Goodell): Statistics. See: Kendall.

Brown's reaction (or test for pregnancy) (Brown, Thomas Kenneth): Medicine. See: Dorland.

Brown's syndrome (Brown, Harold Whaley): Medicine. See: Jablonski.

Brown's syndrome (Brown, Jason W.): Medicine. See: Jablonski.

Brown's typesetting machine (Brown, O. S.): Printing. See: Lockwood.

Broyhan (beer) (Broyhan, Cord): Food and Drink. See: Charnock.

BROYHAN, CORD. d. 1570. German beer brewer. Cited in: Brockhaus Enzyk. Broyhan (beer).

Broz or Brozovich, Josip. See: Tito.

BRUCE, ALEXANDER. 1854-1911. Scottish anatomist. See: Sci., vol. 33 (1911) p. 959. Bruce's tract.

BRUCE, ALEXANDER, 9TH EARL OF ELGIN. 1849-1917. English statesman. See: Dict. Nat. Biog., 3d. suppl. Elgin Commission.

BRUCE, ARCHIBALD. 1777-1818. American physician and mineralogist. See: Dict. Amer. Biog. Brucite.

BRUCE, SIR DAVID. 1855-1931. English physician and bacteriologist. See: Dict. Sci. Biog. Brucella, Brucellosis, Bruce's septicemia.

BRUCE, JAMES. 1730-1794. Scottish explorer. See: Dict. Sci. Biog. Brucea, Brucine.

Bruce('s) spanworm (Bruce, William Speirs): Zoology. See: Webster's 3d.

BRUCE, THOMAS, 7TH EARL OF ELGIN. 1766-1841. English diplomat. See: Dict. Nat. Biog. Elgin Marbles.

BRUCE, WILLIAM SPEIRS. 1867-1921. English explorer and naturalist. See: Dict. Nat. Biog., 3rd suppl. Bruce('s) spanworm.

Brucea (Bruce, James): Botany. See: Charnock.

Brucella (Bruce, Sir David): Medicine. See: Dorland; Stedman; Webster's 3d.

Brucellosis (Bruce, Sir David): Medicine. See: Hendrickson; Stedman; Van Nostrand Sci. Encyc.

Bruce's septicemia (Bruce, Sir David). See: Bang's disease.

Bruce's tract (Bruce, Alexander): Medicine. See: Dorland; Stedman. Also known as: Hoche's tract.

Bruceton method (Derivation undetermined): Statistics. See: Kendall.

BRUCH, KARL WILHELM LUDWIG. 1819-1884. German anatomist. See: World Who's Who Sci. Bruch's glands, Bruch's membrane.

Bruch's glands (Bruch, Karl Wilhelm Ludwig): Medicine. See: Stedman.

Bruch's membrane (Bruch, Karl Wilhelm Ludwig): Anatomy. See: Donath; Drever; Henderson. Also known as: Henle's membrane.

Brucine (Bruce, James): Medicine. See: Hendrickson; Stedman; Webster's 3d.

Brucite (Bruce, Archibald): Earth Sciences. See: Charnock; Thrush; Van Nostrand Sci. Encyc.

BRUCK, ALFRED. b. 1865. German physician. See: Biog. Lex. hervorr. Aerzte., 1880-1930. Bruck's disease.

BRUCK, CARL. 1879-1944. German dermatologist. See: Biog. Lex. hervorr. Aerzte., 1880-1930. Bruck's test.

Bruck-De Lange syndrome (Bruck, F. and De Lange, Cornelia). See: De Lange's syndrome (1).

BRUCK, F. fl. 1889. German physician. (Biography source unavailable.) Bruck-De Lange syndrome.

BRUCKENTHAL, SAMUEL VON. 1721-1803. Hungarian statesman. See: Allg. Deut. Biog. Bruckenthalia.

Bruckenthalia (Bruckenthal, Samuel von): Botany. See: Taylor, N.

Bruckner cylinder (Bruckner, Walter Herbert?): Engineering and Industry. See: Thrush.

Bruckner furnace (Bruckner, Walter Herbert?): Engineering and Industry. See: Thrush.

BRUCKNER, WALTER HERBERT. 1903- . American metallurgist. See: Amer. Men Sci., 9th ed. Bruckner cylinder?, Bruckner furnace?

Bruck's disease (Bruck, Alfred): Medicine. See: Jablonski; Stedman.

Bruck's test (Bruck, Carl): Medicine. See: Stedman.

BRUDENELL, JAMES THOMAS, 7TH EARL OF CARDIGAN. 1797-1868. English soldier. See: Dict. Nat. Biog. Cardigan.

BRUDZINSKI, JOSEF VON. 1874-1917. Polish physician. See: World Who's Who Sci. Brudzinski('s) sign (or reflex).

Brudzinski('s) sign (or reflex) (Brudzinski, Josef von): Medicine. See: Dorland; Hinsie; Stedman.

BRUECKE, ERNST WILHELM VON. 1819-1892. German physiologist. See: Dict. Sci. Biog. Bruecke reagent for proteins, Bruecke reagents for peptones, Bruecke's muscle(s), Bruecke's tunic.

Bruecke reagent for proteins (Bruecke, Ernst Wilhelm von): Chemistry. See: Van Nostrand Chem. Dict.

Bruecke reagents for peptones (Bruecke, Ernst Wilhelm von): Chemistry. See: Van Nostrand Chem. Dict.

Bruecke's muscle(s) (Bruecke, Ernst Wilhelm von): Medicine. See: Donath; Stedman.

Bruecke's tunic (Bruecke, Ernst Wilhelm von): Medicine. See: Stedman.

Brueckner cycle (Brueckner, Eduard): Earth Sciences. See: Huschke; Monkhouse; Moore.

BRUECKNER, EDUARD. 1862-1927. German geographer. See: World Who's Who Sci. Brueckner cycle.

BRUECKNER, JOSEF. fl. 1934. Hungarian physiological chemist. Cited in: Kelly. Brueckner test for ergosterol.

Brueckner test for ergosterol (Brueckner, Josef): Chemistry. See: Van Nostrand Chem. Dict.

BRUEHL, JULIUS WILHELM. 1850-1911. German chemist. See: World Who's Who Sci. Bruehl receiver?

Bruehl receiver (Bruehl, Julius Wilhelm?): Chemistry. See: Hackh; Van Nostrand Chem. Dict.

BRUENAUER, STEFAN ROBERT. b. 1887. Austrian-born physician. See: Biog. Lex. hervorr. Aerzte., 1880-1930. Bruenauer's syndrome.

Bruenauer's syndrome (Bruenauer, Stefan Robert). See: Unna-Thost syndrome.

BRUENING, HEINRICH. 1885-1970. German statesman. See: Encyc. Brit., 1973. Lex Bruening.

Bruenner acid (Derivation undetermined): Chemistry. See: Hackh.

BRUENNICH, MORTEN THRANE. 1737-1823. Danish naturalist. See: Biog. Notes Upon Botanists. Bruennich's murre (or guillemot), Brunnichia.

Bruennich's murre (or guillemot) (Bruennich, Morten Thrane): Zoology. See: Webster's 3d.

BRUENNINGHAUSEN, HERMANN JOSEPH. 1761-1834. German physician. See: Biog. Lex. hervorr. Aerzte. Bruenninghausen's method.

Bruenninghausen's method (Bruenninghausen, Hermann Joseph): Medicine. See: Dorland.

BRUGEAS, C. fl. 1932. French chemist. Cited in: Chem. Abstr., vol. 26, p. 3874. Brugeas test.

Brugeas test (Brugeas, C.): Chemistry. See: Van Nostrand Chem. Dict.

BRUGES, CHARLES ERNEST. fl. 1895. English engineer. Cited in: Royal Soc. Cat. Sci. Pap., 1884-1900. Crimp and Bruges' formula.

BRUGNATELLI, LUIGI. 1860-1928. Italian mineralogist. See: Pogg., vols. 4, 6. Brugnatellite.

Brugnatellite (Brugnatelli, Luigi): Earth Sciences. See: Thrush; Webster's 3d.

BRUGSCH, THEODOR KARL LOUIS. b. 1878. German physician. See: Wer Ist Wer, 8th ed. Brugsch's syndrome.

Brugsch's syndrome (Brugsch, Theodor Karl Louis): Medicine. See: Jablonski; Stedman.

BRUHN, MARTHA EMMA. b. 1872. American educator. Cited in: Mansell. Bruhn method (or lip reading system).

Bruhn method (or lip reading system) (Bruhn, Martha Emma): Education. See: Good. Also known as: Mueller-Walle method.

BRUM, BALTASAR. 1883-1933. Uruguayan jurist, journalist, and political leader. See: Encyc. Brit., 1973. Brum doctrine.

Brum doctrine (Brum, Baltasar): History. Cited in: Webster's Biog. Dict.

BRUMBY, JAMES. 1771-1838. English-born Australian soldier and pastoralist. See: Australian Dict. Biog., 1788-1850. Brumby (wild horse)?

Brumby (wild horse) (Brumby, James?): Generic Word. See: Hendrickson.

BRUMMELL, GEORGE BRYAN. 1778-1840. English fashion arbiter. See: Dict. Nat. Biog. Beau Brummel(l) (or Brummelism).

BRUMPT, EMILE. 1877-1951. French parasitologist. See: Dict. Sci. Biog. Brumpt's white mycetoma.

Brumpt's white mycetoma (Brumpt, Emile): Medicine. See: Stedman.

BRUN, CORNELIUS. No dates. Traveller. (Biography source unavailable.) Brunia.

Brunauer, Emmett and Teller adsorption equation (method or theory) (Brunauer, Stephen; Emmett, Paul Hugh; and Teller Edward): Chemistry. See: Ballentyne; Thrush; Van Nostrand Chem. Dict.

BRUNAUER, STEPHEN. 1903- . Hungarian-born American physical chemist. See: Amer. Men Sci., 9th ed. Brunauer, Emmett and Teller adsorption equation (method or theory).

BRUNELLI, GABRIELE. 1728-1797. Italian botanist. See: Biog. Notes Upon Botanists. Brunellia.

Brunellia (Brunelli, Gabriele): Botany. See: Webster's 3d.

BRUNET, ODETTE. fl. 1948. French psychologist. Cited in: Psych. Abstr., 1950. Brunet tests.

Brunet tests (Brunet, Odette): Psychology. See: English; Hinsie.

BRUNFELS, OTTO. 1489-1534. German botanist. See: Dict. Sci. Biog. Brunfelsia (or Brumsfelsia).

Brunfelsia (or Brumsfelsia) (Brunfels, Otto): Botany. See: Charnock; Webster's 3d.

BRUNHES, S. fl. 1938. French physician. (Biography source unavailable.) Chavany-Brunhes syndrome.

BRUNI, GIUSEPPE. 1873-1946. Italian chemist. See: Diz. Biog. Ital. Bruni-Tornani test.

Bruni-Tornani test (Bruni, Giuseppi and Tornani, E.): Chemistry. See: Van Nostrand Chem. Dict.

Brunia (Brun, Cornelius): Botany. See: Charnock.

BRUNINGHAUS, L. fl. 1910-1930. French chemist. See: Pogg., vol. 6. Bruninghaus optimum.

Bruninghaus optimum (Bruninghaus, L.): Chemistry. See: Hackh.

BRUNN, ALBERT VON. 1849-1895. German anatomist. See: Nature, vol. 3 (1890) p. 66. Brunn's membrane, Brunn's nests.

BRUNNER, HEINRICH. b. 1847. German chemist. See: Pogg., vol. 4. Brunner test for atropine.

Brunner, Johann Conrad von. See: Von Brunner, Johann Conrad.

BRUNNER, K. fl. 1837. Chemist? (Biography source unavailable.) Brunner's yellow.

Brunner reagents (Derivation undetermined): Chemistry. See: Van Nostrand Chem. Dict.

BRUNNER, SAMUEL. 1790-1844. Swiss botanist. See: Biog. Notes Upon Botanists. Brunnera.

Brunner test for atropine (Brunner, Heinrich): Chemistry. See: Van Nostrand Chem. Dict.

Brunner test for fuchsin (Derivation undetermined): Chemistry. See: Van Nostrand Chem. Dict.

Brunner test for glucosides (Derivation undetermined): Chemistry. See: Van Nostrand Chem. Dict.

Brunner test for sulfur (Derivation undetermined): Chemistry. See: Van Nostrand Chem. Dict.

runnera (Brunner, Samuel): Botany. See: Taylor, N.

runnerite (Derivation undetermined): Earth Sciences. See: Thrush.

runneroma (Von Brunner, Johann Conrad): Medicine. See: Stedman.

runnerosis (Von Brunner, Johann Conrad): Medicine. See: Stedman.

runner's glands (Von Brunner, Johann Conrad): Medicine. See: Donath; orland; Gray.

runner's yellow (Brunner, K.): Chemistry. See: Thrush.

runnichia (Bruennich, Morten Thrane): Botany. See: Webster's 3d.

runn's membrane (Brunn, Albert von): Medicine. See: Donath; Dorland; tedman.

runn's nests (Brunn, Albert von): Medicine. See: Dorland; Stedman.

RUNO OF QUERFURT, SAINT. 970?-1009. German archbishop and mis-ionary. See: Holweck. St. (Saint) Bruno's lily.

runonia (Brown, Robert): Botany. See: Charnock; Webster's 3d.

runonianism (or Brownism) (Brown, John): Medicine. See: Stedman.

runs' ataxia (Bruns, Ludwig): Medicine. See: Stedman.

RUNS, JOHN DICKSON. 1836-1883. American physician. Cited in: oyal Soc. Cat. Sci. Pap., 1800-1863. Bruns's disease.

RUNS, LUDWIG. 1858-1916. German neurologist. See: Wer Ist's?, 1906. astian-Bruns law, Bruns' ataxia, Bruns'(s) sign (or syndrome).

runs'(s) sign (or syndrome) (Bruns, Ludwig): Medicine. See: Dorland; Hinsie; ablonski.

RUNSCHWIG, ALEXANDER. 1901- . American surgeon. See: World ho's Who Sci. Brunschwig's operation.

runschwig's operation (Brunschwig, Alexander): Medicine. See: Dorland; tedman.

runs's disease (Bruns, John Dickson): Medicine. See: Dorland.

RUNSTING, LOUIS A., SR. 1900- . American dermatologist. See: irect. Med. Specialists, 1970-1971. Brunsting's disease.

runsting's disease (Brunsting, Louis A., Sr.): Medicine. See: Jablonski.

runsvegia (Brunsvigia) (Brunswick): Botany. See: Charnock; Taylor, N.

RUNSWICK. German royal family. See: Webster's Biog. Dict. Brunsvegia Brunsvigia).

RUNSWICK, FRIEDRICH WILHELM, DUKE OF. 1771-1815. German army fficer. See: Encyc. Brit., 1911. Black Brunswickers, Brunswick manifesto.

runswick manifesto (Brunswick, Friedrich Wilhelm, Duke of): History. See: Morris and Irwin.

runswick reagent for phytosterol (Derivation undetermined): Chemistry. See: /an Nostrand Chem. Dict.

runswick tests for cyanide in plants (Brunswik, Hermann): Chemistry. See: /an Nostrand Chem. Dict.

RUNSWIK, EGON. 1903-1955. American psychologist. See: New Encyc. rit., 1974, Microp. Brunswik ratio.

RUNSWIK, HERMANN. fl. 1921. Austrian chemist. Cited in: Chem. Abstr., vol. 16, p. 3920. Brunswick tests for cyanide in plants.

runswik ratio (Brunswik, Egon): Psychology. See: Chaplin; English; Wolman.

RUNT, DAVID. 1886-1965. English meteorologist. See: Who Was Who, 961-1970. Brunt-Douglas isallobaric wind.

runt-Douglas isallobaric wind (Brunt, David and Douglas, C. K. M.): Earth ciences. See: Huschke.

runton compass (Brunton, David William): Earth Sciences. See: Thrush; Van Nostrand Sci. Encyc.

RUNTON, DAVID WILLIAM. 1849-1927. American mining engineer and nventor. See: Dict. Amer. Biog. Brunton compass, Brunton furnace?, runton sampler.

Brunton furnace (Brunton, David William?): Chemistry. See: Van Nostrand Chem. Dict.

BRUNTON, JOHN. 1835-1899. English physician and surgeon. (Biography source unavailable.) Brunton's otoscope.

Brunton sampler (Brunton, David William): Engineering and Industry). See: Thrush.

Brunton stoker (Brunton, William): Engineering and Industry. See: Auger.

BRUNTON, WILLIAM. 1777-1851. Scottish engineer and inventor. See: Dict. Nat. Biog. Brunton stoker.

Brunton's otoscope (Brunton, John): Medicine. See: Stedman.

BRUSH, CHARLES FRANCIS. 1849-1929. American inventor. See: Dict. Amer. Biog., 1st suppl. Brush electric arc light.

Brush electric arc light (Brush, Charles Francis): Engineering and Industry. Cited in: Webster's Biog. Dict.

BRUSHFIELD, THOMAS. fl. 1924-27. English physician. See: Med. Direct., 1924. Brushfield-Wyatt syndrome, Brushfield's spots.

Brushfield-Wyatt syndrome (Brushfield, Thomas and Wyatt, Walter?): Medicine. See: Jablonski.

Brushfield's spots (Brushfield, Thomas): Medicine. See: Jablonski; Stedman.

Brusians (or Petrobrusian(s)) (Bruys, Pierre de): Religion. See: Canney; Mathews, S.; Webster's 3d.

BRUSILOV, ALEKSEY ALEKSEYEVICH. 1853-1926. Russian army officer. See: New Encyc. Brit., 1974, Microp. Brusilov breakthrough.

Brusilov breakthrough (Brusilov, Aleksey Alekseyevich): History. Cited in: New Encyc. Brit., 1974, Microp.

BRUTON, OGDEN CARR. 1908- . American pediatrician. See: Direct. Med. Specialists, 8th ed. Bruton's disease.

Bruton's disease (Bruton, Ogden Carr): Medicine. See: Jablonski.

Brutus (Brutus, Marcus Junius): Generic Word (treacherous person). See: Hendrickson.

Brutus (chrysanthemum) (Brutus, Marcus Junius): Botany. See: Hendrickson; Partridge.

Brutus cut (Brutus, Marcus Junius): Fashion. See: Hendrickson; Partridge; Picken.

BRUTUS, LUCIUS JUNIUS. fl. 509 B.C. Roman consul. See: Webster's Biog. Dict. June?

BRUTUS, MARCUS JUNIUS. 85-42 B.C. Roman politician and conspirator. See: Encyc. Brit., 1911. Brutus, Brutus (chrysanthemum), Brutus cut.

BRUYERE, P. fl. 1926. French chemist. Cited in: Chem. Abstr., vol. 21, p. 1077. Bruyere test.

Bruyere test (Bruyere, P.): Chemistry. See: Van Nostrand Chem. Dict.

BRUYS, PIERRE DE. d. ca. 1126. French religious reformer. See: Webster's Biog. Dict. Brusians (or Petrobrusian(s)).

Bryan-Chamorro Treaty (Bryan, William Jennings and Chamorro Vargas, Emiliano): History. See: Morris; Morris and Irwin; Smith.

BRYAN, ELMER JOSEPH. b. 1891. American chemist. See: Amer. Men Sci., 6th ed. Bryanizing?

BRYAN, JOHN RAYMOND. b. 1893. American mining engineer. See: Who's Who Engin., 2nd ed. Bryan mill?

BRYAN, KIRK. 1888-1950. American geologist. See: Dict. Sci. Biog. Kirk Bryan Award, Kirk Bryan Fund.

Bryan mill (Bryan, John Raymond?): Engineering and Industry. See: Thrush.

BRYAN, WILLIAM JENNINGS. 1860-1925. American political leader. See: Dict. Amer. Biog. Bryan-Chamorro Treaty, Bryanism.

Bryanism (Bryan, William Jennings): History. See: Mathews, M. M.

Bryanite (O'Bryan, William): Earth Sciences. See: Webster's 3d.

Bryanites (O'Bryan, William): Religion. See: Mathews, S.

Bryanizing (Bryan, Elmer Joseph?): Chemistry. See: Thrush.

BRYANT, DOUGLAS WALLACE. 1913-   . American librarian. See: Who's Who Amer., 1974-75. Bryant memorandum.

Bryant memorandum (Bryant, Douglas Wallace): Library Science. See: Harrod.

BRYANT, SIR THOMAS. 1828-1914. English surgeon. See: Sci., vol. 41 (1915) p. 163. Bryant's ampulla, Bryant's line, Bryant's sign, Bryant's traction, Bryant's triangle.

Bryant's ampulla (Bryant, Sir Thomas): Medicine. See: Stedman.

Bryant's line (Bryant, Sir Thomas): Medicine. See: Dorland; Stedman.

Bryant's sign (Bryant, Sir Thomas): Medicine. See: Stedman.

Bryant's traction (Bryant, Sir Thomas): Medicine. See: Stedman.

Bryant's triangle (Bryant, Sir Thomas): Medicine. See: Dorland; Stedman.

BRYCE, JAMES. fl. 1792-1815. Scottish physician. See: Biog. Lex. hervorr. Aerzte. Bryce's test.

Bryce-Teacher ovum (Bryce, Thomas Hastie and Teacher, John Hammond): Medicine. See: Dorland.

BRYCE, THOMAS HASTIE. 1862-1946. Scottish physician. See: World Who's Who Sci. Bryce-Teacher ovum.

Bryce's test (Bryce, James): Medicine. See: Dorland; Stedman.

BRYNGELSON, BRYNG. 1892-   . American speech pathologist. See: Amer. Men and Women Sci., 12th ed. Bryngelson-Glaspey test.

Bryngelson-Glaspey test (Bryngelson, Bryng and Glaspey, E.): Psychology. See: Wolman.

bryobrittonia (Britton, Elizabeth Gertrude Knight): Botany. Cited in: Dict. Sci. Biog. under "Britton, Nathaniel Lord."

BUCH, CHRISTIAN LEOPOLD VON. 1774-1853. German mineralogist. See: Dict. Sci. Biog. Buchite.

BUCHAN, ALEXANDER. 1829-1907. Scottish meteorologist. See: Dict. Nat. Biog., 2nd suppl. Buchan's weather periods.

BUCHAN, ELSPETH. 1738-1791. Scottish religious leader. See: Dict. Nat. Biog. Buchanites.

BUCHANAN, JAMES. 1791-1868. American president. See: Dict. Amer. Biog. Buchanan's blunder, Buchanier (or Buchananer).

Buchanan's blunder (Buchanan, James): History. See: New Encyc. Brit., 1974, Microp.

Buchanier (or Buchananer) (Buchanan, James): History. See: Mathews, M. M.

Buchanites (Buchan, Elspeth): Religion. See: Brewer; Canney; Latham.

Buchan's weather periods (Buchan, Alexander): Earth Sciences. See: Brewer.

BUCHEM, FRANCIS STEVEN PETER VAN. 1897-   . Dutch internist. See: Who's Who Netherl., 1962-1963. Van Buchem's syndrome.

BUCHER, JOHN EMERY. 1872-1943. American chemist. See: Who Was Who Amer., vol. 5. Bucher process?

BUCHER, KARL. 1847-1930. German economist. See: Internat. Encyc. Soc. Sco. Bucher's stages of economic development.

Bucher process (Bucher, John Emery?): Chemistry. See: Van Nostrand Chem. Dict.

Bucherer carbazole synthesis (Bucherer, Hans Theodor?): Chemistry. See: Van Nostrand Chem. Dict.

BUCHERER, HANS THEODOR. 1869-1949. German chemist. See: World Who's Who Sci. Bucherer carbazole synthesis?, Bucherer hydantoin synthesis, Bucherer reaction.

Bucherer hydantoin synthesis (Bucherer, Hans Theodor): Chemistry. See: Van Nostrand Chem. Dict.

Bucherer reaction (Bucherer, Hans Theodor): Chemistry. See: Ballentyne; Van Nostrand Chem. Dict.

Bucher's stages of economic development (Bucher, Karl): Economics. See: Zadrozny.

BUCHI, A. J. fl. 1937. American mechanical engineer. (Biography source unavailable.) Buchi system.

Buchi system (Buchi, A. J.): Engineering and Industry. See: Auger.

Buchite (Buch, Christian Leopold von): Earth Sciences. See: Webster's 3d.

BUCHMAN, FRANK NATHAN DANIEL. 1878-1961. American evangelist. See: Webster's Biog. Dict. Buchmanism (or Buchmanite).

Buchmanism (or Buchmanite) (Buchman, Frank Nathan Daniel): Religion. See: Brewer; Hendrickson; Partridge.

Buchmann-Meyer pattern (Derivation undetermined): Physics. See: Hughes.

Buchner-Curtius-Schlotterbeck reaction (Buchner, Eduard; Curtius, Theodor; and Schlotterbeck; Fritz): Chemistry. See: Van Nostrand Chem. Dict.

BUCHNER, EDUARD. 1860-1917. German chemist. See: Dict. Sci. Biog. Buchner-Curtius-Schlotterbeck reaction, Buchner extract, Buchner funnel, Buchner number.

Buchner extract (Buchner, Eduard and Buchner, Hans Ernst Angass): Chemistry. See: Stedman.

Buchner funnel (Buchner, Eduard): Chemistry. See: Hackh; Stedman; Thrush.

BUCHNER, HANS ERNST ANGASS. 1850-1902. German bacteriologist. See: World Who's Who Sci. Buchner extract, Buchner's bodies, Buchner's stain, Buchner's theory, Buchner's tuberculin.

BUCHNER, J. G. fl. 18th c. German botanist. (Biography source unavailable.) Buchnera.

Buchner number (Buchner, Eduard): Chemistry. See: Hackh.

Buchnera (Buchner, J. G.): Botany. See: Charnock; Webster's 3d.

Buchnerite (Derivation undetermined): Earth Sciences. See: Thrush.

Buchner's bodies (Buchner, Hans Ernst Angass): Medicine. See: Stedman.

Buchner's stain (Buchner, Hans Ernst Angass): Medicine. See: Dorland; Stedman.

Buchner's theory (Buchner, Hans Ernst Angass): Medicine. See: Dorland.

Buchner's tuberculin (Buchner, Hans Ernst Angass): Medicine. See: Dorland; Stedman.

BUCHOLZ, CHRISTIAN FRIEDRICH. 1770-1818. German chemist. See: Dict. Sci. Biog. Bucholzite, Hagen-Bucholz Foundation.

Bucholzite (Bucholz, Christian Friedrich): Earth Sciences. See: Charnock.

BUCHWALD, HERMANN EDMUND. 1903-   . German physician. Cited in: Kelly. Buchwald's atrophy.

BUCHWALD, JOH. fl. 1907. German chemist. Cited in: Chem. Abstr. Decenn. Index, 1907-1916. Buchwald-Treml test?

Buchwald-Treml test (Buchwald, Joh? and Treml, H.?): Chemistry. See: Van Nostrand Chem. Dict.

Buchwald's atrophy (Buchwald, Hermann Edmund): Medicine. See: Stedman.

BUCK, GURDON. 1807-1877. American surgeon. See: Dict. Amer. Biog. Buck's extension (or extension process), Buck's fascia, Buck's operation.

Buck mortar (Derivation undetermined): Chemistry. See: Hackh.

Buckendale differential (Buckendale, Lawrence Raymond): Engineering and Industry. See: Auger.

BUCKENDALE, LAWRENCE RAYMOND. b. 1892. American automative engineer. See: Who's Who Engin., 2nd ed. Buckendale differential.

Buckett engine (Derivation undetermined): Engineering and Industry. See: Auger.

Buckhorse (Smith, John "Buckhorse"): Generic Word (severe blow). See: Brewer; Hendrickson.

BUCKINGHAM, EDGAR. 1867-1940. American physicist. See: Dict. Sci. Biog. Buckingham's pi theorem.

BUCKINGHAM, JOHN HERBERT. 1912- . American physical chemist. See: Amer. Men Sci., 9th ed. Buckingham potential.

Buckingham potential (Buckingham, John Herbert): Chemistry. See: Internat. Dict. Ap. Math.

Buckingham's pi theorem (Buckingham, Edgar): Physics. See: Ballentyne.

BUCKLAND, WILLIAM. 1784-1856. English geologist. See: Dict. Sci. Biog. Bucklandia, Bucklandite.

Bucklandia (Buckland, William): Earth Sciences. See: Charnock.

Bucklandite (Buckland, William): Earth Sciences. See: Charnock; Thrush.

Buckley gauge (gage) (Buckley, Oliver Ellsworth): Physics. See: Hughes; Internat. Dict. Phys. Elec.; Markus.

Buckley method for obtaining interference patterns with highly-convergent light (Derivation undetermined): Physics. See: Internat. Dict. Phys. Elec.

BUCKLEY, OLIVER ELLSWORTH. 1887- . American physicist. See: World Who's Who Sci. Buckley gauge (gage).

BUCKLEY, SAMUEL BOTSFORD. 1809-1883. American naturalist. See: Dict. Amer. Biog. Buckleya.

BUCKLEY, WILLIAM. 1780-1856. English convict. See: Dict. Nat. Biog. Buckley's chance.

Buckleya (Buckley, Samuel Botsford): Botany. See: Webster's 3d.

Buckley's chance (Buckley, William): Generic Word (remote chance). See: Brewer.

BUCKLIN, JAMES W. 1856-1919. American lawyer. See: Who Was Who Amer., vol. 1. Bucklin plan.

Bucklin plan (Bucklin, James W.): Politics. See: Smith.

Buckman table (Derivation undetermined): Engineering and Industry. See: Thrush.

BUCKMASTER. fl. before 1870. English? tailor. (Biography source unavailable.) Buckmaster's light infantry.

Buckmaster's light infantry (Buckmaster): History. See: Brewer.

Buck's extension (or extension process) (Buck, Gurdon): Medicine. See: Black; Dorland; Stedman.

Buck's fascia (Buck, Gurdon): Medicine. See: Dorland; Stedman.

Buck's operation (Buck, Gurdon): Medicine. See: Dorland.

Bucky camera (Bucky, Gustav P.): Medicine. Cited in: World Who's Who Sci.

Bucky diaphragm (or grid) (Bucky, Gustav P.). See: Potter-Bucky grid (or diaphragm).

BUCKY, GUSTAV P. 1880-1963. German-born American roentgenologist. See: World Who's Who Sci. Bucky camera, Bucky('s) rays, Potter-Bucky grid (or diaphragm).

Bucky('s) rays (Bucky, Gustav P.): Medicine. See: Dorland; Stedman.

BUCY, J. FRED, JR. 1928- . American electronics company executive. See: Who's Who Amer., 1974-1975. Bucy's law.

BUCY, PAUL CLANCY. 1904- . American neurologist. See: Who's Who Among Physicians and Surg. Kluever-Bucy syndrome.

Bucy's law (Bucy, J. Fred, Jr.): Sociology. See: Martin.

BUDAN DE BOISLAURENT, FERDINAND FRANCOIS DESIRE. 1800-1853. French mathematician. See: Dict. Sci. Biog. Budan('s) theorem.

Budan('s) theorem (Budan de Boislaurent, Ferdinand Francois Desire): Mathematics. See: Ballentyne; Internat. Dict. Ap. Math.; James.

BUDAY, KALMAN. 1863-1937. Hungarian physician. See: New York Acad. Med. Portrait Cat. Bogdaen-Buday disease.

Budd-Chiari syndrome (Budd, George and Chiari, Hans): Medicine. See: Jablonski. Also known as: Budd's disease, Budd's jaundice, Chiari's disease, Rokitansky's disease, Von Rokitansky's disease.

BUDD, GEORGE. 1808-1882. English physician. See: Dict. Nat. Biog. Budd-Chiari syndrome, Budd's cirrhosis.

BUDDE, E. b. 1871. Danish sanitary engineer. (Biography source unavailable.) Budde('s) process, Buddeize.

Budde effect (Budde, Emil Arnold?): Chemistry. See: Ballentyne; Hackh; Internat. Dict. Phys. Elec.

BUDDE, EMIL ARNOLD. 1842-1921. German chemist. See: Wer Ist's?, 8th ed. Budde effect?

Budde('s) process (Budde, E.): Medicine. See: Stedman; Winburne.

Buddeize (Budde, E.): Medicine. See: Stedman.

BUDDHA, GAUTAMA. 563-483 B.C. Indian philosopher. See: Encyc. Brit., 1973. Buddha's hand, Buddhism.

Buddha's hand (Buddha, Gautama): Botany. See: Winick.

Buddhism (Buddha, Gautama): Religion. See: Brewer; Canney; Charnock.

BUDDLE, ADAM. d. 1715. English botanist. See: Dict. Nat. Biog. Buddleia (Buddlea).

Buddleia (Buddlea) (Buddle, Adam): Botany. See: Charnock; Partridge; Taylor, N.

Budd's cirrhosis (Budd, George): Medicine. See: Dorland; Stedman.

Budd's disease (Budd, George). See: Budd-Chairi syndrome.

Budd's jaundice (Budd, George). See: Budd-Chiari syndrome.

BUDGE, JULIUS LUDWIG. 1811-1888. German physiologist. See: World Who's Who Sci. Budge's center.

Budge's center (Budge, Julius Ludwig): Medicine. See: Dorland; Stedman.

BUDIN, PIERRE CONSTANT. 1846-1907. French gynecologist. See: Sci., vol. 25 (1907) p. 318. Budin's joint (or obstetrical joint), Budin's pelvimeter, Budin's rule.

Budin's joint (or obstetrical joint) (Budin, Pierre Constant): Medicine. See: Dorland; Stedman.

Budin's pelvimeter (Budin, Pierre Constant): Medicine. See: Stedman.

Budin's rule (Budin, Pierre Constant): Medicine. See: Dorland.

Budnaeans (Budnaeaus, Simon): Religion. See: Canney.

BUDNAEAUS, SIMON. fl. 1572-1584. Polish theologian. See: Nouv. Biog. Univ. Budnaeans.

Bueb process (Bueb, Julius?): Chemistry. See: Hackh; Van Nostrand Chem. Dict.

BUEB, JULIUS. fl. 1895. German chemist. See: Wer Ist's?, 8th ed. Bueb process.

BUECHNER, ERNST. fl. 1888. German chemist. Cited in: New Encyc. Brit., 1974, Microp. Buechner filter (or funnel).

Buechner filter (or funnel) (Buechner, Ernst): Chemistry. See: Van Nostrand Chem. Dict.; Webster's 3d.

BUECHNER, JOHANN ANDREAS. 1783-1852. German chemist and pharmacist. See: World Who's Who Sci. Buechner test of beeswax?

Buechner test for gallic acid and tannin (Derivation undetermined): Chemistry. See: Van Nostrand Chem. Dict.

Buechner test of beeswax (Buechner, Johann Andreas?): Chemistry. See: Van Nostrand Chem. Dict.

Buecklers' dystrophy (Buecklers, Max Hermann Eduard). See: Reis-Buecklers disease.

BUECKLERS, MAX HERMANN EDUARD. 1895- . German ophthalmologist. See: Wer Ist's?, 8th ed. Reis-Buecklers disease.

BUEDINGER, KONRAD. b. 1867. Swiss-born Austrian surgeon. See: Biog. Lex. hervorr. Aerzte., 1880-1930. Buedinger-Ludloff-Laewen disease (or syndrome).

Buedinger-Laewen syndrome (Buedinger, Konrad and Laewen, Arthur). See: Buedinger-Ludloff-Laewen disease (or syndrome).

Buedinger–Ludloff–Laewen disease (or syndrome) (Buedinger, Konrad; Ludloff, Karl; and Laewen, Arthur): Medicine. See: Dorland; Jablonski. Also known as: Buedinger–Laewen syndrome, Haglund–Laewen–Fruend syndrome.

BUELAU, GOTTHARD. 1835-1900. German surgeon. See: Biog. Lex. hervorr. Aerzte. Buelau's method, Buelau's treatment.

Buelau's method (Buelau, Gotthard): Medicine. See: Dorland.

Buelau's treatment (Buelau, Gotthard): Medicine. See: Dorland.

BUELL, HAROLD DOUGLASS. b. 1885. American chemist. See: Amer. Men Sci., 9th ed. Buell test for uranium.

Buell test for uranium (Buell, Harold Douglass): Chemistry. See: Van Nostrand Chem. Dict.

Buelow test for phenylhydrazides (Buelow, Theodor Carl Heinrich): Chemistry. See: Van Nostrand Chem. Dict.

BUELOW, THEODOR CARL HEINRICH. fl. 1886-1900. German chemist. See: Wer Ist's?, 8th ed. Buelow test for phenylhydrazides.

BUENGNER, OTTO VON. 1858-1905. German neurologist. See: Biog. Lex. hervorr. Aerzte, 1880-1930. Buengner's bands (or cell cordons).

Buengner's bands (or cell cordons) (Buengner, Otto von): Medicine. See: Dorland.

Buerger–Gruetz syndrome (Buerger, Max and Gruetz, Otto): Medicine. See: Jablonski.

BUERGER, LEO. 1879-1943. American physician. See: Webster's Biog. Dict. Buerger's disease, Buerger's stain.

BUERGER, MAX. b. 1885. German physician. See: Wer Ist's?, 8th ed. Buerger–Gruetz syndrome.

Buerger's disease (Buerger, Leo): Medicine. See: Dorland; Jablonski; Van Nostrand Sci. Encyc. Also known as: Winiwarter–Buerger syndrome.

Buerger's stain (Buerger, Leo): Medicine. See: Stedman.

Buerker chamber (Buerker, Karl Jakob Sebastian): Chemistry. See: Hackh.

BUERKER, KARL JAKOB SEBASTIAN. 1872-1957. German physiologist. See: World Who's Who Sci. Buerker chamber.

BUETSCHLI, OTTO. 1848-1920. German zoologist and mineralogist. See: Dict. Sci. Biog. Buetschliite, Buetschli's nuclear spindle.

Buetschliite (Buetschli, Otto): Earth Sciences. See: Thrush; Webster's 3d.

Buetschli's nuclear spindle (Buetschli, Otto): Zoology. See: Dorland.

BUETTNER, DAVID SIGMUND AUGUSTE. 1724-1768. German botanist. See: Nouv. Biog. Univ. Buettneria.

Buettneria (Buettner, David Sigmund Auguste): Botany. See: Charnock; Webster's 3d.

BUFFINGTON, ADELBERT RINALDO. 1837-1922. American army officer. See: Webster's Biog. Dict. Buffington–Crozier disappearing gun carriage.

Buffington–Crozier disappearing gun carriage (Buffington, Adelbert Rinaldo and Crozier, William): Weapons. Cited in: Webster's Biog. Dict.

BUFFON, GEORGES LOUIS LECLERC. 1707-1788. French naturalist. See: Dict. Sci. Biog. Buffon's needle problem.

Buffon's needle problem (Buffon, Georges Louis Leclerc): Mathematics. See: James.

BUFFUM, D. fl. 1828. American horticulturist. (Biography source unavailable.) Buffum (pear).

Buffum (pear) (Buffum, D.): Food and Drink. See: Mathews, M. M.

BUG, JOSHUA (NORFOLK HOWARD). fl. 1862. Englishman. (Biography source unavailable.) Norfolk Howard.

Buhl, Andre Charles. See: Boulle, Andre Charles.

Buhl, Ludwig von. See: Von Buhl, Ludwig.

BUHLER, CHARLOTTE BERTHA. b. 1893. German-born American psychologist. See: Amer. Men Sci., 9th ed. Buhler tests (or baby tests).

Buhler tests (or baby tests) (Buhler, Charlotte Bertha): Psychology. See: English; Hinsie.

Buhl's disease (Von Buhl, Ludwig): Medicine. See: Dorland; Jablonski; Stedman.

BUHRER, JACOB. fl. 1911. Inventor. Cited in: Chem. Abstr., vol. 5, p. 1982. Buhrer kiln.

Buhrer kiln (Buhrer, Jacob): Engineering and Industry. See: Thrush.

BUIST, ROBERT COCHRANE. 1860-1939. Scottish obstetrician. See: Who Was Who, 1929-40. Buist's method.

Buist's method (Buist, Robert Cochrane): Medicine. See: Dorland; Stedman.

BUJWID, ODO. 1857-1942. Polish bacteriologist. See: New York Acad. Med. Portrait Cat. Bujwid test?

Bujwid test (Bujwid, Odo?): Chemistry. See: Van Nostrand Chem. Dict.

Bulbeck, Lord. See: Vere, Edward de (Lord Bulbeck and 17th Earl of Oxford).

BULBULIAN, ARTHUR H. 1900- . Turkish-born American medical researcher. See: Amer. Men Sci., 10th ed. Boothby, Lovelace, and Bulbulian mask.

Bulkley diet (Bulkley, Lucius Duncan): Medicine. See: Dorland.

BULKLEY, LUCIUS DUNCAN. 1845-1928. American dermatologist. See: Dict. Amer. Biog. Bulkley diet.

Bull (Bull, Obadiah): Generic Word (blunder). See: Brewer; Phyfe.

BULL, CARROLL GIDEON. 1883-1931. American immunologist. See: World Who's Who Sci. Bull's serum.

BULL, EDWARD. fl. 1798. English engineer. Cited in: Encyc. Brit., 1973, under "Steam." Bull engine.

Bull engine (Bull, Edward): Engineering and Industry. See: Auger.

Bull, John. See: John Bull.

BULL, OBADIAH. fl. 1485-1509. Irish lawyer. (Biography source unavailable.) Bull.

BULL, WILLIAM REX. 1929- . English-born American mineral processer. See: Amer. Men and Women Sci., 12th ed. Bull's kiln?

Bullard Dunn process (Bullard Co. and Dunn, Thomas E.): Engineering and Industry. See: Thrush.

BULLEN, KEITH EDWARD. 1906- . Australian geophysicist. See: World Who's Who Sci. Jeffreys–Bullen curves.

BULLER, ARTHUR HENRY REGINALD. 1874-1944. English-born Canadian botanist. See: Dict. Sci. Biog. Buller phenomenon.

BULLER, FRANK. 1844-1905. Canadian ophthalmic surgeon. See: Leonardo. Buller's bandage (or shield).

Buller phenomenon (Buller, Arthur Henry Reginald): Botany. Cited in: Dict. Sci. Biog.

Buller's bandage (or shield) (Buller, Frank): Medicine. See: Dorland; Stedman.

Buller's rings (Derivation undetermined): Engineering and Industry. See: Thrush.

Bulling test for phenylpropiolic acid (Derivation undetermined): Chemistry. See: Van Nostrand Chem. Dict.

BULLOCK, JEREMIAH. fl. 19th c. American religious leader. (Biography source unavailable.) Bullockite.

Bullock press (Bullock, William A.): Printing. See: Lockwood.

BULLOCK, WILLIAM. fl. 1808-1827. English naturalist. See: Dict. Nat. Biog. Bullock's oriole (or troupial).

BULLOCK, WILLIAM A. 1813-1867. American inventor. See: Dict. Amer. Biog. Bullock press.

Bullockite (Bullock, Jeremiah): Religion. See: Webster's 3d.

Bullock's oriole (or troupial) (Bullock, William): Zoology. See: Gray; Mathews, M. M.; Pennak.

Bullock's pippin (apple) (Derivation undetermined): Botany. See: Mathews, M. M.

Bull's kiln (Bull, William Rex?): Engineering and Industry. See: Thrush.

Bull's serum (Bull, Carroll Gideon): Medicine. See: Stedman.

BULWER, JAMES. d. 1879. English clergyman and naturalist. (Biography source unavailable.) Bulwer's petrel.

BULWER, SIR WILLIAM HENRY LYTTON. 1801-1872. English diplomat. See: Dict. Nat. Biog. Clayton-Bulwer Treaty.

Bulwer's petrel (Bulwer, James): Zoology. See: Webster's 3d.

BULWINKLE, ALFRED LEE. 1883-1947. American legislator. See: Biog. Direct. Amer. Congress. La Follette-Bulwinkle Act.

Bumble (Bumble, Mr.): Generic Word (beadle). See: Brewer; Partridge; Weekley.

BUMBLE, MR. Character in Charles Dickens's novel, "Oliver Twist." See: Benet. Bumble, Bumbledom.

Bumbledom (Bumble, Mr.): Generic Word (fussy officialism). See: Brewer; Partridge; Weekley.

BUMKE, OSWALD CONRAD EDWARD. 1877-1950. German neurologist. See: World Who's Who Sci. Bumke's pupil.

Bumke's pupil (Bumke, Oswald Conrad Edward): Medicine. See: Dorland; Stedman.

BUMPUS, DEAN FRANKLIN. 1912- . American oceanographer. See: Amer. Men Sci., 9th ed. Clarke-Bumpus plankton sampler.

BUNAU-VARILLA, PHILIPPE JEAN. 1860-1940. French engineer. See: Webster's Biog. Dict. Hay-Bunau-Varilla Treaty.

BUNCE, DONALD FAIRBAIRN MAC DOUGAL. 1920- . American anatomist. See: World Who's Who Sci. Bunce double hemostat.

Bunce double hemostat (Bunce, Donald Fairbairn MacDougal): Medicine. Cited in: World Who's Who Sci.

BUNDESMANN. fl. 1936. German chemist. Cited in: Chem. Abstr., vol. 30, p. 1236. Bundesmann test.

Bundesmann test (Bundesmann): Chemistry. See: Hackh.

Bundle of His (His, Wilhelm, Jr.). See: His' bundle.

Bundle of Lenhossek (Lenhossek, Mihaly Michael von). See: Lenhossek's processes.

BUNGE, GUSTAV VON. 1844-1920. German physiologist. See: Dict. Sci. Biog. Bunge-Trantenroth stain, Bunge's law.

BUNGE, PAUL. 1853-1926. German ophthalmologist. See: Wer Ist's?, 1906. Bunge's spoon.

BUNGE, RICHARD. b. 1870. German surgeon. See: Wer Ist's ?, 1906. Bunge's amputation.

Bunge-Trantenroth stain (Bunge, Gustav von and Trantenroth, Adolph Arthur): Medicine. See: Stedman.

Bunge's amputation (Bunge, Richard): Medicine. See: Dorland.

Bunge's law (Bunge, Gustav von): Medicine. See: Dorland.

Bunge's spoon (Bunge, Paul): Medicine. See: Dorland.

BUNIAKOVSKI, VICTOR JAKOVLEVICH. 1804-1889. Russian mathematician. See: World Who's Who Sci. Buniakovski's inequality.

Buniakovski's inequality (Buniakovski, Victor Jakovlevich). See: Schwarz's inequality.

Bunk Carter's law (Derivation undetermined): Sociology. See: Martin.

Bunn chart (Derivation undetermined): Physics. See: Thewlis.

BUNNELL, STERLING. b. 1882. American surgeon. See: Who's Imp. Med., 2nd ed. Bunnell's suture.

BUNNELL, WALLS WILLARD. 1902- . American physician. (Biography source unavailable.) Paul-Bunnell antibody, Paul-Bunnell test (or reaction).

Bunnell's suture (Bunnell, Sterling): Medicine. See: Stedman.

Bunsen battery (Bunsen, Robert Wilhelm Eberhard): Chemistry. See: Partridge.

Bunsen burner (Bunsen, Robert Wilhelm Eberhard): Chemistry. See: Stedman; Van Nostrand Chem. Dict.; Webster's 3d.

Bunsen cell (Bunsen, Robert Wilhelm Eberhard): Chemistry. See: Hackh; Partridge.

Bunsen clamp (Bunsen, Robert Wilhelm Eberhard): Chemistry. See: Hackh.

Bunsen coefficient (Bunsen, Robert Wilhelm Eberhard): Chemistry. See: Dorland; Internat. Dict. Phys. Elec.; Stedman.

Bunsen disk (Bunsen, Robert Wilhelm Eberhard): Chemistry. See: Partridge.

Bunsen eudiometer (Bunsen, Robert Wilhelm Eberhard): Chemistry. See: Hackh.

Bunsen flame (Bunsen, Robert Wilhelm Eberhard): Chemistry. See: Hackh; Partridge.

Bunsen funnel (Bunsen, Robert Wilhelm Eberhard): Chemistry. See: Hackh.

Bunsen gas bottle (Bunsen, Robert Wilhelm Eberhard): Chemistry. See: Hackh.

Bunsen ice calorimeter method for latent heat of fusion (Bunsen, Robert Wilhelm Eberhard): Chemistry. See: Internat. Dict. Phys. Elec.

Bunsen-Kirchhoff law (Bunsen, Robert Wilhelm Eberhard and Kirchoff, Gustav Robert): Chemistry. See: Webster's 3d.

Bunsen lamp (Bunsen, Robert Wilhelm Eberhard): Chemistry. See: Partridge.

Bunsen photometer (Bunsen, Robert Wilhelm Eberhard): Physics. See: Thewlis; Thrush.

Bunsen reaction for acetate (Bunsen, Robert Wilhelm Eberhard): Chemistry. See: Van Nostrand Chem. Dict.

BUNSEN, ROBERT WILHELM EBERHARD. 1811-1899. German chemist. See: Dict. Sci. Biog. Bunsen battery, Bunsen burner, Bunsen cell, Bunsen clamp, Bunsen coefficient, Bunsen disk, Bunsen eudiometer, Bunsen flame, Bunsen funnel, Bunsen gas bottle, Bunsen ice calorimeter method for latent heat of fusion, Bunsen-Kirchhoff law, Bunsen lamp, Bunsen photometer, Bunsen reaction for acetate, Bunsen-Roscoe law, Bunsen screen, Bunsen valve, Bunsenite.

Bunsen-Roscoe law (Bunsen, Robert Wilhelm. Eberhard and Roscoe, Sir Henry Enfield): Physics. See: Chaplin; English; Pennak.

Bunsen screen (Bunsen, Robert Wilhelm Eberhard): Physics. See: Internat. Dict. Phys. Elec.; Van Nostrand Sci. Encyc.

Bunsen valve (Bunsen, Robert Wilhelm Eberhard): Chemistry. See: Hackh.

Bunsenite (Bunsen, Robert Wilhelm Eberhard): Earth Sciences. See: Partridge; Thrush; Webster's 3d.

Bunte buret (Bunte, Hans Hugo Christian): Chemistry. See: Hackh.

BUNTE, HANS HUGO CHRISTIAN. 1848-1925. German chemist. See: World Who's Who Sci. Bunte buret.

BUNTING, HENRY H. fl. 1907. Peruvian? chemist. Cited in: Chem. Abstr., vol. 1, p. 1957. Bunting test.

Bunting test (Bunting, Henry H.): Chemistry. See: Van Nostrand Chem. Dict.

BUNYAN, JOHN. 1628-1688. English preacher and writer. See: Dict. Nat. Biog. Bunyanesque (1).

BUNYAN, JOHN. 1907- . English medical engineer. See: Who's Who Sci. Europe, 1967. Bunyan-Stannard envelope.

BUNYAN, PAUL. Legendary giant lumberjack of Canada and northwest U.S. See: Benet. Bunyanesque (2), Paul Bunyan.

Bunyan-Stannard envelope (Bunyan, John and Stannard): Medicine. See: Dorland.

Bunyanesque (1) (Bunyan, John): Literature. See: Webster's 3d.

Bunyanesque (2) (Bunyan, Paul): Mythology. See: Webster's 3d.

Buonarroti, Michelangelo. See: Michelangelo.

Buononcini, Giovanni Battista. See: Bononcini, Giovanni Battista.

BURALI-FORTI, CESARE. 1861-1931. Italian mathematician. See: Dict. Sci. Biog. Burali-Forti paradox.

Burali-Forti paradox (Burali-Forti, Cesare): Mathematics. See: James.

BURBANK, LUTHER. 1849-1926. American naturalist. See: Dict. Amer. Biog. Burbank plum, Burbank potato.

Burbank plum (Burbank, Luther): Botany. See: Hendrickson.

Burbank potato (Burbank, Luther): Botany. See: Hendrickson.

BURBANK, WILBUR SWETT. 1898- . American geologist. See: World Who's Who Sci. Burbankite.

Burbankite (Burbank, Wilbur Swett): Earth Sciences. See: Thrush.

BURCHARD (BROCARD). d. 1025. Bishop of Worms. See: Allg. Deut. Biog. Brocard.

BURCHARD, H. fl. 19th c. German chemist. (Biography source unavailable.) Liebermann-Burchard test (or reaction).

Burchard incident (Burchard, Samuel Dickinson): History. See: Smith.

Burchard-Liebermann reaction (Burchard, H. and Liebermann, Carl Theodore). See: Liebermann-Burchard test (or reaction).

BURCHARD, SAMUEL DICKINSON. 1812-1891. American clergyman. See: Dict. Amer. Biog. Burchard incident.

Burchard test reaction (Burchard, H.). See: Liebermann-Burchard test (or reaction).

BURCHELL, WILLIAM JOHN. 1782-1863. English naturalist. See: Dict. Nat. Biog. Burchell's zebra.

Burchell's zebra (Burchell, William John): Zoology. See: Webster's 3d.

BURCKHARDT, WALTER. 1905- . German? physician. See: New York Acad. Med. Portrait Cat. Burckhardt's dermatitis.

Burckhardt's dermatitis (Burckhardt, Walter): Medicine. See: Jablonski.

BURDACH, KARL FRIEDRICH. 1776-1847. German physiologist. See: Dict. Sci. Biog. Burdach's column(s) (or tract), Burdach's nucleus.

Burdach's column(s) (or tract) (Burdach, Karl Friedrich): Medicine. See: Donath; Dorland; Stedman.

Burdach's nucleus (Burdach, Karl Friedrich): Medicine. See: Stedman.

BURDIN, CLAUDE. 1790-1873. French mining engineer. See: World Who's Who Sci. Burdin turbine.

Burdin turbine (Burdin, Claude): Engineering and Industry. See: Auger.

Burdizzo forceps (or emasculatome) (Derivation undetermined): Agriculture. See: Winburne.

Bureau-Barriere disease (Bureau, Yves and Barriere, Henri): Medicine. See: Jablonski.

BUREAU, YVES. fl. 1957. French physician. See: Who's Who Sci. Europe, 1967. Bureau-Barriere disease.

Buren, William Holme van. See: Van Buren, William Holme.

Burger-Dorgelo-Ornstein (Orstein) rule (or sum rule for atomic spectra (Burger, Herman Carel; Dorgelo, Hendrik Berend; and Ornstein, Leonard Salomon): Physics. See: Ballentyne; Internat. Dict. Phys. Elec.

BURGER, HERMAN CAREL. 1893-1965. Dutch physicist. See: Dict. Sci. Biog. Burger-Dorgelo-Ornstein (Orstein) rule (or sum rule for atomic spectra).

Burgers' circuit (Burgers, Wilhelm Gerard): Physics. See: Ballentyne.

Burgers dislocation (Burgers, Wilhelm Gerard): Physics. See: Internat. Dict. Phys. Elec.

Burgers material (Burgers, Wilhelm Gerard): Physics. See: Internat. Dict. Ap. Math.

Burgers' vector (Burgers, Wilhelm Gerard): Physics. See: Ballentyne; Hackh; Hughes.

BURGERS, WILHELM GERARD. 1897- . Dutch physical chemist. See: Pogg., vols. 6, 7b. Burgers' circuit, Burgers dislocation, Burgers material, Burgers' vector.

Burgess-Cottrell marital adjustment scale (Burgess, Ernest Watson and Cottrell, Leonard Slater): Sociology. See: Zadrozny.

BURGESS, ERNEST WATSON. b. 1886. Canadian-born American sociologist. See: Amer. Men Sci., 9th ed. Burgess-Cottrell marital adjustment scale.

BURGESS, GEORGE KIMBALL. 1874-1932. American physicist. See: Dict. Amer. Biog., 1st suppl. Waidner-Burgess standard.

Burgess-Kamm test (Burgess, Laurie Lorne and Kamm, Oliver): Chemistry. See: Van Nostrand Chem. Dict.

BURGESS, LAURIE LORNE. b. 1882. American chemist. See: Amer. Men Sci., 2nd ed. Burgess-Kamm test.

Burgess reagent for aromatic compounds (Derivation undetermined): Chemistry. See: Van Nostrand Chem. Dict.

BURGHART, HANS GERNY. 1862-1932. German physician. See: Biog. Lex. hervorr. Aerzte, 1880-1930. Burghart's symptom.

Burghart's symptom (Burghart, Hans Gerny): Medicine. See: Dorland.

Burghley, Lord. See: Cecil, William (Lord Burghley).

Burgoynade (Burgoyne, John): Generic Word. See: Hendrickson; Mathews, M. M.; Partridge.

BURGOYNE, JOHN. 1722-1792. English army officer and dramatist. See: Dict. Nat. Biog. Burgoynade.

BURIAN, RICHARD. b. 1871. German physiologist. See: Biog. Lex. hervorr. Aerzte, 1880-1930. Burian test for xanthine bases.

Burian test for xanthine bases (Burian, Richard): Chemistry. See: Van Nostrand Chem. Dict.

BURIDAN, JEAN. ca. 1295-1356. French philosopher and scientist. See: Dict. Sci. Biog. Buridan's ass.

Buridan's ass (Buridan, Jean): Generic Word (indecision). See: Blumberg; Brewer; Hendrickson.

BURK, DEAN. 1904- . American educator and biochemist. See: Pogg., vols. 6, 7b. Lineweaver-Burk equation.

Burke (Burke, William): Generic Word (suffocate). See: Brewer; Charnock; Hendrickson.

BURKE, EDMUND. 1729-1797. English statesman. See: Dict. Nat. Biog. Burkean.

BURKE, EDWARD RAYMOND. 1881-1968. American legislator. See: Biog. Direct. Amer. Congress. Burke-Wadsworth Bill.

BURKE, MARTHA JANE ("CALAMITY JANE"). 1852?-1903. American army scout. See: Encyc. Amer., 1959 ed. Calamity Jane.

BURKE, RICHARD M. 1903- . American physician. See: Who's Who Among Physicians and Surg. Burke's syndrome.

Burke-Wadsworth Bill (Burke, Edward Raymond and Wadsworth, James Wolcott, Jr.): History. See: Morris.

BURKE, WILLIAM. 1792-1829. Irish criminal. See: Dict. Nat. Biog. Burke.

BURKE, WILLIAM EDMUND. b. 1880. American chemical engineer. See: Amer. Men Sci., 5th ed. Burkeite.

Burkean (Burke, Edmund): Politics. See: Webster's 3d.

Burkeite (Burke, William Edmund): Earth Sciences. See: Thrush; Webster's 3d.

Burke's syndrome (Burke, Richard M.): Medicine. See: Jablonski. Also known as: De Martini-Balestra syndrome.

Burkholder approximation (Burkholder, Donald Lyman): Statistics. See: Kendall.

BURKHOLDER, DONALD LYMAN. 1927- . American mathematician. See: World Who's Who Sci. Burkholder approximation.

BURKITT, DENIS PARSONS. 1911- . English physician. See: Who's Who, 1972-73. Burkitt's lymphoma (or tumor).

Burkitt's lymphoma (or tumor) (Burkitt, Denis Parsons): Medicine. See: Barnhart (New Eng.); Jablonski; Stedman.

BURKWOOD, ALBERT. b. 1890. English nurseryman. (Biography source unavailable.) Burkwood viburnum.

BURKWOOD, ARTHUR. b. 1888. English nurseryman. (Biography source unavailable.) Burkwood viburnum.

Burkwood viburnum (Burkwood, Albert and Burkwood, Arthur): Botany. See: Webster's 3d.

Burleigh's nod (Cecil, William): Generic Word. See: Harvey.

BURLINGAME, ANSON. 1820-1870. American lawyer and diplomat. See: Dict. Amer. Biog. Burlingame Treaty.

Burlingame Treaty (Burlingame, Anson): History. See: Smith.

Burls' formula (Burls, George Arthur): Engineering and Industry. See: Auger.

BURLS, GEORGE ARTHUR. 1866-1939. English engineer. (Biography source unavailable.) Burls' formula.

BURMANN, JOHANNES. 1707-1779. Dutch botanist. See: Nouv. Biog. Univ. Burmannia.

Burmannia (Burmann, Johannes): Botany. See: Charnock; Webster's 3d.

BURMEISTER, HERMANN CARL CONRAD. 1807-1892. German zoologist and traveler. See: World Who's Who Sci. Burmeisteria?

BURMEISTER, HERMANN CARL GUSTAV. b. 1882. German chemist. See: Pogg., vol. 6. Schenk-Burmeister test.

Burmeisteria (Burmeister, Hermann Carl Conrad?): Zoology. See: Pennak.

Burn and Rand theory (Burn, Joshua Harold and Rand, Michael John): Medicine. See: Stedman.

BURN, JOSHUA HAROLD. 1892- . English pharmacologist. See: World Who's Who Sci. Burn and Rand theory.

BURNAM, CURTIS FIELD. 1877-1947. American surgeon. See: World Who's Who Sci. Burnam's test.

Burnam's test (Burnam, Curtis Field): Medicine. See: Dorland; Stedman.

BURNESS, JACK K. No dates. American librarian. (Biography source unavailable.) Jack K. Burness Award.

BURNETT, CHARLES HOYT. 1913- . American physician. See: Amer. Men Sci., 9th ed. Burnett's syndrome.

BURNETT, EARLE SMEAD. b. 1880. American physicist. See: Amer. Men Sci., 10th ed. Burnett method for compressibility determinations.

Burnett equations (Derivation undetermined): Physics. See: Internat. Dict. Ap. Math.

BURNETT, JOHN. 1729-1784. Scottish merchant. See: Dict. Nat. Biog. Burnett Lectures, Burnett Prizes.

Burnett Lectures (Burnett, John): Religion. See: Canney.

Burnett method for compressibility determinations (Burnett, Earle Smead): Physics. Cited in: Amer. Men Sci., 10th ed.

Burnett Prizes (Burnett, John): Religion. See: Latham.

BURNETT, SIR WILLIAM. 1779-1861. Scottish physician. See: Dict. Nat. Biog. Burnettize, Burnett's solution.

Burnettize (Burnett, Sir William): Chemistry. See: Partridge; Webster's 3d.

Burnett's solution (Burnett, Sir William): Chemistry. See: Dorland.

Burnett's syndrome (Burnett, Charles Hoyt): Medicine. See: Jablonski; Stedman.

Burnham scale (Lawson, Harry Lawson Webster, 1st Viscount Burnham): Education. See: Partridge.

Burnham, Viscount. See: Lawson, Harry Lawson Webster (Viscount Burnham).

BURNIER, R. fl. 1912. American? physician. (Biography source unavailable.) Burnier's syndrome.

Burnier's syndrome (Burnier, R.): Medicine. See: Jablonski.

BURNS, ALLAN. 1781-1813. Scottish anatomist. See: Dict. Nat. Biog. Burns' falciform process, Burns' ligament, Burns' space.

Burns' amaurosis (Burns, John): Medicine. See: Dorland.

Burns' falciform process (Burns, Allan): Medicine. See: Stedman.

BURNS, JOHN. 1774-1850. Scottish physician and medical writer. See: Dict. Nat. Biog. Burns' amaurosis.

Burns' ligament (Burns, Allan): Medicine. See: Dorland; Stedman.

BURNS, ROBERT. 1759-1796. Scottish poet. See: Dict. Nat. Biog. Burns stanza (or meter), Burnsian.

Burns' space (Burns, Allan): Medicine. See: Dorland; Stedman.

Burns stanza (or meter) (Burns, Robert): Literature. See: Preminger; Scott; Webster's 3d.

Burnsian (Burns, Robert): Literature. See: Webster's 3d.

BURNSIDE, AMBROSE EVERETT. 1824-1881. American army officer. See: Dict. Amer. Biog. Burnside (carbine), Burnside hat, Sideburns (or Burnsides).

Burnside apparatus (Derivation undetermined): Engineering and Industry. See: Thrush.

Burnside boring machine (Derivation undetermined): Engineering and Industry. See: Thrush.

Burnside (carbine) (Burnside, Ambrose Everett): Weapons. See: Hendrickson; Mathews, M. M.; Quick.

Burnside hat (Burnside, Ambrose Everett): Fashion. See: Hendrickson; Mathews, M. M.

BURNSIDE, WILLIAM. 1852-1927. English mathematician. See: Dict. Sci. Biog. Burnside's formula?

Burnsides (Burnside, Ambrose Everett). See: Sideburns.

Burnside's formula (Burnside, William?): Mathematics. See: Ballentyne.

BUROW, AUGUST. 1809-1874. German surgeon. See: Biog. Lex. hervorr. Aerzte. Burow's operation, Burow's solution, Burow's vein(s).

Burow's operation (Burow, August): Medicine. See: Dorland; Stedman.

Burow's solution (Burow, August): Medicine. See: Dorland; Hackh; Webster's 3d.

Burow's vein(s) (Burow, August): Medicine. See: Donath; Dorland; Stedman.

BURR, AARON. 1756-1836. American army officer and political leader. See: Dict. Amer. Biog. Burr-Hamilton duel, Burrism (or Burrite(s)), Burr's conspiracy.

BURR, GEORGE OSWALD. 1896- . American biochemist. See: World Who's Who Sci. Evans-Burr unit.

Burr-Hamilton duel (Burr, Aaron and Hamilton, Alexander): History. See: Morris and Irwin.

BURR, IRVING WINGATE. 1908- . American mathematician. See: Amer. Men Sci., 11th ed. Burr's distribution.

Burr typesetting-machine (Derivation undetermined): Printing. See: Lockwood.

Burrell apparatus (Burrell, George Arthur): Engineering and Industry. See: Thrush.

Burrell gas detector (Burrell, George Arthur): Engineering and Industry. See: Thrush.

BURRELL, GEORGE ARTHUR. 1882-1957. American chemist. See: World Who's Who Sci. Burrell apparatus, Burrell gas detector, Burrell indicator, Burrell-Oberfell process.

Burrell indicator (Burrell, George Arthur): Engineering and Industry. See: Thrush.

Burrell-Oberfell process (Burrell, George Arthur and Oberfell, George Grover): Chemistry. Cited in: World Who's Who Sci. under "Burrell, George Arthur."

BURRI, ROBERT. b. 1867. Swiss bacteriologist. Cited in: Royal Soc. Cat. Sci. Pap., 1884-1900. Burri's method.

Burri's method (Burri, Robert): Medicine. See: Stedman.

Burrism (or Burrite(s) (Burr, Aaron): History. See: Clapin; Mathews, M. M.

Burrows and Quinn method (Burrows, William Henry and Quinn, Joseph Patrick): Zoology. See: Winburne.

BURROWS, WILLIAM HENRY. b. 1892. American animal surgeon. See: Amer. Men Sci., 6th ed. Burrows and Quinn method.

Burr's conspiracy (Burr, Aaron): History. See: Harbottle; Morris and Irwin; Phyfe.

Burr's distribution (Burr, Irving Wingate): Statistics. See: Kendall.

bursa of Fabricius (Fabrici, Girolamo): Zoology. See: Pennak; Stedman; Webster's 3d.

bursa of Monro (Monro, Alexander): Anatomy. See: Dorland; Stedman.

BURSER, JOACHIM. 1603-1689. German botanist. See: Nouv. Biog. Univ. Bursera.

Bursera (Burser, Joachim): Botany. See: Charnock; Webster's 3d.

Burstein effect (Burstein, Elias): Physics. See: Ballentyne.

BURSTEIN, ELIAS. 1917- . American physicist. See: World Who's Who Sci. Burstein effect.

Bursum Bill (Bursum, Holm Olaf): History. See: Morris.

BURSUM, HOLM OLAF. 1867-1953. American legislator. See: Biog. Direct. Amer. Congress. Bursum Bill.

BURT, EDWIN. fl. 1906. Chemist. Cited in: Chem. Abstr., vol. 1, p. 2198. Burt filter.

Burt filter (Burt, Edwin): Engineering and Industry. See: Thrush.

Burt-McCollum sleeve valve (Derivation undetermined): Engineering and Industry. See: Auger.

Burton-ail (Burton, Glenn Willard): Medicine. See: Webster's 3d.

BURTON, GEORGE DEXTER. 1855-1918. American inventor. See: World Who's Who Sci. Burton stock car.

BURTON, GLENN WILLARD. 1910- . American agronomist. See: World Who's Who Sci. Burton-ail.

BURTON, HENRY. 1799-1849. English physician. Cited in: Kelly. Burton's line.

Burton process (Burton, William Merriam): Chemistry. See: Van Nostrand Chem. Dict.

Burton stock car (Burton, George Dexter): Engineering and Industry. Cited in: World Who's Who Sci.

BURTON, THEODORE ELIJAH. 1851-1929. American legislator. See: Biog. Direct. Amer. Congress. Smoot-Burton Bill.

BURTON, WILLIAM MERRIAM. b. 1865. American chemist. See: Amer. Men Sci., 3-5 eds. Burton process.

Burton's line (Burton, Henry): Medicine. See: Dorland; Stedman.

BURY, CHARLES RUGELEY. b. 1890. English physical chemist. See: Pogg., vol. 7b. Bury('s) theory.

BURY, JUDSON SYKES. 1852-1944. English dermatologist. See: Who Was Who, 1941-1950. Bury's disease.

Bury('s) theory (Bury, Charles Rugeley): Chemistry. See: Ballentyne; Van Nostrand Chem. Dict.

Bury's disease (Bury, Judson Sykes): Medicine. See: Dorland; Jablonski; Stedman.

BUSACCA, ARCHIMEDE. 1893- . Italian physician. (Biography source unavailable.) Busacca's nodule (or floccule).

BUSACCA, ATTILIO. fl. 1921. Italian? physician. (Biography source unavailable.) Busacca's gelatin test.

Busacca's gelatin test (Busacca, Attilio): Medicine. See: Dorland.

Busacca's nodule (or floccule) (Busacca, Archimede): Medicine. See: Jablonski.

Busby (hat or wig) (Busby, Richard): Fashion. See: Charnock; Hendrickson; Partridge.

BUSBY, RICHARD. 1606-1695. English clergyman. See: Dict. Nat. Biog. Busby (hat or wig).

BUSCAINO, VITO MARIA. b. 1887. Italian neurologist and psychiatrist. See: World Who's Who Sci. Buscaino's reaction (or test).

Buscaino's reaction (or test) (Buscaino, Vito Maria): Medicine. See: Dorland.

BUSCH, A. fl. 1903. German chemist. (Biography source unavailable.) Biehringer-Busch test reaction.

Busch-Blume test (Busch, Max Gustav Reinhold and Blume, Gustav): Chemistry. See: Van Nostrand Chem. Dict.

BUSCH, FRIEDRICH. 1851-1931. German meteorologist. See: World Who's Who Sci. Busch lemniscate.

Busch lemniscate (Busch, Friedrich): Earth Sciences. See: Huschke.

BUSCH, MAX GUSTAV REINHOLD. 1865-1941. German chemist. See: Pogg., vols. 4-7a. Busch-Blume test, Busch reagent?

Busch reagent (Busch, Max Gustav Reinhold?): Chemistry. See: Van Nostrand Chem. Dict.

Buschi test (Derivation undetermined): Chemistry. See: Van Nostrand Chem. Dict.

Buschke-Loewenstein tumor (Bushke, Abraham and Loewenstein, Ludwig W.): Medicine. See: Jablonski.

Buschke-Ollendorff syndrome (Bushke, Abraham and Ollendorff, Helene): Medicine. See: Jablonski.

Buschke's disease (1) (Bushke, Abraham): Medicine. See: Jablonski; Stedman.

Buschke's disease (2) (Bushke, Abraham): Medicine. See: Dorland; Jablonski; Stedman. Also known as: Busse-Buschke disease.

Buschke's disease (3) (Bushke, Abraham). See: Madelung's disease.

BUSEMANN, ADOLF. 1901- . German-born American physicist. See: Amer. Men Sci., 10th ed. Busemann second-order theory.

Busemann second-order theory (Busemann, Adolf): Physics. See: Internat. Dict. Ap. Math.

Bush differential (Bush, E.): Engineering and Industry. See: Auger.

BUSH, E. fl. 1938. Engineer. (Biography source unavailable.) Bush differential.

BUSH, LINCOLN. b. 1861. American engineer. See: Who's Who Engin., 1925. Bush track construction, Bush train shed.

Bush track construction (Bush, Lincoln): Engineering and Industry. Cited in: Who's Who Engin., 1925.

Bush train shed (Bush, Lincoln): Engineering and Industry. Cited in: Who's Who Engin., 1925.

BUSHKE, ABRAHAM. 1868-1943. Polish-born German dermatologist. See: World Who's Who Sci. Buschke-Loewenstein tumor, Buschke-Ollendorff syndrome, Buschke's disease (1), Buschke's disease (2), Buschke's disease (3).

BUSHNELL, DAVID. 1742-1824. American inventor. See: Dict. Amer. Biog. Bushnell's turtle.

BUSHNELL, JOHN HORACE, JR. 1925- . American biologist. See: World Who's Who Sci. Bushnell's wasp?

Bushnell's turtle (Bushnell, David): Engineering and Industry (submarine). See: Brewer.

Bushnell's wasp (Bushnell, John Horace, Jr.?): Zoology. See: Pennak.

BUSK, GEORGE. 1807-1886. Russian-born English microscopist. See: Dict. Sci. Biog. Buskia.

Buskia (Busk, George): Zoology. See: Pennak.

BUSQUET, PAUL. 1866-1930. French physician. See: Dict. Biog. Fran. Busquet's disease.

Busquet's disease (Busquet, Paul): Medicine. See: Dorland; Jablonski; Stedman.

BUSS, ARNOLD HERBERT. 1924– . American psychologist. See: World Who's Who Sci. Buss–Durkee inventory.

Buss–Durkee inventory (Buss, Arnold Herbert and Durkee, Ann): Psychology. See: Wolman.

Buss table (Derivation undetermined): Engineering and Industry. See: Thrush.

Busse–Buschke disease (Busse, Otto Emil Franz Ulrich and Bushke, Abraham). See: Buschke's disease (2).

BUSSE, OTTO EMIL FRANZ ULRICH. 1867–1922. German pathologist. See: World Who's Who Sci. Busse–Buschke disease, saccharomyces Busse.

Bussolini test (Derivation undetermined): Chemistry. See: Van Nostrand Chem. Dict.

Bustamante Code of Private International Law (Bustamante y Sirven, Antonio Sanchez de): Law. See: New Encyc. Brit., 1974, Microp.

BUSTAMANTE Y SIRVEN, ANTONIO SANCHEZ DE. 1865–1951. Cuban politician and jurist. See: New Encyc. Brit., 1974, Microp. Bustamante Code of Private International Law.

BUSTAMENTE, ANASTASIO. 1780–1853. Mexican general and political leader. See: Webster's Biog. Dict. Bustamite.

Bustamente furnace (Bustamente, Juan Alonso de): Engineering and Industry. See: Webster's 3d.

BUSTAMENTE, JUAN ALONSO DE. fl. 1642. Spanish metallurgist. See: Encic. Univ. Ilus. Bustamente furnace.

Bustamite (Bustamente, Anastasio): Earth Sciences. See: Thrush; Webster's 3d.

BUSTER BROWN. American comic strip character. See: Benet. Buster Brown collar.

Buster Brown collar (Buster Brown): Fashion. See: Picken.

Butamen process (Derivation undetermined): Chemistry. See: Hackh.

Butchart table (Butchart, W. A.): Engineering and Industry. See: Thrush.

BUTCHART, W. A. fl. 1915–1925. American metallurgist. Cited in: Chem. Abstr., vol. 19, p. 29. Butchart table.

BUTCHER, RICHARD GEORGE HERBERT. 1819–1891. Irish surgeon. See: Biog. Lex. hervorr. Aerzte. Butcher's saw.

Butcher's saw (Butcher, Richard George Herbert): Medicine. See: Dorland.

Bute, 3rd. Earl of. See: Stuart, John (3rd Earl of Bute).

Butea (Butia) (Stuart, John, 3rd Earl of Bute): Botany. See: Dorland; Taylor, N.; Webster's 3d.

Butler Act (Butler, Richard Austen): History. See: Morris and Irwin; Steinberg under "Education Acts."

Butler–Albright syndrome (Butler, Allan Macy and Albright, Fuller). See: Lightwood–Albright syndrome.

BUTLER, ALLAN MACY. 1894– . American pediatrician. See: World Who's Who Sci. Albright–Butler–Bloomberg syndrome, Butler–Albright syndrome, Butler–Lightwood–Albright syndrome.

BUTLER, BENJAMIN FRANKLIN. 1818–1893. American lawyer, army officer, and politician. See: Dict. Amer. Biog. Butlerize.

BUTLER, CHARLES. 1750–1832. English lawyer. See: Dict. Nat. Biog. Butler's ordinance?

BUTLER, CHARLES P. fl. 1895–1911. English astronomer. Cited in: Royal Soc. Cat. Sci. Pap., 1884–1900. Edser and Butler's bands (or Edser–Butler bands), Edser–Butler method of calibrating a spectrometer.

Butler committee (Butler, Sir William Francis): History. See: Montgomery.

BUTLER, DEAN GURDON MONTAGUE. b. 1881. American geologist and mineralogist. See: Amer. Men Sci., 9th ed. Butlerite.

Butler finish (Derivation undetermined): Engineering and Industry. See: Thrush.

BUTLER, JOHN. 1728–1796. American Loyalist. See: Dict. Amer. Biog. Butler's Rangers.

BUTLER, JOHN (LORD DUNBOYNE). d. 1800. Bishop of Cork. See: Dict. Nat. Biog. Dunboyne Establishment.

Butler–Lightwood–Albright syndrome (Butler, Allan Macy; Lightwood, Reginald; and Albright, Fuller). See: Lightwood–Albright syndrome.

BUTLER, RICHARD AUSTEN. 1902– . English politician. See: Webster's Biog. Dict. Butler Act, Butskellism (or Butskell).

BUTLER, SIR WILLIAM FRANCIS. 1838–1910. English army officer. See: Dict. Nat. Biog., 2nd suppl. Butler committee.

Butlerite (Butler, Dean Gurdon Montague): Earth Sciences. See: Thrush; Webster's 3d.

Butlerize (Butler, Benjamin Franklin): Generic Word (steal). See: Mathews, M. M.

Butler's ordinance (Butler, Charles?): Law. See: Black.

Butler's Rangers (Butler, John): History. Cited in: Webster's Biog. Dict.

Butskellism (or Butskell) (Butler, Richard Austen and Gaitskell, Hugh Todd Naylor): Politics. See: Barnhart (New Eng.).

BUTTE, LUCIEN. 1856–1918. French physician. See: Dict. Biog. Fran. Arthaud–Butte reagent.

BUTTERICK, EBENEZER. 1826–1903. American inventor. See: Dict. Amer. Biog. Butterick (patterns).

Butterick (patterns) (Butterick, Ebenezer): Fashion. See: Mathews, M. M.

Butters and Mein distributor (Derivation undetermined): Engineering and Industry. See: Thrush.

Butter's cancer (Derivation undetermined): Medicine. See: Stedman.

BUTTERS, CHARLES. fl. 1906. English engineer. Cited in: Chem. Abstr. Decenn. Index, 1907–1916. Butters' filter.

Butters' filter (Butters, Charles): Engineering and Industry. See: Thrush; Van Nostrand Chem. Dict.

Butterworth filter (Derivation undetermined): Electronics. See: Hughes.

Butterworth shape (Derivation undetermined): Physics. See: Internat. Dict. Phys. Elec.

BUTTGENBACH, HENRI. 1874–1964. Belgian mineralogist. See: Pogg., vols. 6, 7b. Buttgenbachite.

Buttgenbachite (Buttgenbach, Henri): Earth Sciences. See: Thrush; Webster's 3d.

BUTTLAR, RICHARD FREIHERR VON. fl. 1911. German chemist. Cited in: Chem. Abstr., vol. 5, p. 3583. Pauly–Buttlar test reaction for alcohols.

BUXBAUM, JOHANNES CHRISTIAN. 1693–1730. German botanist. See: World Who's Who Sci. Buxbaumia.

Buxbaumia (Buxbaum, Johannes Christian): Botany. See: Webster's 3d.

Buxton's fluid (Derivation undetermined): Chemistry. See: Hackh.

BUYEH (OR BUWAYH). fl. 932. Founder of Persian dynasty. Cited in: New Encyc. Brit., 1974, Microp. under "Buyids." Buyids.

Buyids (Buyeh): History. See: New Encyc. Brit., 1974, Microp.

BUYS BALLOT, CHRISTOPH HENDRIK DIEDERIK. 1817–1890. Dutch meteorologist. See: Dict. Sci. Biog. Buys Ballot('s) law, Buys–Ballot table.

Buys Ballot('s) law (Buys Ballot, Christoph Hendrik Diederik): Earth Sciences. See: Ballentyne; Huschke; Internat. Dict. Phys. Elec.

Buys–Ballot table (Buys Ballot, Christoph Hendrik Diederik): Statistics. See: Kendall.

Buznea–Cernatesco test (Buznea, D. and Cernatescu, Radu): Chemistry. See: Van Nostrand Chem. Dict.

BUZNEA, D. fl. 1927. Rumanian chemist. Cited in: Chem. Abstr., vol. 22, p. 1297. Buznea–Cernatesco test.

BUZZARD, THOMAS. 1831–1919. English physician. See: Who Was Who, 1916–1928. Buzzard's maneuver.

Buzzard's maneuver (Buzzard, Thomas): Medicine. See: Stedman.

by Jove (or Jove) (Jupiter): Generic Word. See: Partridge; Webster's 3d.

by St. Peter (Peter the Apostle, Saint): Generic Word (oath). See: Charnock under "Peter."

by Washington (Washington, George): History. See: Mathews, M. M.

Byerite (Byers, William Newton): Earth Sciences. See: Thrush.

BYERLEY, FRANCIS X. fl. 1894. American chemist. (Biography source unavailable.) Byerlite?

Byerlite (Byerley, Francis X.?): Earth Sciences. See: Thrush.

Byerly Turk (Byerly): Generic Word (oriental horse). See: Hendrickson.

BYERS, WILLIAM NEWTON. 1831-1903. American surveyor and pioneer. See: Webster's Biog. Dict. Byerite.

BYLERLY. fl. 1690. English captain. (Biography source unavailable.) Byerly Turk.

Byler's disease (Derivation undetermined): Medicine. See: Jablonski.

BYNG, JULIAN HEDWORTH GEORGE, VISCOUNT. 1862-1935. English military commander. See: Dict. Nat. Biog., 5th suppl. Bing Boys.

BYNG, LADY MARIE EVELYN MORETON. d. 1949. English authoress and wife of Julian Byng, Governor-General of Canada. Cited in: Dict. Nat. Biog., 5th suppl. under "Byng, Julian Hedworth George Byng, Viscount." Lady Byng Trophy.

Byrd-Dew method (Byrd, Harvey Leonidas and Dew, James Harvie): Medicine. See: Dorland; Stedman.

BYRD, HARVEY LEONIDAS. 1820-1884. American physician. (Biography source unavailable.) Byrd-Dew method.

Byrnes Act (Byrnes, James Francis): Law. See: Smith.

BYRNES, JAMES FRANCIS. 1879- . American jurist. See: Biog. Direct. Amer. Congress. Byrnes Act.

BYRON, GEORGE NOEL GORDON, LORD. 1788-1824. English poet. See: Dict. Nat. Biog. Byronic (or Byronism).

Byronic (or Byronism) (Byron, George Noel Gordon, Lord): Literature. See: Harvey; Hendrickson; Partridge.

BYSTROEM, ANDERS. fl. 1950. Swedish mineral chemist. Cited in: Min. Mag., vol. 29 (1952) p. 977. Bystromite.

Bystromite (Bystroem, Anders): Earth Sciences. See: Thrush.

BYWATERS, ERIC GEORGE LAPTHORNE. 1910- . English physician. See: Who's Who, 1974. Bywaters' syndrome.

Bywaters' syndrome (Bywaters, Eric George Lapthorne): Medicine. See: Jablonski.

C

C & D hot top (Charman, Walter Miller and Darlington, Harry J.): Engineering and Industry. See: Thrush.

C. P. Hemborn dust extractor (Derivation undetermined): Engineering and Industry. See: Thrush.

C. W. Wheeler radial-flow condenser (Wheeler, C. W.): Engineering and Industry. See: Van Nostrand Sci. Encyc.

Cable Act (Cable, John Levi): Law. See: Smith; Zadrozny.

CABLE, JOHN LEVI. 1884-1971. American legislator. See: Biog. Direct. Amer. Congress. Cable Act.

CABOT, ARTHUR TRACY. 1852-1912. American surgeon. See: Dict. Amer. Biog. Cabot's splint.

Cabot-Locke murmur (Derivation undetermined): Medicine. See: Stedman.

CABOT, RICHARD CLARKE. 1868-1939. American physician. See: Webster's Biog. Dict. Cabot('s) ring (or ring bodies).

Cabot('s) ring (or ring bodies) (Cabot, Richard Clarke): Medicine. See: Dorland; Stedman; Webster's 3d.

CABOT, SAMUEL. d. 1885. American ornithologist. See: Sci., 1st ser., vol. 6 (1885) p. 20. Cabot's tern?

CABOTIN. fl. 1628. French actor. See: Dict. Biog. Fran. Cabotinage.

Cabotinage (Cabotin): Generic Word (charlatan). See: Webster's 3d.

Cabot's splint (Cabot, Arthur Tracy): Medicine. See: Dorland; Stedman.

Cabot's tern (Cabot, Samuel?): Zoology. See: Gray.

CABRAL, PEDRO ALVARES. 1460?-1526. Portuguese navigator. See: Encyc. Brit., 1973. Cabralea.

Cabralea (Cabral, Pedro Alvares): Botany. See: Webster's 3d.

Cacchi-Ricci syndrome (Cacchi, Roberto and Ricci, Vincenzo): Medicine. See: Jablonski.

CACCHI, ROBERTO. fl. 1949. French? physician. (Biography source unavailable.) Cacchi-Ricci syndrome.

CACCHIONE, ALDO. fl. 1932. Italian physician. (Biography source unavailable.) De Sanctis-Cacchione syndrome.

Cade('s) insurrection (or rebellion) (Cade, John): History. See: Harvey; Phyfe.

CADE, JOHN. d. 1450. English rebel. See: Dict. Nat. Biog. Cade('s) insurrection (or rebellion), Jack Cade legislation.

CADENET, MARSHAL. fl. 17th c. French army officer. (Biography source unavailable.) Cadenette (braids).

Cadenette (braids) (Cadenet, Marshal): Fashion. See: Picken.

CADET, LOUIS-CLAUDE. 1731-1799. French chemist. See: Dict. Sci. Biog. Cadet's liquid (or fuming liquid).

Cadet's liquid (or fuming liquid) (Cadet, Louis-Claude): Chemistry. See: Dorland; Hackh.

Cadillac (Cadillac, Antoine de la Mothe): Generic Word (expensive car). See: Hendrickson.

CADILLAC, ANTOINE DE LA MOTHE. 1658-1730. French colonial governor. See: Dict. Amer. Biog. Cadillac.

Cadmean (Cadmian) letters (Cadmus): Generic Word. See: Brewer; Charnock; Phyfe.

Cadmean victory (Cadmus): Generic Word. See: Brewer; Harvey; Scott.

Cadmium (Cadmus): Chemistry. See: Weekley.

CADMUS. Mythical King of Phoenicia. See: Jobes. Cadmean (Cadmian) letters, Cadmean victory, Cadmium.

Cadogan bow (Cadogan, William, 1st Earl of): Fashion. See: Picken.

Cadogan (hair style) (Cadogan, William, 1st Earl of): Fashion. See: Brewer; Harvey; Hendrickson.

Cadogan teapot (Cadogan, William, 1st Earl of): Applied Arts. See: Hendrickson.

Cadogan wig (Cadogan, William, 1st Earl of): Fashion. See: Picken.

CADOGAN, WILLIAM, 1ST EARL OF. 1675-1726. English general. See: Dict. Nat. Biog. Cadogan bow, Cadogan (hair style), Cadogan teapot, Cadogan wig.

CADOUDAL, GEORGES. 1771-1804. French royalist conspirator. See: Webster's Biog. Dict. George's conspiracy.

Cadoudal plot (Cadoudal, Georges). See: George's conspiracy.

CADWALADER, CHARLES MEIGS BIDDLE. b. 1885. American scientist. Cited in: Min. Mag., vol. 26 (1943) p. 335. Cadwaladerite.

Cadwaladerite (Cadwalader, Charles Meigs Biddle): Earth Sciences. See: Thrush.

CADY, LOUIS CLYDE. 1900- . American chemist. See: Amer. Men Sci., 9th ed. Cone-Cady reagent.

CAEDMON. fl. 670. English poet. See: Dict. Nat. Biog. Caedmon poems.

Caedmon poems (Caedmon); Literature. Cited in: Webster's Biog. Dict.

Caesalpinia (Cesalpini, Andrea): Botany. See: Charnock; Webster's 3d.

Caesar (Caesar, Gaius Julius): Generic Word (king). See: Funk; Phyfe; Webster's 3d.

Caesar, Augustus. See: Augustus Caesar.

Caesar cipher (or Julius Caesar cipher) (Caesar, Gaius Julius): Generic Word (code). See: Hendrickson; Webster's 3d.

CAESAR, GAIUS JULIUS. 100-44 B.C. Roman Emperor. See: Encyc. Brit., 1973. Caesar, Caesar cipher (or Julius Caesar cipher), Caesar salad, Caesar substitution (or shift), Caesarian (or Caesarean), Caesarian operation (or section), Caesaropapism, Caesar's mushroom (or agaric), Czar (or Tsar), Julian, Julian calendar, July, Kaiser.

Caesar salad (Caesar, Gaius Julius): Food and Drink. See: De Sola.

Caesar substitution (or shift) (Caesar, Gaius Julius): Cryptography. See: Webster's 3d.

Caesarian (or Caesarean) (Caesar, Gaius Julius): History. See: Hendrickson.

Caesarian operation (or section) (Caesar, Gaius Julius): Medicine. See: Attwater; Brewer; Hendrickson.

Caesarism (Caesarist or Caesarize) (Augustus Caesar): Politics. See: Hendrickson; Partridge; Zadrozny.

Caesaropapism (Caesar, Gaius Julius): History. See: Attwater; Mathews, S.; Winick.

Caesar's mushroom (or agaric) (Caesar, Gaius Julius): Botany. See: Hendrickson; Webster's 3d.

Caesia (Cesi, Federico): Botany. See: Charnock.

Caesio (Cesi, Federico?): Biology. See: Charnock.

Caesio, Frederico. See: Cesi, Federico.

CAFFEY, JOHN. 1895- . American pediatrician. See: Direct. Med. Specialists, 1970-1971. Caffey-Silverman syndrome.

Caffey-Silverman syndrome (Caffey, John and Silverman, William Aaron): Medicine. See: Jablonski. Also known as: Caffey-Smyth disease, Caffey's syndrome, De Toni-Caffey syndrome, Roske-De Toni-Caffey-Smyth disease.

Caffey-Smyth disease (Caffey, John and Smyth, Francis Scott). See: Caffey-Silverman syndrome.

Caffey's syndrome (Caffey, John). See: Caffey-Silverman syndrome.

Cagliari or Calliari, Paolo. See: Veronese, Paul.

Caglioti test reaction (Caglioti, Vincenzo): Chemistry. See: Van Nostrand Chem. Dict.

CAGLIOTI, VINCENZO. 1902- . Italian chemist. See: Diz. Encic. Ital. Caglioti test reaction.

CAGNIARD DE LA TOUR, CHARLES. 1777-1859. French engineer and physicist. See: Dict. Sci. Biog. Cagniard-La Tour siren, Cagniardelle (pump).

Cagniard-La Tour siren (Cagniard de la Tour, Charles): Engineering and Industry. Cited in: New Encyc. Brit., 1974, Microp. under "Cagniard de la Tour."

Cagniardelle (pump) (Cagniard de la Tour, Charles): Engineering and Industry. See: Auger. Also known as: Charles de la Tour (pump).

Cahall boiler (Derivation undetermined): Engineering and Industry. See: Auger.

Cahensly agitation (Cahensly, Peter): History. See: Latham.

CAHENSLY, PETER. fl. 1891. German parliamentarian. See: Wer Ist's, 1906. Cahensly agitation, Cahenslyism.

Cahenslyism (Cahensly, Peter): Politics. See: Webster's 3d.

CAHN, L. No dates. American scientist. Cited in: Bailey. Cahnite.

Cahnite (Cahn, L.): Earth Sciences. See: Thrush.

CAILLE, E. fl. 1923. French chemist. Cited in: Chem. Abstr., vol. 17, p. 3518. Caille-Viel solution.

Caille-Viel solution (Caille, E. and Viel, E.): Chemistry. See: Van Nostrand Chem. Dict.

Caillet, Guillaume. See: Cale, Guillaume.

Cailletet and Mathias law (Cailletet, Louis Paul and Mathias, Emile-Ovide-Joseph): Physics. See: Ballentyne; Internat. Dict. Phys. Elec.; Van Nostrand Chem. Dict.

CAILLETET, LOUIS PAUL. 1832-1913. French physicist and industrialist. See: Dict. Sci. Biog. Cailletet and Mathias law, Cailletet process.

Cailletet process (Cailletet, Louis Paul): Physics. See: Thewlis.

CAIN. Biblical son of Adam and Eve. See: Encyc. Amer., 1959. Cain-coloured (beard), Cain complex, Cainites, Cain's apple, curse of Cain, to raise Cain.

Cain-coloured (beard) (Cain): Generic Word (yellowish). See: Barnhart (Eng. Lit.); Brewer; Harvey.

Cain complex (Cain): Psychology. See: Hinsie; Stedman; Wolman.

Cainites (Cain): Religion. See: Brewer; Canney; Latham.

Cain's apple (Cain): Botany. See: Gray.

Cairns' Act (Cairns, Hugh McCalmont): Law. See: Black.

CAIRNS, HUGH MCCALMONT. 1819-1885. Irish lawyer, parliamentary orator and statesman. See: Dict. Nat. Biog. Cairns' Act.

CAIRNS, SIR HUGH WILLIAM BELL. 1896- . English surgeon. See: Who's Who, 1948. Cairns' syndrome.

Cairns' stupor (Derivation undetermined): Medicine. See: Hinsie.

Cairns' syndrome (Cairns, Sir Hugh William Bell): Medicine. See: Jablonski.

Caitanya. See: Chaitanya.

Caitanya sect (Chaitanya): Religion. See: Canney.

Cajal, Santiago Ramon y. See: Ramon y Cajal, Santiago.

Cajal's astrocyte stain (Ramon y Cajal, Santiago): Medicine. See: Dorland; Stedman.

Cajal's cell (Ramon y Cajal, Santiago): Anatomy. See: Donath; Dorland; Stedman.

Cajal's nucleus (Ramon y Cajal, Santiago): Anatomy. See: Donath.

CAJETAN OF THIENE, SAINT. 1480-1547. Italian lawyer and religious reformer. See: Webster's Biog. Dict. Cajetani.

Cajetani (Cajetan of Thiene, Saint): Religion. See: Canney. Also known as: Chietini, Theatines.

CALAMARI, JOSEPH A. fl. 1936. American chemist. Cited in: Chem. Abstr., vol. 30, p. 3577. Rogers-Calamari test for rotenone.

Calamity Jane (Burke, Martha Jane): Generic Word (female desperado). See: Hendrickson.

CALAMY, EDMUND. 1600-1666. English Puritan clergyman. See: Dict. Nat. Biog. Smectymnians.

CALANDRINI, GIOVANNI LUDOVICO. 1703-1758. Italian botanist. See: Nouv. Biog. Univ. Calandrinia.

Calandrinia (Calandrini, Giovanni Ludovico): Botany. See: Taylor, N.; Webster's 3d.

CALANUS. d. 325 B.C. Indian gymnosophist. See: Nouv. Biog. Univ. Calanus.

Calanus (Calanus, the Brahman): Zoology. See: Webster's 3d.

CALBICK, CHESTER JOSEPH. 1903- . American electron microscopist. See: Amer. Men Sci., 9th ed. Davisson-Calbick formula.

calcification lines of Retzius (Retzius, Gustav Magnus). See: Retzius' lines.

CALDANI, LEOPOLDO MARCANTONIO. 1725-1813. Italian anatomist. See: Dict. Sci. Biog. Caldani's ligament.

Caldani's ligament (Caldani, Leopoldo Marcantonio): Medicine. See: Dorland; Stedman.

Caldecott award(s) (or medal) (Caldecott, Randolph): Fine Arts. See: Good; Harrod; Hendrickson.

Caldecott cone (Caldecott, William Arthur): Engineering and Industry. See: Thrush.

CALDECOTT, RANDOLPH. 1846-1886. English artist and illustrator. See: Dict. Nat. Biog. Caldecott award(s) (or medal).

CALDECOTT, WILLIAM ARTHUR. fl. 1894-1908. South African metallurgist. Cited in: Chem. Abstr. Decenn. Index, 1907-1916. Caldecott cone.

CALDER, FRANK. d. 1943. American hockey league president. See: New York Times, Feb. 5, 1943, p. 21, col. 1. Calder Memorial Trophy.

CALDER, JAMES. No dates. Geologist. Cited in: Bailey. Calderite.

Calder Memorial Trophy (Calder, Frank): Recreation and Sports. See: Encyc. Brit. 1973 under "Ice Hockey," p. 1033.

Calderite (Calder, James): Earth Sciences. See: Thrush.

Caldwell crucible (Caldwell, George Chapman): Chemistry. See: Hackh.

CALDWELL, EUGENE WILSON. 1870-1918. American physician. See: World Who's Who Sci. Caldwell liquid interrupter.

CALDWELL, GEORGE CHAPMAN. 1834-1907. American chemist. See: Who Was Who Amer., vol. 1. Caldwell crucible.

CALDWELL, GEORGE W. 1834-1918. American physician. (Biography source unavailable.) Caldwell-Luc operation.

Caldwell liquid interrupter (Caldwell, Eugene Wilson): Medicine. Cited in: World Who's Who Sci.

Caldwell-Luc operation (Caldwell, George W. and Luc, Henri): Medicine. See: Dorland; Stedman. Also known as: Luc's operation.

Caldwell-Moloy classification (Caldwell, William Edgar and Moloy, Howard Carman): Medicine. See: Dorland; Stedman.

CALDWELL, WILLIAM EDGAR. 1880-1943. American obstetrician. See: World Who's Who Sci. Caldwell-Moloy classification.

CALE, GUILLAUME ("JACQUES BONHOMME"). d. 1358. French peasant leader. See: Webster's Biog. Dict. Jacquerie, Jacques Bonhomme.

Calembour(g) (Calembour, Abbe de): Generic Word (pun). See: Brewer; Charnock.

CALEMBOUR, ABBE DE (WIGAN VON THEBEN). Austrian priest who was introduced in "Till Eulenspiegel" and other German tales. (Biography source unavailable.) Calembour(g).

Calepin (Calepino, Ambrogio): Generic Word (dictionary). See: Brewer; Charnock; Harvey.

CALEPINO, AMBROGIO. 1435-1511. Italian lexicographer and Augustinian monk. See: Webster's Biog. Dict. Calepin.

CALEY, EARLE RADCLIFFE. 1900- . American chemist. See: Amer. Men Sci., 9th ed. Caley reagent for sodium, Caley test for calcium, Caley test for lithium, Caley test for oxalic acid.

CALEY, GEORGE. 1770-1829. English botanist. See: Biog. Notes Upon Botanists. Caleya.

Caley reagent for sodium (Caley, Earle Radcliffe): Chemistry. See: Van Nostrand Chem. Dict.

Caley test for calcium (Caley, Earle Radcliffe): Chemistry. See: Van Nostrand Chem. Dict.

Caley test for lithium (Caley, Earle Radcliffe): Chemistry. See: Van Nostrand Chem. Dict.

Caley test for oxalic acid (Caley, Earle Radcliffe): Chemistry. See: Van Nostrand Chem. Dict.

Caleya (Caley, George): Botany. See: Charnock.

CALHOUN, JOHN CALDWELL. 1782-1850. American lawyer. See: Dict. Amer. Biog. Calhounery (Calhounism, Calhounist, or Calhounite).

Calhounery (Calhounism, Calhounist, or Calhounite) (Calhoun, John Caldwell): History. See: Mathews, M. M.

CALIBAN. Character from William Shakespeare's play, "The Tempest." See: Benet. Caliban.

Caliban (Caliban, the character): Generic Word (rude). See: Brewer; Partridge.

Calicrat (Callicrates): Generic Word (ant). See: Stenhouse.

Caliga(e) (sandals or boots) (Caligula): Fashion. See: Brewer; Harvey.

CALIGULA (GAIUS CAESAR). 12 A.D.-41 A.D. Roman emperor. See: Encyc. Brit., 1973. Caliga(e) (sandals or boots), Caligulism(s).

Caligulism(s) (Caligula): Generic Word (cruelty). See: Brewer; Harvey.

CALISAYA. fl. 17th c. Indian who revealed the properties of quinine to the Spaniards. (Biography source unavailable.) Calisaya bark.

Calisaya bark (Calisaya): Botany. See: Webster's 3d.

Call-Exner bodies (Call and Exner, Sigmund): Medicine. See: Stedman.

CALLAGHAN, EUGENE. 1904- . American geologist. See: Amer. Men Sci., 9th ed. Callaghanite.

Callaghanite (Callaghan, Eugene): Earth Sciences. See: Thrush.

CALLAHAN, JOHN R. 1853-1918. American dentist. (Biography source unavailable.) Callahan's method.

Callahan's method (Callahan, John R.): Dentistry. See: Dorland.

Callan-Henderson reagent (Callan, Thomas and Henderson, J. A. Russell): Chemistry. See: Van Nostrand Chem. Dict.

CALLAN, THOMAS. fl. 1929. English? chemist. Cited in: Chem. Abstr., vol. 24, p. 312. Callan-Henderson reagent.

CALLANDER, CURLE LATIMER. 1892-1947. American surgeon. See: Who's Who Among Physicians and Surg. Callander's amputation.

Callander's amputation (Callander, Curle Latimer): Medicine. See: Dorland; Stedman.

CALLAWAY, THOMAS. 1791-1848. English physician. Cited in: Kelly. Callaway's test.

Callaway's test (Callaway, Thomas): Medicine. See: Dorland; Stedman.

CALLEJA, CAMILO. d. 1913. Spanish anatomist. Cited in: New York Acad. Med. Portrait Cat. Calleja's islets.

Calleja's islets (Calleja, Camilo): Medicine. See: Dorland; Stedman.

Callendar and Barnes method for mechanical equivalent of heat (Callendar, Hugh Longbourne and Barnes, Howard Turner): Physics. See: Internat. Dict. Phys. Elec.

Callendar and Griffiths bridge (Callendar, Hugh Longbourne and Griffiths, Ernest Howard): Physics. See: Internat. Dict. Phys. Elec.

Callendar('s) equation (Callendar, Hugh Longbourne): Physics. See: Ballentyne; Internat. Dict. Ap. Math.

CALLENDAR, HUGH LONGBOURNE. 1863-1930. English physicist. See: Dict. Sci. Biog. Callendar and Barnes method for mechanical equivalent of heat, Callendar and Griffiths bridge, Callendar('s) equation, Callendar steam tables.

Callendar steam tables (Callendar, Hugh Longbourne): Engineering and Industry. See: Auger.

CALLIAS. fl. 392 B.C. Athenian soldier and diplomat. See: Webster's Biog. Dict. Peace of Callias.

CALLICRATES. fl. 5th c. B.C. Greek architect. See: Webster's Biog. Dict. Calicrat.

CALLIER, ANDRE. 1877-1938. Belgian amateur physicist. (Biography source unavailable.) Callier coefficient, Callier effect.

Callier coefficient (Callier, Andre): Physics. See: Internat. Dict. Ap. Math.; Internat. Dict. Phys. Elec.; Thewlis.

Callier effect (Callier, Andre): Physics. See: Focal Encyc. Film; Focal Encyc. Photog.

CALLIOPE. Muse of epic poetry. See: Jobes. Calliope (steam organ), Callithumpians.

Calliope (steam organ) (Calliope): Music. See: Brewer; Partridge.

Callippic (Calippic) period (Callippus): Astronomy. See: Brewer; Charnock.

CALLIPPUS. b. ca. 370 B.C. Greek astronomer. See: Dict. Sci. Biog. Callippic (Calippic) period.

CALLISEN, HENDRIK. 1740-1824. Danish surgeon. See: Nouv. Biog. Univ. Callisen's operation.

Callisen's operation (Callisen, Hendrik): Medicine. See: Dorland.

CALLISON, JAMES S. b. 1873. American physician. (Biography source unavailable.) Callison's fluid.

Callison's fluid (Callison, James S.): Medicine. See: Dorland; Stedman.

Callithumpians (Calliope): Generic Word (rowdy students). See: Clapin.

CALLON, PIERRE-JULES. 1815-1875. French mining engineer. See: Dict. Biog. Fran. Callon's rule?

Callon's rule (Callon, Pierre-Jules?): Engineering and Industry. See: Thrush.

Callow cone (Callow, John Michael): Engineering and Industry. See: Thrush.

Callow flotation cell (Callow, John Michael): Engineering and Industry. See: Thrush.

CALLOW, JOHN MICHAEL. 1867-1940. English-born mining engineer. See: World Who's Who Sci. Callow cone, Callow flotation cell, Callow process, Callow screen.

Callow process (Callow, John Michael): Engineering and Industry. See: Thrush.

CALLOW, ROBERT KENNETH. 1901- . English chemist. See: Who's Who, 1974. Rosenheim-Callow test reactions for sterols.

Callow screen (Callow, John Michael): Engineering and Industry. See: Thrush.

Calmberg test for codeine (Derivation undetermined): Chemistry. See: Van Nostrand Chem. Dict.

CALMETTE, ALBERT. 1863-1933. French bacteriologist. See: Dict. Sci. Biog. Calmette-Guerin bacillus (or bacillus Calmette-Guerin), Calmette-Guerin vaccine, Calmette test, Calmette's tuberculin.

Calmette-Guerin bacillus (or bacillus Calmette-Guerin) (Calmette, Albert and Guerin, Camille): Medicine. See: Stedman; Van Nostrand Sci. Encyc.; Webster's 3d.

Calmette-Guerin vaccine (Calmette, Albert and Guerin, Camille): Medicine. See: Stedman.

Calmette test (Calmette, Albert): Medicine. See: Dorland; Stedman. Also known as: Chantemesse reaction.

Calmette's tuberculin (Calmette, Albert): Medicine. See: Stedman.

CALORI, LUIGI. 1807-1896. Italian anatomist. See: Sci., vol. 5 (1897) p. 143; vol. 6 (1897) p. 876. Calori's bursa.

Calori's bursa (Calori, Luigi): Anatomy. See: Dorland; Stedman.

CALOT, JEAN-FRANCOIS. 1861-1944. French surgeon. See: Biog. Lex. hervorr. Aerzte, 1880-1930. Calot's operation, Calot's solution, Calot's treatment, Calot's triangle.

Calot's operation (Calot, Jean-Francois): Medicine. See: Dorland.

Calot's solution (Calot, Jean-Francois): Medicine. See: Dorland.

Calot's treatment (Calot, Jean-Francois): Medicine. See: Dorland.

Calot's triangle (Calot, Jean-Francois): Medicine. See: Dorland.

CALVE, JACQUES. 1875-1954. French surgeon. See: New York Acad. Med. Portrait Cat. Calve-Legg-Perthes syndrome, Calve's syndrome.

Calve-Legg-Perthes syndrome (Calve, Jacques; Legg, Arthur Thornton; and Perthes, George Clemens): Medicine. See: Jablonski. Also known as: Calve-Perthes disease, Legg's disease, Perthes-Calve-Legg-Waldenstroem syndrome, Perthes' disease, Waldenstroem's syndrome.

Calve-Perthes disease (Calve, Jacques and Perthes, George Clemens). See: Calve-Legg-Perthes syndrome.

CALVENA, C. MATIUS. fl. 1st c. B.C. Roman writer on gastronomy. See: Dict. Grk. Rom. Biog. Myth. Manzana.

CALVERT, CAROLINE LOUISA WARING (LOUISA ATKINSON). 1834-1872. Australian author and botanist. See: Dict. Nat. Biog. Atkinsonia, epaeris Calvertiana.

CALVERT, EDWIN GEORGE BLEAKLEY. fl. 1915- . English physician. See: Who's Who, 1972. Calvert's test.

CALVERT, GEORGE, 1ST LORD BALTIMORE. 1580?-1632. English proprietor and colonizer of Maryland. See: Dict. Nat. Biog. Baltimore (butterfly), Baltimore oriole, Baltimore starling, Lord Baltimore cake.

CALVERT, MRS. GEORGE, LADY BALTIMORE. 1580-1632. Wife of George Calvert, Lord Baltimore. (Biography source unavailable.) Lady Baltimore cake.

Calvert's test (Calvert, Edwin George Bleakley): Medicine. See: Dorland.

Calve's syndrome (Calve, Jacques): Medicine. See: Jablonski.

CALVIN, JOHN. 1509-1564. French theologian and reformer. See: Internat. Encyc. Soc. Sci. Calvinism, Calvinistic, Calvinists, Institutes of Calvin.

Calvinism (Calvin, John): Religion. See: Attwater; Hoult; Mathews, S.

Calvinistic (Calvin, John): Generic Word (bleak). See: Partridge.

Calvinists (Calvin, John): Religion. See: Wagner (Names).

CALVO, CARLOS. 1824-1906. Argentine diplomat and jurist. See: Encyc. Brit., 1911. Calvo Doctrine.

Calvo Doctrine (Calvo, Carlos): Law. See: Black; Smith.

Calypso (dance) (Calypso): Dance. See: Webster's 3d.

Calypso (herbs) (Calypso): Botany. See: Webster's 3d.

Calzecchi-Onesti effect (Calzecchi-Onesti, Temistocle?): Physics. See: Ballentyne.

CALZECCHI-ONESTI, TEMISTOCLE. 1853-1922. Italian physicist. See: Dizz. Biog. Ital. Calzecchi-Onesti effect?

CALZOLARI, F. fl. 1923. Italian chemist. Cited in: Chem. Abstr., vol. 19, p. 2317. Calzolari test reaction.

Calzolari test reaction (Calzolari, F.): Chemistry. See: Van Nostrand Chem. Dict.

CAMACHO. Character from Cervantes' novel, "Don Quixote." See: Benet. Camacho's wedding.

Camacho's wedding (Camacho): Generic Word (useless show). See: Brewer.

CAMARGO, MARIE. 1710-1770. Belgian-born French ballerina. See: New Encyc. Brit., 1974, Microp. Camargo Society.

Camargo Society (Camargo, Marie): Dance. See: New Encyc. Brit., 1974, Microp.

Cambridge conspiracy (Richard, Earl of Cambridge): History. See: Steinberg.

Cambridge, Earl of. See: Richard (Earl of Cambridge).

CAMBYSES. Character in Thomas Preston's tragedy, "Cambyses, King of Persia," (1569). See: Benet. Cambyses.

Cambyses (Cambyses, the King): Generic Word (bombastic). See: Harvey.

Camden, 1st Earl. See: Pratt, Charles (1st Earl Camden).

Camden Professor (Camden, William): History. See: Wagner (More Names).

Camden Society (Camden, William): History. See: Barnhart (Eng. Lit.); Brewer; Harvey.

CAMDEN, WILLIAM. 1551-1623. English antiquary and historian. See: Dict. Nat. Biog. Camden Professor, Camden Society.

Camden-Yorke opinion (Pratt, Charles, 1st Earl Camden and Yorke, Charles): Law. See: Morris.

CAMEL, GEORGE JOSEPH. 1661-1706. Moravian botanist. See: World Who's Who Sci. Camellia.

Camellia (Camel, George Joseph): Botany. See: Charnock; Hargrave, Taylor, N.

CAMERA, UGO. fl. 1909. Italian physician. Cited in: New York Acad. Med. Portrait Cat. Camera's syndrome.

Cameraria (Camerarius, Joachim): Botany. See: Charnock.

CAMERARIUS, JOACHIM. 1534-1598. German physician and botanist. See: World Who's Who Sci. Cameraria.

Camera's syndrome (Camera, Ugo): Medicine. See: Jablonski.

Camerer-Arnstein test (Derivation undetermined): Chemistry. See: Van Nostrand Chem. Dict.

CAMERER, JOHANN FRIEDRICH WILHELM. 1842-1910. German physician and physiologist. See: World Who's Who Sci. Camerer's law.

Camerer's law (Camerer, Johann Friedrich Wilhelm): Medicine. See: Dorland.

CAMERON, A. S. fl. 1869. English engineer. (Biography source unavailable.) Cameron pump.

CAMERON, SIR ALAN. 1753-1828. English general. See: Dict. Nat. Biog. Cameron Highlanders.

Cameron dynasty (Cameron, Simon and Cameron, James Donald): History. See: Smith.

Cameron Highlanders (Cameron, Sir Alan): History. See: Brewer; Wagner (More Names).

CAMERON, JAMES DONALD. 1833-1918. American legislator. See: Dict. Amer. Biog. Cameron dynasty.

CAMERON, JOHN. 1579-1625. Scottish theologian. See: Dict. Nat. Biog. Cameronites.

Cameron pump (Cameron, A. S.): Engineering and Industry. See: Auger.

CAMERON, RICHARD. 1648-1680. Scottish religious leader. See: Dict. Nat. Biog. Cameronians.

CAMERON, SIMON. 1799-1889. American financier and legislator. See: Dict. Amer. Biog. Cameron dynasty.

Cameronians (Cameron, Richard): Religion. See: Brewer; Canney; Harbottle.

Cameronites (Cameron, John): Religion. See: Canney; Latham.

Camilla-Pertusi test for saccharin and dulcin (Camilla, Stefano and Pertusi, Camillo Alessandro Giorgio): Chemistry. See: Van Nostrand Chem. Dict.

Camilla-Pertusi test for xanthine bases (Camilla, Stefano and Pertusi, Camillo Allessandro Giorgio): Chemistry. See: Van Nostrand Chem. Dict.

CAMILLA, STEFANO. fl. 1912. Italian chemist. Cited in: Chem. Abstr., vol. 6, p. 1323. Camilla-Pertusi test for saccharin and dulcin, Camilla-Pertusi test for xanthine bases.

Camillians (Camillus de Lellis): Religion. See: Attwater.

CAMILLUS DE LELLIS. 1550-1614. Italian religious leader. See: Holweck. Camillians.

CAMMANN, GEORGE PHILIP. 1804-1863. American physician. See: Webster's Biog. Dict. Cammann's stethoscope.

Cammann's stethoscope (Cammann, George Philip): Medicine. See: Dorland.

Cammett table (Derivation undetermined): Engineering and Industry. See: Thrush.

CAMMIDGE, PERCY JOHN. b. 1872. English physician. See: Who's Who, 1930. Cammidge reaction.

Cammidge reaction (Cammidge, Percy John): Medicine. See: Dorland; Stedman.

CAMP, BURTON HOWARD. b. 1880. American mathematician. See: Pogg., vol. 6. Camp-Meidell inequality, Camp-Paulson approximation.

Camp-Meidell inequality (Camp, Burton Howard and Meidell, Birger Oivind): Statistics. See: Kendall.

Camp-Paulson approximation (Camp, Burton Howard and Paulson, Edward): Statistics. See: Kendall.

Campani's test (Derivation undetermined): Medicine. See: Stedman.

CAMPBELL, MRS. ADALE. fl. 19th c. English duck breeder. (Biography source unavailable.) khaki Campbell.

CAMPBELL, ALBERT. 1862-1954. Irish-born English physicist. See: Pogg., vol. 7b. Campbell bridge, Campbell gauge, Campbell-Larsen potentiometer, Campbell method, Heaviside-Campbell bridge.

CAMPBELL, ALEXANDER. 1788-1866. Irish-born American religious leader. See: Dict. Nat. Biog. Campbellites.

CAMPBELL, ANDREW. 1821-1890. American inventor and manufacturer. See: Dict. Amer. Biog. Campbell press.

CAMPBELL, ARCHIBALD, 3RD DUKE OF ARGYLL. 1682-1761. English botanist. See: Dict. Nat. Biog. Argyllia.

CAMPBELL, ARCHIBALD, 9TH EARL OF ARGYLL. 1629-1685. Scottish nobleman. See: Dict. Nat. Biog. Argyll's rebellion.

CAMPBELL, SIR ARCHIBALD CAMPBELL (LORD BLYTHSWOOD). 1835-1908. Scottish amateur scientist. See: Dict. Nat. Biog., 2nd. suppl. Blythswood engine.

CAMPBELL, ARTHUR J. fl. 1930. American engineer. Cited in: Chem. Abstr., Decenn. Index, 1927-1936. Moore-Campbell kiln.

Campbell bridge (Campbell, Albert): Physics. See: Hughes; Internat. Dict. Phys. Elec.; Markus.

Campbell-Colpitts bridge (Campbell, George Ashley and Colpitts, Edwin Henry): Electronics. See: Internat. Dict. Phys. Elec.; Markus.

CAMPBELL, FRANCIS JOSEPH. 1832-1914. American educator. See: Dict. Amer. Biog. Francis Joseph Campbell citation.

Campbell gauge (Campbell, Albert): Electronics. See: Hughes.

CAMPBELL, GEORGE ASHLEY. 1870-1954. American engineer. See: Amer. Men Sci., 9th ed. Campbell-Colpitts bridge, Campbell's formula.

CAMPBELL, JOHN CAMPBELL. 1779-1861. Scottish-born English jurist. See: Encyc. Brit., 1973. Lord Campbell Act?

CAMPBELL, JOHN MCLEOD. 1800-1872. Scottish theologian. See: Dict. Nat. Biog. Campbellite(s).

CAMPBELL, KENNETH NIELSEN. 1905- . American organic chemist. See: Amer. Men Sci., 10th ed. Hoch-Campbell ethylenimine synthesis.

Campbell-Larsen potentiometer (Campbell, Albert and Larsen, Absalon): Physics. See: Internat. Dict. Phys. Elec.

Campbell method (Campbell, Albert): Physics. See: Internat. Dict. Phys. Elec.; Van Nostrand Sci. Encyc.

CAMPBELL, NORMAN ROBERT. 1880-1949. English physicist and mathematician. See: Pogg., vols. 5, 6. Campbell's theorem.

CAMPBELL, PETER. fl. 1960. English physician. (Biography source unavailable.) Williams-Campbell syndrome.

Campbell press (Campbell, Andrew): Printing. See: Lockwood.

Campbell process (Derivation undetermined): Engineering and Industry. See: Thrush.

Campbell, Robert. See: Macgregor (or Campbell), Robert.

Campbell-Stark test reaction (Derivation undetermined): Chemistry. See: Van Nostrand Chem. Dict.

Campbell-Stokes recorder (Derivation undetermined): Earth Sciences. See: Huschke; Monkhouse; Van Nostrand Sci. Encyc.

Campbell test (Derivation undetermined): Chemistry. See: Van Nostrand Chem. Dict.

CAMPBELL, WILLIAM FRANCIS. 1867-1926. American physician. See: Who's Who Amer. Med. Campbell's ligament.

Campbellite(s) (Campbell, John McLeod): Religion. See: Brewer; Webster's 3d.

Campbellites (Campbell, Alexander): Religion. See: Canney; Jameson; Latham.

Campbell's formula (Campbell, George Ashley): Electronics. See: Ballentyne; Hughes.

Campbell's ligament (Campbell, William Francis): Medicine. See: Dorland; Stedman.

Campbell's theorem (Campbell, Norman Robert): Statistics. See: Kendall.

Campden tablets (Derivation undetermined): Chemistry. See: Hackh.

CAMPER, PETER. 1722-1789. Dutch physician and anatomist. See: Dict. Sci. Biog. Camper's chiasm, Camper's facial angle, Camper's fascia, Camper's ligament, Camper's line.

Camper's chiasm (Camper, Peter): Medicine. See: Dorland; Stedman.

Camper's facial angle (Camper, Peter): Medicine. See: Donath; Dorland; Stedman.

Camper's fascia (Camper, Peter): Medicine. See: Dorland; Stedman.

Camper's ligament (Camper, Peter): Medicine. See: Dorland; Stedman.

Camper's line (Camper, Peter): Medicine. See: Dorland; Stedman.

Campini gas turbine (or engine) (Campini, Secondo): Engineering and Industry. See: Auger; Webster's 3d.

CAMPINI, SECONDO. 1904- . Italian engineer. See: Diz. Encic. Ital. Campini gas turbine (or engine).

CAMPO, ANGEL DEL (CAMPO Y CERDAN). fl. 1909-1930. Spanish chemist. See: Pogg., vol. 6. Campo-Cerdan test reaction.

Campo–Cerdan test reaction (Campo, Angel del): Chemistry. See: Van Nostrand Chem. Dict.

Camps quinoline synthesis (Derivation undetermined): Chemistry. See: Van Nostrand Chem. Dict.

Camurati-Engelmann syndrome (Camurati, Mario and Engelmann, Guido): Medicine. See: Jablonski.

CAMURATI, MARIO. 1896-1948. Italian physician. See: New York Acad. Med. Portrait Cat. Camurati-Engelmann syndrome.

CANADA, WILMA JEANNE. No dates. American radiologist. (Biography source unavailable.) Cronkhite–Canada syndrome.

CANADELL VIDAL, JOSE MARIA. fl. 1949. Spanish physician. (Biography source unavailable.) Vilanova–Canadell syndrome.

canal of Hering (Hering, Ewald): Anatomy. See: Stedman.

canal of Hovius (Hovius, Jacobus): Anatomy. See: Dorland; Stedman.

canal of Lauth (Lauth, Ernst Alexander). See: Lauth's canal.

canal of Petit (Petit, Francois Pourfour du). See: Petit's canal.

canal of Volkmann (Volkmann, Alfred Wilhelm). See: Volkmann's canals.

CANAVAN, MYRTELLE MAY. b. 1879. American neuropathologist. See: Who's Who Amer. Med. Canavan's disease (or sclerosis).

Canavan's disease (or sclerosis) (Canavan, Myrtelle May): Medicine. See: Jablonski; Stedman. Also known as: Van Bogaert–Bertrand syndrome.

CANCRIN, GEORG. 1774-1845. Russian statesman. See: Webster's Biog. Dict. Cancrinite.

Cancrinite (Cancrin, Georg): Earth Sciences. See: Van Nostrand Sci. Encyc.; Webster's 3d.

CANDOLLE, AUGUSTIN-PYRAMUS DE. 1778-1841. Swoss botanist. See: Dict. Sci. Biog. Candollea.

Candollea (Candolle, Augustin-Pyramus de): Botany. See: Webster's 3d.

Candussio reagent for phenolic compounds (Derivation undetermined): Chemistry. See: Van Nostrand Chem. Dict.

Canevari binding (Canevari, Demetrio): Applied Arts. See: Harrod.

CANEVARI, DEMETRIO. 1559-1625. Genoese physician and medical writer. See: Nouv. Biog. Univ. Canevari binding.

Canfield (Canfield, Richard A.): Recreation and Sports. See: Webster's 3d.

CANFIELD, FREDERICK ALEXANDER. 1849-1926. American mining engineer. (Biography source unavailable.) Canfieldite.

Canfield('s) reagent (Canfield, Robert Hawthorne?): Chemistry. See: Thrush; Van Nostrand Chem. Dict.

CANFIELD, RICHARD A. 1855-1914. American gambling house owner and art collector. See: Dict. Amer. Biog. Canfield.

CANFIELD, ROBERT HAWTHORNE. 1894- . American metallurgist. Cited in: Chem. Abstr., vol. 18, p. 1630. Canfield('s) reagent?

Canfieldite (Canfield, Frederick Alexander): Earth Sciences. See: Webster's 3d.

Cannizzarite (Cannizzaro, Stanislao?): Earth Sciences. See: Thrush.

Cannizzaro number (Cannizzaro, Stanislao): Chemistry. See: Hackh.

Cannizzaro('s) reaction (Cannizzaro, Stanislao): Chemistry. See: Ballentyne; Dorland; Stedman; Van Nostrand Chem. Dict.

CANNIZZARO, STANISLAO. 1826-1910. Italian chemist. See: Dict. Sci. Biog. Cannizzarite? Cannizzaro number, Cannizzaro('s) reaction.

CANNON, A. BENSON. b. 1888. American dermatologist. See: Who's Who Among Physicians and Surg. Cannon's nevus.

Cannon and La Paz test (Cannon, Walter Bradford and Paz, Daniel de la): Medicine. See: Stedman.

Cannon, Boehm, and Roith's sphincter (Derivation undetermined): Medicine. See: Stedman.

Cannon hypothalamic theory of emotion (Cannon, Walter Bradford): Medicine. See: Hinsie.

CANNON, JOSEPH GURNEY. 1836-1926. American politician. See: Dict. Amer. Biog. Cannonism.

CANNON, WALTER BRADFORD. 1871-1945. American physiologist. See: Internat. Encyc. Soc. Sci. Cannon and La Paz test, Cannon hypothalamic theory of emotion, Cannon's ring, Cannon's syndrome (or reflex), Cannon's test, Cannon's theory, Rosenbleuth and Cannon test.

Cannonism (Cannon, Joseph Gurney): Politics. See: Morris; Smith; Webster's 3d.

Cannon's nevus (Cannon, A. Benson): Medicine. See: Jablonski.

Cannon's ring (Cannon, Walter Bradford): Medicine. See: Dorland; Stedman.

Cannon's syndrome (or reflex) (Cannon, Walter Bradford): Medicine. See: Jablonski.

Cannon's test (Cannon, Walter Bradford): Medicine. See: Stedman.

Cannon's theory (Cannon, Walter Bradford): Medicine. See: Stedman.

Cant (Cant, Andrew): Generic Word (whining speech). See: Charnock; Hendrickson.

CANT, ANDREW. 1590-1663. Scottish ecclesiastical leader and preacher. See: Dict. Nat. Biog. Cant.

CANTANI, ARNOLDO. 1837-1893. Italian physician. See: World Who's Who Sci. Cantani's diet, Cantani's serum, Cantani's treatment.

Cantani's diet (Cantani, Arnoldo): Medicine. See: Dorland.

Cantani's serum (Cantani, Arnoldo): Medicine. See: Dorland.

Cantani's treatment (Cantani, Arnoldo): Medicine. See: Dorland.

CANTELLI, FRANCESCO PAOLO. b. 1875. Italian mathematician. See: Diz. Encic. Ital. Borel-Cantelli lemmas, Cantelli's inequality, Glivenko-Cantelli lemma.

Cantelli's inequality (Cantelli, Francesco Paolo): Statistics. See: Kendall.

Cantelli's sign (Derivation undetermined): Medicine. See: Stedman.

CANTLIE, JAMES. 1851-1926. Scottish physician. See: Webster's Biog. Dict. Cantlie's foot tetter.

Cantlie's foot tetter (Cantlie, James): Medicine. See: Dorland.

CANTON, JOHN. 1718-1772. English physicist. See: Dict. Sci. Biog. Canton's phosphorus.

Canton's phosphorus (Canton, John): Physics. Cited in: Webster's Biog. Dict.

Cantor-Dedkind axiom (Cantor, Georg and Dedekind, Julius Wilhelm Richard): Mathematics. Cited in: World Who's Who Sci.

CANTOR, GEORG. 1845-1918. German mathematician. See: Dict. Sci. Biog. Cantor-Dedkind axiom, Cantor set (discontinuum or ternary set), Cantor's paradox, Cantor's theorem.

Cantor lectures (Cantor, Theodore Edward): Education. See: Wagner (More Names).

CANTOR, MEYER O. 1907- . American surgeon. See: Who's Imp. Med., 2nd ed. Cantor tube.

Cantor set (discontinuum or ternary set) (Cantor, Georg): Mathematics. See: James.

CANTOR, THEODORE EDWARD. 1809-1859. English naturalist in India. (Biography source unavailable.) Cantor lectures.

Cantor tube (Cantor, Meyer O.): Medicine. See: Dorland; Stedman.

Cantor's paradox (Cantor, Georg): Mathematics. See: New Encyc. Brit., 1974, Microp.

Cantor's theorem (Cantor, Georg): Mathematics. See: New Encyc. Brit., 1974, Microp.

CANULEIUS, CNEIUS. fl. ca. 445 B.C. Roman politician. See: Webster's Biog. Dict. lex Canuleia.

CAPDEPONT, CHARLES. 1867-1917. French dentist. (Biography source unavailable.) Capdepont's syndrome.

Capdepont-Hodge syndrome (Capdepont, Charles and Hodge, Harold Carpenter). See: Capdepont's syndrome.

Capdepont's syndrome (Capdepont, Charles): Medicine. See: Jablonski. Also known as: Capdepont-Hodge syndrome, Fargin-Fayelle syndrome, Stainton-Capdepont syndrome, Stainton's syndrome.

Capel court (Capel, William): Generic Word (stock exchange). See: Brewer.

CAPEL, WILLIAM. fl. 1504. English politician. (Biography source unavailable.) Capel court.

CAPELL, G.M. fl. 1893. American mining engineer. Cited in: Royal Soc. Cat. Sci. Pap., 1884-1900. Capell ventilator (or fan).

Capell ventilator (or fan) (Capell, G. M.): Engineering and Industry. See: Auger; Thrush.

Capet, Hugh. See: Hugh Capet.

Capetian dynasty (Hugh Capet): History. See: Brewer; Phyfe; Webster's 3d.

CAPGRAS, JEAN MARIE JOSEPH. 1873-1950. French psychiatrist. (Biography source unavailable.) Capgras syndrome.

Capgras syndrome (Capgras, Jean Marie Joseph): Psychiatry. See: Chaplin; Hinsie; Jablonski.

CAPITAINE, E. fl. 1889. Engineer. (Biography source unavailable.) Capitaine engine.

Capitaine engine (Capitaine, E.): Engineering and Industry. See: Auger.

CAPLAN, ANTHONY. fl. 1953. English physician. See: Med. Register, 1952. Caplan's syndrome.

Caplan-Colinet syndrome (Caplan, Anthony and Colinet, E.). See: Caplan's syndrome.

Caplan's syndrome (Caplan, Anthony): Medicine. See: Jablonski; Stedman. Also known as: Caplan-Colinet syndrome.

Capone (Capone, Alphonse): Generic Word (mobster). See: Hendrickson.

CAPONE, ALPHONSE. 1898-1947. American gangster. See: Chambers' Biog. Dict. Capone.

Cappeau furnace (Derivation undetermined): Engineering and Industry. See: Thrush.

CAPPELEN, D. fl. 1885. Norwegian scientist. Cited in: Bailey. Cappelenite.

Cappelenite (Cappelen, D.): Earth Sciences. See: Thrush; Webster's 3d.

Cappelin-Smith process (Derivation undetermined): Engineering and Industry. See: Thrush.

CAPPER, ARTHUR. 1865-1951. American editor and legislator. See: Biog. Direct. Amer. Congress. Capper-Volstead Act.

Capper-Volstead Act (Capper, Arthur and Volstead, Andrew John): Law. See: Morris.

CAPPS, JOSEPH ALMARIN. b. 1872. American physician. See: Amer. Men Sci., 8th ed. Capp's reflex.

Capp's reflex (Capps, Joseph Almarin): Medicine. See: Dorland; Stedman.

CAPRANICA, STEFANO. fl. 1877. Italian chemist. Cited in: Royal Soc. Cat. Sci. Pap., 1874-1883; 1800-1883 (suppl.); 1884-1900. Capranica test reaction.

Capranica test reaction (Capranica, Stefano): Chemistry. See: Van Nostrand Chem. Dict.

CAPROTTI, ARTURO. 1881-1938. Italian engineer. See: Diz. Encic. Ital. Caprotti valve gear.

Caprotti valve gear (Caprotti, Arturo): Engineering and Industry. See: Auger.

Capstaff effect (Capstaff, John George): Photography. See: Internat. Dict. Phys. Elec.; Van Nostrand Sci. Encyc.

CAPSTAFF, JOHN GEORGE. 1879-1960. English-born American photography authority. See: World Who's Who Sci. Capstaff effect.

Captain Bligh (Bligh, William): Generic Word (cruel taskmaster). See: Hendrickson.

Captain Cooks (or Cookers) (Cook, James): Generic Word (wild pig). See: Brewer.

Capulet (Juliet): Fashion. See: Picken.

Capulet, Juliet. See: Juliet.

CAPURON, JOSEPH. 1767-1850. French physician. See: Biog. Lex. hervorr. Aerzte. Capuron's points.

Capuron's points (Capuron, Joseph): Medicine. See: Stedman.

CARABELLI, GEORG. 1787-1842. Hungarian dentist. See: World Who's Who Sci. Carabelli('s) tubercle.

Carabelli('s) tubercle (Carabelli, Georg): Dentistry. See: Donath; Dorland; Stedman.

Caraffa, Giovanni Pietro. See: Paul IV.

Carapella's reagent (Derivation undetermined): Chemistry. See: Thrush.

Carassini's spool (Derivation undetermined): Medicine. See: Dorland.

CARATHEODORY, CONSTANTIN. 1873-1950. German mathematician. See: Dict. Sci. Biog. Caratheodory (mathematical) theorem, Caratheodory measure, Caratheodory('s) principle, Caratheodory theorem (in optics).

Caratheodory (mathematical) theorem (Caratheodory, Constantin): Mathematics. See: Internat. Dict. Ap. Math.

Caratheodory measure (Caratheodory, Constantin): Mathematics. See: James.

Caratheodory('s) principle (Caratheodory, Constantin): Mathematics. See: Ballentyne; Internat. Dict. Ap. Math.; Thewlis.

Caratheodory theorem (in optics) (Caratheodory, Constantin): Physics. See: Internat. Dict. Ap. Math.

CARAVAGGIO, MICHELANGELO DA. 1573-1610. Italian painter. See: Encyc. Brit., 1973. Caravaggisti.

Caravaggisti (Caravaggio, Michelangelo da): Fine Arts. See: Osborne.

Carcano reaction for morphine derivatives (Derivation undetermined): Chemistry. See: Van Nostrand Chem. Dict.

CARCASSONNE, BERNARD GAUDERIC. b. 1728. French surgeon. (Biography source unavailable.) Carcassonne's ligament.

Carcassonne's ligament (Carcassonne, Bernard Gauderic); Medicine. See: Dorland.

CARCEL, BERTRAND GUILLAUME. 1750-1812. French clockmaker and inventor. See: Webster's Biog. Dict. Carcel lamp.

Carcel lamp (Carcel, Bertrand Guillaume): Engineering and Industry. See: Partridge.

Cardan, Jerome. See: Cardano, Girolamo.

Cardan joint (Cardano, Girolamo): Engineering and Industry. See: Auger. Also known as: Hooke's coupling.

Cardan-shaft (Cardano, Girolamo): Engineering and Industry. See: Carter; Partridge; Webster's 3d.

Cardan('s) suspension (Cardano, Girolamo): Engineering and Industry. See: Webster's 3d.

Cardanic (Cardano, Girolamo): Mathematics. See: Partridge.

CARDANO, GIROLAMO. 1501-1576. Italian mathematician and physician. See: Dict. Sci. Biog. Cardan joint, Cardan-shaft, Cardan('s) suspension, Cardanic, Cardan's rule, Cardan's solution.

Cardan's rule (Cardano, Girolamo): Mathematics. Cited in: World Who's Who Sci.

Cardan's solution (Cardano, Girolamo): Mathematics. See: Partridge.

Cardanus, Hieronymus. See: Cardano, Girolamo.

CARDARELLI, ANTONIO. 1831-1926. Italian physician. See: Biog. Lex. hervorr. Aerzte, 1880-1930. Cardarelli's aphthae (or disease)? Cardarelli's sign.

Cardarelli's aphthae (or disease) (Cardarelli, Antonio?). See: Riga-Fede syndrome.

Cardarelli's sign (Cardarelli, Antonio): Medicine. See: Dorland; Stedman. Also known as: Oliver-Cardarelli sign, Oliver's sign, Porter's sign.

CARDEN, HENRY DOUGLAS. d. 1872. English surgeon. See: Biog. Lex. hervorr. Aerzte. Carden's amputation.

Carden's amputation (Carden, Henry Douglas): Medicine. See: Dorland; Stedman.

Cardigan (Brudenell, James Thomas, 7th Earl of Cardigan): Fashion. See: Brewer; Funk; Hendrickson.

Cardigan, Earl of. See: Brudenell, James Thomas.

CARDIN, PIERRE. 1922- . Italian-born French designer. See: New Encyc. Brit., 1974, Microp. Cardin's helmet?

Cardin's helmet (Cardin, Pierre?): Fashion. See: Picken.

Cardwell army system (Cardwell, Edward): History. See: Montgomery.

CARDWELL, EDWARD. 1813-1886. English statesman and military reformer. See: Dict. Nat. Biog. Cardwell army system.

Careme (Careme, Marie Antoine): Generic Word (great chef). See: Hendrickson.

CAREME, MARIE ANTOINE. 1784-1833. French chef. See: Nouv. Biog. Univ. Careme.

Carey Act (Carey, Joseph Maull): Law. See: Morris; Smith; Winburne.

Carey Coombs. See: Coombs, Carey.

Carey Coombs murmur (Coombs, Carey Franklin): Medicine. See: Stedman. Also known as: Coombs murmur.

Carey-Foster. See: Foster, George Carey.

Carey-Foster bridge (Foster, George Carey?): Physics. See: Hughes; Internat. Dict. Phys. Elec.; Markus. Also known as: Heydweiller bridge.

Carey-Foster method of calibration (Foster, George Carey?): Physics. See: Internat. Dict. Phys. Elec.

CAREY, HENRY CHARLES. 1793-1879. American economist. See: Internat. Encyc. Soc. Sci. Carey's law of individuality.

CAREY, JOSEPH MAULL. 1845-1924. American legislator. See: Biog. Direct. Amer. Congress. Carey Act.

Carey's law of individuality (Carey, Henry Charles): Sociology. See: Zadrozny.

CARGILE, CHARLES HASTINGS. 1853-1930. American surgeon. See: Who's Who Amer. Med. Cargile membrane.

Cargile membrane (Cargile, Charles Hastings): Medicine. See: Dorland.

Carhart-Clark cell (Carhart, Henry Smith and Clark, Josiah Latimer): Physics. Cited in: Webster's Biog. Dict.

CARHART, HENRY SMITH. 1844-1920. American physicist. See: World Who's Who Sci. Carhart-Clark cell.

Caricum (Caricus): Medicine. See: Charnock.

CARICUS. No dates. Inventor of ointment for ulcers. (Biography source unavailable.) Caricum.

CARINI, ANTONINO. 1872-1950. Italian physician. See: New York Acad. Med. Portrait Cat. Carini's syndrome.

Carini's syndrome (Carini, Antonino): Medicine. See: Jablonski. Also known as: Seeligmann's disease.

Carius furnace (Carius, Ludwig): Chemistry. See: Hackh; Van Nostrand Chem. Dict.

CARIUS, LUDWIG. 1829-1875. German chemist. See: Pogg., vol. 3. Carius furnace, Carius method.

Carius method (Carius, Ludwig): Chemistry. See: Van Nostrand Chem. Dict.; Webster's 3d.

Carl d'or (Karl Wilhelm Ferdinand): Numismatics. See: Charnock.

CARL, G. P. fl. 1939. American psychologist. Cited in: Psych. Abstr., 1939. Carl hollow-square test.

Carl hollow-square test (Carl, G. P.): Psychology. See: English.

Carl Smith's disease (Smith, Carl Henry). See: Smith's disease.

CARLEMAN, TAGE GILLIS TORSTEN. 1892-1949. Swedish mathematician. See: Pogg., vols. 5, 6, 7b. Carleman's criterion.

Carleman's criterion (Carleman, Tage Gillis Torsten): Statistics. See: Kendall.

Carlen's catheter (Carlens, Eric): Medicine. See: Stedman.

CARLENS, ERIC. 1908- . Swedish physician. (Biography source unavailable.) Carlen's catheter.

CARLETON, BUKK G. 1856-1914. American surgeon. See: Who Was Who Amer., vol. 1. Carleton's spots.

Carleton's spots (Carleton, Bukk G.): Medicine. See: Dorland; Jablonski.

CARLETTI, OTTORINO. fl. 1907-1930. Italian chemist. Cited in: Chem. Abstr., vol. 1, p. 1458; vol. 5, p. 1244; vol. 24, p. 4481. Carletti solutions for mineral acids, Carletti test for alpha-naphthol, Carletti test for menthol, eucalyptol, and thymol? Carletti test reaction for pyrogallol.

Carletti solutions for mineral acids (Carletti, Ottorino): Chemistry. See: Van Nostrand Chem. Dict.

Carletti test for alpha-naphthol (Carletti, Ottorino): Chemistry. See: Van Nostrand Chem. Dict.

Carletti test for menthol, eucalyptol, and thymol (Carletti, Ottorino?): Chemistry. See: Van Nostrand Chem. Dict.

Carletti test reaction for pyrogallol (Carletti, Ottorino): Chemistry. See: Van Nostrand Chem. Dict.

Carley float (or raft) (Carley, Horace S.): Engineering and Industry. See: Hendrickson; Partridge.

CARLEY, HORACE S. fl. 1899. American designer and decorator. (Biography source unavailable.) Carley float (or raft).

CARLI, GIOVANNI RINALDO. 1720-1795. Italian economist and antiquary. See: Webster's Biog. Dict. Carli's index.

Carlina (or Carline) (Charlemagne): Botany. See: Charnock.

Carlino (Carline, or Caroline) (Charles I): Numismatics. See: Charnock; Partridge; Webster's 3d.

Carli's index (Carli, Giovanni Rinaldo): Statistics. See: Kendall.

CARLISLE, RICHARD RISLEY. d. 1874. American gymnast and circus performer. See: New York Times, May 27, 1874, p. 1, col. 4. Risley act.

Carlists (Carlos, Don): History. See: Brewer; Harbottle; Latham.

CARLOS, DON. 1788-1855. Infante of Spain and Pretender. See: Encyc. Brit., 1911. Carlists.

Carlovingians (or Carolingians) (Charlemagne): History. See: Brewer; Weekley.

Carl's solution (Derivation undetermined): Chemistry. See: Hackh.

Carlson compass (Derivation undetermined): Engineering and Industry. See: Thrush.

CARLSON, EVANS FORDYCE. 1896-1947. American marine officer. See: Encyc. Brit., 1973. Carlson's Raiders.

Carlson's Raiders (Carlson, Evans Fordyce): History. Cited in: Encyc. Brit., 1973.

Carludovica (Charles IV): Botany. See: Charnock; Webster's 3d.

CARLYLE, THOMAS. 1795-1881. Scottish essayist and historian. See: Dict. Nat. Biog. Carlylese (Carlylism or Carlylean).

Carlylese (Carlylism or Carlylean) (Carlyle, Thomas): Literature. See: Partridge; Webster's 3d.

Carmack Act (Carmack, Edward Ward): Law. See: Black.

CARMACK, EDWARD WARD. 1858-1908. American prohibitionist and legislator. See: Dict. Amer. Biog. Carmack Act.

Carman equation (Carman, Philip Crosbie): Chemistry. See: Thrush.

CARMAN, PHILIP CROSBIE. fl. 1938-1949. English chemist. Cited in: Chem. Abstr., vol. 32, p. 8239. Carman equation.

Carmathians (Hamdan Karmat). See: Karmatians (or Karmatis).

Carmichael crown (Carmichael, John P.): Dentistry. See: Dorland; Stedman.

CARMICHAEL, DUGALD. 1772-1827. Scottish botanist. See: Biog. Notes Upon Botanists. Carmichaelia.

CARMICHAEL, JOHN P. 1856-1946. American dentist. Cited in: New York Acad. Med. Portrait Cat. Carmichael crown.

Carmichaelia (Carmichael, Dugald): Botany. See: Taylor, N.

Carmichel-Bradford process (Derivation undetermined): Engineering and Industry. See: Thrush.

CARNALL, RUDOLF VON. 1804-1874. German mining engineer. See: Dict. Sci. Biog. Carnallite.

Carnallite (Carnall, Rudolf von): Earth Sciences. See: Thrush; Webster's 3d.

Carnarvon, 4th Earl of. See: Herbert, Henry (4th Earl of Carnarvon).

Carnarvon controversy (Herbert, Henry Howard Molyneux, 4th Earl of Carnarvon): History. See: Montgomery.

CARNEGIE, ANDREW. 1835-1919. Scottish-born American industrialist. See: Dict. Amer. Biog. Carnegie library, Carnegie medal, Carnegiea (cactus), Carnegieite.

CARNEGIE, HATTIE. 1889-1956. Austrian-born American designer. See: Who Was Who Amer., vol. 3. Carnegie look.

Carnegie library (Carnegie, Andrew): Library Science. See: Good.

Carnegie look (Carnegie, Hattie): Fashion. See: Picken.

Carnegie medal (Carnegie, Andrew): Literature. See: Harrod.

Carnegiea (cactus) (Carnegie, Andrew): Botany. See: Hendrickson; Mathews, M. M.; Webster's 3d.

Carnegieite (Carnegie, Andrew): Earth Sciences. See: Thrush; Webster's 3d.

CARNET, JULES. b. 1830. French physician. (Biography source unavailable.) Carnett's sign?

Carnett's sign (Carnet, Jules?): Medicine. See: Stedman.

Carney reagent (Carney, Robert John): Chemistry. See: Van Nostrand Chem. Dict.

CARNEY, ROBERT JOHN. b. 1884. American chemist. See: Amer. Men Sci., 3-8 eds. Carney reagent.

CARNOCHAN, JOHN MURRAY. 1817-1887. American surgeon. See: Dict. Amer. Biog. Carnochan's operation.

Carnochan's operation (Carnochan, John Murray): Medicine. See: Dorland.

Carnot('s) cycle (Carnot, Nicolas Leonard Sadi): Physics. See: Auger; Ballentyne; Internat. Dict. Ap. Math.

Carnot efficiency (Carnot, Nicolas Leonard Sadi): Physics. See: Huschke.

Carnot engine (Carnot, Nicolas Leonard Sadi): Engineering and Industry. See: Huschke; Webster's 3d.

Carnot('s) function (Carnot, Nicolas Leonard Sadi): Physics. See: Hackh; Thrush.

CARNOT, LAZARE NICOLAS MARGUERITE. 1753-1823. French military engineer and mathematician. See: Dict. Sci. Biog. Carnot's wall.

CARNOT, MARIE-ADOLPHE. 1839-1920. French mining engineer and chemist. See: World Who's Who Sci. Carnot reaction for potassium, Carnot test for cobalt, Carnotite.

CARNOT, NICOLAS LEONARD SADI. 1796-1832. French physicist. See: Dict. Sci. Biog. Carnot('s) cycle, Carnot efficiency, Carnot engine, Carnot('s) function, Carnot('s) theorem, Carnotization, Carnot's law.

CARNOT, PAUL. b. 1869. French physician. See: Biog. Lex. hervorr. Aerzte, 1880-1930. Carnot's solution, Carnot's test.

Carnot reaction for potassium (Carnot, Marie Adolphe): Chemistry. See: Van Nostrand Chem. Dict.

Carnot test for cobalt (Carnot, Marie Adolphe): Chemistry. See: Van Nostrand Chem. Dict.

Carnot('s) theorem (Carnot, Nicolas Leonard Sadi): Physics. See: Ballentyne; Internat. Dict. Ap. Math.; Internat. Dict. Phys. Elec.

Carnotite (Carnot, Marie-Adolphe): Earth Sciences. See: Thrush; Van Nostrand Sci. Encyc.; Webster's 3d.

Carnotization (Carnot, Nicolas Leonard Sadi): Physics. See: Internat. Dict. Ap. Math.

Carnot's law (Carnot, Nicolas Leonard Sadi): Physics. See: Webster's 3d.

Carnot's solution (Carnot, Paul): Medicine. See: Dorland.

Carnot's test (Carnot, Paul): Medicine. See: Dorland.

Carnot's wall (Carnot, Lazare Nicolas Marguerite): Engineering and Industry. Cited in: World Who's Who Sci.

Carnoy hardening solution (Carnoy, Jean Baptiste?): Chemistry. See: Van Nostrand Chem. Dict.

CARNOY, JEAN BAPTISTE. 1836-1899. Belgian-born biologist. See: World Who's Who Sci. Carnoy hardening solution? Carnoy-Le Brun fluid, Carnoy's fluid.

Carnoy-Le Brun fluid (Carnoy, Jean Baptiste and Lebrun, Hector): Chemistry. See: Van Nostrand Chem. Dict.

Carnoy's fluid (Carnoy, Jean Baptiste): Chemistry. See: Dorland; Hackh; Stedman.

CARO, HEINRICH. 1834-1910. German chemist. See: Dict. Sci. Biog. Caro reagent? Caro test for persulfate ion? Caro test for sulfide? Caro's acid.

Caro reagent (Caro, Heinrich?): Chemistry. See: Van Nostrand Chem. Dict.

Caro test for persulfate ion (Caro, Heinrich?): Chemistry. See: Van Nostrand Chem. Dict.

Caro test for sulfide (Caro, Heinrich?): Chemistry. See: Van Nostrand Chem. Dict.

Carobbio test for zinc or resorcinol (Derivation undetermined): Chemistry. See: Van Nostrand Chem. Dict.

CAROL, WILLEM LAMBERTUS LEONARD. 1879-1945. Dutch physician. Cited in: New York Acad. Med. Portrait Cat. Godfried-Prick-Carol-Prakken syndrome.

Carolath, Prince. See: Schoenaich-Carolath, Emil Rudolf Osman, prinz von.

Carolathine (Schoenaich-Carolath, Emil Rudolf Osman, prinz von): Earth Sciences. See: Charnock.

CAROLI, JACQUES. 1902-   . French physician. See: Who's Who France, 1975-1976. Caroli's disease.

Carolin (1) (Charles XI): Numismatics. See: Webster's 3d.

Carolin (2) (Carolin d'or or Karolin) (Charles VII): Numismatics. See: Charnock; Webster's 3d.

Caroline (Charles I): Literature. See: Barnet; Harvey; Partridge.

Caroline books (Charlemagne): Religion. See: Mathews, S.

Caroline minuscule (Charlemagne): Literature. See: Harvey.

Caroline Ordinance (Charles V): History. See: Harbottle.

Carolinea (Sophia Caroline): Botany. See: Charnock.

Carolingians (Charlemagne). See: Carlovingians.

Caroli's disease (Caroli, Jacques): Medicine. See: Jablonski.

Carolus (Charles I): Numismatics. See: Brewer; Charnock; Partridge.

Carolus Magnus. See: Charlemagne.

CARON, HENRI. fl. 1919-1947. French chemist. Cited in: Chem. Abstr., vol. 13, p. 1435. Caron-Raquet test for manganese, Caron solution.

Caron-Raquet test for manganese (Caron, Henri and Raquet, D.): Chemistry. See: Van Nostrand Chem. Dict.

Caron solution (Caron, Henri): Chemistry. See: Van Nostrand Chem. Dict.

CARONIA, GIUSEPPE. b. 1884. Italian pediatrician. See: Biog. Lex. hervorr. Aerzte, 1880-1930. Caronia's organism.

Caronia's organism (Caronia, Giuseppe): Medicine. See: Dorland.

Caro's acid (Caro, Heinrich): Chemistry. See: Hackh; Webster's 3d.

CARPENE, ANTONIO. 1838-1902. Italian chemist. See: Diz. Encic. Ital. Carpene solution.

Carpene solution (Carpene, Antonio): Chemistry. See: Van Nostrand Chem. Dict.

CARPENTER, GEORGE ALFRED. 1859-1910. English physician. See: Dict. Nat. Biog., 2nd suppl. Carpenter's syndrome.

CARPENTER, SAMUEL D. fl. 1890. American inventor. (Biography source unavailable.) Carpenter typesetting machine.

Carpenter typesetting machine (Carpenter, Samuel D.): Printing. See: Lockwood.

CARPENTER, WILLIAM MARBURY. 1811-1848. American physician and botanist. See: Biog. Notes Upon Botanists. Carpenteria.

Carpenteria (Carpenter, William Marbury): Botany. See: Mathews, M. M.; Webster's 3d.

Carpenter's syndrome (Carpenter, George Alfred): Medicine. See: Jablonski.

CARPENTIER, G. fl. 1921. French chemist. Cited in: Chem. Abstr., vol. 16, p. 538. Thomas-Carpentier reagent.

CARPOCRATES. fl. 2nd c. A.D. Alexandrian Gnostic. See: Encyc. Brit., 1911. Carpocratian(s).

Carpocratian(s) (Carpocrates): Religion. See: Canney; Latham; Webster's 3d.

CARPUE, JOSEPH CONSTANTINE. 1764-1846. English surgeon. See: Dict. Nat. Biog. Carpue's method.

Carpue's method (Carpue, Joseph Constantine): Medicine. See: Dorland; Stedman.

CARR, FRANCIS HOWARD. 1874- . English chemist. See: World Who's Who Sci. Carr-Price reagent, Carr-Price tests (for vitamin A).

Carr-Price reagent (Carr, Francis Howard and Price, E.A.): Chemistry. See: Van Nostrand Chem. Dict.

Carr-Price tests (for vitamin A) (Carr, Francis Howard and Price, E. A.): Chemistry. See: Dorland; Stedman; Van Nostrand Chem. Dict.

CARR-SAUNDERS, ALEXANDER M. 1886- . English educator. See: Internat. Encyc. Soc. Sci. Carr-Saunders theory of population growth.

Carr-Saunders theory of population growth (Carr-Saunders, Alexander M.): Sociology. See: Zadrozny.

CARRARA, GIACOMO. 1864-1925. Italian chemist. See: Pogg., vols. 4-6. Carrara test.

Carrara test (Carrara, Giacomo): Chemistry. See: Van Nostrand Chem. Dict.

CARRE, FERDINAND P. E. 1824-1900. French inventor. See: World Who's Who Sci. Carre machine.

CARRE, H. fl. 1905. French veterinarian. (Biography source unavailable.) Carre's disease.

Carre machine (Carre, Ferdinand P. E.): Engineering and Industry. See: Auger.

CARREL, ALEXIS. 1873-1944. French surgeon and biologist. See: Dict. Sci. Biog. Carrel-Dakin solution, Carrel-Lindbergh pump, Carrel's method, Carrel's mixture, Carrel's treatment.

Carrel-Dakin solution (Carrel, Alexis and Dakin, Henry Drysdale): Chemistry. See: Hackh; Van Nostrand Chem. Dict.; Webster's 3d.

Carrel-Dakin treatment (Carrel, Alexis and Dakin, Henry Drysdale): See: Carrel's treatment.

Carrel-Lindbergh pump (Carrel, Alexis and Lindbergh, Charles Augustus): Medicine. See: Stedman.

Carrel's method (Carrel, Alexis): Medicine. See: Dorland.

Carrel's mixture (Carrel, Alexis): Medicine. See: Dorland; Stedman.

Carrel's treatment (Carrel, Alexis): Medicine. See: Dorland; Stedman. Also known as: Carrel-Dakin treatment, Dakin-Carrel treatment.

Carre's disease (Carre, H.): Medicine. See: Jablonski; Stedman.

CARREZ, CYRILLE. fl. 1909. French physician. Cited in: Kelly. Carrez reagent?

Carrez reagent (Carrez, Cyrille?): Chemistry. See: Van Nostrand Chem. Dict.

Carrick, John Stewart, Earl of. See: Robert III.

Carrier density (Carrier, George Francis?): Physics. See: Internat. Dict. Ap. Math.

CARRIER, GEORGE FRANCIS. 1918- . American engineer. See: World Who's Who Sci. Carrier density?

CARRION, DANIEL A. 1850-1886. Peruvian medical student. See: World Who's Who Sci. Carrion's disease (or fever).

Carrion's disease (or fever) (Carrion, Daniel A.): Medicine. See: Dorland; Jablonski; Stedman.

carry a message to Garcia (Iniguez, Garcia): Generic Word (fulfill a task). See: Mathews, M. M. under "Garcia."

Carry Nation (Nation, Carry Amelia Moore): Generic Word (intolerant temperance agitator). See: Hendrickson.

CARSON, CHRISTOPHER ("KIT"). 1809-1868. American trapper, scout, and Indian agent. See: Dict. Amer. Biog. Kit Carson hitch.

CARSWELL, SIR ROBERT. 1793-1857. English physician. See: Dict. Nat. Biog. Carswell's grapes.

Carswell's grapes (Carswell, Sir Robert): Medicine. See: Dorland; Stedman.

CARTEAUD, ALEXANDRE. 1897- . French physician. (Biography source unavailable.) Gougerot-Carteaud syndrome (or papillomatosis).

CARTER. No dates. American farmer. (Biography source unavailable.) Carter's oats.

CARTER, HENRY VANDYKE. 1831-1907. English-born physician. See: World Who's Who Sci. Carter's black mycetoma, Carter's fever.

CARTER, NICK. Fictional character invented by John R. Coryell (1848-1924). See: Benet. Nick Carter.

CARTER, WILLIAM WESLEY. b. 1869. American plastic surgeon, rhinolaryngologist, and otologist. See: Who's Who Amer. Med. Carter's operation, Carter's splint.

Carter's black mycetoma (Carter, Henry Vandyke): Medicine. See: Stedman.

Carter's fever (Carter, Henry Vandyke): Medicine. See: Dorland; Stedman.

Carter's oats (Carter): Generic Word (exaggerated comparison). See: Mathews, M. M.

Carter's operation (Carter, William Wesley): Medicine. See: Dorland.

Carter's splint (Carter, William Wesley): Medicine. See: Dorland.

Cartesian control (Descartes, Rene du Perron): Physics. See: Markus.

Cartesian coordinate(s) (Descartes, Rene du Perron): Physics. See: Hoult; Huschke; Internat. Dict. Phys. Elec.

Cartesian diver (Descartes, Rene du Perron): Biology. See: Pennak; Webster's 3d.

Cartesian dualism (Descartes, Rene du Perron): Philosophy. See: Morris and Irwin.

Cartesian equation (Descartes, Rene du Perron): Mathematics. See: Webster's 3d.

Cartesian linguistics (Descartes, Rene du Perron): Linguistics. See: Hartmann.

Cartesian oval (Descartes, Rene du Perron): Physics. See: Internat. Dict. Phys. Elec.; Thewlis.

Cartesian (philosophy) (Descartes, Rene du Perron): Philosophy. See: Brewer; Hendrickson; Phyfe.

Cartesian surfaces (Descartes, Rene du Perron): Mathematics. See: Internat. Dict. Ap. Math.

Cartesian tensor (field) (Descartes, Rene du Perron): Mathematics. See: Huschke; Internat. Dict. Ap. Math.; Van Nostrand Sci. Encyc.

Cartesian vector field (Descartes, Rene du Perron): Mathematics. See: Internat. Dict. Ap. Math.

Cartesianism (Descartes, Rene du Perron): Philosophy. See: Attwater; Good; Mathews, S.

Cartier scale (Derivation undetermined): Chemistry. See: Hackh.

cartilage of Santorini (Santorini, Giovanni Domenico). See: Santorini's cartilage.

cartilage of Wrisberg (Wrisberg, Heinrich August). See: Wrisberg's cartilage.

CARTOUCHE (LOUIS DOMINIQUE BOURGUIGNON). 1693-1721. French bandit. See: Webster's Biog. Dict. Cartouche.

Cartouche (Cartouche, the bandit): Generic Word (criminal). Cited in: Webster's Biog. Dict.

CARTWRIGHT, EDMUND. 1743-1823. English inventor. See: Dict. Nat. Biog. Cartwright's parallel motion.

CARTWRIGHT, WILBURN. b. 1892. American legislator. See: Biog. Direct. Amer. Congress. Hayden-Cartwright Act.

Cartwright's parallel motion (Cartwright, Edmund): Engineering and Industry. See: Auger.

CARUS, CARL GUSTAV. 1789-1869. German physiologist. See: World Who's Who Sci. Carus' curve (or circle).

Carus' curve (or circle) (Carus, Carl Gustav): Medicine. See: Dorland; Stedman.

CARUSO, ENRICO. 1873-1921. Italian vocalist. See: Dict. Amer. Biog. sauce Caruso, touch of Caruso.

CARVALLO, EMMANUEL. 1856-1945. French physicist. See: Pogg., vols. 4, 5, 6, 7b. Carvallo paradox.

Carvallo paradox (Carvallo, Emmanuel): Physics. See: Internat. Dict. Phys. Elec.; Van Nostrand Sci. Encyc.

Carvallo's sign (Derivation undetermined): Medicine. See: Stedman.

Carver chair (Carver, John): Applied Arts. See: Hendrickson; Mathews, M.M.

CARVER, HARRY CLYDE. b. 1890. American mathematical statistician. See: Amer. Men Sci., 6th ed. Ord-Carver system.

CARVER, JOHN. 1576-1621. English colonial governor in America. See: Dict. Nat. Biog. Carver chair.

Cary rebellion (Cary, Thomas): History. See: Jameson.

CARY, THOMAS. fl. 1711. American conspirator. Cited in: Encyc. Amer., 1959, under "Cary's Rebellion." Cary rebellion.

Casabona. See: Benincasa, Giuseppe.

CASAGRANDE, ARTHUR. 1902- . Austrian-born American civil engineer. See: Amer. Men Sci., 9th ed. Casagrande liquid limit apparatus.

Casagrande liquid limit apparatus (Casagrande, Arthur): Engineering and Industry. See: Thrush.

CASAL, GASPAR. 1691-1759. Spanish physician. See: World Who's Who Sci. Casal's necklace.

CASALA, AUGUSTO M. fl. 1955. Argentinian physician. (Biography source unavailable.) Casala-Mosto disease.

Casala-Mosto disease (Casala, Augusto M. and Mosto, Santiago J.): Medicine. See: Jablonski.

CASALE, LUIGI. 1882-1927. Italian chemist. See: Diz. Encic. Ital. Casale process.

Casale process (Casale, Luigi): Chemistry. See: Van Nostrand Chem. Dict.; Webster's 3d.

Casal's necklace (Casal, Gaspar): Medicine. See: Dorland; Jablonski; Stedman.

Casanova (Casanova, Giovanni Jacopo): Generic Word (promiscuity). See: Brewer; Hendrickson; Partridge.

CASANOVA, CARLO. fl. 1912. Italian chemist. Cited in: Chem. Abstr., vol. 6, p. 1013. Casanova test reaction.

CASANOVA, GIOVANNI JACOPO. 1725-1798. Italian adventurer. See: Webster's Biog. Dict. Casanova.

Casanova test reaction (Casanova, Carlo): Chemistry. See: Van Nostrand Chem. Dict.

CASARES-LOPEZ, ROMAN. fl. 1936. Spanish chemist. See: Who's Who Sci. Europe, 1967. Casares test.

Casares test (Casares-Lopez, Roman): Chemistry. See: Van Nostrand Chem. Dict.

CASAS Y ARARGORRI, LUIS DE LAS. 1745-1800. Spanish soldier. See: Encic. Univ. Ilus. Casasia.

Casasia (Casas y Arargorri, Luis de las): Botany. See: Webster's 3d.

CASATI, GABRIO. 1798-1873. Italian statesman. See: Nouv. Biog. Univ. Casati Law.

Casati Law (Casati, Gabrio): Education. See: Morris and Irwin.

Casearia (Casearius, Johannes): Botany. See: Webster's 3d.

CASEARIUS, JOHANNES. d. 1678. Dutch clergyman. See: Biog. Notes Upon Botanists. Casearia.

CASENEUVE, M. fl. 1923. French chemist. Cited in: Chem. Abstr., vol. 18, p. 208. Caseneuve test reactions.

Caseneuve test reactions (Caseneuve, M.): Chemistry. See: Van Nostrand Chem. Dict.

Casey cookie (Casey, Hugh J.): Weapons. See: Quick.

CASEY, HUGH J. d. 1961. American army officer. See: New York Times, Ap. 18, 1961, p. 37, col. 4. Casey cookie.

Casimir-Du Pre theory of spin-lattice relaxation (Casimir, Hendrik B. G. and Du Pre, Frits Karel): Physics. See: Internat. Dict. Phys. Elec.

CASIMIR, HENDRIK B. G. 1909- . Dutch physicist. See: World Who's Who Sci. Casimir-Du Pre theory of spin-lattice relaxation.

Casimiroa (Ortega, Casimiro Gomez de): Botany. See: Taylor, N.; Webster's 3d.

Caslick's operation (Derivation undetermined): Medicine. See: Stedman.

Caslon (type) (Caslon, William): Printing. See: Harrod; Lockwood; Partridge.

CASLON, WILLIAM. 1692-1766. English type founder. See: Dict. Nat. Biog. Caslon (type).

CASOLARI, ANGELO ARMANDO. b. 1878. Italian chemist. See: Pogg., vol. 6. Casolori reactions for peroxidase, Casolori solution for thiosulfate.

Casolori reactions for peroxidase (Casolari, Angelo Armando): Chemistry. See: Van Nostrand Chem. Dict.

Casolori solution for thiosulfate (Casolari, Angelo Armando): Chemistry. See: Van Nostrand Chem. Dict.

CASONI, TOMASO. 1880-1933. Italian physician. See: New York Acad. Med. Portrait Cat. Casoni's reaction.

Casoni's reaction (Casoni, Tomaso): Medicine. See: Dorland; Stedman.

Casparian band (or strip) (Caspary, Johann Xavier Robert): Botany. See: Henderson; Webster's 3d.

Casparis reagent (Derivation undetermined): Chemistry. See: Van Nostrand Chem. Dict.

CASPARY, JOHANN XAVIER ROBERT. 1818-1887. German botanist. See: Allg. Deut. Biog. Casparian band (or strip).

CASS. fl. 1887. English dressmaker. (Biography source unavailable.) Cass case.

Cass case (Cass): History. See: Montgomery.

CASS, JOHN W. fl. 1937. American obstetrician. (Biography source unavailable.) Meigs-Cass syndrome.

CASS, LEWIS. 1782-1866. American lawyer. See: Dict. Amer. Biog. Cassism (or Cassite).

Cassal-Gorraus test reaction (Derivation undetermined): Chemistry. See: Van Nostrand Chem. Dict.

CASSANDRA. Mythical Greek prophetess. See: Encyc. Brit., 1973. Cassandra.

Cassandra (Cassandra, the prophetess): Generic Word (unheeded prophetess). See: Brewer; Partridge; Weekley.

Cassegrain antenna (Cassegrain, Giovanni D.): Electronics. See: Hughes; Markus.

CASSEGRAIN, GIOVANNI D. 1625-1712. French physician and astronomer. See: World Who's Who Sci. Cassegrain antenna, Cassegrain-Newtonian telescope, Cassegrain (or Cassegrainian) telescope, Cassegrainian mirror, Herschel-Cassegrain telescope, Schmidt-Cassegrain telescope.

Cassegrain-Newtonian telescope (Cassegrain, Giovanni D. and Newton, Sir Isaac): Physics. See: Satterthwaite.

Cassegrain (or Cassegrainian) telescope (Cassegrain, Giovanni D.): Physics. See: Internat. Dict. Phys. Elec.; Satterthwaite; Thewlis.

Cassegrainian mirror (Cassegrain, Giovanni D.): Physics. See: Huschke.

CASSEL, E. F. fl. 19th c. American engineer. (Biography source unavailable.) Cassel water wheel.

Cassel water wheel (Cassel, E. F.): Engineering and Industry. See: Auger.

Casselberry position (Casselberry, William Evans): Medicine. See: Dorland; Stedman.

CASSELBERRY, WILLIAM EVANS. 1858-1916. American laryngologist. See: Who Was Who Amer., vol. 1. Casselberry position.

CASSELMANN. fl. 1890. German chemist. (Biography source unavailable.) Casselmann's green.

Casselmann's green (Casselmann): Chemistry. See: Webster's 3d.

CASSERI, GIULIO. ca. 1552-1616. Italian anatomist. See: Dict. Sci. Biog. Casserian (ganglion), Casserio's (Casser's) muscle (or perforated muscle), Casserio's (Casser's) nerve (or perforating nerve), Casser's fontanelle.

Casserian (ganglion) (Casseri, Giulio): Anatomy. See: Charnock.

Casserio's (Casser's) muscle (or perforated muscle) (Casseri, Giulio): Anatomy. See: Donath; Stedman.

Casserio's (Casser's) nerve (or perforating nerve) (Casseri, Giulio): Anatomy. See: Donath; Stedman.

Casserius, Julius. See: Casseri, Giulio.

Casser's fontanelle (Casseri, Giulio): Anatomy. See: Stedman.

Cassianism (Cassianus, Joannes Massiliensis): Religion. See: Charnock.

CASSIANUS, JOANNES MASSILIENSIS. ca. 350-ca. 433. French hermit and theologian. See: Encyc. Brit., 1973. Cassianism.

CASSIDY, MAURICE ALAN. fl. 1901-1930. English physician. See: Who's Who, 1930. Cassidy's syndrome.

Cassidy-Scholte syndrome (Cassidy, Maurice Alan and Scholte, A. J.). See: Cassidy's syndrome.

Cassidy's syndrome (Cassidy, Maurice Alan): Medicine. See: Jablonski. Also known as: Biorck-Thorson syndrome, Biorck's syndrome, Cassidy-Scholte syndrome, Hedinger's syndrome, Scholte's syndrome.

Cassin('s) finch (purple finch or pine finch) (Cassin, John): Zoology. See: Mathews, M. M.; Webster's 3d.

CASSIN, JOHN. 1813-1869. American ornithologist. See: Dict. Amer. Biog. Cassin('s) finch (purple finch or pine finch), Cassinite, Cassin's auklet, Cassin's flycatcher, Cassin's jay, Cassin's kingbird, Cassin's sparrow, Cassin's vireo.

Cassini('s) division (Cassini, Gian Domenico): Astronomy. See: Asimov; Satterthwaite.

CASSINI, GIAN DOMENICO. 1625-1712. Italian-born French astronomer. See: Dict. Sci. Biog. Cassini('s) division, oval(s) of Cassini (or Cassinian oval).

Cassinian oval (Cassini, Gian Domenico). See: oval(s) of Cassini.

Cassinite (Cassin, John): Earth Sciences. See: Thrush.

Cassin's auklet (Cassin, John): Zoology. See: Gray; Webster's 3d.

Cassin's flycatcher (Cassin, John): Zoology. See: Mathews, M. M.

Cassin's jay (Cassin, John): Zoology. See: Mathews, M. M.

Cassin's kingbird (Cassin, John): Zoology. See: Mathews, M. M.; Webster's 3d.

Cassin's sparrow (Cassin, John): Zoology. See: Gray.

Cassin's vireo (Cassin, John): Zoology. See: Mathews, M. M.

Cassiope (Cassiopeia): Botany. See: Taylor, I.

CASSIOPEIA. Greek deity of night. See: Jobes. Cassiope.

CASSIRER, RICHARD. 1868-1925. German neurologist. See: World Who's Who Sci. Cassirer's syndrome.

Cassirer's syndrome (Cassirer, Richard): Medicine. See: Jablonski.

Cassism (or Cassite) (Cass, Lewis): History. See: Mathews, M. M.

CASSIUS, ANDREAS. ca. 1605-1673. Danish-born German physician and chemist. See: World Who's Who Sci. purple of Cassius (or Cassius purple).

Cassius purple (Cassius, Andreas). See: purple of Cassius.

CASTAIGNE, JOSEPH. 1871-1951. French physician. See: New York Acad. Med. Portrait Cat. Achard-Castaigne method.

Castaigne method (Castaigne, Joseph). See: Achard-Castaigne method.

Castellana test for borates (Derivation undetermined): Chemistry. See: Van Nostrand Chem. Dict.

Castellanella (Castellani, Marquis Aldo): Medicine. See: Dorland; Stedman.

Castellani-Low sign (Castellani, Marquis Aldo and Low, George Carmichael): Medicine. See: Dorland; Stedman.

CASTELLANI, MARQUIS ALDO. 1879- . Italian-born physician. See: World Who's Who Sci. Castellanella, Castellani-Low sign, Castellania, Castellani's absorption test, Castellani's bronchitis, Castellani's mixture, Castellani's paint, Castellani's syndrome.

Castellani test for sucrose in milk (Derivation undetermined): Chemistry. See: Van Nostrand Chem. Dict.

Castellania (Castellani, Marquis Aldo): Medicine. See: Dorland; Stedman.

Castellani's absorption test (Castellani, Marquis Aldo): Medicine. See: Dorland; Stedman.

Castellani's bronchitis (Castellani, Marquis Aldo): Medicine. See: Dorland; Jablonski; Stedman.

Castellani's mixture (Castellani, Marquis Aldo): Medicine. See: Dorland.

Castellani's paint (Castellani, Marquis Aldo): Medicine. See: Dorland; Stedman; Webster's 3d.

Castellani's syndrome (Castellani, Marquis Aldo): Medicine. See: Jablonski.

Castellanos powder (Derivation undetermined): Engineering and Industry. See: Thrush.

CASTETS, J. fl. 1916. French chemist. Cited in: Chem. Abstr., vol. 10, p. 1486. Castets test reaction.

Castets test reaction (Castets, J.): Chemistry. See: Van Nostrand Chem. Dict.

CASTIGLIANO, (CARLO) ALBERTO. 1847-1884. Italian engineer. See: Dict. Sci. Biog. Castigliano('s) theorem(s).

Castigliano('s) theorem(s) (Castigliano, Carlo Alberto): Engineering and Industry. See: Ballentyne; Internat. Dict. Ap. Math.; Webster's 3d.

CASTIGLIONI, ANGELO. 1905- . Italian chemist. See: Diz. Encic. Ital. Castiglioni test for peroxide in ether, Castiglioni test for pyridine, Castiglioni test reactions for nitrite.

Castiglioni test for peroxide in ether (Castiglioni, Angelo): Chemistry. See: Van Nostrand Chem. Dict.

Castiglioni test for pyridine (Castiglioni, Angelo): Chemistry. See: Van Nostrand Chem. Dict.

Castiglioni test reactions for nitrite (Castiglioni, Angelo): Chemistry. See: Van Nostrand Chem. Dict.

Castilleja (or Castilleia) (Castillejo, Domingo): Botany. See: Taylor, N.; Webster's 3d.

CASTILLEJO, DOMINGO. No dates. Spanish botanist. See: Biog. Notes Upon Botanists. Castilleja (or Castilleia).

Castillite (Castillo, Antonio del?): Earth Sciences. See: Thrush.

CASTILLO, ANTONIO DEL. 1820-1895. Mexican mineralogist. Cited in: Bailey. Castillite?

Castillo, E. B. del. See: Del Castillo, E. B.

CASTILLO, JUAN DIEGO DEL. 1745-1793. Mexican botanist. See: Biog. Notes Upon Botanists. Castilloa (or Castilla).

Castilloa (or Castilla) (Castillo, Juan Diego del): Botany. See: Hendrickson; Taylor, N.; Webster's 3d.

CASTLE, IRENE. 1893-1969. American dancer. See: Webster's Biog. Dict. Irene Castle bob.

CASTLE, VERNON BLYTHE. 1887-1918. American dancer and aviator. See: Dict. Amer. Biog. Castle walk.

Castle walk (Castle, Vernon Blythe): Dance. Cited in: Webster's Biog. Dict.

CASTLE, WILLIAM BOSWORTH. 1897- . American physician. See: World Who's Who Sci. Castle's extrinsic factor, Castle's intrinsic factor.

CASTLEMAN, BENJAMIN. 1906- . American physician. See: World Who's Who Sci. Castleman's tumor (or lymphoma), Rosen-Castleman-Liebow syndrome.

Castleman's tumor (or lymphoma) (Castleman, Benjamin): Medicine. See: Jablonski.

Castle's extrinsic factor (Castle, William Bosworth): Medicine. See: Stedman.

Castle's intrinsic factor (Castle, William Bosworth): Medicine. See: Blumberg; Dorland; Stedman.

Castner cell (Castner, Hamilton Young): Chemistry. See: Webster's 3d.

CASTNER, HAMILTON YOUNG. 1859-1899. American chemist. See: World Who's Who Sci. Castner cell, Castner process (for the preparation of sodium).

Castner process (for the preparation of sodium) (Castner, Hamilton Young): Chemistry. See: Ballentyne; Van Nostrand Chem. Dict.

CASTOR. Mythical son of Leda. See: Jobes. Castor and Pollux (Castor and Pollux, the twins).

Castor and Pollux (Castor and Pollux, the twins): Generic Word (faithful friends). See: Partridge.

CASTRILLO. fl. 1911. Nicaraguan diplomat. (Biography source unavailable.) Knox-Castrillo Convention.

CASTRO, FIDEL. 1927-   . Cuban political leader. See: Encyc. Brit., 1973. Castroism.

Castroism (Castro, Fidel): Politics. See: Hendrickson. Also known as: Fidelism.

CASWELL, JOHN HENRY. fl. 1876. American mineralogist. Cited in: Bailey. Caswellite.

Caswellite (Caswell, John Henry): Earth Sciences. See: Thrush; Webster's 3d.

CAT, CHRISTOPHER. fl. 1703-1733. English tavern-keeper. See: Dict. Nat. Biog. Kit-Kat (Cat) Club.

Catchpenny (Catnach, James): Generic Word (fraudulent). See: Hendrickson.

Catesboea (Catesby, Mark): Botany. See: Charnock.

CATESBY, MARK. 1683-1749. English naturalist. See: Dict. Sci. Biog. Catesboea.

CATHCART, CHARLES MURRAY, 2D EARL CATHCART AND LORD GREENOCK. 1783-1859. English general. See: Dict. Nat. Biog. Greenockite.

CATHELIN, FERNAND. 1873-1945. French urologist. See: World Who's Who Sci. Cathelin's segregator.

Cathelin's segregator (Cathelin, Fernand): Medicine. See: Dorland.

CATHERINE I. 1684-1727. Russian empress. See: Encyc. Brit., 1973. Order of Catherine.

CATHERINE II. Russian empress. 1729-1796. See: Encyc. Brit., 1973. Conspiracy of Catherine.

CATHERINE, SAINT. d. 307. Christian martyr of Alexandria. See: Encyc. Brit., 1973. Catherine-wheel, Order of St. Catherine, Saint Catherine's flower.

Catherine-wheel (Catherine, Saint): Generic Word. See: Attwater; Hendrickson; Partridge.

Catiline (Catilinism or Catilinarian) (Catiline, Lucius Sergius): Generic Word (conspiracy). See: Charnock; Hendrickson; Partridge.

CATILINE, LUCIUS SERGIUS. ca. 108-62 B.C. Roman politician. See: Encyc. Brit., 1973. Catiline (Catilinism or Catilinarian), Catiline's conspiracy.

Catiline's conspiracy (Catiline, Lucius Sergius): History. See: Brewer; Phyfe.

CATLIN, GEORGE. 1796-1872. American painter and writer. See: Dict. Amer. Biog. Catlinite.

Catlinite (Catlin, George): Earth Sciences. See: Hendrickson; Mathews, M. M.; Van Nostrand Sci. Encyc.

CATNACH, JAMES. 1792-1841. English publisher. See: Dict. Nat. Biog. Catchpenny.

Cato (Cato, Marcus Porcius, the censor): Generic Word. See: Brewer.

Cato Conspiracy (Derivation undetermined): History. See: Morris.

CATO, MARCUS PORCIUS, OF UTICA. 95-46 B.C. Roman praetor and philosopher. See: Encyc. Brit., 1973. Catonian (or Catonism).

CATO, MARCUS PORCIUS, THE CENSOR. 234-149 B.C. Roman statesman. See: Encyc. Brit., 1973. Cato, Catonian (or Catonism).

Catonian (or Catonism) (Cato, Marcus Porcius, the censor; or Cato, Marcus Porcius, of Utica): Generic Word (inflexible). See: Charnock; Partridge; Webster's 3d.

CATTAN, ROGER. 1903-1963. French physician. See: Sem. Hop. Inform., 1963, no. 15. Siegal-Cattan-Mamou disease.

CATTANI, GUISEPPINA. d. 1915. Italian pathologist. (Biography source unavailable.) Cattani's serum.

Cattani's serum (Cattani, Guiseppina): Medicine. See: Dorland.

CATTELAIN, EUGENE ALBERT. 1887-1955. French chemist. See: Pogg., vols. 6, 7b. Cattelain test reaction.

Cattelain test reaction (Cattelain, Eugene Albert): Chemistry. See: Van Nostrand Chem. Dict.

Cattell infant scale (Cattell, Ramond Bernard): Psychology. See: Chaplin; Wolman.

CATTELL, RAMOND BERNARD. 1905-   . English-born American psychologist. See: World Who's Who Sci. Cattell infant scale, Cattell's factorial theory of personality.

Cattell's factorial theory of personality (Cattell, Ramond Bernard): Psychology. See: Chaplin.

Cattermole process (Derivation undetermined): Engineering and Industry. See: Thrush.

CATTIER, FELICIEN. b. 1869. Belgian colonial administrator in the Congo. Cited in: Min. Mag., vol. 17 (1946) p. 267. Cattierite.

Cattierite (Cattier, Felicien): Earth Sciences. See: Thrush.

Cattley guava (Cattley, William): Botany. See: Hendrickson.

CATTLEY, WILLIAM. d. 1832. English botanist. See: Biog. Notes Upon Botanists. Cattley guava, Cattleya, Cattleya fly.

Cattleya (Cattley, William): Botany. See: Hendrickson; Partridge; Taylor, N.

Cattleya fly (Cattley, William): Biology. See: Hendrickson.

Catullian (Catullus, Gaius Valerius): Literature. See: Webster's 3d.

CATULLUS, GAIUS VALERIUS. 84?-54 B.C. Roman poet. See: Encyc. Brit., 1973. Catullian.

CAUCHY, AUGUSTIN-LOUIS. 1789-1857. French mathematician. See: Dict. Sci. Biog. Cauchy('s) boundary condition(s), Cauchy convergence test (or integral convergence test), Cauchy('s) dispersion formula (or equation), Cauchy distribution, Cauchy-Euler equation, Cauchy-Hadamard theorem, Cauchy('s) integral formula, Cauch('s) integral theorem, Cauchy-Lipschitz theorem, Cauchy number, Cauchy problem for partial differential equations, Cauchy ratio test, Cauchy relations (in crystal structure), Cauchy relations in elasticity theory, Cauchy-Riemann equation(s), Cauchy-Schwarz inequality, Cauchy sequence, Cauchy's mean, Cauchy's mean value theorem, Cauchy's rule for series, Cauchy's theorem (for a square matrix), Cauchy's theorem (for the existence of a limit), Maclaurin-Cauchy test.

Cauchy('s) boundary condition(s) (Cauchy, Augustin-Louis): Mathematics. See: Ballentyne; Internat. Dict. Phys. Elec.

Cauchy convergence test (or integral convergence test) (Cauchy, Augustin-Louis): Mathematics. See: Internat. Dict. Ap. Math.; Internat. Dict. Phys. Elec.; Van Nostrand Sci. Encyc. Also known as: Maclaurin-Cauchy test.

Cauchy('s) dispersion formula (or equation) (Cauchy, Augustin-Louis): Physics. See: Ballentyne; Thewlis; Van Nostrand Sci. Encyc. Also known as: Cauchy formula (for refractive index).

Cauchy distribution (Cauchy, Augustin-Louis): Statistics. See: Internat. Dict. Ap. Math.; James; Kendall.

Cauchy-Euler equation (Cauchy, Augustin-Louis and Euler, Leonhard). See: Euler-Lagrange equation.

Cauchy formula (for refractive index) (Cauchy, Augustin-Louis). See: Cauchy('s) dispersion formula (or equation).

Cauchy-Hadamard theorem (Cauchy, Augustin-Louis and Hadamard, Jacques Salomon): Mathematics. See: James.

Cauchy('s) integral formula (Cauchy, Augustin-Louis): Mathematics. See: Ballentyne; Internat. Dict. Ap. Math.; James.

Cauchy('s) integral theorem (Cauchy, Augustin-Louis): Mathematics. See: Ballentyne; Internat. Dict. Ap. Math.; James.

Cauchy-Lipschitz theorem (Cauchy, Augustin-Louis and Lipschitz, Rudolf Otto Sigismund). See: Lipschitz condition.

Cauchy number (Cauchy, Augustin-Louis): Physics. See: Huschke; Internat. Dict. Ap. Math.

Cauchy problem for partial differential equations (Cauchy, Augustin-Louis): Mathematics. See: Internat. Dict. Ap. Math.

Cauchy ratio test (Cauchy, Augustin-Louis). See: D'Alembert('s) test (for convergence).

Cauchy relations (in crystal structure) (Cauchy, Augustin-Louis): Physics. See: Internat. Dict. Ap. Math.; Internat. Dict. Phys. Elec.; Thewlis.

Cauchy relations in elasticity theory (Cauchy, Augustin-Louis): Physics. See: Internat. Dict. Ap. Math.

Cauchy-Riemann equation(s) (Cauchy, Augustin-Louis and Riemann, Georg Friedrich Bernhard): Mathematics. See: Ballentyne; Internat. Dict. Ap. Math.; Thewlis.

Cauchy-Schwarz inequality (Cauchy, Augustin-Louis and Schwarz, Hermann Amandus): Mathematics. See: Ballentyne. Also known as: Buniakovski's inequality, Cauchy's inequality, Schwarz's inequality.

Cauchy sequence (Cauchy, Augustin-Louis): Mathematics. See: Internat. Dict. Ap. Math.; James; Van Nostrand Sci. Encyc.

Cauchy's condensation test (Cauchy, Augustin-Louis). See: Cauchy convergence test (or integral convergence test).

Cauchy's inequality (Cauchy, Augustin-Louis). See: Cauchy-Schwarz inequality.

Cauchy's mean (Cauchy, Augustin-Louis): Mathematics. See: Ballentyne.

Cauchy's mean value theorem (Cauchy, Augustin-Louis): Mathematics. See: Ballentyne.

Cauchy's rule for series (Cauchy, Augustin-Louis): Mathematics. See: Ballentyne.

Cauchy's theorem (for a square matrix) (Cauchy, Augustin-Louis): Mathematics. See: Ballentyne.

Cauchy's theorem (for the existence of a limit) (Cauchy, Augustin-Louis): Mathematics. See: Ballentyne.

CAUDLE, MRS. JOB. Character from series of papers by Douglas Jerrold (1846). See: Benet. Caudle lecture.

Caudle lecture (Caudle, Mrs. Job): Generic Word (curtain lecture). See: Brewer; Phyfe.

Cauer filter (Cauer, Wilhelm): Electronics. See: Hughes.

CAUER, WILHELM. 1900-1945. German mathematician. See: World Who's Who Sci. Cauer filter.

Caulinia (Cavolini, Filippo): Botany. See: Charnock.

CAULK, JOHN ROBERTS. 1881-1938. American urologist. See: Who Was Who Amer., vol. 1. Caulk punch.

Caulk punch (Caulk, John Roberts): Medicine. See: Dorland.

CAVALIERI, BONAVENTURA. 1598-1647. Italian mathematician. See: Dict. Sci. Biog. Cavalieri's theorem.

Cavalieri's theorem (Cavalieri, Bonaventura): Mathematics. See: Ballentyne; James.

Cavalli solution (Derivation undetermined): Chemistry. See: Van Nostrand Chem. Dict.

CAVALLINI, GUIDO. fl. 1935. Italian chemist. Cited in: Chem. Abstr., vol. 29, p. 199. Bachstez-Cavallini test reaction.

Cavare-Romberg syndrome (Cavare and Romberg, Moritz Heinrich von). See: Westphal's syndrome.

Cavare-Romberg-Westphal syndrome (Cavare; Romberg, Moritz Heinrich von; and Westphal, Karl Friedrich Otto). See: Westphal's syndrome.

Cavare-Westphal syndrome (Cavare and Westphal, Karl Friedrich Otto). See: Westphal's syndrome.

CAVENDISH. fl. before 1872. Exporter of tobacco. (Biography source unavailable.) Cavendish (tobacco)?

Cavendish. See: Jones, Henry.

Cavendish (1) (treatise on whist) (Jones, Henry): Recreation and Sports. See: Partridge; Weekley.

Cavendish (2) (hand in whist) (Jones, Henry): Recreation and Sports. Cited in: Webster's Biog. Dict.

Cavendish experiment (Cavendish, Henry): Physics. See: Hughes; Internat. Dict. Phys. Elec.; Thewlis.

CAVENDISH FAMILY. fl. from 1550. English nobility. See: Webster's Biog. Dict. Cavendish (tobacco)?

CAVENDISH, HENRY. 1731-1810. English chemist and physicist. See: Dict. Sci. Biog. Cavendish experiment.

CAVENDISH, SPENCER COMPTON, MARQUIS OF HARTINGTON AND 8TH DUKE OF DEVONSHIRE. 1833-1908. English statesman. See: Dict. Nat. Biog., 2d suppl. Hartington Commission.

Cavendish (tobacco) (Cavendish family? or Cavendish, the exporter?): Botany. See: Partridge, Weekley.

CAVINO, GIOVANNI ("PADUAN"). fl. 17th c. Italian forger. (Biography source unavailable.) Paduan coins.

CAVOLINI, FILIPPO. 1756-1810. Italian naturalist. See: World Who's Who Sci. Caulinia, Cavolinite.

Cavolinite (Cavolini, Filippo): Earth Sciences. See: Charnock.

CAWTHORNE, ALBERT. 1871-1958. English librarian. See: Lib. Assoc. Rec., vol. 60 (1958) pp. 102-03. Cawthorne Prize.

Cawthorne Prize (Cawthorne, Albert): Library Science. See: Harrod.

Caxton (book) (Caxton, William): Printing. See: Partridge; Weekley.

Caxton (type) (Caxton, William): Printing. See: Partridge.

CAXTON, WILLIAM. 1422-1491. English printer. See: Dict. Nat. Biog. Caxton (book), Caxton (type), Caxtonian.

Caxtonian (Caxton, William): Printing. See: Webster's 3d.

Cayley algebra (Cayley, Arthur): Mathematics. See: James.

CAYLEY, ARTHUR. 1821-1895. English mathematician. See: Dict. Sci. Biog. Cayley algebra, Cayley-Hamilton theorem, Cayley-Klein parameter(s), Cayley numbers, Cayley's theorem.

Cayley engine (Cayley, Sir George): Engineering and Industry. See: Auger.

CAYLEY, SIR GEORGE. 1773-1857. English aeronautical engineer. See: World Who's Who Sci. Cayley engine.

Cayley-Hamilton theorem (Cayley, Arthur and Hamilton, Sir William Rowan): Mathematics. See: Ballentyne. Also known as: Hamilton-Cayley theorem.

Cayley-Klein parameter(s) (Cayley, Arthur and Klein, Christian Felix): Mathematics. See: Ballentyne; Internat. Dict. Ap. Math.; Internat. Dict. Phys. Elec.

Cayley numbers (Cayley, Arthur): Mathematics. See: Ballentyne; James.

Cayley's theorem (Cayley, Arthur): Mathematics. See: James

CAZENAVE, PIERRE-LOUIS-ALPHEE. 1802-1877. French dermatologist. See: World Who's Who Sci. Cazenave's disease (1), Cazenave's disease (2), Cazenave's vitiligo.

Cazenave's disease (1) (Cazenave, Pierre-Louis-Alphee): Medicine. See: Dorland; Jablonski; Stedman. Also known as: Leloir's disease.

Cazenave's disease (2) (Cazenave, Pierre-Louis-Alphee): Medicine. See: Jablonski.

Cazenave's vitiligo (Cazenave, Pierre-Louis-Alphee): Medicine. See: Jablonski; Stedman. Also known as: alopecia Celsi, area Celsi, Celsus' vitiligo, Jonston's alopecia (or area).

Cazeneuve-Defournel test (Cazeneuve, Paul Jean Baptiste and Defournel): Chemistry. See: Van Nostrand Chem. Dict.

CAZENEUVE, PAUL JEAN BAPTISTE. 1852-1934. French chemist. See: Pogg., vols. 4-6, 7b. Cazeneuve-Defournel test, Cazeneuve reagent for metals, Cazeneuve solution for oxygen.

Cazeneuve reagent for metals (Cazeneuve, Paul Jean Baptiste): Chemistry. See: Van Nostrand Chem. Dict.

Cazeneuve solution for oxygen (Cazeneuve, Paul Jean Baptiste): Chemistry. See: Van Nostrand Chem. Dict.

CAZES, L. fl. 1895. French scientist. Cited in: Royal Soc. Cat. Sci. Pap., 1884-1900. Cazes's stereoscope.

Cazes's stereoscope (Cazes, L.): Photography. See: Focal Encyc. Photog.

CEBES. fl. 5th c. B.C. Greek philosopher. See: Webster's Biog. Dict. table of Cebes.

CECH, EDUARD. 1893-1960. Czech mathematician. See: Dict. Sci. Biog. Stone-Cech compactification.

Cecil gas engine (Cecil, William): Engineering and Industry. See: Auger.

CECIL, ROBERT ARTHUR TALBOT GASCOYNE (3RD MARQUIS OF SALISBURY). 1830-1903. English statesman, scientist and writer. See: Dict. Nat. Biog. Salisbury circular.

CECIL, WILLIAM. 1792-1882. English engineer. Cited in: Royal Soc. Cat. Sci. Pap., 1800-1863. Cecil gas engine.

CECIL, WILLIAM (LORD BURGHLEY). 1520-1598. English statesman. See: Dict. Nat. Biog. Burleigh's nod, Cecil's fast.

CECILIA, SAINT. d. 230? Christian martyr. See: Encyc. Brit., 1973. St. Cecelia Society.

Cecil's fast (Cecil, William): Generic Word (fish dinner). See: Brewer; Harbottle; Hendrickson.

Cecropia (Cecrops): Botany. See: Charnock.

Cecropian (Cecrops): Mythology. See: Weekley.

CECROPS. fl. 1580 B.C. King of Attica. See: Nouv. Biog. Univ. Cecropia, Cecropian.

Cedricite (Derivation undetermined): Earth Sciences. See: Thrush.

Ceelen-Gellerstedt syndrome (Ceelen, Wilhelm and Gellerstedt, Nils): Medicine. See: Jablonski.

CEELEN, WILHELM. 1883-1964. German physician. See: Who's Who Ger., 1956. Ceelen-Gellerstedt syndrome.

CELADON. Character in Honore d'Urfe's romance, "Astree" (1610). See: Benet. Celadon (Celadonique or Celadonism), Celadon (green), Celadonite.

Celadon (Celadonique or Celadonism) (Celadon): Generic Word (sentimental lover). See: Stenhouse.

Celadon (green) (Celadon): Fine Arts. See: Osborne; Partridge; Picken.

Celadonite (Celadon): Earth Sciences. See: Thrush.

CELESTIN, FELIX. 1900- . French physician. (Biography source unavailable.) Celestin tube?

Celestin tube (Celestin, Felix?): Medicine. See: Stedman.

Celestine (Celestine V): Food and Drink. See: Webster's 3d.

CELESTINE V. ca. 1215-1296. Pope. See: Encyc. Brit., 1973. Celestine, Celestines (or Celestinians), Celestinian Hermits.

Celestines (or Celestinians) (Celestine V): Religion. See: Attwater; Brewer; Canney.

Celestinian Hermits (Celestine V): Religion. See: Canney.

cell of Corti (Corti, Alfonso Giacomo Gaspare). See: Corti's cells.

CELLANO. No dates. Hospital patient. (Biography source unavailable.) Cellano (factor).

Cellano (factor) (Cellano): Medicine. See: Dorland.

Cellarius (Cellarius, Henri): Dance. See: Charnock.

CELLARIUS, HENRI. fl. 1847. French professor. (Biography source unavailable.) Cellarius.

CELLI, ANGELO. 1857-1914. Italian physician. See: World Who's Who Sci. Cellia (mosquitoes).

Cellia (mosquitoes) (Celli, Angelo): Medicine. See: Dorland.

CELLINI, BENVENUTO. 1500-1571. Italian goldsmith and sculptor. See: Encyc. Brit., 1973. Cellini's halo.

Cellini's halo (Cellini, Benvenuto): Physics. See: Huschke.

cells of Leydig (Leydig, Franz von). See: Leydig('s) cell(s).

Celsi reaction for gallic and tannic acids (Celsi, Santiago Alejandro): Chemistry. See: Van Nostrand Chem. Dict.

Celsi reaction for malic acid (Celsi, Santiago Alejandro): Chemistry. See: Van Nostrand Chem. Dict.

Celsi reagent for potassium (Celsi, Santiago Alejandro): Chemistry. See: Van Nostrand Chem. Dict.

CELSI, SANTIAGO ALEJANDRO. 1899- . Argentine chemist. See: Gran. Encic. Argentina. Celsi reaction for gallic and tannic acids, Celsi reaction for malic acid, Celsi reagent for potassium, Rossi-Celsi microreagent.

Celsia (Celsius, Olaus): Botany. See: Charnock; Taylor, N.; Webster's 3d.

Celsian (Celsius, Anders): Earth Sciences. See: Webster's 3d.

CELSIUS, ANDERS. 1701-1744. Swedish astronomer. See: Dict. Sci. Biog. Celsian, Celsius degree, Celsius scale (or temperature scale), Celsius thermometer, degree Celsius.

Celsius degree (Celsius, Anders): Physics. See: Dresner.

CELSIUS, OLAUS. 1670-1756. Swedish botanist and orientalist. See: Nouv. Biog. Univ. Celsia.

Celsius scale (or temperature scale) (Celsius, Anders): Physics. See: Ballentyne; Huschke; Monkhouse.

Celsius thermometer (Celsius, Anders): Physics. See: Hendrickson; Partridge.

CELSUS, AULUS CORNELIUS. fl. c. 25 A.D. Roman medical writer. See: Dict. Sci. Biog. Celsus' chancre, Celsus' kerion, Celsus' operation, Celsus' operation, Celsus' papules, Celsus' vitiligo, morbus attonitus Celsi.

Celsus' chancre (Celsus, Aulus Cornelius): Medicine. See: Stedman.

Celsus' kerion (Celsus, Aulus Cornelius): Medicine. See: Stedman.

Celsus' operation (Celsus, Aulus Cornelius): Medicine. See: Stedman.

Celsus' papules (Celsus, Aulus Cornelius): Medicine. See: Stedman.

Celsus' vitiligo (Celsus, Aulus Cornelius): Medicine. See: Stedman. Also known as: alopecia Celsi, area Celsi, Celsus' vitiligo, Jonston's alopecia (or area).

Celsus's disease (Celsus, Aulus Cornelius). See: morbus attonitus Celsi.

Cenco-Petersen molecular model (Central Scientific Company and Petersen, Quentin Richard): Chemistry. Cited in: World Who's Who Sci.

Centers' method for determining class (Centers, Richard): Sociology. See: Zadrozny.

CENTERS, RICHARD. 1912- . American psychologist. See: World Who's Who Sci. Centers' method for determining class.

CEPOLA, BARTOLOMMEO. fl. 15th c. Italian lawyer. See: Webster's Biog. Dict. devices of Cepola.

CERBELAND. fl. 1913. Italian chemist. Cited in: Chem. Abstr., vol. 7, p. 207. Cerbeland tests of hair-dyeing substances.

Cerbeland tests of hair-dyeing substances (Cerbeland): Chemistry. See: Van Nostrand Chem. Dict.

Cerberus (Cerberus, the dog): Generic Word (guardian). See: Brewer.

CERBERUS, THE DOG. Mythical dog who guarded the entrance to infernal regions. See: Jobes. Cerberus.

CERDEIRAS, J. J. fl. 1915. Spanish chemist. Cited in: Chem. Abstr., vol. 11, p. 381. Cerdeiras solution.

Cerdeiras solution (Cerdeiras, J. J.): Chemistry. See: Van Nostrand Chem. Dict.

CERDO. fl. 2nd c. Syrian Gnostic. See: Webster's Biog. Dict. Cerdonians.

Cerdonians (Cerdo): Religion. See: Canney.

Cereal (Ceres): Botany. See: Charnock; Funk; Partridge.

Cerealia (Ceres): Generic Word (Roman festival). See: Brewer.

Cerenkov effect (Cherenkov, Pavel Aleksandrovich): Physics. See: Hackh.

Cerenkov, Pavel Aleksandrovich. See: Cherenkov, Pavel Aleksandrovich.

CERES. Mythical goddess of the generative forces in Nature. See: Encyc. Brit., 1973. Cereal, Cerealia.

Cerinthians (Cerinthus): Religion. See: Canney; Latham; Mathews, S.

CERINTHUS. fl. 1st. c. A.D. Syrian religious leader. See: Encyc. Brit., 1973. Cerinthians.

Cermak-Spirek furnace (Derivation undetermined): Engineering and Industry. See: Thrush.

CERNATESCU, RADU. 1894-1958. Rumanian chemist. See: World Who's Who Sci. (addendum). Buznea-Cernatesco test, Papafil-Cernatesco reagent.

CERRUTI, VALENTINO. 1850-1909. Italian mathematician. See: Sci., vol. 30 (1909) p. 363. problem of Boussinesq and Cerruti?

CERTONCINY, A. fl. 1953. French physician. (Biography source unavailable.) Forestier-Certonciny syndrome.

CERULARIUS, MICHAEL. 1043-1059. Patriarch of Constantinople. See: Webster's Biog. Dict. Schism of Cerularius.

CESALPINI, ANDREA. 1519-1603. Italian physician and botanist. See: Nouv. Biog. Univ. Caesalpinia.

CESARIS-DEMEL, ANTONIO. b. 1866. Italian pathologist. See: Biog. Lex. hervorr. Aerzte, 1880-1930. Cesaris-Demel bodies.

Cesaris-Demel bodies (Cesaris-Demel, Antonio): Medicine. See: Dorland.

CESARO, ERNESTO. 1859-1906. Italian mathematician. See: Dict. Sci. Biog. Cesaro's summation formula.

CESARO, GIUSEPPE RAIMONDO PIO. 1849-1939. Italian-born Belgian mineralogist. See: Pogg., vols. 4-6, 7b. Cesarolite.

Cesarolite (Cesaro, Giuseppe Raimondo Pio): Earth Sciences. See: Thrush; Webster's 3d.

Cesaro's summation formula (Cesaro, Ernesto): Mathematics. See: Ballentyne; James.

CESI, FEDERICO. 1585-1630. Italian botanist. See: Dict. Sci. Biog. Caesia, Caesio?

Cestan-Chenais syndrome (Cestan, Raymond and Chenais, Louis J.): Medicine. See: Dorland; Jablonski; Stedman. Also known as: Cestan's paralysis.

CESTAN, RAYMOND. 1872-1934. French physician. See: Biog. Lex. hervorr. Aerzte, 1880-1930. Cestan-Chenais syndrome, Raymond-Cestan syndrome.

Cestan's paralysis (Cestan, Raymond). See: Cestan-Chenais syndrome.

CEVA, GIOVANNI. 1647-1734. Italian mathematician. See: Dict. Sci. Biog. Ceva's theorem.

Ceva's theorem (Ceva, Giovanni): Mathematics. See: Ballentyne; Webster's 3d.

CHABERT, PHILABERT. 1737-1814. French veterinary surgeon. See: World Who's Who Sci. Chabertia, Chabert's disease.

Chabertia (Chabert, Philabert): Zoology. See: Stedman; Webster's 3d.

Chabert's disease (Chabert, Philabert): Medicine. See: Jablonski.

Chadband (Chadband, the minister): Generic Word (religious hypocrite). See: Brewer; Partridge; Weekley.

CHADBAND, THE MINISTER. Character in Charles Dickens' novel, "Bleak House" (1852-3). See: Benet. Chadband.

Chaddock burner (Derivation undetermined): Chemistry. See: Hackh; Van Nostrand Chem. Dict.

CHADDOCK, CHARLES GILBERT. 1861-1936. American neurologist. See: Webster's Biog. Dict. Chaddock reflex (or sign).

Chaddock reflex (or sign) (Chaddock, Charles Gilbert): Medicine. See: Hinsie; Stedman; Wolman.

Chadwick-Goldhaber effect (Chadwick, Sir James and Goldhaber, Maurice): Physics. See: Hughes; Internat. Dict. Phys. Elec.; Van Nostrand Chem. Dict.

CHADWICK, SIR JAMES. 1891- . English physicist. See: Encyc. Brit., 1973. Chadwick-Goldhaber effect.

CHADWICK, JAMES READ. 1844-1905. American gynecologist. See: Dict. Amer. Biog. Chadwick's sign.

Chadwick's sign (Chadwick, James Read): Medicine. See: Dorland; Stedman. Also known as: Jacquemier's sign, Kluge's sign.

CHAGAS, CARLOS RIBEIRO JUSTINIANO. 1879-1934. Brazilian physician. See: Dict. Sci. Biog. Chagas' disease, Chagoma.

Chagas-Cruz disease (Chagas, Carlos Ribeiro Justiniano and Cruz, Oswaldo). See: Chagas' disease.

Chagas' disease (Chagas, Carlos Ribeiro Justiniano): Medicine. See: Jablonski; Pennak; Stedman. Also known as: Chagas-Cruz disease, Chagas-Mazza disease.

Chagas-Mazza disease (Chagas, Carlos Ribeiro Justiniano and Mazza, Salvador). See: Chagas' disease.

Chagoma (Chagas, Carlos Ribeiro Justiniano): Medicine. See: Stedman.

CHAIKOFF, ISRAEL LYON. 1902- . English-born American physiologist. See: Amer. Men Sci., 5th ed. Gee-Chaikoff reagent.

CHAILLET, JEAN FREDERIC DE. 1747-1839. Swiss? botanist. See: Biog. Notes Upon Botanists. Chailletia.

Chailletia (Chaillet, Jean Frederic de): Botany. See: Charnock.

CHAITANYA (OR CAITANYA). 1485-1527. Indian mystic. See: Webster's Biog. Dict. Caitanya sect.

CHAIX, ACHILLE. b. 1875. French physician. See: Dict. Nat. Contemp., vol. 2, p. 126. Favre-Chaix angiodermatitis.

Chakravarti-Roy test reaction (Chakravarti, Satyendra Nath and Roy, S. N.): Chemistry. See: Van Nostrand Chem. Dict.

CHAKRAVARTI, SATYENDRA NATH. 1903-1945. Indian chemist. See: Pogg. vols. 6, 7b. Chakravarti-Roy test reaction.

CHALL, JEANNE S. 1921- . Polish-born American educational psychologist. See: Amer. Men and Women Sci., 12th ed. (Soc. Behav. Sci.). Dale-Chall readability formula.

CHALLONER, RICHARD. 1691-1781. English Roman Catholic prelate. See: Dict. Nat. Biog. Challoner's Bible.

Challoner's Bible (Challoner, Richard): Religion. See: Attwater.

CHALMERS, G. fl. 1902. Superintendent of Brazilian mine. Cited in: Min. Mag., vol. 13 (1903) p. 366. Chalmersite.

CHALMERS, T. A. fl. 1934. English physicist. Cited in: Chem. Abstr., vol. 28, p. 7148. Szilard-Chalmers method (reaction or process).

Chalmersite (Chalmers, G.): Earth Sciences. See: Webster's 3d.

CHALMOT, GUILLAUME LOUIS JACQUES DE. b. 1870. French? chemist. See: Amer. Chem. J., vol. 23 (1900) p. 447. Chalmot test?

Chalmot test (Chalmot, Guillaume Louis Jacques de?): Chemistry. See: Van Nostrand Chem. Dict.

Cham. See: Ham.

CHAMBERLAIN, JOSEPH. 1836-1914. English statesman. See: Dict. Nat. Biog., 3rd suppl. Bayard-Chamberlain Treaty, Chamberlain scheme.

Chamberlain scheme (Chamberlain, Joseph): History. See: Montgomery.

CHAMBERLAIN, THOMAS. No dates. English distillery owner. (Biography source unavailable.) Old Tom (gin).

CHAMBERLAIN, W. EDWARD. 1891-1947. American radiologist. See: Who's Imp. Med., 2nd ed. Chamberlain's line.

Chamberlain's line (Chamberlain, W. Edward): Medicine. See: Stedman.

CHAMBERLAND, CHARLES EDOUARD. 1851-1908. French bacteriologist. See: Dict. Sci. Biog. Chamberland filter, Chamberland flask.

Chamberland filter (Chamberland, Charles Edouard); Medicine. See: Dorland; Hackh; Stedman. Also known as: Pasteur-Chamberland filter.

Chamberland flask (Chamberland, Charles Edouard): Chemistry. See: Hackh.

Chamberlen forceps (Chamberlen, Peter): Medicine. See: Dorland; Stedman.

CHAMBERLEN, PETER. 1560-1631. English obstetrician. See: Dict. Nat. Biog. Chamberlen forceps.

Chambers-Imrie-Sharpe curve (Derivation undetermined): Electronics. See: Hughes.

CHAMORRO VARGAS, EMILIANO. 1871-1966. Nicaraguan engineer, army officer, and statesman. See: Webster's Biog. Dict. Bryan-Chamorro Treaty.

CHAMOT, EMILE MONNIN. b. 1868. American chemist. See: Pogg., vol. 6. Mason-Chamot micro-test for bromide.

CHAMPERNOWNE, DAVID GAWEN. 1912- . English economist and statistician. See: Who's Who, 1974. Champernowne distributions.

Champernowne distributions (Champernowne, David Gawen): Statistics. See: Kendall.

Champetier de Ribes bag (Champetier de Ribes, Camille Louis Antoine): Medicine. See: Dorland; Stedman.

CHAMPETIER DE RIBES, CAMILLE LOUIS ANTOINE. 1848-1935. French obstetrician. Cited in: Kelly. Champetier de Ribes bag.

Champion-Cregan-Klein syndrome (Champion, Randell; Cregan, James Cyril Fraser; and Klein, David). See: Fevre-Languepin syndrome.

Champion press (Derivation undetermined): Printing. See: Lockwood.

CHAMPION, RANDELL. fl. 1959. English physician. (Biography source unavailable.) Champion-Cregan-Klein syndrome.

Championniere, Just Marie Lucas. See: Lucas-Championniere, Just Marie Marcellin.

Championniere's disease (Lucas-Championniere, Just Marie Marcellin): Medicine. See: Dorland; Stedman.

CHAMPNEY, JOHN. fl. 1801. American horticulturist. (Biography source unavailable.) Champney(a) (rose).

Champney(a) (rose) (Champney, John): Botany. See: Mathews, M. M.; Webster's 3d. Also known as: Noisette rose.

CHAMPOLLION-FIGEAC, JEAN-FRANCOIS. 1790-1832. French Egyptologist. See: World Who's Who Sci. Champollionist.

Champollionist (Champollion-Figeac, Jean-Francois): History. See: Charnock.

CHAMPY, CHRISTIAN. b. 1885. French physician. See: Biog. Lex. hervorr. Aerzte, 1880-1930. Champy fixative?

Champy fixative (Champy, Christian?): Chemistry. See: Van Nostrand Chem. Dict.

CHAN, CHARLIE. Fictional Chinese detective created in novel of Earl Derr Biggers (d. 1933). See: Benet, under "Biggers." Charley (or Charlie).

CHANCE, ALEXANDER M. fl. 1888. English chemist. Cited in: Royal Soc. Cat. Sci. Pap., 1874-1883; 1884-1900. Chance-Claus process.

Chance-Claus process (Chance, Alexander and Claus): Engineering and Industry. See: Thrush; Van Nostrand Chem. Dict.

Chance cone (Chance, Thomas Mitchell?): Engineering and Industry. See: Thrush.

Chance direct acting internal combustion pump (Chance, Thomas Mitchell): Engineering and Industry. Cited in: Who's Who Engin., 1925.

CHANCE, FRANK LEROY. 1877-1924. American baseball player. See: Who's Who Pro. Baseball, 1973. Tinker to Evers to Chance.

Chance process (Chance, Thomas Mitchell): Engineering and Industry. See: Thrush; Webster's 3d.

Chance sand-flotation process (Chance, Thomas Mitchell): Engineering and Industry. See: Thrush.

CHANCE, THOMAS MITCHELL. b. 1887. American mining engineer. See: Who's Who Engin., 1931. Chance cone?, Chance direct acting internal combustion pump, Chance process, Chance sand-flotation process, Chance washer.

Chance washer (Chance, Thomas Mitchell): Engineering and Industry. See: Thrush.

CHANCEL, GUSTAV CHARLES BONAVENTURE. 1822-1890. French chemist. See: Dict. Sci. Biog. Chancel test.

Chancel test (Chancel, Gustav Charles Bonaventure): Chemistry. See: Van Nostrand Chem. Dict.

CHANDLEE, GROVER C. b. 1884. American chemist. See: Amer. Men Sci., 10th ed. Knapper-Craig-Chandlee test.

Chandler Act (Chandler, Walter Clift): Law. See: Smith.

CHANDLER, FREMONT AUGUSTUS. 1893-1954. American orthopedic surgeon. See: Who Was Who Amer., 1951-1960. Chandler's disease.

CHANDLER, SETH CARLO. 1846-1913. American astronomer. See: Dict. Sci. Biog. Chandler wobble.

CHANDLER, WALTER CLIFT. 1887-1967. American legislator. See: Biog. Direct. Amer. Congress. Chandler Act.

Chandler wobble (Chandler, Seth Carlo): Astronomy. See: Barnhart (New Eng.)

Chandler's disease (Chandler, Fremont Augustus): Medicine. See: Jablonski.

Chandrasekhar absorption constants (Chandrasekhar, Subrahmanyan): Physics. See: Thewlis.

Chandrasekhar method of envelopes (Chandrasekhar, Subrahmanyan): Physics. See: Thewlis.

CHANDRASEKHAR, SUBRAHMANYAN. 1910- . Indian-born American astrophysicist. See: World Who's Who Sci. Chandrasekhar absorption constants, Chandrasekhar method of envelopes, Chandrasekhar's limit, Wick-Chandrasekhar method.

Chandrasekhar's limit (Chandrasekhar, Subrahmanyan): Physics. Cited in: World Who's Who Sci.

CHANEL, GABRIELLE. 1883-1971. French dress designer. See: Webster's Biog. Dict. Chanel jacket.

Chanel jacket (Chanel, Gabrielle): Fashion. See: Picken.

Chang-Kao reagent (Chang, Ming-Che and Kao, Chen-Heng): Chemistry. See: Van Nostrand Chem. Dict.

CHANG, MING-CHE. fl. 1935. Chinese chemist. Cited in: Chem. Abstr., vol. 29, p. 7228. Chang-Kao reagent.

CHANG, SHIH-HSU. fl. 1934. Chinese chemist. Cited in: Chem. Abstr., vol. 29, p. 1429. Sah-Chang-Lei test reagent.

CHANTEMESSE, ANDRE. 1851-1919. French bacteriologist. See: World Who's Who Sci. Chantemesse reaction.

Chantemesse reaction (Chantemesse, Andre): Medicine. See: Dorland; Stedman.

CHAOUL, HENRI. 1888-1964. German radiologist. See: Strahlen. (1964) vol. 125, pt. 3, p. 476. Chaoul therapy, Chaoul tube.

Chaoul therapy (Chaoul, Henri): Medicine. See: Dorland.

Chaoul tube (Chaoul, Henri): Medicine. See: Dorland.

Chaperon cell (Derivation undetermined): Chemistry. See: Hackh.

Chaperon resistor (Derivation undetermined): Physics. See: Hughes; Internat. Dict. Phys. Elec.

CHAPLIN, CHARLES SPENCER. 1889- . English motion picture actor. See: Encyc. Brit., 1973. Chaplinesque, Charlie Chaplin moustache, Charlie Chaplin (walk).

Chaplinesque (Chaplin, Charles Spencer): Generic Word. See: Hendrickson; Webster's 3d.

CHAPMAN, ALFRED CHASTON ARTHUR WILLIAM HENRY. fl. 1900. English chemist. See: Pogg., vol. 6. Chapman test for isomeric allyl and propenyl phenols.

CHAPMAN, DAVID LEONARD. 1869-1958. English chemist. See: Dict. Sci. Biog. Chapman equation.

CHAPMAN, DOUGLAS GEORGE. 1920- . American mathematical statistician. See: Amer. Men and Women Sci., 12th ed. Chapman-Kolmogorov equations.

CHAPMAN, EDWARD JOHN. 1821-1904. English mineralogist. See: Dict. Nat. Biog., 2nd suppl. Chapmanite.

Chapman equation (Chapman, David Leonard): Chemistry. See: Ballentyne; Internat. Dict. Phys. Elec.; Van Nostrand Chem. Dict.

CHAPMAN, G. fl. 1936. English chemist. Cited in: Chem. Abstr., vol. 31, p. 68. Giblin-Chapman test.

CHAPMAN, JAMES. d. 1872. English traveler in Africa. See: Pogg. vol. 3. Chapman's zebra.

CHAPMAN, JOHN ("JOHNNY APPLESEED"). 1775-1847. American folk hero. See: Barnhart (Cycl. Names). Johnny Appleseed.

CHAPMAN, JOHN. 1822-1894. English publisher, editor, and physician. See: Dict. Nat. Biog., 1st suppl. Chapman's bag.

Chapman Jones. See: Jones, Henry Chapman.

Chapman Jones plate tester (Jones, Henry Chapman): Photography. See: Focal Encyc. Photog.

Chapman-Jouguet (Jouget) condition (Chapman and Jouguet, Emile): Physics. See: Internat. Dict. Ap. Math.; Internat. Dict. Phys. Elec.; Van Nostrand Sci. Encyc.

Chapman-Jouguet (Jouget) state (Chapman and Jouguet, Emile): Physics. See: Thewlis.

Chapman-Kolmogorov equations (Chapman, Douglas George and Kolmogorov, Andrey Nikolaevich): Statistics. See: Kendall.

Chapman process (Derivation undetermined): Engineering and Industry. See: Thrush.

Chapman rearrangement (Derivation undetermined): Chemistry. See: Van Nostrand Chem. Dict.

Chapman region (Chapman, Sydney): Physics. See: Hughes; Huschke; Van Nostrand Sci. Encyc.

Chapman shield (Derivation undetermined): Engineering and Industry. See: Thrush.

CHAPMAN, SYDNEY. 1888- . English-born American mathematician and geophysicist. See: World Who's Who Sci. Chapman region.

Chapman test for isomeric allyl and propenyl phenols (Chapman, Alfred Chaston Arthur William Henry): Chemistry. See: Van Nostrand Chem. Dict.

Chapmanite (Chapman, Edward John): Earth Sciences. See: Webster's 3d.

Chapman's bag (Chapman, John): Medicine. See: Dorland.

Chapman's zebra (Chapman, James): Zoology. See: Webster's 3d.

Chappius bands (Chappuis, James): Physics. See: Huschke. Also known as: Huggins bands.

Chappius, James. See: Chappuis, James.

CHAPPLE, CHARLES CULLODEN. 1903- . American pediatrician. See: Direct. Med. Specialists, 8th ed. Chapple's clinical sign of congenital hip (or sign (2)), Chapple's sign (1), Chapple's syndrome.

Chapple's clinical sign of congenital hip (or sign (2)) (Chapple, Charles Culloden): Medicine. See: Jablonski.

Chapple's sign (1) (Chapple, Charles Culloden): Medicine. See: Jablonski.

Chapple's syndrome (Chapple, Charles Culloden): Medicine. See: Jablonski.

CHAPPUIS, JAMES. 1854-1896. French radiologist. See: World Who's Who Sci. Chappius 'ni .

CHAPTAL, JEAN-ANTOINE. 1756-1832. French chemist. See: Dict. Sci. Biog. Chaptalia?, Chaptalize.

Chaptalia (Chaptal, Jean-Antoine?): Botany. See: Charnock.

Chaptalize (Chaptal, Jean-Antoine): Chemistry. See: Webster's 3d.

CHAPUT, HENRI. 1857-1919. French surgeon. See: World Who's Who Sci. Chaput's operation.

Chaput's operation (Chaput, Henri): Medicine. See: Dorland; Stedman.

CHARAUX, CAMILLE. 1861-1941. French chemist. See: Pogg., vols. 6, 7b. Charaux test reactions.

Charaux test reactions (Charaux, Camille): Chemistry. See: Van Nostrand Chem. Dict.

Charcot–Boettcher crystalloids (Charcot, Jean-Martin and Boettcher, Arthur): Medicine. See: Stedman.

CHARCOT, JEAN-MARTIN. 1825-1893. French neurologist. See: Dict. Sci. Biog. aneurysm of Charcot, Charcot–Boettcher crystalloids, Charcot–Leyden crystals, Charcot school, Charcot('s) triad, Charcot–Vigouroux sign, Charcot–Weiss–Baker syndrome, Charcot's artery, Charcot's bath, Charcot's disease (arthrosis or joint), Charcot's edema, Charcot's gait, Charcot's intermittent fever, Charcot's syndrome (1) (or sclerosis), Charcot's syndrome (2), Charcot's vertigo, Charcot's zones, Erb–Charcot syndrome, Souques–Charcot geroderma.

Charcot–Leyden crystals (Charcot, Jean Martin and Leyden, Ernst Viktor von): Medicine. See: Dorland; Stedman. Also known as: Charcot–Leyden–Zenker crystals, Charcot–Neumann's crystals, Charcot–Robin crystals, Leyden's crystals.

Charcot–Leyden–Zenker crystals (Charcot, Jean Martin; Leyden, Ernst Viktor von; and Von Zenker, Friedrich Albert). See: Charcot–Leyden crystals.

Charcot–Neumann crystals (Charcot, Jean Martin and Neumann, Alfred). See: Charcot–Leyden crystals.

Charcot–Robin crystals (Charcot, Jean-Martin and Robin). See: Charcot–Leyden crystals.

Charcot school (Charcot, Jean-Martin): Medicine. See: Canney.

Charcot('s) triad (Charcot, Jean-Martin): Medicine. See: Hinsie; Jablonski; Stedman.

Charcot–Vigouroux sign (Charcot, Jean Martin and Vigouroux, Auguste?). See: Vigouroux's sign.

Charcot–Weiss–Baker syndrome (Charcot, Jean Martin; Weiss, Soma; and Baker, James P.): Medicine. See: Jablonski; Stedman.

Charcot's artery (Charcot, Jean-Martin): Medicine. See: Donath; Stedman.

Charcot's bath (Charcot, Jean-Martin): Medicine. See: Dorland.

Charcot's disease (arthrosis or joint) (Charcot, Jean-Martin): Medicine. See: Dorland; Jablonski; Stedman.

Charcot's edema (Charcot, Jean-Martin): Medicine. See: Jablonski.

Charcot's gait (Charcot, Jean-Martin): Medicine. See: Stedman.

Charcot's intermittent fever (Charcot, Jean-Martin): Medicine. See: Stedman.

Charcot's syndrome (1) (or sclerosis) (Charcot, Jean-Martin): Medicine. See: Jablonski.

Charcot's syndrome (2) (Charcot, Jean-Martin): Medicine. See: Dorland; Jablonski; Stedman.

Charcot's vertigo (Charcot, Jean-Martin): Medicine. See: Jablonski; Stedman.

Charcot's zones (Charcot, Jean-Martin): Medicine. See: Stedman.

CHARDIN, DMITRIJ ANDREEVICH. fl. 1893. Russian chemist. Cited in: Royal Soc. Cat. Sci. Pap., 1884-1900. Chardin filter paper?

Chardin filter paper (Chardin, Dmitrij Andreevich?): Chemistry. See: Hackh.

Chardin, Pierre Teilhard de. See: Teilhard de Chardin, Pierre.

CHARDONNET, LOUIS–MARIE–HILAIRE BERNIGAUD, COMTE DE. 1839-1924. French chemist. See: Dict. Sci. Biog. Chardonnet nitrocellulose process.

Chardonnet nitrocellulose process (Chardonnet, Louis–Marie–Hilaire Bernigaud, Comte de): Chemistry. See: Van Nostrand Chem. Dict.

CHARGAFF, ERWIN. 1905- . Austrian-born American chemist. See: World Who's Who Sci. Feigl–Chargav test reaction.

Charitshkov, K. See: Kharichkov, K.

CHARLEMAGNE (CHARLES THE GREAT). 742-814. King of the Franks and Holy Roman Emperor. See: Encyc. Brit., 1973. Carlina (or Carline), Carlovingians (or Carolingians), Caroline books, Caroline minuscule, Charlemagne cycle, Charlemagne's pleiad, Donation of Charles

Charlemagne cycle (Charlemagne): Literature. See: Barnhart (Eng. Lit.).

Charlemagne's pleiad (Charlemagne): History. See: Brewer.

CHARLES I. 1226-1285. King of Naples and Sicily. See: Encyc. Brit., 1973. Carlino (Carline, or Caroline).

CHARLES I. 1600-1649. King of England. See: Dict. Nat. Biog. Caroline, Carolus, Charley (Charlie) (beard), Charleys (or Charlies), King Charles's head, Prince Charles' men?

CHARLES II. 1630-1685. King of England. See: Dict. Nat. Biog. King Charles spaniel?

CHARLES III. 1716-1788. King of Spain. See: Encyc. Brit., 1973. Order of Charles III.

CHARLES IV. 1748-1819. King of Spain. See: Encyc. Brit., 1973. Carludovica.

CHARLES V (Dauphin of Vienne). 1337-1380. King of France. See: Encyc. Brit., 1973. Dolphin.

CHARLES V. 1500-1558. Holy Roman emperor and King of Spain. See: Encyc. Brit., 1973. Caroline Ordinance.

CHARLES VI. 1685-1740. Holy Roman emperor and King of Hungary. See: Encyc. Brit., 1973. Pragmatic Sanction of Charles VI.

CHARLES VII. 1697-1745. Prince of Bavaria and Holy Roman emperor. See: Encyc. Brit., 1973. Carolin (2) (Carolin d'or or Karolin).

CHARLES XI. 1655-1697. King of Sweden. See: Encyc. Brit., 1973. Carolin (1).

CHARLES XIII. 1748-1818. King of Sweden. See: Encyc. Brit., 1973. Order of Charles XIII.

Charles Bonnet's syndrome (Bonnet, Charles). See: Bonnet's syndrome.

CHARLES BORROMEO, SAINT. 1538-1584. Italian nobleman and ecclesiastic. See: Holweck. Oblates of St. Charles.

Charles de la Tour (pump) (Cagniard de la Tour, Charles). See: Cagniardelle (pump).

CHARLES EDWARD STUART, "YOUNG PRETENDER". 1720-1788. Claimant to the throne of England. See: Dict. Nat. Biog. Pretenderism.

Charles F. Adams (destroyers) (Adams, Charles Francis): Weapons. See: Quick.

Charles-Gay-Lussac law (Charles, Jacques-Alexandre-Cesar and Gay-Lussac, Joseph Louis). See: Charles' law.

CHARLES, JACQUES-ALEXANDRE-CESAR. 1746-1823. French physicist. See: Dict. Sci. Biog. Boyle-Charles law, Charles' law, Charlieres.

Charles' law (Charles, Jacques-Alexandre-Cesar): Physics. See: Ballentyne; Hackh; Internat. Dict. Ap. Math. Also known as: Charles-Gay-Lussac law, Gay-Lussac('s) law (of expansion).

Charles Piazzi Smyth's camera (Smyth, Charles Piazzi): Photography. See: Focal Encyc. Photog. under "Camera History."

Charles the Great. See: Charlemagne.

Charles William Ferdinand. See: Karl Wilhelm Ferdinand.

CHARLET, HENRI. b. 1884. French physician. (Biography source unavailable.) Nicolas-Moutot-Charlet syndrome.

Charley (Charlie) (beard) (Charles I? or Fox, Charles James?): Fashion. See: Charnock; Partridge; Webster's 3d.

Charley (or Charlie) (Chan, Charlie): Generic Word (oriental person). See: Webster's 3d.

Charley More (More, Charles): Generic Word (fair dealing). See: Hendrickson.

Charley Noble (Noble, Charles): Generic Word (ship's galley funnel). See: Hendrickson.

Charleys (or Charlies) (Charles I): Generic Word (night-watchman). See: Brewer; Harvey; Hendrickson.

Charlie Chaplin moustache (Chaplin, Charles Spencer): Fashion. See: Hendrickson; Partridge.

Charlie Chaplin (walk) (Chaplin, Charles Spencer): Generic Word. See: Hendrickson

Charlie McCarthy (McCarthy, Charlie, the ventriloquist's dummy): Generic Word (totally dominated person). See: Webster's 3d.

CHARLIER, CARL WILHELM LUDWIG. 1862-1934. Swedish astronomer. See: World Who's Who Sci. Charlier('s) check(s), Charlier distribution, Charlier polynomials, Gram-Charlier series.

Charlier('s) check(s) (Charlier, Carl Wilhelm Ludwig): Mathematics. See: Ballentyne; English; James.

Charlier distribution (Charlier, Carl Wilhelm Ludwig): Statistics. See: Kendall.

Charlier polynomials (Charlier, Carl Wilhelm Ludwig): Statistics. See: Kendall.

Charlier shoe (Derivation undetermined): Agriculture. See: Winburne.

Charlieres (Charles, Jacques-Alexandre-Cesar): Generic Word (balloons). See: Stenhouse.

CHARLIN, C. CARLOS. b. 1886. Chilean physician. See: Biog. Lex. hervorr. Aerzte, 1880-1930. Charlin's syndrome.

Charlin's syndrome (Charlin, C. Carlos): Medicine. See: Jablonski.

CHARLOTTE AUGUSTA. 1796-1817. English princess. See: Dict. Nat. Biog. apple Charlotte, Charlotte russe.

Charlotte Corday cap (Corday, Charlotte): Fashion. See: Picken.

CHARLOTTE ELIZABETH. 1652-1722. German Princess Palatine and Duchess of Orleans. See: Nouv. Biog. Univ. Palatine (cape).

Charlotte russe (Charlotte Augusta): Food and Drink. See: Hendrickson.

CHARLOTTE SOPHIA (PRINCESS OF MECKLENBURG-STRELITZ). 1744-1818. Queen of George III of England. See: Dict. Nat. Biog. Strelitzia.

Charlouis' disease (Charlouis, M.): Medicine. See: Dorland; Jablonski; Stedman. Also known as: Breda's disease.

CHARLOUIS, M. fl. 1881. Dutch physician in Java. Cited in: Kelly. Charlouis' disease.

CHARLTON, ALEX ELIAS. 1908- . American electronics engineer. See: Amer. Men Sci., 11th ed. Charlton photoceramic process.

Charlton photoceramic process (Charlton, Alex Elias): Engineering and Industry. See: Thrush.

CHARLTON, WILLY. b. 1889. German physician. Cited in: Garrison and Morton. Schultz-Charlton reaction (or phenomenon).

CHARMAN, WALTER MILLER. b. 1894. American mechanical engineer. See: Who's Who Engin., 1941. C & D hot top.

CHARMAT, EUGENE. fl. 1907. Inventor. (Biography source unavailable.) Charmat process.

Charmat process (Charmat, Eugene): Food and Drink. See: Webster's 3d.

CHARMOT, GUY DENIS. 1914- . French physician. See: World Who's Who Sci. Charmot's syndrome.

Charmot's syndrome (Charmot, Guy Denis): Medicine. See: Jablonski.

CHARNOCK, JOB. d. 1693. English founder of Calcutta. See: Dict. Nat. Biog. Charnockite.

Charnockite (Charnock, Job): Earth Sciences. See: Thrush; Van Nostrand Sci. Encyc.; Webster's 3d.

Charon (Charon, the ferryman): Generic Word (ferryman). See: Partridge; Weekley.

CHARON, THE FERRYMAN. Mythical conveyor of the dead. See: Jobes. Charon, Charon's staircase, Charon's toll.

Charon's staircase (Charon, the ferryman): Theater. See: Webster's 3d.

Charon's toll (Charon, the ferryman): Generic Word (ferry fare). See: Jobes.

CHARPENTIER COSSIGNY, JOSEPH FRANCOIS. 1730-1809. French naturalist and traveller. See: World Who's Who Sci. Cossignea.

CHARPENTIER, PIERRE MARIE AUGUSTINE. 1852-1916. French physician. See: World Who's Who Sci. Charpentier's bands? Charpentier's law?

Charpentier's bands (Charpentier, Pierre Marie Augustine?): Psychology. See: Chaplin; Drever; English.

Charpentier's law (Charpentier, Pierre Marie Augustine?): Psychology. See: Chaplin; Drever; Wolman.

CHARPIT. fl. 1784. Mathematician. See: Pogg. vol. 4. Charpit equations.

Charpit equations (Charpit): Physics. See: Thewlis.

CHARPY, AUGUSTIN GEORGES ALBERT. 1865-1945. French metallurgist and chemist. See: Dict. Sci. Biog. Charpy machine, Charpy test.

Charpy machine (Charpy, Augustin Georges Albert): Physics. See: Webster's 3d.

Charpy test (Charpy, Augustin Georges Albert): Physics. See: Ballentyne; Hackh; Thewlis.

CHARRIERE, JOSEPH-FREDERIC BENOIT. 1803-1876. Swiss-born French surgeon and instrument maker. See: World Who's Who Sci. Charriere scale.

Charriere scale (Charriere, Joseph-Frederic Benoit): Medicine. See: Dorland; Stedman.

CHARRIN, ALBERT (BENOIT-JEROME). 1857-1907. French pathologist. See: World Who's Who Sci. Charrin's disease.

CHARRIN, SALOMON. fl. 1873. French physician. Cited in: Kelly. Charrin-Winckel disease.

Charrin-Winckel disease (Charrin, Salomon and Winckel, Franz Karl Ludwig Wilhelm von). See: Winckel's disease.

Charrin's disease (Charrin, Albert): Medicine. See: Dorland.

CHARTIER, J. fl. 1853. French mathematician. Cited in: Royal Soc. Cat. Sci. Pap., 1800-1863. Chartier's test?

Chartier's test (Chartier, J.?): Mathematics. See: Ballentyne.

Chasalia (Derivation undetermined): Botany. See: Charnock.

CHASE, IRA CARLETON. 1896-1933. American surgeon and gynecologist. See: Who's Who Amer. Med. Chase's sign.

Chase's sign (Chase, Ira Carleton): Medicine. See: Dorland.

CHASLIN, PHILIPPE. b. 1857. French physician. See: Biog. Lex. hervorr. Aerzte, 1880-1930. Chaslin's gliosis.

Chaslin's gliosis (Chaslin, Philippe): Medicine. See: Jablonski.

CHASSAIGNAC, PIERRE MARIE EDOUARD. 1804-1879. French surgeon. See: World Who's Who Sci. Chassaignac's ecraseur, Chassaignac's paralysis, Chassaignac's space, Chassaignac's tubercle.

Chassaignac's ecraseur (Chassaignac, Pierre Marie Edouard): Medicine. See: Stedman.

Chassaignac's paralysis (Chassaignac, Pierre Marie Edouard): Medicine. See: Jablonski.

Chassaignac's space (Chassaignac, Pierre Marie Edouard): Medicine. See: Stedman.

Chassaignac's tubercle (Chassaignac, Pierre Marie Edouard): Medicine. See: Donath; Dorland; Stedman.

CHASSEPOT, ANTOINE ALPHONSE. 1833-1905. French inventor. See: Webster's Biog. Dict. Chassepot (rifle).

Chassepot (rifle) (Chassepot, Antoine Alphonse): Weapons. See: Partridge; Phyfe; Quick.

CHASTEK, J. S. fl. 1932. American fox rancher. (Biography source unavailable.) Chastek paralysis.

Chastek paralysis (Chastek, J. S.): Medicine. See: Stedman; Webster's 3d.

Chateau Ausone (claret) (Ausonius, Decimus Magnus): Food and Drink. See: Brewer.

CHATEAUBRIAND, FRANCOIS. 1768-1848. French writer and statesman. See: Encyc. Brit., 1973. Chateaubriand (steak).

Chateaubriand (steak) (Chateaubriand, Francois): Food and Drink. See: De Sola; Hendrickson.

CHATENAY, ABEL. 1850-1931. French botanist. See: Biog. Notes Upon Botanists. Chatenay pink.

Chatenay pink (Chatenay, Abel): Botany. See: Webster's 3d.

Chatillon furnace (Derivation undetermined): Chemistry. See: Van Nostrand Chem. Dict.

Chatterton, Thomas. See: Rowley, Thomas.

Chatterton's compound (Derivation undetermined): Chemistry. See: Hackh.

CHATTOCK, ARTHUR PRINCE. 1860-1934. English physicist. See: Pogg., vols. 4-6, 7b. Chattock-Fry tilting micromanometer?, Chattock gauge?

Chattock-Fry tilting micromanometer (Chattock, Arthur Prince? and Fry, J. D.): Physics. See: Thrush.

Chattock gauge (Chattock, Arthur Prince?): Physics. See: Internat. Dict. Phys. Elec.; Thewlis; Van Nostrand Sci. Encyc.

CHAUCER, GEOFFREY. 1340?-1400. English poet. See: Dict. Nat. Biog. Chaucer Society, Chaucer type, Chaucerian (or Chaucerism), Chaucerian stanza, Scottish Chaucerians.

Chaucer Society (Chaucer, Geoffrey): Literature. See: Barnhart (Eng. Lit.); Harvey.

Chaucer type (Chaucer, Geoffrey): Printing. See: Harrod.

Chaucerian (or Chaucerism) (Chaucer, Geoffrey): Literature. See: Partridge; Webster's 3d.

Chaucerian stanza (Chaucer, Geoffrey): Literature. See: Scott.

CHAUDHRY, ANAND P. 1922- . Indian-born American oral pathologist. See: Amer. Men and Women Sci., 12th ed. Gorlin-Chaudhry-Moss syndrome.

Chaudhurei (Chaudhuri, Banawari Lal?): Zoology. See: Pennak.

CHAUDHURI, BANAWARI LAL. fl. 1912. Indian biologist. (Biography source unavailable.) Chaudhurei?

CHAUFFARD, ANATOLE MARIE EMILE. 1855-1932. French physician. See: World Who's Who Sci. Chauffard-Ramond syndrome, Chauffard-Still syndrome, Minkowski-Chauffard syndrome, Troisier-Hanot-Chauffard syndrome.

Chauffard-Ramond syndrome (Chauffard, Anatole Marie Emile and Ramond, Felix). See: Still's syndrome.

Chauffard-Still syndrome (Chauffard, Anatole Marie Emile and Still, Sir George Frederick). See: Still's syndrome.

CHAUSSIER, FRANCOIS. 1746-1828. French physician. See: World Who's Who Sci. Chaussier's areola, Chaussier's line, Chaussier's sign, Chaussier's tube.

Chaussier's areola (Chaussier, Francois): Medicine. See: Dorland; Stedman.

Chaussier's line (Chaussier, Francois): Medicine. See: Dorland; Stedman.

Chaussier's sign (Chaussier, Francois): Medicine. See: Dorland; Stedman.

Chaussier's tube (Chaussier, Francois): Medicine. See: Dorland.

CHAUTARD, PAUL HENRY JOSEPH. fl. 1886. French chemist. Cited in: Royal Soc. Cat. Sci. Pap., 1884-1900. Chautard's test.

Chautard's test (Chautard, Paul Henry Joseph): Medicine. See: Stedman.

CHAUVEAU, JEAN-BAPTISTE AUGUSTE. 1827-1917. French veterinary surgeon. See: Dict. Sci. Biog. Chauveau's bacterium.

Chauveau's bacterium (Chauveau, Jean-Baptiste Auguste): Medicine. See: Dorland; Stedman.

CHAUVIN, NICOLAS. fl. 1815. French soldier. See: Webster's Biog. Dict. Chauvinism.

Chauvinism (Chauvin, Nicolas): Generic Word (exaggerated patriotism). See: Brewer; Funk; Harbottle.

chaux de Theil (Derivation undetermined): Engineering and Industry. See: Thrush.

CHAVANNE, GEORGES. 1875-1941. French chemist. See: Pogg., vols. 6, 7b. Simon-Chavaune test reactions.

Chavany-Brunhes syndrome (Chavany, Jean Alfred Emile and Brunhes, S.): Medicine. See: Jablonski.

CHAVANY, JEAN ALFRED EMILE. 1892-1959. French physician. See: Dict. Nat. Contemp., vol. 3, p. 160. Chavany-Brunhes syndrome, Putti-Chavany syndrome.

CHAVASSIEU, HENRY L. J. fl. 1906. French chemist. Cited in: Chem. Abstr., Decenn. Index, 1907-1916. Morel-Chavassieu test for purines.

CHAVASTELON, RAOUL. fl. 1897. French chemist. Cited in: Royal Soc. Cat. Sci. Pap., 1884-1900. Chavastelon test reaction.

Chavastelon test reaction (Chavastelon, Raoul): Chemistry. See: Van Nostrand Chem. Dict.

CHAYES, HERMAN E. S. 1879-1933. American dentist. See: New York J. Dent., vol. 3, no. 9 (Sept., 1933) p. 209. Chayes' method.

Chayes' method (Chayes, Herman E. S.): Dentistry. See: Stedman.

Cheadle-Moeller-Barlow disease (Cheadle, Walter Butler; Moeller, Julius Otto Ludwig; and Barlow, Sir Thomas). See: Moeller-Barlow disease.

CHEADLE, WALTER BUTLER. 1835-1910. English pediatrician. See: World Who's Who Sci. Cheadle-Moeller-Barlow disease, Cheadle's disease.

Cheadle's disease (Cheadle, Walter Butler). See: Moeller-Barlow disease.

CHEATLE, SIR GEORGE LENTHAL. b. 1865. English surgeon. See: Who's Who, 1930. Cheatle's disease.

Cheatle's disease (Cheatle, Sir George Lenthal): Medicine. See: Jablonski. Also known as: Bloodgood's disease, Cooper's disease, Reclus' syndrome, Schimmelbusch's disease, Tillaux-Phocas disease.

Chebyshev('s) approximation (Chebyshev, Pafnuty Lvovich): Mathematics. See: Ballentyne; Internat. Dict. Ap. Math.

Chebyshev (Tschebyscheff) equation (Chebyshev, Pafnuty Lvovich): Mathematics. See: Internat. Dict. Ap. Math.; Internat. Dict. Phys. Elec.; Van Nostrand Sci. Encyc.

Chebyshev expansion (Chebyshev, Pafnuty Lvovich): Mathematics. See: Internat. Dict. Ap. Math.

Chebyshev filter (Chebyshev, Pafnuty Lvovich): Electronics. See: Hughes.

Chebyshev('s) (Tchebychev) inequality (Chebyshev, Pafnuty Lvovich): Statistics. See: Ballentyne; Internat. Dict. Ap. Math.; Kendall.

Chebyshev net of parametric curves on a surface (Chebyshev, Pafnuty Lvovich): Mathematics. See: James.

CHEBYSHEV, PAFNUTY LVOVICH. 1821-1894. Russian mathematician. See: Dict. Sci. Biog. Bienayme-Chebyshev inequality, Chebyshev('s) approximation, Chebyshev (Tschebyscheff) equation, Chebyshev expansion, Chebyshev filter, Chebyshev('s) (Tchebychev) inequality, Chebyshev net of parametric curves on a surface, Chebyshev (Tschebyscheff) polynomial(s), Chebyshev quadrature formula, Chebyshev response, Chebyshev shape, Chebyshev system (of order n), Chebyshev's theorem, Cramer-Tchebychev inequality, Tchebischeff's parallel motion, Tchebischeff-Hermite polynomials.

Chebyshev (Tschebyscheff) polynomial(s) (Chebyshev, Pafnuty Lvovich): Mathematics. See: Ballentyne; Internat. Dict. Ap. Math.; Internat. Dict. Phys. Elec.

Chebyshev quadrature formula (Chebyshev, Pafnuty Lvovich): Mathematics. See: Internat. Dict. Ap. Math.

Chebyshev response (Chebyshev, Pafnuty Lvovich): Electronics. See: Hughes.

Chebyshev shape (Chebyshev, Pafnuty Lvovich): Electronics. See: Internat. Dict. Phys. Elec.

Chebyshev system (of order n) (Chebyshev, Pafnuty Lvovich): Mathematics. See: Internat. Dict. Ap. Math.

Chebyshev's theorem (Chebyshev, Pafnuty Lvovich): Statistics. See: James.

CHEDIAK, ALEJANDRO. b. 1904. Cuban physician. Cited in: New York Acad, Med. Portrait Cat. Chediak reaction (or test).

Chevkinite (Tscheffkin, Konstantin V.) See: Tscheffkinite.

CHEWINGS, CHARLES. d. 1937. Australian scientist. (Biography source unavailable.) Chewings fescue.

Chewings fescue (Chewings, Charles): Agriculture. See: Webster's 3d., Winburne.

CHEYNE, JOHN. 1777-1836. Scottish medical writer. See: Dict. Nat. Biog. Cheyne-Stokes asthma, Cheyne-Stokes psychosis, Cheyne-Stokes respiration, Cheyne's disease, Cheyne's nystagmus.

Cheyne-Stokes asthma (Cheyne, John and Stokes, William): Medicine. See: Stedman.

Cheyne-Stokes psychosis (Cheyne, John and Stokes, William): Medicine. See: Hinsie; Stedman; Wolman.

Cheyne-Stokes respiration (Cheyne, John and Stokes, William): Medicine. See: Drever; English; Jablonski.

CHEYNE, WILLIAM WATSON. 1852-1932. English surgeon. See: Dict. Nat. Biog., 5th suppl. Cheyne's operation.

Cheyne's disease (Cheyne, John): Medicine. See: Jablonski.

Cheyne's nystagmus (Cheyne, John): Medicine. See: Dorland; Stedman.

Cheyne's operation (Cheyne, William Watson): Medicine. See: Dorland.

Chezy formula (De Chezy, Antoine?): Physics. See: Thrush; Van Nostrand Sci. Encyc.

CHIANG KAI-SHEK. 1887- . Chinese general and statesman. See: Encyc. Brit., 1973. Chinese 7.92 mm Chiang Kai Shek rifle.

Chiari-Frommel syndrome (Chiari, Johann Baptiste and Frommel, Richard Julius Ernst): Medicine. See: Jablonski; Stedman. Also known as: Frommel's disease.

CHIARI, HANS. 1851-1916. Czech physician. See: Wer Ist's, 1905. Arnold-Chiari syndrome (or deformity), Budd-Chiari syndrome, Chiari's net.

CHIARI, JOHANN BAPTIST. 1817-1854. Austrian physician. See: Biog. Lex. hervorr. Aerzte. Chiari-Frommel syndrome.

Chiari's disease (Chiari, Hans). See: Budd-Chiari syndrome.

Chiari's net (Chiari, Hans): Medicine. See: Dorland; Stedman.

CHIAROTTINO, A. fl. 1933. Italian chemist. Cited in: Chem. Abstr., vol. 27, p. 2396. Chiarottino's reagent.

Chiarottino's reagent (Chiarottino, A.): Chemistry. See: Van Nostrand Chem. Dict.

CHICHIBABIN, ALEXEI YEVGENIEVICH. 1871-1945. Russian chemist. See: Dict. Sci. Biog. Bodroux-Chichibabin reaction (or aldehyde synthesis), Chichibabin pyridine synthesis, Chichibabin reaction.

Chichibabin pyridine synthesis (Chichibabin, Alexei Yevgenievich): Chemistry. See: Van Nostrand Chem. Dict.

Chichibabin reaction (Chichibabin, Alexei Yevgenievich): Chemistry. See: Van Nostrand Chem. Dict.

CHICK, HARRIETTE. b. 1875. English physiologist. (Biography source unavailable.) Chick-Martin test.

Chick-Martin test (Chick, Harriette and Martin, Sir Charles James): Medicine. See: Stedman.

Chickele Professor (Chickeley, Henry): History. See: Wagner (More Names).

CHICKELEY, HENRY. 1362-1443. Archbishop of Canterbury. (Biography source unavailable.) Chickele Professor.

chicken Tetrazzini (Tetrazzini, Luisa): Food and Drink. See: De Sola; Hendrickson.

CHIDDEY, ALFRED. fl. 1900. English chemist. Cited in: Royal Soc. Cat. Sci. Pap., 1884-1900. Chiddy's test?

Chiddy's test (Chiddey, Alfred?): Chemistry. See: Thrush.

CH'IEN LUNG (KIEN LUNG). 1711-1799. Chinese emperor. See: Encyc. Brit., 1973. Ch'ien Lung.

Ch'ien Lung (Ch'ien Lung, the emperor): Fine Arts. See: Webster's 3d.

Chien-Shih solution (Chien, Szu-Liang and Shih, Tsai-Min): Chemistry. See: Van Nostrand Chem. Dict.

CHIEN, SZU-LIANG. 1908- . Chinese chemist. Cited in: Chem. Abstr., vol. 31, p. 6130. Chien-Shih solution.

CHIENE, JOHN. 1843-1923. Scottish surgeon. See: Biog. Lex. hervorr. Aerzte, 1880-1930. Chiene's operation.

Chiene's operation (Chiene, John): Medicine. See: Dorland.

Chietini (Paul IV). See: Theatines.

CHIEVITZ, JOHAN HENRIK. 1850-1901. Danish anatomist. See: Sci., vol. 15 (1902) p. 79. Chievitz' layer, Chievitz' organ.

Chievitz' layer (Chievitz, Johan Henrik): Medicine. See: Dorland; Stedman.

Chievitz' organ (Chievitz, Johan Henrik): Medicine. See: Dorland.

Chignon's disease (Derivation undetermined). See: Beigel's disease.

CHILAIDITI, DEMETRIOS. b. 1883. Austrian-born physician. See: Biog. Lex. hervorr. Aerzte, 1880-1930. Chilaiditi's syndrome.

Chilaiditi's syndrome (Chilaiditi, Demetrios): Medicine. See: Jablonski; Stedman.

CHILD, CHARLES MANNING. 1869-1954. American zoologist. See: Dict. Sci. Biog. Childia.

CHILD, CLEMENT DEXTER. 1868-1933. American physicist. See: Pogg., vols. 4-6, 7b. Child-Langmuir equation, Child-Langmuir-Schottky equation, Child's law.

CHILD, FRANCIS JAMES. 1825-1896. American scholar and educator. See: Encyc. Brit., 1973. Childe ballad.

Child-Langmuir equation (Child, Clement Dexter and Langmuir, Irving): Physics. See: Thewlis.

Child-Langmuir-Schottky equation (Child, Clement Dexter; Langmuir, Irving; and Schottky, Walter): Physics. See: Hughes; Internat. Dict. Phys. Elec.

Childe ballad (Child, Francis James): Music. See: Hendrickson.

Childia (Child, Charles Manning): Zoology. See: Pennak.

CHILDREN, JOHN GEORGE. 1777-1852. English chemist. See: Dict. Nat. Biog. Childrenite.

Childrenite (Children, John George): Earth Sciences. See: Charnock; Thrush; Van Nostrand Sci. Encyc.

Child's law (Child, Clement Dexter): Physics. See: Ballentyne; Markus.

CHILON. fl. 556 B.C. Spartan statesman. See: Encyc. Amer., 1959. Chilonian (or Chilonic).

Chilonian (or Chilonic) (Chilon): Generic Word (brief). See: Charnock.

CHIMERA. Mythical fire-breathing monster. See: Jobes. Chimerical.

Chimerical (Chimera): Generic Word (unreal). See: Partridge.

CHIN FANG SHIH. fl. 249 B.C. Chinese priest-magician. (Biography source unavailable.) Fang Shih.

CHINCHON, DONA FRANCISCA HENRIQUEZ DE RIBERA, COUNTESS OF. d. 1641. Vicereine of Peru. (Biography source unavailable.) Chinchona (bark), Quinina (Quinia or Quinine)?

Chinchona (bark) (Chinchon, Dona Francisca Henriquez de Ribera, Countess of): Botany. See: Dorland; Hendrickson; Van Nostrand Sci. Encyc.

Chinese 7.92mm Chiang Kai Shek rifle (Chiang Kai-Shek): Weapons. See: Quick.

CHIO, FELICE. 1813-1871. Italian mathematician. See: Riv. Sci. Ind., vol. 3 (1872) p. 61. Chio's method (for evaluating a determinant).

Chio's method (for evaluating a determinant) (Chio, Felice): Mathematics. See: Internat. Dict. Ap. Math.

Chippendale (furniture) (Chippendale, Thomas): Applied Arts. See: Hendrickson; Partridge; Webster's 3d.

CHIPPENDALE, THOMAS. 1718-1779. English cabinetmaker. See: Dict. Nat. Biog. Chippendale (furniture).

Chireix-Mesny antenna (Derivation undetermined): Physics. See: Hughes; Internat. Dict. Phys. Elec.

Chireix transmitter (Derivation undetermined): Electronics. See: Hughes.

Chisholm effect and the laws of human interaction (Chisholm, Francis Perry): Sociology. See: Martin.

CHISHOLM, FRANCIS PERRY. 1905- . American linguist. (Biography source unavailable.) Chisholm effect and the laws of human interaction.

Chishti (Chishti, Mu'in al-Din Muhammad): Religion. See: Webster's 3d.

CHISHTI, MU'IN AL-DIN MUHAMMAD. d. 1236. Indian saint. (Biography source unavailable.) Chishti.

CHITTENDEN, RUSSELL HENRY. 1856-1943. American chemist and educator. See: Dict. Sci. Biog. Chittenden's standard diet.

Chittenden's standard diet (Chittenden, Russell Henry): Medicine. See: Dorland; Stedman.

CHIZYNSKI, ANTON. fl. 1865. German chemist. Cited in: Royal Soc. Cat. Sci. Pap., 1864-1873. Chizynski test?

Chizynski test (Chizynski, Anton?): Chemistry. See: Van Nostrand Chem. Dict.

CHLADNI, ERNST FLORENZ FRIEDRICH. 1756-1827. German physicist. See: Dict. Sci. Biog. Chladni('s) figures, Chladnite.

Chladni('s) figures (Chladni, Ernst Florenz Friedrich): Physics. See: Ballentyne; Thewlis; Webster's 3d.

Chladnite (Chladni, Ernst Florenz Friedrich): Earth Sciences. See: Thrush; Webster's 3d.

Chlopin test reaction for iridium (Chlopin, Vitalius Gregor): Chemistry. See: Van Nostrand Chem. Dict.

Chlopin test reagent for ozone (Chlopin, Vitalius Gregor?): Chemistry. See: Van Nostrand Chem. Dict.

CHLOPIN, VITALIUS GREGOR. 1890-1950. Russian chemist. See: Pogg., vols. 6, 7b. Chlopin test reaction for iridium, Chlopin test reagent for ozone?

CHLUMSKY, VITEZSLAV. b. 1867. Czech surgeon. See: Biog. Lex. hervorr. Aerzte, 1880-1930. Chlumsky's button, Chlumsky's solution.

Chlumsky's button (Chlumsky, Vitezslav): Medicine. See: Dorland.

Chlumsky's solution (Chlumsky, Vitezslav): Medicine. See: Dorland.

chocolat-Menier (Menier, Emile Justin): Food and Drink. See: Wagner (More Names).

CHODAT, ROBERT. 1865-1934. Swiss botanist. See: Dict. Sci. Biog. Chodat test reaction.

Chodat test reaction (Chodat, Robert): Chemistry. See: Van Nostrand Chem. Dict.

Chodzko's reflex (Derivation undetermined): Medicine. See: Stedman.

CHOISEUL, CESAR, DUC DE (MARECHAL DU PLESSIS-PRASLIN). 1602-1675. French field marshal. See: Nouv. Biog. Univ. Praline.

CHOISY, JACQUES DENIS. 1799-1859. Swiss botanist. See: Biog. Notes Upon Botanists. Choisya.

Choisya (Choisy, Jacques Denis): Botany. See: Taylor, N.

Choleski's method (for inverting a positive definite Hermitian matrix A) (Derivation undetermined): Mathematics. See: Internat. Dict. Ap. Math.

Cholesky method of solving equations (Derivation undetermined): Mathematics. See: Van Nostrand Sci. Encyc.

CHOLEWA, ERASMUS RUDOLPH. b. 1845. German physician. Cited in: Royal Soc. Cat. Sci. Pap., 1884-1900. Itard-Chowlewa sign.

CHOMEL, AUGUST FRANCOIS. 1788-1858. French physician. See: World Who's Who Sci. Chomelia.

Chomelia (Chomel, August Francois): Botany. See: Charnock.

CHONGJO. fl. 1776-1800. King of Korea. (Biography source unavailable.) Yongjong Era.

CHOPART, FRANCOIS. 1743-1795. French surgeon. See: World Who's Who Sci. Chopart's amputation, Chopart's articulation (or joint).

Chopart's amputation (Chopart, Francois): Medicine. See: Dorland; Stedman.

Chopart's articulation (or joint) (Chopart, Francois): Medicine. See: Donath; Stedman; Webster's 3d.

chordae Willisii (Willis, Thomas). See: Willis' cords.

chorea St. Viti (Vitus, Saint). See: Saint Vitus' dance.

CHORIS, LOUIS. 1795-1828. Russian painter and traveler. See: Nouv. Biog. Univ. Chorisia.

Chorisia (Choris, Louis): Botany. See: Taylor, N.

CHORON, YVONNE. fl. 1935. French physician. Cited in: Chem. Abstr., vol. 28, p. 4455. Chevallier-Choron test.

Chouan(s) (Cottereau, Jean): History. See: Harvey; Latham; Webster's 3d.

Chouan, Jean. See: Cottereau, Jean ("Chouan").

CHOUCHAK, D. fl. 1911-1929. Algerian chemist. Cited in: Chem. Abstr., vol. 5, p. 3208. Pouget-Chouchak solution.

CHOW, TSE-SHUI. fl. 1937. Chinese chemist. Cited in: Chem. Abstr., vol. 31, p. 8442. Tseou-Chow test reaction.

CHRETIEN, HENRY. 1870-1956. French mathematician and astronomer. See: World Who's Who Sci. Ritchey-Chretien telescope.

Chretien telescope (Chretien, Henry). See: Ritchey-Chretien telescope.

chriopeops Goodei (Goode, George Brown): Zoology. See: Pennak.

CHRIST, J. fl. 1913. German physician. (Biography source unavailable.) Christ-Siemens-Touraine syndrome.

Christ, Jesus. See: Jesus Christ.

Christ-Siemens-Touraine syndrome (Christ, J.; Siemens, Hermann Werner; and Touraine, M. A.): Medicine. See: Jablonski.

Christadelphian(s) (Jesus Christ): Religion. See: Attwater; Canney; Encyc. Brit., 1973; Jameson; Mathews, S.; Weekley. Also known as: Brothers of Christ, Thomasites.

CHRISTEL, G. fl. 1883. German physician. Cited in: Royal Soc. Cat. Sci. Pap., 1800-1883 (suppl.). Christel reactions.

Christel reactions (Christel, G.): Chemistry. See: Van Nostrand Chem. Dict.

Christen (or Christening) (Jesus Christ): Religion. See: Attwater; Charnock; Mathews, S.; Partridge.

Christendom (Jesus Christ): Religion. See: Attwater; Brewer; Mathews, S.

CHRISTENSEN, ANDERS. 1852-1923. Danish chemist. See: Pogg., vols. 5, 6. Christensen reagent for quinine.

CHRISTENSEN, E. fl. 1928. German? physician. Cited in: Chem. Abstr., vol. 24, p. 5351. Christensen test reaction for hormones and vitamins.

CHRISTENSEN, ERNA. 1906-1967. Danish neurologist. See: Nord. Med., vol. 79 (1968) p. 658. Christensen-Krabbe disease.

Christensen-Krabbe disease (Christensen, Erna and Krabbe, Knud H.). See: Alpers' disease.

Christensen process (Derivation undetermined): Chemistry. See: Van Nostrand Chem. Dict.

Christensen reagent for quinine (Christensen, Anders): Chemistry. See: Van Nostrand Chem. Dict.

Christensen test reaction for hormones and vitamins (Christensen, E.): Chemistry. See: Van Nostrand Chem. Dict.

Christian (Jesus Christ): Religion. See: Attwater; Black; Brewer; Mathews, S.; Partridge.

CHRISTIAN V. 1646-1699. King of Denmark and Norway. See: Encyc. Brit., 1973. Christian Code.

CHRISTIAN VII. 1749-1808. King of Denmark and Norway. See: Encyc. Brit., 1973. Christian d'or.

Christian Code (Christian V): Law. Cited in: Webster's Biog. Dict.

Christian d'or (Christian VII): Numismatics. See: Charnock; Webster's 3d.

CHRISTIAN, HENRY ASBURY. 1876-1951. American internist. See: World Who's Who Sci. Hand-Schueller-Christian syndrome, Weber-Christian syndrome.

Christianity (Jesus Christ): Religion. See: Attwater; Black; Encyc. Brit., 1973; Mathews, S.

Christians (or Disciples) of St. John (or St. John's Christians) (John the Baptist, Saint): Religion. See: Canney; Mathews, S.

Christians of St. Thomas (Thomas the Apostle, Saint). See: Saint Thomas Christians.

Christian's syndrome (Christian, Henry Asbury). See: Hand-Schueller-Christian syndrome.

CHRISTIANSEN, CHRISTIAN. 1843-1917. Danish physicist. See: World Who's Who Sci. Christiansen effect?, Christiansen filter?

Christiansen effect (Christiansen, Christian?): Chemistry. See: Thrush.

Christiansen filter (Christiansen, Christian?): Physics. See: Internat. Dict. Phys. Elec.; Thewlis; Van Nostrand Sci. Encyc.

Christinos (Maria Christina de Borbon): History. See: Brewer; Harbottle; Latham.

CHRISTISON, SIR ROBERT. 1797-1882. Scottish physician. See: Dict. Nat. Biog. Christison's formula.

Christison's formula (Christison, Sir Robert): Medicine. See: Dorland; Stedman. Also known as: Haeser's formula (or coefficient).

Christmas (Jesus Christ): Religion. See: Attwater; Brewer; Encyc. Brit., 1973; Hendrickson; Mathews, S.; Weekley.

Christmas disease (Christmas, Stephen): Medicine. See: Stedman; Webster's 3d.

Christmas factor (Christmas, Stephen): Medicine. See: Stedman.

CHRISTMAS, STEPHEN. fl. 20th c. English hospital patient. (Biography source unavailable.) Christmas disease, Christmas factor.

CHRISTOFFEL, ELWIN BRUNO. 1829-1900. German mathematician. See: Dict. Sci. Biog. Christoffel symbol(s), Riemann-Christoffel curvature tensor, Schwarz-Christoffel transformation.

Christoffel symbol(s) (Christoffel, Elwin Bruno): Mathematics. See: Ballentyne; James; Van Nostrand Sci. Encyc.

Christology (Jesus Christ): Religion. See: Attwater; Mathews, S.

CHRISTOPHER, SAINT. fl. 3d. c. Christian martyr. See: Encyc. Brit., 1973. herb Christopher, images of St. Christopher.

Christ's thorn (Jesus Christ): Botany. See: Charnock; Gray; Winburne.

CHRISTY, EDWIN P. 1815-1862. American actor and singer. See: Dict. Amer. Biog. Christy('s) minstrels.

Christy('s) minstrels (Christy, Edwin P.): Music. See: Harvey; Hendrickson; Mathews, M. M.

CHRISTY, SAMUEL BENEDICT. 1853-1914. American metallurgist. See: Who Was Who Amer., 1897-1942. Christy's equation.

Christy's equation (Christy, Samuel Benedict): Engineering and Industry. See: Thrush.

Chrobak pelvis (Chrobak, Rudolf): Medicine. See: Stedman.

CHROBAK, RUDOLF. 1843-1910. Austrian gynecologist. See: World Who's Who Sci. Chrobak pelvis, Otto-Chrobak syndrome.

Chrustiov's hardness scale (Derivation undetermined): Engineering and Industry. See: Thrush.

Chrysostom, Saint John. See: John Chrysostom, Saint.

CHUBB, CHARLES. d. 1845. English locksmith. See: Dict. Nat. Biog. Chubb('s) lock.

Chubb('s) lock (Chubb, Charles): Engineering and Industry. See: Partridge.

CHUGAEV, LEV ALEKSANDROVICH. 1873-1922. Russian chemist. See: Dict. Sci. Biog. Chugaev reaction (or method), Tschugaev-Orelkin test for ferrous iron, Tschugaev reagent and test for nickel, Tschugaev tests for differentiating borneol and isoborneol, Tschugaev's ring rule.

Chugaev reaction (or method) (Chugaev, Lev Aleksandrovich): Chemistry. See: Ballentyne; Van Nostrand Chem. Dict.

CHUKHROV, FEDOR VASILEVICH. 1908-   . Russian mineralogist and geochemist. See: World Who's Who Sci. Chukhrovite.

Chukhrovite (Chukhrov, Fedor Vasilevich): Earth Sciences. See: Thrush.

CHURCH, ARTHUR HERBERT. 1834-1915. English chemist. See: Encyc. Amer., 1959. Churchite.

Church boiler (Church, William?): Engineering and Industry. See: Auger.

CHURCH, WILLIAM. 1779-1864. American-born mechanical engineer. See: Boase, suppl. Church boiler?

CHURCH, WILLIAM. fl. 1822. American inventor. See: Webster's Biog. Dict. Church's press.

CHURCHILL, JOHN, 1ST DUKE OF MARLBOROUGH. 1560-1722. English statesman and soldier. See: Dict. Nat. Biog. Marlborough spaniels.

CHURCHILL, SIR WINSTON LEONARD SPENCER. 1874-1965. English statesman. See: Encyc. Brit., 1973. Churchillian.

Churchillian (Churchill, Sir Winston Leonard Spencer): Generic Word (eloquence). See: Hendrickson; Partridge; Webster's 3d.

Churchite (Church, Arthur Herbert): Earth Sciences. See: Thrush; Webster's 3d.

Church's press (Church, William): Printing. See: Lockwood.

CHURRIGUERA, JOSE. 1650-1723. Spanish architect. See: Encyc. Brit., 1973. Churrigueresque.

Churrigueresque (Churriguera, Jose): Generic Word (ornate architecture). See: Brewer; Charnock; Hendrickson.

CHVOSTEK, FRANZ. 1835-1884. Austrian surgeon. See: World Who's Who Sci. Chvostek's anemia, Chvostek's habitus, Chvostek's tremor (or sign).

Chvostek's anemia (Chvostek, Franz): Medicine. See: Dorland.

Chvostek's habitus (Chvostek, Franz): Medicine. See: Stedman.

Chvostek's tremor (or sign) (Chvostek, Franz): Medicine. See: Dorland; Jablonski; Stedman.

CIACCIO, GINO GIUSEPPI VINCENZO. 1824-1901. Italian anatomist. See: Sci., vol. 14 (1901) p. 158. Ciaccio's glands.

Ciaccio's glands (Ciaccio, Gino Giuseppi Vincenzo): Medicine. See: Dorland; Stedman.

CIACCO, CARMELO. b. 1877. Italian pathologist. See: Gazz. Internaz. Med. Chir., (Mar. 15, 1929) p. 299. Ciacco's method.

Ciacco's method (Ciacco, Carmelo): Medicine. See: Stedman.

Ciamician-Dennstedt rearrangement (Ciamician, Giacomo Luigi and Dennstedt, Max Eugen Hermann): Chemistry. See: Van Nostrand Chem. Dict.

CIAMICIAN, GIACOMO LUIGI. 1857-1922. Italian chemist. See: Dict. Sci. Biog. Ciamician-Dennstedt rearrangement, Ciamician-Magnanini test.

Ciamician-Magnanini test (Ciamician, Giacomo Luigi and Magnanini, Gaetano): Chemistry. See: Van Nostrand Chem. Dict.

CIARROCCHI, GAETANO. 1857-1924. Italian dermatologist. See: Biog. Lex. hervorr. Aerzte, 1880-1930. Ciarrocchi's disease.

Ciarrocchi's disease (Ciarrocchi, Gaetano): Medicine. See: Dorland.

CICERO, MARCUS TULLIUS. 106-43 B.C. Roman orator, statesman, and philosopher. See: Encyc. Brit., 1973. Cicero (unit), Cicerone, Ciceronian (or Ciceronianism), Ciceronian sentence.

Cicero (unit) (Cicero, Marcus Tullius): Printing. See: Hendrickson.

Cicerone (Cicero, Marcus Tullius): Generic Word (guide). See: Brewer; Funk; Partridge.

Ciceronian (or Ciceronianism) (Cicero, Marcus Tullius): Generic Word (eloquent). See: Good; Hendrickson; Partridge.

Ciceronian sentence (Cicero, Marcus Tullius): Literature. See: Barnet; Scott.

CIMMINO, RAFFAELE. fl. 1896. Italian chemist. Cited in: Royal Soc. Cat. Sci. Pap., 1884-1900. Cimmino reagent?

Cimmino reagent (Cimmino, Raffaele?): Chemistry. See: Van Nostrand Chem. Dict.

Cincinnatus (Cincinnatus, Lucius Quinctius): Generic Word. See: Hendrickson; Partridge; Weekley.

CINCINNATUS, LUCIUS QUINCTIUS. fl. 458 B.C. Roman general and statesman. See: Encyc. Brit., 1973. Cincinnatus, Society of the Cincinnati.

Cinderella (Cinderella, the heroine): Generic Word. See: Webster's 3d.

Cinderella (dance) (Cinderella, the heroine): Generic Word. See: Partridge; Wagner (Names); Webster's 3d.

Cinderella slipper (Cinderella, the heroine): Fashion. See: Mathews, M. M.

CINDERELLA, THE HEROINE. Fairy tale heroine. See: Benet. Cinderella, Cinderella (dance), Cinderella slipper.

CINISELLI, LUIGI. 1803-1878. Italian surgeon. See: Biog. Lex. hervorr. Aerzte. Ciniselli's method.

Ciniselli's method (Ciniselli, Luigi): Medicine. See: Dorland; Stedman.

CINZANO, FRANCESCO. 1783-1859. Italian industrialist. See: Diz. Encic. Ital. Cinzano (wine).

Cinzano (wine) (Cinzano, Francesco): Food and Drink. See: Partridge.

CIPOLLETTI, CESARE. 1843-1908. Italian engineer. See: Diz. Encic. Ital. Cipolletti (Cipoletti) weir.

Cipolletti (Cipoletti) weir (Cipolletti, Cesare): Engineering and Industry. See: Thrush; Webster's 3d; Winburne.

CIPOLLINA, A. fl. 1901. Italian physician. Cited in: Kelly. Cipollina's test.

Cipollina's test (Cipollina, A.): Medicine. See: Stedman.

Circaea (Circe): Botany. See: Charnock; Webster's 3d.

CIRCE. Mythical sorceress deity. See: Encyc. Brit., 1973. Circaea, Circean.

Circean (Circe): Generic Word (attractive woman). See: Partridge; Webster's 3d.

circle of Ulloa (Ulloa, Antonio de). See: Ulloa's ring (bow or circle).

circle of Willis (Willis, Thomas). See: Willis' circle.

circulus Zinnii (Zinn, Johann Gottfried). See: Zinn's vascular circle.

circus Hudsonicus (Hudson, William Henry?): Zoology. See: Pennak.

CIRILLO, DOMINICO. 1739-1799. Italian physician. See: Encyc. Brit., 1911. Cyrilla.

cissoid of Diocles (Diocles): Mathematics. See: Ballentyne; Van Nostrand Sci. Encyc.

cistenides Gouldi (Gould, Augustus Addison?): Zoology. See: Pennak.

cistern of Pecquet (Pecquet, Jean). See: Pecquet's cistern (receptaculum or reservoir).

CITELLI, SALVATORE. 1875-1947. Italian laryngologist. See: Biog. Lex. hervorr. Aerzte, 1880-1930. Citelli's syndrome.

Citelli's syndrome (Citelli, Salvatore): Medicine. See: Dorland; Jablonski.

Citron Flood Compact Act (Citron, William Michael): Law. See: Smith.

CITRON, WILLIAM MICHAEL. 1896- . American legislator. See: Biog. Direct. Amer. Congress. Citron Flood Compact Act.

Ciuffini-Pancoast syndrome (Ciuffini and Pancoast, Henry Khunrath). See: Pancoast's syndrome (apex syndrome or tumor).

Ciusa test reaction (Ciussa, Riccardo?): Chemistry. See: Van Nostrand Chem. Dict.

CIUSSA, RICCARDO. 1877-1965. Italian chemist. See: World Who's Who Sci. Ciusa test reaction?

CIVATTE, ACHILLE. 1877-1956. French dermatologist. See: Ann. de Derm. Syph., vol. 83 (1956) p. 483. Civatte bodies, Civatte's disease.

Civatte bodies (Civatte, Achille): Medicine. See: Stedman.

Civatte's disease (Civatte, Achille): Medicine. See: Dorland; Jablonski; Stedman.

CIVIALE, JEAN. 1792-1867. French surgeon. See: World Who's Who Sci. Civiale's operation.

Civiale's operation (Civiale, Jean): Medicine. See: Dorland.

CIVININI, FILIPPO. 1805-1844. Italian anatomist. See: Biog. Lex. hervorr. Aerzte. Civinini's canal, Civinini's ligament, Civinini's orifice, Civinini's process, Civinini's spine.

Civinini's canal (Civinini, Filippo): Medicine. See: Stedman. Also known as: Huguier's canal.

Civinini's ligament (Civinini, Filippo): Medicine. See: Stedman.

Civinini's orifice (Civinini, Filippo): Medicine. See: Donath.

Civinini's process (Civinini, Filippo): Medicine. See: Donath; Stedman.

Civinini's spine (Civinini, Filippo): Medicine. See: Dorland.

CLADO, SPIRO. 1862-1920. Turkish-born French gynecologist. See: World Who's Who Sci. Clado's anastomosis, Clado's band, Clado's ligament, Clado's points.

Clado's anastomosis (Clado, Spiro): Medicine. See: Dorland; Stedman.

Clado's band (Clado, Spiro): Medicine. See: Dorland; Stedman.

Clado's ligament (Clado, Spiro): Medicine. See: Dorland; Stedman.

Clado's points (Clado, Spiro): Medicine. See: Dorland; Stedman.

Clairant's theorem (Clairaut, Alexis-Claude): Physics. See: Ballentyne.

CLAIRAUT, ALEXIS-CLAUDE. 1713-1765. French mathematician. See: Dict. Sci. Biog. Clairant's theorem, Clairaut and Stokes theorems, Clairaut('s) equation (or differential equation).

Clairaut and Stokes theorems (Clairaut, Alexis-Claude and Stokes, Sir George Gabriel): Physics. See: Thewlis.

Clairaut('s) equation (or differential equation) (Clairaut, Alexis-Claude): Mathematics. See: Ballentyne; Internat. Dict. Ap. Math.; James.

Claisen condensation (Claisen, Ludwig): Chemistry. See: Ballentyne; Hackh; Van Nostrand Chem. Dict.

Claisen flask (Claisen, Ludwig): Chemistry. See: Hackh; Van Nostrand Chem. Dict.; Webster's 3d.

CLAISEN, LUDWIG. 1851-1930. German chemist. See: Dict. Sci. Biog. Claisen condensation, Claisen flask, Claisen reaction for phenylglyoxylic acid, Claisen rearrangement, Claisen-Schmidt condensation, Claisen test for thiophene in benzene.

Claisen reaction for phenylglyoxylic acid (Claisen, Ludwig): Chemistry. See: Van Nostrand Chem. Dict.

Claisen rearrangement (Claisen, Ludwig): Chemistry. See: Ballentyne; Van Nostrand Chem. Dict.

Claisen-Schmidt condensation (Claisen, Ludwig and Schmidt): Chemistry. See: Ballentyne; Van Nostrand Chem. Dict.

Claisen test for thiophene in benzene (Claisen, Ludwig): Chemistry. See: Van Nostrand Chem. Dict.

Clanny lamp (or safety lamp) (Clanny, William Reid): Engineering and Industry. See: Auger; Thrush.

CLANNY, WILLIAM REID. 1776-1850. Irish medical writer and inventor. See: Dict. Nat. Biog. Clanny lamp (or safety lamp).

CLAPEYRON, BENOIT-PIERRE-EMILE. 1799-1864. French civil engineer. See: Dict. Sci. Biog. Clapeyron-Clausius equation, Clapeyron equation of state, Clapeyron('s) theorem.

Clapeyron-Clausius equation (Clapeyron, Benoit-Pierre-Emile and Clausius, Rudolf Julius Emanuel): Physics. See: Huschke; Internat. Dict. Phys. Elec.; Van Nostrand Chem. Dict. Also known as: Clapeyron equation, Clausius-Clapeyron equation.

Clapeyron equation (Clapeyron, Benoit-Pierre-Emile). See: Clapeyron-Clausius equation.

Clapeyron equation of state (Clapeyron, Benoit-Pierre-Emile): Physics. See: Ballentyne.

Clapeyron('s) theorem (Clapeyron, Benoit-Pierre-Emile): Physics. See: Ballentyne; Internat. Dict. Ap. Math.

Clapp('s) favorite (pear) (Clapp, T.): Food and Drink. See: Mathews, M. M.

CLAPP, JAMES KILTON. 1897- . American radio engineer. See: Amer. Men Sci., 10th ed. Clapp oscillator.

Clapp-Jordan formulae (Clapp, Verner Warren and Jordan, Robert Thayer): Library Science. See: Harrod.

Clapp oscillator (Clapp, James Kilton): Electronics. See: Hughes; Internat. Dict. Phys. Elec.; Markus.

CLAPP, T. fl. 1860. American horticulturist. (Biography source unavailable.) Clapp('s) favorite (pear).

CLAPP, VERNER WARREN. 1901- . American librarian. See: Who's Who Amer., 1974-75. Clapp-Jordan formulae.

CLAPTON, EDWARD. fl. 1870. English physician. Cited in: Royal Soc. Cat. Sci. Pap., 1864-1873. Clapton's line.

Clapton's line (Clapton, Edward): Medicine. See: Stedman.

Clara Vere de Vere, Lady. See: Vere de Vere, Lady Clara.

CLARE OF ASSISI, SAINT. 1194-1253. Italian foundress of Franciscan Nuns. See: Holweck. Order of St. Clare, Poor Clares, Saint Claire's disease.

Clarence (carriage) (William IV, Duke of Clarence): Generic Word. See: Charnock; Partridge; Weekley.

Clarence, Duke of. See: Lionel (Duke of Clarence).

Clarence, Duke of. See: William IV (Duke of Clarence).

Clarenceux (Clarencieux) (king of arms) (Lionel, Duke of Clarence): History. See: Brewer; Charnock.

CLARENDON. fl. 19th c. English? printer. (Biography source unavailable.) Clarendon (type).

Clarendon, 1st Earl of. See: Hyde, Edward (1st Earl of Clarendon).

Clarendon, 4th Earl of. See: Villiers, George William Frederick (4th Earl of Clarendon).

Clarendon Code (Hyde, Edward, 1st Earl of Clarendon): History. See: Brewer; Harbottle; Steinberg.

Clarendon Note (Villers, George William Frederick, 4th Earl of Clarendon): History. See: Morris and Irwin.

Clarendon Press (Hyde, Edward, 1st Earl of Clarendon); Printing. See: Barnhart (Eng. Lit.); Harrod; Latham.

Clarendon (type) (Clarendon): Printing. See: Harrod; Partridge; Weekley.

Clareni (Angelus Clarenus): Religion. See: Attwater.

Clareno, Angelo. See: Angelus Clarenus.

Claret, Antonio Maria. See: Claret y Clara, Saint.

CLARET Y CLARA, SAINT. 1807-1870. Spanish priest. See: Webster's Biog. Dict. Claretian(s).

Claretian(s) (Claret y Clara, Saint): Religion. See: Attwater; Webster's 3d.

CLARK, ALONZO. 1807-1887. American physician. See: Nat. Cycl. Amer. Biog., vol. 1, p. 354. Clark's sign.

CLARK, ARTHUR WILLIAM. b. 1879. American chemist. See: Amer. Men Sci., 6th ed. Clark-Willit test.

CLARK, CECIL HENRY DOUGLAS. b. 1890. English chemist. See: Pogg., vol. 7b. Clark rule.

Clark cell (Clark, Josiah Latimer): Electronics. See: Hughes; Markus; Van Nostrand Sci. Encyc. under "Electric Cell." Also known as: Latimer-Clark cell.

Clark circle system (Derivation undetermined): Engineering and Industry. See: Thrush.

Clark degree (Clark, Thomas): Chemistry. See: Dresner; Hackh.

Clark dwarf (or rootstock) (Derivation undetermined): Botany. See: Winburne.

CLARK, ELIOT. b. 1881. American anatomist. See: Amer. Men Sci., 7th ed. Sandison-Clark chamber.

CLARK, JOSHUA REUBEN, JR. 1871-1961. American church official and attorney. See: Who Was Who Amer., vol. 4. Clark memorandum.

CLARK, JOSIAH LATIMER. 1822-1898. English engineer. See: Dict. Sci. Biog. Carhart-Clark cell, Clark cell.

Clark memorandum (Clark, Joshua Reuben, Jr.): History. See: Morris.

Clark process (Clark, Thomas): Chemistry. See: Ballentyne; Thrush.

Clark riffler (Derivation undetermined): Engineering and Industry. See: Thrush.

Clark rule (Clark, Cecil Henry Douglas): Chemistry. See: Thewlis.

CLARK, THOMAS. 1801-1867. Scottish chemist. See: Dict. Sci. Biog. Clark degree, Clark process.

CLARK, WILLIAM. 1770-1838. American general and explorer. See: Dict. Amer. Biog. Clark Expedition, Clarkia, Clark's grebe, Clark's nutcracker (or crow), Lewis and Clark Centennial Exposition.

Clark-Willit test (Clark, Arthur William and Willits, Charles Oliver): Chemistry. See: Van Nostrand Chem. Dict.

CLARKE, ALEXANDER ROSS. 1828-1914. English geodesist. See: World Who's Who Sci. Clarke ellipsoids, Clarke's spheroid.

Clarke-Bumpus plankton sampler (Clarke, George Leonard and Bumpus, Dean Franklin): Biology. See: Pennak.

CLARKE, CECIL. fl. 1923. English physician. (Biography source unavailable.) Clarke-Hadfield syndrome.

CLARKE, SIR CHARLES MANSFIELD. 1782-1857. English physician. See: Dict. Nat. Biog. Clarke's ulcer.

Clarke ellipsoids (Clarke, Alexander Ross): Earth Sciences. Cited in: World Who's Who Sci.

CLARKE, FRANK WIGGLESWORTH. 1847-1931. American chemist. See: Dict. Sci. Biog. Clarkeite.

CLARKE, GEORGE LEONARD. 1905- . American biologist. See: World Who's Who Sci. Clarke-Bumpus plankton sampler.

CLARKE, GEORGE SYDENHAM (1ST LORD SYDENHAM). 1848-1933. English soldier and politician. See: Dict. Nat. Biog., 5th suppl. Clarke's gazelle.

Clarke-Hadfield syndrome (Clarke, Cecil and Hadfield, Geoffrey). See: Andersen's syndrome.

CLARKE, JACOB AUGUSTUS LOCKHART. 1817-1880. English anatomist. See: Dict. Nat. Biog. Clarke's cells, Clarke's collateral bundle, Clarke's column (or nucleus).

CLARKE, JOHN DAVENPORT. 1873-1933. American legislator. See: Biog. Direct. Amer. Congress. Clarke-McNary Act.

Clarke-Jones test reaction (Clarke, S. G. and Jones, B.): Chemistry. See: Van Nostrand Chem. Dict.

Clarke-McNary Act (Clarke, John Davenport and McNary, Charles Linza): Politics. See: Winburne.

Clarke Medal (Clarke, William Branwhite): Earth Sciences. Cited in: Dict. Sci. Biog.

Clarke, Richard W. See: Deadwood Dick.

CLARKE, S. G. fl. 1929. English chemist. Cited in: Chem. Abstr., vol. 23, p. 4637. Clarke-Jones test reaction.

CLARKE, WILLIAM BRANWHITE. 1798-1878. English-born Australian geologist. See: Dict. Sci. Biog. Clarke Medal.

Clarkeite (Clarke, Frank Wigglesworth): Earth Sciences. See: Thrush; Webster's 3d.

Clarke's cells (Clarke, Jacob Augustus Lockhart): Medicine. See: Dorland; Stedman.

Clarke's collateral bundle (Clarke, Jacob Augustus Lockhart): Medicine. See: Dorland; Stedman.

Clarke's column (or nucleus) (Clarke, Jacob Augustus Lockhart): Medicine. See: Donath; Drever; Stedman.

Clarke's gazelle (Clarke, George Sydenham): Zoology. See: Hendrickson; Webster's 3d.

Clarke's spheroid (Clarke, Alexander Ross): Earth Sciences. See: Webster's 3d.

Clarke's ulcer (Clarke, Sir Charles Mansfield): Medicine. See: Dorland; Jablonski; Stedman.

Clarkia (Clark, William): Botany. See: Hendrickson; Partridge; Taylor, N.

Clark's grebe (Clark, William): Biology. See: Mathews, M. M.

Clark's nutcracker (or crow) (Clark, William): Biology. See: Gray; Pennak; Webster's 3d.

Clark's sign (Clark, Alonzo): Medicine. See: Dorland.

Clark's weight rule (Derivation undetermined): Medicine. See: Stedman.

Clarkson boiler (Clarkson, T.): Engineering and Industry. See: Auger.

CLARKSON, T. 1864-1933. Engineer. (Biography source unavailable.) Clarkson boiler.

CLASS, WILLIAM J. 1874-1906. American physician. Cited in: Polk's Med. Reg., 1904. Class's coccus.

CLASSEN, ALEXANDER. 1843-1934. German chemist. See: World Who's Who Sci. Classen switchboard.

Classen switchboard (Classen, Alexander): Chemistry. See: Hackh.

Class's coccus (Class, William J.): Medicine. See: Dorland.

CLAUBERG, KARL WILHELM. b. 1893. German bacteriologist. See: Wer ist Wer, 8th ed. Clauberg('s) test (or unit), Clauberg's culture medium.

Clauberg('s) test (or unit) (Clauberg, Karl Wilhelm): Medicine. See: Dorland; Stedman.

Clauberg's culture medium (Clauberg, Karl Wilhelm): Medicine. See: Dorland.

CLAUDE. 1499-1524. French queen and daughter of Louis XII. See: Nouv. Biog. Univ. Reine-Claude (plums).

Claude Bernard. See: Bernard, Claude.

Claude Bernard-Horner syndrome (Bernard, Claude and Horner, Johann Friedrich). See: Bernard-Horner syndrome.

Claude Bernard's syndrome (Bernard, Claude). See: Bernard-Horner syndrome.

CLAUDE, GEORGES. 1870-1960. French chemist and physicist. See: Dict. Sci. Biog. Claude-Heylandt liquefaction process, Claude process.

Claude glass (Claude Lorrain): Fine Arts. See: Hendrickson; Osborne; Partridge.

CLAUDE, HENRI. 1869-1945. French psychiatrist. See: Biog. Lex. hervorr. Aerzte, 1880-1930. Claude's hyperkinesis sign, Claude's syndrome.

Claude-Heylandt liquefaction process (Claude, Georges and Heylandt, C. W. P.): Chemistry. See: Thewlis.

CLAUDE LORRAIN. 1600-1682. French landscape painter and engraver. See: Encyc. Brit., 1973. Claude glass.

Claude-Loyez syndrome (Claude, Henri and Loyez). See: Claude's syndrome.

Claude process (Claude, Georges): Chemistry. See: Ballentyne; Van Nostrand Chem. Dict.; Webster's 3d.

Claude's hyperkinesis sign (Claude, Henri): Medicine. See: Dorland.

Claude's syndrome (Claude, Henri): Medicine. See: Dorland; Jablonski; Stedman. Also known as: Claude-Loyez syndrome.

CLAUDET, ANTOINE FRANCOIS JEAN. 1797-1867. French-born photographer and inventor in England. Claudetype.

CLAUDET, FREDERICK. fl. 19th c. French chemist. Cited in: Dana. Claudetite.

Claudetite (Claudet, Frederick): Earth Sciences. See: Thrush; Webster's 3d.

Claudetype (Claudet, Antoine Francois Jean): Photography. See: Charnock.

Claudius' cells (Claudius, Friedrich Matthias): Anatomy. See: Donath; Dorland; Henderson.

Claudius' fossa (Claudius, Friedrich Matthias): Anatomy. See: Dorland; Stedman.

CLAUDIUS, FRIEDRICH MATTHIAS. 1822-1869. German anatomist. See: World Who's Who Sci. Claudius' cells, Claudius' fossa.

CLAUDIUS, M. C. fl. 1913. German chemist. Cited in: Chem. Abstr., vol. 7, p. 355. Claudius solution.

Claudius solution (Claudius, M. C.): Chemistry. See: Van Nostrand Chem. Dict.

CLAUS, ADOLPH. 1840-1900. German chemist. See: Pogg., vols. 3, 4. Claus-Risler benzidine tests for chlorine and bromine.

CLAUS, C. F. fl. 1885. English chemist. (Biography source unavailable.) Claus process.

Claus process (Claus, C. F.): Chemistry. See: Webster's 3d.

Claus-Risler benzidine tests for chlorine and bromine (Claus, Adolph and Risler, .): Chemistry. See: Van Nostrand Chem. Dict.

Claus test for anthraquinone (Derivation undetermined): Chemistry. See: Van Nostrand Chem. Dict.

Claus test for water in alcohol (Derivation undetermined): Chemistry. See: Van Nostrand Chem. Dict.

Clausewitz (Clausewitz, Karl von): Generic Word (formidable strategist). See: Hendrickson; Webster's 3d.

CLAUSEWITZ, KARL VON. 1780-1831. Prussian army officer. See: Internat. Encyc. Soc. Sci. Clausewitz.

Clausius-Clapeyron equation (Clausius, Rudolf and Clapeyron, Benoit-Pierre-Emile). See: Clapeyron-Clausius equation.

Clausius condition (Clausius, Rudolf): Physics. See: Internat. Dict. Ap. Math.

Clausius cycle (Clausius, Rudolf). See: Rankine cycle.

Clausius equation (Clausius, Rudolf): Physics. See: Ballentyne; Internat. Dict. Phys. Elec.; Van Nostrand Chem. Dict.

Clausius formulation (or statement) of the second law of thermodynamics (Clausius, Rudolf): Physics. See: Ballentyne; Internat. Dict. Ap. Math.

Clausius inequality (or theorem) (Clausius, Rudolf): Physics. See: Internat. Dict. Ap. Math.; Internat. Dict. Phys. Elec.; Van Nostrand Sci. Encyc. Also known as: inequality of Clausius.

Clausius integral (Clausius, Rudolf): Physics. See: Internat. Dict. Ap. Math.

Clausius law (or law of Clausius) (Clausius, Rudolf): Physics. See: Internat. Dict. Phys. Elec.; Van Nostrand Chem. Dict.; Van Nostrand Sci. Encyc.

Clausius-Mosotti equation (Clausius, Rudolf and Mossotti, Ottaviano Fabrizio): Electronics. See: Ballentyne; Hughes; Internat. Dict. Phys. Elec.

Clausius-Rankine cycle (Clausius, Rudolf and Rankine, William John Macquorn). See: Rankine cycle.

CLAUSIUS, RUDOLF. 1822-1888. German physicist. See: Dict. Sci. Biog. Clapeyron-Clausius equation, Clausius condition, Clausius cycle, Clausius equation, Clausius formulation (or statement) of the second law of thermodynamics, Clausius inequality (or theorem), Clausius integral, Clausius law (or law of Clausius), Clausius-Mosotti equation, Clausius (unit), Clausius' virial theorem, Joule-Clausius velocity.

Clausius (unit) (Clausius, Rudolf): Physics. See: Dresner; Internat. Dict. Ap. Math.; Thrush.

Clausius' virial theorem (Clausius, Rudolf): Physics. See: Ballentyne.

Clay ball (Clay, Henry): History. See: Mathews, M. M.

Clay club (Clay, Henry): History. See: Mathews, M. M.

Clay dinner (Clay, Henry): History. See: Mathews, M. M.

CLAY, HENRY. 1777-1852. American statesman. See: Dict. Amer. Biog. Adams and Clay Republicans, Clay ball, Clay club, Clay dinner, Clay man, Clay party, Clayism, Clayite, Henry Clay flag, Henry Clay whig, Henryite (or Henryism).

Clay man (Clay, Henry): History. See: Mathews, M. M.

Clay party (Clay, Henry): History. See: Mathews, M. M.

Clay process for rosin refining (Derivation undetermined): Chemistry. See: Van Nostrand Chem. Dict.

CLAYBROOK, EDWIN BROWN. b. 1871. American surgeon. See: Who's Who Amer. Med. Claybrook's sign.

Claybrook's sign (Claybrook, Edwin Brown): Medicine. See: Stedman.

CLAYDEN, ARTHUR WILLIAM. 1855-1944. English meteorologist. See: Who Was Who, 1941-1950. Clayden effect.

Clayden effect (Clayden, Arthur William): Photography. See: Focal Encyc. Photog.; Huschke; Internat. Dict. Phys. Elec.

Clayism (Clay, Henry): History. See: Mathews, M. M.

Clayite (Clay, Henry): History. See: Mathews, M. M.

Clayton Antitrust Act (Clayton, Henry De Lamar): Politics. See: Greenwald; Morris; Morris and Irwin.

Clayton-Bulwer Treaty (Clayton, John Middleton and Bulwer, Sir William Henry Lytton): History. See: Harbottle; Jameson; Morris.

Clayton compromise (Clayton, John Middleton): History. See: Barnhart (Cycl. Names).

Clayton gas (Clayton, T. A.): Chemistry. See: Stedman; Webster's 3d.

CLAYTON, HENRY DE LAMAR. 1857-1929. American jurist and legislator. See: Dict. Amer. Biog., 1st suppl. Clayton Antitrust Act.

CLAYTON, JOHN. 1693-1773. American botanist. See: Dict. Amer. Biog. Claytonia.

CLAYTON, JOHN MIDDLETON. 1796-1856. American jurist. See: Dict. Amer. Biog. Clayton-Bulwer Treaty, Clayton compromise.

CLAYTON, T. A. No dates. English chemist. (Biography source unavailable.) Clayton gas.

Claytonia (Clayton, John): Botany. See: Charnock; Mathews, M. M.; Taylor, N.

CLEAVELAND, PARKER. 1780-1858. American mineralogist. See: Dict. Sci. Biog. Cleavelandite.

Cleavelandite (Cleaveland, Parker): Earth Sciences. See: Charnock; Mathews, M. M.; Thrush.

Clebsch-Aronhold symbolic notation (Clebsch, Rudolf Friedrich Alfred and Aronhold, Siegfried Heinrich): Mathematics. Cited in: Dict. Sci. Biog.

Clebsch-Gordan coefficients (Clebsch, Rudolf Friedrich Alfred and Gordan, Paul): Mathematics. See: Ballentyne; Internat. Dict. Ap. Math.; Internat. Dict. Phys. Elec.

Clebsch-Lueroth method (Clebsch, Rudolf Friedrich Alfred and Lueroth, Jakob): Mathematics. See: Dict. Sci. Biog. under "Lueroth, Jakob."

CLEBSCH, RUDOLF FRIEDRICH ALFRED. 1833-1872. German mathematician. See: Dict. Sci. Biog. Clebsch-Aronhold symbolic notation, Clebsch-Gordan coefficients, Clebsch-Lueroth method, Pluecker-Clebsch principle.

Cleemann's sign (Derivation undetermined): Medicine. See: Stedman.

Cleeton and Williams magnetron (Cleeton, Claud Edwin and Williams, Neil Hooker): Physics. See: Internat. Dict. Phys. Elec.

CLEETON, CLAUD EDWIN. 1907- . American physicist. See: Amer. Men Sci., 6th ed. Cleeton and Williams magnetron.

CLEJAT, CHARLES PHILIPPE ANTOINE. b. 1880. French dermatologist. Cited in: Index Cat. Libr. Surg. Gen. Off., 3d ser., vol. 3, 1922. Petges-Clejat syndrome.

CLELAND, W. WALLACE. No dates. Physician. (Biography source unavailable.) Cleland's reagent.

Cleland's reagent (Cleland, W. Wallace): Medicine. See: Stedman.

Clemenceau (aircraft carriers) (Clemenceau, Georges): Weapons. See: Quick.

CLEMENCEAU, GEORGES. 1841-1929. French statesman. See: Encyc. Brit., 1973. Clemenceau (aircraft carriers).

Clemens Romanus. See: Clement I, Saint.

CLEMENS, SAMUEL LANGHORNE. 1835-1910. American writer. See: Dict. Amer. Biog. Martin's plagiarism of Mark Twain.

CLEMENSEN, ERIK CHRISTIAN. 1876?-1941. Danish-born American chemist. See: Cur. Biog., 1941. Clemmensen reduction (or reaction).

CLEMENT I. fl. 40-97 A.D. Bishop of Rome. See: Encyc. Brit., 1973. Clementine (literature or liturgy), Clementine Epistle.

CLEMENT V. 1264-1314. Pope. See: Encyc. Brit., 1973. Clementine(s).

CLEMENT VII. 1342-1394. Antipope. See: Encyc. Brit., 1973. Clementine popes.

CLEMENT VII. 1478-1534. Pope. See: Encyc. Brit., 1973. Clementine League.

CLEMENT VIII. 1536-1605. Pope. See: Encyc. Brit., 1973. Clementine (revision).

CLEMENT XII. 1652-1740. Pope. See: Encyc. Brit., 1973. Clementine instruction.

Clementine(s) (Clement V): Law. See: Charnock; Webster's 3d.; Weekley.

Clementine Epistle (Clement I): Religion. See: Attwater.

Clementine instruction (Clement XII): Religion. See: Attwater.

Clementine League (Clement VII): History. See: Harbottle.

Clementine (literature or liturgy) (Clement I): Religion. See: Attwater; Mathews, S.; Webster's 3d.

Clementine popes (Clement VII, antipope): Religion. See: Attwater.

Clementine (revision) (Clement VIII): Religion. See: Webster's 3d.

Clemmensen reduction (or reaction) (Clemensen, Erik Christian): Chemistry. See: Ballentyne; Hackh; Van Nostrand Chem. Dict.

Cleopatra (Cleopatra, Queen): Generic Word (feminine allurement). See: Hendrickson; Partridge.

Cleopatra (blue) (Cleopatra, Queen): Fine Arts. See: Webster's 3d.

CLEOPATRA, QUEEN. 69-30 B.C. Queen of Egypt. See: Encyc. Brit., 1973. Cleopatra, Cleopatra (blue), Cleopatra's needles.

Cleopatra's needles (Cleopatra, Queen): Fine Arts. See: Latham.

Clerambault, Gaetan-Henri. See: De Clerambault, Gaetan-Henri-Alfred-Edouard-Leon-Marie Gatian.

Clerambault-Kandinskii complex (De Clerambault, Gaetan-Henri-Alfred-Edouard-Leon-Marie Gatian and Kandinskii, Victor Chrisanfovic). See: Kandinskii-Clerambault syndrome.

CLERC, ANTONIN. 1871-1954. French physician. See: Dict. Nat. Contemp Clerc-Levy-Cristesco syndrome.

Clerc-Levy-Cristesco syndrome (Clerc, Antonin; Levy, Robert; and Cristesco, C.): Medicine. See: Jablonski.

CLERET, M. fl. 1910. French physician. (Biography source unavailable.) Launois-Cleret syndrome.

Clerget inversion (or method) (Clerget, T.): Chemistry. See: Hackh; Van Nostrand Chem. Dict.

CLERGET, T. fl. 1843. French chemist. Cited in: Royal Soc. Cat. Sci. Pap., 1800-1863. Clerget inversion (or method).

CLERICI, ENRICO. d. 1938. Italian geologist. See: Atti Pontif. Accad. Sci. Nuovi Lincei, LXXXIV (1931), pp. 480-484. Clerici solution.

Clerici solution (Clerici, Enrico): Chemistry. See: Hackh; Thrush; Van Nostrand Chem. Dict.

Clerihew (verse) (Bentley, Edmund Clerihew): Literature. See: Barnet; Harvey; Preminger.

CLERK, DUGALD. 1854-1932. Scottish engineer. See: Dict. Nat. Biog., 5th suppl. Clerk engine.

Clerk engine (Clerk, Dugald): Engineering and Industry. See: Auger.

Clerk-Maxwell, James. See: Maxwell, James Clerk.

Clerk Maxwell relation (Maxwell, James Clerk). See: Maxwell relation(ship) (between dielectric constant and refractive index).

Clerks of Saint Viator (Viator, Saint): Religion. See: Attwater.

CLEVE, PER TEODOR. 1840-1905. Swedish chemist. See: Dict. Sci. Biog. Cleveite, Cleve's acid, Cleve's salts.

Clevedon positive pressure respirator (Derivation undetermined): Medicine. See: Stedman.

Cleveite (Cleve, Per Teodor): Earth Sciences. See: Partridge; Webster's 3d.

Cleveland flash point tester (Derivation undetermined): Chemistry. See: Van Nostrand Chem. Dict.

CLEVENGER, SHOBAL VAIL. 1843-1920. American neurologist. See: Dict. Amer. Biog. Clevenger's fissure.

Clevenger's fissure (Clevenger, Shobal Vail): Medicine. See: Dorland; Stedman.

Cleve's acid (Cleve, Per Teodor): Chemistry. See: Hackh; Webster's 3d.

Cleve's salts (Cleve, Per Teodor): Chemistry. See: Hackh.

CLIFFORD, STEWART HILTON. 1900- . American physician. See: Direct. Med. Specialists, vol. 8. Clifford's syndrome.

CLIFFORD, WILLIAM KINGDON. 1845-1879. English mathematician. See: Dict. Sci. Biog. Bessel-Clifford differential equation?, Clifford's surfaces.

Clifford's surfaces (Clifford, William Kingdon): Mathematics. Cited in: Dict. Sci. Biog.

Clifford's syndrome (Clifford, Stewart Hilton). See: Ballantyne-Runge syndrome.

CLIFFORT, GEORGE. 1685-1750. Dutch botanist. See: World Who's Who Sci. Cliffortia.

Cliffortia (Cliffort, George): Botany. See: Charnock.

CLIFTON, ROBERT BELLAMY. 1836-1921. English physicist. See: Royal Soc. Proc., ser. A, 1921. Cliftonite.

Cliftonite (Clifton, Robert Bellamy): Earth Sciences. See: Webster's 3d.

Clinique Auguste Lumiere (Lumiere, Auguste Marie Louis): Biology. Cited in: Focal Encyc. Photog. under "Lumiere, Auguste."

Clinton Dawkins committee (Dawkins, Sir Clinton Edward): History. See: Montgomery.

CLINTON, DE WITT. 1769-1828. American statesman. See: Dict. Amer. Biog. Clinton (grape), Clintonia, Clintonian(s) (or Clintonianism), Clintonite.

CLINTON, EDWARD FIENNES DE, 9TH LORD CLINTON AND SAYE, AND 1ST EARL OF LINCOLN. 1512-1585. English nobleman. See: Dict. Nat. Biog. Lincoln's men.

Clinton (grape) (Clinton, De Witt): Botany. See: Mathews, M. M.

CLINTON, HENRY PELHAM FIENNES PELHAM (5TH DUKE OF NEWCASTLE). 1811-1864. English statesman. See: Dict. Nat. Biog. Newcastle Commission.

Clintonia (Clinton, De Witt): Botany. See: Mathews, M. M.; Taylor, N.; Webster's 3d.

Clintonian(s) (or Clintonianism) (Clinton, De Witt): Politics. See: Mathews, M. M.; Smith.

Clintonite (Clinton, De Witt): Earth Sciences. See: Charnock; Mathews, M. M.; Thrush.

CLIO. Greek Muse of poetry and history. See: Jobes. Cliometricians, Clionidae.

Cliometricians (Clio): History. See: Time, (June 17, 1974).

Clionidae (Clio): Zoology. See: Charnock.

CLIQUOT, BARBE-NICOLE PONSARDIN. 1775-1866. French wine producer. See: Dict. Biog. Fran. Cliquot (champagne).

Cliquot (champagne) (Cliquot, Barbe-Nicole Ponsardin): Food and Drink. See: Charnock.

CLIVE, LADY CHARLOTTE. d. 1866. English duchess. (Biography source unavailable.) Clivia.

Clivia (Clive, Lady Charlotte): Botany. See: Taylor, N.; Webster's 3d.

CLOETTA, MAX. 1868-1940. Swiss pharmacologist. See: World Who's Who Sci. Cloetta's mixture.

Cloetta's mixture (Cloetta, Max): Medicine. See: Hinsie.

CLOQUET, HIPPOLYTE. 1787-1840. French anatomist. See: World Who's Who Sci. Cloquet's ganglion, Cloquet's space.

CLOQUET, JULES GERMAIN. 1790-1883. French anatomist. See: World Who's Who Sci. Cloquet's canal, Cloquet's ganglion, Cloquet's hernia, Cloquet's septum (or membrane), Cloquet's sign.

Cloquet's canal (Cloquet, Jules Germain): Anatomy. See: Donath; Dorland; Stedman. Also known as: Stilling's canal.

Cloquet's ganglion (Cloquet, Hippolyte): Anatomy. See: Donath; Dorland; Stedman.

Cloquet's ganglion (Cloquet, Jules Germain): Anatomy. See: Donath.

Cloquet's hernia (Cloquet, Jules Germain): Medicine. See: Dorland; Jablonski; Stedman.

Cloquet's septum (or membrane) (Cloquet, Jules Germain): Anatomy. See: Donath; Stedman.

Cloquet's sign (Cloquet, Jules Germain): Medicine. See: Stedman.

Cloquet's space (Cloquet, Hippolyte): Anatomy. See: Stedman.

CLOSS, KARL. fl. 1942. Swedish physician. (Biography source unavailable.) Danbolt-Closs syndrome.

Closs liver function test (Derivation undetermined): Medicine. See: Stedman.

CLOUDMAN, ARTHUR MOSHER. 1901- . American zoologist. See: Amer. Men Sci., 6th ed. Cloudman's melanoma.

Cloudman's melanoma (Cloudman, Arthur Mosher): Medicine. See: Jablonski; Stedman.

CLOUGH, MILDRED CLARK. b. 1888. American physician. See: Who's Who Among Physicians and Surg. Clough-Richter syndrome.

Clough-Richter syndrome (Clough, Mildred Clark and Richter, Ina M.): Medicine. See: Jablonski.

CLOUSTON, SIR THOMAS SMITH. 1840-1915. Scottish physician. See: World Who's Who Sci. Cloustonite?

Cloustonite (Clouston, Sir Thomas Smith?): Earth Sciences. See: Thrush.

CLUETT, SANFORD LOCKWOOD. 1874-1968. American inventor. See: Webster's Biog. Dict. Sanforize.

Clusia (L'Ecluse, Charles de): Botany. See: Charnock; Webster's 3d.

Clusius, Carolus. See: L'Ecluse, Charles de.

Clusius column (Clusius, Klaus Paul Alfred): Engineering and Industry. See: Hughes; Internat. Dict. Phys. Elec.; Van Nostrand Sci. Encyc.

CLUSIUS, KLAUS PAUL ALFRED. 1903- . German chemist. See: Pogg., vol. 7a. Clusius column.

CLUTTON, HENRY HUGH. 1850-1909. English surgeon. See: Dict. Nat. Biog., 2nd suppl. Clutton's syndrome (or joint).

Clutton's syndrome (or joint) (Clutton, Henry Hugh): Medicine. See: Dorland; Jablonski; Stedman.

CLUYT, AUGER. fl. 1627-1636. Dutch botanist. See: Nouv. Biog. Univ. Cluytia.

Cluytia (Cluyt, Auger): Botany. See: Charnock.

CLYMER, GEORGE E. 1754-1834. American inventor. See: Dict. Amer. Biog. Clymer press.

Clymer press (Clymer, George E.): Printing. See: Lockwood.

CLYTEMNESTRA. Mythical wife of Agamemnon. See: Jobes. Clytemnestra complex.

Clytemnestra complex (Clytemnestra): Psychology. See: Hinsie; Wolman.

CLYTIE. Mythical sea nymph. See: Jobes. Clytie knot.

Clytie knot (Clytie): Fashion. See: Picken.

CO-TUI, FRANK WANG. 1896- . American surgeon. See: Who's Who Among Physicians and Surg. Co-Tui treatment.

Co-Tui treatment (Co-Tui, Frank Wang): Medicine. See: Dorland.

COADE, ELIZABETH. d. 1796. English manufacturer. (Biography source unavailable.) Coade stone.

Coade stone (Coade, Elizabeth): Earth Sciences. See: Briggs; Thrush; Webster's 3d.

COAKLEY, CORNELIUS GODFREY. 1862-1934. American laryngologist. See: Dict. Amer. Biog., 1st suppl. Coakley's operation.

Coakley's operation (Coakley, Cornelius Godfrey): Medicine. See: Dorland.

Coanda effect (Coanda, Henri-Marie): Engineering and Industry. See: Barnhart, (New Eng.); Internat. Dict. Ap. Math.; Thewlis.

COANDA, HENRI-MARIE. 1885- . Rumanian-born aeronautical engineer. See: World Who's Who Sci. Coanda effect.

Coats' disease (or retinitis) (Coats, George): Medicine. See: Dorland; Jablonski; Stedman.

COATS, GEORGE. 1876-1915. English ophthalmologist. See: Biog. Lex. hervorr. Aerzte, 1880-1930. Coats' disease (or retinitis), Coats' ring.

Coats' ring (Coats, George): Medicine. See: Jablonski.

Cobaea (Cobo, Bernabe): Botany. See: Charnock; Taylor, N.; Webster's 3d. Also known as: Rosenbergia.

Cobalt (Kobold?): Earth Sciences. See: Charnock.

COBB, CHARLES W. fl. 1928. American economist. (Biography source unavailable.) Cobb-Douglas production function.

Cobb-Douglas production function (Cobb, Charles W. and Douglas, Paul Howard): Economics. See: Greenwald.

Cobb paper (Derivation undetermined): Printing. See: Lockwood.

Cobb scale (Derivation undetermined): Botany. See: Winburne.

COBB, STANLEY. 1887- . American neuropathologist. See: World Who's Who Sci. Cobb's syndrome.

Cobb's disease (or bacterial wilt of sugarcane) (Derivation undetermined): Botany. See: Winburne.

Cobb's syndrome (Cobb, Stanley): Medicine. See: Jablonski.

Cobden Club (Cobden, Richard): Economics. See: Latham; Montgomery; Phyfe.

COBDEN, RICHARD. 1804-1865. English statesman and economist. See: Dict. Nat. Biog. Cobden Club, Cobden Treaty, Cobdenism.

Cobden Treaty (Cobden, Richard): Economics. See: Morris and Irwin.

Cobdenism (Cobden, Richard): Economics. See: Partridge; Webster's 3d.; Weekley.

COBO, BERNABE. 1582-1657. Spanish naturalist. See: Webster's Biog. Dict. Cobaea.

Cocceian(s) (Cocceius, Johannes): Religion. See: Canney; Weekley.

COCCEIUS, JOHANNES. 1603-1669. Dutch Hebraist and commentator. See: Encyc. Brit., 1973. Cocceian(s).

Cochran boiler (Cochran, J. T.): Engineering and Industry. See: Auger.

Cochran-Cox test (Cochran, William Gemmell and Cox, Gertrude Mary): Statistics. See: Good.

COCHRAN, J. T. fl. 1878. Engineer. (Biography source unavailable.) Cochran boiler.

COCHRAN, JACOB. fl. 1816. American religious leader. (Biography source unavailable.) Cochranism (or Cochranite).

COCHRAN, WILLIAM GEMMELL. 1909- . Scottish statistician. See: World Who's Who Sci. Cochran-Cox test, Cochran's criterion, Cochran's Q-test, Cochran's rule, Cochran's test, Cochran's theorem.

Cochrane rotary engine (Cochrane, Thomas?): Engineering and Industry. See: Auger.

COCHRANE, THOMAS (10TH EARL OF DUNDONALD). 1775-1860. English naval commander. See: Dict. Nat. Biog. Cochrane rotary engine?

Cochranism (or Cochranite) (Cochran, Jacob): Religion. See: Mathews, M. M.

Cochran's criterion (Cochran, William Gemmell): Statistics. See: Kendall.

Cochran's Q-test (Cochran, William Gemmell): Statistics. See: Kendall.

Cochran's rule (Cochran, William Gemmell): Statistics. See: Kendall.

Cochran's test (Cochran, William Gemmell): Statistics. See: Kendall.

Cochran's theorem (Cochran, William Gemmell): Statistics. See: James; Kendall; Van Nostrand Sci. Encyc.

COCK, EDWARD. 1805-1892. English surgeon. See: Encyc. Brit., 1911. Cock's operation, Cock's peculiar tumor.

COCKAYNE, EDWARD ALFRED. 1880-1956. English physician. See: Who Was Who, 1951-1960. Cockayne's syndrome, Weber-Cockayne syndrome.

Cockayne's syndrome (Cockayne, Edward Alfred): Medicine. See: Jablonski; Stedman.

COCKBURN, ALEXANDER JAMES EDMUND. 1802-1880. English judge. See: Dict. Nat. Biog. Cockburn's Act.

Cockburn's Act (Cockburn, Alexander James Edmund): Law. See: Harbottle.

Cockcroft-Walton accelerator (Cockroft, John Douglas and Walton, Ernest Thomas Sinton): Physics. See: Internat. Dict. Phys. Elec.; Markus; Van Nostrand Sci. Encyc.

Cockcroft-Walton experiment (Cockroft, John Douglas and Walton, Ernest Thomas Sinton): Physics. See: Internat. Dict. Phys. Elec.

COCKER, EDWARD. 1631-1675. English engraver and teacher. See: Dict. Nat. Biog. according to Cocker.

COCKERTON. No dates. English auditor. (Biography source unavailable.) Cockerton case (or judgment).

Cockerton case (or judgment) (Cockerton): Law. See: Harbottle; Montgomery.

COCKROFT, JOHN DOUGLAS. 1897-1967. English physicist. See: Dict. Sci. Biog. Cockcroft-Walton accelerator, Cockcroft-Walton experiment.

Cock's operation (Cock, Edward): Medicine. See: Dorland.

Cock's peculiar tumor (Cock, Edward): Medicine. See: Stedman.

CODAZZI, DELFINO. 1824-1873. Italian mathematician. See: Dict. Sci. Biog. Codazzi equations, equations of Gauss and Codazzi, Mainardi-Codazzi relations.

Codazzi equations (Codazzi, Delfino): Mathematics. See: James.

Coddington eyepiece (or lens) (Coddington, Henry): Physics. See: Internat. Dict. Phys. Elec.; Van Nostrand Sci. Encyc.; Webster's 3d.

CODDINGTON, HENRY. d. 1845. English mathematician. See: Dict. Nat. Biog. Coddington eyepiece (or lens), Coddington shape and position factors.

Coddington shape and position factors (Coddington, Henry): Physics. See: Internat. Dict. Ap. Math.; Internat. Dict. Phys. Elec.

Code Frederic (Frederick II): History. See: Harbottle; Latham.

Code Louis (Louis XIV): History. See: Harbottle.

Code Napoleon (Napoleon I): Law. See: Brewer; Harbottle; Latham; Phyfe; Smith. Also known as: Napoleonic Code.

code of Hammurabi (Hammurabi): History. See: Canney; Encyc. Brit., 1973 under "Hammurabi, Code of"; Mathews, S.; Winick.

Code of Justinian (Justinian I, the Great). See: Justinian Code.

CODE, WILLIAM EDWARD. b. 1878. American physician. Cited in: Amer. Med. Direct., 1929. Codeball.

Codeball (Code, William Edward): Recreation and Sports. See: Det. Free Press, (July 25, 1975).

CODIVILLA, ALESSANDRO. 1861-1912. Italian surgeon. See: Castiglioni. Codivilla's extension, Codivilla's operation.

Codivilla's extension (Codivilla, Alessandro): Medicine. See: Dorland; Stedman.

Codivilla's operation (Codivilla, Alessandro): Medicine. See: Dorland; Stedman.

CODMAN, ERNEST AMORY. 1869-1940. American surgeon. See: Who's Who Amer. Med. Codman's sign, Codman's tumor.

Codman's sign (Codman, Ernest Amory): Medicine. See: Dorland; Stedman.

Codman's tumor (Codman, Ernest Amory): Medicine. See: Jablonski; Stedman.

CODRINGTON. No dates. Celebrated English family. (Biography source unavailable.) Codrington (coat).

Codrington (coat) (Codrington): Fashion. See: Charnock.

Coe virus (Derivation undetermined): Medicine. See: Stedman.

COEHN, ALFRED. 1863-1938. German chemist. See: Pogg., vols. 4, 5, 6, 7a. Coehn's rule.

Coehn's rule (Coehn, Alfred): Chemistry. See: Ballentyne.

COEHOORN, MENNO. 1641-1704. Dutch military engineer. See: Encyc. Brit., 1973. Coehorn (or Coehoorn).

Coehorn (or Coehoorn) (Coehoorn, Menno): Weapons. See: Brewer; Partridge; Weekley.

Coelebs (Coelebs, the bachelor): Generic Word. See: Barnhart (Eng. Lit.).

COELEBS, THE BACHELOR. Character in Hannah More's novel, "Coelebs in Search of a Wife" (1809). See: Benet. Coelebs.

COENEN, HERMANN. b. 1875. German physician. See: Biog. Lex. hervorr. Aerzte, 1880-1930. Henle-Coenen test (or sign).

Coffey-Humber method (Coffey, Walter Bernard and Humber, John Davis): Medicine. See: Dorland; Stedman.

COFFEY, ROBERT CALVIN. 1869-1933. American surgeon. See: World Who's Who Sci. Coffey suspension.

Coffey suspension (Coffey, Robert Calvin): Medicine. See: Stedman.

COFFEY, WALTER BERNARD. 1868-1944. American physician. See: Who's Who Among Physicians and Surg. Coffey-Humber method.

Coffinite (Derivation undetermined): Earth Sciences. See: Thrush.

COGAN, DAVID GLENDENNING. 1908- . American physician. See: World Who's Who Sci. Bielschowsky-Lutz-Cogan syndrome, Cogan's dystrophy, Cogan's syndrome (1), Cogan's syndrome (2).

Cogan's dystrophy (Cogan, David Glendenning): Medicine. See: Jablonski.

Cogan's syndrome (1) (Cogan, David Glendenning): Medicine. See: Jablonski; Stedman.

Cogan's syndrome (2) (Cogan, David Glendenning): Medicine. See: Jablonski.

Cogger hand-press (Cogger, J.): Printing. See: Lockwood.

COGGER, J. No dates. Inventor. (Biography source unavailable.) Cogger hand-press.

COGHILL, GEORGE ELLETT. 1872-1941. American anatomist. See: Dict. Sci. Biog. Coghillion sequence.

Coghillion sequence (Coghill, George Ellett): Medicine. See: Good.

Cognacq-Jay Foundation (Cognacq, Theodore Ernest and Cognacq, Marie Louise Jay): Philanthropy. Cited in: Webster's Biog. Dict.

COGNACQ, MARIE LOUISE JAY. 1838-1925. French merchant. See: Webster's Biog. Dict. Cognacq-Jay Foundation.

COGNACQ, THEODORE ERNEST. 1839-1928. French merchant. See: Webster's Biog. Dict. Cognacq-Jay Foundation.

COGSWELL, JOSEPH GREEN. 1786-1871. American librarian. See: Dict. Amer. Biog. Cogswellia.

Cogswellia (Cogswell, Joseph Green): Botany. See: Webster's 3d.

Cohan rule (Derivation undetermined): Law. See: Black.

COHEN, EMIL WILHELM. 1842-1905. Danish-born geologist. See: Webster's Biog. Dict. Cohenite.

COHEN, JEROME ALAN. 1930- . American educator. See: Who's Who Amer., 1972-1973. Cohen's law.

COHEN, LOUIS. 1876-1948. Russian-born American physicist. See: World Who's Who Sci. Austin-Cohen formula, Austin-Cohen law.

Cohen test reaction (Derivation undetermined): Chemistry. See: Van Nostrand Chem. Dict.

Cohenite (Cohen, Emil Wilhelm): Earth Sciences. See: Thrush; Webster's 3d.

Cohen's law (Cohen, Jerome Alan): Sociology. See: Martin.

Cohen's test (for albumin in the urine) (Derivation undetermined): Medicine. See: Stedman.

COHN, HERMANN LUDWIG. 1838-1906. German ophthalmologist. See: Sci., vol. 24 (1906), p. 447. Cohn's test.

COHN, LASSAR. 1858-1922. German chemist. See: Dict. Sci. Biog. Lassar-Cohn reagent for aldehydes.

COHN, MAX. b. 1875. German physician. Cited in: New York Acad. Med. Portrait Cat. Pyle-Cohn disease.

COHNHEIM, JULIUS FRIEDRICH. 1839-1884. German pathologist. See: World Who's Who Sci. Cohnheim's areas (or field), Cohnheim's frog, Cohnheim's theory.

Cohnheim's areas (or field) (Cohnheim, Julius Friedrich): Anatomy. See: Donath; Dorland; Stedman.

Cohnheim's frog (Cohnheim, Julius Friedrich): Medicine. See: Dorland.

Cohnheim's theory (Cohnheim, Julius Friedrich): Medicine. See: Dorland; Stedman.

Cohn's test (Cohn, Hermann Ludwig): Medicine. See: Dorland; Stedman.

coiffure a la Ninon (Lenclos, Ninon de): Fashion. See: Picken.

COINTREAU. French family of wine producers. (Biography source unavailable.) Cointreau (liqueur).

Cointreau (liqueur) (Cointreau): Food and Drink. See: De Sola.

Coissi, Graman. See: Quassi, Graman.

COITER (OR KOYTER), VOLCHER. 1534-1600. Dutch anatomist in Bologna. See: Dict. Sci. Biog. Coiter's (Koyter's) muscle.

Coiter's (Koyter's) muscle (Coiter, Volcher): Anatomy. See: Donath; Dorland; Stedman.

COKE, SIR EDWARD. 1552-1634. English jurist. See: Dict. Nat. Biog. Coke upon Littleton.

COKE, THOMAS WILLIAM (EARL OF LEICESTER). 1752-1842. English landowner. See: Dict. Nat. Biog. Billycock hat.

Coke upon Littleton (Coke, Sir Edward and Littleton, Sir Thomas): Law. See: Harvey; Hendrickson; Partridge.

COKER, ERNEST GEORGE. 1899-1946. English engineer. See: World Who's Who Sci. Coker's extensometer.

Coker's extensometer (Coker, Ernest George): Engineering and Industry. See: Auger.

COLASANTI, GIUSEPPE. b. 1846. Italian chemist. See: Biog. Lex. hervorr. Aerzte, 1880-1930. Colasanti test reaction for thiocyanates?, Colasanti test reaction for thiocyanates and mustard oils?

Colasanti test reaction for thiocyanates (Colasanti, Giuseppe?): Chemistry. See: Van Nostrand Chem. Dict.

Colasanti test reaction for thiocyanates and mustard oils (Colasanti, Giuseppe?): Chemistry. See: Van Nostrand Chem. Dict.

Colbert embroidery (Colbert, Jean Baptiste): Applied Arts. See: Picken.

COLBERT, JEAN BAPTISTE. 1619-1683. French statesman. See: Encyc. Brit., 1973. Colbert embroidery, Colbertine (or Colberteen) (lace), Colbertism.

Colbertine (or Colberteen) (lace) (Colbert, Jean Baptiste): Fashion. See: Charnock; Picken; Webster's 3d.

Colbertism (Colbert, Jean Baptiste): History. See: Webster's 3d.

COLBURN, ALLAN PHILLIP. 1904- . American chemical engineer. See: Amer. Men Sci., 5th ed. Colburn heat-transfer factor.

Colburn heat-transfer factor (Colburn, Allan Phillip): Physics. See: Thewlis.

COLBURN, IRVING WIGHTMAN. 1861-1917. American inventor. See: Dict. Amer. Biog. Colburn process.

Colburn process (Colburn, Irving Wightman): Engineering and Industry. See: Thrush; Van Nostrand Chem. Dict.

COLDEN, CADWALLADER. 1688-1776. Irish-born American botanist, physician and politician. See: Dict. Sci. Biog. Coldenia.

Coldenia (Colden, Cadwallader): Botany. See: Charnock; Mathews, M. M.

Cole and Adie's method (Cole, Sydney William and Adie, William John): Medicine. See: Ballentyne.

Cole-Cecil murmur (Derivation undetermined): Medicine. See: Stedman.

Cole-Cole plot (Derivation undetermined): Physics. See: Hughes; Internat. Dict. Phys. Elec.

COLE, ELBERT CHARLES. 1891- . American biologist. See: World Who's Who Sci. Cole's ferricyanide-methylene blue method.

COLE, FRANK NELSON. 1861-1926. American mathematician. See: Dict. Sci. Biog. Frank Nelson Cole prize.

COLE, GEORGE WATSON. 1850-1939. American bibliographer and librarian. See: Webster's Biog. Dict. Cole size card.

COLE, HAROLD NEWTON. 1884-1966. American dermatologist. See: Bull. Cleveland med. lib. 13, no. 4 (Oct. 1966), 75. Zinsser-Engmann-Cole syndrome.

COLE, HOWARD IRVING. b. 1892. American chemist. See: Amer. Men Sci., 10th ed. Cole microchemical reagent for alkaloids, Cole reagent (for gold).

COLE, LEWIS GREGORY. 1874-1954. American radiologist. See: Who Was Who Amer., 1951-1960. Coles's sign.

Cole microchemical reagent for alkaloids (Cole, Howard Irving): Chemistry. See: Van Nostrand Chem. Dict.

Cole-Rauschkolb-Toomey syndrome (Cole, Harold Newton; Rauschkolb, J. E.; and Toomey, James Joseph?). See: Zinsser-Engman-Cole syndrome.

Cole reagent (for gold) (Cole, Howard Irving): Chemistry. See: Thrush; Van Nostrand Chem. Dict.

Cole size card (Cole, George Watson): Library Science. See: Harrod.

COLE, SYDNEY WILLIAM. 1877-1952. English biochemist. Cited in: Chem. Abstr., vol. 15, p. 1330. Benedict-Hopkins Cole reagent, Cole and Adie's method, Hopkins-Cole (glyoxylic acid) reaction (test or reagent for tryptophane).

Colebrooke Report (Colebrooke, William Mac Bean George): History. See: Morris and Irwin.

COLEBROOKE, WILLIAM MACBEAN GEORGE. 1787-1870. English general and colonial governor. See: Dict. Nat. Biog. Colebrooke Report.

COLEMAN, CLAUDE C. b. 1879. American surgeon. See: Who's Who Among Physicians and Surg. Coleman's syndrome.

Coleman-Shaffer diet (Coleman, Warren and Shaffer, Philip Anderson): Medicine. See: Dorland; Stedman.

COLEMAN, WARREN. 1869-1948. American physician. See: Who Was Who Amer., 1943-1950. Coleman-Shaffer diet.

COLEMAN, WILLIAM TELL. 1824-1893. American mine owner. See: Dict. Amer. Biog. Colemanite.

Colemanite (Coleman, William Tell): Earth Sciences. See: Mathews, M. M.; Thrush; Van Nostrand Sci. Encyc.

Coleman's syndrome (Coleman, Claude C.): Medicine. See: Jablonski.

Colenso controversy (Colenso, John William): Religion. See: Phyfe; Steinberg.

COLENSO, JOHN WILLIAM. 1814-1883. English bishop of Natal. See: Dict. Nat. Biog. Colenso controversy.

COLERIDGE, SAMUEL TAYLOR. 1772-1834. English poet and critic. See: Dict. Nat. Biog. Coleridgean (or Coleridgian).

Coleridgean (or Coleridgian) (Coleridge, Samuel Taylor): Literature. See: Webster's 3d.

Cole's ferricyanide-methylene blue method (Cole, Elbert Charles): Chemistry. See: Ballentyne.

Cole's method for acidity of urine (Derivation undetermined): Chemistry. See: Ballentyne.

Cole's method for amino acids and ammonia in urine (Derivation undetermined): Chemistry. See: Ballentyne.

Cole's syndrome (Cole, Harold Newton). See: Zinsser-Engman-Cole syndrome.

Cole's test for bile pigments (Derivation undetermined): Chemistry. See: Ballentyne.

COLES, W. J. fl. 1910. English engineer. Cited in: Chem. Abstr., Decenn. Index, 1907-1916. Ruggles-Coles dryer.

Coles's sign (Cole, Lewis Gregory): Medicine. See: Dorland; Stedman.

COLETTE, SAINT. 1381-1447. Flemish religious leader. See: Encyc. Brit., 1973. Colettines.

Colettines (Colette, Saint): Religion. See: Attwater.

COLEY, WILLIAM BRADLEY. 1862-1936. American surgeon. See: Who's Who Amer. Med. Coley's fluid, Coley's toxin.

Coley's fluid (Coley, William Bradley): Medicine. See: Dorland.

Coley's toxin (Coley, William Bradley): Medicine. See: Dorland.

COLINET, E. fl. 1953. Belgian physician. (Biography source unavailable.) Caplan-Colinet syndrome.

COLLES, ABRAHAM. 1773-1843. Irish surgeon. See: Dict. Nat. Biog. Colles' fascia, Colles' fracture, Colles' fracture (reverse), Colles' law, Colles' ligament, Colles' space.

Colles-Baumes law (Colles, Abraham and Baumes, Pierre Prosper Francois). See: Colles' law.

Colles' fascia (Colles, Abraham): Medicine. See: Dorland; Stedman.

Colles' fracture (Colles, Abraham): Medicine. See: Jablonski; Partridge; Stedman.

Colles' fracture (reverse) (Colles, Abraham). See: Smith's fracture.

Colles' law (Colles, Abraham): Medicine. See: Dorland; Stedman. Also known as: Baumes' law, Colles-Baumes' law.

Colles' ligament (Colles, Abraham): Anatomy. See: Donath; Stedman.

Colles' space (Colles, Abraham): Medicine. See: Stedman.

COLLET, FREDERIC JUSTIN. b. 1870. French laryngologist. See: Biog. Lex. hervorr. Aerzte, 1880-1930. Collet-Sicard syndrome.

COLLET, PHILIBERT. 1643-1718. French jurist and botanist. See: Nouv. Biog. Univ. Colletia.

Collet-Sicard syndrome (Collet, Frederic Justin and Sicard, Jean Athanase): Medicine. See: Jablonski. Also known as: Collet's syndrome, Sicard's syndrome.

Colletia (Collet, Philibert): Botany. See: Taylor, N.; Webster's 3d.

Collet's syndrome (Collet, Frederic Justin). See: Collet-Sicard syndrome.

COLLIER, JAMES S. 1870-1935. English physician. See: Who Was Who, 1929-1940. Collier's tract.

Collier's tract (Collier, James S.): Medicine. See: Stedman.

COLLIN, ANATOLE. 1831-1923. French instrument maker. (Biography source unavailable.) Collin's osteoclast.

COLLINGS, JESSE. 1831-1920. English statesman. See: Dict. Nat. Biog., 3rd suppl. Jesse Collings Act, Jesse Collings Amendment.

Collinite (Derivation undetermined): Earth Sciences. See: Thrush.

Collins ax (Collins, Samuel W.): Engineering and Industry. See: Mathews, M. M.

Collins dynamometer (Derivation undetermined): Engineering and Industry. See: Winburne.

COLLINS, EDWARD TREACHER. 1862-1919. English ophthalmologist. See: World Who's Who Sci. Treacher Collins' syndrome.

COLLINS, HENRY EDWARD. 1903- . English mining engineer. See: Who's Who, 1972-1973. Collins miner.

COLLINS, JOHN. No dates. English bartender. (Biography source unavailable.) John Collins.

Collins (letter) (Collins, William): Generic Word. See: Brewer; Harvey; Partridge.

Collins machine (Derivation undetermined): Physics. See: Thewlis.

Collins miner (Collins, Henry Edward): Engineering and Industry. See: Thrush.

Collin's osteoclast (Collin, Anatole): Medicine. See: Dorland.

Collins rule (Collins, S. H.): Chemistry. See: Winburne.

COLLINS, S. H. fl. 1910. South African food chemist. Cited in: Chem. Abstr., vol. 5, p. 2505. Collins rule.

COLLINS, SAMUEL W. No dates. American hardware dealer. (Biography source unavailable.) Collins ax.

COLLINS, TOM. No dates. American bartender. (Biography source unavailable.) Tom Collins.

Collins, Tom. See: Furphy, Joseph.

COLLINS, WILLIAM. Character in Jane Austen's novel, "Pride and Prejudice" (1813). See: Benet. Collins (letter).

COLLINS, WILLIAM HENRY. 1878-1937. Canadian geologist. See: Geol. Soc. Amer. Proc., 1937, pp. 157-161. Collinsite.

COLLINS, ZACCHEUS. 1764-1831. American botanist. See: Amer. J. Sci., vol. 23 (1832-33), pp. 398-399. Collinsia.

Collinsia (Collins, Zaccheus): Botany. See: Mathews, M. M.; Taylor, N.; Webster's 3d.

Collinsite (Collins, William Henry): Earth Sciences. See: Thrush; Webster's 3d.

COLLINSON, PETER. 1694-1768. English botanist. See: Dict. Sci. Biog. Collinsonia.

Collinsonia (Collinson, Peter): Botany. See: Charnock; Dorland; Taylor, N.

COLLIP, JAMES BERTRAM. 1892-1965. Canadian biochemist. See: Dict. Sci. Biog. Anderson-Collip test, Collip unit, Noble-Collip procedure.

Collip unit (Collip, James Bertram): Medicine. See: Dorland; Stedman.

Collobrierite (Derivation undetermined): Earth Sciences. See: Thrush.

Collum washer (Derivation undetermined): Engineering and Industry. See: Thrush.

COLONNA, PAUL C. b. 1892. American orthopedic surgeon. See: Who's Who Among Physicians and Surg. Colonna's operation.

Colonna's operation (Colonna, Paul C.): Medicine. See: Dorland.

COLPITTS, EDWIN HENRY. 1872-1949. Canadian-born American electrical engineer. See: Amer. Men Sci., 9th ed. Campbell-Colpitts bridge, Colpitts oscillator?

Colpitts oscillator (Colpitts, Edwin Henry?): Electronics. See: Hughes; Internat. Dict. Phys. Elec.; Markus.

COLSON, RENE. b. 1853. French physicist. See: Pogg., vol. 4. Vogel-Colson-Russell effect.

Colt (revolver) (Colt, Samuel): Weapons. See: Brewer; Charnock; Hendrickson.

COLT, SAMUEL. 1814-1862. American inventor. See: Dict. Amer. Biog. Colt (revolver).

COLUMBA, SAINT. 521-597. Irish missionary. See: Dict. Nat. Biog. Feast of St. Columba.

COLUMBANUS, SAINT. 543-615. Irish missionary. See: Dict. Nat. Biog. Rule of Saint Columbanus.

Columbus (Columbus, Christopher): Generic Word (intrepid discoverer). See: Hendrickson; Partridge; Webster's 3d.

COLUMBUS, CHRISTOPHER. 1451-1506. Italian explorer. See: Encyc. Brit., 1973. Columbus, Columbus('s) crab, Columbus Day, Columbus('s) egg (or egg of Columbus), Knights of Columbus.

Columbus('s) crab (Columbus, Christopher): Zoology. See: Webster's 3d.

Columbus Day (Columbus, Christopher): Generic Word. See: Mathews, M. M.; Smith; Webster's 3d.

Columbus('s) egg (or egg of Columbus) (Columbus, Christopher): Generic Word. See: Brewer; Hendrickson; Phyfe.

column of Bertin (Bertin, Exupere-Joseph). See: Bertin's columns.

Column of Marcus Aurelius (or Antonine Column) (Marcus Aurelius Antoninus): Fine Arts. See: Latham.

column(s) of Morgagni (Morgagni, Giovanni Battista). See: Morgagni's column(s).

column of Tuerck (Tuerck, Ludwig). See: Tuerck's column.

COLUMNA, FABIUS. 1567-1647. Italian botanist. See: World Who's Who Sci. Columnea.

Columnea (Columna, Fabius): Botany. See: Taylor, N.

columns of Goll (Goll, Friedrich). See: Goll's column(s) (tract or column(s) of Goll).

Columns of St. Mark and St. Theodore (Mark, Saint and Theodore Tiro "the General", Saint): Fine Arts. See: Latham.

COMANDUCCI, EZIO. 1873-1922. Italian chemist. See: Pogg., vols. 5, 6, 7b. Commanducci test reaction.

Comaristae (Comartius, Theodore): Religion. See: Canney.

COMARTIUS, THEODORE. d. ca. 1595. Secretary to the States-General. (Biography source unavailable.) Comaristae.

COMBE, ARTHUR DELMAR. 1893-1949. Ugandan geologist. Cited in: Min. Mag., vol. 31 (1958), p. 956. Combeite.

Combeite (Combe, Arthur Delmar): Earth Sciences. See: Thrush.

COMBES, ALPHONSE EDMOND. fl. 1884. French chemist. See: Ber. Deut. Chem. Ges., vol. 29 (1896), pp. 2580-2581. Combes quinoline synthesis.

Combes quinoline synthesis (Combes, Alphonse Edmond): Chemistry. See: Van Nostrand Chem. Dict.

COMBESCURE, JEAN JOSEPH ANTOINE EDOUARD. 1824-1889. French mathematician. See: Pogg., vols. 3, 4. Combescure transformation of a curve, Combescure transformation of a triply orthogonal system of surfaces.

Combescure transformation of a curve (Combescure, Jean Joseph Antoine Edouard): Mathematics. See: James.

Combescure transformation of a triply orthogonal system of surfaces (Combescure, Jean Joseph Antoine Edouard): Mathematics. See: James.

combination principle of Ritz (Ritz, Walter). See: Ritz combination principle.

COMBY, JULES. 1853-1947. French pediatrician. See: World Who's Who Sci. Comby's sign.

Comby's sign (Comby, Jules): Medicine. See: Dorland; Stedman.

COMEL, MARCELLO. 1902- . Italian dermatologist. See: Diz. Encic. Ital. Comel's acrorhigosis.

Comel's acrorhigosis (Comel, Marcello): Medicine. See: Jablonski.

Comessatti test (Derivation undetermined): Medicine. See: Stedman.

COMLY, HUNTER HALL. 1919- . American child psychiatrist. See: Amer. Men Sci., 10th ed. Comly's syndrome.

Comly's syndrome (Comly, Hunter Hall): Medicine. See: Jablonski.

comma Johanninum (or Johannine clause) (John the Evangelist, Saint): Religion. See: Attwater.

comma tract of Schultze (Schultze, Max Johann Sigismund). See: Schultze's fascicle (or comma tract).

Commanducci test reaction (Comanducci, Ezio): Chemistry. See: Van Nostrand Chem. Dict.

COMMELIN, CASPAR. 1668-1731. Dutch botanist. See: World Who's Who Sci. Commelina.

COMMELIN, JEAN. 1629-1692. Dutch botanist. See: World Who's Who Sci. Commelina.

Commelina (Commelin, Caspar and Commelin, Jean): Botany. See: Taylor, N.; Webster's 3d.

COMOLLI, ANTONIO. b. 1879. Italian pathologist. See: Atti Soc. Med.-Chir. Padova, vol. 11, no. 1 (Dec., 1932), p. 107. Comolli's sign.

Comolli's sign (Comolli, Antonio): Medicine. See: Stedman.

Company of Jesus (Jesus Christ). See: Jesuits.

Company of Mary (Mary, Virgin-Mother): Religion. See: Attwater.

Company of St. George (Derivation undetermined): History. See: Harbottle.

Company of St. Paul (Paul the Apostle, Saint?): Religion. See: Attwater.

COMPIN, LOUIS. fl. 1920. French chemist. Cited in: Chem. Abstr., vol. 14, p. 2315. Compin test reaction.

Compin test reaction (Compin, Louis): Chemistry. See: Van Nostrand Chem. Dict.

Compton absorption (Compton, Arthur Holly): Physics. See: Hughes; Internat. Dict. Phys. Elec.; Thrush.

COMPTON, ARTHUR HOLLY. 1892-1962. American physicist. See: Dict. Sci. Biog. Compton absorption, Compton effect (or scattering), Compton electrometer, Compton electron (or recoil electron), Compton-Getting effect, Compton meter, Compton recoil particle, Compton rule, Compton shift, Compton-Simon experiment, Compton wavelength.

Compton effect (or scattering) (Compton, Arthur Holly): Physics. See: Ballentyne; Hughes; Internat. Dict. Ap. Math.

Compton electrometer (Compton, Arthur Holly): Physics. See: Hughes; Thewlis.

Compton electron (or recoil electron) (Compton, Arthur Holly): Physics. See: Hughes; Huschke; Internat. Dict. Phys. Elec.

Compton-Getting effect (Compton, Arthur Holly and Getting, Ivan Alexander): Physics. See: Ballentyne; Thewlis.

COMPTON, HENRY. 1632-1713. English prelate. See: Dict. Nat. Biog. Comptonia.

Compton meter (Compton, Arthur Holly): Physics. See: Internat. Dict. Phys. Elec.; Thrush; Van Nostrand Chem. Dict.

Compton recoil particle (Compton, Arthur Holly): Physics. See: Internat. Dict. Phys. Elec.; Thrush.

Compton rule (Compton, Arthur Holly): Physics. See: Internat. Dict. Phys. Elec.; Van Nostrand Chem. Dict.; Van Nostrand Sci. Encyc.

Compton shift (Compton, Arthur Holly): Physics. See: Internat. Dict. Phys. Elec.; Thrush.

Compton-Simon experiment (Compton, Arthur Holly and Simon, Alfred Walter): Physics. See: Internat. Dict. Phys. Elec.

COMPTON, SPENCER JOSHUA ALWYNE (2ND MARQUIS OF NORTHAMPTON). 1790-1851. English political leader. See: Dict. Nat. Biog. Comptonite.

Compton wavelength (Compton, Arthur Holly): Physics. See: Hughes; Internat. Dict. Phys. Elec.; Thewlis.

Comptonia (Compton, Henry): Botany. See: Charnock; Hendrickson; Taylor, N.

Comptonite (Compton, Spencer Joshua Alwyne): Earth Sciences. See: Charnock; Thrush.

COMSTOCK, ANTHONY. 1844-1915. American reformer. See: Dict. Amer. Biog. Comstockery.

COMSTOCK, HENRY TOMKINS PAIGE. 1820-1870. American prospector. See: Dict. Amer. Biog. Comstocker.

COMSTOCK, JOHN HENRY. 1849-1931. American entomologist. See: World Who's Who Sci. Comstock('s) mealybug.

Comstock('s) mealybug (Comstock, John Henry): Zoology. See: Webster's 3d.

Comstocker (Comstock, Henry Tomkins Paige): Generic Word. See: Hendrickson.

Comstockery (Comstock, Anthony): Generic Word (excessive censorship). See: Brewer; Hendrickson; Mathews, M. M.

COMTE, AUGUSTE. 1798-1857. French mathematician and philosopher. See: Internat. Encyc. Soc. Sci. Comte's stages of social development, Comtian (or Comtean), Comtism.

Comte's stages of social development (Comte, Auguste): Sociology. See: Zadrozny.

Comtian (or Comtean) (Comte, Auguste): Philosophy. See: Webster's 3d.

Comtism (Comte, Auguste): Philosophy. See: Attwater; Partridge; Weekley.

CONANT, CHARLES ARTHUR. 1861-1915. American banking expert. See: Dict. Amer. Biog. Conant (coin).

Conant (coin) (Conant, Charles Arthur): Numismatics. See: Mathews, M. M.

CONCATO, LUIGI MARIA. 1825-1882. Italian physician. See: World Who's Who Sci. Concato's disease.

Concato's disease (Concato, Luigi Maria). See: Bamberger's disease (1).

conchoid of Nicomedes (Nicomedes): Mathematics. See: James; Van Nostrand Sci. Encyc.

Concordat of Francis I (Francis I): History. See: Latham.

Condamine reagent (Derivation undetermined): Chemistry. See: Van Nostrand Chem. Dict.

CONDILLAC, ETIENNE BONNET DE. 1715-1780. French philosopher. See: Internat. Encyc. Soc. Sci. statue of Condillac.

CONDON, EDWARD UHLER. 1902- . American physicist. See: World Who's Who Sci. Condon parabola, Franck-Condon principle, Gamow-Condon-Gurney theory of alpha decay.

Condon parabola (Condon, Edward Uhler): Physics. See: Internat. Dict. Ap. Math.

CONDORELLI, LUIGI. 1899- . Italian pathologist. See: World Who's Who Sci. Condorelli's disease.

Condorelli's disease (Condorelli, Luigi): Medicine. See: Jablonski.

Condum (Condum, Colonel? or Conton, Dr.?): Medicine. See: Hendrickson.

CONDUM, COLONEL. fl. mid-17th c. English army officer. (Biography source unavailable.) Condum?

CONDY, HENRY BOLLMANN. fl. 1862. English physician. (Biography source unavailable.) Condy's fluid.

Condy's fluid (Condy, Henry Bollmann): Medicine. See: Dorland; Hackh; Partridge.

Cone-Cady reagent (Cone, William Homer and Cady, Louis Clyde): Chemistry. See: Van Nostrand Chem. Dict.

cone of Wulzen (Wulzen, Rosalind): Zoology. See: Henderson.

CONE, WILLIAM HOMER. b. 1893. American chemist. See: Amer. Men Sci., 9th ed. Cone-Cady reagent.

Confucian (or Confucianism) (Confucius): Religion. See: Canney; Hendrickson; Partridge.

CONFUCIUS. 551-479 B.C. Chinese philosopher. See: Encyc. Brit., 1973. Confucian (or Confucianism).

Congregation of Saint Joseph (Joseph, Saint). See: Josephites (1).

Congregation of Saint Ottilia (Ottilia, Saint): Religion. See: Attwater.

Congreve (match) (Congreve, William): Weapons. See: Brewer; Charnock; Partridge.

Congreve rocket(s) (Congreve, William): Weapons. See: Brewer; Partridge; Quick.

CONGREVE, WILLIAM. 1772-1828. English inventor. See: Dict. Sci. Biog. Congreve (match), Congreve rocket(s).

CONKLIN, HARRY R. b. 1867. American mining engineer. See: Who's Who Engin., 1925. Conklin process.

Conklin process (Conklin, Harry R.): Engineering and Industry. See: Thrush.

Conkling magnetic separator (Derivation undetermined): Engineering and Industry. See: Thrush.

CONN, HAROLD JOEL. b. 1886. American bacteriologist. See: Amer. Men Sci., 10th ed. Conn stain, Hucker-Conn solution.

CONN, JEROME W. 1907- . American physician. See: Who's Imp. Med., 2d ed. Conn's syndrome.

Conn-Louis syndrome (Conn, Jerome W. and Louis, Lawrence Hua-Hsien). See: Conn's syndrome.

Conn stain (Conn, Harold Joel): Chemistry. See: Van Nostrand Chem. Dict.

Connally-Fulbright resolution (Connally, Thomas Terry and Fulbright, James William): History. See: Morris.

CONNALLY, THOMAS TERRY. 1877-1963. American legislator. See: Biog. Direct. Amer. Congress. Connally-Fulbright resolution, Jones-Connally Farm Relief Act, Smith-Connally Anti-Strike Act.

CONNELL, ARTHUR. 1794-1863. Scottish chemist. See: Royal Soc. Proc., vol. 13 (1864), p. i. Connellite.

CONNELL, FRANK GREGORY. b. 1875. American surgeon. See: Who's Who Amer. Med. Connell's suture.

Connellite (Connell, Arthur): Earth Sciences. See: Charnock; Thrush.

Connell's suture (Connell, Frank Gregory): Medicine. See: Dorland; Stedman.

Conners Foundation (Conners, William James): Philanthropy. Cited in: Webster's Biog. Dict.

CONNERS, WILLIAM JAMES. 1857-1929. American shipowner and newspaper publisher. See: Webster's Biog. Dict. Conners Foundation.

CONNERY, WILLIAM PATRICK, JR. 1888-1937. American legislator. See: Biog. Direct. Amer. Congress. Black-Connery-Perkins Wages and Hours Bill, Wagner-Connery Act.

Conn's syndrome (Conn, Jerome W.): Medicine. See: Jablonski; Stedman. Also known as: Conn-Louis syndrome.

CONOLLY, JOHN. 1794-1866. English physician. See: Dict. Nat. Biog. Conolly's system.

Conolly's system (Conolly, John): Medicine. See: Dorland.

Conrad counterflush coring system (Derivation undetermined): Engineering and Industry. See: Thrush.

Conrad-Limpach synthesis (Conrad, Max and Limpach, Karl Friedrich Leonhard): Chemistry. See: Van Nostrand Chem. Dict.

Conrad machine (Derivation undetermined): Engineering and Industry. See: Thrush.

CONRAD, MAX. 1848-1920. German chemist. See: Pogg., vols. 3, 4, 5. Conrad-Limpach synthesis.

CONRADI, ANDREAS CHRISTIAN. 1809-1869. Norwegian physician. See: Biog. Lex. hervorr. Aerzte. Conradi's line.

Conradi-Drigalski agar (Conradi, Heinrich and Drigalski, Wilhelm von): Medicine. See: Dorland; Stedman. Also known as: Drigalski-Conradi agar.

CONRADI, ERICH. b. 1882. German physician. (Biography source unavailable.) Conradi-Huenermann syndrome.

CONRADI, HEINRICH. b. 1876. German bacteriologist. See: Biog. Lex. hervorr. Aerzte, 1880-1930. Conradi-Drigalski agar.

Conradi-Huenermann syndrome (Conradi, Erich and Huenermann, Carl): Medicine. See: Jablonski. Also known as: Conradi's syndrome.

Conradi's line (Conradi, Andreas Christian): Medicine. See: Dorland; Stedman.

Conradi's syndrome (Conradi, Erich). See: Conradi-Huenermann syndrome.

CONRADSON, PONTUS H. fl. 1912. American chemist. Cited in: Chem. Abstr., vol. 6, p. 3325. Conradson test (or carbon test).

Conradson test (or carbon test) (Conradson, Pontus H.): Chemistry. See: Hackh; Van Nostrand Sci. Encyc.

CONRING, HERMANN. 1606-1681. German scholar and physician. See: World Who's Who Sci. Conringia.

Conringia (Conring, Hermann): Botany. See: Webster's 3d.

Conspiracy of Catherine (Catherine II): History. See: Harbottle.

Conspiracy of Marino Falieri (Falieri, Marino): History. See: Harbottle.

CONSTANTINE I. 280-337. Roman emperor. See: Encyc. Brit., 1911. Constantinian, Constantinian calendar, cross of Constantine, Donation of Constantine, Sacred Constantinian Order.

CONSTANTINE VII (PORPHYROGENITUS). 905-959. Byzantine emperor. See: Encyc. Brit., 1911. Porphyrogenitus.

Constantinesco gear (Constantinesco, George): Engineering and Industry. See: Auger.

CONSTANTINESCO, GEORGE. fl. 1926. English engineer. (Biography source unavailable.) Constantinesco gear.

CONSTANTINESCU, G. fl. 1934. Rumanian chemist. Cited in: Chem. Abstr., vol. 30, p. 3583. Constantinescu test reactions.

Constantinescu test reactions (Constantinescu, G.): Chemistry. See: Van Nostrand Chem. Dict.

Constantinian (Constantine I): History. See: Webster's 3d.

Constantinian calendar (Constantine I): Horology. See: Winick.

CONTARDI, ANGELO. fl. 1925-1928. Italian chemist. See: Pogg., vol. 6. Koerner-Contardi reaction.

CONTINO, ANTONINO. 1878-1951. Italian ophthalmologist. See: Rass. Ital. d'Ottalm., vol. 20, p. 341. Contino's epithelioma, Contino's glaucoma.

Contino's epithelioma (Contino, Antonino): Medicine. See: Jablonski.

Contino's glaucoma (Contino, Antonino): Medicine. See: Jablonski.

CONTON, DR. fl. 17th c. English physician. (Biography source unavailable.) Condum?

Conway cabal (Conway, Thomas): History. See: Jameson; Latham; Smith.

CONWAY, THOMAS. 1735-1800. Irish army officer. See: Dict. Amer. Biog. Conway cabal.

CONWELL, ESTHER MARLY. 1922- . American physicist. See: World Who's Who Sci. Conwell-Weisskopf equation (or formula).

Conwell-Weisskopf equation (or formula) (Conwell, Esther Marly and Weisskopf, Victor Frederick): Physics. See: Ballentyne; Internat. Dict. Ap. Math.; Internat. Dict. Phys. Elec.

Coodies (political party) (Verplanck, Gulian Crommelin, Pseud., Abimeleck Coody): History. See: Clapin; Jameson; Smith.

Coody, Abimeleck. See: Verplanck, Gulian Crommelin.

COOK, ALBERT JOHN. 1842-1916. American naturalist. See: World Who's Who Sci. Cook's petrel?

COOK, ELLEN PARMELEE. 1865- . American chemist. Cited in: Chem. Abstr., vol. 1, p. 55. Bogert-Cook synthesis.

Cook-Ficklen benzene apparatus (Cook, Warren A. and Ficklen, Joseph Burwell III): Chemistry. Cited in: World Who's Who Sci.

Cook formula (Cook, L. W.): Chemistry. See: Hackh; Van Nostrand Chem. Dict.

COOK, JAMES. 1728-1779. English mariner and explorer. See: Dict. Nat. Biog. Captain Cooks (or Cookers).

COOK, L. W. fl. 1922. American chemist. Cited in: Chem. Abstr., vol. 16, p. 1674. Cook formula.

COOK, ROBERT JOHNSON. 1849-1922. American crew coach and publisher. See: Dict. Amer. Biog. Bob Cook stroke.

COOK, THOMAS. 1808-1892. English tourist agent. See: Dict. Nat. Biog., 1st suppl. Cook's tour.

COOK, WARREN A. fl. 1932. American chemist. Cited in: Chem. Abstr., vol. 26, p. 5875. Cook-Ficklen benzene apparatus.

COOKE, A. BENNETT. b. 1869. American physician. See: Who's Who Among Physicians and Surg. Cooke's speculum.

Cooke-Apert-Gallais syndrome (Cooke; Apert, Eugene; and Gallais, Alfred): Medicine. See: Jablonski; Stedman.

Cooke elutriator (Cooke, Strathmore Ridley Barnott): Engineering and Industry. See: Thrush.

Cooke eyepiece (Cooke, Thomas?): Astronomy. See: Satterthwaite.

COOKE, J. fl. 19th c. Inventor. (Biography source unavailable.) Cooke ventilating machine.

COOKE, JOSIAH PARSONS. 1827-1894. American chemist. See: Dict. Sci. Biog. Cookeite.

Cooke-Ponder method (Cooke, William Edmond and Ponder, Eric): Medicine. See: Kelly. Also known as: weighted mean of Cooke and Ponder.

COOKE, STRATHMORE RIDLEY BARNOTT. 1907- . New Zealand-born American metallurgist. See: Amer. Men Sci., 9th ed. Cooke elutriator.

COOKE, THOMAS. 1807-1868. English optician. See: World Who's Who Sci. Cooke eyepiece?, Cooke triplet?

Cooke triplet (Cooke, Thomas?): Physics. See: Internat. Dict. Phys. Elec.

Cooke ventilating machine (Cooke, J.): Engineering and Industry. See: Auger.

COOKE, WILLIAM EDMOND. 1881-1939. English physician. See: Lancet, vol. 2 (July 29, 1939), p. 293. Cooke-Ponder method, Cooke's count (criterion, method, modification, formula or index).

Cookeite (Cooke, Josiah Parsons): Earth Sciences. See: Mathews, M.M.; Thrush; Webster's 3d.

Cooke's count (criterion, method, modification, formula or index) (Cooke, William Edmond): Medicine. See: Dorland; Kelly.

Cooke's speculum (Cooke, A. Bennett): Medicine. See: Stedman.

Cook's petrel (Cook, Albert John?): Biology. See: Gray.

Cook's tour (Cook, Thomas): Generic Word (humorous excursion). See: Hendrickson.

COOKSON, BRYAN. 1874-1909. English astronomer. See: Sci., vol. 30 (1909), p. 476. Cookson floating zenith tube.

Cookson floating zenith tube (Cookson, Bryan): Astronomy. See: Satterthwaite.

COOLEY, CHARLES HORTON. 1864-1929. American sociologist. See: Encyc. Brit., 1973. Cooley's wishes.

Cooley-Lee syndrome (Cooley, Thomas Benton and Lee, Pearl). See: Cooley's anemia (disease, or syndrome).

COOLEY, THOMAS BENTON. 1871-1945. American pediatrician. See: Who's Who Amer. Med. Cooley's anemia (disease, or syndrome), Cooley's trait.

Cooley's anemia (disease or syndrome) (Cooley, Thomas Benton): Medicine. See: Jablonski; Stedman; Winick. Also known as: Cooley-Lee syndrome, Dameshek's syndrome.

Cooley's trait (Cooley, Thomas Benton). See: Silvestroni-Bianco syndrome.

Cooley's wishes (Cooley, Charles Horton): Sociology. See: Zadrozny.

COOLIDGE, CALVIN. 1872-1932. American president. See: Dict. Amer. Biog., 1st suppl. Coolidgean.

Coolidge tube (Coolidge, William David): Chemistry. See: Hackh; Hughes; Van Nostrand Chem. Dict.

COOLIDGE, WILLIAM DAVID. 1873-1974. American physicist. See: World Who's Who Sci. Coolidge tube.

Coolidgean (Coolidge, Calvin): History. See: Webster's 3d.

COOMBS, CAREY FRANKLIN. 1879-1932. English physician. See: Who Was Who, 1929-40. Carey Coombs murmur.

COOMBS, CLYDE HAMILTON. 1912- . American psychologist. See: Amer. Psych. Assoc. Direct., 1960. Coombs' criterion.

Coombs' criterion (Coombs, Clyde Hamilton): Statistics. See: Thrush.

Coombs murmur (Coombs, Carey Franklin). See: Carey-Coombs murmur.

COOMBS, ROBIN ROYSTON AMOS. fl. 20th c. English physician. See: Direct. Brit. Sci., 1966-1967. Coombs' test.

Coombs' test (Coombs, Robin Royston Amos): Medicine. See: Dorland; Stedman.

COOPER. No dates. Bartender. (Biography source unavailable.) Cooper.

Cooper (Cooper, the bartender): Food and Drink. See: Charnock.

COOPER, A. No dates. Physician. (Biography source unavailable.) Cooper's disease.

COOPER, ARTHUR REUBEN. b. 1888. Canadian helminthologist. (Biography source unavailable.) Cooperia (worms).

COOPER, SIR ASTLEY PASTON. 1768-1841. English anatomist and surgeon. See: Dict. Nat. Biog. Cooper's disease, Cooper's droop, Cooper's fascia, Cooper's hernia, Cooper's herniotome, Cooper's ligaments, Cooper's neuralgia, Cooper's reflected tendon, Cooper's testis.

COOPER, DANIEL. 1817-1842. English botanist. See: Dict. Nat. Biog. Cooperia (lily).

Cooper('s) hawk (Cooper, William): Biology. See: Gray; Pennak under "Accipiter cooperi;" Webster's 3d.

COOPER, JOHN GORDON. 1872-1955. American legislator. See: Biog. Direct. Amer. Congress. Hawes-Cooper Act?

COOPER, JOHN THOMAS. 1790-1854. English chemist. See: World Who's Who Sci. Cooper's tube.

COOPER, LEON N. 1930- . American physicist. See: Amer. Men Sci., 10th ed. Bardeen-Cooper-Schrieffer theory of superconductivity, Cooper pair.

Cooper pair (Cooper, Leon N.): Physics. See: Ballentyne; Barnhart (New Eng.).

COOPER, R. A. fl. 1920. South African mineralogist. Cited in: Dana. Cooperite.

Cooper reagent (Cooper, Stewart Rochester): Chemistry. See: Van Nostrand Chem. Dict.

COOPER, STEWART ROCHESTER. b. 1893. American chemist. See: Amer. Men Sci., 6th ed. Cooper reagent, Nichols-Cooper reagent.

COOPER, WILLIAM. 1798-1864. American naturalist. See: Who Was Who Amer., 1607-1896. Cooper('s) hawk.

Cooperia (lily) (Cooper, Daniel): Botany. See: Taylor, N.; Webster's 3d.

Cooperia (worms) (Cooper, Arthur Reuben): Medicine. See: Stedman; Webster's 3d.

Cooperite (Cooper, R. A.): Earth Sciences. See: Thrush; Webster's 3d.

COOPERNAIL, GEORGE PETER. b. 1876. American surgeon. See: Who's Who Amer. Med. Coopernail's sign.

Coopernail's sign (Coopernail, George Peter): Medicine. See: Dorland; Jablonski; Stedman.

Cooper's disease (Cooper, A.). See: Reclus' syndrome.

Cooper's disease (Cooper, Sir Astley Paston). See: Cheatle's disease.

Cooper's droop (Cooper, Sir Astley Paston): Medicine. See: Atlanta J. (Apr. 4, 1974) "World Events Translated - Rapid Changes Spell New Language Angles."

Cooper's fascia (Cooper, Sir Astley Paston): Anatomy. See: Donath; Dorland; Stedman. Also known as: Scarpa's sheath.

Cooper's hernia (Cooper, Sir Astley Paston): Medicine. See: Dorland; Jablonski; Stedman.

Cooper's herniotome (Cooper, Sir Astley Paston): Medicine. See: Stedman.

Cooper's ligaments (Cooper, Sir Astley Paston): Anatomy. See: Donath; Dorland; Stedman.

Cooper's lines (Derivation undetermined): Earth Sciences. See: Thrush.

Cooper's neuralgia (Cooper, Sir Astley Paston): Medicine. See: Jablonski.

Cooper's reflected tendon (Cooper, Sir Astley Paston): Medicine. See: Stedman.

Cooper's testis (Cooper, Sir Astley Paston): Medicine. See: Jablonski.

Cooper's tube (Cooper, John Thomas): Chemistry. Cited in: World Who's Who Sci.

Coote-Hunauld syndrome (Derivation undetermined): See: Naffziger's syndrome.

Coote's syndrome (Derivation undetermined). See: Naffziger's syndrome.

COPAUX, HIPPOLYTE EUGENE. 1872-1934. French chemist. See: Dict. Sci. Biog. Copaux-Kawecki fluoride process.

Copaux-Kawecki fluoride process (Copaux, Hippolyte Eugene and Kawecki, Henry Casimir): Chemistry. See: Thrush.

COPE, EDWARD DRINKER. 1840-1897. American zoologist and naturalist. See: Dict. Amer. Biog. Cope's law?

COPE, RICHARD WHITTAKER. No dates. Inventor. (Biography source unavailable.) Cope's press, Sherwin and Cope's press.

Copeman-Ackermann syndrome (Derivation undetermined): Medicine. See: Jablonski.

Copernican system (or Copernicanism) (Copernicus, Nicholas): Astronomy. See: Brewer; Phyfe; Satterthwaite.

Copernicia (Copernicus, Nicholas): Botany. See: Webster's 3d.

COPERNICUS, NICHOLAS. 1473-1543. Polish astronomer. See: Dict. Sci. Biog. Copernican system (or Copernicanism), Copernicia.

Cope's law (Cope, Edward Drinker?): Biology. See: Winick.

Cope's press (Cope, Richard Whittaker): Printing. See: Lockwood.

COPLEY, SIR GODFREY. d. 1709. English aristocrat. See: Dict. Nat. Biog. Copley medal.

COPLEY, JOHN SINGLETON, LORD LYNDHURST. 1772-1863. American-born English jurist. See: Dict. Nat. Biog. Lord Lyndhurst's Act.

Copley medal (Copley, Sir Godfrey): Science. See: Phyfe.

COPLEY, MICHAEL JOSEPH. 1900- . American chemist. See: Amer. Men Sci., 6th ed. Copley, Phipps and Glasser gauge.

Copley, Phipps and Glasser gauge (Copley, Michael Joseph; Phipps, Thomas Erwin; and Glasser, Julian): Chemistry. See: Internat. Dict. Phys. Elec.

Coppet, Louis Casimir. See: De Coppet, Louis Casimir.

Coppet's law (De Coppet, Louis Casimir): Chemistry. See: Dorland; Hackh; Stedman.

COPSON, RAYMOND LESLIE. 1904- . American chemical engineer. See: Amer. Men Sci., 9th ed. Copson, Walthall, and Hignett process.

Copson, Walthall, and Hignett process (Copson, Raymond Leslie; Walthall, John Henry; and Hignett, Travis Porter): Chemistry. See: Van Nostrand Chem. Dict.

COQUEBERT DE MONTBREY, ANTOINE-FRANCOIS-ERNEST. 1781-1801. French naturalist. See: Michaud. Montbretia.

Corahism (Korah): Generic Word. See: Matthews, M. M.

Corbino disc (disk) (Corbino, Orso Mario): Physics. See: Ballentyne; Markus.

Corbino effect (Corbino, Orso Mario): Physics. See: Thewlis; Van Nostrand Sci. Encyc. Also known as: Hall effect.

CORBINO, ORSO MARIO. 1876-1937. Italian physicist. See: Pogg., vol. 4, 5, 6, 7b. Corbino disc (disk), Corbino effect.

cord of Ocnus (Ocnus). See: rope of Ocnus.

cord of St. Thomas (Aquinas, Saint Thomas): Religion. See: Attwater.

CORDA, AUGUST KARL JOSEPH. 1809-1849. Bohemian botanist. See: World Who's Who Sci. Cordaites.

Cordaites (Corda, August Karl Joseph): Botany. See: Thrush; Webster's 3d.

CORDAY, CHARLOTTE. 1768-1793. French patriot. See: Encyc. Brit., 1973. Charlotte Corday cap.

CORDEAUX, J. H. fl. 1877. English? engineer. (Biography source unavailable.) Cordeaux thread.

Cordeaux thread (Cordeaux, J. H.): Engineering and Industry. See: Auger.

Cordia (Cordus, Valerius): Botany. See: Taylor, N.

CORDIER, PIERRE-LOUIS-ANTOINE. 1777-1861. French geologist. See: Dict. Sci. Biog. Cordierite.

Cordierite (Cordier, Pierre-Louis-Antoine): Earth Sciences. See: Charnock; Van Nostrand Sci. Encyc.; Webster's 3d.

Cordirie process (Derivation undetermined): Engineering and Industry. See: Thrush.

Cordoba (coin) (Cordoba, Francisco Fernandez de): Numismatics. See: Hendrickson; Partridge; Webster's 3d.

CORDOBA, FRANCISCO FERNANDEZ DE. 1475-1526. Spanish explorer. See: Webster's Biog. Dict. Cordoba (coin).

Cords' angiopathy (Cords, Richard): Medicine. See: Jablonski.

CORDS, RICHARD. 1881-1931. German ophthalmologist. See: Biog. Lex. hervorr. Aerzte, 1880-1930. Cords' angiopathy.

CORDUS, VALERIUS. 1515-1544. German botanist. See: Dict. Sci. Biog. Cordia.

Coreau detonnant (Derivation undetermined): Engineering and Industry. See: Thrush.

CORELLI, ARCANGELO. 1653-1713. Italian composer. See: Encyc. Brit., 1973. Corelli Fugue.

Corelli Fugue (Corelli, Arcangelo): Music. See: Scholes.

COREY, ROBERT BRAINARD. 1897-1971. American chemist. See: Who Was Who Amer., 1969-1973. Pauling-Corey helix.

CORI, CARL FERDINAND. 1896- . Czech-born American biochemist. See: World Who's Who Sci. Cori cycle, Cori ester.

Cori cycle (Cori, Carl Ferdinand): Medicine. See: Dorland; Stedman.

Cori ester (Cori, Carl Ferdinand): Medicine. See: Dorland; Stedman.

CORI, GERTY THERESA RADNITZ. 1896-1957. Czech-born American biochemist. See: Dict. Sci. Biog. Cori's disease.

Corino Andrade, M. See: Andrade, Corino M.

Coriolis acceleration (Coriolis, Gaspard Gustave de): Physics. See: Huschke; James; Webster's 3d.

Coriolis effects (or deflection) (Coriolis, Gaspard Gustave de): Physics. See: Hughes; Internat. Dict. Ap. Math.; Internat. Dict. Phys. Elec.

Coriolis' force (Coriolis, Gaspard Gustave de): Physics. See: Ballentyne; Markus; Monkhouse.

CORIOLIS, GASPARD GUSTAVE DE. 1792-1843. French civil engineer. See: Dict. Sci. Biog. Coriolis acceleration, Coriolis effects (or deflection), Coriolis' force, Coriolis parameter.

Coriolis parameter (Coriolis, Gaspard Gustave de): Physics. See: Huschke; Internat. Dict. Ap. Math.

Cori's disease (Cori, Gerty Theresa Radnitz): Medicine. See: Jablonski. Also known as: Forbes' disease.

CORLETT, WILLIAM THOMAS. 1854-1948. American dermatologist. See: Who's Who Amer. Med. Corlett's pyosis.

Corlett's pyosis (Corlett, William Thomas): Medicine. See: Dorland; Stedman. Also known as: Fox's impetigo.

Corliss engine (Corliss, George Henry): Engineering and Industry. See: Auger; Mathews, M. M.; Van Nostrand Sci. Encyc.

CORLISS, GEORGE HENRY. 1817-1888. American inventor. See: Dict. Amer. Biog. Corliss engine, Corliss valve.

Corliss valve (Corliss, George Henry): Engineering and Industry. See: Auger.

Cornelia (Cornelia, the Roman): Generic Word. See: Partridge.

Cornelia de Lange's syndrome (De Lange, Cornelia Catharina). See: De Lange's syndrome (1) and De Lange's syndrome (2).

CORNELIA, THE ROMAN. 2d c. B.C. Roman matron. See: Encyc. Brit., 1973. Cornelia, Cornelian corner.

Cornelian corner (Cornelia, the Roman): Psychology. See: Good.

Cornelian law (or Lex Cornelia) (Sulla, Lucius Cornelius): Law. See: Black; Latham.

Cornelius. See: Sulla, Lucius Cornelius.

CORNELIUS, ERIK. fl. 1906. Swedish inventor. Cited in: Chem. Abstr., vol. 1, p. 2831. Cornelius furnace.

Cornelius furnace (Cornelius, Erik): Engineering and Industry. See: Thrush.

Corner-Allen test (Corner, George Washington and Allen, Willard Myron): Medicine. See: Dorland; Stedman.

Corner and Allen unit (Corner, George Washington and Allen, Willard Myron): Medicine. See: Stedman.

CORNER, EDRED MOSS. 1873-1950. English surgeon. See: Who Was Who, 1941-1950. Corner's tampon.

CORNER, GEORGE WASHINGTON. b. 1889. American anatomist. See: Who's Who Amer. Med. Corner-Allen test , Corner and Allen unit.

Corner's tampon (Corner, Edred Moss): Medicine. See: Dorland; Stedman.

CORNET, GEORGE. 1858-1915. German bacteriologist. See: World Who's Who Sci. Cornet's forceps.

CORNET, JULES. d. 1929. Belgian geologist. See: Bull. Soc. Geogr. Anvers, vol. 33 (1909), pp. 351-53. Cornetite.

Cornetite (Cornet, Jules): Earth Sciences. See: Webster's 3d.

Cornet's forceps (Cornet, George): Medicine. See: Dorland.

CORNIL, LUCIEN. 1888-1952. French physician. See: Presse Med., vol. 60 (1952), p. 1017. Lhermitte-Cornil-Quesnel syndrome, Roussy-Cornil syndrome.

CORNING, JAMES LEONARD. 1855-1923. American neurologist. See: World Who's Who Sci. Corning's anesthesia (or method).

Corning's anesthesia (or method) (Corning, James Leonard): Medicine. See: Dorland.

CORNISH, EDMUND ALFRED. fl. 1937. Australian statistician. (Biography source unavailable.) Cornish-Fisher expansion.

Cornish-Fisher expansion (Cornish, Edmund Alfred and Fisher, Sir Ronald Alymer): Statistics. See: Kendall.

CORNO, RENZO. fl. 1956. Italian physician. (Biography source unavailable.) Corno's disease.

Corno's disease (Corno, Renzo): Medicine. See: Jablonski.

Cornu-Hartman formula (Cornu, Marie Alfred and Hartman, Johannes Franz): Physics. See: Ballentyne.

Cornu-Jellet prism (Cornu, Marie Alfred and Jellett, John Hewitt): Physics. See: Internat. Dict. Phys. Elec.; Van Nostrand Sci. Encyc.

CORNU, MARIE ALFRED. 1841-1902. French physicist. See: Dict. Sci. Biog. Cornu-Hartman formula, Cornu-Jellet prism, Cornu polariscope, Cornu prism, Cornu('s) spiral.

Cornu polariscope (Cornu, Marie Alfred): Physics. See: Internat. Dict. Phys. Elec.

Cornu prism (Cornu, Marie Alfred): Physics. See: Hackh; Thewlis.

Cornu('s) spiral (Cornu, Marie Alfred): Physics. See: Ballentyne; Internat. Dict. Ap. Math.; Internat. Dict. Phys. Elec.

CORNUT, JACQUES PHILLIPE. 1626-1651. French botanist and physician. See: World Who's Who Sci. Cornutia.

Cornutia (Cornut, Jacques Phillipe): Botany. See: Charnock.

CORNWALLIS, CHARLES. 1738-1805. English soldier. See: Dict. Nat. Biog. Cornwallis Code, Cornwallis (masquerade), Cornwallisade.

Cornwallis Code (Cornwallis, Charles): History. See: Morris and Irwin.

Cornwallis (masquerade) (Cornwallis, Charles): Generic Word. See: Mathews, M. M.; Webster's 3d.

Cornwallisade (Cornwallis, Charles): Generic Word (a surrender). See: Mathews, M. M.

Coromant cut (Derivation undetermined): Engineering and Industry. See: Thrush.

Coronadite (Coronado, Francesco Vasquez de): Earth Sciences. See: Webster's 3d.

CORONADO, FRANCESCO VASQUEZ DE. 1510-1554. Spanish explorer. See: Encyc. Brit., 1973. Coronadite.

Corpus Christi (Jesus Christ): Religion. See: Attwater; Canney; Encyc. Brit., 1973; Weekley.

corpus Highmori (Highmore, Nathaniel). See: Highmore's body.

corpuscle(s) of Hassall (or Hassal) (Hassall, Arthur Hill). See: Hassall's (or Hassal's) corpuscles (concentric corpuscles or bodies).

corpuscle of Herbst (Herbst, Ernst Friedrich Gustav). See: Herbst's corpuscle.

corpuscle of Meissner (Meissner, Georg). See: Meissner('s) corpuscle(s).

corpuscle of Ruffini (Ruffini, Angelo). See: Ruffini's corpuscles (nerve endings, organs, or cylinder).

corpuscle of Vater (Vater, Abraham). See: Vater-Pacini corpuscles.

Correa (Correa da Serra, Jose Francisco): Botany. See: Webster's 3d.

CORREA DA SERRA, JOSE FRANCISCO. 1750-1823. Portuguese botanist. See: Encyc. Brit., 1911. Correa.

CORRENS, CARL WILHELM. 1893-   . German mineralogist. See: World Who's Who Sci. Corrensite?

Corrensite (Correns, Carl Wilhelm?): Earth Sciences. See: Thrush.

Correra's line (Derivation undetermined): Medicine. See: Stedman.

Correy gear (Correy, M.): Engineering and Industry. See: Auger.

CORREY, M. No dates. French engineer. (Biography source unavailable.) Correy gear.

CORRIGAN, SIR DOMINIC JOHN. 1802-1880. Irish pathologist. See: Dict. Nat. Biog. Corrigan's cautery, Corrigan's cirrhosis, Corrigan's disease, Corrigan's pulse (or sign), Corrigan's respiration.

Corrigan's cautery (Corrigan, Sir Dominic John): Medicine. See: Dorland; Stedman.

Corrigan's cirrhosis (Corrigan, Sir Dominic John): Medicine. See: Jablonski.

Corrigan's disease (Corrigan, Sir Dominic John): Medicine. See: Dorland; Jablonski; Stedman.

Corrigan's pulse (or sign) (Corrigan, Sir Dominic John): Medicine. See: Dorland; Jablonski; Stedman.

Corrigan's respiration (Corrigan, Sir Dominic John): Medicine. See: Dorland.

Corsini, Lorenzo. See: Clement XII.

Corso solution (Derivation undetermined): Chemistry. See: Van Nostrand Chem. Dict.

CORTI, ALFONSO GIACOMO GASPARE. 1822-1876. Italian anatomist. See: Dict. Sci. Biog. Corti's arch (or arch of Corti), Corti's cells (or cell of Corti), Corti's ganglion, Corti's membrane (or membrane of Corti), Corti's organ (or organ of Corti), Corti's rods (or rods of Corti), Corti's teeth, Corti's tunnel (or canal).

Corti compromise (Corti, Lodovico): History. See: Harbottle.

CORTI, LODOVICO. 1823-1888. Italian diplomat. See: Encyc. Brit., 1973. Corti compromise.

Corti's arch (or arch of Corti) (Corti, Alfonso Giacomo Gaspare): Anatomy. See: Dorland; Drever; Stedman.

Corti's cells (or cell of Corti) (Corti, Alfonso Giacomo Gaspare): Anatomy. See: Donath; Stedman; Webster's 3d.

Corti's ganglion (Corti, Alfonso Giacomo Gaspare): Anatomy. See: Stedman; Webster's 3d.

Corti's membrane (or membrane of Corti) (Corti, Alfonso Giacomo Gaspare): Anatomy. See: Henderson; Stedman; Webster's 3d.

Corti's organ (or organ of Corti) (Corti, Alfonso Giacomo Gaspare): Anatomy. See: Chaplin; Gray; Pennak.

Corti's rods (or rods of Corti) (Corti, Alfonso Giacomo Gaspare): Anatomy. See: Drever; English; Henderson.

Corti's teeth (Corti, Alfonso Giacomo Gaspare). See: Huschke's teeth.

Corti's tunnel (or canal) (Corti, Alfonso Giacomo Gaspare): Anatomy. See: Dorland; Stedman.

Cortusa (Cortusi, Jacobo Antonio): Botany. See: Charnock.

CORTUSI, JACOBO ANTONIO. d. 1593. Italian botanist. See: Nouv. Biog. Univ. Cortusa.

CORVISART, JEAN-NICOLAS. 1755-1821. French physician. See: Dict. Sci. Biog. Corvisart's complex (or disease [1]), Corvisart's disease (2), Corvisart's facies.

Corvisart's complex (or disease [1]) (Corvisart, Jean-Nicolas): Medicine. See: Jablonski.

Corvisart's disease (2) (Corvisart, Jean-Nicolas): Medicine. See: Dorland; Jablonski; Stedman.

Corvisart's facies (Corvisart, Jean-Nicolas): Medicine. See: Dorland; Jablonski; Stedman.

CORY, CHARLES BARNEY. 1857-1921. American ornithologist. See: Dict. Amer. Biog. Cory's shearwater.

Corydon (Corydon, the shepherd): Generic Word (shepherd). See: Charnock; Partridge.

CORYDON, THE SHEPHERD. Character from Virgil's "Eclogue VII." See: Benet. Corydon.

Cory's shearwater (Cory, Charles Barney): Zoology. See: Gray.

Coschwitz' duct (Coschwitz, Georgius Daniel): Medicine. See: Dorland.

COSCHWITZ, GEORGIUS DANIEL. 1679-1729. German physician. See: Nouv. Biog. Univ. Coschwitz' duct.

COSLETT, THOMAS W. fl. 1906. English inventor. Cited in: Chem. Abstr., vol. 1, p. 1340. Coslett treatment, Coslettize (or Coslettizer).

Coslett treatment (Coslett, Thomas W.): Engineering and Industry. See: Thrush.

Coslettize (or Coslettizer) (Coslett, Thomas W.): Engineering and Industry. See: Partridge.

Cosmatesque (or Cosmatic work) (Cosmati family): Fine Arts. See: Partridge.

COSMATI FAMILY. Roman architects, sculptors, and mosaic workers of the 13th c. See: Webster's Biog. Dict. Cosmatesque (or Cosmatic work).

Cossignea (Charpentier Cossigny, Joseph Francois): Botany. See: Charnock.

Cossigny de Palma, Joseph Francois. See: Charpentier Cossigny, Joseph Francois.

COSSIO, PEDRO. 1900-   . Argentinian physician. See: Gran. Encic. Argentina. Cossio's syndrome.

Cossio's syndrome (Cossio, Pedro): Medicine. See: Jablonski.

COSTA, LOUIS MARIE PANTALEON. 1806-1864. Student of hummingbirds. (Biography source unavailable.) Costa's hummingbird.

Costa's hummingbird (Costa, Louis Marie Pantaleon): Biology. See: Gray; Mathews, M. M.; Pennak.

COSTE, JACQUES-MARIE-CYPRIEN-VICTOR. 1807-1873. French naturalist and embryologist. See: World Who's Who Sci. Coste's cell.

Costello-Dent syndrome (Costello, J. M. and Dent, Charles Enrique): Medicine. See: Jablonski.

COSTELLO, J. M. fl. 1963. English physician. (Biography source unavailable.) Costello-Dent syndrome.

COSTEN, JAMES BRAY. 1895-   . American otolaryngologist. See: Who's Who Among Physicians and Surg. Costen's syndrome.

Costen's syndrome (Costen, James Bray): Medicine. See: Dorland; Jablonski; Stedman.

COSTER, DIRK. 1889-1950. Dutch physicist. See: Dict. Sci. Biog. Bohr and Coster notation.

COSTER, LAURENS JANSZOON. 1370-1440. Dutch printer. See: Webster's Biog. Dict. Costeriana.

Costeriana (Coster, Laurens Janszoon): Printing. See: Harrod.

Coste's cell (Coste, Jacques-Marie-Cyprien-Victor): Anatomy. See: Donath.

COSTIGAN, EDWARD PRENTISS. 1874-1939. American legislator. See: Biog. Direct. Amer. Congress. Jones-Costigan Sugar Act.

costmary (Mary, Virgin-Mother): Botany. See: Partridge; Webster's 3d.

COSTON, BENJAMIN FRANKLIN. 1821-1848. American inventor. (Biography source unavailable.) Coston's lights.

Coston's lights (Coston, Benjamin Franklin): Engineering and Industry. See: Quick.

Cotal gear (Cotal, J.): Engineering and Industry. See: Auger.

COTAL, J. No dates. French engineer. (Biography source unavailable.) Cotal gear.

COTARD, JULES. 1840-1887. French neurologist. See: Leopoldina, vol. 25 (1889), pp. 170-171. Cotard's syndrome.

Cotard's syndrome (Cotard, Jules): Medicine. See: Dorland; Hinsie; Jablonski.

COTES, ROGER. 1682-1716. English mathematician and astronomer. See: Dict. Sci. Biog. Cotes' rule, Newton-Cotes formula (or quadrature formula(s).

Cotes' rule (Cotes, Roger): Mathematics. See: Ballentyne.

COTTE, GASTON. 1879-1951. French surgeon. See: Biog. Lex. hervorr. Aerzte, 1880-1930. Cotte's operation.

COTTER, MISS. No dates. Irish woman who obtained the mineral. Cited in: Bailey. Cotterite.

COTTEREAU, JEAN ("CHOUAN"). 1757-1794. French royalist insurgent. See: Webster's Biog. Dict. Chouan(s).

Cotterite (Cotter, Miss): Earth Sciences. See: Thrush.

Cotte's operation (Cotte, Gaston): Medicine. See: Dorland; Stedman.

COTTING, BENJAMIN EDDY. 1812-1898. American surgeon. See: Burrage, p. 164. Cotting's operation.

Cotting's operation (Cotting, Benjamin Eddy): Medicine. See: Dorland; Stedman.

COTTON, AIME AUGUSTE. 1869-1951. French physicist. See: World Who's Who Sci. Cotton balance, Cotton effect, Cotton-Mouton effect.

Cotton balance (Cotton, Aime Auguste): Physics. See: Hughes; Thewlis.

Cotton effect (Cotton, Aime Auguste): Physics. See: Stedman; Van Nostrand Chem. Dict.

COTTON, FREDERIC JAY. 1869-1938. American surgeon. See: World Who's Who Sci. Cotton's fracture.

Cotton-Mouton effect (Cotton, Aime Auguste and Mouton, Henri): Physics. See: Ballentyne; Hughes; Internat. Dict. Phys. Elec.

COTTON, SIDNEY. No dates. Group captain. (Biography source unavailable.) Sidcott suit.

COTTON, STANISLAS. fl. 1869. French chemist. Cited in: Royal Soc. Cat. Sci. Pap., 1864-1873. Cotton test reaction for brucine.

Cotton test reaction for brucine (Cotton, Stanislas): Chemistry. See: Van Nostrand Chem. Dict.

Cotton's fracture (Cotton, Frederic Jay): Medicine. See: Jablonski.

COTTRELL, ALAN HOWARD. 1919- . English metallurgist. See: World Who's Who Sci. Cottrell atmosphere, Cottrell hardening, Cottrell locking.

Cottrell atmosphere (Cottrell, Alan Howard): Physics. See: Thewlis.

COTTRELL, CALVERT BYRON. 1821-1893. American inventor. See: Dict. Amer. Biog. Cottrell presses.

Cottrell effect (Derivation undetermined): Electronics. See: Hughes.

COTTRELL, FREDERICK GARDNER. 1877-1948. American physical chemist. See: Dict. Sci. Biog. Cottrell method, Cottrell operator, Cottrell precipitator, Cottrell process, Lodge-Cottrell process.

Cottrell hardening (Cottrell, Alan Howard): Physics. See: Internat. Dict. Phys. Elec.; Van Nostrand Sci. Encyc.

COTTRELL, LEONARD SLATER. 1899- . American social psychologist. See: Amer. Men Sci., 9th ed. Burgess-Cottrell marital adjustment scale.

Cottrell locking (Cottrell, Alan Howard): Physics. See: Internat. Dict. Phys. Elec.; Van Nostrand Sci. Encyc.

Cottrell method (Cottrell, Frederick Gardner): Chemistry. See: Internat. Dict. Phys. Elec.

Cottrell operator (Cottrell, Frederick Gardner): Chemistry. See: Thrush.

Cottrell precipitator (Cottrell, Frederick Gardner): Chemistry. See: Hackh; Thrush; Van Nostrand Chem. Dict.

Cottrell presses (Cottrell, Calvert Byron): Printing. See: Lockwood.

Cottrell process (Cottrell, Frederick Gardner): Chemistry. See: Webster's 3d.

Cotugno-Boettcher's duct (or pouch) (Cotugno, Domenico Felice Antonio and Boettcher, Arthur). See: Boettcher-Cotugno's duct (or pouch).

COTUGNO, DOMENICO FELICE ANTONIO. 1736-1822. Italian anatomist. See: Dict. Sci. Biog. Boettcher-Cotugno's duct (or pouch), Cotugno's syndrome, Cotunnite, Cotunnius' aqueduct (or canal), Cotunnius' columns, Cotunnius' disease, Cotunnius' liquid, Cotunnius' nerve, Cotunnius' space.

Cotugno's syndrome (Cotugno, Domenico Felice Antonio): Medicine. See: Jablonski.

Cotunnite (Cotugno, Domenico Felice Antonio): Earth Sciences. See: Thrush; Webster's 3d.

Cotunnius. See: Cotugno, Domenico Felice Antonio.

Cotunnius' aqueduct (or canal) (Cotugno, Domenico Felice Antonio): Anatomy. See: Dorland; Stedman.

Cotunnius' columns (Cotugno, Domenico Felice Antonio): Anatomy. See: Stedman.

Cotunnius' disease (Cotugno, Domenico Felice Antonio): Medicine. See: Stedman.

Cotunnius' liquid (Cotugno, Domenico Felice Antonio): Medicine. See: Stedman.

Cotunnius' nerve (Cotugno, Domenico Felice Antonio): Medicine. See: Dorland; Stedman. Also known as: Scarpa's nerve.

Cotunnius' space (Cotugno, Domenico Felice Antonio): Medicine. See: Stedman. Also known as: Boettcher's space.

Cotyttia (festivals) (Cotytto): Generic Word. See: Charnock.

COTYTTO. Thracian goddess of debauchery. See: Oxford Clas. Dict. Cotyttia (festivals).

COUDER, ANDRE. 1897- . French astronomer. See: World Who's Who Sci. Couder telescope.

Couder telescope (Couder, Andre): Astronomy. See: Satterthwaite.

COUE, EMILE. 1857-1926. French physician and pharmacist. See: World Who's Who Sci. Coueism.

Coueism (Coue, Emile): Medicine. See: Hendrickson; Partridge; Webster's 3d.

COUES, ELLIOTT. 1842-1899. American ornithologist. See: Dict. Sci. Biog. Coues' flycatcher.

Coues' flycatcher (Coues, Elliott): Biology. See: Gray.

COUES, GRACE D. d. 1925. Sister of American ornithologist, Elliot Coues. (Biography source unavailable.) Grace's warbler.

Coulmer antenna array (Derivation undetermined): Electronics. See: Markus.

Coulomb barrier (Coulomb, Charles Augustin): Physics. See: Internat. Dict. Ap. Math.; Internat. Dict. Phys. Elec.; Thewlis.

COULOMB, CHARLES AUGUSTIN. 1736-1806. French physicist. See: Dict. Sci. Biog. Coulomb barrier, Coulomb collision, Coulomb damping, Coulomb degeneracy, Coulomb energy, Coulomb excitation, Coulomb field, Coulomb force (or interaction), Coulomb integral, Coulomb law (electrostatics), Coulomb('s) law (for magnetism or electromagnetic), Coulomb potential, Coulomb scattering, Coulomb (unit), Coulomb wave function, Coulombian (or Coulombic), Coulombmeter (or Coulometer), Coulomb's law of friction, Coulometric titration, Coulometry.

Coulomb collision (Coulomb, Charles Augustin): Physics. See: Markus.

Coulomb damping (Coulomb, Charles Augustin): Physics. See: Thrush; Van Nostrand Sci. Encyc.

Coulomb degeneracy (Coulomb, Charles Augustin): Physics. See: Internat. Dict. Ap. Math.; Internat. Dict. Phys. Elec.; Van Nostrand Sci. Encyc.

Coulomb energy (Coulomb, Charles Augustin): Physics. See: Internat. Dict. Ap. Math.; Internat. Dict. Phys. Elec.; Thewlis.

Coulomb excitation (Coulomb, Charles Augustin): Physics. See: Internat. Dict. Ap. Math.; Thewlis; Van Nostrand Sci. Encyc.

Coulomb field (Coulomb, Charles Augustin): Physics. See: Internat. Dict. Ap. Math.; Webster's 3d.

Coulomb force (or interaction) (Coulomb, Charles Augustin): Physics. See: Internat. Dict. Phys. Elec.; Thewlis; Webster's 3d.

Coulomb integral (Coulomb, Charles Augustin): Physics. See: Internat. Dict. Ap. Math.; Thewlis.

Coulomb law (electrostatics) (Coulomb, Charles Augustin): Physics. See: Internat. Dict. Ap. Math.; Van Nostrand Chem. Dict.; Van Nostrand Sci. Encyc.

Coulomb('s) law (for magnetism or electromagnetic) (Coulomb, Charles Augustin): Physics. See: Hughes; Internat. Dict. Phys. Elec.; Van Nostrand Chem. Dict.

Coulomb potential (Coulomb, Charles Augustin): Physics. See: Hughes; Internat. Dict. Ap. Math.; Internat. Dict. Phys. Elec.

Coulomb scattering (Coulomb, Charles Augustin): Physics. See: Hughes; Internat. Dict. Phys. Elec.; Thewlis.

Coulomb (unit) (Coulomb, Charles Augustin): Physics. See: Dresner; Internat. Dict. Ap. Math.; Thewlis.

Coulomb wave function (Coulomb, Charles Augustin): Physics. See: Internat. Dict. Ap. Math.

Coulombian (or Coulombic) (Coulomb, Charles Augustin): Physics. See: Webster's 3d.

Coulombmeter (or Coulometer) (Coulomb, Charles Augustin): Physics. See: Hughes; Internat. Dict. Phys. Elec.; Thewlis. Also known as: Voltameter.

Coulomb's law of friction (Coulomb, Charles Augustin): Physics. See: Ballentyne.

Coulometric titration (Coulomb, Charles Augustin): Physics. See: Webster's 3d.

Coulometry (Coulomb, Charles Augustin): Physics. See: Thewlis; Webster's 3d.

COULSON, ARTHUR LENNOX. 1898- . Indian geologist. (Biography source unavailable.) Coulsonite.

Coulsonite (Coulson, Arthur Lennox): Earth Sciences. See: Thrush; Webster's 3d.

Coulter counter (Coulter, W. H.): Engineering and Industry. See: Thrush.

Coulter('s) pine (Coulter, Thomas): Botany. See: Mathews, M. M.; Webster's 3d.

COULTER, THOMAS. 1793-1843. Irish botanist. See: Dakin. Coulter('s) pine.

COULTER, W. H. No dates. American engineer. (Biography source unavailable.) Coulter counter.

Councilman (hyaline) body (or lesion) (Councilman, William Thomas): Medicine. See: Dorland; Stedman.

COUNCILMAN, WILLIAM THOMAS. 1854-1933. American pathologist. See: Dict. Sci. Biog. Councilman (hyaline) body (or lesion), Councilmania.

Councilmania (Councilman, William Thomas): Medicine. See: Dorland; Stedman.

Count Warwick's powder (Derivation undetermined): Medicine. See: Charnock.

Countess of Huntingdon's Connexion (or Huntingdonians) (Huntingdon, Selina Hastings, Countess of): Religion. See: Brewer; Canney; Latham; Mathews, S.

coup de Jarnac (or Jarnac) (Jarnac, Comte Guy Chabot de): Generic Word (unexpected and decisive blow). See: Brewer; Harvey.

Coupier's blue (Derivation undetermined): Chemistry. See: Hackh.

COUQUET, HENRI CAMILLE. fl. 1900. French chemist. Cited in: Royal Soc. Cat. Sci. Pap., 1884-1900. Pozzi-Escot-Couquet test reaction for palladium.

COURANT, RICHARD. 1888- . Polish-born mathematician. See: World Who's Who Sci. Courant's maximum-minimum principle (or theorem), Courant's minimum-maximum principle (or theorem).

Courant's maximum-minimum principle (or theorem) (Courant, Richard): Mathematics. See: James.

Courant's minimum-maximum principle (or theorem) (Courant, Richard): Mathematics. See: James.

COURMONT, JULES. 1865-1917. French bacteriologist. See: World Who's Who Sci. Arloing-Courmont test.

court of King Petaud (Petaud, King): Generic Word. See: Harvey.

COURTENAY-LATIMER, MARJORIE EILEEN DORIS. 1907- . South African museum director. See: Who's Who S. Africa, 1966. Latimeria.

Courtis growth curve (Courtis, Stuart Appleton): Psychology. See: English.

COURTIS, STUART APPLETON. b. 1874. American educator. See: Amer. Psych. Assoc. Direct., 1960. Courtis growth curve.

Courtzilite (Derivation undetermined): Earth Sciences. See: Thrush.

COURVOISIER, LUDWIG GEORG. 1843-1918. Swiss surgeon. See: World Who's Who Sci. Courvoisier-Terrier syndrome, Courvoisier's law (or sign).

Courvoisier-Terrier syndrome (Courvoisier, Ludwig Georg and Terrier, Louis-Felix): Medicine. See: Dorland; Jablonski.

Courvoisier's law (or sign) (Courvoisier, Ludwig Georg): Medicine. See: Dorland; Stedman.

COUTARD, HENRI. 1876-1950. French roentgenologist. See: Webster's Biog. Dict. Coutard's technique.

Coutard's technique (Coutard, Henri): Medicine. See: Dorland; Stedman.

COUTO, MIGUEL DE OIVEIRA. 1864-1934. Brazilian physician. See: Brasil.-Med., vol. 48, no. 24 (June 16, 1934), p. 457. Couto's disease.

Couto's disease (Couto, Miguel de Oiveira): Medicine. See: Jablonski.

COUVELAIRE, ALEXANDRE. 1873-1948. French obstetrician. See: Biog. Lex. hervorr. Aerzte, 1880-1930. Couvelaire uterus, Couvelaire's syndrome.

Couvelaire uterus (Couvelaire, Alexandre): Medicine. See: Dorland; Stedman.

Couvelaire's syndrome (Couvelaire, Alexandre): Medicine. See: Jablonski.

COVELLI, E. fl. 1907. German chemist. Cited in: Chem. Abstr., vol. 1, p. 1757; vol. 4, p. 883. Covelli test for arsenite, Covelli test for chloral.

COVELLI, NICCOLO. 1790-1829. Italian chemist. See: Webster's Biog. Dict. Covellite (or Covelline).

Covelli test for arsente (Covelli, E.): Chemistry. See: Van Nostrand Chem. Dict.

Covelli test for chloral (Covelli, E.): Chemistry. See: Van Nostrand Chem. Dict.

Covellite (or Covelline) (Covelli, Niccolo): Earth Sciences. See: Partridge; Thrush; Van Nostrand Sci. Encyc.

COVERDALE, MILES. 1488-1568. English bishop and translator. See: Dict. Nat. Biog. Coverdale's Bible.

Coverdale's Bible (Coverdale, Miles): Religion. See: Brewer; Canney.

COVERLEY, SIR ROGER DE. Character described by Joseph Addison in the "Spectator," (1711-1714). See: Harvey. Roger de Coverley (or Sir Roger de Coverley).

COWDEN. No dates. Family name of the propositus. (Biography source unavailable.) Cowden's syndrome.

Cowden's syndrome (Cowden): Medicine. See: Jablonski.

Cowdria (Cowdry, Edmund Vincent): Medicine. See: Dorland; Stedman; Webster's 3d.

COWDRY, EDMUND VINCENT. 1888- . American pathologist. See: World Who's Who Sci. Cowdria, Cowdry's type A inclusion bodies, Cowdry's type B inclusion bodies.

Cowdry's type A inclusion bodies (Cowdry, Edmund Vincent): Medicine. See: Stedman.

Cowdry's type B inclusion bodies (Cowdry, Edmund Vincent): Medicine. See: Stedman.

COWGILL, DONALD OLEN. 1911- . American sociologist. See: Amer. Men Sci., 9th ed (Soc. Behav. Sci.). Cowgill index.

Cowgill index (Cowgill, Donald Olen and Cowgill, Mary S.): Sociology. See: Zadrozny.

COWGILL, MARY S. fl. 20th c. American sociologist. (Biography source unavailable.) Cowgill index.

Cowick Ordinances (Derivation undetermined): History. See: Steinberg.

COWLES, ALFRED. 1865-1939. American lawyer. See: Who Was Who Amer., vol. 1. Cowles Foundation.

COWLES, ALFRED HUTCHINSON. 1858-1929. American engineer and metallurgist. See: Who Was Who Amer., vol. 1. Cowles process.

Cowles Foundation (Cowles, Alfred): Economics. See: Greenwald.

Cowles process (Cowles, Alfred Hutchinson): Engineering and Industry. See: Thrush; Van Nostrand Chem. Dict.

COWLEY, ABRAHAM. 1618-1667. English poet. See: Dict. Nat. Biog. Cowleyan ode (or irregular ode).

Cowleyan ode (or irregular ode) (Cowley, Abraham): Literature. See: Duffy; Scott.

Cowling's rule (Derivation undetermined): Medicine. See: Stedman.

COWPER-COLES, SHERARD OSBORN. d. 1936. English chemist. See: World Who's Who Sci. Sherardizing (or Sherardize).

COWPER, EDWARD ALFRED. fl. 1860. English engineer. See: Electrician, vol. 31 (1893), p. 67. Cowper-Siemens stove, Cowper stove.

Cowper-Siemens stove (Cowper, Edward Alfred and Siemens, Sir Charles William): Engineering and Industry. See: Thrush.

Cowper stove (Cowper, Edward Alfred): Engineering and Industry. See: Auger; Hackh; Thrush.

Cowper-Temple clause (Cowper, William Francis): Education. See: Harbottle; Montgomery.

COWPER, WILLIAM. 1666-1709. English anatomist. See: Dict. Nat. Biog. Cowperian, Cowperitis, Cowper's cyst, Cowper's gland.

COWPER, WILLIAM FRANCIS (BARON MOUNT-TEMPLE). 1811-1888. English statesman. See: Dict. Nat. Biog., 1st suppl. Cowper-Temple clause.

Cowperian (Cowper, William): Medicine. See: Dorland; Stedman.

Cowperitis (Cowper, William): Medicine. See: Dorland; Stedman; Webster's 3d.

Cowper's cyst (Cowper, William): Medicine. See: Dorland; Stedman.

Cowper's gland (Cowper, William): Medicine. See: Gray; Stedman; Van Nostrand Sci. Encyc. Also known as: Mery's gland.

COX. Character in John M. Morton's farce, "Box and Cox" (1847). See: Benet, under "Box." Box and Cox (arrangement).

COX, DAVID ROXBEE. 1924- . English theoretical statistician. See: World Who's Who Sci. Cox's theorem.

COX, GERTRUDE MARY. 1900- . American statistician. See: Amer. Men Sci., 9th ed. Cochran-Cox test.

COX, HERALD REA. 1907- . American virologist. See: World Who's Who Sci. Coxiella.

Cox printing-presses (Derivation undetermined): Printing. See: Lockwood.

COXEY, JACOB SECHLER. 1854-1951. American businessman and politician. See: Webster's Biog. Dict. Coxeyism (or Coxeyite), Coxey's army.

Coxeyism (or Coxeyite) (Coxey, Jacob Sechler): History. See: Mathews, M. M.

Coxey's army (Coxey, Jacob Sechler): History. See: Blumberg; Hendrickson; Smith.

Coxiella (Cox, Herald Rea): Zoology. See: Dorland; Stedman; Webster's 3d.

Cox's theorem (Cox, David Roxbee): Statistics. See: Kendall.

Crabtree effect (Crabtree, Herbert G.): Medicine. See: Stedman.

CRABTREE, HERBERT G. No dates. Physician. (Biography source unavailable.) Crabtree effect.

Crafoord clamp (Crafoord, Clarence): Medicine. See: Stedman.

CRAFOORD, CLARENCE. 1899- . Swedish surgeon. See: Acta Chir. Scand., 1959, suppl. 245, p. 9. Crafoord clamp.

CRAFTS, JAMES MASON. 1839-1917. American organic chemist. See: Dict. Amer. Biog. Crafts' rule, Friedel-Crafts condensation, Friedel-Crafts reaction.

CRAFTS, LEO MELVILLE. 1863-1938. American neurologist. See: Who's Who Amer. Med. Crafts' test.

Crafts' rule (Crafts, James Mason): Chemistry. See: Ballentyne.

Crafts' test (Crafts, Leo Melville): Medicine. See: Dorland.

CRAIG, ALLEN THORNTON. 1904- . American mathematical statistician. See: World Who's Who Sci. Craig's theorem.

Craig-Benson operation (Craig, Earl Burrell and Benson, Francis Colgate, Jr.): Medicine. Cited in: World Who's Who Sci.

CRAIG, CECIL CALVERT. b. 1898. American mathematician. See: Amer. Men and Women Sci., 12th ed. Stevens-Craig distribution.

CRAIG, CHARLES FRANKLIN. 1872-1950. American bacteriologist. See: World Who's Who Sci. Craigia.

CRAIG, EARL BURRELL. b. 1881. American gynecologist. See: Who's Who Among Physicians and Surg. Craig-Benson operation.

Craig effect (Craig, J. I.): Statistics. See: Kendall.

CRAIG, J. I. fl. 1916. Statistician. (Biography source unavailable.) Craig effect.

CRAIG, KENNETH ALEXANDER. 1908- . American chemist. See: Amer. Men Sci., 10th ed. Knapper-Craig-Chandlee test.

Craig method (Derivation undetermined): Chemistry. See: Van Nostrand Chem. Dict.

Craig method (reading) (Derivation undetermined): Education. See: Good.

Craigia (Craig, Charles Franklin): Medicine. See: Dorland.

Craig's theorem (Craig, Allen Thornton): Statistics. See: Kendall.

CRAMER, FRIEDRICH. 1847-1903. German surgeon. See: Biog. Lex. hervorr. Aerzte, 1880-1930. Cramer's splint.

CRAMER, GABRIEL. 1704-1752. Swiss mathematician. See: Dict. Sci. Biog. Cramer('s) rule.

CRAMER, HARALD. 1893- . Swedish mathematician. See: World Who's Who Sci. Cramer-Rao efficiency, Cramer-Rao inequality, Cramer-Tchebychev inequality, Cramer-Von Mises test, Levy-Cramer theorem.

Cramer-Rao efficiency (Cramer, Harald and Rao, Calyampudi Radhakrishna): Statistics. See: Kendall.

Cramer-Rao inequality (Cramer, Harald and Rao, Calyampudi Radhakrishna): Statistics. See: Kendall.

Cramer('s) rule (Cramer, Gabriel): Mathematics. See: Ballentyne; Internat. Dict. Ap. Math.; Internat. Dict. Phys. Elec.; James.

Cramer solution (Cramer, William): Chemistry. See: Van Nostrand Chem. Dict.

Cramer-Tchebychev inequality (Cramer, Harald and Chebyshev, Pafnuty Lvovich): Statistics. See: Kendall.

Cramer-Von Mises test (Cramer, Harald and Mises, Richard von): Statistics. See: Kendall.

CRAMER, WILLIAM. b. 1878. English biochemist. See: Who's Who, 1930. Cramer solution.

Cramer's splint (Cramer, Friedrich): Medicine. See: Dorland; Stedman.

CRAMPTON, C. WARD. b. 1877. American physician. See: Who's Who Amer. Med. Crampton test.

CRAMPTON, PHILIP. 1777-1858. Irish surgeon. See: Dict. Nat. Biog. Crampton's line, Crampton's muscle.

Crampton test (Crampton, C. Ward): Medicine. See: Dorland; Stedman.

Crampton's line (Crampton, Philip): Medicine. See: Dorland; Stedman.

Crampton's muscle (Crampton, Philip): Medicine. See: Dorland; Pennak; Stedman.

CRANDALL, M. L. fl. 20th c. American mining engineer. Cited in: Min. Mag., vol. 18, p. 377. Crandallite.

Crandallite (Crandall, M. L.): Earth Sciences. See: Webster's 3d.

CRANMER, THOMAS. 1489-1556. English reformer. See: Dict. Nat. Biog. Cranmer's Bible.

Cranmer's Bible (Cranmer, Thomas): Religion. See: Brewer; Canney; Phyfe.

Cranston press (Derivation undetermined): Printing. See: Lockwood.

Crapaud, Johnny. See: Marigny, Bernard.

Crapper (Crapper, Thomas): Generic Word (toilet bowl). See: Hendrickson.

CRAPPER, THOMAS. No dates. English inventor. (Biography source unavailable.) Crapper.

Craps (Marigny, Bernard): Generic Word (dice). See: Brewer; Hendrickson.

Crassus (Crassus, Marcus Licinius): Generic Word (rich man). See: Hendrickson.

CRASSUS, MARCUS LICINIUS. 115-53 B.C. Roman financier and politician. See: Webster's Biog. Dict. Crassus.

Crateva (garlic pear) (Cratevas): Botany. See: Charnock.

CRATEVAS. fl. 80 B.C. Greek botanist. See: Nouv. Biog. Univ. Crateva (garlic pear).

CRAVEN, REGINALD. fl. 1931. English chemist. Cited in: Chem. Abstr., vol. 25, p. 4538. Craven test reaction.

Craven test reaction (Craven, Reginald): Chemistry. See: Van Nostrand Chem. Dict.

CRAWFORD, BRIAN HEWSON. fl. 1948-1963. English physiologist. See: Direct. Brit. Sci., 1966-67. Stiles-Crawford effect.

CRAWFORD, D. fl. 1918. English? chemist. Cited in: Chem. Abstr., vol. 13, p. 100. Saul-Crawford test.

CRAWFORD, W. G. fl. 1913. American chemist. Cited in: Chem. Abstr., vol. 6, p. 3246; vol. 7, p. 951. Lenher-Crawford test.

CRAWFURD, JOHN. 1783-1868. Scottish orientalist. See: Dict. Nat. Biog. Crawfurdia.

Crawfurdia (Crawfurd, John): Botany. See: Charnock.

Crawley midget miner (Derivation undetermined): Engineering and Industry. See: Thrush.

Crawley-Wilcox miner (Derivation undetermined): Engineering and Industry. See: Thrush.

CREDE, BENNO CARL. 1847-1929. German surgeon. See: Wer Ist's, 1906. Crede's antiseptic, Crede's ointment.

CREDE, KARL SIEGMUND FRANZ. 1819-1892. German gynecologist. See: World Who's Who Sci. Crede's incubator, Crede's methods (or maneuver).

Crede's antiseptic (Crede, Benno Carl): Medicine. See: Dorland.

Crede's incubator (Crede, Karl Siegmund Franz): Medicine. Cited in: World Who's Who Sci.

Crede's methods (or maneuver) (Crede, Karl Siegmund Franz): Medicine. See: Dorland; Stedman; Webster's 3d.

Crede's ointment (Crede, Benno Carl): Medicine. See: Dorland.

CREDNER, KARL FRIEDRICH HEINRICH. 1809-1876. German geologist. See: World Who's Who Sci. Crednerite.

Crednerite (Credner, Karl Friedrich Heinrich): Earth Sciences. See: Charnock; Thrush; Webster's 3d.

CREGAN, JAMES CYRIL FRASER. fl. 1959. English physician. Cited in: Med. Reg., 1966. Champion-Cregan-Klein syndrome.

CREHORE, DIANA. fl. 19th c. American horticulturist. (Biography source unavailable.) Diana grape.

CREIGHTON, HENRY JERMAIN MAUDE. 1886- . Canadian-born American chemist. See: World Who's Who Sci. Creighton process.

Creighton process (Creighton, Henry Jermain Maude): Chemistry. See: Van Nostrand Chem. Dict.

CREIGHTON, ROBERT. 1639-1734. English precentor and scholar. See: Dict. Nat. Biog. Creyghtonian seventh.

Cremer kiln (Derivation undetermined): Engineering and Industry. See: Thrush.

CREMER, MAX. 1865-1935. German physiologist. See: Pogg., vol. 7a. Cremer test reactions for phloridzin?

Cremer test reactions for phloridzin (Cremer, Max?): Chemistry. See: Van Nostrand Chem. Dict.

CREMONA, ANTONIO LUIGI GAUDENZIO GIUSEPPE. 1830-1903. Italian mathematician. See: Dict. Sci. Biog. Cremona transformation.

Cremona transformation (Cremona, Antonio Luigi Gaudenzio Giuseppe): Mathematics. Cited in: World Who's Who Sci.

Crespi effect (Derivation undetermined): Psychology. See: Chaplin; English; Wolman.

CRESPI, GIO B. fl. 1952. Italian metallurgist. Cited in: Chem. Abstr., Decenn. Index, 1937-46. Crespi hearth.

Crespi hearth (Crespi, Gio B.): Engineering and Industry. See: Thrush.

Cresti test (Derivation undetermined): Chemistry. See: Van Nostrand Chem. Dict.

Creswick (drawing-paper) (Creswick, Thomas?): Printing. See: Lockwood.

CRESWICK, THOMAS. 1811-1869. English landscape painter. See: Dict. Nat. Biog. Creswick (drawing-paper)?

CREUTZFELDT, HANS GERHARD. 1885-1964. German psychiatrist. See: Wer Ist Wer?, 1958. Jakob-Creutzfeldt('s) disease (or syndrome).

Creveld, Simon van. See: Van Creveld, Simon.

CREW, NATHANIEL. 1633-1721. English baron and bishop. See: Dict. Nat. Biog. Crewian oration.

CREWE, JOHN. 1742-1829. English baron. See: Dict. Nat. Biog. Crewe's Act.

Crewe's Act (Crewe, John): History. See: Steinberg.

Crewian oration (Crew, Nathaniel): Literature. See: Brewer; Harvey.

Creyghton, Robert. See: Creighton, Robert.

Creyghtonian seventh (Creighton, Robert): Music. See: Scholes.

Creyx-Levy syndrome (Creyx, Maurice and Levy, Jacques): Medicine. See: Jablonski.

CREYX, MAURICE. fl. 1948. French physician. Cited in: New York Acad. Med. Portrait Cat. Creyx-Levy syndrome.

CRICHTON, SIR ALEXANDER. 1763-1856. Scottish physician. See: Dict. Nat. Biog. Crichtonite.

CRICHTON-BROWNE, SIR JAMES. 1840-1938. Scottish alienist. See: Dict. Nat. Biog., 5th suppl. Crichton-Browne's sign.

Crichton-Browne's sign (Crichton-Browne, Sir James): Medicine. See: Dorland; Stedman.

CRICHTON, JAMES. 1560-1582. Scottish scholar. See: Dict. Nat. Biog. Admirable Crichton.

Crichtonite (Crichton, Sir Alexander): Earth Sciences. See: Charnock; Thrush.

CRICK, FRANCIS HARRY COMPTON. 1916- . English biochemist. See: World Who's Who Sci. Watson-Crick helix (or model).

Criegee reaction (Criegee, Rudolf): Chemistry. See: Ballentyne; Van Nostrand Chem. Dict.

CRIEGEE, RUDOLF. 1902- . German chemist. See: Pogg., vol. 7a. Criegee reaction.

CRIGLER, JOHN FIELDING, JR. 1919- . American physician. See: Direct. Med. Specialists, 1970-71. Crigler-Najjar syndrome.

Crigler-Najjar syndrome (Crigler, John Fielding, Jr. and Najjar, Victor Assad): Medicine. See: Jablonski; Stedman.

CRILE, GEORGE WASHINGTON. 1864-1943. American surgeon. See: World Who's Who Sci. Crile's clamp?

Crile's clamp (Crile, George Washington?): Medicine. See: Stedman.

Crilley and Everson process (Derivation undetermined): Engineering and Industry. See: Thrush.

Crimp and Bruges' formula (Crimp, William Santo and Bruges, Charles Ernest): Engineering and Industry. See: Thrush.

CRIMP, WILLIAM SANTO. d. 1901. English engineer. Cited in: Royal Soc. Cat. Sci. Pap., 1884-1900. Crimp and Bruges' formula.

Crippen (Crippen, Hawley Harvey): Generic Word (murderer). See: Hendrickson; Partridge.

CRIPPEN, HAWLEY HARVEY. 1862-1910. English murderer. See: Encyc. Brit., 1973. Crippen.

CRIPPS, WILLIAM HARRISON. 1850-1923. English surgeon and sportsman. See: Ann. Reg. Cripps's obturator, Cripps's operation.

Cripps's obturator (Cripps, William Harrison): Medicine. See: Dorland.

Cripps's operation (Cripps, William Harrison): Medicine. See: Dorland.

CRISMER, LEON. 1858-1944. Belgian chemist. See: Pogg., vols. 4, 6, 7b. Crismer test (for butter and fats), Crismer test for water in alcohol, chloroform, and ether, Crismer's test (for glucose).

Crismer test (for butter and fats) (Crismer, Leon): Chemistry. See: Winburne.

Crismer test for water in alcohol, chloroform, and ether (Crismer, Leon): Chemistry. See: Van Nostrand Chem. Dict.

Crismer test reaction (Derivation undetermined): Chemistry. See: Van Nostrand Chem. Dict.

Crismer test reaction for hydrogen peroxide (Derivation undetermined): Chemistry. See: Van Nostrand Chem. Dict.

Crismer's test (for glucose) (Crismer, Leon): Chemistry. See: Dorland; Stedman.

CRISP, TOBIAS. 1600-1643. English clergyman. See: Dict. Nat. Biog. Crispians.

Crispians (Crisp, Tobias): Religion. See: Canney.

Crispin (Crispin, Saint): Generic Word (shoemaker). See: Brewer; Charnock; Hendrickson.

CRISPIN, SAINT. d. 285. Christian martyr. See: Holweck. Crispin, Crispinades, Saint (St.) Crispin's Day, St. Crispin's holiday, St. Crispin's lance.

Crispinades (Crispin, Saint): Religion. See: Canney.

CRISTESCO, C. fl. 1938. French physician. (Biography source unavailable.) Clerc-Levy-Cristesco syndrome.

Criswell reagent (Derivation undetermined): Chemistry. See: Van Nostrand Chem. Dict.

CRITCHETT, GEORGE. 1817-1882. English ophthalmologist. See: Dict. Nat. Biog. Critchett's operation.

Critchett's operation (Critchett, George): Medicine. See: Dorland; Stedman.

Crittenden compromise (Crittenden, John Jordan): History. See: Jameson; Latham; Smith.

CRITTENDEN, JOHN JORDAN. 1787-1863. American legislator. See: Dict. Amer. Biog. Crittenden compromise, Crittenden-Montgomery Amendment.

Crittenden-Montgomery Amendment (Crittenden, John Jordan and Montgomery, William): History. See: Morris.

CROASDALE, STUART. 1866-1934. American mining engineer. See: World Who's Who Sci. Pohle-Croasdale process.

CROCCO, LUIGI. 1908- . Italian aeronautical engineer. See: Diz. Encic. Ital. Crocco theorem.

Crocco theorem (Crocco, Luigi): Physics. See: Internat. Dict. Ap. Math.

CROCE, BENEDETTO. 1866-1952. Italian philosopher and statesman. See: Encyc. Brit., 1973. Crocean (or Crocian).

Crocean (or Crocian) (Croce, Benedetto): Philosophy. See: Webster's 3d.

CROCKER, ERNEST CHARLTON. b. 1888. American chemist. See: Amer. Men Sci., 4th ed. Crocker tests for aldehydes.

Crocker, Henry Radcliffe. See: Radcliffe-Crocker, Henry.

Crocker tests for aldehydes (Crocker, Ernest Charlton): Chemistry. See: Van Nostrand Chem. Dict.

Crocker's disease (Radcliffe-Crocker, Henry): Medicine. See: Jablonski.

CROCKETT, DAVID. 1786-1836. American frontiersman. See: Dict. Amer. Biog. Davy Crockett costume, Davy Crockett (mobile launcher), sin to Davy Crockett.

Crockett magnetic separator (Crockett, Robert): Engineering and Industry. See: Thrush.

CROCKETT, ROBERT. fl. 1937. American inventor. Cited in: Chem. Abstr., vol. 31, p. 6934. Crockett magnetic separator.

Crockford (clerical directory) (Crockford, John): Religion. See: Hendrickson; Partridge; Weekley.

CROCKFORD, JOHN. 1823-1865. English publisher. See: Boase, suppl. Crockford (clerical directory).

CROCQ, JEAN B. 1868-1925. Belgian physician. Cited in: Kelly. Crocq's disease.

Crocq's disease (Crocq, Jean B.): Medicine. See: Stedman.

Crocus (blossom) (Crocus, the lover): Botany. See: Harvey.

crocus of Venus (Venus): Chemistry. See: Thrush.

CROCUS, THE LOVER. Mythical Greek youth. See: Jobes. Crocus (blossom).

Croesus (Croesus, King): Generic Word (rich man). See: Hendrickson; Partridge; Webster's 3d.

CROESUS, KING. 591-546 B.C. Lydian king. See: Encyc. Brit., 1973. Croesus.

Croft lily (Croft, Sydney): Botany. See: Webster's 3d.

CROFT, SYDNEY. d. ca. 1940. American horticulturist. (Biography source unavailable.) Croft lily.

CROHN, BURRILL BERNARD. b. 1884. American physician. See: Who's Who Amer. Med. Crohn's disease.

Crohn-Lesniowski disease (Crohn, Burrill Bernard and Lesniowski, Antoni). See: Crohn's disease.

Crohn's disease (Crohn, Burrill Bernard): Medicine. See: Dorland; Jablonski; Stedman. Also known as: Crohn-Lesniowski disease.

CROISSY, CHARLES COLBERT, MARQUIS DE. 1625-1696. French statesman. See: Encyc. Brit., 1973. a la Croissy.

Crolas-Ducker test reaction (Derivation undetermined): Chemistry. See: Van Nostrand Chem. Dict.

CROMIE, JOHN BULLER. 1922- . Irish-born American chest surgeon. See: Direct. Med. Specialists, 1965-1966. Magovern-Cromie prosthesis.

CROMPTON, SAMUEL. 1753-1827. English inventor. See: Dict. Nat. Biog. Crompton's mule.

Crompton's mule (Crompton, Samuel): Engineering and Industry. See: Brewer.

Cromwell current (Cromwell, Townsend): Earth Sciences. See: Van Nostrand Sci. Encyc.

CROMWELL, OLIVER. 1599-1658. Lord protector of England. See: Dict. Nat. Biog. Cromwellian, curse of Cromwell, Oliver (1), Oliver (2), Oliverian, Oliver's skull.

CROMWELL, RICHARD. 1626-1712. Lord Protector of England. See: Dict. Nat. Biog. Dick's hatband.

CROMWELL, THOMAS. 1485-1540. English statesman. See: Dict. Nat. Biog. Cromwell's Bible.

CROMWELL, TOWNSEND. 1922- . American oceanographer. See: Amer. Men Sci., 9th ed. Cromwell current.

Cromwellian (Cromwell, Oliver): History. See: Hendrickson; Partridge; Webster's 3d.

Cromwell's Bible (Cromwell, Thomas): Religion. See: Brewer.

Croner-Cronheim test (Croner, Wilhelm and Cronheim, W.): Chemistry. See: Van Nostrand Chem. Dict.

CRONER, WILHELM. b. 1867. German chemist. Cited in: Kelly. Croner-Cronheim test.

CRONHEIM, W. fl. 1905. German chemist. Cited in: Kelly. Croner-Cronheim test.

Cronin Lowe, E. See: Lowe, E. Cronin.

Cronin Lowe reaction (or test) (Lowe, E. Cronin): Medicine. See: Dorland.

CRONING, JOHANNES. fl. 1943. German metallurgist. Cited in: Chem. Abstr., vol. 39, p. 2481. Croning process.

Croning process (Croning, Johannes): Engineering and Industry. See: Thrush.

Cronkhite–Canada syndrome (Cronkhite, Leonard Wolsey, Jr. and Canada, Wilma Jeanne): Medicine. See: Jablonski; Stedman.

CRONKHITE, LEONARD WOLSEY, JR. 1919- . American physician. See: Who's Who Amer., 1974-75. Cronkhite-Canada syndrome.

CRONSTEDT, AXEL FREDRIK. 1722-1765. Swedish mineralogist and chemist. See: Dict. Sci. Biog. Cronstedtite (or Cronstedite).

Cronstedtite (or Cronstedite) (Cronstedt, Axel Fredrik): Earth Sciences. See: Charnock; Thrush; Webster's 3d.

CROOKE, ARTHUR CARLETON. 1905- . English pathologist. See: World Who's Who Sci. Crooke's granules, Crooke's hyaline change (or degeneration).

Crookes dark space (Crookes, William): Physics. See: Ballentyne; Markus; Thewlis.

Crookes glass (Crookes, William): Chemistry. See: Hackh; Thrush; Webster's 3d.

Crooke's granules (Crooke, Arthur Carleton): Medicine. See: Stedman.

Crooke's hyaline change (or degeneration) (Crooke, Arthur Carleton): Medicine. See: Dorland; Stedman.

Crookes radiometer (Crookes, William): Physics. See: Internat. Dict. Phys. Elec.; Markus; Van Nostrand Chem. Dict.

Crookes tube (Crookes, William): Physics. See: Hughes; Internat. Dict. Phys. Elec.; Van Nostrand Sci. Encyc.

CROOKES, WILLIAM. 1832-1919. English chemist and physicist. See: Dict. Sci. Biog. Crookes dark space, Crookes glass, Crookes radiometer, Crookes tube, Crookesite.

Crookesite (Crookes, William): Earth Sciences. See: Hackh; Thrush.

CROOM, HARDY BRYAN. 1797-1837. American botanist. See: Biog. Notes Upon Botanists. Croomia.

Croomia (Croom, Hardy Bryan): Botany. See: Webster's 3d.

Crosby capsule (Crosby, William Holmes, Jr.): Medicine. See: Stedman.

CROSBY, GEORGE H. fl. 1881. American engineer. (Biography source unavailable.) Crosby indicator mechanism.

Crosby indicator mechanism (Crosby, George H.): Engineering and Industry. See: Auger.

CROSBY, WILLIAM HOLMES, JR. 1914- . American physician. See: Who's Who Amer., 1974-75. Crosby capsule, Crosby's syndrome.

Crosby's syndrome (Crosby, William Holmes, Jr.): Medicine. See: Jablonski.

Cross-Bevan process (Cross, Charles Frederick and Bevan, Edward John): Chemistry. See: Van Nostrand Chem. Dict.

Cross-Bevan reagent for cellulose (Cross, Charles Frederick and Bevan, Edward John): Chemistry. See: Van Nostrand Chem. Dict.

Cross-Bevan solution (Cross, Charles Frederick and Bevan, Edward John): Chemistry. See: Van Nostrand Chem. Dict.

Cross-Bevan test for jute (Cross, Charles Frederick and Bevan, Edward John): Chemistry. See: Van Nostrand Chem. Dict.

CROSS, CHARLES FREDERICK. 1855-1935. English chemist. See: World Who's Who Sci. Cross-Bevan process, Cross-Bevan reagent for cellulose, Cross-Bevan solution, Cross-Bevan test for jute.

CROSS, CHARLES WHITMAN. 1854-1949. American geologist. See: Dict. Sci. Biog. Crossite.

Cross engine (Cross, Roland Claude): Engineering and Industry. See: Auger.

CROSS, HARDY. 1885-1959. American civil engineer. See: World Who's Who Sci. Hardy Cross method.

CROSS, HOWARD BENJAMIN. 1873-1921. American bacteriologist. See: Dutton, 1951, pt. 2, p. 23. Cross stain.

cross of Constantine (Constantine I): Religion. See: Webster's 3d.

Cross process (Cross, Roy): Chemistry. See: Van Nostrand Chem. Dict.

CROSS, ROLAND CLAUDE. 1895- . English engineer. See: Who's Who Brit. Engin., 1968. Cross engine.

CROSS, ROY. 1884-1947. American chemist. See: World Who's Who Sci. Cross process.

Cross stain (Cross, Howard Benjamin): Medicine. See: Stedman.

CROSSER, ROBERT. 1874-1957. American legislator. See: Biog. Direct. Amer. Congress. Wagner-Crosser Railroad Retirement Act.

Crossite (Cross, Charles Whitman): Earth Sciences. See: Thrush; Webster's 3d.

Crossley engine (Crossley, Francis William): Engineering and Industry. See: Auger.

CROSSLEY, FRANCIS WILLIAM. 1839-1897. Irish engineer and philanthropist. See: Crone. Crossley engine.

CROSTI, AGOSTINO. 1896- . Italian dermatologist. See: Hautarzt, vol. 8 (1966), p. 383. Gianotti-Crosti syndrome.

CROSWELL, HARRY. 1778-1858. American publisher. See: Dict. Amer. Biog. Croswell libel case.

Croswell libel case (Croswell, Harry): History. See: Morris.

Crout method (Crout, Prescott Durand?): Mathematics. See: Internat. Dict. Ap. Math.

CROUT, PRESCOTT DURAND. 1907- . American mathematician. See: Amer. Men Sci., 9th ed. Crout method?

CROUZON, OCTAVE. 1874-1938. French neurologist. See: World Who's Who Sci. Crouzon's disease.

Crouzon's disease (Crouzon, Octave): Medicine. See: Dorland; Jablonski; Stedman.

CROVA, ANDRE PROSPER. 1833-1907. French physicist. See: World Who's Who Sci. Crova wavelength?

Crova wavelength (Crova, Andre Prosper?): Physics. See: Internat. Dict. Phys. Elec.

Crow, Jim. See: Jim Crow.

Crowak process (Derivation undetermined): Chemistry. See: Van Nostrand Chem. Dict.

Crowe process (Crowe, Thomas Bennett): Engineering and Industry. See: Thrush; Van Nostrand Chem. Dict.

CROWE, THOMAS BENNETT. 1876-1940. American metallurgical engineer. See: Who Was Who Amer., 1897-1942. Crowe process, Merrill-Crowe process, Mills-Crowe process.

Crowther engine (Crowther, P.): Engineering and Industry. See: Auger.

CROWTHER, SIR GEOFFREY. 1907- . English educator. See: Who's Who, 1959. Crowther report.

CROWTHER, P. fl. 1800. Engineer. (Biography source unavailable.) Crowther engine.

Crowther report (Crowther, Sir Geoffrey): Education. See: Good; Harrod.

Croxdale stretcher tram (Derivation undetermined): Engineering and Industry. See: Thrush.

CROZIER, WILLIAM. 1855-1942. American army officer. See: Webster's Biog. Dict. Buffington-Crozier disappearing gun carriage, Crozier wire-wound gun.

Crozier wire-wound gun (Crozier, William): Weapons. Cited in: Webster's Biog. Dict.

CRUCHET, RENE. 1875-1959. French physician. See: World Who's Who Sci. Cruchet's disease.

Cruchet's disease (Cruchet, Rene): Medicine. See: Dorland.

Crum-Brown, Alexander. See: Brown, Alexander Crum.

Crum-Brown and Gibson rule (Brown, Alexander Crum and Gibson, John?): Chemistry. See: Ballentyne; Van Nostrand Chem. Dict. Also known as: Brown rule, Crum Brown rule.

Crum-Brown and Walker synthesis (or reaction) (Brown, Alexander Crum and Walker, Sir James): Chemistry. See: Ballentyne; Van Nostrand Chem. Dict.

Crum Brown rule (Brown, Alexander Crum). See: Crum-Brown and Gibson rule.

Crum test for manganese (Crum, Walter): Chemistry. See: Van Nostrand Chem. Dict.

CRUM, WALTER. 1796-1867. Scottish chemist. See: Dict. Sci. Biog. Crum test for manganese.

Crummles (Crummles, Vincent): Generic Word (actor). See: Partridge.

CRUMMLES, VINCENT. Character in Charles Dickens' novel "Nicholas Nickleby" (1838-39). See: Benet. Crummles.

CRUSCHMANN, HEINRICH JAKOB WILHELM. 1846-1910. German internist. See: World Who's Who Sci. Cruschmann's spirals.

Cruschmann's spirals (Cruschmann, Heinrich Jakob Wilhelm): Medicine. Cited in: World Who's Who Sci.

Crusoe (Robinson Crusoe): Generic Word (solitary traveler). See: Webster's 3d.

Crusoe, Robinson. See: Robinson Crusoe.

Cruveilhier-Baumgarten murmur (Cruveilhier, Jean and Baumgarten, Paul Clemens von): Medicine. See: Stedman.

Cruveilhier-Baumgarten syndrome (or cirrhosis) (Cruveilhier, Jean and Baumgarten, Paul Clemens von): Medicine. See: Jablonski; Stedman.

CRUVEILHIER, JEAN. 1791-1874. French anatomist. See: Dict. Sci. Biog. Cruveilhier-Baumgarten murmur, Cruveilhier-Baumgarten syndrome (or cirrhosis), Cruveilhier's atrophy, Cruveilhier's disease, Cruveilhier's fascia, Cruveilhier's fossa, Cruveilhier's joint, Cruveilhier's ligaments, Cruveilhier's plexus, Cruveilhier's sign, Cruveilhier's ulcer.

Cruveilhier's atrophy (Cruveilhier, Jean): Medicine. See: Dorland; Jablonski.

Cruveilhier's disease (Cruveilhier, Jean): Medicine. See: Dorland; Stedman. Also known as: Duchenne-Aran disease.

Cruveilhier's fascia (Cruveilhier, Jean): Medicine. See: Stedman.

Cruveilhier's fossa (Cruveilhier, Jean): Medicine. See: Stedman.

Cruveilhier's joint (Cruveilhier, Jean): Medicine. See: Stedman.

Cruveilhier's ligaments (Cruveilhier, Jean): Medicine. See: Stedman.

Cruveilhier's plexus (Cruveilhier, Jean): Medicine. See: Stedman.

Cruveilhier's sign (Cruveilhier, Jean): Medicine. See: Stedman.

Cruveilhier's ulcer (Cruveilhier, Jean): Medicine. See: Jablonski.

CRUZ, OSWALDO. 1871-1917. Brazilian physician. See: World Who's Who Sci. Chagas-Cruz disease.

Cryderman loader (Derivation undetermined): Engineering and Industry. See: Thrush.

CRYER, MATTHEW HENRY. 1840-1921. American surgeon. See: World Who's Who Sci. Cryer's elevator.

Cryer's elevator (Cryer, Matthew Henry): Medicine. See: Dorland.

crypts of Lieberkuehn (Lieberkuehn, Johannes Nathanael). See: Lieberkuehn's gland(s) (crypts or follicles).

CSILLAG, J. fl. 1909. Hungarian? dermatologist. (Biography source unavailable.) Csillag's disease.

Csillag's disease (Csillag, J.). See: Hallopeau's disease (1).

CUBONI, E. fl. 1934. Italian chemist. Cited in: Chem. Abstr., vol. 28, p. 3776. Cuboni test.

Cuboni test (Cuboni, E.): Chemistry. See: Winburne.

CUCCIA, CARMEN LOUIS. 1918- . American engineer. See: Amer. Men Sci., 9th ed. Cuccia coupler.

Cuccia coupler (Cuccia, Carmen Louis): Electronics. See: Hughes; Markus.

Cudbear (dye) (Gordon, Cuthbert): Botany. See: Hendrickson; Stedman.

CUIGNET, FERDINAND LOUIS JOSEPH. b. 1823. French ophthalmologist. Cited in: Kelly. Cuignet's method.

Cuignet's method (Cuignet, Ferdinand Louis Joseph): Medicine. See: Dorland; Stedman.

Cuisenaire-Gattegno rods (Cuisenaire, Georges and Gattegno, Caleb): Education. See: Good.

CUISENAIRE, GEORGES. fl. 1955. French? psychologist. (Biography source unavailable.) Cuisenaire-Gattegno rods.

CULBERTSON, ELY. 1891-1955. American authority on contract bridge. See: Webster's Biog. Dict. Culbertson system.

Culbertson system (Culbertson, Ely): Recreation and Sports. See: Webster's 3d.

CULLEN, THOMAS STEPHEN. 1868-1953. American gynecologist. See: World Who's Who Sci. Cullen's sign.

Cullen's sign (Cullen, Thomas Stephen): Medicine. See: Dorland; Stedman.

CULLER, ELMER AUGUSTINE KURTZ. b. 1889. American psychologist. See: Amer. Men Sci., 9th ed (Soc. Behav. Sci.). Culler's phi process?

Culler's phi process (Culler, Elmer Augustine Kurtz?): Psychology. See: Chaplin; English.

Cullinan diamond (Cullinan, Sir Thomas Major): Earth Sciences. See: Brewer; Hendrickson.

CULLINAN, SIR THOMAS MAJOR. 1862-1936. South African industrialist. See: Encyc. S. Africa, 6th ed. Cullinan diamond.

CULMANN, KARL. 1821-1881. German engineer. See: Dict. Sci. Biog. Culmann's diagram.

Culmann's diagram (Culmann, Karl): Engineering and Industry. See: Webster's 3d.

CULPEPER, JOHN. fl. 1671. English surveyor and political leader. See: Webster's Biog. Dict. Culpeper's rebellion.

Culpeper's rebellion (Culpeper, John): History. See: Morris.

CULVER, DR. fl. before 1716. American physician. (Biography source unavailable.) Culver's root (or physic).

Culver's root (or physic) (Culver, Dr.): Botany. See: Gray; Mathews, M. M.; Stedman.

CUMENGE, EDOUARD. 1828-1902. French mining engineer. See: Dict. Biog. Fran. Cumengeite (or Cumengite).

Cumengeite (or Cumengite) (Cumenge, Edouard): Earth Sciences. See: Thrush; Webster's 3d.

Cumingia (Cumings, Hugh): Zoology. See: Pennak.

CUMINGS, HUGH. 1791-1865. English naturalist. See: World Who's Who Sci. Cumingia.

Cummings apparatus (Derivation undetermined): Chemistry. See: Hackh.

Cummings' sedimentation method (Derivation undetermined): Engineering and Industry. See: Thrush.

CUMMINS, ALBERT BAIRD. 1850-1926. American lawyer and statesman. See: Dict. Amer. Biog. Esch-Cummins Act.

CUNARD, SAMUEL. 1787-1865. English shipowner. See: Dict. Nat. Biog. Cunarder.

Cunarder (Cunard, Samuel): Generic Word. See: Mathews, M. M.

Cunctator, Quintus Fabius. See: Fabius, Quintus.

CUNIASSE, LUCIEN MARIE. b. 1866. French chemist. Cited in: Royal Soc. Cat. Sci. Pap., 1884-1900. Cuniasse solution.

Cuniasse solution (Cuniasse, Lucien Marie): Chemistry. See: Van Nostrand Chem. Dict.

Cunisset's test (Derivation undetermined): Medicine. See: Stedman.

Cunliffe committee (Cunliffe, Walter): Economics. See: Seldon.

CUNLIFFE, WALTER (1ST BARON). 1855-1920. English banker. See: Webster's Biog. Dict. Cunliffe committee.

CUNNINGHAM, ALLAN. 1791-1839. Scottish botanist. See: Dict. Nat. Biog. Cunninghamia?

Cunningham lectureship (Cunningham, William): Religion. See: Canney.

CUNNINGHAM, RICHARD. 1793-1835. Scottish botanist. See: Dict. Nat. Biog. Cunninghamia?

CUNNINGHAM, WILLIAM. fl. 1780. Soldier. (Biography source unavailable.) Cunningham's raid.

CUNNINGHAM, WILLIAM. 1805-1861. Scottish theologian. See: Internat. Encyc. Soc. Sci. Cunningham lectureship.

Cunninghamia (Cunningham, Allan or Cunningham, Richard): Botany. See: Taylor, N.; Webster's 3d.

Cunningham's raid (Cunningham, William): History. See: Jameson.

CUNO, JOHANN CHRISTIAN. 1708-1783. Dutch poet and botanist. See: Nouv. Biog. Univ. Cunonia.

Cunonia (Cuno, Johann Christian): Botany. See: Charnock; Webster's 3d.

CUNY, LOUIS. fl. 1923. French chemist. Cited in: Chem. Abstr., vol. 18, p. 208. Cuny-Poirot test.

Cuny-Poirot test (Cuny, Louis and Poirot, G.): Chemistry. See: Van Nostrand Chem. Dict.

Cup of Tantalus (Tantalus): Recreation and Sports. See: Phyfe.

CUPANI, FRANCESCO. 1657-1711. Sicilian botanist. See: Nouv. Biog. Univ. Cupania.

Cupania (Cupani, Francesco): Botany. See: Charnock.

CUPID. Roman god of love. See: Jobes. Cupid, Cupid's bow, Cupid's cup, Cupid's dart (1), Cupid's darts (2), Cupid's delight, Cupid's golden arrow, Cupid's leaden arrow, Kewpie.

Cupid (Cupid, the Roman god): Generic Word (cherub). See: Webster's 3d.

Cupid's bow (Cupid): Weapons. See: Partridge; Webster's 3d.

Cupid's cup (Cupid): Botany. See: Mathews, M. M.

Cupid's dart (1) (Cupid): Botany. See: Webster's 3d.

Cupid's darts (2) (Cupid): Earth Sciences. See: Webster's 3d.

Cupid's delight (Cupid): Botany. See: Mathews, M. M.; Webster's 3d.

Cupid's golden arrow (Cupid): Generic Word (virtuous love). See: Brewer.

Cupid's leaden arrow (Cupid): Generic Word (sensual passion). See: Brewer.

CURETON, WILLIAM. 1808-1864. English scholar. See: Dict. Nat. Biog. Curetonian.

Curetonian (Cureton, William): Religion. See: Stenhouse.

Curie-Cheveneau balance (Curie, Pierre and Cheneveau, Joseph Gabriel Charles): Physics. See: Thewlis.

Curie constant (Curie, Pierre): Physics. See: Internat. Dict. Phys. Elec.

Curie electroscope (Curie, Pierre): Physics. See: Hackh.

Curie('s) law (Curie, Pierre): Physics. See: Ballentyne; Thewlis; Webster's 3d.

CURIE, MARIE (MARIA SKLODOWSKA). 1867-1934. Polish-born physicist. See: Dict. Sci. Biog. Curie (unit), Curiegram, Curietherapy, Curium, Sklodowskite.

CURIE, PIERRE. 1859-1906. French physicist. See: Dict. Sci. Biog. Curie-Cheveneau balance, Curie constant, Curie electroscope, Curie('s) law, Curie point (or temperature), Curie principle, Curie scale of temperature, Curie (unit), Curie-Weiss law, Curietherapy, Curite, Curium.

Curie point (or temperature) (Curie, Pierre): Physics. See: Ballentyne; Internat. Dict. Ap. Math.; Internat. Dict. Phys. Elec.

Curie principle (Curie, Pierre): Physics. See: Ballentyne.

Curie scale of temperature (Curie, Pierre): Physics. See: Thewlis.

Curie (unit) (Curie, Pierre and Curie, Marie): Physics. See: Ballentyne; Dresner; Internat. Dict. Ap. Math.

Curie-Weiss law (Curie, Pierre and Weiss, Pierre Ernst): Physics. See: Ballentyne; Internat. Dict. Ap. Math.; Internat. Dict. Phys. Elec.

Curiegram (Curie, Marie): Medicine. See: Dorland; Stedman.

Curietherapy (Curie, Pierre and Curie, Marie): Physics. See: Hackh; Webster's 3d.

Curite (Curie, Pierre): Earth Sciences. See: Thrush; Webster's 3d.

Curium (Curie, Pierre and Curie, Marie): Chemistry. See: Thrush; Van Nostrand Chem. Dict.; Van Nostrand Sci. Encyc.

Curlicism (Curll, Edmund): Generic Word (literary indecency). See: Hendrickson; Partridge.

CURLING, THOMAS BLIZARD. 1811-1888. English surgeon. See: World Who's Who Sci. Curling's ulcer.

Curling's ulcer (Curling, Thomas Blizard): Medicine. See: Dorland; Jablonski; Stedman.

CURLL, EDMUND. 1675-1747. English publisher. See: Webster's Biog. Dict. Curlicism.

Curran-Knowles process (Curran, Maurice Donovan and Knowles Fuel Process Corp.): Chemistry. See: Van Nostrand Chem. Dict.

CURRAN, MAURICE DONOVAN. b. 1893. American metallurgist. See: Amer. Men Sci., 9th ed. Curran-Knowles process.

Currier and Ives (prints) (Currier, Nathaniel and Ives, James Merritt): Fine Arts. See: Mathews, M. M.; Osborne.

CURRIER, NATHANIEL. 1813-1888. American lithographer. See: Dict. Amer. Biog. Currier and Ives (prints).

CURRY, MILTON K. fl. 1973. American college president. See: Nat. Faculty Direct., 1975. Curry's caveat.

Curry's caveat (Curry, Milton K.): Sociology. See: Martin.

Curschmann-Batten-Steinert syndrome (Curschmann, Hans; Batten, Frederic Eustace; and Steinert, Hans Gustav Wilhelm): Medicine. See: Jablonski. Also known as: Batten-Steinert syndrome, Batten's disease, Curschmann-Steinert syndrome, Steinert's disease.

CURSCHMANN, HANS. 1875-1950. German neurologist. See: World Who's Who Sci. Curschmann-Batten-Steinert syndrome, Curschmann's sign, Curschmann's solution.

CURSCHMANN, HEINRICH. 1846-1910. German physician. See: Wer Ist's, 1906. Curschmann's disease, Curschmann's mask, Curschmann's spiral, Curschmann's trocar.

Curschmann-Steinert syndrome (Curschmann, Hans and Steinert, Hans Gustav Wilhelm). See: Curschmann-Batten-Steinert syndrome.

Curschmann's disease (Curschmann, Heinrich): Medicine. See: Dorland; Stedman.

Curschmann's mask (Curschmann, Heinrich): Medicine. See: Dorland.

Curschmann's sign (Curschmann, Hans): Medicine. See: Dorland.

Curschmann's solution (Curschmann, Hans): Medicine. See: Dorland.

Curschmann's spiral (Curschmann, Heinrich): Medicine. See: Dorland; Stedman.

Curschmann's trocar (Curschmann, Heinrich): Medicine. See: Dorland.

curse of Cain (Cain): Generic Word. See: Brewer; Hendrickson.

curse of Cromwell (Cromwell, Oliver): History. See: Latham; Phyfe.

CURTIS, ARTHUR HALE. b. 1881. American gynecologist. See: Who's Who Amer. Med. Fitz-Hugh and Curtis syndrome.

CURTIS, CHARLES GORDON. 1860-1953. American inventor. See: World Who's Who Sci. Curtis scavenging system, Curtis stage, Curtis steam turbine.

Curtis completion form (Curtis, James Wylie): Psychology. See: Wolman.

CURTIS, HARVEY LINCOLN. b. 1875. American physicist. See: Amer. Men Sci., 9th ed. Curtis winding (resistor).

CURTIS, JAMES WYLIE. 1913- . American psychologist. See: World Who's Who Sci. Curtis completion form.

CURTIS, P. L. fl. 20th c. American mineral collector. Cited in: Bailey. Curtisite.

Curtis scavenging system (Curtis, Charles Gordon): Engineering and Industry. Cited in: World Who's Who Sci.

Curtis stage (Curtis, Charles Gordon): Engineering and Industry. See: Webster's 3d.

Curtis steam turbine (Curtis, Charles Gordon): Engineering and Industry. See: Auger.

CURTIS, WILLIAM. 1746-1799. English botanist. See: Britten and Boulger. Curtisia.

Curtis winding (resistor) (Curtis, Harvey Lincoln): Electronics. See: Hughes; Internat. Dict. Phys. Elec.; Markus.

Curtisia (Curtis, William): Botany. See: Charnock.

Curtisite (Curtis, P. L.): Earth Sciences. See: Thrush; Webster's 3d.

CURTISS, GLENN HAMMOND. 1878-1930. American inventor and aviator. See: Encyc. Brit., 1973. Navy-Curtiss machine.

Curtius-Frazen test reaction (Curtius, Theodor and Franzen, Hartwig?): Chemistry. See: Van Nostrand Chem. Dict.

CURTIUS, FRIEDRICH. 1896- . German physician. See: Wer Ist's, 10th ed. Curtius' syndrome (1), Curtius' syndrome (2).

Curtius reaction (Curtius, Theodor): Chemistry. See: Hackh; Van Nostrand Chem. Dict.

Curtius rearrangement (Curtius, Theodor): Chemistry. See: Ballentyne; Webster's 3d.

Curtius' syndrome (1) (Curtius, Friedrich): Medicine. See: Jablonski. Also known as: Steiner's syndrome.

Curtius' syndrome (2) (Curtius, Friedrich): Medicine. See: Jablonski.

CURTIUS, THEODOR. 1857-1928. German chemist. See: Dict. Sci. Biog. Buchner-Curtius-Schlotterbeck reaction, Curtius-Frazen test reaction?, Curtius reaction, Curtius rearrangement.

CURTMAN, LOUIS JACOB. 1878-1958. English-born American chemist. See: Amer. Men Sci., 5th ed. Curtman-Plechner test, Curtman reagent for potassium, cesium, rubidium, and ammonium, Curtman solution for nitrite, Lyle-Curtman-Marshall alpha-aminocaproic acid solution, Lyle-Curtman-Marshall benzidine reagent.

Curtman-Plechner test (Curtman, Louis Jacob and Plechner, Walter William): Chemistry. See: Van Nostrand Chem. Dict.

Curtman reagent for potassium, cesium, rubidium, and ammonium (Curtman, Louis Jacob): Chemistry. See: Van Nostrand Chem. Dict.

Curtman solution for nitrite (Curtman, Louis Jacob): Chemistry. See: Van Nostrand Chem. Dict.

curve of Spee (Spee, Ferdinand Graf von): Anatomy. See: Dorland; Stedman. Also known as: Von Spee's curve.

CURZON, GEORGE NATHANIEL. 1859-1925. English statesman. See: Dict. Nat. Biog., 4th suppl. Curzon-Kitchener controversy, Curzon line.

Curzon-Kitchener controversy (Curzon, George Nathaniel and Kitchener, Horatio Herbert): History. See: Montgomery.

Curzon line (Curzon, George Nathaniel): History. See: Hendrickson.

CUSCO, EDOUARD GABRIEL. 1819-1894. French surgeon. See: Biog. Lex. hervorr. Aerzte. Cusco's speculum.

Cusco's speculum (Cusco, Edouard Gabriel): Medicine. See: Dorland; Stedman.

CUSHING, HARVEY WILLIAMS. 1869-1939. American neurosurgeon. See: Dict. Sci. Biog. Cushingoid signs, Cushing's basophilism, Cushing's medulloblastoma, Cushing's phenomenon (or law), Cushing's syndrome (1), Cushing's syndrome (2), Cushing's syndrome (3) (basophilism or disease), Cushing's tumor, Rokitansky-Cushing ulcer.

CUSHING, HAYWARD WARREN. 1854-1934. American surgeon. Cited in: Kelly. Cushing's suture.

Cushingoid signs (Cushing, Harvey Williams): Medicine. See: Stedman.

Cushing's basophilism (Cushing, Harvey Williams): Medicine. See: Stedman.

Cushing's medulloblastoma (Cushing, Harvey Williams): Medicine. See: Jablonski.

Cushing's phenomenon (or law) (Cushing, Harvey Williams): Medicine. See: Stedman.

Cushing's suture (Cushing, Hayward Warren): Medicine. See: Dorland; Stedman.

Cushing's syndrome (1) (Cushing, Harvey Williams): Medicine. See: Jablonski.

Cushing's syndrome (2) (Cushing, Harvey Williams): Medicine. See: Jablonski.

Cushing's syndrome (3) (basophilism or disease) (Cushing, Harvey Williams): Medicine. See: Hinsie; Jablonski; Stedman. Also known as: Itsenko-Cushing syndrome.

Cushing's tumor (Cushing, Harvey Williams): Medicine. See: Jablonski.

CUSSON. fl. 1909. French chemist. Cited in: Chem. Abstr., vol. 3, p. 2877. Cusson test.

CUSSON, PIERRE. 1727-1783. French botanist. See: Dict. Biog. Fran. Cussonia.

Cusson test (Cusson): Chemistry. See: Van Nostrand Chem. Dict.

Cussonia (Cusson, Pierre): Botany. See: Charnock.

CUSTER, GEORGE ARMSTRONG. 1839-1876. American army officer. See: Dict. Amer. Biog. Custer (massacre).

Custer (massacre) (Custer, George Armstrong): History. See: Harbottle; Mathews, M. M.

cut(ting) a Dido (or cut up Didos) (Dido): Generic Word (play a prank). See: Brewer; Hendrickson; Partridge.

Cuthbert duck (or Saint Cuthbert's duck) (Cuthbert, Saint): Zoology. See: Brewer; Partridge; Webster's 3d.

CUTHBERT, SAINT. 635-687. English monk. See: Dict. Nat. Biog. Cuthbert duck (or Saint Cuthbert's duck), patrimony of St. Cuthbert, Saint (St.) Cuthbert's beads.

CUTHBERTSON, JOHN. fl. late 18th c. Dutch inventor. See: World Who's Who Sci. Cuthbertson vacuum pump.

Cuthbertson vacuum pump (Cuthbertson, John): Engineering and Industry. See: Auger.

CUTLER, ALPHEUS. fl. 1853. American theologist. (Biography source unavailable.) Cutlerite.

CUTLER, CASSIUS CHAPIN. 1914- . American physicist. See: Amer. Men Sci., 9th ed. Cutler feed?

Cutler feed (Cutler, Cassius Chapin?): Electronics. See: Hughes; Markus.

CUTLER, HAYDN H. fl. 1938. American physician. Cited in: Chem. Abstr., vol. 32, p. 8544. Cutler-Power-Wilder test.

CUTLER, MANASSEH. 1742-1823. American clergyman and botanist. See: World Who's Who Sci. Cutleria.

Cutler-Power-Wilder test (Cutler, Haydn H.; Power, Marschelle Harnly; and Wilder, Russell Morse): Medicine. See: Stedman.

Cutleria (Cutler, Manasseh): Botany. See: Webster's 3d.

Cutlerite (Cutler, Alpheus): Religion. See: Webster's 3d.

Cutolo reagent (Derivation undetermined): Chemistry. See: Van Nostrand Chem. Dict.

Cutter author marks (Cutter, Charles Ammi): Library Science. See: Harrod.

CUTTER, CHARLES AMMI. 1837-1903. American librarian. See: Dict. Amer. Biog. Cutter author marks, Cutter classification, Cutter number, Cutter-Sanborn three-figure table.

Cutter classification (Cutter, Charles Ammi): Library Science. See: Webster's 3d.

CUTTER, EPHRAIM. 1832-1917. American physician. See: World Who's Who Sci. Wada-Cutter hingeless heart valve?

Cutter number (Cutter, Charles Ammi): Library Science. See: Hendrickson; Webster's 3d.

Cutter-Sanborn three-figure table (Cutter, Charles Ammi and Jones, Kate Emery Sanborn): Library Science. See: Harrod.

CUTTING, BRONSON MURRAY. 1888-1935. American legislator. See: Biog. Direct. Amer. Congress. Hawes-Cutting Act.

Cuverian sinus (Cuvier, Georges): Zoology. See: Gray.

CUVIER, GEORGES. 1769-1832. French naturalist. See: Dict. Sci. Biog. Cuverian sinus, Cuvierian, Cuvierian organ(s), Cuvierian tubule, Cuvier's canal, Cuvier's chinchilla, Cuvier's golden crest, Cuvier's regulus, Cuvier's (Cuvierian) vein(s), duct(s) of Cuvier.

Cuvierian (Cuvier, Georges): Zoology. See: Webster's 3d.

Cuvierian organ(s) (Cuvier, Georges): Zoology. See: Henderson; Van Nostrand Sci. Encyc.; Webster's 3d.

Cuvierian tubule (Cuvier, Georges): Zoology. See: Gray.

Cuvier's canal (Cuvier, Georges): Zoology. See: Gray.

Cuvier's chinchilla (Cuvier, Georges): Zoology. See: Gray.

Cuvier's golden crest (Cuvier, Georges): Zoology. See: Mathews, M. M.

Cuvier's regulus (Cuvier, Georges): Zoology. See: Mathews, M. M.

Cuvier's (Cuvierian) vein(s) (Cuvier, Georges): Medicine. See: Stedman; Webster's 3d.

Cuylen conveyor (Derivation undetermined): Engineering and Industry. See: Thrush.

cyanotic syndrome of Scheid (Derivation undetermined): Psychiatry. See: Hinsie.

cyclid of Dupin (Dupin, Pierre-Charles-Francois): Mathematics. Cited in: Dict. Sci. Biog.

Cyon, Elie de. See: De Cyon, Elie.

Cyon's experiment (De Cyon, Elie): Medicine. See: Dorland.

Cyon's nerve (De Cyon, Elie): Medicine. See: Dorland; Stedman.

Cyrano de Bergerac (Bergerac, Cyrano de): Generic Word. See: Hendrickson.

Cyrano de Bergerac. See: Bergerac, Cyrano de.

Cyrenaic (Aristippus of Cyrene): Philosophy. See: Canney; Hendrickson.

CYRIAX, EDGAR FERDINAND. b. 1874. English physician. Cited in: Med. Reg., 1952. Cyriax's syndrome.

Cyriax's syndrome (Cyriax, Edgar Ferdinand): Medicine. See: Jablonski. Also known as: Davies-Colley's syndrome.

CYRIL, SAINT. 376-444. Bishop of Alexandria. See: Encyc. Brit., 1973. Cyrillian (or Cyrillianism).

CYRIL, SAINT. 827-869. Apostle to the Slavs. See: Encyc. Brit., 1973. Cyrillic (alphabet).

Cyrilla (Cirillo, Dominico): Botany. See: Chamock; Webster's 3d.

Cyrillian (or Cyrillianism) (Cyril, Saint): Religion. See: Webster's 3d.

Cyrillic (alphabet) (Cyril, Saint): Generic Word. See: Brewer; Hendrickson; Webster's 3d.

Cyrillo, Domenico. See: Cirillo, Domenico.

Cytherea. See: Venus.

Cytherea (Venus): Botany. See: Webster's 3d.

Cytherean (Venus): Mythology. See: Webster's 3d.

Cytherella (Venus): Zoology. See: Webster's 3d.

CYTHERIS (Poetic name: LYCORIS). fl. ca. 47 B.C. Roman actress and courtesan. See: Dict. Grk. Rom. Biog. Myth. Lycoris.

Czapek-Dox medium (Czapek, Friedrich Johann Franz and Dox, Arthur Wayland): Botany. See: Webster's 3d. Also known as: Czapek medium.

CZAPEK, FRIEDRICH JOHANN FRANZ. 1868-1921. Czech botanist. See: World Who's Who Sci. Czapek-Dox medium.

Czapek medium (Czapek, Friedrich Johann Franz). See: Czapek-Dox medium.

Czapek tests (Derivation undetermined): Chemistry. See: Van Nostrand Chem. Dict.

CZAPLEWSKI, EUGEN. 1865-1945. Polish bacteriologist. See: World Who's Who Sci. Czaplewski's stain.

Czaplewski's stain (Czaplewski, Eugen): Medicine. See: Stedman.

Czar (or Tsar) (Caesar, Gaius Julius): Generic Word (king). See: Hendrickson.

CZERMAK, JOHANN NEPOMUK. 1828-1873. Czech physiologist. See: Dict. Sci. Biog. Czermak lines, Czermak spaces.

Czermak lines (Czermak, Johann Nepomuk): Dentistry. Cited in: Dict. Sci. Biog.

Czermak spaces (Czermak, Johann Nepomuk): Dentistry. Cited in: Dict. Sci. Biog.

CZERNOTZKY, ADOLF. fl. 1928. German chemist. Cited in: Chem. Abstr., vol. 23, p. 60. Czernotzky test.

Czernotzky test (Czernotzky, Adolf): Chemistry. See: Van Nostrand Chem. Dict.

CZERNY, ADALBERT. 1863-1941. German pediatrician. See: Wer Ist's, 1906. Czerny's anemia (or diathesis).

Czerny-Lembert suture (Czerny, Vincenz and Lembert, Antoine): Medicine. See: Stedman.

CZERNY, VINCENZ. 1842-1916. German surgeon. See: World Who's Who Sci. Czerny-Lembert suture, Czerny's operation, Czerny's suture.

Czerny's anemia (or diathesis) (Czerny, Adalbert): Medicine. See: Dorland; Jablonski.

Czerny's operation (Czerny, Vincenz): Medicine. See: Dorland; Stedman.

Czerny's suture (Czerny, Vincenz): Medicine. See: Dorland; Stedman.

CZOCHRALSKI, JAN. 1885-1953. Polish metallurgist. See: Pogg., vol. 6, 7b. Czochralski (Czockralski) method (or technique), Czochralski's reagent.

Czochralski (Czockralski) method (or technique) (Czochralski, Jan): Engineering and Industry. See: Ballentyne; Thrush.

Czochralski's reagent (Czochralski, Jan): Engineering and Industry. See: Thrush.

Czokor alum-cochineal (Czokor, Johann): Chemistry. See: Van Nostrand Chem. Dict.

CZOKOR, JOHANN. fl. 1880. Austrian physician. Cited in: Kelly. Czokor alum-cochineal.

Czumplitz test reaction (Derivation undetermined): Chemistry. See: Van Nostrand Chem. Dict.

CZYHLARZ, ERNST RITTER VON. fl. 1908. Austrian chemist. Cited in: Chem. Abstr., vol. 2, p. 671. Czyhlarz-Furth test.

Czyhlarz-Furth test (Czyhlarz, Ernst Ritter von and Von Fuerth, Otto): Chemistry. See: Van Nostrand Chem. Dict.

D

DAAE, ANDERS. 1838-1910. Norwegian physician. See: Biog. Lex. hervorr. Aerzte, 1880-1930. Daae's disease?

Daae's disease (Daae, Anders?): Medicine. See: Stedman. Also known as: Palme's disease.

DABNEY, WILLIAM CECIL. 1849-1894. American physician. See: Biog. Lex. hervorr. Aerzte, 1880-1930. Dabney's grippe.

Dabney's grippe (Dabney, William Cecil). See: Sylvest's syndrome.

Daboecia (or Saint Daboec's heath) (Beoc, Saint): Botany. See: Taylor, N.; Webster's 3d.

Daboll (arithmetic) (Daboll, Nathan): Mathematics. See: Mathews, M. M.

DABOLL, NATHAN. 1750-1818. American mathematician. See: Dict. Amer. Biog. Daboll (arithmetic).

D'ACHIARDI, ANTONIO. 1840?-1902. Italian mineralogist. See: Sci., vol. 17 (1903) p. 119. Dachiardite (or Achiardite).

Dachiardite (or Achiardite) (D'Achiardi, Antonio): Earth Sciences. See: Thrush; Webster's 3d.

Da Costa, Antonio Placido. See: Placido da Costa, Antonio.

DA COSTA, JACOB MENDEZ. 1833-1900. American surgeon. See: World Who's Who Sci. Da Costa's syndrome.

D'Acosta, Jose. See: Acosta, Jose de.

DA COSTA, MENDES S. fl. 1925. Swedish? dermatologist. (Biography source unavailable.) Da Costa's syndrome.

Da Costa's syndrome (Da Costa, Jacob Mendez): Medicine. See: Dorland; Hinsie; Jablonski.

Da Costa's syndrome (Da Costa, Mendes S.): Medicine. See: Jablonski. Also known as: Mendes Da Costa syndrome.

DACQUE, EDGAR VIKTOR AUGUST. 1878-1945. German paleontologist and geologist. See: World Who's Who Sci. Dacque's principle.

Dacque's principle (Dacque, Edgar Viktor August): Biology. See: Webster's 3d.

DADANT, CAMILLE PIERRE. 1851-1938. French apiarist. See: World Who's Who Sci. Dadant hive.

DADANT, CHARLES. 1817-1902. French apiarist. Cited in: World Who's Who Sci. under "Dadant, Camille Pierre." Dadant hive.

Dadant hive (Dadant, Camille Pierre and Dadant, Charles): Zoology. See: Winburne.

DADDI, G. fl. 1933. Italian chemist. Cited in: Chem. Abstr., vol. 27, p. 2972. Daddi solution.

Daddi solution (Daddi, G.): Chemistry. See: Van Nostrand Chem. Dict.

DADU. 1544-1603. Hindu religious reformer and poet. See: Webster's Biog. Dict. Dadu Panthis.

Dadu Panthis (Dadu): Religion. See: Canney.

Daedal (or Daedalian) (Daedalus): Generic Word (skillful). See: Charnock; Partridge; Webster's 3d.

Daedalea (Daedalus): Biology. See: Webster's 3d.

DAEDALUS. Mythical Greek architect and sculptor. See: Encyc. Brit., 1973. Daedal (or Daedalian), Daedalea.

Daelen mill (Daelen, R.): Engineering and Industry. See: Thrush.

DAELEN, R. fl. 1870. German engineer. (Biography source unavailable.) Daelen mill.

DAEVES, KARL HEINRICH. b. 1893. German metallurgist. See: Pogg., vol. 6, 7a. Daeves's reagent.

Daeves's reagent (Daeves, Karl Heinrich): Engineering and Industry. See: Thrush.

DAFFY, THOMAS. d. 1680. English clergyman. See: Dict. Nat. Biog. Daffy's elixir.

Daffy's elixir (Daffy, Thomas): Medicine. See: Dorland; Partridge; Weekley.

Dagner condenser (Derivation undetermined): Engineering and Industry. See: Thrush.

DAGNINI, GIUSEPPE. 1866-1928. Italian physician. See: Biog. Lex. hervorr. Aerzte, 1880-1930. Aschner-Dagnini reflex.

DAGNINI, GUIDO. fl. 1935. Italian physician. (Biography source unavailable.) Scaglietti-Dagnini syndrome.

DAGUERRE, LOUIS JACQUES MANDE. 1789-1851. French painter and inventor. See: World Who's Who Sci. Daguerrean, Daguerreotype.

Daguerrean (Daguerre, Louis Jacques Mande): Photography. See: Webster's 3d.

Daguerreotype (Daguerre, Louis Jacques Mande): Photography. See: Focal Encyc. Photog.; Harrod; Van Nostrand Sci. Encyc.

DAHL, ANDREAS. 1751-1789. Swedish botanist. See: World Who's Who Sci. Dahlia.

Dahl-Kirkam telescope (Derivation undetermined): Physics. See: Internat. Dict. Phys. Elec.

DAHL, OLAUS. d. 1897. Linguist. See: Sci., vol. 5 (1897), p. 473. Dahl's law?

Dahlgren (gun) (Dahlgren, John Adolphus Bernard): Weapons. See: Mathews, M. M.; Partridge; Quick.

DAHLGREN, JOHN ADOLPHUS BERNARD. 1809-1870. American naval officer. See: Dict. Amer. Biog. Dahlgren (gun).

Dahlia (Dahl, Andreas): Botany. See: Charnock; Hendrickson; Taylor, N.

Dahlite (Derivation undetermined): Earth Sciences. See: Thrush.

DAHLL, JOHANN. fl. 19th c. Norwegian geologist and mineralogist. Cited in: Bailey. Dahllite.

DAHLL, TELLEF. 1825-1893. Norwegian geologist and mineralogist. See: Pogg., vol. 3, 4. Dahllite.

Dahllite (Dahll, Johann and Dahll, Telef): Earth Sciences. See: Thrush; Webster's 3d.

Dahlmann test (Derivation undetermined): Chemistry. See: Van Nostrand Chem. Dict.

Dahl's acid (Derivation undetermined): Chemistry. See: Hackh.

Dahl's law (Dahl, Olaus?): Linguistics. See: Winick.

DAHLSTROM, DONALD ALBERT. 1920- . American chemical engineer. See: Amer. Men Sci., 9th ed. Dahlstrom's formula.

Dahlstrom's formula (Dahlstrom, Donald Albert): Engineering and Industry. See: Thrush.

Daimler engine (Daimler, Gottlieb Wilhelm): Engineering and Industry. See: Auger.

DAIMLER, GOTTLIEB WILHELM. 1834-1900. German engineer, inventor, and automobile manufacturer. See: World Who's Who Sci. Daimler engine.

Daisy Millerism (Miller, Daisy): Generic Word (unconventional female behavior). See: Mathews, M. M.

DAKEYNE, EDWARD. fl. 1830. English? engineer. (Biography source unavailable.) Dakeyne engine.

Dakeyne engine (Dakeyne, Edward and Dakeyne, James): Engineering and Industry. See: Auger, 2nd ed.

DAKEYNE, JAMES. fl. 1830. English? engineer. (Biography source unavailable.) Dakeyne engine.

Dakin antiseptic (Dakin, Henry Drysdale): Chemistry. See: Hackh.

Dakin-Carrel treatment (Dakin, Henry Drysdale and Carrel, Alexis). See: Carrel's treatment.

DAKIN, HENRY DRYSDALE. 1880-1952. English-born chemist. See: World Who's Who Sci. Carrel-Dakin solution, Dakin antiseptic, Dakin-Carrel treatment, Dakin reaction, Dakin reagent for aldehydes and ketones, Dakin('s) solution, Dakin-West reaction.

Dakin reaction (Dakin, Henry Drysdale): Chemistry. See: Van Nostrand Chem. Dict.

Dakin reagent for aldehydes and ketones (Dakin, Henry Drysdale): Chemistry. See: Van Nostrand Chem. Dict.

Dakin('s) solution (Dakin, Henry Drysdale): Chemistry. See: Van Nostrand Chem. Dict.; Van Nostrand Sci. Encyc.; Webster's 3d.

Dakin-West reaction (Dakin, Henry Drysdale and West, Randolph): Chemistry. See: Van Nostrand Chem. Dict.

DALBERG, NILS E. 1736-1820. Swedish physician and botanist. See: Krok. Dalbergia.

Dalbergia (Dalberg, Nils E.): Botany. See: Taylor, N.; Webster's 3d.

DALBY, W. ERNEST. d. 1936. English engineer. See: World Who's Who Sci. Dalby's diagram.

Dalby's diagram (Dalby, W. Ernest): Engineering and Industry. See: Auger.

Dale-Chall readability formula (Dale, Edgar and Chall, Jeanne S.): Education. See: Good.

DALE, DAVID. 1739-1806. Scottish industrialist and philanthropist. See: Dict. Nat. Biog. Daleites.

DALE, EDGAR. 1900- . American educator. See: Who's Who Amer., 1972-73. Dale-Chall readability formula.

Dale-Feldberg law (Dale, Sir Henry Hallett and Feldberg, Wilhelm Siegmund): Medicine. See: Stedman.

DALE, SIR HENRY HALLETT. 1875-1968. English physiologist. See: World Who's Who Sci. Dale-Feldberg law, Schultz-Dale reaction.

Dale reaction (Dale, Sir Henry Hallett). See: Schultz-Dale reaction.

DALE, SAMUEL. 1659-1739. English botanist and pharmacologist. See: Dict. Nat. Biog. Dalea.

DALE, THOMAS. d. 1619. Colonial administrator in America. See: Dict. Nat. Biog. Dale's Code.

DALE, THOMAS PELHAM. 1821-1892. English chemist. See: Chamber's Dict. Sci. Gladstone-Dale formula, Gladstone-Dale law.

Dalea (Dale, Samuel): Botany. See: Mathews, M. M.

Dalechampia (Dalechamps, Jacques): Botany. See: Charnock.

DALECHAMPS, JACQUES. 1513-1588. French physician and botanist. See: Dict. Sci. Biog. Dalechampia.

Daleites (Dale, David): Religion. See: Canney.

D'Alembert equation (Alembert, Jean Le Rond d'): Mathematics. See: Thewlis.

D'Alembert, Jean Le Rond. See: Alembert, Jean Le Ronde d'.

D'Alembert('s) paradox (Alembert, Jean Le Rond d'): Physics. See: Ballentyne; Huschke; Internat. Dict. Ap. Math.

D'Alembert('s) principle (Alembert, Jean Le Rond d'): Physics. See: Ballentyne; Internat. Dict. Ap. Math.; Internat. Dict. Phys. Elec.

D'Alembert('s) test (for convergence) (Alembert, Jean Le Rond d'): Mathematics. See: Ballentyne; Internat. Dict. Ap. Math.; Van Nostrand Sci. Encyc. Also known as: Cauchy ratio test.

D'Alembertian (Alembert, Jean Le Rond d'): Mathematics. See: Ballentyne; Internat. Dict. Ap. Math.; Internat. Dict. Phys. Elec.

Dalen-Fuchs spots (or nodules) (Dalen, Johan Albin and Fuchs, Ernst): Medicine. See: Jablonski.

DALEN, GUSTAF. fl. 1910. German technologist. Cited in: Mansell. Dalen-Martens machine?

DALEN, JOHAN ALBIN. b. 1866. Swedish physician. See: Biog. Lex. hervorr. Aerzte, 1880-1930. Dalen-Fuchs spots (or nodules).

Dalen-Martens machine (Dalen, Gustaf? and Martens, Adolf?): Engineering and Industry. See: Hackh.

Dale's Code (Dale, Thomas): Law. Cited in: Webster's Biog. Dict.

Dale's pony (Derivation undetermined): Zoology. See: Winburne.

DALI, SALVADOR. 1904- . Spanish painter. See: Encyc. Brit., 1973. Daliesque.

DALIBARD, THOMAS-FRANCOIS. 1703-1779. French physicist and botanist. See: Dict. Sci. Biog. Dalibarda.

Dalibarda (Dalibard, Thomas-Francois): Botany. See: Taylor, N.

Daliesque (Dali, Salvador): Fine Arts. See: Webster's 3d.

Dalitz pair (Dalitz, Richard Henry): Physics. See: Hughes.

Dalitz plot (Dalitz, Richard Henry): Physics. See: Hughes.

DALITZ, RICHARD HENRY. 1925- . Australian-born physicist. See: World Who's Who Sci. Dalitz pair, Dalitz plot.

Dall flow tube (Dall, Horace E.): Engineering and Industry. See: Auger.

DALL, HORACE E. fl. 1938. English? engineer. Cited in: Chem. Abstr., vol. 32, p. 7787. Dall flow tube.

Dall('s) porpoise (Dall, William Healey): Zoology. See: Webster's 3d.

Dall('s) sheep (Dall, William Healey): Zoology. See: Gray; Hendrickson; Mathews, M. M.

DALL, WILLIAM HEALEY. 1845-1927. American naturalist. See: Dict. Sci. Biog. Dall('s) porpoise, Dall('s) sheep, Dallia (blackfish).

DALLAS, ALEXANDER JAMES. 1759-1817. American administrator. See: Dict. Amer. Biog. Dallas' Reports.

DALLAS, CAMPBELL DUNCAN. fl. 1863. Photo-engraver. (Biography source unavailable.) Dallastype.

Dallas-Clarendon Treaty (Dallas, George Mifflin and Villiers, George William Frederick): History. See: Jameson.

DALLAS, GEORGE MIFFLIN. 1792-1864. American statesman and diplomat. See: Dict. Amer. Biog. Dallas-Clarendon Treaty.

Dallas' Reports (Dallas, Alexander James): Law. See: Jameson.

Dallastype (Dallas, Campbell Duncan): Photography. See: Focal Encyc. Photog.; Partridge; Weekley.

Dallia (blackfish) (Dall, William Healey): Zoology. See: Hendrickson; Pennak.

DALLINGER, WILLIAM HENRY. 1842-1909. English biologist. See: World Who's Who Sci. Dallingeria.

Dallingeria (Dallinger, William Henry): Zoology. See: Pennak.

DALMAN, JOHANN WILHELM. 1787-1826. Swedish naturalist. See: Biog. Lex. hervorr. Aerzte. Dalmanites.

Dalmanites (Dalman, Johann Wilhelm): Zoology. See: Webster's 3d.

DAL MONTE, GUIDUBALDO. 1545-1607. Italian astronomer and mathematician. See: World Who's Who Sci. Guidobaldo's first method.

DALRYMPLE, JOHN. 1803-1852. Scottish oculist and surgeon. See: Dict. Nat. Biog. Dalrymple's disease, Dalrymple's sign.

Dalrymple's disease (Dalrymple, John): Medicine. See: Dorland; Jablonski; Stedman.

Dalrymple's sign (Dalrymple, John): Medicine. See: Dorland; Stedman.

Dalton-Henry law (Dalton, John and Henry, Joseph): Chemistry. See: Dorland; Stedman.

DALTON, JOHN. 1766-1844. English chemist. See: Dict. Sci. Biog. Dalton-Henry law, Dalton('s) law (of partial pressure), Dalton (unit), Daltonian, Daltonide (compound), Daltonism, Dalton's law of evaporation, Dalton's law of solubility of gases, Dalton's temperature scale.

Dalton('s) law (of partial pressure) (Dalton, John): Chemistry. See: Ballentyne; Huschke; Internat. Dict. Ap. Math. Also known as: Gibbs-Dalton law.

Dalton (unit) (Dalton, John): Chemistry. See: Dresner; Hackh; Stedman.

Daltonian (Dalton, John): Chemistry. See: Stedman; Webster's 3d.

Daltonide (compound) (Dalton, John): Chemistry. See: Hackh; Van Nostrand Sci. Encyc.; Webster's 3d.

Daltonism (Dalton, John): Generic Word (color-blindness). See: Chaplin; Hendrickson; Phyfe.

Dalton's law of evaporation (Dalton, John): Chemistry. See: Ballentyne.

Dalton's law of solubility of gases (Dalton, John): Chemistry. See: Ballentyne.

Dalton's temperature scale (Dalton, John): Chemistry. See: Ballentyne.

DALY, REGINALD ALDWORTH. 1871-1957. Canadian-born American geologist. See: Dict. Sci. Biog. Dalyite.

DALYELL, JOHN GRAHAM. 1775-1851. Scottish naturalist. See: Dict. Nat. Biog. Dalyellia.

Dalyellia (Dalyell, John Graham): Zoology. See: Pennak; Webster's 3d.

Dalyite (Daly, Reginald Aldworth): Earth Sciences. See: Thrush.

DAM, CARL PETER HENRIK. 1895- . Danish biochemist. See: World Who's Who Sci. Dam unit.

Dam unit (Dam, Carl Peter Henrik): Medicine. See: Stedman.

Dame Durden (Durden, Dame): Generic Word (old-fashioned housewife). See: Brewer.

DAMESHEK, WILLIAM. 1900-1969. Russian-born American physician and hematologist. See: Who Was Who Amer., 1969-1973. Dameshek's syndrome, Estren-Dameshek syndrome.

Dameshek's syndrome (Dameshek, William). See: Cooley's anemia.

Damianites (Damianus): Religion. See: Canney.

DAMIANUS. fl. 570 A.D. Patriarch of Alexandria. See: Holweck. Damianites.

DAMIEN, FATHER (JOSEPH DE VEUSTER). 1840-1889. Belgian Catholic missionary. See: Encyc. Brit., 1973. Father Damien.

DAMIENS, AUGUSTIN AMEDEE. 1866-1946. French chemist. See: Bull. Soc. Chim. France, 1949, fasc. 11/12, p. 771. Damiens reagent.

Damiens' bed of steel (Damiens, Robert Francois): Generic Word (instrument of torture). See: Hendrickson.

Damiens reagent (Damiens, Augustin Amedee): Chemistry. See: Van Nostrand Chem. Dict.

DAMIENS, ROBERT FRANCOIS. 1715-1757. French assassin. See: Encyc. Brit., 1973. Damiens' bed of steel.

DAMMAN, KARL. 1839-1914. German veterinarian. See: Wer Ist's, 1905. Damman's bacillus.

Damman's bacillus (Damman, Karl): Medicine. See: Dorland.

Damoclean (Damocles): History. See: Webster's 3d.

DAMOCLES. fl. 4th c. B.C. Greek courtier. See: Encyc. Brit., 1973. Damoclean, sword of Damocles.

DAMOISEAU, LOUIS HYACINTHE CELESTE. 1815-1890. French physician. See: Dict. Biog. Fran. Damoiseau's curve (or sign).

Damoiseau's curve (or sign) (Damoiseau, Louis Hyacinthe Celeste): Medicine. See: Dorland.

DAMON. fl. 4th c. B.C. Pythagorean philosopher of ancient Greece. See: Encyc. Brit., 1973. Damon and Pythias.

Damon and Pythias (Damon and Pythias, the philosophers): Generic Word (devoted friends). See: Hendrickson; Partridge; Weekley.

DAMOUR, AUGUSTINE-ALEXIS. 1808-1902. French mineralogist. See: World Who's Who Sci. Damourite.

Damourite (Damour, Augustine-Alexis): Earth Sciences. See: Webster's 3d.

DAMPIER, WILLIAM. 1652-1715. English buccaneer and circumnavigator. See: Dict. Nat. Biog. Dampiera.

Dampiera (Dampier, William): Botany. See: Charnock.

DAN. Biblical son of Jacob. See: Webster's Biog. Dict. Danite(s).

DANA, CHARLES LOOMIS. 1852-1935. American physician. See: World Who's Who Sci. Dana's operation, Dana's syndrome.

DANA, GIOVANNI PIETRO MARIA. 1736-1801. Italian physician and naturalist. See: Biog. Lex. hervorr. Aerzte. Danaea.

DANA, JAMES DWIGHT. 1813-1895. American geologist. See: Dict. Sci. Biog. Danalite.

DANA, JAMES FREEMAN. 1793-1827. American chemist. See: Dict. Amer. Biog. Danaite.

Danaea (Dana, Giovanni Pietro Maria): Botany. See: Charnock.

Danaite (Dana, James Freeman): Earth Sciences. See: Mathews, M. M.; Thrush; Webster's 3d.

Danalite (Dana, James Dwight): Earth Sciences. See: Mathews, M. M.; Thrush; Webster's 3d.

Dana's operation (Dana, Charles Loomis): Medicine. See: Dorland; Stedman.

Dana's syndrome (Dana, Charles Loomis): Medicine. See: Jablonski. Also known as: Lichtheim's syndrome, Putnam-Dana syndrome, Putnam's disease.

DANAUS. Mythical King of Argos. See: Jobes. Danaus (butterfly).

Danaus (butterfly) (Danaus): Zoology. See: Webster's 3d.

Danbolt-Closs syndrome (Danbolt, Niels Christian and Closs, Karl). See: Brandt's syndrome.

DANBOLT, NIELS CHRISTIAN. 1900- . Swedish? physician. See: Hautarzt, Berlin, 1970, Jahrg. 21, p. 527. Danbolt-Closs syndrome.

Danbolt's syndrome (Danbolt, Niels Christian). See: Brandt's syndrome.

DANCE, JEAN BAPTISTE HIPPOLYTE. 1797-1832. French physician. See: World Who's Who Sci. Dance's sign.

Dance's sign (Dance, Jean Baptiste Hippolyte): Medicine. See: Dorland; Stedman.

Danchakoff fluid (Derivation undetermined): Chemistry. See: Van Nostrand Chem. Dict.

Dancoff corrections (Dancoff, Sidney M.): Physics. See: Internat. Dict. Ap. Math.

DANCOFF, SIDNEY M. 1913- . American physicist. See: Amer. Men Sci., 7th ed. Dancoff corrections, Tamm-Dancoff method?

DANDEKAR. fl. 1955. Statistician. (Biography source unavailable.) Dandekar's correction.

Dandekar's correction (Dandekar): Statistics. See: Kendall.

DANDELIN, GERMINAL PIERRE. 1794-1847. French-born mathematician. See: Dict. Sci. Biog. Dandelin method, Dandelin sphere.

Dandelin method (Dandelin, Germinal Pierre): Mathematics. See: Internat. Dict. Ap. Math.

Dandelin sphere (Dandelin, Germinal Pierre): Mathematics. See: James.

Dandie Dinmont (terrier) (Dinmont, Dandie): Generic Word. See: Latham; Partridge; Webster's 3d.

Dando (Dando, the hero): Generic Word. See: Brewer.

DANDO, THE HERO. Hero of popular 19th c. songs. (Biography source unavailable.) Dando.

Dandy operation (Dandy, Walter Edward): Medicine. See: Stedman.

Dandy-Walker syndrome (Dandy, Walter Edward and Walker, Arthur Earl): Medicine. See: Hinsie; Jablonski; Stedman.

DANDY, WALTER EDWARD. 1886-1946. American surgeon. See: World Who's Who Sci. Dandy operation, Dandy-Walker syndrome.

Dane test reaction for formaldehyde (Derivation undetermined): Chemistry. See: Van Nostrand Chem. Dict.

DANFORTH, CHARLES HASKELL. 1883-1969. American anatomist and geneticist. See: Dict. Sci. Biog. Danforth's shorttail.

Danforth's shorttail (Danforth, Charles Haskell): Genetics. See: Gray.

D'Angely case (D'Angely, Madame): History. See: Montgomery.

D'ANGELY, MADAME. fl. 1906. English woman who was arrested for indecent behavior. (Biography source unavailable.) D'Angely case.

DANHEISER, MELVIN B. fl. 1920. American metallurgist. Cited in: Chem. Abstr., vol. 15, p. 38. Danheiser solution.

Danheiser solution (Danheiser, Melvin B.): Chemistry. See: Van Nostrand Chem. Dict.

Daniel and Florence Guggenheim Foundation (Guggenheim, Daniel and Guggenheim, Florence Schloss): Philanthropy. Cited in: New Encyc. Brit., 1974, Microp. under "Guggenheim, Meyer and Daniel."

Daniel Boone (Boone, Daniel): Generic Word (resourceful backwoodsman). See: Hendrickson; Partridge.

DANIEL, CHARLES HENRY CLIVE. 1836-1919. English scholar and printer. See: Dict. Nat. Biog., 3d suppl. Daniel Press.

Daniel (come to judgement) (Daniel, the prophet): Generic Word (upright judge). See: Weekley.

Daniel Guggenheim Foundation for the Promotion of Aeronautics (Guggenheim, Daniel): Philanthropy. Cited in: New Encyc. Brit., 1974, Microp. under "Guggenheim, Meyer and Daniel."

Daniel in the lions' den (Daniel, the prophet): Generic Word. See: Partridge.

Daniel Press (Daniel, Charles Henry Clive): Printing. See: Harrod.

DANIEL, THE PROPHET. Hebrew prophet. See: Webster's Biog. Dict. Daniel (come to judgement), Daniel in the lions' den.

Daniell cell (Daniell, John Frederic): Physics. See: Hackh; Hughes; Thewlis.

DANIELL, JOHN FREDERIC. 1790-1845. English chemist and physicist. See: Dict. Sci. Biog. Daniell cell, Daniell (unit).

Daniell (unit) (Daniell, John Frederic): Physics. See: Dorland.

Danielson-Lindemann deflection test (Danielson, Ralph Raymond and Lindemann, Walter C.): Engineering and Industry. See: Thrush.

DANIELSON, RALPH RAYMOND. b. 1892. American ceramic engineer. See: Amer. Men Sci., 9th ed. Danielson-Lindemann deflection test.

Danielssen-Boeck disease (Danielssen, Daniel Cornelius and Boeck, Karl Wilhelm): Medicine. See: Jablonski. Also known as: Danielssen's disease.

DANIELSSEN, DANIEL CORNELIUS. 1815-1894. Norwegian physician. See: World Who's Who Sci. Danielssen-Boeck disease.

Danielssen's disease (Danielssen, Daniel Cornelius). See: Danielssen-Boeck disease.

DANILA, P. fl. 1923. French chemist. Cited in: Chem. Abstr., vol. 17, p. 2437. Danila test reaction.

Danila test reaction (Danila, P.): Chemistry. See: Van Nostrand Chem. Dict.

DANIS, P. fl. 1947. Swiss ophthalmologist. (Biography source unavailable.) Maeder-Danis dystrophy.

Danite(s) (Dan): Religion. See: Harbottle; Mathews, M. M.; Webster's 3d.

DANJON, ANDRE-LOUIS. 1890-1967. French astronomer. See: World Who's Who Sci. Danjon astrolabe (or prismatic astrolabe).

Danjon astrolabe (or prismatic astrolabe) (Danjon, Andre-Louis): Astronomy. See: Satterthwaite.

DANLOS, HENRI-ALEXANDRE. 1844-1912. French dermatologist. See: Biog. Lex. hervorr. Aerzte, 1880-1930. Ehlers-Danlos syndrome.

Danlos' syndrome (Danlos, Henri Alexandre). See: Ehlers-Danlos syndrome.

DANNER, EDWARD. d. 1952. American inventor. Cited in: Chem. Abstr., Decenn. Index, 1917-26. Danner process.

Danner process (Danner, Edward): Engineering and Industry. See: Thrush; Webster's 3d.

D'ANS, J. No dates. Professor. Cited in: Min. Mag., vol. 32, no. 255, p. 952. D'Ansite.

D'Ansite (D'Ans, J.): Earth Sciences. See: Thrush.

DANTE (ALIGHIERI). 1265-1321. Italian poet. See: Encyc. Brit., 1973. Dante chair, Dante Sonata, Dante Symphony, Dantesque (or Dantean), Dantist.

Dante chair (Dante): Applied Arts. See: Webster's 3d.

Dante Sonata (Dante): Music. See: Apel.

Dante Symphony (Dante): Music. See: Apel.

DANTEC, M. fl. 1934. French chemist. Cited in: Chem. Abstr., vol. 30, p. 3587. Dantec test reaction.

Dantec test reaction (Dantec, M.): Chemistry. See: Van Nostrand Chem. Dict.

Dantesque (or Dantean) (Dante): Literature. See: Brewer; Partridge; Webster's 3d.

DANTHOINE, ETIENNE. fl. 19th c. French botanist. Cited in: Biog. Notes Upon Botanists. Danthonia.

Danthonia (Danthoine, Etienne): Botany. See: Webster's 3d.

Dantist (Dante): Literature. See: Webster's 3d.

DANTON, GEORGES JACQUES. 1759-1794. French revolutionist. See: Encyc. Brit., 1973. Dantonesque.

Dantonesque (Danton, Georges Jacques): History. See: Webster's 3d.

DANYSZ, JEAN. 1860-1928. Polish pathologist. See: World Who's Who Sci. Danysz phenomenon (or effect).

Danysz phenomenon (or effect) (Danysz, Jean): Medicine. See: Dorland; Stedman; Webster's 3d.

Danziger test reaction (Derivation undetermined): Chemistry. See: Van Nostrand Chem. Dict.

DAPHNE. Greek mythical nymph. See: Jobes. Daphne (shrub), Daphnean, Daphnia (crustaceans).

Daphne (shrub) (Daphne): Botany. See: Charnock; Partridge.

Daphnean (Daphne): Generic Word (shy). See: Webster's 3d.

Daphnia (crustaceans) (Daphne): Zoology. See: Webster's 3d.

DARANYI, JULIUS VON. b. 1888. Hungarian bacteriologist. See: Biog. Lex. hervorr. Aerzte, 1880-1930. Daranyi's test.

Daranyi's test (Daranyi, Julius von): Medicine. See: Dorland.

Darapskite (Darapsky, Luis): Earth Sciences. See: Thrush; Webster's 3d.

DARAPSKY, LUIS. b. 1857. Chilean scientist. Cited in: Royal Soc. Cat. Sci. Pap., 1884-1900. Darapskite.

DARAZI, AL- (MUHAMMAD IBN-ISMAIL AL-DARAZI). d. 1019. Mohammedan religious leader. See: Webster's Biog. Dict. Druse(s) (or Druzes).

Darbies (Derby): Generic Word (handcuffs). See: Hendrickson.

DARBOUX, JEAN-GASTON. 1842-1917. French mathematician. See: Dict. Sci. Biog. Darboux vector, Darboux's theorem.

Darboux vector (Darboux, Jean-Gaston): Mathematics. See: Internat. Dict. Ap. Math.

Darboux's theorem (Darboux, Jean-Gaston): Mathematics. See: James.

Darby and Joan (Darby, John and Darby, Joan): Generic Word (contented old married couple). See: Brewer; Hendrickson; Latham.

DARBY, JOAN. fl. 18th c. Wife of English printer, John Darby. Cited in: Benet. Darby and Joan.

DARBY, JOHN. d. 1730. English printer. See: Benet. Darby and Joan.

DARBY, JOHN NELSON. 1800-1882. English theologist. See: Dict. Nat. Biog. Darbyite(s) (or Darbyism).

Darby process (Derivation undetermined): Engineering and Industry. See: Thrush.

Darbyite(s) (or Darbyism) (Darby, John Nelson): Religion. See: Canney; Webster's 3d.

D'ARCET, JEAN. 1725-1801. French chemist. See: Dict. Sci. Biog. d'Arcet('s) metal.

d'Arcet('s) metal (d'Arcet, Jean): Chemistry. See: Hackh; Partridge; Stedman. Also known as: Mellotte's (Mellot's) metal, Newton's alloy.

DARCY, HENRI-PHILIBERT-GASPARD. 1803-1858. French railroad engineer. See: World Who's Who Sci. Darcy (unit), Darcy's law.

Darcy (unit) (Darcy, Henri-Philibert-Gaspard): Physics. See: Internat. Dict. Ap. Math.; Internat. Dict. Phys. Elec.; Thrush.

Darcy's law (Darcy, Henri-Philibert-Gaspard): Physics. See: Huschke; Internat. Dict. Ap. Math.; Monkhouse.

Dardanian (Dardanus): Generic Word (Trojan). See: Webster's 3d.

DARDANUS. Legendary ancestor of the Trojans. See: Encyc. Brit., 1973. Dardanian.

DARDELET, HUGHES LOUIS. fl. 1924. French engineer. (Biography source unavailable.) Dardelet screw thread.

Dardelet screw thread (Dardelet, Hughes Louis): Engineering and Industry. See: Auger.

DARDIN, AMY. fl. 1796-1815. American widow. (Biography source unavailable.) Amy's case.

d'Arezzo, Guido. See: Guido (of Arezzo).

d'Arezzo, Guittone. See: Guittone d'Arezzo.

daric (coin) (Darius I): Numismatics. See: Brewer; Charnock; Partridge.

Darier-Ferrand dermatofibrosarcoma (or dermatofibroma) (Darier, Jean Ferdinand and Ferrand, Marcel): Medicine. See: Jablonski.

DARIER, JEAN FERDINAND. 1856-1938. French dermatologist. See: World Who's Who Sci. Darier-Ferrand dermatofibrosarcoma (or dermatofibroma), Darier-Roussy sarcoid, Darier's disease (1), Darier's disease (2), Darier's disease (3), Darier's syndrome.

Darier-Roussy sarcoid (Darier, Jean Ferdinand and Roussy, Gustave): Medicine. See: Jablonski.

Darier's disease (1) (Darier, Jean Ferdinand): Medicine. See: Jablonski.

Darier's disease (2) (Darier, Jean Ferdinand): Medicine. See: Jablonski.

Darier's disease (3) (Darier, Jean Ferdinand). See: Hailey-Hailey disease.

Darier's syndrome (Darier, Jean Ferdinand): Medicine. See: Jablonski. Also known as: White's disease.

DARIUS I. 550-486 B.C. Persian king. See: Encyc. Brit., 1973. Daric (coin).

Darkschewitsch's fibers (Darkshevich, Liveri O.): Medicine. See: Dorland.

Darkschewitsch's (Darkshevitch's) nucleus (Darkshevich, Liveri O.): Medicine. See: Dorland; Stedman.

DARKSHEVICH, LIVERI O. 1858-1925. Russian neurologist. See: World Who's Who Sci. Darkschewitsch's fibers, Darkschewitsch's (Darkshevitch's) nucleus.

DARLEY, FREDERIC LOUDON. 1918- . Venezuelan-born American speech pathologist. See: Amer. Men and Women Sci., 12th ed. Temple-Darley test.

DARLING, DONALD ALLAN. 1915- . American statistician. See: Amer. Men Sci., 11th ed. Anderson-Darling statistic.

DARLING, SAMUEL TAYLOR. 1872-1925. American pathologist. See: World Who's Who Sci. Darling's disease.

DARLING, WENDY. Character from Sir James Barrie's play, "Peter Pan," (1905). See: Benet. Wendy house.

Darlingite (Derivation undetermined): Earth Sciences. See: Thrush.

Darling's disease (Darling, Samuel Taylor): Medicine. See: Dorland; Jablonski; Stedman.

Darlington amplifier (or pair) (Derivation undetermined): Physics. See: Markus; Van Nostrand Sci. Encyc.

DARLINGTON, HARRY J. fl. 1925. American mechanical engineer. Cited in: Chem. Abstr., vol. 25, p. 3610. C & D hot top.

Darlington oak (Darlington, William): Botany. See: Mathews, M. M.

DARLINGTON, WILLIAM. 1782-1863. American botanist. See: Dict. Sci. Biog. Darlington oak, Darlingtonia.

Darlingtonia (Darlington, William): Botany. See: Hendrickson; Taylor, N.; Webster's 3d.

DARMESTETER, ARSENE. 1846-1888. French philologist. See: Encyc. Brit., 1973. Darmesteter's law.

Darmesteter's law (Darmesteter, Arsene): Linguistics. See: Hartmann; Winick.

DARMOIS, GEORGES. 1888-1960. French physicist. See: World Who's Who Sci. Darmois-Koopman's distributions, Darmois-Skitovich theorem.

Darmois-Koopman's distributions (Darmois, Georges and Koopmans, Tjalling Charles): Statistics. See: Kendall.

Darmois-Skitovich theorem (Darmois, Georges and Skitovich, V. P.): Statistics. See: Kendall.

DARNELL, SIR THOMAS. d. 1640? English patriot. See: Dict. Nat. Biog. Darnel's case.

Darnel's case (Darnell, Sir Thomas): History. See: Steinberg.

DARROW, DANIEL CADY. 1895- . American pediatrician. See: Who's Who Among Physicians and Surg. Darrow's solution.

Darrow's solution (Darrow, Daniel Cady): Medicine. See: Dorland.

d'Arsonval current (d'Arsonval, Jacques Arsene): Physics. See: Stedman; Webster's 3d.

d'Arsonval galvanometer (d'Arsonval, Jacques Arsene): Physics. See: Hughes; Internat. Dict. Phys. Elec.; Van Nostrand Chem. Dict.

D'ARSONVAL, JACQUES ARSENE. 1851-1940. French physicist. See: World Who's Who Sci. d'Arsonval current, d'Arsonval galvanometer, d'Arsonval movement, Darsonvalization.

d'Arsonval movement (d'Arsonval, Jacques Arsene): Physics. See: Markus.

Darsonvalization (d'Arsonval, Jacques Arsene): Medicine. See: Stedman.

D'Arusmont, Mme. Frances. See: Wright, Frances.

Darwin barberry (Darwin, Charles Robert): Botany. See: Webster's 3d.; Winburne.

DARWIN, CHARLES GALTON. 1887-1962. English physicist. See: Dict. Sci. Biog. Darwin curve, Darwin-Fowler method.

DARWIN, CHARLES ROBERT. 1809-1882. English naturalist. See: Dict. Sci. Biog. Darwin barberry, Darwin potato, Darwin tulip?, Darwin (unit), Darwinian curvature, Darwinian ear, Darwinian inheritance, Darwinian reflex, Darwinism (or Darwinian theory), Darwinite, Darwin's finches, Darwin's frog, Darwin's point (or tubercle), Darwin's sheep?, Knight-Darwin law.

Darwin curve (Darwin, Charles Galton): Physics. See: Thewlis.

DARWIN, ERASMUS. 1731-1802. English physiologist and poet. See: Dict. Sci. Biog. Darwinia.

Darwin-Fowler method (Darwin, Charles Galton and Fowler, Sir Ralph Howard): Physics. Cited in: Dict. Sci. Biog. under "Darwin, Charles Galton."

DARWIN, GEORGE HOWARD. 1845-1912. English mathematician and astronomer. See: Dict. Sci. Biog. George Darwin Lecture.

Darwin potato (Darwin, Charles Robert): Botany. See: Gray.

Darwin tulip (Darwin, Charles Robert?): Botany. See: Webster's 3d.; Winburne.

Darwin (unit) (Darwin, Charles Robert): Biology. See: Dresner.

Darwinia (Darwin, Erasmus): Botany. See: Charnock.

Darwinian curvature (Darwin, Charles Robert): Biology. See: Gray.

Darwinian ear (Darwin, Charles Robert): Medicine. See: Stedman.

Darwinian inheritance (Darwin, Charles Robert): Anthropology. See: Winick.

Darwinian reflex (Darwin, Charles Robert): Medicine. See: English; Stedman.

Darwinism (or Darwinian theory) (Darwin, Charles Robert): Biology. See: Gray; Pennak; Wolman.

Darwinite (Darwin, Charles Robert): Earth Sciences. See: Thrush.

Darwin's finches (Darwin, Charles Robert): Zoology. See: Blumberg; Pennak.

Darwin's frog (Darwin, Charles Robert): Zoology. See: Webster's 3d.

Darwin's point (or tubercle) (Darwin, Charles Robert): Zoology. See: Pennak; Webster's 3d.; Winick.

Darwin's sheep (Darwin, Charles Robert?): Zoology. See: Webster's 3d.

Darzens condensation (Darzens, Georges Auguste): Chemistry. See: Van Nostrand Chem. Dict.

DARZENS, GEORGES AUGUSTE. 1867-1954. French chemist. See: Pogg., vol. 5, 6, 7b. Darzen's glycidic ester condensation, Darzens condensation, Darzen's procedure, Darzens synthesis of tetralin derivatives, Darzens synthesis of unsaturated ketones.

Darzen's glycidic ester condensation (Darzens, Georges Auguste): Chemistry. See: Ballentyne.

Darzen's procedure (Darzens, Georges Auguste): Chemistry. See: Ballentyne.

Darzens synthesis of tetralin derivatives (Darzens, Georges Auguste): Chemistry. See: Van Nostrand Chem. Dict.

Darzens synthesis of unsaturated ketones (Darzens, Georges Auguste): Chemistry. See: Van Nostrand Chem. Dict.

DASEY. No dates. Irish physician. (Biography source unavailable.) Dasey (cloak).

Dasey (cloak) (Dasey): Fashion. See: Charnock.

Da Silva, Ferreira. See: Silva, Ferreira da.

DASTRE, ALBERT-JULES-FRANCK. 1844-1917. French physiologist. See: World Who's Who Sci. Dastre-Morat law.

Dastre-Morat law (Dastre, Albert-Jules-Franck and Morat, Jean-Pierre): Medicine. See: Dorland; Stedman.

DAUBENTON, LOUIS JEAN MARIE. 1716-1800. French physician and naturalist. See: World Who's Who Sci. Daubentonia, Daubenton's angle, Daubenton's line, Daubenton's plane.

Daubentonia (Daubenton, Louis Jean Marie): Botany. See: Charnock; Taylor, N.; Webster's 3d.

Daubenton's angle (Daubenton, Louis Jean Marie): Medicine. See: Dorland; Stedman.

Daubenton's line (Daubenton, Louis Jean Marie): Medicine. See: Dorland; Stedman.

Daubenton's plane (Daubenton, Louis Jean Marie): Anthropology. See: Dorland; Webster's 3d.

DAUBER, HERRMANN. b. 1823. German mineralogist. See: Pogg., vol. 1. Dauberite.

Dauberite (Dauber, Herrmann): Earth Sciences. See: Thrush.

D'Aubigne, Francoise. See: Maintenon, Francoise D'Aubigne, Marquise de.

DAUBLEBSKY VON STERNECK, ROBERT. 1839-1910. Czechoslovakian geodesist. See: World Who's Who Sci. Von Sterneck-Askania pendulum.

DAUBREE, GABRIEL-AUGUSTE. 1814-1896. French geologist and mineralogist. See: Dict. Sci. Biog. Daubreeite (or Daubreite), Daubreelite.

Daubreeite (or Daubreite) (Daubree, Gabriel-Auguste): Earth Sciences. See: Webster's 3d.

Daubreelite (Daubree, Gabriel-Auguste): Earth Sciences. See: Webster's 3d.

Dauphine twin (or law) (Derivation undetermined): Physics. See: Ballentyne; Thewlis; Thrush.

DAUSSE, MARIE-FRANCOIS BENJAMIN. 1801-1890. French engineer. See: World Who's Who Sci. Dausse's law.

Dausse's law (Dausse, Marie-Francois Benjamin): Engineering and Industry. Cited in: World Who's Who Sci.

DAUTRICHE, H. fl. 1907. French chemist. Cited in: Chem. Abstr., vol. 1, p. 357. Dautriche test.

Dautriche test (Dautriche, H.): Engineering and Industry. See: Thrush; Van Nostrand Chem. Dict.

DAUVE, M. fl. 1909. French chemist. Cited in: Chem. Abstr., vol. 3, p. 2274. Dauve test reaction.

Dauve test reaction (Dauve, M.): Chemistry. See: Van Nostrand Chem. Dict.

DAVAINE, CASIMIR JOSEPH. 1812-1882. French physician. See: Dict. Sci. Biog. Davainea (tapeworms), Davaine's bacillus.

Davainea (tapeworms) (Davaine, Casimir Joseph): Zoology. See: Dorland; Pennak; Webster's 3d.

Davaine's bacillus (Davaine, Casimir Joseph): Zoology. See: Stedman.

DAVALL, EDMUND. 1763-1798. English botanist in Switzerland. See: Dict. Nat. Biog. Davallia (ferns).

Davallia (ferns) (Davall, Edmund): Botany. See: Taylor, N.; Webster's 3d.

DAVANNE, LOUIS-ALPHONSE. 1824-1912. French chemist and photographer. See: World Who's Who Sci. Davanne Medal.

Davanne Medal (Davanne, Louis-Alphonse): Photography. See: Focal Encyc. Photog.

DAVENPORT. fl. 19th c. English furniture-maker. (Biography source unavailable.) Davenport (writing-desk or sofa).

DAVENPORT, IRA ERASTUS. 1839-1911. American spiritualistic medium. See: Dict. Amer. Biog. Davenport-trick.

Davenport-trick (Davenport, Ira Erastus and Davenport, William Henry Harrison): Generic Word. See: Brewer.

DAVENPORT, WILLIAM HENRY HARRISON. 1841-1877. American spiritualistic medium. See: Webster's Biog. Dict. Davenport-trick.

Davenport (writing-desk or sofa) (Davenport): Applied Arts. See: Charnock; Hendrickson; Partridge.

DAVEY, HENRY. 1843-1928. English inventor. See: World Who's Who Sci. Davey's differential.

Davey's differential (Davey, Henry): Engineering and Industry. See: Auger.

David and Goliath (David, the king and Goliath, the giant): Generic Word. See: Partridge.

David and Jonathan (David, the king and Jonathan): Generic Word (close friends). See: Partridge.

DAVID, ARMAND. 1826-1900. French naturalist. See: World Who's Who Sci. Davidia, David's squirrel, Pere David's deer.

DAVID, FERENC (FRANCISCUS DAVIDIS). 1510-1579. Transylvanian theologist. See: New Encyc. Brit., 1973, Microp. Davidist.

DAVID, JACQUES LOUIS. 1748-1825. French painter. See: Encyc. Brit., 1973. Davidian.

DAVID, JEAN PIERRE. 1738-1784. French surgeon. See: World Who's Who Sci. David's disease.

DAVID, LUDWIG. fl. 1925. German chemist. Cited in: Chem. Abstr., vol. 19, p. 2999. David reagent for opium alkaloids, David test for alcohol in essential oils, David tests for barbital and phenobarbital.

David Octavius Hill Medal (Hill, David Octavius): Photography. See: Focal Encyc. Photog.

DAVID OF DINANT. fl. 1200. Belgian scholastic philosopher. See: Webster's Biog. Dict. Davidist(s).

David reagent for opium alkaloids (David, Ludwig): Chemistry. See: Van Nostrand Chem. Dict.

DAVID, SAINT. 490-554. Archibishop and patron saint of Wales. See: Dict. Nat. Biog. St. David's Day.

David Sarnoff Medal (Sarnoff, David): Photography. See: Focal Encyc. Photog. under "Awards (America)."

DAVID, TANNATT WILLIAM EDGEWORTH. 1858-1934. Australian geologist. See: Dict. Sci. Biog. Davidite.

David test for alcohol in essential oils (David, Ludwig): Chemistry. See: Van Nostrand Chem. Dict.

David tests for barbital and phenobarbital (David, Ludwig): Chemistry. See: Van Nostrand Chem. Dict.

DAVID, THE KING. d. ca. 973 B.C. King of Judah and Israel. See: Encyc. Brit., 1973. David and Goliath, David and Jonathan, Davidic, David's harp, magen (or mogen) David.

DAVID, WALTER. b. 1890. German physician. Cited in: Kelly. David's disease.

Davidia (David, Armand): Botany. See: Taylor, N.

Davidian (David, Jacques Louis): Fine Arts. See: Webster's 3d.

Davidic (David, the king): History. See: Webster's 3d.

Davidist (David, Ferenc): Religion. See: Webster's 3d.

Davidist(s) (David of Dinant): Religion. See: Canney; Webster's 3d.

Davidists (or Davidians) (Joris (Joriszoon), David). See: Jorists.

Davidite (David, Tannatt William Edgeworth): Earth Sciences. See: Thrush.

DAVIDOFF, M. VON. d. 1904. German histologist. Cited in: Royal Soc. Cat. Sci. Pap., 1874-1883; 1884-1900. Davidoff's cells.

Davidoff's cells (Davidoff, M. von): Medicine. See: Dorland; Stedman. Also known as: Paneth('s) cells (or granular cells).

David's disease (David, Jean Pierre). See: Pott's disease.

David's disease (David, Walter): Medicine. See: Dorland; Jablonski.

David's harp (David, the king): Botany. See: Webster's 3d.

David's squirrel (David, Armand): Zoology. See: Webster's 3d.

DAVIDSOHN, HERMANN. 1842-1911. German physician. See: Biog. Lex. hervorr. Aerzte, 1880-1930. Davidsohn's sign.

Davidsohn's sign (Davidsohn, Hermann): Medicine. See: Dorland; Stedman.

Davidson current (Davidson, George): Earth Sciences. See: Huschke.

DAVIDSON, EDWARD CLARK. 1894-1933. American surgeon. See: Wayne County Med. Soc. Bull., vol. 24, no. 52 (Aug. 22, 1933) p. 7. Davidson's syringe.

DAVIDSON, GEORGE. 1825-1911. English-born American geodesist and astronomer. See: Dict. Amer. Biog. Davidson current.

DAVIDSON, SIR LEYBOURNE STANLEY PATRICK. 1894- . Scottish physician. See: Who's Who, 1972-73. Davidson's anemia.

DAVIDSON, THOMAS. 1817-1885. English paleontologist. See: World Who's Who Sci. Davidsonite.

Davidsonite (Davidson, Thomas): Earth Sciences. See: Thrush; Webster's 3d.

Davidson's anemia (Davidson, Sir Leybourne Stanley Patrick): Medicine. See: Jablonski. Also known as: Bomford-Rhoads anemia.

Davidson's syringe (Davidson, Edward Clark): Medicine. See: Stedman.

DAVIEL, JACQUES. 1696-1762. French ophthalmologist. See: World Who's Who Sci. Daviel's operation, Daviel's spoon.

Daviel's operation (Daviel, Jacques): Medicine. See: Dorland; Stedman.

Daviel's spoon (Daviel, Jacques): Medicine. See: Dorland; Stedman.

DAVIES-COLLEY, ROBERT. d. 1955. English surgeon. See: Who Was Who, 1951-60. Davies-Colley's syndrome.

Davies-Colley's syndrome (Davies-Colley, Robert). See: Cyriax's syndrome.

Davies' disease (Davies, Jack Neville Phillips): Medicine. See: Jablonski.

Davies engine (Derivation undetermined): Engineering and Industry. See: Auger. Also known as: Bishopp engine.

DAVIES, HUGH. 1739-1821. English botanist. See: Dict. Nat. Biog. Daviesia.

DAVIES, JACK NEVILLE PHILLIPS. 1915- . English-born pathologist. See: World Who's Who Sci. Davies' disease.

DAVIES, THOMAS. 1837-1891. English mineralogist. See: Dict. Nat. Biog., 1st suppl. Daviesite.

Daviesia (Davies, Hugh): Botany. See: Webster's 3d.

Daviesite (Davies, Thomas): Earth Sciences. See: Partridge; Thrush; Webster's 3d.

DAVILA, CARLOS GUILLERMO. 1887- . Chilean newspaper editor and politician. See: Barnhart (Cycl. Names). Davila Plan.

Davila Plan (Davila, Carlos Guillermo): Economics. Cited in: Barnhart (Cycl. Names).

Davilla (Davilla, H. C.): Botany. See: Charnock.

DAVILLA, H. C. No dates. Italian historian. (Biography source unavailable.) Davilla.

Davina (or Davyne) (Davy, Humphry): Earth Sciences. See: Charnock; Thrush.

Da Vinci, Leonardo. See: Leonardo da Vinci.

DAVIS, ALLISON. 1902- . American psychologist and anthropologist. See: Shockley. Davis-Eells games.

Davis bit (or cutter bit) (Derivation undetermined): Engineering and Industry. See: Thrush.

Davis calyx drill (Derivation undetermined): Engineering and Industry. See: Thrush.

Davis concentrator (Davis, Joseph Dana): Chemistry. See: Van Nostrand Chem. Dict.

Davis-Crowe mouth gag (Derivation undetermined): Medicine. See: Stedman.

Davis Cup (Davis, Dwight Filley): Recreation and Sports. See: Hendrickson; Mathews, M. M.

DAVIS, DWIGHT FILLEY. 1879-1945. American statesman and sportsman. See: Who Was Who Amer., 1943-50. Davis Cup.

DAVIS, EDWARD WILSON. 1888- . American metallurgical engineer. See: World Who's Who Sci. Davis magnetic tester.

Davis-Eells games (Davis, Allison and Eells, Kenneth Walter): Psychology. See: English.

Davis furnace (Derivation undetermined): Engineering and Industry. See: Thrush.

Davis-Gibson colour filter (Davis, Raymond and Gibson, Kasson Stanford): Physics. See: Thewlis.

Davis grafts (Davis, John Staige): Medicine. See: Dorland; Stedman.

DAVIS, H. T. No dates. Engineer. (Biography source unavailable.) Davis steering gear.

DAVIS, HENRY WINTER. 1817-1865. American lawyer and political leader. See: Dict. Amer. Biog. Wade-Davis Bill, Wade-Davis Manifesto.

DAVIS, JAMES JOHN. 1873-1947. American legislator. See: Biog. Direct. Amer. Congress. Bacon-Davis Act.

DAVIS, JEFFERSON. 1808-1889. President of the American Confederacy. See: Dict. Amer. Biog. Davisdom (or Jeffdom), Jeff Davis-box(es), Jeff Davis coffee, Jeff Davis Grays, Jeff Davis money, Jefferson Davis's Birthday, Jeffite.

DAVIS, JOHN. 1550?-1605. English navigator. See: Encyc. Brit., 1973. Davis quadrant.

DAVIS, JOHN STAIGE. 1872-1946. American surgeon. See: World Who's Who Sci. Davis grafts.

DAVIS, JOSEPH DANA. b. 1882. American chemist. See: Who's Who Engin., 1925. Davis concentrator.

Davis magnetic tester (Davis, Edward Wilson): Engineering and Industry. See: Thrush.

DAVIS, NELSON L. fl. 1950. American engineer. Cited in: Chem. Abstr., vol. 44, p. 9660. Nelson Davis separator.

Davis oscillating press (Derivation undetermined): Printing. See: Lockwood.

Davis quadrant (Davis, John): Navigation. Cited in: Encyc. Brit., 1973, under "Davis, John."

DAVIS, RAYMOND. b. 1888. American physicist. See: Amer. Men Sci., 9th ed. Davis-Gibson colour filter.

DAVIS, SIR ROBERT HENRY. 1870-1965. English inventor. See: World Who's Who Sci. Davis submersion decompression chamber.

Davis steering gear (Davis, H. T.): Engineering and Industry. See: Auger.

Davis submersion decompression chamber (Davis, Sir Robert Henry): Engineering and Industry. Cited in: World Who's Who Sci.

DAVIS, TOBE COLLER. d. 1962. American merchandiser and fashion consultant. See: Who Was Who Amer., 1961-1968. Tobe formula, Tobe-wise store.

Davis wheel (Derivation undetermined): Engineering and Industry. See: Thrush.

DAVIS, WILLIAM MORRIS. 1850-1934. American geologist and meteorologist. See: Dict. Sci. Biog. Davisian system (of landscape analysis).

Davisdom (or Jeffdom) (Davis, Jefferson): Generic Word (Confederate states). See: Mathews, M. M.

Davisian system (of landscape analysis) (Davis, William Morris): Earth Sciences. Cited in: Dict. Sci. Biog.

DAVISON, JOHN M. d. 1915. American chemist and mineralogist. Cited in: Royal Soc. Cat. Sci. Pap., 1884-1900. Davisonite.

Davisonite (Davison, John M.): Earth Sciences. See: Thrush; Webster's 3d.

Davisson-Calbick formula (Davisson, Clinton Joseph and Calbick, Chester Joseph): Physics. See: Thewlis.

Davisson chart (Davisson, Clinton Joseph): Physics. See: Hughes; Internat. Dict. Ap. Math.; Internat. Dict. Phys. Elec.

DAVISSON, CLINTON JOSEPH. 1881-1958. American physicist. See: Dict. Sci. Biog. Davisson-Calbick formula, Davisson chart, Davisson-Germer experiment.

Davisson-Germer experiment (Davisson, Clinton Joseph and Germer, Lester Halbert): Physics. See: Hughes; Internat. Dict. Phys. Elec.; Van Nostrand Sci. Encyc.

Davite (Davy, Humphry): Earth Sciences. See: Hendrickson; Partridge.

DAVREUX, CHARLES JOSEPH. 1806-1863. Belgian chemist and mineralogist. See: Pogg., vol. 1, 3. Davreuxite.

Davreuxite (Davreux, Charles Joseph): Earth Sciences. See: Thrush.

Davy Crockett costume (Crockett, David): Fashion. See: Picken.

Davy Crockett (mobile launcher) (Crockett, David): Weapons. See: Quick.

DAVY, EDMUND WILLIAM. 1826-1899. Irish physician. See: Pogg., vol. 3, 4. Davy('s) test (or reagent).

DAVY, EDWARD. 1806-1885. English physician. See: World Who's Who Sci. Davy's diamond cement.

Davy experiment (Davy, Humphry): Chemistry. See: Internat. Dict. Phys. Elec.; Van Nostrand Sci. Encyc.

DAVY, HUMPHRY. 1778-1829. English chemist. See: Dict. Sci. Biog. Davina (or Davyne), Davite, Davy experiment, Davy lamp (or safety lamp), Davy Medal, Davy's gray.

Davy Jones (Jonah): Generic Word (spirit of the sea). See: Charnock; Barnhart (Eng. Lit.); Brewer; Latham; Weekley.

Davy Jones' locker (Jonah): Generic Word (grave in the sea). See: Hendrickson; Partridge; Phyfe; Wagner (More Names); Webster's 3d.

Davy lamp (or safety lamp) (Davy, Humphry): Engineering and Industry. See: Phyfe; Thewlis; Thrush.

Davy Medal (Davy, Humphry): Chemistry. See: Hendrickson.

Davy('s) test (or reagent) (Davy, Edmund William): Chemistry. See: Dorland; Stedman; Van Nostrand Chem. Dict.

DAVYDOV, ALEKSANDR SERGEEVICH. 1912- . Russian physicist. See: World Who's Who Sci. Davydov splitting.

Davydov splitting (Davydov, Aleksandr Sergeevich): Physics. See: Van Nostrand Sci. Encyc.

Davy's diamond cement (Davy, Edward): Engineering and Industry. Cited in: World Who's Who Sci.

Davy's gray (Davy, Humphry): Chemistry. See: Webster's 3d.

DAWBARN, ROBERT HUGH MACKAY. 1860-1915. American surgeon. See: Biog. Lex. hervorr. Aerzte, 1880-1930. Dawbarn's sign.

Dawbarn's sign (Dawbarn, Robert Hugh Mackay): Medicine. See: Dorland; Stedman.

Dawes Act (or Severalty Act) (Dawes, Henry Laurens): History. See: Jameson; Morris; Smith, under "Indian."

DAWES, CHARLES GATES. 1865-1951. American lawyer, financier, and politician. See: Encyc. Brit., 1973. Dawes plan.

DAWES, HENRY LAURENS. 1816-1903. American legislator. See: Dict. Amer. Biog. Dawes Act (or Severalty Act).

Dawes' limit (Dawes, William Rutter): Astronomy. See: Webster's 3d.

Dawes plan (Dawes, Charles Gates): History. See: Harvey; Jameson; Smith.

DAWES, WILLIAM RUTTER. 1799-1868. English astronomer. See: Dict. Sci. Biog. Dawes' limit.

DAWKINS, SIR CLINTON EDWARD. 1859-1905. English statesman. See: Who Was Who, 1897-1916. Clinton Dawkins committee.

DAWSON, CHARLES. 1864-1916. English paleontologist. See: Dict. Sci. Biog. eoanthropus Dawsoni.

DAWSON, JAMES ROBERTSON. 1908- . American pathologist. See: Amer. Men Sci., 10th ed. Dawson's encephalitis.

DAWSON, SIR JOHN WILLIAM. 1820-1899. Canadian geologist. See: Dict. Sci. Biog. Dawsonite.

DAWSON, JOSEPH E. fl. 1906. English inventor. Cited in: Chem. Abstr., vol. 2, p. 202. Dawson producer.

Dawson producer (Dawson, Joseph E.): Engineering and Industry. See: Thrush.

Dawsonia (Turner, Dawson): Botany. See: Webster's 3d.

Dawsonite (Dawson, Sir John William): Earth Sciences. See: Thrush; Webster's 3d.

Dawson's encephalitis (Dawson, James Robertson). See: Van Bogaert's encephalitis.

DAY, BENJAMIN. 1838-1916. American printer. See: Webster's Biog. Dict. Ben Day (process) (or Ben Dayed).

DAY, DORIS. 1924- . American singer and actress. See: Who's Who Amer., 1974-75. Doris Day.

Day engine (Day, J.): Engineering and Industry. See: Auger.

DAY, J. fl. 1891. English? engineer. (Biography source unavailable.) Day engine.

Day modulation (Derivation undetermined): Electronics. See: Hughes.

DAY, RICHARD HANCE. 1813-1892. American physician. (Biography source unavailable.) Day's test.

DAY, RICHARD LAWRENCE. 1905- . American pediatrician. See: Amer. Men Sci., 10th ed. Riley-Day syndrome.

Day's test (Day, Richard Hance): Medicine. See: Dorland; Stedman.

de-Stalinization (Stalin, Joseph): Politics. See: Hendrickson.

DEACON, HENRY. 1822-1876. English industrial chemist. See: World Who's Who Sci. Deacon('s) process.

Deacon('s) process (Deacon, Henry): Chemistry. See: Ballentyne; Hackh; Van Nostrand Chem. Dict.

Deacon test reaction for amygdalin (Derivation undetermined): Chemistry. See: Van Nostrand Chem. Dict.

De Acosta, Jose. See: Acosta, Jose de.

Deadwood Dick (Deadwood Dick, the Indian fighter): Generic Word (fearless Indian scout). See: Hendrickson; Partridge.

DEADWOOD DICK, THE INDIAN FIGHTER (CLARKE, RICHARD W.). 1845-1930. English-born American frontiersman. See: Barnhart (Cycl. Names). Deadwood Dick.

DEAGAN, JOHN CALHOUN. 1853-1936. American inventor. (Biography source unavailable.) Deagan nabimba, Deagan steel marimba, Deagan Swiss staff bells, Deagan wooden marimbaphone, Deaganometer.

Deagan nabimba (Deagan, John Calhoun): Music. See: Scholes.

Deagan steel marimba (Deagan, John Calhoun): Music. See: Scholes.

Deagan Swiss staff bells (Deagan, John Calhoun): Music. See: Scholes.

Deagan wooden marimbaphone (Deagan, John Calhoun): Music. See: Scholes.

Deaganometer (Deagan, John Calhoun): Music. See: Scholes.

De Almeida, Floriano Paulo. See: Almeida, Floriano Paulo de.

De Almeida's disease (Almeida, Floriano Paulo de). See: Lutz-Splendore-De Almeida syndrome.

DEAM, CHARLES CLEMON. b. 1865. American botanist. See: Amer. Men Sci., 5th ed. Deamia.

Deamia (Deam, Charles Clemon): Botany. See: Taylor, N.

DEAN, ALBERT FLANDREAU. 1842-1933. American actuary. Cited in: Mansell. Dean schedule.

Dean schedule (Dean, Albert Flandreau): Mathematics. See: Webster's 3d.

De Andrada e Silva, Jose Bonifacio. See: Andrada e Silva, Jose Bonifacio de.

Dearborn (carriage) (Dearborn, Henry): Engineering and Industry. See: Clapin; Mathews, M. M.; Partridge.

DEARBORN, HENRY. 1751-1829. American general and statesman. See: Amer. Biog. Dearborn (carriage).

DEASY, RICHARD. 1812-1883. Irish judge. See: Dict. Nat. Biog. Deasy's Act.

Deasy's Act (Deasy, Richard): History. See: Montgomery.

DEAVER, JOHN BLAIR. 1855-1931. American surgeon. See: World Who's Who Sci. Deaver's incision.

Deaver's incision (Deaver, John Blair): Medicine. See: Dorland.

De Azara, Felix. See: Azara, Felix de.

DE AZUA Y SUAREZ, JUAN. 1859-1922. Spanish dermatologist. See: Mansch. De Azua's pseudoepithelioma.

De Azua's pseudoepithelioma (De Azua y Suarez, Juan): Medicine. See: Jablonski. Also known as: Azua's pseudoepithelioma.

DE BAKEY, MICHAEL ELLIS. 1908- . American surgeon. See: World Who's Who Sci. De Bakey roller pump.

De Bakey roller pump (De Bakey, Michael Ellis): Medicine. See: Van Nostrand Sci. Encyc. under "Artificial Organs."

De Bavay process (Derivation undetermined): Engineering and Industry. See: Thrush.

De Beaumont, Elie. See: Beaumont, Elie de.

DEBEAUNE, FLORIMOND. 1601-1652. French mathematician. See: Dict. Sci. Biog. Beaune's problem.

DE BEURMANN, CHARLES LUCIEN. 1851-1923. French dermatologist. See: World Who's Who Sci. Beurmann-Gougerot disease, Beurmann's disease.

De Blainville, Henri Marie Ducrotay. See: Blainville, Henri Marie Ducrotay.

Deblanchol rotary furnace (Derivation undetermined): Engineering and Industry. See: Thrush.

DEBLER, KARL. 1909- . German? physician. (Biography source unavailable.) Debler's syndrome.

Debler's syndrome (Debler, Karl): Medicine. See: Jablonski.

DE BOER, JAN HENDRIK. 1899- . Dutch chemist. See: World Who's Who Sci. Van Arkel and De Boer process.

De Boer test reactions (Derivation undetermined): Chemistry. See: Van Nostrand Chem. Dict.

De Boisbaudran, Paul Emile Lecoq. See: Boisbaudran, Paul Emile Lecoq de.

De Borda, Jean Charles. See: Borda, Jean Charles de.

De Bordeu, Theophile. See: Bordeu, Theophile de.

De Bordeu theory (Bordeu, Theophile de): Medicine. See: Stedman. Also known as: Bordeu theory.

De Bougainville, Louis Antoine. See: Bougainville, Louis Antoine de.

DEBOUT, EMILE. 1811-1865. French physician. See: Biog. Lex. hervorr. Aerzte. Debout's pills.

Debout's pills (Debout, Emile): Medicine. See: Dorland.

DEBOVE, MAURICE GEORGES. 1845-1920. French physician. See: World Who's Who Sci. Debove's disease, Debove's membrane, Debove's tube.

Debove's disease (Debove, Maurice Georges): Medicine. See: Dorland; Jablonski; Stedman.

Debove's membrane (Debove, Maurice Georges): Medicine. See: Dorland; Henderson.

Debove's tube (Debove, Maurice Georges): Medicine. See: Dorland.

De Boyer, Alexis. See: Boyer, Alexis de.

DEBRAY, JULES HENRI. 1827-1888. French chemist. See: Nature, vol. 38 (1888), p. 396. Debray reagent.

Debray reagent (Debray, Jules Henri): Chemistry. See: Van Nostrand Chem. Dict.

Debre-Fibiger syndrome (Debre, Robert and Fibiger, Johannes Andreas Grib): Medicine. See: Jablonski.

Debre-Marie syndrome (1) (Debre, Robert and Marie, Julien): Medicine. See: Jablonski.

Debre-Marie syndrome (2) (Debre, Robert and Marie, Julien): Medicine. See: Jablonski.

Debre-Mollaret syndrome (Debre, Robert and Mollaret, Pierre). See: Debre's syndrome (1).

Debre phenomenon (Debre, Robert): Medicine. See: Stedman.

DEBRE, ROBERT. b. 1882. French physician. See: Who's Who France, 1961-62. Debre-Fibiger syndrome, Debre-Marie syndrome (1), Debre-Marie syndrome (2), Debre phenomenon, Debre-Semelaigne syndrome, Debre's syndrome (1), Debre's syndrome (2), Fanconi-De Toni-Debre syndrome.

Debre-Semelaigne syndrome (Debre, Robert and Semelaigne, Georges): Medicine. See: Jablonski. Also known as: Kocher-Debre-Semelaigne syndrome.

Debre's syndrome (1) (Debre, Robert): Medicine. See: Jablonski. Also known as: Debre-Mollaret syndrome, Foshay-Mollaret syndrome, Petzetakis' disease.

Debre's syndrome (2) (Debre, Robert): Medicine. See: Jablonski.

DEBRETT, JOHN. d. 1822. English publisher. See: Dict. Nat. Biog. Debrett's Peerage.

Debrett's Peerage (Debrett, John): History. See: Hendrickson; Partridge.

De Broglie atom (Broglie, Louis Victor Pierre Raymond, Duc de): Physics. See: Internat. Dict. Ap. Math.; Internat. Dict. Phys. Elec.

De Broglie (Broglie) equation (or formula) (Broglie, Louis Victor Pierre Raymond, Duc de): Physics. See: Hackh; Webster's 3d.

De Broglie, Louis Victor Pierre Raymond, Duc. See: Broglie, Louis Victor Pierre Raymond, Duc de.

De Broglie('s) theory (or hypothesis) (Broglie, Louis Victor Pierre Raymond, Duc de): Physics. See: Ballentyne; Internat. Dict. Ap. Math.; Internat. Dict. Phys. Elec.

De Broglie wavelength (Broglie, Louis Victor Pierre Raymond, Duc de): Physics. See: Hughes; Internat. Dict. Phys. Elec.; Markus.

DEBS, EUGENE VICTOR. 1855-1926. American labor leader. See: Dict. Amer. Biog. Debsism; Debsite.

Debsism (Debs, Eugene Victor): History. See: Mathews, M. M.

Debsite (Debs, Eugene Victor): History. See: Mathews, M. M.

Debye crystallogram (Debye, Peter Joseph William): Physics. See: Hackh.

Debye dipole theory (Debye, Peter Joseph William): Physics. See: Internat. Dict. Phys. Elec.

Debye effect (Debye, Peter Joseph William): Physics. See: Internat. Dict. Ap. Math.; Markus.

Debye energy (Debye, Peter Joseph William): Physics. See: Internat. Dict. Ap. Math.

Debye equation for complex permittivity (Debye, Peter Joseph William): Physics. See: Internat. Dict. Phys. Elec.

Debye equation (for heat capacity of a solid) (Debye, Peter Joseph William). See: Debye theory of specific heat.

Debye equation for polarization (or total polarization) (Debye, Peter Joseph William): Physics. See: Ballentyne; Internat. Dict. Phys. Elec.

Debye equation for the dispersion of the dielectric constant (Debye, Peter Joseph William): Physics. See: Internat. Dict. Ap. Math.

Debye equation of state (of solids) (Debye, Peter Joseph William): Physics. See: Internat. Dict. Ap. Math.; Internat. Dict. Phys. Elec.

Debye-Falkenhagen effect (Debye, Peter Joseph William and Falkenhagen, Hans): Physics. See: Internat. Dict. Phys. Elec.; Van Nostrand Chem. Dict.; Van Nostrand Sci. Encyc.

Debye frequency (Debye, Peter Joseph William): Physics. See: Internat. Dict. Ap. Math.; Internat. Dict. Phys. Elec.

Debye heat capacity equation (Debye, Peter Joseph William). See: Debye theory of specific heat.

Debye-Hueckel equation (Debye, Peter Joseph William and Hueckel, Erich Armand Arthur Joseph): Physics. See: Ballentyne; Internat. Dict. Phys. Elec.

Debye-Hueckel limiting law (Debye, Peter Joseph William and Hueckel, Erich Armand Arthur Joseph): Physics. See: Internat. Dict. Phys. Elec.; Van Nostrand Chem. Dict.; Van Nostrand Sci. Encyc.

Debye-Hueckel-Onsager equation (Debye, Peter Joseph William; Hueckel, Erich Armand Arthur Joseph; and Onsager, Lars). See: Onsager equation (or conductivity equation).

Debye-Hueckel theory (Debye, Peter Joseph William and Hueckel, Erich Armand Arthur Joseph): Physics. See: Internat. Dict. Ap. Math.; Thewlis; Webster's 3d.

Debye-Hueckel theory of conductivity (of electrolytes) (Debye, Peter Joseph William and Hueckel, Erich Armand Arthur Joseph): Physics. See: Internat. Dict. Phys. Elec.; Van Nostrand Chem. Dict.; Van Nostrand Sci. Encyc.

Debye-Jauncey scattering (Debye, Peter Joseph William and Jauncey, George Eric MacDonnell): Physics. See: Ballentyne; Thewlis.

Debye length (Debye, Peter Joseph William): Physics. See: Hughes; Markus; Thewlis.

DEBYE, PETER JOSEPH WILLIAM. 1884-1966. Dutch physicist. See: Dict. Sci. Biog. Debye crystallogram, Debye dipole theory, Debye effect, Debye energy, Debye equation for complex permittivity, Debye equation for polarization (or total polarization), Debye equation for the dispersion of the dielectric constant, Debye equation of state (of solids), Debye-Falkenhagen effect, Debye frequency, Debye-Hueckel equation, Debye-Hueckel limiting law, Debye-

Hueckel-Onsager equation, Debye-Hueckel theory, Debye-Hueckel theory of conductivity (of electrolytes), Debye-Jauncey scattering, Debye length, Debye-Scherrer-Hull method, Debye-Sears cell, Debye-Sears effect, Debye shielding distance (or length), Debye T^3 law (or approximation), Debye temperature, Debye theory (of crystal vibrations), Debye theory of specific heat, Debye (unit), Debye-Waller factor (or temperature factor), Giauque-Debye method, Langevin-Debye equation.

Debye radius (Debye, Peter Joseph William). See: Debye shielding distance (or length).

Debye-Scherrer-Hull method (Debye, Peter Joseph William; Scherrer, Paul Herman; and Hull, Albert Wallace): Physics. See: Internat. Dict. Phys. Elec.; Van Nostrand Sci. Encyc. Also known as: Debye-Scherrer method.

Debye-Scherrer method (Debye, Peter Joseph William and Scherrer, Paul Herman). See: Debye-Scherrer-Hull method.

Debye-Sears cell (Debye, Peter Joseph William and Sears, Francis Weston): Physics. See: Internat. Dict. Phys. Elec.

Debye-Sears effect (Debye, Peter Joseph William and Sears, Francis Weston): Physics. See: Ballentyne; Internat. Dict. Phys. Elec.; Van Nostrand Sci. Encyc.

Debye shielding distance (or length) (Debye, Peter Joseph William): Physics. See: Internat. Dict. Phys. Elec. Also known as: Debye radius.

Debye T^3 law (or approximation) (Debye, Peter Joseph William): Physics. See: Ballentyne; Internat. Dict. Ap. Math.; Internat. Dict. Phys. Elec.

Debye temperature (Debye, Peter Joseph William): Physics. See: Internat. Dict. Ap. Math.; Thewlis; Van Nostrand Sci. Encyc.

Debye theory (of crystal vibrations) (Debye, Peter Joseph William): Physics. See: Internat. Dict. Ap. Math.; Webster's 3d.

Debye theory of specific heat (Debye, Peter Joseph William): Physics. See: Internat. Dict. Phys. Elec.; Thewlis; Van Nostrand Sci. Encyc. Also known as: Debye equation (for heat capacity of a solid), Debye heat capacity equation.

Debye (unit) (Debye, Peter Joseph William): Physics. See: Ballentyne; Dresner; Internat. Dict. Ap. Math.

Debye-Waller factor (or temperature factor) (Debye, Peter Joseph William and Waller, Ivar): Physics. See: Ballentyne; Thewlis.

DECAISNE, JOSEPH. 1807-1882. French botanist. See: World Who's Who Sci. Decaisnea.

Decaisnea (Decaisne, Joseph): Botany. See: Webster's 3d.

DECAUVILLE, PAUL. 1846-1922. French industrialist. See: Webster's Biog. Dict. Decauville (railway).

Decauville (railway) (Decauville, Paul): Engineering and Industry. See: Partridge; Webster's 3d.; Winick.

DE CHANCOURTOIS, ALEXANDRE EMILE BEGUYER. 1819-1886. French geologist. See: World Who's Who Sci. De Chancourtois screw (telluric screw).

De Chancourtois screw (telluric screw) (De Chancourtois, Alexandre Emile Beguyer): Chemistry. See: Van Nostrand Chem. Dict.

DECHAUME, JEAN. 1896-1968. French physician. See: J. Med. Lyon, 1969, no. 1166, p. 905. Bonnet-Dechaume-Blanc syndrome.

DECHEN, HEINRICH VON. 1800-1889. German geologist and mineralogist. See: Dict. Sci. Biog. Dechenite.

Dechenite (Dechen, Heinrich von): Earth Sciences. See: Thrush; Webster's 3d.

Dechenne process (Derivation undetermined): Engineering and Industry. See: Thrush.

DE CHEZY, ANTOINE. 1718-1798. French mathematician. See: World Who's Who Sci. Chezy formula?

decibel (Bell, Alexander Graham): Physics. See: Huschke; Internat. Dict. Phys. Elec.; Thewlis.

Deckert reagent for zinc (Deckert, Walter): Chemistry. See: Van Nostrand Chem. Dict.

Deckert test for ethylene oxide in air (Deckert, Walter): Chemistry. See: Van Nostrand Chem. Dict.

DECKERT, WALTER. fl. 1932. German chemist. Cited in: Chem. Abstr., vol. 26, p. 5877; vol. 29, p. 3937. Deckert reagent for zinc; Deckert test for ethylene oxide in air.

DECKHARD. fl. before 1853. American manufacturer. (Biography source unavailable.) Deckhard rifle.

Deckhard rifle (Deckhard): Weapons. See: Mathews, M. M.

DE CLERAMBAULT, GAETAN-HENRI-ALFRED-EDOUARD-LEON-MARIE GATIAN. 1872-1934. French psychiatrist. See: World Who's Who Sci. Kandinskii-Clerambault syndrome.

De Coninck test for succinic and malic acids (Derivation undetermined): Chemistry. See: Van Nostrand Chem. Dict.

DE COPPET, LOUIS CASIMIR. 1841-1911. French physicist. See: World Who's Who Sci. Coppet's law.

De Coriolis, Gaspard Gustave. See: Coriolis, Gaspard Gustave de.

De Corvisart des Marets, Jean Nicholas. See: Corvisart, Jean-Nicolas.

DE CYON, ELIE. 1843-1912. Russian physiologist. See: World Who's Who Sci. Cyon's experiment, Cyon's nerve.

Dedekind cut (Dedekind, Julius Wilhelm Richard): Mathematics. See: Internat. Dict. Ap. Math.; James.

DEDEKIND, JULIUS WILHELM RICHARD. 1831-1916. German mathematician. See: Dict. Sci. Biog. Cantor-Dedekind axiom, Dedekind cut, Dedekind-Peirce theorem, Dedekind's definition, Dedekind's test.

Dedekind-Peirce theorem (Dedekind, Julius Wilhelm Richard and Peirce, Charles Sanders?): Mathematics. See: Ballentyne.

Dedekind's definition (Dedekind, Julius Wilhelm Richard): Mathematics. See: Ballentyne.

Dedekind's test (Dedekind, Julius Wilhelm Richard): Mathematics. See: Ballentyne.

DE DION, ALBERT (MARQUIS). 1856-1946. French inventor. See: World Who's Who Sci. De Dion engine.

De Dion engine (De Dion, Albert): Engineering and Industry. See: Auger.

De Dolomieu, Dieudonne. See: Dolomieu, Dieudonne de Gratet de.

DE EDS, FLOYD. b. 1894. American pharmacologist. See: Amer. Men Sci., 10th ed. Eddy-De Eds test.

DEEN, BRASWELL DRUE. 1893- . American legislator. See: Biog. Direct. Amer. Congress. George-Deen Act.

Deen, Izaak Abrahamszoon van. See: Van Deen, Izaak Abrahamszoon.

Deen's test (Van Deen, Izaak Abrahamszoon). See: Van Deen test reaction.

DEER, A., JR. fl. 1925. Austrian chemist. Cited in: Chem. Abstr., vol. ?, p. 3144. Deer reaction for codeine, dionine, morphine, and papaverine.

Deer reaction for codeine, dionine, morphine, and papaverine (Deer, A., Jr.): Chemistry. See: Van Nostrand Chem. Dict.

DEETJEN, HERMANN. 1867-1915. German physician. See: Biog. Lex. Hervorr. Aerzte, 1880-1930. Deetjen's bodies.

Deetjen's bodies (Deetjen, Hermann): Medicine. See: Dorland; Stedman.

DE FAZI, REMO. b. 1891. Italian chemist. See: Diz. Encic. Ital. De Fazi test reaction.

De Fazi test reaction (De Fazi, Remo): Chemistry. See: Van Nostrand Chem. Dict.

DE FILIPPI, FILIPPO. 1814-1867. Italian naturalist. See: World Who's Who Sci. Filippi's gland(s)?

DE FINETTI, BRUNO. 1906- . Italian mathematician. See: Who's Who Europe, 1967. De Finetti's theorem.

De Finetti's theorem (De Finetti, Bruno): Statistics. See: Kendall.

DE FLORES, L. fl. 1923. American chemist. Cited in: Chem. Abstr., vol. ?, p. 3245. De Florez process.

De Florez process (De Flores, L.): Chemistry. See: Van Nostrand Chem. Dict.

DEFOE, DANIEL. 1661-1731. English journalist and novelist. See: Dict. Nat. Biog. Defoe's law.

Defoe's law (Defoe, Daniel): Sociology. See: Martin.

DE FREYCINET, CHARLES-LOUIS DE SAULSES. 1828-1923. French engineer. See: World Who's Who Sci. Freycinet plan.

DE FREYCINET, LOUIS DE SAULSES. 1779-1842. French naval officer and earth scientist. See: World Who's Who Sci. Freycinetia.

DE GARENGEOT, RENE-JACQUES CROISSANT. 1688-1759. French surgeon. See: World Who's Who Sci. Garengeot's key.

DE GAULLE, CHARLES ANDRE JOSEPH MARIE. 1890-1970. French soldier and statesman. See: Encyc. Brit., 1973. Gaullism (or Gaullist).

De Gaullist (De Gaulle, Charles Andre Joseph Marie). See: Gaullism (or Gaullist).

degauss(ing) (Derivation undetermined): Physics. See: Hughes; Markus; Webster's 3d.

Degener cylinder press (Degener, Frederick Otto): Printing. See: Lockwood.

DEGENER, FREDERICK OTTO. d. 1873. American inventor. (Biography source unavailable.) Degener cylinder press.

DEGENER, OTTO. 1899- . American botanist. See: Amer. Men Sci., 10th ed. Degeneriaceae.

Degeneriaceae (Degener, Otto): Botany. Cited in: Amer. Men Sci., 10th ed.

Degener's indicator (Derivation undetermined): Chemistry. See: Hackh.

De Giacomo reagents (Derivation undetermined): Chemistry. See: Van Nostrand Chem. Dict.

De Gimard, Martin Jules Louis Alexander. See: Gimard, Martin Jules Louis Alexander De.

De Gimard's syndrome (Martin de Gimard, Jules-Louis-Alexandre de): Medicine. See: Jablonski. Also known as: Martin de Gimard's syndrome, Sheldon's necrotic purpura.

DE GIMBERNAT, ANTONIO. 1734-1816. Spanish surgeon and anatomist. See: World Who's Who Sci. Gimbernat's ligament.

DE GOBINEAU, COUNT JOSEPH ARTHUR. 1816-1882. French orientalist and social philosopher. See: World Who's Who Sci. Gobinism.

Degos-Delort-Tricot syndrome (Degos, Robert; Delort, J.; and Tricot, Robert): Medicine. See: Jablonski. Also known as: Degos' syndrome, Koehlmeier-Degos syndrome.

DEGOS, ROBERT. 1904- . French dermatologist. See: World Who's Who Sci. Degos-Delort-Tricot syndrome.

Degos' syndrome (Degos, Robert). See: Degos-Delort-Tricot syndrome.

De Graaf, Regnier. See: Graaf, Regnier de.

De Grandmont's operation (Derivation undetermined): Medicine. See: Stedman.

degree Baume (Baume, Antoine): Chemistry. See: Dresner.

degree Celsius (Celsius, Anders): Physics. See: Dresner.

degree Fahrenheit (Fahrenheit, Daniel Gabriel): Physics. See: Dresner.

degree Kelvin (Thomson, William, Lord Kelvin). See: Kelvin (1).

degree Reaumur (Reaumur, Rene Antoine Ferchault de): Physics. See: Dresner.

degrees Rankine (Rankine, William John Macquorn): Physics. See: Dresner; Markus; Thrush.

DE GUA, JEAN PAUL. 1713-1786. French mathematician. See: World Who's Who Sci. De Gua's rule?

De Gua's rule (De Gua, Jean Paul?): Mathematics. See: Ballentyne.

De Haan, Galen Abraham. See: Abrahamsz, Galenus.

De Haas test for beta-naphthol (Derivation undetermined): Chemistry. See: Van Nostrand Chem. Dict.

De Haas–van Alphen effect (Haas, Wander Johannes de and Van Alphen, Pieter Martinus): Physics. See: Ballentyne; Internat. Dict. Phys. Elec.; Thewlis.

De Haas, Wander Johannes. See: Haas, Wander Johannes de.

De Heine press (Derivation undetermined): Printing. See: Lockwood.

De Hevesy, George Charles. See: Hevesy, George Charles de.

DEHIO, KARL KONSTANTINOVITCH. 1851–1927. Russian physician. See: Biog. Lex. hervorr. Aerzte, 1880–1930. Dehio's test.

Dehio's test (Dehio, Karl Konstantinovitch): Medicine. See: Dorland; Stedman.

DEHN, MAX. 1878–1952. German mathematician. See: World Who's Who Sci. Dehn's lemma.

Dehn–Scott test reaction for alkaloids (Dehn, William Maurice and Scott, S. F.): Chemistry. See: Van Nostrand Chem. Dict.

Dehn–Scott test reaction for aromatic amines (Dehn, William Maurice and Scott, S. F.): Chemistry. See: Van Nostrand Chem. Dict.

Dehn–Scott test reaction for phenolic compounds (Dehn, William Maurice and Scott, S. F.): Chemistry. See: Van Nostrand Chem. Dict.

DEHN, WILLIAM MAURICE. b. 1872. American chemist. See: Amer. Men Sci., 5th ed. Dehn–Scott test reaction for alkaloids, Dehn–Scott test reaction for aromatic amines, Dehn–Scott test reaction for phenolic compounds.

Dehne filter (Dehne, P.): Engineering and Industry. See: Thrush.

DEHNE, P. fl. 1908. German chemist. Cited in: Chem. Abstr., vol. 6, p. 141. Dehne filter.

Dehn's lemma (Dehn, Max): Mathematics. Cited in: Dict. Sci. Biog.

De Hondt, Jodocus. See: Hondius, Jodocus.

DEHOTTAY, HENRI. fl. 1927–1934. French? engineer. Cited in: Chem. Abstr., Decenn. Index, 1927–1936. Dehottay process?, Rodio–Dehottay process?

Dehottay process (Dehottay, Henri?): Engineering and Industry. See: Thrush.

Deisler hand press (Derivation undetermined): Printing. See: Lockwood.

Deister table (Derivation undetermined): Engineering and Industry. See: Thrush.

Deiters' cells (Deiters, Otto Friedrich Karl): Anatomy. See: Chaplin; Donath; Drever.

Deiters' formation (Deiters, Otto Friedrich Karl): Medicine. See: Stedman. Also known as: Lenhossek's fibers.

Deiters' nucleus (Deiters, Otto Friedrich Karl): Medicine. See: Dorland; Henderson; Stedman; Webster's 3d.

Deiters nucleus syndrome (Deiters, Otto Friedrich Karl). See: Bonnier's syndrome.

DEITERS, OTTO FRIEDRICH KARL. 1834–1863. German anatomist. See: Phi Beta Pi Q., 1955, vol. 52, no. 1–2, p. 17. Deiters' cells, Deiters' formation, Deiters' nucleus, Deiters' nucleus syndrome, Deiters' process, Deiters' terminal frames.

Deiters' process (Deiters, Otto Friedrich Karl): Medicine. See: Dorland; Stedman.

Deiters' terminal frames (Deiters, Otto Friedrich Karl): Medicine. See: Stedman.

DEJEAN, M. C. fl. 1935. French physician. (Biography source unavailable.) Dejean's syndrome.

Dejean's syndrome (Dejean, M. C.): Medicine. See: Jablonski.

DEJERINE, JOSEPH JULES. 1849–1917. Swiss-born French neurologist. See: World Who's Who Sci. Dejerine-Lichtheim phenomenon, Dejerine-Roussy syndrome, Dejerine-Sottas syndrome, Dejerine-Thomas syndrome, Dejerine's syndrome (1), Dejerine's syndrome (2), Dejerine's hand phenomenon (or reflex), Dejerine's peripheral neurotabes, Dejerine's sign, Landouzy-Dejerine dystrophy (or type).

DEJERINE-KLUMPKE, AUGUSTA. 1859–1927. French neurologist. See: World Who's Who Sci. Dejerine-Klumpke's syndrome (or paralysis).

Dejerine-Klumpke's syndrome (or paralysis) (Dejerine-Klumpke, Augusta): Medicine. See: Jablonski. Also known as: Klumpke's palsy (or paralysis).

Dejerine-Roussy syndrome (Dejerine, Joseph Jules and Roussy, Gustave): Medicine. See: Dorland; Jablonski; Stedman.

Dejerine-Sottas syndrome (Dejerine, Joseph Jules and Sottas, Jules): Medicine. See: Jablonski. Also known as: Dejerine's disease, Gombault's degeneration (or neuritis).

Dejerine-Thomas syndrome (Dejerine, Joseph Jules and Thomas, Andre): Medicine. See: Jablonski.

Dejerine's disease (Dejerine, Joseph Jules). See: Dejerine-Sottas syndrome.

Dejerine's hand phenomenon (or reflex) (Dejerine, Joseph Jules): Medicine. See: Stedman.

Dejerine's peripheral neurotabes (Dejerine, Joseph Jules): Medicine. See: Stedman.

Dejerine's sign (Dejerine, Joseph Jules): Medicine. See: Dorland; Stedman.

Dejerine's syndrome (1) (Dejerine, Joseph Jules): Medicine. See: Jablonski.

Dejerine's syndrome (2) (Dejerine, Joseph Jules): Medicine. See: Jablonski.

De Joinville (ascot) (Joinville, Francois Ferdinand Philippe Louis Marie d'Orleans, Prince de): Fashion. See: Picken.

DE KAY, JAMES ELLSWORTH. 1792–1851. American naturalist. See: Dict. Amer. Biog. De Kay's snake.

De Kay's snake (De Kay, James Ellsworth): Zoology. See: Pennak.

de Khotinsky cement (Khotinsky, Achilles de): Chemistry. See: Hackh; Thrush.

De Koninck ether test (Derivation undetermined): Chemistry. See: Van Nostrand Chem. Dict.

DE KONINCK, LAURENT-GUILLAUME. 1809–1887. Belgian paleontologist. See: World Who's Who Sci. Koninckite.

De Koninck test for manganese (Derivation undetermined): Chemistry. See: Van Nostrand Chem. Dict.

De Koninck test reaction for thiosulfate (Derivation undetermined): Chemistry. See: Van Nostrand Chem. Dict.

Dekorite (Derivation undetermined): Earth Sciences. See: Thrush.

DE KUPFFER, ADOLPH THEODORE. 1799–1865. Russian physicist. See: World Who's Who Sci. Kupfferite.

DELABARRE, CHRISTOPHE-FRANCOIS. 1784–1862. French dentist. See: World Who's Who Sci. Delabarre syrup.

Delabarre syrup (Delabarre, Christophe-Francois): Dentistry. Cited in: World Who's Who Sci.

DELAFIELD, FRANCIS. 1841–1915. American pathologist. See: World Who's Who Sci. Delafield's hematoxylin.

Delafield's hematoxylin (Delafield, Francis): Medicine. See: Dorland; Stedman.

DE LA FOLLIE, LOUIS GUILLAUME. 1739–1780. French chemist. See: World Who's Who Sci. La Follie's finishing.

DELAFOSSE, GABRIEL. 1796–1878. French mineralogist. See: World Who's Who Sci. Delafossite.

Delafossite (Delafosse, Gabriel): Earth Sciences. See: Thrush; Webster's 3d.

DE LAGUNA, ANDRES. 1499–1560. Spanish anatomist and botanist. See: World Who's Who Sci. Lagunaria.

DELAMBRE, JEAN-BAPTISTE JOSEPH. 1749–1822. French astronomer. See: Dict. Sci. Biog. Delambre's analogies.

Delambre's analogies (Delambre, Jean-Baptiste Joseph): Mathematics. See: Ballentyne; James.

Delaney clause (Delaney, James Joseph): Law. See: Stedman.

DELANEY, JAMES JOSEPH. 1901– . American legislator. See: Biog. Direct. Amer. Congress. Delaney clause.

DE LANGE, CORNELIA CATHARINA. 1871–1950. Dutch physician. See: World Who's Who Sci. De Lange's syndrome (1), De Lange's syndrome (2).

De Lange's syndrome (1) (De Lange, Cornelia Catharina): Medicine. See: Hinsie; Jablonski; Stedman. Also known as: Brachman-De Lange syndrome, Cornelia de Lange's syndrome, Lange's syndrome.

De Lange's syndrome (2) (De Lange, Cornelia Catharina): Medicine. See: Jablonski. Also known as: Bruck-De Lange syndrome, Cornelia de Lange syndrome.

De la Peyronie, Francois Gigot. See: La Peyronie, Francois Gigot de.

DE LA PLANTE, GEORGETTE. fl. late 19th c. French dressmaker and modiste. (Biography source unavailable.) Georgette (crepe).

DELAROCHE, F. fl. 1813. French chemist. Cited in: Royal Soc. Cat. Sci. Pap., 1800-1863. law of Delaroche and Berard.

DELAROCHE, FRANCOIS. 1780-1813. Swiss physician and botanist. See: Biog. Lex. hervorr. Aerzte. Rochea.

De la Rue and Miller's law (De la Rue, Warren and Miller, William Allen): Electronics. See: Ballentyne.

DE LA RUE, WARREN. 1815-1889. English astronomer and inventor. See: Dict. Sci. Biog. De la Rue and Miller's law.

DE LATTRE, J. G. fl. 1952. English metallurgist. Cited in: Chem. Abstr., Decenn. Index, 1947-56. De Lattre pickling process.

De Lattre pickling process (De Lattre, J. G.): Engineering and Industry. See: Thrush.

DELAUNAY, CHARLES EUGENE. 1816-1872. French astronomer. See: Dict. Sci. Biog. Delaunay variables.

Delaunay variables (Delaunay, Charles Eugene): Astronomy. See: Thewlis.

DE LAVAL, CARL GUSTAF PATRIK. 1845-1913. Swedish engineer. See: Svenska Maen Och Kvinnor. De Laval turbine (or steam turbine), Laval nozzle.

De Laval turbine (or steam turbine) (De Laval, Carl Gustaf Patrik): Engineering and Industry. See: Auger; Internat. Dict. Ap. Math.

DE LAVAUD, D. SENSAUD. fl. 1928. Engineer. (Biography source unavailable.) De Lavaud suspension and transmission.

De Lavaud process (Derivation undetermined): Engineering and Industry. See: Thrush.

De Lavaud suspension and transmission (De Lavaud, D. Sensaud): Engineering and Industry. See: Auger.

DELAYE, J. B. fl. 1824. French physician. Cited in: Kelly. Delaye's paralysis.

Delaye's paralysis (Delaye, J. B.): Psychiatry. See: Jablonski.

DELBET, PAUL. 1866-1924. French surgeon. See: Biog. Lex. hervorr. Aerzte, 1880-1930. Delbet's sign.

DELBET, PIERRE. 1861-1957. French surgeon. See: World Who's Who Sci. Delbet's solution.

Delbet's sign (Delbet, Paul): Medicine. See: Dorland; Stedman.

Delbet's solution (Delbet, Pierre): Medicine. See: Dorland.

Del Boca, A.D. See: Boca, A. D. del.

Del Boca-Remazzano test (Boca, A. D. del and Remazzano, A. L.): Chemistry. See: Van Nostrand Chem. Dict.

Delboeuf disc (Delboeuf, Joseph Remy Leopold?): Psychology. See: Drever.

DELBOEUF, JOSEPH REMY LEOPOLD. 1831-1896. Belgian philosopher and psychologist. See: World Who's Who Sci. Delboeuf disc?

Delbrueck scattering (Derivation undetermined): Physics. See: Ballentyne; Thewlis; Van Nostrand Sci. Encyc.

DEL CASTILLO, E. B. fl. 1932. Argentinian physician. (Biography source unavailable.) Ahumada-Del Castillo syndrome, Argonz-Del Castillo syndrome, Del Castillo's syndrome.

Del Castillo's syndrome (Del Castillo, E. B.): Medicine. See: Jablonski. Also known as: Sertoli-cell syndrome.

Delepine reaction (Delepine, Stephane-Marcel): Chemistry. See: Ballentyne; Van Nostrand Chem. Dict.

DELEPINE, STEPHANE-MARCEL. 1871-1965. French chemist. See: Dict. Sci. Biog. Delepine reaction, Delepine test for fenchone, Delepine test for methylamine.

Delepine test for fenchone (Delepine, Stephane-Marcel): Chemistry. See: Van Nostrand Chem. Dict.

Delepine test for methylamine (Delepine, Stephane-Marcel): Chemistry. See: Van Nostrand Chem. Dict.

DELESSE, ACHILLE ERNEST OSCAR JOSEPH. 1817-1881. French geologist and mineralogist. See: World Who's Who Sci. Delessite.

Delesseria (Delessert, Jules Paul Benjamin): Botany. See: Webster's 3d.

DELESSERT, JULES PAUL BENJAMIN. 1773-1847. French banker and botanist. See: Encyc. Brit., 1973. Delesseria, Lessertia.

Delessite (Delesse, Achille Ernest Oscar Joseph): Earth Sciences. See: Thrush.

Delff reagents for alkaloids (Delffs, Friedrich Wilhelm Herrmann): Chemistry. See: Van Nostrand Chem. Dict.

Delff test for fumaric acid (Delffs, Friedrich Wilhelm Herrmann): Chemistry. See: Van Nostrand Chem. Dict.

DELFFS, FRIEDRICH WILHELM HERRMANN. 1812-1894. German chemist. See: Pogg., vol. 1, 3. Delff reagents for alkaloids, Delff test for fumaric acid.

DELHAYE, FERNAND. fl. 1929-1948. Belgian geologist. Cited in: Min. Mag., vol. 32, no. 255, p. 953. Delhayelite.

Delhayelite (Delhaye, Fernand): Earth Sciences. See: Thrush.

De Liege, Jacques. See: Jacques de Liege.

Delilah (Delilah, the seductress): Generic Word (temptress). See: Hendrickson; Partridge; Weekley.

DELILAH, THE SEDUCTRESS. Biblical courtesan. See: Encyc. Brit., 1973. Delilah.

DELILLE, ARTHUR. 1876-1950. French physician. See: World Who's Who Sci. Renon-Delille syndrome.

DELISLE, C. No dates. German engineer. (Biography source unavailable.) Delisle thread.

DELISLE, JOSEPH NICOLAS. 1688-1768. French astronomer. See: Dict. Sci. Biog. Delisle's thermometer.

Delisle thread (Delisle, C.): Engineering and Industry. See: Auger.

Delisle's thermometer (Delisle, Joseph Nicolas): Astronomy. Cited in: World Who's Who Sci.

De Littre, Alexis. See: Littre, Alexis de.

Della Porta, Giovanni Battista. See: Porta, Giambattista della.

Della Robbia colors (or blue) (Robbia, Luca della): Fine Arts. See: Picken; Webster's 3d.

Della Robbia, Luca. See: Robbia, Luca della.

Della Robbia ware (Robbia, Luca della): Fine Arts. See: Partridge; Webster's 3d.

Della Robbia work (Robbia, Luca della): Fine Arts. See: Partridge.

Dellinger fadeout (or effect) (Dellinger, John Howard): Electronics. See: Ballentyne; Hughes; Huschke. Also known as: Moegel-Dellinger effect.

DELLINGER, JOHN HOWARD. 1886-1962. American radio engineer and physicist. See: World Who's Who Sci. Dellinger fadeout (or effect).

DELMON, ANGELES. fl. 1918. Argentinian chemist. Cited in: Chem. Abstr., vol. 12, p. 1185. Guglialmelli-Delmon test for carbohydrates.

DELMONICO, LORENZO. 1813-1881. American restaurateur. See: Dict. Amer. Biog. Delmonico potatoes.

Delmonico potatoes (Delmonico, Lorenzo): Food and Drink. See: De Sola; Webster's 3d.

Del Monte, Guidubaldo. See: Dal Monte, Guidubaldo.

DE LOME, DUPUY. fl. 1898. Spanish government official. (Biography source unavailable.) De Lome letter.

De Lome letter (De Lome, Dupuy): History. See: Morris.

DELORE, XAVIER. 1828-1916. French physician. See: Biog. Lex. hervorr. Aerzte. Delore's method.

Delorenzite (De Lorenzo, Giuseppe): Earth Sciences. See: Thrush; Webster's 3d.

DE LORENZO, GIUSEPPE. b. 1871. Italian geologist. See: Pogg., vol. 4. Delorenzite.

Delore's method (Delore, Xavier): Medicine. See: Dorland.

DELORME, EDMOND. 1847-1929. French surgeon. See: World Who's Who Sci. Delorme's operation.

Delorme's operation (Delorme, Edmond): Medicine. See: Dorland.

DELORT, J. fl. 1942. French dermatologist. (Biography source unavailable.) Degos-Delort-Tricot syndrome.

DELPECH, JACQUES MATHIEU. 1777-1832. French orthopedic surgeon. See: World Who's Who Sci. Delpech's abscess, Delpech's operation.

Delpech's abscess (Delpech, Jacques Mathieu): Medicine. See: Dorland; Stedman.

Delpech's operation (Delpech, Jacques Mathieu): Medicine. See: Dorland.

Delphin(e) classics (Louis de France): Literature. See: Barnhart (Eng. Lit.); Partridge; Phyfe; Wagner (More Names).

DELPRAT, G. D. fl. 1901. Australian metallurgist. Cited in: Chem. Abstr., Decenn. Index, 1907-1916. Delprat process, Potter-Delprat process.

Delprat method (Derivation undetermined): Engineering and Industry. See: Thrush.

Delprat process (Delprat, G. D.): Engineering and Industry. See: Thrush.

DEL RIO, ANDRES MANUEL. 1764-1849. Spanish-born mineralogist. See: World Who's Who Sci. Delrioite, Riolite.

Del Rio Hortega, Pio. See: Rio Hortega, Pio del.

Delrioite (Del Rio, Andres Manuel): Earth Sciences. See: Thrush.

DELSARTE, FRANCOIS ALEXANDRE NICOLAS CHERI. 1811-1871. French musician. See: Webster's Biog. Dict. Delsarte (Delsartian) method.

Delsarte (Delsartian) method (Delsarte, Francois Alexandre Nicolas Cheri): Music. See: Hendrickson; Webster's 3d.

DELVAUX DE FENFFE, JEAN CHARLES PHILIPP JOSEPH. b. 1782. Belgian chemist and physicist. See: Pogg., vol. 1. Delvauxene.

Delvauxene (Delvaux de Fenffe, Jean Charles Philipp Joseph): Earth Sciences. See: Charnock; Webster's 3d.

DE MAN, JOHANNES GOVERT. 1850-1930. Dutch zoologist. Cited in: Royal Soc. Cat. Sci. Pap., 1800-1883. Demanian (system or vessel).

Demanian (system or vessel) (De Man, Johannes Govert): Zoology. See: Henderson; Webster's 3d.

Demansia (snake) (Diemen, Antonio van): Zoology. See: Webster's 3d.

DEMANT, V. fl. 1937. Austrian chemist. Cited in: Chem. Abstr., vol. 31, p. 8428. Feigl-Demant test.

DEMARCAY, EUGENE. 1852-1903. French chemist. See: World Who's Who Sci. Demarcay reaction for rhodium.

Demarcay reaction for rhodium (Demarcay, Eugene): Chemistry. See: Van Nostrand Chem. Dict.

De Marignac, Jean Charles Galissard. See: Marignac, Jean Charles Galissard de.

DEMARQUAY, JEAN-NICOLAS. 1814-1875. French surgeon. See: World Who's Who Sci. Demarquay-Richet syndrome, Demarquay's symptom.

Demarquay-Richet syndrome (Demarquay, Jean-Nicolas and Richet, Didier Dominique Alfred): Medicine. See: Jablonski.

Demarquay's symptom (Demarquay, Jean-Nicolas): Medicine. See: Dorland; Stedman.

De Mars turnstile antenna (Derivation undetermined): Physics. See: Internat. Dict. Phys. Elec.

DE MARTINI, A. fl. 1951. Italian physician. (Biography source unavailable.) De Martini-Balestera syndrome.

De Martini-Balestra syndrome (De Martini, A. and Balestra, G.). See: Burke's syndrome.

DEMBER, ALEXIS BERTHOLD. 1912- . German-born American physicist. See: Amer. Men Sci., 10th ed. Dember effect.

Dember effect (Dember, Alexis Berthold): Physics. See: Ballentyne.

Demenge process (Derivation undetermined): Engineering and Industry. See: Thrush.

DEMIANOV, NIKOLAI JAKOVLEVICH. 1861-1938. Russian chemist. See: World Who's Who Sci. Demjanov rearrangement.

DEMIDOV, ANATOLY NIKOLAYEVICH. 1812-1870. Russian traveller and patron of the arts. See: New Encyc. Brit., 1974, Microp. Demidovite.

Demidovite (Demidov, Anatoly Nikolayevich): Earth Sciences. See: Thrush.

Deminrolit apparatus (Derivation undetermined): Engineering and Industry. See: Thrush.

De Mirbel, Charles Francois Brisseau. See: Mirbel, Charles Francois Brisseau de.

Demjanov rearrangement (Demianov, Nikolai Jakovlevich): Chemistry. See: Ballentyne; Van Nostrand Chem. Dict.

Democritean (Democritus): Philosophy. See: Weekley.

DEMOCRITUS. fl. 460-357 B.C. Greek philosopher, physicist and mathematician. See: Dict. Sci. Biog. Democritean.

DE MOIVRE, ABRAHAM. 1667-1754. French-born English mathematician. See: World Who's Who Sci. De Moivre identity, De Moivre-Laplace theorem, De Moivre('s) theorem, Demoivre's formula.

De Moivre identity (De Moivre, Abraham): Mathematics. See: Internat. Dict. Ap. Math.

De Moivre-Laplace theorem (De Moivre, Abraham and Laplace, Pierre Simon): Mathematics. See: Internat. Dict. Ap. Math.; Van Nostrand Sci. Encyc.

De Moivre('s) theorem (De Moivre, Abraham): Mathematics. See: Ballentyne; Internat. Dict. Phys. Elec.; James.

Demoivre's formula (De Moivre, Abraham): Mathematics. See: Stedman.

De Molay (Molay, Jacques de): Philanthropy. See: Webster's 3d.

De Molay, Jacques. See: Molay, Jacques de.

DEMONS, ALBERT-JEAN-OCTAVE. 1842-1920. French physician. See: Dict. Biog. Fran. Demons-Meigs syndrome.

Demons-Meigs syndrome (Demons, Albert-Jean-Octave and Meigs, Joe Vincent). See: Meigs' syndrome.

DE MORGAN, AUGUSTUS. 1806-1871. English mathematician and logician. See: Dict. Sci. Biog. De Morgan formulas, De Morgan's rules, De Morgan's test, De Morgan's theorem.

DE MORGAN, CAMPBELL. 1811-1876. English physician. See: Dict. Nat. Biog. De Morgan's spots.

De Morgan formulas (De Morgan, Augustus): Mathematics. See: James.

De Morgan's rules (De Morgan, Augustus): Mathematics. See: Ballentyne.

De Morgan's spots (De Morgan, Campbell): Medicine. See: Dorland; Jablonski; Stedman.

De Morgan's test (De Morgan, Augustus): Mathematics. See: Ballentyne.

De Morgan's theorem (De Morgan, Augustus): Mathematics. See: Webster's 3d.

De Morsier-Gauthier syndrome (Morsier, Georges de and Gauthier, G.). See: De Morsier's syndrome (2).

De Morsier, Georges. See: Morsier, Georges de.

De Morsier's syndrome (1) (Morsier, Georges de): Medicine. See: Jablonski.

De Morsier's syndrome (2) (Morsier, Georges de): Medicine. See: Jablonski. Also known as: De Morsier-Gauthier syndrome.

DEMOSTHENES. 385?-322 B.C. Athenian statesman. See: Encyc. Brit., 1973. Demosthenes complex, Demosthenic (or Demosthenean).

Demosthenes complex (Demosthenes): Psychology. See: Hinsie.

Demosthenic (or Demosthenean) (Demosthenes): Generic Word (oratorical eloquence). See: Hendrickson; Partridge; Webster's 3d.

Demours' membrane (Demours, Pierre): Medicine. See: Dorland.

DEMOURS, PIERRE. 1702-1795. French ophthalmologist. See: World Who's Who Sci. Demours' membrane.

DEMPSEY, JACK (WILLIAM HARRISON). 1895- . American heavyweight pugilist. See: Encyc. Brit., 1973. Jack Dempsey (fish)?

DEMPSTER, ARTHUR JEFFREY. 1886-1950. Canadian-born American physicist. See: World Who's Who Sci. Dempster mass spectrograph, Dempster positive-ray analysis.

Dempster mass spectrograph (Dempster, Arthur Jeffrey): Physics. See: Internat. Dict. Phys. Elec.; Markus.

Dempster positive-ray analysis (Dempster, Arthur Jeffrey): Physics. See: Hughes; Internat. Dict. Phys. Elec.

DENEKE, THEODOR. b. 1860. German bacteriologist. See: Biog. Lex. hervorr. Aerzte, 1880-1930. Deneke's spirillum (or vibrio).

Deneke's spirillum (or vibrio) (Deneke, Theodor): Medicine. See: Dorland.

Denham's bustard (Derivation undetermined): Zoology. See: Gray.

Deniges arsenic mirror reagent (Deniges, Georges): Chemistry. See: Van Nostrand Chem. Dict.

Deniges benzoyl reagent (Deniges, Georges): Chemistry. See: Van Nostrand Chem. Dict.

Deniges-Chelle reagent for halogens (Deniges, Georges and Chelle, Louis): Chemistry. See: Van Nostrand Chem. Dict.

Deniges-Chelle test for bromine (Deniges, Georges and Chelle, Louis): Chemistry. See: Van Nostrand Chem. Dict.

DENIGES, GEORGES. 1859-1935. French chemist. See: Biog. Lex. hervorr. Aerzte, 1880-1930. Auche-Deniges reagent, Deniges arsenic mirror reagent, Deniges benzoyl reagent, Deniges-Chelle reagent for halogens, Deniges-Chelle test for bromine, Deniges hydrostrychnine solution, Deniges-Lebat test reactions for arsphenamine, Deniges mercuric sulfate reagent, Deniges methylglyoxal reagent, Deniges micro-reaction for cocaine, Deniges micro-reaction for salol, Deniges micro-reaction for strychnine, Deniges micro-reagent, Deniges micro-reagent for alkaline earths, Deniges micro-reagent for barium, Deniges micro-test for novocaine, Deniges phosphate-arsenate reagent, Denige's reagent, Deniges selenate and tellurate reagent, Deniges solution for butyric acid, Deniges sugar reagent, Deniges test for acetoacetic acid, Deniges test (for acetone in urine), Deniges test for allyl alcohol, Deniges test for anilides, Deniges test for benzoic acid, Deniges test for chlorate, Deniges test for chlorobutanol, Deniges test for chromate, Deniges test for cinnamic acid, Deniges test for cyclic aldehydes, Deniges test for ethanol in methanol, Deniges test for ferric ion, Deniges test for formic acid, Deniges test for glycerin, Deniges test for hippuric acid, Deniges test for indole, Deniges test for inositol, Deniges test for isothiocyanates, Deniges test for mercaptans, Deniges test for metaldehyde, Deniges' test (for morphine), Deniges test for nitrite, Deniges test for phosphate and arsenate, Deniges test for salicylate, Deniges test for selenium, Deniges test for sulfate ion in insoluble substances, Deniges test for sulfanilides, Deniges test for tartrate, Deniges test for thiophene in benzene, Deniges' test (for uric acid), Deniges test reaction for alpha and beta naphthol, Deniges test reaction for bismuth, Deniges test reaction for cadmium, Deniges test reaction for carbon disulfide, Deniges test reaction for copper, Deniges test reaction for cresols, Deniges test reaction for cupreine, Deniges test reaction for glycocoll, Deniges test reaction for glycol, Deniges test reaction for hydrogen peroxide, Deniges test reaction for malic acid, Deniges test reaction for nickel, Deniges test reaction for peptides and alpha amino acids, Deniges test reaction for skatol, Deniges test reaction for succinate, Deniges test reaction for tin or stannous salts, Deniges test reactions for manganese, Deniges test reactions for thiourea, Deniges test reagent for acetylene, Deniges test reagent for cobalt, copper, nickel, and manganese, Deniges test reagent for cyanide, Deniges test reagent for ferrous, cadmium, cobalt, magnesium, zinc, and other metal salts, Deniges test reagent for lactic and glycolic acid, Deniges test reagent for mercury salts, Deniges test reagent for phenolic alkaloids, Deniges test reagent for phosphate, Deniges tests for cinchona alkaloids.

Deniges hydrostrychnine solution (Deniges, Georges): Chemistry. See: Van Nostrand Chem. Dict.

Deniges-Lebat test reactions for arsphenamine (Deniges, Georges and Labat, Jean-Andre): Chemistry. See: Van Nostrand Chem. Dict.

Deniges mercuric sulfate reagent (Deniges, Georges): Chemistry. See: Van Nostrand Chem. Dict.

Deniges methylglyoxal reagent (Deniges, Georges): Chemistry. See: Van Nostrand Chem. Dict.

Deniges micro-reaction for cocaine (Deniges, Georges): Chemistry. See: Van Nostrand Chem. Dict.

Deniges micro-reaction for salol (Deniges, Georges): Chemistry. See: Van Nostrand Chem. Dict.

Deniges micro-reaction for strychnine (Deniges, Georges): Chemistry. See: Van Nostrand Chem. Dict.

Deniges micro-reagent (Deniges, Georges): Chemistry. See: Van Nostrand Chem. Dict.

Deniges micro-reagent for alkaline earths (Deniges, Georges): Chemistry. See: Van Nostrand Chem. Dict.

Deniges micro-reagent for barium (Deniges, Georges): Chemistry. See: Van Nostrand Chem. Dict.

Deniges micro-test for novocaine (Deniges, Georges): Chemistry. See: Van Nostrand Chem. Dict.

Deniges phosphate-arsenate reagent (Deniges, Georges): Chemistry. See: Van Nostrand Chem. Dict.

Denige's reagent (Deniges, Georges): Chemistry. See: Hackh.

Deniges selenate and tellurate reagent (Deniges, Georges): Chemistry. See: Van Nostrand Chem. Dict.

Deniges solution for butyric acid (Deniges, Georges): Chemistry. See: Van Nostrand Chem. Dict.

Deniges sugar reagent (Deniges, Georges): Chemistry. See: Van Nostrand Chem. Dict.

Deniges test for acetoacetic acid (Deniges, Georges): Chemistry. See: Van Nostrand Chem. Dict.

Deniges test (for acetone in urine) (Deniges, Georges): Chemistry. See: Dorland.

Deniges test for allyl alcohol (Deniges, Georges): Chemistry. See: Van Nostrand Chem. Dict.

Deniges test for anilides (Deniges, Georges): Chemistry. See: Van Nostrand Chem. Dict.

Deniges test for benzoic acid (Deniges, Georges): Chemistry. See: Van Nostrand Chem. Dict.

Deniges test for chlorate (Deniges, Georges): Chemistry. See: Van Nostrand Chem. Dict.

Deniges test for chlorobutanol (Deniges, Georges): Chemistry. See: Van Nostrand Chem. Dict.

Deniges test for chromate (Deniges, Georges): Chemistry. See: Van Nostrand Chem. Dict.

Deniges test for cinnamic acid (Deniges, Georges): Chemistry. See: Van Nostrand Chem. Dict.

Deniges test for cyclic aldehydes (Deniges, Georges): Chemistry. See: Van Nostrand Chem. Dict.

Deniges test for ethanol in methanol (Deniges, Georges): Chemistry. See: Van Nostrand Chem. Dict.

Deniges test for ferric ion (Deniges, Georges): Chemistry. See: Van Nostrand Chem. Dict.

Deniges test for formic acid (Deniges, Georges): Chemistry. See: Van Nostrand Chem. Dict.

Deniges test for glycerin (Deniges, Georges): Chemistry. See: Van Nostrand Chem. Dict.

Deniges test for hippuric acid (Deniges, Georges): Chemistry. See: Van Nostrand Chem. Dict.

Deniges test for indole (Deniges, Georges): Chemistry. See: Van Nostrand Chem. Dict.

Deniges test for inositol (Deniges, Georges): Chemistry. See: Van Nostrand Chem. Dict.

Deniges test for isothiocyanates (Deniges, Georges): Chemistry. See: Van Nostrand Chem. Dict.

Deniges test for mercaptans (Deniges, Georges): Chemistry. See: Van Nostrand Chem. Dict.

Deniges test for metaldehyde (Deniges, Georges): Chemistry. See: Van Nostrand Chem. Dict.

Deniges' test (for morphine) (Deniges, Georges): Chemistry. See: Dorland.

Deniges test for nitrite (Deniges, Georges): Chemistry. See: Van Nostrand Chem. Dict.

Deniges test for phosphate and arsenate (Deniges, Georges): Chemistry. See: Van Nostrand Chem. Dict.

Deniges test for salicylate (Deniges, Georges): Chemistry. See: Van Nostrand Chem. Dict.

Deniges test for selenium (Deniges, Georges): Chemistry. See: Van Nostrand Chem. Dict.

Deniges test for sulfanilides (Deniges, Georges): Chemistry. See: Van Nostrand Chem. Dict.

Deniges test for sulfate ion in insoluble substances (Deniges, Georges): Chemistry. See: Van Nostrand Chem. Dict.

Deniges test for tartrate (Deniges, Georges): Chemistry. See: Van Nostrand Chem. Dict.

Deniges test for thiophene in benzene (Deniges, Georges): Chemistry. See: Van Nostrand Chem. Dict.

Deniges' test (for uric acid) (Deniges, Georges): Chemistry. See: Dorland; Stedman.

Deniges test reaction for alpha and beta naphthol (Deniges, Georges): Chemistry. See: Van Nostrand Chem. Dict.

Deniges test reaction for bismuth (Deniges, Georges): Chemistry. See: Van Nostrand Chem. Dict.

Deniges test reaction for cadmium (Deniges, Georges): Chemistry. See: Van Nostrand Chem. Dict.

Deniges test reaction for carbon disulfide (Deniges, Georges): Chemistry. See: Van Nostrand Chem. Dict.

Deniges test reaction for copper (Deniges, Georges): Chemistry. See: Van Nostrand Chem. Dict.

Deniges test reaction for cresols (Deniges, Georges): Chemistry. See: Van Nostrand Chem. Dict.

Deniges test reaction for cupreine (Deniges, Georges): Chemistry. See: Van Nostrand Chem. Dict.

Deniges test reaction for glycocoll (Deniges, Georges): Chemistry. See: Van Nostrand Chem. Dict.

Deniges test reaction for glycol (Deniges, Georges): Chemistry. See: Van Nostrand Chem. Dict.

Deniges test reaction for hydrogen peroxide (Deniges, Georges): Chemistry. See: Van Nostrand Chem. Dict.

Deniges test reaction for malic acid (Deniges, Georges): Chemistry. See: Van Nostrand Chem. Dict.

Deniges test reaction for nickel (Deniges, Georges): Chemistry. See: Van Nostrand Chem. Dict.

Deniges test reaction for peptides and alpha amino acids (Deniges, Georges): Chemistry. See: Van Nostrand Chem. Dict.

Deniges test reaction for skatol (Deniges, Georges): Chemistry. See: Van Nostrand Chem. Dict.

Deniges test reaction for succinate (Deniges, Georges): Chemistry. See: Van Nostrand Chem. Dict.

Deniges test reaction for tin or stannous salts (Deniges, Georges): Chemistry. See: Van Nostrand Chem. Dict.

Deniges test reactions for manganese (Deniges, Georges): Chemistry. See: Van Nostrand Chem. Dict.

Deniges test reactions for thiourea (Deniges, Georges): Chemistry. See: Van Nostrand Chem. Dict.

Deniges test reagent for acetylene (Deniges, Georges): Chemistry. See: Van Nostrand Chem. Dict.

Deniges test reagent for cobalt, copper, nickel, and manganese (Deniges, Georges): Chemistry. See: Van Nostrand Chem. Dict.

Deniges test reagent for cyanide (Deniges, Georges): Chemistry. See: Van Nostrand Chem. Dict.

Deniges test reagent for ferrous, cadmium, cobalt, magnesium, zinc, and other metal salts (Deniges, Georges): Chemistry. See: Van Nostrand Chem. Dict.

Deniges test reagent for lactic and glycolic acid (Deniges, Georges): Chemistry. See: Van Nostrand Chem. Dict.

Deniges test reagent for mercury salts (Deniges, Georges): Chemistry. See: Van Nostrand Chem. Dict.

Deniges test reagent for phenolic alkaloids (Deniges, Georges): Chemistry. See: Van Nostrand Chem. Dict.

Deniges test reagent for phosphate (Deniges, Georges): Chemistry. See: Van Nostrand Chem. Dict.

Deniges tests for cinchona alkaloids (Deniges, Georges): Chemistry. See: Van Nostrand Chem. Dict.

Denis-Browne splint (Brown, Denis): Medicine. See: Stedman.

Denis' plasmin (Denis, Prosper-Sylvain): Medicine. See: Dorland.

DENIS, PROSPER-SYLVAIN. 1799-1863. French chemist. See: Biog. Lex. hervorr. Aerzte. Denis' plasmin.

DENIS, WILLEY GLOVER. b. 1879. American biochemist. See: Amer. Men Sci., 4th ed. Benedict-Denis sulfur reagent?, Folin-Denis reagent for phenols, Folin-Denis reagent for tyrosine, Folin-Denis reagent for uric acid.

DENISON, IRVING ALSON. 1896- . American chemist. See: Amer. Men Sci., 5th ed. Denison sampler (or core barrel)?

Denison sampler (or core barrel) (Denison, Irving Alson?): Engineering and Industry. See: Thrush.

DENISON, SIR WILLIAM THOMAS. 1804-1871. English general and governor of New South Wales. See: Dict. Nat. Biog. Denisonia (snake).

Denisonia (snake) (Denison, Sir William Thomas): Zoology. See: Pennak; Stedman; Webster's 3d.

Denk operation (Denk, Wolfgang Karl Josef): Medicine. Cited in: Kelly.

DENK, WOLFGANG KARL JOSEF. 1882- . Austrian surgeon. See: World Who's Who Sci. Denk operation.

DENMAN, GEORGE. 1819-1896. English jurist. See: Dict. Nat. Biog., 1st suppl. Denman's (Lord) Act.

DENMAN, THOMAS. 1773-1815. English obstetrician. See: Dict. Nat. Biog. Denman's spontaneous evolution.

Denman's (Lord) Act (Denman, George): Law. See: Black.

Denman's spontaneous evolution (Denman, Thomas): Medicine. See: Dorland; Stedman.

DENNET. No dates. Manufacturer. (Biography source unavailable.) Dennet (carriage).

Dennet (carriage) (Dennet): Engineering and Industry. See: Charnock.

DENNETT, JOHN. 1790-1852. English inventor. See: World Who's Who Sci. Dennett rocket.

Dennett rocket (Dennett, John): Engineering and Industry. Cited in: World Who's Who Sci.

DENNETT, ROGER HERBERT. 1876-1935. American pediatrician. See: Who's Who Amer. Med. Dennett's diet.

Dennett's diet (Dennett, Roger Herbert): Medicine. See: Dorland.

DENNIE, CHARLES CLAYTON. b. 1884. American dermatologist and syphilologist. See: Who's Who Amer. Med. Dennie–Marfan syndrome.

Dennie–Marfan syndrome (Dennie, Charles Clayton and Marfan, Antonin Bernard Jean): Medicine. See: Jablonski. Also known as: Marfan's syndrome.

DENNING, REYNOLDS MC CONNELL. b. 1916. American mineralogist. See: Amer. Men Sci., 9th ed. Denningite.

Denningite (Denning, Reynolds McConnell): Earth Sciences. See: Thrush.

Dennis–Browne test reaction (Dennis, Louis Munroe and Browne, Arthur Wesley): Chemistry. See: Van Nostrand Chem. Dict.

DENNIS, LOUIS MUNROE. 1863–1936. American chemist. See: World Who's Who Sci. Dennis–Browne test reaction.

Dennis roasting furnace (Dennis, William B.): Engineering and Industry. Cited in: World Who's Who Sci.

DENNIS, WILLIAM B. 1865–1937. American mining engineer. See: World Who's Who Sci. Dennis roasting furnace.

Dennison method (Derivation undetermined): Engineering and Industry. See: Thrush.

Dennisonite (Derivation undetermined): Earth Sciences. See: Thrush.

DENNSTAEDT, AUGUST WILHELM. fl. 19th c. German botanist. See: Hamberger, 11:161, 17:339, 22(1):595. Dennstaedtia.

Dennstaedtia (Dennstaedt, August Wilhelm): Botany. See: Taylor, N.; Webster's 3d.

Dennstedt furnace (Dennstedt, Max Eugen Hermann): Chemistry. See: Hackh.

DENNSTEDT, MAX EUGEN HERMANN. 1852–1931. German chemist. See: Wer 1st's, 1906. Ciamician–Dennstedt rearrangement, Dennstedt furnace.

DENNY–BROWN, DEREK ERNEST. 1901– . New Zealand–born physician in England and America. See: Who's Who Amer., 1974–1975. Denny–Brown's syndrome (1), Denny–Brown's syndrome (2).

Denny–Brown's syndrome (1) (Denny–Brown, Derek Ernest): Medicine. See: Jablonski.

Denny–Brown's syndrome (2) (Denny–Brown, Derek Ernest). See: Hick's syndrome.

Denoel formula (Denoel, Lucien): Engineering and Industry. See: Thrush.

DENOEL, LUCIEN. fl. 1935. Belgian mining engineer. Cited in: Mansell. Denoel formula.

Denonvilliers' aponeurosis (or fascia) (Denonvilliers, Charles Pierre): Medicine. See: Donath; Dorland; Stedman.

DENONVILLIERS, CHARLES PIERRE. 1808–1872. French surgeon. See: World Who's Who Sci. Denonvilliers' aponeurosis (or fascia), Denonvilliers' ligament, Denonvilliers' operation.

Denonvilliers' ligament (Denonvilliers, Charles Pierre): Medicine. See: Donath; Dorland; Stedman.

Denonvilliers' operation (Denonvilliers, Charles Pierre): Medicine. See: Dorland.

De Normanville overdrive (Normanville, E. J. de). See: Laycock De Normanville overdrive.

DENT, CHARLES ENRIQUE. 1911– . English physician. See: World Who's Who Sci. Costello–Dent syndrome.

DENUCE, MAURICE. 1859–1924. French surgeon. See: Biog. Lex. hervorr. Aerzte, 1880–1930. Denuce's ligament.

Denuce's ligament (Denuce, Maurice): Medicine. See: Dorland; Stedman.

DENYS, JOSEPH. 1857–1932. Belgian bacteriologist. Cited in: Kelly. Denys–Leclef phenomenon, Denys' tuberculin.

Denys–Leclef phenomenon (Denys, Joseph and Leclef, J.): Medicine. See: Stedman.

Denys' tuberculin (Denys, Joseph): Medicine. See: Dorland; Stedman.

D'EON DE BEAUMONT, CHARLES GENEVIEVE LOUIS AUGUSTE ANDRE TIMOTHEE. 1728–1810. French diplomat, swordsman, and writer. See: Dict. Nat. Biog. Eonism.

DEPAGE, ANTOINE. 1862–1925. Belgian surgeon. See: World Who's Who Sci. Depage operation.

Depage operation (Depage, Antoine): Medicine. Cited in: Kelly.

DE PAOLINI, I. fl. 1930. Italian chemist. Cited in: Chem. Abstr., vol. 25, p. 1182. De Paolini test.

De Paolini test (De Paolini, I.): Chemistry. See: Van Nostrand Chem. Dict.

DEPAUL, JEAN ANNE HENRI. 1811–1883. French obstetrician. See: World Who's Who Sci. Depaul tube.

Depaul tube (Depaul, Jean Anne Henri): Medicine. Cited in: Kelly.

De Peiresc, Nicolas-Claude Fabri. See: Peiresc, Nicolas-Claude Fabri de.

DEPERET, CHARLES. 1854–1929. French geologist. See: Dict. Sci. Biog. Deperet's law.

Deperet's law (Deperet, Charles): Zoology. See: Webster's 3d.; Winick.

De Petit, Francois Pourfour. See: Petit, Francois Pourfour du.

DE POINCI, M. fl. 17th c. Governor of French West Indies. (Biography source unavailable.) Poinciana.

DE POURTALES, LOUIS FRANCOIS. 1823–1880. Swiss-born naturalist. See: World Who's Who Sci. Pourtalesia (sea urchin).

DE PRONY, BARON GASPARD-CLAIR-FRANCOIS-MARIE RICHE. 1755–1839. French engineer and mathematician. See: World Who's Who Sci. Prony(s) brake (or dynamometer).

DE QUATREFAGES DE BREAU, JEAN LOUIS ARMAND. 1810–1892. French naturalist and anthropologist. See: World Who's Who Sci. Quatrefage's angle.

De Quervain, Fritz. See: Quervain, Fritz de.

De Quervain's thyroiditis (Quervain, Fritz de). See: Quervain's disease (2).

De Rada test (Diaz de Rada, F.): Chemistry. See: Van Nostrand Chem. Dict.

DERBY. fl. 16th c. English lawyer and moneylender. (Biography source unavailable.) Darbies.

Derby, 12th Earl. See: Stanley, Edward, 12th Earl of Derby.

Derby, 13th Earl. See: Stanley, Edward, 13th Earl of Derby.

Derby, 16th Earl. See: Stanley, Sir Frederick Arthur, 16th Earl of Derby.

Derby, 17th Earl. See: Stanley, Edward George Villiers, 17th Earl of Derby.

Derby Day (Stanley, Edward Smith, 12th Earl of Derby): Recreation and Sports. See: Phyfe.

Derby dog (Stanley, Edward Smith, 12th Earl of Derby): Generic Word (irritating interruption). See: Hendrickson; Partridge.

Derby flycatcher (Stanley, Edward, 13th Earl of Derby): Zoology. See: Webster's 3d.

DERBY, GEORGE STRONG. 1875–1931. American ophthalmologist. See: World Who's Who Sci. Derby operation.

Derby hat (Stanley, Edward Smith, 12th Earl of Derby): Fashion. See: Hendrickson; Partridge.

Derby operation (Derby, George Strong): Medicine. Cited in: Kelly.

DERBY, ORVILLE ADELBERT. 1851–1915. American geologist. See: Who Was Who Amer., 1961–1968. Derbylite.

Derby pocket safety ohmmeter (Derivation undetermined): Engineering and Industry. See: Thrush.

Derby (stakes) (Stanley, Edward Smith, 12th Earl of Derby): Recreation and Sports. See: Barnhart (Eng. Lit.); Brewer; Charnock.

Derbyite (and Derby Scheme) (Stanley, Edward George Villiers, 17th Earl of Derby): History. See: Brewer.

Derbylite (Derby, Orville Adelbert): Earth Sciences. See: Thrush; Webster's 3d.

DERCUM, FRANCIS XAVIER. 1856-1931. American neurologist. See: World Who's Who Sci. Dercum's syndrome (or disease).

Dercum's syndrome (or disease) (Dercum, Francis Xavier): Medicine. See: Jablonski; Stedman; Wolman. Also known as: Anders' syndrome.

DE REYNIER, JEAN PIERRE. 1914- . Swiss otologist. See: World Who's Who Sci. Nager-De Reynier syndrome.

DERIAZ, PAUL. fl. 1960. Swiss engineer and inventor. See: New Encyc. Brit., 1974, Microp. Deriaz pump-turbine.

Deriaz pump-turbine (Deriaz, Paul): Engineering and Industry. See: Auger.

DERINGER, HENRY. fl. 1835. American gunsmith. See: Webster's Biog. Dict. Derringer (pistol).

DERN, GEORGE H. b. 1872. American mining engineer. See: Who's Who Engin., 1922-1923. Holt-Dern process (and furnace).

De Rochas, Adolphe-Eugene. See: Beau de Rochas, Adolphe-Eugene.

DE ROCHON, ALEXIS MARIE. 1741-1817. French astronomer and optician. See: World Who's Who Sci. Rochon prism.

DEROME FAMILY. fl. 18th c. French bookbinders. See: Webster's Biog. Dict. Derome style.

Derome style (Derome family): Fine Arts. See: Harrod.

DE ROSSI, MICHELE STEFANO. 1834-1898. Italian geologist. See: Encic. Ital. Rossi-Forel scale (or intensity scale).

Derrick (or Deric) (Derrick, Godfrey): Generic Word (crane). See: Charnock; Clapin; Hendrickson.

DERRICK, GODFREY. fl. ca. 1600. English hangman. (Biography source unavailable.) Derrick (or Deric).

DERRIEN, EUGENE. 1879-1931. French chemist. See: Biog. Lex. hervorr. Aerzte, 1880-1930. Derrien's test.

Derrien's test (Derrien, Eugene): Medicine. See: Dorland.

Derringer (pistol) (Deringer, Henry): Weapons. See: Hendrickson; Partridge; Quick.

DE SAINT-RAT, LOUIS. fl. 1936. French chemist. Cited in: Chem. Abstr., vol. 30, p. 6304. Bertrand-De Saint Rat reagent.

DE SAINT-VENANT, ADHEMAR-JEAN-CLAUDE BARRE. 1797-1886. French mathematician and physicist. See: World Who's Who Sci. Saint-Venant-Mises material, Saint Venant plasticity, Saint-Venant('s) principle, Saint-Venant's compatibility equations, Saint-Venant's problem.

DE SAINT-VINCENT, GREGOIRE. 1584-1667. Flemish mathematician. See: World Who's Who Sci. virtual parabolas of St. Vincent.

De Sanctis-Cacchione syndrome (De Sanctis, Carlo and Cacchione, Aldo): Medicine. See: Jablonski.

DE SANCTIS, CARLO. b. 1888. Italian psychiatrist. See: Who's Who Sci. Europe, 1967. De Sanctis-Cacchione syndrome.

DESARGUES, GIRARD. 1591-1661. French mathematician. See: Dict. Sci. Biog. Arguesian transformation, Desargues('s) theorem.

Desargues('s) theorem (Desargues, Girard): Mathematics. See: James; Osborne; Webster's 3d.

DE SAULES, A. B. No dates. Mine manager. Cited in: Bailey. De Saulesite.

De Saulesite (De Saules, A. B.): Earth Sciences. See: Thrush.

DESAULT, PIERRE JOSEPH. 1744-1795. French surgeon. See: World Who's Who Sci. Desault's apparatus, Desault's bandage, Desault's ligature, Desault's sign.

Desault's apparatus (Desault, Pierre Joseph): Medicine. Cited in: World Who's Who Sci.

Desault's bandage (Desault, Pierre Joseph): Medicine. See: Dorland; Stedman.

Desault's ligature (Desault, Pierre Joseph): Medicine. See: Dorland; Stedman.

Desault's sign (Desault, Pierre Joseph): Medicine. See: Dorland.

De Saussure, Ferdinand. See: Saussure, Ferdinand de.

De Saussure, Horace Benedict. See: Saussure, Horace Benedict de.

DESBASSAYNS DE RICHEMONT, E. fl. 1835. French chemist. Cited in: Royal Soc. Cat. Sci. Pap., 1800-1863. Desbassins de Richemont test.

Desbassins de Richemont test (Desbassayns de Richemont, E.): Chemistry. See: Van Nostrand Chem. Dict.

Descartes' folium (or folium of Descartes) (Descartes, Rene du Perron): Mathematics. See: Ballentyne; Van Nostrand Sci. Encyc.

Descartes' laws (of refraction) (Descartes, Rene du Perron): Physics. See: Ballentyne; Internat. Dict. Phys. Elec.; Van Nostrand Sci. Encyc.

Descartes' organ (Descartes, Rene du Perron): Medicine. See: Donath.

Descartes ray (Descartes, Rene du Perron): Physics. See: Huschke.

DESCARTES, RENE DU PERRON. 1596-1650. French philosopher and mathematician. See: Dict. Sci. Biog. Cartesian control, Cartesian coordinate(s), Cartesian diver, Cartesian dualism, Cartesian equation, Cartesian linguistics, Cartesian oval, Cartesian (philosophy), Cartesian surfaces, Cartesian tensor (field), Cartesian vector field, Cartesianism, Descartes' folium (or folium of Descartes), Descartes' laws (of refraction), Descartes' organ, Descartes ray, Descartes' rule of signs.

Descartes' rule of signs (Descartes, Rene du Perron): Mathematics. See: Internat. Dict. Ap. Math.; James; Van Nostrand Sci. Encyc.

DESCEMET, JEAN. 1732-1810. French physician. See: World Who's Who Sci. Descemetitis, Descemetocele, Descemet's membrane.

Descemetitis (Descemet, Jean): Medicine. See: Dorland; Stedman.

Descemetocele (Descemet, Jean): Medicine. See: Dorland; Stedman.

Descemet's membrane (Descemet, Jean): Medicine. See: Donath; Gray; Henderson.

DESCHAMPS, JOSEPH FRANCOIS-LOUIS. 1740-1824. French surgeon. See: World Who's Who Sci. Deschamps' needle.

Deschamps' needle (Deschamps, Joseph Francois-Louis): Medicine. See: Dorland; Stedman.

Deschampsia (Loiseleur-Deslongchamps, Jean Louis Auguste): Botany. See: Webster's 3d.

Deschapelles coup (Deschapelles, Louis Honore Lebreton): Recreation and Sports. See: Webster's 3d.

DESCHAPELLES, LOUIS HONORE LEBRETON. 1780-1847. French whist and chess player. See: Barnhart (Cycl. Names). Deschapelles coup.

De Schepper process (Derivation undetermined): Chemistry. See: Van Nostrand Chem. Dict.

DES CLOIZEAUX, ALFRED-LOUIS-OLIVIER LEGRAND. 1817-1897. French mineralogist. See: Dict. Sci. Biog. Descloizite.

Descloizite (Des Cloizeaux, Alfred-Louis-Olivier Legrand): Earth Sciences. See: Charnock; Thrush; Webster's 3d.

DESCOURAIN, FRANCOIS. d. 1740. French botanist. (Biography source unavailable.) Descurainia.

Descurainia (Descourain, Francois): Botany. See: Webster's 3d.

DE SENARMONT, HENRI HUREAU. 1808-1862. French physicist. See: World Who's Who Sci. De Senarmont prism, Senarmontite.

De Senarmont prism (De Senarmont, Henri Hureau): Physics. See: Thewlis.

DESFONTAINES, RENE LOUICHE. 1750-1833. French botanist. See: World Who's Who Sci. Fontanesia.

De Siebold, Charles Gaspard. See: Siebold, Carl Caspar von.

De Signeux's dilator (Derivation undetermined): Medicine. See: Stedman.

De Sitter universe (Sitter, Willem de): Astronomy. See: Van Nostrand Sci. Encyc.

De Sitter, Willem. See: Sitter, Willem de.

DESJARDINS, ABEL. fl. 1905. French surgeon. Cited in: Index Cat. Surg. Gen. Off., 3d. ser., vol. 4. Desjardins' point.

Desjardins' point (Desjardins, Abel): Medicine. See: Dorland.

DESLANDRES, HENRI ALEXANDRE. 1853-1948. French astrophysicist. See: Dict. Sci. Biog. laws of Deslandres.

DE SLUSE, RENE FRANCOIS WALTER. 1622-1685. Belgian mathematician. See: World Who's Who Sci. pearls of Sluse.

DESMAREST, ANSELME-GAETAN. 1784-1838. French naturalist. See: World Who's Who Sci. Desmarestia.

Desmarestia (Desmarest, Anselme-Gaetan): Biology. See: Webster's 3d.

Desmarre's dacryoliths (Desmarres, Louis Auguste): Medicine. See: Dorland; Stedman.

DESMARRES, LOUIS AUGUSTE. 1810-1882. French ophthalmologist. See: World Who's Who Sci. Desmarre's dacryoliths.

Desmoisite (Derivation undetermined): Earth Sciences. See: Thrush.

Desmosite (Derivation undetermined): Earth Sciences. See: Thrush.

Desnos' disease (Desnos, Louis): Medicine. See: Dorland.

DESNOS, LOUIS. 1828-1893. French physician. See: Biog. Lex. hervorr. Aerzte. Desnos' disease.

DESOR, PIERRE JEAN EDOUARD. 1811-1882. French geologist. See: Dict. Sci. Biog. Desor's larva.

Desor's larva (Desor, Pierre Jean Edouard): Zoology. See: Gray; Webster's 3d.

DESPARD, EDWARD MARCUS. 1751-1803. Irish conspirator. See: Dict. Nat. Biog. Despard's plot.

Despard's plot (Despard, Edward Marcus): History. See: Harbottle; Steinberg.

Despert fables (Despert, Juliette Louise): Psychology. See: Wolman.

DESPERT, JULIETTE LOUISE. 1892- . French-born American psychiatrist. See: Amer. Psychiat. Assoc. Biog. Direct., 1968. Despert fables.

D'ESPINE, ADOLPHE. 1846-1930. French physician. See: World Who's Who Sci. D'Espine's sign.

D'Espine's sign (D'Espine, Adolphe): Medicine. See: Dorland; Stedman.

Dessauer curves (Dessauer, Friedrich J.): Medicine. Cited in: Kelly.

DESSAUER, FRIEDRICH J. 1881- . German biophysicist. See: World Who's Who Sci. Dessauer curves.

Destriau effect (Destriau, G.): Physics. See: Ballentyne; Hughes; Markus.

DESTRIAU, G. fl. 1947. French physicist. Cited in: Chem. Abstr., vol. 31, p. 6559. Destriau effect.

DESVERGNES, LOUIS. fl. 1929. French chemist. Cited in: Chem. Abstr., vol. 23, p. 1367. Desvergnes test reaction.

Desvergnes test reaction (Desvergnes, Louis): Chemistry. See: Van Nostrand Chem. Dict.

DE TAKATS, GEZA. 1892- . Hungarian-born surgeon in America. See: World Who's Who Sci. De Takats method, De Takats technic, De Takats test.

De Takats method (De Takats, Geza): Medicine. Cited in: Kelly.

De Takats technic (De Takats, Geza): Medicine. Cited in: Kelly.

De Takats test (De Takats, Geza): Medicine. Cited in: Kelly.

DETERMANN, HERMANN AUGUST. b. 1865. German physician. See: Biog. Lex. hervorr. Aerzte, 1880-1930. Determann's syndrome.

Determann's syndrome (Determann, Hermann August): Medicine. See: Jablonski.

DETMOLD, WILLIAM LUDWIG. 1808-1894. German-born surgeon. See: World Who's Who Sci. Detmold's knife.

Detmold's knife (Detmold, William Ludwig): Medicine. Cited in: World Who's Who Sci.

De Toni-Caffey syndrome (De Toni, Giovanni and Caffey, John). See: Caffey-Silverman syndrome.

De Toni-Fanconi syndrome (De Toni, Giovanni and Fanconi, Guido). See: Abderhalden-Fanconi syndrome.

DE TONI, GIOVANNI. 1895- . Italian pediatrician. See: Ciba symposium, vol. 7, no. 2 (1959), p. 50. De Toni-Caffey syndrome, De Toni-Fanconi syndrome, Fanconi-De Toni-Debre syndrome, Roske-De Toni-Caffey-Smyth disease.

De Torquemada, Tomas. See: Torquemada, Tomas de.

De Ulloa, Antonio. See: Ulloa, Antonio de.

DEUTSCHLAENDER, KARL. 1872-1942. German surgeon. See: Biog. Lex. hervorr. Aerzte, 1880-1930. Deutschlaender's disease.

Deutschlaender's disease (Deutschlaender, Karl): Medicine. See: Dorland; Jablonski; Stedman.

DEUTSCHMANN, RICHARD HEINRICH. 1852-1935. German ophthalmologist. See: World Who's Who Sci. Deutschmann serum.

Deutschmann serum (Deutschmann, Richard Heinrich): Medicine. Cited in: World Who's Who Sci.

DEUTZ, J. d. ca. 1784. Dutch patron of botany. (Biography source unavailable.) Deutzia.

Deutzia (Deutz, J.): Botany. See: Partridge; Taylor, N.; Webster's 3d.

Devarda's alloy (Derivation undetermined): Chemistry. See: Hackh.

De Vathaire process (Derivation undetermined): Chemistry. See: Thrush; Van Nostrand Chem. Dict.

De-Vecchis process (Derivation undetermined): Engineering and Industry. See: Thrush.

DEVENTER, HENDRIK VAN. 1651-1724. Dutch obstetrician. See: Nouv. Biog. Univ. Deventer's diameter(s), Deventer's pelvis.

Deventer's diameter(s) (Deventer, Hendrik van): Medicine. See: Dorland; Stedman.

Deventer's pelvis (Deventer, Hendrik van): Medicine. See: Dorland; Stedman.

Devereaux agitator (Devereux, W. G.): Engineering and Industry. See: Thrush.

DEVEREUX, W. G. fl. 1922. American? metallurgist. Cited in: Chem. Abstr., vol. 16, p. 3867. Devereaux agitator.

DEVERGIE, MARIE GUILLAUME ALPHONSE. 1798-1879. French dermatologist. See: World Who's Who Sci. Devergie's disease.

Devergie's disease (Devergie, Marie Guillaume Alphonse). See: Kaposi's disease (2).

De Vermale, Raymond. See: Vermale, Raymond de.

De Veuster, Joseph. See: Damien, Father.

Devic-Gault syndrome (Devic, M. Eugene and Gault, Fernand). See: Devic's syndrome (or disease).

DEVIC, M. EUGENE. d. 1930. French physician. Cited in: Lieber and Olbrich. Devic's syndrome (or disease).

devices of Cepola (Cepola, Bartolommeo): Generic Word (quips of law). See: Brewer.

Devic's syndrome (or disease) (Devic, M. Eugene): Medicine. See: Hinsie; Jablonski; Stedman. Also known as: Devic-Gault syndrome.

De Vieussens, Raymond. See: Vieussens, Raymond de.

DE VIGENERE, BLAISE. 1523-1596. French diplomat and student of cryptography. See: World Who's Who Sci. Vigenere cipher, Vigenere tableau (or square).

DEVILLE, HENRI ETIENNE SAINTE-CLAIRE. 1818-1881. French chemist. See: Dict. Sci. Biog. Devilline (or Devillite), Saint Clair-Blue process.

Deville-Negre engine (Deville, P. and Negre, G.): Engineering and Industry. See: Auger.

DEVILLE, P. No dates. French engineer. (Biography source unavailable.) Deville-Negre engine.

Deville–Pechiney process (Derivation undetermined): Chemistry. See: Van Nostrand Chem. Dict.

Devilline (or Devillite) (Deville, Henri Etienne Sainte–Claire): Earth Sciences. See: Thrush; Webster's 3d.

Devine exclusion (Devine, Sir Hugh Berchmans): Medicine. See: Stedman.

DEVINE, SIR HUGH BERCHMANS. 1878–1959. Australian surgeon. See: Med. J. Australia, vol. 46, no. 21 (1959), p. 777. Devine exclusion.

DE VINNE, THEODORE LOW. 1828–1914. American printer. See: Dict. Amer. Biog. De Vinne (type face).

De Vinne (type face) (De Vinne, Theodore Low): Printing. See: Harrod.

DEVLIN, BERNADETTE JOSEPHINE. 1947– . Irish civil rights leader. Cur. Biog., 1970. Devlinite.

Devlinite (Devlin, Bernadette Josephine): Politics. See: Barnhart (New Eng.).

Devonshire, 8th Duke of. See: Cavendish, Spencer Compton, Marquis of Hartington and 8th Duke of Devonshire.

DEVONSHIRE, A. F. fl. 1935–1939. English? physicist. Cited in: Chem. Abstr. Lennard–Jones and Devonshire theory.

De Vooys process (Vooys, Gerard Jan de). See: Vooys process.

DE VRIES, ANDRE. 1911– . Dutch-born Israeli physician. See: Who's Who Israel, 1952. De Vries' syndrome.

DE VRIES, HUGO MARIE. 1848–1935. Dutch botanist. See: World Who's Who Sci. De Vries' theory.

DEVRIES, RALPH P. fl. 1912. American physicist. Cited in: Chem. Abstr. Decenn. Index, 1907–1916. De Vries test.

De Vries' syndrome (De Vries, Andre): Medicine. See: Jablonski.

De Vries test (Devries, Ralph P.): Engineering and Industry. See: Thrush.

De Vries' theory (De Vries, Hugo Marie): Medicine. See: Dorland.

De Vriese, Willem Hendrik. See: Vriese, Willem Hendrik de.

De Vrij solution (Derivation undetermined): Chemistry. See: Van Nostrand Chem. Dict.

DEW, JAMES HARVIE. 1843–1914. American physician. See: Phys. Surg. Amer. Byrd–Dew method.

DE WALL, RICHARD ALLISON. 1926– . American thoracic surgeon. See: Direct. Med. Specialists, 1975–1976. Lillehei–De Wall apparatus.

Dewar calorimeter (Dewar, James): Chemistry. See: Thewlis.

Dewar flask (or vessel) (Dewar, James): Chemistry. See: Hackh; Hendrickson; Internat. Dict. Phys. Elec.

DEWAR, JAMES. 1842–1923. Scottish chemist. See: Dict. Sci. Biog. Dewar calorimeter, Dewar flask (or vessel), Dewar–Redwood process?

Dewar–Redwood process (Dewar, James? and Redwood, Sir Boverton): Chemistry. See: Thrush.

De Watteville, Baron Oscar. See: Watteville, Baron Oscar de.

DE WECKER, LOUIS. 1832–1904. French ophthalmologist. See: World Who's Who Sci. De Wecker's scissors.

De Wecker's scissors (De Wecker, Louis): Medicine. See: Stedman.

Dewees' sign (Dewees, William Potts): Medicine. See: Dorland; Stedman.

DEWEES, WILLIAM POTTS. 1768–1841. American obstetrician. See: World Who's Who Sci. Dewees' sign.

DEWEY, CHESTER. 1784–1867. American clergyman and scientist. See: Dict. Amer. Biog. Deweylite.

Dewey decimal classification (or system) (Dewey, Melvil): Library Science. See: Harrod; Hendrickson; Mathews, M. M.

DEWEY, JOHN. 1859–1952. American philosopher and educator. See: Internat. Encyc. Soc. Sci. Deweyan.

DEWEY, MELVIL. 1851–1931. American librarian. See: Dict. Amer. Biog., 1st suppl. Dewey decimal classification (or system), Melvil Dewey Medal.

Deweyan (Dewey, John): Education. See: Hendrickson; Webster's 3d.

Deweylite (Dewey, Chester): Earth Sciences. See: Thrush; Webster's 3d.

DEWINDT, JEAN. 20th c. Belgian geologist. Cited in: Bailey. Dewindtite.

Dewindtite (Dewindt, Jean): Earth Sciences. See: Thrush; Webster's 3d.

Dewitt (Dewitt, Cornelius and Dewitt, Jan): Generic Word (lynch). See: Hendrickson; Partridge; Webster's 3d.

DEWITT, CORNELIUS. 1623–1672. Dutch statesman. See: Barnhart (Cycl. Names). Dewitt.

DEWITT, JAN. 1625–1672. Dutch statesman. See: Barnhart (Cycl. Names). Dewitt.

DEWRANCE, JOHN. d. 1861. English engineer. (Biography source unavailable.) Dewrance valve.

Dewrance valve (Dewrance, John): Engineering and Industry. See: Auger.

D'HERELLE, FELIX HUBERT. 1873–1949. Canadian-born bacteriologist. See: Webster's Biog. Dict. Herelleosis, Twort–D'Herelle phenomenon.

D'Herelle phenomenon (D'Herelle, Felix Hubert). See: Twort–D'Herelle phenomenon.

D'HONT, ALFRED (DONATO). 1845–1900. Belgian magnetizer. (Biography source unavailable.) Donatism.

D'HUART, GEORGES. fl. 1929. French metallurgist. Cited in: Chem. Abstr., vol. 23, p. 4658. D'Huart reagent.

D'Huart reagent (D'Huart, Georges): Engineering and Industry. See: Thrush.

D'Huilier's equation (Derivation undetermined): Mathematics. See: Ballentyne.

DIABELLI, ANTONIO. 1781–1858. Austrian composer and music publisher. See: Grove. Diabelli Variations.

Diabelli Variations (Diabelli, Antonio): Music. See: Apel; Scholes.

dial of Ahaz (Ahaz): Horology. See: Brewer.

Diamond albumin test (Diamond, Louis Stanley): Medicine. See: Webster's 3d.

Diamond–Blackfan syndrome (Diamond, Louis Klein and Blackfan, Kenneth D.): Medicine. See: Jablonski. Also known as: Josephs–Diamond–Blackfan anemia (or syndrome), Kaznelson's syndrome.

DIAMOND, HARRY. 1900– . American radio engineer. See: Amer. Men Sci., 6th ed. Diamond–Hinman radiosonde.

Diamond–Hinman radiosonde (Diamond, Harry and Hinman, Wilbur Stanley): Engineering and Industry. See: Huschke.

DIAMOND, LOUIS KLEIN. 1902– . American physician. See: World Who's Who Sci. Diamond–Blackfan syndrome.

DIAMOND, LOUIS STANLEY. 1920– . American parasitologist. See: Amer. Men and Women Sci., 12th ed. Diamond albumin test.

DIAMOND, SOLOMON. 1906– . American psychologist. See: Amer. Psych. Assoc., Direct., 1948. Porteus–Diamond learning machine.

Diana (Diana, the goddess): Generic Word (silver). See: Charnock.

Diana butterfly (Diana, the goddess): Zoology. See: Webster's 3d.

Diana complex (Diana, the goddess): Psychology. See: Chaplin; English.

Diana grape (Crehore, Diana): Botany. See: Mathews, M. M.

Diana monkey (Diana, the goddess): Zoology. See: Charnock; Webster's 3d.

DIANA, THE GODDESS. Roman goddess of the moon. See: Jobes. Diana, Diana butterfly, Diana complex, Diana monkey, Diana's worshippers, Dianella.

DIANANDA, P. H. fl. 1950. Malayan mathematician. Cited in: World Direct. Math. Bartlett and Diananda test.

Diana's worshippers (Diana, the goddess): Generic Word (midnight revellers). See: Brewer.

Dianella (Diana, the goddess): Botany. See: Charnock.

DIAZ DE RADA, F. fl. 1929. Spanish chemist. Cited in: Chem. Abstr., vol. 23, p. 4161. De Rada test.

DIBDIN, WILLIAM JOSEPH. 1850-1925. English chemist. See: World Who's Who Sci. Dibdin's hand photometer.

Dibdin's hand photometer (Dibdin, William Joseph): Chemistry. Cited in: World Who's Who Sci.

Di Birago bridge (Di Birago, Carlo): Engineering and Industry. Cited in: World Who's Who Sci.

DI BIRAGO, CARLO. 1792-1845. Italian engineer. See: World Who's Who Sci. Di Birago bridge.

Dichert reagent (Dickert, M.): Chemistry. See: Van Nostrand Chem. Dict.

DICK, ALLAN B. d. 1926. English mineralogist. Cited in: Royal Soc. Cat. Sci. Pap., 1884-1900. Dickite.

DICK, GEORGE FREDERICK. 1881- . American physician and bacteriologist. See: World Who's Who Sci. Dick method, Dick test, Dick toxin.

DICK, GLADYS HENRY. 1881-1963. American bacteriologist. See: Who Was Who Amer., 1961-1968. Dick method, Dick test, Dick toxin.

Dick method (Dick, George Frederick and Dick, Gladys Henry): Medicine. See: Stedman.

Dick test (Dick, George Frederick and Dick, Gladys Henry): Medicine. See: Dorland; Hendrickson; Stedman.

Dick toxin (Dick, George Frederick and Dick, Gladys Henry): Medicine. See: Dorland; Webster's 3d.

Dicke('s) radiometer (Dicke, Robert Henry): Electronics. See: Hughes; Markus.

DICKE, ROBERT HENRY. 1916- . American physicist. See: Amer. Men Sci., 10th ed. Brans-Dicke theory, Dicke('s) radiometer.

DICKENS, CHARLES JOHN HUFFAM. 1812-1870. English novelist. See: Dict. Nat. Biog. Dickensian.

DICKENS, FRANK. 1899- . English biochemist. See: World Who's Who Sci. Dickens shunt.

Dickens shunt (Dickens, Frank): Medicine. See: Stedman.

Dickensian (Dickens, Charles John Huffam): Literature. See: Hendrickson; Partridge; Webster's 3d.

Dickenson reagent (Derivation undetermined): Chemistry. See: Van Nostrand Chem. Dict.

DICKERT, M. fl. 1911. German chemist. Cited in: Chem. Abstr., vol. 5, p. 1989. Dichert reagent.

DICKINSON, JOHN. fl. 19th c. American clergyman and mineralogist. Cited in: Bailey. Dickinsonite.

DICKINSON, JOSEPH. fl. 1898. English geologist. Cited in: Royal Soc. Cat. Sci. Pap., 1884-1900. Dickinson's fault plane theory.

DICKINSON, WILLIAM HOWSHIP. 1832-1913. English physician. See: World Who's Who Sci. Dickinson's syndrome.

Dickinsonite (Dickinson, John): Earth Sciences. See: Thrush; Webster's 3d.

Dickinson's fault plane theory (Dickinson, Joseph): Earth Sciences. See: Thrush.

Dickinson's syndrome (Dickinson, William Howship). See: Alport's syndrome.

Dickite (Dick, Allan B.): Earth Sciences. See: Thrush; Webster's 3d.

Dickman charging system (Derivation undetermined): Library Science. See: Harrod.

Dick's hatband (Cromwell, Richard): Generic Word (crown of England). See: Phyfe.

DICKSON, JAMES. 1737-1822. Scottish botanist. See: Dict. Nat. Biog. Dicksonia.

Dicksonia (Dickson, James): Botany. See: Charnock; Taylor, N.; Webster's 3d.

Diddle (Diddler, Jeremy): Generic Word (to swindle). See: Partridge; Weekley.

DIDDLER, JEREMY. Chief character in James Kenney's farce, "Raising the Wind," (1803). See: Harvey. Diddle.

Dide-Botcazo syndrome (Derivation undetermined): Medicine. See: Jablonski.

DIDO. Legendary queen of Carthage. See: Jobes. cut(ting) a Dido (or cut up Didos), Dido's problem.

Dido's problem (Dido): Mathematics. See: Internat. Dict. Ap. Math.; James.

DIDOT, FRANCOIS AMBROISE. 1730-1804. French typefounder. See: World Who's Who Sci. Didot system.

Didot system (Didot, Francois Ambroise): Printing. See: Harrod.

Dieckmann reaction (or condensation) (Dieckmann, Walter): Chemistry. See: Ballentyne; Webster's 3d.

Dieckmann synthesis (Dieckmann, Walter): Chemistry. See: Van Nostrand Chem. Dict.

DIECKMANN, WALTER. 1869-1925. German chemist. See: Surrey. Dieckmann reaction (or condensation), Dieckmann synthesis.

DIEFFENBACH, ERNEST. 1811-1855. German naturalist. See: World Who's Who Sci. Dieffenbachia.

DIEFFENBACH, JOHANN FRIEDRICH. 1792-1847. German surgeon. See: World Who's Who Sci. Dieffenbach's amputation, Dieffenbach's method.

Dieffenbachia (Dieffenbach, Ernest): Botany. See: Taylor, N.; Webster's 3d.

Dieffenbach's amputation (Dieffenbach, Johann Friedrich): Medicine. See: Stedman.

Dieffenbach's method (Dieffenbach, Johann Friedrich): Medicine. See: Stedman.

Diego blood group (Derivation undetermined): Medicine. See: Stedman.

Diehl process (Derivation undetermined): Engineering and Industry. See: Thrush.

DIEL, AUGUST FRIEDRICH ADRIAN. 1756-1839. German physician and pomologist. See: World Who's Who Sci. Diels butterbirne (avocado).

Diels-Alder reaction (Diels, Otto Paul Hermann and Alder, Kurt): Chemistry. See: Ballentyne; Van Nostrand Chem. Dict.; Webster's 3d.

Diels butterbirne (avocado) (Diel, August Friedrich Adrian): Botany. Cited in: World Who's Who Sci.

Diels' hydrocarbon (Diels, Otto Paul Hermann): Chemistry. See: Hackh; Stedman.

DIELS, OTTO PAUL HERMANN. 1876-1954. German chemist. See: Dict. Sci. Biog. Diels-Alder reaction, Diels' hydrocarbon.

DIEMEN, ANTONIO VAN. 1593-1645. Dutch merchant and colonial administrator. See: Encyc. Brit., 1973. Demansia (snake).

DIENST, ARTHUR. b. 1871. German gynecologist. See: Biog. Lex. hervorr. Aerzte, 1880-1930. Dienst's test.

Dienst's test (Dienst, Arthur): Medicine. See: Dorland.

DIEREVILLE, N. DE. fl. 17th c. French surgeon in Canada. See: Dict. Biog. Fran. Diervilla.

Dierk's layer (or zone) (Derivation undetermined): Medicine. See: Dorland.

Diervilla (Diereville, N. de): Botany. See: Taylor, N.; Webster's 3d.

Dies Committee (Dies, Martin, Jr.): History. See: Morris.

DIES, MARTIN, JR. 1900- . American lawyer and legislator. See: Biog. Direct. Amer. Congress. Dies Committee.

Diesel cycle (Diesel, Rudolf Christian Karl): Physics. See: Ballentyne; Internat. Dict. Phys. Elec.; Thewlis.

Diesel engine (Diesel, Rudolf Christian Karl): Engineering and Industry. See: Hendrickson; Van Nostrand Sci. Encyc.; Webster's 3d.

Diesel fuel (or oil) (Diesel, Rudolf Christian Karl): Chemistry. See: Hackh.

DIESEL, RUDOLF CHRISTIAN KARL. 1858-1930. German mechanical engineer. See: World Who's Who Sci. Diesel cycle, Diesel engine, Diesel fuel (or oil).

Diesselhorst difference potentiometer (Diesselhorst, Hermann Georg Heinrich?): Physics. See: Internat. Dict. Phys. Elec.

DIESSELHORST, HERMANN GEORG HEINRICH. 1870- . German physicist. See: Pogg., vol. 4, 5, 6, 7a. Diesselhorst difference potentiometer?

Dieterich test reaction for uric acid (Derivation undetermined): Chemistry. See: Van Nostrand Chem. Dict.

DIETERICI, CONRAD HEINRICH. 1858-1929. German physicist. See: Pogg., vols. 4, 5, 6. Dieterici equation, Dieterici's rule.

Dieterici equation (Dieterici, Conrad Heinrich): Physics. See: Ballentyne; Internat. Dict. Ap. Math.; Internat. Dict. Phys. Elec.

Dieterici's rule (Dieterici, Conrad Heinrich): Physics. See: Hackh.

Dietert tester (Derivation undetermined): Engineering and Industry. See: Thrush.

DIETL, JOZEF. 1804-1878. Polish physician. See: World Who's Who Sci. Dietl's crisis.

DIETLEN, JOHANNES. 1879-1955. German physician. See: Biog. Lex. hervorr. Aerzte, 1880-1930. Dietlen's syndrome.

Dietlen's syndrome (Dietlen, Johannes): Medicine. See: Jablonski.

Dietl's crisis (Dietl, Jozef): Medicine. See: Dorland; Jablonski; Stedman.

DIETRICH, DR. fl. 19th c. Austrian scientist. Cited in: Bailey. Dietrichite.

Dietrich fluid (Derivation undetermined): Chemistry. See: Van Nostrand Chem. Dict.

DIETRICH, HANS. 1891-1956. German surgeon. Cited in: Lieber and Olbrich. Dietrich's syndrome.

Dietrichite (Dietrich, Dr.): Earth Sciences. See: Webster's 3d.

Dietrich's syndrome (Dietrich, Hans): Medicine. See: Jablonski.

DIETZ, ROBERT SINCLAIR. 1914- . American geological oceanographer. See: Amer. Men Sci., 10th ed. Emery-Dietz gravity corer.

DIETZE, AUGUST. d. ca 1893. German chemist. Cited in: Bailey. Dietzeite.

Dietze test (Derivation undetermined): Chemistry. See: Van Nostrand Chem. Dict.

Dietzeite (Dietze, August): Earth Sciences. See: Thrush; Webster's 3d.

DIEUDONNE, ADOLF. 1864-1945. German serologist. See: World Who's Who Sci. Dieudonne's medium.

Dieudonne's medium (Dieudonne, Adolf): Medicine. See: Dorland.

DIEULAFOY, GEORGES. 1839-1911. French physician. See: World Who's Who Sci. Dieulafoy's aspirator, Dieulafoy's erosion, Dieulafoy's theory, Dieulafoy's triad.

Dieulafoy's aspirator (Dieulafoy, Georges): Medicine. See: Dorland; Stedman.

Dieulafoy's erosion (Dieulafoy, Georges): Medicine. See: Dorland; Stedman.

Dieulafoy's theory (Dieulafoy, Georges): Medicine. See: Dorland; Stedman.

Dieulafoy's triad (Dieulafoy, Georges): Medicine. See: Dorland.

DI GEORGE, ANGELO MARIO. 1921- . American endocrinologist. See: Amer. Men and Women Sci., 12th ed. DiGeorge's syndrome.

DiGeorge's syndrome (DiGeorge, Angelo Mario): Medicine. See: Jablonski.

DIGHTON, ADAIR. b. 1861. English physician. Cited in: Mansell. Adair Dighton's syndrome.

DI GUGLIELMO, GIOVANNI. 1886-1961. Italian physician. See: Athena (March, 1936), p. 97. Di Guglielmo's disease (1), Di Guglielmo's disease (2).

Di Guglielmo's disease (1) (Di Guglielmo, Giovanni): Medicine. See: Jablonski; Stedman.

Di Guglielmo's disease (2) (Di Guglielmo, Giovanni). See: Mortensen's disease.

DILLE, JAMES MADISON. 1907- . American pharmacologist. See: Amer. Men and Women Sci., 12th ed. Dille-Koppanyi test.

Dille-Koppanyi test (Dille, James Madison and Koppanyi, Theodore): Chemistry. See: Van Nostrand Chem. Dict.

Dillenia (Dillenius, Johann Jacob): Botany. See: Charnock; Webster's 3d.

DILLENIUS, JOHANN JACOB. 1687-1747. German botanist in England. See: Dict. Sci. Biog. Dillenia.

Dillingham Bill (Dillingham, William Paul): History. Cited in: Webster's Biog. Dict.

DILLINGHAM, WILLIAM PAUL. 1843-1923. American lawyer and statesman. See: Dict. Amer. Biog. Dillingham Bill.

DILLON, CLARENCE DOUGLAS. 1909- . American politician and businessman. See: Sobel. Dillon round.

Dillon round (Dillon, Clarence Douglas): Economics. See: Smith.

DILLWYN, LEWIS WESTON. 1778-1855. Welsh naturalist. See: Dict. Nat. Biog. Dillwynia.

Dillwynia (Dillwyn, Lewis Weston): Botany. See: Charnock.

DIMITRI, VINCENTE. 1885-1955. Austrian-born Argentine neurologist. See: Gran Encic. Argentina. Parkes-Weber and Dimitri syndrome, Sturge-Weber-Dimitri syndrome, Weber-Dimitri syndrome.

DIMLER, MARGUERITE C. fl. 1929. American pharmacist. Cited in: Chem. Abstr., vol. 23, p. 4165. Arny-Dimler test.

DIMMER, FRIEDRICH. 1855-1926. Austrian ophthalmologist. See: Biog. Lex. hervorr. Aerzte, 1880-1930. Biber-Haab-Dimmer degeneration, Dimmer's keratitis.

Dimmer's keratitis (Dimmer, Friedrich): Medicine. See: Dorland; Jablonski; Stedman.

Dimond ring (Dimond, Thomas Leone?): Electronics. See: Markus.

DIMOND, THOMAS LEONE. 1903- . American electrical engineer. See: Amer. Men Sci., 10th ed. Dimond ring?

dine with Duke Humphrey (Humphrey, Duke of Gloucester and Earl of Pembroke): Generic Word (not dine). See: Harvey; Hendrickson; Partridge; Phyfe; Weekley.

Dines pressure tube anemometer (Dines, William Henry): Engineering and Industry. See: Monkhouse.

DINES, WILLIAM HENRY. 1855-1927. English meteorologist. See: World Who's Who Sci. Dines pressure tube anemometer.

DINGAAN. fl. 1838. Zulu chieftain. See: Webster's Biog. Dict. Dingaan's day.

Dingaan's day (Dingaan): History. See: Harbottle; Steinberg.

Dingley Act (or Tariff Act) (Dingley, Nelson): History. See: Jameson; Montgomery; Smith.

DINGLEY, NELSON. 1832-1899. American legislator. See: Dict. Amer. Biog. Dingley Act (or Tariff Act), Dingleyism.

Dingleyism (Dingley, Nelson): History. See: Mathews, M. M.

DINGWALL, MARY M. fl. 1950. English physician. (Biography source unavailable.) Neill-Dingwall syndrome.

Dini helicoid surfaces (Dini, Ulisse): Mathematics. Cited in: Dict. Sci. Biog.

DINI, O. No dates. Italian professor who discovered the crystals. Cited in: Bailey. Dinite.

DINI, ULISSE. 1845-1918. Italian mathematician. See: Dict. Biog. Sci. Dini helicoid surfaces.

Dinite (Dini, O.): Earth Sciences. See: Charnock.

DINMONT, DANDIE. Character in Sir Walter Scott's "Guy Mannering" (1815). See: Benet. Dandie Dinmont (terrier).

Dinnyhayser (Hayes, Dinny): Generic Word (knock-out blow). See: Brewer.

DI NOLA, ETTORE. fl. 1909. Italian chemist. Cited in: Chem. Abstr., vol. 3, p. 1312. Bianchi-Nola test, Malatesta-Di Nola reagent for copper, nickel and cobalt, Malatesta-Di Nola test reaction for gold and platinum.

DINOSTRATUS. fl. ca. 350 B.C. Greek mathematician. See: Dict. Sci. Biog. quadratrix of Dinostratus.

DIOCLES. fl. 2d c. B.C. Greek mathematician. See: Dict. Sci. Biog. cissoid of Diocles.

Diodorean (Diodorus Cronus): Philosophy. See: Webster's 3d.

DIODORUS CRONUS. fl. 4th c. B.C. Greek philosopher and jurist. See: Encyc. Brit., 1973. Diodorean.

DIOGENES. 412?-323 B.C. Greek Cynic philosopher. See: Encyc. Brit., 1973. Diogenes crab, Diogenes cup, Diogenic (or Diogenean).

Diogenes crab (Diogenes): Zoology. See: Brewer; Hendrickson; Webster's 3d.

Diogenes cup (Diogenes): Generic Word. See: Brewer; Charnock; Hendrickson.

Diogenic (or Diogenean) (Diogenes): Generic Word (cynical). See: Webster's 3d.; Weekley.

Diomeda (Diomedea) (birds) (Diomedes): Zoology. See: Charnock; Webster's 3d.

Diomedean exchange (Diomedes): Generic Word. See: Brewer.

DIOMEDES. Legendary Greek warrior. See: Encyc. Brit., 1973. Diomeda (Diomedea) (birds), Diomedean exchange.

Dionise (Dionysus): Lapidary. See: Partridge; Webster's 3d.

Dionysia (Dionysus): Religion. See: Webster's 3d.

Dionysian (1) (or Dionysiac) (Dionysus): Generic Word (orgiastic). See: Chaplin; English; Hoult.

Dionysian (2) (Dionysius the Elder and Dionysius the Younger): History. See: Webster's 3d.

Dionysian (3) (Dionysius the Areopagite): Religion. See: Webster's 3d.

Dionysian (period) (Dionysius Exiguus): Horology. See: Webster's 3d.

DIONYSIUS EXIGUUS. fl. 6th c. Roman monk and scholar. See: Webster's Biog. Dict. Dionysian (period).

DIONYSIUS THE AREOPAGITE. fl. 500 A.D. Greek Christian neoplatonist. See: Webster's Biog. Dict. Dionysian (3).

DIONYSIUS THE ELDER. ca. 430-367 B.C. Greek tyrant. See: Webster's Biog. Dict. Dionysian (2).

DIONYSIUS THE YOUNGER. fl. 367-343 B.C. Greek tyrant. See: Webster's Biog. Dict. Dionysian (2).

DIONYSUS. Greek god of wine and earthly enjoyment. See: Jobes. Dionise, Dionysia, Dionysian (1) (or Dionysiac).

Diophantine (equation) (Diophantus of Alexandria): Mathematics. See: Charnock; Van Nostrand Sci. Encyc.

DIOPHANTUS OF ALEXANDRIA. fl. 250 A.D. Greek mathematician. See: Dict. Sci. Biog. Diophantine (equation).

Dioscorea (Dioscorides): Botany. See: Charnock; Hendrickson; Taylor, N.

DIOSCORIDES (PEDANIUS DIOSCORIDES OF ANAZARBUS). fl. 50-70 A.D. Greek physician and botanist. See: Dict. Sci. Biog. Dioscorea.

DIPPEL, JOHANN CONRAD. 1673-1734. German theologian, physician, and alchemist. See: World Who's Who Sci. Dippel's oil.

Dippel's oil (Dippel, Johann Conrad): Chemistry. See: Hackh; Webster's 3d.

Dirac classical electron theory (Dirac, Paul Adrien Maurice): Physics. See: Internat. Dict. Phys. Elec.

Dirac delta function (Dirac, Paul Adrien Maurice): Physics. See: Ballentyne; Internat. Dict. Phys. Elec.; Van Nostrand Sci. Encyc.

Dirac electron theory (Dirac, Paul Adrien Maurice): Physics. See: Internat. Dict. Phys. Elec.; Van Nostrand Sci. Encyc.

Dirac equation (Dirac, Paul Adrien Maurice): Physics. See: Ballentyne; Internat. Dict. Ap. Math.; Thewlis.

Dirac operators (Dirac, Paul Adrien Maurice): Physics. See: Internat. Dict. Phys. Elec.

DIRAC, PAUL ADRIEN MAURICE. 1902- . English physicist. See: World Who's Who Sci. Dirac classical electron theory, Dirac delta function, Dirac electron theory, Dirac equation, Dirac operators, Dirac's constant, Fermi-Dirac distribution function, Fermi-Dirac gas, Fermi-Dirac liquid, Fermi-Dirac-Sommerfield velocity-distribution law, Fermi-Dirac statistics.

Dirac's constant (Dirac, Paul Adrien Maurice): Physics. See: Hughes.

Dirichlet condition (or boundary condition) (Dirichlet, Gustav Peter Lejeune): Mathematics. See: Ballentyne; Internat. Dict. Phys. Elec.; Thewlis.

Dirichlet discontinuous factor (Dirichlet, Gustav Peter Lejeune): Mathematics. See: Internat. Dict. Phys. Elec.; Van Nostrand Sci. Encyc.

Dirichlet distribution (Dirichlet, Gustav Peter Lejeune): Mathematics. See: Kendall.

DIRICHLET, GUSTAV PETER LEJEUNE. 1805-1859. German mathematician. See: Dict. Sci. Biog. Dirichlet condition (or boundary condition), Dirichlet discontinuous factor, Dirichlet distribution, Dirichlet integral, Dirichlet principle, Dirichlet problem, Dirichlet series, Dirichlet theorem, Dirichlet's test for convergence.

Dirichlet integral (Dirichlet, Gustav Peter Lejeune): Mathematics. See: Internat. Dict. Ap. Math.; Internat. Dict. Phys. Elec.; Van Nostrand Sci. Encyc.

Dirichlet principle (Dirichlet, Gustav Peter Lejeune): Mathematics. See: Internat. Dict. Ap. Math.

Dirichlet problem (Dirichlet, Gustav Peter Lejeune): Mathematics. See: Ballentyne.

Dirichlet series (Dirichlet, Gustav Peter Lejeune): Mathematics. See: Internat. Dict. Ap. Math.

Dirichlet theorem (Dirichlet, Gustav Peter Lejeune): Mathematics. See: Ballentyne.

Dirichlet's test for convergence (Dirichlet, Gustav Peter Lejeune): Mathematics. See: Ballentyne.

DIRKSEN, EVERETT MC KINLEY. 1896-1969. American legislator. See: Biog. Direct. Amer. Congress. Dirksen resolution.

Dirksen resolution (Dirksen, Everett McKinley): Politics. See: Smith.

Dische carbazole solution (Dische, Zacharias): Chemistry. See: Van Nostrand Chem. Dict.

Dische reaction (Dische, Zacharias): Chemistry. See: Hackh; Stedman.

DISCHE, ZACHARIAS. 1895- . Austrian biochemist. See: Pogg., vol. 6, 7b. Dische carbazole solution, Dische reaction.

Disciples of Christ (Jesus Christ): Religion. See: Canney; Mathews, S.

DISNEY, JOHN. 1779-1857. English collector of classical antiquities. See: Dict. Nat. Biog. Disney Professor.

Disney Professor (Disney, John): Archeology. See: Wagner (More Names).

DISNEY, WALT (WALTER ELIAS). 1901-1966. American film producer. See: Encyc. Brit., 1973. Disneyan (or Disneyesque).

Disneyan (or Disneyesque) (Disney, Walt): Fine Arts. See: Hendrickson; Webster's 3d.

DISSE, JOSEPH. 1852-1912. German anatomist. See: Biog. Lex. hervorr. Aerzte, 1880-1930. Disse's space(s).

Disse's space(s) (Disse, Joseph): Medicine. See: Dorland; Stedman.

distribution law of Maxwell (Maxwell, James Clerk). See: Maxwell distribution law.

Ditmar reagents (Derivation undetermined): Chemistry. See: Van Nostrand Chem. Dict.

Dittel, Leopold von. See: Von Dittel, Leopold.

Dittel's operation (Von Dittel, Leopold Ritter): Medicine. See: Dorland.

DITTRICH, FRANZ. 1815-1850. German pathologist. See: World Who's Who Sci. Dittrich's plugs, Dittrich's stenosis.

Dittrich's plugs (Dittrich, Franz): Medicine. See: Dorland; Stedman. Also known as: Traube's plugs.

Dittrich's stenosis (Dittrich, Franz): Medicine. See: Stedman.

Dittus-Boelter equation (Dittus, Frederick William and Boelter, Llewellyn Michael Kraus): Physics. See: Thewlis.

DITTUS, FREDERICK WILLIAM. 1897- . German-born American engineer. See: Who's Who Engin., 1959. Dittus-Boelter equation.

DITZ, HUGO. 1876-1944. Austrian chemist. See: Pogg., vol. 5, 6, 7a. Ditz test reactions.

Ditz test reactions (Ditz, Hugo): Chemistry. See: Van Nostrand Chem. Dict.

Dives (Dives, the rich man): Generic Word (wealthy person). See: Hendrickson.

DIVES, THE RICH MAN. Biblical figure. See: Encyc. Amer., 1959. Dives.

DIVISIA, FRANCOIS. 1889-1964. Algerian-born French economist. See: Internat. Encyc. Soc. Sci. Divisia-Roy index, Divisia's index.

Divisia-Roy index (Divisia, Francois and Roy): Economics. See: Kendall.

Divisia's index (Divisia, Francois): Economics. See: Kendall.

DIVRY, PAUL. b. 1889. Belgian physician. See: Biog. Lex. hervorr. Aerzte, 1880-1930. Van Bogaert-Divry syndrome.

Dix, Dorothy. See: Gilmer, Elizabeth Meriwether.

DIX, JOHN ADAMS. 1798-1879. American army officer and political leader. See: Dict. Amer. Biog. Dix's order.

DIXIE. No dates. American slaveholder. (Biography source unavailable.) Dixie('s) (land).

Dixie('s) (land) (Dixie): Generic Word (Southern States of America). See: Harbottle; Hendrickson; Partridge.

DIXON, JEREMIAH. 1733-1779. English surveyor. See: Dict. Sci. Biog. Mason and Dixon's line.

DIXON, WILFRID JOSEPH. 1915- . American mathematical statistician. See: Amer. Men and Women Sci., 12th ed. Dixon's statistics.

Dixon's statistics (Dixon, Wilfrid Joseph): Statistics. See: Kendall.

Dix's order (Dix, John Adams): History. See: Phyfe.

DJALMA, GUIMARAES. fl. 20th c. Brazilian mineralogist. (Biography source unavailable.) Djalmaite.

Djalmaite (Djalma, Guimaraes): Earth Sciences. See: Webster's 3d.

DJURLE, S. fl. 1958. Described the mineral. Cited in: Min. Mag., vol. 33 (1964), p. 1131-32. Djurleite.

Djurleite (Djurle, S.): Earth Sciences. See: Thrush.

DOAN, CHARLES AUSTIN. 1896- . American physician. See: World Who's Who Sci. Wiseman-Doan syndrome.

DOBA, STEPHEN JR. 1907- . American electrical engineer. See: Amer. Men Sci., 10th ed. Doba's network?

Doba's network (Doba, Stephen Jr.?): Electronics. See: Hughes.

Dobbin reagent (Derivation undetermined): Chemistry. See: Van Nostrand Chem. Dict.

DOBBINS, JOE. fl. 20th c. American shop foreman. (Biography source unavailable.) Dobbins' law.

Dobbins' law (Dobbins, Joe): Sociology. See: Martin.

DOBELL, HORACE BENGE. 1828-1917. English physician. See: Webster's Biog. Dict. Dobell('s) solution.

Dobell('s) solution (Dobell, Horace Benge): Medicine. See: Dorland; Van Nostrand Chem. Dict.; Webster's 3d.

Doberman pinscher (Dobermann, Ludwig): Zoology. See: Hendrickson; Webster's 3d.

DOBERMANN, LUDWIG. fl. 1890. German dog breeder. (Biography source unavailable.) Doberman pinscher.

DOBIE, WILLIAM MURRAY. 1828-1915. English physician. Cited in: Kelly. Dobie's globule, Dobie's line (or layer).

Dobie's globule (Dobie, William Murray): Medicine. See: Dorland.

Dobie's line (or layer) (Dobie, William Murray): Medicine. See: Dorland; Henderson; Stedman. Also known as: Krause's membrane.

Doble vane (Doble, William A.): Engineering and Industry. See: Auger.

DOBLE, WILLIAM A. fl. 1889. American mining engineer. Cited in: Royal Soc. Cat. Sci. Pap., 1884-1900. Doble vane.

DOBOS, JOZEF C. d. 1928. Hungarian pastry chef. (Biography source unavailable.) Dobos (torte).

Dobos (torte) (Dobos, Jozef C.): Food and Drink. See: Webster's 3d.

DOBROLYUBSKII, O. K. fl. 1938. Russian chemist. Cited in: Chem. Abstr., vol. 32, p. 4465. Dobrolyubskii test.

Dobrolyubskii test (Dobrolyubskii, O. K.): Chemistry. See: Van Nostrand Chem. Dict.

DOBSON, GEORGE EDWARD. 1848-1895. Irish-born zoologist. See: World Who's Who Sci. Dobsonia (bats).

DOBSON, GORDON MILLER BOURNE. 1889- . English climatologist. See: Pogg., vol. 6. Dobson-Lindemann theory, Dobson spectrophotometer.

Dobson-Lindemann theory (Dobson, Gordon Miller Bourne and Lindemann, Frederick Alexander): Earth Sciences. See: Dict. Sci. Biog. under "Lindemann, Frederick Alexander."

Dobson prop (Derivation undetermined): Engineering and Industry. See: Thrush.

Dobson spectrophotometer (Dobson, Gordon Miller Bourne): Physics. See: Huschke; Van Nostrand Sci. Encyc.

Dobson support system (Derivation undetermined): Engineering and Industry. See: Thrush.

Dobsonia (bats) (Dobson, George Edward): Zoology. See: Pennak.

DOCHEZ, ALPHONSE RAYMOND. 1882-1964. American physician. See: World Who's Who Sci. Dochez' antitoxin (or serum).

Dochez' antitoxin (or serum) (Dochez, Alphonse Raymond): Medicine. See: Stedman.

DOCK, GEORGE. b. 1860. American physician. See: Who's Who Amer. Med. Dock's test breakfast.

Dock's test breakfast (Dock, George): Medicine. See: Dorland.

Dr. Fell (Fell, John): Generic Word. See: Hendrickson; Partridge; Weekley.

Doctor Marianus (Mary, Virgin-Mother): Religion. See: Attwater.

Doctrinaire (Royer-Collard, Pierre Paul "Doctrinaire"): Politics. See: Hendrickson.

DODD, A. SCOTT. fl. 1929. English chemist. Cited in: Chem. Abstr., vol. 23, p. 4645. Dodd test.

Dodd buddle (Derivation undetermined): Engineering and Industry. See: Thrush.

Dodd test (Dodd, A. Scott): Chemistry. See: Van Nostrand Chem. Dict.

Dodecatheon Jeffreyi (Jeffrey, John): Botany. Cited in: World Who's Who Sci. under "Jeffrey, John."

DODGE. fl. 1942. Inventor. (Biography source unavailable.) Dodge weapons carrier.

Dodge continuous sampling plan (Dodge, Harold French): Statistics. See: Kendall.

Dodge crusher (Derivation undetermined): Engineering and Industry. See: Thrush.

DODGE, HAROLD FRENCH. 1893- . American electrical engineer. See: Amer. Men and Women Sci., 12th ed. Dodge continuous sampling plan.

DODGE, HENRY P. b. 1871. American electrical engineer. See: Who's Who Engin., 1925. Dodge process.

Dodge mirror tachistoscope (Dodge, Raymond): Psychology. Cited in: World Who's Who Sci.

Dodge process (Dodge, Henry P.): Engineering and Industry. Cited in: Who's Who Engin., 1925.

Dodge pulverizer (Derivation undetermined): Engineering and Industry. See: Thrush.

DODGE, RAYMOND. 1871-1942. American psychologist. See: World Who's Who Sci. Dodge mirror tachistoscope.

Dodge weapons carrier (Dodge): Weapons. See: Quick.

DODOENS, REMBERT (DODONAEUS). 1517-1585. Dutch botanist. See: Dict. Sci. Biog. Dodonaea.

Dodonaea (Dodoens, Rembert): Botany. See: Charnock; Taylor, N.; Webster's 3d.

Dodsworth-Lyons reagents (Derivation undetermined): Chemistry. See: Van Nostrand Chem. Dict.

DOE, ORLANDO WITHERSPOON. 1843-1890. American physician. See: Hist. Boston City Hosp. Doe's method.

DOEBEREINER, JOHANN WOLFGANG. 1780-1849. German chemist. See: Dict. Sci. Biog. Doebereiner's matchbox (or lamp), Doebereiner's rule, triads of Doebereiner.

Doebereiner's matchbox (or lamp) (Doebereiner, Johann Wolfgang): Chemistry. See: Hackh.

Doebereiner's rule (Doebereiner, Johann Wolfgang): Chemistry. See: Hackh.

Doebner-Miller synthesis (Doebner, Oskar Gustav and Miller, Wilhelm von): Chemistry. See: Ballentyne; Van Nostrand Chem. Dict.

DOEBNER, OSKAR GUSTAV. 1850-1907. German chemist. See: World Who's Who Sci. Doebner-Miller synthesis, Doebner synthesis.

Doebner reagent (Derivation undetermined): Chemistry. See: Van Nostrand Chem. Dict.

Doebner synthesis (Doebner, Oskar Gustav): Chemistry. See: Van Nostrand Chem. Dict.

DOEDERLEIN, ALBERT SIEGMUND GUSTAV. 1860-1941. German obstetrician and gynecologist. See: World Who's Who Sci. Doederlen's bacillus.

Doederlen's bacillus (Doederlein, Albert Siegmund Gustav): Medicine. See: Dorland; Stedman.

DOEGE, KARL HERMAN. b. 1892. American physician. See: Direct. Med. Specialists, 1970-1971. Doege-Potter syndrome.

Doege-Potter syndrome (Doege, Karl Herman and Potter, Roy Pilling): Medicine. See: Jablonski.

Doehle body-panmyelopathic syndrome (Doehle, Paul). See: Hegglin's anomaly.

DOEHLE, PAUL. 1855-1928. German pathologist. See: World Who's Who Sci. Doehle body-panmyelopathic syndrome, Doehle's bodies (or inclusion bodies), Heller-Doehle mesoaortitis.

Doehle's bodies (or inclusion bodies) (Doehle, Paul): Medicine. See: Dorland; Stedman.

DOELLINGER, JOHANN IGNAZ J. 1770-1841. German physician. See: World Who's Who Sci. Doellinger's ring (or tendinous ring).

Doellinger's ring (or tendinous ring) (Doellinger, Johann Ignaz J.): Medicine. See: Dorland; Stedman.

DOERFLER, LEO G. 1919- . American audiologist. See: Amer. Men and Women Sci., 12th ed. Doerfler-Stewart test.

Doerfler-Stewart test (Doerfler, Leo G. and Stewart, Kenneth C.?): Medicine. See: Stedman.

DOERING, GERHARD. 1909- . German neurologist. See: Kuerschner's Deut. Gel. Kal., vol. 8, 1954. Pette-Doering encephalitis.

DOERING, HANS. b. 1886. German physician. Cited in: Mansell. Neisser-Doering phenomenon.

DOERR, ROBERT. 1871-1952. Hungarian-born bacteriologist. See: World Who's Who Sci. Doerr solution.

Doerr solution (Doerr, Robert): Medicine. Cited in: Kelly.

Doe's method (Doe, Orlando Witherspoon): Medicine. See: Stedman.

DOETTINGER, ANNA. fl. 1917. German chemist. Cited in: Chem. Abstr., vol. 12, p. 2503. Weinland-Doettinger test reaction.

DOGBERRY, THE CONSTABLE. Character from William Shakespeare's "Much Ado about Nothing." See: Benet. Dogberrydom.

Dogberrydom (Dogberry, the constable): Generic Word (blundering officialdom). See: Partridge.

DOGGETT, THOMAS. d. 1721. Irish actor. See: Dict. Nat. Biog. Doggett's (Dogget's) Coat and Badge (prize).

Doggett's (Dogget's) Coat and Badge (prize) (Doggett, Thomas): Recreation and Sports (rowing). See: Brewer; Harvey; Latham.

DOGIEL, ALEXANDER STANISLAVOVIC. 1852-1922. Russian histologist. See: Biog. Lex. hervorr. Aerzte, 1880-1930. Dogiel's cells?, Dogiel's corpuscle.

Dogiel's cells (Dogiel, Alexander Stanislavovic?): Medicine. See: Henderson.

Dogiel's corpuscle (Dogiel, Alexander Stanislavovic): Medicine. See: Dorland; Stedman.

Doherty amplifier (Doherty, William Humphrey): Electronics. See: Hughes; Markus; Van Nostrand Sci. Encyc.

Doherty transmitter (Doherty, William Humphrey): Electronics. See: Hughes.

DOHERTY, WILLIAM HUMPHREY. 1907- . American electronics engineer. See: Amer. Men and Women Sci., 12th ed. Doherty amplifier, Doherty transmitter.

Dohmee reagent (Derivation undetermined): Chemistry. See: Van Nostrand Chem. Dict.

DOILY. fl. 17th c. English linen draper. (Biography source unavailable.) Doily (or Doyley).

Doily (or Doyley) (Doily): Generic Word (ornamental mat). See: Brewer; Hendrickson; Partridge.

DOISY, EDWARD ADELBERT. 1893- . American biochemist. See: World Who's Who Sci. Allen-Doisy test, Allen-Doisy unit.

DOKUCHAEV, VASILY VASILIEVICH. 1846-1903. Russian pedologist. See: Dict. Sci. Biog. Dokuchaiev formula.

Dokuchaiev formula (Dokuchaev, Vasily Vasilievich): Agriculture. See: Winburne.

DOLBEAU, HENRI FERDINAND. 1830-1877. French surgeon. See: World Who's Who Sci. Dolbeau's operation.

Dolbeau's operation (Dolbeau, Henri Ferdinand): Medicine. Cited in: World Who's Who Sci.

Dolcinists (Dolcino, Fra.): Religion. See: Canney.

DOLCINO, FRA. d. 1307. Italian religious leader. See: New Catholic Encyc. Dolcinists.

DOLD, HERMANN. b. 1882. German bacteriologist. See: Wer Ist Wer, 8th ed. Dold's reaction (or test).

Dold's reaction (or test) (Dold, Hermann): Medicine. See: Dorland.

Dole-Nyswander program (Dole, Vincent Paul and Nyswander, Marie): Medicine. See: Hinsie.

DOLE, VINCENT PAUL. 1913- . American physician. See: Direct. Med. Specialists, 1970-71. Dole-Nyswander program.

DOLERIS, JACQUES-AMEDEE. 1852-1938. French gynecologist. See: Biog. Lex. hervorr. Aerzte, 1880-1930. Doleris' operation.

Doleris' operation (Doleris, Jacques-Amedee): Medicine. See: Dorland.

Dolezalek electrometer (Dolezalek, Friedrich): Electronics. See: Hackh; Hughes; Thewlis.

DOLEZALEK, FRIEDRICH. 1873-1920. Hungarian-born physico-chemist. See: World Who's Who Sci. Dolezalek electrometer.

DOLGOV, K. A. fl. 1929. Russian chemist. Cited in: Chem. Abstr., Decennial Index, 1927-1936. Tananaev-Dolgov tests for gold, palladium and platinum.

DOLIN, ANTON (Original name: PATRICK HEALEY-KAY). 1904- .
English dancer and choreographer. See: Who's Who, 1975. Markova-Dolin
Ballet, Nemtchinova-Dolin Ballet.

DOLLINGER, ALBERT. b. 1888. German physician. Cited in: Lieber and
Ulbrich. Dollinger-Bielschowsky syndrome.

Dollinger-Bielschowsky syndrome (Dollinger, Albert and Bielschowsky, Max):
Medicine. See: Jablonski. Also known as: Jansky-Bielschowsky syndrome.

DOLLO, LOUIS ANTOINE MARIE JOSEPH. 1857-1931. Belgian paleontologist. See: Dict. Sci. Biog. Dollo's law.

DOLLOND, PETER. 1730-1820. English optician. See: World Who's Who
Sci. Dollond (telescope).

Dollond (telescope) (Dollond, Peter): Astronomy. See: Charnock.

Dollo's law (Dollo, Louis Antoine Marie Joseph): Biology. See: Gray;
Henderson; Winick.

Dolly Varden crab (Varden, Dolly): Zoology. See: Webster's 3d.

Dolly Varden (dress) (Varden, Dolly): Fashion. See: Partridge; Picken;
Webster's 3d.

Dolly Varden pattern (Varden, Dolly): Fashion. See: Picken.

Dolly Varden spotted horse (Varden, Dolly): Zoology. See: Mathews, M. M.

Dolly Varden trout (or char) (Varden, Dolly): Zoology. See: Mathews,
M. M.; Pennak; Webster's 3d.

DOLOMIEU, DIEUDONNE DE GRATET DE. 1750-1801. French geologist and
mineralogist. See: Dict. Sci. Biog. Dolomite.

Dolomite (Dolomieu, Dieudonne de Gratet de): Earth Sciences. See:
Partridge; Van Nostrand Sci. Encyc.; Webster's 3d.

Dolphin (Charles V): Numismatics. See: Wagner (Names).

Dolphins (Alba, Fernando Alvarez de Toledo, Duke): Engineering and Industry.
See: Stenhouse.

Dom Pedro (shoe) (Pedro II): Fashion. See: Picken.

DOMBEY, JOSEPH. 1742-1794. French botanist. See: Dict. Sci. Biog.
Dombeya.

Dombeya (Dombey, Joseph): Botany. See: Charnock; Webster's 3d.

Domeykite (Domeyko, Ignacio): Earth Sciences. See: Webster's 3d.

DOMEYKO, IGNACIO. 1802-1889. Polish-born Chilean mineralogist and
chemist. See: World Who's Who Sci. Domeykite.

DOMINIC, SAINT (DOMINGO DE GUZMAN). 1170-1221. Spanish-born
Roman Catholic priest. See: Encyc. Brit., 1973. Dominican Nuns, Dominican
Rite, Dominicans, Rule of St. Dominic.

Dominican Nuns (Dominic, Saint): Religion. See: Black.

Dominican Rite (Dominic, Saint): Religion. See: Attwater.

Dominicans (Dominic, Saint): Religion. See: Attwater; Brewer; Canney.

DOMINICI, HENRI. 1867-1919. French physician. See: Biog. Lex. hervorr.
Aerzte, 1880-1930. Dominici('s) tube.

Dominici('s) tube (Dominici, Henri): Medicine. See: Dorland; Stedman.

Dominikiewcz test (Dominikiewicz, Mieczyslaw Kazimierz Jozef): Chemistry.
See: Van Nostrand Chem. Dict.

DOMINIKIEWICZ, MIECZYSLAW KAZIMIERZ JOZEF. b. 1882. Polish
chemist. See: Pogg., vol. 6, 7b. Dominikiewcz test.

Don Carlos, Maria Isidro de Borbon. See: Carlos, Don.

DON, DAVID. 1800-1841. Scottish botanist. See: Dict. Nat. Biog.
Donia.

Don Juan (Don Juan, the libertine): Generic Word (seducer). See: English;
Hendrickson; Hinsie.

DON JUAN (TENORIO), THE LIBERTINE. fl. 14th c. Spanish aristocrat.
See: Benet. Don Juan.

Don Pacifico affair (or incident) (Pacifico, David): History. See: Morris and
Irwin; Steinberg.

Don Quixote (Don Quixote, the country gentleman): Generic Word (impractical). See: Webster's 3d.

DON QUIXOTE, THE COUNTRY GENTLEMAN. Character in Miguel de
Cervantes satirical romance, "Don Quixote de la Mancha" (1615). See:
Benet. Don Quixote, Quixotic.

Donaldson colorimeter (Donaldson, R.): Physics. See: Internat. Dict. Phys.
Elec.

DONALDSON, R. fl. 1935. English chemist. Cited in: Chem. Abstr.,
vol. 30, p. 905. Donaldson colorimeter.

Donaldson('s) test (or reagent) (Derivation undetermined): Chemistry. See:
Stedman; Van Nostrand Chem. Dict.

DONAR. Germanic god. See: Jobes. Donarium.

Donarium (Donar): Earth Sciences. See: Charnock.

Donat (or Donet) (Donatus, Aelius): Generic Word (elementary grammar). See:
Barnhart (Eng. Lit.); Harvey; Stenhouse.

DONATH, JULIUS. b. 1849. Austrian physician. See: Biog. Lex. hervorr.
Aerzte, 1880-1930. Donath-Landsteiner cold autoantibody, Donath-Landsteiner
phenomenon, Donath-Landsteiner syndrome, Donath-Landsteiner test.

Donath-Landsteiner cold autoantibody (Donath, Julius and Landsteiner, Karl):
Medicine. See: Stedman.

Donath-Landsteiner phenomenon (Donath, Julius and Landsteiner, Karl): Medicine. See: Stedman.

Donath-Landsteiner syndrome (Donath, Julius and Landsteiner, Karl): Medicine.
See: Jablonski.

Donath-Landsteiner test (Donath, Julius and Landsteiner, Karl): Medicine.
See: Dorland. Also known as: Landsteiner-Donath test.

Donath test reaction for cobalt (Derivation undetermined): Chemistry. See:
Van Nostrand Chem. Dict.

Donath test reaction for quinoline (Derivation undetermined): Chemistry. See:
Van Nostrand Chem. Dict.

Donation of Charles (Charlemagne): History. See: Harbottle.

Donation of Constantine (Constantine I): History. See: Attwater; Barnhart
(Eng. Lit.); Brewer.

Donation of Pepin (Pepin III, the Short): History. See: Brewer.

Donatism (D'Hont, Alfred): Generic Word (form of hypnosis). See: Hinsie.

Donatism (or Donatists) (Donatus the Great): Religion. See: Brewer; Canney;
Mathews, S.

Donatist schism (or Donatism) (Donatus): Religion. See: Attwater.

DONATUS. fl. early 4th c. Bishop of Casae Nigrae in North Africa. See:
Webster's Biog. Dict. Donatist schism (or Donatism).

DONATUS, AELIUS. fl. 4th c. A.D. Roman grammarian. See: Webster's
Biog. Dict. Donat (or Donet).

DONATUS THE GREAT. fl. 315 A.D. Bishop of Carthage. See: Webster's
Biog. Dict. Donatism (or Donatists).

DONAU, JULIUS. b. 1877. Austrian chemist. See: Pogg., vol. 5, 6, 7a.
Donau test reaction.

Donau test reaction (Donau, Julius): Chemistry. See: Van Nostrand Chem.
Dict.

DONDERS, FRANCISCUS CORNELIS. 1818-1889. Dutch ophthalmologist.
See: Dict. Sci. Biog. Donders' glaucoma, Donders' law, Donders' pressure,
Donders' rings, Donders' test.

Donders' glaucoma (Donders, Franciscus Cornelis): Medicine. See: Dorland;
Stedman.

Donders' law (Donders, Franciscus Cornelis): Psychology. See: Chaplin;
Drever; English.

Donders' pressure (Donders, Franciscus Cornelis): Medicine. See: Stedman.

Donders' rings (Donders, Franciscus Cornelis): Medicine. See: Stedman.

Donders' test (Donders, Franciscus Cornelis): Medicine. See: Stedman.

Dongan Charter (Dongan, Thomas): History. See: Harbottle; Latham.

DONGAN, THOMAS. 1634-1715. Earl of Limerick and colonial governor of New York. See: Dict. Amer. Biog. Dongan Charter.

Donia (Don, David): Botany. See: Charnock.

DONIZETTI, GAETANO. 1797-1848. Italian operatic composer. See: Encyc. Brit., 1973. Donizetti Variations.

Donizetti Variations (Donizetti, Gaetano): Music. See: Chujoy.

DONKIN, BRYAN. 1768-1855. English civil engineer and inventor. See: Dict. Nat. Biog. Donkin pantograph.

Donkin pantograph (Donkin, Bryan): Engineering and Industry. See: Auger.

Donnan distribution coefficient (Donnan, Frederick George): Chemistry. See: Thewlis.

Donnan equilibrium (Donnan, Frederick George): Chemistry. See: Hackh; Internat. Dict. Phys. Elec.; Pennak. Also known as: Gibbs-Donnan equilibrium.

DONNAN, FREDERICK GEORGE. 1870-1956. English physical chemist. See: Dict. Sci. Biog. Donnan distribution coefficient, Donnan equilibrium, Donnan potential.

Donnan potential (Donnan, Frederick George): Chemistry. See: Ballentyne; Thewlis.

DONNAY, GABRIELLE HAMBURGER. 1920- . German-born American crystallographer. See: Amer. Men and Women Sci., 12th ed. Donnay-Harker principle.

Donnay-Harker principle (Donnay, Gabrielle Hamburger and Harker, David): Chemistry. See: Ballentyne.

DONNE, ALFRED. 1801-1878. French bacteriologist. See: World Who's Who Sci. Donne's corpuscles, Donne's test.

DONNE, JOHN. 1573-1631. English poet. See: Dict. Nat. Biog. Donnean (Donneish, or Donnesque).

Donne-Mueller test (Donne, Alfred and Mueller, Eduard). See: Donne's test.

Donnean (Donneish, or Donnesque) (Donne, John): Literature. See: Webster's 3d.

DONNELLAN, ANNE. fl. 18th c. Irish philanthropist. (Biography source unavailable.) Donnellan Lectures.

Donnellan Lectures (Donnellan, Anne): Religion. See: Canney.

Donne's corpuscles (Donne, Alfred): Medicine. See: Dorland; Stedman.

Donne's test (Donne, Alfred): Medicine. See: Dorland; Stedman. Also known as: Donne-Mueller test.

DONNISON, DAVID VERNON. 1926- . English administrator. See: Who's Who, 1974. Donnison Report.

Donnison Report (Donnison, David Vernon): Education. See: Good.

DONOHUE, WILLIAM LESLIE. 1906- . Canadian pathologist. See: Amer. Men and Women Sci., 12th ed. Donohue's syndrome.

Donohue's syndrome (Donohue, William Leslie): Medicine. See: Jablonski.

Donovan bodies (Donovan, Charles). See: Leishman-Donovan bodies.

DONOVAN, CHARLES. 1863-1951. Irish surgeon. See: Biog. Lex. hervorr. Aerzte, 1880-1930. Donovania, Donovanosis, Leishman-Donovan body(-ies).

DONOVAN, MICHAEL D. 1809-1876. Irish physician. See: World Who's Who Sci. Donovan's solution.

Donovania (Donovan, Charles): Medicine. See: Dorland.

Donovanosis (Donovan, Charles): Medicine. See: Stedman.

Donovan's solution (Donovan, Michael D.): Medicine. Cited in: World Who's Who Sci.

don't hurry, Hopkins (Hopkins): Generic Word. See: Hendrickson.

Doodia (ferns) (Doody, Samuel): Botany. See: Taylor, N.

DOODY, SAMUEL. 1656-1706. English botanist. See: Dict. Nat. Biog. Doodia (ferns).

Doolittle division-board feeder (Doolittle, Gilbert M.): Engineering and Industry. See: Winburne.

DOOLITTLE, GILBERT M. b. 1846. American apiarist. Cited in: Mansell. Doolittle division-board feeder.

DOOLITTLE, JAMES HAROLD. 1896- . American air-force officer. See: Barnhart (Cycl. Names). Doolittle raid.

DOOLITTLE, M. H. fl. 1878. American scientist. (Biography source unavailable.) Doolittle method (or technique), Wherry-Doolittle method.

Doolittle method (or technique) (Doolittle, M. H.): Statistics. See: English; Internat. Dict. Ap. Math.; Kendall.

Doolittle raid (Doolittle, James Harold): History. See: Quick.

Doppler broadening (Doppler, Johann Christian): Physics. See: Hughes; Internat. Dict. Phys. Elec.; Markus.

Doppler effect(s) (Doppler, Johann Christian): Physics. See: Ballentyne; Internat. Dict. Phys. Elec.; Satterthwaite.

Doppler error (Doppler, Johann Christian): Physics. See: Huschke.

Doppler-Fizeau principle (Doppler, Johann Christian and Fizeau, Armand Hippolyte Louis): Physics. See: Internat. Dict. Phys. Elec.

DOPPLER, JOHANN CHRISTIAN. 1803-1853. Austrian physicist and mathematician. See: Dict. Sci. Biog. Doppler broadening, Doppler effect(s), Doppler error, Doppler-Fizeau principle, Doppler navigation (system), Doppler radar, Doppler shift (or frequency), Doppler width of a spectral line, Doppler width of Breit-Wigner cross-section, Dopplerite.

DOPPLER, KARL. fl. 1928. Austrian surgeon. See: Chirurgen-Verzeichnis, 1938, p. 117. Doppler's operation.

Doppler navigation (system) (Doppler, Johann Christian): Physics. See: Hughes; Markus; Webster's 3d.

Doppler radar (Doppler, Johann Christian): Physics. See: Hughes; Internat. Dict. Phys. Elec.; Van Nostrand Sci. Encyc.

Doppler shift (or frequency) (Doppler, Johann Christian): Physics. See: Focal Encyc. Film; Internat. Dict. Phys. Elec.; Van Nostrand Sci. Encyc.

Doppler width of a spectral line (Doppler, Johann Christian): Physics. See: Internat. Dict. Ap. Math.

Doppler width of Breit-Wigner cross-section (Doppler, Johann Christian): Physics. See: Internat. Dict. Ap. Math.

Dopplerite (Doppler, Johann Christian): Earth Sciences. See: Charnock; Thrush; Webster's 3d.

Doppler's operation (Doppler, Karl): Medicine. See: Dorland.

DOR-DELATTRE, EMILE. fl. 1911. Belgian metallurgist. Cited in: Chem. Abstr., vol. 5, p. 2485. Dor furnace.

Dor furnace (Dor-Delattre, Emile): Engineering and Industry. See: Thrush.

Dorcas (Dorcas, the Christian): Generic Word (model housewife). See: Hendrickson.

Dorcas Societies (Dorcas, the Christian): Philanthropy. See: Latham.

DORCAS, THE CHRISTIAN. Biblical woman of Joppa. See: Barnhart (Cycl. Names). Dorcas, Dorcas Societies, Dorcastry.

Dorcastry (Dorcas, the Christian): Philanthropy. See: Webster's 3d.

DOREE, CHARLES. b. 1875. English chemist. See: Pogg., vol. 6. Doree-Gardner test reaction.

Doree-Gardner test reaction (Doree, Charles and Gardner, John Addyman): Chemistry. See: Van Nostrand Chem. Dict.

Doreite (Derivation undetermined): Earth Sciences. See: Thrush.

DORELLO, PRIMO. b. 1872. Italian anatomist. See: Annuario Univers. Roma 1923/24 p. 181f. Dorello's canal.

Dorello's canal (Dorello, Primo): Anatomy. See: Stedman.

DORENDORF, HANS. b. 1866. German physician. See: Biog. Lex. hervorr. Aerzte, 1880-1930. Dorendorf's sign.

Dorendorf's sign (Dorendorf, Hans): Medicine. See: Dorland; Stedman.

DORFNER, J. fl. 1914. German ceramics engineer. Cited in: Chem. Abstr., Decenn. Index, 1907-1916. Dorfner test.

Dorfner test (Dorfner, J.): Engineering and Industry. See: Thrush.

DORGELO, HENDRIK BEREND. 1894- . Dutch physicist. See: Pogg., vol. 6. Burger-Dorgelo-Ornstein (Orstein) rule (or sum rule for atomic spectra).

DORIOT, GEORGES F. 1899- . French-born American educator and corporation executive. See: Who's Who Amer., 1974-1975. Doron (body armour).

Doris Day (Day, Doris): Generic Word (anti-feminist). See: Barnhart (New Eng.)

Dorn and Sugarman test (Dorn, John H. and Sugarman, Edward J.): Medicine. See: Dorland.

Dorn effect (Derivation undetermined): Physics. See: Ballentyne; Internat. Dict. Phys. Elec.; Thewlis.

DORN, JOHN H. No dates. American obstetrician. (Biography source unavailable.) Dorn and Sugarman test.

Dornier bomber (Dornier, Claude): Weapons. See: Hendrickson.

DORNIER, CLAUDE. 1884-1969. German airplane builder. See: Webster's Biog. Dict. Dornier bomber.

DORNO, CARL W. M. 1865-1942. Swiss climatologist. See: Dict. Sci. Biog. Dorno rays.

Dorno rays (Dorno, Carl W. M.): Medicine. See: Dorland; Stedman.

Doron (body armour) (Doriot, Georges F.): Engineering and Industry. See: Webster's 3d.

Dorothy Dix (Gilmer, Elizabeth Meriwether): Generic Word (counselor). See: Webster's 3d.

Dorothy Perkins' rose (Perkins, Dorothy): Botany. See: Hendrickson.

Dorr agitator (Dorr, John Van Nostrand): Engineering and Industry. See: Thrush.

Dorr classifier (or rake classifier) (Dorr, John Van Nostrand): Engineering and Industry. See: Thrush; Van Nostrand Chem. Dict.

DORR, JOHN VAN NOSTRAND. 1872-1962. American metallurgical engineer. See: Webster's Biog. Dict. Dorr agitator, Dorr classifier (or rake classifier), Dorr thickener.

Dorr('s) rebellion (Dorr, Thomas Wilson): History. See: Blumberg; Harbottle; Jameson.

Dorr thickener (Dorr, John Van Nostrand): Engineering and Industry. See: Thrush; Van Nostrand Chem. Dict.

DORR, THOMAS WILSON. 1805-1854. American lawyer and politician. See: Dict. Amer. Biog. Dorr('s) rebellion, Dorrism (or Dorrite).

Dorrism (or Dorrite) (Dorr, Thomas Wilson): History. See: Mathews, M. M.

Dorronsoro-Fernandez test (Dorronsoro y Ucelayeta, Bernabe and Fernandez, Oledulio): Chemistry. See: Van Nostrand Chem. Dict.

DORRONSORO Y UCELAYETA, BERNABE. b. 1860. Spanish chemist. Cited in: Chem. Abstr., vol. 8, p. 3405. Dorronsoro-Fernandez test.

D'ORSAY, ALFRED GUILLAUME GABRIEL. 1801-1852. French-born artist, dandy, and wit in England. See: Dict. Nat. Biog. D'Orsay (pump), Dossy.

D'Orsay (pump) (D'Orsay, Alfred Guillaume Gabriel): Fashion. See: Hendrickson; Picken; Webster's 3d.

DORSET, MARIAN. 1872-1935. American bacteriologist. See: Dict. Amer. Biog., 1st suppl. Dorset's egg medium, Dorset's stain.

Dorset's egg medium (Dorset, Marian): Medicine. See: Stedman.

Dorset's stain (Dorset, Marian): Medicine. See: Stedman.

DORSEY, HERBERT GROVE. 1876- . American oceanographer and physicist. See: World Who's Who Sci. Dorsey phonelescope.

DORSEY, NOAH ERNEST. b. 1873. American physicist. See: Amer. Men Sci., 3rd ed. Rosa and Dorsey method.

Dorsey phonelescope (Dorsey, Herbert Grove): Physics. Cited in: Webster's Biog. Dict.

DORSTEN, THEODOR. 1492-1552. German botanist and physician. See: Biog. Lex. hervorr. Aerzte. Dorstenia.

Dorstenia (Dorsten, Theodor): Botany. See: Charnock; Webster's 3d.

DORTHES, JACQUES ANSELM. 1759-1794. French physician and naturalist. See: Nouv. Biog. Univ. Orthezia.

DORY, JOHN. fl. 16th c. Privateer and subject of popular song. (Biography source unavailable.) John Dory (fish).

Dositheans (Dositheus): Religion. See: Webster's 3d.

DOSITHEUS. fl. 1st c. Jewish heretic. See: Webster's Biog. Dict. Dositheans.

Dossy (D'Orsay, Alfred Guillaume Gabriel): Generic Word (elegant). See: Hendrickson.

DOSTOEVSKI, FEDOR MIKHAILOVICH. 1821-1881. Russian novelist. See: Encyc. Brit., 1973. Dostoevskian.

Dostoevskian (Dostoevski, Fedor Mikhailovich): Literature. See: Webster's 3d.

DOUBLEDAY, HENRY. 1808-1875. English naturalist. See: World Who's Who Sci. Doubleday's list.

DOUBLEDAY, THOMAS. 1790-1870. English social reformer. See: Boase. Doubleday's theory of population.

Doubleday's list (Doubleday, Henry): Zoology. Cited in: World Who's Who Sci.

Doubleday's theory of population (Doubleday, Thomas): Sociology. See: Zadrozny.

doubting Thomas (Thomas the Apostle, Saint): Generic word (skeptic). See: Brewer; Hendrickson; Webster's 3d.

DOUCAS, CHRISTOPHE. 1890- . Greek dermatologist. See: World Who's Who Sci. Doucas-Kapetanakis disease.

Doucas-Kapetanakis disease (Doucas, Christophe and Kapetanakis, J.). See: Casala-Mosto disease.

Douglas' abscess (Douglas, James): Medicine. See: Stedman.

Douglas agar (Douglas, Stewart Ranken): Medicine. Cited in: Kelly.

Douglas bag (Douglas, Claude Gordon): Medicine. See: Stedman.

DOUGLAS, BEVERLY. b. 1891. American surgeon. See: Who's Imp. Med., 2nd. ed. Douglas graft.

DOUGLAS, C. K. M. fl. 1928. English meteorologist. Cited in: Mansell. Brunt-Douglas isallobaric wind.

DOUGLAS, CLAUDE GORDON. 1882-1963. English physiologist. See: World Who's Who Sci. Douglas bag.

Douglas clematis (Douglas, David): Botany. See: Winburne.

Douglas code (Douglas, Sir Howard): History. Cited in: Webster's Biog. Dict.

DOUGLAS, DAVID. 1798-1834. Scottish botanist in America. See: Dict. Nat. Biog. Douglas clematis, Douglas fir (pine or spruce), Douglas spirea, Douglas squirrel, Douglas waterhemlock, Douglasia (Douglassia).

Douglas Democrat (Douglas, Stephen Arnold): History. See: Mathews, M. M.

Douglas fir (pine or spruce) (Douglas, David): Botany. See: Hendrickson; Webster's 3d.; Winburne.

Douglas' fold (Douglas, James): Medicine. See: Donath; Dorland; Stedman.

Douglas furnace (Derivation undetermined): Engineering and Industry. See: Thrush.

Douglas graft (Douglas, Beverly): Medicine. See: Stedman.

DOUGLAS, SIR HOWARD. 1776-1861. English naval and artillery expert. See: Dict. Nat. Biog. Douglas code.

DOUGLAS, SIR JAMES. 1286-1330. English aristocrat. See: Dict. Nat. Biog. Douglas larder.

DOUGLAS, JAMES. 1525-1581. English statesman. See: Dict. Nat. Biog. Douglas Wars.

DOUGLAS, JAMES. 1675-1742. Scottish anatomist. See: Dict. Sci. Biog. Douglas' abscess, Douglas' fold, Douglas' line, Douglas('s) pouch (cul-de-sac or fossa), Douglasitis.

DOUGLAS, JAMES. 1837-1918. Canadian-born metallurgist. See: World Who's Who Sci. Douglas process.

DOUGLAS, JAMES, 2ND DUKE OF QUEENSBERRY. 1662-1711. Scottish statesman. See: Dict. Nat. Biog. Queensberry plot.

DOUGLAS, JOHN C. 1777-1850. Irish obstetrician. Cited in: Mansell. Douglas' mechanism, Douglas' spontaneous evolution.

DOUGLAS, JOHN SHOLTO, 8TH MARQUIS OF QUEENSBERRY. 1844-1900. English boxing enthusiast. See: Dict. Nat. Biog., 1st suppl. Queensberry rules.

Douglas larder (Douglas, Sir James): History. See: Harbottle.

Douglas' line (Douglas, James): Medicine. See: Donath; Dorland; Stedman.

Douglas' mechanism (Douglas, John C.): Medicine. See: Stedman.

DOUGLAS, PAUL HOWARD. 1892- . American economist. See: Amer. Men Sci. (Soc. Behav. Sci.), 11th ed. Cobb-Douglas production function.

DOUGLAS-PENNANT, GEORGE SHOLTO GORDON, BARON PENRHYN. 1836-1907. English industrialist. See: Dict. Nat. Biog., 2nd suppl. Penrhyn quarry dispute.

Douglas('s) pouch (cul-de-sac or fossa) (Douglas, James): Medicine. See: Dorland; Partridge; Stedman; Webster's 3d.

Douglas' principle of suburbanization (Douglas, H. P.): Sociology. See: Zadrozny.

Douglas process (Douglas, James). See: Hunt and Douglas process.

Douglas spirea (Douglas, David): Botany. See: Mathews, M. M.; Winburne.

Douglas' spontaneous evolution (Douglas, John C.): Medicine. See: Stedman.

Douglas squirrel (Douglas, David): Zoology. See: Hendrickson; Pennak, Webster's 3d.

DOUGLAS, STEPHEN ARNOLD. 1813-1861. American statesman. See: Dict. Amer. Biog. Douglas Democrat, Douglasism (or Douglasite), Lincoln-Douglas debates.

DOUGLAS, STEWART RANKEN. 1871-1936. English bacteriologist. See: World Who's Who Sci. Douglas agar.

Douglas Wars (Douglas, James): History. See: Harbottle.

Douglas waterhemlock (Douglas, David): Botany. See: Winburne.

Douglasia (Douglassia) (Douglas, David): Botany. See: Charnock; Taylor, N.

Douglasism (or Douglasite) (Douglas, Stephen Arnold): History. See: Mathews, M. M.

Douglasitis (Douglas, James): Medicine. See: Stedman.

Douglass formula for teaching load (Douglass, Harl Roy): Education. See: Good.

DOUGLASS, HARL ROY. 1892- . American educator. See: Contemp. Auth., vols. 5-8. Douglass formula for teaching load.

DOVE, HEINRICH WILHELM. 1803-1879. German physicist. See: Dict. Sci. Biog. Dove prism, Dove's law.

Dove prism (Dove, Heinrich Wilhelm): Physics. See: Internat. Dict. Phys. Elec.; Van Nostrand Sci. Encyc.; Webster's 3d.

DOVER, THOMAS. 1660-1742. English physician. See: Dict. Nat. Biog. Dover's powder.

Dover's powder (Dover, Thomas): Medicine. See: Hackh; Partridge; Webster's 3d.

Dove's law (Dove, Heinrich Wilhelm): Earth Sciences. See: Huschke.

Dow cell (Dow, Herbert Henry): Chemistry. See: Thrush.

DOW, CHARLES HENRY. 1851-1902. American statistician. See: Encyc. Brit., 1973. Dow-Jones average (or index), Dow theory.

DOW, HERBERT HENRY. 1866-1930. Canadian-born American chemist. See: World Who's Who Sci. Dow cell.

Dow-Jones average (or index) (Dow, Charles Henry and Jones, Edward D.): Economics. See: Webster's 3d.

Dow-Law planter (Derivation undetermined): Agriculture. See: Winburne.

DOW, NEAL. 1804-1897. American social reformer. See: Dict. Amer. Biog. Neal Dow law.

Dow oscillator (Derivation undetermined): Physics. See: Hughes; Internat. Dict. Phys. Elec.; Markus.

Dow process (Dow, Willard Henry): Chemistry. See: Thrush; Van Nostrand Chem. Dict.

Dow process for magnesium (Dow, Willard Henry): Chemistry. See: Van Nostrand Chem. Dict.

Dow theory (Dow, Charles Henry): Economics. See: Greenwald.

DOW, WILLARD HENRY. 1897-1949. American chemist. See: World Who's Who Sci. Dow process, Dow process for magnesium.

DOWELL, DONALD MAURICE. 1904- . American physician. Cited in: New York Acad. Med. Portrait Cat. Dowell's test.

Dowell process (Derivation undetermined): Chemistry. See: Van Nostrand Chem. Dict.

Dowell's test (Dowell, Donald Maurice): Medicine. See: Dorland.

DOWIE, JOHN ALEXANDER. 1847-1907. Scottish-born American religious leader. See: Dict. Amer. Biog. Dowieism (or Dowieite).

Dowieism (or Dowieite) (Dowie, John Alexander): Religion. See: Mathews, M. M.; Webster's 3d.

DOWN, JOHN LANGDON HAYDON. 1828-1896. English physician. See: World Who's Who Sci. Down's syndrome.

DOWNES, ANDREW J. fl. 1888. American physician. Cited in: Mansell. Downes' separate-urine siphon.

Downes' separate-urine siphon (Downes, Andrew J.): Medicine. See: Stedman.

DOWNEY, JUNE ETTA. 1875-1932. American psychologist. See: Dict. Amer. Biog., 1st suppl. Downey's will-temperament test.

Downey's will-temperament test (Downey, June Etta): Psychology. See: Wolman.

DOWNING, ANDREW JACKSON. 1815-1852. American horticulturist, nurseryman and landscape architect. See: Dict. Amer. Biog. Downingia.

DOWNING, SIR GEORGE. 1623-1684. English diplomat. See: Dict. Nat. Biog. Downing Professor, George Downing.

Downing Professor (Downing, Sir George): Law. See: Wagner (More Names).

Downingia (Downing, Andrew Jackson): Botany. See: Mathews, M. M.; Taylor, N.; Webster's 3d.

Downs cell (Downs, J. C.): Chemistry. See: Van Nostrand Chem. Dict.

DOWNS, J. C. fl. 1924. American chemist. Cited in: Chem. Abstr., vol. 18, p. 2844. Downs cell, Downs process.

Downs process (Downs, J. C.): Chemistry. See: Ballentyne; Thrush.

Down's syndrome (Down, John Langdon Haydon): Medicine. See: Blumberg; Jablonski; Webster's 3d. Also known as: Langdon Down's disease.

Dow's mining salts (Derivation undetermined): Engineering and Industry. See: Thrush.

DOWSEY. No dates. American manufacturer. (Biography source unavailable). Dowsey (pistol).

Dowsey (pistol) (Dowsey): Weapons. See: Partridge.

Dowson gas (Dowson, Joseph Emerson): Engineering and Industry. See: Thrush.

DOWSON, JOSEPH EMERSON. 1844-1940. English inventor. See: World Who's Who Sci. Dowson gas, Dowson producer (or pressure producer).

Dowson producer (or pressure producer) (Dowson, Joseph Emerson): Engineering and Industry. See: Auger; Thrush.

DOX, ARTHUR WAYLAND. b. 1882. American chemist. See: Amer. Men Sci., 9th ed. Czapek-Dox medium, Lyons-Dox test for alkylbarbituric acids.

DOXEY, WALL. 1892-1962. American legislator. See: Biog. Direct. Amer. Congress. Norris-Doxey Act.

DOYEN, EUGENE LOUIS. 1859-1916. French surgeon. See: World Who's Who Sci. Doyen's clamp, Doyen's operation.

Doyen's clamp (Doyen, Eugene Louis): Medicine. See: Dorland.

Doyen's operation (Doyen, Eugene Louis): Medicine. See: Dorland.

DOYERE, LOUIS MICHEL FRANCOIS. 1811-1863. French physiologist. See: World Who's Who Sci. Doyere's cone, Doyere's eminence.

Doyere's cone (Doyere, Louis Michel Francois): Medicine. See: Henderson.

Doyere's eminence (Doyere, Louis Michel Francois): Medicine. See: Dorland; Stedman.

DOYLE, EDWARD. fl. 1825. American lumberman. Cited in: Mansell. Doyle rule, Doyle-Scribner rule.

Doyle rule (Doyle, Edward): Engineering and Industry. See: Winburne.

Doyle-Scribner rule (Doyle, Edward and Scribner): Engineering and Industry. See: Winburne.

DOYNE, ROBERT WALTER. 1857-1896. English ophthalmologist. See: Biog. Lex. hervorr. Aerzte, 1880-1930. Doyne's choroiditis, Doyne's iritis.

Doyne's choroiditis (Doyne, Robert Walter): Medicine. See: Dorland; Jablonski.

Doyne's iritis (Doyne, Robert Walter): Medicine. See: Jablonski.

DOZSA, GYORGY. 1475-1514. Hungarian soldier. See: Encyc. Brit., 1973. Dozsa revolt.

Dozsa revolt (Dozsa, Gyorgy): History. See: Harbottle.

DRACO. fl. 7th c. B.C. Athenian lawgiver. See: Encyc. Brit., 1973. Draconian Laws (or Code), Draconic (or Draconian).

Draconian Laws (or Code) (Draco): History. See: Black; Brewer.

Draconic (or Draconian) (Draco): Generic Word (severe punishment). See: Charnock; Hendrickson; Partridge.

Dracula (Dracula, Count): Generic Word. See: Webster's 3d.

DRACULA, COUNT. Principal character in Bram Stoker's novel, "Dracula" (1897). See: Magill. Dracula.

DRAEGER, ALEXANDER B. d. 1928. German scientist and inventor. Cited in: Chem. Abstr., Decenn. Index, 1907-1916. Draeger breathing apparatus, Draeger escape apparatus, Draeger self-rescuer, Draegerman (miner), Drager respirometer?

Draeger breathing apparatus (Draeger, Alexander B.): Engineering and Industry. See: Thrush.

Draeger escape apparatus (Draeger, Alexander B.): Engineering and Industry. See: Thrush.

Draeger self-rescuer (Draeger, Alexander B.): Engineering and Industry. See: Thrush.

Draegerman (miner) (Draeger, Alexander B.): Engineering and Industry. See: Webster's 3d.

Dragendorff-Brasche test reaction (Derivation undetermined): Chemistry. See: Van Nostrand Chem. Dict.

Dragendorff helleborein reagent (Derivation undetermined): Chemistry. See: Van Nostrand Chem. Dict.

Dragendorff-Husemann test reaction (Derivation undetermined): Chemistry. See: Van Nostrand Chem. Dict.

DRAGENDORFF, JOHANN GEORG NOEL. 1836-1898. German physician and pharmacist. See: World Who's Who Sci. Dragendorff reagent (or alkaloid reagent), Dragendorff's test (for bile pigments).

Dragendorff reagent (or alkaloid reagent) (Dragendorff, Johann Georg Noel): Chemistry. See: Hackh; Van Nostrand Chem. Dict.

Dragendorff test for benzene in petroleum benzine (Derivation undetermined): Chemistry. See: Van Nostrand Chem. Dict.

Dragendorff test reaction for amygdalin (Derivation undetermined): Chemistry. See: Van Nostrand Chem. Dict.

Dragendorff test reactions for various substances (Derivation undetermined): Chemistry. See: Van Nostrand Chem. Dict.

Dragendorff's test (for bile pigments) (Dragendorff, Johann Georg Noel): Medicine. See: Dorland; Stedman.

DRAGER, GLENN ALBERT. 1917-   . American neurologist. See: Amer. Men Sci., 10th ed. Shy-Drager syndrome.

Drager respirometer (Draeger, Alexander B.?): Medicine. See: Stedman.

Drago Doctrine (Drago, Luis Maria): History. See: Hendrickson; Smith.

DRAGO, LUIS MARIA. 1859-1921. Argentine statesman. See: Encyc. Brit., 1973. Drago Doctrine.

Dragstedt-Behrens method (Dragstedt and Behrens, W. V.). See: Behrens' method.

DRAGSTEDT, LESTER REYNOLD. 1893-   . American physician. See: World Who's Who Sci. Dragstedt method, Dragstedt operation, Dragstedt pouch.

Dragstedt method (Dragstedt, Lester Reynold): Medicine. Cited in: Kelly.

Dragstedt operation (Dragstedt, Lester Reynold): Medicine. Cited in: Kelly.

Dragstedt pouch (Dragstedt, Lester Reynold): Medicine. Cited in: Kelly.

DRAIS VON SAUERBRONN, KARL FRIEDRICH CHRISTIAN LUDWIG. 1785-1851. German forester and inventor. See: World Who's Who Sci. Draisine (motorized vehicle).

Draisine (motorized vehicle) (Drais von Sauerbronn, Karl Friedrich Christian Ludwig): Engineering and Industry. See: Webster's 3d.

DRAKE, EDWIN LAURENTINE. 1819-1880. American industrialist. See: Dict. Amer. Biog. Drake's well.

Drake's well (Drake, Edwin Laurentine): Engineering and Industry. See: Thrush.

DRALLE, EDUARD. fl. 1897. German chemist. Cited in: Royal Soc. Cat. Sci. Pap., 1884-1900. Thiele-Dralle reagent.

Draper effect (Draper, John William): Chemistry. See: Ballentyne; Hackh; Thewlis.

DRAPER, HENRY. 1837-1882. American astronomer. See: World Who's Who Sci. Harvard-Draper sequence.

DRAPER, JOHN WILLIAM. 1811-1882. English chemist. See: Dict. Sci. Biog. Draper effect, Grotthuss-Draper law.

Draper law (Draper, John William). See: Grotthus-Draper law.

Drapier's letters (Swift, Jonathan): Literature. See: Barnhart (Eng. Lit.).

DRAVES, CARL ZENO. 1894-   . American chemist. See: Who's Who East, 1974-1975. Draves test.

Draves test (Draves, Carl Zeno): Chemistry. See: Webster's 3d.

Drawcansir (Drawcansir, the tyrant): Generic Word (braggart). See: Barnhart (Eng. Lit.); Brewer; Partridge.

DRAWCANSIR, THE TYRANT. Character in the Duke of Buckingham's, "The Rehearsal," (1671). See: Benet. Drawcansir.

DRECHSEL, FERDINAND HEINRICH EDMUND. 1843-1897. German chemist. See: World Who's Who Sci. Borsche-Drechsel synthesis, Drechsel's test.

Drechsel's test (Drechsel, Ferdinand Heinrich Edmund): Medicine. See: Dorland; Stedman.

Dred Scott. See: Scott, Dred.

Dred Scott Decision (Scott, Dred): History. See: Morris; Mathews, M. M.; Phyfe.

Dred Scott dictum (Scott, Dred): History. See: Mathews, M. M.

Dred-Scottite (Scott, Dred): History. See: Mathews, M. M.

DREE, ETIENNE-MARIE-GILBERT. 1760-1848. French patron of science. See: Dict. Biog. Fran. Dreelite.

Dreelite (Dree, Etienne-Marie-Gilbert): Earth Sciences. See: Charnock.

Dreissensia (Dreyssen): Zoology. See: Webster's 3d.

DRESBACH, MELVIN. 1874-1946. American physician. See: World Who's Who Sci. Dresbach's anemia (or syndrome).

Dresbach's anemia (or syndrome) (Dresbach, Melvin): Medicine. See: Dorland; Jablonski.

Dreschel reagent (Derivation undetermined): Chemistry. See: Van Nostrand Chem. Dict.

DRESSLER. fl. 1854. German physician. Cited in: Kelly. Dressler's syndrome.

DRESSLER, CONRAD. fl. 1912. American engineer. Cited in: Chem. Abstr., vol. 9, p. 259. Dressler kiln.

Dressler kiln (Dressler, Conrad): Engineering and Industry. See: Thrush.

DRESSLER, WILLIAM. 1890- . Polish-born American physician. See: World Who's Who Sci. Dressler's syndrome.

Dressler's syndrome (Dressler): Medicine. See: Jablonski. Also known as: Harley's disease.

Dressler's syndrome (Dressler, William): Medicine. See: Jablonski.

DREW, GEORGE HAROLD. 1881-1913. English marine bacteriologist. See: Sci., vol. 37 (1913), pp. 330, 552-553. Drewite.

Drewite (Drew, George Harold): Earth Sciences. See: Thrush; Van Nostrand Sci. Encyc.

Drewsen test reaction (Drewsen, Viggo): Chemistry. See: Van Nostrand Chem. Dict.

DREWSEN, VIGGO. d. 1930. Danish chemist. See: Forhandlinger Kgl. Norske Vidensk. Selskab, vol. 3 (1930), p. 101. Baeyer-Drewsen indigo synthesis, Baeyer-Drewsen test for acetone, Drewsen test reaction.

DREYER, GEORGES. 1873-1934. English pathologist. See: Dict. Nat. Biog., 5th suppl. Dreyer's formula.

Dreyer's formula (Dreyer, Georges): Medicine. See: Dorland; Stedman.

Dreyer's tuberculin (Derivation undetermined): Medicine. See: Stedman.

Dreyfus affair (or case) (Dreyfus, Alfred): History. See: Barnhart (Eng. Lit.); Harbottle; Morris and Irwin.

DREYFUS, ALFRED. 1859-1935. French army officer. See: Encyc. Brit., 1973. Dreyfus affair (or case), Dreyfusard.

DREYFUS, GILBERT. 1902- . French physician. See: Who's Who France, 1975-1976. Gilbert-Dreyfus' syndrome.

DREYFUS, JULES R. fl. 1938. Swiss? physician. Cited in: Mansell. Dreyfus' syndrome.

Dreyfus' syndrome (Dreyfus, Jules R.): Medicine. See: Jablonski.

Dreyfusard (Dreyfus, Alfred): History. See: Brewer; Hendrickson; Webster's 3d.

Dreyse, Johann Nikolaus von. See: Von Dreyse, Johann Nikolaus.

Dreyse rifle (Von Dreyse, Johann Nikolaus): Weapons. See: Quick; Stenhouse.

DREYSSEN. fl. 19th c. Belgian physician. (Biography source unavailable.) Dreissensia.

DRIFFIELD, V. C. 1848-1915. English chemist and photographer. Cited in: Focal Encyc. Film under "H & D curve." H & D (or Hurter and Driffield) curve, H & D (or Hurter and Driffield) speed (and speed system), Hurter and Driffield Memorial Lecture Award.

Drigalski-Conradi agar (Von Drigalski, Wilhelm and Conradi, Heinrich). See: Conradi-Drigalski agar.

Drigalski, Wilhelm. See: Von Drigalski, Wilhelm.

DRINKER, CECIL KENT. 1887-1956. American physiologist. See: World Who's Who Sci. Drinker method, Schafer (Schaefer)-Nielsen-Drinker method.

Drinker method (Drinker, Cecil Kent): Medicine. See: Stedman; Thrush.

DRINKER, PHILIP. 1894-1972. American industrial hygienist. See: Who Was Who Amer., 1969-1973. Drinker respirator.

Drinker respirator (Drinker, Philip): Medicine. See: Dorland; Stedman.

DROOP, HENRY RICHMOND. ca. 1831-1884. English jurist. See: Boase. Droop quota.

Droop quota (Droop, Henry Richmond): Politics. See: Smith.

DROUOT, THEOPHILE. b. 1803. French oculist. See: Biog. Lex. hervorr. Aerzte. Drouot's plaster.

Drouot's plaster (Drouot, Theophile): Medicine. See: Dorland.

Drude equation (Drude, Paul Karl Ludwig): Physics. See: Ballentyne; Internat. Dict. Ap. Math.; Internat. Dict. Phys. Elec.

DRUDE, PAUL KARL LUDWIG. 1863-1906. German physicist. See: Dict. Sci. Biog. Drude equation, Drude('s) theory of conduction (or electrons in metals).

Drude('s) theory of conduction (or electrons in metals) (Drude, Paul Karl Ludwig): Physics. See: Ballentyne; Internat. Dict. Ap. Math.; Internat. Dict. Phys. Elec.

DRUM, JACK. Character in John Marston's comedy, "Jack Drum's Entertainment," (1600). See: Benet. John (Jack) Drum's entertainment.

DRUMMOND, C. S. fl. 1909. English engineer. (Biography source unavailable.) Gray-Drummond engine.

DRUMMOND, SIR DAVID. 1852-1932. Irish physician. See: World Who's Who Sci. Drummond-Morison operation, Drummond's sign.

DRUMMOND, SIR JACK CECIL. 1891-1952. English biochemist. See: World Who's Who Sci. Rosenheim-Drummond test for vitamin A.

DRUMMOND, JAMES. 1784-1863. Scottish botanical collector. See: Dict. Nat. Biog. Drummond's phlox.

Drummond light (Drummond, Thomas): Engineering and Industry. See: Charnock; Hendrickson; Phyfe.

Drummond-Morison operation (Drummond, Sir David and Morison, James Rutherford): Medicine. See: Dorland; Stedman.

DRUMMOND, THOMAS. 1797-1840. Scottish engineer and administrator. See: Dict. Nat. Biog. Drummond light.

Drummond-Wolff, Henry. See: Wolff, Sir Henry Drummond.

Drummond-Wolff Mission (Wolff, Sir Henry Drummond Charles): History. See: Montgomery.

Drummond's phlox (Drummond, James): Botany. See: Webster's 3d.

Drummond's sign (Drummond, Sir David): Medicine. See: Dorland; Stedman.

Druse(s) (or Druzes) (Darazi, al-): Religion. See: Barnhart (Eng. Lit.); Harvey; Weekley.

DRYANDER, JONAS. 1748-1810. Swedish botanist in England. See: Dict. Nat. Biog. Dryandra.

Dryandra (Dryander, Jonas): Botany. See: Charnock.

Dryasdust (Dryasdust, Dr. Jonas): Generic Word (dull scholar). See: Barnhart (Eng. Lit.); Brewer; Partridge.

DRYASDUST, DR. JONAS. Character created by Sir Walter Scott. See: Benet. Dryasdust.

Drysdale potentiometer (Derivation undetermined): Physics. See: Hughes; Internat. Dict. Phys. Elec.

DRYSDALE, THOMAS MURRAY. 1831-1904. American gynecologist. See: World Who's Who Sci. Drysdale's corpuscles.

Drysdale's corpuscles (Drysdale, Thomas Murray): Medicine. See: Dorland; Stedman.

DUANE, ALEXANDER. 1858-1926. American ophthalmologist. See: Dict. Amer. Biog. Duane's test, Stilling-Tuerk-Duane syndrome.

Duane and Hunt('s) law (Duane, William and Hunt, Franklin Livingston): Physics. See: Hughes; Internat. Dict. Ap. Math.; Van Nostrand Sci. Encyc.

DUANE, WILLIAM. 1872-1935. American physicist. See: Dict. Sci. Biog. Duane and Hunt('s) law.

Duane's syndrome (Duane, Alexander). See: Stilling-Tuerk-Duane syndrome.

Duane's test (Duane, Alexander): Medicine. See: Dorland; Stedman.

DUBAQUIE, J. fl. 1925. French chemist. Cited in: Chem. Abstr., vol. 19, p. 1927. Dubaquie test reaction.

Dubaquie test reaction (Dubaquie, J.): Chemistry. See: Van Nostrand Chem. Dict.

Du Barry costume (Du Barry, Marie Jeanne Becu): Fashion. See: Picken.

DU BARRY, MARIE JEANNE BECU. ca. 1746-1793. Mistress of Louis XV of France. See: Encyc. Brit., 1973. Du Barry costume, rose du Barry.

Dubb's asphalt (Dubbs, J. A.): Chemistry. See: Thrush.

DUBBS, C. P. fl. 1917. American chemist. Cited in: Chem. Abstr., vol. 11, p. 2404. Dubbs process.

DUBBS, J. A. fl. 1913. American chemist. Cited in: Chem. Abstr., vol. 7, p. 1805. Dubb's asphalt.

Dubbs process (Dubbs, C. P.): Chemistry. See: Van Nostrand Chem. Dict.

DUBIN, ISADORE NATHAN. 1913- . American pathologist. See: Direct. Med. Specialists, 1970-1971. Dubin-Johnson syndrome.

Dubin-Johnson syndrome (Dubin, Isadore Nathan and Johnson, Frank B.): Medicine. See: Jablonski; Stedman. Also known as: Dubin-Sprinz syndrome.

Dubin-Sprinz syndrome (Dubin, Isadore Nathan and Sprinz, Helmuth). See: Dubin-Johnson syndrome.

DUBINI, ANGELO. 1813-1902. Italian physician. See: Dict. Sci. Biog. Dubini's disease.

Dubini's disease (Dubini, Angelo): Medicine. See: Dorland; Jablonski; Stedman. Also known as: Guertin's disease.

DUBIS (or DUBOIS), PAUL ANTOINE. 1795-1871. French obstetrician. See: World Who's Who Sci. Dubois abscess (or disease), Dubois' shears.

Dublanc test reaction (Derivation undetermined): Chemistry. See: Van Nostrand Chem. Dict.

Dubois abscess (or disease) (Dubis, Paul Antoine): Medicine. See: Dorland; Jablonski; Stedman.

DU BOIS, DELAFIELD. b. 1880. American physiologist. See: Amer. Men Sci., 5th ed. Meeh-DuBois formula.

DuBois diet (DuBois, Eugene Floyd): Medicine. See: Dorland.

DU BOIS, EUGENE FLOYD. 1882-1959. American physiologist. See: World Who's Who Sci. Aub-DuBois table, DuBois diet, Meeh-DuBois formula.

DUBOIS, EUSTACHE. No dates. French cutler. (Biography source unavailable.) Eustache.

DuBois formula (or method) (DuBois, Delafield and DuBois, Eugene Floyd). See: Meeh-DuBois formula.

DUBOIS, FRANCOIS NOEL ALEXANDER. 1752-1824. French botanist. See: Nouv. Biog. Univ. Duboisia.

Dubois, Jacques. See: Sylvius, Jacobus.

Dubois, Paul Antoine. See: Dubis, Paul Antoine.

DUBOIS, PAUL CHARLES. 1848-1918. Swiss psychiatrist. See: World Who's Who Sci. Dubois's method (or treatment).

Du Bois Raymond's test for convergence (Du Bois-Reymond, Paul David Gustav): Mathematics. See: Ballentyne.

DU BOIS-REYMOND, EMIL HEINRICH. 1818-1896. German physiologist. See: Dict. Sci. Biog. Du Bois-Reymond('s) law, Du Bois-Reymond's key.

Du Bois Reymond('s) law (Du Bois-Reymond, Emil Heinrich): Medicine. See: Dorland; Drever; Stedman.

DU BOIS-REYMOND, PAUL DAVID GUSTAV. 1831-1889. German mathematician. See: Dict. Sci. Biog. Du Bois Raymond's test for convergence.

Du Bois-Reymond's key (Du Bois-Reymond, Emil Heinrich): Medicine. See: Dorland.

Dubois' shears (Dubis, Paul Antoine): Medicine. See: Stedman

Duboisia (Dubois, Francois Noel Alexander): Botany. See: Charnock; Stedman; Webster's 3d.

Dubois's method (or treatment) (Dubois, Paul Charles): Psychiatry. See: Dorland.

Dubos enzyme (Dubos, Rene Jules): Medicine. See: Dorland.

Dubos lysin (Dubos, Rene Jules): Medicine. See: Dorland.

Dubos medium (Dubos, Rene Jules): Medicine. See: Dorland.

DUBOS, RENE JULES. 1901- . French biochemist in America. See: World Who's Who Sci. Dubos enzyme, Dubos lysin, Dubos medium.

DUBOSCQ, JULES. 1817-1886. French optician. See: World Who's Who Sci. Duboscq's colorimeter.

Duboscq's colorimeter (Duboscq, Jules): Medicine. See: Dorland; Stedman.

Dubovitz's syndrome (Dubowitz, Victor): Medicine. See: Jablonski.

DUBOWITZ, VICTOR. 1931- . South African-born physician. See: World Who's Who Sci. Dubovitz's syndrome.

DUBREUIL-CHAMBARDEL, LOUIS. 1879-1927. French dentist. See: Congres (16) Internat. Med., 1909; Album, p. 74. Dubreuil-Chambardel's syndrome.

Dubreuil-Chambardel's syndrome (Dubreuil-Chambardel, Louis): Medicine. See: Jablonski; Stedman.

DUBREUILH, M. W. fl. 1912. French dermatologist. (Biography source unavailable.) Dubreuilh's melanosis.

Dubreuilh's melanosis (Dubreuilh, M. W.). See: Hutchinson's freckle.

DUBRUL, LEON. fl. 1934. French industrial chemist. Cited in: Chem. Abstr., vol. 28, p. 3853. Gilard and Dubrul factors.

Dubsky-Hrdlicka reagent (Dubsky, Jan Vaclav and Hrdlicka, M.): Chemistry. See: Van Nostrand Chem. Dict.

DUBSKY, JAN VACLAV. 1882-1946. Czechoslovakian chemist. See: Pogg., vol. 7b. Dubsky-Hrdlicka reagent, Dubsky-Krametz test reaction, Dubsky-Kuras test reaction, Dubsky-Langer-Stonad reagents, Dubsky-Okac test reaction for bismuth, Dubsky-Okac test reaction for magnesium, Dubsky-Wagner test for aluminum, Dubsky-Wagner tests for magnesium.

Dubsky-Krametz test reaction (Dubsky, Jan Vaclav and Krametz, E.): Chemistry. See: Van Nostrand Chem. Dict.

Dubsky-Kuras test reaction (Dubsky, Jan Vaclav and Kuras, M.): Chemistry. See: Van Nostrand Chem. Dict.

Dubsky-Langer-Stonad reagents (Dubsky, Jan Vaclav; Langer, Alois; and Strnad, M.): Chemistry. See: Van Nostrand Chem. Dict.

Dubsky-Okac test reaction for bismuth (Dubsky, Jan Vaclav and Okac, Arnost): Chemistry. See: Van Nostrand Chem. Dict.

Dubsky-Okac test reaction for magnesium (Dubsky, Jan Vaclav and Okac, Arnost): Chemistry. See: Van Nostrand Chem. Dict.

Dubsky-Wagner test for aluminum (Dubsky, Jan Vaclav and Wagner, E.): Chemistry. See: Van Nostrand Chem. Dict.

Dubsky-Wagner tests for magnesium (Dubsky, Jan Vaclav and Wagner, E.): Chemistry. See: Van Nostrand Chem. Dict.

DU BUAT, PIERRE-LOUIS-GEORGES. 1734-1809. French hydraulic engineer. See: Dict. Sci. Biog. Du Buat's paradox.

Du Buat's paradox (Du Buat, Pierre-Louis-Georges): Engineering and Industry. Cited in: Dict. Sci. Biog.

DUCHEMIN, EMILE MARIN. fl. 1876. French navigator. (Biography source unavailable.) Duchemin's formula?

Duchemin's formula (Duchemin, Emile Marin?): Engineering and Industry. See: Ballentyne; Thrush.

Duchene, Pere. See: Hebert, Jacques Rene.

Duchenne-Erb syndrome (or paralysis) (Duchenne, Guillaume Benjamin Amand and Erb, Wilhelm Heinrich): Medicine. See: Dorland; Jablonski; Stedman. Also known as: Erb-Duchenne paralysis, Erb's palsy.

Duchenne-Griesinger disease (Duchenne, Guillaume Benjamin Amand and Griesinger, Wilhelm). See: Duchenne's dystrophy.

DUCHENNE, GUILLAUME BENJAMIN AMAND. 1806-1875. French physician. See: World Who's Who Sci. Aran-Duchenne disease, Duchenne-Erb syndrome (or paralysis), Duchenne-Landouzy type, Duchenne's disease, Duchenne's dystrophy, Duchenne's paralysis, Duchenne's sign, Duchenne's syndrome, Duchenne's trocar.

Duchenne-Landouzy type (Duchenne, Guillaume Benjamin Amand and Landouzy, Louis Theophil Joseph). See: Landouzy-Dejerine dystrophy.

Duchenne's disease (Duchenne, Guillaume Benjamin Amand): Medicine. See: Dorland; Jablonski; Stedman.

Duchenne's dystrophy (Duchenne, Guillaume Benjamin Amand): Medicine. See: Barnhart (New Eng.); Jablonski. Also known as: Duchenne-Griesinger disease.

Duchenne's paralysis (Duchenne, Guillaume Benjamin Amand): Medicine. See: Dorland; Jablonski; Stedman.

Duchenne's sign (Duchenne, Guillaume Benjamin Amand): Medicine. See: Stedman.

Duchenne's syndrome (Duchenne, Guillaume Benjamin Amand): Medicine. See: Stedman.

Duchenne's trocar (Duchenne, Guillaume Benjamin Amand): Medicine. See: Dorland.

DUCHESNE, ANTOINE-NICOLAS. 1747-1827. French botanist. See: World Who's Who Sci. Duchesnea.

Duchesnea (Duchesne, Antoine-Nicolas): Botany. See: Taylor, N.

DUCKERT, ROGER. fl. 1938. Swiss chemist. Cited in: Chem. Abstr., Decenn. Index, 1937-1946. Wenger-Duckert-Blancpain reagent.

Duckert test reaction for antimony (Derivation undetermined): Chemistry. See: Van Nostrand Chem. Dict.

DUCKHAM, SIR ARTHUR MAC DOUGALL. 1879-1932. English industrialist. See: Who Was Who, 1929-1940. Woodall-Duckham coking retort, Woodall-Duckham kiln.

DUCKWORTH, SIR DYCE. 1840-1928. English physician. See: Dict. Nat. Biog., 4th suppl. Duckworth's phenomenon.

Duckworth's phenomenon (Duckworth, Sir Dyce): Medicine. See: Dorland; Stedman.

DUCREY, AUGUSTO. 1860-1940. Italian dermatologist. See: World Who's Who Sci. Ducrey's bacillus, Ducrey's disease.

Ducrey's bacillus (Ducrey, Augusto): Medicine. See: Dorland; Stedman.

Ducrey's disease (Ducrey, Augusto): Medicine. See: Jablonski.

duct of Bellini (Bellini, Lorenzo). See: Bellini's duct.

duct of Botallus (Botallo, Leonardo). See: Botallo's duct.

duct(s) of Cuvier (Cuvier, Georges): Zoology. See: Henderson; Pennak; Webster's 3d.

duct of Mueller (Mueller, Johannes Peter). See: Mueller's duct.

duct of Rivinus (Rivinus, August Quirinus). See: Rivinus' ducts (or canals).

duct of Santorini (Santorini, Giovanni Domenico). See: Santorini's duct (or canal).

duct of Steno (Stensen, Niels). See: Stensen's duct.

duct of Wharton (Wharton, Thomas). See: Wharton's duct.

duct of Wirsung (Wirsung, Johann Georg). See: Wirsung's canal (or duct).

Duddell arc (Duddell, William du Bois): Electronics. See: Hughes.

DUDDELL, BENEDICTUS. fl. 1729. English oculist. See: Biog. Lex. hervorr. Aerzte. Duddell's membrane.

Duddell oscillograph (Duddell, William du Bois): Electronics. See: Thewlis.

DUDDELL, WILLIAM DU BOIS. 1872-1917. English electrical engineer. See: World Who's Who Sci. Duddell arc, Duddell oscillograph.

Duddell's membrane (Duddell, Benedictus): Medicine. See: Dorland; Stedman.

Dudevant, Amandine Aurore Lucie. See: Sand, Georges.

Dudley apparatus (Dudley, Charles Benjamin?): Chemistry. See: Hackh.

DUDLEY, CHARLES BENJAMIN. 1842-1907. American chemist. See: Dict. Amer. Biog. Dudley apparatus?

Dudley diamond (Dudley, William Ward, 1st Earl of): Earth Sciences. See: Latham; Phyfe; Wagner (Names).

DUDLEY, EMELIUS CLARK. 1850-1928. American gynecologist. See: World Who's Who Sci. Dudley's operation.

DUDLEY, HOMER DANIEL. 1877-1950. American physician. See: N.W. Med., vol. 39 (1940), p. 397. Dudley-Klingenstein syndrome.

Dudley-Klingenstein syndrome (Dudley, Homer Daniel and Klingenstein, Percy): Medicine. See: Jablonski.

Dudley pipet(te) (Derivation undetermined): Chemistry. See: Hackh; Van Nostrand Chem. Dict.

DUDLEY, ROBERT, 1ST EARL OF LEICESTER. 1532-1588. English courtier. See: Dict. Nat. Biog. Leicester's Men.

Dudley rock (Derivation undetermined): Earth Sciences. See: Thrush.

Dudley solution for glucose (Dudley, William Lofland): Chemistry. See: Van Nostrand Chem. Dict.

Dudley test reaction for gallic acid (Derivation undetermined): Chemistry. See: Van Nostrand Chem. Dict.

DUDLEY, WILLIAM LOFLAND. 1859-1914. American chemist. See: World Who's Who Sci. Dudley solution for glucose.

DUDLEY, WILLIAM WARD, 1ST EARL OF. 1817-1885. English aristocrat. See: Boase. Dudley diamond.

Dudley's operation (Dudley, Emelius Clark): Medicine. See: Dorland; Stedman.

DUDZEELE, G. DE. fl. 1923. English? metallurgist. Cited in: Chem. Abstr., vol. 18, p. 1639. Dudzeele process.

Dudzeele process (Dudzeele, G. de): Engineering and Industry. See: Thrush.

DUEHRSSEN, ALFRED. 1863-1933. German obstetrician and gynecologist. See: World Who's Who Sci. Duehrssen's incisions (or method), Duehrssen's operation, Duehrssen's tampon.

Duehrssen's incisions (or method) (Duehrssen, Alfred): Medicine. See: Stedman.

Duehrssen's operation (Duehrssen, Alfred): Medicine. See: Dorland; Stedman.

Duehrssen's tampon (Duehrssen, Alfred): Medicine. See: Dorland.

DUELFER, HANS. 1892-1915. German alpinist. See: Sport Brockhaus. Duelfer rappel.

Duelfer rappel (Duelfer, Hans): Recreation and Sports. See: Webster's 3d.

DUERCK, HERMAN LUDWIG FRIEDRICH FRANZ. 1869-1941. German pathologist. See: World Who's Who Sci. Duerck's nodes.

Duerck's nodes (Duerck, Herman Ludwig Friedrich Franz): Medicine. See: Dorland; Stedman.

DUERFELDT, RICHARD. No dates. Cited in: Bailey. Durfeldtite.

DUFAU, EMIL. b. 1870. French chemist. Cited in: Mansell. Grimbert-Dufau reagent.

DUFAY, LOUIS D. fl. 1910. French photographer. Cited in: Chem. Abstr., Decenn. Index, 1907-1916. Dufay process, Dufaycolor film.

Dufay process (Dufay, Louis D.): Photography. See: Focal Encyc. Film.

Dufaycolor film (Dufay, Louis D.): Photography. See: Focal Encyc. Photog.

DUFF, A. B. fl. 1912. American chemist. Cited in: Chem. Abstr., Decenn. Index, 1907-1916. Duff furnace.

Duff furnace (Duff, A. B.): Engineering and Industry. See: Thrush.

DUFF, JAMES ("JAMIE"). fl. mid 19th c. Scottish eccentric. (Biography source unavailable.) Jamie Duff.

DUFF, JAMES COOPER. 1888- . Scottish chemist. See: Surrey. Duff reaction.

Duff reaction (Duff, James Cooper): Chemistry. See: Van Nostrand Chem. Dict.

DUFF, RICHARD D. 1905- . American chemical engineer. See: Amer. Men Sci., 9th ed. Kershner-Duff solution?

Duffin-Kemmer matrices (Duffin and Kemmer, Nicholas): Physics. See: Internat. Dict. Ap. Math.; Internat. Dict. Phys. Elec.

Duffing equation (Duffing, Georg): Physics. See: Ballentyne.

DUFFING, GEORG. b. 1861. German technologist. Cited in: Mansell. Duffing equation.

DUFFY. No dates. Hospital patient. (Biography source unavailable.) Duffy blood group (antigen or factor).

Duffy blood group (antigen or factor) (Duffy): Medicine. See: Stedman; Webster's 3d.

DUFLOS, ADOLF. 1802-1889. German chemist. See: Allg. Deut. Biog. Duflos test reaction for aniline?

Duflos test reaction for aniline (Duflos, Adolf?): Chemistry. See: Van Nostrand Chem. Dict.

DUFOUR, ALEXANDRE. fl. 1908. French physicist. See: Pogg., vols. 5, 6. Dufour effect.

Dufour effect (Dufour, Alexandre): Physics. See: Internat. Dict. Phys. Elec.; Van Nostrand Chem. Dict.

DUFOUR, JEAN MARIE LEON. 1782-1865. French entomologist. See: World Who's Who Sci. Dufour's gland.

Dufour's gland (Dufour, Jean Marie Leon): Biology. See: Gray; Henderson.

Dufrenite (Dufrenoy, Ours-Pierre-Armand): Earth Sciences. See: Charnock; Thrush; Webster's 3d.

DUFRENOY, OURS-PIERRE-ARMAND. 1792-1857. French mineralogist. See: Dict. Sci. Biog. Dufrenite, Dufrenoysite.

Dufrenoysite (Dufrenoy, Ours-Pierre-Armand): Earth Sciences. See: Charnock; Thrush; Webster's 3d.

DUFT, G. fl. 20th c. Director of mines at Tsumeb, South-West Africa. Cited in: Bailey. Duftite.

Duftite (Duft, G.): Earth Sciences. See: Thrush; Webster's 3d.

DUGAS, LOUIS ALEXANDER. 1806-1884. American physician. See: Biog. Lex. hervorr. Aerzte. Dugas' test.

Dugas' test (Dugas, Louis Alexander): Medicine. See: Dorland; Stedman.

DUGES, ANTOINE-LOUIS. 1797-1838. French physician and zoologist. See: World Who's Who Sci. Dugesia, Dugesiella.

Dugesia (Duges, Antoine-Louis): Zoology. See: Pennak; Webster's 3d.

Dugesiella (Duges, Antoine-Louis): Zoology. See: Pennak.

DUHAMEL DU MONCEAU, HENRI-LOUIS. 1700-1782. French engineer and agriculturist. See: Dict. Sci. Biog. Hamelia.

DUHAMEL, JEAN-MARIE-CONSTANT. 1797-1872. French mathematician. See: Dict. Sci. Biog. Duhamel's integral, Duhamel's theorem.

Duhamel's integral (Duhamel, Jean-Marie-Constant): Mathematics. See: Internat. Dict. Ap. Math.

Duhamel's theorem (Duhamel, Jean-Marie-Constant): Mathematics. See: Ballentyne.

Duhem-Margules equation (Duhem, Pierre Maurice Marie and Margules, Max): Physics. See: Ballentyne; Internat. Dict. Ap. Math.; Internat. Dict. Phys. Elec.

DUHEM, PIERRE-MAURICE-MARIE. 1861-1916. French physicist. See: Dict. Sci. Biog. Duhem-Margules equation, Duhem theorem, Gibbs-Duhem equation.

Duhem theorem (Duhem, Pierre-Maurice-Marie): Physics. See: Internat. Dict. Ap. Math.; Van Nostrand Sci. Encyc.

DUHRING, LOUIS ADOLPHUS. 1845-1913. American dermatologist. See: World Who's Who Sci. Duhring-Sneddon-Wilkinson syndrome, Duhring's disease, Duhring's pruritus.

Duhring rule (Duhring, U.): Chemistry. See: Ballentyne.

Duhring-Sneddon-Wilkinson syndrome (Duhring, Louis Adolphus; Sneddon, Ian Bruce; and Wilkinson, Darrell Sheldon). See: Sneddon-Wilkinson syndrome.

Duhring's disease (Duhring, Louis Adolphus): Medicine. See: Dorland; Jablonski; Stedman. Also known as: Brocq-Duhring disease.

Duhring's pruritus (Duhring, Louis Adolphus): Medicine. See: Jablonski.

DUJARIER, CHARLES. 1870-1931. French surgeon. See: J. Chir., vol. 38, no. 2 (1931), p. 145. Dujarier's clasp.

Dujarier's clasp (Dujarier, Charles): Medicine. See: Dorland.

Dujon, Francois. See: Junius, Franciscus.

Duke of Burgundy fritillary (Philip the Good, Duke of Burgundy?): Zoology. See: Gray.

Duke of Edinburgh's award (Edinburgh, Duke of): Education. See: Good.

Duke of Exeter's daughter (Holland, John, Duke of Exeter): History. See: Brewer; Latham.

Duke's classification (Dukes, Cuthbert Esquire): Medicine. See: Stedman.

DUKES, CLEMENT. 1845-1925. English physician. See: Biog. Lex. hervorr. Aerzte, 1880-1930. Dukes' disease.

DUKES, CUTHBERT ESQUIRE. 1890- . English pathologist. See: Who's Who, 1974. Duke's classification.

Dukes' disease (Dukes, Clement): Medicine. See: Dorland; Jablonski; Stedman. Also known as: Dukes-Filatov disease.

Dukes-Filatov disease (Dukes, Clement and Filatov, Nil Fedorovich). See: Dukes' disease.

Duke's laws (James II): History. See: Smith.

Dulcinea (Dulcinea del Toboso): Generic Word (lady-love). See: Brewer; Partridge; Webster's 3d.

DULCINEA DEL TOBOSO (ALDONZA LORENZO). Heroine of Miguel de Cervantes' novel, "Don Quixote de la Mancha," (1605, 1615). See: Benet. Dulcinea.

Dulcinists (Dulcino of Novara): Religion. See: Brewer; Phyfe.

DULCINO OF NOVARA. d. 1307. Italian sectarian. See: Webster's Biog. Dict. Dulcinists.

DULIN, ROBERT S. fl. 1915. American engineer. Cited in: Mansell. Dulin rotarex?

Dulin rotarex (Dulin, Robert S.?): Engineering and Industry. See: Hackh.

Dulong and Petit's law (Dulong, Pierre Louis and Petit, Alexis Therese): Chemistry. See: Ballentyne; Thrush; Webster's 3d.

DULONG, PIERRE LOUIS. 1785-1838. French chemist and physicist. See: Dict. Sci. Biog. Dulong and Petit's law, Dulong's formula.

Dulong's formula (Dulong, Pierre Louis): Chemistry. See: Thrush.

Dulop diving apparatus (Derivation undetermined): Engineering and Industry. See: Thrush.

Dumas bulb (Dumas, Jean-Baptiste-Andre): Chemistry. See: Hackh.

DUMAS, CHARLES-LOUIS. 1765-1813. French physician. See: World Who's Who Sci. Dumasine?

DUMAS, JEAN-BAPTISTE-ANDRE. 1800-1884. French chemist. See: Dict. Sci. Biog. Dumas bulb, Dumas method for nitrogen, Dumas method for vapor pressure.

Dumas method for nitrogen (Dumas, Jean-Baptiste-Andre): Chemistry. See: Van Nostrand Chem. Dict.

Dumas method for vapor pressure (Dumas, Jean-Baptiste-Andre): Physics. See: Internat. Dict. Phys. Elec.; Van Nostrand Sci. Encyc.

Dumasine (Dumas, Charles-Louis?): Medicine. See: Charnock.

DUMONT, ANDRE-HUBERT. 1809-1857. Belgian geologist. See: World Who's Who Sci. Dumontite.

DUMONT, ARSENE-JEAN-LOUIS. 1849-1902. French anthropologist. See: Dict. Biog. Fran. Dumont's theory of population.

Dumontite (Dumont, Andre-Hubert): Earth Sciences. See: Thrush; Webster's 3d.

DUMONTPALLIER, VICTOR-ALPHONSE-AMEDEE. 1826-1899. French physician. See: World Who's Who Sci. Dumontpallier's pessary, Dumontpallier's test.

Dumontpallier's pessary (Dumontpallier, Victor-Alphonse-Amedee): Medicine. See: Stedman. Also known as: Mayer's pessary.

Dumontpallier's test (Dumontpallier, Victor-Alphonse-Amedee): Medicine. See: Stedman.

Dumont's theory of population (Dumont, Arsene-Jean-Louis): Sociology. See: Zadrozny.

DUMORTIER, VINCENT-EUGENE. 1802-1876. French paleontologist and geologist. See: Dict. Biog. Fran. Dumortierite.

Dumortierite (Dumortier, Vincent-Eugene): Earth Sciences. See: Thrush; Webster's 3d.

Dumoulin process (Derivation undetermined): Engineering and Industry. See: Thrush.

Dun (Dun, Joe): Generic Word. See: Brewer; Hendrickson; Phyfe.

DUN, JOE. fl. ca. 1485-1509. English bailiff. (Biography source unavailable.) Dun.

DUNAEV, S. A. fl. 1929. Russian chemist. Cited in: Chem. Abstr., vol. 23, p. 4422. Dunajewa test.

Dunajewa test (Dunaev, S. A.): Chemistry. See: Van Nostrand Chem. Dict.

DUNBAR, CARL OWEN. 1891- . American geologist. See: World Who's Who Sci. Dunbaria (dragonflies).

DUNBAR, WILLIAM PHILIPPS. 1863-1922. American hygienist. See: World Who's Who Sci. Dunbar's serum.

Dunbaria (dragonflies) (Dunbar, Carl Owen): Zoology. See: Pennak.

Dunbar's serum (Dunbar, William Philipps): Medicine. See: Stedman.

Dunboyne Establishment (Butler, John): Religion. See: Attwater.

Dunboyne, Lord. See: Butler, John (Lord Dunboyne).

DUNCAN, CHARLES HENRY. b. 1866. American physician. See: Who's Who Among Physicians and Surg. Duncan's method.

DUNCAN, DAVID BEATTIE. 1916- . Australian-born American statistician. See: Amer. Men and Women Sci., 12th ed. Duncan's test.

Duncan (grapefruit) (Derivation undetermined): Food and Drink. See: De Sola.

DUNCAN, JAMES MATTHEWS. 1826-1890. Scottish gynecologist. See: Dict. Nat. Biog., 1st suppl. Duncan's folds, Duncan's position, Duncan's mechanism, Duncan's ventricle.

Duncan Phyfe log (Phyfe, Duncan): Applied Arts. See: Mathews, M. M.

Duncan Phyfe (style) (Phyfe, Duncan): Applied Arts. See: Hendrickson; Mathews, M. M.; Webster's 3d.

Duncan's folds (Duncan, James Matthews): Medicine. See: Dorland; Stedman.

Duncan's mechanism (Duncan, James Matthews): Medicine. See: Stedman.

Duncan's method (Duncan, Charles Henry): Medicine. See: Dorland.

Duncan's position (Duncan, James Matthews): Medicine. See: Dorland.

Duncan's test (Duncan, David Beattie): Statistics. See: Kendall.

Duncan's ventricle (Duncan, James Matthews): Medicine. See: Dorland; Stedman. Also known as: Sylvian ventricle, Vieussen's ventricle, Wenzel's ventricle.

Dunce (Duns Scotus, John): Generic Word (stupid person). See: Brewer; Funk; Hendrickson.

Dundonald, 10th Earl of. See: Cochrane, Thomas (10th Earl of Dundonald).

DUNDREARY, LORD. Chief character in Tom Taylor's comedy, "Our American Cousin," (1858). See: Benet. Dundreary whiskers.

Dundreary whiskers (Dundreary, Lord): Fashion. See: Brewer; Partridge; Weekley.

DUNGERN, EMIL FREIHERR VON. b. 1867. German bacteriologist. See: Biog. Lex. hervorr. Aerzte, 1880-1930. Dungern's test.

Dungern's test (Dungern, Emil Freiherr von): Medicine. See: Dorland.

DUNHAM, EDWARD KELLOGG. 1860-1922. American pathologist. See: World Who's Who Sci. Dunham's solution.

DUNHAM, HENRY KENNAN. 1872-1944. American physician. See: World Who's Who Sci. Dunham's fans (cones or triangles).

Dunham's fans (cones or triangles) (Dunham, Henry Kennan): Medicine. See: Dorland.

Dunham's solution (Dunham, Edward Kellogg): Medicine. See: Dorland.

Dunkard series (Derivation undetermined): Earth Sciences. See: Thrush.

DUNKERLEY, STANLEY. d. 1912. English engineer. See: Sci., vol. 36 (1912), p. 431. Dunkerley's formula.

Dunkerley's formula (Dunkerley, Stanley): Engineering and Industry. See: Auger.

Dunlap chronoscope (Dunlap, Knight): Psychology. See: Drever.

DUNLAP, KNIGHT. 1875-1949. American psychologist. See: World Who's Who Sci. Dunlap chronoscope.

DUNLOP, ALEXANDER COLQUHOUN-STIRLING-MURRAY. 1798-1870. Scottish church lawyer and politician. See: Dict. Nat. Biog. Dunlop's Act.

Dunlop test reaction for ferric ion (Derivation undetermined): Chemistry. See: Van Nostrand Chem. Dict.

Dunlop's Act (Dunlop, Alexander Colquhoun-Stirling-Murray): Education. See: Montgomery.

Dunmore, 4th Earl of. See: Murray, John (4th Earl of Dunmore).

Dunmore's Indian scheme (Murray, John): History. See: Jameson.

Dunmore's War (Murray, John): History. See: Jameson; Mathews, M. M.

DUNN, BEVERLY WYLY. 1860-1936. American soldier and ordnance expert. See: Webster's Biog. Dict. Dunnite.

DUNN, THOMAS E. fl. 1936. American chemist. Cited in: Chem. Abstr., vol. 30, p. 687. Bullard-Dunn process.

DUNNACHIE, JAMES. fl. 1876. Scottish ceramics engineer. Cited in: Chem. Abstr., Decenn. Index, 1917-1926. Dunnachie kiln.

Dunnachie kiln (Dunnachie, James): Engineering and Industry. See: Thrush.

DUNNE, JOHN GREGORY. 1932- . American writer. See: Contemp. Auth., vol. 25. Dunne's law.

Dunne's law (Dunne, John Gregory): Sociology. See: Martin.

Dunning colorimeter (Dunning, Henry Armitt Brown): Chemistry. See: Hackh.

DUNNING, HENRY ARMITT BROWN. 1877-1962. American pharmacist. See: Amer. Men Sci., 10th ed. Dunning colorimeter.

DUNNING, JOHN, 1ST BARON ASHBURTON. 1731-1783. English lawyer. See: Dict. Nat. Biog. Dunning's resolution.

Dunning's resolution (Dunning, John, 1st Baron Ashburton): History. See: Steinberg.

Dunnite (Dunn, Beverly Wyly): Weapons. See: Quick.

Dunraven, 4th Earl of. See: Quin, Windham Thomas Wyndham (4th Earl of Dunraven).

Dunraven Conference (Quin, Windham Thomas Wyndham, 4th Earl of Dunraven): History. See: Montgomery.

Dunraven scheme (Quin, Windham Thomas Wyndham, 4th Earl of Dunraven): History. See: Montgomery.

DUNS SCOTUS, JOHN. 1265-1308. Scottish scholastic theologian. See: Dict. Sci. Biog. Dunce, Scotists.

DUPASQUIER, GASPARD ALPHONSE. 1793-1848. French chemist. See: Nouv. Biog. Univ. Dupasquier reagent?

Dupasquier reagent (Dupasquier, Gaspard Alphonse?): Chemistry. See: Van Nostrand Chem. Dict.

Du Petit, Francois Pourfour. See: Petit, Francois Pourfour du.

Dupin indicatrix (Dupin, Pierre-Charles-Francois): Mathematics. See: Internat. Dict. Ap. Math.

DUPIN, PIERRE-CHARLES-FRANCOIS. 1784-1873. French mathematician. See: Dict. Sci. Biog. cyclid of Dupin, Dupin indicatrix, Dupin theorem, Malus-Dupin theorem.

Dupin theorem (Dupin, Pierre-Charles-Francois): Mathematics. See: Internat. Dict. Ap. Math.

DUPLAY, SIMON-EMMANUEL. 1836-1924. French surgeon. See: World Who's Who Sci. Duplay's bursitis (or disease), Duplay's fibroma.

Duplay's bursitis (or disease) (Duplay, Simon-Emmanuel): Medicine. See: Dorland; Jablonski; Stedman.

Duplay's fibroma (Duplay, Simon-Emmanuel): Medicine. See: Jablonski.

Duplessis-Marly, Seigneur. See: Mornay, Philippe de, Seigneur du Plessis-Marly.

DUPLEX, S. fl. 20th c. Australian quarry manager. (Biography source unavailable.) Duplexite.

Duplexite (Duplex, S.): Earth Sciences. See: Webster's 3d.

DUPLOYE, EMILE. 1833-1912. French inventor. See: Webster's Biog. Dict. Duploye method.

Duploye method (Duploye, Emile): Stenography. Cited in: Webster's Biog. Dict.

DU PONT, FRANCIS IRENEE. 1873-1942. American chemist. See: World Who's Who Sci. Dupont process.

Dupont process (Du Pont, Francis Irenee): Chemistry. See: Thrush.

Dupouy test for haloforms (Derivation undetermined): Chemistry. See: Van Nostrand Chem. Dict.

DUPPA, BALDWIN FRANCIS. 1828-1873. French chemist. See: World Who's Who Sci. Duppa-Perkin test reactions, Frankland-Duppa reaction.

Duppa-Perkin test reactions (Duppa, Baldwin Francis and Perkin, Sir William Henry): Chemistry. See: Van Nostrand Chem. Dict.

Dupre equation (Derivation undetermined): Physics. See: Ballentyne.

DUPRE, ERNEST PIERRE. 1862-1921. French physician. See: World Who's Who Sci. Dupre's disease (or syndrome).

DU PRE, FRITS KAREL. 1912- . Dutch-born physicist. See: Amer. Men and Women Sci., 12th ed. Casimir-Du Pre theory of spin-lattice relaxation.

Dupre's disease (or syndrome) (Dupre, Ernest Pierre): Medicine. See: Dorland; Jablonski.

Dupre's muscle (Derivation undetermined): Medicine. See: Stedman.

DUPUIS, EDMUND. 1839-1892. German physician. See: Biog. Lex. hervorr. Aerzte. Dupuis's cannula.

Dupuis's cannula (Dupuis, Edmund): Medicine. See: Dorland.

DUPUY. fl. 1816. French physician. (Biography source unavailable.) Dupuy's syndrome.

DUPUY-DUTEMPS, LOUIS. b. 1871. French ophthalmologist. Cited in: Kelly. Dupuy-Dutemps operation.

Dupuy-Dutemps operation (Dupuy-Dutemps, Louis): Medicine. See: Stedman.

DUPUY, EUGENE LOUIS. fl. 1914-1933. French metallurgist. Cited in: Chem. Abstr. Le Chatelier-Dupuy reagent.

Dupuy's syndrome (Dupuy). See: Frey's syndrome.

DUPUYTREN, GUILLAUME. 1777-1835. French surgeon and anatomist. See: World Who's Who Sci. Dupuytren-Nelaton disease, Dupuytren's abscess, Dupuytren's amputation, Dupuytren's canal, Dupuytren's contracture, Dupuytren's disease, Dupuytren's enterotome, Dupuytren's fascia, Dupuytren's fracture, Dupuytren's hydrocele, Dupuytren's phlegmon, Dupuytren's sign, Dupuytren's splint, Dupuytren's suture, Dupuytren's tourniquet.

Dupuytren-Nelaton disease (Dupuytren, Guillaume and Nelaton, Auguste). See: Nelaton's disease.

Dupuytren's abscess (Dupuytren, Guillaume): Medicine. See: Jablonski.

Dupuytren's amputation (Dupuytren, Guillaume): Medicine. See: Stedman.

Dupuytren's canal (Dupuytren, Guillaume): Medicine. See: Stedman.

Dupuytren's contracture (Dupuytren, Guillaume): Medicine. See: Dorland; Jablonski; Stedman.

Dupuytren's disease (Dupuytren, Guillaume): Medicine. See: Stedman.

Dupuytren's enterotome (Dupuytren, Guillaume): Medicine. See: Stedman.

Dupuytren's fascia (Dupuytren, Guillaume): Medicine. See: Stedman.

Dupuytren's fracture (Dupuytren, Guillaume). See: Pott's fracture.

Dupuytren's hydrocele (Dupuytren, Guillaume): Medicine. See: Stedman.

Dupuytren's phlegmon (Dupuytren, Guillaume): Medicine. See: Jablonski.

Dupuytren's sign (Dupuytren, Guillaume): Medicine. See: Stedman.

Dupuytren's splint (Dupuytren, Guillaume): Medicine. See: Dorland.

Dupuytren's suture (Dupuytren, Guillaume): Medicine. See: Stedman.

Dupuytren's tourniquet (Dupuytren, Guillaume): Medicine. See: Stedman.

Duran-Reynals factor (or permeability factor) (Duran-Reynals, Francisco): Medicine. See: Dorland; Stedman.

DURAN-REYNALS, FRANCISCO. 1899-1958. American bacteriologist. See: Amer. Men Sci., 9th ed. Duran-Reynals factor (or permeability factor).

DURAND, J. fl. 1913. French physician. (Biography source unavailable.) Durand-Nicolas-Favre disease.

Durand-Nicolas-Favre disease (Durand, J.; Nicolas, Joseph; and Favre, Maurice): Medicine. See: Dorland; Jablonski. Also known as: Frei's disease, Nicolas-Favre disease.

DURAND, PAUL. fl. 1955. French? physician. (Biography source unavailable.) Durand-Zunin syndrome, Durand's disease.

Durand-Zunin syndrome (Durand, Paul and Zunin, C.): Medicine. See: Jablonski.

DURANDE, JEAN FRANCOIS. d. 1794. French physician. See: Nouv. Biog. Univ. Durande's remedy.

Durande's remedy (Durande, Jean Francois): Medicine. See: Dorland.

Durand's disease (Durand, Paul): Medicine. See: Jablonski.

Duranta (Durante, Castor): Botany. See: Taylor, N.; Webster's 3d.

DURANTE, CASTOR. d. 1590. Italian physician and botanist. See: World Who's Who Sci. Duranta.

DURANTE, FRANCESCO. 1845-1934. Italian surgeon. See: World Who's Who Sci. Durante's treatment.

DURANTE, GUSTAVE. 1865-1934. French neurologist. See: Gynecologie, annee 33 (Nov., 1934), p. 669. Porak-Durante syndrome.

Durante's disease (Derivation undetermined): Medicine. See: Stedman.

Durante's treatment (Durante, Francesco): Medicine. See: Dorland.

Durbachite (Derivation undetermined): Earth Sciences. See: Thrush.

DURBIN, JAMES. 1923- . English statistician. See: Who's Who Sci. Europe, 1967. Durbin-Watson statistic.

Durbin-Watson statistic (Durbin, James and Watson, Geoffrey Stuart): Statistics. See: Kendall.

DURDEN, DAME. Notable housewife in famous English song. See: Barnhart Cycl. Names). Dame Durden.

DURER, ALBRECHT. 1471-1528. German painter and engraver. See: Encyc. Brit., 1973. Dureresque (or Duereresque).

Dureresque (or Duereresque) (Durer, Albrecht): Fine Arts. See: Webster's 3d.

DURET, HENRI. 1849-1921. French neurosurgeon. See: Biog. Lex. hervorr. Aerzte, 1880-1930. Duret's lesion.

Duret's lesion (Duret, Henri): Medicine. See: Dorland; Stedman.

Durfeldtite (Duerfeldt, Richard): Earth Sciences. See: Thrush.

DURHAM. fl. 1954. American felon found to be criminally insane. (Biography source unavailable.) Durham rule.

Durham, 1st Earl of. See: Lambton, John George (1st Earl of Durham).

DURHAM, ARTHUR EDWARD. 1834-1895. English surgeon. See: Sci., vol. (1895), p. 640. Durham's tube (1).

Durham boat (Durham, Robert): Engineering and Industry. See: Webster's 3d.

DURHAM, HERBERT EDWARD. 1866-1945. English bacteriologist. See: World Who's Who Sci. Durham's tube (2).

Durham('s) Report (Lambton, John George, 1st Earl of Durham): History. See: Harvey; Montgomery; Morris and Irwin.

DURHAM, ROBERT. fl. 18th c. American boat builder. (Biography source unavailable.) Durham boat.

Durham rule (Durham): Law. See: Black; Hoult; Stedman; Wolman.

Durham's tube (1) (Durham, Arthur Edward): Medicine. See: Dorland; Stedman.

Durham's tube (2) (Durham, Herbert Edward): Medicine. See: Dorland.

DURKEE, ANN. 1912- . American psychologist. See: Amer. Psych. Assoc. Direct., 1960. Buss-Durkee inventory.

DURKHEIM, EMILE. 1858-1917. French sociologist. See: Internat. Encyc. Soc. Sci. Durkheimian, Durkheim's law of suicide, Durkheim's stages of societal development.

Durkheimian (Durkheim, Emile): Sociology. See: Webster's 3d.

Durkheim's law of suicide (Durkheim, Emile): Sociology. See: Zadrozny.

Durkheim's stages of societal development (Durkheim, Emile): Sociology. See: Zadrozny.

Duroziez murmur (sign or symptom) (Duroziez, Paul Louis): Medicine. See: Dorland; Stedman.

Duroziez' onomatope (Duroziez, Paul Louis): Medicine. See: Stedman.

DUROZIEZ, PAUL LOUIS. 1826-1897. French physician. See: World Who's Who Sci. Duroziez's disease, Duroziez murmur (sign or symptom), Duroziez' onomatope.

Duroziez's disease (Duroziez, Paul Louis): Medicine. See: Dorland; Jablonski; Stedman.

Durrani (Ahmad Shah Durrani): History. Cited in: Webster's Biog. Dict.

Durrant test reaction (Derivation undetermined): Chemistry. See: Van Nostrand Chem. Dict.

DURVILLE, P. H. G. fl. 1915. German? metallurgist. Cited in: Chem. Abstr., vol. 9, p. 783. Durville process.

Durville process (Durville, P. H. G.): Engineering and Industry. See: Thrush.

DURYEE, ABRAM. 1815-1890. American army officer. See: Webster's Biog. Dict. Duryee's Zouaves.

Duryee's Zouaves (Duryee, Abram): History. Cited in: Webster's Biog. Dict.

Dushman and Found gauge (Dushman, Saul and Found, Clifton Garwin): Physics. See: Internat. Dict. Phys. Elec.

Dushman equation (Dushman, Saul). See: Richardson-Dushman equation.

Dushman-Langmuir equation (Dushman, Saul and Langmuir, Irving): Physics. See: Thewlis.

DUSHMAN, SAUL. 1883-1954. Russian-born American physical chemist. See: World Who's Who Sci. Dushman and Found gauge, Dushman-Langmuir equation, Richardson-Dushman equation.

DUSPIVA, FRANZ. 1895- . German biochemist. See: Who's Who Sci. Europe, 1967. Linderstrom-Lang-Duspiva method.

DUSSERT, DESIRE. b. 1872. French mining engineer. Cited in: Min. Mag., vol. 20. Dussertite.

Dussertite (Dussert, Desire): Earth Sciences. See: Thrush; Webster's 3d.

DUSUQI, IBRAHIM ED-. d. 1278. Religious leader. (Biography source unavailable.) Dusuqiyeh.

Dusuqiyeh (Dusuqi, Ibrahim ed-): Religion. See: Canney.

DUTTON, CLARENCE EDWARD. 1841-1912. American geologist. See: Dict. Sci. Biog. Duttonite.

DUTTON, JOSEPH EVERETT. 1874-1905. English physician. See: World Who's Who Sci. Duttonella, Dutton's disease, Dutton's fever, Dutton's spirochete.

Duttonella (Dutton, Joseph Everett): Medicine. See: Dorland.

Duttonite (Dutton, Clarence Edward): Earth Sciences. See: Thrush.

Dutton's disease (Dutton, Joseph Everett): Medicine. See: Dorland; Jablonski; Stedman.

Dutton's fever (Dutton, Joseph Everett): Medicine. See: Dorland; Jablonski.

Dutton's spirochete (Dutton, Joseph Everett): Medicine. See: Dorland.

DUVAL, CHARLES WARREN. b. 1876. American pathologist. See: Who's Who Amer. Med. Duval's bacillus.

DUVAL, MATHIAS MARIE. 1844-1907. French anatomist. See: Dict. Sci. Biog. Duval's nucleus, Duval's tufted convolution.

Duval's bacillus (Duval, Charles Warren): Medicine. See: Dorland.

Duval's nucleus (Duval, Mathias Marie): Medicine. See: Dorland; Stedman.

Duval's tufted convolution (Duval, Mathias Marie): Medicine. See: Stedman.

Duvdevani dew gage (Derivation undetermined): Earth Sciences. See: Huschke.

DUVERNEY, JOSEPH-GUICHARD. 1648-1730. French anatomist. See: Dict. Sci. Biog. Duverney's fissure, Duverney's foramen, Duverney's gland, Duverney's muscle.

Duverney's fissure (Duverney, Joseph-Guichard): Medicine. See: Stedman.

Duverney's foramen (Duverney, Joseph-Guichard): Medicine. See: Stedman.

Duverney's gland (Duverney, Joseph-Guichard): Medicine. See: Donath; Dorland; Stedman.

Duverney's muscle (Duverney, Joseph-Guichard): Medicine. See: Stedman. Also known as: Horner's muscle.

DU VIGNEAUD, VINCENT. 1901- . American biochemist. See: World Who's Who Sci. Marvel-Du Vigneud reagent.

D'UXELLES, MARQUIS. fl. 17th c. French aristocrat. (Biography source unavailable.) Duxelles sauce.

Duxelles sauce (d'Uxelles, Marquis): Food and Drink. See: Hendrickson.

DUYK, MAURICE. fl. 1901. Belgian chemist. Cited in: Kelly. Duyk solution for glucose.

Duyk solution for glucose (Duyk, Maurice): Chemistry. See: Van Nostrand Chem. Dict.

Duyk test for differentiating fibers (Derivation undetermined): Chemistry. See: Van Nostrand Chem. Dict.

Dvoretsky's stochastic approximation theorem (Dvoretzky, A.): Statistics. See: Kendall.

DVORETZKY, A. fl. 1956. American statistician. Cited in: Mansell. Dvoretsky's stochastic approximation theorem.

DWIGHT, ARTHUR SMITH. 1864-1946. American mining and metallurgical engineer. See: World Who's Who Sci. Dwight-Lloyd machine, Dwight-Lloyd process (or sintering), Dwight-Lloyd roaster.

Dwight-Lloyd machine (Dwight, Arthur Smith and Lloyd, Richard Lewis): Engineering and Industry. See: Thrush; Van Nostrand Chem. Dict.

Dwight-Lloyd process (or sintering) (Dwight, Arthur Smith and Lloyd, Richard Lewis): Engineering and Industry. See: Thrush; Van Nostrand Chem. Dict.; Webster's 3d.

Dwight-Lloyd roaster (Dwight, Arthur Smith and Lloyd, Richard Lewis): Engineering and Industry. See: Thrush.

DWYER, F. P. fl. 1938. Australian chemist. Cited in: Chem. Abstr., vol. 30, p. 6302; vol. 31, p. 65, 3412; vol. 32, p. 73. Dwyer-Murphy reagent, Dwyer reagent for cadmium, Dwyer reagents for magnesium, Dwyer test for cobalt, Dwyer test for magnesium and cadmium.

Dwyer-Murphy reagent (Dwyer, F. P. and Murphy, R. K.): Chemistry. See: Van Nostrand Chem. Dict.

Dwyer reagent for cadmium (Dwyer, F. P.): Chemistry. See: Van Nostrand Chem. Dict.

Dwyer reagents for magnesium (Dwyer, F. P.): Chemistry. See: Van Nostrand Chem. Dict.

Dwyer test for cobalt (Dwyer, F. P.): Chemistry. See: Van Nostrand Chem. Dict.

Dwyer test for magnesium and cadmium (Dwyer, F. P.): Chemistry. See: Van Nostrand Chem. Dict.

DYAR, HARRISON GRAY. 1866-1929. American entomologist. See: Dict. Amer. Biog. Dyar's law.

Dyar's law (Dyar, Harrison Gray): Biology. See: Gray.

Dyck, Sir Anthony Van. See: Vandyke, Sir Anthony.

DYCKERHOFF, WALTER. fl. 1933. German chemist. Cited in: Chem. Abstr., Decenn. Index, 1927-1936. Seailles-Dyckerhoff process.

Dyckia (Salm-Reifferscheid-Dyck, Joseph Franz Maria Anton Hubert Ignatz zu): Botany. See: Taylor, N.

Dyer Act (Dyer, Leonidas Carstarphen): Law. See: Smith.

DYER, LEONIDAS CARSTARPHEN. 1871-1957. American legislator. See: Biog. Direct. Amer. Congress. Dyer Act.

Dyer method (Derivation undetermined): Engineering and Industry. See: Thrush.

DYKE, SIDNEY CAMPBELL. 1886- . English physician. See: Who's Who, 1974. Dyke-Young syndrome.

Dyke-Young syndrome (Dyke, Sidney Campbell and Young, Freida): Medicine. See: Jablonski.

DYMPNA, SAINT. fl. 7th c. Irish princess and Christian martyr. See: Dict. Nat. Biog. Saint Dymphna's disease.

DYSON, FREEMAN JOHN. 1923- . English-born American physicist. See: World Who's Who Sci. Dyson representation?

Dyson representation (Dyson, Freeman John?): Physics. See: Internat. Dict. Ap. Math.

DZIERZON, JOHANN. 1811-1906. German apiculturist. See: World Who's Who Sci. Dzierzon('s) theory.

Dzierzon('s) theory (Dzierzon, Johann): Biology. See: Henderson; Winburne.

DZIERZYNSKY, W. fl. 1913. Polish? physician. (Biography source unavailable.) Dzierzynsky's syndrome.

Dzierzynsky's syndrome (Dzierzynsky, W.): Medicine. See: Jablonski.

E

E. P. Dutton-John Macrae Award (E. P. Dutton Co. and Macrae, John): Library Science. See: Harrod.

EADFRID, BISHOP OF LINDISFARNE. d. 721. English bishop. See: Dict. Nat. Biog. Lindisfarne gospels.

Eadgar's Law (Edgar): History. See: Harbottle.

EAGLE, HARRY. 1905- . American physician. See: World Who's Who Sci. Eagle test.

Eagle test (Eagle, Harry): Medicine. See: Dorland; Stedman.

EALES, HENRI. 1852-1913. English physician. See: Biog. Lex. hervorr. Aerzte. Eales' syndrome (or disease).

Eales' syndrome (or disease) (Eales, Henri): Medicine. See: Jablonski; Stedman.

Earl loco (Derivation undetermined): Botany. See: Winburne.

Earl of Mar's Grey-Breeks (Derivation undetermined): History. See: Brewer.

EARLAND, ARTHUR. d. 1958. English civil servant. Cited in: Mansell. Earlandite.

Earlandite (Earland, Arthur): Earth Sciences. See: Thrush; Webster's 3d.

Earle L fibrosarcoma (or sarcoma) (Earle, Wilton Robinson): Medicine. See: Jablonski; Stedman.

EARLE, WILTON ROBINSON. 1902-1962. American pathologist. See: Amer. Men Sci., 9th ed. Earle L fibrosarcoma (or sarcoma).

Early effect (Early, James M.): Physics. See: Internat. Dict. Phys. Elec.

EARLY, JAMES M. 1922- . American physicist. See: Amer. Men and Women Sci., 12th ed. Early effect.

EARLY, JUBAL ANDERSON. 1816-1894. American army officer. See: Dict. Amer. Biog. Early's raids.

Early's raids (Early, Jubal Anderson): History. See: Morris and Irwin.

EARNSHAW, SAMUEL. 1805-1888. English physicist and mathematician. See: Pogg., vols. 4, 5. Earnshaw('s) theorem.

Earnshaw('s) theorem (Earnshaw, Samuel): Physics. See: Ballentyne; Internat. Dict. Ap. Math.; Internat. Dict. Phys. Elec.; Van Nostrand Sci. Encyc.

EASTLAKE, SIR CHARLES LOCK. 1793-1865. English painter and art critic. See: Dict. Nat. Biog. Eastlake (furniture style).

Eastlake (furniture style) (Eastlake, Sir Charles Lock): Applied Arts. See: Webster's 3d.

Eastman colorimeter (Derivation undetermined): Physics. See: Internat. Dict. Phys. Elec.

EASTMAN, GEORGE. 1854-1932. American inventor and manufacturer. See: World Who's Who Sci. Walker/Eastman roller-slide camera.

Eastman survey instrument (Derivation undetermined): Engineering and Industry. See: Thrush.

Eaton affair (Eaton, Margaret O'Neale): History. See: Morris; Smith.

EATON, CHARLES. fl. 1847. English con artist. (Biography source unavailable.) Billies and Charlies.

Eaton-Lambert syndrome (Eaton, Lealdes McKendree and Lambert, Edward Howard): Medicine. See: Jablonski.

EATON, LEALDES MC KENDREE (LEE M.). 1905-1958. American physician. See: World Who's Who Sci. Eaton-Lambert syndrome.

EATON, MARGARET O'NEALE. 1796-1879. Wife of American Secretary of War, John Henry Eaton. See: Encyc. Brit., 1973. Eaton affair.

EATON, MONROE DAVIS. 1904- . American bacteriologist. See: World Who's Who Sci. Eaton pneumonia (or agent pneumonia).

Eaton pneumonia (or agent pneumonia) (Eaton, Monroe Davis): Medicine. See: Jablonski; Stedman.

Ebbecke's reaction (Derivation undetermined): Medicine. See: Stedman.

Ebbinghaus' curve (of retention) (Ebbinghaus, Hermann): Psychology. See: Chaplin; English; Wolman.

EBBINGHAUS, HERMANN. 1850-1909. German psychologist. See: Internat. Encyc. Soc. Sci. Ebbinghaus' curve (of retention), Ebbinghaus illusion, Ebbinghaus test.

Ebbinghaus illusion (Ebbinghaus, Hermann): Psychology. See: Wolman.

Ebbinghaus test (Ebbinghaus, Hermann): Psychology. See: Dorland; English; Stedman.

EBEL, JOHANN WILHELM. 1784-1861. German theologian. See: Allg. Deut. Biog. Ebelians.

Ebelians (Ebel, Johann Wilhelm): Religion. See: Canney.

Eber solution (Derivation undetermined): Chemistry. See: Van Nostrand Chem. Dict.

Eber test reaction for physostigmine (Derivation undetermined): Chemistry. See: Van Nostrand Chem. Dict.

Eberhard effect (Eberhard, Paul Alexander Julius Gustav): Physics. See: Focal Encyc. Film; Focal Encyc. Photog.; Internat. Dict. Phys. Elec.

EBERHARD, PAUL ALEXANDER JULIUS GUSTAV. 1867-1940. German astronomer. See: World Who's Who Sci. Eberhard effect.

EBERT, HERMANN. 1861-1913. German physicist. See: World Who's Who Sci. Ebert ion-counter.

Ebert ion-counter (Ebert, Hermann): Earth Sciences. See: Huschke.

EBERTH, CARL JOSEPH. 1835-1926. German anatomist. See: Dict. Sci. Biog. Eberthella, Eberth's bacillus, Eberth's body, Eberth's disease, Eberth's lines, Eberth's perithelium.

Eberthella (Eberth, Carl Joseph): Medicine. See: Dorland; Stedman; Webster's 3d.

Eberth's bacillus (Eberth, Carl Joseph): Medicine. See: Stedman.

Eberth's body (Eberth, Carl Joseph): Zoology. See: Gray.

Eberth's disease (Eberth, Carl Joseph): Medicine. See: Jablonski.

Eberth's lines (Eberth, Carl Joseph): Medicine. See: Dorland; Stedman.

Eberth's perithelium (Eberth, Carl Joseph): Medicine. See: Stedman.

Ebner fluid (Derivation undetermined): Chemistry. See: Hackh.

EBNER VON ROFENSTEIN, ANTON GILBERT VIKTOR. 1842-1925. Austrian physician and histologist. See: World Who's Who Sci. Ebner's fibers (or fibrils), Ebner's glands, Ebner's pillar, Ebner's reticulum.

Ebner's fibers (or fibrils) (Ebner von Rofenstein, Anton Gilbert Viktor): Medicine. See: Donath; Dorland.

Ebner's glands (Ebner von Rofenstein, Anton Gilbert Viktor): Medicine. See: Donath; Dorland; Stedman.

Ebner's pillar (Ebner von Rofenstein, Anton Gilbert Viktor): Medicine. See: Donath.

Ebner's reticulum (Ebner von Rofenstein, Anton Gilbert Viktor): Medicine. See: Donath; Dorland; Stedman.

Eboli test reaction (Derivation undetermined): Chemistry. See: Van Nostrand Chem. Dict.

EBSTEIN, WILHELM. 1836-1912. German internist, pathologist and medical historian. See: World Who's Who Sci. Armanni-Ebstein cells, Armanni-Ebstein change (or kidney), Armanni-Ebstein lesion, Ebstein's anomaly (or syndrome), Ebstein's diet, Ebstein's disease, Ebstein's sign, Ebstein's treatment, Pel-Ebstein disease (or symptom).

Ebstein's anomaly (or syndrome) (Ebstein, Wilhelm): Medicine. See: Jablonski; Stedman.

Ebstein's diet (Ebstein, Wilhelm): Medicine. See: Dorland.

Ebstein's disease (Ebstein, Wilhelm): Medicine. See: Dorland; Jablonski.

Ebstein's sign (Ebstein, Wilhelm): Medicine. See: Stedman.

Ebstein's treatment (Ebstein, Wilhelm): Medicine. See: Dorland

Eccles-Jordan circuit (Eccles, William Henry and Jordan, F. W.): Electronics. See: Hughes; Internat. Dict. Phys. Elec.; Markus.

ECCLES, WILLIAM HENRY. b. 1875. English physicist. See: World Who's Who Sci. Eccles-Jordan circuit.

Ecebolians (Ecebolius): Religion. See: Canney.

ECEBOLIUS. fl. ca. 361-363 A.D. Sophist of Constantanople. See: Blunt, under "Ecebolians." Ecebolians.

Echeveria (Echeverria, Atanasio): Botany. See: Taylor, N.

ECHEVERRIA, ATANASIO. fl. 19th c. Mexican botanical illustrator. See: Leon. Echeveria.

Eck, C. L. von Panthaleon van. See: Van Eck, C. L. von Panthaleon.

Eck('s) fistula (Eck, Nikolay Vladimirovich): Medicine. See: Dorland; Stedman; Webster's 3d.

ECK, NIKOLAY VLADIMIROVICH. 1847-1917. Russian physiologist. See: Heart Bull., vol. 9, no. 4 (1960), cover. Eck('s) fistula.

ECKER, ALEXANDER. 1816-1887. German anatomist. See: World Who's Who Sci. Ecker's convolution, Ecker's fissure.

ECKER, ENRIQUE EDUARDO. b. 1887. Dutch West Indian-born American pathologist. See: Amer. Men Sci. 4th ed. Rees-Ecker fluid.

ECKERMANN, CLAES WALTER HARRY VON. b. 1886. Swedish mineralogist. See: Svensk Uppslagsbok. Eckermannite.

Eckermannite (Eckermann, Claes Walter Harry von): Earth Sciences. See: Thrush; Webster's 3d.

Ecker's convolution (Ecker, Alexander): Medicine. See: Dorland.

Ecker's fissure (Ecker, Alexander): Medicine. See: Dorland; Stedman.

Eckerson press (Derivation undetermined): Printing. See: Lockwood.

ECKERT-GREIFENDORFF, MAX. 1865-1938. German cartographer. See: Kuerschner's Gel. Kal., vol. 4, 1931. Eckert projection(s).

Eckert projection(s) (Eckert-Greifendorff, Max): Geography. See: Monkhouse; Webster's 3d.

ECKLIN, THEOPHIL. fl. 1918. Swiss physician. Cited in: Mansell. Ecklin's syndrome (or anemia).

Ecklin's syndrome (or anemia) (Ecklin, Theophil): Medicine. See: Jablonski.

Economo, Constantin Alexander von. See: Von Economo, Constantin Alexander.

Economo's disease (Von Economo, Constantin Alexander): Medicine. See: Dorland; Hinsie; Jablonski. Also known as: Von Economo's disease.

EDDINGTON, ARTHUR STANLEY. 1882-1944. English astronomer. See: Dict. Sci. Biog. Eddington theory, Eddington transfer equation.

Eddington theory (Eddington, Arthur Stanley): Physics. See: Internat. Dict. Phys. Elec.; Thewlis.

Eddington transfer equation (Eddington, Arthur Stanley): Astronomy. See: Thewlis.

EDDOWES, ALFRED. b. 1850. English physician. See: Biog. Lex. hervorr. Aerzte, 1880-1930. Eddowes' syndrome.

Eddowes' syndrome (Eddowes, Alfred). See: Lobstein's syndrome.

EDDY C. W. fl. 1938. American chemist. Cited in: Chem. Abstr., vol. 32, p. 5841. Eddy-De Eds test.

Eddy-De Eds test (Eddy, C. W. and De Eds, Floyd): Chemistry. See: Van Nostrand Chem. Dict.

EDDY, HENRY TURNER. 1844-1921. American mathematician and physicist. See: World Who's Who Sci. Eddy's theorem.

Eddy kite (Eddy, William Abner): Earth Sciences. Cited in: World Who's Who Sci.

EDDY, MARY BAKER. 1821-1910. American religious leader. See: Dict. Amer. Biog. Eddyism.

EDDY, WILLIAM ABNER. 1858-1909. American meteorologist. See: World Who's Who Sci. Eddy kite.

Eddyism (Eddy, Mary Baker): Religion. See: Hendrickson; Mathews, M. M.

Eddy's theorem (Eddy, Henry Turner): Physics. See: Thrush.

EDEBOHLS, GEORGE. 1853-1908. American surgeon. See: Dict. Amer. Biog. Edebohls' operation, Edebohls' position.

Edebohls' operation (Edebohls, George): Medicine. See: Dorland; Stedman.

Edebohls' position (Edebohls, George): Medicine. See: Dorland; Stedman.

EDELEANU, LAZAR. 1861-1941. Romanian chemist. See: Pogg., vol. 6, 7b. Edeleanu process.

Edeleanu process (Edeleanu, Lazar): Chemistry. See: Van Nostrand Chem. Dict; Webster's 3d.

EDELMANN, ADOLF. 1885-1939. Polish-born Austrian physician. See: Biog. Lex. hervorr. Aerzte, 1880-1930. Edelmann's syndrome (1) (or anemia), Edelmann's syndrome (2).

Edelmann's syndrome (1) (or anemia) (Edelmann, Adolf): Medicine. See: Dorland; Jablonski.

Edelmann's syndrome (2) (Edelmann, Adolf): Medicine. See: Jablonski.

Edelstein, Sigismund Zois, Baron von. See: Zois, Sigismund, von Edelstein.

EDEN, ROBERT ANTHONY (1st Earl of Avon). 1897- . English statesman. See: New Encyc. Brit., 1974, Microp. Anthony Eden (hat).

Eden treaty (Eden, William): History. See: Morris and Irwin.

EDEN, WILLIAM. 1744-1814. English statesman. See: Dict. Nat. Biog. Eden treaty.

Eder-Hecht wedge sensitometer (Eder, Joseph Maria and Hecht, Water D.): Photography. See: Focal Encyc. Photog.

EDER, JOSEPH MARIA. 1855-1946. Austrian photochemist. See: Dict. Sci. Biog. Eder-Hecht wedge sensitometer.

EDGAR. 944-975. King of England. See: Dict. Nat Biog. Eadgar's Law.

Edgar (Poe, Edgar Allan): Literature. See: Hendrickson.

Edge Act (Edge, Walter Evans): Politics. See: Smith.

EDGE, WALTER EVANS. 1873-1956. American journalist and diplomat. See: Biog. Direct. Amer. Congress. Edge Act.

EDGEWORTH, FRANCIS YSIDRO. 1845-1926. English economist and statistician. See: Internat. Encyc. Soc. Sci. Edgeworth('s) series, Marshall-Edgeworth-Boley index.

Edgeworth index (Edgeworth, Francis Ysidro). See: Marshall-Edgeworth-Bowley index.

EDGEWORTH, MICHAEL PAKENHAM. 1812-1881. Irish botanist. See: Dict. Nat. Biog. Edgeworthia.

Edgeworth('s) series (Edgeworth, Francis Ysidro): Statistics. See: Internat. Dict. Ap. Math.; Kendall; Van Nostrand Sci. Encyc.

Edgeworthia (Edgeworth, Michael Pakenham): Botany. See: Taylor, N.

EDINBURGH, DUKE OF (PHILIP MOUNTBATTEN). 1921- . Prince consort of England. See: Barnhart (Cycl. Names). Duke of Edinburgh's award.

EDINGER, LUDWIG. 1855-1918. German anatomist. See: World Who's Who Sci. Edinger-Westphal('s) nucleus, Edinger's fibers, Edinger's law, Edinger's nucleus, Edinger's tract (or bundle).

Edinger-Westphal('s) nucleus (Edinger, Ludwig and Westphal, Karl Friedrich Otto): Medicine. See: Donath; Stedman.

Edinger's fibers (Edinger, Ludwig): Medicine. See: Stedman.

Edinger's law (Edinger, Ludwig): Medicine. See: Dorland.

Edinger's nucleus (Edinger, Ludwig): Medicine. See: Dorland.

Edinger's tract (or bundle) (Edinger, Ludwig): Medicine. See: Donath.

EDINGTON. fl. 19th c. Scottish mineral discoverer. Cited in: Bailey. Edingtonite.

Edingtonite (Edington): Earth Sciences. See: Thrush; Webster's 3d.

Edipism (or Oedipism) (Oedipus): Medicine. See: Dorland; Stedman.

Edipus. See: Oedipus.

Edison (Edison, Thomas Alva): Generic Word (inventor). See: Hendrickson.

Edison base (Edison, Thomas Alva): Engineering and Industry. See: Markus.

Edison effect (Edison, Thomas Alva): Electronics. See: Hughes; Internat. Dict. Phys. Elec.; Webster's 3d.

Edison equation (Edison, Thomas Alva). See: Richardson-Dushman equation.

Edison-Hopkinson dynamo (Edison, Thomas Alva and Hopkinson, John): Electronics. Cited in: World Who's Who Sci.

Edison magnetic separator (Edison, Thomas Alva): Engineering and Industry. See: Thrush.

Edison screw thread (Edison, Thomas Alva): Engineering and Industry. See: Auger.

EDISON, THOMAS ALVA. 1847-1931. American inventor. See: Dict. Sci. Biog. Edison, Edison base, Edison effect, Edison equation, Edison-Hopkinson dynamo, Edison magnetic separator, Edison screw thread, Edisonite.

Edison three-wire system (Derivation undetermined): Engineering and Industry. See: Thrush.

Edisonite (Edison, Thomas Alva): Earth Sciences. See: Mathews, M. M.; Thrush.

EDLBACHER, SIEGFRIED AUGUSTIN JOHANN. 1886-1946. Austrian physiological chemist. See: World Who's Who Sci. Edlbacher test reaction.

Edlbacher test reaction (Edlbacher, Siegfried Augustin Johann): Chemistry. See: Van Nostrand Chem. Dict.

EDLEFSEN, GUSTAV JULIUS FRIEDRICH. 1842-1910. German physician. See: Wer Ist's, 1906. Edlefsen's reagent.

Edlefsen test reaction for resorcinol (Derivation undetermined): Chemistry. See: Van Nostrand Chem. Dict.

Edlefsen's reagent (Edlefsen, Gustav Julius Friedrich): Medicine. See: Dorland; Stedman.

Edman method (or reagent) (Edman, Pehr): Chemistry. See: Stedman.

EDMAN, PEHR. 1916- . Swedish chemist. See: Vem Ar Det, 1963. Edman method (or reagent).

EDMUND RICH, SAINT. 1175-1240. English prelate. See: Dict. Nat. Biog. Fathers of St. Edmund.

Edmunds Act (Edmunds, George Franklin): History. See: Black; Jameson; Smith.

EDMUNDS, GEORGE FRANKLIN. 1828-1919. American lawyer and legislator. See: Dict. Amer. Biog. Edmunds Act.

EDMUNDS, H. M. fl. 1921. Inventor. (Biography source unavailable.) Edmunds' method.

Edmunds' method (Edmunds, H. M.): Photography. See: Focal Encyc. Photog.

EDNER, J. fl. 1908. Swiss chemist. Cited in: Chem. Abstr. vol. 2, p. 1327. Tschirch-Edner reagent.

Edom. See: Esau.

Edomite(s) (Esau, the twin): History. See: Hendrickson; Webster's 3d.

EDRIDGE-GREEN, FREDERICK WILLIAM. 1863-1953. English ophthalmologist. See: World Who's Who Sci. Edridge-Green lamp, Edridge-Green theory.

Edridge-Green lamp (Edridge-Green, Frederick William): Medicine. See: Stedman.

Edridge-Green theory (Edridge-Green, Frederick William): Medicine. See: Stedman.

EDSALL, DAVID LINN. 1869-1945. American physician. See: World Who's Who Sci. Edsall's disease.

Edsall's disease (Edsall, David Linn): Medicine. See: Dorland.

Edser and Butler's bands (or Edser-Butler bands) (Edser, Edwin and Butler, Charles P.): Physics. See: Ballentyne; Thewlis.

Edser-Butler method of calibrating a spectrometer (Edser, Edwin and Butler, Charles P.): Physics. See: Internat. Dict. Phys. Elec.

EDSER, EDWIN. d. 1932. English physicist. See: Pogg., vols. 6, 7b. Edser and Butler's bands (or Edser-Butler bands), Edser-Butler method of calibrating a spectrometer.

EDWARD I. 1239-1307. King of England. See: Dict. Nat. Biog. Edwardian conquest, Ordinances of Edward I.

EDWARD IV, DUKE OF YORK. 1442-1483. King of England. See: Dict. Nat. Biog. Yorkists.

EDWARD VI. 1537-1553. King of England and Ireland. See: Dict. Nat. Biog. Edwardian Reformation, Edwardine ordinal.

EDWARD VII. 1841-1910. King of Great Britain and Ireland. See: Dict. Nat. Biog., 2d suppl. Edwardian (style or age).

EDWARD THE CONFESSOR, SAINT. 1004-1066. King of England. See: Dict. Nat. Biog. Saint Edward's crown.

Edwardean (or Edwardsism) (Edwards, Jonathan): Religion. See: Mathews, M. M.; Webster's 3d.

Edwardian conquest (Edward I): History. See: Steinberg.

Edwardian Reformation (Edward VI): History. See: Steinberg.

Edwardian (style or age) (Edward VII): History. See: Barnhart (Eng. Lit.); Brewer; Harvey.

Edwardine ordinal (Edward VI): Religion. See: Attwater.

Edwards' air pump (Edwards, F.): Engineering and Industry. See: Auger.

EDWARDS, ALBA. b. 1872. American statistician. Cited in: Mansell. Edwards' occupational classification.

EDWARDS, ALLEN L. 1914- . American psychologist. See: Amer. Men Sci., 9th ed. (Soc. Behav. Sci.). Edwards personal preference schedule.

EDWARDS, F. fl. 1894. Inventor. (Biography source unavailable.) Edwards' air pump.

Edwards gauge (Derivation undetermined): Physics. See: Internat. Dict. Phys. Elec.

EDWARDS, JOHN HILTON. 1928- . English human geneticist. See: World Who's Who Sci. Edward's syndrome.

EDWARDS, JONATHAN. 1703-1758. American clergyman and theologian. See: Dict. Amer. Biog. Edwardean (or Edwardsism).

EDWARDS, M. L. fl. 20th c. American physician. (Biography source unavailable.) Starr-Edwards ball valve prosthesis.

Edwards' occupational classification (Edwards, Alba): Sociology. See: Zadrozny.

Edwards personal preference schedule (Edwards, Allen L.): Psychology. See: Wolman.

Edwards roaster (Edwards, Thomas): Engineering and Industry. See: Thrush.

Edwards' syndrome (Edwards, John Hilton): Medicine. See: Jablonski.

EDWARDS, THOMAS. fl. 1912. Australian metallurgist. Cited in: Chem. Abstr., vol. 6, p. 215. Edwards roaster.

Edwardsia (Milne-Edwards, Henri): Zoology. See: Pennak; Webster's 3d.

Edwardsiella (Milne-Edwards, Henri): Zoology. See: Pennak.

Edwin Smith medical papyrus (Derivation undetermined): Medicine. See: Winick.

EEGRIWE, EDWIN. fl. 1932. German chemist. Cited in: Chem. Abstr., Decenn. Index, 1927-1936. Eegriwe micro-test for phenol, Eegriwe reagent for silica and fluorine, Eegriwe reagent for tin, Eegriwe reagents for zinc, Eegriwe test for antimony and tungsten, Eegriwe test for free chlorine, Eegriwe test for glycolic acid, Eegriwe test for lactic acid, Eegriwe test for magnesium, Eegriwe test for malic acid, Eegriwe test for nitrite and nitrate, Eegriwe test for orcinol, Eegriwe test for sulfite, Eegriwe test for sulfur dioxide, Eegriwe tests for cobalt, Eegriwe tests for tartrate.

Eegriwe micro-test for phenol (Eegriwe, Edwin): Chemistry. See: Van Nostrand Chem. Dict.

Eegriwe reagent for silica and fluorine (Eegriwe, Edwin): Chemistry. See: Van Nostrand Chem. Dict.

Eegriwe reagent for tin (Eegriwe, Edwin): Chemistry. See: Van Nostrand Chem. Dict.

Eegriwe reagents for zinc (Eegriwe, Edwin): Chemistry. See: Van Nostrand Chem. Dict.

Eegriwe test for antimony and tungsten (Eegriwe, Edwin): Chemistry. See: Van Nostrand Chem. Dict.

Eegriwe test for free chlorine (Eegriwe, Edwin): Chemistry. See: Van Nostrand Chem. Dict.

Eegriwe test for glycolic acid (Eegriwe, Edwin): Chemistry. See: Van Nostrand Chem. Dict.

Eegriwe test for lactic acid (Eegriwe, Edwin): Chemistry. See: Van Nostrand Chem. Dict.

Eegriwe test for magnesium (Eegriwe, Edwin): Chemistry. See: Van Nostrand Chem. Dict.

Eegriwe test for malic acid (Eegriwe, Edwin): Chemistry. See: Van Nostrand Chem. Dict.

Eegriwe test for nitrite and nitrate (Eegriwe, Edwin): Chemistry. See: Van Nostrand Chem. Dict.

Eegriwe test for orcinol (Eegriwe, Edwin): Chemistry. See: Van Nostrand Chem. Dict.

Eegriwe test for sulfite (Eegriwe, Edwin): Chemistry. See: Van Nostrand Chem. Dict.

Eegriwe test for sulfur dioxide (Eegriwe, Edwin): Chemistry. See: Van Nostrand Chem. Dict.

Eegriwe tests for cobalt (Eegriwe, Edwin): Chemistry. See: Van Nostrand Chem. Dict.

Eegriwe tests for tartrate (Eegriwe, Edwin): Chemistry. See: Van Nostrand Chem. Dict.

EELLS, KENNETH WALTER. 1913- . American psychologist. See: Amer. Men and Women Sci., 12th ed. (Soc. Behav. Sci.). Davis-Eells games.

EGER, ERNEST. 1892- . Czech-born American engineer. See: World Who's Who Sci. Eger valve.

Eger valve (Eger, Ernest): Engineering and Industry. Cited in: World Who's Who Sci.

Egeria (Egeria, the nymph): Generic Word (adviser). See: Brewer; Partridge; Webster's 3d.

EGERIA, THE NYMPH. Roman goddess of childbirth. See: Oxford Clas. Dict. Egeria.

Eger's yellow (Derivation undetermined): Chemistry. See: Hackh.

EGERTON, FRANCIS HENRY, 8TH EARL OF BRIDGEWATER. 1756-1829. English clergyman and antiquarian. See: Dict. Nat. Biog. Bridgewater prize, Bridgewater treatises.

EGGENBURGER, F. fl. 1923. German mathematician. Cited in: Kendall and Doig. Polya-Eggenburger distribution.

Eggertz's method (Derivation undetermined): Chemistry. See: Ballentyne.

EGGLESTON, CARY. American physician. b. 1884. See: Who's Who Amer. Med. Eggleston('s) method.

Eggleston('s) method (Eggleston, Cary): Medicine. See: Dorland; Stedman.

eggs Benedict (Benedict, Samuel): Food and Drink. See: Funk; Hendrickson.

EGLESTON, THOMAS. 1832-1900. American mineralogist. See: Dict. Amer. Biog. Eglestonite.

Eglestonite (Egleston, Thomas): Earth Sciences. See: Thrush; Webster's 3d.

Egli's glands (Derivation undetermined): Medicine. See: Stedman.

Egnell's law (Derivation undetermined): Earth Sciences. See: Huschke.

EHISSISIN, CHEIK. fl. time of Crusades. Middle-Eastern chieftain. (Biography source unavailable.) Assassin.

Ehlers-Danlos syndrome (Ehlers, Edward L. and Danlos, Henri Alexander): Medicine. See: Dorland; Jablonski; Stedman. Also known as: Danlos' syndrome, Meekeren-Ehlers-Danlos syndrome.

EHLERS, EDWARD L. 1863-1937. Danish dermatologist. See: World Who's Who Sci. Ehlers-Danlos syndrome.

EHLERS, ERNST HEINRICH. 1835-1925. German zoologist. See: World Who's Who Sci. Ehlersia.

Ehlersia (Ehlers, Ernst Heinrich): Zoology. See: Pennak.

EHN, E. W. fl. 1922. English metallurgist. Cited in: Chem. Abstr., Decenn. Indexes, 1917-1926; 1927-1936. McQuaid-Ehn test.

Ehrenfest('s) adiabatic law (Ehrenfest, Paul): Physics. See: Ballentyne; Internat. Dict. Ap. Math.; Internat. Dict. Phys. Elec.

Ehrenfest model (Ehrenfest, Paul): Statistics. See: Kendall.

EHRENFEST, PAUL. 1880-1933. Austrian physicist. See: Dict. Sci. Biog. Ehrenfest('s) adiabatic law, Ehrenfest model, Ehrenfest relations, Ehrenfest('s) theorem, Ehrenfest's equations.

Ehrenfest relations (Ehrenfest, Paul): Physics. See: Internat. Dict. Ap. Math.

Ehrenfest('s) theorem (Ehrenfest, Paul): Physics. See: Ballentyne; Internat. Dict. Ap. Math.; Thewlis.

Ehrenfest's equations (Ehrenfest, Paul): Physics. See: Ballentyne.

EHRENFRIED, ALBERT. 1880-1951. American surgeon. See: Who Was Who Amer., 1951-1960. Ehrenfried's disease.

Ehrenfried's disease (Ehrenfried, Albert): Medicine. See: Jablonski.

Ehrenhaft effect (Ehrenhaft, Felix): Physics. See: Ballentyne; Thewlis.

EHRENHAFT, FELIX. 1879-1952. Austrian physicist. See: World Who's Who Sci. Ehrenhaft effect.

EHRENRITTER, JOHANN. d. 1790. Austrian anatomist. See: Biog. Lex. hervorr. Aerzte. Ehrenritter's ganglion.

Ehrenritter's ganglion (Ehrenritter, Johann): Medicine. See: Donath; Dorland; Stedman.

EHRET, GEORG DIONYSIUS. 1708-1770. German-born English botanist. See: Dict. Sci. Biog. Ehretia.

EHRET, HEINRICH. 1870- . German physician. Cited in: Kelly. Ehret's phenomenon, Ehret's syndrome.

Ehretia (Ehret, Georg Dionysius): Botany. See: Charnock; Taylor, N.; Webster's 3d.

Ehret's phenomenon (Ehret, Heinrich): Medicine. See: Stedman.

hret's syndrome (Ehret, Heinrich): Medicine. See: Jablonski.

hrhardt powder (Derivation undetermined): Engineering and Industry. See: hrush.

hrlich('s) 606 (arsphenamine) (Ehrlich, Paul): Chemistry. See: Dorland; Hackh; Webster's 3d.

hrlich acid hematoxylin (Ehrlich, Paul): Chemistry. See: Van Nostrand Chem. Dict.

hrlich bacteria stain (Ehrlich, Paul): Chemistry. See: Van Nostrand Chem. Dict.

hrlich('s) benzaldehyde reaction (or solution) (Ehrlich, Paul): Chemistry. See: Hackh; Stedman.

hrlich-Berteim test reaction (Ehrlich, Paul and Bertheim, Alfred): Chemistry. ee: Van Nostrand Chem. Dict.

hrlich bilirubin solution (Ehrlich, Paul): Chemistry. See: Van Nostrand Chem. Dict.

hrlich-Biondi triacid stain (Ehrlich, Paul and Biondi, Domenico): Chemistry. ee: Van Nostrand Chem. Dict.

hrlich('s) diazo reaction (Ehrlich, Paul): Chemistry. See: Dorland; Hackh; tedman.

hrlich('s) diazo reagent (Ehrlich, Paul): Chemistry. See: Hackh; Stedman; an Nostrand Chem. Dict.

hrlich-Hata preparation (Ehrlich, Paul and Hata, Sahachiro): Chemistry. ee: Dorland.

hrlich indican solution (Ehrlich, Paul): Chemistry. See: Van Nostrand Chem. Dict.

hrlich neutral red stain (Ehrlich, Paul): Chemistry. See: Van Nostrand Chem. Dict.

HRLICH, P. fl. 1882. German ophthalmologist. (Biography source unavailable.) Ehrlich-Tuerk line, Ehrlich tumor.

HRLICH, PAUL. 1854-1915. German bacteriologist. See: Dict. Sci. Biog. Kermer-Ehrlich anemia, Ehrlich acid hematoxylin, Ehrlich bacteria stain, hrlich('s) benzaldehyde reaction (or solution), Ehrlich-Berteim test reaction, hrlich bilirubin solution, Ehrlich-Biondi triacid stain, Ehrlich('s) diazo reaction, hrlich('s) diazo reagent, Ehrlich-Hata preparation, Ehrlich indican solution, hrlich neutral red stain, Ehrlich reaction for indole, Ehrlich-Sachs reaction, hrlich('s) 606 (arsphenamine), Ehrlich('s) theory (or side chain theory), hrlich('s) triacid stain, Ehrlich tubercle stain, Ehrlich's anemia, Ehrlich's ematoxylin, Ehrlich's inner body, Ehrlich's phenomenon, Ehrlich's theorem, hrlich's triple stain, Koch-Ehrlich stain.

hrlich reaction for indole (Ehrlich, Paul): Chemistry. See: Van Nostrand Chem. Dict.

hrlich-Sachs reaction (Ehrlich, Paul and Sachs, Franz): Chemistry. See: an Nostrand Chem. Dict.

hrlich('s) theory (or side chain theory) (Ehrlich, Paul): Chemistry. See: Hackh; Stedman; Van Nostrand Chem. Dict.

hrlich('s) triacid stain (Ehrlich, Paul): Chemistry. See: Hackh; Stedman; an Nostrand Chem. Dict.

hrlich tubercle stain (Ehrlich, Paul): Chemistry. See: Van Nostrand Chem. Dict.

hrlich-Tuerk line (Ehrlich, P. and Tuerk, Siegmund): Medicine. See: ablonski. Also known as: Ehrlich's line.

hrlich tumor (Ehrlich, P.): Medicine. See: Jablonski.

hrlich's anemia (Ehrlich, Paul): Medicine. See: Stedman.

hrlich's aniline-oil stain (Ehrlich, Paul). See: Koch-Ehrlich stain.

hrlich's hematoxylin (Ehrlich, Paul): Medicine. See: Stedman.

hrlich's inner body (Ehrlich, Paul): Medicine. See: Stedman. Also known s: Heinz-Ehrlich bodies.

hrlich's line (Ehrlich, P.). See: Ehrlich-Tuerk line.

hrlich's phenomenon (Ehrlich, Paul): Medicine. See: Stedman.

Ehrlich's theorem (Ehrlich, Paul): Medicine. See: Stedman.

Ehrlich's triple stain (Ehrlich, Paul): Medicine. See: Stedman.

EHRMANN, RUDOLF. b. 1879. German internist. See: Biog. Lex. hervorr. Aerzte, 1880-1930. Ehrmann's alcohol test meal.

Ehrmann's alcohol test meal (Ehrmann, Rudolf): Medicine. See: Dorland.

EICHELBERG, GUSTAV. 1891- . Swiss engineer. See: Pogg., vol. 7a. Eichelberg injector.

Eichelberg injector (Eichelberg, Gustav): Engineering and Industry. See: Auger.

EICHHORN, HERMANN VON. 1848-1918. Prussian field marshall. See: Webster's Biog. Dict. Eichhorn military group.

EICHHORN, JOHANN ALBRECHT FRIEDRICH VON. 1779-1856. Prussian official. See: Webster's Biog. Dict. Eichhornia.

Eichhorn-Liebig furnace (Derivation undetermined): Engineering and Industry. See: Thrush.

Eichhorn military group (Eichhorn, Hermann von): History. Cited in: Webster's Biog. Dict.

Eichhornia (Eichhorn, Johann Albrecht Friedrich von): Botany. See: Webster's 3d.

EICHHORST, HERMANN LUDWIG. 1849-1921. Swiss physician. See: World Who's Who Sci. Eichhorst's corpuscles, Eichhorst's disease (or neuritis).

Eichhorst's corpuscles (Eichhorst, Hermann Ludwig): Medicine. See: Dorland; Stedman.

Eichhorst's disease (or neuritis) (Eichhorst, Hermann Ludwig): Medicine. See: Dorland; Jablonski; Stedman.

Eichler amine reagent (Eichler, Hermann): Chemistry. See: Van Nostrand Chem. Dict.

EICHLER, HERMANN. fl. 1934. German chemist. Cited in: Chem. Abstr., Decenn. Index, 1927-1936. Eichler amine reagent, Eichler nitrate reagent, Eichler resorcinol solution, Eichler test for nitrobenzene.

Eichler nitrate reagent (Eichler, Hermann): Chemistry. See: Van Nostrand Chem. Dict.

Eichler resorcinol solution (Eichler, Hermann): Chemistry. See: Van Nostrand Chem. Dict.

Eichler test for nitrobenzene (Eichler, Hermann): Chemistry. See: Van Nostrand Chem. Dict.

EICHSTEDT, KARL FERDINAND. 1816-1892. German dermatologist. See: World Who's Who Sci. Eichstedt's disease.

Eichstedt's disease (Eichstedt, Karl Ferdinand): Medicine. See: Dorland; Jablonski; Stedman.

EICKEN, CARL OTTO VON. 1873-1960. German laryngologist. See: Wer Ist Wer, 8th ed. Eicken's method.

Eicken's method (Eicken, Carl Otto von): Medicine. See: Dorland; Stedman.

EIGER, MARVIN S. 1930- . American pediatrician. See: Direct. Med. Specialists, 1970-1971. Bakwin-Eiger syndrome.

EIJKMAN, CHRISTIAAN. 1858-1930. Dutch physiologist. See: Dict. Sci. Biog. Eijkman('s) test (for coliform bacteria), Eijkman('s) test (reaction for phenol).

Eijkman('s) test (for coliform bacteria) (Eijkman, Christiaan): Medicine. See: Dorland; Webster's 3d.

Eijkman('s) test (reaction for phenol) (Eijkman, Christiaan): Medicine. See: Dorland; Van Nostrand Chem. Dict.

Eiloart test reaction for quinine (Derivation undetermined): Chemistry. See: Van Nostrand Chem. Dict.

Eimbrodt reagent for ammonium ion (Derivation undetermined): Chemistry. See: Van Nostrand Chem. Dict.

EIMER, THEODOR GUSTAV HEINRICH. 1843-1898. Swiss-born German zoologist. See: World Who's Who Sci. Eimeria.

Eimeria (Eimer, Theodor Gustav Heinrich): Zoology. See: Pennak; Webster's 3d.

EINHORN, MAX. 1862-1953. Russian-born American gastroenterologist. See: World Who's Who Sci. Einhorn's saccharimeter, Einhorn's test.

Einhorn's saccharimeter (Einhorn, Max): Medicine. See: Dorland; Stedman.

Einhorn's test (Einhorn, Max): Medicine. See: Dorland.

Einstein (Einstein, Albert): Generic Word (genius). See: Hendrickson; Webster's 3d.

EINSTEIN, ALBERT. 1879-1955. German physicist. See: Dict. Sci. Biog. Bose-Einstein condensation, Bose-Einstein distribution, Bose-Einstein gas, Bose-Einstein liquid, Bose-Einstein particles, Bose-Einstein statistics, Einstein, Einstein characteristic temperature, Einstein-de Haas effect, Einstein-de Haas method, Einstein diffusion equation, Einstein displacement, Einstein('s) equation for specific heat (or heat capacity), Einstein formula in radiation theory, Einstein law of gravitation, Einstein mass-energy equation (or equivalence formula), Einstein mobility equation, Einstein particle equation, Einstein photoelectric equation, Einstein('s) principle (or theory of relativity), Einstein relationship between mobility and diffusion coefficient (or relation for the mobility of an ion), Einstein shift, Einstein specific heat function, Einstein summation convention, Einstein-Szillard pump, Einstein temperature, Einstein theory of specific heats, Einstein transition probabilities, Einstein unified field theories, Einstein unit, Einstein universe, Einstein viscosity formula (or equation), Einsteinian, Einsteinium, Einstein's coefficient of absorption, Einstein's coefficient of induced emission, Einstein's coefficient of spontaneous emission, Einstein's law, Nernst-Einstein relation, Stark-Einstein equation, Stark-Einstein law, Stokes-Einstein equation, Sutherland-Einstein equation.

Einstein characteristic temperature (Einstein, Albert): Physics. See: Thewlis.

Einstein condensation (Einstein, Albert). See: Bose-Einstein condensation.

Einstein-de Haas effect (Einstein, Albert and Haas, Wander Johannes de): Physics. See: Markus; Thewlis; Webster's 3d. Also known as: Richardson effect.

Einstein-de Haas method (Einstein, Albert and Haas, Wander Johannes de): Physics. See: Internat. Dict. Phys. Elec.

Einstein diffusion equation (Einstein, Albert): Physics. See: Internat. Ap. Math.; Thewlis; Van Nostrand Chem. Dict.

Einstein displacement (Einstein, Albert): Physics. See: Satterthwaite; Thewlis.

Einstein energy (Einstein, Albert). See: Einstein mass-energy equation (or equivalence formula).

Einstein('s) equation for specific heat (or heat capacity) (Einstein, Albert): Physics. See: Ballentyne; Internat. Dict. Phys. Elec.; Van Nostrand Chem. Dict.

Einstein formula (for mass-energy equivalence) (Einstein, Albert). See: Einstein mass-energy equation (or equivalence formula).

Einstein formula in radiation theory (Einstein, Albert): Physics. See: Thewlis.

Einstein law of gravitation (Einstein, Albert): Physics. See: Internat. Dict. Phys. Elec.

Einstein law of photochemical equivalence (Einstein, Albert). See: Stark-Einstein law.

Einstein mass-energy equation (or equivalence formula) (Einstein, Albert): Physics. See: Ballentyne; Van Nostrand Sci. Encyc. Also known as: Einstein energy, Einstein formula (for mass-energy equivalence).

Einstein mobility equation (Einstein, Albert): Physics. See: Hughes.

Einstein particle equation (Einstein, Albert): Chemistry. See: Hackh.

Einstein photoelectric equation (Einstein, Albert): Physics. See: Internat. Dict. Ap. Math.; Internat. Dict. Phys. Elec.; Hughes.

Einstein('s) principle (or theory of relativity) (Einstein, Albert): Physics. See: Ballentyne; Hackh; Webster's 3d.

Einstein relationship between mobility and diffusion coefficient (or relation for the mobility of an ion) (Einstein, Albert): Physics. See: Ballentyne; Internat. Dict. Ap. Math.; Internat. Dict. Phys. Elec.

Einstein shift (Einstein, Albert): Physics. See: Internat. Dict. Phys. Elec.; Van Nostrand Sci. Encyc.

Einstein specific heat function (Einstein, Albert): Physics. See: Internat. Dict. Ap. Math.

Einstein summation convention (Einstein, Albert): Physics. See: Ballentyne.

Einstein-Szillard pump (Einstein, Albert and Szilard, Leo): Engineering and Industry. See: Auger.

Einstein temperature (Einstein, Albert): Physics. See: Webster's 3d.

Einstein theory of specific heats (Einstein, Albert): Physics. See: Thewlis.

Einstein transition probabilities (Einstein, Albert): Physics. See: Internat. Dict. Ap. Math.; Internat. Dict. Phys. Elec.; Van Nostrand Sci. Encyc.

Einstein unified field theories (Einstein, Albert): Physics. See: Internat. Dict. Phys. Elec.; Van Nostrand Sci. Encyc.

Einstein unit (Einstein, Albert): Physics. See: Dresner; Internat. Dict. Phys. Elec.; Van Nostrand Sci. Encyc.

Einstein universe (Einstein, Albert): Physics. See: Internat. Dict. Phys. Elec.; Van Nostrand Sci. Encyc.

Einstein viscosity formula (or equation) (Einstein, Albert): Physics. See: Hackh; Internat. Dict. Phys. Elec.; Van Nostrand Sci. Encyc.

Einsteinian (Einstein, Albert): Physics. See: Webster's 3d.

Einsteinium (Einstein, Albert): Physics. See: Hendrickson; Internat. Dict. Phys. Elec.; Van Nostrand Sci. Encyc.

Einstein's coefficient of absorption (Einstein, Albert): Physics. See: Internat. Dict. Phys. Elec.; Van Nostrand Sci. Encyc.

Einstein's coefficient of induced emission (Einstein, Albert): Physics. See: Internat. Dict. Phys. Elec.; Van Nostrand Sci. Encyc.

Einstein's coefficient of spontaneous emission (Einstein, Albert): Physics. See: Internat. Dict. Phys. Elec.; Van Nostrand Sci. Encyc.

Einstein's law (Einstein, Albert): Physics. See: Ballentyne.

Einthoven('s) galvanometer (or string galvanometer) (Einthoven, Willem): Medicine. See: Dorland; Internat. Dict. Phys. Elec.; Stedman; Van Nostrand Chem. Dict.

EINTHOVEN, WILLEM. 1860-1927. Dutch physiologist. See: Dict. Sci. Biog. Einthoven('s) galvanometer (or string galvanometer), Einthoven's law (or equation), Einthoven's triangle.

Einthoven's law (or equation) (Einthoven, Willem): Medicine. See: Stedman.

Einthoven's triangle (Einthoven, Willem): Medicine. See: Stedman.

EIRICH, A. fl. 1912. German inventor. Cited in: Chem. Abstr., vol. 7, p. 3052. Eirich mixer.

Eirich mixer (Eirich, A.): Engineering and Industry. See: Thrush.

EISEN, GUSTAVUS AUGUSTUS. 1847-1940. Swedish-born American biologist. See: World Who's Who Sci. Eisenia, Eiseniella.

EISENHART, LUTHER PFAHLER. 1876-1965. American mathematician. See: Dict. Sci. Biog. Eisenhart models, Eisenhart's theorem.

Eisenhart models (Eisenhart, Luther Pfahler): Statistics. See: Kendall.

Eisenhart's theorem (Eisenhart, Luther Pfahler): Mathematics. Cited in: Dict. Sci. Biog.

Eisenhower Doctrine (Eisenhower, Dwight David): Politics. See: Smith.

EISENHOWER, DWIGHT DAVID. 1890-1969. American president. See: Encyc. Brit., 1973. Eisenhower Doctrine, Eisenhower jacket, Eisenhower-Remon treaty, Eisenhower trophy.

Eisenhower jacket (Eisenhower, Dwight David): Fashion. See: Hendrickson; Picken; Webster's 3d.

Eisenhower-Remon treaty (Eisenhower, Dwight David and Remon, Jose): History. Cited in: Encyc. Brit., 1973.

Eisenhower trophy (Eisenhower, Dwight David): Recreation and Sports. Cited in: Encyc. Brit., 1973.

Eisenia (Eisen, Gustavus Augustus): Zoology. See: Pennak; Webster's 3d.

Eiseniella (Eisen, Gustavus Augustus): Zoology. See: Pennak.

EISENLOHR, KARL. 1847-1896. German physician. See: Biog. Lex. hervorr. Aerzte, 1880-1930. Eisenlohr's syndrome.

Eisenlohr test reaction (Derivation undetermined): Chemistry. See: Van Nostrand Chem. Dict.

Eisenlohr's syndrome (Eisenlohr, Karl): Medicine. See: Jablonski; Stedman.

Eisenmenger syndrome (Eisenmenger, Victor): Medicine. See: Stedman.

EISENMENGER, VICTOR. 1864-1932. German physician. See: Postgrad. Med., vol. 4, no. 3 (1948), following p. 232 (p. 29). Eisenmenger syndrome, Eisenmenger's complex (disease or tetrology).

EISENMENGER, WILLIAM J. 1914- . American physician. See: Direct. Med. Specialists, 1970-1971. Bongiovanni-Eisenmenger syndrome.

Eisenmenger's complex (disease or tetrology) (Eisenmenger, Victor): Medicine. See: Dorland; Jablonski; Stedman.

EISNER, ELMER. 1919- . American physicist. See: Amer. Men Sci., 8th ed. Eisner-Lachs theorem.

Eisner-Lachs theorem (Eisner, Elmer and Sachs, Robert Green): Physics. See: Internat. Dict. Ap. Math.

EISTERT, BERND. 1902- . German chemist. See: Surrey. Arndt-Eistert synthesis.

EITELBERG, ABRAHAM. b. 1847. Austrian physician. See: Geistige Wien, vol. 2 (1893), p. 104f. Eitelberg's test.

Eitelberg's test (Eitelberg, Abraham): Medicine. See: Dorland.

EKBOM, KARL-AXEL. 1907- . Swedish physician. See: Vem Ar Det, 1963. Wittmaack-Ekbom syndrome.

Ekbom's syndrome (Ekbom, Karl Axel). See: Wittmaack-Ekbom syndrome.

EKEBERG, ANDERS GUSTAF. 1767-1813. Swedish chemist and mineralogist. See: Dict. Sci. Biog. Ekebergite.

EKEBERG, CARL GUSTAV. 1716-1784. Swedish traveler and savant. See: Nouv. Biog. Univ. Ekebergia.

Ekebergia (Ekeberg, Carl Gustav): Botany. See: Charnock.

Ekebergite (Ekeberg, Anders Gustaf): Earth Sciences. See: Charnock.

EKEHORN, GUSTAF. 1857-1938. Swedish surgeon. See: Biog. Lex. hervorr. Aerzte, 1880-1930. Ekehorn's operation.

Ekehorn's operation (Ekehorn, Gustaf): Medicine. See: Dorland.

Ekenstein, Willem Alberda van. See: Van Ekenstein, Willem Alberda.

EKKERT, LADISLAUS. fl. 1934. Hungarian chemist. Cited in: Kelly. Ekkert reaction for phenolic compounds, Ekkert test reaction for alcohol, Ekkert test reaction for alkaloids, Ekkert test reaction for barbital, phenobarbital, cinchophen, and neocinchophen, Ekkert test reaction for benzocaine, Ekkert test reaction for betaine, Ekkert test reaction for ethyl urethane, Ekkert test reaction for glycerin, Ekkert test reaction for lactic acid, Ekkert test reaction for levulose (fructose), Ekkert test reaction for papaverine, Ekkert test reaction for phenacaine (holocaine), Ekkert test reaction for pilocarpine, Ekkert test reaction for saccharin, Ekkert test reaction for salicylate, Ekkert test reaction for tartaric acid, Ekkert test reactions for adrenaline and ephedrine, Ekkert test reactions for barbiturates, Ekkert test reactions for cocaine, eucaine, and similar substances, Ekkert test reactions for nitrate and nitrite, Ekkert test reactions for various aromatic compounds.

Ekkert reaction for phenolic compounds (Ekkert, Ladislaus): Chemistry. See: Van Nostrand Chem. Dict.

Ekkert test reaction for alcohol (Ekkert, Ladislaus): Chemistry. See: Van Nostrand Chem. Dict.

Ekkert test reaction for alkaloids (Ekkert, Ladislaus): Chemistry. See: Van Nostrand Chem. Dict.

Ekkert test reaction for barbital, phenobarbital, cinchophen, and neocinchophen (Ekkert, Ladislaus): Chemistry. See: Van Nostrand Chem. Dict.

Ekkert test reaction for benzocaine (Ekkert, Ladislaus): Chemistry. See: Van Nostrand Chem. Dict.

Ekkert test reaction for betaine (Ekkert, Ladislaus): Chemistry. See: Van Nostrand Chem. Dict.

Ekkert test reaction for ethyl urethane (Ekkert, Ladislaus): Chemistry. See: Van Nostrand Chem. Dict.

Ekkert test reaction for glycerin (Ekkert, Ladislaus): Chemistry. See: Van Nostrand Chem. Dict.

Ekkert test reaction for lactic acid (Ekkert, Ladislaus): Chemistry. See: Van Nostrand Chem. Dict.

Ekkert test reaction for levulose (fructose) (Ekkert, Ladislaus): Chemistry. See: Van Nostrand Chem. Dict.

Ekkert test reaction for papaverine (Ekkert, Ladislaus): Chemistry. See: Van Nostrand Chem. Dict.

Ekkert test reaction for phenacaine (holocaine) (Ekkert, Ladislaus): Chemistry. See: Van Nostrand Chem. Dict.

Ekkert test reaction for pilocarpine (Ekkert, Ladislaus): Chemistry. See: Van Nostrand Chem. Dict.

Ekkert test reaction for saccharin (Ekkert, Ladislaus): Chemistry. See: Van Nostrand Chem. Dict.

Ekkert test reaction for salicylate (Ekkert, Ladislaus): Chemistry. See: Van Nostrand Chem. Dict.

Ekkert test reaction for tartaric acid (Ekkert, Ladislaus): Chemistry. See: Van Nostrand Chem. Dict.

Ekkert test reactions for adrenaline and ephedrine (Ekkert, Ladislaus): Chemistry. See: Van Nostrand Chem. Dict.

Ekkert test reactions for barbiturates (Ekkert, Ladislaus): Chemistry. See: Van Nostrand Chem. Dict.

Ekkert test reactions for cocaine, eucaine, and similar substances (Ekkert, Ladislaus): Chemistry. See: Van Nostrand Chem. Dict.

Ekkert test reactions for nitrate and nitrite (Ekkert, Ladislaus): Chemistry. See: Van Nostrand Chem. Dict.

Ekkert test reactions for various aromatic compounds (Ekkert, Ladislaus): Chemistry. See: Van Nostrand Chem. Dict.

Ekman current meter (Ekman, Vagn Walfrid): Earth Sciences. See: Van Nostrand Sci. Encyc.

Ekman dredge (Ekman, Vagn Walfrid): Earth Sciences. See: Pennak.

Ekman layer (Ekman, Vagn Walfrid): Earth Sciences. See: Barnhart (New Eng.); Huschke; Internat. Dict. Ap. Math.

Ekman-Lobstein syndrome (Ekman, Olof Jacob and Lobstein, Johann Friedrich Georg Christian Martin). See: Lobstein's syndrome.

EKMAN, OLOF JACOB. 1764-1839. Swedish physician. See: Biog. Lex. hervorr. Aerzte. Ekman-Lobstein syndrome.

Ekman spiral (Ekman, Vagn Walfrid): Earth Sciences. See: Internat. Dict. Ap. Math.; Van Nostrand Sci. Encyc.

EKMAN, VAGN WALFRID. 1874-1954. Swedish oceanographer. See: Dict. Sci. Biog. Ekman current meter, Ekman dredge, Ekman layer, Ekman spiral.

Ekman's syndrome (Ekman, Olof Jacob). See: Lobstein's syndrome.

ELAUT, LEON JOZEF STEPHAAN. fl. 1929. Belgian anatomist. Cited in: Mansell. Elaut's triangle.

Elaut's triangle (Elaut, Leon Jozef Stephaan): Medicine. See: Stedman.

Elbert Hubbard tie (Hubbard, Elbert Green): Fashion. See: Picken.

Elberta peach (Rumph, Elberta): Botany. See: Hendrickson; Mathews, M. M.

ELBS, KARL JOSEPH XAVER. 1858-1933. German chemist. See: World Who's Who Sci. Elbs oxidation reaction, Elbs reaction, Elbs test for naphthanthraquinone.

Elbs oxidation reaction (Elbs, Karl Joseph Xaver): Chemistry. See: Van Nostrand Chem. Dict.

Elbs reaction (Elbs, Karl Joseph Xaver): Chemistry. See: Ballentyne; Van Nostrand Chem. Dict.

Elbs test for naphthanthraquinone (Elbs, Karl Joseph Xaver): Chemistry. See: Van Nostrand Chem. Dict.

ELDRED, B. E. fl. 1914. American inventor. Cited in: Chem. Abstr., vol. 8, p. 809. Eldred's wire.

Eldred's wire (Eldred, B. E.): Chemistry. See: Hackh.

Eleanor blue (Roosevelt, Eleanor): Fashion. See: Hendrickson; Partridge.

Eleanor Crosses (Eleanor of Castile): History. See: Brewer; Harvey; Steinberg.

Eleanor Farjeon Award (Farjeon, Eleanor): Library Science. See: Harrod.

ELEANOR OF CASTILE. 1244-1290. English queen. See: Dict. Nat. Biog. Eleanor Crosses.

elecampane (Helen of Troy): Botany. See: Charnock.

ELECTRA. Mythical daughter of Agamemnon and Clytemnestra. See: Oxford Clas. Dict. Electra complex.

Electra complex (Electra): Psychology. See: Chaplin; Drever; English.

electronic reactions of Abrams (Abrams, Albert): Medicine. Cited in: World Who's Who Sci.

ELERS, DAVID. fl. 1690-1730. English ceramist. See: Webster's Biog. Dict. Elers ware.

ELERS, JOHN PHILIP. fl. 1690-1730. English ceramist. See: Webster's Biog. Dict. Elers ware.

Elers ware (Elers, John Philip and Elers, David): Engineering and Industry. See: Thrush.

Elfving distribution (Elfving, Erik Gustav): Statistics. See: Kendall.

ELFVING, ERIK GUSTAV. 1908- . Finnish mathematician. See: World Who's Who Sci. Elfving distribution.

Elgin, 7th Earl of. See: Bruce, Thomas.

Elgin, 9th Earl of. See: Bruce, Alexander.

Elgin Commission (Bruce, Alexander, 9th Earl of Elgin): History. See: Montgomery.

Elgin Marbles (Bruce, Thomas, 7th Earl of Elgin): Fine Arts. See: Barnhart (Eng. Lit.); Brewer; Osborne.

Eli (Yale, Elihu): Education. See: Matthews, M.M.

Elian (Lamb, Charles): Literature. See: Webster's 3d.

ELIE DE BEAUMONT, JEAN-BAPTISTE-ARMAND-LOUIS-LEONCE. 1798-1874. French geologist. See: Dict. Sci. Biog. Beaumontage (or Beaumontague).

ELIJAH. fl. 9th c. B.C. Hebrew prophet. See: Encyc. Brit., 1973. Elijah's cup, Elijah's mantle, Elijah's melons.

Elijah's cup (Elijah): Religion. See: De Sola; Hendrickson.

Elijah's mantle (Elijah): Generic Word. See: Partridge.

Elijah's melons (Elijah): Generic Word (stones on Mount Carmel). See: Brewer.

ELIOT. No dates. Writer on needlecraft. (Biography source unavailable.) Eliottine silk.

ELIOTT, GEORGE AUGUSTUS, 1ST BARON HEATHFIELD. 1717-1790. Scottish soldier. See: Dict. Nat. Biog. Eliott's tailors.

Eliottine silk (Eliot): Fashion. See: Picken.

Eliott's tailors (Eliott, George Augustus, 1st Baron Heathfield): History. See: Brewer.

Elisabeth Charlotte of Bavaria. See: Charlotte Elisabeth.

ELIZABETH I. 1533-1603. Queen of England. See: Dict. Nat. Biog. Betsies, Elizabethan (1), Elizabethan Age, Elizabethan collar, Elizabethan (literature), Elizabethan settlement, Elizabethan (style), Queen Elizabeth's men, Queen Elizabeth's pocket-pistol.

ELIZABETH II. 1926- . Queen of England. See: Encyc. Brit., 1973. Elizabethan (2).

Elizabethan (1) (Elizabeth I): History. See: Charnock; Webster's 3d.

Elizabethan (2) (Elizabeth II): History. See: Webster's 3d.

Elizabethan Age (Elizabeth I): History. See: Barnhart (Eng. Lit.); Hendrickson; Webster's 3d.

Elizabethan collar (Elizabeth I): Fashion. See: Webster's 3d.

Elizabethan (literature) (Elizabeth I): Literature. See: Harvey; Partridge; Scott.

Elizabethan settlement (Elizabeth I): History. See: Steinberg.

Elizabethan (style) (Elizabeth I): Fashion. See: Picken; Webster's 3d.

ELIZUR, A. fl. 1959. Israeli psychologist. Cited in: Psych. Abstr., Author Index, 1st suppl. Elizur's test for organicity.

Elizur's test for organicity (Elizur, A.): Psychology. See: Wolman.

Elkesai. See: Elxai.

Elkesaite (Elxai): Religion. See: Webster's 3d.

ELKINGTON, JOSEPH. No dates. English farmer. (Biography source unavailable.) Elkington system.

Elkington system (Elkington, Joseph): Agriculture. See: Winburne.

Elkins Act (Elkins, Stephen): History. See: Morris; Morris and Irwin; Smith.

ELKINS, STEPHEN BENTON. 1841-1911. American legislator and industrialist. See: Biog. Direct. Amer. Congress. Elkins Act, Mann-Elkins Act.

Ellenborough, 1st Baron. See: Law, Edward.

Ellenborough's Act (Law, Edward, 1st Baron Ellenborough): Law. See: Black.

ELLER, ELIAS. 1690-1750. German religious leader. See: Nouv. Biog. Univ. Ellerian sect.

Ellerian sect (Eller, Elias): Religion. See: Canney.

Ellermann-Erlandsen method (Ellermann, Vilhelm and Erlandsen, Alfred): Medicine. See: Dorland; Stedman.

ELLERMANN, VILHELM. 1871-1924. Danish pathologist. See: Biog. Lex. hervorr. Aerzte, 1880-1930. Ellermann-Erlandsen method.

ELLESTAD, REUBEN B. 1900- . American chemist. See: Amer. Men Sci., 10th ed. Ellestadite.

Ellestadite (Ellestad, Reuben B.): Earth Sciences. See: Thrush; Webster's 3d.

ELLETT, ALEXANDER. b. 1894. American physicist. See: World Who's Who Sci. Huntoon and Ellett gauge.

ELLICOTT, ANDREW. 1754-1820. American surveyor. See: Dict. Amer. Biog. Ellicott plan.

Ellicott plan (Ellicott, Andrew): History. Cited in: Webster's Biog. Dict.

ELLIMAN. No dates. Pharmaceutical manufacturer. (Biography source unavailable.) Elliman's (embrocation).

Elliman's (embrocation) (Elliman): Medicine. See: Partridge.

ELLIOT, DANIEL GIRAUD. 1835-1915. American zoologist. See: Dict. Amer. Biog. Elliot's pheasant.

ELLIOT, GEORGE THOMSON. 1851-1935. American dermatologist. See: Who's Who Amer. Med. Elliot's sign.

ELLIOT, GILBERT JOHN MURRAY KYNYNMOND, 4TH EARL OF MINTO. 1845-1914. English statesman and administrator. See: Dict. Nat. Biog., 3d suppl. Morley-Minto reforms.

ELLIOT, JAMES. fl. 1839. Inventor. (Biography source unavailable.) Elliot's stereoscope.

ELLIOT, JOHN WHEELOCK. 1852-1925. American surgeon. See: Who's Who Amer. Med. Elliot's position.

ELLIOT, JONATHAN. 1784-1846. American editor and publicist. See: Dict. Amer. Biog. Elliot's Debates.

ELLIOT, ROBERT HENRY. 1864-1936. English ophthalmologist in India. See: Who Was Who, 1929-1940. Elliot's operation.

Elliot tester (Derivation undetermined): Chemistry. See: Hackh.

Elliot's Debates (Elliot, Jonathan): History. See: Smith.

Elliot's operation (Elliot, Robert Henry): Medicine. See: Dorland; Stedman.

Elliot's pheasant (Elliot, Daniel Giraud): Zoology. See: Webster's 3d.

Elliot's position (Elliot, John Wheelock): Medicine. See: Dorland; Stedman.

Elliot's sign (Elliot, George Thomson): Medicine. See: Dorland.

Elliot's stereoscope (Elliot, James): Photography. See: Focal Encyc. Photog.

ELLIOTT, CHARLES ROBERT. No dates. American gynecologist. (Biography source unavailable.) Elliott treatment.

ELLIOTT, THOMAS RENTON. 1877-1961. English physician. See: World Who's Who Sci. Elliott's law.

Elliott treatment (Elliott, Charles Robert): Medicine. See: Dorland.

Elliott's law (Elliott, Thomas Renton): Medicine. See: Stedman.

ELLIS, ARTHUR W. M. fl. 1912. American physician. Cited in: Kelly. Swift-Ellis treatment.

ELLIS, CALVIN. 1826-1883. American physician. See: Dict. Amer. Biog. Ellis's curve, Ellis's ligament, Ellis's line, Ellis's sign.

Ellis harmonical (Derivation undetermined): Psychology. See: Drever.

ELLIS, JOHN. 1710-1776. English botanist. See: World Who's Who Sci. Ellisia.

ELLIS, RICHARD WHITE BERNARD. 1902- . English physician. See: Contemp. Authors, vol. 15. Ellis-Van Creveld syndrome, Sheldon-Ellis syndrome.

Ellis type glomerulonephritis (or nephritis) (Derivation undetermined): Medicine. See: Stedman.

Ellis-Van Creveld syndrome (Ellis, Richard White Bernard and Van Creveld, Simon): Medicine. See: Jablonski; Stedman.

Ellis vanner (Derivation undetermined): Engineering and Industry. See: Thrush.

Ellisia (Ellis, John): Botany. See: Charnock.

ELLISON, EDWIN HOMER. 1918-1970. American surgeon. See: Amer. Men Sci., 10th ed. Strom-Zollinger-Ellison syndrome, Zollinger-Ellison syndrome, Zollinger-Ellison tumor.

Ellis's curve (Ellis, Calvin): Medicine. See: Dorland.

Ellis's ligament (Ellis, Calvin): Medicine. See: Dorland.

Ellis's line (Ellis, Calvin): Medicine. See: Dorland.

Ellis's sign (Ellis, Calvin): Medicine. See: Dorland.

Ellms-Hauser test (Ellms, Joseph Wilton and Hauser, S. J.): Chemistry. See: Van Nostrand Chem. Dict.

ELLMS, JOSEPH WILTON. b. 1867. American chemical engineer. See: Amer. Men Sci., 2d ed. Ellms-Hauser test.

Ellram reagent for alkaloids, resins, and volatile oils (Derivation undetermined): Chemistry. See: Van Nostrand Chem. Dict.

Ellram test reaction for vanadates and molybdates (Derivation undetermined): Chemistry. See: Van Nostrand Chem. Dict.

Ellsworth-Howard test (Ellsworth, Read McLane and Howard, John Eager): Medicine. See: Stedman.

ELLSWORTH, LINCOLN. 1880-1951. American polar explorer and civil engineer. See: World Who's Who Sci. Amundsen-Ellsworth Nobile Expedition, Amundsen-Ellsworth North Pole Expedition.

ELLSWORTH, READ MC LANE. 1899- . American physician. See: Amer. Men Sci., 5th ed. Ellsworth-Howard test.

ELMENDORF, ARMIN. 1890- . American mechanical engineer. See: Who's Who Engin., 1925. Elmendorf test.

Elmendorf test (Elmendorf, Armin): Engineering and Industry. See: Webster's 3d.

ELMER, CHARLES W. fl. 1937. American manufacturer. (Biography source unavailable.) Perkin-Elmer spectrophotometers.

Elmo, Saint. See: Erasmus, Saint.

ELMORE, A. S. fl. 1907. American engineer. Cited in: Chem. Abstr., vol. 1, p. 1687. Elmore process.

Elmore jig (Derivation undetermined): Engineering and Industry. See: Thrush.

Elmore process (Elmore, A. S.): Engineering and Industry. See: Thrush.

Elmo's fire (Erasmus, Saint). See: Saint Elmo's fire.

Eloisa. See: Heloise.

ELSASSER, WALTER MAURICE. 1904- . German-born American geophysicist. See: World Who's Who Sci. Elsasser's radiation chart.

Elsasser's radiation chart (Elsasser, Walter Maurice): Earth Sciences. See: Huschke; Van Nostrand Sci. Encyc.

ELSBERG, CHARLES ALBERT. 1871-1948. American surgeon. See: Who's Who Amer. Med. Elsberg's solution, Elsberg's test.

Elsberg's solution (Elsberg, Charles Albert): Medicine. See: Dorland.

Elsberg's test (Elsberg, Charles Albert): Medicine. See: Dorland.

ELSCHNIG, ANTON PHILIPP. 1863-1939. Austrian ophthalmologist. See: World Who's Who Sci. Elschnig pearls, Elschnig's bodies, Elschnig's conjunctivitis, Elschnig's spots, Elschnig's syndrome, Koerber-Salus-Elschnig syndrome.

Elschnig pearls (Elschnig, Anton Philipp): Medicine. See: Stedman.

Elschnig's bodies (Elschnig, Anton Philipp): Medicine. See: Dorland.

Elschnig's conjunctivitis (Elschnig, Anton Philipp): Medicine. See: Jablonski.

Elschnig's spots (Elschnig, Anton Philipp): Medicine. See: Dorland; Jablonski; Stedman.

Elschnig's syndrome (Elschnig, Anton Philipp): Medicine. See: Jablonski.

ELSHOLTZ, JOHANN SIGMUND. 1623-1688. German physician and botanist. See: World Who's Who Sci. Elsholtzia.

Elsholtzia (Elsholtz, Johann Sigmund): Botany. See: Taylor, N.; Webster's 3d.

ELSNER, CHRISTOPH FRIEDRICH. 1749-1820. German physician. See: Nouv. Biog. Univ. Elsner's asthma.

ELSNER, MORITZ. 1861-1935. German bacteriologist. See: Biog. Lex. hervorr. Aerzte, 1880-1930. Elsner's medium.

Elsner test reaction (Derivation undetermined): Chemistry. See: Van Nostrand Chem. Dict.

Elsner's asthma (Elsner, Christoph Friedrich). See: Heberden's asthma.

Elsner's equation (Derivation undetermined): Engineering and Industry. See: Thrush.

Elsner's medium (Elsner, Moritz): Medicine. See: Dorland.

Elster and Geitel effect (Elster, Johann Philipp Ludwig Julius and Geitel, Hans Friedrich): Physics. See: Ballentyne.

ELSTER, JOHANN PHILIPP LUDWIG JULIUS. 1854-1920. German physicist. See: Dict. Sci. Biog. Elster and Geitel effect.

ELTESTE, GERHARD. fl. 1928. German chemist. Cited in: Chem. Abstr., vol. 22, p. 4409. Elteste reagent.

Elteste reagent (Elteste, Gerhard): Chemistry. See: Van Nostrand Chem. Dict.

ELXAI. fl. 1st c. A.D. Jewish sectary. See: Nouv. Biog. Univ. Elkesaite.

ELY, LEONARD WHEELER. 1868-1944. American orthopedic surgeon. See: Who's Who Amer. Med. Ely's sign (or test).

Ely's sign (or test) (Ely, Leonard Wheeler): Medicine. See: Dorland.

Elzevir (editions) (Elzevir family): Printing. See: Charnock; Harrod; Phyfe.

ELZEVIR FAMILY. Dutch publishers and printers. fl. 17th c. See: Encyc. Brit., 1973. Elzevir (editions), Elzevir (type).

Elzevir (type) (Elzevir family): Printing. See: Lockwood; Partridge.

ELZHOLZ, ADOLF. 1863-1925. Austrian psychiatrist. See: Biog. Lex. hervorr. Aerzte, 1880-1930. Elzholz bodies, Elzholz' mixture.

Elzholz' bodies (Elzholz, Adolf): Medicine. See: Dorland; Stedman.

Elzholz' mixture (Elzholz, Adolf): Medicine. See: Dorland; Stedman.

Embden ester (Embden, Gustav): Medicine. See: Hackh; Stedman.

EMBDEN, GUSTAV. 1874-1933. German biochemist. See: Dict. Sci. Biog. Embden ester, Embden-Meyerhof pathway, Robison-Embden ester.

Embden-Meyerhof-Parnas pathway (Embden, Gustav; Meyerhof, Otto Fritz; and Parnas, Jakub Karol). See: Embden-Meyerhof pathway.

Embden-Meyerhof pathway (Embden, Gustav and Meyerhof, Otto Fritz): Medicine. See: Stedman. Also known as: Embden-Meyerhof-Parnas pathway.

Embrey vanner (Derivation undetermined): Engineering and Industry. See: Thrush.

Emde decomposition reaction (Emde, Hermann Karl Christian Maximilian): Chemistry. Cited in: World Who's Who Sci.

Emde degradation reaction (Emde, Hermann Karl Christian Maximilian): Chemistry. See: Van Nostrand Chem. Dict.

EMDE, HERMANN KARL CHRISTIAN MAXIMILIAN. 1880-1935. German chemist. See: World Who's Who Sci. Emde decomposition reaction, Emde degradation reaction, Emde test reaction.

Emde test reaction (Emde, Hermann Karl Christian Maximilian): Chemistry. See: Van Nostrand Chem. Dict.

Emden equation (or function) (Emden, Robert): Physics. See: Internat. Dict. Ap. Math.

EMDEN, ROBERT. 1862-1940. Swiss astrophysicist. See: Dict. Sci. Biog. Emden equation (or function).

EMERSON, RALPH WALDO. 1803-1882. American essayist and poet. See: Dict. Amer. Biog. Emersonian.

Emersonian (Emerson, Ralph Waldo): Literature. See: Mathews, M. M.; Webster's 3d.

EMERY, ALBERT HAMILTON. 1834-1926. American engineer and inventor. See: Dict. Amer. Biog. Emery testing machine.

Emery-Dietz gravity corer (Emery, Kenneth Orris and Dietz, Robert Sinclair): Engineering and Industry. See: Thrush.

EMERY, KENNETH ORRIS. 1914- . Canadian-born American marine geologist. See: Amer. Men Sci., 10th ed. Emery-Dietz gravity corer.

Emery testing machine (Emery, Albert Hamilton): Engineering and Industry. See: Auger.

EMIR GHANI, MUHAMMAD UTHMAN AL-. 1793-1853. Mohammedan sect founder. See: Hastings (Encyc. Rel. Ethics) under "Religious Orders (Muslim)," vol. 10, p. 726a. Marghanites.

Emley plastometer (Emley, Warren Edwards): Engineering and Industry. See: Thrush.

EMLEY, WARREN EDWARDS. b. 1886. American engineer. Cited in: Chem. Abstr., vol. 10, p. 675. Emley plastometer.

Emmanuel Movement (Derivation undetermined): Psychology. See: English.

EMMENS, CLIFFORD WALTER. fl. 1941. English endocrinologist. Cited in: Chem. Abstr., vol. 36, p. 1655. Emmens' S/L test.

Emmens' S/L test (Emmens, Clifford Walter): Medicine. See: Stedman.

EMMERICH, RUDOLF. 1852-1914. German bacteriologist. See: Wer Ist's, 1906. Emmerich's bacillus.

Emmerich's bacillus (Emmerich, Rudolf): Medicine. See: Dorland.

EMMERIE, ADRIANUS. fl. 1934. Dutch chemist. Cited in: Chem. Abstr., vol. 29, p. 2211. Emmerie test reactions.

Emmerie test reactions (Emmerie, Adrianus): Chemistry. See: Van Nostrand Chem. Dict.

Emmerling tube (Derivation undetermined): Chemistry. See: Hackh.

Emmerman process (Emmermann, Curt): Photography. See: Van Nostrand Sci. Encyc.

EMMERMANN, CURT. fl. 1936. German inventor. Cited in: Chem. Abstr., Decenn. Index, 1937-1946. Emmerman process.

Emmert's law (Derivation undetermined): Psychology. See: Chaplin; Drever; English.

Emmet engine (Emmet, William LeRoy): Engineering and Industry. See: Auger.

EMMET, ROBERT. 1778-1803. Irish rebel. See: Dict. Nat. Biog. Emmett's rebellion (or insurrection).

EMMET, THOMAS ADDIS. 1828-1919. American gynecologist. See: Dict. Amer. Biog. Emmet's method, Emmet's needle, Emmet's operation.

EMMET, WILLIAM LE ROY. 1859-1941. American electrical engineer. See: World Who's Who Sci. Emmet engine.

Emmet's method (Emmet, Thomas Addis): Medicine. See: Stedman.

Emmet's needle (Emmet, Thomas Addis): Medicine. See: Dorland; Stedman.

Emmet's operation (Emmet, Thomas Addis): Medicine. See: Dorland; Stedman.

EMMETT, PAUL HUGH. 1900- . American chemist. See: World Who's Who Sci. Brunauer, Emmett and Teller adsorption equation (method or theory).

Emmett's rebellion (or insurrection) (Emmet, Robert): History. See: Harbottle; Phyfe.

Emmonite (Emmons, Ebenezer): Earth Sciences. See: Thrush.

EMMONS, EBENEZER. 1799-1863. American geologist. See: Amer. Geol., vol. 7 (1891), pp. 17-21. Emmonite.

EMMONS, NATHANAEL. 1745-1840. American theologian. See: Dict. Amer. Biog. Emmonsism (or Emmonism).

EMMONS, SAMUEL FRANKLIN. 1841-1911. American geologist. See: Dict. Sci. Biog. Emmonsite.

Emmonsism (or Emmonism) (Emmons, Nathanael): Religion. See: Mathews, M. M.

Emmonsite (Emmons, Samuel Franklin): Earth Sciences. See: Thrush; Webster's 3d.

Emory('s) oak (Emory, William Hemsley): Botany. See: Mathews, M. M.; Webster's 3d.

Emory picker (Derivation undetermined): Engineering and Industry. See: Thrush.

EMORY, WILLIAM HEMSLEY. 1811-1887. American soldier and engineer. See: Dict. Amer. Biog. Emory('s) oak, Emory's opuntia.

Emory's opuntia (Emory, William Hemsley): Botany. See: Mathews, M. M.

Empedoclean (Empedocles of Acragas): Philosophy. See: Webster's 3d.

EMPEDOCLES OF ACRAGAS. ca. 492-ca. 432 B.C. Greek philosopher and statesman. See: Dict. Sci. Biog. Empedoclean.

Emperor's Hymn (Francis II): Music. See: Scholes.

empirical Bayes' estimator (Bayes, Thomas): Statistics. See: Kendall.

empirical Bayes' procedure (Bayes, Thomas): Statistics. See: Kendall.

Ems method (Derivation undetermined): Engineering and Industry. See: Thrush.

ENCEL, CHRISTOPHER. fl. 1577. Writer on oak galls. (Biography source unavailable.) Encelia.

Encelia (Encel, Christopher): Botany. See: Mathews, M. M.; Taylor, N.

ENCKE, JOHANN FRANZ. 1791-1865. German astronomer. See: Dict. Sci. Biog. Encke's division.

Encke roots (Derivation undetermined): Mathematics. See: Ballentyne.

Encke's division (Encke, Johann Franz): Astronomy. See: Satterthwaite.

end-feet of Held (Held, Hans): Anatomy. See: Stedman.

Endell plastometer (Derivation undetermined): Engineering and Industry. See: Thrush. Also known as: Gareis-Endell plastometer.

ENDLICH, FREDERIC MILLER. 1851-1899. American mineralogist. See: Pogg., vol. 3. Endlichite.

Endlichite (Endlich, Frederic Miller): Earth Sciences. See: Thrush; Webster's 3d.

Endo agar (or medium) (Endo, Shigeru): Medicine. See: Dorland; Stedman.

ENDO, SHIGERU. 1869-1937. Japanese bacteriologist in Germany. Cited in: Kelly. Endo agar (or medium), Endo's fuchsin agar.

Endo's fuchsin agar (Endo, Shigeru): Medicine. See: Stedman.

ENGEL, CHRISTIAAN. 1912- . Dutch biochemist. See: Who's Who Sci. Europe, 1967. Linderstrom-Lang-Engel method.

ENGEL, ERNST. 1821-1896. German statistician and economist. See: Internat. Encyc. Soc. Sci. Engel's law.

ENGEL, GERHARD. fl. 1864. German physician. Cited in: Kelly. Engel-Von Recklinghausen syndrome.

ENGEL, RUDOLPHE CHARLES. 1850-1916. Alsatian biochemist. See: Pogg., vols. 3, 4, 5, 6. Engel's alkalimetry.

Engel test reactions (Derivation undetermined): Chemistry. See: Van Nostrand Chem. Dict.

Engel-Ville tests (Derivation undetermined): Chemistry. See: Van Nostrand Chem. Dict.

Engel-Von Recklinghausen syndrome (Engel, Gerhard and Recklinghausen, Friedrich Daniel von). See: Recklinghausen's disease (2).

ENGELMANN, GEORGE. 1809-1884. German-born American meteorologist, botanist and physician. See: Dict. Amer. Biog. Engelmann spruce, Engelmannia.

ENGELMANN, GUIDO. b. 1876. Austrian physician. See: Biog. Lex. hervorr. Aerzte, 1880-1930. Camurati-Engelmann syndrome.

Engelmann ivy (Derivation undetermined): Botany. See: Webster's 3d.

Engelmann spruce (Engelmann, George): Botany. See: Mathews, M. M.; Partridge; Webster's 3d.

ENGELMANN, THEODOR WILHELM. 1843-1909. German physiologist. See: Dict. Sci. Biog. Engelmann's basal knobs, Engelmann's disks.

Engelmannia (Engelmann, George): Botany. See: Webster's 3d.

Engelmann's basal knobs (Engelmann, Theodor Wilhelm): Medicine. See: Stedman.

Engelmann's disease (Engelmann, Guido). See: Camurati-Engelmann syndrome.

Engelmann's disks (Engelmann, Theodor Wilhelm): Medicine. See: Dorland.

Engel's alkalimetry (Engel, Rudolphe Charles): Medicine. See: Dorland; Stedman.

Engel's law (Engel, Ernst): Economics. See: Greenwald; Hendrickson; Webster's 3d.

Engel's syndrome (Derivation undetermined): Medicine. See: Jablonski.

ENGLER, ADOLF GUSTAV HEINRICH. 1844-1930. German botanist. See: World Who's Who Sci. Englerophoenix.

ENGLER, CARL OSWALD VIKTOR. 1842-1925. German chemist. See: World Who's Who Sci. Bach-Engler peroxide theory of oxidation, Engler degree, Engler flask, Engler viscosimeter, Engler-Wild test.

Engler degree (Engler, Carl Oswald Viktor): Chemistry. See: Hackh.

Engler flask (Engler, Carl Oswald Viktor): Chemistry. See: Webster's 3d.

Engler viscosimeter (Engler, Carl Oswald Viktor): Chemistry. See: Internat. Dict. Phys. Elec.

Engler-Wild test (Engler, Carl Oswald Viktor and Wild, Wilhelm): Chemistry. See: Van Nostrand Chem. Dict.

Englerophoenix (Engler, Adolf Gustav Heinrich): Botany. See: Webster's 3d.

ENGLISCH, JOSEF. 1835-1915. Austrian physician. See: Biog. Lex. hervorr. Aerzte. Englisch's sinus.

Englisch's sinus (Englisch, Josef): Medicine. See: Stedman.

English Bill (English, William Hayden): History. See: Morris.

ENGLISH, GEORGE LETCHWORTH. 1864-1944. American mineralogist. See: Who Was Who Amer., 1943-1950. Englishite.

ENGLISH, WILLIAM HAYDEN. 1822-1896. American statesman and historian. See: Dict. Amer. Biog. English Bill.

Englishite (English, George Letchworth): Earth Sciences. See: Thrush; Webster's 3d.

ENGMAN, MARTIN FEENEY. 1869-1953. American dermatologist. See: World Who's Who Sci. Engman's disease, Zinsser-Engman-Cole syndrome.

Engman's disease (Engman, Martin Feeney): Medicine. See: Dorland; Jablonski.

Engman's syndrome (Engman, Martin Feeney). See: Zinsser-Engman-Cole syndrome.

Enke blower (Derivation undetermined): Engineering and Industry. See: Auger.

ENNEPER, ALFRED. 1830-1885. German mathematician. See: Pogg., vol. 3. Beltrami-Enneper theorem?

Eno Foundation for Transportation (Eno, William Phelps): Transportation. See: Encyc. Assoc.

ENO, WILLIAM PHELPS. 1858-1945. American highway traffic engineer. See: Who Was Who Amer., 1943-1950. Eno Foundation for Transportation.

ENOCH. Biblical patriarch and father of Methuselah. See: Barnhart (Cycl. Names). Enochic.

Enoch Arden (Arden, Enoch): Generic Word. See: Webster's 3d.

Enoch Arden law (Arden, Enoch): Law. See: Smith; Webster's 3d.

Enochic (Enoch): Religion. See: Webster's 3d.

ENROTH, EMIL EMANUEL. b. 1879. Finnish physician. See: Biog. Lex. hervorr. Aerzte, 1880-1930. Enroth's sign.

Enroth's sign (Enroth, Emil Emanuel): Medicine. See: Stedman.

ENSKOG, DAVID. 1884-1947. Swedish physicist. See: Dict. Sci. Biog. Enskog-Maxwell equations of change, Enskog series for the solutions of the Boltzmann equation, Enskog theory, Enskog theory for the transport phenomena in dense gases.

Enskog-Maxwell equations of change (Enskog, David and Maxwell, James Clerk): Physics. See: Internat. Dict. Ap. Math.

Enskog series for the solutions of the Boltzmann equation (Enskog, David): Physics. See: Internat. Dict. Ap. Math.

Enskog theory (Enskog, David): Physics. See: Thewlis.

Enskog theory for the transport phenomena in dense gases (Enskog, David): Physics. See: Internat. Dict. Ap. Math.; Van Nostrand Sci. Encyc.

ENSLIN. fl. 1904. German ophthalmologist. (Biography source unavailable.) Enslin's triad.

Enslin apparatus (Enslin, O.): Engineering and Industry. See: Thrush.

ENSLIN, O. fl. 1933. German inventor. Cited in: Chem. Abstr., vol. 27, p. 2344. Enslin apparatus.

Enslin's triad (Enslin): Medicine. See: Jablonski.

ENTELLUS. Sicilian hero, famous as a pugilist. See: Harper. Entellus (monkey).

Entellus (monkey) (Entellus): Zoology. See: Partridge.

Ent's bursa (Derivation undetermined): Zoology. See: Gray.

eoanthropus Dawsoni (Dawson, Charles): Anthropology. See: Pennak.

Eon, Chevalier d'. See: D'Eon de Beaumont, Charles.

EON DE L'ESTOILE. d. 1148. Breton fanatic. See: Nouv. Biog. Univ. Eonians.

Eonians (Eon de l'Estoile): Religion. See: Canney.

Eonism (D'Eon de Beaumont, Charles Genevieve Louis Auguste Andre Timothee): Generic Word (transvestism). See: Harvey; Stedman; Winick.

Eotvos balance (or torsion balance) (Eotvos, Roland): Physics. See: Thewlis; Thrush; Van Nostrand Sci. Encyc.

Eotvos equation (Eotvos, Roland): Physics. See: Internat. Dict. Phys. Elec.; Van Nostrand Chem. Dict.; Van Nostrand Sci. Encyc.

Eotvos-Ramsey-Shields law (Eotvos, Roland; Ramsay, Sir William; and Shields, John): Physics. See: Van Nostrand Sci. Encyc. under "surface tension."

EOTVOS, ROLAND. 1848-1919. Hungarian physicist. See: Dict. Sci. Biog. Eotvos balance (or torsion balance), Eotvos equation, Eotvos-Ramsey-Shields law, Eotvos rule, Eotvos (unit).

Eotvos rule (Eotvos, Roland): Physics. See: Ballentyne; Thewlis.

Eotvos (unit) (Eotvos, Roland): Physics. See: Dresner; Thrush; Webster's 3d.

epaeris Calvertiana (Calvert, Caroline Louisa Waring): Botany. Cited in: Webster's Biog. Dict.

EPHRAIM. Biblical son of Joseph. See: Barnhart (Cycl. Names). Ephraimite.

EPHRAIM, FRITZ BRUNO. 1876-1935. German chemist. See: World Who's Who Sci. Ephraim reaction for thallium (thallous) salts, Ephraim reagent for copper, Ephraim test for vanadium.

Ephraim reaction for thallium (thallous) salts (Ephraim, Fritz Bruno): Chemistry. See: Van Nostrand Chem. Dict.

Ephraim reagent for copper (Ephraim, Fritz Bruno): Chemistry. See: Van Nostrand Chem. Dict.

Ephraim test for vanadium (Ephraim, Fritz Bruno): Chemistry. See: Van Nostrand Chem. Dict.

Ephraimite (Ephraim): Religion. See: Webster's 3d.

Epictetan (Epictetian) (Epictetus): Philosophy. See: Charnock; Webster's 3d.

EPICTETUS. ca. 60-ca. 118 A.D. Greek philosopher. See: Encyc. Brit., 1973. Epictetan (Epictetian).

Epicure (Epicurus): Generic Word. See: Charnock; Funk; Hargrave.

Epicureans (or Epicureanism) (Epicurus): Philosophy. See: Canney; Good; Phyfe.

EPICURUS. 342-270 B.C. Greek philosopher. See: Encyc. Brit., 1973. Epicure, Epicureans (or Epicureanism).

Epimenidean (Epimenides): Philosophy. See: Webster's 3d.

EPIMENIDES. fl. 7th c. B.C. Cretan poet and philosopher. See: Encyc. Brit., 1973. Epimenidean.

epistles of Phalaris (Phalaris): History. See: Brewer.

Eppinger test reaction (Derivation undetermined): Chemistry. See: Van Nostrand Chem. Dict.

EPPLEY, MARION. b. 1883. American physical chemist. See: Amer. Men Sci., 10th ed. Eppley pyrheliometer.

Eppley pyrheliometer (Eppley, Marion): Earth Sciences. See: Huschke.

EPSTEIN, ALBERT ARTHUR. b. 1880. American physician. See: Who's Who Among Physicians and Surg. Epstein's nephrosis, Epstein's syndrome.

EPSTEIN, ALOIS. 1849-1918. Czech pediatrician. See: Biog. Lex. hervorr. Aerzte, 1880-1930. Epstein's pearls, Epstein's syndrome (or disease).

EPSTEIN, B. No dates. German physician. (Biography source unavailable.) Epstein's symptom.

Epstein-Barr virus (Epstein, Michael Anthony and Barr, Y. M.): Medicine. See: Barnhart (New Eng.); Stedman.

EPSTEIN, EMIL. fl. 1937. Austrian biochemist. Cited in: Chem. Abstr., Decenn. Index, 1927-1936. Van Bogaert-Scherer-Epstein syndrome.

EPSTEIN, MICHAEL ANTHONY. 1921-   . English physician. See: World Who's Who Sci. Epstein-Barr virus.

Epstein's nephrosis (Epstein, Albert Arthur): Medicine. See: Dorland.

Epstein's pearls (Epstein, Alois): Medicine. See: Dorland; Stedman.

Epstein's symptom (Epstein, B.): Medicine. See: Dorland; Stedman.

Epstein's syndrome (Epstein, Albert Arthur): Medicine. See: Jablonski.

Epstein's syndrome (or disease) (Epstein, Alois): Medicine. See: Dorland; Jablonski; Stedman.

equations of Gauss and Codazzi (Gauss, Carl Friedrich and Codazzi, Delfino): Mathematics. See: Internat. Dict. Ap. Math.

equations of Rodrigues (Rodrigues, Olinde): Mathematics. See: James.

equations of Weierstrass (Weierstrass, Karl Theodor Wilhelm): Mathematics. See: James. Also known as: theorem of Weierstrass.

Era of Nabonassar (Nabonassar): Astronomy. See: Brewer; Charnock; Harvey.

Erasmian (Erasmus, Desiderius): Literature. See: Webster's 3d.

ERASMUS, DESIDERIUS. 1465-1536. Dutch scholar. See: Encyc. Brit., 1973. Erasmian.

ERASMUS (ELMO), SAINT. d. 303. Syrian bishop and patron saint of sailors. See: Holweck. Saint Elmo's fire, Saint Erasmus' disease.

Erastian (Erastus, Thomas): Religion. See: Harvey; Webster's 3d.

Erastianism (Erastus, Thomas): Religion. See: Attwater; Brewer; Charnock.

Erastians (Erastus, Thomas): Religion. See: Canney; Harbottle; Latham.

ERASTUS, THOMAS. 1524-1583. German physician and Protestant controversialist. See: Encyc. Brit., 1973. Erastian, Erastians, Erastianism.

ERATOSTEHENES. ca. 276-ca. 196 B.C. Greek geographer and astronomer. See: Dict. Sci. Biog. seive of Eratosthenes.

Erb-Charcot syndrome (Erb, Wilhelm Heinrich and Charcot, Jean Martin): Medicine. See: Jablonski. Also known as: Erb's disease (syndrome or paralysis), Struempell's disease.

Erb-Goldflam syndrome (or disease) (Erb, Wilhelm Heinrich and Goldflam, Samuel): Medicine. See: Jablonski. Also known as: Erb-Oppenheim-Goldflam syndrome, Erb's syndrome, Hoppe-Goldflam syndrome.

Erb-Landouzy syndrome (Erb, Wilhelm Heinrich and Landouzy, Louis Theophil Joseph). See: Erb's dystrophy.

Erb-Oppenheim-Goldflam syndrome (Erb, Wilhelm Heinrich; Oppenheim, Hermann; and Goldflam, Samuel). See: Erb-Goldflam syndrome (or disease).

ERB, WERNER. fl. 1943. German physician. (Biography source unavailable.) Rotter-Erb syndrome.

ERB, WILHELM HEINRICH. 1840-1921. German neurologist. See: World Who's Who Sci. Erb-Charcot syndrome, Erb-Goldflam syndrome (or disease), Erb's atrophy, Erb's dystrophy, Erb's point, Erb's sign, Erb's spinal paralysis, Duchenne-Erb syndrome (or paralysis), Friedrich-Erb-Arnold syndrome, Gaensslen-Erb syndrome, Nievergelt-Erb syndrome.

ERBEN SIEGMUND. b. 1863. Austrian neurologist. See: Biog. Lex. hervorr. Aerzte, 1880-1930. Erben's phenomenon.

Erben's phenomenon (Erben, Siegmund): Medicine. See: Dorland; Stedman.

Erb's atrophy (Erb, Wilhelm Heinrich): Medicine. See: Dorland; Stedman.

Erb's disease (syndrome or paralysis) (Erb, Wilhelm Heinrich). See: Erb-Charcot syndrome.

Erb's dystrophy (Erb, Wilhelm Heinrich): Medicine. See: Dorland; Jablonski. Also known as: Erb-Landouzy syndrome.

Erb's point (Erb, Wilhelm Heinrich): Medicine. See: Donath; Dorland; Stedman.

Erb's sign (Erb, Wilhelm Heinrich): Medicine. See: Stedman.

Erb's spinal paralysis (Erb, Wilhelm Heinrich): Medicine. See: Stedman.

Erb's syndrome (Erb, Wilhelm Heinrich). See: Erb-Goldflam syndrome (or disease).

Ercles vein (Hercules): Generic Word (bombastic manner). See: Webster's 3d.

ERDELYI, JANOS. fl. 1933. Hungarian chemist. Cited in: Chem. Abstr., Decenn. Index, 1927-1936. Rosenthal-Erdelyi reagent.

ERDHEIM, JAKOB. 1874-1937. Austrian physician. See: Biog. Lex. hervorr. Aerzte, 1880-1930. Erdheim tumor, Erdheim's syndrome, Gsell-Erdheim syndrome.

Erdheim tumor (Erdheim, Jakob): Medicine. See: Stedman.

Erdheim's syndrome (Erdheim, Jakob): Medicine. See: Jablonski. Also known as: Scaglietti-Dagnini syndrome.

Erdman Act (Erdman, Constantine Jacob): History. See: Morris; Smith.

ERDMAN, CONSTANTINE JACOB. 1846-1911. American legislator. See: Biog. Direct. Amer. Congress. Erdman Act.

ERDMANN, AXEL JOAKIM. 1814-1869. Swedish mineralogist. See: Royal Soc. Cat. Sci. Pap. Erdmannite.

Erdmann float (Derivation undetermined): Chemistry. See: Hackh.

ERDMANN, HUGO WILHELM TRAUGOTT. 1862-1910. German chemist. See: World Who's Who Sci. Erdmann('s) reagent (for alkaloids), Erdmann reagent for potassium and rubidium, Volhard-Erdmann thiophene synthesis.

Erdmann reagent (or test for nitrite) (Derivation undetermined): Chemistry. See: Hackh; Van Nostrand Chem. Dict.

Erdmann('s) reagent (for alkaloids) (Erdmann, Hugo Wilhelm Traugott): Chemistry. See: Dorland; Hackh; Stedman.

Erdmann reagent for potassium and rubidium (Erdmann, Hugo Wilhelm Traugott): Chemistry. See: Van Nostrand Chem. Dict.

Erdmannite (Erdmann, Axel Joakim): Earth Sciences. See: Charnock.

EREMEEV, PAVEL VLADIMIROVIC. 1830-1899. Russian mineralogist. See: Royal Soc. Cat. Sci. Pap. Eremeyevite.

Eremeyevite (Eremeev, Pavel Vladimirovic): Earth Sciences. See: Thrush; Webster's 3d. Also known as Jeremejevite.

ERENYI, GYORGY. fl. 1937. Hungarian chemist. Cited in: Chem. Abstr., vol. 32, p. 2050. Erenyi test.

Erenyi test (Erenyi, Gyorgy): Chemistry. See: Van Nostrand Chem. Dict.

ERIC THE RED. fl. 10th c. Norwegian explorer. See: Barnhart (Cycl. Names). Erikite.

ERICHSEN, A. M. fl. 1914. German engineer. Cited in: Chem. Abstr., vol. 8, p. 1952. Erichsen test, Erichsen value.

ERICHSEN, JOHN ERIC. 1818-1896. English surgeon. See: Dict. Nat. Biog., 1st suppl. Erichsen's disease, Erichsen's ligature, Erichsen's sign (or test).

Erichsen test (Erichsen, A. M.): Engineering and Industry. See: Auger; Thewlis; Thrush.

Erichsen value (Erichsen, A. M.): Engineering and Industry. See: Ballentyne.

Erichsen's disease (Erichsen, John Eric): Medicine. See: Dorland; Jablonski.

Erichsen's ligature (Erichsen, John Eric): Medicine. See: Dorland.

Erichsen's sign (or test) (Erichsen, John Eric): Medicine. See: Dorland; Stedman.

ERICSON, LEIF. fl. 1,000 A.D. Norse adventurer. See: Barnhart (Cycl. Names). Leifite.

Ericsson cycle (Derivation undetermined): Physics. See: Internat. Dict. Ap. Math.

Ericsson engine (Ericsson, John): Engineering and Industry. See: Auger.

ERICSSON, JOHN. 1803-1889. Swedish-born American engineer and inventor. See: Dict. Amer. Biog. Ericsson engine.

Erikite (Eric the Red): Earth Sciences. See: Webster's 3d.

ERIKSSON, ALDUR W. fl. 1964. Swedish ophthalmologist. (Biography source unavailable.) Forsius-Eriksson syndrome.

Erlacher-Blount syndrome (Erlacher, Philipp and Blount, Walter Putnam): Medicine. See: Jablonski. Also known as: Blount-Barber syndrome, Blount's syndrome.

ERLACHER, PHILIPP. b. 1886. German physician. See: Biog. Lex. hervorr. Aerzte, 1880-1930. Erlacher-Blount syndrome.

ERLANDSEN, ALFRED. 1878-1918. Danish hygienist. See: Biog. Lex. hervorr. Aerzte, 1880-1930. Ellermann-Erlandsen method.

ERLANG, AGNER KRARUP. 1878-1929. Danish mathematician. See: Hagerups Illus. Kon. Lek. Erlang distribution, Erlang (unit), Erlang's formula.

Erlang distribution (Erlang, Agner Krarup?): Statistics. See: Kendall.

Erlang (unit) (Erlang, Agner Krarup): Statistics. See: Dresner.

Erlang's formula (Erlang, Agner Krarup): Statistics. See: Kendall.

ERLENMEYER, EMIL. 1864-1921. German chemist. See: Surrey. Erlenmeyer-Ploechl azlactone and amino acid synthesis, Erlenmeyer rule?

Erlenmeyer flask (Erlenmeyer, Richard August Carl Emil): Chemistry. See: Dorland; Hackh; Hendrickson.

ERLENMEYER, FRIEDRICH ALBRECHT. 1849-1926. German physician. See: Biog. Lex. hervorr. Aerzte, 1880-1930. Erlenmeyer's mixture.

Erlenmeyer-Ploechl azlactone and amino acid synthesis (Erlenmeyer, Emil and Ploechl, Josef): Chemistry. See: Van Nostrand Chem. Dict.

ERLENMEYER, RICHARD AUGUST CARL EMIL. 1825-1909. German organic chemist. See: Dict. Sci. Biog. Erlenmeyer flask.

Erlenmeyer rule (Erlenmeyer, Emil?): Chemistry. See: Van Nostrand Chem. Dict.

Erlenmeyer's mixture (Erlenmeyer, Friedrich Albrecht): Medicine. See: Dorland.

Erlicki solution (Derivation undetermined): Chemistry. See: Van Nostrand Chem. Dict.

Erlicki stain (Derivation undetermined): Chemistry. See: Van Nostrand Chem. Dict.

ERMATINGER, FRANCIS. 1798-1857. English-born Canadian fur trader. See: Dict. Canadian Biog. Ermatinger money.

Ermatinger money (Ermatinger, Francis): History. See: Mathews, M. M.

Ermengem, Emile Pierre Marie van. See: Van Ermengem, Emile Pierre Marie.

ERNEMANN, HEINRICH. 1850-1928. German camera manufacturer. See: Focal Encyc. Photog. Ernemann Zeitlupe.

Ernemann Zeitlupe (Ernemann, Heinrich): Photography. Cited in: Focal Encyc. Photog.

ERNST, PAUL. 1859-1937. Swiss pathologist. See: Biog. Lex. hervorr. Aerzte, 1880-1930. Babes-Ernst bodies.

EROS. Greek god of love. See: Encyc. Brit., 1973. Eros (instinct), Erotic (or Eroticism).

Eros (instinct) (Eros): Psychology. See: Hinsie; Zadrozny.

Erotic (or Eroticism) (Eros): Generic Word (passion). See: Chaplin; Funk; Partridge.

ERSKINE, JOHN, EARL OF MAR. 1675-1732. Scottish Jacobite leader. See: Dict. Nat. Biog. Mar's year.

Erwinia (Smith, Erwin F.): Zoology. See: Dorland.

erythroplasia of Queyrat (Queyrat, Louis). See: Queyrat's erythroplasia.

Esaki diode (Esaki, Leo): Electronics. See: Hughes; Markus; Van Nostrand Sci. Encyc.

ESAKI, LEO. 1925-   . Japanese physicist. See: World Who's Who Sci. Esaki diode.

Esau (Esau, the twin): Generic Word. See: Partridge; Webster's 3d.

ESAU (or EDOM), THE TWIN. Biblical son of Isaac and Rebekah. See: Webster's Biog. Dict. Edomite(s), Esau.

ESBACH, GEORGES HUBERT. 1843-1890. French physician. See: World Who's Who Sci. Esbach('s) reagent, Esbach tube.

Esbach('s) reagent (Esbach, Georges Hubert): Medicine. See: Dorland; Hackh; Stedman.

Esbach tube (Esbach, Georges Hubert): Medicine. Cited in: World Who's Who Sci.

Esbauch reagents (Derivation undetermined): Chemistry. See: Van Nostrand Chem. Dict.

ESCAICH, A. fl. 1920. French chemist. Cited in: Chem. Abstr., vol. 14, pp. 3039, 3045. Eschaich test for cyanide, Eschaich test for nitrate and nitrite, Eschaich test for phenol.

ESCALLON, ANTONIO. fl. 18th c. Colombian botanist. See: Rees' Cycl., under "Escallonia." Escallonia.

Escallonia (Escallon, Antonio): Botany. See: Charnock; Partridge; Taylor, N.

Escamilla–Lisser syndrome (Escamilla, Roberto Francisco and Lisser, Hans): Medicine. See: Jablonski.

ESCAMILLA, ROBERTO FRANCISCO. 1905– . Mexican-born American endocrinologist. See: Amer. Men Sci., 10th ed. Escamilla–Lisser syndrome.

ESCAT, ETIENNE. 1865–1948. French physician. See: Dict. Nat. Contemp., vol. 2, p. 210. Escat's phlegmon.

Escat's phlegmon (Escat, Etienne): Medicine. See: Jablonski.

Esch Act (Esch, John Jacob): Politics. See: Smith.

Esch–Cummins Act (Esch, John Jacob and Cummins, Albert Baird): Politics. See: Smith.

ESCH, JOHN JACOB. 1861–1941. American lawyer and legislator. See: Biog. Direct. Amer. Congress. Esch Act, Esch–Cummins Act.

ESCH, PETER. 1874–1952. German gynecologist. See: Biog. Lex. hervorr. Aerzte, 1880–1930. Esch's medium.

Eschaich test for cyanide (Escaich, A.): Chemistry. See: Van Nostrand Chem. Dict.

Eschaich test for nitrate and nitrite (Escaich, A.): Chemistry. See: Van Nostrand Chem. Dict.

Eschaich test for phenol (Escaich, A.): Chemistry. See: Van Nostrand Chem. Dict.

Eschbaum test (Derivation undetermined): Chemistry. See: Van Nostrand Chem. Dict.

ESCHERICH, THEODOR. 1857–1911. German physician. See: Dict. Sci. Biog. Escherichia, Escherich's bacillus, Escherich's sign.

Escherichia (Escherich, Theodor): Medicine. See: Dorland; Stedman; Webster's 3d.

Escherich's bacillus (Escherich, Theodor): Medicine. See: Dorland.

Escherich's sign (Escherich, Theodor): Medicine. See: Stedman.

Eschka('s) mixture (Derivation undetermined): Chemistry. See: Hackh; Thrush; Van Nostrand Chem. Dict.

Esch's medium (Esch, Peter): Medicine. See: Dorland.

ESCHSCHOLTZ, JOHANN FRIEDRICH. 1793–1831. German naturalist and traveler. See: Dict. Sci. Biog. Eschscholtzia.

Eschscholtzia (Eschscholtz, Johann Friedrich): Botany. See: Mathews, M. M.; Partridge; Taylor, N.

Eschweiler–Clarke reaction (Derivation undetermined): Chemistry. See: Ballentyne.

Esclangon effect (Esclangon, Ernest Benjamin?): Physics. See: Internat. Dict. Phys. Elec.; Van Nostrand Sci. Encyc.

ESCLANGON, ERNEST BENJAMIN. 1876–1954. French astronomer, mathematician and physicist. See: Dict. Sci. Biog. Esclangon effect?

ESCOBAR Y MENDOZA, ANTONIO. 1589–1669. Spanish Jesuit. See: Encyc. Brit., 1973. Escobarderie, Escobaria.

Escobarderie (Escobar y Mendoza, Antonio): Generic Word (hypocritical duplicity). See: Stenhouse.

Escobaria (Escobar y Mendoza, Antonio): Botany. See: Taylor, N.

Escoffier garnish (Escoffier, Georges Auguste): Food and Drink. See: Hendrickson.

ESCOFFIER, GEORGES AUGUSTE. 1846–1935. French chef. See: Encyc. Brit., 1973. Escoffier garnish, Escoffier sauce.

Escoffier sauce (Escoffier, Georges Auguste): Food and Drink. See: Hendrickson; Partridge.

ESCONTRIA, BLAS. 1847–1906. Mexican engineer and politician. See: Dicc. Biog. Mex. Escontria (cactus).

Escontria (cactus) (Escontria, Blas): Botany. See: Taylor, N.

ESCUDERO, PEDRO. b. 1877. Argentine physician. See: Biog. Lex. hervorr. Aerzte, 1880–1930. Escudero's test.

Escudero's test (Escudero, Pedro): Medicine. See: Dorland.

Esher, 2d Viscount. See: Brett, Reginald Baliol (2d Viscount Esher).

Esher Committee (Brett, Reginald Baliol, 2d. Viscount Esher): History. See: Montgomery.

ESHMUN. Syro-Phoenician sun deity of healing and vital force. See: Jobes. Eshmun (Eshum) complex.

Eshmun (Eshum) complex (Eshmun): Psychology. See: Hinsie; Wolman.

Esmarch bottle (Derivation undetermined): Chemistry. See: Hackh.

Esmarch, Johannes Friedrich August von. See: Von Esmarch, Johannes Friedrich August.

Esmarch mask (Von Esmarch, Johann Friedrich August): Medicine. See: Stedman.

Esmarch's bandage (Von Esmarch, Johann Friedrich August): Medicine. See: Dorland; Stedman; Webster's 3d.

ESMARK, JENS. 1763–1839. Danish mineralogist. See: Hagerups Illus. Kon. Lek. Esmarkite.

Esmarkite (Esmark, Jens): Earth Sciences. See: Charnock.

ESPENSHEID, LOUIS. fl. 1851–1859. American wagon-maker. (Biography source unavailable.) Esponshay (wagon).

Esperanto (Zamenhof, Lazarus Ludwig): Linguistics. See: Hendrickson; Webster's 3d.

ESPILDORA–LUQUE, CRISTOBAL. 1896– . Chilean ophthalmologist. See: Who's Who Latin Amer., pt. 4, 3d ed. Espildor–Luque's syndrome.

Espildora–Luque's syndrome (Espildora–Luque): Medicine. See: Jablonski.

Esponshay (wagon) (Espensheid, Louis): Engineering and Industry. See: Mathews, M. M.

ESPY, JAMES POLLARD. 1785–1860. American meteorologist. See: Dict. Sci. Biog. Espy (ventilator).

Espy (ventilator) (Espy, James Pollard): Engineering and Industry. See: Mathews, M. M.

ESSEEN, CARL–GUSTAF HARALDSSON. 1918– . Swedish mathematician. See: Vem Ar Det, 1963. Esseen-type approximation.

Esseen–type approximation (Esseen, Carl–Gustaf Haraldsson): Statistics. See: Kendall.

Essen coefficient (Derivation undetermined): Electronics. See: Ballentyne.

ESSEN, LOUIS. 1908– . English physicist. See: World Who's Who Sci. Essen-ring quartz clock.

Essen–ring quartz clock (Essen, Louis): Physics. See: Dresner.

ESSER, JOHANNES FREDERICUS SAMUEL. 1877–1946. Dutch surgeon. See: J. Internat. Coll. Surg., vol. 2, p. 735. Esser's operation.

Esser's operation (Esser, Johannes Fredericus Samuel): Medicine. See: Stedman.

ESSIG, GEORGE STURGESS. b. 1875. American dentist. See: Temple Dent. Rev., vol. 19, no. 2 (1949), p. 4. Essig-type splint.

Essig–type splint (Essig, George Sturgess): Dentistry. See: Stedman.

Esterhazi rostelyos (Esterhazy family): Food and Drink. See: De Sola.

ESTERHAZY FAMILY. Hungarian aristocrats. See: Encyc. Brit., 1973. Esterhazi rostelyos.

ESTES, BILLIE SOL. 1925– . American financier. See: Biog. Index, 1961–1964. Billie Sol Estes scandal.

ESTES, CLARENCE. fl. 1917. American chemist. Cited in: Chem. Abstr., vol. 11, p. 675. Estes test reaction.

Estes operation (Estes, William Lawrence, Jr.): Medicine. See: Stedman.

Estes' statistical model of learning (Estes, William Kaye): Psychology. See: Chaplin; Wolman.

Estes test reaction (Estes, Clarence): Chemistry. See: Van Nostrand Chem. Dict.

ESTES, WILLIAM KAYE. 1919– . American psychologist. See: World Who's Who Sci. Estes' statistical model of learning.

ESTES, WILLIAM LAWRENCE, JR. 1885–1940. American surgeon. See: Who's Who Amer. Med. Estes operation.

ESTEVE, J. fl. 1924. French chemist. Cited in: Chem. Abstr., vol. 18, p. 2300. Esteve test.

ESTEVE, PEDRO JACOB. d. 1556. Spanish botanist and physician. See: Nouv. Biog. Univ. Stevia.

Esteve test (Esteve, J.): Chemistry. See: Van Nostrand Chem. Dict.

ESTEY, JACQUES. 1814-1890. American organ-builder. See: Dict. Amer. Biog. Estey organ.

Estey organ (Estey, Jacques): Music. See: Apel under "Harmonium."

ESTHER (Jewish name: HADASSAH). Jewish Old Testament heroine. See: Webster's Biog. Dict. Fast of Esther, Hadassah (Women's Zionist Organization of America).

Esther J. Piercy Award (Piercy, Esther June): Library Science. See: Harrod.

ESTILL, HOWARD WILMOT. b. 1890. American biochemist. See: Amer. Men Sci., 4th ed. Estill-Nugent test.

Estill-Nugent test (Estill, Howard Wilmot and Nugent, Robert Logan): Chemistry. See: Van Nostrand Chem. Dict.

ESTLANDER, JAKOB AUGUST. 1831-1881. Finnish surgeon. See: Biog. Lex. hervorr. Aerzte. Abbe-Estlander operation, Estlander's operation.

Estlander's operation (Estlander, Jakob August): Medicine. See: Dorland; Stedman.

Estren-Dameshek syndrome (Estren, Solomon and Dameshek, William): Medicine. See: Jablonski.

ESTREN, SOLOMON. 1918-   . Russian-born American physician. See: Direct. Med. Specialists, 1970-1971. Estren-Dameshek syndrome.

ETARD, ALEXANDRE LEON. 1852-1910. French chemist. See: Pogg., vols. 3, 4. Etard('s) reaction?

Etard('s) reaction (Etard, Alexandre Leon?): Chemistry. See: Ballentyne; Hackh; Van Nostrand Chem. Dict.

ETERNOD, AUGUSTE-FRANCOIS-CHARLES D'. 1854-1932. Swiss histologist. See: Biog. Lex. hervorr. Aerzte, 1880-1930. Eternod's sinus.

Eternod's sinus (Eternod, Auguste-Francois-Charles d'): Medicine. See: Dorland.

Ethan Allen (submarine) (Allen, Ethan): Military Science. See: Quick.

Etheldreda, St. See: Audrey, St.

Ethelwold, St. See: Aethelwold, St.

Etti test reaction (Derivation undetermined): Chemistry. See: Van Nostrand Chem. Dict.

ETTINGSHAUSEN, ALBERT VON. 1850-1932. German physicist. See: Pogg., vols. 3, 4, 6. Ettingshausen coefficient, Ettingshausen effect, Nernst-Ettingshausen effect.

Ettingshausen coefficient (Ettingshausen, Albert von): Physics. See: Internat. Dict. Ap. Math.

Ettingshausen effect (Ettingshausen, Albert von): Physics. See: Ballentyne; Markus; Thewlis.

EUCKEN, ARNOLD THOMAS. 1884-1950. German physical chemist. See: Dict. Sci. Biog. Eucken correction.

Eucken correction (Eucken, Arnold Thomas): Chemistry. See: Internat. Dict. Ap. Math.

EUCLID. fl. ca. 295 B.C. Greek mathematician. See: Dict. Sci. Biog. Euclidean (or Euclidian), Euclidean construction, Euclidean geometry, Euclidean space, Euclid's (or Euclidean) algorithm.

EUCLID OF MEGARA. fl. ca. 455-380 B.C. Greek philosopher. See: Encyc. Brit., 1973. Megaric(s).

Euclidean (or Euclidian) (Euclid): Mathematics. See: Hendrickson; Partridge; Webster's 3d.

Euclidean construction (Euclid): Mathematics. See: Webster's 3d.

Euclidean geometry (Euclid): Mathematics. See: Ballentyne; Thewlis; Webster's 3d.

Euclidean space (Euclid): Mathematics. See: Internat. Dict. Ap. Math.; Internat. Dict. Phys. Elec.; Thewlis.

Euclid's (or Euclidean) algorithm (Euclid): Mathematics. See: Ballentyne; Internat. Dict. Ap. Math.; Webster's 3d.

EUDES, JEAN. 1601-1680. French devotional writer. See: Nouv. Biog. Univ. Eudists.

Eudists (Eudes, Jean): Religion. See: Attwater; Canney.

Eudoxian(s) (Eudoxius): Religion. See: Brewer; Canney; Webster's 3d.

EUDOXIUS. d. 370. Patriarch of Constantinople and Bishop of Antioch. See: Barnhart (Cycl. Names). Eudoxian(s).

EUGENE OF SAVOY (In full: FRANCOIS EUGENE DE SAVOIE-CARIGNAN). 1663-1736. Austrian general. See: Encyc. Brit., 1973. Eugenia.

Eugenia (Eugene of Savoy): Botany. See: Charnock; Stedman; Taylor, N.; Webster's 3d.

Eugenie (carriage) (Eugenie, Empress): Engineering and Industry. See: Charnock.

EUGENIE, EMPRESS (In full: EUGENIE MARIE DE MONTIJO DE GUZMAN). 1826-1920. Empress of France. See: Encyc. Brit., 1973. Eugenie (carriage), Eugenie hat (or Empress Eugenie hat), Eugenie (style).

Eugenie hat (or Empress Eugenie hat) (Eugenie, Empress): Fashion. See: Hendrickson; Picken.

Eugenie (style) (Eugenie, Empress): Fashion. See: Picken.

Euhemerism (Euhemerus): Mythology. See: Mathews, S.; Partridge; Webster's 3d.

EUHEMERUS. fl. 4th c. B.C. Greek mythographer. See: Encyc. Brit., 1973. Euhemerism.

EULENBURG, ALBERT. 1840-1917. German neurologist. See: World Who's Who Sci. Eulenburg's disease.

Eulenburg's disease (Eulenburg, Albert): Medicine. See: Dorland; Jablonski; Stedman.

Euler circles technique (Euler, Leonhard): Mathematics. See: Good.

Euler('s) constant (Euler, Leonhard). See: Euler-Mascheroni constant.

Euler diagram (Euler, Leonhard): Mathematics. See: Webster's 3d.

Euler('s) equation (Euler, Leonhard): Physics. See: Ballentyne; Internat. Dict. Ap Math.; Thewlis.

Euler('s) equations of motion (Euler, Leonhard): Physics. See: Ballentyne; Internat. Dict. Ap. Math.; Thewlis.

Euler force (or crippling stress) (Euler, Leonhard): Physics. See: Ballentyne; Thrush.

Euler formula (columns) (Euler, Leonhard): Physics. See: Internat. Dict. Ap. Math.; Internat. Dict. Phys. Elec.; Van Nostrand Sci. Encyc.

Euler('s) formula (for a polyhedron) (Euler, Leonhard): Physics. See: Ballentyne; Thewlis.

Euler (Eulerian) integral (Euler, Leonhard): Physics. See: Internat. Dict. Phys. Elec.; Thewlis.

Euler-Lagrange equations (Euler, Leonhard and Lagrange, Joseph Louis, Comte de): Mathematics. See: Ballentyne; Internat. Dict. Ap. Math. Also known as: Cauchy-Euler equation.

EULER, LEONHARD. 1707-1783. Swiss mathematician and physicist. See: Dict. Sci. Biog. Euler circles technique, Euler diagram, Euler('s) equation, Euler('s) equations of motion, Euler force (or crippling stress), Euler formula (columns), Euler('s) formula (for a polyhedron), Euler (Eulerian) integral, Euler-Lagrange equations, Euler-Maclaurin formula, Euler-Mascheroni constant, Euler method for solving an ordinary differential equation (or numerical solution of a differential equation), Euler reciprocity relation (or criterion), Euler-Rodrigues parameter, Euler('s) theorem (for homogeneous functions), Euler theorem on normal curvature, Euler('s) transformation (or algorithm), Euler velocity field, Eulerian (Euler) angle(s), Eulerian coordinates, Eulerian correlation, Eulerian method of analysis (or specification of fluid flow), Eulerian methods of current measurement, Eulerian wind, Euler's definition of the gamma function, Euler's kinematical theorem, Euler's numbers, Euler's relation.

Euler-Maclaurin formula (Euler, Leonhard and Maclaurin, Colin): Mathematics. See: Ballentyne; Internat. Dict. Ap. Math.; Internat. Dict. Phys. Elec.

Euler–Mascheroni constant (Euler, Leonhard and Mascheroni, Lorenzo): Mathematics. See: Internat. Dict. Ap. Math.; Internat. Dict. Phys. Elec.; Van Nostrand Sci. Encyc. Also known as: Euler('s) constant, Mascheroni's constant.

Euler method for solving an ordinary differential equation (or numerical solution of a differential equation) (Euler, Leonhard): Mathematics. See: Internat. Dict. Ap. Math.; Internat. Dict. Phys. Elec.; Van Nostrand Sci. Encyc.

Euler reciprocity relation (or criterion) (Euler, Leonhard): Mathematics. See: Internat. Dict. Ap. Math.; Internat. Dict. Phys. Elec.

Euler–Rodrigues parameter (Euler, Leonhard and Rodrigues, Olinde): Physics. See: Internat. Dict. Ap. Math.; Internat. Dict. Phys. Elec.

Euler('s) theorem (for homogeneous functions) (Euler, Leonhard): Mathematics. See: Ballentyne; Internat. Dict. Ap. Math.; Van Nostrand Sci. Encyc.

Euler theorem on normal curvature (Euler, Leonhard): Physics. See: Internat. Dict. Ap. Math.

Euler('s) transformation (or algorithm) (Euler, Leonhard): Mathematics. See: Ballentyne; Internat. Dict. Ap. Math.

Euler velocity field (Euler, Leonhard): Physics. See: Thrush.

Eulerian (Euler) angle(s) (Euler, Leonhard): Physics. See: Ballentyne; Internat. Dict. Ap. Math.; Thewlis.

Eulerian coordinates (Euler, Leonhard): Physics. See: Huschke; Van Nostrand Sci. Encyc.

Eulerian correlation (Euler, Leonhard): Physics. See: Huschke.

Eulerian method of analysis (or specification of fluid flow) (Eler, Leonhard): Physics. See: Internat. Dict. Ap. Math.; Internat. Dict. Phys. Elec.; Van Nostrand Sci. Encyc.

Eulerian methods of current measurement (Euler, Leonhard): Physics. See: Thrush.

Eulerian wind (Euler, Leonhard): Physics. See: Huschke; Internat. Dict. Ap. Math.

Euler's definition of the gamma function (Euler, Leonhard): Mathematics. See: Ballentyne.

Euler's kinematical theorem (Euler, Leonhard): Physics. See: Ballentyne.

Euler's numbers (Euler, Leonhard): Mathematics. See: Ballentyne.

Euler's relation (Euler, Leonhard): Mathematics. See: Ballentyne.

Eumachia (Eumachus of Neapolis): Botany. See: Charnock.

EUMACHUS OF NEAPOLIS. No dates. Greek writer. See: Dict. Grk. Rom. Biog. Myth. Eumachia.

Eunice Rockwell Oberly Memorial Award (Oberly, Eunice Rockwell): Agriculture. See: Harrod.

Eunomianism (or Eunomians) (Eunomius): Religion. See: Attwater; Canney; Mathews, S.

Eunomio-Theophronians (Theophronius of Cappadocia): Religion. See: Canney.

EUNOMIUS. d. ca. 393. Bishop of Cyzicus. See: Barnhart (Cycl. Names). Eunomianism (or Eunomians).

Eupatorium (Mithridates VI, Eupator): Botany. See: Charnock; Hendrickson under "Mithridatize..;" Taylor, N.

Euphorbia (Euphorbus): Botany. See: Partridge; Weekley.

Euphorbium (Euphorbus): Medicine. See: Partridge.

EUPHORBUS. fl. 1st c. A.D. Greek physician. See: Biog. Lex. hervorr. Aerzte. Euphorbia, Euphorbium.

EUPHUES. Chief character of John Lyly's romance, "Euphues: The Anatomy of Wit" (1578). See: Benet. Euphuism.

Euphuism (Euphues): Literature. See: Brewer; Duffy; Preminger.

Euripidean (Euripides): Literature. See: Webster's 3d.

EURIPIDES. fl. 5th c. B.C. Greek playwright. See: Encyc. Brit., 1974. Euripidean.

EURY, J. fl. 1934. French chemist. Cited in: Chem. Abstr., vol. 28, p. 5368. Eury test.

Eury test (Eury, J.): Chemistry. See: Van Nostrand Chem. Dict.

Eusebian (1) (Eusebius of Caesarea): Religion. See: Webster's 3d.

Eusebian (2) (Eusebius of Nicomedia): Religion. See: Webster's 3d.

Eusebian canons (Eusebius of Caesarea): Religion. See: Webster's 3d.

EUSEBIUS OF CAESAREA (PAMPHILI). 264-340. Palestinian theologian and church historian. See: Encyc. Brit., 1973. Eusebian (1), Eusebian canons.

EUSEBIUS OF NICOMEDIA. d. 341 A.D. Arian bishop. See: Encyc. Brit., 1973. Eusebian (2).

Eustache (Dubois, Eustache): Generic Word (knife). See: Partridge.

EUSTACHI, BARTOLOMEO. 1524-1574. Italian phusician, surgeon, and anatomist. See: Dict. Sci. Biog. Eustachian amygdalae, Eustachian catheter, Eustachian cushion, Eustachian muscle, Eustachian tonsil, Eustachian tube, Eustachian tuber, Eustachian valve, Eustachitis.

Eustachian amygdalae (Eustachi, Bartolomeo): Medicine. See: Donath.

Eustachian catheter (Eustachi, Bartolomeo): Medicine. See: Stedman.

Eustachian cushion (Eustachi, Bartolomeo): Medicine. See: Stedman.

Eustachian muscle (Eustachi, Bartolomeo): Medicine. See: Donath.

Eustachian tonsil (Eustachi, Bartolomeo): Medicine. See: Partridge; Stedman; Webster's 3d.

Eustachian tube (Eustachi, Bartolomeo): Medicine. See: Drever; Gray; Pennak.

Eustachian tuber (Eustachi, Bartolomeo): Medicine. See: Stedman.

Eustachian valve (Eustachi, Bartolomeo): Medicine. See: Gray; Stedman; Webster's 3d. Also known as: Sylvian valve.

Eustachitis (Eustachi, Bartolomeo): Medicine. See: Stedman.

Eustathian (1) (Eustathius of Antioch): Religion. See: Webster's 3d.

Eustathian (2) (Eustathius of Sebaste): Religion. See: Webster's 3d.

EUSTATHIUS OF ANTIOCH. d. ca. 360. Syrian bishop. See: Encyc. Brit., 1973. Eustathian (1).

EUSTATHIUS OF SEBASTE. ca. 300-ca. 380. Armenian semi-Arian bishop. See: Barnhart (Cycl. Names). Eustathian (2).

EUSTIS, ALLAN CHOTARD. b. 1876. American physician. See: Who's Who Amer. Med. Eustis' test.

Eustis' test (Eustis, Allan Chotard): Medicine. See: Dorland.

EUSTON, E. fl. 1914. American chemist. Cited in: Chem. Abstr., vol. 8, p. 3377. Euston process.

Euston process (Euston, E.): Chemistry. See: Van Nostrand Chem. Dict.

EUTERPE. Greek muse of harmony and lyric poetry. See: Jobes. Euterpean.

Euterpean (Euterpe): Generic Word (pertaining to music). See: Charnock; Partridge; Weekley.

EUTYCHES. 375?-454. Greek archimandrite. See: Encyc. Brit., 1973. Eutychianism.

Eutychianism (Eutyches): Religion. See: Attwater; Canney; Charnock.

Evans and Lloyd-Thomas syndrome (Evans, William and Lloyd-Thomas, Hywel Geoffrey): Medicine. See: Jablonski.

EVANS, ARTHUR F. fl. 1913-1955. English engineer. Cited in: Chem. Abstr., vol. 38, p. 1347. Evans pump.

Evans blue (Evans, Herbert McLeon): Medicine. See: Stedman; Webster's 3d.

EVANS, BROOKE. 1797-1862. English nickel refiner. See: Dict. Nat. Biog. Evansite.

Evans-Burr unit (Evans, Herbert McLeon and Burr, George Oswald): Medicine. See: Stedman.

Evans cell (Evans, David J.): Engineering and Industry. See: Thrush.

EVANS, DAVID J. fl. 1933. English inventor. Cited in: Chem. Abstr., vol. 28, p. 1936. Evans cell.

Evans' disease (Evans, William): Medicine. See: Jablonski.

Evans engine (and boiler) (Evans, Oliver): Engineering and Industry. See: Auger.

EVANS, HERBERT MC LEON. 1882-1971. American anatomist and embryologist. See: World Who's Who Sci. Evans blue, Evans-Burr unit.

EVANS, OLIVER. 1755-1819. American inventor. See: Dict. Amer. Biog. Evans engine (and boiler).

Evans pump (Evans, Arthur F.): Engineering and Industry. See: Auger.

EVANS, ROBERT SHERMAN. 1912- . American physician. See: Amer. Men and Women Sci., 12th ed. Evans' syndrome.

Evans' syndrome (Evans, Robert Sherman): Medicine. See: Jablonski.

EVANS, WILLIAM. 1895- . English physician. See: Who's Who, 1974. Evans and Lloyd-Thomas syndrome, Evans' disease.

Evansite (Evans, Brooke): Earth Sciences. See: Thrush; Webster's 3d.

EVE. Biblical name given to first woman. See: Encyc. Brit., 1973. Adam and Eve (orchid), Eve, Eve's cup, Eve's needle (or darning needle), Eve's thread.

Eve (Eve, the first woman): Generic Word (woman). See: Partridge.

EVE, ARTHUR STEWARD. 1862-1948. English physicist. See: World Who's Who Sci. Eve's constant.

EVE, FRANK CECIL. d. 1952. English physician. See: Who Was Who, 1951-1960. Eve('s) method.

EVE, J. fl. 1825. Engineer. (Biography source unavailable.) Eve pump.

Eve('s) method (Eve, Frank Cecil): Medicine. See: Dorland; Stedman; Thrush.

Eve pump (Eve, J.): Engineering and Industry. See: Auger.

even Steven (Steven): Generic Word. See: Hendrickson.

Everett('s) interpolation formula (Everett, Joseph David): Physics. See: Ballentyne; Internat. Dict. Ap. Math.

EVERETT, JOSEPH DAVID. 1831-1904. English physicist. See: Pogg., vols. 3, 4, 5. Everett('s) interpolation formula.

EVERITT, WILLIAM LITTELL. 1900- . American electrical engineer. See: Amer. Men and Women Sci., 12th ed. Everitt's corollaries, Everitt's form of the second law of thermodynamics.

Everitt's corollaries (Everitt, William Littell): Sociology. See: Martin.

Everitt's form of the second law of thermodynamics (Everitt, William Littell): Sociology. See: Martin.

Evers-Bellier test (Evers, Norman and Bellier, Jean): Chemistry. See: Van Nostrand Chem. Dict.

EVERS, NORMAN. b. 1887. English chemist. Cited in: Chem. Abstr., vol. 7, p. 662. Evers-Bellier test.

EVERSBUSCH, OSKAR. 1853-1912. German ophthalmologist. See: Wer Ist's, 1906. Eversbusch's operation.

Eversbusch's operation (Eversbusch, Oskar): Medicine. See: Dorland.

Evershed criterion (Evershed, John): Physics. See: Thewlis.

Evershed effect (Evershed, John): Physics. See: Ballentyne; Satterthwaite; Thewlis.

EVERSHED, JOHN. 1864-1956. English physicist. See: Dict. Sci. Biog. Evershed criterion, Evershed effect.

Everson process (Derivation undetermined): Engineering and Industry. See: Thrush.

EVERTSEN, JACOB. fl. 17th c. Dutch sea captain. (Biography source unavailable.) Jacopever (fish).

Eve's constant (Eve, Arthur Steward): Physics. See: Webster's 3d.

Eve's cup (Eve): Botany. See: Mathews, M. M.

Eve's needle (or darning needle) (Eve): Botany. See: Mathews, M. M.; Webster's 3d.

Eve's thread (Eve): Botany. See: Mathews, M. M.

EVJEN, HAAKON MUUS. 1904- . Norwegian-born American physicist. See: Amer. Men Sci., 6th ed. Evjen method.

Evjen method (Evjen, Haakon Muus): Physics. See: Internat. Dict. Ap. Math.; Internat. Dict. Phys. Elec.

Evrard reagent (Evrard, V.): Chemistry. See: Van Nostrand Chem. Dict.

EVRARD, V. fl. 1929. French chemist. Cited in: Chem. Abstr., vol. 24, p. 311. Evrard reagent.

EWALD, KARL EMIL ANTON. 1845-1915. German physician. See: World Who's Who Sci. Ewald's enema, Ewald's test breakfast (or meal), Ewald's test (of the motility of the stomach).

Ewald-Kornfeld method (Ewald, Paul Peter and Kornfeld): Physics. See: Internat. Dict. Phys. Elec.

Ewald method (Ewald, Paul Peter): Physics. See: Internat. Dict. Phys. Elec.

EWALD, PAUL PETER. b. 1888. German-born physicist. See: World Who's Who Sci. Ewald-Kornfeld method, Ewald method, Ewald sphere.

Ewald reagent (Derivation undetermined): Chemistry. See: Van Nostrand Chem. Dict.

Ewald sphere (Ewald, Paul Peter): Physics. See: Ballentyne.

Ewald's enema (Ewald, Karl Emil Anton): Medicine. See: Dorland.

Ewald's test breakfast (or meal) (Ewald, Karl Emil Anton): Medicine. See: Dorland; Stedman.

Ewald's test (of the motility of the stomach) (Ewald, Karl Emil Anton): Medicine. See: Stedman.

Ewart mill (Ewart, P.): Engineering and Industry. See: Auger.

EWART, P. fl. ca. 1795. Engineer. (Biography source unavailable.) Ewart mill.

EWART, WILLIAM. 1848-1929. English physician. See: Who Was Who, 1929-1940. Ewart's procedure, Ewart's sign.

Ewart's phenomenon (Derivation undetermined): Medicine. See: Jablonski.

Ewart's procedure (Ewart, William): Medicine. See: Stedman.

Ewart's sign (Ewart, William): Medicine. See: Dorland; Stedman. Also known as: Pin's sign.

Ewer and Pick's acid (Derivation undetermined): Chemistry. See: Hackh.

Ewing extensometer (Ewing, James Alfred): Engineering and Industry. See: Auger.

EWING, JAMES. 1866-1943. American pathologist. See: Dict. Sci. Biog. Ewing's sarcoma (angioendothelioma, endothelial sarcoma, or tumor).

EWING, JAMES ALFRED. 1855-1935. Scottish physicist and engineer. See: Dict. Sci. Biog. Ewing extensometer, Ewing theory of ferromagnetism.

EWING, JAMES H. 1798-1827. Physician. (Biography source unavailable.) Ewing's sign.

Ewing theory of ferromagnetism (Ewing, James Alfred): Physics. See: Internat. Dict. Phys. Elec.; Thewlis; Van Nostrand Sci. Encyc.

Ewing's sarcoma (angioendothelioma, endothelial sarcoma, or tumor) (Ewing, James): Medicine. See: Jablonski.

Ewing's sign (Ewing, James H.): Medicine. See: Stedman.

EWINS, ARTHUR JAMES. 1882-1957. English chemist. See: Royal Soc. Biog. Mem. of Fellows. Ewins test reactions.

Ewins test reactions (Ewins, Arthur James): Chemistry. See: Van Nostrand Chem. Dict.

Exeter, Duke of. See: Holland, John (Duke of Exeter).

EXNER, SIGMUND. 1846-1926. Austrian physiologist. See: World Who's Who Sci. Call-Exner bodies, Exner's nerve, Exner's plexus.

Exner's nerve (Exner, Sigmund): Medicine. See: Donath; Dorland.

Exner's plexus (Exner, Sigmund): Medicine. See: Donath; Dorland; Stedman.

Exton reagent (Exton, William Gustav): Chemistry. See: Hackh; Stedman.

Exton-Rose test (Exton, William Gustav and Rose, Anton R.): Medicine. See: Stedman.

EXTON, WILLIAM GUSTAV. 1876-1943. American physician. See: World Who's Who Sci. Exton reagent, Exton-Rose test.

EYDE, SAMUEL. 1866-1940. Norwegian chemist. See: World Who's Who Sci. Birkeland-Eyde method (or process).

Eyermann turbine (Eyermann, Wilhelm Heinrich): Engineering and Industry. See: Auger.

EYERMANN, WILHELM HEINRICH. b. 1872. German engineer. Cited in: Mansell. Eyermann turbine.

Eykman formula (Eykman, Johann Frederik): Chemistry. See: Internat. Dict. Ap. Math.; Internat. Dict. Phys. Elec.; Van Nostrand Chem. Dict.; Van Nostrand Sci. Encyc.

EYKMAN, JOHANN FREDERIK. 1851-1915. German chemist. See: Sci., vol. 42 (1915), p. 242. Eykman formula.

EYRING, CARL FERDINAND. b. 1889. American physicist. See: Amer. Men Sci., 5th ed. Norris-Eyring reverberation formula.

Eyring equation (Eyring, Henry): Physics. See: Ballentyne.

Eyring free volume theory (Eyring, Henry): Physics. See: Internat. Dict. Phys. Elec.

Eyring general energy equation (Eyring, Henry): Physics. See: Internat. Dict. Phys. Elec.

EYRING, HENRY. 1901- . Mexican-born American chemist. See: World Who's Who Sci. Eyring equation, Eyring free volume theory, Eyring general energy equation, Eyring theory of transport processes, Eyring treatment of diffusion, Eyring treatment of viscosity.

Eyring theory of transport processes (Eyring, Henry): Physics. See: Internat. Dict. Ap. Math.; Van Nostrand Sci. Encyc.

Eyring treatment of diffusion (Eyring, Henry): Physics. See: Internat. Dict. Phys. Elec.

Eyring treatment of viscosity (Eyring, Henry): Physics. See: Internat. Dict. Phys. Elec.

EZCURRA, JUAN MANUEL DE. No dates. Argentinian mine manager. Cited in: Min. Mag., vol. 31 (1958), p. 958. Ezcurrite.

Ezcurrite (Ezcurra, Juan Manuel de): Earth Sciences. See: Thrush.

F

f-sum rule of Thomas-Reiche-Kuhn (Thomas, W.?; Reiche, Fritz; and Kuhn, Heinrich Gerhard). See: Kuhn-Thomas-Reiche f-sum rule.

Faber du Faur, Adolf Friedrich von. See: Von Faber du Faur, Adolf Friedrich.

Faber du Faur furnace (Von Faber du Faur, Adolf Friedrich): Engineering and Industry. See: Thrush.

Faber flaws (Faber, T. E.): Physics. See: Ballentyne.

FABER, KNUD HELGE. 1862-1956. Danish physician. See: World Who's Who Sci. Faber's anemia (or syndrome).

FABER, T. E. fl. 1952. English chemist. Cited in: Chem. Abstr., vol. 46, p. 10751. Faber flaws.

FABERGE, PETER CARL. 1846-1920. Russian artist. See: Encyc. Brit., 1973. Faberge (ware).

Faberge (ware) (Faberge, Peter Carl): Applied Arts. See: Hendrickson.

Faber's anemia (or syndrome) (Faber, Knud Helge): Medicine. See: Dorland; Jablonski; Stedman. Also known as: Hayem-Faber syndrome, Kaznelson's syndrome, Witts' anemia.

FABIAN, HANS-JOACHIM. fl. 1939. German geologist. Cited in: Min. Mag., vol. 33 (1964), p. 1132. Fabianite.

Fabian socialism (or Fabianism) (Fabius Maximus Verrucosus, Quintus): Economics. See: Greenwald; Webster's 3d.

Fabian Society (Fabius Maximus Verrucosus, Quintus): History. See: Barnhart (Eng. Lit.); Brewer; Steinberg.

Fabian system (Derivation undetermined): Engineering and Industry. See: Thrush.

Fabian (tactics) (Fabius Maximus Verrucosus, Quintus): Generic Word (delaying tactics). See: Brewer; Charnock; Partridge.

FABIAN Y FUERO, FRANCISCO. 1719-1801. Spanish archbishop and naturalist. See: Encic. Univ. Ilus. Fabiana.

Fabiana (Fabian y Fuero, Francisco): Botany. See: Stedman; Taylor, N.; Webster's 3d.

Fabianite (Fabian, Hans-Joachim): Earth Sciences. See: Thrush.

FABINYI, RUDOLF. 1849-1920. Hungarian chemist. See: Pogg., vols. 3, 4, 5. Fabinyi test.

Fabinyi test (Fabinyi, Rudolf): Chemistry. See: Van Nostrand Chem. Dict.

FABIUS MAXIMUS VERRUCOSUS, QUINTUS (CUNCTATOR). 275-203 B.C. Roman general. See: Barnhart (Cycl. Names). Fabian socialism (or Fabianism), Fabian Society, Fabian (tactics).

Fabraea (fungi) (Fabre, Jean Henri): Botany. See: Webster's 3d.

FABRE, JEAN HENRI. 1823-1915. French entomologist. See: Dict. Sci. Biog. Fabraea (fungi).

FABRE TERSOL, J. fl. 1944. Spanish physician. (Biography source unavailable.) Martorell-Fabre syndrome.

FABRICI, GIROLAMO (FABRICIUS AB AQUAPENDENTE, GERONIMO FABRIZIO). 1533-1619. Italian anatomist and embryologist. See: Dict. Sci. Biog. bursa of Fabricius, Fabricius' ship.

Fabricia (Fabricius, Johann Christian): Botany. See: Charnock.

Fabrician (classification) (Fabricius, Johann Christian): Zoology. See: Henderson.

FABRICIUS, JOHANN CHRISTIAN. 1743-1808. Danish entomologist. See: Dict. Sci. Biog. Fabricia, Fabrician (classification).

Fabricius' ship (Fabrici, Girolamo): Medicine. See: Stedman

FABRY, A. fl. 1872. Belgian engineer. (Biography source unavailable.) Fabry blower.

Fabry and Barot method (Fabry, Charles and Barot, J.): Physics. See: Internat. Dict. Phys. Elec.

Fabry (and) Perot etalon (or interferometer) (Fabry, Charles and Perot, Alfred): Physics. See: Internat. Dict. Phys. Elec.; Thewlis; Van Nostrand Sci. Encyc.

Fabry-Anderson syndrome (Fabry, Johannes and Anderson, William A.). See: Fabry's syndrome.

Fabry blower (Fabry, A.): Engineering and Industry. See: Auger.

FABRY, CHARLES. 1867-1945. French physicist. See: Dict. Sci. Biog. Fabry and Barot method, Fabry (and) Perot etalon (or interferometer), Fabry lens, Fabry-Perot fringes.

FABRY, JOHANNES. 1860-1930. German physician. See: Biog. Lex. hervorr. Aerzte, 1880-1930. Fabry's syndrome.

Fabry lens (Fabry, Charles): Physics. See: Thewlis.

Fabry-Perot fringes (Fabry, Charles and Perot, Alfred): Physics. See: Ballentyne.

Fabry's syndrome (Fabry, Johannes): Medicine. See: Jablonski. Also known as: Fabry-Anderson syndrome, Ruiter-Pompen syndrome, Ruiter-Pompen-Wyers syndrome, Sweeley-Klionsky disease.

FAGEL, CASPAR. 1634-1688. Dutch statesman. See: Nieuw Nederl. Biog. Woordenb. Fagelia.

Fagelia (Fagel, Caspar): Botany. See: Webster's 3d.

Fagergren cell (Fagergren, William): Engineering and Industry. See: Thrush.

FAGERGREN, WILLIAM. fl. 1934. American metallurgist. Cited in: Chem. Abstr., vol. 28, p. 4691. Fagergren cell.

Fages test reaction (Derivation undetermined): Chemistry. See: Van Nostrand Chem. Dict.

FAGET, JEAN CHARLES. 1818-1884. French physician. See: Dict. Amer. Biog. Faget's sign.

Faget's sign (Faget, Jean Charles): Medicine. See: Dorland; Stedman.

Fagin (Fagin, the thief): Generic Word (thief-trainer). See: Partridge; Webster's 3d.

FAGIN, THE THIEF. Character in Charles Dickens' novel, "Oliver Twist" (1837-39). See: Benet. Fagin.

FAGON, GUI-CRESCENT. 1638-1718. French physician and botanist. See: World Who's Who Sci. Fagonia.

Fagonia (Fagon, Gui-Crescent): Botany. See: Charnock.

FAHEY, JOSEPH JOHN. 1901- . American geochemist. See: Amer. Men Sci., 9th ed. Faheyite

Faheyite (Fahey, Joseph John): Earth Sciences. See: Thrush.

Fahnestock clip (Fahnestock James D.): Electronics. See: Markus.

FAHNESTOCK, JAMES D. fl. 1953. American electronics engineer. Cited in: Chem. Abstr., vol. 47, p. 12054. Fahnestock clip.

FAHR, THEODOR. 1877-1945. German neurologist. See: World Who's Who Sci. Fahr's disease.

Fahraeus reaction (or test) (Fahraeus, Robin): Medicine. See: Dorland.

FAHRAEUS, ROBIN. b. 1888. Swedish pathologist and anatomist. See: World Who's Who Sci. Fahraeus reaction (or test).

FAHRENHEIT, DANIEL GABRIEL. 1689-1736. German-Dutch physicist. See: Dict. Sci. Biog. degree Fahrenheit, Fahrenheit degree, Fahrenheit scale (or temperature scale).

Fahrenheit degree (Fahrenheit, Daniel Gabriel): Physics. See: Dresner.

Fahrenheit scale (or temperature scale) (Fahrenheit, Daniel Gabriel): Physics. See: Ballentyne; Focal Encyc. Photog.; Huschke; Internat. Dict. Phys. Elec.

FAHRENWALD, ARTHUR WILLIAM. b. 1890. American metallurgist. See: Amer. Men Sci., 10th ed. Fahrenwald machines.

Fahrenwald machines (Fahrenwald, Arthur William): Engineering and Industry. See: Thrush.

Fahr's disease (Fahr, Theodor): Medicine. See: Hinsie; Jablonski.

Fairbairn and Tate method for vapor pressure (Fairbairn, Sir William? and Tate, Thomas Turner): Physics. See: Internat. Dict. Phys. Elec.

Fairbairn coupling (Fairbairn, Sir William): Engineering and Industry. See: Auger.

FAIRBAIRN, SIR WILLIAM. 1789-1874. Scottish engineer. See: Dict. Nat. Biog. Fairbairn and Tate method for vapor pressure?, Fairbairn coupling.

FAIRBANK, SIR HAROLD ARTHUR THOMAS. b. 1876. English surgeon. See: Who's Who, 1957. Fairbank's disease (or dysostoses).

Fairbank's disease (or dysostoses) (Fairbank, Sir Harold Arthur Thomas): Medicine. See: Jablonski.

FAIRCHILD, JOHN G. b. 1882. American chemist. See: Amer. Men Sci., 9th ed. Fairchildite.

Fairchildite (Fairchild, John G.): Earth Sciences. See: Thrush; Webster's 3d.

FAIRHALL, LAWRENCE TURNER. b. 1888. American chemist. See: Amer. Men Sci., 4th ed. Fairhall test.

Fairhall test (Fairhall, Lawrence Turner): Chemistry. See: Van Nostrand Chem. Dict.

FAJANS, KASIMIR. 1887- . Polish-born American chemist. See: World Who's Who Sci. Fajans method, Fajans' precipitation rule, Fajans rules, Fajans-Soddy law.

Fajans method (Fajans, Kasimir): Chemistry. See: Van Nostrand Chem. Dict.

Fajans' precipitation rule (Fajans, Kasimir): Chemistry. See: Ballentyne.

Fajans rules (Fajans, Kasimir): Chemistry. See: Thewlis.

Fajans-Soddy law (Fajans, Kasimir and Soddy, Frederick): Chemistry. See: Hackh. Also known as: Soddy-Fajans displacement law.

Falcidian Law (Falcidius): Law. See: Black.

Falcidian portion (Falcidius): Law. See: Black.

FALCIDIUS. fl. 40 B.C. Roman tribune. See: Dict. Grk. Rom. Biog. Myth. Falcidian Law, Falcidian portion.

FALCIOLA, PIETRO. fl. 1926. Italian chemist. See: Pogg., vols. 5, 6. Falciola test reaction for cobalt, Falciola test reaction for molybdenum, Falciola test reaction for selenium, Falciola test reaction for tellurium.

Falciola test reaction for cobalt (Falciola, Pietro): Chemistry. See: Van Nostrand Chem. Dict.

Falciola test reaction for molybdenum (Falciola, Pietro): Chemistry. See: Van Nostrand Chem. Dict.

Falciola test reaction for selenium (Falciola, Pietro): Chemistry. See: Van Nostrand Chem. Dict.

Falciola test reaction for tellurium (Falciola, Pietro): Chemistry. See: Van Nostrand Chem. Dict.

Falconer Foundation (Falconer, Richard): Medicine. See: Encyc. Assoc.

FALCONER, MURRAY ALEXANDER. 1910- . New Zealand-born English neurosurgeon. See: World Who's Who Sci. Falconer-Weddell syndrome.

FALCONER, RICHARD. 1947-1964. American university student. (Biography source unavailable.) Falconer Foundation.

Falconer-Weddell syndrome (Falconer, Murray Alexander and Weddell, Graham): Medicine. See: Jablonski.

FALIERI, MARINO. 1278-1355. Doge of Venice. See: Barnhart (Cycl. Names). conspiracy of Marino Falieri.

FALK, ADALBERT (In full: PAUL LUDWIG ADALBERT). 1827-1900. Prussian jurist and statesman. See: Barnhart (Cycl. Names). Falk laws.

FALK, JOHANN PETER. 1727-1774. Swedish botanist and physician. See: Nouv. Biog. Univ. Falkia.

Falk laws (Falk, Adalbert): History. See: Attwater; Harbottle.

FALKENHAGEN, HANS. 1895- . German physicist. See: Wer Ist Wer, 8th ed. Debye-Falkenhagen effect.

Falkia (Falk, Johann Peter): Botany. See: Charnock.

FALKINER FAMILY. fl. 19th and 20th c. Australian sheep breeders. (Biography source unavailable.) Falkiner (shilling).

Falkiner (shilling) (Falkiner family): Numismatics. See: Brewer.

Falkner, William. See: Faulkner, William.

Fallopian aqueduct (or canal) (Falloppio, Gabriele): Medicine. See: Donath; Dorland; Stedman; Webster's 3d. Also known as: Tarin's foramen.

Fallopian arch (or ligament) (Falloppio, Gabriele): Medicine. See: Donath; Dorland; Stedman. Also known as: Poupart's ligament, Vesalius' ligament.

Fallopian hiatus (Falloppio, Gabriele): Medicine. See: Dorland; Stedman.

Fallopian neuritis (Falloppio, Gabriele): Medicine. See: Stedman. Also known as: Bell's palsy.

Fallopian pregnancy (Falloppio, Gabriele): Medicine. See: Stedman.

Fallopian tube (Falloppio, Gabriele): Medicine. See: Henderson; Pennak; Stedman.

Fallopian valve (Falloppio, Gabriele): Medicine. See: Donath.

FALLOPPIO, GABRIELE. 1523-1562. Italian anatomist. See: Dict. Sci. Biog. Fallopian aqueduct (or canal), Fallopian arch (or ligament), Fallopian hiatus, Fallopian neuritis, Fallopian pregnancy, Fallopian tube, Fallopian valve.

FALLOT, ETIENNE LOUIS ARTHUR. 1850-1911. French physician. See: World Who's Who Sci. Fallot's tetralogy (or tetrad), pentalogy of Fallot, trilogy of Fallot.

Fallot's tetralogy (or tetrad) (Fallot, Etienne Louis Arthur): Medicine. See: Dorland; Jablonski; Stedman.

FALLOUX, FREDERIC ALFRED PIERRE. 1811-1886. French politician. See: Encyc. Brit., 1973. Loi Falloux.

FALLS, FREDERICK HOWARD. b. 1885. American obstetrician and gynecologist. See: Who's Who Among Physicians and Surg. Falls's test.

FALLS, HAROLD FRANCIS. 1909- . American ophthalmologist and geneticist. See: Amer. Men and Women Sci., 12th ed. Rundles-Falls syndrome.

Falls's test (Falls, Frederick Howard): Medicine. See: Dorland.

FALRET, JEAN PIERRE. 1794-1870. French psychiatrist. See: World Who's Who Sci. Falret's disease.

Falret's disease (Falret, Jean Pierre): Medicine. See: Jablonski.

FALSTAFF, SIR JOHN. Character in William Shakespeare's plays, "The Merry Woves of Windsor" and "Henry IV." See: Benet. Falstaffian.

Falstaffian (Falstaff, Sir John): Literature. See: Barnhart (Eng. Lit.); Brewer; Partridge.

FALTA, WILHELM. b. 1875. Austrian physician. See: World Who's Who Sci. Falta's syndrome, Falta's triad, Kahn-Falta sign.

Falta's sign (Falta, Wilhelm). See: Kahn-Falta sign.

Falta's syndrome (Falta, Wilhelm): Medicine. See: Jablonski.

Falta's triad (Falta, Wilhelm): Medicine. See: Dorland.

Falter apparatus (Falter, Arthur Henry): Engineering and Industry. See: Thrush.

FALTER, ARTHUR HENRY. fl. 1945. American inventor. Cited in: Chem. Abstr., vol. 39, p. 1030. Falter apparatus.

Fament's process (Derivation undetermined): Chemistry. See: Hackh.

Fanconi-Albertini-Zellweger syndrome (Fanconi, Guido; Albertini, Ambrosius; and Zellweger, Hans Ulrich): Medicine. See: Jablonski.

Fanconi-De Toni-Debre syndrome (Fanconi, Guido; De Toni, Giovanni; and Debre, Robert). See: Abderhalden-Fanconi syndrome.

FANCONI, GUIDO. b. 1892. Swiss pediatrician. See: Rev. Colombiana, vol. 14, no. 1 (1954), p. 57. Abderhalden-Fanconi syndrome, Fanconi-Albertini-Zellweger syndrome, Fanconi-Hegglin syndrome, Fanconi-Petrassi syndrome, Fanconi-Schlesinger syndrome, Fanconi-Tuerler syndrome, Fanconi's anemia (panmyelopathy or refractory anemia), Fanconi's syndrome (1), Fanconi's syndrome (3), Prader-Labhart-Willi-Fanconi syndrome, Wissler-Fanconi syndrome.

Fanconi-Hegglin syndrome (Fanconi, Guido and Hegglin, Robert): Medicine. See: Jablonski. Also known as: Wassermann-positive pneumonia (or pulmonary infiltrations).

Fanconi-Petrassi syndrome (Fanconi, Guido and Petrassi, Gino): Medicine. See: Jablonski.

Fanconi-Schlesinger syndrome (Fanconi, Guido and Schlesinger, Bernard Edward?): Medicine. See: Jablonski.

Fanconi-Tuerler syndrome (Fanconi, Guido and Tuerler, U.): Medicine. See: Jablonski.

Fanconi's anemia (panmyelopathy or refractory anemia) (Fanconi, Guido): Medicine. See: Barnhart (New Eng.); Jablonski; Stedman.

Fanconi's syndrome (1) (Fanconi, Guido): Medicine. See: Jablonski.

Fanconi's syndrome (2) (Fanconi, Guido). See: Abderhalden-Fanconi syndrome.

Fanconi's syndrome (3) (Fanconi, Guido). See: Andersen's syndrome.

FANDAL, DAMIAN CALLERY. 1929- . American educator. See: Lead. Educ., 5th ed. Father Damian Fandal's rules for deans.

FANG, HSIN-YUN. fl. 1935. Chinese chemist. Cited in: Chem. Abstr., vol. 29, p. 6172. Kao-Fang-Sah reagent.

Fang Shih (Chin fang shih): Parapsychology. See: Webster's 3d.

FANKUCHEN, ISIDOR. 1905-1964. American crystallographer. See: Dict. Sci. Biog. Fankuchen Memorial Lectures.

Fankuchen Memorial Lectures (Fankuchen, Isidor): Physics. Cited in: Dict. Sci. Biog.

Fann viscosimeter (Derivation undetermined): Engineering and Industry. See: Thrush.

FANNING, JOHN THOMAS. 1837-1911. American hydraulic engineer. See: Dict. Amer. Biog. Fanning's equation.

Fanning's equation (Fanning, John Thomas): Engineering and Industry. See: Thrush.

Fanny (Hill, Fanny, the fictional character): Generic Word. See: Hendrickson.

Fanny Adams (Adams, Fanny): Food and Drink. See: Brewer, Hendrickson.

Fanny Heath raspberry (Heath, Fanny): Botany. See: Hendrickson.

Fanny Wright (or Wrightism) (Wright, Frances): Sociology. See: Mathews, M. M.

Fano factor (Fano, Robert Mario): Physics. See: Hughes.

FANO, ROBERT MARIO. 1917- . Italian-born American electrical engineer. See: World Who's Who Sci. Fano factor.

FANO, UGO. 1912- . Italian-born American physicist. See: World Who's Who Sci. Spencer-Fano method.

Fantus' antidote (Fantus, Bernard): Medicine. See: Dorland.

FANTUS, BERNARD. 1874-1940. American pharmacologist. See: Who's Who Amer. Med. Fantus' antidote.

FARABEUF, LOUIS HUBERT. 1841-1910. French surgeon. See: World Who's Who Sci. Farabeuf's amputation, Farabeuf's operation, Farabeuf's triangle.

Farabeuf's amputation (Farabeuf, Louis Hubert): Medicine. See: Stedman.

Farabeuf's operation (Farabeuf, Louis Hubert): Medicine. See: Stedman.

Farabeuf's triangle (Farabeuf, Louis Hubert): Medicine. See: Donath; Dorland; Stedman.

Farad (unit of capacitance) (Faraday, Michael): Physics. See: Ballentyne; Dresner; Hughes.

Faraday balance (Faraday, Michael): Physics. See: Thewlis.

Faraday cage (Faraday, Michael): Physics. See: Stedman; Thewlis; Webster's 3d.

Faraday cell (Faraday, Michael): Chemistry. See: Hackh.

Faraday (constant) (Faraday, Michael): Physics. See: Ballentyne; Dresner; Internat. Dict. Ap. Math.

Faraday dark space (Faraday, Michael): Electronics. See: Ballentyne; Internat. Dict. Phys. Elec.; Markus.

Faraday disc (machine) (Faraday, Michael): Physics. See: Internat. Dict. Phys. Elec.; Van Nostrand Sci. Encyc.; Webster's 3d.

Faraday effect (Faraday, Michael): Physics. See: Ballentyne; Internat. Dict. Ap. Math.; Markus.

Faraday ice-bucket (or ice-pail) experiment (Faraday, Michael): Electronics. See: Hughes; Internat. Dict. Phys. Elec.; Van Nostrand Sci. Encyc.

Faraday law of electromagnetic induction (Faraday, Michael): Physics. See: Internat. Dict. Ap. Math.; Internat. Dict. Phys. Elec.; Van Nostrand Sci. Encyc.

Faraday('s) laws (of electrolysis) (Faraday, Michael): Physics. See: Ballentyne; Internat. Dict. Phys. Elec.; Thewlis.

FARADAY, MICHAEL. 1791-1867. English chemist and physicist. See: Dict. Sci. Biog. Farad (unit of capacitance), Faraday balance, Faraday cage, Faraday cell, Faraday (constant), Faraday dark space, Faraday disc (machine), Faraday effect, Faraday ice-bucket (or ice-pail) experiment, Faraday law of electromagnetic induction, Faraday('s) laws (of electrolysis), Faraday rotation isolator, Faraday shield (screen), Faraday tube, Faraday washing bottle, Faraday's wheel, Faradic (current(s), Faradization (or Faradism), Faradmeter.

Faraday rotation isolator (Faraday, Michael): Electronics. See: Markus.

Faraday shield (screen) (Faraday, Michael): Electronics. See: Markus; Van Nostrand Sci. Encyc.; Webster's 3d.

Faraday tube (Faraday, Michael): Electronics. See: Hackh; Hughes.

Faraday washing bottle (Faraday, Michael): Chemistry. See: Hackh.

Faraday's wheel (Faraday, Michael): Physics. See: Dresner.

Faradic (current(s) (Faraday, Michael): Electronics. See: Hughes; Markus; Stedman.

Faradization (or Faradism) (Faraday, Michael): Electronics. See: Hughes; Markus; Stedman.

Faradmeter (Faraday, Michael): Electronics. See: Hughes; Webster's 3d.

FARBER, SIDNEY. 1903- . American pathologist. See: Amer. Men and Women Sci., 12th ed. Farber's syndrome.

Farber-Uzman syndrome (Farber, Sidney and Uzman, L. Lahut). See: Farber's syndrome.

Farber's syndrome (Farber, Sidney): Medicine. See: Jablonski. Also known as: Farber-Uzman syndrome.

FAREY, JOHN. 1766-1826. English geologist and mathematician. See: Dict. Sci. Biog. Farey sequence.

Farey sequence (Farey, John): Mathematics. See: Ballentyne; James.

FARGIN-FAYOLLE, PAUL. b. 1876. French dentist. Cited in: Mansell. Fargin-Fayolle syndrome.

Fargin-Fayolle syndrome (Fargin-Fayolle, Paul). See: Capdepont's syndrome.

FARJEON, ELEANOR. 1881-1965. English writer. See: Webster's Biog. Dict. Eleanor Farjeon Award.

FARMER, ERNEST HOWARD. 1860?-1944. English photographic technician. Cited in: Chem. Abstr., Decenn. Index, 1927-1936. Farmer's reducer.

Farmer's reducer (Farmer, Ernest Howard): Photography. See: Focal Encyc. Photog.; Webster's 3d.

Farnese, Allessandro. See: Paul III.

Farnovians (Farnovius, Stanislaus): Religion. See: Canney.

FARNOVIUS (FARNESIUS), STANISLAUS. d. 1615. Polish religious leader. See: New Schaff-Herzog Encyc. Rel. Know. Farnovians.

Farnsworth image dissector tube (Farnsworth, Philo Taylor): Physics. See: Internat. Dict. Phys. Elec.; Markus.

FARNSWORTH, PHILO TAYLOR. 1906-1971. American research engineer. See: Who Was Who Amer., 1969-1973. Farnsworth image dissector tube.

FARR, WILLIAM. 1807-1883. English medical statistician. See: Dict. Nat. Biog. Farr's law.

Farrant('s) fluid (or solution) (Derivation undetermined): Chemistry. See: Stedman; Van Nostrand Chem. Dict.

Farrar('s) process (Derivation undetermined): Chemistry. See: Hackh; Thrush; Van Nostrand Chem. Dict.

FARRE, ARTHUR. 1811-1887. English obstetrician and gynecologist. See: Dict. Nat. Biog. Farre's line.

FARRE, JOHN RICHARD. 1775-1862. English physician. See: Dict. Nat. Biog. Farre's tubercles.

Farre's line (Farre, Arthur): Medicine. See: Donath; Dorland; Stedman.

Farre's tubercles (Farre, John Richard): Medicine. See: Dorland; Stedman.

FARRINGTON, OLIVER CUMMINGS. 1864-1932. American geologist. See: World Who's Who Sci. Farringtonite?

Farringtonite (Farrington, Oliver Cummings?): Earth Sciences. See: Thrush.

Farr's law (Farr, William): Medicine. See: Dorland; Stedman.

FARSETI, P. No dates. Italian botanist. (Biography source unavailable.) Farsetia.

Farsetia (Farseti, P.): Botany. See: Charnock.

Fast bearing (Fast, Gustave): Engineering and Industry. See: Auger.

FAST, GUSTAVE. 1884-1946. Swedish-born American engineer. See: Who Was Who Amer., 1943-1950. Fast bearing.

Fast of Esther (Esther): Religion. See: Webster's 3d.

Fast of Gedaliah (Gedaliah): Religion. See: Webster's 3d.

Fata Morgana. See: Morgan le Fay.

fata Morgana (Morgan le Fay): Earth Sciences. See: Harvey; Moore; Partridge.

Father Damian Fandal's rules for deans (Fandal, Damian Callery): Sociology. See: Martin.

Father Damien (Damien, Father): Generic Word (selfless man). See: Hendrickson.

Father Hugo's rose (Scallan, Hugh): Botany. See: Webster's 3d.

Father Mathew (Mathew, Theobald): Generic Word (temperance reformer). See: Hendrickson.

Fathers of St. Edmund (Edmund Rich, Saint): Religion. See: Attwater.

FATIMA. 606-632 A.D. Daughter of Mohammad. See: Nouv. Biog. Univ. Fatimids (or Fatimites).

Fatimids (or Fatimites) (Fatima): History. See: Brewer.

FATOU, PIERRE JOSEPH LOUIS. 1878-1929. French mathematician. See: Dict. Sci. Biog. Fatou's theorem (or lemma).

Fatou's theorem (or lemma) (Fatou, Pierre Joseph Louis): Mathematics. See: James.

Fauchard Gold Medal (Fauchard, Pierre): Dentistry. See: Encyc. Assoc.

FAUCHARD, PIERRE. 1678-1761. French dentist. See: World Who's Who Sci. Fauchard Gold Medal, Fauchard's disease.

Fauchard's disease (Fauchard, Pierre): Medicine. See: Jablonski. Also known as: Riggs' disease.

FAUCK, A. fl. 1877. German engineer. Cited in: Mansell. Fauck's boring method.

Fauck's boring method (Fauck, A.): Engineering and Industry. See: Thrush.

FAUGERON, E. G. fl. 1910. Inventor. (Biography source unavailable.) Faugeron kiln.

Faugeron kiln (Faugeron, E. G.): Engineering and Industry. See: Thrush.

FAUJAS DE SAINT-FOND, BARTHELEMY. 1741-1819. French geologist. See: Dict. Sci. Biog. Faujasite.

Faujasite (Faujas de Saint-Fond, Barthelemy): Earth Sciences. See: Charnock; Webster's 3d.

Faun (Faunus): Generic Word (handsome, lustful young man). See: Partridge.

Fauna (Fauna, the nature goddess): Generic Word (animal life). See: Partridge; Weekley.

FAUNA, THE NATURE GODDESS. Mythical sister of Faunus. See: Jobes. Fauna.

Faunalia (Faunus): Generic Word (festival). See: Barnhart (Eng. Lit.)

Fauntleroy (Fauntleroy, Henry): Generic Word (forgery). See: Mathews, M.M.

FAUNTLEROY, HENRY. 1785-1824. English forger. See: Dict. Nat. Biog. Fauntleroy.

FAUNTLEROY, LORD. Hero of Frances Hodgson Burnett's novel, "Little Lord Fauntleroy" (1886). See: Benet. Lord Fauntleroy (suit).

FAUNUS. Roman woodland deity. See: Encyc. Brit., 1973. Faun, Faunalia.

FAUSER, GIACOMO. b. 1892. Italian engineer. See: Diz. Encic. Ital. Fauser process.

Fauser process (Fauser, Giacomo): Chemistry. See: Van Nostrand Chem. Dict.

FAUST, GEORGE TOBIAS. 1908- . American geologist. See: Amer. Men Sci., 9th ed. Faustite.

Faust jig (Derivation undetermined): Engineering and Industry. See: Thrush.

FAUST, JOHANN. d. ca. 1540. German magician and astrologer. See: Barnhart (Cycl. Names). Faustian.

Faustian (Faust, Johann): Generic Word. See: Webster's 3d.

Faustite (Faust, George Tobias): Earth Sciences. See: Thrush.

FAUVEL, SULPICE ANTOINE. 1813-1884. French physician. See: World Who's Who Sci. Fauvel's granules.

FAUVELLE. fl. 1846. French engineer. (Biography source unavailable.) Fauvell (system).

Fauvelle (system) (Fauvelle): Engineering and Industry. See: Thrush.

Fauvel's granules (Fauvel, Sulpice Antoine): Medicine. See: Jablonski.

Favorskii rearrangement (Favorsky, Alexei Yevgrafovich): Chemistry. See: Ballentyne; Van Nostrand Chem. Dict.

FAVORSKY, ALEXEI YEVGRAFOVICH. 1860-1945. Russian chemist. See: Dict. Sci. Biog. Favorskii rearrangement.

Favre-Chaix angiodermatitis (Favre, Maurice and Chaix, Achille): Medicine. See: Jablonski.

FAVRE, MAURICE JULES. 1876-1954. French physician. See: J. Med. Lyon, no. 844 (1955), p. 179. Durand-Nicolas-Favre disease, Favre-Chaix angiodermatitis, Favre-Racouchot disease, Gamna-Favre bodies.

Favre-Racouchot disease (Favre, Maurice and Racouchot, Jean): Medicine. See: Jablonski.

FAVREL, GEORGES. fl. 1908. French chemist. See: Pogg., vols. 5, 6. Favrel test reaction.

Favrel test reaction (Favrel, Georges): Chemistry. See: Van Nostrand Chem. Dict.

Favre's disease (Derivation undetermined): Medicine. See: Jablonski.

FAWKES, GUY. 1570-1606. English conspirator. See: Dict. Nat. Biog. Guy, Guy Fawkes' Day.

FAYOL, HENRI. 1841-1925. Turkish-born French engineer. See: World Who's Who Sci. Fayol's theory.

FAYOLLE, M. fl. 1911. French chemist. Cited in: Chem. Abstr., Decenn. Index, 1907-1916. Villiers-Fayolle reagent for free chlorine.

Fayol's theory (Fayol, Henri): Engineering and Industry. See: Thrush.

Fearon-Mitchell test for alcohols (Fearon, William Robert and Mitchell, David M.): Chemistry. See: Van Nostrand Chem. Dict.

Fearon solution for glyoxylic acid (Fearon, William Robert): Chemistry. See: Van Nostrand Chem. Dict.

Fearon test reaction for cyanate (Fearon, William Robert): Chemistry. See: Van Nostrand Chem. Dict.

Fearon test reaction for vitamin A (Fearon, William Robert): Chemistry. See: Van Nostrand Chem. Dict.

FEARON, WILLIAM ROBERT. 1892-1959. Irish physiologist. See: World Who's Who Sci. Fearon-Mitchell test for alcohols, Fearon solution for glyoxylic acid, Fearon test reaction for cyanate, Fearon test reaction for vitamin A.

Feast of St. Columba (Columba, Saint): Generic Word. See: Wagner (Names).

Feather analysis (Feather, Norman): Physics. See: Hughes; Internat. Dict. Phys. Elec.; Markus.

FEATHER, NORMAN. 1904- . English physicist. See: Who's Who, 1950. Feather analysis.

Febronianism (Hontheim, Johann Nikolaus von): Religion. See: Attwater; Canney; Mathews, S.; Webster's 3d.

Febronius. See: Hontheim, Johann Nikolaus von.

Fechner('s) colors (Fechner, Gustav Theodor): Physics. See: Chaplin; Internat. Dict. Phys. Elec.; Van Nostrand Sci. Encyc.

Fechner fraction (Fechner, Gustav Theodor): Physics. See: Internat. Dict. Ap. Math.; Internat. Dict. Phys. Elec.; Van Nostrand Sci. Encyc.

FECHNER, GUSTAV THEODOR. 1801-1887. German psychologist. See: Dict. Sci. Biog. Fechner('s) colors, Fechner fraction, Fechner-Helmholtz law, Fechnerian, Fechner's law, Fechner's paradox, Fechner's shadow experiment.

Fechner-Helmholtz law (Fechner, Gustav Theodor and Helmholtz, Hermann Ludwig Ferdinand von): Psychology. See: Drever.

Fechner-Weber law (Fechner, Gustav Theodor and Weber, Ernst Heinrich). See: Fechner's law.

Fechnerian (Fechner, Gustav Theodor): Physics. See: Webster's 3d.

Fechner's law (Fechner, Gustav Theodor): Physiology. See: Ballentyne; Chaplin; Drever. Also known as: Fechner-Weber law, Weber-Fecher law.

Fechner's paradox (Fechner, Gustav Theodor): Psychology. See: Chaplin; Drever; Wolman.

Fechner's shadow experiment (Fechner, Gustav Theodor): Psychology. See: Chaplin; English; Wolman.

FEDE, FRANCESCO. 1832-1913. Italian physician. See: World Who's Who Sci. Fede's disease, Riga-Fede syndrome.

FEDER, E. fl. 1907. German chemist. Cited in: Chem. Abstr., vol. 1, p. 1693; vol. 2, p. 1732. Feder solution for aldehydes, Feder test for hydrogen peroxide.

Feder solution for aldehydes (Feder, E.): Chemistry. See: Van Nostrand Chem. Dict.

Feder test for hydrogen peroxide (Feder, E.): Chemistry. See: Van Nostrand Chem. Dict.

FEDERICI, CESARE. 1832-1892. Italian physician. See: Biog. Lex. hervorr. Aerzte. Federici's sign.

Federici's sign (Federici, Cesare): Medicine. See: Dorland

Fede's disease (Fede, Francesco): Medicine. See: Dorland.

Fede's syndrome (Fede, Francesco). See: Riga-Fede syndrome.

Fedora (hat) (Romanoff, Fedora): Fashion. See: Mathews, M. M.

FEER, ADOLF. fl. 1889. Inventor. (Biography source unavailable.) Feertype.

FEER, WALTHER EMIL. 1864-1955. Swiss pediatrician. See: World Who's Who Sci. Feer's disease (or neurosis).

Feer's disease (or neurosis) (Feer, Walther Emil): Medicine. See: Dorland; Jablonski; Stedman. Also known as: Selter-Swift-Feer syndrome, Selter's disease, Swift-Feer syndrome, Swift's disease.

Feertype (Feer, Adolf): Photography. See: Focal Encyc. Photog.

FEGELER, FERDINAND. fl. 1949. German dermatologist. Cited in: Leiber and Olbrich. Fegeler's syndrome.

Fegeler's syndrome (Fegeler, Ferdinand): Medicine. See: Jablonski.

FEHLEISEN, FRIEDRICH. 1854-1924. German-born American physician. See: World Who's Who Sci. Fehleisen's streptococcus.

Fehleisen's streptococcus (Fehleisen, Friedrich): Medicine. See: Dorland.

Fehling, Hermann Christian von. See: Von Fehling, Hermann Christian.

Fehling('s) solution (or reagent) (Von Fehling, Hermann Christian): Chemistry. See: Ballentyne; Hackh; Van Nostrand Chem. Dict.; Van Nostrand Sci. Encyc.; Webster's 3d.

FEHR, OSKAR. b. 1871. German ophthalmologist. See: Biog. Lex. hervorr. Aerzte, 1880-1930. Fehr's dystrophy.

Fehr's dystrophy (Fehr, Oskar). See: Groenouw's dystrophy II.

FEICHTIGER, H. fl. 1943. German physician. Cited in: Leiber and Olbrich. Ullrich-Feichtiger syndrome.

Feigl-Anger test (Feigl, Friedrich and Anger, V.): Chemistry. See: Van Nostrand Chem. Dict.

Feigl-Chargav test reaction (Feigl, Friedrich and Chargaff, Erwin): Chemistry. See: Van Nostrand Chem. Dict.

Feigl–Demant test (Feigl, Friedrich and Demant, V.): Chemistry. See: Van Nostrand Chem. Dict.

Feigl–Frehden test (Feigl, Friedrich and Frehden, O.): Chemistry. See: Van Nostrand Chem. Dict.

FEIGL, FRIEDRICH. b. 1891. Austrian chemist. See: Pogg., vol. 6, 7a, 7b. Feigl–Anger test, Feigl–Chargav test reaction, Feigl–Demant test, Feigl–Frehden test, Feigl–Krumholz test for palladium, Feigl–Leitmeier test, Feigl micro–reaction for copper, Feigl micro–reaction for phosphate, Feigl–Neuber test for mercury, Feigl–Neuber test for tin, Feigl–Neuber tests for copper, Feigl–Pavelka test, Feigl–Pollak reagent for silver, Feigl reagent for copper, Feigl reagent for gold, silver, and palladium, Feigl reagent for sulfides, Feigl test for manganese, cerium, cobalt, and titanium, Feigl test for nickel, Feigl test reaction for antimony, Feigl test reaction for cerium, Feigl test reaction for mercuric salts, Feigl–Zappert–Vasquez test for acetic acid, Feigl–Zappert–Vasquez test for methyl ketones, Krumholz–Feigl–Rajmann reagent for palladium and platinum, Krumholz–Feigl–Rajmann reagent for zirconium, Leitmeier–Feigl test for chromium in minerals, Leitmeier–Feigl test for magnesium in minerals.

Feigl–Krumholz test for palladium (Feigl, Friedrich and Krumholz, P.): Chemistry. See: Van Nostrand Chem. Dict.

Feigl–Leitmeier test (Feigl, Friedrich and Leitmeier, Hans): Chemistry. See: Van Nostrand Chem. Dict.

Feigl micro–reaction for copper (Feigl, Friedrich): Chemistry. See: Van Nostrand Chem. Dict.

Feigl micro–reaction for phosphate (Feigl, Friedrich): Chemistry. See: Van Nostrand Chem. Dict.

Feigl–Neuber test for mercury (Feigl, Friedrich and Neuber, Fritz): Chemistry. See: Van Nostrand Chem. Dict.

Feigl–Neuber test for tin (Feigl, Friedrich and Neuber, Fritz): Chemistry. See: Van Nostrand Chem. Dict.

Feigl–Neuber tests for copper (Feigl, Friedrich and Neuber, Fritz): Chemistry. See: Van Nostrand Chem. Dict.

Feigl–Pavelka test (Feigl, Friedrich and Pavelka, Friedrich): Chemistry. See: Van Nostrand Chem. Dict.

Feigl–Pollak reagent for silver (Feigl, Friedrich and Pollak, Ignaz): Chemistry. See: Van Nostrand Chem. Dict.

Feigl reagent for copper (Feigl, Friedrich): Chemistry. See: Van Nostrand Chem. Dict.

Feigl reagent for gold, silver, and palladium (Feigl, Friedrich): Chemistry. See: Van Nostrand Chem. Dict.

Feigl reagent for sulfides (Feigl, Friedrich): Chemistry. See: Van Nostrand Chem. Dict.

Feigl test for manganese, cerium, cobalt, and tatanium (Feigl, Friedrich): Chemistry. See: Van Nostrand Chem. Dict.

Feigl test for nickel (Feigl, Friedrich): Chemistry. See: Van Nostrand Chem. Dict.

Feigl test reaction for antimony (Feigl, Friedrich): Chemistry. See: Van Nostrand Chem. Dict.

Feigl test reaction for cerium (Feigl, Friedrich): Chemistry. See: Van Nostrand Chem. Dict.

Feigl test reaction for mercuric salts (Feigl, Friedrich): Chemistry. See: Van Nostrand Chem. Dict.

Feigl–Zappert–Vasquez test for acetic acid (Feigl, Friedrich; Zappert, R.; and Vasquez, S.): Chemistry. See: Van Nostrand Chem. Dict.

Feigl–Zappert–Vasquez test for methyl ketones (Feigl, Friedrich; Zappert, R.; and Vasquez, S.): Chemistry. See: Van Nostrand Chem. Dict.

FEIJO, JUAN DA SILVA. fl. 19th c. Spanish naturalist. (Biography source unavailable.) Feijoa.

Feijoa (Feijo, Juan da Silva): Botany. See: Hendrickson; Mathews, M. M.; Taylor, N.

FEIL, ANDRE. b. 1884. French physician. Cited in: Mansell. Klippel–Feil syndrome.

Feinberg law (Derivation undetermined): Politics. See: Zadrozny.

FEISS, HENRY O. fl. 20th c. American orthopedic surgeon. (Biography source unavailable.) Feiss line.

Feiss line (Feiss, Henry O.): Medicine. See: Stedman.

Feist–Benary synthesis (Derivation undetermined): Chemistry. See: Van Nostrand Chem. Dict.

Feist reagent (Derivation undetermined): Chemistry. See: Van Nostrand Chem. Dict.

FEJER, LIPOT. 1880-1959. Hungarian mathematician. See: Dict. Sci. Biog. Fejer's theorem.

Fejer's theorem (Fejer, Lipot): Mathematics. See: Ballentyne; James.

FELDBERG, WILHELM SIEGMUND. 1900- . German-born English physiologist. See: World Who's Who Sci. Dale–Feldberg law.

FELDMAN, DAVID. 1921- . American physicist. See: World Who's Who Sci. Yang–Feldman formalism and the S-matrix.

FELDMAN, HARRY ALFRED. 1914- . American epidemologist. See: World Who's Who Sci. Sabin–Feldman dye test, Sabin–Feldman syndrome.

FELDMAN, SAMUEL. 1877-1947. Polish-born American dermatologist. See: Who's Who Among Physicians and Surg. Graham Little–Lassueur–Feldman syndrome.

FELDSTEIN, ERNEST. b. 1888. French physician. Cited in: Mansell. Klippel–Feldstein syndrome.

Feleki's instrument (Feleky, Hugo von): Medicine. See: Dorland.

FELEKY, HUGO VON. 1861-1932. Hungarian urologist. See: Biog. Lex. hervorr. Aerzte, 1880-1930. Feleki's instrument.

Felici balance (Felici, Noel Joseph): Physics. See: Hughes; Internat. Dict. Phys. Elec.

Felici generator (Felici, Noel Joseph): Physics. See: Hughes.

FELICI, NOEL JOSEPH. 1916- . French physicist. See: World Who's Who Sci. Felici balance, Felici generator.

Felicia (Felix): Botany. See: Taylor, N.

FELIX. No dates. German official. (Biography source unavailable.) Felicia.

FELIX, ARTHUR. 1887-1956. Polish-born bacteriologist. See: World Who's Who Sci. Weil–Felix reaction.

FELIX, ELISA (Stage name: MADEMOISELLE RACHEL). 1820-1858. French actress. See: New Encyc. Brit., 1974, Microp. Rachel (face powder), Raschel knitting.

FELIX, JULES. 1838-1912. French physician. See: Congres (16) Internat. Med., Budapest (1906), Album, p. 46. Felix's antiserum.

Felix's antiserum (Felix, Jules): Medicine. See: Stedman.

FELL. fl. 1868. Engineer. (Biography source unavailable.) Fell system.

FELL, GEORGE EDWARD. 1850-1918. American physician. See: World Who's Who Sci. Fell–O'Dwyer method.

FELL, JOHN. 1625-1686. English clergyman. See: Dict. Nat. Biog. Dr. Fell, Fell types.

Fell–O'Dwyer method (Fell, George Edward and O'Dwyer, Joseph P.): Medicine. See: Stedman.

Fell system (Fell): Engineering and Industry. See: Webster's 3d.

Fell types (Fell, John): Printing. See: Harrod; Hendrickson; Partridge.

FELLEGI, IVAN PETER. 1935- . Hungarian-born Canadian statistician. See: Amer. Men and Women Sci., 12th ed. (Soc. Behav. Sci.). Fellegi's method.

Fellegi's method (Fellegi, Ivan Peter): Statistics. See: Kendall.

FELLENIUS. fl. 1927. Swedish engineer. (Biography source unavailable.) Fellenius' circular arc method.

Fellenius' circular arc method (Fellenius): Earth Sciences. See: Thrush.

FELLER, WILLIAM. 1906- . Yugoslavian-born American mathematician. See: Pogg., vol. 7a. Lindeberg–Feller theorem.

Fels scales of parental behavior (Derivation undetermined): Psychology. See: Wolman.

FELSEN, JOSEPH. b. 1892. American gastroenterologist. See: Who's Who Among Physicians and Surg. Felsen's treatment.

Felsen's treatment (Felsen, Joseph): Medicine. See: Dorland.

FELTON, ALFRED. 1831-1904. English-Australian philanthropist. See: Australian Biog. Dict. Felton bequest.

Felton bequest (Felton, Alfred): Philanthropy. See: Osborne.

FELTON, LLOYD DERR. 1885-1953. American pathologist. See: Who's Who Amer. Med. Felton's method (or serum), Felton's unit.

Felton's method (or serum) (Felton, Lloyd Derr): Medicine. See: Dorland; Stedman.

Felton's unit (Felton, Lloyd Derr): Medicine. See: Dorland; Stedman.

FELTY, AUGUSTUS ROI. 1895- . American physician. See: Direct. Med. Specialists, 8th ed. Felty's syndrome.

Felty's syndrome (Felty, Augustus Roi): Medicine. See: Dorland; Jablonski; Stedman.

FENAROLI, PIERO. fl. 1909. Italian chemist. Cited in: Chem. Abstr., vol. 3, p. 322. Molinari-Fenaroli petroleum reaction.

FENDT, HEINRICH. fl. 1900. German physician. Cited in: Index-Cat. Libr. Surg.-Gen. Off., 2d Ser., vol. 5, 1900. Spiegler-Fendt sarcoid (or sarcomatosis).

Fenianism (or Fenians) (Fingal): Politics. See: Charnock; Wagner (Names).

FENNER, CLARENCE NORMAN. 1870-1949. American petrologist. See: Dict. Sci. Biog. Fenner trend.

Fenner trend (Fenner, Clarence Norman): Earth Sciences. Cited in: Dict. Sci. Biog.

Fenton-Barr test reactions (Fenton, Henry John Horstman and Barr, Guy): Chemistry. See: Van Nostrand Chem. Dict.

FENTON, HENRY JOHN HORSTMAN. 1854-1929. English chemist. See: World Who's Who Sci. Fenton-Barr test reactions, Fenton reagent for ketohexoses, Fenton test for malonic acid, Fenton test reaction for tartaric acid, Ruff-Fenton degradation.

Fenton reagent for ketohexoses (Fenton, Henry John Horstman): Chemistry. See: Van Nostrand Chem. Dict.

Fenton reagent for sodium (Derivation undetermined): Chemistry. See: Van Nostrand Chem. Dict.

Fenton test for malonic acid (Fenton, Henry John Horstman): Chemistry. See: Van Nostrand Chem. Dict.

Fenton test reaction for tartaric acid (Fenton, Henry John Horstman): Chemistry. See: Van Nostrand Chem. Dict.

Fenton's reagent (for oxidizing sugars and alcohols) (Derivation undetermined): Chemistry. See: Hackh.

FENWICK, EDWIN HURRY. 1856-1944. English physician. See: London Hosp. Gaz., vol. 47 (1944), p. 227. Fenwick's ulcer.

FENWICK, SAMUEL. 1821-1902. English physician. See: Biog. Lex. hervorr. Aerzte. Fenwick's disease.

Fenwick's disease (Fenwick, Samuel): Medicine. See: Dorland; Jablonski; Stedman.

Fenwick's ulcer (Fenwick, Edwin Hurry): Medicine. See: Jablonski.

FERBER, RUDOLPH. fl. 19th c. German mineralogist. Cited in: Bailey. Ferberite.

Ferberite (Ferber, Rudolph): Earth Sciences. See: Thrush; Van Nostrand Sci. Encyc.; Webster's 3d.

FERDINAND I. 1503-1564. Holy Roman emperor. See: Encyc. Brit., 1973. Treaty of Ferdinand.

FERE, CHARLES. 1852-1907. French neurologist. See: Sci., vol. 25 (1907), p. 917. Fere's method?

Fere-Langmead lipomatosis (Derivation undetermined): Medicine. See: Jablonski.

Fereol-Graux palsy (Fereol, Louis Henri Felix and Graux, Gaston): Medicine. See: Stedman.

FEREOL, LOUIS HENRI FELIX. 1825-1891. French physician. See: World Who's Who Sci. Fereol-Graux palsy, Fereol's nodes.

Fereol's nodes (Fereol, Louis Henri Felix): Medicine. See: Dorland; Stedman.

Fere's method (Fere, Charles?): Psychology. See: Chaplin.

FERET, RENE. b. 1861. French chemist. Cited in: Chem. Abstr., vol. 4, p. 504. Ferets law.

Ferets law (Feret, Rene): Engineering and Industry. See: Thrush.

Ferguson classification of bridges (Derivation undetermined): Physics. See: Internat. Dict. Phys. Elec.

FERGUSON, HARRY GEORGE. 1884-1960. English industrialist. See: World Who's Who Sci. Ferguson-Teramala transmission, Ferguson transmission.

FERGUSON, JAMES. 1710-1776. Scottish astronomer and instrument maker. See: Dict. Sci. Biog. Ferguson's mechanical paradox.

FERGUSON, ROBERT. 1799-1865. Scottish physician. See: Dict. Nat. Biog. Fergusonite.

Ferguson Smith. See: Smith, John Ferguson.

Ferguson Smith's epithelioma (or keratoacanthoma) (Smith, John Ferguson): Medicine. See: Jablonski.

Ferguson-Teramala transmission (Ferguson, Harry George and Salerni, Piero Giri de Teramala): Engineering and Industry. See: Auger.

Ferguson transmission (Ferguson, Harry George): Engineering and Industry. See: Auger.

Fergusonite (Ferguson, Robert): Earth Sciences. See: Charnock; Partridge; Thrush.

Ferguson's mechanical paradox (Ferguson, James): Engineering and Industry. See: Auger.

FERGUSSON, SIR WILLIAM. 1808-1877. Scottish surgeon. See: Dict. Nat. Biog. Fergusson's incision, Fergusson's speculum.

Fergusson's incision (Fergusson, Sir William): Medicine. See: Dorland; Stedman.

Fergusson's speculum (Fergusson, Sir William): Medicine. See: Dorland; Stedman.

Fermat('s) last theorem (Fermat, Pierre de): Mathematics. See: Ballentyne; Blumberg; Thewlis.

Fermat numbers (Fermat, Pierre de): Mathematics. See: James.

FERMAT, PIERRE DE. 1601-1665. French mathematician. See: Dict. Sci. Biog. Fermat('s) last theorem, Fermat numbers, Fermat('s) principle (or law), Fermat's theorem.

Fermat('s) principle (or law) (Fermat, Pierre de): Physics. See: Ballentyne; Huschke; Van Nostrand Sci. Encyc.

Fermat's theorem (Fermat, Pierre de): Mathematics. See: Ballentyne; James.

Fermi age (Fermi, Enrico): Physics. See: Hughes; Markus; Thewlis.

Fermi age model (Fermi, Enrico): Physics. See: Internat. Dict. Phys. Elec.; Markus; Van Nostrand Sci. Encyc.

FERMI, CLAUDIO. b. 1862. Italian physician. See: Biog. Lex. hervorr. Aerzte, 1880-1930. Fermi vaccine.

Fermi constant (Fermi, Enrico): Physics. See: Ballentyne; Internat. Dict. Ap. Math.; Thewlis.

Fermi-Dirac distribution function (Fermi, Enrico and Dirac, Paul Adrien Maurice): Physics. See: Internat. Dict. Ap. Math.; Internat. Dict. Phys. Elec.; Markus.

Fermi-Dirac gas (Fermi, Enrico and Dirac, Paul Adrien Maurice): Physics. See: Internat. Dict. Ap. Math.; Internat. Dict. Phys. Elec.

Fermi-Dirac liquid (Fermi, Enrico and Dirac, Paul Adrien Maurice): Physics. See: Internat. Dict. Ap. Math.

Fermi-Dirac-Sommerfield velocity-distribution law (Fermi, Enrico; Dirac, Paul Adrien Maurice; and Sommerfeld, Arnold Johannes): Physics. See: Markus.

Fermi-Dirac statistics (Fermi, Enrico and Dirac, Paul Adrien Maurice): Physics. See: Ballentyne; Internat. Dict. Ap. Math.; Markus. Also known as: Fermi statistics.

Fermi distribution (Fermi, Enrico): Physics. See: Hughes; Internat. Dict. Phys. Elec.

Fermi energy (Fermi, Enrico): Physics. See: Internat. Dict. Ap. Math.; Internat. Dict. Phys. Elec.

FERMI, ENRICO. 1901-1954. Italian-born American physicist. See: Dict. Sci. Biog. Fermi age, Fermi age model, Fermi constant, Fermi-Dirac distribution function, Fermi-Dirac gas, Fermi-Dirac liquid, Fermi-Dirac-Sommerfield velocity-distribution law, Fermi-Dirac statistics, Fermi distribution, Fermi energy, Fermi hole, Fermi interaction, Fermi level (or brim), Fermi plot, Fermi potential, Fermi resonance (or perturbations), Fermi selection rules (for beta decay), Fermi surface, Fermi temperature, Fermi theory of beta decay, Fermi theory of cosmic ray acceleration, Fermi (unit), Fermion, Fermi's 'golden' rule, Fermium, Thomas-Fermi differential equation, Thomas-Fermi model.

Fermi hole (Fermi, Enrico): Physics. See: Internat. Dict. Ap. Math.; Internat. Dict. Phys. Elec.

Fermi interaction (Fermi, Enrico): Physics. See: Internat. Dict. Phys. Elec.; Thewlis.

Fermi level (or brim) (Fermi, Enrico): Physics. See: Internat. Dict. Ap. Math.; Internat. Dict. Phys. Elec.; Markus.

Fermi plot (Fermi, Enrico). See: Kurie plot.

Fermi potential (Fermi, Enrico): Physics. See: Hughes; Internat. Dict. Phys. Elec.

Fermi resonance (or perturbations) (Fermi, Enrico): Physics. See: Internat. Dict. Ap. Math.; Internat. Dict. Phys. Elec.; Van Nostrand Sci. Encyc.

Fermi selection rules (for beta decay) (Fermi, Enrico): Physics. See: Ballentyne; Hughes; Markus; Van Nostrand Sci. Encyc.

Fermi statistics (Fermi, Enrico). See: Fermi-Dirac statistics.

Fermi surface (Fermi, Enrico): Physics. See: Internat. Dict. Phys. Elec.; Thewlis.

Fermi temperature (Fermi, Enrico): Physics. See: Hughes; Internat. Dict. Ap. Math.; Internat. Dict. Phys. Elec.

Fermi theory of beta decay (Fermi, Enrico): Physics. See: Internat. Dict. Ap. Math.; Internat. Dict. Phys. Elec.; Thewlis.

Fermi theory of cosmic ray acceleration (Fermi, Enrico): Physics. See: Internat. Dict. Ap. Math.; Internat. Dict. Phys. Elec.

Fermi (unit) (Fermi, Enrico): Physics. See: Ballentyne; Dresner; Internat. Dict. Phys. Elec.

Fermi vaccine (Fermi, Claudio): Medicine. See: Stedman.

Fermion (Fermi, Enrico): Physics. See: Markus; Thewlis; Van Nostrand Sci. Encyc.

Fermi's 'golden' rule (Fermi, Enrico): Physics. See: Ballentyne.

Fermium (Fermi, Enrico): Physics. See: Internat. Dict. Phys. Elec.; Markus; Thrush.

FERMOR, LEWIS LEIGH. 1880-1954. English geologist. See: World Who's Who Sci. Fermorite.

Fermorite (Fermor, Lewis Leigh): Earth Sciences. See: Partridge; Thrush; Webster's 3d.

FERNALD, GRACE MAXWELL. b. 1879. American psychologist. See: Amer. Men Sci., 3d ed. Fernald-Keller approach.

Fernald-Keller approach (Fernald, Grace Maxwell and Keller, Helen Bass): Education. See: Good.

FERNANDEZ, OLEDULIO. fl. 1914. Spanish chemist. Cited in: Chem. Abstr., vol. 8, p. 3405. Dorronsoro-Fernandez test.

FERNANDINI, EULAGIO E. fl. 20th c. Peruvian mine owner. Cited in: Min. Mag., vol. 17 (1916), p. 349. Fernandinite.

Fernandinite (Fernandini, Eulagio E.): Earth Sciences. See: Thrush.

FERNBACH, AUGUSTE. 1860-1939. French microbiologist. See: Ann. Univers., vol. 14 (1939), p. 206. Fernbach (Fernback) flask.

Fernbach (Fernback) flask (Fernbach, Auguste): Chemistry. See: Stedman; Van Nostrand Chem. Dict.

Feronia (Feronia, the fountain goddess): Botany. See: Partridge.

FERONIA, THE FOUNTAIN GODDESS. Italic goddess. See: Encyc. Brit., 1973. Feronia.

FERRAND, MARCEL. 1878-1940. French physician. Cited in: Mansell. Darier-Ferrand dermatofibrosarcoma (or dermatofibroma).

Ferranti effect (Ferranti, Sebastian Ziani de): Electronics. See: Ballentyne.

FERRANTI, SEBASTIAN ZIANI DE. 1864-1930. English electrical engineer. See: Dict. Nat. Biog., 1922-1930. Ferranti effect.

FERRARA, ANDREA. fl. 16th c. Italian broadsword-maker. See: Webster's Biog. Dict. Andrea Ferrara (sword).

Ferrari cement (Ferrari, F.): Engineering and Industry. See: Thrush.

FERRARI, E. fl. 1915. Italian chemist. Cited in: Chem. Abstr., vol. 9, p. 2523. Oddo-Ferrari test reaction for aldehydes.

FERRARI, F. fl. 1923. Italian chemist. Cited in: Chem. Abstr., vol. 17, p. 1315. Ferrari cement.

FERRARI, GIOVANNI BATTISTA. 1584-1653. Italian Jesuit and botanical writer. See: Ascherson and Graebner. Ferraria.

FERRARI, LUDOVICO. 1522-1565. Italian mathematician. See: Dict. Sci. Biog. Ferrari's solution of the quartic.

Ferraria (Ferrari, Giovanni Battista): Botany. See: Charnock.

Ferraris furnace (Derivation undetermined): Engineering and Industry. See: Thrush.

Ferraris screen (Derivation undetermined): Engineering and Industry. See: Thrush.

Ferrari's solution of the quartic (Ferrari, Ludovico): Mathematics. See: James.

Ferraris table (Derivation undetermined): Engineering and Industry. See: Thrush.

Ferraris truss (Derivation undetermined): Engineering and Industry. See: Thrush.

FERRATA, ADOLFO. 1880-1946. Italian physician. See: Biog. Lex. hervorr. Aerzte, 1880-1930. Ferrata's cell.

Ferrata's cell (Ferrata, Adolfo): Medicine. See: Dorland.

FERRATON, LOUIS. b. 1860. French surgeon. Cited in: Index-Cat. Libr. Surg.-Gen. Off., 2d Ser., vol. 5, 1900. Perrin-Ferraton disease.

FERREIN, ANTOINE. 1693-1769. French surgeon and anatomist. See: Dict. Sci. Biog. Ferrein's canal, Ferrein's cords, Ferrein's foramen, Ferrein's ligament, Ferrein's pyramid, Ferrein's tube(s), Ferrein's vasa aberrantia.

Ferrein's canal (Ferrein, Antoine): Medicine. See: Donath; Stedman.

Ferrein's cords (Ferrein, Antoine): Medicine. See: Dorland; Stedman.

Ferrein's foramen (Ferrein, Antoine): Medicine. See: Dorland; Stedman.

Ferrein's ligament (Ferrein, Antoine): Medicine. See: Donath; Dorland; Stedman.

Ferrein's pyramid (Ferrein, Antoine): Medicine. See: Donath; Dorland; Stedman.

Ferrein's tube(s) (Ferrein, Antoine): Medicine. See: Dorland; Stedman. Also known as: Schachowa's tube.

Ferrein's vasa aberrantia (Ferrein, Antoine): Medicine. See: Stedman.

Ferreira Da Silva solution (Derivation undetermined): Chemistry. See: Van Nostrand Chem. Dict.

Ferrel('s) law (Ferrel, William): Earth Sciences. See: Internat. Dict. Phys. Elec.; Monkhouse; Moore.

FERREL, WILLIAM. 1817-1891. American meteorologist. See: Dict. Sci. Biog. Ferrel('s) law.

Ferrers' case (Ferrers, George): Law. See: Steinberg.

FERRERS, GEORGE. 1500?-1579. English politician and poet. See: Webster's Biog. Dict. Ferrers' case.

FERRI, ALPHONSO. 1515-1595. Italian surgeon. See: Nouv. Biog. Univ. Alphonsin (surgical instrument).

FERRIER, DAVID. 1843-1928. Scottish-born neurologist. See: Dict. Sci. Biog. Ferrier's experiment.

FERRIER, PAUL. fl. 1906. French physician. Cited in: Mansell. Ferrier's method (or treatment).

FERRIER, WALTER FREDERICK. fl. 1920. Canadian mineralogist. Cited in: Min. Mag., vol. 18 (1919), p. 378-379. Ferrierite.

Ferrierite (Ferrier, Walter Frederick): Earth Sciences. See: Thrush.

Ferrier's experiment (Ferrier, David): Psychology. See: Drever; Wolman.

Ferrier's method (or treatment) (Ferrier, Paul): Medicine. See: Dorland

Ferriertypes (Derivation undetermined): Printing. See: Wagner (Names).

Ferris bile duct scoop and dilator (Ferris, Deward Olmstead): Medicine. Cited in: World Who's Who Sci.

FERRIS, DEWARD OLMSTEAD. 1907- . Canadian-born American surgeon. See: World Who's Who Sci. Ferris bile duct scoop and dilator.

FERRIS, GEORGE WASHINGTON GALE. 1859-1896. American engineer. See: Dict. Amer. Biog. Ferris wheel.

Ferris wheel (Ferris, George): Engineering and Industry. See: Hendrickson; Mathews, M. M.; Partridge.

Ferro, Alphonsin. See: Ferri, Alphonsin.

Ferruccite (Zambonini, Ferrucci): Earth Sciences. See: Webster's 3d.

FERRY, ERWIN SIDNEY. 1868-1956. American physicist. See: World Who's Who Sci. Ferry-Porter law.

Ferry-Porter law (Ferry, Erwin Sidney and Porter, Thomas Cunningham): Physics. See: Chaplin; Internat. Dict. Phys. Elec.; Stedman. Also known as: Porter's law.

FERSMAN, ALEKSANDR EVGENIEVICH. 1883-1945. Russian mineralogist. See: Dict. Sci. Biog. Fersmanite (or Fersmannite), Fersman's law, Fersmite.

Fersmanite (or Fersmannite) (Fersman, Aleksandr Evgenievich): Earth Sciences. See: Thrush; Webster's 3d.

Fersman's law (Fersman, Aleksandr Evgenievich): Earth Sciences. See: Thrush.

Fersmite (Fersman, Aleksandr Evgenievich): Earth Sciences. See: Thrush; Webster's 3d.

Fery calorimeter (Fery, Charles): Physics. See: Hackh.

FERY, CHARLES. 1865-1935. French physicist. See: World Who's Who Sci. Fery calorimeter, Fery prism, Fery radiation pyrometer, Fery refractometer, Fery spectrograph.

Fery prism (Fery, Charles): Physics. See: Internat. Dict. Phys. Elec.

Fery radiation pyrometer (Fery, Charles): Physics. See: Thrush.

Fery refractometer (Fery, Charles): Physics. See: Hackh.

Fery spectrograph (Fery, Charles): Physics. See: Thewlis.

Fess-Kenyon Act (Fess, Simeon Davison and Kenyon, William Squire): Politics. See: Smith.

FESS, SIMEON DAVISON. 1861-1936. American educator and legislator. See: Biog. Direct. Amer. Congress. Fess-Kenyon Act.

Fessenden oscillator (Fessenden, Reginald Aubrey): Electronics. See: Hughes; Internat. Dict. Phys. Elec.; Van Nostrand Sci. Encyc.

FESSENDEN, REGINALD AUBREY. 1866-1932. Canadian-born American radio engineer. See: Dict. Sci. Biog. Fessenden oscillator.

Feuerbach circle (Feuerbach, Karl Wilhelm): Mathematics. See: Ballentyne.

FEUERBACH, KARL WILHELM. 1800-1834. German mathematician. See: Dict. Sci. Biog. Feuerbach circle.

FEUERBACH, LUDWIG ANDREAS VON. 1804-1872. German philosopher. See: Encyc. Brit., 1973. Feuerbachian.

Feuerbachian (Feuerbach, Ludwig Andreas von): Philosophy. See: Webster's 3d.

FEUERHEERD, E. fl. 1919. English? engineer. (Biography source unavailable.) Feuerheerd pump.

Feuerheerd pump (Feuerheerd, E.): Engineering and Industry. See: Auger.

FEUILLEE, LOUIS. 1660-1732. French monk, traveller and botanist. See: Dict. Sci. Biog. Fevillea (Feuillea).

FEULGEN, ROBERT JOACHIM. 1884-1955. German biochemist. See: Dict. Sci. Biog. Feulgen('s) test (or reaction).

Feulgen('s) test (or reaction) (Feulgen, Robert Joachim): Chemistry. See: Dorland; Hackh; Stedman.

Fevillea (Feuillea) (Feuillee, Louis): Botany. See: Charnock.

FEVOLD, HARRY LEONARD. 1902- . American biochemist. See: World Who's Who Sci. Fevold test.

Fevold test (Fevold, Harry Leonard): Medicine. See: Stedman.

Fevre-Languepin syndrome (Fevre, Marcel Paul Louis Edmond and Languepin, Anne): Medicine. See: Jablonski. Also known as: Champion-Cregan-Klein syndrome.

FEVRE, MARCEL PAUL LOUIS EDMOND. 1897- . French physician. See: Who's Who France, 1961-1962. Fevre-Languepin syndrome.

Feynman diagram (Feynman, Richard Phillips): Physics. See: Ballentyne; Hughes; Internat. Dict. Phys. Elec.

Feynman-Gell-Mann theory (Feynman, Richard Phillips and Gell-Mann, Murray): Physics. See: Internat. Dict. Phys. Elec.

Feynman method (Feynman, Richard Phillips): Physics. See: Internat. Dict. Ap. Math.

Feynman positron theory (Feynman, Richard Phillips): Physics. See: Internat. Dict. Ap. Math.; Internat. Dict. Phys. Elec.

FEYNMAN, RICHARD PHILLIPS. 1918- . American physicist. See: World Who's Who Sci. Feynman diagram, Feynman-Gell-Mann theory, Feynman method, Feynman positron theory, Feynman theory of liquid helium, Hellman-Feynmann theorem, Wheeler-Feynman theory.

Feynman theory of liquid helium (Feynman, Richard Phillips): Physics. See: Internat. Dict. Ap. Math.; Internat. Dict. Phys. Elec.

FEYRTER, FRIEDRICH. 1895- . Austrian pathologist. See: World Who's Who Sci. Feyrter's disease.

Feyrter's disease (Feyrter, Friedrich): Medicine. See: Jablonski.

Fiacre (cab) (Fiacre, Saint): Engineering and Industry. See: Hargrave; Hendrickson.

FIACRE (FIACHRACH), SAINT. 600-670. Irish nobleman. See: Dict. Nat. Biog. Fiacre (cab), Saint Fiacre's disease.

FIAMBERTI, ADAMO MARIO. b. 1894. Italian psychiatrist. See: Diz. Encic. Ital. Fiamberti hypothesis.

Fiamberti hypothesis (Fiamberti, Adamo Mario): Psychiatry. See: Hinsie.

fiber(s) of Mueller (Mueller, Heinrich). See: Mueller's fibers.

fibers of Remak (Remak, Robert). See: Remak's fibers.

fibers of Sharpey (Sharpey, William). See: Sharpey's fibers.

Fibiger-Debre-Von Gierke syndrome (Fibiger, Johannes Andreas Grib; Debre, Robert; and Von Gierke, Edgar Otto Konrad). See: Debre-Fibiger syndrome.

FIBIGER, JOHANNES ANDREAS GRIB. 1867-1928. Danish pathologist. See: World Who's Who Sci. Debre-Fibiger syndrome.

FIBONACCI, LEONARDO. 1180?-1250. Italian mathematician. See: Dict. Sci. Biog. Fibonacci numbers (series or sequence).

Fibonacci numbers (series or sequence) (Fibonacci, Leonardo): Mathematics. See: Barnhart (New Eng.); James; Markus.

FICHTE, JOHANN GOTTLIEB. 1762-1814. German philosopher. See: Encyc. Brit., 1973. Fichtean (or Fichteanism).

Fichtean (or Fichteanism) (Fichte, Johann Gottlieb): Philosophy. See: Webster's 3d.

FICK, ADOLF EUGEN. 1829-1901. German physiologist. See: Dict. Sci. Biog. Fickian diffusion, Fick's law.

FICK, RUDOLPH ARMIN. 1866-1939. German anatomist. See: World Who's Who Sci. Fick's bacillus.

FICKER, PHILIPP MARTIN. 1868-1950. German bacteriologist. See: World Who's Who Sci. Ficker's diagnosticum.

Ficker's diagnosticum (Ficke, Philipp Martin): Medicine. See: Dorland.

Fickian diffusion (Fick, Adolf Eugen): Physics. See: Internat. Dict. Ap. Math.

FICKLEN, JOSEPH BURWELL, III. 1902- . American chemical engineer. See: World Who's Who Sci. Cook-Ficklen benzene apparatus, Ficklen-Ott dust camera, Ficklen-Strong thermal precipitators.

Ficklen-Ott dust camera (Ficklen, Joseph Burwell III and Ott, Lawrence H.): Engineering and Industry. Cited in: World Who's Who Sci.

Ficklen-Strong thermal precipitators (Ficklen, Joseph Burwell III and Strong, William Walker?): Engineering and Industry. Cited in: World Who's Who Sci.

Fick's bacillus (Fick, Rudolph Armin): Medicine. See: Dorland.

Fick's law (Fick, Adolf Eugen): Physics. See: Ballentyne; Hughes; Markus.

fidas Achates (Achates): (faithful companion) Generic Word. See: Brewer; Partridge.

Fidelism (Castro, Fidel). See: Castroism.

Fidler-Maxwell kiln (Derivation undetermined): Engineering and Industry. See: Thrush.

FIEDLER, CARL LUDWIG ALFRED. 1835-1921. German physician. See: World Who's Who Sci. Fiedler's disease, Fiedler's myocarditis (or syndrome).

Fiedler's disease (Fiedler, Carl Ludwig Alfred). See: Weil's disease.

Fiedler's myocarditis (or syndrome) (Fiedler, Carl Ludwig Alfred): Medicine. See: Jablonski. Also known as: Abramov-Fiedler myocarditis.

FIEHE, J. fl. 1909. German chemist. Cited in: Chem. Abstr., vol. 3, pp. 83, 2836. Fiehe reagent for artificial honey, Fiehe test for glucose.

Fiehe reagent for artificial honey (Fiehe, J.): Chemistry. See: Van Nostrand Chem. Dict.

Fiehe test for glucose (Fiehe, J.): Chemistry. See: Van Nostrand Chem. Dict.

Field boiler (Field, E.): Engineering and Industry. See: Auger.

Field codes (Field, David Dudley): Law. See: Latham.

Field cycle (Field, J. F.): Engineering and Industry. See: Auger.

FIELD, DAVID DUDLEY. 1805-1894. American lawyer. See: Dict. Amer. Biog. Field codes.

FIELD, E. fl. 1862. English engineer. (Biography source unavailable.) Field boiler.

FIELD, F. No dates. Mineralogist. Cited in: Bailey. Fieldite.

FIELD, J. F. fl. 1950. English? engineer. (Biography source unavailable.) Field cycle.

FIELDING, GEORGE HUNSLEY. 1801-1871. English anatomist and ophthalmologist. See: Biog. Lex. hervorr. Aerzte. Fielding's membrane.

Fielding's membrane (Fielding, George Hunsley): Medicine. See: Donath; Dorland; Stedman.

Fieldite (Field, F.): Earth Sciences. See: Thrush.

FIELLER, E. C. fl. 1940. English statistician. Cited in: Mansell. Fieller's theorem.

Fieller's theorem (Fieller, E. C.): Statistics. See: Kendall.

FIESCHI, GIUSEPPE MARIA. 1790-1836. Corsican conspirator. See: Encyc. Brit., 1973. Fieschi's plot.

Fieschi's plot (Fieschi, Giuseppe Maria): History. See: Harbottle.

FIESER, LOUIS FREDERICK. 1899- . American chemist. See: World Who's Who Sci. Fieser's (Feiser) solution.

Fieser's (Feiser) solution (Fieser, Louis Frederick): Chemistry. See: Ballentyne; Hackh.

Fiessinger-Leroy-Reiter syndrome (Fiessinger, Noel; Leroy, Emile?; and Reiter, Hans). See: Reiter's disease (or triad).

Fiessinger-Leroy syndrome (Fiessinger, Noel and Leroy, Emile?). See: Reiter's disease (or triad).

FIESSINGER, NOEL. 1881-1946. French physician. See: Dict. Sci. Biog. Fiessinger-Leroy-Reiter syndrome, Fiessinger-Rendu syndrome.

Fiessinger-Rendu syndrome (Fiessinger, Noel and Rendu, Henry Jules Louis Marie). See: Stevens-Johnson syndrome.

Figaro (Figaro, the rogue): Generic Word (witty roguery). See: Brewer.

Figaro sauce (Figaro, the rogue): Food and Drink. See: De Sola; Webster's 3d.

FIGARO, THE ROGUE. Hero of two comedies by Beaumarchais and several operas. See: Benet. Figaro, Figaro sauce.

FIGUEIRA, FERNANDES. d. 1928. Brazilian pediatrician. See: Amer. Acad. Ped., District IX Informe, Wash., 1947, p. 26. Figueira's syndrome.

Figueira's syndrome (Figueira, Fernandes): Medicine. See: Dorland; Stedman.

Figuier's gold purple (Derivation undetermined): Chemistry. See: Thrush.

Filatov-Gillies tubed pedicle (Filatow, Wladimir Petrovich and Gillies, Sir Harold Delf): Medicine. See: Stedman.

FILATOV, NILS FEODOROVICH. 1847-1902. Russian pediatrician. See: World Who's Who Sci. Dukes-Filatov disease, Filatov's disease, Filatov's spots.

Filatov's disease (Filatov, Nils Feodorovich): Medicine. See: Dorland; Jablonski; Stedman. Also known as: Pfeiffer's disease, Tuerk's lymphomatosis.

Filatov's spots (Filatov, Nils Feodorovich): Medicine. See: Stedman. Also known as: Koplik('s) spots.

FILATOW, WLADIMIR PETROVICH. 1875-1956. Russian ophthalmologist. See: Biog. Lex. hervorr. Aerzte, 1880-1930. Filatov-Gillies tubed pedicle.

Filbert (nut) (Philibert, Saint): Botany. See: Charnock; Hargrave; Hendrickson; Partridge; Webster's 3d.

Filhol test (Derivation undetermined): Chemistry. See: Van Nostrand Chem. Dict.

FILIPOVITCH, CASIMIR. fl. 1870. Polish physician. (Biography source unavailable.) Filipovitch's (Filipowicz's) sign.

Filipovitch's (Filipowicz's) sign (Filipovitch, Casimir): Medicine. See: Dorland.

Filippi, Filippo de. See: De Filippi, Filippo.

Filippi's gland(s) (De Filippi, Filippo?): Zoology. See: Gray; Henderson.

Filippo (coin) (Filippo Maria): Numismatics. See: Charnock.

FILIPPO MARIA. 1392-1447. Viscount and Duke of Milan. See: Encic. Ital. Filippo (coin).

FILLMORE, MILLARD. 1800-1874. American president. See: Dict. Amer. Biog. Fillmoreite.

Fillmoreite (Fillmore, Millard): History. See: Mathews, M. M.

FILLOW, A. N. fl. 19th c. American mine owner. Cited in: Bailey. Fillowite.

Fillowite (Fillow, A. N.): Earth Sciences. See: Webster's 3d.

FILOMUSI-GUELFI, GIOELE. b. 1855. Italian physician. Cited in: Royal Soc. Cat. Sci. Pap., 1884-1900. Filomusi-Guelfi test.

Filomusi-Guelfi test (Filomusi-Guelfi, Gioele): Chemistry. See: Van Nostrand Chem. Dict.

Fimmenite (Derivation undetermined): Earth Sciences. See: Thrush.

Finagle factor (Derivation undetermined): Sociology. See: Martin.

Finagle's laws (Derivation undetermined): Sociology. See: Martin.

FINCKH, JOHANN. b. 1873. German psychiatrist. (Biography source unavailable.) Finckh test.

Finckh test (Finckh, Johann): Medicine. See: Dorland; Stedman.

FINDEISEN, THEODOR ROBERT WALTER. 1909-1945. German meteorologist. See: World Who's Who Sci. Bergeron-Findeisen theory.

FINGAL (FINN or FIONN). Gaelic semimythological hero. See: Benet. Fenianism (or Fenians).

FINIKOFF. No dates. Russian surgeon. (Biography source unavailable.) Finikoff's method (or treatment).

Finikoff's method (or treatment) (Finikoff): Medicine. See: Dorland.

FINK, ALBERT. 1827-1897. German-born American railroad engineer. See: Who Was Who Amer., 1607-1896. Fink (or ratfink)?

Fink control (Fink, Pius): Engineering and Industry. See: Auger.

Fink (or ratfink) (Fink, Albert?): Generic Word. See: Hendrickson.

FINK, PIUS. fl. 1857. German engineer. Cited in: Mansell. Fink control.

FINKELSTEIN, HEINRICH. 1865-1942. German pediatrist. See: World Who's Who Sci. Finkelstein's albumin milk.

Finkelstein's albumin milk (Finkelstein, Heinrich): Medicine. See: Dorland.

FINKLEDEY, W. fl. 20th c. German pathologist. (Biography source unavailable.) Warthin-Finkledey cells.

FINKLER, DITTMAR. 1852-1912. German bacteriologist. See: Sci., vol. 45 (1912), p. 449. Finkler-Prior spirillum.

Finkler-Prior spirillum (Finkler, Dittmar and Prior, J.): Medicine. See: Dorland.

FINLAY, CLARE L. d. 1936. English inventor. Cited in: Chem. Abstr., vol. 27, p. 674. Finlay colour (or process).

Finlay colour (or process) (Finlay, Clare L.): Photography. See: Focal Encyc. Photog.; Webster's 3d.

FINN, MICKEY. fl. 19th c. American underworld figure. (Biography source unavailable.) Mickey Finn.

FINNEMAN, K. J. fl. 20th c. Swedish mineralogist. Cited in: Bailey. Finnemanite.

Finnemanite (Finneman, K. J.): Earth Sciences. See: Webster's 3d.

FINNEY, JOHN MILLER TURPIN. 1863-1942. American surgeon. See: Who Was Who Amer., 1943-1950. Finney pyloroplasty, Finney's operation.

Finney pyloroplasty (Finney, John Miller Turpin): Medicine. See: Stedman.

Finney's operation (Finney, John Miller Turpin): Medicine. See: Dorland; Stedman.

FINOCHIETTO, ENRIQUE. 1881-1948. Argentinian surgeon. See: Ann. Surg., vol. 128 (1948), p. 319. Finochietto's stirrup.

Finochietto's stirrup (Finochietto, Enrique): Medicine. See: Dorland.

Finsen bath (Finsen, Niels Ryberg): Medicine. See: Dorland.

Finsen light (or lamp) (Finsen, Niels Ryberg): Electronics. See: Dorland; Hackh; Partridge.

Finsen method (Finsen, Niels Ryberg): Medicine. See: Stedman.

FINSEN, NIELS RYBERG. 1860-1904. Danish physician. See: Dict. Sci. Biog. Finsen bath, Finsen light (or lamp), Finsen method, Finsen unit.

Finsen unit (Finsen, Niels Ryberg): Physics. See: Dresner.

FINSTERER, HANS. 1877-1955. Austrian surgeon. See: World Who's Who Sci. Finsterer's operation.

Finsterer's operation (Finsterer, Hans): Medicine. See: Stedman. Also known as: Hofmeister's operation.

FIOCCA, RUFINO. fl. 1893. Italian physician. (Biography source unavailable.) Fiocca's stain.

Fiocca's stain (Fiocca, Rufino): Medicine. See: Stedman.

FIRM, JOSEPH LANNISON. b. 1837. American inventor. See: Who Was Who Amer., 1961-1968. Firm press.

Firm press (Firm, Joseph Lannison): Printing. See: Lockwood.

First law of Laplace (Laplace, Pierre-Simon, Marquis de). See: Laplace distribution.

FIRTH, JOHN RUPERT. 1890-1960. English linguist. See: Sebeok, vol. 2. Firthian linguistics.

Firthian linguistics (Firth, John Rupert): Linguistics. See: Hartmann.

FISCH, L. fl. 1956. English physician. (Biography source unavailable.) Fisch-Renwick syndrome.

Fisch-Renwick syndrome (Fisch, L. and Renwick, T. K.): Medicine. See: Jablonski.

FISCHER, EMIL HERMANN. 1852-1919. German chemist. See: Dict. Sci. Biog. Fischer indole synthesis, Fischer peptide (or polypeptide) synthesis, Fischer phenylhydrazone and osazone reaction, Fischer reagent for aldehydes and ketones, Fischer's projection formulas, Fischer's test, Kiliani-Fischer synthesis, Penzoldt-Fischer test for aldehydes and phenols.

FISCHER, ERNST SIGISMUND. 1875-1954. Austrian mathematician. See: World Who's Who Sci. Riesz-Fischer theorem.

FISCHER, FRANZ JOSEF EMIL. 1877-1947. German chemist. See: World Who's Who Sci. Ficher-Tropsch process.

FISCHER, H. fl. 1921. German dermatologist. Cited in: Leiber and Olbrich. Fischer's syndrome.

FISCHER, HANS. 1881-1945. German physician. See: Biog. Lex. hervorr. Aerzte, 1880-1930. Neubauer-Fischer test.

Fischer indole synthesis (Fischer, Emil Hermann): Chemistry. See: Ballentyne; Van Nostrand Chem. Dict.

Fischer-Jennings test (Derivation undetermined): Chemistry. See: Van Nostrand Chem. Dict.

FISCHER, KARL. fl. 1935. German chemist. Cited in: Chem. Abstr., vol. 29, p. 6532. Karl Fischer reagent.

FISCHER, LOUIS. 1864-1945. Austrian-born American pediatrician. See: World Who's Who Sci. Fischer's murmur (or cerebral murmur), Fischer's sign, Fischer's symptom.

FISCHER, MARTIN HENRY. 1879-1962. German-born American physician. See: Who Was Who Amer., 1961-1968. Fischer's solution, Fischer's treatment.

FISCHER, NICOLAUS WOLFGANG. 1782-1850. German chemist. See: Dict. Sci. Biog. Fischer's salt.

Fischer oxazole synthesis (Derivation undetermined): Chemistry. See: Van Nostrand Chem. Dict.

Fischer peptide (or polypeptide) synthesis (Fischer, Emil Hermann): Chemistry. See: Ballentyne; Van Nostrand Chem. Dict.

Fischer phenylhydrazine synthesis (Derivation undetermined): Chemistry. See: Van Nostrand Chem. Dict.

Fischer phenylhydrazone and osazone reaction (Fischer, Emil Hermann): Chemistry. See: Van Nostrand Chem. Dict.

Fischer reagent for aldehydes and ketones (Fischer, Emil Hermann): Chemistry. See: Van Nostrand Chem. Dict.

Fischer reagent for beryllium (Derivation undetermined): Chemistry. See: Van Nostrand Chem. Dict.

Fischer reagent for metals (Derivation undetermined): Chemistry. See: Van Nostrand Chem. Dict.

Fischer reagent for water (Derivation undetermined): Chemistry. See: Van Nostrand Chem. Dict.

Fischer reagents for cobalt (Derivation undetermined): Chemistry. See: Van Nostrand Chem. Dict.

Fischer-Speier esterification (method) (Derivation undetermined): Chemistry. See: Ballentyne; Van Nostrand Chem. Dict.

Fischer test for fluoride (Derivation undetermined): Chemistry. See: Van Nostrand Chem. Dict.

Fischer test for hydrogen sulfide (Derivation undetermined): Chemistry. See: Van Nostrand Chem. Dict.

Fischer test reaction for benzaldehyde (Derivation undetermined): Chemistry. See: Van Nostrand Chem. Dict.

Fischer test reaction for cobalt (Derivation undetermined): Chemistry. See: Van Nostrand Chem. Dict.

Fischer test reaction for tertiary amines (Derivation undetermined): Chemistry. See: Van Nostrand Chem. Dict.

Fischer-Tropsch process (Fischer, Franz Josef Emil and Tropsch, Hans): Chemistry. See: Thewlis; Thrush; Van Nostrand Chem. Dict.

FISCHER VON WALDHEIM, GOTTHELF. 1771-1853. German naturalist. See: World Who's Who Sci. Fischerite.

FISCHER, WALTER. fl. 1929. German chemist. Cited in: Krauch and Kunz. Houben-Fischer synthesis.

Fischerite (Fischer von Waldheim, Gotthelf): Earth Sciences. See: Webster's 3d.

Fischer's murmur (or cerebral murmur) (Fischer, Louis): Medicine. See: Dorland; Stedman.

Fischer's needle (Derivation undetermined): Medicine. See: Stedman.

Fischer's projection formulas (Fischer, Emil Hermann): Chemistry. See: Stedman.

Fischer's salt (Fischer, Nicolaus Wolfgang): Chemistry. See: Thrush.

Fischer's sign (Fischer, Louis): Medicine. See: Dorland; Stedman.

Fischer's solution (Fischer, Martin Henry): Medicine. See: Dorland.

Fischer's symptom (Fischer, Louis): Medicine. See: Stedman.

Fischer's syndrome (Fischer, H.): Medicine. See: Jablonski.

Fischer's test (Fisher, Emil Hermann): Chemistry. See: Dorland; Stedman.

Fischer's touraco (Derivation undetermined): Zoology. See: Gray.

Fischer's treatment (Fischer, Martin Henry): Medicine. See: Dorland.

Fischer's whydah (Derivation undetermined): Zoology. See: Gray.

Fishel ketose test reaction (Derivation undetermined): Chemistry. See: Van Nostrand Chem. Dict.

Fisher Act (Fisher, Herbert Albert Laurens): Education. See: Good.

Fisher bed (Fisher, Frederick Richard): Medicine. See: Dorland.

Fisher-Behrens test (Fisher, Ronald Aylmer and Behrens, W. V.). See: Behrens-Fisher test.

Fisher (currency note) (Fisher, Sir Norman Fenwick Warren): Generic Word. See: Partridge; Weekley.

FISHER, FREDERICK RICHARD. 1844-1932. English orthopedist. (Biography source unavailable.) Fisher bed.

FISHER, HERBERT ALBERT LAURENS. 1865-1940. English historian and statesman. See: Encyc. Brit., 1973. Fisher Act.

FISHER, LISELOTTE K. fl. 1940. American psychologist. (Biography source unavailable.) Bolgar-Fisher world test.

FISHER, MILLER. fl. 1956. American physician. Cited in: Leiber and Olbrich. Fisher's syndrome.

Fisher model (Fisher, Ronald Aylmer): Statistics. See: Kendall.

FISHER, SIR NORMAN FENWICK WARREN. 1879-1948. English government official. See: Webster's Biog. Dict. Fisher (currency note).

FISHER, RONALD AYLMER. 1890-1962. English statistician and geneticist. See: Dict. Sci. Biog. Behrens-Fisher problem, Behrens-Fisher test, Cornish-Fisher expansion, Fisher model, Fisher-Yates test, Fisher's 'B' distribution, Fisher's exact test, Fisher's test, Fisher's transformation (of the correlation coefficient), Fisher's z distribution.

Fisher subsieve sizer (Derivation undetermined): Engineering and Industry. See: Thrush.

Fisher-Yates test (Fisher, Ronald Aylmer and Yates, Frank): Statistics. See: Internat. Dict. Ap. Math.; Kendall.

Fisher's 'B' distribution (Fisher, Ronald Aylmer): Statistics. See: Kendall.

Fisher's exact test (Fisher, Ronald Aylmer): Statistics. See: Hoult.

Fisher's syndrome (Fisher, Miller): Medicine. See: Jablonski; Stedman.

Fisher's test (Fisher, Ronald Aylmer): Statistics. See: Chaplin; English.

Fisher's transformation (of the correlation coefficient) (Fisher, Ronald Aylmer): Statistics. See: Kendall. Also known as: inverse Tanh transformation.

Fisher's z distribution (Fisher, Ronald Aylmer): Statistics. See: Ballentyne; James; Van Nostrand Sci. Encyc.

fissure of Rolando (Rolando, Luigi). See: Rolando's fissure.

fissure of Sylvius (Sylvius, Franciscus). See: Sylvian fissure.

Fittig reaction (or synthesis) (Fittig, Rudolph): Chemistry. See: Ballentyne; Hackh; Van Nostrand Chem. Dict.; Van Nostrand Sci. Encyc.; Webster's 3d.

FITTIG, RUDOLPH. 1835-1910. German chemist. See: Dict. Sci. Biog. Fittig reaction (or synthesis), Wuertz-Fitting-Frankland reaction, Wuertz-Fittig reaction.

FITTON, ELIZABETH. fl. late 18th and early 19th c.'s. English botanist. See: Britten and Boulger. Fittonia.

FITTON, SARAH MARY. fl. late 18th and early 19th c.'s. English botanist. See: Britten and Boulger. Fittonia.

Fittonia (Fitton, Elizabeth and Fitton, Sarah Mary): Botany. See: Taylor, N.

FITZ, REGINALD HEBER. 1843-1913. American physician. See: World Who's Who Sci. Fitz's law, Fitz's syndrome.

Fitzgerald contraction (FitzGerald, George Francis). See: Lorentz-Fitzgerald contraction.

FITZGERALD, EDITH. fl. 1926. American educator. Cited in: Mansell. Fitzgerald key.

Fitzgerald factor (FitzGerald, George Francis): Physics. See: Internat. Dict. Phys. Elec.

FITZGERALD, GEORGE FRANCIS. 1851-1901. Irish physicist. See: Dict. Sci. Biog. Fitzgerald Factor, Lorentz-Fitzgerald contraction.

Fitzgerald key (Fitzgerald, Edith): Education. See: Good.

Fitzgerald-Lorentz contraction (hypothesis) (FitzGerald, George Francis and Lorentz, Hendrik Antoon). See: Lorentz-Fitzgerald contraction.

FitzGerald method (or treatment) (FitzGerald, William Henry Hope): Medicine. See: Dorland.

FITZ GERALD, WILLIAM HENRY HOPE. 1872-1939. American physician. Cited in: Mansell. FitzGerald method (or treatment).

FITZHUGH. fl. 1970. American army officer. (Biography source unavailable.) Fitzhugh phenomenon.

Fitz-Hugh and Curtis syndrome (Fitz-Hugh, Thomas, Jr. and Curtis, Arthur Hale). See: Fitz-Hugh's syndrome.

Fitzhugh phenomenon (Fitzhugh): Sociology. See: Martin.

FITZ-HUGH, THOMAS, JR. b. 1894. American physician. See: Amer. Men Sci., 10th ed. Fitz-Hugh's syndrome.

Fitz-Hugh's syndrome (Fitz-Hugh, Thomas, Jr.): Medicine. See: Jablonski. Also known as: Fitz-Hugh and Curtis syndrome, Stojano's syndrome (or sub-costal syndrome).

Fitzroy barometer (Fitzroy, Robert): Navigation. See: Harvey.

FITZROY, ROBERT. 1805-1865. English naval officer and meteorologist. See: Dict. Sci. Biog. Fitzroy barometer, Fitzroya.

Fitzroya (Fitzroy, Robert): Botany. See: Taylor, N.; Webster's 3d.

Fitz's law (Fitz, Reginald Heber): Medicine. See: Dorland.

Fitz's syndrome (Fitz, Reginald Heber): Medicine. See: Dorland; Jablonski

Fitzwilliam affair (Fitzwilliam, William Wentworth): History. See: Morris and Irwin.

FITZWILLIAM, CHARLES WILLIAM WENTWORTH, VISCOUNT MILTON. 1786-1857. English statesman and patron of Botany. See: Dict. Nat. Biog. Miltonia.

FITZWILLIAM, RICHARD. 1745-1816. English viscount. See: Dict. Nat. Biog. Fitzwilliam Virginal Book.

Fitzwilliam Virginal Book (Fitzwilliam, Richard): Music. See: Scholes.

FITZWILLIAM, WILLIAM WENTWORTH. 1748-1833. English statesman. See: Dict. Nat. Biog. Fitzwilliam affair.

FIZEAU, ARMAND-HIPPOLYTE-LOUIS. 1819-1896. French physicist. See: Dict. Sci. Biog. Doppler-Fizeau principle, Fizeau experiment, Fizeau fringes, Fizeau-Laurent surface interferometer?, Fizeau toothed wheel.

Fizeau experiment (Fizeau, Armand-Hippolyte-Louis): Physics. See: Internat. Dict. Phys. Elec.; Thewlis; Van Nostrand Sci. Encyc.

Fizeau fringes (Fizeau, Armand-Hippolyte-Louis): Physics. See: Ballentyne; Thewlis.

Fizeau-Laurent surface interferometer (Fizeau, Armand-Hippolyte-Louis? and Laurent, Leon Louis): Physics. See: Encyc. Brit., 1973 under "Interferometer," vol. 12, p. 355a.

Fizeau toothed wheel (Fizeau, Armand-Hippolyte-Louis): Physics. See: Internat. Dict. Phys. Elec.; Van Nostrand Sci. Encyc.

FIZELY, SANDOR. fl. 20th c. Hungarian mining engineer. Cited in: Bailey. Fizelyite.

Fizelyite (Fizely, Sandor): Earth Sciences. See: Thrush; Webster's 3d.

FLACCUS, L. VALERIUS. fl. 82 B.C. Roman senator. See: Dict. Grk. Rom. Biog. Myth. Lex Valeria.

Flacian (Flacius Illyricus, Matthias): Religion. See: Webster's 3d.

FLACIUS ILLYRICUS, MATTHIAS. 1520-1575. German Protestant theologian. See: Encyc. Brit., 1973. Flacian.

FLACK, MARTIN WILLIAM. 1882-1931. English physiologist. See: Who Was Who, 1929-1940. Hill-Flack sign, Keith and Flack's node.

Flack's node (Flack, Martin William). See: Keith and Flack's node.

FLACOURT, ETIENNE DE. 1607-1660. French governor of Madagascar. See: Barnhart (Cycl. Names). Flacourtia.

Flacourtia (Flacourt, Etienne de): Botany. See: Charnock; Taylor, N.; Webster's 3d.

FLADE, FR. fl. 1911. German metallurgist. Cited in: Chem. Abstr., vol. 5, p. 2356. Flade potential.

Flade potential (Flade, Fr.): Chemistry. See: Ballentyne.

Flajani-Basedow syndrome (Flajani, Giuseppe and Basedow, Karl Adolph von). See: Basedow's disease.

FLAJANI, GIUSEPPE. 1741-1808. Italian surgeon. See: World Who's Who Sci. Flajani-Basedow syndrome.

Flajani's disease (Flajani, Giuseppe). See: Basedow's disease.

FLAJOLOT. fl. 1871. French mineralogist. Cited in: Bailey. Flajolotite.

Flajolotite (Flajolot): Earth Sciences. See: Thrush; Webster's 3d.

Flaminian (Flaminius, Gaius): History. See: Hendrickson; Webster's 3d.

FLAMINIUS, GAIUS. d. 217 B.C. Roman general and statesman. See: Encyc. Brit., 1973. Flaminian.

FLAMMOCK, THOMAS. d. 1497. English lawyer and rebel. See: Dict. Nat. Biog. Flammock's rebellion.

Flammock's rebellion (Flammock, Thomas): History. See: Harbottle; Latham.

FLAMSTEED, JOHN. 1646-1719. English astronomer. See: Dict. Nat. Biog. Flamsteed numbers, Sanson-Flamsteed projection.

Flamsteed numbers (Flamsteed, John): Astronomy. See: Satterthwaite.

FLATAU, EDWARD. 1869-1932. Polish neurologist. See: Biog. Lex. hervorr. Aerzte, 1880-1930. Flatau-Schilder disease, Flatau's law, Redlich-Flatau syndrome?

Flatau-Schilder disease (Flatau, Edward and Schilder, Paul): Medicine. See: Stedman. Also known as: Schilder's disease.

Flatau's law (Flatau, Edward): Medicine. See: Stedman.

FLAUBERT, GUSTAVE. 1821-1880. French novelist. See: Encyc. Brit., 1973. Flaubertian.

Flaubertian (Flaubert, Gustave): Literature. See: Webster's 3d.

FLAVIUS, GNAEUS. fl. 4th c. B.C. Roman statesman. See: Encyc. Brit., 1973. Jus Flavianum.

FLECHSIG, PAUL EMIL. 1847-1929. German neurologist. See: Dict. Sci. Biog. Flechsig's areas, Flechsig's centers, Flechsig's cuticulum, Flechsig's fasciculi (or ground bundles), Flechsig's field, Flechsig's incision, Flechsig's tract.

Flechsig's areas (Flechsig, Paul Emil): Medicine. See: Donath; Dorland; Stedman.

Flechsig's centers (Flechsig, Paul Emil): Medicine. See: Stedman.

Flechsig's cuticulum (Flechsig, Paul Emil): Medicine. See: Dorland.

Flechsig's fasciculi (or ground bundles) (Flechsig, Paul Emil): Medicine. See: Dorland; Stedman.

Flechsig's field (Flechsig, Paul Emil): Medicine. See: Dorland.

Flechsig's incision (Flechsig, Paul Emil): Medicine. See: Donath.

Flechsig's tract (Flechsig, Paul Emil): Medicine. See: Donath; Dorland; Stedman.

FLECK, L. fl. 1951. Polish physician. (Biography source unavailable.) Fleck's phenomenon.

Fleck test reaction (Derivation undetermined): Chemistry. See: Van Nostrand Chem. Dict.

Fleck's phenomenon (Fleck, L.): Medicine. See: Jablonski.

fleece of Stilling (Stilling, Benedikt): Anatomy. See: Stedman.

Fleig blood reagent (Fleig, Charles Auguste): Chemistry. See: Van Nostrand Chem. Dict.

FLEIG, CHARLES AUGUSTE. 1883-1912. French physiologist. See: Montpellier Med., vol. 35 (1912), p. 241. Fleig blood reagent.

Fleig test reactions for carbohydrates (Derivation undetermined): Chemistry. See: Van Nostrand Chem. Dict.

FLEISCHER, BRUNO OTTO. b. 1874. German physician. See: Wer Ist Wer, 8th ed. Fleischer's dystrophy (1), Fleischer's dystrophy (2), Fleischer's ring (or line.

FLEISCHER, MICHAEL. 1908- . American geochemist. See: Amer. Men and Women Sci., 12th ed. Fleischerite.

FLEISCHER, RICHARD. 1848-1909. German physician. See: Biog. Lex. hervorr. Aerzte, 1880-1930. Kayser-Fleischer ring.

Fleischerite (Fleischer, Michael): Earth Sciences. See: Thrush.

Fleischer's dystrophy (1) (Fleischer, Bruno Otto): Medicine. See: Jablonski.

Fleischer's dystrophy (2) (Fleischer, Bruno Otto). See: Groenouw's dystrophy I.

Fleischer's ring (or line) (Fleischer, Bruno Otto): Medicine. See: Jablonski.

Fleischl, Ernst von. See: Von Fleischl Marxow, Ernst.

Fleischl('s) hemometer (Von Fleischl Marxow, Ernst): Medicine. See: Dorland; Hackh; Stedman.

Fleischl's test (Von Fleischl Marxow, Ernst): Medicine. See: Dorland.

FLEISCHMANN, GOTTFRIED. 1777-1853. German anatomist. See: Biog. Lex. hervorr. Aerzte. Fleischmann's bursa.

Fleischmann test (Derivation undetermined): Chemistry. See: Van Nostrand Chem. Dict.

FLEISCHMANN, WILHELM. 1837-1920. German chemist. Cited in: Chem. Abstr., vol. 8, p. 3827. Fleischmann's formula.

Fleischmann's bursa (Fleischmann, Gottfried): Medicine. See; Donath; Dorland; Stedman.

Fleischmann's formula (Fleischmann, Wilhelm): Chemistry. See: Winburne.

FLEISCHNER, FELIX. b. 1893. German physician. Cited in: Mansell. Fleischner's syndrome, Thiemann-Fleischner disease.

Fleischner's syndrome (Fleischner, Felix): Medicine. See: Jablonski.

Fleissner grille (Fleissner von Wastrowitz, Eduard B.): Cryptography. See: Webster's 3d.

FLEISSNER, HANS. fl. 1926. German chemist. Cited in: Chem. Abstr., vol. 20, p. 1677; vol. 21, p. 4047. Apold-Fleissner process, Fleissner process.

Fleissner process (Fleissner, Hans): Engineering and Industry. See: Thrush.

FLEISSNER VON WASTROWITZ, EDUARD B. fl. 1881. Austrian cryptographer. Cited in: Mansell. Fleissner grille.

FLEITMANN, THEODOR. d. 1904. German chemist. See: Pogg., vol. 5. Fleitmann's test.

Fleitmann's test (Fleitmann, Theodor): Chemistry. See: Dorland; Stedman.

Fleming diode (or valve) (Fleming, Sir John Ambrose): Electronics. See: Hughes; Internat. Dict. Phys. Elec.; Webster's 3d.

Fleming engine (Derivation undetermined): Engineering and Industry. See: Auger.

FLEMING, JOHN. 1785-1857. Scottish zoologist and geologist. See: Dict. Sci. Biog. Flemingia.

FLEMING, SIR JOHN AMBROSE. 1849-1945. English electrical engineer. See: Dict. Sci. Biog. Fleming diode (or valve), Fleming's rule.

Fleming tube (Fleming, William R.): Chemistry. See: Hackh; Van Nostrand Chem. Dict.

FLEMING, WILLIAM R. fl. 1913. American chemist. Cited in: Chem. Abstr., vol. 7, p. 1461. Fleming tube.

Flemingia (Fleming, John): Botany. See: Charnock.

Fleming's rule (Fleming, Sir John Ambrose): Electronics. See: Ballentyne; Markus; Thrush.

Flemming('s) solution (or fluid) (Flemming, Walther): Chemistry. See: Hackh; Pennak; Stedman; Van Nostrand Chem. Dict.; Webster's 3d.

FLEMMING, WALTHER. 1843-1905. German anatomist. See: Dict. Sci. Biog. Flemming('s) solution (or fluid), Flemming's triple stain, germinal center of Flemming, intermediate body of Flemming.

Flemming's triple stain (Flemming, Walther): Medicine. See: Stedman.

Flesch index (or formulas) (Flesch, Rudolf): Education. See: Chaplin; English; Wolman.

FLESCH, RUDOLF. 1911- . Austrian-born American language psychologist. See: Amer. Men and Women Sci., 12th ed. (Soc. Behav. Sci.). Flesch index (or formulas).

Fletcher burner (Derivation undetermined): Chemistry. See: Hackh; Van Nostrand Chem. Dict.

Fletcher furnace (Derivation undetermined): Chemistry. See: Hackh.

FLETCHER, HARVEY. b. 1884. American physicist. See: Amer. Men Sci., 9th ed. Fletcher-Munson contours (or curves), Troland and Fletcher theories.

Fletcher-Hopkins test (Fletcher, Sir Walter Morley and Hopkins, Frederick Gowland): Chemistry. See: Van Nostrand Chem. Dict.

FLETCHER, HORACE. 1849-1919. American nutritionist. See: Dict. Amer. Biog. Fletcherism (or Fletcherize).

Fletcher indicatrix (Derivation undetermined): Physics. See: Thewlis.

FLETCHER, JAMES. 1852-1908. Canadian entomologist. See: World Who's Who Sci. Fletcher scale.

Fletcher-Munson contours (or curves) (Fletcher, Harvey and Munson, W. A.): Physics. See: Hughes; Internat. Dict. Phys. Elec.; Markus.

Fletcher scale (Fletcher, James): Zoology. See: Webster's 3d.

FLETCHER, SIR WALTER MORLEY. 1873-1933. English physiologist. See: Dict. Sci. Biog. Fletcher-Hopkins test.

Fletcherism (or Fletcherize) (Fletcher, Horace): Medicine. See: Hendrickson; Hinsie; Stedman; Webster's 3d.

FLETTNER, ANTON. b. 1885. German engineer and inventor. See: Barnhart (Cycl. Names). Flettner control, Flettner rotor.

Flettner control (Flettner, Anton): Engineering and Industry. See: Webster's 3d.

Flettner rotor (Flettner, Anton): Physics. See: Thewlis.

fleur-de-Luce (Louis VII, Le Jeune?): Generic Word. See: Hendrickson; Partridge.

Fleury test reaction for benzoic acid (Derivation undetermined): Chemistry. See: Van Nostrand Chem. Dict.

Fleuss apparatus (or breathing apparatus) (Fleuss, H. A.): Engineering and Industry. See: Auger; Thrush.

FLEUSS, H. A. fl. 1879. Inventor. (Biography source unavailable.) Fleuss apparatus (or breathing apparatus).

Flewelling circuit (Derivation undetermined): Electronics. See: Hughes.

Flexner-Jobling carcinosarcoma (carcinoma or tumor) (Flexner, Simon and Jobling, James Wesley): Medicine. See: Jablonski.

FLEXNER, SIMON. 1863-1946. American pathologist. See: Dict. Sci. Biog. Flexner-Jobling carcinosarcoma (carcinoma or tumor), Flexner's bacillus, Flexner's dysentery, Flexner's serum.

Flexner's bacillus (Flexner, Simon): Medicine. See: Dorland; Stedman.

Flexner's dysentery (Flexner, Simon): Medicine. See: Jablonski.

Flexner's serum (Flexner, Simon): Medicine. See: Dorland; Stedman

Flibbertigibbet (Flibbertigibbet, the fiend): Generic Word (mischievous gossip). See: Brewer.

FLIBBERTIGIBBET, THE FIEND. Character in William Shakespeare's "King Lear." See: Benet. Flibbertigibbet.

FLICK, FULTON BROOKS. 1895- . American chemist. See: Amer. Men Sci., 9th ed. Flick solution.

Flick solution (Flick, Fulton Brooks): Chemistry. See: Van Nostrand Chem. Dict.

FLIERINGA, HENRI JOHAN. b. 1891. Dutch ophthalmologist. See: Who's Who Netherl., 1962-1963. Flieringa's ring.

Flieringa's ring (Flieringa, Henri Johan): Medicine. See: Stedman.

Fliess therapy (or treatment) (Fliess, Wilhelm): Medicine. See: Dorland.

FLIESS, WILHELM. 1858-1928. German physican. See: Biog. Lex. hervorr. Aerzte, 1880-1930. Fliess therapy (or treatment).

Flinders bar (Flinders, Matthew): Navigation. See: Webster's 3d.

Flinders grass (Flinders, Matthew): Botany. See: Webster's 3d.

FLINDERS, MATTHEW. 1774-1814. English mariner. See: World Who's Who Sci. Flinders bar, Flinders grass, Flindersia.

Flindersia (Flinders, Matthew): Botany. See: Partridge; Webster's 3d.

FLINDT, NICOLAJ. 1843-1913. Danish physician. Cited in: Mansell. Flindt's spots.

Flindt's spots (Flindt, Nicolaj): Medicine. See: Dorland.

FLINK, GUSTAF. 1849-1931. Swedish mineralogist. See: Pogg., vols. 4, 5, 6. Flinkite.

Flinkite (Flink, Gustaf): Earth Sciences. See: Webster's 3d.

FLINT, AUSTIN. 1812-1886. American physician. See: World Who's Who Sci. Flint's murmur.

FLINT, AUSTIN JR. 1836-1915. American physiologist. See: Who Was Who Amer., 1897-1942. Flint's arcade, Flint's law.

Flint's arcade (Flint, Austin Jr.): Medicine. See: Dorland; Stedman.

Flint's law (Flint, Austin Jr.): Medicine. See: Dorland.

Flint's murmur (Flint, Austin): Medicine. See: Dorland; Jablonski; Stedman. Also known as: Austin Flint's murmur.

Flip Wilson's law (Wilson, Flip): Sociology. See: Martin.

Flobert (gun) (Flobert, M.): Weapons. See: Mathews, M. M.

FLOBERT, M. 1819-1894. French arms-maker. See: Webster's Biog. Dict. Flobert (gun).

FLOCKS, MILTON. 1914- . American ophthalmologist. See: Direct. Med. Specialists, 1970-1971. Harrington-Flocks test.

FLODIN, HENNING G. fl. 1925. English metallurgist. Cited in: Chem. Abstr., vol. 19, p. 3454. Flodin process.

Flodin process (Flodin, Henning G.): Engineering and Industry. See: Thrush.

FLOERKE, HEINRICH GUSTAV. 1764-1835. German botanist. See: Ule. Floerkea.

Floerkea (Floerke, Heinrich Gustav): Botany. See: Webster's 3d.

Flokite (Vilgerdarson, Floki): Earth Sciences. See: Webster's 3d.

FLOOD, HENRY. 1732-1791. Irish orator and politician. See: Dict. Nat. Biog. Flood's Reform Bill.

Flood reaction (Derivation undetermined): Chemistry. See: Van Nostrand Chem. Dict.

FLOOD, VALENTINE. 1800-1847. Irish surgeon. See: World Who's Who Sci. Flood's ligament.

Flood's equation (Derivation undetermined): Chemistry. See: Ballentyne.

Flood's ligament (Flood, Valentine): Medicine. See: Dorland; Stedman.

Flood's Reform Bill (Flood, Henry): History. See: Harbottle.

FLOQUET, GASTON. 1847-1920. French mathematician. See: Pogg., vols. 3, 4, 5. Floquet theorem.

Floquet theorem (Floquet, Gaston): Mathematics. See: Internat. Dict. Ap. Math.; Internat. Dict. Phys. Elec.; Thewlis.

Flora (Flora, the goddess): Generic Word. See: Partridge.

FLORA, THE GODDESS. Roman goddess of flowers and fertility. See: Jobes. Flora, Floralia, Flora's paint brush.

Floralia (Flora, the goddess): Generic Word (festival). See: Charnock; Webster's 3d.

Flora's paint brush (Flora, the goddess): Botany. See: Gray; Webster's 3d.

FLORENCE, ALBERT. 1851-1927. French physician. See: Biog. Lex. hervorr. Aerzte, 1880-1930. Florence reagent, Florence's crystals, Florence's reaction.

Florence flask (Derivation undetermined): Medicine. See: Stedman.

Florence Nightingale (Nightingale, Florence): Generic Word (selfless nurse). See: Hendrickson; Partridge.

Florence reagent (Florence, Albert): Chemistry. See: Van Nostrand Chem. Dict.

FLORENCE, W. fl. 20th c. Scientist. Cited in: Min. Mag., vol. 12 (1900), p. 244. Florencite.

Florence's crystals (Florence, Albert): Medicine. See: Stedman.

Florence's reaction (Florence, Albert): Medicine. See: Dorland; Stedman

Florencite (Florence, W.): Earth Sciences. See: Thrush; Webster's 3d.

FLOREY, HOWARD WALTER. 1898-1968. Australian-born English pathologist. See: Dict. Sci. Biog. Florey unit.

Florey unit (Florey, Howard Walter): Medicine. See: Dorland; Stedman.

Flourens' theory (or doctrine) (Flourens, Marie Jean Pierre): Medicine. See: Dorland; Stedman.

FLOWER, SIR WILLIAM HENRY. 1831-1899. English surgeon and anatomist. See: Dict. Sci. Biog. Flower's bone, Flower's index.

Flower's bone (Flower, Sir William Henry): Medicine. See: Stedman. Also known as: Wormian bone.

Flower's index (Flower, Sir William Henry): Medicine. See: Dorland.

FLOYD, EDWARD. d. 1648. English Roman Catholic barrister. See: Dict. Nat. Biog. Floyd's case.

Floyd's case (Floyd, Edward): Law. See: Steinberg.

Flueckinger test reactions for alkaloids (Derivation undetermined): Chemistry. See: Van Nostrand Chem. Dict.

Flueckinger tests for phenol and naphthols (Derivation undetermined): Chemistry. See: Van Nostrand Chem. Dict.

FLUERSCHEIM, BERNHARD. b. 1874. German chemist. See: Pogg., vol. 6. Flurscheim's theory of benzene substitution.

FLUHMANN, CHARLES FREDERIC. 1898- . American gynecologist. See: Amer. Men Sci., 10th ed. Fluhmann's test.

Fluhmann's test (Fluhmann, Charles Frederic): Medicine. See: Dorland.

FLUHRER, WILLIAM FRANCIS. 1870-1932. American physician. See: J. Mount Sinai Hosp., vol. 3 (1937), p. 231. Fluhrer's probe.

Fluhrer's probe (Fluhrer, William Francis): Medicine. See: Dorland; Stedman.

Flurscheim's theory of benzene substitution (Fluerscheim, Bernhard): Chemistry. See: Ballentyne.

Flury high egg passage (Derivation undetermined): Medicine. See: Stedman.

Flury low egg passage (Derivation undetermined): Medicine. See: Stedman.

Flury strain (Derivation undetermined): Medicine. See: Stedman.

Flygt pump (Derivation undetermined): Engineering and Industry. See: Thrush.

Foch space (Derivation undetermined): Physics. See: Thewlis.

FOCHIER, ALPHONSE. 1845-1903. French gynecologist. See: Biog. Lex. hervorr. Aerzte, 1880-1930. Fochier's abscess.

Fochier's abscess (Fochier, Alphonse): Medicine. See: Dorland.

Fock, Vladimir Alexandrovitch. See: Fok, Vladimir Alexandrovitch.

FOCKE, HEINRICH. 1890- . German aircraft designer. See: Barnhart (Cycl. Names). Focke-Wulfe fighter (plane).

Focke-Wulfe fighter (plane) (Focke, Heinrich and Wulfe): Weapons. See: Hendrickson.

FODERE, FRANCOIS EMMANUEL. 1764-1835. French physician. See: World Who's Who Sci. Fodere's sign.

Fodere's sign (Fodere, Francois Emmanuel): Medicine. See: Dorland.

FOELLING, IVAR ASBJORN. b. 1888. Norwegian physician. Cited in: Mansell. Foelling's (Folling's) disease.

Foelling's (Folling's) disease (Foelling, Ivar Asbjorn): Medicine. See: Jablonski; Stedman.

FOERSTER, CARL FRIEDRICH RICHARD. 1825-1902. Polish-born German ophthalmologist. See: World Who's Who Sci. Aubert-Foerster phenomenon, Foerster's choroiditis, Foerster's phenomenon, Foerster's photometer, Foerster's uveitis.

FOERSTER, OTFRID. 1873-1941. German neurologist. See: World Who's Who Sci. Foerster-Penfield operation, Foerster's operation, Foerster's syndrome.

Foerster-Penfield operation (Foerster, Otfrid and Penfield, Wilder Graves): Medicine. See: Dorland.

Foerster's choroiditis (Foerster, Carl Friedrich Richard): Medicine. See: Dorland; Jablonski; Stedman.

Foerster's operation (Foerster, Otfrid): Medicine. See: Dorland.

Foerster's phenomenon (Foerster, Carl Friedrich Richard): Medicine. See: Stedman.

Foerster's photometer (Foerster, Carl Friedrich Richard): Medicine. See: Dorland; Stedman.

Foerster's syndrome (Foerster, Otfrid): Medicine. See: Jablonski.

Foerster's uveitis (Foerster, Carl Friedrich Richard): Medicine. See: Stedman.

Foettinger coupling (and transmitter) (Foettinger, Hermann): Engineering and Industry. See: Auger.

FOETTINGER, HERMANN. 1877-1945. German engineer. See: World Who's Who Sci. Foettinger coupling (and transmitter).

Fogarty catheter (Fogarty, T. J.): Medicine. See: Stedman.

FOGARTY, T. J. No dates. American surgeon. (Biography source unavailable.) Fogarty catheter.

FOGEL, CHARLES. fl. 1947. American chemist. Cited in: Chem. Abstr., vol. 41, p. 3694. Fogel gauge.

Fogel gauge (Fogel, Charles): Physics. See: Internat. Dict. Phys. Elec.

Foges test (Derivation undetermined): Chemistry. See: Van Nostrand Chem. Dict.

FOGG, HEMAN CHARLES. b. 1894. American chemist. See: Amer. Men Sci., 6th ed. Rice-Fogg-James reagent.

Foix-Alajouanine syndrome (Foix, Charles and Alajouanine, Theophile): Medicine. See: Jablonski.

FOIX, CHARLES. 1882-1927. French neurologist. See: World Who's Who Sci. Foix-Alajouanine syndrome, Foix's syndrome, Schilder-Foix disease.

Foix's syndrome (Foix, Charles): Medicine. See: Jablonski.

FOK, VLADIMIR ALEKSANDROVITCH. 1898- . Russian theoretical physicist. See: World Who's Who Sci. Hartree-Fock method (or approximation).

FOKKER, ADRIAAN DANIEL. 1887- . Dutch physicist. See: World Who's Who Sci. Fokker-Planck equation.

Fokker (airplane) (Fokker, Anthony Hermann Gerard): Engineering and Industry. See: Partridge; Weekley.

FOKKER, ANTHONY HERMANN GERARD. 1890-1939. Dutch-born aeronautical engineer and inventor. See: World Who's Who Sci. Fokker (airplane).

Fokker-Planck equation (Fokker, Adriaan Daniel and Planck, Max Karl Ernst Ludwig): Physics. See: Ballentyne; Internat. Dict. Ap. Math.; Internat. Dict. Phys. Elec.

fold of Veraguth (Veraguth, Otto): Physiology. See: Hinsie.

FOLDY, LESLIE LAWRENCE. 1919- . Czech-born American mathematical physicist. See: Amer. Men and Women Sci., 12th ed. Foldy-Wouthuysen representation.

Foldy-Wouthuysen representation (Foldy, Leslie Lawrence and Wouthuysen, S. A.): Physics. See: Internat. Dict. Ap. Math.

Foley catheter (Foley, Frederic Eugene Basil): Medicine. See: Stedman.

FOLEY, FREDERIC EUGENE BASIL. 1891-1966. American urologist. See: Direct. Med. Specialists, 8th ed. Foley catheter, Foley's operation.

Foley's operation (Foley, Frederic Eugene Basil): Medicine. See: Stedman.

FOLIA. No dates. Roman inventor. (Biography source unavailable.) Foliatum (beauty cream).

Foliatum (beauty cream) (Folia): Cosmetics. See: Hendrickson.

Folin apparatus (Folin, Otto): Chemistry. See: Hackh; Van Nostrand Chem. Dict.

Folin-Denis reagent for phenols (Folin, Otto and Denis, Willey Glover): Chemistry. See: Van Nostrand Chem. Dict.

Folin-Denis reagent for tyrosine (Folin, Otto and Denis, Willey Glover): Chemistry. See: Van Nostrand Chem. Dict.

Folin-Denis reagent for uric acid (Folin, Otto and Denis, Willey Glover): Chemistry. See: Van Nostrand Chem. Dict.

Folin diet (Folin, Otto): Chemistry. See: Hackh.

Folin-Looney test (Folin, Otto and Looney, Joseph Michael): Chemistry. See: Stedman.

Folin-McEllroy reagent (Folin, Otto and McEllroy, W. S.): Chemistry. See: Van Nostrand Chem. Dict.

Folin mixture (Folin, Otto): Chemistry. See: Van Nostrand Chem. Dict.

Florschuetz' formula (Florschuetz, Georg): Medicine. See: Dorland; Stedman.

FLORSCHUETZ, GEORG. b. 1859. German physician. See: Biog. Lex. hervorr. Aerzte, 1880-1930. Florschuetz' formula.

Flory-Huggins effect (Flory, Paul John and Huggins, Maurice Loyal): Chemistry. See: Internat. Dict. Ap. Math.

FLORY, PAUL JOHN. 1910- . American physical chemist. See: World Who's Who Sci. Flory-Huggins effect.

FLOURENS, MARIE JEAN PIERRE. 1794-1867. French physiologist. See: World Who's Who Sci. Flourens' theory (or doctrine).

FOLIN, OTTO. 1867-1934. Swedish-born American biochemist. See: Dict. Sci. Biog. Folin apparatus, Folin-Denis reagent for phenols, Folin-Denis reagent for tyrosine, Folin-Denis reagent for uric acid, Folin diet, Folin-Looney test, Folin-McEllroy reagent, Folin mixture, Folin's reaction, Folin's test, Ostwald-Folin pipette.

Folin's reaction (Folin, Otto): Chemistry. See: Stedman.

Folin's test (Folin, Otto): Chemistry. See: Dorland; Stedman.

Folius, Caecilius. See: Folli, Cecilio.

FOLLI, CECILIO. 1615-1660. Italian anatomist. See: World Who's Who Sci. Folli's (Folius' or Folian) process.

follicles of Langerhans (Langerhans, Paul): Zoology. See: Henderson.

Folli's (Folius' or Folian) process (Folli, Cecilio): Medicine. See: Dorland; Henderson; Stedman. Also known as: Rau's process.

FOLTZ, JEAN CHARLES EUGENE. 1822-1876. French ophthalmologist. See: Biog. Lex. hervorr. Aerzte. Foltz'(s) valvules (or valve).

Foltz'(s) valvules (or valve) (Foltz, Jean Charles Eugene): Medicine. See: Dorland; Stedman.

FONG, EDWARD EVERETT. 1912- . American radiologist. See: Direct. Med. Specialists, 8th ed. Fong's syndrome.

Fong's syndrome (Fong, Edward Everett). See: Oesterreicher-Turner syndrome.

FONIO, ANTON. b. 1889. Swiss physician. See: Biog. Lex. hervorr. Aerzte, 1880-1930. Fonio's solution.

Fonio's solution (Fonio, Anton): Medicine. See: Stedman.

FONTAINE-BARON, M. fl. 1846. French? engineer. (Biography source unavailable.) Fontaine's turbine.

Fontaine's turbine (Fontaine-Baron, M.): Engineering and Industry. See: Auger.

FONTANA, ARTURO. 1873-1950. Italian dermatologist. Cited in: Mansell. Fontana's stain.

FONTANA, FELICE. 1730-1805. Italian neurologist. See: Dict. Sci. Biog. Fontana's canal, Fontana's mark, Fontana's mask, Fontana's spaces.

Fontana's canal (Fontana, Felice): Medicine. See: Dorland; Stedman.

Fontana's mark (Fontana, Felice): Medicine. See: Stedman.

Fontana's mask (Fontana, Felice): Medicine. See: Dorland.

Fontana's spaces (Fontana, Felice): Medicine. See: Dorland; Henderson; Stedman.

Fontana's stain (Fontana, Arturo): Medicine. See: Stedman.

Fontanesia (Desfontaines, Rene Louiche): Biology. See: Charnock; Taylor, N.

Fontange (head-dress) (Fontanges, Duchesse de): Fashion. See: Brewer; Hendrickson; Picken.

FONTANGES, DUCHESSE DE (MARIE ANGELIQUE DE SCORRAILLE DE ROUSSILLES). 1661-1681. French mistress of Louis XIV. See: Webster's Biog. Dict. Fontange (head-dress).

foot-Lambert (Lambert, Johann Heinrich): Physics. See: Dresner; Focal Encyc. Photog.; Hughes; Markus; Van Nostrand Sci. Encyc.

FOOT, LUNDY. fl. 18th c. Irish tobacconist. (Biography source unavailable.) Lundyfoot (snuff).

FOOTE, ALBERT E. 1846?-1895. American mineralogist. See: Amer. J. Sci., vol. 150 (1895), p. 434. Footeite.

Footeite (Foote, Albert E.): Earth Sciences. See: Thrush; Webster's 3d.

Foraker Act (Foraker, Joseph Benson): Politics. See: Black; Harbottle; Morris.

FORAKER, JOSEPH BENSON. 1846-1917. American legislator. See: Biog. Direct. Amer. Congress. Foraker Act.

Foraky boring method (Derivation undetermined): Engineering and Industry. See: Thrush.

Foraky freezing process (Derivation undetermined): Engineering and Industry. See: Thrush.

foramen of Bochdalek (Bochdalek, Vincenz Alexander). See: Bochdalek's hernia.

foramen of Magendie (Magendie, Francois). See: Magendie's foramen.

foramen of Monro (Monro, Alexander): Anatomy. See: Donath; Stedman; Webster's 3d.

foramen of Winslow (Winslow, Jakob Benignus). See: Winslow's foramen.

foramina of Key and Retzius (Key, Ernst Axel Henrik and Retzius, Magnus G.). See: Retzius' foramina.

FORBES, A. P. fl. 1954. American physician. (Biography source unavailable.) Forbes-Albright syndrome.

Forbes-Albright syndrome (Forbes, A. P. and Albright, Fuller). See: Argonz-Del Castillo syndrome.

Forbes bands (Forbes, James David): Earth Sciences. See: Monkhouse.

FORBES, DAVID. 1828-1876. English geologist. See: World Who's Who Sci. Forbesite.

Forbes' disease (Forbes, Gilbert Burnett). See: Cori's disease.

Forbes' famous law (Forbes, Malcolm Stevenson): Sociology. See: Martin.

FORBES, GILBERT BURNETT. 1915- . American pediatrician. See: World Who's Who Sci. Forbes' disease.

FORBES, JAMES DAVID. 1809-1868. Scottish geologist. See: Dict. Sci. Biog. Forbes bands.

Forbes log (Forbes, Robert Bennet): Navigation. See: Van Nostrand Sci. Encyc.

Forbes Mackenzie Act (Mackenzie, William Forbes): History. See: Montgomery.

FORBES, MALCOLM STEVENSON. 1919- . American publisher and investment counselor. See: Who's Who Amer., 1974-1975. Forbes' famous law.

Forbes primrose (Derivation undetermined): Botany. See: Winburne.

FORBES, ROBERT BENNET. 1804-1889. American sea captain, inventor, and ship-builder. See: Dict. Amer. Biog. Forbes log.

Forbes scale (Forbes, Stephen Alfred): Zoology. See: Webster's 3d.; Winburne.

FORBES, STEPHEN ALFRED. 1844-1930. American entomologist. See: Dict. Sci. Biog. Forbes scale.

FORBES, THOMAS ROGERS. 1911- . American anatomist. See: World Who's Who Sci. Hooker-Forbes test.

Forbesite (Forbes, David): Earth Sciences. See: Thrush; Webster's 3d.

Forbush decrease (Forbush, Scott E.): Physics. See: Markus; Thewlis.

FORBUSH, EDWARD HOWE. 1858-1929. American ornithologist. See: World Who's Who Sci. Forbush's sparrow.

FORBUSH, SCOTT E. 1904- . American physicist. See: World Who's Who Sci. Forbush decrease.

Forbush's sparrow (Forbush, Edward Howe): Zoology. See: Webster's 3d.

FORCHER. No dates. Mineral discoverer. Cited in: Bailey. Forcherite.

Forcherite (Forcher): Earth Sciences. See: Thrush.

FORCHHEIMER, FREDERICK. 1853-1913. American physician. See: World Who's Who Sci. Forchheimer's sign.

Forchheimer's sign (Forchheimer, Frederick): Medicine. See: Dorland; Stedman.

Ford (car) (Ford, Henry): Generic Word (inexpensive car). See: Hendrickson; Partridge.

Ford cup (Derivation undetermined): Engineering and Industry. See: Thrush.

FORD, HENRY. 1863-1947. American inventor. See: Who Was Who Amer., 1943-1950. Ford (car), Fordism (or Fordize).

Fordism (or Fordize) (Ford, Henry): Engineering and Industry. See: Webster's 3d.

FORDNEY, JOSEPH WARREN. 1853-1932. American legislator. See: Biog. Direct Amer. Congress. Fordney-McCumber Tariff (Bill).

Fordney-McCumber Tariff (Bill) (Fordney, Joseph Warren and McCumber, Porter James): Economics. See: Jameson; Morris; Smith.

FORDYCE, JOHN ADDISON. 1858-1925. American dermatologist. See: Who Was Who Amer., 1897-1942. Brooke-Fordyce disease, Fordyce's disease (or spots), Fordyce's lesion (or angiokeratoma), Fox-Fordyce disease.

Fordyce's disease (or spots) (Fordyce, John Addison): Medicine. See: Dorland; Jablonski; Stedman.

Fordyce's lesion (or angiokeratoma) (Fordyce, John Addison): Medicine. See: Jablonski.

FOREL, AUGUSTE-HENRI. 1848-1931. Swiss neurologist. See: Dict. Sci. Biog. Forel's commissure, Forel's decussation, Forel's field, Forel's fornix.

FOREL, FRANCOIS-ALPHONSE. 1841-1912. Swiss physician and naturalist. See: World Who's Who Sci. Forel scale, Rossi-Forel scale (or intensity scale).

Forel scale (Forel, Francois-Alphonse): Earth Sciences. See: Huschke; Thrush.

Forellenstein (Derivation undetermined): Earth Sciences. See: Thrush.

Forel's commissure (Forel, Auguste-Henri): Medicine. See: Donath; Dorland.

Forel's decussation (Forel, Auguste-Henri): Medicine. See: Dorland; Stedman.

Forel's field (Forel, Auguste-Henri): Medicine. See: Dorland.

Forel's fornix (Forel, Auguste-Henri): Medicine. See: Dorland.

Foreman series (Derivation undetermined): Earth Sciences. See: Thrush.

Foreman's method (for the determination of ammonia in urine) (Derivation undetermined): Chemistry. See: Ballentyne.

FORER, BERTRAM ROBIN. 1914- . American psychologist. See: Amer. Men Sci., 9th ed. (Soc. Behav. Sci.) Forer structured sentence completion test.

Forer structured sentence completion test (Forer, Bertram Robin): Psychology. See: Wolman.

Forestier and Rotes-Querol syndrome (Forestier, Jacques and Rotes-Querol, J.): Medicine. See: Jablonski.

Forestier-Certonciny syndrome (Forestier, Jacques and Certonciny, A.): Medicine. See: Jablonski.

FORESTIER, JACQUES. b. 1890. French neurologist. See: Who's Who France, 1961-1962. Forestier and Rotes-Querol syndrome, Forestier-Certonciny syndrome.

FORESTIER, PIERRE-GASPARD. 1775-1847. French physician. See: Biog. Lex. hervorr. Aerzte. Forestiera.

Forestiera (Forestier, Pierre-Gaspard): Botany. See: Taylor, N.; Webster's 3d.

FORLANINI, CARLO. 1847-1918. Italian physician. See: World Who's Who Sci. Forlanini's treatment.

Forlanini's treatment (Forlanini, Carlo): Medicine. See: Dorland.

FORMAD, HENRY F. 1847-1892. American physician. Cited in: Kelly. Formad's kidney.

Formad's kidney (Formad, Henry F.): Medicine. See: Dorland; Jablonski.

FORMAN, FRANCIS GLOSTER. fl. 1937. Australian geologist. See: Who's Who Australia, 1968. Formanite.

Formanek reaction for metals (Derivation undetermined): Chemistry. See: Van Nostrand Chem. Dict.

Formanek's indicator (Derivation undetermined): Chemistry. See: Hackh.

Formanite (Forman, Francis Gloster): Earth Sciences. See: Thrush; Webster's 3d.

forme fruste of Hurler's syndrome (Hurler, Gertrud). See: Scheie's syndrome.

formula of Hormisdas (Hormisdas, Saint): Religion. See: Attwater.

Fornacalia (Fornax): Generic Word (ancient feast). See: Charnock.

FORNAX. Roman goddess of the oven. See: Jobes. Fornacalia.

FORNET, WALTER. b. 1877. German surgeon. See: Biog. Lex. hervorr. Aerzte, 1880-1930. Fornet's reaction.

Fornet's reaction (Fornet, Walter): Medicine. See: Dorland; Stedman.

FORREST, R. W. fl. 1889. Scottish engineer in South Africa. Cited in: New Encyc. Brit., 1974, Microp. under "Johannesburg," p. 230b. MacArthur and Forest cyanide process.

FORRESTER, D. L. fl. 1925. American engineer. Cited in: Chem. Abstr., vol. 19, p. 3450. Forrester machine.

Forrester machine (Forrester, D. L.): Engineering and Industry. See: Thrush.

Forsius-Eriksson syndrome (Forsius, Henrik Runar and Eriksson, Aldur W.): Medicine. See: Jablonski.

FORSIUS, HENRIK RUNAR. 1921- . Finnish ophthalmologist. See: World Who's Who Sci. Forsius-Eriksson syndrome.

Forskohlea (Forsskal, Peter): Botany. See: Charnock.

FORSSELL, GOSTA. 1876-1950. Swedish radiologist. See: World Who's Who Sci. Forssell's sinus(es).

FORSSELL, JARL. 1912-1964. Swedish physician. Cited in: Mansell. Forssell's syndrome.

Forssell's sinus(es) (Forssell, Gosta): Medicine. See: Donath; Dorland; Stedman.

Forssell's syndrome (Forssell, Jarl): Medicine. See: Jablonski.

FORSSKAL, PETER. 1732-1763. Swedish botanist. See: Dict. Sci. Biog. Forskohlea.

Forssman antibody (Forssman, John): Medicine. See: Stedman; Webster's 3d.

Forssman antigen (Forssman, John): Medicine. See: Dorland; Stedman; Webster's 3d.

Forssman antigen-antibody reaction (Forssman, John): Medicine. See: Stedman.

FORSSMAN, HANS AXEL. 1912- . Swedish physician. See: Vem ar Det, 1963. Boerjeson-Forssman-Lehmann syndrome.

FORSSMAN, JOHN. 1868-1947. Swedish pathologist. See: Biog. Lex. hervorr. Aerzte, 1880-1930. Forssman antibody, Forssman antigen, Forssman antigen-antibody reaction, Forssman-Skoog syndrome.

Forssman-Skoog syndrome (Forssman, John and Skoof, Torsten Olof): Medicine. See: Jablonski. Also known as: Forssman's syndrome.

Forssman's syndrome (Forssman, John). See: Forssman-Skoog syndrome.

Forster–Decker amine method (Derivation undetermined): Chemistry. See: Van Nostrand Chem. Dict.

FORSTER, JOHANN REINHOLD. 1729-1798. German traveler and author. See: Dict. Sci. Biog. Forsterite, Forster's shrew, Forster's tern.

Forsterite (Forster, Johann Reinhold): Earth Sciences. See: Charnock; Markus; Thrush.

Forster's shrew (Forster, Johann Reinhold): Zoology. See: Mathews, M. M.

Forster's tern (Forster, Johann Reinhold): Zoology. See: Webster's 3d.

Forsyth mission (Forsyth, Sir Thomas Douglas): History. See: Morris and Irwin.

FORSYTH, SIR THOMAS DOUGLAS. 1827-1886. English official in India. See: Dict. Nat. Biog. Forsyth mission.

FORSYTH, WILLIAM. 1737-1804. Scottish gardener and horticulturist. See: Dict. Nat. Biog. Forsythia.

Forsythia (Forsyth, William): Botany. See: Charnock; Hendrickson; Taylor, N.

Fortin('s) barometer (Fortin, Jean Nicolas): Earth Sciences. See: Huschke; Monkhouse; Winburne.

FORTIN, JEAN NICOLAS. 1750-1831. French instrument maker. See: Dict. Sci. Biog. Fortin('s) barometer.

Fortrat parabola (or diagram) (Fortrat, Rene): Physics. See: Internat. Dict. Phys. Elec.; Thewlis.

FORTRAT, RENE. b. 1886. French physicist. See: Pogg., vols. 5, 6. Fortrat parabola (or diagram).

FORTUNATUS. Hero of a popular European tale. See: Jobes. Fortunatus's cap.

Fortunatus's cap (Fortunatus): Generic Word. See: Charnock.

FORTUNE, ROBERT. 1813-1880. English botanist. See: World Who's Who Sci. Fortunella.

Fortunella (Fortune, Robert): Botany. See: Hendrickson; Taylor, N.; Webster's 3d.

Fortuny tea gowns (Fortuny y Madrazo, Mariano): Fashion. See: Picken.

FORTUNY Y MADRAZO, MARIANO. 1871-1949. Spanish-born painter and designer. See: Diz. Encic. Ital. Fortuny tea gowns.

FOSHAG, WILLIAM FREDERICK. 1894-1956. American geologist. See: World Who's Who Sci. Foshagite.

Foshagite (Foshag, William Frederick): Earth Sciences. See: Thrush; Webster's 3d.

FOSHAY, LEE. 1896- . American microbiologist. See: Amer. Men Sci., 10th ed. Foshay serum.

Foshay–Mollaret syndrome (Foshay and Mollaret, Pierre). See: Debre's syndrome.

Foshay serum (Foshay, Lee): Medicine. See: Dorland; Stedman.

fossa of Morgagni (Morgagni, Giovanni Battista). See: Morgagni's fossa.

fossa of Sylvius (Sylvius, Franciscus). See: Sylvian fossa.

Fosse reagent for urea (Fosse, Richard-Jules): Chemistry. See: Van Nostrand Chem. Dict.

FOSSE, RICHARD-JULES. 1870-1949. French chemist. See: World Who's Who Sci. Fosse reagent for urea.

FOSTER, FENTON G. fl. 1865. American army officer and inventor. (Biography source unavailable.) Foster typesetting machine.

Foster frame (Derivation undetermined): Medicine. See: Stedman.

FOSTER, G. No dates. Traveler and plant collector. (Biography source unavailable.) Fostera.

FOSTER, GEORGE CAREY. 1835-1919. English physicist. See: World Who's Who Sci. Carey-Foster bridge?, Carey-Foster method of calibration.

FOSTER, J. R. No dates. Traveler and plant collector. (Biography source unavailable.) Fostera.

Foster Kennedy. See: Kennedy, Robert Foster.

Foster Kennedy('s) syndrome (Kennedy, Robert Foster): Medicine. See: Dorland; Hinsie; Jablonski; Stedman. Also known as: Gowers-Paton-Kennedy syndrome, Kennedy's syndrome.

Foster networks (Derivation undetermined): Physics. See: Van Nostrand Sci. Encyc.

Foster press (Derivation undetermined): Printing. See: Lockwood.

Foster('s) reactance theorem (Derivation undetermined): Physics. See: Ballentyne; Hughes; Internat. Dict. Ap. Math.

Foster–Seeley discriminator (Foster and Seeley, Stuart William): Electronics. See: Hughes; Markus.

Foster typesetting machine (Foster, Fenton G.): Printing. See: Lockwood.

Fostera (Foster, J. R. and Foster, G.): Botany. See: Charnock.

Foster's formula (Derivation undetermined): Engineering and Industry. See: Thrush.

FOTHERGILL, JOHN. 1712-1780. English physician. See: World Who's Who Sci. Fothergilla, Fothergill's disease, Fothergill's pill.

FOTHERGILL, SAMUEL. fl. 1802. English physician. See: Biog. Lex. hervorr. Aerzte. Fothergill's neuralgia.

FOTHERGILL, WILLIAM EDWARD. 1865-1926. English gynecologist. See: Who Was Who, 1916-1928. Fothergill's operation.

Fothergilla (Fothergill, John): Botany. See: Mathews, M. M.; Taylor, N.; Webster's 3d.

Fothergill's disease (Fothergill, John): Medicine. See: Dorland; Jablonski; Stedman.

Fothergill's neuralgia (Fothergill, Samuel): Medicine. See: Dorland; Hinsie; Jablonski.

Fothergill's operation (Fothergill, William Edward): Medicine. See: Stedman.

Fothergill's pill (Fothergill, John): Medicine. See: Dorland.

Fothergill's sign (Derivation undetermined): Medicine. See: Stedman.

Foucault current (Foucault, Jean Bernard Leon): Physics. See: Ballentyne; Markus; Webster's 3d.

Foucault diffraction (Foucault, Jean Bernard Leon): Physics. See: Internat. Dict. Phys. Elec.

Foucault gyroscope (or gyroscopic compass) (Foucault, Jean Bernard Leon): Physics. See: Internat. Dict. Phys. Elec.

FOUCAULT, JEAN BERNARD LEON. 1819-1868. French physicist. See: Dict. Sci. Biog. Foucault current, Foucault diffraction, Foucault gyroscope (or gyroscopic compass), Foucault knife-edge test, Foucault('s) pendulum, Foucault prism, Foucault rotating mirror.

Foucault knife-edge test (Foucault, Jean Bernard Leon): Physics. See: Internat. Dict. Phys. Elec.; Van Nostrand Sci. Encyc.

Foucault('s) pendulum (Foucault, Jean Bernard Leon): Physics. See: Ballentyne; Internat. Dict. Phys. Elec.; Monkhouse.

Foucault prism (Foucault, Jean Bernard Leon): Physics. See: Hackh; Internat. Dict. Phys. Elec.

Foucault rotating mirror (Foucault, Jean Bernard Leon): Physics. See: Internat. Dict. Phys. Elec.; Van Nostrand Sci. Encyc.

FOUCHET, ANDRE. 1894- . French chemist. Cited in: Kelly. Fouchet('s) reagent (test or solution).

Fouchet('s) reagent (test or solution) (Fouchet, Andre): Chemistry. See: Dorland; Stedman; Van Nostrand Chem. Dict.

FOUCRY, M. fl. 1934. French chemist. Cited in: Kelly. Foucry test reaction.

Foucry test reaction (Foucry, M.): Chemistry. See: Van Nostrand Chem. Dict.

FOULGER, JOHN HENRY. 1898- . English-born American pharmacologist. See: Amer. Men Sci., 5th ed. Foulger('s) test (or reagents).

Foulger('s) test (or reagents) (Foulger, John Henry): Chemistry. See: Ballentyne; Van Nostrand Chem. Dict.

FOULIS, ANDREW. 1712-1775. Scottish printer and publisher. See: Dict. Nat. Biog. Foulis press.

FOWLER, SIR RALPH HOWARD. 1889-1944. English mathematician. See: World Who's Who Sci. Darwin-Fowler method, Fowler function?, Fowler-Nordheim equation, Fowler plot.

Fowler return (Fowler, Sir Henry Hartley): History. See: Montgomery.

FOWLER, SAMUEL. 1779-1844. American physician and mineralogist. See: World Who's Who Sci. Fowlerite.

FOWLER, SAMUEL PAGE. 1800-1888. American antiquarian and naturalist. Cited in: Mansell. Fowler's toad.

Fowler('s) solution (Fowler, Thomas): Medicine. See: Dorland; Partridge; Van Nostrand Chem. Dict.

FOWLER, THOMAS. 1736-1801. English physician. See: World Who's Who Sci. Fowler('s) solution.

Fowlerite (Fowler, Samuel): Earth Sciences. See: Hackh; Thrush; Webster's 3d.

Fowler's operation (Fowler, George Ryerson): Medicine. See: Dorland.

Fowler's position (Fowler, George Ryerson): Medicine. See: Dorland; Stedman.

Fowler's series (Fowler, Alfred): Physics. See: Hackh.

Fowler's toad (Fowler, Samuel Page): Zoology. See: Pennak; Webster's 3d.

FOX, CHARLES JAMES. 1749-1806. English statesman and orator. See: Dict. Nat. Biog. Charley (or Charlie) (beard).

Fox flue (Fox, Samson): Engineering and Industry. See: Auger.

Fox-Fordyce disease (Fox, George Henry and Fordyce, John Addison): Medicine. See: Dorland; Jablonski; Stedman.

FOX, GEORGE HENRY. 1846-1937. American dermatologist. See: World Who's Who Sci. Fox-Fordyce disease.

FOX (or FOXE), JOHN. 1516-1587. English martyrologist. See: Dict. Nat. Biog. Fox's (Foxe's) Book of Martyrs.

FOX, SAMSON. 1838-1903. English inventor. See: Dict. Nat. Biog., 2d suppl. Fox flue.

FOX-STRANGWAYS, WILLIAM THOMAS HORNER. 1795-1865. English botanist. See: Ascherson and Graebner, vol. 3, p. 199. Stranvaesia.

Fox test (Derivation undetermined): Chemistry. See: Van Nostrand Chem. Dict.

FOX, WILLIAM TILBURY. 1836-1879. English dermatologist. See: World Who's Who Sci. Fox's disease, Fox's impetigo.

Fox's (Foxe's) Book of Martyrs (Fox, John): Religion. See: Attwater; Mathews, S.

Fox's disease (Fox, William Tilbury): Medicine. See: Jablonski. Also known as: Goldscheider's disease, Koebner's disease, Weber-Cockayne syndrome.

Fox's impetigo (Fox, William Tilbury): Medicine. See: Dorland; Jablonski; Stedman.

FRAENKEL, ALBERT. 1848-1916. German physician. See: World Who's Who Sci. Fraenkel-Weichselbaum pneumococcus, Fraenkel's disease, Fraenkel's treatment.

FRAENKEL, BERNHARD. 1836-1911. German laryngologist. See: World Who's Who Sci. Fraenkel's speculum, Fraenkel's test.

FRAENKEL, KARL. 1861-1915. German bacteriologist. See: World Who's Who Sci. Fraenken-Gabbet stain.

Fraenkel-Weichselbaum pneumococcus (Fraenkel, Albert and Weichselbaum, Anthon): Medicine. See: Dorland. Also known as: Fraenkel's pneumococcus.

Fraenkel's disease (Fraenkel, Albert): Medicine. See: Jablonski.

Fraenkel's pneumococcus (Fraenkel, Albert). See: Fraenkel-Weichselbaum pneumococcus.

Fraenkel's speculum (Fraenkel, Bernhard): Medicine. See: Dorland; Stedman.

Fraenkel's test (Fraenkel, Bernhard): Medicine. See: Dorland.

Fraenkel's treatment (Fraenkel, Albert): Medicine. See: Dorland.

Fraenken-Gabbet stain (Fraenkel, Karl and Gabbet, Henry Singer): Medicine. See: Stedman.

Fraentzel's murmur (Derivation undetermined): Medicine. See: Stedman.

Frahm('s) reeds (or frequency meter) (Derivation undetermined). See: Environ. Terms; Markus.

FRAMES, P. R. No dates. Mineral collector. Cited in: Bailey. Framesite.

Framesite (Frames, P. R.): Earth Sciences. See: Thrush.

FRANCES OF ROME. 1384-1440. Italian saint. See: Encyc. Brit., 1973. Oblates of St. Frances of Rome.

FRANCESCHETTI, ADOLPHE. 1896- . Swiss ophthalmologist. See: World Who's Who Sci. Franceschetti-Jadassohn syndrome, Franceschetti-Klein-Wildervanck syndrome, Franceschetti's disease, Franceschetti's dystrophy, Franceschetti's syndrome (1), Franceschetti's syndrome (2).

Franceschetti-Jadassohn syndrome (Franceschetti, Adolphe and Jadassohn, Josef). See: Naegeli's syndrome.

Franceschetti-Klein-Wildervanck syndrome (Franceschetti, Adolphe; Klein, David; and Wildervanck, L. S.). See: Wildervanck's syndrome.

Franceschetti-Zwahlen-Klein syndrome (Franceschetti, Adolphe; Zwahlen, P.; and Klein, David). See: Franceschetti's syndrome (2).

Franceschetti-Zwahlen syndrome (Franceschetti, Adolphe and Zwahlen, P.). See: Franceschetti's syndrome (2).

Franceschetti's disease (Franceschetti, Adolphe): Medicine. See: Jablonski.

Franceschetti's dystrophy (Franceschetti, Adolphe): Medicine. See: Jablonski.

Franceschetti's syndrome (1) (Franceschetti, Adolphe): Medicine. See: Jablonski.

Franceschetti's syndrome (2) (Franceschetti, Adolphe): Medicine. See: Jablonski; Stedman. Also known as: Berry's syndrome, Franceschetti-Zwahlen-Klein syndrome, Franceschetti-Zwahlen syndrome, Zwahlen's syndrome.

Francescone (coin) (Francis III): Numismatics. See: Charnock.

FRANCHET, ADRIEN. 1834-1900. French botanist. See: Royal Soc. Cat. Sci. Pap. Franchet cotoneaster?

Franchet cotoneaster (Franchet, Adrien?): Botany. See: Winburne.

FRANCHIMONT, ANTOINE PAUL. 1844-1919. Dutch chemist. See: World Who's Who Sci. Franchimont reaction.

Franchimont reaction (Franchimont, Antoine Paul): Chemistry. See: Van Nostrand Chem. Dict.

FRANCIS I. 1494-1547. King of France. See: Encyc. Brit., 1973. Concordat of Francis I, Francois Premier.

FRANCIS II. 1768-1835. Emperor of Austria. See: Encyc. Brit., 1973. Emperor's Hymn.

FRANCIS III. 1737-1765. French aristocrat. (Biography source unavailable.) Francescone (coin).

Francis' disease (Francis, Edward): Medicine. See: Dorland; Jablonski. Also known as: Ohara's disease.

FRANCIS, EDWARD. 1872-1957. American bacteriologist. See: World Who's Who Sci. Francis' disease.

FRANCIS, JAMES BICHENO. 1815-1892. English hydraulic engineer. See: World Who's Who Sci. Francis turbine.

FRANCIS, JOHN WAKEFIELD. 1789-1861. American physician. See: World Who's Who Sci. Francis' triplex pill.

Francis Joseph Campbell citation (Campbell, Francis Joseph): Library Science. See: Harrod.

FRANCIS OF ASSISI, SAINT. ca. 1182-1226. Italian monk and preacher. See: Encyc. Brit., 1973. Franciscans, Rule of St. Francis.

FRANCIS OF SALES, ST. 1567-1622. French nobleman and ecclesiastic. See: Encyc. Brit., 1973. Oblates of St. Francis de Sales, Salesian(s).

Francis test (Francis, Thomas, Jr.): Medicine. See: Stedman.

FRANCIS, THOMAS, JR. 1900-1969. American epidemiologist. See: World Who's Who Sci. Francis test.

Francis' triplex pill (Francis, John Wakefield): Medicine. See: Dorland.

Francis turbine (Francis, James Bicheno): Engineering and Industry. See: Auger; Thrush.

Francis Xavier, Saint. See: Xavier, Saint Francis.

Francis Xavier's hymn (Xavier, Saint Francis): Religion. See: Attwater.

Franciscans (Francis of Assisi, Saint): Religion. See: Attwater; Canney; Mathews, S.

Francisci furnace (Derivation undetermined): Engineering and Industry. See: Thrush.

Franck-Condon principle (Franck, James and Condon, Edward Uhler): Physics. See: Ballentyne; Internat. Dict. Ap. Math.; Internat. Dict. Phys. Elec.

Franck drawing completion test (Franck, Kate): Psychology. See: Wolman.

Franck-Hertz experiment (Franck, James and Hertz, Gustav Ludwig): Physics. See: Internat. Dict. Phys. Elec.

FRANCK, JAMES. 1882-1964. German physicist. See: Dict. Sci. Biog. Franck-Condon principle, Franck-Hertz experiment, Franck-Rabinowitch hypothesis.

FRANCK, KATE. fl. 1951. Australian psychologist. Cited in: Mansell. Franck drawing completion test.

Franck-Rabinowitch hypothesis (Franck, James and Rabinowitch, Eugene): Physics. See: Thewlis.

FRANCKE, AUGUST HERMANN. 1663-1727. German pietist. See: Encyc. Brit., 1973. Franckesche Stiftungen.

FRANCKE, CARL. fl. 19th c. German mining engineer. Cited in: Bailey. Franckeite.

FRANCKE, ERNEST. fl. 19th c. German mining engineer. Cited in: Bailey. Franckeite.

FRANCKE, KARL ERNST. 1859-1920. German physician. See: Biog. Lex. hervorr. Aerzte, 1880-1930. Francke's needle, Francke's sign, Francke's symptom.

Franckeite (Francke, Carl and Francke, Ernest): Earth Sciences. See: Thrush; Webster's 3d.

Francke's needle (Francke, Karl Ernst): Medicine. See: Dorland; Stedman.

Francke's sign (Francke, Karl Ernst): Medicine. See: Dorland.

Francke's symptom (Francke, Karl Ernst): Medicine. See: Dorland.

Franckesche Stiftungen (Francke, August Hermann): Philanthropy. See: Canney.

FRANCO, FRANCISCO. fl. 16th c. Spanish physician and botanist. See: Biog. Lex. hervorr. Aerzte. Francoa.

FRANCO, FRANCISCO. 1892-1975. Spanish dictator. See: Encyc. Brit., 1973. Francoism.

Francoa (Franco, Francisco): Botany. See: Charnock; Taylor, N.

Francois dysencephaly (Francois, Jules). See: Hallermann-Streiff syndrome.

Francois' dystrophy (1) (Francois, Jules): Medicine. See: Jablonski.

Francois' dystrophy (2) (Francois, Jules): Medicine. See: Jablonski.

Francois-Haustrate syndrome (Francois, Jules and Haustrate): Medicine. See: Jablonski.

FRANCOIS, JULES. fl. 1956. Belgian ophthalmologist. Cited in: Leiber and Olbrich. Francois dysencephaly, Francois' dystrophy (1), Francois' dystrophy (2), Francois-Haustrate syndrome, Francois' syndrome (1), Francois' syndrome (2), Hallermann-Streiff-Francois syndrome.

Francois Premier (Francis I): Fashion. See: Webster's 3d.

Francois reagent for ammonia in methylamine (Derivation undetermined): Chemistry. See: Van Nostrand Chem. Dict.

Francois' syndrome (1) (Francois, Jules): Medicine. See: Jablonski.

Francois' syndrome (2) (Francois, Jules): Medicine. See: Jablonski.

Francoism (Franco, Francisco): Politics. See: Webster's 3d.

Frangipane (or Frangipani) (pastry) (Frangipani, Marquis?): Food and Drink. See: Hendrickson.

Frangipane (perfume) (Frangipani family): Generic Word. See: Charnock; Hendrickson; Partridge.

FRANGIPANI FAMILY. fl. 11th c. Roman aristocrats. See: Barnhart (Cycl. Names). Frangipane (perfume).

FRANGIPANI, MARQUIS. fl. 17th c. French army officer. (Biography source unavailable.) Frangipane (or Frangipani) (pastry)?

FRANK, ALFRED ERICH. b. 1884. German physician. See: Biog. Lex. hervorr. Aerzte, 1880-1930. Frank's capillary toxicosis.

FRANK, FREDERICK CHARLES. fl. 1950. English physicist. See: Direct. Brit. Sci., 1963. Frank-Read source.

FRANK, FRITZ. 1856-1923. German gynecologist. See: Biog. Lex. hervorr. Aerzte, 1880-1930. Frank's operation (1).

FRANK, JACOB. 1712-1791. Polish theologian and mystic. See: Barnhart (Cycl. Names). Frankists.

Frank Nelson Cole prize (Cole, Frank Nelson): Mathematics. Cited in: Dict. Sci. Biog.

Frank-Read source (Frank, Frederick Charles and Read, William Thornton, Jr.): Physics. See: Ballentyne; Internat. Dict. Phys. Elec.; Thewlis.

FRANK, RUDOLF. 1862-1913. Austrian surgeon. See: Sci., vol. 37 (1913), p. 479. Frank's operation (2), Ssabanejew-Frank operation.

Frank test (Derivation undetermined): Chemistry. See: Van Nostrand Chem. Dict.

FRANKE, FELIX. b. 1860. German surgeon. See: Biog. Lex. hervorr. Aerzte, 1880-1930. Franke's operation.

FRANKE, GUSTAV. b. 1878. German physician. Cited in: Mansell. Franke's triad.

FRANKEL, CHARLES. 1917- . American educator and author. See: Who's Who Amer., 1974-1975. Frankel's law.

Frankel's law (Frankel, Charles): Politics. See: Hendrickson.

FRANKENHAEUSER, FERDINAND. 1832-1894. German gynecologist. See: Speert, p. 129. Frankenhaeuser's ganglion, Frankenhaeuser's plexus.

Frankenhaeuser's ganglion (Frankenhaeuser, Ferdinand): Medicine. See: Donath; Dorland; Stedman.

Frankenhaeuser's plexus (Frankenhaeuser, Ferdinand): Medicine. See: Donath.

Frankenia (sea heath) (Frankenius, Johann): Botany. See: Charnock; Webster's 3d.

FRANKENIUS, JOHANN. 1590-1661. Swedish physician and botanist. See: Nouv. Biog. Univ. Frankenia (sea heath).

Frankenstein (Frankenstein, the medical student): Generic Word. See: Funk; Partridge; Webster's 3d.

FRANKENSTEIN, THE MEDICAL STUDENT. Character in the novel by Mary Shelley (1818). See: Benet. Frankenstein.

Franke's operation (Franke, Felix): Medicine. See: Dorland.

Franke's triad (Franke, Gustav): Medicine. See: Jablonski.

Frankfort plane (Derivation undetermined): Medicine. See: Stedman.

Frankists (Frank, Jacob): Religion. See: Canney.

FRANKL-HOCHWART, LOTHAR VON. 1862-1914. Austrian neurologist. See: Sci., vol. 41 (1915), p. 204. Frankl-Hochwart's disease.

Frankl-Hochwart's disease (Frankl-Hochwart, Lothar von): Medicine. See: Dorland; Jablonski.

Frankland-Duppa reaction (Frankland, Edward and Duppa, Baldwin Francis): Chemistry. See: Van Nostrand Chem. Dict.

FRANKLAND, EDWARD. 1825-1899. English-born chemist. See: Dict. Sci. Biog. Frankland-Duppa reaction, Frankland('s) method (or reaction), Wuertz-Fittig-Frankland reaction.

Frankland('s) method (or reaction) (Frankland, Edward): Chemistry. See: Ballentyne; Hackh; Van Nostrand Chem. Dict.

Frankland notation (Derivation undetermined): Chemistry. See: Hackh.

Franklin-Adams charts (Franklin-Adams, John): Astronomy. See: Satterthwaite.

FRANKLIN-ADAMS, JOHN. 1843-1912. English astronomer. Cited in: Mansell. Franklin-Adams charts.

Franklin antenna (Franklin, C. S.?): Electronics. See: Hughes; Internat. Dict. Phys. Elec.; Markus.

FRANKLIN, BENJAMIN. 1706-1790. American statesman, scientist, and philosopher. See: Dict. Sci. Biog. Franklin lightening rod (or conductor), Franklin spectacles, Franklin stove, Franklin (unit), Franklinia (or Franklin tree), Franklinian.

FRANKLIN, C. S. fl. 1920. English electrical engineer. (Biography source unavailable.) Franklin antenna?, Marconi-Franklin antenna.

FRANKLIN, EDWARD CLAUS. 1928- . German-born American physician. See: Amer. Men Sci., 10th ed. Franklin's disease.

Franklin equation (Derivation undetermined): Physics. See: Ballentyne; Internat. Dict. Ap. Math.; Internat. Dict. Phys. Elec.

Franklin('s) ground-squirrel (Franklin, Sir John): Zoology. See: Gray; Mathews, M. M.

Franklin('s) grouse (Franklin, Sir John): Zoology. See: Mathews, M. M.; Webster's 3d.

FRANKLIN, HENRY JAMES. 1883-1958. American zoologist and entomologist. See: Amer. Men Sci., 9th ed., vol. 2. Frankliniella.

FRANKLIN, SIR JOHN. 1786-1847. English explorer. See: World Who's Who Sci. Franklin('s) ground-squirrel, Franklin('s) grouse, Franklin's gull.

Franklin lightening rod (or conductor) (Franklin, Benjamin): Engineering and Industry. See: Hendrickson; Mathews, M. M.

Franklin spectacles (Franklin, Benjamin): Medicine. See: Hendrickson; Mathews, M. M.; Stedman.

Franklin stove (Franklin, Benjamin): Engineering and Industry. See: Hendrickson; Partridge; Webster's 3d.

Franklin (unit) (Franklin, Benjamin): Physics. See: Dresner; Markus; Thewlis.

Franklinia (or Franklin tree) (Franklin, Benjamin): Botany. See: Partridge; Webster's 3d.; Winburne.

Franklinian (Franklin, Benjamin): History. See: Mathews, M. M.; Webster's 3d.

Frankliniella (Franklin, Henry James): Zoology. See: Pennak; Webster's 3d.

Franklin's disease (Franklin, Edward Claus): Medicine. See: Jablonski; Stedman.

Franklin's gull (Franklin, Sir John): Zoology. See: Hendrickson; Partridge; Pennak.

Frank's capillary toxicosis (Frank, Alfred Erich): Medicine. See: Stedman.

Frank's operation (1) (Frank, Fritz): Medicine. See: Dorland.

Frank's operation (2) (Frank, Rudolf): Medicine. See: Dorland.

FRANSERI, ANTONIO. b. 1745. Spanish physician and botanist. See: Encic. Univ. Ilus. Franseria.

Franseria (Franseri, Antonio): Botany. See: Webster's 3d.

FRANZ, CARL AUGUST OTTO. b. 1870. German physician. See: Biog. Lex. hervorr. Aerzte, 1880-1930. Franz's syndrome.

Franz-Keldysh effect (Derivation undetermined): Physics. See: Ballentyne.

FRANZ, RUDOLF. d. 1902. German physicist. See: Sci., vol. 17 (1903), p. 319. Wiedemann-Franz law.

FRANZEN, HARTWIG. 1878-1923. German chemist. See: Pogg., vol. 5. Curtius-Frazen test reaction.

Franzen reagent (Derivation undetermined): Chemistry. See: Van Nostrand Chem. Dict.

Franz's syndrome (Franz, Carl August Otto): Medicine. See: Jablonski.

Frapie hand-press (Derivation undetermined): Printing. See: Lockwood.

FRARY, FRANCIS COWLES. b. 1884. American chemist. See: Amer. Men Sci., 3d ed. Frary's metal.

Frary's metal (Frary, Francis Cowles): Chemistry. See: Hackh.

FRASCH, HERMAN. 1851-1914. German-born American chemist. See: World Who's Who Sci. Frasch process (or sulphur process), Frasch sulfur.

Frasch process (or sulphur process) (Frasch, Herman): Engineering and Industry. See: Ballentyne; Thrush; Van Nostrand Chem. Dict.

Frasch sulfur (Frasch, Herman): Engineering and Industry. See: Thrush.

Fraser clutch (Fraser, William): Engineering and Industry. See: Auger.

Fraser-Darling law (or effect) (Derivation undetermined): Zoology. See: Gray; Pennak.

Fraser fir (or balsam fir) (Fraser, John): Botany. See: Webster's 3d.; Winburne.

FRASER, JOHN. 1750-1811. Scottish botanist. See: Dict. Nat. Biog. Fraser fir (or balsam fir), Fraser magnolia, Fraser thimbleberry, Frasera.

Fraser magnolia (Fraser, John): Botany. See: Winburne.

Fraser method for osmotic pressure (Derivation undetermined): Physics. See: Internat. Dict. Phys. Elec.

Fraser thimbleberry (Fraser, John): Botany. See: Winburne.

FRASER, THOMAS. b. 1893. American mining engineer. See: Amer. Men Sci., 4th ed. Fraser's air-sand process.

FRASER, WILLIAM. fl. 1949. English engineer. (Biography source unavailable.) Fraser clutch.

Frasera (Fraser, John): Botany. See: Dorland; Taylor, N.

Fraser's air-sand process (Fraser, Thomas): Engineering and Industry. See: Thrush.

Fraser's composing machine (Derivation undetermined): Printing. See: Lockwood.

Frases test reaction (Derivation undetermined): Chemistry. See: Van Nostrand Chem. Dict.

Fraude solution (Derivation undetermined): Chemistry. See: Van Nostrand Chem. Dict.

Fraunhofer diffraction (Fraunhofer, Joseph): Physics. See: Ballentyne; Internat. Dict. Ap. Math.; Markus.

FRAUNHOFER, JOSEPH. 1787-1826. German physicist. See: Dict. Sci. Biog. Fraunhofer diffraction, Fraunhofer lines, Fraunhofer region, Fraunhofer (unit).

Fraunhofer lines (Fraunhofer, Joseph): Physics. See: Hackh; Thewlis; Van Nostrand Chem. Dict.

Fraunhofer region (Fraunhofer, Joseph): Physics. See: Internat. Dict. Phys. Elec.; Markus; Van Nostrand Sci. Encyc.

Fraunhofer (unit) (Fraunhofer, Joseph): Physics. See: Dresner.

Frautschy bottles (Frautschy, Jeffery Dean): Engineering and Industry. See: Thrush.

FRAUTSCHY, JEFFERY DEAN. 1919- . American geologist. See: Amer. Men and Women Sci. 12th ed. Frautschy bottles.

FRAZIER, CHARLES HARRISON. 1870-1936. American surgeon. See: World Who's Who Sci. Frazier-Spiller operation, Frazier's needle.

Frazier-Lemke Act (or Farm Bankruptcy Act) (Frazier, Lynn Joseph and Lemke, William): History. See: Morris; Smith.

FRAZIER, LYNN JOSEPH. 1874-1947. American legislator. See: Biog. Direct. Amer. Congress. Frazier-Lemke Act (or Farm Bankruptcy Act).

Frazier-Spiller operation (Frazier, Charles Harrison and Spiller, William Gibson): Medicine. See: Dorland; Stedman.

Frazier's needle (Frazier, Charles Harrison): Medicine. See: Dorland; Stedman.

FREARSON. fl. 1875. English engineer. (Biography source unavailable.) Frearson recess.

Frearson recess (Frearson): Engineering and Industry. See: Auger.

Frederician cut (Derivation undetermined): Engineering and Industry. See: Thrush.

Frederician poets (Frederick II Augustus of Hohenstaufen): Literature. See: Preminger under "Sicilian School."

FREDERICK II (FREDERICK THE GREAT). 1712-1786. King of Prussia. See: Encyc. Brit., 1973. Code Frederic, Friedrichsdor.

FREDERICK II AUGUSTUS OF HOHENSTAUFEN. 1194-1250. Holy Roman emperor. See: Dict. Sci. Biog. Augustal (coin), Frederician poets.

FREDERICK VI. 1768-1839. King of Denmark. See: Encyc. Brit., 1973. Frederick (d'or) (coin).

Frederick (d'or) (coin) (Frederick VI): Numismatics. See: Charnock; Webster's 3d.

Frederick's syndrome (Derivation undetermined): Medicine. See: Jablonski.

FREDERICQ, LOUIS AUGUSTE. 1815-1853. Belgian physician. Cited in: Mansell. Fredericq's sign.

Fredericq's sign (Fredericq, Louis Auguste): Medicine. See: Dorland.

FREDET, PIERRE. 1870-1946. French surgeon. See: Presse Med. (1946, annee 54, p. 579. Fredet-Ramstedt operation.

Fredet-Ramstedt operation (Fredet, Pierre and Ramstedt, Conrad): Medicine. See: Dorland; Stedman.

Fredholm('s) determinant (Fredholm, Erik Ivar): Mathematics. See: Internat. Dict. Ap. Math.; James.

Fredholm equation (Fredholm, Erik Ivar): Mathematics. See: Ballentyne; Internat. Dict. Phys. Elec.; Van Nostrand Sci. Encyc.

FREDHOLM, ERIK IVAR. 1866-1927. Swedish mathematician. See: Dict. Sci. Biog. Fredholm('s) determinant, Fredholm equation, Fredholm method, Fredholm minors, Fredholm theorem (for integral equations).

Fredholm method (Fredholm, Erik Ivar): Mathematics. See: Internat. Dict. Phys. Elec.

Fredholm minors (Fredholm, Erik Ivar): Mathematics. See: James.

Fredholm test reaction (Friedheim, Hugo): Chemistry. See: Van Nostrand Chem. Dict.

Fredholm theorem (for integral equations) (Fredholm, Erik Ivar): Mathematics. See: Internat. Dict. Ap. Math.

FREDIANI, HAROLD ARTHUR. 1911- . American chemist. See: World Who's Who Sci. Frediani micro-test for potassium.

Frediani micro-test for potassium (Frediani, Harold Arthur): Chemistry. See: Van Nostrand Chem. Dict.

FREEDLEY, GEORGE. 1904-1967. American theater historian and curator. See: Who Was Who Amer., 1961-1968. George Freedley Memorial Award.

FREEMAN, E.A. fl. 1938. English physician. (Biography source unavailable.) Freeman-Sheldon syndrome.

Freeman-Nichols roaster (Derivation undetermined): Engineering and Industry. See: Thrush.

Freeman-Sheldon syndrome (Freeman, E.A. and Sheldon, Joseph Harold): Medicine. See: Jablonski.

Freeman time-unit (Derivation undetermined): Photography. See: Drever.

FREESE, FRIEDRICH HEINRICH THEODOR. d. 1876. German physician. See: Ascherson and Graebner. Freesia?

Freesia (Freese, Friedrich Heinrich Theodor? or Fries, Elias Magnus?): Botany. See: Hendrickson; Taylor, N.; Webster's 3d.

FREGE, FRIEDRICH LUDWIG GOTTLOB. 1848-1925. German mathematician. See: Dict. Sci. Biog. Fregean.

Fregean (Frege, Friedrich Ludwig Gottlob): Mathematics. See: Webster's 3d.

Frehden-Fuerst spot-test (Frehden, O. and Fuerst, K.): Chemistry. See: Van Nostrand Chem. Dict.

Frehden-Goldschmidt test for amines (Frehden, O. and Goldschmidt, Leontine): Chemistry. See: Van Nostrand Chem. Dict.

Frehden-Goldschmidt test for protein (Frehden, O. and Goldschmidt, Leontine): Chemistry. See: Van Nostrand Chem. Dict.

FREHDEN, O. fl. 1934. Austrian pharmacologist. Cited in: Chem. Abstr., vol. 29, p. 80. Feigl-Frehden test, Frehden-Fuerst spot-test, Frehden-Goldschmidt test for amines, Frehden-Goldschmidt test for protein.

FREHSE. fl. 1914. German? chemist. Cited in: Chem. Abstr., vol. 8, p. 2581. Sisley-Frehse reagent.

Frei-Hoffman reaction (Frei, Wilhelm Siegmund and Hoffman). See: Frei test.

Frei test (Frei, Wilhelm Siegmund): Medicine. See: Stedman; Webster's 3d. Also known as: Frei-Hoffman reaction.

FREI, WILHELM SIEGMUND. 1885-1943. German dermatologist. See: World Who's Who Sci. Frei test, Frei's disease.

FREIBERG, ALBERT HENRY. 1869-1940. American surgeon. See: Who Was Who Amer., 1897-1942. Freiberg's infraction.

Freiberg amalgamation (Derivation undetermined): Engineering and Industry. See: Thrush.

Freiberg's infraction (Freiberg, Albert Henry). See: Koehler's second disease.

FREIESLEBEN, JOHANN KARL. 1774-1846. German geologist. See: Dict. Sci. Biog. Freieslebenite.

Freieslebenite (Freiesleben, Johann Karl): Earth Sciences. See: Thrush; Webster's 3d.

Frei's disease (Frei, Wilhelm Siegmund). See: Durand-Nicolas-Favre disease.

Freitag hand press (Derivation undetermined): Printing. See: Lockwood.

FREJKA, BEDRICH. 1890- . Czech physician. See: Lek. Listy, (1950), rocnik 5, cislo 3/4, p. 61. Frejka pillow?

Frejka pillow (Frejka, Bedrich?): Medicine. See: Stedman.

FREMEREY-DOHNA, H. fl. 1953. German ophthalmologist. Cited in: Leiber and Olbrich. Ullrich and Fremerey-Dohna syndrome.

FREMONT, CHARLES. 1855-1930. French engineer. Cited in: Mansell. Fremont test, Fremont testing machine.

Fremont cottonwood (Fremont, John Charles): Botany. See: Webster's 3d.

Fremont etching reagent (Derivation undetermined): Engineering and Industry. See: Thrush.

FREMONT, JOHN CHARLES. 1813-1890. American explorer. See: World Who's Who Sci. Fremont cottonwood, Fremontia, Fremontism.

Fremont screwbean (Derivation undetermined): Botany. See: Winburne.

Fremont test (Fremont, Charles): Engineering and Industry. See: Thewlis; Thrush.

Fremont testing machine (Fremont, Charles): Engineering and Industry. See: Auger.

Fremontia (Fremont, John Charles): Botany. See: Taylor, N.; Webster's 3d.

Fremontism (Fremont, John Charles): History. See: Mathews, M.M.

Fremont's pine (or nut pine) (Derivation undetermined): Botany. See: Webster's 3d.

Fremont's squirrel (Derivation undetermined): Zoology. See: Webster's 3d.

FREMY, EDMOND. 1814-1894. French chemist. See: Dict. Sci. Biog. Fremy reagent, Fremy salt.

Fremy reagent (Fremy, Edmond): Chemistry. See: Van Nostrand Chem. Dict.

Fremy salt (Fremy, Edmont): Chemistry. See: Hackh.

FRENCH, HERBERT E. b. 1889. American chemist. See: Amer. Men Sci., 4th ed. Bickel-French test reaction, French-Wittel reagent.

French process (Derivation undetermined): Chemistry. See: Van Nostrand Chem. Dict.

French-Wittel reagent (French, Herbert E. and Wirtel, A.F.): Chemistry. See: Van Nostrand Chem. Dict.

Frenet formulae (Frenet, Jean-Frederic). See: Serret-Frenet formulae.

FRENET, JEAN-FREDERIC. 1816-1900. French mathematician. See: Dict. Sci. Biog. Serret-Frenet formulae.

Frenet-Serret formulas (Frenet, Jean-Frederic and Serret, Joseph Alfred). See: Serret-Frenet formulae.

Frenier sand pump (Derivation undetermined): Engineering and Industry. See: Thrush.

Frenkel defect (Frenkel, Yakov Ilyich): Physics. See: Ballentyne; Internat. Dict. Ap. Math.; Thewlis.

Frenkel exciton (Frenkel, Yakov Ilyich): Physics. See: Ballentyne.

Frenkel-Halsey-Hill isotherm (Derivation undetermined): Physics. See: Internat. Dict. Phys. Elec.

FRENKEL-HEIDEN, HEINRICH S. 1860-1931. German neurologist. See: Biog. Lex. hervorr. Aerzte, 1880-1930. Frenkel's method, Frenkel's movements (or treatment), Frenkel's symptom.

FRENKEL, HENRI. 1864-1934. French ophthalmologist. Cited in: Leiber and Olbrich. Frenkel's syndrome.

Frenkel mixer (Derivation undetermined): Engineering and Industry. See: Thrush.

FRENKEL, YAKOV ILYICH. 1894-1954. Russian physicist. See: Dict. Sci. Biog. Frenkel defect, Frenkel exciton.

Frenkel's method (Frenkel-Heiden, Heinrich S.): Medicine. See: Stedman.

Frenkel's movements (or treatment) (Frenkel-Heiden, Heinrich S.): Medicine. See: Dorland.

Frenkel's symptom (Frenkel-Heiden, Heinrich S.): Medicine. See: Stedman.

Frenkel's syndrome (Frenkel, Henri): Medicine. See: Jablonski.

frenulum of Giacomini (Giacomini, Carlo): Medicine. See: Stedman.

frenulum of Macdowel (MacDowell, Benjamin George). See: McDowell's frenulum.

frenulum of Morgagni (Morgagni, Giovanni Battista): Anatomy. See: Dorland; Stedman.

Frerich, Friedrich Theodor von. See: Von Frerich, Friedrich Theodor.

Frerich's theory (Von Frerich, Friedrich Theodor): Medicine. See: Dorland; Stedman.

FRESENIUS, CARL REMIGIUS. 1818-1897. German chemist. See: Dict. Sci. Biog. Fresenius desiccator, Fresenius nitrogen bulb, Fresenius test reaction for antimony.

Fresenius desiccator (Fresenius, Carl Remigius): Chemistry. See: Hackh.

Fresenius nitrogen bulb (Fresenius, Carl Remigius): Chemistry. See: Hackh.

Fresenius test reaction for antimony (Fresenius, Carl Remigius): Chemistry. See: Van Nostrand Chem. Dict.

FRESNEL, AUGUSTIN JEAN. 1788-1827. French physicist. See: Dict. Sci. Biog. Fresnel biprism, Fresnel coefficient of drag, Fresnel diffraction, Fresnel ellipsoid, Fresnel equations, Fresnel equations for metallic reflection, Fresnel-Huyghens principle, Fresnel integral(s), Fresnel lens, Fresnel mirror(s), Fresnel region, Fresnel rhomb, Fresnel (unit), Fresnel zone, law(s) of Fresnel-Arago.

Fresnel biprism (Fresnel, Augustin Jean): Physics. See: Internat. Dict. Phys. Elec.; Thewlis; Webster's 3d.

Fresnel coefficient of drag (Fresnel, Augustin Jean): Physics. See: Internat. Dict. Phys. Elec.; Van Nostrand Sci. Encyc.

Fresnel diffraction (Fresnel, Augustin Jean): Physics. See: Internat. Dict. Phys. Elec.; Markus; Thewlis.

Fresnel ellipsoid (Fresnel, Augustin Jean): Physics. See: Thewlis; Thrush.

Fresnel equations (Fresnel, Augustin Jean): Physics. See: Internat. Dict. Ap. Math.; Internat. Dict. Phys. Elec.; Thewlis.

Fresnel equations for metallic reflection (Fresnel, Augustin Jean): Physics. See: Internat. Dict. Ap. Math.; Internat. Dict. Phys. Elec.

Fresnel-Huyghens principle (Fresnel, Augustin Jean and Huyghens, Christiaan). See: Huyghens principle.

Fresnel integral(s) (Fresnel, Augustin Jean): Physics. See: Ballentyne; Internat. Dict. Phys. Elec.; Thewlis.

Fresnel lens (Fresnel, Augustin Jean): Physics. See: Focal Encyc. Photog.; Markus; Webster's 3d.

Fresnel mirror(s) (Fresnel, Augustin Jean): Physics. See: Internat. Dict. Phys. Elec.; Thewlis; Van Nostrand Sci. Encyc.

Fresnel region (Fresnel, Augustin Jean): Physics. See: Internat. Dict. Phys. Elec.; Markus; Van Nostrand Sci. Encyc.

Fresnel rhomb (Fresnel, Augustin Jean): Physics. See: Internat. Dict. Phys. Elec.; Thewlis; Webster's 3d.

Fresnel (unit) (Fresnel, Augustin Jean): Physics. See: Dresner; Hughes; Internat. Dict. Ap. Math.

Fresnel zone (Fresnel, Augustin Jean): Physics. See: Ballentyne; Huschke; Markus.

FRESSON, HENRI T. d. 1951. French agricultural engineer. (Biography source unavailable.) Fresson process.

Fresson process (Fresson, Henri T.): Engineering and Industry. See: Webster's 3d.

FREUD, SIGMUND. 1856-1939. German psychoanalyst. See: Dict. Sci. Biog. Freudian (or Freudianism), Freudian fixation, Freudian slip, Freud's cathartic method, Freud's syndrome.

Freudenberg plates (Derivation undetermined): Engineering and Industry. See: Thrush.

FREUDENBERG, WILHELM. b. 1881. German geologist. Cited in: Min. Mag., vol. 32 (1961), p. 957. Freudenbergite.

Freudenbergite (Freudenberg, Wilhelm): Earth Sciences. See: Thrush.

Freudian (or Freudianism) (Freud, Sigmund): Psychology. See: English; Good; Hoult.

Freudian fixation (Freud, Sigmund): Psychology. See: Stedman.

Freudian slip (Freud, Sigmund): Psychology. See: Chaplin; Hendrickson; Wolman.

Freud's cathartic method (Freud, Sigmund): Psychology. See: Dorland.

Freud's syndrome (Freud, Sigmund): Psychology. See: Dorland; Hinsie; Stedman.

FREUND, EMANUELE. b. 1869. German dermatologist. See: Biog. Lex. hervorr. Aerzte, 1880-1930. Freund's dermatitis.

FREUND, ERNST. 1863-1946. Austrian chemist. See: Biog. Lex. hervorr. Aerzte, 1880-1930. Freund-Kaminer reaction.

FREUND, JULES THOMAS. 1890-1960. American immunologist. See: Who Was Who Amer., 1961-1968. Freund's adjuvant.

Freund-Kaminer reaction (Freund, Ernst and Kaminer, Gisa): Medicine. See: Dorland; Stedman.

Freund method (for preparation of cycloparaffins) (Derivation undetermined): Chemistry. See: Ballentyne.

Freund reaction (Derivation undetermined): Chemistry. See: Van Nostrand Chem. Dict.

FREUND, WILHELM ALEXANDER. 1833-1918. German surgeon. See: Wer Ist's, 1906. Freund's anomaly, Freund's law, Freund's operation.

Freundler-Menager reagent (Freundler, Paul Theodore and Menager, Y.): Chemistry. See: Van Nostrand Chem. Dict.

FREUNDLER, PAUL THEODORE. b. 1874. French chemist. See: Pogg., vols. 4, 5, 6. Freundler-Menager reagent.

Freundlich equation (Freundlich, Herbert Max Finley): Chemistry. See: Van Nostrand Chem. Dict.

FREUNDLICH, HERBERT MAX FINLAY. 1880-1941. German-born chemist in America. See: World Who's Who Sci. Freundlich equation, Freundlich isotherm (or adsorption isotherm), Thomson-Freundlich equation.

Freundlich isotherm (or adsorption isotherm) (Freundlich, Herbert Max Finlay): Chemistry. See: Ballentyne; Internat. Dict. Phys. Elec.; Van Nostrand Chem. Dict.

Freund's adjuvant (Freund, Jules Thomas): Medicine. See: Stedman; Webster's 3d.

Freund's anomaly (Freund, Wilhelm Alexander): Medicine. See: Dorland; Jablonski; Stedman.

Freund's dermatitis (Freund, Emanuele): Medicine. See: Jablonski.

Freund's law (Freund, Wilhelm Alexander): Medicine. See: Dorland; Stedman.

Freund's operation (Freund, Wilhelm Alexander): Medicine. See: Dorland; Stedman.

Frey-Baillarger syndrome (Frey, Lucie and Baillarger, Jules Gabriel Francois). See: Frey's syndrome.

FREY, LUCIE. fl. 1923. French physician. Cited in: Leiber and Olbrich. Frey's syndrome.

FREY, MAXIMILIAN RUPPERT FRANZ VON. 1852-1932. Austrian-born physiologist. See: Dict. Sci. Biog. Frey's hairs (or irritation hairs).

FREYA. Scandinavian goddess of fruitfulness and love. See: Jobes. Freyalite.

Freyalite (Freya): Earth Sciences. See: Thrush.

Freycinet, Charles-Louis de Saulses de. See: De Freycinet, Charles-Louis de Saulses.

Freycinet, Louis de Saulses de. See: De Freycinet, Louis de Saulses.

Freycinet plan (De Freycinet, Charles-Louis de Saulses): History. Cited in: World Who's Who Sci.

Freycinetia (De Freycinet, Louis de Saulses): Botany. See: Webster's 3d.

FREYER, SIR PETER JOHNSTON. 1851-1921. English surgeon. See: World Who's Who Sci. Freyer's operation.

Freyer's operation (Freyer, Sir Peter Johnston): Medicine. See: Dorland; Stedman.

Frey's hairs (or irritation hairs) (Frey, Maximilian Ruppert Franz von): Medicine. See: Dorland; Stedman.

Frey's syndrome (Frey, Lucie): Medicine. See: Dorland; Jablonski; Stedman. Also known as: Baillarger's syndrome, Dupuy's syndrome, Frey-Baillarger syndrome.

FREYTAG, GUSTAV. 1816-1895. German novelist, playwright, and historian. See: Encyc. Brit., 1973. Freytag's pyramid.

FREYTAG, HANS. fl. 1938. German chemist. Cited in: Chem. Abstr., vol. 32, p. 3295. Freytag test for sulfonated oils.

Freytag test for sulfonated oils (Freytag, Hans): Chemistry. See: Van Nostrand Chem. Dict.

Freytag test for sulfur dioxide (Derivation undetermined): Chemistry. See: Van Nostrand Chem. Dict.

Freytag's pyramid (Freytag, Gustav): Literature. See: Scott.

FRICKE, JOHANN KARL GEORG. 1790-1841. German surgeon. See: Biog. Lex. hervorr. Aerzte. Fricke's bandage.

Fricke's bandage (Fricke, Johann Karl Georg): Medicine. See: Dorland; Stedman.

FRID, B. I. fl. 1938-1945. Russian chemist. Cited in: Chem. Abstr., vol. 32, p. 76. Alimarin-Frid reagent.

FRIDAY. Servant of Robinson Crusoe in the novel of the same name (1719) by Daniel Defoe. See: Benet. Man Friday.

Friday (Frigg): Generic Word. See: Charnock; Funk; Wagner (Names).

FRIDENBERG, PERCY H. 1868-1960. American ophthalmologist. See: Who Was Who Amer., 1961-1968. Fridenberg's stigmometric card test.

Fridenberg's stigmometric card test (Fridenberg, Percy H.): Medicine. See: Dorland; Stedman.

FRIDERICHSEN, CARL. b. 1886. Danish pediatrician. See: Acta paed., vol. 45, no. 4 (1956), p. 329. Waterhouse-Friderichsen syndrome.

FRIEDEL, CHARLES. 1832-1899. French chemist. See: World Who's Who Sci. Friedel-Crafts condensation, Friedel-Crafts reaction, Friedelin, Friedelite.

Friedel-Crafts condensation (Friedel, Charles and Crafts, James Mason): Chemistry. See: Hackh.

Friedel-Crafts reaction (Friedel, Charles and Crafts, James Mason): Chemistry. See: Ballentyne; Van Nostrand Chem. Dict.; Webster's 3d.

FRIEDEL, GEORGES. 1865-1933. French mineralogist. See: Dict. Sci. Biog. Friedel('s) law.

Friedel('s) law (Friedel, Georges): Physics. See: Ballentyne; Internat. Dict. Phys. Elec.; Thewlis.

Friedelin (Friedel, Charles): Chemistry. See: Hackh; Webster's 3d.

Friedelite (Friedel, Charles): Earth Sciences. See: Thrush; Webster's 3d.

Friedenwald-Ehrlich diazo reagent (Derivation undetermined): Chemistry. See: Van Nostrand Chem. Dict.

FRIEDENWALD, JONAS STEIN. 1897-1955. American ophthalmologist. See: Amer. Men Sci., 9th ed. Friedenwald's syndrome?

Friedenwald's syndrome (Friedenwald, Jonas Stein?): Medicine. See: Jablonski.

FRIEDHEIM, HUGO. fl. 1936. German chemist. Cited in: Chem. Abstr., vol. 30, p. 4427. Fredholm test reaction.

FRIEDLAENDER, KARL. 1847-1887. German physician. See: Allg. Deut. Biog. Friedlaender's disease, Friedlaender's pneumonia (or bacillus pneumonia), Friedlaender's stain for capsules.

FRIEDLAENDER, PAUL. 1857-1923. German chemist. See: Surrey. Friedlaender (Friedlander) synthesis.

Friedlaender picrocarmine solution (Derivation undetermined): Chemistry. See: Van Nostrand Chem. Dict.

Friedlaender (Friedlander) synthesis (Friedlaender, Paul): Chemistry. See: Ballentyne; Van Nostrand Chem. Dict.

Friedlaender's disease (Friedlaender, Karl): Medicine. See: Dorland; Jablonski; Stedman.

Friedlaender's pneumonia (or bacillus pneumonia) (Friedlaender, Karl): Medicine. See: Jablonski; Stedman. Also known as: Klebsiella pneumonia.

Friedlaender's stain for capsules (Friedlaender, Karl): Medicine. See: Stedman.

FRIEDMAN, ARNOLD PHINEAS. 1909- . American neurologist. See: Amer. Men and Women Sci., 12th ed. Friedman-Roy syndrome.

Friedman curve (Friedman, Emanuel A.): Medicine. See: Stedman.

FRIEDMAN, EMANUEL A. 1926- . American physician. See: World Who's Who Sci. Friedman curve.

Friedman-Lapham test (Friedman, Maurice Harold and Lapham, Maxwell Edward). See: Friedman test.

FRIEDMAN, MAURICE HAROLD. 1903- . American physician. See: Amer. Men Sci., 10th ed. Friedman test.

FRIEDMAN, MILTON. 1912- . American economist. See: World Who's Who Sci. Friedmanite, Friedman's test.

Friedman-Roy syndrome (Friedman, Arnold Phineas and Roy, James Evans): Medicine. See: Jablonski.

Friedman test (Friedman, Maurice Harold): Medicine. See: Dorland; Stedman; Webster's 3d.; Winburne. Also known as: Friedman-Lapham test.

Friedmanite (Friedman, Milton): Economics. See: Barnhart (New Eng.).

FRIEDMANN, MAX. 1858-1925. German neurologist. Cited in: Kelly. Friedmann's complex, Friedmann's disease, Friedmann's syndrome (1), Friedmann's syndrome (2).

Friedmann's complex (Friedmann, Max): Medicine. See: Hinsie.

Friedmann's disease (Friedmann, Max): Medicine. See: Hinsie; Jablonski; Wolman.

Friedmann's syndrome (1) (Friedmann, Max): Medicine. See: Jablonski.

Friedmann's syndrome (2) (Friedmann, Max): Medicine. See: Jablonski.

Friedman's test (Friedman, Milton): Statistics. See: Kendall.

FRIEDREICH, NICOLAUS ANTON. 1761-1836. German physician. See: Biog. Lex. hervorr. Aerzte. Friedreich's disease.

FRIEDREICH, NIKOLAUS. 1826-1882. German physician. See: World Who's Who Sci. Friedreich's ataxia (or disease (2), Friedreich's disease (1), Friedreich's foot, Friedreich's phenomenon, Friedreich's sign.

Friedreich's ataxia (or disease (2) (Friedreich, Nikolaus): Medicine. See: Dorland; Jablonski.

Friedreich's disease (Friedreich, Nicolaus Anton): Medicine. See: Jablonski.

Friedreich's disease (1) (Friedreich, Nikolaus): Medicine. See: Dorland; Jablonski; Stedman.

Friedreich's foot (Friedreich, Nikolaus): Medicine. See: Stedman.

Friedreich's phenomenon (Friedreich, Nikolaus): Medicine. See: Stedman.

Friedreich's sign (Friedreich, Nikolaus): Medicine. See: Dorland; Stedman

Friedrich-Erb-Arnold syndrome (Friedrich, N.; Erb, Wilhelm Heinrich; and Arnold, Julius). See: Uehlinger's syndrome.

FRIEDRICH, H. fl. 1924. German surgeon. Cited in: Leiber and Olbrich. Friedrich's syndrome.

FRIEDRICH, N. fl. 1868. German physician. (Biography source unavailable.) Friedrich-Erb-Arnold syndrome.

Friedrichs condenser (Friedrichs, Fritz): Chemistry. See: Hackh.

FRIEDRICHS, FRITZ. b. 1885. German chemist. See: Pogg., vol. 6. Friedrichs condenser, Friedrichs gas bottle.

Friedrichs gas bottle (Friedrichs, Fritz): Chemistry. See: Hackh.

Friedrich's syndrome (Friedrich, H.): Medicine. See: Jablonski.

Friedrichsdor (Frederick II): Numismatics. See: Webster's 3d.

FRIEND, CHARLOTTE. 1921- . American microbiologist. See: Amer. Men and Women Sci., 12th ed. Friend disease, Friend virus, Friend's leukemia.

Friend disease (Friend, Charlotte): Medicine. See: Stedman.

Friend virus (Friend, Charlotte): Medicine. See: Stedman.

Friend's leukemia (Friend, Charlotte): Medicine. See: Jablonski.

FRIES, ELIAS MAGNUS. 1794-1874. Swedish botanist. See: Dict. Sci. Biog. Freesia?

FRIES, JOHN. ca. 1750-1818. American insurgent. See: Dict. Amer. Biog. Fries' rebellion.

FRIES, KARL. 1875- . German chemist. See: Surrey. Fries rearrangement (or reaction), Fries-Vogt test reaction.

Fries rearrangement (or reaction) (Fries, Karl): Chemistry. See: Ballentyne; Van Nostrand Chem. Dict.; Webster's 3d.

Fries' rebellion (Fries, John): History. See: Morris and Irwin; Smith.

Fries' rule (Derivation undetermined): Chemistry. See: Ballentyne; Van Nostrand Chem. Dict.

Fries-Vogt test reaction (Fries, Karl and Vogt, W.): Chemistry. See: Van Nostrand Chem. Dict.

Friess-Pierrou syndrome (Derivation undetermined): Medicine. See: Jablonski.

FRIGG. Norse queen of the gods. See: Jobes. Friday.

Frisbie('s) feeder (Derivation undetermined): Engineering and Industry. See: Auger; Thrush.

Frischer ring (Derivation undetermined): Engineering and Industry. See: Thrush.

Frise aileron (Frise, Leslie G.): Engineering and Industry. See: Webster's 3d.

FRISE, LESLIE G. 1897- . English engineer. (Biography source unavailable.) Frise aileron.

Fritsch-Asherman syndrome (Fritsch, Heinrich and Asherman, Joseph G.): Medicine. See: Jablonski.

FRITSCH, HEINRICH. 1844-1915. German gynecologist. See: World Who's Who Sci. Bozeman-Fritsch catheter, Fritsch-Asherman syndrome, Fritsch's catheter.

FRITSCH, PAUL ERNST MORITZ. 1859-1913. German chemist. See: Pogg., vols. 4, 5. Pomeranz-Fritsch reaction.

FRITSCH, RUDOLFO. fl. 1910. Austrian chemist. Cited in: Kelly. Fritsch test.

Fritsch test (Fritsch, Rudolfo): Chemistry. See: Van Nostrand Chem. Dict.

Fritsch's catheter (Fritsch, Heinrich): Medicine. See: Dorland.

Fritz engine (Fritz, Hans): Engineering and Industry. See: Auger.

FRITZ, HANS. No dates. German engineer. (Biography source unavailable.) Fritz engine.

FRITZMANN, ERNST. b. 1863. German chemist. See: Pogg., vol. 6. Fritzmann test.

Fritzmann test (Fritzmann, Ernst): Chemistry. See: Van Nostrand Chem. Dict.

FROBENIUS, GEORG FERDINAND. 1849-1917. German mathematician. See: Dict. Sci. Biog. Frobenius' method, Frobenius' theorem.

Frobenius' method (Frobenius, Georg Ferdinand): Mathematics. See: Ballentyne; Internat. Dict. Ap. Math.

Frobenius' theorem (Frobenius, Georg Ferdinand): Mathematics. See: James.

FROEBEL, FRIEDRICH. 1782-1852. German educator. See: Encyc. Brit., 1973. Froebel system (or teaching method), Froebelian (or Froebelism), Froebelian gifts, Froebelian kindergarten, Froebelian occupations, Froebel's games.

Froebel system (or teaching method) (Froebel, Friedrich): Education. See: Brewer; Hendrickson.

Froebelian (or Froebelism) (Froebel, Friedrich): Education. See: Partridge; Webster's 3d.; Weekley.

Froebelian gifts (Froebel, Friedrich): Education. See: Good.

Froebelian kindergarten (Froebel, Friedrich): Education. See: Good.

Froebelian occupations (Froebel, Friedrich): Education. See: Good.

Froebel's games (Froebel, Friedrich): Education. See: Good.

FROEHDE, A. fl. 1868. German chemist. Cited in: Kelly. Froehde test reaction for albumin.

Froehde('s) reagent (Derivation undetermined): Chemistry. See: Hackh; Stedman, Van Nostrand Chem. Dict.

Froehde test reaction for albumin (Froehde, A.): Chemistry. See: Van Nostrand Chem. Dict.

FROEHLICH, ALFRED. 1871-1953. Austrian-born pharmacologist in America. See: World Who's Who Sci. Froehlich's dwarf, Froehlich's syndrome (disease or obesity).

FROEHLICH, F. fl. 1839. German physician. (Biography source unavailable.) Froehlich's syndrome.

Froehlich's dwarf (Froehlich, Alfred): Medicine. See: Stedman.

Froehlich's syndrome (Froehlich, F.). See: Obrinsky's syndrome.

Froehlich's syndrome (disease or obesity) (Froehlich, Alfred): Medicine. See: Jablonski; Stedman; Wolman. Also known as: Babinski-Froehlich syndrome, Launois-Cleret syndrome.

FROESCHELS, EMIL. 1883- . Austrian-born otologist in America. See: World Who's Who Sci. Froeschel's symptom.

Froeschel's symptom (Froeschels, Emil): Medicine. See: Dorland.

FROHBERG, MAX HANS. 1901- . German-born Canadian geologist. See: Amer. Men Sci., 9th ed. Frohbergite.

Frohbergite (Frohberg, Max Hans): Earth Sciences. See: Thrush; Webster's 3d.

Frohlich-Bardeen theory (Frohlich, Herbert and Bardeen, John): Physics. See: Internat. Dict. Ap. Math.; Internat. Dict. Phys. Elec.

FROHLICH, HERBERT. 1905- . German-born physicist in England. See: World Who's Who Sci. Frohlich-Bardeen theory.

FROHN, DAMIANUS. b. 1843. German physician. Cited in: Mansell. Frohn's reagent.

Frohn's reagent (Frohn, Damianus): Medicine. See: Dorland; Stedman.

FROIN, GEORGES. b. 1874. French physician. See: Biog. Lex. hervorr. Aerzte, 1880-1930. Froin's syndrome.

Froin's syndrome (Froin, Georges): Medicine. See: Dorland; Hinsie; Jablonski; Stedman. Also known as: Lepine-Froin syndrome, Nonne-Froin syndrome, Nonne's syndrome.

from Maidenkirk to John O'Groats (John O'Groat): Generic Word (from end to end of Scotland). See: Encyc. Brit., 1973 under "John O'Groats."

FROMENT, JULES. 1878-1946. French physician. See: Dict. Nat. Contemp., vol. 2, p. 228. Froment's sign (or paper sign).

Froment process (Derivation undetermined): Engineering and Industry. See: Thrush.

Fromentin boiler feed (Fromentin, E.): Engineering and Industry. See: Auger.

FROMENTIN, E. No dates. French engineer. (Biography source unavailable.) Fromentin boiler feed.

Froment's sign (or paper sign) (Froment, Jules): Medicine. See: Dorland; Stedman.

FROMMANN, CARL. 1831-1892. German anatomist. See: World Who's Who Sci. Frommann's lines.

Frommann's lines (Frommann, Carl): Medicine. See: Dorland.

FROMMEL, RICHARD JULIUS ERNST. 1854-1912. German gynecologist. See: Biog. Lex. hervorr. Aerzte, 1880-1930. Chiari-Frommel syndrome, Frommel's operation.

Frommel's disease (Frommel, Richard Julius Ernst). See: Chiari-Frommel syndrome.

Frommel's operation (Frommel, Richard Julius Ernst): Medicine. See: Dorland; Stedman.

Frommer's dilator (Derivation undetermined): Medicine. See: Stedman.

Frommherz reagent (Derivation undetermined): Chemistry. See: Van Nostrand Chem. Dict.

FRONDEL, CLIFFORD. 1907- . American mineralogist. See: World Who's Who Sci. Frondelite.

Frondelite (Frondel, Clifford): Earth Sciences. See: Thrush; Webster's 3d.

Froriep, August Friedrich von. See: Von Froriep, August Friedrich.

Froriep's ganglion (Von Froriep, August Friedrich): Anatomy. See: Dorland; Stedman.

Froriep's induration (Von Froriep, August Friedrich): Medicine. See: Stedman.

Frost count (Frost, William Dodge): Medicine. See: Winburne.

Frost gravimeter (Derivation undetermined): Engineering and Industry. See: Thrush.

FROST, JAMES. fl. 1811. English inventor. (Biography source unavailable.) Frost's cement.

Frost-Lang operation (Frost, William Adams and Lang, Basil T.): Medicine. See: Stedman.

Frost little-plate method (Frost, William Dodge): Medicine. See: Winburne.

FROST, WILLIAM ADAMS. 1853-1935. English ophthalmologist. See: Brit. J. Ophthal., (Dec., 1935), p. 697. Frost-Lang operation.

FROST, WILLIAM DODGE. 1867-1957. American bacteriologist. See: World Who's Who Sci. Frost count, Frost little-plate method.

Frostathing's Law (Derivation undetermined): History. See: Harbottle.

FROSTIG, MARIANNE B. 1906- . Austrian-born American psychologist. See: Amer. Men and Women Sci., 12th ed. (Soc. Behav. Sci.). Frostig test of visual motor development.

Frostig test of visual motor development (Frostig, Marianne B.): Psychology. See: Wolman.

Frost's cement (Frost, James): Engineering and Industry. See: Thrush.

Froude brake (Froude, William): Engineering and Industry. See: Auger.

Froude method (Froude, William): Physics. See: Thewlis.

Froude momentum theory (Froude, William): Physics. See: Internat. Dict. Ap. Math.

Froude number (Froude, William): Physics. See: Huschke; Internat. Dict. Ap. Math.; Internat. Dict. Phys. Elec.

FROUDE, WILLIAM. 1810-1879. English engineer. See: Dict. Sci. Biog. Froude brake, Froude method, Froude momentum theory, Froude number, Froude's curve.

Froude's curve (Froude, William): Physics. See: Ballentyne; Thrush.

Frue vanner (Derivation undetermined): Engineering and Industry. See: Thrush.

FRUEND, H. fl. 1926. German physician. (Biography source unavailable.) Haglund-Laewen-Fruend syndrome.

FRUGONI, CESARE. b. 1881. Italian physician. See: Biog. Lex. hervorr. Aerzte, 1880-1930. Frugoni's disease, Frugoni's syndrome.

Frugoni's disease (Frugoni, Cesare): Medicine. See: Jablonski.

Frugoni's syndrome (Frugoni, Cesare): Medicine. See: Jablonski.

FRY, J. D. fl. 1914. English inventor. Cited in: Chem. Abstr., vol. 8, p. 1687. Chattock-Fry tilting micromanometer.

Fry reagent (Derivation undetermined): Chemistry. See: Van Nostrand Chem. Dict.

Fryberg and Simons gauge (Fryburg, George C. and Simons, Joseph H.): Physics. See: Internat. Dict. Phys. Elec.

FRYBURG, GEORGE C. 1919- . American physicist. See: Amer. Men and Women Sci., 12th ed. Fryberg and Simons gauge.

FRYER, PERCIVAL JOHN. fl. 1918. English chemist. Cited in: Mansell. Fryer-Weston reagent for fats.

Fryer-Weston reagent for fats (Fryer, Percival John and Weston, Frank Edwin): Chemistry. See: Van Nostrand Chem. Dict.

FUBINI, GUIDO. 1879-1943. Italian mathematician. See: Dict. Sci. Biog. Fubini's theorem.

Fubini's theorem (Fubini, Guido): Mathematics. See: James.

Fuchs' atrophy (Fuchs, Ernst): Medicine. See: Jablonski.

Fuchs' coloboma (Fuchs, Ernst): Medicine. See: Dorland; Stedman.

Fuchs' dimples (or dellen) (Fuchs, Ernst): Medicine. See: Jablonski.

Fuchs' dystrophy (or syndrome) (Fuchs, Ernst): Medicine. See: Jablonski. Also known as: Fuchs-Kraupa syndrome, Kraupa's dystrophy.

FUCHS, ERNST. 1851-1930. Austrian ophthalmologist. See: World Who's Who Sci. Dalen-Fuchs spots (or nodules), Fuchs' atrophy, Fuchs' coloboma, Fuchs' dimples (or dellen), Fuchs' dystrophy (or syndrome), Fuchs' heterochromia, Fuchs' keratitis, Fuchs' spot, Fuchs' stoma, Fuchs' syndrome (1), Fuchs' syndrome (2).

Fuch's gold purple (Derivation undetermined): Engineering and Industry. See: Thrush.

FUCHS, HANS JACOBUS. fl. 1925. German physician. Cited in: Kelly. Fuchs's protein test.

Fuchs' heterochromia (Fuchs, Ernst): Medicine. See: Jablonski.

FUCHS, IMMANUEL LAZARUS. 1833-1902. German mathematician. See: Dict. Sci. Biog. Fuchs theorem, Fuchsian group.

FUCHS, JOHANN NEPOMUK VON. 1774-1856. German chemist and mineralogist. See: Dict. Sci. Biog. Fuchsite.

Fuchs' keratitis (Fuchs, Ernst): Medicine. See: Jablonski.

Fuchs-Kraupa syndrome (Fuchs, Ernst and Kraupa, Ernst). See: Fuchs' dystrophy (or syndrome).

FUCHS, LEONHARD. 1501-1566. German physician and botanist. See: World Who's Who Sci. Fuchsia, Fuchsin (or Fuchsine) (dye).

Fuchs' spot (Fuchs, Ernst): Medicine. See: Jablonski.

Fuchs' stoma (Fuchs, Ernst): Medicine. See: Stedman.

Fuchs' syndrome (1) (Fuchs, Ernst): Medicine. See: Jablonski.

Fuchs' syndrome (2) (Fuchs, Ernst): Medicine. See: Jablonski.

Fuchs theorem (Fuchs, Immanuel Lazarus): Mathematics. See: Internat. Dict. Ap. Math.; Internat. Dict. Phys. Elec.; Van Nostrand Sci. Encyc.

Fuchsia (Fuchs, Leonhard): Botany. See: Brewer; Charnock; Taylor, N.

Fuchsian group (Fuchs, Immanuel Lazarus): Mathematics. See: Hendrickson.

Fuchsin (or Fuchsine) (dye) (Fuchs, Leonhard): Chemistry. See: Dorland; Stedman; Thrush.

Fuchsite (Fuchs, Johann Nepomuk von): Earth Sciences. See: Thrush; Webster's 3d.

Fuchs's protein test (Fuchs, Hans Jacobus): Medicine. See: Dorland.

Fudge (Fudge, Captain): Generic Word (nonsense). See: Charnock; Hendrickson.

FUDGE, CAPTAIN. fl. 17th c. English sea captain. (Biography source unavailable.) Fudge.

FUELLEBORN, FRIEDRICH GEORG HANS. 1866-1933. German parasitologist. See: Wer Ist's, 1906. Fuelleborn's method.

Fuelleborn's method (Fuelleborn, Friedrich Georg Hans): Medicine. See: Dorland.

FUELLING, GEORG. fl. 1963. German physician. (Biography source unavailable.) Weyers-Fuelling syndrome.

FUERBRINGER, PAUL WALTHER. 1849-1930. German physician. See: World Who's Who Sci. Fuerbringer's hand disinfection, Fuerbringer's sign, Fuerbringer's test.

Fuerbringer's hand disinfection (Fuerbringer, Paul Walther): Medicine. See: Stedman.

Fuerbringer's sign (Fuerbringer, Paul Walther): Medicine. See: Dorland.

Fuerbringer's test (Fuerbringer, Paul Walther): Medicine. See: Dorland; Stedman. Also known as: Stuetz's test.

FUERST, K. fl. 1938. Austrian chemist. Cited in: Chem. Abstr., vol. 32, p. 5334. Frehden-Fuerst spot-test.

FUERSTNER, KARL. 1848-1906. German psychiatrist. See: Wer Ist's, 1906. Fuerstner's disease.

Fuerstner's disease (Fuerstner, Karl): Medicine. See: Dorland; Jablonski; Stedman.

Fuerth-Hermann test reaction (Von Fuerth, Otto and Herrmann, Heinz): Chemistry. See: Van Nostrand Chem. Dict.

Fuerth, Otto von. See: Von Fuerth, Otto.

Fuerth's myosin (Von Fuerth, Otto): Medicine. See: Stedman.

FUIREN, GEORGE. 1581-1628. Danish botanist and physician. See: Nouv. Biog. Univ. Fuirena?

Fuirena (Fuiren, George?): Botany. See: Charnock.

FUJITA, AKIJI. fl. 1935. Japanese physician. Cited in: Chem. Abstr., vol. 29, p. 4398. Fujita-Iwatake-Miyata test for ascorbic acid.

Fujita-Iwatake-Miyata test for ascorbic acid (Fujita, Akiji; Iwatake, Danzo; and Miyata, Tadao): Chemistry. See: Van Nostrand Chem. Dict.

FUJIWARA, HIDEKATSU. fl. 1933. Japanese chemist. Cited in: Chem. Abstr., vol. 27, p. 5145. Fujiwara test for strychnine.

FUJIWARA, KYOYETSURO. fl. 1916. Japanese chemist. Cited in: Chem. Abstr., vol. 11, p. 3201. Fujiwara test reaction.

Fujiwara test for strychnine (Fujiwara, Hidekatsu): Chemistry. See: Van Nostrand Chem. Dict.

Fujiwara test reaction (Fujiwara, Kyoyetsuro): Chemistry. See: Van Nostrand Chem. Dict.

Fukai test (Fukai, Toshi): Chemistry. See: Van Nostrand Chem. Dict.

FUKAI, TOSHI. fl. 1928. Japanese chemist. Cited in: Chem. Abstr., vol. 23, p. 1081. Fukai test.

FUKALA, VINCENZ. 1847-1911. Austrian ophthalmologist. See: Biog. Lex. hervorr. Aerzte, 1880-1930. Fukala's operation.

Fukala's operation (Fukala, Vincenz): Medicine. See: Dorland; Stedman.

Fulbright exchange program (or scholarship) (Fulbright, James William): Education. See: Good; Hendrickson; Webster's 3d.

FULBRIGHT, JAMES WILLIAM. 1905- . American legislator. See: Biog. Direct. Amer. Congress. Connally-Fulbright resolution, Fulbright exchange program (or scholarship).

FULCHER, GORDON SCOTT. b. 1884. American physicist. See: Amer. Men Sci., 9th ed. Fulcher spectrum.

Fulcher spectrum (Fulcher, Gordon Scott): Chemistry. See: Hackh.

FULD, ERNST. b. 1873. German internist. See: Biog. Lex. hervorr. Aerzte, 1880-1930. Fuld('s) test (or reagent).

Fuld('s) test (or reagent) (Fuld, Ernst): Chemistry. See: Dorland; Van Nostrand Chem. Dict.

Fullagar engine (Fullagar, H. F.): Engineering and Industry. See: Auger.

FULLAGAR, H. F. fl. 1912. English engineer. (Biography source unavailable.) Fullagar engine.

Fuller Albright's syndrome (Albright, Fuller). See: Albright's syndrome (2).

FULLER, EUGENE. 1858-1930. American urologist. Cited in: Kelly. Fuller's operation.

Fuller rose beetle (Derivation undetermined): Zoology. See: Winburne.

Fuller's grading curve (Derivation undetermined): Engineering and Industry. See: Thrush.

Fuller's operation (Fuller, Eugene): Medicine. See: Dorland.

Fullerton-Cattell law (Derivation undetermined): Psychology. See: Chaplin; Drever; Wolman.

FULTON, CHARLES CLARKE. 1900- . American chemist. See: Amer. Men Sci., 10th ed. Fulton reactions for phenols, Fulton solutions, Fulton test for copper.

Fulton reactions for phenols (Fulton, Charles Clarke): Chemistry. See: Van Nostrand Chem. Dict.

FULTON, ROBERT. 1765-1815. American civil engineer. See: World Who's Who Sci. Fulton's folly.

Fulton solutions (Fulton, Charles Clarke): Chemistry. See: Van Nostrand Chem. Dict.

Fulton test for copper (Fulton, Charles Clarke): Chemistry. See: Van Nostrand Chem. Dict.

FULTON, WESTON MILLER, SR. 1871-1946. American inventor. See: World Who's Who Sci. Fulton's bellows.

Fulton's bellows (Fulton, Weston Miller, Sr.): Engineering and Industry. See: Auger.

Fulton's folly (Fulton, Robert): Generic Word. See: Phyfe.

FUNAKOSHI, OTOZO. fl. 1929. Japanese chemist. Cited in: Chem. Abstr., vol. 23, p. 4644. Funakoshi reagent.

Funakoshi reagent (Funakoshi, Otozo): Chemistry. See: Van Nostrand Chem. Dict.

FUNKENSTEIN, DANIEL HERTZ. 1910- . American psychiatrist. See: Direct. Med. Specialists, 1970-1971. Funkenstein test.

Funkenstein test (Funkenstein, Daniel Hertz): Psychiatry. See: Hinsie; Stedman.

Furphy (Furphy, Joseph? or Furphy, the contractor?): Generic Word (rumor). See: Hendrickson; Partridge.

FURPHY, JOSEPH. 1843-1913. Australian writer. See: Encyc. Brit., 1973. Furphy?

FURPHY THE CONTRACTOR. fl. 1915. Australian rubbish cart supplier. (Biography source unavailable.) Furphy?

Furrer 20mm aircraft cannon (Furrer, Adolf): Weapons. See: Quick.

FURRER, ADOLF. fl. 1933. Swiss inventor. (Biography source unavailable.) Furrer 20mm aircraft cannon.

Furry process (Derivation undetermined): Statistics. See: Kendall.

Furry theorem (Furry, Wendell Hinkle): Physics. See: Internat. Dict. Phys. Elec.

FURRY, WENDELL HINKLE. 1907- . American physicist. See: World Who's Who Sci. Furry theorem.

FURSINA, M. M. fl. 1938. Russian chemist. Cited in: Chem. Abstr., vol. 32, p. 2052. Korenman-Fursina micro-reaction for lithium.

Furst-Ostrum syndrome (Furst, William and Ostrum, Herman William): Medicine. See: Jablonski.

FURST, WILLIAM. fl. 1942. American physician. (Biography source unavailable.) Furst-Ostrum syndrome.

FURTH, JACOB. 1896- . Hungarian-born American pathologist. See: Amer. Men and Women Sci., 12th ed. Furth's tumor.

Furth's tumor (Furth, Jacob): Medicine. See: Jablonski.

G

G wave (Gutenberg, Beno): Earth Sciences. See: Encyc. Brit., 1973 under "Earthquake," vol. 7, p. 859b.

ga-ga (or gaga) (Gauguin, Paul?): Generic Word (mentally unbalanced). See: Hendrickson.

GABBET, HENRY SINGER. fl. 1887. English physician. Cited in: Kelly. Fraenken-Gabbet stain, Gabbet('s) solution (or stain).

Gabbet('s) solution (or stain) (Gabbet, Henry Singer): Medicine. See: Hackh; Stedman.

Gabble ratchet (Gabriel). See: Gabriel('s) hounds (or rachet).

GABRIEL. Biblical messenger of God. See: Barnhart (Cycl. Names). Gabriel('s) hounds (or rachet).

Gabriel ethylenimine method (Gabriel, Siegmund?): Chemistry. See: Van Nostrand Chem. Dict.

Gabriel('s) hounds (or rachet) (Gabriel): Generic Word (wild geese). See: Brewer; Harvey. Also known as: Gabble ratchet.

Gabriel isoquinoline synthesis (Gabriel, Siegmund): Chemistry. See: Van Nostrand Chem. Dict.

GABRIEL, SIEGMUND. 1851-1924. German chemist. See: Dict. Sci. Biog. Gabriel ethylenimine method?, Gabriel isoquinoline synthesis, Gabirel('s) synthesis (or phthalimide synthesis).

Gabriel('s) synthesis (or phthalimide synthesis) (Gabriel, Siegmund): Chemistry. See: Ballentyne; Van Nostrand Chem. Dict.

Gabrielites (Scherling, Gabriel): Religion. See: Wagner (Names).

Gabriel's insurrection (Prosser, Gabriel): History. See: Jameson.

Gabriel's test (Derivation undetermined): Statistics. See: Kendall.

GABUTTI, E. fl. 1908. Italian chemist. Cited in: Chem. Abstr., vol. 2, p. 862. Gabutti reagent for morphine and codeine, Gabutti test for formaldehyde.

Gabutti reagent for morphine and codeine (Gabutti, E.): Chemistry. See: Van Nostrand Chem. Dict.

Gabutti test for formaldehyde (Gabutti, E.): Chemistry. See: Van Nostrand Chem. Dict.

Gaddum and Schild test (Gaddum, John Henry and Schild, Heinz Otto): Medicine. See: Stedman.

GADDUM, JOHN HENRY. 1900- . English biochemist. Cited in: Kelly. Gaddum and Schild test.

GADOLIN, JOHAN. 1760-1852. Finnish chemist and mineralogist. See: Dict. Sci. Biog. Gadolinite, Gadolinium.

Gadolinite (Gadolin, Johan): Earth Sciences. See: Charnock; Thrush; Webster's 3d.

Gadolinium (Gadolin, Johan): Chemistry. See: Hendrickson; Partridge; Van Nostrand Sci. Encyc.

GADSDEN, JAMES. 1788-1858. American diplomat. See: Dict. Amer. Biog. Gadsden Purchase.

Gadsden Purchase (Gadsden, James): History. See: Hendrickson; Latham; Phyfe.

GAEBLER, OLIVER HENRY. 1895- . American biochemist. See: World Who's Who Sci. Breh-Gaebler reagent.

Gaede molecular pump (Gaede, Wolfgang): Engineering and Industry. See: Hughes.

Gaede vacuum (or diffusion) pump (Gaede, Wolfgang): Engineering and Industry. See: Auger; Hughes.

GAEDE, WOLFGANG. 1878-1945. German physicist. See: World Who's Who Sci. Gaede molecular pump, Gaede vacuum (or diffusion) pump.

GAENSLEN, FREDERICK JULIUS. 1877-1937. American surgeon. See: Who Was Who Amer., 1897-1942. Gaenslen's sign (or test).

Gaenslen's sign (or test) (Gaenslen, Frederick Julius): Medicine. See: Dorland; Stedman.

Gaensslen-Erb syndrome (Gaensslen, Max and Erb, Wilhelm Heinrich). See: Minkowski-Chauffard syndrome.

GAENSSLEN, MAX. 1895- . German physician. See: Who's Who Ger., 1956. Gaensslen's disease, Gaensslen's syndrome.

Gaensslen's disease (Gaensslen, Max): Medicine. See: Jablonski.

Gaensslen's syndrome (Gaensslen, Max). See: Minkowski-Chauffard syndrome.

GAERTNER, AUGUST ANTON HIERONYMUS. 1848-1934. German hygienist and bacteriologist. See: World Who's Who Sci. Gaertner's bacillus.

GAERTNER, GUSTAV. 1855-1937. Austrian pathologist. See: World Who's Who Sci. Gaertner's method, Gaertner's phenomenon (or vein phenomenon), Gaertner's tonometer.

Gaertner spectrophotometer (Derivation undetermined): Physics. See: Internat. Dict. Phys. Elec.

Gaertner's bacillus (Gaertner, August Anton Hieronymus): Medicine. See: Dorland; Stedman; Webster's 3d.

Gaertner's method (Gaertner, Gustav): Medicine. See: Stedman.

Gaertner's phenomenon (or vein phenomenon) (Gaertner, Gustav): Medicine. See: Dorland; Stedman.

Gaertner's tonometer (Gaertner, Gustav): Medicine. See: Dorland; Stedman.

GAFFKY, GEORG THEODOR AUGUST. 1850-1918. German bacteriologist. See: Dict. Sci. Biog. Gaffky table (or scale).

Gaffky table (or scale) (Gaffky, Georg Theodor August): Medicine. See: Dorland; Stedman.

Gagarinite (Derivation undetermined): Earth Sciences. See: Thrush.

GAGE, ROBERT B. fl. 1913. American mineral collector. Cited in: Min. Mag., vol. 16 (1913), p. 361. Gageite.

GAGE, THOMAS. 1721-1787. English general and colonial governor. See: Dict. Nat. Biog. Gageite.

GAGE, SIR WILLIAM. d. 1820. English botanist. (Biography source unavailable.) greengage (plum).

Gageite (Gage, Robert B.): Earth Sciences. See: Webster's 3d.

Gageite (Gage, Thomas): History. See: Mathews, M. M.

Gaglio test (Derivation undetermined): Chemistry. See: Van Nostrand Chem. Dict.

GAHN, JOHAN GOTTLIEB. 1745-1818. Swedish chemist and mineralogist. See: Dict. Sci. Biog. Gahnite.

Gahnite (Gahn, Johan Gottlieb): Earth Sciences. See: Charnock; Thrush; Van Nostrand Sci. Encyc.

GAILLARD, ANTONIO. fl. 1909. Spanish chemist. Cited in: Chem. Abstr., vol. 3, p. 585. Gaillard-Parrish chamber, Gaillard tower.

GAILLARD DE MARENTONNEAU. fl. 18th c. French botanist. (Biography source unavailable.) Gaillardia.

GAILLARD, FRANCOIS LUCIEN. 1805-1869. French physician. See: Biog. Lex. hervorr. Aerzte. Gaillard's suture.

Gaillard-Parrish chamber (Gaillard, Antonio and Parrish): Chemistry. See: Van Nostrand Chem. Dict.

Gaillard tower (Gaillard, Antonio): Chemistry. See: Hackh; Van Nostrand Chem. Dict.

Gaillardia (Gaillard de Marentonneau): Botany. See: Mathews, M. M.; Taylor, N.; Webster's 3d.

Gaillard's suture (Gaillard, Francois Lucien): Medicine. See: Dorland.

Gainsborough hat (Gainsborough, Thomas): Fashion. See: Hendrickson; Partridge; Picken.

GAINSBOROUGH, THOMAS. 1727-1788. English painter. See: Dict. Nat. Biog. Gainsborough hat.

GAIRDNER, MEREDITH. d. 1837. Scottish naturalist. Cited in: Mansell. Gairdner's woodpecker.

GAIRDNER, SIR WILLIAM TENNANT. 1824-1907. Scottish physician. See: World Who's Who Sci. Gairdner's disease, Gairdner's test.

Gairdner's disease (Gairdner, Sir William Tennant): Medicine. See: Stedman.

Gairdner's test (Gairdner, Sir William Tennant): Medicine. See: Dorland.

Gairdner's woodpecker (Gairdner, Meredith): Zoology. See: Mathews, M. M.

GAISBOECK, FELIX. 1868-1955. Austrian internist. Cited in: Kelly. Gaisboeck's (Geisboeck's) syndrome (or disease).

Gaisboeck's (Geisboeck's) syndrome (or disease) (Gaisboeck, Felix): Medicine. See: Dorland; Jablonski; Stedman.

GAITSKELL, HUGH TODD NAYLOR. 1906-1963. English political leader. See: Webster's Biog. Dict. Butskellism (or Butskell).

GAIUS. ca. 110-ca. 180 A.D. Roman jurist. See: Encyc. Brit., 1973. Institutes of Gaius.

GAL, UZIEL. No dates. Israeli army officer. (Biography source unavailable.) Uzi 9mm submachine gun.

Galahad (Galahad, Sir): Generic Word (knightly chivalry). See: Partridge.

GALAHAD, SIR. Knight of the Round Table in Arthurian romance. See: Benet. Galahad.

GALANT, IVAN BORISOVICH. 1893- . Russian psychiatrist. See: World Who's Who Sci. Galant's reflex.

Galant's reflex (Galant, Ivan Borisovich): Medicine. See: Stedman.

Galassi's pupillary phenomenon (Derivation undetermined): Medicine. See: Stedman.

GALBIATI, GENNARO. 1776-1844. Italian surgeon. See: Biog. Lex. hervorr. Aerzte. Galbiati's operation.

Galbiati's operation (Galbiati, Gennaro): Medicine. See: Stedman.

GALBRAITH, JOHN KENNETH. 1908- . American economist. See: Amer. Men and Women Sci., 12th ed. (Soc. Behav. Sci.). Galbraithian.

Galbraithian (Galbraith, John Kenneth): Economics. See: Barnhart (New. Eng.).

GALE, W. A. No dates. American? mineralogist. Cited in: Min. Mag., vol. 31 (1958), p. 960. Galeite.

Galeati's glands (Galeazzi, Domenico Gusmano): Medicine. See: Donath; Dorland; Stedman.

GALEAZZI, DOMENICO GUSMANO. 1686-1775. Italian physician. See: Dict. Sci. Biog. Galeati's glands.

GALEAZZI, RICCARDO. 1866-1952. Italian orthopedic surgeon. See: Biog. Lex. hervorr. Aerzte, 1880-1930. Galeazzi's fracture, Galeazzi's sign.

Galeazzi's fracture (Galeazzi, Riccardo): Medicine. See: Dorland; Stedman.

Galeazzi's sign (Galeazzi, Riccardo): Medicine. See: Dorland.

Galeite (Gale, W. A.): Earth Sciences. See: Thrush.

GALEN. 130-200 A.D. Greek physician. See: Dict. Sci. Biog. Galen, Galenian figure, Galenic, Galenical(s), Galenism (or Galenite), Galen's anastomosis (or nerve), Galen's bandage, Galen's doctrine of temperament, Galen's innominate gland, great vein of Galen, vein(s) of Galen (or Galen's vein).

Galen (Galen, the physician): Generic Word (medical man). See: Phyfe.

Galenian figure (Galen): Medicine. See: Webster's 3d.

Galenic (Galen): Medicine. See: Dorland; Stedman; Webster's 3d.

Galenical(s) (Galen): Medicine. See: Brewer; Partridge; Webster's 3d.

Galenism (or Galenite) (Galen): Medicine. See: Charnock; Webster's 3d.

Galenists (Abrahamsz, Galenus): Religion. See: Latham.

Galen's anastomosis (or nerve) (Galen): Medicine. See: Stedman.

Galen's bandage (Galen): Medicine. See: Stedman.

Galen's doctrine of temperament (Galen): Psychology. See: Wolman.

Galen's innominate gland (Galen): Medicine. See: Stedman.

galeopsis Hagenii (Hagen, Carl Gottfried): Botany. Cited in: World Who's Who Sci. under "Hagen, Carl Gottfried."

GALERKIN, BORIS GRIGORIEVICH. 1871-1945. Russian mathematician. See: Dict. Sci. Biog., suppl. Galerkin method?, Galerkin stress functions?

Galerkin method (Galerkin, Boris Grigorievich?): Mathematics. See: Internat. Dict. Ap. Math.

Galerkin stress functions (Galerkin, Boris Grigorievich?): Mathematics. See: Internat. Dict. Ap. Math.

GALETZKA, AMBROSIUS. No dates. Inventor of printing process. (Biography source unavailable.) Ambrogal printing.

Galilean (method) (Galilei, Galileo): Physics. See: English; Webster's 3d.

Galilean relativity (Galilei, Galileo): Physics. See: Internat. Dict. Phys. Elec.

Galilean telescope (Galilei, Galileo): Astronomy. See: Internat. Dict. Phys. Elec.; Satterthwaite; Van Nostrand Sci. Encyc.

Galilean transformation (Galilei, Galileo): Physics. See: Ballentyne; Internat. Dict. Ap. Math.; Internat. Dict. Phys. Elec.

GALILEI, GALILEO. 1564-1642. Italian physicist and astronomer. See: Dict. Sci. Biog. Galilean (method), Galilean relativity, Galilean telescope, Galilean transformation, Galileo (Galilei or Gal) (unit of acceleration), Galileo's case, Galileo's lamp.

Galileo (Galilei or Gal) (unit of acceleration) (Galilei, Galileo): Physics. See: Ballentyne; Dresner; Huschke.

Galileo's case (Galilei, Galileo): History. See: Attwater.

Galileo's lamp (Galilei, Galileo): Physics. See: Phyfe.

Galinsoga (Galinsoga, Mariano M. de): Botany. See: Webster's 3d.

GALINSOGA, MARIANO M. DE. c. 1797. Spanish botanist. (Biography source unavailable.) Galinsoga.

Galitzin, Boris Borisovich. See: Golitsyn, Boris Borisovich.

Galitizin-type seismograph (Golitsyn, Boris Borisovich): Earth Sciences. See: Thrush.

GALL, D. C. fl. 1938. English electrical engineer. See: Pogg., vol. 6. Gall potentiometer (or alternating-current potentiometer), Tinsley-Gall ac polar potentiometer.

GALL, FRANZ JOSEPH. 1758-1828. German neuroanatomist. See: Dict. Sci. Biog. Gall's craniology.

Gall potentiometer (or alternating-current potentiometer) (Gall, D. C.): Engineering and Industry. See: Hughes; Internat. Dict. Phys. Elec.

GALL, SAINT. ca. 550-ca. 645. Irish missionary. See: Encyc. Brit., 1973. Order of St. Gall.

Gallagher-Hollander degradation (Gallagher, Thomas Francis and Hollander, Vincent Paul): Chemistry. See: Van Nostrand Chem. Dict.

GALLAGHER, THOMAS FRANCIS. 1905- . American biochemist. See: Amer. Men Sci., 8th ed. Gallagher-Hollander degradation.

GALLAIS, ALFRED. fl. 1912. French physician. Cited in: Kelly. Cooke-Apert-Gallais syndrome.

GALLAVARDIN, LOUIS. 1875-1957. French physician. See: World Who's Who Sci. Gallavardin's phenomenon.

Gallavardin's phenomenon (Gallavardin, Louis): Medicine. See: Stedman.

Galli Mainini, Carlos. See: Mainini, Carlos.

Galli-Mainini test (Mainini, Carlos): Medicine. See: Dorland; Stedman. Also known as: Mainini test.

GALLIE, WILLIAM EDWARD. 1882-1959. Canadian surgeon. See: World Who's Who Sci. Gallie's transplant.

Gallie's transplant (Gallie, William Edward): Medicine. See: Dorland; Stedman.

Gallio (Gallio, Junius): Generic Word (indifferent). See: Charnock; Harvey; Partridge.

GALLIO, JUNIUS. d. ca. 65 A.D. Roman proconsul. See: Encyc. Brit., 1973. Gallio.

Gallitzin, Demetrius de. See: Golitsyn, Dmitry Alekseyevich.

Gallitzinite (Golitsyn, Dmitry Alekseyevich): Earth Sciences. See: Charnock.

Gallium (Boisbaudran, Paul Emile Lecoq de): Chemistry. See: Hendrickson; Weekley.

GALLO, DON GREGORIO. No dates. Spanish inventor. (Biography source unavailable.) Gregoriara.

Galloway boiler (Derivation undetermined): Engineering and Industry. See: Thrush.

Galloway sinking and walling stage (Galloway, Sir William): Engineering and Industry. See: Thrush.

Galloway stage (Galloway, Sir William): Engineering and Industry. See: Thrush.

GALLOWAY, SIR WILLIAM. d. 1927. English mining engineer. See: World Who's Who Sci. Galloway sinking and walling stage, Galloway stage.

Gall's craniology (Gall, Franz Joseph): Medicine. See: Dorland; Stedman.

Gall's projection (or stereographic projection) (Derivation undetermined): Geography. See: Monkhouse; Moore.

GALLUCHAT, JEAN-CLAUDE. d. 1774. French leather craftsman. (Biography source unavailable.) Galuchat.

GALLUP, GEORGE HORACE. 1901- . American public opinion analyst and statistician. See: Who's Who Amer., 1974-1975. Gallup poll.

Gallup poll (Gallup, George Horace): Politics. See: Brewer; Hendrickson.

GALOIS, EVARISTE. 1811-1832. French mathematician. See: Dict. Sci. Biog. Galois field, Galois group, Galois theory.

Galois field (Galois, Evariste): Mathematics. See: James.

Galois group (Galois, Evariste): Mathematics. See: James.

Galois theory (Galois, Evariste): Mathematics. See: James; Webster's 3d.

Galton bar (Galton, Francis): Psychology. See: Chaplin; Drever; Wolman.

GALTON, FRANCIS. 1822-1911. English anthropologist. See: Dict. Sci. Biog. Galton bar, Galton-Henry method, Galton-McAllister distribution, Galton ogive, Galton-Watson process, Galton('s) whistle, Galtonia, Galtonian, Galtonian curve, Galton's delta, Galton's individual difference problem, Galton's law (of inheritance), Galton's law (of regression), Galton's questionary, Galton's rank order test, Galton's system of classifications of fingerprints.

Galton-Henry method (Galton, Francis and Henry, Edward Richard): Sociology. See: Fairchild.

Galton-McAllister distribution (Galton, Francis and Macalister, Sir Donald): Statistics. See: Kendall.

Galton ogive (Galton, Francis): Statistics. See: Kendall.

Galton-Watson process (Galton, Francis and Watson, Henry William): Statistics. See: Kendall.

Galton('s) whistle (Galton, Francis): Psychology. See: Chaplin; Drever; Wolman.

Galtonia (Galton, Francis): Botany. See: Taylor, N.; Webster's 3d.

Galtonian (Galton, Francis): Science. See: Webster's 3d.

Galtonian curve (Galton, Francis): Statistics. See: Ballentyne.

Galton's delta (Galton, Francis): Medicine. See: Donath; Dorland; Stedman.

Galton's individual difference problem (Galton, Francis): Statistics. See: Kendall.

Galton's law (of inheritance) (Galton, Francis): Genetics. See: Gray; Webster's 3d; Zadrozny.

Galton's law (of regression) (Galton, Francis): Genetics. See: Dorland; Henderson, Stedman.

Galton's questionary (Galton, Francis): Psychology. See: English.

Galton's rank order test (Galton, Francis): Statistics. See: Kendall.

Galton's system of classification of fingerprints (Galton, Francis): Medicine. See: Stedman.

Galuchat (Galluchat, Jean-Claude): Applied Arts. See: Webster's 3d.

GALVANI, LUIGI. 1737-1798. Italian anatomist, physiologist, and physicist. See: Dict. Sci. Biog. Galvanic, Galvanism, Galvanizing (or Galvanization), Galvano (or Galvanomagnetic) effects, Galvanocautery, Galvanochemical, Galvanocontractility, Galvanofaradization, Galvanoglyphy, Galvanography (or Galvanograph), Galvanoionization, Galvanoluminescence, Galvanolysis, Galvanometer, Galvanomuscular, Galvanonarcosis, Galvanonervous, Galvanopalpation, Galvanoplasty (or Galvanoplastic process), Galvanopuncture, Galvanoscope (or Galvanoscopy), Galvanosurgery, Galvanotherapeutics (or Galvanotherapy), Galvanothermometer, Galvanothermy, Galvanotonic (or Galvanotonus), Galvanotropism (or Galvanotaxis), Galvat (unit of current).

Galvanic (Galvani, Luigi): Physics. See: Drever; Funk; Markus.

Galvanism (Galvani, Luigi): Physics. See: Charnock; Hughes; Webster's 3d.

Galvanizing (or Galvanization) (Galvani, Luigi): Physics. See: Thewlis; Van Nostrand Sci. Encyc.; Webster's 3d.

Galvano (or Galvanomagnetic) effects (Galvani, Luigi): Physics. See: Ballentyne; Hughes; Thewlis.

Galvanocautery (Galvani, Luigi): Medicine. See: Dorland; Stedman.

Galvanochemical (Galvani, Luigi): Medicine. See: Dorland; Stedman.

Galvanocontractility (Galvani, Luigi): Medicine. See: Dorland; Stedman.

Galvanofaradization (Galvani, Luigi): Medicine. See: Dorland; Stedman.

Galvanoglyphy (Galvani, Luigi): Printing. See: Lockwood.

Galvanography (or Galvanograph) (Galvani, Luigi): Photography. See: Focal Encyc. Photog.; Lockwood; Webster's 3d.

Galvanoionization (Galvani, Luigi): Medicine. See: Dorland.

Galvanoluminescence (Galvani, Luigi): Physics. See: Hughes; Internat. Dict. Phys. Elec.; Webster's 3d.

Galvanolysis (Galvani, Luigi): Medicine. See: Dorland; Stedman.

Galvanometer (Galvani, Luigi): Electronics. See: Chaplin; Drever; Van Nostrand Sci. Encyc.

Galvanomuscular (Galvani, Luigi): Medicine. See: Dorland; Stedman.

Galvanonarcosis (Galvani, Luigi): Medicine. See: Dorland.

Galvanonervous (Galvani, Luigi): Medicine. See: Dorland; Stedman.

Galvanopalpation (Galvani, Luigi): Medicine. See: Dorland; Stedman.

Galvanoplasty (or Galvanoplastic process) (Galvani, Luigi): Physics. See: Lockwood; Thewlis.

Galvanopuncture (Galvani, Luigi): Medicine. See: Dorland.

Galvanoscope (or Galvanoscopy) (Galvani, Luigi): Medicine. See: Dorland Stedman; Thrush.

Galvanosurgery (Galvani, Luigi): Medicine. See: Dorland; Stedman.

Galvanotherapeutics (or Galvanotherapy) (Galvani, Luigi): Medicine. See: Dorland; Stedman.

Galvanothermometer (Galvani, Luigi): Engineering and Industry. See: Thrush.

Galvanothermy (Galvani, Luigi): Medicine. See: Dorland.

Galvanotonic (or Galvanotonus) (Galvani, Luigi): Medicine. See: Dorland; Stedman.

Galvanotropism (or Galvanotaxis) (Galvani, Luigi): Electronics. See: Drever; Hughes; Pennak.

Galvat (unit of current) (Galvani, Luigi): Physics. See: Dresner.

Gamaleia's spirillum (Gamaleya, Nikolay Fyodorovich): Medicine. See: Dorland.

GAMALEYA, NIKOLAY FYODOROVICH. 1859-1949. Russian bacteriologist. See: Dict. Sci. Biog. Gamaleia's spirillum.

Gambel oak (Gambel, William): Botany. See: Mathews, M. M.; Webster's 3d.

Gambel('s) quail (Gambel, William): Zoology. See: Gray; Pennak; Webster's 3d.

Gambel('s) sparrow (Gambel, William): Zoology. See: Mathews, M. M.; Webster's 3d.

GAMBEL, WILLIAM. 1821-1849. American ornithologist. See: Who Was Who Amer., 1607-1896. Gambel oak, Gambel('s) quail, Gambel('s) sparrow, Gambel's finch, Gambel's goose, Gambel's partridge, Gambel's woodmouse.

Gambel's finch (Gambel, William): Zoology. See: Mathews, M. M.

Gambel's goose (Gambel, William): Zoology. See: Mathews, M. M.

Gambel's partridge (Gambel, William): Zoology. See: Mathews, M. M.

Gambel's woodmouse (Gambel, William): Zoology. See: Mathews, M. M.

GAMGEE, JOSEPH SAMPSON. 1828-1886. English surgeon. See: World Who's Who Sci. Gamgee tissue.

Gamgee tissue (Gamgee, Joseph Sampson): Medicine. See: Carter; Dorland; Stedman.

GAMNA, CARLO. 1886-1950. Italian physician. See: Minerva Med., vol. 2, nos. 33/34 (1950), p. 1. Gamna-Favre bodies, Gamna-Gandy bodies (or nodules), Gamna's disease.

Gamna-Favre bodies (Gamna, Carlo and Favre, Maurice): Medicine. See: Stedman.

Gamna-Gandy bodies (or nodules) (Gamna, Carlo and Gandy, Charles): Medicine. See: Stedman. Also known as: Gandy-Gamna bodies.

Gamna's disease (Gamna, Carlo): Medicine. See: Stedman.

Gamow barrier (radius) (Gamow, George): Physics. See: Markus; Thewlis; Webster's 3d.

Gamow-Condon-Gurney theory of alpha-decay (Gamow, George; Condon, Edward Uhler; and Gurney, Ronald Wilfrid): Physics. See: Internat. Dict. Phys. Elec.

Gamow factor (Gamow, George): Physics. See: Internat. Dict. Phys. Elec.

GAMOW, GEORGE. 1904-1968. Russian-born American physicist. See: Dict. Sci. Biog. Gamow barrier (radius), Gamow-Condon-Gurney theory of alpha-decay, Gamow factor, Gamow-Teller interaction, Gamow-Teller matrix element, Gamow-Teller selection rules.

Gamow-Teller interaction (Gamow, George and Teller, Edward): Physics. See: Internat. Dict. Phys. Elec.

Gamow-Teller matrix element (Gamow, George and Teller, Edward): Physics. See: Internat. Dict. Phys. Elec.

Gamow-Teller selection rules (Gamow, George and Teller, Edward): Physics. See: Hughes; Markus; Van Nostrand Sci. Encyc.

Gamp (Gamp, Sarah): Generic Word (umbrella). See: Brewer; Partridge; Webster's 3d.

GAMP, SARAH. Character in Charles Dickens' novel, "Martin Chuzzlewit," (1843-1844). See: Benet. Gamp.

GAMS, ALFONS. fl. 1910. Swiss chemist. Cited in: Chem. Abstr., vol. 4, p. 3222. Pictet-Gams isoquinoline synthesis.

GAMSTORP, INGRID. fl. 1956. Swedish pediatrician. Cited in: Leiber and Olbrich. Gamstorp's syndrome.

Gamstorp's syndrome (Gamstorp, Ingrid): Medicine. See: Jablonski. Also known as: Westphal's syndrome.

GANASSINI, DOMENICO. fl. 1912. Italian chemist. Cited in: Chem. Abstr., vol. 8, p. 309. Ganassini reagent for hydrogen sulfide, Ganassini test for acrolein, Ganassini test for mercury, Ganassini test for quinotoxine in quinine, Ganassini test for uric acid and zinc.

Ganassini reagent for hydrogen sulfide (Ganassini, Domenico): Chemistry. See: Van Nostrand Chem. Dict.

Ganassini test for acrolein (Ganassini, Domenico): Chemistry. See: Van Nostrand Chem. Dict.

Ganassini test for mercury (Ganassini, Domenico): Chemistry. See: Van Nostrand Chem. Dict.

Ganassini test for quinotoxine in quinine (Ganassini, Domenico): Chemistry. See: Van Nostrand Chem. Dict.

Ganassini test for uric acid and zinc (Ganassini, Domenico): Chemistry. See: Van Nostrand Chem. Dict.

Gandhi (cap) (Gandhi, Mohandas Karamchand): Fashion. See: Hendrickson; Picken; Webster's 3d.

GANDHI, MOHANDAS KARAMCHAND. 1869-1948. Indian nationalist and religious leader. See: Encyc. Brit., 1973. Gandhi (cap), Gandhian (or Gandhism), Irwin-Gandhi pact.

Gandhian (or Gandhism) (Gandhi, Mohandas Karamchand): History. See: Hendrickson; Webster's 3d.

GANDY, CHARLES. b. 1872. French physician. Cited in: Arnim. Gamna-Gandy bodies (or nodules), Gandy-Nanta disease.

Gandy-Gamna bodies (Gandy, Charles and Gamna, Carlo). See: Gamna-Gandy bodies (or nodules).

Gandy-Nanta disease (Gandy, Charles and Nanta, A.?): Medicine. See: Stedman.

GANGI, SALVATORE. fl. 1910. Italian physician. Cited in: Chem. Abstr., vol. 4, p. 2323. Gangi's reaction.

Gangi's reaction (Gangi, Salvatore): Medicine. See: Stedman.

GANGOLPHE, LOUIS. 1858-1920. French surgeon. (Biography source unavailable.) Gangolphe's sign.

Gangolphe's sign (Gangolphe, Louis): Medicine. See: Dorland.

GANGULF, SAINT. 720-760. French aristocrat and warrior. See: Holweck. Jingo?

GANNON, WILLIAM. fl. 1895. English engineer. Cited in: Royal Soc. Cat. Sci. Pap., 1884-1900. Schuster-Gannon method for mechanical equivalent of heat.

GANONG, WILLIAM FRANCIS. 1924- . American physiologist. See: Amer. Men Sci., 10th ed. Lown-Ganong-Levine syndrome.

GANSER, SIGBERT JOSEPH MARIA. 1853-1931. German psychiatrist. See: Wer Ist's, 1906. Ganser('s) syndrome, Ganser's ganglion, Ganser's symptom.

Ganser('s) syndrome (Ganser, Sigbert Joseph Maria): Psychiatry. See: Chaplin; Good; Hinsie.

Ganser's ganglion (Ganser, Sigbert Joseph Maria): Medicine. See: Dorland.

Ganser's symptom (Ganser, Sigbert Joseph Maria): Medicine. See: Dorland.

GANT, FREDERICK JAMES. 1825-1905. English surgeon. See: World Who's Who Sci. Gant's line, Gant's operation.

GANT, SAMUEL GOODWIN. 1869-1944. American surgeon. See: Who Was Who Amer., 1969-1973. Gant's clamp.

Gant's clamp (Gant, Samuel Goodwin): Medicine. See: Dorland; Stedman.

Gant's line (Gant, Frederick James): Medicine. See: Dorland.

Gant's operation (Gant, Frederick James): Medicine. See: Dorland.

Gantt chart (or progress chart) (Gantt, Henry Laurence): Engineering and Industry. See: Clark; Kendall; Thrush.

GANTT, HENRY LAURENCE. 1861-1919. American management scientist and mechanical engineer. See: World Who's Who Sci. Gantt chart (or progress chart).

Gantzner's muscle (or accessory bundle) (Derivation undetermined): Medicine. See: Stedman.

Ganymede(s) (Ganymede, the youth): Generic Word (cup-bearer). See: Brewer; Partridge; Webster's 3d.

GANYMEDE, THE YOUTH. Mythical cup-bearer to the gods. See: Jobes. Ganymede(s).

Ganz transmission (Derivation undetermined): Engineering and Industry. See: Auger.

GAPCHENKO, M. V. fl. 1935. Russian chemist. Cited in: Chem. Abstr., vol. 30, p. 984. Gapchenko-Sheintzis micro-test for bismuth, Gapchenko-Sheintzis micro-test for magnesium, Gapchenko-Sheintzis test for bismuth, Gapchenko-Sheintzis test for titanium.

Gapchenko-Sheintzis micro-test for bismuth (Gapchenko, M. V. and Sheintzis, O. G.): Chemistry. See: Van Nostrand Chem. Dict.

Gapchenko-Sheintzis micro-test for magnesium (Gapchenko, M. V. and Sheintzis, O. G.): Chemistry. See: Van Nostrand Chem. Dict.

Gapchenko-Sheintzis test for bismuth (Gapchenko, M. V. and Sheintzis, O. G.): Chemistry. See: Van Nostrand Chem. Dict.

Gapchenko-Sheintzis test for titanium (Gapchenko, M. V. and Sheintzis, O. G.): Chemistry. See: Van Nostrand Chem. Dict.

GARAMOND, CLAUDE. d. 1561. French type-founder. See: Nouv. Biog. Univ. Garamond (type).

Garamond (type) (Garamond, Claude): Printing. See: Harrod; Lockwood.

GARAND, JOHN CANTIUS. 1888- . Canadian-born American engineer and inventor. See: World Who's Who Sci. Garand rifle.

Garand rifle (Garand, John Cantius): Weapons. See: Hendrickson; Partridge; Quick.

GARBE, WILLIAM. 1908 . Canadian dermatologist. See: Direct. Med. Specialists, vol. 8. Sulzberger-Garbe syndrome (or disease).

GARBY, C. D. fl. 1926. American chemist. Cited in: Chem. Abstr., vol. 20, p. 2965. Garby solution.

Garby solution (Garby, C. D.): Chemistry. See: Van Nostrand Chem. Dict.

Garcia. See: Iniguez, Garcia.

Garcin-Guillain syndrome (Garcin, Raymond and Guillain, Georges). See: Garcin's syndrome.

GARCIN, LAURENT. 1683-1751. French botanist and surgeon. See: World Who's Who Sci. Garcinia.

GARCIN, RAYMOND. 1897- . French physician. Cited in: Mansell. Garcin's syndrome.

Garcinia (Garcin, Laurent): Botany. See: Charnock; Taylor, N.; Webster's 3d.

Garcin's syndrome (Garcin, Raymond): Medicine. See: Jablonski. Also known as: Bertolotti-Garcin syndrome, Garcin-Guillain syndrome, Schmincke's tumor-unilateral cranial paralysis syndrome.

GARDEN, ALEXANDER. ca. 1730-1791. Scottish-born American naturalist and physician. See: World Who's Who Sci. Gardenia.

Gardenia (Garden, Alexander): Botany. See: Charnock; Taylor, N.; Webster's 3d.

GARDINER-BROWN, ALFRED. No dates. English otologist. (Biography source unavailable.) Gardiner-Brown's test.

Gardiner-Brown's test (Gardiner-Brown, Alfred): Medicine. See: Dorland; Stedman.

Gardiner test (Derivation undetermined): Chemistry. See: Van Nostrand Chem. Dict.

GARDNER. fl. 1899. American inventor. Cited in: Singer. Gardner-Serpollet steam car.

Gardner-Bosch syndrome (Gardner, Eldon John; Bosch Hernandez, Juan; and Bosch Millares, Juan). See: Gardner's syndrome.

Gardner crusher (Derivation undetermined): Engineering and Industry. See: Thrush.

GARDNER, EDWARD. fl. late 18th c. Botanist in Nepal. See: Britten and Boulger. Gardneria.

GARDNER, ELDON JOHN. 1909- . American geneticist. See: World Who's Who Sci. Gardner's syndrome.

Gardner gun (Gardner, M. W.): Weapons. See: Partridge.

GARDNER, JOHN ADDYMAN. 1867-1946. English chemist. See: Who Was Who, 1941-1950. Doree-Gardner test reaction.

GARDNER, M. W. fl. 1880. Inventor. (Biography source unavailable.) Gardner gun.

Gardner mobilometer (Derivation undetermined): Engineering and Industry. See: Thrush.

Gardner-Serpollet steam car (Gardner and Serpollet, Leon): Engineering and Industry. Cited in: Carter.

Gardneria (Gardner, Edward): Botany. See: Charnock.

Gardner's syndrome (Gardner, Eldon John): Medicine. See: Jablonski; Stedman. Also known as: Gardner-Bosch syndrome.

GARDOQUI, DIEGO MARIA DE. 1735-1798. Spanish diplomat. See: Dicc. Hist. Espana. Jay-Gardoqui negotiations.

Gareis-Endell plastometer (Derivation undetermined): Engineering and Industry. See: Thrush. Also known as: Endell plastometer.

GAREL, JEAN. 1852-1931. French physician. See: Biog. Lex. hervorr. Aerzte, 1880-1930. Garel's sign.

GARELLI, F. fl. 1933. Italian chemist. Cited in: Chem. Abstr., vol. 28, p. 1295. Garelli-Tettamanzi test reaction.

Garelli-Tettamanzi test reaction (Garelli, F. and Tettamanzi, Angelo): Chemistry. See: Van Nostrand Chem. Dict.

Garel's sign (Garel, Jean): Medicine. See: Dorland; Stedman.

Garengeot, Rene-Jacques Croissant de. See: De Garengeot, Rene-Jacques Croissant.

Garengeot's key (De Garengeot, Rene-Jacques Croissant): Medicine. Cited in: World Who's Who Sci.

GARGANTUA. Hero of Francois Rabelais' satire, "Gargantua and Pantagruel" (1532). See: Benet. Gargantuan.

Gargantuan (Gargantua): Generic Word (enormous). See: Funk; Partridge; Weekley.

Garibaldi biscuit (Garibaldi, Giuseppe): Food and Drink. See: Brewer.

Garibaldi (fish) (Garibaldi, Giuseppe): Zoology. See: Hendrickson; Partridge; Webster's 3d.

GARIBALDI, GIUSEPPE. 1807-1882. Italian patriot and soldier. See: Encyc. Brit., 1973. Baldie, Garibaldi biscuit, Garibaldi (fish), Garibaldi (shirt or jacket), Garibaldini.

Garibaldi (shirt or jacket) (Garibaldi, Giuseppe): Fashion. See: Charnock; Picken; Webster's 3d.

Garibaldini (Garibaldi, Giuseppe): History. See: Harbottle.

GARIDEL, PIERRE-JOSEPH. 1658-1737. French botanist. See: World Who's Who Sci. Garidella.

Garidella (Garidel, Pierre-Joseph): Botany. See: Charnock.

GARIEL, MAURICE. 1812-1878. French physician. (Biography source unavailable.) Gariel's pessary.

Gariel's pessary (Gariel, Maurice): Medicine. See: Dorland; Stedman.

GARLAND, AUGUSTUS HILL. 1832-1899. American politician. See: Dict. Amer. Biog. Garlandite, Garland's case.

GARLAND, GEORGE MINOT. 1848-1926. American physician. See: Biog. Lex. hervorr. Aerzte, 1880-1930. Garland's curve, Garland's triangle.

GARLAND, HUGH. fl. 1953. English neurologist. (Biography source unavailable.) Marinesco-Garland syndrome.

GARLAND, JOSEPH. b. 1893. American physician. See: Direct. Med. Specialists, vol. 8. Bland-White-Garland syndrome.

Garlandite (Garland, Augustus Hill): History. See: Mathews, M. M.

Garland's case (Garland, Augustus Hill): History. See: Jameson.

Garland's curve (Garland, George Minot): Medicine. See: Dorland.

Garland's triangle (Garland, George Minot): Medicine. See: Dorland.

GARMASH, E. P. fl. 1932. Russian chemist. Cited in: Chem. Abstr., vol. 26, p. 3204. Garmask test for strontium.

Garmask test for strontium (Garmash, E. P.): Chemistry. See: Van Nostrand Chem. Dict.

GARNER, JOHN NANCE. 1868-1967. American legislator. See: Biog. Direct. Amer. Congress. Wagner-Garner Bill.

Garnett machine (Derivation undetermined): Engineering and Industry. See: Winburne.

GARNIER, JULES. 1839?-1904. French geologist. See: Sci., vol. 19 (1904), p. 598. Garnierite.

Garnierite (Garnier, Jules): Earth Sciences. See: Thrush; Webster's 3d.

GAROUSSE, M. DE LA. fl. 1737. French? engineer. (Biography source unavailable.) Lagarousse levers (ratchet or wheel).

GARRE, KARL. 1857-1928. Swiss surgeon and bacteriologist. See: Bulloch. Garre's osteomyelitis.

GARRELS, ROBERT MINARD. 1916- . American geologist. See: World Who's Who Sci. Garrelsite.

Garrelsite (Garrels, Robert Minard): Earth Sciences. See: Thrush.

Garre's osteomyelitis (Garre, Karl): Medicine. See: Dorland; Jablonski.

GARRISON, EDWARD H. d. 1931. American jockey. (Biography source unavailable.) Garrison finish.

Garrison finish (Garrison, Edward H.): Generic Word (last-minute victory). See: Hendrickson; Webster's 3d.

GARRISON, WILLIAM LLOYD. 1805-1879. American abolitionist. See: Dict. Amer. Biog. Garrisonian (or Garrisonite), Garrisonism.

Garrisonian (or Garrisonite) (Garrison, William Lloyd): History. See: Mathews, M. M.; Smith; Webster's 3d.

Garrisonism (Garrison, William Lloyd): History. See: Mathews, M. M.; Webster's 3d.

GARROD, SIR ALFRED BARING. 1819-1907. English physician. See: World Who's Who Sci. Garrod's test (for uric acid in blood).

GARROD, ARCHIBALD EDWARD. 1857-1936. English physician. See: World Who's Who Sci. Garrod's pads, Garrod's test (for hematoporphrin in urine).

Garrod's pads (Garrod, Archibald Edward): Medicine. See: Jablonski.

Garrod's test (for hematoporphrin in urine) (Garrod, Archibald Edward): Medicine. See: Dorland.

Garrod's test (for uric acid in blood) (Garrod, Sir Alfred Baring): Medicine. See: Dorland; Stedman.

GARTNER, HERMANN TRESCHOW. 1785-1827. Danish anatomist. See: Biog. Lex. hervorr. Aerzte. Gartner's canal (or duct), Gartner's cyst.

Gartner's canal (or duct) (Gartner, Hermann Treschow): Medicine. See: Dorland; Gray; Stedman. Also known as: Malpighian canal.

Gartner's cyst (Gartner, Hermann Treschow): Medicine. See: Dorland; Stedman.

Garwood distribution (Derivation undetermined): Statistics. See: Kendall.

GASIS, DEMETRIUS. fl. 1909. Greek physician. Cited in: Kelly. Gasis' stain.

Gasis' stain (Gasis, Demetrius): Medicine. See: Stedman.

GASKELL, WALTER HOLBROOK. 1847-1914. English physiologist. See: Dict. Sci. Biog. Gaskell's bridge, Gaskell's clamp, Gaskell's nerves.

Gaskell's bridge (Gaskell, Walter Holbrook): Medicine. See: Dorland; Gray; Henderson. Also known as: His' bundle.

Gaskell's clamp (Gaskell, Walter Holbrook): Medicine. See: Stedman.

Gaskell's nerves (Gaskell, Walter Holbrook): Medicine. See: Stedman.

GASPAR, BELA. 1898- . Rumanian-born American chemist. See: Amer. Men Sci., 9th ed. Gasparcolor.

Gaspar y Arnal reagent for aluminum (Gaspar y Arnal, Teofilo): Chemistry. See: Van Nostrand Chem. Dict.

Gaspar y Arnal reagent for lithium (Gaspar y Arnal, Teofilo): Chemistry. See: Van Nostrand Chem. Dict.

GASPAR Y ARNAL, TEOFILO. fl. 1934. Spanich chemist. See: Pogg., vol. 6. Gaspar y Arnal reagent for aluminum, Gaspar y Arnal reagent for lithium, Gaspar y Arnal test reaction for ammonium, potassium, cesium, and rubidium, Gaspar y Arnal test reaction for phosphate, Gaspar y Arnal test reaction for thallous salts.

Gaspar y Arnal test reaction for ammonium, potassium, cesium, and rubidium (Gaspar y Arnal, Teofilo): Chemistry. See: Van Nostrand Chem. Dict.

Gaspar y Arnal test reaction for phosphate (Gaspar y Arnal, Teofilo): Chemistry. See: Van Nostrand Chem. Dict.

Gaspar y Arnal test reaction for thallous salts (Gaspar y Arnal, Teofilo): Chemistry. See: Van Nostrand Chem. Dict.

Gasparcolor (Gaspar, Bela): Photography. See: Focal Encyc. Photog.

GASSER, JOHANN LUDWIG. 1723-1765. Austrian anatomist. See: Biog. Lex. hervorr. Aerzte. Gasserectomy, Gasserian, Gasserian ganglion.

Gasser-Karrer syndrome (Gasser, Konrad Johann and Karrer, Juerg?): Medicine. See: Jablonski.

GASSER, KONRAD JOHANN. 1912- . Swiss pediatrician. See: Kuerschner's Deut. Gel. Kal., vol. 9, 1961. Gasser-Karrer syndrome, Gasser's syndrome (1), Gasser's syndrome (2), Vahlquist-Gasser syndrome.

Gasserectomy (Gasser, Johann Ludwig): Medicine. See: Dorland; Stedman.

Gasserian (Gasser, Johann Ludwig): Medicine. See: Dorland; Stedman.

Gasserian ganglion (Gasser, Johann Ludwig): Medicine. See: Dorland; Pennak; Stedman.

Gasser's syndrome (1) (Gasser, Konrad Johann): Medicine. See: Jablonski.

Gasser's syndrome (2) (Gasser, Konrad Johann): Medicine. See: Jablonski.

Gassner cell (Derivation undetermined): Chemistry. See: Hackh.

GASTALDI, E. fl. 1913. Italian chemist. Cited in: Chem. Abstr., vol. 7, p. 3292. Pertusi-Gastaldi reagent for cyanide.

Gastaldi synthesis (Derivation undetermined): Chemistry. See: Van Nostrand Chem. Dict.

GASTAUT, HENRI JEAN-PASCAL. 1915- . French biologist. See: World Who's Who Sci. Gastaut's syndrome.

Gastaut's syndrome (Gastaut, Henri Jean-Pascal): Medicine. See: Jablonski.

GASTON. Comic strip character by Frederick B. Opper. Alphonse and Gaston.

Gastornis (Plante, Gaston): Zoology. See: Webster's 3d.

Gatch bed (Gatch, Willis Dew): Medicine. See: Dorland; Stedman.

Gatch method (Gatch, Willis Dew): Medicine. See: Stedman.

GATCH, WILLIS DEW. 1878-1954. American surgeon. See: World Who's Who Sci. Gatch bed, Gatch method.

GATES, ARTHUR IRVING. b. 1890. American psychologist. See: Amer. Men Sci., 9th ed., vol. 3. Gates-MacGinitie reading tests.

Gates canvas table (Derivation undetermined): Engineering and Industry. See: Thrush.

Gates–MacGinitie reading tests (Gates, Arthur Irving and MacGinitie, Walter Harold): Psychology. See: Wolman.

Gatling gun (Gatling, Richard Jordan): Weapons. See: Hendrickson; Phyfe; Quick.

GATLING, RICHARD JORDAN. 1818-1903. American physician and inventor. See: World Who's Who Sci. Gatling gun.

GATTEGNO, CALEB. 1911- . Egyptian-born American educator. See: Lead. Educ., 5th ed. Cuisenaire–Gattegno rods.

Gattermann aldehyde (or ketone) synthesis (Gattermann, Friedrich August Ludwig): Chemistry. See: Ballentyne; Van Nostrand Chem. Dict.

Gattermann carbon monoxide synthesis of aldehydes (Gattermann, Friedrich August Ludwig). See: Gattermann–Koch reaction.

GATTERMANN, FRIEDRICH AUGUST LUDWIG. 1860-1920. German chemist. See: World Who's Who Sci. Gattermann aldehyde (or ketone) synthesis, Gattermann–Koch reaction, Gattermann reaction (or diazo reaction), Gattermann–Skita synthesis.

Gattermann–Koch reaction (Gattermann, Friedrich August Ludwig and Koch, J. A.): Chemistry. See: Ballentyne; Van Nostrand Chem. Dict.; Webster's 3d. Also known as: Gattermann carbon monoxide synthesis of aldehydes.

Gattermann reaction (or diazo reaction) (Gattermann, Friedrich August Ludwig): Chemistry. See: Ballentyne; Van Nostrand Chem. Dict.; Webster's 3d.

Gattermann–Skita synthesis (Gattermann, Friedrich August Ludwig and Skita, Aladar): Chemistry. See: Van Nostrand Chem. Dict.

Gaucher('s) cells (Gaucher, Philippe Charles Ernest): Medicine. See: Dorland; Stedman.

Gaucher hematin solution (Gaucher, L.): Chemistry. See: Van Nostrand Chem. Dict.

GAUCHER, L. fl. 1908. French chemist. Cited in: Chem. Abstr., vol. 2, p. 2270. Gaucher hematin solution.

GAUCHER, PHILIPPE CHARLES ERNEST. 1854-1918. French physician. Cited in: Kelly. Gaucher('s) cells, Gaucher's disease.

Gaucher–Schlagenhaufer syndrome (Gaucher, Philippe Charles Ernest and Schlagenhaufer, Friedrich). See: Gaucher's disease.

Gaucher's disease (Gaucher, Philippe Charles Ernest): Medicine. See: Jablonski; Webster's 3d.; Wolman. Also known as: Gaucher–Schlagenhaufer syndrome.

GAUDEFROY, CHRISTOPHE. fl. 1919. French mineralogist. See: Pogg., vol. 6. Gaudefroyite.

Gaudefroyite (Gaudefroy, Christophe): Earth Sciences. See: Thrush.

GAUDI Y CORNET, ANTONIO. 1852-1926. Spanish architect. See: New Encyc. Brit., 1974, Microp. Gaudian.

Gaudian (Gaudi y Cornet, Antonio): Applied Arts. See: Webster's 3d.

GAUDIN, ANTOINE MARC. 1900- . Smyrna-born American metallurgist and mining engineer. See: Amer. Men Sci., 9th ed. Gaudin's equation.

Gaudin's equation (Gaudin, Antoine Marc): Engineering and Industry. See: Thrush.

gauging by Gunter (Gunter, Edmund): History. See: Mathews, M. M.

GAUGUIN, PAUL. 1848-1903. French painter and sculptor.. See: Encyc. Brit., 1973. ga-ga (or gaga)?

GAULE, JUSTUS. b. 1849. German physiologist. See: Biog. Lex. hervorr. Aerzte, 1880-1930. Gaule's spots.

Gaule's spots (Gaule, Justus): Medicine. See: Jablonski.

Gaullism (or Gaullist) (De Gaulle, Charles Andre Joseph Marie): History. See: Hendrickson; Morris and Irwin; Webster's 3d.

GAULT, FERNAND. 1873-1936. French physician. See: Ann. Otol-Laryngol. (1936), no. 11 p. 1109. Devic–Gault syndrome.

Gaultheria (Gaultier, Jean Francois): Botany. See: Charnock; Taylor, N.; Webster's 3d.

Gaultherin (Gaultier, Jean Francois): Medicine. See: Stedman.

GAULTIER, JEAN FRANCOIS. 1708-1756. Canadian physician and botanist. See: Dict. Amer. Med. Biog. Gaultheria, Gaultherin.

GAUSE, G. F. fl. 20th c. German geneticist. (Biography source unavailable.) Gause's law (principle or rule).

Gause's law (principle or rule) (Gause, G. F.): Genetics. See: Gray; Pennak; Webster's 3d.

GAUSLIN. No dates. American corporation manager. Cited in: Min. Mag., vol. 21. Gauslinite.

Gauslinite (Gauslin): Earth Sciences. See: Thrush.

GAUSS, CARL FRIEDRICH. 1777-1855. German mathematician. See: Dict. Sci. Biog. binomial law of Quetelet–Gauss, degauss(ing), equations of Gauss and Codazzi, Gauss conformal projection, Gauss' error curve, Gauss eyepiece, Gauss formulas, Gauss fundamental theorem of electrostatics, Gauss hypergeometric equation, Gauss hypergeometric function, Gauss law, Gauss law for a magnetic medium, Gauss law for gravitation, Gauss law of normal gravitational force, Gauss–Markov theorem, Gauss' mean value theorem, Gauss method for quadratures, Gauss' multiplication theorem, Gauss optics formulae, Gauss(ian) point (or image point), Gauss principle of "least constraint", Gauss product function, Gauss' reciprocal theorem, Gauss–Seidel method, Gauss' test (for convergence or divergence), Gauss theorem, Gauss theorem on curvature, Gauss (unit of magnetic induction), Gauss–Winckler inequality, Gaussian brackets, Gaussian curvature (of space-time), Gaussian curve, Gaussian distribution, Gaussian integer (or complex integers), Gaussian kernel, Gaussian noise, Gaussian optics, Gaussian positions, Gaussian process (or time series), Gaussian quadrature formula, Gaussian response, Gaussian units, Gaussian wave group, Gaussian well, Gaussistor, Gaussmeter, Newton–Gauss interpolation formula(s).

GAUSS, CARL JOSEPH. 1875-1957. German gynecologist. See: World Who's Who Sci. Gauss' sign.

Gauss conformal projection (Gauss, Carl Friedrich): Geography. See: Monkhouse.

Gauss' error curve (Gauss, Carl Friedrich): Mathematics. See: Ballentyne.

Gauss eyepiece (Gauss, Carl Friedrich): Physics. See: Internat. Dict. Phys. Elec.; Satterthwaite; Van Nostrand Sci. Encyc.

Gauss formulas (Gauss, Carl Friedrich): Mathematics. See: Internat. Dict. Ap. Math.

Gauss' fundamental theorem of electrostatics (Gauss, Carl Friedrich): Physics. See: Ballentyne; James.

Gauss hypergeometric equation (Gauss, Carl Friedrich): Physics. See: Internat. Dict. Ap. Math.; Internat. Dict. Phys. Elec.; Van Nostrand Sci. Encyc.

Gauss hypergeometric function (Gauss, Carl Friedrich): Physics. See: Internat. Dict. Phys. Elec.

Gauss law (Gauss, Carl Friedrich): Electronics. See: Internat. Dict. Ap. Math.; Internat. Dict. Phys. Elec.

Gauss law for a magnetic medium (Gauss, Carl Friedrich): Physics. See: Internat. Dict. Ap. Math.; Internat. Dict. Phys. Elec.

Gauss law for gravitation (Gauss, Carl Friedrich): Physics. See: Internat. Dict. Phys. Elec.

Gauss law of normal gravitational force (Gauss, Carl Friedrich): Physics. See: Internat. Dict. Ap. Math.; Internat. Dict. Phys. Elec.

Gauss–Markov theorem (Gauss, Carl Friedrich and Markov, Andrei Andreevich): Statistics. See: Internat. Dict. Ap. Math.; Kendall.

Gauss' mean value theorem (Gauss, Carl Friedrich): Mathematics. See: James.

Gauss method for quadratures (Gauss, Carl Friedrich): Physics. See: Internat. Dict. Phys. Elec.; Van Nostrand Sci. Encyc.

Gauss' multiplication theorem (Gauss, Carl Friedrich): Mathematics. See: Ballentyne.

Gauss optics formulae (Gauss, Carl Friedrich): Physics. See: Ballentyne.

Gauss(ian) point (or image point) (Gauss, Carl Friedrich): Physics. See: Internat. Dict. Phys. Elec.; Thewlis; Webster's 3d.

Gauss principle of "least constraint" (Gauss, Carl Friedrich): Physics. See: Internat. Dict. Phys. Elec.; Van Nostrand Chem. Dict.; Van Nostrand Sci. Encyc.

Gauss product function (Gauss, Carl Friedrich): Mathematics. See: Ballentyne.

Gauss' reciprocal theorem (Gauss, Carl Friedrich): Mathematics. See: Ballentyne.

Gauss–Seidel method (Gauss, Carl Friedrich and Seidel, Ludwig Philipp von): Mathematics. See: Internat. Dict. Ap. Math.; Kendall.

Gauss' sign (Gauss, Carl Joseph): Medicine. See: Dorland; Stedman.

Gauss' test (for convergence or divergence) (Gauss, Carl Friedrich): Mathematics. See: Ballentyne.

Gauss theorem (Gauss, Carl Friedrich): Physics. See: Internat. Dict. Phys. Elec.; Thewlis; Van Nostrand Sci. Encyc.

Gauss theorem on curvature (Gauss, Carl Friedrich): Physics. See: Internat. Dict. Ap. Math.

Gauss (unit of magnetic induction) (Gauss, Carl Friedrich): Physics. See: Ballentyne; Dresner; Hughes.

Gauss–Winckler inequality (Gauss, Carl Friedrich and Winckler, Anton?): Statistics. See: Kendall.

GAUSSEL, AMANS. 1871-1937. French physician. See: Siecle Med., vol. 10, no. 247 (1937), p. 6. Grasset-Gaussel phenomenon.

Gaussian brackets (Gauss, Carl Friedrich): Mathematics. See: Internat. Dict. Ap. Math.

Gaussian curvature (of space-time) (Gauss, Carl Friedrich): Mathematics. See: Ballentyne; Internat. Dict. Ap. Math.; Internat. Dict. Phys. Elec.

Gaussian curve (Gauss, Carl Friedrich): Statistics. See: Monkhouse; Webster's 3d.; Zadrozny.

Gaussian distribution (Gauss, Carl Friedrich): Statistics. See: Focal Encyc. Film; Hughes; Internat. Dict. Phys. Elec.

Gaussian integer (or complex integers) (Gauss, Carl Friedrich): Mathematics. See: Ballentyne; James.

Gaussian interpolation formulas (Gauss, Carl Friedrich). See: Newton–Gauss interpolation formula(s).

Gaussian kernel (Gauss, Carl Friedrich): Physics. See: Internat. Dict. Ap. Math.; Internat. Dict. Phys. Elec.

Gaussian noise (Gauss, Carl Friedrich): Electronics. See: Hughes; Markus.

Gaussian optics (Gauss, Carl Friedrich): Physics. See: Internat. Dict. Ap. Math.

Gaussian positions (Gauss, Carl Friedrich): Physics. See: Ballentyne.

Gaussian process (or time series) (Gauss, Carl Friedrich): Statistics. See: Huschke.

Gaussian quadrature formula (Gauss, Carl Friedrich): Physics. See: Internat. Dict. Ap. Math.

Gaussian response (Gauss, Carl Friedrich): Electronics. See: Hughes.

Gaussian units (Gauss, Carl Friedrich): Physics. See: Ballentyne; Hughes; Internat. Dict. Ap. Math.

Gaussian wave group (Gauss, Carl Friedrich): Physics. See: Internat. Dict. Ap. Math.; Internat. Dict. Phys. Elec.

Gaussian well (Gauss, Carl Friedrich): Physics. See: Hughes; Internat. Dict. Phys. Elec.; Markus.

Gaussistor (Gauss, Carl Friedrich): Engineering and Industry. See: Hughes.

Gaussmeter (Gauss, Carl Friedrich): Engineering and Industry. See: Hughes; Markus; Thewlis.

GAUSTAD, V. fl. 1949. Swedish physician. (Biography source unavailable.) Gaustad's syndrome.

Gaustad's syndrome (Gaustad, V.): Medicine. See: Jablonski.

GAUTHIER, G. fl. 1960. French physician. (Biography source unavailable.) De-Morsier-Gauthier syndrome.

GAUTIER, ARMAND E. J. 1837-1920. French chemist. See: Dict. Sci. Biog. Gautier receiver?

Gautier receiver (Gautier, Armand E. J.?): Chemistry. See: Hackh.

GAUVAIN, E. ALMORE. b. 1893. American dermatologist. See: Who's Who Among Physicians and Surg. Gauvain's fluid.

Gauvain's fluid (Gauvain, E. Almore): Medicine. See: Dorland.

GAVARD, HYACINTHE. 1753-1802. French anatomist. See: World Who's Who Sci. Gavard's muscle.

Gavard's muscle (Gavard, Hyacinthe): Medicine. See: Donath; Dorland; Stedman.

Gaviola caustic test (Gaviola, Ramon Enrique): Physics. See: Internat. Dict. Ap. Math.

GAVIOLA, RAMON ENRIQUE. 1900- . Argentinian-born American astrophysicist. See: Amer. Men Sci., 9th ed. Gaviola caustic test.

GAWALOWSKI, ANTON CARL WILHELM. 1848-1927. Austrian chemist. See: Pogg., vol. 6. Gawalowski's test, Hager-Gawalowski reagent.

Gawalowski's test (Gawalowski, Anton Carl Wilhelm): Medicine. See: Stedman.

GAY, ALEXANDER H. 1842-1907. Russian anatomist. See: Biog. Lex. hervorr. Aerzte, 1880-1930. Gay's gland.

Gay-Lussac (Gay-Lussac, Joseph Louis): Chemistry. See: Webster's 3d.

Gay-Lussac alcoholometer (Gay-Lussac, Joseph Louis): Chemistry. See: Partridge.

Gay-Lussac hydrometer (Gay-Lussac, Joseph Louis): Chemistry. See: Hackh; Partridge.

GAY-LUSSAC, JOSEPH LOUIS. 1778-1850. French chemist and physicist. See: Dict. Sci. Biog. Gay-Lussac, Gay-Lussac alcoholometer, Gay-Lussac hydrometer, Gay-Lussac law (of combining volumes), Gay Lussac('s) law (of expansion), Gay-Lussac('s) tower, Gaylussacia, Gaylussite.

Gay Lussac law (of combining volumes) (Gay-Lussac, Joseph Louis): Chemistry. See: Ballentyne; Thewlis; Van Nostrand Chem. Dict.

Gay Lussac('s) law (of expansion) (Gay-Lussac, Joseph Louis). See: Charles' law.

Gay-Lussac('s) tower (Gay-Lussac, Joseph Louis): Chemistry. See: Thrush; Van Nostrand Chem. Dict.; Webster's 3d.

GAYET, CHARLES-JULES-ALPHONSE. 1833-1904. French physician. See: Biog. Lex. hervorr. Aerzte, 1880-1930. Gayet's disease.

Gayet-Wernicke syndrome (Gayet, Charles-Jules-Alphonse and Wernicke, Karl). See: Wernicke's encephalopathy.

Gayet's disease (Gayet, Charles Jules Alphonse). See: Wernicke's encephalopathy.

GAYLEY, JAMES. fl. 1911. American mining engineer. Cited in: Mansell. Gayley process.

Gayley process (Gayley, James): Engineering and Industry. See: Thrush.

Gaylussacia (Gay-Lussac, Joseoh Louis): Botany. See: Partridge; Taylor, N.; Webster's 3d.

Gaylussite (Gay-Lussac, Joseph Louis): Earth Sciences. See: Charnock; Thrush; Webster's 3d.

Gay's gland (Gay, Alexander H.): Medicine. See: Stedman.

GAZA, THEODORUS. ca. 1400-1478. Greek scholar. See: Barnhart (Cycl. Names). Gazania.

GAZA, WILHELM VON. b. 1883. German surgeon. See: Biog. Lex. hervorr. Aerzte, 1880-1930. Gaza's operation.

Gazania (Gaza, Theodorus): Botany. See: Taylor, N.; Webster's 3d.

Gaza's operation (Gaza, Wilhelm von): Medicine. See: Dorland.

GEARY, ROBERT CHARLES. 1896- . English statistician. Cited in: Mansell. Geary's ratio.

Geary sampler (Derivation undetermined): Engineering and Industry. See: Thrush.

Geary's ratio (Geary, Robert Charles): Statistics. See: Kendall.

GEBER. fl. 11th c. Arabian alchemist. (Biography source unavailable.) Gibberish.

Gebhardt survey instrument (Derivation undetermined): Engineering and Industry. See: Thrush.

GEDALIAH. fl. 586. Governor of Judah. See: Encyc. Judaica. Fast of Gedaliah.

GEE, ALBERT HALDANE. 1901- . English-born American bacteriologist. See: Amer. Men Sci., 4th ed. Gee-Chaikoff reagent.

Gee-Chaikoff reagent (Gee, Albert Haldane and Chaikoff, Israel Lyon): Chemistry. See: Van Nostrand Chem. Dict.

Gee-Herter disease (Gee, Samuel Jones and Herter, Christian Archibald). See: Herter's syndrome.

Gee-Herter-Heubner syndrome (Gee, Samuel Jones; Herter, Christian Archibald; and Heubner, Otto Johann Leonhard). See: Herter's syndrome.

GEE, SAMUEL JONES. 1839-1911. English physician. See: Dict. Nat. Biog., 2d suppl. Gee's disease.

Gee-Thaysen disease (Gee, Samuel Jones and Thaysen, Thornwald Einar Hess). See: Herter's syndrome.

Gee's disease (Gee, Samuel Jones). See: Herter's syndrome.

Gegenbauer function (Gegenbauer, Leopold Bernhard): Mathematics. See: Internat. Dict. Ap. Math.; Internat. Dict. Phys. Elec.; Van Nostrand Sci. Encyc.

GEGENBAUER, LEOPOLD BERNHARD. 1849-1903. Austrian mathematician. See: World Who's Who Sci. Gegenbauer function, Gegenbauer polynomials.

Gegenbauer polynomials (Gegenbauer, Leopold Bernhard): Mathematics. See: Ballentyne.

GEGENBAUR, CARL. 1826-1903. German anatomist. See: World Who's Who Sci. Gegenbaur's cells.

Gegenbaur's cells (Gegenbaur, Carl): Medicine. See: Dorland.

GEHLEN, ADOLF FERDINAND. 1775-1815. German chemist. See: World Who's Who Sci. Gehlenite.

Gehlenite (Gehlen, Adolf Ferdinand): Earth Sciences. See: Charnock; Thrush; Webster's 3d.

GEHRCKE, ERNST JOHANNES LUDWIG. b. 1878. German physicist. See: Pogg., vols. 5, 6. Lummer-Gehrcke (Gehreke) plate (or interference spectroscope).

Gehuchten, Arthur van. See: Van Gehucten, Arthur.

GEIGEL, RICHARD. 1859-1930. German physician. See: Biog. Lex. hervorr. Aerzte, 1880-1930. Geigel's reflex.

Geigel's reflex (Geigel, Richard): Medicine. See: Dorland; Stedman.

Geiger characteristic (Geiger, Hans Wilhelm): Physics. See: Hughes.

Geiger counter (or tube) (Geiger, Hans Wilhelm): Physics. See: Hendrickson; Markus; Van Nostrand Sci. Encyc. Also known as: Geiger-Mueller counter (or tube).

Geiger formula (Geiger, Hans Wilhelm): Physics. See: Internat. Dict. Phys. Elec.; Van Nostrand Chem. Dict.; Van Nostrand Sci. Encyc.

GEIGER, HANS WILHELM. 1882-1945. German physicist. See: Dict. Sci. Biog. Geiger characteristic, Geiger counter (or tube), Geiger formula, Geiger-Mueller probe, Geiger-Mueller survey meter, Geiger-Nuttall law (rule or relation), Geiger region, Geiger test (or testing), Geiger threshold.

GEIGER, JOHN. fl. ca. 1832. American friend of Audubon. (Biography source unavailable.) Geiger tree.

Geiger-Mueller counter (or tube) (Geiger, Hans Wilhelm and Mueller, Walther). See: Geiger counter (or tube).

Geiger-Mueller probe (Geiger, Hans Wilhelm and Mueller, Walther): Engineering and Industry. See: Thrush.

Geiger-Mueller region (Geiger, Hans Wilhelm and Mueller, Walther). See: Geiger region.

Geiger-Mueller survey meter (Geiger, Hans Wilhelm and Mueller, Walther): Engineering and Industry. See: Thrush.

Geiger-Mueller threshold (Geiger, Hans Wilhelm and Mueller, Walther). See: Geiger threshold.

Geiger-Nuttall law (rule or relation) (Geiger, Hans Wilhelm and Nuttall, John Michael): Physics. See: Markus; Thewlis; Van Nostrand Chem. Dict.

Geiger region (Geiger, Hans Wilhelm): Physics. See: Hughes; Markus; Thewlis. Also known as: Geiger-Mueller region.

Geiger test (or testing) (Geiger, Hans Wilhelm): Engineering and Industry. See: Thrush.

Geiger threshold (Geiger, Hans Wilhelm): Physics. See: Hughes; Markus; Thewlis. Also known as: Geiger-Mueller threshold.

Geiger tree (Geiger, John): Botany. See: Webster's 3d.

Geigy-Hardisty process (Derivation undetermined): Chemistry. See: Ballentyne.

Geikia (Geika) (Geikie, Archibald): Zoology. See: Hendrickson; Partridge; Webster's 3d.

GEIKIE, ARCHIBALD. 1835-1924. Scottish geologist. See: Dict. Sci. Biog. Geikia (Geika), Geikielite.

Geikielite (Geikie, Archibald): Earth Sciences. See: Partridge; Thrush; Webster's 3d.

GEILMANN, WILHELM. b. 1891. German chemist. See: Pogg., vol. 6. Geilmann-Wrigge-Weibke test for rhenium.

Geilmann-Wrigge-Weibke test for rhenium (Geilmann, Wilhelm; Wrigge, F. W.; and Weibke, Friedrich): Chemistry. See: Van Nostrand Chem. Dict.

Geissler bulb (Geissler, Johann Heinrich Wilhelm): Chemistry. See: Hackh; Webster's 3d.

GEISSLER, ERNST. b. 1866. German physician. Cited in: Mansell. Geissler-Oliver testing papers, Geissler('s) test, Geissler test papers.

GEISSLER, JOHANN HEINRICH WILHELM. 1815-1879. German mechanic and glassblower. See: Dict. Sci. Biog. Geissler bulb, Geissler pump, Geissler tube.

Geissler-Oliver testing papers (Geissler, Ernst and Oliver): Chemistry. See: Van Nostrand Chem. Dict.

Geissler pump (Geissler, Johann Heinrich Wilhelm): Engineering and Industry. See: Partridge; Webster's 3d.

Geissler('s) test (Derivation undetermined): Chemistry. See: Dorland; Stedman.

Geissler test papers (Geissler, Ernst): Chemistry. See: Van Nostrand Chem. Dict.

Geissler tube (Geissler, Johann Heinrich Wilhelm): Electronics. See: Hughes; Internat. Dict. Phys. Elec.; Markus.

GEITEL, HANS FRIEDRICH. 1855-1923. German physicist. See: World Who's Who Sci. Elster and Geitel effect.

Gelasian Sacramentary (Gelasius I, Saint): Religion. See: Attwater

GELASIUS I, SAINT. d. 496. Pope. See: Barnhart (Cycl. Names). Gelasian Sacramentary.

GELB, ADHEMAR MAXIMILIAN MAURICE. 1887-1936. Russian-born German psychologist. See: World Who's Who Sci. Gelb-Goldstein color sorting test, Gelb-Goldstein-Weigl-Scheerer object sorting test.

Gelb-Goldstein color sorting test (Gelb, Adhemar Maximilian Maurice and Goldstein, Kurt): Psychology. See: Wolman.

Gelb-Goldstein-Weigl-Scheerer object sorting test (Gelb, Adhemar Maximilian Maurice; Goldstein, Kurt; Weigl, Egon; and Scheerer, Martin): Psychology. See: Wolman.

GELFOND, ALEXANDER OSIPOVICH. 1906-1968. Russian mathematician. See: Dict. Sci. Biog. Gelfond-Schneider theorem.

Gelfond-Schneider theorem (Gelfond, Alexander Osipovich and Schneider, Theodor): Mathematics. See: James.

GELINEAU, JEAN BAPTISTE EDOUARD. b. 1859. French neurologist. Cited in: Kelly. Gelineau's syndrome.

Gelineau's syndrome (Gelineau, Jean Baptiste Edouard): Medicine. See: Hinsie; Jablonski; Stedman.

GELLE, MARIE ERNEST. 1834-1923. French otologist. See: Biog. Lex. hervorr. Aerzte, 1880-1930. Gelle('s) test.

Gelle('s) test (Gelle, Marie Ernest): Medicine. See: Dorland; Stedman.

Gellee, Claude. See: Claude Lorrain.

GELLERSTEDT, NILS. 1896- . Swedish pathologist. Cited in: Arnim. Ceelen-Gellerstedt syndrome.

GELLHORN, GEORGE. 1870-1936. American gynecologist. See: World Who's Who Sci. Gellhorn pessary.

Gellhorn pessary (Gellhorn, George): Medicine. See: Dorland.

GELL-MANN, MURRAY. 1929- . American physicist. See: World Who's Who Sci. Feynman-Gell-Mann theory.

GELY, JULES ARISTIDE. 1806-1861. French surgeon. See: Biog. Lex. hervorr. Aerzte. Gely's suture.

Gely's suture (Gely, Jules Aristide): Medicine. See: Dorland; Stedman.

Gemmho (Ohm, Georg Simon): Physics. See: Dresner.

GENE, CARLO GIUSEPPE. 1800-1847. Italian zoologist. Cited in: Arnim. Gene's gland (or organ).

General Pershing (tank) (Pershing, John Joseph): Weapons. See: Quick.

General Sheridan (airborne assault vehicle) (Sheridan, Philip Henry?): Weapons. See: Quick.

General Sherman sequoia (Sherman, William Tecumseh): Botany. See: Hendrickson under "Sequoia...".

General Sherman (tank) (Sherman, William Tecumseh): Weapons. See: Quick.

General Stuart tank (Stuart, James Ewell Brown "Jeb"?): Weapons. See: Quick.

Gene's gland (or organ) (Gene, Carlo Giuseppe): Zoology. See: Gray; Henderson; Pennak.

Genet affair (Genet, Edmond Charles Edouard): History. See: Morris and Irwin.

GENET, EDMOND CHARLES EDOUARD. 1763-1834. French diplomat. See: Encyc. Brit., 1973. Genet affair.

Gengou-Moreschi phenomenon (Gengou, Octave and Moreschi, Carlo): Medicine. See: Dorland; Stedman. Also known as: Gengou's reaction (or phenomenon).

GENGOU, OCTAVE. 1875-1957. Belgian bacteriologist. See: Bruxelles-med., vol. 37 (1957), p. 939. Bordet and Gengou's potato blood agar, Bordet-Gengou bacillus, Bodet-Gengou phenomenon, Bordet-Gengou test, Gengou-Moreschi phenomenon.

Gengou's reaction (or phenomenon) (Gengou, Octave). See: Gengou-Moreschi phenomenon.

Genlis reagent (Derivation undetermined): Chemistry. See: Van Nostrand Chem. Dict.

GENNARI, FRANCESCO. 1750-1795? Italian anatomist. See: Diz. Encic. Ital. Gennari's band (line or stria).

Gennari's band (line or stria) (Gennari, Francesco): Medicine. See: Dorland; Henderson; Stedman.

Gennaro, Saint. See: Januarius, Saint.

GENNERICH. WILHELM. 1877-1951. German dermatologist. See: Biog. Lex. hervorr. Aerzte, 1880-1930. Gennerich's treatment.

Gennerich's treatment (Gennerich, Wilhelm): Medicine. See: Dorland.

GENSOUL, JOSEPH. 1797-1858. French surgeon. See: World Who's Who Sci. Gensoul's disease.

Gensoul's disease (Gensoul, Joseph). See: Ludwig's angina.

GENTER, A. L. fl. 1913. American metallurgist. Cited in: Chem. Abstr., vol. 12, p. 1540. Genter filter, Genter thickener.

Genter filter (Genter, A. L.): Engineering and Industry. See: Thrush.

Genter thickener (Genter, A. L.): Engineering and Industry. See: Thrush.

GENTH, FREDERICK AUGUSTUS. 1820-1893. German-born American chemist and mineralogist. See: Dict. Sci. Biog. Genthelvite, Genthite.

Genthelvite (Genth, Frederick Augustus): Earth Sciences. See: Thrush; Webster's 3d.

Genthite (Genth, Frederick Augustus): Earth Sciences. See: Thrush; Webster's 3d.

Gentian (Gentius): Botany. See: Charnock; Funk; Hendrickson.

Gentile statistics (Derivation undetermined): Physics. See: Internat. Dict. Ap. Math.

GENTIUS. fl. 180-167 B.C. King of Illyria. See: Nouv. Biog. Univ. Gentian.

gentleman George (Pendleton, George Hunt): Generic Word. See: Frey.

geocronite (Saturn): Earth Sciences. See: Charnock.

GEOFFREY IV, PLANTAGENET. 1113-1150. Count of Anjou. See: Encyc. Brit., 1973. Plantagenet.

GEOFFROY, ETIENNE FRANCOIS. 1672-1731. French chemist and physician. See: Dict. Sci. Biog. Geoffroya.

Geoffroya (Geoffroy, Etienne Francois): Botany. See: Charnock.

Geordie lamp (Stephenson, George). See: Stephenson lamp.

GEORGE I. 1660-1727. King of England. See: Dict. Nat. Biog. Georgian (1).

GEORGE II. 1683-1760. King of England. See: Dict. Nat. Biog. Georgian (1), King George's war.

GEORGE III. 1738-1820. King of England. See: Dict. Nat. Biog. Georgia (moss), Georgian (1).

GEORGE IV. 1762-1830. King of England. See: Dict. Nat. Biog. George the Fourth (peach tree), Georgian (1).

GEORGE V. 1865-1936. King of England. See: Dict. Nat. Biog., 5th suppl. Georgian (2), Georgian poetry (or Georgianism).

George-Barden Act (George, Walter Franklin and Barden, Graham Arthur): Education. See: Good.

George Bill (George, Walter Franklin): Politics. See: Smith.

George Cross (and Medal) (George, Saint): History. See: Brewer; Steinberg.

George Darwin Lecture (Darwin, George Howard): Astronomy. See: Satterthwaite.

George-Deen Act (George, Walter Franklin and Deen, Braswell Drue): Education. See: Good.

George Downing (Downing, Sir George): Generic Word (false man). See: Hendrickson.

George Freedley Memorial Award (Freedley, George): Theater. See: Harrod.

George (half crown or guinea) (George, Saint): Numismatics. See: Webster's 3d.

George Harris Award (Harris, George): Photography. See: Focal Encyc. Photog. under "Awards (America)."

George-Noble (George, Saint): Numismatics. See: Wagner (Names).

George (pendant) (George, Saint): History. See: Brewer; Charnock; Webster's 3d.

GEORGE, SAINT. d. ca. 303. Christian martyr and patron saint of England. See: Encyc. Brit., 1973. George Cross (and Medal), George (half crown or guinea), George-Noble, George (pendant), Order (or Knights) of St. Michael and St. George, Saint George's Day, Saint George's duck, St. George's herb, Saint George's mushroom, Saint George's round.

George the Fourth (peach tree) (George IV): Botany. See: Charnock.

GEORGE, WALTER FRANKLIN. 1878-1957. American legislator. See: Biog. Direct. Amer. Congress. George-Barden Act, George Bill, George-Deen Act.

George Washington (Washington, George): (truthful person) Generic Word. See: Partridge.

George Washington submarine (Washington, George): Weapons. See: Quick.

George's conspiracy (Cadoudal, Georges): History. See: Latham; Phyfe. Also known as: Cadoudal plot, Pichegru's conspiracy.

Georges Sand (chrysanthemum) (Sand, Georges). See: Sand (chrysanthemum).

Georgette (crepe) (De la Plante, Georgette): Fashion. See: Hendrickson; Partridge; Picken.

GEORGI, WALTER. 1889-1920. German bacteriologist. See: Biog. Lex. hervorr. Aerzte, 1880-1930. Sachs-Georgi reaction.

Georgia (moss) (George III): Botany. See: Charnock.

Georgiad (Derivation undetermined): Literature. See: Charnock.

GEORGIADES. fl. 20th c. Greek mine director. Cited in: Min. Mag., vol. 15, p. 421. Georgiadesite.

Georgiadesite (Georgiades): Earth Sciences. See: Thrush; Webster's 3d.

Georgian (1) (George I, II, III, and IV): History. See: Webster's 3d.

Georgian (2) (George V): Fine Arts. See: Hendrickson; Partridge; Webster's 3d.

Georgian poetry (or Georgianism) (George V): Literature. See: Barnet; Preminger; Scott.

GERAGHTY, JOHN TIMOTHY. 1876-1924. American physician. Cited in: Chem. Abstr., Decenn. Index, 1907-1916. Rowntree and Geraghty test.

Gerard bearing (Gerard, P.): Engineering and Industry. See: Auger.

GERARD, JOHN. 1545-1612. English botanist. See: Dict. Sci. Biog. Gerardia.

Gerard-Marchand fracture (Derivation undetermined): Medicine. See: Jablonski.

GERARD, P. fl. 1949. French engineer. (Biography source unavailable.) Gerard bearing.

Gerardia (Gerard, John): Botany. See: Mathews, M. M.; Partridge; Webster's 3d.

Gerasimovskite (Gerasimovsky, V. I.): Earth Sciences. See: Thrush.

GERASIMOVSKY, V. I. No dates. Russian mineralogist. Cited in: Min. Mag., vol. 32 (1961), p. 958. Gerasimovskite.

GERBASI, MICHELE. 1900- . Italian pediatrician. See: Diz. Encic. Ital. Gerbasi's anemia (or syndrome).

Gerbasi's anemia (or syndrome) (Gerbasi, Michele): Medicine. See: Jablonski.

Gerber convention (Gerber, John): Recreation and Sports. See: Webster's 3d.

GERBER, JOHN. fl. 20th c. American bridge player. (Biography source unavailable.) Gerber convention.

GERBER, TRAUGOTT. d. 1743. German naturalist. See: Biog. Lex. hervorr. Aerzte. Gerbera.

Gerbera (Gerber, Traugott): Botany. See: Taylor, N.; Webster's 3d.

Gerdien aspirator (Gerdien, Hans): Physics. See: Huschke.

GERDIEN, HANS. 1877-1951. German physicist. See: World Who's Who Sci. Gerdien aspirator.

GERDY, PIERRE NICOLAS. 1797-1856. French surgeon. See: Nouv. Biog. Univ. Gerdy's fibers, Gerdy's fontanel, Gerdy's hyoid fossa, Gerdy's interatrial loop, Gerdy's ligament, Gerdy's tubercle.

Gerdy's fibers (Gerdy, Pierre Nicolas): Medicine. See: Donath; Dorland; Stedman.

Gerdy's fontanel (Gerdy, Pierre Nicolas): Medicine. See: Stedman.

Gerdy's hyoid fossa (Gerdy, Pierre Nicolas): Medicine. See: Donath; Stedman.

Gerdy's interatrial loop (Gerdy, Pierre Nicolas): Medicine. See: Stedman.

Gerdy's ligament (Gerdy, Pierre Nicolas): Medicine. See: Donath; Stedman.

Gerdy's tubercle (Gerdy, Pierre Nicolas): Medicine. See: Stedman

GERHARDT, CARL JAKOB CHRISTIAN ADOLPH. 1833-1902. German physician. See: World Who's Who Sci. Gerhardt-Semon law, Gerhardt's disease, Gerhardt's dullness, Gerhardt's sign, Gerhardt's syndrome, Gerhardt's test (for acetoacetic acid in urine), Gerhardt's test (for acetone in the urine).

GERHARDT, CHARLES FREDERIC. 1816-1856. French chemist. See: Dict. Sci. Biog. Gerhardtite (Gerhardite), Gerhardt's test for urobilin (or bile pigments) in the urine.

Gerhardt reaction for picric acid (Derivation undetermined): Chemistry. See: Van Nostrand Chem. Dict.

Gerhardt-Semon law (Gerhardt, Carl Jakob Christian Adolph and Semon, Sir Felix): Medicine. See: Dorland; Stedman.

Gerhardtite (Gerhardite) (Gerhardt, Charles Frederic): Earth Sciences. See: Thrush; Webster's 3d.

Gerhardt's disease (Gerhardt, Carl Jakob Christian Adolph). See: Mitchell's syndrome.

Gerhardt's dullness (Gerhardt, Carl Jakob Christian Adolph): Medicine. See: Stedman.

Gerhardt's reaction (Gerhardt, Carl Jakob Christian Adolph). See: Gerhardt's test (for acetoacetic acid in urine).

Gerhardt's sign (Gerhardt, Carl Jakob Christian Adolph): Medicine. See: Dorland; Stedman.

Gerhardt's syndrome (Gerhardt, Carl Jakob Christian Adolph): Medicine. See: Jablonski.

Gerhardt's test (for acetoacetic acid in urine) (Gerhardt, Carl Jakob Christian Adolph): Medicine. See: Ballentyne; Dorland; Stedman. Also known as: Gerhardt's reaction.

Gerhardt's test (for acetone in the urine) (Gerhardt, Carl Jakob Christian Adolph): Medicine. See: Dorland.

Gerhardt's test for urobilin (or bile pigments) in the urine (Gerhardt, Charles Frederic): Medicine. See: Dorland; Stedman.

Gericke, Otto von. See: Guericke, Otto von.

GERLACH, ANDREAS CHRISTIAN. 1811-1877. German veterinary surgeon. See: Biog. Lex. hervorr. Aerzte. Gerlach's valvula.

GERLACH, JOSEPH VON. 1820-1896. German anatomist. See: Allg. Deut. Biog. Gerlach's annular tendon, Gerlach's network, Gerlach's tonsil, Gerlach's valve (or valve of Gerlach).

GERLACH, WALTHER. 1889- . German physicist. See: World Who's Who Sci. Stern-Gerlach experiment (or effect).

Gerlach's annular tendon (Gerlach, Joseph von): Medicine. See: Stedman.

Gerlach's network (Gerlach, Joseph von): Medicine. See: Dorland; Stedman.

Gerlach's tonsil (Gerlach, Joseph von): Medicine. See: Stedman.

Gerlach's valve (or valve of Gerlach): Medicine. See: Donath; Dorland; Stedman.

Gerlach's valvula (Gerlach, Andreas Christian): Medicine. See: Stedman. Also known as: Hueck's ligament.

GERLIER, FELIX. 1840-1914. Swiss physician. See: Biog. Lex. hervorr. Aerzte, 1880-1930. Gerlier's disease.

Gerlier's disease (Gerlier, Felix): Medicine. See: Dorland; Jablonski; Stedman.

GERMER, LESTER HALBERT. 1896-1971. American physicist. See: World Who's Who Sci. Davisson-Germer experiment.

germinal center of Flemming (Flemming, Walther): Medicine. See: Stedman.

GERMUTH, FREDERICK GEORGE. b. 1891. American chemist. See: Amer. Men Sci., 9th ed. Germuth-Mitchell reagent for inorganic salts, Germuth reagent for nitrite, Germuth test reaction for lactate.

Germuth-Mitchell reagent for inorganic salts (Germuth, Frederick George and Mitchell, Clifford): Chemistry. See: Van Nostrand Chem. Dict.

Germuth reagent for nitrite (Germuth, Frederick George): Chemistry. See: Van Nostrand Chem. Dict.

Germuth test reaction for lactate (Germuth, Frederick George): Chemistry. See: Van Nostrand Chem. Dict.

Geronimo (Geronimo, the chief): Generic Word. See: Hendrickson; Webster's 3d.

GERONIMO, THE CHIEF. 1829-1900. American Indian chief. See: Dict. Amer. Biog. Geronimo.

GEROTA, DUMITRU. 1867-1939. Roumanian surgeon. Cited in: Kelly. Gerota's capsule, Gerota's fascia, Gerota's fascitis, Gerota's method.

Gerota's capsule (Gerota, Dumitru): Medicine. See: Dorland; Stedman.

Gerota's fascia (Gerota, Dumitru): Medicine. See: Donath.

Gerota's fascitis (Gerota, Dimitru). See: Ormond's syndrome.

Gerota's method (Gerota, Dumitru): Medicine. See: Dorland; Stedman.

Gerrard solution (Derivation undetermined): Chemistry. See: Van Nostrand Chem. Dict.

GERRY, ELBRIDGE. 1744-1814. American legislator and diplomat. See: Dict. Amer. Biog. Gerrymander.

GERRY, HAROLD TIRRELL. 1908- . American physical chemist. See: Amer. Men Sci., 9th ed. Keyes-Smith-Gerry equation.

Gerrymander (Gerry, Elbridge): Politics. See: Funk; Hendrickson; Smith.

GERSDORFF, VON. fl. 19th c. German mine owner. Cited in: Bailey. Gersdorffite.

Gersdorffite (Gersdorff, von): Earth Sciences. See: Thrush; Van Nostrand Sci. Encyc.; Webster's 3d.

GERSH, ISIDORE. 1907- . American histologist. See: World Who's Who Sci. Altmann-Gersh method.

Gerson diet (Gerson, Max Bernhard): Medicine. See: Dorland. Also known as: Gerson-Herrmannsdorfer diet.

Gerson-Herrmannsdorfer diet (Gerson, Max Bernhard and Herrmannsdorfer, Adolf). See: Gerson diet.

GERSON, MAX BERNHARD. b. 1881. Austrian-born American physician. See: Biog. Lex. hervorr. Aerzte, 1880-1930. Gerson diet.

Gerstenhofer furnace (Derivation undetermined): Engineering and Industry. See: Thrush.

GERSTLEY, J. M. No dates. American borax company owner. Cited in: Min. Mag., vol. 31 (1958), p. 960. Gerstleyite.

Gerstleyite (Gerstley, J. M.): Earth Sciences. See: Thrush.

GERSTMANN, JOSEF. 1887-1969. Austrian neurologist. See: Biog. Lex. hervorr. Aerzte, 1880-1930. Gerstmann('s) syndrome.

Gerstmann('s) syndrome (Gerstmann, Josef): Medicine. See: Good; Hinsie; Jablonski.

Gerstner wave (Derivation undetermined): Physics. See: Huschke.

GERSUNY, ROBERT. 1844-1924. Austrian surgeon. See: World Who's Who Sci. Gersuny's phenomenon (or symptom).

Gersuny's phenomenon (or symptom) (Gersuny, Robert): Medicine. See: Dorland.

GERVASIUS, SAINT. d. 166. Italian martyr and patron of Milan. See: Holweck. Jarvey (or Jarvie)?, Saint Gervasius' disease.

GERVILLE, CHARLES ALEXIS ADRIEN LEHERISSIER DE. 1769-1853. French antiquarian and naturalist. See: Nouv. Biog. Univ. Gervillia?

Gervillia (Gerville, Charles Alexis Adrien Leherissier de?): Botany. See: Charnock.

Geryk pump (Derivation undetermined): Engineering and Industry. See: Auger; Hackh.

GERYON. Monster of Greco-Roman mythology. See: Jobes. Geryonia.

Geryonia (Geryon): Zoology. See: Pennak.

GESELL, ARNOLD LUCIUS. 1880-1961. American psychologist. See: Dict. Sci. Biog. Gesell development scales (or developmental test).

Gesell development scales (or developmental test) (Gesell, Arnold Lucius): Psychology. See: Chaplin; Hinsie; Wolman.

GESNER, KONRAD. 1516-1565. Swiss naturalist. See: Dict. Sci. Biog. Gesneria (or Gesnera).

Gesneria (or Gesnera) (Gesner, Konrad): Botany. See: Charnock; Webster's 3d.

Gesvelst's network (Derivation undetermined): Medicine. See: Stedman.

Getsowa's adenoma (Derivation undetermined): Medicine. See: Stedman.

GETTING, IVAN ALEXANDER. 1912- . American physicist. See: World Who's Who Sci. Compton-Getting effect.

GEUTHER, ANTON. 1833-1889. German chemist. See: Dict. Sci. Biog. Geuther reagent and test?

Geuther reagent and test (Geuther, Anton?): Chemistry. See: Van Nostrand Chem. Dict.

Geyer larkspur (Derivation undetermined): Botany. See: Winburne.

Ghibellines. See: Waiblingen.

GHILARDUCCI, FRANCESCO. 1857-1924. Italian physician. See: Biog. Lex. hervorr. Aerzte, 1880-1930. Ghilarducci's reaction.

Ghilarducci's reaction (Ghilarducci, Francesco): Chemistry. See: Dorland.

Ghon and Sachs bacillus (Ghon, Anton and Sachs, Anton): Medicine. See: Dorland; Stedman.

GHON, ANTON. 1866-1936. Czech pathologist. See: World Who's Who Sci. Ghon and Sachs bacillus, Ghon('s) primary lesion (focus or tubercle).

Ghon('s) primary lesion (focus or tubercle) (Ghon, Anton): Medicine. See: Dorland; Stedman; Webster's 3d.

GHULAM AHMAD, MIRZA. 1839-1908. Indian religious reformer. Cited in: Encyc. Amer., 1959. Ahmadiyyach (Ahmadiya).

GIACOBINI, GENARO. 1889-1954. Argentinian physician. See: Gran Encic. Argentina. Lucherini-Giacobini syndrome?

GIACOMINI, CARLO. 1841-1898. Italian anatomist. See: World Who's Who Sci. frenulum of Giacomini, Giacomini's band.

Giacomini's band (Giacomini, Carlo): Medicine. See: Donath; Dorland; Stedman.

Gianotti-Crosti syndrome (Gianotti, Ferdinando and Crosti, Agostino): Medicine. See: Jablonski.

GIANOTTI, FERDINANDO. 1920- . Italian dermatologist. See: World Who's Who Sci. Gianotti-Crosti syndrome.

GIANUZZI, GIUSEPPE. 1839-1876. Italian physiologist. See: Diz. Encic. Ital. Gianuzzi's crescents (demilunes or cells).

Gianuzzi's crescents (demilunes or cells) (Gianuzzi, Giuseppe): Medicine. See: Donath; Dorland; Stedman. Also known as: Heidenhain's crescents (demilunes or demilune of Heidenhain).

GIARD, ALFRED. 1846-1908. French biologist. See: Dict. Sci. Biog. Giardia, Giardiasis.

Giardia (Giard, Alfred): Zoology. See: Pennak; Stedman; Webster's 3d. Also known as: Lamblia.

Giardiasis (Giard, Alfred): Medicine. See: Dorland; Stedman. Also known as: Lambliasis.

Giauque-Debye method (Giauque, William Francis and Debye, Peter Joseph William): Physics. See: Internat. Dict. Phys. Elec.

GIAUQUE, WILLIAM FRANCIS. 1895- . Canadian-born American chemist. See: World Who's Who Sci. Giauque-Debye method, Giauque's temperature scale.

Giauque's temperature scale (Giauque, William Francis): Physics. See: Ballentyne.

GIB, JOHN. fl. 1681. Scottish mariner and religious leader. Cited in: Blunt. Gibbites.

Gibberish (Geber): Generic Word (unintelligible language). See: Charnock; Hargrave; Hendrickson.

Gibbites (Gib, John): Religion. See: Canney.

GIBBON, JOHN HEYSHAM, JR. 1903- . American surgeon. See: World Who's Who Sci. Landis-Gibbon test.

GIBBON, Q. V. 1813-1894. American surgeon. (Biography source unavailable.) Gibbon's hernia.

Gibbon's hernia (Gibbon, Q. V.): Medicine. See: Dorland.

Gibbs' adsorption equation (or theorem) (Gibbs, Josiah Willard): Physics. See: Ballentyne; Internat. Dict. Phys. Elec.; Thrush.

Gibbs apparatus (Derivation undetermined): Engineering and Industry. See: Thrush.

Gibbs-Dalton law (Gibbs, Josiah Willard and Dalton, John). See: Dalton('s) law (of partial pressure).

Gibbs division surface (Gibbs, Josiah Willard): Physics. See: Internat. Dict. Ap. Math.; Van Nostrand Sci. Encyc.

Gibbs-Donnan equilibrium (Gibbs, Josiah Willard and Donnan, Frederick George). See: Donnan equilibrium.

Gibbs-Duhem equation (Gibbs, Josiah Willard and Duhem, Pierre-Maurice-Marie): Physics. See: Ballentyne; Internat. Dict. Ap. Math.; Internat. Dict. Phys. Elec.

Gibbs formula for the surface tension (Gibbs, Josiah Willard): Physics. See: Internat. Dict. Ap. Math.; Van Nostrand Sci. Encyc.

Gibbs' function (or free energy) (Gibbs, Josiah Willard): Physics. See: Ballentyne; Huschke; Thewlis.

GIBBS, GEORGE, JR. 1815-1873. American ethnologist. See: Dict. Amer. Biog. Gibbs' mole.

GIBBS, GEORGE SR. 1776-1833. American mineralogist. See: Dict. Amer. Biog. Gibbsite.

Gibbs-Hamilton notation (Gibbs, Josiah Willard and Hamilton, William Rowan): Physics. See: Internat. Dict. Phys. Elec.

GIBBS, HARRY DRAKE. 1872-1934. American chemist. See: Amer. Men Sci., 5th ed. Gibbs phthalic anhydride process, Gibbs test.

Gibbs-Helmholtz equation (Gibbs, Josiah Willard and Helmholtz, Hermann Ludwig Ferdinand von): Physics. See: Ballentyne; Internat. Dict. Phys. Elec.; Van Nostrand Chem. Dict.

GIBBS, ISABELLA. fl. 19th c. American woman. (Biography source unavailable.) Isabella grape.

GIBBS, JOSIAH WILLARD. 1839-1903. American physicist. See: Dict. Sci. Biog. Gibbs' adsorption equation (or theorem), Gibbs-Dalton law, Gibbs division surface, Gibbs-Donnan equilibrium, Gibbs-Duhem equation, Gibbs forumula for the surface tension, Gibbs' function (or free energy), Gibbs-Hamilton notation, Gibbs-Helmholtz equation, Gibbs-Konovalov theorems, Gibbs' paradox, Gibbs' phase rule, Gibbs' phenomenon, Gibbs' rule, Gibbs' theorem (1), Gibbs theorem (2), Gibbs (unit).

Gibbs-Konovalov theorems (Gibbs, Josiah Willard and Konovalov, Dmitrij Petrovich?): Physics. See: Internat. Dict. Ap. Math.; Van Nostrand Sci. Encyc.

Gibbs' mole (Gibbs, George, Jr.): Zoology. See: Pennak; Webster's 3d.

Gibbs' paradox, (Gibbs, Josiah Willard): Physics. See: Ballentyne; Internat. Dict. Ap. Math.; Van Nostrand Sci. Encyc.

Gibbs' phase rule (Gibbs, Josiah Willard): Physics. See: Ballentyne; Thewlis; Thrush.

Gibbs' phenomenon (Gibbs, Josiah Willard): Physics. See: Ballentyne; Internat. Dict. Ap. Math.; James.

Gibbs phthalic anhydride process (Gibbs, Harry Drake): Chemistry. See: Van Nostrand Chem. Dict.

Gibbs' rule (Gibbs, Josiah Willard): Physics. See: Ballentyne.

Gibbs test (Gibbs, Harry Drake): Chemistry. See: Van Nostrand Chem. Dict.

Gibbs' theorem (1) (Gibbs, Josiah Willard): Physics. See: Dorland; Stedman.

Gibbs theorem (2) (Gibbs, Josiah Willard): Physics. See: Thewlis.

Gibbs (unit) (Gibbs, Josiah Willard): Physics. See: Dresner.

Gibbsite (Gibbs, George Sr.): Earth Sciences. See: Charnock; Thrush; Webster's 3d.

GIBERT, CAMILLE MELCHIOR. 1797-1866. French dermatologist. See: Nouv. Biog. Univ. Gibert's disease.

Gibert's disease (Gibert, Camille Melchior): Medicine. See: Dorland; Jablonski; Stedman. Also known as: Hebra's disease (or pityriasis).

Giblin-Chapman test (Giblin, John Charles and Chapman, G.): Chemistry. See: Van Nostrand Chem. Dict.

GIBLIN, JOHN CHARLES. fl. 1936. English chemist. Cited in: Chem. Abstr., vol. 31, p. 68. Giblin-Chapman test.

GIBNEY, VIRGIL PENDLETON. 1847-1927. American orthopedist. See: Who Was Who Amer., 1897-1942. Gibney's fixation bandage.

Gibney's fixation bandage (Gibney, Virgil Pendleton): Medicine. See: Dorland; Stedman. Also known as: Gibney's bandage (or fixation bandage).

Gibrat('s) distribution (Gibrat, Robert): Statistics. See: James; Kendall.

GIBRAT, ROBERT. fl. 1931. French statistician. Cited in: Mansell. Gibrat('s) distribution.

GIBSON, CHARLES DANA. 1867-1944. American illustrator. See: Encyc. Brit., 1973. Gibson cocktail, Gibson girl, Gibson waist.

Gibson cocktail (Gibson, Charles Dana): Food and Drink. See: Hendrickson.

GIBSON, EDWARD, LORD ASHBOURNE. 1837-1913. Chancellor of Ireland. See: Dict. Nat. Biog., 3d. suppl. Lord Ashbourne's Act.

GIBSON, GEORGE ALEXANDER. 1854-1913. Scottish physician. See: Edinburgh Royal Soc. Proc., vol. 34 (1913-1914), p. 6. Gibson('s) murmur, Gibson's rule.

Gibson girl (Gibson, Charles Dana): Generic Word (elegant beauty). See: Brewer; Matthews, M. M.; Partridge.

GIBSON, JOHN. 1855-1914. Scottish chemist. See: Edinburgh Royal Soc. Proc., vol. 34 (1913-1914), pp. 285-289. Crum-Brown and Gibson rule?

GIBSON, JOHN LOCKHART. 1860-1944. Australian ophthalmologist. See: Brit. J. Ophthal., vol. 29 (1945), p. 219. Gibson's glioma.

GIBSON, KASSON STANFORD. b. 1890. American physicist. See: Amer. Men Sci., 9th ed. Davis-Gibson colour filter.

Gibson('s) murmur (Gibson, George Alexander): Medicine. See: Dorland; Stedman.

GIBSON, QUENTIN HOWIESON. fl. 1948. English physician. Cited in: Med. Register, 1952. Gibson's disease.

GIBSON, STANLEY. b. 1883. American pediatrician. See: Direct. Med. Specialists, vol. 8. Potts-Smith-Gibson operation.

Gibson waist (Gibson, Charles Dana): Fashion. See: Picken.

GIBSON, WILLIAM. 1788-1868. American surgeon. See: World Who's Who Sci. Gibson's bandage.

Gibsonite (Derivation undetermined): Derivation undetermined. See: Thrush.

Gibson's bandage (Gibson, William): Medicine. See: Dorland; Stedman.

Gibson's disease (Gibson, Quentin Howieson): Medicine. See: Jablonski.

Gibson's glioma (Gibson, John Lockhart): Medicine. See: Jablonski.

Gibson's rule (Gibson, George Alexander): Medicine. See: Dorland.

GIBUS, ANTOINE. fl. 1837. French hat-maker. (Biography source unavailable.) Gibus (opera-hat).

Gibus (opera-hat) (Gibus, Antoine): Fashion. See: Brewer; Hendrickson; Partridge.

GICHTEL, JOHANN GEORG. 1638-1710. German mystic. See: Encyc. Brit., 1973. Gichtelians.

Gichtelians (Gichtel, Johann Georg): Religion. See: Canney.

Gideon Bible (Gideon, the judge): Religion. See: Hendrickson; Mathews, M. M.

Gideon (Society) (Gideon, the judge): Religion. See: Mathews, M. M.; Webster's 3d.

GIDEON, THE JUDGE. fl. 13th c. B.C. Hebrew liberator and religious reformer. See: Encyc. Brit., 1973. Gideon Bible, Gideon (Society).

GIEMSA, BERTHOLD GUSTAV CARL. 1867-1948. German chemotherapeutist. See: World Who's Who Sci. Giemsa reagent, Giemsa('s) stain, Giemsa ultrafilter.

Giemsa reagent (Giemsa, Berthold Gustav Carl): Chemistry. See: Van Nostrand Chem. Dict.

Giemsa('s) stain (Giemsa, Berthold Gustav Carl): Chemistry. See: Dorland; Stedman; Winburne.

Giemsa ultrafilter (Giemsa, Berthold Gustav Carl): Chemistry. See: Hackh.

Gierke, Edgar Otto Konrad von. See: Von Gierke, Edgar Otto Konrad.

GIERKE, HANS PAUL BERNARD. 1847-1886. German anatomist. See: Biog. Lex. hervorr. Aerzte. Gierke's bundle (or respiratory bundle).

Gierke's bundle (or respiratory bundle) (Gierke, Hans Paul Bernard): Medicine. See: Donath; Dorland; Stedman. Also known as: Krause's respiratory bundle.

Gies biuret solution (Gies, William John): Chemistry. See: Van Nostrand Chem. Dict.

GIES, WILLIAM JOHN. 1872-1956. American chemist. See: World Who's Who Sci. Gies biuret solution.

GIESECKE, SIR CHARLES. 1761-1833. Irish mineralogist. Cited in: Mansell. Gieseckite.

Gieseckite (Giesecke, Sir Charles): Earth Sciences. See: Charnock; Thrush.

Giesl ejector (Giesl-Gieslingen, Adolph): Engineering and Industry. See: Auger.

GIESL-GIESLINGEN, ADOLPH. fl. 1935. Austrian engineer. (Biography source unavailable. Giesl ejector.

Gieson, Ira Thompson van. See: Van Gieson, Ira Thompson.

GIFFARD, HENRI. 1825-1882. French engineer and inventor. See: World Who's Who Sci. Giffard injector.

Giffard injector (Giffard, Henri): Engineering and Industry. See: Auger.

GIFFARD, WILLIAM. d. 1731. English midwife. See: Biog. Lex. hervorr. Aerzte. Giffard's maneuver.

Giffard's maneuver (Giffard, William): Medicine. See: Stedman.

GIFFORD, ADAM. 1820-1887. Scottish jurist. See: Dict. Nat. Biog. Gifford Lectureship (or Lectures).

GIFFORD, ALGERNON CHARLES. No dates. Astronomer. See: Pogg., vol. 6. Gifford eyepiece?

Gifford eyepiece (Gifford, Algernon Charles?): Astronomy. See: Satterthwaite.

GIFFORD, HAROLD. 1858-1929. American ophthalmologist. See: Who Was Who Amer., 1897-1942. Gifford's operation, Gifford's reflex, Gifford's sign.

Gifford Lectureship (or Lectures) (Gifford, Adam): Religion. See: Brewer; Harvey.

Gifford's operation (Gifford, Harold): Medicine. See: Dorland; Stedman.

Gifford's reflex (Gifford, Harold): Medicine. See: Dorland; Stedman.

Gifford's sign (Gifford, Harold): Medicine. See: Dorland; Stedman.

gigawatt (Watt, James): Physics. See: Markus.

GIGLI, LEONARDO. 1863-1908. Italian gynecologist. See: Biog. Lex. hervorr. Aerzte, 1880-1930. Gigli's operation, Gigli's saw.

Gigli's operation (Gigli, Leonardo): Medicine. See: Dorland; Stedman. Also known as: Siebold's operation.

Gigli's saw (Gigli, Leonardo): Medicine. See: Dorland; Stedman.

Gilard and Dubrul factors (Gilard, Pierre and Dubrul, Leon): Engineering and Industry. See: Thrush.

GILARD, PIERRE. fl. 1934. French industrial chemist. See: Univ. Liege, vol. 2 (1936), p. 405. Gilard and Dubrul factors.

Gilbert and Sullivan (Gilbert, William Schwenck and Sullivan, Arthur Seymour): Generic Word. See: Hendrickson; Partridge.

GILBERT, AUGUSTIN-NICHOLAS. 1858-1927. French physician. See: Biog. Lex. hervorr. Aerzte, 1880-1930. Gilbert-Behcet syndrome, Gilbert-Lereboullet syndrome.

Gilbert-Behcet syndrome (Gilbert, Augustin-Nicolas and Behcet, Halushi). See: Behcet's syndrome (aphthae or disease).

GILBERT, DAVIES. 1767-1839. English antiquarian and economist. See: Dict. Nat. Biog. Gilbertite.

Gilbert-Dreyfus' syndrome (Dreyfus, Gilbert): Medicine. See: Jablonski.

Gilbert engine (Gilbert, H. S.): Engineering and Industry. See: Auger.

GILBERT, H. S. No dates. Engineer. (Biography source unavailable.) Gilbert engine.

GILBERT, JUDSON BENNETT. 1898-1950. American urologist. Cited in: Kelly. Gilbert's syndrome.

Gilbert-Lereboullet syndrome (Gilbert, Augustin-Nicolas and Lereboullet, Pierre): Medicine. See: Jablonski. Also known as: Gilbert's disease, Meulengracht's icterus.

GILBERT OF SEMPRINGHAM, SAINT. ca. 1083-1189. English priest. See: Encyc. Brit., 1973. Gilbertines.

Gilbert, Sir Robert, 1st Baron Vansittart. See: Vansittart, Sir Robert Gilbert, 1st Baron.

GILBERT, THOMAS. 1720-1798. English reformer. See: Dict. Nat. Biog. Gilbert's Act.

Gilbert (unit) (Gilbert, William): Physics. See: Ballentyne; Dresner; Markus.

GILBERT, WILLIAM. 1544-1603. English physicist. See: Dict. Sci. Biog. Gilbert (unit).

GILBERT, WILLIAM SCHWENCK. 1836-1911. English playwright. See: Dict. Nat. Biog., 2d suppl. Gilbert and Sullivan, Gilbertian.

Gilbertia (Gilibert, Jean Immanuel): Botany. See: Charnock.

Gilbertian (Gilbert, William Schwenck): Generic Word (humorous absurdity). See: Harvey; Partridge; Webster's 3d.

Gilbertines (Gilbert of Sempringham, Saint): Regligion. See: Attwater; Bamhart (Engl. Lit.); Brewer.

Gilbertite (Gilbert, Davies): Earth Sciences. See: Charnock; Thrush.

Gilbert's Act (Gilbert, Thomas): History. See: Steinberg.

Gilbert's disease (Gilbert, Augustin-Nicolas). See: Gilbert-Lereboullet syndrome.

Gilbert's syndrome (Gilbert, Augustin-Nicolas). See: Behcet's syndrome (aphthae or disease).

Gilbert's syndrome (Gilbert, Judson Bennett): Medicine. See: Jablonski.

GILBRETH, FRANK BUNKER. 1868-1924. American engineer and management scientist. See: World Who's Who Sci. therblig.

GILCHRIST, PERCY CARLYLE. 1851-1935. English metallurgist. See: World Who's Who Sci. Thomas-Gilchrist process, Thomas-Gilchrist steel.

GILCHRIST, THOMAS CASPAR. 1862-1927. American physician. See: World Who's Who Sci. Gilchrist's disease (or mycosis).

Gilchrist's disease (or mycosis) (Gilchrist, Thomas Caspar): Medicine. See: Dorland; Jablonski; Stedman.

iles (Giles, the Farmer): Generic Word (farmer). See: Brewer.

iles flask (Derivation undetermined): Chemistry. See: Hackh.

ILES, SAINT. d. 550. French patron of cripples, beggars and blacksmiths. ee: Encyc. Brit., 1973. Saint Giles' disease?

ILES, THE FARMER. Subject of Bloomfield's poem, "The Farmer's Boy," 800). Giles.

ILFORD, HASTINGS. 1861-1941. English physician. See: World Who's ho Sci. Hutchinson-Gilford syndrome.

ilford's syndrome (Gilford, Hastings). See: Hutchinson-Gilford syndrome.

ilia (Gilii, Felipe Luis?): Botany. See: Charnock; Mathews, M. M.; aylor, N.

ILIBERT, JEAN IMMANUEL. 1741-1814. French botanist and physician. See: orld Who's Who Sci. Gilbertia.

ILII, FELIPE LUIS. 1756-1821. Italian physician and botanist. See: Encic. niv. Ilus. Gilia?

ILL, ARTHUR BRUCE. b. 1876. American surgeon. See: Who's Who Amer. ed. Gill('s) operation (or bone-block operation).

ILL, ERIC ROWLAND. 1882-1940. English sculptor and type designer. See: ict. Nat. Biog., 5th suppl. Gill (type-face).

ill-Morrell oscillator (Derivation undetermined): Physics. See: Hughes; ternat. Dict. Phys. Elec.; Markus.

ill('s) operation (or bone-block operation) (Gill, Arthur Bruce): Medicine. ee: Dorland; Stedman.

ill (type-face) (Gill, Eric Rowland): Printing. See: Harrod; Hendrickson; artridge.

ille Wylie, Walker. See: Wylie, Walker Gill.

ILLEN, ARNOLD. fl. 17th c. German botanist. See: Pritzel. Gillenia.

illenia (Gillen, Arnold): Botany. See: Dorland; Taylor, N.; Webster's 3d.

ILLES DE LA TOURETTE, GEORGES EDOUARD ALBERT BRUTUS. 1859-1904. rench physician. See: Barnhart (Cycl. Names). Gilles de la Tourett's ndrome.

illes de la Tourette's syndrome (Gilles de la Tourette, Georges Edouard Albert utus): Medicine. See: Jablonski. Also known as: Brissaud's disease, uinon's disease, Tourette's syndrome.

illes de Retz. See: Retz, Baron de.

illes de Retz (Retz, Baron de): Generic Word (perpetrator of atrocities). ee: Harvey.

ILLESPIE, F. D. fl. 1964. American physician. (Biography source unavail-le.) Gillespie's syndrome.

ILLESPIE, FRANK. fl. 20th c. American mineral collector. Cited in: ailey. Gillespite.

illespie's syndrome (Gillespie, F. D.). See: Meyer-Schwickerath and Weyers ndrome.

illespite (Gillespie, Frank): Earth Sciences. See: Thrush; Webster's 3d.

illet-Hains test reaction (Derivation undetermined): Chemistry. See: an Nostrand Chem. Dict.

ILLETTE, EUGENE PAULIN. 1836-1886. French surgeon. See: Biog. Lex. ervorr. Aerzte. Gillette's suspensory ligament.

illette's suspensory ligament (Gillette, Eugene Paulin): Medicine. See: tedman.

ILLIAM, DAVID TOD. 1844-1923. American gynecologist. See: World ho's Who Sci. Gilliam's operation.

illiam's operation (Gilliam, David Tod): Medicine. See: Dorland; Stedman.

illies' graft (Gilles, Harold Delf): Medicine. See: Dorland.

ILLIES, HAROLD DELF. 1882-1960. New Zealand surgeon. See: Who Was ho, 1951-1960. Filatov-Gillies tubed pedicle, Gillies' graft, Gillies' opera-on.

GILLIES, JOHN. 1747-1836. Scottish-born Chilean physician and botanist. See: Britten and Boulger. Gilliesia.

Gillies' operation (Gillies, Harold Delf): Medicine. See: Dorland; Stedman.

Gillie's process (Derivation undetermined): Engineering and Industry. See: Thrush.

Gilliesia (Gillies, John): Botany. See: Charnock.

GILLINGHAM, ANNA. fl. 1940. American educator. Cited in: Mansell. Gillingham method.

Gillingham method (Gillingham, Anna): Education. See: Good. Also known as: Gillingham-Stillman method.

Gillingham-Stillman method (Gillingham, Anna and Stillman, Bessie Whitmore). See: Gillingham method.

Gillite (Derivation undetermined): Religion. See: Mathews, M. M.

Gillmore (Gilmore) needle (Derivation undetermined): Dentistry. See: Stedman; Thrush.

Gill's hot-rolling machine (Derivation undetermined): Printing. See: Lockwood.

GILMAN, G. H. fl. 1926. American metallurgist. Cited in: Chem. Abstr., vol. 20, p. 3154. Gilman heat-treating machine.

Gilman heat-treating machine (Gilman, G. H.): Engineering and Industry. See: Thrush.

GILMAN, HENRY. b. 1893. American chemist. See: Amer. Men Sci., 4th ed. Gilman-Nelson reagents, Gilman-Sweeney-Heck reaction.

Gilman-Nelson reagents (Gilman, Henry and Nelson, Joseph Frederick): Chemi-stry. See: Van Nostrand Chem. Dict.

Gilman-Sweeney-Heck reaction (Gilman, Henry; Sweeney, Orland Russel; and Heck, Lloyd Leslie): Chemistry. See: Van Nostrand Chem. Dict.

GILMER, ELIZABETH MERIWETHER (Pseud.: DOROTHY DIX). 1870-1951. American journalist and syndicated columnist. See: Who Was Who Amer., 1951-1960. Dorothy Dix.

GILMER, THOMAS LEWIS. 1849-1931. American oral surgeon. See: Who Was Who Amer., 1897-1942. Gilmer('s) wiring (or splint).

Gilmer('s) wiring (or splint) (Gilmer, Thomas Lewis): Medicine. See: Dorland; Stedman.

GILMOUR, G. VAN B. fl. 1925. English chemist. Cited in: Chem. Abstr., vol. 19, p. 1111. Gilmour reagent.

Gilmour reagent (Gilmour, G. Van B.): Chemistry. See: Van Nostrand Chem. Dict.

Gilpin sulky (Moore, Gilpin): Agriculture. See: Winburne.

Gilson('s) fluid (Derivation undetermined): Chemistry. See: Pennak; Van Nostrand Chem. Dict.

GILSON, S. H. No dates. American mineralogist. Cited in: Bailey. Gilsonite.

Gilsonite (Gilson, S. H.): Earth Sciences. See: Mathews, M. M.; Thrush; Van Nostrand Sci. Encyc.

Gilson's gland (Derivation undetermined): Zoology. See: Gray.

Gimard, Martin Jules Louis Alexandre de. See: Martin de Gimard, Jules Louis Alexandre.

Gimbernat, Antonio de. See: De Gimbernat, Antonio.

Gimbernat's ligament (De Gimbernat, Antonio): Anatomy. See: Donath; Dorland; Stedman; Webster's 3d.

Gimlet (Gimlette, Sir T. O.): Food and Drink. See: Hendrickson.

GIMLETTE, SIR T. O. fl. 1879-1917. English naval surgeon. (Biography source unavailable.) Gimlet.

gin Rickey (Rickey, Colonel): Food and Drink. See: Hendrickson.

GINACA, H. fl. 1915. American? inventor. Cited in: Chem. Abstr., vol. 9, p. 338. Ginaca machine.

Ginaca machine (Ginaca, H.): Engineering and Industry. See: Winburne.

Gingoulph, Saint. See: Gangulf, Saint.

GINI, CORRADO. 1884- . Italian economist. See: Internat. Encyc. Soc. Sci. Gini index, Gini's hypothesis, Gini's index of cograduation, Gini's theory of population growth.

Gini index (Gini, Corrado): Sociology. See: Zadrozny.

Gini's hypothesis (Gini, Corrado): Statistics. See: Kendall.

Gini's index of cograduation (Gini, Corrado): Statistics. See: Kendall.

Gini's theory of population growth (Gini, Corrado): Statistics. See: Zadrozny.

GINNINGS, DEFOE CHILDRESS. 1905- . American physicist. See: Amer. Men Sci., 5th ed. Osborne, Stimson and Ginnings method for mechanical equivalent of heat.

GINORI-CONTI, PIERO. 1865-1939. Italian industrialist. See: Diz. Encic. Ital. Ginorite.

Ginorite (Ginori-Conti, Piero): Earth Sciences. See: Webster's 3d.

GIOBERT, GIOVANNI ANTONIO. 1761-1834. Italian chemist. See: Pogg., vol. 1. Giobertite.

Giobertite (Giobert, Giovanni Antonio): Earth Sciences. See: Thrush.

GIORDANO, DAVIDE. 1864-1954. Italian surgeon. See: Castiglioni. Giordano's sphincter.

Giordano's sphincter (Giordano, Davide): Medicine. See: Dorland.

GIORGI, CARLO TOMMASO. fl. 1896. Italian musician. (Biography source unavailable.) Giorgi flute.

Giorgi flute (Giorgi, Carlo Tommaso): Music. See: Partridge; Scholes.

GIORGI, GIOVANNI. 1871-1950. Italian physicist. See: Dict. Sci. Biog. Giorgi system.

Giorgi system (Giorgi, Giovanni): Physics. See: Ballentyne; Hughes; Webster's 3d.

GIORGIONE (GIORGIO BARBARELLI). ca. 1477-1511. Venetian painter. See: Encyc. Brit., 1973. Giorgionesque.

Giorgionesque (Giorgione): Fine Arts. See: Webster's 3d.

Giottesque (adj.) (Giotto di Bondone): Fine Arts. See: Partridge; Webster's 3d; Weekley.

Giottesques (n.) (Giotto di Bondone): Fine Arts. See: Osborne.

GIOTTO DI BONDONE. ca. 1266-1337. Florentine painter, architect, and sculptor. See: Encyc. Brit., 1973. Giottesque (adj.), Giottesques (n.).

GIOVANNINI, SABASTIANO. 1851-1920. Italian dermatologist. See: Biog. Lex. hervorr. Aerzte. Giovannini's disease.

Giovannini's disease (Giovannini, Sabastiano): Medicine. See: Dorland; Jablonski.

GIRALDES, JOAQUIM PEDRO CASADO. 1808-1875. Portuguese-born French surgeon. See: World Who's Who Sci. Giraldes' organ.

Giraldes' organ (Giraldes, Joaquim Pedro Casado): Medicine. See: Donath; Dorland; Henderson.

GIRARD, A. fl. 1925. French chemist. Cited in: Chem. Abstr., vol. 20, p. 725. Girard-Fourneau reagent.

GIRARD, ALFRED CONRAD. 1841-1914. Swiss-born American surgeon. See: Who Was Who Amer., 1897-1942. Girard's method (or treatment).

GIRARD, ANDRE. fl. 1933. French chemist. Cited in: Chem. Abstr., vol. 27, p. 4286. Girard reagent(s).

Girard-Fourneau reagent (Girard, A. and Fourneau, Ernest Francois Auguste): Chemistry. See: Van Nostrand Chem. Dict.

GIRARD, J. fl. 1910. French chemist. Cited in: Chem. Abstr., vol. 3, p. 1098. Volcy-Boucher-Girard test.

Girard reagent(s) (Girard, Andre): Chemistry. See: Hackh; Van Nostrand Chem. Dict.; Webster's 3d.

Girard test reaction (Derivation undetermined): Chemistry. See: Van Nostrand Chem. Dict.

GIRARDIN. No dates. French gardener. (Biography source unavailable.) Girardin (graft).

Girardin (graft) (Girardin): Botany. See: Charnock.

Girard's method (or treatment) (Girard, Alfred Conrad): Medicine. See: Dorland.

girdle of Venus (Venus): Parapsychology. See: Webster's 3d.

GIRDNER, JOHN HARVEY. 1856-1933. American physician. See: World Who's Who Sci. Girdner's probe.

Girdner's probe (Girdner, John Harvey): Medicine. See: Dorland; Stedman.

GIRLING, A. H. fl. 1930. English engineer. (Biography source unavailable.) Girling brake.

Girling brake (Girling, A. H.): Engineering and Industry. See: Auger.

Girond process (Derivation undetermined): Engineering and Industry. See: Thrush.

GISEKE, PAUL DIETRICH. 1745-1796. Dutch botanist. See: Biog. Lex. hervorr. Aerzte. Gisekia.

Gisekia (Giseke, Paul Dietrich): Botany. See: Charnock.

GISH, OLIVER HOLMES. b. 1883. American geophysicist. See: Amer. Men Sci., 4th ed. Gish-Rooney method.

Gish-Rooney method (Gish, Oliver Holmes and Rooney, William Joseph): Earth Sciences. See: Thrush.

GISMONDI, CARLO GIUSEPPE. 1762-1824. Italian mineralogist. See: Nouv. Biog. Univ. Gismondine (or Gismondite).

Gismondine (or Gismondite) (Gismondi, Carlo Giuseppe): Earth Sciences. See: Charnock; Thrush; Webster's 3d.

Giuffrida-Ruggieri('s) stigma (Giuffrida-Ruggieri, Vincenzo): Medicine. See: Dorland; Jablonski; Stedman.

GIUFFRIDA-RUGGIERI, VINCENZO. 1872-1922. Italian anthropologist. See: World Who's Who Sci. Giuffrida-Ruggieri('s) stigma.

Giulio (coin) (Julius II). See: Julio (or Giulio).

Givaudan's method (Derivation undetermined): Photography. See: Focal Encyc. Photog.

Gjer's soaking pit (Derivation undetermined): Engineering and Industry. See: Thrush.

GJESSING, LEIV ROLVSSOEN. 1918- . Norwegian physician. See: World Who's Who Sci. Gjessing's syndrome.

Gjessing's syndrome (Gjessing, Leiv Rolvssoen): Medicine. See: Hinsie; Jablonski.

Gladdenite (Bishop, Gladden): Religion. See: Mathews, M.M.

Gladstone bag (Gladstone, William Ewart): Fashion. See: Brewer; Hendrickson; Picken.

Gladstone (claret) (Gladstone, William Ewart): Food and Drink. See: Brewer; Partridge; Weekley.

Gladstone collar (Gladstone, William Ewart): Fashion. See: Picken.

Gladstone-Dale formula (Gladstone, John Hall and Dale, Thomas Pelham): Chemistry. See: Van Nostrand Chem. Dict.

Gladstone-Dale law (Gladstone, John Hall and Dale, Thomas Pelham): Physics. See: Ballentyne; Internat. Dict. Phys. Elec.; Thewlis.

GLADSTONE, JOHN HALL. 1827-1902. English chemist. See: Dict. Sci. Biog. Gladstone-Dale formula, Gladstone-Dale law.

GLADSTONE, WILLIAM EWART. 1809-1898. English statesman, financier, and orator. See: Dict. Nat. Biog. 1st suppl. Gladstone bag, Gladstone (claret), Gladstone collar, Gladstone's umbrella, Gladstonian, Gladstonian liberal.

Gladstone's umbrella (Gladstone, William Ewart): History. See: Harbottle; Phyfe.

ladstonian (Gladstone, William Ewart): History. See: Webster's 3d.

ladstonian liberal (Gladstone, William Ewart): History. See: Montgomery.

LADWELL. fl. 1908. Surveyor. (Biography source unavailable.) ladwellized.

ladwellized (Gladwell): Engineering and Industry. See: Stenhouse.

LAESSER, KARL. fl. 1910. German veterinarian. Cited in: Mansell. laesser's (Glasser's) disease.

laesser's (Glasser's) disease (Glaesser, Karl): Medicine. See: Jablonski; edman.

lamorgan, Earl of. See: Somerset, Edward (Marquess of Worchester and arl of Glamorgan).

lamorgan Treaty (Somerset, Edward, Marquess of Worcester and Earl of lamorgan): History. See: Harbottle; Latham; Steinberg.

LAN, PAUL. 1846-1898. German physicist. See: Sci., vol. 8 (1898), 367. Glan prism? Glan spectrophotometer?

lan prism (Glan, Paul?): Physics. See: Internat. Dict. Phys. Elec.

lan spectrophotometer (Glan, Paul?): Physics. See: Internat. Dict. Phys. ec.

and of Meibom (Meibom, Heinrich). See: Meibomian gland.

land of Moll (Moll, Jakob Anthoni). See: Moll's gland(s).

land of Tyson (Tyson, Edward). See: Tyson's gland.

LANZMANN, EDUARD. 1887-1959. Swiss physician. See: Neue. Schweiz. og., p. 183. Glanzmann-Riniker syndrome, Glanzmann-Saland syndrome, lanzmann's syndrome (or thrombasthenia).

lanzmann-Naegeli syndrome (Glanzmann, Eduard and Naegeli, Otto?). See: lanzmann's syndrome (or thrombasthenia).

lanzmann-Riniker syndrome (Glanzmann, Eduard and Riniker, Paul): Medicine. ee: Jablonski.

lanzmann-Saland syndrome (Glanzmann, Eduard and Saland, S.): Medicine. ee: Jablonski.

lanzmann's dysporia (Derivation undetermined). See: Andersen's syndrome.

lanzmann's syndrome (or thrombasthenia) (Glanzmann, Eduard): Medicine. ee: Jablonski; Stedman. Also known as: Bernard-Soulier syndrome, lanzmann-Naegeli syndrome, Revol's syndrome.

LAS, JOHN. 1695-1773. Scottish clergyman. See: Dict. Nat. Biog. lassites (or Glasites).

LASER, CHRISTOPHER. 1615-1672? Swiss-born French chemist. See: Dict. i. Biog. Glaserite.

laser furnace (Derivation undetermined): Chemistry. See: Hackh.

LASER, JOHANN HEINRICH. 1629-1675. Swiss anatomist. See: Dict. i. Biog. Glaserian artery, Glaserian fissure.

laserian artery (Glaser, Johann Heinrich): Medicine. See: Dorland; edman.

laserian fissure (Glaser, Johann Heinrich): Medicine. See: Henderson; edman; Webster's 3d.

laserite (Glaser, Christopher): Chemistry. Cited in: Dict. Sci. Biog.

LASGOW, WILLIAM CARR. 1845-1907. American physician. Cited in: elly. Glasgow's sign.

lasgow's sign (Glasgow, William Carr): Medicine. See: Dorland; Stedman.

LASPEY, E. fl. 1941. American? psychologist. (Biography source unavailable.) Bryngelson-Glaspey test.

LASS, CARTER. 1858-1946. American legislator. See: Biog. Direct. mer. Congress. Glass-Steagall Act, Owen-Glass Act.

Glass-Steagall Act (Glass, Carter and Steagall, Henry Bascom): Politics. See: Morris; Morris and Irwin; Smith.

GLASSER, JULIAN. 1912- . American metallurgist. See: Amer. Men Sci., 8th ed. Copley, Phipps and Glasser gauge.

Glassites (or Glasites) (Glas, John): Religion. See: Canney; Mathews, S.; Webster's 3d. Also known as: Sandemanians.

GLASTONBURY, ABBOT OF. No dates. English clergyman. (Biography source unavailable.) Glastonbury chair.

Glastonbury chair (Glastonbury, Abbot of): Applied Arts. See: Partridge; Weekley.

GLAUBER, JOHANN RUDOLPH. 1604-1670. German chemist. See: Dict. Sci. Biog. Glauber('s) salt(s), Glauberite.

Glauber('s) salt(s) (Glauber, Johann Rudolph): Chemistry. See: Brewer; Focal Encyc. Photog.; Hackh.

Glauberite (Glauber, Johann Rudolph): Earth Sciences. See: Thrush; Webster's 3d.

GLAUERT, HERMANN. 1892-1934. English physicist. See: World Who's Who Sci. Glauert number, Prandtl-Glauert rule.

Glauert number (Glauert, Hermann): Physics. See: Thewlis.

GLEDITSCH, JOHN GOTTLEIB. 1714-1786. German botanist. See: World Who's Who Sci. Gleditschia (or Gleditsia).

Gleditschia (or Gleditsia) (Gleditsch, John Gottleib): Botany. See: Charnock; Webster's 3d.

GLEICHEN-RUSSWORM, WILHELM FRIEDRICH VON. 1717-1783. German naturalist. See: Dict. Sci. Biog. Gleichenia.

Gleichenia (Gleichen-Russworm, Wilhelm Friedrich von): Botany. See: Webster's 3d.

Glen Grey Act (Derivation undetermined): History. See: Harbottle.

GLENARD, FRANTZ. 1848-1920. French physician. See: Biog. Lex. hervorr. Aerzte, 1880-1930. Glenard's disease, Glenard's syndrome, Glenard's test, Glenard's theory.

Glenard's disease (Glenard, Frantz): Medicine. See: Dorland.

Glenard's syndrome (Glenard, Franzt): Medicine. See: Jablonski.

Glenard's test (Glenard, Frantz): Medicine. See: Dorland.

Glenard's theory (Glenard, Frantz): Medicine. See: Dorland.

GLENDOWER, OWEN. 1359-1416. Welsh chieftain. See: Dict. Nat. Biog. Glyn Dwr rebellion, Owen Glendower's oak.

GLEY, EMILE. 1857-1930. French physiologist. See: World Who's Who Sci. Gley's cells, Gley's glands.

Gley's cells (Gley, Emile): Medicine. See: Dorland; Stedman.

Gley's glands (Gley, Emile): Medicine. See: Dorland; Stedman.

GLICK, DAVID. 1908- . American biochemist. See: Amer. Men Sci., 10th ed. Linderstrom-Lang-Glick method.

Glick effect (Glick, Paul Charles?): Psychology. See: Hinsie.

GLICK, PAUL CHARLES. 1910- . American sociologist. See: Amer. Men Sci., 9th ed, vol. 3. Glick effect?

GLINSKI, LEO KONRAD. 1870-1918. Polish physician. See: Biog. Lex. hervorr. Aerzte, 1880-1930. Glinski-Simmonds syndrome.

Glinski-Simmonds syndrome (Glinski, Leo Konrad and Simmonds, Morris). See: Simmonds' syndrome.

GLISSON, FRANCIS. 1597-1677. English anatomist, physiologist, and pathologist. See: Dict. Sci. Biog. Glissonitis, Glisson's capsule, Glisson's cirrhosis, Glisson's disease, Glisson's sling, Glisson's sphincter.

Glissonitis (Glisson, Francis): Medicine. See: Stedman.

Glisson's capsule (Glisson, Francis): Medicine. See: Donath; Gray; Henderson.

Glisson's cirrhosis (Glisson, Francis): Medicine. See: Stedman.

Glisson's disease (Glisson, Francis): Medicine. See: Jablonski.

Glisson's sling (Glisson, Francis): Medicine. See: Dorland.

Glisson's sphincter (Glisson, Francis): Medicine. See: Stedman.

Glivenko–Cantelli lemma (Glivenko, Valerij Ivanovich and Cantelli, Francesco Paolo): Statistics. See: Kendall.

GLIVENKO, VALERIJ IVANOVICH. 1897-1940. Russian mathematician. See: Matematika v.SSSR, vol. 2, 1959. Glivenko–Cantelli lemma, Glivenko's theorem.

Glivenko's theorem (Glivenko, Valerij Ivanovich): Statistics. See: Kendall.

GLOCKER, ERNST FRIEDRICH. 1793-1858. German geologist. See: Royal Soc. Cat. Sci. Pap. Glockerite.

Glockerite (Glocker, Ernst Friedrich): Earth Sciences. See: Thrush.

GLOGER, CONSTANTINE WILHELM LAMBERT. 1803-1863. German zoologist and ornithologist. See: World Who's Who Sci. Gloger's law (or rule).

Gloger's law (or rule) (Gloger, Constantine Wilhelm Lambert): Zoology. See: Gray; Pennak; Winick.

Gloucester, Duke of. See: Humphrey, Duke of Gloucester and Earl of Pembroke.

Glover and West coking retort (Glover, Samuel and West, John): Chemistry. See: Van Nostrand Chem. Dict.

GLOVER, JOHN. d. 1902. English chemist. See: Sci., vol. 15 (1902), p. 838. Glover('s) tower.

GLOVER, SAMUEL. fl. 1911. English chemist. Cited in: Chem. Abstr., vol. 5, p. 2546. Glover and West coking retort.

Glover('s) scale (Glover, Townsend): Zoology. See: Gray; Webster's 3d.

GLOVER, THOMAS JOSEPH. b. 1887. Canadian bacteriologist. Cited in: Mansell. Glover's organism.

Glover('s) tower (Glover, John): Chemistry. See: Thrush; Van Nostrand Chem. Dict.; Webster's 3d.

GLOVER, TOWNSEND. 1813-1883. American entomologist. See: World Who's Who Sci. Glover('s) scale.

Glover's organism (Glover, Thomas Joseph): Medicine. See: Dorland.

GLOXIN, BENJAMIN PETER fl. 18th c. German physician and botanist. See: Pritzel. Gloxinia.

Gloxinia (Gloxin, Benjamin Peter): Botany. See: Charnock; Partridge; Webster's 3d.

GLUCK, CHRISTOPH WILLIBALD. 1714-1787. German composer. See: Encyc. Brit., 1973. Gluckists.

Gluckists (Gluck, Christoph Willibald): Music. See: Brewer.

GLUECKSMANN, CARL. fl. 1914. German chemist. Cited in: Chem. Abstr., vol. 8, p. 205. Gluecksmann reaction for pyrogallol.

Gluecksmann reaction for pyrogallol (Gluecksmann, Carl): Chemistry. See: Van Nostrand Chem. Dict.

GLUGE, GOTTLIEB. 1812-1899. German histologist. See: Sci., vol. 9 (1899), p. 229. Gluge's corpuscles.

Gluge's corpuscles (Gluge, Gottlieb): Medicine. See: Dorland; Gray; Stedman.

Glushinskite (Derivation undetermined): Earth Sciences. See: Thrush.

GLUZINSKI, WLADYSLAW ANTONI. 1856-1935. Polish physician. See: Lutte Contre Tuberculose, p. 37. Gluzinski's test.

Gluzinski's test (Gluzinski, Wladyslaw Antoni): Medicine. See: Dorland; Stedman.

GLYCON. No dates. Greek lyric poet. See: Dict. Grk. Rom. Biog. Myth. Glyconic (verse).

Glyconic (verse) (Glycon): Literature. See: Partridge; Preminger.

Glyn Dwr, Owain. See: Glendower, Owen.

Glyn Dwr rebellion (Glendower, Owen): History. See: Steinberg.

GMELIN, CHRISTIAN GOTTLOB. 1792-1860. German chemist. See: World Who's Who Sci. Gmelinite, Gmelin's blue.

GMELIN, JOHANN GEORG. 1709-1755. German botanist. See: Dict. Sci. Biog. Gmelina.

GMELIN, LEOPOLD. 1788-1853. German chemist. See: Dict. Sci. Biog. Gmelin's test (for bile pigments), Tiedemann–Gmelin test reaction for acetate, Tiedemann–Gmelin test reaction for tryptophane.

Gmelina (Gmelin, Johann Georg): Botany. See: Charnock; Webster's 3d.

Gmelinite (Gmelin, Christian Gottlob): Earth Sciences. See: Charnock; Thrush; Webster's 3d.

Gmelin's blue (Gmelin, Christian Gottlob): Chemistry. See: Webster's 3d.

Gmelin's test (for bile pigments) (Gmelin, Leopold): Chemistry. See: Ballentyne; Dorland; Stedman. Also known as: Rosenbach–Gmelin test.

GNATHO. Sycophant in the comedy, "Eunuchus", by Terence. See: Barnhart (Cycl. Names). Gnathonic.

Gnathonic (Gnatho): Generic Word (sycophantic). See: Webster's 3d.; Weekley.

GNEDENKO, BORIS VLADIMIROVICH. 1912- . Russian mathematician. See: World Who's Who Sci. Gnedenko's theorem.

Gnedenko's theorem (Gnedenko, Boris Vladimirovich): Statistics. See: Kendall.

go Nap (Napoleon I): Gerneric Word (aim at highest). See: Partridge.

Goadby solution (Derivation undetermined): Chemistry. See: Van Nostrand Chem. Dict.

Gobelin blue (Gobelin family): Applied Arts. See: Partridge; Picken.

GOBELIN FAMILY. fl. 16th c. French dyers. See: Encyc. Brit., 1973. Gobelin blue, Goebelin stitch, Gobelin tapestry.

Gobelin stitch (Gobelin family): Applied Arts. See: Picken.

Gobelin tapestry (Gobelin family): Applied Arts. See: Brewer; Harvey; Phyfe.

Gobineau, Count Joseph Arthur de. See: De Gobineau, Count Joseph Arthur.

Gobinism (De Gobineau, Count Joseph Arthur): Philosophy. See: Webster's 3d.

Goclenian sorites (Goclenius, Rudolphus): Philosophy. See: Webster's 3d.

GOCLENIUS, RUDOLPHUS. 1572-1621. German logician. See: World Who's Who Sci. Goclenian sorites.

GODARD, BENJAMIN LOUIS PAUL. 1849-1895. French composer. See: Encyc. Brit., 1973. Godard (garnish).

Godard (garnish) (Godard, Benjamin Louis Paul): Food and Drink. See: De Sola.

GODARD, JEAN-LUC. 1930- . French film-maker. See: Cur. Biog. Godardian.

Godardian (Godard, Jean-Luc): Film. See: Barnhart (New Eng.).

GODBE, WILLIAM SAMUEL. 1833-1902. English-born American mine operator and editor. See: Who Was Who Amer., 1607-1896. Godbeite.

Godbeite (Godbe, William Samuel): Religion. See: Mathews, M. M.

GODEFFROY, RICHARD. fl. 1876. German chemist. Cited in: Royal Soc. Cat. Sci. Pap. Godeffroy test reaction for alkaloids?

Godeffroy test reaction for alkaloids (Godeffroy, Richard?): Chemistry. See: Van Nostrand Chem. Dict.

GODELIER, CHARLES PIERRE. 1813-1877. French physician. Cited in: Mansell. Godélier's law.

Godelier's law (Godelier, Charles Pierre): Medicine. See: Dorland; Stedman.

GODET, CHARLES HENRY. 1796?-1879. Swiss botanist. See: Amer. J. Sci., vol. 119 (1880), p. 158. Godetia.

Godetia (Godet, Charles Henry): Botany. See: Partridge; Taylor, N.; Webster's 3d.

Godfrey furnace (Derivation undetermined): Engineering and Industry. See: Thrush.

Godfrey gripper-machine (Derivation undetermined): Printing. See: Lockwood.

GODFRIED, EMANUEL GERARD. fl. 1940. Dutch internist. Cited in: Mansell. Godfried-Prick-Carol-Prakken syndrome.

Godfried-Prick-Carol-Prakken syndrome (Godfried, Emmanuel Gerard; Prick, Joseph Jules Guillaume; Carol, Willem Lambertus Leonard; and Prakken, Jan Roelof): Medicine. See: Jablonski.

GODIVA (OR GODGIFU). fl. 11th c. English wife of Leofric, earl of Mercia. See: Encyc. Brit., 1973. Lady Godiva.

GODMAN, JOHN DAVIDSON. 1794-1830. American anatomist. See: World Who's Who Sci. Godman's fascia.

Godman's fascia (Godman, John Davidson): Medicine. See: Stedman.

Godolphin Barb (horse) (Godolphin, Francis): Zoology. See: Hendrickson under "Byerly Turk..."

GODOLPHIN, FRANCIS. 1678-1766. English aristocrat. See: Dict. Nat. Biog. Godolphin Barb (horse).

GODOY, MANUEL DE. 1767-1851. Spanish statesman. See: Encyc. Brit., 1973. Godoya.

Godoya (Godoy, Manuel de): Botany. See: Charnock.

GODTFREDSEN, ERIK. fl. 1947. Danish radiologist. Cited in: Mansell. Godtfredsen's syndrome.

Godtfredsen's syndrome (Godtfredsen, Erik): Medicine. See: Jablonski.

GODWIN, WILLIAM. 1756-1836. English philosopher, novelist, and historian. See: Encyc. Brit., 1973. Godwinian.

Godwinian (Godwin, William): Philosophy. See: Webster's 3d.

Goebel reagent for metals (Derivation undetermined): Chemistry. See: Van Nostrand Chem. Dict.

Goeckel condenser (Derivation undetermined): Chemistry. See: Hackh.

Goeckerman treatment (Goeckerman, William Henry): Medicine. See: Stedman.

GOECKERMAN, WILLIAM HENRY. 1884-1954. American dermatologist. See: L. A. County Med. Assoc. Bull., vol. 84, no. 24 (1954), p. 1479. Goeckerman treatment.

GOEDEL, KURT. 1906- . Austrian-born American mathematician. See: World Who's Who Sci. Goedel's proof, Neumann-Bernays-Goedel axioms.

Goedel's proof (Goedel, Kurt): Mathematics. See: Asimov.

Goedenhuyse, Joseph. See: Benincasa, Guiseppe.

GOERGEY (VON GOERGOE), ROLF. 1886-1915. Hungarian-born Austrian mineralogist. See: Min. Abstr., vol. 17 (1913-1916) p. 365. Gorgeyite. Also known as: Mikheevite.

GOERNER, PAUL. b. 1879. German chemist. Cited in: Chem. Abstr., vol. 5, p. 1159. Rosenthaler-Goerner test reagents for alkaloids.

GOERTZEL, GERALD. 1919- . American physicist. See: World Who's Who Sci. Goertzel-Greuling approximation, Goertzel-Selengut method.

Goertzel-Greuling approximation (Goertzel, Gerald and Greuling, Eugene): Physics. See: Internat. Dict. Ap. Math.

Goertzel-Selengut method (Goertzel, Gerald and Selengut, David S.): Physics. See: Internat. Dict. Ap. Math.

GOETHE, JOHANN WOLFGANG VON. 1749-1832. German poet, statesman and scientist. See: Dict. Sci. Biog. Goethea, Goethe's bone, Goethian (or Goethean), Goethite (or Gothite).

Goethea (Goethe, Johann Wolfgang von): Botany. See: Charnock.

GOETHERT, BERNHARD HERMANN. 1907- . German-born American aeronautical engineer. See: World Who's Who Sci. Goethert's rule.

Goethert's rule (Goethert, Bernhard Hermann): Physics. See: Internat. Dict. Ap. Math.

Goethe's bone (Goethe, Johann Wolfgang von): Medicine. See: Stedman.

Goethian (or Goethean) (Goethe, Johann Wolfgang von): Generic Word. See: Hendrickson; Partridge; Webster's 3d.

Goethite (or Gothite) (Goethe, Johann Wolfgang von): Earth Sciences. See: Charnock; Thrush; Van Nostrand Sci. Encyc.

GOETHLIN, GUSTAF. b. 1874. Swedish physiologist. See: Biog. Lex. hervorr. Aerzte, 1880-1930. Goethlin's index (or test).

Goethlin solution (Derivation undetermined): Chemistry. See: Hackh.

Goethlin's index (or test) (Goethlin, Gustaf): Medicine. See: Dorland; Stedman.

GOETSCH, EMIL. 1883- . American physician. See: World Who's Who Sci. Goetsch('s) skin reaction (or test).

Goetsch('s) skin reaction (or test) (Goetsch, Emil): Medicine. See: Dorland; Wolman.

GOETTE, ALEXANDER WILHELM. 1840-1922. Russian-born German zoologist. See: Dict. Sci. Biog. Goette's larva.

Goette's larva (Goette, Alexander Wilhelm): Zoology. See: Gray; Henderson; Pennak.

Goetz effect (Goetz, Paul): Earth Sciences. Cited in: World Who's Who Sci.

GOETZ, PAUL (In full: FRIEDRICH WILHELM PAUL). 1891-1954. German geophysicist. See: World Who's Who Sci. Goetz effect.

GOETZEN, COUNT GUSTAV ADOLF VON. b. 1866. German traveler in Africa. Cited in: Mansell. Gotzenite.

GOFFE, JAMES RIDDLE. 1851-1932. American gynecologist. See: Who Was Who Amer., 1897-1942. Goffe's operation.

Goffe's operation (Goffe, James Riddle): Medicine. See: Dorland.

GOFMAN, MOSES. b. 1897. German physician. Cited in: Mansell. Gofman test.

Gofman test (Gofman, Moses): Medicine. See: Stedman.

GOGGIA, CARLO PAOLO. fl. 20th c. Italian physician. Cited in: Mansell. Goggia's sign.

Goggia's sign (Goggia, Carlo Paolo): Medicine. See: Stedman.

GOGTE, G. R. fl. 1940. Indian chemist. Cited in: Chem. Abstr., vol. 34, p. 2829. Gogte synthesis.

Gogte synthesis (Gogte, G. R.): Chemistry. See: Van Nostrand Chem. Dict.

Golay cell (Golay, Marcel Jules Edouard): Engineering and Industry. See: Markus; Thewlis; Van Nostrand Sci. Encyc.

Golay column (Golay, Marcel Jules Edouard): Chemistry. See: Hackh.

GOLAY, MARCEL JULES EDOUARD. 1902- . Swiss-born American physicist. See: Amer. Men Sci., 9th ed. Golay cell, Golay column.

Gol'braikh test for nigrogen (Gol'braikh, Z. E.): Chemistry. See: Van Nostrand Chem. Dict.

GOL'BRAIKH, Z. E. fl. 1938. Russian chemist. Cited in: Chem. Abstr., vol. 32, p. 1612. Gol'braikh test for nitrogen.

Gold slide (Derivation undetermined): Earth Sciences. See: Huschke.

GOLDBACH, CHRISTIAN. 1690-1764. Prussian-born Russian mathematician. See: Dict. Sci. Biog. Goldbach('s) conjecture(s).

Goldbach('s) conjecture(s) (Goldbach, Christian): Mathematics. See: Ballentyne; Blumberg; James.

GOLDBERG, IRMA. fl. 1906. Swiss chemist. Cited in: Pogg., vol. 6 under "Ullmann, Fritz." Jourdan-Ullman-Goldberg synthesis (or acridone synthesis).

GOLDBERG, JOHANN GOTTLIEB. 1727-1756. German keyboard player and pupil of J. S. Bach. See: Grove. Goldberg Variations.

Goldberg-Maxwell-Morris syndrome (Goldberg, Minnie Berelson; Maxwell, Alice Freeland; and Morris, John McLean): Medicine. See: Jablonski. Also known as: Goldberg-Maxwell syndrome, Goldberg-Morris syndrome, Morris' syndrome.

Goldberg-Maxwell syndrome (Goldberg, Minnie Berelson and Maxwell, Alice Freeland). See: Goldberg-Maxwell-Morris syndrome.

GOLDBERG, MINNIE BERELSON. 1900- . American physician. See: Amer. Men Sci., 10th ed. Goldberg-Maxwell-Morris syndrome.

Goldberg-Morris syndrome (Goldberg, Minnie Berelson and Morris, John McLean). See: Goldberg-Maxwell-Morris syndrome.

GOLDBERG, REUBEN LUCIUS. 1883-1970. American cartoonist. See: Barnhart (Cycl. Names). Rube Goldberg.

GOLDBERG, SAMUEL. fl. 1955. American mathematical analyst. See: Amer. Men Sci., 9th ed. WAGR test.

Goldberg Variations (Goldberg, Johann Gottlieb): Music. See: Apel.

Goldberg wedge (Derivation undetermined): Photography. See: Focal Encyc. Photog.

GOLDBERGER, JOSEPH. 1874-1929. American physician. See: Dict. Sci. Biog. Goldberger's diet.

Goldberger's diet (Goldberger, Joseph): Medicine. See: Dorland.

GOLDBLATT, HARRY. 1891- . American pathologist. See: World Who's Who Sci. Goldblatt kidney, Goldblatt's clamp, Goldblatt's hypertension.

Goldblatt kidney (Goldblatt, Harry): Medicine. See: Stedman.

Goldblatt's clamp (Goldblatt, Harry): Medicine. See: Dorland; Stedman.

Goldblatt's hypertension (Goldblatt, Harry): Medicine. See: Dorland; Jablonski.

GOLDBLOOM, RICHARD B. 1924- . Canadian physician. See: Amer. Men and Women Sci., 12th ed. Seriver-Goldbloom-Roy syndrome.

Golden-Kantor syndrome (Golden, Ross and Kantor, John Leonard): Medicine. See: Jablonski.

GOLDEN, ROSS. 1889- . American physician. See: Amer. Men Sci., 10th ed. Golden-Kantor syndrome.

GOLDEN, WILLIAM WOLFE. 1866-1929. American physician. See: W. Va. Med. J., vol. 25, no. 11 (Nov., 1929), p. 676. Golden's sign?

GOLDENHAR, MAURICE. fl. 1952. Swiss physician. Cited in: Mansell. Goldenhar's syndrome.

Goldenhar's syndrome (Goldenhar, Maurice): Medicine. See: Jablonski.

Golden's sign (Golden, William Wolfe?): Medicine. See: Dorland.

GOLDFLAM, SAMUEL VULFOVICH. 1852-1932. Polish neurologist. See: Biog. Lex. hervorr. Aerzte, 1880-1930. Erb-Goldflam syndrome (or disease).

GOLDFUSS, GEORG AUGUST. 1782-1848. German zoologist and paleontologist. See: World Who's Who Sci. Goldfussia?

Goldfussia (Goldfuss, Georg August?): Botany. See: Charnock.

GOLDHABER, MAURICE. 1911- . Austrian-born American physicist. See: World Who's Who Sci. Chadwick-Goldhaber effect.

GOLDHORN, L. B. fl. 1905. American pathologist. Cited in: Kelly. Goldhorn's stain.

Goldhorn's stain (Goldhorn, L. B.): Medicine. See: Stedman.

GOLDICH, SAMUEL STEPHEN. 1909- . American geologist. See: World Who's Who Sci. Goldichite, Goldich's stability series.

Goldichite (Goldich, Samuel Stephen): Earth Sciences. See: Thrush.

Goldich's stability series (Goldich, Samuel Stephen): Earth Sciences. See: Thrush.

Goldie('s) fern (shield fern or wood fern) (Goldie, John): Botany. See: Webster's 3d.

GOLDIE, JOHN. 1793-1886. Scottish-born Canadian naturalist. See: Dict. Canadian Biog. Goldie('s) fern (shield fern or wood fern).

GOLDMAN, MARCUS ISAAC. b. 1891. American geologist. See: Amer. Men Sci., 9th ed. Goldmanite.

Goldmanite (Goldman, Marcus Isaac): Earth Sciences. See: Thrush.

GOLDMANN, HANS. 1899- . Swiss ophthalmologist. See: Kuerschner's Gel. Kal., vol. 9, 1961. Goldmann perimeter, Goldmann's applanation tonometer.

Goldmann perimeter (Goldmann, Hans): Medicine. See: Stedman.

Goldmann's applanation tonometer (Goldmann, Hans): Medicine. See: Stedman.

GOLDSCHEIDER, JOHANN KARL AUGUST EUGEN ALFRED. 1858-1935. German physician. See: World Who's Who Sci. Goldscheider's disease Goldscheider's percussion, Goldscheider's test.

Goldscheider's disease (Goldscheider, Johann Karl August Eugen Alfred). See: Fox's disease.

Goldscheider's percussion (Goldscheider, Johann Karl August Eugen Alfred): Medicine. See: Dorland.

Goldscheider's test (Goldscheider, Johann Karl August Eugen Alfred): Medicine. See: Dorland; Stedman.

Goldschmidt alternator (Derivation undetermined): Electronics. See: Hughes.

Goldschmidt detinning process (Goldschmidt, Hans): Chemistry. See: Van Nostrand Chem. Dict.; Van Nostrand Sci. Encyc.

GOLDSCHMIDT, HANS. 1861-1923. German chemist. See: World Who's Who Sci. Goldschmidt detinning process, Goldschmidt('s) process (or reduction process).

Goldschmidt('s) law (Goldschmidt, Victor Moritz): Physics. See: Ballentyne; Internat. Dict. Ap. Math.; Internat. Dict. Phys. Elec.

GOLDSCHMIDT, LEONTINE. 1913- . Austrian-born American biochemist. See: World Who's Who Sci. Frehden-Goldschmidt test for amines, Frehden-Goldschmidt test for protein.

Goldschmidt process (Derivation undetermined): Chemistry. See: Van Nostrand Chem. Dict.

Goldschmidt('s) process (or reduction process) (Goldschmidt, Hans): Chemistry. See: Thrush; Van Nostrand Chem. Dict.; Van Nostrand Sci. Encyc.

Goldschmidt test for silver halides (Derivation undetermined): Chemistry. See: Van Nostrand Chem. Dict.

GOLDSCHMIDT, VICTOR. 1853-1933. German crystallographer. See: Dict. Sci. Biog. Goldschmidtine, Goldschmidtite.

GOLDSCHMIDT, VICTOR MORITZ. 1888-1947. Swiss-born Norwegian mineralogist and geochemist. See: Dict. Sci. Biog. Goldschmidt('s) law, Goldschmidt's mineralogical phase rule.

Goldschmidtine (Goldschmidt, Victor): Earth Sciences. See: Webster's 3d.

Goldschmidtite (Goldschmidt, Victor): Earth Sciences. See: Webster's 3d.

Goldschmidt's mineralogical phase rule (Goldschmidt, Victor Moritz): Earth Sciences. See: Thrush.

Goldsmith fluid (Derivation undetermined): Chemistry. See: Van Nostrand Chem. Dict.

GOLDSMITH, JOHN NAISH. b. 1874. English chemist. Cited in: Chem. Abstr., vol. 21, p. 1193. Goldsmith test for tung oil.

Goldsmith test for tung oil (Goldsmith, John Naish): Chemistry. See: Van Nostrand Chem. Dict.

GOLDSTEIN, EUGEN. 1850-1930. German physicist. See: Dict. Sci. Biog. Goldstein rays.

GOLDSTEIN, HYMAN ISAAC. 1887-1954. American physician. See: Who's Who Among Physicians and Surg. Goldstein's disease, Goldstein's hematemesis (or heredofamilial angiomatosis), Goldstein's hemoptysis, Goldstein's sign (or toe sign).

GOLDSTEIN, KURT. 1878-1965. German-born American psychologist. See: World Who's Who Sci. Gelb-Goldstein color sorting test, Gelb-Goldstein-Weigl-Scheerer object sorting test, Goldstein-Scheerer cube test, Goldstein-Scheerer stick test, Goldstein's syndrome, Weigl-Goldstein-Scheerer test.

GOLDSTEIN, L. fl. 1874. German physician. Cited in: Kelly. Goldstein solution.

Goldstein rays (Goldstein, Eugen): Physics. See: Dorland.

Goldstein-Reichmann syndrome (Goldstein, Kurt and Reichmann, Frieda). See: Goldstein's syndrome.

Goldstein-Scheerer cube test (Goldstein, Kurt and Scheerer, Martin): Psychology. See: Wolman.

Goldstein-Scheerer stick test (Goldstein, Kurt and Scheerer, Martin): Psychology. See: Wolman.

Goldstein solution (Goldstein, L.): Chemistry. See: Van Nostrand Chem. Dict.

Goldstein's disease (Goldstein, Hyman Isaac): Medicine. See: Dorland.

Goldstein's hematemesis (or heredofamilial angiomatosis) (Goldstein, Hyman Isaac). See: Osler's syndrome (2).

Goldstein's hemoptysis (Goldstein, Hyman Isaac): Medicine. See: Dorland.

Goldstein's sign (or toe sign) (Goldstein, Hyman Isaac): Medicine. See: Dorland; Stedman.

Goldstein's syndrome (Goldstein, Kurt): Medicine. See: Jablonski. Also known as: Goldstein-Reichmann syndrome.

GOLDSTUECK, M. fl. 1924. German chemist. Cited in: Chem. Abstr. vol. 19, p. 23. Goldstueck reagent.

Goldstueck reagent (Goldstueck, M.): Chemistry. See: Van Nostrand Chem. Dict.

GOLDTHWAIT, JOE ERNEST. 1866-1961. American surgeon. See: Who Was Who Amer., 1969-1973. Goldthwait's sign (or symptom).

Goldthwait's sign (or symptom) (Goldthwait, Joel Ernest): Medicine. See: Dorland; Stedman.

GOLDWYN, SAMUEL. 1882- . American motion picture producer. See: Barnhart (Cycl. Names). Goldwynism.

Goldwynism (Goldwyn, Samuel): Generic Word. See: Hendrickson; Webster's 3d.

GOLE, L. fl. 1935. French physician. Cited in: Leiber and Olbrich. Touraine-Solente-Gole syndrome.

Golenkin reagent (Derivation undetermined): Chemistry. See: Van Nostrand Chem. Dict.

Golgi apparatus (complex or internal reticulum) (Golgi, Camillo): Zoology. See: Gray; Henderson; Pennak. Also known as: Holmgren-Golgi canals.

Golgi body (or bodies) (Golgi, Camillo): Medicine. See: Carter; Webster's 3d.

GOLGI, CAMILLO. 1843-1926. Italian histologist. See: Dict. Sci. Biog. Golgi apparatus (complex or internal reticulum), Golgi body (or bodies), Golgi('s) cells, Golgi material (or substance), Golgi-Mazzoni corpuscles, Golgi('s) method, Golgi tendon organ, Golgi zone, Golgiokinesis, Golgiosomes, Golgi's fibers, Golgi's osmiobichromate solution, Golgi's stain, Rezzonico-Golgi threads (or spirals).

Golgi('s) cells (Golgi, Camillo): Anatomy. See: Donath; Dorland; Pennak.

Golgi material (or substance) (Golgi, Camillo): Medicine. See: Webster's 3d.

Golgi-Mazzoni corpuscles (Golgi, Camillo and Mazzoni, Vittorio): Anatomy. See: Drever; Henderson; Wolman.

Golgi('s) method (Golgi, Camillo): Medicine. See: Pennak; Stedman.

Golgi tendon organ (Golgi, Camillo): Physiology. See: Chaplin; English; Wolman.

Golgi zone (Golgi, Camillo): Medicine. See: Stedman.

Golgiokinesis (Golgi, Camillo): Medicine. See: Henderson; Stedman.

Golgiosomes (Golgi, Camillo): Medicine. See: Henderson.

Golgi's fibers (Golgi, Camillo): Medicine. See: Stedman.

Golgi's osmiobichromate solution (Golgi, Camillo): Medicine. See: Stedman.

Golgi's stain (Golgi, Camillo): Medicine. See: Stedman.

Goliard (Golias, Bishop): History. See: Partridge; Encyc. Brit., 1973.

Goliardic verse (Golias, Bishop): Literature. See: Barnet; Barnhart (Eng. Lit.); Partridge; Preminger; Scott.

GOLIAS, BISHOP. Legendary patron of the Latin poets of the Middle Ages. See: Jobes. Goliard, Goliardic verse.

GOLIATH. Biblical giant of the Philistines. See: Encyc. Brit., 1973. David and Goliath, Goliath, Goliath frog, Goliath heron, Goliath (insect genus), Goliath (or Goliath crane).

Goliath (Goliath, the Biblical giant): Generic Word (giant). See: Hendrickson; Webster's 3d.

Goliath (or Goliath crane) (Goliath, the Biblical giant): Engineering and Industry. See: Encyc. Brit., 1973 under "Crane," vol. 6, p. 698a; Partridge.

Goliath frog (Goliath, the Biblical giant): Zoology. See: Gray.

Goliath heron (Goliath, the Biblical giant): Zoology. See: Encyc. Brit. 1973 under "Heron," vol. 11, p. 446a.

Goliath (insect genus) (Goliath, the Biblical giant): Zoology. See: Charnock.

GOLITSYN, BORIS BORISOVICH. 1862-1916. Russian physicist and seismologist. See: Dict. Sci. Biog. Galitizin-type seismograph.

GOLITSYN, DMITRY ALEKSEYEVICH. 1738-1803. Russian mineralogist and naturalist. See: Barnhart (Cycl. Names). Gallitzinite.

GOLL, FRIEDRICH. 1829-1903. Swiss anatomist. See: World Who's Who Sci. Goll's column(s) (tract or column(s) of Goll), Goll's fibers, Goll's nucleus.

GOLLIWOG. Animated doll in Bertha Upton's books written for children. (Biography source unavailable.) Golliwog.

Golliwog (Golliwog, the animated character): Generic Word (grotesque doll or person). See: Webster's 3d.

Goll's column(s) (track or column(s) of Goll) (Goll Friedrich): Anatomy. See: Chaplin; Dorland; Donath; English; Hinsie; Stedman.

Goll's fibers (Goll, Friedrich): Anatomy. See: Dorland; Stedman.

Goll's nucleus (Goll, Friedrich): Anatomy. See: Donath; Dorland; Stedman.

GOLODETZ, L. fl. 1908-1910. German chemist. Cited in: Chem. Abstr., Decenn. Index, 1907-1916. Golodetz test reaction, Unna-Golodetz test reaction.

Golodetz test reaction (Golodetz, L.): Chemistry. See: Van Nostrand Chem. Dict.

GOLSE, JEAN MARIUS JOSEPH. 1886-1959. French pharmaceutical chemist. See: Pogg., vols. 6, 7b. Golse test for mercury oxycyanide, Golse test reaction for arsonic acids.

Golse test for mercury oxycyanide (Gose, Jean Marius Joseph): Chemistry. See: Van Nostrand Chem. Dict.

Golse test reaction for arsonic acids (Golse, Jean Marius Joseph): Chemistry. See: Van Nostrand Chem. Dict.

Goltz' experiment (Goltz, Friedrich Leopold): Physiology. See: Dorland; Stedman.

GOLTZ, FRIEDRICH LEOPOLD. 1834-1902. German physiologist. See: Dict. Sci. Biog. Goltz' experiment.

Goltz-Gorlin syndrome (Goltz, Robert W. and Gorlin, Robert James): Medicine. See: Jablonski.

GOLTZ, ROBERT WILLIAM. 1923- . American physician. See: World Who's Who Sci. Goltz-Gorlin syndrome, Gorlin-Goltz syndrome.

GOLUCHOWSKI, COUNT AGENOR. 1849-1921. Polish-born Austrian diplomat. See: Encyc. Brit., 1973. Goluchowski telegram.

Goluchowski telegram (Goluchowski, Count): History. See: Montgomery.

Gomara (Gomara, Francisco Lopez de?): Botany. See: Charnock.

GOMARA, FRANCISCO LOPEZ DE. 1510-ca. 1560. Spanish historian. See: Webster's Biog. Dict. Gomara?

Gomarists (and Gomarian) (Gomarus, Franciscus): Religion. See: Harbottle; Webster's 3d.

GOMARUS, FRANCISCUS (Orig. surname: GOMMER). 1563-1641. Dutch Calvinistic theologian. See: Encyc. Brit., 1973. Gomarists (and Gomarian).

GOMBAULT, FRANCOIS ALEXIS ALBERT. 1844-1904. French neurologist. See: Biog. Lex. hervorr. Aerzte, 1880-1930. Gombault's degeneration (or neuritis), Gombault's triangle.

Gombault's degeneration (or neuritis) (Gombault, Francois Alexis Albert): See: Dejerine-Sottas syndrome.

Gombault's triangle (Gombault, Francois Alexis Albert): Anatomy. See: Dorland; Stedman. Also known as: Hoche's tract.

Gomberg-Bachmann-Hey reaction (Gomberg, Moses; Bachmann, Werner Emmanuel; and Hey, Donald Holroyde): Chemistry. See: Ballentyne; Van Nostrand Chem. Dict. Also known as: Gomberg-Hey reaction.

Gomberg free radical reaction (Gomberg, Moses): Chemistry. See: Van Nostrand Chem. Dict.

Gomberg-Hey reaction (Gomberg, Moses and Hey, Donald Holroyde). See: Gomberg-Bachmann-Hey reaction.

GOMBERG, MOSES. 1866-1947. American chemist. See: Dict. Sci. Biog. Gomberg-Bachmann-Hey reaction, Gomberg free radical reaction, Gomberg reaction.

Gomberg reaction (Gomberg, Moses): Chemistry. See: Ballentyne.

GOMES, BERNARDINO ANTONIO. 1769-1824. Portugese physician. See: World Who's Who Sci. Gomesa.

Gomesa (Gomes, Bernardino Antonio): Botany. See: Charnock; Taylor N.

Gomez de Ortega, Casimir. See: Ortega, Casimir Gomez de.

Gommer, Franciscus. See: Gomarus, Franciscus.

Gommesson method (Derivation undetermined): Engineering and Industry. See: Thrush.

GOMONT, MAURICE AUGUSTE. d. 1909. French botanist. See: Bull. Soc. Bot. Fr., vol. LVI (1909) p. 449. Gomontia.

Gomontia (Gomont, Maurice Auguste): Botany. See: Webster's 3d.

GOMORI, GEORGE. 1904-1957. Hungarian-born American pathologist. See: Nat. Cycl. Amer. Biog., vol. 42, pp. 552-553. Gomori method (or stain).

Gomori method (or stain) (Gomori, George): Medicine. See: Dorland.

GOMPERTZ, BENJAMIN. 1779-1865. English mathematician, astronomer and actuary. See: Dict. Sci. Biog. Gompertz curve, Gompertz formula, Gompertz('s) law (or hypothesis).

Gompertz curve (Gompertz, Benjamin): Statistics. See: English; James; Kendall.

Gompertz formula (Gompertz, Benjamin): Statistics. See: Good.

Gompertz('s) law (or hypothesis) (Gompertz, Benjamin): Statistics. See: James; Stedman.

Gomphoides Williamsoni (Williamson, Henry Charles): Zoology. See: Pennak.

GONCOURT, EDMOND LOUIS ANTOINE DE. 1822-1896. French novelist and critic. See: Encyc. Brit., 1973. Prix Goncourt.

GONCOURT, JULES ALFRED HUOT DE. 1830-1870. French novelist and critic. See: Encyc. Brit., 1973. Prix Goncourt.

Gonell air elutriator (Gonell, Hans Wolfgang): Engineering and Industry. See: Thrush.

GONELL, HANS WOLFGANG. 1901-1944. German chemical technologist. See: Pogg., vol. 7a. Gonell air elutriator.

GONGORA Y ARGOTE LUIS DE. 1561-1627. Spanish poet. See: Encyc. Brit., 1973. Gongorism.

Gongorism (Gongora y Argote): Generic Word (affected, obscure literary style). See: Barnhart (Eng. Lit.), Harvey, Hendrickson, Partridge, Preminger, Webster's 3d.

GONIN, JULES. 1870-1935. Swiss ophthalmologist. See: World Who's Who Sci. Gonin operation.

Gonin operation (Gonin, Jules): Medicine. See: Dorland; Stedman.

GONNARD, FERDINAND. fl. 1875. French mineralogist. See: Pogg., vol. 4. Gonnarite.

Gonnarite (Gonnard, Ferdinand): Earth Sciences. See: Thrush; Webster's 3d.

Gooch crucible (or filter) (Gooch, Frank Austin): Chemistry. See: Hackh; Stedman; Thrush; Van Nostrand Chem. Dict.; Webster's 3d.

GOOCH, SIR DANIEL. 1816-1889. English engineer. See: World Who's Who Sci. Gooch link motion.

GOOCH, FRANK AUSTIN. 1852-1929. American chemist. See: World Who's Who Sci. Gooch crucible (or filter).

Gooch link motion (Gooch, Sir Daniel): Engineering and Industry. See: Auger.

GOODALL, JOHN FRANCIS. fl. 1940-1972. English physician. See: Med. Direct., 1972. Goodall's disease.

Goodall's disease (Goodall, John Francis). See: Spencer's disease.

GOODE, SIR CHARLES HENRY. 1827-1922. English-born Australian merchant and philanthropist. See: Australian Encyc. Goodletite?

GOODE, GEORGE BROWN. 1851-1896. American zoologist. See: World Who's Who Sci. chriopeops Goodei.

GOODE, JOHN PAUL. 1862-1932. American geographer. See: Dict. Amer. Biog., 1st suppl. Goode's interrupted homolosine projection.

GOODELL, WILLIAM. 1829-1894. American gynecologist. See: Nat. Cycl. Amer. Biog., vol. 27, p. 297. Goodell's sign.

Goodell's sign (Goodell, William): Medicine. See: Dorland.

Goodenia (Goodenough, Samuel): Botany. See: Charnock; Webster's 3d.

GOODENOUGH, FLORENCE LAURA. b. 1886. American psychologist. See: Amer. Men Sci., 9th ed., Soc. and Behav. Goodenough test (draw-a-man test or scale).

GOODENOUGH, SAMUEL. 1743-1827. English bishop and botanist. See: Dict. Nat. Biog. Goodenia.

Goodenough test (draw-a-man test or scale) (Goodenough, Florence Laura): Psychology. See: Chaplin; English; Good; Hinsie; Wolman.

GOODERHAM, WALTER JOSEPH. 1903- . English chemist. See: Who's Who Brit. Sci., 1953. Gooderham's gas analysis.

Gooderham's gas analysis (Gooderham, Walter Joseph): Chemistry. See: Encyc. Brit., 1973 under "Chemistry," vol. 5, p. 440c.

Goode's interrupted homolosine projection (Goode, John Paul): Geography. See: Monkhouse; Moore.

Goodfellow, Robin. See: Puck.

Goodletite (Goode, Sir Charles?): Earth Sciences. See: Thrush.

GOODMAN, EDWARD HARRIS. 1880-1939. American physician. See: J.A.M.A., vol. 113 (1939) p. 76. Goodman-Suzanne reagent.

Goodman-Kruskal tau (Goodman, Leo A. and Kruskal, William Henry): Statistics. See: Kendall.

GOODMAN, LEO A. 1928- . American statistician. See: World Who's Who Sci. Goodman-Kruskal tau.

Goodman-Martinez-Thompson correlation (or GMT correlation) (Derivation undetermined): Statistics. See: Encyc. Brit., 1973 under "Chronology," vol. 5, p. 730b.

Goodman-Suzanne reagent (Goodman, Edward Harris and Stern, Suzanne): Chemistry. See: Van Nostrand Chem. Dict.

GOODPASTURE, ERNEST WILLIAM. 1886-1960. American pathologist. See: World Who's Who Sci. Goodpasture's polychrome stain, Goodpasture's stain for gram-negative bacteria, Goodpasture's syndrome.

Goodpasture's polychrome stain (Goodpasture, Ernest William): Medicine. See: Dorland; Stedman.

Goodpasture's stain for gram-negative bacteria (Goodpasture, Ernest William): Medicine. See: Stedman.

Goodpasture's syndrome (Goodpasture, Ernest William): Medicine. See: Jablonski; Stedman.

Goodrich chain pump (Goodrich, Simon): Engineering and Industry. See: Auger.

GOODRICH, SIMON. 1773-1847. Engineer. (Biography source unavailable.) Goodrich chain pump.

GOODYER, JOHN. 1592-1664. English botanist. See: Britten and Boulger. Goodyera.

Goodyera (Goodyer, John): Botany. See: Charnock; Taylor N., Webster's 3d.

GOORMAGHTIGH, NORBERT. 1890-1960. Belgian physician. See: Who's Who Belgium, 1957-1958. Goormaghtigh's apparatus, Goormaghtigh's cells.

Goormaghtigh's apparatus (Goormaghtigh, Norbert): Medicine. See: Dorland.

Goormaghtigh's cells (Goormaghtigh, Norbert): Anatomy. See: Dorland; Stedman. Also known as: Polkissen of Zimmermann.

GOPALAN, C. fl. 1946-1960. Indian biochemist. Cited in: Chem. Abstr. Gopalan's syndrome.

Gopalan's syndrome (Gopalan, C.): Medicine. See: Jablonski.

GOPPELSROEDER, FRIEDRICH (In full: CHRISTOPH FRIEDRICH). 1837-1919. Swiss chemist. See: World Who's Who Sci. Goppelsroeder reagent.

Goppelsroeder reagent (Goppelsroeder, Friedrich): Chemistry. See: Van Nostrand Chem. Dict.

GORCEIX, HENRIQUE. d. 1919. German-born Brazilian mineralogist. See: Pogg., vols. 3, 4. Gorceixite.

Gorceixite (Gorceix, Henrique): Earth Sciences. See: Thrush; Webster's 3d.

GORDAN, GILBERT S. 1916- . American physician. See: Direct. Med. Specialists, 1965-1966. Gordan-Overstreet syndrome.

Gordan-Overstreet syndrome (Gordan, Gilbert S. and Overstreet, Edmund William): Medicine. See: Jablonski.

GORDAN, PAUL. 1837-1912. German mathematician. See: World Who's Who Sci. Clebsch-Gordon coefficients, Gordan's theorem.

Gordan's theorem (Gordan, Paul): Mathematics. Cited in: World Who's Who Sci.

Gordiacea (Gordius): Zoology. See: Pennak; Stedman.

Gordian knot (or to cut the Gordian knot) (Gordius): Generic Word (solve a problem by a single, incisive act). See: Charnock; Brewer; Funk; Hendrickson; Partridge; Webster's 3d.

GORDIUS. Mythological King of Phyrigia. See: Encyc. Brit., 1973. Gordiacea, Gordian knot (or to cut the Gordian knot).

GORDON, ALEXANDER. 1818-1887. Irish physician. See: Biog. Lex. hervorr. Aerzte. Gordon's splint.

GORDON, ALEXANDER GORDON, 4TH DUKE OF. 1743-1827. Scottish nobleman and sportsman. See: Dict. Nat. Biog. Gordon setter.

GORDON, ALFRED. 1874-1953. American neurologist. See: Who Was Who Amer., 1969-1973. Gordon reflex, Gordon sign, Gordon's symptom.

Gordon Bennett international trophies (Bennett, James Gordon): Sports and Recreation. Cited in: Webster's Biog. Dict.

Gordon Bennett race (Bennett, James Gordon): Sports and Recreation. Cited in: Van Nostrand Sci. Encyc. under "Flight, Artificial."

GORDON, CHARLES GEORGE. 1833-1885. English soldier. See: Dict. Nat. Biog. Gordon's Calvary.

GORDON, CUTHBERT. fl. 18th c. Scotch chemist. Cited in: Mansell. Cudbear (dye).

GORDON, LORD GEORGE. 1751-1793. English agitator. See: Dict. Nat. Biog. Gordon riots.

GORDON, GEORGE. 1806-1879. Scottish naturalist. See: Dict. Nat. Biog. Gordonia.

GORDON, GEORGE PHINEAS. 1810-1878. American inventor. See: Dict. Amer. Biog. Gordon press.

GORDON, JAMES. d. 1781. English gardener. See: Britten and Boulger. Gordonia.

GORDON, LEWIS, fl. 1850. Scottish civil engineer. Cited in: Poorman, p. 249. Gordon's formula (or column formula).

GORDON, MERVYN HENRY. 1872-1953. English bacteriologist. See: Who Was Who, 1951-1960. Gordon's test.

Gordon press (Gordon, George Phineas): Printing. See: Lockwood.

Gordon-Rankine formula (column formula or equation) (Gordon, Lewis and Rankine, William John Macquorn). See: Gordon's formula (or column formula).

Gordon reflex (Gordon, Alfred): Medicine. See: Dorland; Hinsie; Stedman; Wolman.

Gordon riots (Gordon, Lord George): History. See: Attwater; Barnhart (Eng. Lit.); Harvey; Morris and Irwin; Phyfe; Steinberg.

GORDON, ROBERT STANTON. 1922- . American physician. See: Direct. Med. Specialists, 1965-1966. Gordon's disease.

GORDON, SAMUEL GEORGE. 1897-1952. American mineralogist. See: Amer. Min., vol. 38 (1953) pp. 301-308. Gordonite.

Gordon setter (Gordon, Alexander Gordon): Recreation and Sports. See: Hendrickson; Webster's 3d.

Gordon sign (Gordon, Alfred): Medicine. See: Stedman.

GORDON, WALTER. 1893-1940. German physicist. See: Dict. Sci. Biog. Klein-Gordon equation, Schroedinger-Gordon equation.

GORDON, WILLIAM. 1863-1929. English physician. See: Who Was Who, 1929-1940. Gordon's sign.

Gordonia (Gordon, George): Zoology. See: Webster's 3d.

Gordonia (Gordon, James): Botany. See: Partridge; Taylor, N.; Webster's 3d.

Gordonite (Gordon, Samuel George): Earth Sciences. See: Thrush; Webster's 3d.

Gordon's Calvary (Gordon, Charles George): Religion. See: Attwater.

Gordon's disease (Gordon, Robert Stanton): Medicine. See: Jablonski.

Gordon's formula (or column formula) (Gordon, Lewis): Engineering and Industry. See: Ballentyne; Thrush. Also known as: Gordon-Rankine formula (column formula or equation).

Gordon's rule (Derivation undetermined): Engineering and Industry. See: Thrush.

Gordon's sign (Gordon, William): Medicine. See: Dorland.

Gordon's splint (Gordon, Alexander): Medicine. See: Stedman.

Gordon's symptom (Gordon, Alfred): Medicine. See: Stedman.

Gordon's test (Gordon, Mervyn Henry): Medicine. See: Dorland; Stedman.

Gore breed (cattle) (Gore, Christopher): Zoology. See: Mathews, M. M.

GORE, CHRISTOPHER. 1758-1829. American politician. See: Who Was Who Amer., Hist. vol. Gore breed (cattle).

Gore-McLemore resolutions (Gore, Thomas Pryor and McLemore, Jeff): Politics. See: Morris.

Gore pheonomenon (Derivation undetermined): Chemistry. See: Hackh.

GORE, THOMAS PRYOR. 1870-1949. American legislator. See: Biog. Direct. Amer. Congress. Gore-McLemore resolutions.

Gorgeyite (Goergey, Rolf): Earth Sciences. See: Thrush. Also known as: Mikheevite.

GORGON. One of three sisters in Greek mythology capable of turning one into stone. See: Encyc. Brit., 1973. Gorgon (1), Gorgon (2), Gorgonia, Gorgonocephalus.

Gorgon (1) (Gorgon, the mythological figure): Generic Word (repulsive, terrifying woman). See: Webster's 3d.

Gorgon (2) (Gorgon, the mythological figure): Zoology. See: Pennak.

Gorgonia (Gorgon, the mythological figure): Zoology. See: Pennak.

Gorgonocephalus (Gorgon, the mythological figure): Zoology. See: Pennak.

Gorham case (controversy or judgement) (Gorham, George Cornelius): History. See: Brewer; Harvey; Steinberg.

GORHAM, GEORGE CORNELIUS. 1787-1857. English bishop and antiquarian. See: Dict. Nat. Biog. Gorham case (controversy or judgement).

GORHAM, LEMUEL WHITTINGTON. 1885-1968. American physician. See: Amer. Men. Sci., 5th ed. Gorham's sign, Gorham's syndrome (or disease), Gorham's theory.

Gorham's sign (Gorham, Lemuel Whittington): Medicine. See: Kelly.

Gorham's syndrome (or disease) (Gorham, Lemuel Whittington): Medicine. See: Jablonski; Stedman.

Gorham's theory (Gorham, Lemuel Whittington): Medicine. See: Kelly.

Goriaew's rule (Derivation undetermined): Medicine. See: Stedman.

Gorlin-Chaudhry-Moss syndrome (Gorlin, Robert James; Chaudhry, Anand P.; and Moss, Melvin Lionel): Medicine. See: Jablonski.

Gorlin formula (Gorlin, Richard): Medicine. See: Stedman.

Gorlin-Goltz syndrome (Gorlin, Robert James and Goltz, Robert William). See: Gorlin's syndrome.

GORLIN, RICHARD. 1926- . American cardiologist. See: World Who's Who Sci. Gorlin formula.

GORLIN, ROBERT JAMES. 1923- . American physician. See: Amer. Men and Women Sci., 12th ed. Goltz-Gorlin syndrome, Gorlin-Chaudhry-Moss syndrome, Gorlin's syndrome.

Gorlin's syndrome (Gorlin, Robert James): Medicine. See: Jablonski. Also known as: Gorlin-Goltz syndrome.

GORMAN, ARTHUR PUE. 1839-1906. American political leader. See: Dict. Amer. Biog. Wilson-Gorman Tariff (Act).

GORMAN, MARTIN W. 1853-1926. American botanist. Cited in: Mansell. Gormania.

Gormania (Gorman, Martin W.): Botany. See: Taylor, N.

GORTER, JAN DE. 1689-1762. Dutch physician. See: Nouv. Biog. Univ. Gorteria.

Gorteria (Gorter, Jan de): Botany. See: Charnock.

Gorthaeans (or Gortheni) (Gortheus): Religion. See: Canney.

GORTHEUS. No dates. Christian heretic. See: Dict. Christian Biog. Gorthaeans (or Gortheni).

GORTON, SAMUEL. 1592?-1677. American religious sect founder. See: Dict. Amer. Biog. Gortonian (Gortonist or Gortonite).

Gortonian (Gortonist or Gortonite) (Gorton, Samuel): Religion. See: Mathews, M. M.; Webster's 3d.

Goskar dryer (Goskar, T. A.): Engineering and Industry. See: Thrush.

GOSKAR, T. A. fl. 1938. English ceramics chemist. Cited in: Chem. Abstr., vol. 32, p. 3565. Goskar dryer.

GOSLEE, HART JOHN. 1871-1930. American dentist. See: Who Was Who Amer., 1897-1942. Goslee tooth.

Goslee tooth (Goslee, Hart John): Dentistry. See: Dorland.

Goss (china) (Goss, W. H.): Applied Arts. See: Partridge.

GOSS, W. H. fl. ca. 1900. English porcelain maker. (Biography source unavailable.) Goss (china).

GOSSELIN, LEON ATHANASE. 1815-1887. French surgeon. See: Biog. Lex. hervorr. Aerzte. Gosselin's fracture.

Gosselin's fracture (Gosselin, Leon Athanase): Medicine. See: Dorland; Jablonski; Stedman.

GOSSEN, HERMANN HEINRICH. 1810-1858. German economist. See: Internat. Encyc. Soc. Sci. Gossen's laws (or three laws of Gossen).

Gossen's laws (or three laws of Gossen) (Gossen, Hermann Heinrich): Economics. See: Internat. Encyc. Soc. Sci. under "Gossen, Hermann Heinrich"; Seldon.

GOSSETT, WILLIAM SEALY (Pseud.: STUDENT). 1876-1937. English statistician. See: Dict. Sci. Biog. Studentisation, Studentised maximum absolute deviate, Studentised range, 'Student's' hypothesis, Student's t-distribution (or test).

Got, Bertrand de. See: Clement V.

GOTO, E. fl. 1960. Japanese electrical engineer. Cited in: Sci. Abstr. (Elec. Engin.), vol. 63B, (1960) p. 611. Goto pair.

Goto pair (Goto, E.): Electronics. See: Hughes; Markus.

Gottignies kiln (Gottignies, Rodolphe and Gottignies, Louis): Engineering and Industry. See: Thrush.

GOTTIGNIES, LOUIS. fl. 1938-1942. Belgian engineer. Cited in: Chem. Abstr., vol. 36, p. 5326. Gottignies kiln.

GOTTIGNIES, RODOLPHE. fl. 1938-1942. Belgian engineer. Cited in: Chem. Abstr., vol. 36, p. 5326. Gottignies kiln.

GOTTLIEB, BERNHARD. b. 1885. Austrian dentist. See: Biog. Lex. hervorr. Aerzte, 1880-1930. Gottlieb's epithelial attachment.

GOTTLIEB, MURRAY. No dates. Medical librarian? (Biography source unavailable.) Murray Gottlieb Prize.

Gottlieb's epithelial attachment (Gottlieb, Bernhard): Dentistry. See: Dorland.

GOTTRON, HEINRICH ADOLF. b. 1890. German dermatologist. See: New York Acad. Med. Lib. Portrait Cat. Arndt-Gottron disease, Gottron's syndrome.

Gottron's syndrome (Gottron, Heinrich Adolf): Medicine. See: Jablonski.

Gottschaldt figures (Gottschaldt, Kurt): Psychology. See: Chaplin; English; Wolman.

GOTTSCHALDT, KURT. 1902- . German psychologist. See: Who's Who Sci. Europe, 1972. Gottschaldt figures.

GOTTSCHALK, SIGMUND. 1860-1914. German surgeon. See: Biog. Lex. hervorr. Aerzte, 1880-1930. Gottschalk's operation.

Gottschalk's operation (Gottschalk, Sigmund): Medicine. See: Dorland.

GOTTSTEIN, JACOB. 1832-1895. German otologist. See: Biog. Lex. hervorr. Aerzte. Gottstein's fibers, Gottstein's process.

Gottstein's fibers (Gottstein, Jacob): Medicine. See: Dorland.

Gottstein's process (Gottstein, Jacob): Medicine. See: Dorland.

Gotzenite (Goetzen, Count Gustav Adolf von): Earth Sciences. See: Thrush.

GOUAN, ANTOINE. 1733-1821. French botanist. See: World Who's Who Sci. Gouania.

Gouania (Gouan, Antoine): Botany. See: Charnock.

Goudsmit and Uhlenbeck assumption (Goudsmit, Samuel Abraham and Uhlenbeck, George Eugene): Physics. See: Internat. Dict. Ap. Math.; Internat. Dict. Phys. Elec.

Goudsmit Gamma-Sum rule (Goudsmit, Samuel Abraham): Physics. See: Internat. Dict. Ap. Math.; Internat. Dict. Phys. Elec.

GOUDSMIT, SAMUEL ABRAHAM. 1902- . Dutch-born American physicist. See: World Who's Who Sci. Back-Goudsmit effect, Goudsmit and Uhlenbeck assumption, Goudsmit Gamma-Sum rule.

GOUDY, FREDERIC WILLIAM. 1865-1947. American type designer. See: Who Was Who Amer., 1943-1950. Goudy (type faces).

Goudy (type faces) (Goudy, Frederic William): Printing. See: Harrod.

Gougerot-Blum syndrome (Gougerot, Henri and Blum, Paul): Medicine. See: Jablonski.

Gougerot-Carteaud syndrome (or papillomatosis) (Gougerot, Henri and Carteaud, Alexandre): Medicine. See: Jablonski.

Gougerot-Hailey-Hailey disease (Gougerot, Henri; Hailey, Howard; and Hailey, Hugh). See: Hailey-Hailey disease.

GOUGEROT, HENRI. 1881-1955. French physician. See: Biog. Lex. hervorr. Aerzte, 1880-1930. Beurmann-Gougerot disease, Gougerot-Blum syndrome, Gougerot-Carteaud syndrome (or papillomatosis), Gougerot-Hailey-Hailey disease, Gougerot-Ruiter syndrome, Gougerot-Sjoegren syndrome (or disease), Gougerot's syndrome (or trisymptomatic disease).

Gougerot-Houwer-Sjoegren syndrome (Gougerot, Henri; Houwer, A. W. M.; and Sjoegren, Henrik Samuel Conrad). See: Sjoegren's syndrome.

Gougerot-Ruiter syndrome (Gougerot, Henri and Ruiter, M.): Medicine. See: Jablonski.

Gougerot-Sjoegren syndrome (or disease) (Gougerot, Henri and Sjoegren, Henrik Samuel Conrad). See: Sjoegren's syndrome.

Gougerot's syndrome (or trisymptomatic disease) (Gougerot, Henri): Medicine. See: Jablonski.

GOULARD, THOMAS. 1720-1790. French surgeon. See: World Who's Who Sci. Goulard's extract (or Goulard (1)), Goulard's lotion (cerate or Goulard (2)), Goulard's water (or eau de Goulard).

Goulard's extract (or Goulard (1)) (Goulard, Thomas): Medicine. See: Dorland; Hackh; Partridge; Webster's 3d.

Goulard's lotion (cerate or Goulard (2)) (Goulard, Thomas): Medicine. See: Dorland; Partridge.

Goulard's water (or eau de Goulard) (Goulard, Thomas): Medicine. See: Dorland.

GOULD, SIR ALFRED PEARCE. 1852-1922. English surgeon. See: Who Was Who, 1916-1928. Gould's suture.

GOULD, AUGUSTUS ADDISON. 1805-1866. American zoologist. See: Dict. Sci. Biog. cistenides Gouldi?, Gould's turkey?

GOULD, BENJAMIN APTHORP. 1824-1896. American astronomer. See: World Who's Who Sci. Gould's belt.

GOULD, GEORGE MILBRY. 1848-1922. American ophthalmologist and medical lexicographer. See: World Who's Who Sci. Gould's sign.

Gould-Jacobs reaction (Gould, Robert Gordon and Jacobs, Walter Abraham): Chemistry. See: Van Nostrand Chem. Dict.

GOULD, JOHN. 1804-1881. English ornithologist. See: Dict. Sci. Biog. Gouldian finch (or Gouldian).

GOULD, ROBERT GORDON. 1909- . American biochemist. See: Amer. Men Sci., 10th ed. Gould-Jacobs reaction.

Gouldian finch (or Gouldian) (Gould, John): Zoology. See: Webster's 3d.

Gould's belt (Gould, Benjamin Apthorp): Astronomy. See: New Encyc. Brit., 1974, Microp.

Gould's sign (Gould, George Milbry): Medicine. See: Dorland; Stedman.

Gould's suture (Gould, Sir Alfred Pearce): Medicine. See: Dorland; Stedman.

Gould's turkey (Gould, Augustus Addison?): Zoology. See: Encyc. Brit., 1973 under "Turkey," vol. 22, p. 398c.

GOULEY, JOHN WILLIAM SEVERIN. 1832-1920. American surgeon. See: Who Was Who Amer., 1961-1968. Gouley's catheter.

Gouley's catheter (Gouley, John William Severin): Medicine. See: Dorland.

GOUTEREAU, CHARLES. fl. 1898-1923. French meteorologist. Cited in: Kendall and Doig. Goutereau's constant.

Goutereau's constant (Goutereau, Charles): Statistics. See: Kendall.

Gouy balance (Gouy, Georges?): Physics. See: Thewlis.

GOUY, GEORGES (In full: LOUIS-GEORGES). 1854-1926. French physicist. See: Dict. Sci. Biog. Gouy balance?, Gouy layer, Gouy principle.

Gouy layer (Gouy, Georges): Chemistry. See: Hackh; Thrush.

Gouy principle (Gouy, Georges): Physics. See: Thewlis, unabridged ed.

Govenia (Gowen, James Robert): Botany. Cited in: Britten and Boulger.

Gover process (Govers, Francis X.): Chemistry. See: Van Nostrand Chem. Dict.

Governor Winthrop desk (Winthrop, John): Applied Arts. See: Partridge; Webster's 3d.

Governor Wood cherry (Wood, Governor): Botany. See: Hendrickson under "Bing".

GOVERS, FRANCIS X. fl. 1934. American petroleum chemist. Cited in: Chem. Abstr., vol. 28, p. 2520. Gover process.

Gowen cypress (Gowen, James Robert): Botany. See: Webster's 3d.

GOWEN, JAMES ROBERT. d. 1862. English horticulturist. See: Britten and Boulger. Govenia, Gowen cypress.

GOWER, HARRISON P. fl. ca. 1959. American industrialist. Cited in: Hintze, 3d suppl., p. 124. Gowerite.

Gowerite (Gower, Harrison P.): Earth Sciences. See: Thrush.

Gowers' apparatus (or hemometer) (Gowers, Sir William Richard): Medicine. See: Kelly.

Gowers' contraction (Gowers, Sir William Richard): Medicine. See: Dorland; Stedman.

Gowers' disease (Gowers, Sir William Richard): Medicine. See: Stedman.

Gowers-Paton-Kennedy syndrome (Gowers, Sir William Richard; Paton, Leslie; and Kennedy, Foster). See: Foster Kennedy('s) syndrome.

Gowers' phenomenon (Gowers, Sir William Richard): Medicine. See: Blakiston's Gould.

Gowers' process (or intermediate process) (Gowers, Sir William Richard): Medicine. See: Dorland.

Gowers' solution (1) (Gowers, Sir William Richard): Medicine. See: Blakiston's Gould; Kelly.

Gowers' solution (2) (Gowers, Sir William Richard?): Chemistry. See: Van Nostrand Chem. Dict.

Gowers' syndrome (1) (or disease) (Gowers, Sir William Richard): Medicine. See: Jablonski; Stedman.

Gowers' syndrome (2) (or sign) (Gowers, Sir William Richard): Medicine. See: Blakiston's Gould; Jablonski.

Gowers' syndrome (3) (or vasovagal attack of Gowers) (Gowers, Sir William Richard): Medicine. See: Dorland; Hinsie; Jablonski; Stedman.

Gowers' tetanoid chorea (Gowers, Sir William Richard): Medicine. See: Hinsie.

Gowers tract (or column or fasciculus) (Gowers, Sir William Richard): Anatomy. See: Donath; Dorland; Stedman; Webster's 3d.

GOWERS, SIR WILLIAM RICHARD. 1845-1915. English neurologist. See: World Who's Who Sci. Gower solution (2)?, Gowers' apparatus (or hemometer), Gowers' contraction, Gowers' disease (1), Gowers-Paton-Kennedy syndrome, Gowers' phenomenon, Gowers' process (or intermediate process), Gowers' solution (1), Gowers' syndrome (1) (or disease (2)), Gowers' syndrome (2) (or sign), Gowers' syndrome (3) (or vasovagal attack of Gowers), Gowers' tetanoid chorea, Gowers tract (column or fasciculus).

Gowrie, 3d Earl of. See: Ruthven, John, 3d Earl of Gowrie.

Gowrie conspiracy (Ruthven, John, 3rd Earl of Gowrie): History. See: Harbottle; Latham; Steinberg.

GOYA Y LUCIENTES, FRANCISCO JOSE DE. 1746-1828. Spanish painter. See: Encyc. Brit., 1973. Goyescas.

Goyder and Laughton process (Goyder, George Arthur? and Laughton): Engineering and Industry. See: Thrush.

GOYDER, GEORGE ARTHUR. fl. 1893. Australian mining engineer. Cited in: Royal Soc. Cat. Sci. Pap., 1884-1900. Goyder and Laughton process?

GOYDER, GEORGE WOODROFFE. 1826-1898. English-born Australian surveyor and explorer. See: Australian Encyc. Goyder's line of rainfall.

Goyder's line of rainfall (Goyder, George Woodroffe): Earth Sciences. Cited in: Australian Encyc. under "Goyder, George Woodroffe."

Goyescas (Goya y Lucientes, Francisco Jose de): Music. See: Apel.

GOYRAND, JEAN GASPAR BLAISE. 1803-1866. French surgeon. See: Biog. Lex. hervorr. Aerzte. Goyrand's hernia, Goyrand's injury.

Goyrand's hernia (Goyrand, Jean Gaspar Blaise): Medicine. See: Dorland.

Goyrand's injury (Goyrand, Jean Gaspar Blaise): Medicine. See: Stedman.

GRAAF, REGNIER DE. 1641-1673. Dutch anatomist and biologist. See: Dict. Sci. Biog. Graafian follicle(s), Graafian vessels.

Graafian follicle(s) (Graaf, Regnier de): Anatomy. See: Donath; Henderson; Pennak.

Graafian vessels (Graaf, Regnier de): Anatomy. See: Stedman.

GRABAU, L. fl. 1889. German chemist. Cited in: Royal Soc. Cat. Sci. Pap., 1884-1900. Grabau process.

Grabau process (Grabau, L.): Engineering and Industry. See: Thrush.

GRABER, VITUS. 1844-1892. Austrian biologist. See: Neue Deut. Biog. Graber's organ.

Graber's organ (Graber, Vitus): Zoology. See: Gray; Henderson.

GRABHORN, EDWIN E. d. 1968. American founder of fine press. See: New York Times, Dec. 18, 1968, p. 47, col. 2. Grabhorn press.

Grabhorn press (Grabhorn, Edwin E. and Grabhorn, Robert): Library Science. See: Harrod.

GRABHORN, ROBERT. fl. 1920-1949. American founder of fine press. (Biography source unavailable.) Grabhorn press.

GRABLE, BETTY (In full: ELIZABETH RUTH). 1916-1973. American actress. See: Who Was Who Amer., 1969-1973. Grable-bodied seamen.

Grable-bodied seamen (Grable, Betty): Generic Word. See: Hendrickson.

Grace-Arthur. See: Arthur, Grace.

Grace-Arthur performance scale (Arthur, Mary Grace): Psychology. See: Chaplin; English.

Grace('s) card (Grace, Richard?): History. See: Brewer; Charnock.

Grace contract (Grace, Michael): History. See: Latham.

GRACE, MICHAEL. fl. 1889. Businessman. (Biography source unavailable.) Grace contract.

GRACE, RICHARD. 1620?-1691. Irish governor of Athlone. See: Dict. Nat. Biog. Grace('s) card?

Grace's warbler (Coues, Grace D.): Biology. See: Gray; Mathews, M. M.; Webster's 3d.

GRADENIGO, GIUSEPPE. 1859-1926. Italian otorhinolaryngologist. See: Biog. Lex. hervorr. Aerzte, 1880-1930. Gradenigo-Struyken triangle, Gradenigo's syndrome.

Gradenigo-Struyken triangle (Gradenigo, Giuseppe and Struycken, Hubert Johann Leonard?): Medicine. Cited in: Biog. Lex. hervorr. Aerzte, 1880-1930 under "Gradenigo, Giuseppe."

Gradenigo's syndrome (Gradenigo, Giuseppe): Medicine. See: Dorland; Jablonski; Stedman. Also known as: Lannois-Gradenigo's syndrome.

Gradgrind (Gradgrind, Thomas): Generic Word (total materialist). See: Partridge; Webster's 3d.; Weekley.

GRADGRIND, THOMAS. Materialistic hardware merchant in Charles Dickens's novel "Hard Times," (1854). See: Magill. Gradgrind.

GRAEBE, KARL JAMES PETER. 1841-1927. German chemist. See: Dict. Sci. Biog. Graebe-Ullmann synthesis.

Graebe-Ullmann synthesis (Graebe, Karl James Peter and Ullmann, Fritz): Chemistry. See: Van Nostrand Chem. Dict.

Graefe, Albrecht Friedrich Wilhelm Ernst. See: Von Graefe, Albrecht Friedrich Wilhelm Ernst.

Graefe reagent for formaldehyde in milk (Derivation undetermined): Chemistry. See: Van Nostrand Chem. Dict.

Graefe-Sjoegren syndrome (Von Graefe, Albrecht Friedrich Wilhelm Ernst and Sjoegren, Torsten): Medicine. See: Jablonski. Also known as: Hallgren's syndrome, Sjoegren's syndrome.

GRAEFENBERG, ERNST. b. 1881. German gynecologist. Cited in: Chem. Abstr. Graefenberg ring.

Graefenberg ring (Graefenberg, Ernst): Medicine. See: Dorland; Stedman; Van Nostrand Sci. Encyc. under "Contraception."

Graefe's disease (or syndrome) (Von Graefe, Albrecht Friedrich Wilhelm Ernst): Medicine. See: Dorland; Hinsie; Jablonski; Stedman.

Graefe's knife (Von Graefe, Albrecht Friedrich Wilhelm Ernst): Medicine. See: Stedman.

Graefe's operation (Von Graefe, Albrecht Friedrich Wilhelm Ernst): Medicine. See: Stedman.

Graefe's sign (Von Graefe, Albrecht Friedrich Wilhelm Ernst). See: Von Graefe's (or Graefe's) sign.

Graefe's spots (Von Graefe, Albrecht Friedrich Wilhelm Ernst): Medicine. See: Stedman.

Graefe's test (Von Graefe, Albrecht Friedrich Wilhelm Ernst): Medicine. See: Stedman.

GRAEFFE, KARL HEINRICH. 1799-1873. German mathematician. See: Dict. Sci. Biog. Graeffe('s) method (for determining roots of an equation).

Graeffe('s) method (for determining roots of an equation) (Graeffe, Karl Heinrich): Mathematics. See: Ballentyne; Internat. Dict. Ap. Math.; James; Van Nostrand Sci. Encyc. Also known as: Dandelin's method (for determining roots of an equation), Lobachevski's method (for determining roots of an equation).

GRAESBECK, RALPH. 1930- . Finnish biochemist. See: World Who's Who Sci. Imerslund-Graesbeck syndrome.

GRAETZ, LEO. 1856-1941. German physicist. See: World Who's Who Sci. Graetz number, Graetz (or Gratz) rectifier?

Graetz number (Graetz, Leo): Physics. See: Ballentyne; Thewlis.

Graetz (or Gratz) rectifier (Graetz, Leo?): Electronics. See: Hackh; Hughes; Markus.

GRAEUPNER, SIGURD C. 1861-1916. German physician. See: Biog. Lex. hervorr. Aerzte, 1880-1930. Graeupner's method.

Graeupner's method (Graeupner, Sigurd C.): Medicine. See: Dorland; Stedman.

GRAF, ANTON. 1901- . German geophysicist. See: Pogg., vol. 7a. Graf sea gravimeter?

Graf sea gravimeter (Graf, Anton?): Earth Sciences. See: Thrush.

Graf Zeppelin (Zeppelin, Count Ferdinand Graf von). See: Zeppelin.

GRAFFI, ARNOLD. 1910- . German pathologist. See: Pogg., vol. 7a. Graffi's leukemia (mouse chloroleukemia or virus).

Graffi's leukemia (mouse chloroleukemia or virus) (Graffi, Arnold): Medicine. See: Jablonski; Stedman.

Grafton engine (Grafton, H.): Engineering and Industry. See: Auger.

GRAFTON, H. fl. late 19th c. Engineer. (Biography source unavailable.) Grafton engine.

Graham boarding houses (societies and food stores) (Graham, Sylvester): History. See: Hendrickson; Mathews, M. M.

GRAHAM, EVARTS AMBROSE. 1883-1957. American surgeon. See: World Who's Who Sci. Graham's test.

Graham flour (biscuit, bread and cracker) (Graham, Sylvester): Food and Drink. See: Mathews, M. M.; Partridge; Webster's 3d.

GRAHAM, J. A. fl. ca. 1866. American mine owner. (Biography source unavailable.) Grahamite.

GRAHAM, J. L. fl. ca. 1866. American mine owner. (Biography source unavailable.) Grahamite.

GRAHAM, SIR JAMES ROBERT GEORGE. 1792-1861. English statesman. See: Dict. Nat. Biog. Grahamize.

GRAHAM, JOSEPH IVON. b. 1888. English mining engineer. See: Who's Who Brit. Sci., 1953. Graham ratio.

Graham('s) law (or law of diffusion) (Graham, Thomas): Chemistry. See: Asimov; Ballentyne; Thrush; Van Nostrand Sci. Encyc.; Webster's 3d.

Graham Little. See: Little, Ernest Gordon Graham.

Graham Little-Lassueur-Feldman syndrome (Little, Sir Ernest Gordon Graham; Lassueur, Auguste?; and Feldman, Samuel). See: Little's syndrome.

Graham Little's syndrome (Little, Sir Ernest Gordon Graham). See: Little's syndrome.

Graham-Menten reagent (Derivation undetermined): Chemistry. See: Van Nostrand Chem. Dict.

Graham pressure surveying apparatus (Derivation undetermined): Earth Sciences. See: Thrush.

Graham ratio (Graham, Joseph Ivon): Engineering and Industry. See: Thrush.

Graham('s) salt (Graham, Thomas): Chemistry. See: Hackh; Thrush; Webster's 3d.

GRAHAM-SMITH, GEORGE STUART. fl. 1920. English zoologist. Cited in: Mansell. Graham-Smith's infusion, Grahamella.

Graham-Smith's infusion (Graham-Smith, George Stuart): Medicine. See: Kelly.

Graham Steell. See: Steell, Graham.

Graham Steell's murmur (Steell, Graham). See: Steell's murmur.

GRAHAM, SYLVESTER. 1794-1851. American temperance advocate. See: Dict. Amer. Biog. Graham boarding houses (societies and food stores), Graham flour (biscuit, bread and cracker), Grahamism (Graham system and Grahamite).

GRAHAM, THOMAS. 1805-1869. Scottish physical chemist. See: Dict. Sci. Biog. Graham('s) law (or law of diffusion), Graham('s) salt.

Grahamella (Graham-Smith, George Stuart): Zoology. See: Stedman.

Grahamism (Graham system and Grahamite) (Graham, Sylvester): History. See: Mathews, M. M.; Partridge; Webster's 3d.

Grahamite (Graham, J. A. and Graham, J. L.): Earth Sciences. See: Mathews, M. M.; Thrush; Webster's 3d.

Grahamize (Graham, Sir James Robert George): Generic Word (severely edit). See: Hendrickson; Partridge; Weekley.

Graham's test (Graham, Evarts Ambrose): Medicine. See: Dorland.

Gram-Charlier series (type A, B and C) (Gram, Joergen Pedersen and Charlier, Carl Wilhelm Ludwig): Statistics. See: English; Internat. Dict. Ap. Math.; James; Kendall; Van Nostrand Sci. Encyc.

Gram complex (Gram, Hans Christian Joachim): Medicine. See: Webster's 3d.

Gram('s) determinant (or criterion) (Gram, Joergen Pedersen): Mathematics. See: Ballentyne; Internat. Dict. Ap. Math.; Kendall; Van Nostrand Sci. Encyc.

GRAM, HANS CHRISTIAN JOACHIM. 1853-1938. Danish physician. See: Dict. Sci. Biog. Gram complex, Gram-negative, Gram-positive (or Gram-fast), Gram('s) stain (or method), Gram's solution (or iodine solution), Gram's syndrome, Weigert-Gram stain for bacteria in tissues.

GRAM, JOERGEN PEDERSEN. 1850-1916. Danish mathematician. See: Dansk Biog. Lek. Gram-Charlier series (type A, B and C), Gram('s) determinant (or criterion), Gram-Schmidt process.

Gram-negative (Gram, Hans Christian Joachim): Medicine. See: Hackh; Pennak; Webster's 3d.

Gram-positive (or Gram-fast) (Gram, Hans Christian Joachim): Medicine. See: Asimov; Hackh; Pennak; Webster's 3d.

gram-Roentgen (Roentgen, Wilhelm Konrad): Physics. See: Markus.

Gram-Schmidt process (Gram, Joergen Pedersen and Schmidt, Erhard): Mathematics. See: Internat. Dict. Ap. Math.; James.

Gram('s) stain (or method) (Gram, Hans Christian Joachim): Medicine. See: Dorland; Hackh; Pennak; Stedman; Van Nostrand Sci. Encyc.; Webster's 3d.

Gramme armature (Gramme, Zenobe Theophile): Engineering and Industry. Cited in: World Who's Who Sci.

Gramme machine (Gramme, Zenobe Theophile): Engineering and Industry. Cited in: World Who's Who Sci.

Gramme ring (Gramme, Zenobe Theophile): Engineering and Industry. Cited in: World Who's Who Sci.

GRAMME, ZENOBE THEOPHILE. 1826-1901. Belgian electrician. See: Dict. Sci. Biog. Gramme armature, Gramme machine, Gramme ring.

GRAMONT, COMTE PHILIBERT DE. 1621-1707. French courtier. See: Encyc. Brit., 1973. Gramont's memory.

Gramont's memory (Gramont, Comte Philibert de): Generic Word (convenient memory). See: Hendrickson.

Gram's solution (or iodine solution) (Gram, Hans Christian Joachim): Chemistry. See: Hackh; Webster's 3d.

Gram's syndrome (Gram, Hans Christian Joachim): Medicine. See: Jablonski.

GRANCHER, JACQUES JOSEPH. 1843-1907. French physician. See: World Who's Who Sci. Grancher's disease, Grancher's system.

Grancher's disease (Grancher, Jacques Joseph): Medicine. See: Dorland; Jablonski. Also known as: Desnos's pneumonia.

Grancher's system (Grancher, Jacques Joseph): Medicine. See: Dorland.

Grand Guignol (Guignol): Theater. See: Harvey; New Encyc. Brit., 1974, Microp.

grand Marnier (Marnier-Lapostolle): Food and Drink. See: Partridge.

Grand Panjandrum. See: Panjandrum.

GRANDIDIER, ALFRED. 1836-1921. French naturalist and traveler. See: Grand Larousse Encyc. Grandidierite.

Grandidierite (Grandidier, Alfred): Earth Sciences. See: Thrush.

GRANDISON, SIR CHARLES. Character in Samuel Richardson's novel of the same name (1753). See: Magill. Grandisonian.

Grandisonian (Grandison, Sir Charles): Generic Word (model gentleman). See: Partridge; Webster's 3d.

GRANDMOUGIN, EUGENE. 1871-1955. Swiss chemist. See: Pogg., vols. 5, 6, 7b. Grandmougin-Havas reagent.

Grandmougin-Havas reagent (Grandmougin, Eugene and Havas, Emeric): Chemistry. See: Van Nostrand Chem. Dict.

GRANDRY, M. fl. 1867. Belgian physician. Cited in: Royal Soc. Cat. Sci. Pap., 1864-1873. Grandry's corpuscle.

Grandry's corpuscle (Grandry, M.): Zoology. See: Dorland; Gray; Henderson; Stedman.

GRANGER, AMEDEE. 1879-1939. American radiologist. See: Amer. J. Roentg., vol. 34 (1940), p. 601. Granger's line, Granger's sign.

GRANGER, JAMES. 1723-1776. English biographer. See: Dict. Nat. Biog. Grangerize (and Grangerism).

Grangerize (and Grangerism) (Granger, James): Generic Word (extra-illustrate). See: Brewer; Harrod; Harvey; Hendrickson; Lockwood; Webster's 3d.

Granger's line (Granger, Amedee): Medicine. See: Blakiston's Gould; Dorland; Stedman.

Granger's sign (Granger, Amedee): Medicine. See: Dorland.

GRANHOLM, JACKSON WALTER. 1921- . American physicist. See: Amer. Men Sci., 10th ed. Granholm's definition of the kludge.

Granholm's definition of the kludge (Granholm, Jackson Walter): Sociology. See: Martin.

GRANIT, RAGNAR ARTHUR. 1900- . Finnish neurophysiologist. See: World Who's Who Sci. Granit's loop.

Granit's loop (Granit, Ragnar Arthur): Physiology. See: Stedman.

Granny Smith (apple) (Smith, Maria Ann): Botany. See: Brewer.

GRANSTROEM, KARL OTTO. 1901- . Swedish ophthalmologist. See: Vem Ar Det?, 1955. Granstroem's sign.

Granstroem's sign (Granstroem, Karl Otto): Medicine. See: Dorland.

GRANT, CLAUDE WILSON. 1918- . American educational psychologist. See: Amer. Men Sci., vol. 10, Soc. and Behav. Grant's research results.

GRANT, JAMES AUGUSTUS. 1827-1892. English explorer. See: Dict. Nat. Biog., 1st suppl. Grant's gazelle, Grant's zebra.

Grant ranger (Grant, Ulysses Simpson): History. See: Mathews, M. M.

Grant (redwood tree) (Grant, Ulysses Simpson): Botany. See: Mathews, M. M.

GRANT, ROBERT EDMOND. 1793-1874. Scottish comparative anatomist. See: World Who's Who Sci. Grantia.

GRANT, ULYSSES SIMPSON. 1822-1885. American president. See: Dict. Amer. Biog. Grant ranger, Grant (redwood tree), Grantism.

Grantham lobotomy (Derivation undetermined): Medicine. See: Hinsie.

Grantia (Grant, Robert Edmond): Zoology. See: Pennak; Van Nostrand Sci. Encyc. under "Calcarea"; Webster's 3d.

Grantism (Grant, Ulysses Simpson): History. See: Mathews, M. M.

Grant's gazelle (Grant, James Augustus): Zoology. See: Webster's 3d.

Grant's research results (Grant, Claude Wilson): Sociology. See: Martin.

Grant's zebra (Grant, James Augustus): Zoology. See: Webster's 3d.

Granville wilt (Derivation undetermined): Botany. See: Winburne.

GRAS, BASILE. 1836-1901. French general. See: Webster's Biog. Dict. Gras rifle.

Gras rifle (Gras, Basile): Weapons. See: Partridge.

GRASER, ERNST. 1860-1929. German surgeon. See: Biog. Lex. hervorr. Aerzte, 1880-1930. Graser's diverticulum.

Graser's diverticulum (Graser, Ernst): Medicine. See: Dorland; Jablonski.

GRASHEY, HUBERT. 1839-1911. German physician. See: Biog. Lex. hervorr. Aerzte. Grashey's aphasia.

Grashey's aphasia (Grashey, Hubert): Medicine. See: Dorland.

Grashof criterion (Grashof, Franz): Physics. See: Dict. Sci. Biog. under "Grashof, Franz."

GRASHOF, FRANZ. 1826-1893. German technologist. See: Dict. Sci. Biog. Grashof criterion, Grashof Medal, Grashof Monument, Grashof('s) number.

Grashof Medal (Grashof, Franz): Science. See: Dict. Sci. Biog. under "Grashof, Franz."

Grashof Monument (Grashof, Franz): Science. See: Dict. Sci. Biog. under "Grashof, Franz."

Grashof('s) number (Grashof, Franz): Physics. See: Ballentyne; Huschke; Thewlis; Van Nostrand Sci. Encyc.

Grasset-Gaussel phenomenon (Grasset, Joseph and Gaussel Amans). See: Grasset's phenomenon.

GRASSET, JOSEPH. 1849-1918. French physician. See: World Who's Who Sci. Grasset's phenomenon, Grasset's sign, Landouzy-Grasset law.

Grasset's phenomenon (Grasset, Joseph): Medicine. See: Dorland; Stedman. Also known as: Grasset-Gaussel phenomenon.

Grasset's sign (Grasset, Joseph): Medicine. See: Stedman.

GRASSINI. No dates. Italian bread maker. (Biography source unavailable.) Grassini (bread).

Grassini (bread) (Grassini): Food and Drink. See: Charnock.

Grassmann algebra (Grassmann, Hermann Guenther): Mathematics. See: Encyc. Brit., 1973 under "Algebras," vol. 1, p. 619a.

GRASSMANN, HERMANN GUENTHER. 1809-1877. German mathematician and linguist. See: World Who's Who Sci. Grassmann algebra, Grassmann laws of colour vision, Grassmannian, Grassmann's law.

Grassmann laws of colour vision (Grassmann, Hermann Guenther): Physics. See: Thewlis.

Grassmannian (Grassmann, Hermann Guenther): Mathematics. See: Encyc. Brit., 1973 under "Grassmann, Hermann Guenther," vol. 10, p. 707a.

Grassmann's law (Grassmann, Hermann Guenther): Linguistics. See: Hartmann; Webster's 3d.; Winick.

Grassot flux meter (Grassot, M. E.): Physics. See: Thewlis.

GRASSOT, M. E. fl. 1904. French physicist. Cited in: Glazebrook, vol. 2. Grassot flux meter.

GRATEAU, MARCEL. 1852-1936. French hairdresser. (Biography source unavailable.) Marcel (Marcelling or Marcel wave).

GRATIOLET, LOUIS PIERRE. 1815-1865. French anatomist. See: Dict. Sci. Biog. Gratiolet's radiation (or fibers).

Gratiolet's radiation (or fibers) (Gratiolet, Louis Pierre): Anatomy. See: Donath; Dorland; Stedman. Also known as: Wernicke's radiation.

GRATON, LOUIS CARYL. b. 1880. American geologist. See: Amer. Men Sci., 9th ed. Gratonite.

Gratonite (Graton, Louis Caryl): Earth Sciences. See: Thrush.

GRATTAN, HENRY. 1746-1820. Irish statesman. See: Dict. Nat. Biog. Grattan's Parliament.

Grattan's Parliament (Grattan, Henry): History. See: Brewer; Harbottle; Montgomery; Steinberg.

GRAUX, GASTON. fl. 1878. French physician. Cited in: Mansell. Fereol-Graux palsy.

Gravelet, Jean Francois. See: Blondin, Charles.

Graves' disease (Graves, Robert James): Medicine. See: Dorland; English; Stedman; Van Nostrand Sci. Encyc.; Webster's 3d. Also known as: Basedow's disease, Parry's disease.

GRAVES, ROBERT JAMES. 1796-1853. Irish physician. See: World Who's Who Sci. Graves' disease.

GRAVES, SARA STOWELL. fl. 1915. American chemist. Cited in: Kelly. Graves test.

Graves test (Graves, Sara Stowell): Chemistry. See: Van Nostrand Chem. Dict.

Graves' theorem (Derivation undetermined): Mathematics. See: Ballentyne.

Grawitz basophilia (Grawitz, Paul Albert): Medicine. See: Stedman.

Grawitz' cachexia (Grawitz, Paul Albert): Medicine. See: Dorland; Stedman.

GRAWITZ, PAUL ALBERT. 1850-1932. German pathologist. See: World Who's Who Sci. Grawitz basophilia, Grawitz' cachexia, Grawitz' slumbering cells, Grawitz's tumor.

Grawitz' slumbering cells (Grawitz, Paul Albert): Medicine. See: Stedman.

Grawitz's tumor (Grawitz, Paul Albert): Medicine. See: Dorland; Jablonski; Stedman.

GRAY, CHARLES HARRY GRACE. 1896- . American electrical engineer. See: Amer. Men Sci., 9th ed. Gray code?

Gray code (Gray, Charles Harry Grace?): Data Processing. See: Markus; Van Nostrand Sci. Encyc. under "Code."

Gray-Drummond engine (Gray, H. and Drummond, C. S.): Engineering and Industry. See: Auger.

GRAY, H. fl. 1909. English engineer. (Biography source unavailable.) Gray-Drummond engine.

Gray hunting gear (Gray, J. McFarlane): Engineering and Industry. See: Auger.

GRAY, J. MC FARLANE. 1832-1908. Engineer. (Biography source unavailable.) Gray hunting gear.

GRAY, JOHN. fl. 1891. English petroleum chemist. Cited in: Royal Soc. Cat. Sci. Pap., 1884-1900. Gray's tester.

Gray-King coke type (Gray, Thomas and King, James Grieve): Engineering and Industry. See: Thrush.

Gray-King test (Gray, Thomas and King, James Grieve): Engineering and Industry. See: Thrush.

Gray-Leary readability formula (Gray, William Scott and Leary, Bernice Elizabeth): Education. See: Good.

Gray oral reading test (Gray, William Scott): Psychology. See: Wolman.

GRAY, THOMAS. b. 1869. English fuel chemist. Cited in: Mansell. Gray-King coke type, Gray-King test.

GRAY, WILLIAM SCOTT. 1885-1960. American educator. See: Nat. Cycl. Amer. Biog., vol. 48, p. 106. Gray-Leary readability formula, Gray oral reading test.

Gray's tester (Gray, John): Engineering and Industry. See: Thrush.

Great Scott! (Scott, Winfield?): Generic Word. See: Hendrickson.

great vein of Galen (Galen): Medicine. See: Donath; Stedman.

GREATHEAD, JAMES HENRY. 1844-1896. English engineer. See: Encyc. Brit., 1973. Greathead shield.

Greathead shield (Greathead, James Henry): Engineering and Industry. See: Thrush.

GREEFF, CARL RICHARD. b. 1862. German ophthalmologist. See: Biog. Lex. hervorr. Aerzte. Prowazek-Greeff bodies.

GREELEY, HORACE. 1811-1872. American editor and politician. See: Dict. Amer. Biog. Greeleyism (or Greeleyite).

Greeleyism (or Greeleyite) (Greeley, Horace): History. See: Mathews, M. M.

GREEN, E. 1795-1865. English engineer. (Biography source unavailable.) Green's economiser.

Green('s) formula(s) (Green, George): Mathematics. See: Internat. Dict. Phys. Elec.; James.

Green('s) function (Green, George): Mathematics. See: Ballentyne; Huschke; Internat. Dict. Ap. Math.; James; Markus; Van Nostrand Sci. Encyc.

GREEN, GEORGE. 1793-1841. English mathematician. See: World Who's Who Sci. Green tensor, Green('s) formula(s), Green('s) function, Green('s) theorem, Green's dyadic, Green's identity.

GREEN, GEORGE. fl. 1908. English physicist. See: Pogg., vol. 6. Twyman-Green interferometer.

Green Howards (Howard, Sir Charles): History. See: Brewer; Latham.

green salt of Magnus (Magnus, Heinrich Gustav). See: Magnus salt.

Green tensor (Green, George): Mathematics. See: Internat. Dict. Phys. Elec.

Green('s) theorem (Green, George): Mathematics. See: Ballentyne; Huschke; Internat. Dict. Ap. Math.; James; Thewlis; Van Nostrand Sci. Encyc. under "Green function."

Greenacre (Greenacre, James): Generic Word (falling of cargo). See: Hendrickson.

GREENACRE, JAMES. 1785-1837. English murderer. See: Dict. Nat. Biog. Greenacre.

Greenawalt electro chlorination process (Greenawalt, John Eckert): Engineering and Industry. Cited in: Who's Who Engin., 1937.

Greenawalt electrolytic copper extraction process (Greenawalt, William Eckert): Engineering and Industry. See: Chem. Abstr., vol. 17, p. 240.

GREENAWALT, JOHN ECKERT. b. 1867. American metallurgist and electrochemist. See: Who's Who Engin., 1937. Greenawalt electro chlorination process, Greenawalt process (blast roasting process or sintering process), Greenawalt sintering machine (or apparatus), Greenawalt system for the disposal of city refuse.

Greenawalt process (blast roasting process or sintering process) (Greenawalt, John Eckert): Engineering and Industry. See: Thrush.

Greenawalt sintering machine (or apparatus) (Greenawalt, John Eckert): Engineering and Industry. See: Thrush.

Greenawalt system for the disposal of city refuse (Greenawalt, John Eckert): Engineering and Industry. Cited in: Who's Who Engin., 1937.

GREENAWALT, WILLIAM ECKERT. fl. 1883-1937. American electro-metallurgist. See: Who's Who Engin., 1937. Greenawalt electrolytic copper extraction process.

GREENAWAY, KATE. 1846-1901. English artist and book illustrator. See: Dict. Nat. Biog., 2d suppl. Kate Greenaway bonnet, Kate Greenaway dress, Kate Greenaway Medal, Kate Greenaway (style).

GREENBURG, LEONARD. b. 1892. American engineer. See: Amer. Men Sci., 6th ed. Greenburg-Smith impinger.

Greenburg-Smith impinger (Greenburg, Leonard and Smith, George W.): Engineering and Industry. See: Thrush.

GREENE, CHARLES LYMAN. 1863-1929. American physician. See: Who Was Who Amer., 1897-1942. Greene's sign.

Greene's sign (Greene, Charles Lyman): Medicine. See: Dorland.

GREENFIELD, JOSEPH GODWIN. 1844-1958. English neuropathologist. See: J. Path. Bact., vol. 78 (1959), pp. 586-592. Greenfield's disease.

Greenfield's disease (Greenfield, Joseph Godwin): Medicine. See: Hinsie; Jablonski; Stedman. Also known as: Scholz-Bielschowsky-Henneberg syndrome, Scholz's syndrome (or disease), van Bogaert-Nijssen disease, van Bogaert-Nijssen-Peiffer disease, van Bogaert-Nyssen disease, van Bogaert-Nyssen-Peiffer disease.

greengage (plum) (Gage, Sir William): Botany. See: Brewer; Charnock; De Sola.

GREENHOW, EDWARD HEADLAM. 1814-1888. English physician. See: Boase. Greenhow's disease.

Greenhow's disease (Greenhow, Edward Headlam): Medicine. See: Dorland; Jablonski; Stedman.

Greenock, Lord. See: Cathcart, Charles Murray, 2d Earl Cathcart and Lord Greenock.

Greenockite (Cathcart, Charles Murray, 2d Earl Cathcart and Lord Greenock): Earth Sciences. See: Charnock; Thrush; Van Nostrand Sci. Encyc.; Webster's 3d.

GREENOUGH, GEORGE BELLAS. 1778-1855. English geologist. See: Dict. Sci. Biog. Greenovite.

Greenough microscope (or binocular microscope) (Derivation undetermined): Physics. See: Blakiston's Gould; Stedman.

Greenovite (Greenough, George Bellas): Earth Sciences. See: Charnock; Thrush.

Green's dyadic (Green, George): Mathematics. See: Ballentyne.

Green's economiser (Green, E.): Engineering and Industry. See: Auger; Thrush.

Green's identity (Green, George): Mathematics. See: Internat. Dict. Ap. Math.

Green's theorem in space (Green, George). See: Ostrogradski's theorem.

Greenstein-Henyey camera (Greenstein, Jesse Leonard and Henyey, Louis George): Astronomy. See: New Encyc. Brit., 1974, Microp.

GREENSTEIN, JESSE LEONARD. 1909- . American astronomer. See: World Who's Who Sci. Greenstein-Henyey camera.

GREENWELL, ALLAN. b. 1860. English mining engineer. Cited in: Mansell. Greenwell formula?

Greenwell formula (Greenwell, Allan?): Engineering and Industry. See: Thrush.

GREGG, JOHN ROBERT. 1864-1948. Irish inventor of shorthand system. See: Nat. Cycl. Amer. Biog., vol. C, p. 273. Gregg system.

GREGG, NORMAN MC ALLISTER. fl. 1915-1972. Australian ophthalmologist. See: Med. Direct., 1964. Gregg's syndrome.

Gregg system (Gregg, John Robert): Dictation. See: Hendrickson.

Gregg's syndrome (Gregg, Norman McAllister): Medicine. See: Jablonski.

Gregor microchemical reagent (Derivation undetermined): Chemistry. See: Van Nostrand Chem. Dict.

GREGOR, WILLIAM. 1761-1817. English chemist. See: Pogg., vol. 1. Gregorite.

Gregorian (Gregory I, the Great, Saint): Religion. See: Webster's 3d.

Gregorian (Gregory XIII): Religion. See: Webster's 3d.

Gregorian altar (Gregory I, the Great, Saint): Religion. See: Attwater.

Gregorian Armenian Church (or Gregorian) (Gregory the Illuminator, Saint): Religion. See: Attwater; Webster's 3d.

Gregorian calendar (Gregory XIII): Generic Word. See: Attwater; Barnhart (Eng. Lit.); Satterthwaite; Van Nostrand Sci. Encyc. under "Calendar"; Webster's 3d.; Winick.

Gregorian chant (or music) (Gregory I, the Great, Saint): Music. See: Apel; Attwater; New Cath. Encyc.; New Encyc. Brit., 1974, Microp.; Phyfe; Scholes; Webster's 3d.

Gregorian mass (Gregory I, the Great, Saint): Religion. See: Attwater.

Gregorian mode(s) (Gregory I, the Great, Saint): Music. See: Apel under "Church modes"; Webster's 3d.

Gregorian reform (Gregory VII): Religion. See: New Cath. Encyc.; New Encyc. Brit., 1974, Microp.

Gregorian sacramentary (Gregory I, the Great, Saint): Religion. See: Attwater.

Gregorian staff (Gregory I, the Great, Saint): Music. See: Webster's 3d.

Gregorian telescope (Gregory, James): Satterthwaite; Thewlis; Van Nostrand Sci. Encyc.; Webster's 3d.

Gregorian tone (Gregory I, the Great, Saint): Music. See: Webster's 3d.

Gregorian tree (Brandon, Gregory and Richard): Generic Word (gallows). See: Brewer; Hendrickson.

Gregorian water (Gregory I, the Great, Saint): Religion. See: Attwater.

Gregorian (wig) (Gregory): Fashion. See: Oxford Eng. Dict.; Picken.

Gregorian year (or epoch) (Gregory XIII): History. See: Brewer; Hendrickson; Webster's 3d.

Gregoriara (Gallo, Don Gregorio): Recreation and Sports. See: Charnock.

Gregorite (Gregor, William): Chemistry. Cited in: World Who's Who Sci. under "Gregor, William."

GREGORY. fl. by 1670. English barber. (Biography source unavailable.) Gregorian (wig).

GREGORY I, THE GREAT, SAINT. ca. 540-604. Roman-born pope. See: Encyc. Brit., 1973. Gregorian, Gregorian altar, Gregorian chant (or music), Gregorian mass, Gregorian mode(s), Gregorian sacramentary, Gregorian staff, Gregorian tone, Gregorian water, Liturgy of St. Gregory dialogos, Order of St. Gregory The Great.

GREGORY VII (Real name: HILDEBRAND). ca. 1025-1085. Italian-born pope. See: Encyc. Brit., 1973. Gregorian reform, Hildebrandine.

GREGORY XIII (Real name: UGO BUONCOMPAGNI). 1502-1585. Italian-born pope. See: Encyc. Brit., 1973. Gregorian, Gregorian calendar, Gregorian year (or epoch).

Gregory('s) formula (or interpolation formulae) (Gregory, James). See: Gregory-Newton formula (or formula for interpolation).

GREGORY, JAMES. 1638-1675. Scottish mathematician. See: Dict. Sci. Biog. Gregory-Newton formula (or formula for interpolation), Gregorian telescope, Gregory's series, Gregory's theorem.

GREGORY, JAMES. 1753-1821. Scottish physician. See: Dict. Nat. Biog. Gregory('s) powder (or mixture).

Gregory-Newton formula (or formula for interpolation) (Gregory, James and Newton, Sir Isaac): Mathematics. See: Ballentyne; James; Van Nostrand Sci. Encyc. Also known as: Gregory('s) formula (or interpolation formulae), Newton-Gregory interpolation formula.

Gregory('s) powder (or mixture) (Gregory, James): Medicine. See: Dorland; Hackh; Partridge; Stedman; Webster's 3d.

Gregory salt (Gregory, William): Chemistry. See: Hackh.

GREGORY THAUMATURGUS, SAINT. ca. 213-ca. 270. Bishop of Neo-Caesarea. See: Holweck. Thaumaturgus.

GREGORY THE ILLUMINATOR, SAINT. 240-332. Armenian apostle to his own people. See: New Encyc. Brit., 1974, Microp. Gregorian Armenian Church (or Gregorian).

GREGORY, WILLIAM. 1803-1858. Scottish chemist. See: Dict. Sci. Biog. Gregory salt.

Gregory's series (Gregory, James): Mathematics. See: Ballentyne.

Gregory's theorem (Gregory, James): Mathematics. See: Encyc. Brit., 1973 under "Calculus of Differences," vol. 4, p. 601d.

GREIG, DAVID MIDDLETON. 1864-1936. Scottish scientist. See: Edinburgh Med. J. vol. 43, (1936) pp. 531-539. Greig's syndrome.

GREIG, JOSEPH WILSON. 1895- . American petrographer. See: Amer. Men Sci., 10th ed. Greigite.

Greigite (Greig, Joseph Wilson): Earth Sciences. See: Thrush.

Greig's syndrome (Greig, David Middleton): Medicine. See: Jablonski; Wolman.

Greinacher circuit (or connection) (Greinacher, Heinrich): Physics. See: Thewlis. Also known as: Latour circuit.

GREINACHER, HEINRICH. b. 1880. Swiss physicist. See: World Who's Who Sci. Greinacher circuit (or connection).

GREINDL, BARON. fl. 19th c. German? engineer. (Biography source unavailable.) Greindl pump.

Greindl pump (Greindl, Baron): Engineering and Industry. See: Auger.

GREITHER, ALOYS. 1913- . German dermatologist. See: Wer Ist Wer?, 1974-1975. Greither's syndrome.

Greither's syndrome (Greither, Aloys): Medicine. See: Jablonski.

GRELLING, KURT. fl. 1908-1910. German philosopher. Cited in: Mansell. Grelling-Nelson paradox of heterologicality, Grelling's paradox.

Grelling–Nelson paradox of heterologicality (Grelling, Kurt and Nelson): Philosophy. See: Edwards.

Grelling's paradox (Grelling, Kurt): Philosophy. See: Edwards.

GRENACHER, HERMANN (In full: GEORG HERMANN). 1843–1923. German zoologist. See: World Who's Who Sci. Grenacher stain.

Grenacher stain (Grenacher, Hermann): Chemistry. See: Hackh.

GRENANDER, ULF. 1923– . Swedish-born American mathematician. See: World Who's Who Sci. Grenander's uncertainty principle.

Grenander's uncertainty principle (Grenander, Ulf): Statistics. See: Kendall.

Grenet battery (Derivation undetermined): Chemistry. See: Hackh.

GRENINGER, ALDEN BUCHANAN. 1907– . American metallurgist. See: Amer. Men and Women Sci., 12th ed. Greninger chart.

Greninger chart (Greninger, Alden Buchanan): Physics. See: Thewlis.

Grenville Act (Grenville, Richard Temple, Earl Temple?): History. See: Black; Harbottle.

GRENVILLE, RICHARD TEMPLE, EARL TEMPLE. 1711–1779. English politician. See: Dict. Nat. Biog. Grenville Act?

GREPPI, ENRICO. 1896– . Italian hematologist. See: World Who's Who Sci. Rietti–Greppi–Micheli syndrome.

Gresham Professorship of Music (Gresham, Sir Thomas): Music. See: Scholes.

GRESHAM, SIR THOMAS. ca. 1519–1579. English financier. See: Dict. Nat. Biog. Gresham Professorship of Music, Gresham's law (1), Gresham's law (2), sup with Sir Thomas Gresham.

Gresham's law (1) (Gresham, Sir Thomas): Economics. See: Greenwald; Harvey; Seldon; Webster's 3d.; Zadrozny.

Gresham's law (2) (Gresham, Sir Thomas): Sociology. See: Martin.

Grethen bottle (Grethen, Willy?): Chemistry. See: Van Nostrand Chem. Dict.

GRETHEN, WILLY. fl. 1876. German chemist. Cited in: Royal Soc. Cat. Sci. Pap., 1874–1883. Grethen bottle?

GREULING, EUGENE. 1914– . American physicist. See: Amer. Men Sci., 9th ed. Goertzel–Greuling approximation.

Greve's test (or tumor reaction) (Derivation undetermined): Medicine. See: Dorland.

Greville bath (Derivation undetermined): Medicine. See: Stedman.

GREVILLE, CHARLES FRANCIS. 1749–1809. Scottish botanist. See: Britten and Boulger. Grevillea.

Grevillea (Greville, Charles Francis): Botany. See: Partridge; Taylor, N.; Webster's 3d.

GREVY, JULES (In full: FRANCOIS-PAUL-JULES). 1807–1891. French president. See: Encyc. Brit., 1973. Grevy's zebra.

Grevy's zebra (Grevy, Jules): Zoology. See: Gray; Pennak; Webster's 3d.

GREW, NEHEMIAH. 1641–1712. English plant physiologist. See: Dict. Sci. Biog. Grewia.

Grewia (Grew, Nehemiah): Botany. See: Webster's 3d.

GREY, SIR GEORGE. 1812–1898. English colonial governor. See: Dict. Nat. Biog., 1st suppl. Greyia, Grobya?

Grey Turner, George. See: Turner, George Grey.

Grey Turner's sign (Turner, George Grey). See: Turner's (or Grey Turner's sign).

Greyia (Grey, Sir George): Botany. See: Taylor, N.

GRIEBEL, CONSTANT VICTOR EDUARD. 1876– . German chemist. See: Pogg., vol. 6, 7a. Griebel test for hydrogen peroxide.

Griebel test for hydrogen peroxide (Griebel, Constant Victor Eduard): Chemistry. See: Van Nostrand Chem. Dict.

Griebhard's rings (Derivation undetermined): Physics. See: Internat. Dict. Phys. Elec.

GRIESINGER, WILHELM. 1817–1868. German neurologist. See: World Who's Who Sci. Duchenne–Griesinger disease, Griesinger's disease (1), Griesinger's disease (3) (or bilious typhoid of Griesinger), Griesinger's symptom (or sign).

Griesinger's disease (1) (Griesinger, Wilhelm): Medicine. See: Jablonski.

Griesinger's disease (2) (Griesinger, Wilhelm). See: Duchenne–Griesinger disease.

Griesinger's disease (3) (or bilious typhoid of Griesinger) (Griesinger, Wilhelm): Medicine. See: Stedman.

Griesinger's symptom (or sign) (Griesinger, Wilhelm): Medicine. See: Blakiston's Gould; Dorland; Stedman.

Griess–Ilosva reagent (Griess, Peter and Ilosvay de Nagyilosova, Lajos?): Chemistry. See: Hackh.

GRIESS, PETER (In full: JOHANN PETER). 1829–1888. German-born English chemist. See: Dict. Sci. Biog. Griess–Ilosva reagent, Griess phenylenediamine test for nitrite, Griess reaction, Griess reagent and test for nitrite.

Griess phenylenediamine test for nitrite (Griess, Peter): Chemistry. See: Van Nostrand Chem. Dict.

Griess reaction (Griess, Peter): Chemistry. See: Hackh.

Griess reagent and test for nitrite (Griess, Peter): Chemistry. See: Van Nostrand Chem. Dict.

GRIESSMAYER, VICTOR. fl. 1893. German chemist. Cited in: Royal Soc. Cat. Sci. Pap., 1884–1900. Griessmeyer reaction for tannic acid.

Griessmeyer reaction for tannic acid (Griessmayer, Victor): Chemistry. See: Van Nostrand Chem. Dict.

Griffin gas engine (Griffin, Samuel): Engineering and Industry. See: Auger.

Griffin mill (Derivation undetermined): Engineering and Industry. See: Thrush.

GRIFFIN, ROBERT PAUL. 1923– . American legislator. See: Biog. Direct. Amer. Congress. Landrum–Griffin Act.

GRIFFIN, SAMUEL. fl. 1883–1889. English engineer. Cited in: Royal Soc. Cat. Sci. Pap., 1884–1900. Griffin gas engine.

GRIFFITH, ALAN ARNOLD. fl. 1918–1929. English engineer. See: Who's Who Brit. Sci., 1953. Griffith cracks, Griffith('s) theory (theory of brittle fracture or crack theory).

Griffith cracks (Griffith, Alan Arnold): Engineering and Industry. See: Thewlis under "Griffith theory of brittle fracture."

GRIFFITH, SIR RICHARD JOHN. 1784–1878. English geologist and civil engineer. See: Dict. Nat. Biog. Griffith's valuation.

Griffith('s) theory (theory of brittle fracture or crack theory) (Griffith, Alan Arnold): Engineering and Industry. See: Thewlis; Thrush; Van Nostrand Sci. Encyc.

GRIFFITHS, ERNEST HOWARD. 1851–1932. English physicist. See: World Who's Who Sci. Awberg and Griffiths method (for latent heat of vaporization), Callendar and Griffiths bridge, Griffiths method for mechanical equivalent of heat.

Griffiths method for mechanical equivalent of heat (Griffiths, Ernest Howard): Physics. See: Internat. Dict. Phys. Elec.

Griffiths propeller (Griffiths, Robert): Engineering and Industry. See: Auger.

GRIFFITHS, ROBERT. 1805–1883. English inventor. See: World Who's Who Sci. Griffiths propeller.

GRIFFITHS, RUTH. 1909– . English psychologist. Cited in: Mansell. Griffiths' scale.

Griffiths' scale (Griffiths, Ruth): Psychology. See: Wolman.

Griffith's valuation (Griffith, Sir Richard John): History. See: Harbottle; Montgomery.

Grigg Committee (Grigg, Sir James): Library Science. See: Harrod.

GRIGG, SIR JAMES (In full: PERCY JAMES). 1890-1964. English statesman. See: Who Was Who, 1961-1970. Grigg Committee.

Griggi reaction for gallic acid (Derivation undetermined): Chemistry. See: Van Nostrand Chem. Dict.

Grignard degradation (Grignard, Victor): Chemistry. See: Van Nostrand Chem. Dict.

Grignard reaction (Grignard, Victor): Chemistry. See: Ballentyne; Hackh; Van Nostrand Chem. Dict.; Van Nostrand Sci. Encyc.; Webster's 3d.

Grignard reagent (or compound) (Grignard, Victor): Chemistry. See: Asimov; Hackh; Webster's 3d.

GRIGNARD, VICTOR (In full: FRANCOIS AUGUSTE VICTOR). 1871-1935. French chemist. See: Dict. Sci. Biog. Grignard degradation, Grignard reaction, Grignard reagent (or compound).

GRIGNOLO, ANTONIO. 1915-   . Italian ophthalmologist. See: Who's Who Sci. Europe, 1972. Grignolo's syndrome.

Grignolo's syndrome (Grignolo, Antonio): Medicine. See: Jablonski.

Grigoriew reagents (Grigorjew, Pavel Semenovich?): Chemistry. See: Van Nostrand Chem. Dict.

GRIGORJEW, PAVEL SEMENOVICH. b. 1879. Russian physician. See: Biog. Lex. hervorr. Aerzte, 1880-1930. Grigoriew reagents?

Grillo furnace (Derivation undetermined): Engineering and Industry. See: Thrush.

Grillo-Schroeder process (Derivation undetermined): Engineering and Industry. See: Van Nostrand Chem. Dict.

GRIM (OR GRIMM), HERMANN NICLAS. 1641-1711. German scientist. See: Biog. Lex. hervorr. Aerzte. Grimme.

GRIMALDI, JOSEPH. 1779-1837. English pantomimist and clown. See: Dict. Nat. Biog. Joey.

Grimani Breviary (Grimani, Domenico): Fine Arts. See: Osborne under "Bening..."

GRIMANI, DOMENICO. b. 1461. Venetian cardinal. See: Encic. Cattolica. Grimani Breviary.

GRIMAUX, EDOUARD (In full: LOUIS EDOUARD). 1835-1900. French chemist. See: Pogg., vols. 3, 4. Grimaux reagent for nitrate.

Grimaux reagent for nitrate (Grimaux, Edouard): Chemistry. See: Van Nostrand Chem. Dict.

Grimbert-Dufau reagent (Grimbert, Leon Louis and Dufau, Emil): Chemistry. See: Van Nostrand Chem. Dict.

GRIMBERT, LEON LOUIS. 1860-1931. French chemist. See: Pogg., vols. 4, 5, 6. Grimbert-Dufau reagent, Grimbert test reaction for magnesium.

Grimbert test reaction for magnesium (Grimbert, Leon Louis): Chemistry. See: Van Nostrand Chem. Dict.

Grimes golden (apple) (Grimes, Thomas P.): Food and Drink. See: De Sola; Mathews, M. M.

GRIMES, THOMAS P. fl. 18th c. American fruit grower. (Biography source unavailable.) Grimes golden (apple).

GRIMM, HANS. 1910-   . German anthropologist. See: Kuerschner's Deut. Gel. Kal., vol. 9, 1961. Grimm's graves?

GRIMM, HANS AUGUST GEORG. 1887-1958. German physical chemist. See: World Who's Who Sci. Grimm's hydride displacement theorem.

Grimm, Hermann Niclas. See: Grim, Hermann Niclas.

GRIMM, JACOB LUDWIG KARL. 1785-1863. German philologist and mythologist. See: Encyc. Brit., 1973. Grimm's law.

GRIMM, JOHANN FRIEDRICH KARL. 1737-1821. German botanist. See: Nouv. Biog. Univ. Grimmia.

Grimme (Grim, Hermann Niclas): Zoology. See: Webster's 3d.

Grimmia (Grimm, Johann Friedrich Karl): Botany. See: Webster's 3d.

Grimm's graves (Grimm, Hans?): Archaeology. See: Winick.

Grimm's hydride displacement theorem (Grimm, Hans August Georg): Chemistry. Cited in: World Who's Who Sci.

Grimm's law (Grimm, Jacob Ludwig Karl): Linguistics. See: Barnhart (Eng. Lit.); Brewer; Phyfe; Webster's 3d.; Weekley; Winick.

Grimthorpe (Beckett, Sir Edmund, 1st Baron Grimthorpe): Generic Word (restore a building). See: Hendrickson; Partridge; Webster's 3d.

Grimthorpe, 1st Baron. See: Beckett, Sir Edmund, 1st Baron Grimthorpe.

GRINDEL, DAVID HIERONYMOUS. 1776-1836. Russian botanist. See: Biog. Lex. hervorr. Aerzte. Grindelia.

Grindelia (Grindel, David Hieronymous): Botany. See: Dorland; Mathews, M. M.; Stedman; Taylor, N.; Webster's 3d.

GRINDON, JOSEPH, SR. 1858-1950. American dermatologist. See: World Who's Who Sci. Grindon's disease.

Grindon's disease (Grindon, Joseph, Sr.): Medicine. See: Dorland; Jablonski.

Gringo (Ringgold, Major Samuel?): Generic Word. See: Hendrickson.

Grinnell expedition (Grinnell, Henry): Discovery. See: Encyc. Brit., 1973 under "Kane, Elisha Kent," vol. 13, p. 205a.

GRINNELL, FREDERICK. 1836-1905. American mechanical engineer. See: World Who's Who Sci. Grinnell sprinkler.

GRINNELL, HENRY. 1799-1874. American merchant. See: Dict. Amer. Biog. Grinnell expedition, Grinnellia.

Grinnell sprinkler (Grinnell, Frederick): Engineering and Industry. See: Auger.

Grinnellia (Grinnell, Henry): Botany. See: Webster's 3d.

GRISEL, P. fl. 1930. French physician. (Biography source unavailable.) Grisel's disease.

GRISELDA. Paragon of womanly virtue in medieval romances. See: Jobes. Griselda complex.

Griselda complex (Griselda, the medieval heroine): Psychiatry. See: Hinsie; Wolman.

GRISELINI, FRANCESCO. d. 1783. Italian botanist. See: Archo. Stor. Sci., vol. 1 (1919), pp. 1-20. Griselinia.

Griselinia (Griselini, Francesco): Botany. See: Taylor, N.; Webster's 3d.

Grisel's disease (Grisel, P.): Medicine. See: Jablonski.

GRISOLLE, AUGUSTIN. 1811-1869. French physician. See: Biog. Lex. hervorr. Aerzte. Grisolle's sign.

Grisolle's sign (Grisolle, Augustin): Medicine. See: Dorland; Stedman.

GRITTI, ROCCO. 1828-1920. Italian surgeon. See: Biog. Lex. hervorr. Aerzte. Gritti's amputation (or operation).

Gritti's amputation (or operation) (Gritti, Rocco): Medicine. See: Dorland; Stedman.

GROB, E. fl. 20th c. Swiss engineer. (Biography source unavailable.) Grob standard spline.

GROB, MAX. 1901-   . Swiss child surgeon. See: Kuerschner's Deut. Gel. Kal., vol. 8, 1954. Grob's syndrome.

Grob standard spline (Grob, E.): Engineering and Industry. See: Auger.

Grobian (Grobianus): Generic Word (boorish). See: Partridge.

GROBIANUS. Mythical character in German literature of the 15th-16th c. See: Brockhaus. Grobian.

Grob's syndrome (Grob, Max): Medicine. See: Jablonski.

Grobya (Grey, Sir George?): Botany. See: Charnock.

GROCCO, PIETRO. 1856-1916. Italian physician. See: Biog. Lex. hervorr. Aerzte, 1880-1930. Grocco-Poncet disease, Grocco's sign (1), Grocco's sign (2), Grocco's triangle (or sign (3)), Orsi-Grocco method.

Grocco–Poncet disease (Grocco, Pietro and Poncet, Antonin). See: Poncet's disease.

Grocco–Rauchfuss triangle (Grocco, Pietro and Rauchfuss, Karl Andreivich). See: Grocco's triangle (or sign (3)).

Grocco's sign (1) (Grocco, Pietro): Medicine. See: Dorland; Stedman.

Grocco's sign (2) (Grocco, Pietro): Medicine. See: Dorland; Stedman.

Grocco's triangle (or sign (3)) (Grocco, Pietro): Medicine. See: Dorland; Stedman. Also known as: Grocco–Rauchfuss triangle, Rauchfuss's triangle.

GRODZKI, M. fl. 1880. German chemist. Cited in: Royal Soc. Cat. Sci. Pap., 1874–1883. Grodzki test reaction.

Grodzki test reaction (Grodzki, M.): Chemistry. See: Van Nostrand Chem. Dict.

GROENBLAD, ESTER ELISABETH. 1898– . Swedish ophthalmologist. Cited in: Kelly. Groenblad–Strandberg syndrome.

Groenblad–Strandberg syndrome (Groenblad, Ester Elisabeth and Strandberg, James Victor): Medicine. See: Dorland; Jablonski.

Groendal flotation cell (Groendal, Gustaf): Engineering and Industry. See: Thrush.

GROENDAL, GUSTAF (In full: JOHAN GUSTAF). 1859–1932. Swedish industrialist. See: Svenska Maen Och Kvinnor. Groendal flotation cell, Groendal separator.

Groendal separator (Groendal, Gustaf): Engineering and Industry. See: Thrush.

GROENOUW, ARTHUR. 1862–1945. German ophthalmologist. See: Biog. Lex. hervorr. Aerzte, 1880–1930. Groenouw's dystrophy I (or corneal dystrophy (1)), Groenouw's dystrophy II (or corneal dystrophy (2)).

Groenouw's dystrophy I (or corneal dystrophy (1)) (Groenouw, Arthur): Medicine. See: Jablonski; Stedman. Also known as: Fleischer's dystrophy.

Groenouw's dystrophy II (or corneal dystrophy (2)) (Groenouw, Arthur): Medicine. See: Jablonski; Stedman. Also known as: Fehr's dystrophy.

GROENWALL, EUGEN ASSAR ALEXIS. b. 1872. Swedish industrialist. See: Svenska Maen Och Kvinnor. Groenwall process.

Groenwall process (Groenwall, Eugen Assar Alexis): Engineering and Industry. See: Thrush.

GROFFITH, JOSEPH. fl. 1893. English surgeon. (Biography source unavailable.) Groffith's degeneration.

Groffith's degeneration (Groffith, Joseph): Medicine. See: Jablonski.

"Grog." See: Vernon, Admiral Edward "Old Grog."

Grog (Vernon, Admiral Edward "Old Grog"): Food and Drink. See: Charnock; Latham; Partridge.

Groggy (Vernon, Admiral Edward "Old Grog"): (intoxicated) Generic Word. See: Charnock; Funk; Partridge.

Grolier binding (or Grolieresque) (Grolier, Jean, Vicomte d'Aguisy): Applied Arts. See: Harrod; Hendrickson; Lockwood under "Finishing"; Partridge.

GROLIER, JEAN, VICOMTE D'AGUISY. 1479–1565. French bibliophile. See: Encyc. Brit., 1973. Grolier binding (or Grolieresque).

Groos droop (Groos, Ole V.): Mathematics. See: Amer. Doc., vol. 18, no. 1, (1967) p. 46.

GROOS, OLE V. fl. 1967. American librarian? (Biography source unavailable.) Groos droop.

Gross' disease (Gross, Samuel David): Medicine. See: Dorland; Jablonski.

Gross leukemia (virus or leukemia virus) (Gross, Ludwik): Medicine. See: Jablonski; Stedman.

GROSS, LUDWIK. 1904– . Polish-born American physician. See: World Who's Who Sci. Gross leukemia (virus or leukemia virus).

GROSS, ROBERT EDWARD. 1905– . American surgeon. See: World Who's Who Sci. Ladd–Gross syndrome.

GROSS, SAMUEL DAVID. 1805–1884. American surgeon. See: World Who's Who Sci. Gross' disease, Gross's pill.

GROSSFELD, JOHANN GERHARD. 1889–1944. German food chemist. See: Pogg., vols. 6, 7a. Grossfeld reagent for oxalates, Grossfeld test for benzoic acid.

Grossfeld reagent for oxalates (Grossfeld, Johann Gerhard): Chemistry. See: Van Nostrand Chem. Dict.

Grossfeld test for benzoic acid (Grossfeld, Johann Gerhard): Chemistry. See: Van Nostrand Chem. Dict.

GROSSICH, ANTONIO. 1849–1926. Fiume physician. See: Biog. Lex. hervorr. Aerzte, 1880–1930. Grossich's method.

Grossich's method (Grossich, Antonio): Medicine. See: Dorland.

GROSSMAN, MORRIS. b. 1881. American neurologist. (Biography source unavailable.) Grossman's sign.

Grossman test reaction for cobalt (Grossmann, Hermann?): Chemistry. See: Van Nostrand Chem. Dict.

Grossman test reactions for titanium (Grossmann, Hermann?): Chemistry. See: Van Nostrand Chem. Dict.

GROSSMANN, HERMANN (Orig. name: HERMANN ITZIG). b. 1877. German chemist. See: Pogg., vols. 6, 7a. Grossmann–Mannheim reagent, Grossmann reagent, Grossmann–Schueck reagent for metallic salts, Grossmann–Schueck reagent for nickel, Grossman test reaction for cobalt?, Grossman test reactions for titanium?

GROSSMANN, LOUIS ADOLF. 1855– . American meteorologist. See: World Who's Who Sci. Guilbert–Grossmann rules.

Grossmann–Mannheim reagent (Grossmann, Hermann and Mannheim, Julie): Chemistry. See: Chem. Abstr., vol. 12, p. 1372; Van Nostrand Chem. Dict.

Grossmann reagent (Grossmann, Hermann): Chemistry. See: Hackh.

Grossmann–Schueck reagent for metallic salts (Grossmann, Hermann and Schueck, Bernhard): Chemistry. See: Van Nostrand Chem. Dict.

Grossmann–Schueck reagent for nickel (Grossmann, Hermann and Schueck, Bernhard): Chemistry. See: Van Nostrand Chem. Dict.

Grossman's sign (Grossman, Morris): Medicine. See: Dorland.

Gross's pill (Gross, Samuel David): Medicine. See: Dorland.

GROTE, IRVINE WALTER. 1899– . American biochemist. See: Amer. Men and Women Sci., 12th ed. Grote reagent.

Grote reagent (Grote, Irvine Walter): Chemistry. See: Van Nostrand Chem. Dict.

Groth, Paul Heinrich von. See: Von Groth, Paul Heinrich.

Grothit (Von Groth, Paul Heinrich): Earth Sciences. Cited in: World Who's Who Sci.

Grotthus' chain theory (Grotthuss, Christian Johann Dietrich Theodor von): Physics. See: Ballentyne.

Grotthus–Draper law (Grotthuss, Christian Johann Dietrich Theodor von and Draper, John William): Physics. See: Hackh; Hughes; Thewlis; Webster's 3d. Also known as: Draper law, Grotthus law.

Grotthus' law (Grotthuss, Christian Johann Dietrich Theodor von). See: Grotthus–Draper law.

GROTTHUSS, CHRISTIAN JOHANN DIETRICH THEODOR VON. 1785–1822. German physicist. See: World Who's Who Sci. Grotthus' chain theory, Grotthus–Draper law.

GROUT, FRANK FITCH. 1880–1958. American geologist and mineralogist. See: Who Was Who Amer., 1951–1960. Groutite.

Groutite (Grout, Frank Fitch): Earth Sciences. See: Webster's 3d.

Grove('s) cell (Grove, Sir William Robert): Physics. See: Asimov; Dorland; Hackh.

Grove gas cell (Grove, Sir William Robert): Physics. Cited in: Webster's Biog. Dict.

GROVE, SIR WILLIAM ROBERT. 1811-1896. English physicist. See: Dict. Sci. Biog. Grove('s) cell, Grove gas cell.

GROVES, ARTHUR WILLIAM. 1903- . English geologist. See: Who's Who Brit. Sci., 1953. Grovesite.

GROVES, CHARLES EDWARD. 1841-1920. English chemist. Cited in: Royal Soc. Cat. Sci. Pap., 1874-1883. Grove's process?

Grove's process (Groves, Charles Edward?): Chemistry. See: Ballentyne.

Grovesite (Groves, Arthur William): Earth Sciences. See: Thrush.

GRUBBS, FRANK EPHRAIM. 1913- . American mathematical statistician. See: Amer. Men and Women Sci., 12th ed. Grubbs' rule.

Grubbs' rule (Grubbs, Frank Ephraim): Statistics. See: Kendall.

GRUBE, AUGUST WILHELM. 1816-1884. German educator. See: Allg. Deut. Biog. Grube method.

Grube method (Grube, August Wilhelm): Education. See: Good.

GRUBER, GEORG BENNO OTTO. b. 1884. German pathologist. See: World Who's Who Sci. Gruber's syndrome, Gruber's test.

GRUBER, JOSEF. 1827-1900. Austrian otologist. See: Biog. Lex. hervorr. Aerzte. Gruber's bougies, Gruber's method, Gruber's speculum, Gruber's test.

Gruber-Landzert fossa (Gruber, Wenzel Leopold and Landzert, Theodor): Medicine. See: Stedman.

Gruber, Maximilian Franz Maria. See: Von Gruber, Maximilian Franz Maria.

GRUBER, WENZEL LEOPOLD. 1814-1890. Russian anatomist. See: Biog. Lex. hervorr. Aerzte. Gruber-Landzert fossa, Gruber's cul-de-sac, Gruber's hernia.

Gruber-Widal reaction (Von Gruber, Maximilian Franz Maria and Widal, Fernand). See: Widal('s) reaction.

Gruber's bougies (Gruber, Josef): Medicine. See: Dorland.

Gruber's cul-de-sac (Gruber, Wenzel Leopold): Medicine. See: Dorland; Stedman.

Gruber's hernia (Gruber, Wenzel Leopold): Medicine. See: Jablonski.

Gruber's method (Gruber, Josef): Medicine. See: Dorland; Stedman.

Gruber's reaction (Von Gruber, Maximilian Franz Maria). See: Widal('s) reaction.

Gruber's speculum (Gruber, Josef): Medicine. See: Dorland.

Gruber's syndrome (Gruber, Georg Benno Otto): Medicine. See: Jablonski.

Gruber's test (Gruber, Georg Benno Otto): Medicine. See: Kelly

Gruber's test (Gruber, Josef): Medicine. See: Blakiston's Gould; Kelly.

GRUBY, DAVID. 1810-1898. French physician. See: Dict. Sci. Biog. Gruby's disease.

Gruby's disease (Gruby, David): Medicine. See: Dorland; Jablonski; Stedman.

GRUDZINSKI, ZYGMUNT. 1870-1929. Polish roentgenologist. See: Biog. Lex. hervorr. Aerzte, 1880-1930. Grudzinski's osteochondropathy.

Grudzinski's osteochondropathy (Grudzinski, Zygmunt). See: Silfrerskioeld's syndrome.

Gruenbaum, Albert. See: Leyton, Albert Sidney Frankau.

Grueneisen constant (number or gamma) (Grueneisen, Eduard): Physics. See: Ballentyne; Internat. Dict. Phys. Elec.; Thewlis.

GRUENEISEN, EDUARD. 1877-1949. German physicist. See: World Who's Who Sci. Bloch-Grueneisen relationship, Grueneisen constant (number or gamma), Grueneisen first rule, Grueneisen formula, Grueneisen relation (law or second rule), Mie-Grueneisen equation of state.

Grueneisen equation of state (Grueneisen, Eduard). See: Mie-Grueneisen equation of state.

Grueneisen first rule (Grueneisen, Eduard): Physics. See: Thewlis.

Grueneisen formula (Grueneisen, Eduard): Physics. See: Internat. Dict. Phys. Elec.

Grueneisen relation (law or second rule) (Grueneisen, Eduard): Physics. See: Ballentyne; Thewlis.

GRUENEWALD, MATHIAS. b. ca. 1455-1480-1528. German painter. See: New Encyc. Brit., 1974. Mathis der Maler.

Gruenlingite (Grunling, Friedrich): Earth Sciences. See: Webster's 3d.

GRUENWALD, LUDWIG. b. 1863. German rhinologist. Cited in: Kelly. Gruenwald operations, May-Gruenwald staining solution.

Gruenwald operations (Gruenwald, Ludwig): Medicine. See: Kelly.

GRUESS, JOHANNES. b. 1860. German botanist. Cited in: Mansell. Gruess solution for wood and vanillin.

Gruess solution for wood and vanillin (Gruess, Johannes): Chemistry. See: Van Nostrand Chem. Dict.

GRUETZ, OTTO. b. 1886. German dermatologist. See: Who's Who Ger. Buerger-Gruetz syndrome.

GRUNDTVIG, NIKOLAI FREDERIK SEVERIN. 1783-1872. Danish theologian and poet. See: Encyc. Brit., 1973. Grundtvigian (and Grundtvigianism).

Grundtvigian (and Grundtvigianism) (Grundtvig, Nikolai Frederik Severin): Religion. See: Webster's 3d.

GRUNDY, MRS. Character alluded to in Thomas Morton's play "Speed the Plough" (1798). See: Encyc. Brit., 1973. Grundyism, Mrs. Grundy (or Grundy).

Grundyism (Grundy, Mrs.): Generic Word (ultra-conventional behavior). See: Partridge; Webster's 3d.

GRUNER, LOUIS (In full: EMMANUEL LOUIS). 1809-1883. French geologist. See: Pogg., vol. 3. Grunerite (or Gruenerite).

Grunerite (or Gruenerite) (Gruner, Louis): Earth Sciences. See: Webster's 3d.

GRUNLING, FRIEDRICH. 1857-1919. German mineralogist. See: Min. Mag., vol. 20 (Mar. 1923-Dec. 1925) p. 260. Gruenlingite.

GRUTTERINK, ALIDE. fl. 1910-1912. Dutch chemist. Cited in: Chem. Abstr., vol. 6, p. 1210. Grutterink reagents for alkaloids.

Grutterink reagents for alkaloids (Grutterink, Alide): Chemistry. See: Van Nostrand Chem. Dict.

Gruzewska-Roussel test (Gruzewska, S. and Roussel, G.): Chemistry. See: Van Nostrand Chem. Dict.

GRUZEWSKA, S. fl. 1936. French? chemist. Cited in: Chem. Abstr., vol. 30, p. 2216. Gruzewska-Roussel test.

GRYNFELTT, JOSEPH CASIMIR. 1840-1913. French surgeon. See: Biog. Lex. hervorr. Aerzte., 1880-1930. Grynfeltt's triangle.

Grynfeltt's triangle (Grynfeltt, Joseph Casimir): Medicine. See: Dorland; Stedman. Also known as: Lesshaft's triangle.

Gryszkiewicz-Trochimowski and McCombie method (Gryszkiewicz-Trochimowski, Eustachy and McCombie, Hamilton): Chemistry. See: Van Nostrand Chem. Dict.

GRYSZKIEWICZ-TROCHIMOWSKI, EUSTACHY. b. 1888. Polish chemist. See: Pogg., vols. 6, 7b. Gryszkiewicz-Trochimowski and McCombie method.

Gsell-Erdheim syndrome (Gsell, Otto and Erdheim, Jakob): Medicine. See: Jablonski.

GSELL, OTTO ROBERT. 1902- . Swiss internist. See: Brockhaus. Gsell-Erdheim syndrome.

GUALDI, AUGUSTO. fl. 1935. Italian physician. See: Ann. Univers. Roma, 1936-1937, p. 354f. Van der Hoeve-Waardenburg-Gualdi syndrome?

GUARESCHI, ICILIO. 1847-1918. Italian chemist. See: Pogg., vols. 3, 4, 5. Guareschi test for bromine, Guareschi test reaction for phenols.

Guareschi test for bromine (Guareschi, Icilio): Chemistry. See: Van Nostrand Chem. Dict.

Guareschi test reaction for phenols (Guareschi, Icilio): Chemistry. See: Van Nostrand Chem. Dict.

GUARINI, GUARINO. 1624-1683. Italian architect. See: Encic. Ital. Guarinite.

Guarinite (Guarini, Guarino): Earth Sciences. See: Thrush.

GUARNERI. fl. 16th-18th c. Italian family of violin-makers. See: Encyc. Brit., 1973. Guarnerius (or Guarneri) (violin).

Guarnerius (or Guarneri) (violin) (Guarneri): Music. See: Partridge; Webster's 3d.

Guarnieri bodies (Guarnieri, Giuseppe): Medicine. See: Dorland; Stedman; Webster's 3d.

GUARNIERI, GIUSEPPE. 1856-1918. Italian pathologist. See: Biog. Lex. hervorr. Aerzte, 1880-1930. Guarnieri bodies, Guarnieri's gelatin agar.

Guarnieri's gelatin agar (Guarnieri, Giuseppe): Medicine. See: Stedman.

GUASTALLA, LUDOVICA TORELLI, COUNTESS OF. d. ca. 1569. Italian founder of religious sisterhood. Cited in: Encic. Ital. under "Guastalline, Suore." Guastalline.

Guastalline (Guastalla, Ludovica Torelli, Countess of): Religion. See: Webster's 3d.

GUBLER, ADOLPHE MARIE. 1821-1879. French physician. See: World Who's Who Sci. Gubler-Robin typhus, Gubler's icterus, Gubler's line, Gubler's tumor (or sign), Millard-Gubler syndrome.

Gubler-Robin typhus (Gubler, Adolphe Marie and Robin, Albert): Medicine. See: Dorland.

Gubler's icterus (Gubler, Adolphe Marie): Medicine. See: Dorland; Stedman.

Gubler's line (Gubler, Adolphe Marie): Medicine. See: Dorland; Stedman.

Gubler's paralysis (hemiplegia or syndrome) (Gubler, Adolphe Marie). See: Millard-Gubler syndrome.

Gubler's tumor (or sign) (Gubler, Adolphe Marie): Medicine. See: Dorland; Jablonski; Stedman.

GUDDEN, BERNHARD FRIEDRICH ADOLF. 1892-1945. German physicist. See: World Who's Who Sci. Gudden-Pohl effect.

Gudden-Pohl effect (Gudden, Bernhard Friedrich Adolf and Pohl, Robert Wichard): Physics. See: Ballentyne; Hughes; Markus.

Gudden's atrophy (Von Guedden, Johann Bernhard Aloys): Medicine. See: Jablonski.

Gudden's commissure (Von Guedden, Johann Bernhard Aloys): Anatomy. See: Donath; Dorland; Stedman. Also known as: Meynert's commissure.

Gudden's ganglion (Von Guedden, Johann Bernhard Aloys): Anatomy. See: Dorland; Stedman.

Gudden's tract (Von Guedden, Johann Bernhard Aloys): Anatomy. See: Donath.

GUDERMANN, CHRISTOF. 1798-1852. German mathematician. See: Dict. Sci. Biog. Gudermannian.

Gudermannian (Gudermann, Christof): Mathematics. See: Ballentyne; James.

Guedden, Johann Bernhard Aloys von. See: Von Guedden, Johann Bernhard Aloys.

GUEDEL, ARTHUR ERNEST. 1883-1956. American anesthesiologist. See: Nat. Cycl. Amer. Biog., vol. 44, p. 88. Guedel classification.

Guedel classification (Guedel, Arthur Ernest): Medicine. See: Stedman under "general anesthesia."

Guelf. See: Welf.

Guelfi, Gioele. See: Filomusi-Guelfi, Giole.

Guelfs and Ghibellines (Welf and Waiblingen): History. See: Encyc. Brit., 1973.

Guelpa diet (Guelpa, Guglielmo): Medicine. See: Dorland.

GUELPA, GUGLIELMO. 1850-1930. Italian physician in Paris. See: Biog. Lex. hervorr. Aerzte, 1880-1930. Guelpa diet, Guelpa treatment.

Guelpa treatment (Guelpa, Guglielmo): Medicine. See: Dorland.

GUENEAU DE MUSSY, NOEL-FRANCOIS-ODON. 1813-1885. French physician. See: Biog. Lex. hervorr. Aerzte. Gueneau de Mussy's point.

Gueneau de Mussy's point (Gueneau de Mussy, Noel-Francois-Odon): Medicine. See: Dorland; Stedman.

GUENTHER, CARL OSKAR. 1854-1929. German physician. See: Biog. Lex. hervorr. Aerzte, 1880-1930. Guenther's stain.

GUENTHER, HANS. 1884-1956. German physician. See: Biog. Lex. hervorr. Aerzte, 1880-1930. Guenther's syndrome (1) (or disease), Guenther's syndrome (2), Guenther's test.

Guenther's stain (Guenther, Carl Oskar): Medicine. See: Stedman.

Guenther's syndrome (1) (or disease) (Guenther, Hans): Medicine. See: Jablonski; Stedman.

Guenther's syndrome (2) (Guenther, Hans): Medicine. See: Jablonski.

Guenther's test (Guenther, Hans): Medicine. See: Kelly.

GUENZ, JUSTUS. 1714-1789. German anatomist. See: Biog. Lex. hervorr. Aerzte. Guenz' ligament.

Guenz' ligament (Guenz, Justus): Medicine. See: Dorland; Stedman.

GUENZBERG, ALFRED. b. 1861. German physician. See: Biog. Lex. hervorr. Aerzte, 1880-1930. Guenzberg('s) reaction (reagent test or method), Guenzberg's phenomenon, Guenzberg's probe.

Guenzberg('s) reaction (reagent test or method) (Guenzberg, Alfred): Chemistry. See: Dorland; Hackh; Stedman; Van Nostrand Chem. Dict.

Guenzberg's phenomenon (Guenzberg, Alfred): Medicine. Cited in: Biog. Lex. hervorr. Aerzte, 1880-1930.

Guenzberg's probe (Guenzberg, Alfred): Medicine. Cited in: Biog. Lex. hervorr. Aerzte, 1880-1930.

GUERBET, MARCEL. 1861-1938. French chemist. See: Pogg., vols. 5, 6, 7b. Guerbet reaction.

Guerbet reaction (Guerbet, Marcel): Chemistry. See: Ballentyne; Van Nostrand Chem. Dict.

GUERICKE, OTTO VON. 1602-1686. German physicist. See: Dict. Sci. Biog. Von Guericke pump.

GUERIN, ALPHONSE FRANCOIS MARIE. 1816-1895. French surgeon. See: World Who's Who Sci. Guerin's fold (or valve), Guerin's fracture, Guerin's glands, Guerin's sinus.

GUERIN, CAMILLE. 1872-1961. French bacteriologist. See: Grand Larousse Encyc. Calmette-Guerin bacillus, Calmette-Guerin vaccine.

GUERIN, E. fl. 1930. French pharmaceutical chemist. Cited in: Chem. Abstr., vol. 24, p. 4235. Guerin solution for selenium.

GUERIN, GABRIEL (In full: FELIX GABRIEL). 1852-1917. French pharmaceutical chemist. See: Bull. Sciences Pharmacol., vol. 24 (1917), pp. 244-247. Guerin test reactions for guaiacol?, Guerin test for zinc.

GUERIN, HENRI PIERRE PAUL. 1906- . French chemist. See: Who's Who France, 1975-1976. Guerinite.

GUERIN, JULES RENE. 1811-1886. French surgeon. See: World Who's Who Sci. Guerin-Stern syndrome.

GUERIN, MAURICE. fl. 1934. French physician. Cited in: Chem. Abstr. Guerin's tumor (or epithelioma).

GUERIN, P. fl. 1934. French physician. Cited in: Chem. Abstr. Guerin's tumor (or epithelioma).

GUERIN, PIERRE. fl. 1634. French sect founder. Cited in: New Cath. Encyc. under "Illuminism," vol. 7, p. 368a. Guerinists (or Guerinets).

Guerin solution for selenium (Guerin, E.): Chemistry. See: Van Nostrand Chem. Dict.

Guerin-Stern syndrome (Guerin, Jules Rene and Stern, Walter G.): Medicine. See: Jablonski. Also known as: Otto's syndrome, Rocher-Sheldon syndrome.

Guerin test for zinc (Guerin, Gabriel): Chemistry. See: Van Nostrand Chem. Dict.

Guerin test reactions for guaiacol (Guerin, Gabriel?): Chemistry. See: Van Nostrand Chem. Dict.

Guerinists (or Guerinets) (Guerin, Pierre): Religion. See: Brewer.

Guerinite (Guerin, Henri Pierre Paul): Earth Sciences. See: Thrush.

Guerin's fold (or valve) (Guerin, Alphonse Francois Marie): Anatomy. See: Donath; Dorland; Stedman.

Guerin's fracture (Guerin, Alphonse Francois Marie): Medicine. See: Dorland; Jablonski; Stedman. Also known as: Le Fort I fracture.

Guerin's glands (Guerin, Alphonse Francois Marie): Anatomy. See: Dorland; Henderson; Stedman. Also known as: Skene's gland.

Guerin's sinus (Guerin, Alphonse Francois Marie): Medicine. See: Dorland; Stedman.

Guerin's tumor (or epithelioma) (Guerin, M. and Guerin, P.): Medicine. See: Jablonski.

GUERREIRO, CEZAR. fl. 1913. Scientist. Cited in: Chem. Abstr. Machado-Guerreiro test.

GUERTIN, ANDRE. fl. 1881. French physician. Cited in: Mansell. Guertin's disease.

Guertin's disease (Guertin, Andre). See: Dubini's disease.

GUESDE, JULES (Orig. name: MATHIEU BASILE). 1845-1922. French political leader. See: Encyc. Brit., 1973. Guesdism.

Guesdism (Guesde, Jules): Politics. See: Webster's 3d.

Guess, George. See: Sequoyah.

GUETTARD, JEAN-ETIENNE. 1715-1786. French naturalist. See: Dict. Sci. Biog. Guettarda.

Guettarda (Guettard, Jean-Etienne): Botany. See: Charnock; Webster's 3d.

GUEVARA, ANTONIO DE. 1481?-1545. Spanish writer and moralist. See: Encyc. Brit., 1973. Guevarism (or Guevarist).

GUEVARA, ERNESTO "CHE." 1928-1967. Argentinian-born Latin American revolutionary leader. See: New Encyc. Brit., 1974. Guevarist.

Guevarism (or Guevarist) (Guevara, Antonio de): Generic Word (euphuistic writer). See: Hendrickson; Partridge.

Guevarist (Guevara, Ernesto "Che"): Politics. See: Barnhart (New Eng.).

GUFFEY, JOSEPH F. 1870-1959. American legislator. See: Biog. Direct. Amer. Congress. Guffey-Snyder coal Act (bituminous coal stabilization or conservation Act), Guffy-Vinson Act (or bituminous coal Act).

Guffey-Snyder coal Act (bituminous coal stabilization or conservation Act) Guffey, Joseph F. and Snyder, John Buell): Politics. See: Morris; Smith.

Guffy-Vinson Act (or bituminous coal Act) (Guffey, Joseph F. and Vinson, Frederick Moore): Politics. See: Morris; Smith.

GUGGENHEIM, DANIEL. 1856-1930. American industrialist. See: Encyc. Brit., 1973. Daniel and Florence Guggenheim Foundation, Daniel Guggenheim Foundation for the Promotion of Aeronautics, Guggenheim (word game)?

GUGGENHEIM, FLORENCE SCHLOSS. 1863-1944. American philanthropist. See: Nat. Cycl. Amer. Biog., vol. 33, p. 198. Daniel and Florence Guggenheim Foundation.

Guggenheim Museum (or Solomon R. Guggenheim Museum) (Guggenheim, Solomon R.): Fine Arts. See: New Encyc. Brit., 1974, Microp.

GUGGENHEIM, SIMON. 1867-1941. American businessman. See: Nat. Cycl. Amer. Biog., vol. C, p. 50. John Simon Guggenheim Memorial Foundation (or Guggenheim).

GUGGENHEIM, SOLOMON R. 1861-1949. American industrialist. See: Nat. Cycl. Amer. Biog., vol. 39, p. 74. Guggenheim Museum (or Solomon R. Guggenheim Museum), Solomon R. Guggenheim Foundation.

Guggenheim (word game) (Guggenheim, Daniel?): Recreation and Sports. See: Hendrickson.

GUGGISBERG, SIR FREDERICK GORDON. 1869-1930. English governor of the Gold Coast (Ghana). See: Who Was Who, 1929-1940. Guggisberg plan.

Guggisberg plan (Guggisberg, Sir Frederick Gordon): History. See: Morris and Irwin.

Guglialmelli-Delmon test for carbohydrates (Guglialmelli, Luis and Delmon, Angeles): Chemistry. See: Van Nostrand Chem. Dict.

GUGLIALMELLI, LUIS. 1884-1937. Argentinian chemist. See: Pogg., vols. 6, 7b. Guglialmelli-Delmon test for carbohydrates, Guglialmelli reagents for phenols.

Guglialmelli reagents for phenols (Guglialmelli, Luis): Chemistry. See: Van Nostrand Chem. Dict.

Guglielmo, G. di. See: Di Guglielmo, G.

Guibal fan (Guibal, Jules): Engineering and Industry. See: Auger; Thrush.

GUIBAL, JULES. 1813-1888. French mining engineer. See: World Who's Who Sci. Guibal fan.

GUICHENOT, ANTONY. fl. before 1860. French? scientist? (Biography source unavailable.) Guichenotia.

Guichenotia (Guichenot, Antony): Botany. See: Charnock.

Guidi, Guido. See: Vidius.

Guidi's canal (Vidius). See: Vidian canal.

GUIDO OF AREZZO (or ARETINO). 995?-?1050. Benedictine monk and musical reformer. See: Encyc. Brit., 1973. Guidonian, Guidonian hand, Guidonian syllable (or scale).

Guido Ubaldo, Maria. See: Dal Monte, Guidubaldo.

Guidobaldo's first method (Dal Monte, Guidubaldo): Fine Arts. See: Osborne under "Perspective."

Guidonian (Guido of Arezzo): Music. See: Webster's 3d.

Guidonian hand (Guido of Arezzo): Music. See: Apel; Webster's 3d.

Guidonian syllable (or scale) (Guido of Arezzo): Music. See: Hendrickson; Webster's 3d. Also known as: Aretinian syllables.

GUIGNARD, LEON (In full: JEAN-LOUIS-LEON). 1852-1928. French botanist. See: Dict. Sci. Biog. Guignard test for hydrocyanic acid, Guignardia.

Guignard test for hydrocyanic acid (Guignard, Leon): Chemistry. See: Van Nostrand Chem. Dict.

Guignardia (Guignard, Leon): Botany. See: Webster's 3d.

GUIGNET, CHARLES ERNEST. b. 1829. French chemist. See: Pogg., vols. 3, 4. Guignet's green.

Guignet's green (Guignet, Charles Ernest): Chemistry. See: Hackh; Webster's 3d. Also known as: Pannetier's green.

GUIGNOL. Most prominent puppet character in France. See: New Encyc. Brit., 1974, Microp. Grand Guignol, Guignol (puppet theater).

Guignol (puppet theater) (Guignol): Theater. See: New Encyc. Brit., 1974, Microp. under "Guignol."

Guilandina (Guilandini, Melchior): Botany. See: Charnock; Webster's 3d.

GUILANDINI, MELCHIOR (MELCHIOR WIELAND). d. 1589. Prussian botanist in Italy. See: Biog. Lex. hervorr. Aerzte. Guilandina.

GUILBERT, GABRIEL. fl. 1889-1921. French meteorologist. See: Pogg., vol. 5. Guilbert-Grossmann rules.

GUILD, FRANK NELSON. 1870-1939. American mineralogist. See: Amer. Min., vol. 25 (1940), pp. 181-183. Guildite.

GUILD, JOHN. b. 1889. English photometrist. See: Pogg., vols. 6, 7b. Guild type colorimeter.

Guild type colorimeter (Guild, John): Physics. See: Van Nostrand Sci. Encyc. under "Colorimeter."

Guildite (Guild, Frank Nelson): Earth Sciences. See: Thrush; Webster's 3d.

GUILFORD, JOY PAUL. 1897- . American psychologist. See: World Who's Who Sci. Guilford-Martin personnel inventory, Guilford-Zimmerman temperament survey.

Guilford-Martin personnel inventory (Guilford, Joy Paul and Martin, H. G.): Psychology. See: English.

GUILFORD, SIMEON HAYDEN. 1841-1919. American dentist. See: Who Was Who Amer., 1897-1942. Guilford's syndrome.

Guilford–Zimmerman temperament survey (Guilford, Joy Paul and Zimmerman, Wayne S.): Psychology. See: Chaplin; English; Wolman.

Guilford's syndrome (Guilford, Simeon Hayden): Medicine. See: Jablonski.

Guilielma (Guilielma Carolina): Botany. See: Taylor, N.

GUILIELMA CAROLINA. No dates. Queen of Bavaria. (Biography source unavailable.) Guilielma.

Guillain–Barre reflex (Guillain, Georges and Barre, Jean Alexandre): Medicine. See: Dorland; Stedman. Also known as: Reimer's reflex, Weingrow's heel reflex.

Guillain–Barre–Strohl syndrome (Guillain, Georges; Barre, Jean Alexandre; and Strohl, Andre). See: Guillain–Barre syndrome.

Guillain–Barre syndrome (Guillain, Georges and Barre, Jean Alexandre): Medicine. See: Dorland; Hinsie; Jablonski; Stedman; Webster's 3d. Also known as: Guillain–Barre–Strohl syndrome, Landry–Guillain–Barre syndrome, Landry–Kussmaul syndrome, Landry's paralysis (or disease).

GUILLAIN, GEORGES. 1876-1951. French physician. See: World Who's Who Sci. Garcin–Guillain syndrome, Guillain–Barre reflex, Guillain–Barre syndrome.

GUILLAUME, EMILE. fl. 1910. French chemical engineer. Cited in: Chem. Abstr., Decenn. Index, 1907-1916. Guillaume process.

Guillaume process (Guillaume, Emile): Chemistry. See: Van Nostrand Chem. Dict.

Guillemin effect (Guillemin, Ernest Adolph?): Physics. See: Ballentyne; Hughes; Thewlis; Van Nostrand Sci. Encyc. under "Magnetostriction."

GUILLEMIN, ERNEST ADOLPH. 1898- . American engineer. See: World Who's Who Sci. Guillemin effect?, Guillemin line.

Guillemin line (Guillemin, Ernest Adolph): Electronics. See: Hughes; Markus.

GUILLERY, R. fl. 1912-1939. French metallurgist. Cited in: Chem. Abstr. Guillery testing machine.

Guillery testing machine (Guillery, R.): Engineering and Industry. See; Auger.

GUILLOTIN, JOSEPH IGNACE. 1738-1814. French physician. See: Nouv. Biog. Univ. Guillotine.

Guillotine (Guillotin, Joseph Ignace): Generic Word. See: Barnhart (Eng. Lit.); Brewer; Charnock; Hendrickson; Phyfe; Webster's 3d. Also known as: Louison (or Louisette).

GUIMARAES, DJALMA. fl. 20th c. Brazilian mineralogist. Cited in: Hintze, 2d suppl., p. 95. Djalmaite.

GUIMET, JEAN BAPTISTE. 1795-1871. French chemist. See: Encyc. Brit., 1911. Guimet's blue.

Guimet's blue (Guimet, Jean Baptiste): Chemistry. See: Webster's 3d.

GUINARD, AIME. 1856-1911. French surgeon. See: Biog. Lex. hervorr. Aerzte, 1880-1930. Guinard's treatment (or method).

Guinard's treatment (or method) (Guinard, Aime): Medicine. See: Dorland.

GUINIER, ANDRE. 1911- . French physicist. See: Who's Who Sci. Europe, 1972. Guinier–Preston zones.

Guinier–Preston zones (Guinier, Andre and Preston, George Dawson): Physics. See: Thewlis; Van Nostrand Sci. Encyc.

Guinness (Guinness family): Generic Word (stout). See: Hendrickson; Partridge.

GUINNESS FAMILY. fl. from 18th c. Irish brewers. See: Webster's Biog. Dict. according to Guinness, Guinness.

Guinness, Walter Edward. See: Moyne, Walter Edward Guinness, 1st Baron.

GUINON, GEORGES. 1859-1932. French physician. See: Presse Med., vol. 40 (April 6, 1932), p. 541. Guinon's disease.

Guinon's disease (Guinon, Georges). See: Gilles de la Tourette's syndrome.

Guiteras' disease (Guiteras, Juan): Medicine. See: Dorland.

GUITERAS, JUAN. 1852-1925. Cuban physician. See: World Who's Who Sci. Guiteras' disease.

GUITERMAN, FRANKLIN. 1856-1915. American metallurgist. See: New York Times, May 10, 1915, p. 15, col. 4. Guitermanite.

Guitermanite (Guiterman, Franklin): Earth Sciences. See: Webster's 3d.

GUITTONE D'AREZZO. d. 1294. Italian poet. See: Encyc. Brit., 1973. Guittonian.

Guittonian (Guittone d'Arezzo): Literature. See: Webster's 3d.

GULATHING. Probably fl. before 930. Norwegian ruler. (Biography source unavailable.) Gulathing's law.

Gulathing's law (Gulathing): History. See: Harbottle; Norsk Allkunnebok.

Guldberg and Waage's law (or law of Guldberg and Waage) (Guldberg, Cato Maximilian and Waage, Peter): Chemistry. See: Ballentyne; Hackh; Internat. Dict. Ap. Math.; Van Nostrand Chem. Dict.

GULDBERG, CATO MAXIMILIAN. 1836-1902. Norwegian chemist and mathematician. See: Dict. Sci. Biog. Guldberg and Waage's law (or law of Guldberg and Waage), Guldberg–Guye rule, Guldberg rule.

Guldberg–Guye rule (Guldberg, Cato Maximilian and Guye, Philippe–Auguste): Chemistry. See: Hackh.

Guldberg rule (Guldberg, Cato Maximilian): Chemistry. See: Hackh.

Guldner engine (Guldner, Hugo): Engineering and Industry. See: Auger.

GULDNER, HUGO. 1866-1926. German engineer. See: World Who's Who Sci. Guldner engine.

Gull–Sutton disease (Gull, Sir William Whithey and Sutton, Henry): Medicine. See: Dorland; Jablonski; Stedman.

GULL, SIR WILLIAM WITHEY. 1816-1890. English physician. See: World Who's Who Sci. Addison–Gull disease, Gull–Sutton disease, Gull's disease.

Gull's disease (Gull, Sir William Withey): Medicine. See: Dorland; Jablonski; Stedman.

GULLSTRAND, ALLVAR. 1862-1930. Swedish ophthalmologist. See: World Who's Who Sci. Gullstrand's slit lamp.

Gullstrand's slit lamp (Gullstrand, Allvar): Medicine. See: Dorland.

GUMPLOWICZ, LUDWIG VON. 1838-1909. Austrian economist and sociologist. See: Internat. Encyc. Soc. Sci. Gumplowicz's law of wants.

Gumplowicz's law of wants (Gumplowicz, Ludwig von): Sociology. See: Zadrozny.

GUMPRECHT, FERDINAND. b. 1864. German physician. See: Biog. Lex. hervorr. Aerzte, 1880-1930. Gumprecht's shadows (or shadow nuclei).

Gumprecht's shadows (or shadow nuclei) (Gumprecht, Ferdinand): Medicine. See: Dorland; Stedman. Also known as: Klein–Gumprecht shadow nuclei.

Gundelia (Gundelsheimer, Andrew): Botany. See: Charnock.

GUNDELSHEIMER, ANDREW. No dates. German botanist. (Biography source unavailable.) Gundelia.

Gunn effect (Gunn, John Battiscombe): Physics. See: Ballentyne; Barnhart (New Eng.); Hughes; Markus; Thewlis; Van Nostrand Sci. Encyc.

GUNN, JOHN BATTISCOMBE. 1928- . English physicist in Canada and America. See: World Who's Who Sci. Gunn effect.

GUNN, ROBERT MARCUS. 1850-1909. English ophthalmologist. See: Who Was Who, 1897-1916. Gunn's dots, Gunn's sign, Gunn's syndrome (or phenomenon).

Gunnera (Gunnerus, Johan Ernst): Botany. See: Charnock; Partridge; Webster's 3d.

GUNNERUS, JOHAN ERNST. 1718-1773. Norwegian botanist. See: Norsk Biog. Lek. Gunnera.

GUNNING, HENRY CECIL. 1901- . Candian geologist. See: Canadian Who's Who, 1973-1975. Gunningite.

GUNNING, JAN WILLEM. 1827-1901. Dutch chemist. See: Pogg., vol. 3. Gunning('s) reaction (reagent and test).

Gunning('s) reaction (reagent and test) (Gunning, Jan Willem): Chemistry. See: Dorland; Hackh; Stedman.

Gunning splint (Gunning, Thomas Brian): Medicine. See: Dorland; Stedman.

GUNNING, THOMAS BRIAN. 1813-1889. American dentist. Cited in: Kelly. Gunning splint.

Gunningite (Gunning, Henry Cecil): Earth Sciences. See: Thrush.

Gunn's dots (Gunn, Robert Marcus): Medicine. See: Dorland; Stedman. Also known as: Marcus Gunn's dots.

Gunn's sign (Gunn, Robert Marcus): Medicine. See: Dorland; Hinsie; Stedman. Also known as: Marcus Gunn's sign.

Gunn's syndrome (or phenomenon) (Gunn, Robert Marcus): Medicine. See: Dorland; Jablonski; Stedman. Also known as: Marcus Gunn's phenomenon (or syndrome).

GUNTER, EDMUND. 1581-1626. English mathematician. See: Dict. Sci. Biog. according to Gunter, gauging by Gunter, Gunter rig (Gunter (2) or sliding Gunter), Gunter's chain, Gunter's gradient, Gunter's line, Gunter's quadrant, Gunter's scale (or Gunter (1)).

Gunter rig (Gunter (2) or sliding Gunter) (Gunter, Edmund): Navigation. See: Webster's 3d.

Gunter's chain (Gunter, Edmund): Earth Sciences. See: Brewer; Dresner; Hendrickson; Thrush; Webster's 3d.

Gunter's gradient (Gunter, Edmund): Engineering and Industry. Cited in: Partridge.

Gunter's line (Gunter, Edmund): Mathematics. See: Encyc. Brit., 1973 vol. 10, p. 1044b.

Gunter's quadrant (Gunter, Edmund): Navigation. See: Encyc. Brit., 1973 under "Gunter, Edmund"; Hendrickson.

Gunter's scale (or Gunter (1)) (Gunter, Edmund): Engineering and Industry. See: Brewer; Encyc. Brit., 1973 under "Gunter, Edmund," vol. 10, p. 1044b; Partridge.

Guppy (Guppy, Robert John Lechmere): Zoology. See: Encyc. Brit., 1973; Hendrickson.

GUPPY, ROBERT JOHN LECHMERE. 1836-1916. English scientist. See: Bull. U.S. Geol. Survey, vol. 746 (1923), pp. 432-434. Guppy.

GUPTA. fl. 320-480 A.D. Dynasty of Kings in Northern India. See: Webster's Biog. Dict. Gupta art, Gupta dynasty (or period).

Gupta art (Gupta): Fine Arts. See: New Encyc. Brit., 1974, Microp.; Osborne under "Indian Art."

Gupta dynasty (or period) (Gupta): History. See: New Encyc. Brit., 1974, Microp.

GUPTA, JAGANNATH. fl. 1935. Indian chemist. Cited in: Chem. Abstr., vol. 29, p. 7214. Ray-Gupta reagent for metals.

Gurevich effect (Gurevich, V. L.): Physics. See: Ballentyne.

GUREVICH, M. I. fl. 1940. Russian aeronautical designer. Cited in: World Who's Who Sci. under "Mikoyan, Artyom Ivanovich." MIG (fighter plane).

GUREVICH, V. L. fl. 1962. Russian electrical engineer. Cited in: Sci. Abstr. (Elec. Engin.), vol. 65 B, p. 1477. Gurevich effect.

GURLAND, JOHN. 1917- . Candian-born American statistician. See: World Who's Who Sci. Gurland's generalisation of Neyman's distribution.

Gurland's generalisation of Neyman's distribution (Gurland, John): Statistics. See: Kendall.

Gurney boiler (Gurney, Sir Goldsworthy): Engineering and Industry. See: Auger.

Gurney burner (Gurney, Sir Goldsworthy): Engineering and Industry. Cited in: Webster's Biog. Dict.

GURNEY, SIR GOLDSWORTHY. 1793-1875. English inventor. See: World Who's Who Sci. Gurney boiler, Gurney burner, Gurney light, Gurney stove.

GURNEY, JOSEPH JOHN. 1788-1847. English Quaker minister and philanthropist. See: Dict. Nat. Biog. Gurneyite.

Gurney light (Gurney, Sir Goldsworthy): Engineering and Industry. See: Brewer.

Gurney-Mott theory (Gurney, Ronald Wilfried and Mott, Nevill Francis): Photography. See: Focal Encyc. Photog.

GURNEY, RONALD WILFRIED. 1899-1953. English physicist. See: Pogg., vols. 6, 7b. Gamow-Condon-Gurney theory of alpha decay, Gurney-Mott theory.

Gurney stove (Gurney, Sir Goldsworthy): Engineering and Industry. Cited in: World Who's Who Sci.

Gurneyite (Gurney, Joseph John): Earth Sciences. See: Webster's 3d.

GURVICH, ALEKSANDR GAVRILOVICH. 1874- . Russian biologist. See: Dict. Sci. Biog. Gurwitsch ray.

Gurwitsch ray (Gurvich, Aleksandr Gavrilovich): Biology. See: Webster's 3d.

GUSSENBAUER, CARL IGNATZ. 1842-1903. Austrian surgeon. See: World Who's Who Sci. Gussenbauer's clamp, Gussenbauer's operation, Gussenbauer's suture.

Gussenbauer's clamp (Gussenbauer, Carl Ignatz): Medicine. See: Dorland.

Gussenbauer's operation (Gussenbauer, Carl Ignatz): Medicine. See: Dorland.

Gussenbauer's suture (Gussenbauer, Carl Ignatz): Medicine. See: Dorland; Stedman

Gustav-Adolf-Verein (Gustavus II, Adolphus): Religion. See: Canney; Mathews, S.

Gustavia (Gustavus III): Botany. See: Charnock.

Gustavian age (Gustavus III and Gustavus IV): History. See: Preminger under "Swedish poetry."

GUSTAVSON, GABRIEL. 1842-1908. Russian chemist. See: Pogg., vols. 4, 5. Gustavson reaction.

Gustavson reaction (Gustavson, Gabriel): Chemistry. See: Van Nostrand Chem. Dict.

GUSTAVSON, REUBEN GILBERT. b. 1892. American chemist. See: Amer. Men Sci., 9th ed. Hearon-Gustavson reagent.

GUSTAVUS II, ADOLPHUS. 1594-1632. King of Sweden. See: Encyc. Brit., 1973. Gustav-Adolf-Verein.

GUSTAVUS III. 1746-1792. King of Sweden. See: Encyc. Brit., 1973. Gustavia, Gustavian age.

GUSTAVUS IV (GUSTAVUS ADOLPHUS). 1778-1837. King of Sweden. See: Encyc. Brit., 1973. Gustavian age.

Gusto scraper box (Derivation undetermined): Engineering and Industry. See: Thrush.

GUTENBERG, BENO. 1889-1960. German-born American geologist. See: Dict. Sci. Biog. G wave, Gutenberg discontinuity, Gutenberg-Richter scale.

Gutenberg Bible (Gutenberg, Johann): Printing. See: Asimov; Brewer; Hendrickson; Osborne under "Typography." Also known as: Mazarin Bible.

Gutenberg discontinuity (Gutenberg, Beno): Earth Sciences. See: Asimov; Monkhouse.

GUTENBERG, JOHANN. ca. 1398-1468. German inventor. See: Encyc. Brit., 1973. Gutenberg Bible.

Gutenberg-Richter scale (Gutenberg, Beno and Richter, Charles Francis): Earth Sciences. See: Thewlis.

GUTERMAN, HENRY SAMUEL. 1915- . American physician. See: Amer. Men Sci., 8th ed. Guterman's test.

Guterman's test (Guterman, Henry Samuel): Medicine. See: Dorland.

GUTERMUTH, MAX FRIEDRICH. b. 1858. German engineer. Cited in: Mansell. Gutermuth valve?

Gutermuth valve (Gutermuth, Max Friedrich?): Engineering and Industry. See: Auger.

GUTHRIE, CLYDE GRAEME. 1880-1931. American physician. Cited in: Mansell. Guthrie's formula.

GUTHRIE, EDWIN RAY. 1886- . American psychologist. See: Internat. Encyc. Soc. Sci. Guthrie's contiguous conditioning.

GUTHRIE, GEORGE JAMES. 1785-1856. English surgeon. See: World Who's Who Sci. Guthrie's muscle.

GUTHRIE, H. fl. 1877. Engineer. (Biography source unavailable.) Guthrie kiln.

Guthrie kiln (Guthrie, H.): Engineering and Industry. See: Thrush.

GUTHRIE, ROBERT. 1916- . American microbiologist. See: Amer. Men Sci., 10th ed. Guthrie test (or inhibition assay test).

Guthrie test (or inhibition assay test) (Guthrie, Robert): Medicine. See: Blakiston's Gould; Stedman.

Guthrie's contiguous conditioning (Guthrie, Edwin Ray): Psychology. See: Chaplin.

Guthrie's formula (Guthrie, Clyde Graeme): Medicine. See: Dorland.

Guthrie's muscle (Guthrie, George James): Anatomy. See: Donath; Dorland; Stedman.

GUTIERREZ. Noble Spanish family. No dates. (Biography source unavailable.) Gutierrezia.

GUTIERREZ, ROBERT. 1895- . American urologist. See: Direct. Med. Specialists, 1965-1966. Gutierrez's syndrome.

Gutierrezia (Gutierrez): Botany. See: Webster's 3d.

Gutierrez's syndrome (Gutierrez, Robert): Medicine. See: Jablonski.

GUTKNECHT, HERMANN. fl. 1879. German chemist. Cited in: Krauch and Kunz. Gutknecht pyrazine synthesis.

Gutknecht pyrazine synthesis (Gutknecht, Hermann): Chemistry. See: Van Nostrand Chem. Dict.

GUTMANN, AUGUST. b. 1868. German chemist. See: Pogg., vols. 5, 6. Gutmann reagent for halogens, Gutmann reagent for mercury, Gutmann test for thiosulfate.

GUTMANN, C. b. 1872. German physician. (Biography source unavailable.) Michaelis-Gutmann bodies (or calcospherules).

Gutmann reagent for halogens (Gutmann, August): Chemistry. See: Van Nostrand Chem. Dict.

Gutmann reagent for mercury (Gutmann, August): Chemistry. See: Van Nostrand Chem. Dict.

Gutmann test for thiosulfate (Gutmann, August): Chemistry. See: Van Nostrand Chem. Dict.

GUTSCHOVEN, GERARD VAN. 1615-1668. Belgian scientist. Cited in: Mansell. Gutschoven's curve.

Gutschoven's curve (Gutschoven, Gerard van): Mathematics. See: New Encyc. Brit., 1974, Microp.

GUTTMAN, LOUIS. 1916- . Israeli psychologist. See: Biog. Direct. Amer. Psych. Assoc., 1975. Guttman scale (scaling, scalogram technique or analysis).

Guttman scale (scaling, scalogram technique or analysis) (Guttman, Louis): Psychology. See: Chaplin; English; Hoult; Wolman.

GUTTMANN, E. fl. 1931. German physician. (Biography source unavailable.) Bodechtel-Guttmann encephalitis.

GUTZEIT, GREGOIRE. fl. 1929-1938. Swiss chemist. See: Doc. p. servir a l'histoire de l'Univ. de Geneve, vol. 8 (1938), pp. 413-415. Gutzeit-Monnier-Bachoulkova-Brun reagent for magnesium, Gutzeit-Monnier reagent for vanadium and iron, Gutzeit-Wiebel spot test for antimony.

GUTZEIT, HEINRICH WILHELM THEODOR. 1845-1888. German chemist. See: Chem. Ztg., vol. 12 (1888), p. 1553. Gutzeit('s) test (or arsenic test).

GUTZEIT, KURT (In full: ROBERT JULIUS KURT). 1893-1957. German internist. See: Neue Deut. Biog. Gutzeit's food probe.

Gutzeit-Monnier-Bachoulkova-Brun reagent for magnesium (Gutzeit, Gregoire; Monnier, Robert; and Bachoulkova-Brun, R.): Chemistry. See: Van Nostrand Chem. Dict.

Gutzeit-Monnier reagent for vanadium and iron (Gutzeit, Gregoire and Monnier, Robert): Chemistry. See: Van Nostrand Chem. Dict.

Gutzeit('s) test (or arsenic test) (Gutzeit, Heinrich Wilhelm Theodor): Chemistry. See: Dorland; Hackh; Stedman; Van Nostrand Chem. Dict.; Webster's 3d.

Gutzeit-Wiebel spot test for antimony (Gutzeit, Gregoire and Weibel, Raymond): Chemistry. See: Van Nostrand Chem. Dict.

Gutzeit's food probe (Gutzeit, Kurt): Medicine. See: Brockhaus.

Gutzkow's process (Derivation undetermined): Engineering and Industry. See: Thrush.

Guy (Fawkes, Guy): Generic Word (dowdy figure). See: Brewer; Funk; Hendrickson.

GUY, E. F. fl. 1925. American physiologist. Cited in: Chem. Abstr., vol. 19, p. 2234. Leake-Guy fluid.

Guy Fawkes' Day (Fawkes, Guy): Generic Word. See: Barnhart (Eng. Lit.); Wagner (Names); Webster's 3d.

Guy, Saint. See: Vitus, Saint.

Guy test reaction (Guy, William Augustus): Chemistry. See: Van Nostrand Chem. Dict.

GUY, WILLIAM AUGUSTUS. 1810-1885. English physician. See: Dict. Nat. Biog. Guy test reaction.

GUYARD, ANTHONY (Pseud.: HUGO TAMM). fl. 1875. French mineralogist. Cited in: Royal Soc. Cat. Sci. Pap., 1874-1883. Tamm test reaction?

GUYE, PHILIPPE-AUGUSTE. 1862-1922. Swiss chemist. See: World Who's Who Sci. Guldberg-Guye rule.

GUYON, JEAN CASIMIR FELIX. 1831-1920. French surgeon. See: World Who's Who Sci. Guyon's amputation, Guyon's isthmus, Guyon's method; Guyon's sign (1), Guyon's sign (2).

Guyon's amputation (Guyon, Jean Casimir Felix): Medicine. See: Dorland; Stedman.

Guyon's isthmus (Guyon, Jean Casimir Felix): Medicine. See: Stedman.

Guyon's method (Guyon, Jean Casimir Felix): Medicine. See: Stedman.

Guyon's sign (1) (Guyon, Jean Casimir Felix): Medicine. See: Dorland; Stedman.

Guyon's sign (2) (Guyon, Jean Casimir Felix): Medicine. See: Dorland; Stedman.

GUYOT. fl. 1770. French photographer. (Biography source unavailable.) Guyot's table camera.

GUYOT, ALFRED (In full: JOSEPH CHARLES ALFRED). b. 1870. French chemist. See: Pogg., vols. 5, 6. Guyot reagent for ammonia?, Guyot reagent for epinephrine?, Guyot test reaction for formic acid?

GUYOT, ARNOLD HENRY. 1807-1884. Swiss-born American geologist. See: Dict. Sci. Biog. Guyot (submarine mountain).

GUYOT, O. fl. 1925. German chemist. (Biography source unavailable.) Vanino-Guyot reagent.

Guyot reagent for ammonia (Guyot, Alfred?): Chemistry. See: Van Nostrand Chem. Dict.

Guyot reagent for epinephrine (Guyot, Alfred?): Chemistry. See: Van Nostrand Chem. Dict.

Guyot (submarine mountain) (Guyot, Arnold Henry): Earth Sciences. See: Carter; Monkhouse; Webster's 3d.

Guyot test reaction for formic acid (Guyot, Alfred?): Chemistry. See: Van Nostrand Chem. Dict.

Guyot's table camera (Guyot): Photography. See: Focal Encyc. Photog. under "Camera Obscura."

Guy's pill (Derivation undetermined): Medicine. See: Stedman. Also known as: Baillie's pill.

GUZMAN, A. fl. 1800? Spanish naturalist. (Biography source unavailable.) Guzmannia.

GUZMAN, J. fl. 1930. Spanish chemist. Cited in: Chem. Abstr. Arrhenius-Guzman equation?

Guzmannia (Guzman, A.): Botany. See: Charnock; Taylor, N.; Webster's 3d.

GWATHMEY, JAMES TAYLOE. 1863-1944. American surgeon. See: Who Was Who Amer., 1943-1950. Gwathmey's oil-ether anesthesia.

Gwathmey's oil-ether anesthesia (Gwathmey, James Tayloe): Medicine. See: Dorland.

H

H & D (or Hurter and Driffield) curve (Hurter, Ferdinand and Driffield, V. C.): Photography. See: Focal Encyc. Film; Markus; Van Nostrand Sci. Encyc.

H & D (or Hurter and Driffield) speed (and speed system) (Hurter, Ferdinand and Driffield, V. C.): Photography. See: Focal Encyc. Photog.; Van Nostrand Sci. Encyc. under "Sensitivity Determination of Photographic Material"; Webster's 3d.

H disease (Hartnup, Edward). See: Hartnup('s) disease (or syndrome).

H factor of Lewis (Lewis, Sir Thomas): Medicine. See: Stedman.

H line (band or disk) (Hensen, Viktor). See: Hensen's line (band or disk).

HLSP method (Heitler, Walter Heinrich; London, Fritz; Slater, John Clarke; and Pauling, Linus). See: Heitler-London-Slater-Pauling method.

H-R diagram (Hertzsprung, Ejnar and Russell, Henry Norris). See: Hertzsprung-Russell diagram.

H-theorem of Boltzmann and Lorentz (Boltzmann, Ludwig Eduard and Lorentz, Hendrik Antoon): Physics. See: Thewlis.

Haab-Dimmer syndrome (Haab, Otto and Dimmer, Friedrich). See: Biber-Haab-Dimmer degeneration.

HAAB, OTTO. 1850-1931. Swiss ophthalmologist. See: World Who's Who Sci. Biber-Haab-Dimmer degeneration, Haab's magnet, Haab's reflex (or pupil(lary) reflex).

Haab's magnet (Haab, Otto): Medicine. See: Dorland; Stedman.

Haab's reflex (or pupil(lary) reflex) (Haab, Otto): Physiology. See: Chaplin; Dorland; Stedman; Wolman.

HAAG, RUDOLF. 1922-   . German physicist. See: World Who's Who Sci. Haag's theorem.

Haag's theorem (Haag, Rudolf): Physics. See: Internat. Dict. Ap. Math.

HAAKH, HERMANN. fl. 1910. German chemist. Cited in: Chem. Abstr., vol. 4, p. 593. Haakh test reaction.

Haakh test reaction (Haakh, Hermann): Chemistry. See: Van Nostrand Chem. Dict.

Haanel depth rule (Haanel, Eugene Emil Felix Richard): Engineering and Industry. See: Thrush.

HAANEL, EUGENE EMIL FELIX RICHARD. 1841-1927. German-born engineer in Canada and U.S. See: Pogg., vol. 4. Haanel depth rule.

HAAR, ALFRED. 1885-1933. Hungarian mathematician. See: Dict. Sci. Biog. Haar measure.

Haar measure (Haar, Alfred): Mathematics. See: James.

HAARMANN, AUGUST (In full: HERMANN AUGUST). 1840-1913. German metallurgist. See: World Who's Who Sci. Haarmann clamp, Haarmann twin rail roadbed for streetcars.

Haarmann clamp (Haarmann, August): Engineering and Industry. Cited in: World Who's Who Sci.

Haarmann plough (Derivation undetermined): Engineering and Industry. See: Thrush.

Haarmann twin rail roadbed for streetcars (Haarmann, August): Engineering and Industry. Cited in: World Who's Who Sci.

HAAS. pr. fl. 20th c. German? physician. (Biography source unavailable.) Haas' disease.

Haas disease (Haas). See: Panner's disease (2).

Haas effect (Derivation undetermined): Physics. See: Hughes.

Haas hand-press (Haas, Wilhelm): Printing. See: Lockwood under "Hand-Press," p. 256.

Haas' (or Haase's) rule (Derivation undetermined): Medicine. See: Blakiston's Gould; Stedman.

Haas tester (Derivation undetermined): Engineering and Industry. See: Thrush.

HAAS, WANDER JOHANNES DE. 1878-1960. Dutch physicist. See: Dict. Sci. Biog. De Haas-van Alphen effect, Einstein-de Haas effect, Einstein-de Haas method, Shubnikov-de Haas effect.

HAAS, WILHELM. 1741-1800. Swiss type-founder and printer. See: Nouv. Biog. Univ. Haas hand-press.

Haase furnace (Derivation undetermined): Engineering and Industry. See: Thrush.

Haase system (Derivation undetermined): Engineering and Industry. See: Thrush.

HABEL, KARL. 1908-   . American virologist. See: World Who's Who Sci. Habel test.

Habel test (Habel, Karl): Medicine. See: Stedman.

Haber-Bosch process (Haber, Fritz and Bosch, Karl): Chemistry. See: Ballentyne; Hackh; New Encyc. Brit., 1974, Microp.; Thrush; Van Nostrand Chem. Dict.; Webster's 3d. Also known as: Bosch process, Haber process (or ammonia process).

Haber Colloquium (Haber, Fritz): Chemistry. See: Dict. Sci. Biog. under "Haber, Fritz."

HABER, FRITZ. 1868-1934. German chemist. See: World Who's Who Sci. Born-Haber cycle, Haber-Bosch process, Haber Colloquium.

HABER, HENRY. d. ca. 1960. English dermatologist. (Biography source unavailable.) Haber's syndrome.

Haber process (or ammonia process) (Haber, Fritz). See: Haber-Bosch process.

HABERLE, KARL KONSTANTIN. 1764-1832. Austrian botanist. See: Oesterr. Biog. Lex., 1815-1950. Haberlea.

Haberlea (Haberle, Karl Konstantin): Botany. See: Taylor, N.

HABERMANN, RUDOLF. 1884-1941. German dermatologist. See: Deut. Dermatologenkal., 1929, p. 82. Mucha-Habermann syndrome (or disease).

Haber's syndrome (Haber, Henry): Medicine. See: Jablonski.

HABLA, ALOIS. fl. 1925. Czechoslovakian engineer. Cited in: Chem. Abstr., vol. 20, p. 1310. Habla kiln.

Habla kiln (Habla, Alois): Engineering and Industry. See: Thrush.

HABSBURG. Royal house of Austria. See: Encyc. Brit., 1973. Hapsburg jaw (and lip).

HACKENBRUCH, PETER THEODOR. 1865-1924. German surgeon. See: Biog. Lex. hervorr. Aerzte, 1880-1930. Hackenbruch's experience.

Hackenbruch's experience (Hackenbruch, Peter Theodor): Medicine. See: Dorland.

HACKER, ANDREW. 1929-   . American political scientist. See: Who's Who Amer., 1974-1975. Hacker's law, Hacker's law of personnel.

Hacker's law (Hacker, Andrew): Sociology. See: Martin.

Hacker's law of personnel (Hacker, Andrew): Sociology. See: Martin.

HACKWORTH, T. 1786-1850. English? engineer. (Biography source unavailable.) Hackworth valve gear.

Hackworth valve gear (Hackworth, T.): Engineering and Industry. See: Auger.

HADAMARD, JACQUES SALOMON. 1865-1963. French mathematician. See: Dict. Sci. Biog. Cauchy-Hadamard theorem, Hadamard's conjecture, Hadamard's inequality, Hadamard's three-circles theorem.

Hadamard's conjecture (Hadamard, Jacques Salomon): Mathematics. See: James.

Hadamard's inequality (Hadamard, Jacques salomon): Mathematics. See: Ballentyne; James.

Hadamard's three-circles theorem (Hadamard, Jacques Salomon): Mathematics. See: James.

Hadassah (Women's Zionist Organization of America) (Esther): Sociology. See: Encyc. Brit., 1973; Encyc. Judaica.

Hadassah. See: Esther.

HADEN, RUSSEL LANDRAM. 1888-1952. American physician. See: Who Was Who Amer., 1951-1960. Haden's syndrome.

Haden's syndrome (Haden, Russel Landram): Medicine. See: Jablonski.

HADFIELD, GEOFFREY. b. 1889. English pathologist. See: Med. Direct., 1964. Clarke Hadfield syndrome.

Hadfield manganese test (Hadfield, Sir Robert Abbott): Chemistry. See: Webster's 3d.

Hadfield process (Hadfield, Sir Robert Abbott): Chemistry. See: Hackh.

HADFIELD, SIR ROBERT ABBOTT. 1859-1940. English metallurgist. See: Dict. Sci. Biog. Hadfield manganese test, Hadfield process, Hadfield's manganese steel.

Hadfield's manganese steel (Hadfield, Sir Robert Abbott): Chemistry. See: Thrush.

Hadley cell (Hadley, George): Earth Sciences. See: Huschke; Monkhouse.

HADLEY, GEORGE. 1685-1768. English meteorologist. See: World Who's Who Sci. Hadley cell, Hadley regime.

HADLEY, JOHN. 1682-1744. English mathematician and mechanician. See: Dict. Sci. Biog. Hadley's quadrant (or octant).

Hadley regime (Hadley, George): Earth Sciences. See: Huschke.

Hadley's quadrant (or octant) (Hadley, John): Navigation. See: Dict. Sci. Biog. under "Hadley, John."

HADORN, WALTER. fl. 1898-1948. Swiss physician. (Biography source unavailable.) Albright-Hadorn syndrome.

HADOW, SIR HENRY (In full: WILLIAM HENRY). 1859-1937. English educator and music historian. See: Dict. Nat. Biog., 5th suppl. Hadow report.

Hadow report (Hadow, Sir Henry): Education. See: Good.

HADRIAN (PUBLIUS AELIUS HADRIANUS). 76-138 A.D. Roman emperor. See: Encyc. Brit., 1973. Hadrian's Wall.

Hadrian's Wall (Hadrian): History. See: New Encyc. Brit., 1974, Microp.; Steinberg.

HADSEL, ALVAH DENTON. fl. 1935. German? engineer. Cited in: Chem. Abstr., Decenn. Index, 1927-1936. Hadsel mill.

Hadsel mill (Hadsel, Alvah Denton): Engineering and Industry. See: Thrush.

HAECKEL, ERNST HEINRICH. 1834-1919. German biologist. See: Dict. Sci. Biog. Haeckelian (or Haeckelism), Haeckel's gastrea theory, Haeckel's law (or biogenetic law).

Haeckelian (or Haeckelism) (Haeckel, Ernst Heinrich): Biology. See: Webster's 3d.

Haeckel's gastrea theory (Haeckel, Ernst Heinrich): Biology. See: Stedman.

Haeckel's law (or biogenetic law) (Haeckel, Ernst Heinrich): Genetics. See: Dorland; Gray; Henderson; Hinsie; Stedman.

HAEGG, GUNNAR. 1903- . Swedish chemist. See: Pogg., vol. 6. Haeggite.

Haeggite (Haegg, Gunnar): Earth Sciences. See: Thrush.

haemoproteus (Proteus): Zoology. See: Stedman.

HAEN, ANTON DE. 1704-1776. Dutch physician. See: Biog. Lex. hervorr. Aerzte. Haen's pills.

HAENEL, HEINRICH G. (HANS). b. 1874. German neurologist. See: Biog. Lex. hervorr. Aerzte, 1880-1930. Haenel's symptom (syndrome or sign).

Haenel's symptom (syndrome or sign) (Haenel, Heinrich G.): Medicine. See: Dorland; Jablonski; Stedman.

Haenisch and Schroeder process (Derivation undetermined): Earth Sciences. See: Thrush.

Haen's pills (Haen, Anton de): Medicine. See: Dorland.

HAESER, HEINRICH. 1811-1885. German physician. See: Biog. Lex. hervorr. Aerzte. Haeser's formula (or coefficient).

Haeser's formula (or coefficient) (Haeser, Heinrich): Medicine. See: Dorland; Hackh; Stedman. Also known as: Christison's formula, Trapp-Haeser formula, Trapp's formula (or coefficient).

HAFERKAMP, OTTO. 1929- . German pathologist. See: Who's Who Sci. Europe, 1972. Haferkamp's syndrome.

Haferkamp's syndrome (Haferkamp, Otto): Medicine. See: Jablonski.

HAFFKINE, WALDEMAR MORDECAI WOLFF. 1860-1930. Russian bacteriologist. See: Dict. Sci. Biog. Haffkine's vaccine.

Haffkine's vaccine (Haffkine, Waldemar Mordecai Wolff): Medicine. See: Stedman.

Haffner Serenade (Haffner, Sigmund): Music. See: Apel; Scholes.

HAFFNER, SIGMUND. fl. ca. 1770. Austrian burgomaster. Cited in: Grove under "Haffner Serenade." Haffner Serenade, Haffner Symphony.

Haffner Symphony (Haffner, Sigmund): Music. See: Apel; Scholes.

Hagan-Sievert test reaction (Hagen, Harro and Sieverts, Adolf Ferdinand): Chemistry. See: Van Nostrand Chem. Dict.

HAGAR. Abraham's concubine and mother of Ishmael in the Old Testament. See: Hastings (Dict. Bible). Hagarenes.

HAGAR. fl. 19th c.? German printer. (Biography source unavailable.) Hagar press.

Hagar press (Hagar): Printing. See: Lockwood, p. 256.

Hagarenes (Hagar): History. See: Brewer.

Hagedorn and Jensen estimation (of sugar in the blood) (Hagedorn, Hans Christian and Jensen, B. Norman): Medicine. See: Ballentyne.

HAGEDORN, HANS CHRISTIAN. b. 1888. Danish physician. See: Kraks Blaa Bog, 1938. Hagedorn and Jensen estimation (of sugar in the blood), neutral Hagedorn insulin suspension, neutral protamine Hagedorn insulin injection.

Hagedorn needle (Hagedorn, Werner): Medicine. See: Dorland; Stedman.

HAGEDORN, WERNER. 1831-1894. German surgeon. See: World Who's Who Sci. Hagedorn needle, Hagedorn's table.

Hagedorn's table (Hagedorn, Werner): Medicine. See: Kelly.

HAGEMAN. No dates. Hospital patient. (Biography source unavailable.) Hageman factor, Hageman trait.

Hageman factor (Hageman): Medicine. See: Stedman.

Hageman trait (Hageman): Medicine. See: Blakiston's Gould.

Hagen-Bucholz Foundation (Hagen, Carl Gottfried and Bucholz, Christian Friedrich): Medicine. Cited in: World Who's Who Sci. under "Hagen, Carl Gottfried."

HAGEN, CARL GOTTFRIED. 1749-1829. German pharmaceutical chemist. See: World Who's Who Sci. galeopsis Hagenii, Hagen-Bucholz Foundation, Hagenia, mytilus Hagenii.

HAGEN, ERNST (In full: CARL ERNST BESSEL). 1851-1923. German physicist. See: World Who's Who Sci. Hagen-Rubens relation.

HAGEN, GOTTHILF HEINRICH LUDWIG. 1797-1884. German hydraulic engineer. See: World Who's Who Sci. Hagen-Poiseuille flow, Poiseuille-Hagen law.

HAGEN, HARRO. fl. 1932. German chemist. Cited in: Pogg., vol. 7a under "Sieverts, Adolf Ferdinand." Hagan-Sievert test reaction.

Hagen-Poiseuille flow (Hagen, Gotthilf Heinrich Ludwig and Poiseuille, Jean Louis Marie). See: Poiseuille's flow.

Hagen-Rubens relation (Hagen, Ernst and Rubens, Heinrich): Physics. See: Ballentyne.

Hagenia (Hagen, Carl Gottfried): Botany. See: Webster's 3d.

Hager-Gawalowski reagent (Hager, Herman and Gawalowski, Anton Carl Wilhelm): Chemistry. See: Van Nostrand Chem. Dict.

HAGER, HERMAN (In full: HANS HERMAN JULIUS). 1816-1897. German pharmacist. See: World Who's Who Sci. Hager-Gawalowski reagent, Hager reagent, Hager reagent for alkali salts, Hager reagent for alkaloids, Hager reagent for free chlorine, Hager reagent for glucose, Hager test for free chlorine or bromine, Hager test for nitrate and nitrite, Hager test reaction for glycerol, Hager tests for alcohol in volatile oils.

Hager reagent (Hager, Herman): Chemistry. See: Van Nostrand Chem. Dict.

Hager reagent for alkali salts (Hager, Herman): Chemistry. See: Van Nostrand Chem. Dict.

Hager reagent for alkaloids (Hager, Herman): Chemistry. See: Van Nostrand Chem. Dict.

Hager reagent for free chlorine (Hager, Herman): Chemistry. See: Van Nostrand Chem. Dict.

Hager reagent for glucose (Hager, Herman): Chemistry. See: Van Nostrand Chem. Dict.

Hager test for free chlorine or bromine (Hager, Herman): Chemistry. See: Van Nostrand Chem. Dict.

Hager test for nitrate and nitrite (Hager, Herman): Chemistry. See: Van Nostrand Chem. Dict.

Hager test reaction for glycerol (Hager, Herman): Chemistry. See: Van Nostrand Chem. Dict.

Hager tests for alcohol in volatile oils (Hager, Herman): Chemistry. See: Van Nostrand Chem. Dict.

Haglund-Laewen-Fruend syndrome (Haglund, Patrik; Laewen, Arthur; and Fruend, H.). See: Buedinger-Ludloff-Laewen syndrome.

HAGLUND, PATRIK (In full: SIMS EMIL PATRIK). 1870-1937. Swedish physician. See: Svenska Maen Och Kvinnor. Haglund-Laewen-Fruend syndrome, Haglund's disease, Haglund's syndrome.

Haglund's disease (Haglund, Patrik): Medicine. See: Dorland; Jablonski.

Haglund's syndrome (Haglund, Patrik): Medicine. See: Jablonski.

HAGNER, FRANCIS RANDALL. 1873-1940. American surgeon. See: World Who's Who Sci. Hagner's bag, Hagner's operation.

HAGNER, KARL. fl. ca. 1868. German hospital patient. Cited in: Lieber and Olbrich. Hagner's disease.

HAGNER, WILHELM. fl. ca. 1868. German hospital patient. Cited in: Lieber and Olbrich. Hagner's disease.

Hagner's bag (Hagner, Francis Randall): Medicine. See: Dorland.

Hagner's disease (Hagner, Karl and Hagner, Wilhelm): Medicine. See: Jablonski.

Hagner's operation (Hagner, Francis Randall): Medicine. See: Dorland.

Hahn-Banach theorem (Hahn, Hans and Banach, Stefan): Mathematics. See: James.

Hahn emanation technique (Hahn, Otto): Physics. See: Thewlis.

HAHN, EUGENE. 1841-1902. German surgeon. See: Biog. Lex. hervorr. Aerzte, 1880-1930. Hahn's cannula.

HAHN, FRIEDRICH LAZARUS. b. 1888. German analytical chemist. See: Pogg., vols. 5, 6, 7a. Hahn reagent for nitrite, Hahn test for boric acid (boron), Hahn test for bromate, Hahn's oxine reagent (or reagent), Hahn-Wolf-Jaeger reagent.

HAHN, HANS. 1879-1934. Austrian mathematician. See: World Who's Who Sci. Hahn-Banach theorem.

HAHN, JOHANN MICHAEL. 1758-1819. German sect founder. See: Allg. Deut. Biog. Michelianites.

HAHN, MARTIN. fl. 1928. German chemist. Cited in: Chem. Abstr., vol. 22, p. 3716. Hahn-Schutze-Pavlides reagent.

HAHN, OTTO. 1879-1968. German radio chemist. See: Dict. Sci. Biog. Hahn emanation technique, Hahnium.

Hahn reagent for nitrite (Hahn, Friedrich Lazarus): Chemistry. See: Van Nostrand Chem. Dict.

Hahn-Schutze-Pavlides reagent (Hahn, Martin; Schuetz, Franz; and Pavlides, Spiro George): Chemistry. See: Van Nostrand Chem. Dict.

Hahn test for boric acid (boron) (Hahn, Friedrich Lazarus): Chemistry. See: Van Nostrand Chem. Dict.

Hahn test for bromate (Hahn, Friedrich Lazarus): Chemistry. See: Van Nostrand Chem. Dict.

Hahn-Wolf-Jaeger reagent (Hahn, Friedrich Lazarus; Wolf, Hans; and Jaeger, Gustav): Chemistry. See: Van Nostrand Chem. Dict.

HAHNEMANN, SAMUEL (In full: CHRISTIAN FRIEDRICH SAMUEL). 1755-1843. German physician. See: Dict. Sci. Biog. Hahnemannian.

Hahnemannian (Hahnemann, Samuel): Medicine. See: Dorland; Stedman.

Hahner furnace (Derivation undetermined): Earth Sciences. See: Thrush.

Hahnium (Hahn, Otto): Chemistry. See: Asimov; Barnhart (New Eng.)

Hahn's cannula (Hahn, Eugene): Medicine. See: Dorland.

Hahn's oxine reagent (or reagent) (Hahn, Friedrich Lazarus): Chemistry. See: Stedman; Van Nostrand Chem. Dict.

Haidinger('s) brushes (Haidinger, Wilhelm Karl von): Physics. See: Dorland; Stedman; Thewlis.

Haidinger fringes (or interference fringes) (Haidinger, Wilhelm Karl von): Physics. See: Ballentyne; Thewlis; Van Nostrand Sci. Encyc.

HAIDINGER, WILHELM KARL VON. 1795-1871. Austrian mineralogist. See: Dict. Sci. Biog. Haidinger fringes (or interference fringes), Haidinger('s) brushes, Haidingerite, Haidinger's dichroscope.

Haidingerite (Haidinger, Wilhelm Karl von): Earth Sciences. See: Charnock; Thrush; Webster's 3d.

Haidinger's dichroscope (Haidinger, Wilhelm Karl von): Earth Sciences. See: Dict. Sci. Biog. under "Haidinger, Wilhelm Karl von."

HAIGH, B. P. (or P. B.). fl. 1912. English engineer. Cited in: Chem. Abstr. Haigh fatigue testing machine.

Haigh fatigue testing machine (Haigh, B. P.): Engineering and Industry. See: Auger.

HAIGH, H. No dates. Engineer. (Biography source unavailable.) Haigh kiln.

Haigh kiln (Haigh, H.): Engineering and Industry. See: Thrush.

Hail Mary (Mary, Virgin-Mother). See: Ave Maria.

HAILE SELASSIE (Princely title and surname: RAS TAFARI). 1892- Emperor of Ethiopia. See: New Encyc. Brit., 1974, Microp. Ras Tafarian.

Hailey-Hailey disease (Hailey, Howard and Hailey, Hugh): Medicine. See: Jablonski; Stedman. Also known as: Darier's disease, Gougerot-Hailey-Hailey disease, Hailey's disease.

HAILEY, HOWARD (In full: WILLIAM HOWARD). 1898-1967. American dermatologist. See: Nat. Cycl. Amer. Biog., vol. 53, pp. 362-363. Hailey-Hailey disease.

HAILEY, HUGH E. 1909- . American dermatologist. (Biography source unavailable.) Hailey-Hailey disease.

Hailey's disease (Hailey, Howard or Hailey, Hugh). See: Hailey-Hailey disease.

Haines' formula (or coefficient) (Haines, Walter Stanley): Medicine. See: Dorland; Hackh; Stedman.

HAINES, JACKSON. 1840-1879. American figure skater. See: Arlott. Jackson Haines (spin).

Haines' reagent (Haines, Walter Stanley): Medicine. See: Stedman; Van Nostrand Chem. Dict.

HAINES, WALTER STANLEY. 1850-1923. American toxicologist. See: Who Was Who Amer., 1897-1942. Haines' formula (or coefficient), Haines' reagent.

HAKE, BARON VON. d. 1818. German patron of botany. (Biography source unavailable.) Hakea.

Hakea (Hake, Baron von): Botany. See: Taylor, N.; Webster's 3d.

Halban, Josef von. See: Von Halban, Josef.

Halban's disease (Derivation undetermined): Medicine. See: Jablonski.

Halban's sign (Van Halban, Josef): Medicine. See: Dorland.

HALBEISEN, WILLIAM A. 1915- . American dermatologist. See: Direct. Med. Specialists, 1975-1976. Stryker-Halbeisen syndrome.

HALBERSTAEDTER, LUDWIG. b. 1876. German physician. See: Biog. Lex. hervorr. Aerzte, 1880-1930. Halberstaedter-Prowazek bodies.

Halberstaedter-Prowazek bodies (Halberstaedter, Ludwig and Prowazek, Stanislas Josef Mathias Edler von Lanow). See: Prowazek-Greeff bodies.

HALBERTSMA, IR. NICOLAAS ADOLF. b. 1889. Dutch physician. See: Wie is dat?, 1948. Van der Hoeve–Halbertsma–Waardenburg syndrome?

HALBRECHT, I. fl. 1944. Palestinian physician. (Biography source unavailable.) Halbrecht's syndrome.

Halbrecht's syndrome (Halbrecht, I.): Medicine. See: Jablonski.

Haldane chamber (Haldane, John Scott): Medicine. See: Dorland; Stedman.

HALDANE, JAMES ALEXANDER. 1768–1851. Scottish clergyman. See: Dict. Nat. Biog. Haldanite.

HALDANE, JOHN BURDON SANDERSON. 1892–1964. Scottish geneticist. See: Dict. Sci. Biog. Haldane's law (or rule).

HALDANE, JOHN SCOTT. 1860–1936. Scottish physiologist. See: Dict. Sci. Biog. Haldane chamber, Haldane tube, Haldane's apparatus.

Haldane reforms (or army scheme) (Haldane, Richard Burdon, Viscount Haldane): History. See: Montgomery; Steinberg.

HALDANE, RICHARD BURDON, VISCOUNT HALDANE. 1856–1928. English statesman, lawyer and philosopher. See: Dict. Nat. Biog., 4th suppl. Haldane reforms (or army scheme).

HALDANE, ROBERT. 1764–1842. Scottish clergyman. See: Dict. Nat. Biog. Haldanite.

Haldane tube (Haldane, John Scott): Medicine. See: Stedman.

Haldane's apparatus (Haldane, John Scott): Medicine. See: Dorland; Stedman.

Haldane's law (or rule) (Haldane, John Burdon Sanderson): Genetics. See: Gray; Webster's 3d.

Haldanite (Haldane, James Alexander and Haldane, Robert): Earth Sciences. See: Webster's 3d.

Halden solutions (Halden, Wilhelm): Chemistry. See: Van Nostrand Chem. Dict.

HALDEN, WILHELM. b. 1892. Austrian chemist. See: Pogg., vols. 6, 7a. Halden solutions.

HALE, DONALD HERBERT. 1904– . American physicist. See: Amer. Men Sci., 9th ed. Hale gauge?

Hale gauge (Hale, Donald Herbert?): Physics. See: Internat. Dict. Phys. Elec.

HALE, GEORGE ELLERY. 1868–1938. American astronomer. See: Dict. Sci. Biog. Hale telescope.

HALE, SARAH JOSEPHA. 1788–1879. American writer and editor. See: Dict. Amer. Biog. Sarah Josepha Hale Award.

Hale telescope (Hale, George Ellery): Astronomy. See: Asimov.

HALEN, JOHANN. fl. 19th c. German botanist. (Biography source unavailable.) Halenia.

Halenia (Halen, Johann): Botany. See: Webster's 3d.

HALES, SIR EDWARD. d. 1695. English nobleman. See: Dict. Nat. Biog. Hales's case.

Hales' piesimeter (Hales, Stephen): Chemistry. See: Dorland; Stedman.

HALES, STEPHEN. 1677–1761. English physiologist. See: Dict. Sci. Biog. Hales' piesimeter, Halesia.

Halesia (Hales, Stephen): Botany. See: Mathews, M. M.; Taylor, N.; Webster's 3d.

Hales's case (Hales, Sir Edward): History. See: Steinberg.

half-Joe (or half-Johannes) (John V of Portugal). See: Johannes.

Halifax, 1st Earl of. See: Wood, Edward Frederick Lindley, 1st Earl of Halifax and Baron Irwin.

Halimond tube (Derivation undetermined): Engineering and Industry. See: Thrush.

HALL, SIR ALFRED DANIEL. 1864–1942. English agriculturist. See: World Who's Who Sci. Halls crabapple?

Hall angle (Hall, Edwin Herbert): Physics. See: Internat. Dict. Phys. Elec.; Thewlis.

HALL, CHARLES MARTIN. 1863–1914. American chemist. See: Dict. Sci. Biog. Hall–Heroult cell, Hall('s) process.

Hall coefficient (Hall, Edwin Herbert): Physics. See: Internat. Dict. Ap. Math.; Internat. Dict. Phys. Elec.; Hughes; Markus; Thewlis.

Hall condenser (Hall, Samuel): Engineering and Industry. See: Auger.

Hall constant (Hall, Edwin Herbert): Physics. See: Internat. Dict. Phys. Elec. under "Hall coefficient"; Markus.

HALL, DOROTHY. fl. 1922. American chemist. (Biography source unavailable.) Willard–Hall reagent.

HALL, EDWIN HERBERT. 1855–1938. American physicist. See: Dict. Sci. Biog. Hall angle, Hall coefficient, Hall constant, Hall effect, Hall electrolytic cell, Hall formula, Hall generator, Hall mobility, Hall voltage.

Hall effect (Hall, Edwin Herbert): Physics. See: Ballentyne; Hackh; Hughes; Huschke; Markus; Thewlis; Van Nostrand Sci. Encyc.

Hall electrolytic cell (Hall, Edwin Herbert): Physics. See: Encyc. Brit., 1973 under "Electrometallurgy," vol. 8, p. 237b.

Hall formula (Hall, Edwin Herbert): Physics. See: Hackh.

Hall furnace (Hall, William A.): Engineering and Industry. See: Thrush.

HALL, G. R. fl. 20th c. American physician. (Biography source unavailable.) Hall's honeysuckle.

Hall gear (Hall, J. W.): Engineering and Industry. See: Auger.

Hall generator (Hall, Edwin Herbert): Physics. See: Markus.

HALL, HERMAN CHRISTIAN VAN. 1801–1874. Dutch botanist. Cited in: Mansell. Halls panicum.

Hall–Heroult cell (Hall, Charles Martin and Heroult, Paul Louis Touissant): Chemistry. See: Van Nostrand Chem. Dict.

Hall–Heroult process (Hall, Charles Martin and Heroult, Paul Louis Touissant). See: Hall process and Heroult process.

HALL, J. W. fl. 1896. Engineer. (Biography source unavailable.) Hall gear.

HALL, JOHN. fl. 1870. American mineralogist. Cited in: Bailey. Hallite.

HALL, JOHN H. fl. 1811. American inventor. (Biography source unavailable.) Hall rifle.

HALL, JOHN SCOVILLE. 1908– . American astronomer. See: World Who's Who Sci. Hiltner–Hall effect?

HALL, MARSHALL. 1790–1857. English physiologist. See: Dict. Sci. Biog. Hall's disease (or syndrome), Hall's facies, Hall's method.

HALL, MARTHA. fl. 1935. American? chemist. (Biography source unavailable.) Adams–Hall–Bailey reagent.

HALL, MAURICE CROWTHER. 1881–1938. American zoologist. See: World Who's Who Sci. Hall('s) scale.

Hall mobility (Hall, Edwin Herbert): Physics. See: Hughes; Internat. Dict. Phys. Elec.; Markus.

Hall('s) process (Hall, Charles Martin): Chemistry. See: Hackh; Mathews, M. M.; Thrush; Van Nostrand Chem. Dict.; Webster's 3d. Also known as: Hall–Heroult process, Heroult process.

Hall purinometer (Derivation undetermined): Chemistry. See: Hackh.

Hall reheating process (Hall, William A.?): Engineering and Industry. See: Van Nostrand Chem. Dict.

Hall rifle (Hall, John H.): Weapons. See: Quick.

Hall–Rowe wedge (Derivation undetermined): Engineering and Industry. See: Thrush.

HALL, SAMUEL. 1781–1863. English engineer. See: Dict. Nat. Biog. Hall condenser, Hall's pulsometer?

Hall('s) scale (Hall, Maurice Crowther): Zoology. See: Gray; Webster's 3d.

HALL, THOMAS. 1834–1911. American inventor. See: World Who's Who Sci. Hall typewriter.

Hall typewriter (Hall, Thomas): Engineering and Industry. Cited in: World Who's Who Sci. under "Hall, Thomas."

Hall voltage (Hall, Edwin Herbert): Physics. See: Encyc. Brit., 1973 under "Electricity, Conduction of."

HALL, WILLIAM A. fl. 1910. American engineer. Cited in: Chem. Abstr. Hall furnace, Hall reheating process?

HALLADAY. fl. 1876. Engineer. (Biography source unavailable.) Halladay wind wheel.

Halladay wind wheel (Halladay): Engineering and Industry. See: Auger.

Hallam company (Hallam, Lewis): Theater. See: Morris.

HALLAM, LEWIS. ca. 1740–1808. English-born actor in America. See: Dict. Amer. Biog. Hallam company.

HALLAUER, OTTO. b. 1866. Swiss ophthalmologist. Cited in: Index-Cat. Libr. Surg.-Gen. Off., 3d ser., vol. 6, 1926. Hallauer's glasses.

Hallauer's glasses (Hallauer, Otto): Medicine. See: Dorland.

Hallberg effect (Hallberg, Josef Hendrik): Medicine. See: Dorland.

HALLBERG, JOSEF HENDRIK. b. 1874. American electrician. Cited in: Mansell. Hallberg effect.

HALLE, ADRIEN JOSEPH MARIE NOEL. 1859-1947. French physician. Cited in: Index-Cat. Libr. Surg.-Gen. Off., 2d ser., vol. 6, 1901. Halle's point.

HALLE, SIR CHARLES. 1819-1885. German-born English pianist and conductor. See: Encyc. Brit., 1973. Halle concerts.

Halle concerts (Halle, Sir Charles): Music. See: Hunt.

HALLER, ALBIN. 1849-1925. French chemist. See: World Who's Who Sci. Haller-Bauer reaction.

Haller, Albrecht von. See: Von Haller, Albrecht.

Haller-Bauer reaction (Haller, Albin and Bauer, Edouard): Chemistry. See: Van Nostrand Chem. Dict.

HALLER, GOTTFRIED. d. 1886. German zoologist. See: Frankf. Zool. Garten., vol. 27 (1886), p. 200. Haller's organ.

Hallermann-Streiff-Francois syndrome (Hallermann, Wilhelm; Streiff, Enrico Bernard; and Francois, Jules). See: Hallermann-Streiff syndrome.

Hallermann-Streiff syndrome (Hallermann, Wilhelm and Streiff, Enrico Bernard): Medicine. See: Jablonski. Also known as: Francois' dyscephaly, Hallermann-Streiff-Francois syndrome, Hallermann's syndrome, Ullrich and Fremerey-Dohna syndrome.

HALLERMANN, WILHELM. 1901- . German physician. See: Who's Who Sci. Europe, 1972. Hallermann-Streiff syndrome.

Hallermann's syndrome (Hallermann, Wilhelm). See: Hallerman-Streiff syndrome.

Haller's ansa (Von Haller, Albrecht): Anatomy. See: Donath; Dorland; Stedman.

Haller's arch(es) (Von Haller, Albrecht): Anatomy. See: Donath; Dorland; Stedman.

Haller's circle (1) (circulus arteriosus nervi optici) (Von Haller, Albrecht): Anatomy. See: Donath; Dorland; Stedman. Also known as: Zinn's vascular circle.

Haller's circle (2) (plexus venosus areolaris) (Von Haller, Albrecht): Anatomy. See: Dorland; Stedman.

Haller's circle (3) (circulosus callosus) (Von Haller, Albrecht): Anatomy. See: Dorland; Stedman.

Haller's cone(s) (Von Haller, Albrecht): Anatomy. See: Donath; Stedman.

Haller's habenula (Von Haller, Albrecht): Anatomy. See: Donath; Stedman. Also known as: Scarpa's habenula.

Haller's insula (or anulus) (Von Haller, Albrecht): Anatomy. See: Stedman.

Haller's layer (Von Haller, Albrecht): Anatomy. See: Donath.

Haller's line (Von Haller, Albrecht): Anatomy. See: Dorland; Stedman.

Haller's organ (Haller, Gottfried): Zoology. See: Gray; Henderson; Pennak; Van Nostrand Sci. Encyc.

Haller's plexus (Von Haller, Albrecht): Anatomy. See: Stedman.

Haller's rete (or network) (Von Haller, Albrecht): Anatomy. See: Donath; Stedman.

Haller's tripod (Von Haller, Albrecht): Anatomy. See: Stedman.

Haller's tunica vasculosa (Von Haller, Albrecht): Anatomy. See: Stedman.

Haller's unguis (Von Haller, Albrecht): Anatomy. See: Stedman.

Haller's vas aberrans (Von Haller, Albrecht): Anatomy. See: Stedman.

Haller's vascular tissue (Von Haller, Albrecht): Anatomy. See: Stedman.

HALLERVORDEN, JULIUS. 1882-1965. German neurologist. See: Handb. Deut. Wiss. Hallervorden-Spatz syndrome.

Hallervorden-Spatz syndrome (Hallervorden, Julius and Spatz, Hugo): Medicine. See: Jablonski; Stedman. Also known as: Hallervorden syndrome.

Hallervorden syndrome (Hallervorden, Julius). See: Hallervorden-Spatz syndrome.

Halle's point (Halle, Adrien Joseph Marie Noel): Medicine. See: Dorland; Stedman.

Hallett table (Derivation undetermined): Engineering and Industry. See: Thrush.

HALLEY, EDMUND. 1656-1742. English astronomer. See: Dict. Sci. Biog. Halley lecture, Halley's method.

Halley lecture (Halley, Edmund): Astronomy. See: Satterthwaite.

Halley's method (Halley, Edmund): Astronomy. See: Webster's 3d.

HALLEZ, PAUL. b. 1848. French zoologist. Cited in: Mansell. Hallezia?

Hallezia (Hallez, Paul?): Zoology. See: Pennak.

HALLGREN, BERTIL. fl. 1959. Swedish human geneticist. Cited in: Lieber and Olbrich. Alstroem-Hallgren syndrome, Hallgren's syndrome.

Hallgren's syndrome (Hallgren, Bertil). See: Graefe-Sjoegren syndrome.

HALLIDAY, JOHN. fl. 1949. Australian physician. (Biography source unavailable.) Halliday's hyperostosis.

Halliday's hyperostosis (Halliday, John): Medicine. See: Jablonski.

HALLINGER, JOHANN. fl. 1913-1925. German engineer. Cited in: Mansell. Hallinger shield?

Hallinger shield (Hallinger, Johann?): Engineering and Industry. See: Thrush.

HALLION, LOUIS. 1862-1940. French physiologist. See: Biog. Lex. hervorr. Aerzte, 1880-1930. Hallion's test.

Hallion's test (Hallion, Louis): Medicine. See: Dorland. Also known as: Tuffier's test.

Hallite (Hall, John): Earth Sciences. See: Bailey.

Hallock box (Derivation undetermined): Agriculture. See: Winburne.

HALLOPEAU, FRANCOIS HENRI. 1842-1919. French dermatologist. See: World Who's Who Sci. Hallopeau's disease (1), Hallopeau's disease (2) (or acrodermatitis), Hallopeau's syndrome.

Hallopeau-Leredde syndrome (Hallopeau, Francois Henri and Leredde, Emile). See: Hallopeau's syndrome.

Hallopeau's disease (1) (Hallopeau, Francois Henri): Medicine. See: Jablonski. Also known as: Csillag's disease, von Zambusch's disease.

Hallopeau's disease (2) (or acrodermatitis) (Hallopeau, Francois Henri): Medicine. See: Dorland; Jablonski; Stedman.

Hallopeau's syndrome (Hallopeau, Francois Henri): Medicine. See: Jablonski. Also known as: Hallopeau-Leredde syndrome.

Halloran process (Halloran, Ralph A.): Chemistry. See: Van Nostrand Chem. Dict.

HALLORAN, RALPH A. fl. 1928-1940. American engineer. Cited in: Chem. Abstr. Halloran process.

Halloy, d'Omalius d', Jean Baptiste Julien. See: Omalius-d'Halloy, d', Jean Baptiste Julien.

Halloysite (Omalius-d'Halloy, d', Jean Baptiste Julien): Earth Sciences. See: Thrush; Webster's 3d. Also known as: Lenzinite.

Halls crabapple (Hall, Sir Alfred Daniel?): Botany. See: Winburne.

Hall's disease (or syndrome) (Hall, Marshall): Medicine. See: Dorland; Jablonski; Stedman.

Hall's facies (Hall, Marshall): Medicine. See: Stedman.

Hall's factors (Derivation undetermined): Engineering and Industry. See: Thrush.

Hall's honeysuckle (Hall, G. R.): Botany. See: Webster's 3d.

Hall's method (Hall, Marshall): Medicine. See: Stedman. Also known as: Marshall hall's method.

Halls panicum (Hall, Herman Christian van): Botany. See: Winburne.

Hall's pulsometer (Hall, Samuel?): Engineering and Industry. See: Encyc. Brit., 1973 under "Steam," vol. 21, p. 185c.

Hallwachs effect (Hallwachs, Wilhelm Ludwig Franz): Physics. See: Ballentyne; Hughes; Internat. Dict. Phys. Elec.; Markus; Webster's 3d.

HALLWACHS, WILHELM LUDWIG FRANZ. 1859-1922. German physicist. See: Dict. Sci. Biog. Hallwachs effect.

halo of Hevelius (Hevelius, Johannes). See: Hevelian halo.

HALPHEN, GEORGES. fl. 1912. French chemist. Cited in: Chem. Abstr. Halphen reagent (and test) for cottonseed oil, Halphen reagent for linseed oil, Halphen reagent for rosin oil, Halphen test for benzene in alcohol.

Halphen reagent (and test) for cottonseed oil (Halphen, Georges): Chemistry. See: Hackh; Van Nostrand Chem. Dict.

Halphen reagent for linseed oil (Halphe, Georges): Chemistry. See: Van Nostrand Chem. Dict.

Halphen reagent for rosin oil (Halphen, Georges): Chemistry. See: Van Nostrand Chem. Dict.

Halphen test for benzene in alcohol (Halphen, Georges): Chemistry. See: Van Nostrand Chem. Dict.

HALSKE, JOHANN GEORG. 1814-1890. German electrical engineer. See: World Who's Who Sci. Siemens and Halske process.

Halsted forceps (or mosquito forceps) (Halsted, William Stewart): Medicine. See: Blakiston's Gould.

Halsted school of surgery (Halsted, William Stewart): Medicine. See: Blakiston's Gould.

HALSTED, WILLIAM STEWART. 1852-1922. American surgeon. See: Dict. Sci. Biog. Halsted forceps (or mosquito forceps), Halsted school of surgery, Halsted's law, Halsted's operation (1) (inguinal herniorrhaphy or incision(?)), Halsted's operation (2) (or radical mastectomy), Halsted's suture.

Halsted's law (Halsted, William Stewart): Medicine. See: Stedman.

Halsted's operation (1) (inguinal herniorrhaphy or incision(?)) (Halsted, William Stewart): Medicine. See: Blakiston's Gould; Dorland; Stedman.

Halsted's operation (2) (or radical mastectomy) (Halsted, William Stewart): Medicine. See: Blakiston's Gould; Dorland; Stedman.

Halsted's suture (Halsted, William Stewart): Medicine. See: Dorland; Stedman.

Halushi Behcet's syndrome (Behcet, Halushi). See: Behcet's syndrome.

HAM. Son of Noah (Gen 10:6-20). See: Encyc. Brit., 1973. Hamite (1), Hamite (2), Hamitic (or Hamitic languages).

Ham actor (McCullough, Hamish): Theater. See: Brewer.

HAM, THOMAS HALE. 1905- . American physician. See: World Who's Who Sci. Ham's test.

HAMAN. Prime minister of the Persian King Ahasuerus and an enemy of the Jews in the Old Testament. See: Hastings (Dict. Bible). Hamantaschen (Hamantasch or Hamantash).

Hamantaschen (Hamantasch or Hamantash) (Haman): Food and Drink. See: De Sola; Webster's 3d.

HAMBERG, AXEL. 1863-1933. Swedish mineralogist. See: Dict. Sci. Biog. Hambergite.

Hambergite (Hamberg, Axel): Earth Sciences. See: Thrush; Webster's 3d.

HAMBURGER, HARTOG JAKOB. 1859-1924. Dutch physiologist. See: World Who's Who Sci. Hamburger test reaction, Hamburger's interchange, Hamburger's law, Hamburger's phenomenon.

Hamburger test reaction (Hamburger, Hartog Jakob): Chemistry. See: Van Nostrand Chem. Dict.

Hamburger's interchange (Hamburger, Hartog Jakob): Medicine. See: Dorland.

Hamburger's law (Hamburger, Hartog Jakob): Medicine. See: Dorland; Stedman.

Hamburger's phenomenon (Hamburger, Hartog Jakob): Medicine. See: Stedman.

HAMDAN QARMAT. fl. 2d half 9th c. Mohammedan sect leader. See: Hastings (Dict. Rel. Ethics). Karmathians (or Karmatis).

Hamel basis (Hamel, Georg Karl Wilhelm): Mathematics. See: James.

HAMEL, GEORG KARL WILHELM. 1877-1954. German mathematician. See: World Who's Who Sci. Hamel basis.

Hamelia (Duhamel Du Monceau, Henri-Louis): Botany. See: Taylor, N.; Webster's 3d.

HAMER, H. fl. 1924. Dutch chemist. (Biography source unavailable.) Kolthoff-Hamer reagent for zinc in the presence of cadmium, Kolthoff-Hamer reagents for heavy metals.

HAMILTON, ALEXANDER. 1757-1804. Scottish-born American statesman. See: Dict. Amer. Biog. Burr-Hamilton duel, Hamiltonian (or Hamiltonianism), Hamiltonian philosophy of law.

HAMILTON, BENGT LEOPOLD KNUTSSON. b. 1892. Swedish-born American pediatrician. See: Amer. Men Sci., 6th ed. Hamilton-Swartz test.

Hamilton('s) canonical equation (or equations) (Hamilton, Sir William Rowan): Physics. See: Ballentyne; Internat. Dict. Phys. Elec.

Hamilton-Cayley theorem (Hamilton, Sir William Rowan and Cayley, Arthur). See: Cayley-Hamilton theorem.

Hamilton characteristic (Hamilton, Sir William Rowan): Physics. See: Internat. Dict. Ap. Math.

HAMILTON, DAVID JAMES. 1849-1909. Scottish pathologist. See: World Who's Who Sci. Hamilton's method.

HAMILTON, FRANK HASTINGS. 1813-1886. American surgeon. See: World Who's Who Sci. Hamilton's pseudophlegmon, Hamilton's test.

Hamilton-Jacobi equation (or partial differential equation) (Hamilton, Sir William Rowan and Jacobi, Carl Gustav Jacob): Physics. See: Ballentyne; Internat. Dict. Ap. Math.; Internat. Dict. Phys. Elec.

HAMILTON, JAMES. 1769-1829. English foreign language teacher. See: Encyc. Brit., 1973. Hamiltonian system.

Hamilton(ian) operator (Hamilton, Sir William Rowan): Physics. See: Hackh; Internat. Dict. Phys. Elec.

Hamilton('s) principle (Hamilton, Sir William Rowan): Physics. See: Ballentyne; Internat. Dict. Ap. Math.; James; Thewlis; Van Nostrand Sci. Encyc.

Hamilton-Swartz test (Hamilton, Bengt Leopold Knutsson and Schwartz, C.): Medicine. See: Stedman.

Hamilton theorem (Hamilton, Sir William Rowan): Physics. See: Internat. Dict. Ap. Math.

HAMILTON, SIR WILLIAM. 1788-1856. Scottish philosopher. See: Dict. Sci. Biog. Hamiltonism.

HAMILTON, SIR WILLIAM ROWAN. 1805-1865. Irish mathematical physicist. See: World Who's Who Sci. Cayley-Hamilton theorem, Gibbs-Hamilton notation, Hamilton('s) canonical equation (or equations), Hamilton characteristic, Hamilton-Jacobi equation (or partial differential equation), Hamilton(ian) operator, Hamilton('s) principle, Hamilton theorem, Hamiltonian density, Hamiltonian formalism for continuous systems, Hamiltonian (function), Hamiltonian function of optics, Hamiltonian representation, interaction Hamiltonian, Lagrangian and Hamiltonian formalism for continuous systems, perturbation Hamiltonian.

Hamiltonian (or Hamiltonianism) (Hamilton, Alexander): Politics. See: Hendrickson; Mathews, M. M.; Webster's 3d.

Hamiltonian density (Hamilton, Sir William Rowan): Physics. See: Internat. Dict. Ap. Math.

Hamiltonian formalism for continuous systems (Hamilton, Sir William Rowan): Physics. See: Internat. Dict. Ap. Math.

Hamiltonian (function) (Hamilton, Sir William Rowan): Physics. See: Ballentyne; Internat. Dict. Phys. Elec.; James; Thewlis; Van Nostrand Sci. Encyc.

Hamiltonian function of optics (Hamilton, Sir William Rowan): Physics. See: Internat. Dict. Ap. Math.

Hamiltonian philosophy of law (Hamilton, Alexander): Politics. See: Good.

Hamiltonian representation (Hamilton, Sir William Rowan): Physics. See: Van Nostrand Sci. Encyc. under "Representation Theory (Quantum Mechanical)."

Hamiltonian system (Hamilton, James): Linguistics. See: Brewer; Wagner (More Names).

Hamiltonism (Hamilton, Sir William): Philosophy. See: Webster's 3d.

Hamilton's method (Hamilton, David James): Medicine. See: Stedman.

Hamilton's pseudophlegmon (Hamilton, Frank Hastings): Medicine. See: Dorland; Stedman.

Hamilton's test (Hamilton, Frank Hastings): Medicine. See: Stedman.

Hamite (1) (Ham): History. See: Webster's 3d.

Hamite (2) (Ham): Anthropology. See: Encyc. Brit., 1973; Webster's 3d.

Hamitic (or Hamitic languages) (Ham): Linguistics. See: Encyc. Brit., 1973; Weekley.

HAMLET. Tragic hero of William Shakespeare's play "Hamlet" (1600-1601). See: Jobes. Hamlet, Hamlet without the part of the prince.

Hamlet (Hamlet, the fictional character): Generic Word (brooding, indecisive person). See: Webster's 3d.

Hamlet without the part of the prince (Hamlet, the fictional character): Generic Word (principal person at a function is absent). See: Jobès.

HAMLIN, AUGUSTUS CHOATE. 1829-1905. American mineralogist. See: Who Was Who Amer., 1897-1942. Hamlinite.

Hamlinite (Hamlin, Augustus Choate): Earth Sciences. See: Thrush.

HAMMAN, LOUIS. 1877-1946. American physician. See: Who Was Who Amer., 1943-1950. Hamman-Rich syndrome, Hamman('s) syndrome (or disease), Hamman's sign.

Hamman-Rich syndrome (Hamman, Louis and Rich, Arnold): Medicine. See: Dorland; Jablonski; Stedman.

Hamman('s) syndrome (or disease) (Hamman, Louis): Medicine. See: Dorland; Stedman.

Hamman's sign (Hamman, Louis): Medicine. See: Dorland; Stedman.

HAMMARSTEN, OLOF. 1841-1932. Swedish physiological chemist. See: Pogg., vols. 3, 4, 6. Hammarsten('s) reagent (or solution).

Hammarsten('s) reagent (or solution) (Hammarsten, Olof): Medicine. See: Dorland; Kelly; Stedman; Van Nostrand Chem. Dict.

Hammer-Aitoff projection (Von Hammer, Ernst Hermann Heinrich and Aitoff, David). See: Hammer projection.

Hammer, Ernst Hermann Heinrich von. See: Van Hammer, Ernst Hermann Heinrich von.

Hammer projection (Von Hammer, Ernst Hermann Heinrich): Geography. See: Monkhouse. Also known as: Aitoff-Hammer projection, Hammer-Aitoff projection.

HAMMERSCHLAG, ALBERT. 1863-1935. Austrian physician. See: Biog. Lex. hervorr. Aerzte, 1880-1930. Hammerschlag's method.

Hammerschlag's method (Hammerschlag, Albert): Medicine. See: Dorland; Stedman.

Hammett acidity function (Hammett, Louis Plack): Chemistry. See: Van Nostrand Sci. Encyc.

Hammett equation (Hammett, Louis Plack): Physics. See: Ballentyne.

HAMMETT, LOUIS PLACK. 1894- . American chemist. See: World Who's Who Sci. Hammett acidity function, Hammett equation, Hammett-Sottery test for aluminum.

Hammett-Sottery test for aluminum (Hammett, Louis Plack and Sottery, Constantine Theodore): Chemistry. See: Van Nostrand Chem. Dict.

HAMMICK, DALZIEL LLEWELLYN. 1887-1966. English chemist. See: Pogg., vols. 6, 7b. Hammick-Illingworth rule, Hammick reaction.

Hammick-Illingworth rule (Hammick, Dalziel Llewellyn and Illingworth, Walter S.): Chemistry. See: Ballentyne.

Hammick reaction (Hammick, Dalziel Llewellyn): Chemistry. See: Van Nostrand Chem. Dict.

Hamming (Hamming, G.?): Statistics. See: Kendall.

Hamming code (Hamming, Richard Wesley): Electronics. See: Markus.

HAMMING, G. fl. 1947-1949. Dutch? statistician. Cited in: Kendall and Doig. Hamming?

HAMMING, RICHARD WESLEY. 1915- . American mathematician. See: Amer. Men and Women Sci., 12th ed. Hamming code.

HAMMOND, LAURENS. 1895- . American inventor. See: Webster's Biog. Dict. Hammond organ.

Hammond organ (Hammond, Laurens): Music. See: Apel; Hughes.

HAMMOND, WILLIAM ALEXANDER. 1823-1900. American neurologist. See: Dict. Amer. Biog. Hammond's disease (or syndrome).

Hammond's disease (or syndrome) (Hammond, William Alexander): Medicine. See: Dorland; Jablonski.

HAMMURABI. ca. 1792-1750 B.C. King of Babylonia. See: Encyc. Brit., 1973. code of Hammurabi.

Hampden (or village Hampden) (Hampden, John): Generic Word (defender of people's liberties). See: Partridge.

HAMPDEN, JOHN. 1594-1643. English parliamentary leader. See: Dict. Nat. Biog. Hampden (or village Hampden), Hampden's case.

Hampden's case (Hampden, John): History. See: Steinberg.

Hampson meter (Hampson, William): Medicine. See: Stedman under "dose, erythema."

Hampson unit (Hampson, William): Medicine. See: Stedman.

HAMPSON, WILLIAM. 1854-1926. English inventor. See: World Who's Who Sci. Hampson meter, Hampson unit, Linde-Hampson method.

HAMPTON, AUBREY OTIS. 1900-1955. American radiologist. See: Who Was Who Amer., 1951-1960. Hampton hump, Hampton line, Hampton maneuver, Hampton technique.

Hampton hump (Hampton, Aubrey Otis): Medicine. See: Stedman.

Hampton line (Hampton, Aubrey Otis): Medicine. See: Stedman.

Hampton maneuver (Hampton, Aubrey Otis): Medicine. See: Stedman.

Hampton technique (Hampton, Aubrey Otis): Medicine. See: Stedman.

Ham's test (Ham, Thomas Hale): Medicine. See: Stedman.

HAMSTED, ADRIAN. fl. 1561. Dutch Anabaptist leader. (Biography source unavailable.) Adrianists.

Hamstorn's syndrome (Derivation undetermined): Medicine. See: Jablonski.

HAMZA, SHEIKH. fl. early 16th c. Dervish. (Biography source unavailable.) Hamzavis.

Hamzavis (Hamza, Sheikh): Religion. See: Canney.

Hanafites (Abu-Hanifah): Law. Cited in: Webster's Biog. Dict.

Hanbal, Ibn. See: Ahmad B. Muhammad B. Hanbal.

Hanbali (Ahmad B. Muhammad B. Hanbal): Law. See: Webster's 3d.

HANCOCK, ALBANY. 1806-1873. English zoologist. See: Nature, vol. 9 (1874), pp. 43-44. Hancockia.

Hancock boiler (Hancock, Walter): Engineering and Industry. See: Auger.

HANCOCK, E. P. fl. 1900. American mineralogist. Cited in: Bailey. Hancockite.

HANCOCK, HENRY. 1809-1880. English surgeon. See: Boase.

HANCOCK, HENRY R. fl. 1910. Australian engineer. Cited in: Chem. Abstr., vol. 4, p. 2629. Hancock jig.

Hancock jig (Hancock, Henry R.): Engineering and Industry. See: Thrush.

HANCOCK, JOHN. 1737-1793. American patriot. See: Dict. Amer. Biog. Hancockorian, John Hancock.

HANCOCK, WALTER. 1799-1852. English engineer. See: Dict. Nat. Biog. Hancock boiler.

Hancockia (Hancock, Albany): Zoology. See: Pennak.

Hancockite (Hancock, E. P.): Earth Sciences. See: Mathews, M. M.; Webster's 3d.

Hancockorian (Hancock, John): History. See: Mathews, M. M.

Hancock's amputation (Hancock, Henry): Medicine. See: Stedman.

HAND, ALFRED. 1868-1949. American pediatrician. See: New York Times, Sept. 3, 1949, p. 13, col. 7. Hand-Schueller-Christian syndrome (or disease).

Hand-Rowland disease (Hand, Alfred, Jr. and Rowland, Russell S.). See: Hand-Schueller-Christian syndrome (or disease).

Hand-Schueller-Christian syndrome (or disease) (Hand, Alfred, Jr.; Schueller, Artur; and Christian, Henry): Medicine. See: Dorland; Jablonski; Stedman; Webster's 3d. Also known as: Christian's syndrome, Hand-Rowland disease, Hand's disease (or syndrome), Schueller-Christian disease, Schueller's disease.

Handel and Haydn Society (Handel, George Frederick and Haydn, Joseph): Music. See: Latham.

Handel commemorations (Handel, George Frederick): Music. See: Scholes.

Handel festival (Handel, George Frederick): Music. See: Latham.

HANDEL, GEORGE FREDERICK. 1685-1759. German-born English composer. See: Dict. Nat. Biog. Handel and Haydn Society, Handel commemorations, Handel festival, Handel Society, Handel variations, Handelian, Tweedledum and Tweedledee.

Handel Society (Handel, George Frederick): Music. See: Latham; Scholes.

Handel variations (Handel, George Frederick): Music. See: Apel.

Handelian (Handel, George Frederick): Music. See: Webster's 3d.

HANDLEY, WILLIAM SAMPSON. b. 1872. English surgeon. See: Biog. Lex. hervorr. Aerzte, 1880-1930. Handley's method.

Handley's method (Handley, William Sampson): Medicine. See: Dorland.

Handmaids of Mary (Mary, Virgin-Mother): Religion. See: Attwater.

Hand's disease (or syndrome) (Hand, Alfred, Jr.). See: Hand-Schueller-Christian syndrome (or disease).

Handy-Andy (Rooney, Handy Andy): Generic Word (handyman). See: Webster's 3d.

HANFMANN, EUGENIA. fl. 1937-1975. American psychologist. See: Biog. Direct. Amer. Psych. Assoc., 1975. Hanfmann-Kasanin concept formation test.

Hanfmann-Kasanin concept formation test (Hanfmann, Eugenia and Kasanin, Jacob Sergi): Psychology. See: Chaplin; Wolman.

HANGER, FRANKLIN M. 1894-   . American physician. See: World Who's Who Sci. Hanger's test.

Hanger's test (Hanger, Franklin M.): Medicine. See: Dorland; Stedman.

HANHART, ERNST. fl. 1936-1950. Swiss internist. Cited in: Mansell. Hanhart's disease, Hanhart's nanism (or syndrome (3)), Hanhart's syndrome (1), Hanhart's syndrome (2), Richner-Hanhart syndrome.

Hanhart's disease (Hanhart, Ernst): Medicine. See: Jablonski.

Hanhart's nanism (or syndrome (3)) (Hanhart, Ernst): Medicine. See: Jablonski.

Hanhart's syndrome (1) (Hanhart, Ernst): Medicine. See: Jablonski.

Hanhart's syndrome (2) (Hanhart, Ernst): Medicine. See: Jablonski.

Hanhart's syndrome (4) (Hanhart, Ernst). See: Richner-Hanhart syndrome.

HANKE, MILTON THEODORE. b. 1893. American chemist. See: Amer. Men Sci., 4th ed. Koessler-Hanke estimation of imidazoles.

Hankel function(s) (Hankel, Hermann): Mathematics. See: Ballentyne; Internat. Dict. Ap. Math.; Internat. Dict. Phys. Elec.; James; Thewlis. Also known as: Bessel functions of the third kind.

HANKEL, HERMANN. 1839-1873. German mathematician. See: Dict. Sci. Biog. Hankel function(s), Hankel transform, Hankel's integral.

Hankel transform (Hankel, Hermann): Mathematics. See: Internat. Dict. Ap. Math.; Thewlis.

Hankel's integral (Hankel, Hermann): Mathematics. See: Ballentyne.

HANKINS, GEORGE ALEXANDER. fl. 1923. English engineer. Cited in: Mansell. Hankins scratch test.

Hankins scratch test (Hankins, George Alexander): Engineering and Industry. See: Auger.

HANKS, HENRY G. 1826-1907. American mineralogist. See: Who Was Who Amer., 1897-1942. Hanksite.

Hanksite (Hanks, Henry G.): Earth Sciences. See: Thrush; Webster's 3d.

HANLON, C. ROLLINS. 1913-   . American surgeon. See: Direct. Med. Specialists, 1970-1971. Blalock-Hanlon operation.

Hanlon-Lees troupe (Hanlon, Thomas and Lees, John): Theater. See: Hartnoll.

HANLON, THOMAS. fl. 19th c. English actor. (Biography source unavailable.) Hanlon-Lees troupe.

HANN, F. VON. fl. 1918. Hungarian physician. Cited in: Lieber and Olbrich. Hann's disease.

HANN, JULIUS FERDINAND VON. 1839-1921. Austrian meteorologist. See: Dict. Sci. Biog. Hanning.

Hannah (Snell, Hannah): Military Science. See: Brewer.

HANNAY, JAMES BALLANTINE. b. 1855. Scottish chemist. See: Pogg., vol. 3. Hannay test reaction, Hannayite.

Hannay test reaction (Hannay, James Ballantine): Chemistry. See: Van Nostrand Chem. Dict.

Hannayite (Hannay, James Ballantine): Earth Sciences. See: Thrush; Webster's 3d.

HANNIBAL. 247-183 B.C. Carthaginian general. See: Encyc. Brit., 1973. Hannibalic (or Hannibalian).

Hannibalic (or Hannibalian) (Hannibal): History. See: Webster's 3d.

Hanning (Hann, Julius Ferdinand von): Statistics. See: Kendall.

HANNOVER, ADOLPH. 1814-1894. Danish anatomist. See: World Who's Who Sci. Hannover's canal.

Hannover's canal (Hannover, Adolph): Anatomy. See: Dorland; Stedman.

Hann's disease (Hann, F. von): Medicine. See: Jablonski.

Hanot-Chauffard syndrome (Hanot, Victor Charles and Chauffard, Anatole Marie Emile). See: Troisier-Hanot-Chauffard syndrome.

Hanot-Kiener syndrome (Hanot, Victor Charles): Medicine. See: Jablonski.

Hanot-MacMahon-Thannhauser syndrome (Hanot, Victor Charles; MacMahon, Harold Edward; and Thannhauser, Siegfried Josef): Medicine. See: Jablonski. Also known as: MacMahon-Thannhauser syndrome, Thannhauser-Magendantz syndrome.

Hanot-Roessle syndrome (Hanot, Victor Charles and Roessle, Robert): Medicine. See: Jablonski.

HANOT, VICTOR CHARLES. 1844-1896. French physician. See: World Who's Who Sci. Hanot-Kiener syndrome, Hanot-MacMahon-Thannhauser syndrome, Hanot-Roessle syndrome, Hanot's cirrhosis, Troisier-Hanot-Chauffard syndrome.

Hanot's cirrhosis (Hanot, Victor Charles): Medicine. See: Dorland; Jablonski; Stedman.

HANOVER. Electoral house of Germany and royal family of England. See: Encyc. Brit., 1973. Hanoverian succession.

Hanoverian succession (Hanover): History. See: Steinberg.

HANRAHAN, MAY. fl. mid-20th c. American benefactress to sailors. (Biography source unavailable.) Aunt May.

HANSARD, LUKE. 1752-1828. English printer. See: Dict. Nat. Biog. Hansard (official reports of the English Parliament) (and Hansardize).

Hansard (official reports of the English Parliament) (and Hansardize) (Hansard, Luke and Hansard, Thomas Curson): Politics. See: Brewer; Lockwood; Partridge; Steinberg; Webster's 3d.

HANSARD, THOMAS CURSON. 1776-1833. English printer. See: Dict. Nat. Biog. Hansard (official reports of the English Parliament) (and Hansardize).

HANSEN, CHRISTIAN JOHANNES. b. 1886. German chemist. See: Pogg., vols. 6, 7a. Hansen reagent?

HANSEN, GERHARD HENRIK ARMAUER. 1841-1912. Norwegian bacteriologist. Hansen's bacillus, Hansen's disease (or Hansenosis).

Hansen hybrid plums (Hansen, Niels Ebbesen): Botany. Cited in: Webster's Biog. Dict. under "Hansen, Niels Ebbesen."

HANSEN, NIELS EBBESEN. 1866-1950. Danish-born American horticulturist. See: World Who's Who Sci. Hansen hybrid plums, Hansen squirreltail?

HANSEN, PETER ANDREAS. 1795-1874. Danish astronomer. See: World Who's Who Sci. Hansen's integral formula?

Hansen reagent (Hansen, Christian Johannes?): Chemistry. See: Van Nostrand Chem. Dict.

Hansen squirreltail (Hansen, Niels Ebbesen?): Botany. See: Winburne.

Hansen's bacillus (Hansen, Gerhard Henrik Armauer): Medicine. See: Dorland; Stedman; Webster's 3d.

Hansen's disease (or Hansenosis) (Hansen, Gerhard Henrik Armauer): Medicine. See: Jablonski; Stedman; Webster's 3d.

Hansen's integral formula (Hansen, Peter Andreas?): Mathematics. See: Ballentyne.

HANSGIRG, FRITZ. fl. 1935. German chemical engineer. Cited in: Chem. Abstr. Hansgirg process.

Hansgirg process (Hansgirg, Fritz): Engineering and Industry. See: Thrush; Van Nostrand Chem. Dict.

Hansom (or Hansom cab) (Hansom, Joseph Aloysius): Generic Word. See: Brewer; Hargrave; Harvey; Hendrickson; Latham; Webster's 3d.

HANSOM, JOSEPH ALOYSIUS. 1803-1882. English architect and inventor. See: Dict. Nat. Biog. Hansom (or Hansom cab).

HANSON, ADOLPH MELANCHTON. 1888-1959. American physician. See: World Who's Who Sci. Hanson unit.

Hanson lily (Derivation undetermined): Botany. See: Winburne.

HANSON, TIMOTHY. fl. ca. 1720. American farmer. (Biography source unavailable.) Timoth (or Timothy grass and hay), Timothy trimmer.

Hanson unit (Hanson, Adolph Melanchton): Medicine. See: Dorland; Stedman.

HANSTROEM, BERTIL. b. 1891. Swedish zoologist. See: Vem Ar Det?, 1933. Hanstrom's organ.

Hanstrom's organ (Hanstroem, Bertil): Zoology. See: Gray.

HANTZSCH, ARTHUR RUDOLF. 1857-1935. German chemist. See: Dict. Sci. Biog. Auld-Hantzsch test, Hantzsch pyridine synthesis, Hantzsch synthesis (or pyrrole synthesis), Hantzsch-Widman name.

Hantzsch pyridine synthesis (Hantzsch, Arthur Rudolf): Chemistry. See: Van Nostrand Chem. Dict.

Hantzsch synthesis (or pyrrole synthesis) (Hantzsch, Arthur Rudolf): Chemistry. See: Ballentyne; Van Nostrand Chem. Dict.

Hantzsch-Widman name (Hantzsch, Arthur Rudolf and Widman, Oskar): Chemistry. See: Van Nostrand Sci. Encyc. under "Organic Chemical Nomenclature."

HANUS, JOSEF. 1872-1955. Czech chemist. See: Pogg., vols. 6, 7b. Hanus reagent for cinnamaldehyde, Hanus reagent for vanillin, Hanus solution (solution for determining iodine number or method), Hanusite.

Hanus reagent for cinnamaldehyde (Hanus, Josef): Chemistry. See: Van Nostrand Chem. Dict.

Hanus reagent for vanillin (Hanus, Josef): Chemistry. See: Van Nostrand Chem. Dict.

Hanus solution (solution for determining iodine number or method) (Hanus, Josef): Chemistry. See: Hackh; Van Nostrand Chem. Dict.

Hanusite (Hanus, Josef): Earth Sciences. See: Webster's 3d.

HAPKE, FRANZ. fl. 1910. German physician. Cited in: Kelly. Hapke's phenomenon.

Hapke's phenomenon (Hapke, Franz): Medicine. See: Dorland; Stedman.

Hapsburg family. See: Habsburg.

Hapsburg jaw (and lip) (Habsburg): Medicine. See: Stedman.

HARADA, E. fl. 1926. Japanese ophthalmologist. (Biography source unavailable.) Harada's disease (or syndrome).

Harada's disease (or syndrome) (Harada, E.): Medicine. See: Jablonski; Stedman.

HARBITZ, FRANCIS. 1867-1950. Norwegian physician. See: Biog. Lex. hervorr. Aerzte, 1880-1930. Harbitz-Mueller disease, Raeder-Harbitz syndrome.

Harbitz-Mueller disease (Harbitz, Francis and Mueller, Carl): Medicine. See: Jablonski.

HARBONG. No dates. Hindu rajah. (Biography source unavailable.) Harbong ka raj.

Harbong ka raj (Harbong): Generic Word (civil disorders). See: Charnock.

HARCOURT, AUGUSTUS GEORGE VERNON. 1834-1919. English chemist. See: Dict. Sci. Biog. Harcourt lamp.

Harcourt lamp (Harcourt, Augustus George Vernon): Physics. See: Internat. Dict. Phys. Elec.

HARDAUL LALA. No dates. Hindu chieftain. (Biography source unavailable.) Hardaur (or Hardour).

Hardaur (or Hardour) (Hardaul Lala): Sociology. See: Charnock.

HARDEN, SIR ARTHUR. 1865-1940. English biochemist. See: Dict. Sci. Biog. Harden-Norris diacetyl reaction, Harden-Young ester.

Harden-Norris diacetyl reaction (Harden, Sir Arthur and Norris, Dorothy): Chemistry. See: Van Nostrand Chem. Dict.

Harden-Young ester (Harden, Sir Arthur and Young, William John): Chemistry. See: Hackh; Stedman.

HARDENBERG, FRANZISKA VON. No dates. Austrian noblewoman. (Biography source unavailable.) Hardenbergia.

Hardenbergia (Hardenberg, Franziska von): Botany. See: Taylor, N.; Webster's 3d.

HARDER, JOHANN JACOB. 1656-1711. Swiss anatomist. See: World Who's Who Sci. Harderian (or Harder's) gland.

Harderian (or Harder's) gland (Harder, Johann Jacob): Zoology. See: Dorland; Gray; Henderson; Pennak; Stedman.

Hardgrove number (Hardgrove, Ralph M.): Engineering and Industry. See: Thrush.

HARDGROVE, RALPH M. b. 1891. American mechanical engineer. See: Who's Who Engin., 1937. Hardgrove number, Hardgrove test.

Hardgrove test (Hardgrove, Ralph M.): Engineering and Industry. See: Thrush.

HARDING, HAROLD EDWARD. fl. 1934-1972. English pathologist. See: Med. Direct., 1972. Harding-Passey melanoma.

Harding-Passey melanoma (Harding, Harold Edward and Passey, Richard Douglas): Medicine. See: Jablonski; Stedman.

HARDINGE, HARLOWE. b. 1894. American mechanical engineer. See: Who's Who Engin., 1922-1923. Hardinge mill, Hardinge thickener.

Hardinge mill (Hardinge, Harlowe): Engineering and Industry. See: Thrush.

Hardinge thickener (Hardinge, Harlowe): Engineering and Industry. See: Thrush.

Hardwick conveyor loader head (Derivation undetermined): Engineering and Industry. See: Thrush.

Hardwicke, 1st Earl of. See: Yorke, Philip, 1st Earl of Hardwicke.

HARDWICKE, THOMAS. 1757-1835. English artillery officer in India. See: Britten and Boulger. Hardwickia.

Hardwicke's Act (Yorke, Philip, 1st Earl of Hardwicke). See: Lord Hardwicke's Act.

Hardwickia (Hardwicke, Thomas): Botany. See: Webster's 3d.

Hardy brake (Hardy, John George): Engineering and Industry. See: Auger.

Hardy Cross. See: Cross, Hardy.

Hardy Cross method (Cross, Hardy): Engineering and Industry. See: Thrush.

HARDY, SIR GEORGE FRANCIS. d. 1914. English actuary. See: Who Was Who, 1897-1916. Hardy summation method.

HARDY, GODFREY HAROLD. 1877-1947. English mathematician. See: World Who's Who Sci. Hardy-Weinberg law (or formula).

HARDY, JOHN GEORGE. 1851-1914. Austrian engineer. See: Oesterr. Biog. Lex., 1815-1950. Hardy brake.

HARDY, LOUIS PHILLIPE ALFRED. 1811-1893. French physician. See: Biog. Lex. hervorr. Aerzte. Behier-Hardy symptom.

Hardy-Schulze rule (Hardy, Sir William Bate and Schulze, Hans). See: Schulze-Hardy rule.

Hardy summation method (Hardy, Sir George Francis): Statistics. See: Kendall.

Hardy-Weinberg law (or formula) (Hardy, Godfrey Harold and Weinberg, Wilhelm): Genetics. See: Encyc. Brit., 1973 under "Anthropology," vol. 2, p. 53b; Gray; Pennak.

HARDY, SIR WILLIAM BATE. 1864-1934. English biologist. See: World Who's Who Sci. Schulze-Hardy rule.

HARE, EDWARD SELLECK. 1812-1838. English physician. (Biography source unavailable.) Hare's syndrome.

HARE, ROBERT. 1781-1858. American chemist. See: Dict. Sci. Biog. Hare's apparatus.

Hare system (or plan) (Hare, Thomas): Politics. See: Smith; Webster's 3d.

HARE, THOMAS. 1806-1891. English political reformer. See: Dict. Nat. Biog., 1st suppl. Hare system (or plan).

Hare's apparatus (Hare, Robert): Chemistry. See: Webster's 3d.

Hare's syndrome (Hare, Edward Selleck). See: Pancoast's syndrome (apex syndrome or tumor).

Hargrave kite (Hargrave, Lawrence): Recreation and Sports. See: Webster's 3d.

HARGRAVE, LAWRENCE. 1850-1915. Australian pioneer in aviation. See: Dict. Australian Biog. Hargrave kite.

HARGREAVE, CHARLES J. fl. 19th c. English mathematician. Cited in: Royal Soc. Cat. Sci. Pap., 1800-1863. Hargreave's equation.

Hargreaves-Bird cell (Hargreaves, James and Bird, T.): Chemistry. See: Hackh; Van Nostrand Chem. Dict.

Hargreave's equation (Hargreave, Charles J.): Mathematics. See: Ballentyne.

HARGREAVES, GEORGE WALTER. 1903- . American pharmaceutical chemist. See: Amer. Men Sci., 9th ed. Hargreaves test reaction.

HARGREAVES, JAMES. 1834-1915. English chemist. See: World Who's Who Sci. Hargreaves-Bird cell.

Hargreaves test reaction (Hargreaves, George Walter): Chemistry. See: Van Nostrand Chem. Dict.

Haring cell (Haring, Horace Egbert): Chemistry. See: Thrush.

HARING, HORACE EGBERT. b. 1895. American electrochemist. See: Amer. Men Sci., 9th ed. Haring cell.

HARINGTON, JOHN, 1ST BARON HARINGTON OF EXTON. d. 1613. English nobleman. See: Dict. Nat. Biog. Harrington (farthing).

HARISON, MR. fl. 19th c. American horticulturist. (Biography source unavailable.) Harison's yellow rose.

Harison's yellow rose (Harison, Mr.): Botany. See: Webster's 3d.

HARKAVY, JOSEPH. b. 1890. American physician. See: Direct. Med. Specialists, 1975-1976. Harkavy's syndrome.

Harkavy's syndrome (Harkavy, Joseph): Medicine. See: Jablonski.

HARKER, ALFRED. 1859-1939. English petrologist. See: Dict. Sci. Biog. Harkerite.

HARKER, DAVID. 1906- . American chemist. See: World Who's Who Sci. Donnay-Harker principle, Harker-Kasper inequalities, Patterson-Harker method.

Harker-Kasper inequalities (Harker, David and Kasper, John Simon): Physics. See: Internat. Dict. Phys. Elec.

Harkerite (Harker, Alfred): Earth Sciences. See: Thrush.

Harkins and Jura method (Harkins, William Draper and Jura, George): Chemistry. See: Thrush.

Harkins theory (Harkins, William Draper): Chemistry. See: Hackh.

HARKINS, WILLIAM DRAPER. 1873-1951. American physical chemist. See: Dict. Sci. Biog. Harkins and Jura method, Harkins theory.

Harkness Ballet (Harkness, Rebekah Semple West): Dance. See: Chujoy.

HARKNESS, REBEKAH SEMPLE WEST. 1915- . American composer and sponsor of dance. See: Cur. Biog., Yearbook, 1974. Harkness Ballet.

Harkort test (Harktort, Herman): Engineering and Industry. See: Thrush.

HARKTORT, HERMAN. fl. 1914. German ceramics chemist. Cited in: Chem. Abstr., Decenn. Index, 1907-1916. Harkort test.

HARLAN, RICHARD. 1796-1843. American physician and naturalist. See: Dict. Sci. Biog. Harlan's hawk (or buzzard).

HARLAND, SYDNEY CROSS. fl. 1940. English botanist. See: Who's Who Sci. Europe, 1972. Harlands box?

Harlands box (Harland, Sydney Cross?): Botany. See: Winburne.

Harlan's hawk (or buzzard) (Harlan, Richard): Zoology. See: Mathews, M. M.; Webster's 3d.

Harleian collection (or manuscripts) (Harley, Robert, 1st Earl of Oxford and Harley, Edward, 2d Earl of Oxford): Literature. See: Brewer; Phyfe.

Harleian Miscellany (Harley, Robert, 1st Earl of Oxford and Harley, Edward, 2d Earl of Oxford): Literature. See: Brewer.

Harleian Society (Harley, Robert, 1st Earl of Oxford and Harley, Edward, 2d Earl of Oxford): Sociology. See: Brewer.

Harleian style (Harley, Robert, 1st Earl of Oxford and Harley, Edward, 2d Earl of Oxford): Library Science. See: Harrod; Lockwood; Webster's 3d.

HARLEQUIN. Personification of the discordant elements of life. See: Jobes. Harlequin bloom, Harlequin costume, Harlequin (1), Harlequin (2) (pattern), Harlequinade.

Harlequin (1) (Harlequin): Generic Word (buffoon). See: Charnock; Scott; Webster's 3d.

Harlequin (2) (pattern) (Harlequin): Fashion. See: Picken; Webster's 3d.

Harlequin bloom (Harlequin): Generic Word (laughing at trouble). See: Jobes.

Harlequin costume (Harlequin): Fashion. See: Picken; Webster's 3d.

Harlequinade (Harlequin): Theater. See: Hargrave; Webster's 3d.

Harley approximation (Harley, B. I.): Statistics. See: Kendall.

HARLEY, B. I. fl. 1957. English statistician. Cited in: Kendall and Doig. Harley approximation.

HARLEY, EDWARD, 2ND EARL OF OXFORD. 1689-1741. English book collector. See: Dict. Nat. Biog. Harleian collection (or manuscripts), Harleian Miscellany, Harleian Society, Harleian style.

HARLEY, GEORGE. 1829-1896. English physician. See: Boase. Harley's disease.

HARLEY, ROBERT, 1ST EARL OF OXFORD. 1661-1724. English statesman. See: Dict. Nat. Biog. Harleian collection (or manuscripts), Harleian Miscellany, Harleian Society, Harleian style.

Harley's disease (Harley, George). See: Dressler's syndrome.

HARMAN, EUGENE S. fl. 1950. American engineer. Cited in: Chem. Abstr., Decenn. Index, 1947-1956. Harman process.

Harman method (Harman, Theodore Carter): Physics. Cited in: World Who's Who Sci. under "Harman, Theodore Carter."

Harman process (Harman, Eugene S.): Engineering and Industry. See: Thrush.

HARMAN, THEODORE CARTER. 1929- . American physicist. See: World Who's Who Sci. Harman method.

HARMAR, JOSIAH. 1753-1813. American soldier. See: Dict. Amer. Biog. Harmar's defeat.

Harmar's defeat (Harmar, Josiah): History. See: Jameson.

Harmensen, James. See: Arminius, Jacobus.

HARMONIA. Daughter of Aries and Aphrodite in Greek mythology. See: Jobes. Harmonia's necklace (or Harmonia).

Harmonia's necklace (or Harmonia) (Harmonia): Generic Word (unlucky gift). See: Brewer.

HARMS, CLAUS. 1778-1855. German divine. See: Encyc. Brit., 1911. ninety-five theses of Harms.

HARNACK, AXEL (In full: CARL GUSTAV AXEL). 1851-1888. German mathematician. See: Pogg., vols. 3, 4. Harnack's theorem.

Harnack's theorem (Harnack, Axel): Mathematics. See: Ballentyne.

HARNASCH, HANS MAX EMIL. 1907- . German physician. Cited in: Index-Cat. Libr. Surg.-Gen. Off., 4th ser., vol. 7, 1942. Harnasch's disease.

Harnasch's disease (Harnasch, Hans Max Emil): Medicine. See: Jablonski.

HARNER, HAROLD RUSSELL. 1901- . American chemist. See: Amer. Men Sci., 7th ed. Musgrave-Harner turbidimeter.

Harness Prize (Harness, William): Literature. See: Latham.

HARNESS, WILLIAM. 1790-1869. English clergyman and writer. See: Dict. Nat. Biog. Harness Prize.

HARNISCH, OTTO ERNST RICHARD. 1901- . German hydrobiologist. See: Pogg., vol. 7a. Harnischia?

Harnischia (Harnisch, Otto Ernst Richard?): Zoology. See: Pennak.

Harold Jeffreys Lecture (Jeffreys, Sir Harold): Astronomy. See: Satterthwaite.

Harriet Lane (Lane, Harriet): Generic Word (Australian canned meat). See: Brewer; Hendrickson.

HARRINGTON. fl. ca. 1834. Irish friend of T. Thomson. Cited in: Bailey. Harringtonite.

HARRINGTON, DAVID O. 1904- . American ophthalmologist. See: Direct. Med. Specialists, 1975-1976. Harrington-Flocks test.

HARRINGTON, ETHEL REGAN. b. 1891. American pediatrician. Cited in: Mansell. Helmholz-Harrington syndrome.

Harrington (farthing) (Harington, John, 1st Baron Harington of Exton): Numismatics. See: Brewer.

Harrington–Flocks test (Harrington, David O. and Flocks, Milton): Medicine. See: Stedman.

Harringtonite (Harrington): Earth Sciences. See: Charnock.

Harris and Ray test (Harris, Leslie Julius and Ray, Surendra N.): Medicine. See: Stedman. Also known as: Harris test.

Harris buck (or Harrisbuck) (Harris, Sir William Cornwallis): Zoology. See: Partridge; Webster's 3d.

Harris convention (Harris, Townsend): History. See: Morris and Irwin.

HARRIS, EDWARD. 1799-1863. American naturalist. Cited in: Royal Soc. Cat. Sci. Pap., 1800-1863. Harris('s) hawk (or buzzard, Harris('s) sparrow, Harris's woodpecker.

HARRIS, EDWARD GRANT. 1924- . American theoretical physicist. See: Amer. Men Sci., 11th ed. Harris instability.

Harris flow (Harris, Lawrence Arnold?): Physics. See: Hughes; Van Nostrand Sci. Encyc.

HARRIS, GEORGE. No dates. American photographer? (Biography source unavailable.) George Harris Award.

Harris('s) hawk (or buzzard) (Harris, Edward): Zoology. See: Mathews, M. M; Pennak; Webster's 3d.

Harris' hematoxylin (Harris, Henry Fauntleroy): Medicine. See: Stedman; Van Nostrand Chem. Dict.

HARRIS, HENRY. fl. 1920. English engineer. Cited in: Chem. Abstr., Decenn. Index, 1917-1926. Harris process.

HARRIS, HENRY ALBERT. b. 1886. English anatomist. Cited in: Index-Cat. Libr. Surg.-Gen. Off., 4th ser., vol. 7, 1942. Harris' lines.

HARRIS, HENRY FAUNTLEROY. 1867-1926. American physician. See: J. A. M. A., vol. 86 (1926), p. 1088. Harris' hematoxylin.

Harris instability (Harris, Edward Grant): Physics. See: Hughes.

HARRIS, JOHN (In full: WILLIAM JOHN). 1903- . New Zealand librarian in Nigeria and Ghana. See: Who's Who Librarianship, 1972. John Harris Award.

HARRIS, LAWRENCE ARNOLD. 1923- . Canadian-born American physicist. See: World Who's Who Sci. Harris flow?

HARRIS, LESLIE JULIUS. 1898- . English biological chemist. See: Pogg., vol. 6. Harris and Ray test.

Harris' lines (Harris, Henry Albert): Anatomy. See: Stedman.

HARRIS, LOUIS. 1921- . American public opinion analyst. See: Who's Who Amer., 1970-1971. Harris poll.

HARRIS, MALCOLM LA SALLE. 1862-1936. American surgeon. See: World Who's Who Sci. Harris separator (or segregator).

Harris' migraine (Harris, Wilfred John): Medicine. See: Jablonski; Stedman. Also known as: Horton's neuralgia.

Harris poll (Harris, Louis): Sociology. See: Hendrickson.

Harris process (Harris, Henry): Engineering and Industry. See: Thrush; Van Nostrand Chem. Dict.

HARRIS, SEALE. 1870-1957. American physician. See: Who Was Who Amer., 1951-1960. Harris' syndrome.

Harris separator (or segregator) (Harris, Malcolm La Salle): Medicine. See: Dorland; Stedman.

Harris('s) sparrow (Harris, Edward): Zoology. See: Mathews, M. M.; Webster's 3d.

Harris' syndrome (Harris, Seale): Medicine. See: Jablonski.

Harris test (Harris, Leslie Julius). See: Harris and Ray test.

HARRIS, TOWNSEND. 1804-1878. American diplomat. See: Dict. Amer. Biog. Harris convention.

HARRIS, WILFRED JOHN. 1869-1960. English physician. See: Who Was Who, 1951-1960. Harris' migraine.

HARRIS, WILLIAM. 1860-1920. Scottish-born Jamaican botanist. See: Britten and Boulger. Harrisella, Harrisia.

HARRIS, SIR WILLIAM CORNWALLIS. 1807-1848. English engineer and traveller. See: Dict. Nat. Biog. Harris buck (or Harrisbuck).

HARRISBERGER, LEE (In full: EDGAR LEE). 1924- . American mechanical engineer. See: Amer. Men and Women Sci., 12th ed. Harrisberger's laws of the laboratory.

Harrisberger's laws of the laboratory (Harrisberger, Lee): Sociology. See: Martin.

Harriscolor process (Derivation undetermined): Photography. See: Focal Encyc. Photog.

Harrisella (Harris, William): Botany. Cited in: Britten and Boulger.

Harrisia (Harris, William): Botany. See: Partridge; Taylor, N.; Webster's 3d.

HARRISON, BIRGE (In full: LOVELL BIRGE). 1854-1929. American landscape painter. See: Dict. Amer. Biog. Harrison red.

Harrison boiler (or steam boiler) (Harrison, Joseph): Engineering and Industry. See: Auger.

HARRISON, BYRON PATTON. 1881-1941. American legislator. See: Biog. Direct. Amer. Congress. Harrison Narcotic Act.

HARRISON, CHARLES VICTOR. 1907- . English pathologist. See: World Who's Who Sci. Harrison–Vaughan disease.

HARRISON, EDWARD. 1766-1838. English physician. See: World Who's Who Sci. Harrison's groove.

HARRISON, HAROLD EDWARD. 1908- . American physician. See: World Who's Who Sci. Harrison spot test?

HARRISON, JOSEPH. 1810-1874. American mechanical engineer. See: Dict. Amer. Biog. Harrison boiler (or steam boiler).

Harrison Land Act (Harrison, William Henry "Tippecanoe"): Politics. See: Morris.

Harrison Narcotic Act (Harrison, Byron Patton): Politics. See: Hackh.

HARRISON, PETER JEFFREY. 1935- . English mathematical statistician. See: Who's Who Sci. Europe, 1972. Harrison's method.

Harrison red (Harrison, Birge): Fine Arts. See: Webster's 3d.

HARRISON, SAMUEL BEALEY. 1802-1867. English-born Canadian statesman. See: Macmillan Dict. Canadian Biog. Sydenham–Harrison resolution.

Harrison spot test (Harrison, Harold Edward?): Medicine. See: Blakiston's Gould; Stedman.

Harrison–Vaughan disease (Harrison, Charles Victor and Vaughan, Janet M.). See: Vaughan's disease.

HARRISON, WILLIAM HENRY "TIPPECANOE." 1773-1841. American president. See: Dict. Amer. Biog. Harrison Land Act, Harrisonian (or Harrisonite), Tippecanoe and Tyler Too, Tippecanoe(s).

Harrisonian (or Harrisonite) (Harrison, William Henry "Tippecanoe"): History. See: Mathews, M. M.

Harrison's groove (Harrison, Edward): Medicine. See: Dorland; Stedman.

Harrison's method (Harrison, Peter Jeffrey): Statistics. See: Kendall.

Harris's woodpecker (Harris, Edward): Zoology. See: Mathews, M. M.; Webster's 3d.

Harrop kiln (Derivation undetermined): Engineering and Industry. See: Thrush.

Harrower inkblots (Harrower, Molly R.): Psychology. See: Wolman.

HARROWER (Or HARROWER-ERICKSON), MOLLY R. 1906- . American psychologist. See: Biog. Direct. Amer. Psych. Assoc., 1975. Harrower inkblots.

Harry Tate (airplane) (Tate, Harry): History. See: Hargrave.

HART, CECIL. d. 1940. Canadian hockey coach. See: New York Times, July 17, 1940, p. 21, col. 2. Hart Memorial Trophy.

HART, EDWARD WATSON. fl. 1942-1972. English pediatrician. See: Med. Direct., 1972. Hart's syndrome.

HART, HARRY. b. 1848. English mechanician. See: Pogg., vol. 3. Hart's parallel motion.

HART, HENRY GEORGE. 1808-1878. English soldier. See: Dict. Nat. Biog. Hart's Army List.

Hart Memorial Trophy (Hart, Cecil): Recreation and Sports. See: Arlott.

HARTEL, FRITZ. fl. 1913. German surgeon. Cited in: Index-Cat. Libr. Surg.-Gen. Off., 3d ser., vol. 6, 1926. Hartel technique.

Hartel technique (Hartel, Fritz): Medicine. See: Dorland; Stedman.

Harter Act (Harter, Michael Daniel): Politics. See: Black; Clark; Smith.

HARTER, MICHAEL DANIEL. 1846-1896. American legislator. See: Biog. Direct. Amer. Congress. Harter Act.

Hartig net (Hartig, Robert): Botany. See: Henderson.

HARTIG, ROBERT (In full: HEINRICH JULIUS ADOLPH ROBERT). 1839-1901. German botanist. See: World Who's Who Sci. Hartig net.

Hartington Commission (Cavendish, Spencer Compton, Marquis of Hartington and 8th Duke of Devonshire): History. See: Montgomery.

Hartington, Marquis of. See: Cavendish, Spencer Compton, Marquis of Hartington and 8th Duke of Devonshire.

HARTL, F. fl. 1903. German chemist. (Biography source unavailable.) Vanino-Hartl test reaction.

HARTLAUB, GUSTAV (In full: CARL JOHANN GUSTAV). 1814-1900. German ornithologist. See: World Who's Who Sci. Hartlaub's touraco (or turaco).

Hartlaub's touraco (or turaco) (Hartlaub, Gustav): Zoology. See: Encyc. Brit., 1973 under "Turaco"; Gray.

Hartleian (or Hartleyan) (Hartley, David): Philosophy. See: Weekley; Webster's 3d.

Hartley bands (Hartley, Sir Walter Noel): Physics. See: Huschke.

HARTLEY, DAVID. 1705-1757. English philosopher. See: Internat. Encyc. Soc. Sci. Hartleian (or Hartleyan).

HARTLEY, ERNALD GEORGE JUSTINIAN. fl. 1906. English physicist. Cited in: Chem. Abstr. Berkeley and Hartley method.

Hartley formula for time-frequency duality (Hartley, Ralph Vinton Lyon): Electronics. See: Internat. Dict. Phys. Elec.

HARTLEY, FRED ALLAN, JR. 1902-1969. American legislator. See: Biog. Direct. Amer. Congress. Taft-Hartley Act.

Hartley gravimeter (Derivation undetermined): Physics. See: Thrush.

Hartley oscillator (Hartley, Ralph Vinton Lyon): Electronics. See: Hughes; Internat. Dict. Phys. Elec.; Markus; Thewlis; Van Nostrand Sci. Encyc.

HARTLEY, SIR PERCIVAL. 1881-1957. English biochemist. See: World Who's Who Sci. Hartley's broth.

Hartley principle (or law) (Hartley, Ralph Vinton Lyon): Electronics. See: Hughes; Markus; Van Nostrand Sci. Encyc.

HARTLEY, RALPH VINTON LYON. b. 1888. American physicist. See: World Who's Who Sci. Hartley formula for time-frequency duality, Hartley oscillator, Hartley principle (or law), Hartley (unit).

Hartley test reaction (Hartley, Sir Walter Noel): Chemistry. See: Van Nostrand Chem. Dict.

Hartley (unit) (Hartley, Ralph Vinton Lyon): Electronics. See: Hughes; Internat. Dict. Phys. Elec.; Markus; Van Nostrand Sci. Encyc.

HARTLEY, SIR WALTER NOEL. 1846-1913. Irish physicist. See: Pogg., vols. 4, 5. Hartley bands, Hartley test reaction.

Hartley's broth (Hartley, Sir Percival): Medicine. Cited in: World Who's Who Sci. under "Hartley, Sir Percival."

Hartman eustachian catheters (Hartmann, Arthur): Medicine. Cited in: Laughlin.

HARTMAN, LE ROY LEO. 1893-1951. American dentist. See: Nat. Cycl. Amer. Biog., vol. E, p. 341. Hartman's solution.

HARTMANN, ALEXIS FRANK. 1898- . American pediatrician. Cited in: Kelly. Shaffer-Hartmann method.

HARTMANN, ARTHUR. 1849-1931. German laryngologist. See: Biog. Lex. hervorr. Aerzte, 1880-1930. Hartman eustachian catheters, Hartmann's curette.

Hartmann boiler (Hartmann, Otto Hermann). See: Schmidt-Hartmann boiler.

Hartmann diaphragm (Hartmann, Johannes Franz): Physics. See: Internat. Dict. Phys. Elec.; Van Nostrand Sci. Encyc. under "Hartmann test."

Hartmann dispersion formula (Hartmann, Johannes Franz): Physics. See: Ballentyne; Internat. Dict. Phys. Elec.; Thewlis.

HARTMANN, EMANUEL. fl. 19th c. American botanist. (Biography source unavailable.) Hartmannia.

Hartmann flow (Hartmann, Julius Fredrik Georg): Physics. See: Internat. Dict. Phys. Elec.

HARTMANN, FRITZ. 1871-1937. German physician. See: Biog. Lex. hervorr. Aerzte, 1880-1930. Hartmann's apraxia.

HARTMANN, JOHANNES FRANZ. 1865-1936. German astronomer. See: World Who's Who Sci. Cornu-Hartman formula, Hartmann diaphragm, Hartmann dispersion formula, Hartmann microphotometer, Hartmann test(s) (or method), Hartmann wavelength formula.

HARTMANN, JULIUS FREDRIK GEORG. 1881-1951. Danish physicist. See: Pogg., vols. 6, 7b. Hartmann flow, Hartmann number, Hartmann oscillator, Hartmann-Trolle modification of the Galton whistle.

Hartmann lines (Hartmann, Louis?): Engineering and Industry. See: Thrush. Also known as: Lueder(s) bands (or lines), Piobert effect (or lines).

HARTMANN, LOUIS. b. 1851. French metallurgist. Cited in: Mansell. Hartmann lines?

HARTMANN, MAX. 1876-1971. German protozoologist. See: World Who's Who Sci. Hartmannella.

Hartmann microphotometer (Hartmann, Johannes Franz): Physics. Cited in: World Who's Who Sci.

Hartmann number (Hartmann, Julius Fredrik Georg): Physics. See: Internat. Dict. Phys. Elec.

Hartmann oscillator (Hartmann, Julius Fredrik Georg): Physics. See: Encyc. Brit., 1973 under "Sound," vol. 20, p. 940b; Thewlis.

HARTMANN, OTTO HERMANN. fl. 1930. German inventor. Cited in: Chem. Abstr., vol. 24, p. 486. Schmidt-Hartmann boiler.

HARTMANN, ROBERT. 1831-1893. German anatomist. See: Biog. Lex. hervorr. Aerzte. Hartmann's pouch.

Hartmann test (Derivation undetermined): Chemistry. See: Van Nostrand Chem. Dict.

Hartmann test(s) (or method) (Hartmann, Johannes Franz): Physics. See: Ballentyne; Thewlis; Van Nostrand Sci. Encyc.

Hartmann-Trolle modification of the Galton whistle (Hartmann, Julius Fredrik Georg and Trolle, B.): Physics. See: Van Nostrand Sci. Encyc. under "Ultrasonics."

Hartmann wavelength formula (Hartmann, Johannes Franz): Physics. See: Thewlis.

Hartmannella (Hartmann, Max): Zoology. See: Pennak.

Hartmannia (Hartmann, Emanuel): Botany. See: Webster's 3d.

Hartmann's apraxia (Hartmann, Fritz): Medicine. See: Jablonski.

Hartmann's curette (Hartmann, Arthur): Medicine. See: Dorland; Stedman.

Hartmann's pouch (Hartmann, Robert): Anatomy. See: Dorland; Stedman.

Hartman's solution (Hartman, LeRoy Leo): Dentistry. See: Dorland; Hackh; Stedman.

Hartnell governor (Hartnell, Wilson): Engineering and Industry. See: Auger.

HARTNELL, WILSON. fl. 1882. Engineer. (Biography source unavailable.) Hartnell governor.

HARTNESS, JAMES. 1861-1934. American inventor. See: Dict. Amer. Biog., 1st suppl. Hartness lathe.

Hartness lathe (Hartness, James): Engineering and Industry. See: Auger.

Hartnup('s) disease (or syndrome) (Hartnup, Edward): Medicine. See: Hinsie; Jablonski; Stedman; Wolman. Also known as: H disease, Hart's syndrome.

HARTNUP, EDWARD. fl. ca. 1951. English? hospital patient. (Biography source unavailable.) Hartnup('s) disease (or syndrome).

HARTOG, J. fl. 18th c. Dutch traveler. (Biography source unavailable.) Hartogia.

Hartogia (Hartog, J.): Botany. See: Charnock; Webster's 3d. Also known as: Schrebera.

HARTREE, DOUGLAS RAYNER. 1897-1958. English physicist. See: Dict. Sci. Biog. Hartree equation, Hartree-Fock method (or approximation), Hartree harmonics, Hartree lines, Hartree method (or approximation), Hartree system, Hartree (units).

Hartree equation (Hartree, Douglas Rayner): Physics. See: Ballentyne; Hughes; Van Nostrand Sci. Encyc.

Hartree-Fock method (or approximation) (Hartree, Douglas Rayner and Fok, Vladimir Alexandrovitch): Physics. See: Internat. Dict. Ap. Math.; Van Nostrand Sci. Encyc.

Hartree harmonics (Hartree, Douglas Rayner): Physics. See: Internat. Dict. Phys. Elec.

artree lines (Hartree, Douglas Rayner): Physics. See: Internat. Dict. Phys. Elec.

artree method (or approximation) (Hartree, Douglas Rayner): Physics. See: ternat. Dict. Ap. Math.; Internat. Dict. Phys. Elec.; Thewlis.

artree system (Hartree, Douglas Rayner): Physics. See: Ballentyne.

artree (units) (Hartree, Douglas Rayner): Physics. See: Dresner; Internat. ct. Ap. Math.; Internat. Dict. Phys. Elec.

ARTRIDGE, HAMILTON. b. 1886. English physicist. See: Pogg., vols. 7b. Hartridge unit.

artridge unit (Hartridge, Hamilton): Physics. See: Hackh.

art's Army List (Hart, Henry George): History. See: Dict. Nat. Biog. under art, Henry George."

art's parallel motion (Hart, Harry): Engineering and Industry. See: Auger.

art's syndrome (Hart, Edward Watson): Medicine. See: Jablonski. Also own as: H disease, Hartnup's disease.

artung governor (Hartung, H.): Engineering and Industry. See: Auger.

ARTUNG, H. fl. 1893. German engineer. (Biography source unavailable.) artung governor.

arvard–Draper sequence (Harvard University and Draper, Henry): Astronomy. ee: Thewlis.

arveian (Harvey, William): Medicine. See: Webster's 3d.

ARVEY. No dates. English? saucier. (Biography source unavailable.) arvey (sauce).

arvey and West valve (Harvey, N. and West, William): Engineering and dustry. See: Auger.

arvey (apple) (Harvey, Gabriel): Botany. See: Charnock.

ARVEY, EDMUND NEWTON. 1887-1959. American physiologist. See: orld Who's Who Sci. lucibacterium Harveyi.

ARVEY, FRED. 1835-1901. English-born American restaurateur. Cited in: ansell. Harvey House (Fred Harvey system or Harvey restaurants).

ARVEY, GABRIEL. ca. 1545-1630. English writer. See: Dict. Nat. Biog. arvey (apple).

ARVEY, HAYWARD AUGUSTUS. 1824-1893. American manufacturer. See: ct. Amer. Biog. Harvey process, Harveyize(d) (steel).

arvey House (Fred Harvey system or Harvey restaurants) (Harvey, Fred): od and Drink. See: Mathews, M. M.

ARVEY, N. fl. 1839. English engineer. (Biography source unavailable.) arvey and West valve.

arvey process (Harvey, Hayward Augustus): Engineering and Industry. See: athews, M. M.; Thrush.

arvey (sauce) (Harvey): Food and Drink. See: Charnock

ARVEY, WILLIAM. 1578-1657. English physician. See: Dict. Sci. Biog. arveian.

ARVEY, WILLIAM. 1578-1657. English physician. See: Dict. Sci. Biog. arveian.

arveyize(d) (steel) (Harvey, Hayward Augustus): Engineering and Industry. ee: Mathews, M. M.; Partridge; Thrush.

ASBROUCK, JONATHAN. d. 1846. American jurist and gardener. (Biog-phy source unavailable.) Jonathan (apple).

ASCHE, RUDOLPH LEONARD. 1896- . American chemical engineer. ee: World Who's Who Sci. Koppers-Hasche process?

aselwander engine (Haselwander, Friedrich August): Engineering and Industry. ee: Auger.

ASELWANDER, FRIEDRICH AUGUST. 1859-1932. German engineer. See: eue Deut. Biog. Haselwander engine.

asenclever furnace (Hasenclever, Robert Wilhelm): Engineering and Industry. ee: Thrush.

asenclever-Helbig furnace (Hasenclever, Robert William? and Helbig, Albin erthold?): Engineering and Industry. See: Thrush.

ASENCLEVER, ROBERT WILHELM. 1841-1902. German engineer. See: eue Deut. Biog. Hasenclever furnace, Hasenclever-Helbig furnace?

asenclever turntable (Derivation undetermined): Engineering and Industry. ee: Thrush.

HASHIM. Great grandfather of Mohammed. See: Gibb and Kramers under "Muhammad." Hashimite (or Hashemite).

Hashimite (or Hashemite) (Hashim): History. See: Webster's 3d.

HASHIMOTO, HAKARU. 1881-1934. Japanese surgeon. (Biography source unavailable.) Hashimoto's disease (struma or thyroiditis).

Hashimoto's disease (struma or thyroiditis) (Hashimoto, Hakaru): Medicine. See: Dorland; Jablonski; Stedman.

Hashmon. See: Hasmon.

HASMON (HASHMON). Ancestor of the Maccabees. See: Hastings (Dict. Bible) under "Hasmoneans." Hasmonaean (or Asmonaean).

Hasmonaean (or Asmonaean) (Hasmon): History. See: Hastings (Dict. Bible); Webster's 3d.

HASNER, JOSEPH RITTER VON ARTHA. 1819-1892. Czechoslovakian physi-cian. See: Biog. Lex. hervorr. Aerzte. Hasner's valve (fold or valve of Hasner).

Hasner's valve (fold or valve of Hasner) (Hasner, Joseph Ritter von Artha): Anatomy. See: Donath; Dorland; Stedman; Webster's 3d. Also known as: Huschke's valve, Rosenmueller's valve.

Hass cyclopropane reaction (Hass, Henry Bohn): Chemistry. See: Van Nostrand Chem. Dict.

HASS, HENRY BOHN. 1902- . American chemist. See: World Who's Who Sci. Hass cyclopropane reaction.

HASSALL, ARTHUR HILL. 1817-1894. English physician. See: Biog. Lex. hervorr. Aerzte. Hassall-Henle bodies (or warts), Hassall's (or Hassal's) cor-puscles (concentric corpuscles, bodies or corpuscle(s) of Hassall).

Hassall-Henle bodies (or warts) (Hassall, Arthur Hill and Henle, Friedrich): Medicine. See: Jablonski; Stedman. Also known as: Henle's warts.

Hassall joint (Hassall, William): Engineering and Industry. See: Thrush.

HASSALL, WILLIAM. fl. 19th c. Engineer. (Biography source unavailable.) Hassall joint.

Hassall's (or Hassal's) corpuscles (concentric corpuscles, bodies or corpuscle(s) of Hassall) (Hassall, Arthur Hill): Anatomy. See: Donath; Dorland; Henderson; Pennak; Stedman; Webster's 3d. Also known as: Virchow-Hassall bodies.

HASSELBALCH, KARL ALBERT. 1874-1962. Danish biochemist and physician. See: Danmarks hist. bla bog. Henderson-Hasselbalch equation.

Hasselbalch's equation (Hasselbalch, Karl). See: Henderson-Hasselbalch equa-tion.

HASSELQUIST, FREDRIK. 1722-1752. Swedish naturalist. See: Encyc. Brit., 1911. Hasselquistia.

Hasselquistia (Hasselquist, Fredrik): Botany. See: Charnock.

Hasseltia (Van Hasselt): Botany. See: Charnock.

HASTE, F. C. fl. 1900. Engineer. (Biography source unavailable.) Haste valve.

HASTE, J. fl. 19th c. Engineer. (Biography source unavailable.) Haste's safety valve.

Haste valve (Haste, F. C.): Engineering and Industry. See: Auger.

Haste's safety valve (Haste, J.): Engineering and Industry. See: Auger.

HASTIE, J. d. 1894. English engineer. (Biography source unavailable.) Hastie steering gear.

Hastie steering gear (Hastie, J.): Engineering and Industry. See: Auger.

HASTINGS, CHARLES SHELDON. 1848-1932. American physicist. See: World Who's Who Sci. Brashear-Hastings prism.

Hastings, Selina. See: Huntingdon, Selina Hastings, Countess of.

Hasting's stain (Hastings, Thomas Wood): Medicine. See: Stedman.

HASTINGS, THOMAS WOOD. 1873-1942. American physician. See: Who Was Who Amer., 1969-1973. Hasting's stain.

HASTINGS, WARREN. 1732-1818. English administrator in India. See: Dict. Nat. Biog. impeachment of Hastings.

HATA, SAHACHIRO. 1873-1938. Japanese physician and chemist. See: World Who's Who Sci. Ehrlich-Hata preparation, Hata's phenomenon.

Hata's phenomenon (Hata, Sahachiro): Medicine. See: Dorland; Stedman.

Hatch Act (1887) (Hatch, William Henry?): Politics. See: Good.

Hatch Act (1939) (Hatch, Carl Atwood): Politics. See: Morris; Smith; Zadrozny under "Federal Corrupt Practices Act."

HATCH, CARL ATWOOD. 1889-1963. American legislator. See: Biog. Direct. Amer. Congress. Hatch Act (1939).

HATCH, FREDERICK HENRY. 1864-1932. English mining engineer and geologist. See: Who Was Who, 1929-1940. Hatchite.

HATCH, WILLIAM HENRY. 1833-1896. American legislator. See: Biog. Direct. Amer. Congress. Hatch Act (1887)?.

HATCHETT, CHARLES. 1765?-1847. English chemist. See: Dict. Sci. Biog. Hatchettine (or Hatchettite), Hatchettolite.

Hatchettine (or Hatchettite) (Hatchett, Charles): Earth Sciences. See: Webster's 3d.

Hatchettolite (Hatchett, Charles): Earth Sciences. See: Webster's 3d.

Hatchite (Hatch, Frederick Henry): Earth Sciences. See: Webster's 3d.

HATFIELD, HENRY S. fl. 1910. English electrochemist. Cited in: Chem. Abstr. Hatfield process.

Hatfield process (Hatfield, Henry S.): Engineering and Industry. See: Thrush.

HATFIELD, THEOPHILUS DAVID. fl. 1900. American horticulturist. Cited in: Mansell. Hatfield yew.

Hatfield time yield (Hatfield, William Herbert): Engineering and Industry. See: Thrush.

HATFIELD, WILLIAM HERBERT. 1882-1943. English metallurgist. See: Pogg., vol. 6. Hatfield time yield.

Hatfield yew (Hatfield, Theophilus David): Botany. See: Webster's 3d.

HATSCHEK, BERTHOLD. 1854-1941. Austrian zoologist. See: Dict. Sci. Biog. Hatschek's fossa, Hatschek's nephridium, Hatschek's pit, Hatschek's theory.

Hatschek's fossa (Hatschek, Berthold): Zoology. See: Gray.

Hatschek's nephridium (Hatschek, Berthold): Zoology. See: Gray; Henderson.

Hatschek's pit (Hatschek, Berthold): Zoology. See: Henderson; Pennak.

Hatschek's theory (Hatschek, Berthold): Zoology. See: Gray.

HATT, PAUL KITCHENER. 1914-1953. Canadian-born American sociologist. See: Who Was Who Amer., 1951-1960. North-Hatt scale.

HATTEM, PONTIAAN VAN. ca. 1641-1706. Dutch religious leader. See: Nieuw Nederl. Biog. Woordenb. Hattemists.

Hattemists (Hattem, Pontiaan van): Religion. See: Canney.

Hattersley composing machine (Hattersley, Robert): Printing. See: Lockwood.

HATTERSLEY, ROBERT. 1829-1889. English inventor. See: Boase. Hattersley composing machine.

HATTON, JAMES. 1841-1907. English printer and bookbinder. Cited in: Dict. Cat. Hist. Print. Hatton machine?

Hatton machine (Hatton, James?): Printing. See: Lockwood.

HAUDEK, MARTIN. 1880-1931. Austrian roentgenologist. See: Biog. Lex. hervorr. Aerzte, 1880-1930. Haudek's syndrome (niche or sign).

Haudek's syndrome (niche or sign) (Haudek, Martin): Medicine. See: Dorland; Jablonski; Stedman.

Hauer, Franz von. See: Von Hauer, Franz.

Hauerite (Von Hauer, Franz): Earth Sciences. See: Thrush; Webster's 3d.

HAUFF, FRIEDRICH WILHELM ALBERT. 1863-1935. German chemist. See: Neue Deut. Biog. hydramine of Hauff?, ortol of Hauff?

HAUGE, HANS NIELSEN. 1771-1824. Norwegian Lutheran divine. See: Encyc. Brit., 1973. Haugianer (or Haugians).

HAUGEN, GILBERT NELSON. 1859-1933. American banker and politician. See: Who Was Who Amer., 1897-1942. McNary-Haugen Bill (or Farm Relief Bill).

HAUGHTON, JOHN LESLIE. b. 1885. English metallurgist. See: Pogg., vols. 6, 7b. Rosenhain-Haughton reagent.

HAUGHTON, SAMUEL. 1821-1897. Irish scientist. See: Dict. Nat. Biog., 1st suppl. Haughtonite?

Haughtonite (Haughton, Samuel?): Earth Sciences. See: Thrush.

Haugianer (or Haugians) (Hauge, Hans Nielsen): Religion. Cited in: Encyc. Brit., 1973 under "Hauge, Hans Nielsen."

Haupt furnace (Derivation undetermined): Engineering and Industry. See: Thrush.

HAUPT, HUGO (In full: ADOLPH HUGO). 1874-1954. German chemist. See: Pogg., vol. 7a. Ludwig-Haupt reagent.

Hauschka-Klein ascites tumor (Hauschka, Theodore Spaeth and Klein, Edmund): Medicine. See: Jablonski.

HAUSCHKA, THEODORE SPAETH. 1908- . Austrian-born American biologist. See: World Who's Who Sci. Hauschka-Klein ascites tumor.

HAUSDORFF, FELIX. 1868-1942. German mathematician. See: Dict. Sci. Biog. Hausdorff maximal principle, Hausdorff paradox, Hausdorff space.

Hausdorff maximal principle (Hausdorff, Felix). See: Zorn's lemma.

Hausdorff paradox (Hausdorff, Felix): Mathematics. See: James.

Hausdorff space (Hausdorff, Felix): Mathematics. See: Internat. Dict. Ap. Math.; James; Van Nostrand Sci. Encyc.

HAUSER, GUSTAV. 1856-1935. German bacteriologist. See: Biog. Lex. Hervorr. Aerzte, 1880-1930. Hauser's stain.

Hauser-Herzfeld test (Hauser, Otto and Herzfeld, H.): Chemistry. See: Van Nostrand Chem. Dict.

Hauser-Lewite reagent (Hauser, Otto and Lewite, A.): Chemistry. See: Van Nostrand Chem. Dict.

HAUSER, OTTO. 1877-1915. German chemist. See: Pogg., vol. 6. Hauser-Herzfeld test, Hauser-Lewite reagent.

HAUSER, S. J. fl. 1914. American chemical engineer. Cited in: Chem. Abstr., vol. 8, p. 880. Ellms-Hauser test.

Hauser's stain (Hauser, Gustav): Medicine. See: Kelly; Stedman.

Hauserr DK9/51 drilling machine (Derivation undetermined): Engineering and Industry. See: Thrush.

HAUSHOFER, KARL VON. 1839-1895. German mineralogist. See: Pogg., vols. 3, 4. Haushofer test reaction.

Haushofer test reaction (Haushofer, Karl von): Chemistry. See: Van Nostrand Chem. Dict.

HAUSMANN, JOHANN FRIEDRICH LUDWIG. 1782-1859. German mineralogist. See: World Who's Who Sci. Hausmannite.

Hausmannite (Hausmann, Johann Friedrich Ludwig): Earth Sciences. See: Charnock; Thrush; Webster's 3d.

Haussler test reaction (Derivation undetermined): Chemistry. See: Van Nostrand Chem. Dict.

HAUSSMANN, BARON GEORGES EUGENE. 1809-1891. French administrator. See: Encyc. Brit., 1973. Haussmannize (or Haussmannization).

Haussmannize (or Haussmannization) (Haussmann, Baron Georges Eugene): Generic Word (extensive urban reconstruction). See: Brewer; Hendrickson; Partridge.

HAUSTRATE. fl. 20th c. Continental physician. (Biography source unavailable.) Francois-Haustrate syndrome.

Hauy('s) law (or law of Hauy) (Hauy, Rene Just): Physics. See: Internat. Dict. Phys. Elec.; Thrush; Van Nostrand Chem. Dict.; Van Nostrand Sci. Encyc.

HAUY, RENE JUST. 1743-1822. French mineralogist and pioneer crystallographer. See: Dict. Sci. Biog. Hauy('s) law (or law of Hauy), Hauynite (or Hauyne), Hauynitite (and Hauynophyre).

Hauynite (or Hauyne) (Hauy, Rene Just): Earth Sciences. See: Charnock; Thrush; Webster's 3d.

Hauynitite (and Hauynophyre) (Hauy, Rene Just): Earth Sciences. See: Thrush.

Hauzeur furnace (Derivation undetermined): Earth Sciences. See: Thrush.

HAVAS, EMERIC. fl. 1913-1938. Hungarian chemist. Cited in: Chem. Abstr., vol. 7, p. 43. Grandmougin-Havas reagent.

Havelock (1) (cap cover for neck protection) (Havelock, Sir Henry): Fashion. See: Brewer; Hendrickson; Mathews, M. M.; Partridge; Stenhouse; Webster's 3d.

avelock (2) (sleeveless cloak) (Havelock, Sir Henry): Fashion. See: enhouse.

AVELOCK, SIR HENRY. 1795-1857. English soldier. See: Dict. Nat. og. Havelock (1) (cap cover for neck protection), Havelock (2) (sleeveless oak).

avelock law (Havelock, Thomas Henry): Physics. See: Internat. Dict. Phys. ec. under "Kerr constant."

AVELOCK, THOMAS HENRY. 1877-1968. English physicist. See: Pogg., ls. 5, 6, 7b. Havelock law.

AVEN, HALE. 1902- . American neurologist. See: Nat. Cycl. Amer. og., vol. I, pp. 429-430. Haven's syndrome.

aven's syndrome (Haven, Hale). See: Naffziger's syndrome.

AVERS, CLOPTON. ca. 1655-1702. English anatomist. See: Dict. Sci. og. Havers' glands, Haversian canal(s), Haversian fringes, Haversian mella(ae), Haversian spaces, Haversian system.

avers' glands (Havers, Clopton): Anatomy. See: Stedman.

aversian canal(s) (Havers, Clopton): Anatomy. See: Donath; Gray; enderson; Stedman; Webster's 3d. Also known as: Leeuwenhoek's canal.

aversian fringes (Havers, Clopton): Anatomy. See: Henderson.

aversian lamella(ae) (Havers, Clopton): Anatomy. See: Donath; Stedman.

aversian spaces (Havers, Clopton): Anatomy. See: Stedman.

aversian system (Havers, Clopton): Anatomy. See: Gray; Pennak; Stedman; an Nostrand Sci. Encyc. under "Bone."

AVET, ARMAND ETIENNE MAURICE. 1795-1820. French botanist. See: ichaud. Havetia.

avetia (Havet, Armand Etienne Maurice): Botany. See: Charnock.

awes-Cooper Act (Hawes, Harry Bartow and Cooper, John Gordon?): Politics. e: Fairchild; Smith.

awes-Cutting Act (Hawes, Harry Bartow and Cutting, Bronson Murray): Poli- cs. See: Morris.

AWES, HARRY BARTOW. 1869-1947. American legislator. See: Biog. rect. Amer. Congress. Hawes-Cooper Act, Hawes-Cutting Act.

awes-Pallister-Landor syndrome (Hawes, Sir Richard Brunel; Pallister, Richard an; and Landor, J. V.). See: Strachan-Scott syndrome.

AWES, SIR RICHARD BRUNEL. fl. 1926-1964. English physician. See: ed. Direct., 1964. Hawes-Pallister-Landor syndrome.

AWKINS, CAESAR HENRY. 1798-1884. English surgeon. See: World Who's ho Sci. Hawkins' keloid.

AWKINS, JAKE. fl. early 19th c. American rifle manufacturer. (Biography urce unavailable.) Hawkins (or Hawken) (rifle or gun).

AWKINS, JOHN HENRY WILLIS. 1797-1858. American social reformer. e: Nat. Cycl. Amer. Biog., vol. 11, p. 370. Hawkins' whetstone (rum).

awkins' keloid (Hawkins, Caesar Henry). See: Alibert's disease (1).

awkins (or Hawken) (rifle or gun) Hawkins, Jake): Weapons. See: athews, M. M.; Partridge.

awkins' whetstone (rum) (Hawkins, John Henry Willis): History. See: athews, M. M.; Partridge.

AWKSHAW. Detective character in Tom Taylor's play "The Ticket of Leave an" (1863). (Biography source unavailable.) Hawkshaw.

awkshaw (Hawkshaw, the detective): Generic Word (detective). See: ebster's 3d.

AWKSLEY. fl. ca. 1895. English solicitor. (Biography source unavailable.) awksley telegrams.

awksley telegrams (Hawksley): History. See: Montgomery.

AWLEY, JAMES EDWIN. 1897- . Canadian mineralogist. See: Amer. en Sci., 9th ed. Hawleyite.

awley-Smoot Tariff Act (Hawley, Willis Chatman and Smoot, Reed): Politics. e: Jameson; Morris; Morris and Irwin; Smith. Also known as: Smoot-Hawley riff Act.

AWLEY, WILLIS CHATMAN. 1864-1941. American legislator. See: Biog. rect. Amer. Congress. Hawley-Smoot Tariff Act.

awleyite (Hawley, James Edwin): Earth Sciences. See: Thrush.

HAWNT, J. S. fl. 1964. Irish committee chairman. (Biography source un- available.) Hawnt Report.

Hawnt Report (Hawnt, J. S.): Library Science. See: Harrod.

HAWORTH, ADRIAN HARDY. 1767-1833. English botanist and entomologist. See: Dict. Sci. Biog. Haworthia.

Haworth formulas (or structures) (Haworth, Sir Walter Norman): Chemistry. See: Asimov; Stedman; Van Nostrand Sci. Encyc. under "Carbohydrate Metabolism."

Haworth methylation reaction (Haworth, Sir Walter Norman): Chemistry. See: Van Nostrand Chem. Dict.

HAWORTH, ROBERT DOWNS. 1898- . English chemist. See: Pogg., vols. 6, 7b. Haworth synthesis.

Haworth synthesis (Haworth, Robert Downs): Chemistry. See: Van Nostrand Chem. Dict.

HAWORTH, SIR WALTER NORMAN. 1883-1950. English chemist. See: World Who's Who Sci. Haworth formulas (or structures), Haworth methylation reaction.

Haworthia (Haworth, Adrian Hardy): Botany. See: Taylor, N.; Webster's 3d.

Hawthorne, Jerry, the fictional character. See: Jerry.

HAXTHAUSEN, HOLGER. 1892-1958. Danish dermatologist. See: Biog. Lex. hervorr. Aerzte, 1880-1930. Blegvad-Haxthausen syndrome, Haxthausen's syndrome (or hyperkeratosis).

Haxthausen's syndrome (or hyperkeratosis) (Haxthausen, Holger): Medicine. See: Jablonski.

Hay bridge (Hay, C. E.): Electronics. See: Hughes; Internat. Dict. Phys. Elec.; Markus.

Hay-Bunau-Varilla Treaty (Hay, John Milton and Bunau-Varilla, Philippe Jean): History. See: Encyc. Brit. under "Panama Canal," vol. 17, p. 209b; Jameson; Morris; Smith.

HAY, C. E. fl. 1912. English? engineer. Cited in: Glazebrook, vol. 2. Hay bridge.

Hay-Herran Treaty (or Convention) (Hay, John Milton and Herran, Tomas): History. See: Encyc. Brit., 1973 under "Panama Canal," vol. 17, p. 209b; Morris and Irwin; Smith.

HAY, JOHN MILTON. 1838-1905. American diplomat, journalist and histo- rian. See: Dict. Amer. Biog. Hay-Bunau-Varilla Treaty, Hay-Herran Treaty (or Convention), Hay-Pauncefote Treaty, Logan-Hay medal.

HAY, MATTHEW. 1855-1932. Scottish physician. See: Who Was Who, 1929-1940. Hay's test (for bile salts).

Hay mist projector (Derivation undetermined): Engineering and Industry. See: Thrush.

Hay-Pauncefote Treaty (Hay, John Milton and Pauncefote, Julian, 1st Baron Pauncefote): History. See: Harbottle; Jameson; Montgomery; Morris; Smith; Steinberg.

HAY, WILLIAM HOWARD. 1866-1940. American physician. Cited in: Mansell. Hayism.

HAYDEN, CARL TRUMBULL. b. 1877. American legislator. See: Biog. Direct. Amer. Congress. Hayden-Cartwright Act.

Hayden-Cartwright Act (Hayden, Carl Trumbull and Cartwright, Wilburn): Politics. See: Smith.

HAYDEN, FERDINAND VANDEVEER. 1829-1887. American geologist. See: Pogg., vol. 3. Hayden poisonvetch?

HAYDEN, HORACE H. 1769-1844. American dentist and geologist. See: World Who's Who Sci. Haydenite.

HAYDEN, JOSEPH LE ROY. fl. 1918. American electrical engineer. Cited in: Mansell. Hayden process?

Hayden poisonvetch (Hayden, Ferdinand Vandeveer?): Botany. See: Winburne.

Hayden process (Hayden, Joseph Le Roy?): Engineering and Industry. See: Thrush.

Haydenite (Hayden, Horace H.): Earth Sciences. See: Charnock; Thrush.

HAYDN, JOSEPH (In full: FRANZ JOSEPH). 1732-1809. Austrian composer. See: Encyc. Brit., 1973. Handel and Haydn Society, Haydn quartets, Haydn variations, Haydnverein.

Haydn quartets (Haydn, Joseph): Music. See: Apel.

Haydn variations (Haydn, Joseph): Music. See: Apel.

Haydnverein (Haydn, Joseph): Music. See: Scholes.

Hayem–Faber syndrome (Hayem, Georges and Faber, Knud Helge). See: Faber's syndrome.

HAYEM, GEORGES. 1841-1933. French physician. See: World Who's Who Sci. Hayem–Faber syndrome, Hayem('s) solution, Hayem–Widal anemia, Hayem–Widal syndrome, Hayem's disease, Hayem's hematoblast, Jaksch–Hayem–Luzet syndrome.

Hayem('s) solution (Hayem, Georges): Medicine. See: Dorland; Hackh; Stedman; Van Nostrand Chem. Dict.

Hayem–Widal anemia (Hayem, Georges and Widal, Georges Fernand Isidore): Medicine. See: Stedman.

Hayem–Widal syndrome (Hayem, Georges and Widal, Georges Fernand Isidore): Medicine. See: Dorland; Jablonski; Stedman. Also known as: Abrami's disease, Widal–Abrami syndrome, Widal's disease (or syndrome).

Hayem's disease (Hayem, Georges): Medicine. See: Dorland; Stedman.

Hayem's hematoblast (Hayem, Georges): Medicine. See: Stedman.

HAYES. fl. 1933. American engineer? (Biography source unavailable.) Hayes transmission.

HAYES, AUGUSTUS ALLEN. 1806-1882. American chemist. See: World Who's Who Sci. Hayesine.

Hayes–Binet scale (Hayes, Samuel Perkins and Binet, Alfred): Psychology. See: Good.

HAYES, DINNY. No dates. Australian prize-fighter. (Biography source unavailable.) Dinnyhayser.

HAYES, SAMUEL PERKINS. 1874-1958. American psychologist. See: World Who's Who Sci. Hayes–Binet scale.

Hayes transmission (Hayes): Engineering and Industry. See: Auger.

Hayesine (Hayes, Augustus Allen): Earth Sciences. See: Charnock.

HAYGARTH, JOHN. 1740-1827. English physician. See: World Who's Who Sci. Haygarth's nodes (or nodosities).

Haygarth's nodes (or nodosities) (Haygarth, John): Medicine. See: Dorland; Stedman.

Hayism (Hay, William Howard): Medicine. See: Hendrickson.

HAYLOCKE, M. No dates. English botanist? (Biography source unavailable.) Haylockia.

Haylockia (Haylocke, M.): Botany. See: Charnock.

HAYNE, ROBERT YOUNG. 1791-1839. American statesman. See: Dict. Amer. Biog. Webster–Hayne debates.

Haynes alloy (Haynes, Elwood): Chemistry. See: Hackh.

HAYNES, ELWOOD. 1857-1925. American inventor. See: World Who's Who Sci. Haynes alloy.

HAYNES, IRVING SAMUEL. 1861-1946. American surgeon. See: Who Was Who Amer., 1943-1950. Haynes' operation.

HAYNES, JAMES RICHARD. 1909- . American physicist. See: Amer. Men Sci. 9th ed. Haynes–Shockley experiment.

Haynes' operation (Haynes, Irving Samuel): Medicine. See: Dorland; Stedman.

Haynes–Shockley experiment (Haynes, James Richard and Shockley, William Bradford): Physics. See: Internat. Dict. Phys. Elec.

Hays Code (and Office) (Hays, William): Mass Media. See: Hendrickson.

Hay's test (for bile salts) (Hay, Matthew): Medicine. See: Ballentyne; Dorland; Stedman.

HAYS, WILLIAM HARRISON. 1879-1954. American motion picture executive. See: Nat. Cycl. Amer. Biog., vol. A, pp. 354-355. Hays Code (and Office).

Hayters clay (Derivation undetermined): Earth Sciences. See: Thrush.

HAYWARD, CARLE REED. b. 1880. American metallurgist. See: Amer. Men Sci., 9th ed. Hayward–Schleicher process, Hayward–Wright process?

Hayward–Schleicher process (Hayward, Carle Reed and Schleicher, Henry M.): Engineering and Industry. See: Van Nostrand Chem. Dict.

Hayward–Wright process (Hayward, Carle Reed? and Wright): Chemistry. See: Van Nostrand Chem. Dict.

HAZELETT, CLARENCE WILLIAM. 1892-1956. American inventor and manufacturer. See: Nat. Cycl. Amer. Biog., vol. 43, p. 226. Hazelett process.

Hazelett process (Hazelett, Clarence William): Engineering and Industry. See: Thrush.

HAZELTINE, ALAN (In full: LOUIS ALAN). b. 1886. American physicist and mathematician. See: World Who's Who Sci. Hazeltine neutralization.

Hazeltine neutralization (Hazeltine, Alan): Physics. See: Hughes.

HAZEN, ALLEN. 1869-1930. American hydraulic engineer. See: Nat. Cycl. Amer. Biog., vol. 28, p. 342. Hazen and Williams formula, Hazen's law?

Hazen and Williams formula (Hazen, Allen and Williams, Gardner Stewart): Engineering and Industry. See: Thrush.

HAZEN, HENRY ALLEN. 1849-1900. American meteorologist. See: World Who's Who Sci. Hazen thermometer shelter.

Hazen method (Hazen, Richard?): Earth Sciences. See: Huschke.

HAZEN, RICHARD. fl. 1952. American? earth scientist. (Biography source unavailable.) Hazen method?

Hazen thermometer shelter (Hazen, Henry Allen): Earth Sciences. Cited in: Nat. Cycl. Amer. Biog., vol. 8, p. 115.

Hazen's law (Hazen, Allen?): Engineering and Industry. See: Thrush.

Head governor (Head, Jeremiah): Engineering and Industry. See: Auger.

HEAD, SIR HENRY. 1861-1940. English neurologist. See: World Who's Who Sci. Head–Holmes syndrome, Head's areas, Head's lines (or zones).

Head–Holmes syndrome (Head, Henry and Holmes, Gordon Morgan): Medicine. See: Jablonski.

HEAD, JEREMIAH. 1835-1899. English engineer. See: Boase. Head governor.

Head's areas (Head, Sir Henry): Medicine. See: Dorland; Stedman.

Head's lines (or zones) (Head, Sir Henry): Medicine. See: Stedman.

Head's syndrome (Head, Henry). See: Head–Holmes syndrome.

HEALEY, ARTHUR DANIEL. 1889-1948. American legislator. See: Biog. Direct. Amer. Congress. Walsh–Healey Act.

HEALEY, JAMES HUESTON. 1924- . American ceramics engineer. See: Amer. Men Sci., 10th ed. Healy–Sullivan process.

Healey–Kay, Patrick. See: Dolin, Anton.

Healy picture completion test (Healy, William): Psychology. See: Chaplin; Drever; English; Wolman.

Healy–Sullivan process (Healy, James Hueston and Sullivan, John Daniel): Engineering and Industry. See: Thrush.

HEALY, WILLIAM. 1869-1962. English-born American psychologist. See: World Who's Who Sci. Healy picture completion test.

Hearon–Gustavson reagent (Hearon, William Montgomery and Gustavson, Reuben Gilbert): Chemistry. See: Van Nostrand Chem. Dict.

HEARON, WILLIAM MONTGOMERY. 1914- . American chemist. See: Amer. Men and Women Sci., 12th ed. Hearon–Gustavson reagent.

Hearst charges (Hearst, William Randolph): History. See: Jameson.

HEARST, WILLIAM RANDOLPH. 1863-1951. American journalist and newspaper publisher. See: Nat. Cycl. Amer. Biog., vol. 39, pp. 7-9. Hearst charges, William Randolph Hearst Foundation.

HEATH, CHRISTOPHER. 1835-1905. English surgeon. See: World Who's Who Sci. Heath's operation.

HEATH, FANNY. fl. 1881. American immigrant. (Biography source unavailable.) Fanny Heath raspberry.

Heath reagent (Derivation undetermined): Chemistry. See: Van Nostrand Chem. Dict.

Heath Robinson (or Heath Robinsonian) (Robinson, Heath): Generic Word (mechanical contraption). See: Brewer.

Heath Robinson. See: Robinson, W. Heath.

Heath's operation (Heath, Christopher): Medicine. See: Dorland.

HEATON, GEORGE. 1808-1879. American surgeon. See: Med. Rec., N.Y. vol. 16 (1879), p. 95. Heaton's operation.

Heaton pump (Heaton, T.): Engineering and Industry. See: Auger.

HEATON, T. fl. 1844. English engineer. (Biography source unavailable.) Heaton pump.

Heaton's operation (Heaton, George): Medicine. See: Dorland; Stedman.

Heaviside bridge (or mutual inductance bridge) (Heaviside, Oliver): Electronics. See: Internat. Dict. Phys. Elec.; Markus; Thewlis.

Heaviside–Campbell bridge (Heaviside, Oliver and Campbell, Albert): Electronics. See: Hughes; Internat. Dict. Phys. Elec.; Markus.

Heaviside equations (Heaviside, Oliver): Electronics. See: Ballentyne.

Heaviside–Kennelly layer (Heaviside, Oliver and Kennelly, Arthur Edwin). See: Kennelly–Heaviside layer.

Heaviside layer (Heaviside, Oliver). See: Kennelly–Heaviside layer.

Heaviside–Lorentz system of units (or units) (Heaviside, Oliver and Lorentz, Hendrik Antoon): Physics. See: Ballentyne; Hughes.

HEAVISIDE, OLIVER. 1850–1925. English physicist and electrical engineer. See: Dict. Sci. Biog. Heaviside bridge (or mutual inductance bridge), Heaviside–Campbell bridge, Heaviside equations, Heaviside–Lorentz system of units (or units), Heaviside operational calculus, Heaviside unit function, Heaviside's expansion theorem, Kennelly–Heaviside layer.

Heaviside operational calculus (Heaviside, Oliver): Mathematics. See: Internat. Dict. Ap. Math.

Heaviside unit function (Heaviside, Oliver): Electronics. See: Hughes; Internat. Dict. Ap. Math.

Heaviside's expansion theorem (Heaviside, Oliver): Mathematics. See: Ballentyne.

HEBB, DONALD OLDING. 1904– . Canadian psychologist. See: World Who's Who Sci. Hebb's theory of perceptual learning.

Hebbenet. See: Hubbenet.

Hebb's theory of perceptual learning (Hebb, Donald Olding): Psychology. See: Chaplin; Wolman.

HEBE. Cupbearer to the gods in Greek mythology. See: Jobes. Hebe.

Hebe (Hebe, the mythological figure): Generic Word (barmaid or waitress). See: Partridge.

HEBENSTREIT, ERNST BENJAMIN GOTTLIEB. 1753–1803. German physician. See: Biog. Lex. hervorr. Aerzte. Hebenstreitia?

HEBENSTREIT, PANTALEON. 1667–1750. German musician. See: Grove. Pantaleon (Pantaleone or Pantalon) (dulcimer).

Hebenstreitia (Hebenstreit, Ernst Benjamin Gottlieb?): Botany. See: Charnock.

HEBERDEN, WILLIAM, SR. 1710–1801. English physician. See: World Who's Who Sci. Heberden's asthma, Heberden's nodes (nodosities or sign).

Heberden's asthma (Herberden, William Sr.): Medicine. See: Dorland; Jablonski; Stedman. Also known as: Elsner's asthma, Rougnon de Magny's disease, Rougnon–Heberden disease.

Heberden's nodes (nodosities or sign) (Heberden, William, Sr.): Medicine. See: Dorland; Jablonski; Stedman; Webster's 3d. Also known as: Rosenbach's disease.

Heberlein brake (Heberlein, Jakob): Engineering and Industry. See: Auger.

HEBERLEIN, F. fl. 1913. American chemist. Cited in: Chem. Abstr. Huntington–Heberlein process, Huntington–Heberlein roasting process.

HEBERLEIN, JAKOB. 1825–1881. German engineer. See: Neue Deut. Biog. Heberlein brake.

HEBERT, ALEXANDRE. fl. 1907. French chemist. Cited in: Mansell. Herbert–Heim test.

HEBERT, JACQUES RENE (PERE DUCHENE). 1755–1794. French revolutionist. See: Encyc. Brit., 1911. Hebertistes.

Hebertistes (Hebert, Jacques Rene): History. See: Morris and Irwin.

Hebra, Ferdinand Ritter von. See: Von Hebra, Ferdinand Ritter.

Hebra's disease (or pityriasis) (Von Hebra, Ferdinand Ritter). See: Gibert's disease and Kaposi's disease (2).

Hebra's syndrome (Von Hebra, Ferdinand Ritter): Medicine. See: Jablonski.

HECATE. Moon goddess in Greek mythology. See: Jobes. Hecate.

Hecate (Hecate, the goddess): Generic Word (witch). See: Partridge.

Hechenbelikner concentrator (Hechenbleikner, Ingenuin): Engineering and Industry. See: Van Nostrand Chem. Dict.

HECHENBLEIKNER, INGENUIN. 1883–1933. Austrian-born American chemist. See: Nat. Cycl. Amer. Biog., vol. 24, pp. 238–239. Hechenbelikner concentrator.

HECHT, ADOLF FRANZ. b. 1876. Austrian physician. See: Biog. Lex. hervorr. Aerzte, 1880–1930. Hecht reagent (and test) for mucus, Hecht's phenomenon.

Hecht cones (Hecht, Hermann Carl Wilhelm): Chemistry. See: Thrush.

HECHT, HERMANN CARL WILHELM. 1860–1932. German ceramics chemist. See: Neue Deut. Biog. Hecht cones, Hecht's porcelain.

HECHT, HUGO. b. 1883. Czechoslovakian physician. See: Deut. Dermatologenkal., 1929. Hecht's test.

HECHT, J. G. H. d. 1837. Prussian counselor. (Biography source unavailable.) Hechtia.

Hecht reagent (and test) for mucus (Hecht, Adolf Franz): Medicine. See: Kelly; Van Nostrand Chem. Dict.

HECHT, VICTOR. fl. 1910. Austrian pathologist. Cited in: Lieber and Olbrich. Hecht's pneumonia.

HECHT, WALTER D. 1896– . Austrian scientist. See: Kuerschner's Deut. Gel. Kal., vol. 9, 1961. Eder–Hecht wedge sensitometer.

Hechtia (Hecht, J. G. H.): Botany. See: Taylor, N.; Webster's 3d.

Hecht's phenomenon (Hecht, Adolf Franz): Medicine. See: Dorland.

Hecht's pneumonia (Hecht, Victor): Medicine. See: Jablonski.

Hecht's porcelain (Hecht, Hermann Carl Wilhelm): Chemistry. See: Thrush.

Hecht's test (Hecht, Hugo): Medicine. See: Dorland; Stedman.

HECK, JOHN W. fl. 1965. Surgeon. (Biography source unavailable.) Heck's disease.

HECK, LLOYD LESLIE. 1903– . American chemist. See: Amer. Men Sci., 5th ed. Gilman–Sweeney–Heck reaction.

HECKEL, WILHELM. 1856–1909. German instrument maker. See: Neue Deut. Biog. Heckelphone.

Heckelphone (Heckel, Wilhelm): Music. See: Apel under "Oboe"; Scholes; Webster's 3d.

HECKER, ISAAC THOMAS. 1819–1888. American Roman Catholic clergyman. See: Dict. Amer. Biog. Heckerism.

HECKER, KARL VON. 1827–1882. German obstetrician. See: Biog. Lex. hervorr. Aerzte. Hecker's law.

Heckerism (Hecker, Isaac Thomas): Religion. See: Webster's 3d.

Hecker's law (Hecker, Karl von): Medicine. See: Dorland; Stedman.

Heck's disease (Heck, John W.): Medicine. See: Jablonski.

HECTOR. Leader of the Trojans in their war against the Greeks. See: Jobes. Hector (or to Hector).

Hector (or to Hector) (Hector, the Trojan leader): Generic Word (bully). See: Charnock; Funk; Hendrickson; Partridge; Stenhouse.

HECTOR, DAVID STEFANUS. b. 1862. Swedish chemist. See: Vem Ar Det?, 1918. Hector's base.

HECTOR, GRAHAM. fl. 1569. Scottish robber chieftain. Cited in: Dict. Nat. Biog. under "Percy, Thomas, 7th Earl of Northumberland." Hector's cloak.

HECTOR, SIR JAMES. 1834–1907. New Zealand geologist. See: Who Was Who, 1897–1916. Hectorite.

Hectorite (Hector, Sir James): Earth Sciences. See: Bailey.

Hector's base (Hector, David Stefanus): Chemistry. See: Hackh.

Hector's cloak (Hector, Graham): Generic Word (receiving evil one prepares for another). See: Jobes.

Heczko solution (Heczko, Theodor Georg): Chemistry. See: Van Nostrand Chem. Dict.

HECZKO, THEODOR GEORG. 1897– . Austrian chemist. See: Pogg., vol. 6. Heczko solution.

HEDBLOM, CARL ARTHUR. 1879–1934. American surgeon. See: Who Was Who Amer., 1897–1942. Hedblom's syndrome.

Hedblom's syndrome (Hedblom, Carl Arthur): Medicine. See: Jablonski.

HEDENBERG, LUDWIG. fl. 19th c. Swedish mineralogist. Cited in: Bailey. Hedenbergite.

Hedenbergite (Hedenberg, Ludwig): Earth Sciences. See: Charnock; Partridge; Thrush; Webster's 3d.

HEDERICH, H. fl. 1947. Physician. (Biography source unavailable.) Piulachs-Hederich syndrome.

HEDGE, ALICE N. fl. 1950. American? physician. (Biography source unavailable.) Stanbury-Hedge defect.

HEDINGER, CHRISTOPH ERNST. 1917- . Swiss pathologist. See: Who's Who Sci. Europe, 1972. Hedinger's syndrome.

Hedinger's syndrome (Hedinger, Christoph Ernst). See: Cassidy's syndrome.

HEDSTROEM, ERIK GUSTAV. b. 1869. Swedish dental scientist. Cited in: Mansell. Hedstroem file.

Hedstroem file (Hedstroem, Erik Gustav): Dentistry. See: Stedman.

heel of Achilles (Achilles, the Greek hero). See: Achilles tendon.

HEEP, URIAH. Character in Charles Dickens's novel David Copperfield (1849-1850). See: Harvey. Uriah Heep.

HEERFORDT, CHRISTIAN FREDERIK. b. 1871. Danish oculist. See: Dansk Biog. Lek. Heerfordt's syndrome.

Heerfordt's syndrome (Heerfordt, Christian Frederik): Medicine. See: Dorland; Jablonski; Stedman.

HEERMANN, ADOLPHUS L. b. ca. 1827-1865. American physician and ornithologist. See: Who Was Who Amer., Hist. vol. Heermann's gull.

HEERMANN, PAUL. 1868-1945. German textile chemist. See: Pogg., vols. 6, 7a. Heermann reagent.

Heermann reagent (Heermann, Paul): Chemistry. See: Van Nostrand Chem. Dict.

Heermann's gull (Heermann, Adolphus L.): Zoology. See: Mathews, M. M.; Webster's 3d.

HEERWAGEN, FRIEDRICH. b. 1864. German physicist. See: Pogg., vol. 4. Heerwagen pipet.

Heerwagen pipet (Heerwagen, Friedrich): Chemistry. See: Hackh.

Hefner-Alteneck, Friedrich von. See: Von Hefner-Alteneck, Friedrich.

Hefner lamp (Von Hefner-Alteneck, Friedrich): Physics. See: Hackh; Thewlis; Van Nostrand Sci. Encyc.

Hefner (Hefner candle or Hefnerkerze) (unit) (Von Hefner-Alteneck, Friedrich): Physics. See: Ballentyne; Dresner; Webster's 3d.

HEGAR, ALFRED. 1830-1914. German gynecologist. See: World Who's Who Sci. Hegar's dilators, Hegar's method, Hegar's sign.

Hegar's dilators (Hegar, Alfred): Medicine. See: Dorland; Stedman.

Hegar's method (Hegar, Alfred): Medicine. See: Dorland; Stedman.

Hegar's sign (Hegar, Alfred): Medicine. See: Dorland; Stedman.

HEGEL, GEORG WILHELM FRIEDRICH. 1770-1831. German philosopher. See: Internat. Encyc. Soc. Sci. Hegelian dialectic, Hegelian triad, Hegelian (2), Hegelianism (or Hegelian (1)).

HEGELER, EDWARD CARL. 1835-1910. German-born American metallurgist. See: Nat. Cycl. Amer. Biog., vol. 23, p. 60. Hegeler furnace, Hegeler producer?, Hegeler roaster?

Hegeler furnace (Hegeler, Edward Carl): Engineering and Industry. See: Thrush.

Hegeler producer (Hegeler, Edward Carl?): Engineering and Industry. See: Thrush.

Hegeler roaster (Hegeler, Edward Carl?): Engineering and Industry. See: Thrush.

Hegelian (2) (Hegel, Georg Wilhelm Friedrich): Generic Word (transcendent). See: Partridge.

Hegelian dialectic (Hegel, Georg Wilhelm Friedrich): Philosophy. See: Barnhart (Eng. Lit.); Good.

Hegelian triad (Hegel, Georg Wilhelm Friedrich): Philosophy. See: Webster's 3d.

Hegelianism (or Hegelian (1)) (Hegel, Georg Wilhelm Friedrich): Philosophy. See: Edwards; Good; Webster's 3d.

HEGGLIN, ROBERT MARQUARD. 1907- . Swiss internist. See: Kuerschner's Deut. Gel. Kal., vol. 9, 1961. Fanconi-Hegglin syndrome, Hegglin's anomaly (or anomaly of constitutional changes in neutrophils and platelets), Hegglin's syndrome.

Hegglin's anomaly (or anomaly of constitutional changes in neutrophils and platelets) (Hegglin, Robert Marquard): Medicine. See: Jablonski; Stedman. Also known as: Doehle body panmyelopathic syndrome, May-Hegglin syndrome.

Hegglin's syndrome (Hegglin, Robert Marquard): Medicine. See: Jablonski

HEGLER, ROBERT. fl. 1887-1897. German botanist. Cited in: Royal Soc. Cat. Sci. Pap., 1884-1900. Hegler test reaction.

Hegler test reaction (Hegler, Robert): Chemistry. See: Van Nostrand Chem. Dict.

Hehner cylinder (Hehner, Otto?): Chemistry. See: Van Nostrand Sci. Encyc. under "Color Comparators (Visual)."

Hehner number (Hehner, Otto): Chemistry. See: Hackh; Stedman; Van Nostrand Chem. Dict.

HEHNER, OTTO. 1853-1924. English? chemist. (Biography source unavailable.) Bechi-Hehner solution?, Hehner cylinder?, Hehner number, Hehner test for formaldehyde and phenol, Hehner test for formaldehyde in milk.

Hehner test for formaldehyde and phenol (Hehner, Otto): Chemistry. See: Van Nostrand Chem. Dict.

Hehner test for formaldehyde in milk (Hehner, Otto): Chemistry. See: Van Nostrand Chem. Dict.

Heiberg-Esmarch maneuver (Heiberg, Jacob Munch and Von Esmarch, Johann Friedrich August): Medicine. See: Dorland.

HEIBERG, JACOB MUNCH. 1843-1888. Norwegian surgeon. See: Biog. Lex. hervorr. Aerzte. Heiberg-Esmarch maneuver.

HEICHELHEIM, RUDOLF. No dates. German physician. (Biography source unavailable.) Heichelheim's test.

Heichelheim's test (Heichelheim, Rudolf): Medicine. See: Dorland.

HEIDEGGER, MARTIN. 1889- . German philosopher. See: New Encyc. Brit., 1974. Heideggerian.

Heideggerian (Heidegger, Martin): Philosophy. See: Webster's 3d.

HEIDENHAIN, ADOLF. 1893- . German neurologist. Cited in: Index-Cat. Libr. Surg.-Gen. Off., 4th ser., vol. 7, 1942. Heidenhain's syndrome.

HEIDENHAIN, HEINRICH. fl. 1896. German-born American? chemist. Cited in: Royal Soc. Cat. Sci. Pap., 1884-1900. Heidenhain reagent for carbon dioxide.

Heidenhain pouch (Heidenhain, Rudolf Peter Heinrich): Medicine. See: Stedman.

Heidenhain reagent for carbon dioxide (Heidenhain, Heinrich): Chemistry. See: Van Nostrand Chem. Dict.

HEIDENHAIN, RUDOLF PETER HEINRICH. 1834-1897. German physiologist. See: Dict. Sci. Biog. Biondi-Heidenhain mixture, Biondi-Heidenhain stain, Heidenhain pouch, Heidenhain's crescents (demilunes or demilune of Heidenhain), Heidenhain's law, Heidenhain's stain (or iron-hematoxylin).

Heidenhain's crescents (demilunes or demilune of Heidenhain) (Heidenhain, Rudolf Peter Heinrich): Anatomy. See: Donath; Stedman; Webster's 3d. Also known as: Gianuzzi's demilunes (or crescents).

Heidenhain's law (Heidenhain, Rudolf Peter Heinrich): Medicine. See: Dorland; Stedman.

Heidenhain's stain (or iron-hematoxylin) (Heidenhain, Rudolf Peter Heinrich): Medicine. See: Dorland; Stedman

Heidenhain's syndrome (Heidenhain, Adolf): Medicine. See: Jablonski.

HEIL, ALBRECHT. fl. 1907. German electrical engineer. Cited in: Chem. Abstr., Decenn. Index, 1907-1916. Heil oscillator.

Heil oscillator (Heil, Albrecht): Electronics. See: Hughes; Van Nostrand Sci. Encyc.

HEILBRONNER, KARL. 1869-1914. Dutch physician. See: Biog. Lex. hervorr. Aerzte. Heilbronner's thigh.

eilbronner's thigh (Heilbronner, Karl): Medicine. See: Dorland.

EILE, BERNHARD. fl. 1908. German surgeon. See: Deut. Chirurgenkal., 926, p. 125. Heile's operation.

eile's operation (Heile, Bernhard): Medicine. See: Stedman.

EILMEYER, LUDWIG. 1899- . German physician. See: World Who's ho Sci. Heilmeyer-Schoener erythroblastosis.

eilmeyer-Schoener erythroblastosis (Heilmeyer, Ludwig and Schoener, W.): edicine. See: Jablonski.

EIM DE BALSAC, FREDERIC. b. 1869. French scientist. Cited in: Mansell. erbert-Heim test.

EIM, ERNST LUDWIG. 1747-1834. German physician. See: Biog. Lex. ervorr. Aerzte. Heim-Kreysig sign, Heimia, Heim's pill.

eim-Kreysig sign (Heim, Ernst Ludwig and Kreysig, Friedrich Ludwig): Medi-ine. See: Dorland; Stedman. Also known as: Kreysig's sign.

EIM, WERNER GEORGE. 1929- . American biologist. See: World Who's ho Sci. Heim's cage?

eimia (Heim, Ernst Ludwig): Botany. Cited in: Biog. Lex. hervorr. Aerzte.

EIMLICH, HENRY JAY. 1920- . American surgeon. See: Direct. Med. pecialists, 1975-1976. Heimlich maneuver.

eimlich maneuver (Heimlich, Henry Jay): Medicine. See: People, Nov. 18, 974.

EIMROD, GEORGE WILLIAM. 1876-1917. American chemist. See: Pogg., ols. 4, 5. Heimrod-Levine test.

eimrod-Levine test (Heimrod, George William and Levene, Phoebus Aaron heodore): Chemistry. See: Van Nostrand Chem. Dict.

eim's cage (Heim, Werner George?): Biology. See: Hackh.

eim's pill (Heim, Ernst Ludwig): Medicine. See: Dorland.

eine-Borel theorem (Heine, Eduard and Borel, Felix Edouard Emile): Mathe-atics. See: Internat. Dict. Ap. Math.; James. Also known as: Borel overing theorem.

EINE, EDUARD (In full: HEINRICH EDUARD). 1821-1881. German mathe-atician. See: Dict. Sci. Biog. Heine-Borel theorem, Heine formula.

eine formula (Heine, Eduard): Mathematics. See: Internat. Dict. Phys. lec.; Van Nostrand Sci. Encyc. under "Legendre Differential Equation."

EINE, HEINRICH. 1799-1856. German poet and writer. See: Encyc. Brit., 973. Heinesque.

eine, Jakob von. See: Von Heine, Jakob.

EINE, LEOPOLD. 1870-1940. German ophthalmologist. See: Biog. Lex. ervorr. Aerzte, 1880-1930. Heine's operation.

eine-Medin disease (Von Heine, Jakob and Medin, Oskar): Medicine. ee: Dorland; Hinsie; Jablonski; Stedman. Also known as: Little's paralysis.

eineke-Mikulicz pyloroplasty (Heinecke, Walter Hermann and Von Mikulicz-adecki, Johann): Medicine. See: Dorland; Stedman.

EINEKE, WALTER HERMANN. 1834-1901. German surgeon. See: Biog. ex. hervorr. Aerzte. Heineke-Mikulicz pyloroplasty.

eine's operation (Heine, Leopold): Medicine. See: Dorland; Stedman.

einesque (Heine, Heinrich): Literature. See: Webster's 3d.

einis constant (Heinis, Hugo): Psychology. See: Chaplin; English; Wolman.

EINIS, HUGO. b. 1883. Swiss psychologist. See: Doc. p. servir a histoire de l'Univ. de Geneve, vol. 8 (1938), p. 415. Heinis constant, einis law of mental growth.

einis law of mental growth (Heinis, Hugo): Psychology. See: Chaplin; nglish; Wolman.

einkel bomber (Heinkel, Ernst): Engineering and Industry. See: Hendrickson nder "Messerschmitt..."

EINKEL, ERNST. 1885-1958. German airplane designer. See: Neue eut. Biog. Heinkel bomber.

EINRICH, EBERHARDT WILLIAM. 1918- . American geologist. See: mer. Men Sci., 10th ed. Heinrichite.

einrichite (Heinrich, Eberhardt William): Earth Sciences. See: Thrush.

einrici motor (Derivation undetermined): Engineering and Industry. See: uger.

Heintz test for potassium (Heintz, Wilhelm Heinrich?): Chemistry. See: Van Nostrand Chem. Dict.

Heintz test for sulfite (Heintz, Wilhelm Heinrich?): Chemistry. See: Van Nostrand Chem. Dict.

HEINTZ, WILHELM HEINRICH. 1807-1880. German chemist. See: World Who's Who Sci. Heintz test for potassium?, Heintz test for sulfite?

HEINTZMANN, H. F. fl. 1951. Belgian engineer. Cited in: Mansell. Toussaint-Heintzmann arch?

Heinz bodies (or granules) (Heinz, Robert): Medicine. See: Blakiston's Gould; Dorland; Stedman.

Heinz-Ehrlich bodies (Heinz, Robert and Ehrlich, Paul). See: Ehrlich's inner body.

HEINZ, ROBERT. 1865-1924. German pathologist. See: World Who's Who Sci. Heinz bodies (or granules), Heinz-Ehrlich bodies.

HEINZLER, J. fl. 1920. German chemist. Cited in: Chem. Abstr. Weinland-Heinzler reagent.

Heisenberg equation of motion (Heisenberg, Werner Karl): Physics. See: Internat. Dict. Phys. Elec.

Heisenberg force (Heisenberg, Werner Karl): Physics. See: Ballentyne; Hughes; Internat. Dict. Ap. Math.; Van Nostrand Sci. Encyc.

Heisenberg picture (Heisenberg, Werner Karl): Physics. See: Internat. Dict. Ap. Math.

Heisenberg('s) principle (or uncertainty principle) (Heisenberg, Werner Karl): Physics. See: Ballentyne; Hackh; Hughes; Thrush; Van Nostrand Sci. Encyc.; Webster's 3d.

Heisenberg representation (Heisenberg, Werner Karl). See: Born-Heisenberg representation.

Heisenberg theory of ferromagnetism (Heisenberg, Werner Karl): Physics. See: Thewlis; Van Nostrand Sci. Encyc.

HEISENBERG, WERNER KARL. 1901- . German physicist. See: World Who's Who Sci. Born-Heisenberg representation, Heisenberg equation of motion, Heisenberg force, Heisenberg picture, Heisenberg('s) principle (or uncertainty principle), Heisenberg theory of ferromagnetism.

HEISER, VICTOR GEORGE. b. 1873. American physician. See: Biog. Lex. hervorr. Aerzte. Heiser's treatment.

Heiser's treatment (Heiser, Victor George): Medicine. See: Dorland.

Heising modulation (Heising, Raymond Alphonsus): Physics. See: Hughes; Internat. Dict. Phys. Elec.; Markus; Van Nostrand Sci. Encyc. under "Modula-tion."

HEISING, RAYMOND ALPHONSUS. 1888-1965. American engineer and physicist. See: World Who's Who Sci. Heising modulation.

HEISLER, CHARLES LOUIS. 1863-1931. American engineer. See: Nat. Cycl. Amer. Biog., vol. 25, pp. 399-400. Heisler pump.

Heisler pump (Heisler, Charles Louis): Engineering and Industry. See: Auger.

Heisman trophy (Heismann, John William): Recreation and Sports. See: Hendrickson.

HEISMANN, JOHN WILLIAM. b. 1869. American football coach. Cited in: Mansell. Heisman trophy.

HEISRATH, FRIEDRICH. 1850-1904. German ophthalmologist. See: Biog. Lex. hervorr. Aerzte, 1880-1930. Heisrath's operation.

Heisrath's operation (Heisrath, Friedrich): Medicine. See: Dorland; Stedman.

HEISTER, LORENZ. 1683-1758. German anatomist. See: Dict. Sci. Biog. Heister's diverticulum, Heister's valve(s) (or valve of Heister), Heisteria.

Heisteria (Heister, Lorenz): Botany. See: Charnock.

Heister's diverticulum (Heister, Lorenz): Anatomy. See: Dorland; Stedman.

Heister's valve(s) (or valve of Heister) (Heister, Lorenz): Anatomy. See: Donath; Pennak; Stedman; Webster's 3d.

Heitler-London-Slater-Pauling method (or HLSP method) (Heitler, Walter Heinrich; London, Fritz; Slater, John Clarke; and Pauling, Linus): Physics. See: Internat. Dict. Ap. Math.

Heitler-London theory (theory of valence, covalence theory or method) (Heitler, Walter Heinrich and London, Fritz): Physics. See: Ballentyne; Internat. Dict. Ap. Math.; Internat. Dict. Phys. Elec.; Thewlis; Van Nostrand Chem. Dict.

Heitler–London theory of the hydrogen molecule (Heitler, Walter Heinrich and London, Fritz): Physics. See: Van Nostrand Sci. Encyc. under "Hydrogen Molecule..."

HEITLER, WALTER HEINRICH. 1904– . German-born physicist. See: World Who's Who Sci. Bethe–Heitler theory, Heitler–London–Slater–Pauling method (or HLSP method), Heitler–London theory of the hydrogen molecule, Heitler–London theory (theory of valence, covalence theory or method).

HEJNA, ROBERT F. fl. 1960. American speech pathologist. Cited in: Nat. Union Cat., 1956-1967. Hejna test.

Hejna test (Hejna, Robert F.): Psychology. See: Wolman.

HEKTOEN, LUDVIG. 1863-1951. American pathologist. See: Dict. Sci. Biog. Hektoen phenomenon.

Hektoen phenomenon (Hektoen, Ludvig): Medicine. See: Dorland.

HE LA. fl. 1951. American hospital patient. (Biography source unavailable.) He La cells.

He La cells (He La): Medicine. See: Stedman.

HELBERGER, BRUNO. fl. 1936. German pianist. Cited in: Thompson, O. under "Hellertion." Hellertion (electric piano).

HELBIG, ALBIN BERTHOLD. b. 1869. German engineer. Cited in: Mansell. Hasenclever–Helbig furnace?

HELD, HANS. b. 1866. German anatomist. See: Biog. Lex. hervorr. Aerzte, 1880-1930. end-feet of Held, Held's bundle, Held's decussation.

Held's bundle (Held, Hans): Anatomy. See: Dorland; Stedman.

Held's decussation (Held, Hans): Anatomy. See: Stedman.

Hele–Shaw cell (Hele–Shaw, Henry Selby): Engineering and Industry. See: Internat. Dict. Ap. Math.

Hele–Shaw clutch (Hele–Shaw, Henry Selby): Engineering and Industry. See: Auger.

Hele–Shaw gear (Hele–Shaw, Henry Selby): Engineering and Industry. See: Auger.

HELE–SHAW, HENRY SELBY. 1854-1941. English engineer. See: World Who's Who Sci. Hele–Shaw cell, Hele–Shaw clutch, Hele–Shaw gear.

HELEN. The most beautiful woman of Greece in legend. See: Encyc. Brit., 1973. elecampane, Helen.

Helen (Helen of Troy): Generic Word (beautiful woman). See: Partridge.

Helena Rubinstein prize (Rubinstein, Helena): Fine Arts. See: Osborne.

HELFERICH, BURCKHARDT. b. 1887. German chemist. See: World Who's Who Sci. Helferich method.

Helferich method (Helferich, Burckhardt): Chemistry. See: Van Nostrand Chem. Dict.

HELFGAT, I. I. fl. 1929. German? chemist. Cited in: Chem. Abstr., vol. 23, p. 3050. Sterkin–Helfgat solution.

HELIOS. Early Greek god of the sun. See: Encyc. Brit., 1973. Helium.

Helium (Helios, the sun god): Chemistry. See: Encyc. Brit., 1973; Partridge.

HELL, KARL MAGNUS VON. 1849-1926. German chemist. See: Pogg., vols. 4, 5, 6. Hell–Volhard–Zelinsky reaction.

Hell–Volhard–Zelinsky reaction (Hell, Karl Magnus von; Volhard, Jacob; and Zelinski, Nikolai Dimitrievich): Chemistry. See: Ballentyne; Van Nostrand Chem. Dict.

Helladic (Hellen): History. See: Osborne.

HELLAND, AMUND THEODOR. 1846-1918. Norwegian geologist. See: Norsk Biog. Lek. Hellandite.

Hellandite (Helland, Amund Theodor): Earth Sciences. See: Webster's 3d.

HELLAT, PETER. 1857-1912. Russian otologist. See: Biog. Lex. hervorr. Aerzte, 1880-1930. Hellat's sign.

Hellat's sign (Hellat, Peter): Medicine. See: Dorland.

HELLEN. Legendary King of Phthia in Greek mythology. See: Jobes. Helladic, Hellenes (2), Hellenic (and Hellene(s) (1)), Hellenism (1), Hellenism (2), Hellenist, Hellenistic (or Hellenestic Age).

HELLENDALL, HUGO. b. 1872. German gynecologist. See: Biog. Lex. hervorr. Aerzte, 1880-1930. Hellendall's sign.

Hellendall's sign (Hellendall, Hugo): Medicine. See: Dorland.

Hellenes (2) (Hellen): History. See: Brewer.

Hellenic (and Hellene(s) (1)) (Hellen): History. See: Brewer; Osborne; Webster's 3d.

Hellenism (1) (Hellen): Generic Word. See: Charnock; Webster's 3d.

Hellenism (2) (Hellen): Literature. See: Preminger under "Hebraism–Hellenism"; Webster's 3d.

Hellenist (Hellen): Generic Word. See: Charnock; Webster's 3d.

Hellenistic (or Hellenestic Age) (Hellen): History. See: Charnock; Encyc. Brit., 1973; Osborne; Webster's 3d.

HELLER, ARNOLD LUDWIG GOTTHILF. 1840-1913. German pathologist. See: World Who's Who Sci. Heller–Doehle mesoaortitis, Heller's plexus.

HELLER, CARL GEORGE. 1913– . American physiologist. See: World Who's Who Sci. Heller–Nelson syndrome.

Heller–Doehle mesoaortitis (Heller, Arnold Ludwig Gotthilf and Doehle, Paul): Medicine. See: Jablonski.

HELLER, ERNST. 1877-1964. German surgeon. See: Biog. Lex. hervorr. Aerzte, 1880-1930. Heller esophagomyotomy.

Heller esophagomyotomy (Heller, Ernst): Medicine. See: Stedman.

HELLER, JOHANN FLORIAN. 1813-1871. Austrian pathologist. See: World Who's Who Sci. Heller's test (1) (for albumin), Heller's test (2) (for blood), Heller's test (3) (for sugar).

HELLER, JULIUS. 1864-1931. German dermatologist. See: Biog. Lex. hervorr. Aerzte, 1880-1930. Heller's disease.

HELLER, KAMILL. 1823-1917. Austrian zoologist. See: Oesterr. Biog. Lex., 1815-1950. Helleri?

Heller–Nelson syndrome (Heller, Carl George and Nelson, Warren O.): Medicine. See: Jablonski.

HELLER, THEODOR O. b. 1869. German neuropsychiatrist. See: Psych. Register, 1932, p. 607f. Heller's disease (syndrome or dementia).

Heller–Zappert syndrome (Heller, Theodor and Zappert, Julius). See: Heller's disease (syndrome or dementia).

Helleri (Heller, Kamill?): Zoology. See: Webster's 3d.

Heller's disease (Heller, Julius): Medicine. See: Jablonski.

Heller's disease (syndrome or dementia) (Heller, Theodor O.): Medicine. See: Chaplin; English; Hinsie; Jablonski. Also known as: Heller–Zappert syndrome.

Heller's plexus (Heller, Arnold Ludwig Gotthilf): Anatomy. See: Stedman.

Heller's test (1) (for albumin) (Heller, Johann Florian): Medicine. See: Ballentyne; Dorland; Stedman.

Heller's test (2) (for blood) (Heller, Johann Florian): Medicine. See: Dorland; Stedman.

Heller's test (3) (for sugar) (Heller, Johann Florian). See: Moore's test.

HELLERSBERG, ELISABETH F. b. 1893. German-born American psychologist. See: Amer. Psych. Assoc. Direct., 1948. Horn–Hellersberg drawing completion test.

HELLERSTROEM, SVEN CURT ALFRED. 1901– . Swedish dermatologist. See: Svenska Maen Och Kvinnor. Hellerstroem's disease.

Hellerstroem's disease (Hellerstroem, Sven Curt Alfred): Medicine. See: Jablonski.

Hellertion (electric piano) (Helberger, Bruno and Lertes, Peter): Music. See: Partridge; Scholes.

HELLIN, DYONISY. 1867-1935. Polish pathologist. See: Warsz. Czas. lek., vol. 12 (1935), p. 789. Hellin's law (or ratio).

Hellin's law (or ratio) (Hellin, Dyonisy): Medicine. See: Dorland; English; Good; Kelly; Stedman.

Hellman–Feynmann theorem (Hellmann, Hans and Feynman, Richard Phillips): physics. See: Thewlis.

HELLMANN, HANS. 1903- . German physicist. See: Pogg., vol. 6. Hellman–Feynmann theorem.

HELLWAG, CHRISTOPH FRIEDRICH. 1754-1835. German linguist. Cited in: Mansell. Hellwag's vowel triangle.

Hellwag's vowel triangle (Hellwag, Christoph Friedrich): Linguistics. See: Wolman.

Helly–Bray theorem (Helly, Eduard? and Bray, Hubert Evelyn?): Statistics. See: Kendall. Also known as: Helly's second theorem.

HELLY, EDUARD. 1884-1943. Austrian-born American mathematician. See: Neue Deut. Biog. Helly–Bray theorem?, Helly's first theorem (or lemma).

Helly('s) fluid (Helly, Konrad): Medicine. See: Pennak; Stedman; Van Nostrand Chem. Dict.; Webster's 3d.

HELLY, KONRAD. b. 1875. Swiss pathologist. See: Biog. Lex. hervorr. Aerzte, 1880-1930. Helly('s) fluid.

Helly's first theorem (or lemma) (Helly, Eduard): Statistics. See: Kendall.

Helly's second theorem (Helly, Eduard?). See: Helly–Bray theorem.

Helmert criterion (Helmert, Friedrich Robert). See: Abbe–Helmert criterion.

Helmert distribution (Helmert, Friedrich Robert): Statistics. See: Kendall.

HELMERT, FRIEDRICH ROBERT. 1843-1917. German geodesist. See: Dict. Sci. Biog. Abbe–Helmert criterion, Helmert distribution, Helmert transformation, Helmert's formula (or equation).

Helmert transformation (Helmert, Friedrich Robert): Statistics. See: Kendall.

Helmert's formula (or equation) (Helmert, Friedrich Robert): Physics. See: Ballentyne; Hackh.

Helmholtz' axis ligament (Helmholtz, Hermann Ludwig Ferdinand von): Medicine. See: Dorland; Stedman.

Helmholtz coil(s) (Helmholtz, Hermann Ludwig Ferdinand von): Physics. See: Hughes; Internat. Dict. Phys. Elec.; Thewlis; Thrush; Webster's 3d.

Helmholtz derivative (Helmholtz, Hermann Ludwig Ferdinand von): Physics. See: Internat. Dict. Ap. Math.

Helmholtz' differential equation (Helmholtz, Hermann Ludwig Ferdinand von): Mathematics. See: James.

Helmholtz double layer (or layer) (Helmholtz, Hermann Ludwig Ferdinand von): Physics. See: Ballentyne; Hackh; Webster's 3d.

Helmholtz('s) equation (or partial differential equation) (Helmholtz, Hermann Ludwig Ferdinand von): Physics. See: Ballentyne; Huschke.

Helmholtz equation for vorticity (Helmholtz, Hermann Ludwig Ferdinand von): Physics. See: Internat. Dict. Ap. Math.

Helmholtz flow (Helmholtz, Hermann Ludwig Ferdinand von): Physics. See: Internat. Dict. Phys. Elec.

Helmholtz formulation of Huygens principle (Helmholtz, Hermann Ludwig Ferdinand von): Physics. See: Internat. Dict. Ap. Math.

Helmholtz function (or free energy) (Helmholtz, Hermann Ludwig Ferdinand von): Physics. See: Ballentyne; Huschke; Internat. Dict. Ap. Math.; Internat. Dict. Phys. Elec.; Thewlis.

Helmholtz–Gibbs theory (Helmholtz, Hermann Ludwig Ferdinand von and Gibbs, Josiah Willard). See: Gibbs–Helmholtz equation.

HELMHOLTZ, HERMANN LUDWIG FERDINAND VON. 1821-1894. German physicist. See: Dict. Sci. Biog. Fechner–Helmholtz law, Gibbs–Helmholtz equation, Helmholtz' axis ligament, Helmholtz coil(s), Helmholtz derivative, Helmholtz' differential equation, Helmholtz double layer (or layer), Helmholtz('s) equation (or partial differential equation), Helmholtz equation for vorticity, Helmholtz flow, Helmholtz formulation of Huygens principle, Helmholtz function (or free energy), Helmholtz instability, Helmholtz reciprocal theorem, Helmholtz('s) relation (or equation for optical magnification), Helmholtz resonator, Helmholtz theory of accommodation, Helmholtz theory of hearing, Helmholtz (unit), Helmholtz wave(s), Helmholtz's equation (for a reversible electrolyte cell), Helmholtz's theorem (for fluids), Ketteler–Helmholtz formula, law of Helmholtz, Smith–Helmholtz law, Thevenin–Helmholtz theorem, Young–Helmholtz theory.

Helmholtz instability (Helmholtz, Hermann Ludwig Ferdinand von): Physics. See: Huschke; Internat. Dict. Ap. Math.; Internat. Dict. Phys. Elec.; Van Nostrand Sci. Encyc.

Helmholtz–Ketteler formula (Helmholtz, Hermann Ludwig Ferdinand von and Ketteler, Eduard). See: Ketteler–Helmholtz formula.

Helmholtz–Lagrange formula (Helmholtz, Hermann Ludwig Ferdinand von and Lagrange, Joseph Louis). See: Helmholtz('s) relation (or equation for optical magnification).

Helmholtz reciprocal theorem (Helmholtz, Hermann Ludwig Ferdinand von): Physics. See: Internat. Dict. Phys. Elec.; Van Nostrand Sci. Encyc.

Helmholtz('s) relation (or equation for optical magnification) (Helmholtz, Hermann Ludwig Ferdinand von): Physics. See: Ballentyne; Internat. Dict. Ap. Math.; Van Nostrand Sci. Encyc. Also known as: Helmholtz–Lagrange formula, Lagrange–Helmholtz equation, Lagrange theorem (1), Smith–Helmholtz equation.

Helmholtz resonator (Helmholtz, Hermann Ludwig Ferdinand von): Physics. See: Auger; Hughes; Markus; Thewlis; Van Nostrand Sci. Encyc.; Webster's 3d.

Helmholtz('s) theorem (Helmholtz, Hermann Ludwig Ferdinand von). See: Thevenin's theorem.

Helmholtz theory (or theory of color vision) (Helmholtz, Hermann Ludwig Ferdinand von). See: Young–Helmholtz theory.

Helmholtz theory of accommodation (Helmholtz, Hermann Ludwig Ferdinand von): Medicine. See: Dorland; Stedman.

Helmholtz theory of hearing (Helmholtz, Hermann Ludwig Ferdinand von): Physics. See: Chaplin; Stedman.

Helmholtz (unit) (Helmholtz, Hermann Ludwig Ferdinand von): Physics. See: Dresner.

Helmholtz wave(s) (Helmholtz, Hermann Ludwig Ferdinand von): Physics. See: Huschke; Internat. Dict. Ap. Math.; Van Nostrand Sci. Encyc.

Helmholtz's equation (for a reversible electrolyte cell) (Helmholtz, Hermann Ludwig Ferdinand von): Physics. See: Ballentyne.

Helmholtz's theorem (for fluids) (Helmholtz, Hermann Ludwig Ferdinand von): Physics. See: Ballentyne.

Helmholz–Harrington syndrome (Helmholz, Henry Frederic and Harrington, Ethel R.): Medicine. See: Jablonski.

HELMHOLZ, HENRY FREDERIC. b. 1882. American pediatrician. See: Biog. Lex. hervorr. Aerzte, 1880-1930. Helmholz–Harrington syndrome.

Helmont, Jean Baptiste van. See: Van Helmont, Jean Baptiste.

HELOISE. 1101-1164. French abbess and wife of Abelard. See: Nouv. Biog. Univ. Heloise and Abelard.

Heloise and Abelard (Heloise, the abbess and Abailard, Pierre): Generic Word. (hapless lovers). See: Partridge under "Eloisa."

Helquin. See: Harlequin.

HELSON, HARRY. 1898- . American psychologist. See: World Who's Who Sci. Helson–Judd effect.

Helson–Judd effect (Helson, Harry and Judd, Deane Brewster): Psychology. See: Wolman under "Helson, Harry."

Helvidians (Helvidius): Religion. See: Canney.

HELVIDIUS. fl. ca. 383. Roman heretic. See: Dict. Christian Biog. Helvidians.

HELWEG, HANS KRISTIAN SAXTORPH. 1847-1901. Danish physician. See: Biog. Lex. hervorr. Aerzte, 1880-1930. Helweg's bundle.

Helweg's bundle (Helweg, Hans Kristian Saxtorph): Anatomy. See: Donath; Dorland; Stedman.

HELWIG, ELSON BOWMAN. 1907- . American physician. See: Amer. Men and Women Sci., 12th ed. Helwig's disease.

Helwig's disease (Helwig, Elson Bowman): Medicine. See: Jablonski.

hemoglobin Gower-1 (Derivation undetermined): Medicine. See: Stedman.

hemoglobin Gower-2 (Derivation undetermined): Medicine. See: Stedman.

Hempel column (Hempel, Walter): Chemistry. See: Webster's 3d.

Hempel gas buret (burette or apparatus) (Hempel, Walter): Chemistry. See: Hackh; Van Nostrand Chem. Dict.

HEMPEL, HENRY ADOLPH. b. 1836. German-born printer in America. See: Lockwood. Hempel quoin.

Hempel palladium tube (Hempel, Walter): Chemistry. See: Hackh.

Hempel quoin (Hempel, Henry Adolph): Printing. See: Glaister; Lockwood.

HEMPEL, WALTER. 1851-1916. German chemist. See: World Who's Who Sci. Hempel column, Hempel gas buret (burette or apparatus), Hempel palladium tube.

HEMPT, HANS. fl. 1932. German bacteriologist. Cited in: Chem. Abstr., Decenn. Index, 1927-1936. Hempt vaccine?

Hempt vaccine (Hempt, Hans?): Medicine. See: Stedman.

Hench–Aldrich test (or index) (Hench, Philip Showalter and Aldrich, Martha): Medicine. See: Dorland.

HENCH, PHILIP SHOWALTER. 1896-1965. American physician. See: World Who's Who Sci. Hench–Aldrich test (or index), Hench–Rosenberg syndrome.

Hench–Rosenberg syndrome (Hench, Philip Showalter and Rosenberg, Edward F.): Medicine. See: Jablonski.

HENCKY, HEINRICH. 1885-1951. German physicist. See: Pogg., vols. 6, 7a. Hencky–Prandtl net, Huber–Mises–Hencky theory.

Hencky–Prandtl net (Hencky, Heinrich and Prandtl, Ludwig): Physics. See: Internat. Dict. Ap. Math.

HENDERSON, A. L. d. 1900. English photographer. See: Focal Encyc. Photog. Henderson Award (and Medal).

Henderson Award (and Medal) (Henderson, A. L.): Photography. See: Focal Encyc. Photog. under "Awards (Britain)."

HENDERSON, EDWARD PORTER. fl. 1920-1960. American mineralogist. See: Amer. Men Sci., 10th ed. Hendersonite.

Henderson equation (or equation for pH) (Henderson, Lawrence Joseph): Chemistry. See: Ballentyne; Van Nostrand Chem. Dict.

Henderson equation (for continuous mixture boundaries) (Henderson, P.): Chemistry. See: Ballentyne.

Henderson–Hasselbalch equation (Henderson, Lawrence Joseph and Hasselbalch, Karl): Medicine. See: Stedman. Also known as: Hasselbalch's equation.

HENDERSON, J. A. RUSSELL. fl. 1929. English chemist. Cited in: Chem. Abstr., vol. 24, p. 312. Callan–Henderson reagent.

Henderson–Jones syndrome (or disease) (Henderson, Melvin Starkey and Jones, Hugh T.). See: Reichel's syndrome.

HENDERSON, LAWRENCE JOSEPH. 1878-1942. American biological chemist. See: Dict. Sci. Biog. Henderson equation (or equation for pH), Henderson–Hasselbalch equation.

HENDERSON, MELVIN STARKEY. 1883-1954. American orthopedic surgeon. See: Who Was Who Amer., 1951-1960. Henderson–Jones syndrome (or disease).

HENDERSON, P. fl. 1907. German? chemist. Cited in: Chem. Abstr., vol. 1, p. 2766; vol. 2, p. 2893. Henderson equation (for continuous mixture boundaries).

Henderson process (Derivation undetermined): Chemistry. See: Hackh; Thrush; Van Nostrand Chem. Dict.

HENDERSON, YANDELL. 1873-1944. American physiologist. See: Dict. Sci. Biog. Henderson's test.

Hendersonite (Henderson, Edward Porter): Earth Sciences. See: Thrush.

Henderson's test (Henderson, Yandell): Medicine. See: Dorland.

HENDRICKSON, ELLWOOD ROBERT. 1921- . American environmental engineer. See: Amer. Men and Women Sci., 12th ed. Hendrickson's law.

Hendrickson's law (Hendrickson, Ellwood Robert): Sociology. See: Martin.

Hendschel (railway timetable) (Hendschel, U.): Transportation. See: Stenhouse.

HENDSCHEL, U. fl. 1844-1870. German map maker. Cited in: Mansell. Hendschel (railway timetable).

HENGLEIN, MARTIN. b. 1882. German mineralogist. See: Pogg., vols. 6, 7a. Hengleinite.

Hengleinite (Henglein, Martin): Earth Sciences. See: Thrush.

Henglin's courser (Derivation undetermined). Zoology. See: Gray.

HENING, WILLIAM WALLER. 1768-1828. American legislative writer. See: Dict. Amer. Biog. Hening's Statutes.

Hening's Statutes (Hening, William Waller): History. See: Jameson.

HENKE, WILHELM. 1834-1896. German anatomist. See: Biog. Lex. hervorr. Aerzte. Henke's space.

Henke's space (Henke, Wilhelm): Anatomy. See: Dorland; Stedman.

HENKIN, LEON ALBERT. 1921- . American mathematician. See: Amer. Men and Women Sci., 12th ed. Henkin's completeness theorem.

Henkin's completeness theorem (Henkin, Leon Albert): Philosophy. See: Edwards.

HENLE, ADOLF. b. 1864. German surgeon. See: Biog. Lex. hervorr. Aerzte, 1880-1930. Henle–Coenen test (or sign).

Henle–Coenen test (or sign) (Henle, Adolf and Coenen, Hermann): Medicine. See: Dorland.

HENLE, FRANZ WILHELM. 1876-1944. German chemist. See: Pogg., vols. 5, 6, 7a. Henle reagent.

HENLE, FRIEDRICH GUSTAV JACOB. 1809-1885. German anatomist and pathologist. See: Dict. Sci. Biog. Hassall–Henle bodies (or warts), Henle's ampulla, Henle's bundle, Henle's fenestrated membrane, Henle's fiber layer, Henle's fissures, Henle's glands, Henle's layer, Henle's ligament, Henle's loop (ansa or loop of Henle), Henle's membrane (or membrane of Henle), Henle's nervous layer, Henle's reaction, Henle's sheath (or sheath of Henle), Henle's spine, Henle's tubules (or tubules of Henle).

Henle reagent (Henle, Franz Wilhelm): Chemistry. See: Van Nostrand Chem. Dict.

Henle's ampulla (Henle, Friedrich Gustav Jacob): Anatomy. See: Stedman.

Henle's bundle (Henle, Friedrich Gustav Jacob): Anatomy. See: Donath.

Henle's fenestrated membrane (Henle, Friedrich Gustav Jacob): Anatomy. See: Dorland; Stedman.

Henle's fiber layer (Henle, Friedrich Gustav Jacob): Anatomy. See: Dorland; Stedman.

Henle's fissures (Henle, Friedrich Gustav Jacob): Anatomy. See: Stedman.

Henle's glands (Henle, Friedrich Gustav Jacob): Anatomy. See: Donath; Stedman.

Henle's layer (Henle, Friedrich Gustav Jacob): Anatomy. See: Donath; Gray; Henderson; Stedman.

Henle's ligament (Henle, Friedrich Gustav Jacob): Anatomy. See: Stedman.

Henle's loop (ansa or loop of Henle) (Henle, Friedrich Gustav Jacob): Anatomy. See: Donath; Dorland; Gray; Pennak; Stedman; Webster's 3d.

Henle's membrane (or membrane of Henle) (Henle, Friedrich Gustav Jacob): Anatomy. See: Henderson; Stedman; Webster's 3d. Also known as: Bruch's membrane.

Henle's nervous layer (Henle, Friedrich Gustav Jacob): Anatomy. See: Stedman.

Henle's reaction (Henle, Friedrich Gustav Jacob): Medicine. See: Stedman.

Henle's sheath (or sheath of Henle) (Henle, Friedrich Gustav Jacob): Anatomy. See: Donath; Dorland; Henderson; Stedman; Webster's 3d. Also known as: sheath of Key and Retzius.

Henle's spine (Henle, Friedrich Gustav Jacob): Anatomy. See: Stedman.

Henle's tubules (or tubules of Henle) (Henle, Friedrich Gustav Jacob): Anatomy. See: Stedman.

Henle's warts (Henle, Friedrich Gustav Jacob). See: Hassall–Henle bodies (or warts).

HENNEBERG, LEBRECHT (In full: ERNST LEBRECHT). b. 1850. German mechanician. See: Pogg., vols. 3, 4, 5. Henneberg method?, surface of Henneberg.

Henneberg method (Henneberg, Lebrecht?): Engineering and Industry. See: Internat. Dict. Ap. Math.

HENNEBERG, RICHARD. b. 1868. German physician. See: Kuerschner's Deut. Gel. Kal., vol. 9, 1961. Scholz–Bielschowsky–Henneberg syndrome.

HENNEBERT, CAMILLE. b. 1867. Belgian otologist. See: Rev. hebd. Lar. Otol. Rhinol., Paris, vol. ii (1907) No. 29. Hennebert's sign (or syndrome).

Hennebert's sign (or syndrome) (Hennebert, Camille): Medicine. See: Dorland; Jablonski.

HENNEBIQUE, FRANCOIS. 1842-1927. French structural engineer. (Biography source unavailable.) Hennebique (reinforced concrete).

Hennebique (reinforced concrete) (Hennebique, Francois): Engineering and Industry. See: Webster's 3d.

Hennig purifier (Derivation undetermined): Engineering and Industry. See: Thrush.

Henning fluid (Derivation undetermined): Chemistry. See: Van Nostrand Chem. Dict.

HENNING, FRITZ GUSTAV HERMANN. 1877-1958. German physicist. See: Pogg., vols. 5, 6, 7a. Henning method for latent heat of vaporization, Holburn and Henning method for specific heat at constant pressure.

Henning method for latent heat of vaporization (Henning, Fritz Gustav Hermann): Physics. See: Internat. Dict. Phys. Elec.

HENOCH, EDUARD HEINRICH. 1820-1910. German pediatrician. See: Biog. Lex. hervorr. Aerzte. Henoch's angina, Henoch's disease (1) (or chorea), Schoenlein-Henoch purpura (disease or syndrome).

Henoch-Schoenlein purpura (Henoch, Eduard Heinrich and Schoenlein, Johann Lukas). See: Schoenlein-Henoch purpura (disease or syndrome).

Henoch's angina (Henoch, Eduard Heinrich): Medicine. See: Stedman.

Henoch's disease (1) (or chorea) (Henoch, Eduard Heinrich): Medicine. See: Jablonski.

Henoch's disease (2) (or purpura) (Henoch, Heinrich). See: Schoenlein-Henoch purpura (disease or syndrome).

Henri Deux faience (Henry II of France): Applied Arts. See: Webster's 3d.

Henri Quatre (whiskers) (Henry IV of France): Fashion. See: Stenhouse.

Henriade (Henry IV of France): History. See: Phyfe.

Henrician (Henry of Lausanne): Religion. See: Latham; Webster's 3d.

Henrician (and Henrician reformation) (Henry VIII): History. See: Steinberg; Webster's 3d.

Henricians (Henry IV, Holy Roman Emperor): History. See: Latham.

Henrietta (or Henrietta cloth) (Henrietta Maria of England): Fashion. See: Picken; Webster's 3d.

HENRIETTA MARIA. 1609-1669. Queen consort of Charles I of England. See: Dict. Nat. Biog. Henrietta (or Henrietta cloth), Queen Henrietta's Men.

HENRY. fl. 19th c. Scottish gunsmith. (Biography source unavailable.) Martini-Henry (rifle)?

Henry (Henry, Joseph): Physics. See: Ballentyne; Dresner; Thewlis; Van Nostrand Sci. Encyc.; Webster's 3d.

HENRY II. 1519-1559. King of France. See: Encyc. Brit., 1973. Henri Deux faience.

HENRY II, COUNT OF ANJOU. 1133-1189. King of England. See: Dict. Nat. Biog. Angevin empire.

HENRY III. 1551-1589. King of France. See: Encyc. Brit., 1973. Articles of Henry.

HENRY IV. 1050-1106. King of Germany and Holy Roman emperor. See: Encyc. Brit., 1973. Henricians.

HENRY IV (HENRY OF NAVARRE). 1553-1610. King of France. See: Encyc. Brit., 1973. Henri Quatre (whiskers), Henriade, plume-of-Navarre.

HENRY VII, EARL OF RICHMOND. 1457-1509. King of England. See: Dict. Nat. Biog. another Richmond in the field.

HENRY VIII. 1491-1547. King of England. See: Dict. Nat. Biog. Henrician (and Henrician reformation).

Henry alcohol reactions (Henry, Louis): Chemistry. See: Van Nostrand Chem. Dict.

HENRY, BENJAMIN TYLER. 1821-1898. American gunsmith. See: Nat. Cycl. Amer. Biog., vol. 10, p. 476. Henry rifle (.44 cal. rifle or carbine), Martini-Henry (rifle)?

Henry Clay flag (Clay, Henry): History. See: Mathews, M. M.

Henry Clay whig (Clay, Henry): History. See: Mathews, M. M.

HENRY, SIR EDWARD RICHARD. 1850-1931. English government official. See: Dict. Nat. Biog., 5th suppl. Galton-Henry method, Henry system.

HENRY, JOHN. b. ca. 1776-d. ca. 1820. Irish-born adventurer in America. See: Dict. Amer. Biog. Henry letters.

HENRY, JOHN. 1818-1889. Irish-born American printer. See: Lockwood. Henry press.

HENRY, JOSEPH. 1797-1878. American physicist. See: Dict. Sci. Biog. Dalton-Henry law, Henry, yrneh.

Henry('s) law (or law of Henry) (Henry, William): Chemistry. See: Ballentyne; Hackh; Internat. Dict. Phys. Elec.; Thewlis; Van Nostrand Sci. Encyc.; Webster's 3d.

Henry letters (Henry, John): History. See: Smith.

HENRY, LOUIS. 1864-1913. Belgian chemist. See: Pogg., vols. 3, 4, 5. Henry alcohol reactions, Henry reaction.

HENRY OF LAUSANNE. fl. 1st half of 12th c. French heresiarch. See: Encyc. Brit., 1911. Henrician.

Henry press (Henry, John): Printing. See: Lockwood.

Henry reaction (Henry, Louis): Chemistry. See: Van Nostrand Chem. Dict.

Henry rifle (.44 cal. rifle or carbine) (Henry, Benjamin Tyler): Weapons. See: Hendrickson; Mathews, M. M.; Quick.

Henry system (Henry, Sir Edward Richard): Sociology. See: Webster's 3d.

HENRY, WILLIAM. 1775-1836. English chemist. See: Dict. Sci. Biog. Henry('s) law (or law of Henry).

Henryite (or Henryism) (Clay, Henry): History. See: Mathews, M. M.

HENSELEIT, KURT. fl. 1932. German biochemist. Cited in: Chem. Abstr., vol. 26, pp. 4846, 5624. Krebs-Henseleit cycle.

HENSEN, VIKTOR. 1835-1924. German physiologist. See: World Who's Who Sci. Hensen's canal (or duct), Hensen's cell(s), Hensen's node (or knot), Hensen's (or H) line (band or disk), Hensen's stripe.

Hensen's canal (or duct) (Hensen, Viktor): Anatomy. See: Donath; Dorland; Stedman.

Hensen's cell(s) (Hensen, Viktor): Anatomy. See: Donath; Dorland; Gray; Henderson; Stedman.

Hensen's (or H) line (band or disk) (Hensen, Viktor): Anatomy. See: Henderson; Pennak; Stedman.

Hensen's node (or knot) (Hensen, Viktor): Anatomy. See: Gray; Pennak; Stedman. Also known as: Hubrecht's protochordal knot.

Hensen's stripe (Hensen, Viktor): Anatomy. See: Dorland; Stedman.

HENSHAW, RUSSELL. No dates. American physician. (Biography source unavailable.) Henshaw test.

Henshaw test (Henshaw, Russell): Medicine. See: Dorland.

HENSING, FRIEDRICH W. 1719-1745. German anatomist. See: Biog. Lex. hervorr. Aerzte. Hensing's ligament.

Hensing's ligament (Hensing, Friedrich W.): Anatomy. See: Dorland; Stedman.

Henslovian (Henslow, John Stevens): Botany. See: Gray.

Henslovian membrane (Henslow, John Stevens): Botany? See: Gray.

HENSLOW, JOHN STEVENS. 1796-1861. English botanist and geologist. See: Dict. Sci. Biog. Henslovian, Henslovian membrane, Henslow's sparrow (or bunting).

Henslow's sparrow (or bunting) (Henslow, John Stevens): Zoology. See: Gray; Mathews, M. M.; Webster's 3d.

Hentenian (Hentenius, John): Religion. See: Webster's 3d.

HENTENIUS, JOHN. 1500-1566. Flemish theologian. See: Biog. Nat. de Belgique. Hentenian.

HENYEY, LOUIS GEORGE. 1910- . American astronomer. See: World Who's Who Sci. Greenstein-Henyey camera.

Hepar test (Derivation undetermined): Chemistry. See: Van Nostrand Chem. Dict.

Hepburn Act (Hepburn, William Peters): Politics. See: Black; Jameson under "Interstate Commerce Law"; Morris; Smith.

HEPBURN, WILLIAM PETERS. 1833-1916. American legislator. See: Dict. Amer. Biog. Hepburn Act.

HEPP, E. fl. 1912. German chemist. Cited in: Chem. Abstr., vol. 6, p. 2435. Fischer-Hepp rearrangement.

Hepplewhite (furniture style) (Hepplewhite, George): Applied Arts. See: Hendrickson; Barnhart (Eng. Lit.); Partridge; Webster's 3d.

HEPPLEWHITE, GEORGE. d. 1786. English cabinetmaker. See: Encyc. Brit., 1911. Hepplewhite (furniture style).

Hepplewhite–Gray lamp (Derivation undetermined): Engineering and Industry. See: Thrush.

Heraclean (or Heracleian) (Hercules): Mythology. See: Webster's 3d.

Heraclean stone (Hercules). See: Hercules stone.

HERACLEON OF ALEXANDRIA. fl. 2d c. A.D. Gnostic Christian. See: Encyc. Brit., 1973. Heracleonite.

Heracleonite (Heracleon of Alexandria): Religion. See: Webster's 3d.

Heracles. See: Hercules.

Heracles complex (Hercules): Psychiatry. See: Hinsie.

Heracleum (Hercules): Botany. See: Webster's 3d.

Heraclidae (or Heracleidae) (Hercules): History. See: Encyc. Brit., 1973.

Heraclitean (Heraclitic or Heracliteanism) (Heraclitus, the philosopher): Philosophy. See: Good; Webster's 3d.

HERACLITUS. ca. 540–ca. 480 B.C. Greek philosopher of Ephesus. See: Encyc. Brit., 1973. Heraclitean (Heraclitic or Heracliteanism).

HERAPATH, WILLIAM BIRD. 1820–1868. English chemist. See: Dict. Sci. Biog. Herapathite.

Herapathite (Herapath, William Bird): Earth Sciences. See: Webster's 3d.

herb Christopher (Christopher, Saint): Botany. See: Brewer; Webster's 3d.

herb of St. Barbara. See: Barbarea.

herb of St. Martin (Martin of Tours, Saint): Botany. Cited in: Laughlin.

herb Robert (Robert, Saint): Botany. See: Webster's 3d. Also known as: Wren's flower.

HERBART, JOHANN FRIEDRICH. 1776–1841. German philosopher and educator. See: Encyc. Brit., 1973. Herbartian, Herbartian method, Herbartian movement, Herbartianism (or Herbartian psychology).

Herbartian (Herbart, Johann Friedrich): Philosophy. See: Webster's 3d.

Herbartian method (Herbart, Johann Friedrich): Education. See: Good.

Herbartian movement (Herbart, Johann Friedrich): Education. See: Good.

Herbartianism (or Herbartian psychology) (Herbart, Johann Friedrich): Psychology. See: Chaplin; Drever; English; Mathews, S.; Webster's 3d.; Wolman.

l'herbe de St. Main (Mevan, Saint): Botany. See: Butler's Lives of the Saints.

HERBERT, EDWARD GEISLER. b. 1869. English engineer. Cited in: Mansell. Herbert hardness tester (or pendulum).

Herbert hardness tester (or pendulum) (Herbert, Edward Geisler): Engineering and Industry. See: Auger; Thewlis.

Herbert–Heim test (Hebert, Alexandre and Heim de Balsac, Frederic): Chemistry. See: Van Nostrand Chem. Dict.

HERBERT, HENRY, 9TH EARL OF PEMBROKE. 1693–1751. English architect. See: Dict. Nat. Biog. Pembroke table?

HERBERT, HENRY HOWARD MOLYNEUX, 4TH EARL OF CARNARVON. 1831–1890. English statesman. See: Dict. Nat. Biog. Carnarvon controversy.

HERBERT, HERBERT. 1865–1942. English ophthalmic surgeon. See: Who Was Who, 1941–1950. Herbert's operation, Herbert's pits.

Herbert T. Kalmus Award (Kalmus, Herbert Thomas): Photography. See: Focal Encyc. Photog. under "Awards (America)."

Herbert's duplex sand mixer (Derivation undetermined): Engineering and Industry. See: Thrush.

Herbert's operation (Herbert, Herbert): Medicine. See: Dorland; Stedman.

Herbert's pits (Herbert, Herbert): Medicine. See: Jablonski.

HERBST, ERNST FRIEDRICH GUSTAV. 1803–1893. German physician. See: Biog. Lex. hervorr. Aerzte, 1880–1930. Herbst's corpuscle(s) (bodies or corpuscle of Herbst).

Herbst's corpuscle(s) (bodies or corpuscle of Herbst) (Herbst, Ernst Friedrich Gustav): Zoology. See: Blakiston's Gould; Dorland; Gray; Henderson; Stedman; Webster's 3d.

Herculean (Hercules): Generic Word (extremely difficult): See: Charnock; Funk; Webster's 3d.

Herculean knot (Hercules): History. See: Brewer.

Herculean rule-cutter (Hercules): Printing. See: Lockwood.

HERCULES (HERACLES). Greek legendary hero. See: Encyc. Brit., 1973. awakening of Hercules, Ercles vein, Heraclean (or Heracleian), Heracles complex, Heracleum, Heraclidae (or Heracleidae), Herculean, Herculean knot, Herculean rule-cutter, Hercules (1), Hercules (2) (pile driving machine), Hercules allheal, Hercules beetle, Hercules braid, Hercules' club (1), Hercules club (2), Hercules (or Heraclean) stone, Hercules powder (and coal powder 2), Herculeus morbus, infant Hercules.

Hercules (1) (Hercules): Generic Word (one of great physicial strength). See: Webster's 3d.

Hercules (2) (pile driving machine) (Hercules): Engineering and Industry. See: Partridge.

Hercules' allheal (Hercules): Botany. See: Webster's 3d.

Hercules beetle (Hercules): Zoology. See: Pennak; Webster's 3d.

Hercules braid (Hercules): Fashion. See: Picken.

Hercules' club (1) (Hercules): Botany. See: Blumberg; Gray; Mathews, M. M.; Webster's 3d.

Hercules club (2) (Hercules): Zoology. See: Webster's 3d.

Hercules powder (and coal powder 2) (Hercules): Engineering and Industry. See: Mathews, M. M.; Thrush.

Hercules (or Heraclean) stone (Hercules): Earth Sciences. See: Thrush; Webster's 3d.

Herculeus morbus (Hercules): Medicine. See: Hinsie.

Hercus and Laby method for heat transmission of gases (Hercus, Eric Oswald and Laby, Thomas Howell): Physics. See: Internat. Dict. Phys. Elec.

HERCUS, ERIC OSWALD. b. 1891. Australian physicist. See: Who's Who Brit. Sci., 1953. Hercus and Laby method for heat transmission of gases, Laby and Hercus method for mechanical equivalent of heat.

Herd('s) grass (Herd, John): Botany. See: Hendrickson under "Timothy Grass, Herd's Grass."; Webster's 3d. Also known as: Timothy (grass and hay).

HERD, JOHN. fl. 18th c. American farmer. (Biography source unavailable.) Herd('s) grass.

HERDER, BARON SIEGMUND. 1776–1838. German mining official. See: Neue Deut. Biog., vol. 8, p. 594. Herderite.

Herderite (Herder, Baron Siegmund): Earth Sciences. See: Charnock; Thrush; Webster's 3d.

Herdic (Herdic, Peter): Generic Word (horse-drawn omnibus). See: Mathews, M. M.; Webster's 3d.

HERDIC, PETER. 1824–1888. American inventor. See: Dict. Amer. Biog. Herdic.

Herelleosis (D'Herelle, Felix Hubert): Medicine. See: Stedman.

heresy of Berengarius (Berengar of Tours): Religion. See: Attwater.

HERFF, OTTO VON. 1856–1916. Swiss gynecologist. See: Biog. Lex. hervorr. Aerzte, 1880–1930. Herff's clamp.

Herff's clamp (Herff, Otto von): Medicine. See: Dorland.

Hering afterimage (or image) (Hering, Ewald): Physiology. See: Chaplin; Drever; English; Webster's 3d.; Wolman.

Hering–Breuer reflex (Hering, Heinrich Ewald and Breuer, Josef): Physiology. See: Stedman.

HERING, EWALD (In full: KARL EWALD CONSTANTIN). 1834–1918. German physiologist. See: Dict. Sci. Biog. canal of Hering, Hering afterimage (or image), Hering illusion, Hering('s) grays, Hering('s) window, Hering theory (or theory of color vision), Hering's test, Semon–Hering theory, Traube–Hering waves (or curves).

Hering('s) grays (Hering, Ewald): Physics. See: Chaplin; Drever; English; Wolman.

HERING, HEINRICH EWALD. 1866–1948. German physiologist. See: World Who's Who Sci. Hering–Breuer reflex, Hering's sinus nerve.

Hering illusion (Hering, Ewald): Physiology. See: Drever; Wolman.

Hering theory (or theory of color vision) (Hering, Ewald): Physiology. See: Chaplin; Drever; English; Van Nostrand Sci. Encyc.; Wolman.

Hering('s) window (Hering, Ewald): Physiology. See: Drever; Wolman.

Hering's sinus nerve (Hering, Heinrich Ewald): Anatomy. See: Dorland; Stedman

Hering's test (Hering, Ewald): Physiology. See: Dorland; Stedman.

Hering's theory of color blindness (Hering, Ewald). See: Hering theory (or theory of color vision).

HERITIER DE BRUTELLE, CHARLES LOUIS L'. 1746-1800. French botanist. See: Nouv. Biog. Univ. Heritiera.

Heritiera (Heritier de Brutelle, Charles Louis l'): Botany. See: Charnock.

HERLITZ, GILLIS (In full: CARL GILLIS). 1902-   . Swedish pediatrician. See: Vem Ar Det?, 1975. Herlitz's syndrome.

Herlitz's syndrome (Herlitz, Gillis): Medicine. See: Jablonski.

Herm (Hermes or Hermaen (2)) (Hermes, the god): Fine Arts. See: Charnock; Encyc. Brit., 1973; Osborne.

Hermaea (Hermes, the God?): Zoology. See: Pennak.

Hermaean (1) (Hermes, the god): Mythology. See: Webster's 3d.

HERMAN, EUFEMIUSZ. fl. 1937-1954. Polish physician. Cited in: Mansell. Herman's syndrome.

HERMANN, CARL HEINRICH. 1898-1961. German physicist. See: Dict. Sci. Biog. Hermann-Mauguin symbols.

Hermann('s) fluid (Hermann, Friedrich): Medicine. See: Stedman; Van Nostrand Chem. Dict.; Webster's 3d.

HERMANN, FRIEDRICH. 1859-1920. German anatomist. Cited in: Mansell. Hermann('s) fluid.

HERMANN, GOTTFRIED (In full: JOHANN GOTTFRIED JAKOB). 1772-1848. German classical philologist. See: Encyc. Brit., 1973. Hermann's law?

Hermann-Mauguin symbols (Hermann, Carl Heinrich and Maugin, Charles): Physics. See: Ballentyne; Van Nostrand Sci. Encyc.

HERMANN, PAUL. 1646-1695. German botanist. See: World Who's Who Sci. Hermannia, Mahernia.

Hermannia (Hermann, Paul): Botany. See: Charnock; Hendrickson.

Hermann's law (Hermann, Gottfried?): Literature. See: Encyc. Brit., 1973 under "Hexameter," vol. 11, p. 468b.

HERMANS, PETRUS HENDRIK. 1898-   . Dutch chemical technologist. See: Pogg., vol. 6. Hermans test for nitrite.

Herman's syndrome (Herman, Eufemiusz): Medicine. See: Jablonski.

Hermans test for nitrite (Hermans, Petrus Hendrik): Chemistry. See: Van Nostrand Chem. Dict.

HERMANSEN, AXEL. 1871-1933. Danish engineer. See: Dansk Biog. Lek. Hermansen furnace.

Hermansen furnace (Hermansen, Axel): Engineering and Industry. See: Thrush.

HERMANSKY, F. fl. 1959. Czechoslovakian internist. (Biography source unavailable.) Hermansky-Pudlak syndrome.

Hermansky-Pudlak syndrome (Hermansky, F. and Pudlak, P.): Medicine. See: Jablonski.

HERMAPHRODITE. Son of Hermes and Aphrodite in Greek mythology. See: Encyc. Brit., 1973. Hermaphrodite.

Hermaphrodite (Hermaphrodite, the Greek god): Generic Word. See: Charnock; Partridge; Pennak; Stedman; Van Nostrand Sci. Encyc.; Webster's 3d.

Hermeneutics (Hermeneutic or Hermeneutical) (Hermes, the god): Generic Word. See: Charnock.

HERMES. Greek god. See: Encyc. Brit., 1973. Herm (Hermes or Hermaen (2)), Hermaea?, Hermaean (1), Hermeneutics (Hermeneutic or Hermeneutical), Hermes (missile), Hermesite, Hermodactyl.

HERMES, GEORGE. 1775-1831. German theologian and philosopher. See: Encyc. Brit., 1973. Hermesianism.

Hermes (missile) (Hermes, the god): Engineering and Industry. See: Markus.

HERMES TRISMEGISTOS. Greek name for the Egyptian god Thoth. See: Encyc. Brit., 1973. Hermetic (1) (or Hermetical), Hermetic (2) (or Hermetically sealed), Hermetic art (or philosophy), Hermetic books, Hermetic powder, Hermeticism, Hermetism (or Hermeticism).

Hermesianism (Hermes, George): Religion. See: Attwater; Canney; Mathews, S.

Hermesite (Hermes, the god): Earth Sciences. See: Thrush.

Hermetic (1) (or Hermetical) (Hermes Trismegistos): Parapsychology. See: Charnock; Partridge; Webster's 3d.

Hermetic (2) (or Hermetically sealed) (Hermes Trismegistos): Generic Word (airtight). See: Brewer; Funk; Stenhouse; Webster's 3d.

Hermetic art (or philosophy) (Hermes Trismegistos): Generic Word (alchemy). See: Brewer; Harvey under "Hermes Trismegistus."

Hermetic books (Hermes Trismegistos): Parapsychology. See: Barnhart (Eng. Lit.); Brewer; Canney; Harvey; Phyfe.

Hermetic powder (Hermes Trismegistos): Parapsychology. See: Brewer.

Hermeticism (Hermes Trismegistos): Literature. See: Preminger.

Hermetism (or Hermeticism) (Hermes Trismegistos): Parapsychology. See: Webster's 3d.

HERMITE, CHARLES. 1822-1901. French mathematician. See: Dict. Sci. Biog. Hermite distribution, Hermite equation, Hermite functions, Hermite interpolation formula, Hermite polynomials, Hermitian, Hermitian conjugate, Hermitian manifold, Hermitian matrix, Hermitian operator, Hermitian product, Hermitian scalar product, Hermitian space, Tchebychev-Hermite polynomials.

Hermite distribution (Hermite, Charles): Statistics. See: Kendall.

Hermite equation (Hermite, Charles): Mathematics. See: Thewlis; Van Nostrand Sci. Encyc.

Hermite functions (Hermite, Charles): Mathematics. See: Kendall under "Hh_n function."

Hermite interpolation formula (Hermite, Charles): Mathematics. See: Internat. Dict. Ap. Math.

Hermite polynomials (Hermite, Charles): Mathematics. See: Ballentyne; Internat. Dict. Ap. Math.; Internat. Dict. Phys. Elec.; Van Nostrand Sci. Encyc.

Hermitian (Hermite, Charles): Mathematics. See: Internat. Dict. Phys. Elec.; Van Nostrand Sci. Elec. under "Form."

Hermitian conjugate (Hermite, Charles): Mathematics. See: Internat. Dict. Ap. Math.; Internat. Dict. Phys. Elec.

Hermitian manifold (Hermite, Charles): Mathematics. See: Encyc. Brit., 1973 under "Riemannian geometry," vol. 19, p. 325b.

Hermitian matrix (Hermite, Charles): Mathematics. See: Ballentyne; Internat. Dict. Ap. Math.; Internat. Dict. Phys. Elec.

Hermitian operator (Hermite, Charles): Mathematics. See: Ballentyne; Internat. Dict. Ap. Math.; Internat. Dict. Phys. Elec.

Hermitian product (Hermite, Charles): Mathematics. See: Internat. Dict. Phys. Elec.

Hermitian scalar product (Hermite, Charles): Mathematics. See: Internat. Dict. Ap. Math.

Hermitian space (Hermite, Charles): Mathematics. See: Internat. Dict. Ap. Math.

Hermits of St. Augustine (Augustine, Saint). See: Augustinian friars.

Hermits of St. Jerome (Jerome, Saint): Religion. See: Attwater.

Hermits of St. Paul (Paul of Thebes, Saint): Religion. See: Attwater.

Hermodactyl (Hermes, the god): Botany. See: Charnock; Webster's 3d.

HERMOGENES. fl. 2d c. A.D. Greek rhetorician. See: Encyc. Brit., 1911. Hermogenian.

Hermogenian (Hermogenes): Linguistics. See: Webster's 3d.

HERNANDEZ, FRANCISCO. 1517-1587. Spanish botanist. See: Dict. Sci. Biog. Hernandia.

HERNANDEZ, J. FERRER. fl. 1911. Spanish chemist. Cited in: Chem. Abstr., vol. 5, p. 2045. Hernandez test paper.

Hernandez test paper (Hernandez, J. Ferrer): Chemistry. See: Van Nostrand Chem. Dict.

Hernandia (Hernandez, Francisco): Botany. See: Charnock; Webster's 3d.

HERO (HERON) OF ALEXANDRIA. fl. ca. 62 A.D. Greek geometer and mechanician. See: Dict. Sci. Biog. Heron's (or Hero's) formula, Heron's fountain, Hero's turbine.

HEROD THE GREAT. 73-4 B.C. King of Judaea under Roman rule. See: Encyc. Brit., 1973. Herodian (1), Herodian(s) (2), out-herod Herod.

Herodian (1) (Herod the Great): History. See: Webster's 3d.

Herodian(s) (2) (Herod the Great): History. See: Attwater; Phyfe; Webster's 3d.

Herodotean (Herodotus): History. See: Webster's 3d.

HERODOTUS. fl. 5th c. B.C. Greek historian. See: Encyc. Brit., 1973. Herodotean.

Heron of Alexandria. See: Hero of Alexandria.

Heron's (or Hero's) formula (Hero of Alexandria): Mathematics. See: Ballentyne; James.

Heron's fountain (Hero of Alexandria): Engineering and Industry. Cited in: Encyc. Brit., 1973 under "Hero of Alexandria," vol. 11, p. 437b.

HEROPHILUS. fl. 300 B.C. Greek anatomist and surgeon. See: Dict. Sci. Biog. torcular Herophili (or Herophilus' wine press).

Herophilus' wine press (Herophilus). See: torcular Herophili.

Hero's turbine (Hero of Alexandria): Engineering and Industry. See: Auguer.

Heroult furnace (Heroult, Paul Louis Touissant): Engineering and Industry. See: Thrush; Van Nostrand Sci. Encyc.

HEROULT, PAUL LOUIS TOUISSANT. 1863-1914. French metallurgist. See: Dict. Sci. Biog. Hall-Heroult cell, Heroult furnace, Heroult process.

Heroult process (Heroult, Paul Louis Toussaint). See: Hall process.

HERRAN, TOMAS. 1846-1904. Colombian diplomat. See: Dicc. Biog. y Bibliog. Colombia. Hay-Herran Treaty (or Convention).

Herrenschmidt furnace (Derivation undetermined): Chemistry. See: Van Nostrand Chem. Dict.

Herrenschmidt process (Derivation undetermined): Chemistry. See: Thrush.

HERRENSCHWAND, FRIEDRICH VON. b. 1881. German physician. See: Biog. Lex. hervorr. Aerzte, 1880-1930. Herrenschwand's syndrome.

Herrenschwand's syndrome (Herrenschwand, Friedrich von): Medicine. See: Jablonski.

HERRERA. fl. 19th c. Mineralogist. Cited in: Bailey. Herrerite.

Herrerite (Herrera): Earth Sciences. See: Thrush.

Herreshoff boiler (Herreshoff, James Brown and Herreshoff, John Brown): Engineering and Industry. See: Auger.

Herreshoff furnace (Herreshoff, James Brown): Engineering and Industry. See: Thrush.

HERRESHOFF, JAMES BROWN. 1834-1930. American inventor. See: Dict. Amer. Biog. Herreshoff boiler, Herreshoff furnace.

HERRESHOFF, JOHN BROWN. 1841-1915. American designer. See: Dict. Amer. Biog. Herreshoff boiler.

HERRICK, JAMES BRYAN. 1861-1954. American physician. See: World Who's Who Sci. Herrick's syndrome (or anemia).

Herrick's syndrome (or anemia) (Herrick, James Bryan): Medicine. See: Dorland; Jablonski.

Herring-Binet test (Herring, John Peabody and Binet, Alfred). See: Herring revision.

Herring bodies (Herring, Percy Theodore): Physiology. See: Dorland; Stedman.

HERRING, JOHN PEABODY. b. 1882. American psychologist. See: Amer. Men Sci., 4th ed. Herring revision.

HERRING, PERCY THEODORE. 1872-1967. English physiologist. See: Who Was Who, 1961-1970. Herring bodies.

Herring revision (Herring, John Peabody): Psychology. See: Drever; English; Wolman. Also known as: Herring-Binet test.

Herringer-Huelster effect (Derivation undetermined): Physics. See: Van Nostrand Sci. Encyc. under "Phase focusing in magnetrons."

HERRMANN, HEINZ. fl. 1935. German chemist. Cited in: Chem. Abstr., vol. 30, p. 54. Fuerth-Hermann test reaction.

HERRMANNSDORFER, ADOLF. b. 1889. German surgeon. See: Biog. Lex. hervorr. Aerzte, 1880-1930. Gerson-Herrmannsdorfer diet.

Herrmannsdorfer diet (Herrmannsdorfer, Adolf). See: Gerson-Herrmannsdorfer diet.

Hers' disease (Hers, H. G.): Medicine. See: Jablonski; Stedman.

HERS, H. G. fl. 1959. French biochemist. Cited in: Nat. Union Cat., 1956-1967. Hers' disease.

Hersch cell (Hersch, Paul): Physics. See: Thewlis.

HERSCH, PAUL. fl. 1950. English chemist. Cited in: Chem. Abstr., Decenn. Index, 1947-1956. Hersch cell.

Herschel-Cassegrain telescope (Herschel, Sir William and Cassegrain, Giovanni D.): Astronomy. See: Satterthwaite.

Herschel condition (Herschel, Sir John Frederick William?): Physics. See: Internat. Dict. Ap. Math.

Herschel effect (Herschel, Sir John Frederick William): Photography. See: Focal Encyc. Photog.; Van Nostrand Sci. Encyc.; Webster's 3d.

HERSCHEL, SIR JOHN FREDERICK WILLIAM. 1792-1871. English astronomer. See: Dict. Sci. Biog. Herschel condition?, Herschel effect, Herschel system, Herschel (unit), Herschelite.

Herschel system (Herschel, Sir John Frederick William): History. See: Harbottle.

Herschel (unit) (Herschel, Sir John Frederick William): Physics. See: Dresner.

HERSCHEL, SIR WILLIAM. 1738-1822. German-born English astronomer. See: Dict. Sci. Biog. Herschel-Cassegrain telescope, Herschelian, Herschelian telescope.

Herschelian (Herschel, Sir William): Astronomy. See: Webster's 3d.

Herschelian telescope (Herschel, Sir William): Astronomy. See: Charnock; Satterthwaite; Thewlis; Webster's 3d.

Herschelite (Herschel, Sir John Frederick William): Earth Sciences. See: Charnock; Thrush; Webster's 3d.

Herschkind furnace (Derivation undetermined): Engineering and Industry. See: Van Nostrand Chem. Dict.

HERSMAN, C. F. fl. 1894. American physician. Cited in: Kelly. Hersman's disease.

Hersman's disease (Hersman, C. F.): Medicine. See: Jablonski.

HERTER, CHRISTIAN ARCHIBALD. 1865-1910. American physician. See: World Who's Who Sci. Herter's syndrome (disease or infantilism).

Herter's syndrome (disease or infantilism) (Herter, Christian Archibald): Medicine. See: Dorland; Jablonski; Stedman. Also known as: Gee-Herter disease (infantilism or syndrome), Gee-Herter-Heubner syndrome, Gee's disease, Gee-Thaysen disease, Heubner-Herter syndrome.

Hertford, 1st Marquis of. See: Seymour-Conway, Francis, 1st Marquis of Hertford.

Hertford ambulance (Seymour-Conway, Francis, 1st Marquis of Hertford): History. Cited in: Dict. Nat. Biog. under "Wallace, Sir Richard."

Hertford-Wallace collection (Seymour-Conway, Francis, 1st Marquis of Hertford and Wallace, Sir Richard). See: Wallace collection.

Hertwig-Magendie syndrome (phenomenon or sign) (Von Hertwig, Richard Carl Wilhelm Theodor and Magendie, Francois): Medicine. See: Dorland; Hinsie; Jablonski; Stedman; Wolman. Also known as: Magendie-Hertwig phenomenon (sign or syndrome).

HERTWIG, OSKAR (In full: WILHELM AUGUST OSKAR). 1849-1922. German physiologist. See: Dict. Sci. Biog. Hertwig-Magendie phenomenon; Hertwig's sheath.

HERTWIG, PAULA. b. 1889. German biologist. See: Biog. Lex. hervorr. Aerzte, 1880-1930. Hertwig-Weyers syndrome.

Hertwig, Richard Carl Wilhelm von. See: Von Hertwig, Richard Carl Wilhelm.

Hertwig-Weyers syndrome (Hertwig, Paula and Weyers, Helmut): Medicine. See: Jablonski.

Hertwigia (Von Hertwig, Richard Carl Wilhelm Theodor): Zoology. See: Pennak.

Hertwig's sheath (Hertwig, Oskar): Anatomy. See: Dorland; Stedman.

Hertz antenna (Hertz, Heinrich Rudolph): Physics. See: Hughes; Internat. Dict. Phys. Elec. under "Antenna, doublet"; Markus.

Hertz effect (Hertz, Gustav Ludwig): Physics. See: Ballentyne.

HERTZ, GUSTAV LUDWIG. b. 1887. German physicist. See: World Who's Who Sci. Franck-Hertz experiment, Hertz effect.

HERTZ, HEINRICH RUDOLPH. 1857-1894. German physicist. See: Dict. Sci. Biog. Hertz antenna, Hertz(ian) oscillator, Hertz (unit), Hertz(ian) vector, Hertzian dipole, Hertzian experiments, Hertzian radiator, Hertzian waves (and radiation), Hertzian telegraphy, Hertz's law?

Hertz(ian) oscillator (Hertz, Heinrich Rudolph): Physics. See: Hughes; Webster's 3d.

Hertz (unit) (Hertz, Heinrich Rudolph): Physics. See: Dresner; Hughes; Markus; Thewlis; Van Nostrand Sci. Encyc.; Webster's 3d.

Hertz(ian) vector (Hertz, Heinrich Rudolph): Physics. See: Ballentyne; Internat. Dict. Ap. Math.; Internat. Dict. Phys. Elec.; Markus; Thewlis.

Hertzian (Hertz, Heinrich Rudolph): Physics. See: Webster's 3d.

Hertzian dipole (Hertz, Heinrich Rudolph): Physics. See: Hughes; Thewlis.

Hertzian experiments (Hertz, Heinrich Rudolph): Physics. See: Stedman.

Hertzian radiator (Hertz, Heinrich Rudolph): Physics. See: Hughes.

Hertzian telegraphy (Hertz, Heinrich Rudolph): Telegraphy. See: Webster's 3d.

Hertzian waves (and radiation) (Hertz, Heinrich Rudolph): Physics. See: Ballentyne; Hughes; Internat. Dict. Phys. Elec.; Van Nostrand Sci. Encyc.; Webster's 3d.

Hertz's law (Hertz, Heinrich Rudolf?): Physics. See: Ballentyne.

HERTZSPRUNG, EJNAR. 1873-1967. Danish astronomer. See: Dict. Sci. Biog. Hertzsprung-Russell (or H-R) diagram.

Hertzsprung-Russell (or H-R) diagram (Hertzsprung, Ejnar and Russell, Henry Norris): Astronomy. See: Satterthwaite; Thewlis; Van Nostrand Sci. Encyc. under "Spectral Class." Also known as: Russell diagram.

HERXHEIMER, KARL. 1861-1944. German dermatologist. See: World Who's Who Sci. Herxheimer reaction, Herxheimer's disease, Herxheimer's fever, Herxheimer's fibers (or spirals).

Herxheimer reaction (Herxheimer, Karl): Medicine. See: Dorland; Hinsie; Stedman; Webster's 3d. Also known as: Jarisch-Herxheimer reaction.

Herxheimer's disease (Herxheimer, Karl): Medicine. See: Jablonski. Also known as: Pick-Herxheimer syndrome, Pick's disease, Taylor's disease.

Herxheimer's fever (Herxheimer, Karl): Medicine. See: Dorland, 25th ed.

Herxheimer's fibers (or spirals) (Herxheimer, Karl): Medicine. See: Dorland.

HERYNG, THEODOR. 1847-1925. Polish laryngologist. See: Biog. Lex. hervorr. Aerzte, 1880-1930. Heryng's benign ulcer, Heryng's sign.

Heryng's benign ulcer (Heryng, Theodor): Medicine. See: Blakiston's Gould.

Heryng's sign (Heryng, Theodor): Medicine. See: Dorland; Stedman. Also known as: Voltolini-Heryng sign, Voltolini's sign.

Herz reaction (Herz, Richard): Chemistry. See: Van Nostrand Chem. Dict.

HERZ, RICHARD. 1867-1936. German organic chemist. See: Pogg., vols. 6, 7a. Herz reaction.

Herzberg continuum (Herzberg, Gerhard): Physics. See: Van Nostrand Sci. Encyc.

HERZBERG, GERHARD. 1904- . German-born Canadian physicist. See: World Who's Who Sci. Herzberg continuum.

HERZBERG, WILHELM. fl. 1888-1907. German paper chemist. Cited in: Mansell. Herzberg's stain.

Herzberger dispersion formula (Herzberger, Maximillian Jakob): Physics. See: Internat. Dict. Ap. Math.

HERZBERGER, MAXIMILLIAN JAKOB. 1899- . German-born physicist in America and Switzerland. See: World Who's Who Sci. Herzberger dispersion formula.

Herzberg's stain (Herzberg, Wilhelm): Chemistry. See: Hackh.

HERZENBERG, ROBERT. fl. ca. 1934. German? mineralogist in Bolivia. Cited in: Hintze, 2d suppl., p. 150. Herzenbergite.

Herzenbergite (Herzenberg, Robert): Earth Sciences. See: Thrush.

HERZFELD, H. fl. 1910. German chemist. Cited in: Pogg., vol. 6 under "Hauser, Otto." Hauser-Herzfeld test.

HERZIG, JOSEF. 1853-1924. Austrian chemist. See: Pogg., vols. 4, 5. Herzig-Meyer method (or determination of alkimides).

Herzig-Meyer method (or determination of alkimides) (Herzig, Josef and Meyer, Hans Johannes Leopold): Chemistry. See: Ballentyne; Van Nostrand Chem. Dict.

Herzog reagent for lysine and ornithine (Herzog, Reginald Oliver?): Chemistry. See: Van Nostrand Chem. Dict.

HERZOG, REGINALD OLIVER. 1878-1935. Austrian chemist. See: Pogg., vols. 5, 6. Herzog reagent for lysine and ornithine?, Herzog test reaction for histidine.

HERZOG, RICHARD FRANZ KARL. 1911- . Austrian-born American physicist. See: Pogg., vol. 7a. Mattauch-Herzog mass spectrograph (and geometry).

Herzog test reaction for histidine (Herzog, Reginald Oliver): Chemistry. See: Van Nostrand Chem. Dict.

HESCHL, RICHARD LADISLAUS. 1824-1881. Austrian anatomist. See: World Who's Who Sci. Heschl's gyri (or convolutions).

Heschl's gyri (or convolutions) (Heschl, Richard Ladislaus): Anatomy. See: Donath; Dorland; Stedman.

HESIOD. fl. 8th c. B.C. Greek poet. See: Encyc. Brit., 1973. Hesiodic.

Hesiodic (Hesiod): Literature. See: Webster's 3d.

HESIONE. Trojan princess of Greek mythology. See: Jobes. Hesione.

Hesione (Hesione, the princess): Zoology. See: Webster's 3d.

HESLOP, ADAM. fl. 1790. English engineer. (Biography source unavailable.) Heslop engine.

Heslop engine (Heslop, Adam): Engineering and Industry. See: Auger.

HESS, ALFRED FABIAN. 1875-1933. American physician. See: World Who's Who Sci. Hess test.

HESS, CARL VON. 1863-1923. German ophthalmologist. See: Biog. Lex. hervorr. Aerzte, 1880-1930. Hess image.

Hess diagram (Hess, Victor Francis?): Physics. See: Thewlis.

HESS, HENRI (In full: Germain Henri). 1801-1850. Swiss-born physicist in Russia. See: Dict. Sci. Biog. Hess('s) law, Hessite.

Hess image (Hess, Carl von): Physiology. See: Webster's 3d.

Hess-Ives photometer (Hess, Walter Rudolf? and Ives, Frederick Eugene?): Physics. See: Van Nostrand Sci. Encyc.

Hess('s) law (Hess, Henri): Chemistry. See: Ballentyne; Hackh; Internat. Dict. Ap. Math.; Thewlis; Van Nostrand Sci. Encyc. under "Thermochemistry"; Webster's 3d.

Hess rays (Hess, Victor Francis): Physics. See: Hackh.

Hess test (Hess, Alfred Fabian). See: Rumpel-Leede test.

HESS, VICTOR FRANCIS. 1883-1964. Austrian-born American physicist. See: World Who's Who Sci. Hess diagram?, Hess rays.

Hess viscometer (Hess Walter Rudolf): Chemistry. See: Hackh.

HESS, WALTER RUDOLF. b. 1881. Swiss physiologist. See: World Who's Who Sci. Hess-Ives photometer, Hess viscometer, trophotropic zone of Hess.

HESSE. fl. 1896. German? engineer. (Biography source unavailable.) Oddesse pump.

HESSE, LUDWIG OTTO. 1811-1874. German mathematician. See: Dict. Sci. Biog. Hesse normal form, Hessian (functional determinant).

Hesse normal form (Hesse, Ludwig Otto): Mathematics. See: Internat. Dict. Ap. Math.

HESSE, OSWALD (In full: JULIUS OSWALD). 1835-1917. German chemist. See: Pogg., vols. 3, 4, 5. Hesse test for pyrocatechnic acid?

HESSE, RICHARD. 1868-1944. German zoologist. See: Kuerschner's Deut. Gel. Kal., vol. 4, 1931. Hesse's cell.

Hesse test for pyrocatechnic acid (Hesse, Oswald?): Chemistry. See: Van Nostrand Chem. Dict.

HESSELBACH, FRANZ KASPAR. 1759-1816. German surgeon. See: World Who's Who Sci. Hesselbach's fascia, Hesselbach's hernia, Hesselbach's ligament (or band), Hesselbach's triangle (or triangle of Hesselbach).

Hesselbach's fascia (Hesselbach, Franz Kaspar): Anatomy. See: Dorland; Stedman.

Hesselbach's hernia (Hesselbach, Franz Kaspar): Medicine. See: Dorland; Jablonski; Stedman.

Hesselbach's ligament (or band) (Hesselbach, Franz Kaspar): Anatomy. See: Donath; Stedman.

Hesselbach's triangle (or triangle of Hesselbach) (Hesselbach, Franz Kaspar): Medicine. See: Dorland; Stedman; Webster's 3d.

Hesselman engine (Hesselman, Knut Jonas Elias): Engineering and Industry. See: Auger.

HESSELMAN, KNUT JONAS ELIAS. b. 1877. Swedish engineer. See: Svenska Maen Och Kvinnor. Hesselman engine.

HESSENBERG, GERHARD WILHELM. 1874-1925. German mathematician. See: Pogg., vols. 5, 6. Hessenberg method?

Hessenberg method (Hessenberg, Gerhard Wilhelm?): Mathematics. See: Internat. Dict. Ap. Math.

Hesse's cell (Hesse, Richard): Zoology. See: Gray.

Hessian (functional determinant) (Hesse, Ludwig Otto): Mathematics. See: Encyc. Brit., 1973 under "Invariants," vol. 12, p. 462b; Internat. Dict. Ap. Math.; Internat. Dict. Phys. Elec.; James.

Hessite (Hess, Henri): Earth Sciences. See: Thrush; Van Nostrand Sci. Encyc.; Webster's 3d.

HESYCHIUS. fl. 5th or 6th c. A.D. Greek scholar of Alexandria. See: Encyc. Brit., 1973. Hesychius (extant Greek lexicon).

Hesychius (extant Greek lexicon) (Hesychius, the scholar): Linguistics. See: Charnock.

HEUBLEIN, ARTHUR CARL. 1879-1932. American radiologist. See: Nat. Cycl. Amer. Biog. vol. 31, p. 91. Heublein method.

Heublein method (Heublein, Arthur Carl): Medicine. See: Dorland.

Heubner-Herter syndrome (Heubner, Otto and Herter, Christian Archibald). See: Herter's syndrome.

HEUBNER, OTTO (In full: JOHANN OTTO LEONHARD). 1843-1926. German pediatrician. See: World Who's Who Sci. Heubner-Herter syndrome, Heubner-Schilder syndrome, Heubner's disease.

Heubner-Schilder syndrome (Heubner, Otto? and Schilder, Paul). See: Schilder's disease.

Heubner's disease (Heubner, Otto): Medicine. See: Dorland; Stedman.

HEUCHER, JOHANN HEINRICH VON. 1677-1747. German botanist. See: Pogg., vol. 1. Heuchera.

Heuchera (Heucher, Johann Heinrich von): Botany. See: Taylor, N.; Webster's 3d.

HEULAND, HENRY. 1777-1856. English mineralogical collector. See: Pogg., vol. 1. Heulandite.

Heulandite (Heuland, Henry): Earth Sciences. See: Charnock; Van Nostrand Sci. Encyc.; Webster's 3d.

Heumann indigo synthesis (Heumann, Karl): Chemistry. See: Van Nostrand Chem. Dict.

HEUMANN, KARL. 1850-1893. Swiss chemist. See: Pogg., vols. 3, 4. Heumann indigo synthesis.

Heurlinger equations (Heurlinger, Torsten Valter Fredrik): Physics. See: Ballentyne.

HEURLINGER, TORSTEN VALTER FREDRIK. b. 1893. Swedish physicist. See: Pogg., vol. 6. Heurlinger equations.

Heusinger valve gear (Heusinger von Waldegg, Edmund): Engineering and Industry. See: Auger. Also known as: Waldegg gear.

HEUSINGER VON WALDEGG, EDMUND. 1817-1886. German engineer. See: Neue Deut. Biog. Heusinger valve gear.

Heusler alloys (Heusler, Fritz): Chemistry. See: Ballentyne; Hackh; Hughes; Thewlis; Webster's 3d.

HEUSLER, FRITZ. 1866-1947. German mining engineer and chemist. See: Neue Deut. Biog. Heusler alloys.

Hevelian halo (Hevelius, Johannes): Astronomy. See: Huschke; Van Nostrand Sci. Encyc.

HEVELIUS, JOHANNES. 1611-1687. German astronomer. See: Dict. Sci. Biog. Hevelian halo, Hevelius's parhelia.

Hevelius's parhelia (Hevelius, Johannes): Astronomy. See: Huschke.

HEVESY, GYORGY. 1885-1966. Hungarian chemist. See: Dict. Sci. Biog. Von Hevesy-Loegstrup test reaction.

Hewera-Bermejo test reaction (Derivation undetermined): Chemistry. See: Van Nostrand Chem. Dict.

HEWETT, DONNEL FOSTER. b. 1881. American geologist. See: World Who's Who Sci. Hewettite.

Hewettite (Hewett, Donnel Foster): Earth Sciences. See: Thrush; Webster's 3d.

HEWLETT, RICHARD TANNER. 1865-1940. English bacteriologist. See: Brit. Med. J., vol. 2 (1940), p. 400. Hewlett's stain.

Hewlett's stain (Hewlett, Richard Tanner): Medicine. See: Stedman.

Hexhlet sampler (Derivation undetermined): Engineering and Industry. See: Thrush.

HEY, DONALD HOLROYDE. 1904- . English chemist. See: Who's Who Brit. Sci., 1953. Gomberg-Bachmann-Hey reaction.

HEY, WILLIAM. 1736-1819. English surgeon. See: World Who's Who Sci. Hey's amputation (or operation), Hey's internal derangement, Hey's hernia, Hey's ligament.

HEYD, CHARLES GORDON. b. 1884. American surgeon. See: Amer. Men Sci., 9th ed. Heyd's syndrome.

Heyd's syndrome (Heyd, Charles Gordon): Medicine. See: Dorland; Jablonski.

HEYDWEILLER, ADOLF. 1856-1926. German physicist. See: Pogg., vols. 4, 5, 6. Heydweiller bridge.

Heydweiller bridge (Heydweiller, Adolf): Physics. See: Internat. Dict. Phys. Elec. Also known as: Carey-Foster bridge.

HEYLANDT, C. W. P. fl. 1929. German chemist. Cited in: Chem. Abstr., vol. 24, p. 5899. Claude-Heylandt liquefaction process?

HEYMANN, ERICH. 1901-1949. German-born American chemist. See: Pogg., vols. 6, 7a. Wolf-Heymann test.

HEYMANS, CORNEILLE JEAN FRANCOIS. 1892-1968. Belgian physiologist. See: World Who's Who Sci. Heymans' law (or law of inhibition).

Heymans' law (or law of inhibition) (Heymans, Corneille Jean Francois): Physiology. See: Chaplin; Drever; English; Wolman.

Heyn-Bauer reagent (Heyn, Emil and Bauer, Oswald): Chemistry. See: Van Nostrand Chem. Dict.

HEYN, EMIL (In full: FRIEDRICH EMIL). 1867-1922. German metallurgist. See: Pogg., vol. 6. Heyn-Bauer reagent, Heyn stresses, Heyn's reagent.

Heyn stresses (Heyn, Emil): Chemistry. See: Van Nostrand Sci. Encyc.

Heyn's reagent (Heyn, Emil): Chemistry. See: Thrush.

HEYNSIUS, ADRIAN. 1831-1885. Dutch physician. See: Biog. Lex. hervorr. Aerzte, 1880-1930. Heynsius' test.

Heynsius' test (Heynsius, Adrian): Medicine. See: Dorland; Stedman.

Hey's amputation (or operation) (Hey, William): Medicine. See: Dorland; Stedman.

Hey's hernia (Hey, William): Medicine. See: Dorland; Stedman.

Hey's internal derangement (Hey, William): Medicine. See: Stedman.

Hey's ligament (Hey, William): Anatomy. See: Dorland; Stedman.

HIBBERT, GEORGE. 1757-1837. English merchant and botanist. See: Dict. Nat. Biog. Hibbertia.

HIBBERT, HAROLD. b. 1877. English-born Canadian chemist. See: Pogg., vol. 6. Sudborough-Hibbert test reaction.

Hibbert Lectures (Hibbert, Robert): Religion. See: Canney; Latham.

HIBBERT, ROBERT. 1770-1849. English merchant and philanthropist. See: Dict. Nat. Biog. Hibbert Lectures.

Hibbert standard (Hibbert, Walter): Electronics. See: Hughes.

HIBBERT, WALTER. b. 1852. English engineer. Cited in: Mansell. Hibbert standard.

Hibbertia (Hibbert, George): Botany. See: Charnock; Taylor, N.; Webster's 3d.

Hibbs frame (Hibbs, Russell Aubra): Medicine. See: Dorland.

Hibbs' operation (Hibbs, Russell Aubra): Medicine. See: Dorland; Stedman.

HIBBS, RUSSELL AUBRA. 1869-1932. American surgeon. See: World Who's Who Sci. Hibbs frame, Hibbs' operation.

HIBON, P. fl. 1956. French? mineralogist. Cited in: Hintze, 2d suppl., p. 723. Hibonite.

Hibonite (Hibon, P.): Earth Sciences. See: Thrush.

HIBSCH, JOSEPH EMMANUEL. 1882-1940. Czech mineralogist. See: Pogg., vols. 3 to 6. Hibschite.

Hibschite (Hibsch, Joseph Emmanuel): Earth Sciences. See: Webster's 3d.

Hick reagent (Hicks, Edwin Francis): Chemistry. See: Van Nostrand Chem. Dict.

HICKMAN, KENNETH CLAUDE DEVERAUX. 1896- . American chemist. See: World Who's Who Sci. Hickman pump.

Hickman pump (Hickman, Kenneth Claude Deveraux): Chemistry. See: Hackh.

Hickoryism (Jackson, Andrew "Old Hickory"): History. See: Mathews, M. M.

HICKS, BRAXTON (In full: JOHN BRAXTON). 1823-1897. English gynecologist. See: Boase. Braxton Hicks' sign, Hicks' version.

HICKS, EDWIN FRANCIS. b. 1872. American chemist. See: Amer. Men Sci., 4th ed. Hick reagent.

HICKS, ELIAS. 1748-1830. American Quaker minister. See: Dict. Amer. Biog. Hicksite(s).

HICKS, ERIC PERRIN. fl. 1913-1964. English physician. See: Med. Direct., 1964. Hicks' syndrome.

Hicks formula (Hicks, William Mitchinson): Physics. See: Internat. Dict. Ap. Math.

Hicks' hydrometer (Derivation undetermined): Chemistry. See: Thrush.

Hicks' sign (Hicks, Braxton). See: Braxton Hicks sign.

Hicks' syndrome (Hicks, Eric Perrin): Medicine. See: Jablonski. Also known as: Dennys-Brown's syndrome, Thevenard's disease.

Hicks' version (Hicks, Braxton): Medicine. See: Stedman. Also known as: Braxton Hicks' version.

HICKS, WILLIAM MITCHINSON. 1850-1934. English physicist. See: Pogg., vols. 3 to 6. Hicks formula.

Hicksite(s) (Hicks, Elias): Religion. See: Canney; Jameson; Mathews, M. M.; Mathews, S.; Phyfe; Webster's 3d.

HIDDEN, WILLIAM EARL. 1832-1918. American mineralogist. See: Who Was Who Amer., 1897-1942. Hiddenite.

Hiddenite (Hidden, William Earl): Earth Sciences. See: Mathews, M. M.; Webster's 3d.

hidradenitis of Verneuil (Verneuil, Aristide Auguste Stanislas): Medicine. See: Dorland; Stedman.

Hielmite (Hjelm, Peter Jacob). See: Hjelmite.

HIERACAS (HIERAX). fl. 4th c. Egyptian ascetic. See: Dict. Christian Biog. Hieracites.

Hieracites (Hieracas): Religion. See: Canney; Webster's 3d.

HIGASHI, OTOTAKA. fl. 1954. Japanese physician. (Biography source unavailable.) Arakawa-Higashi syndrome, Chediak-Higashi syndrome.

HIGGINSON, ALFRED. d. ca. 1885. English surgeon. See: Liverpool Lit. Phil. Soc. Proc. vol. 39 (1885), pp. 40-41. Higginson's syringe.

Higginson's syringe (Higginson, Alfred): Medicine. See: Dorland.

HIGHLEY, JOHN. fl. ca. 1737. American colonist. (Biography source unavailable.) Highley's copper.

Highley's copper (Highley, John): Numismatics. See: Mathews, M. M.

HIGHMORE, NATHANIEL. 1613-1685. English anatomist. See: Dict. Sci. Biog. antrum of Highmore (or Highmore's antrum), Highmore's body (or corpus Highmori).

Highmore's antrum (Highmore, Nathaniel). See: antrum of Highmore.

Highmore's body (or corpus Highmori) (Highmore, Nathaniel): Medicine. See: Dorland; Henderson; Stedman.

HIGNETT, TRAVIS PORTER. 1907- . American chemical engineer. See: Amer. Men Sci., 9th ed. Copson, Walthall, and Hignett process.

Hilaria (Saint-Hilaire, Auguste de): Botany. See: Webster's 3d.

HILARY OF POITIERS, SAINT. ca. 315-367. French bishop. See: Encyc. Brit., 1973. Hilary sitting, Hilary term, Hilarymas.

Hilary sitting (Hilary of Poitiers, Saint): Law. See: Webster's 3d.

Hilary term (Hilary of Poitiers, Saint): Law. See: Brewer; Hargrave; Weekley; Webster's 3d.

Hilarymas (Hilary of Poitiers, Saint): Generic Word. See: Webster's 3d.

Hilbert basis theorem (Hilbert, David): Mathematics. See: New Encyc. Brit., 1974, Microp.

HILBERT, DAVID. 1862-1943. German mathematician. See: Dict. Sci. Biog. Hilbert basis theorem, Hilbert parallelotype, Hilbert program, Hilbert-Schmidt theory of integral equations with symmetric kernels, Hilbert space, Hilbert symbols, Hilbert transform; Hilbert's fifth problem.

Hilbert parallelotype (Hilbert, David): Mathematics. See: James.

Hilbert program (Hilbert, David): Philosophy. See: Edwards.

Hilbert-Schmidt theory of integral equations with symmetric kernels (Hilbert, David and Schmidt, Erhard): Mathematics. See: Internat. Dict. Ap. Math.; James. Also known as: Schmidt-Hilbert method.

Hilbert space (Hilbert, David): Mathematics. See: Internat. Dict. Ap. Math.; James; Thewlis; Van Nostrand Sci. Encyc.

Hilbert symbols (Hilbert, David): Philosophy. See: Edwards.

Hilbert transform (Hilbert, David): Mathematics. See: Ballentyne; Internat. Dict. Ap. Math.

Hilbert transformer (Derivation undetermined): Electronics. See: Hughes.

Hilbert's fifth problem (Hilbert, David): Mathematics. See: New Encyc. Brit., 1974, Microp.

Hildebrand. See: Gregory VII.

Hildebrand electrode (Hildebrand, Joel Henry): Chemistry. See: Hackh; Internat. Dict. Phys. Elec.

HILDEBRAND, JOEL HENRY. b. 1881. American chemist. See: World Who's Who Sci. Hildebrand electrode, Hildebrand rule, Hildebrand's law.

Hildebrand rule (Hildebrand, Joel Henry): Chemistry. See: Hackh; Thewlis; Van Nostrand Sci. Encyc.

Hildebrandine (Gregory VII): Religion. See: Webster's 3d.

Hildebrand's law (Hildebrand, Joel Henry): Sociology. See: Martin.

HILDEBRANDT, FRITZ. b. 1887. German pharmacologist. See: Biog. Lex. hervorr. Aerzte, 1880-1930. Hildebrandt's test.

Hildebrandt's test (Hildebrandt, Fritz): Medicine. See: Dorland.

HILDENBRAND, JOHANN VALENTIN EDLER VON. 1763-1818. Austrian physician. See: Biog. Lex. hervorr. Aerzte, 1880-1930. Hildenbrand's disease.

Hildenbrand's disease (Hildenbrand, Johann Valentin Edler von): Medicine. See: Dorland; Jablonski.

Hiley's formula (Derivation undetermined): Engineering and Industry. See: Thrush.

HILFERTY, M. M. fl. 1931. American scientist. (Biography source unavailable.) Wilson-Hilferty transformation.

HILGARD, EUGENE WOLDEMAR. 1833-1916. German-born American geologist. See: World Who's Who Sci. Hilgardite.

Hilgardite (Hilgard, Eugene Woldemar): Earth Sciences. See: Thrush; Webster's 3d.

HILGER, ALBERT. 1839-1905. German chemist. See: Pogg., vols. 3, 4, 5. Hilger-Rothenfusser reagent, Hilger test reaction for malic acid, Hilger test for selenite and tellurite.

HILGER, JEROME ANDREW. 1912- . American otorhinolaryngologist. See: Direct. Med. Specialists, 1975-1976. Hilger's syndrome.

Hilger-Rothenfusser reagent (Hilger, Albert and Rothenfusser, S.): Chemistry. See: Van Nostrand Chem. Dict.

Hilger test reaction for malic acid (Hilger, Albert): Chemistry. See: Van Nostrand Chem. Dict.

Hilger test reaction for selenite and tellurite (Hilger, Albert): Chemistry. See: Van Nostrand Chem. Dict.

Hilger's syndrome (Hilger, Jerome Andrew): Medicine. See: Jablonski.

HILL, ARCHIBALD VIVIAN. b. 1886. English physiologist. See: World Who's Who Sci. Hill's equation.

Hill cloud lens (Hill, R.): Photography. See: Focal Encyc. Photog.

HILL, DAVID OCTAVIUS. 1802-1870. Scottish painter and photographer. See: Dict. Nat. Biog. David Octavius Hill Medal.

Hill('s) determinant (Hill, George William): Mathematics. See: Ballentyne; Internat. Dict. Phys. Elec.

HILL, FANNY. Fictional character from John Cleland's novel "Fanny Hill" (1749). (Biography source unavailable.) Fanny.

Hill-Flack sign (Hill, Sir Leonard Erskine and Flack, Martin William). See: Hill's sign.

HILL, GEORGE WILLIAM. 1838-1914. American mathematical astronomer. See: Dict. Sci. Biog. Hill('s) determinant.

HILL, JAMES JEROME. 1838-1916. American railroad promoter. See: Dict. Amer. Biog. Jim Hill mustard.

HILL, SIR LEONARD ERSKINE. b. 1866. English physiologist. Cited in: Kelly. Hill's sign.

HILL, R. fl. 20th c. Photographer. (Biography source unavailable.) Hill cloud lens.

Hill reaction (Hill, Robin): Chemistry. See: Stedman; Webster's 3d.

HILL, ROBIN. fl. 1925. English chemist. Cited in: Chem. Abstr., Decenn. Index, 1917-1926. Hill reaction.

Hillebrand test for vanadium in rocks (Hillebrand, William Francis): Chemistry. See: Van Nostrand Chem. Dict.

HILLEBRAND, WILLIAM FRANCIS. 1853-1925. American chemist. See: World Who's Who Sci. Hillebrand test for vanadium in rocks, Hillebrandite.

Hillebrandite (Hillebrand, William Francis): Chemistry. See: Thrush; Webster's 3d.

HILLEL. fl. 30 B.C.-9 A.D. Jewish teacher. See: Encyc. Brit., 1973. Hillel Foundation, Hillelite.

Hillel Foundation (Hillel): Education. See: Good.

Hillelite (Hillel): Religion. See: Webster's 3d.

HILLIS, DAVID S. fl. 20th c. American? physician. (Biography source unavailable.) Hillis maneuver.

Hillis maneuver (Hillis, David S.): Medicine. See: Stedman.

Hill's equation (Hill, Archibald Vivian): Physiology. See: Stedman.

Hill's sign (Hill, Sir Leonard Erskine): Medicine. See: Stedman. Also known as: Hill-Flack sign.

HILPERT, SIEGFRIED (In full: RICHARD SIEGFRIED). 1883-1951. German chemist. See: Pogg., vols. 5, 6, 7a. Hilpert-Wolf reagent.

Hilpert-Wolf reagent (Hilpert, Siegfried and Wolf, Ludwig): Chemistry. See: Van Nostrand Chem. Dict.

HILT, CARL. fl. 1885. English mining engineer. Cited in: Royal Soc. Cat. Sci. Pap., 1884-1900. Hilt's law?

Hiltner-Hall effect (Hiltner, William Albert and Hall, John Scoville?): Astronomy. See: Ballentyne; Thewlis.

HILTNER, WILLIAM ALBERT. 1914- . American astronomer. See: World Who's Who Sci. Hiltner-Hall effect.

HILTON, JOHN. 1804-1878. English surgeon. See: World Who's Who Sci. Hilton's law, Hilton's method, Hilton's muscle, Hilton's sac.

Hilton's law (Hilton, John): Physiology. See: Dorland; Stedman.

Hilton's method (Hilton, John): Medicine. See: Stedman.

Hilton's muscle (Hilton, John): Medicine. See: Dorland.

Hilton's sac (Hilton, John): Anatomy. See: Dorland; Stedman.

Hilt's law (Hilt, Carl?): Engineering and Industry. See: Hackh; Thrush.

HIMELFARB, ALBERT J. 1909- . American physician. See: Direct. Med. Specialists, 1974/75. Weinberg-Himelfarb syndrome.

HIMYAR. Legendary ancient King in Yemen. See: New Encyc. Brit., 1974, Microp. Himyarite.

Himyarite (Himyar): History. See: Webster's 3d.

Hinckley system (Derivation undetermined): Agriculture. See: Winburne.

Hind effect (Hind, S. R.): Engineering and Industry. See: Thrush.

HIND, S. R. fl. 1930. English ceramics chemist. Cited in: Chem. Abstr., Decenn. Index, 1927-1936. Hind effect.

Hindenburg (airship) (Hindenburg, Paul von): Engineering and Industry. See: Encyc. Brit., 1973 under "Airship," vol. 1, p. 472a.

Hindenburg line (Hindenburg, Paul von): History. See: Jameson; Quick.

HINDENBURG, PAUL VON. 1847-1934. German field marshal. See: Encyc. Brit., 1973. Hindenburg (airship), Hindenburg line, Hindenburg plan (or program).

Hindenburg plan (or program) (Hindenburg, Paul von): History. See: Morris and Irwin; New Encyc. Brit., 1974, Microp.

HINDENLANG, KARL. 1854-1884. German physician. (Biography source unavailable.) Hindenlang's test.

Hindenlang's test (Hindenlang, Karl): Medicine. See: Dorland; Stedman.

HINDERER, WALTER. fl. 1931. German chemist. Cited in: Chem. Abstr., vol. 25, p. 4813. Schmidt-Hinderer test for metals.

HINDLEY, HENRY. 1710-1771. English clockmaker. (Biography source unavailable.) Hindley('s) worm gear (or screw).

Hindley('s) worm gear (or screw) (Hindley, Henry): Engineering and Industry. See: Auger; Webster's 3d.

HINDS, ASHER CROSBY. 1863-1919. American parliamentarian. See: Dict. Amer. Biog. Hinds' Precedents.

Hinds' Precedents (Hinds, Asher Crosby): Politics. See: Smith.

Hinds walnut (Derivation undetermined): Botany. See: Winburne.

HINES, MARION. b. 1889. American neurologist. See: World Who's Who Sci. strip area of Hines.

HINKEMANN. Character in Ernst Toller's play of the same name (1923). (Biography source unavailable.) Hinkemann.

Hinkemann (Hinkemann, the character): Generic Word (castrated male). See: Hinsie.

Hinkle's pill (Derivation undetermined): Medicine. See: Stedman.

HINMAN, FRANK. b. 1880. American urologist. See: Amer. Men Sci., 9th ed. Hinman's reflux.

Hinman tube (Derivation undetermined): Chemistry. See: Hackh.

HINMAN, WILBUR STANLEY. 1906- . American electrical engineer. See: Amer. Men Sci., 9th ed. Diamond-Hinman radiosonde.

Hinman's reflux (Hinman, Frank): Medicine. See: Jablonski.

Hinoki falsecypress (Derivation undetermined): Botany. See: Winburne.

Hinsberg indole synthesis (Hinsberg, Oscar Heinrich Daniel): Chemistry. See: Van Nostrand Chem. Dict.

HINSBERG, OSCAR HEINRICH DANIEL. b. 1857. German chemist. See: Pogg., vol. 4. Autenrieth-Hinsberg test reaction, Hinsberg indole synthesis, Hinsberg separation (or test reaction for primary and secondary amines), Hinsberg test reaction for o-diamines.

Hinsberg separation (or test reaction for primary and secondary amines) (Hinsberg, Oscar Heinrich Daniel): Chemistry. See: Ballentyne; Van Nostrand Chem. Dict.

Hinsberg test reaction for o-diamines (Hinsberg, Oscar Heinrich Daniel): Chemistry. See: Van Nostrand Chem. Dict.

HINSIE, LELAND EARL. b. 1893. American psychiatrist. See: Amer. Men Sci., 10th ed. Strongin-Hinsie-Peck test.

HINTIKKA, JAAKKO (In full: KAARLO JAAKKO JUHANI). 1929- . Finnish philosopher. See: Dict. Scandinavian Biog. Hintikka's paradox.

Hintikka's paradox (Hintikka, Jaakko): Philosophy. See: Edwards.

Hinton test (Hinton, William Augustus): Medicine. See: Dorland; Stedman; Webster's 3d.

HINTON, WILLIAM AUGUSTUS. 1883-1959. American physician. See: J. A. M. A., vol. 171 (1959), p. 1241. Hinton test.

HINTZE, CARL A. F. 1851-1916. German mineralogist. See: Neue Deut. Biog. Hintzeite (or Heintzite).

Hintzeite (or Heintzite) (Hintze, Carl A. F.): Earth Sciences. See: Thrush; Webster's 3d.

HIORTDAHL, THORSTEIN HALLAGER. 1839-1926. Norwegian chemist. See: Norsk Biog. Lek. Hiortdahlite.

Hiortdahlite (Hiortdahl, Thorstein Hallager): Earth Sciences. See: Webster's 3d.

Hipp chronoscope (Hipp, Matthaus): Horology. See: Chaplin; Drever; English; Wolman. Also known as: Wheatstone-Hipp chronoscope.

HIPP, MATTHAUS. 1813-1893. German scientist. See: Neue Deut. Biog. Hipp chronoscope.

Hippel-Czermak syndrome (Hippel, Eugen von and Czermak). See: Hippel-Lindau syndrome (or disease).

HIPPEL, EUGEN VON. 1867-1939. German ophthalmologist. See: Biog. Lex. hervorr. Aerzte, 1880-1930. Hippel-Lindau syndrome (or disease).

Hippel-Lindau syndrome (or disease) (Hippel, Eugen von and Lindau, Arvid): Medicine. See: Dorland; Jablonski; Stedman. Also known as: Hippel-Czermak syndrome, Hippel's disease, Lindau's disease (or tumor), Von Hippel-Lindau disease.

Hippel's disease (Hippel, Eugen von). See: Hippel-Landau syndrome (or disease).

Hippocras (or Ipocras) (Hippocrates of Cos): Food and Drink. See: Charnock; Partridge; Wagner (Names); Webster's 3d.

Hippocratea (Hippocrates of Cos): Botany. See: Charnock; Webster's 3d.

Hippocrates cap (or bandage) (Hippocrates of Cos): Medicine. See: Stedman.

Hippocrates' cord (Hippocrates of Cos): Anatomy. See: Stedman. Also known as: Achilles tendon.

HIPPOCRATES OF COS. ca. 460 B.C.-ca. 370 B.C. Greek physician. See: Dict. Sci. Biog. aphorisms of Hippocrates, Hippocras (or Ipocras), Hippocratea, Hippocrates cap (or bandage), Hippocrates' cord, Hippocrates' sleeve, Hippocratic, Hippocratic facies (or face), Hippocratic finger(s), Hippocratic nails, Hippocratic oath, Hippocratic (or Hippocratean) school, Hippocratic succussion (and succussion sound), Hippocratic treatises (or collections), Hippocratism.

Hippocrates' sleeve (Hippocrates of Cos): Medicine. See: Brewer; Partridge; Phyfe.

Hippocratic (Hippocrates of Cos): Medicine. See: Webster's 3d.

Hippocratic facies (or face) (Hippocrates of Cos): Medicine. See: Phyfe; Stedman; Webster's 3d.

Hippocratic finger(s) (Hippocrates of Cos): Medicine. See: Jablonski; Stedman; Webster's 3d.

Hippocratic nails (Hippocrates of Cos): Medicine. See: Stedman.

Hippocratic oath (Hippocrates of Cos): Medicine. See: Brewer; Harvey; Hendrickson; Phyfe; Stedman; Webster's 3d.

Hippocratic (or Hippocratean) school (Hippocrates of Cos): Medicine. See: Barnhart (Eng. Lit.) under "Hippocrates"; Brewer; Stedman; Webster's 3d.

Hippocratic succussion (and succussion sound) (Hippocrates of Cos): Medicine. See: Stedman.

Hippocratic treatises (or collections) (Hippocrates of Cos): Medicine. See: Barnhart (Eng. Lit.) under "Hippocrates"; Stedman.

Hippocratism (Hippocrates of Cos): Medicine. See: Charnock; Stedman; Webster's 3d.

HIPPOLYTE. Amazon in Greek mythology. See: Jobes. Hippolyte.

Hippolyte (Hippolyte, the Amazon): Zoology. See: Webster's 3d.

Hipponactean (Hipponax): Literature. See: Webster's 3d.

HIPPONAX. fl. 6th c. B.C. Greek poet. See: Encyc. Brit., 1911. Hipponactean.

HIRSCH, J. S. No dates. Physician. (Biography source unavailable.) Hirsch's syndrome.

HIRSCH, MAX. fl. 1922. German chemist. Cited in: Chem. Abstr., vol. 6, p. 2279. Hirsch test reaction for osmium.

HIRSCH, PAUL. b. 1885. German chemist. See: Pogg., vol. 6. Tillmans-Hirsch test reaction for ascorbic acid.

Hirsch test reaction for osmium (Hirsch, Max): Chemistry. See: Van Nostrand Chem. Dict.

Hirschback method (Derivation undetermined): Engineering and Industry. See: Thrush.

HIRSCHBERG, JULIUS. 1843-1925. German ophthalmologist. See: World Who's Who Sci. Hirschberg's method.

HIRSCHBERG, LEONARD KEENE. b. 1877. American physician. Cited in: Kelly. Hirschberg test reaction for sugar, Hirschberg's reflex.

Hirschberg test reaction for sugar (Hirschberg, Leonard Keene): Chemistry. See: Van Nostrand Chem. Dict.

Hirschberg's method (Hirschberg, Julius): Medicine. See: Dorland; Stedman.

Hirschberg's reflex (Hirschberg, Leonard Keene): Medicine. See: Dorland; Stedman.

HIRSCHFELD, FELIX. b. 1863. German physician. See: Biog. Lex. hervorr. Aerzte, 1880-1930. Hirschfeld's disease.

HIRSCHFELD, HANS. 1873-1929. German physician. See: Sang, Paris, vol. 3 (1929), p. 51. Hirschfeld reagent for pus.

HIRSCHFELD, ISADOR. b. 1881. American dentist. Cited in: Index-Cat. Libr. Surg.-Gen. Off., 4th ser., vol. 7, 1942. Hirschfeld's canals.

Hirschfeld reagent for pus (Hirschfeld, Hans): Medicine. See: Van Nostrand Chem. Dict.

HIRSCHFELDER, JOSEPH OAKLAND. 1854-1920. American pathologist. See: World Who's Who Sci. Hirschfelder's tuberculin.

Hirschfelder's tuberculin (Hirschfelder, Joseph Oakland): Medicine. See: Dorland; Stedman.

Hirschfeld's canals (Hirschfeld, Isador): Dentistry. See: Dorland; Stedman.

Hirschfeld's disease (Hirschfeld, Felix): Medicine. See: Dorland; Jablonski.

Hirsch's syndrome (Hirsch, J. S.): Medicine. See: Jablonski.

Hirschsohn cottonseed oil reagent (Hirschsohn, Eduard): Chemistry. See: Van Nostrand Chem. Dict.

HIRSCHSOHN, EDUARD. fl. 1884. Russian chemist. Cited in: Royal Soc. Cat. Sci. Pap., 1884-1900. Hirschsohn cottonseed oil reagent, Hirschsohn myrrh reagent, Hirschsohn reagent for volatile oils, Hirschsohn test reaction for chloresterol.

Hirschsohn myrrh reagent (Hirschsohn, Eduard): Chemistry. See: Van Nostrand Chem. Dict.

Hirschsohn reagent for volatile oils (Hirschsohn, Eduard): Chemistry. See: Van Nostrand Chem. Dict.

Hirschsohn test reaction for chloresterol (Hirschsohn, Eduard): Chemistry. See: Van Nostrand Chem. Dict.

HIRSCHSPRUNG, HARALD. 1830-1916. Danish pediatrician. See: Biog. Lex. hervorr. Aerzte. Hirschsprung's disease.

Hirschsprung's disease (Hirschsprung, Harald): Medicine. See: Dorland; Jablonski; Stedman. Also known as: Mya's disease.

His' bundle (band or bundle of His) (His, Wilhelm, Jr.): Anatomy. See: Donath; Dorland; Gray; Henderson; Pennak; Stedman. Also known as: Gaskell's bridge, Keith's bundle, Kent-His bundle, Kent's bundle.

His' canal (or duct) (His, Wilhelm, Sr.): Anatomy. See: Donath; Dorland; Stedman.

His' copula (His, Wilhelm, Sr.): Anatomy. See: Stedman.

His' isthmus (His, Wilhelm, Sr.): Anatomy. See: Stedman.

His' rule (His, Wilhelm, Sr.): Medicine. See: Dorland; Stedman.

His' spaces (His, Wilhelm, Sr.): Anatomy. See: Donath; Dorland; Stedman.

His' spindle (His, Wilhelm, Jr.): Medicine. See: Dorland; Stedman.

His-Tawara system (His, Wilhelm, Jr. and Tawara, K. Sunao): Medicine. See: Stedman.

HIS, WILHELM, JR. 1863-1934. Swiss-born anatomist in Germany. See: Dict. Sci. Biog. His' bundle (band or bundle of His), His' spindle, His-Tawara system, Werner-His disease.

HIS, WILHELM, SR. 1831-1904. Swiss-born anatomist in Germany. See: Dict. Sci. Biog. His' canal (or duct), His' copula, His' isthmus, His' rule, His' spaces, His's cells.

HISINGER, WILHELM. 1766-1852. Swedish geologist. See: Dict. Sci. Biog. Hisingerite.

Hisingerite (Hisinger, Wilhelm): Earth Sciences. See: Thrush; Webster's 3d.

HISLOP, STEPHEN. 1817-1863. English missionary to India and amateur geologist. See: Boase. Hislopite.

Hislopite (Hislop, Stephen): Earth Sciences. See: Webster's 3d.

HISS, ALGER. 1904- . American public official. See: New Encyc. Brit., 1974, Microp. Hiss trials.

His's cells (His, Wilhelm, Sr.): Anatomy. See: Gray.

HISS, PHILIP HANSON. 1868-1913. American bacteriologist. See: Nat. Cycl. Amer. Biog. vol. 16, p. 235. Hiss' stain.

Hiss' stain (Hiss, Philip Hanson): Medicine. See: Stedman.

Hiss trials (Hiss, Alger): Politics. See: Smith.

HITCHCOCK, ALFRED JOSEPH. 1899- . English film director. See: New Encyc. Brit., 1974, Microp. Hitchcock ending.

Hitchcock chair (or Hitchcock) (Hitchcock, Lambert H.): Applied Arts. See: Hendrickson; Mathews, M. M.; Webster's 3d.

Hitchcock ending (Hitchcock, Alfred Joseph): Mass Media. See: Hendrickson.

HITCHCOCK, FRANK LAUREN. 1875-1957. American mathematician. See: Pogg., vols. 6, 7b. Hitchcock method, Hitchcock transportation problem?

HITCHCOCK, LAMBERT H. 1795-1852. American furniture manufacturer. See: Boger. Hitchcock chair (or Hitchcock).

Hitchcock method (Hitchcock, Frank Lauren): Mathematics. See: Internat. Dict. Ap. Math.

Hitchcock transportation problem (Hitchcock, Frank Lauren?): Mathematics. See: Internat. Dict. Ap. Math.

Hitler (Hitler, Adolf): Generic Word (tyrant). See: Hendrickson; Partridge.

HITLER, ADOLF. 1889-1945. German dictator. See: New Encyc. Brit., 1974. Hitler, Hitler Youth Movement, Hitlerism (Hitlerian and Hitlerite).

Hitler Youth Movement (Hitler, Adolf): History. See: New Encyc. Brit., 1974, Microp.

Hitlerism (Hitlerian and Hitlerite) (Hitler, Adolf): History. See: Brewer; Webster's 3d.

Hittorf dark space (Hittorf, Johann Wilhelm): Physics. See: Internat. Dict. Phys. Elec.; Thewlis.

HITTORF, JOHANN WILHELM. 1824-1914. German physicist. See: Dict. Sci. Biog. Hittorf dark space, Hittorf method (for transport number), Hittorf number, Hittorf principle, Hittorf tube.

Hittorf method (for transport number) (Hittorf, Johann Wilhelm): Physics. See: Internat. Dict. Phys. Elec.

Hittorf number (Hittorf, Johann Wilhelm): Physics. See: Hackh; Thrush; Van Nostrand Chem. Dict.

Hittorf principle (Hittorf, Johann Wilhelm): Physics. See: Internat. Dict. Phys. Elec.; Van Nostrand Sci. Encyc.

Hittorf tube (Hittorf, Johann Wilhelm): Physics. See: Hackh; Hughes; Internat. Dict. Phys. Elec.

HITZIG, EDUARD (In full: JULIUS EDUARD). 1838-1907. German neuro-physiologist. See: Dict. Sci. Biog. Hitzig's girdle, Hitzig's syndrome?

Hitzig's girdle (Hitzig, Eduard): Medicine. See: Dorland; Drever; Stedman; Wolman.

Hitzig's syndrome (Hitzig, Eduard?): Medicine. See: Jablonski.

HJARRE, ALBERT. 1897-1958. Swedish veterinarian. See: Vem Ar Det?, 1955. Hjarre's disease.

Hjarre-Wramby disease (Hjarre, Albert and Wramby, G. O.). See: Hjarre's disease.

Hjarre's disease (Hjarre, Albert): Medicine. See: Jablonski; Stedman. Also known as: Hjarre-Wramby disease.

HJELM, PETER JACOB. 1746-1813. Swedish chemist. See: New Encyc. Brit., 1974, Microp. Hjelmite (or Hielmite).

Hjelmite (or Hielmite) (Hjelm, Peter Jacob): Earth Sciences. See: Webster's 3d.

HJELMSLEV, LOUIS. 1899- . Danish linguist. See: Danmarks hist. Bla bog. Hjelmslevian.

Hjelmslevian (Hjelmslev, Louis): Linguistics. See: Webster's 3d.

HLAVACSEK, KORNEL. fl. 1926. Czechoslovakian engineer. Cited in: Hintze, vol. I, part 3, half 2, p. 4402. Kornelite.

HOADLEY, BENJAMIN, BISHOP OF BANGOR. 1676-1761. Welsh churchman. See: Dict. Nat. Biog. Bangorian controversy.

Hoare-Laval plan (Hoare, Sir Samuel John Gurney, 2d Baronet Hoare and Viscount Templewood, and Laval, Pierre): History. See: Steinberg.

HOARE, SIR SAMUEL JOHN GURNEY, 2D BARONET HOARE AND VISCOUNT TEMPLEWOOD. 1880-1959. English statesman. See: Dict. Nat. Biog., 7th suppl. Hoare-Laval plan.

HOBART, FLOYD B. 1897- . American chemical engineer. See: Amer. Men Sci., 9th ed. Braley-Hobart test.

HOBBES, THOMAS. 1588-1679. English philosopher. See: Dict. Nat. Biog. Hobbesian, Hobbes's voyage, Hobbism.

Hobbesian (Hobbes, Thomas): Philosophy. See: Webster's 3d.

Hobbes's voyage (Hobbes, Thomas): Generic Word (leap in the dark). See: Phyfe.

Hobbism (Hobbes, Thomas): Philosophy. See: Brewer; Webster's 3d.

Hobbs Act (or Law) (Hobbs, Samuel Francis): Politics. See: Smith; Zadrozny.

HOBBS, SAMUEL FRANCIS. 1887-1952. American legislator. See: Biog. Direct. Amer. Congress. Hobbs Act (or Law).

HOBBS, WILLIAM HERBERT. 1864-1953. American geologist. See: World Who's Who Sci. Hobbs's theory.

Hobbs's theory (Hobbs, William Herbert): Earth Sciences. See: Huschke.

HOBHOUSE, JOHN CAM, BARON BROUGHTON DE GYFFORD. 1786-1869. English statesman. See: Dict. Nat. Biog. Hobhouse's Acts.

HOBHOUSE, LEONARD TRELAWNEY. 1864-1929. English sociologist and philosopher. See: Internat. Encyc. Soc. Sci. Hobhouse's stages of political organization.

Hobhouse's Acts (Hobhouse, John Cam, Baron Broughton de Gyfford): History. See: Montgomery.

Hobhouse's stages of political organization (Hobhouse, Leonard Trelawney): Sociology. See: Zadrozny.

HOBOKEN, NICOLAAS. 1632-1678. Dutch anatomist and physician. See: Biog. Lex. hervorr. Aerzte. Hoboken's valves.

Hoboken's valves (Hoboken, Nicolaas): Medicine. See: Dorland; Stedman.

HOBSON, RICHMOND PEARSON. 1870-1937. American soldier. See: Who Was Who Amer., 1897-1942. Hobsonize (or Hobsonizing).

HOBSON, THOMAS. ca. 1544-1631. English livery stable owner. See: Dict. Nat. Biog. Hobson's choice.

Hobsonize (or Hobsonizing) (Hobson, Richmond Pearson): Generic Word (to kiss). See: Hendrickson; Mathews, M. M.

Hobson's choice (Hobson, Thomas): Generic Word (no choice at all). See: Brewer; Funk; Hendrickson; Partridge; Phyfe; Weekley; Webster's 3d.

Hoch-Campbell ethylenimine synthesis (Hoch, J. and Campbell, Kenneth Nielsen): Chemistry. See: Van Nostrand Chem. Dict.

HOCH, J. fl. 1934. French chemist. Cited in: Krauch and Kunz. Hoch-Campbell ethylenimine synthesis.

HOCHE, ALFRED ERICH. 1865-1945. German psychiatrist. See: World Who's Who Sci. Hoche's bandelette, Hoche's tract.

ochenegg, Julius von. See: Von Hochenegg, Julius.

ochenegg's operation (Von Hochenegg, Julius): Medicine. See: Dorland.

ochenegg's symptom (Von Hochenegg, Julius): Medicine. See: Dorland.

ochenegg's ulcer (Von Hochenegg, Julius): Medicine. See: Jablonski.

oche's bandelette (Hoche, Alfred Erich): Anatomy. See: Dorland.

oche's tract (Hoche, Alfred Erich): Anatomy. See: Dorland; Stedman. Also known as: Gombault's triangle.

OCHSINGER, KARL. b. 1860. Austrian pediatrician. See: Biog. Lex. ervorr. Aerzte, 1880-1930. Hochsinger's phenomenon.

ochsinger's phenomenon (Hochsinger, Karl): Medicine. See: Dorland; tedman.

ock engine (Hock, Julius): Engineering and Industry. See: Auger.

OCK, JULIUS. fl. 19th c. Austrian engineer. Cited in: Royal Soc. Cat. ci. Pap., 1884-1900. Hock engine.

ocus-Pocus (Ochus-Bochus?): Generic Word (to cheat). See: Charnock.

ODARA, MENAHEM. d. 1926. Turkish physician. Cited in: Royal Soc. at. Sci. Pap., 1884-1900. Hodara's disease.

lodara's disease (Hodara, Menahem): Medicine. See: Dorland; Jablonski.

ODGE, HAROLD CARPENTER. 1904- . American pharmacologist. See: mer. Men Sci., 10th ed. Capdepont-Hodge syndrome.

ODGE, HUGH LENOX. 1796-1873. American gynecologist. See: Dict. mer. Biog. Hodge's forceps, Hodge's pessary.

ODGEN, JOHN THOMPSON. 1826-1882. American surgeon. See: Dict. mer. Biog. Hodgen's splint.

odgen's splint (Hodgen, John Thompson): Medicine. See: Dorland; Stedman.

odges bivariate sign test (Hodges, Joseph Lawson, Jr.): Statistics. See: endall.

lodge's forceps (Hodge, Hugh Lenox): Medicine. See: Dorland; Stedman.

ODGES, JOSEPH LAWSON, JR. 1922- . American statistician. See: mer. Men Sci., 10th ed. Hodges bivariate sign test.

odge's pessary (Hodge, Hugh Lenox): Medicine. See: Dorland; Stedman.

odgkin-Key murmur (Hodgkin, Thomas? and Key, Charles Aston): Medicine. ee: Stedman.

odgkin-Paltauf-Sternberg disease (Hodgkin, Thomas; Paltauf, Richard; and ternberg, Carl von). See: Hodgkin's disease (granuloma or syndrome).

ODGKIN, THOMAS. 1798-1866. English physician. See: Dict. Nat. iog. Hodgkin-Key murmur, Hodgkin's disease (granuloma or syndrome), odgkin's paragranuloma.

odgkin's disease (granuloma or syndrome) (Hodgkin, Thomas): Medicine. See: orland; Stedman; Van Nostrand Sci. Encyc.; Webster's 3d. Also nown as: Bonfils' disease, Hodgkin-Paltauf-Sternberg disease, Pel-Ebstein isease (or symptom), Sternberg's disease.

odgkin's paragranuloma (Hodgkin, Thomas): Medicine. See: Dorland; tedman.

ODGKINSON, H. H. fl. ca. 1914. American mineralogist. Cited in: ailey. Hodgkinsonite.

odgkinsonite (Hodgkinson, H. H.): Earth Sciences. See: Thrush; Webster's d.

ODGSON, JOHN LAWRENCE. fl. 1929. English engineer. Cited in: Mansell. Hodgson's micromanometer.

ODGSON, JOSEPH. 1788-1869. English physician. See: World Who's ho Sci. Hodgson's disease.

odgson's disease (Hodgson, Joseph): Medicine. See: Dorland; Jablonski; tedman.

odgson's micromanometer (Hodgson, John Lawrence): Engineering and Industry. ee: Thrush.

oe press(es) (Hoe, Robert and Hoe, Richard M.): Printing. See: Lockwood.

HOE, RICHARD M. 1812-1886. American inventor. See: Dict. Amer. Biog. Hoe press(es), Hoe (rotary printing press).

HOE, ROBERT. 1784-1883. English-born American printer. See: Dict. Amer. Biog. Hoe press(es).

Hoe (rotary printing printing press) (Hoe, Richard M.): Printing. See: Jameson; Mathews, M. M.

Hoechst's peptone (Derivation undetermined): Medicine. See: Stedman.

HOECHTLEN, FRIEDRICH. b. 1878. German chemist. Cited in: Mansell. Holmann-Hoechtlen reagent.

Hoeffding 'C1' statistic (Hoeffding, Wassily): Statistics. See: Kendall.

HOEFFDING, WASSILY. 1914- . Russian-born American mathematician. See: Amer. Men Sci., 10th ed. Hoeffding 'C1' statistic.

HOEGBOEM, ARVID GUSTAF. b. 1857. Swedish scientist. See: Svenskt Biog. Handlex. Hoegbomite.

Hoegbomite (Hoegboem, Arvid Gustaf): Earth Sciences. See: Thrush; Webster's 3d.

HOEGYES, ENDRE. 1847-1906. Hungarian physician. See: Biog. Lex. hervorr. Aerzte, 1880-1930. Hoegyes' vaccine.

Hoegyes' vaccine (Hoegyes, Endre): Medicine. See: Dorland; Stedman.

HOEHNE, OTTOMAR. 1871-1932. German gynecologist. See: Biog. Lex. hervorr. Aerzte, 1880-1930. Hoehne's sign.

HOEHNEL, FRANZ XAVER RUDOLF RITTER VON. 1852-1920. German botanist. See: Ber. Deut. Bot. Ges., vol. 38 (1920), Nekr., pp. 119-126. Hoehnel reagent for silk, Hoehnel reagents for wood.

Hoehnel reagent for silk (Hoehnel, Franz Xaver Rudolf Ritter von): Chemistry. See: Van Nostrand Chem. Dict.

Hoehnel reagents for wood (Hoehnel, Franz Xaver Rudolf Ritter von): Chemistry. See: Van Nostrand Chem. Dict.

Hoehne's sign (Hoehne, Ottomar): Medicine. See: Dorland.

Hoelder('s) condition (Hoelder, Otto Ludwig): Mathematics. See: Ballentyne; Internat. Dict. Ap. Math.; James.

HOELDER, HERMANN FRIEDRICH. 1819-1906. German physician. See: Biog. Lex. hervorr. Aerzte. Virchow-Holder angle?

Hoelder('s) inequality (Hoelder, Otto Ludwig): Mathematics. See: Ballentyne; Internat. Dict. Ap. Math.; James.

HOELDER, OTTO LUDWIG. 1859-1937. German mathematician. See: Dict. Sci. Biog. Hoelder('s) condition, Hoelder('s) inequality, Hoelder's definition of the sum of a divergent series, Jordan-Hoelder theorem.

Hoelder's definition of the sum of a divergent series (Hoelder, Otto Ludwig): Mathematics. See: James.

Hoene-Wronski, Jozef Maria. See: Wronski, Jozef Maria.

HOENEL, F. fl. 1938. German chemist. Cited in: Chem. Abstr., vol. 32, p. 877. Krumholz-Hoenel reagents for mercury, copper, iron, and cadmium.

HOEPFNER, CARL. 1857-1900. German chemical engineer. See: Neue Deut. Biog. Hoepfner (or Hopfner) process.

Hoepfner (or Hopfner) process (Hoepfner, Carl): Chemistry. See: Hackh; Thrush.

Hoeppli phenomenon (Hoeppli, Reinhard J. C.): Medicine. See: Stedman.

HOEPPLI, REINHARD J. C. 1893- . German parasitologist. See: Kuerschner's Deut. Gel. Kal., vol. 4, 1931. Hoeppli phenomenon.

HOERLEIN, HEINRICH (In full: PHILIPP HEINRICH). 1882-1954. German medicinal chemist. See: Pogg., vol. 7a. Hoerlein-Weber disease.

Hoerlein-Weber disease (Hoerlein, Heinrich and Weber, Gustav): Medicine. See: Jablonski.

HOERNES, MORITZ. 1815-1868. Austrian paleontologist. See: Oesterr. Biog. Lex., 1815-1950. Hoernesite (or Hornesite).

Hoernesite (or Hornesite) (Hoernes, Moritz): Earth Sciences. See: Thrush; Webster's 3d.

HOESCH, KURT. 1882-1932. German chemist. See: Pogg., vols. 5, 6. Hoesch reaction (or synthesis), Houben-Hoesch synthesis.

Hoesch reaction (or synthesis) (Hoesch, Kurt): Chemistry. See: Ballentyne; Van Nostrand Chem. Dict.

Hoet-Abaza syndrome (Hoet, Joseph Jules and Abaza, Alphonse?): Medicine. See: Jablonski.

HOET, JOSEPH JULES. 1925- . Belgian physician. See: Who's Who Sci. Europe, 1972. Hoet-Abaza syndrome.

HOEVE, JAN VAN DER. b. 1878. Dutch physician. See: Wie is dat?, 1948. Van der Hoeve-Halbertsma-Waardenburg syndrome, Van der Hoeve's syndrome (or triad).

Hofacker and Sadler's law(s) (Hofacker, Johann Daniel and Sadler, Michael): Genetics. See: Dorland; Gray; Stedman.

HOFACKER, JOHANN DANIEL. 1788-1828. German obstetrician. See: Biog. Lex. hervorr. Aerzte. Hofacker and Sadler's law(s).

Hofbauer cell (Hofbauer, J. Isfred Isidore): Medicine. See: Dorland; Stedman.

HOFBAUER, J. ISFRED ISIDORE. 1878-1961. American gynecologist. See: New York Times, March 15, 1961, p. 39, col. 4. Hofbauer cell.

HOFER, HANS. fl. 1899-1902. German chemist. Cited in: Royal Soc. Cat. Sci. Pap., 1884-1900. Hofer-Moest reaction.

Hofer-Moest reaction (Hofer, Hans and Moest, Martin): Chemistry. See: Van Nostrand Chem. Dict.

Hoff convergence method (Hoff, Wilhelm?): Engineering and Industry. See: Internat. Dict. Ap. Math.

Hoff, Jacobus Hendricus van't. See: van't Hoff, Jacobus Hendricus.

HOFF, WILHELM. 1883-1945. German aerodynamics engineer. See: Pogg., vol. 7a. Hoff convergence method?

HOFFA, ALBERT. 1859-1907. German surgeon. See: World Who's Who Sci. Hoffa-Kastert syndrome, Hoffa's operation.

Hoffa-Kastert syndrome (Hoffa, Albert and Kastert, Josef): Medicine. See: Jablonski. Also known as: Hoffa's syndrome.

Hoffa-Lorenz operation (Hoffa, Albert and Lorenz, Adolf). See: Hoffa's operation.

Hoffa's operation (Hoffa, Albert): Medicine. See: Dorland; Stedman. Also known as: Hoffa-Lorenz operation.

Hoffa's syndrome (Hoffa, Albert). See: Hoffa-Kastert syndrome.

Hoffer test reaction (Derivation undetermined): Chemistry. See: Van Nostrand Chem. Dict.

Hoffman (Hoffmann) electrometer (or binant electrometer) (Hoffmann, Gerhard): Physics. See: Hughes; Internat. Dict. Phys. Elec.; Thewlis.

Hoffman frame (Derivation undetermined): Agriculture. See: Winburne.

HOFFMAN, JACOB. 1900- . American physician. Cited in: Index-Cat. Libr. Surg.-Gen. Off., 5th ser., vol. 1, 1959. Mazer-Hoffman test.

Hoffman press (Derivation undetermined): Printing. See: Lockwood, p. 256.

HOFFMANN, AUGUST. 1887-1929. German physician. See: Biog. Lex. hervorr. Aerzte, 1880-1930. Bouveret-Hoffmann syndrome.

Hoffmann bearing (Hoffmann, E. G.): Engineering and Industry. See: Auger.

HOFFMANN, CHRISTIAN (or CHRISTOPHER). 1815-1884. German sect founder. See: Allg. Deut. Biog. Hoffmannites.

Hoffmann clamp (Hoffmann, Friedrich?): Chemistry. See: Hackh.

HOFFMANN, E. G. fl. 1901. Engineer. (Biography source unavailable.) Hoffmann bearing.

Hoffmann electrolytic apparatus (Hoffmann, Friedrich): Chemistry. See: Hackh.

HOFFMANN, ERICH. 1868-1958. German dermatologist. See: World Who's Who Sci. Hoffmann-Zurhelle syndrome.

HOFFMANN, FRIEDRICH. 1660-1742. German physician and chemist. See: Dict. Sci. Biog. Hoffmann clamp?, Hoffmann electrolytic apparatus, Hoffmann's anodyne, Hoffmann's drops.

HOFFMANN, GEORG FRANZ. 1766-1821. German botanist. See: Biog. Lex. hervorr. Aerzte. Hoffmannia.

HOFFMANN, GERHARD. 1880-1945. German physicist. See: Pogg., vols. 5, 6, 7a. Hoffman (Hoffmann) electrometer (or binant electrometer).

HOFFMANN, JOHANN. 1857-1919. German neurologist. See: World Who's Who Sci. Charcot-Marie-Tooth-Hoffmann syndrome, Hoffmann's phenomenon, Hoffmann's sign (1), Hoffmann's sign (2) (or reflex), Hoffmann's syndrome, Werdnig-Hoffmann disease (or syndrome).

Hoffmann kiln (Derivation undetermined): Engineering and Industry. See: Thrush.

HOFFMANN, MORITZ. 1622-1698. German anatomist. See: World Who's Who Sci. Hoffmann's duct.

HOFFMANN, WALTHER. 1910- . German plant breeding scientist. See: Who's Who Sci. Europe, 1972. Hoffman's anthocyaninless?

HOFFMANN-WELLENHOF, GEORG. b. 1843. Austrian bacteriologist. Cited in: Kelly. Hoffmann's bacillus.

Hoffmann-Zurhelle syndrome (Hoffmann, Erich and Zurhelle, Emil): Medicine. See: Jablonski.

Hoffmannia (Hoffmann, Georg Franz): Botany. See: Taylor, N.

Hoffmannites (Hoffmann, Christian): Religion. See: Canney.

Hoffmann's anodyne (Hoffmann, Friedrich): Medicine. See: Dorland; Webster's 3d.

Hoffmann's atrophy (or muscular atrophy) (Hoffmann, Johann). See: Werdnig-Hoffmann disease (or syndrome).

Hoffmann's bacillus (Hoffmann-Wellenhof, Georg): Medicine. See: Dorland; Stedman.

Hoffmann's drops (Hoffmann, Friedrich): Medicine. See: Stedman; Webster's 3d.

Hoffmann's duct (Hoffmann, Moritz): Anatomy. See: Dorland; Stedman. Also known as: Wirsung's canal.

Hoffmann's phenomenon (Hoffmann, Johann): Medicine. See: Stedman.

Hoffmann's sign (1) (Hoffmann, Johann): Medicine. See: Dorland; Stedman.

Hoffmann's sign (2) (or reflex) (Hoffmann, Johann): Medicine. See: Hinsie; Stedman; Wolman. Also known as: Troemner's (or Troemmer's) reflex (or sign).

Hoffmann's syndrome (Hoffmann, Johann): Medicine. See: Jablonski.

HOFFMANNSEGG, JOHANN CENTURIUS. 1766-1849. German naturalist. See: Nour. Biog. Univ. Hoffmanseggia.

Hoffman's anthocyaninless (Hoffmann, Walther?): Botany. See: Gray.

Hoffmanseggia (Hoffmannsegg, Johann Centurius): Botany. See: Charnock.

HOFLUND, SVEN. 1906- . Swedish physician. See: Vem Ar Det?, 1975. Hoflund's syndrome.

Hoflund's syndrome (Hoflund, Sven): Medicine. See: Jablonski.

Hofmann amine separation (Hofmann, August Wilhelm von): Chemistry. See: Ballentyne.

HOFMANN, AUGUST WILHELM VON. 1818-1892. German chemist. See: Dict. Sci. Biog. Hofmann amine separation, Hofmann degradation, Hofmann exhaustive methylation reaction, Hofmann-Martius rearrangement, Hofmann mustard oil reaction, Hofmann rearrangement (or reaction), Hofmann rule, Hofmann test reaction for benzene, Hofmann test reactions for aniline, Hofmann test reactions for primary amines, Hofmann test reagent for carbon disulfide?, Hofmannite, Hofmann's violets.

Hofmann degradation (Hofmann, August Wilhelm von): Chemistry. See: Ballentyne; Van Nostrand Chem. Dict.

Hofmann exhaustive methylation reaction (Hofmann, August Wilhelm von): Chemistry. See: Ballentyne.

HOFMANN, H. No dates. German obstetrician. (Biography source unavailable.) Hofmann's test (or reaction).

Hofmann-Hoechtlen reagent (Hofmann, Karl Andreas and Hoechtlen, Friedrich): Chemistry. See: Van Nostrand Chem. Dict.

HOFMANN, KARL ANDREAS. 1870-1940. German chemist. See: Pogg., vols. 6, 7a. Hofmann-Hoechtlen reagent, Hofmann-Sand reaction, Hofmann-Storm reagent, Hofmann test reagent for titanic acid?

ofmann–Martius rearrangement (Hofmann, August Wilhelm von and Martius, Carl Alexander von): Chemistry. See: Van Nostrand Chem. Dict.

OFMANN, MELCHIOR. ca. 1498–ca. 1543. German Anabaptist leader. See: New Encyc. Brit., 1974, Microp. Melchiorists.

ofmann method for vapor pressure (Derivation undetermined): Physics. See: nternat. Dict. Phys. Elec.

ofmann mustard oil reaction (Hofmann, August Wilhelm von): Chemistry. See: Ballentyne.

ofmann rearrangement (or reaction) (Hofmann, August Wilhelm von): Chemistry. See: Ballentyne; Hackh; Van Nostrand Chem. Dict.

ofmann rule (Hofmann, August Wilhelm von): Chemistry. See: Van Nostrand hem. Dict.

ofmann–Sand reaction (Hofmann, Karl Andreas and Sand, Julius): Chemistry. See: Van Nostrand Chem. Dict.

ofmann–Storm reagent (Hofmann, Karl Andreas and Storm, Douglas): Chemistry. See: Van Nostrand Chem. Dict.

ofmann test reaction for benzene (Hofmann, August Wilhelm von): Chemistry. See: Van Nostrand Chem. Dict.

ofmann test reactions for aniline (Hofmann, August Wilhelm von): Chemistry. an Nostrand Chem. Dict.

ofmann test reactions for primary amines (Hofmann, August Wilhelm von): hemistry. See: Van Nostrand Chem. Dict.

ofmann test reagent for carbon disulfide (Hofmann, August Wilhelm von?): hemistry. See: Van Nostrand Chem. Dict.

ofmann test reagent for titanic acid (Hofmann, Karl Andreas?): Chemistry. See: Van Nostrand Chem. Dict.

ofmannite (Hofmann, August Wilhelm von): Earth Sciences. See: Thrush.

ofmann's test (or reaction) (Hofmann, H.): Medicine. See: Dorland.

ofmann's violets (Hofmann, August Wilhelm von): Chemistry. See: Blumberg; orland; Webster's 3d.

OFMEISTER, FRANZ. 1850–1922. Austro-German physiological chemist. See: Oesterr. Biog. Lex., 1815–1950. Hofmeister reactions for aliphatic mino acids, Hofmeister series.

OFMEISTER, FRANZ VON. 1867–1926. German surgeon. See: Biog. Lex. ervorr. Aerzte, 1880–1930. Hofmeister–Polya anastomosis, Hofmeister's opera- on.

ofmeister–Polya anastomosis (Hofmeister, Franz von and Polya, Jeno). See: ofmeister's operation and Polya's operation.

ofmeister reactions for aliphatic amino acids (Hofmeister, Franz): Chemistry. See: Van Nostrand Chem. Dict.

ofmeister series (Hofmeister, Franz): Chemistry. See: Ballentyne; Hackh; edman; Thrush; Van Nostrand Sci. Encyc.; Webster's 3d.

ofmeister's operation (Hofmeister, Franz von): Medicine. See: Dorland; edman. Also known as: Finsterer's operation.

ogan (seed) (Hogan, William): Botany. See: Mathews, M. M.

OGAN, WILLIAM. fl. 1848. American grower. (Biography source unavail- ble.) Hogan (seed).

oganas process (Derivation undetermined): Engineering and Industry. See: hrush.

ogarth Act (Hogarth, William): Law. See: New Encyc. Brit., 1974, Microp.

ogarth chair (Hogarth, William): Applied Arts. See: Webster's 3d.

ogarth Club (Hogarth, William): Fine Arts. See: Latham.

OGARTH, WILLIAM. 1697–1764. English painter and engraver. See: Dict. at. Biog. Hogarth Act, Hogarth chair, Hogarth Club, Hogarthian, Hogarth's ne.

ogarthian (Hogarth, William): Fine Arts. See: Hendrickson; Partridge; ebster's 3d.

ogarth's line (Hogarth, William): Fine Arts. See: Webster's 3d.

OGBEN, LANCELOT T. 1895– . English physiologist and medical statis- cian. See: World Who's Who Sci. Hogben test.

Hogben test (Hogben, Lancelot T.): Medicine. See: Stedman.

Hohenheim, Theophrastus Bombastus von. See: Paracelsus, Philippus Aureolus.

Hohenstaufen (dynasty) (Hohenstaufen family): History. See: Webster's 3d.

HOHENSTAUFEN (STAUFER) FAMILY. fl. 1138–1254. German royal dynasty. See: New Encyc. Brit., 1974, Microp. Hohenstaufen (dynasty).

Hohenstaufen, Friedrich von. See: Swabia, Friedrich von Hohenstaufen, Duke of.

Hohenzollern (Hohenzollern family): History. See: Webster's 3d.

HOHENZOLLERN FAMILY. fl. 11th–20th c. German royal dynasty. See: Encyc. Brit., 1973. Hohenzollern, Hohenzollernism.

Hohenzollernism (Hohenzollern family): History. See: Webster's 3d.

Hohmann orbit (or transfer ellipses) (Hohmann, Walter): Engineering and Industry. See: New Encyc. Brit., 1974, Microp.; Van Nostrand Sci. Encyc. under "Space Vehicle Guidance."

HOHMANN, THOMAS. fl. before 1929. Chilean mining engineer. Cited in: Bailey. Hohmannite.

HOHMANN, WALTER. 1880–1945. German engineer. See: Neue Deut. Biog. Hohmann orbit (or transfer ellipses).

Hohmannite (Hohmann, Thomas): Earth Sciences. See: Thrush; Webster's 3d.

HOIGNE, ROLF VICTOR. 1923– . Swiss physician. See: Who's Who Sci. Europe, 1967. Nicolau–Hoigne syndrome.

HOILAND, EINAR. 1907– . Norwegian geophysicist. See: World Who's Who Sci. Hoiland's circulation theorem.

Hoiland's circulation theorem (Hoiland, Einar): Earth Sciences. See: Huschke.

HOLBEIN, HANS, THE YOUNGER. ca. 1497–1543. German painter and designer. See: Encyc. Brit., 1973. Holbein-stitch, Holbein work.

Holbein-stitch (Holbein, Hans, the younger): Applied Arts. See: Picken; Webster's 3d.

Holbein work (Holbein, Hans, the younger): Applied Arts. See: Picken.

HOLBERG, LUDVIG HOLBERG, BARON. 1684–1754. Danish man of letters. See: Encyc. Brit., 1973. Holberg suite.

Holberg suite (Holberg, Ludvig Holberg, Baron): Music. See: Apel.

HOLBOELL, CARL PETER. 1795–1856. Danish ornithologist. See: Dansk Biog. Lek. Holboell's grebe.

Holboell's grebe (Holboell, Carl Peter): Zoology. See: Webster's 3d.

Holborn and Henning method for specific heat at constant pressure (Holborn, Ludwig Christian Friedrich and Henning, Fritz Hermann Gustav): Physics. See: Internat. Dict. Phys. Elec.

Holborn–Kurlbaum pyrometer (Holborn, Ludwig Christian Friedrich and Kurlbaum, Ferdinand): Engineering and Industry. See: Hackh.

HOLBORN, LUDWIG CHRISTIAN FRIEDRICH. 1860–1926. German physicist. See: Dict. Sci. Biog. Holborn and Henning method for specific heat at constant pressure, Holborn–Kurlbaum pyrometer.

HOLBROOK, JOHN EDWARDS. 1794–1871. American naturalist. See: World Who's Who Sci. Holbrookia.

Holbrookia (Holbrook, John Edwards): Zoology. See: Mathews, M. M.; Pennak.

HOLDEN, ALBERT FAIRCHILD. 1867–1913. American mining engineer. See: Nat. Cycl. Amer. Biog., vol. 22, p. 230. Holdenite.

HOLDEN, LUTHER. 1815–1905. English anatomist. See: Dict. Nat. Biog., 2d suppl. Holden's line.

Holdenite (Holden, Albert Fairchild): Earth Sciences. See: Thrush; Webster's 3d.

Holden's line (Holden, Luther): Anatomy. See: Dorland; Stedman.

Holger Nielsen method (Nielsen, Holger). See: Nielsen method.

HOLL, MORITZ. 1852–1920. Austrian surgeon. See: Biog. Lex. hervorr. Aerzte, 1880–1930. Holl's ligament.

HOLLAENDER, EUGEN. 1867–1932. German physician. See: Biog. Lex. hervorr. Aerzte, 1880–1930. Hollaender–Simons syndrome.

Hollaender–Simons syndrome (Hollaender, Eugen and Simons, Arthur). See: Simon's disease (or syndrome).

HOLLAND, JOHN, DUKE OF EXETER. 1395-1447. English nobleman. See: Dict. Nat. Biog. Duke of Exeter's daughter.

HOLLAND, SIR THOMAS HENRY. 1868-1947. English geologist. See: World Who's Who Sci. Hollandite.

HOLLANDER, FRANKLIN. 1899-1966. American physiologist. See: Nat. Cycl. Amer. Biog., vol. 51, pp. 308-309. Hollander test.

Hollander test (Hollander, Franklin): Medicine. See: Stedman.

HOLLANDER, VINCENT PAUL. 1917- . American biochemist. See: Amer. Men Sci., 8th ed. Gallagher–Hollander degradation.

Hollandite (Holland, Sir Thomas Henry): Earth Sciences. See: Thrush; Webster's 3d.

Hollenhorst plaques (Hollenhorst, Robert William): Medicine. See: Stedman.

HOLLENHORST, ROBERT WILLIAM. 1913- . American ophthalmologist. See: Amer. Men and Women Sci., 12th ed. Hollenhorst plaques.

Hollerith card (Hollerith, Hermann): Data Processing. See: Hoult.

Hollerith code (Hollerith, Hermann): Data Processing. See: Internat. Dict. Phys. Elec.; Markus; Van Nostrand Sci. Encyc. under "Digital Computer."

HOLLERITH, HERMANN. 1860-1929. American inventor. See: World Who's Who Sci. Hollerith card, Hollerith code, Hollerith machine, Hollerith (system).

Hollerith machine (Hollerith, Hermann): Data Processing. See: Good; Webster's 3d.

Hollerith (system) (Hollerith, Hermann): Data Processing. See: Good; Van Nostrand Sci. Encyc.

Holley carburettor (Holley, Earl and Holley, George Malvin): Engineering and Industry. See: Auger.

HOLLEY, EARL. fl. 1904. American engineer. Cited in: Nat. Cycl. Amer. Biog. under "Holley, George Malvin," vol. 53, pp. 253-254. Holley carburettor.

HOLLEY, GEORGE MALVIN. 1878-1963. American automotive pioneer. See: Nat. Cycl. Amer. Biog., vol. 53, pp. 253-254. Holley carburettor.

HOLLOWAY, GEORGE. 1825-1886. English manufacturer. See: Boase. Holloway societies.

HOLLOWAY, JOHN. fl. 1913. American? engineer. Cited in: Chem. Abstr. Holloway process?

Holloway process (Holloway, John?): Engineering and Industry. See: Thrush.

Holloway societies (Holloway, George): Sociology. See: Encyc. Brit., 1973 under "Fraternal Organizations."

Holl's ligament (Holl, Moritz): Anatomy. See: Stedman.

HOLLY, BIRDSILL. No dates. Engineer. (Biography source unavailable.) Holly pump.

Holly pump (Holly, Birdsill): Engineering and Industry. See: Auger.

HOLMAN, JACK PHILIP. 1934- . American mechanical engineer. See: Amer. Men and Women Sci., 12th ed. Holman's first homily.

Holman's first homily (Holman, Jack Philip): Sociology. See: Martin.

HOLMBERG, ANDERS. fl. 1924-1951. American? engineer. Cited in: Chem. Abstr. Holmberg system.

Holmberg system (Holmberg, Anders): Engineering and Industry. See: Thrush.

HOLME. fl. ca. 1836. English scientist. Cited in: Bailey. Holmite.

Holme mud sampler (Derivation undetermined): Engineering and Industry. See: Thrush.

Holme suction grab (Derivation undetermined): Engineering and Industry. See: Thrush.

Holmes–Adie syndrome (Holmes, Gordon M. and Adie, William J.). See: Adie's syndrome.

HOLMES, ARTHUR. 1890-1965. English geologist. See: Dict. Sci. Biog. Holmes' classification.

Holmes' classification (Holmes, Arthur): Earth Sciences. See: Thrush.

Holmes' disease (Holmes, Gordon Morgan): Medicine. See: Jablonski.

HOLMES, ERIC GORDON. 1897- . English neurologist. See: Med. Direct., 1964. Stewart–Holmes sign.

HOLMES, GORDON MORGAN. 1876-1965. English neurologist. See: Who Was Who, 1961-1970. Adie–Holmes syndrome, Head–Holmes syndrome, Holmes' disease, Holmes's phenomenon (or rebound phenomenon of Gordon Holmes), Holmes' syndrome.

Holmes–Manley process (Holmes, Ralph C. and Manley, Frederick T.): Chemistry. See: Van Nostrand Chem. Dict.

HOLMES, OLIVER WENDELL, SR. 1809-1894. American man of letters. See: Dict. Amer. Biog. Holmes viewers.

HOLMES, RALPH C. fl. 1926-1931. American chemist. Cited in: Chem. Abstr., vol. 25, p. 808. Holmes–Manley process.

HOLMES, SHERLOCK. Prototype master detective in stories by Sir Arthur Conan Doyle written from 1891 to 1904. See: New Encyc. Brit., 1974, Microp. Holmesian, Sherlock, Sherlock Holmes, Sherlockian.

Holmes' syndrome (Holmes, Gordon Morgan): Medicine. See: Jablonski.

HOLMES, TIMOTHY. 1825-1907. English surgeon. See: Dict. Nat. Biog., 2d suppl. Holmes's operation.

Holmes viewers (Holmes, Oliver, Wendell, Sr.): Photography. See: Focal Encyc. Photog. under "Stereoscopic Photography."

Holmesian (Holmes, Sherlock): Literature. See: Webster's 3d.

Holmes's operation (Holmes, Timothy): Medicine. See: Dorland.

Holmes's phenomenon (or rebound phenomenon of Gordon Holmes) (Holmes, Gordon Morgan): Medicine. See: Dorland; Hinsie.

HOLMGREN, EMIL ALGOT. 1866-1922. Swedish histologist. See: Svenska Maen Och Kvinnor. Holmgren–Golgi canals.

HOLMGREN, FRITHIOF (In full: ALARIK FRITHIOF). 1831-1897. Swedish physiologist. See: Dict. Sci. Biog. Holmgren test (or yarn test), Holmgren wools.

Holmgren–Golgi canals (Holmgren, Emil Algot and Golgi, Camillo). See: Golgi apparatus.

Holmgren test (or yarn test) (Holmgren, Frithiof): Psychology. See: Chaplin; English; Hinsie; Webster's 3d.; Wolman.

Holmgren wools (Holmgren, Frithiof): Psychology. See: Drever; Wolman.

Holmite (Holme): Earth Sciences. See: Charnock.

HOLMQUIST, PER JOHAN. 1866-1946. Swedish geologist. See: Svenska Maen Och Kvinnor. Holmquistite.

Holmquistite (Holmquist, Per Johan): Earth Sciences. See: Thrush; Webster's 3d.

HOLMSKIOLD, THEODOR. 1732-1793. Danish physician and naturalist. See: Nouv. Biog. Univ. Holmskioldia.

Holmskioldia (Holmskiold, Theodor): Botany. See: Taylor, N.

HOLT, CHARLES CARTER. 1921- . American economist. See: Amer. Men Sci., 10th ed., Soc. and Behav. Holt's method.

Holt–Dern process (and furnace) (Holt, Theodore P. and Dern, George H.): Engineering and Industry. See: Van Nostrand Chem. Dict.

HOLT, MARY CLAYTON. fl. 1950-1972. English pediatrician. See: Med. Direct., 1972. Holt–Oram syndrome.

Holt–Oram syndrome (Holt, Mary Clayton and Oram, Samuel): Medicine. See: Jablonski; Stedman.

HOLT, THEODORE P. fl. 1924. American mining engineer. Cited in: Chem. Abstr., vol. 18, p. 2490. Holt–Dern process (and furnace).

Holte method (Holte, Per Gunnar): Physics. See: Internat. Dict. Ap. Math.

HOLTE, PER GUNNAR. 1920- . Swedish physicist. See: World Who's Who Sci. Holte method.

HOLTEN, CAI. b. 1894. Danish physician. See: Biog. Lex. hervorr. Aerzte, 1880-1930. Holten's test.

olten's test (Holten, Cai): Medicine. See: Dorland.

OLTER, HEINZ. 1904- . Danish biochemist. See: Who's Who Sci. rope, 1967. Linderstrom-Lang-Holter method (1), Linderstrom-Lang-Holter ethod (2), Linderstrom-Lang-Weil-Holter methods.

OLTERMANN, BERNARD OTTO. 1838-1885. German-born miner and pioneer onsor of photography in Australia. See: Australian Encyc. Holtermann col-ction, Holtermann nugget.

oltermann collection (Holtermann, Bernard Otto): Photography. See: Focal ncyc. Photog. under "Australia."

oltermann nugget (Holtermann, Bernard Otto): Earth Sciences. See: Encyc. it. under "Gold," vol. 10, p. 536b.

OLTERMUELLER, K. fl. 1960. German pediatrician. (Biography source un-vailable.) Holtermueller-Wiedemann syndrome.

oltermueller-Wiedemann syndrome (Holtermueller, K. and Wiedemann, Hans dolf): Medicine. See: Jablonski.

OLTHOUSE, CARSTEN. 1810-1901. English surgeon. See: Biog. Lex. ervorr. Aerzte. Holthouse's hernia.

olthouse's hernia (Holthouse, Carsten): Medicine. See: Dorland; Stedman.

olton test (Derivation undetermined): Chemistry. See: Van Nostrand Chem. ct.

olt's method (Holt, Charles Carter): Statistics. See: Kendall.

oltz machine (Holtz, Wilhelm). See: Toepler-Holtz machine.

OLTZ, WILHELM. 1836-1913. German physicist. See: World Who's Who i. Toepler-Holtz machine.

OLTZAPFFEL, CHARLES. 1806-1847. English mechanical engineer. Cited : Royal Soc. Cat. Sci. Pap., 1800-1863. Holtzapffel gauge.

oltzapffel gauge (Holtzapffel, Charles): Engineering and Industry. See: uger.

oltzman inkblot technique (Holtzman, Wayne Harold): Psychology. See: olman.

OLTZMAN, WAYNE HAROLD. 1923- . American psychologist. See: mer. Men Sci., 10th ed., Soc. And Behav. Holtzman inkblot technique.

OLTZMANN, CARL HEINRICH ALEXANDER. 1811-1865. German physicist. e: Pogg., vol. 1. Holtzmann mechanical generator?

oltzmann mechanical generator (Holtzmann, Carl Heinrich Alexander?): Engi-ering and Industry. See: Thrush.

OLUB, JIRI. fl. 1962. Czechoslovakian engineer. (Biography source un-ailable.) Holub process.

olub process (Holub, Jiri): Engineering and Industry. See: Auger.

OLVECK, FERNAND. 1890-1941. French physicist. See: World Who's Who i. Holweck-Lejay inverted pendulum (or apparatus).

olweck-Lejay inverted pendulum (or apparatus) (Holveck, Fernand and Lejay, erre R. P.): Physics. See: Thrush.

OLZER, HANS. fl. 1933. German chemist. Cited in: Chem. Abstr., vol. ?, p. 2108. Holzer-Reif test reaction.

olzer-Reif test reaction (Holzer, Hans and Reif, Wilhelm): Chemistry. See: an Nostrand Chem. Dict.

OLZKNECHT, GUIDO. 1872-1931. Austrian radiologist. See: World Who's ho Sci. Holzknecht meter, Holzknecht unit, Holzknecht's space, Holzknecht's omach, Holzknecht's syndrome.

olzknecht meter (Holzknecht, Guido): Medicine. See: Stedman under "dose ythema."

olzknecht unit (Holzknecht, Guido): Medicine. See: Dorland; Stedman.

olzknecht's space (Holzknecht, Guido): Medicine. See: Dorland.

olzknecht's stomach (Holzknecht, Guido): Medicine. See: Dorland.

olzknecht's syndrome (Holzknecht, Guido): Medicine. See: Jablonski.

OLZMANN, WALTER. fl. 1909. German physician. Cited in: Kelly. uch-Holzmann reaction.

olzwarth gas turbine (Holzwarth, Hans): Engineering and Industry. See: uger; Encyc. Brit., 1973 under "Turbine," vol. 22, p. 342a.

HOLZWARTH, HANS. 1877-1933. German engineer. See: Neue Deut. Biog. Holzwarth gas turbine.

HOMANS, JOHN. 1836-1903. American surgeon. See: World Who's Who Sci. John Homans professorship of surgery.

HOMANS, JOHN. 1877-1954. American surgeon. See: New York Times, June 8, 1954, p. 27, col. 2. Homans' sign.

Homans' sign (Homans, John): Medicine. See: Stedman; Webster's 3d.

HOMBERG, WILHELM. 1652-1715. German-French chemist. See: Dict. Sci. Biog. Homberg's phosphorus.

Homberg's phosphorus (Homberg, Wilhelm): Chemistry. See: Thrush.

HOME, SIR EVERARD. 1756-1832. English surgeon. See: Dict. Sci. Biog. Home's lobe.

HOMEN, ERNST ALEXANDER. 1851-1926. Finnish physician. See: Biog. Lex. hervorr. Aerzte, 1880-1930. Homen's syndrome.

Homen's syndrome (Homen, Ernst Alexander): Medicine. See: Jablonski.

HOMER. fl. 8th c. B.C. Greek poet. See: Encyc. Brit., 1973. Homer sometimes nods (or sometimes Homer nods), Homeria, Homeric (or Homerian), Homeric combat, Homeric dialect, Homeric epigrams, Homeric epithet, Homeric Hymns, Homeric laughter, Homeric simile, Homeric times, Homeric verse, Homeridae, Homerist.

Homer sometimes nods (or sometimes Homer nods) (Homer, the poet): Generic Word (best of us make mistakes). See: Hendrickson.

Homeria (Homer): Botany. See: Webster's 3d.

Homeric (or Homerian) (Homer): Literature. See: Webster's 3d.

Homeric combat (Homer): Generic Word (unreserved fighting). See: Partridge; Weekley.

Homeric dialect (Homer): Literature. See: Encyc. Brit., 1973 under "Homer", vol. 11, p. 634b.

Homeric epigrams (Homer): Literature. See: Preminger under "Lyric."

Homeric epithet (Homer): Literature. See: Scott.

Homeric Hymns (Homer): Literature. See: Encyc. Brit., 1973; Harvey under "Homer"; Phyfe; Preminger under "Lyric."

Homeric laughter (Homer): Generic Word (hearty, unreserved laughter). See: Hendrickson; Partridge; Weekley.

Homeric simile (Homer): Literature. See: Barnet; Preminger under "Simile"; Scott; Webster's 3d.

Homeric times (Homer): Generic Word. See: Phyfe.

Homeric verse (Homer): Literature. See: Phyfe.

Homeridae (Homer): Literature. See: Encyc. Brit., 1973 under "Homer," vol. 11, p. 630b.

Homerist (Homer): Literature. See: Webster's 3d.

Home's lobe (Home, Sir Everard): Medicine. See: Stedman.

HOMMEL, WOLDEMAR. b. 1878. German petrographer. Cited in: Mansell. Hommel's classification.

Hommel's classification (Hommel, Woldemar): Earth Sciences. See: Thrush.

HONDIUS (DE HONDT), JODOCUS. 1563-1611. Flemish engraver and cartographer. See: World Who's Who Sci. Mercator-Hondius atlas.

Honigmann process (Derivation undetermined): Engineering and Industry. See: Thrush.

HONTHEIM, JOHANN NIKOLAUS VON (Pseud., FEBRONIUS). 1701-1790. German theologian and historian. See: Encyc. Brit., 1973. Febronianism.

HOOD, JOHN. 1720-1783. Irish surveyor and inventor. See: Dict. Nat. Biog. Hood's compass.

Hoodlum (Muldoon): Generic Word. See: Clapin.

Hood's compass (Hood, John): Navigation. Cited in: World Who's Who Sci.

HOOFT, C. fl. 1962. Belgian pediatrician. See: Who's Who Sci. Europe, 1972. Hooft's syndrome.

Hooft's syndrome (Hooft, C.): Medicine. See: Jablonski.

Hoogoliet test paper for chloride (Derivation undetermined): Chemistry. See: Van Nostrand Chem. Dict.

Hook, Weller van. See: van Hook, Weller.

Hooke('s) law (Hooke, Robert): Physics. See: Hackh; Internat. Dict. Phys. Elec.; James; Thewlis; Thrush; Van Nostrand Sci. Encyc.; Webster's 3d.

HOOKE, ROBERT. 1635-1703. English experimental physicist. See: Dict. Sci. Biog. Hooke('s) law, Hookean solid, Hooke's coupling (joint or universal joint).

Hookean solid (Hooke, Robert): Physics. See: Thewlis.

Hooker (Hooker, Joseph?): Generic Word (prostitute). See: Hendrickson.

HOOKER, ALBERT HUNTINGTON. 1865-1936. American electrochemist. See: Nat. Cycl. Amer. Biog., vol. 28, pp. 232-233. Hooker cell.

Hooker cell (Hooker, Albert Huntington): Chemistry. See: Webster's 3d.

HOOKER, CHARLES WRIGHT. 1910-   . American anatomist. See: Amer. Men Sci., 9th ed. Hooker-Forbes test.

Hooker-Forbes test (Hooker, Charles Wright and Forbes, Thomas Rogers): Medicine. See: Stedman.

HOOKER, JOSEPH. 1814-1879. American Union general. See: Dict. Amer. Biog. Hooker?

HOOKER, SIR JOSEPH DALTON. 1817-1911. English botanist. See: World Who's Who Sci. Hooker's sea lion?

Hooker process (Derivation undetermined): Engineering and Industry. See: Thrush.

Hooker reaction (Hooker, Samuel Cox): Chemistry. See: Van Nostrand Chem. Dict.

HOOKER, SAMUEL COX. 1864-1935. American chemist. See: Dict. Amer. Biog., 1st suppl. Hooker reaction.

Hooker telescope (Derivation undetermined): Astronomy. Cited in: Encyc. Brit., 1973 under "Telescope," vol. 21, p. 791a.

Hooker typesetting machine (Derivation undetermined): Printing. See: Lockwood.

HOOKER, WILLIAM. 1779-1832. English botanical painter. See: Britten and Boulger. Hooker's green.

HOOKER, SIR WILLIAM JACKSON. 1785-1865. English botanist. See: Dict. Sci. Biog. Hookeria, Hooker's orchid.

Hookeria (Hooker, Sir William Jackson): Botany. See: Webster's 3d.

Hooker's green (Hooker, William): Fine Arts. See: Webster's 3d.

Hooker's orchid (Hooker, Sir William Jackson): Botany. See: Webster's 3d.

Hooker's sea lion (Hooker, Sir Joseph Dalton?): Zoology. Cited in: Encyc. Brit., 1973 under "Carnivore," vol. 4, p. 936b.

Hooke's coupling (joint or universal joint) (Hooke, Robert): Engineering and Industry. See: Auger; Encyc. Brit., 1973 under "Linkages," vol. 14, p. 79a. Also known as: Cardan joint.

Hooligan (and Hooliganism) (Hooligan, Patrick): Generic Word. See: Harvey; Hendrickson; Partridge; Webster's 3d.

HOOLIGAN, PATRICK. fl. 1898. Irishman in Southwark, England. (Biography source unavailable.) Hooligan (and Hooliganism).

HOOPER, CLAUDE E. 1898-1954. American statistician. See: Who Was Who Amer., 1951-1960. Hooper rating.

Hooper jig (Derivation undetermined): Engineering and Industry. See: Thrush.

HOOPER, JOHN. fl. 18th c. English apothecary. (Biography source unavailable.) Hooper's pills.

Hooper rating (Hooper, Claude E.): Mass Media. See: Clark; Hendrickson.

Hooper's pills (Hooper, John): Medicine. See: Dorland.

Hoope's aluminum (Hoopes, William): Engineering and Industry. See: Thrush.

Hoopes conductivity bridge (Hoopes, William?): Physics. See: Internat. Dict. Phys. Elec.

Hoope's process (Hoopes, William): Engineering and Industry. See: Thrush; Van Nostrand Chem. Dict.

HOOPES, WILLIAM. 1867-1924. American electrical engineer. See: Nat. Cycl. Amer. Biog., vol. 19, p. 413. Hoope's aluminum, Hoopes conductivity bridge?, Hoope's process.

Hoorne, Jan van. See: van Hoorne, Jan.

Hoover (Hoover, W. H.): Generic Word (vacuum cleaner). See: Hendrickson under "Hoover..."

Hoover apron (Hoover, Herbert Clark): Fashion. See: Mathews, M. M.; Picken; Webster's 3d.

Hoover cart (Hoover, Herbert Clark): Generic Word. See: Hendrickson.

HOOVER, CHARLES FRANKLIN. 1865-1927. American physician. See: World Who's Who Sci. Hoover's sign (1), Hoover's sign (2).

HOOVER, CHARLES RUGLAS. 1885-1942. American chemist. See: World Who's Who Sci. Hoover test reaction.

Hoover Commission(s) (Hoover, Herbert Clark): Politics. See: Encyc. Brit., 1973 under "Hoover, Herbert C.," vol. 11, p. 677a; Smith.

Hoover debt moratorium (Hoover, Herbert Clark): Politics. See: Morris and Irwin.

HOOVER, HERBERT CLARK. 1874-1964. American president. See: Encyc. Brit., 1973. Hoover apron, Hoover cart, Hoover Commission(s), Hoover debt moratorium, Hoover hog, Hoover Library (and Institution) on War, Revolution and Peace, Hoover Plans, Hoover relief policy, Hoovercrat, Hooverette, Hooverian (and Hooverism), Hooverize, Hooverville.

Hoover hog (Hoover, Herbert Clark): History. See: Mathews, M. M.

HOOVER, J(OHN) EDGAR. 1895-1972. American lawyer and criminologist. See: Encyc. Brit., 1973. J. Edgar Hoover.

Hoover Library (and Institution) on War, Revolution and Peace (Hoover, Herbert Clark): History. See: Encyc. Brit., 1973 under "Hoover, Herbert Clark," vol. 11, p. 675d.

Hoover Plans (Hoover, Herbert Clark): Politics. Cited in: Laughlin.

Hoover relief policy (Hoover, Herbert Clark): Politics. See: Morris and Irwin.

Hoover test reaction (Hoover, Charles Ruglas): Chemistry. See: Van Nostrand Chem. Dict.

HOOVER, W. H. 1849-1932. American industrialist. See: Webster's Biog. Dict. Hoover.

Hoovercrat (Hoover, Herbert Clark): Politics. See: Mathews, M. M.; Smith; Webster's 3d.

Hooverette (Hoover, Herbert Clark): Fashion. See: Mathews, M. M.

Hooverian (and Hooverism) (Hoover, Herbert Clark): Politics. See: Mathews, M. M.; Webster's 3d.

Hooverize (Hoover, Herbert Clark): Generic Word (economize on food). See: Hendrickson; Webster's 3d.

Hoover's sign (1) (Hoover, Charles Franklin): Medicine. See: Dorland; Hinsie; Stedman.

Hoover's sign (2) (Hoover, Charles Franklin): Medicine. See: Stedman.

Hooverville (Hoover, Herbert Clark): Generic Word (slum). See: Hendrickson; Mathews, M. M.; Webster's 3d.

Hope('s) apparatus (and experiment) (Hope, Thomas Charles): Physics. See: Dict. Sci. Biog.; Thewlis.

Hope diamond (Hope, Henry Philip?): Applied Arts. See: Latham; New Encyc. Brit., 1974, Microp.; Phyfe.

HOPE, FREDERICK WILLIAM. 1797-1862. English entomologist. See: Dict. Nat. Biog. Hope Professor.

HOPE, HENRY PHILIP. d. 1839. English traveller and art collector. See: Dict. Nat. Biog. Hope diamond?

HOPE, JOHN. 1725-1786. Scottish physician and botanist. See: World Who's Who Sci. Hopea, Hope's mixture.

Hope press (Derivation undetermined): Printing. See: Lockwood.

ope Professor (Hope, Frederick William): Zoology. See: Wagner (More ames).

OPE, THOMAS CHARLES. 1766-1844. Scottish chemist. See: Dict. Sci. og. Hope('s) apparatus (and experiment), Hopeite.

opea (Hope, John): Botany. See: Webster's 3d.

opeite (Hope, Thomas Charles): Earth Sciences. See: Thrush; Webster's 3d.

ope's mixture (Hope, John): Medicine. See: Dorland.

OPF, EBERHARD. 1902- . Austrian-born American mathematician. See: ew Encyc. Brit., 1974, Microp. Wiener and Hopf equation, Wiener-Hopf chnique.

OPF, GUSTAV. 1900- . German dermatologist. See: Wer Ist Wer?, 74-1975. Hopf's keratosis.

opfield bands (Hopfield, John Joseph): Physics. See: Huschke.

OPFIELD, JOHN JOSEPH. 1891-1953. American physicist. See: Pogg., ls. 6, 7b. Hopfield bands.

opf's keratosis (Hopf, Gustav): Medicine. See: Jablonski.

OPKINS. No dates. American debtor. (Biography source unavailable.) n't hurry, Hopkins.

OPKINS, ANDREW DELMAR. b. 1857. American entomologist. See: Amer. en Sci., 5th ed. Hopkin's law (or bioclimatic law).

opkins-Cole (glyoxylic acid) reaction (test or reagent for tryptophane) opkins, Sir Frederick Gowland and Cole, Sydney William): Chemistry. See: llentyne; Pennak; Van Nostrand Chem. Dict.; Stedman.

opkins condenser (Hopkins, Cyril George): Chemistry. See: Van Nostrand em. Dict.

OPKINS, CYRIL GEORGE. 1866-1919. American agricultural chemist. See: orld Who's Who Sci. Hopkins condenser, Hopkins' distilling tube, Hopkins' mestone tester.

opkins' distilling tube (Hopkins, Cyril George): Chemistry. Cited in: World ho's Who Sci.

OPKINS, SIR FREDERICK GOWLAND. 1861-1947. English biochemist. See: ct. Sci. Biog. Benedict-Hopkins-Cole reagent, Fletcher-Hopkins test, Hopkins-ole (glyoxylic acid) reaction (test or reagent for tryptophane), Hopkins reaction r lactic acid.

opkin's law (or bioclimatic law) (Hopkins, Andrew Delmar): Biology. See: ray; Pennak.

opkins' limestone tester (Hopkins, Cyril George): Chemistry. Cited in: orld Who's Who Sci.

opkins reaction for lactic acid (Hopkins, Sir Frederick Gowland): Chemistry. e: Ballentyne.

OPKINS, SAMUEL. 1721-1803. American clergyman. See: Dict. Amer. og. Hopkinsians (Hopkinsianism or Hopkintonian).

OPKINS, SEWELL HEPBURN. 1906- . American zoologist. See: World ho's Who Sci. Hopkinsia?

opkinsia (Hopkins, Sewell Hepburn?): Zoology. See: Pennak.

opkinsians (Hopkinsianism or Hopkintonian) (Hopkins, Samuel): Religion. See: ewer; Latham; Mathews, M. M.; Mathews, S.; Webster's 3d.

OPKINSON, BERTRAM. 1874-1918. English engineer and physicist. See: orld Who's Who Sci. Hopkinson pressure bar.

opkinson chain machine (Derivation undetermined): Engineering and Industry. e: Thrush.

OPKINSON, EDWARD. fl. 1886. English electrical engineer. Cited in: yal Soc. Cat. Sci. Pap., 1884-1900. Hopkinson's coefficient.

OPKINSON, JOHN. 1849-1898. English physicist and electrical engineer. e: Dict. Sci. Biog. Edison-Hopkinson dynamo, Hopkinson rate theory, opkinson's coefficient.

opkinson pressure bar (Hopkinson, Bertram): Engineering and Industry. See: ger.

opkinson rate theory (Hopkinson, John): Engineering and Industry. See: Van ostrand Sci. Encyc. under "Electric Rates."

opkinson's coefficient (Hopkinson, John and Hopkinson, Edward): Electronics. e: Ballentyne.

HOPMANN, CARL MELCHIOR. 1844-1925. German rhinologist. See: Biog. Lex. hervorr. Aerzte, 1880-1930. Hopmann's papilloma (or polyp).

Hopmann's papilloma (or polyp) (Hopmann, Carl Melchior): Medicine. See: Dorland; Jablonski; Stedman.

Hoppe-Goldflam syndrome (or disease) (Hoppe, Hermann Henry and Goldflam, Samuel). See: Erb-Goldflam syndrome.

HOPPE, HERMANN HENRY. 1867-1929. American neurologist. See: Arch. Neurol. Psychiatr., Chic., vol. 23 (1930), p. 548. Hoppe-Goldflam syndrome (or disease).

Hoppe-Saylor test reaction for phenol (Hoppe-Seyler, Felix): Chemistry. See: Van Nostrand Chem. Dict.

HOPPE-SEYLER, FELIX (In full: ERNST FELIX IMMANUEL). 1825-1895. German physiologist and chemist. See: Dict. Sci. Biog. Hoppe-Saylor test reaction for phenol?, Hoppe-Seyler test.

Hoppe-Seyler test (Hoppe-Seyler, Felix): Medicine. See: Dorland; Stedman.

HORACE (QUINTUS HORATIUS FLACCUS). 65-8 B.C. Roman poet. See: Encyc. Brit., 1973. Horatian (1), Horatian (2), Horatian ode, Horatian satire.

Horatian (1) (Horace): Literature. See: Webster's 3d.

Horatian (2) (Horace): Generic Word. See: Partridge.

Horatian ode (Horace): Literature. See: Barnet; Duffy; New Encyc. Brit., 1974, Microp.; Preminger under "Ode"; Scott.

Horatian satire (Horace): Literature. See: Barnet; New Encyc. Brit., 1974, Microp.

Horatio Alger story (Alger, Horatio Jr.): Generic Word. See: Hendrickson, Mathews, M. M.

Horatio diamond (Derivation undetermined): Earth Sciences. See: Thrush.

HORE-BELISHA, LESLIE. 1893-1957. English statesman. See: Encyc. Brit., 1973. Belisha beacon (or Hore-Belisha).

Hore-Belisha (traffic beacon) (Hore-Belisha, Leslie): See: Belisha beacon.

HORGAN, EDMUND J. b. 1884. American surgeon. See: Physicians Mayo Clinic, 1937, p. 638f. Lyon and Horgan method (or operation).

horizontal cell of Cajal (Ramon y Cajal, Santiago): Medicine. See: Dorland; Stedman.

Horley-Sedgley water finder (Derivation undetermined): Engineering and Industry. See: Thrush.

HORMISDAS, SAINT. d. 523. Pope. See: Encyc. Brit., 1973. formula of Hormisdas.

Horn art aptitude inventory (Horn, C. A.): Psychology. Cited in: Cum. Auth. Index to Psych. Index, 1894-1935, and Psych. Abstr., 1927-1958.

HORN, C. A. fl. 1953. American psychologist. (Biography source unavailable.) Horn art aptitude inventory, Tomkins-Horn picture arrangement test.

HORN, C. C. fl. 1948. American psychologist. (Biography source unavailable.) Horn-Hellersberg drawing completion test.

HORN, C. TEN. No dates. Dutch surgeon. (Biography source unavailable.) Horn's (Ten Horn's) sign.

Horn-Hellersberg drawing completion test (Horn, C. C. and Hellersberg, Elisabeth F.): Psychology. See: Wolman.

Horn of Ammon (Ammon, Jupiter). See: Ammon's horn.

Hornblower engine (Hornblower, Jonathan Carter): Engineering and Industry. See: Auger.

HORNBLOWER, JONATHAN CARTER. 1753-1815. English engineer. See: World Who's Who Sci. Hornblower engine.

HORNEMANN, FRIEDRICH K. 1772-1801. German explorer in Africa. See: Encyc. Brit., 1973. Hornemann's redpoll.

Hornemann's redpoll (Hornemann, Friedrich K.): Zoology. See: Webster's 3d.

HORNER, JACK. fl. 1500's. English steward. (Biography source unavailable.) Jack Horner, Jack Horner pie.

HORNER, JOHANN FRIEDRICH. 1831-1886. Swiss ophthalmologist. See: World Who's Who Sci. Horner-Trantas spots, Horner's law, Horner's syndrome (or symptom complex).

Horner–Trantas spots (Horner, Johann Friedrich? and Trantas, Alexios): Medicine. See: Jablonski. Also known as: Trantas' dots.

HORNER, WILLIAM EDMONDS. 1793–1853. American anatomist. See: World Who's Who Sci. Horner's muscle (or muscle of Horner), Horner's teeth.

HORNER, WILLIAM GEORGE. 1786–1837. English mathematician. See: Dict. Sci. Biog. Horner's method.

Horner's law (Horner, Johann Friedrich): Physiology. See: Chaplin; Drever; English; Wolman.

Horner's method (Horner, William George): Mathematics. See: Ballentyne; Internat. Dict. Ap. Math.; Internat. Dict. Phys. Elec.; James; Webster's 3d.

Horner's muscle (or muscle of Horner) (Horner, William Edmonds): Anatomy. See: Donath; Dorland; Stedman. Also known as: Duverney's muscle.

Horner's syndrome (or symptom complex) (Horner, Johann Friedrich): Medicine. See: Dorland; Hinsie; Stedman; Wolman; Webster's 3d. Also known as: Bernard–Horner syndrome, Claude Bernard–Horner syndrome.

Horner's teeth (Horner, William Edmonds): Dentistry. See: Stedman.

Horn's (Ten Horn's) sign (Horn, C. Ten): Medicine. See: Dorland; Stedman.

Hornsby–Akroyd engine (Hornsby, Richard and Akroyd Stuart, H.): Engineering and Industry. See: Auger.

HORNSBY, RICHARD. fl. 19th c. English? engineer. (Biography source unavailable.) Hornsby–Akroyd engine.

HORNSEY, JOHN W. fl. 1928. American engineer. Cited in: Chem. Abstr., vol. 22, p. 2350. Hornsey process.

Hornsey process (Hornsey, John W.): Engineering and Industry. See: Thrush.

horopter circle of Johannes Mueller (Mueller, Johannes Peter). See: Vieth–Mueller circle.

Horoszkiewicz–Marx test (Horoszkiewicz, Stefan von and Marx, H.): Chemistry. See: Van Nostrand Chem. Dict.

HOROSZKIEWICZ, STEFAN VON. fl. 1906. Polish physician. See: Univ. Poznanski, 1924, p. 264f. Horoszkiewicz–Marx test.

Horrocks' maieutic (Horrocks, Peter): Medicine. See: Dorland.

HORROCKS, PETER. 1852–1901. English obstetrician. See: Biog. Lex. hervorr. Aerzte, 1880–1930. Horrocks' maieutic.

HORSEY. No dates. English? inventor. (Biography source unavailable.) Horsey pouch.

Horsey pouch (Horsey): Generic Word. See: Partridge.

HORSFORD, EBEN NORTON. 1818–1893. American chemist. See: Dict. Sci. Biog. Horsfordite.

Horsfordite (Horsford, Eben Norton): Earth Sciences. See: Thrush; Webster's 3d.

HORSLEY, SIR VICTOR ALEXANDER HADEN. 1857–1916. English surgeon and physiologist. See: Dict. Sci. Biog. Horsley's bone wax (or wax), Horsley's operation, Horsley's test.

Horsley's bone wax (or wax) (Horsley, Sir Victor Alexander Haden): Medicine. See: Dorland; Stedman.

Horsley's operation (Horsley, Sir Victor Alexander Haden): Medicine. See: Stedman.

Horsley's test (Horsley, Sir Victor Alexander Haden): Medicine. See: Dorland; Stedman.

Hortega('s) cell(s) (Rio–Hortega, Pio del): Medicine. See: Donath; Dorland; Gray; Henderson; Stedman. Also known as: Rio–Hortega's glia.

Hortega del Rio, Pio. See: Rio–Hortega, Pio del.

HORTON, BAYARD TAYLOR. 1895– . American physician. See: Direct. Med. Specialists, 1975–1976. Horton's disease (1), Horton's neuralgia (headache, cephalgia, disease (2), or syndrome).

Horton–Magath–Brown disease (Horton, Bayard Taylor; Magath, Thomas Byrd; and Brown, George Elgie). See: Horton's disease (1).

HORTON, SILAS R. fl. 19th c. American mineralogist. Cited in: Hintze, vol. 2, p. 23. Hortonolite.

Hortonolite (Horton, Silas R.): Earth Sciences. See: Thrush; Webster's 3d.

Horton's disease (1) (Horton, Bayard Taylor): Medicine. See: Jablonski. Also known as: Horton–Magath–Brown syndrome.

Horton's neuralgia (headache, cephalgia, disease (2), or syndrome) (Horton, Bayard Taylor): Medicine. See: Dorland; Hinsie; Jablonski; Stedman. Also known as: Bing–Horton syndrome, Bing's erythroprosopalgia (or syndrome), Harris' neuralgia.

Horvitz & Thompson estimator (Horvitz, Daniel Goodman and Thompson, Donovan Jerome): Statistics. See: Kendall.

HORVITZ, DANIEL GOODMAN. 1921– . American statistician. See: Amer. Men Sci., 11th ed. Horvitz & Thompson estimator.

HORWOOD, EDWARD J. fl. 1912. English engineer. Cited in: Chem. Abstr. Horwood process.

Horwood process (Horwood, Edward J.): Engineering and Industry. See: Hackh; Thrush.

HOSACK, DAVID. 1769–1835. American physician. See: Dict. Sci. Biog. Hosackia.

Hosackia (Hosack, David): Botany. See: Hendrickson; Taylor, N.; Webster's 3d.

Hosemann, Andreas. See: Osiander, Andreas.

Hoshida reagent (Derivation undetermined): Chemistry. See: Van Nostrand Chem. Dict.

Hoskin furnace (Derivation undetermined): Engineering and Industry. See: Hackh.

Hoskold formula (Hoskold, Henry Davis): Engineering and Industry. See: Thrush.

HOSKOLD, HENRY DAVIS. fl. 1889–1902. English engineer. Cited in: Mansell. Hoskold formula.

Hospitallers (or Brother Hospitaler) of St. John of God (John of God, Saint): Religion. See: Attwater; Webster's 3d.

HOST, NICOLAUS THOMAS. 1761–1834. Austrian botanist. See: Oesterr. Biog. Lex., 1815–1950. Hosta.

Hosta (Host, Nicolaus Thomas): Botany. See: Taylor, N. under "Plantain-Lily."

Hotchkiss (1) (cannon) (Hotchkiss, Benjamin Berkeley): Weapons. See: Mathews, M. M.; Quick.

HOTCHKISS, BENJAMIN BERKELEY. 1826–1885. American inventor. See: World Who's Who Sci. Hotchkiss (1) (cannon), Hotchkiss machine gun (or Hotchkiss (2)), Hotchkiss magazine rifle (or Hotchkiss (3)).

HOTCHKISS, LUCIUS WALES. 1859–1926. American surgeon. See: Who Was Who Amer., 1897–1942. Hotchkiss' operation.

Hotchkiss machine gun (or Hotchkiss (2)) (Hotchkiss, Benjamin Berkeley): Weapons. See: Encyc. Brit., 1973 under "Machine Gun," vol. 14, p. 522b; Partridge; Quick.

Hotchkiss magazine rifle (or Hotchkiss (3)) (Hotchkiss, Benjamin Berkeley): Weapons. See: Partridge.

Hotchkiss' operation (Hotchkiss, Lucius Wales): Medicine. See: Dorland.

Hotchkiss superdip (Hotchkiss, William Otis): Engineering and Industry. See: Thrush.

HOTCHKISS, WILLIAM OTIS. b. 1878. American engineer and geologist. See: Who's Who Engin., 1922–1923. Hotchkiss superdip.

HOTELLING, HAROLD. 1895– . American statistician. See: World Who's Who Sci. Hotelling–Kelly method of factor analysis, Hotelling's T.

Hotelling–Kelly method of factor analysis (Hotelling, Harold and Kelly): Statistics. See: Good.

Hotelling's T (Hotelling, Harold): Statistics. See: Internat. Dict. Ap. Math.; Kendall; Van Nostrand Sci. Encyc.

HOTIS, RALPH P. 1890–1935. American agricultural marketing specialist. Cited in: Mansell. Hotis test.

Hotis test (Hotis, Ralph P.): Agriculture. See: Webster's 3d.; Winburne.

"Hotspur." See: Percy, Sir Henry "Hotspur."

Hotspur (Percy, Sir Henry "Hotspur"): Generic Word (fiery-tempered person). See: Brewer.

HOTTON, PETER. 1648-1709. Dutch botanist and physician. See: Biog. Lex. hervorr. Aerzte. Hottonia.

Hottonia (Hotton, Peter): Botany. See: Webster's 3d.

Hotz-Anagnostakis operation (Hotz, Ferdinand Carl and Anagnostakis, Andreas): Medicine. See: Stedman.

HOTZ, FERDINAND CARL. 1843-1908. American ophthalmologist. See: Dict. Amer. Biog. Hotz-Anagnostakis operation.

Houben-Fischer synthesis (Houben, Josef and Fischer, Walter): Chemistry. See: Van Nostrand Chem. Dict.

Houben-Hoesch synthesis (Houben, Josef and Hoesch, Kurt): Chemistry. See: Ballentyne.

HOUBEN, JOSEF. 1875-1940. German organic chemist. See: World Who's Who Sci. Houben-Fischer synthesis, Houben-Hoesch synthesis.

Houdini (Houdini, Harry): Generic Word (magician). See: Hendrickson.

HOUDINI, HARRY (Real name: EHRICH WEISS). 1875-1926. American magician. See: Dict. Amer. Biog. Houdini, pull a Houdini (or do a Houdini).

HOUDRY, EUGENE J. 1892-1962. French-born American engineer. See: World Who's Who Sci. Houdry process.

Houdry process (Houdry, Eugene J.): Engineering and Industry. See: Van Nostrand Chem. Dict.; Van Nostrand Sci. Encyc. under "Gasoline"; Webster's 3d.

Houghton current (Derivation undetermined): Botany. See: Winburne.

HOUGHTON, ELIJAH MARK. 1867-1937. American physician. See: Nat. Cycl. Amer. Biog., vol. 31, pp. 168-169. Houghton's test.

Houghton's test (Houghton, Elijah Mark): Medicine. See: Dorland; Stedman.

HOUMY, COMTESSE DE. No dates. French noblewoman. (Biography source unavailable.) a la Houmy (style).

HOUNSFIELD, LESLIE HAYWOOD. fl. 1930. English engineer. Cited in: Chem. Abstr., Decenn. Index, 1927-1936. Hounsfield tensometer.

Hounsfield tensometer (Hounsfield, Leslie Haywood): Engineering and Industry. See: Auger.

HOURI. Beautiful woman who awaits the devout Muslim in paradise. See: Encyc. Brit., 1973. Houri.

Houri (Houri, the damsel): Generic Word (dark-eyed, beautiful woman). See: Brewer.

Houssay animal (or phenomenon) (Houssay, Bernardo Alberto): Medicine. See: Dorland; Stedman.

HOUSSAY, BERNARDO ALBERTO. b. 1887. Argentinian physiologist. See: World Who's Who Sci. Houssay animal (or phenomenon), Houssay's syndrome (or phenomenon in man).

Houssay-Biasotti syndrome (Houssay, Bernardo Alberto and Biasotti, Alfredo): See: Houssay's syndrome (or phenomenon in man).

Houssay's syndrome (or phenomenon in man) (Houssay, Bernardo Alberto): Medicine. See: Jablonski; Stedman. Also known as: Houssay-Biasotti syndrome.

HOUSTON, JOHN. 1802-1845. Irish physician. See: Dict. Nat. Biog. Houston's muscle, Houston's valve (fold or valve of Houston).

HOUSTON, SAMUEL. 1793-1863. American soldier and politician. See: Dict. Amer. Biog. Houstonize.

HOUSTON, WILLIAM. ca. 1695-1733. English physician and botanist. See: Dict. Nat. Biog. Houstonia.

Houstonia (Houston, William): Botany. See: Charnock; Mathews, M. M.; Partridge; Taylor, N.; Webster's 3d.

Houstonize (Houston, Samuel): History. See: Mathews, M. M.

Houston's muscle (Houston, John): Anatomy. See: Dorland; Stedman.

Houston's valve (fold or valve of Houston) (Houston, John): Anatomy. See: Donath; Dorland; Stedman; Webster's 3d. Also known as: Kohlrausch's folds (or valves).

HOUTTUYN, MARTINUS. b. 1720. Dutch physician. See: Biog. Woordenb. der Nederl. (Aa). Houttuynia.

Houttuynia (Houttuyn, Martinus): Botany. See: Charnock.

HOUWER, A. W. M. fl. 20th c. Dutch physician. (Biography source unavailable.) Gougerot-Houwer-Sjoegren syndrome.

HOUZEAU, AUGUSTE. 1829-1911. French chemist. See: World Who's Who Sci. Houzeau reagents for ozone.

Houzeau reagents for ozone (Houzeau, Auguste): Chemistry. See: Van Nostrand Chem. Dict.

HOVDA, OLAF. b. 1875. American physicist. See: Amer. Men Sci., 4th ed. Stewart-Hovda relationship.

HOVEN (TEN HOVE), DAVID. d. 1787. Dutch senator. (Biography source unavailable.) Hovenia.

Hovenia (Hoven, David): Botany. See: Charnock; Taylor, N.; Webster's 3d.

HOVIUS, JACOBUS. 1710-1786. Dutch anatomist. See: Biog. Lex. hervorr. Aerzte. canal of Hovius, Hovius' membrane, Hovius' plexus.

Hovius' membrane (Hovius, Jacobus): Medicine. See: Kelly.

Hovius' plexus (Hovius, Jacobus): Medicine. See: Kelly. Also known as: Leber's plexus.

Hovorka-Sykora reagent (Hovorka, Vaclav and Sykora, Vaclav): Chemistry. See: Van Nostrand Chem. Dict.

HOVORKA, VACLAV. fl. 1938-1952. Czechoslovakian chemist. Cited in: Chem. Abstr., vol. 32, p. 4460? Hovorka-Sykora reagent.

HOW, HENRY. 1827-1879. Canadian mineralogist. Cited in: Mansell. Howlite.

HOWARD, BENJAMIN DOUGLAS. 1840-1900. American physician. See: Med.-Chir. Trans., London, vol. 84 (1901), p. cx. Howard's method.

Howard boiler (Howard, J. and Howard, F.): Engineering and Industry. See: Auger.

HOWARD, BURTON JAMES. b. 1872. American bacteriologist. See: Amer. Men Sci., 8th ed. Howard chamber?

Howard chamber (Howard, Burton James?): Biology. See: Hackh.

HOWARD, SIR CHARLES. d. 1765. English soldier. See: Dict. Nat. Biog. Green Howards.

HOWARD, EDGAR. 1858-1951. American legislator. See: Biog. Direct. Amer. Congress. Wheeler-Howard Act.

HOWARD, F. fl. 19th c. English engineer. (Biography source unavailable.) Howard boiler.

HOWARD, HENRY FITZALAN, 15TH DUKE OF NORFOLK. 1847-1917. English statesman. See: Dict. Nat. Biog., 3d suppl. Norfolk Commission.

HOWARD, J. fl. 19th c. English engineer. (Biography source unavailable.) Howard boiler.

HOWARD, JOHN EAGER. 1902- . American physician. See: World Who's Who Sci. Ellsworth-Howard test.

HOWARD, LELAND OSSIAN. 1857-1950. American entomologist. See: Dict. Sci. Biog. Howard method for worm count?, Howard scale?

Howard Libbey (redwood) (Libbey, Howard): Botany. See: Hendrickson under "Sequoia..."

HOWARD, LUKE. 1772-1864. English meteorologist. See: World Who's Who Sci. Howardite.

Howard method for worm count (Howard, Leland Ossian?): Agriculture.

Howard, Norfolk. See: Bug, Joshua.

Howard scale (Howard, Leland Ossian?): Zoology. See: Winburne.

HOWARD, THOMAS, 14TH EARL OF ARUNDEL. 1586-1646. English art collector. See: Dict. Nat. Biog. Arundel prints, Arundel Society (and Club), Arundelian (or Arundel) marbles.

Howardite (Howard, Luke): Earth Sciences. See: Webster's 3d.

Howard's method (Howard, Benjamin Douglas): Medicine. See: Dorland; Stedman.

Howe factor (Howe, Horace Albert?): Physics. See: Hughes.

HOWE, HORACE ALBERT. 1922-   . American physicist. See: Amer. Men Sci., 9th ed. Howe factor?

HOWE, JOHN. 1855-1922. Australian champion shearer. See: Australian Encyc. Jackie Howe (shirt).

Howe link motion (Howe, William): Engineering and Industry. See: Auger.

HOWE, PERCY. 1864-1950. American dentist. See: World Who's Who Sci. Howe's silver precipitation method.

Howe truss (Howe, William): Engineering and Industry. See: Webster's 3d.

HOWE, WILLIAM. 1803-1852. American inventor. See: Dict. Amer. Biog. Howe link motion, Howe truss.

Howell (1) (duplicate bridge game) (Howell, Edwin C.): Recreation and Sports. See: Webster's 3d.

HOWELL, EDWIN C. d. 1907. American journalist and whist expert. Cited in: Mansell. Howell (1) (duplicate bridge game), Howell settlement, Howell system (movement or Howell (2)).

HOWELL, J. T. fl. 1915. American engineer. (Biography source unavailable.) White-Howell furnace?

HOWELL, JOHN ADAMS. 1840-1918. American soldier and inventor. See: Dict. Amer. Biog. Howell (revolver)?

Howell-Jolly bodies (Howell, William Henry and Jolly, Justin M. J.): Medicine. See: Dorland; Stedman; Webster's 3d. Also known as: Howell's bodies, Jolly bodies.

Howell (revolver) (Howell, John Adams?): Weapons. See: Partridge.

Howell settlement (Howell, Edwin C.): Recreation and Sports. See: Webster's 3d.

Howell system (movement or Howell (2)) (Howell, Edwin C.): Recreation and Sports. See: Webster's 3d.

Howell unit (Howell, William Henry): Medicine. See: Stedman.

HOWELL, WILLIAM HENRY. 1860-1945. American physiologist. See: Dict. Sci. Biog. Howell-Jolly bodies, Howell unit.

Howell's bodies (Howell, William Henry). See: Howell-Jolly bodies.

Howe's silver precipitation method (Howe, Percy): Dentistry. See: Stedman.

Howlite (How, Henry): Earth Sciences. See: Webster's 3d.

HOWSHIP, JOHN. 1781-1841. English anatomist. See: Biog. Lex. hervorr. Aerzte. Howship-Romberg syndrome (symptom or sign), Howship's lacuna (or lacunae).

Howship-Romberg syndrome (symptom or sign) (Howship, John and Romberg, Moritz H.): Medicine. See: Dorland; Jablonski; Stedman. Also known as: Howship's symptom, Romberg-Howship sign, Romberg's sign (or symptom) (2).

Howship's lacuna (or lacunae) (Howship, John): Anatomy. See: Donath; Dorland; Gray; Stedman; Webster's 3d.

Howship's symptom (Howship, John). See: Howship-Romberg syndrome (symptom or sign).

HOY, THOMAS. fl. 1788-1809. English gardener. See: Britten and Boulger. Hoya.

Hoya (Hoy, Thomas): Botany. See: Taylor, N.

HOYER, HEINRICH F. 1834-1907. Polish anatomist and histologist. See: Biog. Lex. hervorr. Aerzte. Hoyer's canals.

Hoyer's canals (Hoyer, Heinrich F.): Medicine. See: Stedman.

Hoyle (Hoyle, Edmond). See: according to Hoyle.

HOYLE, EDMOND. 1672-1769. English whist expert. See: Dict. Nat. Biog. according to Hoyle (or Hoyle), Hoyle's laws.

Hoyle's laws (Hoyle, Edmond): Recreation and Sports. See: Harvey under "Hoyle, Edmond."

HOYT, CYRIL J. 1905-   . American psychologist. See: Amer. Men Sci., 10th ed., Soc. and Behav. Hoyt formula.

Hoyt formula (Hoyt, Cyril J.): Statistics. See: English; Wolman.

HOZAY, JEAN. fl. 1953. French neurologist. (Biography source unavailable.) Van Bogaert-Hozay syndrome.

Hozay's syndrome (Hozay, Jean). See: Van Bogaert-Hozay syndrome.

HRDLICKA, M. fl. 1937. Czechoslovakian chemist. Cited in: Chem. Abstr., vol. 31, p. 4225. Dubsky-Hrdlicka reagent.

Hubam clover (or sweetclover) (Hughes, Harold De Mott and Alabama): Botany. See: Webster's 3d.; Winburne.

HUBBARD, BERNARD ROSECRANS. 1889-1962. American Jesuit priest, explorer and photographer. See: Who Was Who Amer., 1961-1968. Hubbard cloth.

Hubbard cloth (Hubbard, Bernard Rosecrans): Fashion. See: Picken.

Hubbard distributor (Hubbard, Prevost?): Engineering and Industry. See: Thrush.

HUBBARD, ELBERT GREEN. 1856-1915. American author, editor and publisher. See: Dict. Amer. Biog. Elbert Hubbard tie.

HUBBARD, PREVOST. b. 1881. American chemical engineer. See: Amer. Men Sci., 9th ed. Hubbard distributor?

HUBBENET (HEBBENET). fl. 1860. French? physician. (Biography source unavailable.) Hubbenet's spots.

Hubbenet's spots (Hubbenet). See: Bitot's spots.

Hubble Atlas of Galaxies (Hubble, Edwin Powell): Astronomy. See: Encyc. Brit., 1973 under "Nebula," vol. 16, p. 173a; Monkhouse under "Atlas."

Hubble constant (Hubble, Edwin Powell): Astronomy. See: Internat. Dict. Phys. Elec.; Satterthwaite; Van Nostrand Sci. Encyc.

HUBBLE, EDWIN POWELL. 1889-1953. American astronomer. See: Dict. Sci. Biog. Hubble Atlas of Galaxies, Hubble constant, Hubble radius, Hubble('s) law (effect or law of red shifts), Hubble's distance scale.

Hubble('s) law (effect or law of red shifts) (Hubble, Edwin Powell): Astronomy. See: Ballentyne; Encyc. Brit., 1973 under "Nebula," vol. 16, p. 180c; Internat. Dict. Phys. Elec.; Satterthwaite; Thewlis; Van Nostrand Sci. Encyc.

Hubble radius (Hubble, Edwin Powell): Astronomy. See: Asimov.

Hubble's distance scale (Hubble, Edwin Powell): Astronomy. See: Encyc. Brit., 1973 under "Nebula," vol. 16, p. 178Bc.

HUBBS, CLARK LEAVITT. b. 1894. American zoologist. See: Amer. Men and Women Sci., 12th ed. novumbra Hubbsi.

HUBER, JOHANN JACOB. 1707-1778. Swiss anatomist. See: Dict. Sci. Biog. Huber's ganglion.

HUBER, MAKSYMILIAN TYTUS. 1872-1950. Polish engineer. See: Dict. Sci. Biog. Huber-Mises-Hencky theory.

Huber-Mises-Hencky theory (Huber, Maksymilian Tytus; Mises, Richard von; and Hencky, Heinrich): Engineering and Industry. See: Dict. Sci. Biog. under "Huber, M. T."

Huber solution (Derivation undetermined): Chemistry. See: Van Nostrand Chem. Dict.

Huber's ganglion (Huber, Johann Jacob): Anatomy. See: Stedman.

HUBERT, ANDRE. fl. 1894. Swiss chemist. Cited in: Royal Soc. Cat. Sci. Pap., 1884-1900. Pictet-Hubert reaction.

HUBERT, SAINT. b. ca. 656-d. ca. 727. Belgian bishop. See: Holweck. Order of St. Hubert, Saint Hubert's disease.

HUBRECHT, AMBROSIUS ARNOLD WILLEM. 1858-1915. Dutch zoologist and comparative anatomist. See: Dict. Sci. Biog. Hubrecht's protochordal knot.

Hubrecht's protochordal knot (Hubrecht, Ambrosius Arnold Willem): Anatomy. See: Stedman. Also known as: Hensen's node.

HUCHARD, HENRI. 1844-1910. French physician. See: World Who's Who Sci. Huchard's disease.

Huchard's disease (Huchard, Henri): Medicine. See: Dorland; Stedman.

Hucker-Conn solution (Hucker, George James and Conn, Harold Joel): Medicine. See: Stedman.

HUCKER, GEORGE JAMES. b. 1893. American bacteriologist. See: Amer. Men Sci., 8th ed. Hucker-Conn solution.

JDIBRAS. Hero of Samuel Butler's poem "Hudibras" (1663-1678). See: Jobes. dibrastic (or Hudibrastic verse).

dibrastic (or Hudibrastic verse) (Hudibras, the literary character): Literature. e: Barnet; Charnock; Preminger; Webster's 3d.

JDSON, ARTHUR CYRIL. 1875-1962. English ophthalmologist. See: Who as Who, 1961-1970. Hudson-Staehli line.

dson Award (Hudson, Claude Silbert): Chemistry. Cited in: Nat. Acad. i. Biog. Mem., vol. 32 (1958), p. 189.

JDSON, CLAUDE SILBERT. 1881-1952. American chemist. See: World no's Who Sci. Hudson Award, Hudson isorotation rule(s) (or rule), Hudson ctone rule, Levene-Hudson isorotation rule.

JDSON, HERBERT EDSON, JR. 1910- . American civil engineer and emist. See: Amer. Men Sci., 11th ed. Hudson-Jardi design (rain intensity uge).

dson isorotation rule(s) (or rule) (Hudson, Claude Silbert): Chemistry. See: ckh; Van Nostrand Chem. Dict.

dson-Jardi design (rain intensity gauge) (Hudson, Herbert Edson, Jr.? and rdi y Barras, Ramon?): Earth Sciences. See: Van Nostrand Sci. Encyc. der "Precipitation Gauge."

dson lactone rule (Hudson, Claude Silbert): Chemistry. See: Van Nostrand em. Dict.

dson-Staehli line (Hudson, Arthur Cyril and Staehli, Jean): Medicine. See: blonski; Stedman. Also known as: Hudson's line, Staehli's line.

JDSON, WILLIAM. 1733-1793. English botanist. See: Dict. Sci. Biog. dsonia.

JDSON, WILLIAM HENRY. 1841-1922. Argentinian-born English naturalist d author. See: Webster's Biog. Dict. circus Hudsonicus?

dsonia (Hudson, William): Botany. See: Charnock; Mathews, M. M.; ebster's 3d.

dson's line (Hudson, Arthur Cyril). See: Hudson-Staehli line.

JEAT, G. J. fl. 1931. Dutch pediatrician. Cited in: Kelly. Pelger-eat anomaly (or phenomenon).

ebl number (Derivation undetermined): Chemistry. See: Hackh; Thrush.

ebl solution (Derivation undetermined): Chemistry. See: Hackh; Van ostrand Chem. Dict.

ebl-Waller reagent (Derivation undetermined): Chemistry. See: Van Nostrand em. Dict.

JEBNER, ADOLF. fl. 19th c. German mine superintendent. Cited in: iley. Huebnerite (or Hubnerite).

JEBNER, OTTO. fl. 1956. German cell pathologist. (Biography source available.) Nierhoff-Huebner syndrome.

ebnerite (or Hubnerite) (Huebner, Adolf): Earth Sciences. See: Thrush; ebster's 3d.

JECK, ALEXANDER FRIEDRICH. 1802-1842. German anatomist. See: orld Who's Who Sci. Hueck's ligament.

JECKEL, ERICH ARMAND ARTHUR JOSEPH. 1896- . German physicist. e: Pogg., vol. 6. Debye-Hueckel equation, Debye-Hueckel limiting law, ebye-Hueckel-Onsager equation, Debye-Hueckel theory, Debye-Hueckel eory of conductivity (of electrolytes).

JECKEL, WALTER KARL FRIEDRICH. 1895- . German physical chemist. e: Pogg., vol. 6. Hund-Mulliken-Hueckel method?

eck's ligament (Hueck, Alexander Friedrich): Anatomy. See: Dorland; edman. Also known as: Gerlach's valvula.

UEFNER, CARL GUSTAV VON. 1840-1908. German physiologist. See: og. Lex. hervorr. Aerzte, 1880-1930. Huefner (Huebner) rhomb, Hufner's quation.

efner (Huebner) rhomb (Huefner, Carl Gustav von): Physics. See: Internat. ict. Phys. Elec.; Thewlis.

efner spectrophotometer (Von Huefner, Carl Gustav): Physics. See: Internat. ict. Phys. Elec.

UEGEL, BARON VON. fl. ca. 1915? German mineralogist. Cited in: iley. Huegelite.

Huegelite (Huegel, Baron von): Earth Sciences. See: Thrush.

Huelsemann incident (or letter) (Huelsemann, Johann Georg): History. See: Dict. Amer. Hist.; Morris and Irwin.

HUELSEMANN, JOHANN GEORG. fl. 1850. Austrian diplomat in America. Cited in: Mansell. Huelsemann incident (or letter).

HUENEFELD, FRIEDRICH LUDWIG. 1799-1882. German chemist. See: Biog. Lex. hervorr. Aerzte. Huenefeld('s) solution.

Huenefeld('s) solution (Huenefeld, Friedrich Ludwig): Medicine. See: Dorland; Hackh; Van Nostrand Chem. Dict.

HUENERMANN, CARL. fl. 1937. German physician. (Biography source unavailable.) Conradi-Huenermann syndrome.

Huenermann's syndrome (Huenermann, Carl). See: Conradi-Huenermann syndrome.

HUEPPE, FERDINAND. 1852-1938. German bacteriologist. See: World Who's Who Sci. Hueppe's disease.

Hueppe's disease (Hueppe, Ferdinand): Medicine. See: Dorland.

Huernia (Huernius, Justus): Botany. See: Charnock; Taylor, N.

HUERNIUS, JUSTUS. fl. 18th c.? Dutch botanist in South Africa. (Biography source unavailable.) Huernia.

Huerthle cell (Huerthle, Karl W.): Medicine. See: Dorland; Stedman.

Huerthle cell adenoma (Huerthle, Karl W.): Medicine. See: Stedman.

Huerthle cell tumor (or carcinoma) (Huerthle, Karl W.): Medicine. See: Stedman.

HUERTHLE, KARL W. 1860-1945. German histologist. See: Biog. Lex. hervorr. Aerzte, 1880-1930. Huerthle cell, Huerthle cell adenoma, Huerthle cell tumor (or carcinoma).

HUETER, KARL. 1838-1882. German surgeon. See: Biog. Lex. hervorr. Aerzte. Hueter's maneuver, Hueter's sign, Vogt-Hueter point.

Hueter's maneuver (Hueter, Karl): Medicine. See: Dorland; Stedman.

Hueter's sign (Hueter, Karl): Medicine. See: Dorland; Stedman.

Huettig equation (Huettig, Gustav Franz): Physics. See: Ballentyne.

HUETTIG, GUSTAV FRANZ. 1890-1957. Austrian chemist. See: Pogg., vols. 6, 7a. Huettig equation.

HUFNAGEL, CHARLES ANTHONY. 1916- . American surgeon. See: Amer. Men and Women Sci., 12th ed. Hufnagel valve.

Hufnagel valve (Hufnagel, Charles Anthony): Medicine. See: Dorland; Stedman.

Hufner's equation (Huefner, Carl Gustav von): Medicine. See: Stedman.

HUGGENBERGER, ARNOLD U. b. 1895. Swiss engineer. Cited in: Mansell. Huggenberger extensometer.

Huggenberger extensometer (Huggenberger, Arnold U.): Engineering and Industry. See: Auger; Encyc. Brit., 1973 under "Strain Gauge," vol. 21, p. 285c.

Huggins bands (Huggins, Sir William): Physics. See: Huschke. Also known as: Chappuis' bands.

HUGGINS, CHARLES BRENTON. 1901- . American surgeon. See: World Who's Who Sci. Huggins-Miller-Jensen test, Huggins' operation.

HUGGINS, MAURICE LOYAL. 1897- . American chemist. See: World Who's Who Sci. Flory-Huggins effect.

Huggins-Miller-Jensen test (Huggins, Charles Brenton; Miller, Gerald M.; and Jensen, Elwood Vernon): Medicine. See: Stedman.

Huggins' operation (Huggins, Charles Brenton): Medicine. See: Dorland; Stedman.

Huggins test (Huggins, Charles Brenton). See: Huggins-Miller-Jensen test.

HUGGINS, SIR WILLIAM. 1824-1910. English astronomer. See: Dict. Sci. Biog. Huggins bands.

HUGH CAPET. ca. 938-996. King of France. See: Encyc. Brit., 1973. Capetian dynasty.

HUGHES, DUDLEY MAYS. 1848-1927. American legislator. See: Biog. Direct. Amer. Congress. Smith-Hughes Act.

HUGHES, HAROLD DE MOTT. b. 1882. American agronomist. See: Amer. Men Sci., 10th ed. Hubam clover (or sweetclover).

HUGHES, JOHN PATTESON. fl. 1952-1972. English physician. See: Med. Direct., 1972. Hughes-Stovin syndrome.

Hughes-Stovin syndrome (Hughes, John Patteson and Stovin, Peter George Ingle): Medicine. See: Jablonski.

Hughes virus (Derivation undetermined): Medicine. See: Stedman.

HUGHES, WILLIAM C. 1844-1908. English optician and inventor. See: Focal Encyc. Film. Kelvin-Hughes projector, Kelvin-Hughes system of rapid processing?

Hughlings Jackson. See: Jackson, John Hughlings.

Hughlings Jackson's syndrome (Jackson, John Hughlings). See: Jackson's syndrome.

HUGILL, W. fl. 1926. English chemist. Cited in: Chem. Abstr., vol. 20, p. 1733. Rees-Hugill flask.

HUGO, AUGUSTUS JOANNES. fl. 1732. Botanist. Cited in: Mansell. Hugonia.

Hugo, King. See: "King Hugo."

HUGO, VICTOR MARIE. 1802-1885. French writer. See: Encyc. Brit., 1973. Hugoesque.

Hugoesque (Hugo, Victor Marie): Literature. See: Webster's 3d.

HUGON, PIERRE. fl. 1865. French engineer. (Biography source unavailable.) Hugon's engine.

Hugonia (Hugo, Augustus Joannes): Botany. See: Charnock.

Hugoniot curve (Hugoniot, Henri): Physics. See: Thewlis; Thrush.

Hugoniot equation (Hugoniot, Henri): Physics. See: Thewlis.

HUGONIOT, HENRI (In full: PIERRE HENRI). 1851-1887. French engineer. See: Dict. Sci. Biog. Hugoniot curve, Hugoniot equation, Rankine-Hugoniot relations.

Hugon's engine (Hugon, Pierre): Engineering and Industry. See: Auger.

HUGUENIN, GUSTAVE. 1841-1920. Swiss physician. See: Biog. Lex. hervorr. Aerzte, 1880-1930. Huguenin's edema.

Huguenin's edema (Huguenin, Gustave): Medicine. See: Dorland.

Huguenot(s) (Hugues, Besancon? or King Hugo?): History. See: Charnock; Encyc. Brit., 1973; Harbottle; Partridge; Webster's 3d.

HUGUES, BESANCON. d. 1532. Swiss political leader. (Biography source unavailable.) Huguenot(s)?

Huguier-Jersild syndrome (Huguier, Pierre Charles and Jersild, Olaf): Medicine. See: Jablonski. Also known as: Jersild's syndrome.

HUGUIER, PIERRE CHARLES. 1804-1874. French surgeon. See: World Who's Who Sci. Huguier-Jersild syndrome, Huguier's canal, Huguier's circle, Huguier's sinus, Huguier's theory.

Huguier's canal (Huguier, Pierre Charles): Anatomy. See: Dorland; Stedman.

Huguier's circle (Huguier, Pierre Charles): Anatomy. See: Dorland; Stedman.

Huguier's sinus (Huguier, Pierre Charles): Anatomy. See: Stedman.

Huguier's theory (Huguier, Pierre Charles): Medicine. See: Stedman.

HUHNER, MAX. 1873-1947. American urologist. See: World Who's Who Sci. Huhner test.

Huhner test (Huhner, Max): Medicine. See: Dorland; Stedman; Webster's 3d.

HUIZINGA, DERK. 1840-1903. Dutch physiologist. See: Nederl. Tijdschr. v. geneesk., Amsterdam, vol. 39 (1903, 2R), d. 1, pp. 1193-1196. Huizinga reagent for ozone.

Huizinga reagent for ozone (Huizinga, Derk): Chemistry. See: Van Nostrand Chem. Dict.

HULETT, GEORGE AUGUSTUS. 1867-1955. American physical chemist. See: Who Was Who Amer., 1951-1960. Hulett still.

Hulett still (Hulett, George Augustus): Chemistry. See: Hackh.

HULL, ALBERT WALLACE. 1880-1966. American physicist. See: World Who's Who Sci. Debye-Scherrer-Hull method, Hull magnetron.

Hull cell (Hull, R. O.): Chemistry. See: Thrush.

HULL, CLARK LEONARD. 1884-1952. American psychologist. See: World Who's Who Sci. Hull's mathematico-deductive theory of learning.

HULL, ISAAC. 1773-1843. American naval officer. See: Dict. Amer. Biog. Hull's victory.

Hull magnetron (Hull, Albert Wallace): Physics. See: Internat. Dict. Phys. Elec.

HULL, R. O. fl. 1939-1953. American electrochemist. Cited in: Mansell. Hull cell.

Hull (to defeat) (Hull, William): History. See: Mathews, M. M.

HULL, WILLIAM. 1753-1825. American soldier. See: Dict. Amer. Biog. Hull (to defeat).

Hull's mathematico-deductive theory of learning (Hull, Clark Leonard): Psychology. See: Chaplin; Wolman.

Hull's triad (Derivation undetermined): Medicine. See: Stedman.

Hull's victory (Hull, Isaac): History. See: Mathews, M. M.

HULSE, JOHN. 1708-1790. English clergyman. See: Dict. Nat. Biog. Hulsean lectures, Hulsean prizes, Hulsean professorship.

Hulsean lectures (Hulse, John): Religion. See: Brewer; Canney; Latham; Weekley.

Hulsean prizes (Hulse, John): Cited in: Webster's Biog. Dict. under "Hulse, John."

Hulsean professorship (Hulse, John): Religion. See: Harvey under "Hulse, John."

Hulsite (Brooks, Alfred Hulse): Earth Sciences. See: Webster's 3d.

HULTKRANTZ, JOHAN VILHELM. 1862-1938. Swedish physician. See: Biog. Lex. hervorr. Aerzte. Hultkrantz's syndrome?

Hultkrantz's syndrome (Hultkrantz, Johan Vilhelm?). See: Scheuthauer-Marie-Sainton syndrome.

HUMBER, JOHN DAVIS. 1895- . American physician. See: Who's Who Among Physicians and Surg. Coffey-Humber method.

Humble detaching hook (Derivation undetermined): Engineering and Industry. See: Thrush.

Humbold penetrometer (Derivation undetermined): Engineering and Industry. See: Hackh.

HUMBOLDT, BARON ALEXANDER (In full: FRIEDRICH HEINRICH ALEXANDER) VON. 1769-1859. German naturalist, traveler and statesman. See: Dict. Sci. Biog. Humboldt current, Humboldt('s) lily, Humboldtilite, Humboldtine (or humboldtite (2)), Humboldtite (1).

Humboldt current (Humboldt, Baron Alexander von): Earth Sciences. See: Asimov; Huschke; Van Nostrand Sci. Encyc.

Humboldt jig (Derivation undetermined): Engineering and Industry. See: Thrush.

Humboldt('s) lily (Humboldt, Baron Alexander von): Botany. See: Webster's 3d.; Winburne.

HUMBOLDT, BARON WILHELM FREIHERR VON. 1767-1835. German philologist, diplomat and man of letters. See: New Encyc. Brit., 1974, Microp. Humboldtism.

Humboldtilite (Humboldt, Baron Alexander von): Earth Sciences. See: Thrush.

Humboldtine (or Humboldtite (2)) (Humboldt, Baron Alexander von): Earth Sciences. See: Charnock; Thrush; Webster's 3d.

Humboldtism (Humboldt, Baron Wilhelm Freiherr von). See: Whorfian hypotesis.

Humboldtite (1) (Humboldt, Baron Alexander von): Earth Sciences. See: Charnock; Webster's 3d.

HUME, SIR ABRAHAM. 1749-1838. English scientist. See: Dict. Nat. Biog. Humite.

HUME, LADY AMELIA (nee EGERTON). 1751-1809. English botanical student. See: Britten and Boulger. Humea.

HUME, DAVID. 1711-1776. Scottish philosopher. See: Internat. Encyc. Soc. Sci. Humism (or Humean empiricism).

HUME, JOSEPH. 1777-1855. English physician and radical politician. See: Dict. Nat. Biog. Joey (or Joe).

Hume-Rothery rule(s) (Hume-Rothery, William): Chemistry. See: Ballentyne; Hackh; Internat. Dict. Ap. Math.; Van Nostrand Chem. Dict.; Thewlis; Van Nostrand Sci. Encyc.

HUME-ROTHERY, WILLIAM. 1899-1968. English metallurgist. See: Dict. Sci. Biog. Hume-Rothery rule(s).

Humea (Hume, Lady Amelia): Botany. See: Taylor, N.

HUMFREY, JOHN CHARLES WILLIS. fl. 1912-1919. English engineer. Cited in: Mansell. Humfrey machine, Humfrey reagent.

Humfrey machine (Humfrey, John Charles Willis): Engineering and Industry. See: Auger.

Humfrey reagent (Humfrey, John Charles Willis): Chemistry. See: Van Nostrand Chem. Dict.

Humism (or Humean empiricism) (Hume, David): Philosophy. See: Urmson; Weekley.

Humite (Hume, Sir Abraham): Earth Sciences. See: Charnock.

HUMM, DONCASTER GEORGE. 1887-1959. American psychologist. See: Amer. Men Sci., 9th ed., Soc. and Behav. Humm-Wadsworth temperament scale.

Humm-Wadsworth temperament scale (Humm, Doncaster George and Wadsworth, Guy Woodbridge, Jr.): Psychology. See: Chaplin; English; Wolman.

HUMPHREY, DUKE OF GLOUCESTER AND EARL OF PEMBROKE. 1391-1447. English statesman and patron of arts. See: Dict. Nat. Biog. dine with Duke Humphrey.

Humphrey gas pump (Humphrey, Herbert Alfred): Engineering and Industry. See: Auger.

HUMPHREY, GEORGE. 1889-1966. English psychologist. See: World Who's Who Sci. Humphrey's paradox?

HUMPHREY, HERBERT ALFRED. 1868-1951. English engineer. See: Who Was Who, 1951-1960. Humphrey gas pump.

HUMPHREY, IRVIN W. fl. 1938. American chemist. Cited in: Chem. Abstr., vol 32, p. 4366. Humphrey process.

Humphrey process (Humphrey, Irvin W.): Chemistry. See: Van Nostrand Chem. Dict.

HUMPHREYS, CURTIS JUDSON. 1898- . American physicist. See: World Who's Who Sci. Humphreys series.

Humphreys engine (or constant compression engine) (Humphreys, I. B.): Engineering and Industry. See: Auger.

HUMPHREYS, I. B. fl. 20th c. Engineer. (Biography source unavailable.) Humphreys engine (or constant compression engine).

Humphrey's paradox (Humphrey, George?): Physiology. See: English.

Humphreys series (Humphreys, Curtis Judson): Physics. See: Thewlis.

Humphries equation (Derivation undetermined): Physics. See: Van Nostrand Sci. Encyc.

HUMPHRY, GEORGE MURRAY. 1820-1896. English surgeon. See: Dict. Nat. Biog., 1st suppl. Humphry's ligament.

Humphry's ligament (Humphry, George Murray): Anatomy. See: Stedman.

HUMPTY-DUMPTY. Character in Mother Goose nursery rhyme. See: Jobes. Humpty-Dumpty.

Humpty-Dumpty (Humpty-Dumpty, the nursery rhyme character): Generic Word. See: Harvey.

Hund coupling cases (Hund, Friedrich): Physics. See: Internat. Dict. Ap. Math.; Thewlis.

HUND, FRIEDRICH. 1896- . German physicist. See: Wer Ist Wer?, 1974-1975. Hund coupling cases, Hund-Mulliken-Huckel method, Hund('s) rule(s).

Hund-Mulliken-Huckel method (Hund, Friedrich; Mulliken, Robert Sanderson; and Hueckel, Walter Karl Friedrich?): Physics. See: Internat. Dict. Ap. Math.

Hund('s) rule(s) (Hund, Friedrich): Physics. See: Ballentyne; Hackh; Hughes; Internat. Dict. Phys. Elec.; Van Nostrand Chem. Dict.; Thewlis.

hung higher than Gilderoy's kite (MacGregor, Patrick "Gilderoy"): Generic Word (very severe punishment). See: Hendrickson.

HUNG HSIU-CH'UAN (Assumed title: T'AI P'ING). 1814-1864. Chinese revolutionary. See: Encyc. Brit., 1973. Taiping rebellion.

HUNG, SEE-LU. fl. 1927. American? scientist. Cited in: Mansell. Hung's method?

Hung's method (Hung, See-Lu?): Medicine. See: Stedman. Also known as: Wilson's method.

HUNNEMAN, JOHN. d. 1839. English botanist. See: Britten and Boulger. Hunnemannia.

Hunnemannia (Hunneman, John): Botany. See: Taylor, N.

HUNNER, GUY LEROY. 1868-1957. American surgeon. See: Who Was Who Amer., 1951-1960. Hunner's stricture, Hunner's ulcer.

Hunner's stricture (Hunner, Guy Leroy): Medicine. See: Stedman.

Hunner's ulcer (Hunner, Guy Leroy): Medicine. See: Dorland; Jablonski; Stedman.

HUNSDIEKER, HEINZ. fl. 1942. German chemist. Cited in: Chem. Abstr. Hunsdieker reaction.

Hunsdieker reaction (Hunsdieker, Heinz): Chemistry. See: Ballentyne.

Hunt and Douglas process (Hunt, Thomas Sterry and Douglas, James): Engineering and Industry. See: Thrush. Also known as: Douglas process.

HUNT, ANDREW DICKSON, JR. 1915- . American pediatrician. See: Amer. Men and Women Sci., 12th ed. Hunt's epilepsy.

HUNT, BERTRAM. fl. 1885. English chemist. Cited in: Royal Soc. Cat. Sci. Pap., 1884-1900. Hunt's process.

Hunt continuous filter (Derivation undetermined): Engineering and Industry. See: Thrush.

HUNT, FRANKLIN LIVINGSTON. 1883- . American physicist. See: World Who's Who Sci. Duane and Hunt('s) law.

HUNT, HOWARD FRANCIS. 1918- . American psychologist. See: World Who's Who Sci. Hunt-Minnesota test (for organic brain damage).

HUNT, JAMES RAMSAY. 1872-1937. American neurologist. See: World Who's Who Sci. Hunt's atrophy, Hunt's neuralgia, Hunt's paradoxical phenomenon, Hunt's paralysis (or syndrome (3)), Hunt's syndrome (1), Hunt's syndrome (2).

Hunt-Minnesota test (for organic brain damage) (Hunt, Howard Francis): Psychology. See: Chaplin; English; Wolman.

HUNT, REED. 1870-1948. American pharmacologist. See: World Who's Who Sci. Hunt's reaction (or test).

Hunt-Stein theorem (Derivation undetermined): Statistics. See: Kendall.

HUNT, THOMAS STERRY. 1826-1892. American chemist and geologist. See: Dict. Sci. Biog. Hunt and Douglas process, Huntilite.

HUNT, WILLIAM EDWARD. 1921- . American neurosurgeon. See: Amer. Men and Women Sci., 12th ed. Tolosa-Hunt syndrome.

HUNTER, CHARLES. fl. 20th c. Canadian? physician. (Biography source unavailable.) Hunter('s) syndrome (or group).

Hunter-Hurler syndrome (Hunter, Charles and Hurler, Gertrud). See: Hurler's syndrome and Hunter's syndrome.

HUNTER, JAMES DE GRAAFF. b. 1881. English-born Australian geodesist. See: World Who's Who Sci. Hunter short base?

HUNTER, JOHN. 1728-1793. English surgeon and anatomist. See: Dict. Sci. Biog. Hunterian, Hunterian Oration, Hunter's bundle, Hunter's canal, Hunter's chancre (or induration), Hunter's operation.

Hunter short base (Hunter, James de Graaff?): Earth Sciences. See: Thewlis.

Hunter('s) syndrome (or group) (Hunter, Charles): Medicine. See: Jablonski; Stedman; Wolman.

HUNTER, WALTER DAVID. 1875-1925. American entomologist. See: Dict. Amer. Biog. Hunter's butterfly?

HUNTER, WILLIAM. 1718-1783. English anatomist. See: Dict. Sci. Biog. Hunterian, Hunter's glossitis, Hunter's gubernaculum, Hunter's ligament, Hunter's line, Hunter's membrane.

HUNTER, WILLIAM. 1755-1812. English botanist in Bengal. See: Britten and Boulger. Hunteria.

Hunteria (Hunter, William): Botany. See: Charnock.

Hunterian (Hunter, John or Hunter, William): Medicine. See: Weekley.

Hunterian chancre (Hunter, John). See: Hunter's chancre (or induration).

Hunterian Oration (Hunter, John): Medicine. See: Harvey.

Hunter's bundle (Hunter, John): Anatomy. See: Donath.

Hunter's butterfly (Hunter, Walter David?): Zoology. See: Pennak under "Vanessa."

Hunter's canal (Hunter, John): Anatomy. See: Donath; Dorland; Stedman; Webster's 3d.

Hunter's chancre (or induration) (Hunter, John): Medicine. See: Jablonski; Stedman. Also known as: Hunterian chancre.

Hunter's glossitis (Hunter, William): Medicine. See: Dorland; Jablonski; Stedman.

Hunter's gubernaculum (Hunter, William): Anatomy. See: Stedman.

Hunter's hartebeest (Derivation undetermined): Zoology. See: Encyc. Brit., 1973 under "Antelope," vol. 2, p. 23a.

Hunter's ligament (Hunter, William): Anatomy. See: Dorland; Stedman.

Hunter's line (Hunter, William): Anatomy. See: Dorland; Stedman.

Hunter's membrane (Hunter, William): Anatomy. See: Donath; Stedman.

Hunter's operation (Hunter, John): Medicine. See: Dorland; Stedman.

Huntilite (Hunt, Thomas Sterry): Earth Sciences. See: Thrush.

HUNTINGDON, SELINA HASTINGS, COUNTESS OF. 1707-1791. English religious revival leader. See: Encyc. Brit., 1973. Countess of Huntingdon's Connexion (or Huntingdonians).

Huntingdonians (Huntingdon, Selina Hastings, Countess of). See: Countess of Huntingdon's Connexion.

Huntington dresser (Derivation undetermined): Engineering and Industry. See: Thrush.

HUNTINGTON, ELLSWORTH. 1876-1947. American geographer and explorer. See: Internat. Encyc. Soc. Sci. Huntington's principle of selectivity in migration.

HUNTINGTON, GEORGE. 1850-1916. American neurologist. See: Bull. Johns Hopkins Hosp., vol. 54 (1934), pp. 53-76. Huntington's chorea (or disease).

Huntington-Heberlein process (Hungtington, T. and Heberlein, F.): Engineering and Industry. See: Thrush.

Huntington-Heberlein roasting process (Huntington, T. and Heberlein, F.): Engineering and Industry. See: Thrush.

Huntington mill (Derivation undetermined): Engineering and Industry. See: Hackh; Thrush.

HUNTINGTON, T. fl. 1913. American? engineer. Cited in: Chem. Abstr. Huntington-Heberlein process, Huntington-Heberlein roasting process.

HUNTINGTON, WILLIAM. 1745-1813. English preacher. See: Dict. Nat. Biog. Huntingtonians.

Huntingtonians (Huntington, William): Religion. See: Canney.

Huntington's chorea (or disease) (Huntington, George): Medicine. See: Dorland; Hinsie; Jablonski; Stedman; Van Nostrand Sci. Encyc.; Wolman. Also known as: Lund-Huntington chorea.

Huntington's principle of selectivity in migration (Huntington, Ellsworth): Sociology. See: Zadrozny.

HUNTLEY, CAROLYN COKER. 1924- . American pediatrician. See: Amer. Men and Women Sci., 12th ed. Wiskott-Aldrich-Huntley syndrome.

HUNTLEY, J. T. No dates. English? botanist. (Biography source unavailable.) Huntleya.

Huntleya (Huntley, J. T.): Botany. See: Charnock.

Huntoon and Ellett gauge (Huntoon, Robert Dewitt and Ellett, Alexander): Physics. See: Internat. Dict. Phys. Elec.

HUNTOON, ROBERT DEWITT. 1909- . American physicist. See: Amer. Men Sci., 10th ed. Huntoon and Ellett gauge.

Hunt's atrophy (Hunt, James Ramsay): Medicine. See: Dorland; Stedman.

Hunt's epilepsy (Hunt, Andrew Dickson, Jr.): Medicine. See: Jablonski.

Hunt's neuralgia (Hunt, James Ramsay): Medicine. See: Dorland; Stedman.

Hunt's paradoxical phenomenon (Hunt, James Ramsay): Medicine. See: Dorland; Stedman.

Hunt's paralysis (or syndrome (3)) (Hunt, James Ramsay): Medicine. See: Jablonski; Stedman. Also known as: Ramsay Hunt's paralysis.

Hunt's process (Hunt, Bertram): Engineering and Industry. See: Thrush.

Hunt's reaction (or test) (Hunt, Reed): Medicine. See: Dorland; Stedman.

Hunt's syndrome (1) (Hunt, James Ramsay): Medicine. See: Hinsie; Jablonski; Stedman; Wolman. Also known as: Ramsay Hunt's syndrome.

Hunt's syndrome (2) (Hunt, James Ramsay): Medicine. See: Dorland; Jablonski; Stedman. Also known as: Ramsay Hunt's syndrome.

HUPPERT, HUGO (In full: KARL HUGO). 1832-1904. German physician. See: Biog. Lex. hervorr. Aerzte. Huppert's disease, Huppert's reagent.

Huppert's disease (Huppert, Hugo). See: Kahler's disease.

Huppert's reagent (Huppert, Hugo): Chemistry. See: Hackh

HURLBUT, CORNELIUS SEARLE, JR. 1906- . American mineralogist. See: Amer. Men Sci., 10th ed. Hurlbutite.

Hurlbutite (Hurlbut, Cornelius Searle, Jr.): Earth Sciences. See: Thrush.

HURLER, GERTRUD. fl. 1919. Austrian pediatrician. Cited in: Kelly. Hurler's syndrome (disease or polydystrophy).

Hurler's syndrome (disease or polydystrophy) (Hurler, Gertrud): Medicine. See: Dorland; Hinsie; Jablonski; Stedman; Wolman. Also known as: Hunter-Hurler syndrome, Hunter's syndrome, Johnie McL's syndrome, Pfaundler-Hurler syndrome, Sheldon-Ellis syndrome, Thompson's syndrome.

HURST, EDWARD WESTON. fl. 1920-1964. English physician in Australia. See: Med. Direct., 1964. Hurst's disease.

HURST, H. fl. 1910. English chemist. Cited in: Chem. Abstr. 4, p. 1389. Thompson-Hurst test.

Hurst's disease (Hurst, Edward Weston): Medicine. See: Jablonski.

Hurter and Driffield curve (Hurter, Ferdinand and Driffield, V. C.). See: H and D curve.

Hurter and Driffield Memorial Lecture Award (Hurter, Ferdinand and Driffield, V. C.): Photography. See: Focal Encyc. Photog. under "Awards (Britain)."

Hurter and Driffield speed (and speed system) (Hurter, Ferdinand and Driffield, V.C.). See: H & D speed (and speed system).

HURTER, FERDINAND. 1844-1898. Swiss chemist. See: Dict. Hist. Biog. Suisse. H & D (or Hurter and Driffield) curve, H & D (or Hurter and Driffield) speed (and speed system), Hurter and Driffield Memorial Lecture Award.

HURTLEY, WILLIAM HOLDSWORTH. 1865-1936. English biochemist. See: Biochem. J., Lond., vol. 30 (1936), p. 1787. Hurtley's test (for acetoacetic acid in urine).

Hurtley's test (for acetoacetic acid in urine) (Hurtley, William Holdsworth): Chemistry. See: Ballentyne.

HURWITZ, ADOLF. 1859-1919. Swiss mathematician. See: Dict. Sci. Biog. Hurwitz criterion, Hurwitz polynomial.

Hurwitz criterion (Hurwitz, Adolf): Mathematics. See: Internat. Dict. Ap. Math.; Van Nostrand Sci. Encyc.

Hurwitz polynomial (Hurwitz, Adolf): Mathematics. See: Internat. Dict. Ap. Math.

HUSCHKE, EMIL. 1797-1858. German anatomist. See: Dict. Sci. Biog. Huschke's auditory teeth, Huschke's canal, Huschke's cartilage, Huschke's foramen, Huschke's valve.

Huschke's auditory teeth (Huschke, Emil): Anatomy. See: Donath; Stedman.

Huschke's canal (Huschke, Emil): Anatomy. See: Dorland.

Huschke's cartilage (Huschke, Emil): Anatomy. See: Donath; Stedman.

Huschke's foramen (Huschke, Emil): Anatomy. See: Dorland; Stedman.

Huschke's valve (Huschke, Emil): Anatomy. See: Donath; Dorland; Stedman. Also known as: Hasner's valve (fold, or valve of Hasner), Rosenmueller's valve.

HUSEMANN, AUGUST. d. 1877. German chemist. See: Pogg., vol. 3. Husemann's reaction.

Husemann's reaction (Husemann, August): Chemistry. See: Kelly.

HUSLER, JOSEF. b. 1885. German physician. See: Biog. Lex. hervorr. Aerzte, 1880-1930. Braun-Husler reaction (or test).

HUSS (HUS), JOHN. ca. 1370-1415. Bohemian religious reformer. See: Encyc. Brit., 1973. Hussites (and Hussitism).

HUSSERL, EDMUND. 1859-1938. German philosopher. See: New Encyc. Brit., 1974. Husserlian.

Husserlian (Husserl, Edmund): Philosophy. See: Webster's 3d.

Hussites (and Hussitism) (Huss, John): Religion. See: Attwater; Canney; Harbottle; Mathews, S.; Webster's 3d.

HUTCHESON, FRANCIS. 1694-1746. Scottish philosopher. See: Dict. Nat. Biog. Hutchesonian.

Hutchesonian (Hutcheson, Francis): Philosophy. See: Webster's 3d.

Hutchin('s) goose (or brant) (Hutchins, Thomas): Zoology. See: Mathews, M. M.; Webster's 3d.

HUTCHINS, ELLEN. 1785-1815. Irish botanist. See: Britten and Boulger. Hutchinsia.

HUTCHINS, THOMAS. d. 1790. English attache of the Hudson's Bay Co. (Biography source unavailable.) Hutchin('s) goose (or brant).

Hutchinsia (Hutchins, Ellen): Botany. See: Taylor, N.

HUTCHINSON, ANNE. ca. 1591-1643. English-born American religious reformer. See: Dict. Amer. Biog. Hutchinsonians.

HUTCHINSON, ARTHUR. 1866-1937. English mineralogist. See: World Who's Who Sci. Hutchinsonite.

Hutchinson-Boeck granulomatosis (Hutchinson, Sir Jonathan and Boeck, Cesar Peter Moeller). See: Besnier-Boeck-Schaumann syndrome.

Hutchinson-Gilford syndrome (or disease) (Hutchinson, Sir Jonathan and Gilford, Hastings): Medicine. See: Jablonski; Stedman. Also known as: Gilford's syndrome.

HUTCHINSON, JOHN. 1674-1737. English philosopher and religious writer. See: Dict. Nat. Biog. Hutchinsonians.

HUTCHINSON, SIR JONATHAN. 1828-1913. English surgeon. See: World Who's Who Sci. Hutchinson-Boeck granulomatosis, Hutchinson-Gilford syndrome (or disease), Hutchinson-Weber-Peutz syndrome, Hutchinson's crescentic notch, Hutchinson's disease (1), Hutchinson's disease (2), Hutchinson's disease (3), Hutchinson's facies, Hutchinson's freckle, Hutchinson's mask, Hutchinson's patch, Hutchinson's prurigo, Hutchinson's pupil, Hutchinson's teeth (or incisor), Hutchinson's triad.

HUTCHINSON, JONATHAN, JR. 1859-1933. English ophthalmic surgeon. See: Who Was Who, 1929-1940. Siegrist-Hutchinson syndrome.

Hutchinson letters scandal (Hutchinson, Thomas): History. See: Morris.

HUTCHINSON, THOMAS. 1711-1780. American colonial administrator. See: Dict. Amer. Biog. Hutchinson letters scandal.

Hutchinson-Weber-Peutz syndrome (Hutchinson, Sir Jonathan; Weber, Frederick Parkes; and Peutz, J. L. A.). See: Peutz-Jeghers syndrome.

Hutchinsonians (Hutchinson, Anne): Religion. See: Harvey.

Hutchinsonians (Hutchinson, John): Religion. See: Canney.

Hutchinsonite (Hutchinson, Arthur): Earth Sciences. See: Thrush; Webster's 3d.

Hutchinson's crescentic notch (Hutchinson, Sir Jonathan): Medicine. See: Stedman.

Hutchinson's disease (1) (Hutchinson, Sir Jonathan): Medicine. See: Dorland; Jablsonki; Stedman.

Hutchinson's disease (2) (Hutchinson, Sir Jonathan): Medicine. See: Dorland; Jablonski; Stedman. Also known as: Tay's choroiditis (or disease).

Hutchinson's disease (3) (Hutchinson, Sir Jonathan): Medicine. See: Jablonski.

Hutchinson's facies (Hutchinson, Sir Jonathan): Medicine. See: Dorland; Stedman.

Hutchinson's freckle (Hutchinson, Sir Jonathan): Medicine. See: Jablonski. Also known as: Dubreauilh's melanosis.

Hutchinson's mask (Hutchinson, Sir Jonathan): Medicine. See: Dorland; Stedman.

Hutchinson's patch (Hutchinson, Sir Jonathan): Medicine. See: Stedman.

Hutchinson's prurigo (Hutchinson, Sir Jonathan): Medicine. See: Jablonski.

Hutchinson's pupil (Hutchinson, Sir Jonathan): Medicine. See: Dorland; Stedman.

Hutchinson's teeth (or incisor) (Hutchinson, Sir Jonathan): Medicine. See: Dorland; Jablonski; Stedman; Webster's 3d.

Hutchinson's triad (Hutchinson, Sir Jonathan): Medicine. See: Dorland; Jablonski; Stedman; Webster's 3d.

HUTCHISON, SIR ROBERT GRIEVE. 1871-1960. English pediatrician. See: Who Was Who, 1951-1960. Hutchison (Hutchinson's) syndrome (or disease).

Hutchison (Hutchinson's) syndrome (or disease) (Hutchison, Sir Robert Grieve): Medicine. See: Dorland; Jablonski; Stedman. Also known as: Abercrombie's tumor, Parker's syndrome, Pepper's disease (or syndrome), Smith's syndrome.

Huter, Jakob. See: Hutter, Jakob.

Hutinel-Pick syndrome (Hutinel, Victor Henri and Pick, Friedel). See: Pick's disease (cirrhosis or syndrome).

HUTINEL, VICTOR HENRI. 1849-1933. French physician. See: Biog. Lex. hervorr. Aerzte, 1880-1930. Hutinel-Pick syndrome, Hutinel's cirrhosis (or disease (2)), Hutinel's disease (1).

Hutinel's cirrhosis (or disease (2)) (Hutinel, Victor Henri): Medicine. See: Jablonski.

Hutinel's disease (1) (Hutinel, Victor Henri): Medicine. See: Jablonski.

HUTTER, JAKOB. d. 1536. Tyrolian Anabaptist leader. See: New Cath. Encyc. Hutterite(s) (Huterites, Hutites or Hutterian brethren).

Hutterite(s) (Huterites, Hutites or Hutterian brethren) (Hutter, Jakob): Religion. See: Canney; New Encyc. Brit., 1974, Microp.; Webster's 3d.

HUTTON, COLIN OSBORNE. 1910-1971. New Zealand-born American geologist. See: Who Was Who Amer., 1969-1973. Huttonite.

HUTTON, FREDERICK WOLLASTON. 1836-1905. New Zealand biologist. See: Dict. Nat. Biog., 2d suppl. Hutton's vireo?

HUTTON, JAMES. 1726-1797. Scottish geologist. See: Dict. Sci. Biog. Huttonian (or Huttonianism).

Huttonian (or Huttonianism) (Hutton, James): Earth Sciences. See: Webster's 3d.; Weekley.

Huttonite (Hutton, Colin Osborne): Earth Sciences. See: Thrush; Webster's 3d.

Hutton's vireo (Hutton, Frederick Wollaston?): Zoology. See: Gray.

Huwood loader (Derivation undetermined): Engineering and Industry. See: Thrush.

Huwood slicer (Derivation undetermined): Engineering and Industry. See: Thrush.

Huxleian (or Huxleyan) (Huxley, Aldous Leonard): Literature. See: Webster's 3d.

Huxleian (or Huxleyan) (Huxley, Thomas Henry): Biology. See: Webster's 3d.

HUXLEY, ALDOUS LEONARD. 1894-1963. English novelist and critic. See: Encyc. Brit., 1973. Huxleian (or Huxleyan).

Huxley-Brook reagent (Derivation undetermined): Chemistry. See: Van Nostrand Chem. Dict.

HUXLEY, THOMAS HENRY. 1825-1895. English biologist. See: Dict. Sci. Biog. Huxleian (or Huxleyan), Huxley's anastomosis?, Huxley's layer (membrane or sheath).

Huxley's anastomosis (Huxley, Thomas Henry?): Zoology. See: Gray.

Huxley's layer (membrane or sheath) (Huxley, Thomas Henry): Anatomy. See: Donath; Dorland; Gray; Henderson; Stedman.

HUYGENS (HUYGHENS), CHRISTIAAN. 1629-1695. Dutch physicist. See: Dict. Sci. Biog. Huygens (Huyghenian) eyepiece, Huygens' formula, Huygens' ocular, Huygens' pendulum, Huygens' principle Huygens reverse wave, Huygens(s) wavelets, Huygens' zone, Huyghens' construction, tractrix of Huygens.

Huygens (Huyghenian) eyepiece (Huygens, Christiaan): Physics. See: Internat. Dict. Phys. Elec.; Satterthwaite; Thewlis; Webster's 3d.

Huygens' formula (Huygens, Christiaan): Mathematics. See: James.

Huygens-Fresnel principle (Huygens, Christiaan and Fresnel, Augustin Jean). See: Huyghens principle.

Huygens' ocular (Huygens, Christiaan): Physics. See: Hackh; Stedman.

Huygens' pendulum (Huygens, Christiaan): Physics. See: Internat. Dict. Ap. Math.

Huygens' principle (Huygens, Christiaan): Physics. See: Ballentyne; Internat. Dict. Ap. Math.; Internat. Dict. Phys. Elec.; James; Thewlis; Van Nostrand Sci. Encyc. Also known as: Fresnel-Huygens principle.

Huygens reverse wave (Huygens, Christiaan): Physics. See: Internat. Dict. Phys. Elec.

Huygen('s) wavelets (Huygens, Christiaan): Physics. See: Huschke; Internat. Dict. Ap. Math.

Huygens' zone (Huygens, Christiaan): Mathematics. See: Internat. Dict. Ap. Math.

Huyghens construction (Huygens, Christiaan): Physics. See: Hughes.

HUYSSE, ARY CORNELIS. b. 1871. Dutch microchemist. Cited in: Mansell. Huysse reagent for potassium, rubidium, and cesium?, Huysse test for indium?

Huysse reagent for potassium, rubidium, and cesium (Huysse, Ary Cornelis?): Chemistry. See: Van Nostrand Chem. Dict.

Huysse test for indium (Huysse, Ary Cornelis?): Chemistry. See: Van Nostrand Chem. Dict.

Hvid engine (Hvid, R. M.): Engineering and Industry. See: Auger.

HVID, R. M. fl. 1913. English engineer. (Biography source unavailable.) Hvid engine.

Hyacinth (and Hyacinthus) (Hyacinthus): Botany. See: Charnock; Encyc. Brit., 1973; Funk; Partridge; Taylor, N.

Hyacinthia (Hyacinthus): Mythology. See: Barnhart (Eng. Lit.).

HYACINTHUS. Beloved of Apollo in Greek mythology. See: Encyc. Brit., 1973. Hyacinth (and Hyacinthus), Hyacinthia.

hyatid of Morgagni (Morgagni, Giovanni Battista). See: Morgagnian cyst.

Hyatt billiard ball (Hyatt, John Wesley): Recreation and Sports. Cited in: World Who's Who Sci.

HYATT, JOHN WESLEY. 1837-1920. American inventor. See: Dict. Amer. Biog. Hyatt billiard ball, Hyatt roller bearings.

Hyatt roller bearings (Hyatt, John Wesley): Engineering and Industry. See: Van Nostrand Sci. Encyc. under "Bearings."

HYBINETTE, NOAK VICTOR. b. 1867. French? engineer. Cited in: Mansell. Hybinette process.

Hybinette process (Hybinette, Noak Victor): Engineering and Industry. See: Thrush; Van Nostrand Chem. Dict.

HYDE. Evil side of the split-personality character in Robert Louis Stevenson's story, "The Strange Case of Dr. Jekyll and Mr. Hyde," (1886). See: Harvey. Jekyll and Hyde.

HYDE, EDWARD, 1ST EARL OF CLARENDON. 1609-1674. English statesman and historian. See: Dict. Nat. Biog. Clarendon Code, Clarendon Press.

HYDE, JAMES MACDONALD. b. 1873. American metallurgist. See: Who's Who Engin., 1922-1923. Hyde pneumatic flotation machine, Hyde process.

HYDE, JAMES NEVINS. 1840-1910. American dermatologist. See: Dict. Amer. Biog. Hyde's syndrome (or disease).

Hyde pneumatic flotation machine (Hyde, James Macdonald): Engineering and Industry. Cited in: Who's Who Engin., 1922-1923.

Hyde process (Hyde, James Macdonald): Engineering and Industry. See: Thrush.

Hyde's syndrome (or disease) (Hyde, James Nevins): Medicine. See: Dorland; Jablonski; Stedman.

HYDRA. Gigantic monster in Greek mythology. See: Encyc. Brit., 1973. Hydra.

Hydra (Hydra, the monster): Generic Word (multiple evil or danger). See: Partridge.

hydramine of Hauff (Hauff, Friedrich Wilhelm Albert?): Photography. See: Focal Encyc. Photog. under "Development History."

Hygeian (1) (Hygieia): Mythology. See: Webster's 3d.

HYGIEIA. Goddess of health in Greek mythology. See: Encyc. Brit., 1973. Hygeian (1), Hygiene (Hygeian (2) or Hygienic).

Hygiene (Hygeian (2) or Hygienic) (Hygieia): Generic Word. See: Charnock; Encyc. Brit., 1973; Partridge; Stedman.

Hylleraas coordinate(s) (Hylleraas, Egil Andersen): Physics. See: Ballentyne; Internat. Dict. Phys. Elec.

HYLLERAAS, EGIL ANDERSEN. 1898-1965. Norwegian physicist. See: Dict. Sci. Biog. Hylleraas coordinate(s).

HYMEN. Son of Apollo in Greek mythology. See: New Encyc. Brit., 1974, Microp. Hymen (1), Hymen (2), Hymeneal (or Hymenean).

Hymen (1) (Hymen, the god): Anatomy. See: Charnock; Partridge.

Hymen (2) (Hymen, the god): Mythology. See: New Encyc. Brit., 1974, Microp.

Hymeneal (or Hymenean) (Hymen, the god): Generic Word (marriage). See: Charnock; Partridge.

HYNES, WALTER ALOYSIUS. 1897- . German chemist. Cited in: Chem. Abstr. Hynes-Yanowski micro reagent, Yanowski-Hynes microreagent.

Hynes-Yanowski micro reagent (Hynes, Walter Aloysius and Yanowski, Leo K.): Chemistry. See: Van Nostrand Chem. Dict.

HYPATIA. d. 415. Greek mathematician and philosopher. See: Encyc. Brit., 1973. Hypatia.

Hypatia (Hypatia, the mathematician): Generic Word (learned, beautiful woman). See: Partridge.

HYPERION. One of the Titans in Greek mythology. See: Encyc. Brit., 1973. Hyperion.

Hyperion (Hyperion, the Titan): Generic Word (manly beauty). See: Phyfe.

hypermetamorphosis of Wernicke (Wernicke, Karl): Medicine. See: Stedman.

HYRTL, JOSEPH. 1811-1894. Austrian anatomist. See: Dict. Sci. Biog. Hyrtl's canal, Hyrtl's epitympanic recess, Hyrtl's foramen, Hyrtl's loop (or anastomosis), Hyrtl's plexus, Hyrtl's muscle, Hyrtl's sphincter.

Hyrtl's canal (Hyrtl, Joseph): Anatomy. See: Donath.

Hyrtl's epitympanic recess (Hyrtl, Joseph): Anatomy. See: Stedman.

Hyrtl's foramen (Hyrtl, Joseph): Anatomy. See: Stedman.

Hyrtl's loop (or anastomosis) (Hyrtl, Joseph): Anatomy. See: Stedman.

Hyrtl's muscle (Hyrtl, Joseph): Anatomy. See: Donath.

Hyrtl's plexus (Hyrtl, Joseph): Anatomy. See: Donath.

Hyrtl's sphincter (Hyrtl, Joseph): Anatomy. See: Stedman.

iamb (and Iambic verse) (Iambe): Literature. See: Funk; New Encyc. Brit., 1974, Microp.; Wagner (More Names).

IAMBE. Old maid-servant in Greek mythology. See: Jobes. Iamb (and Iambic verse).

IBRAHIM IBN-AL-AGHLAB (IBRAHIM I). 756-812. Arab amir. See: Webster's Biog. Dict. Aghlabids (or Aghlabite) (dynasty).

IBRAHIM, MURAD JUSSUF BEY. 1877-1953. Egyptian-born physician. See: Biog. Lex. hervorr. Aerzte, 1880-1930. Beck-Ibrahim's disease.

Ibrahim's disease (Ibrahim, Murad Jussuf Bey). See: Beck-Ibrahim's disease.

IBSEN, HENRIK JOHAN. 1828-1906. Norwegian dramatist and poet. See: Encyc. Brit., 1973. Ibsenism (Ibsenian and Ibsenite), Ibsenity.

Ibsenism (Ibsenian and Ibsenite) (Ibsen, Henrik Johan): Literature. See: Brewer; Webster's 3d.

Ibsenity (Ibsen, Henrik Johan): Literature. See: Partridge; Weekley.

Icarian (Icarus): Generic Word (foolhardy). See: Barnhart (Eng. Lit.); Charnock; Partridge; Webster's 3d.; Weekley.

ICARUS. Son of Daedelus in Greek mythology. See: Jobes. Icarian.

Ida and George Eliot Prize Essay Award (Eliot, George and Eliot, Ida): Library Science. See: Harrod.

Iddings' classification (Iddings, Joseph Paxson): Earth Sciences. See: Thrush.

IDDINGS, JOSEPH PAXSON. 1857-1920. American geologist. See: Dict. Sci. Biog. Iddings' classification, Iddingsite.

Iddingsite (Iddings, Joseph Paxson): Earth Sciences. See: Thrush; Webster's 3d.

IDES, EVERT YSBRANDZOON. fl. 1695. Dutch traveler. See: Biog. Woordenb. der Nederl. (Aa). Idesia.

Idesia (Ides, Evert Ysbrandzoon): Botany. See: Taylor, N.

idiopathic Marie-Bamberger syndrome (Marie, Pierre and Bamberger, Eugen). See: Uehlinger's syndrome.

idiopathic Pierre Marie-Bamberger syndrome (Marie, Pierre and Bamberger, Eugen). See: Uehlinger's syndrome.

Ieyasu. See: Iyeyasu.

Igewsky's reagent (Derivation undetermined): Chemistry. See: Thrush.

IGNARO. Character in Edmund Spenser's poem "The Faerie Queene" (1589-1596. See: Jobes. Ignaro.

Ignaro (Ignaro, the literary character): Generic Word (ignoramus). See: Webster's 3d.

Ignatia (Ignatius Azevedo, Saint): Botany. See: Stedman; Webster's 3d.

Ignatian (Ignatius of Antioch, Saint): Religion. See: Webster's 3d.

Ignatian(s) (Ignatius of Loyola, Saint). See: Jesuits.

Ignatian spirituality (Ignatius of Loyola, Saint): Religion. See: New Cath. Encyc.

IGNATIUS AZEVEDO, SAINT. 1528-1570. Portuguese-born missionary in Brazil. See: Holweck. Ignatia, Saint Ignatius('s) bean.

Ignatius epistles (Ignatius of Antioch, Saint): Religion. See: Encyc. Brit., 1973 under "Polycarp," vol. 18, p. 197b.

IGNATIUS OF ANTIOCH, SAINT. d. ca. 110. Christian bishop and theologian. See: Encyc. Brit., 1973. Ignatian, Ignatius epistles, Saint Ignatius' itch.

IGNATIUS OF LOYOLA, SAINT. 1491-1556. Spanish soldier and founder of Jesuits. See: New Cath. Encyc. Ignatian spirituality, Ignatian(s).

ignotus Baker (Baker, Charles Fuller): Zoology. Cited in: World Who's Who Sci.

IHLE, M. fl. 19th c. Bohemian superintendent of mines. Cited in: Hintze, vol. I, pt. 3, half 2, p. 4423. Ihleite.

Ihleite (Ihle, M.): Earth Sciences. See: Webster's 3d.

IKA. fl. 19th c. German optical designer. (Biography source unavailable.) Zeiss-Ikon camera.

Ilbert Bill (Ilbert, Sir Courtenay-Peregrine): History. See: Harbottle; Morris and Irwin; Steinberg.

ILBERT, SIR COURTENAY-PEREGRINE. 1841-1924. English parliamentarian. See: Dict. Nat. Biog., 4th suppl. Ilbert Bill.

ILES, MALVERN WELLS. 1852-1890. American mineralogist. See: Who Was Who Amer., 1961-1968. Ilesite.

Ilesite (Iles, Malvern Wells): Earth Sciences. See: Webster's 3d.

Ilgner flywheel (Ilgner, Howard Frederick?): Engineering and Industry. See: Thrush.

ILGNER, HOWARD FREDERICK. b. 1889. American electrical engineer. See: Who's Who Engin., 1922-1923. Ilgner flywheel?, Ilgner system?, Ward-Leonard-Ilgner system?

Ilgner system (Ilgner, Howard Frederick?): Engineering and Industry. See: Thrush.

Ilinski-Knorre reagent for cobalt and nickel (Ilinski, Mikhail and Knorre, Georg Karl von): Chemistry. See: Van Nostrand Chem. Dict.

ILINSKI, MIKHAIL ALEKSANDROVICH. 1856-1941. Russian chemist. See: World Who's Who Sci. Ilinski-Knorre reagent for cobalt and nickel.

ILKOVIK, D. fl. 1935-1972. Czechoslovakian physicist. See: Who's Who Sci. Europe, 1972. Ilkovik equation.

Ilkovik equation (Ilkovik, D.): Physics. See: Ballentyne.

ILLINGWORTH, WALTER S. fl. 1929. English chemist. Cited in: Pogg., vol. 6 under "Hammick, Dalziel Llewellyn." Hammick-Illingworth rule.

ILOSVAY DE NAGYILOSOVA, LAJOS. 1851-1936. Hungarian chemist. See: Pogg., vols. 4, 5, 6. Griess-Ilosva reagent?, Ilosvay reagent for acetylene, Ilosvay reagent for hydrogen peroxide.

Ilosvay reagent for acetylene (Ilosvay de Nagyilosova, Lajos): Chemistry. See: Van Nostrand Chem. Dict.

Ilosvay reagent for hydrogen peroxide (Ilosvay de Nagyilosova, Lajos): Chemistry. See: Van Nostrand Chem. Dict.

ILSEMANN, J. C. d. 1822. German mining commissioner. Cited in: Bailey. Ilsemannite.

Ilsemannite (Ilsemann, J. C.): Earth Sciences. See: Thrush; Webster's 3d.

images of St. Christopher (Christopher, Saint): Religion. See: Attwater.

Imerslund-Graesbeck syndrome (Imerslund, Olga and Graesbeck, Ralph): Medicine. See: Jablonski. Also known as: Imerslund-Najman-Graesbeck syndrome.

Imerslund-Najman-Graesbeck (Imerslund, Olga; Najman; and Graesbeck, Ralph). See: Imerslund-Graesbeck syndrome.

IMERSLUND, OLGA. fl. 1960. Scandinavian physician. (Biography source unavailable.) Imerslund-Graesbeck syndrome.

IMHOFF, JOHN LEONARD. 1923- . American industrial engineer. See: Amer. Men and Women Sci. Imhoff's law.

IMHOFF, KARL. 1876-1965. German engineer. See: Neue Deut. Biog. Imhoff sludge, Imhoff tank.

Imhoff sludge (Imhoff, Karl): Agriculture. See: Hackh; Winburne.

Imhoff tank (Imhoff, Karl): Engineering and Industry. See: Thrush; Van Nostrand Sci. Encyc.; Webster's 3d.

Imhoff's law (Imhoff, John Leonard): Sociology. See: Martin.

IMLACH, FRANCIS. 1819-1891. Scottish anatomist and surgeon. Cited in: Mansell. Imlach's fat-pad, Imlach's ring.

Imlach's fat-pad (Imlach, Francis): Anatomy. See: Dorland; Stedman.

Imlach's ring (Imlach, Francis): Anatomy. See: Stedman.

IMMELMANN, MAX. 1890-1916. German aviator. See: Neue Deut. Biog. Immelmann (Immelman) (turn).

Immelmann (Immelman) (turn) (Immelmann, Max): Aeronautics. See: Partridge; Webster's 3d.

impeachment of Hastings (Hastings, Warren): History. See: Phyfe.

Imperata (Imperato, Ferrante): Botany. See: Webster's 3d.

IMPERATO, FERRANTE. ca. 1550-ca. 1631. Italian apothecary. See: World Who's Who Sci. Imperata.

IMPEY, SIR ELIJAH. 1732-1809. English jurist. See: Dict. Nat. Biog. Impeyan (or Impeyan pheasant).

IMPEY, LADY MARY. d. 1818. English noblewoman. Cited in: Dict. Nat. Biog. under "Impey, Sir Elijah." Impeyan (or Impeyan pheasant).

Impeyan (or Impeyan pheasant) (Impey, Sir Elijah and Impey, Lady Mary): Zoology. See: Partridge; Webster's 3d.

IMRAY, JOHN. fl. 1874. English engineer. (Biography source unavailable.) Imray pump.

Imray pump (Imray, John): Engineering and Industry. See: Auger.

INCARVILLE, PIERRE D'. 1706-1757. French Jesuit missionary in China. Cited in: Mansell. Incarvillea.

Incarvillea (Incarville, Pierre d'): Botany. See: Taylor, N.; Webster's 3d.

incomplete Horner's syndrome (Horner, Johann Friedrich). See: Raeder's syndrome.

incomplete Laurence-Moon-Biedl syndrome (Laurence, John Zachariah; Moon, Robert Charles; and Biedl, Arthur). See: Carpenter's syndrome.

infant Hercules (Hercules): Medicine. See: Stedman.

INFELD, LEOPOLD. 1898-1968. Polish physicist. See: World Who's Who Sci. Born-Infeld theory.

INGERSOLL, GEORGE GOLDTHWAIT. 1796-1863. American minister. Cited in: Mansell. Ingersoll lectureship.

Ingersoll glarimeter (Ingersoll, Leonard Rose): Engineering and Industry. See: Thrush.

Ingersoll lectureship (Ingersoll, George Goldthwait): Religion. See: Canney.

INGERSOLL, LEONARD ROSE. 1880-1958. American physicist. See: Who Was Who Amer., 1951-1960. Ingersoll glarimeter.

Ingersoll lifeboat (Ingersoll, Oliver Roland): Engineering and Industry. See: Nat. Cycl. Amer. Biog. under "Ingersoll, Oliver Roland," vol. 23, p. 357.

INGERSOLL, OLIVER ROLAND. b. 1837. American inventor and manufacturer. See: Nat. Cycl. Amer. Biog., vol. 23, p. 357. Ingersoll lifeboat.

INGERSOLL, ROBERT GREEN. 1833-1899. American lawyer and agnostic. See: Dict. Amer. Biog. Ingersollian (Ingersollism and Ingersollite).

INGERSOLL, ROBERT HAWLEY. 1859-1928. American industrialist. See: Dict. Amer. Biog. Ingersoll (watch).

INGERSOLL, SIMON. 1818-1894. American inventor. See: Who Was Who Amer., Hist. vol. Leyner-Ingersoll drill.

Ingersoll (watch) (Ingersoll, Robert Hawley): Generic Word. See: Partridge.

Ingersollian (Ingersollism and Ingersollite) (Ingersoll, Robert Green): History. See: Mathews, M. M.

INGHAM, BENJAMIN. 1712-1772. English evangelist. See: Dict. Nat. Biog. Inghamites.

Inghamites (Ingham, Benjamin): Religion. See: Canney; Latham.

INGRASSIA, GIOVANNI FILIPPO. 1510-1580. Sicilian anatomist. See: Dict. Sci. Biog. Ingrassia's process (or wing).

Ingrassia's process (or wing) (Ingrassia, Giovanni Filippo): Anatomy. See: Donath; Stedman.

INGRES, JEAN AUGUSTE DOMINIQUE. 1780-1867. French painter. See: Encyc. Brit., 1973. papier Ingres (or Ingres paper).

Ingres paper (Ingres, Jean Auguste Dominique). See: Papier Ingres.

INIGUEZ, GARCIA. 1839-1898. Cuban general. See: Dicc. Biog. Cubano, vol. 2. carry a message to Garcia.

Institutes of Calvin (Calvin, John): Religion. See: Harbottle.

Institutes of Gaius (Gaius): Law. See: Black.

Institutes of Justinian (Justinian I, the Great): Law. See: Black.

interaction Hamiltonian (Hamilton, Sir William Rowan): Physics. See: Internat. Dict. Phys. Elec.

interglobular space of Owen (Owen, Sir Richard): Anatomy. See: Stedman.

intermediate body of Flemming (Flemming, Walther): Medicine. See: Stedman.

international Ohm (Ohm, Georg Simon): Physics. See: Dresner; Thewlis; Van Nostrand Sci. Encyc.

international Watt (Watt, James): Physics. See: Dresner; Webster's 3d.

inverse Tanh transformation (Derivation undetermined). See: Fisher's transformation.

inverted Marcus Gunn syndrome (Gunn, Robert Marcus). See: Marin Amat's syndrome.

inverted Marfan's syndrome (Marfan, Antonin Bernard Jean). See: Marchesani's syndrome.

IO. Daughter of Inachus in Greek mythology. See: Encyc. Brit., 1973. Io (or Io moth).

Io (or Io moth) (Io, the Greek heroine): Zoology. See: Mathews, M. M.

IONESCU, ALEX. fl. 1921. Rumanian chemist. Cited in: Pogg., vol. 5 under "Minovici, Stefan." Minovici-Ionescu micro-reagent.

Ioxia (Ixion): Botany. See: Charnock.

Ipatiev reaction (Ipatiev, Vladimir Nikolaevich): Chemistry. See: Hackh; Van Nostrand Chem. Dict.

IPATIEV, VLADIMIR NIKOLAEVICH. 1867-1952. Russian chemist. See: Dict. Sci. Biog. Ipatiev reaction.

Ipocras (Hippocrates of Cos). See: Hippocras.

IRELAND, JOHN. 1761-1842. English educator. See: Dict. Nat. Biog. Ireland Scholarship.

Ireland Scholarship (Ireland, John): Literature. See: Harvey.

Irene Castle bob (Castle, Irene): Fashion. See: Picken.

IRGANG, S. fl. 1954. French physician. (Biography source unavailable.) Kaposi-Irgang disease.

IRIARTE, BERNARDO DE. 1734-1814. Spanish diplomat and amateur botanist. Cited in: Mansell. Iriartea.

Iriartea (Iriarte, Bernardo de): Botany. See: Webster's 3d.

Iridium (Iris): Chemistry. See: Encyc. Brit., 1973; Partridge.

IRIS. Personification of the rainbow and messenger of the gods in Greek mythology. See: New Encyc. Brit., 1974, Microp. Iridium, Iris (and Iridaceae).

Iris (and Iridaceae) (Iris): Botany. See: Encyc. Brit., 1973; Funk.

IRMINGER, CARL LUDVIG CHRISTIAN. 1802-1888. Danish admiral. See: Dansk Biog. Lek. Irminger current.

Irminger current (Irminger, Carl Ludvig Christian): Earth Sciences. See: New Encyc. Brit., 1974, Microp.; Van Nostrand Sci. Encyc.

IRVIN, LESLIE LEROY. 1895-1966. American parachute manufacturer. See: Who Was Who Amer., 1961-1968. Irvin suit.

Irvin suit (Irvin, Leslie Leroy): Fashion. See: Partridge.

IRVINE, A. RAY, JR. 1917- . American ophthalmologist. See: Direct. Med. Specialists, 1975-1976. Irvine's syndrome.

Irvine's syndrome (Irvine, A. Ray, Jr.): Medicine. See: Stedman.

IRVING, EDWARD. 1792-1834. Scottish clergyman. See: Dict. Nat. Biog. Irvingite(s) (and Irvinism).

IRVING, ROLAND DUER. 1847-1888. American geologist. See: Pogg., vol. 3. Irvingite.

Irvingite (Irving, Roland Duer): Earth Sciences. See: Hintze, 1st suppl., p. 234.

Irvingite(s) (and Irvinism) (Irving, Edward): Religion. See: Attwater; Canney; Charnock; Harvey; Latham; Mathews, S.; Steinberg.

Irwin, Baron. See: Wood, Edward Frederick Lindley, 1st Earl of Halifax and Baron Irwin.

Irwin consistometer (Irwin, J. T.): Engineering and Industry. See: Thrush.

Irwin distribution (Irwin, Joseph Oscar): Statistics. See: Kendall.

Irwin-Gandhi pact (Wood, Edward Frederick Lindley, 1st Earl of Halifax and Baron Irwin; and Gandhi, Mohandas Karamchand): Politics. See: Encyc. Brit., 1973 under "India-Pakistan" vol. 12, p. 155c.

IRWIN, J. T. fl. 1940. American? or Canadian? engineer. Cited in: Chem. Abstr. Irwin consistometer, Irwin slump test.

IRWIN, JOSEPH OSCAR. 1898- . English mathematician. See: Who's Who Brit. Sci., 1953. Irwin distribution.

Irwin loop (Irwin, Malcolm Robert?): Zoology. See: Pennak.

IRWIN, MALCOLM ROBERT. 1897- . American zoologist and geneticist. See: World Who's Who Sci. Irwin loop?

Irwin slump test (Irwin, J. T.): Engineering and Industry. See: Thrush.

ISAAC II (ISAAC ANGELUS). ca. 1155-1204. Byzantine emperor. See: Encyc. Brit., 1973. Angelici?

Isaac Newton telescope (Newton, Isaac): Astronomy. See: Satterthwaite.

Isabel (Isabella or Isabelline) (Isabella Clara Eugenia of Austria): Generic Word (pale buff color). See: Brewer; Charnock; Hendrickson; Partridge; Wagner (Names); Weekley.

ISABELLA I, THE CATHOLIC. 1451-1504. Queen of Castile, Spain. See: Encyc. Brit., 1973. Isabelline style, Order of Isabella the Catholic.

ISABELLA II. 1830-1904. Queen of Spain. See: Encyc. Brit., 1973. Isabellino.

ISABELLA CLARA EUGENIA OF AUSTRIA. 1566-1633. Infanta of Spain. See: New Encyc. Brit., 1974, Microp. Isabel (Isabella or Isabelline).

Isabella grape (Gibbs, Isabella): Botany. See: Webster's 3d.

Isabelline style (Isabella I, the Catholic): Architecture. See: Osborne.

Isabellino (Isabella II): Numismatics. See: Charnock.

ISAIAH. fl. 740-701 B.C. Hebrew prophet in the Old Testament. See: New Encyc. Brit., 1974. Isaianic.

Isaianic (Isaiah): Religion. See: Stenhouse.

ISAMBERT, EMILE. 1827-1876. French physician. See: Biog. Lex. hervorr. Aerzte. Isambert's disease.

Isambert's disease (Isambert, Emile): Medicine. See: Dorland; Jablonski.

Iscariot, Judas. See: Judas Iscariot.

ISHERWOOD, BENJAMIN FRANKLIN. 1822-1915. American naval engineer. See: Dict. Amer. Biog. Isherwood system.

Isherwood system (Isherwood, Benjamin Franklin): Engineering and Industry. See: Webster's 3d.

ISHIBASHI, MASAYOSHI. fl. 1934. Japanese chemist. Cited in: Chem. Abstr., vol. 29, p. 1358. Ishibashi-Mori test.

Ishibashi-Mori test (Ishibashi, Masayoshi and Mori, Shun): Chemistry. See: Van Nostrand Chem. Dict.

ISHIHARA, SHINOBU. b. 1879. Japanese ophthalmologist. See: World Who's Who Sci. Ishihara test (and color plates).

Ishihara test (and color plates) (Ishihara, Shinobu): Medicine. See: Chaplin; English; Good; Stedman; Webster's 3d; Wolman.

ISHII, KIKUJIRO. 1866-1945. Japanese diplomat. See: Encyc. Brit., 1973. Lansing-Ishii Agreement.

ISHMAEL. Son of Abraham and Hagar in the Old Testament. See: Hastings (Dict. Bible.) Ishmael (or Ishmaelite), Ismaelism.

Ishmael (or Ishmaelite) (Ishmael, the Biblical figure): Generic Word (outcast). See: Brewer; Harvey; Partridge.

ISHTAR. Sumerian-Akkadian goddess. See: Encyc. Brit., 1973. Istar variations.

ISIDORE OF SEVILLE, SAINT. b. ca. 560-636. Spanish bishop, theologian and historian. See: Encyc. Brit., 1973. Isidorian, Isidorian Decretals.

Isidorian (Isidore of Seville, Saint): Religion. See: Weekley.

Isidorian Decretals (Isidore of Seville, Saint): Religion. See: Barnhart (Eng. Lit.); Brewer.

ISING. fl. 1925. Statistician. (Biography source unavailable.) Ising-Stevens distribution.

ISING, ERNEST. 1900- . German-born American physicist. See: Amer. Men and Women Sci. Ising model.

Ising model (Ising, Ernest): Physics. See: Ballentyne; Van Nostrand Sci. Encyc.

Ising problem (Derivation undetermined): Mathematics. See: New Encyc. Brit., 1974, Microp.

Ising-Stevens distribution (Ising and Stevens, W. L.): Statistics. See: Kendall.

island of Reil (Reil, Johann Christian). See: Reil's island (or insula).

islets of Langerhans (or Langerhans' islands) (Langerhans, Paul): Anatomy. See: Donath; Dorland; Henderson; Pennak; Stedman; Webster's 3d.

Ismaelism (Ishmael): Religion. See: Webster's 3d.

ISMAIL (Arabic: ISMA'IL). d. 760. Shiite sect leader. See: Webster's Biog. Dict. Isma'ilism (Isma'ili or Ismailian(s)).

Isma'ilism (Isma'ili or Ismailian(s)) (Ismail): Religion. See: Encyc. Brit., 1973; Stenhouse; Webster's 3d.

ISMENE. Daughter of Oedipus. See: Jobes. Ismene (herbs).

Ismene (herbs) (Ismene): Botany. See: Webster's 3d.

ISOCRATES. 436-338 B.C. Athenian writer and orator. See: Encyc. Brit., 1973. Isocratic (style).

Isocratic (style) (Isocrates): Literature. See: Barnet.

ISRAEL, JAMES A. 1848-1926. German surgeon. See: Biog. Lex. hervorr. Aerzte, 1880-1930. Israel's stain.

ISRAELS, MARTIN CYRIL GORDON. 1906- . English physician. See: World Who's Who Sci. Israels-Wilkinson anemia.

Israel's stain (Israel, James A.): Medicine. See: Stedman.

Israels-Wilkinson anemia (Israels, Martin Cyril Gordon and Wilkinson, John F.). See: Wilkinson's anemia.

ISSACHAR. Ninth son of Jacob in the Bible. See: Encyc. Brit., 1973. Issacharite.

Issacharite (Issachar): History. See: Webster's 3d.

ISSOGLIO, GIOVANNI. 1879-1948. Italian chemist. See: Pogg., vols. 6, 7b. Issoglio test.

Issoglio test (Issoglio, Giovanni): Chemistry. See: Hackh.

Istar. See: Ishtar.

Istar variations (Ishtar): Music. See: Apel.

Itard-Cholewa sign (Itard, Jean-E.-Marie Gaspard and Cholewa, Erasmus Rudolph): Medicine. See: Stedman.

ITARD, JEAN-E.-MARIE GASPARD. 1774-1838. French otologist. See: World Who's Who Sci. Itard-Cholewa sign, Itard's catheter.

Itard's catheter (Itard, Jean-E.-Marie Gaspard): Medicine. See: Dorland; Stedman.

ITHURIEL. Angel in search of Satan in John Milton's work "Paradise Lost" (1667). See: Magill. Ithuriel's spear (1), Ithuriel's spear (2).

Ithuriel's spear (1) (Ithuriel): Generic Word (touchstone of truth). See: Partridge.

Ithuriel's spear (2) (Ithuriel): Botany. See: Mathews, M. M.

ITO, HAYAZO. b. 1865. Japanese pathologist. See: Biog. Lex. hervorr. Aerzte, 1880-1930. Ito-Reenstierna test.

ITO, MINOR. fl. 1954. Japanese physician. (Biography source unavailable.) Ito's nevus.

Ito-Reenstierna test (Ito, Hayazo and Reenstierna, John Libert): Medicine. See: Dorland.

Ito's nevus (Ito, Minor): Medicine. See: Jablonski; Stedman.

Itsenko-Cushing syndrome (Itsenko, N. N. and Cushing, Harvey Williams). See: Cushing's syndrome (3).

ITSENKO, N. N. fl. 1946. Russian physician. (Biography source unavailable.) Itsenko-Cushing syndrome.

ITTNER, MARTIN HILL. 1870-1945. American chemist. See: World Who's Who Sci. Ittner process, Ittner test for cyanides?

Ittner process (Ittner, Martin Hill): Chemistry. See: Van Nostrand Chem. Dict.

Ittner test for cyanides (Ittner, Martin Hill?): Chemistry. See: Van Nostrand Chem. Dict.

Itzig, Hermann. See: Grossmann, Hermann.

Iuba I and Iuba II. See: Juba I and Juba II.

Iugurtha. See: Jugurtha.

Iuno. See: Juno.

IVAN OF CRONSTADT. d. 1909. Russian sect leader. (Biography source unavailable.) Ivannites.

Ivannites (Ivan of Cronstadt): Religion. See: Mathews, S. under "Russian Sects."

IVANOV, DIMITRE IVANOV. b. 1894. Bulgarian chemist. See: World Who's Who Sci. Ivanov reagent (and reaction).

Ivanov reagent (and reaction) (Ivanov, Dimitre Ivanov): Chemistry. See: Ballentyne.

IVANOV-SMOLENSKY, ANATOLIY GEORGIEVICH. 1895- . Russian psychiatrist and pathophysiologist. See: World Who's Who Sci. Ivanov-Smolensky technique.

Ivanov-Smolensky technique (Ivanov-Smolensky, Anatoliy Georgievich): Psychology. See: Drever.

IVANOV, V. N. fl. 1923. Russian chemist. Cited in: Chem. Abstr. Iwanow iridium chloride solution?, Iwanow reagent?, Iwanow test for rhodium.

IVEMARK, BIORN I. 1925- . Swedish pediatric pathologist. See: Who's Who Sci. Europe, 1972. Ivemark's syndrome.

Ivemark's syndrome (Ivemark, Biorn I.): Medicine. See: Jablonski; Stedman.

Ives colorimeter (Ives, Frederick Eugene): Physics. See: Internat. Dict. Phys. Elec.; Van Nostrand Sci. Encyc. under "Colorimeter."

IVES, FREDERICK EUGENE. 1856-1937. American inventor. See: World Who's Who Sci. Hess-Ives photometer?, Ives colorimeter, Ives process.

IVES, JAMES MERRITT. 1824-1895. American lithographer. See: Dict. Amer. Biog. Currier and Ives (prints).

Ives process (Ives, Frederick Eugene): Photography. See: Lockwood.

Ives, Saint. See: Ivo Helory, Saint.

Iwakura mission (Iwakura Tomomi, Prince): History. See: Morris and Irwin.

IWAKURA TOMOMI, PRINCE. 1825-1883. Japanese statesman. See: Encyc. Brit., 1973. Iwakura mission.

Iwan auger shoe (Derivation undetermined): Engineering and Industry. See: Thrush.

Iwan-pattern earth auger (or earth auger) (Derivation undetermined): Engineering and Industry. See: Thrush.

IWANOFF, WLADIMIR P. b. 1861. Russian ophthalmologist. See: Biog. Lex. hervorr. Aerzte, 1880-1930. Iwanoff's cysts.

Iwanoff's cysts (Iwanoff, Wladimir P.). See: Blessig-Iwanoff cyst.

Iwanow iridium chloride solution (Ivanov, V. N.?): Chemistry. See: Van Nostrand Chem. Dict.

Iwanow reagent (Ivanov, V. N.?): Chemistry. See: Van Nostrand Chem. Dict.

Iwanow test for rhodium (Ivanov, V. N.): Chemistry. See: Van Nostrand Chem. Dict.

IWATAKE, DANZO. fl. 1935. Japanese physician. Cited in: Chem. Abstr., vol. 29, p. 4398. Fujita-Iwatake-Miyata test for ascorbic acid.

IXION. Father of Centaurs in Greek mythology. See: Encyc. Brit., 1973. Ioxia.

IYEYASU. 1542-1616. Japanese general and statesman. See: Webster's Biog. Dict. legacy of Iyeyasu.

IZAR, GUIDO. b. 1883. Italian pathologist. See: Biog. Lex. hervorr. Aerzte, 1880-1930. Izar's reagent.

Izar's reagent (Izar, Guido): Medicine. See: Dorland.

IZOD, E. G. fl. 1906. English mechanical engineer. (Biography source unavailable.) Izod impact test (or test).

Izod impact test (or test) (Izod, E. G.): Engineering and Industry. See: Auger; Thrush; Webster's 3d.

J

J. B. King (King, J. B., the millionaire?): Generic Word (world traveler). See: Hendrickson.

J. Edgar Hoover (Hoover, J. Edgar): Generic Word (top lawman). See: Hendrickson under "Hoover..."

JRS (Jensen, Carl O.). See: Jensen's sarcoma.

JABLAKOFF, M. fl. 1912. Chemist. Cited in: Chem. Abstr., vol. 6, p. 2334. Jablokoff test.

Jablochkoff's candles (Jablochkov, Paul): Engineering and Industry. See: Blumberg.

JABLOCHKOV (or JABLOCHKOFF), PAUL. 1847-1894. Russian electrical engineer. See: World Who's Who Sci. Jablochkoff's candles.

Jablokoff test (Jablakoff, M.): Chemistry. See: Van Nostrand Chem. Dict.

JABOULAY, MATHIEU. 1860-1913. French surgeon. See: World Who's Who Sci. Jaboulay pyloroplasty, Jaboulay's amputation (or operation), Jaboulay's button, Jaboulay's method.

Jaboulay pyloroplasty (Jaboulay, Mathieu): Medicine. See: Stedman.

Jaboulay's amputation (or operation) (Jaboulay, Mathieu): Medicine. See: Stedman.

Jaboulay's button (Jaboulay, Mathieu): Medicine. See: Dorland.

Jaboulay's method (Jaboulay, Mathieu): Medicine. See: Stedman.

Jaccod, Maurice. See: Jacod, Maurice.

Jaccod's syndrome (Jacod, Maurice). See: Jacod's syndrome.

JACCOUD, SIGISMOND (In full: FRANCOIS-SIGISMOND). 1830-1913. French physician. See: World Who's Who Sci. Jaccoud's disease (or arthritis), Jaccoud's fever, Jaccoud's sign.

Jaccoud's disease (or arthritis) (Jaccoud, Sigismond): Medicine. See: Jablonski.

Jaccoud's fever (Jaccoud, Sigismond): Medicine. See: Dorland.

Jaccoud's sign (Jaccoud, Sigismond): Medicine. See: Dorland.

Jack Brag (Brag, Jack): Generic Word (braggart). See: Brewer.

Jack Cade legislation (Cade, John): Generic Word (pressure from without). See: Brewer.

Jack Dempsey (fish) (Dempsey, Jack?): Zoology. See: Gray.

Jack Horner (Horner, Jack, the steward): Generic Word. See: Hendrickson; Jobes.

Jack Horner pie (Horner, Jack): Recreation and Sports. See: Webster's 3d.

Jack Johnson (howitzer and shell) (Johnson, Jack): Weapons. See: Hendrickson; Partridge.

Jack K. Burness Award (Burness, Jack K.): Library Science. See: Harrod.

Jack Ketch (Ketch, John): Generic Word (executioner). See: Hendrickson; Latham; Partridge; Webster's 3d.

Jack Rose (cocktail) (Jacqueminot, Vicomte Jean Francois): Food and Drink. See: Hendrickson.

JACK THE CLIPPER. No dates. American hair clipper. (Biography source unavailable.) Jack the Clipper.

Jack the Clipper (Jack the Clipper, the American hair snipper) (Jack the Clipper): Generic Word. See: Hinsie.

Jackie Howe (shirt) (Howe, John): Fashion. See: Brewer.

JACKS. fl. 19th c. Scottish settler in Monterey, California. (Biography source unavailable.) Jacks' Monterey (or Jacks') cheese.

Jacks' Monterey (or Jacks') cheese (Jacks): Food and Drink. See: De Sola.

JACKSON. fl. 18th c.? American slave trader in colonial times. (Biography source unavailable.) Jackson white.

JACKSON, ANDREW "OLD HICKORY." 1767-1845. American president. See: Dict. Amer. Biog. Hickoryism, Jackson ball, Jackson banquet, Jackson cracker (firecracker), Jackson Day, Jackson Day dinner, Jackson Purchase, Jacksonian, Jacksonian democracy, Jacksonism (or Jacksonianism), Jacksonite(s), Jacksonize.

Jackson ball (Jackson, Andrew): History. See: Mathews, M. M.

Jackson banquet (Jackson, Andrew): History. See: Mathews, M. M.

JACKSON, CHEVALIER Q. 1865-1958. American otolaryngologist. See: World Who's Who Sci. Jackson's safety triangle, Jackson's sign.

Jackson cracker (firecracker) (Jackson, Andrew): History. See: Mathews, M. M.

Jackson Day (Jackson, Andrew): History. See: Mathews, M. M.; Smith.

Jackson Day dinner (Jackson, Andrew): Politics. See: Mathews, M. M.

JACKSON, GEORGE. 1780?-1811. English botanist. See: Britten and Boulger. Jacksonia.

Jackson Haines (spin) (Haines, Jackson): Recreation and Sports. See: Webster's 3d.

JACKSON, JABEZ NORTH. 1868-1935. American surgeon. See: World Who's Who Sci. Jackson's membrane (or veil).

JACKSON, JAMES, JR. 1810-1834. American physician. See: Dict. Amer. Biog. under "Jackson, James, Sr." Jackson's sign.

JACKSON, JOHN HARRY. 1915- . American metallurgist. See: World Who's Who Sci. Jackson reaction for titanium?

JACKSON, JOHN HUGHLINGS. 1835-1911. English neurologist. See: Dict. Sci. Biog. Jacksonian epilepsy (or Jackson's epilepsy), Jackson's law, Jackson's rule, Jackson's sign, Jackson's syndrome.

Jackson-MacKenzie syndrome (Jackson, John Hughlings and MacKenzie, Sir Stephen). See: Jackson's syndrome.

Jackson Purchase (Jackson, Andrew): History. See: Mathews, M. M.

Jackson reaction for titanium (Jackson, John Harry?): Chemistry. See: Van Nostrand Chem. Dict.

JACKSON, THOMAS "STONEWALL." 1824-1863. American Confederate general. See: Dict. Amer. Biog. Stonewall, Stonewall brigade, Stonewall Guard.

Jackson white (Jackson): Sociology. See: Webster's 3d.

JACKSON, WILLIAM. 1751-1815. English bishop. See: Dict. Nat. Biog. Jacksonian Professor?

Jacksonia (Jackson, George): Botany. See: Webster's 3d.

Jacksonian (Jackson, Andrew): History. See: Mathews, M. M.; Webster's 3d.

Jacksonian democracy (Jackson, Andrew): Politics. See: Hendrickson; Mathews, M. M.; Smith.

Jacksonian epilepsy (or Jackson's epilepsy) (Jackson, John Hughlings): Medicine. See: Dorland; Hinsie; Jablonski; Stedman; Webster's 3d.; Wolman. Also known as: Bravais-Jackson epilepsy.

Jacksonian Professor (Jackson, William?): Physics. See: Wagner (More Names).

Jacksonism (or Jacksonianism) (Jackson, Andrew): History. See: Good; Mathews, M. M.; Webster's 3d.

Jacksonite(s) (Jackson, Andrew): History. See: Clapin; Mathews, M. M.

Jacksonize (Jackson, Andrew): History. See: Mathews, M. M.; Partridge.

Jackson's law (Jackson, John Hughlings): Physiology. See: Dorland; Drever; English; Hinsie; Stedman; Wolman.

Jackson's membrane (or veil) (Jackson, Jabez North): Anatomy. See: Donath; Dorland; Stedman.

Jackson's rule (Jackson, John Hughlings): Medicine. See: Dorland; Stedman.

Jackson's safety triangle (Jackson, Chevalier Q.): Medicine. See: Dorland.

Jackson's sign (Jackson, Chevalier Q.): Medicine. See: Dorland; Stedman.

Jackson's sign (Jackson, James, Jr.): Medicine. See: Dorland.

Jackson's sign (Jackson, John Hughlings): Medicine. See: Dorland; Stedman.

Jackson's syndrome (Jackson, John Hughlings): Medicine. See: Dorland; Hinsie; Jablonski; Stedman; Wolman. Also known as: Hughlings Jackson's syndrome, Jackson-MacKenzie syndrome, MacKenzie's syndrome.

Jackstraw (Straw, Jack): Generic Word (worthless person). See: Hendrickson.

JACOB. Biblical son of Isaac and Rebekah. See: Encyc. Brit., 1973. Jacob's ladder (plant), Jacob's ladder (ship's rope ladder), Jacob's ladder (sun phenomenon), Jacob's rod(s), Jacob's stone (1), Jacob's stones (2)?, St. Jacob's dipper.

JACOB, ARTHUR. 1790-1874. Irish ophthalmologist. See: World Who's Who Sci. Jacob's coat, Jacob's membrane, Jacob's ulcer.

JACOB BEN MAHIR IBN TIBBON. ca. 1236-ca. 1304. Arabic mathematician, astronomer and translator. See: World Who's Who Sci. Jacob's staff.

JACOB, FRANCOIS. 1920- . French geneticist. See: World Who's Who Sci. Jacob-Monod (theory).

Jacob-Monod (theory) (Jacob, Francois and Monod, Jacques Lucien): Genetics. See: Barnhart (New Eng.).

JACOB, OCTAVE. b. 1867. French physician. See: Biog. Lex. hervorr. Aerzte, 1880-1930. Jacob's disease?

JACOB OF EDESSA (ZANZALUS). d. 578. Syrian monk. See: Encyc. Brit., 1973. Jacobite, Zanzalians.

Jacobaea (or St. James wort) (James the Greater, Saint): Botany. See: Charnock.

JACOBAEUS, HANS CHRISTIAN. 1879-1937. Swedish physician. See: World Who's Who Sci. Jacobaeus operation.

Jacobaeus operation (Jacobaeus, Hans Christian): Medicine. See: Dorland; Stedman.

Jacobean (James I): Fine and Applied Arts. See: Barnet; Partridge; Scott; Webster's 3d.

Jacobean (James the Greater, Saint): Religion. See: Webster's 3d.

Jacobean embroidery (James I): Applied Arts. See: Picken.

Jacobean lily (or St. James lily) (James the Greater, Saint): Botany. See: Webster's 3d.

JACOBI, CARL GUSTAV JAKOB. 1804-1851. German mathematician. See: Dict. Sci. Biog. Hamilton-Jacobi equation (or partial differential equation), Jacobi ellipsoid, Jacobi-fraction (or J-fraction), Jacobi-matrix (or J-matrix), Jacobi method, Jacobi('s) elliptic function(s), Jacobi('s) polynomial(s), Jacobi theorem in optics, Jacobian curve, Jacobian integral, Jacobian of two or more functions in as many variables, Jacobian (or Jacobian determinant), Jacobi's identity, Jacobi's theorem, Jacobi's theta functions.

JACOBI, EDUARD. 1862-1915. German dermatologist. See: Biog. Lex. hervorr. Aerzte, 1880-1930. Jacobi's disease.

Jacobi ellipsoid (Jacobi, Carl Gustav Jakob): Physics. See: Thewlis.

Jacobi('s) elliptic function(s) (Jacobi, Carl Gustav Jakob): Mathematics. See: James; Van Nostrand Sci. Encyc.

Jacobi-fraction (or J-fraction) (Jacobi, Carl Gustav Jakob): Mathematics. See: Encyc. Brit., 1973 under "Continuity," vol. 6, p. 422c.

Jacobi-matrix (or J-matrix) (Jacobi, Carl Gustav Jakob): Mathematics. See: Encyc. Brit., 1973 under "Continuity," vol. 6, p. 422c.

Jacobi method (Jacobi, Carl Gustav Jakob): Mathematics. See: Internat. Dict. Ap. Math.

Jacobi('s) polynomial(s) (Jacobi, Carl Gustav Jakob): Mathematics. See: Ballentyne; Internat. Dict. Ap. Math.; James; Thewlis; Van Nostrand Sci. Encyc.

Jacobi theorem in optics (Jacobi, Carl Gustav Jakob): Mathematics. See: Internat. Dict. Ap. Math.

Jacobian (or Jacobian determinant) (Jacobi, Carl Gustav Jakob): Mathematics. See: Ballentyne; Huschke; Thewlis; Van Nostrand Sci. Encyc.; Webster's 3d.

Jacobian curve (Jacobi, Carl Gustav Jakob): Mathematics. See: Encyc. Brit., 1973 under "Algebraic Geometry," vol. 1, p. 615b.

Jacobian integral (Jacobi, Carl Gustav Jakob): Astronomy. See: Encyc. Brit., 1973 under "Celestina," vol. 5, p. 136c.

Jacobian of two or more functions in as many variables (Jacobi, Carl Gustav Jakob): Mathematics. See: James.

Jacobi's disease (Jacobi, Eduard): Medicine. See: Jablonski.

Jacobi's identity (Jacobi, Carl Gustav Jakob): Mathematics. See: Ballentyne; Encyc. Brit., 1973 under "Groups, Continuous," vol. 10, p. 957a.

Jacobi's theorem (Jacobi, Carl Gustav Jakob): Mathematics. See: James.

Jacobi's theta functions (Jacobi, Carl Gustav Jakob): Mathematics. See: Ballentyne.

Jacobite (Jacob of Edessa): Religion. See: Attwater; Brewer; Mathews, S.

Jacobite(s) (or Jacobitism) (James II): History. See: Barnhart (Eng. Lit.); Brewer; Hargrave; Latham; Steinberg; Webster's 3d.

Jacob's coat (Jacob, Arthur): Medicine. See: Blumberg.

Jacob's disease (Jacob, Octave?): Medicine. See: Jablonski.

JACOBS, EUGENE C. fl. 1951. American physician. Cited in: Chem. Abstr., Decenn. Index, 1947-1956. Jacobs' syndrome.

Jacob's ladder (plant) (Jacob): Botany. See: Gray; Phyfe; Webster's 3d.

Jacob's ladder (ship's rope ladder) (Jacob): Navigation. See: Brewer; Charnock; Webster's 3d.

Jacob's ladder (sun phenomenon) (Jacob): Earth Sciences. See: Huschke.

Jacob's membrane (Jacob, Arthur): Anatomy. See: Donath.

Jacobs process (Derivation undetermined): Engineering and Industry. See: Thrush.

Jacob's rod(s) (Jacob): Botany. See: Webster's 3d.

Jacobs-Singer separatory flask (Derivation undetermined): Chemistry. See: Van Nostrand Chem. Dict.

Jacob's staff (Jacob ben Mahir ibn Tibbon): Engineering and Industry. See: Blumberg.

Jacob's staff (1) (James the Greater, Saint): Generic Word (pilgrim staff). See: Brewer; Webster's 3d.

Jacob's staff (2) (James the Greater, Saint): Navigation. See: Charnock; Webster's 3d.; Winick.

Jacob's staff (3) (James the Greater, Saint): Navigation. See: Brewer; Webster's 3d.

Jacob's staff (4) (James the Greater, Saint): Navigation. See: Brewer; Webster's 3d.

Jacob's staff (5) (James the Greater, Saint): Generic Word (staff with sword or dagger inside). See: Webster's 3d.

Jacob's staff(s) (6) (James the Greater, Saint): Botany. See: Gray; Webster's 3d.

Jacob's-staff(s) (7) (James the Greater, Saint): Botany. See: Webster's 3d.

Jacob's stone (1) (Jacob): History. See: Hendrickson.

Jacob's stones (2) (Jacob, the Old Testament figure?): Earth Sciences. See: Thrush.

Jacobs' syndrome (Jacobs, Eugene C.): Medicine. See: Jablonski.

Jacob's ulcer (Jacob, Arthur): Medicine. See: Dorland; Jablonski; Stedman. Also known as: Krompecher's tumor (or carcinoma).

JACOBS, WALTER ABRAHAM. b. 1883. American chemist. See: World Who's Who Sci. Gould-Jacobs reaction.

JACOBSEN, OSKAR GEORG FRIEDRICH. 1840-1889. German chemist. See: Pogg., vols. 3, 4. Jacobsen reagent?, Jacobsen rearrangement (or reaction).

Jacobsen reagent (Jacobsen, Oskar Georg Friedrich?): Chemistry. See: Van Nostrand Chem. Dict.

Jacobsen rearrangement (or reaction) (Jacobsen, Oskar George Friedrich): Chemistry. See: Ballentyne; Van Nostrand Chem. Dict.

JACOBSON, JACOB. No dates. French ophthalmologist. (Biography source unavailable.) Jacobson's solution.

JACOBSON, JULIUS. 1828-1889. German ophthalmologist. See: Biog. Lex. hervorr. Aerzte. Jacobson's retinitis.

JACOBSON, LUDVIG LEVIN. 1783-1843. Danish anatomist. See: World Who's Who Sci. Jacobson's anastomosis, Jacobson's canal, Jacobson's cartilage (or turbinal), Jacobson's commissure, Jacobson's groove, Jacobson's nerve, Jacobson's organ, Jacobson's plexus, Jacobson's reflex.

JACOBSON, PAUL HEINRICH. 1859-1923. German organic chemist. See: Pogg., vols. 3, 4, 5, 6. Prager-Jacobson classification.

Jacobson's anastomosis (Jacobson, Ludvig Levin): Anatomy. See: Donath; Dorland; Stedman.

Jacobson's canal (Jacobson, Ludvig Levin): Anatomy. See: Dorland; Stedman.

Jacobson's cartilage (or turbinal) (Jacobson, Ludvig Levin): Anatomy. See: Donath; Dorland; Henderson; Stedman; Webster's 3d.

Jacobson's commissure (Jacobson, Ludvig Levin): Zoology. See: Gray.

Jacobson's groove (Jacobson, Ludvig Levin): Anatomy. See: Donath.

Jacobson's nerve (Jacobson, Ludvig Levin): Anatomy. See: Dorland; Henderson; Stedman; Webster's 3d. Also known as: Andersch's nerve.

Jacobson's organ (Jacobson, Ludvig Levin): Anatomy. See: Donath; Dorland; Gray; Henderson; Pennak; Stedman; Webster's 3d.

Jacobson's plexus (Jacobson, Ludvig Levin): Anatomy. See: Donath; Dorland; Stedman.

Jacobson's reflex (Jacobson, Ludvig Levin): Physiology. See: Stedman.

Jacobson's retinitis (Jacobson, Julius): Medicine. See: Dorland.

Jacobson's solution (Jacobson, Jacob): Medicine. See: Dorland.

JACOBSTHAL, ERWIN WOLFGANG JAKOB. b. 1879. German bacteriologist. See: Biog. Lex. hervorr. Aerzte, 1880-1930. Jacobsthal's test.

Jacobsthal's test (Jacobsthal, Erwin Wolfgang Jakob): Medicine. See: Dorland.

Jacobus (coin) (James I): Numismatics. See: Black; Brewer; Wagner (Names); Webster's 3d.

JACOBY, MARTIN JOHANN. b. 1872. German biochemist. See: Pogg., vols. 6, 7a. Jacoby reagent for pepsin and trypsin.

Jacoby reagent for pepsin and trypsin (Jacoby, Martin Johann): Chemistry. See: Van Nostrand Chem. Dict.

JACOD, MAURICE. b. 1880. French physician. Cited in: Mansell. Jacod's syndrome (or triad).

Jacod's syndrome (or triad) (Jacod, Maurice): Medicine. See: Jablonski. Also known as: Jaccod's syndrome, Negri-Jacod syndrome, Silvio Negri's syndrome.

JACONET. No dates. French manufacturer. (Biography source unavailable.) Jaconet (muslin fabric)?

Jaconet (muslin fabric) (Jaconet, the manufacturer?): Fashion. See: Charnock.

Jacopever (fish) (Evertsen, Jacob): Zoology. See: Webster's 3d.

Jacquard (1) (or Jacquard apparatus) (Jacquard, Joseph Marie): Engineering and Industry. See: Charnock; Partridge; Webster's 3d.

Jacquard (2) (or Jacquard fabric) (Jacquard, Joseph Marie): Fashion. See: Picken; Webster's 3d.

Jacquard board (and cards) (Jacquard, Joseph Marie): Engineering and Industry. See: Webster's 3d.

JACQUARD, JOSEPH MARIE. 1752-1834. French inventor. See: Encyc. Brit., 1911. Jacquard (1) (or Jacquard apparatus), Jacquard (2) (or Jacquard fabric), Jacquard board (and cards), Jacquard knitting, Jacquard loom, Jacquard weave.

Jacquard knitting (Jacquard, Joseph Marie): Engineering and Industry. See: Picken; Webster's 3d.

Jacquard loom (Jacquard, Joseph Marie): Engineering and Industry. See: Hendrickson; Phyfe; Picken; Webster's 3d.

Jacquard weave (Jacquard, Joseph Marie): Engineering and Industry. See: Clark; Picken; Webster's 3d.

JACQUART, HENRI. b. 1881. French physician. Cited in: Kelly. Jacquart's facial angle.

Jacquart's facial angle (Jacquart, Henri): Medicine. See: Stedman. Also known as: Topinard's angle.

Jacquemart reagent (Derivation undetermined): Chemistry. See: Van Nostrand Chem. Dict.

JACQUEMET, MARCEL. 1872-1908. French anatomist. Cited in: Index-Cat. Libr. Surg.-Gen. Off., 3rd Ser., vol. 7, 1928. Jacquemet's recess.

Jacquemet's recess (Jacquemet, Marcel): Anatomy. See: Stedman.

JACQUEMIER, JEAN MARIE. 1806-1879. French obstetrician. See: World Who's Who Sci. Jacquemier's sign.

Jacquemier's sign (Jacquemier, Jean Marie): Medicine. See: Dorland; Stedman.

JACQUEMIN, EMILE. fl. 1873. French chemist. Cited in: Royal Soc. Cat. Sci. Pap., 1864-1873. Jacquemin('s) test (or test for phenol), Jacquemin test for fibers.

Jacquemin('s) test (or test for phenol) (Jacquemin, Emile): Chemistry. See: Stedman; Van Nostrand Chem. Dict.

Jacquemin test for fibers (Jacquemin, Emile): Chemistry. See: Van Nostrand Chem. Dict.

JACQUEMINOT, VICOMTE JEAN FRANCOIS. 1787-1865. French soldier. See: Nouv. Biog. Univ. Jack Rose (cocktail), Jacqueminot (or General Jacqueminot) (rose), Jacqueminot (raspberry red color).

Jacqueminot (raspberry red color) (Jacqueminot, Vicomte Jean Francois): Botany. See: Webster's 3d.

Jacqueminot (or General Jacqueminot) (rose) (Jacqueminot, Vicomte Jean Francois): Botany. See: Partridge; Webster's 3d.

JACQUEMONT, VICTOR. 1801-1832. French botanist and explorer. See: World Who's Who Sci. Jaquemontia.

Jacquerie (Cale, Guillaume): History. See: Charnock; Harbottle; Harvey.

Jacques Bonhomme (Cale, Guillaume): Generic Word (French peasant). See: Latham.

JACQUES DE LIEGE. No dates. Liege cutler? (Biography source unavailable.) Jockteleg (knife)?

JACQUES, PAUL. fl. 1895. French physician. Cited in: Royal Soc. Cat. Sci. Pap., 1884-1900. Jacques's plexus.

Jacques's plexus (Jacques, Paul): Anatomy. See: Stedman.

Jacquet chronometer (Jacquet, Edouard Auguste?): Engineering and Industry. See: Drever.

JACQUET, EDOUARD AUGUSTE. fl. 1896. French navigator. Cited in: Royal Soc. Cat. Sci. Pap., 1884-1900. Jacquet chronometer?

JACQUET, LUCIEN (In full: LEONARD MARIE LUCIEN). 1860-1914. French physician. See: Biog. Lex. hervorr. Aerzte, 1880-1930. Jacquet's erythema, Jacquet's syndrome.

JACQUET, PIERRE ARMAND. 1906-1967. French electrochemist. See: Dict. Sci. Biog. Jacquet's method.

Jacquet's erythema (Jacquet, Lucien): Medicine. See: Blakiston's Gould; Stedman.

Jacquet's method (Jacquet, Pierre Armand): Engineering and Industry. See: Thrush.

Jacquet's syndrome (Jacquet, Lucien): See: Christ-Siemens-Touraine syndrome.

Jacquett, Richard. See: Ketch, Jack.

JACQUIN, BARON NIKOLAUS JOSEPH VON. 1727-1817. Austrian botanist. See: Dict. Sci. Biog. Jacquinia.

Jacquinia (Jacquin, Baron Nikolaus Joseph von): Botany. See: Charnock.

JADASSOHN, JOSEF. 1863-1936. German dermatologist. See: Biog. Lex. hervorr. Aerzte, 1880-1930. Borst-Jadassohn epithelioma (or type intraepidermal epithelioma), Franceschetti-Jadassohn syndrome, Jadassohn-Lewandowski syndrome, Jadassohn-Tieche nevus, Jadassohn's disease, Jadassohn's nevus, Jadassohn's test.

Jadassohn-Lewandowski syndrome (Jadassohn Josef and Lewandowski, Felix): Medicine. See: Jablonski.

Jadassohn-Tieche nevus (Jadassohn, Josef and Tieche, Max): Medicine. See: Jablonski.

Jadassohn's disease (Jadassohn, Josef): Medicine. See: Dorland; Jablonski.

Jadassohn's nevus (Jadassohn, Josef): Medicine. See: Jablonski.

Jadassohn's test (Jadassohn, Josef): Medicine. See: Dorland; Kelly.

JADELOT, JEAN FRANCOIS NICOLAS. 1791-1830. French physician. See: Biog. Lex. hervorr. Aerzte. Jadelot's lines (or furrows).

Jadelot's lines (or furrows) (Jadelot, Jean Francois Nicolas): Medicine. See: Dorland.

Jaderin wire (Jaederin, Edvard): Earth Sciences. See: Thewlis.

JAEDERIN, EDVARD. 1852-1923. Swedish geodesist and topographer. See: Pogg., vols. 4, 5, 6. Jaderin wire.

JAEGER, ALPHONS OTTO. 1886-1953. German-born American chemist. See: World Who's Who Sci. Jaeger converter.

Jaeger blower (Jaeger, C. H.): Engineering and Industry. See: Auger.

JAEGER, C. H. fl. 1892. German engineer. (Biography source unavailable.) Jaeger blower.

Jaeger converter (Jaeger, Alphons Otto): Engineering and Industry. See: Thrush; Van Nostrand Chem. Dict.

JAEGER, FRANS MAURITS. 1877-1945. Dutch physical chemist. See: Dict. Sci. Biog. Jaeger method for surface tension.

JAEGER, GUSTAV. 1832-1917. German naturalist and hygienist. See: Biog. Lex. hervorr. Aerzte, 1880-1930. Jaeger stocking, Jaegers.

JAEGER, GUSTAV. 1865-1938. German physicist. See: Pogg., vol. 6. Hahn-Wolf-Jaeger reagent.

JAEGER (JEZEK), KARL. 1903- . Austrian engineer. See: Pogg., vol. 7a. Jezek method.

Jaeger method for surface tension (Jaeger, Frans Maurits): Physics. See: Internat. Dict. Phys. Elec.

Jaeger-Steinwehr method for mechanical equivalent of heat (Jaeger, Wilhelm Ludwig and Steinwehr, Hellmuth von): Physics. See: Internat. Dict. Phys. Elec.

Jaeger stocking (Jaeger, Gustav): Fashion. See: Picken.

Jaeger test reaction for cholesterol (Derivation undetermined): Chemistry. See: Van Nostrand Chem. Dict.

JAEGER VON JAXTTHAL, EDUARD. 1818-1884. Austrian oculist. See: Biog. Lex. hervorr. Aerzte. Jaeger's test types.

JAEGER, WILHELM LUDWIG. 1862-1937. German physicist. See: Pogg., vols. 4, 5, 6, 7a. Jaeger-Steinwehr method for mechanical equivalent of heat.

Jaegers (Jaeger, Gustav): Generic Word (woolen underwear). See: Hendrickson; Partridge; Stenhouse.

Jaeger's test types (Jaeger von Jaxtthal, Eduard): Medicine. See: Dorland.

JAFFE, E. fl. 1935. Italian chemist. Cited in: Chem. Abstr. Jaffe reagent for gold and silver, Jaffe test for sulfur oils, Jaffe test reaction for bismuth and antimony, Jaffe test reaction for boric acid, Jaffe test reaction for ferric salts, Jaffe test reaction for mercury, Jaffe test reaction for molybdenum, Jaffe test reaction for vanadium, Tortelli-Gaffe test.

JAFFE, HENRY LEWIS. 1896- . American pathologist. See: Direct. Med. Specialists, 1975-1976. Jaffe-Lichtenstein syndrome.

Jaffe-Lichtenstein syndrome (Jaffe, Henry Lewis and Lichtenstein, Louis): Medicine. See: Jablonski. Also known as: Jaffe-Lichtenstein-Uehlinger syndrome.

JAFFE, MAX. 1841-1911. German biochemist. See: World Who's Who Sci. Jaffe's test for indican, Jaffe's test of creatinine.

Jaffe reagent for gold and silver (Jaffe, E.): Chemistry. See: Van Nostrand Chem. Dict.

Jaffe test for sulfur oils (Jaffe, E.): Chemistry. See: Van Nostrand Chem. Dict.

Jaffe test reaction for bismuth and antimony (Jaffe, E.): Chemistry. See: Van Nostrand Chem. Dict.

Jaffe test reaction for boric acid (Jaffe, E.): Chemistry. See: Van Nostrand Chem. Dict.

Jaffe test reaction for ferric salts (Jaffe, E.): Chemistry. See: Van Nostrand Chem. Dict.

Jaffe test reaction for mercury (Jaffe, E.): Chemistry. See: Van Nostrand Chem. Dict.

Jaffe test reaction for molybdenum (Jaffe, E.): Chemistry. See: Van Nostrand Chem. Dict.

Jaffe test reaction for vanadium (Jaffe, E.): Chemistry. See: Van Nostrand Chem. Dict.

Jaffe's test for indican (Jaffe, Max): Chemistry. See: Ballentyne; Dorland; Stedman.

Jaffe's test of creatinine (Jaffe, Max): Chemistry. See: Ballentyne.

Jagiello. See: Ladislas II.

Jagiellon (Jagellon or Jagellonian) (dynasty) (Wladyslaw II Jagiello): History. See: New Encyc. Brit., 1974, Microp.; Webster's 3d.

JAHN, HERMANN ARTHUR. 1907- . German-born? English mathematical physicist. See: Who's Who Sci. Europe, 1967. Jahn Teller rule (or effect).

Jahn Teller rule (or effect) (Jahn, Hermann Arthur and Teller, Edward): Physics. See: Ballentyne; Thewlis.

JAHNKE. fl. 1930. German? physician. (Biography source unavailable.) Jahnke's syndrome.

Jahnke's syndrome (Jahnke). See: Sturge-Weber syndrome.

Jahns governor (Jahns, W.): Engineering and Industry. See: Auger.

JAHNS, W. fl. 1912. Engineer. (Biography source unavailable.) Jahns governor.

Jain iconography (Mahavira, Vardahamana Jnatiputra): Fine Arts. See: Osborne.

Jainism (Mahavira, Vardahamana Jnatiputra): Religion. See: Encyc. Brit., 1973; Mathews, S.

Jakes (Ajax): (privy) Generic Word. See: Partridge.

JAKOB, ALFONS. 1884-1931. German physician. See: Biog. Lex. hervorr. Aerzte, 1880-1930. Jakob-Creutzfeldt('s) disease (or syndrome).

Jakob-Creutzfeldt('s) disease (or syndrome) (Jakob, Alfons and Creutzfeldt, Hans Gerhard): Medicine. See: Dorland; Hinsie; Jablonski. Also known as: Creutzfeldt-Jakob disease, Jakob's pseudosclerosis (or disease).

Jakob's pseudosclerosis (or disease) (Jakob, Alfons). See: Jakob-Creutzfeldt('s) disease (or syndrome).

Jakobson, Ludvig Levin. See: Jacobson, Ludvig Levin.

Jaksch-Hayem-Luzet syndrome (Jaksch-Wartenhorst, Rudolf von; Hayem, Georges; and Luzet, Charles). See: Jaksch's syndrome (anemia or disease).

Jaksch-Hayem syndrome (Jaksch-Wartenhorst, Rudolf von and Hayem, Georges). See: Jaksch's syndrome (anemia or disease).

JAKSCH-WARTENHORST, RUDOLF VON. 1855-1947. Austrian physician. See: Biog. Lex. hervorr. Aerzte, 1880-1930. Jaksch's syndrome (anemia or disease), Jaksch's test (1), Jaksch's test (2), Jaksch's test (3) (glucose).

Jaksch's syndrome (anemia or disease) (Jaksch-Wartenhorst, Rudolf von): Medicine. See: Dorland; Jablonski; Stedman. Also known as: Jaksch-Hayem syndrome, Jaksch-Hayem-Luzet syndrome, von Jaksch's anemia.

Jaksch's test (1) (Jaksch-Wartenhorst, Rudolf von): Medicine. See: Dorland; Stedman.

Jaksch's test (2) (Jaksch-Wartenhorst, Rudolf von): Medicine. See: Dorland; Stedman.

Jaksch's test (3) (glucose) (Jaksch-Wartenhorst, Rudolf von). See: Fischer's test (glucose).

JALAGUIER, ADOLPHE. 1853-1924. French surgeon. See: Bull. Soc. Nat. Chir., Paris, vol. 56 (1930) pp. 53-72. Battle-Jalaguier-Kammerer incision.

JALAL-UD-DIN RUMI (MOHAMMED IBN MOHAMMED MOULAVI BALKHI). 1207-1273. Persian Sufi poet. See: Encyc. Brit., 1973. Mowlawiyeh (Mevlevi, Mevelavites, Maulavi or Maulawiyyah) (whirling dervishes).

JAMES I. 1566-1625. King of England, Scotland and Ireland. See: Dict. Nat. Biog. Baby Stuart cap, Jacobean, Jacobean embroidery, Jacobus (or James), King James'('s) version (or Bible).

JAMES II (DUKE OF YORK). 1633-1701. King of England, Scotland and Ireland. See: Dict. Nat. Biog. Duke's laws, Jacobite(s) (or Jacobitism).

JAMES IV. 1473-1513. King of Scotland. See: Dict. Nat. Biog. Jemmy (sheep's head).

JAMES, CHARLES. 1880-1928. English-born American chemist. See: World Who's Who Sci. James separation method, Rice-Fogg-James reagent.

James (coin) (James I). See: Jacobus.

James concentrator (Derivation undetermined): Engineering and Industry. See: Thrush.

JAMES, EDWIN. 1797-1861. American botanist and geologist. See: Dict. Amer. Biog. Jamesia.

JAMES FRANCIS EDWARD STUART "OLD PRETENDER." 1688-1766. Claimant to the throne of England. See: Dict. Nat Biog. Pretenderism.

JAMES, G. C. W. fl. 1953. American physician. (Biography source unavailable.) Swyer-James syndrome.

JAMES, HENRY. 1843-1916. American writer in England. See: Dict. Amer. Biog. Jamesian (or Jamesean).

JAMES, JESSE WOODSON. 1847-1882. American desperado. See: Encyc. Brit., 1973. Jesse James.

James Jig (Derivation undetermined): Engineering and Industry. See: Thrush.

James-Lange-Sutherland theory (James, William; Lange, Carl Georg; and Sutherland, George Fraser?). See: James-Lange theory (of the emotions).

James-Lange theory (of the emotions) (James, William and Lange, Carl Georg): Psychology. See: Chaplin; Drever; English; Hinsie; Webster's 3d; Wolman. Also known as: James-Lange-Sutherland theory.

James Norris Memorial Trophy (Norris, James D.): Recreation and Sports. See: Encyc. Brit., 1973 under "Ice Hockey," p. 1033.

James of Compostela, Saint. See: James the Greater, Saint.

James'('s) powder (James, Robert): Chemistry. See: Hackh; Webster's 3d.

JAMES, ROBERT. 1705-1776. English physician. See: Dict. Nat. Biog. James'('s) powder, James tea?

James separation method (James, Charles): Chemistry. Cited in: World Who's Who Sci.

James table (Derivation undetermined): Engineering and Industry. See: Thrush.

James tea (James, Robert?): Botany. See: Hackh.

JAMES THE GREATER, SAINT (SAINT JAMES OF COMPOSTELA). d. ca. 44 A.D. Apostle of Jesus. See: New Encyc. Brit., 1974, Microp. Jacobaea (or St. James wort), Jacobean, Jacobean lily (or St. James lily), Jacob's staff (1), Jacob's staff (2), Jacob's staff (3), Jacob's staff (4), Jacob's staff (5), Jacob's staff(s) (6), Jacob's-staff(s) (7), liturgy of St. James, Order of St. James of the Sword.

JAMES, WILLIAM. 1842-1910. American psychologist and philosopher. See: Internat. Encyc. Soc. Sci. James-Lange theory (of the emotions), Jamesian (or Jamesean).

Jamesia (James, Edwin): Botany. See: Taylor, N.

Jamesian (or Jamesean) (James, Henry): Literature. See: Webster's 3d.

Jamesian (or Jamesean) (James, William): Psychology and Philosophy. See: Webster's 3d.

JAMESON, JAMES SLIGO. 1856-1888. English naturalist and traveler. See: Dict. Nat. Biog. Jameson's snake?

JAMESON, SIR LEANDER STARR. 1853-1917. English physician and statesman in South Africa. See: Dict. Nat. Biog., 3d suppl. Jameson Raid.

Jameson Raid (Jameson, Sir Leander Starr): History. See: Brewer; Harbottle; Harvey; Montgomery; Morris and Irwin; Steinberg.

JAMESON, ROBERT. 1774-1854. Scottish mineralogist. See: Dict. Sci. Biog. Jamesonite.

Jamesonite (Jameson, Robert): Earth Sciences. See: Thrush; Webster's 3d.

Jameson's snake (Jameson, James Sligo?): Zoology. See: Stedman.

Jamie Duff (Duff, James): Generic Word (professional mourner). See: Hendrickson.

Jamin effect (Jamin, Jules Celestin): Physics. See: Hackh; Van Nostrand Sci. Encyc.

JAMIN, JULES CELESTIN. 1818-1886. French physicist. See: World Who's Who Sci. Jamin effect, Jamin's chain.

Jamin's chain (Jamin, Jules Celestin): Botany. See: Gray.

JAMPEL, ROBERT STEVEN. 1926. American ophthalmologist. See: Amer. Men and Women Sci., 12th ed. Schwartz-Jampel syndrome.

Jan Steen household (Steen, Jan Havickszoon): Generic Word (untidy household). See: Osborne.

JANBON, MARCEL MARIE JOSEPH. 1898- . French physician. See: Who's Who Sci. Europe, 1967. Janbon's syndrome.

Janbon's syndrome (Janbon, Marcel Marie Joseph): Medicine. See: Jablonski.

JANDRIER, EDMOND. fl. 1892. French chemist. Cited in: Royal Soc. Cat. Sci. Pap., 1884-1900. Barbet-Jandrier reagent for formaldehyde, Barbet-Jandrier test, Jandrier test for cotton, Jandrier test for oxycelluloses.

Jandrier test for cotton (Jandrier, Edmond): Chemistry. See: Van Nostrand Chem. Dict.

Jandrier test for oxycelluloses (Jandrier, Edmond): Chemistry. See: Van Nostrand Chem. Dict.

Jane Addams Award (Addams, Jane): Sociology. See: Harrod.

Janeite (Austen, Jane): Literature. See: Webster's 3d.

JANET, PIERRE MARIE FELIX. 1859-1947. French psychologist and neurologist. See: World Who's Who Sci. Janet's disease, Janet's test.

Janet's disease (Janet, Pierre Marie Felix): Medicine. See: Dorland; Hinsie; Jablonski; Stedman; Wolman.

Janet's test (Janet, Pierre Marie Felix): Medicine. See: Dorland; Hinsie; Stedman.

JANEWAY, EDWARD GAMALIEL. 1841-1911. American physician. See: Dict. Amer. Biog. Janeway's pill, Janeway's spots (or lesion), Janeway's sphygmomanometer.

Janeway's pill (Janeway, Edward Gamaliel): Medicine. See: Dorland.

Janeway's sphygmomanometer (Janeway, Edward Gamaliel): Medicine. See: Dorland.

Janeway's spots (or lesion) (Janeway, Edward Gamaliel): Medicine. See: Dorland; Jablonski; Stedman.

Janiceps (Janus): Medicine. See: Stedman; Webster's 3d.

Janiform (Janus): Generic Word. See: Webster's 3d.

JANIN, JOSEPH. b. 1864. French physician. Cited in: Mansell. Janin's tetanus.

Janin's tetanus (Janin, Joseph): Medicine. See: Dorland; Jablonski. Also known as: Rose's tetanus.

Janko keyboard (Janko, Paul von): Music. See: Scholes; Webster's 3d.

JANKO, PAUL VON. 1856-1919. Hungarian pianist. See: Grove. Janko keyboard.

Jannasch-Biedermann reagent (Jannasch, Paul Erhardt and Biedermann, Karl): Chemistry. See: Van Nostrand Chem. Dict.

JANNASCH, PAUL ERHARDT. 1841-1921. German chemist. See: Pogg., vols. 3, 4, 5. Jannasch-Biedermann reagent, Jannasch reagent.

Jannasch reagent (Jannasch, Paul Erhardt): Chemistry. See: Van Nostrand Chem. Dict.

JANNEK, JOSEF. b. 1886. German chemist. Cited in: Chem. Abstr., vol. 8, p. 881. Meyer-Jennek test.

Janney coupler (Janney, Eli Hamilton): Engineering and Industry. See: Webster's 3d.

JANNEY, ELI HAMILTON. 1831-1912. American inventor. See: Dict. Amer. Biog. Janney coupler.

Janney flotation cell (Janney, T. A.): Engineering and Industry. See: Thrush.

JANNEY, R. fl. early 20th c. English engineer. (Biography source unavailable.) Williams and Janney gear.

JANNEY, T. A. fl. 1920. Canadian or American engineer. Cited in: Chem. Abstr., vol. 14, p. 2157. Janney flotation cell.

Janney-Williams transmission (Janney, R. and Williams, H. D.). See: Williams and Janney gear.

JANNIN, L. fl. 1922-1927. French metallurgical engineer. Cited in: Chem. Abstr. Jannin wear test.

Jannin wear test (Jannin, L.): Engineering and Industry. See: Auger.

JANOSIK, JAN. 1856-1927. Czechoslovakian anatomist. See: Biog. Lex. hervorr. Aerzte, 1880-1930. Janosik's embryo.

Janosik's embryo (Janosik, Jan): Medicine. See: Dorland.

JANSEN, ALBERT. 1859-1933. German otologist. See: Monatschr. f. Ohrenheilk. Laryngo-Rhinol., vol. 64 (1930), p. 124ff. Jansen's operation.

Jansen burner (Derivation undetermined): Chemistry. See: Van Nostrand Chem. Dict.

JANSEN, CORNELIUS OTTO. 1585-1638. Dutch theologian and sect leader. See: Encyc. Brit., 1973. Jansenism (or Jansenists), Jansenist style.

JANSEN, MURK. 1867-1935. Dutch orthopedic surgeon. See: J. Bone Joint Surg., vol. 17 (1935), p. 510. Jansen's syndrome, Jansen's test.

Jansenism (or Jansenists) (Jansen, Cornelius Otto): Religion. See: Attwater; Canney; Encyc. Brit., 1973; Harvey; Mathews, S.; Phyfe; Webster's 3d.

Jansenist style (Jansen, Cornelius Otto): Applied Arts. See: Harrod.

Jansen's operation (Jansen, Albert): Medicine. See: Dorland; Stedman.

Jansen's syndrome (Jansen, Murk): Medicine. See: Jablonski. Also known as: Murk Jansen's syndrome.

Jansen's test (Jansen, Muck): Medicine. See: Dorland.

Jansky-Bielschowsky syndrome (or disease) (Jansky, Jan and Bielschowsky, Max). See: Dollinger-Bielschowsky syndrome.

JANSKY, JAN. 1873-1921. Czechoslovakian physician. See: World Who's Who Sci. Jansky-Bielschowsky syndrome (or disease), Jansky's classification.

JANSKY, KARL GUTHE. 1905-1950. American radio engineer. See: World Who's Who Sci. Jansky (unit).

Jansky (unit) (Jansky, Karl Guthe): Physics. See: Asimov under "Jansky, Karl G."

Jansky's classification (Jansky, Jan): Medicine. See: Dorland; Stedman.

JANSON, ANTON. 1620-1687. Dutch type founder. See: Webster's Biog. Dict. Janson (type face).

Janson (type face) (Janson, Anton): Printing. Cited in: Glaister under "Janson, Anton."

Janssen Medal (Janssen, Pierre Jules Cesar): Photography. See: Focal Encyc. Photog. under "Awards, (France)."

JANSSEN, PIERRE JULES CESAR. 1824-1907. French astronomer. See: Dict. Sci. Biog. Janssen Medal.

JANUARIUS, SAINT (Ital.: SAN GENNARO). 272?-305? Italian prelate. See: Webster's Biog. Dict. Miracle of St. Januarius.

January (Janus): Generic Word. See: Brewer; Charnock; Funk; Webster's 3d.; Weekley.

JANUS. Ancient Italian deity. See: Encyc. Brit., 1973. Janiceps, Janiform, January, Janus green B?, Janus (or Janus antenna array), Janus (or Janus technique), Janus-faced (Janus or Janus-like), Janus syndrome, Janusian thinking.

Janus (or Janus antenna array) (Janus): Electronics. See: Hughes; Markus.

Janus (or Janus technique) (Janus): Electronics. See: Internat. Dict. Phys. Elec.; Markus.

Janus-faced (Janus or Janus-like) (Janus): Generic Word. See: Partridge; Webster's 3d.

Janus green B (Janus, the god?): Medicine. See: Stedman.

Janus syndrome (Janus, the god). See: Bret's syndrome.

Janusian thinking (Janus): Generic Word. See: Blakiston's Gould.

Janvillier reagent for antipyrine and aminopyrine (Javillier, Maurice): Chemistry. See: Van Nostrand Chem. Dict.

JAPHETH. One of Noah's sons in the Old Testament. See: Encyc. Brit., 1973. Japhetic, Japhetic (languages).

Japhetic (Japheth): Generic Word (Indo-European family). See: Brewer; Charnock; Harvey; Webster's 3d.

Japhetic (languages) (Japheth): Linguistics. See: Webster's 3d.

JAPP, FRANCIS ROBERT. 1848-1925. Scottish chemist. See: World Who's Who Sci. Japp-Klingemann reaction.

Japp-Klingemann reaction (Japp, Francis Robert and Klingemann, Felix): Chemistry. See: Ballentyne; Van Nostrand Chem. Dict.

Jaquemontia (Jacquemont, Victor): Botany. See: Charnock; Taylor, N.

JAQUET, ALFRED. 1865-1937. Swiss pharmacologist. See: Biog. Lex. hervorr. Aerzte, 1880-1930. Jaquet's apparatus.

Jaquet's apparatus (Jaquet, Alfred): Medicine. See: Dorland.

JARCHO, JULIUS. 1882-1963. American obstetrician. See: World Who's Who Sci. Jarcho's pressometer.

JARCHO, SAUL. 1906- . American physician. See: Amer. Men and Women Sci., 12th ed. Jarcho's syndrome.

Jarcho's pressometer (Jarcho, Julius): Medicine. See: Dorland.

Jarcho's syndrome (Jarcho, Saul): Medicine. See: Jablonski.

JARDI Y BARRAS, RAMON. b. 1881. Spanish scientist. See: Who's Who Sci. Europe, 1967. Hudson-Jardi design (rain intensity gauge)?

JARED. Ancestor of the Jaredites according to the Book of Mormon. (Biography source unavailable.) Jaredite.

Jaredite (Jared): Religion. See: Webster's 3d.

JARISCH, ADOLF. 1850-1902. Austrian dermatologist. See: Biog. Lex. hervorr. Aerzte, 1880-1930. Jarisch-Herxheimer reaction, Jarisch's ointment.

JARISCH, ADOLF. fl. 1937. German pharmacologist. Cited in: Chem. Abstr. Bezold-Jarisch reflex.

Jarisch-Herxheimer reaction (Jarisch, Adolf and Herxheimer, Karl). See: Herxheimer reaction.

Jarisch's ointment (Jarisch, Adolf): Medicine. See: Dorland.

JARJAVAY, JEAN FRANCOIS. 1815-1868. French physician. See: World Who's Who Sci. Jarjavay's ligaments (or muscle).

Jarjavay's ligaments (or muscle) (Jarjavay, Jean Francois): Anatomy. See: Dorland; Stedman.

JARNAC, COMTE GUY CHABOT DE. fl. 1547. French soldier. See: Webster's Biog. Dict. coup de Jarnac (or Jarnac).

Jarno taper (Derivation undetermined): Engineering and Industry. See: Thrush; Van Nostrand Sci. Encyc.

JAROTZKY, ALEXANDER. b. 1866. Russian physician. See: Biog. Lex. hervorr. Aerzte, 1880-1930. Jarotzky's diet.

Jarotzky's diet (Jarotzky, Alexander): Medicine. See: Dorland.

JARVEY (or JERVIS). fl. 18th c. Irish driver. (Biography source unavailable.) Jarvey (or Jarvie).

Jarvey (or Jarvie) (Jarvey, the driver? or Gervasius, Saint?): Generic Word (hackney-coachman). See: Stenhouse; Weekley.

Jarvis' snare (Jarvis, William Chapman): Medicine. See: Dorland; Stedman.

JARVIS, WILLIAM CHAPMAN. 1855-1895. American laryngologist. See: World Who's Who Sci. Jarvis' snare.

JASON. Leader of the Argonauts in Greek mythology. See: New Encyc. Brit., 1974, Microp. Jason.

Jason (Jason, the Argonaut): Generic Word (zealous searcher). See: Partridge.

Jastrow cylinders (Jastrow, Joseph): Physiology. See: Drever; Wolman.

Jastrow illusion (Jastrow, Joseph): Physiology. See: English; Wolman.

JASTROW, JOSEPH. 1863-1944. American psychologist. See: World Who's Who Sci. Jastrow cylinders, Jastrow illusion.

JAUNCEY, GEORGE ERIC MAC DONNELL. 1888-1947. Australian-born American physicist. See: World Who's Who Sci. Debye-Jauncey scattering.

JAVAL, LOUIS EMILE. 1839-1907. French ophthalmologist. See: World Who's Who Sci. Javal's ophthalmometer.

Javal's ophthalmometer (Javal, Louis Emile): Medicine. See: Dorland.

JAVILLIER, MAURICE (In full: JEAN-MAURICE). 1875-1955. French chemist. See: World Who's Who Sci. Bertrand-Javillier test reaction for zinc, Janvillier reagent for antipyrine and aminopyrine.

JAWOROWSKI, ADAM. fl. 1894-1897. Polish chemist. Cited in: Royal Soc. Cat. Sci. Pap., 1884-1900. Jaworowski reagent for albumin?, Jaworowski reagent for alkaloids, Jaworowski reagent for ammonia?, Jaworowski test for cobalt in presence of nickel, Jaworowski test for copper.

Jaworowski reagent for albumin (Jaworowski, Adam?): Chemistry. See: Van Nostrand Chem. Dict.

Jaworowski reagent for alkaloids (Jaworowski, Adam): Chemistry. See: Van Nostrand Chem. Dict.

Jaworowski reagent for ammonia (Jaworowski, Adam?): Chemistry. See: Van Nostrand Chem. Dict.

Jaworowski test for cobalt in presence of nickel (Jaworowski, Adam): Chemistry. See: Van Nostrand Chem. Dict.

Jaworowski test for copper (Jaworowski, Adam): Chemistry. See: Van Nostrand Chem. Dict.

JAWORSKI, WALERY. 1849-1924. Polish physician. See: Biog. Lex. hervorr. Aerzte, 1880-1930. Jaworski's bodies.

Jaworski's bodies (Jaworski, Walery): Medicine. See: Dorland; Stedman.

JAY, ANTONY. 1930- . English student of corporations. Cited in: Nat. Union Cat., 1968-1972. Jay's first law, Jay's hierarchical syndrome, Jay's law of administrators, Jay's law of economy, Jay's laws of hierarchy, Jay's laws of leadership.

Jay-Gardoqui negotiations (Jay, John and Gardoqui, Diego Maria de): History. See: Morris and Irwin.

JAY, JOHN. 1745-1829. American jurist and statesman. See: Dict. Amer. Biog. Jay-Gardoqui negotiations, Jay('s) Treaty.

Jay, Marie Louise. See: Cognacq, Marie Louise nee Jay.

Jay('s) Treaty (Jay, John): History. See: Encyc. Brit., 1973; Harbottle; Jameson; Latham; Morris and Irwin; Smith.

JAYLE, GAETAN E. 1904- . French ophthalmologist. Cited in: Index-Cat. Libr. Surg.-Gen. Off., 5th Ser., vol. 1, 1959. Jayle-Ourgaud syndrome.

Jayle-Ourgaud syndrome (Jayle, Gaetan E. and Ourgaud, A. G.): Medicine. See: Jablonski.

Jay's first law (Jay, Antony): Sociology. See: Martin.

Jay's hierarchical syndrome (Jay, Antony): Sociology. See: Martin.

Jay's law of administrators (Jay, Antony): Sociology. See: Martin.

Jay's law of economy (Jay, Antony): Sociology. See: Martin.

Jay's laws of hierarchy (Jay, Antony): Sociology. See: Martin.

Jay's laws of leadership (Jay, Antony): Sociology. See: Martin.

JEAMES (or JAMES PLUSH). Character in William Makepeace Thackeray's story, "The Diary of Jeames de la Pluche," (1845-1846). See: Harvey. Jeames.

Jeames (Jeames, the footman): Generic Word (footman). See: Partridge; Weekley.

JEAN, FERDINAND. fl. 1872. French chemist. Cited in: Royal Soc. Cat. Sci. Pap., 1864-1873. Jean test for soap in lubricating oils?

Jean Paul, pseud. See: Richter, Johann Paul Friedrich.

Jean test for soap in lubricating oils (Jean, Ferdinand?): Chemistry. See: Van Nostrand Chem. Dict.

Jeanes teacher (Jeans, Anna T.): Education. See: Good.

Jeanne d'Arc. See: Joan of Arc, Saint.

Jeanpaulia (Richter, Johann Paul Friedrich): Botany. See: Webster's 3d.

JEANS, ANNA T. 1822-1907. American philanthropist. See: Dict. Amer. Biog. Jeanes teacher.

JEANS, SIR JAMES HOPWOOD. 1877-1946. English mathematical physicist and astronomer. See: Dict. Sci. Biog. Jeans length, Jeans viscosity equation, Rayleigh-Jeans law (and equation).

Jeans law (Jeans, Sir James Hopwwod). See: Rayleigh-Jeans law.

Jeans length (Jeans, Sir James Hopwood): Physics. See: New Encyc. Brit., 1974, Microp.

Jeans viscosity equation (Jeans, Sir James Hopwood): Physics. See: Ballentyne; Internat. Dict. Phys. Elec.

JEANSELME, EDOUARD. 1858-1935. French dermatologist. See: Bull. Soc. Franc. Hist. Med., vol. 33 (1939), pp. 145-192. Jeanselme's nodules.

Jeanselme's nodules (Jeanselme, Edouard): Medicine. See: Dorland; Jablonski; Stedman. Also known as: Lutz-Jeanselme syndrome, Steiner's tumor.

Jebawi, Sa'ad-ed-Din ed-. See: Sa'ad al-Din al-Jabani.

Jebawiyeh. See: Sa'adiyeh (or Jebawiyeh).

JEFF. Cartoon character created by Harry Conway Fisher in 1907. See: Mansell. Mutt and Jeff.

Jeff Davis-box(es) (Davis, Jefferson): Generic Word (army wagons). See: Clapin; Mathews, M. M.

Jeff Davis coffee (Davis, Jefferson): Food and Drink. See: Mathews, M. M.

Jeff Davis Grays (Davis, Jefferson): Generic Word (Confederate regiment). See: Mathews, M. M.

Jeff Davis money (Davis, Jefferson): Generic Word (Confederate money). See: Mathews, M. M.

JEFFCOTT, HENRY HOMAN. d. 1937. Irish engineer. See: World Who's Who Sci. Jeffcott tachometer.

Jeffcott tachometer (Jeffcott, Henry Homan): Engineering and Industry. See: Thrush.

Jeffdom (Davis, Jefferson). See: Davisdom.

JEFFERIS, WILLIAM WALTER. 1820-1906. American mineralogist. See: Nat. Cycl. Amer. Biog., vol. 15, pp. 372-373. Jefferisite.

Jefferisite (Jefferis, William Walter): Earth Sciences. See: Thrush; Webster's 3d.

Jefferson('s) Bible (Jefferson, Thomas): Religion. See: Hendrickson; Mathews, M. M.

Jefferson Davis's Birthday (Davis, Jefferson): Generic Word. See: Webster's 3d.

Jefferson Day (Jefferson, Thomas): Generic Word. See: Mathews, M. M.; Smith; Webster's 3d.

JEFFERSON, SIR GEOFFREY. b. 1886. English neurosurgeon. See: Who's Who Brit. Sci., 1953. Jefferson's syndrome.

Jefferson (plum) (Jefferson, Thomas): Botany. See: Mathews, M. M.

Jefferson Republican party (Jefferson, Thomas): History. See: Smith.

Jefferson shoe (or boot) (Jefferson, Thomas): Fashion. See: Mathews, M. M.

Jefferson Territory (or Jefferson) (Jefferson, Thomas): History. See: Mathews, M. M.; Smith.

JEFFERSON, THOMAS. 1743-1826. American president and renaissance man. See: Dict. Amer. Biog. Jefferson Day, Jefferson (plum), Jefferson('s) Bible, Jefferson shoe (or boot), Jefferson Territory (or Jefferson), Jeffersonia, Jeffersonian (and Jeffersonianism), Jeffersonian classification, Jeffersonian democracy, Jeffersonian Democrat, Jeffersonian mobocracy, Jeffersonian Republican, Jefferson Republican party, Jeffersonian simplicity, Jeffersonite, Jefferson's giant sloth, Jefferson's Manual, Jefferson's salamander?

Jeffersonia (Jefferson, Thomas): Botany. See: Dorland; Mathews, M. M.; Taylor, N.; Webster's 3d.

Jeffersonian (and Jeffersonianism) (Jefferson, Thomas): Politics. See: Mathews, M. M.; Partridge; Webster's 3d.

Jeffersonian classification (Jefferson, Thomas): Library Science. See: Mathews, M. M.

Jeffersonian democracy (Jefferson, Thomas): Politics. See: Smith.

Jeffersonian Democrat (Jefferson, Thomas): Politics. See: Mathews, M. M.

Jeffersonian mobocracy (Jefferson, Thomas): History. See: Mathews, M. M.

Jeffersonian Republican (Jefferson, Thomas): Politics. See: Mathews, M. M.

Jeffersonian simplicity (Jefferson, Thomas): Generic Word. See: Mathews, M. M.

Jeffersonite (Jefferson, Thomas): Earth Sciences. See: Charnock; Mathews, M. M.; Thrush; Webster's 3d.

Jefferson's giant sloth (Jefferson, Thomas): Zoology. See: Mathews, M. M.

Jefferson's Manual (Jefferson, Thomas): Politics. See: Mathews, M. M.; Smith.

Jefferson's salamander (Jefferson, Thomas?): Zoology. See: Pennak.

Jefferson's syndrome (Jefferson, Sir Geoffrey): Medicine. See: Jablonski.

Jeffing (Derivation undetermined): Recreation and Sports. See: Lockwood.

Jeffite (Davis, Jefferson): History. See: Mathews, M. M.

JEFFREY, JOHN. 1826-1853. Scottish gardener and botanical explorer. See: World Who's Who Sci. Dodecatheon Jeffreyi, Jeffrey('s) pine.

Jeffrey('s) pine (Jeffrey, John): Botany. See: Mathews, M. M.; Webster's 3d.

Jeffreys-Bullen curves (Jeffreys, Sir Harold and Bullen, Keith Edward): Earth Sciences. See: Dict. Sci. Biog. under "Gutenberg, Beno," vol. 5, p. 596.

JEFFREYS, SIR HAROLD. b. 1891. English astronomer and geophysicist. See: World Who's Who Sci. Harold Jeffreys Lecture, Jeffreys-Bullen curves, Wentzel-Kramers-Brillouin-Jeffreys approximation (or method).

JEGHERS, HAROLD. 1904- . American physician. See: Amer. Men and Women Sci., 12th ed. Peutz-Jeghers syndrome.

Jeghers' syndrome (Jeghers, Harold). See: Peutz-Jeghers syndrome.

JEHN, CARL JOSEF. b. 1845. German chemist. Cited in: Royal Soc. Cat. Sci. Pap., 1884-1900. Jehn test reaction for polyvalent alcohols.

Jehn test reaction for polyvalent alcohols (Jehn, Carl Josef): Chemistry. See: Van Nostrand Chem. Dict.

JEHOSHAPHAT. fl. early 9th c. B.C. King of Juah. See: Encyc. Brit., 1973. jumping Jehoshaphat.

JEHOVAH (YAHWEH). Covenant God of the Hebrew people. See: Jobes. Jehovah complex, Jehovah's Witnesses.

Jehovah complex (Jehovah): Psychology. See: Drever.

Jehovah's Witnesses (Jehovah): Religion. See: Brewer; Black; Encyc. Brit., 1973; Webster's 3d.

Jehu (Jehu, the chariot driver): Generic Word (reckless driver). See: Barnhart (Eng. Lit.); Charnock; Webster's 3d.

JEHU, THE CHARIOT DRIVER. d. ca. 816 B.C. King of Israel. See: Encyc. Brit., 1973. Jehu.

Jekyll and Hyde (Jekyll, Dr. Henry and Hyde, Edward): Generic Word (dual personality). See: Brewer; Partridge; Stenhouse; Webster's 3d.

JEKYLL, DR. HENRY. Good side of the split-personality character in Robert Louis Stevenson's story, "The Strange Case of Dr. Jekyll and Mr. Hyde," (1886). See: Magill. Jekyll and Hyde.

JELINEK, BOHDAN. fl. 1938. Czechoslovakian chemist. Cited in: Chem. Abstr., vol. 32, p. 884. Jelinek test for mustard gas.

Jelinek test for mustard gas (Jelinek, Bohdan): Chemistry. See: Van Nostrand Chem. Dict.

JELKS, JOHN LEMUEL. 1870-1945. American surgeon. See: World Who's Who Sci. Jelks' operation.

Jelks' operation (Jelks, John Lemuel): Medicine. See: Stedman.

JELLETT, JOHN HEWETT. 1817-1888. Irish physicist. See: Pogg., vol. 3. Cornu-Jellet prism.

JELLINEK, STEFAN. b. 1871. Austrian physician. See: Biog. Lex. hervorr. Aerzte, 1880-1930. Jellinek's sign.

Jellinek's sign (Jellinek, Stefan): Medicine. See: Dorland; Stedman.

jelly of Wharton (Wharton, Thomas). See: Wharton's jelly.

JELLYBY, MRS. Character in Charles Dickens's novel, "Bleak House," (1852-1853). See: Magill. Mrs. Jellyby.

Jemimaite (Wilkinson, Jemima): Religion. See: Mathews, M. M.

Jemmy (sheep's head) (James IV): Food and Drink. See: Brewer.

JENDRASSIK, ALADAR. fl. 1923. Hungarian chemist. Cited in: Chem. Abstr., vol. 17, p. 3517. Jendrassik solution.

JENDRASSIK, ERNO. 1858-1921. Hungarian physician. See: Biog. Lex. hervorr. Aerzte, 1880-1930. Jendrassik('s) reinforcement (reinforcement of reflexes or maneuver).

Jendrassik gas turbine (Jendrassik, Gyorgy): Engineering and Industry. See: Auger.

JENDRASSIK, GYORGY. 1898-1954. Hungarian engineer. See: Magyar Eletr. Lek. Jendrassik gas turbine.

Jendrassik('s) reinforcement (reinforcement of reflexes or maneuver) (Jendrassik, Erno): Physiology. See: Dorland; English; Hinsie; Stedman; Wolman.

Jendrassik solution (Jendrassik, Aladar): Chemistry. See: Van Nostrand Chem. Dict.

Jenkins'('s) ear (Jenkins, Robert). See: War of Jenkins'('s) ear.

JENKINS, GWILYM MEIRION. fl. 1953-1963. English statistician. See: Direct. Brit. Sci. Box-Jenkins model.

JENKINS, ROBERT. fl. 1731-1745. English mariner. See: Dict. Nat. Biog. War of Jenkins'('s) ear (or Jenkins'('s) ear (incident)).

JENNER, EDWARD. 1749-1823. English physician. See: Dict. Sci. Biog. Jenner vaccination (or Jennerization), Jennerian, Jennerian vaccine.

JENNER, HARLEY DEMING. 1907- . Canadian physician. Cited in: Kelly. Jenner-Kay test, Jenner-Kay unit.

Jenner-Kay test (Jenner, Harley Deming and Kay, Herbert Davenport): Medicine. See: Stedman.

Jenner-Kay unit (Jenner, Harley Deming and Kay, Herbert Davenport): Medicine. See: Stedman.

JENNER, LOUIS LEOPOLD. 1866-1904. English physician. See: Biog. Lex. hervorr. Aerzte, 1880-1930. Jenner('s) stain.

Jenner('s) stain (Jenner, Louis Leopold): Medicine. See: Dorland; Hackh; Stedman; Van Nostrand Chem. Dict.

Jenner vaccination (or Jennerization) (Jenner, Edward): Medicine. See: Dorland; Stedman.

JENNER, SIR WILLIAM. 1815-1898. English physician. See: Dict. Nat. Biog., 1st suppl. Jenner's emphysema.

Jennerian (Jenner, Edward): Medicine. See: Dorland; Stedman; Webster's 3d.

Jennerian vaccine (Jenner, Edward): Medicine. See: Dorland; Stedman.

Jenner's emphysema (Jenner, Sir William): Medicine. See: Stedman.

Jenny Lind bed (Lind, Jenny): Applied Arts. See: Webster's 3d.

Jenny Lind boot (Lind, Jenny): Fashion. Cited in: Mathews, M. M.

Jenny Lind carriage (Lind, Jenny): Generic Word. See: Mathews, M. M.

Jenny Lind costume (Lind, Jenny): Fashion. See: Picken.

Jenny Lind (fishing fly) (Lind, Jenny): Recreation and Sports. Cited in: Mathews, M. M.

Jenny Lind house (Lind, Jenny): History. See: Mathews, M. M.

Jenny Lind polka (Lind, Jenny): Dance. Cited in: Mathews, M. M.

Jenny Lind table (Lind, Jenny): Applied Arts. Cited in: Mathews, M. M.

JENSEN, B, NORMAN. fl. 1923. Danish biochemist. Cited in: Kelly. Hagedorn and Jensen estimation (of sugar in the blood).

JENSEN, CARL OLUF. 1864-1934. Danish veterinarian and pathologist. See: Hospitalstidende, vol. 77 (1934), pp. 1005-1010. Jensen's sarcoma (or tumor).

JENSEN, EDMUND. 1861-1950. Danish ophthalmologist. Cited in: Mansell. Jensen's disease.

JENSEN, EINAR. fl. 1937. Danish? geologist. Cited in: Chem. Abstr., vol. 31, p. 5713. Jensen test for manganese.

JENSEN, ELWOOD VERNON. 1920- . American biochemist. See: Amer. Men Sci. 10th ed. Huggins-Miller-Jensen test.

Jensen governor (Jensen, P.): Engineering and Industry. See: Auger.

JENSEN, JOHAN LUDVIG WILLIAM VALDEMAR. 1859-1925. Danish mathematician. See: Dict. Sci. Biog. Jensen's inequality.

JENSEN, LLOYD B. 1896- . American bacteriologist. See: Amer. Men Sci., 10th ed. Jensen-Urbain reagent.

Jensen, Orla. See: Orla-Jensen, Sigurd.

JENSEN, P. fl. 1859. Engineer. Cited in: Royal Soc. Cat. Sci. Pap., 1864-1873. Jensen governor.

Jensen test for manganese (Jensen, Einar): Chemistry. See: Van Nostrand Chem. Dict.

Jensen-Urbain reagent (Jensen, Lloyd B. and Urbain, Walter Mathias): Chemistry. See: Van Nostrand Chem. Dict.

Jensen's classification (Orla-Jensen, Sigurd): Medicine. See: Dorland.

Jensen's disease (Jensen, Edmund): Medicine. See: Jablonski; Stedman.

Jensen's inequality (Jensen, Johan Ludvig William Valdemar): Mathematics. See: James; Kendall.

Jensen's sarcoma (or tumor) (Jensen, Carl Oluf): Medicine. See: Dorland; Jablonski; Stedman.

Jensen's solution (Orla-Jensen, Sigurd): Medicine. See: Kelly.

JENSON, NICOLAS. ca. 1420-1480. French printer. See: Encyc. Brit., 1973. Jenson (type face).

Jenson (type face) (Jenson, Nicolas): Printing. See: Harrod.

JENTAUD. fl. 1860-1862. French engineer. (Biography source unavailable.) Jentaud steering.

Jentaud steering (Jentaud): Engineering and Industry. See: Auger.

JEPPE, CARL WILHELM BICCARD. b. 1891. German? engineer in South Africa. Cited in: Mansell. Jeppe's tables?

Jeppe's tables (Jeppe, Carl Wilhelm Biccard?): Engineering and Industry. See: Thrush.

Jeroboam (chamber pot) (Jeroboam I): Generic Word. See: Webster's 3d.

Jeremejevite (Eremeev, Pavel V.). See: Eremeyevite.

Jeremiad (Jeremiah): Generic Word (doleful complaint). See: Partridge; Scott; Webster's 3d.

JEREMIAH. b. pr. after 650 B.C.-d. ca. 570 B.C. Hebrew prophet. See: New Encyc. Brit., 1974. Jeremiah, Jeremiad, Jeremianic (or Jeremian), Jerry-built (or Jerry-builder).

JEREMIAH. No dates. English builder? (Biography source unavailable.) Jerry-built (or Jerry-builder).

Jeremiah (Jeremiah, the prophet): Generic Word (doleful prophet). See: Brewer; Webster's 3d.

Jeremianic (or Jeremian) (Jeremiah): Religion. See: Webster's 3d.

JEROBOAM I. d. 912? B.C. King of northern kingdom of Israel. See: Encyc. Brit., 1973. Jeroboam (chamber pot), Jeroboam (wine bottle).

Jeroboam (wine bottle) (Jeroboam I): Generic Word. See: Harvey; Hendrickson; Partridge; Stenhouse; Webster's 3d.

JEROME, SAINT (EUSEBIUS HIERONYMUS). ca. 347-ca. 420. Early Christian Church father. See: Encyc. Brit., 1973. Hermits of St. Jerome, Jeromian.

Jeromian (Jerome, Saint): Religion. See: Webster's 3d.

JERRY. Character from Pierce Egan's "Life in London," (1821). See: Harvey. Tom and Jerry.

Jerry-built (or Jerry-builder) (Jeremiah, the prophet? or Jeremiah, the English builder?): Generic Word (cheap construction). See: Hargrave; Hendrickson; Wagner (Names); Webster's 3d.

JERSILD, OLAF (In full: Peter Christian Olaf). 1867-1950. Danish dermatologist. See: Ugeskr. Laeg. vol. 112 (June 15, 1950), pp. 877-878. Huguier-Jersild syndrome.

Jersild's syndrome (Jersild, Olaf). See: Huguier-Jersild syndrome.

Jervell and Lange-Nielsen syndrome (Jervell, Anton and Lange-Nielsen, Fred): Medicine. See: Jablonski; Stedman.

JERVELL, ANTON. 1901-   . Norwegian physician. See: Hvem er Hvem?, 1973. Jervell and Lange-Nielsen syndrome.

JESIONEK, ALBERT. 1870-1935. German dermatologist. See: Biog. Lex. hervorr. Aerzte, 1880-1930. Jesionek lamp.

Jesionek lamp (Jesionek, Albert): Medicine. See: Dorland.

JESSE. Father of David and ancestor of Jesus in the Bible. See: Encyc. Brit., 1973. Jesse (branched candlestick), Jesse (Jessie or Jessy), Jesse tree, Jesse-window.

Jesse (Jessie or Jessy) (Jesse): Generic Word (severe scolding). See: Webster's 3d.

Jesse (branched candlestick) (Jesse): Religion. See: Charnock.

Jesse Collings Act (Collings, Jesse): History. See: Montgomery.

Jesse Collings Amendment (Collings, Jesse): History. See: Montgomery.

Jesse James (James, Jesse Woodson): Generic Word (outlaw). See: Hendrickson.

Jesse tree (Jesse): Religion. See: Harvey; Webster's 3d.

Jesse-window (Jesse): Religion. See: Attwater; Webster's 3d.; Weekley.

Jesuats (Jesus Christ): Religion. See: Attwater.

Jesuit (dress) (Jesus Christ): Fashion. See: Stenhouse.

Jesuitic (or Jesuitical) (Jesus Christ): Generic Word (deceitful). See: Charnock; Hargrave; Stenhouse; Webster's 3d.; Weekley.

Jesuits (or Society of Jesus) (Jesus Christ): Religion. See: Attwater; Barnhart (Eng. Lit.); Encyc. Brit., 1973 under "Jesus, Society of"; Latham; Mathews, S. under "Jesus Society of"; Steinberg; Webster's 3d. Also known as: Company of Jesus, Ignatians.

Jesus-bird (Jesus Christ): Zoology. See: Gray.

Jesus bug (Jesus Christ): Zoology. See: Webster's 3d.

JESUS CHRIST. b. between 8 and 4 B.C. - d. ca. 29 A.D. Founder of Christianity. See: Encyc. Brit., 1973. Anima Christi, Anno Domini, Christadelphian(s), Christen (or Christening), Christendom, Christian, Christianity, Christmas, Christology, Christ's thorn, Corpus Christi, Crisscross, Disciples of Christ, Jesuats, Jesuit (dress), Jesuitic (or Jesuitical), Jesuits (or Society of Jesus), Jesus-bird, Jesus bug, Jesus freak, Jesus movement (or revolution), Jesus paper, Jesus people, Jesu's Psalter (or Jesus Psalter), Jesus shop, lacrima (lachryma) Christi (wine), Lumen Christi, manus Christi, Militia of Jesus Christ, Order of Christ, Order of Jesus, palma Christi, Poor Handmaids of Jesus, Prayer of Jesus, Sacred Heart of Jesus, Sister of the Holy Names of Jesus and Mary, Sisters of the Holy Child Jesus, Sisters of the Poor Child Jesus, Sisters of the Sacred Hearts of Jesus and Mary, Supreme Order of Christ, Vicar of Jesus Christ.

Jesus freak (Jesus Christ): Religion. See: Barnhart (New Eng.).

Jesus movement (or revolution) (Jesus Christ): Religion. See: Barnhart (New Eng.)

Jesus paper (Jesus Christ): Fine Arts. See: Brewer.

Jesus people (Jesus Christ): Religion. See: Barnhart (New Eng.).

Jesu's Psalter (or Jesus Psalter) (Jesus Christ): Religion. See: Attwater.

Jesus shop (Jesus Christ): Religion. See: Barnhart (New Eng.).

JEUNE, MATHIS. 1910-   . French pediatrician. See: Who's Who France, 1975-1976. Jeune's disease.

Jeunehomme Concerto (Jeunehomme, Mlle.): Music. See: Scholes.

JEUNEHOMME, MLLE. fl. 1777. French pianist. (Biography source unavailable.) Jeunehomme Concerto.

Jeune's disease (Jeune, Mathis): Medicine. See: Jablonski.

Jevons effect (Jevons, William Stanley): Earth Sciences. See: Huschke.

JEVONS, WILLIAM STANLEY. 1835-1882. English economist and logician. See: Dict. Sci. Biog. Jevons effect.

JEWETT, EUGENE LYON. 1900-   . American surgeon. Cited in: Kelly. Jewett nail.

Jewett nail (Jewett, Eugene Lyon): Medicine. See: Dorland.

JEZEBEL. fl. 9th c. B.C. Phoenician princess and wife of King Ahab of Israel. See: Jobes. Jezebel, Jezebel (or painted Jezebel).

Jezebel (Jezebel, the princess): Electronics. See: Markus.

Jezebel (or painted Jezebel) (Jezebel, the princess): Generic Word (wanton woman). See: Hendrickson; Partridge; Phyfe; Webster's 3d.

JEZEK, BOHUSLAV. b. 1877. Czech mineralogist. See: Vestnik statniho geolog. ustava CSR, vol. 22 (1947), p. 260f. Jezekite.

Jezek, Karl. See: Jaeger, Karl.

Jezek method (Jaeger, Karl): Engineering and Industry. See: Internat. Dict. Ap. Math.

Jezekite (Jezek, Bohuslav): Earth Sciences. See: Webster's 3d.

Jezreelites (White, James): Religion. See: Brewer; Canney.

JILEK, ANTONIN. b. 1889. Czech chemist. See: Pogg., vol. 6. Lukas-Jilek test reaction.

JIM CROW. Character in Thomas D. Rice's Negro song-and-dance routine of the same name (1833). See: Barnhart (Cycl. Names). Jim Crow, Jim Crow (bending machine), Jim Crow car(s), Jim Crow (comb), Jim Crow law, Jim Crow (planing-machine), Jim Crow school, Jim Crow (song and dance), Jim Crowism.

Jim Crow (Jim Crow, the character): Generic Word. See: Hendrickson; Mathews, M. M.; Webster's 3d.

Jim Crow (bending machine) (Jim Crow): Engineering and Industry. See: Thrush; Webster's 3d.

Jim Crow car(s) (Jim Crow): Generic Word. See: Hendrickson; Mathews, M. M.

Jim Crow (comb) (Jim Crow): Generic Word. See: Mathews, M. M.

Jim Crow law (Jim Crow): Generic Word. See: Mathews, M. M.; Smith.

Jim Crow (planing-machine) (Jim Crow): Engineering and Industry. See: Mathews, M. M.; Webster's 3d.

Jim Crow school (Jim Crow): Generic Word (racially segregated school). See: Mathews, M. M.

Jim Crow (song and dance) (Jim Crow): Dance. See: Latham; Mathews, M. M.; Phyfe.

Jim Crowism (Jim Crow): Generic Word (racial discrimination). See: Mathews, M. M.; Webster's 3d.

Jim Hill mustard (Hill, James Jerome): Botany. See: Webster's 3d.

Jimmy Valentine (Valentine, Jimmy, the fictional character): Generic Word (master burglar and safe opener). See: Partridge.

Jina. See: Mahavira, Vardhamana Jnatiputra.

JINDAL, S. J. fl. 1925. English? chemist. Cited in: Chem. Abstr. Jindal test reaction.

Jindal test reaction (Jindal, S. J.): Chemistry. See: Van Nostrand Chem. Dict.

Ingo (Gangulf, Saint?): Generic Word. See: Charnock; Phyfe; Stenhouse.

Innah (or Jinnah cap) (Jinnah, Mohammed Ali): Fashion. See: Picken; Webster's 3d.

JINNAH, MOHAMMED ALI. 1876-1948. Pakistani statesman. See: Encyc. Brit., 1973. Jinnah (or Jinnah cap).

JIRASEK, ARNOLD. b. 1887. Czechoslovakian physician. See: Biog. Lex. hervorr. Aerzte, 1880-1930. Jirasek-Zuelzer-Wilson syndrome.

Jirasek-Zuelzer-Wilson syndrome (Jirasek, Arnold; Zuelzer, Wolf W.; and Wilson, James L.): Medicine. See: Jablonski. Also known as: Zuelzer-Wilson syndrome.

JIRINA, M. fl. 1952. Czechoslovakian mathematician. Cited in: Kendall and Doig. Jirina sequential procedure.

Jirina sequential procedure (Jirina, M.): Statistics. See: Kendall.

Jnatiputra. See: Mahavira, Vardhamana Jnatiputra.

JOACHIM OF FIORE (FLORIS). ca. 1135-1202. Italian mystic and sect founder. See: Encyc. Brit., 1973. Joachimites (and Joachimism).

Joachimites (and Joachimism) (Joachim of Fiore): Religion. See: Canney; Latham; Mathews, S.; Webster's 3d.

JOACHIMSTHAL, FERDINAND. 1818-1861. German mathematician. See: Dict. Sci. Biog. surface of Joachimsthal.

JOAN. fl. 853-855. Mythical female Pope. See: Encyc. Brit., 1973. Pope Joan (card game).

Joan of Arc (Joan of Arc, Saint): Generic Word (fearless, inspired woman). See: Partridge.

Joan of Arc costume (Joan of Arc, Saint): Fashion. See: Picken.

JOAN OF ARC, SAINT. ca. 1412-1431. French national heroine. See: Encyc. Brit., 1973. Joan of Arc, Joan of Arc costume.

Joanna Southcott's box (Southcott, Joanna): Religion. See: Brewer.

Joannes (Southcott, Joanna). See: Southcottians.

JOANNY. fl. 1922. French physician. (Biography source unavailable.) Meri-Joanny syndrome.

JOB. Old Testament hero who epitomizes patience. See: Jobes. Job (Job, the Patriarch), Jobation (or Jawbation), Job's cat, Job's comforter(s), Job's comforter (boil), Job's news, Job's oxen, Job's post, Job's tears (chrysolite grains), Job's tears (grass), Job's turkey, patience of Job, poor as Job.

Job (Job, the Patriarch) (Job): Generic Word. See: Brewer; Partridge; Weekley.

Jobation (or Jawbation) (Job): Generic Word (scolding). See: Brewer; Charnock; Partridge; Weekley.

JOBERT DE LAMBALLE, ANTOINE JOSEPH. 1799-1867. French surgeon. See: World Who's Who Sci. Jobert de Lamballe's fossa, Jobert de Lamballe's operation, Jobert de Lamballe's suture.

Jobert de Lamballe's fossa (Jobert de Lamballe, Antoine Joseph): Anatomy. See: Dorland; Stedman.

Jobert de Lamballe's operation (Jobert de Lamballe, Antoine Joseph): Medicine. See: Stedman.

Jobert de Lamballe's suture (Jobert de Lamballe, Antoine Joseph): Medicine. See: Dorland; Stedman.

JOBLING, JAMES WESLEY. 1876-1961. American pathologist. See: Who Was Who Amer., 1961-1968. Flexner-Jobling carcinosarcoma (carcinoma or tumor).

Job's cat (Job): Generic Word (poverty). See: Mathews, M. M.

Job's comforter(s) (Job): Generic Word. See: Blumberg; Brewer; Hendrickson; Partridge; Phyfe; Webster's 3d.

Job's comforter (boil) (Job): Medicine. See: Webster's 3d.

Job's news (Job): Generic Word (bad news). See: Jobes.

Job's oxen (Job): Generic Word. See: Mathews, M. M.

Job's post (Job): Generic Word (bringer of bad news). See: Brewer.

Job's tears (chrysolite grains) (Job): Earth Sciences. See: Picken; Thrush.

Job's tears (grass) (Job): Botany. See: Blumberg; Charnock; Gray; Picken; Webster's 3d.; Winburne.

Job's turkey (Job): Generic Word (poverty). See: Hendrickson; Mathews, M. M.; Partridge; Phyfe.

JOCASTA. Mother-wife of Oedipus in Greek mythology. See: Jobes. Jocasta complex.

Jocasta complex (Jocasta): Psychology. See: English; Hinsie; Wolman.

JOCHMANN, GEORG. 1874-1915. German physician. See: Biog. Lex. hervorr. Aerzte, 1880-1930. Mueller-Jochmann test(s).

Jochmann's test (Jochmann, Georg). See: Mueller-Jochmann test.

Jockteleg (knife) (Jacques de Liege?): Generic Word. See: Partridge.

JODLBAUER, ALBERT. b. 1871. German pharmaceutical chemist. See: Pogg., vol. 6. Jodlbauer reagent?

Jodlbauer reagent (Jodlbauer, Albert?): Chemistry. See: Van Nostrand Chem. Dict.

Joe (La Trobe, Charles Joseph): Generic Word (policeman in Australia). See: Brewer.

Joe Brown's pets (Brown, Joseph Emerson): History. See: Mathews, M. M.

Joe Louis (Louis, Joe): Generic Word (peerless boxer). See: Hendrickson.

Joe Manton (shotgun) (Manton, Joseph): Weapons. See: Harvey; Partridge. Also known as: Manton (gun or pistol).

Joe Miller (Miller, Joseph): Generic Word (stale joke). See: Barnhart (Eng. Lit.); Brewer; Hendrickson; Partridge; Webster's 3d.

Joe-Pye weed (Pye, Joseph): Botany. See: Clapin; Gray; Hendrickson.

JOERGENSEN, ERIK. 1848-1896. Norwegian inventor. See: Norsk Biog. Lek. Krag-Joergensen rifle.

Joergensen solution (Derivation undetermined): Chemistry. See: Van Nostrand Chem. Dict.

Joest bodies (Joest, Ernst): Medicine. See: Dorland; Stedman.

JOEST, ERNST. 1873-1926. German veterinary pathologist. See: World Who's Who Sci. Joest bodies.

Joey (Grimaldi, Joseph): Generic Word (circus clown). See: Hendrickson; Partridge; Webster's 3d.

Joey (or Joe) (Hume, Joseph): Numismatics. See: Brewer; Charnock; Partridge; Webster's 3d.

JOFFREY, ROBERT (ABDULLAH JAFFA ANVER BEY KHAN). 1930- . American dancer, choreographer, teacher and director. See: Curr. Biog., Nov., 1967, pp. 201-203. Robert Joffrey Ballet (or Joffrey Ballet).

JOFFROY, ALEX. 1844-1908. French physician. See: World Who's Who Sci. Joffroy's reflex, Joffroy's sign (1) (exophthalmic goiter), Joffroy's sign (2) (brain disease).

Joffroy's reflex (Joffroy, Alex): Medicine. See: Dorland; Stedman.

Joffroy's sign (1) (exophthalmic goiter) (Joffroy, Alex): Medicine. See: Stedman.

Joffroy's sign (2) (brain disease) (Joffroy, Alex): Medicine. See: Stedman.

JOHANN BAPTIST JOSEPH FABIAN SEBASTIAN. 1782-1859. Archduke of Austria. See: Oesterr. Biog. Lex., 1815-1950. Johannite.

Johannes (Joannes, half-Johannes, half-Joe or Johnny) (John V): Numismatics. See: Charnock; Partridge; Webster's 3d.

Johannine (John the Evangelist, Saint): Religion. See: Webster's 3d.

Johannine clause (John the Evangelist, Saint). See: comma Johanninum.

Johannite (Johann Baptist Joseph Fabian Sebastian): Earth Sciences. See: Thrush; Webster's 3d.

JOHANNSEN, ALBERT. 1871-1962. American geologist. See: Dict. Sci. Biog. Johannsenite, Johannsen's classification (and number).

Johannsenite (Johannsen, Albert): Earth Sciences. See: Thrush; Webster's 3d.

Johannsen's classification (and number) (Johannsen, Albert): Earth Sciences. See: Thrush.

Johannson reagent (Derivation undetermined): Chemistry. See: Van Nostrand Chem. Dict.

JOHANSEN, KNUD WINSTRUP. 1901- . Danish engineer. See: Who's Who Sci. Europe, 1972. Johansen theory.

Johansen theory (Johansen, Knud Winstrup): Engineering and Industry. See: Internat. Dict. Ap. Math. under "Rupture line theory."

Johansson block (combination gauge block or Jo block) (Johansson, Carl Edvard): Engineering and Industry. See: Webster's 3d.

JOHANSSON, CARL EDVARD. 1864-1943. Swedish engineer. See: Svenska Maen Och Kvinnor. Johansson block (combination gauge block or Jo block).

JOHANSSON, SVEN CHRISTIAN. b. 1880. Swedish surgeon. See: Svenska Maen Och Kvinnor. Larsen-Johansson syndrome (or disease).

JOHN. No dates. English? gardener. (Biography source unavailable.) John (pear).

JOHN (JOHANNES) V. 1689-1750. King of Portugal. See: Webster's Biog. Dict. Johannes (Joannes, half-Johannes, half-Joe or Johnny).

John B. hat (Stetson, John Batterson). See: Stetson hat.

JOHN BULL. Character in John Arbuthnot's satire, "Law is a Bottomless Pit," (1712). See: Harvey. John Bull (1), John Bull (2) (drill stand).

John Bull (1) (John Bull): Generic Word (Englishman). See: Charnock; Encyc. Brit., 1973; Hargrave; Partridge; Wagner (Names).

John Bull (2) (drill stand) (John Bull): Engineering and Industry. See: Thrush.

JOHN CHRYSOSTOM, SAINT. 344-407. Doctor of the Church. See: Holweck. Liturgy of St. John Chrysostom.

John Collins (Collins, John). See: Tom Collins.

John Dory (fish) (Dory, John): Food and Drink. See: Hendrickson; Partridge. Also known as: St. Peter's cock.

John (Jack) Drum's entertainment (Drum, Jack): Generic Word. See: Brewer.

John Hancock (Hancock, John, first signer of the Declaration of Independence): Generic Word (signature). See: Brewer; Hendrickson; Partridge; Webster's 3d.

John Harris Award (Harris, John): Library Science. See: Harrod.

John Henry (Derivation undetermined): Generic Word (signature): See: Hendrickson under "John Hancock..."

John Homans professorship of surgery (Homans, John): Medicine. Cited in: World Who's Who Sci.

JOHN, JOHANN FRIEDRICH. 1782-1847. German chemist. See: Pogg., vol. 1. Johnite.

JOHN, JOSEPH. 1938- . Indian-born American physicist. See: Amer. Men and Women Sci., 12th ed. Johnniac (computer)?

John Knox cap (Knox, John): Generic Word (mortar-board). See: Brewer.

JOHN (JOAN) MAURICE OF NASSAU. 1604-1679. Dutch general and administrator in Brazil. See: New Encyc. Brit., 1974. Mauritia.

John Odges (borehole) (Derivation undetermined): Engineering and Industry. See: Thrush.

JOHN OF GAUNT, DUKE OF LANCASTER. 1340-1399. English founder of house of Lancaster. See: Dict. Nat. Biog. Lancastrian(s).

JOHN OF GOD, SAINT (JUAN CIUDAD). 1495-1550. Spanish religous order founder. See: Encyc. Brit., 1973. Hospitallers (or Brother Hospitaler) of St. John of God.

JOHN O'GROAT. fl. ca. 1500. Dutch-born settler in Scotland. (Biography source unavailable.) from Maidenkirk to John O'Groats, John O'Groat's house (or from land's end to John O'Groat's house), John O'Groats sandstone.

John O'Groat's house (or from land's end to John O'Groat's house) (John O'Groat): Generic Word (from one end of Britain to the other). See: Encyc. Brit., 1973; Hargrave; Hendrickson.

John O'Groats sandstone (John O'Groat): Earth Sciences. See: Thrush.

John Paul Jones's raids (Jones, John Paul): History. See: Morris and Irwin.

John (pear) (John): Botany. See: Charnock.

JOHN, PETER WILLIAM MEREDITH. 1923- . Welsh-born American mathematical statistician. See: Amer. Men and Women Sci., 12th ed. John's cyclic incomplete block designs.

John Roberts (Roberts, John): Generic Word (large tankard). See: Brewer.

John Simon Guggenheim Memorial Foundation (or Guggenheim) (Guggenheim, Simon): Philanthropy. Cited in: Nat. Cycl. Amer. Biog., vol. C, p. 50 under "Guggenheim, Simon."

JOHN THE BAPTIST, SAINT. b. before 4 B.C. - d. 28-30 A.D. Forerunner of Jesus in the New Testament. See: Encyc. Brit., 1973. Christians (or Disciples) of St. John (or St. John's Christians), Knights Hospitallers of St. John of Jerusalem, Knights of St. John, Saint John's bread, Saint John's dance?, Saint John's eve, St. John's evil (or disease)?, Saint John's fire, Saint John's wort, Saint John the Baptist's Day.

JOHN THE EVANGELIST, SAINT. d. ca. 101 A.D. One of Christ's apostles. See: Holweck. comma Johanninum (or Johannine clause), Johannine.

JOHN, WALTER, JR. 1924- . American physicist. See: World Who's Who Sci. U-coefficient of John?

JOHNE, ALBERT (In full: HEINRICH ALBERT). 1839-1910. German veterinarian. See: World Who's Who Sci. Johne's bacillus, Johne's disease, Johne's stain, Johnin.

Johne's bacillus (Johne, Albert): Medicine. See: Dorland; Stedman; Webster's 3d.

Johne's disease (Johne, Albert): Medicine. See: Dorland; Jablonski; Stedman; Webster's 3d.; Winburne.

Johne's stain (Johne, Albert): Medicine. See: Stedman.

Johnie McL.'s disease (Derivation undetermined). See: Hurler's syndrome.

Johnin (Johne, Albert): Medicine. See: Stedman; Webster's 3d.

Johnite (John, Johann Friedrich): Earth Sciences. See: Thrush.

Johnniac (computer) (John, Joseph?): Engineering and Industry. See: Internat. Dict. Phys. Elec.

Johnny Appleseed (Chapman, John): Generic Word (planter). See: Hendrickson.

Johnny Appleseed. See: Chapman, John.

Johnny Mitchell trains (Mitchell, John): History. See: Thrush.

John's cyclic incomplete block designs (John, Peter William Meredith): Statistics. See: Kendall.

John's wort (John the Baptist, Saint). See: Saint John's wort.

JOHNSEN, ALFRED. 1887-1930. Danish engineer. See: Kraks Blaa Bog., 1930. Johnsen (or Johnson)-Rahbek effect.

Johnsen (or Johnson)-Rahbek effect (Johnsen, Alfred and Rahbek, Knud): Electronics. See: Ballentyne; Thewlis.

Johnson /30 cal. machine gun Model 1941 (Johnson, Melvin Maynard, Jr.): Weapons. See: Quick.

JOHNSON, ALBERT. 1869-1957. American legislator. See: Biog. Direct. Amer. Congress. Johnson restrictive immigration bill.

Johnson and Lark-Horowitz effect (or formula) (Johnson, Vivian Annabelle and Lark-Horowitz, Karl): Electronics. See: Hughes; Van Nostrand Sci. Encyc.

JOHNSON, ANDREW. 1808-1875. American president. See: Dict. Amer. Biog. Johnsonian (Johnsonite and Johnsonize).

Johnson concentrator (Derivation undetermined): Engineering and Industry. See: Thrush.

Johnson Debt Default Act (Johnson, Hiram Warren): Politics. See: Morris.

JOHNSON, FRANK B. 1919- . American pathologist. See: Direct. Med. Specialists, 1970-1971. Dubin-Johnson syndrome.

JOHNSON, FRANK CHAMBLISS. 1894-1934. American pediatrician. (Biography source unavailable.) Stevens-Johnson syndrome.

JOHNSON, SIR GEORGE. 1818-1896. English physician. See: Dict. Nat. Biog., 1st Suppl. Johnson's test.

Johnson grass (Johnson, William): Botany. See: Mathews, M. M.; Webster's 3d.; Winburne.

JOHNSON, HIRAM WARREN. 1866-1945. American legislator. See: Biog. Direct. Amer. Congress. Johnson Debt Default Act.

JOHNSON, JACK (In full: JOHN ARTHUR). 1878-1946. American Negro boxer. See: Encyc. Brit., 1973. Jack Johnson (howitzer and shell).

JOHNSON, JOHN. 1706-1791. English sect founder. See: Dict. Nat. Biog. Johnsonian Baptists.

JOHNSON, JOHN BERTRAND. b. 1877. Swedish-born American physicist. See: Pogg., vols. 6, 7b. Johnson noise.

JOHNSON, LORAND VICTOR. 1905- . American ophthalmic surgeon. See: Nat. Cycl. Amer. Biog., vol. L, pp. 539-540. Johnson's syndrome.

JOHNSON, MELVIN MAYNARD, JR. 1909-1965. American inventor. See: Who Was Who Amer., 1961-1968. Johnson .30 cal. machine gun Model 1941.

Johnson milling machine (Johnson, R.): Engineering and Industry. See: Auger.

Johnson-Neyman method (Johnson, Palmer Oliver and Neyman, Jerzy): Statistics. See: Good.

Johnson noise (Johnson, John Bertrand): Electronics. See: Ballentyne; Hughes; Markus; Thewlis; Van Nostrand Sci. Encyc. under "Noise"; Webster's 3d.

JOHNSON, NORMAN LLOYD. fl. 1949. English statistician. Cited in: Mansell. Johnson's system.

JOHNSON, PALMER OLIVER. b. 1892. American statistician. See: Amer. Men Sci., 6th ed. Johnson-Neyman method.

JOHNSON, R. fl. 1818. Engineer. (Biography source unavailable.) Johnson milling machine.

Johnson restrictive immigration bill (Johnson, Albert): Politics. See: Jameson.

JOHNSON, SAMUEL. 1709-1784. English author and lexicographer. See: Dict. Nat. Biog. Johnsonese, Johnsonian, Johnsoniana, Johnson's dictionary.

JOHNSON, TREAT BALDWIN. 1875-1947. American chemist. See: Who Was Who Amer., 1943-1950. Wheeler-Johnson test.

JOHNSON, VIVIAN ANNABELLE. 1912- . American physicist. See: Amer. Men and Women Sci., 12th ed. Johnson and Lark-Horowitz effect (or formula).

JOHNSON (JOHNSTON), WILLIAM. d. 1859. American farmer. (Biography source unavailable.) Johnson grass.

JOHNSON, WILLIAM EUGENE "PUSSYFOOT." 1862-1945. American reformer. See: Who Was Who Amer., 1943-1950. Pussyfoot.

Johnsonese (Johnson, Samuel): Generic Word (rambling, polysyllabic writing style). See: Hendrickson; Scott; Webster's 3d.

Johnsonian (Johnson, Samuel): Literature. See: Hendrickson; Webster's 3d.

Johnsonian (Johnsonite and Johnsonize) (Johnson, Andrew): History. See: Mathews, M. M.

Johnsonian Baptists (Johnson, John): Religion. See: Canney.

Johnsoniana (Johnson, Samuel): Literature. See: Webster's 3d.

Johnson's dictionary (Johnson, Samuel): Linguistics. See: Barnhart (Eng. Lit.); Lockwood.

Johnson's syndrome (Johnson, Lorand Victor): Medicine. See: Jablonski.

Johnson's system (Johnson, Norman Lloyd): Statistics. See: Kendall.

Johnson's test (Johnson, Sir George): Medicine. See: Dorland; Stedman.

JOHNSTON, CHRISTOPHER. d. 1891. American physician. (Biography source unavailable.) Johnston's (or Johnstonian) organ.

JOHNSTON, SIR HARRY HAMILTON. 1858-1927. English administrator, explorer and author. See: World Who's Who Sci. Okapia Johnstoni?

Johnston vanner (Derivation undetermined): Engineering and Industry. See: Thrush.

JOHNSTONE. No dates. Hangman. (Biography source unavailable.) Johnstone (or St. Johnstone's tippet).

Johnstone (or St. Johnstone's tippet) (Johnstone): Generic Word (halter). See: Brewer.

JOHNSTONE, ALEXANDER. fl. 1888. Scottish geologist. Cited in: Royal Soc. Cat. Sci. Pap., 1884-1900. Johnstone test.

Johnstone test (Johnstone, Alexander): Chemistry. See: Van Nostrand Chem. Dict.

Johnston's (or Johnstonian) organ (Johnston, Christopher): Zoology. See: Gray; Henderson; Pennak; Webster's 3d.

JOHNSTRUP, FREDERIK. 1818-1894. Danish mineralogist. See: Danmarks hist. Bla Bog. Johnstrupite.

Johnstrupite (Johnstrup, Fredrik): Earth Sciences. See: Thrush; Webster's 3d.

JOINVILLE, FRANCOIS FERDINAND PHILIPPE LOUIS MARIE D'ORLEANS, PRINCE DE. 1818-1900. French naval officer and writer. See: Encyc. Brit., 1973. De Joinville (ascot).

JOLIFFE, NORMAN HAYHURST. 1901-1961. American physician. See: Nat. Cycl. Amer. Biog., vol. 45, pp. 44-45. Joliffe's syndrome.

Joliffe's syndrome (Joliffe, Norman Hayhurst): Medicine. See: Jablonski.

JOLLES, ADOLF. 1864-1944. German chemist. See: Pogg., vols. 4, 5, 6, 7a. Jolles formal reagent, Jolles reagent for albumin in urine, Jolles' test.

Jolles formal reagent (Jolles, Adolf): Chemistry. See: Van Nostrand Chem. Dict.

Jolles reagent for albumin in urine (Jolles, Adolf): Chemistry. See: Van Nostrand Chem. Dict.

Jolles' test (Jolles, Adolf): Chemistry. See: Dorland; Stedman.

Jolly balance (Von Jolly, Philipp Johann Gustav): Physics. See: Hackh; Thrush; Webster's 3d.

Jolly bodies (Jolly, Justin). See: Howell-Jolly bodies.

JOLLY, FRIEDRICH. 1844-1904. German neurologist. See: World Who's Who Sci. Jolly's reaction.

JOLLY, JUSTIN. 1870-1953. French histologist. See: World Who's Who Sci. Jolly bodies.

Jolly, Philipp Johann Gustav von. See: Von Jolly, Philipp Johann Gustav.

Jolly's reaction (Jolly, Friedrich): Medicine. See: Dorland; Stedman.

Joly balance (Joly, John): Engineering and Industry. See: Auger.

Joly block photometer (block screen or screen) (Joly, John): Physics. See: Internat. Dict. Phys. Elec.; Thewlis; Van Nostrand Sci. Encyc.

JOLY, JOHN. 1857-1933. Irish physicist and geologist. See: Dict. Sci. Biog. Joly balance, Joly block photometer (block screen or screen), Joly steam calorimeter.

Joly steam calorimeter (Joly, John): Physics. See: Van Nostrand Sci. Encyc.

Jominy test (Jominy, Walter Edwin): Engineering and Industry. See: Auger; Thrush; Van Nostrand Sci. Encyc.

JOMINY, WALTER EDWIN. b. 1893. American metallurgical engineer. See: Amer. Men Sci., 10th ed. Jominy test.

JONAH. Hebrew prophet in the Old Testament. See: New Encyc. Brit., 1974, Microp. Davy Jones, Davy Jones' locker, Jonah, Jonah crab, Jonah's gourd.

Jonah (Jonah, the prophet): Generic Word (bearer of bad luck). See: Brewer; Harvey; Hendrickson; Partridge; Webster's 3d.; Weekley.

Jonah crab (Jonah): Zoology. See: Pennak.

Jonah's gourd (Jonah): Botany. See: Brewer.

JONAS, JANOS. fl. 1936. Hungarian chemist. Cited in: Chem. Abstr., vol. 31, p. 1323. Szebelledy-Jonas test.

JONAS, SIEGFRIED. b. 1874. Austrian physician. See: Biog. Lex. hervorr. Aerzte, 1880-1930. Jonas' symptom.

Jonas' symptom (Jonas, Siegfried): Medicine. See: Dorland.

JONATHAN. Biblical son of King Saul. See: Webster's Biog. Dict. David and Jonathan.

Jonathan (apple) (Hasbrouck, Jonathan): Botany. See: De Sola; Hendrickson; Partridge; Webster's 3d.; Winburne

JONCQUET, DENIS. d. 1671. French botanist. Cited in: Mansell. Joncquetia.

Joncquetia (Joncquet, Denis): Botany. See: Charnock.

JONES. Character in story by Richard Doyle (1870's). See: Benet, under "Brown, Jones and Robinson." Brown, Jones, and Robinson.

Jones Act (1) (Jones, Wesley Livsey): Politics. See: Morris.

Jones Act (2) (or Prohibition Law) (Jones, Wesley Livsey): Politics. See: Jameson; Morris. Also known as: Jones-Volstead Act, Volstead-Jones Act.

Jones Act (3) (Jones, William Atkinson): Politics. See: Morris; Smith.

Jones Act (4) (or Law) (Jones, William Atkinson): Politics. See: Jameson; Morris; Morris and Irwin; Smith.

JONES, B. fl. 1929. English chemist. Cited in: Chem. Abstr., vol. 23, p. 4637. Clarke-Jones test reaction.

JONES, CLEMENS. fl. 1887. American metallurgist. Cited in: Royal Soc. Cat. Sci. Pap., 1884-1900. Jones reductor.

Jones-Connally Farm Relief Act (Jones, Marvin and Connally, Thomas Terry): Politics. See: Morris.

Jones-Costigan Sugar Act (Jones, Marvin and Costigan, Edward Prentiss): Politics. See: Morris.

Jones' disease (Jones, William Alfred?): Medicine. See: Jablonski.

JONES, E. C. fl. 1915. American engineer. Cited in: Chem. Abstr., vol. 9, pp. 2584, 3357. Jones process.

JONES, EDWARD. 1856-1920. American statistician. (Biography source unavailable.) Dow-Jones average (or index).

JONES, ERNST (In full: ALFRED ERNST). b. 1879. Canadian psychiatrist. See: Biog. Lex. hervorr. Aerzte, 1880-1930. Ross-Jones test.

JONES, HENRY (Pseud.: CAVENDISH). 1831-1899. English writer on whist. See: Dict. Nat. Biog., 1st supp. Cavendish (1) (treatise on whist), Cavendish (2) (hand in whist).

Jones, Henry Bence. See: Bence Jones, Henry.

JONES, HENRY CHAPMAN. 1855(?)-1932. English chemist and photographer. See: Who Was Who, 1929-1940. Chapman Jones plate tester.

JONES, HOWARD ALGERNON. 1898- . American chemist. See: Amer. Men Sci., 10th ed. Jones-Smith test.

JONES, HUGH T. b. 1892. American orthopedic surgeon. (Biography source unavailable.) Reichel-Jones-Henderson syndrome.

JONES, HUMPHREY OWEN. 1876-1912. English chemist. See: Pogg., vol. 5. Jones-Tasker test reaction.

JONES, JESSE LEE. fl. 1915. American metallurgist. Cited in: Mansell. Jones reagent.

JONES, JOHN. 1729-1791. American surgeon. See: World Who's Who Sci. Jones's nasal splint.

JONES, JOHN PAUL. 1747-1792. Scottish-born American revolutionary naval officer. See: Dict. Amer. Biog. John Paul Jones's raids, Paul Jones.

JONES, JOHN VIRIAMU. 1856-1901. English physicist. See: Dict. Nat. Biog., 2nd suppl. Ayrton-Jones current balance.

JONES, KATE EMERY SANBORN. b. 1860. American librarian. See: Who Was Who Amer., vol. 4. Cutter-Sanborn three-figure table.

JONES, L. B. fl. 1915. American engineer. Cited in: Chem. Abstr., vol. 9, pp. 2584, 3357. Jones process.

Jones' law (Jones, Thomas Franklin, Jr.): Sociology. See: Martin.

Jones' law of hierarchical limits (Jones, Thomas Franklin, Jr.): Sociology. See: Martin.

JONES, MARVIN (In full: JOHN MARVIN). 1886- . American legislator. See: Biog. Direct. Amer. Congress. Bankhead-Jones Farm Tennant Act, Jones-Connally Farm Relief Act, Jones-Costigan Sugar Act.

Jones process (Jones, E. C. and Jones, L. B.): Chemistry. See: Van Nostrand Chem. Dict.

Jones reagent (Jones, Jesse Lee): Chemistry. See: Hackh.

Jones reductor (Jones, Clemens): Engineering and Industry. See: Hackh; Van Nostrand Chem. Dict.; Webster's 3d.

Jones riffle (Derivation undetermined): Engineering and Industry. See: Thrush.

JONES, SIR ROBERT. 1858-1933. English orthopedic surgeon. See: Dict. Nat. Biog., 5th suppl. Jones's position, Jones's splint.

Jones signature press (Derivation undetermined): Printing. See: Lockwood.

Jones-Smith test (Jones, Howard Algernon and Smith, Charles Meldrum): Chemistry. See: Van Nostrand Chem. Dict.

Jones splitter (Derivation undetermined): Engineering and Industry. See: Thrush.

Jones symbols (Derivation undetermined): Mathematics. See: Ballentyne.

Jones-Tasker test reaction (Jones, Humphrey Owen and Tasker, H. S.): Chemistry. See: Van Nostrand Chem. Dict.

JONES, THOMAS DUCKETT. 1899-1954. American physician. See: Amer. Men Sci., 8th ed. T. Duckett Jones Memorial Award.

JONES, THOMAS FRANKLIN, JR. 1916- . American university administrator. See: Leaders Educ., 4th ed., 1971. Jones' law, Jones' law of hierarchical limits, Tom Jones' first law.

Jones-Volstead Act (Jones, Wesley Livsey and Volstead, Andrew Joseph). See: Jones Act (or Prohibition Law).

JONES, WESLEY LIVSEY. 1863-1932. American legislator. See: Biog. Direct. Amer. Congress. Jones Act (1), Jones Act (2) (or Prohibition Law), Jones-White Act.

Jones-White Act (Jones, Wesley Livsey and White, Wallace, Humphrey, Jr.): Politics. See: Morris.

JONES, SIR WILLIAM. 1746-1794. English Orientalist and jurist. See: Dict. Nat. Biog. Jonesia.

JONES, WILLIAM ALFRED. b. 1892. Canadian radiologist. See: Direct. Med. Specialists, 1965-1966. Jones' disease?

JONES, WILLIAM ATKINSON. 1849-1918. American legislator. See: Biog. Direct. Amer. Congress. Jones Act (3), Jones Act (4) (or Law).

Jones zone (Derivation undetermined): Physics. See: Ballentyne.

JONESCU, ANNA. fl. 1909. Rumanian chemist. Cited in: Chem. Abstr., vol. 3, pp. 1781, 2184. Jonescu test.

Jonescu test (Jonescu, Anna): Chemistry. See: Van Nostrand Chem. Dict.

Jonesia (Jones, Sir William): Botany. See: Charnock.

Jones's nasal splint (Jones, John): Medicine. See: Dorland.

Jones's position (Jones, Sir Robert): Medicine. See: Dorland.

Jones's splint (Jones, Sir Robert): Medicine. See: Dorland.

JONKERS, GARRIT HENDRIK. fl. 1946-1961. Dutch ophthalmologist. Cited in: Mansell. Waardenburg-Jonkers disease.

ONNESCO, THOMA. 1860-1926. Rumanian physician. See: Biog. Lex. rvorr. Aerzte, 1880-1930. Jonnesco's fold, Jonnesco's fossa, Jonnesco's eration, Jonnesco's spinal anesthesia.

nnesco's fold (Jonnesco, Thoma): Medicine. See: Dorland.

nnesco's fossa (Jonnesco, Thoma): Anatomy. See: Donath; Dorland; edman.

nnesco's operation (Jonnesco, Thoma): Medicine. See: Dorland; Stedman.

nnesco's spinal anesthesia (Jonnesco, Thoma): Medicine. See: Dorland.

ONSON, BEN. ca. 1573-1637. English dramatist. See: Dict. Nat. Biog. nsonian, tribe of Ben.

nsonian (Jonson, Ben): Literature. See: Webster's 3d.

ONSTON, JOHNS. 1603-1675. Scottish physician in Poland. See: Dict. i. Biog. Jonston's alopecia (or area).

nston's alopecia (or area) (Jonston, Johns): Medicine. See: Dorland; edman. Also known as: Cazenave's vitiligo, Celsus' alopecia (area or iligo).

ONVAL, N. J. fl. 1841. French engineer. (Biography source unavailable.) nval turbine.

nval turbine (Jonval, N. J.): Engineering and Industry. See: Auger.

os Ballet (Jooss, Kurt): Dance. See: Chujoy.

OOSS, KURT. 1901-   . German choreographer, dancer and director of nce company. See: Wer Ist Wer?, 1974-1975. Joos Ballet.

OOSTEN, HUGO J. fl. 1925-1954. Dutch soil engineer. Cited in: ansell. Joosten process.

osten process (Joosten, Hugo J.): Engineering and Industry. See: Thrush.

plin jig (Derivation undetermined): Engineering and Industry. See: Thrush.

ORAM. Son of Tou in the Old Testament. See: Hastings (Dict. Bible.) rum.

ORDAN. fl. ca. 1864. German physician. Cited in: Dana, p. 88. rdanite.

ORDAN, ALEXIS (In full: CLAUDE THOMAS ALEXIS). 1814-1897. French tanist. See: Dict. Sci. Biog. Jordanism, Jordanon.

rdan algebra (Jordan, Pascual): Mathematics. See: New Encyc. Brit., 74, Microp.

ORDAN, CAMILLE (In full: MARIE ENNEMOND CAMILLE). 1838-1922. ench mathematician. See: Dict. Sci. Biog. Jordan content, Jordan curve, rdan curve theorem, Jordan-Hoelder theorem, Jordan matrix (and form), rdan method, Jordan normal form, Jordan's condition for convergence of urier series.

rdan chest (Jordan, Joseph): Engineering and Industry. See: Webster's 3d.

rdan content (Jordan, Camille): Mathematics. See: James.

rdan cosmological theory (Jordan, Pascual): Physics. See: Van Nostrand i. Encyc.

rdan curve (Jordan, Camille): Mathematics. See: English; Internat. Dict. . Math.; James; Webster's 3d.

rdan curve theorem (Jordan, Camille): Mathematics. See: James; Van ostrand Sci. Encyc.

ORDAN, DAVID STARR. 1851-1931. American zoologist. See: Dict. Sci. og. Jordan's law (1), Jordans' law (2) (or rule), Jordanella floridae?

ORDAN, EDWARD BRENT, JR. 1906-   . American physicist. See: Amer. en Sci., 10th ed. Bainbridge-Jordan mass spectrograph.

ORDAN, F. W. fl. 1919-1920. English engineer. Cited in: Pogg., vol. under "Eccles, William Henry." Eccles-Jordan circuit.

rdan-Hoelder theorem (Jordan, Camille and Hoelder, Otto Ludwig): Mathe-atics. See: Internat. Dict. Ap. Math.

ORDAN, JOSEPH. fl. 1859. American inventor. (Biography source unavail-le.) Jordan chest, Jordan refiner (or engine).

JORDAN, KARL (In full: HEINRICH ERNST KARL). 1861-1954. English entomologist. See: Who's Who Brit. Sci., 1953. Jordan's organ?

Jordan lag (Jordan, Pascual?): Physics. See: Thewlis.

Jordan matrix (and form) (Jordan, Camille): Mathematics. See: Internat. Dict. Ap. Math.; James.

Jordan method (Jordan, Camille): Mathematics. See: Internat. Dict. Ap. Math.

Jordan normal form (Jordan, Camille): Mathematics. See: Internat. Dict. Ap. Math.

JORDAN, PASCUAL (In full: ERNST PASCUAL). 1902-   . Graman physicist. See: World Who's Who Sci. Jordan algebra, Jordan cosmological theory, Jordan lag?, Jordan-Wigner commutation rules.

Jordan refiner (or engine) (Jordan, Joseph): Engineering and Industry. See: Van Nostrand Chem. Dict.; Webster's 3d.

JORDAN, ROBERT THAYER. 1922-   . American librarian. See: Who's Who Libr. Service, 4th ed. Clapp-Jordan formulae.

Jordan sunshine recorder (Derivation undetermined): Earth Sciences. See: Huschke; Van Nostrand Sci. Encyc.

Jordan-Wigner commutation rules (Jordan, Pascual and Wigner, Eugene): Physics. See: Internat. Dict. Phys. Elec.

Jordanella floridae (Jordan, David Starr?): Zoology. See: Pennak.

Jordanism (Jordan, Alexis): Botany. See: Gray.

Jordanite (Jordan): Earth Sciences. See: Thrush; Webster's 3d.

Jordanon (Jordan, Alexis): Biology. See: Dict. Sci. Biog.; Henderson; Webster's 3d.

Jordan's condition for convergence of Fourier series (Jordan, Camille): Math-ematics. See: James.

Jordan's law (1) (Jordan, David Starr): Biology. See: Gray; Webster's 3d.

Jordans' law (2) (or rule) (Jordan, David Starr): Zoology. See: Gray; Pennak.

Jordan's organ (Jordan, Karl?): Zoology. See: Henderson.

JORIS (JORISZOON), DAVID. ca. 1502-1556. Dutch Anabaptist leader. See: Encyc. Brit., 1973. Jorists.

JORISSEN, ARMAND. 1853-1920. Belgian pharmacist. See: J. Pharm. Belg., vol. 3 (1921), pp. 121-157. Jorissen reagent for glycosides and alka-loids, Jorissen reagent for nitrite?, Jorissen test for titanium?

Jorissen reagent for glycosides and alkaloids (Jorissen, Armand): Chemistry. See: Van Nostrand Chem. Dict.

Jorissen reagent for nitrite (Jorissen, Armand?): Chemistry. See: Van Nostrand Chem. Dict.

Jorissen reagent for peroxide in ether (Jorissen, Willem Paulinus?): Chemistry. See: Van Nostrand Chem. Dict.

Jorissen test for formaldehyde (Jorissen, Willem Paulinus?): Chemistry. See: Hackh; Van Nostrand Chem. Dict.

Jorissen test for titanium (Jorissen, Armand?): Chemistry. See: Van Nostrand Chem. Dict.

JORISSEN, WILLEM PAULINUS. 1869-1940. Dutch chemist. See: Pogg., vols. 4, 5, 6. Jorissen reagent for peroxide in ether?, Jorissen test for form-aldehyde?

JORISSENNE, GUSTAV. b. 1846. Belgian physician. Cited in: Kelly. Jorissenne's sign.

Jorissenne's sign (Jorissenne, Gustav): Medicine. See: Dorland; Stedman.

Jorists (Joris, David): Religion. See: Canney; Webster's 3d. Also known as: Davidists (or Davidians).

JORKINS. Character from Charles Dickens' novel, "David Copperfield" (1849-50). See: Harvey. Spenlow and Jorkins.

Jorum (Joram): Generic Word (large drinking bowl). See: Brewer; Partridge; Webster's 3d.

Josef (Joseph or Josup) (elephant fish) (Joseph): Zoology. See: Webster's 3d.

Josefite (Joseph ?): Earth Sciences. See: Thrush.

JOSEPH. Old Testament patriarch. See: New Encyc. Brit., 1974, Microp. Josef (Joseph or Josup) (elephant fish), Joseph (Joseph, the Patriarch), Joseph's coat, Joseph's coat (amaranth), Joseph (riding coat or cloak), Josie (or flying Josie).

JOSEPH (Or: JOSEPH AUGUST). b. 1872. Austrian archduke and regent of Hungary. See: Webster's Biog. Dict. Josefite?

Joseph (Joseph, the Patriarch) (Joseph): Generic Word (one unable to be seduced). See: Brewer.

JOSEPH II. 1741-1790. Austrian emperor. See: New Encyc. Brit., 1974. Josephinism.

Joseph A. Sprague Memorial Award (Sprague, Joseph A.): Photography. See: Focal Encyc. Photog. under "Awards (America)."

Joseph-and-Mary (flower) (Joseph, Saint and Mary, Virgin-Mother): Botany. See: Webster's 3d.

JOSEPH, ANTONE. fl. 1845. Portuguese-born American citizen. (Biography source unavailable.) Joseph illness.

JOSEPH, HEINRICH. b. 1875. German zoologist. See: Kuerschner's Deut. Gel. Kal., vol. 4, 1931. Joseph's cell.

Joseph illness (Joseph, Antone): Medicine. See: Time, Oct. 13, 1975.

JOSEPH OF VOLOKOLAMSK. 1439-1515. Leader in the Russian orthodox church. See: New Encyc. Brit., 1974, Microp. Josephite.

JOSEPH, RENE. 1907-   . French pediatrician. Cited in: Mansell. Joseph's syndrome?

Joseph (riding coat or cloak) (Joseph): Fashion. See: Harvey; Hendrickson; Partridge; Picken; Webster's 3d.

JOSEPH, SAINT. fl. 1st c. A.D. Father of Jesus in the New Testament. See: Holweck. Joseph-and-Mary, Josephite Fathers (Missionaries, Josephites (2), or St. Joseph's Society of the Sacred Heart), Josephites (1) (or Congregation of St. Joseph), Saint Joseph's lily, St. Joseph's rod, Sisters of St. Joseph.

Joseph W. Lippincott Award (Lippincott, Joseph Wharton): Library Science. See: Harrod.

JOSEPHINE (In full: MARIE ROSE JOSEPHINE TASCHER DE LA PAGERIE DE BEAUHARNAIS). 1763-1814. French empress. See: Encyc. Brit., 1973. Josephine knot, Josephinia, Lapageria.

Josephine knot (Josephine): Fashion. See: Picken.

Josephine('s) lily (Josephine). See: Lapageria.

Josephinia (Josephine): Botany. See: Charnock.

Josephinism (Joseph II): Religion. See: Attwater; New Cath. Encyc.

Josephite (Joseph of Volokolamsk): Religion. See: Webster's 3d.

Josephite (Smith, Joseph, the younger): Religion. See: Mathews, M. M.

Josephite Fathers (Missionaries, Josephites (2), or St. Joseph's Society of the Sacred Heart) (Joseph, Saint): Religion. See: New Cath. Encyc.

Josephites (1) (or Congregation of St. Joseph) (Joseph, Saint): Religion. See: Attwater.

Joseph's cell (Joseph, Heinrich): Zoology. See: Gray.

Joseph's coat (Joseph): Generic Word (multi-colored coatlike garment). See: Picken.

Joseph's coat (amaranth) (Joseph): Botany. See: Blumberg; Winburne.

Josephs-Diamond-Blackfan anemia (or syndrome) (Josephs, Hugh Wilson; Diamond, Louis Klein; and Blackfan, Kenneth D.). See: Diamond-Blackfan syndrome.

JOSEPHS, HUGH WILSON. b. 1892. American padiatrician. See: Amer. Men Sci., 10th ed. Josephs-Diamond-Blackfan anemia (or syndrome).

Joseph's syndrome (Joseph, Rene?): Medicine. See: Jablonski; Wolman.

JOSEPHSON, BRIAN DAVID. 1940-   . Welsh physicist. See: Direct. Brit. Sci., 1971-1972. Josephson effect (and junction).

Josephson effect (and junction) (Josephson, Brian David): Physics. See: Ballentyne; Barnhart (New Eng.); New Encyc. Brit., 1974, Microp.; Thewlis.

Josh (Shaw, Henry Wheeler): Generic Word (to kid). See: Hendrickson.

Joshi effect (Joshi, Shridhar S.): Physics. See: Ballentyne; Hughes; Thewlis; Van Nostrand Sci. Encyc.

JOSHI, SHRIDHAR S. 1898-   . Indian physical chemist. See: Pogg., vols. 6, 7b. Joshi effect.

JOSHUA. Old Testament Israelite chieftain. See: New Encyc. Brit., 1974, Microp. Joshua tree.

Joshua tree (Joshua): Botany. See: Partridge; Webster's 3d.; Winburne.

JOSIAH. ca. 640-609 B.C. King of Judah. See: New Encyc. Brit., 1974, Microp. Josianic.

Josianic (Josiah): Religion. See: Webster's 3d.

Josie (or flying Josie) (Joseph): Fashion. See: Picken; Webster's 3d.

JOSSIN. fl. before 1860's. Botanist. (Biography source unavailable.) Jossinia.

Jossinia (Jossin): Botany. See: Charnock.

JOST, ADOLF. b. 1874. German psychologist. Cited in: Mansell. Jost's law.

Jost-Lehmann representation (Derivation undetermined): Physics. See: Internat. Dict. Ap. Math.

Jost's law (Jost, Adolf): Psychology. See: Chaplin; Drever; English; Wolman.

JOSUE, OTTO. 1869-1923. French physician. See: Biog. Lex. hervorr. Aerzte. Roger-Josue test.

JOUGUET, EMILE (In full: JACQUES CHARLES EMILE). b. 1871. French physicist. See: Pogg., vols. 5, 6. Chapman-Jouguet (or Jouget) condition, Chapman-Jouguet (or Jouget) state.

Joukowski airfoils (or airfoil profile) (Schukowski, Nikolai Egorovic): Engineering and Industry. See: Internat. Dict. Ap. Math.; James under "Joukowski transformation."

Joukowski condition (Schukowski, Nikolai Egorovic): Engineering and Industry. See: Internat. Dict. Ap. Math.

Joukowski, Nikolaj Egorovic. See: Schukowski, Nikolai Egorovic.

Joukowski transformation (Schukowski, Nikolai Egorovic): Engineering and Industry. See: James.

Joukowski's proof (Schukowski, Nikolai Egorovic): Aviation. See: Van Nostrand Sci. Encyc. under "Circulation (Aerodynamic)."

Joule (Joule, James Prescott): Physics. See: Dresner; Focal Encyc. Photog.; Thewlis; Van Nostrand Chem. Dict.; Van Nostrand Sci. Encyc.; Webster's 3d.

Joule air engine (Joule, James Prescott): Engineering and Industry. See: Auger.

Joule-Clausius velocity (Joule, James Prescott and Clausius, Rudolf Julius Emanuel): Physics. See: Internat. Dict. Phys. Elec.

Joule('s) cycle (Joule, James Prescott): Physics. See: Thewlis; Van Nostrand Sci. Encyc.; Webster's 3d. Also known as: Brayton cycle.

Joule effect (1) (Joule or Joulean heat) (Joule, James Prescott): Physics. See: Hughes; Markus; Thewlis; Webster's 3d.

Joule effect (2) (or Joule magnetostriction effect) (Joule, James Prescott): Physics. See: Ballentyne; Hackh; Hughes; Internat. Dict. Phys. Elec.; Thewlis.

Joule effect (3) (Joule, James Prescott). See: Joule-Thomson (or Joule-Kelvin) effect.

Joule('s) equivalent (unit or constant) (Joule, James Prescott): Physics. See: Hackh; Hughes; Huschke; Thewlis; Webster's 3d.

Joule experiment (Joule, James Prescott): Physics. See: Internat. Dict. Phys. Elec.; Thewlis.

Joule (or Joulean) heat (Joule, James Prescott). See: Joule effect (1).

oule heating (of a plasma) (Joule, James Prescott): Physics. See: Internat.
ct. Phys. Elec.

OULE, JAMES PRESCOTT. 1818-1889. English physicist. See: Dict. Sci.
og. Joule, Joule air engine, Joule-Clausius velocity, Joule effect (1)
oule or Joulean heat), Joule effect (2) (or Joule magnetostriction effect),
ule experiment, Joule heating (of a plasma), Joule-Rowland method for me-
anical equivalent of heat, Joule-Thomson coefficient, Joule('s) cycle, Joule('s)
uivalent (unit or constant), Joule('s) law (1) (electric heating), Joule('s)
w (2) (or law of energy content), Joule('s) law (3) (molecular heat), Joule-
omson inversion temperature, Joule-Thomson (or Joule-Kelvin) effect, Joule-
omson valve.

ule-Kelvin effect (Joule, James Prescott and Thomson, William, Lord Kelvin).
e: Joule-Thomson effect.

ule('s) law (1) (electric heating) (Joule, James Prescott): Physics. See:
llentyne; Hackh; Hughes; Internat. Dict. Ap. Math.; Thewlis; Van Nostrand
i. Encyc.; Webster's 3d.

ule('s) law (2) (or law of energy content) (Joule, James Prescott): Physics.
ee: Hackh; Hughes; Thewlis; Webster's 3d. Also known as: Mayer's hypoth-
is.

ule('s) law (3) (molecular heat) (Joule, James Prescott): Physics. See:
ackh; Van Nostrand Chem. Dict. Also known as: Kopp('s) law, Woestyn's
w (or rule).

ule-Rowland method for mechanical equivalent of heat (Joule, James Prescott
d Rowland, Henry Augustus): Physics. See: Internat. Dict. Phys. Elec.

ule-Thomson coefficient (Joule, James Prescott and Thomson, William, Lord
elvin): Physics. See: Hughes; Internat. Dict. Ap. Math.; Internat. Dict.
ys. Elec.; Thewlis.

ule-Thomson (or Joule-Kelvin) effect (Joule, James Prescott and Thomson,
illiam, Lord Kelvin): Physics. See: Ballentyne; Hackh; Hughes; Thewlis;
an Nostrand Sci. Encyc.; Webster's 3d.

ule-Thomson inversion temperature (Joule, James Prescott and Thomson,
illiam, Lord Kelvin): Physics. See: Internat. Dict. Phys. Elec.; Thewlis.

ule-Thomson valve (Joule, James Prescott and Thomson, William, Lord Kelvin):
ysics. See: Thewlis.

OURDAIN, ANSELME-LOUIS-BERNARD-BERCHILLET. 1734-1816. French
rgeon. See: Biog. Lex. hervorr. Aerzte. Jourdain's disease.

urdain's disease (Jourdain, Anselme-Louis-Bernard-Berchillet): Medicine. See:
rland.

OURDAN, FRIEDRICH. fl. 1879-1883. German chemist. Cited in: Royal
c. Cat. Sci. Pap., 1874-1883. Jourdan-Ullmann-Goldberg synthesis.

urdan-Ullmann-Goldberg synthesis (or acridone synthesis) (Jourdan, Friedrich;
llmann, Fritz; and Goldberg, Irma): Chemistry. See: Krauch and Kunz;
an Nostrand Chem. Dict.

ve (Jupiter): Generic Word (tin). See: Charnock.

vellana (Jovellanos, Gaspar Melchior de): Botany. See: Charnock.

OVELLANOS, GASPAR MELCHIOR DE. 1744-1811. Spanish statesman and
thor. See: Encyc. Brit., 1973. Jovellana.

ve's beard (Jupiter, the god). See: Jupiter's beard.

ve's-flower(s) (Jupiter): See: Webster's 3d.

ve's fruit(s) (Jupiter): Botany. See: Gray; Webster's 3d.

vial (Jupiter): Generic Word (merry). See: Charnock; Hargrave; Partridge;
yfe; Webster's 3d.

vian (Jupiter): Generic Word (imperious superiority). See: Partridge;
ebster's 3d.

OVIGNOT, CHARLES. fl. 1909. French scientist. Cited in: Chem. Abstr.,
ecenn. Index, 1907-1916. Jovignot test.

vignot test (Jovignot, Charles): Engineering and Industry. See: Auger;
ewlis.

vite (Jupiter): Weapons. See: Matthews, M.M.

OY, DAVID. 1825-1903. English engineer. See: Who Was Who, 1897-1916.
y's valve gear.

JOY, LAURA. fl. 19th c. Friend of Wochler. Cited in Bailey. Laurite.

Joyce atomizer (Joyce, J. R.): Engineering and Industry. See: Auger.

JOYCE, J. R. fl. 1949-1953. English? engineer. Cited in: Chem. Abstr.
Joyce atomizer.

JOYCE, JAMES AUGUSTINE. 1882-1941. Irish writer. See: New Encyc.
Brit., 1974. Joycean.

Joycean (Joyce, James Augustine): Literature. See: Webster's 3d.

joys of Mary (Mary, Virgin-Mother): Religion. See: Attwater.

Joy's valve gear (Joy, David): Engineering and Industry. See: Auger.

JUBA I. ca. 85-46 B.C. King of Numidia. See: Encyc. Brit., 1973.
Jubaea?

JUBA II. ca. 50 B.C.-24 A.D. King of Numidia. See: Encyc. Brit., 1973.
Jubaea?

Jubaea (Juba I? or Juba II?): Botany. See: Taylor, N.

Juckes chain grate (Juckes, J.): Engineering and Industry. See: Auger.

JUCKES, J. fl. 1841. English engineer. (Biography source unavailable.)
Juckes chain grate.

JUDAH. In the Bible, the 4th son of Jacob. See: Hastings (Dict. Bible).
Judahite, Judaic (or Judaical), Judaism (and Judaize).

Judahite (Judah): History. See: Webster's 3d.

Judaic (or Judaical) (Judah): Generic Word (Jews). See: Charnock.

Judaism (and Judaize) (Judah): Religion. See: Charnock; Encyc. Brit., 1973.

Judas (or Judas Iscariot): Generic Word (traitor). See: Hendrickson; Partridge;
Webster's 3d; Weekley.

Judas Bible (Judas Iscariot): Printing. See: Brewer.

Judas-bird (Judas Iscariot): Zoology. See: Gray.

Judas-colored (hair) (or Judas) (Judas Iscariot): Generic Word (reddish-brown).
See: Brewer; Partridge; Webster's 3d. Also known as: Cain-colored (hair) (or
Cain).

Judas ear (Judas Iscariot). See: Jew's-ear.

Judas goat (or Judas) (Judas Iscariot): Generic Word. See: Winburne;
Webster's 3d.

JUDAS ISCARIOT. d. ca. 30. Traitor of the twelve apostles of Jesus. See:
Encyc. Brit., 1973. Jew's-ear, Judas Bible, Judas-bird, Judas-colored (hair)
(or Judas), Judas goat (or Judas), Judas kiss, Judas (or Judas Iscariot), Judas
tree, Judas window (hole or slit).

Judas kiss (Judas Iscariot): Generic Word (simulated affection). See: Brewer;
Hendrickson.

Judas tree (Judas Iscariot): Botany. See: Brewer; Gray; Partridge; Phyfe;
Wagner (More Names); Webster's 3d.

Judas window (hole or slit) (Judas Iscariot): Generic Word (peephole). See:
Hendrickson; Webster's 3d.

JUDD, DEANE BREWSTER. 1900- . American physicist. See: Pogg., vol.
6. Helson-Judd effect.

judgment of Paris (Paris): Generic Word (treacherous problem). See: Jobes.

JUDSON, EGBERT PUTNAM. 1812-1893. American inventor. See: Webster's
Biog. Dict. Judson powder.

Judson powder (Judson, Egbert Putnam): Engineering and Industry. See:
Webster's 3d.

JUDY. Puppet character of English name origin. See: Jobes. Punch and
Judy.

JUENGLING, OTTO. 1884-1944. German physician. See: Biog. Lex. hervorr. Aerzte, 1880-1930. Juengling's disease (2), Perthes-Juengling disease.

Juengling's disease (1) (or polycystic osteitis) (Juengling, Otto). See: Perthes-
Juengling disease.

Juengling's disease (2) (Juengling, Otto?). See: Besnier-Boeck-Schaumann syndrome.

JUERGENS RUDOLF. 1897-1961. German hematologist. See: Blut, vol. 7 (July, 1961) pp. 165-166. Juergens' syndrome, Willebrand-Juergens syndrome.

Juergens' syndrome (Juergens, Rudolf): Medicine. See: Jablonski.

Juerst ebullioscope (Juerst, R.?): Chemistry. See: Hackh; Van Nostrand Chem. Dict.

JUERST, R. fl. 1911. American chemist. Cited in: Chem. Abstr. Juerst ebullioscope?

Juglans (Jupiter): Botany. See: Webster's 3d.

Juglar (business cycle) (Juglar, Clement): Economics. See: Webster's 3d.

JUGLAR CLEMENT (In full: JOSEPH CLEMENT). 1819-1905. French economist. See: Encyc. Soc. Sci. Juglar (business cycle.)

JUGURTHA. ca. 160-104 B.C. King of Numidia. See: Encyc. Brit., 1973. Jugurthine.

Jugurthine (Jugurtha): History. See: Webster's 3d.

JUHEL-RENOY, EDOUARD (In full: JEAN-EDOUARD). 1855-1894. French physician. See: Pagel. Juhel-Renoy's syndrome.

Juhel-Renoy's syndrome (Juhel-Renoy, Edouard): Medicine. See: Jablonski.

Jukes family (Jukes, the fictious family): Sociology: See: Pennak; Zadrozny.

JUKES, THE FICTIOUS FAMILY. Fictious family of criminal and feeble-minded tendencies. See: Dugdale. Jukes Family.

Jules Verne garnish (Verne, Jules): Food and Drink. See: De Sola.

Julian (Caesar, Gaius Julius): History. See: Webster's 3d.

Julian calendar (Caesar, Gaius Julius): Horology. See: Phyfe; Satterthwaite; Thewlis.

Julian day (Scaliger, Julius Caesar): Astronomy. See: Asimov; Satterthwaite; Van Nostrand Sci. Encyc.

Julianist(s) (Julianus the Monophysite): Religion. See: Latham; Webster's 3d.

JULIANUS THE MONOPHYSITE. fl. 511. Bishop of Halicarnassus. See: Dict. Christian Biog. under "Julianus (47)." Julianist(s).

JULIEN (or JULIENNE). No dates. Cook? (Biography source unavailable.) Julienne (soup or strips).

JULIEN, HENRY. d. 1920. Belgian geologist. Cited in: Hintze, lst suppl., p. 239. Julienite.

Julien Marie-See syndrome (Marie, Julien and See, Georges). See: Marie-See syndrome.

Julien Marie's syndrome (Marie, Julien). See: Marie's syndrome.

Julienite (Julien, Henry): Earth Sciences. See: Thrush; Webster's 3d.

Julienne (soup or strips) (Julien (or Julienne): Food and Drink. See: Charnock; Hendrickson; Phyfe.

Julien's organ (Jullien, John): Zoology. See: Gray.

JULIET (CAPULET). Heroine of Shakespeare's play "Romeo and Juliet," (1594-1595). See Harvey. capulet, Juliet cap, Juliet (slipper), Romeo and Juliet.

Juliet cap (Juliet): Fashion. See: Picken; Webster's 3d.

Juliet (slipper) (Juliet): Fashion. See: Picken; Webster's 3d.

Julio (or Giulio) (Julius II): Numismatics. See: Charnock: Webster's 3d.

JULIUS II. 1445-1513. Pope. See: Encyc. Brit., 1973. Julio (or Giulio), Pope Julius.

JULIUS, PAUL. 1862-1931. Austrian chemist. See: Pogg., vol. 6. Julius test reaction.

Julius test reaction (Julius, Paul): Chemistry. See: Van Nostrand Chem. Dict.

JULIUSBERG, FRITZ. b. 1872. German physician. See: Biog. Lex. hervorr. Aerzte, 1880-1930. Kaposi-Juliusberg dermatitis (or syndrome).

JULLIARD, GUSTAVE. 1836-1911. Belgian surgeon. See: Biog. Lex. hervor Aerzte, 1880-1930. Julliard's mask.

Julliard's mask (Julliard, Gustave): Medicine. See: Dorland; Stedman.

JULLIEN, JOHN. 1873-1928. Swiss zoologist. See: Bull. Soc. Lepidopt. Geneve, vol. 6, no. 2 (1929) pp. 45-62. Julien's organ.

July (Caesar, Gaius Julius): Generic Word. See: Brewer; Charnock; Funk.

jumping Jehoshaphat (Jehoshaphat): Generic Word. Cited in: Hendrickson under "Jezebel..."

June (Juno? or Brutus, Lucius Junius?): Generic Word. See: Charnock; Ency Brit., 1973; Funk; Hendrickson; Webster's 3d; Weekley.

JUNET, ROBERT MAURICE. 1907- . Swiss internist. See: Doc. p. servir l' histoire de l'Univ. de Geneve, vol. 10, 1948; vol. 11, 1953; vol. 12, 1959 Troell-Junet syndrome.

Jung association test (Jung, Carl Gustav): Psychology. See: Wolman.

JUNG, CARL GUSTAV. 1875-1961. Swiss psychologist and psychiatrist. See: Internat. Encyc. Soc. Sci. Jung association test, Jungian, Jungian archetypes, Jungian (or Jung's) analytical psychology (analysis or psychoanalysis).

JUNG, KARL GUSTAV. 1793-1864. Swiss anatomist. See: Biog. Lex. hervorr. Aerzte. Jung's muscle.

JUNGERMANN, LUDWIG. 1572-1653. German botanist. See: Allg. Deut. Biog. Jungermannia.

Jungermannia (Jungermann, Ludwig): Botany. See: Webster's 3d.

JUNGHANS, PAUL. b. 1885. German physician. Cited in: Index-Cat. Libr. Surg.-Gen. Off., 3d Ser., vol. 7, 1928. Wolff-Junghans test.

Jungian (Jung, Carl Gustav): Psychology. See: Webster's 3d.

Jungian (or Jung's) analytical psychology (analysis or psychoanalysis) (Jung, Carl Gustav): Psychology. See: Chaplin; Dorland; English; Stedman.

Jungian archetypes (Jung, Carl Gustav): Psychology. See: Preminger under "Nature."

Jungmann solution (Derivation undetermined): Chemistry. See: Van Nostrand Chem. Dict.

Jung's muscle (Jung, Karl Gustav): Anatomy. See: Donath; Dorland; Stedman.

JUNIUS. fl. 1769-1772. Pseudonymous English author. See: Encyc. Brit., 1973. Letters of Junius.

JUNIUS, FRANCISCUS. 1589-1677. German-born philologist and antiquary in England. See: Encyc. Brit., 1973. Junius Manuscript.

Junius Letters (Junius). See: Letters of Junius.

Junius Manuscript (Junius, Franciscus): Literature. See: Barnhart (Eng. Lit.)

JUNIUS, PAUL. b. 1871. German ophthalmologist. See: Kuerschner's Deut. Gel. Kal., vol. 4, 1931. Kuhnt-Junius degeneration (or disease).

Junker apparatus (bottle or inhaler) (Junker, F. E.): Medicine. See: Dorland.

JUNKER, F. E. fl. 1868. English physician. Cited in: Royal Soc. Cat. Sci. Pap., 1864-1873. Junker apparatus (bottle or inhaler).

Junkers bomber (Junkers, Hugo): Engineering and Industry. See: Hendrickson under "Messerschmitt..."

Junkers' gas calorimeter (Junkers, Hugo): Physics. See: Van Nostrand Sci. Encyc.

JUNKERS, HUGO. 1859-1935. German airplane designer and engineer. See: World Who's Who Sci. Junkers bomber, Junkers' gas colorimeter.

JUNO (EPITHETS: MONETA, SATURNIA). Ancient Roman goddess. See: Encyc. Brit., 1973. June?, Junoesque (or Juno), Junonia, Juno's bird, Money, Saturnia.

JUNOD, VICTOR THEODORE. 1809-1882. French physician. See: World Who's Who Sci. Junod's boot.

Junod's boot (Junod, Victor Theodore): Medicine. See: Dorland; Stedman.

Junoesque (or Juno) (Juno): Generic Word (regal, stately woman). Funk; Partridge; Webster's 3d.

...nonia (Juno): Zoology. See: Webster's 3d.

...no's bird (Juno): Zoology. See: Webster's 3d.

...PITER. Ancient Roman deity. See: Encyc. Brit., 1973. by Jove (or ...ve), Jove, Jove's-flower(s), Jove's fruit(s), Jovial, Jovian, Jovite, Juglans, ...piter's beard (or Jove's beard), Mount of Jupiter.

...piter's beard (or Jove's beard) (Jupiter): Botany. See: Gray; Webster's 3d.

...RA, GEORGE. 1911- . American physical chemist. See: Amer. Men. ...., 7th ed. Harkins and Jura method.

...RIN, JAMES. 1684-1750. English physician. See: World Who's Who Sci. ...rin('s) law (or rule).

...rin('s) law (or rule) (Jurin, James): Physics. See: Ballentyne; Van Nostrand ... Encyc.; Webster's 3d

...s Flavianum (Flavius, Gnaeus): Law. See: Black.

...s Papirianum (Papirius, Sextus): Law. See: Black; Charnock. Also known ... Lex Papiria.

...SSE. fl. 20th c.? French physician. (Biography source unavailable.) ...nbaud-Jusse syndrome.

...ssiaea (or Jussieua) (Jussieu, Bernard de): Botany. See: Charnock; Taylor, ...; Webster's 3d.

...ssiaean (or Jussieuan) (Jussieu, Bernard de and Jussieu, Antoine Laurent de): ...tany. See: Webster's 3d.

...SSIEU, ANTOINE LAURENT DE. 1748-1836. French botanist. See: World ...no's Who Sci. Jussiaean (or Jussieuan).

JUSSIEU, BERNARD DE. 1699-1777. French botanist. See: World Who's Who Sci. Jussiaea (or Jussieua), Jussiaean (or Jussieuan), Jussieu system.

Jussieu system (Jussieu, Bernard de): Botany. Cited in: World Who's Who Sci.

JUSTICE, JAMES. d. ca. 1762. Scottish gardener. See: Britten and Boulger. Justicia.

Justicia (Justice, James): Botany. See: Charnock; Taylor, N.

Justin-Mueller cuprosodic reagent (Justin-Mueller, Edward): Chemistry. See: Van Nostrand Chem. Dict.

JUSTIN-MUELLER, EDWARD. b. 1867. French chemist. See: Pogg., vol. 6. Justin-Mueller cuprosodic reagent.

JUSTINIAN I, THE GREAT. 483-565. Byzantine emperor. See: Encyc. Brit., 1973. Institutes of Justinian, Justinian code, Justinianist, pandects of Justinian.

Justinian code (Justinian I, the Great): Law. See: Charnock; Latham; New Encyc. Brit., 1974, Microp; Phyfe.

Justinianist (Justinian I, the Great): Law. See: Black.

JUSTUS, JAKOB. b. 1866. Hungarian dermatologist. See: Jaznigi. Justus' test.

Justus' test (Justus, Jakob): Medicine. See: Dorland; Stedman.

JUTRAS, ALBERT. fl. 1930-1968. Canadian radiologist. See: Canadian Med. Direct., 1968. Roy-Jutras syndrome.

JUVENAL (DECIMUS JUNIUS JUVENALIS). ca. 60-ca. 148. Roman satirist and Poet. See: Encyc. Brit., 1973. Juvenalian (satire).

Juvenalian (satire) (Juvenal): Literature. See: Barnet; Partridge.

K

K.D.B. process (Keller-Dorian, Albert and Berthon, Rodolphe): Photography. See: Focal Encyc. Photog. under "Keller-Dorian, Albert."

KABIR. 1938?-1518. Hindu mystic poet. See: Encyc. Brit., 1973. Kabirpanthi (or Kabir Panthis).

Kabirpanthi (or Kabir Panthis) (Kabir): Religion. See: Canney; Webster's 3d.

KADENACY, MICHEL. fl. 20th c.? Engineer. (Biography source unavailable.) Kadenacy principle.

Kadenacy principle (Kadenacy, Michel): Engineering and Industry. See: Auger.

KADER, BRONISLAW. 1863-1937. Polish surgeon. See: Polska Gaz. lek, vol. 16 (Dec. 12, 1937) pp. 980-981. Kader-Senn operation.

Kader-Senn operation (Kader, Bronislaw): Medicine. See: Dorland; Stedman; Also known as: Kader's operation.

Kader's operation (Kader, Bronislaw). See: Kader-Senn operation.

KAEDING, HENRY B. 1877-1913. American mining engineer. Cited in: Chem. Abstr. Kaeding('s) petrel.

Kaeding('s) petrel (Kaeding, Henry B.): Zoology. See: Mathews, M.M.; Webster's 3d.

KÁEMMERER, A. fl. 1842. Russian scientist. Cited in: Royal Soc. Cat. Sci. Pap., 1800-1863. Káemmererite.

Kaemmererite (Kaemmerer, A.): Earth Sciences. See: Webster's 3d.

KAEMPFER, ENGELBERT. 1651-1716. German physician. See: Dict. Sci. Biog. Kaempferol (or Kampferol).

Kaempferol (or Kampferol) (Kaempfer, Engelbert): Chemistry. See: Webster's 3d.

KAERBER, GERHARD HERMANN. 1901- . German physician. See: Wer Ist's?, 1951. Spearman-Kaerber method.

Kaerber's method (Kaerber, Gerhard Hermann). See: Spearman-Kaerber method.

Kaes' layer (Kaes, Theodor). See: Bechterev's band.

KAES, THEODOR. 1852-1913. German neurologist. See: Biog. Lex. hervorr. Aerzte., 1880-1930. Kaes' layer.

KAFKA, VICTOR. 1881-1955. German physician. See: World Who's Who Sci. Kafka's test (or reaction).

Kafka's test (or reaction) (Kafka, Victor): Medicine. See: Dorland.

KAHLBAUM, KARL LUDWIG. 1828-1899. German physician. See: World Who's Who Sci. Kahlbaum's disease.

Kahlbaum's disease (Kahlbaum, Karl Ludwig): Medicine. See: Dorland.

KAHLENBERG, LOUIS ALBERT BERTHOLD. 1870-1941. American chemist. See: Dict. Sci. Biog. Steinle-Kahlenberg test reaction.

Kahler-Bozzolo disease (Kahler, Otto and Bozzolo, Camillo). See: Kahler's disease (or syndrome).

KAHLER, FRITZ. fl. 1953. German geologist. Cited in: Min. Mag., vol. 30 (1953-1955) p. 736. Kahlerite.

KAHLER, OTTO. 1849-1893. German physcian. See: Biog. Lex. hervorr. Aerzte, 1880-1930. Kahler's disease (or syndrome).

Kahlerite (Kahler, Fritz): Earth Sciences. See: Thrush.

Kahler's disease (or syndrome) (Kahler, Otto): Medicine. See: Dorland; Jablonski; Stedman. Also known as: Huppert's disease, Kahler-Bozzolo disease, Rustitskii's disease.

Kahle's solution (Derivation undetermined): Chemistry. See: Hackh.

KAHN, EUGEN. b. 1887. German psychologist. See: Psych. Reg., 1932, p. 209f. Kahn test of symbol arrangement?

Kahn-Falta sign (Kahn, Friedel and Falta, Wilhelm): Medicine. See: Stedman. Also known as: Falta's sign.

KAHN, FRIEDEL. fl. 1912. German physician. Cited in: Chem. Abstr., vol. 6, p. 884. Kahn-Falta sign.

KAHN, HERBERT. fl. 1925. German physician. Cited in: Kelly. Kahn's albumin A reaction (or test).

KAHN, REUBEN LEON. b. 1887. American bacteriologist. See: World Who's Who Sci. Kahn test (reaction or Kahn).

Kahn test (reaction or Kahn) (Kahn, Reuben Leon): Medicine. See: Dorland; Stedman; Webster's 3d.

Kahn test of symbol arrangement (Kahn, Eugen?): Psychology. See: Wolman.

Kahn's albumin A reaction (or test) (Kahn, Herbert): Medicine. See: Dorland.

Kaiser (Caesar, Gaius Julius): Generic Word (king). See: Hendrickson; Webster's 3d.

Kaiser effect (Derivation undetermined): Physics. See: Ballentyne.

KAISER, J. fl. 1911. English librarian. Cited in: Mansell. Kaiser's system.

Kaiser-Ponsold edetic acid test (Kaiser, Wolfram Karl): Chemistry. Cited in: World Who's Who Sci.

Kaiser test for wood pulp (Derivation undetermined): Chemistry. See: Van Nostrand Chem. Dict.

KAISER, WOLFRAM KARL. 1923- . German physician. See: World Who's Who sci. Kaiser-Ponsold edetic acid test.

KAISERLING, CARL. 1869-1942. German pathologist. See: Biog. Lex. hervorr. Aerzte, 1880-1930. Kaiserling('s) solution (or method).

Kaiserling('s) solution (or method) (Kaiserling, Carl): Medicine. See: Dorland; Hackh; Stedman.

Kaiser's system (Kaiser, J.): Library Science. See: Harrod.

Kakiemon. See: Sakaida Kakiemon.

Kakiemon (porcelain style) (Sakaida Kakiemon): Applied Arts. See: Encyc. Brit., 1973 under "Pottery and Porcelain," vol. 18, p. 359d; Webster's 3d.

KALAN, JAMES E. fl. 1973. American mathematician. (Biography source unavailable.) Kalan's corollary.

KALANIANAOLE, JONAH KUHIO. 1871-1922. Hawaiian politician. See: Dict. Amer. Biog. Kuhio Day.

Kalanos. See: Calanus.

Kalan's corollary (Kalan, James E.): Sociology. See: Martin.

KALISCHER, SIEGFRIED. 1862- . German physician. Cited in: Royal Soc. Cat. Sci. Pap., 1884-1900. Sturge-Kalischer-Weber syndrome.

Kalischer's syndrome (Kalischer, Siegfried). See: Sturge-Weber syndrome.

lkowskite (or Kalkowskyn) (Kalkowsky, Ernst Louis): Earth Sciences. See: ush; Webster's 3d.

LKOWSKY, ERNST LOUIS. 1851-1938. German mineralogist. See: Min. g., vol. 25 (Mar. 1938-Sept. 1940) p. 293. Kalkowskite (or Kalkowskyn).

LLAB. fl. 1862. Austrian postal official. (Biography source unavailable.) llabize.

llabize (Kallab): Generic Word (open mail illegally). See: Charnock.

llikak family (Kallikak, Martin): Sociology. See: Pennak; Zadrozny.

LLIKAK, MARTIN. Pseudonymous ancestor of a much-studied feeble-minded nily in psychology. See: Goddard. Kallikak family.

LLING, BO MICHAEL STURE. b. 1892. Swedish metallurgist. See: nska Maen Och Kvinnor. Kalling's solution.

lling's solution (Kalling, Bo Michael Sture): Engineering and Industry. See: ush.

lliope. See: Calliope.

LLMANN, FRANZ JOSEF. 1897-1965. German-born American geneticist and chiatrist. See: Who Was Who Amer., 1961-1968. Kallmann's syndrome.

llmann's syndrome (Kallmann, Franz Josef): Medicine. See: Jablonski; dman.

LM, PEHR. 1716-1779. Swedish botanist. See: Dict. Sci. Biog. Kalmia.

mia (Kalm, Pehr): Botany. See: Mathews, M. M.; Partridge; Taylor, N.; bster's 3d.

LMUS, HERBERT THOMAS. 1881-1963. American physicist and metallurgist. e: World Who's Who Sci. Herbert T. Kalmus Award.

LUZA, THEODOR FRANZ EDUARD. 1885-1954. German mathematical physi- t. See: Dict. Sci. Biog. Kaluza theory.

luza theory (Kaluza, Theodor Franz Eduard): Physics. See: Hughes; Internat. ct. Phys. Elec.

mel, George Joseph. See: Camel, George Joseph.

MINER, GISA. 1883-1941. Austrian physician. Cited in: Index-Cat. Libr. g.-Gen. Off., 4th Ser., vol. 9, 1945. Freund-Kaminer reaction.

MLET, JONAS. 1914- . American chemist. See: Amer. Men Sci., h ed. Kamlet reaction, Kamlet reagent.

mlet reaction (Kamlet, Jonas): Chemistry. See: Van Nostrand Chem. Dict.

mlet reagent (Kamlet, Jonas): Chemistry. See: Van Nostrand Chem. Dict.

MM, OLIVER. b. 1888. American chemist. See: Amer. Men. Sci., 3rd . Burgess-Kamm test.

MMERER, FREDERIC. 1856-1928. American Surgeon. See: World Who's o Sci. Battle-Jalaguier-Kammerer incision.

MPSCHULTE, WILLY. fl. 1906. German chemist. Cited in: Mansell. nchot-Kampschulte test.

NAVEL, ALLEN BUCKNER. 1874-1938. American surgeon. See: World o's Who Sci. Kanavel's sign.

navel's sign (Kanavel, Allen Buckner): Medicine. See: Dorland.

ndinskii-Clérambault syndrome (Kandinskii, Viktor Kh and De Clérambault, aetan-Henri-Alfred-Edouard-Leon-Marie Gatian): Medicine. See: Jablonski. so known as: Clerambault-Kandinskii complex.

NDINSKII, VICTOR CHRISANFOVIC. 1825-1890? Russian psychiatrist. e: Allg. Z. Psychiat., vol. 46 (1890), p. 550-551. Kandinskii-Clerambault drome.

NE, ROBERT JOHN. 1809-1890. Irish chemist. See: Dict. Sci. Biog. neite.

neite (Kane, Robert John): Earth Sciences. See: Charnock.

NER, E. A. fl. 1956-1966. Russian physicist. Cited in: Chem. Abstr. bel-Kaner resonance.

ANG-HSI. 1654-1722. Chinese emperor. See: Encyc. Brit., 1973. ang-hsi (ceramic or porcelain ware).

ang-hsi (ceramic or porcelain ware) (K'ang-Hsi): Applied Arts. See: Web- r's 3d.

KANNER, LEO. 1894- . Austrian-born American child psychiatrist. See: Direct. Med. Specialists, 1975-1976. Kanner's syndrome.

Kanner's syndrome (Kanner, Leo): Medicine. See: Jablonski; Stedman. Also known as: Asperger's psychopathy.

KANO FAMILY. fl. 1453-1674. Japanese painters. See: Webster's Biog. Dict. Kano School.

Kano School (Kano family): Fine Arts. See: Osborne.

KANT, EDGAR. 1902- . Estonian geographer. Cited in: Mansell. Kant's index of concentration.

KANT, IMMANUEL. 1724-1804. German philosopher. See: Internat. Encyc. Soc. Sci. Kantianism (Kantism or Kantian).

Kantianism (Kantism or Kantian) (Kant, Immanuel): Philosophy. See: Attwater; New Encyc. Brit., 1974; Partridge; Webster's 3d.

KANTOR, JOHN LEONARD. 1890-1947. American roentgenologist. See: Nat. Cycl. Amer. Biog., vol. 36, p. 246. Golden-Kantor syndrome.

Kant's index of concentration (Kant, Edgar): Geography. See: Monkhouse.

KAO, CHEN-HENG. fl. 1935. Chinese chemist. Cited in: Chem. Abstr., vol. 29, pp. 7228, 6172^9; vol. 30, pp. 8074^7, 2875^5. Chang-Kao reagent, Kao-Fang-Sah reagent, Kao-Tao-Sah reagent, Tung-Kao-Sah reagent, Wang-Kao-Sak reagent.

Kao-Chen reagent (Kao, Chung-Hsi and Chen, Kuang-Hsu): Chemistry. See: Van Nostrand Chem. Dict.

KAO, CHUNG-HSI. fl. 1935. Chinese chemist. Cited in: Chem. Abstr., vol. 29, p. 4691^5; vol. 30, pp. 8074^7, 2875^5. Kao-Chen reagent, Kao-Tao-Sah reagent, Tung-Kao-Sah reagent, Wang-Kao-Sak reagent.

Kao-Fang-Sah reagent (Kao, Chen-Heng; Fang, Hsin-Yun; and Sah, Peter P. T.) Chemistry. See: Van Nostrand Chem. Dict.

Kao-Tao-Sah reagent (Kao, Chung-Hsi; Tao, Tuan-Ko; Kao, Cheng-Heng; and Sah, Peter P. T.): Chemistry. See: Van Nostrand Chem. Dict.

KAPETANAKIS J. fl. 1953. Swiss? physician. (Biography source unavailable.) Doucas-Kapetanakis disease.

Kapitza balance (Kapitza, Peter): Physics. See: Thewlis.

Kapitza liquefier (Kapitza, Peter): Physics. See: Thewlis.

KAPITZA, PETER. 1894- . Russian physicist. See: Encyc. Brit., 1973. Kapitza balance, Kapitza liquefier.

KAPLAN, DAVID MICHAEL. 1876-1952. American physician. See: Nat. Cycl. Amer. Biog., vol. 39, p. 548. Kaplan's test.

KAPLAN, EUGENE. fl. 1947-1976. American physician. See: Direct. Med. Specialists, 1975-1976. Zuelzer-Kaplan syndrome (1), Zuelzer-Kaplan syndrome (2).

KAPLAN, HENRY SEYMOUR. 1918- . American radiologist. See: World Who's Who Sci. Kaplan lymphoma.

KAPLAN, HERBERT. 1929- . American physician. See: Direct. Med. Specialists, 1975-1976. Kaplan-Klatskin syndrome.

Kaplan-Klatskin syndrome (Kaplan, Herbert and Klatskin, Gerald): Medicine. See: Jablonski.

Kaplan lymphoma (Kaplan, Henry Seymour): Medicine. See: Jablonski.

Kaplan turbine (Kaplan, Victor): Engineering and Industry. See: Auger; Thrush; Van Nostrand Sci. Eneyc. under "Hydraulic Turbine."

KAPLAN, VICTOR (In full: H.C. VICTOR). 1876-1934. Austrian engineer. See: Oesterr. Biog. Lex., 1815-1950. Kaplan turbine.

Kaplan's test (Kaplan, David Michael): Medicine. See: Dorland; Stedman.

Kaposi-Besnier-Libman-Sacks syndrome (Kaposi, Moritz; Besnier, Ernest; and Libman, Emanuel). See: Libman-Sacks syndrome (or disease).

Kaposi-Irgang disease (Kaposi, Moritz and Irgang, S.): Medicine. See: Jablonski.

Kaposi-Juliusberg dermatitis (or syndrome) (Kaposi, Moritz and Juliusberg, Fritz). See: Kaposi's varicelliform eruption.

Kaposi-Kohn, Moritz. See: Kaposi, Moritz.

KAPOSI, MORITZ. 1837-1902. Hungarian-born Austrian dermatologist. See: World Who's Who Sci. Kaposi-Besnier-Libman-Sacks syndrome, Kaposi-Irgang disease, Kaposi-Spiegler sarcomatosis, Kaposi's dermatosis (or xeroderma), Kaposi's disease (1), Kaposi's disease (2), Kaposi's disease (3), Kaposi's sarcoma (angiomatosis, disease (4), or sarcomatosis), Kaposi's varicelliform eruption (dermatitis or eczema).

Kaposi-Spiegler sarcomatosis (Kaposi, Moritz and Spiegler, Edward). See: Baefverstedt's syndrome.

Kaposi's dermatosis (or xeroderma) (Kaposi, Moritz): Medicine. See: Jablonski; Stedman.

Kaposi's disease (1) (Kaposi, Moritz): Medicine. See: Jablonski. Also known as: Wise-Rein disease.

Kaposi's disease (2) (Kaposi, Moritz): Medicine. See: Jablonski. Also known as: Devergie's disease, Hebra's disease, Tarral-Besnier disease.

Kaposi's disease (3) (Kaposi, Moritz): Medicine. See: Jablonski.

Kaposi's disease (4) (Kaposi, Moritz). See: Kaposi's sarcoma.

Kaposi's sarcoma (angiomatosis, disease (4), or sarcomatosis) (Kaposi, Moritz): Medicine. See: Dorland; Jablonski; Stedman.

Kaposi's varicelliform eruption (dermatitis or eczema) (Kaposi, Moritz): Medicine. See: Jablonski; Stedman. Also known as: Kaposi-Juliusberg dermatitis (or syndrome).

KAPP, GISBERT. 1852-1922. German engineer in England. See: World Who's Who Sci. Kapp line.

Kapp line (Kapp, Gisbert): Physics. See: Ballentyne; Dresner.

KAPPELER, OTTO. 1841-1909. German surgeon. See: Biog. Lex. hervorr. Aerzte, 1880-1930. Kappeler's maneuver.

Kappeler's maneuver (Kappeler, Otto): Medicine. See: Dorland.

KAPTEYN, JACOBUS CORNELIUS. 1851-1922. Dutch astronomer. See: Dict. Sci. Biog. Kapteyn selected areas, Kapteyn universe, Kapteyn distribution, Kapteyn's transformation.

Kapteyn selected areas (Kapteyn, Jacobus Cornelius): Astronomy. See: Satterthwaite; Thewlis.

Kapteyn universe (Kapteyn, Jacobus Corenelius): Astronomy. See: Thewlis.

Kapteyn's distribution (Kapteyn, Jacobus Corenelius): Statistics. See: Kendall.

Kapteyn's transformation (Kapteyn, Jacobus Cornelius): Statistics. See: Kendall.

Karaglanov sulfite test (Karaoglanov, Zachari): Chemistry. See: Van Nostrand Chem. Dict.

KARAOGLANOV, ZACHARI. 1878-1943. Bulgarian chemist. See: Pogg., vol. 7b. Karaglanov sulfite test, Karoglanov test.

KARAVODINE. fl. 1908. French engineer. (Biography source unavailable.) Karavodine engine.

Karavodine engine (Karavodine): Engineering and Industry. See: Auger.

Karell diet (Karell, Philip Jakob): Medicine. See: Dorland; Stedman.

KARELL, PHILIP JAKOB. 1806-1886. Russian physician. See: Biog. Lex. hervorr. Aerzte. Karell diet, Karell's treatment (or cure).

Karell's treatment (or cure) (Karell, Philip Jakob): Medicine. See: Dorland.

Karl d'or (Karl Wilehlm Ferdinand). See: Carl d'or.

Karl Fischer reagent (Fischer, Karl): Chemistry. See: Hackh; Webster's 3d.

KARL WILHELM FERDINAND. 1735-1806. Duke of Brunswick and Lueneburg. See: Allg. Deut. Biog. Carl d'or.

Karman boundary layer theorem (Von Karman, Theodore): Physics. See: Thewlis.

Karman (or von Karman's) constant (Von Karman, Theodore): Physics. See: Huschke; Internat. Dict. Phys. Elec.; Van Nostrand Sci. Encyc.

Karman-Friedrich equations (Von Karman, Theodore and Friedrich): Mathematics. See: Internat. Dict. Ap. Math.

Karman similarity theory (Von Karman, Theodore): Physics. See: Thewlis.

Karman, Theodore von. See: Von Karman, Theodore.

Karman-Tsien relation (Von Karman, Theodore and Tsien, Hsue-Shen): Physics. See: Internat. Dict. Ap. Math.; Thewlis.

Karman vortex street (street of vortices, street of eddies or vortices) (Von Karman, Theodore): Physics. See: Huschke; Internat. Dict. Ap. Math.; Internat. Dict. Phys. Elec.; Thewlis; Van Nostrand Sci. Encyc.

Karmat. See: Hamdan Qarmat.

Karmathians (or Karmatis) (Hamdan Qarmat): Religion. See: Barnhart (Eng. Lit.); Brewer; Harbottle; Harvey.

Karn test (Karns, George Melvin): Chemistry. See: Van Nostrand Chem. Dict.

Karnaugh map (Karnaugh, Maurice?): Electronics. See: Hughes; Markus.

KARNAUGH, MAURICE. 1924- . American electrical engineer. See: Amer. Men Sci., 10th ed. Karnaugh map?

KARNS, GEORGE MELVIN. 1899- . American chemist. See: Amer. Men Sci., 9th ed. Karn test.

Karoglanov test (Karaoglanov, Zachari): Chemistry. See: Van Nostrand Chem. Dict.

Karolin (Charles Philipp). See: Carolin (or Carolin d'or).

Karpinskite (Karpinsky, Alexandr Petrovich): Earth Sciences. See: Thrush.

KARPINSKY, ALEXANDR PETROVICH. 1847-1936. Russian geologist. See: Dict. Sci. Biog. Karpinskite, Karpinskyite.

Karpinskyite (Karpinsky, Alexandr Petrovich): Earth Sciences. See: Thrush.

KARRAM, MUHAMMAD IBN. No dates. Arabian sect leader. (Biography source unavailable.) Karramiyya.

Karramiyya (Karram, Muhammad ibn): Religion. See: Canney.

KARRER, JUERG. 1919- . Swiss physician. Cited in: Index-Cat. Libr. Surg.-Gen. Off., 5th Ser., vol. 1, 1959. Gasser-Karrer syndrome?

KARTAGENER, MANES. 1897- . Swiss physician. See: Who's Who Switz. 1970-1971. Kartagener's disease, Kartagener's syndrome (or triad).

Kartagener's disease (Kartagener, Manes): Medicine. See: Jablonski.

Kartagener's syndrome (or triad) (Kartagener, Manes): Medicine. See: Dorland; Jablonski; Stedman.

Karwinskia (Karwinsky von Karwin, Wilhelm): Botany. See: Webster's 3d.

KARWINSKY VON KARWIN, WILHELM. d. 1855. German traveler. (Biography source unavailable.) Karwinskia.

KASABACH, HAIG HAIGOUNI. 1898-1943. American physician. See: Amer. J. Roentg. vol. 50 (Nov., 1943) pp. 691-692. Kasabach-Merritt syndrome.

Kasabach-Merritt syndrome (Kasabach, Haig Haigouni and Merritt, Katherine K.): Medicine. See: Jablonski.

KASANIN, JACOB SERGI. 1897-1946. American psychologist. See: Grinstein, vol. 2, 1957. Hanfmann-Kasanin concept formation test.

Kaschin, Nikolai Ivanovich. See: Kashin, Nikolai Ivanovich.

KASERER, HERMANN IGNAZ PHILIPP JOSEF. 1877-1955. Austrian chemist. See: Pogg., 7a. Kaserer reagent.

Kaserer reagent (Kaserer, Hermann Ignaz Philipp Josef): Chemistry. See: Van Nostrand Chem. Dict.

Kashin-Bek disease (Kashin, Nikolai Ivanovich and Bek, E. V.): Medicine. See: Jablonski; Stedman.

KASHIN, NIKOLAI IVANOVICH. 1825-1872. Russian physician. See: Biog. Lex. hervorr. Aerzte. Kashin-Bek disease.

KASPER, JOHN SIMON. 1915- . American physical chemist. See: Amer. Men and Women Sci., 12th ed. Harker-Kasper inequalities.

KASSNER, GEORG. fl. 1885-1900. German chemist. Cited in: Royal Soc. Cat. Sci. Pap., 1884-1900. Kassner mixture.

Kassner mixture (Kassner, Georg): Chemistry. See: Van Nostrand Chem. Dict.

KAST, ALFRED. 1856-1903. German internist. See: Biog. Lex. hervorr. Aerzte, 1880-1930. Maffucci-Kast syndrome.

Kast furnace (Derivation undetermined): Engineering and Industry. See: Thrush.

ASTENBEIN, KARL. fl. 1869. Inventor in England. See: Glaister. stenbein typesetting machine (or machine).

stenbein typesetting machine (or machine) (Kastenbein, Karl): Printing. See: ckwood.

ASTERT, JOSEF. 1910- . German orthopedic surgeon. See: Chirurgen- rz., 1958. Hoffa-Kastert syndrome.

ASTLE, JOSEPH HOEING. 1864-1916. American chemist. See: Pogg., ls. 4, 5. Kastle reagent for bromine and iodine, Kastle-Shedd reagent.

stle reagent for bromine and iodine (Kastle, Joseph Hoeing): Chemistry. e: Van Nostrand Chem. Dict.

stle-Shedd reagent (Kastle, Joseph Hoeing and Shedd, Oliver March): emistry. See: Van Nostrand Chem. Dict.

st's syndrome (Kast, Alfred). See: Maffucci's syndrome.

t, Christopher ("Kit"). See: Cat, Christopher.

ATAKOUZINOS, D. fl. 1930. Greek chemist. Cited in: Chem. Abstr., l. 27, p. 3163. Katakouzinos test reaction.

takouzinos test reaction (Katakouzinos, D.): Chemistry. See: Van Nostrand em. Dict.

te Greenaway bonnet (Greenaway, Kate): Fashion. See: Picken.

te Greenaway dress (Greenaway, Kate): Fashion. See: Picken.

te Greenaway Medal (Greenaway, Kate): Library Science. See: Harrod.

te Greenaway (style) (Greenaway, Kate): Fashion. See: Barnhart (Eng. .); Picken; Webster's 3d.

ATER, HENRY. 1777-1835. English scientist. See: Dict. Sci. Biog. ter('s) pendulum.

ter('s) pendulum (Kater, Henry): Physics. See: Auger; Thewlis; Thrush; an Nostrand Sci. Encyc.; Webster's 3d.

terfelto (Katerfelto, Gustavus): Generic Word (quack). See: Brewer.

ATERFELTO, GUSTAVUS. d. 1799. London quack. (Biography source available.) Katerfelto.

threin's test (Derivation undetermined): Medicine. See: Stedman. Also own as: Marechal's test, Smith's test, Trousseau's test.

tt, Christopher ("Kit"). See: Cat, Christopher.

tz and Braly questionnaire (Katz, Daniel L. and Braly, Kenneth Walter): ychology. See: English.

ATZ, DANIEL L. 1903- . American psychologist. See: Amer. Psych. soc. Biog. Direct., 1970. Katz and Braly questionnaire.

tz formula (Katz, Johann Rudolf): Medicine. See: Dorland.

ATZ, JOHANN RUDOLF. 1880-1938. German chemist. See: Pogg., vol. Katz formula.

ATZENSTEIN, MORITZ. 1872-1932. German surgeon. See: Biog. Lex. her- rr. Aerzte, 1880-1930. Katzenstein's test.

tzenstein's test (Katzenstein, Mortiz): Medicine. See: Dorland.

uertz engine (Kauertz, Eugen): Engineering and Industry. See: Auger.

AUERTZ, EUGEN. No dates. German engineer. (Biography source unavail- le.) Kauertz engine.

AUFFMAN, ANGELICA (In full: MARIA ANNA ANGELICA). 1741-1807. iss-born painter in England. See: Encyc. Brit., 1973. Kauffman screen.

uffman screen (Kauffman, Angelica): Fine Arts. See: Partridge.

AUFFMANN, FRIEDRICH. b. 1893. German internist. See: Biog. Lex. rvorr. Aerzte, 1880-1930. Kauffmann's test.

uffmann's test (Kauffmann, Friedrich): Medicine. See: Dorland.

ufler configuration of biphenyl (Kaufler, Felix): Chemistry. See: Van ostrand Chem. Dict.

AUFLER, FELIX. b. 1878. Austrian chemist. Cited in: Royal Soc. Cat. i. Pap., 1884-1900. Kaufler configuration of biphenyl.

AUFMANN, EDUARD. 1860-1931. German physician. See: Biog. Lex. rvorr. Aerzte, 1880-1930. Parrot-Kaufmann syndrome.

KAUFMANN, FRITZ. b. 1875. German neurologist. (Biography source unavailable.) Kaufmann's treatment (or method).

KAUFMANN, LUDWIG. fl. 1895. German chemist. Cited in: Royal Soc. Cat. Sci. Pa., 1884-1900. Wislicenus-Kaufmann test reaction.

KAUFMANN, RUDOLF. 1871-1927. German physician. See: Wien Med. Wchnschr. vol. 77 (1927) p. 920. Kaufmann's stain.

Kaufmann's disease (Kaufmann, Eduard). See: Parrot's disease (2).

Kaufmann's stain (Kaufmann, Rudolf): Medicine. See: Stedman.

Kaufmann's treatment (or method) (Kaufmann, Fritz): Medicine. See: Dorland.

KAUTZSCH, KARL FREIDRICH. b. 1879. German chemist. Cited in: Chem. Abstr. Abderhalden-Kautzsch test reaction.

KAVALIER, F. fl. 1837. Czechoslovakian chemist. (Biography source unavailable). Kavalier glass.

Kavalier glass (Kavalier, F.): Engineering and Industry. See: Thrush.

KAWAI, GINNOSUKE. fl. 1926. Japanese physician. Cited in: Kelly. Kawai test for blood.

Kawai reaction for eugenol (Kawai, Sin'iti): Chemistry. See: Van Nostrand Chem. Dict.

KAWAI, SIN'ITI. fl. 1926-1931. Japanest chemist. See: Pogg., vols. 6, 7b. Kawai reaction for eugenol.

Kawai test for blood (Kawai, Ginnosuke): Chemistry. See: Van Nostrand Chem. Dict.

KAWECKI, HENRY CASIMER. 1912- . American metallurgist. See: Amer. Men Sci., 8th ed. Copaux-Kawecki fluoride process.

KAY, HERBERT DAVENPORT. b. 1893. English biochemist. See: Who's Who Sci. Europe, 1972. Jenner-Kay test, Jenner-Kay unit.

Kay test (Kay, Herbert Davenport). See: Jenner-Kay test.

KAYSER, BERNHARD. 1869-1954. German ophthalmologist. See: Biog. Lex. hervorr. Aerzte, 1880-1930. Kayser-Fleischer ring, Kayser's disease.

KAYSER, EMANUEL (In full: FRIEDRICH HEINRICH EMANUEL). 1845-1927. German geologist. See: Pogg., vols. 3, 4, 6. Kayserite.

Kayser-Fleischer ring (Kayser, Bernhard and Fleischer, Richard): Medicine. See: Dorland; Hinsie; Jablonski; Stedman.

KAYSER, HEINRICH. 1976-1940. German physician. See: Biog. Lex. hervorr. Aerzte, 1880-1930. Brion-Kayser disease.

KAYSER, HEINRICH GUSTAV JOHANNES. 1853-1940. German physicist. See: Dict. Sci. Biog. Kayser (unit).

Kayser (unit) (Kayser, Heinrich Gustav Johannes): Physics. See: Ballentyne; Dresner; Van Nostrand Sci. Encyc.

Kayserite (Kayser, Emanuel): Earth Sciences. See: Thrush.

Kayser's disease (Kayser, Bernhard): Medicine. See: Dorland.

KAZANJAN, VARAZTAD HOVHANNES. b. 1879. Armenian-born American otorhinolaryngologist. See: Direct. Med. Specialists, 1965-1966. Kazanjian's operation.

Kazanjian's operation (Kazanjan, Varaztad Hovhannes): Medicine. See: Stedman.

KAZNELSON, PAUL. fl. 1916-1922. Czechoslovakian physician. Cited in: Kelly. Kaznelson's syndrome?

Kaznelson's syndrome (Kaznelson, Paul?). See: Diamond-Blackfan syndrome and Faber's anemia.

KEARNEY, DENIS. 1847-1907. Irish-born American labor leader. See: Dict. Amer. Biog. Kearneyism (or Kearneyites).

Kearneyism (or Kearneyites) (Kearney, Denis): History. See: Clapin; Mathews, M. M.

Keate Award (Keate, Robert William): History. See: Encyc. Brit., 1973 under "South Africa," vol. 20, p. 970c; Harbottle.

KEATE, ROBERT WILLIAM. 1814-1873. English colonial governor. See: Boase. Keate Award.

KEATING, EDWARD. 1875-1965. American legislator. See: Biog. Direct. Amer. Congress. Keating-Owen Act.

KEATING-HART, WALTER-VALENTIN. 1870-1922. French physician. See: Biog. Lex. hervorr. Aerzte, 1880-1930. Keating-Hart's method.

Keating-Hart's method (Keating-Hart, Walter-Valentin): Medicine. See: Dorland; Stedman.

Keating-Owen Act (Keating, Edward and Owen, Robert Latham): Politics. See: Smith.

KEATS, JOHN. 1795-1821. English poet. See: Dict. Nat. Biog. Keatsian.

Keatsian (Keats, John): Literature. See: Webster's 3d.

KEBER, GOTTHARD AUGUST FERDINAND. 1816-1871. German zoologist. See: Biog. Lex. hervorr. Aerzte. Keber's organ (or organ of Keber).

Keber's organ (or organ of Keber) (Keber, Gotthard August Ferdinand): Zoology. See: Gray; Henderson; Pennak; Van Nostrand Sci. Encyc.

KEDAR. Son of Ishmael in the Old Testament (Gen. 25:13). See: Buttrick. Kedar's tents.

Kedar's tents (Kedar): Generic Word (the secular world). See: Brewer.

KEELER, LEONARDE. 1903-1949. American criminologist. See: Who Was Who Amer., 1943-1950. Keeler polygraph.

Keeler polygraph (Keeler, Leonarde): Sociology. See: Chaplin; English; Webster's 3d.

Keeley cure (Keeley, Leslie E.): Medicine. See: Dorland; Mathews, M. M.; Stedman.

Keeley institute (Keeley, Leslie E.): Medicine. See: Mathews, M. M.

KEELEY, LESLIE E. 1834-1900. American physician. See: World Who's Who Sci. Keeley cure, Keeley institute.

KEELY, JOHN ERNST WORRELL. 1827-1898. American inventor and imposter. See: Dict. Amer. Biog. Keely motor, Keelyism (or Keelyist).

Keely motor (Keely, John Ernst Worrell): Engineering and Industry. See: Mathews, M. M.; Phyfe.

Keelyism (or Keelyist) (Keely, John Ernst Worrell): Generic Word (hoax). See: Mathews, M. M.

Keen tester (Keen, William Herbert): Engineering and Industry. See: Hackh.

KEEN, WILLIAM HERBERT. b. 1882. American metallurgist. See: Who's Who Engin., 1922-1923. Keen tester.

KEEN, WILLIAM WILLIAMS. 1837-1932. American surgeon. See: Encyc. Brit., 1973. Keen's operation, Keen's sign.

KEENAN, PHILIP CHILDS. 1908- . American astronomer. See: Amer. Men and Women Sci., 12th ed. MKK system.

KEENE, RICHARD WYNNE. 1810-1877. English sculptor. See: Boase. Keene's cement.

Keene's cement (Keene, Richard Wynne): Engineering and Industry. See: Thrush; Webster's 3d.

Keen's operation (Keen, William Williams): Medicine. See: Dorland; Stedman.

Keen's sign (Keen, William Williams): Medicine. See: Dorland; Stedman.

Keepen, Vladimir Petrovich. See: Koeppen, Wladimir Peter.

Keesom energy (Keesom, Willem Hendrik): Physics. See: Internat. Dict. Ap. Math.

Keesom potential (Keesom, Willem Hendrik): Physics. See: Internat. Dict. Ap. Math.

Keesom relationship (or equation) (Keesom, Willem Hendrik): Physics. See: Hughes; Internat. Dict. Phys. Elec.; Van Nostrand Chem. Dict.

KEESOM, WILLEM HENDRIK. 1876-1956. Dutch physicist. See: Dict. Sci. Biog. Keesom energy, Keesom potential, Keesom relationship (or equation).

KEHOE, HENRY. fl. ca. 1893. American mineralogist. Cited in: Hintze, vol. I, pt. 4, half 2, p. 965. Kehoeite.

Kehoeite (Kehoe, Henry): Earth Sciences. See: Thrush; Webster's 3d.

KEHR, HANS. 1862-1916. German surgeon. See: Biog. Lex. hervorr. Aerzte, 1880-1930. Kehr's incision, Kehr's sign.

Kehrer-Adie syndrome (Kehrer, Ferdinand Adalbert and Adie, William John). See: Adie's syndrome.

KEHRER, FERDINAND ADALBERT. b. 1883. German physician. See: Biog. Lex. hervorr. Aerzte, 1880-1930. Kehrer-Adie syndrome.

Kehr's incision (Kehr, Hans): Medicine. See: Dorland; Stedman.

Kehr's sign (Kehr, Hans): Medicine. See: Dorland; Stedman.

Keil furnace (Derivation undetermined): Engineering and Industry. See: Thrush.

Keith and Flack's node (Keith, Sir Arthur and Flack, Martin): Anatomy. See: Donath; Dorland; Stedman. Also known as: Keith's node, Koch's node.

KEITH, SIR ARTHUR. 1866-1955. Scottish anatomist. See: Dict. Sci. Biog. Keith and Flack's node, Keith's bundle.

KEITH, GEORGE. ca. 1639-1716. Scottish-born religious leader in America. See: Dict. Amer. Biog. Keithian(s) (or Keithan Quaker).

KEITH, NATHANIEL SHEPARD. 1838-1925. American electro-metallurgist. See: World Who's Who Sci. Keith process.

KEITH, NORMAN MACDONNELL. b. 1885. American physician. See: World Who's Who Sci. Keith's diet.

KEITH, PATRICK. 1769-1840. English botanist. See: Britten and Boulger. Keithia.

Keith process (Keith, Nathaniel Shepard): Engineering and Industry. See: Thrush.

Keithia (Keith, Patrick): Botany. See: Charnock.

Keithian(s) (or Keithan Quaker) (Keith, George): Religion. See: Canney; Mathews, M. M.; Morris.

Keith's bundle (Keith, Sir Arthur): Anatomy. See: Dorland; Stedman. Also known as: His bundle.

Keith's diet (Keith, Norman MacDonnell): Medicine. See: Dorland.

Keith's node (Keith, Sir Arthur). See: Keith and Flack node.

Kekule benzene formula (Kekule von Stradonitz, August): Chemistry. See: Ballentyne; Hackh; Webster's 3d.

Kekule structure(s) (Kekule von Stradonitz, August): Chemistry. See: Asimov; Internat. Dict. Ap. Math.; Van Nostrand Sci. Encyc. under "Benzene."

KEKULE VON STRADONITZ, (FRIEDRICH) AUGUST. 1829-1896. German chemist. See: Dict. Sci. Biog. Kekule benzene formula (formula or ring), Kekule structure(s).

KELDYS, MSTISLAV VSEVOLODOVICH. 1911- . Russian mathematician. See: Turkevich. Keldyshite?

Keldyshite (Keldys, Mstislav Vsevolodovich?): Earth Sciences. See: Thrush.

Kelev strain vaccine (Derivation undetermined): Medicine. See: Stedman.

Kell blood group (Kell, Mrs.): Medicine. See: Stedman.

KELL, MRS. fl. 1946. Patient. (Biography source unavailable.) Kell blood group.

Keller automatic roaster (Derivation undetermined): Engineering and Industry. See: Thrush.

KELLER, CURT. 1904- . Swiss engineer. Cited in: Mansell. Ackeret-Keller gas turbine.

KELLER-DORIAN, ALBERT. 18??-1924. French photo-engraver and manufacturer. See: Focal Encyc. Photog. K.D.B. process.

Keller furnace (Derivation undetermined): Engineering and Industry. See: Thrush.

KELLER, HARRY FREDERICK. b. 1861. American mineralogist. See: Amer. Men Sci., 1st ed. Kellerite.

KELLER, HELEN BASS. fl. 1921-1950. American reading teacher. Cited in: Mansell. Fernald-Keller approach.

KELLER, KARL. 1839-1928. German engineer. See: Deux. Biog. Jahrb., vol. 10, 1928. Keller system.

KELLER, PHILIPP. b. 1891. German dermatologist. See: Biog. Lex. hervorr. Aerzte, 1880-1930. Keller's test.

Keller solution (Keller, Fred): Chemistry. See: Van Nostrand Chem. Dict.

Keller system (Keller, Karl): Engineering and Industry. See: Thrush.

llering (Derivation undetermined): Engineering and Industry. See: Thrush.

llerite (Keller, Harry Frederick): Earth Sciences. See: Thrush.

ller's test (Keller, Philipp): Medicine. See: Dorland.

lley-Salisbury method (Kelley, Truman Lee and Salisbury, Frank Seely): atistics. See: Good; Kendall and Doig.

LLEY, TRUMAN LEE. 1884-1961. American psychometrician. See: Internat. cyc. Soc. Sci. Kelley-Salisbury method, Kelley's constant process.

LLEY, WILLIAM VAN DOREN. 1876-1934. American inventor. See: Focal cyc. Film. Kelleycolor two-colour subtractive process.

lleycolor two-colour subtractive process (Kelley, William Van Doren): otography. See: Focal Encyc. Film.

lley's constant process (Kelley, Truman Lee): Psychology. See: Chaplin; glish; Wolman.

LLIE, GEORGE. fl. 1797. Scottish anatomist. See: Biog. Lex. hervorr. rzte. Monro-Kellie doctrine.

LLING, GEORG. b. 1866. German physician. See: Biog. Lex. hervorr. rzte, 1880-1930. Kelling's test.

lling's test (Kelling, Georg): Medicine. See: Dorland; Stedman.

LLMAN, EDITH. fl. 1943. American physicist. Cited in: Mansell. MKK stem.

LLNER, CARL. fl. 1849. German oculist. Cited in: Mansell. Kellner epiece.

llner eyepiece (Kellner, Carl): Physics. See: Internat. Dict. Phys. Elec.; ewlis; Satterthwaite.

LLOGG, ALBERT. 1813-1887. American botanist. See: Dict. Sci. Biog. llogg('s) oak.

llogg-Briand Pact (Kellogg, Frank Billings and Briand, Aristide): History. e: Morris and Irwin; Jameson; Smith. Also known as: Briand-Kellogg Treaty, llogg Pact.

LLOGG, FRANK BILLINGS. 1856-1937. American diplomat. See: New cyc. Brit., 1974, Microp. Kellogg-Briand Pact.

llogg('s) oak (Kellogg, Albert): Botany. See: Mathews, M. M.; Webster's .

llogg Pact (Kellogg, Frank Billings). See: Kellogg-Briand Pact.

llogg rule (or equation) (Derivation undetermined): Physics. See: Ballentyne; ternat. Dict. Phys. Elec.

LLOGG, WILL KEITH. 1860-1951. American industrialist and philanthropist. e: New Encyc. Brit., 1974, Microp. W. K. Kellogg Foundation.

ELLY. fl. 20th c. American statistician. (Biography source unavailable.) otelling-Kelly method of factor analysis.

lly Act (Kelly, Melville Clyde): Politics. See: Morris.

ELLY, ADAM BROWN. 1865-1941. Scottish laryngologist. See: Brit. Med. ., vol. 2 (1941) p. 33. Paterson and Brown Kelly syndrome (Paterson-Kelly ndrome (or webs), or Paterson's syndrome.

elly ball test (Derivation undetermined): Engineering and Industry. See: hrush.

elly drive (Derivation undetermined): Engineering and Industry. See: Thrush.

elly filter (Derivation undetermined): Engineering and Industry. See: Thrush; an Nostrand Chem. Dict.

elly forceps (Kelly, Howard Atwood): Medicine. See: Blakiston's Gould.

elly gang (Kelly, Ned): History. See: Harbottle.

ELLY, HOWARD ATWOOD. 1858-1943. American gynecologist. See: ncyc. Brit., 1973. Kelly forceps, Kelly's operation, Kelly's rectal speculum.

elly (joint or stem) (Derivation undetermined): Engineering and Industry. See: hrush.

ELLY, MELVILLE CLYDE. 1883-1935. American legislator. See: Biog. irect. Amer. Congress. Kelly Act.

ELLY, MICHAEL J. 1857-1894. American professional baseball player. See: ict. Amer. Biog. slide, Kelly, slide.

KELLY, NED (EDWARD). 1855-1880. Australian bushranger. See: Encyc. Brit., 1973. Kelly gang, Ned Kelly (or as game as Ned Kelly).

Kelly process (Kelly, William): Engineering and Industry. See: Morris and Irwin.

Kelly sedimentation tube (Kelly, William J.): Engineering and Industry. See: Thrush.

KELLY, WILLIAM. 1811-1888. American inventor. See: World Who's Who Sci. Kelly process.

KELLY, WILLIAM J. fl. 1924. American engineer. Cited in: Chem. Abstr., vol. 18, p. 3126. Kelly sedimentation tube.

Kelly's operation (Kelly, Howard Atwood): Medicine. See: Dorland; Stedman.

Kelly's rectal speculum (Kelly, Howard Atwood): Medicine. See: Dorland; Stedman.

Kelly's syndrome (Kelly, Adam Brown). See: Plummer-Vinson syndrome.

KELM, E. F. fl. 1936. American chemist. Cited in: Chem. Abstr., vol. 32, p. 4100[5]. Kelm-Wilkinson test.

Kelm-Wilkinson test (Kelm, E. F. and Wilkinson, John Anderson): Chemistry. See: Van Nostrand Chem. Dict.

KELSEY, HARLAN. b. 1872. American horticulturist and landscape architect. See: Who Was Who Amer., 1969-1973. Kelsey locust.

KELSEY, JOHN. fl. 19th c. American botanist. (Biography source unavailable.) Kelsey plum.

Kelsey locust (Kelsey, Harlan): Zoology. See: Webster's 3d.

Kelsey plum (Kelsey, John): Botany. See: De Sola.

Kelvin (1) (unit) (Thomson, William, Lord Kelvin): Physics. See: Dresner; Thewlis.

Kelvin (2) (unit) (Thomson, William, Lord Kelvin): Physics. See: Dresner.

Kelvin (3) (unit) (Thomson, William, Lord Kelvin): Physics. See: Dresner; Thrush.

Kelvin balance (or ampere-balance) (Thomson, William, Lord Kelvin): Physics. See: Hughes; Markus; Webster's 3d.

Kelvin('s) circulation theorem (Thomson, William, Lord Kelvin): Physics. See: Huschke; Internat. Dict. Ap. Math.; Internat. Dict. Phys. Elec.

Kelvin clamp (Thomson, William, Lord Kelvin): Physics. See: Thewlis.

Kelvin compass (Thomson, William, Lord Kelvin): Navigation. See: Encyc. Brit., 1973 under "Compass," vol. 6, p. 227c.

Kelvin degree (Thomson, William, Lord Kelvin). See: Kelvin (2).

Kelvin double bridge (or bridge) (Thomson, William, Lord Kelvin): Electronics. See: Hughes; Internat. Dict. Phys. Elec.; Markus; Thewlis; Van Nostrand Sci. Encyc. under "Bridge (Electrical)".

Kelvin effect (2) (Thomson, William, Lord Kelvin). See: Thomson effect (or heat).

Kelvin electrometer (Thomson, William, Lord Kelvin): Physics. See: Hughes; Internat. Dict. Phys. Elec.

Kelvin equation for surface tension (Thomson, William, Lord Kelvin): Physics. See: Internat. Dict. Phys. Elec.

Kelvin galvanometer (or astatic galvanometer) (Thomson, William, Lord Kelvin): Electronics. See: Hackh; Internat. Dict. Phys. Elec.

Kelvin-Hughes projector (Thomson, William, Lord Kelvin? and Hughes, William C.): Photography. See: Markus.

Kelvin-Hughes system of rapid processing (Thomson, William, Lord Kelvin? and Hughes, William C.?): Photography. See: Focal Encyc. Photog. under "Rapid Access System."

Kelvin('s) law (Thomson, William, Lord Kelvin): Physics. See: Internat. Dict. Phys. Elec.; Thrush; Webster's 3d.

Kelvin, Lord. See: Thomson, William, Lord Kelvin.

Kelvin material (Thomson, William, Lord Kelvin): Physics. See: Internat. Dict. Ap. Math.

Kelvin method of measuring galvanometer resistance (Thomson, William, Lord Kelvin): Physics. See: Internat. Dict. Phys. Elec.

Kelvin model (Thomson, William, Lord Kelvin): Physics. See: Internat. Dict. Ap. Math.

Kelvin skin effect (or effect (1)) (Thomson, William, Lord Kelvin): Physics. See: Ballentyne; Hughes.

Kelvin temperature scale (temperature or Kelvin) (Thomson, William, Lord Kelvin): Physics. See: Ballentyne; Hughes; Internat. Dict. Phys. Elec.; Markus; Thewlis; Thrush.

Kelvin('s) theorem (Thomson, William, Lord Kelvin): Physics. See: Ballentyne; Thewlis.

Kelvin tide predictor (Thomson, William, Lord Kelvin): Earth Sciences. See: Encyc. Brit., 1973 under "Mathematical Instruments," vol. 14, p. 1083b.

Kelvin-Varley slide (Thomson, William, Lord Kelvin and Varley, Cromwell Fleetwood): Electronics. See: Hughes; Internat. Dict. Phys. Elec.

Kelvin wave (Thomson, William, Lord Kelvin): Earth Sciences. See: Monkhouse.

Kelvin-White sounding machine (Thomson, William, Lord Kelvin and White, James): Earth Sciences. See: Encyc. Brit., 1973 under "Sounding," vol. 20, p. 952d.

Kelvinator (Thomson, William, Lord Kelvin): Generic Word. See: Hendrickson.

Kelvin's coupling (Thomson, William, Lord Kelvin): Engineering and Industry. See: Auger.

Kelvin's equation (Thomson, William, Lord Kelvin): Physics. See: Ballentyne.

Kelvin's problem (Thomson, William, Lord Kelvin): Physics. See: New Encyc. Brit., 1974, Microp.

Kelvin's statement (of the second law of thermodynamics) (Thomson, William, Lord Kelvin): Physics. See: Ballentyne.

Kelvin's warming engine (Thomson, William, Lord Kelvin): Engineering and Industry. See: Auger.

KEMAL ATATURK, MUSTAFA. 1881-1938. Turkish general and statesman. See: Encyc. Brit., 1973. Kemalism.

Kemalism (Kemal Ataturk, Mustafa): Politics. See: Webster's 3d.

KEMBLE, JOHN. ca. 1599-1679. English. See: Dict. Nat. Biog. Kemble pipe.

Kemble pipe (Kemble, John): Generic Word. See: Partridge; Weekley.

KEMMER, NICHOLAS. 1911- . Swiss-born Scottish physicist. See: Direct Brit. Sci. Duffin-Kemmer matrices.

KEMP, JAMES FURMAN. 1859-1926. American geologist. See: World Who's Who Sci. Kempite.

Kempite (Kemp, James Furman): Earth Sciences. See: Webster's 3d.

KEMPNER, WALTER. 1903- . American physician. See: World Who's Who Sci. Kempner's rice-fruit diet.

Kempner's rice-fruit diet (Kempner, Walter): Medicine. See: Dorland; Stedman.

KENDALL, AMOS. 1789-1869. American postmaster general. See: Dict. Amer. Biog. Kendall vs United States.

KENDALL, DAVID GEORGE. 1918- . English mathematical statistician. See: Direct. Brit. Sci., 1966-1967. Kendall's terminology.

KENDALL, EDWARD CALVIN. b. 1886. American biochemist. See: World Who's Who Sci. Kendall-Sherman test, Kendall's compound A, Kendall's compound B, Kendall's compound E, Kendall's compound F.

Kendall effect (Derivation undetermined): Electronics. See: Internat. Dict. Phys. Elec.; Markus.

Kendall equation for viscosity (Kendall, James Pickering): Chemistry. See: Internat. Dict. Phys. Elec.

KENDALL, JAMES PICKERING. b. 1889. English chemist. See: Pogg., vols. 5, 6, 7b. Kendall equation for viscosity.

KENDALL, MAURICE GEORGE. 1907- . English statistician. See: Direct. Brit. Sci., 1971-1972. Kendall's Q?, Kendall's 'S' score, Kendall's tau (coefficient of rank correlation (tau) or r).

Kendall-Sherman test (Kendall, Edward Calvin and Sherman Henry Clapp): Chemistry. See: Van Nostrand Chem. Dict.

Kendall vs United States (Kendall, Amos): History. See: Jameson.

Kendall's compound A (Kendall, Edward Calvin): Chemistry. See: Stedman.

Kendall's compound B (Kendall, Edward Calvin): Chemistry. See: Stedman. Also known as: Reichstein's substance H.

Kendall's compound E (Kendall, Edward Calvin): Chemistry. See: Stedman. Also known as: Reichstein's substance FA, Wintersteiner's compound F.

Kendall's compound F (Kendall, Edward Calvin): Chemistry. See: Stedman.

Kendall's Q (Kendall, Maurice George?): Statistics. See: Hoult.

Kendall's 'S' score (Kendall, Maurice George): Statistics. See: Kendall.

Kendall's tau (coefficient of rank correlation (tau) or r) (Kendall, Maurice George): Statistics. See: Hoult; Kendall; Van Nostrand Sci. Encyc.

Kendall's terminology (Kendall, David George): Statistics. See: Kendall.

KENDRICK, PEARL LUELLA. b. 1890. American public health scientist. See: Amer. Men Sci., 5th ed. Kendrick's test.

Kendrick's test (Kendrick, Pearl Luella): Medicine. See: Stedman.

KENNARD, EARL HESSE. b. 1885. American physicist. See: Pogg., vols. 5, 6. Kennard packet.

Kennard packet (Kennard, Earl Hesse): Physics. See: Ballentyne.

Kennedy (Kennedy, the Murder Victim): Generic Word (poker iron). See: Charnock.

Kennedy bar (Kennedy, Edward): Dentistry. See: Stedman.

Kennedy('s) (critical velocity) (Kennedy, Robert Gregg): Engineering and Industry. See: Thrush.

KENNEDY, EDWARD. b. 1883. American dentist. Cited in: Mansell. Kennedy bar.

KENNEDY, JOHN. 1759-1842. English nurseryman. See: Britten and Boulger. Kennedya.

KENNEDY, JOHN FITZGERALD. 1917-1963. American president. See: Encyc. Brit., 1973. Kennedy round.

KENNEDY, ROBERT FOSTER. 1884-1952. American neurologist. See: Neurology, vol. 2 (July-Aug. 1952) pp. 360-362. Foster Kennedy('s) syndrome).

KENNEDY, ROBERT GREGG. 1851-1920. Scottish engineer in India. See: Who Was Who, 1916-1928. Kennedy('s) (critical velocity).

Kennedy round (Kennedy, John Fitzgerald): Economics. See: Greenwald; Morris and Irwin; Seldon.

KENNEDY, ROY JAMES. 1897- . American physicist. See: Amer. Men Sci., 5th ed. Kennedy-Thorndike experiment, Kennedy's theorem?

KENNEDY, THE MURDER VICTIM. No dates. Victim murdered with a poker. (Biography source unavailable.) Kennedy.

KENNEDY, THOMAS. fl. 1854. English? engineer. (Biography source unavailable.) Kennedy water meter.

Kennedy-Thorndike experiment (Kennedy, Roy James and Thorndike, Edward Moulton): Physics. See: Van Nostrand Sci. Encyc.

Kennedy water meter (Kennedy, Thomas): Engineering and Industry. See: Auger.

KENNEDY, WILLIAM QUARRIER. 1903- . English geologist. See: Direct. Brit. Sci., 1971-1972. Kennedyite.

Kennedya (Kennedy, John): Botany. See: Partridge; Webster's 3d.

Kennedyite (Kennedy, William Quarrier): Earth Sciences. See: Thrush.

Kennedy's syndrome (Kennedy, Robert Foster). See: Foster Kennedy('s) syndrome.

Kennedy's theorem (Kennedy, Roy James?): Physics. See: Ballentyne.

KENNELLY, ARTHUR EDWIN. 1861-1939. Irish-English electrical engineer in America. See: Dict. Sci. Biog. Kennelly-Heaviside layer.

Kennelly-Heaviside layer (Kennelly, Arthur Edwin and Heaviside, Oliver): Physics. See: Ballentyne; Hughes; Huschke; Internat. Dict. Phys. Elec.; Monkhouse; Thewlis; Van Nostrand Sci. Encyc.; Webster's 3d. Also known as: Heaviside-Kennelly layer, Heaviside layer.

Kenneth Roberts Memorial Award (Roberts, Kenneth): Literature. Cited in: aughlin.

KENNY, ELIZABETH (SISTER KENNY). 1886-1952. Australian nurse. See: World Who's Who Sci. Kenny('s) method (or treatment).

KENNY, FREDERIC MARSHAL. 1929- . American pediatrician. See: Amer. Men and Women Sci., 12th ed. Kenny's syndrome.

Kenny('s) method (or treatment) (Kenny, Elizabeth): Medicine. See: Dorland; tedman; Webster's 3d.

Kenny's syndrome (Kenny, Frederic Marshal): Medicine. See: Jablonski.

KENT, ALBERT FRANK STANLEY. 1863-1958. English physiologist. See: World Who's Who Sci. Kent's bundle.

Kent bugle (or royal Kent bugle) (Kent, Edward, Duke of). Music. See: Partridge; Webster's 3d.

KENT, EDWARD, DUKE OF. 1767-1820. Father of Queen Victoria. See: Dict. Nat. Biog. Kent bugle (or royal Kent bugle).

KENT, GRACE HELEN. b. 1875. American psychologist. See: Amer. Men Sci., 6th ed. Kent-Rosanoff test (series or list), Kent series of emergency scales or EGY test).

Kent-His bundle (Kent, Albert Frank Stanley and His, Wilhelm, Jr.). See: His' bundle.

Kent roller mill (Derivation undetermined): Engineering and Industry. See: Thrush.

Kent-Rosanoff test (series or list) (Kent, Grace Helen and Rosanoff, Aaron oshua): Psychology. See: Chaplin; Drever; English; Wolman.

Kent series of emergency scales (or EGY test) (Kent, Grace Helen): Psychology. See: Chaplin; English; Wolman.

KENT, WILLIAM. d. ca. 1828. Dutch gardener and traveler of the Orient. ee: Britten and Boulger. Kentia.

Kentia (Kent, William): Botany. See: Webster's 3d.

Kentmann reagent (Derivation undetermined): Chemistry. See: Van Nostrand Chem. Dict.

Kent's bundle (Kent, Albert Frank Stanley). See: His' bundle.

Kentsmithite (Smith, J. Kent): Earth Sciences. See: Thrush.

Kenyon-Slaney Clause (Kenyon-Slaney, William Slaney): Education. See: Tarbottle; Montgomery.

KENYON-SLANEY, WILLIAM SLANEY. 1847-1908. English politician. See: Dict. Nat. Biog. 2d suppl. Kenyon-Slaney Clause.

KENYON, WILLIAM SQUIRE. 1869-1933. American jurist and legislator. ee: Dict. Amer. Biog. Fess-Kenyon Act, Webb-Kenyon Act.

Keogh plans (Derivation undetermined): Business. See: Fam. Circle, April, 976, p. 78.

Kepler belt (Derivation undetermined): Fashion. See: Picken.

KEPLER, EDWIN JOHN. b. 1894. American physician. See: Physicians ayo Clinic, 1937, p. 726f. Robinson-Kepler-Power test.

Kepler('s) equation (Kepler, Johannes): Mathematics. See: Ballentyne; nternat. Dict. Ap. Math.

Kepler eyepiece (Kepler, Johannes): Astronomy. See: Satterthwaite.

KEPLER, JOHANNES. 1571-1630. German astronomer. See: Dict. Sci. Biog. epler eyepiece, Kepler('s) equation, Kepler('s) laws (or laws of planetary otion), Keplerian, Keplerian telescope.

Kepler('s) laws (or laws of panetary motion) (Kepler, Johannes): Astronomy. ee: Ballentyne; James; Satterthwaite; Thewlis; Van Nostrand Sci. Encyc.; Webster's 3d.

Keplerian (Kepler, Johannes): Astronomy. See: Webster's 3d.

Keplerian telescope (Kepler, Johannes): Astronomy. See: Webster's 3d.

KER, JOHN (3D DUKE OF ROXBURGHE). 1740-1804. Scottish book collector. ee: Dict. Nat. Biog. Roxburghe binding, Roxburghe Club.

KER, WILLIAM. d. 1814. English gardener. See: Britten and Boulgar. erria.

KERANDEL, JEAN FRANCOIS. 1873-1934. French physician. See: Bull. Soc. Path. Exot., Paris, vol. 27 (1934) pp. 703-705. Kerandel's symptom.

Kerandel's symptom (Kerandel, Jean Francois): Medicine. See: Dorland; Stedman.

KERBOSCH, MATTHIEU GERARD JACQUES MARIE. fl. 1910. Dutch chemist. Cited in: Mansell. Kerbosch reagent.

Kerbosch reagent (Kerbosch, Matthieu Gerard Jacques Marie): Chemistry. See: Van Nostrand Chem. Dict.

KERCKRING, THEODOR. 1640-1693. Dutch anatomist. See: World Who's Who Sci. Kerckring's ossicle, Kerckring's valves (folds or valve(s) of Kerckring).

Kerckring's ossicle (Kerckring, Theodor): Anatomy. See: Dorland; Stedman.

Kerckring's valves (folds or valve(s) of Kerckring) (Kerckring, Theodor): Anatomy. See: Donath; Dorland; Stedman; Webster's 3d.

KERLEY, PETER JAMES. 1900- . English radiologist. See: Med. Direct., 1972. B lines of Kerley.

Kern anastigmat (Derivation undetermined): Photography. See: Focal Encyc. Photog. under "Lens History."

KERN, SERGIUS. fl. 1880. Russian metullurgist in London? Cited in: Royal Soc. Cat. Sci. Pap., 1874-1883. Kern test reaction?

Kern test reaction (Kern, Sergius?): Chemistry. See: Van Nostrand Chem. Dict.

KERNIG, VLADIMIR MICHAILOVICH. 1840-1917. Russian physician. See: Pagel. Kernig's sign.

Kernig's sign (Kernig, Vladimir Michailovich): Medicine. See: Dorland; Hinsie; Stedman.

Kerr cell (or cell shutter) (Kerr, John): Physics. See: Focal Encyc. Photog. under "High Speed Photography"; Hughes; Internat. Dict. Phys. Elec.; Markus; Thewlis; Webster's 3d.

KERR, CLARK. 1911- . American university administrator. See: Leaders in Educ., 4th ed., 1971. Kerr-Martin law, Kerr's first law, Kerr's second law.

Kerr constant (Kerr, John): Physics. See: Hackh; Internat. Dict. Phys. Elec.; Thrush; Van Nostrand Chem. Dict.

Kerr effect (1) (or electro-optical effect) (Kerr, John): Physics. See: Ballentyne; Internat. Dict. Ap. Math.; Internat. Dict. Phys. Elec.; Thewlis; Van Nostrand Sci. Encyc.; Webster's 3d.

Kerr effect (2) (or magneto-optical effect) (Kerr, John): Physics. See: Ballentyne; Hughes; Internat. Dict. Ap. Math.; Markus; Van Nostrand Sci. Encyc.; Thewlis.

KERR, HARRY HYLAND. b. 1881. American surgeon. See: Biog. Lex. hervorr. Aerzte, 1880-1930. Parker-Kerr suture.

KERR, JOHN. 1824-1907. Scottish physicist. See: Dict. Sci. Biog. Kerr cell (or cell shutter), Kerr constant, Kerr effect (1) (or electro-optical effect), Kerr effect (2) (or magneto-optical effect).

Kerr-Martin law (Kerr, Clark and Martin, Thomas L., Jr.): Sociology. See: Martin.

KERR, WASHINGTON CARUTHERS. 1827-1885. American geologist. See: World Who's Who Sci. Kerrite.

Kerria (Ker, William): Botany. See: Partridge; Taylor, N.; Webster's 3d.

Kerrite (Kerr, Washington Caruthers): Earth Sciences. See: Mathews, M. M.; Partridge; Thrush.

Kerr's first law (Kerr, Clark): Sociology. See: Martin.

Kerr's second law (Kerr, Clark): Sociology. See: Martin.

Kershner-Adams syndrome (Kershner, Richard Dudley and Adams, William Elias): Medicine. See: Jablonski.

Kershner-Duff solution (Kershner, Karl Kenneth and Duff, Richard D.?): Chemistry. See: Chem. Abstr., vol. 26, p. 4007; Van Nostrand Chem. Dict.

KERSHNER, KARL KENNETH. fl. 1932. American metallurgist. Cited in: Mansell. Kershner-Duff solution.

KERSHNER, RICHARD DUDLEY. 1923- . American physician. See: Direct. Med. Specialists, 1975-1976. Kershner-Adams syndrome.

Kerst alternating-gradient stabilization (Kerst, Donald William): Physics. See: Van Nostrand Sci. Encyc. under "Cyclotron."

KERST, DONALD WILLIAM. 1911- . American physicist. See: World Who's Who Sci. Kerst alternating-gradient stabilization.

KERSTEN, KARL MORITZ. 1803-1850. German mineralogist. See: Pogg., vo. 1. Kerstenite.

KERSTEN, MARTIN. 1906- . German physicist. See: World Who's Who Sci. Kersten theory.

Kersten theory (Kersten, Martin): Physics. See: Thewlis.

Kerstenite (Kersten, Karl Moritz): Earth Sciences. See: Thrush.

KERSTING, R. fl. 1863. German chemist. Cited in: Royal Soc. Cat. Sci. Pap., 1800-1863. Kersting test for nitrite.

Kersting test for nitrite (Kersting, R.): Chemistry. See: Van Nostrand Chem. Dict.

KERZIN, N. A. fl. 20th c. Russian scientist. Cited in: Hintze, 1st suppl., p. 252. Kerzinite.

Kerzinite (Kerzin, N. A.): Earth Sciences. See: Thrush.

Kessler abrasion tester (Kessler, Daniel William): Engineering and Industry. See: Thrush.

KESSLER, DANIEL WILLIAM. b. 1883. American building engineer. See: Amer. Men Sci., 9th ed. Kessler abrasion tester.

KESTEN, HOMER DAVIES. 1896- . American pathologist. See: Amer. Men Sci., 10th ed. Kesten's process?

Kesten's process (Kesten, Homer Davies?): Statistics. See: Kendall.

Kestner evaporator (Kestner, Paul): Engineering and Industry. See: Auger.

KESTNER, PAUL. fl. 1906. French engineer. Cited in: Chem. Abstr. Kestner evaporator.

Ket, Robert. See: Kett, Robert.

KETCH, JOHN. d. 1686. English executioner. See: Encyc. Brit., 1973. Jack Ketch.

KETELEER, J. B. fl. 19th c. Belgian gardener. (Biography source unavailable.) Keteleeria.

Keteleeria (Keteleer, J. B.): Botany. See: Taylor, N.; Webster's 3d.

KETT, ROBERT. d. 1549. English rebel. See: Dict. Nat. Biog. Kett's rebellion.

Ketteler dispersion formula (Ketteler, Eduard). See: Ketteler-Helmholtz formula.

KETTELER, EDUARD. 1836-1900. German physicist. See: Pogg., vols. 3, 4. Ketteler-Helmholtz formula.

Ketteler-Helmholtz formula (Ketteler, Eduard and Helmholtz, Hermann Ludwig Ferdinand von): Physics. See: Ballentyne. Also known as: Helmholtz-Ketteler formula, Ketteler dispersion formula, Sellmeier equation (or dispersion formula).

Kettering aerial torpedo (Kettering, Charles Franklin): Weapons. See: Quick.

KETTERING, CHARLES FRANKLIN. 1876-1958. American inventor. See: Dict. Sci. Biog. Kettering aerial torpedo, Kettering engine.

Kettering engine (Kettering, Charles Franklin): Engineering and Industry. See: Auger.

KETTNER, RADIM. 1891- . Czechoslovakian geologist. See: Turkevich and Turkevich. Kettnerite.

Kettnerite (Kettner, Radim): Earth Sciences. See: Thrush.

Kett's rebellion (Kett, Robert): History. See: Harbottle; Steinberg.

KEULS, M. fl. 1952. Dutch? statistician. Cited in: Kendall and Doig. Newman-Keuls test.

Kewpie (Cupid): Generic Word. See: Mathews, M. M.

KEY, CHARLES ASTON. 1793-1849. English surgeon. See: World Who's Who Sci. Hodgkin-Key murmur.

KEY, ERNST AXEL HENRIK. 1832-1901. Swedish anatomist. See: Biog. Lex. hervorr. Aerzte. Key-Retzius corpuscles, Key-Retzius foramina (or foramina of Key and Retzius, sheath of Key and Retzius.

Key-Retzius corpuscles (Key, Ernst Axel Henrik and Retzius, Magnus G.): Anatomy. See: Stedman.

Key-Retzius foramina (or foramina of Key and Retzius) (Key, Ernst Axel Henrik and Retzius, Magnus G.). See: Retzius' foramina.

Keyes equation (Keyes, Frederick George): Physics. See: Van Nostrand Sci. Encyc.

KEYES, FREDERICK GEORGE. b. 1885. Canadian-born American physical chemist. See: Pogg., vols. 5, 6. Keyes equation, Keyes-Smith-Gerry equation.

Keyes-Smith-Gerry equation (Keyes, Frederick George; Smith, Leighton Bruerton; and Gerry, Harold Tirrell): Physics. See: Internat. Dict. Ap. Math.

Keynes-effect theory (Keynes, John Maynard Keynes, 1st Baron): Economics. See: Greenwald.

KEYNES, JOHN MAYNARD KEYNES, 1ST BARON. 1883-1946. English economist. See: Internat. Encyc. Soc. Sci. Keynes-effect theory, Keynes plan, Keynesian economics (Keynesian or Keynesianism).

Keynes plan (Keynes, John Maynard Keynes, 1st Baron): Economics. See: Greenwald.

Keynesian economics (Keynesian or Keynesianism) (Keynes, John Maynard Keynes, 1st Baron): Economics. See: Greenwald; Webster's 3d.

khaki Campbell (Campbell, Mrs. Adale): Zoology. See: Webster's 3d.

Khammurabi. See: Hammurabi.

KHARICHKOV, K. fl. 1906-1914. Russian chemist. Cited in: Chem. Abstr., Decenn. Index, 1907-1916. Kharichkov reagent for organic bases, Kharichkov test for copper, cobalt, and naphthenic acid, Kharichkov test for ferrous salts, Kharichkov test for hydrogen peroxide.

Kharichkov reagent for organic bases (Kharichkov, K.): Chemistry. See: Van Nostrand Chem. Dict.

Kharichkov test for copper, cobalt, and naphthenic acid (Kharichkov, K.): Chemistry. See: Van Nostrand Chem. Dict.

Kharichkov test for ferrous salts (Kharichkov, K.): Chemistry. See: Van Nostrand Chem. Dict.

Kharichkov test for hydrogen perioxide (Kharichkov, K.): Chemistry. See: Van Nostrand Chem. Dict.

Khinchin(e), Aleksandr Yakovlevich. See: Khintchin, Aleksandr Yakovlevich.

KHINTCHIN(E), ALEKSANDR YAKOVLEVICH. 1894-1959. Russian mathematician. See: Dict. Sci. Biog. Khintchine's theorem, Pollaczek-Khintchine formula, Wiener-Khintchine theorem.

Khintchine' theorem (Khintchine(e), Aleksandr Yakovlevich): Mathematics. See: Ballentyne; James; Kendall.

KHOTINSKY, ACHILLES DE. 1850-1933. Russian-born American instrument designer. (Biography source unavailable.) de Khotinsky cement.

KHWARIZMI, AL (MUHAMMAD IBN-MUSA AL-KHWARIZMI). 780-850 A.D. Arab mathematician. See: Dict. Sci. Biog. algorism.

KICK, FRIEDRICH. 1840-1915. German technologist. Cited in: Mansell. Kick's Law?

Kick's law (Kirk, Friedrich?): Engineering and Industry. See: Ballentyne; Thrush.

KICKX, JEAN. 1775-1831. Belgian botanist. See: Biog. Nat. de Belgique. Kickxia.

KICKX, JEAN, THE YOUNGER. 1803-1864. Belgian botanist. See: Biog. Nat. Belg. Kickxia.

Kickxia (Kickx, Jean and Kickx, Jean, the younger): Botany. See: Webster's 3d.

Kidd blood group (Kidd, Mrs.): Medicine. See: Stedman.

KIDD, MRS. fl. 1951. Patient. (Biography source unavailable.) Kidd blood group.

Kidder press (Kidder, Wellington Parker): Printing. See: Lockwood.

KIDDER, WELLINGTON PARKER. 1853-1924. American engineer and inventor. See: World Who's Who Sci. Kidder press.

KIEFER, JACK CARL. 1924- . American mathematical statistician. See: Amer. Men Sci., 10th ed. Kiefer-Wolfowitz process.

Kiefer-Wolfowitz process (Kiefer, Jack Carl and Wolfowitz, Jacob): Statistics. See: Kendall.

Kieffer's stain (Derivation undetermined): Medicine. See: Stedman.

Kiel graft (Derivation undetermined): Medicine. See: Stedman.

KIEN, ALPHONSE-MARIE-JOSEPH. fl. 1865. Strasbourg physician. Cited in: Mansell. Kussmaul-Kien respiration.

Kien Lung. See: Ch'ien Lung.

Kienbock meter (Kienboeck, Robert): Medicine. See: Stedman under "dose erythema."

KIENBOECK, ROBERT. 1871-1954. Austrian roentgenologist. See: World Who's Who Sci. Kienbock meter, Kienboeck's atrophy, Kienboeck's disease, Kienboeck's dislocation (or luxation), Kienboeck's syringomyelia, Kienboeck's unit.

Kienboeck's atrophy (Kienboeck, Robert): Medicine. See: Dorland; Jablonski; Stedman. Also known as: Sudeck's atrophy.

Kienboeck's disease (Kienboeck, Robert): Medicine. See: Dorland; Jablonski; Stedman.

Kienboeck's dislocation (or luxation) (Kienboeck, Robert): Medicine. See: Jablonski; Stedman.

Kienboeck's syringomyelia (Kienboeck, Robert): Medicine. See: Jablonski.

Kienboeck's unit (Kienboeck, Robert): Medicine. See: Dorland; Stedman.

KIENER, PAUL LOUIS ANDRE. 1841-1895. French histologist. See: Pagel. Hanot-Kiener syndrome?

KIERNAN, FRANCIS. 1800-1874. Irish-born English physician. See: World Who's Who Sci. Kiernan's space.

Kiernan's space (Kiernan, Francis): Anatomy. See: Donath; Dorland; Stedman.

KIESER, DIETRICH GEORG. 1779-1862. German physican. See: Biog. Lex. hervorr. Aerzte. Kieserite.

KIESER, WILLIBALD. fl. 1939. German physician. (Biography source unavailable.) Turner-Kieser syndrome.

Kieserite (Kieser, Dietrich Georg): Earth Sciences. See: Thrush; Webster's 3d. Also known as: Martinsite.

KIESOW, FRIEDRICH. 1858-1941. Italian psychologist. See: Psych. Rev., vol. 48 (1941) p. 268. Kiesow's painless cheek-area?

Kiesow's painless cheek-area (Kiesow, Friedrich?): Physiology. See: Drever.

KIESSELBACH, WILHELM. 1839-1902. German laryngologist. See: Biog. Lex. hervorr. Aerzte, 1880-1930. Kiesselbach's area.

Kiesselbach's area (Kiesselbach, Wilhelm): Anatomy. See: Donath; Dorland; Stedman. Also known as: Little's area.

Kikuchi lines (Kikushi, Seishi?): Physics. See: Ballentyne; Hackh; Markus; Thewlis; Van Nostrand Sci. Encyc.

KIKUSHI, SEISHI. fl. 1930. Japanese physicist. Cited in: Chem. Abstr. Kikuchi lines?

KILHAM. fl. 19th c.? American physician. (Biography source unavailable.) Kilham Hill (apple).

KILHAM, ALEXANDER. 1762-1798. English clergyman. See: Dict. Nat. Biog. Kilhamites.

Kilham Hill (apple) (Kilham): Botany. See: Mathews, M. M.

Kilhamites (Kilham, Alexander): Religion. See: Canney; Latham.

KILIAN, HERMAN FRIEDRICH. 1800-1863. German gynecologist. See: Biog. Lex. hervorr. Aerzte. Kilian's line, Kilian's pelvis.

Kiliani-Fischer synthesis (Kiliani, Heinrich and Fischer, Emil): See: Kiliani reaction (or synthesis).

KILIANI, HEINRICH. b. 1855. German chemist. See: Pogg., vol. 3. Kiliani reaction (or synthesis), Kiliani reagent for digitalis glucosides.

Kiliani reaction (or synthesis) (Kiliani, Heinrich): Chemistry. See: Ballentyne; Hackh; Van Nostrand Chem. Dict. Also known as: Kiliani-Fischer synthesis.

Kiliani reagent for digitalis glucosides (Kiliani, Heinrich): Chemistry. See: Van Nostrand Chem. Dict.

Kilian's line (Kilian, Hermann Friedrich): Anatomy. See: Donath; Dorland; Stedman.

Kilian's pelvis (Kilian, Hermann Friedrich): Medicine. See: Dorland; Jablonski; Stedman.

KILLIAN, GUSTAV. 1860-1921. German laryngologist. See: World Who's Who Sci. Killian's bundle (or muscle), Killian's operation.

Killian's bundle (or muscle) (Killian, Gustav): Anatomy. See: Donath; Stedman.

Killian's operation (Killian, Gustav): Medicine. See: Dorland; Stedman.

Killingia (or Kyllingia) (Kylling, Peder): Botany. See: Charnock.

KILOH, LESLIE GORDON. fl. 1938-1964. Australian physician. See: Med. Direct., 1964. Kiloh-Nevin syndrome (1), Kiloh-Nevin syndrome (2).

Kiloh-Nevin syndrome (1) (Kiloh, Leslie Gordon and Nevin, Samuel): Medicine. See: Jablonski.

Kiloh-Nevin syndrome (2) (Kiloh, Leslie Gordon and Nevin, Samuel): Medicine. See: Jablonski.

kiloroentgen (Roentgen, Wilhelm Konrad): Physics. See: Stedman.

kilowatt (Watt, James): Physics. See: Van Nostrand Sci. Encyc.

KILPATRICK, HUGH JUDSON. 1836-1881. American soldier. See: Dict. Amer. Biog. Kilpatrick's Raid.

Kilpatrick's Raid (Kilpatrick, Hugh Judson): History. See: Jameson.

KILROY. No dates. American ship inspector. (Biography source unavailable.) Kilroy?, Kilroy was here?.

Kilroy (Kilroy, the ship inspector?): Generic Word (world traveler). See: Hendrickson.

Kilroy was here (Kilroy, the ship inspector?): Generic Word. See: Hendrickson.

Kimberley, 1st Earl of. See: Wodehouse, John, 1st Earl of Kimberley.

KIMMELSTIEL, PAUL. 1900-1970. German-born American physician. See: Who Was Who Amer., 1969-1973. Kimmelstiel-Wilson syndrome (or disease).

Kimmelstiel-Wilson syndrome (or disease) (Kimmelstiel, Paul and Wilson, Clifford): Medicine. See: Dorland; Jablonski; Stedman.

KIMPFLIN, GEORGES. fl. 1907. French chemist. Cited in: Chem. Abstr., vol. 1, p. 1873. Kimpflin test.

Kimpflin test (Kimpflin, Georges): Chemistry. See: Van Nostrand Chem. Dict.

KIMPTON, ARTHUR RONALD. b. 1881. American surgeon. (Biography source unavailable.) Kimpton-Brown tube.

Kimpton-Brown tube (Kimpton, Arthur Ronald and Brown): Medicine. See: Dorland.

Kind-Chaudron process (Derivation undetermined): Engineering and Industry. See: Thrush.

KINDBERG, MICHEL LEON. 1883-1945. French physician. See: Presse Med., vol. 53 (July 28, 1945) pp. 413-414. Loehr-Kindberg syndrome.

KINDLER, WERNER. 1895- . German otorhinolaryngologist. See: Z. Laryngo. Rhino. Oto. und Ihre Grenzgebiete, vol. 44 (Feb., 1965), [69]. Zange-Kindler syndrome.

Kind's plug (Derivation undetermined): Engineering and Industry. See: Thrush.

King Alfred's candle (Alfred the Great): Horology. See: Webster's 3d.

King-Armstrong unit (King, Earl Judson and Armstrong, A. R.): See: King unit.

King Charles spaniel (Charles II?): Zoology. See: Webster's 3d.

King Charles's head (Charles I): Generic Word (obsession). See: Brewer; Webster's 3d.

KING, D. fl. 1957? Australian geologist. Cited in: Hintze, 2d suppl, p. 740. Kingite.

King detaching hook (Derivation undetermined): Engineering and Industry. See: Thrush.

KING, EARL JUDSON. 1901-1962. Canadian biochemist. See: Pogg., vols. 6, 7b. King unit.

King George's war (George II): History. See: Jameson; Latham; Morris.

KING, GILBERT WILLIAM. 1914-   . American chemical physicist. See: Amer. Men and Women Sci., 12th ed. King report.

"KING HUGO." Spirit who was patron of the Huguenots. Cited in: Encyc. Brit., 1973. Huguenots?

KING, J. B. No dates. Millionaire turned hobo. (Biography source unavailable.) J. B. King?

KING, JAMES GRIEVE. b. 1891. English fuel chemist. See: Who's Who Brit. Sci., 1953. Gray-King coke type, Gray-King test.

King James('s) version (or Bible) (James I): Religion. See: Encyc. Brit., 1973 under "English Literature," vol. 8, p. 573a; Wagner (Names).

King Philip's war (Philip, "King"): History. See: Phyfe.

King report (King, Gilbert William): Library Science. See: Harrod.

King Richard's ransom (Richard I, the Lion-Hearted): History. See: Steinberg.

King Tut (Tutankhamen): Generic Word. See: Hendrickson.

King unit (King, Earl Judson): Chemistry. See: Stedman. Also known as: King-Armstrong unit.

King ventilating system (Derivation undetermined): Agriculture. See: Winburne.

King William pine (William IV of England): Botany. See: Webster's 3d.

King William's War (William III of Orange): History. See: Jameson; Latham; Morris. Also known as: War of William and Mary.

Kingite (King, D.): Earth Sciences. See: Thrush.

KINGSBURY, ALBERT. 1863-1943. American engineer. See: Who Was Who Amer., 1943-1950. Kingsbury bearing (or thrust bearing).

KINGSBURY, ARTHUR W. G. fl. 1957. English mineralogist. Cited in: Min. Mag., vol. 33 (1964) p. 937. Arthurite.

Kingsbury bearing (or thrust bearing) (Kingsbury, Albert): Engineering and Industry. See: Auger; Van Nostrand Sci. Encyc.

KINGSLEY, NORMAN WILLIAM. 1829-1913. American dentist. See: Who Was Who Amer., 1897-1916. Kingsley splint (or reversed Kingsley splint).

Kingsley splint (or reversed Kingsley splint) (Kingsley, Norman William): Dentistry. See: Blakiston's Gould; Stedman.

KINGSTON, JOHN. fl. 1837. English? engineer. (Biography source unavailable.) Kingston valve.

Kingston valve (Kingston, John): Engineering and Industry. See: Auger.

Kinkaid Act (or Home Act) (Kinkaid, Moses Pierce): History. See: Morris; Winburne.

KINKAID, MOSES PIERCE. 1854-1922. American legislator. See: Who Was Who Amer., 1897-1916. Kinkaid Act (or Home Act), Kinkaider.

Kinkaider (Kinkaid, Moses Pierce): History. See: Hendrickson; Webster's 3d; Winburne.

KINKEAD, R. W. fl. 1926. English chemist. Cited in: Chem. Abstr., vol. 20, p. 2416. Kinkead test.

Kinkead test (Kinkead, R. W.): Chemistry. See: Van Nostrand Chem. Dict.

KINNEAR. fl. 1857. Scottish scientist. (Biography source unavailable.) Kinnear pattern.

Kinnear pattern (Kinnear): Photography. See: Focal Encyc. Photog. under "Britain."

KINNERSLEY, HENRY WULFF. fl. 1933. English biochemist. Cited in: Chem. Abstr. Kinnersley-Peters test for vitamin B1 (thiamine).

Kinnersley-Peters test for vitamin B1 (thiamine) (Kinnersley, Henry Wulff and Peters, Sir Rudolph Albert): Chemistry. See: Van Nostrand Chem. Dict.

Kinnier Wilson's disease (Wilson, Samuel Alexander Kinnier). See: Wilson's disease (or syndrome).

KINSEY, ALFRED CHARLES. 1894-1956. American zoologist. See: Internat. Encyc. Soc. Sci. Kinsey Report.

Kinsey Report (Kinsey, Alfred Charles): Sociology. See: Hendrickson.

KINZIE, CORA ELSIE. fl. 1931. American teacher of the deaf. Cited in: Mansell. Kinzie method.

KINZIE, ROSE. fl. 1931. American teacher of the deaf. Cited in: Mansell under "Kinzie, Cora." Kinzie method.

Kinzie method (Kinzie, Cora and Kinzie, Rose): Education. See: Good.

KIPLING, RUDYARD (In full: JOSEPH RUDYARD). 1865-1936. English writer. See: Dict. Nat. Biog. 5th suppl. Kiplingese (or Kiplingesque).

Kiplingese (or Kiplingesque) (Kipling, Rudyard): Literature. See: Webster's 3d.

Kipp('s) generator (or apparatus) (Kipp, Petrus Jacobus): Chemistry. See: Hackh; Thrush; Van Nostrand Chem. Dict.; Webster's 3d.

KIPP, PETRUS JACOBUS. d. 1864. Dutch druggist and chemist. (Biography source unavailable.) Kipp('s) generator (or apparatus).

Kipp relay (Derivation undetermined): Electronics. See: Hughes; Markus.

Kirby's quest (Kirkeby, John de). See: Kirkby's quest.

KIRCHHEIMER, FRANZ. 1911-   . German geologist. See: Pogg., vol. 7a. metakirchheimerite.

Kirchhoff formula for vapor pressure (Kirchhoff, Gustave Robert): Physics. See: Internat. Dict. Phys. Elec.; Thewlis.

Kirchhoff formulation of Huygens principle (Kirchhoff, Gustave Robert): Physics. See: Internat. Dict. Ap. Math.

Kirchhoff geometric optics theorem (Kirchhoff, Gustave Robert): Physics. See: Internat. Dict. Ap. Math.

KIRCHHOFF, GUSTAVE ROBERT. 1824-1887. German physicist. See: Dict. Sci. Biog. Bunsen-Kirchhoff law; Kirchhoff formula for vapor pressure (or vapor pressure formula), Kirchhoff formulation of Huygens principle, Kirchhoff geometric optics theorem, Kirchhoff's approximation, Kirchhoff's equation(s) (or equation for the heat of reaction), Kirchhoff's equation for heat of sublimation, Kirchhoff('s) laws (1) (law(s) of radiation, law of emission, or optical law of Kirchhoff), Kirchhoff('s) laws (2) (laws of (electrical) networks or laws of current), Stewart-Kirchhoff law.

Kirchhoff('s) laws (1) (law(s) of radiation, law of emission, or optical law of Kirchhoff) (Kirchhoff, Gustave Robert): Physics. See: Ballentyne; Huschke; Internat. Dict. Ap. Math.; Satterthwaite; Thrush; Thewlis; Van Nostrand Chem. Dict.

Kirchhoff('s) laws (2) (laws of (electrical) networks or laws of current) (Kirchhoff, Gustave Robert): Physics. See: Ballentyne; Internat. Dict. Phys. Elec.; Markus; Thewlis; Van Nostrand Sci. Encyc.; Webster's 3d.

Kirchhoff's approximation (Kirchhoff, Gustave Robert): Physics. See: Ballentyne.

Kirchhoff's equation(s) (or equation for the heat of reaction) (Kirchhoff, Gustave Robert): Physics. See: Ballentyne; Hackh; Internat. Dict. Ap. Math.; Van Nostrand Chem. Dict.

Kirchhoff's equation for heat of sublimation (Kirchhoff, Gustave Robert): Physics. See: Ballentyne.

KIRCHNER, WILHELM. 1849-1935. Austrian otologist. See: Biog. Lex. hervorr. Aerzte. Kirchner's diverticulum.

Kirchner's diverticulum (Kirchner, Wilhelm): Medicine. See: Dorland.

Kirk Bryan Award (Bryan, Kirk): Earth Sciences. Cited in: Dict. Sci. Biog.

Kirk Bryan Fund (Bryan, Kirk): Earth Sciences. Cited in: Dict. Sci. Biog.

KIRK, NORMAN THOMAS. 1888-1960. Army surgeon. See: World Who's Who Sci. Kirk's amputation.

KIRKALDY, DAVID. 1820-1897. Scottish metallurgist. See: Dict. Sci. Biog. Kirkaldy's machine.

Kirkaldy's machine (Kirkaldy, David): Engineering and Industry. See: Auger.

Kirkby's (or Kirby's) quest (Kirkeby, John de): Law. See: Black; Steinberg.

KIRKE, PERCY. 1646-1691. English soldier. See: Dict. Nat. Biog. Kirke's Lambs.

KIRKEBY, JOHN DE. d. 1290. English bishop and treasurer of Edward I. See: Dict. Nat. Biog. Kirkby's (or Kirby's) quest.

Kirkendall effect (Kirkendall, Ernest Oliver): Physics. See: Ballentyne; Thewlis; Van Nostrand Sci. Encyc. Also known as: Smigelkas effect.

KIRKENDALL, ERNEST OLIVER. 1914- . American metallurgist. See: Amer. Men Sci., 10th ed. Kirkendall effect.

Kirke's Lambs (Kirke, Percy): History. See: Harbottle; Harvey; Latham.

KIRKPATRICK JAMES C. fl. late 19th c. American hotel manager. (Biography source unavailable.) oysters Kirkpatrick.

Kirk's amputation (Kirk, Norman Thomas): Medicine. See: Dorland; Stedman.

KIRKUP, RALPH H. fl. 1931. English? engineer. Cited in: Chem. Abstr. Kirkup table?

Kirkup tables (Kirkup, Ralph H.?): Engineering and Industry. See: Thrush.

Kirkwood approximation (Kirkwood, John Gamble): Physics. See: Internat. Dict. Phys. Elec.

KIRKWOOD, DANIEL. 1814-1895. American astronomer. See: Dict. Sci. Biog. Kirkwood('s) gaps.

Kirkwood equation for the dielectric constant (or formula) (Kirkwood, John Gamble): Physics. See: Internat. Dict. Ap. Math.; Thewlis.

Kirkwood('s) gaps (Kirkwood, Daniel): Astronomy. See: Asimov; Satterthwaite.

KIRKWOOD, JOHN GAMBLE. 1907-1959. American theoretical chemist. See: Dict. Sci. Biog. Kirkwood approximation, Kirkwood equation for the dielectric constant (or formula).

Kirlian photography (Kirlian, Semyon and Kirlian, Valentina): Physics. See: Time, March 4, 1974, p. 70.

KIRLIAN, SEMYON. fl. 1930's. Russian electronics expert. (Biography source unavailable.) Kirlian photography.

KIRLIAN, VALENTINA. fl. 1930. Russian electronics expert. (Biography source unavailable.) Kirlian photography.

KIRMISSON, EDOUARD. 1848-1927. French surgeon. See: Biog. Lex. hervorr. Aerzte, 1880-1930. Kirmisson's operation.

Kirmisson's operation (Kirmisson, Edouard): Medicine. See: Dorland.

KIROV, SERGEI MIRONOVICH. 1888-1934. Russian revolutionary leader. See: Encyc. Brit., 1973. Kirovite.

Kirovite (Kirov, Sergei Mironovich): Earth Sciences. See: Webster's 3d.

KIRSCHMANN, AUGUST. 1860-1932. German psychologist. See: Pogg., vol. 5. Kirschmann's contrast law.

Kirschmann's contrast law (Kirschmann, August): Physics. See: Drever.

KIRSCHNER, MARTIN. 1879-1942. German surgeon. See: Biog. Lex. hervorr. Aerzte, 1880-1930. Kirschner's wire (or apparatus).

Kirschner value (Derivation undetermined): Chemistry. See: Van Nostrand Chem. Dict.

Kirschner's wire (or apparatus) (Kirschner, Martin): Medicine. See: Dorland; Stedman.

KIRSTEIN, ALFRED. 1863-1922. German physician. See: Biog. Lex. hervorr. Aerzte, 1880-1930. Kirstein's method.

Kirstein's method (Kirstein, Alfred): Medicine. See: Dorland.

KIRTLAND, JARED POTTER. 1793-1877. American naturalist. See: World Who's Who Sci. Kirtland's owl, Kirtland's warbler.

Kirtland's owl (Kirtland, Jared Potter): Zoology. See: Webster's 3d.

Kirtland's warbler (Kirtland, Jared Potter): Zoology. See: Gray; Mathews, M. M.; Pennak.

KIRWAN, RICHARD. 1733-1812. Irish chemist and earth scientist. See: Dict. Sci. Biog. Kirwanite.

Kirwanite (Kirwan, Richard): Earth Sciences. See: Charnock.

KISCH, BRUNO. 1890-1966. German physiologist. See: Biog. Lex. hervorr. Aerzte, 1880-1930. Kisch's reflex.

Kisch's reflex (Kisch, Bruno): Medicine. See: Dorland; Stedman.

Kishner cyclopropane synthesis (Kizhner, Nikolay Mateveyevich): Chemistry. See: Van Nostrand Chem. Dict.

Kishner, Nikolay Matveyevich. See: Kizhner, Nikolay Mateyevich.

Kit Carson hitch (Carson, Christopher): Generic Word. See: Mathews, M. M.

Kit-Kat (Cat) Club (Cat, Christopher): History. See: Harbottle; Hendrickson; Latham.

KITAHARA, S. fl. 1936. Japanese ophthalmologist. (Biography source unavailable.) Masuda-Kitahara disease.

Kitahara's disease (Kitahara, S.). See: Masuda-Kitahara disease.

KITAIBEL, PAUL. 1757-1817. Hungarian botanist, chemist and mineralogist. See: Dict. Sci. Biog. Kitaibelia.

Kitaibelia (Kitaibel, Paul): Botany. See: Charnock.

KITASATO, SHIBASABURO. 1852-1931. Japanese bacteriologist. See: Dict. Sci. Biog. Kitasato bacillus, Kitasato's filter.

Kitasato's bacillus (Kitasato, Shibasaburo): Medicine. See: Stedman.

Kitasato's filter (Kitasato, Shibasaburo): Medicine. See: Dorland; Stedman.

KITCHENER, HORATIO HERBERT. 1850-1916. English field-marshall. See: Dict. Nat. Biog., 3rd suppl. Curzon-Kitchener controversy.

Kitchin cycle (or Kitchin) (Kitchin, Joseph Armstrong): Economics. See: Greenwald; Webster's 3d.

KITCHIN, JOSEPH ARMSTRONG. 1910- . American Political scientist. See: Amer. Men Sci., 9th ed. Soc. and Behav. Sci. Kitchin cycle (or Kitchin).

Kite apparatus (Kite, Joseph Hiram): Medicine. See: Dorland.

KITE, JOSEPH HIRAM. b. 1891. American orthopedic surgeon. See: Direct. Med. Specialists, 1965-1966. Kite apparatus.

KITSON, ARTHUR. fl. 1891. American engineer. Cited in: Royal Soc. Cat. Sci. Pap., 1884-1900. Kitson light?

Kitson light (Kitson, Arthur?): Engineering and Industry. Cited in: Laughlin.

KITTEL, M. J. fl. 1902. German physician. Cited in: Mansell. Kittel's treatment.

Kittel's treatment (Kittel, M. J.): Medicine. See: Dorland.

KITTLITZ, BARON FRIEDRICH HEINRICH VON. 1799-1874. German officer, ornithologist and traveler. See: Allg. Deut. Biog. Kittlitz's murrelet.

Kittlitz's murrelet (Kittlitz, Baron Friedrich Heinrich von): Zoology. See: Gray; Webster's 3d.

KITTRICH, MIROSLAV. No dates. Physician. (Biography source unavailable.) Kittrich's method.

Kittrich's method (Kittrich, Miroslav): Medicine. See: Stedman.

KIZHNER, NIKOLAY MATVEYEVICH. 1867-1935. Russian organic chemist. See: Who Was Who USSR. Kishner cyclopropane synthesis, Wolff-Kishner reduction (or reaction).

Kjeldahl apparatus (or condenser) (Kjeldahl, Johan Gustav Christoffer): Chemistry. See: Hackh; Stedman; Van Nostrand Chem. Dict.

Kjeldahl flask (Kjeldahl, Johan Gustav Chrisoffer): Chemistry. See: Hackh; Van Nostrand Chem. Dict.; Webster's 3d.

KJELDAHL, JOHAN GUSTAV CHRISTOFFER. 1849-1900. Danish chemist. See: Dict. Sci. Biog. Kjeldahl apparatus (or condenser), Kjeldahl flask, Kjeldahl method (nitrogen method or Kjeldahlization.

Kjeldahl method (nitrogen method or Kjeldahlization (Kjeldahl, Johan Gustave Christoffer): Chemistry. See: Dorland; Hackh; Stedman; Van Nostrand Sci. Encyc.; Webster's 3d.

KJELLAND, CHRISTIAN. b. 1871. Norwegian obstetrician. (Biography source unavailable.) Kjelland's forceps.

Kjelland's forceps (Kjelland, Christian): Medicine. See: Dorland; Stedman.

KJELLGREN, BENGT RAGNAR FRITIOF. b. 1894. Swedish-born American engineer. See: Amer. Men Sci., 8th ed. Sawyer-Kjellgren process.

KJERSTAD, CONRAD LUND. b. 1883. American psychologist. See: Amer. Men. Sci., 4th ed. Kjersted-Robinson law.

Kjersted-Robinson law (Kjerstad, Conrad Lund and Robinson, Edward Stevens): Psychology. See: Chaplin; English; Wolman.

KLAPP, RUDOLPH. 1873-1949. German surgeon. See: Biog. Lex. hervorr. Aerzte, 1880-1930. Klapp's method, Klapp's suction cups.

Klapp's method (Klapp, Rudolph): Medicine. See: Dorland; Stedman.

Klapp's suction cups (Klapp, Rudolph): Medicine. See: Stedman.

KLAPROTH, MARTIN HEINRICH. 1743-1817. German chemist. See: Dict. Sci. Biog. Klaprothia, Klaprothite.

Klaprothia (Klaproth, Martin Heinrich): Botany. See: Charnock.

Klaprothite (Klaproth, Martin Heinrich): Earth Sciences. See: Webster's 3d.

KLATSKIN, GERALD. 1910- . American internist. See: Amer. Men and Women Sci., 12th ed. Kaplan-Klatskin syndrome.

KLATT, BERTHOLD. 1885-1958. German zoologist. See: Kuerschner's Deut. Gel. Kal., vol. 4, 1931. Klattia?

Klattia (Klatt, Berthold?): Zoology. See: Pennak.

KLAUDER, JOSEPH VICTOR. 1888-1962. American dermatologist. See: New York Times, Apr. 5, 1962, p. 33, col. 2. Klauder's disease, Klauder's syndrome.

Klauder's disease (Klauder, Joseph Victor). See: Rosenbach's disease.

Klauder's syndrome (Klauder, Joseph Victor). See: Stevens-Johnson syndrome.

KLAUSNER, ERWIN. b. 1883. Czech physician. See: Biog. Lex. hervorr. Aerzte, 1880-1930. Klausner's reaction (or test).

Klausner's reaction (or test) (Klausner, Erwin): Medicine. See: Dorland; Stedman.

KLEBELSBERG, KUNO. 1875-1932. Hungarian statesman. See: Magyar Eletr. Lex. Klebelsbergite.

Klebelsbergite (Klebelsberg, Kuno): Earth Sciences. See: Thrush.

Klebs' disease (Klebs, Edwin): Medicine. See: Jablonski.

KLEBS, EDWIN (In full: THEODOR ALBRECHT EDWIN). 1834-1913. German pathologist. See: World Who's Who Sci. Klebs' disease, Klebs-Loeffler bacillus, Klebs' tuberculin, Klebsiella, Klebsiella pneumonia.

Klebs-Loeffler bacillus (Klebs, Edwin and Loeffler, Friedrich A. J.): Medicine. See: Dorland; Stedman; Webster's 3d. Also known as Loeffler's bacillus.

Klebs' tuberculin (Klebs, Edwin): Medicine. See: Stedman.

Klebsiella (Klebs, Edwin): Zoology. See: Dorland; Stedman; Webster's 3d.

Klebsiella pneumonia (Klebs, Edwin). See: Friedlaender's pneumonia.

Kleeman condenser (Derivation undetermined): Engineering and Industry. See: Thrush.

KLEEMAN, RICHARD DANIEL. 1878-1932. Australian-born American physicist. See: Pogg., vols. 5, 6, 7b. Bragg-Kleeman rule.

Kleene-Mostowski hierarchy (Kleene, Stephen Cole and Mastowski, Andrzej): Philosophy. See: Edwards under "Mathematiccs, Foundations of," vol. 5, p. 207.

KLEENE, STEPHEN COLE. 1909- . American mathematician. See: Amer. Men Sci., 9th ed. Kleene-Mostowski hierarchy.

Kleig eyes (Kliegel, John H.). See: Klieg eyes (or conjunctivitis).

Kleig light (Kliegel, John H.): See: Klieg light.

KLEIJN, ADRIANUS PAULUS HUIBERTUS ANTONIE DE. fl. 1936. Dutch otorhinolaryngologist. Cited in: Mansell. van der Hoevede-de Kleyn syndrome?

KLEIN, ABRAHAM ALBERT. b. 1889. American chemist. See: Amer. Men., 9th ed. Klein turbidimeter.

Klein bottle (Klein, Felix): Mathematics. See: James; Webster's 3d.

KLEIN, CARL (In full: JOHANN FRIEDRICH CARL). 1842-1907. German mineralogist. See: World Who's Who Sci. Klein('s) solution (mineral solution or liquid), Kleinite.

KLEIN, CHRISTIAN FELIX. 1849-1925. German mathematician. See: World Who's Who Sci. Cayley-Klein parameter(s).

KLEIN, DAVID. 1908- . Swiss human geneticist. See: Who's Who Sci. Europe, 1972. Champion-Cregan-Klein syndrome, Franceschetti-Zwahlen-Klein syndrome, Klein-Waardenburg syndrome, Wildervanck-Waardenburg-Franceschetti-Klein syndrome.

KLEIN, EDMUND. 1921- . Austrian-born Canadian dermatologist. See: Amer. Men Sci., 11th ed. Hauschka-Klein ascites tumor.

KLEIN, EDWARD EMANUEL. 1844-1925. Hungarian bacteriologist in England. See: Biog. Lex. hervorr. Aerzte, 1880-1930. Klein's bacillus, Klein's muscle, Klein's stain?

KLEIN, FELIX (In full: CHRISTIAN FELIX). 1849-1925. German mathematician. See: Dict. Sci. Biog. Cayley-Klein parameter, Klein bottle.

Klein-Gordon equation (Klein, Oskar Benjamin and Gordon, Walter): Physics. See: Ballentyne; Hughes; Internat. Dict. Ap. Math.; Internat. Dict. Phys. Elec., Thewlis.

Klein-Gumprecht shadow nuclei (Klein and Gumprecht, Ferdinand). See: Gumprecht shadow nuclei.

KLEIN, JACOB THEODORE. 1685-1759. German zoologist. See: Dict. Sci. Biog. Kleinia.

KLEIN, MELANIE. 1882-1960. German psychologist. See: Internat. Encyc. Soc. Sci. Kleinian.

Klein-Nishina formula (Klein, Oskar Benjamin and Nishina, Yoshio): Physics. See: Ballentyne; Internat. Dict. Phys. Elec.; Markus; Thewlis.

KLEIN, OSKAR BENJAMIN. 1894- . Swedish physicist. See: Pogg., vols. 6, 7b. Klein-Gordon equation, Klein-Nishina formula, Klein paradox, Klein-Rydberg method (or construction).

Klein paradox (Klein, Oscar Benjamin): Physics. See: Internat. Dict. Phys. Elec.

Klein-Rydberg method (or construction) (Klein, Oskar Benjamin and Rydberg, Ragner): Physics. See: Hughes; Internat. Dict. Ap. Math.; Internat. Dict. Phys. Elec.

Klein('s) solution (mineral solution or liquid) (Klein, Carl): Chemistry. See: Hackh; Thrush; Van Nostrand Chem. Dict.

Klein solution for nitrate (Derivation undetermined): Chemistry. See: Van Nostrand Chem. Dict.

Klein turbidimeter (Klein, Abraham Albert): Engineering and Industry. See: Thrush.

Klein-Waardenburg syndrome (Klein, David and Waardenburg, P. Johannes): Medicine. See: Jablonski. Also known as: Klein's syndrome, Van der Hoeve-Halbertsma-Waardenburg syndrome, Van der Hoeve-Waardenburg-Gualdi syndrome.

Kleine-Levine syndrome (Kleine, Willi and Levin, Max): Medicine. See: Hinsie; Jablonski.

KLEINE, WILLI. fl. 1925. German psychiatrist. (Biography source unavailable.) Kleine-Levin syndrome.

Kleinenberg mixture (Kleinenberg, Nicolaus?): Chemistry. See: Hackh.

KLEINENBERG, NICOLAUS. 1842-1897. Russian biologist. See: Dict. Sci. Biog. Kleinenberg mixture?

KLEINHOFF. No dates. German botanic gardens director. (Biography source unavailable.) Kleinhovia.

Kleinhovia (Kleinhoff): Botany. See: Charnock.

Kleinia (Klein, Jacob Theodore): Botany. See: Charnock.

Kleinian (Klein, Melanie): Psychology. See: Barnhart (New Eng.)

Kleinite (Klein, Carl): Earth Sciences. See: Thrush; Webster's 3d.

KLEINMANN, HANS. 1895- . German chemist. See: Pogg., vols. 6, 7a., Kleinmann-Pangritz reagent.

Kleinmann-Pangritz reagent (Kleinmann, Hans and Pangritz, Fritz): Chemistry. See: Van Nostrand Chem. Dict.

Klein's bacillus (Klein, Edward Emanuel): Medicine. See: Dorland.

Klein's muscle (Klein, Edward Emanuel): Anatomy. See: Stedman. Also known as: Bovero's muscle.

Klein's stain (Klein, Edward Emanuel?): Medicine. See: Stedman.

Klein's syndrome (Klein, David). See: Klein-Waardenburg syndrome.

KLEINSCHMIDT, AUGUSTUS. b. 1818. German physician. Cited in: Mansell. Kleinschmidt's glands.

KLEINSCHMIDT, HANS ADOLF. b. 1885. German pediatrician. See: World Who's Who Sci. Kleinschmidt's syndrome.

Kleinschmidt's glands (Kleinschmidt, Augustus): Anatomy. See: Stedman. Also known as: Krause's glands.

Kleinschmidt's syndrome (Kleinschmidt, Hans Adolf): Medicine. See: Jablonski.

Kleist, E. Georg von. See: Von Kleist, E. Georg.

KLEIST, KARL. b. 1879. German physician. See: Biog. Lex. hervorr. Aerzte, 1880-1930. Kleist's apraxia.

Kleistian jar (Von Kleist, Ewald Georg): Physics. See: Webster's 3d.

Kleist's apraxia (Kleist, Karl). See: Mayer-Gross' apraxia.

KLEMM, PAUL. 1861-1921. Latvian physician. See: Biog. Lex. hervorr. Aerzte, 1880-1930. Klemm's tetanus.

Klemm's tetanus (Klemm, Paul): Medicine. See: Dorland; Jablonski. Also known as: Rose's tetanus.

Klemon test (Derivation undetermined): Chemistry. See: Van Nostrand Chem. Dict.

KLEMPERER, FELIX. 1866-1931. German physician. See: Biog. Lex. hervorr. Aerzte, 1880-1930. Klemperer's tuberculin.

KLEMPERER, GEORG. 1865-1946. German physician. See: Biog. Lex. hervorr. Aerzte, 1880-1930. Klemperer's tuberculin.

Klemperer's tuberculin (Klemperer, Georg and Klemperer, Friedrich): Medicine. See: Dorland; Stedman.

Kleyne, Adrianus de. See: Kleijn, Adrianus Paulus Huibertus Antonie de.

Klieg (Kleig) eyes (or conjunctivitie) (Kliegel, John H.): Medicine. See: Hendrickson; Mathews, M. M.; Stedman; Webster's 3d.

Klieg (Kleig) light (Kliegel, John H.): Engineering and Industry. See: Hendrickson; Mathews, M. M.; Partridge; Webster's 3d.

KLIEGEL, ANTON T. 1872-1927. German-born American lighting equipment manufacturer. See: Webster's Biog. Dict. Klieg eyes (or conjunctivitis), Klieg light.

KLIEGEL, JOHN H. 1869-1959. German-born American lighting equipment. manufacturer. See: Webster's Biog. Dict. Klieg (Kleig) eyes (or conjunctivitis, Klieg (Kleig) light).

KLIMMER, OTTO-RUDOLF. 1911- . German physician. See: Wer Ist Wer?, 1974-1975. Klimmer's vaccine.

Klimmer's vaccine (Klimmer, Otto-Rudolf): Medicine. See: Stedman.

KLIMOV, IVAN ALEKSANDROVICH. b. 1865. Russian physician. Cited in: Mansell. Klimow's test.

Klimow's test (Klimov, Ivan Aleksandrovich): Medicine. See: Dorland.

KLINE, BENJAMIN SCHOENBRUN. b. 1886. American pathologist. See: Amer. Men Sci., 4th ed. Kline-Young test.

Kline reaction (or test) (Kline, Benjamin). See: Kline-Young test.

Kline-Young test (Kline, Benjamin Schoenbrun and Young, Anna M.): Medicine. See: Dorland; Stedman; Webster's 3d. Also known as: Kline reaction (or test).

KLINEFELTER, HARRY FITCH, JR. 1912- . American physician. See: Amer. Men and Women Sci., 12th ed. Klinefelter's syndrome.

Klinefelter-Reifenstein-Albright (Klinefelter, Harry Fitch, Jr.; Reifenstein, Edward C., Jr.; and Albright, Fuller). See: Klinefelter's syndrome.

Klinefelter's syndrome (Klinefelter, Harry): Medicine. See: Dorland; Hinsie; Jablonski; Stedman; Wolman. Also known as: Klinefelter-Reifenstein-Albright syndrome.

KLING, ANDRE. fl. 1905-1931. French chemist. See: Pogg., vols. 5, 6. Kling reagent.

Kling reagent (Kling, Andre): Chemistry. See: Van Nostrand Chem. Dict.

KLINGEMANN, FELIX. b. 1863. German chemist. Cited in: Royal Soc. Cat. Sci. Pap., 1884-1900. Japp-Klingemann reaction.

KLINGENSTEIN, PERCY. 1896- . American physician. See: Direct. Med. Specialists, 1965-1966. Dudley-Klingenstein syndrome.

KLINGER, HEINZ KARL ERNST. 1907- . German physician. (Biography source unavailable.) Klinger's disease.

Klinger's disease (Klinger, Heinz Karl Ernst). See: Wegener's granulomatosis.

KLIONSKY, BERNARD LEON. 1925- . American pathologist. See: Amer. Men and Women Sci., 12th ed. Sweeley-Klionsky disease.

Klippel-Feil syndrome (Klippel, Maurice and Feil, Andre): Medicine. See: Dorland; Hinsie; Jablonski; Stedman.

Klippel-Feldstein syndrome (Klippel, Maurice and Feldstein, Ernest): Medicine. See: Jablonski.

KLIPPEL, MAURICE. 1858-1942. French neurologist. See: Biog. Lex. hervorr. Aerzte, 1880-1930. Klippel-Feil syndrome, Klippel-Feldstein syndrome, Klippel-Trenaunay syndrome, Klippel's disease.

Klippel-Trenaunay syndrome (Klippel, Maurice and Trenaunay, Paul): Medicine. See: Jablonski; Stedman.

Klippel-Trenaunay-Weber syndrome (Klippel, Maurice; Trenaunay, Paul; and Weber, Frederich Parkes). See: Klippel-Trenaunay syndrome.

Klippel's disease (Klippel, Maurice): Medicine. See: Jablonski; Stedman.

KLIPSTEIN, AUGUST VON. 1801-1894. German mineralogist. See: Pogg., vol. 1. Klipsteinite.

Klipsteinite (Klipstein, August von): Earth Sciences. See: Thrush.

KLOCKMANN, FRIEDRICH FERDINAND HERMANN. 1858-1937. German mineralogist. See: Pogg., vol. 5. Klockmannite.

Klockmannite (Klockmann, Friedrich Ferdinand Hermann): Earth Sciences. See: Thrush; Webster's 3d.

Kloepfer's syndrome (Derivation undetermined): Medicine. See: Jablonski.

Klooster, Hendrik Sjoerd van. See: Van Klooster, Hendrik Sjoerd.

KLOPFER, BRUNO. 1900- . German-born American psychologist. See: Amer. Men Sci., 10th ed., Soc. and Behav. Klopfer system.

Klopfer system (Klopfer, Bruno): Psychology. See: Wolman.

KLOPSTOCK, FRIEDRICH GOTTLIEB. 1724-1803. German poet in Denmark. See: Encyc. Brit., 1973. Klopstockianism.

Klopstockianism (Klopstock, Friedrich Gottlieb): Literature. See: Preminger under "Norske Selskab, Det."

KLOSTERMANN, MAX. fl. 1927. German physician. Cited in: Chem. Abstr., vol. 21, p. 1284. Necke-Schmidt-Klostermann reagent for lead.

KLOTZ, HENRI PIERRE. 1910- . French endocrinologist. See: Who's Who France, 1975-1976. Klotz's syndrome.

Klotz's syndrome (Klotz, Henri Pierre): Medicine. See: Jablonski.

Kluever-Bucy syndrome (Kluever, Heinrich and Bucy, Paul): Medicine. See: Chaplin; Hinsie; Jablonski; Wolman. Also known as: Kluever-Bucy-Terzian syndrome.

Kluever-Bucy-Terzian syndrome (Kluver, Heinrich; Bucy, Paul; and Terzian, H.). See: Kluever-Bucy syndrome.

KLUEVER, HEINRICH. 1897- . German-born American neurologist. See: Amer. Men. Sci., 8th ed. Kluever-Bucy syndrome.

KLUG, F. A. No dates. German? scientist. (Biography source unavailable.) Klugia.

KLUGE, KARL ALEXANDER FERDINAND. 1782-1844. German obstetrician. See: Biog. Lex. hervorr. Aerzte. Kluge's sign.

Kluge's sign (Kluge, Karl Alexander Ferdinand). See: Jacquemier's sign.

Klugia (Klug, F. A.): Botany. See: Charnock.

Klumpke. See: Dejerine-Klumpke, Augusta.

Klumpke's palsy (or paralysis) (Dejerine-Klumpke, Augusta). See: Dejerine-Klumpke's syndrome (or paralysis).

Knapp Foundation (Knapp, Joseph Palmer): Philanthropy. See: Harrod.

KNAPP, HERMAN JAKOB. 1832-1911. American ophthalmologist. See: World Who's Who Sci. Knapp's forceps, Kanpp's operation, Knapp's streaks (or striae).

KNAPP, JOSEPH PALMER. 1864-1951. American publisher. See: Who Was Who Amer., 1951-1960. Knapp Foundation.

KNAPP, KARL. fl. 1870. German chemist. Cited in: Kelly. Knapp('s) test (or solution).

Knapp('s) test (or solution) (Knapp, Karl): Chemistry. See: Dorland; Stedman; Van Nostrand Chem. Dict.

Knapper-Craig-Chandlee test (Knapper, J. S.; Craig, Kenneth Alexander; and Chandlee, Grover C.): Chemistry. See: Van Nostrand Chem. Dict.

KNAPPER, J. S. fl. 1933. American chemist. Cited in: Chem. Abstr., vol. 27, p. 5673. Knapper-Craig-Chandlee test.

Knapp's forceps (Knapp, Herman Jakob): Medicine. See: Dorland; Stedman.

Knapp's operation (Knapp, Herman Jakob): Medicine. See: Dorland.

Knapp's streaks (or striae) (Knapp, Herman Jakob): Medicine. See: Dorland; Jablonski; Stedman.

KNAUS, HERMANN HUBERT. b. 1892. Austrian physiologist. See: World Who's Who Sci. Knaus' reaction, Ogino-Knaus rule.

Knaus' reaction (Knaus, Hermann Hubert): Medicine. See: Stedman.

KNAUTH, CHRISTIAN. 1654-1716. German botanist. See: World Who's Who Sci. Knautia.

Knautia (Knauth, Christian): Botany. See: Charnock; Webster's 3d.

KNEBEL, KARL LUDWIG VON. 1744-1834. German poet and translator. See: Encyc. Brit., 1973. Knebelite.

Knebelite (Knebel, Karl Ludwig von): Earth Sciences. See: Charnock; Thrush; Webster's 3d.

KNECHT, EDMUND. 1861-1925. English chemist. See: Pogg., vols. 5, 6. Knecht reagent, Knecht test reaction for copper, Knecht test reagent for titanium.

Knecht reagent (Knecht, Edmund): Chemistry. See: Van Nostrand Chem. Dict.

Knecht test reaction for copper (Knecht, Edmund): Chemistry. See: Van Nostrand Chem. Dict.

Knecht test reagent for titanium (Knecht, Edmund): Chemistry. See: Van Nostrand Chem. Dict.

KNEIFF, F. G. d. 1832. German physician and botanist. (Biography source unavailable.) Kneiffia.

Kneiffia (Kneiff, F. G.): Botany. See: Webster's 3d.

KNEIPP, SEBASTIAN. 1821-1897. German priest. See: Webster's Biog. Dict. Kneippism (or Kneipp's cure).

Kneippism (or Kneipp's cure) (Kneipp, Sebastian): Medicine. See: Dorland; Webster's 3d.

Knickerbocker (1) (Knickerbockic or Knickerbockerdom) (Knickerbocker, Diedrich): Generic Word (New Yorker). See: Matthews, M. M.; Phyfe; Webster's 3d.

Knickerbocker (2) (Knickerbocker, Diedrich): Fashion. See: Webster's 3d.

Knickerbocker club (Knickerbocker, Diedrich): Sociology. See: Harvey.

KNICKERBOCKER, DIEDRICH. Imaginary author of Washington Irving's book, "The History of New York," (1809). See: Harvey. Knickerbocker (1) (Knickerbockic or Knickerbockerdom), Knickerbocker (2), Knickerbocker club, Knickerbocker school, Knickerbockers (Nickerbockers or Knickers).

Knickerbocker school (Knickerbocker, Diedrich): Literature. See: New Encyc. Brit., 1974, Microp.

Knickerbockers (Nickerbockers or Knickers) (Knickerbocker, Diedrich): Fashion. See: Charnock; Webster's 3d.

Kniffin system (Kniffin, William): Agriculture. See: Webster's 3d; Winburne.

KNIFFIN, WILLIAM. fl. 19th c. American horticulturist. (Biography source unavailable.) Kniffin system.

KNIGA, A. G. fl. 1936. Russian chemist. Cited in: Chem. Abstr., vol. 31, p. 7000. Kniga test.

Kniga test (Kniga, A. G.): Chemistry. See: Van Nostrand Chem. Dict.

Knight bucket (Knight, S. N.): Engineering and Industry. See: Auger.

KNIGHT, C. W. No dates. English? engineer. (Biography source unavailable.) Knight sleeve valve (or sleeve valve design).

Knight-Darwin law (Knight, Thomas Andrew and Darwin, Charles): Genetics. See: Gray.

Knight machine (geotropism) (Knight, Thomas Andrew): Biology. Cited in: World Who's Who Sci.

Knight of Pythias (Pythias): Sociology. See: Webster's 3d.

KNIGHT, S. N. fl. 1870. Engineer. (Biography source unavailable.) Knight bucket.

Knight shift (Knight, Walter David, Jr.): Physics. See: Ballentyne; Hughes; Internat. Dict. Phys. Elec.; Thewlis.

Knight sleeve valve (or sleeve valve design) (Knight, C. W.): Engineering and Industry. See: Auger; Van Nostrand Sci. Encyc. under "Otto Engine."

KNIGHT, THOMAS ANDREW. 1759-1838. English plant physiologist. See: Dict. Sci. Biog. Knight-Darwin law, Knight machine (geotropism), Knightia.

KNIGHT, WALTER DAVID, JR. 1919- . American physicist. See: Amer. Men and Women Sci., 12th ed. Knight shift.

Knightia (Knight, Thomas Andrew): Botany. See: Webster's 3d.

Knights Hospitallers of St. John of Jerusalem (John the Baptist, Saint): Religion. See: Attwater; Webster's 3d.

Knights of Columbus (Columbus, Christopher): Religion. See: Jameson; Mathews, S.; Webster's 3d.

Knights of St. John (John the Baptist, Saint): Religion. See: Attwater.

Knights of St. Lazare (Lazarus, Saint): History. See: Harbottle.

Knights of Saint Patrick (Patrick, Saint). See: Order of Saint Patrick.

Knights of the Maccabees (Maccabees): Sociology. See: Webster's 3d.

KNIPHOF, JOHANN HIERONYMUS. 1704-1765. German botanist and physician. See: Biog. Lex. hervorr. Aerzte. Kniphofia.

Kniphofia (Kniphof, Johann): Botany. See: Taylor, N.; Webster's 3d.

KNIPPERDOLLING, BERNHARD. d. 1536. German Anabaptist leader. See: Webster's Biog. Dict. Knipperdollings.

Knipperdollings (Knipperdolling, Bernhard): Religion. See: Brewer; Canney; Harvey.

Knobellite (Derivation undetermined): Earth Sciences. See: Thrush.

KNOEPFELMACHER, WILHELM. b. 1866. Austrian pediatrician. See: Biog. Lex. hervorr. Aerzte, 1880-1930. Knoepfelmacher's butter meal.

Knoepfelmacher's butter meal (Knoepfelmacher, Wilhelm): Medicine. See: Dorland.

KNOEVENAGEL, EMIL. 1865-1921. German chemist. See: Pogg., vols. 4, 5, 6. Knoevenagel reaction (or condensation).

Knoevenagel reaction (or condensation) (Knoevenagel, Emil): Chemistry. See: Ballentyne; Van Nostrand Chem. Dict.; Webster's 3d.

KNOLL, PHILIPP. 1841-1900. Austrian physiologist. See: Biog. Lex. hervorr. Aerzte, 1880-1930. Knoll's glands.

Knoll's glands (Knoll, Philipp): Anatomy. See Stedman.

KNOOP, FRANZ. 1875-1946. German physiologist. See: Pogg., vols. 6, 7a. Knoop's theory (or beta-oxidation theory).

KNOOP, FREDERICK. fl. 1939. American metallurgist. Cited in: Chem. Abstr., Decennial Index, 1937-1946. Knoop hardness test (tester, number or hardness).

Knoop hardness test (tester, number or hardness) (Knoop, Frederick): Engineering and Industry. See: Auger; Encyc. Brit., 1973 under "Hardness Testing," vol. 11, p. 94b; Stedman; Webster's 3d.

Knoop's theory (or beta-oxidation theory) (Knoop, Franz): Chemistry. See: Ballentyne; Stedman.

KNOP, ADOLF. d. 1893. German mineralogist. See: Chem. Ztg., vol. 17 (1893) pp. 1932-1933. Knopite.

KNOP, JOHANN AUGUST LUDWIG WILHELM. 1817-1891. See: Pogg., vols. 1, 3, 4. Knop's solution.

Knop test reaction for silicic acid (Derivation undetermined): Chemistry. See: Van Nostrand Chem. Dict.

KNOPF, SIGARD ADOLPHUS. 1857-1940. German-born American physician. See: World Who's Who Sci. Knopf's treatment (or method).

Knopf's treatment (or method) (Knopf, Sigard Adolphus): Medicine. See: Dorland.

Knopite (Knop, Adolf): Earth Sciences. See: Webster's 3d.

Knop's solution (Knop, Johann August Ludwig Wilhelm): Chemistry. See: Hackh; Webster's 3d.

Knorr air brake (Knorr, Georg): Engineering and Industry. Cited in: Webster's Biog. Dict.

Knorr alkalimeter (Knorr, Ludwig?): Chemistry. See: Hackh.

KNORR, EDUARD. fl. 1900-1901. German chemist. Cited in: Royal Soc. Cat. Sci. Pap., 1884-1900. Koenigs-Knorr synthesis.

Knorr flask (Knorr, Ludwig): Chemistry. See: Van Nostrand Chem. Dict.

KNORR, GEORG. 1859-1911. German engineer. See: Biog. Jahrb. Deut. Nekr., 1911. Knorr air brake.

KNORR, GEORG WOLFGANG. 1705-1761. German collector of petrified objects. See: Dict. Sci. Biog. Knorria.

KNORR, LUDWIG. 1859-1921. German chemist. See: World Who's Who Sci. Knorr alkalimeter?, Knorr flask, Knorr Pyrazole synthesis, Knorr quinoline synthesis, Knorr reagent for alkaloids, Knorr test reaction for pyrazoline bases, Paal-Knorr pyrrole synthesis, Paal-Knorr synthesis of thiophenes.

Knorr pyrazole synthesis (Knorr, Ludwig): Chemistry. See: Van Nostrand Chem. Dict.

Knorr pyrrole synthesis (Knorr, Ludwig). See: Paal-Knorr pyrrole synthesis.

Knorr quinoline synthesis (Knorr, Ludwig): Chemistry. See: Van Nostrand Chem. Dict.

Knorr reagent for alkaloids (Knorr, Ludwig): Chemistry. See: Van Nostrand Chem. Dict.

Knorr test reaction for pyrazoline bases (Knorr, Ludwig): Chemistry. See: Van Nostrand Chem. Dict.

KNORRE, GEORG VON. b. 1859. German chemist. Cited in: Pogg., vols. 2, 3, 4. Ilinski-Knorre reagent for cobalt and nickel.

Knorria (Knorr, Georg Wolfgang): Botany. See: Webster's 3d.

KNOTT, CARGILL GILSTON. 1856-1922. Scottish seismologist and applied mathematician. See: Dict. Sci. Biog. Knott's equations?

Knott engine (Knott, J. H.): Engineering and Industry. See: Auger.

KNOTT, J. H. fl. 1863. English engineer. (Biography source unavailable.) Knott engine.

Knott's equations (Knott, Cargill Gilston?): Physics. See: Hughes.

KNOWLES, HOWARD BRABOOK. b. 1888. American chemist. See: Amer. Men. Sci., 8th ed. Knowles reagent.

KNOWLES, LUCIUS JAMES. 1819-1884. American inventor. See: Dict. Amer. Biog. Knowles safety steam-boiler feed regulator.

Knowles reagent (Knowles, Howard Brabook): Chemistry. See: Van Nostrand Chem. Dict.

Knowles safety steam-boiler feed regulator (Knowles, Lucius James): Engineering and Industry. Cited in: World Who's Who Sci.

Knox and Osborne furnace (Derivation undetermined): Engineering and Industry. See: Thrush.

Knox-Castrillo Convention (Knox, Philander Chase and Castrillo): Politics. See: Morris.

Knox cube test (Knox, Howard Andrew): Psychology. See: Drever; English; Hinsie; Wolman.

KNOX, HOWARD ANDREW. b. 1885. American psychiatrist. Cited in: Mansell. Knox cube test.

KNOX, JOHN. 1505-1573. Scottish religious reformer. See: Dict. Nat. Biog. John Knox cap, Knox's liturgy.

KNOX, PHILANDER CHASE. 1853-1921. American politician. See: Dict. Amer. Biog. Knox-Castrillo Convention.

KNOX, ROBERT. ca. 1640-1720. Scottish traveler and writer. See: Dict. Amer. Biog. Knoxia.

KNOX, RONALD ARBUTHNOTT. 1888-1957. English Roman Catholic prelate and writer. See: Encyc. Brit., 1973. Knox('s) version.

Knox('s) version (Knox, Ronald Arbuthnott): Religion. See: Attwater; Brewer.

Knoxia (Knox, Robert): Botany. See: Charnock.

Knox's liturgy (Knox, John): Religion. See: Encyc. Brit., 1973 under "Knox, John," vol. 13, p. 435 b.

Knudsen absolute manometer (gauge or pressure gauge) (Knudsen, Martin Hans Christian): Physics. See: Encyc. Brit., 1973 under "Vacuum," vol. 22, p. 840b; Internat. Dict. Phys. Elec.; Thewlis; Van Nostrand Sci. Encyc.

Knudsen cosine law (or rule) (Knudsen, Martin Hans Christian): Physics. See: Ballentyne; Internat. Dict. Phys. Elec.; Thewlis.

Knudsen flow (or diffusion) (Knudsen, Martin Hans Christian): Physics. See: Ballentyne; Encyc. Brit., 1973 under "Diffusion," vol. 7, p. 423a; Thewlis, Van Nostrand Sci. Encyc.

Knudsen formula for gas flow (Knudsen, Martin Hans Christian): Physics. See: Ballentyne; Internat. Dict. Phys. Elec.

Knudsen gas (Knudsen, Martin Hans Christian): Physics. See: Internat. Dict. Ap. Math.

KNUDSEN, MARTIN HANS CHRISTIAN. 1871-1949. Danish physicist and hydrographer. See: Dict. Sci. Biog. Knudsen absolute manometer (gauge or pressure gauge), Knudsen cosine law (or rule), Knudsen flow (or diffusion), Knudsen formula for gas flow, Knudsen gas, Knudson leaf gauge, Knudsen method for vapor pressure of metals, Knudsen number, Knudsen's tables.

Knudsen method for vapor pressure of metals (Knudsen, Martin Hans Christian): Physics. See: Internat. Dict. Phys. Elec.

Knudsen number (Knudsen, Martin Hans Christian): Physics. See: Encyc. Brit., 1973 under "Vacuum," vol. 22, p. 838a; Internat. Dict. Phys. Elec.; Thewlis.

Knudsen's tables (Knudsen, Martin Hans Christian): Earth Sciences. See: Huschke; Thrush; Van Nostrand Sci. Encyc.

Knudson leaf gauge (Knudsen, Martin Hans Christian): Physics. See: Internat. Dict. Phys. Elec.

Knut-Vik square (Vik, Knut?): Statistics. See: Kendall.

Kobellite (Von Kobell, Franz): Earth Science. See: Charnock; Webster's 3d.

KOBELT, GEORGE LUDWIG. 1804-1857. German physician. See: Biog. Lex. hervorr. Aerzte. Kobelt's cyst, Kobelt's network, Kobelt's tubes.

Kobelt's cyst (Kobelt, George Ludwig): Anatomy. See: Stedman. Also known as: Morgagnian cyst.

Kobelt's network (Kobelt, George Ludwig): Anatomy. See: Stedman.

Kobelt's tubes (Kobelt, George Ludwig): Anatomy. See: Dorland; Stedman.

KOBER, PHILIP ADOLPH. b. 1884. American chemist. See: Amer. Men Sci., 9th ed. Kober test?

KOBER, SALOMON. fl. 1935. German physician. Cited in: Chem. Abstr., Decenn. Index, 1927-1936. Kober test.

Kober test (Kober, Philip Adolph?): Chemistry. See: Van Nostrand Chem. Dict.

Kober test (Kober, Salomon): Medicine. See: Stedman.

KOBERT, RUDOLF (In full: EDUARD RUDOLF). 1854-1918. German physiological chemist. See: Pogg., vols. 4, 5. Kobert test reaction for allyl compounds? Kobert's test.

Kobert test reaction for allyl compounds (Kobert, Rudolf?): Chemistry. See: Van Nostrand Chem. Dict.

Kobert's test (Kobert, Rudolf): Medicine. See: Dorland; Stedman.

Koble flask (Derivation undetermined): Chemistry. See: Van Nostrand Chem. Dict.

KOBOLD. German folklore earth spirit. See: Jobes. Cobalt?

Kobuladze reagent (Derivation undetermined): Chemistry. See: Van Nostrand Chem. Dict.

KOBY, FREDERIC EDOUARD. fl. 1923. French ophthalmologist. See: Index-Cat. Libr. Surg.-Gen. Off., 4th ser., vol. 9, 1945. Koby's cataract.

Koby's cataract (Koby, Frederic Edouard): Medicine. See: Jablonski.

Koch('s) bacillus (1) (mycobacterium tuberculosis) (Koch, Robert): Medicine. See: Dorland; Hackh; Stedman; Webster's 3d.

Koch-Ehrlich stain (Koch, Robert and Ehrlich, Paul): Medicine. See: Stedman; Van Nostrand Chem. Dict.

Koch equation (Derivation undetermined): Physics. See: Internat. Dict. Ap. Math.

Koch flask (Koch, Robert): Medicine. See: Hackh.

Koch freezing process (Derivation undetermined): Engineering and Industry. See: Thrush.

KOCH, G. fl. 1870. German chemist. (Biography source unavailable.) Weber-Koch test?

KOCH, J. A. fl. 1897. German chemist. (Biography source unavailable.) Gattermann-Koch reaction.

Koch('s) phenomenon (Koch, Robert): Medicine. See: Dorland; Stedman; Webster's 3d.

Koch resistance (Derivation undetermined): Physics. See: Hughes.

KOCH, ROBERT (In full: HEINRICH HERMANN ROBERT). 1843-1910. German pioneer bacteriologist. See: Dict. Sci. Biog. Koch('s) bacillus (1) (mycobacterium tuberculosis), Koch-Ehrlich stain, Koch flask, Koch('s) phenomenon, Koch solution, Koch-Weeks bacillus, Koch-Weeks conjunctivitis, Koch's blue bodies?, Koch's law (or postulates), Koch's lymph, Koch's new tuberculin, Koch's old tuberculin, Koch's vibrio (or bacillus (2)).

Koch solution (Koch, Robert): Medicine. See: Van Nostrand Chem. Dict.

KOCH, WALTER. b. 1880. German surgeon. See: Biog. Lex. hervorr. Aerzte, 1880-1930. Koch's node.

Koch-Weeks conjunctivitis (Koch, Robert and Weeks, John Elmer): Medicine. See: Stedman.

KOCH, WILHELM DANIEL JOSEF. 1771-1849. German botanist. See: Nouv. Biog. Univ. Kochia.

Kocher-Debre-Semelaigne syndrome (Kocher, Theodor; Debre, Robert; and Semelaigne, Georges). See: Debre-Semelaigne syndrome.

KOCHER, THEODOR (In full: EMIL THEODOR). 1841-1917. Swiss surgeon. See: World Who's Who Sci. Kocher-Debre-Semelaigne syndrome, Kocher's forceps, Kocher's incision, Kocher's operation, Kocher's sign.

Kocher's forceps (Kocher, Theodor): Medicine. See: Dorland; Stedman.

Kocher's incision (Kocher, Theodor): Medicine. See: Stedman.

Kocher's operation (Kocher, Theodor): Medicine. See: Dorland; Stedman.

Kocher's sign (Kocher, Theodor): Medicine. See: Stedman.

Kochia (Koch, Wilhelm Daniel Josef): Botany. See: Taylor, N.; Webster's 3d.

Koch's acid (Derivation undetermined): Chemistry. See: Hackh.

Koch's bacillus (2) (Koch, Robert). See: Koch's vibrio.

Koch's blue bodies (Koch, Robert?): Medicine. See: Stedman.

Koch's law (or postulates) (Koch, Robert): Medicine. See: Dorland; Stedman; Webster's 3d.

Koch's lymph (Koch, Robert): Medicine. See: Dorland; Stedman.

Koch's new tuberculin (Koch, Robert): Medicine. See: Stedman.

Koch's node (Koch, Walter): Anatomy. See: Dorland; Stedman. Also known as: Keith and Flack node.

Koch's old tuberculin (Koch, Robert): Medicine. See: Dorland; Stedman.

Koch's vibrio (or bacillus (2)) (Koch, Robert): Medicine. See: Stedman; Van Nostrand Sci. Encyc.

KOCHUBEY, P. A. VON. fl. 19th c. Russian count. (Biography source unavailable.) Kotschubeite.

KOCKS, JOSEPH. 1846-1916. German surgeon. See: Biog. Lex. hervorr. Aerzte, 1880-1930. Kocks' operation.

Kocks' operation (Kocks, Joseph): Medicine. See: Dorland; Stedman.

KOEBERLE, EUGENE. 1828-1915. French surgeon. See: World Who's Who Sci. Koeberlé's forceps.

Koeberle's forceps (Koeberle, Eugene): Medicine. See: Dorland; Stedman.

KOEBERLIN, C. L. fl. 19th c. German clergyman and amateur botanist. (Biography source unavailable.) Koeberlinia.

Koeberlinia (Koeberlin, C. L.): Botany. See: Webster's 3d.

KOEBNER, HEINRICH. 1838-1904. German dermatologist. See: Biog. Lex. hervorr. Aerzte. Koebner's disease, Koebner's response (or phenomenon).

Koebner's disease (Koebner, Heinrich): Medicine. See: Dorland; Jablonski. Also known as: Fox's disease.

Koebner's response (or phenomenon) (Koebner, Heinrich): Medicine. See: Jablonski; Stedman.

KOECHLIN, RUDOLF. 1862-1939. Austrian mineralogist. See: Oesterr. Biog. Lex., 1815-1950. Koechlinite.

Koechlinite (Koechlin, Rudolf): Earth Sciences. See: Thrush; Webster's 3d.

KOEHLER, ALBAN. 1874-1947. German roentgenologist. See: Biog. Lex. hervorr. Aerzte, 1880-1930. Koehler-Stieda-Pellegrini syndrome, Koehler's first disease (or disease), Koehler's second disease.

KOEHLER, AUGUST KARL JOHANN VALENTIN. 1866-1948. German microscopist. See: Dict. Sci. Biog. Koehler('s) illumination.

Koehler furnace (Derivation undetermined): Engineering and Industry. See: Thrush.

Koehler('s) illumination (Koehler, August Karl Johann Valentin): Physics. See: Focal Encyc. Film; Focal Encyc. Photog; Stedman.

Koehler lamp (Derivation undetermined): Engineering and Industry. See: Thrush.

Koehler-Mouchet disease (Koehler, Alban and Mouchet, Albert). See: Koehler's first disease (or disease).

Koehler-Restorff phenomenon (Koehler, Wolfgang and Restorff, Hedwig von): Psychology. See: English; Wolman.

Koehler-Stieda-Pellegrini syndrome (Koehler, Alban; Stieda, Alfred; and Pellegrini, Augusto). See: Stieda-Pellegrini syndrome.

KOEHLER, WOLFGANG. 1887-1967. German-born American psychologist. See: Internat. Encyc. Soc. Sci. Koehler-Restorff phenomenon.

Koehler's first disease (or disease) (Koehler, Alban): Medicine. See: Dorland; Jablonski; Stedman. Also known as: Koehler-Mouchet disease, Panner's disease.

Koehler's second disease (Koehler, Alban): Medicine. See: Jablonski. Also known as: Freiberg's infraction.

Koehlmeier-Degos syndrome (Koehlmeier, W. and Degos, Robert). See: Degos-Delort-Tricot syndrome.

KOEHLMEIER, W. fl. 1940-1941. German dermatologist. (Biography source unavailable.) Koehlmeier-Degos syndrome.

KOEHN, MANFRED. b. 1894. German soil chemist. See: Pogg., vol. 7a. Koehn pipette.

Koehn pipette (Koehn, Manfred): Engineering and Industry. See: Thrush.

KOELLE, JOHANN LUDWIG CHRISTIAN. 1763-1797. German physician and botanist. See: Biog. Lex. hervorr. Aerzte. Koellia.

Koellia (Koelle, Johann Ludwig Christian): Botany. See: Webster's 3d.

Koelliker, Rudolf Albert von. See: Von Koelliker, Rudolf Albert.

Koelliker's canal (Von Koelliker, Rudolf Albert): Zoology. See: Henderson.

Koelliker's cells (Von Koelliker, Rudolf Albert): Anatomy. See: Donath; Dorland.

Koelliker's dental crest (Von Koelliker, Rudolf Albert): Anatomy. See: Stedman.

Koelliker's gland (Von Koelliker, Rudolf Albert): Anatomy. See: Dorland; Stedman. Also known as: Bowman's gland.

Koelliker's layer (Von Koelliker, Rudolf Albert): Anatomy. See: Donath; Dorland; Stedman.

Koelliker's nucleus (Von Koelliker, Rudolf Albert): Anatomy. See: Dorland.

Koelliker's pit (Von Koelliker, Rudolf Albert): Zoology. See: Henderson.

Koelliker's reticulum (Von Koelliker, Rudolf Albert): Anatomy. See: Stedman.

KOELPIN, ALEXANDER BERNHARD. 1739-1801. German physician and botanist. See: Biog. Lex. hervorr. Aerzte. Koelpinia.

Koelpinia (Koelpin, Alexander Bernhard): Botany. See: Charnock.

KOELREUTER, JOSEF GOTTLIEB. 1733-1806. German botanist. See: Dict. Sci. Biog. Koelreuteria.

Koelreuteria (Koelreuter, Josef Gottlieb): Botany. See: Charnock; Taylor, N.; Webster's 3d.

Koenecke's reaction (or test) (Derivation undetermined): Medicine. See: Dorland.

KOENEN, ADOLF VON. 1837-1915. German geologist. See: Pogg., vols. 3, 4. Koenenite.

Koenenite (Koenen, Adolf von): Earth Sciences. See: Thrush; Webster's 3d.

KOENIG, ARTHUR. 1856-1901. German physicist. See: Pogg., vol. 4. Koenig-Martens spectrophotometer.

KOENIG, CHARLES DIETRICH EBERHARD. 1774-1851. German-born botanist in England. See: Boase. Koeniga.

KOENIG, CHARLES JOSEPH. b. 1868. French otologist. Cited in: Mansell. Koenig's rods.

Koenig cylinders (Koenig, Karl Rudolph): Physics. See: Chaplin; Drever; English; Wolman.

KOENIG, FRANZ. 1832-1910. German surgeon. See: Biog. Lex. hervorr. Aerzte. Koenig's disease, Koenig's operation, Koenig's syndrome.

KOENIG, FRIEDRICH. 1775-1833. German printer. See: Allg. Deut. Biog. Koenig machine.

KOENIG, JOHANN GERHARD. 1729-1785. German botanist and physician. See: Biog. Lex. hervorr. Aerzte. Koenigia.

KOENIG, KARL RUDOLPH (OR RODOLPHE). 1832-1901. German-born physicist in Paris. See: Dict. Sci. Biog. Koenig cylinders.

Koenig machine (Koenig, Friedrich): Printing. See: Lockwood.

Koenig-Martens spectrophotometer (Koenig, Arthur and Martens, Adolf): Physics. See: Internat. Dict. Phys. Elec.

Koenig reagent (Derivation undetermined): Chemistry. See: Van Nostrand Chem. Dict.

Koeniga (Koenig, Charles Dietrich Eberhard): Botany. See: Charnock.

Koenigia (Koenig, Johann Gerhard): Botany. See: Charnock.

Koenig's disease (Koenig, Franz): Medicine. See: Jablonski. Also known as: Paget's quiet necrosis of bone.

Koenigs-Knorr synthesis (Koenigs, Wilhelm and Knorr, Eduard): Chemistry. See: Van Nostrand Chem. Dict.

Koenig's operation (Koenig, Franz): Medicine. See: Dorland; Stedman.

Koenig's rods (Koenig, Charles Joseph): Medicine. See: Dorland.

Koenig's syndrome (Koenig, Franz): Medicine. See: Jablonski; Stedman.

KOENIGS, WILHELM. 1851-1906. German chemist. See: Pogg., vols. 4, 5. Koenigs-Knorr synthesis.

KOENLEIN. No dates. German? superintendent. Cited in: Bailey. Konlite (Konleinite or Koenlinite).

Koenleinite (Koenlein). See: Konlite.

Koepe hoist (Derivation undetermined): Engineering and Industry. See: Thrush.

Koepe sheave (Derivation undetermined): Engineering and Industry. See: Thrush.

Koepe system (Derivation undetermined): Engineering and Industry. See: Thrush.

Koepe winder (Derivation undetermined): Engineering and Industry. See: Thrush.

KOEPPE, LEONHARD. b. 1884. German physician. See: Biog. Lex. hervorr. Aerzte, 1880-1930. Koeppe's disease (1), Koeppe's disease (2), Koeppe's nodules.

Koeppen climatic classification (Koeppen, Wladimir Peter): Earth Sciences. See: Monkhouse; New Encyc. Brit., 1974, Microp.; Van Nostrand Sci. Encyc. under "Climatic Classification."

Koeppen-Supan line (Koeppen, Wladimir Peter and Supan, Alexander Georg): Earth Sciences. See: Huschke.

KOEPPEN, WLADIMIR PETER. 1846-1940. German meteorologist. See: World Who's Who Sci. Koeppen climatic classification, Koeppen-Supan line.

Koeppe's disease (1) (Koeppe, Leonhard): Medicine. See: Jablonski.

Koeppe's disease (2) (Koeppe, Leonhard): Medicine. See: Jablonski.

Koeppe's nodules (Koeppe, Leonhard): Medicine. See: Jablonski.

KOERBER, HERMANN. b. 1878. German ophthalmologist. Cited in: Mansell. Koerber-Salus-Elschnig syndrome.

Koerber-Salus-Elschnig syndrome (Koerber, Hermann; Salus, Robert; and Elschnig, Anton): Medicine. See: Jablonski.

Koerner-Contardi reaction (Koerner, Guglielmo and Contardi, Angelo): Chemistry. See: Van Nostrand Chem. Dict.

KOERNER, GUGLIELMO (WILHELM). 1839-1925. Italian chemist. See: Pogg., vols. 5, 6. Koerner-Contardi reaction.

KOERNER, WILHELM. 1839-1925. German chemist. See: World Who's Who Sci. Korner('s) method (or absolute method).

Koerte-Ballance operation (Koerte, Werner and Ballance, Sir Charles Alfred): Medicine. See: Stedman.

KOERTE, WERNER. 1853-1937. German surgeon. See: Biog. Lex. hervorr. Aerzte, 1880-1930. Koerte-Ballance operation.

KOERTING, ERNST. 1842-1915. German engineer. Cited in: Mansell. Korting engine.

Koessler-Hanke estimation of imidazoles (Koessler, Karl Konrad and Hanke, Milton Theodore): Chemistry. See: Van Nostrand Chem. Dict.

KOESSLER, KARL KONRAD. b. 1880. Austrian-born American chemist. See: Amer. Men Sci., 4th ed. Koessler-Hanke estimation of imidazoles.

Koester effect (Koester, Werner Otto): Chemistry. See: Ballentyne.

KOESTER, HUGO. b. 1858. Swedish physician. See: Biog. Lex. hervorr. Aerzte, 1880-1930. Koester's reagent.

KOESTER, KARL. 1843-1904. German pathologist. See: Biog. Lex. hervorr. Aerzte, 1880-1930. Koester's nodule.

KOESTER, WERNER OTTO. 1896- . German metallurgist. See: Pogg., vols. 6, 7a. Koester effect.

Koester's nodule (Koester, Karl): Medicine. See: Dorland.

Koester's reagent (Koester, Hugo): Medicine. See: Biog. Lex. hervorr. Aerzte, 1880-1930.

KOETTIG, OTTO. fl. 1849-1854. German chemist. Cited in: Royal Soc. Cat. Sci. Pap., 1800-1863. Koettigite.

Koettigite (Koettig, Otto): Earth Sciences. See: Thrush; Webster's 3d.

Koettstorfer number (Derivation undetermined): Chemistry. See: Stedman.

KOFFERATH, WALTER. fl. 1921. German physician. (Biography source unavailable.) Kofferath's syndrome.

Kofferath's syndrome (Kofferath, Walter): Medicine. See: Jablonski.

KOFLER, LUDWIG. 1891-1951. German pharmacologist. See: Pogg., vols. 6, 7a. Kofler's quinone?

Kofler's quinone (Kofler, Ludwig?): Chemistry. See: Stedman.

KOFOID, CHARLES ATWOOD. 1865-1947. American zoologist. See: World Who's Who Sci. Kofoid horizontal net, Kofoid self-closing bucket, Kofoidia.

Kofoid horizontal net (Kofoid, Charles Atwood): Zoology. Cited in: New Encyc. Brit., 1974, Microp.

Kofoid self-closing bucket (Kofoid, Charles Atwood): Zoology. Cited in: New Encyc. Brit., 1974, Microp.

Kofoida (Kofoid, Charles Atwood): Zoology. See: Pennak.

KOGAKUBACHI, MASASHIKA SHIMONOSE. d. 1911. Japanese inventor. (Biography source unavailable.) Shimose (or Shimose powder).

KOGOJ, FRANJO. b. 1894. Yugoslavian dermatologist. See: Biog. Lex. hervorr. Aerzte, 1880-1930. spongiform pustule of Kogoj.

KOHAUT, FRANCIS. No dates. Botanist? (Biography source unavailable.) Kohautia.

Kohautia (Kohaut, Francis): Botany. See: Charnock.

KOHLER, MICHAEL. fl. 19th c. Swiss naturalist. (Biography source unavailable.) Kohleria.

Kohleria (Kohler, Michael): Botany. See: Webster's 3d.

Kohlrausch bridge (Kohlrausch, Friedrich Wilhelm Georg): Physics. See: Hackh.

Kohlrausch flask (or volumetric flask) (Kohlrausch, Rudolf Hermann Arndt): Chemistry. See: Van Nostrand Chem. Dict.; Webster's 3d.

KOHLRAUSCH, FRIEDRICH WILHELM GEORG. 1840-1910. German physicist. See: Dict. Sci. Biog. Kohlrausch bridge, Kohlrausch law (1) (law of electrolytic conduction or law of independent migration of ions), Kohlrausch law (2) (square root law or law of electrolytic conduction).

Kohlrausch law (1) (law of electrolytic conduction or law of independent migration of ions) (Kohlrausch, Friedrich Wilhelm Georg): Chemistry. See: Ballentyne; Hackh; Thewlis; Van Nostrand Sci. Encyc.; Webster's 3d.

Kohlrausch law (2) (square root law or law of electrolytic conduction) (Kohlrausch, Friedrich Wilhelm Georg): Chemistry. See: Ballentyne; Thewlis.

KOHLRAUSCH, OTTO LUDWIG BERNHARD. 1811-1854. German physician. See: Biog. Lex. hervorr. Aerzte. Kohlrausch's folds (or valves), Kohlrausch's muscle.

KOHLRAUSCH, RUDOLF HERMANN ARNDT. 1809-1858. German physicist. See: Dict. Sci. Biog. Kohlrausch flask (or volumetric flask).

Kohlrausch's folds (or valves) (Kohlrausch, Otto Ludwig Bernhard): Anatomy. See: Donath; Dorland; Stedman. Also known as: Houston's valves.

Kohlrausch's muscle (Kohlrausch, Otto Ludwig Bernhard): Anatomy. See: Stedman.

KOHLSCHUETTER, ARNOLD. b. 1883. German astronomer. See: World Who's Who Sci. Schwarzschild-Kohlschuetter formulas.

KOHN, CHARLES ALEXANDER. fl. 1886-1900. English chemist. Cited in: Royal Soc. Cat. Sci. Pap., 1884-1900. Kohn test for glycerin.

KOHN, HANS N. b. 1866. German pathologist. See: Biog. Lex. hervorr. Aerzte, 1880-1930. Kohn's pore.

Kohn, Moriz. See: Kaposi, Moritz.

Kohn test for glycerin (Kohn, Charles Alexander): Chemistry. See: Van Nostrand Chem. Dict.

Kohn's pore (Kohn, Hans N.): Anatomy. See: Dorland; Stedman.

KOHNSTAMM, OSKAR. 1871-1917. German physician. See: Deut. Biog. Jahrb., 1917-1920. Kohnstamm('s) phenomenon (and test).

Kohnstamm('s) phenomenon (and test) (Kohnstamm, Oskar): Physiology. See: Dorland; Hinsie; Stedman.

Kohs block design test (block designs or blocks) (Kohs, Samuel Calmin): Psychology. See: Chaplin; English; Webster's 3d; Wolman.

KOHS, SAMUEL CALMIN. b. 1890. American psychologist. See: Amer. Men Sci., 9th ed., Soc. and Behav. Kohs block design test (block designs or blocks).

Kojewnikoff, Alexis J. See: Kozhevnikov, Alekseiyakovlevich.

KOK III, ADAM. 1811-1875. Griqua chieftain in South Africa. See: New Encyc. Brit., 1974, Microp. Treaty with Adam Kok.

KOKTA, JAROSLAV. fl. 1948. Czechoslovak mineralogist. Cited in: Hintze, 2d suppl., p. 198. Koktaite.

Koktaite (Kokta, Jaroslav): Earth Sciences. See: Webster's 3d.

Kolb machine (Derivation undetermined): Physics. See: Van Nostrand Sci. Encyc.

KOLBE, HERMANN (In full: ADOLF WILHELM HERMANN). 1818-1884. German chemist. See: Dict. Sci. Biog. Kolbe reaction (or electrolysis reaction), Kolbe-Schmitt reaction (or synthesis), Kolbe synthesis.

Kolbe reaction (or electrolysis reaction) (Kolbe, Hermann): Chemistry. See: Ballentyne; Van Nostrand Chem. Dict.

Kolbe-Schmitt reaction (or synthesis) (Kolbe, Hermann and Schmitt, Rudolf): Chemistry. See: Van Nostrand Chem. Dict.; Webster's 3d.

Kolbe synthesis (Kolbe, Hermann): Chemistry. See: Ballentyne; Webster's 3d.

KOLBECK, FRIEDRICH. d. 1943. German mineralogist. Cited in: Hintze, 1st suppl., p. 198. Kolbeckite.

Kolbeckite (Kolbeck, Friedrich): Earth Sciences. See: Thrush; Webster's 3d.

KOLISCH, RUDOLF. 1867-1922. Austrian physician. See: Biog. Lex. hervorr. Aerzte, 1880-1930. Kolisch solution.

Kolisch solution (Kolisch, Rudolf): Chemistry. See: Van Nostrand Chem. Dict.

Kolk, Jacob Ludwig Conrad Schroeder. See: Van der Kolk, Jacob Ludwig Conrad Schroeder.

KOLKWITZ, RICHARD. b. 1873. German biologist. See: Handb. der Deut. Wissensch. Kolkwitzia.

Kolkwitzia (Kolkwitz, Richard): Botany. See: Taylor, N.; Webster's 3d.

KOLLE, WILHELM. 1868-1935. German bacteriologist. See: World Who's Who Sci. Kolle's serum.

Kolle's serum (Kolle, Wilhelm): Medicine. See: Stedman.

Kolliker, Rudolf Albert von. See: Von Koelliker, Rudolf Albert.

KOLLMANN, ARTHUR. b. 1858. German urologist. See: Biog. Lex. hervorr. Aerzte, 1880-1930. Kollmann's dilator.

Kollmann's dilator (Kollmann, Arthur): Medicine. See: Dorland.

KOLMER, E. fl. 1931. German? chemist. Cited in: Chem. Abstr., vol. 25, p. 1758. Pavelka-Kolmer test for cadmium.

KOLMER, JOHN ALBERT. 1886-1962. American pathologist. See: Who Was Who Amer., 1961-1968. Kolmer's test (or reaction).

Kolmer's test (or reaction) (Kolmer, John Albert): Medicine. See: Dorland; Stedman; Webster's 3d.

Kolmogoroff('s) similarity hypotheses (Kolmogorov, Andrey Nikolaevich): Physics. See: Huschke; Internat. Dict. Ap. Math.

KOLMOGOROV, ANDREY NIKOLAEVICH. 1903- . Russian mathematician. See: World Who's Who Sci. Chapman-Kolmogorov equations, Kolmogoroff('s) similarity hypotheses, Kolmogorov axioms, Kolmogorov-Smirnov test (or method), Kolmogorov space, Kolmogorov's equations, Kolmogorov's inequality, Kolmogorov's theorem.

Kolmogorov axioms (Kolmogorov, Andrey Nikolaevich): Statistics. See: Kendall.

Kolmogorov-Smirnov test (or method) (Kolmogorov, Andrey Nikolaevich and Smirnov, Nikolai Vasilevich): Statistics. See: Good; Hoult; Kendall.

Kolmogorov space (Kolmogorov, Andrey Nikolaevich): Mathematics. See: James.

Kolmogorov's equations (Kolmogorov, Andrey Nikolaevich): Statistics. See: Kendall.

Kolmogorov's inequality (Kolmogorov, Andrey Nikolaevich): Statistics. See: Kendall.

Kolmogorov's theorem (Kolmogorov, Andrey Nikolaevich): Statistics. See: Kendall.

Kolovratite (Tschirwinsky, Kolovrat): Earth Sciences. See: Thrush.

Kolthoff buffer solution (Kolthoff, Isaac Maurits): Chemistry. See: Thrush.

Kolthoff-Hamer reagent for zinc in the presence of cadmium (Kolthoff, Isaac Maurits and Hamer, H.): Chemistry. See: Van Nostrand Chem. Dict.

Kolthoff-Hamer reagents for heavy metals (Kolthoff, Isaac Maurits and Hamer, H.): Chemistry. See: Van Nostrand Chem. Dict.

KOLTHOFF, ISAAC MAURITS. b. 1894. Dutch-born American chemist. See: Pogg., vols. 5, 6, 7b. Kolthoff buffer solution, Kolthoff-Hamer reagent for zinc in the presence of cadmium, Kolthoff-Hamer reagents for heavy metals, Kolthoff-Naponen test for nitrate, Kolthoff reactions for beryllium, Kolthoff reagent and reaction for magnesium, Kolthoff reagent for barium, strontium, and lead, Kolthoff reagent for free chlorine in water, Kolthoff reagent for metals, Kolthoff reagents for sodium, Kolthoff-Stansby reagent for fluorine, Kolthoff test for aluminum, Kolthoff test for copper in water, Kolthoff test for cyanide.

Kolthoff-Naponen test for nitrate (Kolthoff, Isaac Maurits and Noponen, George Edward): Chemistry. See: Van Nostrand Chem. Dict.

Kolthoff reactions for beryllium (Kolthoff, Isaac Maurits): Chemistry. See: Van Nostrand Chem. Dict.

Kolthoff reagent and reaction for magnesium (Kolthoff, Isaac Maurits): Chemistry. See: Van Nostrand Chem. Dict.

Kolthoff reagent for barium, strontium, and lead (Kolthoff, Isaac Maurits): Chemistry. See: Van Nostrand Chem. Dict.

Kolthoff reagent for free chlorine in water (Kolthoff, Isaac Maurits): Chemistry. See: Van Nostrand Chem. Dict.

Kolthoff reagent for metals (Kolthoff, Isaac Maurits): Chemistry. See: Van Nostrand Chem. Dict.

Kolthoff reagents for sodium (Kolthoff, Isaac Maurits): Chemistry. See: Van Nostrand Chem. Dict.

Kolthoff-Stansby reagent for fluorine (Kolthoff, Isaac Maurits and Stansby, Maurice Earl): Chemistry. See: Van Nostrand Chem. Dict.

Kolthoff test for aluminum (Kolthoff, Isaac Maurits): Chemistry. See: Van Nostrand Chem. Dict.

Kolthoff test for copper in water (Kolthoff, Isaac Maurits): Chemistry. See: Van Nostrand Chem. Dict.

Kolthoff test for cyanide (Kolthoff, Isaac Maurits): Chemistry. See: Van Nostrand Chem. Dict.

KOMAROVSKII, A. S. fl. 1930's. Russian chemist. Cited in: Chem. Abstr., Decenn. Index, 1927-1936; 1937-1946. Komarovskii-Korenmann spot test for cerium, Komarovskii-Poluektov test for copper, Komarovskii-Poluektov test for germanium, Komarovskii-Poluektov test for indium, Komarovskii-Poluektov test for molybdenum, Komarovskii-Poluektov test reaction for beryllium, Komarovskii-Shapiro reagent for niobium and tantalum.

Komarovskii-Korenmann spot test for cerium (Komarovskii, A. S. and Korenman, Israil Mironovic): Chemistry. See: Van Nostrand Chem. Dict.

Komarovskii-Poluektov test for copper (Komarovskii, A. S. and Poluektov, N. S.): Chemistry. See: Van Nostrand Chem. Dict.

Komarovskii-Poluektov test for germanium (Komarovskii, A. S. and Poluektov, N. S.): Chemistry. See: Van Nostrand Chem. Dict.

Komarovskii-Poluektov test for indium (Komarovskii, A. S. and Poluektov, N. S.): Chemistry. See: Van Nostrand Chem. Dict.

Komarovskii-Poluektov test for molybdenum (Komarovskii, A. S. and Poluektov, N. S.): Chemistry. See: Van Nostrand Chem. Dict.

Komarovskii-Poluektov test reaction for beryllium (Komarovskii, A. S. and Poluektov, N. S.): Chemistry. See: Van Nostrand Chem. Dict.

Komarovskii-Shapiro reagent for niobium and tantalum (Komarovskii, A. S. and Shapiro, M. Ya.): Chemistry. See: Van Nostrand Chem. Dict.

Kondakoff rule (Kondakov, Ivan Lavrentievich): Chemistry. See: Van Nostrand Chem. Dict.

KONDAKOV, IVAN LAVRENTIEVICH. 1857-1931. Russian chemist. See: Dict. Sci. Biog. Kondakoff rule.

KONDOLEON, EMMANUEL. 1879-1939. Greek surgeon. See: Biog. Lex. hervorr. Aerzte, 1880-1930. Kondoleon operation.

Kondoleon operation (Kondoleon, Emmanuel): Medicine. See: Dorland; Stedman.

Kondratieff (cycle) (Kondratieff, Nikolai D.): Economics. See: Greenwald; Webster's 3d.

KONDRATIEFF, NIKOLAI D. b. 1892. Russian economist. See: Internat. Encyc. Soc. Sci. Kondratieff (cycle).

KONIG. No dates. Mathematician. (Biography source unavailable.) Zermelo-Konig paradox.

Koninck, Laurent-Guillaume de. See: De Koninck, Laurent-Guillaume.

Koninckite (De Koninck, Laurent-Guillaume): Earth Sciences. See: Thrush; Webster's 3d.

KONJETZNY, GEORG ERNST. b. 1880. German physician. See: Biog. Lex. hervorr. Aerzte, 1880-1930. Konjetzny's gastritis.

Konjetzny's gastritis (Konjetzny, Georg Ernst): Medicine. See: Jablonski.

Konlite (Konleinite or Koenlinite) (Koenlein): Earth Sciences. See: Thrush.

KONOVALOV, DMITRY PETROVICH. 1856-1929. Russian chemist. See: Dict. Sci. Biog. Gibbs-Konovalov theorems?, Konowaloff('s) rule, Konowaloff test reaction for primary and secondary nitro compounds.

Konowaloff('s) rule (Konovalov, Dmitry Petrovich): Chemistry. See: Ballentyne; Van Nostrand Sci. Encyc.

Konowaloff test reaction for primary and secondary nitro compounds (Konovalov, Dmitry Petrovich): Chemistry. See: Van Nostrand Chem. Dict.

KONSULOFF, STEFAN GEORGIEV. b. 1885. Bulgarian zoologist. See: Alman. Sofijsk Univers., 1888/1928, pp. 272-276. Konsuloff's test?

Konsuloff's test (Konsuloff, Stefan Georgiev?): Medicine. See: Dorland.

KONYUS (or KONUS), A. A. fl. 1924-1939. Russian economist. Cited in: Inter. Encyc. Soc. Sci. Konyus conditions, Konyus index (or index number).

Konyus conditions (Konyus, A. A.): Statistics. See: Kendall.

Konyus index (or index number) (Konyus, A. A.): Statistics. See: Kendall. Also known as: Laspeyres-Konyus index, Paasche-Konyus index.

Kooman's array (Derivation undetermined): Electronics. See: Hughes.

KOOPMANS, TJALLING CHARLES. 1910- . Dutch-born American economist. See: World Who's Who Sci. Darmois-Koopman's distributions.

Kopecky elutriator (Kopecky, Josef): Engineering and Industry. See: Thrush.

KOPECKY, JOSEF. b. 1865. Czechoslovakian soil physicist. Cited in: Mansell. Kopecky elutriator.

KOPLIK, HENRY. 1858-1927. American pediatrician. See: World Who's Who Sci. Koplik('s) spots, Koplik's stigma of degeneration.

Koplik('s) spots (Koplik, Henry): Medicine. See: Dorland; Jablonski; Stedman; Van Nostrand Sci. Encyc. under "Measles."; Webster's 3d. Also known as: Filatov's spots.

Koplik's stigma of degeneration (Koplik, Henry): Medicine. See: Stedman.

Kopp gear (Kopp, Jean E.): Engineering and Industry. See: Auger.

KOPP, HERMANN FRANZ MORITZ. 1817-1892. German chemist. See: Dict. Sci. Biog. Kopp('s) law, Koppite, Neumann-Kopp rule.

KOPP, JEAN E. No dates. Swiss engineer. (Biography source unavailable.) Kopp gear.

KOPP, JOHANN HEINRICH. 1777-1858. German physician. See: World Who's Who Sci. Kopp's asthma.

Kopp('s) law (Kopp, Hermann Franz Moritz): Chemistry. See: Ballentyne; Hackh; Thewlis; Van Nostrand Sci. Encyc. Also known as: Joule('s) law (3) (molecular heat), Woestyn's law (or rule).

Kopp-Neumann law (Kopp, Hermann Franz Moritz and Neumann, Franz Ernst). See: Neumann-Kopp rule.

Kopp solution (Derivation undetermined): Chemistry. See: Van Nostrand Chem. Dict.

KOPPANYI, THEODORE. 1901- . Hungarian-born American pharmacologist. See: World Who's Who Sci. Dille-Koppanyi test.

Koppers-Becker oven (Koppers, Heinrich and Becker, Joseph): Engineering and Industry. See: Thrush.

Koppers-Hasche process (Koppers, Heinrich and Hasche, Rudolph Leonard): Engineering and Industry. See: Thrush.

KOPPERS, HEINRICH. fl. early 20th c. German engineer. (Biography source unavailable.) Koppers-Becker oven, Koppers-Hasche process, Koppers oven (or retorts), Koppers process.

Koppers oven (or retorts) (Koppers, Heinrich): Engineering and Industry. See: Thrush; Van Nostrand Chem. Dict.; Van Nostrand Sci. Encyc. under "Destructive Distillation Products."

Koppers process (Koppers, Heinrich): Chemistry. See: Van Nostrand Chem. Dict.

Koppeschaar solution (or reagent) (Koppeschaar, Willem Fredrik): Chemistry. See: Hackh; Van Nostrand Chem. Dict.

KOPPESCHAAR, WILLEM FREDRIK. fl. 1876. Dutch chemist. Cited in: Kelly. Koppeschaar solution (or reagent).

Koppite (Kopp, Hermann Franz Moritz): Earth Sciences. See: Webster's 3d.

Kopp's asthma (Kopp, Johann Heinrich): Medicine. See: Dorland; Stedman. Also known as: Millar's asthma, Wichmann's asthma.

KORAH. Great-grandson of Levi in the Old Testament. See: Hastings (Dict. Bible). Corahism, Korahite.

Korahite (Korah): History. See: Webster's 3d.

KORANYI, FRIEDRICH VON. 1828-1913. Hungarian physician. See: Biog. Lex. hervorr. Aerzte. Koranyi's method.

Koranyi's method (Koranyi, Friedrich von): Medicine. See: Dorland; Stedman.

KORDINA. fl. 1888. Austrian engineer. (Biography source unavailable.) Kordina blast pipe.

Kordina blast pipe (Kordina): Engineering and Industry. See: Auger.

Korenman-Fursina micro-reaction for lithium (Korenman, Israil Mironovic and Fursina, M. M.): Chemistry. See: Van Nostrand Chem. Dict.

KORENMAN, ISRAIL MIRONOVIC. 1904- . Russian chemist. See: Pogg., vols. 6, 7b. Komarovskii-Korenmann spot test for cerium, Korenman-Fursina micro-reaction for lithium, Korenman-Lubashevick test for copper, Korenman micro-chemical test for iodide, Korenman micro-chemical tests for permanganate, Korenman reagent for free ammonia in pyridine, Korenman reagent for heavy metals, Korenman test for bromate, Korenman test reaction for ferricyanides.

Korenman-Lubashevick test for copper (Korenman, Israil Mironovic and Lukashevich, E. N.): Chemistry. See: Van Nostrand Chem. Dict.

Korenman micro-chemical test for iodide (Korenman, Israil Mironovic): Chemistry. See: Van Nostrand Chem. Dict.

Korenman micro-chemical tests for permanganate (Korenman, Israil Mironovic): Chemistry. See: Van Nostrand Chem. Dict.

Korenman reagent for free ammonia in pyridine (Korenman, Israil Mironovic): Chemistry. See: Van Nostrand Chem. Dict.

Korenman reagent for heavy metals (Korenman, Israil Mironovic): Chemistry. See: Van Nostrand Chem. Dict.

Korenman test for bromate (Korenman, Israil Mironovic): Chemistry. See: Van Nostrand Chem. Dict.

Korenman test reaction for ferricyanides (Korenman, Israil Mironovic): Chemistry. See: Van Nostrand Chem. Dict.

Koreshan (or Koreshanity) (Teed, Koresh R.): Religion. See: Webster's 3d.

Korff's fibers (Derivation undetermined): Anatomy. See: Stedman.

Korfmann arch saver (Derivation undetermined): Engineering and Industry. See: Thrush.

Korfmann power loader (Derivation undetermined): Engineering and Industry. See: Thrush.

Korin, Ogata. See: Ogata Korin.

Korin school (of Japanese painters) (Ogata Korin): Fine Arts. See: Osborne.

Kornelite (Hlavacsek, Kornel): Earth Sciences. See: Thrush; Webster's 3d.

Korner('s) method (or absolute method) (Koerner, Wilhelm): Chemistry. See: Ballentyne; Van Nostrand Chem. Dict.

KORNERUP, ANDREAS NICOLAUS. 1857-1881. Danish geologist. See: Dansk Biog. Lek. Kornerupine.

Kornerupine (Kornerup, Andreas Nicolaus): Earth Sciences. See: Thrush; Webster's 3d.

KORNZWEIG, ABRAHAM LEON. 1900- . American physician. See: Amer. Med. Direct., 18th ed. Bassen-Kornzweig syndrome.

KOROTKOFF, NIKOLAI SERGIEVICH. b. 1874. Russian physician. Cited in: Kelly. Korotkoff sounds, Korotkoff's test.

Korotkoff sounds (Korotkoff, Nikolai Sergievich): Medicine. See: Dorland; Stedman.

Korotkoff's test (Korotkoff, Nikolai Sergievich): Medicine. See: Dorland; Stedman.

KOROVNIKOV, A. F. fl. 1936. Russian physician. (Biography source unavailable.) Korovnikov's disease.

Korovnikov's disease (Korovnikov, A. F.): Medicine. See: Jablonski.

KORSAKOFF, SERGEI SERGIEVICH. 1854-1900. Russian psychiatrist. See: World Who's Who Sci. Korsakoff's (Korsakov's) psychosis (or syndrome).

Korsakoff's (Korsakov's) psychosis (or syndrome) (Korsakoff, Sergei Sergievich): Medicine. See: Dorland; Hinsie; Jablonski; Stedman; Webster's 3d. Also known as: Meynert's amentia.

Korte's laws (Derivation undetermined): Physiology. See: Chaplin; Wolman.

Korting engine (Koerting, Ernst): Engineering and Industry. See: Auger.

KORZHINSKII, DIMITRII SERGEEVICH. 1899- . Russian geologist. See: Turkevich and Turkevich. Korzhinskite (or Korshinskite).

Korzhinskite (or Korshinkite) (Korzhinskii, Dimitrii Sergeevich): Earth Sciences. See: Thrush.

Koschewnikoff (or Koschewnikow), Alexei J. See: Kozhevnikov, Aleksei Yakovlevich.

KOSCHMIEDER, HARALD (In full: HANS HARALD). 1897- . German meteorologist. See: Pogg., vols. 6, 7a. Koschmieder's law?

Koschmieder's law (Koschmieder, Harald?): Earth Sciences. See: Huschke.

Kosciusko rebellion (Kosciuszko, Tadeusz): History. Cited in: Laughlin.

KOSCIUSZKO, TADEUSZ. 1746-1817. Polish revolutionary leader. See: Encyc. Brit., 1973. Kosciusko rebellion.

Koshevnikoff, Alexei Jakovlevich. See: Kozhevnikov, Aleksei Yakovlevich.

Kossa, Julius von. See: Von Kossa, Julius.

KOSSEL, ALBRECHT (In full: KARL MARTIN LEONHARD ALBRECHT). 1853-1927. German physiological chemist. See: Dict. Sci. Biog. Kossel's test.

Kossel effect (Kossel, Walther): Physics. See: Thewlis.

Kossel lines (Kossel, Walther): Physics. See: Ballentyne; Hackh; Thewlis under "Kossel effect."

Kossel press (Kossel, Walther?): Physics. See: Hackh.

Kossel-Sommerfeld displacement law (or law) (Kossel, Walther and Sommerfeld, Arnold Johannes): Physics. See: Ballentyne; Hughes; Internat. Dict. Ap. Math.; Internat. Dict. Phys. Elec. Also known as: Sommerfel-Kossel displacement law (or law).

KOSSEL, WALTHER. 1888-1956. German physicist. See: Dict. Sci. Biog. Kossel effect, Kossel lines, Kossel press?, Kossel-Sommerfeld displacement law (or law).

Kossel's test (Kossel, Albrecht): Medicine. See: Dorland.

Kossuth hat (Kossuth, Lajos): Fashion. See: Mathews, M. M.; Partridge; Picken; Webster's 3d.

KOSSUTH, LAJOS. 1802-1894. Hungarian patriot. See: Encyc. Brit., 1973. Kossuth hat; Kossuthists; Order of Kossuth.

Kossuthists (Kossuth, Lajos): History. See: Harbottle.

Kostanecki-Robinson reaction (or chromone synthesis) (Kostanecki, Stanislaw and Robinson, Sir Robert): Chemistry. See: Krauch and Kunz; Van Nostrand Chem. Dict.

KOSTANECKI, STANISLAW. 1860-1910. Polish chemist. See: Dict. Sci. Biog. Kostanecki-Robinson reaction (or chromone synthesis).

KOSTELETZKY, VINCENT FRANZ. ca. 1800-1887. Bohemian botanist. Cited in: Mansell. Kosteletzkya.

Kosteletzkya (Kosteletzky, Vincent Franz): Botany. See: Webster's 3d.

Koster, Laurens Janszoon. See: Coster, Laurens Janszoon.

Koster's blue spruce (Derivation undetermined): Botany. See: Winburne.

Kostinsky effect (Kostinsky, Sergey Konstantinovich): Photography. See: Focal Encyc. Photog.; Hughes; Van Nostrand Sci. Encyc.

KOSTINSKY, SERGEY KONSTANTINOVICH. 1867-1936. Russian astronomer. See: Dict. Sci. Biog. Kostinsky effect.

KOSTMANN, ROLF. 1909- . Swedish physician. See: Vem Ar Det? 1975. Kostmann's syndrome.

Kostmann's syndrome (Kostmann, Rolf): Medicine. See: Jablonski.

KOSZEWSKI, BOHDAN JULIUSZ. 1918- . Polish-born? physician in Switzerland. Cited in: Mansell. Koszewski's syndrome.

Koszewski's syndrome (Koszewski, Bohdan Juliusz): Medicine. See: Jablonski.

KOTO, BUNDJIRO. 1856-1935. Japanese geologist and petrographer. See: Dict. Sci. Biog. Kotoite.

Kotoite (Koto, Bundjiro): Earth Sciences. See: Webster's 3d.

Kotschubeite (Kochubey, P. A. von): Earth Sciences. See: Webster's 3d.

KOTTMANN, KURT. 1877-1952. German physician. Cited in: Kelly. Kottmann's test (or reaction).

Kottmann's test (or reaction) (Kottmann, Kurt): Medicine. See: Dorland.

Kotze konimeter (Kotze, Sir Robert Nelson): Earth Sciences. See: Thrush.

KOTZE, SIR ROBERT NELSON. 1870-1953. South African mining engineer. See: Std. Encyc. So. Afr. Kotze konimeter.

Kourbatoff('s) reagent(s) (Kurbatov, V. I.): Chemistry. See: Hackh; Thrush; Van Nostrand Chem. Dict.

KOUTEK, JAROMIR. 1902- . Czechoslovakian geologist. See: Turkevich and Turkevich. Koutekite.

Koutekite (Koutek, Jaromir): Earth Sciences. See: Thrush.

KOVALEVSKI, ALEKSANDR ONUFRIEVICH. 1840-1901. Russian embryologist. See: Dict. Sci. Biog. Kovalevski's canal, Kowalevskia?

Kovalevski's canal (Kovalevski, Aleksandr Onufrievich): Zoology. See: Dorland; Henderson.

KOVALEVSKY, MAKSIM MAKSIMOVICH. 1851-1916. Russian historian, anthropologist and sociologist. See: Encyc. Soc. Sci. Kovalevsky's stages of society.

Kovalevsky's stages of society (Kovalevsky, Maksim Maksimovich): Sociology. See: Zadrozny.

Kowalevskia (Kovalevski, Aleksandr Onufrievich?): Zoology. See: Pennak.

KOWALEWSKY, ARNOLD. fl. 1885. Russian physician. Cited in: Kelly. Kowalewsky solution.

Kowalewsky solution (Kowalewsky, Arnold): Chemistry. See: Van Nostrand Chem. Dict.

KOWARSKI, ALBERT. fl. 1906-1913. German physician. Cited in: Kelly. Kowarski's test.

Kowarski's test (Kowarski, Albert): Medicine. See: Dorland; Stedman.

KOYANAGI, YOSHIZO. b. 1880. Japanese physician. See: Biog. Lex. hervorr. Aerzte, 1880-1930. Vogt-Koyanagi syndrome (or disease).

Koyter, Volcher. See: Coiter, Volcher.

Kozeny equation (Kozeny, Josef Alexander). Engineering and Industry. See: Thrush.

KOZENY, JOSEF ALEXANDER. b. 1889. German engineer. See: Kuerschner's Deut. Gel. Kal., vol. 4, 1931. Kozeny equation.

KOZHEVNIKOV, ALEKSEI YAKOVLEVICH. 1836-1902. Russian neurologist. See: World Who's Who Sci. Kozhevnikov's syndrome (epilepsy or disease).

Kozhevnikov's syndrome (epilepsy or disease) (Kozhevnikov, Aleksei Yakovlevich): Medicine. See: Dorland; Jablonski; Stedman.

KOZŁOWSKI, BOGUMIL. 1907- . Polish physician. See: Lodzkie Towarzystwo Naukowe. Sprawozdania z Czynnosci i Posiedzen, vol. 5 (1951), pp. 59-62. Kozłowski's degeneration.

Kozłowski's degeneration (Kozłowski, Bogumil): Medicine. See: Jablonski.

KRABBE, KNUD H. 1885-1961. Danish neurologist. See: World Who's Who Sci. Christensen-Krabbe disease, Krabbe's disease (or leukodystrophy), Krabbe's syndrome (1), Krabbe's syndrome (2).

Krabbe's disease (or leukodystrophy) (Krabbe, Knud H.): Medicine. See: Dorland; Jablonski; Stedman.

Krabbe's syndrome (1) (Krabbe, Knud H.): Medicine. See: Jablonski.

Krabbe's syndrome (2) (Krabbe, Knud H.): Medicine. See: Jablonski; Stedman.

KRAEMER, RICHARD. b. 1878. Austrian ophthalmologist. See: Biog. Lex. hervorr. Aerzte, 1880-1930. Kraemer's disease.

Kraemer-Sarnon test (Derivation undetermined): Chemistry. See: Ballentyne.

Kraemer's disease (Kraemer, Richard): Medicine. See: Jablonski.

KRAEPELIN, EMIL. 1856-1926. German psychiatrist. See: Internat. Encyc. Soc. Sci. Kraepelin ergograph, Kraepelinian, Morel-Kraepelin disease.

Kraepelin ergograph (Kraepelin, Emil): Physiology. See: Drever.

Kraepelinian (Kraepelin, Emil): Psychiatry. See: Webster's 3d.

Kraft method of degradation of acids (Derivation undetermined): Chemistry. See: Van Nostrand Chem. Dict. under "Degradation of acids..."

Krag-Joergensen rifle (Krag, Ole Herman Johannes and Joergensen, Erik): Weapons. See: Quick.

KRAG, OLE HERMAN JOHANNES. 1837-1916. Norwegian inventor. See: Norak Biog. Lek. Krag-Joergensen rifle.

KRAMER, FRANZ. b. 1878. German neurologist and psychiatrist. See: Biog. Lex. hervorr. Aerzte. Kramer-Pollnow disease.

KRAMER, JOHANN GEORG HEINRICH. d. 1742. German botanist. See: World Who's Who Sci. Krameria.

Kramer-Pollnow disease (Kramer, Franz and Pollnow, Hans): Medicine. See: Jablonski.

KRAMER, WILHELM HEINRICH. fl. 1756-1766. German botanist. Cited in: Mansell. Krameria.

Krameria (Kramer, Johann Georg Heinrich): Botany. See: Charnock; Dorland; Stedman; Webster's 3d.

KRAMERS, HENDRIK ANTHONY. 1894-1952. Dutch physicist. See: Dict. Sci. Biog. Kramers-Kronig dispersion formula (or relations), Kramers theorem, Wentzel-Kramers-Brillouin-Jeffreys approximation (or method).

Kramers-Kronig dispersion formula (or relations) (Kramers, Hendrik Anthony and Laer Kronig, Ralph de): Physics. See: Internat. Dict. Phys. Elec.

Kramers theorem (Kramers, Hendrik Anthony): Physics. See: Ballentyne; Thewlis.

KRAMETZ, E. fl. 1936. Czechoslovakian chemist. Cited in: Chem. Abstr., Decenn. Index, 1927-1936. Dubsky-Krametz test reaction.

KRANTZ, AUGUST. 1809-1872. German mineralogist. Cited in: Royal Soc. Cat. Sci. Pap., 1864-1873. Krantzite.

Krantzite (Krantz, August): Earth Sciences. See: Thrush; Webster's 3d.

KRASE, NORMAN WILLIAM. 1895- . American chemical engineer. See: Pogg., vols. 6, 7b. Krase process.

Krase process (Krase, Norman William): Chemistry. See: Van Nostrand Chem. Dict.

KRASKE, PAUL. 1851-1930. German surgeon. See: Biog. Lex. hervorr. Aerzte, 1880-1930. Kraske's operation.

Kraske's operation (Kraske, Paul): Medicine. See: Dorland; Stedman.

KRASNOVA, V. S. fl. 1936. Russian chemist. Cited in: Chem. Abstr., vol. 30, p. 7492. Bogoslovskii-Krasnova test.

KRATCHOVIL, JOSEF. 1878-1958. Czechoslovak petrographer. Cited in: Mansell. Kratochvilite.

Kratochvilite (Kratchovil, Josef): Earth Sciences. See: Thrush; Webster's 3d.

Kratzmann cesium chloride solution (Kratzmann, E.): Chemistry. See: Van Nostrand Chem. Dict.

KRATZMANN, E. fl. 1914. German chemist. Cited in: Chem. Abstr., vol. 8, p. 2740. Kratzmann cesium chloride solution.

KRAUPA, ERNST. fl. 1920. German ophthalmologist. Cited in: Mansell. Kraupa's syndrome.

Kraupa's syndrome (Kraupa, Ernst). See: Fuch's dystrophy (or syndrome).

KRAUS, EDWARD HENRY. 1875-1973. American mineralogist. See: Who Was Who Amer., 1969-1973. Krausite.

Kraus' reaction (Kraus, Rudolf): Medicine. See: Stedman.

KRAUS, RUDOLF. 1868-1932. Austrian bacteriologist. See: World Who's Who Sci. Kraus' reaction.

KRAUSE, ARLINGTON COLTON. 1896- . American ophthalmologist. See: Direct. Med. Specialists, 1975-1976. Krause's syndrome.

KRAUSE, FEDOR. 1857-1937. German surgeon. See: World Who's Who Sci. Krause's method (or graft), Krause's operation.

KRAUSE, KARL CHRISTIAN FRIEDRICH. 1781-1832. German philosopher. See: New Encyc. Brit., 1974, Microp. Krausism.

KRAUSE, KARL FRIEDRICH THEODOR. 1797-1868. German anatomist. See: Biog. Lex. hervorr. Aerzte. Krause's glands, Krause's median puboprostatic ligament, Krause's muscle, Krause's valve.

Krause-Reese syndrome (Krause, Arlington Colton and Reese, Algeron B.) See: Krause's syndrome.

Krause rolling mill (Derivation undetermined): Engineering and Industry. See: Thrush.

KRAUSE, WILHELM. 1833-1910. German anatomist. See: World Who's Who Sci. Krause's bone, Krause's corpuscles (or end bulbs), Krause's membrane, Krause's respiratory bundle.

Krause's bone (Krause, Wilhelm): Anatomy. See: Stedman.

Krause's corpuscles (or end bulbs) (Krause, Wilhelm): Anatomy. See: Dorland; Pennak; Webster's 3d.

Krause's glands (Krause, Karl Friedrich Theodor): Anatomy. See: Donath; Dorland; Henderson; Stedman. Also known as: Kleinschmidt's glands.

Krause's median puboprostatic ligament (Krause, Karl Friedrich Theodor): Anatomy. See: Dorland; Stedman.

Krause's membrane (Krause, Wilhelm): Anatomy. See: Dorland; Henderson; Pennak; Stedman; Webster's 3d. Also known as: Dobie's line.

Krause's method (or graft) (Krause, Fedor): Medicine. See: Stedman.

Krause's muscle (Krause, Karl Friedrich Theodor): Anatomy. See: Dorland; Stedman. Also known as: Bovero's muscle.

Krause's operation (Krause, Fedor): Medicine. See: Dorland; Stedman.

Krause's respiratory bundle (Krause, Wilhelm): Anatomy. See: Dorland; Stedman. Also known as: Gierke's respiratory bundle.

Krause's syndrome (Krause, Arlington Colton): Medicine. See: Jablonski. Also known as: Krause-Reese syndrome.

Krause's valve (Krause, Karl Friedrich Theodor). See: Beraud's valve.

Krausism (Krause, Karl Christian Friedrich): Philosophy. See: Edwards.

Krausite (Kraus, Edward Henry): Earth Sciences. See: Thrush; Webster's 3d.

KRAUSKOPF, FRANCIS CRAIG. b. 1877. American chemist. See: Amer. Men. Sci., 4th ed. Krauskopf-Purdy reagent, Krauskopf-Swartz test for molybdenum.

Krauskopf-Purdy reagent (Krauskopf, Francis Craig and Purdy, L. H.): Chemistry. See: Van Nostrand Chem. Dict.

Krauskopf-Swartz test for molybdenum (Krauskopf, Francis Craig and Swartz, Carl Errett): Chemistry. See: Van Nostrand Chem. Dict.

Krauss test (Krauss, William Ernest?): Medicine. See: Stedman.

KRAUSS, WILLIAM ERNEST. 1899- . American biochemist. See: World Who's Who Sci. Krauss test?

KRAUT, HEINRICH ALBRECHT. 1893- . German chemist. See: Pogg., vols. 6, 7a. Kraut('s) reagent?

Kraut('s) reagent (Kraut, Henrich Albrecht?): Chemistry. See: Hackh; Van Nostrand Chem. Dict.

KREBS, CARL. b. 1892. Danish pathologist. See: Biog. Lex. hervorr. Aerzte, 1880-1930. Krebs' leukocyte index, Krebs 2 tumor (or carcinoma).

Krebs cycle (Krebs, Sir Hans Adolf): Biochemistry. See: Pennak; Stedman; Van Nostrand Sci. Encyc.; Webster's 3d.

KREBS, SIR HANS ADOLF. 1900- . German-born English biochemist. See: World Who's Who Sci. Krebs cycle, Krebs-Ringer solution, Krebs urea cycle (or ornithine cycle).

Krebs-Henseleit cycle (Krebs, Sir Hans Adolf and Henseleit, Kurt). See: Krebs' urea cycle.

Krebs' leukocyte index (Krebs, Carl): Medicine. See: Dorland.

Krebs-Ringer solution (Krebs, Sir Hans Adolf and Ringer, Sidney): Medicine. See: Stedman.

Krebs 2 tumor (or carcinoma) (Krebs, Carl): Medicine. See: Jablonski.

Krebs urea cycle (or ornithine cycle) (Krebs, Sir Hans Adolf): Biochemistry. See: Stedman. Also known as: Krebs-Henseleit cycle.

KREIBIG, WILHELM. fl. 1949. German ophthalmologist. Cited in: Index-Cat. Libr. Surg.-Gen. Off., 5th Ser., vol. 1, 1959. Kreibig's opticomalacia.

Kreibig's opticomalacia (Kreibig, Wilhelm): Medicine. See: Jablonski.

KREIS, HANS. 1861-1931. German chemist. See: Pogg., vols. 4, 5, 6. Kreis-Studinger reagent, Kreis test (or reagent for detecting rancidity).

Kreis-Studinger reagent (Kreis, Hans and Studinger, Josef): Chemistry. See: Van Nostrand Chem. Dict.

Kreis test (or reagent for detecting rancidity) (Kreis, Hans): Chemistry. See: Hackh; Van Nostrand Chem. Dict.; Winburne.

Kremer, Gerhard. See: Mercator, Gerhardus.

KREMERS, PETER. fl. 1865. German chemist. Cited in: Royal Soc. Cat. Sci. Pap., 1864-1873. Kremersite.

Kremersite (Kremers, Peter): Earth Sciences. See: Thrush; Webster's 3d.

KRENNER, JOZSEF SANDOR. 1839-1920. Hungarian mineralogist. See: Magyar Eletr. Lek. Krennerite.

Krennerite (Krenner, Jozsef Sandor): Earth Sciences. See: Thrush; Van Nostrand Sci. Encyc.; Webster's 3d.

KRETSCHMANN, FRIEDERICK. 1858-1934. German otologist. See: Biog. Lex. hervorr. Aerzte, 1880-1930. Kretschmann's space.

Kretschmann's space (Kretschmann, Friederick): Medicine. See: Dorland; Stedman.

KRETSCHMER, ERNST. 1888-1964. German psychiatrist. See: Internat. Encyc. Soc. Sci. Kretschmer type(s) (or personality types), Kretschmer's syndrome.

Kretschmer type(s) (or personality types) (Kretschmer, Ernst): Psychology. See: Dorland; English; Zadrozny.

Kretschmer's syndrome (Kretschmer, Ernst): Medicine. See: Jablonski.

KRETZ, RICHARD. 1865-1920. German pathologist. See: Biog. Lex. hervorr. Aerzte, 1880-1930. Kretz's granules, Kretz's paradox.

Kretz's granules (Kretz, Richard): Medicine. See: Dorland.

Kretz's paradox (Kretz, Richard): Medicine. See: Dorland.

KREUGER, HENRIK. b. 1882. Swedish builder. See: Svenska Maen Och Kvinnor. Kreuger's ratio.

Kreuger's ratio (Kreuger, Henrik): Engineering and Industry. See: Thrush.

KREUTZER, CARL. fl. 1939-1948. German engineer. (Biography source unavailable. Kreutzer roof.

KREUTZER, RODOLPHE. 1766-1831. French violinist and composer. See: Encyc. Brit., 1973. Kreutzer Sonata.

Kreutzer roof (Kreutzer, Carl): Engineering and Industry. See: Thrush.

Kreutzer Sonata (Kreutzer, Rodolphe): Music. See: Apel; Barnhart (Eng. Lit.); Hendrickson; Scholes.

KREYSIG, FRIEDRICH LUDWIG. 1770-1839. German physician. See: Biog. Lex. hervorr. Aerzte. Heim-Kreysig sign.

Kreysig's sign (Kreysig, Friedrich Ludwig). See: Heim-Kreysig sign.

KRIDA, ARTHUR. b. 1888. American surgeon. See: Nu Sigma Nu Bull., vol. 30 (1940-1941), p. 136. Bakwin-Krida syndrome.

Kries, Johannes Adolf von. See: Von Kries, Johannes Adolf.

KRIEWITZ, O. fl. 1899. German chemist. Cited in: Royal Soc. Cat. Sci. Pap., 1884-1900. Kriewitz-Prins reaction.

Kriewitz-Prins reaction (Kriewitz, O. and Prins, Hendrik Jacobus). See: Prins reaction.

KRIG (or KREIG), DAVID. fl. 18th c. American plant collector. (Biography source unavailable.) Krigia.

Krigia (Krig, David): Botany. See: Webster's 3d.

Krishaber's disease (Krishnaber, Maurice): Medicine. See: Dorland; Jablonski.

KRISHNA. One of the principal Hindu gods. See: Jobes. Krishnaism.

KRISHNABER, MAURICE. 1836-1883. Hungarian physician in France. See: Biog. Lex. hervorr. Aerzte. Krishaber's disease.

Krishnaism (Krishna): Religion. See: Webster's 3d.

KRISTELLER, SAMUEL. 1820-1900. German gynecologist. See: Biog. Lex. hervorr. Aerzte, 1880-1930. Kristeller technique.

Kristeller technique (Kristeller, Samuel): Medicine. See: Dorland; Stedman.

KROEHNKE, B. fl. 19th c. German mineralogist. Cited in: Hintze, vol. 1, part 3, half 2, p. 4458. Kroehnkite.

Kroehnkite (Kroehnke, B.): Earth Sciences. See: Thrush; Webster's 3d.

KROENIG, BERNHARD. 1863-1918. German gynecologist. See: Biog. Lex. hervorr. Aerzte, 1880-1930. Kroenig's method.

KROENIG, GEORG. 1856-1911. German physician. See: Biog. Lex. hervorr. Aerzte, 1880-1930. Kroenig's area (or field), Kroenig's isthmus, Kroenig's steps.

Kroenig's area (or field) (Kroenig, Georg): Anatomy. See: Donath; Dorland; Stedman.

Kroenig's isthmus (Kroenig, Georg): Medicine. See: Dorland; Stedman.

Kroenig's method (Kroenig, Bernhard): Medicine. See: Dorland; Stedman.

Kroenig's steps (Kroenig, Georg): Medicine. See: Dorland; Stedman.

KROENLEIN, RUDOLF ULRICH. 1847-1910. Swiss surgeon. See: Biog. Lex. hervorr. Aerzte, 1880-1930. Kroenlein's hernia, Kroenlein's operation.

Kroenlein's hernia (Kroenlein, Rudolf Ulrich): Medicine. See: Dorland; Jablonski; Stedman.

Kroenlein's operation (Kroenlein, Rudolf Ulrich): Medicine. See: Dorland; Stedman.

KROGH, AUGUST (In full: SCHACK AUGUST STEENBERG). 1874-1949. Danish physiologist. See: Dict. Sci. Biog. Krogh's law.

Krogh's law (Krogh, August): Physiology. See: Gray.

Krohn compensator (Derivation undetermined): Engineering and Industry. See: Auger.

Krohnke process (Derivation undetermined): Engineering and Industry. See: Thrush.

Kroll process (or process for producing titanium sponge) (Kroll, Wilhelm): Engineering and Industry. See: Thrush; Van Nostrand Chem. Dict.

KROLL, WILHELM. b. 1889. German metallurgist. See: Pogg., vol. 6. Betterton-Kroll process, Kroll process (or process for producing titanium sponge).

KROMAYER, ERNST L. F. 1862-1933. German dermatologist. See: Biog. Lex. hervorr. Aerzte, 1880-1930. Kromayer('s) lamp.

Kromayer('s) lamp (Kromayer, Ernst L. F.): Medicine. See: Dorland; Internat. Dict. Phys. Elec.; Stedman.

KROMPECHER, EDMUND. 1870-1926. Hungarian pathologist. See: Biog. Lex. hervorr, Aerzte, 1880-1930. Krompecher's tumor (or carcinoma).

Krompecher's tumor (or carcinoma) (Krompecher, Edmund): Medicine. See: Dorland; Jablonski; Stedman. Also known as: Jacob's ulcer.

KRONBERGER, HANS. b. 1884. German physician. Cited in: Kelly. Kronberger solution.

Kronberger solution (Kronberger, Hans): Chemistry. See: Van Nostrand Chem. Dict.

Kronecker delta (Kronecker, Leopold): Mathematics. See: Ballentyne; Internat. Dict. Ap. Math.; Internat. Dict. Phys. Elec.; James.

KRONECKER, HUGO (In full: KARL HUGO). 1839-1914. German physiologist. See: World Who's Who Sci. Kronecker's solution.

KRONECKER, LEOPOLD. 1823-1891. German mathematician. See: Dict. Sci. Biog. Kronecker delta, Kronecker product (or product of matrices), Kronecker product of design.

Kronecker product (or product of matrices) (Kronecker, Leopold): Mathematics. See: Ballentyne; Kendall.

Kronecker product of design (Kronecker, Leopold): Mathematics. See: Kendall.

Kronecker's solution (Kronecker, Hugo): Medicine. See: Dorland; Stedman.

Kronig-Penney model (Laer Kronig, Ralph de and Penney, William George): Physics. See: Ballentyne; Hughes; Internat. Dict. Phys. Elec.

Kronig, Ralph. See: Laer de Kronig, Ralph.

Kronman-Bibikova micro-chemical reaction for rhenium (Kronman, E. S. and Bibikova, V.): Chemistry. See: Van Nostrand Chem. Dict.

KRONMAN, E. S. fl. 1933. Russian chemist. Cited in: Chem. Abstr., vol. 27, p. 681. Kronman-Bibikova micro-chemical reaction for rhenium.

KRUBER, JOHN JULIUS. No dates. Botanist? (Biography source unavailable). Krubera.

Krubera (Kruber, John Julius): Botany. See: Charnock.

Krueger instrument stop (Derivation undetermined): Dentistry. See: Stedman.

KRUGER, PAUL. 1825-1904. South African statesman. See: New Encyc. Brit., 1974. Kruger telegram.

Kruger telegram (Kruger, Paul): History. See: Brewer; Montgomery; Steinberg.

KRUH, O. fl. 1935. German chemist. Cited in: Chem. Abstr., vol. 29, p. 5374. Krumholz-Kruh test for cadmium.

KRUISHEER, C. I. fl. 1932. Dutch chemist. Cited in: Chem. Abstr., vol. 26, p. 5031. Kruisheer test for iodide.

Kruisheer test for iodide (Kruisheer, C. I.): Chemistry. See: Van Nostrand Chem. Dict.

KRUKENBERG, ADOLPH. 1816-1877. German anatomist. See: Biog. Lex. hervorr. Aerzte. Krukenberg's veins.

KRUKENBERG, FRIEDRICH ERNST. 1871-1946. German pathologist. Cited in: Kelly. Krukenberg('s) tumor, Krukenberg's spindle.

KRUKENBERG, HERMANN. b. 1863. German surgeon. See: Z. Orthop. Chir., vol. 60 (1933) pp. 273-278. Krukenberg's arm (or hand).

Krukenberg('s) tumor (Krukenberg, Friedrich Ernst): Medicine. See: Dorland; Jablonski; Stedman; Webster's 3d.

Krukenberg's arm (or hand) (Krukenberg, Hermann): Medicine. See: Dorland.

Krukenberg's spindle (Krukenberg, Friedrich Ernst): Medicine. See: Dorland; Jablonski; Stedman. Also known as: Axenfeld-Krunkenberg spindle.

Krukenberg's veins (Krukenberg, Adolph): Anatomy. See: Dorland; Stedman.

Krumholz-Feigl-Rajmann reagent for palladium and platinum (Krumholz, P.; Feigl, Friedrich; and Rajmann, E.): Chemistry. See: Van Nostrand Chem. Dict.

Krumholz-Feigl-Rajmann reagent for zirconium (Krumholz, P.; Feigl, Friedrich; and Rajmann, E.): Chemistry. See: Van Nostrand Chem. Dict.

Krumholz-Hoenel reagents for mercury, copper, iron, and cadmium (Krumholz, P. and Hoenel, F.): Chemistry. See: Van Nostrand Chem. Dict.

Krumholz-Kruh test for cadmium (Krumholz, P. and Kruh, O.): Chemistry. See: Van Nostrand Chem. Dict.

KRUMHOLZ, P. fl. 1935. German chemist. Cited in: Chem. Abstr. Feigl-Krumholz test for palladium, Krumholz-Feigl-Rajmann reagent for palladium and platinum, Krumholz-Feigl-Rajmann reagent for zirconium, Krumholz-Hoenel reagents for mercury, copper, iron, and cadmium, Krumholz-Kruh test for cadmium, Krumholz-Sanchez reagent.

Krumholz-Sanchez reagent (Krumholz, P. and Vasquez Sanchez, J.): Chemistry. See: Van Nostrand Chem. Dict.

Krupp ball mill (Krupp family): Engineering and Industry. See: Thrush.

KRUPP FAMILY. fl. 1587 to present. German munitions manufacturer. See: New Encyc. Brit., 1974. Krupp ball mill, Krupp gun (rifle and cannon), Krupp process, Krupp-Renn (process), Krupp washing process, Kruppize, Krupp's disease.

Krupp gun (rifle and cannon) (Krupp family): Weapons. See: Partridge; Quick.

Krupp process (Krupp family): Engineering and Industry. See: Thrush. Also known as: Bell-Krupp process.

Krupp-Renn (process) (Krupp family and Renn): Engineering and Industry. See: Thrush.

KRUPP VON BOHLEN UND HALBACH. 1870-1950. German heiress of iron and steel works. See: Encyc. Brit., 1973. Big Bertha (1) (or Bertha) (gun), Big Bertha (2), Big Bertha (3), Big Bertha (4).

Krupp washing process (Krupp family): Engineering and Industry. See: Thrush.

Kruppize (Krupp family): Engineering and Industry. See: Thrush.

Krupp's disease (Krupp family): Engineering and Industry. See: Hackh.

KRUSE, WALTHER. 1864-1943. German bacteriologist. See: World Who's Who Sci. Kruse's brush, Shiga-Kruse disease.

Kruse's brush (Kruse, Walther): Medicine. See: Dorland; Stedman.

Kruskal limit (Kruskal, Martin David): Physics. See: Hughes; Internat. Dict. Phys. Elec.

KRUSKAL, MARTIN DAVID. 1925- . American mathematical physicist. See: Amer. Men and Women Sci., 12th ed. Goodman-Kruskal tau, Kruskal limit.

Kruskal statistic (Kruskal, William Henry): Statistics. See: Kendall.

Kruskal-Wallis test (Kruskal, William Henry and Wallis, Wilson Allen): Statistics. See: Hoult.

KRUSKAL, WILLIAM HENRY. 1919- . American mathematical statistician. See: Amer. Men and Women Sci., 12th ed. Kruskal statistic, Kruskal-Wallis test.

Krylov method (Derivation undetermined): Mathematics. See: Internat. Dict. Ap. Math.

Kryzhanovskite (Kryzhanovsky, Vladimer I.): Earth Sciences. See: Thrush.

KRYZHANOVSKY, VLADIMER I. 1881-1947. Russian mineralogist. Cited in: Hintze, 2d suppl., p. 204. Kryzhanovskite.

KUBIERSCHKY, KONRAD. fl. 1885-1896. German applied chemist. Cited in: Royal Soc. Cat. Sci. Pap., 1884-1900. Kubierschky tower.

Kubierschky tower (Kubierschky, Konrad): Chemistry. See: Van Nostrand Chem. Dict.

KUBINA, HANS. fl. 1927. Czechoslovakian? chemist. See: Kuerschner's Deut. Gel. Kal., vol. 4, 1931. Kubina-Plichta test reaction for bismuth.

Kubina-Plichta test reaction for bismuth (Kubina, Hans and Plichta, J.): Chemistry. See: Van Nostrand Chem. Dict.

KUCEROV, MIKHAIL GRIGOREVICH. fl. 1884-1907. Russian chemist. Cited in: Royal Soc. Cat. Sci. Pap., 1884-1900. Kucherov reaction.

Kuchenreuter (gun) (Derivation undetermined): Weapons. See: Stenhouse.

Kucherov reaction (Kucerov, Mikhail Grigorevich): Chemistry. See: Van Nostrand Chem. Dict.

KUDER, G. FREDERIC. fl. 1934-1975. American psychologist. See: Biog. Direct. Amer. Psych. Assoc., 1975. Kuder preference record, Kuder-Richardson coefficients of equivalence (or formulas).

Kuder preference record (Kuder, G. Frederic): Psychology. See: Chaplin; Encyc. Brit., under "Psychological Tests and Measurements," vol. 18, p. 735c; English; Wolman.

Kuder-Richardson coefficients of equivalence (or formulas) (Kuder, G. Frederic and Richardson, Marion Webster): Statistics. See: Chaplin; English; Good; Kendall; Wolman.

Kuehl cement (Kuehl, Hans Heinrich Gustav Christian): Engineering and Industry. See: Thrush.

KUEHL, HANS HEINRICH GUSTAV CHRISTIAN. b. 1879. German cement chemist. See: Pogg., vols. 5, 6, 7a. Kuehl cement.

KUEHNE, HANS. fl. 1949. German chemist. Cited in: Chem. Abstr., Decenn. Index, 1947-1956. Mueller-Kuehne process.

KUEHNE, WILHELM FRIEDRICH. 1837-1900. German physiologist and histologist. See: Dict. Sci. Biog. Kuehne's fiber, Kuehne's phenomenon, Kuehne's plate, Kuehne's spindle, Kuhne's granule?

Kuehne's fiber (Kuehne, Wilhelm Friedrich): Physiology. See: Dorland; Stedman.

Kuehne's phenomenon (Kuehne, Wilhelm Friedrich): Physiology. See: Dorland; Stedman.

Kuehne's plate (Kuehne, Wilhelm Friedrich): Anatomy. See: Dorland; Stedman.

Kuehne's spindle (Kuehne, Wilhelm Friedrich): Anatomy. See: Dorland; Stedman.

KUELZ, RUDOLPH EDUARD. 1845-1895. German physician. See: Biog. Lex. hervorr. Aerzte, 1880-1930. Kuelz' test, Kuelz's cylinder.

Kuelz' test (Kuelz, Rudolph Eduard): Medicine. See: Dorland; Stedman.

Kuelz's cylinder (Kuelz, Rudolph Eduard): Medicine. See: Dorland; Stedman.

KUEMMELL, HERMANN. 1852-1937. German surgeon. See: Biog. Lex. hervorr. Aerzte, 1880-1930. Kuemmell-Verneuil disease, Kuemmell's point.

Kuemmell-Verneuil disease (Kuemmell, Hermann and Verneuil, Aristide August Stanislaus): Medicine. See: Dorland; Jablonski; Stedman. Also known as: Kuemmell's disease (kyphosis or spondylitis).

Kuemmell's disease (kyphosis or spondylitis) (Kuemmell, Hermann). See: Kuemmell-Verneuil disease.

Kuemmell's point (Kuemmell, Hermann): Medicine. See: Dorland.

KUENTSCHER, GERHARD. 1902- . German surgeon. See: Deutsches Chirurgen Verzeichnis, 1938, p. 378. Kuentscher's nail.

Kuentscher's nail (Kuentscher, Gerhard): Medicine. See: Dorland; Stedman.

Kuess' disease (Kuess, Georges): Medicine. See: Jablonski.

KUESS, EMIL. 1815-1871. Strasburg physiologist. See: Biog. Lex. hervorr. Aerzte. Kuess' experiments.

Kuess' experiments (Kuess, Emil): Medicine. See: Dorland; Stedman.

KUESS, GEORGES. 1877-1967. French physician. See: Who's Who France, 7th ed. Kuess' disease.

KUESTER, ERNST G. 1839-1930. German surgeon. See: Biog. Lex. hervorr. Aerzte. Kuester's operation.

KUESTER, HERMANN. fl. 1910. German gynecologist. See: Gynaekol.-Verzeich., 1939, p. 268f. Mayer-Rokitansky-Kuester syndrome.

Kuester's operation (Kuester, Ernst G.): Medicine. See: Dorland; Stedman.

KUESTNER, HEINZ. 1897- . German gynecologist. See: Biog. Lex. hervorr. Aerzte, 1880-1930. Prausnitz-Kuestner reaction (test or antibody).

KUESTNER, OTTO ERNST. 1849-1931. German gynecologist. See: Index-Cat. Libr. Surg.-Gen. Off., 4th Ser., vol. 9, 1945. Kuestner's law, Kuestner's sign.

Kuestner's law (Kuestner, Otto Ernst): Medicine. See: Dorland.

Kuestner's sign (Kuestner, Otto Ernst): Medicine. See: Dorland; Stedman.

KUEVER, RUDOLPH ANDREW. b. 1886. American pharmacist. Cited in: Mansell. Kuever solution?

Kuever solution (Kuever, Rudolph Andrew?): Chemistry. See: Van Nostrand Chem. Dict.

Kufs' disease (Kufs, H.): Medicine. See: Jablonski; Stedman; Wolman.

KUFS, H. 1871-1955. German psychiatrist. (Biography source unavailable.) Kufs' disease.

KUGEL, MAURICE ALEXANDER. 1899-1946. American physician. See: New York Times, March 11, 1946, p. 25, col. 4. Kugel-Stoloff syndrome, Kugel's artery?

Kugel-Stoloff syndrome (Kugel, Maurice Alexander and Stoloff, E. Gordon): Medicine. See: Jablonski.

KUGELBERG, ERIC KLAS HENRIK. 1913- . Swedish neurologist. See: Who's Who Sci. Europe, 1972. Wohlfart-Kugelberg-Welander disease.

Kugelberg-Welander disease (Kugelberg, Eric Klas Henrik and Welander, Lisa). See: Wohlfart-Kugelberg-Welander disease.

Kugel's artery (Kugel, Maurice Alexander?): Medicine. See: Dorland.

Kuhio Day (Kalanianaole, Jonah Kuhio): Generic Word. See: Webster's 3d.

KUHL, HEINRICH. 1797-1821. German naturalist. Cited in: Mansell. Kuhlia.

Kuhlia (Kuhl, Heinrich): Zoology. See: Webster's 3d.

Kuhlmann-Anderson test (Kuhlmann, Frederick and Anderson, Rose Gustava): Psychology. See: Chaplin; English.

Kuhlmann-Binet test (Kuhlmann, Frederick and Binet, Alfred): Psychology. See: English; Wolman.

KUHLMANN, FREDERICK. 1876-1941. American psychologist. See: Amer. J. Ment. Defic., vol. 45 (1940-1941) pp. 3-7. Kuhlmann-Anderson test, Kuhlmann-Binet test.

KUHN, ADAM. 1741-1817. American physician and botanist. See: Dict. Amer. Biog. Kuhnia.

KUHN, CHARLES. fl. 1928. European chemist. Cited in: Chem. Abstr., vol. 23, p. 3944. Kuhn reagent.

KUHN, ERNST. 1873-1920. German physician. See: Biog. Lex. hervorr. Aerzte, 1880-1930. Kuhn's mask.

KUHN, FRANZ. 1866-1929. German surgeon. See: Biog. Lex. hervorr. Aerzte, 1880-1930. Kuhn's tube.

Kuhn reagent (Kuhn, Charles): Chemistry. See: Van Nostrand Chem. Dict.

KUHN, RICHARD JOHANN. 1900-1967. German chemist. See: Dict. Sci. Biog. Kuhn-Roth method.

Kuhn-Roth method (Kuhn, Richard Johann and Roth, Hubert): Chemistry. See: Van Nostrand Chem. Dict.

Kuhn-Thomas-Reiche f-sum rule (or f-sum rule of Thomas-Reiche-Kuhn) (Kuhn, Werner; Reiche, Fritz; and Thomas, W.?): Physics. See: Ballentyne.

KUHN, WERNER. 1899-1963. Swiss physical chemist. See: Dict. Sci. Biog. Kuhn-Thomas-Reiche f-sum rule.

KUHNE, HEINRICK. No dates. German histologist. (Biography source unavailable.) Kuhne's methylene blue.

uhne's granule (Kuehne, Wilhelm Friedrich?): Anatomy. See: Gray.

uhne's methylene blue (Kuhne, Heinrick): Chemistry. See: Dorland; Stedman.

uhnia (Kuhn, Adam): Botany. See: Charnock; Webster's 3d.

uhn's mask (Kuhn, Ernst): Medicine. See: Dorland; Stedman.

uhn's tube (Kuhn, Franz): Medicine. See: Dorland.

UHNT, HERMANN. 1850-1925. German ophthalmologist. See: Biog. Lex. ervorr. Aerzte, 1880-1930. Kuhnt-Junius degeneration (or disease), Kuhnt's peration, Kuhnt's spaces.

uhnt-Junius degeneration (or disease) (Kuhnt, Hermann and Junius, Paul): edicine. See: Stedman.

uhnt's operation (Kuhnt, Hermann): Medicine. See: Dorland; Stedman.

uhnt's spaces (Kuhnt, Hermann): Anatomy. See: Stedman.

UIPER, NICOLAAS H. 1920- . Dutch statistician. See: Who's Who Sci. urope, 1967. Kuiper statistic.

uiper statistic (Kuiper, Nicolaas H.): Statistics. See: Kendall.

ukersite (Derivation undetermined): Earth Sciences. See: Thrush.

UL'BERG, LEONID M. fl. 1930-1935. Russian chemist. Cited in: Chem. bstr., Decenn. Index, 1927-1936. Kul'berg-Matveeo test for hydrogen eroxide, Kul'berg test reaction for cerium, Kul'berg test reaction for cobalt, ul'berg test reaction for zinc.

ul'berg-Matveeo test for hydrogen peroxide (Kul'berg, Leonid M. and Matveev, .): Chemistry. See: Van Nostrand Chem. Dict.

ul'berg test reaction for cerium (Kul'berg, Leonid M.): Chemistry. See: Van ostrand Chem. Dict.

ul'berg test reaction for cobalt (Kul'berg, Leonid M.): Chemistry. See: Van ostrand Chem. Dict.

ul'berg test reaction for zinc (Kul'berg, Leonid M.): Chemistry. See: Van ostrand Chem. Dict.

ulchitsky cells (Kulchitsky, Nicholas): Medicine. See: Dorland; Stedman.

ULCHITSKY, NICHOLAS. 1856-1925. Russian histologist. See: Brit. Med. ., Lond., vol. 1 (1925), p. 340. Kulchitsky cells.

ULENKAMPFF, C. fl. 1956. German physician. (Biography source unavail-ble.) Kulenkampff-Tarnow syndrome.

ULENKAMPFF, DIETRICH. b. 1880. German surgeon. See: Biog. Lex. ervorr. Aerzte, 1880-1930. Kulenkampff's anesthesia.

ulenkampff-Tarnow syndrome (Kulenkampff, C. and Tarnow, G.): Medicine. ee: Jablonski.

ulenkampff's anesthesia (Kulenkampff, Dietrich): Medicine. See: Dorland; tedman.

ullbach-Liebler information number (Kullback, Solomon and Leibler, Richard rthur?): Statistics. See: Kendall.

ULLBACK, SOLOMON. 1907- . American mathematical statistician. See: mer. Men Sci., 10th ed. Kullbach-Liebler information number.

ullenberg corer (Kullenberg, E. Boerje): Earth Sciences. See: Van Nostrand ci. Encyc.

ULLENBERG, E. BOERJE. 1906- . Swedish oceanographer. See: Vem r Det ?, 1975. Kullenberg corer.

UMMER, ERNST EDUARD. 1810-1893. German mathematician. See: Dict. ci. Biog. Kummer's transformation (or test for convergence).

ummer's transformation (or test for convergence): Mathematics. See: allentyne; James.

UNDRAT, HANS. 1845-1893. German pathologist. See: World Who's Who ci. Kundrat's disease (or lymphosarcoma).

undrat's disease (or lymphosarcoma) (Kundrat, Hans): Medicine. See: Dorland; ablonski.

KUNDT, AUGUST. 1839-1894. German physicist. See: Dict. Sci. Biog. Kundt('s) constant, Kundt effect, Kundt method, Kundt('s) rule (1) (or law of bnormal dispersion), Kundt('s) tube, Kundt's dust figures, Kundt's rule (2)?, Kundt's rule (3)?

Kundt('s) constant (Kundt, August): Physics. See: Hackh; Hughes; Internat. Dict. Phys. Elec.; Van Nostrand Sci. Encyc.

Kundt effect (Kundt, August): Physics. See: Hackh; Internat. Dict. Phys. Elec.

Kundt method (Kundt, August): Physics. See: Van Nostrand Sci. Encyc.

Kundt('s) rule (1) (or law of abnormal dispersion) (Kundt, August): Physics. See: Ballentyne; Hackh; Hughes; Thewlis; Van Nostrand Sci. Encyc.

Kundt('s) tube (Kundt, August): Physics. See: Hackh; Hughes; Thewlis; Van Nostrand Sci. Encyc.; Webster's 3d.

Kundt's dust figures (Kundt, August): Physics. See: Dict. Sci. Biog.

Kundt's rule (2) (Kundt, August?): Physiology. See: Chaplin; Drever; English.

Kundt's rule (3) (Kundt, August?): Physiology. See: Chaplin; Drever; English.

KUNKEL, HENRY GEORGE. 1916- . American physician. See: Amer. Men Sci., 9th ed. Bearn-Kunkel syndrome.

KUNZ, GEORGE FREDERICK. 1856-1932. American mineralogist and gem ex-pert. See: World Who's Who Sci. Kunzite.

Kunz-Kraus reagent for cyanogen (Kunz-Krause, Hermann): Chemistry. See: Van Nostrand Chem. Dict.

KUNZ-KRAUSE, HERMANN (In full: JOHANN WILHELM HERMANN). 1861-1936. German pharmaceutical chemist. See: Pogg., vols. 4, 5, 6, 7a. Kunz-Kraus reagent for cyanogen, Kunz-Krause reagent for dicyanogen.

Kunz-Krause reagent for dicyanogen (Kunz-Krause, Hermann): Chemistry. See: Van Nostrand Chem. Dict.

Kunzite (Kunz, George Frederick): Earth Sciences. See: Encyc. Brit., 1973; Partridge; Van Nostrand Sci. Encyc.; Webster's 3d.

Kupffer, Adolph Theodore de. See: De Kupffer, Adolph Theodore.

Kupffer('s) cells (Kupffer, Karl Wilhelm von): Anatomy. See: Donath; Dorland; Pennak; Stedman; Webster's 3d.

KUPFFER, KARL WILHELM VON. 1829-1902. German anatomist. See: Biog. Lex. hervorr. Aerzte. Kupffer('s) cells, Kupffer's canal, Kupffer's vesicle.

Kupfferite (De Kupffer, Adolph Theodore): Earth Sciences. See: Webster's 3d.

Kupffer's canal (Kupffer, Karl Wilhelm von): Zoology. See: Gray.

Kupffer's vesicle (Kupffer, Karl Wilhelm von): Zoology. See: Gray.

Kupletskite (or Koupletskite) (Kupletsky, Boris Mikhailovich and Bonshtedt (Kupletskaya), Elza Maksimova): Earth Sciences. See: Thrush.

KUPLETSKY, BORIS MIKHAILOVICH. fl. 20th c. Russian petrographer. Cited in: Hintze, 2d suppl., p. 746. Kupletskite (or Koupletskite).

KUPRESSOFF, J. fl. 1870. Russian physician. Cited in: Kelly. Kupressoff's center.

Kupressoff's center (Kupressoff, J.): Anatomy. See: Donath; Dorland.

KURAS, M. fl. 1935. Rumanian chemist. Cited in: Chem. Abstr., Decenn. Index, 1927-1936. Dubsky-Kuras test reaction, Spacu-Kuras reagent.

KURATOWSKI, KAZIMIERZ. 1896- . Polish mathematician. See: Who's Who Sci. Europe, 1972. Kuratowski's lemma.

Kuratowski's lemma (Kuratowski, Kazimierz): Mathematics. See: James.

KURBATOV, V. I. fl. 1906. Russian chemist. Cited in: Chem. Abstr., Decenn. Index, 1907-1916. Kourbatoff('s) reagent(s).

KURCHATOV, IGOR VASILIEVICH. 1903-1960. Russian physicist. See: Dict. Sci. Biog. Kurchatovium.

Kurchatovium (Kurchatov, Igor Vasilievich): Chemistry. See: Barnhart (New Eng.); Van Nostrand Sci. Encyc. under "Element 104."

KURELLA, ERNST GOTTFRIED. 1725-1799. German physician. See: Biog. Lex. hervorr. Aerzte. See: Kurella's powder.

Kurella's powder (Kurella, Ernst Gottfried): Medicine. See: Dorland.

KURIE, FRANZ NEWELL DEVEREUX. 1907- . American physicist. See: Amer. Men Sci., 10th ed. Kurie plot.

Kurie plot (Kurie, Franz Newell Devereux): Physics. See: Ballentyne; Hughes; Internat. Dict. Phys. Elec.; Thewlis; Van Nostrand Sci. Encyc.; Webster's 3d. Also known as: Fermi plot.

KURLBAUM, FERDINAND. 1857-1927. German physicist. See: Dict. Sci. Biog. Holborn-Kurlbaum pyrometer, Kurlbaum method, Lummer and Kurlbaum's bolometer.

Kurlbaum method (Kurlbaum, Ferdinand): Physics. See: Thrush.

KURLOFF, MIKHAIL G. b. 1859. Russian physician. See: Biog. Lex. hervorr. Aerzte, 1880-1930. Kurloff's bodies.

Kurloff's bodies (Kurloff, Mikhail G.): Medicine. See: Dorland; Stedman.

KURNAKOV, NIKOLAI SEMYONOVICH. 1860-1941. Russian mineralogist. See: Dict. Sci. Biog. Kurnakovite (or Kurnakowit).

Kurnakovite (or Kurnakowit) (Kurnakov, Nikolai Semyonovich): Earth Sciences. See: Thrush; Webster's 3d.

Kurowski reagent (Derivation undetermined): Chemistry. See: Van Nostrand Chem. Dict.

Kurrol's salt (Derivation undetermined): Chemistry. See: Hackh.

Kurt Meyer method (Meyer, Kurt Otto Heinrich): Chemistry. See: Van Nostrand Chem. Dict.

KURTH, HEINRICH. 1860-1901. German bacteriologist. See: Biog. Lex. hervorr. Aerzte, 1880-1930. Kurthia.

Kurthia (Kurth, Heinrich): Zoology. See: Dorland.

KURZ, JAROMIR. 1895- . Czechoslovakian ophthalmologist. See: Turkevich and Turkevich. Kurz's syndrome.

KURZ (or KURTZ), KARL. b. 1881. German physicist. See: Pogg., vols. 5, 7a. Barkhausen-Kurz oscillator (or oscillations).

Kurzia latissima (Derivation undetermined): Zoology. See: Pennak.

KURZROK, RAPHAEL. b. 1895. Austrian-born American obstetrician. See: Amer. Men. Sci., 10th ed. Kurzrok-Ratner test.

Kurzrok-Ratner test (Kurzrok, Raphael and Ratner, Sarah?): Medicine. See: Stedman.

Kurz's syndrome (Kurz, Jaromir): Medicine. See: Jablonski.

Kussevitsky, Sergei Alexandrovich. See: Koussevitzky, Serge.

KUSSMAUL, ADOLF. 1822-1902. German physician. See: World Who's Who Sci. Kussmaul('s) breathing (or respiration), Kussmaul-Landry paralysis, Kussmaul-Meier syndrome, Kussmaul's aphasia, Kussmaul's coma, Kussmaul's pulse (or sign), Kussmaul's symptom.

Kussmaul('s) breathing (or respiration) (Kussmaul, Adolf): Medicine. See: Jablonski; Webster's 3d. Also known as: Kussmaul-Kien respiration.

Kussmaul-Kien respiration (Kussmaul, Adolph and Kien, Alphonse). See: Kussmaul breathing (or respiration).

Kussmaul-Landry paralysis (Kussmaul, Adolf and Landry, Jean Baptiste Octave). See: Landry's paralysis.

Kussmaul-Meier syndrome (Kussmaul, Adolf and Maier, Rudolf Robert): Medicine. See: Jablonski. Also known as: Kussmaul's disease.

Kussmaul's aphasia (Kussmaul, Adolf): Medicine. See: Jablonski; Stedman.

Kussmaul's coma (Kussmaul, Adolf): Medicine. See: Dorland; Jablonski; Stedman.

Kussmaul's disease (Kussmaul, Adolf). See: Kussmaul-Meier syndrome.

Kussmaul's pulse (or sign) (Kussmaul, Adolf): Medicine. See: Jablonski; Stedman.

Kussmaul's symptom (Kussmaul, Adolf): Medicine. See: Dorland; Stedman.

Kutta-Joukowski law (or hypothesis) (Kutta, Martin Wilhelm and Schukowski, Nikolaj Egorovic): Physics. See: Internat. Dict. Ap. Math; Thewlis.

KUTTA, MARTIN WILHELM. 1867-1944. German mathematician. See: Pogg. vols. 4, 5. Kutta-Joukowski law (or hypothesis), Runge-Kutta method.

KUTTER, WILHELM R. 1818-1888. German engineer. Cited in: Mansell. Kutter's formula.

Kutter's formula (Kutter, Wilhelm R.): Engineering and Industry. See: Thrush.

KUTZELNIGG, ARTUR. 1904- . German chemist. See: Pogg., vols. 6, 7a. Kutzlnigg test for isobutyl alcohol.

Kutzlnigg test for isobutyl alcohol (Kutzelnigg, Artur): Chemistry. See: Van Nostrand Chem. Dict.

KVEIM, MORTON ANSGAR. b. 1892. Norwegian physician. (Biography source unavailable.) Kveim test.

Kveim test (Kveim, Morton Ansgar): Medicine. See: Stedman. Also known as: Nickerson-Kveim test.

Kvellite (Derivation undetermined): Earth Sciences. See: Thrush.

KWINT, L. A. fl. 1925-1931. German? psychiatrist. Cited in: Cam. Auth. Index to Psych. Index, 1894-1935, and Psych. Abstr., 1927-1958. Kwint psychomotor test.

Kwint psychomotor test (Kwint, L. A.): Psychology. See: English; Wolman.

KYAN, JOHN HOWARD. 1774-1850. Irish inventor. See: World Who's Who Sci. Kyanize (or Kyan's process).

Kyanize (or Kyan's process) (Kyan, John Howard): Engineering and Industry. See: Charnock; Partridge; Thrush; Weekley.

KYLE, BARBARA. fl. 1949. English? librarian. Cited in: Libr. Lit., 1949-1951. Kyle classification.

Kyle classification (Kyle, Barbara): Library Science. See: Harrod.

KYLLING, PEDER. ca. 1640-1696. Danish botanist. See: Danmarks hist. Bla bog. Killingia (or Kyllingia).

KYRLE, JOHN, THE MAN OF ROSS. 1637-1724. English philanthropist. See: Dict. Nat. Biog. Kyrle Society.

KYRLE, JOSEF. 1880-1926. Austrian dermatologist. See: Biog. Lex. hervorr. Aerzte, 1880-1930. Kyrle's disease.

Kyrle Society (Kyrle, John, the Man of Ross): Philanthropy. See: Harvey.

Kyrle's disease (Kyrle, Josef): Medicine. See: Jablonski.

L

a Reine (symphony) (Marie Antoinette): Music. See: Scholes.

AAR (or LAER), PIETER VAN (Nickname: Il BAMBOCCIO). ca. 1592-1642. Dutch painter. See: Webster's Biog. Dict. bambocciades (bambocciate or bambochades), bamboche.

ABADIE, JEAN DE. 1610-1674. French religious reformer. See: Encyc. Brit., 1973. Labadists (or Labadism).

abadists (or Labadism) (Labadie, Jean de): Religion. See: Canney; Latham; Mathews, S. C.; Wagner (Names); Webster's 3d.

aban dance notation system (or Labanotation) (Laban, Rudolf von): Dance. See: Chujoy; Hendrickson; Webster's 3d.

ABAN, RUDOLF VON. 1879-1958. Slovac teacher and theorist. See: New Encyc. Brit., 1974, Microp. Laban dance notation system (or Labanotation).

ABARRAQUE, ANTOINE GERMAINE. 1777-1850. French apothecary. See: World Who's Who Sci. Labarraque('s) solution.

abarraque('s) solution (Labarraque, Antoine Germaine): Chemistry. See: Dorland; Hackh; Stedman; Webster's 3d.

ABAT, JEAN-ANDRE. b. 1877. French chemist. Cited in: Chem. Abstr., Decenn. Index, 1927-1936. Deniges-Lebat test reactions for arsphenamine.

ABAT, JEAN BAPTISTE. 1663-1738. French Dominican Missionary. See: Nouv. Biog. Univ. Labatia.

abatia (Labat, Jean Baptiste): Botany. See: Charnock.

ABBE, ERNEST MARCEL. 1870-1939. French physician. See: Biog. Lex. ervorr. Aerzte, 1880-1930. Labbe's syndrome (or neurocirculatory syndrome).

ABBE, LEON. 1832-1916. French surgeon. See: World Who's Who Sci. Labbe's triangle, Labbe's vein.

abbe's syndrome (or neurocirculatory syndrome): Medicine. See: Jablonski; tedman.

abbe's triangle (Labbe, Leon): Anatomy. See: Donath; Dorland.

abbe's vein (Labbe, Leon): Anatomy. See: Donath; Dorland; Stedman.

aBel tube (Derivation undetermined): Chemistry. See: Hackh.

ABHART, A. fl. 1956. Swiss physician. (Biography source unavailable.) rader-Labhart-Willi-Fanconi syndrome.

ABICHE, JACQUES VINCENT. d. ca. 1888. French pharmacist. See: Dursel. Labiche reagent?

abiche reagent (Labiche, Jacques Vincent?): Chemistry. See: Van Nostrand Chem. Dict.

ABORDE, JEAN-BAPTISTE-VINCENT. 1831-1903. French physician. See: World Who's Who Sci. Laborde('s) method, Laborde's forceps, Laborde's sign.

aborde('s) method (Laborde, Jean-Baptiste-Vincent): Medicine. See: Dorland; Stedman; Thrush.

aborde's forceps (Laborde, Jean-Baptiste-Vincent): Medicine. See: Dorland; Stedman.

aborde's sign (Laborde, Jean-Baptiste-Vincent): Medicine. See: Dorland.

abouchere (betting system) (Labouchere, Henri du Pre): Recreation and Sports. See: Webster's 3d.

LABOUCHERE, HENRI DU PRE. 1831-1912. English journalist and political leader. See: Encyc. Brit., 1973. Labouchere (betting system).

LABOULBENE, JEAN-JOSEPH-ALEXANDRE. 1825-1898. French physician and entomologist. See: World Who's Who Sci. Laboulbenia.

Laboulbenia (Laboulbene, Jean-Joseph-Alexandre): Botany. See: Webster's 3d.

Labountsovite (Labunzov, A. N. and Labunzova-Kostyleva, E. E.). See: Labuntzovite.

La Bour centrifugal pump (La Bour, Harry E.): Engineering and Industry. See: Thrush.

LA BOUR, HARRY E. fl. 1938-1942. American engineer. Cited in: Chem. Abstr., Decenn. Index, 1937-1946. La Bour centrifugal pump.

Labuntzovite (Labuntsovite or Labountsovite) (Labunzov, A. N. and Labunzova-Kostyleva, E. E.): Earth Sciences. See: Thrush.

LABUNZOV, A. N. fl. 20th c. Russian scientist. Cited in: Hintze, 2d suppl., p. 628. Labuntzovite (Labuntsovite or Labountsovite).

LABUNZOVA-KOSTYLEVA, E. E. fl. 20th c. Russian scientist. Cited in: Hintze, 2d suppl., p. 628. Lubuntzovite (Labuntsovite or Labountsovite).

Laby and Hercus method for mechanical equivalent of heat (Laby, Thomas Howell and Hercus, Eric Oswald): Physics. See: Internat. Dict. Phys. Elec.

LABY, THOMAS HOWELL. 1880-1946. Australian physicist. See: World Who's Who Sci. Hercus and Laby method for heat transmission of gases, Laby and Hercus method for mechanical equivalent of heat.

Lacey Act (Lacey, John Fletcher): Law. See: Black.

LACEY, JOHN FLETCHER. 1841-1913. American legislator. See: Biog. Direct. Amer. Congress. Lacey Act.

LACHENAL, WERNHARD DE. 1736-1800. Swiss botanist. See: Dict. Hist. Biog. Suisse. Lachenalia.

Lachenalia (Lachenal, Wernhard de): Botany. See: Charnock; Taylor, N.; Webster's 3d.

LACHMAN, ARTHUR. b. 1873. American chemist. See: Pogg., vols. 4, 5, 6. Lachman process.

Lachman process (Lachman, Arthur): Chemistry. See: Van Nostrand Chem. Dict.

LA COSTE, LUCIEN J. B. fl. 1934. French? seismologist. (Biography source unavailable.) La Coste pendulum, LaCoste-Romberg gravimeter, La Coste seismograph.

La Coste pendulum (La Coste, Lucien J. B.): Earth Sciences. See: Encyc. Brit., 1973 under "Seismology," vol. 20, p. 177c.

LaCoste-Romberg gravimeter (La Coste, Lucien J. B. and Romberg, Frederick Ernst): Earth Sciences. See: Encyc. Brit., 1973 under "Gravitation," vol. 10, p. 723a; Thrush.

La Coste seismograph (La Coste, Lucien J. B.): Earth Sciences. See: Encyc. Brit., 1973 under "Gravitation," vol. 10, p. 722d.

LA COUR, DAN BARFOD. 1876-1942. Danish geodesist. See: Pogg., vol. 6, 7b. LaCour magnetometer.

LaCour magnetometer (LaCour, Dan Barfod): Earth Sciences. See: Thrush.

lacrima (lachryma) Christi (wine) (Jesus Christ): Food and Drink. See: De Sola; Partridge; Weekley.

LACROIX, ALFRED (In full: Francois Antoine Alfred). 1863-1948. French mineralogist. See: Dict. Sci. Biog. Lacroix test?, Lacroixite.

Lacroix test (Lacroix, Alfred?): Chemistry. See: Van Nostrand Chem. Dict.

Lacroixite (Lacroix, Alfred): Earth Sciences. See: Thrush; Webster's 3d.

lactobacillus Leichmannii (Leichmann, Georg?): Zoology. See: Stedman.

LADD-FRANKLIN, CHRISTINE. 1847-1930. American psychologist and logician. See: World Who's Who Sci. Ladd-Franklin theory (or theory of color vision), Ladd-Franklin's principle of the syllogism.

Ladd-Franklin theory (or theory of color vision) (Ladd-Franklin, Christine): Physiology. See: Chaplin; Drever; English; Internat. Dict. Phys. Elec.; Stedman.

Ladd-Franklin's principle of the syllogism (Ladd-Franklin, Christine): Philosophy. See: Edwards.

Ladd-Gross syndrome (Ladd, William Edwards and Gross, Robert Edward): Medicine. See: Jablonski.

LADD, WILLIAM EDWARDS. b. 1880. American surgeon. See: Amer. Men Sci., 10th ed. Ladd-Gross syndrome, Ladd's syndrome.

Ladd's syndrome (Ladd, William Edwards): Medicine. See: Jablonski.

LADENBURG, ALBERT. 1842-1911. German chemist. See: Dict. Sci. Biog. Ladenburg flask, Ladenburg formula, Ladenburg test for omicron-diamines.

Ladenburg F value (Ladenburg, Rudolf Walther): Physics. See: Internat. Dict. Phys. Elec.

Ladenburg flask (Ladenburg, Albert): Chemistry. See: Hackh; Van Nostrand Chem. Dict.; Webster's 3d.

Ladenburg formula (Ladenburg, Albert): Chemistry. See: Hackh.

Ladenburg law (or law of Ladenburg) (Ladenburg, Rudolf Walther): Physics. See: Hackh; Van Nostrand Sci. Encyc.

LADENBURG, RUDOLF WALTHER. 1882-1952. German-born American physicist. See: Dict. Sci. Biog. Ladenburg F value, Ladenburg law (or law of Ladenburg).

Ladenburg test for omicron-diamines (Ladenburg, Albert): Chemistry. See: Van Nostrand Chem. Dict.

LADENDORFF, AUGUST. fl. 1884. German physician. Cited in: Mansell. Ladendorff's test.

Ladendorff's test (Ladendorff, August): Medicine. See: Dorland; Stedman.

Ladies of Mary (Mary, Virgin-Mother): Religion. See: Attwater.

LADIN, LOUIS JULIUS. b. 1862. American obstetrician. See: Hartshorn. Ladin's sign (or test).

Ladino white clover (Derivation undetermined): Botany. See: Winburne.

Ladin's sign (or test) (Ladin, Louis Julius): Medicine. See: Dorland; Stedman. Also known as: Ladinski's sign (or test).

Ladinski, Louis Julius. See: Ladin, Louis Julius.

Ladinski's sign (or test) (Ladin, Louis Julius). See: Ladin's sign (or test).

Lady altar (Mary, Virgin-Mother): Religion. See: Webster's 3d.

Lady Amherst's pheasant (Amherst, Sarah Elizabeth): Zoology. See: Webster's 3d.

Lady Astor (Astor, Nancy Langhorne): Food and Drink. See: Stenhouse.

Lady Baltimore cake (Calvert, Mrs. George, Lady Baltimore): Food and Drink. See: De Sola; Webster's 3d.

Lady Bareacres (Bareacres, Countess of) Generic Word. See: Partridge.

Lady Bountiful (Bountiful, Lady): Generic Word (charitable). See: Latham; Partridge; Webster's 3d.

Lady Byng Trophy (Byng, Lady Marie Evelyn Moreton): Recreation and Sports. See: Encyc. Brit., 1973 under "Ice Hockey," p. 1033.

Lady chapel (Mary, Virgin-Mother): Religion. See: Encyc. Brit., 1973; Webster's 3d.

Lady Clara Vere de Vere (Vere de Vere, Lady Clara, the fictional character): Generic Word (disdainful aristocrat). See: Partridge.

Lady Day (Mary, Virgin-Mother): Religion. See: Webster's 3d.

Lady Godiva (Godiva): Generic Word (undraped woman). See: Hendrickson.

Lady Margaret foundations (Beaufort, Margaret): Education. See: Harvey.

Ladybug (Ladybird beetle or Lady beetle) (Mary, Virgin-Mother): Zoology. See: Encyc. Brit., 1973; Webster's 3d.

Lady's bedstraw (or Our Lady's bedstraw) (Mary, Virgin-Mother): Botany. See: Webster's 3d.

Lady's-mantle(s) (Mary, Virgin-Mother): Botany. See: Encyc. Brit., 1973; Webster's 3d.

Laelia (Laelius, Gaius? or Laelius, Gaius "Sapiens"?): Botany. See: Hendrickson; Taylor, N.; Webster's 3d.

LAELIUS, GAIUS. d. ca. 165 B.C. Roman statesman. See: Dict. Grk. Rom. Biog. Myth. Laelia?

LAELIUS, GAIUS "SAPIENS." fl. 2d c. B.C. Roman statesman. See: Dict. Grk. Rom. Biog. Myth. Laelia?

LAENNEC, RENE THEOPHILE HYACINTHE. 1781-1826. French physician. See: Dict. Sci. Biog. Laennec's catarrh, Laennec's cirrhosis, Laennec's pearls, Laennec's suffocative catarrh, Laennec's thrombus.

Laennec's catarrh (Laennec, Rene Theophile Hyacinthe): Medicine. See: Dorland; Stedman.

Laennec's cirrhosis (Laennec, Rene Theophile Hyacinthe): Medicine. See: Jablonski; Stedman; Van Nostrand Sci. Encyc.; Webster's 3d. Also known as: Morgagni-Laennec syndrome.

Laennec's pearls (Laennec, Rene Theophile Hyacinthe): Medicine. See: Dorland; Stedman.

Laennec's suffocative catarrh (Laennec, Rene Theophile Hyacinthe): Medicine. See: Stedman.

Laennec's thrombus (Laennec, Rene Theophile Hyacinthe): Medicine. See: Stedman.

LAER KRONIG, RALPH DE. 1904- . German physicist. See: Pogg., vol. 6. Kramers-Kronig dispersion formula, Kronig-Penney model.

Laer, Pieter van. See: Laar, Pieter van.

LAEWEN, ARTHUR. b. 1876. German physician. See: Biog. Lex. hervorr. Aerzte, 1880-1930. Buedinger-Ludloff-Laewen disease (or syndrome), Laewen's irrigation tube.

Laewen's irrigation tube (Laewen, Arthur): Medicine. Cited in: Biog. Lex. hervorr. Aerzte, 1880-1930.

La Farge cement (Derivation undetermined): Engineering and Industry. See: Thrush.

Lafayette (1) (butterfish) (Lafayette, Marie Joseph Paul Yves Roch Gilbert du Motier, Marquis de): Zoology. See: Webster's 3d.

Lafayette (2) (or Lafayette fish) (spot) (Lafayette, Marie Joseph Paul Yves Roch Gilbert due Motier, Marquis de): Zoology. See: Charnock; Clapin; Partridge.

Lafayette Escadrille (Lafayette, Marie Joseph Paul Yves Roch Gilbert du Motier, Marquis de): History. See: Jameson.

Lafayette formation (Derivation undetermined): Earth Sciences. See: Thrush.

LAFAYETTE, MARIE JOSEPH PAUL YVES ROCH GILBERT DU MOTIER, MARQUIS DE. 1757-1834. French soldier and statesman. See: Encyc. Brit., 1973. Lafayette Escadrille, Lafayette (1) (butterfish), Lafayette (submarine), Lafayette (2) (or Lafayette fish) (spot).

Lafayette (submarine) (Lafayette, Marie Joseph Paul Yves Roch Gilbert du Motier, Marquis de): Navigation. See: Encyc. Brit., 1973 under "Submarine," vol. 21, p. 340c.

Laffer-Ascher syndrome (Laffer, W. B. and Ascher, Karl Wolfgang). See: Ascher's syndrome.

LAFFER, W. B. fl. 1909. American physician. (Biography source unavailable.) Laffer-Ascher syndrome.

LAFFITTE (LAFITTE), JEAN. ca. 1780-ca. 1825. French pirate. See: Encyc. Brit., 1973. Lafittes.

Lafittes (Laffitte, Jean): History. See: Matthews, M. M.

La Follette-Bulwinkle Act (La Follette, Robert Marion, Jr. and Bulwinkle, Alfred Lee): Politics. See: Smith.

A FOLLETTE, ROBERT MARION, JR. 1895-1953. American legislator. See: og. Direct. Amer. Congress. La Follette–Bulwinkle Act.

A FOLLETTE, ROBERT MARION, SR. 1855-1925. American legislator. See: og. Direct. Amer. Congress. LaFollette Seamen's Act, Lloyd–LaFollette Act?

aFollette Seamen's Act (LaFollette, Robert Marion, Sr.): Politics. See: mith.

a Follie, Louis Guillaume. See: De la Follie, Louis Guillaume.

a Follie's finishing (De la Follie, Louis Guillaume): Chemistry. Cited in: 'orld Who's Who Sci.

AFOND, EUGENE C. 1909– . American oceanographer. See: World Who's Who Sci. Lafond's tables.

afond's tables (Lafond, Eugene C.): Earth Sciences. See: Huschke; Thrush.

afora bodies (Lafora, Gonzalo Rodriguez): Medicine. See: Stedman.

AFORA, GONZALO RODRIGUEZ. b. 1886. Spanish neurologist. See: iog. Lex. hervorr. Aerzte, 1880-1930. Lafora bodies, Unverricht–Lafora isease.

agarousse levers (ratchet or wheel) (Garousse, M. de la): Engineering and dustry. See: Auger.

AGERMAN, ALEXANDER. 1836-1904. Swedish inventor. See: Svenska Maen Och Kvinnor. Lagerman typotheter.

agerman typotheter (Lagerman, Alexander): Printing. See: Lockwood.

AGERSTROEM, MAGNUS. 1691-1759. Swedish naturalist and merchant. ee: Svenska Maen Och Kvinnor. Lagerstroemia.

agerstroemia (Lagerstroem, Magnus): Botany. See: Charnock; Taylor, N.; 'ebster's 3d.

agrange bracket (Lagrange, Joseph Louis): Mathematics. See: Internat. Dict. p. Math.; Internat. Dict. Phys. Elec.; Thewlis.

agrange bracket of optics (Lagrange, Joseph Louis): Physics. See: Internat. ict. Ap. Math.

agrange density (Lagrange, Joseph Louis): Mathematics. See: Internat. Dict. p. Math.; Internat. Dict. Phys. Elec.; Van Nostrand Sci. Encyc.

agrange differential equation (Lagrange, Joseph Louis): Mathematics. See: allentyne.

agrange('s) equations (of motion) (Lagrange, Joseph Louis): Physics. See: allentyne; Internat. Dict. Phys. Elec.; Thewlis.

agrange field equations (Lagrange, Joseph Louis): Mathematics. See: Internat. ict. Ap. Math.; Internat. Dict. Phys. Elec.

agrange–Helmholtz equation (Lagrange, Joseph Louis and Helmholtz, Hermann udwig Ferdinand von). See: Helmholtz('s) relation (or equation for optical agnification).

agrange('s) identity (Lagrange, Joseph Louis): Mathematics. See: Ballentyne; ternat. Dict. Ap. Math.; Internat. Dict. Phys. Elec.; Van Nostrand Sci. ncyc. under "Differential Equation (Integral Solution of)."

AGRANGE, JOSEPH LOUIS. 1736-1813. French mathematician, physicist nd astronomer. See: Dict. Sci. Biog. Euler–Lagrange equations, Lagrange racket, Lagrange bracket of optics, Lagrange density, Lagrange('s) equations (of ation), Lagrange field equations, Lagrange theorem (1), Lagrange('s) identity, agrange('s) multipliers (or method of multipliers), Lagrange's differential equation, agrange's form of the remainder for Taylor's theorem, Lagrange's interpolation ormula (or formula of (for) interpolation), Lagrange's theorem (2), Lagrange's heorem (3) (or theorem in group theory), Lagrange's theorem (4) of divisibility, agrangian and Hamiltonian formalism for continuous systems, Lagrangian coordi- ates, Lagrangian correlation, Lagrangian description of flow, Lagrangian dif- erentiation, Lagrangian equations, Lagrangian equilibrium point, Lagrangian ormalism for field systems, Lagrangian (function), Lagrangian method of analysis, agrangian method of current measurement, Lagrangian wave.

agrange('s) multipliers (or method of multipliers) (Lagrange, Joseph Louis): Mathematics. See: Ballentyne; Internat. Dict. Ap. Math.; James; Van Nostrand Sci. Encyc.

AGRANGE, PIERRE-FELIX. 1857-1928. French ophthalmologist. See: Biog. ex. hervorr. Aerzte, 1880-1930. Legrange's operation.

agrange theorem (1) (Lagrange, Joseph Louis). See: Helmholtz('s) relation or equation for optical magnification).

Lagrange's form of the remainder for Taylor's theorem (Lagrange, Joseph Louis): Mathematics. See: James.

Lagrange's interpolation formula (or formula of (for) interpolation) (Lagrange, Joseph Louis): Mathematics. See: Ballentyne; James; Van Nostrand Sci. Encyc.

Lagrange's operation (Lagrange, Pierre-Felix): Medicine. See: Dorland; Stedman.

Lagrange's theorem (2) (Lagrange, Joseph Louis): Mathematics. See: Ballentyne.

Lagrange's theorem (3) (or theorem in group theory) (Lagrange, Joseph Louis): Mathematics. See: Ballentyne; James.

Lagrange's theorem (4) of divisibility (Lagrange, Joseph Louis): Mathematics. See: Ballentyne.

Lagrangian and Hamiltonian formalism for continuous systems (Lagrange, Joseph Louis and Hamilton, Sir William Rowan): Mathematics. See: Internat. Dict. Ap. Math.

Lagrangian coordinates (Lagrange, Joseph Louis): Earth Sciences. See: Huschke; Internat. Dict. Ap. Math.; Van Nostrand Sci. Encyc.

Lagrangian correlation (Lagrange, Joseph Louis): Physics. See: Huschke; Internat. Dict. Ap. Math.

Lagrangian description of flow (Lagrange, Joseph Louis): Physics. See: Van Nostrand Sci. Encyc.

Lagrangian differentiation (Lagrange, Joseph Louis): Mathematics. See: Internat. Dict. Ap. Math.

Lagrangian equations (Lagrange, Joseph Louis): Physics. See: Huschke.

Lagrangian equilibrium point (Lagrange, Joseph Louis): Physics. See: Internat. Dict. Ap. Math.

Lagrangian formalism for field systems (Lagrange, Joseph Louis): Mathematics. See: Internat. Dict. Ap. Math.

Lagrangian (function) (Lagrange, Joseph Louis): Mathematics. See: Ballentyne; James; Thewlis; Van Nostrand Sci. Encyc.

Lagrangian method of analysis (Lagrange, Joseph Louis): Physics. See: Internat. Dict. Ap. Math.

Lagrangian method of current measurement (Lagrange, Joseph Louis): Earth Sciences. See: Thrush.

Lagrangian wave (Lagrange, Joseph Louis): Earth Sciences. See: Huschke.

LA GUARDIA, FIORELLO HENRY. 1882-1947. American legislator. See: Biog. Direct. Amer. Congress. Norris–La Guardia Act.

Laguerre('s) differential equation (or equation) (Laguerre, Edmond Nicolas): Mathematics. See: James; Thewlis; Van Nostrand Sci. Encyc.

LAGUERRE, EDMOND NICOLAS. 1834-1886. French mathematician. See: Dict. Sci. Biog. associated Laguerre functions, associated Laguerre polynomials, Laguerre polynomial(s), Laguerre('s) differential equation (or equation).

Laguerre polynomial(s) (Laguerre, Edmond Nicolas): Mathematics. See: Ballen- tyne; Internat. Dict. Ap. Math.; Internat. Dict. Phys. Elec.; James; Kendall.

Laguna, Andres de. See: De Laguna, Andres.

Lagunaria (De Laguna, Andres): Botany. See: Taylor, N.

LAILLER, AMAND FREDERIC. fl. 1884-1897. French pharmacist. See: Oursel. Lailler reagent?

Lailler reagent (Lailler, Amand Frederic?): Chemistry. See: Van Nostrand Chem. Dict.

LAIN, EVERETT SAMUEL. b. 1876. American dermatologist. (Biography source unavailable.) Lain's disease.

LAINER, ALEXANDER. 1858-1923. Austrian chemist. See: Lex., Oesterr. Biog. 1815-1950. Lainer (or Lanier) effect.

Lainer (or Lanier) effect (Lainer, Alexander): Photography. See: Focal Encyc. Photog.; Van Nostrand Sci. Encyc.

Lain's disease (Lain, Everett Samuel): Medicine. See: Dorland.

LAIS. Several courtesans in ancient Greece (5th and 4th c. B.C.) See: Encyc. Brit., 1973. Lais.

Lais (Lais, the courtesan): Generic Word (beautiful woman). See: Partridge.

LAKE, RICHARD. 1861-1949. English otorhinolaryngologist. See: World Who's Who Sci. Lake's pigment.

Lake's pigment (Lake, Richard): Medicine. See: Dorland.

LAKI, KOLOMAN. 1909- . Hungarian-born American physiologist. See: Amer. Men Sci., 10th ed. Laki-Lorand factor.

Laki-Lorand factor (Laki, Koloman and Lorand, Lazlo): Physiology. See: Stedman.

Laland firethorn (Derivation undetermined): Botany. See: Winburne.

Lalande cell (De Lalande). See: Edison-Lelande cell.

Lalique (glassware) (Lalique, Rene): Applied Arts. See: Partridge.

LALIQUE, RENE. 1860-1945. French jeweller and glassmaker. See: Encyc. Brit., 1973. Lalique (glassware).

LALLA ROOKH. Character in Thomas Moore's story of the same name (1817). See: Harvey. Lalla Rookh (mantle).

Lalla Rookh (mantle) (Lalla Rookh): Fashion. See: Charnock.

LALLEMAND, CLAUDE FRANCOIS. 1790-1854. French surgeon. See: World Who's Who Sci. Lallemand's bodies.

Lallemand's bodies (Lallemand, Claude Francois): Anatomy. See: Donath; Dorland; Stedman. Also known as: Trousseau-Lallemand bodies.

LALOUETTE, PIERRE. 1711-1742. French physician. See: Biog. Lex. hervorr. Aerzte. Lalouette's (Lallouette's) pyramid(s).

Lalouette's (Lallouette's) pyramid(s) (Lalouette, Pierre): Anatomy. See: Donath; Dorland; Stedman. Also known as: Morgagni's appendix.

LAMAN. Son of the Jewish prophet Lehi in the Book of Mormon (Jacob 3:5). (Biography source unavailable.) Lamanite.

Lamanite (Laman): Religion. See: Mathews, M. M.; Webster's 3d.

LAMARCK, JEAN BAPTISTE PIERRE ANTOINE DE MONET, CHEVALIER DE. 1744-1829. French naturalist. See: Dict. Sci. Biog. Lamarckia, Lamarckian theory (Lamarckianism or Lamarckian), Monetia.

Lamarckia (Lamarck, Jean Baptiste Pierre Antoine de Monet, Chavalier de): Botany. See: Taylor, N.

Lamarckian theory (Lamarckianism or Lamarckian) (Lamarck, Jean Baptiste Pierre Antoine de Monet, Chevalier de): Genetics. See: Encyc. Brit., 1973; Van Nostrand Sci. Encyc.; Webster's 3d.

LAMAZE, FERNAND. 1890-1957. French obstetrician. Cited in: Mansell. Lamaze (method).

Lamaze (method) (Lamaze, Fernand): Medicine. See: Barnhart (New Eng.)

LAMB, CHARLES (Pseud., ELIA). 1775-1834. English essayist and critic. See: Dict. Amer. Biog. Elian.

Lamb constant L (Lamb, Willis Eugene, Jr.): Physics. See: Internat. Dict. Ap. Math.

LAMB, E. H. fl. 20th c. Engineer. (Biography source unavailable.) Lamb's extensometer.

Lamb engine (Lamb, John): Engineering and Industry. See: Auger.

LAMB, JOHN. fl. 1842. English engineer. (Biography source unavailable.) Lamb engine.

Lamb-Retherford shift (Lamb, Willis Eugene, Jr. and Retherford, Robert). See: Lamb shift.

Lamb shift (Lamb, Willis Eugene, Jr.): Physics. See: Ballentyne; Internat. Dict. Ap. Math.; Internat. Dict. Phys. Elec.; Thewlis; Van Nostrand Sci. Encyc. Also known as: Lamb-Retherford shift.

LAMB, WILLIS EUGENE, JR. 1913- . American physicist. See: World Who's Who Sci. Lamb constant L, Lamb shift.

LAMBARDE, WILLIAM. 1536-1601. English historian. See: Dict. Nat. Biog. Lambard's archaion, Lambard's archaionomia, Lambard's eirenarcha.

Lambard's archaion (Lambarde, William): Law. See: Black.

Lambard's archaionomia (Lambarde, William): Law. See: Black.

Lambard's eirenarcha (Lambarde, William): Law. See: Black.

Lambert (Lambert, Daniel): Generic Word (immensity). See: Hendrickson.

Lambert (Lambert, Johann Heinrich): Physics. See: Ballentyne; Dresner; Focal Encyc. Photog.; Hughes; Van Nostrand Sci. Encyc.: Webster's 3d.

LAMBERT, ALEXANDER. 1861-1939. American physician. See: J. A. M. A., vol. 112 (1939) p. 2079. Lambert's treatment.

LAMBERT, AYLMER BOURKE. 1761-1842. English botanist. See: World Who's Who Sci. Lambert cherry?, Lambert crazyweed?, Lambert mottle?, Lambert pine.

Lambert-Bouguer law of absorption (Lambert, Johann Heinrich and Bouguer, Pierre). See: Bouguer's law.

Lambert chart (Lambert, Johann Heinrich): Geography. See: Van Nostrand Sci. Encyc. under "Lambert projection."

Lambert cherry (Lambert, Aylmer Bourke?): Botany. See: Hendrickson under "Bing."

Lambert('s) cosine law (law (1), law of emission or law of illumination) (Lambert, Johann Heinrich): Physics. See: Ballentyne; Hughes; Huschke; Internat. Dict. Phys. Elec.; Van Nostrand Sci. Encyc.; Webster's 3d.

Lambert crazyweed (Lambert, Aylmer Bourke?): Botany. See: Winburne.

LAMBERT, DANIEL. 1770-1809. English jailkeeper. See: Encyc. Brit., 1973. Lambert.

Lambert-Eaton syndrome (Lambert, Edward H. and Eaton, Lee M.). See: Eaton-Lambert syndrome.

LAMBERT, EDWARD HOWARD. 1915- . American physiologist. See: World Who's Who Sci. Eaton-Lambert syndrome.

LAMBERT, JOHANN HEINRICH. 1728-1777. German mathematician, physicist, astronomer, and philosopher. See: World Who's Who Sci. Bouguer-Lambert law of absorption, foot-Lambert, Lambert, Lambert chart, Lambert line, Lambert projection (conformal conic projection or conformal projection), Lambert track, Lambert('s) cosine law (law (1), law of emission or law of illumination), Lambert' azimuthal equal-area (or equivalent azimuthal projection), Lambert's blue, Lambert's diagrams, Lambert's formula, Lambert's zenithal equal area projection.

Lambert('s) law (2) (law of absorption or law of Lambert) (Lambert, Johann Heinrich). See: Bouguer's law.

Lambert line (Lambert, Johann Heinrich): Geography. See: Internat. Dict. Ap. Math.; Van Nostrand Sci. Encyc. under "Lambert projection."

Lambert mottle (Lambert, Aylmer Bourke?): Botany. See: Winburne.

Lambert pine (Lambert, Aylmer Bourke): Botany. See: Webster's 3d.

Lambert projection (conformal conic projection or conformal projection) (Lambert, Johann Heinrich): Geography. See: Huschke; Internat. Dict. Ap. Math.; Thewlis; Van Nostrand Sci. Encyc.; Webster's 3d.

LAMBERT (LANTBERT), SAINT. ca. 636-ca. 708. Belgian saint. See: Holweck. St. Lambert's Day.

Lambert track (Lambert, Johann Heinrich): Navigation. See: Van Nostrand Sci. Encyc. under "Track."

Lambert's azimuthal equal-area (or equivalent azimuthal projection) (Lambert, Johann Heinrich): Geography. See: Moore.

Lambert's blue (Lambert, Johann Heinrich): Chemistry. See: Webster's 3d.

Lambert's diagrams (Lambert, Johann Heinrich): Philosophy. See: Edwards.

Lambert's formula (Lambert, Johann Heinrich): Earth Sciences. See: Huschke; Van Nostrand Sci. Encyc.

Lambert's treatment (Lambert, Alexander): Medicine. See: Dorland.

Lambert's zenithal equal area projection (Lambert, Johann Heinrich): Geography. See: Monkhouse.

LAMBIOTTE, AUGUSTE. fl. 1943. French engineer. Cited in: Chem. Abstr., Decenn. Index, 1937-1946. Lambiotte process.

Lambiotte process (Lambiotte, Auguste): Engineering and Industry. See: Thrush.

LAMBL, WILHELM DUSAN. 1824-1895. Austrian physician. See: Biog. Lex. hervorr. Aerzte. Lamblia, Lambliasis.

Lamblia (Lambl, Wilhelm Dusan). See: Giardia.

Lambliasis (Lambl, Wilhelm Dusan). See: Giardiasis.

LAMBLING, ANDRE. 1899- . French physician. See: Who's Who France, 1975-1976. Lambling's syndrome.

Lambling's syndrome (Lambling, Andre): Medicine. See: Jablonski.

LAMBOTTE, ALBIN. 1866-1912. Belgian surgeon. See: Seyn. Lambotte's method.

Lambotte's method (Lambotte, Albin): Medicine. See: Dorland; Stedman.

LAMBRECHT, WILHELM. fl. 1926-1930. German scientist. Cited in: Chem. Abstr., Decenn. Index, 1927-1936. Lambrecht's polymeter?

Lambrecht's polymeter (Lambrecht, Wilhelm?): Earth Sciences. See: Hackh.

Lamb's extensometer (Lamb, E. H.): Engineering and Industry. See: Auger.

Lambton flight (Derivation undetermined): Engineering and Industry. See: Thrush.

LAMBTON, JOHN GEORGE, 1ST EARL OF DURHAM. 1792-1840. English statesman. See: Dict. Nat. Biog. Durham('s) Report.

Lame curves (Lame, Gabriel): Mathematics. See: Encyc. Brit., 1973 under "Curves, Special," vol. 6, p. 920b.

Lame('s) elastic constants (or constants) (Lame, Gabriel): Mathematics. See: Ballentyne; Internat. Dict. Ap. Math.; Internat. Dict. Phys. Elec.; James.

Lame equation (generalized) (Lame, Gabriel): Mathematics. See: Internat. Dict. Ap. Math.

LAME, GABRIEL. 1795-1870. French mathematician and engineer. See: Dict. Sci. Biog. Lame curves, Lame equation (generalized), Lame relations, Lame('s) elastic constants (or constants), Lame theory of thick walled cylinders, Lame's functions.

Lame relations (Lame, Gabriel): Mathematics. See: Internat. Dict. Ap. Math.

Lame theory of thick walled cylinders (Lame, Gabriel): Physics. See: Internat. Dict. Ap. Math.

La Mer generator (La Mer, Victor Kuhn): Engineering and Industry. See: Redman.

LA MER, VICTOR KUHN. 1895- . American chemist. See: World Who's Who Sci. La Mer generator.

Lame's functions (Lame, Gabriel): Mathematics. See: Ballentyne.

Lamia (Lamia, the demon): Generic Word (sorceress). See: Partridge.

LAMIA, THE DEMON. Female demon who devoured children. See: Encyc. Brit., 1973. Lamia.

Laming process (Derivation undetermined): Engineering and Industry. See: Thrush.

Lami's theorem (Derivation undetermined): Physics. See: Ballentyne.

La Mont boiler (La Mont, Walter D.): Engineering and Industry. See: Auger.

LA MONT, WALTER D. d. 1943. American engineer. (Biography source unavailable.) La Mont boiler.

Lamotte comparator (La Motte, Frank Linton?): Engineering and Industry. See: Thrush.

LA MOTTE, FRANK LINTON. fl. 1932-1941. American chemist. Cited in: Chem. Abstr., Decenn. Index., 1937-1946. Lamotte comparator?

LAMOURETTE, ADRIEN. 1742-1794. French bishop of Lyons and politician. See: Nouv. Biog. Univ. Lamourette's kiss (or baiser de Lamourette).

Lamourette's kiss (or baiser de Lamourette) (Lamourette, Adrien): Generic Word (short-lived reconciliation). See: Harbottle; Harvey; Phyfe.

Lampadite (Lampadius, Wilhelm August): Earth Sciences. See: Webster's 3d.

LAMPADIUS, WILHELM AUGUST. 1772-1842. German chemist. See: Allg. Deut. Biog. Lampadite.

Lampetians (Lampetius): Religion. See: Canney.

LAMPETIUS. fl. 458. Euchite bishop. See: Dict. Christian Biog. Lampetians.

LAMY, MAURICE EMILE JOSEPH. 1895- . French physician. See: Who's Who France, 1975-1976. Maroteaux-Lamy syndrome.

Lancaster gun (Derivation undetermined): Weapons. See: Wagner (More Names).

LANCASTER, H. O. fl. 1950. English statistician. (Biography source unavailable.) Lancaster's partition of chi-squares.

Lancaster, John of Gaunt, Duke of. See: John of Gaunt.

LANCASTER, JOSEPH. 1778-1838. English educator. See: Dict. Nat. Biog. Lancasterian (or Lancastrian) (system, system of education or method of monitorial instruction).

Lancaster rifle (Derivation undetermined): Weapons. See: Wagner (More Names).

Lancasterian (or Lancastrian) (system, system of education or method of monitorial instruction) (Lancaster, Joseph): Education. See: Brewer; Canney; Good; Partridge; Webster's 3d.

Lancaster's partition of chi-squares (Lancaster, H. O.): Statistics. See: Kendall.

Lancastrian(s) (John of Gaunt, Duke of Lancaster): History. See: Steinberg; Webster's 3d.

Lancefield('s) classification (group, grouping, method or differentiation) (Lancefield, Rebecca Craighill): Medicine. See: Dorland; Kelly; Stedman; Webster's 3d.

LANCEFIELD, REBECCA CRAIGHILL. 1895- . American bacteriologist. See: Amer. Men and Women Sci., 12th ed. Lancefield('s) classification (group, grouping, method or differentiation), Lancefield's reaction.

Lancefield's reaction (Lancefield, Rebecca Craighill): Medicine. See: Kelly.

LANCEREAUX, ETIENNE. 1829-1910. French physician. See: World Who's Who Sci. Lancereaux's diabetes, Lancereaux's law of thrombosis, Lancereaux's treatment.

Lancereaux's diabetes (Lancereaux, Etienne): Medicine. See: Dorland; Jablonski; Kelly.

Lancereaux's law of thrombosis (Lancereaux, Etienne): Medicine. See: Blakiston's Gould.

Lancereaux's treatment (Lancereaux, Etienne): Medicine. See: Dorland.

Lanchester 9mm submachine gun Mark 1 (Lanchester, G. H.): Weapons. See: Quick.

LANCHESTER, G. H. fl. 1941. English arms designer. (Biography source unavailable.) Lanchester 9mm submachine gun Mark 1.

LANCISI, GIOVANNI MARIA. 1654-1720. Italian physician. See: Dict. Sci. Biog. Lancisi's sign, Lancisi's striae (streaks, nerves or nerve of Lancisi).

Lancisi's sign (Lancisi, Giovanni Maria): Medicine. See: Stedman.

Lancisi's striae (streaks, nerves or nerve of Lancisi) (Lancisi, Giovanni Maria): Anatomy. See: Donath; Dorland; Stedman; Webster's 3d.

LANCZOS, CORNELIUS. 1893- . Hungarian-born Irish physicist and applied mathematician. See: World Who's Who Sci. Lanczos method of biorthogonalization.

Lanczos method of biorthogonalization (Lanczos, Cornelius): Mathematics. See: Internat. Dict. Ap. Math.

LAND, EDWIN HERBERT. 1909- . American inventor. See: World Who's Who Sci. Polaroid Land photographic process (and camera).

Landau damping (Landau, Lev Davidovich): Physics. See: Internat. Dict. Phys. Elec.; Thewlis.

LANDAU, EDMUND. 1877-1938. German mathematician. See: Dict. Sci. Biog. Bohr-Landau theorem, Landau style.

Landau fluctuations (Landau, Lev Davidovich): Physics. See: Ballentyne; Thewlis.

Landau formula (diamagnetism or theory (1)) (Landau, Lev Davidovich): Physics. See: Hughes; Internat. Dict. Ap. Math.; Internat. Dict. Phys. Elec.

LANDAU, LEOPOLD. 1848-1920. German gynecologist and obstetrician. See: Biog. Lex. hervorr. Aerzte, 1880-1930. Landau reflex (position, posture or response)?

LANDAU, LEV DAVIDOVICH. 1908-1968. Soviet theoretical physicist. See: Dict. Sci. Biog. Landau damping, Landau fluctuations, Landau formula (diamagnetism or theory (1)), Landau theory (2) (or theory of liquid helium II).

Landau reflex (position, posture or response) (Landau, Leopold?): Medicine. See: Blakiston's Gould; Hinsie.

Landau style (Landau, Edmund): Mathematics. See: Dict. Sci. Biog. under "Landau, Edmund."

Landau('s) test (or color test) (Landau, Wilhelm): Medicine. See: Dorland.

Landau theory (2) (or theory of liquid helium II) (Landau, Lev Davidovich): Physics. See: Hughes; Internat. Dict. Phys. Elec.

LANDAU, WILHELM. fl. 1913. German? physician. Cited in: Kelly. Landau('s) test (or color test).

LANDE, ALFRED. b. 1888. German-born American physicist. See: Pogg., vols. 5, 6, 7a. Lande gamma-permanence rule (spectroscopy), Lande interval rule, Lande splitting factor (or g-factor).

Lande gamma-permanence rule (spectroscopy) (Lande, Alfred): Physics. See: Internat. Dict. Phys. Elec.

Lande interval rule (Lande, Alfred): Physics. See: Internat. Dict. Ap. Math.; Thewlis.

Lande splitting factor (or g-factor) (Lande, Alfred): Physics. See: Ballentyne; Hughes; Internat. Dict. Ap. Math.; Internat. Dict. Phys. Elec.; Thewlis; Van Nostrand Chem. Dict.

LANDEN, JOHN. 1719-1790. English mathematician. See: World Who's Who Sci. Landen's point, Landen's transformations (or theorem).

Landen's point (Landen, John): Mathematics. Cited in: World Who's Who Sci.

Landen's transformations (or theorem) (Landen, John): Mathematics. Cited in: Dict. Sci. Biog. under "Legendre, Adrien Marie"; World Who's Who Sci.

Lander gauge (Lander, James J.): Physics. See: Internat. Dict. Phys. Elec.

LANDER, JAMES J. 1914-   . American physical chemist. See: Amer. Men Sci., 10th ed. Lander gauge.

LANDERER, ALBERT. 1854-1904. German surgeon. See: Biog. Lex. hervorr. Aerzte, 1880-1930. Landerer's treatment.

Landerer's treatment (Landerer, Albert): Medicine. See: Dorland.

Landerite (Landero, Carlos F. de): Earth Sciences. See: Thrush.

LANDERO, CARLOS F. DE. fl. 1886-1897. Mexican scientist. Cited in: Hintze, 1st suppl., p. 279. Royal Soc. Cat. Sci. Pap., 1884-1900. Landerite.

LANDES, KENNETH KNIGHT. 1899-   . American geologist. See: World Who's Who Sci. Landesite.

Landesite (Landes, Kenneth Knight): Earth Sciences. See: Thrush; Webster's 3d.

LANDING, BENJAMIN HARRISON. 1920-   . American physician. See: World Who's Who Sci. Landing-Oppenheimer syndrome.

Landing-Oppenheimer syndrome (Landing, Benjamin Harrison and Oppenheimer, Ella H.): Medicine. See: Jablonski.

Landini cadence (or sixth) (Landini, Francesco): Music. See: Apel.

LANDINI, FRANCESCO. 1325-1397. Italian composer. See: New Encyc. Brit., 1974, Microp. Landini cadence (or sixth).

Landino, Francesco. See: Landini, Francesco.

LANDIS, EUGENE MARKLEY. 1901-   . American physiologist. See: World Who's Who Sci. Landis-Gibbon test.

Landis-Gibbon test (Landis, Eugene Markley and Gibbon, John Heysham, Jr.): Medicine. See: Blakiston's Gould; Kelly.

Landmann's tuberculin (Derivation undetermined): Medicine. See: Stedman.

LANDOLFI, NICOLA. fl. 1845. Italian physician. See: Biog. Lex. hervorr. Aerzte. Landolfi's paste, Landolfi's sign?

Landolfi's paste (Landolfi, Nicola): Medicine. See: Dorland.

Landolfi's sign (Landolfi, Nicola?): Medicine. See: Stedman.

LANDOLPHE, JEAN FRANCOIS. 1747-1825. French ship captain. See: Nouv. Biog. Univ. Landolphia.

Landolphia (Landolphe, Jean Francois): Botany. See: Webster's 3d.

Landolt band (or fringe) (Landolt, Hans Heinrich): Physics. See: Ballentyne; Internat. Dict. Phys. Elec.

Landolt('s) circles (or ring) (Landolt, Edmund): Medicine. See: Chaplin; Webster's 3d.

LANDOLT, EDMUND. 1846-1926. French ophthalmologist. See: Biog. Lex. hervorr. Aerzte, 1880-1930. Landolt('s) circles (or ring), Landolt's bodies (or fibre), Landolt's broken C test, Landolt's operation, Landolt's ophthalmotrope, Landolt's prism, Landolt's stereoscope.

LANDOLT, HANS HEINRICH. 1831-1910. Swiss-born German physical chemist. See: Dict. Sci. Biog. Landolt band (or fringe), Landolt reaction.

Landolt reaction (Landolt, Hans Heinrich): Chemistry. See: Van Nostrand Chem. Dict.

Landolt's bodies (or fibre) (Landolt, Edmund): Anatomy. See: Donath; Dorland; Henderson; Stedman.

Landolt's broken C test (Landolt, Edmund): Medicine. See: Blakiston's Gould.

Landolt's operation (Landolt, Edmund): Medicine. See: Biog. Lex. hervorr. Aerzte, 1880-1930.

Landolt's ophthalmotrope (Landolt, Edmund): Medicine. See: Biog. Lex. hervorr. Aerzte, 1880-1930.

Landolt's prism (Landolt, Edmund): Medicine. See: Biog. Lex hervorr. Aerzte, 1880-1930.

Landolt's stereoscope (Landolt, Edmund): Medicine. See: Biog. Lex. hervorr. Aerzte, 1880-1930.

LANDOR, J. V. fl. 1936. English physician. (Biography source unavailable.) Hawes-Pallister-Landor syndrome.

Landouzy-Dejerine dystrophy (or type) (Landouzy, Louis Theophil Joseph and Dejerine, Joseph Jules): Medicine. See: Dorland; Jablonski; Stedman.

Landouzy-Grasset law (Landouzy, Louis Theophil Joseph and Grasset, Joseph): Medicine. See: Blakiston's Gould; Dorland; Stedman.

LANDOUZY, LOUIS THEOPHIL JOSEPH. 1845-1917. French physician. See: World Who's Who Sci. Duchenne-Landouzy type, Erb-Landouzy syndrome, Landouzy-Dejerine dystrophy (or type), Landouzy-Grasset law, Landouzy's disease, Landouzy's syndrome (or sciatica).

Landouzy's disease (Landouzy, Louis Theophil Joseph). See: Weil's disease (or icterus).

Landouzy's syndrome (or sciatica) (Landouzy, Louis Theophil Joseph): Medicine. See: Jablonski

Landrum-Griffin Act (Landrum, Phillip Mitchell and Griffin, Robert Paul): Politics. See: Smith.

LANDRUM, PHILLIP MITCHELL. 1909-   . American legislator. See: Biog. Dict. Amer. Congress. Landrum-Griffin Act.

Landry-Guillain-Barre syndrome (Landry, Jean Baptiste Octave and Guillain, Georges; and Barre, Jean Alexandre). See: Landry's paralysis.

LANDRY, JEAN BAPTISTE OCTAVE. 1826-1865. French physician. See: World Who's Who Sci. Landry's paralysis (or disease).

Landry-Kussmaul syndrome (Landry, Jean Baptiste Octave and Kussmaul, Adolf). See: Landry's paralysis.

Landry's paralysis (or disease) (Landry, Jean Baptiste Octave): Medicine. See: Dorland; Hinsie; Jablonski; Stedman; Webster's 3d. Also known as: Guillain-Barre syndrome, Guillain-Barre-Strohl syndrome, Landry-Guillain-Barre syndrome, Landry-Kussmaul syndrome, Kussmaul-Landry paralysis.

Landsberger method (and apparatus) (Landsberger, Willy?): Chemistry. See: Hackh; Internat. Dict. Phys. Elec.; Van Nostrand Chem. Dict.; Van Nostrand Sci. Encyc. under "Boiling Point Elevation." Also known as: Sakurai-Landsberger apparatus.

LANDSBERGER, WILLY. b. 1876. German chemist. Cited in: Mansell. Landsberger method (and apparatus)?

LANDSCHUETZ, CHRISTOPH. fl. 1949-1957. German medical researcher. Cited in: Chem. Abstr. Landschutz tumor.

Landschutz tumor (Landschuetz, Christoph): Medicine. See: Stedman.

LANDSEER, SIR EDWIN HENRY. 1802-1873. English animal painter. See: Encyc. Brit., 1973. Landseer Newfoundland (dog).

Landseer Newfoundland (dog) (Landseer, Sir Edwin Henry): Zoology. See: Webster's 3d.

Landsteiner-Donath test (Landsteiner, Karl and Donath, Julius). See: Donath-Landsteiner test.

LANDSTEINER, KARL. 1868-1943. Austrian-born pathologist. See: Dict. Sci. Biog. Donath-Landsteiner cold autoantibody, Donath-Landsteiner phenomenon, Donath-Landsteiner syndrome, Donath-Landsteiner test, Landsteiner('s) method.

Landsteiner('s) method (Landsteiner, Karl): Medicine. See: Dorland.

LANDSTROEM, JOHN. 1869-1910. Swedish surgeon. See: Biog. Lex. hervorr. Aerzte, 1880-1930. Landstroem's muscle.

Landstroem's muscle (Landstroem, John): Anatomy. See: Donath; Dorland; Stedman.

LANDZERT, THEODOR. fl. 19th c. German anatomist. See: Ber. enckenberg Naturf., 1890, pp. 5-6. Gruber-Landzert fossa, Landzert's fossa.

Landzert's fossa (Landzert, Theodor): Anatomy. See: Stedman.

LANE, HARRIET. d. ca. 1875. Australian? murder victim. (Biography source unavailable.) Harriet Lane.

LANE, HENRY M. fl. 1904-1922. American engineer. Cited in: Chem. Abstr., vol. 8, p. 405. Lane system?

LANE, JOHN EDWARD. 1872-1933. American dermatologist. See: Arch. of Derm. vol. 29 (1934), pp. 106-111. Lane's disease.

LANE, JONATHAN HOMER. 1819-1880. American physicist. See: Dict. Sci. Biog. Lane('s) law.

Lane-Lannelongue operation (Lane, Sir William Arbuthnot and Lannelongue, Odilon Marc): Medicine. See: Dorland; Stedman.

Lane('s) law (Lane, Jonathan Homer): Physics. See: Ballentyne; Thewlis.

Lane mill (Derivation undetermined): Engineering and Industry. See: Thrush.

Lane system (Lane, Henry M.?): Chemistry. See: Van Nostrand Chem. Dict.

LANE, SIR WILLIAM ARBUTHNOT. 1856-1943. English surgeon. See: World Who's Who Sci. Lane-Lannelongue operation, Lane's band (or kink), Lane's disease, Lane's plates.

Lane's band (or kink) (Lane, Sir William Arbuthnot): Medicine. See: Dorland; Jablonski; Stedman.

Lane's disease (Lane, John Edward): Medicine. See: Jablonski.

Lane's disease (Lane, Sir William Arbuthnot): Medicine. See: Dorland; Jablonski; Stedman.

Lane's plates (Lane, Sir William Arbuthnot): Medicine. See: Dorland; Stedman.

LANG, BASIL THORN. 1880-1928. English ophthalmologist. See: Brit. Med. J., vol. 1 (1928), p. 211. Frost-Lang operation.

LANG, J. fl. 1879. English engineer. (Biography source unavailable.) Lang's lay (or lay rope).

LANG, VICTOR VON. 1838-1921. Austrian physicist. See: Pogg., vols. 3-6. Langite.

LANGBEIN, A. fl. 19th c. German chemist. (Biography source unavailable.) Langbeinite.

Langbeinite (Langbein, A.): Earth Sciences. See: Thrush; Webster's 3d.

Langdale, Lord. See: Bickersteth, Henry, Lord Langdale.

Langdon Down. See: Down, John Langdon Haydon.

Langdon Down's disease (Down, John Langdon Haydon). See: Down's syndrome.

LANGE, CARL. b. 1883. German physician. See: Biog. Lex. hervorr. Aerzte, 1880-1930. Lange('s) solution, Lange's test (or colloidal gold reaction).

LANGE, CARL GEORG. 1834-1900. Danish psychologist. See: Dict. Sci. Biog. James-Lange theory (of the emotions).

Lange, Cornelia de. See: De Lange, Cornelia Catharina.

LANGE, FRITZ. 1864-1952. German orthopedic surgeon. See: Biog. Lex. hervorr. Aerzte, 1880-1930. Lange's operation.

LANGE, FRITZ. fl. 1923. German chemist. Cited in: Chem. Abstr., Decenn. Index, 1917-1926. Simon and Lange vacuum calorimeter.

LANGE-NIELSEN, FREDRIK. fl. 1957. Norwegian? physician. (Biography source unavailable.) Jervell and Lange-Nielsen syndrome.

Lange('s) solution (colloidal gold) (Lange, Carl): Chemistry. See: Dorland; Hackh; Stedman.

Lange solution (for mercerized cotton) (Derivation undetermined): Chemistry. See: Von Nostrand Chem. Dict.

LANGEN, EUGEN. 1833-1895. German engineer. See: World Who's Who Sci. Otto-Langen engine.

LANGENBECK, BERNHARD RUDOLPH KONRAD VON. 1810-1887. German surgeon. See: World Who's Who Sci. Langenbeck's amputation, Langenbeck's incision, Langenbeck's triangle.

LANGENBECK, CONRAD JOHANN MARTIN. 1776-1851. German surgeon and ophthalmologist. See: World Who's Who Sci. Langenbeck's nerve.

Langenbeck's amputation (Langenbeck, Bernhard Rudolph Konrad von): Medicine. See: Stedman.

Langenbeck's incision (Langenbeck, Bernhard Rudolph Konrad von): Medicine. See: Dorland; Stedman.

Langenbeck's nerve (Langenbeck, Conrad Johann Martin): Anatomy. See: Stedman.

Langenbeck's triangle (Langenbeck, Bernhard Rudolph Konrad von): Anatomy. See: Donath; Dorland; Stedman.

LANGENDORFF, OSCAR. 1853-1908. German physiologist. See: Biog. Lex. hervorr. Aerzte, 1880-1930. Langendorff's method.

Langendorff's method (Langendorff, Oscar): Physiology. See: Stedman.

Langenhan (F.L. Seibstader) .32 cal. ACP automatic pistol (Langenhan, Fritz): Weapons. See: Quick.

LANGENHAN, FRITZ. fl. 20th c. German inventor. (Biography source unavailable.) Langenhan (F.L. Seibstader) .32 cal. ACP automatic pistol.

LANGER, ALOIS. fl. 1938. Czechoslovakian chemist. Cited in: Chem. Abstr., vol. 32, p. 4472[4]. Dubsky-Langer-Stonad reagents.

LANGER, KARL RITTER VON. 1819-1887. Austrian anatomist. See: Biog. Lex. hervorr. Aerzte. Langer's arch (axillary arch or muscle), Langer's lines (or fissure lines).

Langerhans' cells (1) (epidermal) (Langerhans, Paul): Anatomy. See: Dorland; Donath; Drever; Henderson; Stedman.

Langerhans' cells (2) (centroacinar) (Langerhans, Paul): Anatomy. See: Stedman.

Langerhans' cells (3) (or stellar corpuscles) (Langerhans, Paul): Anatomy. See: Dorland, 24th ed.

Langerhans' islands (Langerhans, Paul?). See: islets of Langerhans.

LANGERHANS, PAUL. 1847-1888. German pathological anatomist. See: Dict. Sci. Biog. follicles of Langerhans, islets of Langerhans (or Langerhans' islands), Langerhans' cells (1) (epidermal), Langerhans' cells (2) (centroacinar), Langerhans' cells (3) (or stellar corpuscles), Langerhansian hormone.

Langerhansian hormone (Langerhans, Paul): Medicine. See: Stedman.

Langer's arch (axillary arch or muscle) (Langer, Karl Ritter von): Anatomy. See: Donath; Dorland; Stedman.

Langer's lines (or fissure lines) (Langer, Karl Ritter von): Medicine. See: Dorland; Kelly; Stedman.

Lange's operation (Lange, Fritz): Medicine. See: Dorland.

Lange's syndrome (De Lange, Cornelia Catharina). See: De Lange's syndrome (1).

Lange's test (or colloidal gold reaction) (Lange, Carl): Medicine. See: Dorland; Hinsie; Stedman. Also known as: Zsigmondy's test.

Langevin-Debye equation (Langevin, Paul and Debye, Peter Joseph William): Physics. See: Ballentyne.

Langevin formula (Langevin, Paul): Physics. See: Hackh; Internat. Dict. Phys. Elec.; Van Nostrand Chem. Dict.

Langevin function (Langevin, Paul): Physics. See: Ballentyne; Internat. Dict. Ap. Math.; Internat. Dict. Phys. Elec. under "Langevin formula."

Langevin ion (Langevin, Paul): Physics. See: Hughes; Huschke.

LANGEVIN, PAUL. 1872-1946. French physicist. See: Dict. Sci. Biog. Langevin-Debye equation, Langevin formula, Langevin function, Langevin ion, Langevin-Pauli formula, Langevin theory of diamagnetism (theory (1) or diamagnetism equation), Langevin theory of paramagnetic susceptibility (or theory (2)).

Langevin-Pauli formula (Langevin, Paul and Pauli, Wolfgang): Physics. See: Internat. Dict. Ap. Math.

Langevin theory of diamagnetism (theory (1) or diamagnetism equation) (Langevin, Paul): Physics. See: Ballentyne; Hughes; Internat. Dict. Ap. Math.; Internat. Dict. Phys. Elec.; Thewlis.

Langevin theory of paramagnetic susceptibility (or theory (2) (Langevin, Paul): Physics. See: Hughes; Internat. Dict. Ap. Math.; Internat. Dict. Phys. Elec.

Langhans' cells (1) (cytotrophoblastic cells) (Langhans, Theodor): Medicine. See: Donath; Dorland; Henderson; Stedman.

Langhans' cells (2) (or giant cells) (Langhans, Theodor): Medicine. See: Dorland; Stedman.

Langhans' layer (or layer of Langhans) (Langhans, Theodor): Medicine. See: Donath; Dorland; Stedman; Webster's 3d.

Langhan's stria (Langhans, Theodor): Medicine. See: Stedman.

LANGHANS, THEODOR. 1839-1915. German anatomist. See: World Who's Who Sci. Langhans' cells (1) (cytotrophoblastic cells), Langhans' cells (2) (or giant cells), Langhans' layer (or layer of Langhans), Langhan's stria.

LANGHELD, KURT. 1880-1913. German chemist. See: Pogg., vol. 5. Langheld test reaction.

Langheld test reaction (Langheld, Kurt): Chemistry. See: Van Nostrand Chem. Dict.

Langite (Lang, Victor von): Earth Sciences. See: Thrush; Webster's 3d.

LANGLEY, JOHN NEWPORT. 1852-1925. English physiologist. See: Dict. Nat. Biog. Langley's ganglion, Langley's granules, Langley's nerve, Langley's test.

LANGLEY, SAMUEL PIERPONT. 1834-1906. American astronomer and airplane pioneer. See: Dict. Sci. Biog. Langley (unit).

Langley (unit) (Langley, Samuel Pierpont): Physics. See: Ballentyne; Dresner; Huschke; Van Nostrand Sci. Encyc.

Langley's ganglion (Langley, John Newport): Anatomy. See: Dorland.

Langley's granules (Langley, John Newport): Anatomy. See: Dorland; Stedman.

Langley's nerve (Langley, John Newport): Anatomy. See: Dorland.

Langley's test (Langley, John Newport): Medicine. See: Stedman.

Langmuir('s) adsorption isotherm (Langmuir, Irving): Physics. See: Ballentyne; Internat. Dict. Ap. Math.; Internat. Dict. Phys. Elec.; Thrush; Van Nostrand Sci. Encyc. under "Adsorption."

Langmuir-Blodgett film (Langmuir, Irving and Blodgett, Katherine Burr): Physics. See: Internat. Dict. Phys. Elec.

Langmuir dark space (Langmuir, Irving): Physics. See: Hughes; Internat. Dict. Phys. Elec.; Markus.

Langmuir frequency (Langmuir, Irving): Physics. See: Hughes; Van Nostrand Sci. Encyc.

LANGMUIR, IRVING. 1881-1957. American physical chemist. See: Dict. Sci. Biog. Child-Langmuir equation, Child-Langmuir-Schottky equation, Dushman-Langmuir equation, Langmuir-Blodgett film, Langmuir dark space, Langmuir frequency, Langmuir law, Langmuir method for the rate of vaporization of metals, Langmuir probe, Langmuir('s) adsorption isotherm, Langmuir theory (2), Langmuir trough, Langmuir vacuum pump (or condensation pump), Lewis-Langmuir atom, Lewis-Langmuir formula, Lewis-Langmuir theory (or theory of atomic structure).

Langmuir law (Langmuir, Irving): Physics. See: Hughes; Thewlis.

Langmuir method for the rate of vaporization of metals (Langmuir, Irving): Physics. See: Van Nostrand Sci. Encyc.

Langmuir probe (Langmuir, Irving): Physics. See: Barnhart (New Eng.); Hughes; Markus.

Langmuir theory (1) (Langmuir, Irving). See: Lewis-Langmuir theory (or theory of atomic structure).

Langmuir theory (2) (Langmuir, Irving): Physics. See: Hackh.

Langmuir trough (Langmuir, Irving): Engineering and Industry. See: Thrush.

Langmuir vacuum pump (or condensation pump) (Langmuir, Irving): Engineering and Industry. See: Auger; Van Nostrand Sci. Encyc. under "Diffusion Pump."

LANGRISHE, SIR HERCULES. 1731-1811. Irish parliamentarian. See: Dict. Nat. Biog. Langrishe's Act.

Langrishe's Act (Langrishe, Sir Hercules): History. See: Steinberg.

Lang's lay (or lay rope) (Lang, J.): Engineering and Industry. See: Auger; Thrush. Also known as: Albert's lay.

LANGSDORFF, GEORG HEINRICH VON. 1797-1852. German physician. See: World Who's Who Sci. Langsdorffia.

Langsdorffia (Langsdorff, Georg Heinrich von): Botany. See: Webster's 3d.

Langstroth frame (Langstroth, Lorenzo Lorraine): Agriculture. See: Winburne.

LANGSTROTH, LORENZO LORRAINE. 1810-1895. American apiarist. See: Who Was Who Amer., Hist. vol. Langstroth frame.

LANGUEPIN, ANNE. fl. 1962. French pediatrician. (Biography source unavailable.) Fevre-Languepin syndrome.

Lanham Act (1) (Lanham, Fritz Garland): Politics. See: Good; Smith.

Lanham Act (2) (or trademark Act) (Lanham, Fritz Garland): Politics. See: Clark.

LANHAM, FRITZ GARLAND. 1880-1965. American legislator. See: Biog. Direct. Amer. Congress. Lanham Act (1), Lanham Act (2) (or trademark Act).

LANKESTER, SIR EDWIN RAY. 1847-1930. English morphologist. See: World Who's Who Sci. Lankesterella ranarum.

Lankesterella ranarum (Lankester, Sir Edwin Ray): Medicine. See: Dorland.

LANNELONGUE, ODILON MARC. 1840-1911. French surgeon. See: World Who's Who Sci. Lane-Lannelongue operation, Lannelongue-Osgood-Schlatter syndrome, Lannelongue's foramina, Lannelongue's ligament, Lannelongue's method, Lannelongue's operation (2).

Lannelongue-Osgood-Schlatter syndrome (Lannelongue, Odilon Marc; Osgood, Robert Bayley; and Schlatter, Carl). See: Osgood-Schlatter syndrome.

Lannelongue's foramina (Lannelongue, Odilon Marc): Anatomy. See: Stedman.

Lannelongue's ligament (Lannelongue, Odilon Marc): Anatomy. See: Stedman.

Lannelongue's method (Lannelongue, Odilon Marc): Medicine. See: Index-Cat. Libr. Surg.-Gen. Off., 2d Ser., vol. 9, 1904.

Lannelongue's operation (1) (Lannelongue, Odilon Marc). See: Lane-Lannelongue operation.

Lannelongue's operation (2) (Lannelongue, Odilon Marc): Medicine. See: Dorland.

Lannelongue's tibia (or disease) (Lannelongue, Odilon Marc). See: Osgood-Schlatter syndrome.

Lannois-Gradenigo syndrome (Lannois, Maurice? and Gradenigo, Giuseppe). See: Gradenigo's syndrome.

LANNOIS, MAURICE. b. 1856. French otorhinolaryngologist. See: Biog. Lex. hervorr. Aerzte, 1880-1930. Lannois-Gradenigo syndrome?

Lansing-Ishii Agreement (Lansing, Robert and Ishii, Kikujiro): History. See: Jameson; Morris; Smith.

LANSING, ROBERT. 1864-1928. American statesman. See: Encyc. Brit., 1973. Lansing-Ishii Agreement.

Lanston machine (or monotype) (Lanston, Tolbert): Printing. See: Lockwood.

LANSTON, TOLBERT. 1844-1913. American inventor. See: World Who's Who Sci. Lanston machine (or monotype).

LANTERMAN, A. J. fl. 1877. American anatomist in Strasbourg. Cited in: Royal Soc. Cat. Sci. Pap., 1800-1863; 1874-1883. Lantermann's segments, Schmidt-Lanterman incisures (or clefts).

Lantermann's segments (Lanterman, A. J.): Medicine. See: Stedman.

Lanterman's clefts (or incisures) (Lanterman, A. J.). See: Schmidt-Lanterman incisures (or clefts).

LANZ, HENRY CHARLES. 1915- . English-born American medical physicist. See: Amer. Men Sci., 10th ed. Linderstrom-Lang-Lanz method.

LANZ, OTTO. 1865-1935. Swiss-born surgeon in Amsterdam. See: Biog. Lex. hervorr. Aerzte, 1880-1930. Lanz's line (or point).

Lanz's line (or point) (Lanz, Otto): Anatomy. See: Donath; Stedman.

LAOCOON. Ancient Greek priest of Apollo. See: New Encyc. Brit., 1974, Microp. Laocoon.

Laocoon (Laocoon, the priest): Generic Word (heroic struggler with difficulties). See: Webster's 3d.

LAODICE. fl. 248 B.C. Wife of Antiochus II of Syria. See: Dict. Grk. Rom. Biog. Myth. Laodician (or Laodicean).

Laodician (or Laodicean) (Laodice): Generic Word (indifferent or indecise). See: Hendrickson; Jobes.

Lapageria (Josephine): Botany. See: Hendrickson; Taylor, N.; Webster's 3d. Also known as: Josephine('s) lily.

La Pagerie, Marie Josephine Rose Tascher de. See: Josephine.

La Paz, Daniel. See: Paz, Daniel de la.

La Peirouse, Philippe Picot. See: Peirouse, Philippe Picot, Baron de la.

LA PEROUSE, JEAN FRANCOIS DE GALAUP DE. 1741-1788. French sailor and explorer. See: World Who's Who Sci. Lapeyrousia (or Lapeirousia)?

a Peyronie, Francois. See: Peyronie, Francois de la.

A PEYRONIE, FRANCOIS GIGOT DE. 1678-1747. French surgeon. See: World Who's Who Sci. Peyronie's disease.

Lapeyrousia (or Lapeirousia) (La Perouse, Jean Francois de Galaup de? or eirouse, Philippe Picot, Baron de la?): Botany. See: Taylor, N.; Webster's M.

LAPHAM, MAXWELL EDWARD. 1899- . American obstetrician. See: Miss. Doct., vol. 18 (1940-1941), p. 704. Friedman-Lapham test.

LAPICQUE, LOUIS. 1866-1952. French physiologist. See: Dict. Sci. Biog. Lapicque's law.

Lapicque's law (Lapicque, Louis): Medicine. See: Dorland; Stedman.

Laplace azimuth stations (or station) (Laplace, Pierre-Simon, Marquis de): Earth Sciences. See: Thewlis; Webster's 3d.

Laplace distribution (or first law of Laplace) (Laplace, Pierre-Simon, Marquis de): Statistics. See: Kendall.

Laplace('s) equation (or differential equation) (Laplace, Pierre-Simon, Marquis de): Mathematics. See: Ballentyne; Huschke; James; New Encyc. Brit., 1974, Microp.; Thewlis; Van Nostrand Sci. Encyc.; Webster's 3d.

LAPLACE, ERNEST. 1861-1924. American surgeon. See: World Who's Who Sci. Laplace's forceps.

Laplace expansion (or development) (of a determinant) (Laplace, Pierre-Simon, Marquis de): Mathematics. See: Internat. Dict. Ap. Math., Internat. Dict. Phys. Elec.; James; Van Nostrand Sci. Encyc. under "Determinate Structure."

Laplace formula (Laplace, Pierre-Simon, Marquis de): Mathematics. See: Internat. Dict. Ap. Math.

Laplace('s) law (1) (Laplace, Pierre-Simon, Marquis de): Physics. See: Hughes; Internat. Dict. Phys. Elec.

Laplace law of succession (Laplace, Pierre-Simon, Marquis de): Statistics. See: Kendall.

Laplace-Levy theorem (Laplace, Pierre Simon, Marquis de and Levy, Paul Pierre): Statistics. See: Kendall.

LAPLACE, PIERRE-SIMON, MARQUIS DE. 1749-1827. French mathematician, astronomer and physicist. See: New Encyc. Brit., 1974. De Moivre-Laplace theorem, Laplace azimuth stations (or station), Laplace distribution (or first law of Laplace), Laplace expansion (or development) (of a determinant), Laplace formula, Laplace law of succession, Laplace-Levy theorem, Laplace('s) equation (or differential equation), Laplace('s) law (1), Laplace('s) pressure (intrinsic pressure or law (2)), Laplace('s) theorem, Laplace-Stieltjes transform, Laplace('s) transform (or transformation), Laplace transform theorems, Laplace's coefficients, Laplace's equation (for the velocity of sound) (or Laplacian speed of sound), Laplace's integrals, Laplace's principle, Laplace's theory of chemical combination, Laplacian curve, Laplacian (1) (Laplacian operator or Laplace operator), Laplacian (2) (negative of buckling), second law of Laplace.

Laplace('s) pressure (intrinsic pressure or law (2)) (Laplace, Pierre-Simon, Marquis de): Physics. See: Encyc. Brit., 1973 under "Surface Tension," vol. 1, p. 445d; Stedman.

Laplace-Stieltjes transform (Laplace, Pierre-Simon, Marquis de and Stieltjes, Thomas Jean): Mathematics. See: Thewlis.

Laplace('s) theorem (Laplace, Pierre-Simon, Marquis de): Statistics. See: Kendall; Van Nostrand Sci. Encyc.

Laplace('s) transform (or transformation) (Laplace, Pierre-Simon, Marquis de): Mathematics. See: Ballentyne; Huschke; James; Kendall; Thewlis; Van Nostrand Sci. Encyc.

Laplace transform theorems (Laplace, Pierre-Simon, Marquis de): Mathematics. See: Internat. Dict. Ap. Math.

Laplace's coefficients (Laplace, Pierre-Simon, Marquis de): Mathematics. See: Ballentyne.

Laplace's equation (for the velocity of sound) (or Laplacian speed of sound) (Laplace, Pierre-Simon, Marquis de): Mathematics. See: Ballentyne; Huschke.

Laplace's forceps (Laplace, Ernest): Medicine. See: Stedman.

Laplace's integrals (Laplace, Pierre-Simon, Marquis de): Mathematics. See: Ballentyne.

Laplace's principle (Laplace, Pierre-Simon, Marquis de): Mathematics. See: Ballentyne.

Laplace's theory of chemical combination (Laplace, Pierre-Simon, Marquis de): Chemistry. See: Ballentyne.

Laplacian (1) (Laplacian operator or Laplace operator) (Laplace, Pierre-Simon, Marquis de): Mathematics. See: Ballentyne; Hughes; Huschke; Internat. Dict. Ap. Math.; Van Nostrand Sci. Encyc.; Webster's 3d.

Laplacian (2) (negative of buckling) (Laplace, Pierre-Simon, Marquis de): Physics. See: Hughes; Internat. Dict. Phys. Elec.; Thewlis.

Laplacian curve (Laplace, Pierre-Simon, Marquis de): Statistics. See: English.

LA POINTE, JACQUES ROBERT. 1927- . American chemical engineer. See: Who's Who Engin., 1959. LaPointe picker?

LaPointe picker (LaPointe, Jacques Robert?): Engineering and Industry. See: Thrush.

LAPORTE. fl. 19th c. Botanist. (Biography source unavailable.) Laportea.

LAPORTE, OTTO. 1902- . German-born American physicist. See: World Who's Who Sci. Laporte('s) rule (or selection rule).

Laporte('s) rule (or selection rule) (Laporte, Otto): Physics. See: Ballentyne; Internat. Dict. Ap. Math.; Thewlis.

Laportea (Laporte): Botany. See: New Encyc. Brit., 1974, Microp.; Webster's 3d.

LAPRADE, F. fl. 1905. French chemist. Cited in: Chem. Abstr., Decenn. Index, 1907-1916. Aloy-Laprade reagent.

La Ramee, Pierre de. See: Ramus, Petrus.

Lardennois' button (Lardennois, Henri): Medicine. See: Dorland.

LARDENNOIS, HENRI. b. 1872. French surgeon. Cited in: Index-Cat. Libr. Surg.-Gen. Off., 2d Ser., vol. 9, 1904. Lardennois' button.

LARDEREL, FRANCESCO GIACOMO DE. 1789-1858. Italian industrialist. See: Encic. Ital. Larderellite.

Larderellite (Larderel, Francesco Giacomo de): Earth Sciences. See: Thrush; Webster's 3d.

Lardizabala (Lardizabala y Uribe, Don Manuel de): Botany. See: Charnock; New Encyc. Brit., 1974, Microp.

LARDIZABALA Y URIBE, DON MANUEL DE. 1744-1824. Spanish government minister. See: Michaud. Lardizabala.

LARK-HOROWITZ, KARL. 1893-1958. Austrian-born American physicist. See: World Who's Who Sci. Johnson and Lark-Horowitz effect (or formula).

Larmor frequency (or precession frequency) (Larmor, Sir Joseph): Physics. See: Hughes; Markus; Thewlis; Webster's 3d.

LARMOR, SIR JOSEPH. 1857-1942. Irish mathematician and physicist. See: Dict. Sci. Biog. Larmor frequency (or precession frequency), Larmor orbit, Larmor precession, Larmor radius, Larmor('s) theorem (1), Larmor's formula (or theorem (2)).

Larmor orbit (Larmor, Sir Joseph): Physics. See: Markus.

Larmor precession (Larmor, Sir Joseph): Physics. See: Ballentyne; Hughes; Internat. Dict. Phys. Elec.; Thewlis; Van Nostrand Sci. Encyc.; Webster's 3d.

Larmor radius (Larmor, Sir Joseph): Physics. See: Hughes; Internat. Dict. Phys. Elec.

Larmor('s) theorem (1) (Larmor, Sir Joseph): Physics. See: Hackh; Internat. Dict. Phys. Elec.; Webster's 3d.

Larmor's formula (or theorem (2)) (Larmor, Sir Joseph): Physics. See: Ballentyne; Webster's 3d.

LA ROSA, LEOPOLDO. fl. 1932-1954. Italian chemist. Cited in: Chem. Abstr., vol. 27, p. 1840. LaRosa test reaction.

LaRosa test reaction (LaRosa, Leopoldo): Chemistry. See: Van Nostrand Chem. Dict.

Larousse (Larousse, Pierre Athanase): Generic Word (dictionary). See: Hendrickson; New Encyc. Brit., 1974, Microp.

LAROUSSE, PIERRE ATHANASE. 1817-1875. French grammarian, lexicographer and encyclopedist. See: New Encyc. Brit., 1974, Microp. Larousse.

LAROYENNE, LUCIEN. 1831-1902. French surgeon. See: Biog. Lex. hervorr. Aerzte, 1880-1930. Laroyenne's operation.

Laroyenne's operation (Laroyenne, Lucien): Medicine. See: Dorland; Stedman.

Larrea (Larrea, J. A. Hernandez de): Botany. See: Mathews, M. M.; Taylor, N.; Webster's 3d.

LARREA, J. A. HERNANDEZ DE. fl. 18th c. Spanish patron of science. (Biography source unavailable.) Larrea.

LARREY, BARON DOMINIQUE JEAN. 1766-1842. French surgeon. See: World Who's Who Sci. Larrey-Weil disease, Larrey's amputation (or operation), Larrey's bandage, Larrey's cleft (or triangle), Larrey's ligation, Larrey's point.

Larrey-Weil disease (Larrey, Baron Dominique Jean and Weil, Adolf). See: Weil's disease.

Larrey's amputation (or operation) (Larrey, Baron Dominique Jean): Medicine. See: Dorland; Stedman.

Larrey's bandage (Larrey, Baron Dominique Jean): Medicine. See: Dorland.

Larrey's cleft (or triangle) (Larrey, Baron Dominique Jean): Anatomy. See: Donath; Stedman.

Larrey's ligation (Larrey, Baron Dominique Jean): Medicine. See: Stedman.

Larrey's point (Larrey, Baron Dominique Jean): Anatomy. See: Donath.

LARSEN, ABSALON (In full: SOREN ABSALON). b. 1871. Danish electrical engineer. See: Dansk Biog. Lek. Campbell-Larsen potentiometer, Larsen potentiometer.

Larsen, Christian Magnus Falsen Sinding. See: Sinding-Larsen, Christian Magnus Falsen.

LARSEN, ESPER SIGNIUS, JR. 1879-1961. American petrologist and geologist. See: Dict. Sci. Biog. Larsen method for age determination of rocks, Larsenite.

Larsen-Johansson syndrome (or disease) (Sinding-Larsen, Christian Magnus Falsen and Johansson, Sven Christian): Medicine. See: Blakiston's Gould; Dorland; Jablonski. Also known as: Sinding Larsen-Johansson syndrome (or disease).

LARSEN, LOREN JOSEPH. 1914- . American orthopedic surgeon. See: Dir. Med. Specialists, 1975-1976. Larsen's syndrome.

Larsen method for age determination of rocks (Larsen, Esper Signius, Jr.): Earth Sciences. See: Dict. Sci. Biog. under "Larsen, Esper S., Jr," p. 42b; World Who's Who Sci.

Larsen potentiometer (Larsen, Absalon): Electronics. See: Glazebrook, vol. 2, p. 424b.; Internat. Dict. Phys. Elec.

Larsenite (Larsen, Esper Signius, Jr.): Earth Sciences. See: Thrush; Webster's 3d.

Larsen's pile (Derivation undetermined): Engineering and Industry. See: Thrush.

Larsen's spiles (Derivation undetermined): Engineering and Industry. See: Thrush.

Larsen's syndrome (Larsen, Loren Joseph): Medicine. See: Jablonski.

LARSON, HARDY WILLIAM. 1899- . American chemist. See: Amer. Men Sci., 10th ed. Larson test reaction.

Larson ledge finder (Derivation undetermined): Engineering and Industry. See: Thrush.

Larson test reaction (Larson, Hardy William): Chemistry. See: Van Nostrand Chem. Dict.

LARSSON, TAGE KONRAD LEOPOLD. 1905- . Swedish scientist. See: Vem Ar Det?, 1955. Sjoegren-Larsson syndrome.

Lasche unit (Derivation undetermined): Chemistry. See: Hackh.

Lasco, Johannes a. See: Laski, Jan, the younger.

LASEGUE, ERNEST CHARLES. 1816-1883. French physician. See: World Who's Who Sci. Lasegue('s) sign, Lasegue's disease, Lasegue's syndrome.

Lasegue('s) sign (Lasegue, Ernest Charles): Medicine. See: Dorland; Hinsie; Stedman.

Lasegue's disease (Lasegue, Ernest Charles): Medicine. See: Dorland; Jablonski; Stedman.

Lasegue's syndrome (Lasegue, Ernest Charles): Medicine. See: Stedman.

Lashley jumping stand (Lashley, Karl Spencer): Psychology. See: English; Wolman.

LASHLEY, KARL SPENCER. 1890-1958. American psychologist. See: Internat. Encyc. Soc. Sci. Lashley jumping stand.

LASKI, JAN, THE YOUNGER (JOHANNES A LASCO). 1499-1560. Polish-born religious reformer. See: Encyc. Brit., 1973. Alascans.

LASKOWSKY, N. fl. 1878. German? chemist. Cited in: Royal Soc. Cat. Sci. Pap., 1874-1883. Sabanin-Laskowsky test reaction.

LASPEYRES, ETIENNE. 1834-1913. German statistician and economist. See: Encyc. Soc. Sci. Laspeyres' index, Laspeyres-Konyus index.

Laspeyres' index (Laspeyres, Etienne): Statistics. See: Kendall; New Encyc. Brit., 1974, Microp.

LASPEYRES, JACOB HEINRICH. 1768-1809. German zoologist. Cited in: Mansell. Laspeyresia.

Laspeyres-Konyus index (Laspeyres, Etienne and Konyus, A. A.): See: Konyus index number (or index).

Laspeyresia (Laspeyres, Jacob Heinrich): Zoology. See: Pennak; Webster's 3d.

LASSAIGNE, JEAN-LOUIS. 1800-1859. French chemist. See: World Who's Who Sci. Lassaigne reaction (or test) for nitrogen, Lassaigne solution for differentiating wool and silk.

Lassaigne reaction (or test) for nitrogen (Lassaigne, Jean-Louis): Chemistry. See: New Encyc. Brit., 1974, Microp.; Van Nostrand Chem. Dict.

Lassaigne solution for differentiating wool and silk (Lassaigne, Jean-Louis): Chemistry. See: Van Nostrand Chem. Dict.

LASSALLE, FERDINAND. 1825-1864. German socialist. See: New Encyc. Brit., 1974. Lassallean socialists.

Lassallean Socialists (Lassalle, Ferdinand): History. See: Morris.

Lassar-Cohn. See: Cohn, Lassar.

Lassar-Cohn reagent for aldehydes (Cohn, Lassar): Chemistry. See: Van Nostrand Chem. Dict.

LASSAR, OSKAR. 1849-1907. German dermatologist. See: World Who's Who Sci. Lassar's mild resorcin paste, Lassar's plain poste, Lassar's shower-bath, Lassar's zinc paste.

Lassar's mild resorcin paste (Lassar, Oskar): Medicine. See: Dorland; Stedman.

Lassar's plain paste (Lassar, Oskar): Medicine. See: Stedman.

Lassar's shower-bath (Lassar, Oskar): Medicine. Cited in: World Who's Who Sci.

Lassar's zinc paste (Lassar, Oskar): Medicine. See: Stedman.

LASSUEUR, AUGUSTE. 1874-1949. Swiss physician. See: Revue Medic. Suisse Rom., vol. 70 (Aug. 25, 1950), pp. 494-498. Graham Little-Lassueur-Feldman syndrome?

Lassueur-Graham Little triad (Lassueur, Auguste? and Little, Ernest Gordon Graham). See: Little's syndrome.

LASTHENIA. Classical Greek woman who follwed the Platonic philosophy. See: Dict. Grk. Rom. Biog. Myth. Lasthenia.

Lasthenia (Lasthenia, the Greek woman): Botany. See: Hendrickson; Taylor, N.

LATARJET, ANDRE. b. 1877. French anatomist. See: Biog. Lex. hervorr. Aerzte, 1880-1930. Latarjet's nerve, Latarjet's vein (or vein of Latarjet).

Latarjet's nerve (Latarjet, Andre): Anatomy. See: Stedman.

Latarjet's vein (or vein of Latarjet) (Latarjet, Andre): Anatomy. See: Stedman. Also known as Mayo's vein (or vein of Mayo).

late Hurler's syndrome (Hurler, Gertrud). See: Scheie's syndrome.

LATHAM, PETER MERE. 1789-1875. English physician. See: Dict. Nat. Biog. Latham's circle.

Latham's circle (Latham, Peter Mere): Medicine. See: Dorland.

Latimer-Clark. See: Clark, Latimer.

Latimer-Clark cell (Clark, Josiah Latimer). See: Clark cell.

Latimeria (Courtenay-Latimer, Marjorie Eileen Doris): Zoology. See: Pennak; Webster's 3d.

Latona. See: Leto.

Latour circuit (Latour, Marius). See: Greinacher circuit (or connection).

LATOUR, MARIUS. fl. 1901. Belgian engineer. See: World Who's Who Sci. Bethenod-Latour alternator, Latour circuit.

LATREILLE, PIERRE-ANDRE. 1762-1833. French entomologist. See: Dict. Sci. Biog. Latreille's segment.

Latreille's segment (Latreille, Pierre-Andre): Zoology. See: Gray.

LA TROBE, CHARLES JOSEPH. 1801-1875. English-born administrator in Australia. See: Dict. Nat. Biog. Joe.

LATROBE, CHRISTIAN IGNATIUS. 1758-1836. English minister and musical composer. See: Dict. Nat. Biog. Latrobite.

LATROBE, JOHN HAZLEHURST BONEVAL. 1803-1891. American inventor and lawyer. See: Dict. Amer. Biog. Latrobe (stove).

Latrobe (stove) (Latrobe, John Hazlehurst Boneval): Engineering and Industry. See: Mathews, M. M.

Latrobite (Latrobe, Christian Ignatius): Earth Sciences. See: Thrush.

LATZKO, WILHELM. b. 1863. Austrian gynecologist and obstetrician. See: Biog. Lex. hervorr. Aerzte, 1880-1930. Latzko's cesarean section.

Latzko's cesarean section (Latzko, Wilhelm): Medicine. See: Stedman.

LAUBACH, FRANK CHARLES. 1884-1970. American missionary and educator. See: Who Was Who Amer., 1969-1973. Laubach reading method.

Laubach reading method (Laubach, Frank Charles): Education. See: Good.

LAUBER, HANS. b. 1876. Swiss-born ophthalmologist in Austria. See: Biog. Lex. hervorr. Aerzte, 1880-1930. Lauber's disease.

Lauber's disease (Lauber, Hans): Medicine. See: Jablonski.

LAUBMANN, HEINRICH. 1865-1951. German mineralogist. See: Geolog. Bavarica, vol. 14 (1952), p. 177f. Laubmannite.

Laubmannite (Laubmann, Heinrich): Earth Sciences. See: Thrush; Webster's 3d.

Laud Commission (Laud, William): History. See: Morris.

LAUD, WILLIAM. 1573-1645. English prelate. See: Dict. Nat. Biog. Laud Commission, Laudian professor, Laudian(s) (Laudean(s) or Laudianism).

Laudian(s) (Laudean(s) or Laudianism) (Laud, William): History. See: Steinberg; Webster's 3d.

Laudian Professor (Laud, William): Linguistics. See: Wagner (More Names).

LAUDON (or LOUDON), BARON GIDEON ERNST FREIHERR VON. 1717-1790. Austrian field marshal. See: New Encyc. Brit., 1974, Microp. Laudon symphony.

Laudon symphony (Laudon, Baron Gideon Ernst Freiherr von): Music. See: Apel; Scholes.

Laue equations (or conditions) (Laue, Max Theodor Felix von): Physics. See: Ballentyne; Hackh; Internat. Dict. Ap. Math.; Internat. Dict. Phys. Elec.; Thewlis.

LAUE, MAX THEODOR FELIX VON. 1880-1960. German physicist. See: Dict. Sci. Biog. Laue equations (or conditions), Laue pattern (diagram or photograph), Laue photograph(ic) method (method or photography), Laue spot, Laueite (or Laueit).

Laue pattern (diagram or photograph) (Laue, Max Theodor Felix von): Physics. See: Hughes; Markus; Thrush; Van Nostrand Chem. Dict.; Webster's 3d.

Laue photograph(ic) method (method or photography) (Laue, Max Theodor Felix von): Physics. See: Hackh; Internat. Dict. Phys. Elec.; Thewlis; Van Nostrand Chem. Dict.; Van Nostrand Sci. Encyc.

Laue spot (Laue, Max Theodor Felix von): Physics. See: Webster's 3d.

Laueite (or Laueit) (Laue, Max Theodor Felix von): Earth Sciences. See: Thrush.

Laugeria (Laugier, Robert de): Botany. See: Charnock.

LAUGHLEN, GEORGE FRANKLIN. b. 1888. Canadian pathologist. Cited in: Chem. Abstr., Decenn. Index, 1937-1946. Laughlen's test (and reagent).

Laughlen's test (and reagent) (Laughlen, George Franklin): Medicine. See: Dorland; Kelly.

LAUGHTON. fl. 1905. Australian mining engineer. (Biography source unavailable.) Goyder and Laughton process.

LAUGIER, ROBERT DE. fl. 1788. Chemist and botanist in Vienna. (Biography source unavailable.) Laugeria.

LAUGIER, STANISLAS. 1799-1872. French surgeon. See: World Who's Who Sci. Laugier's hernia, Laugier's sign.

Laugier's hernia (Laugier, Stanislas): Medicine. See: Dorland; Jablonski; Stedman.

Laugier's sign (Laugier, Stanislas): Medicine. See: Dorland; Stedman.

LAUMONIER, JEAN-BAPTISTE-PHILIPPE-NICOLAS-RENE. 1749-1818. French surgeon. See: Biog. Lex. hervorr. Aerzte. Laumonier's ganglion.

Laumonier's ganglion (Laumonier, Jean-Baptiste-Philippe-Nicolas-Rene): Anatomy. See: Donath; Dorland; Stedman.

LAUMONT, FRANCOIS PIERRE NICOLAS GILLET DE. 1747-1834. French mineralogist. See: Encyc. Brit., 1911. Laumontite (Laumonite or Lomonite).

Laumontite (Laumonite or Lomonite) (Laumont, Francois Pierre Nicolas Gillet de): Earth Sciences. See: Charnock; Thrush; Webster's 3d. Also known as: leonhardite.

Launois-Bensaude syndrome (Launois, Pierre Emile and Bensaude, Raoul?). See: Madelung's disease.

Launois-Cleret syndrome (Launois, Pierre Emile and Cleret, M.). See: Froehlich's syndrome.

LAUNOIS, PIERRE EMILE. 1856-1914. French physician. See: World Who's Who Sci. Launois-Bensaude syndrome, Launois-Cleret syndrome, Launois' syndrome.

Launois' syndrome (Launois, Pierre Emile): Medicine. See: Jablonski.

LAURA. 1308?-1348. French noblewoman. See: Webster's Biog. Dict. Laura.

Laura (Laura, the Frenchwoman): Generic Word (inspiring woman). See: Hendrickson; New Encyc. Brit., 1974, Microp.

Laura (barnacles) (Derivation undetermined): Zoology. See: Pennak.

LAURA, GIOVANNI BATTISTA. fl. 1872-1877. Italian anatomist. Cited in: Royal Soc. Cat. Sci. Pap., 1874-1883. Laura's nucleus.

Laura Ingalls Wilder medal (Wilder, Laura Ingalls): Library Science. See: Harrod.

Laura's nucleus (Laura, Giovanni Battista): Anatomy. See: Stedman.

Laurence-Biedl syndrome (Laurence, John Zacharias and Biedl, Arthur). See: Laurence-Moon-Biedl syndrome.

LAURENCE, JOHN ZACHARIAS. 1830-1874. English physician. See: World Who's Who Sci. Laurence-Moon-Biedl syndrome.

Laurence-Moon-Biedl-Bardet syndrome (Laurence, John Zacharias; Moon, Robert Charles; Biedl, Arthur; and Bardet, Georges). See: Laurence-Moon-Biedl syndrome.

Laurence-Moon-Biedl syndrome (Laurence, John Zacharias; Moon, Robert Charles; and Biedl, Arthur): Medicine. See: Dorland; Hinsie; Jablonski; Stedman; Wolman. Also known as: Laurence-Biedl syndrome, Laurence-Moon-Biedl-Bardet syndrome.

Laurencia (Laurencie, M. de la): Botany. See: Webster's 3d.

LAURENCIE, M. DE LA. fl. 19th c. French naturalist. (Biography source unavailable.) Laurencia.

Laurent('s) acid (Laurent, Auguste): Chemistry. See: Hackh; Webster's 3d.

LAURENT, AUGUSTE. 1807-1853. French organic chemist. See: Dict. Sci. Biog. Laurent('s) acid.

Laurent('s) expansion (or series) (Laurent, Pierre Alphonse): Mathematics. See: Ballentyne; Internat. Dict. Phys. Elec.; James; Thewlis.

Laurent half-shade plate (Laurent, Leon Louis): Physics. See: Internat. Dict. Phys. Elec.

LAURENT, LEON LOUIS. 1840-1909. French optical instrument maker. See: Pogg., vol. 3. Fizeau-Laurent surface interferometer, Laurent half-shade plate, Laurent polarimeter.

LAURENT, PIERRE ALPHONSE. 1813-1854. French mathematician and optician. See: Dict. Sci. Biog. Laurent process, Laurent('s) expansion (or series).

Laurent polarimeter (Laurent, Leon Louis): Physics. See: Internat. Dict. Phys. Elec.

Laurent process (Laurent, Pierre Alphonse): Statistics. See: Kendall.

LAURER, JOHANN FRIEDRICH. 1798-1873. German pharmacologist. See: Biog. Lex. hervorr. Aerzte. Laurer's canal.

Laurer-Stieda canal (Laurer, Johann Friedrich and Stieda, Alfred?). See: Laurer's canal.

Laurer's canal (Laurer, Johann Friedrich): Zoology. See: Henderson; Pennak; Stedman; Webster's 3d. Also known as: Laurer-Stieda canal.

Laurite (Joy, Laura): Earth Sciences. See: Hendrickson.

LAURITSEN, CHARLES CHRISTIAN. 1892-1968. Danish-born American physicist. See: World Who's Who Sci. Lauritsen electroscope.

Lauritsen electroscope (Lauritsen, Charles Christian and Lauritsen, Thomas): Physics. See: Hughes; Markus; Webster's 3d.

LAURITSEN, THOMAS. 1915- . Danish-born American physicist. See: World Who's Who Sci. Lauritsen electroscope.

Laury furnace (Laury, Napoleon Arthur): Chemistry. See: Van Nostrand Chem. Dict.

LAURY, NAPOLEON ARTHUR. b. 1879. American chemical engineer. Cited in: Mansell. Laury furnace.

LAUSEN, CARL. b. 1889. American mining engineer. See: Amer. Men Sci., 5th ed. Lausenite.

Lausenite (Lausen, Carl): Earth Sciences. See: Thrush; Webster's 3d.

Lautarite (Lautaro): Earth Sciences. See: Thrush.

LAUTARO. fl. 19th c. Chilean official. Cited in: Hintze, vol. I, pt. 3, half 1, pp. 2744-2745. Lautarite.

LAUTH, CHARLES. 1836-1913. English chemist. See: Pogg., vols. 4, 5. Lauth test for hydrogen sulfide?, Lauth tests for aromatic amines, Lauth's violet.

LAUTH, ERNEST ALEXANDRE. 1803-1837. Alsatian anatomist and physiologist. See: World Who's Who Sci. Lauth's canal (sinus or canal of Lauth).

Lauth mill (Derivation undetermined): Engineering and Industry. See: Thrush.

Lauth test for hydrogen sulfide (Lauth, Charles?): Chemistry. See: Van Nostrand Chem. Dict.

Lauth tests for aromatic amines (Lauth, Charles): Chemistry. See: Van Nostrand Chem. Dict.

LAUTH, THOMAS. 1758-1826. German anatomist and surgeon. Lauth's ligament.

Lauth's canal (sinus or canal of Lauth) (Lauth, Ernest Alexandre): Anatomy. See: Donath; Dorland; Stedman. Also known as: Schlemm's canal.

Lauth's ligament (Lauth, Thomas): Anatomy. See: Dorland; Stedman.

Lauth's violet (Lauth, Charles): Chemistry. See: Dorland; Stedman.

Lavailliere (shoes) (Derivation undetermined): Fashion. See: Stenhouse.

Laval (Laval, Pierre): Generic Word (traitor). See: Hendrickson.

Laval, Carl Gustaf Patrik de. See: De Laval, Carl Gustaf Patrik.

Laval nozzle (De Laval, Carl Gustaf Patrik): Engineering and Industry. See: Thewlis.

LAVAL, PIERRE. 1883-1945. French statesman. See: Encyc. Brit., 1973. Hoare-Laval plan, Laval.

Lavaliere (Lavalliere or Lavalier) (La Valliere, Louise Francoise de la Baume Le Blanc, Duchesse de): Fashion. See: Hendrickson; Partridge; Picken; Webster's 3d.

Lavaliere (or Lavalier) microphone (or cord) (La Valliere, Louise Francoise de la Baume Le Blanc, Duchesse de): Mass Media. See: Hendrickson; Hughes

LA VALLIERE, LOUIS CESAR DE LA BAUME LE BLANC, DUC DE. 1708-1780. French bibliophile. See: Nouv. Biog. Univ. maroquin Lavalliere.

LA VALLIERE, LOUISE FRANCOISE DE LA BAUME LE BLANC, DUCHESSE DE. 1644-1710. French mistress of Louis XIV. See: Encyc. Brit., 1973. Lavaliere (Lavalliere or Lavalier), Lavaliere (or Lavalier) microphone (or cord).

LAVATER BROTHERS. fl. 18th c. Swiss physicians. (Biography source unavailable.) Lavatera.

Lavatera (Lavater brothers): Botany. See: Charnock; Taylor, N.; Webster's 3d.

LAVDOVSKY, MICHAIL DORIMENTOW. 1846-1902. Russian histologist. See: Biog. Lex. hervorr. Aerzte, 1880-1930. Lavdovsky's nucleoid.

Lavdovsky's nucleoid (Lavdovsky, Michail Dorimentow): Anatomy. See: Dorland; Stedman.

LAVERAN, CHARLES LOUIS ALPHONSE. 1845-1922. French physician. See: Dict. Sci. Biog. Laverania, Laveran's bodies (or corpuscles), Laveran's stain.

Laverania (Laveran, Charles Louis Alphonse): Zoology. See: Dorland; Webster's 3d.

Laveran's bodies (or corpuscles) (Laveran, Charles Louis Alphonse): Anatomy. See: Blakiston's Gould; Dorland; Kelly.

Laveran's stain (Laveran, Charles Louis Alphonse): Medicine. See: Stedman.

LAVES, FRITZ HENNING. 1906- . German crystallographer. See: World Who's Who Sci. Laves phases.

Laves phases (Laves, Fritz Henning): Physics. See: Ballentyne.

Lavoisera (Lavoisier, Antoine-Laurent): Botany. See: Charnock.

LAVOISIER, ANTOINE-LAURENT. 1743-1794. French chemist, geologist and social reformer. See: Dict. Sci. Biog. Lavoisera.

LAVOYE, M. fl. 1922. Belgian pharmaceutical chemist. Cited in: Chem. Abstr., vol. 16, p. 882. Lavoye test for metals.

Lavoye test for metals (Lavoye, M.): Chemistry. See: Van Nostrand Chem. Dict.

law (2) of Malus (Malus, Etienne Louis). See: Malus' theorem.

Law cell (Derivation undetermined): Electronics. See: Hackh.

LAW, EDWARD, 1ST BARON ELLENBOROUGH. 1750-1818. English jurist. See: Dict. Nat. Biog. Ellenborough's Act.

LAW, JOHN. 1671-1729. Scottish financier and speculator. See: Dict. Nat. Biog. Law's Bubble.

law of Behring (Behring). See: Behring's law.

law of Berthelot-Nernst (Berthelot, Pierre Eugene Marcellin and Nernst, Walther Hermann): Chemistry. See: Van Nostrand Chem. Dict.

law of Berthollet (Berthollet, Claude Louis). See: Berthollet's law.

law of Bichat (Bichat, Marie Francois Xavier): Anatomy. See: Hinsie; Wolman.

law of Boltzmann (Boltzmann, Ludwig Eduard): Physics. See: Hackh; Van Nostrand Chem. Dict.

law of Boyle-Mariotte (Boyle, Robert and Mariotte, Edme). See: Boyle's law.

law of Delaroche and Berard (Delaroche, F. and Berard, Jacques Etienne): Chemistry. Cited in: World Who's Who Sci.

law of Dulong and Petit (Dulong, Pierre Louis and Petit, Alexis Therese). See: Dulong-Petit rule (or law).

law(s) of Fresnel-Arago (Fresnel, Augustin Jean and Arago, Dominique-Francois-Jean): Physics. See: Internat. Dict. Phys. Elec.; Van Nostrand Chem. Dict.; Van Nostrand Sci. Encyc.

law of Guldberg and Waage (Guldberg, Cato Maximilian and Waage, Peter). See: Guldberg and Waage's law.

law of Helmholtz (Helmholtz, Hermann Ludwig Ferdinand von). See: law of Thomson.

law of Henry (Henry, William). See: Henry('s) law.

law of Kopp (Kopp, Hermann Franz Moritz). See: Kopp('s) law.

law of Ladenburg (Ladenburg, Rudolf Walther). See: Ladenburg law.

law of Lambert (Lambert, Johann Heinrich). See: Bouguer-Lambert law of absorption.

law of Le Chatelier (Le Chatelier, Henry Louis). See: Le Chatelier('s) law.

law of Mitscherlich (Mitscherlich, Eilhardt). See: Mitscherlich('s) law.

law of Moseley (Moseley, Henry Gwyn Jeffreys). See: Moseley('s) law.

law of Nasse (Nasse, Christian Friedrich): Medicine. Cited in: World Who's Who Sci.

law of Neumann (Neumann, Franz Ernst). See: Neumann's law (2).

law of Ostwald (Ostwald, Wilhelm). See: Ostwald dulution law.

law of Oudeman (Oudemans, Anthonie Cornelis): Chemistry. See: Internat. Dict. Phys. Elec. Also known as: law of Landolt-Oudeman.

law of Pascal (Pascal, Blaise). See: Pascal law.

law of Paschen (Paschen, Friedrich). See: Paschen('s) law.

law of Retgers (Retgers, Jan Willem). See: Retgers' law.

law of Richter (Richter, Jeremias Benjamin). See: Richter's law.

law of Robin (Robin, G.). See: Robin's law.

law of Stefan and Boltzmann (Stefan, Josef and Boltzmann, Ludwig Eduard). See: Stefan-Boltzmann law.

...w of Thomson (or Thomson's rule) (Thomson, William, Lord Kelvin): Physics. ...ee: Van Nostrand Sci. Encyc. under "Thomson..." Also known as: law of ...elmholtz.

AWACZECK, FRANZ. b. 1880. German engineer. Cited in: Mansell. ...awaczeck machine.

...awaczeck machine (Lawaczeck, Franz): Engineering and Industry. See: ...uger.

...AWFORD, JOHN BOWRING. 1858-1934. Canadian-born English ophthalmol-...gist. See: World Who's Who Sci. Lawford's syndrome?

...awford's syndrome (Lawford, John Bowring?). See: Sturge-Weber syndrome.

...AWLER, JAMES. fl. 18th c.? American cultivator. (Biography source un-...vailable.) Lawler wheat.

...awler wheat (Lawler, James): Botany. See: Mathews, M. M.

...AWLEY, D. N. fl. 1938-1956. English statistician. Cited in: Kendall ...nd Doig. Wilks-Lawley U statistic.

...AWRENCE, ABBOTT. 1792-1855. American merchant, statesman and philan-...ropist. See: Dict. Amer. Biog. Lawrence Scientific School.

...awrence Awards (Lawrence, Ernest Orlando): Physics. See: Dict. Sci. Biog. ...nder "Lawrence, Ernest Orlando," vol. 8, p. 96b.

...awrence Berkeley Laboratory (Lawrence, Ernest Orlando): Physics. See: Dict. ...ci. Biog. under "Lawrence, Ernest Orlando," vol. 8, 96b.

...AWRENCE, D(AVID) H(ERBERT). 1885-1930. English novelist. See: Dict. ...at. Biog., 4th suppl. Lawrencian (Lawrentian or Laurentian).

...AWRENCE, ERNEST ORLANDO. 1901-1958. American physicist. See: ...ict. Sci. Biog. Lawrence Awards, Lawrence Berkeley Laboratory, Lawrence ...all of Science, Lawrence Livermore Laboratory (or Radiation Laboratory), ...awrence tube?, Lawrencium.

...AWRENCE, GEORGE NEWBOLD. 1806-1895. American ornithologist. See: ...orld Who's Who Sci. Lawrence's flycatcher, Lawrence's goldfinch, Lawrence's ...arbler.

...awrence Hall of Science (Lawrence, Ernest Orlando): Physics. See: Dict. ...ci. Biog. under "Lawrence Ernest Orlando," vol. 8, 96b.

...awrence Livermore Laboratory (or Radiation Laboratory) (Lawrence, Ernest ...rlando): Physics. See: Dict. Sci. Biog. under "Lawrence, Ernest Orlando," ...ol. 8, 96b.

...AWRENCE, ROBERT DANIEL. fl. 1912-1964. English physician. See: Med. ...irect., 1964. Lawrence's syndrome.

...AWRENCE, SAINT. d. 258. Christian deacon and martyr. See: Holweck. ...zy as Lawrence, St. Lawrence's tears.

...awrence Scientific School (Lawrence, Abbott): Philanthropy. See: Encyc. ...it., 1973 under "Higher Education," vol. 11, p. 482d.

...awrence tube (Lawrence, Ernest Orlando?): Electronics. See: Focal Encyc. ...lm; Hughes; Internat. Dict. Phys. Elec.; Markus.

...awrence's flycatcher (Lawrence, George Newbold): Zoology. See: ...athews, M. M.

...awrence's goldfinch (Lawrence, George Newbold): Zoology. See: ...athews, M. M.; Webster's 3d.

...awrence's syndrome (Lawrence, Robert Daniel): Medicine. See: Jablonski.

...awrence's warbler (Lawrence, George Newbold): Zoology. See: Gray; ...athews, M. M.

...awrencian (Lawrentian or Laurentian) (Lawrence, D(avid) H(erbert): Literature. ...e: Webster's 3d.

...awrencite (Smith, John Lawrence): Earth Sciences. See: Thrush; Webster's ...d.

...awrencium (Lawrence, Ernest Orlando): Chemistry. See: Encyc. Brit., 1973; ...endrickson; Van Nostrand Sci. Encyc.

...aw's Bubble (Law, John): History. See: Harbottle; Phyfe.

...ws of Deslandres (Deslandres, Henri Alexandre): Physics. See: Internat. ...ct. Phys. Elec.; Van Nostrand Chem. Dict.

...ws of Manu (Manu): Mythology. See: Harvey.

...AWSON, ANDREW COWPER. 1861-1952. Scottish-born American geologist. ...e: Dict. Sci. Biog. Lawsonite.

Lawson('s) cedar (cypress, false cypress or Lawsoniana) (Lawson, George?): Botany. See: Mathews, M. M.; Webster's 3d.

Lawson (furniture style) (Lawson, Thomas William): Applied Arts. See: Webster's 3d.

LAWSON, GEORGE. 1827-1895. Canadian botanist. See: Royal Soc. of Canada. Proc. & Trans., vol. 2 (1896), App. B, 6 pp. Lawson('s) cedar (cypress, false cypress or Lawsoniana)?

LAWSON, HARRY LAWSON WEBSTER, 1ST VISCOUNT BURNHAM. 1862-1933. English newspaper proprietor and public worker. See: Dict. Nat. Biog., 5th suppl. Burnham scale.

LAWSON, ISAAC. d. 1747. Scottish physician and botanist. See: Dict. Nat. Biog. Lawsonia.

LAWSON, THOMAS WILLIAM. 1857-1925. American financier. See: Dict. Amer. Biog. Lawson (furniture style).

Lawsonia (Lawson, Isaac): Botany. See: Charnock; Hendrickson; Stedman under "henna"; Taylor, N.; Webster's 3d.

Lawsonite (Lawson, Andrew Cowper): Earth Sciences. See: Thrush; Webster's 3d.

LAXMAN, ERIK. 1737-1796. Finnish botanist in Russia. See: Finsk Biog. Handb. Laxmannia, Laxmannite.

Laxmannia (Laxman, Erik): Botany. See: Charnock.

Laxmannite (Laxman, Erik). See: vauquelinite.

LAY, GEORGE TRADESCANT. d. 1845. English naturalist. See: Britten and Boulger. Layia.

Laycock De Normanville overdrive (Laycock Engineering Company and Normanville, E. J. de): Engineering and Industry. See: Auger. Also known as: De Normanville overdrive.

layer of Langhans (Langhans, Theodor). See: Langhans' layer.

Layia (Lay, George Tradescant): Botany. See: Taylor, N.; Webster's 3d.

Lazar (Lazarus or Lazarone) (Lazarus, Saint): Generic Word (beggar or leper). See: Brewer; Charnock; Hendrickson; Jobes; Partridge; Webster's 3d.

Lazar house (Lazaret or Lazaretto) (Lazarus, Saint): Generic Word (sanctuary for those with contagious diseases). See: Brewer; Charnock; Hargrave; Hendrickson; Jobes; Stenhouse.

Lazaret (Lazarus, Saint): Generic Word (quarantined ship or building). See: Partridge.

Lazarists (Lazarus the beggar, Saint). See: Vincentians.

Lazarium (Lazarus of Bethany): Religion. Cited in: Butler's Lives of the Saints under "St. Lazarus."

Lazarus (Lazarus of Bethany): Generic Word. See: Hendrickson; Jobes.

LAZARUS OF BETHANY. Friend of Jesus whom he raised from the dead. See: Holweck. Lazarium, Lazarus.

LAZARUS, SAINT. Beggar whom Christ mentioned in a parable. See: Holweck. Knights of St. Lazare, Lazar house (Lazaret or Lazaretto), Lazar (Lazarus or Lazarone), Lazaret, Lazarists, Order (Hospitallers) of St. Lazarus of Jerusalem (or Lazarites), Order of Saints Maurice and Lazarus, poor as Lazarus.

lazy as Lawrence (Lawrence, Saint): Generic Word. See: Hendrickson. Also known as: lazy as Lawrence's (or David Larence's) dog.

lazy as Lawrence's (or David Larence's) dog. See: lazy as Lawrence.

lazy as Ludlam's dog (Ludlam, Mrs.): Generic Word (extremely lazy). See: Hendrickson. Also known as: lazy as Lawrence's (or David Larence's) dog.

Lea Act (Lea, Clarence Frederick): Politics. See: Encyc. Brit., 1973 under "Labour Law," vol. 13, p. 544c.

Lea and Nurse permeability apparatus (Lea, Frederick Measham and Nurse, Ronald Walter Brown): Engineering and Industry. See: Thrush.

LEA, CLARENCE FREDERICK. 1874-1964. American legislator. See: Biog. Dict. Amer. Congress. Lea Act, Lea-Wagner Act, Lea-Wheeler Act (1940), Wheeler-Lea Act (1938).

LEA, FREDERICK MEASHAM. 1900- . English chemist. See: Watford Building Research Station. Bibliog., 1954, 4 pp. Lea and Nurse permeability apparatus.

LEA, MATTHEW CAREY. 1823-1897. American chemist. See: Dict. Amer. Biog. Lea reagent for cyanides, Lea test for hyposulfurous acid.

Lea('s) oak (Lea, Thomas Gibson): Botany. See: Webster's 3d.

Lea reagent for cyanides (Lea, Matthew Carey): Chemistry. See: Van Nostrand Chem. Dict.

Lea test for hyposulfurous acid (Lea, Matthew Carey): Chemistry. See: Van Nostrand Chem. Dict.

LEA, THOMAS GIBSON. 1785-1844. American botanist. Cited in: Mansell. Lea('s) oak.

Lea–Wagner Act (Lea, Clarence Frederick and Wagner, Robert Ferdinand): Politics. See: Smith.

Lea–Wheeler Act (1940) (Lea, Clarence Frederick and Wheeler, Burton Kendall): Politics. See: Smith.

LEACH, ALBERT ERNEST. 1864-1910. American chemist. See: World Who's Who Sci. Leach test for formaldehyde in milk.

Leach('s) petrel (Leach, William Elford): Zoology. See: Gray; Hendrickson under "Petrel..."; Webster's 3d.

Leach test for formaldehyde in milk (Leach, Albert Ernest): Chemistry. See: Van Nostrand Chem. Dict.

LEACH, WILLIAM ELFORD. 1790-1836. English naturalist. See: World Who's Who Sci. Leach('s) petrel.

LEAKE, CHAUNCEY DEPEW. 1896- . American physiologist. See: Amer. Men and Women Sci., 12th ed. Leake–Guy fluid (and method).

Leake–Guy fluid (and method) (Leake, Chauncey Depew and Guy, E. F.): Chemistry. See: Blakiston's Gould; Van Nostrand Chem. Dict.

Lean engine (Lean, John): Engineering and Industry. See: Auger.

LEAN, JOHN. fl. 1815. English engineer. Cited in: Royal Soc. Cat. Sci. Pap., 1800-1863. Lean engine.

LEAR. Legendary British King, whom Shakespeare took as central character of his tragedy, "King Lear," (ca. 1605). See: New Encyc. Brit., 1974, Microp. Lear complex.

Lear complex (Lear): Psychiatry. See: Stedman.

LEARY. fl. 19th c.? American manufacturer. (Biography source unavailable.) stovepipe Leary (hat).

LEARY, BERNICE ELIZABETH. fl. 1934. American educator. Cited in: Mansell. Gray–Leary formula.

LEAVIS, FRANK RAYMOND. 1895- . English literary critic. See: New Encyc. Brit., 1974, Microp. Leavisite.

Leavisite (Leavis, Frank Raymond): Literature. See: Barnhart (New Eng.).

LEAVITT, ERASMUS DARWIN. 1836-1916. American mechanical engineer. See: Dict. Amer. Biog. Leavitt pump.

LEAVITT, FRANK MC DOWELL. 1856-1928. American inventor. See: Dict. Amer. Biog. Bliss–Leavitt torpedo.

Leavitt pump (Leavitt, Erasmus Darwin): Engineering and Industry. See: Auger.

LE BECK, HENRY JULIUS. fl. 1798-1802. English? naturalist. Cited in: Royal Soc. Cat. Sci. Pap., 1800-1863. Lebeckia?

Lebeckia (LeBeck, Henry Julius?): Botany. See: Charnock.

LEBEDEV, PETR NIKOLAEVICH. 1866-1912. Russian physicist. See: Dict. Sci. Biog. P. N. Lebedev Physical Institute.

Lebedev process (Lebedev, Sergei Vasilievich): Chemistry. See: Van Nostrand Chem. Dict.

LEBEDEV, SERGEI VASILIEVICH. 1874-1934. Russian chemist. See: World Who's Who Sci. Lebedev process.

LE BEL, JOSEPH ACHILLE. 1847-1930. French chemist. See: Dict. Sci. Biog. Van't Hoff–LeBel theory.

LEBEL, NICOLAS. 1838-1891. French army officer. See: Webster's Biog. Dict. Lebel (rifle).

Lebel (rifle) (Lebel, Nicolas): Weapons. See: Latham; Partridge.

LeBel–Van't Hoff rule (LeBel, Joseph Achille and Van't Hoff, Jacobus Hendricus): See: Van't Hoff–LeBel theory.

LEBER, M. fl. 1933. German? chemist. Cited in: Chem. Abstr. vol. 27, p. 3161. Volmar–Leber reagent.

LEBER, THEODOR. 1840-1917. German ophthalmologist. See: Biog. Lex. hervorr. Aerzte, 1880-1930. Leber's amaurosis (or amaurosis congenita of Leber), Leber's corpuscles, Leber's disease (atrophy, hereditary optic atrophy or optic atrophy), Leber's idiopathic stellate retinopathy, Leber's plexus.

Leber's amaurosis (or amaurosis congenita of Leber) (Leber, Theodor): Medicine. See: Jablonski; Stedman.

Leber's corpuscles (Leber, Theodor): Medicine. See: Dorland.

Leber's disease (atrophy, hereditary optic atrophy or optic atrophy) (Leber, Theodor): Medicine. See: Hinsie; Jablonski; Stedman.

Leber's idiopathic stellate retinopathy (Leber, Theodor): Medicine. See: Stedman.

Leber's plexus (Leber, Theodor): Anatomy. See: Donath; Dorland; Stedman. Also known as: Hovius' plexus.

LEBERT, HERMANN. 1813-1878. German pathologist and naturalist. See: World Who's Who Sci. Lebertia.

Lebertia (Lebert, Hermann): Zoology. See: Pennak.

Lebesgue convergence theorem (Lebesgue, Henri Leon): Mathematics. See: James.

LEBESGUE, HENRI LEON. 1875-1941. French mathematician. See: Dict. Sci. Biog. Lebesgue convergence theorem, Lebesgue integral, Lebesgue measure, Lebesgue–Stieltjes integral, Riemann–Lebesgue lemma.

Lebesgue integral (Lebesgue, Henri Leon): Mathematics. See: Internat. Dict. Ap. Math.; Internat. Dict. Phys. Elec.; James.

Lebesgue measure (Lebesgue, Henri Leon): Mathematics. See: Internat. Dict. Ap. Math.; James.

Lebesgue–Stieltjes integral (Lebesgue, Henri Leon and Stieltjes, Thomas Jan): Mathematics. See: Internat. Dict. Ap. Math.; James; Van Nostrand Sci. Encyc. Also known as: Stieltjes integral.

Leblanc air pump (Leblanc, Maurice): Engineering and Industry. See: Auger.

Leblanc balancing machine (Leblanc, Maurice): Engineering and Industry. See: Auger.

LEBLANC, MAURICE. 1857-1923. French electrical engineer. See: World Who's Who Sci. Leblanc air pump, Leblanc balancing machine, Leblanc–Thearle balancing machine.

LEBLANC, NICOLAS. 1742-1806. French chemist. See: Dict. Sci. Biog. Leblanc process (or soda process).

Leblanc process (or soda process) (Leblanc, Nicolas): Chemistry. See: Ballentyne; Hackh; Van Nostrand Chem. Dict.; Webster's 3d.

Leblanc–Thearle balancing machine (Leblanc, Maurice and Thearle, Ernest Lathrop): Engineering and Industry. See: Auger.

Lebon engine (Lebon, Philippe): Engineering and Industry. See: Auger.

LEBON, PHILIPPE. 1767-1804. French chemist and inventor. See: World Who's Who Sci. Lebon engine.

LE BRETON, MANUEL. No dates. French botanist. (Biography source unavailable.) Lebretonia.

Lebretonia (LeBreton, Manuel): Botany. See: Charnock.

LEBRUN, HECTOR. b. 1866. French biologist. See: Liber Mem. Gand, vol. 2 (1913), p. 398f. Carnoy–LeBrun fluid.

LE CAT, CLAUDE NICOLAS. 1700-1768. French surgeon. See: Dict. Sci. Biog. Lecat's gulf.

Lecat's gulf (LeCat, Claude Nicolas): Anatomy. See: Donath; Dorland.

LeChatelier bottle (LeChatelier, Henry Louis?): Chemistry. See: Van Nostrand Chem. Dict.

LeChatelier–Braun principle (LeChatelier, Henry Louis and Braun, Ferdinand Karl?). See: LeChatelier('s) law.

LeChatelier couple (LeChatelier, Henry Louis): Engineering and Industry. See: Thrush.

LeChatelier–Dupuy reagent (LeChatelier, Henry Louis and Dupuy, Eugene L.): Chemistry. See: Van Nostrand Chem. Dict.

LE CHATELIER, FRANCOIS. fl. 1927. French metallurgist. Cited in: Chem. Abstr., Decenn. Indexes, 1917-1926; 1927-1936. Portevin–LeChatelier effect.

LE CHATELIER, HENRY LOUIS. 1850-1936. French chemist. See: Dict. Sci. Biog. LeChatelier bottle?, LeChatelier couple, LeChatelier–Dupuy reagent, LeChatelier–Lemoine reagent, LeChatelier soundness test, LeChatelier('s) law (principle or law of LeChatelier), LeChatelier theorem, Lechatelierite.

LeChatelier('s) law (principle or law of LeChatelier) (LeChatelier, Henry Louis): Chemistry. See: Ballentyne; Internat. Dict. Phys. Elec.; Martin; New Encyc. Brit., 1974, Microp.; Van Nostrand Chem. Dict.; Van Nostrand Sci. Encyc. under "Chatelier..."; Webster's 3d. Also known as: LeChatelier-Braun principle.

LeChatelier-Lemoine reagent (LeChatelier, Henry Louis and Lemoine, Jacques): Chemistry. See: Van Nostrand Chem. Dict.

LeChatelier soundness test (LeChatelier, Henry Louis): Engineering and Industry. See: Thrush.

LeChatelier theorem (LeChatelier, Henry Louis): Physics. See: Internat. Dict. Ap. Math. under "Chatelier..."

Lechatelierite (LeChatelier, Henry Louis): Earth Sciences. See: Thrush; Webster's 3d.

LECHE, JOHAN. 1704-1764. Swedish botanist and physician. See: Biog. Lex. hervorr. Aerzte. Lechea.

Lechea (Leche, Johan): Botany. See: Charnock; Webster's 3d.

LECHENAULT. No dates. French botanist and traveler. (Biography source unavailable.) Lechenaultia.

Lechenaultia (Lechenault): Botany. See: Charnock.

LECHER, ERNST. 1856-1926. Austrian physicist. See: World Who's Who Sci. Lecher-line oscillator, Lecher oscillator, Lecher wires (or line).

Lecher-line oscillator (Lecher, Ernst): Electronics. See: Markus.

Lecher oscillator (Lecher, Ernst): Electronics. See: Van Nostrand Sci. Encyc.

Lecher wires (or line) (Lecher, Ernst): Electronics. See: Hughes; Markus; Van Nostrand Sci. Encyc.; Webster's 3d.

Leclanche cell (Leclanche, Georges): Chemistry. See: Hackh; Hughes; Internat. Dict. Phys. Elec.; Markus; Webster's 3d.

LECLANCHE, GEORGES. 1839-1882. French chemist. See: World Who's Who Sci. Leclanche cell.

LECLEF, J. fl. 1894. French physician. Cited in: Royal Soc. Cat. Sci. Pap., 1884-1900. Denys-Leclef phenomenon.

LECLERE, ANDRE. fl. 1886-1914. French chemist. Cited in: Chem. Abstr., vol. 8, p. 308. Leclere test for nitrite in presence of nitrate.

Leclere test for nitrite in presence of nitrate (Leclere, Andre): Chemistry. See: Van Nostrand Chem. Dict.

LECLUSE, CHARLES DE (CAROLUS CLUSIUS). 1526-1609. French physician and botanist. See: Dict. Sci. Biog. Clusia.

Lecocq reaction for molybdenum (Boisbaudran, Paul Emile Lecoq de?): Chemistry. See: Van Nostrand Chem. Dict.

LE CONTE, JOHN LAWRENCE. 1825-1883. American naturalist. See: World Who's Who Sci. LeConte's sparrow (or bunting), LeConte's thrasher (or mockthrush), Lecontite.

LeConte's sparrow (or bunting) (LeConte, John Lawrence): Zoology. See: Gray; Mathews, M. M.; Pennak; Webster's 3d.

LeConte's thrasher (or mockthrush) (LeConte, John Lawrence): Zoology. See: Gray; Mathews, M. M.

Lecontite (LeConte, John Lawrence): Earth Sciences. See: Thrush; Webster's 3d.

Lecoq de Boisbaudran, Paul Emil. See: Boisbaudran, Paul Emil Lecoq de.

Lecq decking system (Derivation undetermined): Engineering and Industry. See: Thrush.

LEDDERHOSE, GEORG. 1855-1925. German physician. See: Biog. Lex. hervorr. Aerzte, 1880-1930. Ledderhose's syndrome.

Ledderhose's syndrome (Ledderhose, Georg): Medicine. See: Jablonski.

LEDEBOUR, KARL FRIEDRICH VON. 1785-1851. German botanist in Russia. See: Webster's Biog. Dict. Ledeburia.

LEDEBUR, ADOLF. 1837-1906. German metallurgist. See: Encic. Ital. Ledeburite.

Ledeburia (Ledebour, Karl Friedrich von): Botany. See: Charnock.

Ledeburite (Ledebur, Adolf): Earth Sciences. See: Thrush; Van Nostrand Sci. Encyc.; Webster's 3d.

LE DENTU, JEAN-FRANCOIS-AUGUSTE. 1841-1926. French surgeon. See: World Who's Who Sci. LeDentu's suture.

LeDentu's suture (LeDentu, Jean-Francois-Auguste): Medicine. See: Dorland.

LEDER, MAX. 1912- . Swiss dermatologist. Cited in: Index-Cat. Libr. Surg.-Gen. Off., 4th Ser., vol. 9, 1945. Miescher-Leder granulomatosis.

LEDERER, BARON. d. 1842. Austrian consul at New York. Cited in: Dana, p. 437. Ledererite (or Lederite).

Lederer-Brill syndrome (Lederer, Max and Brill, Nathan Edwin). See: Lederer's anemia (or disease).

LEDERER, LEONHARD. fl. 1894. German chemist. Cited in: Royal Soc. Cat. Sci. Pap., 1884-1900. Lederer-Manasse reaction.

Lederer-Manasse reaction (Lederer, Leonhard and Manasse, Otto): Chemistry. See: Ballentyne; Krauch and Kunz; Van Nostrand Chem. Dict. Also known as: Baekeland-Lederer-Manasse phenol-formaldehyde polycondensation.

LEDERER, MAX. 1885-1952. American pathologist. See: J.A.M.A., vol. 150 (Nov. 22, 1952), p. 1234. Lederer's anemia (or disease).

Ledererite (or Lederite) (Lederer, Baron): Earth Sciences. See: Charnock; Funk & Wagnalls New Std. Dict. Eng. Lang.

Lederer's anemia (or disease) (Lederer, Max): Medicine. See: Dorland; Jablonski; Stedman. Also known as: Lederer-Brill syndrome.

LEDRAN, HENRI FRANCOIS. 1685-1770. French surgeon. See: World Who's Who Sci. Ledran's suture.

Ledran's suture (Ledran, Henri Francois): Medicine. See: Dorland.

LEDUC, ANATOLE (In full: SYLVESTRE ANATOLE). 1856-1937. French physicist. See: Pogg., vols. 4, 5, 6. Amagat-Leduc rule, Righi-Leduc effect.

Leduc current (and interrupter) (Leduc, Stephane A. N.): Electronics. See: Dorland; Hughes; Markus; Stedman.

Leduc effect (Leduc, Anatole). See: Righi-Leduc effect.

Leduc law (Leduc, Anatole). See: Amagat-Leduc rule.

LEDUC, STEPHANE A. N. 1853-1939. French physician. See: Dict. Nat. Contemp. Leduc current (and interrupter).

Lee board (Derivation undetermined): Engineering and Industry. See: Thrush.

Lee Commission (Lee of Fareham, Arthur Hamilton Lee, 1st Viscount): Politics. See: New Encyc. Brit., 1974, Microp.

Lee configuration (Derivation undetermined): Electronics. See: Thrush.

Lee-Enfield rifle (or .303 rifles) (Lee, James Paris and Enfield, England): Weapons. See: Partridge; Quick; Webster's 3d.

LEE, FRANK ANDREW. 1901- . American chemist. See: Amer. Men Sci., 5th ed. Lynn-Lee reagents.

LEE, J. F. No dates. English academician. Cited in: Dana, p. 356. Leelite.

LEE, JAMES. 1715-1795. English botanist. See: World Who's Who Sci. Leea.

LEE, JAMES PARIS. 1831-1904. Scottish-born American inventor. See: World Who's Who Sci. Lee-Enfield rifle (or .303 rifles), Lee-Metford rifle, Lee-Straight-Pull (magazine rifle).

LEE, MARIA. fl. early 1800's. American boardinghouse proprietor. (Biography source unavailable.) black Maria (police van).

Lee-Metford rifle (Lee, James Paris and Metford, William Ellis): Weapons. See: Latham; Partridge.

Lee-Norse miner (Derivation undetermined): Engineering and Industry. See: Thrush.

LEE OF FAREHAM, ARTHUR HAMILTON LEE, 1ST VISCOUNT. 1868-1947. English statesman. See: Who Was Who, 1941-1950. Lee Commission.

LEE, PEARL. fl. 1927. American physician. (Biography source unavailable.) Cooley-Lee syndrome.

Lee process (Derivation undetermined): Engineering and Industry. See: Thrush.

LEE, ROBERT. 1793-1877. English gynecologist and obstetrician. See: World Who's Who Sci. Lee's ganglion, Lee's polyp.

LEE, ROBERT EDWARD. 1807-1870. American Civil War General. See: Dict. Amer. Biog. Lee's Birthday.

LEE, ROGER IRVING. b. 1881. American physician. See: Amer. Men Sci., 10th ed. Lee-White method.

Lee-Straight Pull (magazine rifle) (Lee, James Paris): Weapons. Cited in: World Who's Who Sci. under "Lee, James Paris."

LEE, TSUNG DAO. 1926- . Chinese-born American physicist. See: World Who's Who Sci. Lee wave?

Lee wave (Lee, Tsung Dao?): Physics. See: Van Nostrand Sci. Encyc.

Lee-White method (Lee, Roger Irving and White, Paul Dudley): Medicine. See: Kelly; Stedman.

Leea (Lee, James): Botany. See: Charnock; Taylor, N.

Leebar separator (Derivation undetermined): Engineering and Industry. See: Thrush.

LEEDE, CARL STOCKBRIDGE. b. 1882. American physician. Cited in: Kelly. Rumpel-Leede test (sign or phenomenon).

Leelite (Lee, J. F.): Earth Sciences. See: Charnock.

LEERS, JOHANN DANIEL. 1727-1772. German botanist. See: Arch. Gesch. Naturw. Tech., vol. 2 (1909-1910) pp. 146-148. Leersia.

Leersia (Leers, Johann Daniel): Botany. See: Webster's 3d.

Lee's Birthday (Lee, Robert Edward): Generic Word. See: Webster's 3d.

Lee's ganglion (Lee, Robert): Anatomy. See: Donath; Stedman.

LEES, JOHN. fl. ca. 1859. English acrobat. (Biography source unavailable.) Hanlon-Lees troupe.

Lee's polyp (Lee, Robert): Medicine. See: Jablonski.

LEESON, CHARLES ROLAND. 1926- . English-born American anatomist. See: Amer. Men and Women Sci., 12th ed. Leeson disk?

Leeson disk (Leeson, Charles Roland? and Leeson, Thomas Sydney?): Physics. See: Thewlis.

LEESON, THOMAS SYDNEY. 1926- . English-born Canadian anatomist. See: Amer. Men and Women Sci., 12th ed. Leeson disk?

LEET, LEWIS DON. 1901- . American seismologist. See: World Who's Who Sci. Leet seismograph.

Leet seismograph (Leet, Lewis Don): Earth Sciences. See: Thrush.

Leeuwen, Johanna Van. See: Van Leeuwen, Johanna.

LEEUWENHOEK, ANTONY VAN. 1632-1723. Dutch microscopist. See: Dict. Sci. Biog. Leeuwenhoekia australiensis, Leeuwenhoek's canal, Leeuwenhoek's little animals.

Leeuwenhoekia australiensis (Leeuwenhoek, Antony van): Zoology. See: Dorland.

Leeuwenhoek's canal (Leeuwenhoek, Antony van). See: Haversian canals.

Leeuwenhoek's little animals (Leeuwenhoek, Antony van): Zoology. See: Blumberg.

LEFEVRE, PAUL. fl. 1924. French dermatologist. (Biography source unavailable.) Papillon-Lefevre syndrome.

LeFort I fracture (LeFort, Leon Clement). See: Guerin's fracture.

LeFort II fracture (LeFort, Leon Clement): Medicine. See: Stedman.

LeFort III fracture (LeFort, Leon Clement): Medicine. See: Stedman.

LE FORT, LEON CLEMENT. 1829-1893. French surgeon. See: World Who's Who Sci. LeFort I fracture, LeFort II fracture, LeFort III fracture, LeFort's amputation, LeFort's operation, LeFort's suture.

LeFort's amputation (LeFort, Leon Clement): Medicine. See: Stedman.

LeFort's operation (LeFort, Leon Clement): Medicine. See: Blakiston's Gould; Dorland; Kelly.

LeFort's suture (LeFort, Leon Clement): Medicine. See: Dorland.

legacy of Iyeyasu (Iyeyasu): History. See: Harbottle.

LEGAL, EMMO. 1859-1922. German physician. See: Biog. Lex. hervorr. Aerzte, 1880-1930. Legal's disease, Legal's test.

Legal's disease (Legal, Emmo): Medicine. See: Blakiston's Gould; Dorland; Jablonski; Kelly.

Legal's test (Legal, Emmo): Medicine. See: Blakiston's Gould; Dorland; Kelly; Stedman.

LE GASCON. fl. 1630-1658. French bookbinder. See: Grand Larousse Encyc. LeGascon binding.

LeGascon binding (LeGascon): Applied Arts. See: Lockwood.

LEGENDRE, ADRIEN MARIE. 1752-1833. French mathematician. See: Dict. Sci. Biog. associated Legendre functions (or equation), Legendre functions (or functions of the second kind), Legendre('s) differential equation (or equation), Legendre('s) polynomial(s), Legendre transformation, Legendre's coefficients, Legendre's elliptic integrals (normal forms or standard (normal) elliptic integrals of the first, second and third kinds), Legendre's necessary condition (or conditions), Legendre's symbol, Legendre's theorem.

Legendre('s) differential equation (or equation) (Legendre, Adrien Marie): Mathematics. See: James; Thewlis; Van Nostrand Sci. Encyc.

Legendre functions (or functions of the second kind) (Legendre, Adrien Marie): Mathematics. See: Encyc. Brit., 1973 under "Spherical Harmonics," vol. 21, p. 15a; Internat. Dict. Ap. Math.; James.

LEGENDRE, GASTON-LUCIEN-JOSEPH. b. 1887. French physician. Cited in: Index-Cat. Libr. Surg.-Gen. Off., 3rd ser., vol. 7, 1928. Legendre's sign.

Legendre('s) polynomial(s) (Legendre, Adrien Marie): Mathematics. See: Internat. Dict. Ap. Math.; Internat. Dict. Phys. Elec.; James; Kendall.

Legendre transformation (Legendre, Adrien Marie): Mathematics. See: Dict. Sci. Biog. under "Legendre, Adrien Marie," p. 136a.

Legendre's coefficients (Legendre, Adrien Marie): Mathematics. See: Ballentyne.

Legendre's elliptic integrals (normal forms or standard (normal) elliptic integrals of the first, second and third kinds) (Legendre, Adrien Marie): Mathematics. See: Ballentyne; Encyc. Brit., 1973 under "Elliptic Functions," vol. 8, p. 297a; Van Nostrand Sci. Encyc. under "Integral (Elliptic)."

Legendre's necessary condition (or conditions) (Legendre, Adrien Marie): Mathematics. See: Dict. Sci. Biog. under "Legendre, Adrien-Marie," vol. 8, p. 135b; James.

Legendre's sign (Legendre, Gaston-Lucien-Joseph): Medicine. See: Stedman.

Legendre's symbol (Legendre, Adrien Marie): Mathematics. See: Encyc. Brit., 1973 under "Numbers, Theory of," vol. 16, p. 747b; James.

Legendre's theorem (Legendre, Adrien Marie): Mathematics. See: Dict. Sci. Biog. under "Legendre, Adrien Marie," pp. 135-136.

LEGER, EUGENE. fl. 1885-1931. French chemist. See: Pogg., vols. 5, 6. Leger test reaction for bismuth.

Leger, Saint. See: Leodigar, Saint.

Leger test reaction for bismuth (Leger, Eugene): Chemistry. See: Van Nostrand Chem. Dict.

LEGG, ARTHUR THORNTON. 1874-1939. American surgeon. See: J.A.M.A., vol. 113 (1939), p. 525. Calve-Legg-Perthes syndrome, Legg's operation.

Legg-Calve-Perthes disease (Legg, Arthur Thornton; Calve, Jacques; and Perthes, Georg Clemens). See: Calve-Legg-Perthes syndrome.

Legg-Perthes disease (Legg, Arthur Thornton and Perthes, Georg Clemens). See: Calve-Legg-Perthes syndrome.

Legg's disease (Legg, Arthur Thornton). See: Calve-Legg-Perthes syndrome.

Legg's operation (Legg, Arthur Thornton): Medicine. See: Kelly; Stedman.

Legion of Mary (Mary, Virgin-Mother): Religion. See: Attwater.

LEGLER, LUDWIG. fl. 1884-1886. German scientist. Cited in: Royal Sci. Cat. Sci. Pap., 1884-1900. Legler test for formaldehyde?

Legler test for formaldehyde (Legler, Ludwig?): Chemistry. See: Van Nostrand Chem. Dict.

LEGRAND. fl. 20th c. Belgian mine owner. Cited in: Min. Mag., vol. 23 (March 1932-Sept. 1934), pp. 175-178. Legrandite.

Legrandite (Legrand): Earth Sciences. See: Thrush; Webster's 3d.

LEGREE, SIMON. Character in Harriet Beecher Stowe's novel, "Uncle Tom's Cabin," (1852). See: Hart. Simon Legree.

LEGUAT, FRANCOIS. 1638-1735. French Huguenot traveler. See: Dict. Nat. Biog. Leguatia.

Leguatia (Leguat, Francois): Zoology. See: Webster's 3d.

Lehman-Filhes method (Lehmann-Filhes, Rudolf): Mathematics. See: Internat. Dict. Ap. Math.

LEHMANN. fl. 20th c.? Physician. (Biography source unavailable.) Lehmann-Ribbing-Mueller syndrome.

Lehmann acoumeter (Derivation undetermined): Physics. See: Drever.

Lehmann alternatives (Lehmann, Erich Leo): Statistics. See: Kendall.

LEHMANN, ERICH LEO. 1917- . French-born American mathematical statistician. See: Amer. Men and Women Sci., 12th ed. Lehmann alternatives, Lehmann's test.

LEHMANN-FILHES, RUDOLF. 1885-1914. German astronomer and mathematician. See: Pogg., vols. 3, 4, 5. Lehman-Filhes method.

LEHMANN, KARL. fl. 1929-1931. German engineer. Cited in: Chem. Abstr., vol. 25, p. 5006. Lehmann process.

Lehmann lovegrass (Derivation undetermined): Botany. See: Winburne.

LEHMANN, ORLA J.O.L. fl. 1961. Swedish physician. See: Legit. Laekare, 1974. Boerjeson-Forssman-Lehmann syndrome.

Lehmann process (Lehmann, Karl): Engineering and Industry. See: Thrush.

Lehmann representation (Derivation undetermined): Physics. See: Internat. Dict. Ap. Math.

Lehmann-Ribbing-Mueller syndrome (Lehmann; Ribbing, Seved; and Mueller, Walther). See: Ribbing's syndrome.

Lehmann's test (Lehmann, Erich Leo): Statistics. See: Kendall.

LEHUNT, CAPT. fl. 19th c. Irish? landowner. Cited in: Hintze, vol. 2, p. 1691. Lehuntite.

Lehuntite (Lehunt, Capt.): Earth Sciences. See: Charnock.

LEI, HSING-HAN. fl. 1933. Chinese chemist. Cited in: Chem. Abstr., vol. 27, p. 4222; vol. 29, p. 1429. Sah-Chang-Lei test reagent, Sah-Lei reagents.

LEIBLEIN, VALENTIN. fl. 1821. German zoologist. Cited in: Mansell. Leiblein's gland?

Leiblein's gland (Leiblein, Valentin?): Zoology. See: Gray.

LEIBLER, RICHARD ARTHUR. 1914- . American mathematician. See: Amer. Men Sci., 10th ed. Kullbach-Liebler information number?

Leibnitz('s) theorem (formula or rule) (Leibniz, Gottfried Wilhelm, Baron von): Mathematics. See: Ballentyne; James; Thewlis; Van Nostrand Sci. Encyc.

Leibnitz's monads (Leibniz, Gottfried Wilhelm, Baron von): Physics. See: Ballentyne.

Leibnitz's test (for alternating series) (Leibniz, Gottfried Wilhelm, Baron von): Mathematics. See: Ballentyne.

LEIBNIZ, GOTTFRIED WILHELM, BARON VON. 1646-1716. German mathematician and philosopher. See: Dict. Sci. Biog. Leibnitz('s) theorem (formula or rule), Leibnitz's monads, Leibnitz's test (for alternating series), Leibniz' law, Leibniz program, Leibnizian (Leibnitzian or Leibnizianism), Leibnizian rationalism, Leibnizo-Wolffian philosophy (or philosophical system).

Leibniz' law (Leibniz, Gottfried Wilhelm, Baron von): Philosophy. See: Edwards.

Leibniz program (Leibniz, Gottfried Wilhelm, Baron von): Philosophy. See: Dict. Sci. Biog. under "Leibniz, Gottfried Wilhelm," p. 159b.

Leibnizian (Leibnitzian or Leibnizianism) (Leibniz, Gottfried Wilhelm, Baron von): Philosophy. See: Webster's 3d.

Leibnizian rationalism (Leibniz, Gottfried Wilhelm, Baron von): Philosophy. See: Urmson.

Leibnizo-Wolffian philosophy (or philosophical system) (Leibniz, Gottfried Wilhelm, Baron von and Wolff, Christian von): Philosophy. See: Dict. Sci. Biog. under "Leibniz, Gottfried Wilhelm," vol. 8, p. 159a.

Leibowicz, Jankiew. See: Frank, Jacob.

Leicester, 1st Earl of. See: Dudley, Robert, 1st Earl of Leicester.

Leicester, Earl of. See: Coke, Thomas William, Earl of Leicester.

Leicester, Earl of. See: Montfort, Simon de, Earl of Leicester.

Leicester's Men (Dudley, Robert, 1st Earl of Leicester): Theater. See: Barnhart (Eng. Lit.).

LEICHHARDT, FRIEDRICH WILHELM LUDWIG. 1813-1848. German explorer in Australia. See: Dict. Nat. Biog. Leichhardt's pine (or tree).

Leichhardt's pine (or tree) (Leichhardt, Friedrich Wilhelm Ludwig): Botany. See: Webster's 3d.

LEICHMANN, GEORG. b. 1866. German scientist. Cited in: Royal Soc. Cat. Sci. Pap., 1884-1900. lactobacillus Leichmannii?

LEICHTENSTERN, OTTO MICHAEL LUDWIG. 1845-1900. German physician. See: Biog. Lex. hervor. Aerzte, 1880-1930. Leichtenstern's phenomenon (or sign), Leichtenstern's (Lichtenstern's) syndrome, Struempell-Leichtenstern encephalitis (or disease).

Leichtenstern's phenomenon (or sign) (Leichtenstern, Otto Michael Ludwig): Medicine. See: Blakiston's Gould; Dorland; Stedman.

Leichtenstern's (Lichtenstern's) syndrome (Leichtenstern, Otto Michael Ludwig): Medicine. See: Jablonski; Kelly.

Leichtlin camas (Leichtlin, Max?): Botany. See: Winburne.

Leichtlin lily (Leichtlin, Max?): Botany. See: Winburne.

LEICHTLIN, MAX. fl. 1886-1900. American? botanist. Cited in: Royal Soc. Cat. Sci. Pap., 1884-1900. Leichtlin camas?, Leichtlin lily?

LEIDENFROST. fl. 1829. American? scientist. Cited in: Royal Soc. Cat. Sci. Pap., 1800-1863. Leidenfrost('s) phenomenon.

Leidenfrost('s) phenomenon (Leidenfrost): Physics. See: Ballentyne; Thewlis.

LEIDY, JOSEPH. 1823-1891. American biologist and paleontologist. See: Dict. Sci. Biog. Leidyi.

Leidyi (Leidy, Joseph): Zoology. See: Pennak.

Leif Ericson. See: Ericson, Leif.

Leifite (Ericson, Leif): Earth Sciences. See: Thrush; Webster's 3d.

LEIGH, DENIS (In full: ARCHIBALD DENIS). 1915- . English neuropathologist. See: Who's Who Sci. Europe, 1967. Leigh's disease (or encephalomyelopathy).

Leigh light (Leigh-Mallory, Sir Trafford Leigh): Engineering and Industry. See: Partridge.

LEIGH-MALLORY, SIR TRAFFORD LEIGH. 1892-1944. English air force officer. See: Who Was Who, 1941-1950. Leigh light.

Leigh's disease (or encephalomyelopathy) (Leigh, Denis): Medicine. See: Jablonski; Wolman.

LEIGHTON DONOSO, TOMAS RAFAEL. 1894- . Chilean mineralogist and mining engineer. See: Dicc. Biog. de Chile. Leightonite.

Leightonite (Leighton Donoso, Tomas Rafael): Earth Sciences. See: Thrush; Webster's 3d.

LEINER, CARL. 1871-1930. Bohemian-born dermatologist in Austria. See: Biog. Lex. hervorr. Aerzte, 1880-1930. Leiner's dermatitis (or disease), Leiner's test.

Leiner's dermatitis (Leiner, Carl): Medicine. See: Dorland; Jablonski; Stedman.

Leiner's test (Leiner, Carl): Medicine. See: Dorland; Stedman.

LEIPNIK, ROY BERGH. 1924- . American mathematician. See: Amer. Men and Women Sci., 12th ed. Madow-Leipnik distribution.

Leishman-Donovan body(-ies) (or Leishmania Donovani) (Leishman, Sir William Boog and Donovan, Charles): Zoology. See: Dorland; Stedman.

LEISHMAN, SIR WILLIAM BOOG. 1865-1926. English medical officer. See: World Who's Who Sci. Leishman-Donovan body(-ies) (or Leishmania Donovani), Leishmania, Leishmaniasis (or Leishmaniosis), Leishman's chrome cells, Leishman's method, Leishman's stain.

Leishmania (Leishman, Sir William Boog): Zoology. See: Dorland; Pennak; Stedman; Webster's 3d.

Leishmaniasis (or Leishmaniosis) (Leishman, Sir William Boog): Medicine. See: Dorland; New Encyc. Brit., 1974, Microp.; Stedman; Van Nostrand Sci. Encyc.

Leishman's chrome cells (Leishman, Sir William Boog): Medicine. See: Stedman.

Leishman's method (Leishman, Sir William Boog): Medicine. See: Stedman.

Leishman's stain (Leishman, Sir William Boog): Medicine. See: Stedman.

LEISLER, JACOB. 1640-1691. German-born American politician. See: Dict. Amer. Biog. Leisler's rebellion.

Leisler's rebellion (Leisler, Jacob): History. See: Morris.

Leiter international performance test (or scale) (Leiter, Russell Graydon): Psychology. See: Chaplin; English; Good; Wolman.

LEITER, RUSSELL GRAYDON. 1901- . American psychologist. See: Biog. Direct. Amer. Psych. Assoc., 1975. Leiter international performance test (or scale).

Leitmeier-Feigl test for chromium in minerals (Leitmeier, Hans and Feigl, Friedrich): Chemistry. See: Van Nostrand Chem. Dict.

Leitmeier-Feigl test for magnesium in minerals (Leitmeier, Hans and Feigl, Friedrich): Chemistry. See: Van Nostrand Chem. Dict.

LEITMEIER, HANS. b. 1885. Austrian petrographer. See: Pogg., vols. 6, 7a. Feigl-Leitmeier test, Leitmeier-Feigl test for chromium in minerals, Leitmeier-Feigl test for magnesium in minerals, Leitmeier test for manganese in minerals.

Leitmeier test for manganese in minerals (Leitmeier, Hans): Chemistry. See: Van Nostrand Chem. Dict.

LEITNER, EDWARD F. *fl.* 19th c. American botanist. (Biography source unavailable.) Leitneria.

LEITNER, STEFAN J. 1903- . Swiss physician. See: Who's Who Switz. 1950-1951. Leitner's syndrome.

Leitneria (Leitner, Edward F.): Botany. See: New Encyc. Brit., 1974, Microp.; Webster's 3d.

Leitner's syndrome (Leitner, Stefan J.): Medicine. See: Jablonski.

LEITZ, ERNST. *fl.* 20th c. German-born optical manufacturer (in America?). (Biography source unavailable.) Leitz tyndallometer.

Leitz tyndallometer (Leitz, Ernst): Physics. See: Thrush.

LEJAY, PIERRE R. P. 1895-1958. French geophysicist. See: Ann. de Geophys., vol. 15 (1959), pp. 125-133. Holweck-Lejay inverted pendulum (or apparatus).

LEJEUNE, A. *fl.* 1929. Belgian chemist. Cited in: Chem. Abstr., vol. 23, p. 4276. Lejeune solution.

LEJEUNE, JEROME JEAN LOUIS MARIE. 1926- . French human geneticist. See: World Who's Who Sci. Lejeune's syndrome.

Lejeune's syndrome (Lejeune, Jerome Jean Louis Marie): Medicine. See: Jablonski.

Lejeune solution (Lejeune, A.): Chemistry. See: Van Nostrand Chem. Dict.

LELEUSE. No dates. Swiss friend of Candolle. (Biography source unavailable.) Leusea.

LELIEVRE, CLAUDE H. 1752-1835. French mineralogist. See: World Who's Who Sci. Lievrite.

Lelli reagent (Derivation undetermined): Chemistry. See: Van Nostrand Chem. Dict.

LELLMANN, EUGENE KARL. 1856-1893. German chemist. See: Pogg., vols. 3, 4. Lellmann test.

Lellmann test (Lellmann, Eugene Karl): Chemistry. See: Van Nostrand Chem. Dict.

LELOIR, HENRI CAMILLE C. 1855-1896. French dermatologist. See: World Who's Who Sci. Leloir's disease.

Leloir's disease (Leloir, Henri Camille C.): Medicine. See: Dorland; Jablonski; Stedman. Also known as: Cazenave's disease.

LEMAIRE, CHARLES ANTOINE. 1801-1871. French horticulturist. See: Merrill and Walker. Lemaireocereus.

Lemaireocereus (Lemaire, Charles Antoine): Botany. See: Webster's 3d.

LeMaistre, Isaac-Louis de Sacy. See: Sacy, Isaac-Louis LeMaistre de.

LEMALE, CHARLES. *fl.* 1894. French engineer. (Biography source unavailable.) Armengaud and Lemale gas turbine.

LEMAN. *fl.* 18th c. French botanist. (Biography source unavailable.) Lemanea.

Lemanea (Leman): Botany. See: Charnock; Webster's 3d.

LEMBERG, JOHANN THEODOR. 1842-1902. German mineralogist. See: Zentralb. f. Mineralogie, 1902, p. 246f. Lemberg('s) solution, Lemberg's reaction.

Lemberg('s) solution (Lemberg, Johann Theodor): Chemistry. See: Thrush; Van Nostrand Sci. Encyc.

Lemberg's reaction (Lemberg, Johann Theodor): Chemistry. See: Thrush.

LEMBERT, ANTOINE. 1802-1851. French surgeon. See: World Who's Who Sci. Czerny-Lembert suture, Lembert suture.

Lembert suture (Lembert, Antoine): Medicine. See: Dorland; Stedman.

LEMIELLE, TH. *fl.* 1840. Belgian mining engineer. Cited in: Royal Soc. Cat. Sci. Pap., 1800-1863. Lemielle ventilating machine (or ventilator).

Lemielle ventilating machine (or ventilator) (Lemielle, Th.): Engineering and Industry. See: Auger.

Le Mithonard solution (Derivation undetermined): Chemistry. See: Van Nostrand Chem. Dict.

LEMKE, WILLIAM. 1878-1950. American legislator. See: Biog. Direct. Amer. Congress. Frazier-Lemke Act (or Farm Bankruptcy Act).

LEMLI, LUC. *fl.* 1964. American? pediatrician. (Biography source unavailable.) Smith-Lemli-Opitz syndrome.

lemniscate of Bernoulli (Bernoulli, Jakob): Mathematics. See: Ballentyne; James; Van Nostrand Sci. Encyc.

Lemoine circle(s) (Lemoine, Emile Michel Hyacinthe): Mathematics. See: Dict. Sci. Biog under "Lemoine, Emile M.H.," p. 176b.

Lemoine deutzia (Lemoine, Emile): Botany. See: Winburne.

LEMOINE, EMILE. *fl.* 1890-1899. French botanist. Cited in: Mansell. Lemoine deutzia.

LEMOINE, EMILE MICHEL HYACINTHE. 1840-1912. French mathematician. See: Dict. Sci. Biog. Lemoine circle(s).

LEMOINE, JACQUES. *fl.* 1916-1936. French metallurgist. Cited in: Chem. Abstr. LeChatelier-Lemoine reagent.

Lemoine mockorange (Lemoine, Victor): Botany. See: Winburne.

LEMOINE, VICTOR. 1823-1911. German botanist. See: Brockhaus. Lemoine mockorange.

LEMON, SIR CHARLES. 1784-1868. English geologist and exotic plant collector. See: Boase. Lemonia.

LEMON, HARVEY BRACE. 1885- . American physicist. See: World Who's Who Sci. Brace-Lemon spectrophotometer.

Lemonia (Lemon, Sir Charles): Botany. See: Charnock.

LE MONNIER, JEAN CHARLES HENRI. *fl.* 1757. French bookbinder. See: Encic. Ital. Lemonnier style.

Lemonnier style (LeMonnier, Jean Charles Henri): Applied Arts. See: Glaister; Harrod.

LEMOULT, PAUL AIME LOUIS. 1871-1916. French chemist. See: Pogg., vols. 4, 5. Lemoult test reaction.

Lemoult test reaction (Lemoult, Paul Aime Louis): Chemistry. See: Van Nostrand Chem. Dict.

Lenard effect (Lenard, Philipp): Physics. See: Huschke.

LENARD, PHILIPP. 1862-1947. German physicist. See: Dict. Sci. Biog. Lenard effect, Lenard ray(s), Lenard tube.

Lenard ray(s) (Lenard, Philipp): Physics. See: Hackh; Internat. Dict. Phys. Elec.; Van Nostrand Chem. Dict.; Van Nostrand Sci. Encyc.; Webster's 3d.

Lenard tube (Lenard, Philipp): Physics. See: Hughes; Markus.

LENCI, FRANCESCO. *fl.* 1912-1918. Italian chemist. Cited in: Chem. Abstr. Tarugi-Lenci reaction for amino and imino groups, Tarugi-Lenci reaction for para-benzoquinone and 2, 6-dibromoquinone.

LENCLOS, NINON DE (Orig.: ANNE DE LENCLOS). 1620-1705. French courtesan. See: New Encyc. Brit., 1974, Microp. coiffure a la Ninon, Ninon.

LENHARTZ, HERMANN. 1854-1910. German physician. See: Biog. Lex. hervorr. Aerzte, 1880-1930. Lenhartz treatment.

Lenhartz treatment (Lenhartz, Hermann): Medicine. See: Dorland.

Lenher-Crawford test (Lenher, Victor and Crawford, W. G.): Chemistry. See: Van Nostrand Chem. Dict.

LENHER, VICTOR. 1873-1927. American chemist. See: World Who's Who Sci. Lenher-Crawford test.

LENHOSSEK, JOSEPH VON. 1818-1888. Hungarian anatomist. See: Biog. Lex. hervorr. Aerzte. Lenhossek's fibers.

LENHOSSEK, MIHALY MICHAEL VON. 1863-1937. Hungarian anatomist. See: World Who's Who Sci. Lenhossek's processes (bundle or bundle of Lenhossek).

Lenhossek's fibers (Lenhossek, Joseph von): Anatomy. See: Dorland; Stedman. Also known as: Deiters' formation.

Lenhossek's processes (bundle or bundle of Lenhossek) (Lenhossek, Mihaly Michael von): Anatomy. See: Stedman.

Lenin (Lenin, Nikolai): Navigation. See: New Encyc. Brit., 1974, Microp.

LENIN, NIKOLAI (Orig. name: VLADIMIR ILICH ULYANOV). 1870-1924. Founder of Russian Communist party. See: New Encyc. Brit., 1974. Lenin, Leniniana, Leninism (or Leninist), Lenin's testament, Order of Lenin.

Leniniana (Lenin, Nikolai): Photography. See: Focal Encyc. Photog. under "Ocup, Peter Adolfovich."

Leninism (or Leninist) (Lenin, Nikolai): Politics. See: Hendrickson; New Encyc. Brit., 1974, Microp.; Partridge; Webster's 3d.

Lenin's testament (Lenin, Nikolai): Politics. See: New Encyc. Brit., 1974, Microp.

LENNANDER, KARL GUSTAF. 1857-1908. Swedish surgeon. See: Biog. Lex. hervorr. Aerzte, 1880-1930. Lennander's operation.

Lennander's operation (Lennander, Karl Gustaf): Medicine. See: Dorland.

Lennard-Jones and Devonshire theory (Lennard-Jones, Sir John Edward and Devonshire, A. F.): Physics. See: Internat. Dict. Phys. Elec.

LENNARD-JONES, SIR JOHN EDWARD. 1894-1954. English physicist and chemist. See: Dict. Sci. Biog. Lennard-Jones and Devonshire theory, Lennard-Jones potential, Lennard-Jones (6, 12) potential.

Lennard-Jones potential (Lennard-Jones, Sir John Edward): Physics. See: Ballentyne; Van Nostrand Chem. Dict.

Lennard-Jones (6, 12) potential (Lennard-Jones, Sir John Edward): Physics. See: Dict. Sci. Biog. under "Lennard-Jones, Sir John Edward," p. 186a.

LENNHOFF, RUDOLF. 1866-1933. German physician. See: Biog. Lex. hervorr. Aerzte, 1880-1930. Lennhoff's index, Lennhoff's sign.

Lennhoff's index (Lennhoff, Rudolf): Medicine. See: Dorland.

Lennhoff's sign (Lennhoff, Rudolf): Medicine. See: Dorland.

LENNOX, DAVID. fl. 1890-1904. American manufacturer. Cited in: Nat. Cycl. Amer. Biog. under "Norris, John Windsor," vol. L, pp. 646-647. Lennox sand drier.

Lennox sand drier (Lennox, David): Engineering and Industry. See: Thrush.

Lennox('s) syndrome (Lennox, William Gordon): Medicine. See: Jablonski; Wolman.

LENNOX, WILLIAM GORDON. 1884-1960. American physician. See: Who Was Who Amer., 1961-1968. Lennox('s) syndrome.

Lenoble-Aubineau syndrome (Lenoble, E. and Aubineau, Ernest Rene Emile): Medicine. See: Jablonski.

LENOBLE, E. fl. 1906. French physician. (Biography source unavailable.) Lenoble-Aubineau syndrome.

LENOIR, CAMILLE-ALEXANDRE-HENRI. b. 1867. French anatomist. Cited in: Index-Cat. Libr. Surg.-Gen. Off., 2d Ser., vol. 9, 1904. Lenoir's facet.

Lenoir engine (or gas engine) (Lenoir, Jean Joseph Etienne): Engineering and Industry. See: Asimov; Auger.

LENOIR, JEAN JOSEPH ETIENNE. 1822-1900. French engineer. See: World Who's Who Sci. Lenoir engine (or gas engine).

Lenoir's facet (Lenoir, Camille-Alexandre-Henri): Anatomy. See: Stedman.

Lente insulin solution (Derivation undetermined): Medicine. See: Blakiston's Gould; Stedman.

Lentulo plugger (Derivation undetermined): Dentistry. See: Stedman.

LENZ, HARALD OTHMAR. 1798-1870. German botanist. Cited in: Grand Larousse Encyc. Lenzites.

LENZ, HEINRICH FRIEDRICH EMIL (or EMIL KHRISTIANOVICH). 1804-1865. Russian physicist. See: Dict. Sci. Biog. Lenz('s) law (1) (electromagnetic induction), Lenz's law (2) (thermal action of a current).

Lenz('s) law (1) (electromagnetic induction) (Lenz, Heinrich Friedrich Emil): Physics. See: Ballentyne; Markus; Thewlis; Thrush; Van Nostrand Sci. Encyc.; Webster's 3d.

Lenz-Richter test reactions for per-salts (Lenz, Wilhelm Georg Lebrecht): Chemistry. See: Van Nostrand Chem. Dict.

Lenz-Schoorl test (Lenz, Wilhelm Georg Lebrecht and Schoorl, Nicolaas): Chemistry. See: Van Nostrand Chem. Dict.

LENZ, VON (LENZIUS). fl. ca. 1816. German mineralogist. (Biography source unavailable.) Lenzinite.

LENZ, WIDUKIND. 1919- . German physician. See: Who's Who Sci. Europe, 1972. Lenz's syndrome?

LENZ, WILHELM GEORG LEBRECHT. 1852-1916. German pharmaceutical chemist. See: Pogg., vols. 4, 5. Lenz-Richter test reactions for per-salts, Lenz-Schoorl test.

Lenzinite (Lenz, von): Earth Sciences. See: Charnock. Also known as: halloysite.

Lenzites (Lenz, Harald Othmar): Botany. See: Webster's 3d.

LENZMAN, RICHARD. 1856-1927. German physician. See: Biog. Lex. hervorr. Aerzte, 1880-1930. Lenzman's point.

Lenzman's point (Lenzman, Richard): Anatomy. See: Donath; Dorland.

Lenz's law (2) (thermal action of a current) (Lenz, Heinrich Friedrich Emil). See: Joule's law.

LEO I THE GREAT, SAINT. ca. 390-461. Italian pope. See: New Encyc. Brit., 1974, Microp. Leonine sacramentary, Tome of St. Leo (or Leo's Tome).

LEO IV, SAINT. ca. 800-855. Italian pope. See: New Encyc. Brit., 1974, Microp. Leonine.

LEO XIII. 1810-1903. Italian pope. See: New Encyc. Brit., 1974. Leonine, Leonine union.

LEO, HANS. 1854-1927. German physician. See: Biog. Lex. hervorr. Aerzte, 1880-1930. Leo's test.

Leon firedamp tester (Leon, Gustave): Engineering and Industry. See: Thrush.

LEON, GUSTAVE. 1863-1916. French? engineer. See: World Who's Who Sci. Leon firedamp tester.

LEON, KARL ISKAR. No dates. Swedish inventor. (Biography source unavailable.) Leon mine.

Leon mine (Leon, Karl Iskar): Weapons. See: Quick.

LEONARD, ARTHUR GRAY. 1865-1932. American geologist. See: Who Was Who Amer., 1897-1942. Leonard series?, Leonardite.

Leonard series (Leonard, Arthur Gray?): Earth Sciences. See: Encyc. Brit., 1973 under "Permian System," vol. 17, p. 637a.

LEONARD, WARD (In full: HARRY WARD). 1861-1915. American electrical engineer. See: Dict. Amer. Biog. Ward Leonard double-arm circuit breaker, Ward Leonard system (or control).

Leonardesque (Leonardo da Vinci): Fine Arts. See: Webster's 3d.

LEONARDI, GIUSEPPE. fl. 1947-1951. Italian physician. Cited in: Chem. Abstr., Decenn. Index, 1947-1956. Magrassi-Leonardi syndrome?

Leonardite (Leonard, Arthur Gray): Earth Sciences. See: Thrush.

LEONARDO DA VINCI. 1452-1519. Italian painter, sculptor, architect, engineer and scientist. See: Encyc. Brit., 1973. Leonardesque.

Leonardo of Pisa. See: Fibonacci, Leonardo.

LEONE, TEODORO. fl. 1884. Italian chemist. Cited in: Royal Soc. Cat. Sci. Pap., 1884-1900. Leone test.

Leone test (Leone, Teodoro): Chemistry. See: Van Nostrand Chem. Dict.

LEONHARD, KARL CAESAR VON. 1779-1862. German mineralogist. See: Allg. Deut. Biog. Leonhardite.

Leonhardite (Leonhard, Karl Caesar von): Earth Sciences. See: Charnock; Thrush; Webster's 3d. Also known as: laumontite.

Leonine (Leo IV, Saint): History. See: Webster's 3d.

Leonine (Leo XIII): Religion. See: Webster's 3d.

Leonine sacramentary (Leo I the Great, Saint): Religion. See: Attwater.

Leonine union (Leo XIII): Religion. See: Attwater.

Leonine verse (or rhyme) (Leonius): Literature. See: Barnhart (Eng. Lit.); Brewer; Harvey; Preminger; Scott.

Leonite (Strippelmann, Leo): Earth Sciences. See: Thrush; Webster's 3d.

LEONIUS. fl. 12 c. French ecclesiastic. See: Michaud. Leonine verse (or rhyme).

LEOPOLD I. 1790-1865. King of the Belgians. See: New Encyc. Brit., 1974, Microp. Leopold (coin), Order of Leopold I.

LEOPOLD II. 1747-1792. Holy Roman Emperor and Duke of Tuscany. See: New Encyc. Brit., 1974, Microp. Leopoldine Code, Leopoldone (coin), Order of Leopold II.

LEOPOLD III. 1351-1386. Duke of Austria. See: Nouv. Biog. Univ. Leopoldine line.

Leopold (coin) (Leopold I): Numismatics. See: Charnock.

LEOPOLD, GERHARD (In full: Christian Gerhard). 1846-1911. German physician. See: Biog. Lex. hervorr. Aerzte, 1880-1930. Leopold's law, Leopold's maneuvers.

Leopold-Levi's syndrome (Levi, Leopold): Medicine. See: Jablonski.

Leopoldi furnace (Derivation undetermined): Engineering and Industry. See: Thrush.

Leopoldina (Maria Leopoldina): Botany. See: Webster's 3d.

Leopoldine Code (Leopold II): History. See: New Encyc. Brit., 1974, Microp.

Leopoldine line (Leopold III): History. See: Encyc. Brit., 1973 under "Austria, Empire of," vol. 2, p. 827d.

Leopoldone (coin) (Leopold II): Numismatics. See: Charnock.

Leopold's law (Leopold, Gerhard): Medicine. See: Dorland; Stedman.

Leopold's maneuvers (Leopold, Gerhard): Medicine. See: Stedman.

Leo's test (Leo, Hans): Medicine. See: Dorland; Stedman.

Leo's Tome (Leo I the Great, Saint). See: Tome of St. Leo.

Leotard (and Leotards) (Leotard, Jules): Fashion. See: Hendrickson; Webster's 3d

LEOTARD, JULES. 1830-1870. French acrobat. Cited in: Grand Larousse Encyc. Leotard (and Leotards).

LEOTTA, NICOLO. b. 1878. Italian surgeon. See: Biog. Lex. hervorr. Aerzte, 1880-1930. Leotta's sign, Leotta's syndrome.

Leotta's sign (Leotta, Nicolo): Medicine. See: Dorland.

Leotta's syndrome (Leotta, Nicolo): Medicine. See: Jablonski.

LEPAGE, PIERRE HIPPOLYTE. d. ca. 1886. Belgian pharmaceutical chemist. See: J. de Pharm. Antwerp., vol. 42 (1886), pp. 242-244. Lepage reagent.

Lepage reagent (Lepage, Pierre Hippolyte): Chemistry. See: Van Nostrand Chem. Dict.

Lepine-Froin syndrome (Lepine, Jean? and Froin, Georges). See: Froin's syndrome.

LEPINE, JEAN. b. 1876. French physician. Cited in: Royal Soc. Cat. Sci. Pap., 1884-1900. Lepine-Froin syndrome?

Le Pois, Willem. See: Piso, Willem.

LERCH, OTTO. fl. 1898-1919. American physician. Cited in: Mansell. Lerch's percussion.

LERCHE, JOHANN JACOB. 1708-1780. Russian physician. See: Biog. Lex. hervorr. Aerzte. Lerchea.

Lerchea (Lerche, Johann Jacob): Botany. See: Charnock.

Lerch's percussion (Lerch, Otto): Medicine. See: Dorland.

LEREBOULLET, PIERRE. 1874-1944. French physician. See: Biog. Lex. hervorr. Aerzte, 1880-1930. Gilbert-Lereboullet syndrome.

Lerebours lens (Lerebours, Noel-Marie-Paymal): Photography. See: Focal Encyc. Photog.

LEREBOURS, NOEL-MARIE-PAYMAL. 1807-1873. French optician and photographer. Cited in: Mansell. Lerebours lens.

LEREDDE, EMILE. b. 1866. French dermatologist. See: Biog. Lex. hervorr. Aerzte, 1880-1930. Hallopeau-Leredde syndrome.

LERI, ANDRE. 1875-1930. French physician. See: Biog. Lex. hervorr. Aerzte, 1880-1930. Leri-Weill syndrome, Leri's disease (1), Leri's disease (2), Leri's pleonosteosis, Leri's sign, Marie-Leri syndrome.

Leri-Joanny syndrome (Leri, Andre and Joanny). See: Leri's disease.

Leri-Weill syndrome (Leri, Andre and Weill, Jean): Medicine. See: Jablonski. Also known as: Leri's syndrome.

LERICHE, RENE. 1879-1955. French surgeon. See: World Who's Who Sci. Leriche's operation, Leriche's syndrome (1), Sudeck-Leriche syndrome.

Leriche's operation (Leriche, Rene): Medicine. See: Dorland; Stedman.

Leriche's syndrome (1) (Leriche, Rene): Medicine. See: Dorland; Jablonski; Stedman.

Leriche's syndrome (2) (Leriche, Rene). See: Sudeck's atrophy.

Leri's disease (1) (Leri, Andre): Medicine. See: Jablonski. Also known as: Leri-Joanny syndrome.

Leri's disease (2) (Leri, Andre): Medicine. See: Jablonski.

Leri's pleonosteosis (Leri, Andre): Medicine. See: Jablonski; Stedman.

Leri's sign (Leri, Andre): Medicine. See: Dorland; Stedman.

Leri's syndrome (Leri, Andre). See: Leri-Weill syndrome.

Lermoliev, Ivan, pseud. See: Morelli, Giovanni.

LERMOYEZ, MARCEL. 1858-1929. French otolaryngologist. See: Biog. Lex. hervorr. Aerzte, 1880-1930. Lermoyez's syndrome.

Lermoyez's syndrome (Lermoyez, Marcel): Medicine. See: Dorland; Jablonski; Stedman. Also known as: symptomatic Meniere's syndrome.

LEROUX, LAURENT CHARLES PIERRE. 1730-1792. French obstetrician. See: Biog. Lex. hervorr. Aerzte. Leroux's method.

Leroux's method (Leroux, Laurent Charles Pierre): Medicine. See: Dorland.

LeRoy clock (LeRoy, Julien): Horology. See: Thewlis.

LEROY, EMILE. b. 1873. French physician. Cited in: Index-Cat. Libr. Surg.-Gen. Off., 2d ser., vol. 9, 1904. Fiessinger-Leroy-Reiter syndrome?

LE ROY, GEORGES A. fl. 1889-1916. French chemist. Cited in: Chem. Abstr., vol. 10, p. 1564; Royal Soc. Cat. Sci. Pap., 1884-1900. LeRoy reagent, LeRoy test for free chlorine in hydrochloric acid.

LE ROY, JULIEN. 1686-1759. French horologist. See: World Who's Who Sci. LeRoy clock.

LeRoy reagent (LeRoy, Georges A.): Chemistry. See: Van Nostrand Chem. Dict.

LeRoy test for free chlorine in hydrochloric acid (LeRoy, Georges A.): Chemistry. See: Van Nostrand Chem. Dict.

LERTES, PETER. fl. 1936. German radio specialist. Cited in: Thompson, O. under "Hellertion." Hellertion.

LESCH, MICHAEL. 1939- . American pediatrician. See: Direct. Med. Specialists, 1975-1976. Lesch-Nyhan syndrome.

Lesch-Nyhan syndrome (Lesch, Michael and Nyhan, William L.): Medicine. See: Jablonski; Stedman.

LESCHKE, ERICH FRIEDRICH WILHELM. 1887-1933. German physician. See: Biog. Lex. hervorr. Aerzte, 1880-1930. Leschke's syndrome.

Leschke's syndrome (Leschke, Erich Friedrich Wilhelm): Medicine. See: Dorland; Jablonski.

LESER, EDMUND. 1853-1916. German surgeon. See: Biog. Lex. hervorr. Aerzte, 1880-1930. Leser-Trelat sign.

Leser-Trelat sign (Leser, Edmund and Trelat, Ulysse): Medicine. See: Dorland. Also known as: Trelat's sign (2).

LESIEUR, CHARLES. 1876-1919. French physician. See: Biog. Lex. hervorr. Aerzte, 1880-1930. Lesieur-Privey sign.

Lesieur-Privey sign (Lesieur, Charles and Privey, Paul): Medicine. See: Dorland; Kelly.

LESLEY, J. PETER. 1819-1903. American geologist. See: Dict. Sci. Biog. Lesleya.

LESLEY, JOHN, JR. fl. ca. 1867. American farmer. (Biography source unavailable.) Lesleyite.

Lesleya (Lesley, J. Peter): Botany. See: Webster's 3d.

Lesleyite (Lesley, John, Jr.): Earth Sciences. See: Thrush; Webster's 3d.

Leslie box (Leslie, William Russel?): Agriculture. See: Winburne.

LESLIE, WILLIAM RUSSEL. b. 1891. Canadian horticulturist. See: Amer. Men Sci., 4th ed. Leslie box?

LESNIOWSKI, ANTONI. b. 1867. Polish physician. See: Biog. Lex. hervorr. Aerzte, 1880-1930. Crohn-Lesniowski disease.

LESPEDEZ (or ZESPEDEZ). fl. 1795. Spanish governor of Florida. (Biography source unavailable.) Lespedeza.

Lespedeza (Lespedez): Botany. See: Charnock; Encyc. Brit., 1973; Hendrickson; Mathews, M. M.

Lesquerella (Lesquereux, Leo): Botany. See: Webster's 3d.

LESQUEREUX, LEO. 1806-1889. Swiss-born American paleobotanist. See: Dict. Sci. Biog. Lesquerella.

Lesser's triangle (Derivation undetermined): Anatomy. See: Blakiston's Gould; Dorland; Stedman.

Lessertia (Delessert, Jules Paul Benjamin): Botany. See: Charnock.

LESSHAFT, PYOTR FRANTSOVICH. 1836-1909. Russian anatomist. See: Biog. Lex. hervorr. Aerzte, 1880-1930. Lesshaft's triangle.

Lesshaft's triangle (Lesshaft, Pyotr Frantsovich): Anatomy. See: Donath; Dorland; Stedman. Also known as: Grynfeltt's triangle.

Lessing process (Lessing, Rudolf): Engineering and Industry. See: Thrush.

Lessing ring(s) (Lessing, Rudolf): Engineering and Industry. See: Hackh; Thrush; Van Nostrand Chem. Dict.

LESSING, RUDOLF. 1878-1964. English coal engineer. See: Who's Who Brit. Sci., 1953. Lessing process, Lessing ring(s).

Lessingite (Levinson-Lessing, Franz Yulevich): Earth Sciences. See: Thrush; Webster's 3d.

LESSON, RENE PRIMEVERE. 1794-1849. French naval pharmacist. See: Dict. Sci. Biog. Lessonia.

Lessonia (Lesson, Rene Primevere): Botany. See: Webster's 3d.

LESTIBOUDOIS, GASPARD (In full: THEMISTOCLE GASPARD). 1797-1876. French botanist and physician. See: World Who's Who Sci. Lestibudesia.

Lestibudesia (Lestiboudois, Gaspard): Botany. See: Charnock.

let George do it (Amboise, Georges d'): Generic Word. See: Hendrickson.

LETO (or LATONA). Personification of darkness in classical mythology. See: Jobes. Latonian, Leto's (or Latona's) children.

Latonian (Leto): Mythology. See: Weekley.

Leto's (or Latona's) children (Leto): Generic Word (sun and moon). See: Jobes.

LETTERER, ERICH. 1895-   . German pathologist. See: Who's Who Sci. Europe, 1972. Abt-Letterer-Siwe syndrome.

Letterer-Siwe disease (Letterer, Erich and Siwe, Sture August). See: Abt-Letterer-Siwe syndrome.

Letterer's reticulosis (Letterer, Erich). See: Abt-Letterer-Siwe syndrome.

LETTERMAN, JONATHAN. 1824-1872. American army surgeon. See: Dict. Amer. Biog. Letterman needlegrass?

Letterman needlegrass (Letterman, Jonathan?): Botany. See: Winburne.

Letters of Junius (Junius): History. See: Harbottle; Phyfe; Scott; Steinberg.

LETTS, EDMUND ALBERT. 1852-1918. English chemist. See: World Who's Who Sci. Letts synthesis.

Letts synthesis (Letts, Edmund Albert): Chemistry. See: Van Nostrand Chem. Dict.

LETTS, THOMAS. 1803-1873. English publisher. See: Dict. Nat. Biog. Letts's Diaries.

LETTSOM, JOHN COAKLEY. 1744-1815. English physician. See: Dict. Nat. Biog. Lettsomia.

LETTSOM, WILLIAM GARROW. 1804-1887. English mineralogist. See: Boase. Lettsomite.

Lettsomia (Lettsom, John Coakley): Botany. See: Charnock.

Lettsomite (Lettsom, William Garrow): Earth Sciences. See: Webster's 3d.

Letts's Diaries (Letts, Thomas): Printing. See: Dict. Nat. Biog.

LEUCHTENBERG, MAXIMILIAN JOSEF, DUKE OF. 1817-1852. Viceroy of Italy. See: Nouv. Biog. Univ. Leuchtenbergite.

Leuchtenbergite (Leuchtenberg, Maximilian Josef, Duke of): Earth Sciences. See: Charnock; Thrush; Webster's 3d.

LEUCHTER, M. fl. 1911. German chemist. Cited in: Chem. Abstr., vol. 6, p. 200. Leuchter reagent for hydrogen peroxide, Leuchter reagents for pine oil and turpentine oil?

Leuchter reagent for hydrogen peroxide (Leuchter, M.): Chemistry. See: Van Nostrand Chem. Dict.

Leuchter reagents for pine oil and turpentine oil (Leuchter, M.?): Chemistry. See: Van Nostrand Chem. Dict.

Leucippian philosophy (Leucippus): Philosophy. Cited in: Carter.

LEUCIPPUS. fl. 5th c. B.C. Greek philosopher. See: New Encyc. Brit., 1974, Microp. Leucippian philosophy.

Leuckart reaction (Leuckart, Rudolf): Chemistry. See: Ballentyne; Van Nostrand Chem. Dict.

LEUCKART, RUDOLF. 1854-1889. German chemist. See: Pogg., vols. 3, 4. Leuckart reaction, Leuckart thiophenol reaction.

Leuckart thiophenol reaction (Leuckart, Rudolf): Chemistry. See: Van Nostrand Chem. Dict.

LEUDET, THEODOR-EMILE. 1825-1887. French physician. See: Biog. Lex. hervorr. Aerzte. Leudet's tinnitus.

Leudet's tinnitus (Leudet, Theodor-Emile): Medicine. See: Dorland; Stedman.

LEUNBACH, JONATHAN HUGH. b. 1884. Danish physician. (Biography source unavailable.) Leunbach's paste.

Leunbach's paste (Leunbach, Jonathan Hugh): Medicine. See: Dorland.

Leupold engine (Leupold, Jacob): Engineering and Industry. See: Auger.

LEUPOLD, JACOB. 1674-1727. German engineer. See: World Who's Who Sci. Leupold engine.

Leusea (Leleuse): Botany. See: Charnock.

Leuwenhoek, Antony van. See: Leeuwenhoek, Antony van.

LEVADITI, CONSTANTIN. 1874-1928. Roumanian bacteriologist. See: Dict. Sci. Biog. Levaditi method.

Levaditi method (Levaditi, Constantin): Medicine. See: Dorland; Stedman.

Levene-Beatty reagent for amino acids (Levene, Phoebus Aaron Theodore and Beatty, W. A.): Chemistry. See: Van Nostrand Chem. Dict.

Levene-Hudson isorotation (Levene, Phoebus Aaron Theodore and Hudson, Claude Silbert): Chemistry. See: Van Nostrand Chem. Dict.

LEVENE, PHOEBUS AARON THEODOR. 1869-1940. Russian-born American biochemist. See: Dict. Sci. Biog. Heimrod-Levine test, Levene-Beatty reagent for amino acids, Levene-Hudson isorotation rule.

Levenstein process (Derivation undetermined): Chemistry. See: Van Nostrand Chem. Dict.

LEVENTHAL, MICHAEL LEO. 1901- . American gynecologist. See: Dir. Med. Specialists, 1965-1966. Stein-Leventhal syndrome.

Lever Act (Lever, Asbury Francis): Politics. See: Dict. Amer. Hist., vol. 3, p. 265; Jameson.

LEVER, ASBURY FRANCIS. 1875-1940. American legislator. See: Biog. Direct. Amer. Congress. Lever Act, Smith-Lever Act.

LEVER, WALTER FREDERICK. 1909- . German-born American physician. See: World Who's Who Sci. Lever's adenoacanthoma.

Lever's adenoacanthoma (Lever, Walter Frederick): Medicine. See: Jablonski.

LEVI. Third son of Jacob in the Old Testament (Gen. 29:34). See: Hastings (Dict. Bible). Levite.

Levi axiom (Levi, Howard?): Mathematics. See: Van Nostrand Sci. Encyc. under "Geometry."

Levi-Civita tensor density (Levi-Civita, Tullio): Mathematics. See: Internat. Dict. Phys. Elec.

LEVI-CIVITA, TULLIO. 1873-1941. Italian mathematician. See: Dict. Sci. Biog. Levi-Civita tensor density.

LEVI, HOWARD. 1916- . American mathematician. See: Amer. Men and Women Sci., 12th ed. Levi axiom?

LEVI, LEOPOLD. 1868-1933. French endocrinologist. See: Presse Med., vol. 42 (Feb. 10, 1934) p. 244. Leopold-Levi's syndrome, Lorain-Levi syndrome (or infantilism).

Leviathan (Leviathan, the aquatic animal): Generic Word (large and monstrous). See: Partridge.

LEVIATHAN, THE AQUATIC ANIMAL. Biblical creature in Jewish mythology. See: New Encyc. Brit., 1974, Microp. Leviathan.

LEVIN, ABRAHAM LOUIS. 1880-1940. Polish-born American physician. See: World Who's Who Sci. Levin (or Levine) tube.

LEVIN, MAX. 1901- . Russian-born American neurologist. See: Direct. Med. Specialists, 1975-1976. Kleine-Levin syndrome.

Levin (or Levine) tube (Levin, Abraham Louis): Medicine. See: Dorland; Stedman; Webster's 3d.

Levine-Bien reagents for differentiating carotene and oils rich in vitamin A (Levine, Victor Emanuel and Bien, George E.): Chemistry. See: Van Nostrand Chem. Dict.

Levine-Bien tests for carotene (Levine, Victor Emanuel and Bien, George E.): Chemistry. See: Van Nostrand Chem. Dict.

LEVINE, MAX. b. 1889. Polish-born American bacteriologist. See: Biog. Lex. hervorr. Aerzte, 1880-1930. Levinea?, Levin's solution, Levin's medium, Levin's agar.

Levine-Richman reagent for terpenes (Levine, Victor Emanuel and Richman, Eudice): Chemistry. See: Van Nostrand Chem. Dict.

Levine-Richman test to differentiate irradiated from non-irradiated sterols (Levine, Victor Emanuel and Richman, Eudice): Chemistry. See: Van Nostrand Chem. Dict.

LEVINE, SAMUEL ALBERT. 1891-1966. Polish-born American physician. See: World Who's Who Sci. Lown-Gannong-Levine syndrome, Samuel A. Levine professorship of medicine, Samuel Levine Cardiac Center.

Levine test for carbohydrates (Levine, Victor Emanuel): Chemistry. See: Van Nostrand Chem. Dict.

Levine test for phenols (Levine, Victor Emanuel): Chemistry. See: Van Nostrand Chem. Dict.

LEVINE, VICTOR EMANUEL. 1892-1963. Russian-born American biochemist. See: Pogg., vols. 6, 7b. Levine-Bien reagents for differentiating carotene and oils rich in vitamin A, Levine-Bien tests for carotene, Levine-Richman reagent for terpenes, Levine-Richman test to differentiate irradiated from non-irradiated sterols, Levine test for carbohydrates, Levine test for phenols.

Levinea (Levine, Max?): Zoology. See: Stedman.

Levin's agar (Levine, Max): Medicine. See: Kelly.

Levin's medium (Levine, Max): Medicine. See: Kelly.

Levin's solution (Levine, Max): Medicine. See: Kelly.

LEVINSON-LESSING, FRANZ YULEVICH. 1861-1939. Russian geologist. See: Dict. Sci. Biog. Lessingite, Loewinson-Lessing classification.

Levinthal-Cole-Lillie bodies (Derivation undetermined): Medicine. See: Stedman.

Levis (Strauss, Levi): Fashion. See: Hendrickson; Mathews, M. M.; Picken.

Levi's syndrome (Levi, Leopold). See: Lorain-Levi syndrome (or infantilism).

Levite (Levi): Religion. See: New Encyc. Brit., 1974, Microp.; Webster's 3d.

LEVRET, ANDRE. 1703-1780. French obstetrician. See: World Who's Who Sci. Levret's forceps, Levret's law.

Levret's forceps (Levret, Andre): Medicine. See: Stedman.

Levret's law (Levret, Andre): Medicine. See: Stedman.

LEVY, ARMAND (In full: SERVE-DIEU ABAILARD). 1795-1841. French mineralogist. See: Dict. Sci. Biog. Levynite (or Levyne).

Levy-Cramer theorem (Levy, Paul Pierre and Cramer, Harald): Statistics. See: Kendall.

LEVY, GABOR BELA. 1913- . Hungarian-born American chemist. See: Amer. Men Sci., 10th ed. Levy unit.

LEVY, GABRIELLE. 1886-1935. French neurologist. See: J. Nerv. Ment. Dis., vol. 81 (1935) p. 725. Roussy-Levy syndrome (or disease).

Levy inkblots (or movement scale) (Derivation undetermined): Psychology. See: English; Wolman.

LEVY, JACQUES. fl. 1948. French physician. (Biography source unavailable.) Creyx-Levy syndrome.

Levy-Pareto distribution (Levy, Paul Pierre and Pareto, Vilfredo): Statistics. See: Kendall.

LEVY, PAUL PIERRE. 1886-1971. French mathematician. See: Pogg., vols. 5, 6, 7b. Laplace-Levy theorem, Levy-Cramer theorem, Levy-Pareto distribution, Levy's theorem, Lindeberg-Levy theorem.

Levy reagents for alkaloids and phenols (Derivation undetermined): Chemistry. See: Van Nostrand Chem. Dict.

LEVY, ROBERT. fl. 1938. French physician. (Biography source unavailable.) Clere-Levy-Cristesco syndrome.

Levy unit (Levy, Gabor Bela): Chemistry. See: Hackh.

Levynite (or Levyne) (Levy, Armand): Earth Sciences. See: Charnock; Thrush; Webster's 3d.

Levy's theorem (Levy, Paul Pierre): Statistics. See: Kendall.

Lew board (Derivation undetermined): Engineering and Industry. See: Thrush.

Lewandowski-Lutz syndrome (Lewandowsky, Felix and Lutz, Wilhelm): Medicine. See: Jablonski.

Lewandowski's periporitis (Lewandowsky, Felix): Medicine. See: Jablonski.

Lewandowski's tuberculid (or disease) (Lewandowsky, Felix): Medicine. See: Dorland; Jablonski.

LEWANDOWSKY, FELIX. 1879-1921. German dermatologist. See: Biog. Lex. hervorr. Aerzte, 1880-1930. Jadassohn-Lewandowski syndrome, Lewandowski-Lutz syndrome, Lewandowski's periporitis, Lewandowski's tuberculid (or disease).

LEWANIKA I. ca. 1843-ca. 1916. King of the Barotse (Africa). See: Encyc. Africa. Lochner treaty (or Lochner-Lewanika treaty).

LEWERENZ, ALFRED SPEIR. 1897- . American educator. Cited in: Mansell. Lewerenz readability formula.

Lewerenz readability formula (Lewerenz, Alfred Speir): Education. See: Good.

LEWIN, KURT. 1890-1947. German-born American social psychologist. See: Internat. Encyc. Soc. Sci. Lewinian.

LEWIN, LOUIS. 1850-1929. German biological chemist. See: Deut. Med. Wchnschr. vol. 56 (1930) p. 151. anhalonium Lewinii, Lewin reagent for aldehydes, Lewin reagent for proteins?

Lewin reagent for aldehydes (Lewin, Louis): Chemistry. See: Van Nostrand Chem. Dict.

Lewin reagent for proteins (Lewin, Louis?): Chemistry. See: Van Nostrand Chem. Dict.

Lewinian (Lewin, Kurt): Psychology. See: Chaplin; English.

Lewis acid (Lewis, Gilbert Newton): Chemistry. See: Van Nostrand Sci. Encyc.; Webster's 3d.

Lewis-Adams formula (Lewis, Gilbert Newton and Adams, Elliot Quincy): Chemistry. See: Hackh.

Lewis and Clark Centennial Exposition (Lewis, Meriwether and Clark, William): History. See: Jameson; Mathews, M. M.

Lewis and Clark Expedition (Lewis, Meriwether and Clark, William): History. See: Encyc. Brit., 1973; Jameson; Morris.

Lewis' barberry (Lewis, Meriwether): Botany. See: Mathews, M. M.

Lewis base (Lewis, Gilbert Newton): Chemistry. See: Webster's 3d.

Lewis blood group (Lewis, Mrs. H. D. G.): Medicine. See: Blakiston's Gould; Stedman.

Lewis bolt (Derivation undetermined): Engineering and Industry. See: Thrush.

Lewis' carcinoma (Derivation undetermined): Medicine. See: Jablonski.

Lewis color theory (Lewis, Gilbert Newton): Physics. See: Hackh.

Lewis concept (Lewis, Gilbert Newton): Chemistry. See: Stedman under "base", Van Nostrand Sci. Encyc. under "Reactions, Chemical."

Lewis' disease (Lewis, George Michael): Medicine. See: Jablonski.

Lewis' equation (Lewis, Gilbert Newton). See: Nernst-Lindemann equation.

Lewis flax (Lewis, Meriwether?): Botany. See: Winburne.

LEWIS, GEORGE MICHAEL. fl. 1954-1972. English pediatrician. See: Med. Direct., 1972. Lewis' disease.

LEWIS, GILBERT NEWTON. 1875-1946. American chemist. See: Dict. Sci. Biog. Broensted and Lewis treatment of acids, Lewis acid, Lewis-Adams formula, Lewis base, Lewis color theory, Lewis concept, Lewis' equation, Lewis-Langmuir atom, Lewis-Langmuir formula, Lewis-Langmuir theory (of atomic structure), Lewis number?, Lewis-Randall rule, Lewis symbols, Lewis' theory, Lewis's atom.

Lewis grass (Lewis, Meriwether): Botany. Cited in: Mathews, M. M.

Lewis gun (or machine gun) (Lewis, Isaac Newton): Weapons. See: Quick; Webster's 3d.

LEWIS, MRS. H. D. G. fl. 1946. English hospital patient. (Biography source unavailable.) Lewis blood group.

Lewis hole (Derivation undetermined): Engineering and Industry. See: Thrush.

LEWIS, ISAAC NEWTON. 1858-1931. American soldier and inventor. See: World Who's Who Sci. Lewis gun (or machine gun).

Lewis-Langmuir atom (Lewis, Gilbert Newton and Langmuir, Irving): Chemistry. See: Van Nostrand Chem. Dict.

Lewis-Langmuir formula (Lewis, Gilbert Newton and Langmuir, Irving): Chemistry. See: Internat. Dict. Phys. Elec.

Lewis-Langmuir theory (of atomic structure) (Lewis, Gilbert Newton and Langmuir, Irving): Chemistry. See: Hackh; Van Nostrand Chem. Dict.; Webster's 3d. Also known as: Langmuir theory (1).

LEWIS, MERIWETHER. 1774-1809. American explorer. See: Dict. Amer. Biog. Lewis and Clark Centennial Exposition, Lewis and Clark Expedition, Lewis' barberry, Lewis flax?, Lewis grass, Lewis' trout, Lewis'('s) woodpecker, Lewisia (or Leuisia).

LEWIS, MORGAN. 1754-1844. American soldier and politician. See: Dict. Amer. Biog. Lewisite(s).

Lewis number (Lewis, Gilbert Newton?): Physics. See: Ballentyne.

Lewis phenomenon (Derivation undetermined): Medicine. See: Stedman.

Lewis pin (Derivation undetermined): Engineering and Industry. See: Thrush.

Lewis-Randall rule (Lewis, Gilbert Newton and Randall, Merle): Physics. See: Ballentyne.

Lewis-Rayleigh afterglow (Lewis and Strutt, John William, 3d Baron Rayleigh): Physics. See: Thewlis.

Lewis symbols (Lewis, Gilbert Newton): Physics. See: Hackh.

Lewis' theory (Lewis, Gilbert Newton): Physics. See: Ballentyne; Hackh.

LEWIS, SIR THOMAS. 1881-1945. English cardiologist. See: World Who's Who Sci. H factor of Lewis.

Lewis' trout (Lewis, Meriwether): Zoology. Cited in: Mathews, M. M.

Lewis (wedge) (Derivation undetermined): Engineering and Industry. See: Thrush.

LEWIS, WILLIAM BEVAN. 1847-1929. English physiologist. See: World Who's Who Sci. Bevan-Lewis cells.

LEWIS, WILLIAM JAMES. 1847-1926. English mineralogist. See: Who Was Who, 1916-1928. Lewisite.

LEWIS, WINFORD LEE. 1878-1943. American chemist. See: World Who's Who Sci. Lewisite.

Lewis'('s) woodpecker (Lewis, Meriwether): Zoology. See: Gray; Mathews, M. M.; Pennak; Webster's 3d.

Lewisia (or Leuisia) (Lewis, Meriwether): Botany. See: Charnock; Taylor, N.; Webster's 3d.

Lewisite(s) (Lewis, Morgan): History. See: Clapin; Jameson; Mathews, M. M.

Lewisite (Lewis, William James): Earth Sciences. See: Webster's 3d.

Lewisite (Lewis, Winford Lee): Chemistry. See: Dorland; Stedman; Webster's 3d.

LEWISOHN, RICHARD. 1875-1961. American surgeon. See: New York Times, Aug. 13, 1961, p. 89, col. 2. Lewisohn's method.

Lewisohn's method (Lewisohn, Richard): Medicine. See: Dorland.

Lewis's atom (Lewis, Gilbert Newton): Physics. See: Hackh.

LEWITE, A. fl. 1910. German chemist. Cited in: Pogg., vol. 6 under "Hauser, Otto." Hauser-Lewite reagent.

Lex Bruening (Bruening, Heinrich): History. Cited in: Webster's Biog. Dict.

Lex Canuleia (Canuleius, Cneius): Law. Cited in: Webster's Biog. Dict.

Lex Cornelia (Sulla, Lucius Cornelius). See: Cornelian law (or Lex Cornelia).

Lex Papiria (Papirius, Sextus). See: Jus Papirianum.

Lex Valeria (Flaccus, L. Valerius): History. See: New Encyc. Brit., 1974, Microp.

Lexaschova spot test for chromium (Derivation undetermined): Chemistry. See: Van Nostrand Chem. Dict.

LEXER, ERICH. 1867-1937. German surgeon. See: Biog. Lex. hervorr. Aerzte, 1880-1930. Lexer's operation.

Lexer's operation (Lexer, Erich): Medicine. See: Dorland.

Lexis distribution (Lexis, Wilhelm Hector Richard Albrecht): Statistics. See: Good.

Lexis ratio (Lexis, Wilhelm Hector Richard Albrecht): Statistics. See: Good; Kendall.

Lexis sample (or universe) (Lexis, Wilhelm Hector Richard Albrecht): Statistics. See: Internat. Encyc. Soc. Sci. under "Lexis, Wilhelm", Zadrozny.

Lexis theory (Lexis, Wilhelm Hector Richard Albrecht): Statistics. See: Kendall.

Lexis variation (Lexis, Wilhelm Hector Richard Albrecht): Statistics. See: Kendall.

LEXIS, WILHELM HECTOR RICHARD ALBRECHT. 1837-1914. German mathematician. See: Internat. Encyc. Soc. Sci. Lexis distribution, Lexis ratio, Lexis sample (or universe), Lexis theory, Lexis variation, Poisson-Lexis distribution.

LEY, HEINRICH. 1872-1938. German chemist. See: Pogg., vols. 4-6, 7a. Ley reagent for honey?

Ley reagent for honey (Ley, Heinrich?): Chemistry. See: Van Nostrand Chem. Dict.

LEYCESTER, WILLIAM. No dates. Bengal judge. (Biography source unavailable.) Leycesteria

Leycesteria (Leycester, William): Botany. See: Taylor, N.

Leyden('s) crystals (Leyden, Ernst Viktor von). See: Charcot-Leyden crystals.

LEYDEN, ERNST VIKTOR VON. 1832-1910. German physician. See: World Who's Who Sci. Charcot-Leyden crystals, Leyden-Moebius syndrome, Leydenia gemmipara, Leyden's disease, Leyden's duct, Leyden's neuritis, Leyden's paralysis (1) (or syndrome), Leyden's paralysis (2), Westphal-Leyden syndrome.

Leyden-Moebius syndrome (Leyden, Ernst Viktor von and Moebius, Paul Julius): Medicine. See: Jablonski.

Leydenia gemmipara (Leyden, Ernst Viktor von): Zoology. See: Stedman.

Leyden's ataxia (Leyden, Ernst Viktor von). See: Westphal-Leyden syndrome.

Leyden's disease (Leyden, Ernst Viktor von): Medicine. See: Dorland; Kelly; Stedman.

Leyden's duct (Leyden, Ernst Viktor von): Anatomy. See: Donath.

Leyden's neuritis (Leyden, Ernst Viktor von): Medicine. See: Jablonski; Kelly; Stedman.

Leyden's paralysis (1) (or syndrome) (Leyden, Ernst Viktor von): Medicine. See: Jablonski; Kelly. Also known as: Weber-Leyden syndrome, Weber's syndrome (sign, symptom or paralysis).

Leyden's paralysis (2) (Leyden, Ernst Viktor von): Medicine. See: Jablonski.

Leydig('s) cell(s) (Leydig, Franz von): Anatomy. See: Dorland; Donath; Stedman; Webster's 3d. Also known as: Gley's cells.

LEYDIG, FRANZ VON. 1821-1908. German zoologist. See: Dict. Sci. Biog. Leydig('s) cell(s), Leydigarche, Leydigia?, Leydig's cylinders, Leydig's duct, Leydig's organ(s).

Leydigarche (Leydig, Franz von): Medicine. See: Stedman.

Leydigia (Leydig, Franz von?): Zoology. See: Pennak.

Leydig's cylinders (Leydig, Franz von): Anatomy. See: Dorland.

Leydig's duct (Leydig, Franz von): Anatomy. See: Dorland; Stedman.

Leydig's organ(s) (Leydig, Franz von): Zoology. See: Gray; Henderson.

Leyner-Ingersoll drill (Leyner, J(ohn) George and Ingersoll, Simon). See: water Leyner.

LEYNER, J(OHN) GEORGE. 1860-1920. American inventor. See: Nat. Cycl. Amer. Biog., vol. 25, pp. 207-208. water Leyner.

LEYS, ALEXANDRE. fl. 1896-1900. French chemist. Cited in: Royal Soc. Cat. Sci. Pap., 1884-1900. Leys reagent for aldehydes?

Leys reagent for aldehydes (Leys, Alexandre?): Chemistry. See: Van Nostrand Chem. Dict.

LEYTON, ALBERT SIDNEY FRANKAU (Alternate name: ALBERT GRUENBAUM). 1869-1921. English physician. See: World Who's Who Sci. Gruenbaum's test.

L'Heritier de Brutelle, Charles Louis. See: Heritier de Brutelle, Charles Louis l'.

Lhermitte-Cornil-Quesnel syndrome (Lhermitte, Jean; Cornil, Lucien; and Quesnel, Maurice?): Medicine. See: Jablonski.

LHERMITTE, JEAN. b. 1877. French physician. See: Biog. Lex. hervorr. Aerzte, 1880-1930. Lhermitte-Cornil-Quesnel syndrome, Lhermitte-McAlpine syndrome, Lhermitte-Trelles syndrome, Lhermitte's sign, Lhermitte's syndrome.

Lhermitte-McAlpine syndrome (Lhermitte, Jean and McAlpine, Douglas): Medicine. See: Jablonski.

Lhermitte-Trelles syndrome (Lhermitte, Jean and Trelles, Julio Oscar?): Medicine. See: Jablonski.

Lhermitte's sign (Lhermitte, Jean): Medicine. See: Blakiston's Gould; Dorland; Stedman.

Lhermitte's syndrome (Lhermitte, Jean): Medicine. See: Jablonski.

L'Hopital('s) (L'Hospital) rule (L'Hospital, Guillaume-Francois-Antoine de): Mathematics. See: Ballentyne; Internat. Dict. Ap. Math.; Internat. Dict. Phys. Elec.; James.

L'HOSPITAL (L'HOPITAL), GUILLAUME-FRANCOIS-ANTOINE DE. 1661-1704. French mathematician. See: Dict. Sci. Biog. L'Hopital('s) (L'Hospital) rule.

L'Huilier's theorem (L'Huillier, Simon-Antoine-Jean): Mathematics. See: James.

L'HUILLIER (or LHUILIER), SIMON-ANTOINE-JEAN. 1750-1840. Swiss mathematician. See: Dict. Sci. Biog. L'Huilier's theorem.

LIAGORA. Greek mythical sea nymph. (Biography source unavailable.) Liagora (algae).

Liagora (algae) (Liagora): Botany. See: Webster's 3d.

LIAN, CAMILLE CONSTANT. b. 1882. French physician. See: Who's Who France, 1961-1962. Lian-Siguier-Welti syndrome, Lian's point.

Lian-Siguier-Welti syndrome (Lian, Camille Constant; Siguier, Fred; and Welti, Jean Jacques): Medicine. See: Jablonski.

Lian's point (Lian, Camille Constant): Medicine. See: Stedman.

Liapounov's inequality (Liapunov, Aleksandr Mikhailovich): Statistics. See: Kendall.

Liapounov's theorem (Liapunov, Aleksandr Mikhailovich): Statistics. See: Kendall.

LIAPUNOV, ALEKSANDR MIKHAILOVICH. 1857-1918. Russian mathematician. See: World Who's Who Sci. Liapounov's inequality, Liapounov's theorem, Liapunov function.

Liapunov function (Liapunov, Aleksandr Mikhailovich): Mathematics. See: Thewlis.

LIBBEY, EDWARD DRUMMOND. 1854-1925. American inventor and manufacturer. See: Who Was Who Amer., 1897-1942. Libbey-Owens process.

LIBBEY, HOWARD. fl. 19th c. American industrialist. (Biography source unavailable.) Howard Libbey (redwood).

Libbey-Owens process (Libbey, Edward Drummond and Owens, Michael Joseph). See: Colburn process.

LIBERALLI, CARLOS H. fl. 1932-1938. Brazilian pharmaceutical chemist. Cited in: Chem. Abstr., vol. 32, p. 4105; vol. 26, p. 3200. Liberalli reaction for polyphenols, Liberalli reagent.

Liberalli reaction for polyphenols (Liberalli, Carlos H.): Chemistry. See: Van Nostrand Chem. Dict.

Liberalli reagent (Liberalli, Carlos H.): Chemistry. See: Van Nostrand Chem. Dict.

LIBERMAN, YEVSEY GRIGOR'EVICH. 1897- . Soviet economist and statistician. See: Prom. Pers. USSR. Libermanism.

Libermanism (Liberman, Yevsey Grigor'evich): Economics. See: Barnhart (New Eng.).

LIBERT, MARIE ANNE. 1782-1865. Belgian botanist. See: Seyn. Libertia.

Libertia (Libert, Marie Anne): Botany. See: Taylor, N.

LIBMAN, EMANUEL. 1872-1946. American physician. See: World Who's Who Sci. Libman-Sacks syndrome (or disease).

Libman-Sacks syndrome (or disease) (Libman, Emanuel and Sacks, Benjamin): Medicine. See: Blakiston's Gould; Dorland; Jablonski; Stedman. Also known as: Kaposi-Besnier-Libman-Sacks syndrome, Osler-Libman-Sacks disease.

Liborius' method (Liborius, Paul): Medicine. See: Stedman.

LIBORIUS, PAUL. fl. 1886. Russian bacteriologist. Cited in: Royal Soc. Cat. Sci. Pap., 1884-1900. Liborius' method.

Lichtenberg figure(s) (Lichtenberg, Georg Christoph): Physics. See: Hackh; Thewlis; Webster's 3d.

LICHTENBERG, GEORG CHRISTOPH. 1742-1799. German physicist and satirist. See: Dict. Sci. Biog. Lichtenberg figure(s), Lichtenberg's alloy.

Lichtenberg's alloy (Lichtenberg, Georg Christoph): Chemistry. See: Dict. Sci. Biog. under "Lichtenberg, Georg Christoph." Also known as: Newton's alloy (or metal).

LICHTENSTEIN, LOUIS. 1906- . American pathologist. See: Direct. Med. Specilists, 1975-1976. Jaffe-Lichtenstein syndrome (or disease).

LICHTENSTEIN, MARTIN HEINRICH CARL. 1780-1857. German zoologist and traveler in Dutch South Africa. See: Allg. Deut. Biog. Lichtenstein's hartebeest?, Lichtenstein's oriole?

Lichtenstein's hartebeest (Lichtenstein, Martin Heinrich Carl?): Zoology. See: Encyc. Brit., 1973 under "Antelope," vol. 2 p. 23a.

Lichtenstein's oriole (Lichtenstein, Martin Heinrich Carl?): Zoology. See: Gray.

LICHTHARDT, GEORGE HENRY PHILIP. b. 1877. American chemist. See: Amer. Men Sci., 4th ed. Lichthardt test solution for caramel.

Lichthardt test solution for caramel (Lichthardt, George Henry Philip): Chemistry. See: Van Nostrand Chem. Dict.

LICHTHEIM, LUDWIG. 1845-1928. German physician. See: World Who's Who Sci. Lichtheim's aphasia, Lichtheim's plaque, Lichtheim's syndrome, Lichtheim's test.

Lichtheim's aphasia (Lichtheim, Ludwig): Medicine. See: Jablonski.

Lichtheim's plaque (Lichtheim, Ludwig): Medicine. See: Dorland.

Lichtheim's syndrome (Lichtheim, Ludwig). See: Dana's syndrome.

Lichtheim's test (Lichtheim, Ludwig): Medicine. See: Hinsie.

LIDDELL, EDWARD GEORGE TANDY. fl. 1926-1972. English physiologist. See: Med. Direct., 1972. Liddell-Sherrington reflex.

Liddell-Sherrington reflex (Liddell, Edward George Tandy and Sherrington, Sir Charles Scott): Physiology. See: Stedman.

Lidford Law (Derivation undetermined): Law: Black.

LIDOV, ALEKSANDR PAVLOVIC. 1853-1919. Russian chemist. Cited in: Royal Soc. Cat. Sci. Pap., 1884-1900. Lidow reagent?, Lidow test for proteins.

Lidow reagent (Lidov, Aleksandr Pavlovic?): Chemistry. See: Van Nostrand Chem. Dict.

Lidow test for proteins (Lidov, Aleksandr Pavlovic): Chemistry. See: Van Nostrand Chem. Dict.

Lie algebra (Lie, Sophus): Mathematics. See: Hughes.

Lie group (Lie, Sophus): Mathematics. See: James; Van Nostrand Sci. Encyc.

Lie ring (Lie, Sophus): Mathematics. See: Internat. Dict. Ap. Math.

LIE, SOPHUS (In full: MARIUS SOPHUS). 1842-1899. Norwegian mathematician. See: Dict. Sci. Biog. Lie algebra, Lie group, Lie ring.

LIEBEN, ADOLF. 1836-1914. Austrian chemist. See: Pogg., vols. 3, 4, 5. Lieben iodoform reaction, Lieben solution (or reagent), Lieben's test.

Lieben iodoform reaction (Lieben, Adolf): Chemistry. See: Van Nostrand Chem. Dict.

Lieben solution (or reagent) (Lieben, Adolf): Chemistry. See: Hackh; Van Nostrand Chem. Dict.

LIEBENER. fl. 19th c. French? mineralogist. Cited in: Hintze, vol. II, p. 871. Liebenerite.

Liebenerite (Liebener): Earth Sciences. See: Webster's 3d.

Lieben's test (Lieben, Adolf): Medicine. See: Dorland; Stedman.

Lieber code (Lieber, Francis): Military Science. See: Encyc. Brit., 1973 under "Military Government," vol. 15, p. 449c.

LIEBER, FRANCIS. 1800-1872. German-born American political philosopher. See: Dict. Amer. Biog. Lieber code.

LIEBERKUEHN, JOHANNES NATHANAEL. 1711-1756. German anatomist. See: Dict. Sci. Biog. Lieberkuehn (reflector), Lieberkuehn's gland(s) (crypts or follicles).

Lieberkuehn (reflector) (Lieberkuehn, Johannes Nathanael): Biology. See: Stedman.

Lieberkuehn's gland(s) (crypts or follicles) (Lieberkuehn, Johannes Nathanael): Anatomy. See: Donath; Dorland; Stedman; Webster's 3d.

Liebermann-Burchard test (or reaction) (Liebermann, Carl Theodore and Burchard, H.): Chemistry. See: Ballentyne; Stedman; Webster's 3d. Also known as: Burchard-Liebermann reaction, Burchard test reaction, Liebermann test for certain sterols.

LIEBERMANN, CARL THEODORE. 1842-1914. German chemist. See: Dict. Sci. Biog. Liebermann-Burchard test (or reaction), Liebermann reaction for proteins, Liebermann reagent for thiophene, Liebermann('s) reaction (nitroso-reaction or test for phenols).

LIEBERMANN, LEO VON S. 1852-1926. Hungarian physician. See: Biog. Lex. hervorr. Aerzte, 1880-1930. Liebermann's test.

Liebermann('s) reaction (nitroso-reaction or test for phenols) (Liebermann, Carl Theodore): Chemistry. See: Ballentyne; Hackh; Van Nostrand Chem. Dict.

Liebermann reaction for proteins (Liebermann, Carl Theodore): Chemistry. See: Van Nostrand Chem. Dict.

Liebermann reagent for thiophene (Liebermann, Carl Theodore): Chemistry. See: Van Nostrand Chem. Dict.

Liebermann test for certain sterols (Liebermann, Carl Theodore). See: Liebermann-Burchard test (or reaction).

Liebermann's test (Liebermann, Leo von S.): Medicine. See: Dorland; Stedman.

LIEBERMEISTER, KARL VON. 1833-1901. German physician. See: Biog. Lex. hervorr. Aerzte. Liebermeister's rule.

Liebermeister's rule (Liebermeister, Karl von): Medicine. See: Dorland; Stedman.

Liebig combustion (Liebig, Baron Justus von): Chemistry. See: Van Nostrand Chem. Dict.

Liebig condenser (Liebig, Baron Justus von): Chemistry. See: Hackh; Van Nostrand Chem. Dict.; Webster's 3d. Also known as: Dariot condenser.

Liebig('s) (extract of beef) (Liebig, Baron Justus von): Chemistry. See: Dorland; Hackh; Partridge; Stenhouse.

LIEBIG, BARON JUSTUS VON. 1803-1873. German chemist. See: Dict. Sci. Biog. Liebig combustion, Liebig condenser, Liebig('s) (extract of beef), Liebig potash bulb, Liebig reflux, Liebigia, Liebigite, Liebig's law (of the minimum), Liebig's test (or reaction for cystine), Liebig's theory.

Liebig potash bulb (Liebig, Baron Justus von): Chemistry. See: Hackh.

Liebig reflux (Liebig, Baron Justus von): Chemistry. See: Dict. Sci. Biog. under "Mohr, Carl Friedrich," vol. 9, p. 445b.

Liebigia (Liebig, Baron Justus von): Botany. See: Charnock.

Liebigite (Liebig, Baron Justus von): Earth Sciences. See: Thrush; Webster's 3d.

Liebig's law (of the minimum) (Liebig, Baron Justus von): Botany. See: Gray; Henderson; Winburne.

Liebig's test (or reaction for cystine) (Liebig, Baron Justus von): Chemistry. See: Dorland; Stedman; Van Nostrand Chem. Dict.

Liebig's theory (Liebig, Baron Justus von): Chemistry. See: Dorland; Stedman.

LIEBMANN, ALBERT. b. 1869. German physicist. Cited in: Mansell. Liebmann effect?

Liebmann effect (Liebmann, Albert?): Physiology. See: English; Van Nostrand Sci. Encyc.

LIEBMANN, HEINRICH (In full: KARL OTTO HEINRICH). 1874-1939. German mathematician. See: Pogg., vols. 4, 5, 6, 7a. Liebmann method.

Liebmann method (Liebmann, Heinrich): Mathematics. See: Internat. Dict. Ap. Math.

LIEBOW, AVERILL ABRAHAM. 1911- . Austrian-born American pathologist. See: Amer. Men and Women Sci., 12th ed. Rosen-Castleman-Liebow syndrome.

LIECK, HERBERT. fl. 1936. Scandinavian chemist. Cited in: Chem. Abstr., vol. 30, p. 4894. Lund-Lieck test reaction.

LIENARD, ALFRED MARIE. 1869-1958. French physicist. See: Pogg., vol. 6, 7b. Lienard-Wiechert potentials.

Lienard-Wiechert potentials (Lienard, Alfred Marie and Wiechert, Emil?): Physics. See: Ballentyne.

LIEOU, YOUNG CHOEN. fl. 1928-1942. French physician. Cited in: Lieber and Olbrich. Barre-Lieou syndrome.

LIEPMANN, HUGO CARL. 1863-1925. German neurologist. See: World Who's Who Sci. Liepmann's apraxia (or disease).

Liepmann's apraxia (or disease) (Liepmann, Hugo Carl): Medicine. See: Dorland; Jablonski.

LIESEGANG, RAPHAEL EDUARD. 1869-1947. German chemist. (Biography source unavailable.) Liesegang rings, Liesegang solution, Liesegang test for iron and copper.

Liesegang rings (Liesegang, Raphael Eduard): Chemistry. See: Ballentyne; Hackh; Thewlis; Van Nostrand Sci. Encyc.; Webster's 3d.

Liesegang solution (Liesegang, Raphael Eduard): Chemistry. See: Van Nostrand Chem. Dict.

Liesegang test for iron and copper (Liesegang, Raphael Eduard): Chemistry. See: Van Nostrand Chem. Dict.

LIEUTAUD, JOSEPH. 1703-1780. French physician. See: Dict. Sci. Biog. Lieutaud's sinus, Lieutaud's triangle (or trigone), Lieutaud's uvula.

Lieutaud's sinus (Lieutaud, Joseph): Anatomy. See: Dorland.

Lieutaud's triangle (or trigone) (Lieutaud, Joseph): Anatomy. See: Donath; Stedman.

Lieutaud's uvula (Lieutaud, Joseph): Anatomy. See: Dorland; Stedman.

Lievrite (Lelievre, Claude H.): Earth Sciences. See: Charnock; Webster's 3d.

life of Riley (Riley, James Whitcomb): Generic Word (life of ease). See: Hendrickson.

LIFSCHUETZ, ISAAC. fl. 1885-1909. German chemist. Cited in: Chem. Abstr., vol. 3, p. 1473. Lifschuetz test reaction for oleic acid.

Lifschuetz test reaction for oleic acid (Lifschuetz, Isaac): Chemistry. See: Van Nostrand Chem. Dict.

ligament of Lockwood (Lockwood, Charles Barrett). See: Lockwood's ligament.

ligament of Treitz (Treitz, Wenzel). See: Treitz's muscle (or ligament).

ligament of Winslow (Winslow, Jakob Benignus). See: Winslow's ligament.

ligament of Zinn (Zinn, Johann Gottfried). See: Zinn's ligament.

LIGAT, DAVID. 1873-1954. English surgeon. Cited in: Chem. Abstr., Decenn. Index, 1917-1926. Ligat's test.

Ligat's test (Ligat, David): Medicine. See: Dorland.

LIGEA. Siren in ancient Greek mythology. See: Jobes. Ligyda (or Ligia).

light-Watt (Watt, James): Physics. See: Dresner.

Lightwood-Albright syndrome (Lightwood, Reginald and Albright, Fuller): Medicine. See: Jablonski. Also known as: Albright's syndrome, Butler-Albright syndrome, Butler-Lightwood-Albright syndrome, Lightwood's syndrome.

LIGHTWOOD, REGINALD. fl. 1924-1972. English pediatrician. See: Med. Direct., 1972. Lightwood-Albright syndrome.

Lightwood's syndrome (Lightwood, Reginald). See: Lightwood-Albright syndrome.

Lignac-Fanconi syndrome (Lignac, Georges Otto Emile and Fanconi, Guido). See: Abderhalden-Fanconi syndrome.

LIGNAC, GEORGES OTTO EMILE. 1891-1954. Dutch pediatrician. See: Nederl. Tijdschr. v. geneesk., vol. 98 (Sept. 18, 1954), pp. 2650-2651. Lignac-Fanconi syndrome.

Lignac's disease (Lignac, Georges Otto Emile). See: Abderhalden-Fanconi syndrome.

LIGNIERES, JOSE. 1868-1933. Argentinian bacteriologist. See: Gran Encic. Argentina. Lignieres' test.

Lignieres' test (Lignieres, Jose): Medicine. See: Dorland.

LIGUORI, SAINT ALFONSO MARIA DE'. 1696-1787. Italian prelate. See: Encyc. Brit., 1973. Liguorians (or Ligorians).

Liguorians (or Ligorians) (Liguori, Saint Alfonso Maria de'): Religion. See: Canney; Wagner (Names).

Ligyda (or Ligia) (Ligea): Zoology. See: Pennak.

like Billio (Billio, Joseph): Generic Word (enthusiasm). See: Brewer.

LIKERT, RENSIS. 1903- . American social scientist. See: World Who's Who Sci. Likert scale (or procedure).

Likert scale (or procedure) (Likert, Rensis): Psychology. See: Chaplin; English; Wolman.

Lilendahl-Petersen reagent (Liliendahl-Petersen, N. A. J.): Chemistry. See: Van Nostrand Chem. Dict.

LILIENDAHL-PETERSEN, N. A. J. fl. 1918. Swedish? chemist. Cited in: Chem. Abstr., vol. 12, p. 2583. Lilendahl-Petersen reagent.

LILIENTHAL, HOWARD. 1861-1946. American surgeon. See: World Who's Who Sci. Lilienthal's costotome, Lilienthal's incision, Lilienthal's operation, Lilienthal's probe.

Lilienthal's costotome (Lilienthal, Howard): Medicine. See: Blakiston's Gould.

Lilienthal's incision (Lilienthal, Howard): Medicine. See: Kelly.

Lilienthal's operation (Lilienthal, Howard): Medicine. See: Blakiston's Gould; Kelly.

Lilienthal's probe (Lilienthal, Howard): Medicine. See: Dorland; Stedman.

LILLEHEI, CLARENCE WALTON. 1918- . American thoracic surgeon. See: Direct. Med. Specialists, 1975-1976. Lillehei-de Wall apparatus.

Lillehei-de Wall apparatus (Lillehei, Clarence Walton and De Wall, Richard Allison): Medicine. See: Van Nostrand Sci. Encyc. under "Artificial Organs."

LILLEHEI, RICHARD CARLTON. 1927- . American surgeon. See: Amer. Men and Women Sci., 12th ed. Lillehei sigmamotor pump?

Lillehei sigmamotor pump (Lillehei, Richard Carlton?): Medicine. See: Van Nostrand Sci. Encyc. under "Artificial Organs."

Lillian Russell costume (Russell, Lillian): Fashion. See: Picken.

Lillian Russell (dessert) (Russell, Lillian): Food and Drink. See: Hendrickson.

LILLIE, RALPH DOUGALL. 1896- . American pathologist. See: World Who's Who Sci. Lillie's allocrhome stain, Lillie's azure-eosin stain.

LILLIE, RALPH STAYNER. 1875-1952. Canadian biologist in the United States. See: World Who's Who Sci. Nernst-Lillie theory.

Lillie's allocrhome stain (Lillie, Ralph Dougall): Medicine. See: Stedman.

Lillie's azure-eosin stain (Lillie, Ralph Dougall): Medicine. See: Stedman.

Lilly controller (Derivation undetermined): Engineering and Industry. See: Thrush.

limacon of Pascal (Pascal, Blaise). See: Pascal's limacon (or snail).

LIMNOREIA. Greek nereid. See: New Cent. Clas. Handb. Limnoria (isopod crustaceans).

Limnoria (isopod crustaceans) (Limnoreia): Zoology. See: Webster's 3d.

LIMPACH, KARL FRIEDRICH LEONHARD. b. 1852. German chemist. See: Pogg., vol. 4. Conrad-Limpach synthesis.

Lincoln, 1st Earl of (Clinton family). See: Clinton, Edward Fiennes de, 9th Lord Clinton and Saye, and 1st Earl of Lincoln.

LINCOLN, ABRAHAM. 1809-1865. American president. See: Dict. Amer. Biog. Abe Lincoln bug, Lincoln badge (club and meeting), Lincoln Brotherhood, Lincoln coffee, Lincoln-Douglas debates, Lincoln flag, Lincoln hireling, Lincoln navy, Lincoln platform, Lincoln penny (or cent), Lincoln Portrait, Lincoln pup, Lincoln rocker, Lincoln skin, Lincoln spy, Lincoln troops, Lincolndom, Lincolnesque, Lincolnian, Lincolniana, Lincolnite (or Lincolnism), Lincoln's birthday.

Lincoln badge (club and meeting) (Lincoln, Abraham): Politics. See: Mathews, M. M.

Lincoln Brotherhood (Lincoln, Abraham): History. See: Jameson; Mathews, M. M.

Lincoln coffee (Lincoln, Abraham): History. See: Mathews, M. M.

Lincoln-Douglas debates (Lincoln, Abraham and Douglas, Stephen Arnold): History. See: Morris and Irwin; New Encyc. Brit., 1974, Microp.

Lincoln flag (Lincoln, Abraham): History. See: Mathews, M. M.

LINCOLN, FREDERICK CHARLES. 1892-1960. American ornithologist. See: Amer. Men Sci., 9th ed. Lincoln index.

Lincoln hireling (Lincoln, Abraham): History. See: Mathews, M. M.

Lincoln index (Lincoln, Frederick Charles): Statistics. See: Kendall; Pennak.

Lincoln navy (Lincoln, Abraham): History. See: Mathews, M. M.

Lincoln-Oseretsky motor development scale (Lincoln, Robert Stanley and Oseretsky, N. I.): Psychology. See: Wolman.

Lincoln penny (or cent) (Lincoln, Abraham): Numismatics. See: Mathews, M. M.

Lincoln platform (Lincoln, Abraham): History. See: Mathews, M. M.

Lincoln Portrait (Lincoln, Abraham): Music. See: Apel.

Lincoln pup (Lincoln, Abraham): History. See: Mathews, M. M.

LINCOLN, ROBERT STANLEY. 1923- . American psychologist. See: Amer. Men Sci., 9th ed., Soc. and Behav. Sci. Lincoln-Oseretsky motor development scale.

Lincoln rocker (Lincoln, Abraham): Applied Arts. See: Webster's 3d.

Lincoln skin (Lincoln, Abraham): History. See: Mathews, M. M.

Lincoln spy (Lincoln, Abraham): History. See: Mathews, M. M.

LINCOLN, THOMAS. 1812-1883. American naturalist. (Biography source unavailable.) Lincoln's sparrow (or finch).

LINCOLN, THOMAS DE. fl. 1331-1348. English serjeant to the king and landlord. Cited in: Encyc. Brit., 1973 under "Inns of Court and Chancery," vol. 12, p. 267a. Lincoln's inn.

Lincoln troops (Lincoln, Abraham): History. See: Mathews, M. M.

Lincolndom (Lincoln, Abraham): History. See: Mathews, M. M.

Lincolnesque (Lincoln, Abraham): History. See: Webster's 3d.

Lincolnia (Derivation undetermined): Botany. See: Charnock.

Lincolnian (Lincoln, Abraham): History. See: Mathews, M. M.; Webster's 3d.

Lincolniana (Lincoln, Abraham): History. See: Mathews, M. M.; Webster's 3d.

Lincolnite (or Lincolnism) (Lincoln, Abraham): Politics. See: Mathews, M. M.; Webster's 3d.

Lincoln's birthday (Lincoln, Abraham): Generic Word. See: Mathews, M. M.; Webster's 3d.

Lincoln's inn (Lincoln, Thomas de): History. See: Latham.

Lincoln's men (Clinton, Edward Fiennes de, 9th Lord Clinton and Saye, and 1st Earl of Lincoln): Theater. See: Hartnoll.

Lincoln's sparrow (or finch) (Lincoln, Thomas): Zoology. See: Gray; Mathews, M. M.; Pennak; Webster's 3d.

LIND, JENNY (JOHANNA MARIA LIND). 1820-1887. Swedish operatic soprano. See: Encyc. Brit., 1973. Jenny Lind bed, Jenny Lind boot, Jenny Lind carriage, Jenny Lind costume, Jenny Lind (fishing fly), Jenny Lind house, Jenny Lind polka, Jenny Lind table.

Lindabrides (Lindabrides, the emperor's daughter): Generic Word (mistress). See: Harvey.

LINDABRIDES, THE EMPEROR'S DAUGHTER. Character in the "Mirror of Knighthood," a Spanish romance translated by Richard Percival (late 16th c.). See: Barnhart (Cycl. Names). Lindabrides.

LINDACKER, JOSEPH. fl. 19th c. Austrian chemist. Cited in: Hintze, vol. I, pt. 4, half 2, p. 1080. Lindackerite.

Lindackerite (Lindacker, Joseph): Earth Sciences. See: Thrush; Webster's 3d.

Lindane (insecticide) (Linden, Teunis van der): Chemistry. See: Webster's 3d.

LINDAU, ARVID VILHELM. 1892- . Swedish pathologist. See: Svenska Maen Och Kvinnor. Hippel-Lindau syndrome (or disease).

Lindau's disease (or tumor) (Lindau, Arvid Vilhelm). See: Hippel-Lindau syndrome (or disease).

LINDBERGH, CHARLES AUGUSTUS. 1902-1974. American aviator. See: New Encyc. Brit., 1974. Carrel-Lindbergh pump, Lindbergh flask, Lindbergh jacket, Lindbergh law, Lindy (hop).

Lindbergh flask (Lindbergh, Charles Augustus): Medicine. See: Blakiston's Gould.

Lindbergh jacket (Lindbergh, Charles Augustus): Fashion. See: Picken.

Lindbergh law (Lindbergh, Charles Augustus): Law. See: Hendrickson; Smith.

Linde ammonia compressor (Linde, Carl Paul Gottfried von): Engineering and Industry. See: Auger.

LINDE, CARL PAUL GOTTFRIED VON. 1842-1934. German engineer. See: Dict. Sci. Biog. Linde ammonia compressor, Linde-Hampson method, Linde method, Linde process (or liquefaction process).

Linde drill (Derivation undetermined): Engineering and Industry. See: Thrush.

Linde-Hampson method (Linde, Carl Paul Gottfried von and Hampson, William): Physics. Cited in: Van Nostrand Sci. Encyc. under "Helium Liquefiers."

LINDE, JONAS OTTO. 1898- . Swedish physicist. See: Who's Who Sci. Europe, 1967. Linde's rule.

Linde method (Linde, Carl Paul Gottfried von): Physics. See: Internat. Dict. Phys. Elec.

LINDE, OTTO ZUR. 1873-1938. German pharmacognosist. See: Kuerschner's Deut. Gel. Kal., vol. 4, 1931. Linde test for glycerin?

Linde process (or liquefaction process) (Linde, Carl Paul Gottfried von): Engineering and Industry. See: Thewlis; Webster's 3d.

Linde test for glycerin (Linde, Otto zur?): Chemistry. See: Van Nostrand Chem. Dict.

Lindeberg-Feller theorem (Lindeberg, Jarl Waldemar and Feller, William): Statistics. See: Kendall.

LINDEBERG, JARL WALDEMAR. 1876-1932. Finnish mathematician. See: Pogg., vols. 5, 6, 7b. Lindeberg-Feller theorem, Lindeberg-Levy theorem.

Lindeberg-Levy theorem (Lindeberg, Jarl Waldemar and Levy, Paul Pierre): Statistics. See: Kendall.

Lindeck potentiometer (Lindeck, Stephan August): Physics. See: Hughes; Internat. Dict. Phys. Elec.

LINDECK, STEPHAN AUGUST. 1864-1911. German physicist. See: Pogg., vols. 4, 5. Lindeck potentiometer.

LINDELOEF, ERNST LEONHARD. 1870-1946. Finnish mathematician. See: Dict. Sci. Biog. Lindeloef('s) space (or theorem), Phragmen-Lindeloef function.

Lindeloef('s) space (or theorem) (Lindeloef, Ernst Leonhard): Mathematics. See: James.

LINDELOF, FRIEDRICH VON. No dates. German patron of botany. (Biography source unavailable.) Lindelofia.

Lindelofia (Lindelof, Friedrich von): Botany. See: Taylor, N.

LINDEMANN, AUGUST. b. 1880. German surgeon. See: Index-Cat. Libr. Surg.-Gen. Off., 4th Ser., vol. 9, 1945. Lindemann's (Lindeman's) cannula, Lindemann's method.

LINDEMANN, CHARLES LIONEL. 1885-1970. English scientist. See: Who Was Who, 1961-1970. Lindemann glass.

Lindemann-Danielson test (Lindemann, Walter C. and Danielson, Ralph Raymond). See: Danielson-Lindemann deflection test.

Lindemann electrometer (Lindemann, Frederick Alexander, 1st Viscount Cherwell): Physics. See: Hughes; Internat. Dict. Phys. Elec.; Thewlis.

LINDEMANN, FREDERICK ALEXANDER, 1ST VISCOUNT CHERWELL. 1886-1957. German-born English physicist. See: Dict. Sci. Biog. Dobson-Lindemann theory, Lindemann electrometer, Lindemann glass, Lindemann melting-point formula, Nernst-Lindemann equation, Nernst-Lindemann theory of specific heats.

Lindemann glass (Lindemann, Frederick Alexander, 1st Viscount Cherwell): Physics. See: Hughes; Markus; Thewlis; Thrush.

Lindemann melting-point formula (Lindemann, Frederick Alexander, 1st Viscount Cherwell): Physics. See: Thewlis.

LINDEMANN, WALTER C. fl. 1920-1932. American ceramics chemist. (Biography source unavailable.) Danielson-Lindemann deflection test.

Lindemann's (Lindeman's) cannula (Lindemann, August): Medicine. See: Dorland; Stedman.

Lindemann's method (Lindemann, August): Medicine. See: Dorland.

LINDEN, TEUNIS VAN DER. fl. 1910. Dutch chemist. See: Pogg., vol. 6. Lindane (insecticide).

LINDER, ERNEST. fl. 1908. English chemist. Cited in: Chem. Abstr., vol. 2, p. 2199. Linder test for mineral acids in gases.

Linder, Johann. See: Lindestolpe, Johann.

Linder test for formaldehyde (Derivation undetermined): Chemistry. See: Van Nostrand Chem. Dict.

Linder test for mineral acids in gases (Linder, Ernest): Chemistry. See: Van Nostrand Chem. Dict.

Lindera (Lindestolpe, Johann): Botany. See: Charnock; New Encyc. Brit., 1974, Microp.; Webster's 3d.

LINDERN, FRANZ BALTHASAR VON. 1682-1755. Strasbourg physician. See: Biog. Lex. hervorr. Aerzte. Lindernia.

Lindernia (Lindern, Franz Balthasar von): Botany. See: Charnock.

Linderstrom-Lang – Duspiva method (Linderstrom-Lang, Kaj Ulrik and Duspiva, Franz): Chemistry. See: Blakiston's Gould.

Linderstrom-Lang – Engel method (Linderstrom-Lang, Kaj Ulrik and Engel, Christiaan): Chemistry. See: Blakiston's Gould.

Linderstrom-Lang – Glick method (Linderstrom-Lang, Kaj Ulrik and Glick, David): Chemistry. See: Blakiston's Gould.

Linderstrom-Lang – Holter method (for protease) (Linderstrom-Lang, Kaj Ulrik and Holter, Heinz): Chemistry. See: Blakiston's Gould.

Linderstrom-Lang – Holter method (for reducing sugars) (Linderstrom-Lang, Kaj Ulrik and Holter, Heinz): Chemistry. See: Blakiston's Gould.

LINDERSTROM-LANG, KAJ ULRIK. 1896-1959. Danish biochemist. See: Pogg., vols. 6, 7b. Linderstrom-Lang – Duspiva method, Linderstrom-Lang – Engel method, Linderstrom-Lang – Glick method, Linderstrom-Lang – Holter method (for protease), Linderstrom-Land – Holter method (for reducing sugars), Linderstrom-Lang – Lanz method, Linderstrom-Lang method, Linderstrom-Lang – Weil – Holter methods.

Linderstrom-Lang – Lanz method (Linderstrom-Lang, Kaj Ulrik and Lanz, Henry Charles): Chemistry. See: Blakiston's Gould.

Linderstrom-Lang method (Linderstrom-Lang, Kaj Ulrik): Chemistry. See: Blakiston's Gould.

Linderstrom-Lang – Weil – Holter methods (Linderstrom-Lang, Kaj Ulrik; Weil, Leopold; and Holter, Heinz): Chemistry. See: Blakiston's Gould.

Linde's rule (Linde, Jonas Otto): Physics. See: Ballentyne.

LINDESTOLPE (or LINDER), JOHANN. 1678-1724. Swedish botanist and physician. See: Svenska Maen Och Kvinnor. Lindera.

LINDGREN, WALDEMAR. 1860-1939. Swedish-born American economic geologist. See: Encyc. Brit., 1973. Lindgrenite.

Lindgrenite (Lindgren, Waldemar): Earth Sciences. See: Thrush; Webster's 3d.

Lindinosite (Derivation undetermined): Earth Sciences. See: Thrush.

Lindisfarne, Bishop of. See: Eadfrid, Bishop of Lindisfarne.

Lindisfarne gospels (Eadfrid, Bishop of Lindisfarne): Fine Arts. See: Harrod; Harvey; New Encyc. Brit., 1974, Microp.

Lindley butterflybush (Lindley, John?): Botany. See: Winburne.

LINDLEY, JOHN. 1799-1865. English botanist. See: Dict. Sci. Biog. Lindley butterflybush?, Lindleya, Lindleyan (system of classification).

Lindley Murray (Murray, Lindley): Generic Word (competent grammarian). See: Partridge.

Lindleya (Lindley, John): Botany. Cited in: World Who's Who Sci.

Lindleyan (system of classification) (Lindley, John): Botany. See: Webster's 3d.

LINDMARK, JOHN GUNNAR. b. 1876. Swedish engineer. See: Svenska Maen Och Kvinnor. Lindmark turbine.

Lindmark turbine (Lindmark, John Gunnar): Engineering and Industry. See: Auger.

Lindner bodies (Lindner, Karl David): Medicine. See: Stedman.

LINDNER, KARL DAVID. 1883-1961. Austrian ophthalmologist. See: Biog. Lex. hervorr. Aerzte, 1880-1930. Lindner bodies.

LINDO, DAVID. fl. 1878-1888. English chemist. Cited in: Royal Soc. Cat. Sci. Pap. Lindo test for nitrate.

Lindo test for nitrate (Lindo, David): Chemistry. See: Van Nostrand Chem. Dict.

LINDSTROEM, GUSTAF. 1838-1916. Swedish mineralogist. See: Svenska Maen Och Kvinnor. Lindstromite (or Lindstroemite).

Lindstromite (or Lindstroemite) (Lindstroem, Gustaf): Earth Sciences. See: Thrush; Webster's 3d.

Lindy (hop) (Lindbergh, Charles Augustus): Dance. See: Hendrickson; Webster's 3d.

LINDZEY, GARDNER EDMOND. 1920- . American psychologist. See: Amer. Men Sci., 10th ed. Allport-Vernon-Lindzey study of values.

line of Mars (Mars): Parapsychology. See: Webster's 3d.

line of Mercury (Mercury): Parapsychology. See: Webster's 3d.

line of Saturn (Saturn): Parapsychology. See: Webster's 3d.

lines of Retzius (Retzius, Gustav Magnus). See: Retzius' lines.

Lineweaver-Burk equation (Lineweaver, Hans and Burk, Dean): Chemistry. See: Stedman.

LINEWEAVER, HANS. 1907- . American chemist. See: Amer. Men and Women Sci., 12th ed. Lineweaver-Burk equation.

LING, PER HENRIK. 1776-1839. Swedish hygienist. See: Encyc. Brit., 1911. Ling's method (or Lingism).

LINGELSHEIM, WALTER (In full: HUGO AUGUST WALTER). b. 1866. German bacteriologist. Cited in: Royal Soc. Cat. Sci. Pap., 1884-1900. Lingelsheimia.

Lingelsheimia (Lingelsheim, Walter): Zoology. See: Stedman.

Ling's method (or Lingism) (Ling, Per Henrik): Medicine. See: Stedman.

LINKE, FRANZ (In full: KARL WILHELM FRANZ). 1878-1944. German meteorologist. See: Pogg., vols. 4-6, 7a. Linke scale?

Linke scale (Linke, Franz?): Earth Sciences. See: Huschke; Monkhouse; Van Nostrand Sci. Encyc.

LINKENBACH, CARL. b. 1842. German metallurgist. Cited in: Mansell. Linkenbach table.

Linkenbach table (Linkenbach, Carl): Engineering and Industry. See: Thrush.

Linley gearbox (Derivation undetermined): Engineering and Industry. See: Auger.

Linnaea (Linnaeus, Carl): Botany. See: Hendrickson; Taylor, N.; Webster's 3d.

Linnaean Society (Linnaeus, Carl): Natural History. See: Asimov; Harvey.

Linnaean species (Linnaeus, Carl): Botany. See: Webster's 3d.

Linnaean system (or classification of plants) (Linnaeus, Carl): Botany. See: Hendrickson; Phyfe; Winburne.

Linnaeite (or Linneite) (Linnaeus, Carl): Earth Sciences. See: Thrush; Webster's 3d.

LINNAEUS (or VON LINNE), CARL. 1707-1778. Swedish botanist. See: Dict. Sci. Biog. Linnaea, Linnaean Society, Linnaean species, Linnaean system (or classification of plants), Linnaeite (or Linneite), Linnaeus' racial classifications.

Linnaeus' racial classifications (Linnaeus, Carl): Anthropology. See: Zadrozny.

Linne, Carl von. See: Linnaeus.

LINNEBACH, ADOLF. fl. 19th c. German stage designer. (Biography source unavailable.) Linnebach effect, Linnebach lantern (or projector).

Linnebach effect (Linnebach, Adolf): Engineering and Industry. See: Focal Encyc. Film.

Linnebach lantern (or projector) (Linnebach, Adolf): Engineering and Industry. See: New Encyc. Brit., 1974, Microp.

LINSEIS, MAX. fl. 1950-1959. German chemist. Cited in: Chem. Abstr. Linseis plastometer.

Linseis plastometer (Linseis, Max): Engineering and Industry. See: Thrush.

LINTNER, CARL JOSEPH LUDWIG. 1855-1926. German chemist. See: Pogg., vol. 6. Lintner reaction for diastase, Lintner reaction for salicylic acid.

Lintner reaction for diastase (Lintner, Carl Joseph Ludwig): Chemistry. See: Van Nostrand Chem. Dict.

Lintner reaction for salicylic acid (Lintner, Carl Joseph Ludwig): Chemistry. See: Van Nostrand Chem. Dict.

LINTON, LAURA ALBERTA. 1853-1915. American chemist and physician. See: Nat. Cycl. Amer. Biog., vol. 12, pp. 62-63. Lintonite.

Lintonite (Linton, Laura Alberta): Earth Sciences. See: Mathews, M. M.; Thrush; Webster's 3d.

Lion of St. Mark (Mark, Saint): Fine Arts. See: Latham.

LIONEL, DUKE OF CLARENCE. 1338-1368. Son of Edward III. See: Dict. Nat. Biog. Clarenceux (Clarencieux) (king of arms).

Liouville equation (Liouville, Joseph): Physics. See: Van Nostrand Sci. Encyc.

Liouville function (Liouville, Joseph): Mathematics. See: James.

LIOUVILLE, JOSEPH. 1809-1882. French mathematician. See: Dict. Sci. Biog. Liouville equation, Liouville function, Liouville-Neumann series, Liouville number, Liouville surface, Liouville's theorem (1) (for a function), Liouville's theorem (2) (statistical mechanics), Sturm-Liouville equation.

Liouville-Neumann series (Liouville, Joseph and Neumann, Karl Gottfried?): Mathematics. See: Internat. Dict. Ap. Math.; James; Van Nostrand Sci. Encyc. Also known as: Neumann('s) series.

Liouville number (Liouville, Joseph): Mathematics. See: James.

Liouville surface (Liouville, Joseph): Mathematics. See: Internat. Dict. Ap. Math.

Liouville's theorem (1) (for a function) (Liouville, Joseph): Mathematics. See: Ballentyne; Internat. Dict. Ap. Math.; Internat. Dict. Phys. Elec.; James.

Liouville's theorem (2) (statistical mechanics) (Liouville, Joseph): Physics. See: Ballentyne; Internat. Dict. Ap. Math.; Internat. Dict. Phys. Elec.

LIPOWITZ, A. fl. 1841-1869. German chemist. Cited in: Royal Soc. Cat. Sci. Pap., 1800-1863. Lipowitz('s) alloy (or metal), Lipowitz test for nondrying oils?

Lipowitz('s) alloy (or metal) (Lipowitz, A.): Chemistry. See: Hackh; Hughes; Partridge.

Lipowitz test for nondrying oils (Lipowitz, A.?): Chemistry. See: Van Nostrand Chem. Dict.

LIPP, ANDREAS. 1855-1916. German chemist. See: Pogg., vols. 3, 4, 5. Lipp solution?

Lipp solution (Lipp, Andreas?): Chemistry. See: Van Nostrand Chem. Dict.

LIPPES, JACOB. 1924- . American obstetrician and gynecologist. See: Direct. Med. Specialists, 1975-1976. Lippes loop.

Lippes loop (Lippes, Jacob): Medicine. See: Barnhart (New Eng.).

LIPPI, AUGUSTE. 1678-1704. French physician and traveler. Cited in: Grand Larousse Encyc. Lippia.

Lippia (Lippi, Auguste): Botany. See: Webster's 3d.

LIPPICH, FERDINAND FRANZ. 1838-1913. Austrian physicist. See: Pogg., vols. 3, 4. Lippich prism.

Lippich prism (Lippich, Ferdinand Franz): Physics. See: Internat. Dict. Phys. Elec.

LIPPINCOTT, JOSEPH WHARTON. fl. early 20th c. American publisher. (Biography source unavailable.) Joseph W. Lippincott Award.

LIPPMANN, EDUARD. 1838-1919. Austrian chemist. See: Pogg., vols. 4, 5. Lippmann-Pollack test reaction.

Lippmann electrode (Lippmann, Gabriel Jonas): Physics. See: Hackh.

Lippmann('s) electrometer (or capillary electrometer) (Lippmann, Gabriel Jonas): Physics. See: Dict. Sci. Biog. under "Lippmann, Gabriel," p. 387; Dorland.

Lippmann emulsion (Lippmann, Gabriel Jonas): Photography. See: Focal Encyc. Photog.

Lippmann fringes (Lippmann, Gabriel Jonas): Physics. See: Van Nostrand Sci. Encyc.

LIPPMANN, GABRIEL JONAS. 1845-1921. French physicist. See: Dict. Sci. Biog. Lippmann electrode, Lippmann('s) electrometer (or capillary electrometer), Lippmann emulsion, Lippmann fringes, Lippmann process.

Lippmann-Pollack test reaction (Lippmann, Eduard and Pollak, Jacob): Chemistry. See: Van Nostrand Chem. Dict.

Lippmann process (Lippmann, Gabriel Jonas): Photography. See: Focal Encyc. Film; Focal Encyc. Photog.; Webster's 3d.

Lipschitz algebra (Lipschitz, Rudolf Otto Sigismund): Mathematics. See: Dict. Sci. Biog. under "Lipschitz, Rudolf...," p. 389.

Lipschitz condition (Lipschitz, Rudolf Otto Sigismund): Mathematics. See: Ballentyne; Internat. Dict. Ap. Math.; James; Kendall. Also known as: Cauchy-Lipschitz theorem.

LIPSCHITZ, RUDOLF OTTO SIGISMUND. 1832-1903. German mathematician. See: Dict. Sci. Biog. Lipschitz algebra, Lipschitz condition.

LIPSCHUETZ, ALEXANDER. b. 1883. German physician. See: Biog. Lex. hervorr. Aerzte, 1880-1930. Lipschuetz law of puberty.

LIPSCHUETZ, BENJAMIN. 1878-1931. Austrian dermatologist. See: World Who's Who Sci. Lipschuetz body (or bodies), Lipschuetz bouillon, Lipschuetz cell, Lipschuetz's erythema, Lipschuetz's ulcer.

Lipschuetz body (or bodies) (Lipschuetz, Benjamin): Medicine. See: Blakiston's Gould; Dorland.

Lipschuetz bouillon (Lipschuetz, Benjamin): Medicine. See: Kelly.

Lipschuetz cell (Lipschuetz, Benjamin): Medicine. See: Dorland; Stedman.

Lipschuetz law of puberty (Lipschuetz, Alexander): Medicine. See: Stedman.

Lipschuetz's erythema (Lipschuetz, Benjamin): Medicine. See: Jablonski. Also known as: Afzelius' erythema.

Lipschuetz's ulcer (Lipschuetz, Benjamin): Medicine. See: Jablonski; Stedman.

LIPSCOMB, WILLIAM NUNN, JR. 1919- . American physical chemist. See: Amer. Men Sci., 10th ed. Lipscombite.

Lipscombite (Lipscomb, William Nunn, Jr.): Earth Sciences. See: Thrush.

LIPSON, HENRY SOLOMON. 1910- . English physicist. See: Who's Who Sci. Europe, 1967. Beevers-Lipson strips.

Lipton Cup (Lipton, Sir Thomas Johnstone, 1st Baronet): Recreation and Sports. Cited in: Laughlin.

LIPTON, SIR THOMAS JOHNSTONE, 1ST BARONET. 1850-1931. English merchant and yachtsman. See: Dict. Nat. Biog., 5th suppl. Lipton Cup.

LISFRANC, JACQUES. 1790-1847. French surgeon. See: World Who's Who Sci. Lisfranc's amputation (or operation), Lisfranc's joint, Lisfranc's ligament, Lisfranc's tubercle.

Lisfranc's amputation (or operation) (Lisfranc, Jacques): Medicine. See: Dorland; Stedman.

Lisfranc's joint (Lisfranc, Jacques): Anatomy. See: Donath; Dorland; Stedman.

Lisfranc's ligament (Lisfranc, Jacques): Anatomy. See: Dorland; Stedman.

Lisfranc's tubercle (Lisfranc, Jacques): Anatomy. See: Donath; Dorland; Stedman.

LISKA, JAROSLAV. fl. 1929. Czechoslovakian? chemist. Cited in: Chem. Abstr., vol. 23, p. 5430. Liska test reaction.

Liska test reaction (Liska, Jaroslav): Chemistry. See: Van Nostrand Chem. Dict.

LISON, LUCIEN. 1907- . Belgian chemist. Cited in: Chem. Abstr., Decenn. Index, 1927-1936. Lison solution for peroxidases, Lison's test.

Lison solution for peroxidases (Lison, Lucien): Chemistry. See: Van Nostrand Chem. Dict.

Lison's test (Lison, Lucien): Medicine. See: Kelly.

Lissajous figure(s) (or curve) (Lissajous, Jules Antoine): Physics. See: Hackh; Hughes; Markus; Thewlis; Van Nostrand Sci. Encyc.; Webster's 3d. Also known as: Bowditch curves.

LISSAJOUS, JULES ANTOINE. 1822-1880. French physicist. See: Dict. Sci. Biog. Lissajous figure(s) (or curve).

LISSAUER, HEINRICH. 1861-1891. German neurologist. See: World Who's Who Sci. Lissauer's angle, Lissauer's paralysis (dementia or atrophy), Lissauer's tract, Lissauer's zone.

Lissauer's angle (Lissauer, Heinrich): Medicine. See: Dorland.

Lissauer's paralysis (dementia or atrophy) (Lissauer, Heinrich): Medicine. See: Dorland; Jablonski.

Lissauer's tract (Lissauer, Heinrich): Anatomy. See: Donath; Dorland; Stedman; Webster's 3d.

Lissauer's zone (Lissauer, Heinrich): Anatomy. See: Donath.

LISSER, HANS. b. 1888. American physician. See: Amer. Men Sci., 10th ed. Escamilla-Lisser syndrome.

Lister comb (Lister, Samuel Cunliffe, 1st Baron Masham): Engineering and Industry. See: Encyc. Brit., 1973 under "Wool," vol. 23, p. 663a.

LISTER, JOSEPH (1ST BARON LISTER OF LYME REGIS). 1827-1912. English surgeon. See: Dict. Sci. Biog. Listerella, Listeria, Lister's antiseptic, Lister's dressing, Lister's method (or Listerism), Lister's operation.

LISTER, MARTIN. 1638?-1712. English physician and zoologist. See: Dict. Sci. Biog. Listera (orchids).

LISTER, SAMUEL CUNLIFFE, 1ST BARON MASHAM. 1815-1906. English inventor and manufacturer. See: Dict. Nat. Biog., 2d suppl. Lister comb.

Listera (orchids) (Lister, Martin): Botany. See: Webster's 3d.

Listerella (Lister, Joseph): Zoology. See: Dorland; Stedman.

Listeria (Lister, Joseph): Zoology. See: Dorland; Stedman; Webster's 3d.

Lister's antiseptic (Lister, Joseph): Medicine. See: Dorland.

Lister's dressing (Lister, Joseph): Medicine. See: Dorland; Kelly; Stedman.

Lister's method (or Listerism) (Lister, Joseph): Medicine. See: Stedman; Webster's 3d.

Lister's operation (Lister, Joseph): Medicine. See: Kelly.

LISTING, JOHANN BENEDIKT. 1808-1882. German physicist. See: Pogg., vols. 1, 3. Listing's law, Listing's reduced (or schematic) eye.

Listing's law (Listing, Johann Benedikt): Physiology. See: Dorland; English; Stedman.

Listing's reduced (or schematic) eye (Listing, Johann Benedikt): Physiology. See: Drever; Stedman.

LISTON, ROBERT. 1794-1847. English surgeon. See: World Who's Who Sci. Liston's forceps, Liston's knives, Liston's operation, Liston's shears, Liston's splint.

Liston's forceps (Liston, Robert): Medicine. See: Dorland; Stedman.

Liston's knives (Liston, Robert): Medicine. See: Dorland; Stedman.

Liston's operation (Liston, Robert): Medicine. See: Dorland.

Liston's shears (Liston, Robert): Medicine. See: Stedman.

Liston's splint (Liston, Robert): Medicine. See: Stedman.

LISZT, FRANZ. 1811-1886. Hungarian pianist and composer. See: New Encyc. Brit., 1974. Lisztian.

Lisztian (Liszt, Franz): Music. See: Webster's 3d.

LITTEN, MORITZ. 1845-1907. German physician. See: Biog. Lex. hervorr. Aerzte, 1880-1930. Litten's sign (or phenomenon).

Litten's sign (or phenomenon) (Litten, Moritz): Medicine. See: Dorland; Hinsie; Stedman.

Little Bo Peep. See: Bo Peep, Little.

little Brodricks (Brodrick, William St. John Fremantle): History. See: Montgomery.

Little Company of Mary (Mary, Virgin-Mother): Religion. See: Attwater.

LITTLE, SIR ERNEST GORDON GRAHAM. 1867-1950. English physician. See: Who Was Who, 1941-1950. Little's syndrome.

LITTLE, JAMES LAWRENCE. 1836-1885. American physician. See: Biog. Lex. hervorr. Aerzte. Little's area?

LITTLE, WILLIAM JOHN. 1810-1894. English surgeon. See: World Who's Who Sci. Little's disease, Little's paralysis, Stromeyer-Little operation.

Littlefield Ballet (Littlefield, Catherine): Dance. See: Chujoy.

LITTLEFIELD, CATHERINE. 1908-1951. American choreographer, ballerina and teacher. See: New York Times, Nov. 20, 1951, p. 31, col. 1. Littlefield Ballet.

LITTLER, WILLIAM. fl. 1750. English potter. (Biography source unavailable.) Littler's blue.

Littler's blue (Littler, William): Chemistry. See: Thrush.

Little's area (Little, James Lawrence?). See: Kiesselbach's area.

Little's disease (Little, William John): Medicine. See: Dorland; Hinsie; Jablonski; Stedman; Webster's 3d.

Little's paralysis (Little, William John): Medicine. See: Stedman. Also known as: Heine-Medin disease.

Little's syndrome (Little, Sir Ernest Gordon Graham): Medicine. See: Jablonski. Also known as: Graham Little-Lassueur-Feldman syndrome, Graham Little's syndrome, Lassueur-Graham Little triad, Piccardi-Lassueur-Little syndrome.

LITTLETON, JESSE TALBOT. 1887-1966. American physicist. See: Pogg., vols. 6, 7b. Littleton softening point.

Littleton softening point (Littleton, Jesse Talbot): Engineering and Industry. See: Thrush.

LITTLETON, SIR THOMAS. 1422-1481. English jurist and legal writer. See: Dict. Nat. Biog. Coke upon Littleton.

LITTON, SAMUEL. 1779-1847. Irish botanist. See: Britten and Boulger. Littonia.

Littonia (Litton, Samuel): Botany. See: Taylor, N.

LITTRE, ALEXIS. 1658-1726. French anatomist. See: World Who's Who Sci. Littre's gland(s), Littre's hernia, Littre's operation.

Littre's gland(s) (Littre, Alexis): Anatomy. See: Donath; Dorland; Stedman; Webster's 3d.

Littre's hernia (Littre, Alexis): Medicine. See: Dorland; Jablonski; Stedman.

Littre's operation (Littre, Alexis): Medicine. See: Dorland; Stedman.

LITTROW, JOSEPH JOHANN VON. 1781-1840. Austrian astronomer and mathematician. See: Pogg., vol. 1. Littrow mirror, Littrow mounting (of prism and plane mirror), Littrow prism, Littrow spectrograph (or spectroscope).

Littrow mirror (Littrow, Joseph Johann von): Physics. See: Thewlis.

Littrow mounting (of prism and plane mirror) (Littrow, Joseph Johann von): Physics. See: Hughes; Internat. Dict. Phys. Elec.; Van Nostrand Sci. Encyc.

Littrow prism (Littrow, Joseph Johann von): Physics. See: Hackh; Van Nostrand Sci. Encyc.

Littrow spectrograph (or spectroscope) (Littrow, Joseph Johann von): Physics. See: Satterthwaite; Van Nostrand Sci. Encyc.; Webster's 3d.

Liturgy of St. Basil. See: Basilian liturgy.

Liturgy of St. Gregory dialogos (Gregory I, the Great, Saint): Religion. See: Attwater.

Liturgy of St. James (James the Greater, Saint): Religion. See: Attwater; New Encyc. Brit., 1974.

Liturgy of St. John Chrysostom (John Chrysostom, Saint): Religion. See: Attwater.

LITZMANN, KARL KONRAD THEODOR. 1815-1890. German gynecologist. See: Biog. Lex. hervorr. Aerzte. Litzmann obliquity.

Litzmann obliquity (Litzmann, Karl Konrad Theodor): Medicine. See: Dorland; Stedman.

LIVEING, GEORGE DOWNING. 1827-1924. English chemist. See: Dict. Nat. Biog., 4th Suppl. Liveingite.

Liveingite (Liveing, George Downing): Earth Sciences. See: Thrush; Webster's 3d.

LIVI, RIDOLFO. 1856-1920. Italian physician. See: Biog. Lex. hervorr. Aerzte, 1880-1930. Livi's index.

LIVIERATO, PANAGINO. 1860-1936. Italian physician. See: Biog. Lex. hervorr. Aerzte, 1880-1930. Livierato's sign, Livierato's test.

Livierato's sign (Livierato, Panagino): Medicine. See: Dorland.

Livierato's test (Livierato, Panagino): Medicine. See: Dorland.

LIVINGSTON, BURTON EDWARD. 1875-1948. American plant physiologist. See: Amer. Men Sci., 7th ed. Livingstone sphere.

LIVINGSTONE, DAVID. 1813-1873. Scottish missionary and explorer in Africa. See: Dict. Nat. Biog. Livingstone's touraco?, Livingstonite.

Livingstone sphere (Livingston, Burton Edward): Botany. See: Huschke.

Livingstone's touraco (Livingstone, David?): Zoology. See: Gray.

Livingstonite (Livingstone, David): Earth Sciences. See: Thrush; Webster's 3d.

Livi's index (Livi, Ridolfo): Medicine. See: Dorland.

Livistona (Murray, Patrick): Botany. See: Taylor, N.

LJUNG, HARVEY ALBERT. 1905- . American analytical chemist. See: Amer. Men and Women Sci., 12th ed. Ljung test.

Ljung test (Ljung, Harvey Albert): Chemistry. See: Van Nostrand Chem. Dict.

LJUNGBERG, ERIK JOHAN. 1843-1915. Swedish engineer. See: Svenska Maen Och Kvinnor. Ljungberg process.

Ljungberg process (Ljungberg, Erik Johan): Engineering and Industry. See: Thrush.

LJUNGGREN, GUSTAF AXEL CARLSSON. 1894-1966. Swedish chemist. See: Pogg., vols. 6, 7b. Ljungren solution.

Ljungren solution (Ljunggren, Gustaf Axel Carlsson): Chemistry. See: Van Nostrand Chem. Dict.

LJUNGSTROEM, BIRGER. 1872-1948. Swedish engineer. See: Svenska Maen Och Kvinnor. Ljungstrom turbine (or steam turbine).

Ljungstrom turbine (or steam turbine) (Ljungstroem, Birger): Engineering and Industry. See: Auger; Internat. Dict. Ap. Math.

Llewellin setter (Purcell-Llewellin): Zoology. See: Webster's 3d.

Lloyd Davies formula (Derivation undetermined): Engineering and Industry. See: Thrush.

LLOYD GEORGE, DAVID. 1863-1945. English statesman. See: New Encyc. Brit., 1974. Lloyd George raspberry, Lloyd-Georgian (or Lloyd-Georgeite).

Lloyd George raspberry (Lloyd George, David): Botany. See: Hendrickson.

Lloyd-Georgian (or Lloyd-Georgeite) (Lloyd George, David): Politics. See: Webster's 3d.

LLOYD, HUMPHREY. 1800-1881. Irish physicist. See: Dict. Sci. Biog. Lloyd mirror, Lloyd mirror effect in acoustics.

LLOYD, JAMES TILGHMAN. 1857-1944. American legislator. See: Biog. Dict. Amer. Congress. Lloyd-La Follette Act.

LLOYD, JOHN URI. 1849-1936. American pharmacist. See: Dict. Sci. Biog. Lloyd('s) reagent (for alkaloids).

Lloyd-La Follette Act (Lloyd, James Tilghman and La Follette, Robert Marion?): Politics. See: Smith.

Lloyd mirror (Lloyd, Humphrey): Physics. See: Internat. Dict. Phys. Elec.; Van Nostrand Sci. Encyc.

Lloyd mirror effect in acoustics (Lloyd, Humphrey): Physics. See: Internat. Dict. Phys. Elec.

Lloyd Morgan's canon (Morgan, Lloyd). See: Morgan's canon (or principle).

LLOYD, PUTNAM C. fl. 1929. American physician. (Biography source unavailable.) Lloyd's syndrome.

Lloyd('s) reagent (for alkaloids) (Lloyd, John Uri): Chemistry. See: Stedman; Van Nostrand Chem. Dict.

LLOYD, RICHARD LEWIS. b. 1870. American mining engineer. See: Who's Who Engin., 1925. Dwight-Lloyd machine, Dwight-Lloyd process (or sintering), Dwight-Lloyd roaster.

LLOYD-THOMAS, HYWEL GEOFFREY LLOYD. fl. 1945-1972. English cardiologist. See: Med. Direct., 1972. Evans and Lloyd-Thomas syndrome.

Lloyd's syndrome (Lloyd, Putnam C.): Medicine. See: Jablonski.

Llull, Ramon. See: Lull, Ramon.

Lobacevskii method (Lobachevsky, Nikolai Ivanovich): Mathematics. See: Internat. Dict. Ap. Math.

Lobachevskian geometry (Lobachevsky, Nikolai Ivanovich): Mathematics. See: Dict. Sci. Biog.; Van Nostrand Sci. Encyc. under "Geometry."

LOBACHEVSKY, NIKOLAI IVANOVICH. 1792-1856. Russian mathematician. See: New Encyc. Brit., 1974. Lobacevskii method, Lobachevskian geometry.

Lobbert lagging (Derivation undetermined): Engineering and Industry.

L'OBEL (or LOBEL), MATTHIAS DE. 1538-1616. Flemish botanist. See: Dict. Sci. Biog. Lobelia, Lobel's catchfly.

Lobelia (L'Obel, Matthias de): Botany. See: Dorland; Encyc. Brit., 1973; Stedman; Taylor, N.; Webster's 3d.

Lobel's catchfly (L'Obel, Matthias de): Botany. See: Webster's 3d.

LOBO, JORGE. fl. 1931. Brazilian physician. (Biography source unavailable.) Lobo's disease.

Lobo micro-test for mercurous ion (Lobo, Rodolfo): Chemistry. See: Van Nostrand Chem. Dict.

LOBO, RODOLFO. fl. 1936. Argentinian chemist. Cited in: Chem. Abstr., vol. 30, p. 6672. Lobo micro-test for mercurous ion.

Lobo's disease (Lobo, Jorge): Medicine. See: Jablonski.

LOBRY DE BRUYN, CORNELIS ADRIAAN. 1857-1904. Dutch chemist. See: Pogg., vols. 4, 5. Lobry de Bruyn-van Ekenstein rearrangement (transformation or conversion).

Lobry de Bruyn-Van Ekenstein rearrangement (transformation or conversion) (Lobry de Bruyn, Cornelis Adriaan and Van Ekenstein, Willem Alberda): Chemistry. See: Ballentyne, Stedman; Van Nostrand Chem. Dict.

LOBSTEIN, JOHANN GEORG C. F. M. 1777-1835. German pathologist. See: World Who's Who Sci. Lobstein's cancer, Lobstein's ganglion, Lobstein's pityriasis, Lobstein's syndrome.

Lobstein's cancer (Lobstein, Johann Georg C. F. M.): Medicine. See: Dorland.

Lobstein's ganglion (Lobstein, Johann Georg C. F. M.): Medicine. See: Dorland; Stedman.

Lobstein's pityriasis (Lobstein, Johann Georg C. F. M.): Medicine. See: Stedman.

Lobstein's syndrome (Lobstein, Johann Georg C. F. M.): Medicine. See: Dorland; Jablonski; Stedman. Also known as: Eddowes' syndrome, Ekman-Lobstein syndrome, Ekman's syndrome, Spurway-Eddowes syndrome.

LOCHER, J. fl. 1874. German chemist. Cited in: Partington, vol. 4, p. 808. Meyer-Locher test for alcohols.

LOCHNER, FRANK ELLIOTT. fl. 1890. English company representative. See: Brelsford, p. 62. Lochner treaty.

Lochner treaty (Lochner, Frank Elliott): History. See: Morris and Irwin.

LOCKE, FRANK SPILLER. 1871-1949. English physiologist. Cited in: Royal Soc. Cat. Sci. Pap., 1884-1900. Locke-Ringer solution, Locke's solution.

LOCKE, JOHN. 1632-1704. English philosopher. See: New Encyc. Brit., 1974. Lockean (or Lockeanism).

Locke-Ringer solution (Locke, Frank Spiller and Ringer, Sidney): Medicine. See: Blakiston's Gould; Stedman.

Lockean (or Lockeanism) (Locke, John): Philosophy. See: Webster's 3d.

LOCKENVITZ, ARTHUR ERNEST. 1902- . American applied physicist. See: Amer. Men and Women Sci., 12th ed. Lockenvitz leaf gauge.

Lockenvitz leaf gauge (Lockenvitz, Arthur Ernest): Physics. See: Internat. Dict. Phys. Elec.

Locke's solution (Locke, Frank Spiller): Medicine. See: Dorland; Hackh; Stedman; Webster's 3d.

LOCKWOOD, CHARLES BARRETT. 1858-1914. English surgeon. See: Who Was Who, 1897-1916. Lockwood's ligament (or ligament of Lockwood), Lockwood's sign.

Lockwood's ligament (or ligament of Lockwood) (Lockwood, Charles Barrett): Medicine. See: Dorland; Stedman.

Lockwood's sign (Lockwood, Charles Barrett): Medicine. See: Dorland.

LODDIGES, CONRAD. d. 1826. English nurseryman. See: Merrill and Walker. Loddigesia.

Loddigesia (Loddiges, Conrad): Zoology. Webster's 3d.

LODE, WALTER. 1898- . German applied physicist. See: Kuerschner's Deut. Gel. Kal., vol. 9, 1961. Lode's variables.

Lode's variables (Lode, Walter): Mathematics. See: Internat. Dict. Ap. Math.

Lodge corollary (Lodge, Henry Cabot): History. See: Morris.

Lodge-Cottrell process (Lodge, Lionel and Cottrell, Frederick Gardner): Engineering and Industry. See: Hackh.

LODGE, HENRY CABOT. 1850-1924. American legislator and author. See: New Encyc. Brit., 1974, Microp. Lodge corollary.

LODGE, LIONEL. fl. 1925-1942. English? chemist. Cited in: Chem. Abstr. Lodge-Cottrell process.

LODGE, SIR OLIVER JOSEPH. 1851-1940. English physicist. See: Pogg., vols. 3-6, 7b. Lodge valve.

Lodge valve (Lodge, Sir Oliver Joseph): Electronics. See: Hughes.

Lodi reagents for bleaching chemicals in flour (Lodi, Vera): Chemistry. See: Van Nostrand Chem. Dict.

LODI, VERA. fl. 1934. Italian chemist. Cited in: Chem. Abstr., vol. 28, p. 4493. Lodi reagents for bleaching chemicals in flour.

Loeb collection (Loeb, Morris?): Chemistry. See: Hackh.

LOEB, LEO. 1869-1959. American pathologist. See: Dict. Sci. Biog. Loeb's deciduoma.

LOEB, MORRIS. 1863-1912. American chemist and philanthropist. See: Dict. Amer. Biog. Loeb collection?

LOEBICH, OTTO. 1902- . German chemist. Cited in: Chem. Abstr., vol. 20, p. 1773. Loebich reagent for perchloric acid.

Loebich reagent for perchloric acid (Loebich, Otto): Chemistry. See: Van Nostrand Chem. Dict.

Loeffler('s) blood culture medium (blood serum or mixture) (Loeffler, Friedrich August Johannes): Medicine. See: Dorland; Hackh; Stedman.

Loeffler boiler (Loeffler, Stephan): Engineering and Industry. See: Auger.

LOEFFLER, FRIEDRICH AUGUST JOHANNES. 1852-1915. German bacteriologist. See: Dict. Sci. Biog. Klebs-Loeffler bacillus, Loeffler('s) blood culture medium (blood serum or mixture), Loeffler('s) methylene blue (or alkaline methylene blue), Loeffleria, Loeffler's caustic solution, Loeffler's medium (1) (for B. diphtheriae), Loeffler's medium (2) (for typhoid-paratyphoid group), Loeffler's stain (flagella stain or method).

Loeffler('s) methylene blue (or alkaline methylene blue) (Loeffler, Friedrich August Johannes): Medicine. See: Dorland; Hackh; Kelly; Stedman.

LOEFFLER, STEPHAN. d. 1929. Austrian engineer. See: Kuerschner's Deut. Gel. Kal., vol. 4, 1931. Loeffler boiler.

LOEFFLER, WILHELM. b. 1887. Swiss physician. See: Biog. Lex. hervorr. Aerzte, 1880-1930. Loeffler's disease (eosinophilia or syndrome), Loeffler's endocarditis.

Loeffleria (Loeffler, Friedrich August Johannes): Medicine. See: Stedman.

Loeffler's bacillus (Loeffler, Friedrich August Johannes). See: Klebs-Loeffler bacillus.

Loeffler's caustic solution (Loeffler, Friedrich August Johannes): Medicine. See: Stedman.

Loeffler's disease (eosinophilia or syndrome) (Loeffler, Wilhelm): Medicine. See: Jablonski; Stedman; Webster's 3d.

Loeffler's endocarditis (Loeffler, Wilhelm): Medicine. See: Jablonski; Stedman.

Loeffler's medium (1) (for B. diphtheriae) (Loeffler, Friedrich August Johannes): Medicine. See: Kelly.

Loeffler's medium (2) (for typhoid-paratyphoid group) (Loeffler, Friedrich August Johannes): Medicine. See: Kelly.

Loeffler's stain (flagella stain or method) (Loeffler, Friedrich August Johannes): Medicine. See: Dorland; Kelly; Stedman.

LOEFGREN, SVEN HALVAR. 1910- . Swedish physician. See: Vem Ar Det?, 1975. Loefgren's syndrome.

Loefgren's syndrome (Loefgren, Sven Halvar): Medicine. See: Jablonski.

LOEGSTRUP, MARIE. fl. 1926. Swedish chemist. Cited in: Chem. Abstr., vol. 21, p. 543. Von Hevesy-Loegstrup test reaction.

LOEHLEIN, HERMANN. 1847-1901. German gynecologist. See: Biog. Lex. hervorr. Aerzte, 1880-1930. Loehlein's diameter.

LOEHLEIN, MAX HERMANN FRIEDRICH. 1877-1921. German physician. See: Biog. Lex. hervorr. Aerzte, 1880-1930. Lohlein-Baehr lesion, Loehlein's nephritis.

Loehlein's diameter (Loehlein, Hermann): Medicine. See: Dorland.

Loehlein's nephritis (Loehlein, Max Hermann Friedrich): Medicine. See: Jablonski.

LOEHR, HANNS. 1891-1949. German physician. See: Index-Cat. Libr. Surg.-Gen. Off., 5th Ser., vol. 1, 1959. Loehr-Kindberg syndrome.

Loehr–Kindberg syndrome (Loehr, Hanns and Kindberg, Michel Leon): Medicine. See: Jablonski.

LOENEN, JOHANNES JACOBUS GUILIELMUS VAN. fl. 1835. Dutch physician. See: Biog. Woordenb. der Nederl. (Aa). Loenen's sign?

Loenen's sign (Loenen, Johannes Jacobus Guilielmus van?). See: Ladin's sign.

LOESCH, FRIEDRICH. fl. 1875. German zoologist and physician. Cited in: Kelly. Loeschia.

Loeschia (Loesch, Friedrich): Zoology. See: Stedman; Webster's 3d.

Loevit, Moritz. See: Loewit, Moritz.

Loevit's cells (Loewit, Moritz): Medicine. See: Dorland; Stedman.

Loew–Bokorny reagent (Loew, Oscar and Bokorny, Thomas): Chemistry. See: Van Nostrand Chem. Dict.

LOEW, OSCAR (In full: CARL BENEDICT OSCAR). 1844–1941. German chemist. See: Pogg., vols. 3, 4, 5, 6, 7a. Loew–Bokorny reagent, Loew theory.

Loew theory (Loew, Oscar): Chemistry. See: Hackh.

LOEWE, FRIEDRICH (In full: CARL FRIEDRICH). 1874–1955. German optician. See: Pogg., vols. 5, 6, 7a. Loewe's ring.

LOEWE, JULIUS FRIEDRICH FERDINAND FRANZ. b. 1823. German chemist. See: Pogg., vols. 1, 3. Loewe's test (or reagent).

LOEWE, KARL J. d. 1890. German chemist. (Biography source unavailable.) Loeweite.

Loeweite (Loewe, Karl J.): Earth Sciences. See: Thrush; Webster's 3d.

LOEWENBERG, BENJAMIN BENNO. 1836–1905. German–born French laryngologist. See: World Who's Who Sci. Loewenberg's canal (or scala), Loewenberg's forceps.

Loewenberg's canal (or scala) (Loewenberg, Benjamin Benno): Anatomy. See: Donath; Dorland; Stedman.

Loewenberg's forceps (Loewenberg, Benjamin Benno): Medicine. See: Dorland; Stedman.

LOEWENSTEIN, ERNST. 1878–1950. Austrian–born American pathologist. See: Biog. Lex. hervorr. Aerzte, 1880–1930. Loewenstein–Jensen medium, Loewenstein's medium, Loewenstein's ointment, Loewenstein's solution.

Loewenstein–Jensen medium (Loewenstein, Ernst and Orla–Jensen, Sigurd): Medicine. See: Blakiston's Gould.

LOEWENSTEIN, LUDWIG W. fl. 1939. German–born American dermatologist. (Biography source unavailable.) Buschke–Loewenstein tumor.

Loewenstein's medium (Loewenstein, Ernst): Medicine. See: Dorland.

Loewenstein's ointment (Loewenstein, Ernst): Medicine. See: Dorland.

Loewenstein's solution (Loewenstein, Ernst): Medicine. See: Kelly.

LOEWENTHAL, LEONARD JOSEPH ALPHONSE. fl. 1925–1964. South African dermatologist. See: Med. Direct., 1964. Loewenthal's purpura.

LOEWENTHAL, WILHELM. 1850–1894. German physician. See: Biog. Lex. hervorr. Aerzte, 1880–1930. Loewenthal's bundle (or tract), Loewenthal's reaction, Loewenthal's test (or reagent).

Loewenthal's bundle (or tract) (Loewenthal, Wilhelm): Anatomy. See: Dorland; Stedman. Also known as: Marchi's tract (or bundle).

Loewenthal's purpura (Loewenthal, Leonard Joseph Alphonse). See: Casala–Mosto disease.

Loewenthal's reaction (Loewenthal, Wilhelm): Medicine. See: Dorland; Stedman.

Loewenthal's test (or reagent) (Loewenthal, Wilhelm): Medicine. See: Stedman; Van Nostrand Chem. Dict.

Loewe's ring (Loewe, Friedrich). See: Maxwell's spot.

Loewe's test (or reagent) (Loewe, Julius Friedrich Ferdinand Franz): Chemistry. See: Dorland; Kelly; Stedman; Van Nostrand Chem. Dict.

LOEWI, OTTO. 1873–1961. German–born American pharmacologist. See: Dict. Sci. Biog. Loewi's reaction (symptom or test).

LOEWIG, KARL JACOB. 1803–1890. German chemist. See: Pogg., vols. 1, 3. Lowig process?

Loewinson–Lessing classification (Levinson–Lessing, Franz Yulevich): Earth Sciences. See: Thrush.

Loewinson–Lessing, Franz Yulevich. See: Levinson–Lessing, Franz Yulevich.

Loewi's reaction (symptom or test) (Loewi, Otto): Medicine. See: Dorland.

LOEWIT, MORITZ. 1851–1918. Austrian pathologist. See: Ber. Naturw.–Medizin. Ver. Innsbruck, vol. 37 (1917–1920), pp. 24–31. Loevit's cells, Loewitt's bodies (or lymphocytes).

Loewitt's bodies (or lymphocytes) (Loewit, Moritz): Medicine. See: Dorland.

LOEWY, ADOLPH. fl. 1885–1907. German physiologist. Cited in: Royal Soc. Cat. Sci. Pap., 1884–1900. Loewy–Neuberg test reaction.

Loewy–Neuberg test reaction (Loewy, Adolph and Neuberg, Carl): Chemistry. See: Van Nostrand Chem. Dict.

Loftin–White circuit (Derivation undetermined): Electronics. See: Markus.

LOGAN. fl. 1946. American legislator. (Biography source unavailable.) Walter–Logan Act.

Logan Act (Logan, George): Politics. See: Nat. Cycl. Amer. Biog. under "Logan, George," vol. 8, p. 255.

Logan black law (Logan, John Alexander): History. See: Mathews, M. M.

LOGAN, GEORGE. 1753–1821. American physician and politician. See: Dict. Amer. Biog. Logan Act.

Logan–Hay Medal (Logan, Stephen Trigg and Hay, John Milton): Sociology. Cited in: Encyc. Assoc. under "Abraham Lincoln Association."

LOGAN, JAMES. 1674–1751. Irish–born American scientist. See: Dict. Amer. Biog. Logania.

LOGAN, JAMES HARVEY. 1841–1921. American lawyer and horticulturist. See: Dict. Amer. Biog. Loganberry.

LOGAN, JAMES JOHN (Indian name: TAH–GAH–JUTE). ca. 1725–1780. American Indian leader. See: Dict. Amer. Biog. Logan's lament.

LOGAN, JOHN ALEXANDER. 1826–1886. American soldier and politician. See: Dict. Amer. Biog. Logan black law.

Logan slabbing machine (Derivation undetermined): Engineering and Industry. See: Thrush.

LOGAN, STEPHEN TRIGG. 1800–1880. American jurist. See: Dict. Amer. Biog. Logan–Hay Medal.

Logan tent (Logan, Sir William Edmond): Applied Arts. See: Webster's 3d.

LOGAN, SIR WILLIAM EDMOND. 1798–1875. Canadian geologist. See: Dict. Nat. Biog. Logan tent, Logan's line.

Loganberry (Logan, James Harvey): Botany. See: De Sola; Hendrickson; Mathews, M. M.; Taylor, N.; Webster's 3d.

Logania (Logan, James): Botany. See: Webster's 3d.

Logan's bow (Derivation undetermined): Medicine. See: Stedman.

Logan's lament (Logan, James John): History. See: Hendrickson.

Logan's line (Logan, Sir William Edmond): Earth Sciences. See: Dict. Sci. Biog. under "Billings, Elkanah," vol. 2, p. 129a; New Encyc. Brit., 1974, Microp.

Logie (Logie, David): Applied Arts. See: Partridge.

LOGIE, DAVID. fl. ca. 1860. Inventor. (Biography source unavailable.) Logie.

Lohlein–Baehr lesion (Loehlein, Max Hermann Friedrich and Baehr, George?): Medicine. See: Stedman.

LOHMANN, HANS. d. 1934. German zoologist. See: Kuerschner's Deut. Gel. Kal., vol. 4, 1931. Lohmannella.

LOHMANN, HERMAN J. fl. 1911. American engineer. Cited in: Chem. Abstr., Decenn. Index, 1907–1916. Lohmannizing.

Lohmannella (Lohmann, Hans): Zoology. See: Pennak.

Lohmannizing (Lohmann, Herman J.): Engineering and Industry. See: Thrush.

LOHNSTEIN, THEODOR. 1866–1918. German physician. See: Biog. Lex. hervorr. Aerzte, 1880–1930. Lohnstein's saccharimeter.

Lohnstein's saccharimeter (Lohnstein, Theodor): Medicine. See: Dorland; Stedman.

LOHUIZEN, CATO H. J. VAN. fl. 1922. Dutch physician. (Biography source unavailable.) Van Lohuizen's disease.

Loi Berenger (Berenger, Rene): Law. See: Harbottle.

Loi Falloux (Falloux, Frederic Alfred Pierre): Education. Cited in: Webster's Biog. Dict.

Loiseau furnace (Loiseau, Oscar): Engineering and Industry. See: Thrush.

LOISEAU, OSCAR. fl. 1909–1911. Belgian engineer. Cited in: Chem. Abstr., Decenn. Index, 1907–1916. Loiseau furnace.

LOISELEUR-DESLONGCHAMPS, JEAN LOUIS AUGUSTE. 1774–1849. French botanist. See: World Who's Who Sci. Deschampsia, Loiseleuria.

Loiseleuria (Loiseleur-Deslongchamps, Jean Louis Auguste): Botany. See: Taylor, N.

LOMB, HENRY. 1828–1908. German-born American optician. See: Webster's Biog. Dict. Bausch and Lomb dust counter.

LOMBARD, ETIENNE. 1869–1920. French physician. See: Biog. Lex. hervorr. Aerzte, 1880–1930. Lombard voice-reflex test?, Lombard's phenomenon.

Lombard voice-reflex test (Lombard, Etienne?): Medicine. See: Stedman.

LOMBARDI, ANTONIO. fl. 1910. Italian physican. Cited in: Index-Cat. Libr. Surg.-Gen. Off., 3d Ser., vol. 7, 1928. Lombardi's sign.

Lombardi's sign (Lombardi, Antonio): Medicine. See: Dorland.

Lombard's phenomenon (Lombard, Etienne): Medicine. See: Biog. Lex. hervorr. Aerzte, 1880–1930.

Lombrosian (criminology) (Lombroso, Cesare): Sociology. See: Webster's 3d.; Zadrozny.

LOMBROSO, CESARE. 1836–1909. Italian physician and criminologist. See: Internat. Encyc. Soc. Sci. Lombrosian (criminology).

London('s) equation for intermolecular attraction (dispersion effect or dipole theory) (London, Fritz Wolfgang): Physics. See: Ballentyne; Van Nostrand Sci. Encyc. under "Molecular Attraction"; Van Nostrand Sci. Encyc.

London equation (for superconductors) (London, Fritz Wolfgang and London, Heinz): Physics. See: Ballentyne; Internat. Dict. Phys. Elec.; Markus.

London forces (London, Fritz Wolfgang): Physics. See: Hughes; Internat. Dict. Phys. Elec.; Van Nostrand Sci. Encyc.; Webster's 3d.

LONDON, FRITZ WOLFGANG. 1900–1954. German-born American physicist. See: Dict. Sci. Biog. Heitler–London–Slater–Pauling method (or HLSP method), Heitler–London theory of the hydrogen molecule, Heitler–London theory (theory of valence, covalence theory of method), London('s) equation for intermolecular attraction (dispersion effect or dipole theory), London equation (for superconductors), London forces, Van der Waals–London interaction.

LONDON, HEINZ. 1907–1970. German-born English physicist. See: Dict. Sci. Biog. London equation (for superconductors), London order parameter, London penetration depth.

London order parameter (London, Heinz): Physics. See: Dict. Sci. Biog. under "London, Fritz," p. 476a.

London penetration depth (London, Heinz): Physics. See: Ballentyne.

LONG, JOHN HARPER. 1856–1918. American biochemist. See: World Who's Who Sci. Long's formula (or coefficient).

LONGHI, GIOVANNI. fl. 1892. Italian physician. See: Archiv. Ital. de Otolog., vol. 1 (1893), p. 197f. Avellis–Longhi syndrome?

LONGI, ANTONIO. fl. 1884–1897. Italian chemist. Cited in: Royal Soc. Cat. Sci. Pap., 1884–1900. Longi test.

Longi test (Longi, Antonio): Chemistry. See: Van Nostrand Chem. Dict.

Longinian (Longinus, Dionysius Cassius): Literature. See: Webster's 3d.

LONGINUS. fl. early 1st c. Roman soldier who pierced Christ's side with a spear. See: Dict. Christian Biog. Lounge?

LONGINUS, DIONYSIUS CASSIUS. ca. 213–273. Greek philosopher and rhetorician. See: Dict. Grk. Rom. Biog. Myth. Longinian.

Longmaid–Henderson process (Derivation undetermined): Engineering and Industry. See: Thrush.

LONGMIRE, WILLIAM POLK, JR. 1913– . American surgeon. See: Amer. Men and Women Sci., 12th ed. Longmire's operation.

Longmire's operation (Longmire, William Polk, Jr.): Medicine. See: Dorland; Stedman.

Long's formula (or coefficient) (Long, John Harper): Medicine. See: Dorland; Stedman.

LONGSTRETH, EDWARD. 1839–1905. American engineer. See: Who Was Who Amer., Hist. vol. Longstreth medal.

Longstreth medal (Longstreth, Edward): Photography. Cited in: Bull. Almanac, 1975; Cited in: Focal Encyc. Photog. under "Britain," p. 121b.

LONGWORTH, ALICE ROOSEVELT. b. 1884. American writer and society woman. See: Amer. Women, vol. 3, 1939–1940. Alice blue.

Lonicera (Lonicerus, Adam): Botany. See: Taylor, N.; Webster's 3d.

LONICERUS (LONITZER), ADAM. 1528–1586. German botanist. See: Dict. Sci. Biog. Lonicera.

Lonitzer, Adam. See: Lonicerus, Adam.

Loo board (Derivation undetermined): Engineering and Industry. See: Thrush.

Loof reagent for arsenic (Derivation undetermined): Chemistry. See: Van Nostrand Chem. Dict.

Loof test for nitrate in water (Derivation undetermined): Chemistry. See: Van Nostrand Chem. Dict.

LOOMIS, ALFRED LEBBEUS. 1830–1895. American physician. See: Nat. Cycl. Amer. Biog., vol. 8, p. 223. Loomis' mixture.

LOOMIS, FRANCIS WHEELER. b. 1889. American physicist. See: World Who's Who Sci. Loomis–Wood diagram.

Loomis' mixture (Loomis, Alfred Lebbeus): Medicine. See: Dorland.

Loomis–Wood diagram (Loomis, Francis Wheeler and Wood, Robert Williams): Physics. See: Internat. Dict. Phys. Elec.

LOONEY, JOSEPH MICHAEL. 1896– . American biochemist. See: Amer. Men Sci., 10th ed. Folin–Looney test.

loop of Henle (Henle, Friedrich Gustav Jacob). See: Henle's loop (or ansa).

Looser–Debray–Milkman syndrome (Looser, Emil; Debray; and Milkman, Louis Arthur). See: Milkman–Looser syndrome.

LOOSER, EMIL. 1877–1936. Swiss physician. See: Index-Cat. Libr. Surg.-Gen. Off., 4th Ser., vol. 9, 1945. Looser's zones, Milkman–Looser syndrome.

Looser–Milkman syndrome (Looser, Emil and Milkman, Louis Arthur). See: Milkman–Looser syndrome.

Looser's zones (Looser, Emil): Medicine. See: Jablonski; Stedman.

LOPEZ, EMILIANO. fl. 20th c. Chilean mineral collector. Cited in: Hintze, 2d suppl., p. 225. Lopezite.

opez filibustering expeditions (Lopez, Narcisco): History. See: Morris and ...win..

LOPEZ, JEANNE A. fl. 1946. American biochemist. Cited in: Chem. Abstr., vol. 40, p. 2181. Lowry-Lopez-Bessey method.

LOPEZ, NARCISCO. ca. 1798-1851. Venezuelan-born Cuban revolutionist. See: Nouv. Biog. Univ. Lopez filibustering expeditions.

LOPEZ, THOMAS. fl. 16th c. Spanish colonial official. (Biography source unavailable.) Lopezia.

Lopezia (Lopez, Thomas): Botany. See: New Encyc. Brit., 1974, Microp. under "Onagraceae"; Taylor, N.; Webster's 3d.

Lopezite (Lopez, Emiliano): Earth Sciences. See: Thrush; Webster's 3d.

Lorain-Levi syndrome (Lorain, Paul Joseph and Levi, Leopold): Medicine. See: Jablonski. Also known as: Levi's syndrome, Lorrain's syndrome.

LORAIN, PAUL JOSEPH. 1827-1875. French physician. See: World Who's Who Sci. Lorain-Levi syndrome, Lorain's disease.

Lorain's disease (Lorain, Paul Joseph): Medicine. See: Stedman.

Lorain's syndrome (Lorain, Paul Joseph). See: Lorain-Levi syndrome.

LORAND, EOTVOS. fl. 19th c. Hungarian physicist. Cited in: Hintze, vol. I, pt. 1, p. 982. Lorandite.

LORAND, LAZLO. 1923- . Hungarian-born American physiologist. See: Amer. Men Sci., 10th ed. Laki-Lorand factor.

Lorandite (Lorand, Eotvos): Earth Sciences. See: Thrush; Webster's 3d.

l'Orange nozzle (L'Orange, Prosper): Engineering and Industry. See: Auger.

L'ORANGE, PROSPER. 1876-1939. German? engineer. Cited in: Mansell. l'Orange nozzle.

LORANSKI, A. M. fl. ca. 1899. Russian mine inspector. Cited in: Hintze, 1st suppl., p. 301. Loranskite.

Loranskite (Loranski, A. M.): Earth Sciences. See: Thrush; Webster's 3d.

Lord Acton's Law (Acton, John Emerick Edward Dalberg): Sociology. See: Martin.

Lord Anson's pea (Anson, George?): Botany. Cited in: Gray.

Lord Ashbourne's Act (Gibson, Edward, Lord Ashbourne): History. See: Harbottle; Montgomery.

Lord Baltimore cake (Calvert, George, 1st Lord Baltimore): Food and Drink. See: Webster's 3d.

Lord blowpipe reagent (Lord, Nathaniel Wright): Chemistry. See: Van Nostrand Chem. Dict.

Lord Campbell Act (Campbell, John Campbell?): Law. See: Black.

Lord Falkland's rule (Derivation undetermined): Sociology. See: Martin.

Lord Fauntleroy (suit) (Fauntleroy, Lord): Fashion. See: Picken; Webster's 3d.

LORD, G. W. fl. 20th c.? English? engineer. (Biography source unavailable.) Lord mill.

Lord Hardwicke's Act (Yorke, Philip, 1st Earl of Hardwicke): History. See: Harbottle.

Lord Langdale's Act (Bickersteth, Henry, Lord Langdale): Law. See: Black.

Lord Lyndhurst's Act (Copley, John Singleton, Lord Lyndhurst): Law: See: Black.

Lord Macdonald's breed (Derivation undetermined): Generic Word (parasites). See: Brewer.

Lord Martin (pear) (Derivation undetermined): Botany. See: Charnock.

Lord mill (Lord, G. W.): Engineering and Industry. See: Auger.

LORD, NATHANIEL WRIGHT. 1854-1911. American chemist. See: World Who's Who Sci. Lord blowpipe reagent.

Lord Nelson (battleship) (Nelson, Horatio, Viscount Nelson): Military Science. See: Quick.

Lorelei (Lorelei, the water nymph): Generic Word. See: Webster's 3d.

LORELEI, THE WATER NYMPH. Siren of German legend. See: Jobes. Lorelei.

Lorentz condition (Lorentz, Hendrik Antoon): Physics. See: Internat. Dict. Phys. Elec.

Lorentz contraction (Lorentz, Hendrik Antoon). See: Lorentz-Fitzgerald contraction.

Lorentz derivative (Lorentz, Hendrik Antoon): Physics. See: Internat. Dict. Ap. Math.

Lorentz double refraction (Lorentz, Hendrik Antoon): Physics. See: Internat. Dict. Phys. Elec.

Lorentz equation of motion (Lorentz, Hendrik Antoon): Physics. See: Internat. Dict. Phys. Elec.

Lorentz factor (or polarization factor) (Lorentz, Hendrik Antoon): Physics. See: Ballentyne; Internat. Dict. Phys. Elec.; Thewlis.

Lorentz field (Lorentz, Hendrik Antoon): Physics. See: Van Nostrand Sci. Encyc.

Lorentz-Fitzgerald contraction (Lorentz, Hendrik Antoon and FitzGerald, George Francis): Physics. See: Satterthwaite; Van Nostrand Sci. Encyc.; Webster's 3d. Also known as: Fitzgerald contraction, Fitzgerald-Lorentz contraction (hypothesis), Lorentz contraction.

Lorentz force (Lorentz, Hendrik Antoon): Physics. See: Ballentyne; Internat. Dict. Ap. Math.; Internat. Dict. Phys. Elec.; Thewlis.

Lorentz frame (Lorentz, Hendrik Antoon): Physics. See: Hughes under "Lorentz contraction"; Van Nostrand Sci. Encyc.

Lorentz gas (Lorentz, Hendrik Antoon): Physics. See: Internat. Dict. Ap. Math.; Internat. Dict. Phys. Elec.

Lorentz gauge (Lorentz, Hendrik Antoon): Physics. See: Ballentyne.

LORENTZ, HENDRIK ANTOON. 1853-1928. Dutch physicist. See: Dict. Sci. Biog. H-theorem of Boltzmann and Lorentz, Heaviside-Lorentz system of units, Lorentz condition, Lorentz derivative, Lorentz double refraction, Lorentz equation of motion, Lorentz factor (or polarization factor), Lorentz field, Lorentz-Fitzgerald contraction, Lorentz force, Lorentz frame, Lorentz gas, Lorentz gauge, Lorentz invariance (or invariant), Lorentz-Lorenz formula, Lorentz-Lorenz law (or equation), Lorentz-Lorenz relation for dielectric constant, Lorentz theory of the electron, Lorentz transformation(s), Lorentz (unit), Lorentz's theory of light sources.

Lorentz invariance (or invariant) (Lorentz, Hendrik Antoon): Physics. See: Internat. Dict. Phys. Elec.; Thewlis; Van Nostrand Sci. Encyc.

Lorentz-Lorenz formula (Lorentz, Hendrik Antoon and Lorenz, Ludwig Valentin): Physics. See: Van Nostrand Chem. Dict.; Thewlis.

Lorentz-Lorenz law (or equation) (Lorentz, Hendrik Antoon and Lorenz, Ludwig Valentin): Physics. See: Ballentyne; Hackh; Internat. Dict. Ap. Math.; Van Nostrand Chem. Dict.

Lorentz-Lorenz relation for dielectric constant (Lorentz, Hendrik Antoon and Lorenz, Ludwig Valentin): Physics. See: Internat. Dict. Phys. Elec.

Lorentz theory of the electron (Lorentz, Hendrik Antoon): Physics. See: Internat. Dict. Phys. Elec.

Lorentz transformation(s) (Lorentz, Hendrik Antoon): Physics. See: Ballentyne; Internat. Dict. Ap. Math.; Satterthwaite; Thewlis; Van Nostrand Sci. Encyc.; Webster's 3d.

Lorentz (unit) (Lorentz, Hendrik Antoon): Physics. See: Ballentyne; Dresner; Internat. Dict. Phys. Elec.; Thewlis.

Lorentz's theory of light sources (Lorentz, Hendrik Antoon): Physics. See: Ballentyne.

LORENZ, ADOLF. 1854-1946. Austrian orthopedic surgeon. See: World Who's Who Sci. Hoffa-Lorenz operation, Lorenz' method, Lorenz' operation, Lorenz' sign.

LORENZ, CHARLOTTE. 1895- . German statistician. See: Kuerschner's Deut. Gel. Kal., vol. 6, 1940-1941. Lorenz curve.

Lorenz curve (Lorenz, Charlotte): Economics. See: Greenwald; Monkhouse; Webster's 3d.

Lorenz instrument landing system (Derivation undetermined): Electronics. See: Markus.

LORENZ, LUDWIG VALENTIN. 1829-1891. Danish physicist. See: Dict. Sci. Biog. Lorentz-Lorenz formula, Lorentz-Lorenz law (or equation), Lorentz-Lorenz relation for dielectric constant, Lorenz number (or constant), Wiedemann-Frenz-Lorenz law.

Lorenz' method (Lorenz, Adolf): Medicine. See: Stedman.

Lorenz number (or constant) (Lorenz, Ludwig Valentin): Physics. See: Ballentyne; Internat. Dict. Phys. Elec.; Thewlis.

Lorenz' operation (Lorenz, Adolf): Medicine. See: Dorland; Stedman.

Lorenz' sign (Lorenz, Adolf): Medicine. See: Dorland; Stedman.

LORENZEN, CHRISTIAN. fl. 1905-1932. German engineer. (Biography source unavailable.) Lorenzen gas turbine.

Lorenzen gas turbine (Lorenzen, Christian): Engineering and Industry. See: Auger.

LORENZINI, STEFANO. fl. 1678. Italian physician. See: World Who's Who Sci. Lorenzini's ampulla(-ae) (or ampullae of Lorenzini).

Lorenzini's ampulla(-ae) (or ampullae of Lorenzini) (Lorenzini, Stefano): Zoology. See: Gray; Henderson; Pennak.

LORETA, PIETRO. 1831-1889. Italian surgeon. See: World Who's Who Sci. Loreta's operation (or operation of Loreta), Loretin.

Loreta's operation (or operation of Loreta) (Loreta, Pietro): Medicine. See: Dorland; Stedman.

Loretin (Loreta, Pietro): Medicine. See: Dorland; Stedman.

LORETTE, LOUIS. 1846-1925. French horticulturist. Cited in: Mansell. Lorette pruning system.

Lorette pruning system (Lorette, Louis): Botany. See: Webster's 3d.

LORGE, IRVING. 1905-1961. American psychologist. See: Who Was Who Amer., 1961-1968. Lorge readability formula, Thorndike-Lorga list.

Lorge readability formula (Lorge, Irving): Psychology. See: Good.

LORIN. fl. 1900. French engineer. (Biography source unavailable.) Lorin engine.

Lorin engine (Lorin): Engineering and Industry. See: Auger.

LORING, EDWARD GREELY. 1837-1888. American oculist. See: Dict. Amer. Biog. Loring's ophthalmoscope.

Loring's ophthalmoscope (Loring, Edward Greely): Medicine. See: Dorland.

LORRAIN, MAURICE. b. 1867. French physician. Cited in: Index-Cat. Libr. Surg.-Gen. Off., 2d ser., vol. 9, 1904. Struempell-Lorrain syndrome.

LORTAT-JACOB, ETIENNE MARIE. 1902- . French dermatologist. See: Who's Who France, 1975-1976. Lortat-Jacob's disease.

Lortat-Jacob's disease (Lortat-Jacob, Etienne Marie): Medicine. See: Jablonski.

LOSCHMIDT, JOSEPH (In full: JOHANN JOSEPH). 1821-1895. Austrian physicist and chemist. See: Dict. Sci. Biog. Loschmidt number.

Loschmidt number (Loschmidt, Joseph): Physics. See: Ballentyne; Hughes; Thewlis; Van Nostrand Chem. Dict.; Van Nostrand Sci. Encyc.; Webster's 3d. Also known as: Avogadro's constant.

LOSEV, O. V. fl. 1940. Russian physicist. Cited in: Chem. Abstr., Decenn. Index, 1937-1946. Lossev effect (or radiation)?

LOSEY, SAMUEL R. ca. 1833-1906. American mineral collector. Cited in: Hintze, 1st suppl., p. 303. Loseyite.

Loseyite (Losey, Samuel R.): Earth Sciences. See: Thrush; Webster's 3d.

LOSSEN, HERMAN FRIEDRICH. 1842-1909. German surgeon. See: Biog. Lex. hervorr. Aerzte, 1880-1930. Lossen's rule.

Lossen rearrangement (Lossen, Wilhelm): Chemistry. See: Ballentyne; Van Nostrand Chem. Dict.; Webster's 3d.

LOSSEN, WILHELM. 1838-1906. German chemist. See: Pogg., vols. 3, 4, 5. Lossen rearrangement.

Lossen's rule (Lossen, Herman Friedrich): Medicine. See: Dorland.

Lossev effect (or radiation) (Losev, O. V.?): Electronics. See: Hughes; Markus.

LO SURDO, ANTONINO. 1880-1949. Italian physicist. See: Pogg., vol. 6. Lo Surdo tube.

Lo Surdo tube (Lo Surdo, Antonino): Physics. See: Thewlis.

LOT. Nephew of Abraham in the Old Testament. See: Hastings (Dict. Bible). Lot's wife.

LOTHARIO. Seducer in Nicholas Rowe's play, "The Fair Penitent," (1703). See: Harvey. Lothario (or gay Lothario).

Lothario (or gay Lothario) (Lothario): Generic Word (libertine). See: Brewer; Charnock; Funk; Partridge; Webster's 3d.

LOTHIAN, JOHN. fl. 1909. English pharmaceutical chemist. Cited in: Chem. Abstr., vol. 3, p. 1441. Lothian test reaction for alkaloids.

Lothian test reaction for alkaloids (Lothian, John): Chemistry. See: Van Nostrand Chem. Dict.

Lot's wife (Lot): Generic Word (curious woman). See: Partridge.

LOUDERBACK, GEORGE DAVIS. 1874-1957. American geologist. See: World Who's Who Sci. Louderback (tilted fault block).

Louderback (tilted fault block) (Louderback, George Davis): Earth Sciences. See: New Encyc. Brit., 1974, Microp.; Webster's 3d.

Loudon, Gideon Ernst Freiherr von. See: Laudon, Gideon Ernst Freiherr von.

LOUDON, JOHN CLAUDIUS. 1783-1843. Scottish horticultural writer. See: Dict. Nat. Biog. Loudonia.

Loudonia (Loudon, John Claudius): Botany. See: Charnock.

LOUGHLIN, GERALD FRANCIS. 1880-1946. American geologist. See: World Who's Who Sci. Loughlinite.

Loughlinite (Loughlin, Gerald Francis): Earth Sciences. See: Thrush; Webster's 3d.

LOUIS VII, LE JEUNE. ca. 1120-1180. King of France. See: Encyc. Brit., 1973. fleur-de-luce?

LOUIS IX (SAINT LOUIS). 1214-1270. King of France. See: Encyc. Brit., 1973. Order of St. Louis, Pragmatic Sanction of Louis IX.

LOUIS XIII. 1601-1643. King of France. See: Encyc. Brit., 1973. Louis (d'or) (coin), Louis XIII collar, Louis Treize (style).

Louis XIII collar (Louis XIII): Fashion. See: Picken.

LOUIS XIV. 1638-1715. King of France. See: Encyc. Brit., 1973. Code Louis, Louis Quatorze (style).

LOUIS XV. 1710-1774. King of France. See: New Encyc. Brit., 1974, Microp. Louis (XV) heel, Louis Quinze (style).

Louis (XV) heel (Louis XV): Fashion. See: Hendrickson; Picken; Webster's 3d.

LOUIS XVI. 1754-1793. King of France. See: New Encyc. Brit., 1974. Louis Seize (style).

Louis' angle (or angle of Louis) (Louis, Pierre-Charles-Alexandre): Anatomy. See: Donath; Dorland; Henderson; Stedman. Also known as Ludwig's angle.

LOUIS, ANTOINE. 1723-1792. French physician. See: World Who's Who Sci. Louison (or Louisette).

LOUIS-BAR, DENISE. fl. 1941. European physician. (Biography source unavailable.) Louis-Bar's syndrome.

ouis-Bar's syndrome (Louis-Bar, Denise): Medicine. See: Jablonski; Stedman. lso known as: Boder-Sedgwick syndrome.

OUIS DE FRANCE (DE BOURBON). 1661-1711. French dauphin. See: ouv. Biog. Univ. Delphin(e) classics.

ouis (d'or) (coin) (Louis XIII): Numismatics. See: Charnock; Partridge; ebster's 3d.

OUIS, JOE (JOSEPH LOUIS BARROW). 1914- . American boxer. See: ncyc. Brit., 1973. Joe Louis.

ouis' law (Louis, Pierre-Charles-Alexandre): Medicine. See: Dorland; edman.

OUIS, LAWRENCE HUA-HSIEN. 1908- . Chinese-born American bio- emist. See: Amer. Men Sci., 9th ed. Conn-Louis syndrome.

OUIS PHILIPPE. 1773-1850. King of France. See: Encyc. Brit., 1973. uis Philippe (costume).

ouis Philippe (costume) (Louis Philippe): Fashion. See: Picken.

OUIS, PIERRE-CHARLES-ALEXANDRE. 1787-1872. French physician. See: orld Who's Who Sci. Louis' angle (or angle of Louis), Louis' law.

ouis Quatorze (style) (Louis XIV): Fine and Applied Arts. See: Hendrickson; ebster's 3d.

ouis Quinze (style) (Louis XV): Fine and Applied Arts. See: Hendrickson; ebster's 3d.

ouis, Saint. See: Louis IX.

ouis Seize (style) (Louis XVI): Fine and Applied Arts. See: Hendrickson; ebster's 3d.

ouis Treize (style) (Louis XIII): Fine and Applied Arts. See: Hencrickson; ew Encyc. Brit., 1974, Microp.; Webster's 3d.

OUISA AUGUSTA W. AMELIA OF MECKLENBERG-STRELITZ. 1776-1810. ueen of Prussia. See: Encyc. Brit., 1911. Order of Louisa.

ouison (or Louisette) (Louis, Antoine). See: Guillotine.

ounge (Longinus?): Generic Word. See: Hendrickson.

utchinski colorimetric phenol determination (Luchinskii, G. P.): Chemistry. e: Van Nostrand Chem. Dict.

OUTERELL, SIR GEOFFREY. fl. ca. 1340. English gentleman. (Biography urce unavailable.) Luttrell Psalter.

OUTIT, JOHN FREEMAN. 1910- . English experimental pathologist. See: ed. Direct., 1964. Loutit's anemia.

utit's anemia (Loutit, John Freeman): Medicine. See: Jablonski.

VE, AUGUSTUS EDWARD HOUGH. 1863-1940. English mathematician and ophysicist. See: Dict. Sci. Biog. Love wave, Love's numbers.

ve wave (Love, Augustus Edward Hough): Physics. See: Huschke; Thewlis; rush; Webster's 3d.

velace (Lovelace, Robert): Generic Word (libertine). See: Brewer; rtridge; Weekley.

OVELACE, ROBERT. Character in Samuel Richardson's novel, "Clarissa rlowe," (1747-48). See: Harvey. Lovelace.

OVELACE, WILLIAM RANDOLPH II. 1907- . American surgeon. See: rect. Med. Specialists, vol. 8. Boothby, Lovelace, and Bulbulian mask.

VEN, OTTO CHRISTIAN. 1835-1904. Swedish physician. See: Biog. x. hervorr. Aerzte. Loven reflex.

ven reflex (Loven, Otto Christian): Medicine. See: Stedman.

VEN, SVEN LUDWIG. 1809-1895. Swedish zoologist. See: Dict. Sci. g. Lovenella, Lovenia, Loven's larva.

venella (Loven, Sven Ludwig): Zoology. See: Pennak.

venia (Loven, Sven Ludwig): Zoology. See: Pennak.

ven's larva (Loven, Sven Ludwig): Zoology. See: Gray.

Love's numbers (Love, Augustus Edward Hough): Earth Sciences. Cited in: Dict. Sci. Biog. under "Love, Augustus Edward Hough."

LOVESTONE, JAY. fl. 1923-1934. American union leader expelled from the Communist party. Cited in: Mansell. Lovestonite.

Lovestonite (Lovestone, Jay): Politics. See: Webster's 3d.

LOVIBOND, JOSEPH WILLIAMS. 1833-1918. English physicist. See: Who Was Who, 1916-1928. Lovibond subtractive system, Lovibond tintometer.

Lovibond subtractive system (Lovibond, Joseph Williams): Physics. See: Focal Encyc. Photog. under "Colour Measurement."

Lovibond tintometer (Lovibond, Joseph Williams): Physics. See: Internat. Dict. Phys. Elec.; Thewlis; Thrush; Van Nostrand Sci. Encyc.

LOVITON, LEON. fl. 1885-1910. French chemist. Cited in: Chem. Abstr., vol. 4, p. 431. Loviton reagent.

Loviton reagent (Loviton, Leon): Chemistry. See: Van Nostrand Chem. Dict.

LOVITS (LOWITZ), JOHANN TOBIAS. 1757-1804. Russian chemist. See: Dict. Sci. Biog. arc(s) of Lowitz (or Lowitz arcs).

LOW, GEORGE CARMICHAEL. 1872-1952. English physician. See: World Who's Who Sci. Castellani-Low sign.

Lowden drier (Lowden, H. W.?): Engineering and Industry. See: Thrush.

LOWDEN, H. W. fl. 1923. English engineer. Cited in: Chem. Abstr., Decenn. Index, 1917-1926. Lowden drier?

LOWE. fl. 1823. Scientist. (Biography source unavailable.) Lowe index.

Lowe anthracite (Lowe, Thaddeus S. C.): Engineering and Industry. See: World Who's Who Sci.

LOWE, CHARLES UPTON. 1921- . American pediatrician. See: Amer. Men and Women Sci., 12th ed. Lowe's syndrome.

LOWE, E. CRONIN. No dates. English physician. (Biography source un- available.) Cronin Lowe reaction (or test).

Lowe index (Lowe): Statistics. See: Kendall.

LOWE, JAMES. 1798-1866. English inventor. See: Dict. Nat. Biog. Lowe propeller (or screw propeller).

Lowe propeller (or screw propeller) (Lowe, James): Engineering and Industry. See: Auger; Dict. Nat. Biog. under "Lowe, James."

Lowe-Terrey-MacLachlan syndrome (Lowe, Charles Upton; Terrey, Mary; and MacLachlan, Elsie A.). See: Lowe's syndrome.

LOWE, THADDEUS S. C. 1832-1913. American inventor. See: Who Was Who Amer., 1897-1942. Lowe anthracite, new Lowe coke oven system.

LOWELL, JAMES RUSSELL (Pseud.: "HOSEA BIGLOW") 1819-1891. American poet, essayist, and diplomat. See: Dict. Amer. Biog. Biglow papers.

LOWELL, MOSES. fl. 18th c. American shipbuilder. (Biography source un- available.) Moses (boat)?

LOWENHERZ, L. fl. 1873. German engineer. (Biography source unavail- able.) Lowenherz thread.

Lowenherz thread (Lowenherz, L.): Engineering and Industry. See: Auger.

LOWENTHAL, ARMAND. 1919- . Belgian neurologist. See: Who's Who Sci. Europe, 1972. Lowenthal's sclerosis.

Lowenthal's sclerosis (Lowenthal, Armand): Medicine. See: Jablonski.

lower Mars (Mars): Parapsychology. See: Webster's 3d.

LOWER, RICHARD. 1631-1691. English physiologist. See: Dict. Sci. Biog. Lower's rings, Lower's tubercle (or tubercle of Lower).

Lower's rings (Lower, Richard): Anatomy. See: Donath; Dorland; Stedman.

Lower's tubercle (or tubercle of Lower) (Lower, Richard): Anatomy. See: Donath; Dorland; Stedman.

Lowe's syndrome (Lowe, Charles Upton): Medicine. See: Jablonski; Stedman; Wolman. Also known as: Lowe-Terrey-MacLachlan syndrome.

Lowig process (Loewig, Karl Jacob?): Chemistry. See: Hackh.

Lowitz arcs (Lovits, Johann Tobias). See: arc(s) of Lowitz.

Lowitz, Johann Tobias. See: Lovits, Johann Tobias.

Lowman balance board (Lowman, Charles Le Roy): Medicine. See: Dorland.

LOWMAN, CHARLES LE ROY. b. 1879. American orthopedic surgeon. See: Direct. Med. Specialists, 1975-1976. Lowman balance board.

LOWN, BERNARD. 1921- . American physician. See: Amer. Med. Direct., 1963. Lown-Ganong-Levine syndrome.

Lown-Ganong-Levine syndrome (Lown, Bernard; Ganong, William Francis; and Levine, Samuel A.): Medicine. See: Jablonski.

Lowndean Professor (Lowndes, Thomas): Astronomy. See: Wagner (More Names).

LOWNDES, THOMAS. •1692-1748. English founder of astronomical professorship. See: Dict. Nat. Biog. Lowndean Professor.

LOWRY, CUTHBERT B. fl. 1906. American chemist. Cited in: Chem. Abstr., vol. 1, p. 255. Lowry process.

Lowry-Lopez-Bessey method (Lowry, Oliver Howe; Lopez, Jeanne A.; and Bessey, Otto Arthur): Medicine. See: Blakiston's Gould.

LOWRY, OLIVER HOWE. 1910- . American pharmacologist and biochemist. See: Amer. Men Sci., 10th ed. Lowry-Lopez-Bessey method.

Lowry process (Lowry, Cuthbert B.): Engineering and Industry. See: Encyc. Brit., 1973 under "Wood," vol. 23, p. 643b; Webster's 3d.

LOWRY, THOMAS MARTIN. 1874-1936. English chemist. See: World Who's Who Sci. Broensted-Lowry definition (or theory) of acids and bases.

LOWY, OTTO. b. 1879. American pathologist. (Biography source unavailable.) Lowy's test.

Lowy's test (Lowy, Otto): Medicine. See: Dorland.

LOYEZ. No dates. French? physician. (Biography source unavailable.) Claude-Loyez syndrome.

Loyola, Saint Ignatius of. See: Ignatius of Loyola.

LUBARSCH, OTTO. 1860-1933. German pathologist. See: Biog. Lex. hervorr. Aerzte, 1880-1930. Lubarsch's crystals, Lubarsch's syndrome.

Lubarsch-Pick syndrome (Lubarsch, Otto and Pick, Ludwig). See: Lubarsch's syndrome.

Lubarsch's crystals (Lubarsch, Otto): Medicine. See: Dorland; Stedman.

Lubarsch's syndrome (Lubarsch, Otto): Medicine. See: Jablonski. Also known as: Lubarsch-Pick syndrome.

Lubavitcher school (Schneersohn, Joseph Isaac, Lubavitcher rabbi): Education. See: Good.

Lubbock atomizer (Lubbock, Isaak): Engineering and Industry. See: Auger.

LUBBOCK, ISAAK. fl. 1930. German-born English? engineer. (Biography source unavailable.) Lubbock atomizer.

Lubetzky code (Lubetzky, Seymour): Library Science. See: Harrod.

LUBETZKY, SEYMOUR. 1898- . American librarian. See: Who's Who Libr. Service, 4th ed., 1966. Lubetzky code.

LUBS, HERBERT AUGUSTUS, JR. 1929- . American physician. See: Direct. Med. Specialists, 1975-1976. Lubs' syndrome.

Lubs' syndrome (Lubs, Herbert Augustus, Jr.): Medicine. See: Jablonski.

LUC, HENRI. 1855-1925. French laryngologist. See: World Who's Who Sci. Caldwell-Luc operation, Ogston-Luc operation.

LUCAE, AUGUST (In full: JOHANN CONSTANIN AUGUST). 1835-1911. German otologist. See: Biog. Lex hervorr. Aerzte. Lucae's probe.

Lucae's probe (Lucae, August): Medicine. See: Dorland.

Lucan (or Lukan) (Luke, Saint): Religion. See: Webster's 3d.

LUCANUS (or LUCIANUS). fl. 2d c. Christian heretic. See: Dict. Christian Biog. under "Lucanus (1)." Lucianists.

Lucas Brotherhood (Brethren or Brotherhood of St. Luke) (Luke, Saint): Fine Arts. See: New Encyc. Brit., 1974 under "Nazarenes."

LUCAS-CHAMPIONNIERE, JUST MARIE MARCELLIN. 1843-1913. French surgeon. See: World Who's Who Sci. Championniere's disease.

LUCAS, CYRIL EDWARD. 1909- . English marine biologist. See: World Who's Who Sci. Lucas sounder?

Lucas engine (Lucas, R.): Engineering and Industry. See: Auger.

Lucas' groove (Lucas, Richard Clement): Anatomy. See: Stedman.

LUCAS, HENRY. d. 1663. English founder of the Lucasian Professorship. See: Dict. Nat. Biog. Lucasian Professor.

LUCAS, HOWARD JOHNSON. 1885-1963. American chemist. See: Pogg., vols. 6, 7b. Lucas theory.

LUCAS, R. fl. 1907. English? engineer. (Biography source unavailable.) Lucas engine.

LUCAS, RICHARD CLEMENT. 1846-1915. English anatomist and surgeon. See: World Who's Who Sci. Lucas' groove, Lucas' sign.

Lucas' sign (Lucas, Richard Clement): Medicine. See: Dorland.

Lucas sounder (Lucas, Cyril Edward?): Earth Sciences. See: Thrush.

Lucas theory (Lucas, Howard Johnson): Chemistry. See: Hackh; Van Nostrand Chem. Dict.

Lucasian Professor (Lucas, Henry): Mathematics. See: Wagner (More Names).

LUCATELLO, LUIGI. 1863-1926. Italian physician. See: Biog. Lex. hervorr. Aerzte, 1880-1930. Lucatello's pneumonia, Lucatello's sign.

Lucatello's pneumonia (Lucatello, Luigi): Medicine. Cited in: Biog. Lex. hervorr. Aerzte, 1880-1930.

Lucatello's sign (Lucatello, Luigi): Medicine. See: Dorland.

Luce and Rozan process (Derivation undetermined): Engineering and Industry. See: Thrush. Also known as: Rozan process.

Lucherini-Giacobini syndrome (Lucherini, Tommaso and Giacobini, Genaro?): Medicine. See: Jablonski.

LUCHERINI, TOMMASO. b. 1891. Italian physician. Cited in: Index-Cat. Libr. Surg.-Gen. Off., 5th ser., vol. 1, 1959. Lucherini-Giacobini syndrome, Lucherini's syndrome.

Lucherini's syndrome (Lucherini, Tommaso): Medicine. See: Jablonski.

LUCHINSKII, G. P. fl. 1938. Russian chemist. Cited in: Chem. Abstr., vol. 32, p. 519. Loutchinski colorimetric phenol determination.

LUCIAN. ca. 120-ca. 180. Greek satirist. See: New Encyc. Brit., 1974. Lucianic.

Lucian (Lucian, the protagonist): Generic Word (personification of an age's follies). See: Brewer.

LUCIAN, THE PROTAGONIST. Character in Lucius Apuleius's story, "The Golden Ass," (2d c.). See: Jobes. Lucian.

LUCIANI, LUIGI. 1840-1919. Italian physiologist. See: Dict. Sci. Biog. Luciani's triad.

Lucianic (Lucian): Generic Word (witty). See: Partridge; Webster's 3d.

Luciani's triad (Luciani, Luigi): Medicine. See: Dorland; Jablonski.

Lucianists (Lucanus): Religion. See: Latham.

lucibacterium Harveyi (Harvey, Edmund Newton): Medicine. See: Stedman.

Lucifer (Lucifer, the devil): Generic Word (devil). See: Webster's 3d.

LUCIFER OF CAGLIARI. d. ca. 370. Bishop in Cagliari, Sardinia. See: Encyc. Brit., 1973. Luciferian(s) (2).

LUCIFER, THE DEVIL. Name of Satan before his fall. See: New Encyc. Brit., 1974, Microp. Lucifer, Luciferian (1).

Luciferian (1) (Lucifer, the devil): Generic Word (proud). See: Webster's 3d.

Luciferian(s) (2) (Lucifer of Cagliari): Religion. See: Canney; Webster's 3d.

Lucina (Lucina, the goddess): Generic Word (midwife). See: Webster's 3d.

LUCINA, THE GODDESS. Roman goddess of childbirth. See: Jobes. Lucina.

LUCIUS. fl. ca. 156. Legendary first Christian King in Britain. See: Dict. Nat. Biog. Lucius legend.

Lucius legend (Lucius): Religion. See: Attwater.

LUCKE, BALDUIN. 1889-1954. German-born American pathologist. See: Who Was Who Amer., 1951-1960. Lucke's tumor (or renal adenocarcinoma), Lucke's virus.

Lucke's tumor (or renal adenocarcinoma) (Lucke, Balduin): Medicine. See: Jablonski.

Lucke's virus (Lucke, Balduin): Medicine. See: Stedman.

Luckhart furnace (Derivation undetermined): Engineering and Industry. See: Thrush.

LUCKIESH, MATTHEW. b. 1883. American physicist. See: Pogg., vol. 6. Luckiesh-Moss visibility meter.

Luckiesh-Moss visibility meter (Luckiesh, Matthew and Moss, Frank Kendall): Engineering and Industry. See: Thrush.

LUCKOW, CARL. fl. 1885. German electrochemist. Cited in: Royal Soc. Cat. Sci. Pap., 1884-1900. Luckow test reaction for aluminum?

Luckow test reaction for aluminum (Luckow, Carl?): Chemistry. See: Van Nostrand Chem. Dict.

Lucopetrians (Lycopetrus): Religion. See: Canney.

Lucretia (or Lucrece) (Lucretia, the Roman): Generic Word (chaste wife). See: Partridge; Weekley.

LUCRETIA, THE ROMAN. fl. ca. 509 B.C. Legendary Roman noblewoman. See: New Encyc. Brit., 1974, Microp. Lucretia (or Lucrece).

Lucretian (Lucretius): Generic Word (poetically philosophic). See: Partridge; Webster's 3d.

LUCRETIUS (TITUS LUCRETIUS CARUS). ca. 99-55 B.C. Roman philosophical poet. See: Encyc. Brit., 1973. Lucretian.

Luc's operation (Luc, Henri). See: Caldwell-Luc operation.

Lucullan (Lucullian) feast (banquet or dinner) (Lucullus, Lucius Licinius): Generic Word (sumptuous meal). See: Hendrickson; Partridge; Webster's 3d.

Lucullite (marble) (Lucullus, Lucius Licinius): Earth Sciences. See: Charnock; Thrush; Webster's 3d.

LUCULLUS, LUCIUS LICINIUS. ca. 117-ca. 58 B.C. Roman general and gourmet. See: Encyc. Brit., 1973. Lucullan (Lucullian) feast (banquet or dinner), Lucullite (marble).

Lucy light (or Saint Lucy's Day) (Lucy, Saint): Generic Word. See: Webster's 3d.

LUCY, SAINT. d. ca. 301. Sicilian virgin and martyr. See: Holweck. Lucy light (or Saint Lucy's Day), Lucy's warbler?

Lucy Stoner (Stone, Lucy): Sociology. See: Hendrickson.

Lucy's warbler (Lucy, Saint?): Zoology. See: Gray.

LUDD, NED. Mythical leader of Luddites in England, 1811-1816. See: Jobes. Luddism (or Ludditism), Luddites.

Luddism (or Ludditism) (Ludd, Ned): History. See: Webster's 3d.

Luddites (Ludd, Ned): History. See: Brewer; Harvey; Phyfe.

LUDER, JOSEPH. fl. 1950-1972. English pediatrician. See: Med. Direct., 1972. Luder-Sheldon syndrome.

Luder-Sheldon syndrome (Luder, Joseph and Sheldon, Wilfrid): Medicine. See: Jablonski.

LUDLAM, HENRY. 1824-1880. English mineralogist. See: Dict. Nat. Biog. Ludlamite.

LUDLAM, MRS. No dates. English sorceress. (Biography source unavailable.) lazy as Ludlam's dog.

Ludlamite (Ludlam, Henry): Earth Sciences. See: Thrush; Webster's 3d.

LUDLOFF, KARL. 1864-1945. German orthopedic surgeon. See: Biog. Lex. hervorr. Aerzte, 1880-1930. Buedinger-Ludloff-Laewen disease (or syndrome), Ludloff's disease, Ludloff's signs.

Ludloff's disease (Ludloff, Karl): Medicine. See: Kelly.

Ludloff's signs (Ludloff, Karl): Medicine. See: Dorland; Stedman.

LUDLOW, LOUIS LEON. 1873-1950. American legislator. See: Biog. Direct. Amer. Congress. Ludlow Resolution.

Ludlow Resolution (Ludlow, Louis Leon): Politics. See: Morris.

LUDLOW, ROGER. 1590-ca. 1664. English pioneer in America. See: Dict. Amer. Biog. Ludlow's Code.

Ludlow typecasting machine (or caster) (Ludlow, Washington I.): Printing. See: Glaister; New Encyc. Brit., 1974, Microp.

LUDLOW, WASHINGTON I. fl. 1911. American typographer. (Biography source unavailable.) Ludlow typecasting machine (or caster).

Ludlow's Code (Ludlow, Roger): History. See: Dict. Amer. Biog. under "Ludlow, Roger"; Latham.

LUDOLF, JOHANN HIOB. 1649-1711. German mathematician. (Biography source unavailable.) Ludolf's number.

Ludolf's number (Ludolf, Johann Hiob): Mathematics. See: Hackh.

LUDOVISI. Ancient Italian family of Bologna. See: Encic. Ital. Ludovisi throne.

Ludovisi throne (Ludovisi): Fine Arts. See: Osborne.

LUDWIG. fl. 19th c. German? chemist. (Biography source unavailable.) Ludwig effect (or phenomenon).

LUDWIG, CARL FRIEDRICH WILHELM. 1816-1895. German anatomist and physiologist. See: Dict. Sci. Biog. Ludwig's ganglion, Ludwig's labyrinth, Ludwig's stromuhr.

LUDWIG, CHRISTIAN GOTTLIEB. 1709-1773. German botanist and physician. See: Biog. Lex. hervorr. Aerzte. Ludwigia (or Ludvigia).

LUDWIG, DANIEL. 1625-1680. German anatomist. See: Biog. Lex. hervorr. Aerzte. Ludwig's angle.

Ludwig effect (or phenomenon) (Ludwig). See: Soret effect (or principle).

LUDWIG, ERNST. 1842-1915. Austrian chemist. See: Pogg., vols. 3, 4, 5. Ludwig reagent, Ludwigite.

Ludwig-Haupt reagent (Ludwig, W. and Haupt, Hugo): Chemistry. See: Van Nostrand Chem. Dict.

Ludwig reagent (Ludwig, Ernst): Chemistry. See: Van Nostrand Chem. Dict.

LUDWIG, T. fl. before 1922. German? industrial chemist. Cited in: Glazebrook, vol. 5, p. 473. Ludwig's chart.

LUDWIG, W. fl. 1907. German chemist. Cited in: Chem. Abstr., vol. 1, pp. 453, 2149. Ludwig-Haupt reagent.

LUDWIG, WILHELM FRIEDRICH VON. 1790-1865. German surgeon. See: Biog. Lex. hervorr. Aerzte. Ludwig's angina.

Ludwigia (or Ludvigia) (Ludwig, Christian Gottlieb): Botany. See: Charnock; Taylor, N.; Webster's 3d.

Ludwigite (Ludwig, Ernst): Earth Sciences. See: Thrush; Webster's 3d.

Ludwig's angina (Ludwig, Wilhelm Friedrich von): Medicine. See: Dorland; Jablonski; Stedman; Van Nostrand Sci. Encyc.; Webster's 3d. Also known as: Gensoul's disease.

Ludwig's angle (Ludwig, Daniel): Anatomy. See: Dorland; Stedman. Also known as: Louis' angle (or angle of Louis).

Ludwig's chart (Ludwig, T.): Engineering and Industry. See: Thrush.

Ludwig's ganglion (Ludwig, Carl Friedrich Wilhelm): Anatomy. See: Donath; Dorland; Stedman.

Ludwig's labyrinth (Ludwig, Carl Friedrich Wilhelm): Anatomy. See: Stedman.

Ludwig's stromuhr (Ludwig, Carl Friedrich Wilhelm): Medicine. See: Stedman.

Ludwik hardness test (and tester) (Ludwik, Paul): Engineering and Industry. See: Auger; Thrush.

LUDWIK, PAUL. 1878-1934. Austrian engineer. See: Oesterrich. Biog. Lex., 1815-1950. Ludwik hardness test (and tester).

LUECKE, GEORGE ALBERT. 1829-1894. German surgeon. See: Biog. Lex. hervorr. Aerzte. Luecke's test.

Luecke's test (Luecke, George Albert): Medicine. See: Dorland; Stedman.

Lueder(s) bands (or line(s)) (Lueders, W.): Physics. See: Ballentyne; Internat. Dict. Ap. Math.; Thewlis; Thrush; Van Nostrand Sci. Encyc.; Webster's 3d. Also known as: Hartmann lines, Piobert effect (or lines).

LUEDERS, W. fl. 1859. German scientist. (Biography source unavailable.) Lueder(s) bands (or line(s)).

Luelling cherry (Luelling, Henderson): Botany. See: Hendrickson under "Bing."

LUELLING, HENDERSON. 1809-1878. American nurseryman. See: Who Was Who Amer., Hist. vol. Luelling cherry.

LUER. d. 1883. German instrument maker in France. (Biography source unavailable.) Luer('s) syringe.

Luer('s) syringe (Luer): Medicine. See: Dorland; Webster's 3d.

LUEROTH, JAKOB. 1844-1910. German mathematician. See: Dict. Sci. Biog. Clebsch-Lueroth method, Lueroth quartic, Lueroth theorem.

Lueroth quartic (Lueroth, Jakob): Mathematics. Cited in: Dict. Sci. Biog.

Lueroth theorem (Lueroth, Jakob): Mathematics. Cited in: Dict. Sci. Biog.

LUETSCHER, JOHN ARTHUR. 1913- . American physician. See: Amer. Men and Women Sci., 12th ed. Luetscher's syndrome.

Luetscher's syndrome (Luetscher, John Arthur): Medicine. See: Jablonski.

Lufbery (Lufberry) circle (Lufbery, Raoul Gervais Victor): Military Science. See: Quick; Webster's 3d.

LUFBERY, RAOUL GERVAIS VICTOR. 1885-1918. French-American aviator. See: Dict. Amer. Biog. Lufbery (Lufberry) circle.

LUFF, ARTHUR PEARSON. 1855-1938. English chemist. See: Who Was Who, 1929-1940. Luff reagent?

Luff reagent (Luff, Arthur Pearson?): Chemistry. See: Van Nostrand Chem. Dict.

LUFT, ROLF. 1914- . Swedish endocrinologist. See: Who's Who Sci. Europe, 1972. Luft's syndrome.

Luft's syndrome (Luft, Rolf): Medicine. See: Jablonski.

Luger automatic pistol (Luger, Georg): Weapons. See: Quick.

LUGER, GEORG. fl. 20th c. German engineer. (Biography source unavailable.) Luger automatic pistol.

LUGOL, JEAN GUILLAUME AUGUSTE. 1786-1851. French physician. See: World Who's Who Sci. Lugol's solution.

Lugol's solution (Lugol, Jean Guillaume Auguste): Medicine. See: Dorland; Stedman; Webster's 3d.

Luhea (Van der Luhe, Charles): Botany. See: Charnock.

Lukas-Jilek test reaction (Lukas, Johann and Jilek, Antonin): Chemistry. See: Van Nostrand Chem. Dict.

LUKAS, JOHANN. b. 1882. Bohemian chemist. See: Pogg., vol. 6. Lukas-Jilek test reaction.

LUKASHEVICH, E. N. fl. 1936. Russian chemist. Cited in: Chem. Abstr., vol. 31, p. 2960. Korenman-Lubashevick test for copper.

Luke-Images (Luke, Saint): Religion. See: Holweck under "Luke, Saint."

LUKE, SAINT. fl. 1st c. Evangelist, physician and companion of St. Paul. See: Holweck. Lucan (or Lukan), Lucas Brotherhood (Brethren or Brotherhood of St. Luke), Luke-Images, St. Lucas Guild, St. Lucas thrush, St. Luke's summer.

Lulio, Raimundo. See: Lull, Ramon.

LULL, RAMON. ca. 1234-1316. Catalan philosopher and mystic. See: Encyc. Brit., 1973. Lullists.

Lullists (Lull, Ramon): Religion. See: Hastings (Encyc. Rel. Ethics); Mathews, S.

Lully, Raymond. See: Lull, Ramon.

LUM, E. A. fl. 1933. English chemist. Cited in: Chem. Abstr., vol. 27, p. 5681. Brown-Lum test reaction, Lum's test (for glucose).

Lumen Christi (Jesus Christ): Religion. See: Attwater.

Lumiere apparatus (Lumiere, Louis Jean and Lumiere, Auguste Marie Louis): Photography. See: Focal Encyc. Film under "Lumiere, Louis..."; New Encyc. Brit., 1974, Microp.

LUMIERE, AUGUSTE MARIE LOUIS. 1862-1954. French photographic inventor and chemist. See: Pogg., vols. 5, 6. Clinique Auguste Lumiere, Lumiere apparatus, Lumiere Autochrome plate (and process), Lumiere's magazine camera.

Lumiere autochrome plate (and process) (Lumiere, Louis Jean and Lumiere, Auguste Marie Louis): Photography. See: Encyc. Brit., 1973, under "Photography," vol. 17, p. 958a; Focal Encyc. Film under "Lumiere, Louis..."

LUMIERE, LOUIS JEAN. 1864-1948. French photographic inventor. See: World Who's Who Sci. Lumiere apparatus, Lumiere Autochrome plate (and process), Lumiere's magazine camera.

Lumiere's magazine camera (Lumiere, Louis Jean and Lumiere, Auguste Marie Louis): Photography. See: Focal Encyc. Photog. under "Camera History."

Lummer and Kurlbaum's bolometer (Lummer, Otto Richard and Kurlbaum, Ferdinand): Physics. See: Dict. Sci. Biog. under "Lummer, Otto"; Encyc. Brit., 1973 under "Bolometer," vol. 3, p. 890d.

Lummer-Brodhun cube (or photometer) (Lummer, Otto Richard and Brodhun, Eugen): Physics. See: Internat. Dict. Phys. Elec.; Thewlis; Thrush.

Lummer fringes (Lummer, Otto Richard): Physics. See: Dict. Sci. Biog.

Lummer-Gehrcke (Gehreke) plate (or interference spectroscope) (Lummer, Otto Richard and Gehrcke, Ernst Johannes Ludwig): Physics. See: Dict. Sci. Biog. under "Lummer, Otto"; Internat. Dict. Phys. Elec.; Thewlis.

LUMMER, OTTO RICHARD. 1860-1925. German physicist. See: Dict. Sci. Biog. Lummer and Kurlbaum's bolometer, Lummer-Brodhun cube (or photometer), Lummer fringes, Lummer-Gehrcke (Gehreke) plate (or interference spectroscope).

LUMPP, HERMANN. fl. 1910. German chemist. Cited in: Chem. Abstr., vol. 4, p. 1725. Schmidt-Lumpp reagent.

Lum's test (for glucose) (Lum, E. A.): Medicine. See: Kelly.

LUMSDEN, THOMAS WILLIAM. 1874-1953. English physician. See: World Who's Who Sci. Lumsden's center.

Lumsden's center (Lumsden, Thomas William): Medicine. See: Dorland.

LUNAN, JOHN. fl. 1814. Jamaican botanist. Cited in: Mansell. Lunan nut?, Lunanea.

Lunan nut (Lunan, John?): Botany. See: Encyc. Brit., 1973 under "Nut," vol. 16, p. 798.

Lunanea (Lunan, John): Botany. See: Charnock.

LUND, HELGE. fl. 1936. Scandinavian chemist. Cited in: Chem. Abstr., vol. 30, p. 4894. Lund-Lieck test reaction.

Lund-Huntington chorea? (Lund, Johann Christian? and Huntington, George). See: Huntington's chorea.

LUND, JOHANN CHRISTIAN. 1830-1906. Scandinavian physician. See: Norges laeger, Kobro I, Krist., vol. 2 (1915) p. 61. Lund-Huntington chorea?

Lund-Lieck test reaction (Lund, Helge and Lieck, Herbert): Chemistry. See: Van Nostrand Chem. Dict.

LUND, R. fl. 1910. Scandinavian chemist. Cited in: Chem. Abstr., vol. 4, p. 2682. Lund solutions.

Lund solutions (Lund, R.): Chemistry. See: Van Nostrand Chem. Dict.

LUNDBORG, HERMANN BERNHARD. 1868-1943. Swedish physician. See: Svenska Maen Och Kvinnor. Lundborg-Unverricht syndrome.

Lundborg-Unverricht syndrome (Lundborg, Hermann and Unverricht, Heinrich). See: Unverricht's disease.

Lunden conductive tile flooring (Lunden, Samuel Eugene): Engineering and Industry. See: Thrush.

LUNDEN, SAMUEL EUGENE. 1897- . American architect. See: Who's Who Amer., 1952-1953. Lunden conductive tile flooring.

LUNDQUIST, EUGENE EDWARD. 1907- . American aeronautical engineer. See: Amer. Men Sci., 10th ed. Lundquist series criterion.

Lundquist series criterion (Lundquist, Eugene Edward): Engineering and Industry. See: Internat. Dict. Ap. Math.

LUNDVALL, HALVAR CARL OSSIAN. b. 1883. Swedish neurologist. Cited in: Mansell. Lundvall's blood crisis.

Lundvall's blood crisis (Lundvall, Halvar Carl Ossian): Medicine. See: Dorland.

Lundyfoot (snuff) (Foot, Lundy): Generic Word. See: Partridge; Weekley.

Luneburg geometry (Luneburg, Rudolf Karl): Physics. See: Internat. Dict. Ap. Math.

Luneburg (Luneberg) lens (Luneburg, Rudolf Karl): Physics. See: Internat. Dict. Ap. Math.; Markus.

LUNEBURG, RUDOLF KARL. 1903-1949. German-born American physicist. See: Amer. Men Sci., 7th ed. Luneburg geometry, Luneburg (Luneberg) lens.

LUNELUND, HARALD. b. 1882. Finnish physicist. See: Pogg., vols. 5, 6. Stark-Lunelund effect.

LUNGE, GEORGE. 1839-1923. German chemist. See: Dict. Sci. Biog. Lunge nitrometer, Lunge solution.

Lunge nitrometer (Lunge, Georg): Chemistry. See: Hackh.

Lunge solution (Lunge, Georg): Chemistry. See: Van Nostrand Chem. Dict.

LUNN, SALLY. fl. late 18th c. English baker. (Biography source unavailable.) Sally Lunn (tea cake).

Lupercalia (Lupercus): Mythology. See: Canney.

LUPERCUS. Ancient Italian rustic deity. See: Jobes. Lupercalia.

LURIA, ALEXANDER ROMANOVICH. 1902- . Russian psychologist. See: World Who's Who Sci. Luria technique.

Luria technique (Luria, Alexander Romanovich): Psychology. See: Chaplin; English; Wolman.

Lurmann front (Derivation undetermined): Engineering and Industry. See: Thrush.

LUSCHKA, HUBERT VON. 1820-1875. German anatomist. See: Biog. Lex. hervorr. Aerzte. Luschka's bursa, Luschka's cartilage, Luschka's crypt, Luschka's cystic glands (or lacunae), Luschka's ducts, Luschka's foramina (or foramen), Luschka's gland, Luschka's ligament, Luschka's nerve, Luschka's sinus, Luschka's subpharyngeal cartilage, Luschka's tonsil, Luschka's tubercle.

Luschka's bursa (Luschka, Hubert von): Anatomy. See: Stedman.

Luschka's cartilage (Luschka, Hubert von): Anatomy. See: Stedman.

Luschka's crypt (Luschka, Hubert von): Anatomy. See: Dorland.

Luschka's cystic glands (or lacunae) (Luschka, Hubert von): Anatomy. See: Dorland; Kelly; Stedman.

Luschka's ducts (Luschka, Hubert von): Anatomy. See: Blakiston's Gould; Donath; Kelly; Stedman.

Luschka's foramina (or foramen) (Luschka, Hubert von): Anatomy. See: Donath; Dorland; Stedman. Also known as: Retzius' foramina.

Luschka's gland (Luschka, Hubert von): Anatomy. See: Donath; Stedman.

Luschka's ligament (Luschka, Hubert von): Anatomy. See: Stedman.

Luschka's nerve (Luschka, Hubert von): Anatomy. See: Stedman.

Luschka's sinus (Luschka, Hubert von): Anatomy. See: Stedman.

Luschka's subpharyngeal cartilage (Luschka, Hubert von): Anatomy. See: Blakiston's Gould.

Luschka's tonsil (Luschka, Hubert von): Anatomy. See: Blakiston's Gould; Donath; Kelly; Stedman.

Luschka's tubercle (Luschka, Hubert von): Anatomy. See: Blakiston's Gould.

Lush (Lushington): Generic Word (drunkard). See: Charnock.

LUSHINGTON. fl. 19th c.? English brewer. (Biography source unavailable.) Lush.

LUSSI, GUSTAVE. 1898- . Swiss figure skater. (Biography source unavailable.) Lutz (jump).

LUST, FRANZ ALEXANDER. b. 1880. German pediatrician. See: Kuerschner's Deut. Gel. Kal., vol. 4, 1931. Lust's sign.

LUSTIG, ALESSANDRO. 1857-1937. Italian pathologist and bacteriologist. See: World Who's Who Sci. Lustig's plague serum.

Lustig's plague serum (Lustig, Alessandro): Medicine. See: Stedman.

Lust's sign (Lust, Franz Alexander): Medicine. See: Stedman.

LUTEMBACHER, RENE. 1884-1916. French cardiologist. See: World Who's Who Sci. Lutembacher's syndrome (complex or disease).

Lutembacher's syndrome (complex or disease) (Lutembacher, Rene): Medicine. See: Dorland; Jablonski; Stedman.

LUTHER, MARTIN. 1483-1546. German religious reformer. See: New Encyc. Brit., 1974. Lutheran window, Lutheranism (or Lutheran Church), Lutherism, Martinist.

LUTHERAN. fl. ca. 1945. English blood donor. (Biography source unavailable.) Lutheran blood group.

Lutheran blood group (Lutheran): Medicine. See: Blakiston's Gould; Stedman.

Lutheran window (Luther, Martin): Architecture. See: Webster's 3d.

Lutheranism (or Lutheran Church) (Luther, Martin): Religion. See: Attwater; Mathews, S.; New Encyc. Brit., 1974, Microp.; Wagner (Names); Webster's 3d.

Lutherism (Luther, Martin): Religion. See: Webster's 3d.

Luttrell Psalter (Louterell, Sir Geoffrey): Fine Arts. See: Harrod.

LUTZ, ADOLFO. 1855-1940. Brazilian bacteriologist. See: Index-Cat. Libr. Surg.-Gen. Off., 4th Ser., vol. 9, 1945. Bielschowsky-Lutz-Cogan syndrome, Lutz-Jeanselme syndrome, Lutz-Splendore-De Almeida syndrome.

Lutz-Jeanselme syndrome (Lutz, Adolfo and Jeanselme, Edouard). See: Jeanselme's nodules.

Lutz (jump) (Lussi, Gustave): Recreation and Sports. See: Webster's 3d.

LUTZ, LOUIS. fl. 1926-1931. French pharmacologist. See: Pogg., vol. 6. Lutz reagent for tannin.

Lutz-Miescher disease (Lutz, Wilhelm and Miescher, Guido): Medicine. See: Jablonski.

LUTZ, OSKAR. 1871-1950. Russian chemist. See: Pogg., vols. 4, 5, 6, 7a. Lutz test reaction for iron.

Lutz reagent for tannin (Lutz, Louis): Chemistry. See: Van Nostrand Chem. Dict.

Lutz-Splendore-De Almeida syndrome (Lutz, Adolfo; Splendore, Alphonso; and Almeida, Floriano Paulo de): Medicine. See: Jablonski. Also known as: De Almeida's disease, Lutz's disease.

Lutz test reaction for iron (Lutz, Oskar): Chemistry. See: Van Nostrand Chem. Dict.

LUTZ, WILHELM. 1888-1958. Swiss dermatologist. See: Biog. Lex. hervorr. Aerzte, 1880-1930. Lewandowski-Lutz syndrome, Lutz-Miescher disease.

Lutz's disease (Lutz, Adolfo). See: Lutz-Splendore-De Almeida syndrome.

Luxemburg effect (Derivation undetermined): Electronics. See: Hughes; Markus; Van Nostrand Sci. Encyc.

LUYS, GEORGES. b. 1870. French urologist. See: World Who's Who Sci. Luys' operation, Luys' segregator (or separator).

LUYS, JULES BERNARD. 1828-1895. French neurologist. See: World Who's Who Sci. Luys' median centre, Luys' nucleus (or body of Luys).

Luys' median centre (Luys, Jules Bernard): Anatomy. See: Donath.

Luys' nucleus (or body of Luys) (Luys, Jules Bernard): Anatomy. See: Donath; Dorland; Hinsie; Stedman.

Luys' operation (Luys, Georges): Medicine. See: Kelly.

Luys' segregator (or separator) (Luys, Georges): Medicine. See: Dorland; Kelly; Stedman.

LUZET, CHARLES. b. 1863. French physician. Cited in: Index-Cat. Libr. Surg.-Gen. Off., 2d Ser., vol. 9, 1904. Jaksch-Hayem-Luzet syndrome.

LUZIN, NIKOLAI NIKOLAIEVICH. 1883-1950. Russian mathematician. See: Dict. Sci. Biog. Luzin's theorem.

Luzin's theorem (Luzin, Nikolai Nikolaievich): Mathematics. See: James.

Lyall angelica (Lyall, David): Botany. See: Winburne.

LYALL, DAVID. d. 1895. Scottish naturalist. See: Royal Soc. Cat. Sci. Pap., 1884-1900. Lyall angelica.

LYCASTE. Daughter of Priam, King of Troy. (Biography source unavailable.) Lycaste (orchids).

Lycaste (orchids) (Lycaste): Botany. See: New Encyc. Brit., 1974, Microp.; Taylor, N.

LYCOPETRUS. Early Christian heretic. See: Dict. Christian Biog. under "Euchites," p. 261, col. a. Lucopetrians.

Lycoris (Cytheris): Botany. See: Hendrickson; Taylor, N.

Lycoris. See: Cytheris.

Lycurgus (Lycurgus, the lawgiver): Generic Word (severe-lawmaker). See: Partridge.

LYCURGUS, THE LAWGIVER. fl. 9th c. B.C. Spartan lawgiver. See: New Encyc. Brit., 1974, Microp. Lycurgus, Lycurgus's Laws.

Lycurgus's Laws (Lycurgus, the Lawgiver): History. See: Phyfe.

LYDDANE, RUSSELL HANCOCK. 1913- . American physicist. See: Amer. Men and Women Sci., 12th ed. Lyddane-Sachs-Teller relation.

Lyddane-Sachs-Teller relation (Lyddane, Russell Hancock; Sachs, Robert Green; and Teller, Edward): Physics. See: Ballentyne.

LYDGATE, JOHN. ca. 1370-ca. 1451. English poet. See: Dict. Nat. Biog. Lydgatian line.

Lydgatian line (Lydgate, John): Literature. See: Webster's 3d.

LYELL, ALAN. fl. 1950-1972. English dermatologist. See: Med. Direct., 1972. Lyell's syndrome.

Lyell's syndrome (Lyell, Alan): Medicine. See: Jablonski.

Lyle-Curtman-Marshall alpha-aminocaproic acid solution (Lyle, William Gordon; Curtman, Louis J. and Marshall, J. T. W.): Chemistry. See: Van Nostrand Chem. Dict.

Lyle-Curtman-Marshall benzidine reagent (Lyle, William Gordon; Curtman, Louis J. and Marshall, J. T. W.): Chemistry. See: Van Nostrand Chem. Dict.

LYLE, DAVID ALEXANDER. 1845-1937. American army officer. See: Nat. Cycl. Amer. Biog., vol. 28, p. 376. Lyle gun.

LYLE, DONALD JOHNSON. 1895- . American ophthalmologist. See: Direct. Med. Specialists, 1965-1966. Lyle's syndrome.

Lyle gun (Lyle, David Alexander): Weapons. See: Webster's 3d.

LYLE, WILLIAM GORDON. b. 1892. American physician. Cited in: Chem. Abstr., Decenn. Index, 1907-1916. Lyle-Curtman-Marshall alpha-aminocaproic acid solution, Lyle-Curtman-Marshall benzidine reagent.

Lyle's syndrome (Lyle, Donald Johnson): Medicine. See: Jablonski.

Lyman alpha line (Lyman, Theodore): Physics. See: New Encyc. Brit., 1974, Microp.

Lyman ghosts (Lyman, Theodore): Physics. See: Thewlis.

LYMAN, S. fl. before 1847. American horticulturist. (Biography source unavailable.) Lyman's long summer (apple).

Lyman series (Lyman, Theodore): Physics. See: Hughes; Internat. Dict. Ap. Math.; Internat. Dict. Phys. Elec.; Thewlis.

LYMAN, THEODORE. 1874-1954. American physicist. See: Dict. Sci. Biog. Lyman alpha line, Lyman ghosts, Lyman series.

Lyman's long summer (apple) (Lyman, S.): Botany. See: Mathews, M. M.

Lyncean (or Lynx-eyed) (Lynceus): Generic Word (sharp-sighted). See: Partridge; Webster's 3d.

LYNCEUS. One of the Argonauts in Greek mythology. See: Jobes. Lyncean (or Lynx-eyed).

Lynch (Lynch, Charles): Generic Word (hang). See: Hendrickson; Partridge; Webster's 3d.

LYNCH ARRIBALZAGA, FELIX. 1854-1894. Argentinian entomologist. See: Gran Encic. Argentina. Lynchia.

LYNCH, CHARLES. 1736-1796. American planter and justice of the peace. See: Dict. Amer. Biog. Lynch, Lynch law.

Lynch law (Lynch, Charles): History. See: Jameson; Phyfe; Zadrozny.

Lynchia (Lynch Arribalzaga, Felix): Zoology. See: Pennak.

Lyndhurst, Lord. See: Copley, John Singleton (Lord Lyndhurst).

Lynen furnace (Lynen, G. H.?): Engineering and Industry. See: Thrush.

LYNEN, G. H. fl. 1914. American? engineer. Cited in: Chem. Abstr., Decenn. Index, 1907-1916. Lynen furnace?

LYNN, ELDIN VERNE. 1886-1955. American chemist. See: Pogg., vols. 6, 7b. Lynn-Lee reagents.

Lynn-Lee reagents (Lynn, Eldin Verne and Lee, Frank Andrew): Chemistry. See: Van Nostrand Chem. Dict.

Lyon and Horgan method (or operation) (Lyon, James Alexander and Horgan, Edmund J.): Medicine. See: Dorland; Stedman.

LYON, BETHUEL BOYD VINCENT. 1880-1953. American physician. See: J.A.M.A., vol. 152 (July 4, 1953), pp. 952-953. Meltzer-Lyon test.

Lyon hypothesis (Lyon, Mary Frances): Genetics. See: Stedman; Wolman.

LYON, JAMES ALEXANDER. 1882-1955. American cardiologist. See: World Who's Who Sci. Lyon and Horgan method (or operation).

LYON, JOHN. d. ca. 1818. Scottish botanist in America. (Biography source unavailable.) Lyonia (shrubs).

LYON, MARY FRANCES. 1925- . English geneticist. See: Who's Who Brit. Scientists, 1971-1972. Lyon hypothesis.

LYON, WILLIAM SCRUGHAM. 1852-1916. American botanist. Cited in: Mansell. Lyonothamnus (or Lyon's shrub).

LYONET, PIERRE. 1707-1789. French-Dutch naturalist. See: Dict. Sci. Biog. Lyonettidae, Lyonnet's glands.

Lyonettidae (Lyonet, Pierre): Zoology. See: Pennak.

Lyonia (shrubs) (Lyon, John): Botany. See: New Encyc. Brit., 1974, Microp.; Taylor, N.; Webster's 3d.

Lyonnet's glands (Lyonet, Pierre): Zoology. See: Henderson.

Lyonothamnus (or Lyon's shrub) (Lyon, William Scrugham): Botany. See: Bailey, L. H.; Taylor, N.

Lyons–Dox test for alkylbarbituric acids (Lyons, Edward and Dox, Arthur W.): Chemistry. See: Van Nostrand Chem. Dict.

LYONS, EDWARD. b. 1890. American chemist. See: Amer. Men Sci., 9th ed. Lyons–Dox test for alkylbarbituric acids, Lyons test for iron.

Lyons test for iron (Lyons, Edward): Chemistry. See: Van Nostrand Chem. Dict.

LYOT, BERNARD FERDINAND. 1897–1952. French astronomer. See: Dict. Sci. Biog. Lyot birefringent filter.

Lyot birefringent filter (Lyot, Bernard Ferdinand): Astronomy. See: Satterthwaite.

LYSANDER. d. 395 B.C. Spartan general. See: New Encyc. Brit., 1974, Microp. Lysandria.

Lysandria (Lysander): History. See: Charnock.

LYSENKO, TROFIM DENISOVICH. 1898–   . Russian biologist and agronomist. See: World Who's Who Sci. Lysenkoism.

Lysenkoism (Lysenko, Trofim Denisovich): Genetics. See: New Encyc. Brit., 1974, Microp.; Pennak; Webster's 3d. Also known as: Michurinism.

LYSHOLM, ALF JAMES RUDOLF. b. 1893. Swedish engineer. See: Svenska Maen Och Kvinnor. Lysholm compressor, Lysholm–Smith converter, Lysholm turbine.

Lysholm compressor (Lysholm, Alf James Rudolf): Engineering and Industry. See: Auger.

LYSHOLM, ERIK LORENZ RUDOLF. 1891–1947. Swedish radiologist. See: Brit. Med. J., vol. 2 (Oct. 18, 1947), p. 634. Lysholm grid, Lysholm projection, Lysholm's line.

Lysholm grid (Lysholm Erik Lorenz Rudolf): Medicine. See: Blakiston's Gould; Hughes.

Lysholm projection (Lysholm, Erik Lorenz Rudolf): Medicine. See: Blakiston's Gould.

Lysholm–Smith converter (Lysholm, Alf James Rudolf and Smith, Jan): Engineering and Industry. See: Auger.

Lysholm turbine (Lysholm, Alf James Rudolf): Engineering and Industry. See: Auger.

Lysholm's line (Lysholm, Erik Lorenz Rudolf): Medicine. See: Blakiston's Gould.

Lysimachia (Lysimachus): Botany. See: Charnock; Webster's 3d.

LYSIMACHUS. fl. 5th or 4th c. B.C.? Greek physician. See: Dict. Grk. Rom. Biog. Myth. Lysimachia.

LYSTER, F. J. fl. 1914. English engineer. Cited in: Chem. Abstr., vol. 8, p. 3552. Lyster process.

Lyster process (Lyster, F. J.): Engineering and Industry. See: Thrush.

LYTTELTON, ALFRED. 1857–1913. English statesman. See: Dict. Nat. Biog., 3d. suppl. Lyttelton Constitution, Lyttelton incident.

Lyttelton Constitution (Lyttelton, Alfred): Politics. See: Montgomery.

Lyttelton incident (Lyttelton, Alfred): Politics. See: Montgomery.

Lyttkens' correction (Lyttkens, Ejnar): Statistics. See: Kendall.

LYTTKENS, EJNAR. fl. 1962. Swedish scientist. (Biography source unavailable.) Lyttkens' correction.

Lytton Report (or Commission) (Lytton, Victor Alexander George Robert Lytton, 2nd Earl of): History. See: Morris; New Encyc. Brit., 1974, Microp.

LYTTON, VICTOR ALEXANDER GEORGE ROBERT LYTTON, 2ND EARL OF. 1876–1947. English statesman. See: Who Was Who, 1941–1950. Lytton Report (or Commission).

M

MIG (fighter plane) (Mikoyan, Artyom Ivanovich and Gurevich, M. I.): Weapons. See: Hendrickson.

MKK-system (Morgan, William Wilson; Keenan, Philip Childs; and Kellman, Edith): Astronomy. See: Satterthwaite.

MA, TSU-SHENG. 1911- . Chinese-born American chemist. See: World Who's Who Sci. Sah-Ma reagent for alcohols, Sah-Ma reagent for organic halogens, Sah-Ma reagent for phenols.

Maas borehole compass (Maas, Guenther Heinrich Julius Max?): Earth Sciences. See: Thrush.

MAAS, GUENTHER HEINRICH JULIUS MAX. 1871-1905. German geologist. See: Arnim. Maas borehole compass?, Maas survey?

Maas survey (Maas Guenther Heinrich Julius Max?): Earth Sciences. See: Thrush.

MAASS, THEODOR A. fl. 1903. German chemist. Cited in: Mansell. Spiegel-Maass test.

McAbee (explosives) (Derivation undetermined): Engineering and Industry. See: Thrush.

Macabee gopher trap (Derivation undetermined): Agriculture. See: Winburne.

Macabre (or Macaber) (Maccabees): Generic Word. See: Charnock; Webster's 3d.

Macadam (or Macadamize) (McAdam, John Loudon): Engineering and Industry. See: Hendrickson; Thrush; Webster's 3d.

MAC ADAM, DAVID LEWIS. 1910- . American optics researcher. See: World Who's Who Sci. Brown-MacAdam colorimeter, MacAdam system.

MACADAM, JOHN. 1827-1865. Scottish-born Australian chemist. See: Dict. Nat. Biog. Macadamia (nut).

MC ADAM, JOHN LOUDON. 1756-1836. Scottish engineer. See: Dict. Nat. Biog. Macadam (or Macadamize).

MacAdam system (MacAdam, David Lewis): Physics. See: Thrush.

Macadamia (nut) (Macadam, John): Botany. See: De Sola; New Encyc. Brit., 1974, Microp.; Webster's 3d.

MC AFEE, ALMER MC DUFFIE. b. 1886. American petroleum chemist. See: Amer. Men Sci., 4th ed. McAfee process.

McAfee process (McAfee, Almer McDuffie): Chemistry. See: Van Nostrand Chem. Dict.

MACAIRE, ROBERT. Character in Benjamin Antier, Saint-Amand and Paulyanthe's play, "L'Auberge des Adrets," (1823). See: Harvey and Heseltine. Robert Macaire.

MACALISTER, SIR DONALD. fl. 1879. English mathematician. (Biography source unavailable.) Galton-McAllister distribution.

McAll Mission (M'All, Robert Whitaker): Religion. See: Mathews, S.

M'ALL, ROBERT WHITAKER. 1821-1893. English independent minister. See: Boase. McAll Mission.

MC ALPINE, DOUGLAS. b. 1890. English neurologist. See: Who's Who, 1975. Lhermitte-McAlpine syndrome.

MC ARDLE, BRIAN. fl. 1936-1972. English neurologist. See: Med. Direct., 1972. McArdle's disease.

McArdle-Schmid-Pearson syndrome (McArdle, Brian; Schmid, Rudi; and Pearson, Carl M.). See: McArdle's disease.

McArdle's disease (McArdle, Brian): Medicine. See: Jablonski; Stedman. Also known as: McArdle-Schmid-Pearson syndrome.

MacArthur and Forest cyanide process (MacArthur, John S.; Forrest, R. W; and Forrest, W.): Engineering and Industry. See: Thrush.

MacArthur clusterpalm (Derivation undetermined): Botany. See: Winburne.

MC ARTHUR, DUNCAN. 1772-1839. American soldier and legislator. See: Dict. Amer. Biog. McArthur's raid.

MAC ARTHUR, JOHN S. fl. ca. 1889-1915. Scottish engineer in South Africa. Cited in: Chem. Abstr., Decenn. Index, 1907-1916. MacArthur and Forest cyanide process.

MC ARTHUR, LOUIS LINN. 1858-1934. American surgeon. See: Who Was Who Amer., 1897-1942. McArthur's method.

McArthur's method (McArthur, Louis Linn): Medicine. See: Dorland; Stedman.

McArthur's raid (McArthur, Duncan): History. See: Jameson.

MACARTNEY, GEORGE (1ST EARL MACARTNEY). 1737-1806. Irish-born English diplomat. See: Dict. Nat. Biog. Macartney (pheasant or cock), Macartney rose.

Macartney (pheasant or cock) (Macartney, George): Zoology. See: Partridge; Webster's 3d.

Macartney rose (Macartney, George): Botany. See: Webster's 3d.; Winburne.

MACAULAY, FREDERICK ROBERTSON. b. 1882. American economist. See: Amer. Men Sci., 9th ed., (Soc. Behav. Sci.). Macaulay's formula.

Macauley method (Macaulay, William Herrick): Engineering and Industry. See: Internat. Dict. Ap. Math.

MACAULAY, THOMAS BABINGTON (1ST BARON MACAULAY). 1800-1859. English writer and statesman. See: Dict. Nat. Biog. Macaulayan (or Macaulayism), Macaulay's minute on education.

MACAULAY, WILLIAM HERRICK. 1853-1936. English applied mathematician. See: Pogg., vol. 5. Macauley method.

Macaulayan (or Macaulayism) (Macaulay, Thomas Babington): Literature. See: Webster's 3d.

Macaulay's formula (Macaulay, Frederick Robertson): Statistics. See: Kendall.

Macaulay's minute on education (Macaulay, Thomas Babington): Education. See: Morris and Irwin.

McBain-Baker (Bakr) balance (McBain, James William and Bakr, Abu Mohamed): Chemistry. See: Hackh; Royal Soc. Obit. Not. of Fellows, vol. 8, 1952-1953, p. 535.

McBain centrifuge (McBain, James William): Chemistry. See: Hackh.

MC BAIN, JAMES WILLIAM. 1882-1953. Canadian-born American physical chemist. See: Who Was Who Amer., 1951-1960. McBain-Baker (Bakr) balance, McBain centrifuge.

Macbeth illuminometer (Macbeth, Norman?): Engineering and Industry. See: Thrush.

MACBETH, NORMAN. fl. 1909-1923. American illumination engineer. Cited in: Chem. Abstr., Decenn. Index, 1917-1926. Macbeth illuminometer?

C BURNEY, CHARLES. 1845-1913. American surgeon. See: Dict. Amer. iog. McBurney's incision, McBurney's operation, McBurney's point.

cBurney's incision (McBurney, Charles): Medicine. See: Dorland; Stedman.

cBurney's operation (McBurney, Charles): Medicine. See: Stedman.

cBurney's point (McBurney, Charles): Anatomy. See: Donath; Dorland; edman; Webster's 3d.

cCaa apparatus (McCaa, George S.): Engineering and Industry. See: Thrush.

cCaa breathing device (McCaa, George S.): Engineering and Industry. See: rush.

C CAA, GEORGE S. b. 1884. American mining safety engineer. (Biogphy source unavailable.) McCaa apparatus, McCaa breathing device.

ACCABAEUS, JUDAS. d. 161 B.C. Jewish patriot. See: New Encyc. it., 1974, Microp. Maccabean (or Maccabaean) (1).

accabean (or Maccabaean) (1) (Maccabaeus, Judas): History. See: Webster's d.

accabean (or Maccabaean) (2) (Maccabees): History. See: Webster's 3d.

accabee(s) (Maccabees family): Sociology. See: Webster's 3d.

ACCABEES. fl. 2d and 1st c. B.C. Jewish priestly family in Palestine. ee: New Encyc. Brit., 1974. Knights of the Maccabees, Macabre (or acaber), Maccabean (or Maccabaean) (2), Maccabee(s).

acCallum test reaction (Derivation undetermined): Chemistry. See: Van ostrand Chem. Dict.

AC CALLUM, WILLIAM GEORGE. 1874-1944. Canadian pathologist in the nited States. See: Who Was Who Amer., 1943-1950. MacCallum's modificion, MacCallum's patch, MacCallum's stain (or method).

acCallum's modification (MacCallum, William George): Medicine. See: elly.

acCallum's patch (MacCallum, William George): Medicine. See: akiston's Gould.

acCallum's stain (or method) (MacCallum, William George): Medicine. See: akiston's Gould; Kelly.

C CANCE, ANDREW. 1889- . Scottish engineer. See: Who's Who, 75. McCance reagent.

cCance reagent (McCance, Andrew): Engineering and Industry. See: Hackh.

cCarran Act (McCarran, Patrick Anthony): Politics. See: Morris.

C CARRAN, PATRICK ANTHONY. 1876-1954. American legislator. See: og. Dict. Amer. Congress. McCarran Act, McCarran-Walter Act.

cCarran-Walter Act (McCarran, Patrick Anthony and Walter, Francis Eugene): litics. See: Morris.

C CARTER, J. fl. 19th c. Irish engineer. (Biography source unavailable.) cCarter jet condenser.

cCarter jet condenser (McCarter, J.): Engineering and Industry. See: ger.

C CARTHY, CHARLIE. Ventriloquist's dummy made famous by Edgar Bergen 903- .). (Biography source unavailable.) Charlie McCarthy.

C CARTHY, DANIEL J. 1874-1958. American neurologist. See: Who Was ho Amer., 1943-1950. McCarthy's reflexes.

cCarthy hearings (McCarthy, Joseph Raymond): Politics. See: Morris and vin.

C CARTHY, JOSEPH RAYMOND. 1908-1957. American legislator. See: cyc. Brit., 1973. McCarthy hearings, McCarthyism.

cCarthyism (McCarthy, Joseph Raymond): Generic Word (accusation without oof). See: Brewer; Hendrickson; Hoult; Webster's 3d.

cCarthy's reflexes (McCarthy, Daniel J.): Medicine. See: Stedman.

ACCHIA, OSVALDO. fl. 1927. Italian chemist. Cited in: Chem. Abstr., . 21, p. 3030. Macchia test for alkaline earths.

acchia test for alkaline earths (Macchia, Osvaldo): Chemistry. See: Van ostrand Chem. Dict.

McClellan cap (McClellan, George Brinton): Fashion. See: Mathews, M. M.

MC CLELLAN, GEORGE BRINTON. 1826-1885. American Union general. See: Dict. Amer. Biog. McClellan cap, McClellan saddle.

McClellan saddle (McClellan, George Brinton): Generic Word. See: Mathews, M. M.; Webster's 3d.

MC CLINTOCK, ALFRED HENRY. 1822-1881. Irish physician. See: Album Amer. Gynec. Soc., Phila., 1918, p. 306. McClintock's sign.

MC CLINTOCK, EMORY. 1840-1916. American mathematician and actuary. See: Dict. Amer. Biog. McClintock's tables.

McClintock's sign (McClintock, Alfred Henry): Medicine. See: Dorland; Kelly; Stedman.

McClintock's tables (McClintock, Emory): Business. See: Webster's 3d.

McCollum Award (McCollum, Elmer Vernon): Chemistry. Cited in: World Who's Who Sci.

McCollum case (McCollum, Vashti Cromwell): Education. See: Good.

MC COLLUM, ELMER VERNON. 1879-1967. American physiological chemist. See: World Who's Who Sci. McCollum Award, Prebluda-McCollum reaction for vitamin B$_1$ (thiamine).

MC COLLUM, VASHTI CROMWELL. fl. 1948-1951. American plaintiff against religious classes in public schools. See: Mansell. McCollum case.

MC COMB, HAROLD EDGAR. 1886-1952. American geophysicist. See: Pogg., vols. 6, 7b. McComb-Romberg seismograph.

McComb-Romberg seismograph (McComb, Harold Edgar and Romberg, Arnold?): Earth Sciences. See: Van Nostrand Sci. Encyc. under "Earthquake."

MAC CONKEY, ALFRED THEODORE. 1861-1931. English bacteriologist. See: World Who's Who Sci. MacConkey's bile salt agar, MacConkey's bouillon.

MacConkey's bile salt agar (MacConkey, Alfred Theodore): Medicine. See: Dorland.

MacConkey's bouillon (MacConkey, Alfred Theodore): Medicine. See: Dorland.

MC CORMICK, CYRUS HALL. 1809-1884. American inventor. See: Dict. Amer. Biog. McCormick's reaper.

McCormick's reaper (McCormick, Cyrus Hall): Agriculture. See: Winburne.

MC COWN, JOHN PORTER. 1815-1879. American Confederate general. See: Boatner. McCown's longspur (or bunting).

McCown's longspur (or bunting) (McCown, John Porter): Zoology. See: Gray; Mathews, M. M.; Webster's 3d.

MC COY, ELIJAH. 1844-1929. American inventor. See: Dict. Amer. Biog. real McCoy?

MC COY, HERBERT NEWBY. 1870-1945. American chemist and physicist. See: World Who's Who Sci. McCoy number.

MC COY, KID (Real name: NORMAN SELBY). 1873-1940. American boxer. See: New Encyc. Brit., 1974, Microp. real McCoy?

McCoy number (McCoy, Herbert Newby): Physics. See: Thrush.

MAC CULLAGH, JAMES. 1809-1847. Irish mathematician and physicist. See: Dict. Sci. Biog. MacCullagh's formula?

MacCullagh's formula (MacCullagh, James?): Physics. See: Ballentyne.

MC CULLOUGH, HAMISH. 1835-1885. American actor. (Biography source unavailable.) Ham actor.

MC CUMBER, PORTER JAMES. 1858-1933. American lawyer and legislator. See: Biog. Direct. Amer. Congress. Fordney-McCumber Tariff Bill.

McCune-Albright syndrome (McCune, Donovan James and Albright, Fuller). See: Albright's syndrome (2).

MC CUNE, DONOVAN JAMES. 1902- . American pediatrician. See: Amer. Men and Women Sci., 12th ed. Albright-McCune-Sternberg syndrome.

MC DADE, JAMES EDWARD. b. 1872. American reading teacher. Cited in: Mansell. McDade plan.

McDade plan (McDade, James Edward): Education. See: Good.

MC DONALD, ELLICE. 1876-1955. American gynecologist, biochemist and pathologist. See: World Who's Who Sci. McDonald's maneuver, McDonald's solution.

Macdonald Training Fund (Macdonald, Sir William Christopher): Education. See: Encyc. Brit., 1973 under "Home Economics," vol. 11, p. 621b.

MACDONALD, SIR WILLIAM CHRISTOPHER. 1831-1917. Canadian manufacturer and philanthropist. See: Macmillan Dict. Canadian Biog. Macdonald Training Fund.

McDonald's maneuver (McDonald, Ellice): Medicine. See: Dorland; Stedman.

McDonald's solution (McDonald, Ellice): Medicine. See: Kelly.

MAC DONNELL, SIR ANTONY PATRICK (BARON MAC DONNELL). 1844-1925. Irish-born English administrator in India and statesman. See: Dict. Nat. Biog., 4th suppl. MacDonnell incident.

MacDonnell incident (MacDonnell, Sir Antony Patrick): Politics. See: Montgomery.

MC DOUGALL. fl. 19th c. English engineer. (Biography source unavailable.) McDougall furnace.

McDougall furnace (McDougall): Engineering and Industry. See: Webster's 3d.

MAC DOWELL, BENJAMIN GEORGE. 1820-1885. Irish anatomist and surgeon. See: Index-Cat. Libr. Surg.-Gen. Off., 1st Ser., vol. 8, 1887. McDowell's frenulum (or frenulum of Macdowel).

MC DOWELL, EPHRAIM. 1771-1830. American surgeon. See: Encyc. Brit., 1973. McDowell's operation.

McDowell's frenulum (or frenulum of Macdowel) (MacDowell, Benjamin George): Anatomy. See: Donath; Stedman.

McDowell's operation (McDowell, Ephraim): Medicine. See: Dorland.

MC DUFFIE, JOHN. 1883-1950. American legislator. See: Biog. Direct. Amer. Congress. Tydings-McDuffie Act.

Macedonians (or Macedonianism) (Macedonius): Religion. See: Brewer; Canney; Mathews, S.

MACEDONIUS. d. ca. 362. Bishop of Constantinople. See: Encyc. Brit., 1973. Macedonians (or Macedonianism).

MC ELLROY, W. S. fl. 1918. American biochemist. Cited in: Chem. Abstr., vol. 12, p. 1059. Folin-McEllroy reagent.

MACEWEN, SIR WILLIAM. 1848-1924. Scottish surgeon. See: World Who's Who Sci. Macewen's operation, Macewen's sign (or symptom), Macewen's triangle.

Macewen's operation (Macewen, Sir William): Medicine. See: Dorland; Stedman.

Macewen's sign (or symptom) (Macewen, Sir William): Medicine. See: Stedman.

Macewen's triangle (Macewen, Sir William): Medicine. See: Dorland; Stedman.

McFadden Act (McFadden, Louis Thomas): Politics. See: Smith.

MC FADDEN, LOUIS THOMAS. 1876-1936. American legislator. See: Biog. Direct. Amer. Congress. McFadden Act.

MC FADYEN, JOHN S. fl. 1936. English chemist. (Biography source unavailable.) McFadyen-Stevens aldehyde synthesis.

McFadyen-Stevens aldehyde synthesis (McFadyen, John S. and Stevens, Thomas Stevens): Chemistry. See: Van Nostrand Chem. Dict.

MACFARLANE, THOMAS. 1834-1907. Scottish-born Canadian mining engineer. See: Macmillan Dict. Canadian Biog. Macfarlanite.

Macfarlanite (Macfarlane, Thomas): Earth Sciences. See: Thrush.

McGavin method (Derivation undetermined): Medicine. See: Stedman.

MacGeorge borehole tube (Derivation undetermined): Engineering and Industry. See: Thrush.

MacGeorge's method (Derivation undetermined): Engineering and Industry. See: Thrush.

McGill fence (McGill, James?): Electronics. See: Markus.

MC GILL, JAMES. 1744-1813. Scottish-born Canadian fur-trader, merchant and philanthropist. See: Dict. Canadian Biog. McGill fence?

McGill metals (Derivation undetermined): Chemistry. See: Hackh.

MAC GILLIVRAY, WILLIAM. 1796-1852. Scottish naturalist. See: Dict. Nat. Biog. MacGillivray's warbler.

MacGillivray's warbler (MacGillivray, William): Zoology. See: Gray; Webster's 3d.

MAC GINTIE, WALTER HAROLD. 1928- . American psychologist. See: Amer. Men. Sci., 11th ed. Gates-MacGintie reading tests.

McGinty (sheaves) (Derivation undetermined): Engineering and Industry. See: Thrush.

MC GOON, DWIGHT CHARLES. 1925- . American heart surgeon. See: World Who's Who Sci. McGoon's technique.

McGoon's technique (McGoon, Dwight Charles): Medicine. See: Stedman.

MC GOVERN, J. J. d. 1915. American mine foreman. See: Amer. Min., vol. 12 (1927), p. 374. Mcgovernite (or Macgovernite).

Mcgovernite (or Macgovernite) (McGovern, J. J.): Earth Sciences. See: Thrush; Webster's 3d.

MC GRAW, THEODORE ANDREWS. 1839-1921. American surgeon. See: Who Was Who Amer., 1897-1942. McGraw's ligature.

McGraw's ligature (McGraw, Theodore Andrews): Medicine. See: Dorland.

MAC GREGOR, JOHN (Pseud.: ROB ROY). 1825-1892. English traveller and writer. See: Dict. Nat. Biog. Rob Roy (canoe).

MAC GREGOR, PATRICK "GILDEROY." d. 1636. Scottish outlaw. (Biography source unavailable.) hung higher than Gilderoy's kite.

MACGREGOR (or CAMPBELL), ROBERT ("ROB ROY"). 1671-1734. Scottish highlands freebooter. See: Dict. Nat. Biog. Rob Roy (cocktail).

McGuffey('s) reader (McGuffey, William Holmes): Education. See: Hendrickson; Mathews, M. M.

MC GUFFEY, WILLIAM HOLMES. 1800-1873. American educator and linguist. See: Dict. Amer. Biog. McGuffey('s) reader.

Mach angle (Mach, Ernst): Physics. See: Internat. Dict. Ap. Math.; Internat. Dict. Phys. Elec.; Van Nostrand Sci. Encyc.; Webster's 3d.

Mach cone (Mach, Ernst): Physics. See: Internat. Dict. Ap. Math.; Internat. Dict. Phys. Elec.; Webster's 3d.

Mach criterion (Mach, Ernst): Physics. See: Internat. Dict. Phys. Elec.

MACH, ERNST. 1838-1916. Austrian physicist and philosopher. See: Dict. Sci. Biog. Mach angle, Mach cone, Mach criterion, Mach line (or surface), Mach number, Mach rotation frame, Mach('s) principle, Mach wave, Machism, Machmeter, Mach's bands.

Mach line (or surface) (Mach, Ernst): Physics. See: Ballentyne; Internat. Dict. Ap. Math.

Mach number (Mach, Ernst): Physics. See: Ballentyne; Huschke; Hughes; Internat. Dict. Ap. Math.; Markus; Thewlis.

Mach('s) principle (Mach, Ernst): Physics. See: Asimov; Hughes; Van Nostrand Sci. Encyc.

MACH, RENE SIGMUND. 1904- . Swiss internist. See: Who's Who Switz., 1970-1971. Mach's syndrome.

Mach rotation frame (Mach, Ernst): Physiology. See: Drever.

Mach wave (Mach, Ernst): Physics. See: Internat. Dict. Phys. Elec.; Webster's 3d.

MACHACEK, G. F. fl. 1953. American physician. (Biography source unavailable.) Bloom-Torre-Machacek syndrome.

Machado-Guerreiro test (Machado and Guerreiro, Cezar). Medicine. See: Blakiston's Gould; Stedman.

MACHE, HEINRICH. 1876-1954. Austrian physicist. See: Pogg., vols. 4, 5, 6, 7a. Mache (unit).

Mache (unit) (Mache, Heinrich): Physics. See: Dresner; Hackh; Internat. Dict. Phys. Elec.; Thrush.

Machiavel (Machiavelli, Niccolo): Generic Word (knave or devious statesman). See: Charnock; Partridge.

MACHIAVELLI, NICCOLO. 1469-1527. Italian statesman and political philosopher. See: New Encyc. Brit., 1974. Machiavel, Machiavellian (principles).

Machiavellian (principles) (Machiavelli, Niccolo): Generic Word (cunning). See: Funk; Hendrickson; Partridge; Phyfe; Webster's 3d.

Machism (Mach, Ernst): Philosophy. See: Webster's 3d.

Machmeter (Mach, Ernst): Physics. See: Webster's 3d.

MACHOVER, KAREN ALPER. 1902- . American psychologist. See: Biog. Direct. Amer. Psych. Assoc., 1975. Machover test (or draw-a-person test).

Machover test (or draw-a-person test) (Machover, Karen Alper): Psychology. See: Chaplin; English.

Mach's bands (Mach, Ernst): Physiology. See: Dict. Sci. Biog. under "Mach, Ernst," p. 596b.

Mach's syndrome (Mach, Rene Sigmund): Medicine. See: Jablonski.

MC ILROY, ROBERT JOSEPH. 1911- . New Zealand chemist. See: Who's Who New Zealand, 1964. McIlroy test for copper.

McIntire (furniture style) (McIntire, Samuel): Applied Arts. See: Webster's 3d.

MC INTIRE, SAMUEL. 1757-1811. American architect and woodcarver. See: Dict. Amer. Biog. McIntire.

Macintosh (Mackintosh) (Macintosh, Charles): Generic Word (waterproof fabric and raincoat). See: Funk; Hendrickson; Webster's 3d.

McIntosh (apple) (McIntosh, John): Botany. See: Hendrickson; Mathews, M.M; Winburne.

Macintosh blockers (Macintosh, Charles): Medicine. See: Stedman.

MACINTOSH, CHARLES. 1766-1843. Scottish chemist. See: Dict. Nat. Biog. Macintosh (Mackintosh), Macintosh blockers.

MC INTOSH, JOHN. fl. 1796. Canadian farmer. (Biography source unavailable.) McIntosh (apple).

McIlroy test for copper (McIlroy, Robert Joseph): Chemistry. See: Van Nostrand Chem. Dict.

MACK, LUDWIG. fl. 1896. German scientist. Cited in: Mansell. Mack's cement.

MAC KAY, A. M. fl. early 20th c. Scottish whiskey importer. (Biography source unavailable.) real McCoy?

MC KAY, GORDON. 1821-1903. American inventor and industrialist. See: Dict. Amer. Biog. McKay (shoe or process).

MAC KAY, JOHN WILLIAM. 1831-1902. Irish-born American miner and financier. See: Dict. Amer. Biog. Mackayite.

Mackay-Marg tonometer (Mackay, Ralph Stuart and Marg, Elwin): Medicine. See: Stedman.

MACKAY, RALPH STUART. 1924- . American biophysicist. See: Amer. Men and Women Sci., 12th ed. Mackay-Marg tonometer.

McKay (shoe or process) (McKay, Gordon): Engineering and Industry. See: Bracken; Webster's 3d. Also known as: Blake (shoe).

Mackayite (MacKay, John William): Earth Sciences. See: Thrush; Webster's 3d.

McKay's bunting (Derivation undetermined): Zoology. See: Gray.

MAC KEE, GEORGE MILLER. b. 1878. American dermatologist. See: Amer. Men Sci., 8th ed. McKees' line?

McKees line (MacKee, George Miller?): Medicine. See: Stedman.

MAC KELLAR, THOMAS. 1812-1899. American typographer and poet. See: Dict. Amer. Biog. MacKellar's brevier No. 16.

MacKellar's brevier No. 16 (MacKellar, Thomas): Printing. See: Lockwood, 551-2.

McKendrick test (or reaction) (Derivation undetermined): Medicine. See: Dorland.

McKenna duties (McKenna, Reginald): History. See: Morris and Irwin; Steinberg under "Free Trade."

MC KENNA, REGINALD. 1863-1943. English statesman. See: Who Was Who, 1941-1950. McKenna duties.

MACKENRODT, ALWIN KARL. 1859-1925. German gynecologist. See: World Who's Who Sci. Mackenrodt's incision, Mackenrodt's ligament, Mackenrodt's method.

Mackenrodt's incision (Mackenrodt, Alwin Karl): Medicine. See: Dorland; Stedman.

Mackenrodt's ligament (Mackenrodt, Alwin Karl): Anatomy. See: Stedman.

Mackenrodt's method (Mackenrodt, Alwin Karl): Medicine. See: Stedman.

Mackenzie amalgam (Derivation undetermined): Chemistry. See: Hackh.

Mackenzie, Edward Montagu Stuart. See: Wharncliffe, Edward Montagu Stuart, 1st Earl of.

Mackenzie equation (Derivation undetermined): Physics. See: Internat. Dict. Phys. Elec.

MACKENZIE, SIR JAMES. 1853-1925. Scottish physician. See: World Who's Who Sci. Mackenzie's disease, Mackenzie's polygraph.

MACKENZIE, JAMES K. fl. 1949. Australian chemist. (Biography source unavailable.) Mackenzie-Shuttleworth equation.

MACKENZIE, RICHARD JAMES. 1821-1854. Scottish surgeon. See: World Who's Who Sci. Mackenzie's amputation.

Mackenzie-Shuttleworth equation (Mackenzie, James K. and Shuttleworth, Roy): Engineering and Industry. See: Thrush.

MAC KENZIE, SIR STEPHEN. 1844-1909. English physician. See: Dict. Nat. Biog., 2d suppl. Jackson-MacKenzie syndrome.

MACKENZIE, WILLIAM FORBES, 1807-1862. Scottish politician. See: Dict. Nat. Biog. Forbes MacKenzie Act.

Mackenzie-Wishart envelope (Derivation undetermined): Photography. See: Focal Encyc. Photog.

Mackenzie's amputation (Mackenzie, Richard James): Medicine. See: Stedman.

Mackenzie's disease (Mackenzie, Sir James): Medicine. See: Dorland.

Mackenzie's polygraph (Mackenzie, Sir James): Medicine. See: Stedman.

MacKenzie's syndrome (MacKenzie, Sir Stephen). See: Jackson-MacKenzie syndrome.

Mackey test (Mackey, William McD.): Engineering and Industry. See: Hackh.

MACKEY, WILLIAM MC D. fl. 1915-1923. English engineer. Cited in: Chem. Abstr., Decenn. Index, 1917-1926. Mackey test.

MACKIE, ALEXANDER. fl. 19th c. Scientist. (Biography source unavailable.) Mackie line.

Mackie line (Mackie, Alexander): Photography. See: Focal Encyc. Photog.; also under "Solarization"; Webster's 3d.

McKinley Act (or Tariff Act) (McKinley, William): Politics. See: Jameson; Latham; Smith.

McKinley prosperity (McKinley, William): History. See: Mathews, M. M.

MC KINLEY, WILLIAM. 1843-1901. American president. See: Dict. Amer. Biog. McKinley Act (or Tariff Act), McKinley prosperity, McKinleyism (or McKinleyite).

McKinleyism (or McKinleyite) (McKinley, William): Politics. See: Mathews, M. M.; Webster's 3d.

MACKINTOSH, JAMES BUCKTON. d. 1891. American chemist. See: J. Amer. Chem. Soc., vol. 13 (1891), pp. 153-154. Mackintoshite.

Mackintoshite (Mackintosh, James Buckton): Earth Sciences. See: Thrush; Webster's 3d.

MC KITTRICK, LELAND STERLING. b. 1892. American physician. See: Direct. Med. Specialists, 1965-1966. McKittrick-Wheelock syndrome.

McKittrick-Wheelock syndrome (McKittrick, Leland Sterling and Wheelock, Frank Cawthorne, Jr.): Medicine. See: Jablonski.

McKittrite (Derivation undetermined): Earth Sciences. See: Thrush.

Mackler's glaze (Derivation undetermined): Engineering and Industry. See: Thrush.

Mack's cement (Mack, Ludwig): Engineering and Industry. See: Thrush; Webster's 3d.

Macky effect (Macky, W. A.?): Earth Sciences. See: Huschke.

MACKY, W. A. fl. 1930. New Zealand? meteorologist. Cited in: Mansell. Macky effect?

MAC LACHLAN, ELSIE A. fl. 1952. American medical researcher. Cited in: Chem. Abstr., Decenn. Index, 1947-1956. Lowe-Terrey-MacLachlan syndrome.

MACLAGAN, NOEL FRANCIS. fl. 1925-1966. English pathologist. See: Direct. Brit. Sci., 1966-1967. Maclagan's thymol turbidity test.

Maclagan's thymol turbidity test (Maclagan, Noel Francis): Medicine. See: Dorland.

Mac-Lane system (Derivation undetermined): Engineering and Industry. See: Thrush.

Maclaurin-Cauchy test (Maclaurin, Colin and Cauchy, Augustin-Louis): Mathematics. See: Ballentyne.

MACLAURIN, COLIN. 1698-1746. Scottish mathematician. See: World Who's Who Sci. Braikenridge-Maclaurin theorem, Euler-Maclaurin formula, Maclaurin-Cauchy test, Maclaurin('s) theorem (or series), Maclaurin's ellipsoids, trisectrix of Maclaurin.

McLaurin process (MacLaurin, Robert): Engineering and Industry. See: Hackh.

MAC LAURIN, ROBERT. fl. 1917-1933. English engineer. Cited in: Chem. Abstr., Decenn. Index, 1917-1926. McLaurin process.

Maclaurin('s) theorem (or series) (Maclaurin, Colin): Mathematics. See: Ballentyne; Huschke; James; Thewlis; Van Nostrand Sci. Encyc.

Maclaurin's ellipsoids (Maclaurin, Colin): Mathematics. See: World Who's Who Sci.

MAC LEAN, CHARLES. 1788-1824. English physician. See: Dict. Nat. Biog. MacLean-Maxwell disease.

MAC LEAN, DONALD. fl. 1934-1936. English? engineer. Cited in: Chem. Abstr., Decenn. Index, 1927-1936. Maclean separator?

MC LEAN, FRANKLIN CHAMBERS. b. 1888. American physiologist. See: World Who's Who Sci. McLean's formula (or index).

MacLean-Maxwell disease (MacLean, Charles and Maxwell, James Laidlow, senior): Medicine. See: Dorland; Stedman.

Maclean separator (MacLean, Donald?): Engineering and Industry. See: Thrush.

McLean's formula (or index) (McLean, Franklin Chambers): Medicine. See: Dorland; Kelly; Stedman.

MAC LEAY, ALEXANDER. 1767-1848. English entomologist and colonial statesman in Australia. See: Dict. Nat. Biog. Macleaya.

Macleaya (MacLeay, Alexander): Botany. See: Webster's 3d.

MC LEMORE, JEFF (In full: ATKINS JEFFERSON). 1857-1929. American legislator. See: Biog. Direct. Amer. Congress. Gore-McLemore resolutions.

MAC LENNAN, ALEXANDER. 1872-1953. Scottish surgeon. See: Who Was Who, 1951-1960. MacLennan's operation, MacLennan's skin grafting, MacLennan's syndrome.

MacLennan's operation (MacLennan, Alexander): Medicine. See: Kelly.

MacLennan's skin grafting (MacLennan, Alexander): Medicine. See: Kelly.

MacLennan's syndrome (MacLennan, Alexander). See: Thaysen's syndrome.

MACLEOD, DONALD BANNERMAN. 1887-1972. New Zealand physicist. See: Pogg., vols. 6, 7b. Macleod equation.

Macleod equation (Macleod, Donald Bannerman): Physics. See: Van Nostrand Sci. Encyc.

McLeod gauge (McLeod, Herbert): Physics. See: Hackh; Hughes; Internat. Dict. Phys. Elec.; Webster's 3d.

MC LEOD, HERBERT. 1841-1923. English chemist. See: Who Was Who, 1916-1928. McLeod gauge, McLeod (unit).

MACLEOD, RODERICK. 1795-1852. Scottish physician. See: Dict. Nat. Biog. Macleod's rheumatism.

McLeod (unit) (McLeod, Herbert): Physics. See: Dresner.

MACLEOD, WILLIAM MATHIESON. fl. 1934-1972. English pneumologist. See: Med. Direct., 1972. Macleod's syndrome.

Macleod's rheumatism (Macleod, Roderick): Medicine. See: Dorland; Stedman.

Macleod's syndrome (Macleod, William Mathieson): Medicine. See: Jablonski; Stedman.

McLetchie-Aikens disease (Derivation undetermined): Medicine. See: Jablonski.

MC LUCKIE, COLIN. fl. 1930-1942. English mining apparatus engineer. Cited in: Chem. Abstr., Decenn. Index, 1927-1936. McLuckie gas detector.

McLuckie gas detector (McLuckie, Colin): Engineering and Industry. See: Thrush.

MC LUHAN, MARSHALL (In full: HERBERT MARSHALL). 1911- . Canadian electronic communications theorist. See: New Encyc. Brit., 1974, Microp. McLuhanism (McLuhanite or McLuhanize).

McLuhanism (McLuhanite or McLuhanize) (McLuhan, Marshall): Mass Media. See: Barnhart (New Eng.).

Maclura (Maclure, William): Botany. See: Mathews, M. M.; Webster's 3d.

MACLURE, WILLIAM. 1763-1840. Scottish-born American geologist. See: Dict. Sci. Biog. Maclura, Maclurite (Maclureite), Maclurite (mollusks).

Maclurite (Maclureite) (Maclure, William): Earth Sciences. See: Charnock; Thrush.

Maclurite (mollusks) (Maclure, William): Zoology. See: New Encyc. Brit., 1974, Microp.; Webster's 3d.

McMahon Act (McMahon, James O'Brien): Politics. See: Morris and Irwin.

MC MAHON, BERNARD. ca. 1775-1816. Irish-born American horticulturist. See: Dict. Amer. Biog. Mahonia.

MAC MAHON, HAROLD EDWARD. 1901- . American hepatologist. See: Direct. Med. Specialists, 1975-1976. Hanot-MacMahon-Thannhauser syndrome.

MC MAHON, SIR HENRY (In full: ARTHUR HENRY). 1862-1949. English administrator. See: Who Was Who, 1941-1950. McMahon line.

MC MAHON, JAMES O'BRIEN. 1903-1952. American legislator. See: Biog. Direct. Amer. Congress. McMahon Act.

McMahon line (McMahon, Sir Henry): Politics. See: Encyc. Brit., 1973 under "North East Frontier Agency," vol. 16, p. 621b.

MacMahon-Thannhauser syndrome (MacMahon, Harold Edward and Thannhauser, Siegfried Josef). See: Hanot-MacMahon-Thannhauser syndrome.

MC MEEKING, J. G. fl. 1959. English administrator. (Biography source unavailable.) McMeeking report.

McMeeking report (McMeeking, J. G.): Education. See: Harrod.

MC MICHAEL, PAUL. fl. 1928. American petroleum chemist. Cited in: Chem. Abstr., Decenn. Index, 1927-1936. McMichael viscosity?

MAC MICHAEL, R. F. fl. 1916-1920. American ceramics chemist. Cited in: Chem. Abstr., Decenn. Index, 1917-1926. MacMichael viscometer (or torsional viscometer).

MacMichael viscometer (or torsional viscometer) (MacMichael, R. F.): Engineering and Industry. See: Chem. Abstr., vol. 14, p. 2567; Thrush.

McMichael viscosity (McMichael, Paul?): Engineering and Industry. See: Thrush.

MAC MILLAN, DONALD BAXTER. 1874-1970. American Arctic explorer. See: Nat. Cycl. Amer. Biog., vol. E, pp. 42-43. McMillan expedition.

McMillan expedition (MacMillan, Donald Baxter): Exploration. See: Jameson.

ACMILLAN, JOHN. 1670-1753. Scottish religious leader. See: Dict. at. Biog. Macmillanites.

C MILLAN, JOHN LOUDON. 1859-1946. American manufacturer and ventor. See: Nat. Cycl. Amer. Biog., vol. 35, pp. 236-237. McMillan pesetting-machine.

cMillan typesetting-machine (McMillan, John Loudon): Printing. See: ockwood.

acmillanites (Macmillan, John): Religion. See: Brewer; Canney.

AC MUNN, CHARLES ALEXANDER. 1852-1911. English pathologist. See: ho Was Who, 1897-1916. MacMunn's test.

acMunn's test (MacMunn, Charles Alexander): Medicine. See: Dorland.

cMurray test (McMurray, Thomas Porter): Medicine. See: Stedman.

C MURRAY, THOMAS PORTER. 1887-1949. English orthopedic surgeon. ee: Brit. Med. J., vol. 2 (Nov. 26, 1949), pp. 1236-1239. McMurray test, cMurray's operation, McMurray's sign.

cMurray's operation (McMurray, Thomas Porter): Medicine. See: Kelly.

cMurray's sign (McMurray, Thomas Porter): Medicine. See: Blakiston's ould.

acNab('s) cypress (MacNab, James): Botany. See: Webster's 3d.; inburne.

AC NAB, JAMES. 1810-1878. Scottish botanist. Cited in: Royal Soc. at. Sci. Pap., 1874-1883. MacNab('s) cypress.

McNabb Doctrine (McNabb family): Law. See: Black.

C NABB FAMILY. No dates. American mountaineers. (Biography source navailable.) McNabb Doctrine.

'Naghten (McNaughten) rule (or test) (M'Naughten, Daniel): Law. See: lack; Dorland; English; Hinsie; Hoult; Stedman.

C NAIR, ARNOLD DUNCAN MC NAIR, 1ST BARON. 1885- . English dministrator. See: Who's Who, 1975. McNair Report.

McNair Report (McNair, Arnold Duncan McNair, 1st Baron): Education. See: ncyc. Brit., 1973 under "Higher Education," vol. 11, p. 483b.

C NALLY, JAMES OSBORNE. 1903- . American electrical engineer. ee: Amer. Men and Women Sci., 12th ed. McNally tube?

McNally-Norton jig (McNally Pittsburgh Manufacturing Corp. and Norton, ertram): Engineering and Industry. See: Thrush.

McNally tube (McNally, James Osborne?): Electronics. See: Hughes; Markus.

McNally-Vissac dryer (McNally Pittsburgh Manufacturing Corporation and issac, Gustave Andre): Engineering and Industry. See: Thrush.

McNamara clamp (Derivation undetermined): Engineering and Industry. See: hrush.

C NARY, CHARLES LINZA. 1874-1944. American legislator. See: Biog. irect. Amer. Congress. Clarke-McNary Act, McNary-Haugen Bill (or farm elief Bill).

McNary-Haugen Bill (or farm relief Bill) (McNary, Charles Linza and Haugen, Gilbert N.): Politics. See: Jameson; Morris; Smith; Winburne.

C NAUGHT, JOHN. fl. 1873. English engineer. (Biography source un-vailable.) McNaughted engine.

McNaughted engine (McNaught, John): Engineering and Industry. See: uger.

M'NAUGHTEN, DANIEL. d. 1865. English criminal. See: Boase. M'Naghten (McNaughten) rule (or test).

MAC NEAL, WARD J. 1881-1946. American bacteriologist. See: World ho's Who Sci. MacNeal's tetrachrome stain, Novy and MacNeal's blood gar.

MacNeal's tetrachrome stain (MacNeal, Ward J.): Medicine. See: Stedman.

C NEMAR, QUINN. 1900- . American psychologist and statistician. ee: World Who's Who Sci. McNemar's test, Terman-McNemar test of mental bility.

McNemar's test (McNemar, Quinn): Statistics. See: Kendall.

McNulty grip (Derivation undetermined): Engineering and Industry. See: Auger.

Macon('s) Bill no. 2 (Macon, Nathaniel): History. See: Jameson; Morris.

MACON, NATHANIEL. 1757-1837. American legislator. See: Dict. Amer. Biog. Macon('s) Bill no. 2.

MC PHAIL, MURCHIE KILBURN. 1907- . Canadian physiologist. See: World Who's Who Sci. McPhail test.

McPhail test (McPhail, Murchie Kilburn): Medicine. See: Stedman.

MC PHEETERS, HERMAN OSCAR. 1891- . American surgeon. See: Wisconsin Med. J., vol. 42 (1943), p. 701. McPheeters' test, McPheeters' treatment (or sponge heart).

McPheeters' test (McPheeters, Herman Oscar): Medicine. See: Kelly.

McPheeters' treatment (or sponge heart) (McPheeters, Herman Oscar): Medicine. See: Dorland; Kelly.

McQuaid-Ehn test (McQuaid, Harry W. and Ehn, E. W.): Engineering and Industry. See: Thrush; Van Nostrand Sci. Encyc.

MC QUAID, HARRY W. fl. 1923-1965. English metallurgical engineer. Cited in: Chem. Abstr. McQuaid-Ehn test.

MACQUARIE, LACHLAN. 1761-1824. English general and governor of New South Wales. See: Dict. Nat. Biog. Macquarie perch, Macquarie pine, Macquarie style.

Macquarie perch (Macquarie, Lachlan): Zoology. See: Webster's 3d.

Macquarie pine (Macquarie, Lachlan): Botany. See: Webster's 3d.

Macquarie style (Macquarie, Lachlan): Architecture. See: Brewer.

MacQuarrie('s) test (for mechanical ability) (MacQuarrie, Thomas William): Psychology. See: Chaplin; Dorland.

MAC QUARRIE, THOMAS WILLIAM. fl. 1927. American psychologist. Cited in: Mansell. MacQuarrie('s) test (for mechanical ability).

MACQUER, PIERRE JOSEPH. 1718-1784. French chemist. See: Dict. Sci. Biog. Macquer's salt.

Macquer's salt (Macquer, Pierre Joseph): Chemistry. See: Charnock.

MacQuisten tube process (Derivation undetermined): Engineering and Industry. See: Thrush.

MACRAE, JOHN. 1866-1944. American publisher. See: Who Was Who Amer., 1943-1950. E. P. Dutton-John Macrae Award.

Macri reagent (Macri, V.?): Chemistry. See: Van Nostrand Chem. Dict.

Macri test reaction for manganese (Macri, V.): Chemistry. See: Van Nostrand Chem. Dict.

MACRI, V. fl. 1918. Italian chemist. Cited in: Chem. Abstr., Decenn. Index, 1917-1926. Macri reagent?, Macri test reaction for manganese.

MACRO, COX. 1683-1767. English antiquary. See: Dict. Nat. Biog. Macro plays.

Macro plays (Macro, Cox): Literature. See: Barnhart (Eng. Lit.).

macroblast of Naegeli (Naegeli, Otto?): Medicine. See: Stedman under "erythroblast."

MAC WILLIAM, JOHN ALEXANDER. 1857-1937. English physician. See: World Who's Who Sci. MacWilliam's test.

MacWilliam's test (MacWilliam, John Alexander): Medicine. See: Dorland; Stedman.

Madame Bovary (Bovary, Emma): Generic Word. See: Hendrickson.

MADARAS, JULIUS D. fl. 1941-1955. American engineer. Cited in: Chem. Abstr., Decenn. Index, 1937-1946. Madaras system.

Madaras system (Madaras, Julius D.): Engineering and Industry. See: Thrush.

Maddox double prism (Maddox, Ernest Edmund): Medicine. See: Dorland; Stedman.

MADDOX, ERNEST EDMUND. 1860-1933. English ophthalmologist. See: World Who's Who Sci. Maddox double prism, Maddox rod (test).

Maddox rod (test) (Maddox, Ernest Edmund): Medicine. See: Dorland; English; Webster's 3d.; Wolman.

MADDRELL, ROBERT. fl. 1845-1848. English? chemist. Cited in: Royal Soc. Cat. Sci. Pap., 1800-1863. Maddrell salt.

Maddrell salt (Maddrell, Robert): Chemistry. See: Hackh.

Madeleine (pastry) (Paulmier, Madeleine): Food and Drink. See: De Sola; Hendrickson.

Madelung constant (Madelung, Erwin): Physics. See: Ballentyne; Internat. Dict. Phys. Elec.; New Encyc. Brit., 1974, Microp.; Thrush.

Madelung energy (Madelung, Erwin): Physics. See: Thewlis.

MADELUNG, ERWIN. b. 1881. German physicist. See: Pogg., vols. 5, 6, 7a. Madelung constant, Madelung energy, Madelung expression for electrical potential due to infinite linear array.

Madelung expression for electrical potential due to infinite linear array (Madelung, Erwin): Physics. See: Internat. Dict. Ap. Math.

MADELUNG, OTTO WILHELM. 1846-1926. German surgeon. See: Biog. Lex. hervorr. Aerzte, 1880-1930. Madelung's deformity (or subluxation), Madelung's disease (or neck), Madelung's operation, Marfan-Madelung syndrome.

Madelung synthesis (Madelung, Walter Otto): Chemistry. See: Van Nostrand Chem. Dict.

MADELUNG, WALTER OTTO. b. 1879. German organic chemist. See: Pogg., vols. 5, 6. Madelung synthesis.

Madelung's deformity (or subluxation) (Madelung, Otto Wilhelm): Medicine. See: Dorland; Jablonski; Stedman.

Madelung's disease (or neck) (Madelung, Otto Wilhelm): Medicine. See: Dorland; Jablonski; Stedman. Also known as: Buschke's disease, Launois-Bensaude syndrome.

Madelung's operation (Madelung, Otto Wilhelm): Medicine. See: Dorland; Stedman.

MADHVA (MADHAVACHARYA or ANANDATIRTHA). ca. 1199-ca. 1278. Hindu philosopher. See: New Encyc. Brit., 1974, Microp. Madhvas.

Madhvas (Madhva): Religion. See: Canney.

MADISON, JAMES. 1751-1836. American president. See: Dict. Amer. Biog. Madisonian (or Madisonism), Madison's Journal, Madison's war.

Madisonian (or Madisonism) (Madison, James): Politics. See: Mathews, M.M; Webster's 3d.

Madison's Journal (Madison, James): History. See: Smith.

Madison's war (Madison, James): History. See: Mathews, M. M.

MADLENER, MAX. b. 1868. German gynecologist. See: Munch. Med. Wchnschr., vol. 85 (1938), p. 65. Madlener operation.

Madlener operation (Madlener, Max): Medicine. See: Kelly; Stedman.

Madonna (Mary, Virgin-Mother): Fine Arts. See: Charnock; Webster's 3d.

Madonna lily (Mary, Virgin-Mother): Botany. See: Webster's 3d.; Winburne.

Madonnina (Mary, Virgin-Mother): Numismatics. See: Charnock.

Madow-Leipnik distribution (Madow, William Gregory and Leipnik, Roy Bergh): Statistics. See: Kendall.

MADOW, WILLIAM GREGORY. 1911- . American statistician. See: Amer. Men Sci., 10th ed. Madow-Leipnik distribution.

MADSEN, THORVALD JOHANNES MARIUS. 1870-1957. Danish bacteriologist. See: World Who's Who Sci. Arrhenius-Madsen theory.

Mae West (lifejacket) (West, Mae): Generic Word. See: Brewer; Hendrickson; Partridge; Quick; Webster's 3d.

Mae West silhouette (West, Mae): Fashion. See: Picken.

Maecenas (Maecenas, the statesman): Generic Word (generous patron of literature). See: Brewer; Partridge; Webster's 3d.

MAECENAS, THE STATESMAN. ca. 70-8 B.C. Roman statesman and patron of literature. See: Dict. Grk. Rom. Biog. Myth. Maecenas, Maecenatism, Mecaenatianum (wine).

Maecenatism (Maecenas, the statesman): Generic Word (patronage). See: Webster's 3d.

Maeder-Danis dystrophy (Maeder, G. and Danis, P.): Medicine. See: Jablonski.

MAEDER, G. fl. 1947. Swiss ophthalmologist. (Biography source unavailable.) Maeder-Danis dystrophy.

MAELZEL, JOHANN NEPOMUK. 1772-1838. German musician. See: Grove. Maelzel's metronome.

Maelzel's metronome (Maelzel, Johann Nepomuk): Music. See: Apel; Scholes; Webster's 3d.

MAETERLINCK, MAURICE POLYDORE MARIE BERNARD. 1862-1949. Belgian poet, dramatist and essayist. See: New Encyc. Brit., 1974, Microp. Maeterlinckian.

Maeterlinckian (Maeterlinck, Maurice Polydore Marie Bernard): Literature. See: Webster's 3d.

MAFFUCCI, ANGELO. 1847-1903. Italian physician. See: Biog. Lex. hervorr. Aerzte, 1880-1930. Maffucci's syndrome.

Maffucci-Kast syndrome (Maffucci, Angelo and Kast, Alfred). See: Maffucci's syndrome.

Maffucci's syndrome (Maffucci, Angelo): Medicine. See: Jablonski; Stedman. Also known as: Kast's syndrome, Maffucci-Kast syndrome.

MAGATH, THOMAS BYRD. 1895- . American parasitologist. See: Index-Cat. Med. Veter. Zool., vol. 10, 1948. Horton-Magath-Brown disease.

Magdalen(e) (Mary Magdalene, Saint): Generic Word (reformed prostitute). See: Harvey; Partridge; Webster's 3d.

MAGEE, KENNETH RAYMOND. 1926- . American neurologist. See: World Who's Who Sci. Shy-Magee disease.

Magellan (Magellan, Ferdinand): Generic Word (world traveler). See: Webster's 3d.

Magellan barberry (Magellan, Ferdinand): Botany. See: Winburne.

MAGELLAN, FERDINAND. 1480-1521. Portuguese navigator. See: Encyc. Brit., 1973. Magellan, Magellan barberry, Magellan fuchsia, Magellan (Magellanic) penguins, Magellania?, Magellanic clouds.

Magellan fuchsia (Magellan, Ferdinand): Botany. See: Winburne.

Magellan (Magellanic) penguins (Magellan, Ferdinand): Zoology. See: Encyc. Brit., 1973 under "Penguins," vol. 17, p. 552a.

Magellania (Magellan, Ferdinand?): Zoology. See: Pennak.

Magellanic clouds (Magellan, Ferdinand): Earth Sciences. See: Phyfe; Thewlis; Van Nostrand Sci. Encyc.

magen (or mogen) David (David, the king): Religion. See: Webster's 3d. Also known as: shield of David, star of David.

MAGENDANTZ, HEINZ. b. 1899. American physician. See: Amer. Med. Direct., 1963. Thannhauser-Magendantz syndrome.

MAGENDIE, FRANCOIS. 1783-1855. French physiologist. See: Dict. Sci. Biog. Bell-Magendie law, Hertwig-Magendie syndrome (phenomenon or sign), Magendie's foramen, Magendie's spaces.

Magendie-Hertwig phenomenon (sign or syndrome) (Magendie, Francois and Von Hertwig, Richard). See: Hertwig-Magendie syndrome (phenomenon or sign).

Magendie's foramen (Magendie, Francois): Anatomy. See: Donath; Dorland; Henderson; Stedman.

Magendie's law (Magendie, Francois). See: Bell-Magendie law.

Magendie's spaces (Magendie, Francois): Anatomy. See: Donath; Dorland; Stedman.

MAGGI, GIAN ANTONIO. 1856-1937. Italian physicist. See: Pogg., vols. 3, 4, 5, 6, 7b. Maggi-Righi-Leduc effect.

Maggi-Righi-Leduc effect (Maggi, Gian Antonio; Righi, Augusto; and Leduc, Sylvestre Anatole). See: Righi-Leduc effect.

MAGINOT, ANDRE. 1877-1932. French statesman. See: Encyc. Brit., 1973. Maginot line, Maginot (mentality).

Maginot line (Maginot, Andre): Military Science. See: Barnhart (Eng. Lit.); Harvey; Webster's 3d.

Maginot (mentality) (Maginot, Andre): Generic Word (delusionary defense). See: Hendrickson; Partridge.

MAGITOT, EMILE. 1833-1897. French oral surgeon. See: World Who's Who Sci. Magitot's disease.

Magitot's disease (Magitot, Emile): Medicine. See: Dorland; Jablonski; Stedman.

MAGNAN, VALENTIN J. J. 1835-1916. French psychiatrist. See: Biog. Lex. hervorr. Aerzte. Magnan's sign, Magnan's trombone movement.

MAGNANINI, GAETANO. b. 1866. Italian chemist. See: Pogg., vols. 4, 5, 6. Ciamician-Magnanini test.

Magnan's sign (Magnan, Valentin J. J.): Medicine. See: Dorland; Stedman.

Magnan's trombone movement (Magnan, Valentin J. J.): Medicine. See: Dorland; Stedman.

MAGNOL, PIERRE. 1638-1715. French physician and botanist. See: World Who's Who Sci. Magnolia.

Magnolia (Magnol, Pierre): Botany. See: Charnock; Hendrickson; Taylor, N.; Webster's 3d.

Magnus effect (Magnus, Heinrich Gustav): Physics. See: Ballentyne; Internat. Dict. Phys. Elec.; New Encyc. Brit., 1974, Microp.; Thewlis; Webster's 3d.

MAGNUS, HEINRICH GUSTAV. 1802-1870. German chemist and physicist. See: Dict. Sci. Biog. Magnus effect, Magnus rule, Magnus salt.

MAGNUS, RUDOLF. 1873-1927. German physiologist. See: Dict. Sci. Biog. Magnus' sign of death.

Magnus rule (Magnus, Heinrich Gustav): Chemistry. See: Hackh; Van Nostrand Chem. Dict.

Magnus salt (Magnus, Heinrich Gustav): Chemistry. See: Hackh.

Magnus' sign of death (Magnus, Rudolf): Medicine. See: Stedman.

MAGNUSSON, NILS HARALD. b. 1890. Swedish geologist. See: Svenska Maen Och Kvinnor. Magnussonite.

Magnussonite (Magnusson, Nils Harald): Earth Sciences. See: Thrush.

Magovern-Cromie prosthesis (Magovern, George Jerome and Cromie, John Buller). Medicine. See: Stedman.

MAGOVERN, GEORGE JEROME. 1923- . American chest and heart surgeon. See: World Who's Who Sci. Magovern-Cromie prosthesis.

MAGRASSI, FLAVIANO. 1908- . Italian pathologist. See: Who's Who Sci. Europe, 1972. Magrassi-Leonardi syndrome.

Magrassi-Leonardi syndrome (Magrassi, Flaviano and Leonardi, Giuseppe?): Medicine. See: Jablonski.

MAGUIRE, CONNOR (or CORNELIUS) (2d BARON OF ENNISKILLEN). 1616-1645. Irish rebel. See: Dict. Nat. Biog. Molly Maguires.

Magus, Simon. See: Simon Magus.

Magyary-Kossa, Gyula. See: Von Kossa, Julius.

Mahalanobis distance (or generalized distance) (Mahalanobis, Prasanta Chandra): Statistics. See: Internat. Dict. Ap. Math.; Kendall; Van Nostrand Sci. Encyc.

MAHALANOBIS, PRASANTA CHANDRA. 1893- . Indian statistician. See: Who's Who Brit. Sci., 1953. Mahalanobis distance (or generalized distance).

MAHAN, ALFRED THAYER. 1840-1914. American naval officer and historian. See: Dict. Nat. Biog. Mahan (destroyers).

Mahan (destroyers) (Mahan, Alfred Thayer): Weapons. See: Quick.

MAHAVIRA, VARDHAMANA JNATIPUTRA. fl. 6th c. B.C. Indian religious leader. See: Webster's Biog. Dict. Jain iconography, Jainism.

MAHER, J. J. E. 1857-1931. American physician. (Biography source unavailable.) Maher's disease.

Mahernia (Hermann, Paul): Botany. See: Charnock; Hendrickson.

Maher's disease (Maher, J. J. E.): Medicine. See: Dorland; Stedman.

MAHIEU, THOMAS (TOMMASO MAIOLI). fl. 1572. French bibliophile. See: Webster's Biog. Dict. Maioli style (book decoration).

Mahir ibn Tibbon, Jacob ben. See: Jacob ben Mahir ibn Tibbon.

Mahler bomb calorimeter (Mahler, P.): Engineering and Industry. See: Thrush.

MAHLER, P. fl. 1922. French engineer. Cited in: Chem. Abstr., vol. 17, p. 2041. Mahler bomb calorimeter.

MAHLER, RICHTER A. fl. 1895. German obstetrician. Cited in: Kelly. Mahler's sign.

Mahler's sign (Mahler, Richter A.): Medicine. See: Dorland; Stedman.

Mahmoudi (or Mamoudi) (coin) (Mahmud II): Numismatics. See: Charnock.

MAHMUD II. 1785-1839. Ottoman sultan of Turkey. See: Encyc. Brit., 1973. Mahmoudi (or Mamoudi) (coin).

Mahometan (Mohammad). See: Mohammedanism.

MAHONE, WILLIAM. 1826-1895. American Confederate general, legislator and engineer. See: Dict. Amer. Biog. Mahonists (Mahoneism or Mahoneites).

Mahonia (McMahon, Bernard): Botany. See: Taylor, N.; Webster's 3d.

Mahonists (Mahoneism or Mahoneites) (Mahone, William): History. See: Clapin; Mathews, M. M.

Mahound (Mohammed): Generic Word (idol). See: Charnock.

MAIA. Roman goddess of spring. See: Jobes. May.

Maid Marian (Maid Marian, the character): Generic Word (impudent, masculine woman). See: Charnock; Jobes, Phyfe.

Maid Marian (dance) (Maid Marian, the character): Dance. See: Charnock.

MAID MARIAN, THE CHARACTER. Participant in May Day games. See: Jobes. Maid Marian, Maid Marian (dance).

MAIER, RUDOLF ROBERT. 1824-1888. German physician. See: World Who's Who Sci. Kussmaul-Maier syndrome, Maier's sinus.

Maier's sinus (Maier, Rudolf Robert): Medicine. See: Dorland; Stedman.

MAILLARD, LOUIS CAMILLE. 1878-1936. French biochemist. See: Pogg., vols. 5, 6, 7b. Maillard reaction.

Maillard reaction (Maillard, Louis Camille): Chemistry. See: Hackh.

Maimonidean (Maimonides, Moses): Philosophy. See: Webster's 3d.

MAIMONIDES, MOSES. 1135-1204. Jewish philosopher. See: New Encyc. Brit., 1974. Maimonidean.

Main, Saint. See: Mevan, Saint.

MAIN, THOMAS FORREST. fl. 1937-1972. English psychiatrist. See: Med. Direct., 1972. Main's syndrome.

MAIN, THOMAS JOHN. 1818-1885. English mathematician and engineer. See: Dict. Nat. Biog. Main's machine?

Mainardi-Codazzi relations (Mainardi, Gasparo and Codazzi, Delfino): Mathematics. See: Internat. Dict. Ap. Math.

MAINARDI, GASPARO. 1800-1879. Italian mathematician. See: Pogg., vol. 3. Mainardi-Codazzi relations.

MAINE, SIR HENRY JAMES SUMNER. 1822-1888. English jurist. See: Internat. Encyc. Soc. Sci. Mainean shift.

Mainean shift (Maine, Sir Henry James Sumner): Anthropology. See: Winick.

MAININI, CARLOS. 1879-1943. Argentinian physician. See: Gran Encic. Argentina. Galli-Mainini test.

Mainini test (Mainini, Carlos). See: Galli-Mainini test.

MAINKA, CARL. 1874-1943. German geophysicist. See: Pogg., vols. 5, 6, 7a. Mainka seismograph.

Mainka seismograph (Mainka, Carl): Earth Sciences. See: Van Nostrand Sci. Encyc. under "Earthquake."

Main's machine (Main, Thomas John?): Printing. See: Lockwood.

Main's syndrome (Main, Thomas Forrest): Psychiatry. See: Hinsie.

Maintenon (Maintenon, Francoise D'Aubigne, Marquise de): Generic Word (mistress). See: Hendrickson.

MAINTENON, FRANCOISE D'AUBIGNE, MARQUISE DE. 1635-1719. French mistress of Louis XIV. See: Encyc. Brit., 1973. a la Maintenon, Maintenon.

Maioli style (book decoration) (Mahieu, Thomas): Applied Arts. See: Harrod.

Maioli, Tommaso. See: Mahieu, Thomas.

MAIRE, MAURICE. fl. 1906. French chemist. Cited in: Chem. Abstr. Decenn. Index, 1906-1917. Blaise-Maire reaction.

MAISONNEUVE, JULES GERMAIN FRANCOIS. 1809-1897. French surgeon. See: World Who's Who Sci. Maisonneuve's bandage, Maisonneuve's urethrotome.

Maisonneuve's bandage (Maisonneuve, Jules Germain Francois): Medicine. See: Dorland.

Maisonneuve's urethrotome (Maisonneuve, Jules Germain Francois): Medicine. See: Blakiston's Gould; Dorland.

MAISSIAT, JACQUES HENRI. 1805-1878. French anatomist. See: Biog. Lex. hervorr. Aerzte. Maissiat's band.

Maissiat's band (Maissiat, Jacques Henri): Anatomy. See: Donath; Stedman.

MAITLAND, JOHN. 1732-1779. Scottish officer serving in America. See: Valentine. Maitland's powder-ship.

MAITLAND, SIR PEREGRINE. 1777-1854. English general and colonial administrator. See: Dict. Nat. Biog. Maitland treaties.

Maitland treaties (Maitland, Sir Peregrine): History. See: Encyc. Brit., 1973 under "Orange Free State," vol. 16, p. 1025c.

Maitland's powder-ship (Maitland, John): History. See: Jameson.

MAIXNER, EMMERICH. 1847-1920. Czech physician. See: Biog. Lex. hervorr. Aerzte, 1880-1930. Maixner's cirrhosis.

Maixner's cirrhosis (Maixner, Emmerich): Medicine. See: Dorland; Jablonski.

MAJOCCHI, DOMENICO. 1849-1929. Italian dermatologist. See: Biog. Lex. hervorr. Aerzte, 1880-1930. Majocchi's disease.

Majocchi's disease (Majocchi, Domenico): Medicine. See: Dorland; Jablonski; Stedman.

Major Mitchell (cockatoo) (Mitchell, Sir Thomas Livingstone): Zoology. See: Gray; Webster's 3d.

Majorana effect (Majorana, Ettore): Physics. See: Ballentyne; Van Nostrand Sci. Encyc.

MAJORANA, ETTORE. 1906-1938. Italian physicist. See: Dict. Sci. Biog. Majorana effect, Majorana force, Majorana neutrino (or particle), Majorana operator.

Majorana force (Majorana, Ettore): Physics. See: Ballentyne; Hughes; Internat. Dict. Ap. Math.; Van Nostrand Sci. Encyc.

Majorana neutrino (or particle) (Majorana, Ettore): Physics. See: Internat. Dict. Phys. Elec.; Markus.

Majorana operator (Majorana, Ettore): Physics. See: Internat. Dict. Phys. Elec.

MAKAI, ENDRE. fl. 1928. Hungarian surgeon. (Biography source unavailable.) Rothmann-Makai disease.

Makarov-Zemlianski-Prokin method (Makarov-Zemlianski, Ya. Ya. and Prokin, S. S.): Chemistry. See: Ballentyne.

MAKAROV-ZEMLIANSKI, YA. YA. fl. 1937. Russian chemist. Cited in: Chem. Abstr., Decenn. Index, 1937-1946. Makarov-Zemlianski-Prokin method.

MAKEHAM, WILLIAM MATTHEW. d. 1892. English statistician. See: World Who's Who Sci. Makeham's formula for bonds, Makeham's law (or hypothesis).

Makeham's formula for bonds (Makeham, William Matthew): Mathematics. See: James.

Makeham's law (or hypothesis) (Makeham, William Matthew): Mathematics. See: James; Stedman; Webster's 3d.

MAKINS, SIR GEORGE. 1853-1933. English surgeon. See: Who Was Who, 1929-1940. Makins' murmur.

Makins' murmur (Makins, Sir George): Medicine. See: Dorland.

Makinson and Treacy gauge (Makinson, R. E. B. and Treacy, Peter B.): Physics. See: Internat. Dict. Phys. Elec.

MAKINSON, R. E. B. fl. 1949-1970. Australian physicist. Cited in: Internat. Physics Astr. Direct., 1969-1970. Makinson and Treacy gauge.

Maklakoff applanation tonometer (Maklakoff, C.): Medicine. See: Stedman.

MAKLAKOFF, C. No dates. Russian ophthalmologist. (Biography source unavailable.) Maklakoff applanation tonometer.

Maksutov-Bouwers telescope (Maksutov, Dmitriy Dmitrievich and Bouwers, Albert). See: Maksutov camera.

Maksutov camera (Maksutov, Dmitriy Dmitrievich): Astronomy. See: Satterthwaite. Also known as: Maksutov-Bouwers telescope.

Maksutov corrector (Maksutov, Dmitriy Dmitrievich): Astronomy. See: Internat. Dict. Phys. Elec.

MAKSUTOV, DMITRIY DMITRIEVICH. 1894- . Russian optician. See: World Who's Who Sci. Maksutov camera, Maksutov corrector, Schmidt-Maksutov telescope.

MALACARNE, MICHELE VINCENZO GIACINTO. 1744-1816. Italian surgeon and anatomist. See: Biog. Lex. hervorr. Aerzte. Malacarne's pyramid, Malacarne's space.

Malacarne's pyramid (Malacarne, Michele Vincenzo Giacinto): Anatomy. See: Donath; Dorland; Stedman.

Malacarne's space (Malacarne, Michele Vincenzo Giacinto): Anatomy. See: Donath.

MALACHY, SAINT. 1094-1148. Irish prelate. See: Encyc. Brit., 1973. Prophecies of St. Malachy.

Malakhovskii, Vladislav. See: Warnerke, Leon.

MALAN, DANIEL FRANCOIS. 1874-1959. South African political leader. See: Encyc. Brit., 1973. Malania.

Malania (Malan, Daniel Francois): Zoology. See: Webster's 3d.

MALAPROP, MRS. Character in Richard Sheridan's comedy, "The Rivals," (1775). See: Harvey. Malapropism.

Malapropism (Malaprop, Mrs.): Generic Word (misuse of similar-sound words). See: Barnhart (Eng. Lit.); Funk; Scott.

Malassez' epithelial rests (Malassez, Louis Charles): Medicine. See: Stedman.

MALASSEZ, LOUIS CHARLES. 1842-1909. French physiologist. See: World Who's Who Sci. Malassez' epithelial rests, Malassezia furfur, Malassez's disease, Malassez's stain.

Malassezia furfur (Malassez, Louis Charles): Zoology. See: Blakiston's Gould; Dorland; Stedman.

Malassez's disease (Malassez, Louis Charles): Medicine. See: Jablonski.

Malassez's stain (Malassez, Louis Charles): Medicine. See: Stedman.

Malatesta-Di Nola reagent for copper, nickel and cobalt (Malatesta, Giuseppe and Di Nola, Ettore): Chemistry. See: Van Nostrand Chem. Dict.

Malatesta-Di Nola test reaction for gold and platinum (Malatesta, Giuseppe and Di Nola, Ettore): Chemistry. See: Van Nostrand Chem. Dict.

MALATESTA, GIUSEPPE. fl. 1913-1915. Italian chemist. Cited in: Chem. Abstr., vol. 9, p. 2200; vol. 8, p. 1397. Malatesta-Di Nola reagent for copper, nickel and cobalt, Malatesta-Di Nola test reaction for gold and platinum.

Malbrouck (monkey) (Malbrouk): Zoology. See: Webster's 3d.

MALBROUK. Probably a Crusader hero of an old French song. See: Harvey and Heseltine. Malbrouck (monkey).

MALCOLM, WILLIAM. fl. 18th c. English horticulturist. (Biography source unavailable.) Malcomia.

Malcomia (Malcolm, William): Botany. See: Taylor, N.

MALERBA, PASQUALE. 1849-1917. Italian physician. See: Biog. Lex. hervorr. Aerzte, 1880-1930. Malerba's test.

Malerba's test (Malerba, Pasquale): Medicine. See: Dorland; Stedman.

MALESHERBES, CHRETIEN GUILLAUME DE LAMOIGNON DE. 1721-1794. French statesman. See: Encyc. Brit., 1973. Malesherbia.

Malesherbia (Malesherbes, Chretien Guillaume de Lamoignon de): Botany. See: Webster's 3d.

MALET, CLAUDE FRANCOIS DE. 1754-1812. French general. See: Encyc. Brit., 1973. Malet's plot.

Malet's plot (Malet, Claude Francois de): History. See: Harbottle.

MALFATTI, GIAN FRANCESCO. 1731-1807. Italian mathematician. See: Dict. Sci. Biog. Malfatti resolvent, Malfatti's problem (or question).

Malfatti resolvent (Malfatti, Gian Francesco): Mathematics. See: Dict. Sci. Biog. under "Malfatti, Gian Francesco."

Malfatti's problem (or question) (Malfatti, Gian Francesco): Mathematics. See: Dict. Sci. Biog. under "Malfatti, Gian Francesco."

MALGAIGNE, JOSEPH FRANCOIS. 1806-1865. French surgeon. See: World Who's Who Sci. Malgaigne's amputation, Malgaigne's apparatus, Malgaigne's fossa (or triangle), Malgaigne's fracture, Malgaigne's hernia, Malgaigne's hooks, Malgaigne's luxation.

Malgaigne's amputation (Malgaigne, Joseph Francois): Anatomy. See: Dorland; Stedman.

Malgaigne's apparatus (Malgaigne, Joseph Francois): Medicine. See: Stedman.

Malgaigne's fossa (or triangle) (Malgaigne, Joseph Francois): Anatomy. See: Donath; Stedman.

Malgaigne's fracture (Malgaigne, Joseph Francois): Medicine. See: Jablonski.

Malgaigne's hernia (Malgaigne, Joseph Francois): Medicine. See: Dorland.

Malgaigne's hooks (Malgaigne, Joseph Francois): Medicine. See: Dorland; Stedman.

Malgaigne's luxation (Malgaigne, Joseph Francois): Medicine. See: Stedman.

MALHERBE, ALBERT. 1845-1915. French surgeon. See: Biog. Lex. hervorr. Aerzte, 1880-1930. Malherbe's epithelioma.

Malherbe-Chenantais epithelioma (Malherbe, Albert and Chenantais, J. E.). See: Malherbe's epithelioma.

Malherbe's epithelioma (Malherbe, Albert): Medicine. See: Jablonski. Also known as: Malherbe-Chenantais epithelioma.

MALIK IBN-ANAS. ca. 715-795. Moslem jurist. See: Encyc. Brit., 1973. Maliki (school), Malikite (or Malekite).

Maliki (school) (Malik ibn-Anas): Law. See: Webster's 3d.

Malikite (or Malekite) (Malik ibn-Anas): Law. See: Webster's 3d.

Malinche (Marina): Dance. See: Webster's 3d.

MALINOWSKI, E. fl. 19th c. Russian civil engineer. (Biography source unavailable.) Malinowskite.

Malinowskite (Malinowski, E.): Earth Sciences. See: Thrush; Webster's 3d.

Malintzin. See: Marina.

Malitzkii-Tubakaiev micro-test for sodium (Malitzkii, V. P. and Tubakaiev, V. A.): Chemistry. See: Van Nostrand Chem. Dict.

MALITZKII, V. P. fl. 1930. Russian? chemist. Cited in: Chem. Abstr., vol. 24, p. 3966. Malitzkii-Tubakaiev micro-test for sodium.

MALL, FRANKLIN PAINE. 1862-1917. American anatomist and embryologist. See: Dict. Sci. Biog. Mall's formula, periportal space of Mall.

MALLABY-DEELEY, SIR HARRY MALLABY, 1ST BARONET. 1863-1937. English parliamentarian. See: Who Was Who, 1929-1940. Mallaby-Deeleys.

Mallaby-Deeleys (Mallaby-Deeley, Sir Harry Mallaby, 1st Baronet): Generic Word (ready-wear clothes). See: Brewer; Partridge.

MALLADRA, ALESSANDRO. 1868-1945. Italian geologist. See: Diz. Encic. Ital. Malladrite.

Malladrite (Malladra, Alessandro): Earth Sciences. See: Thrush; Webster's 3d.

MALLARD, ERNEST (In full: FRANCOIS ERNEST). 1833-1894. French mineralogist. See: Dict. Sci. Biog. Mallardite.

Mallardite (Mallard, Ernest): Earth Sciences. See: Thrush; Webster's 3d.

Mallery's cow (Derivation undetermined): Generic Word (disappearance without a clue). See: Brewer.

MALLET, JOHN WILLIAM. 1832-1912. American chemist. See: Pogg., vols. 3, 4, 5. Mallet test reaction for tungsten.

Mallet test reaction for tungsten (Mallet, John William): Chemistry. See: Van Nostrand Chem. Dict.

Malliana (pears) (Derivation undetermined): Botany. See: Stenhouse.

MALLON, MARY. d. 1938. Irish cook. See: New York Times, Nov. 12, 1938, p. 17, col. 7. typhoid Mary.

Mallory battery (Derivation undetermined): Electronics. See: Hughes.

Mallory bodies (Mallory, Frank Burr): Medicine. See: Dorland; Stedman.

MALLORY, FRANK BURR. 1862-1941. American pathologist. See: World Who's Who Sci. Mallory bodies, Mallory leukemia?, Mallory's aniline blue stain, Mallory's stain for actinomyces, Mallory's triple stain, Mosse-Marchand-Mallory cirrhosis.

MALLORY, G(EORGE) KENNETH. 1900- . American pathologist. See: Amer. Men and Women Sci., 12th ed. Mallory-Weiss syndrome.

Mallory leukemia (Mallory, Frank Burr?): Medicine. See: Stedman.

Mallory-Weiss syndrome (Mallory, G(eorge) Kenneth and Weiss, Soma): Medicine. See: Jablonski; Stedman.

Mallory's aniline blue stain (Mallory, Frank Burr): Medicine. See: Dorland; Stedman.

Mallory's stain for actinomyces (Mallory, Frank Burr): Medicine. See: Dorland; Stedman.

Mallory's triple stain (Mallory, Frank Burr): Medicine. See: Dorland; Stedman.

Mall's formula (Mall, Franklin Paine): Medicine. See: Dorland; Stedman.

MALM, J. L. fl. 1913-1918. American? engineer. Cited in: Chem. Abstr., Decenn. Index, 1907-1916. Malm process.

Malm process (Malm, J. L.): Engineering and Industry. See: Thrush.

MALOWAN, SIEGFRIED LAURENS. b. 1892. Austrian chemist. See: Pogg., vols. 6, 7a. Malowan test reaction.

Malowan test reaction (Malowan, Siegfried Laurens): Chemistry. See: Van Nostrand Chem. Dict.

MALPIGHI, MARCELLO. 1628-1694. Italian anatomist and physiologist. See: Dict. Sci. Biog. Malpighia, Malpighian body (bodies), Malpighian canal, Malpighian capsule, Malpighian cell, Malpighian corpuscle, Malpighian glomerulus (or tuft), Malpighian layer, Malpighian nodule, Malpighian pyramid(s), Malpighian stigmas, Malpighian tubule(s), Malpighi's saccules.

Malpighia (Malpighi, Marcello): Botany. See: Taylor, N.; Webster's 3d.

Malpighian body (bodies) (Malpighi, Marcello): Anatomy. See: Dorland; Pennak; Stedman.

Malpighian canal (Malpighi, Marcello): Anatomy. See: Stedman. Also known as: Gartner's canal.

Malpighian capsule (Malpighi, Marcello): Anatomy. See: Stedman. Also known as: Bowman's capsule, Mueller's capsule.

Malpighian cell (Malpighi, Marcello): Anatomy. See: Gray; Webster's 3d.

Malpighian corpuscle (Malpighi, Marcello): Anatomy. See: Dorland; Gray; Stedman.

Malpighian glomerulus (or tuft) (Malpighi, Marcello): Anatomy. See: Stedman; Webster's 3d.

Malpighian layer (Malpighi, Marcello): Anatomy. See: Henderson; Stedman; Webster's 3d. Also known as: rete Malpighii.

Malpighian nodule (Malpighi, Marcello): Anatomy. See: Gray.

Malpighian pyramid(s) (Malpighi, Marcello): Anatomy. See: Henderson; Stedman; Webster's 3d.

Malpighian stigmas (Malpighi, Marcello): Anatomy. See: Stedman.

Malpighian tubule(s) (Malpighi, Marcello): Zoology. See: Gray; Pennak; Stedman; Van Nostrand Sci. Encyc.

Malpighi's saccules (Malpighi, Marcello): Anatomy. See: Donath.

Malter effect (Malter, Louis): Physics. See: Ballentyne.

MALTER, LOUIS. 1907-   . American physicist. See: Amer. Men and Women Sci., 12th ed. Malter effect.

MALTHUS, THOMAS ROBERT. 1766-1834. English economist and demographer. See: Inter. Encyc. Soc. Sci. Malthusian theory (of population).

Malthusian theory (of population) (Malthus, Thomas Robert): Sociology. See: Fairchild; Hoult; Seldon.

Malus-Dupin theorem (Malus, Etienne Louis and Dupin, Pierre-Charles-Francois). See: Malus' theorem.

MALUS, ETIENNE LOUIS. 1775-1812. French engineer and physicist. See: Dict. Sci. Biog. Malus' law (or cosine squared law), Malus theorem.

Malus' law (or cosine squared law) (Malus, Etienne Louis): Physics. See: Ballentyne; Internat. Dict. Ap. Math.

Malus' theorem (Malus, Etienne Louis): Physics. See: Ballentyne. Also known as: Malus-Dupin theorem.

MALY, RICHARD (In full: LEO RICHARD). 1839-1894. Austrian physiological chemist. See: Biog. Lex. hervorr. Aerzte. Maly's test.

Maly's test (Maly, Richard): Medicine. See: Dorland. Also known as: Van der Velden's test for free hydrochloric acid.

MAMERCUS, AEMILIUS. fl. 391. Roman praetor. (Biography source unavailable.) Aemilian Law.

Mammon (Mammon, the god): Generic Word (wealth). See: Charnock; Phyfe.

MAMMON, THE GOD. Syrian god of riches and worldliness. See: Jobes. Mammon, Mammonist.

Mammonist (Mammon, the god): Generic Word. See: Charnock.

MAMOU, HENRY. 1903-   . French endocrinologist. See: Who's Who France, 1975-1976. Siegal-Cattan-Mamou disease.

Man Friday (Friday): Generic Word (right-hand man). See: Webster's 3d.

Man of Ross. See: Kyrle, John.

MANASSE, ERNESTO. 1875-1922. Italian mineralogist. See: Diz. Encic. Ital. Manasseite.

MANASSE, OTTO. b. 1861. German chemist. Cited in: Royal Soc. Cat. Sci. Pap., 1884-1900. Lederer-Manasse reaction.

MANASSEH. Elder son of Joseph in the Old Testament (Gen 41:50-52). See: Hastings (Dict. Bible). Manassite.

MANASSEH. d. ca. 639 B.C. King of Judah. See: Encyc. Brit., 1973. Prayer of Manasses.

Manasseite (Manasse, Ernesto): Earth Sciences. See: Webster's 3d.

Manassite (Manasseh): History. See: Webster's 3d.

MANCHESTER, BENJAMIN. 1911-   . American physician. See: Amer. Men and Women Sci., 12th ed. Manchester method for measuring capillary blood prothrombin.

Manchester method for measuring capillary blood prothrombin (Manchester, Benjamin): Medicine. Cited in: Amer. Men and Women Sci., 12th ed.

Manchester ovoid (Derivation undetermined): Medicine. See: Stedman.

Manchot-Kampschulte test (Manchot, Wilhelm and Kampschulte, Willy): Chemistry. See: Van Nostrand Chem. Dict.

Manchot-Scherer reagent (Manchot, Wilhelm and Scherer, Otto): Chemistry. See: Van Nostrand Chem. Dict.

MANCHOT, WILHELM. 1869-1945. German chemist. See: Pogg., vols. 4, 5, 6, 7a. Manchot-Kampschulte test, Manchot-Scherer reagent.

MANDEL, JOHN ALFRED. 1865-1929. American physiological chemist. See: Pogg., vol. 6. Mandel-Neuberg reagent for aldo- and ketoacids, Mandel's test.

Mandel-Neuberg reagent for aldo- and ketoacids (Mandel, John Alfred and Neuberg, Carl): Chemistry. See: Van Nostrand Chem. Dict.

MANDELBAUM, MAIER. b. 1881. German bacteriologist. Cited in: Index-Cat. Libr. Surg.-Gen. Off., 3rd Ser., vol. 7, 1928. Mandelbaum's reaction.

Mandelbaum's reaction (Mandelbaum, Maier): Medicine. See: Dorland; Stedman.

MANDELIN, KARL F. fl. 1881-1885. Russian chemist. Cited in: Royal Soc. Cat. Sci. Pap., 1874-1883. Mandelin('s) reagent (for alkaloids).

Mandelin('s) reagent (for alkaloids) (Mandelin, Karl F.): Chemistry. See: Hackh; Stedman; Van Nostrand Chem. Dict.

Mandel's test (Mandel, John Alfred): Medicine. See: Dorland; Stedman.

Mandel'shtam effect (Mandel'stam, Leonid Isaakovic): Physics. See: Ballentyne.

MANDEL'STAM, LEONID ISAAKOVIC. 1879-1944. Russian physicist. See: Pogg., vols. 5, 6, 7b. Mandel'shtam effect.

Mandevilla (Mandeville, John Henry): Botany. See: Taylor, N.

MANDEVILLE, JOHN HENRY. d. 1861. English diplomat. See: Boase. Mandevilla.

MANDL, LOUIS. 1812-1881. Hungarian physician in Paris. See: Biog. Lex. hervorr. Aerzte. Mandl's solution.

Mandl's solution (Mandl, Louis): Medicine. See: Dorland.

Mandousin (sword) (Derivation undetermined): Weapons. See: Wagner (More Names).

Mandozy (Mendoza, Daniel): Generic Word (term of endearment). See: Charnock.

MANDT, MARTIN WILHELM VON. 1800-1858. German physician and naturalist. See: Biog. Lex. hervorr. Aerzte. Mandt's guillemot.

Mandt's guillemot (Mandt, Martin Wilhelm von): Zoology. See: Webster's 3d.

MANEA, A. fl. 1909. Rumanian chemist. Cited in: Chem. Abstr., vol. 3, p. 490. Manea test reaction.

Manea test reaction (Manea, A.): Chemistry. See: Van Nostrand Chem. Dict.

Manes. See: Mani.

Manetti (rose) (Manetti, Saverio): Botany. See: Partridge; Webster's 3d.

MANETTI, SAVERIO. 1723-1785. Italian botanist. See: Nouv. Biog. Univ. Manetti (rose), Manettia.

Manettia (Manetti, Saverio): Botany. See: Taylor, N.; Webster's 3d.

Mangent-Marion reagent for ammonia (Manget, Charles Marie Ferdinand and Marion, F.): Chemistry. See: Van Nostrand Chem. Dict.

Mangent-Marion test for formaldehyde (Manget, Charles Marie Ferdinand and Marion, F.): Chemistry. See: Van Nostrand Chem. Dict.

MANGET, CHARLES MARIE FERDINAND. b. 1855. French chemist. Cited in: Royal Soc. Cat. Sci. Pap., 1884-1900. Mangent-Marion reagent for ammonia, Mangent-Marion test for formaldehyde.

MANGIN, ALPHONSE FRANCOIS EUGENE. 1825-1885. French physicist. See: Genie Civil, vol. 8 (1885-1886), p. 47. Mangin mirror.

MANGIN, LOUIS-ALEXANDRE. 1852-1937. French botanist. See: World Who's Who Sci. Mangin solutions for cellulose?

Mangin mirror (Mangin, Alphonse Francois Eugene): Physics. See: Thewlis.

Mangin solutions for cellulose (Mangin, Louis-Alexandre?): Chemistry. See: Van Nostrand Chem. Dict.

Mangini solution for alkaloids (Derivation undetermined): Chemistry. See: Van Nostrand Chem. Dict.

MANGOLDT, HANS HERMANN FRIEDRICH HOFRAT. 1857-1909. German surgeon. See: Biog. Jahrb. Deut. Nekr., vol. 14, 1909. Mangoldt's epithelial grafting.

Mangoldt's epithelial grafting (Mangoldt, Hans Hermann Friedrich Hofrat): Medicine. See: Dorland.

MANI (MANES or MANICHAEUS). ca. 215-ca. 274. Iranian founder of sect. See: Encyc. Brit., 1973. Manichaeism (or Manichaean).

Manichaeism (or Manichaean) (Mani): Religion. See: Attwater; Canney; Harvey; Mathews, S.; New Encyc. Brit., 1974, Microp.; Webster's 3d.

MAN'KOVSKIY, BORIS NIKITICH. 1883-1962. Russian neuropathologist. See: Who Was Who USSR. Mankowsky's syndrome.

Mankowsky's syndrome (Man'kovskiy, Boris Nikitich): Medicine. See: Jablonski.

MANLEY, FREDERICK T. fl. 1926-1931. American chemist. Cited in: Chem. Abstr., vol. 25, p. 808. Holmes-Manley process.

MANLY, CHARLES MATTHEWS. 1876-1927. American mechanical engineer. See: World Who's Who Sci. Manly gear.

Manly gear (Manly, Charles Matthews): Engineering and Industry. See: Auger.

Mann Act (Mann, James Robert): Politics. See: Morris.

Mann-Bollman fistula (Mann, Frank Charles and Bollman, Jesse Louis): Medicine. See: Dorland; Stedman.

Mann-Elkins Act (Mann, James Robert and Elkins, Stephen Benton): Politics. See: Morris; Smith.

MANN, FRANK CHARLES. 1887-1962. American surgeon and physiologist. See: J.A.M.A., vol. 182, no. 6 (Nov. 10, 1962), p. 695. Mann-Bollman Fistula, Mann-Williamson operation (or ulcer).

MANN, HENRY BERTHOLD. 1905- . Austrian-born American mathematician. See: World Who's Who Sci. Mann-Whitney test.

MANN, JAMES ROBERT. 1856-1922. American legislator. See: Dict. Amer. Biog. Mann Act, Mann-Elkins Act.

MANN, LUDWIG. 1866-1936. German neurologist. See: Biog. Lex. hervorr. Aerzte, 1880-1930. Mann's syndrome, Wernicke-Mann hemiplegia (or type).

MANN, MARGARET. fl. 1894-1968. American librarian. See: Who Was Who Amer., 1969-1973. Margaret Mann Citation.

Mann test paper for water in ether or alcohol (Derivation undetermined): Chemistry. See: Van Nostrand Chem. Dict.

Mann-Whitney test (Mann, Henry Berthold and Whitney, Donald Ransom). See: Wilcoxon's test.

Mann-Williamson operation (or ulcer) (Mann, Frank Charles and Williamson, Carl Sneed): Medicine. See: Dorland; Stedman.

Mannehim process (Derivation undetermined): Engineering and Industry. See: Thrush.

MANNERHEIM, BARON CARL GUSTAF EMIL. 1867-1951. Finnish marshal and patriot. See: Encyc. Brit., 1973. Mannerheim line.

Mannerheim line (Mannerheim, Baron Carl Gustaf Emil): Military Science. Cited in: Encyc. Brit., 1973.

Mannesmann process (Mannesmann, Reinhard M.): Engineering and Industry. See: Thrush; Webster's 3d.

MANNESMANN, REINHARD M. 1856-1922. German industrialist and inventor. See: Deut. Biog. Jahrb., vol. 4, 1922. Mannesmann process.

MANNHEIM, JULIE. b. 1890. German chemist. Cited in: Mansell. Grossmann-Mannheim reagent.

MANNICH, CARL. 1877-1947. German chemist. See: World Who's Who Sci. Mannich reaction.

Mannich reaction (Mannich, Carl): Chemistry. See: Ballentyne; Hackh; Van Nostrand Chem. Dict.; Webster's 3d.

MANNING, ROBERT. fl. 1876-1897. English civil engineer. See: Inst. Civ. Eng. Proc., vol. 131 (1898) pp. 370-371. Manning's formula (or equation)?

Manning's formula (or equation) (Manning, Robert?): Engineering and Industry. See: New Encyc. Brit., 1974, Microp., under "Roughness"; Thrush.

MANNKOPF, EMIL WILHELM. 1836-1918. German physician. See: Biog. Lex. hervorr. Aerzte. Mannkopf's sign.

Mannkopf's sign (Mannkopf, Emil Wilhelm): Medicine. See: Dorland; Stedman.

MANNLICHER, FERDINAND. 1848-1904. Austrian engineer. See: New Encyc. Brit., 1974, Microp. Mannlicher (pistol), Mannlicher (rifle).

Mannlicher (pistol) (Mannlicher, Ferdinand): Weapons. See: Partridge.

Mannlicher (rifle) (Mannlicher, Ferdinand): Weapons. See: Partridge.

Mann's syndrome (Mann, Ludwig): Medicine. See: Jablonski.

MANOILOFF, EWSTATIE. fl. 1905-1915. Russian physician. Cited in: Index-Cat. Libr. Surg.-Gen. Off., 2d Ser., vol. 10, 1905. Manoiloff's (Manoilov's) reaction.

Manoiloff's (Manoilov's) reaction (Manoiloff, Ewstatie): Medicine. See: Dorland.

Manoletina (Sanchez, Manuel R.): Recreation and Sports. See: Webster's 3d.

MANOUVRIER, LEONCE PIERRE. 1850-1927. French anthropologist. See: World Who's Who Sci. Manouvrier's skelic index.

Manouvrier's skelic index (Manouvrier, Leonce Pierre): Anthropology. See: Winick.

Mansard (roof) (Mansart, Francois): Architecture. See: Brewer; Briggs; Partridge; Thrush; Webster's 3d.

MANSART, FRANCOIS. 1598-1667. French architect. See: Osborne. Mansard (roof).

Mansbridge capacitor (Mansbridge, G. F.): Electronics. See: Hughes.

MANSBRIDGE, G. F. fl. 1908-1920. English electrical engineer. Cited in: Glazebrook, vol. 2. Mansbridge capacitor.

Manseau reagent for opium alkaloids (Derivation undetermined): Chemistry. See: Van Nostrand Chem. Dict.

Mansfield, 1st Earl of. See: Murray, William (1st Earl of Mansfield).

MANSFIELD, GEORGE ROGERS. 1875-1947. American geologist. See: Who Was Who Amer., 1969-1973. Mansfieldite.

Mansfieldite (Mansfield, George Rogers): Earth Sciences. See: Thrush; Webster's 3d.

Mansfield's judgment (Murray, William, 1st Earl of Mansfield): History. See: Steinberg.

Manson effect (Manson, Mahlon E.): Engineering and Industry. See: Thrush.

MANSON, MAHLON E. fl. 1923-1936. American? chemist. (Biography source unavailable.) Manson effect.

MANSON, SIR PATRICK. 1844-1922. English parasitologist. See: Dict. Sci. Biog. Mansonella, Mansonelliasis, Mansonia, Manson's disease (or schistosoma), Manson's eye worm, Manson's pyosis.

Mansonella (Manson, Sir Patrick): Zoology. See: Stedman; Webster's 3d. Also known as: Ozzard's filarial parasite.

Mansonelliasis (Manson, Sir Patrick): Medicine. See: Stedman. Also known as: Ozzard's filariasis.

Mansonia (Manson, Sir Patrick): Zoology. See: Pennak; Stedman; Webster's 3d.

Manson's disease (or schistosoma) (Manson, Sir Patrick): Medicine. See: Dorland; Stedman; Webster's 3d.

Manson's eye worm (Manson, Sir Patrick): Medicine. See: Stedman; Winburne.

Manson's pyosis (Manson, Sir Patrick): Medicine. See: Stedman.

Manton (gun or pistol) (Manton, Joseph). See: Joe Manton (shotgun).

MANTON, JOSEPH. ca. 1766-1835. English gunmaker. See: Dict. Nat. Biog. Joe Manton (shotgun).

MANTOUX, CHARLES. 1887-1947. French physician. See: World Who's Who Sci. Mantoux test.

Mantoux test (Mantoux, Charles): Medicine. See: Dorland; Stedman; Webster's 3d.

MANU. Progenitor of the human race in ancient Hindu mythology. See: Jobes. Laws of Manu.

MANUEL I. 1469-1521. King of Portugal. See: Encyc. Brit., 1973. Manueline (style).

Manueline (style) (Manuel I): Architecture. See: Osborne.

manus Christi (Jesus Christ): Food and Drink. See: Charnock.

MANUTIUS, ALDUS. 1449-1515. Italian printer and scholar. See: New Encyc. Brit., 1974, Microp. Aldine Club, Aldine (editions), Aldine leaves, Aldine press, Aldine style, Aldine type.

MANZ, WILHELM. 1833-1911. German ophthalmologist. See: Biog. Lex. hervorr. Aerzte. Manz's disease, Manz's glands (or utricular glands).

Manzana (Calvena, C. Matius): Agriculture. See: Webster's 3d.

MANZONI, ALESSANDRO FRANCESCO TOMMASO ANTONIO. 1785-1873. Italian poet. See: Encyc. Brit., 1973. Manzoni Requiem.

Manzoni Requiem (Manzoni, Alessandro Francesco Tommaso Antonio): Music. See: Apel. Also known as: Verdi's Requiem.

Manz's disease (Manz, Wilhelm): Medicine. See: Dorland.

Manz's glands (or utricular glands) (Manz, Wilhelm): Anatomy. See: Donath; Dorland.

MANZULLO, ALFREDO. 1909- . Argentinian immunologist. See: World Who's Who Sci. Manzullo's test.

Manzullo's test (Manzullo, Alfredo): Medicine. See: Dorland.

Mao flu (Mao Tse-Tung): Medicine. See: Barnhart (New Eng.).

Mao jacket(s) (Mao Tse-Tung): Fashion. See: Barnhart (New Eng.); Picken.

MAO TSE-TUNG. 1893- . Chinese leader. See: New Encyc. Brit., 1974. Mao flu, Mao jacket(s), Mao Tse-Tung thought propaganda teams, Maoism.

Mao Tse-Tung thought propaganda teams (Mao Tse-Tung): Politics. See: New Encyc. Brit., 1974, Microp.

Maoism (Mao Tse-Tung): Politics. See: Barnhart (New Eng.); New Encyc. Brit., 1974, Microp.

MAPP, MARCUS. 1632-1701. German botanist and physician. See: Biog. Lex. hervorr. Aerzte. Mappia.

Mappia (Mapp, Marcus): Botany. See: Charnock.

Mar, Earl of. See: Erskine, John (Earl of Mar).

MARA. Scandinavian hag of nightmare. See: Jobes. nightmare.

MARAGLIANO, EDOARDO. 1849-1940. Italian physician. See: Biog. Lex. hervorr. Aerzte., 1880-1930. Maragliano's antiserum, Maragliano's tuberculin.

Maragliano's antiserum (Maragliano, Edoardo): Medicine. See: Stedman.

Maragliano's tuberculin (Maragliano, Edoardo): Medicine. See: Stedman.

MARANON, GREGORIO. 1887-1960. Spanish endocrinologist. See: World Who's Who Sci. Maranon's lipomatosis, Maranon's sign (or reaction), Maranon's syndrome (1), Maranon's syndrome (2), Maranon's syndrome (3).

Maranon's lipomatosis (Maranon, Gregorio): Medicine. See: Jablonski.

Maranon's sign (or reaction) (Maranon, Gregorio): Medicine. See: Dorland.

Maranon's syndrome (1) (Maranon, Gregorio): Medicine. See: Jablonski.

Maranon's syndrome (2) (Maranon, Gregorio): Medicine. See: Jablonski.

Maranon's syndrome (3) (Maranon, Gregorio): Medicine. See: Dorland.

Maranta (Maranta, Bartolomeo): Botany. See: Charnock; Taylor, N.; Webster's 3d.

MARANTA, BARTOMOMEO. d. 1571. Italian physician and botanist. See: World Who's Who Sci. Maranta.

MARATTI, GIOVANNI FRANCESCO. d. 1777. Italian botanist. See: Diz. Encic. Ital. Marattia.

Marattia (Maratti, Giovanni Francesco): Botany. See: Webster's 3d.

Marauder (Merode, Count Jean de?): Generic Word. See: Charnock.

MARBE, KARL. 1869-1953. German philosopher and psychologist. See: World Who's Who Sci. Marbe's law.

Marbe's law (Marbe, Karl): Psychology. See: Wolman.

MARBLE, W. H. fl. 1921. American? metallurgist. Cited in: Chem. Abstr., Decenn. Index, 1917-1926. Marble's reagent.

Marble's reagent (Marble, W. H.): Engineering and Industry. See: Thrush.

MARCACCI, ARTURO. 1854-1915. Italian physician. See: Biog. Lex. hervorr. Aerzte, 1880-1930. . Marcacci's muscle.

Marcacci's muscle (Marcacci, Arturo): Medicine. See: Stedman.

Marcan (or Markan) (Mark, Saint): Religion. See: Webster's 3d.

Marcel (Marcelling or Marcel wave) (Grateau, Marcel): Fashion. See: Hendrickson; Partridge; Picken; Webster's 3d.

Marcellians (or Marcellianism) (Marcellus): Religion. See: Canney; Charnock; Latham.

MARCELLINA. fl. ca. 156. Christian heretic in Rome. See: Dict. Christian Biog. Marcellinians (or Marcellinists).

Marcellinians (or Marcellinists) (Marcellina): Religion. See: Canney; Latham.

MARCELLUS. d. 374. Bishop of Ancyra in Galatia. See: Dict. Christian Biog. Marcellians (or Marcellianism).

MARCELLUS II. 1501-1555. Italian pope. See: Encyc. Brit., 1973. Marcellus Mass.

Marcellus Mass (Marcellus II): Music. See: Apel. Also known as: Missa Papae Marcelli.

MARCET, FRANCIS (FRANCOIS). 1803-1883. English-Swiss physicist and natural historian. See: Pogg., vols. 2, 3. Marcetia?

Marcetia (Marcet, Francis?): Botany. See: Charnock.

Marcgraf, Georg. See: Markgraf, Georg.

Marcgravia (Markgraf, George): Botany. See: Webster's 3d.

March (Mars): Generic Word. See: Brewer; Charnock; Funk; Webster's 3d.

MARCHAND, FELIX JACOB. 1846-1928. German pathologist. See: World Who's Who Sci. Marchand-Waterhouse-Friderichsen syndrome, Marchand's adrenals, Marchand's wandering cell, Mosse-Marchand-Mallory cirrhosis.

MARCHAND, RICHARD FELIX. 1813-1850. German chemist. See: Dict. Sci. Biog. Marchand tube.

Marchand tube (Marchand, Richard Felix): Chemistry. See: Hackh; Van Nostrand Chem. Dict.

Marchand-Waterhouse-Friderichsen syndrome (Marchand, Felix Jacob; Waterhouse, Rupert; and Friderichsen, Carl). See: Waterhouse-Friderichsen syndrome.

Marchand's adrenals (Marchand, Felix Jacob): Anatomy. See: Donath.

Marchand's wandering cell (Marchand, Felix Jacob): Medicine. See: Donath; Dorland; Stedman.

MARCHANT, GERARD T. JOSEPH. 1850-1903. French surgeon. See: Biog. Lex. hervorr. Aerzte, 1880-1930. Marchant's zone.

MARCHANT, NICOLAS. d. 1678. French botanist. See: Dict. Sci. Biog. Marchantia.

Marchantia (Marchant, Nicolas): Botany. See: Van Nostrand Sci. Encyc. under "Bryophytes"; Webster's 3d.

Marchant's zone (Marchant, Gerard T. Joseph): Medicine. See: Stedman.

MARCHESANI, OSWALD. 1900-1952. German ophthalmologist. See: Kuerschner's Deut. Gel. Kal. vol. 7, 1950. Marchesani's syndrome.

Marchesani's syndrome (Marchesani, Oswald): Medicine. See: Jablonski; Stedman. Also known as: inverted Marfan's syndrome, Weill-Marchesani syndrome.

MARCHI, VITTORIO. 1851-1908. Italian physiologist. See: Dict. Sci. Biog. Marchi's fluid, Marchi's globules, Marchi's method, Marchi's reaction, Marchi's tract (or bundle).

Marchiafava-Bignami syndrome (Marchiafava, Ettore and Bignami, Amico): Medicine. See: Jablonski. Also known as: Marchiafava's disease.

MARCHIAFAVA, ETTORE. 1847-1935. Italian pathologist. See: Dict. Sci. Biog. Marchiafava-Bignami syndrome, Marchiafava-Micheli syndrome (or anemia).

Marchiafava-Micheli syndrome (or anemia) (Marchiafava, Ettore and Micheli, Ferdinando): Medicine. See: Dorland; Jablonski; Stedman. Also known as: Marchiafava-Nazari-Micheli syndrome, Marchiafava's hemolytic anemia (or syndrome), Struebing-Marchiafava syndrome.

Marchiafava-Nazari-Micheli syndrome (Marchiafava, Ettore; Nazari, A.; and Micheli, Ferdinando). See: Marchiafava-Micheli syndrome (or anemia).

Marchiafava's disease (Marchiafava, Ettore). See: Marchiafava-Bignami syndrome.

Marchiafava's hemolytic anemia (or syndrome) (Marchiafava, Ettore). See: Marchiafava-Micheli syndrome (or anemia).

Marchioness (Marchioness, the character): Literature. See: Charnock.

MARCHIONESS, THE CHARACTER. Character in Charles Dickens' novel, "The Old Curiosity Shop," (1840-1841). See: Magill. Marchioness.

Marchi's fluid (Marchi, Vittorio): Medicine. See: Kelly; Stedman.

Marchi's globules (Marchi, Vittorio): Medicine. See: Dorland.

Marchi's method (Marchi, Vittorio): Medicine. See: Kelly; Stedman.

Marchi's reaction (Marchi, Vittorio): Medicine. See: Dorland; Kelly; Stedman.

Marchi's tract (or bundle) (Marchi, Vittorio): Anatomy. See: Donath; Dorland; Stedman. Also known as: Loewenthal's bundle (or tract).

Marcia C. Noyes Award (Noyes, Marcia C.): Library Science. See: Harrod.

MARCIAN. fl. mid-6th c. Christian heretic. See: Dict. Christian Biog. under "Euchites," p. 261a. Marcianists.

Marcianists (Marcian): Religion. See: Canney.

MARCILLE, MAURICE. 1871-1941. French surgeon. See: Mem. Acad. de Chir., vol. 67 (1941), p. 646. Marcille's triangle.

Marcille's triangle (Marcille, Maurice): Anatomy. See: Stedman.

MARCION. fl. 2d c. Asia Minor heretic. See: Encyc. Brit., 1973. Marcionites (or Marcionism).

Marcionites (or Marcionism) (Marcion): Religion. See: Attwater; Barnhart (Eng. Lit.); Harvey; Mathews, S.

MARCKWALD, MAX. 1844-1923. German surgeon. (Biography source unavailable.) Marckwald's operation.

Marckwald's operation (Marckwald, Max): Medicine. See: Stedman. Also known as: Simon's operation.

Marco Polo. See: Polo, Marco.

Marco Polo('s) sheep (Polo, Marco): Zoology. See: Webster's 3d.

Marconi (Marconi, Marchese Guglielmo): Telegraphy. See: Webster's 3d.

Marconi antenna (Marconi, Marchese Guglielmo): Electronics. See: Hughes; Markus; Van Nostrand Sci. Encyc.

Marconi-Franklin antenna (Marconi, Marchese Guglielmo and Franklin, C.S.): Electronics. See: Van Nostrand Sci. Encyc.

MARCONI, MARCHESE GUGLIELMO. 1874-1937. Italian electrical engineer and inventor. See: Dict. Sci. Biog. Marconi, Marconi antenna, Marconi-Franklin antenna, Marconigram, Marconigraph.

Marconi radio (or wireless) message (Marconi, Marchese Guglielmo). See: Marconigram.

Marconigram (Marconi, Marchese Guglielmo): Telegraphy. See: Hughes; Partridge; Webster's 3d. Also known as: Marconi radio (or wireless) message.

Marconigraph (Marconi, Marchese Guglielmo): Telegraphy. See: Webster's 3d.

Marcosians (Marcus): Religion. See: Canney.

MARCUS. fl. mid-2d c. Christian Gnostic. See: Dict. Christian Biog. Marcosians.

MARCUS AURELIUS ANTONINUS. 121-180. Roman emperor and philosopher. See: Encyc. Brit., 1973. Column of Marcus Aurelius (or Antonine Column).

Marcus Gunn. See: Gunn, Robert Marcus.

Marcus Gunn's dots (Gunn, Robert Marcus). See: Gunn's dots.

Marcus Gunn's phenomenon (or syndrome) (Gunn, Robert Marcus). See: Gunn's syndrome (or phenomenon).

Marcus Gunn's sign (Gunn, Robert Marcus). See: Gunn's sign.

MARCY, RANDOLPH BARNES. 1812-1887. American soldier. See: Dict. Amer. Biog. Marcylite.

Marcylite (Marcy, Randolph Barnes): Earth Sciences. See: Mathews, M. M.

MARECHAL, LOUIS-EUGENE. fl. 1868. French physician. Cited in: Mansell. Marechal's test.

Marechal Niel (rose) (Niel, Adolphe): Botany. See: Partridge.

Marechal's test (Marechal, Louis-Eugene): Medicine. See: Dorland; Kelly; Stedman. Also known as: Kathrein's test.

MAREK, J. fl. 1907. German veterinarian. (Biography source unavailable.) Marek's disease.

Marek's disease (Marek, J.): Medicine. See: Jablonski.

Mareng cell (Martin, Glenn Luther): Engineering and Industry. See: Webster's 3d.

MAREY, ETIENNE JULES. 1830-1904. French physiologist. See: Dict. Sci. Biog. Marey('s) tambour, Marey's law, Marey's single negative.

Marey(s) tambour (Marey, Etienne Jules): Physiology. See: Dict. Sci. Biog.; Drever.

Marey's law (Marey, Etienne Jules): Physiology. See: Dorland; Stedman; Webster's 3d.

Marey's single negative (Marey, Etienne Jules): Photography. See: Focal Encyc. Photog. under "Chronophotography."

Marfan-Achard syndrome (Marfan, Antonin Bernard Jean and Achard, Emile Charles). See: Marfan's syndrome (1) (or abiotrophy).

MARFAN, ANTONIN BERNARD JEAN. 1858-1942. French pediatrician. See: World Who's Who Sci. Dennie-Marfan syndrome, inverted Marfan's syndrome, Marfan-Madelung syndrome, Marfan's syndrome (1) (or abiotrophy).

Marfan-Madelung syndrome (Marfan, Antonin Bernard Jean and Madelung, Otto Wilhelm): Medicine. See: Jablonski.

Marfan's syndrome (1) (or abiotrophy) (Marfan, Antonin Bernard Jean): Medicine. See: Dorland; Jablonski; Stedman. Also known as: Marfan-Achard syndrome.

Marfan's syndrome (2) (Marfan, Antonin Bernard Jean). See: Dennie-Marfan syndrome.

MARG, ELWIN. 1918- . American visual scientist. See: World Who's Who Sci. Mackay-Marg tonometer.

Margaret Mann Citation (Mann, Margaret): Library Science. See: Harrod.

MARGARET OF ANJOU. 1430-1482. French-born queen of Henry VI of England. See: New Encyc. Brit., 1974, Microp. Margaret Professor.

Margaret Professor (Margaret of Anjou): Religion. See: Wagner (More Names).

Margaret Scoggin Scholarship (Scoggin, Margaret Clara): Library Science. See: Harrod.

Marghanites (Emir Ghani, Muhammad Uthman al-): Religion. See: Canney.

MARGUERRE, KARL. 1906- . German engineer. See: Pogg., vol. 7a. Marguerre large deflection theory.

Marguerre large deflection theory (Marguerre, Karl): Mathematics. See: Internat. Dict. Ap. Math.

Margules('s) equation (Margules, Max): Earth Sciences. See: Huschke.

MARGULES, MAX. 1856–1920. Ukrainian-born meteorologist in Austria and Germany. See: Dict. Sci. Biog. Duhem-Margules equation, Margules('s) equation.

MARIA CHRISTINA DE BORBON. 1806–1878. Queen dowager of Spain. See: Webster's Biog. Dict. Christinos.

MARIA LEOPOLDINA. 1797–1826. Austrian archduchess and wife of Dom Pedro I of Brazil. Cited in: Nouv. Biog. Univ. under "Pedro I." Leopoldina.

MARIA LUISA (ALOYSIA) TERESA. 1751–1819. Queen of Spain. See: Webster's Biog. Dict. Aloysia, Order of Maria Louisa.

Maria Monk (Monk, Maria): Religion. See: Attwater.

MARIA THERESA. 1717–1780. Archduchess of Austria. See: Encyc. Brit., 1973. Maria Theresa dollar(s), Maria Theresa (symphony), Order of Maria Theresa, Virgin Mary's Bodyguard.

MARIA THERESA. d. 1807. Sicilian-born princess and wife of Francis II of Austria. Cited in: Nouv. Biog. Univ. under "Francois II." Theresienmesse (or Theresa Mass).

Maria Theresa dollar(s) (Maria Theresa): Numismatics. See: Stenhouse; Webster's 3d.

Maria Theresa (symphony) (Maria Theresa): Music. See: Apel; Scholes.

Maria Wood, the pleasure barge (Wood, Maria): History. See: Latham.

Marialite (Rath, Marie von): Earth Sciences. See: Thrush; Van Nostrand Sci. Encyc.; Webster's 3d.

Mariamettes (Mary, Virgin-Mother): Religion. See: Attwater.

Marian (Mary I): History. See: Webster's 3d.

Marian (Mary, Virgin-Mother): Religion. See: Webster's 3d.

Marian. See: Maid Marian.

Marian exiles (Mary I): History. See: Steinberg.

Marian persecution (or reaction) (Mary I): History. See: Phyfe; Steinberg.

Marian priests (Mary I): History. See: Attwater.

MARIANA, JUAN DE. 1536–1624. Spanish historian. See: Encyc. Brit., 1911. Marianne?

Marianists (Mary, Virgin-Mother): Religion. See: Encyc. Brit., 1973.

Marianne (Mariana, Juan de?): Generic Word (France). See: Harvey.

Marians (Mary, Virgin-Mother): Religion. See: Attwater.

Mariavites (Mary, Virgin-Mother): Religion. See: Attwater; New Catholic Encyc.

Marica (Marica, the goddess): Botany. See: Webster's 3d.

MARICA, THE GODDESS. Goddess associated with a sacred grove at Minturnae in central Italy. See: Dict. Grk. Rom. Biog. Myth. Marica.

MARIE ANTOINETTE. 1755–1793. Austrian-born queen of France. See: New Encyc. Brit., 1973, Microp. La Reine (symphony), Marie Antoinette (dress style).

Marie Antoinette (dress style) (Marie Antoinette): Fashion. See: Picken.

Marie-Bamberger syndrome (Marie, Pierre and Bamberger, Eugen): Medicine. See: Jablonski; Stedman. Also known as: Bamberger's disease, Hagner's disease, Pierre Marie-Bamberger syndrome, Pierre Marie's syndrome.

Marie Davy cell (Marie-Davy, Edme Hippolyte): Chemistry. See: Hackh.

MARIE-DAVY, EDME HIPPOLYTE. 1820–1893. French physicist. See: World Who's Who Sci. Marie Davy cell.

MARIE, JULIEN. 1899– . French pediatrician. See: Who's Who Sci. Europe, 1972. Debre-Marie syndrome, Marie-See syndrome, Marie's syndrome.

Marie-Leri syndrome (Marie, Pierre and Leri, Andre): Medicine. See: Jablonski.

MARIE, PIERRE. 1853–1940. French physician. See: World Who's Who Sci. Bekhterev-Struempell-Marie syndrome, Brissaud-Marie syndrome, Charcot-Marie-Tooth-Hoffmann syndrome, idiopathic Marie-Bamberger syndrome, Marie-Bamberger syndrome, Marie-Leri syndrome, Marie's anarthria, Marie's sign, Marie's syndrome (or ataxia), Scheuthauer-Marie-Sainton syndrome.

Marie-Robinson syndrome (Derivation undetermined): Medicine. See: Stedman.

Marie-Sainton disease (Marie, Pierre and Sainton, Raymond). See: Scheuthauer-Marie-Sainton syndrome.

Marie-See syndrome (Marie, Julien and See, Georges): Medicine. See: Jablonski. Also known as: Julien Marie-See syndrome.

Marie-Struempell disease (Marie, Pierre and Struempell, Ernst Adolph Gustav Gottfried von). See: Bekhterev-Struempell-Marie syndrome.

Mariengroschen (Mary, Virgin-Mother): Numismatics. See: Webster's 3d.

Marie's anarthria (Marie, Pierre): Medicine. See: Jablonski. Also known as: Pierre Marie's anarthria.

Marie's disease (Marie, Pierre). See: Bekhterev-Struempell-Marie syndrome.

Marie's sign (Marie, Pierre): Medicine. See: Jablonski.

Marie's syndrome (Marie, Julien): Medicine. See: Jablonski. Also known as: Julien Marie's syndrome.

Marie's syndrome (or ataxia) (Marie, Pierre): Medicine. See: Hinsie; Jablonski; Stedman. Also known as: Nonne-Marie syndrome, Nonne-Pierre Marie syndrome, Pierre Marie's syndrome.

MARIGNAC, JEAN CHARLES GALISSARD DE. 1817–1894. Swiss chemist. See: Pogg., vols. 2, 3, 4. Marignac salt.

Marignac salt (Marignac, Jean Charles Galissard de): Chemistry. See: Hackh.

MARIGNY, BERNARD ("JOHNNY CRAPAUD"). 1785–1868. American planter, official, and social leader. See: Dict. Amer. Biog. Craps.

Marigold (Mary, Virgin-Mother? or Mary I of England?): Botany. See: Brewer; Encyc. Brit., 1973; Funk; Hendrickson; Phyfe; Wagner (Names); Webster's 3d.

MARIN AMAT, MANUEL. b. 1879. Spanish ophthalmologist. See: Rev. cubana de oftal., Habana, vol. i (1919), pp. 487–492. Marin Amat('s) syndrome.

Marin Amat('s) syndrome (Marin Amat, Manuel): Medicine. See: Hinsie; Jablonski. Also known as: inverted Marcus Gunn syndrome.

MARINA (Indian name: MALINTZIN). ca. 1501–ca. 1550. Mexican Indian princess, interpreter and mistress to Cortes. See: New Encyc. Brit., 1974, Microp. Malinche.

Marinesco-Garland syndrome (Marinesco, Georges and Garland, Hugh). See: Marinesco-Sjoegren syndrome.

MARINESCO, GEORGES. 1863–1938. Rumanian pathologist. See: World Who's Who Sci. Marinesco-Sjoegren syndrome, Marinescu's succulent hand.

Marinesco-Sjoegren syndrome (Marinesco, Georges and Sjoegren, Torsten): Medicine. See: Hinsie; Jablonski. Also known as: Marinesco-Garland syndrome, Torsten Sjoegren's syndrome.

Marinescu's succulent hand (Marinesco, Georges): Medicine. See: Dorland; Stedman.

MARINI, GIOVANNI BATTISTA. 1569–1625. Italian poet. See: Encyc. Brit., 1911. Marinism (or Marinismo).

Marinism (or Marinismo) (Marini, Giovanni Battista): Literature. See: Barnhart (Eng. Lit.); Harvey; Partridge; Preminger.

MARINO, LUIGI. d. 1922. Italian chemist. See: Pogg., vols. 5, 6. Marino test reaction.

Marino test reaction (Marino, Luigi): Chemistry. See: Van Nostrand Chem. Dict.

Mariola (Mary, Virgin-Mother): Religion. See: Charnock.

Mariolatry (Mary, Virgin-Mother): Religion. See: Attwater; Webster's 3d.

Mariology (Mary, Virgin-Mother): Religion. See: Attwater; Webster's 3d.

MARION, F. fl. 1900. French chemist. Cited in: Royal Soc. Cat. Sci. Pap., 1884–1900. Mangent-Marion reagent for ammonia, Mangent-Marion test for formaldehyde.

MARION, GEORGES. b. 1869. French urologist. See: Arnim. Marion's disease?

Marion's disease (Marion, Georges?): Medicine. See: Jablonski.

Mariotte bottle (Mariotte, Edme): Physics. See: Webster's 3d.

MARIOTTE, EDME. ca. 1620-1684. French physicist. See: Dict. Sci. Biog. Boyle-Mariotte law, Mariotte bottle, Mariotte tube, Mariotte's experiment, Mariotte's spot (or blind spot).

Mariotte tube (Mariotte, Edme): Physics. See: Thrush.

Mariotte's experiment (Mariotte, Edme): Physiology. See: Dorland; Stedman.

Mariotte's law (Mariotte, Edme). See: Boyle's law.

Mariotte's spot (or blind spot) (Mariotte, Edme): Anatomy. See: Donath; Dorland; Stedman.

Marists (Mary, Virgin-Mother): Religion. See: Attwater; Canney; Encyc. Brit., 1973.

Marivaudage (Marivaux, Pierre Carlet de Chamblain de): Generic Word (affected writing style). See: Brewer; Harvey; Hendrickson; Partridge; Scott.

MARIVAUX, PIERRE CARLET DE CHAMBLAIN DE. 1688-1763. French novelist. See: Encyc. Brit., 1973. Marivaudage.

MARJOLIN, JEAN NICOLAS. 1780-1850. French physician. See: World Who's Who Sci. Marjolin's ulcer.

Marjolin's ulcer (Marjolin, Jean Nicolas): Medicine. See: Dorland; Jablonski; Stedman.

MARJORIBANKS, EDWARD (BARON OF TWEEDMOUTH). 1849-1909. English politician. See: Dict. Nat. Biog. Tweedmouth committee.

Mark boundary conditions (Mark, Carson): Physics. See: Internat. Dict. Ap. Math.

MARK, CARSON (In full: JORDAN CARSON). 1913- . Canadian-born American mathematical physicist. See: Amer. Men and Women Sci., 12th ed. Mark boundary conditions.

MARK, SAINT. One of Jesus's twelve apostles and early Christian evangelist. See: Holweck. Columns of St. Mark and St. Theodore, Lion of St. Mark, Marcan (or Markan), St. Mark's Eve, Saint Mark's fly.

Mark Tapley (Tapley, Mark): Generic Word (invincible cheerfulness). See: Brewer; Partridge.

MARKEE, JOSEPH ELDRIDGE. 1903-1970. American anatomist. See: World Who's Who Sci. Markee test.

Markee test (Markee, Joseph Eldridge): Medicine. See: Dorland; Stedman.

MARKGRAF (or MARCGRAF), GEORGE. 1610-1644. German naturalist and traveler in South America. See: Dict. Sci. Biog. Marcgravia.

Markham throwing belt (Derivation undetermined): Engineering and Industry. See: Thrush.

MARKOE, THOMAS MASTERS. 1819-1901. American surgeon. See: Who Was Who Amer., 1897-1942. Markoe's abscess.

Markoe's abscess (Markoe, Thomas Masters): Medicine. See: Jablonski.

MARKOV, ANDREI ANDREEVICH. 1856-1922. Russian mathematician. See: Pogg., vols. 3, 4, 5, 6. Gauss-Markov theorem, Markov estimate, Markov inequality, Markov (Markoff) chain, Markov (Markoff) process, Poisson-Markov process.

Markov (Markoff) chain (Markov, Andrei Andreevich): Statistics. See: Barnhart (New Eng.); Kendall; Van Nostrand Sci. Encyc.; Webster's 3d.

Markov estimate (Markov, Andrei Andreevich): Statistics. See: Kendall.

Markov inequality (Markov, Andrei Andreevich): Statistics. See: Kendall.

Markov (Markoff) process (Markov, Andrei Andreevich): Statistics. See: Ballentyne; Internat. Dict. Ap. Math.; Kendall; Van Nostrand Sci. Encyc.; Wolman.

MARKOVA, ALICIA (LILIAN ALICIA MARKS). 1910- . English prima ballerina. See: Encyc. Brit., 1973. Markova-Dolin Ballet.

Markova-Dolin Ballet (Markova, Alicia and Dolin, Anton): Dance. See: Chujoy.

Markovnikov (Markownikoff) rule (or replacement rule) (Markovnikov, Vladimir Vasilevich): Chemistry. See: Ballentyne; Hackh; New Encyc. Brit., 1974, Microp.; Van Nostrand Sci. Encyc.; Webster's 3d.

MARKOVNIKOV, VLADIMIR VASILEVICH. 1838-1904. Russian organic chemist. See: Dict. Sci. Biog. Markovnikov (Markownikoff) rule (or replacement rule).

Markovnikovite (Derivation undetermined): Earth Sciences. See: Thrush.

Marks, Lilian Alicia. See: Markova, Alicia.

Markus-Adie syndrome (Markus and Adie, William John). See: Adie's syndrome.

Markus' syndrome (Derivation undetermined). See: Adie's syndrome.

Markush Doctrine (Derivation undetermined): Law. See: Black.

MARLATT, CHARLES LESTER. 1863-1954. American entomologist. See: World Who's Who Sci. Marlatt whitefly.

Marlatt whitefly (Marlatt, Charles Lester): Zoology. See: Winburne.

Marlborough, 1st Duke of. See: Churchill, John (1st Duke of Marlborough).

Marlborough, 4th Duke of. See: Spencer, George (4th Duke of Marlborough).

Marlborough foot (furniture style) (Spencer, George, 4th Duke of Marlborough): Applied Arts. See: Webster's 3d.

Marlborough leg (furniture style) (Spencer, George, 4th Duke of Marlborough): Applied Arts. See: Webster's 3d.

Marlborough spaniels (Churchill, John, 1st Duke of Marlborough): Zoology. See: Wagner (More Names).

MARLES, HENRY. fl. 1919. English? engineer. (Biography source unavailable.) Marles steering gear.

Marles steering gear (Marles, Henry): Engineering and Industry. See: Auger.

Marlovian (Marlowe, Christopher): Literature. See: Webster's 3d.

MARLOW, FRANK WILLIAM. 1858-1942. American ophthalmologist. See: Who Was Who Amer., 1943-1950. Marlow's test.

MARLOW, J. H. fl. 1921-1926. English ceramics engineer. Cited in: Chem. Abstr., vol. 16, p. 4316. Marlow kiln.

Marlow kiln (Marlow, J. H.): Engineering and Industry. See: Thrush.

MARLOWE, CHRISTOPHER. 1564-1593. English dramatist. See: Dict. Nat. Biog. Marlovian.

Marlow's test (Marlow, Frank William): Medicine. See: Dorland.

Marme('s) reagent (or solution) (Marme, Wilhelm Heinrich Theodor Ernst): Chemistry. See: Hackh; Van Nostrand Chem. Dict.

MARME, WILHELM HEINRICH THEODOR ERNST. 1832-1897. German pharmacological chemist. See: Arch. Exper. Path., vol. 40 (1898) 6 pp. Marme('s) reagent (or solution).

Marmes man (Marmes, R. J.): Archaeology. See: Barnhart (New Eng.).

MARMES, R. J. fl. 1965. American rancher. (Biography source unavailable.) Marmes man.

MARMO, SERAFINO. No dates. Italian obstetrician. (Biography source unavailable.) Marmo's method.

MARMOREK, ALEXANDER. 1865-1923. Austrian physician in Paris. See: World Who's Who Sci. Marmorek's serum.

Marmorek's serum (Marmorek, Alexander): Medicine. See: Stedman.

Marmo's method (Marmo, Serafino): Medicine. See: Dorland.

MARNIER-LAPOSTOLLE. No dates. French manufacturer. (Biography source unavailable.) grand Marnier.

MARO (ST. JOHN MARON). fl. 685-707. Patriarch of Antioch and of Maronites. See: Dict. Christian Biog. under "Maro (2)." Maronite(s)?

MARON. Legendary priest of Apollo and King of Thrace. See: Dict. Grk. Rom. Biog. Myth. Maronean (wine).

MARON (MARO), SAINT. d. ca. 423. Syrian monk. See: Encyc. Brit., 1973. Maronite(s)?

Maronean (wine) (Maron): Food and Drink. See: Charnock.

Maronite(s) (Maron, Saint? or Maro?): Religion. See: Brewer; New Encyc. Brit., 1974, Microp.; Hendrickson; Webster's 3d.

maroquin Lavalliere (La Valliere, Louis Cesar de la Baume Le Blanc, Duc de): Applied Arts. See: Grand Larousse Encyc.

Maroteaux-Lamy syndrome (1) (Maroteaux, Pierre and Lamy, Maurice): Medicine. See: Jablonski; Stedman.

Maroteaux-Lamy syndrome (2) (Maroteaux, Pierre and Lamy, Maurice): Medicine. See: Jablonski.

MAROTEAUX, PIERRE. 1926- . French physician. See: Who's Who Sci. Europe, 1972. Maroteaux-Lamy syndrome (1), Maroteaux-Lamy syndrome (2).

Marprelate controversy (Martin Marprelate): Religion. See: Brewer.

Marquardt porcelain (Derivation undetermined): Engineering and Industry. See: Thrush.

Marquis, Frederick James. See: Woolton, Frederick James Marquis, 1st Earl.

Marquis of Queensberry rules (Douglas, John Sholto). See: Queensberry rules.

Marquis' reagent (or solution) (Derivation undetermined): Chemistry. See: Stedman; Van Nostrand Chem. Dict.

MARR, JOHN EDWIN. 1857-1933. English geologist. See: Dict. Nat. Biog., 5th suppl. Marrite.

Marriner process (Derivation undetermined): Engineering and Industry. See: Thrush.

MARRIOTT, WILLIAMS MC KIM. 1885-1936. American physician. See: Who Was Who Amer., 1897-1942. Marriott's method.

Marriott's method (Marriott, Williams McKim): Medicine. See: Dorland.

MARRIS, HENRY FAIRLEY. fl. 1917. English physician. Cited in: Mansell. Marris' test.

Marris' test (Marris, Henry Fairley): Medicine. See: Stedman.

MARRISON, LESLIE WILLIAM. 1901- . English chemist. See: Who's Who Brit. Sci., 1953. Marrison test for phosphate and arsenate.

Marrison test for phosphate and arsenate (Marrison, Leslie William): Chemistry. See: Van Nostrand Chem. Dict.

Marrite (Marr, John Edwin): Earth Sciences. See: Webster's 3d.

Marrow-bones (Mary, Virgin-Mother): Religion. See: Stenhouse.

Marry (Mary, Virgin-Mother): Generic Word (obsolete expletive). See: Charnock; Hargrave; Partridge; Stenhouse; Webster's 3d.

MARS. Roman god of war and agriculture. See: New Encyc. Brit., 1974, Microp. line of Mars, lower Mars, March, Mars brown, Martial, Martial (pear), triangle of Mars.

Mars brown (Mars): Chemistry. See: Webster's 3d.

Mar's year (Erskine, John, Earl of Mar): History. See: Brewer; Harvey.

MARSAUT, J. B. fl. 1879-1883. French mining engineer. Cited in: Royal Soc. Cat. Sci. Pap., 1874-1883. Marsaut lamp.

Marsaut lamp (Marsaut, J. B.): Engineering and Industry. See: Thrush.

MARSDEN, ALEXANDER EDWIN. 1832-1902. English surgeon. See: Dict. Nat. Biog., 2d suppl. Marsden's paste.

Marsden chart (Derivation undetermined): Earth Sciences. See: Huschke.

MARSDEN, WILLIAM. 1754-1836. Irish antiquarian and orientalist. See: Dict. Nat. Biog. Marsdenia.

Marsdenia (Marsden, William): Botany. See: Charnock; Webster's 3d.

Marsden's paste (Marsden, Alexander Edwin): Medicine. See: Dorland.

MARSH, C. W. fl. 1893. Australian geologist. Cited in: Hintze, vol. 1, pt. 2, p. 2325. Marshite.

MARSH, CHARLES DWIGHT. 1855-1932. American biologist. See: Nat. Cycl. Amer. Biog., vol. 27, pp. 207-208. Marshia.

MARSH, CHARLES WESLEY. 1834-1881. American inventor. See: Nat. Cycl. Amer. Biog., vol. 11, p. 268. Marsh harvester.

Marsh funnel (Derivation undetermined): Engineering and Industry. See: Thrush.

Marsh harvester (Marsh, Charles Wesley): Agriculture. Cited in: Nat. Cycl. Amer. Biog., vol. 11, p. 268.

MARSH, SIR HENRY. 1790-1860. Irish physician. See: Dict. Nat. Biog. Marsh's disease.

MARSH, JAMES ERNEST. 1794-1846. English chemist. See: Dict. Nat. Biog. Marsh('s) test (for arsenic).

Marsh solution (Derivation undetermined): Chemistry. See: Van Nostrand Chem. Dict.

Marsh('s) test (for arsenic) (Marsh, James Ernest): Chemistry. See: Ballentyne; Hackh; Stedman.

Marshak boundary conditions (Marshak, Robert Eugene): Physics. See: Internat. Dict. Ap. Math.

MARSHAK, ROBERT EUGENE. 1916- . American physicist. See: World Who's Who Sci. Marshak boundary conditions.

Marshal rebellion (Marshal, Richard): History. See: Steinberg.

MARSHAL, RICHARD (3RD EARL OF PEMBROKE). d. 1234. English aristocrat. See: Dict. Nat. Biog. Marshal rebellion.

MARSHALL, ALFRED. 1842-1924. English economist. See: Dict. Nat. Biog., 4th suppl. Marshall-Edgeworth-Bowley index, Marshallian.

Marshall apparatus (Marshall, Eli Kennerly, Jr.): Medicine. See: Hackh.

Marshall-Edgeworth-Bowley index (Marshall, Alfred; Edgeworth, Francis Ysidro; and Bowley, Arthur Lyon): Statistics. See: Kendall. Also known as: Bowley index, Edgeworth index.

MARSHALL, ELI KENNERLY, JR. b. 1889. American pharmacologist and physiologist. See: World Who's Who Sci. Marshall apparatus, Marshall's method.

MARSHALL, F. C. fl. 1879. English engineer. (Biography source unavailable.) Marshall valve gear.

MARSHALL, GEORGE CATLETT. 1880-1959. American army officer. See: Encyc. Brit., 1973. Marshall plan, Marshall Scholars.

Marshall Hall. See: Hall, Marshall.

Marshall Hall's method (Hall, Marshall). See: Hall's method.

MARSHALL, HUGH. b. 1868. Scottish chemist. See: Pogg., vol. 4. Marshall reaction for manganese.

MARSHALL, J. T. W. fl. 1915. American chemist. Cited in: Chem. Abstr., Decenn. Index, 1907-1916. Lyle-Curtman-Marshall alpha-aminocaproic acid solution, Lyle-Curtman-Marshall benzidine reagent.

MARSHALL, JOHN. 1818-1891. English anatomist. See: World Who's Who Sci. Marshall's oblique vein, Marshall's vestigial fold.

MARSHALL, MOSES. 1758-1813. American botanist. See: Nat. Cycl. Amer. Biog., vol. 20, p. 455. Marshallia.

Marshall plan (Marshall, George Catlett): Economics. See: Greenwald; Morris and Irwin; New Encyc. Brit., 1974, Microp.; Smith; Steinberg.

Marshall reaction for manganese (Marshall, Hugh): Chemistry. See: Van Nostrand Chem. Dict.

MARSHALL, ROBERT. fl. early 19th c. American clergyman. (Biography source unavailable.) Marshallite.

Marshall Scholars (Marshall, George Catlett): History. See: Encyc. Assoc.

MARSHALL, STEPHEN. ca. 1594-1655. English Presbyterian preacher and leader. See: Dict. Nat. Biog. Smectymnians.

Marshall valve gear (Marshall, F. C.): Engineering and Industry. See: Auger.

MARSHALL, WALLACE. fl. 1932. American scientist. (Biography source unavailable.) Marshall-White syndrome.

Marshall–White syndrome (Marshall, Wallace and White, Cleveland): Medicine. See: Jablonski. Also known as: Bier's spots.

Marshallia (Marshall, Moses): Botany. See: Taylor, N.

Marshallian (Marshall, Alfred): Economics. See: Webster's 3d.

Marshallite (Marshall, Robert): Religion. See: Mathews, M. M.

Marshall's method (Marshall, Eli Kennerly, Jr.): Medicine. See: Stedman.

Marshall's oblique vein (Marshall, John): Anatomy. See: Donath; Dorland; Stedman.

Marshall's vestigial fold (Marshall, John): Anatomy. See: Donath; Dorland; Stedman.

Marshia (Marsh, Charles Dwight): Zoology. See: Pennak.

Marshite (Marsh, C. W.): Earth Sciences. See: Thrush; Webster's 3d.

Marsh's disease (Marsh, Sir Henry): Medicine. See: Dorland.

MARSIGLI, COUNT LUIGI FERDINANDO. 1658-1730. Italian naturalist, geographer and soldier. See: World Who's Who Sci. Marsilea.

Marsilea (Marsigli, Count Luigi Ferdinando): Botany. See: Taylor, N.; Webster's 3d.

MARSSON, THEODOR FRIEDRICH. 1816-1892. German botanist. See: Allg. Deut. Biog. Marssonia.

Marssonia (Marsson, Theodor Friedrich): Botany. See: Webster's 3d.

MARTEGIANI, CARLO. fl. 1919. Italian anatomist. Cited in: Index-Cat. Libr. Surg.-Gen. Off., 4th Ser., vol. 10, 1948. Martegiani's funnel (or area).

Martegiani's funnel (or area) (Martegiani, Carlo): Anatomy. See: Stedman.

Martenite (Derivation undetermined): Earth Sciences. See: Thrush.

Martenot (or Ondium Martenot) (Martenot, Maurice): Music. See: Scholes; Webster's 3d.

MARTENOT, MAURICE. 1898-   . French scientist and musician. See: Who's Who France, 1975-1976. Martenot (or Ondium Martenot).

MARTENS, ADOLF. 1850-1914. German metallurgist. See: Dict. Sci. Biog. Dalen-Martens machine?, Koenig-Martens spectrophotometer, Martens' hardness test, Martens test?, Martensite, Pensky-Martens tester (or apparatus).

Martens densitometer (Martens, Friedrich Franz): Physics. See: Hackh.

MARTENS, FRIEDRICH FRANZ. 1873-1939. German physicist. See: Pogg., vols. 4, 5, 6, 7a. Martens densitometer, Martens illuminator, Martens photometer, Martens spectroscope, Martens wedge.

Martens' hardness test (Martens, Adolf): Engineering and Industry. See: Auger.

Martens illuminator (Martens, Friedrich Franz): Physics. See: Hackh.

Martens photometer (Martens, Friedrich Franz): Physics. See: Glazebrook, vol. 4, "Photometry and Illumination," p. 441.

Martens spectroscope (Martens, Friedrich Franz): Physics. See: Hackh.

Martens test (Martens, Adolf?): Engineering and Industry. See: Hackh.

Martens wedge (Martens, Friedrich Franz): Physics. See: Internat. Dict. Phys. Elec.

Martensite (Martens, Adolf): Engineering and Industry. See: Thrush; Van Nostrand Sci. Encyc.; Webster's 3d.

Martha (Martha, Saint): Generic Word (domestically preoccupied). See: Hendrickson.

MARTHA, SAINT. Sister of Mary and Lazarus in the New Testament. See: Hastings (Dict. Bible). Martha, way of Martha.

Martha Washington armchair (Washington, Martha): Applied Arts. See: Webster's 3d.

Martha Washington geranium (Washington, Martha): Botany. See: Webster's 3d.

Martha Washington table (or sewing cabinet) (Washington, Martha): Applied Arts. See: Mathews, M. M.; Webster's 3d.

MARTIA. fl. before 300 B.C. Queen of the Britons. (Biography source unavailable.) Martian laws.

Martial (Mars): Generic Word (related to war). See: Charnock; Partridge; Webster's 3d.

Martial (pear) (Mars): Botany. See: Charnock.

Martian laws (Martia): History. See: Brewer; Harbottle.

MARTIN, A. fl. 1846. German physician. (Biography source unavailable.) Bosviel-Martin syndrome.

MARTIN, AL. H. fl. 1915. American chemical engineer. Cited in: Chem. Abstr., Decenn. Index, 1907-1916. Pennock and Martin sulfur crucible?

Martin-Albright syndrome (Martin, Eric and Albright, Fuller): Medicine. See: Jablonski. Also known as: Albright's syndrome.

MARTIN, AUGUST E. 1847-1933. German gynecologist. See: Biog. Lex. hervorr. Aerzte, 1880-1930. Martin's pelvimeter, Martin's tube.

Martin B-10 (bomber) (Martin, Glenn Luther): Weapons. See: Encyc. Brit., 1973 under "Air Power," vol. 1, p. 460, illus.

Martin B-61 Matador (missile) (Martin, Glenn Luther): Weapons. Cited in: Encyc. Brit., 1973 under "Air Power," vol. 1, p. 466 Id.

Martin-Berthelot principle (Martin, Thomas Lyle, Jr. and Berthelot, Pierre Eugene Marcellin): Sociology. See: Martin.

MARTIN BROTHERS. fl. 18th c. French furniture makers and decorators. Cited in: Boger. vernis Martin (or Martin varnish).

MARTIN, SIR CHARLES JAMES. 1866-1955. English physiologist. See: Who Was Who, 1951-1960. Chick-Martin test, Martin's centrifuge?, Martin's filter?, Martin's flask?

MARTIN DE GIMARD, JULES-LOUIS-ALEXANDRE DE. b. 1858. French physician. Cited in: Mansell. De Gimard's syndrome.

Martin de Gimard's syndrome (Martin de Gimard, Jules-Louis-Alexandre de). See: De Gimard's syndrome.

Martin drunk (Martin of Tours, Saint): Generic Word (very intoxicated). See: Brewer; Hendrickson.

MARTIN DU PAN, CHARLES. 1878-1948. Swiss physician. See: Revue Medic. Suisse Rom., vol. 68 (1948), pp. 242-248. Martin du Pan-Rutishauser disease.

Martin du Pan-Rutishauser disease (Martin du Pan, Charles and Rutishauser, E.): Medicine. See: Jablonski.

Martin effect (Martin, Thomas Lyle, Jr.): Sociology. See: Martin.

MARTIN, ERIC. 1900-   . Swiss internist. See: Who's Who Switz., 1970-1971. Martin-Albright syndrome.

MARTIN, GLENN LUTHER. 1886-1955. American airplane manufacturer. See: New Encyc. Brit., 1974, Microp. Mareng cell, Martin B-10 (bomber), Martin B-61 Matador (missile).

MARTIN, H. G. fl. 1943. American psychologist. Cited in: Cum. Auth. Index to Psych. Index, 1894-1935, and Psych. Abstr., 1927-1958. Guilford-Martin personnel inventory.

MARTIN, HENRY AUSTIN. 1824-1884. American surgeon. See: Dict. Amer. Biog. Martin's bandage, Martin's disease.

MARTIN MARPRELATE. Fictitious writer of Puritan attacks on the established English church (1588-89). See: Harvey. Marprelate controversy, Martinists.

Martin mass dichotomy (Martin, Thomas Lyle, Jr.): Sociology. See: Martin.

MARTIN OF TOURS, SAINT. ca. 316-397. French monastic and bishop. See: New Encyc. Brit., 1974, Microp. all my eye and Betty Martin?, herb of St. Martin, Martin drunk, Martin-pecheur, Martin (Martinet or Martlet) (swallow), Martineta, Martinete, Martinmas, St. Martin's beads, Saint Martin's bird, Saint Martin's evil, St. Martin's goose, Saint Martin's summer.

Martin-pecheur (Martin of Tours, Saint): Zoology. Cited in: Partridge.

MARTIN, PIERRE BLAISE EMILE. 1824-1915. French engineer. See: Rev. Gen. Sci., vol. 26 (1915), pp. 427-430. Siemens-Martin process, Siemens-Martin steel.

Martin (plate) (Derivation undetermined): Engineering and Industry. See: Thrush.

Martin process (Martin, Pierre Blaise Emile). See: Siemens-Martin process.

Martin process for starch (Derivation undetermined): Chemistry. See: Van Nostrand Chem. Dict.

Martin (Martinet or Martlet) (swallow) (Martin of Tours, Saint): Zoology. See: Charnock; Hendrickson; Partridge; Van Nostrand Sci. Encyc.; Webster's 3d.

MARTIN, THOMAS CHARLES. 1864-1926. American physician. See: J.A.M.A., vol. 87 (1926), p. 1053. Martin's speculum.

MARTIN, THOMAS LYLE, JR. 1921- . American electrical engineer and university administrator. See: Amer. Men and Women Sci., 12th ed. Kerr-Martin law, Martin-Berthelot principle, Martin effect, Martin mass dichotomy, Martin's corollary to Vail's second axiom, Martin's law of committees, Martin's law of communication, Martin's laws of academia, Martin's laws of academic status, Martin's laws of hierarchical function, Martin's minimax maxim, Martin's plagiarism of H. L. Mencken, Martin's plagiarism of Mark Twain.

Martin varnish (Martin brothers). See: vernis Martin (or Martin varnish).

Martindale dust respirator (Derivation undetermined): Engineering and Industry. See: Thrush.

Martinet (Martinet, Jean): Generic Word (strict disciplinarian). See: Brewer; Funk; Hendrickson; Partridge; Webster's 3d.

Martinet dioxindole synthesis (Martinet, Joseph): Chemistry. See: Van Nostrand Chem. Dict.

MARTINET, JEAN. d. 1672. French army officer. See: Webster's Biog. Dict. Martinet.

MARTINET, JOSEPH (In full: MARIE E. JOSEPH). b. 1888. French chemist. See: Pogg., vols. 5, 6. Martinet dioxindole synthesis, Martinet reagent?

Martinet reagent (Martinet, Joseph?): Chemistry. See: Van Nostrand Chem. Dict.

Martineta (Martin of Tours, Saint): Zoology. See: Webster's 3d.

Martinete (Martin of Tours, Saint): Zoology. See: Webster's 3d.

MARTINEZ COMPANON Y BUJANDA, BALTASAR JAIME. 1737-1797. Spanish-born bishop in Peru and Colombia. See: New Catholic Encyc. Martinezia.

Martinezia (Martinez Companon y Bujanda, Baltasar Jaime): Botany. See: Taylor, N.

MARTINI. No dates. Italian or Spanish bartender. (Biography source unavailable.) Martini (cocktail)?

MARTINI, ARDOINO. fl. 1926-1931. Argentinian chemist. See: Pogg., vol. 6. Martini micro-test for antimony, bismuth, and gold, Martini micro-test for chromium, Martini micro-test for phosphate and arsenate, Martini micro-test for sodium, Martini micro-tests for cobalt, Martini micro-tests for copper, Martini micro-tests for iron, zinc, and indium, Martini micro-tests for molybdenum, Martini micro-tests for nickel, Martini micro-tests for tungsten, Martini reagent.

Martini (cocktail) (Martini, the bartender?): Food and Drink. See: Hendrickson; Partridge.

MARTINI, FREDERIC DE. 1833-1897. Hungarian-born Swiss mechanical engineer. See: Dict. Hist. Biog. Suisse. Martini-Henry (rifle).

Martini-Henry (rifle) (Martini, Frederic de and Henry, Benjamin Tyler? or Henry, Scottish gunsmith?): Weapons. See: Hendrickson under "Henry Rifle..;" Partridge; Wagner (More Names); Weekley.

Martini micro-test for antimony, bismuth, and gold (Martini, Ardoino): Chemistry. See: Van Nostrand Chem. Dict.

Martini micro-test for chromium (Martini, Ardoino): Chemistry. See: Van Nostrand Chem. Dict.

Martini micro-test for copper (Martini, Ardoino): Chemistry. See: Van Nostrand Chem. Dict.

Martini micro-test for iron, zinc, and indium (Martini, Ardoino): Chemistry. See: Van Nostrand Chem. Dict.

Martini micro-test for phosphate and arsenate (Martini, Ardoino): Chemistry. See: Van Nostrand Chem. Dict.

Martini micro-test for sodium (Martini, Ardoino): Chemistry. See: Van Nostrand Chem. Dict.

Martini micro-tests for cobalt (Martini, Ardoino): Chemistry. See: Van Nostrand Chem. Dict.

Martini micro-tests for molybdenum (Martini, Ardoino): Chemistry. See: Van Nostrand Chem. Dict.

Martini micro-tests for nickel (Martini, Ardoino): Chemistry. See: Van Nostrand Chem. Dict.

Martini micro-tests for tungsten (Martini, Ardoino): Chemistry. See: Van Nostrand Chem. Dict.

Martini reagent (Martini, Ardoino): Chemistry. See: Van Nostrand Chem. Dict.

Martini (rifle) (Martini, Frederic de). See: Martini-Henry (rifle).

MARTINIERE, ANTOINE-AUGUSTIN-BRUZEN DE LA. 1662-1746. Dutch geographer and historian. See: Michaud. Bossioea?

Martinist (Luther, Martin): Religion. See: Webster's 3d.

Martinists (Martin Marprelate): Religion. See: Barnhart (Eng. Lit.).

Martinists (Saint-Martin, Louis Claude de): Religion. See: Latham.

Martinmas (Martin of Tours, Saint): Generic Word. See: Harvey; Hendrickson; Phyfe; Webster's 3d.

Martinotti('s) cell(s) Martinotti, Giovanni): Medicine. See: Dorland; Henderson; Stedman.

MARTINOTTI, GIOVANNI. 1857-1928. Italian physician. See: Biog. Lex. hervorr. Aerzte, 1880-1930. Martinotti('s) cell(s).

MARTINS. fl. ca. 1845. German mine official. Cited in: Hintze, vol. I, pt. 2, p. 2156. Martinsite.

Martin's bandage (Martin, Henry Austin): Medicine. See: Dorland; Stedman.

Martin's centrifuge (Martin, Sir Charles James?): Engineering and Industry. See: Hackh.

Martin's corollary to Vail's second axiom (Martin, Thomas Lyle, Jr. and Vail, Charles Rowe): Sociology. See: Martin.

Martin's disease (Martin, Henry Austin): Medicine. See: Dorland; Stedman.

Martin's filter (Martin, Sir Charles James?): Medicine. See: Hackh.

Martin's flask (Martin, Sir Charles James?): Medicine. See: Hackh.

Martin's law of committees (Martin, Thomas Lyle, Jr.): Sociology. See: Martin.

Martin's law of communication (Martin, Thomas Lyle, Jr.): Sociology. See: Martin.

Martin's laws of academia (Martin, Thomas Lyle, Jr.): Sociology. See: Martin.

Martin's laws of academic status (Martin, Thomas Lyle, Jr.): Sociology. See: Martin.

Martin's laws of hierarchical function (Martin, Thomas Lyle, Jr.): Sociology. See: Martin.

Martin's minimax maxim (Martin, Thomas Lyle, Jr.): Sociology. See: Martin.

Martin's pelvimeter (Martin, August E.): Medicine. See: Stedman.

Martin's plagiarism of H. L. Mencken (Martin, Thomas Lyle, Jr. and Mencken, Henry Louis): Sociology. See: Martin.

Martin's plagiarism of Mark Twain (Martin, Thomas Lyle, Jr. and Clemens, Samuel Langhorne): Sociology. See: Martin.

Martin's speculum (Martin, Thomas Charles): Medicine. See: Stedman.

Martin's tube (Martin, August E.): Medicine. See: Dorland; Stedman.

Martinsite (Martins): Earth Sciences. See: Thrush. Also known as: Kieserite.

Martius disc (Martius, Goetz?): Physiology. See: Drever.

MARTIUS, GOETZ. b. 1853. German physiological psychologist. Cited in: Royal Soc. Cat. Sci. Pap., 1884-1900. Martius disc?

MARTIUS, KARL ALEXANDER. 1838-1920. German chemist. See: Deut. Biog. Jahrb., vol. 2, 1917-1920. Hofmann-Martius rearrangement, Martius yellow.

Martius yellow (Martius, Karl Alexander): Chemistry. See: Webster's 3d.

Martorell-Fabre syndrome (Martorell, Fernando and Fabre Tersol, J.). See: Takayasu's syndrome (or disease).

MARTORELL, FERNANDO. 1906- . Spanish physician. See: World Who's Who Sci. Martorell-Fabre syndrome, Martorell's syndrome (1).

Martorell's syndrome (1) (Martorell, Fernando): Medicine. See: Jablonski.

Martorell's syndrome (2) (Martorell, Fernando). See: Takayasu's syndrome (or disease).

MARTYN, JOHN. 1699-1768. English botanist and scholar. See: Dict. Nat. Biog. Martynia.

Martynia (Martyn, John): Botany. See: Mathews, M. M.; Partridge; Webster's 3d.

Maruyama Okyo. See: Okyo.

Maruyama School (Okyo): Fine Arts. See: Osborne.

MARVEL, CARL SHIPP. b. 1894. American chemist. See: World Who's Who Sci. Marvel-Du Vigneud reagent.

Marvel-Du Vigneud reagent (Marvel, Carl Shipp and Du Vigneaud, Vincent): Chemistry. See: Van Nostrand Chem. Dict.

MARVIN, CHARLES FREDERICK. 1858-1943. American meteorologist. See: World Who's Who Sci. Marvin sunshine recorder.

Marvin sunshine recorder (Marvin, Charles Frederick): Earth Sciences. See: Huschke; Van Nostrand Sci. Encyc.

Marx circuit (Marx, Erwin): Electronics. See: Thewlis.

Marx effect (Marx, Erich Anselm): Physics. See: Ballentyne; Van Nostrand Sci. Encyc.

MARX, ERICH ANSELM. b. 1874. German radiophysicist. See: Pogg., vols. 4, 5, 6. Marx effect.

MARX, ERWIN (In full: OTTO ERWIN). b. 1893. German electrical engineer. See: Pogg., vol. 6. Marx circuit.

MARX, H. fl. 1906. German physician. Cited in: Kelly. Horoszkiewicz-Marx test.

MARX, KARL HEINRICH. 1818-1883. German political philosopher. See: Internat. Encyc. Soc. Sci. Marxian theory of population, Marxism (Marxian or Marxist).

Marxian theory of population (Marx, Karl Heinrich): Sociology. See: Zadrozny.

Marxism (Marxian or Marxist) (Marx, Karl Heinrich): Philosophy. See: Brewer; Encyc. Brit., 1973; Hoult; Partridge; Smith; Webster's 3d.

Marx's stain (Derivation undetermined): Medicine. See: Stedman.

MARY I (TUDOR). 1516-1558. Queen of England. See: Dict. Nat. Biog. Bloody Mary (cocktail), Marian, Marian exiles, Marian persecution (or reaction), Marian priests, Marigold?

MARY II (STUART). 1662-1694. Queen of England. See: Dict. Nat. Biog. Mary Stuart cap, War of William and Mary, William and Mary furniture style.

MARY MAGDALENE, SAINT. Woman whom Jesus healed of evil spirits. See: Webster's Biog. Dict. Magdalen(e), Maudlin, Orders of St. Mary Magdalene, sweet Maudlin?

Mary, sister of Moses. See: Miriam.

MARY STUART. 1542-1587. Queen of Scotland. See: Dict. Nat. Biog. Queen Mary's thistle.

Mary Stuart cap (Mary II): Fashion. See: Picken.

MARY, VIRGIN-MOTHER (Epithets: VIRGIN MARY, OUR LADY, MADONNA, SAINT MARY, REGINA, MATER CARA). fl. early 1st c. Mother of Jesus. See: New Encyc. Brit., 1974. Ave Maria (or Hail Mary), Ave Maria lace, bain-Marie?, Company of Mary, costmary, Doctor Marianus, Handmaids of Mary, Joseph and Mary (flower), joys of Mary, Ladies of Mary, Lady altar, Lady chapel, Lady Day, Ladybug (Ladybird beetle or Lady beetle), Lady's bedstraw, Lady's-mantle(s), Legion of Mary, Little Company of Mary, Madonna, Madonna lily, Madonnina, Mariamettes, Marian, Marianists, Marians, Mariavites, Mariengroschen, Marigold?, Mariola, Mariolatry, Mariology, Marists, Marrowbones, Marry, Marybud, Mother Carey's chicken(s)?, Mother Carey's goose?, Oblates of Mary Immaculate, Our Lady's mint, Our Lady's thistle (or Lady's thistle), Regina Medal, St. (Saint) Mary's thistle, Santa Maria tree?, Saturday Office of the Blessed Virgin Mary, Servants of Mary, Sister of the Holy Names of Jesus and Mary, Sister of the Immaculate Heart of Mary, Sisters of Marie Auxiliatrice, Sisters of Marie Reparatrice, Sisters of St. Mary, Sisters of the Sacred Hearts of Jesus and Mary, Virgin Mary's honeysuckle, Virginal.

Mary Walkers (Walker, Mary Edwards): Fashion. See: Clapin.

Marybud (Mary, Virgin-Mother): Botany. See: Encyc. Brit., 1973 under "Marsh marigold," vol. 14, p. 962; Webster's 3d.

MASANIELLO (Properly: TOMMASO ANIELLO). ca. 1620-1647. Neapolitan fisherman. See: Encyc. Brit., 1973. revolt of Masaniello.

MASCAGNI, PAOLO. 1752-1815. Italian anatomist. See: World Who's Who Sci. Mascagnite (or Mascagnine).

Mascagnite (or Mascagnine) (Mascagni, Paolo): Earth Sciences. See: Charnock; Webster's 3d.

MASCHERONI, LORENZO. 1750-1800. Italian mathematician. See: World Who's Who Sci. Euler-Mascheroni constant.

Mascheroni's constant (Mascheroni, Lorenzo). See: Euler-Mascheroni constant.

MASCHKE, OTTO FRIEDRICH RUDOLF. d. 1900. German chemist. See: Schles. Gesellsch. f. vaterl. Kultur, Breslau. Jahresb., 1900, Nekr., pp. 9-11. Maschke's test.

Maschke's test (Maschke, Otto Friedrich Rudolf): Medicine. See: Stedman.

MASDEVALL, JOSE. d. 1801. Spanish physician and botanist. See: Biog. Lex. hervorr. Aerzte. Masdevallia.

Masdevallia (Masdevall, Jose): Botany. See: New Encyc. Brit., 1974, Microp.; Taylor, N.; Webster's 3d.

Masham, 1st Baron. See: Lister, Samuel Cunliffe, 1st Baron Masham.

Mashburn complex coordinator (or apparatus) (Mashburn, Neely Cornelius): Physiology. See: Chaplin; English; Wolman.

MASHBURN, NEELY CORNELIUS. b. 1886. American physician. Cited in: Index-Cat. Libr. Surg.-Gen. Off., 4th Ser., vol. 10, 1948. Mashburn complex coordinator (or apparatus).

MASINI, GIULIO. 1874-1937. Italian physician. See: Otorinolar. Ital., vol. 7 (1937), p. 285. Masini's sign.

Masini's sign (Masini, Giulio): Medicine. See: Stedman.

Maskelynite (Story-Maskelyne, Nevil): Earth Sciences. See: Webster's 3d.

MASLOW, ABRAHAM HAROLD. 1908-1970. American psychologist. See: World Who's Who Sci. Maslow's theory of personality.

Maslow's theory of personality (Maslow, Abraham Harold): Psychology. See: Wolman.

Masoch, Leopold von Sacher-. See: Sacher-Masoch, Leopold von.

Masochism (Sacher-Masoch, Leopold von): Generic Word. See: Funk; Hendrickson; Partridge; Stedman; Webster's 3d.

Mason and Dixon's line (Mason, Charles and Dixon, Jeremiah): History. See: Clapin; Mathews, M. M.; Phyfe.

MASON, C. J. fl. 1813. English ceramics chemist and manufacturer. (Biography source unavailable.) Mason's ironstone china.

Mason-Chamot micro-test for bromide (Mason, Clyde Walter and Chamot, Emile Monnin): Chemistry. See: Van Nostrand Chem. Dict.

MASON, CHARLES. 1730-1787. English astronomer and surveyor. See: Dict. Nat. Biog. Mason and Dixon's line.

MASON, CLYDE WALTER. 1898- . American chemist. See: Pogg., vol. 6. Mason-Chamot micro-test for bromide.

Mason jar (or fruit jar) (Mason, John L.): Food and Drink. See: De Sola; Hendrickson; Mathews, M. M.

MASON, JOHN L. fl. 1857. American inventor. (Biography source unavailable.) Mason jar (or fruit jar), Masonite.

MASON, MAX. 1877-1961. American mathematician. See: World Who's Who Sci. Mason's theorem?

Masonite (Mason, John L.): Earth Sciences. See: Charnock; Webster's 3d.

Mason's ironstone china (Mason, C. J.): Engineering and Industry. See: Thrush.

Mason's theorem (Mason, Max?): Mathematics. See: Ballentyne.

Masotti field (Mossotti, Ottaviano Fabrizio): Physics. See: Internat. Dict. Ap. Math.; Internat. Dict. Phys. Elec.

MASSELON, JULIEN. 1844-1917. French ophthalmologist. See: Biog. Lex. hervorr. Aerzte, 1880-1930. Masselon's spectacles.

MASSELON, RENE. b. 1874. French psychiatrist. Cited in: Mansell. Masselon test?

Masselon test (Masselon, Rene?): Psychology. See: Drever.

Masselon's spectacles (Masselon, Julien): Medicine. See: Dorland; Stedman.

Massena, Andre. See: Rivoli, Andre Massena, Duc de.

Massena partridge (or quail) (Rivoli, Andre Massena Duc de): Zoology. See: Mathews, M. M.; Webster's 3d.

Massenet (garnish) (Massenet, Jules Emile Frederic): Food and Drink. See: De Sola.

MASSENET, JULES EMILE FREDERIC. 1842-1912. French composer. See: Encyc. Brit., 1973. Massenet (garnish).

MASSET, ALFRED A. b. 1870. French physician. (Biography source unavailable.) Masset's test.

Masset's test (Masset, Alfred A.): Medicine. See: Dorland; Stedman.

MASSEY, CHESTER DANIEL. 1850-1926. Canadian manufacturer and philanthropist. See: Macmillan Dict. Canadian Biog. Massey Foundation.

Massey formula (Massey, Sir Harrie Stewart Wilson): Physics. See: Hughes; Internat. Dict. Phys. Elec.

Massey Foundation (Massey, Chester Daniel): Philanthropy. Cited in: Webster's Biog. Dict.

MASSEY, SIR HARRIE STEWART WILSON. 1908- . Australian-born English physicist. See: World Who's Who Sci. Massey formula.

MASSHOFF, WILLY. (In full: JOHANN WILHELM). 1908- . German pathologist. See: Wer Ist Wer?, 1971-1973. Masshoff's syndrome.

Masshoff's syndrome (Masshoff, Willy): Medicine. See: Jablonski.

MASSIEU, FRANCOIS. 1832-1896. French physicist. See: World Who's Who Sci. Massieu function.

Massieu function (Massieu, Francois): Physics. See: Ballentyne; Internat. Dict. Phys. Elec.

MASSINI, PAUL. fl. 1910. Swiss chemist. Cited in: Chem. Abstr., vol. 4, p. 1947. Schmidlin-Massini test reaction.

Massini's maneuver (Derivation undetermined): Medicine. See: Dorland.

MASSOL, LEON. 1837-1909. Swiss bacteriologist. See: Biog. Lex. hervorr. Aerzte, 1880-1930. Massol's bacillus.

Massol's bacillus (Massol, Leon): Medicine. See: Dorland.

Masson disk (disc) (Masson, W.): Psychology. See: Chaplin; Drever; English.

MASSON, FRANCIS. 1741-1805. Scottish botanist. See: Dict. Nat. Biog. Massonia.

MASSON, PIERRE (In full: CLAUDE LAURENT PIERRE). b. 1880. French-born Canadian pathologist. Cited in: Index-Cat. Libr. Surg.-Gen. Off., 4th Ser., vol. 10, 1948. Barre-Masson syndrome, Masson('s) stain (tetrachrome stain or method).

Masson('s) stain (tetrachrome stain or method) (Masson, Pierre): Medicine. See: Index-Cat. Libr. Surg.-Gen. Off., 4th Ser., vol. 10, 1948; Kelly.

MASSON, W. fl. 1845. Scientist. Cited in: Southall. Masson disk (disc).

Massonia (Masson, Francis): Botany. See: Charnock.

MASSUMI, RASHID A. Iranian-born American physician. See: Direct. Med. Specialists, 1965-1966. Prinzmetal-Massumi syndrome.

MAST. fl. 1967. American •Amish family. Cited in: Lieber and Olbrich. Mast syndrome.

Mast syndrome (Mast): Medicine. See: Hinsie.

MASTER, ARTHUR MATTHEW. 1895- . American cardiologist. See: Nat. Cycl. Amer. Biog., vol. I, pp. 416-418. Master's test (or two-step exercise test).

Master's test (or two-step exercise test) (Master, Arthur Matthew): Medicine. See: Stedman.

MASTERS, WILLIAM HOWELL. 1915- . American physician. See: World Who's Who Sci. Allen-Masters syndrome.

MASUDA. fl. 1936. Japanese ophthalmologist. (Biography source unavailable.) Masuda-Kitahara disease.

Masuda-Kitahara disease (Masuda and Kitahara, S.): Medicine. See: Jablonski. Also known as: Kitahara's disease.

MASUGI, MATAZO. fl. 1933. Japanese pathologist. (Biography source unavailable.) Masugi's nephritis.

Masugi's nephritis (Masugi, Matazo): Medicine. See: Jablonski; Stedman.

Mata Hari (Mata Hari, the spy): Generic Word (seductive female spy). See: Hendrickson.

MATA HARI, THE SPY (Real name: MARGARETHA GEERTRUIDA ZELLE). 1876-1917. Dutch dancer, courtesan and spy. See: New Encyc. Brit., 1974, Microp. Mata Hari.

Matas band (Matas, Rudolph): Medicine. See: Dorland.

Matas' operation (Matas, Rudolph): Medicine. See: Dorland; Stedman.

MATAS, RUDOLPH. 1860-1957. American surgeon. See: World Who's Who Sci. Matas band, Matas' operation.

MATEFY, LADISLAUS. b. 1889. Hungarian physician. (Biography source unavailable.) Matefy test (or reaction).

Matefy test (or reaction) (Matefy, Ladislaus): Medicine. See: Dorland.

MATHER, THOMAS. 1878-1937. English electrical engineer. See: World Who's Who Sci. Ayrton-Mather shunt.

Mathes' mastitis (Mathes, Paul): Medicine. See: Jablonski.

MATHES, PAUL. 1871-1923. Austrian physician. See: Biog. Lex. hervorr. Aerzte, 1880-1930. Mathes' mastitis.

Matheson joint (Derivation undetermined): Engineering and Industry. See: Thrush.

Mathew Brady Award (Brady, Mathew B.): Photography. See: Focal Encyc. Photog. under "Larsen, Lisa."

MATHEW, THEOBALD. 1790-1856. Irish priest and social reformer. See: Encyc. Brit., 1973. Father Mathew.

MATHEWS, ALBERT PRESCOTT. b. 1871. American biochemist. See: Pogg., vol. 6. Vilter-Spies-Mathews test reaction.

MATHEWS, CHESTER ORA. 1895- . American psychologist. See: World Who's Who Sci. Woodworth-Mathews personal data sheet.

MATHEWS, JOSEPH MCDOWELL. b. 1847. American physician. See: Who Was Who Amer., 1961-1968. Mathew's speculum.

Mathew's speculum (Mathews, Joseph McDowell): Medicine. See: Stedman.

Mathewson's device (Derivation undetermined): Engineering and Industry. See: Thrush.

MATHIAS, EMILE-OVIDE-JOSEPH. 1861-1942. French physicist. See: World Who's Who Sci. Cailletet and Mathias law.

Mathiasism (Matthias, Robert): Religion. See: Mathews, M. M.

MATHIEU, ALBERT. 1855-1917. French physician. See: Biog. Lex. hervorr. Aerzte, 1880-1930. Mathieu's disease.

MATHIEU, EMILE LEONARD. 1835-1890. French mathematician. See: Pogg., vols. 3, 4. Mathieu equation(s)

Mathieu equation(s) (Mathieu, Emile Leonard): Mathematics. See: Internat. Dict. Phys. Elec.; Thewlis; Van Nostrand Sci. Encyc.

MATHIEU-PLESSY, E. fl. 1885. French chemist. Cited in: Royal Soc. Cat. Sci. Pap., 1884-1900. Plessy's green?

Mathieu's disease (Mathieu, Albert). See: Weil's disease.

Mathis der Maler (Gruenewald, Mathias): Music. See: Apel.

Mathurin(es) (Mathurin, Saint): Religion. See: Encyc. Brit., 1973 under "Trinitarians"; Webster's 3d.

MATHURIN, SAINT. d. before 388. French priest. See: Holweck. Mathurin(es), Saint Mathurin's disease.

MATIGNON, CAMILLE ARTHEME. 1867-1934. French chemist. See: Pogg., vols. 4, 5, 6. Matignon test reaction for vanadium.

Matignon test reaction for vanadium (Matignon, Camille Artheme): Chemistry. See: Van Nostrand Chem. Dict.

Matius, C. Calvena. See: Calvena, C. Matius.

MATSCH, LEANDER WILLIAM. 1902- . American electrical engineer. See: Amer. Men and Women Sci., 12th ed. Matsch's law, Matsch's maxim.

Matsch's law (Matsch, Leander William): Sociology. See: Martin.

Matsch's maxim (Matsch, Leander William): Sociology. See: Martin.

MATSON, DONALD DARROW. 1913-1969. American neurosurgeon. See: Who Was Who Amer., 1969-1973. Matson operation.

Matson operation (Matson, Donald Darrow): Medicine. See: Stedman.

MATSUI, MOTOOKI. fl. 1920. Japanese chemist. See: Bull. Chem. Soc. Japan, vol. 10, no. 8 (1935), pp. 2-6. Matsui-Nakazawa test for cobalt.

Matsui-Nakazawa test for cobalt (Matsui, Motooki and Nakazawa, Tadasu): Chemistry. See: Van Nostrand Chem. Dict.

Mattan (jewel) (Mattan, Rajah of): Applied Arts. See: Wagner (Names).

MATTAN, RAJAH OF. No dates. Indian? ruler (Biography source unavailable.) Mattan (jewel).

Mattauch-Herzog mass spectrograph (and geometry) (Mattauch, Josef Heinrich Elizabeth and Herzog, Richard Franz): Physics. See: Van Nostrand Sci. Encyc. under "Mass Spectrometry"; Cited in: World Who's Who Sci.

MATTAUCH, JOSEF HEINRICH ELIZABETH. 1895- . Austrian physicist. See: World Who's Who Sci. Mattauch-Herzog mass spectrograph (and geometry), Mattauch's rule.

Mattauch's rule (Mattauch, Josef Heinrich Elizabeth): Physics. See: World Who's Who Sci. under "Mattauch, Josef."

MATTEUCCI, FELICE. 1808-1887. Italian inventor. See: Diz. Encic. Ital. Barsanti-Matteucci gas engine.

Matteuccia (Matteuci, Carlo): Botany. See: Webster's 3d.

MATTEUCI, CARLO. 1811-1868. Italian physicist. See: World Who's Who Sci. Matteuccia, Matteuci effect.

Matteuci effect (Matteuci, Carlo): Physics. See: Ballentyne.

Matthean (or Matthaean) (Matthew, Saint): Religion. See: Webster's 3d.

MATTHEW, SAINT. One of Jesus' twelve apostles in the New Testament. See: Encyc. Brit., 1973. Matthean (or Matthaean), St. Matthew Passion.

Matthew, Thomas. See: Rogers, John.

Matthew's Bible (Rogers, John, pseud., Thomas Matthew): Religion. See: Barnhart (Eng. Lit.): Brewer; Mathews, S.

Matthews, Robert. See: Matthias, Robert.

MATTHIAS, BERND TEO. 1918- . German-born American physicist. See: World Who's Who Sci. Matthias' rules.

MATTHIAS (MATTHEWS), ROBERT. fl. ca. 1831. American religious cult founder. (Biography source unavailable.) Mathiasism.

Matthias' rules (Matthias, Bernd Teo): Chemistry. See: Ballentyne.

MATTHIESSEN, AUGUSTUS. 1831-1870. English chemist and physicist. See: Dict. Nat. Biog. Matthiessen('s) rule (or hypothesis), Matthiessen's standard.

Matthiessen('s) rule (or hypothesis) (Matthiessen, Augustus): Physics. See: Ballentyne; Hackh; Hughes; Thewlis; Van Nostrand Sci. Encyc.

Matthiessen's standard (Matthiessen, Augustus): Physics. See: Ballentyne.

Matthiola (Mattioli, Pietro Andrea Gregorio): Botany. See: Charnock; Taylor, N.; Webster's 3d.

Mattioli-Foggia and Raso syndrome (Mattioli-Foggia, Cesare and Raso, Mario): Medicine. See: Jablonski.

MATTIOLI-FOGGIA, CESARE. fl. 1949. Italian pathologist. (Biography source unavailable.) Mattioli-Foggia and Raso syndrome.

MATTIOLI, PIETRO ANDREA GREGORIO. 1501-1577. Italian physician and botanist. See: World Who's Who Sci. Matthiola.

MATTUSCHKA, COUNT HEINRICH GOTTFRIED VON. 1734-1779. German botanist. See: Allg. Deut. Biog. Matuschkaea.

Matuschkaea (Mattuschka, Count Heinrich Gottfried von): Botany. See: Charnock.

MATVEEV, L. fl. 1936. Russian chemist. Cited in: Chem. Abstr., vol. 30, p. 7492. Kul'berg-Matveeo test for hydrogen peroxide.

Matzenauer-Polland syndrome (Matzenauer, Rudolf and Polland, Rudolf): Medicine. See: Jablonski.

MATZENAUER, RUDOLF. b. 1861. Austrian dermatologist. See: Biog. Lex. hervorr. Aerzte. Matzenauer-Polland syndrome.

MAUCHART, BURKHARD DAVID. 1696-1751. German anatomist. See: World Who's Who Sci. Mauchart's ligaments.

Mauchart's ligaments (Mauchart, Burkhard David): Anatomy. See: Donath; Dorland; Stedman.

MAUCHER, WILHELM. d. 1930. German mineral dealer. (Biography source unavailable.) Maucherite.

Maucherite (Maucher, Wilhelm): Earth Sciences. See: Thrush; Webster's 3d.

Maud, John. See: Redcliffe-Maud, John Primatt, Baron.

Maud report (Redcliffe-Maud, John Primatt, Baron). See: Redcliffe-Maud report.

Maudlin (Mary Magdalene, Saint): Generic Word (sentimental or foolishly drunk). See: Brewer; Charnock; Funk; Hendrickson; Partridge; Webster's 3d.

MAUGERI, SALVATORE. 1905- . Italian physician. See: Who's Who Sci. Europe, 1972. Maugeri's syndrome.

Maugeri's syndrome (Maugeri, Salvatore): Medicine. See: Jablonski.

MAUGIN, CHARLES-VICTOR. 1878-1937. French crystallographer. See: World Who's Who Sci. Hermann-Mauguin symbols.

Maulavi. See: Jalal-Ud-Din Rumi (Mohammed ibn Mohammed Moulavi Balkhi).

MAUMENE, EDME JULES. 1818-1891. French chemist. See: Pogg., vols. 3, 4. Maumene number, Maumene's test.

Maumene number (Maumene, Edme Jules): Chemistry. See: Hackh; Van Nostrand Chem. Dict.

Maumene's test (Maumene, Edme Jules): Medicine. See: Dorland; Stedman.

Maumet (or Mammet) (Mohammed): Generic Word (doll). See: Charnock; Hendrickson; Webster's 3d.

Maumetry (or Mawmetry) (Mohammed): Generic Word (idolatry). See: Charnock; Webster's 3d.

MAUNOIR, JEAN PIERRE. 1768-1861. Swiss surgeon. See: World Who's Who Sci. Maunoir's hydrocele.

Maunoir's hydrocele (Maunoir, Jean Pierre): Medicine. See: Jablonski.

MAUPEOU, RENE NICOLAS CHARLES AUGUSTIN DE. 1714-1792. French statesman. See: New Encyc. Brit., 1974, Microp. Maupeou's reforms.

Maupeou's reforms (Maupeou, Rene Nicolas Charles Augustin de): History. See: Morris and Irwin.

MAUPERTUIS, PIERRE LOUIS MOREAU DE. 1698-1759. French astronomer and mathematician. See: Dict. Sci. Biog. Maupertuis' principle (or theorem).

Maupertuis' principle (or theorem) (Maupertuis, Pierre Louis Moreau de): Mathematics. See: Ballentyne; Internat. Dict. Ap. Math.

Maurandia (Maurandy, Catharina Pancratia): Botany. See: Charnock; Taylor, N.; Webster's 3d.

MAURANDY, CATHARINA PANCRATIA. fl. 18th c. Spanish botanist. (Biography source unavailable.) Maurandia.

MAURER, GEORG. 1909-   . German physician in Sumatra. (Biography source unavailable.) Maurer's dots (or clefts).

Maurer's dots (or clefts) (Maurer, Georg): Medicine. See: Dorland; Stedman; Webster's 3d.

MAURI, ANTONIO. No dates. Botanist. (Biography source unavailable.) Mauria.

Mauria (Mauri, Antonio): Botany. See: Charnock.

MAURIAC, CHARLES MARIE TAMARELLE. 1832-1905. French physician. See: World Who's Who Sci. Mauriac's syndrome.

MAURIAC, PIERRE (In full: LEONARD PIERRE). b. 1882. French physician. See: Biog. Lex. hervorr. Aerzte, 1880-1930. Mauriac's syndrome.

Mauriac's syndrome (Mauriac, Charles Marie Tamarelle): Medicine. See: Jablonski.

Mauriac's syndrome (Mauriac, Pierre): Medicine. See: Jablonski. Also known as: Pierre Mauriac's syndrome.

MAURICE, FREDERICK DENISON (In full: JOHN FREDERICK DENISON). 1805-1872. English theologian. See: Dict. Nat. Biog. Maurice hostels.

Maurice hostels (Maurice, Frederick Denison): Sociology. See: Canney.

MAURICE (MAURITIUS), SAINT. d. ca. 286. Christian martyr. See: Encyc. Brit., 1973. Order of Saints Maurice and Lazarus.

MAURICEAU, FRANCOIS. 1637-1709. French obstetrician. See: World Who's Who Sci. Mauriceau's lance, Mauriceau's maneuver (or method).

Mauriceau's lance (Mauriceau, Francois): Medicine. See: Dorland; Stedman.

Mauriceau's maneuver (or method) (Mauriceau, Francois): Medicine. See: Dorland; Stedman.

Maurists (Maurus, Saint): Religion. See: Attwater; Encyc. Brit., 1973; Harvey; Mathews, S.; Webster's 3d.

Mauritia (John Maurice of Nassau): Botany. See: Charnock; Webster's 3d.

Mauritz von Nassau-Siegen. See: John Maurice of Nassau.

MAURUS, SAINT. ca. 501-ca. 584. Roman-born abbott in France? See: Holweck. Maurists.

MAUSER, PETER PAUL. 1838-1914. German inventor. See: Webster's Biog. Dict. Mauser (rifle).

Mauser (rifle) (Mauser, Peter Paul and Mauser, Wilhelm): Weapons. See: Hendrickson; Partridge; Quick.

MAUSER, WILHELM. 1834-1882. German inventor. See: Webster's Biog. Dict. Mauser (rifle).

Mausoleum (Mausolus): Generic Word (great, gloomy structure). See: Brewer; Charnock; Funk; Hendrickson; Osborne.

MAUSOLUS. d. ca. 353 B.C. King of Caria. See: Encyc. Brit., 1973. Mausoleum.

MAUTHNER, LUDWIG. 1840-1894. German ophthalmologist. See: World Who's Who Sci. Mauthner's cell(s), Mauthner's fiber, Mauthner's sheath, Mauthner's test.

Mauthner's cell(s) (Mauthner, Ludwig): Zoology. See: Dorland; Henderson; Stedman.

Mauthner's fiber (Mauthner, Ludwig): Zoology. See: Stedman.

Mauthner's sheath (Mauthner, Ludwig): Anatomy. See: Donath; Dorland; Stedman.

Mauthner's test (Mauthner, Ludwig): Physiology. See: Dorland; Stedman.

Maverick (Maverick, Samuel Augustus): Generic Word (non-conformist). See: Brewer; Hendrickson; Mathews, M. M.; Webster's 3d.

MAVERICK, SAMUEL AUGUSTUS. 1803-1870. American pioneer in Texas. See: Webster's Biog. Dict. Maverick.

MAWALD. fl. 20th c. German engineer? (Biography source unavailable.) Mawald pump.

Mawald pump (Mawald): Engineering and Industry. See: Auger.

Mawas brasilin solution (Mawas, Jacques): Chemistry. See: Van Nostrand Chem. Dict.

MAWAS, JACQUES. b. 1885. French pharmaceutical chemist and ophthalmologist. See: Arnim. Mawas brasilin solution.

MAWWORM. Character in Isaac Bickerstaffe's play, "The Hypocrite," (1769). See: Harvey under "Bickerstaffe, Isaac." Mawworm.

Mawworm (Mawworm, the fictional character): Generic Word (hypocrite). See: Charnock; Partridge.

Max Bendix string quartet (Bendix, Max): Music. Cited in: Webster's Biog. Dict.

Max d'or (or Maximilian) (Maximilian Joseph): Numismatics. See: Charnock.

MAXCY, KENNETH FULLER. 1889-1966. American bacteriologist. See: World Who's Who Sci. Maxcy's disease.

Maxcy's disease (Maxcy, Kenneth Fuller): Medicine. See: Dorland; Jablonski.

Maxim automobile (Maxim, Hiram Percy): Engineering and Industry. See: Hendrickson.

Maxim gun (or machine gun) (Maxim, Sir Hiram Stevens): Weapons. See: Hendrickson; Partridge; Quick. Also known as: Vickers-Maxim gun, Vickers gun.

MAXIM, HIRAM PERCY. 1869-1936. American inventor. See: World Who's Who Sci. Maxim automobile, Maxim silencer(s).

MAXIM, SIR HIRAM STEVENS. 1840-1916. American-born English inventor. See: World Who's Who Sci. Maxim gun (or machine gun).

MAXIM, HUDSON. 1853-1927. American inventor and explosives expert. See: Dict. Amer. Biog. Maxim-Schupphaus smokeless powder, Maximite.

Maxim-Schupphaus smokeless powder (Maxim, Hudson and Schupphaus, Robert C.): Engineering and Industry. Cited in: Encyc. Brit., 1973, vol. 14, p. 1134b under "Maxim, Hudson."

Maxim silencer(s) (Maxim, Hiram Percy): Engineering and Industry. See: Encyc. Brit., 1973; Hendrickson.

Maximianists (Maximianus): Religion. See: Canney.

MAXIMIANUS. fl. 391. Carthaginian deacon. See: Dict. Christian Biog. under "Maximianus (2)," p. 868-869. Maximianists.

MAXIMILIAN I. 1459-1519. Holy Roman Emperor. See: Encyc. Brit., 1973. Maximilian armour.

MAXIMILIAN I (JOSEPH). 1756-1825. King of Bavaria. See: Encyc. Brit., 1973. Military Order of Maximilian Joseph.

MAXIMILIAN II (JOSEPH). 1811-1864. King of Bavaria. See: Encyc. Brit., 1973. Order of Maximilian.

Maximilian armour (Maximilian I): Military Science. See: Encyc. Brit., 1973 under "Armour, Body."

MAXIMILIAN JOSEPH. 1727-1777. Elector of Bavaria. See: Nouv. Biog. Univ. Max d'or (or Maximilian).

Maximite (Maxim, Hudson): Engineering and Industry. See: Webster's 3d.

MAXIMOW, ALEXANDER ALEXANDROVICH. 1874-1928. Russian-born histologist in Germany and the United States. See: Anat. Anz., vol. 67 (1929), pp. 360-368. Maximow fluid.

Maximow fluid (Maximow, Alexander Alexandrovich): Chemistry. See: Van Nostrand Chem. Dict.

Maximus Planudes. See: Planudes, Maximus.

Maximus, Quintus Fabius. See: Fabius, Quintus.

Maxton screen (Derivation undetermined): Engineering and Industry. See: Thrush.

MAXWELL, ALICE FREELAND. 1890-1961. American obstetrician and gynecologist. See: J.A.M.A., vol. 177 (July 8-Sept. 30, 1961), pp. 161-162. Goldberg-Maxwell-Morris syndrome.

Maxwell-Boltzmann distribution law (Maxwell, James Clerk and Boltzmann, Ludwig): Physics. See: Ballentyne; Internat. Dict. Ap. Math.; Internat. Dict. Phys. Elec.; Van Nostrand Sci. Encyc. Also known as: Boltzmann distribution law.

Maxwell-Boltzmann statistics (Maxwell, James Clerk and Boltzmann, Ludwig): Physics. See: Ballentyne; Kendall; Markus. Also known as: Boltzmann statistics.

Maxwell-Boltzmann transport equation (Maxwell, James Clerk and Boltzmann, Ludwig). See: Boltzmann transport equation.

Maxwell bridge (Maxwell, James Clerk): Electronics. See: Hughes; Internat. Dict. Phys. Elec.; Thewlis.

Maxwell d-c commutator bridge (Maxwell, James Clerk): Electronics. See: Markus.

Maxwell('s) demon(s) (Maxwell, James Clerk): Physics. See: Ballentyne; Clumberg; English; Internat. Dict. Phys. Elec.

Maxwell disk(s) (Maxwell, James Clerk): Physics. See: Chaplin; Wolman; Webster's 3d.

Maxwell distribution (Maxwell, James Clerk): Statistics. See: Kendall.

Maxwell distribution law (or distribution law of Maxwell) (Maxwell, James Clerk): Physics. See: Internat. Dict. Ap. Math.; Van Nostrand Chem. Dict.; Van Nostrand Sci. Encyc.

Maxwell effect (Maxwell, James Clerk): Physics. See: Ballentyne; Internat. Dict. Phys. Elec.

Maxwell('s) equations (or field equations) (Maxwell, James Clerk): Physics. See: Ballentyne; Hughes; Internat. Dict. Phys. Elec.; Thewlis.

Maxwell fisheye (Maxwell, James Clerk): Physics. See: Internat. Dict. Ap. Math.

MAXWELL, JAMES CLERK. 1831-1879. Scottish physicist. See: Dict. Sci. Biog. Abbe-Maxwell theorem, Enskog-Maxwell equations of change, Maxwell-Boltzmann distribution law, Maxwell-Boltzmann statistics, Maxwell-Boltzmann transport equation, Maxwell bridge, Maxwell d-c commutator bridge, Maxwell('s) demon(s), Maxwell disk(s), Maxwell distribution, Maxwell distribution law (or distribution law of Maxwell), Maxwell effect, Maxwell('s) equations (or field equations), Maxwell fisheye, Maxwell('s) law (of viscosity), Maxwell material, Maxwell model, Maxwell modulus, Maxwell-Mohr method, Maxwell primaries, Maxwell relation(s), Maxwell relation(ship) (between dielectric constant and refractive index), Maxwell stress functions, Maxwell stress tensor, Maxwell theorem for isotherms, Maxwell triangle (or color triangle), Maxwell turns, Maxwell (unit), Maxwell-Wagner effect, Maxwell-Wagner mechanism, Maxwell-Wien bridge, Maxwellian, Maxwellian fluid, Maxwellian molecules, Maxwellian view (or viewing system), Maxwell's circuital theorems, Maxwell's circulating current, Maxwell's rule, Maxwell's spot (or ring), Maxwell's theorem, Maxwell's theory of light, reciprocity theorem of Maxwell and Betti.

MAXWELL, JAMES LAIDLOW, SENIOR. 1836-1921. English physician in Formosa. See: Biog. Lex. hervorr. Aerzte. MacLean-Maxwell disease.

Maxwell('s) law (of viscosity) (Maxwell, James Clerk): Physics. See: Huschke; Thewlis.

Maxwell material (Maxwell, James Clerk): Physics. See: Internat. Dict. Ap. Math.

Maxwell model (Maxwell, James Clerk): Physics. See: Internat. Dict. Ap. Math.

Maxwell modulus (Maxwell, James Clerk): Physics. See: Thewlis.

Maxwell-Mohr method (Maxwell, James Clerk and Mohr, Otto): Engineering and Industry. See: Internat. Dict. Ap. Math.

MAXWELL, PATRICK WILLIAM. 1856-1917. Irish ophthalmologist. Cited in: Index Medicus, 2d Ser., vol. 15, 1917. Maxwell's ring.

Maxwell primaries (Maxwell, James Clerk): Physics. See: Ballentyne.

Maxwell relation(s) (Maxwell, James Clerk): Physics. See: Internat. Dict. Ap. Math.; Internat. Dict. Phys. Elec.; Thewlis.

Maxwell relation(ship) (between dielectric constant and refractive index) (Maxwell, James Clerk): Physics. See: Hughes; Internat. Dict. Phys. Elec.; Van Nostrand Sci. Encyc. Also known as: Clerk Maxwell relation.

Maxwell stress functions (Maxwell, James Clerk): Mathematics. See: Internat. Dict. Ap. Math.

Maxwell stress tensor (Maxwell, James Clerk): Physics. See: Ballentyne.

Maxwell theorem for isotherms (Maxwell, James Clerk): Physics. See: Internat. Dict. Ap. Math.

Maxwell triangle (or color triangle) (Maxwell, James Clerk): Physics. See: Chaplin; Thewlis; Van Nostrand Sci. Encyc.; Webster's 3d.

Maxwell turns (Maxwell, James Clerk): Electronics. See: Hughes.

Maxwell (unit) (Maxwell, James Clerk): Physics. See: Ballentyne; Dresner; Thewlis; Van Nostrand Sci. Encyc.; Webster's 3d.

Maxwell-Wagner effect (Maxwell, James Clerk and Wagner, Karl Willy): Physics. See: Thewlis.

Maxwell-Wagner mechanism (Maxwell, James Clerk and Wagner, Karl Willy): Physics. See: Internat. Dict. Phys. Elec.

Maxwell-Wien bridge (Maxwell, James Clerk and Wien, Max Carl): Electronics. See: Internat. Dict. Phys. Elec.

Maxwellian (Maxwell, James Clerk): Physics. See: Webster's 3d.

Maxwellian fluid (Maxwell, James Clerk): Physics. See: Internat. Dict. Phys. Elec.; Van Nostrand Sci. Encyc.

Maxwellian molecules (Maxwell, James Clerk): Physics. See: Internat. Dict. Ap. Math.

Maxwellian view (or viewing system) (Maxwell, James Clerk): Physics. See: Thewlis; Van Nostrand Sci. Encyc.

Maxwell's circuital theorems (Maxwell, James Clerk): Electronics. See: Hughes.

Maxwell's circulating current (Maxwell, James Clerk): Electronics. See: Hughes.

Maxwell's ring (Maxwell, Patrick William). See: Maxwell's spot.

Maxwell's rule (Maxwell, James Clerk): Physics. See: Ballentyne; Thrush; Webster's 3d.

Maxwell's spot (or ring) (Maxwell, James Clerk): Physiology. See: Dorland; Stedman. Also known as: Loewe's ring.

Maxwell's theorem (Maxwell, James Clerk): Physics. See: Ballentyne.

Maxwell's theory of light (Maxwell, James Clerk): Physics. See: Ballentyne.

May (Maia): Generic Word. See: Charnock; Funk; Webster's 3d.; Weekley.

MAY, CHARLES HENRY. 1861-1943. American ophthalmologist. See: World Who's Who Sci. May's sign (or test).

May-Gruenwald staining solution (May, Richard and Gruenwald, Ludwig): Medicine. See: Kelly.

May-Hegglin syndrome (May, Richard and Hegglin, Robert). See: Hegglin's anomaly.

MAY, RICHARD. 1863-1936. German physician. See: Munchen. Med Wchnschr., vol. 84 (1937), p. 430. May-Gruenwald staining solution, May-Hegglin syndrome.

Maybach carburettor (Maybach, Wilhelm): Engineering and Industry. See: Auger.

MAYBACH, WILHELM. 1847-1929. German pioneer automobile builder. See: New Encyc. Brit., 1974, Microp. Maybach carburettor.

MAYDL, KAREL. 1853-1903. Bohemian surgeon. See: World Who's Who Sci. Maydl's hernia, Maydl's method, Maydl's operation.

Maydl's hernia (Maydl, Karel): Medicine. See: Dorland; Jablonski; Stedman.

Maydl's method (Maydl, Karel): Medicine. See: Stedman.

Maydl's operation (Maydl, Karel): Medicine. See: Dorland; Stedman.

Mayer (Mayer, Julius Robert): Physics. See: Dresner; Van Nostrand Sci. Encyc.

MAYER, ALFRED MARSHALL. 1836-1897. American physicist. See: Dict. Sci. Biog. Mayer's law.

MAYER, AUGUST FRANZ JOSEPH KARL. 1787-1865. German anatomist. See: Biog. Lex hervorr. Aerzte. Mayer-Rokitansky-Kuester syndrome.

MAYER, CARL. 1862-1932. Austrian neurologist. See: Biog. Lex. hervorr. Aerzte. Mayer's reflex.

Mayer curve (Derivation undetermined): Engineering and Industry. See: Thrush.

MAYER, FERDINAND F. fl. late 19th c. American pharmaceutical chemist. See: Pharmaceut. Rundschau, vol. 12 (1894), p. 130 f. Mayer-Tanret test, Mayer('s) test (or reagent for alkaloids).

MAYER, FRIEDRICH. fl. 1917. German chemist. Cited in: Chem. Abstr., vol. 11, p. 2870. Mayer-Schramm test for copper.

Mayer-Gross apraxia (Mayer-Gross, Willy): Medicine. See: Jablonski. Also known as: Kleist's apraxia.

MAYER-GROSS, WILLY. b. 1889. German neurologist. See: Biog. Lex. hervorr. Aerzte, 1880-1930. Mayer-Gross apraxia.

Mayer hemacalcium solution (Mayer, Paul): Chemistry. See: Van Nostrand Chem. Dict.

Mayer('s) hemalum (solution) (Mayer, Paul): Chemistry. See: Hackh; Van Nostrand Chem. Dict.

Mayer hypothesis (Mayer, Julius Robert). See: Joule('s) law (2) (or law of energy content).

MAYER, JOSEPH EDWARD. 1904- . American physicist. See: World Who's Who Sci. Born-Mayer equation, Mayer theory of condensation.

MAYER, JULIUS ROBERT. 1814-1878. German physicist and physiologist. See: Dict. Sci. Biog. Mayer, Mayer hypothesis.

MAYER, KARL WILHELM. 1795-1868. German gynecologist. See: Biog. Lex. hervorr. Aerzte. Mayer's pessary.

MAYER, PAUL. 1848-1923. German chemist. See: Anat. Anz., vol. 58 (1924-1925), pp. 88-93. Mayer hemacalcium solution, Mayer('s) hemalum (solution), Mayer picrocarmine solution.

Mayer picrocarmine solution (Mayer, Paul): Chemistry. See: Van Nostrand Chem. Dict.

Mayer reaction for cholesterol (Derivation undetermined): Chemistry. See: Van Nostrand Chem. Dict.

Mayer-Rokitansky-Kuester syndrome (Mayer, August Franz Joseph Karl; Rokitansky, Karl Freiherr von; and Kuester, Hermann): Medicine. See: Jablonski.

Mayer-Schramm test for copper (Mayer, Friedrich and Schramm, W. H.): Chemistry. See: Van Nostrand Chem. Dict.

Mayer-Tanret test (Mayer, Ferdinand F. and Tanret, Charles Joseph): Medicine. See: Stedman.

Mayer('s) test (or reagent for alkaloids) (Mayer, Ferdinand F.): Chemistry. See: Dorland; Hackh; Stedman; Van Nostrand Chem. Dict.

Mayer theory of condensation (Mayer, Joseph Edward): Physics. See: Internat. Dict. Phys. Elec.

Mayer-Vietoris sequence (Mayer, Walther and Vietoris, Leopold): Mathematics. See: Encyc. Brit., 1973 under "Topology, Algebraic," vol. 22, p. 81.

MAYER, WALTHER. b. 1887. Austrian-born American mathematician. See: Pogg., vol. 6. Mayer-Vietoris sequence.

Mayer's law (Mayer, Alfred Marshall): Physics. Cited in: Dict. Sci. Biog.

Mayer's pessary (Mayer, Karl Wilhelm). See: Dumontpallier's pessary.

Mayer's reflex (Mayer, Carl): Medicine. See: Stedman.

MAYNARD, CHARLES JOHNSON. 1845-1929. American ornithologist. See: World Who's Who Sci. Maynard's cuckoo.

MAYNARD, EDWARD. 1813-1891. American dentist. See: World Who's Who Sci. Maynard rifle.

Maynard rifle (Maynard, Edward): Weapons. See: Mathews, M. M.

Maynard's cuckoo (Maynard, Charles Johnson): Zoology. See: Mathews, M. M.; Webster's 3d.

MAYO, CHARLES HORACE. 1865-1939. American physician. See: World Who's Who Sci. Mayo scissors, Mayo's method, Mayo's operation, Mayo's treatment.

Mayo curved surgical scissors (Mayo Marc Antoine Louis): Medicine. Cited in: Carter.

MAYO, MARC ANTOINE LOUIS. No dates. French surgeon. (Biography source unavailable.) Mayo curved surgical scissors.

MAYO-ROBSON, SIR ARTHUR WILLIAM. 1853-1933. English surgeon. See: Ann. Register. Mayo-Robson's point, Mayo-Robson's position.

Mayo-Robson's point (Mayo-Robson, Sir Arthur William): Medicine. See: Dorland; Stedman.

Mayo-Robson's position (Mayo-Robson, Sir Arthur William): Medicine. See: Dorland; Stedman.

Mayo scissors (Mayo, Charles Horace and Mayo, William James): Medicine. See: Carter.

MAYO, WILLIAM JAMES. 1861-1939. American surgeon. See: Who Was Who Amer., vol. 1. Mayo scissors, Mayo's anemic spot, Mayo's operation, Mayo's vein, Quenu-Mayo operation.

MAYOR, MATHIAS LOUIS. 1775-1847. Swiss surgeon. See: World Who's Who Sci. Mayor's hammer.

Mayor's hammer (Mayor, Mathias Louis): Medicine. See: Dorland.

Mayo's anemic spot (Mayo, William James): Medicine. See: Jablonski.

Mayo's method (Mayo, Charles Horace): Medicine. See: Dorland; Stedman.

Mayo's operation (Mayo, Charles Horace and Mayo, William James): Medicine. See: Dorland; Stedman.

Mayo's treatment (Mayo, Charles Horace): Medicine. See: Stedman.

Mayo's vein (Mayo, William James): Anatomy. See: Stedman. Also known as: Latarjet's vein.

MAYOU, MARMADUKE STEPHEN. 1876-1934. English ophthalmologist. See: Who Was Who, 1929-1940. Batten-Mayou syndrome.

MAYR, CARL. 1881-1951. Austrian analytical chemist. See: Pogg., vols. 6, 7a. Mayr solution.

MAYR, GUSTAV. 1830-1908. Austrian zoologist. See: Marcellia, vol. 7 (1908), pp. 134-139. Mayrian furrow.

Mayr solution (Mayr, Carl): Chemistry. See: Van Nostrand Chem. Dict.

MAYRHOFER, ADOLF MARTIN. b. 1881. Austrian microchemist. See: Pogg., vols. 6, 7a. Mayrhoffer reagent.

Mayrhoffer reagent (Mayrhofer, Adolf Martin): Chemistry. See: Van Nostrand Chem. Dict.

Mayrian furrow (Mayr, Gustav): Zoology. See: Gray.

May's sign (or test) (May, Charles Henry): Medicine. See: Dorland.

Mazarin Bible (Mazarin, Jules): Printing. See: Harrod; Lockwood; Phyfe. Also known as: Gutenberg Bible.

Mazarin (cake) (Mazarin, Jules): Food and Drink. See: De Sola.

MAZARIN, HORTENSE MANCINI, DUCHESSE DE. 1646-1699. Italian-French political and society leader. See: Nouv. Biog. Univ. Mazarine hood.

AZARIN, JULES (GIULIO MAZZARINI). 1602-1661. Italian-born French cardinal and statesman. See: New Encyc. Brit., 1974. a la Mazarine, Mazarin Bible, Mazarin (cake), Mazarin (liqueur), Mazarin(e) (serving dish), Mazarinade(s), Mazarine (blue).

Mazarin (liqueur) (Mazarin, Jules): Food and Drink. See: De Sola.

Mazarin(e) (serving dish) (Mazarin, Jules): Food and Drink. See: De Sola; Webster's 3d.

Mazarinade(s) (Mazarin, Jules): Literature. See: Brewer; Scott.

Mazarine (blue) (Mazarin, Jules): Chemistry. See: Wagner (Names); Webster's 3d.; Weekley.

Mazarine hood (Mazarin, Hortense Mancini, Duchesse de): Fashion. See: Partridge; Picken; Webster's 3d.

Mazdaism (Mazdeism) (Ahura Mazda): Religion. See: Canney; Webster's 3d. Also known as: Zoroastrianism.

MAZDAK. fl. late 5th c. Persian religious reformer. See: New Encyc. Brit., 1974, Microp. Mazdakism (Mazdakite or Mazdakean).

Mazdakism (Mazdakite or Mazdakean) (Mazdak): Religion. See: Encyc. Brit., 1973; Webster's 3d.

MAZEPA, IVAN STEPANOVICH. ca. 1640-1709. Cossack leader in Russian Ukraine. See: Encyc. Brit., 1973. Mazeppa (symphonic poem).

Mazeppa (symphonic poem) (Mazepa, Ivan Stepanovich): Music. See: Apel.

MAZER, CHARLES. b. 1881. American physician. See: Index-Cat. Libr. Surg.-Gen. Off., 4th Ser., vol. 10, 1928. Mazer-Hoffman test.

Mazer-Hoffman test (Mazer, Charles and Hoffman, Jacob): Medicine. See: Dorland.

MAZUIR, A. fl. 1920. Italian chemist. Cited in: Chem. Abstr., vol. 14, 1091. Mazuir reaction for tin.

Mazuir reaction for tin (Mazuir, A.): Chemistry. See: Van Nostrand Chem. Dict.

Mazur-Banach game (Mazur, Stanislaw-Mieczyslaw and Banach, Stefan): Mathematics. See: James.

MAZUR, STANISLAW MIECZYSLAW. fl. 1935. Polish mathematician. See: Sprawozd. Towarystowa Nauk. Lwowie, vol. 17 (1937), p. 96f. Mazur-Banach game.

MAZZA, SALVADOR. 1886-1946. Argentinian physician. See: Index-Cat. Med. Veter. Zool., vol. 10, 1948. Chagas-Mazza disease.

Mazzei letter (Mazzei, Philip): History. See: Jameson.

MAZZEI, PHILIP. 1730-1816. Italian physician and merchant. See: Webster's Biog. Dict. Mazzei letter.

MAZZINI, GIUSEPPE. 1805-1872. Italian patriot. See: Encyc. Brit., 1973. Mazzinian.

MAZZINI, LOUIS Y. b. 1894. American serologist. Cited in: Chem. Abstr., Decenn. Index, 1937-1946. Mazzini's test.

Mazzinian (Mazzini, Giuseppe): History. See: Webster's 3d.

Mazzini's test (Mazzini, Louis Y.): Medicine. See: Dorland; Kelly.

MAZZONI, VITTORIO. 1880-1940. Italian physiologist. Cited in: Index-Cat. Libr. Surg.-Gen. Off., 2d Ser., vol. 10, 1905. Golgi-Mazzoni corpuscle, Mazzoni's corpuscle(s).

Mazzoni's corpuscle(s) (Mazzoni, Vittorio): Anatomy. See: Donath; Dorland; Stedman.

MEACHAM, LARNED AMES. 1908- . American electrical engineer. See: Amer. Men Sci., 9th ed. Meacham bridge oscillator.

Meacham bridge oscillator (Meacham, Larned Ames): Electronics. See: Van Nostrand Sci. Encyc.

MEAD, RICHARD. 1673-1754. English physician. See: Encyc. Brit., 1973. Meadia.

Meadia (Mead, Richard): Botany. See: Taylor, N.

MEARNE, SAMUEL. fl. 1660-1683. English bookbinder. Cited in: Glaister. Mearne style (book decoration).

Mearne style (book decoration) (Mearne, Samuel): Printing. See: Harrod.

MEARNS, EDGAR ALEXANDER. 1856-1916. American naturalist and army surgeon. See: Dict. Amer. Biog. Mearns('s) quail, Mearns's coyote, Mearns's woodpecker.

Mearns('s) quail (Mearns, Edgar Alexander): Zoology. See: Mathews, M. M.; Pennak; Webster's 3d.

Mearns's coyote (Mearns, Edgar Alexander): Zoology. See: Mathews, M. M.

Mearns's woodpecker (Mearns, Edgar Alexander): Zoology. See: Mathews, M. M.

Meaurio reagent (Meaurio, Victor L.): Chemistry. See: Van Nostrand Chem. Dict.

MEAURIO, VICTOR L. fl. 1917. Argentinian chemist. Cited in: Chem. Abstr., vol. 12, p. 1221. Meaurio reagent.

Mecaenatianum (wine) (Maecenas, the statesman): Food and Drink. See: Charnock.

mechanical Ohm (Ohm, Georg Simon): Physics. See: Dresner; Internat. Dict. Phys. Elec.; Thewlis; Van Nostrand Sci. Encyc.

Mechitar, Peter. See: Mekitar, Peter.

MECKE, PAUL. fl. 1899. German? pharmaceutical chemist. Cited in: Royal Soc. Cat. Sci. Pap., 1884-1900. Mecke('s) reagent (or solution).

Mecke('s) reagent (or solution) (Mecke, Paul): Medicine. See: Stedman; Van Nostrand Chem. Dict.

MECKE, REINHARD. b. 1895. German chemist and physicist. See: Pogg., vols. 6, 7a. Birge-Mecke rule.

MECKEL, JOHANN FRIEDRICH, THE ELDER. 1724-1774. German anatomist. See: World Who's Who Sci. Meckelectomy, Meckel's band (or ligament), Meckel's cave (or cavity), Meckel's ganglion, Meckel's groove, Meckel's vein.

MECKEL, JOHANN FRIEDRICH, THE YOUNGER. 1781-1833. German anatomist and surgeon. See: Dict. Sci. Biog. Meckelian ossicle, Meckel's cartilage (or rod), Meckel's diverticulum, Meckel's plane, Meckel's tract?

Meckelectomy (Meckel, Johann Friedrich, the elder): Medicine. See: Stedman.

Meckelian ossicle (Meckel, Johann Friedrich, the younger): Anatomy. See: Gray.

Meckel's cartilage (or rod) (Meckel, Johann Friedrich, the younger): Anatomy. See: Donath; Dorland; Henderson; Stedman; Webster's 3d.

Meckel's cave (or cavity) (Meckel, Johann Friedrich, the elder): Anatomy. See: Donath; Dorland; Stedman; Webster's 3d.

Meckel's diverticulum (Meckel, Johann Friedrich, the younger): Anatomy. See: Donath; Dorland; Jablonski; Stedman; Webster's 3d.

Meckel's ganglion (Meckel, Johann Friedrich, the elder): Anatomy. See: Donath; Dorland; Stedman; Webster's 3d.

Meckel's groove (Meckel, Johann Friedrich, the elder): Anatomy. See: Donath.

Meckel's plane (Meckel, Johann Friedrich, the younger): Anatomy. See: Dorland; Stedman.

Meckel's tract (Meckel, Johann Friedrich, the younger?): Anatomy. See: Encyc. Brit., 1973 under "Gastrointestinal Tract," vol. 10, p. 23 d.; Gray.

Meckel's vein (Meckel, Johann Friedrich, the elder): Anatomy. See: Donath.

Mecklenburg-Strelitz, Charlotte Sophia, Princess of. See: Charlotte Sophia.

MECKLENBURG, WERNER. b. 1880. German chemist. See: Pogg., vols. 5, 6, 7a. Biltz-Mecklenburg test reaction.

Medal of St. Benedict (Benedict of Nursia, Saint.): Religion. See: Attwater.

Meddlesome Mattie (Meddlesome Matty, the fictional character): Generic Word (busybody). See: Webster's 3d.

MEDDLESOME MATTY. Subject of a poem of the same name by Ann Taylor (d. 1866) American writer. See: Stevenson. Meddlesome Mattie.

MEDEA. An enchantress in Greek mythology. See: New Encyc. Brit., 1974, Microp. Medea complex, Medea's kettle (or cauldron), Medeola.

Medea complex (Medea): Psychiatry. See: Hinsie.

Medea's kettle (or cauldron) (Medea): Generic Word (restore youth). See: Brewer.

Medeola (Medea): Botany. See: Mathews, M. M.; Partridge; Taylor, N.

Medicean (Medici, Giovanni de): History. See: Hendrickson; Partridge; Webster's 3d.

Medici blue (Medici, Giovanni de): Fashion. See: Webster's 3d.

Medici collar (Medici, Giovanni de): Fashion. See: Picken.

MEDICI, GIOVANNI DE (GIOVANNI DI BICCI). 1360-1429. Florentine merchant and founder of powerful Italian family. See: Encyc. Brit., 1973. Medicean, Medici blue, Medici collar, Medici lace.

Medici, Giulio de. See: Clement VII.

Medici lace (Medici, Giovanni de): Fashion. See: Picken.

MEDIN, OSKAR. 1847-1927. Swedish physician. See: World Who's Who Sci. Heine-Medin disease, Medin's disease.

MEDINGER, PIERRE. fl. 1916. Luxemburg chemist. Cited in: Chem. Abstr., vol. 10, p. 27. Medinger reagent.

Medinger reagent (Medinger, Pierre): Chemistry. See: Van Nostrand Chem. Dict.

Medinilla (Medinilla y Pineda, Jose de): Botany. See: Webster's 3d.

MEDINILLA Y PINEDA, JOSE DE. fl. 1820. Spanish governor of the Mariana Islands. (Biography source unavailable.) Medinilla.

Medin's disease (Medin, Oskar): Medicine. See: Dorland; Stedman.

Medjidie (order) (Abdul-Medjid): History. See: Latham; Weekley.

Medjidite (Abdul-Medjid): Earth Sciences. See: Charnock.

MEDUSA. Gorgon who could turn a beholder into stone by her glance. See: Dict. Grk. Rom. Biog. Myth. Medusa (coelenterate), Medusa's head, Medusoid.

Medusa (coelenterate) (Medusa): Zoology. See: Van Nostrand Sci. Encyc.; Webster's 3d.

Medusa's head (Medusa): Botany. See: Webster's 3d.; Winburne.

Medusoid (Medusa): Zoology. See: Van Nostrand Sci. Encyc.

Meeh-Du Bois formula (Meeh, Kuno: Du Bois, Delafield; and Du Bois, Eugene Floyd): Physiology. See: Stedman. Also known as: Du Bois formula (or method).

MEEH, K. fl. 1879. German physiologist. Cited in: Royal Soc. Cat. Sci. Pap., 1874-1883. Meeh-Du Bois formula, Meeh's formula.

MEEHAN, AUGUSTUS F. b. 1874. American industrialist. See: Who's Who Engin., 1925. Meehanite.

Meehanite (Meehan, Augustus F.): Engineering and Industry. See: Thrush.

Meeh's formula (Meeh, K.): Physiology. See: Kelly.

Meeker harrow (Derivation undetermined): Agriculture. See: Winburne.

Meekeren-Ehlers-Danlos syndrome (Meekeren, Job Janszoon van; Ehlers, Edvard; and Danlos, Henri Alexander). See: Ehlers-Danlos syndrome.

MEEKEREN, JOB JANSZOON VAN. fl. mid-17th c. See: Nederl. Tijdschr. v. geneesk., vol. 67 (1923, pt. 1), pp. 456-479. Meekeren-Ehlers-Danlos syndrome.

Meerburg-Filipps micro-test for copper (Derivation undetermined): Chemistry. See: Van Nostrand Chem. Dict.

MEERWEIN, HANS LEBRECHT. 1879-1965. German chemist. See: Pogg., vol. 7a. Meerwein-Ponndorf-Verley reduction (or reaction), Meerwein reaction (or condensation), Wagner-Meerwein rearrangement.

Meerwein-Ponndorf reaction (Meerwein, Hans Lebrecht and Ponndorf, Wolfgang). See: Meerwein-Ponndorf-Verley reduction (or reaction).

Meerwein-Ponndorf-Verley reduction (or reaction) (Meerwein, Hans Lebrecht; Ponndorf, Wolfgang; and Verley, Albert): Chemistry. See: Ballentyne; Van Nostrand Chem. Dict.; Webster's 3d. Also known as: Meerwein-Ponndorf reaction.

Meerwein reaction (or condensation) (Meerwein, Hans Lebrecht): Chemistry. See: Ballentyne; Van Nostrand Chem. Dict.

MEES, R. A. fl. 1919-1936. Dutch scientist. Cited in: Chem. Abstr., vol. 14, p. 429. Mees' stripe.

Mees' stripe (Mees, R. A.): Medicine. See: Stedman.

MEESEMAECKER, R. fl. 1930. Dutch? chemist. Cited in: Chem. Abstr., vol. 24, p. 1657. Meesemaecker test reaction for ergosterol.

Meesemaecker test reaction for ergosterol (Meesemaecker, R.): Chemistry. See: Van Nostrand Chem. Dict.

MEESMANN, ALOIS. b. 1888. German ophthalmologist. See: Handb. der Deut. Wissensch. Meesmann's dystrophy.

Meesmann-Wilke disease (Meesmann, Alois and Wilke, Fr.). See: Meesmann's dystrophy.

Meesmann's dystrophy (Meesmann, Alois): Medicine. See: Jablonski. Also known as: Meesmann-Wilke disease.

megaloblast of Sabin (Sabin, Florence Rena): Medicine. Cited in: Stedman under "erythroblast."

Megaric(s) (Euclid of Megara): Philosophy. See: Canney; Harvey.

megaroentgen (Roentgen, Wilhelm Konrad): Physics. See: Markus.

megawatt (Watt, James): Physics. See: Markus.

MEGLIN, JEAN ANTOINE. 1756-1824. French physician. See: World Who's Who Sci. Meglin's point.

Meglin's point (Meglin, Jean Antoine): Anatomy. See: Donath; Stedman.

MEGNIN, JEAN PIERRE. 1828-1905. French veterinarian. See: Index-Cat. Med. Veter. Zool., vol. 10, 1948. Megninia.

Megninia (Megnin, Jean Pierre): Zoology. See: Pennak; Webster's 3d.

MEHLER, GUSTAV FERDINAND. 1835-1895. German mathematician. See: Pogg., vols. 3, 4. Mehler's integrals?

Mehler's integrals (Mehler, Gustav Ferdinand?): Mathematics. See: Ballentyne.

Mehlis('s) gland(s) (Mehlis, Karl Friedrich Eduard?): Zoology. See: Gray; Henderson; Pennak; Stedman; Webster's 3d.

MEHLIS, KARL FRIEDRICH EDUARD. 1796-1832. German physician. See: Biog. Lex. hervorr. Aerzte. Mehlis('s) gland(s)?

MEHRING, JOHANNES. fl. 1857. Beekeeper. (Biography source unavailable.) Mehring press.

Mehring press (Mehring, Johannes): Agriculture. See: Winburne.

MEHU, CAMILLE JEAN MARIE. 1835-1887. French physician. See: Bull. Acad. Med. Paris, vol. 18 (1887), pp. 697-701. Mehu solution.

Mehu solution (Mehu, Camille Jean Marie): Chemistry. See: Van Nostrand Chem. Dict.

MEIBOM, HEINRICH. 1638-1700. German anatomist. See: World Who's Who Sci. Meibomian conjunctivitis, Meibomian cyst, Meibomian gland, Meibomian sty, Meibomitis (or Meibomianitis).

Meibomian conjunctivitis (Meibom, Heinrich): Medicine. See: Stedman.

Meibomian cyst (Meibom, Heinrich): Medicine. See: Jablonski; Stedman.

Meibomian gland (Meibom, Heinrich): Anatomy. See: Gray; Stedman; Webster's 3d.

Meibomian sty (Meibom, Heinrich): Medicine. See: Stedman.

Meibomitis (or Meibomianitis) (Meibom, Heinrich): Medicine. See: Stedman.

Meibomius, Heinrich. See: Meibom, Heinrich.

EIDELL, BIRGER OIVIND. b. 1882. Norwegian mathematician. See: Pogg., vol. 6. Camp-Meidell inequality.

Meier art judgment test (Meier, Norman Charles): Psychology. See: Chaplin; Wolman.

MEIER, GEORG. b. 1875. German physician. See: Biog. Lex. hervorr. Aerzte, 1880-1930. Porges-Meier reaction (or test).

MEIER, NORMAN CHARLES. 1893-1967. American psychologist. See: Who Was Who Amer., 1961-1968. Meier art judgment test.

MEIER, R. fl. 1866. German physician. (Biography source unavailable.) Kussmaul-Meier syndrome.

MEIGE, HENRY. 1866-1940. French physician. See: Biog. Lex. hervorr. Aerzte, 1880-1930. Brissaud-Meige syndrome, Nonne-Milroy-Meige syndrome.

Meige-Milroy syndrome (Meige, Henry and Milroy, William Forsyth). See: Nonne-Milroy-Meige syndrome.

MEIGEN, ERNST WILHELM GUSTAV. 1873-1934. German chemist. See: Pogg., vols. 4, 5, 6. Meigen's reaction.

Meigen's reaction (Meigen, Ernst Wilhelm Gustav): Chemistry. See: Thrush.

Meige's disease (Meige, Henry). See: Nonne-Milroy-Meige syndrome.

MEIGS, ARTHUR VINCENT. 1850-1912. American physiologist. See: World Who's Who Sci. Meigs'('s) capillaries, Meigs's test.

Meigs('s) capillaries (Meigs, Arthur Vincent): Anatomy. See: Donath; Dorland.

Meigs-Cass syndrome (Meigs, Joe Vincent and Cass, John W.). See: Meigs' syndrome.

MEIGS, JOE VINCENT. 1892-1963. American surgeon. See: World Who's Who Sci. Meigs' syndrome.

Meigs' syndrome (Meigs, Joe Vincent): Medicine. See: Dorland; Jablonski; Stedman. Also known as: Demons-Meigs syndrome, Meigs-Cass syndrome.

Meigs's test (Meigs, Arthur Vincent): Medicine. See: Dorland.

MEIJI (MUTSUHITO). 1852-1912. Emperor of Japan. See: Encyc. Brit., 1973. Meiji era (or period).

Meiji era (or period) (Meiji): History. See: Morris and Irwin.

Meinesz, Felix Andries Vening-. See: Vening-Meinesz, Felix Andries.

Meinesz zone (Vening-Meinesz, Felix Andries): Earth Sciences. See: Monkhouse.

MEINHOF, CARL. 1857-1944. German specialist in African languages. See: New Encyc. Brit., 1974, Microp. Meinhof's law.

Meinhof's law (Meinhof, Carl): Linguistics. See: Winick.

MEINICKE, ERNST. 1878-1945. German physician. See: Biog. Lex. hervorr. Aerzte, 1880-1930. Meinicke reactions (or test).

Meinicke reactions (or test) (Meinicke, Ernst): Medicine. See: Dorland; Stedman.

MEINZER, OSCAR EDWARD. b. 1876. American geologist. See: Amer. Men Sci., 4th ed. Meinzer (unit).

Meinzer (unit) (Meinzer, Oscar Edward): Earth Sciences. See: Encyc. Brit., 1973 under "Permeability (Fluid)," vol. 17, p. 633c.

Meisen mixture (Meisen, Valdemar): Medicine. See: Dorland.

MEISEN, VALDEMAR. 1878-1934. Danish surgeon. See: Biog. Lex. hervorr. Aerzte, 1880-1930. Meisen mixture.

MEISENBACH, GEORG. 1841-1912. Swiss printer. See: Glaister. Meisenbach negative (process).

Meisenbach negative (process) (Meisenbach, Georg): Printing. See: Lockwood under "Zincotypes."

MEISER, WILHELM OTTMAR. b. 1882. German chemist. Cited in: Chem. Abstr., vol. 16, p. 3904. Bosch-Meiser urea process.

MEISSL, EMERICH. fl. 1879-1882. German chemist. Cited in: Royal Soc. Cat. Sci. Pap., 1874-1883. Reichert-Meissl number (or value).

MEISSNER, ALEXANDER. 1883-1958. Austrian electrical engineer. See: Pogg., vols. 6, 7a. Meissner oscillator (or circuit)?

Meissner('s) corpuscle(s) (Meissner, Georg): Anatomy. See: Chaplin; Dorland; Pennak; Stedman; Webster's 3d. Also known as: Wagner's corpuscles.

Meissner effect (Meissner, Walther): Physics. See: Ballentyne; Hughes; Internat. Dict. Phys. Elec.; Markus; Thewlis. Also known as: Meissner-Ochsenfeld effect.

Meissner flame test (Meissner, Herbert): Chemistry. See: Van Nostrand Chem. Dict.

MEISSNER, GEORG. 1829-1905. German physiologist and anatomist. See: Dict. Sci. Biog. Meissner('s) corpuscle(s), Meissner's plexus.

MEISSNER, HERBERT. fl. 1930. German chemist. Cited in: Chem. Abstr., vol. 24, p. 3966. Meissner flame test.

Meissner-Ochsenfeld effect (Meissner, Walther and Ochsenfeld, Robert). See: Meissner effect.

Meissner oscillator (or circuit) (Meissner, Alexander?): Electronics. See: Hughes; Markus, Van Nostrand Sci. Encyc.

MEISSNER, WALTHER (In full: FRITZ WALTHER). b. 1882. German physicist. See: Pogg., vols. 5, 6, 7a. Meissner effect.

Meissner's plexus (Meissner, Georg): Anatomy. See: Donath; Dorland; Pennak; Stedman; Webster's 3d. Also known as: Remak's plexus.

Meiwa kumquat (Derivation undetermined): Botany. See: Winburne.

Meker burner (Meker, Georges): Chemistry. See: Hackh; Van Nostrand Chem. Dict.; Webster's 3d.

MEKER, GEORGES. fl. 1897-1914. French chemist. Cited in: Chem. Abstr., Decenn. Index, 1907-1916. Meker burner.

Mekhitarists (or Mechitarists) (Mekitar, Peter Manoug): Religion. See: Attwater; Canney; Encyc. Brit., 1973; Latham; Mathews, S.; Webster's 3d.

MEKITAR (MECHITAR), PETER MANOUG. 1676-1749. Armenian religious reformer. See: Webster's Biog. Dict. Mekhitarists (or Mechitarists).

Melampod(ium) (Melampus): Botany. See: Brewer; Charnock.

MELAMPUS. Famous soothsayer and physician of Greek legend. See: Funk & Wagnalls. Melampod(ium).

MELANCHTHON SCHWARZERDT, PHILIPP. 1497-1560. German theologian and religious reformer. See: Encyc. Brit., 1911. Philippism (or Philippist).

Melba (dessert) (Melba, Dame Nellie): Food and Drink. See: Webster's 3d.

MELBA, DAME NELLIE (Real name: HELEN PORTER MITCHELL). 1861-1931. Australian operatic soprano. See: Dict. Nat. Biog., 5th suppl. Melba (dessert), Melba sauce, Melba toast, peche (or peach) Melba.

Melba sauce (Melba, Dame Nellie): Food and Drink. See: Webster's 3d.

Melba toast (Melba, Dame Nellie): Food and Drink. See: Hendrickson; Webster's 3d.

Melchiorists (Hofmann, Melchior): Religion. See: Canney.

Melchizedek (order) (Melchizedek, the priest): Religion. See: Webster's 3d.

MELCHIZEDEK, THE PRIEST. Biblical priest-king in Gen. 14:18 ff. See: Encyc. Brit., 1974. Melchizedek (order).

Meldola('s) blue (Meldola, Raphael): Chemistry. See: Webster's 3d.

MELDOLA, RAPHAEL. 1849-1915. English chemist and naturalist. See: Pogg., vols. 1-5. Meldola('s) blue, Meldola test.

Meldola test (Meldola, Raphael): Chemistry. See: Van Nostrand Chem. Dict.

MELEAGER. One of the Argonauts in Greek mythology. See: Jobes. Meleagris.

Meleagris (Meleager): Zoology. See: Charnock.

MELENEY, FRANK LAMONT. 1889-1963. American surgeon. See: Who Was Who Amer., 1961-1968. Meleney's synergistic gangrene.

Meleney's synergistic gangrene (Meleney, Frank Lamont): Medicine. See: Stedman.

Meletian schism (1) (Meletius of Lycopolis): Religion. See: Attwater; Encyc. Brit., 1973 under "Meletius of Lycopolis;" Webster's 3d.

Meletian schism (2) (Meletius, Saint): Religion. See: Attwater; Encyc. Brit., 1973 under "Meletius, Saint;" Webster's 3d.

MELETIUS OF LYCOPOLIS. fl. early 4th c. Bishop in upper Egypt. See: Encyc. Brit., 1973. Meletian schism (1).

MELETIUS, SAINT. d. 381. Greek ecclesiastic and bishop of Antioch in Syria. See: Encyc. Brit., 1973. Meletian schism (2).

Melicerta (Melicertes): Zoology. See: Pennak; Webster's 3d.

MELICERTES. Greek sea-god. See: Jobes. Melicerta.

MELKERSSON, ERNST GUSTAF. 1898-1932. Swedish physician. See: Hygiea, Stockh., vol. 94 (1932), pp. 929-934. Melkersson-Rosenthal syndrome.

Melkersson-Rosenthal syndrome (Melkersson, Ernst and Rosenthal, Curt): Medicine. See: Hinsie; Jablonski; Stedman. Also known as: Melkersson's syndrome, Miescher's cheilitis.

Melkersson's syndrome (Melkersson, Ernst). See: Melkersson-Rosenthal syndrome.

MELLIN, ROBERT HJALMAR. 1854-1933. Swedish mathematician. See: Pogg., vols. 3-6. Mellin transform(s) (or inversion formulas).

Mellin transform(s) (or inversion formulas) (Mellin, Robert Hjalmar): Mathematics. See: Ballentyne; Internat. Dict. Phys. Elec.; James; Kendall.

MELLONI, MACEDONIO. 1798-1854. Italian physicist. See: Pogg., vol. 2. Melloni thermopile (or pile).

Melloni thermopile (or pile) (Melloni, Macedonio): Physics. See: Thewlis.

MELLUS. fl. 1874. Bishop in Malabar, India. Cited in: New Catholic Encyc. under "Malabar Rite," p. 94. Mellusians.

Mellusians (Mellus): Religion. See: Attwater.

MELNICK, JOHN CHARLES. 1928- . American roentgenologist. See: Direct. Med. Specialists, 1975-1976. Melnick-Needles syndrome.

Melnick-Needles syndrome (Melnick, John Charles and Needles, Carl F.): Medicine. See: Jablonski.

MELOTTE, GEORGE W. 1835-1915. American dentist. (Biography source unavailable.) Melotte's (Mellot's) metal.

Melotte's (Mellot's) metal (Melotte, George W.): Dentistry. See: Dorland; Hackh. Also known as: D'Arcet metal, Newton's alloy.

Melpomene (Melpomene, the Muse): Literature. See: Partridge.

MELPOMENE, THE MUSE. Greek Muse of tragedy. See: Jobes. Melpomene.

Meltzer-Auer test (Meltzer, Samuel and Auer, John): Medicine. See: Stedman.

Meltzer-Lyon test (Meltzer, Samuel and Lyon, Bethel Boyd Vincent): Medicine. See: Dorland; Stedman.

MELTZER, SAMUEL JAMES. 1851-1920. American physiologist. See: Dict. Sci. Biog. Meltzer-Auer test, Meltzer-Lyon test, Meltzer's law, Meltzer's method (or anesthesia), Meltzer's reaction, Meltzer's treatment.

Meltzer's law (Meltzer, Samuel James): Physiology. See: Dorland; Stedman.

Meltzer's method (or anesthesia) (Meltzer, Samuel James): Medicine. See: Dorland; Kelly.

Meltzer's reaction (Meltzer, Samuel James): Physiology. See: Stedman.

Meltzer's treatment (Meltzer, Samuel James): Medicine. See: Dorland; Kelly.

MELUSINE. Heroine of a local legend attached to the house of Lusignan of France. See: Jobes. Melusines (cakes), un cri de Melusine.

Melusines (cakes) (Melusine): Food and Drink. See: Brewer.

Melvil Dewey Medal (Dewey, Melvil): Library Science. See: Harrod.

Melzer reactions for alkaloids (Derivation undetermined): Chemistry. See: Van Nostrand Chem. Dict.

membrane of Corti (Corti, Alfonso Giacomo Gaspare). See: Corti's membrane.

membrane of Henle (Henle, Friedrich Gustav Jacob). See: Henle's membrane.

MEMNON. King of the Ethiopians in Greek mythology. See: Encyc. Brit., 1973. Memnonides (or Memnonians).

Memnonides (or Memnonians) (Memnon): Mythology. See: Charnock.

MENAGER, Y. fl. 1926. French chemist. Cited in: Chem. Abstr., vol. 20, p. 2472. Freundler-Menager reagent.

MENANDER. fl. early 2d c. Samaritan false teacher. See: Dict. Christian Biog. Menandrians.

Menandrians (Menander): Religion. See: Canney.

MENCKEN, HENRY LOUIS. * 1880-1956. American journalist and satirist. See: Who Was Who Amer., 1951-1960. Martin's plagiarism of H. L. Mencken, Menckenese, Menckenian.

Menckenese (Mencken, Henry Louis): Literature. See: Webster's 3d.

Menckenian (Mencken, Henry Louis): Literature. See: Webster's 3d.

MENDE, IRMGARD. fl. 1926. German physician. (Biography source unavailable.) Mende's syndrome.

MENDEL, JOHANN GREGOR. 1822-1884. Austrian botanist. See: Dict. Sci. Biog. Mendel tulip, Mendel's law(s), Mendelian (Mendelianist or Mendelist), Mendelian character, Mendelian factor (or unit), Mendelian population, Mendelian ratio, Mendelism, Mendelize.

MENDEL, KURT. 1874-1946. German neurologist. See: Biog. Lex. hervorr. Aerzte, 1880-1930. Bekhterev-Mendel reflex, Mendel's instep reflex.

Mendel tulip (Mendel, Johann Gregor): Botany. See: Winburne.

MENDELEEV, DMITRY IVANOVICH. 1834-1907. Russian chemist. See: Dict. Sci. Biog. Mendeleev group, Mendeleev system, Mendeleev's (Mendeleeff's) law, Mendeleev's (Mendeleef's, Mendeleyev's) periodic table or chart, Mendelevium, Mendelyeevite.

Mendeleev group (Mendeleev, Dmitry Ivanovich): Chemistry. See: Hackh; Thrush.

Mendeleev system (Mendeleev, Dmitry Ivanovich): Chemistry. See: Hackh.

Mendeleev's (Mendeleeff's) law (Mendeleev, Dmitry Ivanovich): Chemistry. See: Hackh; Stedman; Webster's 3d.

Mendeleev's (Mendeleef's, Mendeleyev's) periodic table or chart (Mendeleev, Dmitry Ivanovich): Chemistry. See: Ballentyne; Blumberg; Hackh.

Mendelevium (Mendeleev, Dmitry Ivanovich): Chemistry. See: Internat. Dict. Phys. Elec.; Thrush; Van Nostrand Sci. Encyc.; Webster's 3d.

Mendelian (Mendelianist or Mendelist) (Mendel, Johann Gregor): Genetics. See: Henderson; Webster's 3d.; Winick.

Mendelian character (Mendel, Johann Gregor): Genetics. See: Stedman; Webster's 3d.

Mendelian factor (or unit) (Mendel, Johann Gregor): Genetics. See: Webster's 3d.

Mendelian population (Mendel, Johann Gregor): Genetics. See: Gray; Henderson.

Mendelian ratio (Mendel, Johann Gregor): Genetics. See: Dorland; English; Fairchild; Stedman; Webster's 3d.

Mendelism (Mendel, Johann Gregor): Genetics. See: English; Hinsie; Pennak; Van Nostrand Sci. Encyc.; Webster's 3d.

Mendelize (Mendel, Johann Gregor): Genetics. See: Webster's 3d.

Mendel's instep reflex (Mendel, Kurt): Medicine. See: Dorland; Stedman.

Mendel's law(s) (Mendel, Johann Gregor): Genetics. See: Good; Stedman; Webster's 3d.; Winburne.

MENDELSOHN, MARTIN. 1860-1930. German physician. See: Biog. Lex. hervorr. Aerzte, 1880-1930. Mendelsohn's test.

Mendelsohn's test (Mendelsohn, Martin): Medicine. See: Dorland.

MENDELSON, CURTIS LESTER. 1913- . American obstetrician and gynecologist. See: Amer. Men Sci., 10th ed. Mendelson's syndrome.

endelson's syndrome (Mendelson, Curtis Lester): Medicine. See: Jablonski; tedman.

MENDELSSOHN, FELIX (In full: JAKOB LUDWIG FELIX MENDELSSOHN-ARTHOLDY). 1809-1847. German musician. See: New Encyc. Brit., 1974. Mendelssohn Scholarship, Mendelssohn Society.

Mendelssohn Scholarship (Mendelssohn, Felix): Music. See: Scholes.

Mendelssohn Society (Mendelssohn, Felix): Music. See: Morris.

Mendelyeevite (Mendeleev, Dmitry Ivanovich): Earth Sciences. See: Webster's d.

Mendes Da Costa, S. See: Da Costa, Mendes S.

Mendes Da Costa syndrome (Da Costa, Mendes S.). See: Da Costa's syndrome.

Mende's syndrome (Mende, Irmgard): Medicine. See: Jablonski.

MENDHEIM, G. fl. 1910. German engineer. Cited in: Chem. Abstr., Decenn. Index, 1907-1916. Mendheim kiln.

Mendheim kiln (Mendheim, G.): Engineering and Industry. See: Thrush.

Mendius reaction (Mendius, William?): Chemistry. See: Ballentyne.

MENDIUS, WILLIAM. fl. 1931-1945. American? engineer. Cited in: Chem. Abstr., Decenn. Index, 1937-1946. Mendius reaction?

MENDOZA, DANIEL. 1764-1836. English boxer. See: Dict. Nat. Biog. Mandozy.

MENEGHINI, GIUSEPPE GIOVANNI ANTONIO. 1811-1889. Italian mineral-gist. See: Encic. Ital. Meneghinite (or Menaghinite).

Meneghinite (or Menaghinite) (Meneghini, Giuseppe Giovanni Antonio): Earth Sciences. See: Thrush; Van Nostrand Sci. Encyc.; Webster's 3d.

MENELAUS OF ALEXANDRIA. fl. late 1st c. Greek mathematician. See: Dict. Sci. Biog. Menelaus' theorem.

Menelaus' theorem (Menelaus of Alexandria): Mathematics. See: Ballentyne; James; Webster's 3d.

MENETRIER, PIERRE. 1859-1935. French physician. See: Biog. Lex. hervorr. Aerzte, 1880-1930. Menetrier's disease (or syndrome).

Menetrier's disease (or syndrome) (Menetrier, Pierre): Medicine. See: Jablonski; Stedman.

MENGE, KARL. 1864-1945. German gynecologist. See: Biog. Lex. hervorr. Aerzte, 1880-1930. Menge's pessary.

Menge's pessary (Menge, Karl): Medicine. See: Dorland; Stedman.

Menghini needle (Derivation undetermined): Medicine. See: Stedman.

MENIER, EMILE JUSTIN. 1826-1881. French chocolate manufacturer and politician. See: Webster's Biog. Dict. chocolat-Menier.

MENIERE, PROSPER. ca. 1801-1862. French physician. See: World Who's Who Sci. Meniere's disease (or syndrome), Meniere's syndrome (symptomatic).

Meniere's disease (or syndrome) (Meniere, Prosper): Medicine. See: Dorland; Jablonski; Stedman; Van Nostrand Sci. Encyc.; Webster's 3d.

Meniere's syndrome (symptomatic) (Meniere, Prosper). See: Lermoyez's syn-drome.

Menippean satire (Menippus): Literature. See: Barnet; New Encyc. Brit., 1974, Microp.

MENIPPUS. fl. 3rd c. B.C. Greek cynic philosopher and satirist. See: Encyc. Brit., 1911. Menippean satire.

Meniscus-Schmidt camera (Schmidt, Bernhard Voldemar): Astronomy. See: Satterthwaite.

Meniscus-Schmidt telescope (Schmidt, Bernhard Voldemar): Astronomy. See: Satterthwaite. Also known as: Schmidt-Maksutov telescope.

MENKES, JOHN H. 1928- . Austrian-born American pediatric neurologist. See: Amer. Men and Women Sci., 12th ed. Menkes' syndrome (1), Menkes' syndrome (2).

Menkes' syndrome (1) (Menkes, John H.): Medicine. See: Jablonski.

Menkes' syndrome (2) (Menkes, John H.): Medicine. See: Jablonski.

Mennel reagent (Mennell, H.): Chemistry. See: Van Nostrand Chem. Dict.

MENNELL, H. fl. 1935. English? textile chemist. Cited in: Chem. Abstr., vol. 20, p. 2753. Mennel reagent.

MENNO SIMONS. 1496-1559. Dutch religious reformer. See: New Encyc. Brit., 1974, Microp. Mennonites (or Mennonitism).

Mennonites (or Mennonitism) (Menno Simons): Religion. See: Attwater; Jameson; Latham; Mathews, S.; Webster's 3d.

MENTEN, MAUD LENORE. 1879-1960. American physician. See: New York Times, July 21, 1960, p. 27, col. 3. Menten's solution, Michaelis-Menten constant, Michaelis-Menten hypothesis.

Menten's solution (Menten, Maud Lenore): Medicine. See: Kelly.

MENTOR. In Greek legend, the trusted friend of Odysseus. See: Dict. Grk. Rom. Biog. Myth. Mentor.

Mentor (Mentor, the Greek): Generic Word (trusted advisor). See: Funk; Partridge; Phyfe.

MENTZEL, C. fl. 19th c. German chemist. (Biography source unavailable.) Arnold-Mentzel reagent for hydrogen peroxide, Arnold-Mentzel reagent for ozone, Arnold-Mentzel reagent for ozone in water, Arnold-Mentzel reagents for milk, Arnold-Mentzel test for formaldehyde.

MENTZEL, CHRISTIAN. 1622-1701. German physician, botanist and scholar. See: Allg. Deut. Biog. Mentzelia.

Mentzelia (Mentzel, Christian): Botany. See: Taylor, N.; Webster's 3d. Also known as: Bartonia, Nuttallia (2).

MENZEL, P. fl. 1891. German physician. Cited in: Royal Soc. Cat. Sci. Pap., 1884-1900. Menzel's disease.

Menzel's disease (Menzel, P.): Medicine. See: Jablonski.

MENZER, ARTHUR AUGUST LUDWIG. b. 1871. German bacteriologist. Cited in: Royal Soc. Cat. Sci. Pap., 1884-1900. Menzer's serum.

Menzer's serum (Menzer, Arthur August Ludwig): Medicine. See: Kelly; Stedman.

MENZIES, ARCHIBALD. 1754-1842. Scottish botanist. See: Dict. Nat. Biog. Menzies larkspur, Menzies spruce, Menzies tolmiea, Menziesia, Minniebush.

Menzies cone separator (Menzies, William C.): Engineering and Industry. See: Thrush.

Menzies era (Menzies, Sir Robert Gordon): Politics. See: Morris and Irwin.

Menzies larkspur (Menzies, Archibald): Botany. See: Webster's 3d.; Winburne.

MENZIES, SIR ROBERT GORDON. b. 1894. Australian statesman. See: New Encyc. Brit., 1974. Menzies era.

Menzies spruce (Menzies, Archibald): Botany. See: Mathews, M. M.; Webster's 3d.

Menzies tolmiea (Menzies, Archibald): Botany. See: Winburne.

MENZIES, WILLIAM C. fl. 1935. Canadian? engineer. Cited in: Chem. Abstr., Decenn. Index, 1927-1936. Menzies cone separator.

Menziesia (Menzies, Archibald): Botany. See: Taylor, N.; Webster's 3d.

MEPHISTOPHELES. Familiar spirit of Faust. See: New Encyc. Brit., 1974, Microp. Mephistophelian (and Mephistopheles).

Mephistophelian (and Mephistopheles) (Mephistopheles): Generic Word (diaboli-cal). See: Charnock; Partridge; Webster's 3d.; Weekley.

Mepstead pump (Derivation undetermined): Engineering and Industry. See: Auger.

MERAT, FRANCOIS VICTOR. 1780-1851. French physician and botanist. See: Nouv. Biog. Univ. Meratia.

Meratia (Merat, Francois Victor): Botany. See: Webster's 3d.

MERCALLI, GIUSEPPE. 1850-1914. Italian seismologist and geologist. See: Davison. Mercalli scale, Mercallite.

Mercalli scale (Mercalli, Giuseppe): Earth Sciences. See: Monkhouse; Thewlis; Webster's 3d.

Mercallite (Mercalli, Giuseppe): Earth Sciences. See: Thrush; Webster's 3d.

Mercator Atlas (Mercator, Gerhardus): Geography. See: Monkhouse under "atlas."

Mercator('s) chart (Mercator, Gerhardus): Geography. See: Charnock; James; Webster's 3d.

MERCATOR, GERHARDUS (GERHARD KREMER). 1512-1594. Flemish cartographer. See: Dict. Sci. Biog. Mercator Atlas, Mercator('s) chart, Mercator-Hondius Atlas, Mercator('s) projection, Mercator sailing, Mercatorial.

Mercator-Hondius Atlas (Mercator, Gerhardus and Hondius, Jodocus): Geography. See: Monkhouse under "atlas."

MERCATOR, ISIDORE. fl. ca. 850. Forger of papal briefs. See: New Catholic Encyc. pseudo-Isidore (decretals).

Mercator('s) projection (Mercator, Gerhardus): Geography. See: Internat. Dict. Ap. Math.; Monkhouse; Moore; Thrush; Van Nostrand Sci. Encyc.; Webster's 3d.

Mercator sailing (Mercator, Gerhardus): Navigation. See: Van Nostrand Sci. Encyc.

Mercatorial (Mercator, Gerhardus): Geography. See: Webster's 3d.

MERCER, JOHN. 1791-1866. English calico printer and chemist. See: Dict. Nat. Biog. Mercerize (Mercerization or Mercer process).

Mercerize (Mercerization or Mercer process) (Mercer, John): Chemistry. See: Hackh; Hendrickson; Webster's 3d.

Merchiston, Laird of. See: Napier, John (Laird of Merchiston).

MERCIER, LOUIS AUGUSTE. 1811-1882. French urologist. See: World Who's Who Sci. Mercier's bar, Mercier's barrier, Mercier's sound, Mercier's valve.

Mercier's bar (Mercier, Louis Auguste): Anatomy. See: Donath; Stedman.

Mercier's barrier (Mercier, Louis Auguste): Anatomy. See: Stedman.

Mercier's sound (Mercier, Louis Auguste): Anatomy. See: Stedman.

Mercier's valve (Mercier, Louis Auguste): Anatomy. See: Stedman.

Merck reagent for alkaloids (Derivation undetermined): Chemistry. See: Van Nostrand Chem. Dict.

Merck test for alcohols (Derivation undetermined): Chemistry. See: Van Nostrand Chem. Dict.

Merck test for iodine (Derivation undetermined): Chemistry. See: Van Nostrand Chem. Dict.

Mercurial (Mercury): Generic Word (active). See: Charnock; Stenhouse; Webster's 3d.

Mercurialis (Mercury): Botany. See: Charnock; Webster's 3d.

MERCURIO, GERONIMO SCIPIONE. fl. late 16th c. Italian obstetrician. See: Biog. Lex. hervorr. Aerzte. Mercurio's position.

Mercurio's position (Mercurio, Geronimo Scipione): Medicine. See: Dorland; Stedman.

MERCURY. Roman god of commerce. See: New Encyc. Brit., 1974, Microp. line of Mercury, Mercurial, Mercurialis, Mercury, Mount of Mercury, staff of Mercury.

Mercury (Mercury, the god): Chemistry. See: Markus; New Encyc. Brit., 1974, Microp.; Webster's 3d.

MEREDITH, GEORGE. 1828-1909. English novelist and poet. See: Dict. Nat. Biog. Meredithian.

Meredithian (Meredith, George): Literature. See: Partridge; Webster's 3d.

MERENDINO, K. ALVIN AURELIUS. 1914- . American surgeon. See: World Who's Who Sci. Merendino's technique.

Merendino's technique (Merendino, K. Alvin Aurelius): Medicine. See: Stedman.

Mergenthaler linotype (or machine) (Mergenthaler, Ottmar): Printing. See: Lockwood; Mathews, M. M.

MERGENTHALER, OTTMAR. 1854-1899. German-born American inventor. See: Dict. Amer. Biog. Mergenthaler linotype (or machine).

MERGET, ANTOINE EUGENE. fl. 1886. French scientist. See: Rev. Gen. Bot., vol. 6 (1894), pp. 145-152. Merget test for mercury vapor.

Merget test for mercury vapor (Merget, Antoine Eugene): Chemistry. See: Van Nostrand Chem. Dict.

MERGNER, JOHN L. fl. 1955. American mineralogist. Cited in: Amer. Min., vol. 40 (1955), pp. 326-327. Reedmergnerite.

MERICA, PAUL DYER. 1889-1957. American metallurgist. See: World Who's Who Sci. Merica reagent.

Merica reagent (Merica, Paul Dyer): Chemistry. See: Van Nostrand Chem. Dict.

MERIMEE, JEAN-FRANCOIS LEONORE. 1765-1836. French painter and chemist. See: Bryan. Merimee's yellow.

Merimee's yellow (Merimee, Jean-Francois Leonore): Fine Arts. See: Webster's 3d.

Merkel(s) corpuscle(s) (Merkel, Friedrich Siegmund): Anatomy. See: Chaplin; Dorland; Drever; Stedman. Also known as: Merkel-Ranvier corpuscle.

MERKEL, FRIEDRICH SIEGMUND. 1845-1919. German anatomist. See: World Who's Who Sci. Merkel(s) corpuscle(s), Merkel's scheme.

MERKEL, JULIUS. fl. 1885. German psychologist. Cited in: Royal Soc. Cat. Sci. Pap., 1884-1900. Merkel's law.

MERKEL, KARL LUDWIG. 1812-1876. German anatomist and laryngologist. See: Biog. Lex. hervorr. Aerzte. Merkel's filtrum, Merkel's fossa, Merkel's muscle.

Merkel-Ranvier corpuscle (Merkel, Friedrich Siegmund and Ranvier, Louis-Antoine). See: Merkel('s) corpuscle(s).

Merkel's filtrum (Merkel, Karl Ludwig): Anatomy. See: Dorland; Stedman.

Merkel's fossa (Merkel, Karl Ludwig): Anatomy. See: Stedman.

Merkel's law (Merkel, Julius): Psychology. See: Chaplin; Drever; English.

Merkel's muscle (Merkel, Karl Ludwig): Anatomy. See: Donath; Dorland; Stedman.

Merkel's scheme (Merkel, Friedrich Siegmund): Medicine. See: Kelly.

MERLIN. Enchanter and wise man in Arthurian legend. See: New Encyc. Brit., 1974, Microp. Merlin's grass.

Merlin's grass (Merlin): Botany. See: Webster's 3d.

MERODES, COUNT JEAN DE. ca. 1588-1633. Flemish-Austrian general. See: Allg. Deut. Biog. Marauder?

MEROVECH. fl. ca. 450. King of Salian Franks. See: New Encyc. Brit., 1974, Microp. Merovingian (dynasty or age), Merovingian (script).

Merovingian (dynasty or age) (Merovech): History. See: Barnhart (Eng. Lit.); New Encyc. Brit., 1974, Microp.; Webster's 3d.

Merovingian (script) (Merovech): Linguistics. See: Charnock; New Encyc. Brit., 1974, Microp.

MERRIAM, CLINTON HART. 1855-1942. American naturalist. See: World Who's Who Sci. Merriam's chipmunk, Merriam's life zones, Merriam's turkey.

MERRIAM, JOHN CAMPBELL. 1869-1945. American paleontologist. See: World Who's Who Sci. Merriamia.

Merriamia (Merriam, John Campbell): Zoology. See: Pennak.

Merriam's chipmunk (Merriam, Clinton Hart): Zoology. See: Mathews, M. M.

Merriam's life zones (Merriam, Clinton Hart): Biology. See: Winburne.

Merriam's turkey (Merriam, Clinton Hart): Zoology. See: Mathews, M. M.

Merrill alphabeting numbers (Merrill, William Stetson): Library Science. See: Harrod.

MERRILL, CHARLES WASHINGTON. 1869-1956. American engineer. See: Who Was Who Amer., 1951-1960. Merrill-Crowe process, Merrill filter?

Merrill-Crowe process (Merrill, Charles Washington and Crowe, Thomas Bennett): Engineering and Industry. See: Thrush; Van Nostrand Chem. Dict. Also known as: Merrill process.

Merrill filter (Merrill, Charles Washington?): Engineering and Industry. See: Thrush.

MERRILL, FRANK DOW. 1903-1955. American army officer. See: New Encyc. Brit., 1974, Microp. Merrill's Marauders.

MERRILL, GEORGE PERKINS. 1854-1929. American geologist. See: Who Was Who Amer., 1897-1942. Merrillite?

MERRILL, LEWIS. ca. 1834-1896. American Union army officer in Civil War. See: Boatner. Merrill's Horse.

MERRILL, MAUD AMANDA. b. 1888. American psychologist. See: Amer. Men Sci., 6th ed. Terman-Merrill tests.

Merrill process (Merrill, Charles Washington). See: Merrill-Crowe process.

MERRILL, WILLIAM STETSON. b. 1886. American cataloger. See: Libr. J., vol. 57 (1932), p. 657. Merrill alphabeting numbers.

Merrillite (Merrill, George Perkins?): Earth Sciences. See: Thrush.

Merrill's Horse (Merrill, Lewis): History. See: Boatner.

Merrill's Marauders (Merrill, Frank Dow): History. See: Nat. Cycl. Amer. Biog., vol. 46, p. 134.

Merriman test (Merriman, Thaddeus): Engineering and Industry. See: Thrush.

MERRIMAN, THADDEUS. 1876-1939. American engineer. See: Nat. Cycl. Amer. Biog., vol. 29, pp. 95-97. Merriman test.

MERRINGTON, M. P. M. fl. 1937-1967. English statistician. See: Direct. Brit. Sci., 1966-1967. Merrington-Pearson approximation.

Merrington-Pearson approximation (Merrington, M. P. M. and Pearson, Egon Sharpe): Statistics. See: Kendall.

Merrit plate (Derivation undetermined): Engineering and Industry. See: Thrush.

MERRITT, KATHARINE KROM. b. 1886. American pediatrician. See: Direct. Med. Specialists, 1965-1966. Kasabach-Merritt syndrome.

Merry-Andrew (Borde, Andrew): Generic Word (buffoon). See: Charnock; Hargrave; Harvey.

Mersenne('s) law (Mersenne, Marin): Physics. See: Ballentyne; Thewlis.

MERSENNE, MARIN. 1588-1648. French mathematician and natural philosopher. See: Dict. Sci. Biog. Mersenne('s) law, Mersenne number(s).

Mersenne number(s) (Mersenne, Marin): Mathematics. See: Asimov; James.

Mersiburg process (Derivation undetermined): Chemistry. See: Van Nostrand Chem. Dict.

MERTENS, FRANZ CARL JOSEF. 1840-1927. Polish-born Austrian mathematician. See: Pogg., vols. 3, 4, 5, 6. Mertens' theorem?

MERTENS, FRANZ KARL. d. 1831. German botanist. Cited in: Royal Soc. Cat. Sci. Pap., 1800-1863. Mertensia.

MERTENS, ROBERT. b. 1894. German zoologist. See: World Who's Who Sci. Mertensian mimicry.

Mertens' theorem (Mertens, Franz Carl Josef?): Mathematics. See: Ballentyne.

Mertensia (Mertens, Franz Karl): Botany. See: New Encyc. Brit., 1974, Microp.; Taylor, N.; Webster's 3d.

Mertensian mimicry (Mertens, Robert): Zoology. See: New Encyc. Brit., 1974, Microp.

Merton nut (Merton, Sir Thomas Ralph): Physics. See: Thewlis.

MERTON, SIR THOMAS RALPH. b. 1888. English physicist. See: Pogg., vol. 6. Merton nut.

Merwig. See: Merovech.

MERWIN, HERBERT E. 1878-1963. American petrologist. See: Who Was Who Amer., 1961-1968. Merwinite.

Merwinite (Merwin, Herbert E.): Earth Sciences. See: Thrush; Webster's 3d.

MERY, JEAN. 1645-1722. French anatomist and physicist. See: Dict. Sci. Biog. Mery's glands.

Mery's glands (Mery, Jean): Anatomy. See: Donath; Dorland; Stedman. Also known as: Cowper's gland.

MERZ, GEORG. 1793-1867. German optics scientist. See: Pogg., vol. 2. Merz slit?

Merz slit (Merz, Georg?): Physics. See: Thewlis.

MERZBACHER, LUDWIG. b. 1875. German neurologist. See: Biog. Lex. hervorr. Aerzte, 1880-1930. Pelizaeus-Merzbacher disease.

MESMER, FRANZ (FRIEDRICH) ANTON. 1734-1815. Austrian physician in Paris. See: Internat. Encyc. Soc. Sci. Mesmerism (or Mesmerize).

Mesmerism (or Mesmerize) (Mesmer, Franz Anton): Generic Word (hypnotism). See: Brewer; Hargrave; Harvey; Webster's 3d.

MESNAGER, AUGUSTINE-CHARLES-MARIE. 1862-1933. French civil engineer. See: World Who's Who Sci. Mesnager notch, Mesnager test.

Mesnager notch (Mesnager, Augustine-Charles-Marie): Engineering and Industry. See: Thrush.

Mesnager test (Mesnager, Augustine-Charles-Marie): Engineering and Industry. See: Thewlis.

MESNARD, PIERRE-HENRI. 1910- . French pharmaceutical chemist. See: Who's Who Sci. Europe, 1972. Mesnard reagent.

Mesnard reagent (Mesnard, Pierre-Henri): Chemistry. See: Van Nostrand Chem. Dict.

Mesny circuit (Mesny, Rene Marie): Electronics. See: Markus; Van Nostrand Sci. Encyc.

MESNY, RENE MARIE. 1874-1949. French physicist. See: Pogg., vol. 6. Mesny circuit.

MESROB, SAINT. ca. 350-440. Armenian bishop and scholar. See: New Encyc. Brit., 1974, Microp. Mesropian alphabet.

Mesropian alphabet (Mesrob, Saint): Linguistics. See: Webster's 3d.

Messalina (Messalina, Valeria): Generic Word (lascivious woman): See: Hendrickson; Phyfe.

MESSALINA, VALERIA. ca. 22-48. Wife of the Roman emperor Claudius I. See: New Encyc. Brit., 1974, Microp. Messalina, Messaline.

Messaline (Messalina, Valeria): Fashion. See: Hendrickson.

Messerschmitt (fighter aircraft) (Messerschmitt, Willy): Weapons. See: Hendrickson; Partridge.

MESSERSCHMITT, WILLY. 1898- . German aircraft designer and manufacturer. See: New Encyc. Brit., 1974, Microp. Messerschmitt (fighter aircraft).

MESSTER, OSKAR EDUARD. 1866-1943. German cinematographer. See: Sadoul. Oskar Messter Medal.

metakirchheimerite (Kirchheimer, Franz): Earth Sciences. See: Thrush.

Metcalfe bean (Metcalfe, J. K.): Botany. See: Webster's 3d.; Winburne.

METCALFE, J. K. fl. late 19th c. American grower. (Biography source unavailable.) Metcalfe bean.

METCHNIKOFF, ELIE (ILIA ILICH MECHNIKOV). 1845-1916. Russian-born French bacteriologist. See: World Who's Who Sci. Metchnikoff's theory.

Metchnikoff's theory (Metchnikoff, Elie): Medicine. See: Dorland; Stedman.

METFORD, WILLIAM ELLIS. 1824-1899. English inventor. See: World Who's Who Sci. Lee-Metford rifle.

method of Saint Sulpice (Sulpice II, Saint): Religion. See: Attwater.

method of Verde and Wick (Verde, Mario, and Wick, Gian Carlo): Physics. See: Internat. Dict. Ap. Math.

METHUEN, PAUL. 1672-1757. English diplomat. See: Dict. Nat. Biog. Methuen Treaty.

Methuen Treaty (Methuen, Paul): History. See: Latham.

Methuselah (Methuselah, the patriarch): Generic Word (aged man). See: Hendrickson; Partridge.

METHUSELAH, THE PATRIARCH. In Genesis, an ancestor of Noah. See: Hastings (Dict. Bible). Methuselah, Methuselah (wine bottle).

Methuselah (wine bottle) (Methuselah, the patriarch): Food and Drink. See: Webster's 3d.

METON. fl. 5th c. B.C. Greek astronomer. See: Dict. Sci. Biog. Metonic cycle.

Metonic cycle (Meton): Astronomy. See: Charnock; Partridge; Phyfe; Satterthwaite; Webster's 3d.

METTE, EMIL LUDWIG PAUL. b. 1867. German physician. Cited in: Index-Cat. Libr. Surg.-Gen. Off., 2d Ser., vol. 10, 1905. Mett's test.

Mettenian gland (Mettenius, Georg Heinrich?): Botany. See: Gray.

METTENIUS, GEORG HEINRICH. 1823-1866. German botanist. See: Dict. Sci. Biog. Mettenian gland?

METTERNICH, PRINCE KLEMENS WERZEL N. LOTHAR FUERST VON. 1773-1859. Austrian statesman and diplomat. See: New Encyc. Brit., 1974. Metternichian.

Metternichian (Metternich, Prince Klemens Werzel N. Lothar Fuerst von): History. See: Webster's 3d.

Mett's test (Mette, Emil Ludwig Paul): Medicine. See: Dorland.

METZ, LUDWIG (In full: HANS EDMUND LUDWIG). 1900-1944. German chemist. See: Pogg., vols. 6, 7a. Woehler-Metz test reaction.

MEULENGRACHT, EINAR. b. 1887. Danish internist. See: Biog. Lex. hervorr. Aerzte, 1880-1930. Meulengracht's diet, Meulengracht's icterus, Meulengracht's method.

Meulengracht's diet (Meulengracht, Einar): Medicine. See: Dorland.

Meulengracht's icterus (Meulengracht, Einar). See: Gilbert-Lereboullet syndrome.

Meulengracht's method (Meulengracht, Einar): Medicine. See: Dorland.

MEUSNIER DE LA PLACE, JEAN-BAPTISTE-MARIE-CHARLES. 1754-1793. French engineer. See: Dict. Sci. Biog. Meusnier('s) (Meunier) theorem.

Meusnier('s) (Meunier) theorem (Meusnier de la Place, Jean-Baptiste-Marie-Charles): Mathematics. See: Ballentyne; Internat. Dict. Ap. Math.; James.

MEVAN (MEEN, MAIN), SAINT. b. ca. 540-611. Welsh-born abbot in Brittany. See: Baring-Gould and Fisher. l'herbe de St. Main, Saint Main's (or St. Meen's) evil.

Mevelava. See: Jalal-Ud-Din Rumi (Mohammed ibn Mohammed Moulavi Balkhi).

MEYEN, FRANZ JULIUS FERDINAND. d. 1840. German botanist and naturalist. See: Allg. Deut. Biog. Meyenia?

Meyenburg-Altherr-Uehlinger syndrome (Meyenburg, Hans von; Altherr, Franz; and Uehlinger, Erwin): Medicine. See: Jablonski. Also known as: Meyenburg's disease (2).

MEYENBURG, HANS VON. b. 1877. Swiss pathologist. See: Biog. Lex. hervorr. Aerzte, 1880-1930. Meyenburg-Altherr-Uehlinger syndrome, Meyenburg's complex, Meyenburg's disease (1).

Meyenburg's complex (Meyenburg, Hans von): Medicine. See: Stedman.

Meyenburg's disease (1) (Meyenburg, Hans von): Medicine. See: Jablonski.

Meyenburg's disease (2) (Meyenburg, Hans von). See: Meyenburg-Altherr-Uehlinger syndrome.

Meyenia (Meyen, Franz Julius Ferdinand?): Zoology. See: Pennak.

MEYER, ADOLF. 1866-1950. Swiss-born American psychiatrist and neurologist. See: Internat. Encyc. Soc. Sci. Meyer-Archambault loop, Meyer's theory.

Meyer-Archambault loop (Meyer, Adolf and Archambault, La Salle): Anatomy. See: Stedman.

Meyer atomic volume curve (Meyer, Lothar): Chemistry. See: Ballentyne.

MEYER-BETZ, FRIEDRICH. fl. 1910. German physician. Cited in: Chem. Abstr., Decenn. Index, 1907-1916. Meyer-Betz's syndrome.

Meyer-Betz's syndrome (Meyer-Betz, Friedrich): Medicine. See: Jablonski.

MEYER, E. fl. 1908. German engineer. Cited in: Chem. Abstr., vol. 2, p. 1376. Meyer hardness number, Meyer hardness test.

MEYER, EDMUND V. 1864-1931. German laryngologist. See: Biog. Lex. hervorr. Aerzte. Meyer's cartilages.

MEYER, GEORG. fl. 1883. German chemist. Cited in: Royal Soc. Cat. Sci. Pap., 1884-1900. Meyer reaction.

MEYER, GEORG C. fl. 1906. German chemist. Cited in: Chem. Abstr., vol. 1, p. 1103. Meyer test reaction for potassium.

MEYER, GEORG HERMANN VON. 1815-1892. German anatomist. See: Biog. Lex. hervorr. Aerzte. Meyer's line, Meyer's sinus.

MEYER, HANS HORST. 1853-1939. German pharmacologist. See: Pogg., vols. 3, 4, 6. Meyer-Overton theory of narcosis.

MEYER, HANS JOHANNES LEOPOLD. b. 1871. Austrian chemist. See: Pogg., vols. 4, 5, 6. Herzig-Meyer method (or determination of alkimides).

Meyer hardness number (Meyer, E.): Engineering and Industry. See: Thewlis.

Meyer hardness test (Meyer, E.): Engineering and Industry. See: Auger.

Meyer "hydraulic" theory (Meyer, Max Frederick): Physics. See: Internat. Dict. Phys. Elec.

MEYER, J. J. 1804-1877. Engineer. (Biography source unavailable.) Meyer valve gear.

Meyer-Jennek test (Meyer, Julius and Jannek, Josef): Chemistry. See: Van Nostrand Chem. Dict.

MEYER, JULIUS (In full: ADOLF JULIUS). b. 1876. German electrochemist. See: Pogg., vols. 5, 6. Meyer-Jennek test.

MEYER, KURT OTTO HEINRICH. 1883-1952. German chemist. See: Pogg., vols. 5, 6, 7a. Kurt Meyer method, Meyer-Schuster rearrangement.

Meyer-Locher test for alcohols (Meyer, Victor and Locher, J.): Chemistry. See: Van Nostrand Chem. Dict.

MEYER, LOTHAR (In full: JULIUS LOTHAR). 1830-1895. German chemist. See: Dict. Sci. Biog. Meyer atomic volume curve.

MEYER, MAX FREDERICK. b. 1873. German-born American psychologist. See: World Who's Who Sci. Meyer "hydraulic" theory.

MEYER, OSKAR EMIL. 1834-1909. German physicist. See: Pogg., vols. 3, 4, 5. Meyer viscosity equation (or formula (2)), Meyer's formula (1), Meyer's theory?, Meyer's value?

MEYER, OSKAR HERMANN ALBIN. 1902-   . German iron and steel analyst. See: Pogg., vol. 6. Meyer's tube?

Meyer-Overton theory of narcosis (Meyer, Hans Horst and Overton, Ernst): Medicine. See: Stedman.

Meyer reaction (Meyer, Georg): Chemistry. See: Krauch and Kunz; Van Nostrand Chem. Dict.

Meyer('s) reagent (or test for blood) (Meyer, Willy): Medicine. See: Dorland; Stedman; Van Nostrand Chem. Dict.

Meyer reagent for thorium (Meyer, Richard Joseph?): Chemistry. See: Van Nostrand Chem. Dict.

MEYER, RICHARD JOSEPH. b. 1865. German chemist. See: Pogg., vol. 5. Meyer reagent for thorium?, Meyer-Schulz solution.

Meyer-Schulz solution (Meyer, Richard Joseph and Schultz, Wilhelm): Chemistry. See: Van Nostrand Chem. Dict.

Meyer-Schuster rearrangement (Meyer, Kurt and Schuster, Kurt): Chemistry. See: Van Nostrand Chem. Dict.

Meyer-Schwickerath and Weyers syndrome (Meyer-Schwickerath, Gerhard and Weyers, Helmut): Medicine. See: Jablonski. Also known as: Gillespie's syndrome.

MEYER-SCHWICKERATH, GERHARD. 1920-   . German ophthalmologist. See: Wer Ist Wer?, 1973. Meyer-Schwickerath and Weyers syndrome.

Meyer test reaction for potassium (Meyer, Georg C.): Chemistry. See: Van Nostrand Chem. Dict.

MEYER, THEODOR. fl. 1908-1926. German engineer. Cited in: Mansell. Prandtl-Meyer expansion, Prandtl-Meyer function.

Meyer valve gear (Meyer, J. J.): Engineering and Industry. See: Auger.

MEYER, VICTOR. 1848-1897. German chemist. See: Dict. Sci. Biog. Meyer-Locher test for alcohols, Meyer's law, Victor Meyer method for vapor pressure, Victor Meyer synthesis.

Meyer viscosity equation (or formula (2)) (Meyer, Oskar Emil): Chemistry. See: Hackh; Van Nostrand Chem. Dict.

MEYER, WILHELM (In full: HANS WILHELM). 1824-1885. Danish otologist. See: Biog. Lex. hervorr. Aerzte. Meyer's disease.

MEYER, WILLY. 1858-1932. German-born American surgeon. See: World Who's Who Sci. Meyer('s) reagent (or test for blood), Meyer's solution for treatment of thromboangitis obliterans.

MEYERBEER, GIACOMO. 1791-1863. German musical composer. See: Grove. a la Meyerbeer.

MEYERHOF, OTTO FRITZ. 1884-1951. German biochemist. See: Dict. Sci. Biog. Embden-Meyerhof pathway.

MEYERHOFFER, WILHELM. 1864-1906. German chemist. See: Pogg., vol. ?. Meyerhofferite?

Meyerhofferite (Meyerhoffer, Wilhelm?): Earth Sciences. See: Thrush.

Meyer's cartilages (Meyer, Edmund V.): Anatomy. See: Stedman.

Meyer's contrast experiment (Derivation undetermined): Psychology. See: Drever.

Meyer's disease (Meyer, Wilhelm): Medicine. See: Dorland; Jablonski; Stedman.

Meyer's formula (1) (Meyer, Oskar Emil): Chemistry. See: Hackh.

Meyer's law (Meyer, Victor): Chemistry. See: Hackh.

Meyer's line (Meyer, Georg Hermann von): Anatomy. See: Dorland; Stedman.

Meyer's sinus (Meyer, Georg Hermann von): Anatomy. See: Donath; Stedman.

Meyer's solution for treatment of thromboangitis obliterans (Meyer, Willy): Medicine. See: World Who's Who Sci.

Meyer's theory (Meyer, Adolf): Psychiatry. See: Dorland.

Meyer's theory (Meyer, Oskar Emil?): Chemistry. See: Hackh.

Meyer's tube (Meyer, Oskar Hermann Albin?): Engineering and Industry. See: Hackh.

Meyer's value (Meyer, Oskar Emil?): Chemistry. See: Hackh.

MEYNERT, THEODOR HERMANN. 1833-1892. German physician in Vienna. See: World Who's Who Sci. Meynert's anemia, Meynert's bundle (retroflex bundle or fasciculus), Meynert's cells, Meynert's commissure, Meynert's decussation, Meynert's fibers, Meynert's layer.

Meynert's anemia (Meynert, Theodor Hermann). See: Korsakov's syndrome.

Meynert's bundle (retroflex bundle or fasciculus) (Meynert, Theodor Hermann): Anatomy. See: Donath; Dorland; Stedman.

Meynert's cells (Meynert, Theodor Hermann): Anatomy. See: Stedman.

Meynert's commissure (Meynert, Theodor Hermann): Anatomy. See: Donath; Dorland; Stedman. Also known as: Gudden's commissure.

Meynert's decussation (Meynert, Theodor Hermann): Anatomy. See: Donath; Stedman.

Meynert's fibers (Meynert, Theodor Hermann): Anatomy. See: Stedman.

Meynert's layer (Meynert, Theodor Hermann): Anatomy. See: Stedman.

MEYNET, PAUL C. H. 1831-1892. French physician. Cited in: Index-Cat. Libr. Surg.-Gen. Off., 1st Ser., vol. 9, 1888. Meynet's nodosities.

Meynet's nodosities (Meynet, Paul C. H.): Medicine. See: Dorland; Stedman.

Mho (Ohm, Georg Simon): Physics. See: Dresner; Thewlis. Also known as: Siemens.

MIBELLI, VITTORIO. 1860-1910. Italian dermatologist. See: Biog. Lex. hervorr. Aerzte, 1880-1930. Mibelli's disease (1), Mibelli's disease (2).

Mibelli's disease (1) (Mibelli, Vittorio): Medicine. See: Jablonski.

Mibelli's disease (2) (Mibelli, Vittorio): Medicine. See: Jablonski; Stedman.

Micah Rood's apples (Rood, Micah): Food and Drink. See: Brewer.

Micawber (Micawberish or Micawberism) (Micawber, Wilkins): Generic Word (incurable optimist). See: Brewer; Partridge; Webster's 3d.

MICAWBER, WILKINS. Character in Charles Dickens's novel "David Copperfield," (1850). See: Harvey. Micawber (Micawberish or Micawberism).

MICHAEL, ARTHUR. 1853-1942. American organic chemist. See: Dict. Sci. Biog. Michael('s) reaction (or condensation).

Michael('s) reaction (or condensation) (Michael, Arthur): Chemistry. See: Ballentyne; Hackh; Van Nostrand Chem. Dict.; Webster's 3d.

MICHAEL THE ARCHANGEL, SAINT. One of the principal angels. See: Holweck. Michaelmas (Day), Order of St. Michael, Order (or Knights) of St. Michael and St. George, St. Michael's pear.

MICHAELIS, AUGUST (In full: K. A. AUGUST). 1847-1916. German chemist. See: Pogg., vols. 3, 4, 5. Michaelis reaction.

Michaelis constant (Michaelis, Leonor): Chemistry. See: Stedman. Also known as: Michaelis-Menten constant.

Michaelis equation (Michaelis, Leonor): Chemistry. See: Van Nostrand Sci. Encyc.

MICHAELIS, GUSTAV ADOLPH. 1798-1848. German obstetrician. See: World Who's Who Sci. Michaelis('s) rhomboid (or area).

Michaelis-Gutmann bodies (or calcospherules) (Michaelis, Leonor and Gutmann, C.): Medicine. See: Blakiston's Gould; Stedman.

MICHAELIS, LEONOR. 1875-1949. German-born American chemist. See: World Who's Who Sci. Michaelis constant, Michaelis equation, Michaelis-Gutmann bodies (or calcospherules), Michaelis-Menten hypothesis, Michaelis' stain, Michaelis' test.

Michaelis-Menten constant (Michealis, Leonor and Menten, Maud Lenore). See: Michaelis constant.

Michaelis-Menten hypothesis (Michaelis, Leonor and Menten, Maud Lenore): Chemistry. See: Stedman.

Michaelis reaction (Michaelis, August): Chemistry. See: Ballentyne.

Michaelis('s) rhomboid (or area) (Michaelis, Gustav Adolph): Anatomy. See: Donath; Dorland.

Michaelis' stain (Michaelis, Leonor): Medicine. See: Kelly.

Michaelis' test (Michaelis, Leonor): Medicine. See: Kelly.

Michaelmas (Day) (Michael the Archangel, Saint): Generic Word. See: Barnhart (Eng. Lit.); Brewer; Harvey; Phyfe.

Michaelson actinograph (Michelson, Albert Abraham?): Physics. See: Compend. Meteorol., pp. 53-54; Huschke.

MICHAUX, ANDRE. 1746-ca. 1802. French botanist. See: Dict. Sci. Biog. Michauxia, Michaux's galingale, Michaux's sandwart.

Michauxia (Michaux, Andre): Botany. See: Taylor, N.

Michaux's galingale (Michaux, Andre): Botany. See: Mathews, M. M.

Michaux's sandwart (Michaux, Andre): Botany. See: Mathews, M. M.

MICHEL, FRANZ. fl. 1911. Luxembourg chemist. Cited in: Chem. Abstr., vols. 5, p. 2477; 6, p. 3435. Michel reagent for blood, Michel reagent for differentiating oxyhemoglobin and co-hemoglobin.

MICHEL, GASTON. 1875-1937. French surgeon. See: Rev. Med de Nancy, vol. 65 (April 1, 1937), pp. 282-287. Michel's clamps.

MICHEL, LOUIS. 1923- . French physicist. See: Who's Who Sci. Europe, 1972. Michel parameter.

MICHEL, M. fl. 1919. French chemist. Cited in: Chem. Abstr., vol. 14, p. 3386. Berthelot-Michel test reaction (for alpha and beta naphthol), Berthelot-Michel test reaction (for dihydroxybenzene).

MICHEL, MARIUS (Name used by JEAN MICHEL). 1821-1890. French book designer. See: Glaister. Michel style.

Michel parameter (Michel, Louis): Physics. See: Internat. Dict. Phys. Elec.

Michel reagent for blood (Michel, Franz): Chemistry. See: Van Nostrand Chem. Dict.

Michel reagent for differentiating oxyhemoglobin and co-hemoglobin (Michel, Franz): Chemistry. See: Van Nostrand Chem. Dict.

Michel style (Michel, Marius): Library Science. See: Harrod.

Michelangelesque (or Michelangelism) (Michelangelo): Fine Arts. See: Partridge; Webster's 3d.

MICHELANGELO (Full name: MICHELANGELO DI LODOVICO BUONARROTI SIMONI). 1475-1564. Italian artist. See: New Encyc. Brit., 1974. bar of Michelangelo, Michelangelesque (or Michelangelism).

MICHELI, FERDINANDO. 1872-1937. Italian physician. See: Lotta contro la tuberculosi, vol. 8 (1938), pp. 677-86. Marchiafava-Micheli syndrome (or anemia), Rietti-Greppi-Micheli syndrome?

MICHELI, PIER ANTONIO. 1679-1737. Italian botanist. See: Dict. Sci. Biog. Michelia.

Micheli-Rietti syndrome (Micheli, Ferdinando? and Rietti, Fernando). See: Rietti-Greppi-Micheli syndrome.

Michelia (Micheli, Pier Antonio): Botany. See: Taylor, N.; Webster's 3d.

Michelianites (Hahn, Johann Michael): Religion. See: Canney.

MICHELL, ANTHONY GEORGE MALDON. 1870-1959. Australian engineer. See: Who Was Who, 1951-1960. Michell bearing, Michell engine.

Michell bearing (Michell, Anthony George Maldon): Engineering and Industry. See: Auger.

Michell engine (Michell, Anthony George Maldon): Engineering and Industry. See: Auger.

MICHELL, JOHN HENRY. d. 1940. Australian mathematician. See: World Who's Who Sci. Beltrami-Michell compatibility equations.

Michel's clamps (Michel, Gaston): Medicine. See: Dorland.

MICHELSON, ALBERT ABRAHAM. 1852-1931. German-born American physicist. See: Dict. Sci. Biog. Michaelson actinograph?, Michelson interferometer, Michelson lamp, Michelson-Morley experiment, Michelson rotating mirror, Michelson stellar interferometer.

Michelson interferometer (Michelson, Albert Abraham): Physics. See: Markus; Van Nostrand Sci. Encyc. under "Interferometers."

Michelson lamp (Michelson, Albert Abraham): Physics. See: Thewlis.

Michelson-Morley experiment (Michelson, Albert Abraham and Morley, Edward Williams): Physics. See: Internat. Dict. Phys. Elec.; Satterthwaite; Thewlis; Van Nostrand Sci. Encyc.; Webster's 3d.

Michelson rotating mirror (Michelson, Albert Abraham): Physics. See: Van Nostrand Sci. Encyc.

Michelson stellar interferometer (Michelson, Albert Abraham): Astronomy. See: Internat. Dict. Phys. Elec.; Thewlis

MICHENER, CHARLES EDWARD. 1907- . Canadian geologist. See: Amer. Men Sci., 7th ed. Michenerite.

Michenerite (Michener, Charles Edward): Earth Sciences. See: Thrush.

MICHIE, A. C. fl. 1920. German? engineer. Cited in: Chem. Abstr., Decenn. Index, 1917-1926. Michie sludge test?

Michie sludge test (Michie, A. C.?): Engineering and Industry. See: Thrush.

Michler('s) ketone (Michler, Wilhelm T.): Chemistry. See: Hackh; Van Nostrand Chem. Dict.; Webster's 3d.

MICHLER, WILHELM T. d. 1889. German chemist. See: Chem. Ges. Ber., vol. 22 (1889), pp. 867-873. Michler('s) ketone, Michler's hydrol.

Michler's hydrol (Michler, Wilhelm T.): Chemistry. See: Hackh.

MICHOTTE, L. J. fl. 1950. Belgian? physician. Cited in: Chem. Abstr., Decenn. Index, 1947-1956. Michotte's syndrome.

Michotte's syndrome (Michotte, L. J.). See: Baastrup's syndrome.

MICHURIN, IVAN VLADIMIROVICH. 1855-1935. Russian horticulturist and geneticist. See: World Who's Who Sci. Michurinism.

Michurinism (Michurin, Ivan Vladimirovich): Genetics. See: Brewer; Pennak; Webster's 3d. Also known as: Lysenkoism.

Mickey Finn (Finn, Mickey): Generic Word (powdered drug). See: Brewer; De Sola; Hendrickson.

MICON, FRANCISCO. b. 1528. Spanish physician and botanist. See: Biog. Lex. hervorr. Aerzte. Miconia.

Miconia (Micon, Francisco): Botany. See: Taylor, N.; Webster's 3d.

micro-Astrup method (Astrup, Tage?): Medicine. See: Stedman.

microroentgen (Roentgen, Wilhelm Konrad): Physics. See: Markus.

microwatt (Watt, James): See: Physics. See: Markus.

MIDAS. A legendary wealthy King of Phrygia in Asia Minor. See: New Encyc. Brit., 1974, Microp. Midas (monkey), Midas syndrome, Midas (touch).

Midas (monkey) (Midas): Zoology. See: Charnock.

Midas syndrome (Midas): Psychiatry. See: Hinsie.

Midas (touch) (Midas): Generic Word (very rich). See: Hendrickson; Partridge.

Middeldorpf, Albrecht Theodor von. See: Von Middeldorpf, Albrecht Theodor.

MIDDELDORPF, K. fl. 1885. German pathologist. (Biography source unavailable.) Middeldorpf's tumor.

Middeldorpf's splint (Von Middeldorpf, Albrecht Thedor): Medicine. See: Dorland.

Middeldorpf's triangle (Von Middeldorpf, Albrecht Theodor): Medicine. See: Dorland.

Middeldorpf's tumor (Middeldorpf, K.): Medicine. See: Jablonski.

MIDDENDORF, ALEKSANDR FEDOROVICH. 1815-1894. Russian biogeographer. See: Dict. Sci. Biog. Middendorff daylily.

Middendorff daylily (Middendorf, Aleksandr Fedorovich): Botany. See: Winburne.

MIDDLETON, GEOFFREY. 1896- . English chemist. See: Pogg., vol. 6. Middleton reagent.

Middleton reagent (Middleton, Geoffrey): Chemistry. See: Van Nostrand Chem. Dict.

MIDIAN. Son of Abraham and Keturah in Gen. 25:2. See: Hastings (Dict. Bible). Midianite.

Midianite (Midian): History. See: New Encyc. Brit., 1974, Microp.; Webster's 3d.

Midlin hypothesis (Mindlin, Raymond David): Engineering and Industry. See: Thrush.

Mie functions (Mie, Gustav): Physics. See: Internat. Dict. Ap. Math.

Mie-Grueneisen equation of state (Mie, Gustav and Grueneisen, Eduard): Physics. See: Ballentyne; Internat. Dict. Ap. Math. Also known as: Grueneisen equation of state.

MIE, GUSTAV. 1868-1957. German physicist. See: Pogg., vol. 7a. Mie functions, Mie-Grueneisen equation of state, Mie scattering, Mie theory.

Mie scattering (Mie, Gustav): Physics. See: Huschke; Internat. Dict. Ap. Math.; Van Nostrand Sci. Encyc.

Mie theory (Mie, Gustav): Physics. See: Huschke; Internat. Dict. Ap. Math.

Miehle (press) (Miehle, Robert): Printing. See: Harrod; Lockwood.

MIEHLE, ROBERT. d. 1932. American inventor. Cited in: Glaister. Miehle (press).

MIEHLKE, ADOLF. 1917- . German otorhinolaryngologist. See: Who's Who Sci. Europe, 1972. Miehlke-Partsch syndrome.

Miehlke-Partsch syndrome (Miehlke, Adolf and Partsch, C. J.): Medicine. See: Jablonski.

MIERS, SIR HENRY ALEXANDER. 1858-1942. English mineralogist. See: Dict. Sci. Biog. Miersite.

Miersite (Miers, Sir Henry Alexander): Earth Sciences. See: Thrush; Webster's 3d.

Mierzejewski effect (Mierzejewski, Johann Lucian): Medicine. See: Dorland.

MIERZEJEWSKI, JOHANN LUCIAN. 1839-1908. Russian neurologist and psychiatrist. See: Biog. Lex. hervorr. Aerzte, 1880-1930. Mierzejewski effect.

Miescher degradation (Miescher, Karl): Chemistry. See: Van Nostrand Chem. Dict.

MIESCHER, FRIEDRICH (In full: JOHANN FRIEDRICH). 1844-1895. Swiss physiologist. See: Dict. Sci. Biog. Miescher pipet?

MIESCHER, GUIDO. 1877-1961. Swiss dermatologist. See: Biog. Lex. hervorr. Aerzte, 1880-1930. Lutz-Miescher disease, Miescher-Leder granulomatosis, Miescher's cheilitis, Miescher's syndrome (1), Miescher's trichofolliculoma.

MIESCHER (MIESCHER-HIS), JOHANN FRIEDRICH. 1811-1887. Swiss pathologist. See: Biog. Lex. hervorr. Aerzte. Miescheria, Miescher's tubes.

MIESCHER, KARL. b. 1892. German organic chemist. See: Kuerschner's Deut. Gel. Kal., vol. 9, 1961. Miescher degradation.

Miescher-Leder granulomatosis (Miescher, Guido and Leder, Max): Medicine. See: Jablonski. Also known as: Miescher's syndrome (2).

Miescher pipet (Miescher, Friedrich?): Chemistry. See: Hackh.

Miescheria (Miescher, Johann Friedrich): Zoology. See: Dorland, 25th ed.

Miescher's cheilitis (Miescher, Guido). See: Melkersson-Rosenthal syndrome.

Miescher's syndrome (1) (Miescher, Guido): Medicine. See: Jablonski.

Miescher's syndrome (2) (Miescher, Guido). See: Miescher-Leder granulomatosis.

Miescher's trichofolliculoma (Miescher, Guido): Medicine. See: Jablonski.

Miescher's tubes (Miescher, Johann Friedrich): Medicine. See: Dorland; Henderson; Stedman. Also known as: Rainey tubes.

MIGNON. Child character in Johann Goethe's novel "Wilhelm Meister's Apprenticeship," (1795-1796). See: Magill. Mignon delusion.

Mignon delusion (Mignon): Psychology. See: Chaplin; English; Hinsie.

MIGRAY, EMOD VON. fl. 1933. Hungarian chemist. Cited in: Chem. Abstr., vol. 27, p. 1592. Migray test.

Migray test (Migray, Emod von): Chemistry. See: Van Nostrand Chem. Dict.

MIGUEL, DOM. 1802-1866. Portuguese pretender to throne. See: New Encyc. Brit., 1974, Microp. Miguelite wars.

Miguelite wars (Miguel, Dom): History. See: Morris and Irwin.

MIGULA, WALTER (In full: EMIL FRIEDRICH WALTER). 1863-1938. German naturalist. See: Chronica Bot., vol. 5 (1939), p. 285. Migula's classification, Migula's solution (1) (glucose nitrate), Migula's solution (2) (hay infusion).

Migula's classification (Migula, Walter): Zoology. See: Dorland.

Migula's solution (1) (glucose nitrate) (Migula, Walter): Medicine. See: Kelly.

Migula's solution (2) (hay infusion) (Migula, Walter): Medicine. See: Kelly.

MIKAN, JOSEF BOHUMIR (Or GOTTFRIED). 1742-1814. Czech botanist. See: Nature, Lond. vol. 150 (1942), pp. 628-629. Mikania.

Mikania (Mikan, Josef Bohumir): Botany. See: Webster's 3d.

MIKHEEV, V. I. fl. 20th c. Russian mineralogist. Cited in: Hintze, suppl. 2, p. 588. Mikheevite.

Mikheevite (Mikheev, V. I.): Earth Sciences. See: Thrush. Also known as: Gorgeyite.

MIKITY, VICTOR G. 1919- . American radiologist. See: Direct. Med. Specialists, 1974-1975. Wilson-Mikity syndrome.

MIKOYAN, ARTYOM IVANOVICH. 1905- . Russian aeronautical designer. See: World Who's Who Sci. MIG (fighter plane).

Mikulicz' cells (Von Mikulicz-Radecki, Johann): Medicine. See: Dorland; Kelly; Stedman.

Mikulicz' clamp (Von Mikulicz-Radecki, Johann): Medicine. See: Stedman.

Mikulicz' dictum (Von Mikulicz-Radecki, Johann): Medicine. See: Kelly.

Mikulicz' drain (Von Mikulicz-Radecki, Johann): Medicine. See: Dorland; Kelly; Stedman.

Mikulicz' kenotribe (Von Mikulicz-Radecki, Johann): Medicine. See: Kelly.

Mikulicz' line (Von Mikulicz-Radecki, Johann): Medicine. See: Kelly.

Mikulicz' mask (Von Mikulicz-Radecki, Johann): Medicine. See: Stedman.

Mikulicz' method (Von Mikulicz-Radecki, Johann): Medicine. See: Stedman.

Mikulicz' operation (1) (exsection of sternocleidomastoid muscles) (Von Mikulicz-Radecki, Johann): Medicine. See: Dorland; Stedman.

Mikulicz' operation (2) (colectomy) (Von Mikulicz-Radecki, Johann): Medicine. See: Dorland; Stedman.

Mikulicz' pad (Von Mikulicz-Radecki, Johann): Medicine. See: Stedman.

Mikulicz-Radecki, Johann von. See: Von Mikulicz-Radecki, Johann.

Mikulicz-Vladimiroff amputation (or operation) (Von Mikulicz-Radecki, Johann and Wladimiroff, Alexander Alex): Medicine. See: Stedman. Also known as: Vladimiroff-Mikulicz amputation.

Mikulicz's disease (or syndrome) (Von Mikulicz-Radecki, Johann): Medicine. See: Dorland; Jablonski; Stedman.

Mikulicz's resection of the intestine (Von Mikulicz-Radecki, Johann): Medicine. Cited in: World Who's Who Sci.

MILANKOVICH, MILUTIN. 1879-1958. Yugoslav astronomer, geophysicist, and mathematician. See: Pogg., vols. 5, 6. Milankovich solar radiation curve.

Milankovich solar radiation curve (Milankovich, Milutin): Earth Sciences. See: Fairbridge, p. 534.

Milbank Memorial Fund (Anderson, Elizabeth Milbank): Philanthropy. Cited in: Webster's Biog. Dict.

MILEDH (or MIL). Legendary conqueror of Ireland. See: Jobes. Milesian(s).

MILES, CATHERINE COX. b. 1890. American psychologist. See: Amer. Men Sci., 6th ed. Terman-Miles attitude-interest blank.

Miles clip (Miles, Robert M.): Medicine. See: Newsweek, Nov. 11, 1974, p. 28.

Miles' operation (or resection) (Miles, William Ernest): Medicine. See: Dorland; Stedman.

MILES, ROBERT M. 1918- . American surgeon. See: Direct. Med. Specialists, 1970-71. Miles clip.

MILES, WILLIAM ERNEST. 1869-1947. English surgeon. See: Who Was Who, 1941-1950. Miles' operation (or resection).

Milesian(s) (Miledh): Mythology. See: Barnhart (Eng. Lit.); Charnock; New Encyc. Brit., 1974, Microp.; Webster's 3d.

Milesian tales (or fables) (Aristeides of Miletus): Literature. See: Barnhart (Eng. Lit.); Charnock.

Milford-Astor machine (Derivation undetermined): Engineering and Industry. See: Thrush.

MILIAN, GASTON. 1871-1945. French dermatologist. See: Bull. Acad. Med. Paris, vol. 129 (Sept. 4-Oct. 16, 1945), pp. 552-556. Milian's ear sign, Milian's erythema (or syndrome).

Milian's ear sign (Milian, Gaston): Medicine. See: Blakiston's Gould.

Milian's erythema (or syndrome) (Milian, Gaston): Medicine. See: Dorland; Jablonski; Stedman.

Military Order of Maximilian Joseph (Maximilian I): History. Cited in: Encyc. Brit. under "Knighthood," vol. 13, p. 408 c.

Militia of Jesus Christ (Jesus Christ): Religion. See: Attwater.

Milkman–Looser syndrome (Milkman, Louis Arthur and Looser, Emil): Medicine. See: Jablonski. Also known as: Looser-Debray-Milkman syndrome, Looser-Milkman syndrome, Milkman's syndrome.

MILKMAN, LOUIS ARTHUR. 1895-1951. American physician. See: Med. Soc. Rep., Scranton, vol. 38 (1944), pp. 5-7. Milkman-Looser syndrome.

Milkman's syndrome (Milkman, Louis Arthur). See: Milkman-Looser syndrome.

MILL, JOHN STUART. 1806-1873. English philosopher. See: Internat. Encyc. Soc. Sci. Mill's canons (or methods).

Milla (or Millea) (Milla, Julian): Botany. See: Charnock; Taylor, N.; Webster's 3d.

MILLA, JULIAN. No dates. Spanish gardener. (Biography source unavailable.) Milla (or Millea).

MILLAR (or MILLER), ANDREW. fl. 18th c. English press gang leader. (Biography source unavailable.) Andrew.

MILLAR, JOHN. 1733-1805. Scottish physician. See: World Who's Who Sci. Millar's asthma.

MILLARD, AUGUSTE. 1830-1915. French internist. See: Biog. Lex. hervorr. Aerzte, 1880-1930. Millard-Gubler syndrome.

MILLARD, EDGAR J. fl. 1889. English chemist. Cited in: Royal Soc. Cat. Sci. Pap., 1884-1900. Millard test reaction for hypophosphite.

Millard–Gubler syndrome (Millard, Auguste and Gubler, Adolphe Marie): Medicine. See: Dorland; Hinsie; Jablonski; Stedman. Also known as: Gubler's paralysis (hemiplegia or syndrome), Millard's syndrome, Weber-Gubler syndrome.

MILLARD, HENRY B. 1832-1893. American physician. See: N.Y. Med. J., vol. 58 (1893), p. 379. Millard's test.

Millard test reaction for hypophosphite (Millard, Edgar J.): Chemistry. See: Van Nostrand Chem. Dict.

Millard's syndrome (Millard, Auguste). See: Millard-Gubler syndrome.

Millard's test (Millard, Henry B.): Medicine. See: Dorland; Stedman.

Millar's asthma (Millar, John): Medicine. See: Dorland; Stedman. Also known as: Kopp's asthma.

MILLER, A. A. fl. 20th c. Engineer. (Biography source unavailable.) Miller control.

Miller–Abbott tube (Miller, Thomas Grier and Abbott, William Osler): Medicine. See: Dorland; Stedman; Webster's 3d. Also known as: Abbott-Miller tube, Abbott's tube.

Miller analogies test (Miller, Wilford Stanton): Psychology. See: Chaplin; Wolman.

MILLER, ARTHUR R. 1915- . American physical oceanographer. See: Amer. Men Sci., 11th ed. Spilhaus-Miller sea sampler.

Miller boiler (Miller, Joseph A.): Engineering and Industry. See: Auger.

Miller–Bravais indices (Miller, William Hallowes and Bravais, Auguste). See: Bravais-Miller indices.

Miller bridge (Miller, John Milton): Electronics. See: Internat. Dict. Phys. Elec.

Miller control (Miller, A. A.): Engineering and Industry. See: Auger.

MILLER, DAISY. Fictional character from short story of the same name by Henry James (1879). See: Benet. Daisy Millerism.

Miller differential (Miller, Dorr): Engineering and Industry. See: Auger.

MILLER, DORR. fl. 20th c. Engineer. (Biography source unavailable.) Miller differential.

Miller effect (Miller, John Milton): Electronics. See: Ballentyne; Hughes; Internat. Dict. Phys. Elec.; Markus.

Miller Fisher. See: Fisher, Miller.

MILLER, FRANCIS BOWYER. fl. 1870. Australian? metallurgical engineer. Cited in: Royal Soc. Cat. Sci. Pap., 1864-1873. Miller process.

MILLER, GERALD M. fl. 1949. American chemist. Cited in: Chem. Abstr., vol. 43, p. 4368h. Huggins-Miller-Jensen test.

Miller index (or indices) (Miller, William Hallowes): Physics. See: Ballentyne; Internat. Dict. Phys. Elec.; Thewlis; Thrush; Webster's 3d.

Miller integrator (or integrating circuit) (Miller, John Milton): Electronics. See: Hughes; Internat. Dict. Phys. Elec.; Markus.

MILLER, JOHN ELVIS. 1888- . American legislator. See: Biog. Direct. Amer. Congress. Miller-Tydings Act (or Enabling Act).

MILLER, JOHN MILTON. b. 1882. American radio engineer. See: Amer. Men. Sci., 4th ed. Miller bridge, Miller effect, Miller integrator (or integrating circuit), Miller-Pierce oscillator?

MILLER, JOSEPH (JOSIAS). 1684-1738. English actor and wit. See: Dict. Nat. Biog. Joe Miller.

MILLER, JOSEPH A. fl. 1868. American engineer. Cited in: Royal Soc. Cat. Sci. Pap., 1864-1873. Miller boiler.

MILLER, PHILIP. 1691-1771. English gardener and botanist. See: Dict. Nat. Biog. Milleria.

Miller–Pierce oscillator (Miller, John Milton? and Pierce, George Washington): Electronics. See: Hughes.

Miller process (Miller, Francis Bowyer): Engineering and Industry. See: New Encyc. Brit., 1974, Microp.

Miller reagent for cerium (Derivation undetermined): Chemistry. See: Van Nostrand Chem. Dict.

Miller reagent for fluorine (Derivation undetermined): Chemistry. See: Van Nostrand Chem. Dict.

MILLER, ROBERT WARWICK. 1921- . American pediatrician and epidemiologist. See: Amer. Men and Women Sci., 12th ed. Miller's syndrome.

MILLER, STANLEY LLOYD. 1930- . American biochemist. See: World Who's Who Sci. Stanley Miller's apparatus.

MILLER, THOMAS GRIER. b. 1886. American physician. See: Amer. Men Sci., 4th ed. Miller-Abbott tube.

Miller–Tydings Act (or Enabling Act) (Miller, John Elvis and Tydings, Millard Evelyn): Politics. See: Morris; Smith.

MILLER, WILFORD STANTON. b. 1883. American psychologist. See: Amer. Men Sci., 4th ed. Miller analogies test.

MILLER, WILHELM VON. d. 1899. German chemist. See: Chem. Ztg., vol. 23 (1889), pp. 195-196. Doebner-Miller synthesis.

MILLER, WILLIAM. 1782-1849. American sect founder. See: Dict. Amer. Biog. Millerites (or Millerism).

MILLER, WILLIAM ALLEN. 1817-1870. English chemist. See: World Who's Who Sci. De la Rue and Miller's law.

MILLER, WILLIAM HALLOWES. 1801-1880. English mineralogist and crystallographer. See: Dict. Sci. Biog. Bravais-Miller indices, Miller index (or indices), Millerite, Miller's law.

Milleria (Miller, Philip): Botany. See: Charnock.

Millerite (Miller, William Hallowes): Earth Sciences. See: Thrush; Van Nostrand Sci. Encyc.; Webster's 3d.

Millerites (or Millerism) (Miller, William): Religion. See: Jameson under "Adventists..;" Mathews, M. M.; Mathews, S.; Webster's 3d.

Miller's law (Miller, William Hallowes): Physics. See: Ballentyne.

Miller's syndrome (Miller, Robert Warwick): Medicine. See: Jablonski.

MILLES, GEORGE. 1902- . American pathologist. See: Amer. Men and Women Sci., 12th ed. Milles' syndrome?

Milles syndrome (Milles, George?). See: Sturge-Weber syndrome.

MILLETT, CHARLES. fl. 19th c. English official in the Far East. (Biography source unavailable.) Millettia.

Millettia (Millett, Charles): Botany. See: Webster's 3d.

Milligan annihilation method (Milligan, William Liddell?): Psychiatry. See: Hinsie.

Milligan bottle (Milligan, Lowell Haines): Chemistry. See: Van Nostrand Chem. Dict.

ILLIGAN, LOWELL HAINES. b. 1894. American chemical technologist. e: Pogg., vol. 6. Milligan bottle.

ILLIGAN, WILLIAM LIDDELL. fl. 1938-1964. English psychiatrist. See: ed. Direct., 1964. Milligan annihilation method?

ILLIKAN, CLARK HAROLD. 1915- . American neurologist. See: World ho's Who Sci. Millikan-Siekert syndrome.

illikan electrometer (Millikan, Robert Andrews): Physics. See: Hughes.

illikan meter (Millikan, Robert Andrews): Physics. See: Hughes; Van ostrand Sci. Encyc.

illikan oil drop experiment (Millikan, Robert Andrews): Physics. See: ternat. Dict. Phys. Elec.

ILLIKAN, ROBERT ANDREWS. 1868-1954. American physicist. See: Dict. i. Biog. Millikan electrometer, Millikan meter, Millikan oil drop experiment, illikan's rays.

illikan-Siekert syndrome (Millikan, Clark Harold and Siekert, Robert G.): edicine. See: Jablonski.

illikan's rays (Millikan, Robert Andrews): Physics. See: Hackh.

ILLINGTON, GEORGE. 1904- . English radio electrician and applied athematician. Cited in: Mansell. Millington reverberation formula.

illington reverberation formula (Millington, George): Physics. See: illentyne.

ILLINGTON, SIR THOMAS. 1628-1704. English physician. See: World ho's Who Sci. Millingtonia.

illingtonia (Millington, Sir Thomas): Botany. See: Webster's 2d.

illiroentgen (Roentgen, Wilhelm Konrad): Physics. See: Markus; Thrush.

ILLIS, F. T. fl. 20th c. American mineral collector. Cited in: Hintze, ol. I, pt. 4, half 2, p. 948. Millisite.

illisite (Millis, F. T.): Earth Sciences. See: Thrush; Webster's 3d.

illiwatt (Watt, James): Physics. See: Markus.

ILLMAN, SIDNEY. 1908- . Russian-born American physicist. See: Amer. en and Women Sci., 12th ed. Millman tube.

illman tube (Millman, Sidney): Electronics. See: Hughes.

illner reagent for aluminum (Millner, Theodor): Chemistry. See: Van ostrand Chem. Dict.

ILLNER, THEODOR. fl. 1938. German chemist. Cited in: Chem. Abstr., l. 32, p. 6970. Millner reagent for aluminum.

ILLON, AUGUSTE NICOLAS EUGENE. 1812-1867. French chemist. See: ct. Sci. Biog. Millon-Nasse test, Millon('s) reaction (or test), Millon('s) agent (or fluid), Millon test for salicylic acid and phenol, Millon's base.

illon-Nasse test (Millon, Auguste Nicolas Eugene and Nasse, Otto Johann edrich): Chemistry. See: Stedman.

illon('s) reaction (or test) (Millon, Auguste Nicolas Eugene): Chemistry. e: Ballentyne; Dorland; Hackh; Pennak; Stedman; Van Nostrand Chem. Dict.

illon('s) reagent (or fluid) (Millon, Auguste Nicolas Eugene): Chemistry. e: Dorland; Hackh; Pennak; Stedman; Webster's 3d.

illon test for salicylic acid and phenol (Millon, Auguste Nicolas Eugene): emistry. See: Van Nostrand Chem. Dict.

illon's base (Millon, Auguste Nicolas Eugene): Chemistry. See: Ballentyne; ackh.

ILLS, BERNARD YARNTON. 1920- . Australian astronomer. See: Who's ho, 1974-1975. Mills Cross antenna (or radio telescope).

ills Bill (Mills, Roger Quarles): History. See: Latham.

ills boat disengaging gear (Mills, Sir William): Engineering and Industry. ted in: World Who's Who Sci.

ills bomb (or grenade) (Mills, Sir William): Weapons. See: New Encyc. it., 1974, Microp.; Partridge; Quick.

ill's canons (or methods) (Mill, John Stuart): Philosophy. See: Blumberg; haplin; Webster's 3d; Wolman.

MILLS, CHARLES KARSNER. 1845-1931. American neurologist. See: World Who's Who Sci. Mills' disease.

Mills Cross antenna (or radio telescope) (Mills, Bernard Yarnton): Astronomy. See: New Encyc. Brit., 1974, Microp.; Van Nostrand Sci. Encyc. under "Telescopes (Astronomical)."

Mills-Crowe process (Mills, Louis D. and Crowe, Thomas Bennett): Engineering and Industry. See: Thrush.

MILLS, DAVID G. fl. ca. 1850. American merchant. Cited in: Dict. Amer. Biog. under "Mills, Robert." Mills's money.

Mills' disease (Mills, Charles Karsner): Medicine. See: Dorland; Jablonski; Stedman.

MILLS, HIRAM FRANCIS. 1836-1921. American engineer. See: Dict. Amer. Biog. Mills-Reincke phenomenon.

MILLS, J. P. fl. 1926. English? statistician. Cited in: Kendall and Doig. Mills' ratio.

MILLS, LOUIS D. fl. 1920. American engineer. Cited in: Chem. Abstr., Decenn. Index, 1917-1926. Mills-Crowe process.

Mills-Packard chamber (Mills, W. G. and Packard, C. T.): Chemistry. See: Van Nostrand Chem. Dict.

Mills' ratio (Mills, J. P.): Statistics. See: Kendall.

Mills-Reincke phenomenon (Mills, Hiram Francis and Reincke, Johann Julius): Medicine. See: Dorland.

MILLS, ROBERT. 1809-1888. American merchant and planter. See: Dict. Amer. Biog. Mills's money.

MILLS, ROGER QUARLES. 1832-1911. American senator. See: Dict. Amer. Biog. Mills Bill.

MILLS, W. G. fl. 1914. English engineer. Cited in: Chem. Abstr., vol. 8, p. 3621. Mills-Packard chamber.

MILLS, SIR WILLIAM. 1856-1932. English industrialist and inventor. See: Dict. Nat. Biog., 5th suppl. Mills boat disengaging gear, Mills bomb (or grenade).

Mills's money (Mills, Robert and Mills, David G.): History. See: Mathews, M. M.

MILNE, EDWARD ARTHUR. 1896-1950. English astrophysicist. See: Dict. Sci. Biog. Milne equation, Milne theory, Milne's problem.

MILNE-EDWARDS, HENRI. 1800-1885. French zoologist. See: Dict. Sci. Biog. Edwardsia, Edwardsiella.

Milne equation (Milne, Edward Arthur): Physics. See: Dict. Sci. Biog.

MILNE, JOHN. 1850-1913. English seismologist. See: Dict. Sci. Biog. Milne-Shaw seismograph.

Milne method (for solving an ordinary differential equation) (Milne, William Edmund): Mathematics. See: Internat. Dict. Ap. Math.; Internat. Dict. Phys. Elec.

Milne-Shaw seismograph (Milne, John and Shaw, J. J.): Earth Sciences. See: Glazebrook, vol. 3, p. 741; Van Nostrand Sci. Encyc. under "Earthquake."

Milne theory (Milne, Edward Arthur): Physics. See: Internat. Dict. Phys. Elec.

MILNE, WILLIAM EDMUND. 1890- . American mathematician. See: Amer. Men Sci., 10th ed. Milne method (for solving an ordinary differential equation).

MILNER, SIR ALFRED. 1854-1925. English administrator in South Africa. See: Dict. Nat. Biog., 4th suppl. Milner's kindergarten.

Milner's kindergarten (Milner, Sir Alfred): History. See: Brewer.

Milne's problem (Milne, Edward Arthur): Physics. See: Internat. Dict. Ap. Math.

MILORI, A. fl. 19th c. French color maker. (Biography source unavailable.) Milori blue, Milori green.

Milori blue (Milori, A.): Chemistry. See: Hackh; Webster's 3d.

Milori green (Milori, A.): Chemistry. See: Webster's 3d.

Milquetoast (Milquetoast, Caspar): Generic Word (timid person). See: Webster's 3d.

MILQUETOAST, CASPAR. Comic strip character created by H. T. Webster (d. 1952), American cartoonist. See: Webster, H. T. Milquetoast.

MILROY, GAVIN. 1805–1886. English medical writer. See: Dict. Nat. Biog. Milroy Lectureship.

MILROY, JOHN ALEXANDER. d. 1934. Irish biochemist. See: Who Was Who, 1929–1940. Milroy reagent.

Milroy Lectureship (Milroy, Gavin): Medicine. See: Dict. Nat. Biog. under "Milroy, Gavin."

Milroy reagent (Milroy, John Alexander): Chemistry. See: Van Nostrand Chem. Dict.

MILROY, WILLIAM FORSYTH. 1855–1942. American physician. See: Who Was Who Amer., 1943–1950. Nonne–Milroy–Meige syndrome.

Milroy's disease (Milroy, William Forsyth). See: Nonne–Milroy–Meige syndrome.

MILTON, JOHN. 1608–1674. English poet. See: Dict. Nat. Biog. Miltonic (or Miltonian), Miltonic sonnet, Miltonism.

MILTON, JOHN LAWS. 1820–1898. English dermatologist. See: Biog. Lex. hervorr. Aerzte. Milton's disease (or urticaria).

Milton, Viscount. See: Fitzwilliam, Charles William Wentworth (Viscount Milton).

Miltonia (Fitzwilliam, Charles William Wentworth, Viscount Milton): Botany. See: Partridge; Taylor, N.; Webster's 3d.

Miltonic (or Miltonian) (Milton, John): Literature. See: Partridge; Webster's 3d.

Miltonic sonnet (Milton, John): Literature. See: Scott.

Miltonism (Milton, John): Literature. See: Webster's 3d.

Milton's disease (or urticaria) (Milton, John Laws). See: Quincke's edema (or disease).

MINDERER, RAYMOND. ca. 1570–1621. German physician. See: World Who's Who Sci. spirit of Mindererus.

MINDES, JONATHAN. fl. 1900–1912. German? pharmacist. Cited in: Mansell. Mindes reagent.

Mindes reagent (Mindes, Jonathan): Chemistry. See: Chem. Abstr., vol. 6, p. 1203; Van Nostrand Chem. Dict.

MINDLIN, RAYMOND DAVID. 1906–   . American civil engineer. See: World Who's Who Sci. Midlin hypothesis.

Minerva (Minerva, the goddess): Generic Word (wisdom). See: Partridge.

Minerva (azalea) (Minerva, the goddess): Botany. Cited in: Partridge.

Minerva jacket (Minerva, the goddess): Medicine. See: Stedman.

Minerva machine (Minerva, the goddess?): Printing. See: Lockwood.

Minerva press (Minerva, the goddess): Printing. See: Weekley.

MINERVA, THE GODDESS. Roman goddess of widom. See: Dict. Grk. Rom. Biog. Myth. Minerva, Minerva (azalea), Minerva jacket, Minerva machine?, Minerva press, Minervalia.

Minervalia (Minerva, the goddess): Mythology. See: Charnock

MINGUZZI, CARLO. 1910–1953. Italian mineralogist. Cited in: Chem. Abstr., Decenn. Index, 1937–1946. Minguzzite.

Minguzzite (Minguzzi, Carlo): Earth Sciences. See: Thrush.

Minie (Minnie) ball (or bullet) (Minie, Claude Etienne): Weapons. See: Hendrickson; Partridge; Quick; Webster's 3d.

MINIE, CLAUDE ETIENNE. 1810–1879. French inventor and soldier. See: Nouv. Biog. Univ. Minie (Minnie) ball (or bullet), Minie rifle.

Minie rifle (Minie, Claude Etienne): Weapons. See: Partridge; Phyfe; Weekley.

MININ, A. V. No dates. Russian surgeon. (Biography source unavailable.) Minin light.

Minin light (Minin, A. V.): Medicine. See: Dorland.

Minkowski–Chauffard–Gaensslen syndrome (Minkowski, Oskar; Chauffard, Anatole Marie Emile; and Gaensslen, Max). See: Minkowski–Chauffard syndrome.

Minkowski–Chauffard syndrome (Minkowski, Oskar and Chauffard, Anatole Marie Emile): Medicine. See: Dorland; Jablonski. Also known as: Gaensslen–Erb syndrome, Gaensslen's syndrome, Minkowski–Chauffard–Gaensslen syndrome.

Minkowski distance function (Minkowski, Hermann): Mathematics. See: James.

Minkowski electrodynamics for moving bodies (Minkowski, Hermann): Mathematics. See: Internat. Dict. Ap. Math.

MINKOWSKI, HERMANN. 1864–1909. Russian-born German mathematician. See: Dict. Sci. Biog. Minkowski distance function, Minkowski electrodynamics for moving bodies, Minkowski('s) inequality, Minkowski space (or world).

Minkowski('s) inequality (Minkowski, Hermann): Mathematics. See: Ballentyne; Internat. Dict. Ap. Math.; James.

MINKOWSKI, OSKAR. 1858–1931. Russian pathologist in Germany. See: World Who's Who Sci. Minkowski–Chauffard syndrome, Minkowski's figure, Naunyn–Minkowski method.

Minkowski space (or world) (Minkowski, Hermann): Mathematics. See: Ballentyne; Internat. Dict. Ap. Math.; New Encyc. Brit., 1974, Microp.; Van Nostrand Sci. Encyc.

Minkowski's figure (Minkowski, Oskar): Medicine. See: Dorland.

Minkowski's method (Minkowski, Oscar). See: Naunyn–Minkowski method.

Minniebush (Menzies, Archibald): Botany. See: Mathews, M. M.; Webster's 3d.

Minoan (civilization) (Minos): History. See: Brewer; New Encyc. Brit., 1974, Microp.; Webster's 3d.

MINOR, LAZAR SALOMOVICH. 1855–1942. Russian pathologist. See: Vopr. Neurokhir., vol. 8 (1944), p. 64. Minor's disease, Minor's sign.

Minor–Oppenheim syndrome (Minor, Lazar Salomovich and Oppenheim, Hermann). See: Minor's disease.

Minor's disease (Minor, Lazar Salomovich): Medicine. See: Dorland; Jablonski. Also known as: Minor–Oppenheim syndrome.

Minor's sign (Minor, Lazar Salomovich): Medicine. See: Dorland.

MINOS. Legendary King of Crete. See: Dict. Grk. Rom. Biog. Myth. Minoan (civilization).

MINOT, FRANCIS. 1821–1899. American physician. See: World Who's Who Sci. Minot–Von Willebrand syndrome.

MINOT, GEORGE RICHARDS. 1885–1950. American physician. See: Dict. Sci. Biog. Minot methods, Minot–Murphy diet (or treatment), Minot treatments.

Minot methods (Minot, George Richards): Medicine. See: Kelly.

Minot–Murphy diet (or treatment) (Minot, George Richards and Murphy, William Parry): Medicine. See: Dorland; Kelly.

Minot treatments (Minot, George Richards): Medicine. See: Kelly.

Minot–Von Willebrand syndrome (Minot, Francis and Willebrand, Erik Adolf von). See: Willebrand–Juergens syndrome.

Minovici–Ionescu micro-reagent (Minovici, Stefan and Ionescu, Alex): Chemistry. See: Van Nostrand Chem. Dict.

Minovici reagent (Minovici, Stefan): Chemistry. See: Van Nostrand Chem. Dict.

MINOVICI, STEFAN. b. 1867. Rumanian chemist. See: Pogg., vols. 5, 6. Minovici–Ionescu micro-reagent, Minovici reagent.

Mint (Mintha): Botany. See: New Encyc. Brit., 1974, Microp.; Wagner (More Names).

MINTHA (or MENTHA). In Greek mythology, a nymph transformed by Persephone, her rival, into a plant. See: Dict. Grk. Rom. Biog. Myth. Mint.

Minto, 4th Earl of. See: Elliot, Gilbert John Murray Kynynmond (4th Earl of Minto).

MINTON, HERBERT. 1793-1858. English pottery manufacturer. See: Dict. Nat. Biog. Minton ware.

Minton oven (Minton, R. H.?): Engineering and Industry. See: New Encyc. Brit., 1974, Microp.; Thrush.

MINTON, R. H. fl. 1920. American ceramics chemist. Cited in: Chem. Abstr., Decenn. Index, 1917-1926. Minton oven?

MINTON, THOMAS. d. 1836. English pottery manufacturer. Cited in: New Encyc. Brit., 1974, Microp. under "Minton ware." Minton ware.

Minton ware (Minton, Herbert and Minton, Thomas): Applied Arts. See: New Encyc. Brit., 1974, Microp.; Webster's 3d.

Miquelets (Miquelot de Prats): History. See: Charnock.

MIQUELOT (MIGUEL) DE PRATS. fl. 15th c. Spanish leader of partisan troops. Cited in: Grand Larousse Encyc. Miquelets.

Miracle of St. Januarius (Januarius, Saint): Religion. See: Attwater.

MIRANDA, FRANCISCO DE. ca. 1750-1816. Venezuelan revolutionary. See: New Encyc. Brit., 1974, Microp. Miranda plot (or expedition).

Miranda plot (or expedition) (Miranda, Francisco de): History. See: Jameson; Morris and Irwin.

MIRAULT, GERMANICUS. 1796-1879. French surgeon. See: Biog. Lex. Hervorr. Aerzte. Mirault's operation (1) (for tongue cancer), Mirault's operation (2) (for harelip).

Mirault's operation (1) (for tongue cancer) (Mirault, Germanicus): Medicine. See: Blakiston's Gould; Kelly.

Mirault's operation (2) (for harelip) (Mirault, Germanicus): Medicine. See: Kelly.

MIRBEL, CHARLES FRANCOIS BRISSEAU DE. 1776-1854. French botanist. See: Dict. Sci. Biog. Mirbelia.

Mirbelia (Mirbel, Charles Francois Brisseau de): Botany. See: Charnock.

Mirchamp's sign (Derivation undetermined): Medicine. See: Stedman.

MIRIAM (MARY). In the Bible, Moses' sister to whom is ascribed a treatise on alchemy. See: McKenzie. bain-Marie?

MIRIZZI, PABLO LUIS. b. 1893. Argentinian physician. See: Gran Encic. Argentina. Mirizzi's syndrome.

Mirizzi's syndrome (Mirizzi, Pablo Luis): Medicine. See: Jablonski.

MISES, RICHARD VON. 1883-1953. Austrian-born American mathematician. See: Dict. Sci. Biog. Cramer-Von Mises test, Huber-Mises-Hencky theory, Mises yield condition, Saint-Venant-Mises material, Von Mises distribution.

Mises yield condition (Mises, Richard von): Physics. See: Internat. Dict. Appl. Math.

Missa Papae Marcelli (Marcellus II). See: Marcellus Mass.

Mrs. Grundy (or Grundy) (Grundy, Mrs.): Generic Word (conventionally proper person). See: Barnhart (Eng. Lit.); Latham; Partridge; Phyfe; Scott; Webster's 3d.

Mrs. Jellyby (Jellyby, Mrs.): Generic Word. See: Brewer.

Mrs. Partington (Partington, Mrs., the literary character): Generic Word (knack of misusing words). See: Partridge.

Mrs. Warren's profession (Warren, Mrs.): Generic Word (prostitution). See: Partridge.

MITCHELL, CHARLES AINSWORTH. 1867-1948. English analytical chemist. See: Analyst, vol. 73 (1948) pp. 55-57. Mitchell solution for gallic acid.

MITCHELL, CLIFFORD. 1854-1939. American physician. See: World Who's Who Sci. Germuth-Mitchell reagent for inorganic salts, Mitchell's test.

MITCHELL, DAVID M. fl. 1932. English chemist. Cited in: Chem. Abstr., vol. 26, p. 4011. Fearon-Mitchell test for alcohols.

Mitchell grass (Mitchell, Sir Thomas Livingstone): Botany. See: Webster's 3d.

Mitchell, Helen Porter. See: Melba, Dame Nellie.

MITCHELL, JAMES FARNANDIS. 1871-1961. American surgeon. See: Who Was Who Amer., 1961-1968. Mitchell's solution.

MITCHELL, JOHN. d. 1768. English-born American botanist, physician and cartographer. See: Dict. Amer. Biog. Mitchella.

MITCHELL, JOHN. 1870-1919. American labor leader. See: Dict. Amer. Biog. Johnny Mitchell trains.

MITCHELL, JOHN T. fl. 1891. American? bridge expert. Cited in: Mansell. Mitchell movement.

Mitchell movement (Mitchell, John T.): Recreation and Sports. See: Webster's 3d.

MITCHELL, SILAS WEIR. 1829-1914. American neurologist, poet, and novelist. See: Dict. Amer. Biog. Mitchell's skin, Mitchell's symptom, Mitchell's syndrome (1), Mitchell's syndrome (2), Mitchell's treatment (or rest cure).

Mitchell slicing system (Derivation undetermined): Engineering and Industry. See: Thrush.

Mitchell solution for gallic acid (Mitchell, Charles Ainsworth): Chemistry. See: Van Nostrand Chem. Dict.

Mitchell test reaction for nitrate and saponin (Derivation undetermined): Chemistry. See: Van Nostrand Chem. Dict.

MITCHELL, SIR THOMAS LIVINGSTONE. 1792-1855. English explorer in Australia. See: New Encyc. Brit., 1974, Microp. Major Mitchell (cockatoo), Mitchell grass.

Mitchella (Mitchell, John): Botany. See: Mathews, M. M.; Partridge; Taylor, N.; Webster's 3d.

Mitchell's skin (Mitchell, Silas Weir): Medicine. See: Dorland.

Mitchell's solution (Mitchell, James Farnandis): Medicine. See: Dorland.

Mitchell's symptom (Mitchell, Silas Weir): Medicine. See: Stedman.

Mitchell's syndrome (1) (Mitchell, Silas Weir): Medicine. See: Jablonski. Also known as: Gerhardt's disease, Weir-Mitchell's disease.

Mitchell's syndrome (2) (Mitchell, Silas Weir). See: Bernard-Horner syndrome.

Mitchell's test (Mitchell, Clifford): Medicine. See: Kelly.

Mitchell's treatment (or rest cure) (Mitchell, Silas Weir): Medicine. See: Dorland; Kelly; Stedman. Also known as: Weir Mitchell's treatment.

MITHRA (MITHRAS). Persian god of light and defender of truth. See: Funk & Wagnalls. Mithraeum, Mithraism (or Mithraic).

Mithraeum (Mithra): Religion. See: Webster's 3d.

Mithraism (or Mithraic) (Mithra): Religion. See: Canney; Harvey; Mathews, S. under "Mystery Religions;" New Encyc. Brit., 1974, Microp.; Webster's 3d.

Mithridate (or Mithridatum) (Mithridates VI, Eupator): Generic Word (antidote against poison). See: Brewer; Charnock; Harvey; Hendrickson; Stenhouse; Webster's 3d.

Mithridatea (Mithridates VI, Eupator): Botany. See: Webster's 3d.

MITHRIDATES VI, EUPATOR. ca. 132-63 B.C. King of Pontus. See: Encyc. Brit., 1973. Eupatorium, Mithridate (or Mithridatum), Mithridatea, Mithridatize (Mithridatism or Mithridatic).

Mithridatize (Mithridatism or Mithridatic) (Mithridates VI, Eupator): Generic Word (gradually induced immunity against poisons). See: Dorland; Hendrickson; Partridge; Stedman; Webster's 3d.

Mitis green (Mitis, Ignatz): Chemistry. See: Webster's 3d.

MITIS, IGNATZ. d. 1842. German manufacturer. Cited in: Royal Soc. Cat. Sci. Pap., 1800-1863. Mitis green.

MITSCHERLICH, ALEXANDER. 1836-1918. German chemist. See: Pogg., vols. 3, 4, 5, 6. Mitscherlich process, Mitscherlich pulp.

Mitscherlich desiccator (Mitscherlich, Eilhardt?): Chemistry. See: Hackh.

MITSCHERLICH, EILHARDT. 1794-1863. German chemist. See: Dict. Sci. Biog. Mitscherlich desiccator?, Mitscherlich eudiometer?, Mitscherlich('s) (Misterlich) law (of isomorphism), Mitscherlichite.

Mitscherlich eudiometer (Mitscherlich, Eilhardt?): Chemistry. See: Hackh.

Mitscherlich('s) (Misterlich) law (of isomorphism) (Mitscherlich, Eilhardt): Chemistry. See: Ballentyne; Hackh; Van Nostrand Sci. Encyc.; Webster's 3d.

Mitscherlich process (Mitscherlich, Alexander): Chemistry. Cited in: Dict. Sci. Biog. under "Mitscherlich, Eilhardt."

Mitscherlich pulp (Mitscherlich, Alexander): Chemistry. See: Hackh.

Mitscherlichite (Mitscherlich, Eilhardt): Earth Sciences. See: Webster's 3d.

MITSUDA, KENSUKE. b. 1876. Japanese physician. See: Japanese Biog. Encyc. and Who's Who, 1964-1965. Mitsuda reaction (or test).

Mitsuda reaction (or test) (Mitsuda, Kensuke): Medicine. See: Stedman.

MITSUKURI, KAKICHI. 1857-1909. Japanese zoologist. See: Dobutsugaku Zasshi, vol. 22 (1910), pp. 99-110. Mitsukurina.

Mitsukurina (Mitsukuri, Kakichi): Zoology. See: Webster's 3d.

MITSUNOBU, TOSA. 1434-1525. Japanese painter. See: Encyc. World Art under "Japanese Art," vol. 8, p. 871. Tosa School.

MITTENDORF, WILLIAM F. fl. 1886. American physician. Cited in: Index-Cat. Libr. Surg.-Gen. Off., 2d Ser., vol. 10, 1905. Mittendorf's dot?

Mittendorf's dot (Mittendorf, William F.?): Medicine. See: Blakiston's Gould.

Mittenzwey eyepiece (Mittenzwey, Moritz): Astronomy. See: Satterthwaite.

MITTENZWEY, MORITZ. fl. 1864-1886. German optician. Cited in: Royal Soc. Cat. Sci. Pap., 1884-1900. Mittenzwey eyepiece.

MITTY, WALTER. Character from James Thurber's short story "The Secret Life of Walter Mitty" (1939). See: Hart under "Secret Life of Walter Mitty." Walter Mitty.

MIXA, A. fl. 19th c. Czech mine inspector. Cited in: Hintze, vol. 1, pt. 4, half 2, p. 969. Mixite.

Mixite (Mixa, A.): Earth Sciences. See: Webster's 3d.

MIXTER, SAMUEL JASON. 1855-1926. American surgeon. See: Who Was Who Amer., 1897-1942. Mixter treatment, Paul-Mixter tube.

Mixter treatment (Mixter, Samuel Jason): Medicine. See: Kelly.

Miyagawa bodies (Miyagawa, Yoneji): Medicine. See: Stedman.

MIYAGAWA, YONEJI. 1885-1959. Japanese bacteriologist. See: World Who's Who Sci. Miyagawa bodies, Miyagawanella.

Miyagawanella (Miyagawa, Yoneji): Zoology. See: Dorland; Stedman; Webster's 3d.

MIYASHIRO, AKIHO. fl. 1957. Japanese mineralogist. Cited in: Min. Mag., vol. 33 pt. 2 (1963-1964), p. 1144. Miyashiroite.

Miyashiroite (Miyashiro, Akiho): Earth Sciences. See: Thrush.

MIYATA, TADAO. fl. 1935. Japanese physician. Cited in: Chem. Abstr., vol. 29, p. 4398. Fujita-Iwatake-Miyata test for ascorbic acid.

MO-TZU (MO-TI). 470?-391? B.C. Chinese philosopher. See: New Encyc. Brit., 1974, Microp. Mohism (or Moism).

Mobius resistor (Moebius, August Ferdinand): Mathematics. See: Markus.

MOBY DICK. Giant sperm whale in Herman Melville's novel of the same name (1851). See: Magill. Moby Dick baloon?

Moby Dick baloon (Moby Dick): Earth Sciences. See: Huschke; Van Nostrand Sci. Encyc. under "Baloon."

MODESTUS, SAINT. Christian martyr. See: Holweck. Saint Modestus disease.

Moe gage (Derivation undetermined): Engineering and Industry. See: Thrush.

MOE, JOHN H. 1905- . American surgeon. See: Amer. Men and Women Sci., 12th ed. Moe plate.

Moe plate (Moe, John H.): Medicine. See: Dorland.

MOEBIUS, AUGUST FERDINAND. 1790-1868. German mathematician. See: Dict. Sci. Biog. Mobius resistor, Moebius function, Moebius strip (or band), Moebius transformation.

Moebius function (Moebius, August Ferdinand): Mathematics. See: James.

MOEBIUS, PAUL JULIUS. 1853-1907. German neurologist. See: World Who's Who Sci. Leyden-Moebius syndrome, Moebius' sign, Moebius syndrome (1), Moebius' syndrome (2).

Moebius process (Derivation undetermined): Engineering and Industry. See: Thrush.

Moebius' sign (Moebius, Paul Julius): Medicine. See: Dorland; Kelly; Stedman.

Moebius strip (or band) (Moebius, August Ferdinand): Mathematics. See: Asimov; Ballentyne; James; Webster's 3d.

Moebius syndrome (1) (Moebius, Paul Julius): Medicine. See: Dorland; Jablonski.

Moebius' syndrome (2) (Moebius, Paul Julius): Medicine. See: Blakiston's Gould; Jablonski; Stedman.

Moebius transformation (Moebius, August Ferdinand): Mathematics. See: Internat. Dict. Phys. Elec.; James.

MOECKEL, KURT. fl. 1910. German physician. Cited in: Chem. Abstr., Decenn. Index, 1907-1916. Moeckel's method.

Moeckel's method (Moeckel, Kurt): Medicine. See: Kelly.

Moegel-Dellinger effect (Moegel, Hans and Dellinger, John Howard). See: Dellinger fadeout (or effect).

MOEGEL, HANS (In full: ERNST HANS). 1900- . German electrotechnician. See: Pogg., vols. 6, 7a. Moegel-Dellinger effect.

MOEHLAU, RICHARD (In full: BERNHARD JULIUS RICHARD). 1857-1940. German chemist. See: Pogg., vols. 4, 5, 7a. Moehlau test reaction for p-diamines?

Moehlau test reaction for p-diamines (Moehlau, Richard?): Chemistry. See: Van Nostrand Chem. Dict.

MOEHRING, PAUL HEINRICH GERHARD. 1710-1792. German physician and naturalist. See: Biog. Lex hervorr. Aerzte. Moehringia.

Moehringia (Moehring, Paul Heinrich Gerhard): Botany. See: Charnock; Webster's 3d.

MOELLER, ALFRED. b. 1868. German bacteriologist. Cited in: Index-Cat. Libr. Surg.-Gen. Off., 3rd Ser., vol. 7, 1928. Moeller's grass bacillus, Moeller's reaction, Moeller's stain.

Moeller and Pfeiffer dryer (Moeller, Gustav and Pfeifer, P.): Engineering and Industry. See: Thrush.

Moeller-Barlow disease (Moeller, Julius Otto Ludwig and Barlow, Sir Thomas): Medicine. See: Dorland; Jablonski. Also known as: Barlow's disease, Cheadle-Moeller-Barlow disease, Cheadle's disease, Moeller's disease.

Moeller Boeck. See: Boeck, Caesar Peter Moeller.

Moeller Boeck's disease (Boeck, Caesar Peter Moeller). See: Besnier-Boeck-Schaumann syndrome.

Moeller chart (Moeller, Fritz): Earth Sciences. See: Huschke.

MOELLER, EGGERT. fl. 1928. Danish-born American? physician. Cited in: Chem. Abstr., vol. 23, pp. 1171, 1669. Moeller's test.

MOELLER, FRITZ. 1906- . German meteorologist. See: World Who's Who Sci. Moeller chart.

MOELLER, GUSTAV. fl. 1897-1933. German engineer. Cited in: Chem. Abstr., Decenn. Index, 1927-1936. Moeller and Pfeiffer dryer.

MOELLER, HERMANN. fl. 1891. German botanist. Cited in: Royal Soc. Cat. Sci. Pap., 1884-1900. Moeller's method.

MOELLER, JULIUS OTTO LUDWIG. 1819-1887. German physician. See: Biog. Lex. hervorr. Aerzte. Moeller-Barlow disease, Moeller's glossitis.

MOELLER, SAM. b. 1880. German physician. Cited in: Index-Cat. Libr. Surg.-Gen. Off., 3rd Ser., vol. 7, 1928. Moeller's test.

Moeller's disease (Moeller, Julius Otto Ludwig). See: Moeller-Barlow disease.

Moeller's glossitis (Moller, Julius Otto Ludwig): Medicine. See: Dorland; Jablonski; Stedman.

Moeller's grass bacillus (Moeller, Alfred): Medicine. See: Stedman.

Moeller's method (Moeller, Hermann): Botany. See: Kelly.

Moeller's reaction (Moeller, Alfred): Medicine. See: Dorland.

Moeller's stain (Moeller, Alfred): Medicine. See: Stedman.

Moeller's test (Moeller, Eggert): Medicine. See: Kelly.

Moeller's test (Moeller, Sam): Medicine. See: Kelly.

MOEN, PHILIP LOUIS. 1824–1890. American manufacturer. See: Nat. Cycl. Amer. Biog., vol. 6, p. 205. Washburn and Moen wire gauge.

MOENCH, CONRAD. 1744–1805. German botanist. See: Dict. Sci. Biog. Moenchia.

Moenchia (Moench, Conrad): Botany. See: Charnock.

MOENCKEBERG, JOHANN GEORG. 1877–1925. German pathologist. See: Deut. Med. Wchnschr., vol. 51 (1925), p. 833. Moenckeberg's arteriosclerosis (calcification, degeneration, or sclerosis).

Moenckeberg's arteriosclerosis (calcification, degeneration, or sclerosis) (Moenckeberg, Johann Georg): Medicine. See: Dorland; Jablonski; Stedman.

MOERNER, CARL THORE. 1864–1940. Swedish physician. See: Svenska Maen Och Kvinnor. Moerner-Sjoeqvist method, Moerner's method.

MOERNER, KARL AXEL HAMPUS. 1854–1917. Swedish chemist. See: Svenska Maen Och Kvinnor. Moerner reagent for tyrosine, Moerner test reaction for quinone?

Moerner reagent for tyrosine (Moerner, Karl Axel Hampus): Chemistry. See: Van Nostrand Chem. Dict.

Moerner-Sjoeqvist method (Moerner, Carl Thore and Sjoeqvist, John August). See: Sjoeqvist's method.

Moerner test reaction for quinone (Moerner, Karl Axel Hampus?): Chemistry. See: Van Nostrand Chem. Dict.

Moerner's method (Moerner, Carl Thore): Medicine. See: Kelly.

MOERSCH, FREDERICK PAUL. b. 1889. American neurologist. See: Amer. Men Sci., 10th ed. Moersch-Woltmann syndrome.

Moersch-Woltmann syndrome (Moersch, Frederick Paul and Woltmann, Henry W.): Medicine. See: Jablonski.

MOESSBAUER, RUDOLF LUDWIG. 1929– . German physicist. See: World Who's Who Sci. Mossbauer effect.

MOEST, MARTIN. fl. 1899–1902. Swiss? chemist. Cited in: Mansell. Hofer-Moest reaction.

MOFFAT, JAMES. 1870–1944. Scottish theologian and biblical scholar. See: Dict. Nat. Biog. Moffat's translation.

Moffat's translation (Moffat, James): Religion. See: Brewer.

MOFFATT, M. R. fl. 1907. German physician? Cited in: Kelly. Moffatt-Spiro test?

Moffatt-Spiro test (Moffatt, M. R.? and Spiro, Karl?): Chemistry. See: Kelly; Van Nostrand Chem. Dict.

Moffet ore hearth (Derivation undetermined): Engineering and Industry. See: Thrush.

MOGENSEN, FREDRIK. fl. 1947. Swedish mineralogist. Cited in: Chem. Abstr., Decenn. Index, 1947–1956. Mogensenite.

Mogensenite (Mogensen, Fredrik): Earth Sciences. See: Thrush.

MOHAMMED (MUHAMMAD). ca. 570–632. Arabian prophet. See: Encyc. Brit., 1973. Mahound, Maumet (or Mammet), Maumetry (or Mawmetry), Mohammedan law, Mohammedanism (or Muhammadanism).

Mohammedan law (Mohammed): Law. See: Black.

Mohammedanism (or Muhammadanism) (Mohammed): Religion. See: Attwater; Barnhart (Eng. Lit.); Canney; Mathews, S. under "Mohammed;" Webster's 3d.

Mohism (or Moism) (Mo-tzu): Philosophy. See: New Encyc. Brit., 1974, Microp.; Webster's 3d.

MOHLER, EDMOND. fl. 1890. French chemist. Cited in: Royal Soc. Cat. Sci. Pap., 1884–1900. Mohler solution for tartaric acid.

Mohler solution for tartaric acid (Mohler, Edmond): Chemistry. See: Van Nostrand Chem. Dict.

Mohm (Ohm, Georg Simon): Physics. See: Dresner.

MOHOROVICIC, ANDRIJA. 1857–1936. Croatian geologist. See: Dict. Sci. Biog. Mohorovicic discontinuity.

Mohorovicic discontinuity (Mohorovicic, Andrija): Earth Sciences. See: Monkhouse; Thewlis; Thrush.

Mohr balance (Mohr, Friedrich): Chemistry. See: Internat. Dict. Phys. Elec.; Thrush; Webster's 3d. Also known as: Mohr-Westphal balance, Westphal balance.

Mohr circle for inertia (Mohr, Otto): Engineering and Industry. See: Internat. Dict. Ap. Math.

Mohr circle for strain (Mohr, Otto): Engineering and Industry. See: Internat. Dict. Ap. Math.

Mohr circle (for stress) (Mohr, Otto): Engineering and Industry. See: Internat. Dict. Ap. Math.; Thrush.

Mohr condenser (Mohr, Friedrich): Chemistry. See: Hackh.

Mohr cubic centimetre (Mohr, Friedrich): Chemistry. See: Dresner.

Mohr envelope (Mohr, Otto): Engineering and Industry. See: Thrush.

MOHR, ERNST W. M. b. 1873. German organic chemist. See: Pogg., vols. 4, 5. Sachse-Mohr theory.

MOHR, F. No dates. Engineer. (Biography source unavailable.) Mohr's dome.

MOHR, FRANCIS. fl. 1849. American pharmaceutical chemist. Cited in: Index-Cat. Libr. Surg.-Gen. Off., 1st Ser., vol. 9, 1888. Mohr's test.

MOHR, FRIEDRICH (In full: KARL FRIEDRICH). 1806–1879. German pharmacist. See: Dict. Sci. Biog. Mohr balance, Mohr condenser, Mohr cubic centimetre, Mohr('s) litre (liter), Mohr pinchcock, Mohr pipette, Mohr test for iron and chloride determination, Mohr's salt.

Mohr('s) litre (liter) (Mohr, Friedrich): Chemistry. See: Ballentyne; Hackh; Van Nostrand Chem. Dict.

MOHR, OTTO (In full: CHRISTIAN OTTO). 1835–1918. German engineer. See: Dict. Sci. Biog. Maxwell-Mohr method, Mohr circle for inertia, Mohr circle for strain, Mohr circle (for stress), Mohr envelope, Mohr yield condition, Mohr's theory, Williot-Mohr diagram.

Mohr pinchcock (Mohr, Friedrich): Chemistry. See: Webster's 3d.

Mohr pipette (Mohr, Friedrich): Chemistry. See: Hackh; Van Nostrand Chem. Dict.

Mohr test for iron and chloride determination (Mohr, Friedrich): Chemistry. See: Dict. Sci. Biog.

Mohr-Westphal balance (Mohr, Friedrich and Westphal, Wilhelm Heinrich). See: Mohr balance.

Mohr yield condition (Mohr, Otto): Engineering and Industry. See: Internat. Dict. Ap. Math.

MOHRENHEIM, BARON JOSEPH JAKOB FREIHERR VON. 1759–1799. Austrian surgeon. See: Biog. Lex. hervorr. Aerzte. Mohrenheim's fossa (or space).

Mohrenheim's fossa (or space) (Mohrenheim, Baron Joseph Jakob Freiherr von): Anatomy. See: Donath; Dorland; Stedman.

Mohr's dome (Mohr, F.): Engineering and Industry. See: Thrush.

Mohr's salt (Mohr, Friedrich): Chemistry. See: Hackh; Thrush; Webster's 3d.

Mohr's test (Mohr, Francis): Medicine. See: Dorland; Stedman.

Mohr's theory (Mohr, Otto): Engineering and Industry. See: Thrush.

Mohs' chemosurgery technique (Mohs, Frederic Edward): Medicine. See: Kelly; Stedman.

MOHS, FREDERIC EDWARD. 1910– . American surgeon. See: World Who's Who Sci. Mohs' chemosurgery technique.

MOHS, FRIEDRICH. 1773–1839. German mineralogist. See: Dict. Sci. Biog. Mohs scale, Mohsite?

Mohs scale (Mohs, Friedrich): Earth Sciences. See: Auger; Thrush; Van Nostrand Sci. Encyc.; Webster's 3d.

Mohsite (Mohs, Friedrich?): Earth Sciences. See: Thrush.

MOINEAU. No dates. French engineer. (Biography source unavailable.) Mono pump.

MOIR, JAMES. 1874-1929. Scottish-born chemist in South Africa. See: Pogg., vol. 6. Moir reagent, Moir test for niobium, tantalum, and titanium, Moir tests for molybdenum.

Moir reagent (Moir, James): Chemistry. See: Van Nostrand Chem. Dict.

Moir test for niobium, tantalum, and titanium (Moir, James): Chemistry. See: Van Nostrand Chem. Dict.

Moir tests for molybdenum (Moir, James): Chemistry. See: Van Nostrand Chem. Dict.

Moissan furnace (Moissan, Henri): Engineering and Industry. See: Hackh.

MOISSAN, HENRI (In full: FERDINAND FREDERIC HENRI). 1852-1907. French chemist. See: Dict. Sci. Biog. Moissan furnace, Moissan process, Moissanite.

Moissan process (Moissan, Henri): Engineering and Industry. See: Hackh; Thrush; Van Nostrand Chem. Dict.

Moissanite (Moissan, Henri): Earth Sciences. See: Thrush; Webster's 3d.

Moitch eucalyptus (Derivation undetermined): Botany. See: Winburne.

Moivre, Abraham de. See: De Moivre, Abraham.

MOJON, BENEDETTO. 1784-1849. Italian anatomist and physiologist. See: Biog. Lex. hervorr. Aerzte. Mojon's method.

MOJONNIER BROTHERS. fl. early 20th c. American dairy chemical engineers. See: Mansell. Mojonnier tube.

Mojonnier tube (Mojonnier Brothers): Chemistry. See: Van Nostrand Chem. Dict.

Mojon's method (Mojon, Benedetto): Medicine. See: Dorland.

MOKRANTZA, MOMCILO ST. fl. 1933. Jugoslavian chemist. Cited in: Chem. Abstr., vol. 27, p. 2531. Mokrantza reagent.

Mokrantza reagent (Mokrantza, Momcilo St.): Chemistry. See: Van Nostrand Chem. Dict.

MOLAY, JACQUES DE. 1243?-1314. French grand master of the Knights Templar. See: Encyc. Brit., 1973. De Molay.

MOLESCHOTT, JACOB. 1822-1893. German physician. See: World Who's Who Sci. Moleschott tests for cholesterol.

Moleschott tests for cholesterol (Moleschott, Jacob): Medicine. See: Kelly; Van Nostrand Chem. Dict.

MOLIERE (Real name: JEAN BAPTISTE POQUELIN). 1622-1673. French actor and playwright. See: New Encyc. Brit., 1974, Microp. Molieres (shoes).

Molieres (shoes) (Moliere): Fashion. See: Stenhouse.

MOLINA, JUAN IGNACIO. 1740-1829. Chilean naturalist. See: World Who's Who Sci. Molinia (or Molinaea).

MOLINA, LUIS. 1535-1600. Spanish Jesuit and theologian. See: New Encyc. Brit., 1974, Microp. Molinism (or Molinists) (1).

MOLINARI, ETTORE. 1867-1926. Italian chemist. See: Pogg., vol. 5. Molinari-Fenaroli petroleum reaction.

Molinari-Fenaroli petroleum reaction (Molinari, Ettore and Fenaroli, Piero): Chemistry. See: Van Nostrand Chem. Dict.

Molinia (or Molinaea) (Molina, Juan Ignacio): Botany. See: Charnock; Taylor, N.; Webster's 3d.

Molinism (or Molinists) (1) (Molina, Luis): Religion. See: Attwater; Brewer; Canney; Mathews, S.; Webster's 3d.

Molinism (or Molinists) (2) (Molinos, Miguel de): Religion. See: Latham; Webster's 3d.

MOLINOS, MIGUEL DE. 1628-1696. Spanish priest and mystic. See: New Encyc. Brit., 1974, Microp. Molinism (or Molinists) (2).

MOLINS, DESMOND W. fl. 1937-1962. English engineer and manufacturer. (Biography source unavailable.) Molins machine.

Molins machine (Molins, Desmond W.): Engineering and Industry. See: Auger.

MOLISCH, HANS. 1856-1937. Austrian botanist and chemist. See: World Who's Who Sci. Molisch reagent for albumin, Molisch solution, Molisch('s) test (for sugars), Molisch test for wood fibers?

Molisch reagent for albumin (Molisch, Hans): Chemistry. See: Van Nostrand Chem. Dict.

Molisch solution (Molisch, Hans): Medicine. See: Kelly.

Molisch('s) test (for sugars) (Molisch, Hans): Chemistry. See: Dorland; Stedman; Van Nostrand Chem. Dict.

Molisch test for wood fibers (Molisch, Hans?): Chemistry. See: Van Nostrand Chem. Dict.

MOLL, JAKOB ANTHONI. 1832-1914. Dutch anatomist and ophthalmologist. See: Biog. Lex. hervorr. Aerzte, 1880-1930. Moll's gland(s).

Moll thermopile (Moll, Willem Jan Henri): Physics. See: Huschke.

MOLL, WILLEM JAN HENRI. b. 1876. Dutch physicist. See: Pogg., vol. 6. Moll thermopile.

MOLLARET, PIERRE. 1898- . French neurologist. See: Who's Who Sci. Europe, 1967. Debre-Mollaret syndrome, Foshay-Mollaret syndrome, Mollaret's meningitis.

Mollaret's meningitis (Mollaret, Pierre): Medicine. See: Jablonski.

MOLLER, CHRISTIAN. 1904- . Danish physicist. See: Pogg., vol. 6. Moller scattering.

Moller scattering (Moller, Christian): Physics. See: Ballentyne.

MOLLERUP, A. M. fl. 1881. Engineer. (Biography source unavailable.) Mollerup lubricator.

Mollerup lubricator (Mollerup, A. M.): Engineering and Industry. See: Auger.

MOLLGAARD, HOLGER CHRISTIAN. b. 1885. Danish surgeon. See: World Who's Who Sci. Mollgaard treatment.

Mollgaard treatment (Mollgaard, Holger Christian): Medicine. See: Dorland.

MOLLIEN, COMTE NICOLAS FRANCOIS. 1758-1850. French statesman and financier. See: New Encyc. Brit., 1974, Microp. Mollienisia (or Molly).

Mollienisia (or Molly) (Mollien, Comte Nicolas Francois): Zoology. See: Hendrickson; Pennak; Webster's 3d.

Mollier diagram (chart or steam table) (Mollier, Richard): Engineering and Industry. See: Auger; Internat. Dict. Phys. Elec.; Thewlis; Van Nostrand Sci. Encyc.

Mollier equation (Mollier, Richard): Engineering and Industry. See: Internat. Dict. Ap. Math.

MOLLIER, RICHARD. 1863-1935. German mechanical engineer. See: Dict. Sci. Biog. Mollier diagram (chart or steam table), Mollier equation.

MOLLISON, THEODORE. 1874-1952. German anthropologist. See: Z. f. Morphologie u. Anthropologie, vol. 45 (1953), pp. 416-432. Mollison's tincture?

Mollison's tincture (Mollison, Theodore?): Archaeology. See: Winick.

Moll's gland(s) (Moll, Jakob Anthoni): Anatomy. See: Donath; Dorland; Stedman.

MOLLWEIDE, KARL BRANDAN. 1774-1825. German mathematician and astronomer. See: Dict. Sci. Biog. Mollweide('s) projection.

Mollweide('s) projection (Mollweide, Karl Brandan): Geography. See: Monkhouse; Moore; Webster's 3d.

Molly (Mollien, Comte Nicolas Francois). See: Mollienisia.

Molly Maguires (Maguire, Connor): History. See: Encyc. Brit., 1973; Harbottle; Phyfe; Webster's 2d.

Molmutian (Molmutin(e)) Laws (Molmutius, Dunvallo): Law. See: Black; Brewer; Charnock.

OLMUTIUS, DUNVALLO. fl. 400 B.C.? Legendary King of the Britons. iography source unavailable.) Molmutian (Molmutin(e)) Laws.

OLOCH (MOLECH). Semitic god to whom children were sacrificed. See: ew Encyc. Brit., 1974, Microp. Moloch, Moloch (lizard).

oloch (Moloch, the Semitic god): Generic Word (tyranny demanding human crifice). See: Partridge; Phyfe; Webster's 3d.

oloch (lizard) (Moloch, the Semitic god): Zoology. See: New Encyc. it., 1974, Microp.; Pennak; Webster's 3d.

OLONEY, JOHN BROMLEY. 1924- . American cancer researcher. See: mer. Men and Women Sci., 12th ed. Moloney's leukemia (or virus).

oloney's leukemia (or virus) (Moloney, John Bromley): Medicine. See: ablonski; Stedman.

olotov breadbasket (Molotov, Vyacheslav Mikhailovich): Weapons. See: ewer; Hendrickson; Quick.

olotov cocktail (Molotov, Vyacheslav Mikhailovich): Weapons. See: ewer; Hendrickson; Webster's 3d.

OLOTOV, VYACHESLAV MIKHAILOVICH (Orig. surname: SKRYABIN). , 1890. Russian statesman. See: New Encyc. Brit., 1974, Microp. olotov breadbasket, Molotov cocktail.

OLOY, HOWARD CARMAN. 1903-1953. American obstetrician and gyne- ologist. See: World Who's Who Sci. Caldwell-Moloy classification.

OLPADIA. Greek minor goddess. (Biography source unavailable.) olpadonia (or Molpadia).

olpadonia (or Molpadia) (Molpadia): Zoology. See: Pennak; Webster's 3d.

OLTKE, JOACHIM GODSKE. 1746-1818. Danish statesman. See: Dansk og. Lek. Moltke linden?, Moltkia.

oltke linden (Moltke, Joachim Godske?): Botany. See: Winburne.

oltkia (Moltke, Joachim Godske): Botany. See: Taylor, N.

olyneux problem (Molyneux, William): Philosophy. See: Edwards.

OLYNEUX, WILLIAM. 1656-1698. Irish philosopher and astronomer. See: ict. Nat. Biog. Molyneux problem.

OMBURG, FRIEDRICH (FRITZ) AUGUST. 1870-1939. German surgeon. See: og. Lex. hervorr. Aerzte, 1880-1930. Momburg's belt, Momburg's method.

omburg's belt (Momburg, Friedrich August): Medicine. See: Dorland.

omburg's method (Momburg, Friedrich August): Medicine. See: Stedman.

omertz-Lintz system (Derivation undetermined): Engineering and Industry. See: hrush.

OMUS. Minor Greek god of mockery. See: Jobes. Momus.

omus (Momus, the Greek god): Generic Word (carping critic). See: ewer; Jobes; Partridge.

ONA LISA (In full: LISA DI ANTON MARIA GHERARDINI or LA IACONDA). fl. ca. 1495. Florentine noblewoman. See: Webster's Biog. ict. Mona Lisa (smile).

ona Lisa (smile) (Mona Lisa): Generic Word (enigmatic). See: Hendrickson; ew Encyc. Brit., 1974, Microp.; Partridge.

onakow, Constantin von. See: Von Monakow, Constantin.

onakow's fasciculus (Von Monakow, Constantin): Anatomy. See: Dorland.

onakow's nucleus (Von Monakow, Constantin): Anatomy. See: Stedman.

onakow's syndrome (Von Monakow, Constantin): Medicine. See: Jablonski; edman.

onakow's tract (bundle or fibers) (Von Monakow, Constantin): Anatomy. ee: Donath; Dorland; Stedman; Webster's 3d.

onarda (Monardes, Nicolas Bautista): Botany. See: Taylor, N.; Webster's d.

MONARDES, NICOLAS BAUTISTA. 1493-1588. Spanish physician and bota- ist. See: Dict. Sci. Biog. Monarda.

MONCKHOVEN, DESIRE CHARLES EMMANUEL VAN. 1834-1882. Belgian photographic chemist. See: Pogg., vol. 4. Monkhoven's intensifier.

MONCRIEFF, ALAN AIRD. 1901- . English pediatrician. See: Med. Direct., 1964. Moncrieff-Wilkinson syndrome.

Moncrieff-Wilkinson syndrome (Moncrieff, Alan Aird and Wilkinson, Richard Hanwell): Medicine. See: Jablonski.

Mond gas (Mond, Ludwig): Chemistry. See: Hackh; Partridge; Webster's 3d.

MOND, LUDWIG. 1839-1909. German-born English chemist and industrialist. See: Dict. Sci. Biog. Mond gas, Mond process (for nickel), Mond producer.

Mond process (for nickel) (Mond, Ludwig): Chemistry. See: Ballentyne; Hackh; Thrush; Van Nostrand Chem. Dict.

Mond producer (Mond, Ludwig): Engineering and Industry. See: Thrush.

Mondini's malformation (Derivation undetermined): Medicine. See: Jablonski.

MONDONESI, FILIPPO. No dates. Italian physician. (Biography source unavailable.) Mondonesi's reflex.

Mondonesi's reflex (Mondonesi, Filippo): Medicine. See: Stedman.

MONDOR, HENRI JEAN JUSTIN. 1885-1962. French surgeon. See: Arnim. Mondor's disease.

Mondor's disease (Mondor, Henri Jean Justin): Medicine. See: Jablonski; Stedman.

Mondragon 7 mm semiautomatic rifle (Mondragon, Manuel): Weapons. See: Quick.

MONDRAGON, MANUEL. 1858-1922. Mexican general. See: Dicc. Porrua de Hist. Biog y Geog. de Mexico. Mondragon 7 mm semiautomatic rifle.

Mondrian (art style) (Mondrian, Piet): Fine Arts. See: Hendrickson.

MONDRIAN, PIET (Real name: PIETER CORNELIS MONDRIAAN). 1872-1944. Dutch painter. See: New Encyc. Brit., 1974. Mondrian (art style).

MONEKEY, CHARLES. fl. ca. 1856. American inventor. Cited in: Nat. Cycl. Amer. Biog., vol. 15, p. 216. Monkey wrench.

Monel metal (Monell, Ambrose): Engineering and Industry. See: New Encyc. Brit., 1974, Microp.; Partridge; Thrush; Van Nostrand Sci. Encyc.

MONELL, AMBROSE. d. 1921. American manufacturer. See: Who Was Who Amer., 1897-1942. Monel metal.

Monell process (Derivation undetermined): Engineering and Industry. See: Thrush.

Monetia (Lamarck, Jean Baptiste Pierre Antoine de Monet, Chevalier de): Botany. See: Charnock.

Money (Juno): Generic Word. See: Charnock; Hargrave; New Encyc. Brit., 1974, Microp.

MONGE, CARLOS. b. 1884. Peruvian physician. See: World Who's Who Sci. Monge's disease.

MONGE, GASPARD. 1746-1818. French mathematician. See: Dict. Sci. Biog. Monge's form for equation of surface, Monge's theorem, surface of Monge.

Monge's disease (Monge, Carlos): Medicine. See: Dorland; Jablonski.

Monge's form for equation of surface (Monge, Gaspard): Mathematics. See: Internat. Dict. Ap. Math.

Monge's theorem (Monge, Gaspard): Mathematics. See: Ballentyne.

MONHEIM, VICTOR. fl. 1848-1865. German mineralogist. Cited in: Royal Soc. Cat. Sci. Pap., 1800-1863. Monheimite?

Monheimite (Monheim, Victor?): Earth Sciences. See: Thrush.

MONIEZ, ROMAIN-LOUIS. 1852-1936. French physician. See: Bull. Acad. Med. Paris, vol. 115 (March 24, 1936), pp. 477-78. Moniezia.

Moniezia (Moniez, Romain-Louis): Zoology. See: Pennak; Webster's 3d.

MONIMA. d. 72 B.C. Ionian wife of Mithridates VI. See: Dict. Grk. Rom. Biog. Myth. Monimia.

Monimia (Monima): Botany. See: Webster's 3d.

MONK, MARIA. 1817?-1850. Canadian imposter. See: Webster's Biog. Dict. Maria Monk.

Monkey wrench (Monekey, Charles): Generic Word (adjustable wrench). See: Hendrickson.

Monkhoven's intensifier (Monckhoven, Desire Charles Emmanuel van): Photography. See: Van Nostrand Sci. Encyc. under "Intensification."

Monmouth, Duke of. See: Scott, James (Duke of Monmouth).

Monmouth's rebellion (Scott, James, Duke of Monmouth): History. See: Barnhart (Eng. Lit.); Brewer; Steinberg.

MONNIER, ALFRED. d. 1917. Swiss chemist. See: Arnim. Monnier reagent for metals and citric acid?

MONNIER, JEAN-BAPTISTE. fl. 1927-1936. French engineer. Cited in: Chem. Abstr., Decenn. Index, 1927-1936. Monnier kiln.

Monnier kiln (Monnier, Jean-Baptiste): Engineering and Industry. See: Thrush.

Monnier process (Derivation undetermined): Engineering and Industry. See: Thrush.

Monnier reagent for metals and citric acid (Monnier, Alfred?): Chemistry. See: Van Nostrand Chem. Dict.

MONNIER, ROBERT. fl. 1933-1934. Swiss chemist. Cited in: Chem. Abstr., vol. 28, p. 3332; vol. 27, p. 2649. Gutzeit-Monnier-Bachoulkova-Brun reagent for magnesium, Gutzeit-Monnier reagent for vanadium and iron.

Mono pump (Moineau): Engineering and Industry. See: Auger.

MONOD, JACQUES LUCIEN. 1910- . French biochemist. See: World Who's Who Sci. Jacob-Monod (theory).

MONRAD, MARCUS JAKOB. 1816-1897. Norwegian philosopher. See: New Encyc. Brit., 1974, Microp. Monradite?

Monradite (Monrad, Marcus Jakob?): Earth Sciences. See: Charnock.

MONRO, ALEXANDER (SECUNDUS). 1733-1817. Scottish anatomist. See: Dict. Sci. Biog. bursa of Monro, foramen of Monro, Monro-Richter line, Monro's doctrine, Monro's gland, Monro's sulcus (or groove).

Monro-Kellie doctrine (Monro, Alexander and Kellie, George). See: Monro's doctrine.

Monro-Richter line (Monro, Alexander and Richter, August Gottlieb): Anatomy. See: Dorland; Stedman. Also known as: Monro's line, Richter-Monro line.

Monroe calculating machine (Monroe, Jay Randolph): Engineering and Industry. Cited in: Webster's Biog. Dict.

Monroe crucible (Derivation undetermined): Chemistry. See: Van Nostrand Chem. Dict.

Monroe diagnostic reading test (Monroe, Marion): Psychology. See: Wolman.

Monroe Doctrine (or Monroeism) (Monroe, James): Politics. See: Mathews, M. M.; Montgomery; Morris; New Encyc. Brit., 1974, Microp.; Smith.

MONROE, JAMES. 1758-1831. American president. See: Dict. Amer. Biog. Monroe Doctrine (or Monroeism), Monroe-Pinkney Treaty, Monroite.

MONROE, JAY RANDOLPH. 1883-1937. American manufacturer. See: Nat. Cycl. Amer. Biog., vol. 27, p. 481. Monroe calculating machine.

MONROE, MARION. 1898- . American psychologist. See: Amer. Psych. Assoc., Direct., 1960. Monroe diagnostic reading test.

Monroe-Pinkney Treaty (Monroe, James and Pinkney, William): History. See: Morris.

Monroite (Monroe, James): History. See: Mathews, M. M.

Monro's doctrine (Monro, Alexander): Medicine. See: Stedman. Also known as: Monro-Kellie doctrine.

Monro's foramen (Monro, Alexander). See: foramen of Monro.

Monro's gland (Monro, Alexander): Anatomy. See: Donath; Stedman.

Monro's line (Monro, Alexander). See: Monro-Richter line.

Monro's sulcus (or groove) (Monro, Alexander): Anatomy. See: Donath; Stedman.

Monsel salt (Derivation undetermined): Chemistry. See: Hackh.

Monsel solution (Derivation undetermined): Chemistry. See: Hackh.

Monson curve (Monson, George S.): Medicine. See: Stedman.

MONSON, GEORGE S. 1869-1933. American dentist. See: Who Was Who Amer., 1897-1942. Monson curve.

Montagu-Chelmsford report (Montagu, Edwin Samuel and Thesiger, Frederic John Napier (1st Viscount Chelmsford): Politics. See: Steinberg.

MONTAGU, EDWIN SAMUEL. 1879-1924. English statesman. See: Encyc. Brit., 1973. Montagu-Chelmsford report.

MONTAGU, JOHN (4TH EARL OF SANDWICH). 1718-1792. English diplomat. See: Dict. Nat. Biog. Sandwich.

MONTAIGNE, MICHEL EYQUEM DE. 1533-1592. French essayist. See: New Encyc. Brit., 1974. Montaignesque.

Montaignesque (Montaigne, Michel Eyquem de): Literature. See: Webster's 3d.

Montanism (or Montanists) (Montanus): Religion. See: Attwater; Canney; Mathews, S.; New Encyc. Brit., 1974, Microp.; Phyfe.

MONTANUS. fl. 2nd. c. A.D. Asia Minor heretic. See: New Encyc. Brit., 1974, Microp. Montanism (or Montanists).

Montbretia (Coquebert de Montbrey, Antoine-Francois- Ernest): Botany. See: Webster's 3d.

Monte, Guidubaldo dal. See: Dal Monte, Guidubaldo.

MONTEGGIA, GIOVANNI BATTISTA. 1762-1815. Italian surgeon. See: Biog. Lex. hervorr. Aerzte. Monteggia's fracture.

Monteggia's fracture (Monteggia, Giovanni Battista): Medicine. See: Dorland; Jablonski; Stedman.

MONTEITH (MONTEIGH). fl. 17th c. Scottish eccentric. (Biography source unavailable.) Monteith (punch-bowl).

Monteith (handkerchief) (Monteith, Henry): Fashion. See: Picken.

MONTEITH, HENRY. fl. early 19th c. Scottish dyer. Cited in: Singer, vol. 4. Monteith (handkerchief).

Monteith (punch-bowl) (Monteith): Generic Word. See: Brewer; De Sola; Webster's 3d.

MONTEQUI (DIAZ DE PLAZA), RODRICA. fl. 1927. Spanish chemist. Cited in: Chem. Abstr., vol. 21, p. 2858. Montequi reagent for zinc.

Montequi reagent for zinc (Montequi, Rodrica): Chemistry. See: Van Nostrand Chem. Dict.

Montespan (Montespan, Francoise-Athenais de Rochechouart, Marquise de): Generic Word (mistress). See: Hendrickson.

MONTESPAN, FRANCOISE-ATHENAIS DE ROCHECHOUART, MARQUISE DE. 1641-1707. French mistress of Louis XIV. See: New Encyc. Brit., 1974, Microp. Montespan.

MONTESSORI, MARIA. 1870-1952. Italian physician and educator. See: Internat. Encyc. Soc. Sci. Montessori method (or Montessorian).

Montessori method (or Montessorian) (Montessori, Maria): Education. See: Brewer; Encyc. Brit., 1973; Good; Webster's 3d.

MONTEZUMA II. ca. 1466- ca. 1520. Aztec ruler at the time of the Spanish conquest of Mexico. See: New Encyc. Brit., 1974, Microp. Montezuma cypress.

Montezuma cypress (Montezuma II): Botany. See: Webster's 3d.

MONTFORT, SIMON DE (EARL OF LEICESTER). ca. 1208-1265. English statesman and soldier. See: Dict. Nat. Biog. Montfortians.

Montfortians (Montfort, Simon de): History. See: Steinberg.

Montgolfier (balloon) (Montgolfier, Joseph Michel and Montgolfier, Jacques Etienne): Aviation. See: Partridge; Webster's 3d.

Montgolfier hydraulic ram (Montgolfier, Joseph Michel): Engineering and Industry. See: Auger.

MONTGOLFIER, JACQUES ETIENNE. 1745-1799. French inventor. See: New Encyc. Brit., 1974, Microp. Montgolfier (balloon)

MONTGOLFIER, JOSEPH MICHEL. 1740-1810. French inventor. See: New Encyc. Brit., 1974, Microp. Montgolfier hydraulic ram, Montgolfier (balloon).

MONTGOMERY, ARTHUR. 1909- . American geologist. See: Amer. Men and Women Sci., 12th ed. Montgomeryite.

Montgomery beret (Montgomery of Alamein, Sir Bernard Law Montgomery, 1st Viscount): Fashion. See: Picken.

Montgomery Charter (Montgomery, John): History. See: Latham.

MONTGOMERY, HAROLD CLARKE. 1907- . American acoustical physicist. See: Amer. Men Sci., 9th ed. Montgomery noise transmission effect?

Montgomery jig (Derivation undetermined): Engineering and Industry. See: Thrush.

MONTGOMERY, JOHN. fl. 1730. English colonial governor in America. (Biography source unavailable.) Montgomery Charter.

Montgomery noise transmission effect (Montgomery, Harold Clarke?): Electronics. See: Van Nostrand Sci. Encyc.

MONTGOMERY OF ALAMEIN, SIR BERNARD LAW MONTGOMERY, 1ST VISCOUNT. b. 1887. English field marshal. See: New Encyc. Brit., 1974, Microp. Montgomery beret.

MONTGOMERY, RAYMOND BRAISLIN. 1910- . American meteorologist and oceanographer. See: Amer. Men Sci., 9th ed. Montgomery stream function.

Montgomery stream function (Montgomery, Raymond Braislin): Earth Sciences. See: Huschke.

MONTGOMERY, WILLIAM. 1818-1870. American legislator. See: Biog. Direct. Amer. Congress. Crittenden-Montgomery amendment.

MONTGOMERY, WILLIAM FETHERSTON. 1797-1859. Irish gynecologist. See: World Who's Who Sci. Montgomery's gland(s); Montgomery's tubercle.

Montgomeryite (Montgomery, Arthur): Earth Sciences. See: Webster's 3d.

Montgomery's gland(s) (Montgomery, William Fetherston): Anatomy. See: Donath; Dorland; Henderson; Stedman.

Montgomery's tubercle (Montgomery, William Fetherston): Anatomy. See: Stedman.

Monthier blue (Derivation undetermined): Chemistry. See: Hackh.

MONTI, E. fl. 1920. Italian manufacturer. Cited in: Chem. Abstr., Decenn. Index, 1927-1936. Monti process.

MONTI, GIUSEPPE. 1682-1760. Italian botanist. See: Nouv. Biog. Univ. Montia.

Monti process (Monti, E.): Agriculture. See: Winburne.

Montia (Monti, Giuseppe): Botany. See: Taylor, N.; Webster's 3d.

MONTICELLI, TEODORO. 1759-1845. Italian naturalist. See: Diz. Encic. Ital. Monticellite.

Monticellite (Monticelli, Teodoro): Earth Sciences. See: New Encyc. Brit., 1974, Microp.; Thrush; Webster's 3d.

MONTIGNIE, EMILE ANDRE LOUIS. b. 1894. French chemist. See: Pogg., vol. 6. Montignie test for ergosterol, Montignie test reaction for hydrazines, Montignie test reaction for molybdenum, Montignie test reaction for sterols.

Montignie test for ergosterol (Montignie, Emile Andre Louis): Chemistry. See: Van Nostrand Chem. Dict.

Montignie test reaction for hydrazines (Montignie, Emile Andre Louis): Chemistry. See: Van Nostrand Chem. Dict.

Montignie test reaction for molybdenum (Montignie, Emile Andre Louis): Chemistry. See: Van Nostrand Chem. Dict.

Montignie test reaction for sterols (Montignie, Emile Andre Louis): Chemistry. See: Van Nostrand Chem. Dict.

MONTIGNY, JOSEPH. fl. 1867. Belgian inventor. (Biography source unavailable.) Montigny mitrailleuse.

Montigny mitrailleuse (Montigny, Joseph): Weapons. See: Quick.

Montroydite (Sharpe, Montroyd): Earth Sciences. See: Webster's 3d.

MONTT, MANUEL. 1809-1880. Chilean statesman. See: Encyc. Brit., 1973. Montt-Varistas (political party).

Montt-Varistas (political party) (Montt, Manuel and Varas, Antonio): History. See: Harbottle.

MOOD, ALEXANDER MC FARLANE. 1913- . American applied mathematician. See: Amer. Men and Women Sci., 12th ed. Mood-Brown estimation (of a line), Mood-Brown median test, Mood's W-test.

Mood-Brown estimation (of a line) (Mood, Alexander McFarlane and Brown, George William): Statistics. See: Kendall.

Mood-Brown median test (Mood, Alexander Mc Farlane and Brown, George William): Statistics. See: Kendall.

Mood's W-test (Mood, Alexander Mc Farlane): Statistics. See: Kendall.

MOODY, LEWIS FERRY. 1880-1953. American hydraulic engineer. See: World Who's Who Sci. Moody turbine.

Moody turbine (Moody, Lewis Ferry): Engineering and Industry. See: Auger.

MOOERS, CALVIN NORTHRUP. 1919- . American mathematician. See: Amer. Men and Women Sci., 12th ed. Mooers' law.

Mooers' law (Mooers, Calvin Northrup): Library Science. See: Harrod.

MOOG, ROBERT ARTHUR. 1934- . American engineering physicist. Cited in: Chem. Abstr., Auth. Index, 1962-1966. Moog synthesizer.

Moog synthesizer (Moog, Robert Arthur): Music. See: Barnhart (New Eng.); Time, Feb. 24, 1975.

MOON, HENRY. fl. 19th c. English surgeon. (Biography source unavailable.) Moon's molars.

MOON, ROBERT C. 1844-1914. American ophthalmologist. See: New York Times, Feb. 14, 1914, p. 11, col. 5. Laurence-Moon-Biedl syndrome, Laurence-Moon-Biedl-Bardet syndrome.

Moon type (Moon, William): Education. See: Good; Harrod.

MOON, WILLIAM. 1818-1894. English clergyman and inventor. See: Dict. Nat. Biog., 1st suppl. Moon type.

Mooney problem check list (Mooney, Ross L.): Psychology. See: Hinsie; Wolman.

MOONEY, ROSS L. fl. 1950. American? psychologist. (Biography source unavailable.) Mooney problem check list.

Moon's molars (Moon, Henry): Dentistry. See: Dorland; Stedman.

MOORBY, WILLIAM HENRY. fl. 1898. English physicist. Cited in: Royal Soc. Cat. Sci. Pap., 1884-1900. Reynolds and Moorby method for mechanical equivalence of heat.

MOORCROFT, WILLIAM. ca. 1765-1825. English physician and traveler. See: Dict. Nat. Biog. Moorcroftia.

Moorcroftia (Moorcroft, William): Botany. See: Charnock.

Moore and Neill sampler (Moore, Hilary B. and Neill, Robert G.): Earth Sciences. See: Thrush.

MOORE, BERNARD J. fl. 1930. American engineer. Cited in: Chem. Abstr., Decenn. Index, 1927-1936. Moore-Campbell kiln.

Moore-Campbell kiln (Moore, Bernard J. and Campbell, Arthur J.): Engineering and Industry. See: Thrush.

MOORE, CHARLES HEWITT. 1821-1870. English surgeon. See: Biog. Lex. hervorr. Aerzte. Moore's method.

Moore code (Moore, Daniel Mc Farlane?): Telegraphy. See: Markus.

MOORE, DANIEL MC FARLANE. 1869-1936. American electrical engineer. See: Who Was Who Amer., 1897-1942. Moore code?, Moore tube.

MOORE, DAVID GILLIS. 1925- . American geologist. See: World Who's Who Sci. Moore free corer.

MOORE, EDWARD MOTT. 1814-1902. American surgeon. See: Dict. Amer. Biog. Moore's fracture.

MOORE, ELIAKIM HASTINGS. 1862-1932. American mathematician. See: Dict. Sci. Biog. Moore-Smith convergence (or set), Moore-Smith sequence.

Moore filter press (Moore, George?): Engineering and Industry. See: Thrush.

MOORE, FRANCIS. 1657-1714. English astrologer and almanac-maker. See: Dict. Nat. Biog. "Old Moore" (almanac).

Moore free corer (Moore, David Gillis): Earth Sciences. See: Thrush.

MOORE, GEORGE. fl. 1917. American engineer. Cited in: Chem. Abstr., Decenn. Index, 1917-1926. Moore filter press?

MOORE, GIDEON EMMET. 1842-1895. American chemist. See: J. Amer. Chem. Soc., vol. 17 (1895), p. 662. Mooreite.

MOORE, GILPIN. fl. 1875. Inventor. (Biography source unavailable.) Gilpin sulky.

MOORE, HILARY B. fl. 1930. English biologist. Cited in: Chem. Abstr., vol. 24, p. 2642. Moore and Neill sampler.

MOORE, HUGH KELSEA. 1872-1939. American chemical engineer. See: World Who's Who Sci. Allen-Moore cell.

MOORE, JOHN BASSETT. 1860-1947. American jurist and publicist. See: Internat. Encyc. Soc. Sci. Moore's Digest.

MOORE, JOHN WILLIAM. fl. 1869-1900. Irish physician and scientist. Cited in: Royal Soc. Cat. Sci. Pap., 1884-1900. Moore's test?

MOORE, MATTHEW THIBAUD. 1901-   . American neuropsychiatrist. See: Amer. Men and Women Sci., 12th ed. Moore's syndrome.

MOORE, ROBERT FOSTER. 1878-1963. English ophthalmologist. See: Who Was Who, 1961-1970. Moore's lightning striae.

MOORE, ROBERT LEE. b. 1882. American mathematician. See: World Who's Who Sci. Moore space.

MOORE, ROBERT THOMAS. 1882-1958. American zoologist. See: World Who's Who Sci. Moore's turkey?

Moore-Smith convergence (or set) (Moore, Eliakim Hastings and Smith, Herman Lyle): Mathematics. See: James.

Moore-Smith sequence (Moore, Eliakim Hastings and Smith, Herman Lyle): Mathematics. See: James.

Moore space (Moore, Robert Lee): Mathematics. See: James.

Moore test for mercury (Moore, William Cabler): Chemistry. See: Van Nostrand Chem. Dict.

Moore tube (Moore, Daniel Mc Farlane): Electronics. See: Encyc. Brit., 1973 under "Lighting."

MOORE, WILLIAM CABLER. b. 1884. American chemist. See: Pogg., vol. 6. Moore test for mercury.

Mooreite (Moore, Gideon Emmet): Earth Sciences. See: Thrush; Webster's 3d.

MOOREN, ALBERT. 1828-1899. German oculist. See: Biog. Lex. hervorr. Aerzte. Mooren's ulcer.

Mooren's ulcer (Mooren, Albert): Medicine. See: Dorland; Jablonski; Stedman.

Moore's Digest (Moore, John Bassett): Law. See: Smith.

Moore's fracture (Moore, Edward Mott): Medicine. See: Dorland; Jablonski; Stedman.

Moore's lightning striae (Moore, Robert Foster): Medicine. See: Stedman.

Moore's method (Moore, Charles Hewitt): Medicine. See: Stedman.

Moore's syndrome (Moore, Matthew Thibaud): Medicine. See: Dorland; Jablonski.

Moore's test (Moore, John William?): Medicine. See: Dorland; Stedman. Also known as: Heller's test (3) (for sugar).

Moore's turkey (Moore, Robert Thomas?): Zoology. See: Encyc. Brit., 1973 under "Turkey," p. 398c.

Moorhead foreign body locator (Moorhead, John Joseph). See: Berman-Moorhead locator.

MOORHEAD, JOHN JOSEPH. b. 1874. American surgeon. See: Who's Who Among Physicians and Surg. Berman-Moorhead locator.

MOORHOUSE, JAMES. 1826-1915. Australian bishop. See: Dict. Nat. Biog., 3d suppl. Moorhouse Lectureship.

Moorhouse Lectureship (Moorhouse, James): Religion. See: Canney.

Mooser bodies (Mooser, Hermann): Medicine. See: Stedman.

MOOSER, HERMANN. b. 1891. Swiss pathologist. See: Kuerschner's Deut. Gel. Kal., vol. 9, 1961. Mooser bodies, Neil-Mooser reaction.

MOOTS, CHARLES WILLIAM. 1869-1933. American surgeon. See: Nat. Cycl. Amer. Biog., vol. A, p. 168. Moots's rule.

Moots's rule (Moots, Charles William): Medicine. See: Dorland.

MORAES, LUCIANO JACQUES DE. fl. 1950. Brazilian geologist. Cited in: Chem. Abstr., Decenn. Index, 1947-1956. Moraesite.

Moraesite (Moraes, Luciano Jacques de): Earth Sciences. See: Thrush.

Moran and Proctor sampler (Derivation undetermined): Engineering and Industry. See: Thrush.

MORAN, PATRICK ALFRED PIERCE. fl. 1942-1967. Australian statistician. See: Direct. Brit. Scientists, 1966-1967. Moran's test statistic.

MORAND, SAUVEUR FRANCOIS. 1697-1773. French surgeon. See: World Who's Who Sci. Morand's disease, Morand's foot, Morand's foramen, Morand's spur.

Morand's disease (Morand, Sauveur Francois): Medicine. See: Dorland.

Morand's foot (Morand, Sauveur Francois): Medicine. See: Dorland; Stedman.

Morand's foramen (Morand, Sauveur Francois): Anatomy. See: Donath; Dorland.

Morand's spur (Morand, Sauveur Francois): Medicine. See: Dorland; Stedman.

Moran's test statistic (Moran, Patrick Alfred Pierce): Statistics. See: Kendall.

MORAT, JEAN-PIERRE. 1846-1920. French physiologist. See: Dict. Sci. Biog. Dastre-Morat law.

Morax-Axenfeld conjunctivitis (Morax, Victor and Axenfeld, Karl Theodor Paul Polykarpus): Medicine. See: Dorland; Jablonski; Stedman. Also known as: Axenfeld's conjunctivitis.

Morax-Axenfeld diplobacillus (Morax, Victor and Axenfeld, Karl Theodor Paul Polykarpus): Medicine. See: Dorland; Stedman.

MORAX, VICTOR. 1866-1935. French ophthalmologist. See: World Who's Who Sci. Morax-Axenfeld conjunctivitis, Morax-Axenfeld diplobacillus, Moraxella.

Moraxella (Morax, Victor): Zoology. See: Dorland; Stedman.

morbus attonitus Celsi (Celsus, Aulus Cornelius): Medicine. See: Hinsie. Also known as: Celsus's disease.

morbus Petzetakis (Petzetakis, M.). See: Debre's syndrome (1).

Mordell cycle (Mordell, Donald Louis): Engineering and Industry. See: Auger.

MORDELL, DONALD LOUIS. 1920-   . Canadian engineer. See: Canad. Who's Who, 1964-1966. Mordell cycle.

Mordkin Ballet (Mordkin, Mikhail): Dance. See: Chujoy.

MORDKIN, MIKHAIL. 1882-1944. Russian dancer, choreographer and teacher. See: Webster's Biog. Dict. Mordkin Ballet.

MORDVILKO, ALEKSANDR KONSTANTOVIC. 1867-1938. Russian entomologist. See: Ann. Entom. Soc. Amer., vol. 33 (1940), pp. 490-494. Mordwilkoja.

Mordwilkoja (Mordvilko, Aleksandr Konstantovic): Zoology. See: Webster's 3d.

MORE, CHARLES. fl. 1840. Maltese tavern owner. (Biography source unavailable.) Charley More.

MORE, ROBERT. 1703-1780. English naturalist. See: Dict. Nat. Biog. Morea (or Moraea).

Morea (or Moraea) (More, Robert): Botany. See: Charnock; Webster's 3d.

MOREAU, PIERRE. fl. ca. 1626-1649. French printer. See: Grand Larousse Encyc. Pierre Morean's ronde (script).

MOREHOUSE, LOUIE H. fl. 1939-1943. American engineer. Cited in: Chem. Abstr., vol. 37, p. 1284. Morehouse mill.

Morehouse mill (Morehouse, Louie H.): Engineering and Industry. See: Thrush.

MOREL, ALBERT. b. 1875. French physiological chemist. See: Pogg., vol. 6. Morel-Chavassieu test for purines.

MOREL, AUGUSTIN BENOIT. 1809-1873. French psychiatrist. See: World Who's Who Sci. Morel-Kraepelin disease, Morel's delerium, Morel's ear.

Morel-Chavassieu test for purines (Morel, Albert and Chavassieu, Henry L. J.): Chemistry. See: Van Nostrand Chem. Dict.

MOREL, FERDINAND. 1888-1957. Swiss psychiatrist and neurologist. See: Doc. p. Servir a l'histoire de l'Univ. de Geneve, vol. 12, 1959. Morel-Wildi syndrome, Morgagni-Stewart-Morel syndrome, Stewart-Morel syndrome.

Morel-Kraepelin disease (Morel, Augustin Benoit and Kraepelin, Emil): Medicine. See: Dorland; Stedman.

Morel-Wildi syndrome (Morel, Ferdinand and Wildi, Erwin): Medicine. See: Jablonski.

MORELLI, F. d. 1918. Italian physician. (Biography source unavailable.) Morelli's test (or reaction).

MORELLI, GIOVANNI (Pseud.: IVAN LERMOLIEV). 1816-1891. Italian art critic. See: Encyc. Brit., 1973. Morellian criticism.

Morellian criticism (Morelli, Giovanni): Fine Arts. See: Osborne.

Morelli's test (or reaction) (Morelli, F.): Medicine. See: Dorland; Stedman.

Morel's delerium (Morel, Augustin Benoit): Psychiatry. See: Kelly.

Morel's ear (Morel, Augustin Benoit): Anatomy. See: Dorland; Stedman.

MORENO. fl. ca. 1851. Spanish scientist. Cited in: Hintze, vol. 1, pt. 3, half 2, p. 4355. Morenosite.

Morenosite (Moreno): Earth Sciences. See: Thrush; Webster's 3d.

MORERA, GIACINTO. 1856-1909. Italian mathematician. See: Diz. Encic. Ital. Morera stress functions, Morera('s) theorem.

Morera stress functions (Morera, Giacinto): Mathematics. See: Internat. Dict. Ap. Math.

Morera('s) theorem (Morera, Giacinto): Mathematics. See: Internat. Dict. Ap. Math.; James.

MORESCHI, CARLO. 1876-1921. Italian pathologist. See: Biog. Lex. hervorr. Aerzte, 1880-1930. Gengou-Moreschi phenomenon.

Morestin's sphincteral accessory nerve (Derivation undetermined): Medicine. See: Stedman.

MORETTI, E. No dates. Italian physician. (Biography source unavailable.) Moretti's test.

MORETTI, JOSEPH L. 1783-1853. Italian chemist and botanist. See: Michaud. Morettia.

Morettia (Moretti, Joseph L.): Botany. See: Charnock.

Moretti's test (Moretti, E.): Medicine. See: Dorland.

MOREY, H. L. Fictitious recipient of forged letter in James A. Garfield's 1880 presidential campaign. Cited in: Dict. Amer. Hist. Morey letter.

Morey letter (Morey, H. L.): History. See: Jameson; Mathews, M. M.; Phyfe; Smith.

MORGAGNI, GIOVANNI BATTISTA. 1682-1771. Italian physician. See: Dict. Sci. Biog. frenulum of Morgagni, Morgagni-Laennec syndrome, Morgagni-Turner syndrome, Morgagni-Turner-Albright syndrome, Morgagnian cyst, Morgagni's appendix, Morgagni's cartilage, Morgagni's caruncle, Morgagni's cataract, Morgagni's column(s), Morgagni's concha, Morgagni's crypt (or sinuses), Morgagni's foramen, Morgagni's fossa, Morgagni's glands, Morgagni's globules (or spheres), Morgagni's hernia, Morgagni's lacuna(ae), Morgagni's liquor, Morgagni's nodule, Morgagni's pouch, Morgagni's prolapse, Morgagni's sinus, Morgagni's syndrome, Morgagni's tubercle, Morgagni's valve, sinus of Morgagni syndrome.

Morgagni-Laennec syndrome (Morgagni, Giovanni Battista and Laennec, Rene Theophile Hyacinthe). See: Laennec's cirrhosis.

Morgagni-Stewart-Morel syndrome (Morgagni, Giovanni Battista; Stewart, Douglas Hunt; and Morel, Ferdinand). See: Morgagni's syndrome.

Morgagni-Turner-Albright syndrome (Morgagni, Giovanni Battista; Turner, Henry Hubert; and Albright, Fuller). See: Turner's syndrome.

Morgagni-Turner syndrome (Morgagni, Giovanni Battista and Turner, Henry Hubert). See: Turner's syndrome.

Morgagnian cyst (Morgagni, Giovanni Battista): Anatomy. See: Stedman. Also known as: hydatid of Morgagni, Kobelt's cyst.

Morgagni's appendix (Morgagni, Giovanni Battista): Anatomy. See: Stedman. Also known as: Lalouette's pyramid(s).

Morgagni's cartilage (Morgagni, Giovanni Battista): Anatomy. See: Dorland; Stedman. Also known as: cartilage of Wrisberg.

Morgagni's caruncle (Morgagni, Giovanni Battista): Anatomy. See: Dorland; Stedman.

Morgagni's cataract (Morgagni, Giovanni Battista): Anatomy. See: Dorland; Stedman.

Morgagni's column(s) (Morgagni, Giovanni Battista): Anatomy. See: Donath; Dorland; Stedman. Also known as: columns of Morgagni.

Morgagni's concha (Morgagni, Giovanni Battista): Anatomy. See: Donath; Stedman.

Morgagni's crypt (or sinuses) (Morgagni, Giovanni Battista): Anatomy. See: Donath; Dorland; Stedman.

Morgagni's foramen (Morgagni, Giovanni Battista): Anatomy. See: Donath; Dorland; Stedman.

Morgagni's fossa (Morgagni, Giovanni Battista): Anatomy. See: Dorland; Stedman. Also known as: fossa of Morgagni.

Morgagni's glands (Morgagni, Giovanni Battista): Anatomy. See: Dorland; Stedman.

Morgagni's globules (or spheres) (Morgagni, Giovanni Battista): Anatomy. See: Stedman.

Morgagni's hernia (Morgagni, Giovanni Battista): Medicine. See: Dorland; Jablonski.

Morgagni's lacuna(ae) (Morgagni, Giovanni Battista): Anatomy. See: Donath; Stedman.

Morgagni's liquor (Morgagni, Giovanni Battista): Anatomy. See: Stedman.

Morgagni's nodule (Morgagni, Giovanni Battista): Anatomy. See: Stedman. Also known as: corpora Arantii.

Morgagni's pouch (Morgagni, Giovanni Battista): Anatomy. See: Donath.

Morgagni's prolapse (Morgagni, Giovanni Battista): Medicine. See: Stedman.

Morgagni's sinus (Morgagni, Giovanni Battista): Anatomy. See: Stedman.

Morgagni's syndrome (Morgagni, Giovanni Battista): Medicine. See: Jablonski; Stedman. Also known as: Morgagni-Stewart-Morel syndrome, Stewart-Morel syndrome.

Morgagni's tubercle (Morgagni, Giovanni Battista): Anatomy. See: Stedman. Also known as: tubercle of Morgagni, tubercle of Zuckerkandl.

Morgagni's valve (Morgagni, Giovanni Battista): Anatomy. See: Stedman.

MORGAN. fl. 1852-1855. French? pharmacist. Cited in: Royal Soc. Cat. Sci. Pap., 1800-1863. Morgan test reaction?

Morgan equation (Morgan, John Livingston Rutgers): Chemistry. See: Hackh; Internat. Dict. Phys. Elec.

Morgan (excitement) (Morgan, William): History. See: Mathews, M. M.; Partridge; Phyfe.

MORGAN, HARRY DE RIEMER. d. 1931. English physician. See: Lancet, vol. 1 (Jan. 31, 1931), p. 273. Morgan's bacillus.

Morgan (horse) (Morgan, Justin): Zoology. See: Hendrickson; Mathews, M.M.; Webster's 3d.

MORGAN, HUGH. fl. 16th c. English horticulturist. (Biography source unavailable.) Morgania.

MORGAN, JOHN HUNT. 1825-1864. American Confederate army officer. See: Dict. Amer. Biog. Morgan's Raiders.

MORGAN, JOHN LIVINGSTON RUTGERS. 1872-1935. American physical chemist. See: Who Was Who Amer., 1897-1942. Morgan equation.

MORGAN, JOHN PIERPONT. 1837-1913. American financier. See: Dict. Amer. Biog. Morganite.

MORGAN, JUSTIN. 1747-1798. American schoolteacher and horse breeder. See: Dict. Amer. Biog. Morgan (horse).

MORGAN LE FAY (MORGANA). Fairy enchantress and sister of King Arthur in Arthurian legend. See: New Encyc. Brit., 1974, Microp. fata Morgana.

MORGAN, LEWIS HENRY. 1818-1881. American ethnologist. See: Internat. Encyc. Soc. Sci. Morgan's stages of society.

MORGAN, LLOYD (In full: CONWAY LLOYD). 1852-1936. English zoologist and psychologist. See: Internat. Encyc. Soc. Sci. Morgan's canon (or principle).

Morgan-Marshall test (Derivation undetermined): Engineering and Industry. See: Thrush.

Morgan school (Morgan, Thomas Hunt): Genetics. Cited in: Encyc. Brit., 1973 under "Morgan, Thomas Hunt."

Morgan test reaction (Morgan): Chemistry. See: Van Nostrand Chem. Dict.

MORGAN, THOMAS HUNT. 1866-1945. American geneticist. See: World Who's Who Sci. Morgan school, Morgan (unit).

Morgan (unit) (Morgan, Thomas Hunt): Genetics. See: Dresner.

MORGAN, WILLIAM. ca. 1774-1826? American Freemason. See: Dict. Amer. Biog. Morgan (excitement), Morganize.

MORGAN, WILLIAM WILSON. 1906-   . American astrophysicist. See: Amer. Men and Women Sci., 12th ed. MKK-system.

Morgania (Morgan, Hugh): Botany. See: Charnock.

Morganite (Morgan, John Pierpont): Earth Sciences. See: Thrush; Webster's 3d. Also known as: Vorobyevite.

Morganize (Morgan, William): Generic Word (kill secretly). See: Mathews, M. M.; Webster's 3d.

Morgan's bacillus (Morgan, Harry de Riemer): Medicine. See: Dorland; Stedman.

Morgan's canon (or principle) (Morgan, Lloyd): Zoology. See: English; Gray; Pennak.

Morgan's Raiders (Morgan, John Hunt): History. See: Blumberg.

Morgan's stages of society (Morgan, Lewis Henry): Sociology. See: Zadrozny.

MORI, SHUN. fl. 1934. Japanese chemist. Cited in: Chem. Abstr., vol. 29, p. 1358. Ishibashi-Mori test.

MORIN, A. fl. before 1921. Engineer. (Biography source unavailable.) Morin hardness test.

MORIN, ARTHUR JULES. 1795-1880. French physicist. See: World Who's Who Sci. Boyelle-Morin apparatus?

Morin hardness test (Morin, A.): Engineering and Industry. See: Auger.

MORIN, LOUIS. ca. 1636-1715. French physician and botanist. See: Michaud. Morina.

Morina (Morin, Louis): Botany. See: Taylor, N.

MORINEAU. fl. 19th c. French mine director. Cited in: Hintze, vol. 1, part 4, half 1, p. 628. Morinite.

Morinite (Morineau): Earth Sciences. See: Thrush; Webster's 3d.

Morisette reamer (or expansion reamer) (Derivation undetermined): Engineering and Industry. See: Thrush.

MORISON, JAMES. 1770-1840. English quack. See: Dict. Nat. Biog. Morison's pill.

MORISON, JAMES. 1816-1893. Scottish minister and theologian. See: Dict. Nat. Biog. Morisonians.

MORISON, JAMES RUTHERFORD. 1853-1939. English surgeon. See: Who Was Who, 1929-1940. Drummond-Morison operation, Morison's method (or paste), Morison's pouch, Morison's space.

Morisonians (Morison, James): Religion. See: Canney.

Morison's method (or paste) (Morison, James Rutherford): Medicine. See: Dorland; Kelly.

Morison's pill (Morison, James): Generic Word (panacea for social ills). See: Partridge; Weekley.

Morison's pouch (Morison, James Rutherford): Medicine. See: Dorland; Stedman.

Morison's space (Morison, James Rutherford): Medicine. See: Kelly.

MORITZ, FRIEDRICH HEINRICH LUDWIG. 1861-1938. German physician. See: Biog. Lex. hervorr. Aerzte. Moritz reaction (or test).

Moritz reaction (or test) (Moritz, Friedrich Heinrich Ludwig): Medicine. See: Dorland. Also known as: Rivalta's reaction.

Morkill's formula (Derivation undetermined): Engineering and Industry. See: Thrush.

MORLEY, EDWARD WILLIAMS. 1838-1923. American chemist and physicist. See: World Who's Who Sci. Michelson-Morley experiment.

MORLEY, JOHN (VISCOUNT MORLEY). 1838-1923. English statesman and writer. See: Dict. Nat. Biog., 4th suppl. Morley-Minto reforms.

Morley-Minto reforms (Morley, John and Elliot, Gilbert John Murray Kynmond): History. See: Steinberg.

Mormon cricket (Moroni): Zoology. See: Pennak; Van Nostrand Sci. Encyc.

Mormons (or Mormonism) (Moroni): Religion. See: Latham; Mathews, M. M.; Mathews, S.; New Encyc. Brit., 1974, Microp.

MORNA. Legendary eponymous ancestor of Morna clan. See: Jobes. Morna.

Morna (Morna, the heroine): Botany. See: Charnock.

MORNAY, PHILIPPE DE, SEIGNEUR DU PLESSIS-MARLY. 1549-1623. French Huguenot leader. See: Encyc. Brit., 1973. sauce Mornay.

MORO, ERNST. 1874-1951. Austrian pediatrician. See: World Who's Who Sci. Moro reflex.

Moro reflex (Moro, Ernst): Physiology. See: Chaplin; Good; Hinsie.

MORON. Fictional character from Moliere's play, "La Princesse d'Elide," (1664). (Biography source unavailable.) Moron.

Moron (Moron, the fictional character): Generic Word (fool). See: Hendrickson.

MORONI. Angel or prophet who revealed religious message to Joseph Smith. See: New Encyc. Brit., 1974, Microp. Book of Mormon, Mormon cricket, Mormons (or Mormonism).

MORPHEUS. In Greek mythology, one of the sons of Somneus, the god of sleep. See: New Encyc. Brit., 1974, Microp. Morpheus, Morphine (Morphia or Morphina).

Morpheus (Morpheus, god of sleep): Generic Word (sleep-inducer). See: Webster's 3d.

Morphine (Morphia or Morphina) (Morpheus, god of sleep): Botany. See: Charnock; Partridge; Webster's 3d.

MORQUIO, LOUIS (LUIS). 1867-1935. Uruguayan physician. See: World Who's Who Sci. Morquio-Silfverskioeld syndrome, Morquio's disease (or syndrome).

Morquio–Silfverskioeld syndrome (Morquio, Louis and Silfverskioeld, Nils). See: Silfverskioeld's syndrome.

Morquio–Ullrich syndrome (Morquio, Louis and Ullrich, Otto). See: Morquio's disease (or syndrome).

Morquio's disease (or syndrome) (mucopolysaccharidosis) (Morquio, Louis): Medicine. See: Dorland; Jablonski; Stedman. Also known as: Brailsford–Morquio syndrome, Morquio–Ullrich syndrome.

Morquio's disease (heart block) (Derivation undetermined): Medicine. See: Jablonski.

MORREN, CHARLES FRANCOIS ANTOINE. 1807–1858. Belgian naturalist. See: Pogg., vol. 2. Morren's gland(s).

Morren's gland(s) Morren, Charles Francois Antoine): Zoology. See: Gray; Henderson.

Morres solution (Morres, Wilhelm): Chemistry. See: Van Nostrand Chem. Dict.

MORRES, WILHELM. fl. 1912. German chemist. Cited in: Chem. Abstr., vol. 6, p. 895. Morres solution.

Morrill Act(s) (Morrill, Justin Smith): Politics. See: Good; Morris; Winburne.

MORRILL, JUSTIN SMITH. 1810–1898. American legislator. See: Dict. Amer. Biog. Morrill Act(s), Morrill Tariff.

Morrill Tariff (Morrill, Justin Smith): Politics. See: Jameson; Morris.

MORRIS, ARTHUR JOSEPH. b. 1881. American financier. See: Nat. Cycl. Amer. Biog., vol. E, p. 160. Morris plan banks (or company).

Morris chair (or armchair) (Morris, William): Applied Arts. See: Hendrickson; Partridge; Webster's 3d.

Morris (furniture style) (Morris, William): Applied Arts. See: Webster's 3d.

MORRIS, HAROLD PAUL. 1900– . American biochemist. See: Amer. Men and Women Sci., 12th ed. Morris hepatoma.

Morris hepatoma (Morris, Harold Paul): Medicine. See: Jablonski.

MORRIS, JOHN MC LEAN. 1914– . American surgeon. See: Amer. Men and Women Sci., 12th ed. Goldberg–Maxwell–Morris syndrome.

MORRIS, JOSEPH. fl. 1860. Welsh-born American convert to Mormonism. (Biography source unavailable.) Morrisite.

Morris (motor car) (Nuffield, William Richard Morris, 1st Viscount): Engineering and Industry. See: Partridge.

Morris' note (Morris, Robert): History. See: Mathews, M. M.

Morris plan banks (or company) (Morris, Arthur Joseph): Economics. See: Mack; Clark.

MORRIS, RICHARD. 1845–1891. English inventor. See: Boase. Morris tube (or aiming tube).

MORRIS, ROBERT. 1734–1806. American financier and statesman. See: Dict. Amer. Biog. Morris' note.

MORRIS, ROBERT TUTTLE. 1857–1945. American surgeon. See: Who Was Who Amer., 1943–1950. Morris's appendix, Morris's point.

Morris syndrome (Morris, John McLean). See: Goldberg–Maxwell–Morris syndrome.

Morris tube (or aiming tube) (Morris, Richard): Weapons. See: Partridge.

MORRIS, WILLIAM. 1834–1896. English artist, poet, and pamphleteer. See: Dict. Nat. Biog., 1st suppl. Morris chair (or armchair), Morris (furniture style).

MORRIS, WILLIAM. No dates. English explorer. (Biography source unavailable.) anglesea Morris.

Morris, William Richard. See: Nuffield, Richard William Morris, 1st Viscount.

Morrisite (Morris, Joseph): Religion. See: Mathews, M. M.; Webster's 3d.

MORRISON, ASHTON BYROM. 1922– . American pathologist. See: Amer. Men and Women Sci., 12th ed. Verner–Morrison syndrome.

Morrison crown (Morrison, William Newton): Dentistry. See: Dorland.

MORRISON, FRANK BARRON. 1887–1958. American animal husbandry scientist. See: Who Was Who Amer., 1951–1960. Morrison standard.

MORRISON, HENRY CLINTON. 1871–1945. American educator. See: Who Was Who Amer., 1943–1950. Morrison plan.

MORRISON OF LAMBETH, BARON HERBERT STANLEY MORRISON. 1888–1965. English statesman. See: Who Was Who, 1961–1970. Morrison (shelter or mousetrap).

Morrison plan (Morrison, Henry Clinton): Education. See: Good.

MORRISON, RICHARD JAMES (Pseud.: ZADKIEL). 1795–1874. English inventor and astrologist. See: Dict. Nat. Biog. Zadkiel.

Morrison (shelter or mousetrap) (Morrison of Lambeth, Baron Herbert Stanley Morrison): Generic Word (bomb shelter). See: Partridge.

Morrison standard (Morrison, Frank Barron): Agriculture. See: Winburne.

MORRISON, WILLIAM NEWTON. 1842–1896. American dentist. Cited in: Index Medicus, vol. 4 (1882), p. 429. Morrison crown.

Morris's appendix (Morris, Robert Tuttle): Medicine. See: Dorland.

Morris's point (Morris, Robert Tuttle): Medicine. See: Dorland.

Morrone, Pietro de. See: Celestine V, Saint.

Morrow–Brooke syndrome (Morrow, Prince Albert and Brooke, Henry Ambrose Grundy): Medicine. See: Jablonski.

Morrow honeysuckle (Morrow, James?): Botany. See: Winburne.

MORROW, J. fl. 1904. English? engineer. (Biography source unavailable.) Morrow's extensometer.

MORROW, JAMES. 1820–1865. American? scientist. Cited in: Mansell. Morrow honeysuckle?

MORROW, PRINCE ALBERT. 1846–1913. American dermatologist. See: World Who's Who Sci. Morrow–Brooke syndrome.

Morrow's extensometer (Morrow, J.): Engineering and Industry. See: Auger.

Morse and Bowie gauge (Morse, Richard Stetson and Bowie, Robert McNeil): Physics. See: Internat. Dict. Phys. Elec.

Morse buret (Morse, Harmon Northrop?): Chemistry. See: Hackh.

Morse chain (Morse, Frank Lincoln): Engineering and Industry. See: Auger.

Morse code (or alphabet) (Morse, Samuel Finley Breese): Telegraphy. See: Hendrickson; Mathews, M. M.; Markus; Webster's 3d.

Morse curve (Morse, Philip McCord): Physics. See: Internat. Dict. Ap. Math.; Thewlis.

Morse equation (or rule) (Morse, Philip McCord): Physics. See: Ballentyne; Internat. Dict. Phys. Elec.; Thewlis.

Morse finger (Morse, Samuel Finley Breese): Medicine. See: Stedman.

MORSE, FRANK LINCOLN. 1864–1935. American manufacturer. See: Who Was Who Amer., 1897–1942. Morse chain.

Morse function (Morse, Marston): Mathematics. See: Internat. Dict. Ap. Math.

MORSE, HARMON NORTHROP. 1848–1920. American chemist. See: World Who's Who Sci. Morse buret?

MORSE, L. G. E. fl. early 20th c. English? engineer. (Biography source unavailable.) Morse test.

MORSE, MARSTON (In full: HAROLD CALVIN MARSTON). b. 1892. American mathematician. See: World Who's Who Sci. Morse function.

MORSE, PHILIP MC CORD. 1903– . American physicist. See: World Who's Who Sci. Morse curve, Morse equation (or rule).

MORSE, RICHARD STETSON. 1911– . American physicist. See: Amer. Men Sci., 8th ed. Morse and Bowie gauge.

MORSE, SAMUEL FINLEY BREESE. 1791–1872. American artist and inventor. See: World Who's Who Sci. Morse code (or alphabet), Morse finger, Morse thump?

MORSE, SIDNEY EDWARDS. 1835-1871. American journalist and inventor. See: Who Was Who Amer., 1607-1896. Morse's folly.

MORSE, STEPHEN A. fl. ca. 1864. American inventor. Cited in: Nat. Cycl. Amer. Biog., vol. 29, p. 303, col. 1. Morse taper.

Morse taper (Morse, Stephen A.): Engineering and Industry. See: Van Nostrand Sci. Encyc.

Morse test (Morse, L. G. E.): Engineering and Industry. See: Auger.

Morse thump (Morse, Samuel Finley Breese?): Electronics. See: Van Nostrand Sci. Encyc.

Morse's folly (Morse, Sidney Edwards): Architecture. See: Nat. Cycl. Amer. Biog., vol. 13, p. 354.

MORSIER, GEORGES DE. b. 1894. Swiss neurologist. See: Who's Who Switz., 1970-1971. De Morsier's syndrome (1), De Morsier's syndrome (2).

MORT, PAUL R. 1894-1962. American educator. See: Who Was Who Amer., 1961-1968. Mort plan.

Mort plan (Mort, Paul R.): Education. See: Good.

Mortara formula (Mortara, Giorgio): Statistics. See: Kendall.

MORTARA, GIORGIO. b. 1885. Italian statistician. See: World Who's Who Sci. Mortara formula.

MORTENSEN, OLE. fl. 1948. Danish physician. (Biography source unavailable.) Mortensen's disease.

Mortensen's disease (Mortensen, Ole): Medicine. See: Jablonski. Also known as: Di Guglielmo's disease, Revol's disease.

MORTH, HERMINE. fl. 1932. German? chemist. Cited in: Chem. Abstr., vol. 26, p. 3749. Pavelka-Morth reaction for thallium.

MORTIMER. fl. ca. 1887. English patient of Sir Jonathan Hutchinson. (Biography source unavailable.) Mortimer's disease (or malady).

Mortimer's disease (or malady) (Mortimer): Medicine. See: Jablonski; Stedman.

MORTON, ALEXANDER. fl. 1871-1896. Scottish engineer. Cited in: Royal Soc. Cat. Sci. Pap., 1874-1883. Morton condenser.

Morton condenser (Morton, Alexander): Engineering and Industry. See: Auger.

Morton('s) current (Morton, William James): Medicine. See: Dorland; Stedman.

MORTON, D. fl. 1882. Engineer. (Biography source unavailable.) Morton valve gear.

MORTON, DUDLEY J. 1884-1960. American orthopedic surgeon. See: Nat. Cycl. Amer. Biog., vol. F, p. 460. Morton's syndrome.

MORTON, JOHN. ca. 1420-1500. English archbishop and statesman. See: Dict. Nat. Biog. Morton's fork (crotch or crutch).

Morton('s) neuralgia (disease, foot, metatarsalgia, syndrome or toe) (Morton, Thomas George): Medicine. See: Black; Dorland; Jablonski; Stedman; Webster's 3d.

MORTON, RICHARD. 1637-1698. English physician. See: Dict. Nat. Biog. Morton's cough.

MORTON, SAMUEL GEORGE. 1799-1851. American physician and anthropologist. See: World Who's Who Sci. Morton's plane?

MORTON, THOMAS GEORGE. 1835-1903. American surgeon. See: World Who's Who Sci. Morton('s) neuralgia (disease, foot, metatarsalgia, syndrome or toe).

Morton valve gear (Morton, D.): Engineering and Industry. See: Auger.

MORTON, WILLIAM JAMES. 1845-1920. American neurologist. See: World Who's Who Sci. Morton('s) current.

Morton's cough (Morton, Richard): Medicine. See: Dorland.

Morton's fork (crotch or crutch) (Morton, John): History. See: Blumberg; Brewer; Harbottle.

Morton's plane (Morton, Samuel George?): Anatomy. See: Stedman.

Morton's syndrome (Morton, Dudley J.): Medicine. See: Jablonski; Stedman.

MORVAN, AUGUSTIN MARIE. 1819-1897. French physician. See: Biog. Lex. hervorr. Aerzte. Morvan's chorea, Morvan's disease.

Morvan's chorea (Morvan, Augustin Marie): Medicine. See: Dorland; Jablonski; Stedman.

Morvan's disease (Morvan, Augustin Marie): Medicine. See: Dorland; Jablonski; Stedman.

Mosaic law (or code) (Moses, the prophet): Religion. See: Attwater; Hendrickson.

MOSANDER, CARL GUSTAF. 1797-1858. Swedish chemist and mineralogist. See: Dict. Sci. Biog. Mosandrite.

Mosandrite (Mosander, Carl Gustaf): Earth Sciences. See: Thrush; Webster's 3d.

MOSCHCOWITZ, ALEXIS VICTOR. 1865-1933. American surgeon. See: Who Was Who Amer., 1897-1942. Moschcowitz' operation.

MOSCHCOWITZ, ELI. 1879-1964. American physician. See: Amer. Men Sci., 5th ed. Moschcowitz's syndrome, Moschcowitz's test.

Moschcowitz' operation (Moschcowitz, Alexis Victor): Medicine. See: Dorland; Stedman.

Moschcowitz-Singer-Symmers syndrome (Moschcowitz, Eli; Singer, Harold Douglas?; and Symmers, Douglas). See: Moschcowitz's syndrome.

Moschcowitz's syndrome (Moschcowitz, Eli): Medicine. See: Jablonski. Also known as: Baehr-Schiffrin disease, Moschcowitz-Singer-Symmers syndrome.

Moschcowitz's test (Moschcowitz, Eli): Medicine. See: Dorland.

Moscrop engine recorder (Moscrop, J. B.): Engineering and Industry. See: Auger.

MOSCROP, J. B. fl. 1884. English? engineer. (Biography source unavailable.) Moscrop engine recorder.

Moseley diagram (or plots) for x-ray levels (Moseley, Henry Gwyn Jeffreys): Physics. See: Internat. Dict. Ap. Math.; Internat. Dict. Phys. Elec.; Thewlis.

Moseley formula (for the energy of K x-rays) (Moseley, Henry Gwyn Jeffreys): Physics. See: Hackh; Van Nostrand Chem. Dict.

MOSELEY, HENRY GWYN JEFFREYS. 1877-1915. English physicist. See: Dict. Sci. Biog. Moseley diagram (or plots) for x-ray levels, Moseley formula (for the energy of K x-rays), Moseley number, Moseley('s) law, Moseley series, Moseley spectrum.

Moseley('s) law (Moseley, Henry Gwyn Jeffreys): Ballentyne; Internat. Dict. Ap. Math.; Internat. Dict. Phys. Elec.; Thewlis; Van Nostrand Sci. Encyc.

Moseley number (Moseley, Henry Gwyn Jeffreys): Physics. See: Hackh; Internat. Dict. Phys. Elec.

Moseley series (Moseley, Henry Gwyn Jeffreys): Physics. See: Hackh.

Moseley spectrum (Moseley, Henry Gwyn Jeffreys): Physics. See: Hackh.

MOSELY, ALFRED. 1855-1917. English educator. See: Who Was Who, 1916-1928. Mosely commission of inquiry (or industrial commission).

Mosely commission of inquiry (or industrial commission) (Mosely, Alfred): Education. See: Good; Montgomery.

MOSER, PAUL. 1865-1924. German pediatrician. See: Biog. Lex. hervorr. Aerzte, 1880-1930. Moser's serum.

Moser's serum (Moser, Paul): Medicine. See: Dorland.

MOSES (MOSHE). fl. 13th c. B.C. Hebrew prophet. See: New Encyc. Brit., 1974. Mosaic law (or code), Moses' cradle (bassinet), Moses (boat)?, Moses' rod.

MOSES. fl. ca. 1910. American mine supervisor. Cited in: Hintze, vol. 1, pt. 2, p. 2619. Mosesite.

Moses (boat) (Moses, the prophet? or Lowell, Moses?): Engineering and Industry. See: Brewer; Hendrickson; Partridge.

Moses' cradle (bassinet) (Moses, the prophet): Applied Arts. See: Hendrickson.

MOSES, LINCOLN ELLSWORTH. 1921- . American statistician. See: World Who's Who Sci. Moses test.

Moses' rod (Moses, the prophet): Religion. See: Brewer; Hendrickson.

...oses test (Moses, Lincoln Ellsworth): Statistics. See: Kendall.

...osesite (Moses): Earth Sciences. See: Thrush.

...OSETIG-MOORHOF, ALBERT VON. 1838-1907. Austrian surgeon. See: ...og. Lex. hervorr. Aerzte. Mosetig-Moorhof's method.

...osetig-Moorhof's method (Mosetig-Moorhof, Albert von): Medicine. See: ...orland; Stedman.

...osher drain (Mosher, Harris Peyton): Medicine. See: Stedman.

...OSHER, HARRIS PEYTON. 1867-1954. American surgeon. See: Who Was ...ho Amer., 1951-1960. Mosher drain.

...OSLER, KARL FRIEDRICH. 1831-1911. German physician. See: Biog. ...ex. hervorr. Aerzte. Mosler's diabetes.

...osler's diabetes (Mosler, Karl Friedrich): Medicine. See: Dorland; ...edman.

...OSNIER, A. fl. 1895-1897. French chemist. Cited in: Royal Soc. Cat. ...ci. Pap., 1884-1900. Mosnier reagent.

...osnier reagent (Mosnier, A.): Chemistry. See: Van Nostrand Chem. Dict.

...osny-Beaufume lipomatosis (Derivation undetermined): Medicine. See: ...ablonski.

...oss combustion chamber (Moss, Sanford Alexander): Engineering and Industry. ...ee: Auger.

...OSS, FRANK KENDALL. 1898- . American physicist. See: Amer. ...en. Sci., 5th ed. Luckiesh-Moss visibility meter.

...OSS, GERALD. 1931- . American surgeon and biomedical engineer. ...ee: Amer. Men and Women Sci., 12th ed. Moss tube(s).

...OSS, MELVIN LIONEL. 1923- . American anatomist. See: Amer. Men ...nd Women Sci., 12th ed. Gorlin-Chaudhry-Moss syndrome.

...OSS, SANFORD ALEXANDER. b. 1872. American engineer. See: Nat. ...ycl. Amer. Biog., vol. F, p. 348. Moss combustion chamber.

...oss tube(s) (Moss, Gerald): Medicine. See: Stedman.

...OSS, WILLIAM LORENZO. 1876-1957. American physician. See: Dict. ...ci. Biog. Moss's grouping or (classification).

...ossbauer effect (Moessbauer, Rudolf Ludwig): Physics. See: Ballentyne; ...ughes; Markus.

...OSSE, ALPHONSE. fl. 1879. French physician. See: Arnim. Mosse-...Marchand-Mallory cirrhosis.

...osse-Marchand-Mallory cirrhosis (Mosse, Alphonse; Marchand, Felix Jacob; ...nd Mallory, Frank Burr): Medicine. See: Jablonski.

...OSSE, MAX. b. 1873. German physician. See: Biog. Lex. hervorr. ...erzte, 1880-1936. Mosse's syndrome (or polycythemia).

...osse's syndrome (or polycythemia) (Mosse, Max): Medicine. See: Jablonski.

...OSSO, ANGELO. 1846-1910. Italian physiologist. See: Dict. Sci. Biog. ...osso's balance, Mosso's ergograph, Mosso's sphygmomanometer.

...osso's balance (Mosso, Angelo): Physiology. See: Drever.

...osso's ergograph (Mosso, Angelo): Physiology. See: Dorland; Stedman.

...osso's sphygmomanometer (Mosso, Angelo): Physiology. See: Dorland; ...tedman.

...OSSOTTI, OTTAVIANO FABRIZIO. 1791-1863. Italian astronomer and ...hysicist. See: Pogg., vol. 2. Clausius-Mosotti equation, Masotti field.

...oss's grouping or (classification) (Moss, William Lorenzo): Medicine. See: ...orland.

...OST, AUGUST. b. 1867. German physician. See: Biog. Lex. hervorr. ...erzte. Most's bath.

...OSTO, SANTIAGO J. fl. 1955. Argentinian dermatologist. (Biography ...ource unavailable.) Casala-Mosto disease.

...OSTOWSKI, ANDRZEJ. fl. 1967-1968. Polish logician. See: Turkevich ...nd Turkevich. Kleene-Mostowski hierarchy.

...ost's bath (Most, August): Medicine. See: Dorland.

MOSZKOWICZ, LUDWIG. 1873-1945. Austrian surgeon. See: Biog. Lex. hervorr. Aerzte, 1880-1930. Moszkowicz test.

Moszkowicz test (Moszkowicz, Ludwig): Medicine. See: Dorland; Stedman.

MOTAIS, ERNST. 1845-1913. French ophthalmologist. See: Biog. Lex. hervorr. Aerzte, 1880-1930. Motais' operation.

Motais' operation (Motais, Ernst): Medicine. See: Dorland; Stedman.

Mother Carey's chicken(s) (Mary, Virgin-Mother?): Generic Word (stormy petrel). See: Blumberg; Gray; Partridge; Pennak; Phyfe; Weekley.

Mother Carey's goose (Mary, Virgin-Mother?): Zoology. See: Gray.

MOTHER HUBBARD. Character in Sarah C. Martin's nursery rhyme (1805). See: Jobes. Mother Hubbard bit?, Mother Hubbard costume, Mother Hubbard (dress).

Mother Hubbard bit (Mother Hubbard?): Engineering and Industry. See: Thrush.

Mother Hubbard costume (Mother Hubbard): Fashion. See: Picken.

Mother Hubbard (dress) (Mother Hubbard): Fashion. See: Partridge; Picken; Webster's 3d.

Mother Shipton (1) (Shipton, Ursula): Generic Word. See: Hendrickson.

Mother Shipton (2) (Shipton, Ursula): Zoology. See: Gray.

MOTT, SIR FREDERICK WALKER. 1853-1926. English neurologist. See: World Who's Who Sci. Mott's law.

MOTT, SIR NEVILL FRANCIS. 1905- . English nuclear physicist. See: Pogg., vol. 6. Gurney-Mott theory, Mott scattering formula, Mott-Wannier exciton.

Mott scattering formula (Mott, Sir Nevill Francis): Physics. See: Internat. Dict. Phys. Elec.; Thewlis.

Mott-Smith gravimeter (Derivation undetermined): Physics. See: Thrush.

Mott-Wannier exciton (Mott, Sir Nevill Francis and Wannier, Gregory Hugh): Physics. See: Van Nostrand Sci. Encyc. under "Exciton."

MOTTELSON, BEN R. fl. 1955. Danish physicist. See: Who's Who Sci. Europe, 1967. Bohr-Modelson theory.

Mott's law (Mott, Sir Frederick Walker): Medicine. See: Dorland.

motu proprio of Pius X (Pius X): Religion. See: Attwater.

Motzu. See: Mo-tzu.

Mouchard (Mouchy, Antoine de): Generic Word (spy). See: Charnock.

MOUCHET, ALBERT. b. 1869. French surgeon. See: Arnim. Koehler-Mouchet disease, Mouchet's syndrome.

Mouchet's syndrome (Mouchet, Albert): Medicine. See: Jablonski. Also known as: Albert Mouchet's syndrome.

MOUCHY, ANTOINE DE. 1494-1574. French theologian. See: Nouv. Biog. Univ. Mouchard.

MOULE, JOHN. fl. 1857. English? photographer. (Biography source unavailable.) Moule's photogen.

Moule's photogen (Moule, John): Photography. See: Focal Encyc. Photog. under "Artificial Light History."

Moulin test reaction for mercury (Derivation undetermined): Chemistry. See: Van Nostrand Chem. Dict.

MOULTON, ALEXANDER ERIC. 1920- . English engineer and manufacturer. See: Who's Who, 1975. Moulton spring.

Moulton spring (Moulton, Alexander Eric): Engineering and Industry. See: Auger.

MOUNIER-KUHN, PIERRE. fl. 1932-1972. French otorhinolaryngologist. See: Who's Who Sci. Europe, 1972. Mounier-Kuhn's syndrome.

Mounier-Kuhn's syndrome (Mounier-Kuhn, Pierre): Medicine. See: Jablonski.

MOUNT, LESTER ADRAN. 1910- . American neurosurgeon. See: Amer. Men and Women Sci., 12th ed. Mount's syndrome.

Mount of Apollo (Apollo): Palmistry. See: Webster's 3d.

Mount of Jupiter (Jupiter): Parapsychology. See: Webster's 3d.

Mount of Mercury (Mercury): Parapsychology. See: Webster's 3d.

Mount of Saturn (Saturn): Parapsychology. See: Webster's 3d.

Mount of Venus (Venus): Parapsychology. See: Webster's 3d.

Mount-Temple, Baron. See: Cowper, William Francis (Baron Mount-Temple).

Mountbatten, Philip. See: Edinburgh, Duke of.

Mount's syndrome (Mount, Lester Adran): Medicine. See: Jablonski.

MOUTIER, JULES. b. 1829. French physicist. See: Diz. Encic. Ital. Moutier law.

Moutier law (Moutier, Jules): Physics. See: Internat. Dict. Ap. Math.

MOUTON, HENRI. fl. 1897-1913. French physicist. Cited in: Chem. Abstr., Decenn. Index, 1907-1916. Cotton-Mouton effect.

MOUTOT, HENRY. b. 1880. French dermatologist. (Biography source unavailable.) Nicolas-Moutot-Charlet syndrome.

Mowatt Committee (Mowatt, Sir Francis): History. See: Montgomery.

MOWATT, SIR FRANCIS. 1837-1919. English civil servant. See: Dict. Nat. Biog., 3d suppl. Mowatt Committee.

Mowlawa, Jelal-ed-Din. See: Jalal-Ud-Din Rumi.

Mowlawiyeh (Mevlevi, Mevelavites, Maulavi or Maulawiyyah) (whirling dervishes) (Jalal-Ud-Din Rumi): Religion. See: Canney; Hastings (Dict. Rel. Ethics); Winick.

Moyes rose (Derivation undetermined): Botany. See: Winburne.

Moyne commission (Moyne, Walter Edward Guiness, 1st Baron): History. See: Morris and Irwin.

MOYNE, WALTER EDWARD GUINESS, 1ST BARON. 1880-1944. English statesman. See: Who Was Who, 1941-1950. Moyne commission.

Mozee, Phoebe Ann Oakley. See: Oakley, Annie.

MUCH, HANS CHRISTIAN R. 1880-1932. German physician. See: World Who's Who Sci. Much-Holzmann reaction, Much-Weiss stain, Much's bacillus.

Much-Holzmann reaction (Much, Hans Christian R. and Holzmann, Walter): Medicine. See: Dorland; Stedman. Also known as: Much's reaction.

Much-Weiss stain (Much, Hans Christian R. and Weiss, Leonhard): Medicine. See: Stedman. Also known as: Weiss stain.

Mucha-Habermann syndrome (Mucha, Viktor and Habermann, Rudolf): Medicine. See: Jablonski. Also known as: Mucha's disease, Wise's disease.

MUCHA, VIKTOR. 1877-1919. Austrian dermatologist. See: Biog. Lex. hervorr. Aerzte. Mucha-Habermann syndrome.

Mucha's disease (Mucha, Viktor). See: Mucha-Habermann syndrome.

Much's bacillus (Much, Hans Christian R.): Medicine. See: Dorland; Stedman.

Much's reaction (Much, Hans Christian R.). See: Much-Holzmann reaction.

MUCK, H. fl. ca. 1878. German mineralogist. Cited in: Hintze, vol. 1, pt. 4, half 2, p. 1411. Muckite.

MUCK, OTTO. 1871-1942. German physician. See: Biog. Lex. hervorr. Aerzte. Muck's test (or reaction).

Muckite (Muck, H.): Earth Sciences. See: Webster's 3d.

MUCKLE, THOMAS JAMES. fl. 1954-1972. Canadian pediatrician. See: Med. Direct., 1972. Muckle-Wells syndrome.

Muckle-Wells syndrome (Muckle, Thomas James and Wells, Michael Vernon): Medicine. See: Stedman.

Muck's test (or reaction) (Muck, Otto): Medicine. See: Dorland.

Mudge Citation (Mudge, Isadore Gilbert): Library Science. See: Harrod.

MUDGE, ISADORE GILBERT. 1875-1957. American librarian. See: Who Was Who Amer., 1951-1960. Mudge Citation.

MUEHLENBECK, H. GUSTAVE. d. 1845. Alsatian physician. Cited in: Mansell. Muehlenbeckia.

Muehlenbeckia (Muehlenbeck, H. Gustave): Botany. See: Taylor, N.; Webster's 3d.

MUELLER-BRESLAU, HEINRICH FRANZ BERNHARD. 1851-1925. German structural engineer. See: Dict. Sci. Biog. Mueller-Breslau principle.

Mueller-Breslau principle (Mueller-Breslau, Heinrich Franz Bernhard): Mathematics. See: Internat. Dict. Ap. Math.

Mueller bridge (Derivation undetermined): Physics. See: Internat. Dict. Phys. Elec.

MUELLER, CARL ARNOLDUS. b. 1886. Norwegian internist. Cited in: Index-Cat. Libr. Sur.-Gen. Off., 5th Ser., vol. 1, 1959. Harbitz-Mueller disease.

MUELLER, EDUARD. 1876-1928. German physician. See: Biog. Lex. hervorr. Aerzte, 1880-1930. Donne-Mueller test, Mueller-Jochmann test(s), Mueller's sign, Mueller's test.

Mueller electronic tonometer (Derivation undetermined): Medicine. See: Stedman.

MUELLER, ERNST. 1881-1945. German chemist. See: Pogg., vols. 6, 7a. Sonn-Mueller method.

Mueller('s) fluid (Mueller, Hermann F.): Chemistry. See: Dorland; Stedman; Van Nostrand Chem. Dict.

MUELLER, FRANZ (BARON DE REICHENSTEIN). 1740-1825. Hungarian mineralogist and chemist. See: Dict. Sci. Biog. Muller's glass.

MUELLER, FRIEDRICH VON. 1858-1941. German physician. See: Biog. Lex. hervorr. Aerzte, 1880-1930. Mueller's sign, Mueller's steatoma.

MUELLER, FRITZ (In full: JOHANN FRIEDRICH THEODOR). 1882-1897. German zoologist. See: Dict. Sci. Biog. Muellerian (Mullerian) mimicry, Muellerius, Mueller's body, Mueller's law, Mullerian association.

MUELLER, GEORG ELIAS. 1850-1934. German psychophysicist. See: Internat. Encyc. Soc. Sci. Mueller-Schumann law (or paradigm of associative inhibition), Mueller-Urban method, Mueller-Urban weights (or weighting).

MUELLER, HEINRICH. 1820-1864. German anatomist. See: World Who's Who Sci. Mueller's fibres, Mueller's muscle, Mueller's trigone.

MUELLER, HERMANN F. 1866-1898. German histologist. See: Biog. Lex. hervorr. Aerzte, 1880-1930. Mueller('s) fluid.

Mueller-Jochmann test(s) (Mueller, Eduard and Jochmann, Georg): Medicine. See: Dorland; Kelly. Also known as: Jochmann's test.

MUELLER, JOHANNES PETER. 1801-1858. German anatomist, physiologist, and pathologist. See: Internat. Encyc. Soc. Sci. Mueller('s) law (of specific nerve energies), Muellerian eminence, Mueller's capsule, Mueller's duct, Mueller's experiment, Mueller's ganglion, Mueller's larva, Vieth-Mueller circle, Vieth-Mueller torus.

Mueller-Kuehne process (Mueller and Kuehne, Hans): Chemistry. See: Van Nostrand Chem. Dict.

Mueller('s) law (of specific nerve energies) (Mueller, Johannes Peter): Physiology. See: Stedman; Van Nostrand Sci. Encyc.

MUELLER-LYER, FRANZ KARL. 1857-1916. German psychiatrist and sociologist. See: Encyc. Soc. Sci. Mueller-Lyer illusion.

Mueller-Lyer illusion (Mueller-Lyer, Franz Karl): Psychology. See: Chaplin; Drever; English; Wolman.

Mueller-Oppenheim diagnosis (or reaction) (Mueller, Rudolf and Oppenheim, Maurice): Medicine. See: Kelly.

MUELLER, PETER. 1836-1922. Swiss gynecologist and obstetrician. See: Biog. Lex. hervorr. Aerzte. Mueller's maneuver?, Mueller's method?

Mueller reagent for blood (Derivation undetermined): Chemistry. See: Van Nostrand Chem. Dict.

Mueller-Ribbing-Clement syndrome (Mueller, Walther; Ribbing, Seved; and Clement). See: Ribbing's syndrome.

MUELLER, RUDOLF. 1877-1934. Austrian physician. See: Biog. Lex. hervorr. Aerzte, 1880-1930. Mueller-Oppenheim diagnosis (or reaction), Mueller's reaction (or test).

Mueller-Schumann law (or paradigm of associative inhibition) (Mueller, Georg Elias and Schumann, Friedrich): Psychology. See: English; Good; Wolman.

Mueller test for carbon in organic compounds (Derivation undetermined): Chemistry. See: Van Nostrand Chem. Dict.

Mueller-Urban method (Mueller, Georg Elias and Urban, Frank): Psychology. See: Chaplin; English; Wolman.

Mueller-Urban weights (or weighting) (Mueller, Georg Elias and Urban, Frank): Psychology. See: Chaplin; English; Wolman. Also known as: Urban's weights.

MUELLER-WALLE, JULIUS (In full: ERNST WILHELM JULIUS). b. 1857. German educator for the deaf. Cited in: Mansell. Mueller-Walle method.

Mueller-Walle method (Mueller-Walle, Julius): Education. See: Good. Also known as: Bruhn method.

MUELLER, WALTHER. b. 1888. German orthopedic surgeon. See: Biog. Lex. hervorr. Aerzte, 1880-1930. Lehmann-Ribbing-Mueller syndrome, Mueller-Ribbing-Clement syndrome, Mueller-Weiss disease.

MUELLER, WALTHER. fl. 1928. German physicist. Cited in: Chem. Abstr., Decenn. Index, 1927-1936. Geiger-Mueller counter (or tube), Geiger-Mueller probe, Geiger-Mueller region, Geiger-Mueller survey meter, Geiger-Mueller threshold.

Mueller-Weiss disease (Mueller, Walther and Weiss, Konrad): Medicine. See: Jablonski.

Muellerian bodies (Mueller, Fritz). See: Mueller's body.

Muellerian duct (Mueller, Johannes Peter). See: Mueller's duct.

Muellerian eminence (Mueller, Johannes Peter): Anatomy. See: Henderson.

Muellerian (Mullerian) mimicry (Mueller, Fritz): Zoology. See: Gray; Pennak; Webster's 3d.

Muellerius (Mueller, Fritz): Zoology. See: Stedman; Webster's 3d.

Mueller's body (Mueller, Fritz): Zoology. See: Gray. Also known as: Muellerian bodies.

Mueller's capsule (Mueller, Johannes Peter): Anatomy. See: Donath; Dorland; Stedman. Also known as: Bowman's capsule, Malpighian capsule.

Mueller's duct (Mueller, Johannes Peter): Anatomy. See: Donath; Dorland; Stedman. Also known as: Muellerian duct.

Mueller's experiment (Mueller, Johannes Peter): Medicine. See: Dorland; Stedman.

Mueller's fibres (Mueller, Heinrich): Anatomy. See: Dorland; Henderson; Stedman.

Mueller's ganglion (Mueller, Johannes Peter): Anatomy. See: Donath.

Mueller's larva (Mueller, Johannes Peter): Anatomy. See: Gray; Henderson; Pennak; Webster's 3d.

Mueller's law (Mueller, Fritz): Zoology. See: Henderson.

Mueller's maneuver (Mueller, Peter?): Medicine. See: Stedman.

Mueller's method (obstetrics) (Mueller, Peter?): Medicine. See: Stedman.

Mueller's method (sclera resection) (Derivation undetermined): Medicine. See: Stedman.

Mueller's muscle (Mueller, Heinrich): Anatomy. See: Donath; Dorland; Stedman.

Mueller's reaction (or test) (Mueller, Rudolf): Medicine. See: Dorland; Kelly; Stedman.

Mueller's sign (Mueller, Eduard): Medicine. See: Kelly.

Mueller's sign (Mueller, Friedrich von): Medicine. See: Dorland; Stedman.

Mueller's steatoma (Mueller, Friedrich von): Medicine. See: Stedman.

Mueller's test (Mueller, Eduard): Medicine. See: Dorland; Stedman.

Mueller's trigone (Mueller, Heinrich): Anatomy. See: Dorland; Stedman.

MUENCH, HUGO, JR. 1894-1972. American physician and statistician. See: Who Was Who Amer., vol. 5. Reed-Muench method.

MUENCHMEYER, ERNST. 1846-1880. German physician. (Biography source unavailable.) Muenchmeyer's disease (or syndrome).

Muenchmeyer's disease (or syndrome) (Muenchmeyer, Ernst): Medicine. See: Dorland; Jablonski.

Muencke pump (Muencke, Robert?): Chemistry. See: Hackh.

MUENCKE, ROBERT. fl. 1884-1892. German chemist. Cited in: Royal Soc. Cat. Sci. Pap., 1884-1900. Muencke pump?

MUENZER, EGMONT. 1865-1924. German physician. See: Biog. Lex. hervorr. Aerzte, 1880-1930. Muenzer's bundle (or tract).

MUENZER, FRANZ THEODOR. fl. 1927-1931. German psychiatrist. See: Kuerschner's Deut. Gel. Kal., vol. 4, 1931. Muenzer-Rosenthal syndrome.

Muenzer-Rosenthal syndrome (Muenzer, Franz Theodor and Rosenthal, Curt): Medicine. See: Jablonski.

Muenzer's bundle (or tract) (Muenzer, Egmont): Medicine. See: Dorland.

Mueseler lamp (Derivation undetermined): Engineering and Industry. See: Thrush.

Muff (Muff, Sir Harry): Generic Word (awkward at sports). See: Brewer.

MUFF, SIR HARRY. Character in Dudley's musical interlude, "The Rival Candidates," (1774). (Biography source unavailable.) Muff.

MUGGLETON, LODOWICKE (LODOVIC). 1609-1698. English sect leader. See: Dict. Nat. Biog. Muggletonians.

Muggletonians (Muggleton, Lodowicke): Religion. See: Barnhart (Eng. Lit.); Canney; Harvey; Webster's 3d.

Muhammad. See: Mohammed.

Muhammad ibn Musa. See: Al-Khwarizmi.

MUHLENBERG, GOTTHILF HENRY ERNST. 1753-1815. American botanist. See: World Who's Who Sci. Muhlenberg('s) turtle, Muhlenbergia, Muhlenbergs smartweed.

Muhlenberg('s) turtle (Muhlenberg, Gotthilf Henry Ernst): Zoology. See: Pennak; Webster's 3d.

Muhlenbergia (Muhlenberg, Gotthilf Henry Ernst): Botany. See: Webster's 3d.

Muhlenbergs smartweed (Muhlenberg, Gotthilf Henry Ernst): Botany. See: Winburne.

MUIR, JOHN. 1838-1914. Scottish-born American naturalist and conservationist. See: New Encyc. Brit., 1974, Microp. Muir peach dwarf?

MUIR, MATTHEW MONCRIEFF PATTISON. 1848-1931. Scottish chemist. See: Dict. Sci. Biog. Muir solution.

Muir peach dwarf (Muir, John?): Agriculture. See: Winburne.

Muir solution (Muir, Matthew Moncrieff Pattison): Chemistry. See: Van Nostrand Chem. Dict.

MULDER, GERARDUS JOHANNES. 1802-1880. Dutch chemist. See: Dict. Sci. Biog. Mulder('s) test (or solution for glucose).

MULDER, JOHANNES. 1769-1810. Dutch anatomist. See: Biog. Lex. hervorr. Aerzte. Mulder's angle.

Mulder('s) test (or solution for glucose) (Mulder, Gerardus Johannes): Medicine. See: Dorland; Stedman; Van Nostrand Chem. Dict.

Mulder's angle (Mulder, Johannes): Medicine. See: Dorland; Stedman.

MULDOON. fl. ca. 1868. American gang leader. (Biography source unavailable.) Hoodlum.

MULES, J. H. W. fl. 20th c. Australian grazier. Cited in: Australian Encyc. under "Blowflies," vol. 2, p. 37a. Mules operation.

Mules operation (Mules, J. H. W.): Medicine. See: Webster's 3d.; Winburne.

Mules' operation (Mules, Philip Henry): Medicine. See: Dorland; Stedman.

MULES, PHILIP HENRY. 1843-1905. English ophthalmologist. See: Biog. Lex. hervorr. Aerzte, 1880-1930. Mules' operation.

MULLER (or MUELLER), FRANZ. fl. ca. 1865. English? murderer. (Biography source unavailable.) Muellerize, Muller (hat).

Muller (hat) (Muller, Franz): Fashion. See: Hendrickson; Partridge.

Mullerian association (Mueller, Fritz): Zoology. See: Gray.

Muellerize (Muller, Franz): Applied Arts. See: Charnock

Muller's glass (Mueller, Franz): Earth Sciences. See: Thrush.

Muller's organ (Derivation undetermined): Zoology. See: Gray.

MULLIGAN. No dates. Irish immigrant in America. (Biography source unavailable.) Mulligan stew.

MULLIGAN, JAMES. fl. 1876. American bookkeeper. Cited in: Dict. Amer. Hist. Mulligan letters.

Mulligan letters (Mulligan, James): History. See: Jameson; Mathews, M. M.; Phyfe; Smith.

Mulligan stew (Mulligan): Food and Drink. See: Hendrickson.

Mullikan-Barker test reaction (Mulliken, Samuel Parsons and Barker, Elliott R.): Chemistry. See: Van Nostrand Chem. Dict.

Mullikan-Scudder test for methanol (Mulliken, Samuel Parsons and Scudder, Heyward): Chemistry. See: Van Nostrand Chem. Dict.

MULLIKEN, ROBERT SANDERSON. 1896- . American physicist. See: World Who's Who Sci. Hund-Mulliken-Hueckel method.

MULLIKEN, SAMUEL PARSONS. 1864-1934. American chemist. See: Pogg., vol. 6. Mullikan-Barker test reaction, Mullikan-Scudder test for methanol, Mulliken's classification.

Mulliken's classification (Mulliken, Samuel Parsons): Chemistry. See: Hackh.

Mulliner Manuscript (Mulliner, Thomas): Music. See: Scholes.

MULLINER, THOMAS. fl. ca. 1550. English organist. See: Dict. Nat. Biog. Mulliner Manuscript.

Mulready envelope (Mulready, William): Printing. See: Brewer.

MULREADY, WILLIAM. 1786-1863. English painter. See: Dict. Nat. Biog. Mulready envelope.

Mum(m) (malt liquor) (Mumme, Christiern or Christoph): Food and Drink. See: Charnock; Wagner (Names).

MUMME, CHRISTIERN or CHRISTOPH. fl. 1492. German brewer. (Biography source unavailable.) Mum(m) (malt liquor).

MUNCH-PETERSEN, CARL J. 1896- . Danish neurologist. See: Kraks Bla Bog., 1948. Munch-Petersen's encephalitis.

Munch-Petersen's encephalitis (Munch-Petersen, Carl J.). See: Redlich's encephalitis.

Munchausen (or Munchausenism) (Munchausen, Baron Karl Friedrich Hieronymus, Freiherr von): Generic Word (fantastic lie or exaggerated tale-teller). See: Hendrickson; Partridge; Webster's 3d.

MUNCHAUSEN, BARON KARL FRIEDRICH HIERONYMUS, FREIHERR VON. 1720-1797. German hunter and soldier. See: New Encyc. Brit., 1974, Microp. Munchausen (or Munchausenism), Munchausen('s) syndrome.

Munchausen('s) syndrome (Munchausen, Baron Karl Friedrich Hieronymus, Freiherr von): Medicine. See: Hinsie; Jablonski; Stedman.

MUNDELLA, ANTHONY JOHN. 1825-1897. English statesman and educator. See: Dict. Nat. Biog., 1st suppl. A. J. Mundella's Act.

MUNDT, KARL EARL. 1900-1973. American legislator. See: Biog. Direct. Amer. Congress. Smith-Mundt Act.

MUNK, FRITZ. b. 1879. German physician. See: Biog. Lex. hervorr. Aerzte, 1880-1930. Munk's disease.

Munk's disease (Munk, Fritz): Medicine. See: Dorland.

MUNRO, JOHN CUMMINGS. 1858-1910. American surgeon. See: Who Was Who Amer., 1897-1942. Munro's point.

MUNRO, WILLIAM DELMAR. 1916- . American mathematician. See: Amer. Men and Women Sci., 12th ed. Robbins-Munro process.

MUNRO, WILLIAM JOHN. fl. 1898. English? physician. Cited in: Royal Soc. Cat. Sci. Pap., 1884-1900. Munro's microabscess (or abscess)?

MUNROE, CHARLES EDWARD. 1849-1938. American chemist and inventor. See: World Who's Who Sci. Munroe effect.

Munroe effect (Munroe, Charles Edward): Chemistry. See: Webster's 3d.

Munro's microabscess (or abscess) (Munro, William John?): Medicine. See: Stedman.

Munro's point (Munro, John Cummings): Medicine. See: Dorland; Stedman.

MUNSELL, ALBERT HENRY. 1858-1918. American painter. See: Who Was Who Amer., 1897-1942. Munsell chroma, Munsell colours (color system or scale), Munsell value.

Munsell chroma (Munsell, Albert Henry): Physics. See: Van Nostrand Sci. Encyc.

Munsell colours (color system or scale) (Munsell, Albert Henry): Physics. See: Drever; English; Hughes.

MUNSELL, HAZEL EDITH. 1891- . American chemist. Cited in: Index-Cat. Libr. Surg.-Gen. Off., 5th Ser., vol. 1, 1959. Sherman-Munsell unit.

Munsell value (Munsell, Albert Henry): Physics. See: Internat. Dict. Phys. Elec.

MUNSON, EDWARD LYMAN. 1868-1947. American army physician. See: Who Was Who Amer., 1943-1950. Munson (shoes).

MUNSON, JAMES EUGENE. 1835-1906. American inventor. See: World Who's Who Sci. Munson system (shorthand), Munson typesetting-machine.

Munson (shoes) (Munson, Edward Lyman): Applied Arts. See: Mathews, M. M.

Munson system (Munson, Thomas Volney): Botany. See: Webster's 3d.

Munson system (shorthand) (Munson, James Eugene): Dictation. See: Nat. Cycl. Amer. Biog., vol. 12, p. 497.

MUNSON, THOMAS VOLNEY. 1843-1913. American viticulturist. See: Dict. Amer. Biog. Munson system.

Munson typesetting-machine (Munson, James Eugene): Printing. See: Lockwood.

MUNSON, W. A. 1902- . American engineer. See: Amer. Men Sci., 9th ed. Fletcher-Munson contours (or curves).

MUNTEANU-MURGOCI, GHEORGHE. d. 1925. Rumanian geologist. See: Bull. Soc. Roman Geolog., vol. 3 (1937), pp. 1-49. Muntenite.

Muntenite (Munteanu-Murgoci, Gheorghe): Earth Sciences. See: Thrush.

MUNTZ, GEORGE FREDERICK. 1794-1857. English metal manufacturer and politician. See: Dict. Nat. Biog. Muntz('s) metal.

Muntz('s) metal (Muntz, George Frederick): Chemistry. See: Carter; Hackh; Partridge; Thrush; Webster's 3d.

MURAKAMI, TAKEJIRO. fl. 1918-1926. Japanese metallurgist. See: Pogg., vol. 6. Murakami's reagent.

Murakami's reagent (Murakami, Takejiro): Chemistry. See: Thrush.

MURAOUR, HENRI. fl. 1914-1930. French chemist. See: Pogg. vol. 6. Muraour relationship.

Muraour relationship (Muraour, Henri): Mathematics. See: Internat. Dict. Ap. Math.

Murasakite (Derivation undetermined): Earth Sciences. See: Thrush.

MURATORI, ANTONIO (In full: LODOVICO ANTONIO). 1672-1750. Italian scholar and pioneer historiographer. See: New Encyc. Brit., 1974, Microp. Muratorian, Muratorian canon.

Muratorian (Muratori, Antonio): History. See: Webster's 3d.

Muratorian canon (Muratori, Antonio): Religion. See: Attwater; Mathews, S.; New Encyc. Brit., 1974, Microp.

Murcheson letter (Murchison, Charles F.): History. See: Jameson.

MURCHISON, CHARLES. 1830-1879. English physician. See: Dict. Nat. Biog. Murchison's pill.

MURCHISON, CHARLES F. Fictitious letter writer to Lord Sackville-West, English minister at Washington in 1888. Cited in: Dict. Amer. Hist. Murcheson letter.

MURCHISON, SIR RODERICK IMPEY. 1792-1871. English geologist. See: World Who's Who Sci. Murchisonite.

Murchisonite (Murchison, Sir Roderick Impey): Earth Sciences. See: Thrush.

Murchison's pill (Murchison, Charles): Medicine. See: Dorland.

Murcott honey orange (Smith, Charles Murcott): Botany. See: Hendrickson under "Temple Orange..."

Murcott Smith, Charles. See: Smith, Charles Murcott.

MURDOCH, JOSEPH. b. 1890. American mineralogist. See: World Who's Who Sci. Murdochite.

Murdochite (Murdoch, Joseph): Earth Sciences. See: Thrush.

Murdock slide valve (Murdock, William): Engineering and Industry. See: Auger.

MURDOCK, WILLIAM. 1754-1839. English inventor. See: World Who's Who Sci. Murdock slide valve.

MURET, PAUL-LOUIS. b. 1878. French physician. Cited in: Index.-Cat. Libr. Surg.-Gen. Off., 3d. Ser., vol. 7, 1928. Quenu-Muret sign.

Murgatroyd belt (Murgatroyd, J. B.?): Engineering and Industry. See: Thrush.

MURGATROYD, J. B. fl. 1937-1948. English glass technologist. Cited in: Chem. Abstr., Decenn. Index, 1937-1946. Murgatroyd belt?

MURILLO, BARTOLOME ESTEBAN. 1618-1682. Spanish painter. See: New Encyc. Brit., 1974, Microp. Murillo (color).

Murillo (color) (Murillo, Bartolome Esteban): Fine Arts. See: Webster's 3d.

Murk Jansen. See: Jansen, Murk.

Murk Jansen's syndrome (Jansen, Murk). See: Jansen's syndrome.

MURLESS, BRIAN CHARLES. fl. 1929-1964. South African obstetrician. See: Med. Direct., 1964. Murless head extractor.

Murless head extractor (Murless, Brian Charles): Medicine. See: Stedman.

Murphree efficiency factor (Murphree, Eger Vaughan): Chemistry. See: Van Nostrand Chem. Dict.

MURPHREE, EGER VAUGHAN. 1898- . American petroleum engineer. See: Amer. Men Sci., 8th ed. Murphree efficiency factor.

MURPHY. No dates. Irishman. (Biography source unavailable.) Murphy (game).

Murphy bed (Murphy, William L.): Generic Word. See: Webster's 3d.

MURPHY, EDSEL. No dates. American? creator of law. (Biography source unavailable.) Murphy's law(s)?, Murphy's laws of college publishing?

Murphy (game) (Murphy): Generic Word (thief's switch maneuver). See: Barnhart (New Eng.).

MURPHY, JAMES BUMGARDNER. 1884-1950. American pathologist. See: World Who's Who Sci. Murphy-Sturm lymphosarcoma.

MURPHY, JOHN BENJAMIN. 1857-1916. American surgeon. See: World Who's Who Sci. Fowler-Murphy treatment, Murphy's button, Murphy's kidney punch, Murphy's method.

MURPHY, R. K. fl. 1937. Australian chemist. Cited in: Chem. Abstr., vol. 32, p. 73. Dwyer-Murphy reagent.

MURPHY, ROBERT CUSHMAN. b. 1887. American zoologist. See: World Who's Who Sci. Murphy's law.

Murphy-Sturm lymphosarcoma (Murphy, James Bumgardner and Sturm, Ernst): Medicine. See: Jablonski.

MURPHY, WILLIAM L. fl. 20th c. American inventor. (Biography source unavailable.) Murphy bed.

MURPHY, WILLIAM PARRY. 1892- . American physician. See: World Who's Who Sci. Minot-Murphy diet (or treatment).

Murphy's button (Murphy, John Benjamin): Medicine. See: Dorland; Stedman.

Murphy's kidney punch (Murphy, John Benjamin): Medicine. See: Stedman.

Murphy's law(s) (Murphy, Edsel?): Sociology. See: Martin.

Murphy's law (Murphy, Robert Cushman): Zoology. See: Gray.

Murphy's laws of college publishing (Murphy, Edsel?): Sociology. See: Martin.

Murphy's method (Murphy, John Benjamin): Medicine. See: Stedman.

MURRAY, ANDREW. 1812-1878. Scottish naturalist. See: Dict. Nat. Biog. Murray pine.

Murray cod (Murray, Sir John?): Zoology. See: Van Nostrand Sci. Encyc.

Murray-Curvex machine (Derivation undetermined): Engineering and Industry. See: Thrush.

Murray Gottlieb Prize (Gottlieb, Murray): Library Science. See: Harrod.

MURRAY, HENRY ALEXANDER. b. 1893. American psychologist. See: World Who's Who Sci. Murray's personology.

MURRAY, JOHANNES ANDREAS. 1740-1791. Swedish botanist. See: World Who's Who Sci. Murraya.

MURRAY, JOHN (4TH EARL OF DUNMORE). 1732-1809. Scottish colonial administrator in America. See: Dict. Nat. Biog. Dunmore's indian scheme, Dunmore's War.

MURRAY, SIR JOHN. 1841-1914. Canadian-born Scottish oceanographer. See: World Who's Who Sci. Murray cod?

MURRAY, LINDLEY. 1745-1826. American grammarian. See: Dict. Amer. Biog. Lindley Murray.

Murray loop (test) (Derivation undetermined): Electronics. See: Hughes; Markus; Van Nostrand Sci. Encyc.

MURRAY, PATRICK, BARON OF LIVINGSTON. fl. 1680. Scottish botanist. See: Britten and Boulger. Livistona.

Murray pine (Murray, Andrew): Botany. See: Webster's 3d.

MURRAY, WILLIAM, 1ST EARL OF MANSFIELD. 1705-1793. English judge. See: Dict. Nat. Biog. Mansfield's judgment.

Murraya (Murray, Johannes Andreas): Botany. See: Taylor, N.; Webster's 3d.

Murrayite (Derivation undetermined): Zoology. See: Pennak.

Murray's personology (Murray, Henry Alexander): Psychology. See: Chaplin.

MURRI, AUGUSTO. 1841-1932. Italian physician. See: Diz. Encic. Ital. Murri's disease, Murri's law.

Murri's disease (Murri, Augusto): Medicine. See: Dorland.

Murri's law (Murri, Augusto): Medicine. See: Dorland.

MURTHY, M. N. fl. 1957. Indian statistician. Cited in: Kendall and Doig. Murthy's estimator.

Murthy's estimator (Murthy, M. N.): Statistics. See: Kendall.

Musa (Musa, Antonius): Botany. See: Charnock; Hendrickson; Taylor, N.

MUSA, ANTONIUS. fl. ca. 25. Roman physician. See: Nouv. Biog. Univ. Musa.

Muschamp coal miner (Derivation undetermined): Engineering and Industry. See: Thrush.

muscle of Horner (Horner, William Edmonds). See: Horner's muscle.

Musgrave-Harner turbidimeter (Musgrave, John Reichert and Harner, Harold Russell): Engineering and Industry. See: Thrush.

MUSGRAVE, JOHN REICHERT. 1906- . American chemist. See: Amer. Men and Women Sci., 12th ed. Musgrave-Harner turbidimeter.

MUSHET, ROBERT FORESTER. 1811-1891. Scottish metallurgist. See: Dict. Nat. Biog. Mushet('s) steel.

Mushet('s) steel (Mushet, Robert Forester): Engineering and Industry. See: Thrush; Webster's 3d.

MUSSCHE, JEAN HENRI. 1765-1834. Belgian horticulturist and botanist. See: Biog. Nat. de Belgique. Musschia.

Musschia (Mussche, Jean Henri): Botany. See: Charnock.

MUSSET, ALFRED (In full: LOUIS-CHARLES-) DE. 1810-1857. French poet and playwright. See: New Encyc. Brit., 1974, Microp. Musset's sign.

Musset's sign (Musset, Alfred de): Medicine. See: Dorland; Stedman.

MUSSIN-PUSCHKIN, APOLLO A. M. d. ca. 1805. Russian chemist. Cited in: Royal Soc. Cat. Sci. Pap., 1800-1863. Puschkinia.

MUSSO, ALFRED. fl. 1929. French? metallurgical engineer. Cited in: Chem. Abstr., Decenn. Index, 1927-1936. Musso process.

Musso process (Musso, Alfred): Engineering and Industry. See: Thrush.

Mustel organ (Mustel, Victor): Music. See: Apel.

MUSTEL, VICTOR. 1815-1890. French musical instrument maker. See: Grove. Mustel organ.

Muthmann('s) liquid (or reagent for separating minerals) (Muthmann, Wilhelm?): Chemistry. See: Thrush; Van Nostrand Chem. Dict.

MUTHMANN, WILHELM (In full: FRIEDRICH WILHELM). 1861-1913. German chemist. See: Pogg., vols. 4, 5. Muthmann('s) liquid (or reagent for separating minerals?), Muthmannite.

Muthmannite (Muthmann, Wilhelm): Earth Sciences. See: Thrush; Webster's 3d.

MUTIS, JOSE CELESTINO BRUNO. 1731-1808. Spanish botanist in Colombia. See: New Encyc. Brit., 1974, Microp. Mutisia.

Mutisia (Mutis, Jose Celestino Bruno): Botany. See: Charnock; Taylor, N.; Webster's 3d.

Mutt and Jeff (Mutt, Augustus and Jeff, cartoon characters): Generic Word (short-tall couple). See: Hendrickson.

MUTT, AUGUSTUS. Cartoon character created by Harry Conway Fisher in 1907. See: Mansell. Mutt and Jeff.

MYA, GIUSEPPE. 1857-1911. Italian physician. See: Biog. Lex. hervorr. Aerzte, 1880-1930. Mya's disease.

Mya's disease (Mya, Giuseppe): Medicine. See: Dorland; Stedman. Also known as: Hirschsprung's disease.

Myatt's pine (strawberry) (Derivation undetermined): Botany. See: Charnock.

Myerholtz' muscle (Derivation undetermined): Medicine. See: Stedman.

Myers-Briggs type indicator (Myers, I. B. and Briggs): Psychology. See: Wolman.

MYERS, I. B. fl. 1962. Psychologist. (Biography source unavailable.) Myers-Briggs type indicator.

Myers rating (Derivation undetermined): Earth Sciences. See: Huschke.

MYERS, VICTOR CARYL. 1883-1948. American biochemist. See: World Who's Who Sci. Pfiffner-Myers reagent.

MYGIND, FRANCIS VON.. No dates. German nobleman. (Biography source unavailable.) Myginda.

Myginda (Mygind, Francis von): Botany. See: Charnock.

MYHRMAN, GUSTAF CHRISTOFER. 1903- . Swedish physician. See: Vem Ar Det?, 1951. Myhrman-Zetterholm disease.

Myhrman-Zetterholm disease (Myhrman, Gustaf and Zetterholm, Sten Gunnar): Medicine. See: Jablonski.

MYLIUS, FRANZ BENNO. 1854-1931. German chemist. See: Pogg., vols. 4, 5, 6. Mylius salt test, Mylius test.

Mylius gear box (Derivation undetermined): Engineering and Industry. See: Auger.

Mylius salt test (Mylius, Franz Benno): Chemistry. See: Van Nostrand Chem. Dict.

Mylius test (Mylius, Franz Benno): Chemistry. See: Thrush.

Mynot-Plymey process (Derivation undetermined): Agriculture. See: Winburne.

MYRICK, F. M. fl. ca. 1910. American mineral discoverer. Cited in: Hintze, suppl. 1, p. 380. Myrickite.

Myrickite (Myrick, F. M.): Earth Sciences. See: Thrush.

MYRMIDON. A son of Zeus in Greek mythology. See: Dict. Grk. Rom. Biog. Myth. Myrmidons.

Myrmidons (Myrmidon): Mythology. See: Barnhart (Eng. Lit.); Harvey.

Myrrh (Myrrha): Botany. See: Harvey.

MYRRHA. In Greek mythology, daughter of Cinyras, king of Cyprus. Myrrh.

mytilus Hagenii (Hagen, Carl Gottfried): Zoology. Cited in: World Who's Who Sci. under "Hagen, Carl Gottfried."

N

NABARRO, FRANK REGINALD NUNES. 1916- . English-born physicist in South Africa. See: World Who's Who Sci. Peierls-Nabarro force.

NABOKOV, VLADIMIR. 1899- . Russian writer, critic and lepidopterist. See: New Encyc. Brit., 1974, Microp. Nabokov's pug.

Nabokov's pug (Nabokov, Vladimir): Zoology. See: Hendrickson.

NABONASSAR (NABU-NASIR). d. 733 B.C. Babylonian king. See: Dict. Grk. Rom. Biog. Myth. Era of Nabonassar.

NABOTH, MARTIN. 1675-1721. German anatomist and physician. See: Biog. Lex. hervorr. Aerzte. Nabothian cyst (gland or follicle).

NABOTH OF JEZREEL. fl. ca. 9th c. B.C. Old Testament vineyard owner. See: Hastings (Dict. Bible). Naboth's vineyard.

Nabothian cyst (gland or follicle) (Naboth, Martin): Medicine. See: Dorland; Stedman; Webster's 3d.

Naboth's vineyard (Naboth of Jezreel): Generic Word (taking an indefensible person's possession). See: Barnhart (Eng. Lit.); Partridge.

NACHMANN, MARCEL. fl. 1925. Swiss chemist. Cited in: Chem. Abstr., vol. 20, p. 1588. Zetsche-Nachmann reagent.

NADER, RALPH. 1934- . American lawyer and consumer advocate. See: Who's Who Amer., 1974-1975. Naderism.

Naderism (Nader, Ralph): Generic Word (consumerism). See: Barnhart (New Eng.)

Nadi reaction (Derivation undetermined): Medicine. See: Stedman.

NAEGELE, FRANZ KARL. 1777-1851. German obstetrician. See: World Who's Who Sci. Naegele obliquity, Naegele's pelvis, Naegele's rule.

Naegele obliquity (Naegele, Franz Karl): Medicine. See: Dorland; Stedman.

Naegele's pelvis (Naegele, Franz Karl): Anatomy. See: Donath; Dorland; Jablonski; Stedman.

Naegele's rule (Naegele, Franz Karl): Medicine. See: Dorland; Stedman.

NAEGELI, KARL. 1895-1942. Swiss organic chemist. See: Pogg., vols. 6, 7a. Naegeli test reaction for aldehydes and ketones?

NAEGELI, KARL WILHELM VON. 1817-1891. German botanist. See: World Who's Who Sci. Naegeli solution?, Naegelia.

NAEGELI, OSKAR. 1885-1959. Swiss dermatologist. See: Biog. Lex. hervorr. Aerzte, 1880-1930. Naegeli's syndrome (or incontinentia pigmenti).

NAEGELI, OTTO. 1871-1938. Swiss hematologist. See: World Who's Who Sci. Glanzmann-Naegeli syndrome?, macroblast of Naegeli?, Naegeli's leukemia, Naegeli's maneuver (or method).

Naegeli solution (Naegeli, Karl Wilhelm von?): Chemistry. See: Van Nostrand Chem. Dict.

Naegeli test reaction for aldehydes and ketones (Naegeli, Karl?): Chemistry. See: Van Nostrand Chem. Dict.

Naegelia (Naegeli, Karl Wilhelm von): Botany. See: Taylor, N.; Webster's 3d.

Naegeli's leukemia (Naegeli, Otto): Medicine. See: Jablonski.

Naegeli's maneuver (or method) (Naegeli, Otto): Medicine. Cited in: Kelly; World Who's Who Sci.

Naegeli's syndrome (or incontinentia pigmenti) (Naegeli, Oskar): Medicine. See: Jablonski. Also known as: Franceschetti-Jadassohn syndrome.

NAFFZIGER, HOWARD CHRISTIAN. 1884-1961. American surgeon. See: Who Was Who Amer., 1961-1968. Naffziger operation, Naffziger('s) syndrome.

Naffziger operation (Naffziger, Howard Christian): Medicine. See: Dorland; Stedman.

Naffziger('s) syndrome (Naffziger, Howard Christian): Medicine. See: Dorland; Jablonski; Stedman. Also known as: Adson's syndrome, Coote-Hanauld syndrome, Coote's syndrome, Haven's syndrome, Nonne's syndrome.

Nagaika (Nogai): Generic Word (whip). See: Weekley.

NAGANT. fl. 19th c. Belgian inventor. (Biography source unavailable.) Nagant 7.62mm revolver.

Nagant 7.62mm revolver (Nagant): Weapons. See: Quick.

NAGEL, WILLIBALD. 1870-1911. German physiologist. See: Biog. Lex. hervorr. Aerzte, 1880-1930. Nagel's adaptometer?, Nagel's test.

Nagel's adaptometer (Nagel, Willibald?): Physiology. See: Drever.

Nagel's test (Nagel, Willibald): Physiology. See: Dorland; Stedman.

Nagel's turbine (Derivation undetermined): Engineering and Industry. See: Auger.

Nageotte bracelets (Nageotte, Jean): Medicine. See: Dorland.

Nageotte cells (Nageotte, Jean): Medicine. See: Stedman.

NAGEOTTE, JEAN. b. 1866. French histologist. See: Biog. Lex. hervorr. Aerzte, 1880-1930. Babinski-Nageotte syndrome, Nageotte bracelets, Nageotte cells, Nageotte radicular nerve.

Nageotte radicular nerve (Nageotte, Jean): Medicine. See: Dorland.

Nager-De Reynier syndrome (Nager, Felix Robert and De Reynier, Jean Pierre): Medicine. See: Jablonski.

NAGER, FELIX ROBERT. b. 1877. Swiss otorhinolaryngologist. Cited in: Index-Cat. Libr. Surg.-Gen. Off., 5th Ser., vol. 1, 1959. Nager-De Reynier syndrome.

Nagler effect (Nagler, Joseph): Medicine. See: Dorland.

NAGLER, F. P. O. fl. 1939. Australian bacteriologist. Cited in: Chem. Abstr., Decenn. Index, 1937-1946. Nagler's reaction (test or method).

NAGLER, FORREST. 1885-1952. American hydraulic engineer. See: Amer. Men Sci., 6th ed. Nagler runner.

NAGLER, JOSEPH. No dates. Austrian radiologist. (Biography source unavailable.) Nagler effect.

Nagler runner (Nagler, Forrest): Engineering and Industry. See: Van Nostrand Sci. Encyc. under "Hydraulic Turbine."

Nagler's reaction (test or method) (Nagler, F. P. O.): Medicine. See: Dorland; Kelly.

Nagyagite (Derivation undetermined): Earth Sciences. See: Van Nostrand Sci. Encyc.

NAHNSEN, GEORG. fl. 1891-1895. German electrotechnologist. Cited in: Royal Soc. Cat. Sci. Pap., 1884-1900. Nahnsen process.

Nahnsen process (Nahnsen, Georg): Engineering and Industry. See: Thrush.

NAIMAN, BARNET. 1900- . American chemist. See: Amer. Men Sci., 6th ed. Naiman reagent for vitamin B1 (thiamine), Naiman test reagent for bismuth.

Naiman reagent for vitamin B₁ (thiamine) (Naiman, Barnet): Chemistry. See: Van Nostrand Chem. Dict.

Naiman test reagent for bismuth (Naiman, Barnet): Chemistry. See: Van Nostrand Chem. Dict.

NAJAS (NAIAS). In Greek mythology, nymph of the springs. (Biography source unavailable.) Najas.

Najas (Najas, nymph of the springs): Botany. See: Charnock.

NAJJAR, VICTOR ASSAD. 1914- . Lebanese-born American pediatrician. See: Amer. Men and Women Sci., 12th ed. Crigler-Najjar syndrome.

NAJMAN. No dates. Scandinavian physician. (Biography source unavailable.) Imerslund-Najman-Graesbeck syndrome.

Nakamura's gland (Derivation undetermined): Zoology. See: Gray.

NAKANISHI, KAMETARO. fl. 1900. Japanese physician. Cited in: Royal Soc. Cat. Sci. Pap., 1884-1900. Nakanishi's method.

Nakanishi's method (Nakanishi, Kametaro): Medicine. See: Kelly; Stedman.

NAKAZAWA, TADASU. fl. 1920. Japanese chemist. Cited in: Chem. Abstr., vol. 15, p. 813. Matsui-Nakazawa test for cobalt.

NAKAZONO, T. fl. 1926. Japanese chemist. Cited in: Brit. Chem. Abstr. 1926 A, 141. Wada-Nakazano reagent.

Nambu 8mm automatic pistol model 1904 (Nambu, Kijiro): Weapons. See: Quick.

NAMBU, KIJIRO. No dates. Japanese army officer. (Biography source unavailable.) Nambu 8mm automatic pistol model 1904.

Namby-Pamby (Philips, Ambrose "Namby-Pamby"): Generic Word (sentimental and effeminate). See: Charnock; Partridge; Picken; Webster's 3d.

NAMDEO (NAMA). fl. 12th or 13th c. Hindu dyer. Cited in: Encyc. Brit., 1911, Index. Namdeo sect.

Namdeo sect (Namdeo): Religion. See: Canney.

NANAK, BABA. 1469-1539. Indian spiritual teacher. See: New Encyc. Brit., 1974, Microp. Nanakpanthi sect.

Nanakpanthi sect (Nanak, Baba): Religion. See: Canney.

nanowatt (Watt, James): Physics. See: Markus.

Nansen bottle (Nansen, Fridtjof): Earth Sciences. See: Huschke; Thrush; Van Nostrand Sci. Encyc.; Webster's 3d.

Nansen cast (Nansen, Fridtjof): Earth Sciences. See: Huschke.

NANSEN, FRIDTJOF. 1861-1930. Norwegian explorer and statesman. See: World Who's Who Sci. Nansen bottle, Nansen cast, Nansen possport, Nansen-Pettersson water bottle.

Nansen passport (Nansen, Fridtjof): History. See: Smith; Webster's 3d.

Nansen-Pettersson water bottle (Nansen, Fridtjof and Pettersson, Sven Otto): Earth Sciences. See: Thrush.

NANTA, A. fl. 1923-1924. French physician. Cited in: Index Medicus, 3d Ser., vol. 4, 1924. Gandy-Nanta disease?

Nap (Napoleon I): Recreation and Sports. See: Partridge.

NAPALKOV, A. V. fl. 1957-1962. Russian neurophysiologist. (Biography source unavailable.) Napalkov phenomenon.

Napalkov phenomenon (Napalkov, A.V.): Psychology. See: Hinsie.

NAPIER. fl. 19th c. English printers. (Biography source unavailable.) Napier machines.

NAPIER, DAVID. 1790-1869. Scottish marine-engineer. See: Dict. Nat. Biog. Napier press?

NAPIER, JOHN, LAIRD OF MERCHISTON. 1550-1617. Scottish mathematician. See: Dict. Sci. Biog. Napierian (or Naperian), Napierian logarithm(s), Napier's analogies, Napier's bones (or rods), Napier's rule(s), Neper (or Napier) (unit).

NAPIER, LIONEL EVERARD. b. 1888. English? physician in India. See: Index-Cat. Med. Veter. Zool., vol. 11, 1950. Napier's aldehyde test.

Napier machines (Napier): Printing. See: Lockwood.

Napier press (Napier, David?): Printing. See: Lockwood.

Napier (unit) (Napier, John). See: Neper (unit).

NAPIERALSKI, BERNARD. fl. 1893. Swiss chemist. Cited in: Royal Soc. Cat. Sci. Pap., 1884-1900. Bischler-Napieralski reaction.

Napierian (or Naperian) (Napier, John, Laird of Merchiston): Mathematics. See: Webster's 3d.

Napierian logarithm(s) (Napier, John, Laird of Merchiston): Mathematics. See: Hackh; Internat. Dict. Ap. Math.; James; Markus; Webster's 3d.

Napier's aldehyde test (Napier, Lionel Everard): Medicine. See: Stedman.

Napier's analogies (Napier, John, Laird of Merchiston): Mathematics. See: James; Webster's 3d.

Napier's bones (or rods) (Napier, John, Laird of Merchiston): Mathematics. See: Blumberg; Brewer; Charnock; Webster's 3d.

Napier's rule(s) (Napier, John, Laird of Merchiston): Mathematics. See: Ballentyne; James; Webster's 3d.

Napoleon (Napoleon I): Generic Word (masterly strategist). See: Partridge; Webster's 3d.

NAPOLEON I (In full: NAPOLEON BONAPARTE). 1769-1821. French general and emperor. See: New Encyc. Brit., 1974, Microp. Bonapartea, Bonapartism (or Bonapartist), Code Napoleon, go Nap, Nap, Napoleon, Napoleon (beard), Napoleon blue (color), Napoleon (boot), Napoleon brandy, Napoleon (card game), Napoleon cherry, Napoleon (coin), Napoleon collar, Napoleon (clover), Napoleon (cypress spurge), Napoleon (pastry)?, Napoleon weaver?, Napoleonic bee, Napoleonic (Napoleonism or Napoleonist), Napoleonic costume, Napoleonic powder cask plot, Napoleonic Wars, Napoleonite, Napoleonize, Napoleon's bell(s), Napoleon's willow, Ode to Napoleon.

NAPOLEON III (CHARLES LOUIS NAPOLEON BONAPARTE). 1808-1873. French emperor. See: New Encyc. Brit., 1974. Bonapartism, Napoleon III style, Napoleon (gun).

Napoleon III style (Napoleon III): Applied Arts. See: New Encyc. Brit., 1974.

Napoleon (beard) (Napoleon I): Fashion. See: Stenhouse.

Napoleon blue (color) (Napoleon I): Fashion. See: Webster's 3d.

Napoleon (boot) (Napoleon I): Fashion. See: Picken; Webster's 3d.

Napoleon brandy (Napoleon I): Food and Drink. See: De Sola.

Napoleon (card game) (Napoleon I): Recreation and Sports. See: New Encyc. Brit., 1974, Microp.; Webster's 3d.

Napoleon cherry (Napoleon I): Botany. See: Hendrickson under "Bing."

Napoleon (clover) (Napoleon I): Botany. See: Webster's 3d.

Napoleon (coin) (Napoleon I): Numismatics. See: Charnock; Webster's 3d.

Napoleon collar (Napoleon I): Fashion. See: Picken.

Napoleon (cypress spurge) (Napoleon I): Botany. See: Webster's 3d.

Napoleon (gun) (Napoleon III): Weapons. See: Mathews, M. M.

Napoleon (pastry) (Napoleon I?): Food and Drink. See: De Sola; Hendrickson; Webster's 3d.

Napoleon weaver (Napoleon I?): Zoology. See: Gray.

Napoleonic (Napoleonism or Napoleonist) (Napoleon I): History. See: Barnhart (New Eng.); Webster's 3d.

Napoleonic bee (Napoleon I): History. See: Phyfe.

Napoleonic Code (Napoleon I). See: Code Napoleon.

Napoleonic costume (Napoleon I): Fashion. See: Picken.

Napoleonic powder cask plot (Napoleon I): History. Cited in: Laughlin.

Napoleonic Wars (Napoleon I): History. See: Latham; Steinberg under "French Revolutionary and Napoleonic Wars."

Napoleonite (Napoleon I): Earth Sciences. See: Thrush; Van Nostrand Sci. Encyc.

Napoleonize (Napoleon I): Generic Word (rule like Napoleon). See: Hendrickson.

Napoleon's bell(s) (Napoleon I): Botany. See: Webster's 3d.

Napoleon's willow (Napoleon I): Botany. See: Gray; Webster's 3d.

NARATH, ALBERT. 1864-1924. German-born? Dutch surgeon. See: Deut. Z. f. Chir., vol. clxxxix (1924), pp. 1-3. Narath's operation.

Narath's operation (Narath, Albert): Medicine. See: Dorland; Stedman.

NARAYANA. Hindu supreme spirit floating on the primeval waters. See: Jobes. Swami-Narayan sect.

Narcissan (Narcissus): Mythology. See: Webster's 3d.

Narcissism (or Narcissistic) (Narcissus): Generic Word (excessive self-love). See: Chaplin; Partridge; Stedman; Webster's 3d.

NARCISSUS. Beautiful youth of Greco-Roman mythology who fell in love with his image. See: New Encyc. Brit., 1974, Microp. Narcissan, Narcissism (or Narcissistic), Narcissus, Narcissus (plant).

Narcissus (Narcissus, of Greco-Roman mythology): Generic Word (fop). See: Stenhouse.

Narcissus (plant) (Narcissus): Botany. See: Taylor, N.; Webster's 3d.

NARSES. ca. 480-574. Byzantine general. See: New Encyc. Brit., 1974, Microp. Narses.

Narses (Narses, Byzantine general): Generic Word (eunuch). See: Latham.

NASINI, RAFFAELLO. 1854-1931. Italian chemist. See: Pogg., vols. 4, 5, 6. Nasinite.

Nasinite (Nasini, Raffaello): Earth Sciences. See: Thrush.

NASLEDOV, B. N. fl. 20th c. Russian mineralogist. Cited in: Hintze, suppl. 3, p. 222. Nasledovite.

Nasledovite (Nasledov, B. N.): Earth Sciences. See: Thrush.

NASMYTH, ALEXANDER. d. 1848. Scottish dentist. Cited in: Royal Soc. Cat. Sci. Pap., 1800-1863. Nasmyth's membrane (or cuticle).

Nasmyth('s) hammer (Nasmyth, James): Engineering and Industry. See: Auger; Thrush.

NASMYTH, JAMES. 1808-1890. Scottish engineer. See: Dict. Sci. Biog. Nasmyth('s) hammer, Nasmyth steam arm.

Nasmyth steam arm (Nasmyth, James): Engineering and Industry. See: Hendrickson.

Nasmyth's membrane (or cuticle) (Nasmyth, Alexander): Anatomy. See: Donath; Henderson; Stedman; Webster's 3d.

NASON, FRANK LEWIS. 1856-1928. American geologist. See: Who Was Who Amer., 1897-1942. Nasonite.

Nasonite (Nason, Frank Lewis): Earth Sciences. See: Thrush; Webster's 3d.

NASSAU, HORTENSE VAN. fl. 18th c. Sister of Prince Charles Henri Nicolas Othon de Nassau-Siegen. (Biography source unavailable.) rose Hortensia.

NASSE, CHRISTIAN FRIEDRICH. 1778-1851. German physician. See: World Who's Who Sci. law of Nasse.

NASSE, OTTO JOHANN FRIEDRICH. 1839-1903. German pharmaceutical and physiological chemist. See: Pogg., vols. 3, 4. Millon-Nasse test, Nasse reagent for albumin.

Nasse reagent for albumin (Nasse, Otto Johann Friedrich): Chemistry. See: Van Nostrand Chem. Dict.

NASSER, GAMAL ABDEL. 1918-1970. Egyptian president. See: New Encyc. Brit., 1974. Nasserism.

Nasserism (Nasser, Gamal Abdel): Politics. See: Hendrickson.

Nat Turner's Insurrection (Turner, Nat): History. See: Smith.

NATANSON, J. fl. 1863. German pharmaceutical chemist. Cited in: Royal Soc. Cat. Sci. Pap., 1864-1873. Natanson test for iron?

Natanson test for iron (Natanson, J.?): Chemistry. See: Van Nostrand Chem. Dict.

NATHAN, W. S. fl. 1935. English chemist. Cited in: Chem. Abstr., Decenn. Index, 1927-1936. Baker-Nathan effect.

Nathusius furnace (Nathusius, Hans): Engineering and Industry. See: Thrush.

NATHUSIUS, HANS. fl. 1910-1929. German engineer. Cited in: Chem. Abstr., Decenn. Index, 1907-1916. Nathusius furnace.

NATION, CARRY AMELIA MOORE. 1846-1911. American temperance advocate. See: Dict. Amer. Biog. Carry Nation.

NATIVELLE, ADOLPHE (In full: CLAUDE ADOLPHE). 1812-1889. French pharmacist. See: Grand Larousse Encyc. Nativelle's digitalin.

Nativelle's digitalin (Nativelle, Adolphe): Medicine. See: Stedman.

Nattier blue (Nattier, Jean-Marc): Fine Arts. See: Partridge; Webster's 3d.

NATTIER, JEAN-MARC. 1685-1766. French painter. See: New Encyc. Brit., 1974, Microp. Nattier blue.

Naumanite (Naumannite) (Naumann, Karl Friedrich): Earth Sciences. See: Thrush; Webster's 3d.

NAUMANN, KARL FRIEDRICH. 1797-1873. German mineralogist. See: Dict. Sci. Biog. Naumanite (Naumannite).

NAUNDORFF, CHARLES GUILLAUME. 1785-1845. French imposter. See: Nouv. Biog. Univ. Naundorff claimant.

Naundorff claimant (Naundorff, Charles Guillaume): History. See: Harbottle.

NAUNYN, BERNARD. 1839-1925. German physician. See: World Who's Who Sci. Naunyn-Minkowski method, Naunyn's centre.

Naunyn-Minkowski method (Naunyn, Bernard and Minkowski, Oscar): Medicine. See: Dorland. Also known as: Minkowski's method.

Naunyn's centre (Naunyn, Bernard): Anatomy. See: Donath.

Navarre, Henry of. See: Henry IV of France.

NAVARRO, ENRIQUE. fl. 1926. Spanish chemist. Cited in: Chem. Abstr., vol. 20, p. 2227. Navarro reagents for alkaloids.

Navarro reagents for alkaloids (Navarro, Enrique): Chemistry. See: Van Nostrand Chem. Dict.

NAVASHIN, SERGEY GAVRILOVICH. 1857-1930. Russian plant physiologist. See: Dict. Sci. Biog. Navashin('s) solution.

Navashin('s) solution (Navashin, Sergey Gavrilovich): Chemistry. See: Hackh; Van Nostrand Chem. Dict.

NAVIER, CLAUDE-LOUIS-MARIE. 1785-1836. French engineer. See: Dict. Sci. Biog. Navier-Stokes equation(s), Navier's hypothesis.

Navier-Stokes equation(s) (Navier, Claude-Louis-Marie and Stokes, Sir George Gabriel): Physics. See: Ballentyne; Huschke; Internat. Dict. Ap. Math.

Navier's hypothesis (Navier, Claude-Louis-Marie): Engineering and Industry. See: Thrush.

Navy-Curtiss machine (Curtiss, Glenn Hammond): Engineering and Industry. See: Jameson.

Naylor spiralarm (Derivation undetermined): Engineering and Industry. See: Thrush.

NAZARI, A. fl. 1911. Italian physician. (Biography source unavailable.) Marchiafava-Nazari-Micheli syndrome.

Neal Dow law (Dow, Neal): History. See: Mathews, S.

NEBECOURT. No dates. French? physician. (Biography source unavailable.) Nebecourt's syndrome.

Nebecourt's syndrome (Nebecourt): Medicine. See: Jablonski.

NEBER, PETER. 1883-1960. German organic chemist. See: Pogg., vols. 6, 7a. Neber reaction.

Neber reaction (Neber, Peter): Chemistry. See: Krauch and Kunz; Van Nostrand Chem. Dict.

Nebuchadnezzar (Nebuchadnezzar II): Generic Word (oversize wine bottle). See: De Sola; Webster's 3d.

NEBUCHADREZZAR (or NEBUCHADNEZZAR) II. ca. 630-562 B.C. King of the Chaldean empire. See: New Encyc. Brit., 1974. Nebuchadnezzar.

NECHELES, HEINRICH. 1897- . German-born American gastroenterologist. See: Amer. Men and Women Sci., 12th ed. Necheles tube?

Necheles tube (Necheles, Heinrich?): Medicine. See: Stedman.

Neck, M. See: Van Neck, M.

NECKE, ALBERT. fl. 1927. German physician. Cited in: Chem. Abstr., vol. 21, p. 1284. Necke-Schmidt-Klostermann reagent for lead.

Necke-Schmidt-Klostermann reagent for lead (Necke, Albert; Schmidt, Paul; and Klostermann, Max): Chemistry. See: Van Nostrand Chem. Dict.

Necker cube (Necker, Louis): Psychology. See: Chaplin; New Encyc. Brit., 1974, Microp.; Wolman.

NECKER, LOUIS. 1730-1804. Swiss physicist and mathematician. See: World Who's Who Sci. Necker cube.

NECKER, NOEL-JOSEPH. 1729-1793. Flemish physician and botanist. See: Nouv. Biog. Univ. Neckera.

Neckera (Necker, Noel-Joseph): Botany. See: Charnock.

Ned Kelly (or as game as Ned Kelly) (Kelly, Ned): Generic Word. See: Hendrickson.

NEEDHAM, JOHN TURBERVILLE. 1713-1781. English naturalist. See: Dict. Sci. Biog. Needhamia (or Needhama), Needham's sac (or organ)?

Needhamia (or Needhama) (Needham, John Turberville): Botany. See: Charnock.

Needham's sac (or organ) (Needham, John Turberville?): Zoology. See: Henderson; Pennak.

NEEDLES, CARL F. 1935- . American pediatrician. See: Direct. Med. Specialists, 1974-1975. Melnick-Needles syndrome.

NEEFF, CHRISTOPHER ERNST. 1782-1849. German physician. See: Biog. Lex. hervorr. Aerzte. Neef's hammer.

Neef's hammer (Neeff, Christopher Ernst): Medicine. See: Dorland.

NEEL, AXEL VALDEMAR. 1878-1952. Danish physician. See: Kraks Bla Bog, 1951. Bing-Neel syndrome.

NEEL, LOUIS EUGENE FELIX. 1904- . French physicist. See: World Who's Who Sci. Neel temperature (or point).

Neel temperature (or point) (Neel, Louis Eugene Felix): Physics. See: Ballentyne; Thewlis; Van Nostrand Sci. Encyc.

NEELSEN, FRIEDRICH CARL ADOLF. 1854-1894. German pathologist. See: Biog. Lex. hervorr. Aerzte, 1880-1930. Ziehl-Neelsen stain.

NEF, JOHN ULRIC. 1862-1915. Swiss-born American chemist. See: Dict. Sci. Biog. Nef ketone ethynation, Nef reaction (or aci-nitroalkane cleavage).

Nef ketone ethynation (Nef, John Ulric): Chemistry. See: Krauch and Kunz.

Nef reaction (or aci-nitroalkane cleavage) (Nef, John Ulric): Chemistry. See: Ballentyne.

NEFTEL, WILLIAM BASIL. 1830-1906. American neurologist. See: Who Was Who Amer., 1961-1968. Neftel's disease.

Neftel's disease (Neftel, William Basil): Medicine. See: Stedman.

NEGRE, G. No dates. French engineer. (Biography source unavailable.) Deville-Negre engine.

NEGRI, ADELCHI. 1876-1912. Italian pathologist. See: Dict. Sci. Biog. Negri bodies.

Negri bodies (Negri, Adelchi): Medicine. See: Dorland; Stedman.

Negri-Jacod syndrome (Negri, Silvio and Jacod, Maurice). See: Jacod's syndrome.

NEGRI, SILVIO. fl. 1935. Italian physician. (Biography source unavailable.) Negri-Jacod syndrome.

NEGRO, CAMILLO. 1861-1927. Italian neurologist. See: Biog. Lex. hervorr. Aerzte, 1880-1930. Negro's phenomenon, Negro's sign.

Negro's phenomenon (Negro, Camillo): Medicine. See: Dorland; Stedman.

Negro's sign (Negro, Camillo): Medicine. See: Dorland.

Negus (Negus, Colonel Francis): Food and Drink. See: Charnock; Hendrickson, Partridge.

NEGUS, COLONEL FRANCIS. d. 1732. English soldier. See: Dict. Nat. Biog. Negus.

NEHER, HENRY VICTOR. 1929- . American physicist. See: Amer. Men and Women Sci., 12th ed. Neher tetrode amplifier?

Neher tetrode amplifier (Neher, Henry Victor?): Electronics. See: Van Nostrand Sci. Encyc.

Nehru jacket (coat or suit) (Nehru, Jawaharlal): Fashion. See: Barnhart (New Eng.); Picken.

NEHRU, JAWAHARLAL. 1889-1964. Indian prime minister. See: New Encyc. Brit., 1974. Nehru jacket (coat or suit).

NEHRU, MOTILAL. 1861-1931. Indian Nationalist leader. See: New Encyc. Brit., 1974, Microp. Nehru report.

Nehru report (Nehru, Motilal): Politics. See: Morris and Irwin.

Neil-Robertson stretcher (Derivation undetermined): Medicine. See: Thrush.

NEILE, WILLIAM. 1637-1670. English mathematician. See: Dict. Nat. Biog. Neil's parabola.

NEILL, CATHERINE ANNIE. 1921- . English-born American cardiologist. See: Amer. Men and Women Sci., 12th ed. Neill-Dingwall syndrome.

Neill-Dingwall syndrome (Neill, Catherine Annie and Dingwall, Mary M.): Medicine. See: Jablonski.

NEILL, MATHER HUMPHREY. 1882-1930. American physician. See: Amer. Men Sci., 4th ed. Neill-Mooser reaction.

Neill-Mooser reaction (Neill, Mather Humphrey and Mooser, Hermann): Medicine. See: Dorland; Stedman.

NEILL, PATRICK. 1776-1851. Scottish botanist. See: Dict. Nat. Biog. Neillia.

NEILL, ROBERT G. fl. 1930-1948. English biologist. Cited in: Chem. Abstr., vol. 24, p. 2642. Moore and Neill sampler.

Neillia (Neill, Patrick): Botany. See: Charnock.

Neil's parabola (Neile, William): Mathematics. See: Ballentyne.

NEISSER, ALBERT LUDWIG SIEGMUND. 1855-1916. German dermatologist. See: Dict. Sci. Biog. Neisseria(e), Neisser's coccus, Neisser's syringe.

Neisser-Doering phenomenon (Neisser, Ernst and Doering, Hans): Medicine. See: Dorland; Stedman.

NEISSER, ERNST. b. 1863. German physician. See: Biog. Lex. hervorr. Aerzte, 1880-1930. Neisser-Doering phenomenon.

NEISSER, MAX. 1869-1938. German bacteriologist. See: World Who's Who Sci. Neisser-Wechsberg phenomenon, Neisser's stain.

Neisser-Wechsberg phenomenon (Neisser, Max and Wechsberg, Friedrich): Medicine. See: Dorland; Stedman.

Neisseria(e) (Neisser, Albert Ludwig Siegmund): Medicine. See: Dorland; Stedman; Van Nostrand Sci. Encyc.; Webster's 3d.

Neisser's coccus (Neisser, Albert Ludwig Siegmund): Medicine. See: Stedman.

isser's stain (Neisser, Max): Medicine. See: Stedman.

isser's syringe (Neisser, Albert Ludwig Siegmund): Medicine. See: Dorland.

LATON, AUGUSTE. 1807-1873. French surgeon. See: World Who's Who . Nelaton's catheter, Nelaton's disease, Nelaton's dislocation, Nelaton's e, Nelaton's probe, Nelaton's sphincter (or fibers), Nelaton's tumor, laton's ulcer.

laton's catheter (Nelaton, Auguste): Medicine. See: Dorland; Stedman.

laton's disease (Nelaton, Auguste): Medicine. See: Jablonski. Also known Dupuytren-Nelaton disease.

laton's dislocation (Nelaton, Auguste): Medicine. See: Stedman.

laton's line (Nelaton, Auguste): Anatomy. See: Donath; Dorland; Stedman. so known as: Roser-Nelaton line.

laton's probe (Nelaton, Auguste): Medicine. See: World Who's Who Sci.

laton's sphincter (or fibers) (Nelaton, Auguste): Anatomy. See: Donath; dman.

laton's tumor (Nelaton, Auguste): Medicine. See: Stedman.

laton's ulcer (Nelaton, Auguste): Medicine. See: Jablonski.

lissen blowpipe reagent (Derivation undetermined): Chemistry. See: Van strand Chem. Dict.

lly Bly (Seaman, Elizabeth Cochrane): Generic Word. See: Hendrickson.

LSON. fl. 20th c. Philosopher. (Biography source unavailable.) Grelling- lson paradox of heterologicality.

lson Act (Nelson, Knute): Politics. See: Smith.

lson Davis separator (Davis, Nelson L.): Engineering and Industry. See: rush.

LSON, EDWARD WILLIAM. 1855-1934. American naturalist. See: Dict. er. Biog., 1st suppl. Nelson's oriole, Nelson's sharp-tailed sparrow (or ch).

LSON, HORATIO, VISCOUNT NELSON. 1758-1805. English naval hero. e: Dict. Nat. Biog. Lord Nelson (battleship), Nelson Mass (or Nelsonmesse), lson Monument, Nelson's blood.

lson hydrogen gauge (Derivation undetermined): Physics. See: Internat. ct. Phys. Elec.

LSON, JAMES BOWMAN. fl. 1945-1967. English physicist. See: Direct. t. Sci., 1966-1967. Nelson-Riley function.

LSON, JOSEPH FREDERICK. 1899- . American chemist. See: Amer. en Sci., 7th ed. Gilman-Nelson reagents.

LSON, KNUTE. 1843-1923. American legislator. See: Biog. Direct. er. Congress. Nelson Act.

lson Mass (or Nelsonmesse) (Nelson, Horatio, Viscount Nelson): Music. e: Apel; Scholes.

lson Monument (Nelson, Horatio, Viscount Nelson): Fine Arts. See: rnhart (Eng. Lit.).

lson-Riley function (Nelson, James Bowman and Riley, Dennis Parker): ysics. See: Ballentyne.

LSON, WARREN OTTO. 1906-1964. American endocrinologist. See: Who as Who Amer., 1961-1968. Heller-Nelson syndrome.

lson's ascites (Derivation undetermined): Medicine. See: Jablonski.

lson's blood (Nelson, Horatio, Viscount Nelson): Generic Word (rum). See: ndrickson.

lson's oriole (Nelson, Edward William): Zoology. See: Mathews, M. M.; ebster's 3d.

lson's sharp-tailed sparrow (or finch) (Nelson, Edward William): Zoology. e: Mathews, M. M.

emertea (or Nemertinea) (Nemertes): Zoology. See: Pennak; Webster's 3d.

NEMERTES. One of the Nereids (sea gods) in Greek mythology. See: Dict. Grk. Rom. Biog. Myth. Nemertea (or Nemertinea), Nemertopsis.

Nemertinea (or Nemertine) (Nemertes, the sea god). See: Nemertea.

Nemertopsis (Nemertes): Zoology. See: Pennak.

Nemesia (Nemesis): Mythology. See: Charnock.

NEMESIS. Goddess of retributive justice in Greek mythology. See: Jobes. Nemesia, Nemesis.

Nemesis (Nemesis, the Greek goddess): Generic Word (agent of retribution). See: Brewer; Funk; Webster's 3d.

NEMIROVICH-DANCHENKO, VLADIMIR IVANOVICH. 1858-1943. Russian stage director, playwright and writer. See: New Encyc. Brit., 1974, Microp. Stanislavsky and Nemirovich-Danchenko Lyric Theatre Ballet Company.

Nemtchinova-Dolin Ballet (Nemtchinova, Vera and Dolin, Anton): Dance. See: Chujoy.

NEMTCHINOVA, VERA. 1903- . Russian-born ballerina and teacher. (Biography source unavailable.) Nemtchinova-Dolin Ballet.

NENADKEVICH, KONSTANTIN AVTONOMOVICH. fl. 1909-1931. Russian mineralogist and geochemist. See: Pogg., vol. 6. Nenadkevichite.

Nenadkevichite (Nenadkevich, Konstantin Avtonomovich): Earth Sciences. See: Thrush.

NENCKI, MARCELI VON. 1847-1901. Polish physician and biochemist. See: Dict. Sci. Biog. Nencki reaction, Nencki's test.

Nencki reaction (Nencki, Marceli von): Chemistry. See: Van Nostrand Chem. Dict.

Nencki's test (Nencki, Marceli von): Chemistry. See: Dorland; Stedman.

NENNI, PIETRO. b. 1891. Italian Socialist leader. See: New Encyc. Brit., 1974, Microp. Nenni telegram.

Nenni telegram (Nenni, Pietro): Politics. See: Brewer.

Neper, John. See: Napier, John, Laird of Merchiston.

Neper (or Napier) (unit) (Napier, John, Laird of Merchiston): Physics. See: Ballentyne; Dresner; Hughes; Markus; Thewlis; Van Nostrand Sci. Encyc.

NEPHI. Son of the Jewish prophet Lehi in the Book of Mormon. (Biography source unavailable.) Nephite.

Nephite (Nephi): Religion. See: Mathews, M. M.; Webster's 3d.

NEPTUNE. Ancient Italian divinity of moisture. See: Jobes. Neptune green, Neptune (or Neptunian), Neptune (pan), Neptune powder?, Neptune shell, Neptunea, Neptune's girdle, Neptune's goblet (or cup), Neptunian (Neptunist or Neptunism), Neptunic (classification)?, Neptunite.

Neptune (or Neptunian) (Neptune): Generic Word (ocean). See: Webster's 3d.

Neptune green (Neptune): Chemistry. See: Webster's 3d.

Neptune (pan) (Neptune): Business. See: Webster's 3d.

Neptune powder (Neptune, the god?): Engineering and Industry. See: Thrush.

Neptune shell (Neptune): Zoology. See: Pennak; Webster's 3d.

Neptunea (Neptune): Zoology. See: Pennak.

Neptune's girdle (Neptune): Medicine. See: Stedman.

Neptune's goblet (or cup) (Neptune): Zoology. See: Gray; Pennak; Webster's 3d.

Neptunian (Neptunist or Neptunism) (Neptune): Earth Sciences. See: Brewer; Thrush; Webster's 3d.

Neptunic (classification) (Neptune, the god?): Earth Sciences. See: Thrush.

Neptunite (Neptune): Earth Sciences. See: Thrush; Webster's 3d.

Nereid (Nereus): Mythology. See: Webster's 3d.

Nereis (Nereus): Zoology. See: Pennak; Webster's 3d.

Nereocystis (Nereus): Botany. See: Webster's 3d.

NEREUS. Greek god of the sea. See: New Encyc. Brit., 1974, Microp. Nereid, Nereis, Nereocystis, Nerine, Nerita.

NERI, B. b. 1882. Italian neurologist. (Biography source unavailable.) Neri's sign.

Neri-Barre syndrome (Neri, V. and Barre, M. J.). See: Barre-Lieou syndrome.

NERI, V. fl. 1924. Italian physician. (Biography source unavailable.) Neri-Barre syndrome.

Nerine (Nereus): Botany. See: Taylor, N.; Webster's 3d.

Neri's sign (Neri, B.): Medicine. See: Stedman.

Nerita (Nereus): Zoology. See: Webster's 3d.

Nernst approximation formula (Nernst, Walther Hermann): Physics. See: Ballentyne; Van Nostrand Sci. Encyc.

Nernst body (Nernst, Walther Hermann): Engineering and Industry. See: Thrush.

Nernst bridge (or high-frequency capacitance bridge) (Nernst, Walther Hermann): Electronics. See: Internat. Dict. Phys. Elec.; Markus; Thewlis.

Nernst calorimeter (Nernst, Walther Hermann): Physics. See: Thewlis; Van Nostrand Sci. Encyc.

Nernst effect (Nernst, Walther Hermann): Physics. See: Ballentyne; Internat. Dict. Phys. Elec.; Thewlis; Van Nostrand Sci. Encyc.; Webster's 3d. Also known as: Nernst-Ettingshausen effect.

Nernst-Einstein relation (Nernst, Walther Hermann and Einstein, Albert): Physics. See: Encyc. Brit., 1973 under "Diffusion."

Nernst equation (for E.M.F.) (Nernst, Walther Hermann): Physics. See: Ballentyne; Thewlis; Van Nostrand Sci. Encyc.

Nernst-Ettingshausen effect (Nernst, Walther Hermann and Ettingshausen, Albert von). See: Nernst effect.

Nernst filament (Nernst, Walther Hermann): Physics. See: Van Nostrand Sci. Encyc.

Nernst film (Nernst, Walther Hermann): Physics. See: Thrush.

Nernst heat theorem (Nernst, Walther Hermann): Physics. See: Ballentyne; Thewlis; Van Nostrand Sci. Encyc.; Webster's 3d.

Nernst lamp (or glower) (Nernst, Walther Hermann): Physics. See: Internat. Dict. Phys. Elec.; Thewlis; Van Nostrand Sci. Encyc.; Webster's 3d.

Nernst law (or distribution law) (Nernst, Walther Hermann): Physics. See: Ballentyne; Hackh; Internat. Dict. Ap. Math.

Nernst-Lillie theory (Nernst, Walther Hermann and Lillie, Ralph Stayner). See: Nernst('s) theory.

Nernst-Lindemann equation (Nernst, Walther Hermann and Lindemann, Frederick Alexander): Physics. See: Ballentyne.

Nernst-Lindemann theory of specific heats (Nernst, Walther Hermann and Lindemann, Frederick Alexander): Physics. See: Thewlis.

Nernst principle of superposition (Nernst, Walther Hermann): Physics. See: Van Nostrand Sci. Encyc.

Nernst-Simon statement of the third law of thermodynamics (Nernst, Walther Hermann and Simon, Sir Francis Eugene): Physics. See: Ballentyne.

Nernst solution pressure (Nernst, Walther Hermann): Physics. See: Ballentyne.

Nernst('s) theory (Nernst, Walther Hermann): Medicine. See: Dorland; Hackh; Stedman. Also known as: Nernst-Lillie theory.

Nernst-Thomson rule (Nernst, Walther Hermann and Thomson, Sir Joseph John): Physics. See: Ballentyne; Van Nostrand Sci. Encyc.

Nernst unit (Nernst, Walther Hermann): Physics. See: Hackh.

NERNST, WALTHER HERMANN. 1864-1941. German physical chemist. See: World Who's Who Sci. law of Berthelot-Nernst, Nernst approximation formula, Nernst body, Nernst bridge (or high-frequency capacitance bridge), Nernst calorimeter, Nernst effect, Nernst-Einstein relation, Nernst equation (for E.M.F.), Nernst filament, Nernst film, Nernst heat theorem, Nernst lamp (or glower), Nernst law (or distribution law), Nernst-Lindemann equation, Nernst-Lindemann theory of specific heats, Nernst principle of superposition, Nernst-Simon statement of the third law of thermodynamics, Nernst solution pressure, Nernst('s) theory, Nernst-Thomson rule, Nernst unit, Nernst zero of potential, Nernst's law.

Nernst zero of potential (Nernst, Walther Hermann): Physics. See: Ballentyne.

Nernst's law (Nernst, Walther Hermann): Physics. See: Thrush.

NERO (LUCIUS DOMITIUS AHENOBARBUS). 37-68. Roman emperor. See: New Encyc. Brit., 1974. Nero (Neronian, Neronic, or Neronize), Nero's crown.

Nero (Neronian, Neronic, or Neronize) (Nero): Generic Word (cruel tyrant). See: Brewer; Hendrickson; Webster's 3d.

Nerole, Princess of. See: Tremoille, Anna Maria de la (Princess of Nerole).

Neroli oil (Tremoille, Anna Maria de la): Botany. See: Partridge; Stedman; Webster's 3d.

Nero's crown (Nero): Botany. See: Gray; Hendrickson. Also known as: Adam's apple tree.

nerve of Lancisi (Lancisi, Giovanni Maria). See: Lancisi's striae (streaks, nerves or nerve of Lancisi).

nerve of Wrisberg (Wrisberg, Heinrich August). See: Wrisberg's nerve.

NESMAYANOV, ALEXANDR NIKOLAEVITCH. 1899- . Russian organic chemist. See: World Who's Who Sci. Nesmeyanov reaction.

Nesmeyanov reaction (Nesmayanov, Alexandr Nikolaevitch): Chemistry. See: Ballentyne; Krauch and Kunz.

NESS, HELGE. 1861-1928. American horticulturist. See: Amer. Men Sci., 4th ed. Nessberry.

Nessberry (Ness, Helge): Botany. See: Webster's 3d.

NESSELRODE, COUNT KARL ROBERT VASILIEVICH. 1780-1862. Russian statesman. See: New Encyc. Brit., 1974, Microp. Nesselrode (pudding or pie).

Nesselrode (pudding or pie) (Nesselrode, Count Karl Robert Vasilievich): Food and Drink. See: De Sola; Mathews, M. M.; Webster's 3d.

NESSLER, JULIUS. 1827-1905. German agricultural chemist. See: World Who's Who Sci. Nessler(s) reagent, Nessler reagent for wine, Nessler(s) test, Nessler tube, Nesslerize (or Nesslerization).

Nessler(s) reagent (Nessler, Julius): Chemistry. See: Dorland; Hackh; Stedman; Van Nostrand Chem. Dict.; Webster's 3d.

Nessler reagent for wine (Nessler, Julius): Chemistry. See: Van Nostrand Chem. Dict.

Nessler(s) test (Nessler, Julius): Chemistry. See: Hackh; Van Nostrand Chem. Dict.

Nessler tube (Nessler, Julius): Chemistry. See: Van Nostrand Chem. Dict.; Webster's 3d.

Nesslerize (or Nesslerization) (Nessler, Julius): Chemistry. See: Stedman; Webster's 3d.

Nessus (Nessus, the Centaur): Generic Word (inescapable misfortune). See: Jobes.

NESSUS, THE CENTAUR. Centaur in Greek mythology. See: Dict. Grk. Rom. Biog. Myth. Nessus.

Nestor (Nestor, the King): Generic Word (wise old man). See: Hendrickson; Phyfe; Webster's 3d.

Nestor (or Nestorine) parrot (Nestor, the King): Zoology. See: Webster's 3d.

NESTOR, THE KING. In Greek legend, King of Pylos. See: New Encyc. Brit., 1974, Microp. Nestor, Nestor (or Nestorine) parrot.

Nestorians (or Nestorianism) (Nestorius): Religion. See: Attwater; Canney; Mathews, S.; Webster's 3d.

NESTORIUS. d. ca. 451. Patriarch of Constantinople. See: New Encyc. Brit., 1974. Nestorians (or Nestorianism).

NETHERTON, EARL WELDON. b. 1893. American dermatologist. See: Direct. Med. Specialists, 1965-1966. Netherton's disease.

Netherton's disease (Netherton, Earl Weldon): Medicine. See: Jablonski.

NETTLESHIP, EDWARD. 1845-1913. English dermatologist and ophthalmic surgeon. See: World Who's Who Sci. Nettleship's syndrome.

Nettleship's syndrome (Nettleship, Edward): Medicine. See: Dorland; Jablonski; Stedman.

Nettleton method (Derivation undetermined): Engineering and Industry. See: Thrush.

eubauer-Fischer test (Neubauer, Otto and Fischer, Hans): Medicine. See: rland.

NEUBAUER, JOHANN ERNST. 1742-1777. German anatomist. See: Biog. x. hervorr. Aerzte. Neubauer's artery.

EUBAUER, OTTO. b. 1874. German physician. See: Biog. Lex. hervorr. erzte, 1880-1930. Neubauer-Fischer test, Neubauer probe.

eubauer probe (Neubauer, Otto): Medicine. Cited in: Biog. Lex. hervorr. erzte, 1880-1930.

eubauer's artery (Neubauer, Johann Ernst): Anatomy. See: Donath; Dorland; edman.

EUBER, FRITZ. fl. 1923-1938. German chemist. Cited in: Chem. Abstr., l. 17, p. 2687. Feigl-Neuber test for mercury, Feigl-Neuber test for tin, eigl-Neuber tests for copper.

EUBER, GUSTAV ADOLF. 1850-1932. German surgeon. See: World Who's ho Sci. Neuber's treatment, Neuber's tubes.

EUBER, HEINZ AUGUST PAUL. 1906-   . German engineer. See: Who's ho Sci. Europe, 1972. Neuber-Papkovich stress functions?

euber-Papkovich stress functions (Neuber, Heinz August Paul? and Papkovich, etr Fedorovich): Mathematics. See: Internat. Dict. Ap. Math.

euberg-Behren reagent for isolating sugars (Neuberg, Carl and Behrens, Martin): hemistry. See: Van Nostrand Chem. Dict.

NEUBERG, CARL. 1877-1956. German biochemist. See: Pogg., vols. 4, 5, , 7a. Loewy-Neuberg test reaction, Mandel-Neuberg reagent for aldo- nd keto acids, Neuberg-Behren reagent for isolating sugars, Neuberg ester, euberg reaction for formaldehyde, Neuberg reagent for aliphatic alcohols and mino acids.

euberg ester (Neuberg, Carl): Chemistry. See: Hackh.

Neuberg-Rauchwerger test reaction (Derivation undetermined): Chemistry. ee: Van Nostrand Chem. Dict.

Neuberg reaction for formaldehyde (Neuberg, Carl): Chemistry. See: Van Nostrand Chem. Dict.

Neuberg reagent for aliphatic alcohols and amino acids (Neuberg, Carl): Chemistry. See: Van Nostrand Chem. Dict.

Neuber's treatment (Neuber, Gustav Adolf): Medicine. See: Dorland.

Neuber's tubes (Neuber, Gustav Adolf): Medicine. See: Dorland.

Neufeld capsular swelling (or reaction) (Neufeld, Fred): Medicine. See: Dorland; Stedman.

NEUFELD, FRED. 1861-1945. German bacteriologist. See: World Who's Who Sci. Neufeld capsular swelling (or reaction).

Neuhauser-Berenberg syndrome (Neuhauser, Edward Blaine and Berenberg, William): Medicine. See: Jablonski.

NEUHAUSER, EDWARD BLAINE. 1908-   . American physician. See: Amer. Men Sci., 9th ed. Neuhauser-Berenberg syndrome.

Neukomm's test (Derivation undetermined): Medicine. See: Stedman.

NEUMANN, ALFRED. fl. 1928. German physician. Cited in: Chem. Abstr., vol. 22, p. 1166. Charcot-Neumann crystals.

Neumann band (lamellae or lines) (Neumann, Franz Ernst): Earth Sciences. See: Thrush; Van Nostrand Sci. Encyc.

Neumann-Bernays-Goedel axioms (Neumann, John von; Bernays, Paul; and Goedel, Kurt): Mathematics. See: New Encyc. Brit., 1974, Microp.

Neumann boundary conditions (Neumann, Karl Gottfried?): Mathematics. See: Internat. Dict. Phys. Elec.

NEUMANN, ERNST F. C. 1834-1918. German pathologist. See: Biog. Lex. hervorr. Aerzte. Neumann's cells, Neumann's sheath, Neumann's syn- drome, Rouget-Neumann sheath.

Neumann formula for Legendre functions of the second kind (Neumann, Franz Ernst): Mathematics. See: James.

NEUMANN, FRANZ ERNST. 1798-1895. German mineralogist, physicist, and mathematician. See: World Who's Who Sci. Neumann band (lamellae or lines), Neumann formula for Legendre functions of the second kind, Neumann- Kopp rule, Neumann('s) (Neuman) principle, Neumann's expansion?, Neumann's formula, Neumann's law (1), Neumann's law (2) (or law of Neumann), Wood- Neumann scale?

Neumann function (1) (Neumann, Karl Gottfried): Mathematics. See: Internat. Dict. Ap. Math.; James; Thewlis.

Neumann('s) function (2) (or problem) (Neumann, Karl Gottfried): Mathematics. See: Ballentyne; Internat. Dict. Ap. Math.; James.

NEUMANN, HEINRICH. 1873-1939. Austrian otologist. See: Biog. Lex. hervorr. Aerzte, 1880-1930. Neumann's method.

NEUMANN, ISIDOR EDLER VON HEILWART. 1832-1906. Austrian dermatol- ogist. See: Biog. Lex. hervorr. Aerzte. Neumann's aphthosis, Neumann's disease.

NEUMANN, JOHN VON. 1903-1957. Hungarian-born American mathemati- cian and scientist. See: Internat. Encyc. Soc. Sci. Neumann-Bernays- Goedel axioms, Von Neumann algebras, Von Neumann matrix, Von Neumann spike?, Von Neumann-Wigner rule, Von Neumann's ratio.

NEUMANN, KARL GOTTFRIED. 1832-1925. German mathematician. See: Dict. Sci. Biog. Liouville-Neumann series?, Neumann boundary conditions?, Neumann function (1), Neumann('s) function (2) (or problem).

Neumann-Kopp rule (Neumann, Franz Ernst and Kopp, Hermann Franz Moritz): Physics. See: Ballentyne. Also known as: Kopp-Neumann law.

Neumann('s) (Neuman) principle (Neumann, Franz Ernst): Earth Sciences. See: Ballentyne; Hughes; Internat. Dict. Phys. Elec.

Neumann reversion reaction (Derivation undetermined): Chemistry. See: Van Nostrand Chem. Dict.

Neumann('s) series (Neumann, Karl Gottfried?). See: Liouville-Neumann series.

Neumann's aphthosis (Neumann, Isidor Edler von Heilwart). See: Stevens- Johnson syndrome.

Neumann's cells (Neumann, Ernst F. C.): Anatomy. See: Donath; Dorland; Stedman.

Neumann's disease (Neumann, Isidor Edler von Heilwart): Medicine. See: Dorland; Jablonski; Stedman.

Neumann's expansion (Neumann, Franz Ernst?): Mathematics. See: Ballentyne.

Neumann's formula (Neumann, Franz Ernst): Physics. See: Ballentyne.

Neumann's law (1) (Neumann, Franz Ernst): Physics. See: Ballentyne.

Neumann's law (2) (or law of Neumann) (Neumann, Franz Ernst): Chemistry. See: Dorland; Stedman; Van Nostrand Chem. Dict.

Neumann's method (Neumann, Heinrich): Medicine. See: Dorland.

Neumann's method for organic phosphorus (Derivation undetermined): Chemistry. See: Ballentyne.

Neumann's sheath (Neumann, Ernst F. C.): Anatomy. See: Dorland; Stedman.

Neumann's syndrome (Neumann, Ernst F. C.): Medicine. See: Jablonski.

Neureither, F. von. See: Von Neureither, F.

Neusser, Edmund von. See: Von Neusser, Edmund.

Neusser's granules (Von Neusser, Edmund): Medicine. See: Dorland; Stedman.

neutral Hagedorn insulin suspension (Hagedorn, Hans Christian): Medicine. See: Stedman.

neutral protamine Hagedorn insulin injection (Hagedorn, Hans Christian): Medi- cine. See: Stedman.

NEVE, ERNEST FREDERIC. 1861-1946. English physician in Kashmir. See: Who Was Who, 1941-1950. Neve's cancer.

Neve's cancer (Neve, Ernest Frederic): Medicine. See: Jablonski.

Nevile and Winther's acid (Nevile, R. H. C. and Winther, Adolf): Chemistry. See: Webster's 3d.

NEVILE, R. H. C. fl. 1880. English chemist. Cited in: Royal Soc. Cat. Sci. Pap., 1874-1883. Nevile and Winther's acid.

Neville boiler (Neville, J.): Engineering and Industry. See: Auger.

NEVILLE, J. fl. 1826. English? engineer. (Biography source unavailable.) Neville boiler.

Neville method of interpolation (Derivation undetermined): Mathematics. See: Internat. Dict. Ap. Math.

NEVIN, SAMUEL. 1905- . English neurologist. See: Med. Direct., 1972. Kiloh-Nevin syndrome, Nevin's syndrome.

Nevin's syndrome (Nevin, Samuel): Medicine. See: Jablonski.

NEVIUS, REUBEN DENTON. 1827-1913. American botanist. See: Biog. Notes Upon Botanists. Neviusia.

Neviusia (Nevius, Reuben Denton): Botany. See: Taylor, N.

Nevski, Alexander. See: Alexander Nevski.

new Lowe coke oven system (Lowe, Thaddeus S. C.): Engineering and Industry. See: World Who's Who Sci.

NEWALL, J. W. fl. 1902. Engineer. (Biography source unavailable.) Newall tolerance system.

Newall tolerance system (Newall, J. W.): Engineering and Industry. See: Auger.

Newaygo screen (Derivation undetermined): Engineering and Industry. See: Thrush.

NEWBERY, J. COSMO. fl. ca. 1880. Australian mineralogist. Cited in: Hintze, vol. 1, pt. 4, half 2, p. 805. Newberyite (or Newberite).

NEWBERY, JOHN. 1713-1767. English publisher. See: Dict. Nat. Biog. Newbery Medal (awards).

Newbery Medal (awards) (Newbery, John): Literature. See: Good; Harrod.

Newberyite (or Newberite) (Newbery, J. Cosmo): Earth Sciences. See: Thrush; Webster's 3d.

Newcastle, 5th Duke of. See: Clinton, Henry Pelham Fiennes Pelham (5th Duke of Newcastle).

Newcastle Commission (Clinton, Henry Pelham Fiennes Pelham): Education. See: Montgomery; Steinberg under "Education Acts."

Newcomen engine (Newcomen, Thomas): Engineering and Industry. See: Auger.

NEWCOMEN, MATTHEW. 1610?-1669. English Noncomformist divine. See: Dict. Nat. Biog. Smectymnians.

NEWCOMEN, THOMAS. 1663-1729. English blacksmith and inventor. See: Dict. Sci. Biog. Newcomen engine.

Newdigate Prize (Newdigate, Sir Roger): Literature. See: Barnhart (Eng. Lit.)

NEWDIGATE, SIR ROGER. 1719-1806. English antiquary. See: Dict. Nat. Biog. Newdigate Prize.

Newell lock (Newell, M.): Engineering and Industry. See: Auger; New Encyc. Brit., 1974, Microp.

NEWELL, M. fl. 19th c. American inventor. (Biography source unavailable.) Newell lock.

Newell solution (Derivation undetermined): Chemistry. See: Van Nostrand Chem. Dict.

Newell's shearwater (Derivation undetermined): Zoology. See: Gray.

Newhouse crusher (Newhouse, Ray C.): Engineering and Industry. See: Thrush.

NEWHOUSE, RAY C. fl. 1945. American engineer. Cited in: Chem. Abstr., Decenn. Index, 1937-1946. Newhouse crusher.

NEWLAND, ABRAHAM. 1730-1807. English bank cashier. See: Dict. Nat. Biog. Abraham Newland(s).

Newlands Act (Newlands, Francis Griffith): Politics. See: Morris.

NEWLANDS, FRANCIS GRIFFITH. 1848-1917. American legislator. See: Biog. Direct. Amer. Congress. Newlands Act.

NEWLANDS, JOHN ALEXANDER REINA. 1837-1898. English chemist. See: Dict. Sci. Biog. Newland's law of octaves.

Newland's law of octaves (Newlands, John Alexander Reina): Chemistry. See: Ballentyne.

NEWMAN, ARTHUR SAMUEL. 1862-1943. English designer of photographic and cinematographic apparatus. See: Focal Encyc. Photog. Newman Lecture, Newman Memorial Award (or plaque).

Newman barometer (Derivation undetermined): Physics. See: Thewlis.

NEWMAN, D. fl. 1939. English statistician. Cited in: Kendall and Doig. Newman-Keuls test.

NEWMAN, JOHN HENRY. 1801-1890. English theologian. See: Dict. Nat. Biog. Newmanism (or Newmanite).

Newman-Keuls test (Newman, D. and Keuls, M.): Statistics. See: Kendall.

Newman Lecture (Newman, Arthur Samuel): Photography. Cited in: Focal Encyc. Photog. under "Newman, Arthur Samuel."

Newman limestone (Derivation undetermined): Earth Sciences. See: Thrush.

Newman Memorial Award (or plaque) (Newman, Arthur Samuel): Photography. See: Focal Encyc. Photog. under "Awards (Britain)."

Newmanism (or Newmanite) (Newman, John Henry): Religion. See: Webster's 3d.

Newmann hearth (Derivation undetermined): Engineering and Industry. See: Thrush.

NEWSOM, SIR JOHN H. fl. 1963. English educator. See: London Times, Oct. 17, 1963, p. 6, col. c. Newsom Report.

Newsom Report (Newsom, Sir John H.): Education. See: Harrod.

Newson's boring method (Derivation undetermined): Engineering and Industry. See: Thrush.

Newton('s) approximation method (or method for solution of equations) (Newton, Isaac): Mathematics. See: Ballentyne; Internat. Dict. Ap. Math.; Internat. Dict. Phys. Elec. Also known as: Newton-Raphson method.

Newton-Cotes formula (or quadrature formulas) (Newton, Isaac and Cotes, Roger): Mathematics. See: Ballentyne; Internat. Dict. Ap. Math.; Van Nostrand Sci. Encyc.

Newton('s) equation (for conjugate distances) (or Newtonian lens equation) (Newton, Isaac): Physics. See: Ballentyne; Internat. Dict. Ap. Math.; Internat. Dict. Phys. Elec.

Newton-Gauss interpolation formula(s) (Newton, Isaac and Gauss, Carl Friedrich): Mathematics. See: Ballentyne; Internat. Dict. Ap. Math.

Newton-Gregory interpolation formula (Newton, Sir Isaac and Gregory, James). See: Gregory-Newton formula (or formula for interpolation).

NEWTON, HENRY JOTHAM. 1823-1895. American inventor. See: World Who's Who Sci. Newton's camera.

Newton('s) interpolation formula(s) (or formula for interpolation) (Newton, Isaac): Mathematics. See: Ballentyne; Internat. Dict. Ap. Math.; Van Nostrand Sci. Encyc. Also known as: Gregory-Newton interpolation formula.

NEWTON, ISAAC. 1642-1727. English mathematician and astronomer. See: Dict. Sci. Biog. Cassegrain-Newtonian telescope, Isaac Newton telescope, Newton('s) approximation method (or method for solution of equations), Newton-Cotes formula (or quadrature formulas), Newton('s) equation (for conjugate distances) (or Newtonian lens equation), Newton-Gauss interpolation formula(s), Newton('s) interpolation formula(s) (or formula for interpolation), Newton('s) law of cooling, Newton('s) law of gravitation, Newton('s) law of resistance (fluid resistance or fluid friction), Newton('s) laws of motion, Newton('s) rings, Newton-Stirling interpolation formula(s), Newton('s) theory of light (or emission theory), Newton (unit), Newtonian, Newtonian fluid (liquid or viscosity), Newtonian focus, Newtonian force, Newtonian friction law (or Newton's formula for the stress), Newtonian mechanics, Newtonian (philosophy) (or Newtonianism), Newtonian potential (function), Newtonian relativity, Newtonian telescope, Newton's alloy (or metal), Newton's disk, Newton's equation (for the velocity of sound) (or Newtonian speed of sound), Newton's fits, Newton's identities (for sums of powers of roots), Newton's inequality, Newton's law of colour mixture, Newton's law of hydrodynamic resistance, Newton's law of motion for rotation, Newton's law of similarity, Newton's theory of lift, Newton's three-eighths rule, non-Newtonian flow, non-Newtonian liquids, old Newton, trident of Newton.

Newton('s) law of cooling (Newton, Isaac): Physics. See: Ballentyne; Thewlis; Van Nostrand Sci. Encyc.; Webster's 3d.

Newton('s) law of gravitation (Newton, Isaac): Physics. See: Ballentyne; Satterthwaite; Thewlis.

Newton('s) law of resistance (fluid resistance or fluid friction) (Newton, Isaac): Physics. See: Ballentyne; Internat. Dict. Ap. Math.; Van Nostrand Sci. Encyc.

Newton('s) laws of motion (Newton, Isaac): Physics. See: Huschke; Internat. Dict. Phys. Elec.; Satterthwaite; Thewlis.

Newton-Raphson method (Newton, Sir Isaac and Raphson, Joseph). See: Newton('s) approximation method (or method for solution of equations).

Newton('s) rings (Newton, Isaac): Physics. See: Ballentyne; Focal Encyc. Photog.; Thewlis; Van Nostrand Sci. Encyc.; Webster's 3d.

Newton–Stirling interpolation formula(s) (Newton, Isaac and Stirling, James): Mathematics. See: Stirling formula for interpolation.

Newton('s) theory of light (or emission theory) (Newton, Isaac): Physics. See: Ballentyne; Internat. Dict. Phys. Elec.

Newton (unit) (Newton, Isaac): Physics. See: Dresner; Van Nostrand Sci. Encyc.; Webster's 3d.

Newtonian (Newton, Isaac): Generic Word (simple grandeur). See: Partridge.

Newtonian–Cassegrain telescope (Newton, Isaac and Cassegrain, Giovanni D.). See: Cassegrain–Newtonian telescope.

Newtonian fluid (liquid or viscosity) (Newton, Isaac): Physics. See: Huschke; Internat. Dict. Ap. Math.; Internat. Dict. Phys. Elec.; Thewlis; Webster's 3d.

Newtonian focus (Newton, Isaac): Astronomy. See: Satterthwaite.

Newtonian force (Newton, Isaac): Physics. See: Webster's 3d.

Newtonian friction law (or Newton's formula for the stress) (Newton, Isaac): Physics. See: Huschke; Van Nostrand Sci. Encyc.

Newtonian mechanics (Newton, Isaac): Physics. See: Huschke; Internat. Dict. Ap. Math.; Internat. Dict. Phys. Elec; Webster's 3d.

Newtonian (philosophy) (or Newtonianism) (Newton, Isaac): Astronomy. See: Brewer; Webster's 3d.

Newtonian potential (function) (Newton, Isaac): Mathematics. See: James; Van Nostrand Sci. Encyc.; Webster's 3d.

Newtonian relativity (Newton, Isaac): Physics. See: Internat. Dict. Ap. Math.

Newtonian telescope (Newton, Isaac): Astronomy. See: Satterthwaite; Thewlis; Van Nostrand Sci. Encyc.; Webster's 3d.

Newton's alloy (or metal) (Newton, Isaac): Earth Sciences. See: Partridge; Thrush. Also known as: D'Arcet's metal, Lichtenberg's alloy, Melotte's (Melott's) metal.

Newton's camera (Newton, Henry Jotham): Photography. See: Focal Encyc. Photog. under "Camera History," p. 139.

Newton's disk (Newton, Isaac): Physics. See: Dorland; Stedman; Webster's 3d.

Newton's equation (for the velocity of sound) (or Newtonian speed of sound) (Newton, Isaac): Physics. See: Ballentyne; Huschke.

Newton's fits (Newton, Isaac): Physics. See: Blumberg.

Newton's identities (for sums of powers of roots) (Newton, Isaac): Mathematics. See: Ballentyne; James.

Newton's inequality (Newton, Isaac): Mathematics. See: James.

Newton's law of colour mixture (Newton, Isaac): Physics. See: Drever.

Newton's law of hydrodynamic resistance (Newton, Isaac): Physics. See: Van Nostrand Sci. Encyc.

Newton's law of motion for rotation (Newton, Isaac): Physics. See: Van Nostrand Sci. Encyc. under "Gyroscope."

Newton's law of similarity (Newton, Isaac): Physics. See: Van Nostrand Sci. Encyc. under "Similitude."

Newton's theory of lift (Newton, Isaac): Physics. See: Ballentyne.

Newton's three-eighths rule (Newton, Isaac): Mathematics. See: Ballentyne; James.

Neyman allocation (Neyman, Jerzy): Statistics. See: Kendall.

NEYMAN, JERZY. 1894– . Rumanian-born American statistician. See: World Who's Who Sci. Bates–Neyman model, Johnson–Neyman method, Neyman allocation, Neyman model, Neyman–Pearson theory (or hypothesis), Neyman-shortest unbiassed confidence intervals, Neyman's psi^2 test.

Neyman model (Neyman, Jerzy): Statistics. See: Kendall.

Neyman–Pearson theory (or hypothesis) (Neyman, Jerzy and Pearson, Egon Sharpe): Statistics. See: Internat. Dict. Ap. Math; Kendall; Wolman.

Neyman-shortest unbiassed confidence intervals (Neyman, Jerzy): Statistics. See: Kendall.

Neyman's psi^2 test (Neyman, Jerzy): Statistics. See: Kendall.

NICANDER (NIKANDER or NIKANDROS). Ancient Greek poet of Colophon. See: Dict. Grk. Rom. Biog. Myth. Nicandra.

Nicandra (Nicander): Botany. See: Taylor, N.

NICHIREN. 1222–1282. Japanese saint and prophet. See: Encyc. Brit., 1973. Nichiren (sect).

Nichiren (sect) (Nichiren): Religion. See: Canney; Webster's 3d.

NICHOLAS IV. 1227–1292. Italian pope. See: Encyc. Brit., 1973. Pope Nicholas' taxation.

NICHOLAS OF MYRA, SAINT. d. ca. 352. Bishop in Asia Minor. See: New Encyc. Brit., 1974, Microp. Saint Nicholas bishop, Saint Nicholas's clerk (1), Saint Nicholas's clerk (2), Santa Claus, Santa Claus suit.

Nicholls' technique (Derivation undetermined): Earth Sciences. See: Thrush.

Nichols chart (Derivation undetermined): Computer Science. See: Van Nostrand Sci. Encyc.

Nichols–Cooper reagent (Nichols, Melvin Lorrel and Cooper, Stewart Rochester): Chemistry. See: Van Nostrand Chem. Dict.

NICHOLS, ERNEST FOX. 1869–1924. American physicist. See: Dict. Sci. Biog. Nichols radiometer.

NICHOLS, MARK LOVEL. 1888–1971. American agricultural engineer. See: Who Was Who Amer., 1969–1973. Nichols terrace.

Nichols medal (Nichols, William Henry): Chemistry. See: Hackh.

NICHOLS, MELVIN LORREL. b. 1894. American chemist. See: Pogg., vol. 6. Nichols–Cooper reagent.

Nichols radiometer (Nichols, Ernest Fox): Physics. See: Van Nostrand Sci. Encyc.

Nichols terrace (Nichols, Mark Lovel): Agriculture. See: Webster's 3d.; Winburne.

NICHOLS, WILLIAM HENRY. 1852–1930. American industrial chemist. See: Who Was Who Amer., 1897–1942. Nichols medal.

NICHOLSON. fl. ca. 1918. American mining engineer. Cited in: Hintze, vol. I, pt. 3, half 1, p. 3016. Nicholsonite.

NICHOLSON. No dates. American inventor. (Biography source unavailable.) Nicholson (pavement).

Nicholson (pavement) (Nicholson): Engineering and Industry. See: Mathews, M. M.

NICHOLSON, WILLIAM. 1753–1815. English scientist. See: World Who's Who Sci. Nicholson's hydrometer, Nicholson's projected machine?

Nicholsonite (Nicholson): Earth Sciences. See: Thrush.

Nicholson's hydrometer (Nicholson, William): Physics. See: Webster's 3d.

Nicholson's projected machine (Nicholson, William?): Printing. See: Lockwood, p. 447.

Nick Carter (Carter, Nick): Generic Word (resourceful detective). See: Partridge.

Nickerson–Kveim test (Nickerson and Kveim, Morton A.). See: Kveim test.

NICKLES, JEROME (In full: FRANCOIS JOSEPH JEROME). 1821–1869. French chemist. See: Pogg., vols. 2, 3. Nickle's test.

Nickle's test (Nickles, Jerome): Chemistry. See: Dorland; Stedman.

NICLAUSSE, ALBERT. fl. 1890–1907. French engineer. Cited in: Chem. Abstr., Decenn. Index, 1907–1916. Niclausse boiler.

Niclausse boiler (Niclausse, Albert): Engineering and Industry. See: Auger.

Nicodemite (Nicodemus): Religion. See: Webster's 3d.

NICODEMUS. Jewish ruler who came to Jesus by night. See: Hastings (Dict. Bible). Nicodemite, Nicodemus complex.

Nicodemus complex (Nicodemus): Psychology. See: Partridge.

Nicol prism (Nicol, William): Physics. See: Hughes; Stedman; Thewlis; Thrush; Van Nostrand Sci. Encyc.

NICOL, WILLIAM. 1768–1851. Scottish physicist and geologist. See: Dict. Sci. Biog. Nicol prism.

NICOLAIER, ARTHUR. b. 1862. German physician. See: World Who's Who Sci. Nicolaier's bacillus.

Nicolaier's bacillus (Nicolaier, Arthur): Medicine. See: Dorland; Stedman.

Nicolaitan(s) (Nicolaus): Religion. See: Hastings (Dict. Rel. Ethics), Mathews, S.; Webster's 3d.

Nicolas-Favre disease (Nicolas, Joseph and Favre, Maurice). See: Durand-Nicolas-Favre disease.

NICOLAS, JOSEPH. b. 1868. French physician. See: Biog. Lex. hervorr. Aerzte, 1880-1930. Durand-Nicolas-Favre disease, Nicolas-Moutot-Charlet syndrome.

Nicolas-Moutot-Charlet syndrome (Nicolas, Joseph; Moutot, Henry; Charlet, Henri): Medicine. See: Jablonski.

Nicolau-Hoigne syndrome (Nicolau, Stefan Gheorge and Hoigne, Rolf Victor): Medicine. See: Jablonski.

NICOLAU, STEFAN GHEORGE. b. 1874. Rumanian dermatologist. See: World Who's Who Sci. Nicolau-Hoigne syndrome.

NICOLAUS (NICOLAS). Proselyte of Antioch in the New Testament. See: Hastings (Dict. Bible). Nicolaitan(s).

NICOLLE, CHARLES JULES HENRI. 1866-1936. French bacteriologist. See: World Who's Who Sci. Nicolle's stain for capsules, Nicolle's white mycetoma, Nicollia.

Nicolle's stain for capsules (Nicolle, Charles Jules Henri): Medicine. See: Stedman.

Nicolle's white mycetoma (Nicolle, Charles Jules Henri): Medicine. See: Stedman.

Nicollia (Nicolle, Charles Jules Henri): Zoology. See: Dorland.

NICOMEDES. fl. 2d c. B.C. Greek mathematician. See: Encyc. Brit., 1973. conchoid of Nicomedes.

NICOT, JEAN. 1530?-1600. French diplomat and scholar. See: Dict. Sci. Biog. Nicotian, Nicotiana, Nicotine.

Nicotian (Nicot, Jean): Generic Word (tobacco). See: Partridge.

Nicotiana (Nicot, Jean): Botany. See: Encyc. Brit., 1973; Taylor, N.; Webster's 3d.

Nicotine (Nicot, Jean): Chemistry. See: Funk; Hendrickson; Stenhouse; Winburne.

NIEL, ADOLPHE. 1802-1869. French marshal. See: Encyc. Brit., 1973. Marechal Niel (rose).

NIELSEN, ARTHUR CHARLES. 1897- . American business executive. See: Who's Who Amer., 1974-1975. Nielson rating.

NIELSEN, HERMAN. 1882-1960. Danish physician. See: Kraks Bla Bog, 1959. Nielsen's disease.

NIELSEN, HOLGER. 1866-1955. Danish army officer. See: Danmarks hist. bla bog. Nielsen method, Schafer-Nielsen-Drinker method.

NIELSEN, JOHANNES MYGAARD. 1890-1969. Danish-born American neurologist and psychiatrist. See: Who Was Who Amer., 1969-1973. Nielsen's syndrome.

Nielsen method (Nielsen, Holger): Medicine. See: Stedman; Webster's 3d. Also known as: Holger-Nielsen method.

Nielsen's disease (Nielsen, Herman): Medicine. See: Jablonski.

Nielsen's syndrome (Nielsen, Johannes Mygaard): Medicine. See: Jablonski.

Nielson rating (Nielsen, Arthur Charles): Mass Media. See: Hendrickson; Time, vol. 95 (May 25, 1970), p. 98.

NIEMANN, ALBERT. 1880-1921. German surgeon. See: World Who's Who Sci. Niemann-Pick cell, Niemann-Pick disease.

Niemann-Pick cell (Niemann, Albert and Pick, Ludwig). See: Pick cell.

Niemann-Pick disease (Niemann, Albert and Pick, Ludwig): Medicine. See: Hinsie; Jablonski; Stedman; Webster's 3d. Also known as: Niemann's disease.

Niemann's disease (Niemann, Albert). See: Niemann-Pick disease.

Niementowski quinazoline reaction (Niementowski, Stephan Dominik Ritter von): Chemistry. See: Van Nostrand Chem. Dict.

Niementowski quinoline synthesis (Niementowski, Stephan Dominik Ritter von): Chemistry. See: Krauch and Kunz; Van Nostrand Chem. Dict.

NIEMENTOWSKI, STEPHAN DOMINIK RITTER VON. 1866-1925. Polish chemist. See: Pogg., vols. 4, 5, 6. Niementowski quinazoline reaction, Niementowski quinoline synthesis.

NIEMEYER, FELIX VON. 1820-1871. German physician. See: Biog. Lex. hervorr. Aerzte. Niemeyer's pill.

Niemeyer's pill (Niemeyer, Felix von): Medicine. See: Dorland.

NIER, ALFRED OTTO CARL. 1911- . American physicist. See: World Who's Who Sci. Nier mass spectrograph.

Nier mass spectrograph (Nier, Alfred Otto Carl): Physics. See: Internat. Dict. Phys. Elec.

NIEREMBERG, JUAN EUSEBIO. 1595?-1658. Spanish Jesuit naturalist and author. See: Encyc. Brit., 1911. Nierembergia.

Nierembergia (Nieremberg, Juan Eusebio): Botany. See: Webster's 3d.

NIERENSTEIN, MAXIMILIAN. b. 1877. English chemist. See: Pogg., vols. 5, 6. Nierenstein reaction, Nierenstein reagent for tannins.

Nierenstein reaction (Nierenstein, Maximilian): Chemistry. See: Hackh; Van Nostrand Chem. Dict.

Nierenstein reagent for tannins (Nierenstein, Maximilian): Chemistry. See: Van Nostrand Chem. Dict.

NIERHOFF, H. fl. 1956. German pediatrician. (Biography source unavailable.) Nierhoff-Huebner syndrome.

Nierhoff-Huebner syndrome (Nierhoff, H. and Huebner, Otto): Medicine. See: Jablonski.

NIETZKI, RUDOLF. 1847-1917. German-born chemist in Switzerland. See: World Who's Who Sci. Nietzki's rule.

Nietzki's rule (Nietzki, Rudolf): Chemistry. See: Ballentyne.

NIETZSCHE, FRIEDRICH WILHELM. 1844-1900. German philosopher. See: New Encyc. Brit., 1974. Nietzscheanism (Nietzcheism or Nietzchean).

Nietzscheanism (Nietzcheism or Nietzchean) (Nietzsche, Friedrich Wilhelm): Philosophy. See: Hendrickson; Partridge; Webster's 3d.

Nieuwenburg-Brobbel micro-test for malic acid (Nieuwenburg, Cornelis Johannes and Brobbel, L. M.): Chemistry. See: Van Nostrand Chem. Dict.

NIEUWENBURG, CORNELIS JOHANNES VAN. b. 1889. Dutch chemist. See: Pogg., vol. 6. Nieuwenburg-Brobbel micro-test for malic acid.

Nievergelt-Erb syndrome (Nievergelt, Kurt and Erb, Wilhelm Heinrich). See: Nievergelt's syndrome.

NIEVERGELT, KURT. 1913- . Swiss physician. (Biography source unavailable.) Nievergelt's syndrome.

Nievergelt's syndrome (Nievergelt, Kurt): Medicine. See: Jablonski. Also known as: Nievergelt-Erb syndrome.

NIEWENGLOWSKI, GASTON HENRI. fl. 1896. French scientist. Cited in: Royal Soc. Cat. Sci. Pap., 1884-1900. Niewenglowski rays.

Niewenglowski rays (Niewenglowski, Gaston Henri): Physics. See: Dorland; Stedman.

NIGGLI, PAUL. 1888-1953. Swiss mineralogist. See: Encyc. Brit., 1973. Niggliite, Niggli's classification.

Niggliite (Niggli, Paul): Earth Sciences. See: Thrush; Webster's 3d.

Niggli's classification (Niggli, Paul): Earth Sciences. See: Thrush.

Nightingale (Nightingale, Florence): Generic Word (hospital bed-jacket). See: Partridge.

NIGHTINGALE, FLORENCE. 1820-1910. English nurse. See: Dict. Nat. Biog., 2d suppl. Florence Nightingale, Nightingale.

nightmare (Mara): Generic Word. See: Charnock.

Nigyl micro-test for lignin (Derivation undetermined): Chemistry. See: Van Nostrand Chem. Dict.

NIJBOER, BERNARD ROELOF ANDRIES. 1915- . Dutch theoretical physicist. See: Who's Who Sci. Europe, 1972. Nijboer-Zernike aberration functions.

Nijboer–Zernike aberration functions (Nijboer, Bernard Roelof Andries and Zernike, Frits): Mathematics. See: Internat. Dict. Ap. Math.

Nijssen, Rene. See: Nyssen, Rene.

NIKE. Greek goddess of victory. See: New Encyc. Brit., 1974, Microp. Nike (missile).

Nike (missile) (Nike): Weapons. See: Markus; New Encyc. Brit., 1974, Microp.

NIKIFOROFF, MIKHAIL NIKIFOROVICH. b. 1858. Russian dermatologist. Cited in: Index-Cat. Libr. Surg.-Gen. Off., 2d Ser., vol. 11, 1906. Nikiforoff stain (or borax–carmine), Nikiforoff's method.

Nikiforoff stain (or borax–carmine) (Nikiforoff, Mikhail Nikiforovich): Medicine. See: Hackh; Van Nostrand Chem. Dict.

Nikiforoff's method (Nikiforoff, Mikhail Nikiforovich): Medicine. See: Dorland; Stedman.

Nikolskii, Petr Vasilevich. See: Nikolsky, Pyotr Vasilyevich.

NIKOLSKY, PYOTR VASILYEVICH. 1858–1940. Russian dermatologist. See: Biog. Lex. hervorr. Aerzte, 1880–1930. Nikolsky's sign.

Nikolsky's sign (Nikolsky, Pyotr Vasilyevich): Medicine. See: Dorland; Jablonski; Stedman.

NIKON. 1605–1681. Russian ecclesiastical prelate. See: New Encyc. Brit., 1974, Microp. Nikonianism.

Nikonianism (Nikon): Religion. See: Mathews, S. under "Russian Sects."

Nilson test reaction (Derivation undetermined): Chemistry. See: Van Nostrand Chem. Dict.

Nimanandis (Nimavats or Nimbaditya sect) (Nimbarka): Religion. See: Canney.

NIMBARKA (NIMBADITYA OR NIYAMANANDA). fl. 12th or 13th c. Indian philosopher and astronomer. See: New Encyc. Brit., 1974, Microp. Nimanandis (Nimavats or Nimbaditya sect).

NIMROD. A mighty hunter mentioned in the Old Testament (Gen. 10: 8–12). See: Encyc. Brit., 1973. Nimrod (Nimrodian or Nimroded).

Nimrod (Nimrodian or Nimroded) (Nimrod): Generic Word (great hunter). See: Brewer; Partridge; Stenhouse.

NIMSHI. Grandfather of King Jehu in the Old Testament. See: Hastings (Dict. Bible). Nimshi.

Nimshi (Nimshi, the grandfather): Generic Word (fool). See: Clapin.

ninety–five theses of Harms (Harms, Claus): Religion. See: Mathews, S.

Ninon (Lenclos. Ninon de): Fashion. See: Partridge.

NIOBE. Daughter of Tantalus in Greek mythology. See: New Encyc. Brit., 1974, Microp. Niobe (or Niobean), Niobids, Niobium.

Niobe (or Niobean) (Niobe): Generic Word (maternal sorrow). See: Brewer; Partridge.

NIOBES, STEPHANUS. fl. 6th c. Alexandrian professor. Cited in: Dict. Christ. Biog. under "Niobites." Niobites.

Niobids (Niobe): Fine Arts. See: Osborne.

Niobites (Niobes, Stephanus): Religion. See: Latham.

Niobium (Niobe): Chemistry. See: Partridge; Van Nostrand Sci. Encyc.; Webster's 3d.

NIPHER, FRANCIS EUGENE. 1847–1927. American physicist. See: World Who's Who Sci. Nipher shield.

Nipher shield (Nipher, Francis Eugene): Earth Sciences. See: Huschke.

Nipkow disc (disk) (Nipkow, Paul Gottlieb): Engineering and Industry. See: Focal Encyc. Film; Hughes; Thewlis; Webster's 3d.

NIPKOW, PAUL GOTTLIEB. 1860–1940. German engineer. See: World Who's Who Sci. Nipkow disc (disk).

NIRANKAL. Indian deity. (Biography source unavailable.) Nirankaris.

Nirankaris (Nirankal): Religion. See: Canney.

NISBET, WILLIAM. 1759–1822. English physician. See: World Who's Who Sci. Nisbet's chancre.

Nisbet's chancre (Nisbet, William): Medicine. See: Dorland; Jablonski; Stedman.

NISHINA, YOSHIO. 1890–1951. Japanese physicist. See: World Who's Who Sci. Klein–Nishina formula.

Nissen hut (Nissen, Peter Norman): Military Sciences. See: Partridge; Quick; Webster's 3d.

NISSEN, PETER NORMAN. 1871–1930. English mining engineer. See: Who Was Who, 1929–1940. Nissen hut, Nissen stamp?

Nissen stamp (Nissen, Peter Norman?): Engineering and Industry. See: Thrush.

Nissl('s) bodies (or substance) (Nissl, Franz): Anatomy. See: Chaplin; Donath; Stedman.

Nissl degeneration (Nissl, Franz): Medicine. See: Dorland; Stedman.

NISSL, FRANZ. 1860–1919. German neurologist. See: Dict. Sci. Biog. Nissl('s) bodies (or substance), Nissl degeneration, Nissl's stain.

Nissl's stain (Nissl, Franz): Medicine. See: Dorland; Stedman.

Nissolia (Nissolle, Guillaume): Botany. See: Charnock.

NISSOLLE, GUILLAUME. 1647–1734. French botanist. See: Nouv. Biog. Univ. Nissolia.

NITABUCH, RAISSA. fl. 19th c. German physician. (Biography source unavailable.) Nitabuch's stria (or layer).

Nitabuch's stria (or layer) (Nitabuch, Raissa): Medicine. See: Dorland; Stedman.

NITCHIE, EDWARD BARTLETT. 1876–1917. American teacher of the deaf. See: Dict. Amer. Biog. Nitchie method.

Nitchie method (Nitchie, Edward Bartlett): Education. See: Good.

Nithsdale (riding hood) (Nithsdale, Winifred Maxwell, Countess of): Fashion. See: Picken.

NITHSDALE, WINIFRED MAXWELL, COUNTESS OF. d. 1749. Scottish noblewoman. See: Webster's Biog. Dict. Nithsdale (riding hood).

NITZSCH, CHRISTIAN LUDWIG. 1782–1837. German naturalist. See: Biog. Lex. hervorr. Aerzte. Nitzschia.

Nitzschia (Nitzsch, Christian Ludwig): Zoology. See: Pennak; Webster's 3d.

NIVEN, WILLIAM. 1850–1937. Scottish–born American mineralogist. See: World Who's Who Sci. Nivenite.

Nivenite (Niven, William): Earth Sciences. See: Thrush; Webster's 3d.

Nixon Doctrine (Nixon, Richard Milhous): Politics. See: Barnhart (New Eng.).

NIXON, IVOR G. fl. 1923. English chemist. Cited in: Chem. Abstr., vol. 17, p. 2091. Nixon reagent.

Nixon reagent (Nixon, Ivor G.): Chemistry. See: Van Nostrand Chem. Dict.

NIXON, RICHARD MILHOUS. 1913– . American president. See: New Encyc. Brit., 1974, Microp. Nixon Doctrine, Nixonologist, Nixonomics.

Nixonologist (Nixon, Richard Milhous): Politics. See: The Atlanta Journal, April 4, 1974 under "World Events Translated–Rapid Changes Spell New Language Angles."

Nixonomics (Nixon, Richard Milhous): Politics. See: Barnhart (New Eng.)

Noachian (or Noachic) (Noah): History. See: Webster's 3d.

Noachite (Noah): Sociology. See: Webster's 3d.

NOAH (or NOE). Patriarch in the Old Testament. See: New Encyc. Brit., 1974, Microp. Noachian (or Noachic), Noachite, Noahide (or Noachian) laws, Noah's ark (cloud band), Noah's ark (flower), Noah's ark (monkshood), Noah's ark (shell), Noah's ark (toy), Noah's nightcap.

Noahide (or Noachian) laws (Noah): Religion. See: New Encyc. Brit., 1974, Microp.

Noah's ark (cloud band) (Noah): Navigation. See: Brewer; Webster's 3d.

Noah's ark (flower) (Noah): Botany. See: Mathews, M. M.; Webster's 3d.

Noah's ark (monkshood) (Noah): Botany. See: Webster's 3d.

Noah's ark (shell) (Noah): Zoology. See: Gray; Pennak; Webster's 3d.

Noah's ark (toy) (Noah): Generic Word. See: Partridge; Webster's 3d.; Weekley.

Noah's nightcap (Noah): Botany. See: Partridge.

NOBEL, ALFRED BERNHARD. 1833-1896. Swedish chemist and engineer. See: Encyc. Brit., 1973. Nobel blastometer, Nobel elutriator?, Nobel oil, Nobel Prizes, Nobelium, Nobel's explosive.

Nobel blastometer (Nobel, Alfred Bernhard): Engineering and Industry. See: Thrush.

Nobel elutriator (Nobel, Alfred Bernhard?): Engineering and Industry. See: Thrush.

Nobel oil (Nobel, Alfred Bernhard): Chemistry. See: Hackh.

Nobel Prizes (Nobel, Alfred Bernhard): Philanthropy. See: Barnhart (Eng. Lit.); Encyc. Brit., 1973.

Nobelium (Nobel, Alfred Bernhard): Chemistry. See: Thrush; Van Nostrand Sci. Encyc.

Nobel's explosive (Nobel, Alfred Bernhard): Chemistry. See: Hackh.

NOBILE, UMBERTO. 1885- . Italian aero-nautical engineer and Arctic explorer. See: Encyc. Brit., 1973. Amundsen-Ellsworth-Nobile expedition.

NOBILI, LEOPOLDO. 1784-1835. Italian physicist. See: Dict. Sci. Biog. Nobili's rings (or figures).

Nobili's rings (or figures) (Nobili, Leopoldo): Physics. See: Charnock; Webster's 3d.

NOBLE, SIR ANDREW. 1831-1915. Scottish physicist. See: World Who's Who Sci. Trouton-Noble experiment.

NOBLE, CHARLES. fl. ca. 1840. English seaman. (Biography source unavailable.) Charley Noble.

NOBLE, CHARLES PERCY. 1863-1935. American gynecologist. See: Who Was Who Amer., 1897-1942. Noble's position.

Noble-Collip procedure (Noble, R. L. and Collip, James Bertram): Medicine. See: Stedman.

NOBLE, LEVI F. b. 1882. American geologist. See: Amer. Men Sci., 9th ed. Nobleite.

NOBLE, R. L. fl. 1942-1965. Canadian physician. (Biography source unavailable.) Noble-Collip procedure.

Nobleite (Noble, Levi F.): Earth Sciences. See: Thrush.

Noble's position (Noble, Charles Percy): Medicine. See: Dorland; Stedman.

NOCARD, EDMOND ISIDORE ETIENNE. 1850-1903. French veterinarian and biologist. See: World Who's Who Sci. Nocardia, Preisz-Nocard bacillus.

Nocardia (Nocard, Edmond Isidore Etienne): Zoology. See: Dorland; Stedman; Webster's 3d.

NOCHT, BERNHARD A. E. 1857-1927. German hygienist. See: Biog. Lex. hervorr. Aerzte, 1880-1930. Nocht's stain.

Nocht's stain (Nocht, Bernhard A. E.): Medicine. See: Stedman.

node of Ranvier (Ranvier, Louis Antoine). See: Ranvier's node (or constriction).

node of Rouviere (Rouviere, Henri): Anatomy. See: Stedman.

NOERLUND, NIELS ERIK. b. 1885. Danish mathematician. See: World Who's Who Sci. Noerlund's definition.

Noerlund's definition (Noerlund, Niels Erik): Mathematics. See: Ballentyne.

NOETHER, EMMY (In full: AMALIE EMMY). 1882-1935. German mathematician. See: Encyc. Brit., 1973. Noetherian ring.

Noetherian ring (Noether, Emmy): Mathematics. See: James.

Noetians (Noetus): Religion. See: Latham.

NOETUS. d. ca. 200. Asia Minor heretic. See: Dict. Christian Biog. Noetians.

NOGAI. fl. 13th c. Russian khan. (Biography source unavailable.) Nagaika.

NOGUCHI, HIDEYO. 1876-1928. Japanese-born American bacteriologist. See: World Who's Who Sci. Noguchi test, Noguchia.

Noguchi test (Noguchi, Hideyo): Medicine. See: Stedman.

Noguchia (Noguchi, Hideyo): Zoology. See: Stedman.

NOIRE, HENRI. fl. 1905. French radiologist. Cited in: Index-Cat. Libr. Surg.-Gen. Off., 2d Ser., vol. 11, 1906. Sabouraud-Noire instrument.

NOISETTE, PHILIPPE. fl. ca. 1820. French horticulturist in America. (Biography source unavailable.) Noisette (rose).

Noisette (rose) (Noisette, Philippe): Botany. See: Partridge; Webster's 3d.; Winburne. Also known as: Champney rose.

Nola, Ettore. See: Di Nola, Ettore.

NOLAN, THOMAS BRENNAN. 1901- . American geologist. See: World Who's Who Sci. Nolanite.

Nolanite (Nolan, Thomas Brennan): Earth Sciences. See: Thrush.

NOLIN, P. C. fl. 1755. French botanist and cleric. (Biography source unavailable.) Nolina.

Nolina (Nolin, P. C.): Botany. See: Webster's 3d.

non-Newtonian flow (Newton, Isaac): Physics. See: Thrush.

non-Newtonian liquids (Newton, Isaac): Physics. See: Ballentyne; Thewlis.

Nonius (Nunez Salaciense, Pedro): Navigation. See: Partridge.

Nonne-Apelt reaction (Nonne, Max and Apelt, Friedrich): Medicine. See: Dorland; Stedman.

Nonne-Froin syndrome (Nonne, Max and Froin, Georges). See: Froin's syndrome.

Nonne-Marie syndrome (Nonne, Max and Marie, Pierre). See: Marie's syndrome (or ataxia).

NONNE, MAX. 1861-1939. German neurologist. See: Biog. Lex. hervorr. Aerzte, 1880-1930. Nonne-Apelt reaction, Nonne-Froin syndrome, Nonne-Marie syndrome, Nonne-Milroy-Meige syndrome, Nonne's syndrome.

Nonne-Milroy-Meige syndrome (Nonne, Max; Milroy, William F.; and Meige, Henri): Medicine. See: Jablonski. Also known as: Meige-Milroy syndrome, Meige's disease, Milroy's disease, Nonne-Milroy syndrome (or disease).

Nonne-Milroy syndrome (or disease) (Nonne, Max and Milroy, William F.). See: Nonne-Milroy-Meige syndrome.

Nonne-Pierre Marie syndrome (Nonne, Max and Marie, Pierre). See: Marie's syndrome (or ataxia).

NONNENBRUCH, WILHELM. 1887-1955. German physician. See: Biog. Lex. hervorr. Aerzte, 1880-1930. Nonnenbruch's syndrome.

Nonnenbruch's syndrome (Nonnenbruch, Wilhelm): Medicine. See: Jablonski.

Nonne's compression syndrome (Nonne, Max). See: Froin's syndrome.

Nonne's syndrome (Nonne, Max). See: Naffziger's syndrome.

NOONAN, JACQUELINE ANNE. fl. 1959-1963. American cardiologist. See: Direct. Med. Specialists, 1974-1975. Noonan's syndrome.

Noonan's syndrome (Noonan, Jacqueline Anne): Medicine. See: Lieber and Olbrich; Stedman.

Noorden, Carl Harko von. See: Von Noorden, Carl Harko.

Noorden treatment (Von Noorden, Carl Harko): Medicine. See: Dorland.

NOOTH, JOHN MERVIN. fl. 18th c. English scientist. See: New Encyc. Brit., 1974, Microp. Nooth's apparatus.

Nooth's apparatus (Nooth, John Mervin): Chemistry. See: Charnock.

NOPONEN, GEORGE EDWARD. 1908- . American chemist. Cited in: Mansell. Kolthoff-Naponen test for nitrate.

NORBERT, SAINT. ca. 1080-1134. German ecclesiastic in France. See: New Encyc. Brit., 1974, Microp. Norbertine(s).

Norbertine(s) (Norbert, Saint): Religion. See: Attwater; Mathews, S.; New Encyc. Brit., 1974, Microp.; Webster's 3d.

NORDAU, MAX SIMON. 1849-1923. German physician and author. See: New Encyc. Brit., 1974, Microp. Nordau's disease.

ordauism (Nordau, Max Simon). See: Nordau's disease.

ordau's disease (Nordau, Max Simon): Medicine. See: Dorland; Jablonski. so known as: Nordauism.

ORDBY, GENE M. 1926-   . American civil engineer and university dministrator. See: Amer. Men and Women Sci., 12th ed. Nordby's nostrum.

ordby's nostrum (Nordby, Gene M.): Sociology. See: Martin.

orden bombsight (Norden, Carl Lukas): Weapons. See: Quick.

ORDEN, CARL LUKAS. 1880-1965. Dutch-born American aeronautical onsultant. See: Nat. Cycl. Amer. Biog., vol. 52, p. 345. Norden bomb-ght.

ordenfelt (machine gun) (Nordenfelt, Thorsten Wilhelm): Weapons. See: artridge.

ORDENFELT, THORSTEN WILHELM. 1842-1920. Swedish engineer. See: orld Who's Who Sci. Nordenfelt (machine gun), Maxim-Nordenfelt machine un.

ordenskjoeld line (Nordenskjoeld, Otto): Earth Sciences. See: Huschke.

ORDENSKJOELD, OTTO (In full: NILS OTTO GUSTAF). 1869-1928. wedish explorer and geographer. See: World Who's Who Sci. Nordenskjoeld ne.

ORDHEIM, LOTHAR WOLFGANG. 1899-   . German-born physicist. See: orld Who's Who Sci. Fowler-Nordheim equation.

ORDHEIM, ROLF. fl. 1954. Norwegian? metallurgist. Cited in: Chem. bstr., Decenn. Index, 1947-1956. Nordheim's rule.

ordheim's rule (Nordheim, Rolf): Chemistry. See: Ballentyne.

ORDLANDER, BIRGER W. 1896-   . Swedish-born American chemist. See: mer. Men Sci., 9th ed. Nordlander test.

ordlander test (Nordlander, Birger W.): Chemistry. See: Van Nostrand hem. Dict.

ORDMANN, ALEXANDER VON. 1803-1866. Finnish naturalist. See: oyal Soc. Cat. Sci. Pap., 1864-1873. Nordmann('s) fir.

ordmann('s) fir (Nordmann, Alexander von): Botany. See: Webster's 3d.; inburne.

ORDSIECK, ARNOLD THEODORE. 1911-   . American physicist. See: mer. Men Sci., 9th ed. Bloch-Nordsieck method.

ordstrand, Robert Alexander van. See: Van Nordstrand, Robert Alexander.

ordstrandite (Van Nordstrand, Robert Alexander): Earth Sciences. See: hrush.

orfolk, 15th Duke of. See: Howard, Henry Fitzalan, 15th Duke of Norfolk.

orfolk Commission (Howard, Henry Fitzalan, 15th Duke of Norfolk): History. ee: Montgomery.

orfolk Howard (Bug, Joshua (Norfolk Howard)): Generic Word (bedbug). See: endrickson; Partridge; Wagner (More Names).

ORMAN, ALBERT. fl. 1900. American photographer. Cited in: Royal Soc. at. Sci. Pap., 1884-1900. Norman's rule?

orman brick (Derivation undetermined): Engineering and Industry. See: Thrush.

ORMAN, RONALD MELVILLE. fl. 1941-1964. English physician. See: ed. Direct., 1964. Norman-Wood syndrome.

orman slabs (Derivation undetermined): Engineering and Industry. See: hrush.

orman Tomlinson Award (Tomlinson, Norman): Library Science. See: Harrod.

orman-Wood syndrome (Norman, Ronald Melville and Wood, Norman): Medi-ne. See: Jablonski.

ORMANVILLE, E. J. DE. b. 1882. English engineer. Cited in: Mansell. aycock De Normanville overdrive.

orman's rule (Norman, Albert?): Photography. See: Focal Encyc. Photog.

ORMET, LEON. b. 1877. French physician. Cited in: Index-Cat. Libr. urg.-Gen. Off., 2d Ser., vol. 11, 1906. Normet's solution.

ormet's solution (Normet, Leon): Medicine. See: Dorland.

NORRIE, GORDON. 1855-1941. Danish ophthalmologist. See: Danmarks hist. bla bog. Norrie's disease.

Norrie's disease (Norrie, Gordon): Medicine. See: Jablonski; Stedman.

Norris Amendment (Norris, George William): Politics. See: Smith.

Norris' corpuscles (Norris, Richard): Anatomy. See: Dorland; Stedman.

NORRIS, DOROTHY. fl. 1911. English chemist. Cited in: Chem. Abstr., vol. 5, p. 3465. Harden-Norris diacetyl reaction.

Norris-Doxey Act (Norris, George William and Doxey, Wall): Politics. See: Winburne.

Norris-Eyring reverberation formula (Norris, Ralph Forbush? and Eyring, Carl Ferdinand): Physics. See: Ballentyne.

NORRIS, GEORGE WILLIAM. 1861-1944. American legislator. See: Biog. Direct. Amer. Congress. Norris Amendment, Norris-Doxey Act, Norris-LaGuardia Act.

NORRIS, JAMES D. 1906-1966. American business executive and hockey enthusiast. See: Who Was Who Amer., 1961-1968. James Norris Memorial Trophy.

NORRIS, JOHN. 1734-1777. English benefactor. See: Dict. Nat. Biog. Norrisian Professor.

Norris-LaGuardia Act (Norris, George William and LaGuardia, Fiorello Henry): Politics. See: Clark; Smith.

NORRIS, RALPH FORBUSH. b. 1892. American acoustics engineer. See: Amer. Men Sci., 5th ed. Norris-Eyring reverberation formula?

NORRIS, RICHARD. 1831-1916. English physiologist. See: Brit. Med. J., vol. 2 (1916), p. 825. Norris' corpuscles.

Norrisian Professor (Norris, John): Religion. See: Wagner (More Names).

NORSETH, KEITH. fl. ca. 1961. American engineering geologist. Cited in: Min. Mag., vol. 32, pt. 2 (1959-1961), p. 973. Norsethite.

Norsethite (Norseth, Keith): Earth Sciences. See: Thrush.

Norsk-Staal process (Derivation undetermined): Engineering and Industry. See: Thrush.

NORTH, CECIL CLARE. 1878-1961. American sociologist. See: Who Was Who Amer., 1961-1968. North-Hatt scale.

North-Hatt scale (North, Cecil Clare and Hatt, Paul Kitchener): Sociology. See: Hoult.

Northampton, 2nd Marquis. See: Compton, Spencer Joshua Alwyne (2nd Marquis of Northampton).

Northey pump (Derivation undetermined): Engineering and Industry. See: Auger.

NORTHRUP, EDWIN FITCH. 1866-1940. American electrothermic engineer. See: World Who's Who Sci. Ajax-Northrup furnace.

NORTHUP, C. H. fl. ca. 1897. American mineral collector. Cited in: Hintze, vol. 1, pt. 3, half 1, p. 2802. Northupite.

Northupite (Northup, C. H.): Earth Sciences. See: Thrush; Webster's 3d.

NORTON, BERTRAM. fl. 1930-1936. English engineer. Cited in: Chem. Abstr., Decenn. Index, 1927-1936. McNally-Norton jig.

Norton('s) theorem (Derivation undetermined): Electronics. See: Ballentyne; Hughes; Van Nostrand Sci. Encyc.

NORY. fl. 19th c. English scientist. (Biography source unavailable.) Nory (tables).

Nory (tables) (Nory): Mathematics. See: Charnock.

NOSE, KARL WILHELM. 1753-1835. German geologist and physician. See: Biog. Lex. hervorr. Aerzte. Noselite (or Nosean).

Noselite (or Nosean) (Nose, Karl Wilhelm): Earth Sciences. See: Webster's 3d.

nosey Parker (Parker, Matthew): Generic Word (busybody). See: Hendrickson; Partridge; Webster's 3d.

NOSTRADAMUS (MICHEL DE NOTREDAME). 1503-1566. French physician and prophet. See: Encyc. Brit., 1973. Nostradamus.

Nostradamus (Nostradamus, the prophet): Generic Word (prophet). See: Hendrickson; Partridge.

not Pygmalion likely! (Pygmalion): Generic Word (definitely unlikely). See: Partridge.

NOTHNAGEL, HERMANN (In full: CARL WILHELM HERMANN). 1841-1905. Austrian physician. See: World Who's Who Sci. Nothnagel's acroparesthesia, Nothnagel's bodies, Nothnagel's sign, Nothnagel's syndrome (1), Nothnagel's syndrome (2), Nothnagel's test.

Nothnagel's acroparesthesia (Nothnagel, Hermann): Medicine. See: Jablonski.

Nothnagel's bodies (Nothnagel, Hermann): Anatomy. See: Dorland.

Nothnagel's sign (Nothnagel, Hermann): Medicine. See: Dorland; Kelly.

Nothnagel's syndrome (1) (Nothnagel, Hermann): Medicine. See: Jablonski.

Nothnagel's syndrome (2) (Nothnagel, Hermann): Medicine. See: Dorland; Jablonski; Stedman.

Nothnagel's test (Nothnagel, Hermann): Medicine. See: Dorland; Stedman.

NOVACEK, RADIM. 1905-1942. Czechoslovakian mineralogist. See: Pogg., vol. 6. Novacekite.

Novacekite (Novacek, Radim): Earth Sciences. See: Thrush.

NOVAK, JIRI. 1902- . Czechoslovakian mineralogist. See: Turkevich and Turkevich. Novakite.

Novakite (Novak, Jiri): Earth Sciences. See: Thrush.

Novatianism (or Novatian) (Novatianus): Religion. See: Attwater; Mathews, S.; Webster's 3d.

NOVATIANUS. fl. ca. 200-ca. 258. Antipope and founder of sect. See: Encyc. Brit., 1973. Novatianism (or Novatian).

NOVELLI, ARMANDO. 1901- . Argentinian chemist. See: Gran Encic. Argentina. Novelli reagent.

Novelli reagent (Novelli, Armando): Chemistry. See: Van Nostrand Chem. Dict.

NOVICOW, JACQUES. fl. 1900-1912. French sociologist. Cited in: Cum. Auth. Index to Psych. Index, 1894-1935, and Psych. Abstr., 1927-1958. Novicow's stages of societal development.

Novicow's stages of societal development (Novicow, Jacques): Sociology. See: Zadrozny.

NOVIKOFF, ALEX BENJAMIN. 1913- . Russian-born American biochemist. See: World Who's Who Sci. Novikoff's hepatoma.

Novikoff's hepatoma (Novikoff, Alex Benjamin): Medicine. See: Jablonski.

Novikov gear (or gearing system) (Novikov, M. L.): Engineering and Industry. See: Auger; Chironis. Also known as: Wildhaber-Novikov gear.

NOVIKOV, M. L. d. 1956. Russian engineer. (Biography source unavailable.) Novikov gear (or gearing system).

novumbra Hubbsi (Hubbs, Clark Leavitt): Zoology. See: Pennak.

Novy and MacNeal's blood agar (Novy, Frederick George and MacNeal, Ward J.): Medicine. See: Dorland; Stedman.

NOVY, FREDERICK GEORGE. 1864-1957. American bacteriologist. See: World Who's Who Sci. Novy and MacNeal's blood agar, Novy's bacillus, Novy's rat disease, Vaughan-Novy test.

Novy's bacillus (Novy, Frederick George): Medicine. See: Dorland.

Novy's rat disease (Novy, Frederick George): Medicine. See: Dorland.

NOWOPOKROWSKY. fl. 1912. Russian botanist. Cited in: Chem. Abstr., vol. 6, p. 1165. Nowopokrowsky reagent.

Nowopokrowsky reagent (Nowopokrowsky): Chemistry. See: Van Nostrand Chem. Dict.

NOYES, JOHN HUMPHREY. 1811-1886. American social reformer. See: Dict. Amer. Biog. Noyesism (or Noyesite).

NOYES, MARCIA C. fl. 1933. American medical librarian. See: Med. Libr. Assn. Bull. vol. 22 (Aug., 1933), p. 7. Marcia C. Noyes Award.

Noyesism (or Noyesite) (Noyes, John Humphrey): Sociology. See: Mathews, M. M.

NUCK, ANTON. 1650-1692. Dutch anatomist. See: World Who's Who Sci. Nuck's canal (or diverticulum), Nuck's hydrocele.

Nuck's canal (or diverticulum) (Nuck, Anton): Anatomy. See: Donath; Dorland; Stedman.

Nuck's hydrocele (Nuck, Anton): Medicine. See: Dorland; Stedman.

nucleus of Pander (Pander, Christian Heinrich). See: Pander's nucleus.

NUEL, JEAN-PIERRE. 1847-1920. Belgian physician. See: Biog. Lex. hervorr. Aerzte, 1880-1930. Nuel's space.

Nuel's space (Nuel, Jean-Pierre): Anatomy. See: Donath; Dorland; Stedman.

Nuffield Foundation (Nuffield, William Richard Morris, 1st Viscount): Education Cited in: New Encyc. Brit, 1974, Microp.

Nuffield Institute for Medical Research (Nuffield, William Richard Morris, 1st Viscount): Medicine. Cited in: New Encyc. Brit., 1974, Microp.

Nuffield Trust (Nuffield, William Richard Morris, 1st Viscount): Philanthropy. Cited in: New Encyc. Brit., 1974, Microp.

NUFFIELD, WILLIAM RICHARD MORRIS, 1ST VISCOUNT. 1877-1963. English automobile manufacturer. See: Who Was Who, 1961-1970. Morris (motor car), Nuffield Foundation, Nuffield Institute for Medical Research, Nuffield Trust.

NUGENT, ROBERT LOGAN. 1902- . American chemist. See: Amer. Men Sci., 5th ed. Estill-Nugent test.

NUHN, ANTON. 1814-1889. German anatomist. See: Biog. Lex. hervorr. Aerzte. Nuhn's gland(s).

Nuhn's gland(s) (Nuhn, Anton): Anatomy. See: Donath; Dorland; Stedman. Also known as: Blandin's gland.

NUNEZ SALACIENSE, PEDRO. ca. 1492-1577. Portuguese mathematician and geographer. See: Dict. Sci. Biog. Nonius.

NUNN, JOSEPH. No dates. American inventor. (Biography source unavailable.) Baker-Nunn camera.

Nunn's gorged corpuscles (Derivation undetermined): Medicine. See: Stedman.

NURSE, RONALD WALTER BROWN. 1913- . English physicist. See: Who's Who Sci. Europe, 1967. Lea and Nurse permeability apparatus.

NUSSBAUM, JOHANN NEPOMUK VON. 1829-1890. German surgeon. See: Allg. Deut. Biog. Nussbaum's bracelet, Nussbaum's narcosis.

NUSSBAUM, MORITZ. 1850-1915. German histologist. See: Biog. Lex. hervorr. Aerzte, 1880-1950. Nussbaum's cells, Nussbaum's experiment.

Nussbaum's bracelet (Nussbaum, Johann Nepomuk von): Medicine. See: Dorland; Stedman.

Nüssbaum's cells (Nussbaum, Moritz): Anatomy. See: Donath.

Nussbaum's experiment (Nussbaum, Moritz): Medicine. See: Dorland; Stedman

Nussbaum's narcosis (Nussbaum, Johann Nepomuk von): Medicine. See: Dorland; Stedman.

Nusse and Grafer PIV/6 drilling machine (Derivation undetermined): Engineering and Industry. See: Thrush.

NUSSELT, ERNST KRAFT WILHELM. 1882-1957. German physicist. See: Dict. Sci. Biog. Nusselt number.

Nusselt number (Nusselt, Ernst Kraft Wilhelm): Physics. See: Ballentyne; Huschke; Internat. Dict. Ap. Math.; Thewlis; Van Nostrand Sci. Encyc.

Nuttall blister beetle (Nuttall, Thomas): Zoology. See: Webster's 3d.; Winburne.

NUTTALL, GEORGE HENRY FALKINER. 1862-1937. American-born English biologist. See: World Who's Who Sci. Nuttallia, Nuttall's bulb, Nuttall's stain for capsules, Nuttall's test for blood stains.

NUTTALL, JOHN MICHAEL. d. 1958. English physicist. (Biography source unavailable.) Geiger-Nuttall law (rule or relation).

Nuttall(s) oak (Nuttall, Thomas): Botany. See: Webster's 3d.

Nuttall saltbush (Nuttall, Thomas?): Botany. See: Winburne.

NUTTALL, THOMAS. 1786-1859. English botanist and ornithologist in America. See: Dict. Sci. Biog. Nuttall blister beetle, Nuttall saltbush?, Nuttall(s) oak, Nuttallia, Nuttalline?, Nuttallite, Nuttall's dogwood, Nuttall's little hare, Nuttall's poorwill, Nuttall's sparrow, Nuttall's tern, Nuttall's whippoorwill, Nuttall's woodpecker, Nuttalornis borealis?

Nuttallia (Nuttall, George Henry Falkiner). See: Babesia.

Nuttallia (Nuttall, Thomas). See: Mentzelia.

Nuttallina (Nuttall, Thomas?): Zoology. See: Pennak.

Nuttallite (Nuttall, Thomas): Earth Sciences. See: Charnock.

Nuttall's bulb (Nuttall, George Henry Falkiner): Medicine. See: Kelly.

Nuttall's dogwood (Nuttall, Thomas): Botany. See: Mathews, M. M.

Nuttall's little hare (Nuttall, Thomas): Zoology. See: Mathews, M. M.

Nuttall's poorwill (Nuttall, Thomas): Zoology. See: Mathews, M. M.

Nuttall's sparrow (Nuttall, Thomas): Zoology. See: Mathews, M. M.

Nuttall's stain for capsules (Nuttall, George Henry Falkiner). See: Welch's stain.

Nuttall's tern (Nuttall, Thomas): Zoology. See: Mathews, M. M.

Nuttall's test for blood stains (Nuttall, George Henry Falkiner): Medicine. See: Kelly.

Nuttall's whippoorwill (Nuttall, Thomas): Zoology. See: Mathews, M. M.

Nuttall's woodpecker (Nuttall, Thomas): Zoology. See: Mathews, M. M.

Nuttalornis borealis (Nuttall, Thomas?): Zoology. See: Pennak.

Nutting colorimeter (Nutting, Perley Gilman): Physics. See: Internat. Dict. Phys. Elec.

Nutting equation (Derivation undetermined): Physics. See: Internat. Dict. Ap. Math.

NUTTING, PERLEY GILMAN. 1873-1949. American physicist. See: Nat. Cycl. Amer. Biog., vol. D, p. 218. Nutting colorimeter.

NYE, GERALD P. 1892-1971. American legislator. See: Biog. Direct. Amer. Congress. Nye munitions investigation.

Nye munitions investigation (Nye, Gerald P.): Politics. See: Morris.

Nygaard-Brown syndrome (Nygaard, Kaare Kristiaan and Brown, George Elgie): Medicine. See: Jablonski.

NYGAARD, KAARE KRISTIAAN. fl. 1937. American physician. See: Physicians Mayo Clinic, 1937, p. 1057 f. Nygaard-Brown syndrome.

NYHAN, WILLIAM LEO. 1926- . American physician. See: World Who's Who Sci. Lesch-Nyhan syndrome.

NYLANDER, CLAES WILHELM. 1835-1902. Swedish chemist. (Biography source unavailable.) Almen-Nylander test, Nylander('s) reagent (or solution), Nylander test.

Nylander('s) reagent (or solution) (Nylander, Claes Wilhelm): Chemistry. See: Dorland; Hackh; Stedman; Van Nostrand Chem. Dict.

Nylander test (Nylander, Claes Wilhelm): Chemistry. See: Hackh.

Nyquist criterion (or stability criterion) (Nyquist, Harry): Electronics. See: Internat. Dict. Phys. Elec.; Van Nostrand Sci. Encyc.

Nyquist diagram(s) (Nyquist, Harry): Electronics. See: Internat. Dict. Phys. Elec.; Markus; Van Nostrand Sci. Encyc. under "Frequency Response."

Nyquist formula (Nyquist, Harry): Electronics. See: Thewlis.

Nyquist frequency (Nyquist, Harry): Mathematics. See: Internat. Dict. Ap. Math.; Kendall; Van Nostrand Sci. Encyc.

NYQUIST, HARRY. b. 1889. Swedish-born American communications engineer. See: Amer. Men Sci., 7th ed. Nyquist criterion (or stability criterion), Nyquist diagram(s), Nyquist formula, Nyquist frequency, Nyquist interval (limit or rate), Nyquist locus, Nyquist rule, Nyquist-Shannon theorem, Nyquist('s) theorem.

Nyquist interval (limit or rate) (Nyquist, Harry): Electronics. See: Hughes; Internat. Dict. Phys. Elec.; Kendall.

Nyquist locus (Nyquist, Harry): Mathematics. See: Internat. Dict. Ap. Math.

Nyquist rule (Nyquist, Harry): Electronics. See: Ballentyne.

Nyquist-Shannon theorem (Nyquist, Harry and Shannon, Claude Elwood): Statistcs. See: Kendall.

Nyquist('s) theorem (Nyquist, Harry): Electronics. See: Ballentyne; Internat. Dict. Ap. Math.; Internat. Dict. Phys. Elec.; Thewlis.

NYSSEN, RENE. fl. 1936. Belgian neurologist. (Biography source unavailable.) Van Bogaert-Nyssen-Peiffer disease.

NYSTEN, PIERRE HUMBERT. 1771-1818. Belgian physician in France. See: World Who's Who Sci. Nysten's law.

Nysten's law (Nysten, Pierre Humbert): Medicine. See: Dorland; Stedman.

NYSWANDER, MARIE. 1919- . American psychiatrist. See: Biog. Direct. Amer. Psych. Assoc., 1973. Dole-Nyswander program.

O. Henry. See: Porter, William Sydney.

O. Henry ending (Porter, William Sydney, pseud., O. Henry): Literature. See: Hendrickson.

O.K. (Van Buren, Martin): Generic Word. See: Hendrickson.

OAKES. No dates. Australian? cattle rancher. (Biography source unavailable.) Oakes's oath.

Oakes's oath (Oakes): Generic Word (unreliable testimony). See: Brewer.

OAKLEY, ANNIE (Real name: PHOEBE ANNE OAKLEY MOZEE). 1860-1926. American markswoman. See: Encyc. Brit., 1973. Annie Oakley(s), Annie Oakley (costume).

Oates('s) plot (Oates, Titus): History. See: Attwater; Phyfe.

OATES, TITUS. 1649-1705. English Anglican priest and inventor of Popish Plot. See: Dict. Nat. Biog. Oates('s) plot.

Obadiah (Prim, Obadiah): Generic Word (Quaker). See: Harvey.

OBAL, ADALBERT. fl. 1951. German ophthalmologist. Cited in: Chem. Abstr., Decenn. Index, 1947-1956. Obal's syndrome.

Obal's syndrome (Obal, Adalbert): Medicine. See: Jablonski.

Obbenite (Philipsz, Obbe). See: Ubbonites.

O'BEIRNE, JAMES. 1786-1862. Irish surgeon. See: Lancet, vol. 1 (1862), p. 114. O'Beirne's sphincter, O'Beirne's tube.

O'Beirne's sphincter (O'Beirne, James): Anatomy. See: Donath; Dorland; Stedman.

O'Beirne's tube (O'Beirne, James): Medicine. See: Dorland.

OBER, FRANK ROBERTS. 1881-1960. American surgeon. See: Who Was Who Amer., 1961-1968. Ober's incision, Ober's operation, Ober's sign (or test), Ober's technic.

OBERFELL, GEORGE GROVER. b. 1885. American chemist. See: Amer. Men Sci., 9th ed. Burrell-Oberfell process.

OBERHAUSER, FERDINAND. 1895- . German chemist in Chile. See: Pogg., vol. 6. Oberhauser test for silica.

Oberhauser test for silica (Oberhauser, Ferdinand): Chemistry. See: Van Nostrand Chem. Dict.

OBERHOFFER, PAUL. 1882-1927. German steel chemist. See: Pogg., vol. 6. Oberhoffer solution.

Oberhoffer solution (Oberhoffer, Paul): Chemistry. See: Van Nostrand Chem. Dict.

OBERHOLSER, HENRY CHURCH. b. 1870. American ornithologist. See: Amer. Men Sci., 1st ed. Oberholseria.

Oberholseria (Oberholser, Henry Church): Zoology. See: Pennak.

OBERLIN, JEAN FREDERIC (JOHANN FRIEDRICH). 1740-1826. Alsatian clergyman. See: New Encyc. Brit., 1974, Microp. Oberlinvereine (or Oberlin Associations).

Oberlinvereine (or Oberlin Associations) (Oberlin, Jean Frederic): Philanthropy. See: Canney.

OBERLY, EUNICE ROCKWELL. fl. 1922. American librarian. (Biography source unavailable.) Eunice Rockwell Oberly Memorial Award.

OBERMEIER, OTTO HUGO FRANZ. 1843-1873. German physician. See: World Who's Who Sci. Obermeier's spirillum.

Obermeier's spirillum (Obermeier, Otto Hugo Franz): Medicine. See: Dorland; Stedman.

OBERMUELLER, KUNO. b. 1861. German physician. Cited in: Index-Cat. Libr. Surg.-Gen. Off., 2d Ser., vol. 12, 1907. Obermueller's test.

Obermueller's test (Obermueller, Kuno): Medicine. See: Dorland; Hackh; Stedman.

OBERNETTER, JOHANN BAPTIST. 1840-1887. German photographer and photographic publisher. See: Focal Encyc. Photog. Vogel-Obernetter silver eosin plate.

Ober's incision (Ober, Frank Roberts): Medicine. See: Kelly.

Ober's operation (Ober, Frank Roberts): Medicine. See: Dorland; Kelly; Stedman.

Ober's sign (or test) (Ober, Frank Roberts): Medicine. See: Dorland; Kelly.

Ober's technic (Ober, Frank Roberts): Medicine. See: Kelly.

OBERST, MAXIMILIAN. 1849-1925. German surgeon. See: Biog. Lex. hervorr. Aerzte, 1880-1930. Oberst's method, Oberst's operation.

OBERSTEINER, HEINRICH. 1847-1922. Austrian neurologist. See: Biog. Lex. hervorr. Aerzte, 1880-1930. Obersteiner-Redlich area.

Obersteiner-Redlich area (Obersteiner, Heinrich and Redlich, Emil): Medicine. See: Dorland; Stedman.

Oberst's method (Oberst, Maximilian): Medicine. See: Dorland.

Oberst's operation (Oberst, Maximilian): Medicine. See: Dorland.

Oblate of St. Benedict (Benedict of Nursia, Saint): Religion. See: Attwater.

Oblates of Mary Immaculate (Mary, Virgin-Mother): Religion. See: Attwater; Encyc. Brit., 1973.

Oblates of St. Charles (Charles Borromeo, Saint): Religion. See: Attwater.

Oblates of St. Francis de Sales (Francis of Sales, St.): Religion. See: Attwater.

Oblates of St. Frances of Rome (Frances of Rome): Religion. See: Attwater.

Oblomovism (Oblovmov, Ilya Ilyitch): Generic Word (utter laziness). See: Barnhart (New Eng.).

OBLOVMOV, ILYA ILYITCH. Main character in Ivan Goncharov's novel "Oblovmov," (1858). See: Magill. Oblomovism.

O'Brien airway needle (Derivation undetermined): Medicine. See: Stedman.

O'Brien akinesia (O'Brien, Cecil Starling): Medicine. See: Dorland; Kelly.

O'BRIEN, AMBROSE J. fl. 1909. Sports enthusiast. (Biography source unavailable.) O'Brien Trophy.

O'BRIEN, CECIL STARLING. b. 1889. American ophthalmologist. See: Amer. Men Sci., 8th ed. O'Brien akinesia, O'Brien's cataract.

O'Brien furnace (Derivation undetermined): Engineering and Industry. See: Thrush.

O'Brien Trophy (O'Brien, Ambrose J.): Recreation and Sports. See: Encyc. Brit., 1973 under "Ice Hockey," p. 1033.

O'Brien's cataract (O'Brien, Cecil Starling): Medicine. See: Jablonski.

OBRINSKY, WILLIAM. 1913- . American physician. See: Amer. Men and Women Sci., 12th ed. Obrinsky's syndrome.

Obrinsky's syndrome (Obrinsky, William): Medicine. See: Jablonski. Also known as: Froehlich's syndrome.

O'BRYAN, WILLIAM. 1778-1868. English-born American preacher. See: Dict. Amer. Biog. Bryanite, Bryanites.

Obsidian (Obsius): Earth Sciences. See: Hendrickson; New Encyc. Brit., 1974, Microp.; Partridge.

OBSIUS (OBSIDIUS). Early Roman traveler in Ethiopia. See: Dict. Grk. Rom. Biog. Myth. Obsidian.

Occam, William of. See: Ockam, William of.

OCHSENFELD, ROBERT. fl. 1933-1956. German physicist. Cited in: Chem. Abstr., Decenn. Indexes, 1937-1946; 1947-1956. Meissner-Ochsenfeld effect.

OCHSNER, ALBERT JOHN. 1858-1925. American surgeon. See: World Who's Who Sci. Ochsner's method (or treatment), Ochsner's operation, Ochsner's ring, Ochsner's solution, Ochsner's trocar.

OCHSNER, ALTON (In full: EDWARD WILLIAM ALTON). 1896- . American surgeon. See: Direct. Med. Specialists, 1965-1966. Ochsner's operation, Ochsner's test, Ochsner's theory.

Ochsner's method (or treatment) (Ochsner, Albert John): Medicine. See: Dorland; Stedman.

Ochsner's operation (Ochsner, Albert John): Medicine. See: Kelly.

Ochsner's operation (Ochsner, Alton): Medicine. See: Kelly.

Ochsner's ring (Ochsner, Albert John): Anatomy. See: Donath; Dorland.

Ochsner's solution (Ochsner, Albert John): Medicine. See: Dorland.

Ochsner's test (Ochsner, Alton): Medicine. See: Kelly.

Ochsner's theory (Ochsner, Alton): Medicine. See: Kelly.

Ochsner's trocar (Ochsner, Albert John): Medicine. See: Kelly.

OCHUS-BOCHUS. No dates. European magician. (Biography source unavailable.) Hocus-Pocus?

OCKHAM, WILLIAM OF. ca. 1285-1349. English scholastic philosopher. See: New Encyc. Brit., 1974. Ockhamism (Ockhamist or Occamism), Ockham's (Occam's) razor.

Ockhamism (Ockhamist or Occamism) (Ockham, William of): Philosophy. See: Webster's 3d.

Ockham's (Occam's) razor (Ockham, William of): Philosophy. See: Chaplin; Blumberg; Greenwald.

OCNUS. In Greek mythology, personification of delay and fruitless effort. See: Jobes. rope (or cord) of Ocnus.

O'CONNELL, DANIEL. 1775-1847. Irish national leader. See: Dict. Nat. Biog. O'Connell's tail.

O'Connell's tail (O'Connell, Daniel): History. See: Harbottle.

Ocrate process (Derivation undetermined): Engineering and Industry. See: Thrush.

Octavianus, Gaius. See: Augustus Caesar.

Oddesse pump (Oddie, F. T. and Hesse): Engineering and Industry. See: Auger.

ODDI, RUGGERO. 1864-1913. Italian physician. See: Dict. Sci. Biog. Oddi's sphincter.

ODDIE, F. T. No dates. Engineer. (Biography source unavailable.) Oddesse pump.

Oddi's sphincter (Oddi, Ruggero): Anatomy. See: Donath; Henderson; Stedman.

ODDO, BERNARDO. b. 1882. Italian chemist. See: Pogg., vols. 5, 6. Oddo-Ferrari test reaction for aldehydes.

Oddo-Ferrari test reaction for aldehydes (Oddo, Bernardo and Ferrari, E.): Chemistry. See: Van Nostrand Chem. Dict.

Ode to Napoleon (Napoleon I): Music. See: Apel.

ODELBERG, AXEL AXELSSON. b. 1892. Swedish physician. See: Svenska Maen Och Kvinnor. Odelberg's disease, Van Neck-Odelberg syndrome.

Odelberg's disease (Odelberg, Axel Axelsson). See: Van Neck's disease.

Oden balance (Oden, Sven Ludvig Alexander): Engineering and Industry. See: Thrush.

ODEN, SVEN LUDVIG ALEXANDER. 1887-1934. Swedish agricultural chemist. See: Pogg., vols. 5, 6. Oden balance.

Odilia, Saint. See: Ottilia, Saint.

ODIN. One of the principal gods in Norse mythology. See: Jobes. Odin oath, Odin's tree, Odin's wagon, Wednesday.

Odin oath (Odin): Mythology. See: Jobes.

Odin's tree (Odin): Generic Word (gallows). See: Jobes.

Odin's wagon (Odin): Generic Word (wind). See: Jobes.

ODIORNE, GEORGE STANLEY. 1920- . American educator. See: Who's Who Amer., 1974-1975. Odiorne's law.

Odiorne's law (Odiorne, George Stanley): Sociology. See: Odiorne.

O'Donaghue formula (Derivation undetermined): Engineering and Industry. See: Thrush.

O'Donahue's theory (Derivation undetermined): Engineering and Industry. See: Thrush.

O'DWYER, JOSEPH P. 1841-1898. American physician. See: World Who's Who Sci. Fell-O'Dwyer method, O'Dwyer's method, O'Dwyer's tube.

O'DWYER, WILLIAM. 1890-1964. American mayor of N.Y.C. See: Who Was Who Amer., 1961-1968. O'Dwyerism?

O'Dwyerism (O'Dwyer, William?): Politics. See: Stenhouse.

O'Dwyer's method (O'Dwyer, Joseph P.): Medicine. See: Stedman.

O'Dwyer's tube (O'Dwyer, Joseph P.): Medicine. See: Dorland; Stedman.

Oechelhauser engine (Oechelhauser, Wilhelm von): Engineering and Industry. See: Auger.

OECHELHAUSER, WILHELM VON. 1820-1902. German industrialist and Shakesperian scholar. See: Webster's Biog. Dict. Oechelhauser engine.

OEDER, GEORG CHRISTIAN VON. 1728-1791. German botanist and physician in Denmark. See: Biog. Lex. hervorr. Aerzte. Oedera.

Oedera (Oeder, Georg Christian von): Botany. See: Charnock.

Oedipal (or Oedipean) (Oedipus): Psychiatry. See: Hinsie; Stedman; Webster's 3d.

Oedipal (Oedipus) period (or phase) (Oedipus): Psychiatry. See: Hinsie; Stedman.

OEDIPUS. Theban King in Greek mythology. See: New Encyc. Brit., 1974, Microp. Edipism (or Oedipism), Oedipal (or Oedipean), Oedipal (Oedipus) period (or phase), Oedipus, Oedipus (Edipus) complex.

Oedipus (Oedipus, the Theban King): Generic Word (riddle-solver). See: Partridge.

Oedipus (Edipus) complex (Oedipus): Psychiatry. See: Chaplin; English; Hinsie; Stedman; Webster's 3d.; Winick.

OEHL, EUSEBIO. 1827-1903. Italian anatomist. See: Biog. Lex. hervorr. Aerzte. Oehl's layer, Oehl's muscles.

OEHLER, JOHANNES (HANS). b. 1879. German physician. See: Handb. der Deut. Wissensch., 1949. Oehler's symptom.

Oehler's symptom (Oehler, Johannes): Medicine. See: Dorland; Stedman.

Oehl's layer (Oehl, Eusebio): Anatomy. See: Donath; Dorland; Stedman.

Oehl's muscles (Oehl, Eusebio): Anatomy. See: Stedman.

Oehman and Payne-Gallwey instrument (Derivation undetermined): Engineering and Industry. See: Thrush.

Oehman's survey instrument (Derivation undetermined): Engineering and Industry. See: Thrush.

OERSTED, ANDERS SANDOE. 1816-1872. Danish naturalist. See: World Who's Who Sci. Oerstedia.

Oersted experiment (Oersted, Hans Christian): Physics. See: Van Nostrand Sci. Encyc.

OERSTED, HANS CHRISTIAN. 1777-1851. Danish physicist and chemist. See: Dict. Sci. Biog. Oersted experiment, Oersted medal, Oersted (unit).

Oersted medal (Oersted, Hans Christian): Physics. See: Encyc. Brit., 1973 under "Oersted, Hans Christian."

Oersted (unit) (Oersted, Hans Christian): Physics. See: Ballentyne; Dresner; Thewlis; Van Nostrand Sci. Encyc.; Webster's 3d.

Oerstedia (Oersted, Anders Sandoe): Zoology. See: Pennak.

OERTEL, MAX JOSEPH. 1835-1897. German physician. See: Biog. Lex. hervorr. Aerzte. Oertel's treatment.

Oertel's treatment (Oertel, Max Joseph): Medicine. See: Dorland.

Oesterheld method (Derivation undetermined): Engineering and Industry. See: Thrush.

OESTERREICHER, K. fl. 1929. Austrian physician. (Biography source unavailable.) Oesterreicher-Turner syndrome.

Oesterreicher-Turner syndrome (Oesterreicher, K. and Turner, John W. Aldren): Medicine. See: Jablonski. Also known as: Fong's syndrome, Oesterreicher's syndrome, Touraine's syndrome, Turner-Kieser syndrome, Turner's syndrome.

Oesterreicher's syndrome (Oesterreicher, K.). See: Oesterreicher-Turner syndrome.

OESTREICHER, A. No dates. Austrian? physician. (Biography source unavailable.) Oestreicher's reaction.

Oestreicher's reaction (Oestreicher, A.): Medicine. See: Dorland.

Oetling freezing method (Derivation undetermined): Engineering and Industry. See: Thrush.

OFFA. d. 796. King of Mercians in Anglo-Saxon England. See: Dict. Nat. Biog. Offa's dyke.

Offa's dyke (Offa): History. See: Columbia-Viking Desk Encyc.; Steinberg.

OFFORD, HAROLD REGINALD. 1903- . Canadian-born American plant pathologist. See: Amer. Men Sci., 8th ed. Offord reagent.

Offord reagent (Offord, Harold Reginald): Chemistry. See: Van Nostrand Chem. Dict.

OFFRET, ALBERT JULES JOSEPH. fl. 1891-1896. French mineralogist. Cited in: Royal Soc. Cat. Sci. Pap., 1884-1900. Offretite.

Offretite (Offret, Albert Jules Joseph): Earth Sciences. See: Thrush. Also known as: Phillipsite.

Ogam (Ogham, Ogum) alphabet (Ogma): Linguistics. See: Brewer; Encyc. Brit., 1973; Harvey; Partridge; Scott.

OGATA KORIN. 1653?-1716. Japanese artist. See: Webster's Biog. Dict. Korin school (of Japanese painters).

OGATA, M. No dates. Japanese physician. (Biography source unavailable.) Ogata's method.

OGATA, MASAKI. fl. 1893. Japanese physician. (Biography source unavailable.) Ogata's broth.

Ogata's broth (Ogata, Masaki): Medicine. See: Kelly.

Ogata's method (Ogata, M.): Medicine. See: Dorland.

OGBURN, (SIHON) CICERO. 1900- . American chemist. See: Pogg., vol. 6. Ogburn test reactions for certain platinum-group metals.

Ogburn test reactions for certain platinum-group metals (Ogburn, Cicero): Chemistry. See: Van Nostrand Chem. Dict.

OGDEN, FRANK NEVIN. 1895- . American physician. See: Amer. Med. Direct., 1950. Zuelzer-Ogden syndrome.

OGILVIE, SIR HENEAGE (In full: WILLIAM HENEAGE). fl. 1910-1964. English physician. See: Med. Direct., 1964. Ogilvie's syndrome.

Ogilvie's syndrome (Ogilvie, Sir Heneage): Medicine. See: Jablonski.

Ogino-Knaus rule (Ogino, Kyusaka and Knaus, Hermann Hubert): Medicine. See: Stedman.

OGINO, KYUSAKA. b. 1881. Japanese physician. Cited in: Kelly. Ogino-Knaus rule.

OGMA. Irish sun deity. See: Jobes. Ogam (Ogham, Ogum) alphabet.

OGSTON, SIR ALEXANDER. 1844-1929. Scottish surgeon. See: World Who's Who Sci. Ogston-Luc operation, Ogston's line, Ogston's operation.

Ogston-Luc operation (Ogston, Sir Alexander and Luc, Henri): Medicine. See: Dorland; Stedman.

Ogston's line (Ogston, Sir Alexander): Medicine. See: Dorland; Stedman.

Ogston's operation (Ogston, Sir Alexander): Medicine. See: Dorland; Stedman.

OGUCHI, CHUTA. 1875-1945. Japanese ophthalmologist. See: Biog. Lex. hervorr. Aerzte, 1880-1930. Oguchi's disease.

Oguchi's disease (Oguchi, Chuta): Medicine. See: Dorland; Jablonski; Stedman.

Ogygian (Ogygus): Generic Word (very ancient). See: Charnock; Partridge; Webster's 3d.

OGYGUS. Legendary King of Attica. See: Jobes. Ogygian.

O'Hara forceps (or clamp) (O'Hara, Michael, Jr.): Medicine. See: Dorland; Stedman.

O'Hara furnace (Derivation undetermined): Engineering and Industry. See: Thrush.

O'HARA, MICHAEL, JR. 1869-1926. American surgeon. Cited in: Kelly. O'Hara forceps (or clamp).

O'HARA, SHOICHIRO (or HACHIRO?). fl. 1930? or fl. 1954? Japanese physician. (Biography source unavailable.) O'Hara's disease.

O'Hara's bureaucratic ethic (Derivation undetermined): Sociology. See: Martin.

O'Hara's disease (O'Hara, Shoichiro (or Hachiro?). See: Francis' disease.

O'Higgins' disease (Derivation undetermined): Medicine. See: Jablonski.

Ohm (Ohm, Georg Simon): Physics. See: Ballentyne; Dresner; Thewlis; Van Nostrand Sci. Encyc.; Webster's 3d.

OHM, GEORG SIMON. 1787-1854. German physicist. See: Dict. Sci. Biog. Abohm, acoustic(al) Ohm, gemmho, international Ohm, mechanical Ohm, Mho, Mohm, Ohm, Ohm('s) law, Ohm law in hydromagnetics, Ohma, Ohmad, Ohmic loss, Ohmmeter(s), Ohm's law (acoustic), reciprocal Ohm, Secohm, specific acoustical Ohm, thermal Ohm.

Ohm('s) law (Ohm, Georg Simon): Physics. See: Ballentyne; Thewlis; Thrush; Van Nostrand Sci. Encyc.; Webster's 3d.

Ohm law in hydromagnetics (Ohm, Georg Simon): Physics. See: Internat. Dict. Phys. Elec.

OHM, REINHARD AUGUST MARIA BERTRAM. b. 1875. German physician. Cited in: Index-Cat. Libr. Surg.-Gen. Off., 2d Ser., vol. 12, 1907. Ohm's instrument.

Ohma (Ohm, Georg Simon): Physics. See: Dresner.

Ohmad (Ohm, Georg Simon): Physics. See: Dresner.

Ohmic loss (Ohm, Georg Simon): Electronics. See: Hughes.

Ohmmeter(s) (Ohm, Georg Simon): Physics. See: Hughes; Internat. Dict. Phys. Elec.; Markus; Van Nostrand Sci. Encyc.

Ohm's instrument (Ohm, Reinhard August Maria Bertram): Medicine. See: Stedman.

Ohm's law (acoustic) (Ohm, Georg Simon): Physics. See: Ballentyne; English; Webster's 3d.

Oisin, legendary Irish bard. See: Ossian.

OKAC, ARNOST. fl. 1931-1950. Czechoslovakian chemist. See: Who's Who Sci. Europe, 1972. Dubsky-Okac test reaction for bismuth, Dubsky-Okac test reaction for magnesium.

Okapia Johnstoni (Johnston, Sir Harry Hamilton?): Zoology. See: Pennak.

OKEN, LORENZ (Real surname: OCKENFUSS). 1779-1851. German naturalist and philosopher. See: Dict. Sci. Biog. Okenite, Oken's body.

Okenite (Oken, Lorenz): Earth Sciences. See: Thrush; Webster's 3d.

Oken's body (Oken, Lorenz): Medicine. See: Dorland.

Okill gauge (Okill, J.): Engineering and Industry. See: Auger.

OKILL, J. fl. 1938. English engineer. (Biography source unavailable.) Okill gauge.

OKOSHI, M. fl. 1955. Japanese engineer. (Biography source unavailable.) Okoshi wear machine.

Okoshi wear machine (Okoshi, M.): Engineering and Industry. See: Auger.

OKUMA, KIYOSHI. fl. 1926. Japanese chemist. Cited in: Chem. Abstr., vol. 20, p. 3000. Suitsu-Okuma test reaction.

OKUN, ARTHUR M. 1928- . American economist. See: Who's Who Amer., 1974-1975. Okun's law.

Okun's law (Okun, Arthur M.): Economics. See: Newsweek, July 14, 1975.

OKYO (MARUYAMA OKYO or MARUYAMA MASATAKA). 1733-1795. Japanese painter. See: New Encyc. Brit., 1974, Microp. Maruyama School.

Olaf Bloch Memorial Award (Bloch, Olaf F.): Photography. See: Focal Encyc. Photog. under "Awards, Britain."

OLBERS, HEINRICH WILHELM MATTHAEUS. 1758-1840. German physician and astronomer. See: Dict. Sci. Biog. Olber's paradox.

Olber's paradox (Olbers, Heinrich Wilhelm Matthaeus): Astronomy. See: Ballentyne; Blumberg; Satterthwaite; Thewlis.

Old Adam (Adam). Religion. See: Partridge.

Old Braggs" (or "The Braggs") (Bragg, Philip): History. See: Brewer under Regimental and Divisional Nicknames (British)."

Old Moore" (almanac) (Moore, Francis): Printing. See: Dict. Nat. Biog.

Old Newton (Newton, Isaac): Generic Word (gravitational force). See: Partridge.

Old Nick (Old Nick, the spirit): Generic Word (devil). See: Charnock; Jobes.

OLD NICK, THE SPIRIT. An ancient evil spirit of waters in Northern mythology. See: Hazlitt. Old Nick.

Old Tom (gin) (Chamberlain, Thomas): Food and Drink. See: Brewer; Wagner (Names).

Oldbuck (Oldbuck, Jonathan): Generic Word (antiquary). See: Charnock.

OLDBUCK, JONATHAN. Character in Sir Walter Scott's "Antiquary," (1816). See: Harvey under "Antiquary." Oldbuck.

Oldham(s) coupling (Oldham, John): Engineering and Industry. See: Auger; Van Nostrand Sci. Encyc.; Webster's 3d.

OLDHAM, JOHN. 1779-1840. Irish engineer. See: Dict. Nat. Biog. Oldham(s) coupling.

Oldham stone duster (Derivation undetermined): Engineering and Industry. See: Thrush.

OLDHAM, THOMAS. 1816-1878. Irish geologist. See: Dict. Sci. Biog. Oldhamite.

Oldhamite (Oldham, Thomas): Earth Sciences. See: Thrush; Webster's 3d.

Olin book number (Olin, Charles R.): Library Science. See: Harrod.

OLIN, CHARLES R. fl. 1893. American librarian. Cited in: Libr. J., vol. 18 (May, 1893), pp. 144-45. Olin book number.

Oliver (1) (Cromwell, Oliver): Generic Word (hammer). See: Hendrickson; Partridge.

Oliver (2) (Cromwell, Oliver): Generic Word (full moon). See: Hendrickson; Partridge.

Oliver-Cardarelli sign (Oliver, William Silver and Cardarelli, Antonio). See: Cardarelli's sign.

Oliver (dogcart) (Oliver, Capt. Richard Aldworth?): Generic Word. See: Charnock.

OLIVER, GEORGE. 1841-1915. English physiologist. See: Dict. Sci. Biog. Oliver reagent for bile acids in urine, Oliver's tests.

OLIVER, GEORGE WATSON. 1857-1923. Scottish-born American botanist. See: Biog. Notes Upon Botanists. Oliveranthus.

Oliver reagent for bile acids in urine (Oliver, George): Medicine. See: Van Nostrand Chem. Dict.

OLIVER, CAPT. RICHARD ALDWORTH. 1811-1889. English naval officer. See: Boase. Oliver (dogcart)?

OLIVER, WILLIAM. 1695-1764. English physician. See: Dict. Nat. Biog Bath Oliver (biscuit).

OLIVER, WILLIAM SILVER. 1836-1908. English physician. See: Biog. Lex. hervorr. Aerzte, 1880-1930. Oliver-Cardarelli sign.

Oliveranthus (Oliver, George Watson): Botany. See: Taylor, N.

Oliverian (Cromwell, Oliver): History. See: Webster's 3d.

Oliver's sign (Oliver, William Silver). See: Oliver-Cardarelli sign.

Oliver's skull (Cromwell, Oliver): Generic Word (chamber pot). See: Hendrickson; Partridge.

Oliver's tests (Oliver, George): Medicine. See: Dorland; Stedman.

OLIVIER, SIMON CORNELIS JOHANNES. b. 1879. Dutch chemist. See: Pogg., vol. 6. Olivier test reaction for nitro compounds.

Olivier test reaction for nitro compounds (Olivier, Simon Cornelis Johannes): Chemistry. See: Van Nostrand Chem. Dict.

Olland cycle (Derivation undetermined): Earth Sciences. See: Huschke.

OLLENDORFF, HELENE. fl. 1928. German dermatologist. (Biography source unavailable.) Buschke-Ollendorff syndrome.

Ollier-Klippel-Trenaunay syndrome (Ollier, Leopold; Klippel, Maurice; and Trenaunay, Paul). See: Klippel-Trenaunay syndrome.

OLLIER, LEOPOLD (In full: Louis Xavier Edouard). 1830-1900. French surgeon. See: World Who's Who Sci. Ollier-Klippel-Trenaunay syndrome, Ollier's layer, Ollier's method (or graft), Ollier's method of treating compound fractures, Ollier's syndrome (or disease), Ollier's theory (or law).

Ollier's layer (Ollier, Leopold): Medicine. See: Dorland; Stedman.

Ollier's method (or graft) (Ollier, Leopold). See: Thiersch's method.

Ollier's method of treating compound fractures (Ollier, Leopold): Medicine. See: Kelly.

Ollier's syndrome (or disease) (Ollier, Leopold): Medicine. See: Dorland; Jablonski; Stedman.

Ollier's theory (or law) (Ollier, Leopold): Medicine. See: Dorland; Stedman.

Olney bulrush (Derivation undetermined): Botany. See: Winburne.

Olney Doctrine (Olney, Richard): History. See: Harbottle.

Olney-Pauncefote Treaty (Olney, Richard and Pauncefote, Julian, 1st Baron Pauncefote): History. See: Jameson.

OLNEY, RICHARD. 1835-1917. American statesman. See: Dict. Amer. Biog. Olney Doctrine, Olney-Pauncefote Treaty.

Olsen ductility test (Olsen, Thorsten Y.): Engineering and Industry. See: Thrush.

OLSEN, OLAF. fl. 1957. Swedish ophthalmologist. (Biography source unavailable.) Alstroem-Olsen syndrome.

OLSEN, THORSTEN Y. fl. 1921. American engineer. Cited in: Chem. Abstr., Decenn. Index, 1917-1926. Olsen ductility test, Olsen's testing machine.

Olsen's testing machine (Olsen, Thorsten Y.): Engineering and Industry. See: Hackh.

Olshausen, Robert von. See: Von Olshausen, Robert.

Olshausen's method (Von Olshausen, Robert): Medicine. See: Dorland; Stedman.

OLSHEVSKY, DIMITRY EUGENE. 1900- . Polish-born American physicist. See: Amer. Men Sci., 6th ed. Olshevsky tube.

Olshevsky tube (Olshevsky, Dimitry Eugene): Medicine. See: Dorland.

OLSON, HARRY FERDINAND. 1902- . American acoustical engineer. See: World Who's Who Amer. Olson microphone.

Olson microphone (Olson, Harry Ferdinand): Electronics. See: Hughes.

OLSZEWSKI, JERZY. 1913-1966. Polish-born Canadian neurologist. See: Amer. Men Sci., 10th ed. Steele-Richardson-Olszewski syndrome.

O'MAHONEY, JOSEPH CHRISTOPHER. 1884-1962. American legislator. See: Biog. Direct. Amer. Congress. O'Mahoney-Ramspeck Act.

O'Mahoney-Ramspeck Act (O'Mahoney, Joseph Christopher and Ramspeck, Robert C. Word): Politics. See: Smith.

OMALIUS-D'HALLOY, D', JEAN BAPTISTE JULIEN. 1783-1875. Belgian geologist. See: Pogg., vols. 2, 3. Halloysite.

OMAR KHAYYAM. d. 1123. Persian poet and astronomer. See: Encyc. Brit., 1973. Omar Khayyam quatrain, Omar stanza, Omarian.

Omar Khayyam quatrain (Omar Khayyam): Literature. See: Preminger.

Omar stanza (Omar Khayyam): Literature. See: Webster's 3d.

Omarian (Omar Khayyam): Literature. See: Webster's 3d.

Omayya. See: Umayyah.

OMBREDANNE, LOUIS. 1871-1956. French physician. See: Biog. Lex. hervorr. Aerzte, 1880-1930. Ombredanne's mask, Ombredanne's operation, Ombredanne's syndrome.

Ombredanne's mask (Ombredanne, Louis): Medicine. See: Dorland.

Ombredanne's operation (Ombredanne, Louis): Medicine. See: Dorland.

Ombredanne's syndrome (Ombredanne, Louis): Medicine. See: Jablonski.

OMODEI-ZORINI, ATTILIO. 1897- . Italian physiologist. See: Who's Who Italy, 1957. Omodei-Zorini syndrome.

Omodei-Zorini syndrome (Omodei-Zorini, Attilio): Medicine. See: Jablonski.

ONAN. A son of Judah in the Old Testament. See: Hastings (Dict. Bible). Onanism (or Onanist).

Onanism (or Onanist) (Onan): Generic Word (coitus interruptus). See: Dorland; Hendrickson; Stedman; Webster's 3d.

ONANOFF, JACQUES. b. 1859. French physician. Cited in: Index-Cat. Libr. Surg.-Gen. Off., 2d Ser., vol. 12, 1907. Onanoff's sign (or reflex).

Onanoff's sign (or reflex) (Onanoff, Jacques): Medicine. See: Stedman.

Ondine, water nymph. See: Undine.

Ondine's (or Undine's) curse (Undine): Medicine. See: Jablonski.

one for Ripley (Ripley, Robert Leroy): Generic Word (strange phenomenon). See: Hendrickson.

O'NEILL, FRANK. fl. 1911-1935. American glass technologist. Cited in: Chem. Abstr., Decenn. Indexes, 1907-1916; 1917-1926. O'Neill machine.

O'Neill hardness test (O'Neill, Hugh): Engineering and Industry. See: Auger.

O'NEILL, HUGH. 1899- . English metallurgist. See: Who's Who Brit. Sci., 1953. O'Neill hardness test.

O'NEILL, HUGH (2ND EARL OF TYRONE). ca. 1540-1616. Irish Roman Catholic rebel. See: Dict. Nat. Biog. Tyrone's revolt.

O'Neill machine (O'Neill, Frank): Engineering and Industry. See: Thrush.

O'Neill's revolt (O'Neill, Hugh). See: Tyrone's revolt.

ONIS, LUIS DE. fl. 1819. Spanish minister. Cited in: Dict. Amer. Hist., vol. 1. Adams-Onis Treaty.

ONISHI, YOSHIAKIRA. b. 1865. Japanese physician. See: Biog. Lex. hervorr. Aerzte, 1880-1930. Takayasu-Onishi syndrome.

Onsager equation (or conductivity equation) (Onsager, Lars): Chemistry. See: Ballentyne; Van Nostrand Chem. Dict. Also known as: Debye-Hueckel-Onsager equation.

Onsager equation for dielectric constant (formula or theory of dielectrics) (Onsager, Lars): Physics. See: Ballentyne; Internat. Dict. Ap. Math.; Internat. Dict. Phys. Elec.; Thewlis.

ONSAGER, LARS. 1903- . Norwegian-born American chemist. See: World Who's Who Sci. Onsager equation (or conductivity equation), Onsager equation for dielectric constant (formula or theory of dielectrics), Onsager('s) relations (reciprocal relations or reciprocity theorem).

Onsager('s) relations (reciprocal relations or reciprocity theorem) (Onsager, Lars): Physics. See: Ballentyne; Internat. Dict. Ap. Math.; Thewlis.

OPALSKI, ADAM. 1897-1963. Polish physician. (Biography source unavailable.) Opalski's syndrome.

Opalski's syndrome (Opalski, Adam): Medicine. See: Jablonski.

operation of Loreta (Loreta, Pietro). See: Loreta's operation.

OPHELIA. Tragic character in William Shakespeare's play "Hamlet" (1600-1601). See: Magill. Ophelia (rose).

Ophelia (rose) (Ophelia): Botany. See: Partridge.

OPIE, EUGENE LINDSAY. 1873-1971. American pathologist. See: World Who's Who Sci. Opie paradox.

Opie paradox (Opie, Eugene Lindsay): Medicine. See: Dorland.

OPITZ, HANS. b. 1888. German pediatrician. See: Biog. Lex. hervorr. Aerzte, 1880-1930. Opitz's disease.

OPITZ, JOHN MARIUS. 1935- . German-born American pediatrician. See: Amer. Men and Women Sci., 12th ed. Smith-Lemli-Opitz syndrome.

OPITZ VON BOBERFELD, MARTIN. 1597-1639. German poet, critic and metrical reformer. See: New Encyc. Brit., 1974, Microp. Opitzian school (of metrical reform).

Opitzian school (of metrical reform) (Opitz von Boberfeld, Martin): Literature. See: Preminger.

Opitz's disease (Opitz, Hans): Medicine. See: Dorland; Jablonski.

Oppenauer oxidation (or reaction) (Oppenauer, Rupert V.): Chemistry. See: Ballentyne; Van Nostrand Chem. Dict.; Webster's 3d.

OPPENAUER, RUPERT V. fl. 1937. Austrian chemist. Cited in: Chem. Abstr., Decenn. Index, 1937-1946. Oppenauer oxidation (or reaction).

OPPENHEIM, HERMANN. 1858-1919. German neurologist. See: World Who's Who Sci. Erb-Oppenheim-Goldflam syndrome, Minor-Oppenheim syndrome, Oppenheim('s) reflex, Oppenheim's disease, Oppenheim's gait, Oppenheim's syndrome?, Ziehen-Oppenheim syndrome (or disease).

OPPENHEIM, MAURICE. 1876-1949. American dermatologist. See: World Who's Who Sci. Mueller-Oppenheim diagnosis (or reaction), Oppenheim-Urbach syndrome (or disease).

Oppenheim('s) reflex (Oppenheim, Hermann): Medicine. See: Hinsie; Stedman.

Oppenheim-Urbach syndrome (or disease) (Oppenheim, Maurice and Urbach, Erich): Medicine. See: Dorland; Jablonski.

Oppenheimer case (Oppenheimer, J. Robert): Politics. See: Morris and Irwin.

OPPENHEIMER, ELLA HUTZLER. 1897- . American pathologist. See: Amer. Men and Women Sci., 12th ed. Landing-Oppenheimer syndrome.

OPPENHEIMER, ISAAC. 1855-1928. American physician. (Biography source unavailable.) Oppenheimer treatment.

OPPENHEIMER, J. ROBERT. 1904-1967. American physicist. See: Dict. Sci. Biog. Born-Oppenheimer approximation, Born-Oppenheimer method, Oppenheimer case, Oppenheimer-Phillips process (or reaction).

Oppenheimer-Phillips process (or reaction) (Oppenheimer, J. Robert and Phillips, Melba): Physics. See: Ballentyne; Thewlis; Van Nostrand Sci. Encyc.

Oppenheimer treatment (Oppenheimer, Isaac): Medicine. See: Dorland; Hinsie; Stedman.

Oppenheim's disease (Oppenheim, Hermann): Medicine. See: Jablonski.

Oppenheim's gait (Oppenheim, Hermann): Medicine. See: Stedman.

Oppenheim's syndrome (Oppenheim, Hermann?): Medicine. See: Jablonski.

OPPLER, BRUNO. fl. 1895. German physician. Cited in: Kelly. Boas-Oppler bacillus.

ORAM, SAMUEL. 1913- . English cardiologist. See: Who's Who Sci. Europe, 1972. Holt-Oram syndrome.

Orange, William III, Prince of. See: William III of Orange.

Orangeism (or Orangemen) (William III of Orange): History. See: Attwater; Brewer; Latham.

Orbeli effect (Orbeli, Leon Abgarovich): Medicine. See: Dorland; Stedman.

ORBELI, LEON ABGAROVICH. 1882-1958. Russian physiologist. See: Dict. Sci. Biog. Orbeli effect.

ORCEL, JEAN FRANCOIS. 1896- . French mineralogist. See: Pogg., vol. 6. Orcelite.

Orcelite (Orcel, Jean Francois): Earth Sciences. See: Thrush.

Ord-Carver system (Ord, John Allyn? and Carver, Harry Clyde): Statistics. See: Kendall.

ORD, JOHN ALLYN. 1912- . American physicist and mathematician. See: Amer. Men and Women Sci., 12th ed. Ord-Carver system?

ORD, WILLIAM MILLER. 1834-1902. English surgeon. See: World Who's Who Sci. Ord's operation.

Order of Catherine (Catherine I): History. See: Wagner (More Names).

Order of Charles III (Charles III): History. See: Latham.

Order of Charles XIII (Charles XIII): History. See: Latham.

Order of Christ (Jesus Christ): Religion. See: Latham.

Order of Isabella the Catholic (Isabella I, the Catholic): History. See: Latham

Order of Jesus (Jesus Christ): Religion. See: Latham.

Order of Kossuth (Kossuth, Lajos): History. Cited in: Encyc. Brit., 1973 under "Knighthood," vol. 13, p. 409b.

Order of Lenin (Lenin, Nikolai): Sociology. See: Encyc. Brit., 1973 under "Medals and Decoration," vol. 15, p. 65c.

Order of Leopold I (Leopold I): Sociology. See: Encyc. Brit., 1973 under "Knighthood," vol. 13, p. 408c.

Order of Leopold II (Leopold II): Sociology. See: Latham.

Order of Louisa (Louisa Augusta W. Amelia of Mecklenberg-Strelitz): History. See: Latham.

Order of Maria Louisa (Maria Luisa Teresa): History. See: Latham.

Order of Maria Theresa (Maria Theresa): History. See: Encyc. Brit., 1973; Latham.

Order of Maximilian (Maximilian II): History. See: Latham.

Order of Medjidie (Abdul-Medjid I.): History. Cited in: Webster's Biog. Dict.

Order of Pius (Pius IV): Religion. See: Attwater.

Order of St. Andrew (Andrew, Saint): History. See: Harbottle; Latham.

Order of St. Augustine (Augustine, Saint). See: Augustinian friars.

Order of Saint Benedict (Benedict of Nursia, Saint). See: Benedictines.

Order of St. Catherine (Catherine, Saint): Religion. See: Brewer.

Order of St. Clare (Clare of Assisi, Saint): Religion. See: Brewer.

Order of St. Gall (Gall, Saint): Religion. See: Latham.

Order of St. George (Derivation undetermined): History. See: Latham.

Order of St. Gregory The Great (Gregory I, the Great, Saint): Religion. See: Attwater.

Order of St. Hubert (Hubert, Saint): History. See: Harbottle.

Order of St. James of the Sword (James the Greater, Saint): History. See: Latham.

Order (Hospitallers) of St. Lazarus of Jerusalem (or Lazarites) (Lazarus, Saint): Religion. See: Attwater; Latham; New Cath. Encyc.

Order of St. Louis (Louis IX): History. See: Latham.

Order of St. Michael (Michael the Archangel, Saint): History. See: Latham.

Order (or Knights) of St. Michael and St. George (Michael the Archangel, Saint and George, Saint): History. See: Black; Brewer; Latham.

Order (or Knights) of Saint Patrick (Patrick, Saint): History. See: Black; Brewer; Harbottle.

Order of St. Silvester (Silvester I, Saint): Religion. See: Attwater.

Order of St. Stanislaus (Stanislaus, Saint): Sociology. See: Latham.

Order of Saints Maurice and Lazarus (Maurice, Saint and Lazarus, Saint): History. Cited in: Attwater under "Order of St. Lazarus of Jerusalem."

Order of Tiron (Bernard of Tiron, Saint): Religion. See: Attwater.

Orders of Saint Anthony (Anthony, Saint): Religion. See: Mathews, S.

Orders of St. Mary Magdalene (Mary Magdalene, Saint): Religion. See: Mathews, S.

Ordinances of Edward I (Edward I): History. See: Black.

ORDONEZ, EZEQUIEL. 1867-1950. Mexican geologist. See: World Who's Who Sci. Ordonezite.

ORDONEZ, J. HERNANDO. 1910- . Colombian physician. See: Amer. Men and Women Sci., 12th ed. Ordonez melanosis.

Ordonez melanosis (Ordonez, J. Hernando): Medicine. See: Jablonski.

Ordonezite (Ordonez, Ezequiel): Earth Sciences. See: Thrush.

Ord's operation (Ord, William Miller): Medicine. See: Dorland; Stedman.

ORELKIN, B. fl. 1910. Russian chemist. Cited in: Chem. Abstr. vol. 9, p. 1442. Tschugaev-Orelkin test for ferrous iron.

ORESTES. Son of Agnememnon in Greek mythology. See: New Encyc. Brit., 1974, Microp. Orestes complex, Pylades and Orestes.

Orestes complex (Orestes): Psychiatry. See: English.

ORFF, CARL. 1895- . German composer. See: New Encyc. Brit., 1974, Microp. Orff method.

Orff method (Orff, Carl): Music. See: Good.

Orford, 4th Earl of. See: Walpole, Horace (4th Earl of Orford).

organ of Corti (Corti, Alfonso Giacomo Gaspare). See: Corti's organ.

organ of Johnston (Johnston, Christopher). See: Johnston's organ.

organ of Keber (Keber, Gotthard August Ferdinand). See: Keber's organ.

organ of Ruffini (Ruffini, Angelo). See: Ruffini's corpuscles (nerve endings, organs, or cylinder).

organ of Tomosvary (Tomosvary, Odon?). See: Tomosvary's organ.

organs of Zuckerkandl (Zuckerkandl, Emil). See: Zuckerkandl's bodies.

orgue de Barbarie (Barbieri): Music. See: Scholes.

ORIGEN (ORIGENES ADAMANTIUS). ca. 185-254. Christian writer, teacher and heretic of Alexandria. See: New Encyc. Brit., 1974. Origenism (Origenist or Origenian), Origenistic controversies.

Origenism (Origenist or Origenian) (Origen): Religion. See: Attwater; Latham, Webster's 3d.

Origenistic controversies (Origen): Religion. See: Mathews, S.

ORLA-JENSEN, SIGURD. b. 1870. Danish bacteriologist. See: Kraks Blaa Bog, 1935. Jensen's classification, Jensen's solution, Loewenstein-Jensen medium?

ORLANDO. Christian hero in medieval romances. See: Jobes. Orlando.

Orlando (Orlando, the knight): Generic Word (gallant knight). See: Partridge.

Orleanists (Orleans, Philippe d'Orleans): History. See: Latham; Phyfe.

ORLEANS, PHILIPPE D'ORLEANS. 1640-1701. French younger brother of Louis XIV. See: New Encyc. Brit., 1974. Orleanists.

Orloff diamond (Orlov, Grigory Grigoryevich): Applied Arts. See: Latham; New Encyc. Brit., 1974, Microp.; Phyfe.

Orloff (horses) (Orlov, Count Aleksey Grigoryevich): Zoology. See: Webster's 3d.

Orloso test reaction for phenols (Derivation undetermined): Chemistry. See: Van Nostrand Chem. Dict.

ORLOV, COUNT ALEKSEY GRIGORYEVICH. 1737-1808. Russian nobleman. See: New Encyc. Brit., 1974. Orloff (horses).

ORLOV (ORLOFF), GRIGORY GRIGORYEVICH. 1734-1783. Russian states-man. See: New Encyc. Brit., 1974, Microp. Orloff diamond.

Orlovius flask (Derivation undetermined): Chemistry. See: Hackh.

Orlow-Horst reaction for alkaloids (Derivation undetermined): Chemistry. See: Van Nostrand Chem. Dict.

Orlow-Ormont reagent for mercury (Derivation undetermined): Chemistry. See: Van Nostrand Chem. Dict.

Orlow test reaction for ruthenium (Derivation undetermined): Chemistry. See: Van Nostrand Chem. Dict.

ORM (ORMIN). fl. ca. 1200. Danish-born monk in England. See: Dict. Nat. Biog. Ormulum.

ORMOND, JOHN KELSO. b. 1886. American urologist. See: Direct. Med. Specialists, 1974-1975. Ormond's syndrome.

Ormond's syndrome (Ormond, John Kelso): Medicine. See: Jablonski. Also known as: Gerota's fascitis.

Ormulum (Orm): Religion. See: Phyfe.

Ornansite (Derivation undetermined): Earth Sciences. See: Thrush.

ORNSTEIN, LEONARD SALOMON. 1880-1941. Dutch-born American physicist. See: Dict. Sci. Biog. Burger-Dorgelo-Ornstein (Orstein) rule (or sum rule for atomic spectra), Ornstein-Uhlenbeck process.

Ornstein-Uhlenbeck process (Ornstein, Leonard Salomon and Uehlenbeck, George Eugene): Statistics. See: Kendall.

O'Rourke car switcher (Derivation undetermined): Engineering and Industry. See: Thrush.

OROWAN, EGON. 1902- . Hungarian-born American physicist. See: Amer. Men and Women Sci., 12th ed. Taylor-Orowan dislocation?

Orpharion (Orpheus and Arion): Music. See: Partridge; Webster's 3d.

Orphean (or Orphic) (Orpheus): Mythology. See: Charnock; Webster's 3d.

Orpheon (or Orpheonist) (Orpheus): Music. See: Webster's 3d.

ORPHEUS. Ancient Greek legendary hero. See: New Encyc. Brit., 1974, Microp. Orpharion, Orphean (or Orphic), Orpheon (or Orpheonist), Orphibaryton, Orphic mysteries, Orphic poems (or Orphica), Orphics (or Orphicism), Orphism.

Orphibaryton (Orpheus): Music. See: Partridge.

Orphic mysteries (Orpheus): Religion. See: Phyfe.

Orphic poems (or Orphica) (Orpheus): Religion. See: Charnock; Phyfe.

Orphics (or Orphicism) (Orpheus): Religion. See: Canney; Harvey.

Orphism (Orpheus): Fine Arts. See: Osborne; Webster's 3d.

Orr-Sommerfeld equation (Orr, William McFadden? and Sommerfeld, Arnold): Physics. See: Internat. Dict. Ap. Math.

ORR, WILLIAM MCFADDEN. fl. 1888-1909. Irish mathematician. See: Pogg., vols. 4, 5. Orr-Sommerfeld equation?

Orrery (Boyle, Charles, 4th Earl of Orrery): Astronomy. See: Brewer; Charnock; New Encyc. Brit., 1974, Microp.; Webster's 3d.

Orrery, 4th Earl of. See: Boyle, Charles (4th Earl of Orrery).

Orsat apparatus (or gas-analysis instrument) (Orsat, H.?): Chemistry. See: Hackh; Thrush.

ORSAT, H. fl. 1875. French scientist. Cited in: Royal Soc. Cat. Sci. Pap., 1874-1883. Orsat apparatus (or gas-analysis instrument)?

ORSI, FRANCESCO. 1828-1900. Italian physician. See: Biog. Lex. hervorr. Aerzte. Orsi-Grocco method.

Orsi-Grocco method (Orsi, Francesco and Grocco, Pietro): Medicine. See: Dorland; Stedman.

Orsini('s) conspiracy (assassination attempt or bombs) (Orsini, Felice): History. See: Harbottle; Morris and Irwin; Phyfe.

ORSINI, FELICE. 1819-1858. Italian revolutionist. See: Encyc. Brit., 1973. Orsini('s) conspiracy (assassination attempt or bombs).

ORSON. Character in the anonymous French romance, "Valentine and Orson," (1495). See: Harvey. Orson.

Orson (Orson, the character): Generic Word (rough, valiant fellow). See: Partridge.

ORTEGA, CASIMIRO GOMEZ DE. 1730-1810. Spanish botanist. See: Michaud. Casimiroa.

ORTH, JOHANNES J. 1847-1923. German pathologist. See: Biog. Lex. hervorr. Aerzte. Orth('s) stain, Orth's fluid.

Orth('s) stain (Orth, Johannes J.): Medicine. See: Hackh; Stedman.

Orthezia (Dorthes, Jacques Anselm): Botany. See: Webster's 3d.

ORTHMANN, ERNST GOTTLOB. 1858-1922. German physician. See: Biog. Lex. hervorr. Aerzte. Orthmann's tumor.

Orthmann's tumor (Orthmann, Ernst Gottlob). See: Brenner's tumor.

Orth's fluid (Orth, Johannes J.): Medicine. See: Stedman.

Ortley pippin (apple) (Derivation undetermined): Botany. See: Partridge.

Ortliberians (Ortlieb): Religion. See: Canney.

ORTLIEB. fl. 1210. Strassburg heretic. Cited in: Hastings (Encyc. Rel. Ethics), vol. 2, p. 842b. Ortliberians.

ORTMANN, ARNOLD EDWARD. 1863-1927. German-born American zoogeographer. See: Pogg., vols. 4, 6, 7a suppl. Ortmann's coastal regions.

Ortmann's coastal regions (Ortmann, Arnold Edward): Earth Sciences. See: Thrush.

ORTNER, NORBERT. b. 1865. Austrian physician. See: Biog. Lex. hervorr. Aerzte. Ortner's syndrome.

Ortner's syndrome (Ortner, Norbert): Medicine. See: Jablonski.

ORTODOSCU, ANDREI P. fl. 1923. Rumanian? chemist. Cited in: Chem. Abstr., vol. 17, p. 3145. Ortodoscu-Ressy micro-test for antimony and tin.

Ortodoscu-Ressy micro-test for antimony and tin (Ortodoscu, Andrei P. and Ressy, Marcelle): Chemistry. See: Van Nostrand Chem. Dict.

ortol of Hauff (Hauff, Friedrich Wilhelm Albert?): Photography. See: Focal Encyc. Photog. under "Development History."

Orton cones (Orton, Edward, Jr.): Engineering and Industry. See: Thewlis; Thrush.

ORTON, EDWARD, JR. 1863-1932. American ceramics engineer. See: Who Was Who Amer., vol. 1. Orton cones.

Orton hypothesis (Orton, Samuel Torrey): Medicine. See: Good.

ORTON, SAMUEL TORREY. 1879-1948. American neuropsychiatrist. See: Who Was Who Amer., vol. 2. Orton hypothesis.

Orvietan (Derivation undetermined): Generic Word (antidote). See: Charnock.

ORWELL, GEORGE (Real name: ERIC BLAIR). 1903-1950. English novelist. See: New Encyc. Brit., 1974. Orwellian (or Orwellism).

Orwellian (or Orwellism) (Orwell, George): Generic Word (totalitarian society). See: Barnhart (New Eng.).

os sylvii (Sylvius, Jacobus). See: Sylvius' bone.

OSANN, ALFRED (In full: CARL ALFRED). 1859-1923. German petrographer and mineralogist. See: Pogg., vols. 4, 5, 6. Osannite, Osann's classification.

Osannite (Osann, Alfred): Earth Sciences. See: Thrush.

Osann's classification (Osann, Alfred): Earth Sciences. See: Thrush.

OSBECK, PETER. 1723-1805. Swedish naturalist. See: Svenska Maen Och Kvinnor. Osbeckia.

Osbeckia (Osbeck, Peter): Botany. See: Charnock.

Osborn-Shaw process (Derivation undetermined): Engineering and Industry. See: Thrush. Also known as: Shaw process.

Osborne judgment (Derivation undetermined): Politics. See: Steinberg.

OSBORNE, NATHAN S. fl. 1899-1931. American physicist. See: Pogg., vol. 6. Osborne, Stimson and Jennings method for mechanical equivalent of heat.

Osborne, Stimson and Jennings method for mechanical equivalent of heat (Osborne, Nathan S.; Stimson, Harold Frederic; and Ginnings, Defoe Childress): Physics. See: Internat. Dict. Phys. Elec.

Oscar (Asche, Oscar): Generic Word (money). See: Hendrickson; Partridge.

Oscar (Oscarizing or Oscar-Wilding) (Wilde, Oscar): Generic Word (homosexual). See: Hendrickson under "Oscar..."

Oscar (award) (Wilde, Oscar): Mass Media. See: Brewer.

Oscar (trophy) (Pierce, Oscar): Mass Media. See: Hendrickson.

OSEEN, CARL WILHELM. b. 1879. Swedish mathematician. See: Pogg., vols. 4, 5, 6. Oseen method (or approximation).

Oseen method (or approximation) (Oseen, Carl Wilhelm): Physics. See: Internat. Dict. Ap. Math.; Thewlis.

OSERETSKY, N. I. fl. 1926-1931. Russian psychologist. Cited in: Cum. Auth. Index to Psych. Index, 1894-1935, and Psych. Abstr., 1927-1958. Lincoln-Oseretsky motor development scale, Oseretsky scale.

Oseretsky scale (Oseretsky, N. I.): Psychology. See: English.

OSGOOD, ROBERT BAYLEY. 1873-1956. American orthopedic surgeon. See: World Who's Who Sci. Osgood-Schlatter syndrome (or disease).

Osgood–Schlatter syndrome (or disease) (Osgood, Robert Bayley and Schlatter, Carl): Medicine. See: Dorland; Jablonski; Stedman. Also known as: Lannelongue–Osgood–Schlatter syndrome, Lannelongue's disease, Schlatter's disease.

OSGOOD, WILLIAM R. 1895– . American mechanical engineer. See: Amer. Men and Women Sci., 12th ed. Ramberg–Osgood parameters.

OSHIMA, KINTARO. fl. 1901–1918. Japanese chemist. Cited in: Chem. Abstr. Decenn. Indexes, 1907–1916, 1917–1926. Oshima–Tollens method for detection of methylpentose or methylpentosan, Tollens–Oshima test.

Oshima–Tollens method for detection of methylpentose or methylpentosan (Oshima, Kintaro and Tollens, Bernhard Christian Gottfried): Chemistry. Cited in: Chem. Abstr., vol. 12, p. 1276.

OSIANDER, ANDREAS (Real name: HOSEMANN). 1498–1552. German Lutheran theologian. See: Encyc. Brit., 1973. Osiandrian(s).

OSIANDER, FRIEDRICH BENJAMIN. 1759–1822. German physician. See: World Who's Who Sci. Osiander's maneuver.

Osiander's maneuver (Osiander, Friedrich Benjamin). See: Saxtorph's maneuver.

Osiandrian(s) (Osiander, Andreas): Religion. See: Canney; Webster's 3d.

Oskar Messter Medal (Messter, Oskar Eduard): Photography. See: Focal Encyc. Photog. under "Awards (Germany)."

Osler–Libman–Sacks disease (Osler, Sir William; Libman, Emanuel; and Sacks, Benjamin). See: Libman–Sacks syndrome (or disease).

Osler–Vaquez disease (Osler, Sir William and Vaquez, Louis Henri). See: Vaquez–Osler disease.

OSLER, SIR WILLIAM. 1849–1919. Canadian-born physician in America and England. See: World Who's Who Sci. Osler–Libman–Sacks disease, Oslerize, Osler's node(s), Osler's phenomenon, Osler's sign, Osler's syndrome (1), Osler's syndrome (2) (or disease), Vaquez–Osler disease.

Oslerize (Osler, Sir William): Generic Word (useless after age 40). See: Hendrickson.

Osler's node(s) (Osler, Sir William): Medicine. See: Dorland; Jablonski; Stedman.

Osler's phenomenon (Osler, Sir William): Medicine. See: Dorland.

Osler's sign (Osler, Sir William): Medicine. See: Dorland; Stedman.

Osler's syndrome (1) (Osler, Sir William): Medicine. See: Jablonski.

Osler's syndrome (2) (or disease) (Osler, Sir William): Medicine. See: Dorland; Jablonski; Stedman. Also known as: Babington's disease, Goldstein's hematemesis (or heredofamilial angiomatosis), Rendu–Osler syndrome, Rendu–Weber–Osler syndrome.

OSMAN (or OTHMAN) I. 1259–1326. Founder of the Ottoman Empire. See: Encyc. Brit., 1973. Osmanli, Ottoman (couch), Ottoman (empire).

Osmanli (Osman I.): History. See: Encyc. Brit., 1973; Webster's 3d.

Osmunda (or Osmund) (Osmunder): Botany. See: Charnock Taylor, N.; Webster's 3d.

OSMUNDER. In Saxon mythology, a name for the god Thor. (Biography source unavailable.) Osmunda (or Osmund).

OSSIAN (or OISIN). Legendary Irish warrior and bard. See: New Encyc. Brit., 1974, Microp. Ossianic.

Ossianic (Ossian): Literature. See: Barnhart (Eng. Lit.); Partridge.

OSTERTAG, ROBERT VON. 1864–1940. German veterinarian. See: Biog. Lex. hervorr. Aerzte. Ostertagia.

Ostertagia (Ostertag, Robert von): Zoology. See: Dorland; Webster's 3d.

OSTROGRADSKI, MIKHAIL VASILIEVICH. 1801–1862. Russian mathematician. See: Dict. Sci. Biog. Ostrogradski's theorem.

Ostrogradski's theorem (Ostrogradski, Mikhail Vasilievich): Mathematics. See: James. Also known as: Gauss' theorem, Green's theorem in space.

Ostromisslensky butadiene synthesis (Ostromisslensky, Ivan): Chemistry. See: Krauch and Kunz.

OSTROMISSLENSKY (OSTROMUISLENSKII or OSTROMYSSLENSKY), IVAN. fl. 1910. Russian chemist. See: Pogg., vol. 5. Ostromisslensky butadiene synthesis, Ostromisslensky test reaction for ethylene compounds, Ostromyslenskii reaction.

Ostromisslensky test reaction for ethylene compounds (Ostromisslensky, Ivan): Chemistry. See: Van Nostrand Chem. Dict.

Ostromyslenskii reaction (Ostromisslensky, Ivan): Chemistry. See: Van Nostrand Chem. Dict.

OSTROWSKI, N. No dates. Russian patron of botany. (Biography source unavailable.) Ostrowskia.

Ostrowskia (Ostrowski, N.): Botany. See: Taylor, N.

OSTRUM, HERMAN WILLIAM. b. 1893. Russian-born American roentgenologist. See: Direct. Med. Specialists, 1965–1966. Furst–Ostrum syndrome.

Ostwald colors (Ostwald, Wilhelm): Chemistry. See: Chaplin; English.

Ostwald dilution law (Ostwald, Wilhelm): Chemistry. See: Ballentyne; Internat. Dict. Ap. Math.; Thewlis.

Ostwald equation (Ostwald, Wilhelm): Chemistry. See: Hackh.

Ostwald–Folin pipette (Ostwald, Wilhelm? and Folin, Otto): Chemistry. See: Van Nostrand Chem. Dict.

Ostwald pipette (Ostwald, Wilhelm?): Chemistry. See: Van Nostrand Chem. Dict.

Ostwald process (Ostwald, Wilhelm): Chemistry. See: Van Nostrand Chem. Dict.

Ostwald rule (Ostwald, Wilhelm): Chemistry. See: Van Nostrand Chem. Dict.

Ostwald solubility coefficient (Ostwald, Wilhelm): Chemistry. See: Ballentyne.

Ostwald statement of the second law of thermodynamics (Ostwald, Wilhelm): Physics. See: Internat. Dict. Ap. Math.

OSTWALD, WILHELM. 1853–1932. German physical chemist. See: World Who's Who Sci. Ostwald colors, Ostwald dilution law, Ostwald equation, Ostwald–Folin pipette? Ostwald pipette? Ostwald process, Ostwald rule, Ostwald solubility coefficient, Ostwald statement of the second law of thermodynamics, Ostwald's adsorption isotherm, Ostwald's basicity rule, Ostwald's theory of indicators.

Ostwald's adsorption isotherm (Ostwald, Wilhelm): Chemistry. See: Ballentyne.

Ostwald's basicity rule (Ostwald, Wilhelm): Chemistry. See: Ballentyne.

Ostwald's theory of indicators (Ostwald, Wilhelm): Chemistry. See: Ballentyne; Hackh.

OSWALD, SAINT. d. 992. English monk and bishop. See: Holweck. Oswald's law, Oswald's law hundred.

Oswald's law (Oswald, Saint): Law. See: Black.

Oswald's law hundred (Oswald, Saint): Law. See: Black.

OSZACKI, ALEXANDER. b. 1883. Polish physician. See: Arnim. Oszacki reagent.

Oszacki reagent (Oszacki, Alexander): Chemistry. See: Van Nostrand Chem. Dict.

OTA, M. T. fl. 1939. Japanese physician. (Biography source unavailable.) Ota's nevus.

OTANI, MORISUKE. fl. 1920. Japanese physician. Cited in: Chem. Abstr., Decenn. Index, 1917–1926. Otani's test.

Otani's test (Otani, Morisuke): Medicine. See: Dorland; Stedman.

Ota's nevus (Ota, M. T.): Medicine. See: Jablonski.

OTHELLO. Character in William Shakespeare's tragedy, "Othello," (1604–1605). See: New Encyc. Brit., 1974, Microp. Othello syndrome.

Othello syndrome (Othello): Psychiatry. See: Stedman.

Othman. See: Osman I.

OTHMER, DONALD FREDERICK. 1904– . American chemical engineer. See: World Who's Who Sci. Othmer process.

Othmer process (Othmer, Donald Frederick): Chemistry. See: Van Nostrand Chem. Dict.

OTIS, ARTHUR SINTON. b. 1886. American psychologist. See: Amer. Men Sci., 6th ed. Otis quick scoring mental ability test, Otis self-administering test of intelligence.

Otis quick scoring mental ability test (Otis, Arthur Sinton): Psychology. See: Wolman.

Otis self-administering test of intelligence (Otis, Arthur Sinton): Psychology. See: Wolman.

OTT, ISAAC. 1847-1916. American physiologist. See: World Who's Who Sci. Ott's test.

OTT, LAWRENCE H. fl. 1935-1950. American engineer. Cited in: Chem. Abstr., vol. 29, p. 7542. Ficklen-Ott dust camera.

OTTA, FREDERICK. No dates. German botanist. (Biography source unavailable.) Ottoa.

OTTILIA (Or ODILIA), SAINT. ca. 660-720. Frankish saint. See: Holweck. Congregation of Saint Ottilia.

OTTO I, THE GREAT. 912-973. King of Germany and Holy Roman emperor. See: Encyc. Brit., 1973. Ottonian.

OTTO, ADOLPH WILHELM. 1786-1845. German surgeon. See: Biog. Lex. hervorr. Aerzte. Otto-Chrobak syndrome, Otto's syndrome.

Otto (bicycle) (Derivation undetermined): Engineering and Industry. See: Partridge.

OTTO, CARL. fl. 1915-1955. German metallurgical engineer. Cited in: Chem. Abstr., Decenn. Indexes to 1937-1946. Otto coke oven.

Otto-Chrobak syndrome (Otto, Adolph Wilhelm and Chrobak, Rudolf): Medicine. See: Dorland; Jablonski. Also known as: Otto's disease (or pelvis).

Otto coke oven (Otto, Carl): Chemistry. See: Van Nostrand Chem. Dict.

Otto cycle (Otto, Nikolaus August): Engineering and Industry. See: Auger; Thewlis; Van Nostrand Sci. Encyc.; Webster's 3d.

Otto engine (or silent engine) (Otto, Nikolaus August): Engineering and Industry. See: Auger; Van Nostrand Sci. Encyc.; Webster's 3d.

OTTO, FRIEDRICH JULIUS. 1809-1870. German chemist. See: Pogg., vol. 2. Stas-Otto method?

Otto-Langen engine (Otto, Nikolaus August and Langen, Eugen): Engineering and Industry. See: Auger.

OTTO, NIKOLAUS AUGUST. 1832-1891. German engineer. See: New Encyc. Brit., 1974, Microp. Otto cycle, Otto engine (or silent engine), Otto-Langen engine.

OTTO, WILLIAM TOD. 1816-1905. American jurist. See: Dict. Amer. Biog. Otto's reports.

Ottoa (Otta, Frederick): Botany. See: Charnock.

Ottoman (couch) (Osman I.): Applied Arts. See: Hendrickson; Partridge.

Ottoman (empire) (Osman I.): History. See: Encyc. Brit., 1973; Webster's 3d.

Ottonian (Otto I, the Great): History. See: Webster's 3d.

Otto's disease (or pelvis) (Otto, Adolph Wilhelm). See: Otto-Chrobak syndrome.

Otto's reports (Otto, William Tod): Law. See: Jameson.

Otto's syndrome (Otto, Adolph Wilhelm). See: Guerin-Stern syndrome.

Ott's test (Ott, Isaac): Medicine. See: Dorland; Stedman.

Ouchterlony method (Ouchterlony, Orjan Thomas Gunnarsson): Medicine. See: Stedman.

OUCHTERLONY, ORJAN THOMAS GUNNARSSON. 1914- . Swedish bacteriologist. See: Who's Who Sci. Europe, 1972. Ouchterlony method, Ouchterlony technique.

Ouchterlony technique (Ouchterlony, Orjan Thomas Gunnarsson): Medicine. See: Stedman.

OUDEMANS, ANTHONIE CORNELIS. 1831-1895. Dutch chemist. See: Pogg., vols. 3, 4. law of Oudeman.

OUDET, DAME. No dates. French cultivator. (Biography source unavailable.) Amadot (pear).

Oudin current (Oudin, Paul): Medicine. See: Dorland; Stedman.

OUDIN, PAUL. 1851-1923. French physician. See: Biog. Lex. hervorr. Aerzte. Oudin current, Oudin resonator.

Oudin resonator (Oudin, Paul): Medicine. See: Dorland.

Our Lady's mint (Mary, Virgin-Mother): Botany. See: Webster's 3d.

Our Lady's thistle (or Lady's thistle) (Mary, Virgin-Mother): Botany. See: Webster's 3d.

Ourania. See: Urania.

OURGAUD, A. G. fl. 1955. French ophthalmologist. (Biography source unavailable.) Jayle-Ourgaud syndrome.

OUSTINOFF, HELEN FICKWEILER. 1909- . American librarian. See: Who's Who Libr. Service, 1966. Oustinoff system.

Oustinoff system (Oustinoff, Helen Fickweiler): Library Science. See: Harrod.

out-herod Herod (Herod the Great): Generic Word. See: Charnock; Harvey; Partridge; Stenhouse; Weekley.

Ouvaroff, Count Serge Semenovitch. See: Uvarov, Count Serge Semenovitch.

Ouvarovite (Uvarov, Count Serge Semenovitch). See: Uvarovite.

oval(s) of Cassini (or Cassinian oval) (Cassini, Gian Domenico): Mathematics. See: Ballentyne; James; Van Nostrand Sci. Encyc.

OVER, EDWIN. 1903- . American mineral collector. Cited in: Hintze, 1st suppl., pp. 293-294. Overite.

Overbeck test for cotton (Derivation undetermined): Chemistry. See: Van Nostrand Chem. Dict.

OVERHAUSER, ALBERT WARNER. 1925- . American physicist. See: Amer. Men and Women Sci., 12th ed. Overhauser effect.

Overhauser effect (Overhauser, Albert Warner): Physics. See: Ballentyne.

Overite (Over, Edwin): Earth Sciences. See: Thrush; Webster's 3d.

Overman Act (Overman, Lee Slater): Politics. See: Morris.

OVERMAN, LEE SLATER. 1854-1930. American legislator. See: Dict. Amer. Biog. Overman Act.

OVERSTREET, EDMUND WILLIAM. 1908- . American gynecologist and obstetrician. See: Amer. Men and Women Sci., 12th ed. Gordan-Overstreet syndrome.

OVERSTROM, CONRAD. fl. 1941. American engineer. Cited in: Chem. Abstr., vol. 35, p. 5358. Overstrom table.

OVERSTROM, GEORGE. fl. 1941. American engineer. Cited in: Chem. Abstr., vol. 35, p. 5358. Overstrom table.

OVERSTROM, GUSTAV A. fl. 1941. American engineer. Cited in: Chem. Abstr., vol. 35, p. 5358. Overstrom table.

Overstrom table (Overstrom, Gustav A.; Overstrom, Conrad; and Overstrom, George): Engineering and Industry. See: Thrush.

OVERTON, CHARLES ERNEST. 1865-1933. English-born cell physiologist in Germany and Sweden. See: Dict. Sci. Biog. Overton coefficient, Overton's lipoid (or lipide) theory of plasma permeability.

Overton coefficient (Overton, Charles Ernest): Chemistry. See: Hackh.

OVERTON, ERNST (In full: C. ERNST). b. 1865. German anesthesiologist. Cited in: Index-Cat. Libr. Surg.-Gen. Off., 2nd ser., vol. 12, 1907. Meyer-Overton theory of narcosis.

OVERTON, ROBERT. fl. 1640-1688. English soldier. See: Dict. Nat. Biog. Overton's plot.

Overton's lipoid (or lipide) theory of plasma permeability (Overton, Charles Ernest): Physiology. See: Dict. Sci. Biog.

Overton's plot (Overton, Robert): History. See: Harbottle.

OVID (PUBLIUS OVIDIUS NASO). 43 B.C.?-17 A.D. Roman poet. See: Encyc. Brit., 1973. Ovidian.

Ovidian (Ovid): Literature. See: Partridge; Webster's 3d.

OVINGTON, EARLE. 1879-1936. American aeronautical engineer. See: Who Was Who Amer., 1897-1942. Ovington high-frequency apparatus.

Ovington high-frequency apparatus (Ovington, Earle): Electronics. Cited in: Webster's Biog. Dict.

Ovoco (Ovoca) classifier (Derivation undetermined): Engineering and Industry. See: Hackh; Thrush.

Ovshinsky effect (Ovshinsky, Stanford Robert): Electronics. See: Barnhart (New Eng.); Hughes.

OVSHINSKY, STANFORD ROBERT. 1922- . American electro-chemist. See: Amer. Men and Women Sci., 12th ed. Ovshinsky effect.

Owen 9 mm Parabellum submachine gun Mk 1/42 (Owen, Evelyn Ernest): Weapons. See: Quick.

Owen bridge (Owen, David): Electronics. See: Hughes; Internat. Dict. Phys. Mec.; Markus.

OWEN, DAVID. b. 1875. English electrical engineer. See: Who's Who Brit. Sci., 1953. Owen bridge.

OWEN, EVELYN ERNEST. 1915-1949. Australian inventor. See: Australian Encyc. Owen 9 mm Parabellum submachine gun Mk 1/42.

Owen-Glass Act (Owen, Robert Latham and Glass, Carter): Politics. See: Morris.

Owen Glendower's oak (Glendower, Owen): History. See: Brewer.

Owen process (Derivation undetermined): Engineering and Industry. See: Thrush.

OWEN, SIR RICHARD. 1804-1892. English anatomist and zoologist. See: Dict. Nat. Biog. interglobular space of Owen, Owenia (1), Owenia (2), Owen's lines.

OWEN, ROBERT. 1771-1858. Welsh socialist and philanthropist. See: Internat. Encyc. Soc. Sci. Owenites (or Owenism).

OWEN, ROBERT LATHAM. 1856-1947. American legislator. See: Biog. Direct. Amer. Congress. Keating-Owen Act, Owen-Glass Act.

OWEN, WILLIAM FITZWILLIAM. 1774-1857. English admiral. See: Dict. Nat. Biog. Owen's protectorate.

Owenia (1) (Owen, Sir Richard): Zoology. See: Pennak.

Owenia (2) (Owen, Sir Richard): Botany. See: Webster's 3d.

Owenites (or Owenism) (Owen, Robert): Sociology. See: Canney; Webster's 3d.

Owen's borehole surveying instrument (Derivation undetermined): Engineering and Industry. See: Thrush.

Owens dust recorder (or jet dust counter) (Owens, John S.): Engineering and Industry. See: Huschke; Thrush; Van Nostrand Sci., Encyc.

OWENS, JOHN S. fl. 1923-1940. English pollution chemist. Cited in: Chem. Abstr., vol. 17, p. 2066. Owens dust recorder (or jet dust counter).

Owen's lines (Owen, Sir Richard): Anatomy. See: Stedman. Also known as: Retzius' lines.

Owens machine (Owens, Michael Joseph): Engineering and Industry. See: Thrush.

OWENS, MICHAEL JOSEPH. 1859-1923. American inventor and glass manufacturer. See: Dict. Amer. Biog. Libbey-Owens process, Owens machine, Owens process.

Owens process (Owens, Michael Joseph): Engineering and Industry. See: Thrush.

Owen's protectorate (Owen, William Fitzwilliam): History. See: Morris and Irwin.

Ower anemometer (Ower, Ernest): Engineering and Industry. See: Thrush.

OWER, ERNEST. 1894- . English physicist. See: Pogg., vol. 6. Ower anemometer.

OWREN, PAUL A. 1905- . Norwegian hematologist. See: World Who's Who Sci. Owren's syndrome (1) (or crisis), Owren's syndrome (2) (or disease).

Owren's syndrome (1) (or crisis) (Owren, Paul A.): Medicine. See: Jablonski.

Owren's syndrome (2) (or disease) (Owren, Paul A.): Medicine. See: Jablonski; Stedman.

Oxford, 1st Earl of. See: Harley, Robert, 1st Earl of Oxford.

Oxford, 2nd Earl of. See: Harley, Edward, 2nd Earl of.

Oxford, 16th Earl of. See: Vere, John de (16th Earl of Oxford).

Oxford, 17th Earl of. See: Vere, Edward de (17th Earl of Oxford).

Oxford, 20th Earl of. See: Vere, Aubrey de (20th Earl of Oxford).

The Oxford Blues (Vere, Aubrey de, 20th Earl of Oxford): History. See: Brewer; Wagner (More Names).

OXFORD, EDWARD. fl. 1840. English deranged youth. Cited in: Dict. Nat. Biog., 1st suppl., under "Victoria," p. 1284. Oxford's assault.

Oxfordian (Vere, Edward de, 17th Earl of Oxford): Literature. See: Webster's 3d.

Oxford's assault (Oxford, Edward): History. See: Phyfe.

Oxford's men (Vere, John de, 16th Earl of Oxford): Theater. See: Hartnoll.

Oxland-Hocking furnace (Derivation undetermined): Engineering and Industry. See: Thrush.

oysters Kirkpatrick (Kirkpatrick, James C.): Food and Drink. See: Hendrickson.

oysters Rockefeller (Rockefeller, John Davison): Food and Drink. See: De Sola; Hendrickson.

OZZARD, A. T. fl. 1890. English? zoologist. Cited in: Royal Soc. Cat. Sci. Pap., 1884-1900. Ozzard's filarial parasite, Ozzard's filariasis.

Ozzard's filarial parasite (Ozzard, A.T.): See: Mansonella.

Ozzard's filariasis (Ozzard, A. T.): See: Mansonelliasis.

P

P. N. Lebedev Physical Institute (Lebedev, Petr Nikolaevich): Physics. See: New Encyc. Brit., 1974, Microp. under "Lebedev, Pyotr Nikolayevich."

PAAL, CARL LUDWIG. 1860-1935. German applied chemist. See: Pogg., vols. 4, 5, 6. Paal-Knorr synthesis (or pyrrole synthesis), Paal-Knorr synthesis of thiophenes.

Paal-Knorr synthesis (or pyrrole synthesis) (Paal, Carl Ludwig and Knorr, Ludwig): Chemistry. See: Ballentyne; Van Nostrand Chem. Dict.

Paal-Knorr synthesis of thiophenes (Paal, Carl Ludwig and Knorr, Ludwig): Chemistry. See: Ballentyne.

Paas' disease (Paas, Hermann?): Medicine. See: Dorland; Stedman.

PAAS, HERMANN. 1900- . German physician. See: Wer Ist's?, 1971/73. Paas' disease?

PAASCHE, HERMANN. 1851-1925. German economist. See: Arnim. Paasche index, Paasche-Konyus index.

Paasche index (Paasche, Hermann): Statistics. See: Kendall; New Encyc. Brit., 1974, Microp.

Paasche-Konyus index (Paasche, Hermann and Konyus, A. A.). See: Konyus index (or index number).

Paaw (or Pauw), Peter. See: Pavius, Petrus.

PACCANARI, NICCOLO. 1773-? Italian monk. See: New Catholic Encyc. under "Paccanarists." Baccanarists.

Paccanarists (Paccanari, Niccolo). See: Baccanarists.

PACCHIONI, ANTONIO. 1665-1726. Italian anatomist. See: World Who's Who Sci. Pacchionian (Pacchioni's) bodies (corpuscles, glands or granulations), Pacchionian (Pacchioni's) depressions (or foveolae), Pacchionian (Pacchioni's) foramen.

Pacchionian (Pacchioni's) bodies (corpuscles, glands or granulations) (Pacchioni, Antonio): Anatomy. See: Donath; Dorland; Stedman; Webster's 3d.

Pacchionian (Pacchioni's) depressions (or foveolae) (Pacchioni, Antonio): Anatomy. See: Donath; Dorland; Stedman.

Pacchionian (Pacchioni's) foramen (Pacchioni, Antonio): Anatomy. See: Donath; Stedman.

Pacheco's parrot disease virus (Derivation undetermined): Medicine. See: Stedman.

Pachomian(s) (Pachomius, Saint): Religion. See: Attwater; Webster's 3d.

PACHOMIUS, SAINT. b. ca. 290-346. Egyptian monk. See: New Encyc. Brit., 1974, Microp. Pachomian(s), Rule of Saint Pachomius.

PACHON, MICHEL VICTOR. 1867-1938. French physiologist. See: Biog. Lex. hervorr. Aerzte. Pachon's method, Pachon's test.

Pachon's method (Pachon, Michel Victor): Medicine. See: Dorland; Stedman.

Pachon's test (Pachon, Michel Victor): Medicine. See: Stedman.

Pachuca tank (Derivation undetermined): Chemistry. See: Van Nostrand Chem. Dict.

PACI, AGOSTINO. 1845-1902. Italian surgeon. See: Biog. Lex. hervorr. Aerzte. Paci's operation.

PACIFICO, DAVID. 1784-1854. Portuguese Jew and English citizen. See: Dict. Nat. Biog. Don Pacifico affair (or incident).

PACINI, ALBERT. fl. 1937. American pharmaceutical chemist. Cited in: Chem. Abstr., vol. 31, p. 8630. Pacini-Taras test for vitamin A in oils.

PACINI, FILIPPO. 1812-1883. Italian anatomist. See: Biog. Lex. hervorr. Aerzte. Pacinian (or Pacini's) corpuscles (or bodies), Pacinitis.

Pacini-Taras test for vitamin A in oils (Pacini, Albert and Taras, M. H.): Chemistry. See: Van Nostrand Chem. Dict.

Pacinian (or Pacini's) corpuscles (or bodies) (Pacini, Filippo): Anatomy. See: Dorland; Pennak; Stedman; Webster's 3d. Also known as: Vater-Pacini corpuscles, Vater's corpuscles.

Pacinitis (Pacini, Filippo): Medicine. See: Stedman.

Paci's operation (Paci, Agostino): Medicine. See: Stedman.

PACKARD, C. T. fl. 1914. English engineer. Cited in: Chem. Abstr., vol. 8, p. 3621. Mills-Packard chamber.

Paddy (or Pat) (Patrick, Saint): Generic Word (Irishman). See: Wagner (Names); Weekley.

PADE, HENRI EUGENE. b. 1863. French mathematician. See: Pogg., vols. 4, 5. Pade table.

PADE, LEON. fl. 1884. French chemist. Cited in: Royal Soc. Cat. Sci. Pap., 1884-1900. Arnaud-Pade reagent.

Pade table (Pade, Henri Eugene): Mathematics. See: Internat. Dict. Ap. Math.

PADELOUP, ANTOINE MICHEL. 1685-1758. French bookbinder. See: Grand Larousse Encyc. Padeloup style.

Padeloup style (Padeloup, Antoine Michel): Library Science. See: Harrod.

PADGETT, EARL C. 1893-1946. American surgeon. See: World Who's Who Sci. Padgett's dermatome.

Padgett's dermatome (Padgett, Earl C.): Medicine. See: Dorland.

PADMOS, ADRIAAN A. fl. 1951. Dutch chemist. Cited in: Chem. Abstr., vol. 45, p. 9821 d. Padmos method.

Padmos method (Padmos, Adriaan A.): Engineering and Industry. See: Thrush.

Paduan coins (Cavino, Giovanni "Paduan"): Numismatics. See: Charnock.

Paean (Apollo): Generic Word (exultant song or cheer). See: Partridge; Preminger; Webster's 3d.

PAEON. Greek god of healing. See: Jobes. Peony (or Paeonia).

Paeon (metrical unit) (Apollo): Literature. See: Preminger; Webster's 3d.

PAESSLER, H. fl. 1906. German physician. Cited in: Index Medicus, 2d Ser., vol. 4, 1906. Romberg-Paessler syndrome.

Paganini etudes (Paganini, Niccolo): Music. See: Apel.

PAGANINI, NICCOLO. 1782-1840. Italian violinist. See: New Encyc. Brit., 1974, Microp. Paganini etudes, Paganini variations.

Paganini variations (Paganini, Niccolo): Music. See: Apel.

PAGE, HERBERT WILLIAM. 1845-1926. English surgeon. See: Who Was Who, 1916-1928. Page's disease.

PAGE, IRVINE HEINLY. 1901- . American physician. See: World Who's Who Sci. Page's syndrome.

_GE, RUTH. 1903?- . American dancer, choreographer and director. _e: Cur. Biog., 1962. Page-Stone Ballet Company.

_ge-Stone Ballet Company (Page, Ruth and Stone, Bentley): Dance. See: _ujoy.

_AGENSTECHER, ALEXANDER. 1828-1879. German ophthalmologist. See: _orld Who's Who Sci. Pagenstecher's circle, Pagenstecher's ointment, _genstecher's thread.

_AGENSTECHER, JOHANN SAMUEL FRIEDRICH. 1783-1856. Swiss chemist. _e: Pogg., vol. 2. Pagenstecher-Schoenbein cyanide paper?

_genstecher-Schoenbein cyanide paper (Pagenstecher, Johann Samuel Friedrich? _d Schoenbein, Christian Friedrich): Chemistry. See: Van Nostrand Chem. _ct.

_genstecher's circle (Pagenstecher, Alexander): Medicine. See: Dorland; _edman.

_genstecher's ointment (Pagenstecher, Alexander): Medicine. See: Dorland.

_genstecher's thread (Pagenstecher, Alexander): Medicine. See: Dorland; _edman.

_ge's disease (Page, Herbert William): Medicine. See: Dorland.

_ge's syndrome (Page, Irvine Heinly): Medicine. See: Jablonski.

_get-Berger test (Paget, Marcel and Berger, Raoul): Chemistry. See: Van _ostrand Chem. Dict.

_AGET, LORD GEORGE AUGUSTUS FREDERICK. 1818-1880. English soldier. _ee: Dict. Nat. Biog. Paget's Irregular Horse?

_AGET, SIR JAMES. 1814-1899. English surgeon and pathologist. See: Dict. _at. Biog., 1st suppl. Paget-Schroetter syndrome, Pagetoid epithelioma, _agetoid osteitis, Paget's abscess, Paget's cells, Paget's disease, Paget's disease _extramammary), Paget's disease (juvenile), Paget's disease (mammary, cancer, _arcinoma, or nipple), Paget's quiet necrosis of bone.

_AGET, MARCEL. fl. 1938-1972. French biochemist. See: Who's Who Sci. _urope, 1972. Paget-Berger test.

_get process (Derivation undetermined): Photography. See: Webster's 3d.

_get-Schroetter syndrome (Paget, Sir James and Schroetter von Kristelli, _eopold): Medicine. See: Jablonski. Also known as: Von Schroetter's _yndrome.

_getoid epithelioma (Paget, Sir James). See: Arning's carcinoid.

_getoid osteitis (Paget, Sir James): Medicine. See: Stedman. Also known _s: Recklinghausen's disease (2) (osteitis fibrosa cystica).

_get's abscess (Paget, Sir James): Medicine. See: Dorland; Jablonski; _tedman.

_get's cells (Paget, Sir James): Medicine. See: Dorland; Stedman.

_get's disease (Paget, Sir James): Medicine. See: Dorland; Hinsie; _ablonski; Stedman; Van Nostrand Sci. Encyc. Also known as: Pozzi's senile _seudorickets.

_get's disease (extramammary) (Paget, Sir James): Medicine. See: Jablonski.

_get's disease (juvenile) (Paget, Sir James): Medicine. See: Jablonski.

_get's disease (mammary, cancer, carcinoma, or nipple) (Paget, Sir James): _edicine. See: Jablonski.

_get's Irregular Horse (Paget, Lard George Augustus Frederick?): History. _ee: Brewer.

_get's quiet necrosis of bone (Paget, Sir James). See: Koenig's disease.

_PAGETT. Character in Rudyard Kipling's work "Departmental Ditties," (1886). _ee: Harvey. Pagett, M.P.

_Pagett, M.P. (Pagett): Generic Word (omniscient traveller). See: Partridge.

_ahlavi (or Pahlevi) (Reza Shah Pahlavi): Numismatics. See: Webster's 3d.

_PAHLEN, PETER LUDWIG. 1745-1826. Russian conspirator. See: Grand _arousse Encyc. Pahlen's conspiracy.

_ahlen's conspiracy (Pahlen, Peter Ludwig): History. See: Harbottle.

_PAIGE, SIDNEY. b. 1880. American geologist. See: World Who's Who _ci. Paigeite.

_Paigeite (Paige, Sidney): Earth Sciences. See: Thrush; Webster's 3d.

PAIN, ARTHUR CHARLES DAVY. fl. 1952. English mineral collector. Cited in: Min. Mag., vol. 31 (1957), p. 420. Painite.

Paine's syndrome (Derivation undetermined): Medicine. See: Jablonski.

Painite (Pain, Arthur Charles Davy): Earth Sciences. See: Thrush.

PAISLEY, IAN RICHARD KYLE. 1926- . Irish Protestant church leader. See: Who's Who, 1975. Paisleyism (or Paisleyite).

Paisleyism (or Paisleyite) (Paisley, Ian Richard Kyle): Religion. See: Barnhart (New Eng.).

Paixhan (cannon) (Paixhans, Henri Joseph): Weapons. See: Charnock; Mathews, M. M.

PAIXHANS, HENRI JOSEPH. 1783-1854. French artillery officer. See: World Who's Who Sci. Paixhan (cannon).

PAJON, CLAUDE. 1626-1685. French Protestant theologian. See: Nouv. Biog. Univ. Pajonism.

Pajonism (Pajon, Claude): Religion. See: Webster's 3d.

PAJOT, CHARLES. 1816-1896. French obstetrician. See: Biog. Lex. hervorr. Aerzte. Pajot's hook, Pajot's law, Pajot's maneuver, Pajot's method.

Pajot's hook (Pajot, Charles): Medicine. See: Dorland; Stedman.

Pajot's law (Pajot, Charles): Medicine. See: Dorland.

Pajot's maneuver (Pajot, Chales). See: Saxtorph's maneuver.

Pajot's method (Pajot, Charles): Medicine. See: Dorland.

PAL, JACOB. 1863-1936. Hungarian-born Austrian physician. See: Biog. Lex. hervorr. Aerzte. Pal's stain.

PALADE, GEORGE EMIL. 1903- . Rumanian-born American cytologist. See: World Who's Who Sci. Palade's granule.

Palade's granule (Palade, George Emil): Biology. See: Gray.

PALAMAS, GREGORIUS. 1296?-1359. Greek mystic. See: New Encyc. Brit., 1974, Microp. Palamite(s).

PALAMEDES. Greek legendary hero of the Trojan war. See: New Encyc. Brit., 1974, Microp. Palamedes.

Palamedes (Palamedes, the hero): Generic Word (ingenious person). See: Brewer.

Palamite(s) (Palamas, Gregorius): Religion. See: Latham; Webster's 3d.

Palatine (cape) (Charlotte Elizabeth): Fashion. See: Picken; Webster's 3d.

PALAU, ANTONIO. d. 1793. Spanish botanist. See: Biog. Notes Upon Botanists. Palavia.

Palavia (Palau, Antonio): Botany. See: Charnock.

PALES. Ancient Italian deity. See: Jobes. Palilia.

PALFYN, JEAN. 1650-1730. Belgian surgeon and anatomist. See: World Who's Who Sci. Palfyn's sinus.

Palfyn's sinus (Palfyn, Jean): Medicine. See: Stedman.

PALGRAVE, SIR ROBERT HARRY INGLIS. 1827-1919. English banker and economist. See: Who Was Who, 1916-1928. Palgrave's index?

Palgrave's index (Palgrave, Sir Robert Harry Inglis?): Statistics. See: Kendall.

Palilia (Pales): Mythology. See: Brewer under "Pales."

PALINURUS. Pilot of Aeneas in Virgil's "Aeneid." See: Jobes. Palinurus, Palinurus (spiny lobster), Panuliris.

Palinurus (Palinurus, the pilot): Generic Word (frustrated person). See: Partridge.

Palinurus (spiny lobster) (Palinurus): Zoology. See: Webster's 3d.

PALISSY, BERNARD. 1510-1589. French potter. See: Encyc. Brit., 1973. Palissy ware.

Palissy ware (Palissy, Bernard): Applied Arts. See: Brewer; Webster's 3d.

Palladian (Athena): Generic Word (wisdom or learning). See: Webster's 3d.

Palladian architecture (or Palladianism) (Palladio, Andrea): Architecture. See: Briggs; Osborne.

Palladian motif (Palladio, Andrea): Architecture. See: Briggs.

Palladian window (Palladio, Andrea): Architecture. See: Webster's 3d.

PALLADIO, ANDREA. 1508-1580. Italian architect. See: New Encyc. Brit., 1974, Microp. Palladian architecture (or Palladianism), Palladian motif, Palladian window.

Palladium (Athena): Generic Word (safeguard). See: Charnock, Partridge.

Pallas Athene. See: Athena.

Pallas('s) cat (Pallas, Peter Simon): Zoology. See: Gray; Webster's 3d.

PALLAS, PETER SIMON. 1741-1811. German naturalist and traveler. See: World Who's Who Sci. Pallas('s) cat, Pallasia, Pallasite, Pallas's cormorant, Pallas's sandgrouse, Pallas's sea-eagle.

Pallasia (Pallas, Peter Simon): Botany. See: Charnock.

Pallasite (Pallas, Peter Simon): Earth Sciences. See: Webster's 3d.

Pallas's cormorant (Pallas, Peter Simon): Zoology. See: Webster's 3d.

Pallas's sandgrouse (Pallas, Peter Simon): Zoology. See: Webster's 3d.

Pallas's sea-eagle (Pallas, Peter Simon): Zoology. See: Gray.

PALLISTER, RICHARD ALAN. fl. 1932-1972. English physician. See: Med. Direct., 1972. Hawes-Pallister-Landor syndrome.

PALLOTTI, VINCENZO MARIA. 1795-1850. Italian secular priest. See: Encic. Cattolica. Pallottine Fathers.

Pallottine Fathers (Pallotti, Vincenzo Maria): Religion. See: Attwater; Encyc. Brit., 1973.

PALM, C. fl. 1936-1957. Swedish statistician. Cited in: Kendall and Doig. Palm function.

Palm function (Palm, C.): Statistics. See: Kendall.

palma Christi (Jesus Christ): Botany. See: Partridge; Weekley.

Palmer acid test for peptic ulcer (Palmer, Walter Lincoln): Medicine. See: Stedman.

Palmer Act (Palmer, Roundell?): Law. See: Black.

PALMER, ALEXANDER MITCHELL. 1872-1936. American legislator and attorney general. See: Who Was Who Amer., 1897-1942. Palmer raids.

PALMER, AUSTIN NORMAN. 1859-1927. American penman and educator. See: Webster's Biog. Dict. Palmer method.

PALMER, EDWARD. 1831-1911. American botanist. See: Dict. Sci. Biog. Palmerella.

PALMER, HOWARD E. fl. 1908. American chemist. Cited in: Chem. Abstr., vol. 2, p. 43. Browning-Palmer test.

Palmer method (Palmer, Austin Norman): Education. See: Good.

Palmer raids (Palmer, Alexander Mitchell): History. See: Morris.

PALMER, ROUNDELL (1ST EARL OF SELBOURNE). 1812-1895. English jurist. See: Dict. Nat. Biog. Palmer Act?

Palmer scan (Derivation undetermined): Electronics. See: Markus.

PALMER, WALTER LINCOLN. 1896- . American physician. See: World Who's Who Sci. Palmer acid test for peptic ulcer.

Palmer water-spray apparatus (Derivation undetermined): Engineering and Industry. See: Thrush.

Palmerella (Palmer, Edward): Botany. See: Taylor, N.

Palmerston, 3rd Viscount. See: Temple, Henry John (3rd Viscount Palmerston).

Palmerstonism (Temple, Henry John, 3rd Viscount Palmerston): History. See: Charnock.

Palmerston's follies (Temple, Henry John, 3rd Viscount Palmerston): History. See: Brewer.

PALMIERI, LUIGI. 1807-1896. Italian meteorologist and physicist. See: World Who's Who Sci. Palmierite.

Palmierite (Palmieri, Luigi): Earth Sciences. See: Thrush; Webster's 3d.

Palmquist apparatus (Derivation undetermined): Chemistry. See: Hackh.

Palo-Travis analyser (Palo and Travis, Pierce Mason): Engineering and Industry. See: Thrush.

Pal's stain (Pal, Jacob): Medicine. See: Dorland.

PALTAUF, ARNOLD. 1860-1893. German physician. See: Biog. Lex. hervorr. Aerzte. Paltauf's infantilism (or nanism).

PALTAUF, RICHARD. 1858-1924. Austrian pathologist. See: Biog. Lex. hervorr. Aerzte. Hodgkin-Paltauf-Sternberg disease, Paltauf-Sternberg disease, Paltauf's stain.

Paltauf-Sternberg disease (Paltauf, Richard and Sternberg, Carl von). See: Hodgkin's disease (granuloma or syndrome).

Paltauf's infantilism (or nanism) (Paltauf, Arnold): Medicine. See: Dorland; Stedman.

Paltauf's stain (Paltauf, Richard): Medicine. See: Stedman.

PAMFIL, G. P. fl. 1925. Rumanian chemist. Cited in: Chem. Abstr., vol. 19, p. 22. Pamfil-Wonnesch reagent.

Pamfil-Wonnesch reagent (Pamfil, G. P. and Wonnesch, M.): Chemistry. See: Van Nostrand Chem. Dict.

PAMPHILUS. fl. 12th c.? Unknown author of the erotic love poem, "Pamphilus, seu De Amore." See: Harvey. Pamphlet.

Pamphlet (Pamphilus): Generic Word. See: Hendrickson; New Encyc. Brit., 1974, Microp.; Webster's 3d.

PAN. Greek woodland spirit. See: Jobes. Pan('s) pipes (or Panpipe), Pandean harmonica, Panic, Panisc (or Panisk).

Pan, Peter. See: Peter Pan.

Pan('s) pipes (or Panpipe) (Pan): Music. See: Apel; Good; Webster's 3d.

PANACEA. Greek goddess of health. See: Jobes. Panacea.

Panacea (Panacea, the goddess): Generic Word (cure-all). See: Brewer.

Panas' operation (Panas, Photinos): Medicine. See: Dorland; Stedman.

PANAS, PHOTINOS. 1832-1903. French ophthalmologist. See: Biog. Lex. hervorr. Aerzte. Panas' operation.

Panasynk solution (Panasyuk, V. I.): Chemistry. See: Van Nostrand Chem. Dict.

PANASYUK (PANASSJUK OR PANASYNK), V. I. fl. 1932. Russian chemist. Cited in: Chem. Abstr., vol. 27, p. 4188. Panasynk solution.

PANCHENKO (or PANTSCHENKO), G.A. fl. 1929. Russian chemist. Cited in: Chem. Abstr., Decenn. Index, 1927-1936. Tananaev-Panchenko test for tungstate, Tananaev-Panchenko test for vanadium, Tananaev-Penchenko test for titanium and uranium.

PANCOAST, HENRY KHUNRATH. 1875-1939. American radiologist. See: Who Was Who Amer., 1897-1942. Pancoast's syndrome (apex syndrome or tumor).

PANCOAST, JOSEPH. 1805-1882. American surgeon. See: Dict. Amer. Biog. Pancoast's drain, Pancoast's operation, Pancoast's suture.

Pancoast-Tobias syndrome (Pancoast, Henry Khunrath and Tobias, Jose Wenceslav). See: Pancoast's syndrome (apex syndrome or tumor).

Pancoast's drain (Pancoast, Joseph): Medicine. See: Dorland.

Pancoast's operation (Pancoast, Joseph): Medicine. See: Dorland; Stedman.

Pancoast's suture (Pancoast, Joseph): Medicine. See: Stedman.

Pancoast's syndrome (apex syndrome or tumor) (Pancoast, Henry Khunrath): Medicine. See: Dorland; Jablonski; Stedman. Also known as: Ciuffini-Pancoast syndrome, Hare's syndrome, Pancoast-Tobias syndrome, Tobias' syndrome.

PANDARUS. A renowned archer in Homer's "Iliad." See: Jobes. Pandarus, Pander (Panderer or Pandar).

Pandarus (Pandarus, the archer): Zoology. See: Pennak; Webster's 3d.

Pandean harmonica (Pan): Music. See: Partridge; Webster's 3d.

Pandean pipes (Pan, the god). See: Pan('s) pipes (or Panpipe).

pandects of Justinian (Justinian I, the Great): Law. See: Barnhard (Eng. Lit.); Brewer; Latham; Phyfe.

Pander (Panderer or Pandar) (Pandarus): Generic Word (procurer). See: Charnock; Funk; Webster's 3d.

PANDER, CHRISTIAN HEINRICH. 1794-1865. German anatomist and embryologist. See: World Who's Who Sci. Pander's island (or isthmus), Pander's layer, Pander's nucleus.

Pander's island (or isthmus) (Pander, Christian Heinrich): Anatomy. See: Dorland.

ander's layer (Pander, Christian Heinrich): Anatomy. See: Dorland.

ander's nucleus (Pander, Christian Heinrich): Medicine. See: Dorland; Stedman.

ANDION. King of Athens in Greek mythology. See: Jobes. Pandion.

andion (Pandion, the King): Zoology. See: Pennak; Webster's 3d.

ANDORA. First woman in Greek mythology. See: Jobes. Pandora (mollusks), Pandora's box, Pandorea.

andora (mollusks) (Pandora): Zoology. See: Pennak; Webster's 3d.

andora's box (Pandora): Generic Word (proliferation of troubles). See: Brewer; Partridge; Webster's 3d.

andorea (Pandora): Botany. See: Taylor, N.; Webster's 3d.

ANDY, KALMAN. b. 1868. Hungarian neurologist. See: Biog. Lex. hervorr. Aerzte. Pandy's reaction (or test).

andy's reaction (or test) (Pandy, Kalman): Chemistry. See: Dorland; Stedman.

aneth('s) cells (or granular cells) (Paneth, Josef): Anatomy. See: Donath; Dorland; Henderson; Stedman. Also known as: Davidoff's cells.

ANETH, FRIEDRICH ADOLF. 1887-1958. German physicist. See: World Who's Who Sci. Paneth('s) rule (or adsorption rule), Paneth technique.

ANETH, JOSEF. 1857-1890. Austrian physiologist. See: Biog. Lex. hervorr. Aerzte. Paneth('s) cells (or granular cells).

aneth('s) rule (or adsorption rule) (Paneth, Friedrich Adolf): Physics. See: Ballentyne; Hackh; Internat. Dict. Phys. Elec.

aneth technique (Paneth, Friedrich Adolf): Physics. See: Van Nostrand Chem. Dict.

angloss (or Panglossian) (Pangloss, Dr.): Generic Word (ultimate optimist). See: Partridge; Webster's 3d.

ANGLOSS, DR. Optimistic tutor of Candide in Voltaire's satire, "Candide," (1759). See: Harvey and Heseltine. Pangloss (or Panglossian).

ANGRITZ, FRITZ. 1900- . German chemist. Cited in: Pogg., vol. 6 under "Kleinmann, Hans." Kleinmann-Pangritz reagent.

anic (Pan): Generic Word (sudden fear). See: Charnock; Hargrave; Partridge; Webster's 3d.

aninean (Panini): Linguistics. See: Webster's 3d.

ANINI. fl. 6th or 5th c. B.C. Sanskrit grammarian. See: New Encyc. Brit., 1974, Microp. Paninean.

anisc (or Panisk) (Pan): Mythology. See: Webster's 3d.

ANIZZA, BARTOLOMEO. 1785-1867. Italian anatomist. See: World Who's Who Sci. Panizza's foramen, Panizza's plexus.

anizza's foramen (Panizza, Bartolomeo): Zoology. See: Gray.

anizza's plexus (Panizza, Bartolomeo): Anatomy. See: Dorland.

ANJANDRUM (or GRAND PANJANDRUM). Burlesque title of an imaginary personage in some nonsense lines by Samuel Foote (d. 1777), English actor and playwright. See: Harvey. Panjandrum.

anjandrum (Panjandrum): Generic Word (powerful or pretentious official). See: Webster's 3d.

ANNER, HANS JESSEN. 1871-1930. Danish roentgenologist. See: Biog. Lex. hervorr. Aerzte. Panner's disease (1), Panner's disease (2).

anner's disease (1) (Panner, Hans Jessen). See: Koehler's first disease.

anner's disease (2) (Panner, Hans Jessen): Medicine. See: Jablonski; Stedman. Also known as: Haas' disease.

ANNETIER, ANTOINE C. d. 1859. French painter and chemist. (Biography source unavailable.) Pannetier's green, Pannetier's reds.

annetier's green (Pannetier, Antoine C.): Chemistry. See: Webster's 3d. Also known as: Guignet's green (1).

annetier's reds (Pannetier, Antoine C.): Chemistry. See: Thrush.

ANSCH, ADOLF. 1841-1887. German anatomist. See: Anat. Anz., vol. 2 (1887), pp. 719-721. Pansch's fissure.

Pansch's fissure (Pansch, Adolf): Anatomy. See: Dorland; Stedman.

PANTAGRUEL. Gigantic son of Gargantua in Francois Rabelais' novel, "Pantagruel," (1533). See: Jobes. Pantagruelian (or Pantagruelism).

Pantagruelian (or Pantagruelism) (Pantagruel): Generic Word (coarse humor with a serious intent). See: Partridge; Webster's 3d.

Pantaleon (Pantaleone or Pantalon) (dulcimer) (Hebenstreit, Pantaleon): Music. See: Apel; Charnock; Partridge; Webster's 3d.

PANTALEONE, SAINT. d. 305. Roman physician from Asia-Minor. See: Holweck. Pantalets (or Pantalettes), Pantaloon (or Pantalone), Pantaloonery, Pantaloons (or Pants), Panties, Pantywaist.

Pantalets (or Pantalettes) (Pantaleone, Saint): Fashion. See: Webster's 3d.

Pantaloon (or Pantalone) (Pantaleone, Saint): Literature (clown). See: Harvey; Webster's 3d.

Pantaloonery (Pantaleone, Saint): Generic Word (buffoonery). See: Webster's 3d.

Pantaloons (or Pants) (Pantaleone, Saint): Fashion. See: Funk; Hendrickson; Picken; Webster's 3d.

Panties (Pantaleone, Saint): Fashion. See: Hendrickson; Webster's 3d.

Pantywaist (Pantaleone, Saint): Generic Word (sissy). See: Hendrickson; Webster's 3d.

Panuliris (Palinurus): Zoology. See: Webster's 3d.

PANUM, PETER LUDWIG. 1820-1885. Danish physiologist. See: Pogg., vols. 2, 3. Panum's area, Panum's casein.

Panum's area (Panum, Peter Ludwig): Physiology. See: Stedman; Wolman.

Panum's casein (Panum, Peter Ludwig): Medicine. See: Dorland; Stedman.

PANURGE. Character in Rabelais' work "Pantagruel," (ca. 1532). See: Harvey. Panurge.

Panurge (Panurge, the character): Generic Word (cunning buffoon). See: Partridge.

Panza, Sancho. See: Sancho Panza.

Panzer-Forderer snaking conveyor (Derivation undetermined): Engineering and Industry. See: Thrush.

Pap test (or smear) (Papanicolaou, George Nicholas). See: Papanicolaou (Pap) test (stain, smear, or examination).

Papafil-Cernatesco reagent (Papafil, M. and Cernatescu, Radu): Chemistry. See: Van Nostrand Chem. Dict.

PAPAFIL, M. fl. 1930. Rumanian? chemist. Cited in: Chem. Abstr., Decenn. Index, 1927-1936. Papafil-Cernatesco reagent.

PAPANICOLAOU, GEORGE NICHOLAS. 1883-1962. Greek-born American anatomist and cytologist. See: Dict. Sci. Biog. Papanicolaou stain, Papanicolaou (Pap) test (stain, smear, or examination).

Papanicolaou stain (Papanicolaou, George Nicholas): Medicine. See: Dorland; Stedman.

Papanicolaou (Pap) test (stain, smear, or examination) (Papanicolaou, George Nicholas): Medicine. See: Hendrickson; Stedman; Webster's 3d.

PAPEZ, JAMES WENCESLAS. 1883-1958. American anatomist. See: Who Was Who Amer., 1951-1960. Papez's circle, Papez's theory of emotion.

Papez's circle (Papez, James Wenceslas): Psychology. See: Hinsie.

Papez's theory of emotion (Papez, James Wenceslas): Psychology. See: Hinsie.

papier Ingres (or Ingres paper) (Ingres, Jean Auguste Dominique): Fine Arts. See: Lockwood.

papilla of Vater (Vater, Abraham). See: Vater's ampulla.

PAPILLON. fl. 1924. French dermatologist. (Biography source unavailable.) Papillon-Lefevre syndrome.

PAPILLON-LEAGE. fl. 1954. French stomatologist. (Biography source unavailable.) Papillon-Leage and Psaume syndrome.

Papillon-Leage and Psaume syndrome (Papillon-Leage and Psaume, Jean): Medicine. See: Jablonski.

Papillon-Lefevre syndrome (Papillon and Lefevre, Paul): Medicine. See: Jablonski.

PAPIN, DENIS. 1647?-1712. French physicist. See: Encyc. Brit., 1973. Papin pump, Papin's digester.

Papin pump (Papin, Denis): Engineering and Industry. See: Auger.

Papin's digester (Papin, Denis): Physics. See: Dorland; Stedman.

Papiria, Lex (Papirius, Sextus (or Publius). See: Jus Papirianum.

PAPIRIUS, SEXTUS (or PUBLIUS). No dates. Early Roman jurist. See: Dict. Grk. Rom. Biog. Myth. Jus Papirianum.

PAPKOVICH, PETR FEDOROVICH. 1887-1946. Russian shipbuilding engineer. See: Who Was Who USSR. Neuber-Papkovich stress functions.

PAPPE, KARL WILHELM LUDWIG. 1803-1862. German botanist. See: Biog. Notes Upon Botanists. Pappea.

Pappea (Pappe, Karl Wilhelm Ludwig): Botany. See: Webster's 3d.

PAPPENHEIM, ARTHUR. 1870-1916. German internist. See: World Who's Who Sci. Pappenheim's method, Unna-Pappenheim stain.

Pappenheim pump (Derivation undetermined): Engineering and Industry. See: Auger.

Pappenheim's method (Pappenheim, Arthur): Medicine. See: Dorland; Kelly; Stedman.

PAPPERITZ, ERWIN (In full: JOHANN ERWIN). 1857-1938. German mathematician. See: Pogg., vols. 4, 5, 6. Riemann-Papperitz equation.

Papperitz's equation (Papperitz, Erwin). See: Riemann-Papperitz equation.

PAPPUS OF ALEXANDRIA. fl. ca. 300. Greek mathematician. See: Encyc. Brit., 1973. Pappus' theorems (or theorems of Pappus).

Pappus' theorems (or theorems of Pappus) (Pappus of Alexandria): Mathematics. See: Ballentyne; Internat. Dict. Phys. Elec.; James.

PAQUELIN, CLAUDE ANDRE. 1836-1905. French physician. See: Biog. Lex. hervorr. Aerzte. Paquelin's cautery.

Paquelin's cautery (Paquelin, Claude Andre): Medicine. See: Dorland; Stedman.

Paracelsian (Paracelsus, Philippus Aureolus): Generic Word (visionary). See: Partridge.

Paracelsian method (or school) (Paracelsus, Philippus Aureolus): Medicine. See: Dorland; Stedman; Webster's 3d.

Paracelsists (Paracelsus, Philippus Aureolus): Religion. See: Canney.

PARACELSUS, PHILIPPUS AUREOLUS (THEOPHRASTUS BOMBASTUS VON HOHENHEIM). 1493?-1541. Swiss alchemist and physician. See: Encyc. Brit., 1973. Paracelsian method (or school), Paracelsists.

Paradisea (Paradisi, Giovanni?): Botany. See: Taylor, N.

PARADISI, GIOVANNI. 1760-1826. Italian writer and politician. See: Michaud. Paradisea?

PARE, AMBROISE. 1510?-1590. French surgeon. See: Dict. Sci. Biog. Pare's suture.

PARENTI, GIAN CARLO. fl. 1936. Italian physician. Cited in: Index. Cat. Libr. Surg.-Gen. Off., 5th Ser., vol. 1, 1959. Parenti's disease.

Parenti's disease (Parenti, Gian Carlo): Medicine. See: Jablonski.

Pare's suture (Pare, Ambroise): Medicine. See: Dorland; Stedman.

Paretian optimum (Pareto, Vilfredo): Economics. See: Greenwald.

Pareto curve/distribution (Pareto, Vilfredo): Statistics. See: Kendall.

Pareto index (Pareto, Vilfredo): Statistics. See: Kendall.

PARETO, VILFREDO. 1848-1923. Italian-born Swiss economist and sociologist. See: Internat. Encyc. Soc. Sci. Levy-Pareto distribution, Paretian optimum, Pareto curve/distribution, Pareto index, Pareto's law.

Pareto's law (Pareto, Vilfredo): Economics. See: Greenwald; Webster's 3d.

Parham band (Parham, Frederick William): Medicine. See: Dorland.

PARHAM, FREDERICK WILLIAM. 1856-1927. American surgeon. See: Who Was Who Amer., 1897-1942. Parham band.

Parian verse (Archilochus of Paros): Literature. See: Wagner (More Names).

PARILLO. No dates. Spanish physician. (Biography source unavailable.) Sarsaparilla?

PARINAUD, HENRI. 1844-1905. French ophthalmologist. See: Biog. Lex. hervorr. Aerzte, 1880-1930. Parinaud's conjunctivitis (conjunctivoadenitis or oculoglandular syndrome), Parinaud's operation, Parinaud's syndrome (or ophthalmoplegia).

Parinaud's conjunctivitis (conjunctivoadenitis or oculoglandular syndrome) (Parinaud, Henri): Medicine. See: Dorland; Jablonski; Stedman.

Parinaud's operation (Parinaud, Henri): Medicine. See: Kelly.

Parinaud's syndrome (or ophthalmoplegia) (Parinaud, Henri): Medicine. See: Dorland; Jablonski; Stedman.

PARIS. In Greek mythology, son of Priam, King of Troy. See: Jobes. judgment of Paris, Paris (plant), Parisian wedding.

PARIS, JOSE J. d. 1849. Columbian mine owner and philanthropist. Cited in: Dana, 9th ed. Parisite.

Paris (plant) (Paris): Botany. See: Charnock.

Parisian wedding (Paris): History. See: Jobes.

Parisite (Paris, Jose J.): Earth Sciences. See: Webster's 3d.

PARK, HENRY. 1744-1831. English surgeon. See: Dict. Nat. Biog. Park's aneurysm.

PARK, MUNGO. 1771-1806. Scottish surgeon and explorer in Africa. See: Encyc. Brit., 1973. Parkia.

PARK, WILLIAM HALLOCK. 1863-1939. American bacteriologist. See: Who Was Who Amer., 1897-1942. Park-Williams bacillus, Park-Williams fixative.

Park-Williams bacillus (Park, William Hallock and Williams, Anna Wessels): Medicine. See: Dorland; Stedman.

Park-Williams fixative (Park, William Hallock and Williams, Anna Wessels): Medicine. See: Stedman.

PARKE, JAMES (BARON WENSLEYDALE). 1782-1868. English judge. See: Dict. Nat. Biog. Wensleydale case.

PARKER, C. H. fl. 1928. English metallurgical engineer. Cited in: Chem. Abstr., Decenn. Index, 1927-1936. Parker process.

PARKER, C. S. fl..1824. Scottish scientist. Cited in: Royal Soc. Cat. Sci. Pap., 1800-1863. Parkeria.

PARKER, EARL RANDALL. 1912- . American metallurgist. See: World Who's Who Sci. Parker-Washburn boundary.

PARKER, EDWARD MASON. 1860-1941. American surgeon. See: Nat. Cycl. Amer. Biog., vol. 30, p. 455. Parker-Kerr suture.

PARKER, GEORGE HOWARD. 1864-1955. American zoologist. See: Who Was Who Amer., 1897-1942. Parker's fluid.

PARKER, HERBERT MYERS. 1910- . English-born American physicist. See: World Who's Who Sci. Parker (unit).

PARKER, JAMES SOUTHWORTH. 1867-1933. American legislator. See: Biog. Direct. Amer. Congress. Watson-Parker Act.

Parker-Kerr suture (Parker, Edward Mason and Kerr, Harry Hyland): Medicine. See: Stedman.

PARKER, MATTHEW. 1504-1575. English prelate. See: Dict. Nat. Biog. nosey Parker.

Parker process (Parker, C. H.): Engineering and Industry. See: Thrush.

PARKER, RALPH ROBINSON. 1888-1949. American zoologist. See: Who Was Who Amer., vol. 2. Spencer-Parker vaccine.

PARKER, ROBERT LUELING. b. 1893. Swiss mineralogist. See: Pogg. vols. 6, 7a. Parkerite.

PARKER, ROBERT WILLIAM. d. 1913. English physician. See: Brit. Med. J., vol. i (1913), p. 588. Parker's syndrome.

PARKER, THEODORE. 1810-1860. American clergyman. See: Dict. Amer. Biog. Parkerism.

Parker (unit) (Parker, Herbert Myers): Physics. See: Dresner.

Parker-Washburn boundary (Parker, Earl Randall and Washburn, Jack): Physics. See: Internat. Dict. Phys. Elec.

PARKER, WILLARD. 1800-1884. American surgeon. See: Dict. Amer. Biog. Parker's incision.

Parkeria (Parker, C. S.): Botany. See: Webster's 3d.

Parkerism (Parker, Theodore): Religion. See: Mathews, M. M.

Parkerite (Parker, Robert Lueling): Earth Sciences. See: Thrush; Webster's 3d.

Parker's fluid (Parker, George Howard): Medicine. See: Dorland; Stedman.

Parker's incision (Parker, Willard): Medicine. See: Dorland; Stedman.

Parker's syndrome (Parker, Robert William). See: Hutchinson's disease.

PARKES, ALBERT E. fl. 1920. English? chemist. Cited in: Chem. Abstr., Decenn. Index, 1917-1926. Parkes reagent.

PARKES, ALEXANDER. 1813-1890. English chemist. See: Dict. Nat. Biog. Parkes process, Parkesine.

Parkes process (Parkes, Alexander): Chemistry. See: Ballentyne; Thrush; Webster's 3d.

Parkes reagent (Parkes, Albert E.): Chemistry. See: Van Nostrand Chem. Dict.

Parkes Weber. See: Weber, Frederick Parkes.

Parkes Weber and Dimitri syndrome (Weber, Frederick Parkes and Dimitri, Vicente). See: Sturge-Weber syndrome.

Parkes Weber's syndrome (Weber, Frederick Parkes). See: Klippel-Trenaunay syndrome.

Parkesine (Parkes, Alexander): Chemistry. See: Hackh.

Parkia (Park, Mungo): Botany. See: Webster's 3d.

Parkin (gingerbread) (Derivation undetermined): Food and Drink. See: Partridge; Webster's 3d.

PARKINSON, CYRIL NORTHCOTE. 1909- . English satirical writer. See: Who's Who, 1975. Parkinson's law(s), Parkinson's law of delay, Parkinson's law of triviality, Parkinson's laws of committee size.

PARKINSON, JAMES. 1755-1824. English physician. See: Dict. Sci. Biog. Parkinsonian, Parkinson's facies, Parkinson's disease (or syndrome).

PARKINSON, JOHN. 1567-1650. English botanist. See: Dict. Nat. Biog. Parkinsonia.

PARKINSON, SIR JOHN. b. 1885. English cardiologist. See: Who's Who, 1975. Wolff-Parkinson-White syndrome.

Parkinsonia (Parkinson, John): Botany. See: Charnock; Taylor, N.; Webster's 3d.

Parkinsonian (Parkinson, James): Medicine. See: Stedman; Webster's 3d.

Parkinsonism (Parkinson, James). See: Parkinson's disease (or syndrome).

Parkinson's disease (or syndrome) (Parkinson, James): Medicine. See: Dorland; Jablonski; Stedman; Van Nostrand Sci. Encyc. Also known as: Parkinsonism.

Parkinson's facies (Parkinson, James): Medicine. See: Dorland; Stedman.

Parkinson's law(s) (Parkinson, Cyril Northcote): Sociology. See: Brewer; Martin; Smith.

Parkinson's law of delay (Parkinson, Cyril Northcote): Sociology. See: Martin.

Parkinson's law of triviality (Parkinson, Cyril Northcote): Sociology. See: Martin.

Parkinson's laws of committee size (Parkinson, Cyril Northcote): Sociology. See: Martin.

Parkman crab (or crabapple) (Parkman, Francis): Botany. See: Webster's 3d.

PARKMAN, FRANCIS. 1823-1893. American historian. See: Dict. Amer. Biog. Parkman crab (or crabapple).

PARKMAN, GEORGE. 1791-1849. American physician. Cited in: Index-Cat. Libr. Surg.-Gen. Off., 1st Ser., vol. 10, 1889. Parkman('s) wren.

Parkman('s) wren (Parkman, George): Zoology. See: Mathews, M. M.

Park's aneurysm (Park, Henry): Medicine. See: Dorland; Stedman.

PARLATORE, FILIPPO. 1816-1877. Italian botanist. See: Biog. Lex. hervorr. Aerzte. Parlatoria.

Parlatoria (Parlatore, Filippo): Zoology. See: Webster's 3d.

PARMELEE, CULLEN WARNER. b. 1874. American ceramics engineer. See: Who's Who Engin., 1937. Talwalkar-Parmelee plasticity index.

Parmenidean (Parmenides): Philosophy. See: Webster's 3d.

PARMENIDES. fl. 5th c. B.C. Greek philosopher. See: Encyc. Brit., 1973. Parmenidean.

Parmentier(e) (or a la Parmentier) (Parmentier, Antoine-Auguste): Food and Drink. See: De Sola; Webster's 3d.

PARMENTIER, ANTOINE-AUGUSTE. 1737-1813. French chemist and economist. See: Dict. Sci. Biog. Parmentier(e) (or a la Parmentier), Parmentiera, potage Parmentier.

Parmentiera (Parmentier, Antoine-Auguste): Botany. See: Webster's 3d.

PARNAS, JAKUB KAROL. 1884-1949. Polish biochemist. See: Dict. Sci. Biog. Embden-Meyerhof-Parnas pathway.

PARNELL, CHARLES STEWART. 1846-1891. Irish Nationalist leader. See: Dict. Nat. Biog. Parnell Commission, Parnellite(s) (or Parnellite party).

Parnell Commission (Parnell, Charles Stewart): History. See: Harbottle; Montgomery; Steinberg.

Parnellite(s) (or Parnellite party) (Parnell, Charles Stewart): History. See: Harbottle; Latham; Webster's 3d.

PARONA, FRANCESCO. fl. 1878-1884. Italian surgeon. Cited in: Index. Cat. Libr. Surg.-Gen. Off., 1st Ser., vol. 10, 1889. Parona's space.

Parona's space (Parona, Francesco): Medicine. See: Stedman.

Parr apparatus (Parr, Samuel Wilson): Chemistry. See: Hackh; Van Nostrand Chem. Dict.

Parr calorimeter (Parr, Samuel Wilson): Chemistry. See: Thrush.

Parr formula (Parr, Samuel Wilson): Earth Sciences. See: Thrush.

PARR, SAMUEL WILSON. 1857-1931. American chemist. See: Dict. Amer. Biog. Parr apparatus, Parr calorimeter, Parr formula, Parr turbidimeter, Parr's classification of coal.

Parr turbidimeter (Parr, Samuel Wilson): Chemistry. See: Van Nostrand Sci. Encyc.

Parri alcohol reagent (Parri, Walter): Chemistry. See: Van Nostrand Chem. Dict.

Parri reagent for metals (Parri, Walter): Chemistry. See: Van Nostrand Chem. Dict.

Parri test reaction for alkaloids (Parri, Walter): Chemistry. See: Van Nostrand Chem. Dict.

Parri test reaction for phenols (Parri, Walter): Chemistry. See: Van Nostrand Chem. Dict.

Parri test reactions for cinnamic, succinic, and malic acids (Parri, Walter): Chemistry. See: Van Nostrand Chem. Dict.

PARRI, WALTER. fl. 1924-1946. Italian chemist. Cited in: Chem. Abstr. Decenn. Indexes, 1917-1926. Parri alcohol reagent, Parri reagent for metals, Parri test reaction for alkaloids, Parri test reaction for phenols, Parri test reactions for cinnamic, succinic, and malic acids.

Parrish arm (Derivation undetermined): Engineering and Industry. See: Thrush.

Parrish shaker (Derivation undetermined): Engineering and Industry. See: Thrush.

PARROT, FRIEDRICH (In full: JOHANN JACOB FRIEDRICH WILHELM). 1792-1841. German naturalist and traveler. See: Allg. Deut. Biog. Parrotia.

PARROT, JOSEPH MARIE JULES. 1829-1883. French physician. See: Biog. Lex. hervorr. Aerzte. Parrot's atrophy, Parrot's cicatrix, Parrot's disease (1) (paralysis or pseudoparalysis), Parrot's disease (2), Parrot's nodes (or sign), Parrott's ulcer.

Parrot-Kaufmann syndrome (Parrot, Joseph Marie Jules and Kaufmann, Eduard). See: Parrot's disease (2).

Parrotia (Parrot, Friedrich): Botany. See: Bailey, L. H.

Parrot's atrophy (Parrot, Joseph Marie Jules): Medicine. See: Dorland; Jablonski.

Parrot's cicatrix (Parrot, Joseph Marie Jules): Medicine. See: Jablonski.

Parrot's disease (1) (paralysis or pseudoparalysis) (Parrot, Joseph Marie Jules): Medicine. See: Dorland; Jablonski; Stedman. Also known as: Bednar-Parrot disease, Wegner's disease (or osteochondritis).

Parrot's disease (2) (Parrot, Joseph Marie Jules): Medicine. See: Dorland; Jablonski; Stedman. Also known as: Kaufmann's disease, Parrot-Kaufmann syndrome.

Parrot's nodes (or sign) (Parrot, Joseph Marie Jules): Medicine. See: Dorland; Jablonski.

Parrott gun(s) (Parrott, Robert Parker): Weapons. See: Mathews, M. M.; Partridge; Quick.

Parrott rifle (Parrott, Robert Parker): Weapons. See: Mathews, M. M.

PARROTT, ROBERT PARKER. 1804-1877. American soldier and inventor. See: Dict. Amer. Biog. Parrott gun(s), Parrott rifle.

Parrott's ulcer (Parrot, Joseph Marie Jules): Medicine. See: Dorland; Stedman.

Parr's classification of coal (Parr, Samuel Wilson): Earth Sciences. See: Thrush.

Parry arcs (Parry, Sir William Edward?): Earth Sciences. See: Huschke.

PARRY, CALEB HILLIER. 1755-1822. English physician. See: Dict. Nat. Biog. Parry-Romberg syndrome, Parry's syndrome (or disease).

PARRY, CHARLES CHRISTOPHER. 1823-1890. American botanist. See: Dict. Amer. Biog. Parry grama, Parry larkspur, Parry lily, Parry pinyon (or pine).

Parry grama (Parry, Charles Christopher): Botany. See: Winburne.

Parry larkspur (Parry, Charles Christopher): Botany. See: Winburne.

Parry lily (Parry, Charles Christopher): Botany. See: Winburne.

Parry pinyon (or pine) (Parry, Charles Christopher): Botany. See: Webster's 3d.

Parry Report (Parry, Thomas): Library Science. See: Harrod.

Parry-Romberg syndrome (Parry, Caleb Hillier and Romberg, Moritz Heinrich). See: Romberg's syndrome.

PARRY, THOMAS. 1904- . English educator. See: Who's Who, 1975. Parry Report.

PARRY, SIR WILLIAM EDWARD. 1790-1855. English Arctic explorer. See: Dict. Nat. Biog. Parry arcs?

Parry's syndrome (or disease) (Parry, Caleb Hillier). See: Basedow's disease.

Parseval (airship) (Parseval, August Franz Max von): Aviation. See: Webster's 3d.

PARSEVAL, AUGUST FRANZ MAX VON. 1861-1942. German aeronautical engineer. See: Pogg., vols. 4, 5, 6. Parseval (airship).

PARSEVAL-DESCHENES, MARC-ANTOINE. 1755-1836. French mathematician. See: Dict. Sci. Biog. Parseval equation, Parseval's identity, Parseval's theorem.

Parseval equation (Parseval-Deschenes, Marc-Antoine): Mathematics. See: Internat. Dict. Ap. Math.

Parseval's identity (Parseval-Deschenes, Marc-Antoine): Mathematics. See: Ballentyne.

Parseval's theorem (Parseval-Deschenes, Marc-Antoine): Mathematics. See: Ballentyne; Huschke; James.

Parshall (flume) (Parshall, Ralph Leroy): Engineering and Industry. See: Webster's 3d.; Winburne.

PARSHALL, RALPH LEROY. b. 1881. American civil and hydraulic engineer. See: Amer. Men Sci., 5th ed. Parshall (flume).

Parson Brown orange (Brown, Nathan L.): Food and Drink. See: Hendrickson under "Temple Orange."

Parson language sample (Derivation undetermined): Psychology. See: Wolman.

PARSONAGE, MAURICE JOHN. fl. 1939-1972. English neurologist. See: Med. Direct., 1972. Parsonage-Turner syndrome.

Parsonage-Turner syndrome (Parsonage, Maurice John and Turner, John W. Aldren): Medicine. See: Jablonski.

PARSONS, ARTHUR LEONARD. 1873-1957. Canadian mineralogist. See: Pogg., vol. 6. Parsonsite.

PARSONS, SIR CHARLES ALGERNON. 1854-1931. English engineer. See: Pogg., vol. 6. Parsons steam turbine.

Parsons' disease (Parsons, James). See: Basedow's disease.

PARSONS, JAMES. 1705-1770. English physician. See: Dict. Nat. Biog. Parson's disease.

Parsons steam turbine (Parsons, Sir Charles Algernon): Engineering and Industry. See: Auger.

Parsonsite (Parsons, Arthur Leonard): Earth Sciences. See: Thrush; Webster's 3d.

PARTINGTON, MRS. Central character of Benjamin Shillaber's "The Life and Sayings of Mrs. Partington," (1851). See: Hart. Mrs. Partington.

PARTSCH, C. J. fl. 1963. German physician. (Biography source unavailable.) Miehlke-Partsch syndrome.

PARTSCH, CARL. b. 1855. German physician. See: Biog. Lex. hervorr. Aerzte, 1880-1930. Partsch operation?

PARTSCH, FRITZ JOSEPH GEORG. b. 1887. German surgeon. See: Kuerschner's Deut. Gel. Kal., vol. 4, 1931. Partsch method of gastrostomy.

Partsch method of gastrostomy (Partsch, Fritz Joseph Georg): Medicine. See: Kelly.

Partsch operation (Partsch, Carl?): Medicine. See: Stedman.

PARTSCH, PAUL MARIA. 1791-1856. Austrian geologist and mineralogist. See: Pogg., vols. 2, 7a suppl. Partschin.

Partschin (Partsch, Paul Maria): Earth Sciences. See: Charnock.

PARTZ, A. fl. 1881. French scientist. Cited in: Royal Soc. Cat. Sci. Pap., 1874-1883. Partz cell?

Partz cell (Partz, A.?): Chemistry. See: Hackh.

PASCAL, BLAISE. 1623-1662. French mathematician, physicist and philosopher. See: Dict. Sci. Biog. Pascal distribution, Pascal law (law of Pascal or principle of Pascal), Pascal('s) triangle, Pascal (unit), Pascalin, Pascal's theorem, Pascal's vases.

Pascal distribution (Pascal, Blaise): Statistics. See: Kendall.

Pascal law (law of Pascal or principle of Pascal) (Pascal, Blaise): Physics. See: Internat. Dict. Phys. Elec.; James under "Pascal, Blaise;" Van Nostrand Sci. Encyc.; Van Nostrand Sci. Encyc.

PASCAL, PAUL VICTOR HENRI. b. 1880. French chemist. See: Pogg., vols. 5, 6. Pascal rules.

Pascal rules (Pascal, Paul Victor Henri): Physics. See: Internat. Dict. Phys. Elec.

PASCAL, STEFAN. fl. 17th c. French father of Plaise Pascal. Cited in: Dict. Sci. Biog. under "Pascal, Blaise." Pascal's limacon (or snail or limacon of Pascal).

Pascal('s) triangle (Pascal, Blaise): Mathematics. See: Ballentyne; James; Van Nostrand Sci. Encyc.

Pascal (unit) (Pascal, Blaise): Physics. See: Ballentyne; Dresner; Thewlis.

Pascalin (Pascal, Blaise): Mathematics. See: Charnock.

Pascal's limacon (snail or limacon of Pascal) (Pascal, Stefan): Mathematics. See: Ballentyne; James; Van Nostrand Sci. Encyc. under "Limacon."

Pascal's theorem (Pascal, Blaise): Mathematics. See: Ballentyne; James.

Pascal's vases (Pascal, Blaise): Physics. See: Webster's 3d.

Pasch axioms (Pasch, Moritz): Mathematics. See: Van Nostrand Sci. Encyc. under "Geometry."

PASCH, MORITZ. 1843-1930. German mathematician. See: Pogg., vols. 3-6. Pasch axioms.

PASCHEFF, CONSTANTIN. b. 1873. Bulgarian ophthalmologist. See: Biog. Lex. hervorr. Aerzte. Pascheff's conjunctivitis, Pascheff's folliculoma.

ascheff's conjunctivitis (Pascheff, Constantin): Medicine. See: Jablonski; edman.

ascheff's folliculoma (Pascheff, Constantin): Medicine. See: Jablonski.

aschen–Back effect (Paschen, Friedrich and Back, Ernst E. A.) Physics. See: allentyne; Internat. Dict. Phys. Elec.; Thewlis; Van Nostrand Chem. Dict.; ebster's 3d.

aschen bodies (corpuscles or granules) (Paschen, Enrique): Medicine. See: orland; Stedman. Also known as: Prowazek bodies.

aschen bolometer (Paschen, Friedrich): Physics. See: Internat. Dict. Phys. ec.

aschen circle (Paschen, Friedrich): Physics. See: Thewlis.

ASCHEN, ENRIQUE. 1860-1936. German physician. See: Lancet, vol. 2 Oct. 31, 1936), pp. 1072-1073. Paschen bodies (corpuscles or granules).

ASCHEN, FRIEDRICH (In full: LOUIS CARL HEINRICH FRIEDRICH). 1865-47. German physicist. See: Pogg., vols. 4, 5, 6, 7a. Paschen–Back fect, Paschen bolometer, Paschen circle, Paschen galvanoscope, Paschen('s) w, Paschen mounting, Paschen series.

aschen galvanoscope (Paschen, Friedrich): Physics. See: Hackh.

aschen('s) law (Paschen, Friedrich): Electronics. See: Ballentyne; Van ostrand Sci. Encyc.; Webster's 3d.

aschen mounting (Paschen, Friedrich): Physics. See: Internat. Dict. Phys. ec. Also known as: Paschen-Runge mounting.

aschen-Runge mounting (Paschen, Friedrich and Runge, Carl David Tolme). e: Paschen mounting.

aschen series (Paschen, Friedrich): Physics. See: Internat. Dict. Ap. Math.; ternat. Dict. Phys. Elec.; Thewlis. Also known as: Ritz–Paschen series.

ASCHUTIN, VICTOR VASILIEVICH. 1845-1901. Russian pathologist. See: og. Lex. hervorr. Aerzte. Paschutin's degeneration.

aschutin's degeneration (Paschutin, Victor Vasilievich): Medicine. See: orland.

ASHKOV, V. A. d. 1902. Russian religious leader. (Biography source un-ailable.) Pashkovist.

ashkovist (Pashkov, V. A.): Religion. See: Webster's 3d.

ASINI, AGOSTINO. fl. 1928-1936. Italian dermatologist. See: Arnim. asini-Pierini syndrome, Pasini's syndrome.

asini-Pierini syndrome (Pasini, Agostino and Pierini, Luigi E.): Medicine. e: Jablonski.

asini's syndrome (Pasini, Agostino): Medicine. See: Jablonski.

ASQUALINI, RUDOLFO QUIRINO. 1909- . Argentinian physician. See: ran Encic. Argentina. Pasqualini's syndrome.

asqualini's syndrome (Pasqualini, Rudolfo Quirino): Medicine. See: Jablonski.

asquinade (Pasquino): Generic Word (lampoon). See: Brewer; Charnock; endrickson.

ASQUINO. fl. late 15th c. Italian tradesman. See: Harvey under Pasquinade." Pasquinade.

ASSAVANT, GUSTAV (In full: PHILIPP GUSTAV). 1815-1893. German urgeon. See: Biog. Lex. hervorr. Aerzte. Passavant's cushion (ridge, bar or ad).

assavant's cushion (ridge, bar or pad) (Passavant, Gustav): Anatomy. See: onath; Dorland; Stedman.

ASSBURG, EMIL. fl. 1907-1930. German chemist. Cited in: Chem. bstr., Decenn. Index, 1907-1916. Passburg process.

assburg process (Passburg, Emil): Agriculture. See: Winburne.

ASSERINI, MARIO TORQUATO LUIGI. b. 1891. Italian chemist. See: ogg., vol. 6. Passerini reaction.

asserini reaction (Passerini, Mario Torquato Luigi): Chemistry. See: Krauch nd Kunz; Van Nostrand Chem. Dict.

ASSEY, RICHARD DOUGLAS. fl. 1919-1964. English pathologist. See: ed. Direct., 1964. Harding-Passey melanoma.

ASSOUANT, P. fl. 1951. French physician. (Biography source unavailable.) imbaud-Passouant-Vallat syndrome.

PASSOW, ARNOLD VON. 1888-1966. German ophthalmologist. See: Docum. Ophthal., vol. 33, no. 1 (1972), p. 12 f. Passow's syndrome.

Passow's syndrome (Passow, Arnold von): Medicine. See: Jablonski.

Pasteur–Chamberland filter (Pasteur, Louis and Chamberland, Charles Edouard). See: Chamberland filter.

Pasteur effect (or reaction) (Pasteur, Louis): Chemistry. See: Dorland; Hackh; Stedman; Webster's 3d.

Pasteur filter (Pasteur, Louis): Chemistry. See: Hackh; Van Nostrand Chem. Dict.

Pasteur flask (Pasteur, Louis): Chemistry. See: Hackh; Van Nostrand Chem. Dict.

Pasteur Institute (Pasteur, Louis): Medicine. See: Hendrickson.

PASTEUR, LOUIS. 1822-1895. French chemist. See: Dict. Sci. Biog. Pasteur-Chamberland filter, Pasteur effect (or reaction), Pasteur filter, Pasteur flask, Pasteur Institute, Pasteur salt solution, Pasteur vaccine (and treatment), Pasteurella, Pasteuria, Pasteurian (or Pasteurism), Pasteurization, Pasteur's solu-tion (fluid or liquid), Pasteur's theory (or method).

Pasteur salt solution (Pasteur, Louis): Chemistry. See: Van Nostrand Chem. Dict.

Pasteur vaccine (and treatment) (Pasteur, Louis): Medicine. See: Hendrickson; Stedman; Webster's 3d.

Pasteur Vallery-Radot. See: Vallery-Radot, Pasteur.

Pasteurella (Pasteur, Louis): Zoology. See: Dorland; Pennak; Stedman; Webster's 3d.

Pasteuria (Pasteur, Louis): Zoology. See: Dorland; Stedman.

Pasteurian (or Pasteurism) (Pasteur, Louis): Medicine. Cited in: Partridge; Webster's 3d.

Pasteurization (Pasteur, Louis): Chemistry. See: Dorland; Stedman; Thewlis; Van Nostrand Chem. Dict.; Webster's 3d.

Pasteur's solution (fluid or liquid) (Pasteur, Louis): Chemistry. See: Dorland.

Pasteur's theory (or method) (Pasteur, Louis): Medicine. See: Dorland; Stedman.

PASTIA, C. fl. 20th c. Roumanian physician. (Biography source unavailable.) Pastia's sign (or lines).

Pastia's sign (or lines) (Pastia, C.): Medicine. See: Dorland; Stedman.

Paston Letters (Paston, William): History. See: Barnhart (Eng. Lit.); Encyc. Brit., 1973; Steinberg.

PASTON, WILLIAM. 1378-1444. English judge. See: Dict. Nat. Biog. Paston Letters.

PATAU, KLAUS. fl. 1960. German? physician. (Biography source unavail-able.) Patau's syndrome.

Patau's syndrome (Patau, Klaus): Medicine. See: Jablonski. Also known as: Bartholin-Patau syndrome.

Patch differential (Patch, Harry M.): Engineering and Industry. See: Auger.

PATCH, HARRY M. fl. before 1951. American? engineer. (Biography source unavailable.) Patch differential.

PATEIN, GUSTAV CONSTANT. 1857-1928. French physician. See: Pogg., vols. 4, 5, 6. Patein solution for milk, Patein's albumin.

Patein solution for milk (Patein, Gustav Constant): Chemistry. See: Van Nostrand Chem. Dict.

Patein's albumin (Patein, Gustav Constant): Medicine. See: Dorland; Stedman.

PATELLA, VINCENZO. 1856-1928. Italian physician. See: Biog. Lex. hervorr. Aerzte, 1880-1930. Patella's disease.

Patella's disease (Patella, Vincenzo): Medicine. See: Dorland.

PATERA, ADOLF. d. 1894. Austrian metallurgical engineer. See: Royal Soc. Cat. Sci. Pap., 1884-1900. Patera process.

Patera process (Patera, Adolf): Engineering and Industry. See: Hackh; Thrush; Van Nostrand Chem. Dict.

PATERNO DI SESSA, EMANUELE. 1847-1935. Italian chemist. See: Pogg., vols. 3-6. Paternoite.

Paternoite (Paterno di Sessa, Emanuele): Earth Sciences. See: Thrush; Webster's 3d.

Paterson and Brown Kelly syndrome (Paterson, Donald Rose and Kelly, Adam Brown). See: Plummer-Vinson syndrome.

PATERSON, DONALD GILDERSLEEVE. b. 1892. American psychologist. See: Amer. Men Sci., 9th ed., (Soc. Behav. Sci.) Pintner-Paterson scale of performance tests.

PATERSON, DONALD ROSE. 1863-1939. English otolaryngologist. See: J. Lar. Otol., vol. 54 (1939), pp. 437-440. Paterson and Brown Kelly syndrome, Paterson-Kelly syndrome, Paterson's syndrome.

Paterson-Kelly syndrome (Paterson, Donald Rose and Kelly, Adam Brown). See: Plummer-Vinson syndrome.

Paterson plan (Paterson, William): History. See: Smith.

PATERSON, ROBERT. 1814-1889. Scottish physician. See: Edinburgh Med. J., vol. 34 (1888-1889), p. 1159. Paterson's corpuscles.

PATERSON, WILLIAM. 1745-1806. Irish-born American jurist. See: Dict. Amer. Biog. Paterson plan.

PATERSON, WILLIAM. 1755-1810. Scottish-born Australian administrator and botanist. See: Dict. Nat. Biog. Paterson's curse.

Paterson's corpuscles (Paterson, Robert): Medicine. See: Stedman.

Paterson's curse (Paterson, William): Botany. See: Webster's 3d.

Paterson's syndrome (Paterson, Donald Rose). See: Plummer-Vinson syndrome.

PATHE, CHARLES. 1863-1957. French industrialist and film manufacturer. See: Focal Encyc. Film. Pathe-KOK projector, Pathe Rural 17.5 mm. films, Pathecolour.

Pathe-KOK projector (Pathe, Charles): Photography. See: Focal Encyc. Photog. under "Cine History," p. 221.

Pathe Rural 17.5 mm. films (Pathe, Charles): Photography. See: Focal Encyc. Photog. under "Cine History," p. 222.

Pathecolour (Pathe, Charles): Photography. See: Focal Encyc. Photog. under "Cine History," p. 223.

patience of Job (Job): Generic Word. See: Hendrickson.

PATITZ, JOHN FREDERICK MAX. 1866-1937. German-born American engineer. See: Nat. Cycl. Amer. Biog., vol. 27, p. 86. Patitz turbine.

Patitz turbine (Patitz, John Frederick Max): Engineering and Industry. See: Auger.

Patman Bonus Bill (Patman, Wright): Politics. See: Morris.

PATMAN, WRIGHT. b. 1893. American legislator. See: Biog. Direct. Amer. Congress. Patman Bonus Bill, Robinson-Patman Act.

PATON, LESLIE. b. 1872. English physician. See: Biog. Lex. hervorr. Aerzte, 1880-1930. Gowers-Paton-Kennedy syndrome.

PATRASSI, GINO. 1904- . Italian physician. See: Who's Who Sci. Europe, 1972. Fanconi-Patrassi syndrome.

PATRICK, HUGH TALBOT. 1860-1938. American neurologist. See: Who Was Who Amer., 1897-1942. Patrick's test.

PATRICK, SAINT. 389?-461? English-born missionary in Ireland. See: Dict. Nat. Biog. Brothers of St. Patrick, Order (or Knights) of Saint Patrick, Paddy (or Pat), Saint Patrick's cabbage, Saint Patrick's cross, Saint Patrick's Day.

Patrick's test (Patrick, Hugh Talbot): Medicine. See: Dorland; Stedman.

PATRIDGE, E. E. fl. 19th c. American sportsman. (Biography source unavailable.) Patridge sight.

Patridge sight (Patridge, E. E.): Recreation and Sports. See: Webster's 3d.

Patrimony of St. Cuthbert (Cuthbert, Saint): Religion. See: Attwater.

Patrimony of St. Peter (Peter the Apostle, Saint): Religion. See: Attwater.

Patronite (Rizo-Patron, Antenor): Earth Sciences. See: Thrush.

PATSCHOVSKY, NORBERT. fl. 1919-1931. German botanist. See: Kuerschner's Deut. Gel. Kal., vol. 4, 1931. Patschowsky solution.

Patschowsky solution (Patschovsky, Norbert): Chemistry. See: Van Nostrand Chem. Dict.

PATTERSON, ARTHUR LINDO. 1902-1966. New Zealand-born American crystallographer. See: World Who's Who Sci. Patterson function, Patterson-Harker method; Patterson map.

Patterson function (Patterson, Arthur Lindo): Physics. See: Thewlis; Van Nostrand Sci. Encyc. under "Crystal Structure Determination."

Patterson-Harker method (Patterson, Arthur Lindo and Harker, David): Physics. See: Internat. Dict. Phys. Elec.

Patterson map (Patterson, Arthur Lindo): Physics. See: Internat. Dict. Phys. Elec.; Thewlis.

PATTINSON, HUGH LEE. 1796-1858. English metallurgist. See: World Who's Who Sci. Pattinson process (for desilvering lead), Pattinson's pots.

Pattinson process (for desilvering lead) (Pattinson, Hugh Lee): Engineering and Industry. See: Ballentyne; Hackh; Thrush; Webster's 3d.

Pattinson's pots (Pattinson, Hugh Lee): Engineering and Industry. See: Thrush.

Pattison engine (Pattison, John): Engineering and Industry. See: Auger.

PATTISON, JOHN. fl. 1857. Engineer. (Biography source unavailable.) Pattison engine.

PATTON, GEORGE SMITH. 1885-1945. American general. See: Dict. Amer. Biog., 3d suppl. Patton tank.

Patton tank (Patton, George Smith): Weapons. See: Quick.

PAUL III (ALLESSANDRO FARNESE). 1468-1549. Pope. See: Encyc. Brit., 1911. Paul (coin).

PAUL IV (GIOVANNI PIETRO CARAFFA, BISHOP OF THEATE). 1476-1559. Pope. See: Webster's Biog. Dict. Theatines.

Paul-Bunnell antibody (Paul, John Rodman and Bunnell, Walls Willard): Medicine. See: Webster's 3d.

Paul-Bunnell test (or reaction) (Paul, John Rodman and Bunnell, Walls Willard): Medicine. See: Dorland; Webster's 3d.

Paul Bunyan (Bunyan, Paul): Generic Word. See: Webster's 3d.

PAUL, CHARLES THEODORE CONSTANTIN. 1833-1896. French physician. See: Biog. Lex. hervorr. Aerzte. Paul's sign.

Paul (coin) (Paul III): Numismatics. See: Charnock.

Paul floc (or water) test (Paul, Ira M.?): Engineering and Industry. See: Thrush.

PAUL, FRANK THOMAS. 1851-1941. English surgeon. See: Brit. Med. J., vol. 1 (Feb. 1, 1941), pp. 176-177. Paul-Mixter tube.

PAUL, GUSTAV. 1859-1935. Austrian physician. See: Biog. Lex. hervorr. Aerzte, 1880-1930. Paul's reaction (or test).

PAUL, HANS. fl. ca. 1812. German mine supervisor. Cited in: Hintze, suppl. 3, p. 251. Paulite.

PAUL, IRA M. fl. 1929. American? chemical engineer. Cited in: Chem. Abstr., Decenn. Index, 1927-1936. Paul floc (or water) test?

PAUL, JOHN RODMAN. 1893-1971. American physician. See: Who Was Who Amer., 1969-1973. Paul-Bunnell antibody, Paul-Bunnell test (or reaction).

Paul Jones (Jones, John Paul): Dance. See: Brewer; Hendrickson; Webster's 3d.

Paul-Mixter tube (Paul, Frank Thomas and Mixter, Samuel Jason): Medicine. See: Dorland.

PAUL OF SAMOSATA. fl. 260. Bishop of Antioch in Syria. See: Encyc. Brit., 1973. Paulianist, Paulicians?

PAUL OF THEBES, SAINT (PAUL THE HERMIT). ca. 230-ca. 343. Egyptian hermit. See: Holweck. Hermits of St. Paul, Paulites.

Paul Pry (Pry, Paul): Generic Word (busybody). See: Partridge; Webster's 3d.

PAUL, R. W. fl. 1935. English scientist. Cited in: Kelly. Bragg-Paul pulsator.

PAUL THE APOSTLE, SAINT (SAUL OF TARSUS). d. ca. 67. Christian missionary to the Gentiles. See: Holweck. Company of St. Paul? Paulicians? Pauline (or Paulinian), Pauline privilege, Paulinism (Paulinist or Paulism), Paulists, Peter-Paul goblet illusion? Regular Clerk of Saint Paul, rob Peter to pay Paul, Saint Paul (oratorio), Saint Paul's speedwell?

aul the Hermit. See: Paul of Thebes, Saint.

aul Veronese green (Veronese, Paul): Fine Arts. See: Webster's 3d.

auli exclusion principle (Pauli, Wolfgang): Physics. See: Internat. Dict. hys. Elec.; Thewlis; Van Nostrand Chem. Dict.; Van Nostrand Sci. Encyc. nder "Atomic Structure."

auli g-permanence rule (Pauli, Wolfgang): Physics. See: Internat. Dict. hys. Elec.

auli g-sum rule (Pauli, Wolfgang): Physics. See: Internat. Dict. Phys. Elec.

auli rule (Pauli, Wolfgang): Physics. See: Hackh.

auli selection rules (Pauli, Wolfgang): Physics. See: Van Nostrand Sci. ncyc. under "Forbidden Transition."

auli spin matrices (or operators) (Pauli, Wolfgang): Physics. See: Ballentyne; nternat. Dict. Ap. Math.; Internat. Dict. Phys. Elec.

auli spin susceptibility (Pauli, Wolfgang): Physics. See: Ballentyne; Internat. ict. Phys. Elec.

auli term (Pauli, Wolfgang): Physics. See: Internat. Dict. Phys. Elec.

auli-Weisskopf equation (Pauli, Wolfgang and Weisskopf, Victor Frederick): hysics. See: Internat. Dict. Phys. Elec.

AULI, WOLFGANG. 1900-1958. Austrian-born Swiss physicist. See: Dict. ci. Biog. Langevin-Pauli formula, Pauli exclusion principle, Pauli g-permanence ule, Pauli g-sum rule, Pauli rule, Pauli selection rules, Pauli spin matrices (or perators), Pauli spin susceptibility, Pauli term, Pauli-Weisskopf equation.

aulianist (Paul of Samosata): Religion. See: Webster's 3d.

aulicians (Paul of Samosata? or Paul the Apostle?): Religion. See: Attwater; arnhart (Eng. Lit.); Harvey.

aulin altimeter (Paulin, Gaston Ludger?): Earth Sciences. See: Thrush.

AULIN, GASTON LUDGER. 1934- . Canadian meteorologist. See: Amer. Men and Women Sci., 12th ed. Paulin altimeter?

auline (or Paulinian) (Paul the Apostle, Saint): Religion. See: Webster's 3d.

auline privilege (Paul the Apostle, Saint): Religion. See: Attwater; Webster's 3d.

auling concentrator (Pauling, Harry): Chemistry. See: Van Nostrand Chem. ict.

auling-Corey helix (Pauling, Linus Carl and Corey, Robert Brainard): Chemistry. ee: Stedman.

PAULING, HARRY. fl. 1920. German chemical engineer. Cited in: Chem. Abstr., Decenn. Index, 1917-1926. Pauling concentrator.

PAULING, LINUS CARL. 1901- . American chemist and physicist. See: World Who's Who Sci. Heitler-London-Slater-Pauling method (or HLSP method), Pauling-Corey helix, Pauling('s) rule, Pauling structure, Pauling's theory.

Pauling('s) rule (Pauling, Linus Carl): Chemistry. See: Internat. Dict. Phys. Elec.; Thrush.

Pauling structure (Pauling, Linus Carl): Chemistry. See: Hackh.

Pauling's theory (Pauling, Linus Carl): Chemistry. See: Stedman.

Paulinism (Paulinist or Paulism) (Paul the Apostle, Saint): Religion. See: Webster's 3d.

Paulism (Paul the Apostle, Saint). See: Paulinism.

Paulists (Paul the Apostle, Saint): Religion. See: Attwater; Webster's 3d.

Paulite (Paul, Hans): Earth Sciences. See: Thrush.

Paulites (Paul of Thebes, Saint): Religion. See: Attwater.

PAULLI, SIMON. 1603-1680. Danish botanist and anatomist. See: Dict. Sci. Biog. Paullinia?

Paullinia (Paulli, Simon?): Botany. See: Charnock; Taylor, N.; Webster's 3d.

PAULMIER, MADELEINE. fl. 19th c. French pastry cook. (Biography source unavailable.) Madeleine (pastry).

Paulownia (Anna Paulowna): Botany. See: Taylor, N.; Webster's 3d.

Paul's reaction (or test) (Paul, Gustav): Medicine. See: Dorland; Stedman.

Paul's sign (Paul, Charles Theodore Constantin): Medicine. See: Dorland.

PAULSEN, AXEL. fl. ca. 1890. Figure skater. (Biography source unavailable.) Axel (skating jump).

PAULSON, EDWARD. 1915- . American mathematician. See: Amer. Men Sci., 9th ed. Camp-Paulson approximation.

Pauly-Buttlar test reaction for alcohols (Pauly, Hermann and Buttlar, Richard Freiherr von): Chemistry. See: Van Nostrand Chem. Dict.

PAULY, HERMANN. 1870-1950. German chemist. See: Pogg., vols. 4, 5, 6, 7a. Pauly-Buttlar test reaction for alcohols, Pauly reaction (or protein reaction).

Pauly reaction (or protein reaction) (Pauly, Hermann): Chemistry. See: Stedman; Van Nostrand Chem. Dict.

PAUNCEFOTE, SIR JULIAN (1ST BARON PAUNCEFOTE). 1828-1902. English diplomat. See: Dict. Nat. Biog., 2d suppl. Hay-Pauncefote Treaty, Olney-Pauncefote Treaty.

Pausania (Pausanias): History. See: Charnock.

PAUSANIAS. fl. 479 B.C. Spartan general. See: Encyc. Brit., 1973. Pausania.

PAUTRIER, LUCIEN MARIUS ADOLPHE. 1876-1959. French dermatologist. Cited in: Index-Cat. Libr. Surg.-Gen. Off., 5th Ser., vol. 1, 1959. Brocq-Pautrier glossitis (or syndrome), Pautrier-Woringer syndrome, Pautrier's abscess (or microabscess).

Pautrier-Woringer syndrome (Pautrier, Lucien Marius Adolphe and Woringer, Frederic): Medicine. See: Jablonski.

Pautrier's abscess (or microabscess) (Pautrier, Lucien Marius Adolphe): Medicine. See: Jablonski; Stedman.

PAUZAT, JEAN EUGENE. fl. 1887. French physician. Cited in: Index-Cat. Libr. Surg.-Gen. Off., 1st Ser., vol. 10, 1889. Pauzat's disease.

Pauzat's disease (Pauzat, Jean Eugene): Medicine. See: Dorland; Jablonski; Stedman.

PAVELKA, FRIEDRICH. 1901- . Czechoslovakian-born chemist in Italy. See: Pogg., vols. 6, 7a. Feigl-Pavelka test, Pavelka-Kolmer test for cadmium, Pavelka-Morth reaction for thallium, Pavelka spot test for titanium, zirconium, and thorium, Pavelka spot tests for lead, Pavelka test for fluoride.

Pavelka-Kolmer test for cadmium (Pavelka, Friedrich and Kolmer, E.): Chemistry. See: Van Nostrand Chem. Dict.

Pavelka-Morth reaction for thallium (Pavelka, Friedrich and Morth, Hermine): Chemistry. See: Van Nostrand Chem. Dict.

Pavelka spot test for titanium, zirconium and thorium (Pavelka, Friedrich): Chemistry. See: Van Nostrand Chem. Dict.

Pavelka spot tests for lead (Pavelka, Friedrich): Chemistry. See: Van Nostrand Chem. Dict.

Pavelka test for fluoride (Pavelka, Friedrich): Chemistry. See: Van Nostrand Chem. Dict.

Pavia (Pavius, Petrus): Botany. See: Webster's 3d.

PAVIUS, PETRUS (PETER PAAW OR PAUW). 1564-1617. Dutch botanist and physician. See: Nieuw Nederl. Biog. Woordenb. Pavia.

PAVLIDES, SPIRO GEORGE. 1901- . German chemist. Cited in: Chem. Abstr., vol. 22, p. 3716. Hahn-Schutze-Pavlides reagent.

PAVLOV, IVAN PETROVICH. 1849-1936. Russian physiologist. See: Internat. Encyc. Soc. Sci. Pavlov method, Pavlov pouch (or stomach), Pavlovian conditioning, Pavlovianism, Pavlov's experiment, Pavlov's reflex, Pavlov's theory of schizophrenia.

Pavlov method (Pavlov, Ivan Petrovich): Physiology. See: Dorland; Stedman.

Pavlov pouch (or stomach) (Pavlov, Ivan Petrovich): Physiology. See: Dorland; Stedman.

PAVLOV (or PAVLOFF), VLADIMIR ALEKSANDROVICH. b. 1863. Russian histologist. See: Arnim. Pavlov's tract.

Pavlovian conditioning (Pavlov, Ivan Petrovich): Psychology. See: Chaplin; Wolman.

Pavlovianism (Pavlov, Ivan Petrovich): Psychology. See: Chaplin; English.

Pavlov's experiment (Pavlov, Ivan Petrovich): Physiology. See: Drever.

Pavlov's reflex (Pavlov, Ivan Petrovich): Physiology. See: Stedman.

Pavlov's theory of schizophrenia (Pavlov, Ivan Petrovich): Psychology. See: Hinsie.

Pavlov's tract (Pavlov, Vladimir Aleksandrovich): Medicine. See: Stedman.

Pavlovsky's gland (Derivation undetermined): Zoology. See: Gray.

Pavolini reagent for metals (Pavolini, Tito Gabriele Vittorio): Chemistry. See: Van Nostrand Chem. Dict.

Pavolini test reaction for ferrous, cuprous, cobalt, and nickel ions (Pavolini, Tito Gabriele Vittorio): Chemistry. See: Van Nostrand Chem. Dict.

PAVOLINI, TITO GABRIELE VITTORIO. 1898- . Italian chemist. See: Pogg., vol. 6. Pavolini reagent for metals, Pavolini test reaction for ferrous, cuprous, cobalt, and nickel ions.

PAVON, JOSE ANTONIO. d. 1844. Spanish botanist. See: Biog. Notes Upon Botanists. Pavonia.

Pavonia (Pavon, Jose Antonio): Botany. See: Taylor, N.; Webster's 3d.

Pavonite (Peacock, Martin Alfred): Earth Sciences. See: Thrush; Webster's 3d.

PAVY, FREDERICK WILLIAM. 1829-1911. English physician. See: World Who's Who Sci. Pavy('s) solution (or reagent), Pavy's disease.

Pavy('s) solution (or reagent) (Pavy, Frederick William): Chemistry. See: Dorland; Hackh; Stedman; Van Nostrand Chem. Dict.

Pavy's disease (Pavy, Frederick William): Medicine. See: Dorland; Jablonski; Stedman.

PAWLIK, KAREL J. 1849-1914. Bohemian obstetrician. See: Biog. Lex. hervorr. Aerzte, 1880-1930. Pawlik's fold, Pawlik's grip, Pawlik's triangle.

Pawlik's fold (Pawlik, Karel J.): Medicine. See: Dorland.

Pawlik's grip (Pawlik, Karel J.): Medicine. See: Dorland; Stedman.

Pawlik's triangle (Pawlik, Karel J.): Anatomy. See: Donath; Dorland.

PAWSEY, JOSEPH LADE. 1908- . Australian electrical physicist. See: Who's Who Brit. Sci., 1953. Pawsey stub?

Pawsey stub (Pawsey, Joseph Lade?): Electronics. See: Hughes.

PAXTON, FRANCIS VALENTINE. d. 1924. English physician. (Biography source unavailable.) Paxton's disease.

Paxton's disease (Paxton, Francis Valentine). See: Beigel's disease.

PAYEN, ANSELME. 1795-1871. French chemist and botanical writer. See: Dict. Sci. Biog. Payena.

Payena (Payen, Anselme): Botany. See: Webster's 3d.

Payne-Aldrich tariff (Payne, Sereno Elisha and Aldrich, Nelson Wilmarth): Politics. See: Smith.

PAYNE, ERNEST E. M. fl. 1934. English? chemist. Cited in: Chem. Abstr., Decenn. Index, 1927-1936. Payne('s) process?

PAYNE, M. d. 1937. Engineer. (Biography source unavailable.) Payne thermostat.

Payne('s) process (Payne, Ernest E. M.?): Chemistry. See: Hackh; Thrush; Van Nostrand Chem. Dict.

PAYNE, ROGER. 1739-1797. English bookbinder. See: Dict. Nat. Biog. Payne style.

Payne sentence completion blank (Derivation undetermined): Psychology. See: Wolman.

PAYNE, SERENO ELISHA. 1843-1914. American legislator. See: Dict. Amer. Biog. Payne-Aldrich tariff.

Payne style (Payne, Roger): Library Science. See: Harrod.

Payne thermostat (Payne, M.): Engineering and Industry. See: Auger.

PAYNE, WILLIAM. fl. 1776-1830. English artist. See: Dict. Nat. Biog. Payne's gray.

Payne's gray (Payne, William): Fine Arts. See: Webster's 3d.

PAYR, ERWIN. 1871-1946. German surgeon. See: World Who's Who Sci. Payr's clamp, Payr's membrane, Payr's method, Payr's sign, Payr's syndrome (or disease).

Payr's clamp (Payr, Erwin): Medicine. See: Dorland; Stedman.

Payr's membrane (Payr, Erwin): Medicine. See: Stedman.

Payr's method (Payr, Erwin): Medicine. See: Dorland.

Payr's sign (Payr, Erwin): Medicine. See: Dorland; Stedman.

Payr's syndrome (or disease) (Payr, Erwin): Medicine. See: Dorland; Jablonski.

PAYTON. fl. 1867. Engineer. (Biography source unavailable.) Payton's water meter.

Payton's water meter (Payton): Engineering and Industry. See: Auger.

PAZ, DANIEL DE LA. fl. 1911. Philippine? physiologist. Cited in: Chem. Abstr., Decenn. Index, 1907-1916. Cannon and La Paz test.

Peabody Fund (Peabody, George): Philanthropy. See: Phyfe.

PEABODY, GEORGE. 1795-1869. American philanthropist. See: Dict. Amer. Biog. Peabody Fund.

Peabody picture vocabulary test (Derivation undetermined): Psychology. See: Wolman.

Peace of Callias (Callias): History. Cited in: Webster's Biog. Dict.

Peachey process (Peachey, Stanley J.): Chemistry. See: Van Nostrand Chem. Dict.

PEACHEY, STANLEY J. fl. 1915. English chemist. Cited in: Chem. Abstr., Decenn. Index, 1907-1916. Peachey process.

PEACOCK, MARTIN ALFRED. 1898-1950. Scottish-born Canadian mineralogist. See: World Who's Who Sci. Pavonite.

Peake ripper (Derivation undetermined): Engineering and Industry. See: Thrush.

PEALE, ALBERT CHARLES. 1849-1913. American geologist. See: Who Was Who Amer., 1897-1942. Pealite.

PEALE, TITIAN RAMSAY. 1799-1885. American naturalist and artist. See: Dict. Amer. Biog. Peale's egret, Peale's falcon.

Peale's egret (Peale, Titian Ramsay): Zoology. See: Mathews, M. M.

Peale's falcon (Peale, Titian Ramsay): Zoology. See: Mathews, M. M.; Webster's 3d.

Pealite (Peale, Albert Charles): Earth Sciences. See: Thrush.

PEAN, JULES-EMILE. 1830-1898. French surgeon. See: World Who's Who Sci. Pean's forceps, Pean's operation, Pean's position.

PEANO, GIUSEPPE. 1858-1932. Italian mathematician. See: Pogg., vols. 4, 5, 6. Peano space (or curve), Peano's postulates (or axioms).

Peano space (or curve) (Peano, Giuseppe): Mathematics. See: James.

Peano's postulates (or axioms) (Peano, Giuseppe): Mathematics. See: Ballentyne; James.

Pean's forceps (Pean, Jules-Emile): Medicine. See: Dorland; Stedman.

Pean's operation (Pean, Jules-Emile): Medicine. See: Dorland.

Pean's position (Pean, Jules-Emile): Medicine. See: Dorland.

PEARCE, LOUISE. 1885-1959. American physician. See: World Who's Who Sci. Brown-Pearce tumor (carcinoma or epithelioma).

PEARCE, RICHARD. 1837-1927. English-American metallurgist. See: Dict. Amer. Biog. Pearceite.

Pearce turret furnace (Derivation undetermined): Engineering and Industry. See: Thrush.

Pearceite (Pearce, Richard): Earth Sciences. See: Thrush.

PEARL, RAYMOND. 1879-1940. American biologist. See: World Who's Who Sci. Pearl-Reed (Read) curve.

Pearl-Reed (Read) curve (Pearl, Raymond and Reed, Lowell Jacob): Statistics. See: Ballentyne; Kendall.

pearls of Sluse (De Sluse, Rene Francois Walter): Mathematics. Cited in: World Who's Who Sci.

Pearson air elutriator (Pearson, Joseph Cleaveland): Engineering and Industry. See: Thrush.

PEARSON, CARL M. 1919- . American physician. See: World Who's Who Sci. McArdle-Schmid-Pearson syndrome.

Pearson(s) (Pearsonian) coefficient (of correlation) (Pearson, Karl): Mathematics. See: James; Kendall; Webster's 3d.

Pearson criterion (Pearson, Karl): Statistics. See: Kendall.

rson curve (Pearson, Karl): Statistics. See: Kendall.

rson('s) distribution(s) (Pearson, Karl): Statistics. See: Ballentyne; James; a Nostrand Sci. Encyc.

ARSON, EGON SHARPE. 1895- . English statistician. See: World o's Who Sci. Merrington-Pearson approximation, Neyman-Pearson theory (or othesis).

ARSON, JOSEPH CLEAVELAND. b. 1879. American concrete and cement hnologist. See: Amer. Men Sci., 4th ed. Pearson air elutriator.

ARSON, KARL. 1857-1936. English scientist. See: Internat. Encyc. Soc. . Pearson(s) (Pearsonian) coefficient (of correlation), Pearson criterion, rson curve, Pearson('s) distribution(s), Pearson measure of skewness, Poisson-rson formula.

rson measure of skewness (Pearson, Karl): Statistics. See: Kendall.

rson system of probability functions (Pearson, Karl). See: Pearson('s) ribution(s).

ry expedition (Peary, Robert Edwin): Exploration. See: Jameson.

ARY, ROBERT EDWIN. 1856-1920. American Arctic explorer. See: Dict. er. Biog. Peary expedition.

AUCELLIER, A. fl. 1873. French engineer. See: World Who's Who Sci. ucellier's cell.

AUCELLIER, CHARLES-NICOLAS. 1832-1913. French engineer. See: w Encyc. Brit., 1974, Microp. Peaucellier linkage.

ucellier linkage (Peaucellier, Charles-Nicolas): Engineering and Industry. e: Auger.

ucellier's cell (Peaucellier, A.): Mathematics. See: James.

avey (grip) (Peavey, Joseph): Engineering and Industry. See: Mathews, M. M.; tridge; Webster's 3d.

AVEY, JOSEPH. fl. ca. 1875. American inventor. (Biography source un-ailable.) Peavey (grip).

CHE, K. fl. 1912. Austrian chemist. Cited in: Chem. Abstr., Decenn. ex, 1907-1916. Peche test for cyanide?

che (or peach) Melba (Melba, Dame Nellie): Food and Drink. See: Funk; tridge; Webster's 3d.

he test for cyanide (Peche, K.?): Chemistry. See: Van Nostrand Chem. t.

chmann condensation (Von Pechmann, Hans): Chemistry. See: Van Nostrand em. Dict.

chmann, Hans von. See: Von Pechmann, Hans.

chmann pyrazole synthesis (Von Pechmann, Hans): Chemistry. See: Van strand Chem. Dict.

CK, GEORGE WILBUR. 1840-1916. American journalist, humorist and itician. See: Dict. Amer. Biog. Peck's bad boy.

CK, ROBERT E. fl. 1959. American psychologist. Cited in: Cum. Auth. ex to Psych. Abstr., 1st suppl., 1959-1963. Strongin-Hinsie-Peck test.

CKHAM, STEPHEN FARNUM. fl. 1884-1900. American chemist. Cited in: yal Soc. Cat. Sci. Pap., 1884-1900. Peckhamite.

ckhamite (Peckham, Stephen Farnum): Earth Sciences. See: Mathews, M.M.

ck's bad boy (Peck, George Wilbur): Generic Word (enfant terrible). See: rnhart, (New Eng.).

cksniff (or Pecksniffian) (Pecksniff, Seth): Generic Word (hypocrite). See: ewer; Charnock; Partridge; Webster's 3d.

CKSNIFF, SETH. Character in Charles Dickens' novel, "Martin Chuzzlewit," 343-1844). See: Harvey. Pecksniff (or Pecksniffian).

CLET, JEAN-CLAUDE-EUGENE. 1793-1857. French physicist. See: World ho's Who Sci. Peclet('s) number.

clet('s) number (Peclet, Jean-Claude-Eugene): Physics. See: Ballentyne; schke; Thewlis.

CQUET, JEAN. 1622-1674. French physician and anatomist. See: World ho's Who Sci. Pecquet's cistern (receptaculum or reservoir), Pecquet's duct.

cquet's cistern (receptaculum or reservoir) (Pecquet, Jean): Anatomy. See: onath; Dorland; Stedman.

Pecquet's duct (Pecquet, Jean): Anatomy. See: Donath; Stedman. Also known as: Van Hoorne's canal.

Pedersen device (Pedersen, John D.): Weapons. See: Quick; Webster's 3d.

PEDERSEN, HARALD CHRISTIAN. 1888-1945. Norwegian metallurgist. See: Norsk Biog. Lek. Pedersen process.

PEDERSEN, JOHN D. fl. 1929. American arms designer. Cited in: Chem. Abstr., Decenn. Index, 1927-1936. Pedersen device.

PEDERSEN, PEDER OLUF. 1874-1941. Danish electrotechnologist. See: Pogg., vols. 5, 6. Pedersen potentiometer.

Pedersen potentiometer (Pedersen, Peder Oluf): Electronics. See: Internat. Dict. Phys. Elec.

Pedersen process (Pedersen, Harald Christian): Engineering and Industry. See: Thrush; Van Nostrand Chem. Dict.

Pedersen's speculum (Derivation undetermined): Medicine. See: Stedman.

PEDRETTI, G. fl. 1931. Italian chemist. Cited in: Chem. Abstr., vol. 25, p. 4568. Pedretti tests for hair dye intermediates.

Pedretti tests for hair dye intermediates (Pedretti, G.): Chemistry. See: Van Nostrand Chem. Dict.

PEDRO II. 1825-1891. Emperor of Brazil. See: Webster's Biog. Dict. Dom Pedro (shoe).

Pedro Ximenes (wine) (Ximenes, Pedro). See: Peter-see-me (Peter or Pedro Ximenes) (wine).

PEEK, ROBERT LEE, JR. 1898- . American physicist and statistician. See: Amer. Men Sci., 7th ed. Peek's inequality.

Peek's inequality (Peek, Robert Lee, Jr.): Statistics. See: Kendall.

PEEL, SIR ROBERT. 1788-1850. English statesman. See: Dict. Nat. Biog. Bobby, Peeler(s), Peelites.

Peeler(s) (Peel, Sir Robert): Generic Word (policeman). See: Brewer; Hendrickson; Latham.

Peelites (Peel, Sir Robert): Politics. See: Brewer; Harbottle; Latham.

Peeping Tom (Tom of Coventry): Generic Word (voyeur). See: Hinsie; Webster's 3d.

PEHRSON, A. P. fl. 1928. English metallurgist. Cited in: Chem. Abstr., Decenn. Index, 1927-1936. Pehrson-Prentice process?

Pehrson-Prentice process (Pehrson, A. P.? and Prentice, John?): Engineering and Industry. See: Thrush.

Peierls-Nabarro force (Peierls, Rudolf Ernst and Nabarro, Frank Reginald Nunes): Physics. See: Van Nostrand Sci. Encyc.

PEIERLS, RUDOLF ERNST. 1907- . German-born English physicist. See: Pogg., vols. 6, 7a. Peierls-Nabarro force, Peierls stress (or force).

Peierls stress (or force) (Peierls, Rudolf Ernst): Physics. See: Thewlis.

PEIFFER, JURGEN. 1922- . Dutch neuropathologist. See: Who's Who Sci. Europe, 1972. Van Bogaert-Nyssen-Peiffer disease.

PEIRCE, BENJAMIN. 1809-1880. American mathematician and astronomer. See: World Who's Who Sci. Peirce criterion.

PEIRCE, CHARLES SANDERS. 1839-1914. American mathematician, physicist and logician. See: Dict. Sci. Biog. Dedekind-Peirce theorem?, Peircean.

Peirce criterion (Peirce, Benjamin): Mathematics. Cited in: World Who's Who Sci.

PEIRCE, S. E. fl. 1914. English physicist. Cited in: Pogg., vol. 5 under "Bragg, Sir William Henry." Bragg-Pierce law.

Peirce-Smith process (and converter) (Derivation undetermined): Engineering and Indsutry. See: Thrush.

Peircean (Peirce, Charles Sanders): Philosophy. See: Webster's 3d.

PEIRESC, NICOLAS-CLAUDE FABRI DE. 1580-1637. French naturalist and antiquarian. See: Dict. Sci. Biog. Pereskia (Peireskia).

PEIROUSE, PHILIPPE PICOT, BARON DE LA. 1744-1818. French naturalist. See: Michaud. Lapeyrousia (or Lapeirousia)?

Peisistratus. See: Pisistratus.

Peissenberg ram (Derivation undetermined): Engineering and Industry. See: Thrush.

PEKELHARING, CORNELIS ADRIANUS. 1848-1922. Dutch physiologist. See: Biog. Lex. hervorr. Aerzte. Pekelharing's theory.

Pekelharing's theory (Pekelharing, Cornelis Adrianus): Medicine. See: Dorland.

Pel-Ebstein disease (or symptom) (Pel, Pieter Klaases and Ebstein, Wilhelm). See: Hodgkin's disease (granuloma or syndrome).

PEL, PIETER KLAASES. 1852-1919. Dutch physician. See: Biog. Lex. hervorr. Aerzte. Pel-Ebstein disease (or symptom), Pel's crises.

PELAGIA. Legendary saint who is a combination of Pelagia, the virgin-martyr of Antioch and Pelagia, the Penitent of Jerusalem. See: Holweck. Pelagia legend.

Pelagia legend (Pelagia): Religion. See: Attwater.

Pelagianism (or Pelagians) (Pelagius): Religion. See: Attwater; Barnhart (Eng. Lit.); Canney; Harvey; Webster's 3d.

PELAGIUS. 360?-420? English monk. See: New Encyc. Brit., 1974, Microp. Pelagianism (or Pelagians).

Pelatan-Clèrici process (Derivation undetermined): Engineering and Industry. See: Thrush.

Pelatan furnace (Derivation undetermined): Engineering and Industry. See: Thrush.

PELE. Polynesian fire goddess of volcanoes. See: Jobes. Pele's hair, Pele's tears.

Pele's hair (Pele): Earth Sciences. See: Monkhouse; Thrush; Webster's 3d.

Pele's tears (Pele): Earth Sciences. See: Monkhouse.

Pelger-Hueat anomaly (or phenomenon) (Pelger, Karel and Hueat, G. J.): Medicine. See: Jablonski; Stedman. Also known as: Pelger's nuclear anomaly.

PELGER, KAREL. 1885-1931. Dutch physician. See: Nederl. Tijdschr. v. geneesk vol. 75 (Aug. 1, 1931) pp. 4106-4108. Pelger-Hueat anomaly (or phenomenon).

Pelger's nuclear anomaly (Pelger, Karel). See: Pelger-Hueat anomaly (or phenomenon).

Peligot blue (Peligot, Eugene Melchior): Chemistry. See: Hackh; Webster's 3d.

PELIGOT, EUGENE MELCHIOR. 1811-1890. French chemist. See: World Who's Who Sci. Peligot blue, Peligot medal? Peligot salt, Peligot tube.

Peligot medal (Peligot, Eugene Melchior?): Photography. See: Focal Encyc. Photog. under "Awards (France)."

Peligot salt (Peligot, Eugene Melchior): Chemistry. See: Hackh.

Peligot tube (Peligot, Eugene Melchior): Chemistry. See: Hackh.

PELIZAEUS, FRIEDRICH. 1850-1917. German neurologist. See: World Who's Who Sci. Pelizaeus-Merzbacher syndrome.

Pelizaeus-Merzbacher syndrome (Pelizaeus, Friedrich and Merzbacher, Ludwig): Medicine. See: Jablonski.

PELL, JOHN. 1610-1685. English mathematician. See: Dict. Nat. Biog. Pellian equation.

PELLEGRINI, AUGUSTO. b. 1877. Italian surgeon. Cited in: Index-Cat. Libr. Surg.-Gen. Off., 5th Ser., vol. 1, 1959. Stieda-Pellegrini syndrome.

Pellegrini-Stieda disease (Pellegrini, Augusto and Stieda, Alfred). See: Stieda-Pellegrini syndrome.

Pellegrini's disease (Pellegrini, Augusto). See: Stieda-Pellegrini syndrome.

PELLET, HENRI JEAN BAPTISTE. b. 1848. French chemist. See: Pogg., vol. 3. Pellet('s) process, Pellet solution.

Pellet('s) process (Pellet, Henri Jean Baptiste): Printing. See: Focal Encyc. Photog. under "Printing Processes (obsolete);" Harrod.

Pellet solution (Pellet, Henri Jean Baptiste): Chemistry. See: Van Nostrand Chem. Dict.

PELLETIER, PIERRE JOSEPH. 1788-1842. French chemist. See: World Who's Who Sci. Pelletierine.

Pelletierine (Pelletier, Pierre Joseph): Chemistry. See: Stedman; Webster's 3d.

Pellett clover (Pellett, Frank Chapman): Botany. See: Webster's 3d.

PELLETT, FRANK CHAPMAN. 1879-1951. American apiculturist. See: Who Was Who Amer., vol. 3. Pellett clover.

Pellian equation (Pell, John): Mathematics. See: Ballentyne; James.

Pellin-Broca prism (Pellin, Philibert L. and Broca, Andre Elie): Physics. See: Van Nostrand Sci. Encyc.

PELLIN, PHILIBERT L. fl. 1899. French physicist. Cited in: Royal Soc. Cat Sci. Pap., 1884-1900. Pellin-Broca prism.

PELLION, A. M. J. ALPHONSE. fl. early 19th c. French naval officer. (Biography source unavailable.) Pellionia.

Pellionia (Pellion, A. M. J. Alphonse): Botany. See: Taylor, N.

PELLIZZI, G. B. fl. 1910. Italian physician. (Biography source unavailable.) Pellizzi's syndrome.

Pellizzi's syndrome (Pellizzi, G. B.): Medicine. See: Jablonski; Stedman.

PELLOGGIO, PIETRO. fl. 1870. Italian chemist. Cited in: Royal Soc. Cat. Sci. Pap., 1874-1883. Peloggio test.

PELMAN, CHRISTOPHER LOUIS. fl. 1902. American memory teacher. Cited in: Libr. Congress Cat. Printed Cards. Pelman method (or Pelmanism).

Pelman method (or Pelmanism) (Pelman, Christopher Louis): Sociology. See: Stenhouse.

Peloggio test (Pelloggio, Pietro): Chemistry. See: Van Nostrand Chem. Dict.

Pelouze synthesis (Pelouze, Theophile Jules): Chemistry. See: Van Nostrand Chem. Dict.

PELOUZE, THEOPHILE JULES. 1807-1867. French chemist. See: World Who's Who Sci. Pelouze synthesis.

Pel's crises (Pel, Pieter Klaases): Medicine. See: Dorland; Jablonski; Stedman

Peltier cooling (Peltier, Jean Charles Athanase): Physics. See: Thewlis.

Peltier effect (Peltier, Jean Charles Athanase): Physics. See: Ballentyne; Internat. Dict. Phys. Elec.; Thewlis; Van Nostrand Chem. Dict.

PELTIER, JEAN CHARLES ATHANASE. 1785-1845. French physicist and meteorologist. See: World Who's Who Sci. Peltier cooling, Peltier effect.

PELTON, LESTER ALLEN. 1829-1908. American engineer. See: New Encyc. Brit., 1974, Microp. Pelton wheel.

Pelton wheel (Pelton, Lester Allen): Engineering and Industry. See: Auger; Van Nostrand Sci. Encyc. under "Hydraulic Turbine;" Webster's 3d.

PELVET, N. fl. 1866-1869. French naturalist and physician. Cited in: Royal Soc. Cat. Sci. Pap., 1864-1873. Pelvetia.

Pelvetia (Pelvet, N.): Botany. See: Webster's 3d.

Pembroke, 3rd Earl of. See: Marshal, Richard (3rd Earl of Pembroke).

Pembroke, 9th Earl of. See: Herbert, Henry (9th Earl of Pembroke).

Pembroke table (Herbert, Henry, 9th Earl of Pembroke?): Applied Arts. See: Brewer; New Encyc. Brit., 1974, Microp.

PENA, PIERRE. fl. 1570-1605. French botanist. Cited in: Index-Cat. Libr. Surg.-Gen. Off., 1st Ser., vol. 10, 1889. Penaea.

Penaea (Pena, Pierre): Botany. See: Webster's 3d.

Penberthy anoloader (Derivation undetermined): Engineering and Industry. See: Thrush.

PENDA. 577?-655. Anglo-Saxon King of Mercia. See: Dict. Nat. Biog. Penny.

PENDE, NICOLA. b. 1880. Italian physician. See: World Who's Who Sci. Pende's sign, Pende's syndrome.

Pende's sign (Pende, Nicola): Medicine. See: Dorland.

Pende's syndrome (Pende, Nicola): Medicine. See: Jablonski.

Pendleton Act (Pendleton, George Hunt): Politics. See: Jameson; Morris.

PENDLETON, GEORGE HUNT ("GENTLEMAN GEORGE"). 1825-1889. American legislator. See: Dict. Amer. Biog. gentleman George, Pendleton Act, Pendletonian.

ndletonian (Pendleton, George Hunt): Politics. See: Mathews, M. M.

ndragon (Uther Pendragon): Mythology. See: Brewer.

NDRED, VAUGHAN. 1869-1946. English physician. Cited in: Garrison d Morton. Pendred's syndrome.

ndred's syndrome (Pendred, Vaughan): Medicine. See: Jablonski; Stedman.

NELOPE. Wife of Odysseus in Greek mythology. See: New Encyc. Brit., 74, Microp. Penelope, Penelops, Penelope's web (or Penelopize).

nelope (Penelope): Generic Word (chaste wife). See: Partridge.

nelope's web (or Penelopize) (Penelope): Generic Word (endless labor). See: rvey; Mathews, M. M.

nelops (Penelope): Mythology. See: Jobes.

nfield reagent (Penfield, Samuel Lewis): Chemistry. See: Van Nostrand em. Dict.

NFIELD, SAMUEL LEWIS. 1856-1906. American mineralogist. See: Pogg., ls. 4, 5. Penfield reagent, Penfield scale, Penfieldite.

nfield scale (Penfield, Samuel Lewis): Chemistry. See: Van Nostrand Chem. ct.

NFIELD, WILDER GRAVES. b. 1891. American-born Canadian surgeon. e: World Who's Who Sci. Foerster-Penfield operation, Penfield's syndrome.

nfieldite (Penfield, Samuel Lewis): Earth Sciences. See: Thrush.

nfield's syndrome (Penfield, Wilder Graves): Medicine. See: Jablonski.

NIAKOFF, VLADIMIR "POPSKI." 1897-1951. English army officer. See: ho Was Who, 1951-1960. Popski's Private Army.

nn engine (Penn, John): Engineering and Industry. See: Auger.

NN, HARRY SAMUEL. b. 1891. Russian-born American surgeon. See: mer. Men Sci., 8th ed. Penn sero-flocculation reaction.

NN, JOHN. 1805-1878. English engineer. See: Dict. Nat. Biog. nn engine.

nn sero-flocculation reaction (Penn, Harry Samuel): Medicine. See: Dorland.

nnanite (Pennantite) (Pennant, Thomas Welsh): Earth Sciences. See: Thrush; ebster's 3d.

NNANT, THOMAS WELSH. 1726-1798. Naturalist. See: World Who's ho Sci. Pennanite (Pennantite), Pennant's marten.

nnant's marten (Pennant, Thomas Welsh): Zoology. See: Webster's 3d.

NNEY, WILLIAM GEORGE. 1909- . English physicist. See: World ho's Who Sci. Kronig-Penney model.

nning effect (Penning, Frans Michel): Physics. See: Ballentyne.

NNING, FRANS MICHEL. b. 1894. Dutch physicist. See: Pogg., vol. . Penning effect, Penning gauge (pressure gauge or discharge), Penning ion urce.

nning gauge (pressure gauge or discharge) (Penning, Frans Michel): Physics. ee: Hughes; Thewlis; Van Nostrand Sci. Encyc.

nning ion source (Penning, Frans Michel): Physics. See: Hughes.

nnock and Martin (sulfur) crucible (Pennock, John Downer? and Martin, Al. .?): Chemistry. See: Van Nostrand Chem. Dict.

NNOCK, JOHN DOWNER. b. 1860. American chemical engineer. See: mer. Men Sci., 1st ed. Pennock and Martin (sulfur) crucible?

nny (Penda): Numismatics. See: Steinberg.

nrhyn, Baron. See: Douglas-Pennant, George Sholto Gordon, Baron Penrhyn.

nrhyn quarry dispute (Douglas-Pennant, George Sholto Gordon, Baron nrhyn): Politics. See: Montgomery.

PENROSE, CHARLES BINGHAM. 1862-1925. American gynecologist. See: Vho Was Who Amer., vol. 1. Penrose drain.

nrose drain (Penrose, Charles Bingham): Medicine. See: Dorland; Stedman.

PENROSE, RICHARD ALEXANDER FULLERTON. 1863-1931. American geolo-gist. See: Dict. Amer. Biog. Penroseite.

nroseite (Penrose, Richard Alexander Fullerton): Earth Sciences. See: hrush; Webster's 3d.

PENRUDDOCK, JOHN. 1619-1655. English royalist. See: Dict. Nat. Biog. Penruddock's rising.

Penruddock's rising (Penruddock, John): History. See: Steinberg.

PENSKY, B. fl. 1892-1895. German physicist. Cited in: Royal Soc. Cat. Sci. Pap., 1884-1900. Abel-Pensky apparatus? Pensky-Marten tester?

Pensky-Marten tester (Pensky, B.? and Martens, A.): Engineering and Industry. See: Thrush.

pentagram of Pythagoras (Pythagoras of Samos): Mathematics. See: James.

pentalogy of Fallot (Fallot, Etienne Louis Arthur): Medicine. See: Stedman.

PENTLAND, JOSEPH BARCLAY. 1797-1873. Irish traveler. See: Dict. Nat. Biog. Pentlandite.

Pentlandite (Pentland, Joseph Barclay): Earth Sciences. See: Thrush; Van Nostrand Sci. Encyc.; Webster's 3d.

PENTZ, CHARLES J. fl. 18th c. Swedish botanist. (Biography source un-available.) Pentzia.

Pentzia (Pentz, Charles J.): Botany. See: Charnock; Webster's 3d.

Penzoldt-Fischer test for aldehydes and phenol (Penzoldt, Franz and Fischer, Emil): Chemistry. See: Van Nostrand Chem. Dict.

PENZOLDT, FRANZ. 1849-1927. German chemist and physician. See: Biog. Lex. hervorr. Aerzte. Penzoldt-Fischer test for aldehydes and phenol, Penzoldt test for stomach absorption, Penzoldt's test for acetone, Penzoldt's test (or reagent) for glucose.

Penzoldt test for stomach absorption (Penzoldt, Franz): Medicine. See: Kelly.

Penzoldt's test for acetone (Penzoldt, Franz): Medicine. See: Dorland; Kelly; Stedman.

Penzoldt's test (or reagent) for glucose (Penzoldt, Franz): Medicine. See: Dorland; Kelly; Stedman.

Peony (or Paeonia) (Paeon): Botany. See: Brewer; Partridge; Taylor, N.; Webster's 3d.

PEPIN III, THE SHORT. 714?-768. King of the Franks. See: New Encyc. Brit., 1974, Microp. donation of Pepin.

Pepper treatment (Pepper, William): Medicine. See: Dorland.

PEPPER, WILLIAM. 1843-1898. American internist. See: Dict. Amer. Biog. Pepper treatment.

PEPPER, WILLIAM, JR. 1874-1947. American physician. See: World Who's Who Sci. Pepper's disease (or syndrome).

Pepper's disease (or syndrome) (Pepper, William, Jr.). See: Hutchinson's disease.

PEPYS, SAMUEL. 1633-1703. English navy official and diarist. See: Dict. Nat. Biog. Pepysian.

Pepysian (Pepys, Samuel): Literature. See: Charnock; Webster's 3d.

PERALT, JOSEPH. No dates. Spanish botanist. (Biography source unavail-able.) Peraltia.

Peraltia (Peralt, Joseph): Botany. See: Charnock.

Percy cautery (method or treatment) (Percy, James Fulton): Medicine. See: Dorland; Kelly.

PERCY, SIR HENRY "HOTSPUR." 1364-1403. English warrior. See: Dict. Nat. Biog. Hotspur.

PERCY, JAMES FULTON. 1864-1946. American surgeon. See: Who Was Who Amer., vol. 2. Percy cautery (method or treatment).

PERCY, JOHN. 1817-1889. English metallurgist. See: Dict. Nat. Biog. Percylite.

Percy Society (Percy, Thomas): Literature. See: Barnhart (Eng. Lit.); Harvey.

PERCY, THOMAS. 1729-1811. English antiquary, bishop and poet. See: Dict. Nat. Biog. Percy Society, Percy's reliques.

Percylite (Percy, John): Earth Sciences. See: Charnock; Webster's 3d.

Percy's reliques (Percy, Thomas): Literature. See: Barnhart (Eng. Lit.); Brewer.

Perdicaris affair (Perdicaris, Jon): History. See: Jameson.

PERDICARIS, JON. d. 1925. American citizen in Morocco. See: Dict. Amer. Hist., vol. 4, p. 253. Perdicaris affair.

Pere David's deer (David, Armand): Zoology. See: Gray; Pennak; Webster's 3d.

Pereira bark (Pereira, Jonathan): Botany. See: Webster's 3d.

PEREIRA, JONATHAN. 1804-1853. English pharmacologist. See: Dict. Nat. Biog. Pereira bark.

PEREIRA, JOSE G. fl. 1913. Spanish chemist. Cited in: Chem. Abstr., vol. 7, p. 3284. Pereira test for hydrogen.

Pereira test for hydrogen (Pereira, Jose G.): Chemistry. See: Van Nostrand Chem. Dict.

Pereskia (Peireskia) (Peiresc, Nicolas-Claude Fabri de): Botany. See: Taylor, N.; Webster's 3d.

PERETZ, ISAAC LEIB. ca. 1852-1915. Polish Jewish writer. See: Encyc. Brit., 1973. Peretz shule.

Peretz shule (Peretz, Isaac Leib): Education. See: Good.

PEREZ, BERNARD. 1836-1903. French physician. Cited in: Index-Cat. Libr. Surg.-Gen. Off., 1st Ser., vol. 10, 1889. Perez reflex.

PEREZ, GEORGE V. d. 1920. Canary Islands physician. Cited in: Index Medicus, 2d Ser., vol. 18, 1920. Perez' sign.

Perez reflex (Perez, Bernard): Medicine. See: Stedman.

Perez' sign (Perez, George V.): Medicine. See: Dorland; Stedman.

PERI. Malevolent sprite in Persian mythology. See: Jobes. Peri.

Peri (Peri, the sprite): Generic Word (beautiful girl). See: Brewer.

PERICLES. d. 429 B.C. Greek statesman of Athens. See: Encyc. Brit., 1973. Pericles (or Periclean).

Pericles (or Periclean) (Pericles): Generic Word (intellectual splendor). See: Partridge; Webster's 3d.

PERIGNON, PIERRE. 1638-1715. French Benedictine monk and winegrower. See: Brockhaus Enzyk. Perignon (wine).

Perignon (wine) (Perignon, Pierre): Food and Drink. See: Encyc. Brit., 1973.

periodic acid–Schiff stain (Schiff, Hugo): Chemistry. See: Stedman.

periportal space of Mall (Mall, Franklin Paine): Anatomy. See: Stedman.

Perique (tobacco) (Chenet, Pierre): Agriculture. See: Hendrickson; Partridge; Webster's 3d.

PERKIEWICZ, MAX. fl. 1935. German engineer. Cited in: Chem. Abstr., Decenn. Index, 1927-1936. Perkiewicz method for preventing kiln scum.

Perkiewicz method for preventing kiln scum (Perkiewicz, Max): Engineering and Industry. See: Thrush.

Perkin-Elmer spectrophotometers (Perkin, Richard Scott and Elmer, Charles W.): Physics. Cited in: Van Nostrand Sci. Encyc. under "Polarimetry and Spectro-polarimetry."

Perkin, Jr., reaction (Perkin, William Henry, Jr.): Chemistry. See: Van Nostrand Chem. Dict.

Perkin method for alicyclic compounds (Perkin, Sir William Henry): Chemistry. See: Van Nostrand Chem. Dict.

Perkin('s) reaction (Perkin, Sir William Henry): Chemistry. See: Ballentyne; Hackh; Van Nostrand Chem. Dict.

Perkin rearrangement (Perkin, Sir William Henry): Chemistry. See: Van Nostrand Chem. Dict.

PERKIN, RICHARD SCOTT. 1906- . American manufacturer. See: Nat. Cycl. Amer. Biog., vol. K, p. 270. Perkin-Elmer spectrophotometers.

PERKIN, SIR WILLIAM HENRY. 1838-1907. English chemist. See: Dict. Nat. Biog., 2d suppl. Duppa-Perkin test reactions, Perkin method for alicyclic compounds, Perkin('s) reaction, Perkin rearrangement, Perkin's mauve (purple or violet).

PERKIN, WILLIAM HENRY, JR. 1860-1929. English organic chemist. See: Dict. Nat. Biog., 4th suppl. Perkin, Jr., reaction.

Perkinism (Perkins, Elisha): Medicine. See: Charnock; Dorland; Mathews, M. M.; Stedman.

Perkins Act (Perkins, Carl Dewey): Education. See: Good.

Perkins (beer) (Derivation undetermined): Food and Drink. See: Charnock.

Perkins boiler (1) (and engine) (Perkins, Jacob): Engineering and Industry. See: Auger.

Perkins boiler (2) (Perkins, Loftus): Engineering and Industry. See: Auger.

PERKINS, CARL DEWEY. 1912- . American legislator. See: Biog. Direct. Amer. Congress. Perkins Act.

PERKINS, DOROTHY. fl. 20th c. American horticulturist's wife. (Biography source unavailable.) Dorothy Perkins' rose.

PERKINS, ELISHA. 1741-1799. American physician. See: Dict. Amer. Biog. Perkinism.

PERKINS, HENRY AUGUSTUS. 1873-1959. American physicist. See: Amer. Men. Sci., 9th ed. Perkin's phenomenon.

PERKINS, JACOB. 1766-1849. American engineer. See: Dict. Amer. Biog. Perkins boiler (1) (and engine).

PERKINS, LOFTUS. 1834-1891. English engineer. See: Dict. Nat. Biog. Perkins boiler (2).

Perkin's mauve (purple or violet) (Perkin, Sir William Henry): Chemistry. See: Hackh; Webster's 3d.

Perkin's phenomenon (Perkins, Henry Augustus): Physics. See: Ballentyne.

PERKINS, RANDOLPH. 1871-1936. American legislator. See: Biog. Direct. Amer. Congress. Black-Connery-Perkins wages and hours bill.

PERKINS, ROBERT CYRIL LAYTON. 1866-1955. English entomologist. See: Royal Soc. Biog. Mem. of Fellows, vol. 2 (1956), pp. 229-236. Perkinsiella.

Perkinsiella (Perkins, Robert Cyril Layton): Zoology. See: Webster's 3d.

Perks' distribution (Perks, W.): Statistics. See: Kendall.

PERKS, W. fl. 1932-1952. American? insurance actuary. (Biography source unavailable.) Perks' distribution.

PERLIA, RICHARD. fl. 1893. German ophthalmologist. Cited in: Index-Cat. Libr. Surg.-Gen. Off., 2d Ser., vol. 13, 1908. Perlia's nucleus.

Perlia's nucleus (Perlia, Richard): Anatomy. See: Donath; Dorland; Stedman. Also known as: Spitzka's nucleus.

PERLS, MAX. 1843-1881. German pathologist. See: Biog. Lex. hervorr. Aerzte. Perls' test.

Perls' test (Perls, Max): Medicine. See: Dorland; Stedman.

Pernettia (Pernetty, Antoine Joseph). See: Pernettya.

PERNETTY, ANTOINE JOSEPH. 1716-1801. French traveler and naturalist. See: Michaud. Pernettya.

Pernettya (Pernetty, Antoine Joseph): Botany. See: Taylor, N.; Webster's 3d.

Pernety, Antoine Joseph. See: Pernetty, Antoine Joseph.

Pernod (Pernod, Henri-Louis): Food and Drink. See: Hendrickson.

PERNOD, HENRI-LOUIS. fl. 20th c. French manufacturer. Cited in: Brockhaus Enzyk. Pernod.

PERNOT, CHARLES. fl. ca. 1877. French? engineer. (Biography source unavailable.) Pernot furnace.

Pernot furnace (Pernot, Charles): Engineering and Industry. See: Thrush; Webster's 3d.

PERNY, PAUL H. d. 1907. French missionary and Chinese scholar. Cited in: Royal Soc. Cat. Sci. Pap., 1800-1863. Pernyi moth (and silkworm).

Pernyi moth (and silkworm) (Perny, Paul H.): Zoology. See: Webster's 3d.

Perofskite (Perovski, Count Leon Alekseivich). See: Perovskite.

PERON, JUAN DOMINGO. 1895-1974. Argentine politician. See: New Encyc. Brit., 1974, Microp. Peronism (or Peronist).

Peronism (or Peronist) (Peron, Juan Domingo): Politics. See: Morris and Irwin; Webster's 3d.

PERONNET, MARCEL. fl. 1934-1936. French chemist. Cited in: Chem. Abstr., Decenn. Indexes, 1927-1936, 1937-1946. Peronnet-Truhaut reaction for aldehydes, Peronnet-Truhaut reaction for amino acids and uric acid.

Peronnet–Truhaut reaction for aldehydes (Peronnet, Marcel and Truhaut, Rene): Chemistry. See: Van Nostrand Chem. Dict.

Peronnet–Truhaut reaction for amino acids and uric acid (Peronnet, Marcel and Truhaut, Rene): Chemistry. See: Van Nostrand Chem. Dict.

PEROT, ALFRED. 1863–1925. French physicist. See: World Who's Who Sci. Fabry (and) Perot etalon (or interferometer), Fabry–Perot fringes, Perot lamp.

Perot lamp (Perot, Alfred): Physics. See: Hackh.

PEROVSKI, COUNT LEON ALEKSEIVICH. 1792–1856. Russian statesman. See: Michaud. Perovskite (Perowskite, Perofskite).

Perovskite (Perowskite, Perofskite) (Perovski, Count Leon Alekseivich): Earth Sciences. See: Charnock; Thrush; Van Nostrand Sci. Encyc.

PERRIER, CARLO. 1886–1948. Italian mineralogist. See: Diz. Encic. Ital. Perrierite.

Perrierite (Perrier, Carlo): Earth Sciences. See: Thrush.

PERRIN, AMI. d. 1561. Swiss political leader. See: New Encyc. Brit., 1974, Microp. Perrinist.

Perrin equation (or determination of the Avogadro constant) (Perrin, Jean Baptiste): Chemistry. See: Hackh; Van Nostrand Sci. Encyc.

Perrin–Ferraton disease (Perrin, Maurice and Ferraton, Louis): Medicine. See: Dorland.

PERRIN, JEAN BAPTISTE. 1870–1942. French physicist and chemist. See: Dict. Sci. Biog. Perrin equation (or determination of the Avogadro constant), Perrin rule.

PERRIN, MAURICE. 1826–1889. French surgeon. See: World Who's Who Sci. Perrin–Ferraton disease.

PERRIN, RENE JEAN LOUIS. 1897– . French metallurgist. See: Who's Who France, 1975–1976. Perrin's process.

Perrin rule (Perrin, Jean Baptiste): Physics. See: Van Nostrand Sci. Encyc.

PERRINE, HENRY. 1797–1840. American physician and naturalist. See: Dict. Amer. Biog. Perrine lemon.

Perrine lemon (Perrine, Henry): Botany. See: Webster's 3d.

Perrinist (Perrin, Ami): Politics. See: Webster's 3d.

Perrin's process (Perrin, Rene Jean Louis): Engineering and Industry. See: Thrush.

PERRONCITO, ALDO. 1882–1929. Italian histologist. See: Biog. Lex. hervorr. Aerzte. Perroncito's apparatus (or spirals).

Perroncito's apparatus (or spirals) (Perroncito, Aldo): Medicine. See: Dorland.

PERROT, LOUIS JEROME. 1798–1878. French inventor. See: Grand Larousse Encyc. Perrotine.

Perrotine (Perrot, Louis Jerome): Engineering and Industry. See: Grand Larousse Encyc.

PERRY, ANTOINETTE ("TONY"). 1888–1946. American actor and producer. See: Who Was Who Amer., vol. 2. Tony (award).

Perry hat (Perry, Oliver Hazard): Fashion. See: Mathews, M. M.

Perry indicator (Perry, John): Engineering and Industry. See: Auger.

PERRY, JAMES. fl. 19th c. English inventor. (Biography source unavailable.) Perryan (pen).

PERRY, JOHN. 1850–1920. Irish engineer. See: Pogg., vols. 3, 4, 5. Perry indicator.

Perry mantle (Perry, Oliver Hazard): Fashion. See: Mathews, M. M.

PERRY, MATTHEW CALBRAITH. 1794–1858. American naval officer. See: Dict. Amer. Biog. Perry's expedition to Japan.

PERRY, OLIVER HAZARD. 1785–1819. American naval officer. See: Dict. Amer. Biog. Perry hat, Perry mantle, Perry shoes, Perry wig.

Perry shoes (Perry, Oliver Hazard): Fashion. See: Mathews, M. M.

Perry wig (Perry, Oliver Hazard): Fashion. See: Mathews, M. M.

Perryan (pen) (Perry, James): Engineering and Industry. See: Charnock.

Perry's expedition to Japan (Perry, Matthew Calbraith): History. See: Dict. Amer. Hist., vol. 4, p. 253.

PERS, R. fl. 1932–1934. French? meteorologist. Cited in: Meteorolog. and Geoastrophys. Abstr., Cum. Index, vol. 1–10, 1950–1959. Pers sunshine recorder?

Pers sunshine recorder (Pers, R.?): Earth Sciences. See: Huschke.

PERSEPHONE. In Greek mythology, goddess of the underworld. See: Jobes. Persephone (crabs), Pherephattia, Proserpinaca.

Persephone (crabs) (Persephone): Zoology. See: Pennak.

Pershbecker furnace (Derivation undetermined): Engineering and Industry. See: Thrush.

PERSHING, JOHN JOSEPH. 1860–1948. American army commander. See: New Encyc. Brit., 1974, Microp. General Pershing (tank), Pershing (missile).

Pershing (missile) (Pershing, John Joseph): Weapons. See: Markus; Quick; Van Nostrand Sci. Encyc. under "Rockets and Launch Vehicles."

PERSON, ALFRED. fl. 1935. German photographer. Cited in: Chem. Abstr., Decenn. Index, 1927–1936. Person process.

Person process (Person, Alfred): Photography. See: Van Nostrand Sci. Encyc.

PERSOZ, JEAN FRANCOIS. 1805–1868. French technical chemist. See: World Who's Who Sci. Persoz('s) reagent (or solution).

Persoz('s) reagent (or solution) (Persoz, Jean Francois): Chemistry. See: Hackh; Van Nostrand Chem. Dict.

Perthes–Calve–Legg–Waldenstroem syndrome (Perthes, Georg Clemens; Calve, Jacques; Legg, Arthur Thornton; Waldenstroem, Henning). See: Calve–Legg–Perthes syndrome.

Perthes' disease (Perthes, Georg Clemens). See: Calve–Legg–Perthes syndrome.

PERTHES, GEORG CLEMENS. 1869–1927. German surgeon. See: World Who's Who Sci. Calve–Legg–Perthes syndrome, Perthes' incision, Perthes–Juengling disease, Perthes' method, Perthes' test.

Perthes' incision (Perthes, Georg Clemens): Medicine. See: Dorland; Stedman.

Perthes, Jacques Boucher de Crevecoeur de. See: Boucher de Crevecoeur de Perthes, Jacques.

Perthes–Juengling disease (Perthes, Georg Clemens and Juengling, Otto): Medicine. See: Jablonski. Also known as: Juengling's disease (or polycystic osteitis).

Perthes' method (Perthes, Georg Clemens): Medicine. See: Dorland; Stedman.

Perthes' test (Perthes, Georg Clemens): Medicine. See: Dorland; Stedman.

PERTIK, OTTO. 1852–1913. Hungarian pathologist. See: Biog. Lex. hervorr. Aerzte. Pertik's diverticulum.

Pertik's diverticulum (Pertik, Otto): Anatomy. See: Donath; Dorland; Stedman.

perturbation Hamiltonian (Hamilton, Sir William Rowan): Physics. See: Internat. Dict. Phys. Elec.

PERTUSI, CAMILLO ALESSANDRO GIORGIO. b. 1877. Italian chemist. See: Pogg., vol. 6. Camilla–Pertusi test for saccharin and dulcin, Camilla–Pertusi test for xanthine bases, Pertusi–Gastaldi reagent for cyanide, Pertusi reaction for fluoride.

Pertusi–Gastaldi reagent for cyanide (Pertusi, Camillo Alessandro Giorgio and Gastaldi, E.): Chemistry. See: Van Nostrand Chem. Dict.

Pertusi reaction for fluoride (Pertusi, Camillo Alessandro Giorgio): Chemistry. See: Van Nostrand Chem. Dict.

Peruginesque (Perugino): Fine Arts. See: Webster's 3d.

PERUGINO (PIETRO DI CRISTOFORO VANNUCCI). ca. 1446–1523. Italian painter. See: New Encyc. Brit., 1974, Microp. Peruginesque.

PERUTZ, ALFRED. b. 1885. Austrian dermatologist. See: Biog. Lex. hervorr. Aerzte. Perutz reaction.

PERUTZ, OTTO. 1847–1922. German photographic manufacturer. See: Focal Encyc. Photog. Perutz perchromo plates.

Perutz perchromo plates (Perutz, Otto): Photography. See: Focal Encyc. Photog. under "Miethe, Adolf."

Perutz reaction (Perutz, Alfred): Medicine. See: Dorland.

Pescara engine (Pescara, R.): Engineering and Industry. See: Auger.

PESCARA, R. fl. 20th c. Engineer. (Biography source unavailable.) Pescara engine.

PESCHEL, OSKAR FERDINAND. 1826-1875. German geographer and geomorphologist. See: Allg. Deut. Biog. Peschel's law?

Peschel's law (Peschel, Oskar Ferdinand?): Anthropology. See: Winick.

Peset-Beundia reagent (Peset, Juan and Beundia, Rogelio): Chemistry. See: Van Nostrand Chem. Dict.

PESET, JUAN. fl. 1916. Spanish chemist. Cited in: Chem. Abstr., vol. 11, p. 2018. Peset-Beundia reagent.

Pestalozzi Foundation of America (Pestalozzi, Johann Heinrich): Philanthropy. Cited in: Nat. Cycl. Amer. Biog., vol. H, p. 72.

PESTALOZZI, JOHANN HEINRICH. 1746-1827. Swiss educational reformer. See: Encyc. Brit., 1973. Pestalozzi Foundation of America, Pestalozzi World Foundation, Pestalozzianism (or Pestalozzian system).

Pestalozzi World Foundation (Pestalozzi, Johann Heinrich): Philanthropy. Cited in: Nat. Cycl. Amer. Biog., vol. H, p. 72.

Pestalozzianism (or Pestalozzian system) (Pestalozzi, Johann Heinrich): Education. See: Good; Phyfe.

Petagna (Petagna, Vincenzo): Botany. See: Charnock.

PETAGNA, VINCENZO. 1734-1810. Italian botanist. See: Nouv. Biog. Univ. Petagna.

Petain (Petain, Henri Philippe): Generic Word (traitor). See: Hendrickson.

PETAIN, HENRI PHILIPPE. 1856-1951. French army commander. See: Encyc. Brit., 1973. Petain.

PETAUD, KING. Proverbial leader of the community of beggars in France. See: Harvey and Heseltine. court of King Petaud.

PETENERA. fl. 19th c. Spanish singer. (Biography source unavailable.) Petenera (song).

Petenera (song) (Petenera): Music. See: Partridge.

Peter-boat (Peter the Apostle, Saint): Generic Word (fishing boat). See: Charnock.

PETER, KARL. b. 1870. German anatomist. See: Biog. Lex. hervorr. Aerzte. Peter's line.

PETER, LAURENCE JOHNSTON. 1919- . Canadian-born American educator. See: Who's Who Amer., 1974-1975. The Peter principle, Peter's law of compulsive incompetence, Peter's nuance, Peter's paradox, Peter's perfect people palliative, Peter's placebo, Peter's pretty pass, Peter's spiral.

Peter-man (Peter the Apostle, Saint): Generic Word (fisherman). See: Charnock; Partridge; Webster's 3d.

PETER OF ALCANTARA, SAINT. 1499-1652. Spanish Franciscan monk. See: Holweck. Alcantarines.

PETER OF CHELCIC. fl. ca. 1456. Bohemian? religious partisan. Cited in: Hastings (Dict. Rel. Ethics), vol. 6, p. 888a. Brethren of Chelcic.

Peter of Morrone. See: Celestine V, Saint.

PETER PAN. Boy hero of Sir James M. Barrie's play of the same name, (1904). See: New Encyc. Brit., 1974, Microp. Peter Pan, Peter Pan collar.

Peter Pan (Peter Pan): Generic Word (perpetual child). See: Hendrickson; Webster's 3d.

Peter Pan collar (Peter Pan): Fashion. See: Picken.

Peter-Paul goblet illusion (Peter the Apostle, Saint? and Paul the Apostle, Saint?): Psychology. See: Chaplin.

Peter (portmanteau) (Peter the Apostle, Saint): Fashion. Cited in: Charnock; Partridge.

Peter principle (Peter, Laurence Johnston): Sociology. See: Martin.

Peter (safe) (Peter the Apostle, Saint): Generic Word. Cited in: Hendrickson.

Peter-see-me (Peter or Pedro Ximenes) (wine) (Ximenes, Pedro): Food and Drink. See: Brewer; Charnock; Partridge.

Peter Stubs' gauge (Stubs, Peter). See: Stubs' iron gauge.

PETER THE APOSTLE, SAINT. d. 67? Disciple of Jesus. See: Holweck. by St. Peter, Patrimony of St. Peter, Peter-boat, Peter-man, Peter-Paul goblet illusion?, Peter (portmanteau), Peter (safe), Peter's fish, Peter's pence, Petrel, Petrine (or Petrinism), rob Peter to pay Paul, Sacred Congregation of the Venerable Fabric of St. Peter's, St. Peter's chains, St. Peter's chair, St. Peter's fingers, St. Peter's fish (or cock), St. Peter's keys, Saint Peter's sandstone? St. Peter's wort, Saint Peter's wreath, Samphire (or Sampire), Sampietrini.

Peter Thomson dress (Thomson, Peter): Fashion. See: Picken.

Peter (wine) (Ximenes, Pedro). See: Peter-see-me (Peter or Pedro Ximenes) (wine).

PETERFI, TIBOR. 1883-1953. Hungarian histologist. See: Biog. Lex. hervorr. Aerzte. Peterfi's micromanipulator.

Peterfi's micromanipulator (Peterfi, Tibor): Medicine. See: Donath.

PETERMAN; MYNIE GUSTAV. 1896- . American physician. See: World Who's Who Sci. Peterman test.

Peterman test (Peterman, Mynie Gustav): Medicine. See: Dorland; Stedman.

PETERS, ALBERT. b. 1862. German ophthalmologist. See: Biog. Lex. hervorr. Aerzte. Peters' anomaly.

Peters' anomaly (Peters, Albert): Medicine. See: Jablonski.

PETERS, CHARLES CLINTON. b. 1881. American psychologist and statistician. See: Amer. Men Sci., 6th ed. Peters' method.

Peter's fish (Peter the Apostle, Saint): Zoology. See: Partridge; Phyfe.

Peter's grass (or cress) (Peter the Apostle, Saint). See: Samphire (or Sampire).

PETERS, HUBERT. 1859-1934. Austrian physician. See: Biog. Lex. hervorr. Aerzte. Peter's ovum.

Peter's law of compulsive incompetence (Peter, Laurence Johnston): Sociology. See: Martin.

Peter's line (Peter, Karl): Anatomy. See: Donath.

Peters' method (Peters, Charles Clinton): Statistics. See: Kendall.

Peter's nuance (Peter, Laurence Johnston): Sociology. See: Martin.

Peter's ovum (Peters, Hubert): Medicine. See: Dorland; Stedman.

Peter's paradox (Peter, Laurence Johnston): Sociology. See: Martin.

Peter's pence (Peter the Apostle, Saint): Religion. See: Attwater; Charnock; Harbottle; Phyfe; Steinberg.

Peter's perfect people palliative (Peter, Laurence Johnston): Sociology. See: Martin.

Peter's placebo (Peter, Laurence Johnston): Sociology. See: Martin.

Peter's pretty pass (Peter, Laurence Johnston): Sociology. See: Martin.

Peters' Reports (Peters, Richard): Law. See: Jameson.

PETERS, RICHARD. 1744-1828. American jurist. See: Dict. Amer. Biog. Peters' Reports.

PETERS, SIR RUDOLPH ALBERT. fl. 1914-1972. English biochemist. See: Direct. Brit. Sci., 1971-1972. Kinnersley-Peters test for vitamin B1 (thiamine).

Peters snapweed (Derivation undetermined): Botany. See: Winburne.

Peter's spiral (Peter, Laurence Johnston): Sociology. See: Martin.

Petersen air elutriator (Petersen, Louis S.?): Engineering and Industry. See: Thrush.

PETERSEN, CHRISTIAN FERDINAND. 1845-1908. German surgeon. See: Biog. Jahrb. Deut. Nekr., vol. 13, 1908. Petersen's bag.

Petersen coil (Petersen, Waldemar): Electronics. See: Webster's 3d.

Petersen grab (Derivation undetermined): Engineering and Industry. See: Thrush.

PETERSEN, HUGO. fl. 1906-1936. German chemist. Cited in: Chem. Abstr., Decenn. Index, 1927-1936. Peterson concentrator, Peterson tower process.

PETERSEN, LOUIS S. fl. 1931. American cement technologist. Cited in: Chem. Abstr., Decenn. Index, 1937-1946. Petersen air elutriator?

PETERSEN, QUENTIN RICHARD. 1924- . American chemist. See: World Who's Who Sci. Cenco-Petersen molecular model.

PETERSEN, WALDEMAR. 1880-1946. German electrical engineer. See: Pogg., vol. 7a. Petersen coil.

Petersen's bag (Petersen, Christian Ferdinand): Medicine. See: Dorland; Stedman.

Petersham (cloth) (Stanhope, Charles Stanhope, 3d earl Harrington and Lord Petersham): Fashion. See: Partridge; Picken; Webster's 3d.

Petersham great-coat (or jacket) (Stanhope, Charles Stanhope, 3d Earl Harrington and Lord Petersham): Fashion. See: Charnock; Partridge; Picken; Webster's 3d.

Petersham, Lord. See: Stanhope, Charles (Lord Petersham).

Petersham (ribbon) (Stanhope, Charles Stanhope, 3d Earl Harrington and Lord Petersham): Fashion. See: Partridge; Webster's 3d.

Peterson concentrator (Petersen, Hugo): Chemistry. See: Van Nostrand Chem. Dict.

Peterson dredge (Peterson, Melvin Norman Adolph?): Zoology. See: Pennak.

PETERSON, JOEL BIGELOW. 1897- . American chemist. See: Amer. Men Sci., 7th ed. Peterson reagent.

PETERSON, MELVIN NORMAN ADOLPH. 1929- . American oceanographer. See: Amer. Men and Women Sci., 12th ed. Peterson dredge?

Peterson reagent (Peterson, Joel Bigelow): Chemistry. See: Van Nostrand Chem. Dict.

Peterson tower process (Petersen, Hugo): Chemistry. See: Van Nostrand Chem. Dict.

Peterwort (Peter the Apostle, Saint). See: Saint Peter's wort.

Petges-Clejat syndrome (Petges, Gabriel and Clejat, Charles Philippe Antoine): Medicine. See: Jablonski.

PETGES, GABRIEL. b. 1872. French dermatologist. See: Biog. Lex. hervorr. Aerzte. Petges-Clejat syndrome.

PETIT, ALEXIS THERESE. 1791-1820. French physicist. See: World Who's Who Sci. Dulong and Petit's law.

PETIT, ANTOINE. 1718-1794. French surgeon and anatomist. See: Nouv. Biog. Univ. Petit's ligaments.

Petit-Dufrenoy, Ours Pierre Armand. See: Dufrenoy, Ours Pierre Armand Petit.

PETIT, FRANCOIS-POURFOUR DU. 1664-1741. French anatomist and surgeon. See: Nouv. Biog. Univ. Petit's canal, Petit's sinus, Petit's syndrome.

PETIT, JEAN LOUIS. 1674-1750. French surgeon. See: World Who's Who Sci. Petit's hernia, Petit's herniotomy, Petit's triangle (or lumbar triangle).

PETIT, PAUL. b. 1889. French anatomist and gynecologist. Cited in: Index-Cat. Libr. Surg.-Gen. Off., 2d Ser., vol. 13, 1908. Petit's aponeurosis.

Petit's aponeurosis (Petit, Paul): Anatomy. See: Stedman.

Petit's canal (Petit, Francois-Pourfour du): Anatomy. See: Donath; Dorland; Stedman.

Petit's hernia (Petit, Jean Louis): Medicine. See: Dorland; Jablonski; Stedman.

Petit's herniotomy (Petit, Jean Louis): Medicine. See: Stedman.

Petit's ligaments (Petit, Antoine): Anatomy. See: Stedman.

Petit's sinus (Petit, Francois-Pourfour du): Anatomy. See: Dorland; Stedman. Also known as: Valsalva's sinus.

Petit's syndrome (Petit, Francois-Pourfour du): Medicine. See: Jablonski.

Petit's triangle (or lumbar triangle) (Petit, Jean Louis): Anatomy. See: Donath; Dorland; Stedman.

PETIVER, JAMES. 1663-1718. English botanist and entomologist. See: Dict. Nat. Biog. Petiveria.

Petiveria (Petiver, James): Botany. See: Charnock; Webster's 3d.

PETRARCH (FRANCESCO PETRARCA). 1304-1374. Italian poet. See: New Encyc. Brit., 1974, Microp. Petrarchan conceits, Petrarchan sonnet, Petrarchism.

Petrarchan conceits (Petrarch): Literature. See: Barnet.

Petrarchan sonnet (Petrarch): Literature. See: Scott.

Petrarchism (Petrarch): Literature. See: Preminger.

PETRASSI, GINO. fl. 1944. Italian internist. Cited in: Lieber and Olbrich. Fanconi-Petrassi syndrome.

PETRE, ROBERT JAMES, 8TH BARON. 1713-1743. English patron of botany. See: Biog. Notes Upon Botanists. Petrea.

Petrea (Petre, Robert James, 8th Baron): Botany. See: Taylor, N.; Webster's 3d.

Petrel (Peter the Apostle, Saint): Zoology. See: Hendrickson; Weekley.

PETREN, KARL. 1869-1927. Swedish physician. See: Svenska Maen Och Kvinnor. Petren's diet, Petren's treatment (or method).

PETRENKO-KRITSCHENKO, PAVEL IVANOVICH. b. 1866. German chemist. See: Pogg., vols. 4, 5, 6. Petrenko-Kritshenko piperidone synthesis.

Petrenko-Kritshenko piperidone synthesis (Petrenko-Kritschenko, Pavel Ivanovich): Chemistry. See: Van Nostrand Chem. Dict.

Petren's diet (Petren, Karl): Medicine. See: Dorland.

Petren's treatment (or method) (Petren, Karl): Medicine. See: Dorland.

PETREQUIN, THEODORE JOSEPH ELEONORD. 1810-1876. French surgeon. See: Biog. Lex. hervorr. Aerzte. Petrequin's ligament.

Petrequin's ligament (Petrequin, Theodore Joseph Eleonord): Anatomy. See: Donath; Dorland;

Petri dishes (Petri, Julius Richard): Microbiology. See: Dorland; Stedman.

PETRI, JULIUS RICHARD. 1852-1921. German bacteriologist. See: World Who's Who Sci. Petri dishes.

PETRI, LIONELLO. 1875-1946. Italian plant pathologist. See: Revista di biologia, vol. 39 (1947), pp. 231-244. Petri's infectious mottling.

Petrine (or Petrinism) (Peter the Apostle, Saint): Religion. See: Webster's 3d.

Petri's infectious mottling (Petri, Lionello): Botany. See: Winburne.

Petrobrusian(s) (Bruys, Pierre de). See: Brusians (or Petrobrusian(s)).

Petroff, Aleksandr Dmitrievich. See: Petrov, Aleksandr Dmitrievich.

Petroff equation (Petrov, Nikolay Pavlovich): Engineering and Industry. See: Hackh.

Petroff medium (Petroff, Strashimer Alburtus): Medicine. See: Van Nostrand Chem. Dict.

Petroff, Nikolay Pavlovich. See: Petrov, Nikolay Pavlovich.

Petroff reagent (Petrov, Aleksandr Dmitrievich): Chemistry. See: Hackh.

Petroff, S. See: Petrov, S.

PETROFF, STRASHIMER ALBURTUS. 1883-1948. Bulgarian-born American bacteriologist. See: Who Was Who Amer., vol. 2. Petroff medium.

Petronian (Petronius, Gaius): History. See: Webster's 3d.

PETRONIUS, GAIUS. d. 66. Roman director of entertainments at Nero's court. See: Dict. Grk. Rom. Biog. Myth. Petronian.

PETROV, ALEKSANDR DMITRIEVICH. 1895- . Russian organic chemist. See: World Who's Who Sci. Petroff reagent.

PETROV, NIKOLAY PAVLOVICH. 1836-1920. Russian mechanical engineer. See: Dict. Sci. Biog. Petroff equation.

PETROV, S. fl. 1910. Russian chemist. Cited in: Chem. Abstr., vol. 5, p. 1036. Tanatar-Petrov test reaction.

PETROVSKII, A. YA. fl. 1929. Russian chemist. Cited in: Chem. Abstr., vol. 23, p. 3872. Petrovskii test.

Petrovskii test (Petrovskii, A. Ya.): Chemistry. See: Van Nostrand Chem. Dict.

Petruschka hat (Petrushka): Fashion. See: Picken.

PETRUSCHKY, JOHANNES. b. 1863. German bacteriologist. See: Biog. Lex. hervorr. Aerzte. Petruschky's litmus whey, Petruschky's spinalgia.

Petruschky's litmus whey (Petruschky, Johannes): Medicine. See: Dorland.

Petruschky's spinalgia (Petruschky, Johannes): Medicine. See: Dorland.

PETRUSHKA. Puppet and eternal clown in Slavic legend. Cited in: New Encyc. Brit., 1974, Microp. Petrushka hat, Petrushka chord.

Petrushka chord (Petrushka): Music. See: Apel.

Pette–Doering encephalitis (Pette, Heinrich Wilhelm and Doering, Gerhard): Medicine. See: Jablonski.

PETTE, HEINRICH WILHELM. b. 1887. German neurologist. See: Kuerschner's Deut. Gel.-Kal., vol. 4, 1931. Pette-Doering encephalitis.

PETTENKOFER, MAX JOSEF VON. 1818-1901. German chemist. See: Dict. Sci. Biog. Pettenkofer reagent for free carbon dioxide in water, Pettenkofer('s) test (or reaction).

Pettenkofer reagent for free carbon dioxide in water (Pettenkofer, Max Josef von): Chemistry. See: Van Nostrand Chem. Dict.

Pettenkofer('s) test (or reaction) (Pettenkofer, Max Josef von): Chemistry. See: Hackh; Stedman.

PETTERSSON, SVEN OTTO. 1848-1941. Swedish chemist. See: World Who's Who Sci. Nansen-Pettersson water bottle.

PETTIT, AUGUSTE. 1869-1939. French physician. See: Presse Med., vol. 47 (Nov. 1, 1939), p. 1473. Bachman and Pettit test.

Petty school (Petty, Sir William): Education. See: Good.

PETTY, SIR WILLIAM. 1623-1687. English statistician and economist. See: Internat. Encyc. Soc. Sci. Petty school, Petty's law.

Petty's law (Petty, Sir William): Economics. See: Seldon.

PETZ, W. K. d. 1873. Hungarian geologist. (Biography source unavailable.) Petzite.

Petzetakis' disease (Petzetakis, M.). See: Debre's syndrome (1).

PETZETAKIS, M. fl. 1950. Greek physician. (Biography source unavailable.) Petzetakis' disease, Petzetakis-Takos syndrome, Petzetaki's test (or reaction)?

Petzetakis-Takos syndrome (Petzetakis, M. and Takos): Medicine. See: Jablonski.

Petzetaki's test (or reaction) (Petzetakis, M.?): Medicine. See: Dorland.

Petzite (Petz, W. K.): Earth Sciences. See: Van Nostrand Sci. Encyc.; Webster's 3d.

Petzval('s) condition (Petzval, Josef Miksa): Physics. See: Internat. Dict. Ap. Math.; Van Nostrand Sci. Encyc.

PETZVAL, JOSEF MIKSA. 1807-1891. Hungarian mathematician. See: Pogg., vol. 2. Petzval('s) condition, Petzval lens, Petzval studio camera, Petzval sum, Petzval surface, Petzval-Voightlaender lens.

Petzval lens (Petzval, Josef Miksa): Photography. See: Focal Encyc. Photog.; Webster's 3d.

Petzval studio camera (Petzval, Josef Miksa): Photography. See: Focal Encyc. Photog. under "Camera History."

Petzval sum (Petzval, Josef Miksa): Physics. See: Focal Encyc. Photog.; Internat. Dict. Ap. Math.

Petzval surface (Petzval, Josef Miksa): Physics. See: Internat. Dict. Ap. Math.; Van Nostrand Sci. Encyc.

Petzval-Voightlaender lens (Petzval, Josef Miksa and Voightlaender, Peter Wilhelm Friedrich): Photography. Cited in: Focal Encyc. Photog. under "Angerer, Ludwig."

PEUTINGER, KONRAD. 1465-1547. German humanist and antiquary. See: Encyc. Brit., 1911. Peutingerian table.

Peutingerian table (Peutinger, Konrad): History. See: Brewer; Charnock; Encyc. Brit., 1973.

PEUTZ, J. L. A. fl. 1921. Dutch physician. (Biography source unavailable.) Peutz-Jeghers syndrome.

Peutz-Jeghers syndrome (Peutz, J. L. A. and Jeghers, Harold): Medicine. See: Jablonski; Stedman. Also known as: Hutchinson-Weber-Peutz syndrome, Jeghers' syndrome, Peutz-Touraine syndrome, Peutz's syndrome.

Peutz-Touraine syndrome (Peutz, J. L. A. and Touraine, Henri). See: Peutz-Jeghers syndrome.

Peutz's syndrome (Peutz, J. L. A.). See: Peutz-Jeghers syndrome.

PEYER, JOHANN KONRAD. 1653-1712. Swiss anatomist. See: Biog. Lex. hervorr. Aerzte. Peyer's patch(es) (or gland(s)).

Peyerian gland (Peyer, Johann Konrad). See: Peyer's patch(es) (or gland(s)).

Peyer's patch(es) (or gland(s)) (Peyer, Johann Konrad): Anatomy. See: Donath; Dorland; Stedman; Webster's 3d. Also known as: Peyerian gland.

Peyronie's disease (La Peyronie, Francois Gigot de): Medicine. See: Dorland; Jablonski; Stedman. Also known as: Van Buren's disease.

PEYROT, JEAN JOSEPH. 1843-1918. French surgeon. See: Biog. Lex. hervorr. Aerzte. Peyrot's thorax.

Peyrot's thorax (Peyrot, Jean Joseph): Medicine. See: Dorland; Stedman.

PEYSER, THEODORE ALBERT. 1873-1937. American legislator. See: Biog. Direct. Amer. Congress. Wagner-Peyser Act.

Pezzer catheter (Pezzer, O. de): Medicine. See: Stedman.

PEZZER, O. DE. fl. 1885. French physician. Cited in: Index-Cat. Libr. Surg.-Gen. Off., 1st Ser., vol. 10, 1889. Pezzer catheter.

PFAFF, CHRISTIAN HEINRICH. 1773-1852. German physician, chemist and physicist. See: Pogg., vol. 2. Pfaff test reaction for malic acid.

Pfaff(ian) differential equation (expression or problem) (Pfaff, Johann Friedrich): Mathematics. See: Ballentyne; Internat. Dict. Phys. Elec.; James; Van Nostrand Sci. Encyc.

PFAFF, JOHANN FRIEDRICH. 1765-1825. German mathematician. See: Dict. Sci. Biog. Pfaff(ian) differential equation (expression or problem).

Pfaff test reaction for malic acid (Pfaff, Christian Heinrich): Chemistry. See: Van Nostrand Chem. Dict.

PFANNENSTIEL, JOHANN (In full: HERMANN JOHANN). 1862-1909. German gynecologist. See: Biog. Lex. hervorr. Aerzte. Pfannenstiel's incision, Pfannenstiel's syndrome.

Pfannenstiel's incision (Pfannenstiel, Johann): Medicine. See: Dorland; Stedman.

Pfannenstiel's syndrome (Pfannenstiel, Johann): Medicine. See: Jablonski.

PFAU, ALEXANDRE STANISLAS. d. 1938. Swiss chemist. See: Helvetica Chim. Acta, vol. 21 (1938), pp. 1562-1570. Saint Pfau-Plattner azulene synthesis.

Pfaundler-Hurler syndrome (Pfaundler, Meinhard von and Hurler, Gertrud). See: Hurler's syndrome (disease or polydystrophy).

PFAUNDLER, MEINHARD VON. 1872-1947. German physician. See: Biog. Lex. hervorr. Aerzte. Pfaundler-Hurler syndrome, Pfaundler's reaction.

Pfaundler's reaction (Pfaundler, Meinhard von): Medicine. See: Dorland; Stedman.

PFEIFER, P. fl. 1897-1933. German engineer. Cited in: Chem. Abstr., Decenn. Index, 1927-1936. Moeller and Pfeiffer dryer.

PFEIFER, VICTOR. 1846-1921. German physician. Cited in: Index-Cat. Libr. Surg.-Gen. Off., 2d Ser., vol. 13, 1908. Pfeifer-Weber-Christian syndrome.

Pfeifer-Weber-Christian syndrome (Pfeifer, Victor; Weber, Frederick Parkes; and Christian, Henry Asbury). See: Weber-Christian syndrome.

PFEIFFER, EMIL. 1846-1921. German physician. See: World Who's Who Sci. Pfeiffer's disease.

PFEIFFER, PAUL. 1875-1951. German chemist. See: Dict. Sci. Biog. Pfeiffer test for phenols?

PFEIFFER, RICHARD FRIEDRICH JOHANN. 1858-1945. German bacteriologist. See: World Who's Who Sci. Pfeifferella, Pfeiffer's bacillus, Pfeiffer's blood agar, Pfeiffer's phenomenon (or reaction).

Pfeiffer test for phenols (Pfeiffer, Paul?): Chemistry. See: Van Nostrand Chem. Dict.

Pfeifferella (Pfeiffer, Richard Friedrich Johann): Zoology. See: Dorland; Stedman; Webster's 3d.

Pfeiffer's bacillus (Pfeiffer, Richard Friedrich Johann): Medicine. See: Dorland; Stedman; Webster's 3d. Also known as: Koch-Weeks bacillus.

Pfeiffer's blood agar (Pfeiffer, Richard Friedrich Johann): Medicine. See: Stedman.

Pfeiffer's disease (Pfeiffer, Emil). See: Filatov's disease.

Pfeiffer's phenomenon (or reaction) (Pfeiffer, Richard Friedrich Johann): Medicine. See: Dorland; Stedman.

Pfeilring reagent (Derivation undetermined): Chemistry. See: Hackh; Van Nostrand Chem. Dict.

PFIFFNER, JOSEPH JOHN. 1903- . American biochemist. See: Amer. Men and Women Sci., 12th ed. Pfiffner-Myers reagent.

Pfiffner–Myers reagent (Pfiffner, Joseph John and Myers, Victor Caryl): Chemistry. See: Van Nostrand Chem. Dict.

PFITZER, ERNST. 1846-1906. German botanist. See: Biog. Jahrb. Deut. Nekr., vol. 11, 1906. Pfitzer's juniper.

Pfitzer's juniper (Pfitzer, Ernst): Botany. See: Webster's 3d.

Pfitzinger reaction (Pfitzinger, Wilhelm): Chemistry. See: Ballentyne; Krauch und Kunz; Van Nostrand Chem. Dict.

PFITZINGER, WILHELM. fl. 1886. German chemist. Cited in: Royal Soc. Cat. Sci. Pap., 1884-1900. Pfitzinger reaction.

PFLUEGER, EDUARD FRIEDRICH WILHELM. 1829-1910. German physiologist. See: World Who's Who Sci. Pflueger's cords, Pflueger's laws, Pflueger's tubes.

Pflueger's cords (Pflueger, Eduard Friedrich Wilhelm): Physiology. See: Henderson.

Pflueger's laws (Pflueger, Eduard Friedrich Wilhelm): Physiology. See: Dorland; Stedman.

Pflueger's tubes (Pflueger, Eduard Friedrich Wilhelm): Anatomy. See: Donath; Dorland; Stedman.

PFUHL, EDUARD. 1852-1905. German physician. See: Biog. Lex. hervorr. Aerzte. Pfuhl's sign.

Pfuhl's sign (Pfuhl, Eduard): Medicine. See: Dorland; Stedman.

PFUND, AUGUST HERMAN. b. 1879. American physicist. See: Amer. Men Sci., 7th ed. Pfund series.

Pfund series (Pfund, August Herman): Physics. See: Hughes; Internat. Dict. Phys. Elec.; Thewlis.

Phaebe (Phoebe): Dance. See: Charnock.

PHAEDRA. In Greek mythology, lover of her stepson, Hippolytus. See: Jobes. Phaedra complex.

Phaedra complex (Phaedra): Psychology. See: Hinsie.

PHAETHON. In Greek mythology, son of Helios and Clymene. See: Jobes. Phaeton, Phaeton's bird.

Phaeton (carriage) (Phaethon): Generic Word. See: Brewer; Harvey; New Encyc. Brit., 1974, Microp.; Partridge.

Phaeton, the god. See: Phaethon.

Phaeton's bird (Phaethon): Zoology. See: Brewer; Jobes.

PHALAECUS. fl. ca. 4th c. B.C. Greek poet. See: Dict. Grk. Rom. Biog. Myth. Phalecian (or Phalaecean).

PHALARIS. fl. 570-554 B.C. Tyrant in Sicily. See: Dict. Grk. Rom. Biog. Myth. epistles of Phalaris.

Phalecian (or Phalaecean) (Phalaecus): Literature. See: Charnock; Preminger.

Pheidias, the sculptor. See: Phidias.

PHELPS, ABEL MIX. 1851-1902. American surgeon. See: Nat. Cycl. Amer. Biog., vol. 12, p. 233. Phelps' operation.

Phelps' operation (Phelps, Abel Mix): Medicine. See: Stedman.

PHELYPEAUX (PHELIPEAUX). Ancient and illustrious French family. See: Nouv. Biog. Univ. Phelypoea.

Phelypoea (Phelypeaux): Botany. See: Charnock.

Phenomenon of Wedensky (Wedensky, Nikolay Yevgen'yevich): Medicine. See: Stedman.

Pherecratean (or Pherecratic) (Pherecrates): Literature. See: Partridge; Preminger.

PHERECRATES. fl. 437 B.C. Greek poet and playwright. See: Dict. Grk. Rom. Biog. Myth. Pherecratean (or Pherecratic).

Pherephatta. See: Persephone.

Pherephattia (Persephone): Mythology. See: Charnock.

Phidian (sculpture) (Phidias): Fine Arts. See: Webster's 3d.; Weekley.

PHIDIAS. d. 432 B.C. Greek sculptor. See: New Encyc. Brit., 1974, Microp. Phidian (sculpture).

Philadelphian (Ptolemy II, Philadelphus): History. See: Charnock.

Philadelphus (Ptolemy II, Philadelphus?): Botany. See: Charnock

Philander (Philander, Kornelius): Zoology. See: Hendrickson; Webster's 3d.

PHILANDER, KORNELIUS. No dates. Dutch naturalist. (Biography source unavailable.) Philander.

Philandering (Philander or Philanderer) (Philandrus): Generic Word (male flirt). See: Charnock; Partridge.

PHILANDRUS. In Greek mythology, hero suckled by a she-goat. See: Jobes. Philandering (Philander or Philanderer).

PHILIBERT, SAINT. 608-686. French abbot. See: Holweck. Filbert (nut).

PHILIP II OF MACEDON. 382-336 B.C. Greek King and military leader. See: New Encyc. Brit., 1974, Microp. appeal from Philip drunk to Philip sober, Philip (coin), Philippei (Philippi or Philippic), Philippic(s), Philippize.

Philip (coin) (Philip II of Macedon): Numismatics. See: Charnock; Partridge.

PHILIP, "KING" (METACOMET). d. 1676. American Indian chief. See: Dict. Amer. Biog. King Philip's war.

PHILIP, SIR ROBERT WILLIAM. 1857-1939. Scottish physician. See: Dict. Nat. Biog., 5th suppl. Philip's glands.

PHILIP THE GOOD, DUKE OF BURGUNDY. 1396-1467. Founder of the Burgundian state. See: New Encyc. Brit., 1974, Microp. Duke of Burgundy fritillary? Philippus (coin)?

PHILIPP, ERNST. b. 1893. German gynecologist. See: Biog. Lex. hervorr. Aerzte. Ruge-Philipp test.

PHILIPPE, CLAUDIEN. 1866-1903. French anatomist. (Biography source unavailable.) Philippe's triangle.

Philippei (Philippi or Philippic) (Philip II of Macedon): Numismatics. See: Charnock; Stenhouse.

Philippe's triangle (Philippe, Claudien): Anatomy. See: Stedman.

Philippic(s) (Philip II of Macedon): Generic Word (bitter invective). See: Barnhart (Eng. Lit.); Hendrickson; Partridge; Webster's 3d.

Philippism (or Philippist) (Melanchthon Schwarzerdt, Philipp): Religion. See: Webster's 3d.

Philippize (Philip II of Macedon): Generic Word (speak corruptly). See: Partridge; Webster's 3d.

PHILIPPUS (coin) (Philip the Good, Duke of Burgundy?): Numismatics. See: Webster's 3d.

PHILIPS, AMBROSE "NAMBY-PAMBY." 1675?-1749. English poet. See: Dict. Nat. Biog. Namby-Pamby.

Philip's glands (Philip, Sir Robert William): Medicine. See: Dorland; Stedman.

Philips ionization gauge (Derivation undetermined): Physics. See: Internat. Dict. Phys. Elec.

Philips liquefier (Derivation undetermined): Physics. See: Thewlis.

Philips pressure gauge (Derivation undetermined): Physics. See: Thewlis.

Philipsia (Phillipsia) (Derivation undetermined): Zoology. See: Charnock; Pennak.

PHILIPSZ, OBBE. d. 1568. Dutch religious leader. See: Biog. Woordenb. der Nederl. (Aa.) Ubbonites (or Obbenite).

Philistidios (coin) (Philistus): Numismatics. See: Stenhouse.

PHILISTUS. fl. ca. 3rd c. B.C.? Syracusan queen. See: Dict. Grk. Rom. Biog. Myth. Philistidios (coin).

Phillipite (Derivation undetermined): Earth Sciences. See: Thrush.

PHILLIPS, ALBAN WILLIAM HOUSEGO. 1914- . English economist. See: Who's Who, 1974-1975. Phillips curve.

Phillips catheter (Phillips, Charles Victor Joseph?): Medicine. See: Stedman.

PHILLIPS, CHARLES VICTOR JOSEPH. 1809-1870. Belgian surgeon. See: Biog. Nat. de Belgique. Phillips catheter?

Phillips code (Phillips, Walter Polk): Telegraphy. See: Webster's 3d.

Phillips curve (Phillips, Alban William Housego): Economics. See: Barnhart (New Eng.).

Phillips entry wing construction (Phillips, Horatio Fredrick): Engineering and Industry. Cited in: World Who's Who Sci.

PHILLIPS, HENRY. fl. 1935. American mechanical engineer. (Biography source unavailable.) Phillips recess (or screw).

PHILLIPS, HORATIO FREDRICK. 1845-1912. English inventor. Cited in: Royal Soc. Cat. Sci. Pap., 1884-1900. Phillips entry wing construction.

PHILLIPS, MELBA NEWELL. 1907- . American theoretical physicist. See: Amer. Men Sci., 10th ed. Oppenheimer-Phillips process (or reaction).

Phillips recess (or screw) (Phillips, Henry): Engineering and Industry. See: Auger; Markus.

PHILLIPS, ROSS. fl. 1928. American chemist. Cited in: Chem. Abstr., vol. 22, p. 3633. Phillips-Williams test for nickel.

PHILLIPS, WALTER POLK. 1846-1920. American telegrapher and journalist. See: Dict. Amer. Biog. Phillips code.

PHILLIPS, WILLIAM. 1775-1828. English mineralogist and geologist. See: Dict. Nat. Biog. Phillipsite.

Phillips-Williams test for nickel (Phillips, Ross and Williams, John F.): Chemistry. See: Van Nostrand Chem. Dict.

Phillipsite (Phillips, William): Earth Sciences. See: Thrush; Van Nostrand Sci. Encyc.; Webster's 3d. Also known as: Offretite.

Phillipson's reflex (Derivation undetermined): Physiology. See: Stedman.

Phillyra, mother of Chiron. See: Philyra.

Phillyrea (Philyra): Botany. See: Charnock.

PHILO JUDAEUS (PHILO OF ALEXANDRIA). fl. late 1st c. B.C. Hellenistic Jewish philosopher of Alexandria. See: Dict. Christian Biog. Philonism (or Philonist).

PHILO OF TARSUS. No dates. Asia-Minor physician. See: Biog. Lex. hervorr. Aerzte. Philonium.

Philomel (or Philomela) (Philomela): Generic Word (nightingale). See: Charnock; Partridge.

PHILOMELA. Daughter of an Athenian King in Greek mythology. See: Jobes. Philomel (or Philomela).

Philonism (or Philonist) (Philo Judaeus): Philosophy. See: New Encyc. Brit., 1974, Microp.; Webster's 3d.

Philonium (Philo of Tarsus): Medicine. See: Charnock.

Philoxenian Version (Philoxenus): Religion. See: Encyc. Brit., 11th ed. under "Bible," p. 882.

PHILOXENUS. fl. 485-523. Persian-born Christian leader of the Eastern Church. See: Dict. Christian Biog. Philoxenian Version.

PHILYRA. In Greek mythology, the mother of Chiron. See: Dict. Grk. Rom. Biog. Myth. Phillyrea.

Phintias. See: Pythias.

PHIPPS, THOMAS ERWIN. 1895- . American chemist. See: Amer. Men Sci., 6th ed. Copley, Phipps and Glasser gauge.

Phipson test for cinnamic acid (Phipson, Thomas Lamb): Chemistry. See: Van Nostrand Chem. Dict.

PHIPSON, THOMAS LAMB. b. 1833. English chemist in Belgium. See: Pogg., vols. 2, 3. Phipson test for cinnamic acid.

Phleger corer (Phleger, Fred B.?): Engineering and Industry. See: Thrush.

PHLEGER, FRED B. 1909- . American oceanographer. See: World Who's Who Sci. Phleger corer?

PHOCAS, B. GERASIME. 1861-1937. French surgeon. See: Biog. Lex. hervorr. Aerzte. Tillaux-Phocas disease.

Phoebad (Apollo): Generic Word (prophetess). See: Partridge.

PHOEBE. A Greek Titan and aspect of Diana. See: Jobes. Phaebe.

Phoebus (or Phoebean) (Apollo): Mythology. See: Partridge; Webster's 3d.

Phoebus Apollo. See: Apollo.

Photinians (Photinus): Religion. See: Canney.

PHOTINUS. fl. ca. 349. Galatian heretic. See: Dict. Christian Biog. Photinians.

PHOTIUS. 820?-891. Patriarch of Constantinople. See: Encyc. Brit., 1973. Schism of Photius.

PHRAGMEN, LARS EDVARD. 1863-1937. Swedish mathematician. See: Svenska Maen Och Kvinnor. Phragmen-Lindeloef function.

Phragmen-Lindeloef function (Phragmen, Lars Edvard and Lindeloef, Ernst Leonard): Mathematics. See: James.

PHRYNE. fl. 4th c. B.C. Greek hetaera. See: Dict. Grk. Rom. Biog. Myth. Phryne.

Phryne (Phryne, the hetaera): Generic Word (prostitute). See: Hendrickson; Partridge.

PHYFE, DUNCAN. 1768-1854. Scottish-born American cabinet maker. See: Dict. Amer. Biog. Duncan Phyfe log, Duncan Phyfe (style).

PHYLLIS. In Greek mythology, a Thracian princess and personification of dawn or spring. See: Jobes. Phyllis (or Phillis).

Phyllis (or Phillis) (Phyllis, the princess): Generic Word (country maiden). See: Partridge.

PHYSICK, PHILIP SYNG. 1768-1837. American surgeon. See: Dict. Amer. Biog. Physick's operation, Physick's pouches.

Physick's operation (Physick, Philip Syng): Medicine. See: Stedman.

Physick's pouches (Physick, Philip Syng): Medicine. See: Stedman.

PIAGET, JEAN. 1896- . Swiss child psychologist. See: World Who's Who Sci. Piagetian.

Piagetian (Piaget, Jean): Psychology. See: Barnhart (New Eng.)

PIAST. Legendary Polish peasant of the 9th c. Cited in: New Encyc. Brit., 1974, Microp. Piast.

Piast (Piast, the peasant): History. See: Charnock; Encyc. Brit., 1973.

PIAZZA, PIETRO. fl. 1855. Italian chemist. Cited in: Royal Soc. Cat. Sci. Pap., 1800-1863. Tassinari-Piazza test.

Piazza's test (Derivation undetermined): Medicine. See: Dorland; Stedman.

PIC, ADRIEN. b. 1863. Algerian physician. See: Biog. Lex. hervorr. Aerzte. Bard-Pic syndrome.

PICARD, EMILE (In full: CHARLES EMILE). 1856-1941. French mathematician. See: World Who's Who Sci. Picard('s) method, Picard's theorems.

PICARD, HUGH F. K. fl. 1898. English? metallurgist. Cited in: Royal Soc. Cat. Sci. Pap., 1884-1900. Sulman and Picard processes.

Picard('s) method (Picard, Emile): Mathematics. See: Ballentyne; Internat. Dict. Ap. Math.; James.

PICARD OF FLANDERS. fl. early 15th c. Belgian religious leader. (Biography source unavailable.) Picards.

Picards (Picard of Flanders): Religion. See: Brewer.

Picard's theorems (Picard, Emile): Mathematics. See: James.

PICCARD, JEAN-FELIX. b. 1884. Swiss-born American chemist and aeronautical engineer. See: Pogg., vols. 5, 6. Piccard test reaction.

Piccard test reaction (Piccard, Jean-Felix): Chemistry. See: Van Nostrand Chem. Dict.

PICCARDI, GEROLAMO. fl. 1912. Italian physician. Cited in: Index-Cat. Libr. Surg.-Gen. Off., 3rd Ser., vol. 8, 1929. Piccardi-Lassueur-Little syndrome?

Piccardi-Lassueur-Little syndrome (Piccardi, Gerolamo?; Lassueur, Auguste?; and Little, Ernest Gordan Graham). See: Little's syndrome.

PICCHINI, LUIGI. fl. 1885. Italian physician. Cited in: Index-Cat. Libr. Surg.-Gen. Off., 1st Ser., vol. 11, 1890. Picchini's syndrome?

Picchini's syndrome (Picchini, Luigi?): Medicine. See: Stedman.

Piccini, Nicola. See: Piccinni, Niccola.

PICCININI, ANTONIO. fl. 1892-1903. Italian chemist. See: Pogg., vols. 4, 5. Piccinini reagent for potassium and sodium?

Piccinini reagent for potassium and sodium (Piccinini, Antonio?): Chemistry. See: Van Nostrand Chem. Dict.

Piccinists (Piccinni, Niccola): Music. See: Apel under "Alceste."

PICCINNI, NICCOLA. 1728-1800. Italian operatic composer. See: New Encyc. Brit., 1974. Piccinists.

PICHE, ALBERT. d. 1907. French meteorologist. See: Bull. Soc. Sci. Pau, 2d Ser., vol. 35 (1907), pp. 243-250. Piche evaporimeter.

Piche evaporimeter (Piche, Albert): Earth Sciences. See: Van Nostrand Sci. Encyc.

PICHEGRU, CHARLES (In full: JEAN-CHARLES). 1761-1804. French general. See: New Encyc. Brit., 1974, Microp. Pichegru's conspiracy.

Pichegru's conspiracy (Pichegru, Charles): History. See: Harbottle. Also known as: Cadoudal plot, George's conspiracy.

PICK, ARNOLD. 1851-1924. Czechoslovakian psychiatrist and neurologist. See: Biog. Lex. hervorr. Aerzte. Pick's atrophy (disease, hallucinations or vision), Pick's bundle.

Pick cell (Pick, Ludwig): Medicine. See: Dorland; Stedman. Also known as: Niemann-Pick cell.

PICK, FRIEDEL. 1867-1926. Czechoslovakian physician. See: Biog. Lex. hervorr. Aerzte. Pick's disease (cirrhosis or syndrome).

Pick-Herxheimer syndrome (Pick, Philipp Josef and Herxheimer, Karl). See: Herxheimer's disease.

PICK, LUDWIG. 1868-1935. German physician. See: Biog. Lex. hervorr. Aerzte. Lubarsch-Pick syndrome, Niemann-Pick disease, Pick cell, Pick's retinitis.

PICK, PHILIPP JOSEF. 1834-1910. Czechoslovakian dermatologist. See: Biog. Lex. hervorr. Aerzte. Pick-Herxheimer syndrome, Pick's liniment.

Pickard core barrel (Pickard, George Lawson?): Engineering and Industry. See: Thrush.

Pickard crank (Pickard, James): Engineering and Industry. See: Auger.

PICKARD, GEORGE LAWSON. 1913- . Welsh-born Canadian oceanographer. See: World Who's Who Sci. Pickard core barrel?

PICKARD, JAMES. fl. 1780. English engineer. Cited in: Lilley. Pickard crank.

Picken dressmaker's gauge (Picken, Mary): Fashion. See: Picken.

PICKEN, MARY. fl. 20th c. American dressmaker. (Biography source unavailable.) Picken dressmaker's gauge.

PICKERING, CHARLES. 1805-1878. American naturalist and physician. See: Dict. Amer. Biog. Pickering's hyla (or tree frog).

PICKERING, EDWARD CHARLES. 1846-1919. American astronomer. See: Pogg., vols. 3, 4, 5. Pickering-Fowler series?

Pickering-Fowler series (Pickering, Edward Charles? and Fowler, Alfred): Physics. See: Thewlis. Also known as: Pickering series.

Pickering governor (Pickering, Thomas R.): Engineering and Industry. See: Auger; Webster's 3d.

PICKERING, JOHN. 1777-1846. American scientist. See: Dict. Amer. Biog. Pickeringite.

Pickering series (Pickering, Edward Charles?). See: Pickering-Fowler series.

PICKERING, THOMAS R. fl. 1862. American engineer. (Biography source unavailable.) Pickering governor.

PICKERING, TIMOTHY. 1745-1829. American statesman. See: Dict. Amer. Biog. Pickeronian (or Pickeroon).

Pickeringite (Pickering, John): Earth Sciences. See: Webster's 3d.

Pickering's hyla (or tree frog) (Pickering, Charles): Zoology. See: Mathews, M. M.; Webster's 3d.

Pickeronian (or Pickeroon) (Pickering, Timothy): Politics. See: Mathews, M.M.

Pickford projective pictures test (Pickford, R. W.): Psychology. See: Wolman.

PICKFORD, R. W. 1903- . Scottish psychologist. See: Internat. Direct. Psych., 1966. Pickford projective pictures test.

Pickle (Beukel, William): Food and Drink. See: Charnock, Hendrickson.

PICKRELL, KENNETH LE ROY. 1910- . American physician. See: Amer. Men and Women Sci., 12th ed. Pickerell spray (or method).

Pickrell spray (or method) (Pickrell, Kenneth Le Roy): Medicine. See: Dorland.

Pick's atrophy (disease, hallucinations or vision) (Pick, Arnold): Medicine. See: Dorland; Hinsie; Jablonski; Webster's 3d.

Pick's bundle (Pick, Arnold): Anatomy. See: Stedman.

Pick's disease (Pick, Philipp Josef). See: Herxheimer's disease.

Pick's disease (cirrhosis or syndrome) (Pick, Friedel): Medicine. See: Dorland; Jablonski; Stedman; Webster's 3d. Also known as: Hutinel-Pick syndrome.

Pick's liniment (Pick, Philipp Josef): Medicine. See: Dorland.

Pick's retinitis (Pick, Ludwig): Medicine. See: Jablonski.

Pickwick (Pickwick, Samuel): Generic Word (cigar). See: Partridge.

PICKWICK, SAMUEL. Character in the Charles Dickens' novel, "Pickwick Papers," (1836-1837). See: Harvey. Pickwick, Pickwickian, Pickwickian sense.

Pickwickian (Pickwick, Samuel): Generic Word (generosity of character). See: Partridge; Webster's 3d.

Pickwickian sense (Pickwick, Samuel): Generic Word (distorted meaning). See: Barnhart (Eng. Lit.); Partridge; Phyfe.

PICOT, GEORGES. fl. 1916. French diplomat. (Biography source unavailable.) Sykes-Picot agreement.

picowatt (Watt, James): Physics. See: Markus.

Pic's syndrome (Pic, Adrien). See: Bard-Pic syndrome.

PICTET, AME. 1857-1937. Swiss chemist. See: Pogg., vols. 3-6, 7a. Pictet-Gams isoquinoline synthesis, Pictet-Hubert reaction, Pictet-Spengler isoquinoline synthesis.

Pictet crystals (Pictet, Raoul): Chemistry. See: Hackh.

Pictet-Gams isoquinoline synthesis (Pictet, Ame and Gams, Alfons): Chemistry. See: Van Nostrand Chem. Dict.

Pictet-Hubert reaction (Pictet, Ame and Hubert, Andre): Chemistry. See: Van Nostrand Chem. Dict.

Pictet method (Pictet, Raoul). See: Cailletet-Pictet method.

PICTET, RAOUL. 1846-1929. Swiss physicist. See: World Who's Who Sci. Cailletet-Pictet method, Pictet crystals.

Pictet-Spengler isoquinoline synthesis (Pictet, Ame and Spengler, Theodore): Chemistry. See: Van Nostrand Chem. Dict.

Piderit drawings (Piderit, Th.): Psychology. See: English; Wolman.

PIDERIT, TH. fl. 1859-1915. German psychologist. Cited in: Cum. Author Index to Psych. Index, 1894-1935 and Psych. Abstr., 1927-1958. Piderit drawings.

PIDGEON, LLOYD MONTGOMERY. 1903- . Canadian chemist. See: Amer. Men and Women Sci., 12th ed. Pidgeon process.

Pidgeon process (Pidgeon, Lloyd Montgomery): Chemistry. See: Van Nostrand Chem. Dict.

Pielstick engine (Pielstick, Gustav E.): Engineering and Industry. See: Auger.

PIELSTICK, GUSTAV E. d. 1961. German? engineer. (Biography source unavailable.) Pielstick engine.

PIER, MATTHIAS. b. 1882. German coal and oil technologist. See: Pogg., vol. 7a. Pier process.

Pier process (Pier, Matthias): Chemistry. See: Van Nostrand Chem. Dict.

Pierce electron gun (Pierce, John Robinson): Electronics. Cited in: New Encyc. Brit., 1974, Microp.

PIERCE, FRANKLIN. 1804-1869. American president. See: Dict. Amer. Biog. Pierce (political faction).

PIERCE, GEORGE WASHINGTON. 1872-1956. American electrical engineer. See: World Who's Who Sci. Miller-Pierce oscillator, Pierce oscillator.

PIERCE, JERRY ALBERT. b. 1886. American pharmaceutical chemist. See: Amer. Men Sci., 7th ed. Pierce reagent.

PIERCE, JOHN ROBINSON. 1910- . American communications engineer. See: World Who's Who Sci. Pierce electron gun.

PIERCE, NEWTON BARRIS. 1856-1917. American plant pathologist. See: Who Was Who Amer., vol. 1. Pierce's disease.

PIERCE, OSCAR. fl. 20th c. American farmer. (Biography source unavailable.) Oscar (trophy).

Pierce oscillator (Pierce, George Washington?): Electronics. See: Hughes; Van Nostrand Sci. Encyc.

Pierce (political faction) (Pierce, Franklin): Politics. See: Mathews, M. M.

Pierce reagent (Pierce, Jerry Albert): Chemistry. See: Van Nostrand Chem. Dict.

PIERCE, S. E. fl. 1914. English physicist. Cited in: Chem. Abstr., vol. 9, p. 21. Bragg-Pierce law.

Pierce's disease (Pierce, Newton Barris): Botany. See: Webster's 3d.; Winburne.

PIERCY, ESTHER JUNE. 1905-   . American librarian. See: Who's Who Libr. Service, 1955. Esther J. Piercy Award.

PIERINI, LUIGI E. fl. 1936. Italian dermatologist. (Biography source unavailable.) Pasini-Pierini syndrome.

Pierre Marie. See: Marie, Pierre.

Pierre Marie-Bamberger syndrome (Marie, Pierre and Bamberger, Eugen). See: Marie-Bamberger syndrome.

Pierre-Marie's anarthria (Marie, Pierre). See: Marie's anarthria.

Pierre Marie's disease (Marie, Pierre). See: Bekhterev-Struempell-Marie syndrome.

Pierre Marie's syndrome (Marie, Pierre). See: Marie's syndrome (or ataxia) and Marie-Bamberger syndrome.

Pierre Mauriac. See: Mauriac, Pierre.

Pierre Mauriac's syndrome (Mauriac, Pierre). See: Mauriac's syndrome.

Pierre Morean's ronde (script) (Moreau, Pierre): Printing. See: Lockwood, p. 538.

Pierre Robin. See: Robin, Pierre.

Pierre Robin syndrome (Robin, Pierre): Medicine. See: Hinsie; Jablonski; Stedman. Also known as: Robin triad, Robin's syndrome.

PIERRETTE. Female Pierot and stock character in old French pantomime. (Biography source unavailable.) Pierrette costume.

Pierrette costume (Pierrette): Fashion. See: Picken.

PIERROT. Stock comic character in old French pantomime. See: Harvey and Heseltine. Pierrot, Pierrot (blouse).

Pierrot (Pierrot, the character): Generic Word (buffoon). See: Webster's 3d.

Pierrot (blouse) (Pierrot, the character): Fashion. See: Picken.

PIERROU. fl. 20th c. French physician. (Biography source unavailable.) Friess-Pierrou syndrome.

PIERSOL, GEORGE ARTHUR. 1856-1924. American anatomist. See: Who Was Who Amer., vol. 1. Piersol's point.

Piersol's point (Piersol, George Arthur): Anatomy. See: Donath.

PIETRANTONI, LUIGI. fl. 1948. Italian otolaryngologist. Cited in: Index-Cat. Libr. Surg. Gen. Off., 5th Ser., vol. 1, 1959. Pietrantoni's syndrome.

Pietrantoni's syndrome (Pietrantoni, Luigi): Medicine. See: Jablonski.

PIETSCH, ERICH. 1902-   . German chemist. See: Pogg., vols. 6, 7a. Pietsch-Roman reagent.

Pietsch-Roman reagent (Pietsch, Erich and Roman, Wadim): Chemistry. See: Van Nostrand Chem. Dict.

Piette coke oven (Piette, Olivier): Engineering and Industry. See: Van Nostrand Chem. Dict.

PIETTE, OLIVIER. fl. 1912-1931. Canadian? engineer. Cited in: Chem. Abstr., Decenn. Indexes, 1907-1916, 1917-1926, 1927-1936. Piette coke oven.

Pigem's question (Derivation undetermined): Psychology. See: Hinsie.

Pignet('s) formula (or index) (Pignet, Maurice-Charles-Joseph): Medicine. See: Dorland; Webster's 3d.

PIGNET, MAURICE-CHARLES-JOSEPH. b. 1871. French physician. See: Biog. Lex. hervorr. Aerzte. Pignet('s) formula (or index).

PIGOT, GEORGE (BARON PIGOT). 1719-1777. English governor of Madras. See: Dict. Nat. Biog. Pigott diamond.

Pigott diamond (Pigot, George): Applied Arts. See: Phyfe.

Pigott forgeries (Pigott, Richard): History. See: Brewer; Montgomery.

Pigott incident (Pigott, Sir Thomas Digby): Politics. See: Montgomery.

PIGOTT, RICHARD. 1828?-1889. Irish journalist and forger. See: Dict. Nat. Biog. Pigott forgeries.

PIGOTT, SIR THOMAS DIGBY. 1840-1927. English administrator. See: Who Was Who, 1916-1928. Pigott incident.

PIGOU, ARTHUR CECIL. 1877-1959. English economist. See: Internat. Encyc. Soc. Sci. Pigou-effect theory.

Pigou-effect theory (Pigou, Arthur Cecil): Economics. See: Greenwald.

PIKE, NICHOLAS. 1818-1905. American naturalist. Cited in: Royal Soc. Cat. Sci. Pap., 1884-1900. Pike's tern.

Pike process (Pike, Robert D.): Engineering and Industry. See: Thrush.

PIKE, ROBERT D. fl. 1954. American metallurgical engineer. Cited in: Chem. Abstr., vol. 48, p. 1229 f. Pike process.

PIKE, ZEBULON MONTGOMERY. 1779-1813. American general and explorer. See: Dict. Amer. Biog. Pikes (regiment).

Pikes (regiment) (Pike, Zebulon Montgomery): History. See: Mathews, M. M.

Pike's tern (Pike, Nicholas): Zoology. See: Mathews, M. M.

PILATE, PONTIUS. fl. early 1st c. Roman procurator of Judea. See: New Encyc. Brit., 1974, Microp. Pilate voice, Pontius Pilate's bodyguard, Puncheon.

Pilate voice (Pilate, Pontius): Generic Word (ranting voice). See: Brewer.

Pilcher bag (Pilcher, Lewis Stephen): Medicine. See: Dorland.

PILCHER, LEWIS STEPHEN. 1845-1934. American surgeon. See: Dict. Amer. Biog., 1st suppl. Pilcher bag.

Pilger tube-reducing process (Derivation undetermined): Engineering and Industry. See: Thrush.

PILHASHY, BENJAMIN M. fl. 1899-1910. American chemist. Cited in: Royal Soc. Cat. Sci. Pap., 1884-1900. Pilhashy test for formaldehyde.

Pilhashy test for formaldehyde (Pilhashy, Benjamin M.): Chemistry. See: Van Nostrand Chem. Dict.

PILKINGTON, ALFRED C. fl. 1910. English glass technologist. Cited in: Chem. Abstr., Decenn. Index, 1907-1916. Pilkington twin process.

Pilkington twin process (Pilkington, W. W. and Pilkington, Alfred C.): Engineering and Industry. See: Thrush.

PILKINGTON, W. W. fl. 1915. English glass technologist. Cited in: Chem. Abstr., Decenn. Indexes, 1907-1916, 1917-1926, 1927-1936. Pilkington twin process.

PILLAT, ARNOLD. b. 1891. Austrian ophthalmologist. See: Who's Who Sci. Europe, 1972. Pillat's dystrophy.

Pillat's dystrophy (Pillat, Arnold): Medicine. See: Jablonski.

PILLOID, CHARLES J. fl. 1920. American? engineer. (Biography source unavailable.) Pilloid sleeve valve.

Pilloid sleeve valve (Pilloid, Charles J.): Engineering and Industry. See: Auger.

Piloty alloxazine synthesis (Piloty, Oskar): Chemistry. See: Van Nostrand Chem. Dict.

PILOTY, OSKAR. 1866-1915. German chemist. See: Pogg., vols. 4, 5. Piloty alloxazine synthesis, Piloty-Robinson pyrrole synthesis.

Piloty-Robinson pyrrole synthesis (Piloty, Oskar; Robinson Gertrud Maud; and Robinson, Robert): Chemistry. See: Van Nostrand Chem. Dict.

PILTZ, JAN. 1871-1930. Austrian neurologist. See: Biog. Lex. hervorr. Aerzte. Piltz reflex, Westphal-Piltz phenomenon, Westphal-Piltz reflex.

Piltz reflex (Piltz, Jan): Physiology. See: Dorland; Stedman.

Piltz sign (Piltz, Jan). See: Westphal-Piltz phenomenon.

Piltz–Westphal phenomenon (Piltz, Jan and Westphal, Alexander Karl Otto). See: Westphal-Piltz phenomenon.

Pilz furnace (Pilz, Hans?): Engineering and Industry. See: Thrush.

PILZ, HANS. fl. 1939. German metallurgical engineer. Cited in: Chem. Abstr., Decenn. Index, 1937-1946. Pilz furnace?

PIMPERNEL. Character in Baroness Emmuska Orczy's novel, "The Scarlet Pimpernel," (1905). See: Kunitz under "Orczy, Emmuska, Baroness, pp. 1054-1055. Pimpernel.

Pimpernel (Pimpernel, the character): Generic Word (chivalrous hero). See: Webster's 3d.

PINARD, ADOLPHE. 1844-1934. French obstetrician. See: Biog. Lex. hervorr. Aerzte. Pinard's maneuver, Pinard's sign.

Pinard's maneuver (Pinard, Adolphe): Medicine. See: Stedman.

Pinard's sign (Pinard, Adolphe): Medicine. See: Dorland; Stedman.

Pinchbeck (1) (Pinchbeck, Christopher): Generic Word (counterfeit). See: Hendrickson; Stenhouse; Webster's 3d.

Pinchbeck (2) (Pinchbeck, Christopher): Applied Arts. See: Charnock; Hendrickson; Webster's 3d.

PINCHBECK, CHRISTOPHER. 1670?-1732. English watchmaker and toymaker. See: Dict. Sci. Biog. Pinchbeck (1), Pinchbeck (2).

PINCHOT, GIFFORD. 1865-1946. American political leader. See: New Encyc. Brit., 1974, Microp. Ballinger-Pinchot controversy.

PINCKNEY, CHARLES. 1757-1824. American statesman. See: Dict. Amer. Biog. Pinckney plan.

PINCKNEY, CHARLES COTESWORTH. 1746-1825. American statesman. See: Dict. Amer. Biog. Pinckneya.

Pinckney plan (Pinckney, Charles): History. See: Jameson.

PINCKNEY, THOMAS. 1750-1828. American statesman. See: Dict. Amer. Biog. Pinckney's Treaty.

Pinckneya (Pinckney, Charles Cotesworth): Botany. See: Webster's 3d.

Pinckney's Treaty (Pinckney, Thomas): History. See: Morris; Smith.

PINDAR. 522?-443 B.C. Greek lyric poet. See: Encyc. Brit., 1911. Pindaric (verse or ode), Pindarics, Pindarism.

Pindaric (verse or ode) (Pindar): Literature. See: Brewer; Partridge; Preminger; Scott; Webster's 3d.

Pindarics (Pindar): Literature. See: Partridge; Webster's 3d.

Pindarism (Pindar): Literature. See: Barnhart (Eng. Lit.).

PINEL, PHILIPPE. 1745-1826. French psychiatrist. See: Internat. Encyc. Soc. Sci. Pinel's system.

Pinel's system (Pinel, Philippe): Medicine. See: Stedman; Wolman.

PINERUA Y ALVAREZ, EUGENIO. fl. 1897-1911. Spanish chemist. See: Pogg., vol. 5; Cited in: Royal Soc. Cat. Sci. Pap., 1884-1900. Alvarez cholic acid reagent, Alvarez nitrate reagent, Alvarez reaction for aconitine, Alvarez reagent for cobalt, nickel, and zinc, Alvarez reagent for nickel, Alvarez reagent for organic acids, Alvarez reagent for organic compounds, Alvarez reagent for osmic acid, Alvarez reagent for potassium, Alvarez test for pyruvic acid.

PINES, DAVID. 1924- . American physicist. See: Amer. Men and Women Sci., 12th ed. Bohm and Pines method.

Pinkerton (Pinkerton, Allan): Generic Word (private detective). See: Hendrickson; Mathews, M. M.; Partridge.

PINKERTON, ALLAN. 1819-1884. Scottish-born American detective. See: Dict. Amer. Biog. Pinkerton, Pinkertonian (or Pinkertonianism).

Pinkertonian (or Pinkertonianism) (Pinkerton, Allan): History. See: Mathews, M. M.

PINKHOF, J. fl. 1919. Dutch chemist. Cited in: Chem. Abstr., Decenn. Index, 1917-1926. Pinkhof titration.

Pinkhof titration (Pinkhof, J.): Chemistry. See: Ballentyne.

PINKNEY, WILLIAM. 1764-1822. American legislator and diplomat. See: Biog. Direct. Amer. Congress. Monroe-Pinkney Treaty.

Pinkus' disease (Pinkus, Felix): Medicine. See: Jablonski; Stedman.

Pinkus' disease (Pinkus, Hermann Karl Benno): Medicine. See: Jablonski.

Pinkus' epithelioma (Pinkus, Hermann Karl Benno): Medicine. See: Jablonski.

PINKUS, FELIX. b. 1868. German dermatologist. See: Biog. Lex. hervorr. Aerzte. Pinkus' disease.

PINKUS, HERMANN KARL BENNO. 1905- . German-born American dermatologist. See: Amer. Men and Women Sci., 12th ed. Pinkus' disease, Pinkus' epithelioma, Pinkus' tumor.

Pinkus' tumor (Pinkus, Hermann Karl Benno): Medicine. See: Jablonski.

PINNER, ADOLF. 1842-1909. German chemist. See: Pogg., vols. 3, 4, 5. Pinner amidine synthesis, Pinner method.

Pinner amidine synthesis (Pinner, Adolf): Chemistry. See: Van Nostrand Chem. Dict.

Pinner method (Pinner, Adolf): Chemistry. See: Van Nostrand Chem. Dict.

PINNO. fl. 19th c. German mining official. (Biography source unavailable.) Pinnoite.

Pinnoite (Pinno): Earth Sciences. See: Webster's 3d.

PINOL AGUADE, JOAQUIN. 1917- . Spanish dermatologist and venereologist. See: Who's Who Sci. Europe, 1972. Vilanova-Pinol Aguade syndrome.

PINS, EMIL. 1845-1913. Austrian physician. See: Biog. Lex. hervorr. Aerzte. Pins' sign, Pins' syndrome.

Pins' sign (Pins, Emil). See: Ewart's sign.

Pins' syndrome (Pins, Emil): Medicine. See: Dorland; Stedman.

Pintner-Paterson scale of performance tests (Pintner, Rudolf and Paterson, Donald Gildersleeve): Psychology. See: Wolman.

PINTNER, RUDOLF. 1884-1942. English-born American psychologist. See: World Who's Who Sci. Pintner-Paterson scale of performance tests.

Pintsch gas (Pintsch, Julius): Engineering and Industry. See: Hackh.

PINTSCH, JULIUS. fl. 19th c. German manufacturer. Cited in: Encyc. Brit., 1973, vol. 14, p. 3a. Pintsch gas.

Piobert effect (or lines) (Piobert, Guillaume?): Physics. See: Hackh; Thrush. Also known as: Hartmann lines, Lueder('s) bands (or line(s)).

PIOBERT, GUILLAUME. 1793-1871. French physicist. See: Pogg., vol. 2. Piobert effect (or lines)?

PIORKOWSKI, MAX. b. 1859. German bacteriologist. Cited in: Chem. Abstr., Decenn. Index, 1907-1916. Piorkowski's medium, Piorkowski's stain (or method) for metachromatic granules, Piorkowski's test.

Piorkowski's medium (Piorkowski, Max): Medicine. See: Dorland; Cited in: Kelly.

Piorkowski's stain (or method) for metachromatic granules (Piorkowski, Max): Medicine. See: Dorland; Stedman.

Piorkowski's test (Piorkowski, Max): Medicine. Cited in: Kelly.

PIOTROWSKI, ALEKSANDR. b. 1878. German neurologist. See: Now. psychiatr. vol. 3/4 (1933), pp. 1-8. Piotrowski's reflex (or sign).

Piotrowski system (Piotrowski, Zygmunt A.): Psychology. See: Kelly; Wolman.

PIOTROWSKI, ZYGMUNT A. fl. 1937. American psychiatrist. Cited in: Kelly. Piotrowski system.

Piotrowski's reflex (or sign) (Piotrowski, Aleksandr): Physiology. See: Dorland; Stedman.

PIPER, HANS EDMUND. 1877-1915. German physiologist. See: Biog. Lex. hervorr. Aerzte. Piper's law.

Piper's forceps (Derivation undetermined): Medicine. See: Stedman.

Piper's law (Piper, Hans Edmund): Psychology. See: Chaplin; Kelly.

PIPPARD, ALFRED BRIAN. 1920- . English physicist. See: World Who's Who Sci. Pippard coherence length.

Pippard coherence length (Pippard, Alfred Brian): Physics. See: Ballentyne.

PIQUER, ANDRES. 1711-1772. Spanish physician and botanist. See: Nouv. Biog. Univ. Piqueria.

Piqueria (Piquer, Andres): Botany. See: Taylor, N.; Webster's 3d.

Pirakoff, Nikolai I. See: Pirogoff, Nikolai.

Pirandellian (Pirandello, Luigi): Literature. See: Webster's 3d.

PIRANDELLO, LUIGI. 1867-1936. Italian novelist and dramatist. See: New Encyc. Brit., 1974, Microp. Pirandellian.

Pirani gauge (or pressure gauge) (Pirani, Marcello Stefano): Physics. See: Internat. Dict. Phys. Elec.; Thewlis; Webster's 3d.

PIRANI, MARCELLO STEFANO. b. 1880. German physicist. See: Pogg., vols. 5, 6, 7a. Pirani gauge (or pressure gauge).

PIRIA, RAFFAELE. 1815-1865. Italian chemist. Cited in: Royal Soc. Cat. Sci. Pap., 1800-1863. Piria reaction, Piria's test.

Piria reaction (Piria, Raffaele): Chemistry. See: Krauch and Kunz; Van Nostrand Chem. Dict.

Piria's test (Piria, Raffaele): Chemistry. See: Stedman.

PIRIE, GEORGE A. fl. 20th c. Scottish radiologist. (Biography source unavailable.) Pirie's bone.

PIRIE, GEORGE R. fl. 1919. English pathologist. Cited in: Chem. Abstr., vol. 13 p. 3229. Pirie's syndrome.

Pirie's bone (Pirie, George A.): Anatomy. See: Stedman.

Pirie's syndrome (Pirie, George R.). See: Debre-Fibiger syndrome.

Piringer, Alexandra. See: Piringer-Kuchinka, Alexandra.

PIRINGER-KUCHINKA, ALEXANDRA. 1912- . Austrian pathologist. See: Kuerschner's Deut. Gel. Kal., vol. 9, 1961. Piringer-Kuchinka's syndrome.

Piringer-Kuchinka's syndrome (Piringer-Kuchinka, Alexandra): Medicine. See: Jablonski. Also known as: Piringer's lymphadenitis.

Piringer's lymphadenitis (Piringer-Kuchinka, Alexandra). See: Piringer-Kuchinka syndrome.

PIROGOFF, NIKOLAI IVANOVICH. 1810-1881. Russian surgeon. See: World Who's Who Sci. Pirogoff's amputation (or operation), Pirogoff's angle, Pirogoff's triangle.

Pirogoff's amputation (or operation) (Pirogoff, Nikolai Ivanovich): Medicine. See: Dorland; Stedman.

Pirogoff's angle (Pirogoff, Nikolai Ivanovich): Anatomy. See: Dorland; Stedman.

Pirogoff's triangle (Pirogoff, Nikolai Ivanovich): Anatomy. See: Stedman.

PIRQUET, CLEMENS FREIHERR VON. 1874-1929. Austrian pediatrician. See: Biog. Lex. hervorr. Aerzte. Pirquet('s) test (or reaction).

Pirquet('s) test (or reaction) (Pirquet, Clemens Freiherr von): Medicine. See: Dorland; Stedman; Webster's 3d.

PIRSSON, LOUIS VALENTINE. 1860-1919. American mineralogist and geologist. See: Encyc. Brit., 1973. Pirssonite.

Pirssonite (Pirsson, Louis Valentine): Earth Sciences. See: New Encyc. Brit., 1974, Microp.; Webster's 3d.

PISANI, FELIX. d. 1920. French chemist and mineralogist. Cited in: Royal Soc. Cat. Sci. Pap., 1884-1900. Pisanite.

Pisanite (Pisani, Felix): Earth Sciences. See: Webster's 3d.

Pisano, Leonardo. See: Fibonacci, Leonardo.

PISCHINGER. fl. 19th c.? Austrian manufacturer. (Biography source unavailable.) Pischinger torte.

Pischinger torte (Pischinger): Food and Drink. See: De Sola.

Pisistratean (Pisistratus): History. See: Webster's 3d.

PISISTRATUS. d. 527 B.C. Tyrant of Athens. See: Encyc. Brit., 1973. Pisistratean.

PISO, LUCIUS CALPURNIUS FRUGI. fl. 149 B.C. Roman tribune. See: Dict. Grk. Rom. Biog. Myth. Piso's justice?

PISO, WILLEM. 1611-1678. Dutch physician, traveler and botanist. See: World Who's Who Sci. Pisonia.

Pisonia (Piso, Willem): Botany. See: Webster's 3d.

Piso's justice (Piso, Lucius Calpurnius Frugi?): Generic Word (verbally right, but morally wrong justice). See: Brewer.

PITCAIRN, WILLIAM. 1711-1791. English physician and botanist. See: Dict. Nat. Biog. Pitcairnia.

Pitcairnia (Pitcairn, William): Botany. See: Webster's 3d.

PITFIELD, ROBERT LUCAS. 1870-1942. American physician. See: Who Was Who Amer., vol. 5. Smith-Pitfield stain.

Pitfield stain (Pitfield, Robert Lucas). See: Smith-Pitfield stain.

PITKIN, GEORGE PHILO. 1885-1943. American surgeon. Cited in: Index-Cat. Libr. Surg.-Gen. Off., 5th Ser., vol. 1, 1959. Pitkin's solution.

Pitkin's solution (Pitkin, George Philo): Medicine. See: Dorland.

PITMAN, SIR ISAAC. 1813-1897. English phonographer. See: Dict. Nat. Biog., 1st suppl. Pitman (shorthand system).

Pitman (shorthand system) (Pitman, Sir Isaac): Dictation. See: Hendrickson; New Encyc. Brit., 1974, Microp.

PITOT, HENRI. 1695-1771. French physicist and engineer. See: World Who's Who Sci. bathypitotmeter, Pitot tube.

Pitot tube (Pitot, Henri): Engineering and Industry. See: Auger; Thewlis; Van Nostrand Sci. Encyc.

PITRES, A. fl. 1895. French neurologist. Cited in: Cum. Auth. Index Psych. Index, 1894-1935 and Psych. Abstr., 1927-1958. Pitres' rule.

Pitres' area (Pitres, Jean-Albert): Anatomy. See: Stedman.

PITRES, JEAN-ALBERT. 1848-1927. French physician. See: Biog. Lex. hervorr. Aerzte. Pitres' area, Pitres' section, Pitres' sign.

Pitres' rule (Pitres, A.): Psychology. See: Hinsie.

Pitres' section (Pitres, Jean-Albert): Anatomy. See: Dorland; Stedman.

Pitres' sign (Pitres, Jean-Albert): Medicine. See: Dorland; Stedman.

Pitt diamond (Pitt, Thomas "Diamond Pitt"): Applied Arts. See: Phyfe.

Pitt press (Pitt, William): Printing. See: Lockwood.

PITT, THOMAS "DIAMOND PITT." 1653-1726. English merchant. See: Dict. Nat. Biog. Pitt diamond.

PITT, WILLIAM. 1759-1806. English statesman. See: Dict. Nat. Biog. Pitt press, Pitt's India Bill, Pitt's pictures.

PITTARELLI, EMILIO. fl. 1928-1936. Italian chemist. Cited in: Chem. Abstr., Decenn. Indexes, 1927-1936, 1937-1946. Pittarelli reaction for creatinine, Pittarelli test for ascorbic acid (vitamin C), Pittarelli test for glucose.

PITTARELLI, MARIO. fl. 1936. Italian chemist. Cited in: Chem. Abstr., vol. 31, p. 7489. Pittarelli test for ascorbic acid (vitamin C).

Pittarelli reaction for creatinine (Pittarelli, Emilio): Medicine. See: Kelly.

Pittarelli test for ascorbic acid (vitamin C) (Pittarelli, Emilio and Pittarelli, Mario): Chemistry. See: Van Nostrand Chem. Dict.

Pittarelli test for glucose (Pittarelli, Emilio): Medicine. See: Kelly.

Pittler pump (Pittler, W. von): Engineering and Industry. See: Auger.

PITTLER, W. VON. fl. 1900. German engineer. (Biography source unavailable.) Pittler pump.

Pittman Act (Pittman, Key): Politics. See: Jameson under "Coinage Laws."

PITTMAN, KEY. 1872-1940. American legislator. See: Biog. Direct. Amer. Congress. Pittman Act, Pittman Resolution, Pittman-Robertson Act.

Pittman Resolution (Pittman, Key): Politics. See: Morris.

Pittman-Robertson Act (Pittman, Key and Robertson, A. Willis): Politics. See: Winburne.

Pitt's India Bill (Pitt, William): History. See: Harbottle.

Pitt's pictures (Pitt, William): History. See: Brewer.

Piulachs-Hederich syndrome (Piulachs Oliva, Pedro and Hederich, H.): Medicine. See: Jablonski.

PIULACHS OLIVA, PEDRO. fl. 1945-1947. Spanish physician. Cited in: Index-Cat. Libr. Surg.-Gen. Off., 5th Ser., vol. 1, 1959. Piulachs-Hederich syndrome.

PIUS IV (Real name: GIOVANNI ANGELO DE MEDICI). 1499-1565. Italian pope. See: Encyc. Brit., 1911. Order of Pius.

IUS X (Real name: GIUSEPPE MELCHIORRE SARTO). 1835-1914. See: ncyc. Brit., 1911. motu proprio of Pius X.

LACIDO DA COSTA, ANTONIO. 1848-1916. Portuguese oculist. See: World Who's Who Sci. Placido's disk (disc).

Placido's disk (disc) (Placido da Costa, Antonio): Medicine. See: Dorland; Drever; Stedman.

Placzek function (Placzek, Georg): Physics. See: Internat. Dict. Ap. Math.

LACZEK, GEORG. 1905-1955. German nuclear physicist. See: Pogg., ol. 6. Placzek function.

Plaffeiite (Derivation undetermined): Earth Sciences. See: Thrush.

PLANCHE. fl. ca. 1908. French worker. Cited in: Hintze, suppl. 1, . 469. Plancheite.

Plancheite (Planche): Earth Sciences. See: Webster's 3d.

Planck (Planck, Max Karl Ernst Ludwig): Physics. See: Dresner.

Planck('s) constant (Planck, Max Karl Ernst Ludwig): Physics. See: Ballentyne; Huschke; Internat. Dict. Phys. Elec.; Thewlis; Van Nostrand Sci. Encyc.

Planck distribution law (Planck, Max Karl Ernst Ludwig). See: Planck radiation ormula.

Planck equation (Planck, Max Karl Ernst Ludwig). See: Planck radiation ormula.

Planck formulation of the second law of thermodynamics (Planck, Max Karl rnst Ludwig): Physics. See: Internat. Dict. Ap. Math.

Planck function (Planck, Max Karl Ernst Ludwig): Physics. See: Internat. Dict. Ap. Math.

Planck-Kelvin formulation of the second law of thermodynamics (Planck, Max Karl Ernst Ludwig and Kelvin, William Thomson, 1st Baron): Physics. See: nternat. Dict. Ap. Math.

Planck('s) law (Planck, Max Karl Ernst Ludwig): Physics. See: Hughes; Huschke; Internat. Dict. Phys. Elec.

PLANCK, MAX KARL ERNST LUDWIG. 1858-1947. German physicist. See: New Encyc. Brit., 1974. Boltzmann-Planck equation, Fokker-Planck equation, Planck, Planck('s) constant, Planck formulation of the second law of thermo-dynamics, Planck function, Planck-Kelvin formulation of the second law of thermodynamics, Planck('s) law, Planck radiation formula, Planckian color, Planckian locus, Planckian radiation, Planck's quantum theory.

Planck radiation formula (Planck, Max Karl Ernst Ludwig): Physics. See: Thewlis; Van Nostrand Sci. Encyc. Also known as: Planck distribution law, Planck equation.

Planckian color (Planck, Max Karl Ernst Ludwig): Physics. See: Van Nostrand Sci. Encyc.

Planckian locus (Planck, Max Karl Ernst Ludwig): Physics. See: Markus; Van Nostrand Sci. Encyc.

Planckian radiation (Planck, Max Karl Ernst Ludwig): Physics. See: Van Nostrand Sci. Encyc.; Webster's 3d.

Planck's quantum theory (Planck, Max Karl Ernst Ludwig): Physics. See: Ballentyne.

PLANER, JOHANN JACOB. 1743-1789. German botanist. See: Michaud. Planer tree.

Planer tree (Planer, Johann Jacob): Botany. See: Mathews, M. M.

Plantagenet (Geoffrey IV, Plantagenet): History. See: Webster's 3d.

Plantagenet, Richard. See: Richard (Duke of York).

Plante battery (or cell) (Plante, Gaston): Electronics. See: Markus; Webster's 3d.

PLANTE, GASTON. 1834-1889. French physician and physicist. See: World Who's Who Sci. Gastornis, Plante battery (or cell).

PLANTIN, CHRISTOPHE. 1520?-1589. French-born printer, bookbinder and publisher in Antwerp. See: Encyc. Brit., 1911. Plantin press, Plantin (type face).

Plantin press (Plantin, Christophe): Printing. See: Lockwood.

Plantin (type face) (Plantin, Christophe): Printing. See: Harrod.

Planudean version (Planudes, Maximus): Literature. Cited in: Preminger under "Pattern Poetry."

PLANUDES, MAXIMUS. 1260?-1330? Byzantine monk and scholar. See: Encyc. Brit., 1973. Planudean version.

PLATEAU, JOSEPH ANTOINE FERDINAND. 1801-1883. Belgian physicist. See: World Who's Who Sci. Plateau problem, Talbot-Plateau disc, Talbot-Plateau law.

Plateau problem (Plateau, Joseph Antoine Ferdinand): Mathematics. See: James.

PLATO. 427?-347 B.C. Greek philosopher. See: Internat. Encyc. Soc. Sci. Plato unit? Platonia, Platonic, Platonic Academy, Platonic bodies (or solids), Platonic love, Platonic year (or cycle), Platonism (or Platonist), Platon-ization.

Plato unit (Plato?): Chemistry. See: Hackh.

Platonia (Plato): Botany. See: Webster's 3d.

Platonic (Plato): Generic Word (theoretical). See: Partridge; Webster's 3d.

Platonic Academy (Plato): Philosophy. See: New Encyc. Brit., 1974, Microp.

Platonic bodies (or solids) (Plato): Mathematics. See: Brewer; Webster's 3d.

Platonic idealism (Plato). See: Platonism (or Platonist).

Platonic love (Plato): Generic Word (non-sexual love). See: Barnet; Brewer; Harvey; Webster's 3d.

Platonic year (or cycle) (Plato): Astronomy. See: Brewer; Harvey; Phyfe.

Platonism (or Platonist) (Plato): Philosophy. See: Canney; Good; Mathews, S. Also known as: Platonic idealism.

Platonization (Plato): Psychology. See: English; Hinsie.

Platt Amendment (Platt, Orville Hitchcock): Politics. See: Jameson; Morris; Smith.

PLATT, JOHN EDWARD. fl. 1899. English surgeon. Cited in: Index-Cat. Libr. Surg.-Gen. Off., 2d Ser., vol. 13, 1908. Putti-Platt operation (or procedure)?

PLATT, ORVILLE HITCHCOCK. 1827-1905. American legislator. See: Dict. Amer. Biog. Platt Amendment.

PLATTNER, KARL FRIEDRICH. 1800-1858. German metallurgist. See: Encyc. Brit., 1911. Plattner('s) process, Plattnerite.

PLATTNER, PLACIDUS ANDREAS. 1904- . Swiss organic chemist. See: Pogg., vol. 7a. Pfau-Plattner azulene synthesis.

Plattner('s) process (Plattner, Karl Friedrich): Chemistry. See: Hackh; Thrush; Webster's 3d.

Plattnerite (Plattner, Karl Friedrich): Earth Sciences. See: Thrush under "lead dioxide...;" Webster's 3d.

Plausen mill (Plauson, Hermann): Chemistry. See: Hackh; Kingzett.

PLAUSON, HERMANN. fl. 1930. German chemist. Cited in: Chem. Abstr., vol. 24, p. 3677. Plausen mill.

PLAUT, HUGO CARL. 1858-1928. German physician. See: Biog. Lex. hervorr. Aerzte. Plaut-Vincent stomatitis, Plaut's bacillus.

Plaut-Vincent stomatitis (Plaut, Hugo Carl and Vincent, Jean Hyacinthe). See: Vincent's infection (disease or stomatitis).

Plaut's bacillus (Plaut, Hugo Carl): Medicine. See: Stedman. Also known as: Vincent's bacillus.

Plaut's ulcer (or angina) (Plaut, Hugo Carl). See: Vincent's infection (disease or stomatitis).

Player cast steel truck (Player, John): Engineering and Industry. Cited in: Nat. Cycl. Amer. Biog.

PLAYER, J. HART. fl. 1896. English? inventor. (Biography source unavailable.) Playertype.

PLAYER, JOHN. b. 1847. English-born American inventor. See: Nat. Cycl. Amer. Biog., vol. 11, p. 323. Player cast steel truck.

Playertype (Player, J. Hart): Photography. See: Focal Encyc. Photog.

PLAYFAIR, JOHN. 1748-1819. Scottish mathematician and geologist. See: World Who's Who Sci. Playfair's axiom, Playfair's law.

PLAYFAIR, WILLIAM SMOULT. 1836-1903. English physician. See: World Who's Who Sci. Playfair's treatment.

Playfair's axiom (Playfair, John): Mathematics. See: Ballentyne; Blumberg.

Playfair's law (Playfair, John): Earth Sciences. See: Monkhouse.

Playfair's treatment (Playfair, William Smoult): Medicine. See: Dorland.

pleased as Punch (Punch): Generic Word (self-delight). See: Jobes.

Pleasure curve (Pleasure, Max A.): Dentistry. See: Stedman.

PLEASURE, MAX A. d. 1965. American dentist. See: New York Times, Dec. 7, 1965, p. 47, col. 2. Pleasure curve.

PLECHNER, WALTER WILLIAM. 1903- . American chemical engineer. See: Amer. Men Sci., 6th ed. Curtman-Plechner test.

PLEHN, ALBERT. 1861-1935. German physician. See: Biog. Lex. hervorr. Aerzte. Plehn's karyochromatophil granules.

Plehn's karyochromatophil granules (Plehn, Albert): Medicine. See: Dorland; Stedman. Also known as: Schuegner's granules.

PLENCK, JOSEF JAKOB EDLER VON. ca. 1733-1807. Austrian physician and botanist. See: Biog. Lex. hervorr. Aerzte. Plenck's solution.

Plenck's solution (Plenck, Josef Jakob Edler von): Medicine. See: Dorland.

PLESCH, JOHANN. b. 1878. German physician in England. See: Biog. Lex. hervorr. Aerzte. Plesch's percussion, Plesch's test.

Plesch's percussion (Plesch, Johann): Medicine. See: Dorland.

Plesch's test (Plesch, Johann): Medicine. See: Dorland.

Plessis-Marly, Seigneur de. See: Mornay, Philippe de, Seigneur du Plessis-Marly.

Plessis-Praslin, Marechal du. See: Choiseul, Cesar, Duc de (Marechal du Plessis-Praslin).

Plessy, E. Mathieu. See: Mathieu-Plessy, E.

Plessy's green (Mathieu-Plessy, E.?): Chemistry. See: Thrush.

Plews process (Derivation undetermined): Engineering and Industry. See: Thrush.

plexus of Meissner (Meissner, Georg). See: Meissner's plexus.

PLICHTA, J. fl. 1927. Czechoslovakian chemist. Cited in: Chem. Abstr., vol. 21, p. 3851; vol. 22, p. 1927. Kubina-Plichta test reaction for bismuth.

PLIMMER, HENRY GEORGE. 1857-1918. English protozoologist. See: Who Was Who, 1916-1928. Plimmer's bodies, Plimmer's method, Plimmer's salt (or broth).

PLIMMER, ROBERT HENRY ADERS. b. 1877. English chemist. See: Pogg., vol. 6. Plimmer's method for the quantitative estimation of urea, Scott-Plimmer reagent.

Plimmer's bodies (Plimmer, Henry George): Medicine. See: Dorland; Kelly; Stedman.

Plimmer's method (Plimmer, Henry George): Medicine. See: Kelly.

Plimmer's method for the quantitative estimation of urea (Plimmer, Robert Henry Aders): Medicine. See: Kelly.

Plimmer's salt (or broth) (Plimmer, Henry George): Medicine. See: Dorland; Kelly.

Plimsoll('s) Act (Plimsoll, Samuel): History. See: Harbottle; Montgomery.

Plimsoll mark (or line) (Plimsoll, Samuel): Navigation. See: Clark; Hendrickson; Steinberg; Webster's 3d.

PLIMSOLL, SAMUEL. 1824-1898. English shipping reform leader. See: Dict. Nat. Biog., 1st suppl. Plimsoll('s) Act, Plimsoll mark (or line), Plimsolls.

Plimsolls (Plimsoll, Samuel): Fashion. See: Hendrickson; Partridge.

PLOECHL, JOSEF. fl. 1884. German chemist. Cited in: Royal Soc. Cat. Sci. Pap., 1884-1900. Erlenmeyer-Ploechl azlactone and amino acid synthesis.

Plotinism (or Plotinian) (Plotinus): Philosophy. See: Webster's 3d.

PLOTINUS. ca. 205-270. Roman Neoplatonic philosopher. See: Encyc. Brit., 1973. Plotinism (or Plotinian).

PLOTNIKOV, IVAN. 1878-1955. Croatian physicist. See: Pogg., vols. 5, 6. Plotnikow effect.

Plotnikow effect (Plotnikov, Ivan): Physics. See: Hackh.

Plott hound (Plott, Jonathan): Zoology. See: Webster's 3d.

PLOTT, JONATHAN. fl. 1750. American dog breeder. (Biography source unavailable.) Plott hound.

Plotz bacillus (Plotz, Harry): Medicine. See: Dorland; Stedman.

PLOTZ, HARRY. 1890-1947. American bacteriologist. See: World Who's Who Sci. Plotz bacillus.

PLOWDEN, LADY BRIDGET HORATIA. fl. 1933-1975. English educator. See: Who's Who, 1974-1975. Plowden report (1967).

PLOWDEN, EDWIN NOEL PLOWDEN, BARON. 1907- . English administrator. See: Who's Who, 1974-1975. Plowden report (1964).

Plowden report (1964) (Plowden, Edwin Noel Plowden, Baron): Politics. See: Steinberg.

Plowden report (1967) (Plowden, Lady Bridget Horatia): Education. See: Harrod.

PLOWRIGHT, CHARLES BAGGE. d. 1910. English mycologist. See: Transact. Norfolk Norwich Naturalists' Soc., vol. 9 (1910), pp. 245-282. Plowrightia.

Plowrightia (Plowright, Charles Bagge): Botany. Cited in: Van Nostrand Sci. Encyc. under "Diseases of Plants."

PLUCHE, NOEL ANTOINE. 1688-1761. French naturalist and writer. See: Nouv. Biog. Univ. Pluchea.

Pluchea (Pluche, Noel Antoine): Botany. See: Webster's 3d.

Plucker tube (Pluecker, Julius): Physics. See: Hackh; Webster's 3d.

Pluecker-Clebsch principle (Pluecker, Julius and Clebsch, Rudolf Friedrich Alfred): Mathematics. Cited in: Dict. Sci. Biog.

Pluecker equations (Pluecker, Julius): Mathematics. See: Focal Encyc. Film.

PLUECKER, JULIUS. 1801-1868. German mathematician and physicist. See: Encyc. Brit., 1973. Plucker tube, Pluecker-Clebsch principle, Pluecker equations, Pluecker's abridged notation.

Pluecker's abridged notation (Pluecker, Julius): Mathematics. See: James.

PLUGGE, PIETER CORNELIS. 1847-1897. Dutch pharmacologist. See: Pogg., vols. 3, 4. Plugge solution for gum ammoniac, Plugge test for cerium, Plugge test for nitrite, Plugge('s) test (for phenol).

Plugge solution for gum ammoniac (Plugge, Pieter Cornelis): Chemistry. See: Van Nostrand Chem. Dict.

Plugge test for cerium (Plugge, Pieter Cornelis): Chemistry. See: Van Nostrand Chem. Dict.

Plugge test for nitrite (Plugge, Pieter Cornelis): Chemistry. See: Van Nostrand Chem. Dict.

Plugge('s) test (for phenol) (Plugge, Pieter Cornelis): Chemistry. See: Dorland; Van Nostrand Chem. Dict.

PLUMBE, SAMUEL. fl. 1830. English dermatologist. Cited in: Index-Cat. Libr. Surg.-Gen. Off., 1st Ser., vol. 16, 1895. Plumbism, Willan-Plumbe syndrome.

Plumbism (Plumbe, Samuel). See: Remak's paralysis.

plume-of-Navarre (Henry IV, King of France and King of Navarre): Botany. See: Webster's 3d.

PLUME, THOMAS. 1630-1704. English divine. See: Dict. Nat. Biog., 1st suppl. Plumian professorship.

Plumeria (Plumier, Charles): Botany. See: Webster's 3d.

Plumian professorship (Plume, Thomas): Astronomy. See: Harvey.

PLUMIER, CHARLES. 1646-1704. French botanist. See: World Who's Who Sci. Plumeria.

Plumiera (Plumier, Charles). See: Plumeria.

Plummer block (Derivation undetermined): Engineering and Industry. See: Partridge; Weekley.

PLUMMER, HENRY STANLEY. 1874-1936. American surgeon. See: World Who's Who Sci. Plummer-Vinson syndrome, Plummer's dilator (or bag), Plummer's disease (or adenoma), Plummer's test, Plummer's treatment.

Plummer–Vinson syndrome (Plummer, Henry Stanley and Vinson, Porter Paisley): Medicine. See: Dorland; Jablonski; Stedman; Webster's 3d. Also known as: Kelly's syndrome, Paterson and Brown Kelly syndrome, Paterson-Kelly syndrome (or webs), Paterson's syndrome.

Plummer's dilator (or bag) (Plummer, Henry Stanley): Medicine. See: Stedman.

Plummer's disease (or adenoma) (Plummer, Henry Stanley): Medicine. See: Dorland; Jablonski; Stedman.

Plummer's test (Plummer, Henry Stanley): Medicine. See: Kelly.

Plummer's treatment (Plummer, Henry Stanley): Medicine. See: Kelly.

Plunket reaction for potassium (Plunkett, William?): Chemistry. See: Van Nostrand Chem. Dict.

PLUNKETT, CHARLES PESHALL. 1864–1931. American naval officer. See: Dict. Amer. Biog. Plunkett guns.

Plunkett guns (Plunkett, Charles Peshall): Weapons. See: Quick.

PLUNKETT, WILLIAM. No dates. English chemist. See: Chem. Soc. J., vol. 45 (1884), p. 618. Plunket reaction for potassium?

PLUTARCH. 46?–120? Greek biographer. See: Encyc. Brit., 1973. Plutarch (or Plutarchan).

Plutarch (or Plutarchan) (Plutarch): Generic Word (biographer). See: Webster's 3d.

PLUTO. Roman god of the subterranean world of the dead. See: Jobes. Pluto monkey, Plutonian (or Plutonic), Plutonic rocks (or Pluton), Plutonist (Plutonic or Plutonism).

Pluto monkey (Pluto): Zoology. See: Webster's 3d.

Plutocrat (Plutus): Generic Word (power through wealth). See: Brewer.

Plutonian (or Plutonic) (Pluto): Generic Word (infernal and gloomy). See: Webster's 3d.

Plutonic rocks (or Pluton) (Pluto): Earth Sciences. See: Brewer; Moore; Van Nostrand Sci. Encyc.; Webster's 3d.

Plutonist (Plutonic or Plutonism) (Pluto): Earth Sciences. See: Charnock; Partridge; Webster's 3d.

PLUTUS. Greek god of riches. See: Jobes. Plutocrat, rich as Plutus.

POCAHONTAS. 1595?–1617. American Indian princess. See: Dict. Amer. Biog. Pocahontas costume.

Pocahontas costume (Pocahontas): Fashion. See: Picken.

POCH, PELAYO. fl. 1923. Spanish chemist. Cited in: Chem. Abstr., vol. 17, p. 2090. Poch test for chlorate.

Poch test for chlorate (Poch, Pelayo): Chemistry. See: Van Nostrand Chem. Dict.

Pochhammer–Barnes equation (Pochhammer, Leo August and Barnes, Ernest W.): Mathematics. See: Van Nostrand Sci. Encyc. under "Gauss hypergeometric equation."

POCHHAMMER, LEO AUGUST. 1841–1920. German mathematician. See: Pogg., vols. 3, 4. Pochhammer-Barnes equation.

Pockels (Pockel's) effect (Pockels, Friedrich Carl Alwin): Physics. See: Ballentyne; Internat. Dict. Phys. Elec.; Thewlis.

POCKELS, FRIEDRICH CARL ALWIN. 1865–1913. German physicist. See: Pogg., vols. 4, 5, 6. Pockels (Pockel's) effect.

Podmore factor (Podmore, Henry Leveson): Engineering and Industry. See: Thrush.

PODMORE, HENRY LEVESON. 1912–   . English glass and ceramics chemist. See: Direct. Brit. Sci., 1966–1967. Podmore factor.

PODSNAP, JOHN. Character in Charles Dickens' novel "Our Mutual Friend," (1864–1865). See: Harvey. Podsnappery.

Podsnappery (Podsnap, John): Generic Word (complacent philistine). See: Brewer; Partridge; Webster's 3d; Weekley.

POE, EDGAR ALLAN. 1809–1849. American poet and writer. See: Dict. Amer. Biog. Edgar.

POEHL, ALEXANDER VASILIEVICH. 1850–1908. Russian physiological chemist. See: Biog. Lex. hervorr. Aerzte. Poehl's test.

Poehl's test (Poehl, Alexander Vasilievich): Medicine. See: Dorland; Stedman. Also known as: Bierinck's reaction.

poesie Bernesia (Berni, Francesco). See: Bernesque poetry.

POETSCH, F. H. fl. 1883. German mining engineer. Cited in: Royal Soc. Cat. Sci. Pap., 1884–1900. Poetsch process.

Poetsch process (Poetsch, F. H.): Engineering and Industry. See: Thrush; Webster's 3d.

POETZL, OTTO. b. 1877. Austrian psychiatrist. See: Biog. Lex. hervorr. Aerzte. Poetzl phenomenon, Poetzl syndrome.

Poetzl phenomenon (Poetzl, Otto): Psychology. See: Chaplin.

Poetzl syndrome (Poetzl, Otto): Medicine. See: Wolman.

POGGENDORF, ADOLF. fl. 1931. German chemist. Cited in: Chem. Abstr., Decenn. Index, 1927–1936. Rupp-Poggendorf reagent.

Poggendorff (Poggendorf) cell (Poggendorff, Johann Christian): Physics. See: Hackh; Van Nostrand Chem. Dict.

Poggendorff (Poggendorf) compensation method (Poggendorff, Johann Christian): Physics. See: Hackh; Thewlis; Van Nostrand Sci. Encyc.

Poggendorff illusion (Poggendorff, Johann Christian): Physiology. See: Chaplin; Drever; Webster's 3d.

POGGENDORFF, JOHANN CHRISTIAN. 1796–1877. German physicist and chemist. See: World Who's Who Sci. Poggendorff (Poggendorf) cell, Poggendorff (Poggendorf) compensation method, Poggendorff (Poggendorf) illusion.

Poggiana (Poggio-Bracciolini, Gian Francesco): Literature. See: Stenhouse.

POGGIO-BRACCIOLINI, GIAN FRANCESCO. 1380–1459. Italian Humanist. See: New Encyc. Brit., 1974. Poggiana.

Pogram (Derivation undetermined): Generic Word (dissenter). See: Charnock.

POHL, JULIUS HEINRICH. b. 1861. German pharmacologist. See: Biog. Lex. hervorr. Aerzte. Pohl('s) test (or reagent for globulins).

POHL, ROBERT WICHARD. b. 1884. German experimental physicist. See: Pogg., vols. 5, 6, 7a. Gudden-Pohl effect, Pohl's commutator?

Pohl('s) test (or reagent for globulins) (Pohl, Julius Heinrich): Medicine. See: Dorland; Van Nostrand Chem. Dict.

Pohle-Croasdale process (Pohle, K. A.? and Croasdale, Stuart): Engineering and Industry. See: Thrush.

POHLE, K. A. fl. 1932. German metallurgical engineer. Cited in: Chem. Abstr., Decenn. Index, 1927–1936. Pohle-Croasdale process

Pohlhausen method (Derivation undetermined): Physics. See: Internat. Dict. Ap. Math.

Poincare-Birkhoff fixed-point theorem (Poincare, Henri and Birkhoff, George David): Mathematics. See: James.

Poincare conjecture (Poincare, Henri): Mathematics. See: James; New Encyc. Brit., 1974, Microp.

Poincare duality theorem (Poincare, Henri): Mathematics. See: James.

Poincare electron theory (Poincare, Henri): Physics. See: Internat. Dict. Phys. Elec.

POINCARE, HENRI (In full: JULES-HENRI). 1854–1912. French mathematician and physicist. See: World Who's Who Sci. Poincare-Birkhoff fixed-point theorem, Poincare conjecture, Poincare duality theorem, Poincare electron theory, Poincare invariant, Poincare recurrence theorem.

Poincare invariant (Poincare, Henri): Mathematics. See: Internat. Dict. Ap. Math.

Poincare recurrence theorem (Poincare, Henri): Mathematics. See: James.

Poinciana (De Poinci, M.): Botany. See: Hendrickson; Webster's 3d.

POINSETT, JOEL ROBERTS. 1779–1851. American legislator and diplomat. See: Dict. Amer. Biog. Poinsettia.

Poinsettia (Poinsett, Joel Roberts): Botany. See: Encyc. Brit., 1973; Hendrickson; Webster's 3d.

Poinsot ellipsoid (Poinsot, Louis): Mathematics. See: Internat. Dict. Ap. Math.

POINSOT, LOUIS. 1777–1859. French mathematician. See: World Who's Who Sci. Poinsot ellipsoid, Poinsot motion.

Poinsot motion (Poinsot, Louis): Mathematics. See: Internat. Dict. Phys. Elec.

POIRET, PAUL. 1879-1944. French fashion designer. See: New Encyc. Brit., 1974, Microp. Poiret twill.

Poiret twill (Poiret, Paul): Fashion. See: Picken.

POIRIER, PAUL-JULIEN. 1853-1907. French surgeon and anatomist. See: Biog. Lex. hervorr. Aerzte. Poirier's gland, Poirier's line.

Poirier's gland (Poirier, Paul-Julien): Anatomy. See: Donath; Dorland; Stedman.

Poirier's line (Poirier, Paul-Julien): Anatomy. See: Dorland; Stedman.

POIROT, G. fl. 1923. French chemist. Cited in: Chem. Abstr., vol. 18, p. 208. Cuny-Poirot test.

Poise (Poiseuille, Jean-Leonard-Marie): Physics. See: Ballentyne; Dresner.

Poiseuille (Poiseuille, Jean-Leonard-Marie): Physics. See: Dresner.

Poiseuille('s) equation (or viscosity coefficient) (Poiseuille, Jean-Leonard-Marie): Physics. See: Stedman; Thewlis; Van Nostrand Sci. Encyc.

Poiseuille flow (Poiseuille, Jean-Leonard-Marie): Physics. See: Huschke; Internat. Dict. Phys. Elec.; Thewlis. Also known as: Hagen-Poiseuille flow.

Poiseuille-Hagen law (Poiseuille, Jean-Leonard-Marie and Hagen, Gotthilf Heinrich Ludwig). See: Poiseuille's law.

POISEUILLE, JEAN-LEONARD-MARIE. 1799-1869. French physiologist. See: World Who's Who Sci. Poise, Poiseuille, Poiseuille('s) equation (or viscosity coefficient), Poiseuille flow, Poiseuille('s) law, Poiseuille's space.

Poiseuille('s) law (Poiseuille, Jean-Leonard-Marie): Physics. See: Dorland; Internat. Dict. Phys. Elec.; Stedman; Webster's 3d. Also known as: Poiseuille-Hagen law.

Poiseuille's space (Poiseuille, Jean-Leonard-Marie): Physiology. See: Donath; Dorland; Stedman.

Poisson('s) bracket (Poisson, Simeon-Denis): Mathematics. See: Ballentyne; Internat. Dict. Ap. Math.; Internat. Dict. Phys. Elec.

Poisson('s) constant (or law) (Poisson, Simeon-Denis): Mathematics. See: Ballentyne; Huschke; Internat. Dict. Ap. Math.

Poisson distribution (Poisson, Simeon-Denis): Mathematics. See: Huschke; James; Kendall; Van Nostrand Sci. Encyc.

Poisson equation (Poisson, Simeon-Denis): Mathematics. See: Huschke; Internat. Dict. Phys. Elec.; Van Nostrand Sci. Encyc.

Poisson index of dispersion (Poisson, Simeon-Denis): Statistics. See: Kendall.

Poisson('s) integral (Poisson, Simeon-Denis): Mathematics. See: Internat. Dict. Ap. Math.; James.

Poisson, Jeanne Antoinette. See: Pompadour, Jeanne Antoinette Poisson, Marquise de.

Poisson-Lexis distribution (Poisson, Simeon-Denis and Lexis, Wilhelm Hector Richard Albrecht): Statistics. See: Kendall.

Poisson-Markov process (Poisson, Simeon-Denis and Markov, Andrei Andreevic): Statistics. See: Kendall.

Poisson parentheses (Poisson, Simeon-Denis): Mathematics. See: New Encyc. Brit., 1974, Microp.

Poisson-Pearson formula (Poisson, Simeon-Denis and Pearson, Karl): Statistics. See: Stedman.

Poisson process (Poisson, Simeon-Denis): Statistics. See: Kendall.

Poisson('s) ratio (Poisson, Simeon-Denis): Mathematics. See: Internat. Dict. Ap. Math.; James; Thrush; Van Nostrand Sci. Encyc.

POISSON, SIMEON-DENIS. 1781-1840. French mathematician. See: World Who's Who Sci. Poisson('s) bracket, Poisson('s) constant (or law), Poisson distribution, Poisson equation, Poisson index of dispersion, Poisson('s) integral, Poisson-Lexis distribution, Poisson-Markov process, Poisson parentheses, Poisson-Pearson formula, Poisson process, Poisson('s) ratio, Poisson variation, Poisson's integral formula (for Bessel functions), Poisson's law of large numbers, Poisson's sum formula.

Poisson variation (Poisson, Simeon-Denis): Statistics. See: Kendall.

Poissonades (Pompadour, Jeanne Antoinette Poisson, Marquise de): Literature. See: Hendrickson.

Poisson's integral formula (for Bessel functions) (Poisson, Simeon-Denis): Mathematics. See: Ballentyne.

Poisson's law of large numbers (Poisson, Simeon-Denis): Statistics. See: Kendall.

Poisson's sum formula (Poisson, Simeon-Denis): Mathematics. See: Ballentyne.

Poitevins (Ramnulf I, Count of Poitou): History. See: Steinberg.

Poitou, Count of. See: Ramnulf I, Count of Poitou.

POIVRE, PIERRE. 1719-1786. French trader. See: New Encyc. Brit., 1974, Microp. Poivrea.

Poivrea (Poivre, Pierre): Botany. See: Charnock.

Pol, Balthasar van der. See: Van der Pol, Balthasar.

Polaises reaction (Derivation undetermined): Chemistry. See: Hackh.

POLAND, ALFRED. 1820-1872. English physician. See: Biog. Lex. hervorr. Aerzte. Poland's syndactyly.

Poland's syndactyly (Poland, Alfred): Medicine. See: Jablonski.

POLANYI, MICHAEL. b. 1891. Hungarian-born English physical chemist. See: World Who's Who Sci. Polanyi's law of responsibility.

Polanyi's law of responsibility (Polanyi, Michael): Sociology. See: Martin.

Polaroid Land photographic process (and camera) (Polaroid Corporation and Land, Edwin Herbert): Photography. See: Focal Encyc. Photog.; Van Nostrand Sci. Encyc.

Polecat (Polk, James Knox). See: Polkism (Polkery, Polkite or Polkocracy).

POLENSKE, EDUARD. fl. 1889-1912. German chemist. Cited in: Royal Soc. Cat. Sci. Pap., 1884-1900. Polenske number (or value).

Polenske number (or value) (Polenske, Eduard): Chemistry. See: Hackh; Stedman; Van Nostrand Chem. Dict.; Webster's 3d.

POLGAR, FRANZ. fl. 1927. Hungarian roentgenologist. (Biography source unavailable.) Barsony-Polgar syndrome.

POLI, GIUSEPPE SAVERIO. 1746-1825. Italian naturalist. See: Nouv. Biog. Univ. Polian vesicle(s).

Polian vesicle(s) (Poli, Giuseppe Saverio): Zoology. See: Henderson; Van Nostrand Sci. Encyc.

Polinices (Polynices, the warrior): Zoology. See: Webster's 3d.

POLITZER, ADAM. 1835-1920. Austrian otologist. See: World Who's Who Sci. Politzer bag, Politzer method (treatment or Politzerization), Politzer's luminous cone, Politzer's speculum, Politzer's test.

Politzer bag (Politzer, Adam): Medicine. See: Dorland; Stedman; Webster's 3d.

Politzer method (treatment or Politzerization) (Politzer, Adam): Medicine. See: Dorland; Stedman.

Politzer's luminous cone (Politzer, Adam): Medicine. See: Dorland; Stedman. Also known as: Wilde's triangle (or cone of light), Woelde's triangle.

Politzer's speculum (Politzer, Adam): Medicine. See: Dorland.

Politzer's test (Politzer, Adam): Medicine. See: Dorland.

Polk-at (Polk, James Knox). See: Polkism (Polkery, Polkite or Polkocracy).

Polk corn (Polk, James Knox): Botany. See: Mathews, M. M.

Polk Doctrine (Polk, James Knox): History. See: Morris.

Polk game (Polk, James Knox): Politics. See: Mathews, M. M.

POLK, JAMES KNOX. 1795-1849. American president. See: Dict. Amer. Biog. Polk corn, Polk Doctrine, Polk game, Polkism (Polkery, Polkite or Polkocracy).

Polkism (Polkery, Polkite or Polkocracy) (Polk, James Knox): Politics. See: Mathews, M. M.

polkissen of Zimmermann (Zimmermann, Karl Wilhelm). See: Goormaghtigh's cells.

POLLACCI, EGIDIO. 1833-1913. Italian pharmacologist. See: Pogg., vols. 3, 4, 5. Pollacci solution for albumin, Pollacci test for iodic acid.

Pollacci solution for albumin (Pollacci, Egidio): Chemistry. See: Van Nostrand Chem. Dict.

Pollacci test for iodic acid (Pollacci, Egidio): Chemistry. See: Van Nostrand Chem. Dict.

Pollack's cement (Derivation undetermined): Chemistry. See: Hackh.

POLLACZEK, FELIX. b. 1892. Austrian-born French mathematician. See: World Who's Who Sci. Pollaczek-Khintchine formula, Pollaczek's formula.

Pollaczek-Khintchine formula (Pollaczek, Felix and Khintchin, Aleksandr Yakovlevich): Statistics. See: Kendall.

Pollaczek's formula (Pollaczek, Felix): Statistics. See: Kendall.

POLLAK, IGNAZ. fl. 1927. Austrian chemist. Cited in: Chem. Abstr., vol. 21, p. 2633. Feigl-Pollak reagent.

POLLAK, JACOB. 1872-1938. Austrian chemist. See: Pogg., vols. 5, 6, 7a. Lippmann-Pollack test reaction.

POLLAND, RUDOLF. b. 1876. Austrian dermatologist. See: Biog. Lex. hervorr. Aerzte. Matzenauer-Polland syndrome.

Pollard test (Pollard, W. Branch): Chemistry. See: Van Nostrand Chem. Dict.

POLLARD, W. BRANCH. fl. 1919. English analytical chemist. Cited in: Chem. Abstr., vol. 13, p. 1194. Pollard test.

POLLATSCHEK, OTTO. No dates. Austrian physician. (Biography source unavailable.) Porges-Pollatschek test (or reaction).

Pollio, Marcus Vitruvius. See: Vitruvius (Marcus Vitruvius Pollio).

POLLNOW, HANS. fl. 1932. German neurologist and psychiatrist. (Biography source unavailable.) Kramer-Pollnow disease.

Pollucite (Pollux): Earth Sciences. See: Thrush; Van Nostrand Sci. Encyc.; Webster's 3d.

POLLUX. One of the Dioscuri with Castor and a demigod of Greek mythology. See: Jobes. Castor and Pollux, Pollucite.

POLLYANNA. Fatuous heroine of Eleanor H. Porter's novel, "Pollyanna," (1913). See: Hart. Pollyanna (or Pollyannaish).

Pollyanna (or Pollyannaish) (Pollyanna): Generic Word (overly optimistic). See: Mathews, M. M.; Webster's 3d.

POLO, MARCO. 1254?-1324? Italian traveler. See: Encyc. Brit., 1911. Marco Polo('s) sheep.

POLONOVSKI, MAX. b. 1861. French chemist. See: Pogg., vols. 5, 6. Polonovski reaction.

POLONOVSKI, MICHEL. 1889-1954. French chemist. See: Pogg., vol. 6. Polonovski reaction.

Polonovski reaction (Polonovski, Michel and Polonovski, Max): Chemistry. See: Ballentyne; Krauch and Kunz.

POLUEKTOV, N. S. fl. 1935. Russian chemist. Cited in: Chem. Abstr., Decenn. Indexes, 1927-1936; 1937-1946; 1947-1956. Komarovskii-Poluektov test for copper, Komarovskii-Poluektov test for germanium, Komarovskii-Poluektov test for indium, Komarovskii-Poluektov test for molybdenum, Komarovskii-Poluektov test reaction for beryllium, Poluetkov micro-test for rhenium, Poluetkov test for gallium, Poluetkov test for germanium, Poluetkov test for potassium, Poluetkov test for rhenium.

Poluetkov micro-test for rhenium (Poluektov, N. S.): Chemistry. See: Van Nostrand Chem. Dict.

Poluetkov, N. S. See: Poluektov, N. S.

Poluetkov test for gallium (Poluektov, N. S.): Chemistry. See: Van Nostrand Chem. Dict.

Poluetkov test for germanium (Poluektov, N. S.): Chemistry. See: Van Nostrand Chem. Dict.

Poluetkov test for potassium (Poluektov, N. S.): Chemistry. See: Van Nostrand Chem. Dict.

Poluetkov test for rhenium (Poluektov, N. S.): Chemistry. See: Van Nostrand Chem. Dict.

Polya-Aeppli distribution (Polya, George and Aeppli): Statistics. See: Kendall.

Polya-Eggenburger distribution (Polya, George and Eggenburger, F.): Statistics. See: Kendall.

Polya frequency function of order two (Polya, George): Statistics. See: Kendall.

POLYA, GEORGE. b. 1887. Hungarian-born American mathematician. See: World Who's Who Sci. Polya-Aeppli distribution, Polya-Eggenburger distribution, Polya frequency function of order two, Polya process, Polya's distribution.

POLYA, JENO. 1876-1944. Hungarian surgeon. See: World Who's Who Sci. Hofmeister-Polya anastomosis, Polya's operation (or gastrectomy), Polya's operation for femoral hernia, Reichel-Polya stomach resection.

Polya process (Polya, George): Statistics. See: Kendall.

Polya's distribution (Polya, George): Statistics. See: Kendall.

Polya's operation (or gastrectomy) (Polya, Jeno): Medicine. See: Dorland; Stedman.

Polya's operation for femoral hernia (Polya, Jeno): Medicine. See: Kelly.

POLYCRATES OF SAMOS. d. ca. 522 B.C. Greek tyrant and pirate. See: Encyc. Brit., 1973. Polycratism.

Polycratism (Polycrates of Samos): Psychology. See: Hinsie.

POLYMNIA. One of the Greek muses. See: New Encyc. Brit., 1974, Microp. Polymnia.

Polymnia (Polymnia): Botany. See: Webster's 3d.

POLYNICES, THE WARRIOR. Legendary Theban warrior prince. See: Jobes. Polinices.

Polypheme (Polyphemus): Generic Word (giant). See: Partridge.

POLYPHEMUS. In Greek mythology, the most famous of the Cyclops. See: Jobes. Polypheme, Polyphemus moth.

Polyphemus moth (Polyphemus): Zoology. See: Webster's 3d.

POMERANCHUK, ISAAK YAKOVLEVICH. 1913- . Russian physicist. See: World Who's Who Sci. Pomeranchuk theorem.

Pomeranchuk theorem (Pomeranchuk, Isaak Yakovlevich): Physics. See: Thewlis.

POMERANZ, CESAR. 1860-1926. Austrian chemist. See: Pogg., vols. 4, 5. Pomeranz-Fritsch reaction.

Pomeranz-Fritsch reaction (Pomeranz, Cesar and Fritsch, Paul Ernst Moritz): Chemistry. See: Krauch and Kunz; Van Nostrand Chem. Dict.

POMERENE, ATLEE. 1863-1937. American lawyer and legislator. See: Dict. Amer. Biog., 2d suppl. Webb-Pomerene Act.

Pomeroy Circular (Pomeroy, Samuel Clarke): Politics. See: Dict. Amer. Hist.; Smith.

POMEROY, RALPH HAYWARD. 1867-1925. American gynecologist. Cited in: Index-Cat. Libr. Surg.-Gen. Off., 2d Ser., vol. 13, 1908. Pomeroy's operation?

POMEROY, SAMUEL CLARKE. 1816-1891. American legislator. See: Dict. Amer. Biog. Pomeroy Circular.

Pomeroy's operation (Pomeroy, Ralph Hayward?): Medicine. See: Stedman.

POMMERY, MADAME. fl. early 18th c. French vineyard owner. (Biography source unavailable.) Pommery (wine vaults).

Pommery (wine vaults) (Pommery, Madame): Food and Drink. See: Wagner (Names).

POMONA. Roman fruit tree goddess. See: Jobes. Pomona, Pomona (green).

Pomona (Pomona, the goddess): Generic Word (fruit). See: Brewer.

Pomona (green) (Pomona): Botany. See: Partridge.

Pompadour (Pompadour, Jeanne Antoinette Poisson, Marquise de): Generic Word (mistress). See: Hendrickson.

Pompadour (architectural style) (Pompadour, Jeanne Antoinette Poisson, Marquise de): Architecture. See: Charnock.

Pompadour (bird) (Pompadour, Jeanne Antoinette Poisson, Marquise de): Zoology. See: Webster's 3d.

Pompadour (claret purple or puce-color) (Pompadour, Jeanne Antoinette Poisson, Marquise de): Fashion. See: Brewer; Wagner (Names).

Pompadour (fabric and textile design) (Pompadour, Jeanne Antoinette Poisson, Marquise de): Fashion. See: Webster's 3d.

Pompadour fantasy (Pompadour, Jeanne Antoinette Poisson, Marquise de): Psychology. See: Hinsie.

Pompadour(s) (foot regiment) (Pompadour, Jeanne Antoinette Poisson, Marquise de): Military Science. See: Charnock; Wagner (More Names).

Pompadour green (Pompadour, Jeanne Antoinette Poisson, Marquise de): Fashion. See: Webster's 3d.

Pompadour (hairstyle) (Pompadour, Jeanne Antoinette Poisson, Marquise de): Fashion. See: Picken; Webster's 3d.

POMPADOUR, JEANNE ANTOINETTE POISSON, MARQUISE DE. 1721-1764. French mistress of Louis XV. See: Encyc. Brit., 1973. a la Pompadour, Poissonades, Pompadour, Pompadour (architectural style), Pompadour (bird), Pompadour (claret purple or puce-color), Pompadour (fabric and textile design), Pompadour fantasy, Pompadour(s) (foot regiment), Pompadour green, Pompadour (hairstyle), rose Pompadour.

POMPE, J. C. fl. 1932. Dutch physician. (Biography source unavailable.) Pompe's disease.

POMPEN, ARNOLD WILLEM MARIA. fl. 1933-1947. Dutch dermatologist. Cited in: Index-Cat. Libr. Surg.-Gen. Off., 5th Ser., vol. 1, 1959. Ruiter-Pompen-Wyers syndrome.

Pompe's disease (Pompe, J. C.): Medicine. See: Jablonski; Stedman; Wolman.

Poncelet (Poncelet, Jean Victor): Physics. See: Dresner; Webster's 3d.

PONCELET, JEAN VICTOR. 1788-1867. French mathematician and engineer. See: Encyc. Brit., 1973. Poncelet, Poncelet wheel.

Poncelet wheel (Poncelet, Jean Victor): Engineering and Industry. See: Auger; Thrush; Webster's 3d.

PONCET, ANTONIN. 1849-1913. French surgeon. See: Biog. Lex. hervorr. Aerzte. Poncet's disease, Poncet's operations.

Poncet's disease (Poncet, Antonin): Medicine. See: Jablonski. Also known as: Grocco-Poncet disease.

Poncet's operations (Poncet, Antonin): Medicine. See: Dorland; Stedman.

PONDER, ERIC. 1898- . Indian-born American physiologist. See: Amer. Men Sci., 7th ed. Cooke-Ponder method, Ponder's stain.

Ponder's stain (Ponder, Eric): Chemistry. See: Hackh.

PONFICK, EMIL (In full: CLEMENS EMIL). 1844-1913. German pathologist. See: World Who's Who Sci. Ponfick's shadow(s).

Ponfick's shadow(s) (Ponfick, Emil): Anatomy. See: Donath; Dorland; Stedman. Also known as: Traube's corpuscles.

PONNDORF, WOLFGANG. fl. 1915. German chemist. Cited in: Chem. Abstr., Decenn. Indexes, 1907-1916; 1917-1926. Meerwein-Ponndorf-Verley reduction (or reaction).

PONS, C. fl. 1910. Dutch pharmacist. Cited in: Chem. Abstr., vol. 5, p. 1121. Pons reagent.

Pons reagent (Pons, C.): Chemistry. See: Van Nostrand Chem. Dict.

pons Varolii (Varolius, Constantius): Anatomy. See: Donath; Henderson; Stedman.

PONSOLD, WERNER. fl. 1960. German physician. Cited in: Chem. Abstr. Kaiser-Ponsold edetic acid test.

PONTEDERA, GIULIO. 1688-1757. Italian botanist and classicist. See: World Who's Who Sci. Pontederia.

Pontederia (Pontedera, Giulio): Botany. See: Webster's 3d.

PONTIAC. 1720?-1769. American Ottawa Indian chief. See: Dict. Amer. Biog. Pontiac's rebellion.

Pontiac's rebellion (Pontiac): History. See: Morris.

Pontius Pilate's bodyguard (Pilate, Pontius): History. See: Brewer; Wagner (More Names). Also known as: the Braggs, old Braggs.

PONZI, CHARLES. d. 1949. American swindler. See: New York Times, Jan. 19, 1949, p. 56, col. 3. Ponzi scheme.

Ponzi scheme (Ponzi, Charles): Business. See: Det. News, June 27, 1974; Encyc. Brit., 1973 under "Fraud," p. 818; Time, July 8, 1974, pp. 45-46.

PONZIO, GIACOMO. b. 1870. Italian organic chemist. See: Pogg., vols. 4, 5, 6. Ponzio reaction.

Ponzio reaction (Ponzio, Giacomo): Chemistry. See: Krauch and Kunz; Van Nostrand Chem. Dict.

Ponzo illusion (Ponzo, Mario): Psychology. See: Wolman.

PONZO, MARIO. fl. 1929. Italian psychologist. See: Psych. Register, 1929, pp. 505-509. Ponzo illusion.

Poo(h)-Ba(h) (Pooh-Bah): Generic Word (multiple office-holder). See: Partridge; Stenhouse; Webster's 3d.

POOH-BAH. Character in Gilbert and Sullivan's opera, "The Mikado," (1885). See: Magill. Poo(h)-Ba(h).

POOL, EUGENE HILLHOUSE. 1874-1949. American surgeon. See: World Who's Who Sci. Pool-Schlesinger sign, Pool's phenomenon.

Pool-Schlesinger sign (Pool, Eugene Hillhouse and Schlesinger, Hermann). See: Schlesinger sign.

Pool's phenomenon (Pool, Eugene Hillhouse): Medicine. See: Dorland; Stedman.

poor as Job (Job): Generic Word. See: Brewer

poor as Lazarus (Lazarus, Saint): Generic Word. See: Brewer.

Poor Clares (Clare of Assisi, Saint): Religion. See: Attwater; Canney; Webster's 3d.

Poor Handmaids of Jesus (Jesus Christ): Religion. See: Attwater.

POOTH, PETER. fl. 1916. Swiss chemist. Cited in: Chem. Abstr., vol. 10, p. 2675. Pooth test reaction for aromatic aldehydes.

Pooth test reaction for aromatic aldehydes (Pooth, Peter): Chemistry. See: Van Nostrand Chem. Dict.

POPE, ALEXANDER. 1688-1744. English poet. See: Dict. Nat. Biog. Popian (or Popean).

Pope Joan (card game) (Joan): Recreation and Sports. See: Partridge.

Pope Julius (Julius II): Recreation and Sports. See: Charnock.

Pope Nicholas' taxation (Nicholas IV): History. See: Black.

POPE, WILLIAM JACKSON. 1870-1939. English chemist. See: World Who's Who Sci. Barlow and Pope theory.

POPESCU, ALIN. fl. 1915. Rumanian pharmaceutical chemist. Cited in: Chem. Abstr., vol. 10, p. 646. Vintilescu-Popescu test.

Popham colony (Popham, George): History. See: Jameson.

POPHAM, GEORGE. 1550-1608. English colonist in America. See: Dict. Amer. Biog. Popham colony.

Popian (or Popean) (Pope, Alexander): Literature. See: Webster's 3d.

POPOV, P. fl. 1936. Russian chemist. Cited in: Chem. Abstr., vol. 30, pp. 2518, 2524. Popov test for cadmium, Popov test for nitrate.

Popov test for cadmium (Popov, P.): Chemistry. See: Van Nostrand Chem. Dict.

Popov test for nitrate (Popov, P.): Chemistry. See: Van Nostrand Chem. Dict.

Popski's Private Army (Peniakoff, Vladimir "Popski"): Military Science. See: Brewer.

Poquelin, Jean Baptiste. See: Moliere.

PORAK, CHARLES. 1845-1921. French obstetrician. See: Biog. Lex. hervorr. Aerzte. Porak-Durante syndrome.

Porak-Durante syndrome (Porak, Charles and Durante, Gustave). See: Vrolik's syndrome (or disease).

Porges-Meier reaction (or test) (Porges, Otto and Meier, Georg): Medicine. See: Dorland; Kelly; Stedman.

Porges method (Porges, Otto): Medicine. See: Stedman.

PORGES, OTTO. b. 1879. Austrian-born American bacteriologist. See: World Who's Who Sci. Porges-Meier reaction (or test), Porges method, Porges-Pollatschek test (or reaction), Porges-Salomon test.

Porges-Pollatschek test (or reaction) (Porges, Otto and Pollatschek, Otto): Medicine. See: Dorland.

Porges-Salomon test (Porges, Otto and Salomon, Hugo): Medicine. See: Dorland; Stedman.

Porphyrian tree (Porphyry): Philosophy. See: Harvey.

Porphyrogenitus (Constantine VII): Generic Word. See: Brewer.

Porphyrogenitus. See: Constantine VII, Porphyrogenitus.

PORPHYRY. ca. 234-305. Greek scholar and Neoplatonic philosopher. See: New Encyc. Brit., 1974, Microp. Porphyrian tree.

ORRO, EDUARDO. 1842-1902. Italian obstetrician. See: Biog. Lex. hervorr. Aerzte. Porro operation (or hysterectomy).

ORRO, IGNAZIO. 1801-1875. Italian physicist. See: World Who's Who ci. Porro prism, Porro-Steinheil lens.

orro operation (or hysterectomy) (Porro, Eduardo): Medicine. See: Dorland; tedman.

orro prism (Porro, Ignazio): Physics. See: Internat. Dict. Phys. Elec.; an Nostrand Sci. Encyc.; Webster's 3d.

orro-Steinheil lens (Porro, Ignazio and Steinheil, Adolph): Photography. See: ocal Encyc. Photog.

ORSON, RICHARD. 1759-1808. English classical scholar and philologist. ee: Dict. Nat. Biog. Porson's Law (or Canon).

orson's Law (or Canon) (Porson, Richard): Literature. See: Preminger.

orta cipher (Porta, Giambattista della): Linguistics. See: Webster's 3d.

ORTA, GIAMBATTISTA DELLA. ca. 1535-1615. Italina physicist. See: orld Who's Who Sci. Porta cipher.

ORTE. fl. ca. 1850. Italian scientist. Cited in: Dana, p. 458. Portite.

ORTEOUS, JOHN. d. 1736. Scottish city official of Edinburgh. See: ict. Nat. Biog. Porteous riots.

orteous riots (Porteous, John): History. See: Barnhart (Eng. Lit.); Brewer; arbottle.

ORTER. fl. 18th c.? American tavern owner. (Biography source unavail-le.) Porterhouse steak.

ORTER. fl. 1882. English printer. (Biography source unavailable.) Porter's pe-composing machine.

orter-Allen steam engine (Porter, Charles Talbot and Allen, John T. F.). ee: Allen steam engine.

orter (apple) (Porter, Samuel?): Botany. See: Mathews, M. M.

ORTER, CHARLES EDWIN, JR. 1926- . American physicist. See: Amer. en Sci., 10th ed. Porter-Thomas distribution.

ORTER, CHARLES TALBOT. 1826-1910. American mechanical engineer. See: ebster's Biog. Dict. Porter-Allen steam engine, Porter governor.

ORTER, CURT CULWELL. 1914- . American biochemist. See: Amer. en and Women Sci., 12th ed. Porter-Silber chromogens.

orter governor (Porter, Charles Talbot): Engineering and Industry. See: uger.

ORTER, SAMUEL. 1810-1901. American teacher of the deaf. See: Dict. mer. Biog. Porter (apple)?

orter-Silber chromogens (Porter, Curt Culwell and Silber, Robert Howard): edicine. See: Stedman.

ORTER, THOMAS CUNNINGHAM. fl. 1892-1899. English scientist. Cited : Royal Soc. Cat. Sci. Pap., 1884-1900. Ferry-Porter law.

orter-Thomas distribution (Porter, Charles Edwin, Jr. and Thomas, Richard arland): Physics. See: Internat. Dict. Ap. Math.

ORTER, WILLIAM BRANCH. b. 1888. American physician. See: Amer. en Sci., 8th ed. Porter's syndrome.

ORTER, WILLIAM HENRY. 1790-1861. Irish surgeon. See: Dict. Nat. Biog. orter's fascia, Porter's sign.

ORTER, WILLIAM HENRY. 1853-1933. American physician. See: Who Was ho Amer., vol. 1. Porter's tests.

ORTER, WILLIAM SYDNEY (Pseud.: O. HENRY). 1862-1910. American uthor. See: Dict. Amer. Biog. O. Henry ending.

orterhouse steak (Porter): Food and Drink. See: Clapin.

orter's fascia (Porter, William Henry): Medicine. See: Stedman.

orter's law (Porter, Thoms Cunningham). See: Ferry-Porter law.

orter's sign (Porter, William Henry): Medicine. See: Dorland; Stedman.

orter's syndrome (Porter, William Branch): Medicine. See: Jablonski.

orter's tests (Porter, William Henry): Medicine. See: Dorland; Stedman.

orter's type-composing machine (Porter): Printing. See: Lockwood, p. 563.

orteus-Diamond learning machine (Porteus, Stanley David and Diamond, olomon): Psychology. Cited in: World Who's Who Sci.

Porteus maze test (Porteus, Stanley David): Psychology. See: Chaplin; Wolman.

PORTEUS, STANLEY DAVID. b. 1883. Australian-born psychologist in Hawaii. See: World Who's Who Sci. Porteus-Diamond learning machine, Porteus maze test.

PORTEVIN, ALBERT MARCEL GERMAIN RENE. 1880-1962. French metallurgist. See: Pogg., vols. 5, 6. Portevin-Le Chatelier effect.

Portevin-Le Chatelier effect (Portevin, Albert Marcel Germain Rene and Le Chatelier, Francois): Chemistry. See: Ballentyne.

Portinari, Beatrice. See: Beatrice.

Portite (Porte): Earth Sciences. See: Charnock.

Portland, 3rd Duke of. See: Bentinck, William Henry Cavendish (3rd Duke of Portland).

Portland vase (Bentinck, William Henry Cavendish, 3d Duke of Portland): Fine Arts. See: Harvey; Latham; Phyfe.

POSADAS, ALEJANDRO. 1870-1920. Argentine parasitologist. See: Gran Encic. Argentina. Posadas-Wernicke disease.

Posadas' disease (Posadas, Alejandro). See: Posadas-Wernicke disease.

Posadas-Wernicke disease (Posadas, Alejandro and Wernicke, Robert): Medicine. See: Dorland; Stedman. Also known as: Posadas' disease.

POSEIDON. God of the sea in Greek religion. See: New Encyc. Brit., 1974, Microp. Poseidon (rocket), Poseidoniastae.

Poseidon (rocket) (Poseidon): Engineering and Industry. Cited in: Van Nostrand Sci. Encyc. under "Rockets & Launch Vehicles."

Poseidoniastae (Poseidon): History. See: Canney.

POSNER, ADOLPH. 1906- . Polish-born American ophthalmologist. See: Direct. Med. Specialists, 1974-1975. Posner-Schlossman syndrome.

POSNER, CARL. 1854-1928. German physician. See: Biog. Lex. hervorr. Aerzte. Posner's test (or reaction), Quensel-Posner cadmium-methylene blue stain?

Posner, E. I. See: Pozner, E. I.

Posner-Schlossman syndrome (Posner, Adolph and Schlossman, Abraham): Medicine. See: Jablonski. Also known as: Terrien-Veil syndrome.

Posner test (Pozner, E. I.): Chemistry. See: Van Nostrand Chem. Dict.

Posner's test (or reaction) (Posner, Carl): Medicine. See: Dorland.

POSTELS, ALEXANDER PHILIPOV. 1801-1871. Estonian botanist. See: Biog. Notes Uoon Botanists. Postelsia?

Postelsia (Postels, Alexander Philipov?): Botany. See: Van Nostrand Sci. Encyc. under "Algae."

potage Parmentier (Parmentier, Antoine-Auguste): Food and Drink. See: De Sola.

potage Rossini (Rossini, Gioachinno Antonio): Food and Drink. See: De Sola.

POTAIN, PIERRE CARL EDOUARD. 1825-1901. French physician. See: World Who's Who Sci. Potain's apparatus, Potain's disease, Potain's sign, Potain's solution, Potain's syndrome.

Potain's apparatus (Potain, Pierre Carl Edouard): Medicine. See: Dorland.

Potain's disease (Potain, Pierre Carl Edouard): Medicine. See: Dorland.

Potain's sign (Potain, Pierre Carl Edouard): Medicine. See: Dorland; Stedman.

Potain's solution (Potain, Pierre Carl Edouard): Medicine. See: Dorland.

Potain's syndrome (Potain, Pierre Carl Edouard): Medicine. See: Dorland.

POTEMKIN, GRIGORI ALEKSANDROVICH. 1739-1791. Russian statesman. See: Encyc. Brit., 1973. Potemkin village.

Potemkin village (Potemkin, Grigori Aleksandrovich): Generic Word (false front). See: Webster's 3d.

POTH, DUNCAN OSLER. 1908- . American dermatologist. See: Direct. Med. Specialists, 1974-1975. Poth's keratosis.

Poth's keratosis (Poth, Duncan Osler): Medicine. See: Jablonski.

POTIPHAR. Biblical Egyptian official in the story of Joseph. See: Hastings (Dict. Bible). Potiphar's wife.

Potiphar's wife (Potiphar): Generic Word. See: Jobes; Partridge.

POTT, PERCIVALL. 1713–1788. English surgeon. See: Dict. Nat. Biog. Pott's abscess, Pott's aneurysm, Pott's disease (caries or curvature), Pott's fracture, Pott's gangrene, Pott's paraplegia (or paralysis), Pott's puffy tumor.

POTTENGER, FRANCIS MARION. 1869–1961. American physician. See: Who Was Who Amer., vol. 4. Pottenger's sign.

Pottenger's sign (Pottenger, Francis Marion): Medicine. See: Dorland; Jablonski.

POTTER. fl. 19th c. American minister. (Biography source unavailable.) Potter baptist.

Potter baptist (Potter): Religion. See: Mathews, M. M.

Potter-Bucky grid(s) (Potter, Hollis Elmer and Bucky, Gustav): Medicine. See: Focal Encyc. Photog. under "Medical Radiography;" Hughes; Markus. Also known as: Bucky diaphragm (or grid).

POTTER, C. V. fl. 1901. Australian metallurgist. Cited in: Singer, vol. 5. Potter-Delprat process.

POTTER, CARYL ASHBY. 1886–1933. American physician. Cited in: Kelly. Potter treatment.

Potter-Delprat process (Potter, C. V. and Delprat, G. D.): Engineering and Industry. See: Thrush.

POTTER, EDITH LOUISE. 1901– . American pathologist. See: World Who's Who Sci. Potter's disease, Potter's facies.

POTTER, HOLLIS ELMER. b. 1880. American radiologist. See: Amer. Men. Sci., 8th ed. Potter-Bucky grid(s).

POTTER, IRVING WHITE. 1868–1956. American obstetrician. See: New York Times, Sept. 18, 1956, p. 35, col. 1. Potter's version (of delivery).

POTTER, ROY PILLING. b. 1879. American radiologist. See: Direct. Med. Specialists, 1965–1966. Doege-Potter syndrome.

Potter treatment (Potter, Caryl Ashby): Medicine. See: Dorland.

Potter's disease (Potter, Edith Louise): Medicine. See: Jablonski.

Potter's facies (Potter, Edith Louise): Medicine. See: Jablonski.

Potter's version (of delivery) (Potter, Irving White): Medicine. See: Dorland; Stedman.

Pott's abscess (Pott, Percivall): Medicine. See: Stedman.

Pott's aneurysm (Pott, Percivall): Medicine. See: Dorland; Jablonski; Stedman.

Pott's disease (caries or curvature) (Pott, Percivall): Medicine. See: Dorland; Jablonski; Stedman; Webster's 3d. Also known as: David's disease.

Pott's fracture (Pott, Percivall): Medicine. See: Dorland; Jablonski; Stedman; Webster's 3d. Also known as: Dupuytren's fracture.

Pott's gangrene (Pott, Percivall): Medicine. See: Dorland; Jablonski; Stedman.

Pott's operation (or anastomosis) (Potts, Willis John): Medicine. See: Dorland; Stedman. Also known as: Potts-Smith-Gibson operation.

Pott's paraplegia (or paralysis) (Pott, Percivall): Medicine. See: Dorland; Jablonski; Stedman.

Pott's puffy tumor (Pott, Percivall): Medicine. See: Dorland; Jablonski; Stedman.

Potts-Smith-Gibson operation (Potts, Willis John; Smith, Sidney; and Gibson, Stanley): Medicine. See: Pott's operation (or anastomosis).

POTTS, WILLIS JOHN. 1895– . American surgeon. See: World Who's Who Sci. Pott's operation (or anastomosis).

Pouget-Chouchak solution (Pouget, Isidore and Chouchak, D.): Chemistry. See: Van Nostrand Chem. Dict.

POUGET, ISIDORE. fl. 1899–1908. Algerian chemist. See: Pogg., vol. 5. Pouget-Chouchak solution.

POULENC, CAMILLE. b. 1864. French chemist. See: Pogg., vol. 5. Poulenc test for nitrate?

Poulenc test for nitrate (Poulenc, Camille?): Chemistry. See: Van Nostrand Chem. Dict.

POULET, ALFRED. 1848–1888. French physician. Cited in: Index-Cat. Libr. Surg.-Gen. Off., 1st Ser., vol. 11, 1890. Poulet's disease.

Poulet's disease (Poulet, Alfred): Medicine. See: Dorland; Stedman.

Poulsen arc (or arc converter) (Poulsen, Valdemar): Electronics. See: Hughes; Webster's 3d.

Poulsen gold medal (Poulsen, Valdemar): Electronics. Cited in: World Who's Who Sci.

POULSEN, VALDEMAR. 1869–1942. Danish electrical engineer. See: World Who's Who Sci. Poulsen arc (or arc converter), Poulsen gold medal.

Poulter method (Poulter, Thomas Charles): Earth Sciences. See: Thrush.

POULTER, THOMAS CHARLES. 1897– . American geophysicist. See: World Who's Who Sci. Poulter method.

POUPART, FRANCOIS. 1661–1708. French anatomist and surgeon. See: World Who's Who Sci. Poupart's ligament, Poupart's line.

Poupart's ligament (Poupart, Francois): Anatomy. See: Donath; Dorland; Stedman; Webster's 3d. Also known as: Fallopian arch, Vesalius' ligament.

Poupart's line (Poupart, Francois): Anatomy. See: Donath; Dorland; Stedman.

Pourbaix diagram (Pourbaix, Marcel): Chemistry. See: Ballentyne.

POURBAIX, MARCEL. 1904– . Belgian electrochemist. See: World Who's Who Sci. Pourbaix diagram.

POURRET, PIERRE ANDRE. fl. early 19th c. French botanist. See: Toulouse Soc. Sci. Bull., vol. 2 (1874), pp. 1–148. Pourretia.

Pourretia (Pourret, Pierre Andre): Botany. See: Charnock.

Pourtales, Louis Francois de. See: De Pourtales, Louis Francois.

Pourtalesia (sea urchin) (De Pourtales, Louis Francois): Zoology. Cited in: World Who's Who Sci.

Pousepp, Louis. See: Puusepp, Lyudvig Martinovich.

POUTEAU, CLAUDE. 1725–1775. French surgeon. See: Nouv. Biog. Univ. Pouteau's fracture.

Pouteau's fracture (Pouteau, Claude): Medicine. See: Jablonski.

POUZERGUES, J. fl. 1932. French chemist. Cited in: Chem. Abstr., vol. 26, pp. 2391, 3202. Sazerac-Pouzergues tests.

Powell bands (Powell, Cecil Frank?): Physics. See: Internat. Dict. Phys. Elec.

POWELL, CECIL FRANK. 1903–1969. English physicist. See: World Who's Who Sci. Powell bands?

POWELL, ENOCH (In full: JOHN ENOCH). 1912– . English politician. See: Who's Who, 1974–1975. Powellism (or Powellite).

POWELL, JOHN WESLEY. 1834–1902. American geologist and ethnologist. See: Dict. Amer. Biog. Powellite.

POWELL, W. fl. 1915. English wood chemist. Cited in: Chem. Abstr., Decenn. Index, 1907–1916; 1917–1926. Powellizing process.

Powellism (or Powellite) (Powell, Enoch): Politics. See: Barnhart (New Eng.).

Powellite (Powell, John Wesley): Earth Sciences. See: Thrush; Webster's 3d.

Powellizing process (Powell, W.): Engineering and Industry. See: Thrush.

POWER, MARSCHELLE HARNLY. b. 1894. American physiological chemist. See: Amer. Men Sci., 10th ed. Cutler-Power-Wilder test, Robinson-Kepler-Power test.

POYNINGS, SIR EDWARD. 1459–1521. English soldier and diplomat. See: Dict. Nat. Biog. Poynings' Law (or Act).

Poynings' Law (or Act) (Poynings, Sir Edward): History. See: Harbottle; Steinberg.

POYNTING, JOHN HENRY. 1852–1914. English physicist. See: World Who's Who Sci. Poynting-Robertson effect, Poynting('s) theorem.

Poynting-Robertson effect (Poynting, John Henry and Robertson, Howard Percy): Physics. See: Internat. Dict. Phys. Elec.; Van Nostrand Sci. Encyc.

Poynting('s) theorem (Poynting, John Henry): Physics. See: Ballentyne; Hughes; Internat. Dict. Ap. Math.

POZNER, E. I. fl. 1927. Russian chemist. Cited in: Chem. Abstr., vol. 21, p. 3851. Posner test.

Pozzi-Escot-Couquet test reaction for palladium (Pozzi-Escot, Emmanuel and Couquet, Henri Camille): Chemistry. See: Van Nostrand Chem. Dict.

...ZZI-ESCOT, EMMANUEL (In full: MARIUS EMMANUEL). b. 1880. ...nch-born chemist in Peru. See: Pogg., vols. 5, 6. Pozzi-Escot-Couquet ...t reaction for palladium, Pozzi-Escot micro-reagent for yttrium, erbium, ...dymium, and praseodymium, Pozzi-Escot micro-test for sulfate, Pozzi-Escot ...t for bromine, Pozzi-Escot test for nickel in presence of cobalt, Pozzi-Escot ...t for thiosulfate, Pozzi-Escot test for tungsten or molybdenum, Pozzi-Escot ...t reaction for chlorate, Pozzi-Escot test reaction for copper, Pozzi-Escot test ...ction for gold, Pozzi-Escot test reaction for rotenone, Pozzi-Escot test re-...ions for cobalt.

...zzi-Escot micro-reagent for yttrium, erbium, neodymium, and praseodymium ...ozzi-Escot, Emmanuel): Chemistry. See: Van Nostrand Chem. Dict.

...zzi-Escot micro-test for sulfate (Pozzi-Escot, Emmanuel): Chemistry. See: ...n Nostrand Chem. Dict.

...zzi-Escot test for bromine (Pozzi-Escot, Emmanuel): Chemistry. See: Van ...ostrand Chem. Dict.

...zzi-Escot test for nickel in presence of cobalt (Pozzi-Escot, Emmanuel): ...emistry. See: Van Nostrand Chem. Dict.

...zzi-Escot test for thiosulfate (Pozzi-Escot, Emmanuel): Chemistry. See: ...n Nostrand Chem. Dict.

...zzi-Escot test for tungsten or molybdenum (Pozzi-Escot, Emmanuel): Chemistry. ...e: Van Nostrand Chem. Dict.

...zzi-Escot test reaction for chlorate (Pozzi-Escot, Emmanuel): Chemistry. ...e: Van Nostrand Chem. Dict.

...zzi-Escot test reaction for copper (Pozzi-Escot, Emmanuel): Chemistry. See: ...n Nostrand Chem. Dict.

...zzi-Escot test reaction for gold (Pozzi-Escot, Emmanuel): Chemistry. See: ...n Nostrand Chem. Dict.

...zzi-Escot test reaction for rotenone (Pozzi-Escot, Emmanuel): Chemistry. ...e: Van Nostrand Chem. Dict.

...zzi-Escot test reactions for cobalt (Pozzi-Escot, Emmanuel): Chemistry. See: ...n Nostrand Chem. Dict.

...OZZI, SAMUEL JEAN. 1846-1918. French gynecologist and anatomist. ...World Who's Who Sci. Pozzi's muscle, Pozzi's senile pseudorickets, ...zzi's syndrome.

...zzi's muscle (Pozzi, Samuel Jean): Anatomy. See: Stedman.

...zzi's senile pseudorickets (Pozzi, Samuel Jean). See: Paget's disease.

...zzi's syndrome (Pozzi, Samuel Jean): Medicine. See: Jablonski.

...ADER, ANDREA. 1919- . Swiss pediatrician. See: Who's Who Switz., ...70-1971. Prader-Willi syndrome.

...ader-Labhart-Willi-Fanconi syndrome (Prader, Andrea; Labhart, A.; Willi, ...einrich; and Fanconi, Guido). See: Prader-Willi syndrome.

...ader-Willi syndrome (Prader, Andrea and Willi, Heinrich): Medicine. See: ...ablonski; Stedman. Also known as: Prader-Labhart-Willi-Fanconi syndrome.

...AGER, BERNHARD LUDWIG. 1867-1934. German organic chemist. See: ...gg., vol. 6. Prager-Jacobson classification.

...ager-Jacobson classification (Prager, Bernhard Ludwig and Jacobson, Paul): ...hemistry. See: Chem. Abstr., Decenn. Index, 1927-1936; Hackh.

...agmatic Sanction of Charles VI (Charles VI): History. See: Harbottle.

...agmatic Sanction of Louis IX (Louis IX): History. See: Harbottle.

...RAKKEN, JAN ROELOF. 1897- . Dutch dermatologist. See: Who's Who ...ci. Europe, 1972. Godfried-Prick-Carol-Prakken syndrome.

...aline (Choiseul, Cesar, Duc de): Food and Drink. See: Hendrickson; ...artridge; Webster's 3d.

...andtl-Glauert rule (Prandtl, Ludwig and Glauert, Hermann): Physics. See: ...ternat. Dict. Ap. Math.

...RANDTL, LUDWIG. 1875-1953. German physicist. See: World Who's Who ...ci. Hencky-Prandtl net, Prandtl-Glauert rule, Prandtl-Meyer expansion, ...andtl-Meyer function, Prandtl number, Prandt-Reuss material, Prandtl stress ...unction.

...andtl-Meyer expansion (Prandtl, Ludwig and Meyer, Theodor): Physics. See: ...ternat. Dict. Ap. Math.; Thewlis.

...andtl-Meyer function (Prandtl, Ludwig and Meyer, Theodor): Physics. See: ...ternat. Dict. Ap. Math.

...andtl number (Prandtl, Ludwig): Physics. See: Huschke; Internat. Dict. Ap. ...ath.; Internat. Dict. Phys. Elec.; Thewlis; Van Nostrand Sci. Encyc.

Prandtl-Reuss material (Prandtl, Ludwig and Reuss): Physics. See: Internat. Dict. Ap. Math.

Prandtl stress function (Prandtl, Ludwig): Physics. See: Internat. Dict. Ap. Math.

PRANNATH. fl. early 18th c. Indian religious sect founder. See: Hastings (Encyc. Rel. Ethics). Prannathi sect.

Prannathi sect (Prannath): Religion. See: Canney.

PRATESI, F. fl. 1965. Spanish physician. (Biography source unavailable.) Pratesi's syndrome.

Pratesi's syndrome (Pratesi, F.): Medicine. See: Jablonski.

Pratt and Whitney key (Pratt, Francis Ashbury and Whitney, Amos): Engineering and Industry. See: Van Nostrand Sci. Encyc. under "Key."

PRATT, CHARLES, 1ST EARL CAMDEN. 1714-1794. English jurist and political leader. See: Dict. Nat. Biog. Camden-Yorke opinion.

PRATT, FRANCIS ASHBURY. 1827-1902. American inventor. See: Dict. Amer. Biog. Pratt and Whitney key.

Pratt isostasy (Pratt, John Henry): Earth Sciences. See: New Encyc. Brit., 1974, Microp.; Thrush.

PRATT, JOHN HENRY. d. 1871. English geophysicist and mathematician. See: Dict. Nat. Biog. Pratt isostasy.

PRATT, JOSEPH HERSEY. 1872-1956. American physician. See: Bull. Hist. Med., vol. 30 (Sept.-Oct. 1956), pp. 473-474. Pratt's method, Pratt's symptom.

PRATT, THOMAS WILLIS. 1812-1875. American civil engineer. See: Dict. Amer. Biog. Pratt truss.

Pratt truss (Pratt, Thomas Willis): Engineering and Industry. See: Encyc. Brit., 1973 under "Truss;" Thrush.

Pratt's method (Pratt, Joseph Hersey): Medicine. See: Stedman.

Pratt's symptom (Pratt, Joseph Hersey): Medicine. See: Dorland; Stedman.

PRAUSNITZ, CARL WILLY. b. 1876. German bacteriologist. See: Biog. Lex. hervorr. Aerzte. Prausnitz-Kuestner reaction (test or antibody).

Prausnitz-Kuestner reaction (test or antibody) (Prausnitz, Carl Willy): Medicine. See: Dorland; Stedman.

PRAVAZ, CHARLES GABRIEL. 1791-1853. French physician. See: World Who's Who Sci. Pravaz's syringe.

Pravaz's syringe (Pravaz, Charles Gabriel): Medicine. See: Dorland.

Praxean (Praxeas): Religion. See: Webster's 3d.

PRAXEAS. fl. 2d c. Asia Minor heretic. See: Dict. Christian Biog. Praxean.

PRAXITELES. fl. 4th c. B.C. Greek sculptor. See: Encyc. Brit., 1973. Praxiteles curve.

Praxiteles curve (Praxiteles): Fine Arts. See: Winick.

Prayer of Jesus (Jesus Christ): Religion. See: Attwater.

Prayer of Manasses (Manasseh): Religion. See: Attwater; Encyc. Brit., 1973.

Pray's letters (Derivation undetermined): Psychology. See: Drever.

Pre-Raphaelite Brotherhood (Raphael): Fine Arts. See: Barnhart (Eng. Lit.); Brewer; Preminger.

Pre-Urbanite hymns (Urban VIII): Religion. See: Attwater.

PREBLUDA, HARRY JACOB. 1911- . American chemist. See: Amer. Men and Women Sci., 12th ed. Prebula-McCollum reaction for vitamin B_1 (thiamine).

Prebula-McCollum reaction for Vitamin B_1 (thiamine) (Prebluda, Harry Jacob and McCollum, Elmer Vernon): Chemistry. See: Kelly; Van Nostrand Chem. Dict.

Preece (Preece, Sir William Henry): Physics. See: Dresner.

PREECE, SIR WILLIAM HENRY. 1834-1913. English electrical engineer. See: World Who's Who Sci. Preece.

PREGL, FRITZ. 1869-1930. Austrian physiological chemist. See: Biog. Lex. hervorr. Aerzte. Pregl's solution, Pregl's test.

Pregl's solution (Pregl, Fritz): Medicine. See: Dorland.

Pregl's test (Pregl, Fritz): Medicine. See: Dorland.

Prehnite (Van Prehn, Col.): Earth Sciences. See: Thrush; Van Nostrand Sci. Encyc.; Webster's 3d.

PREISER, GEORG KARL FELIX. 1879-1913. German orthopedic surgeon. Cited in: Index Medicus, 2d Ser., vol. 12, 1914. Preiser's disease.

Preiser's disease (Preiser, Georg Karl Felix): Medicine. See: Dorland; Jablonski.

PREISZ, HUGO VON. 1860-1940. Hungarian bacteriologist. See: Biog. Lex. hervorr. Aerzte. Preisz-Nocard bacillus.

Preisz-Nocard bacillus (Preisz, Hugo von and Nocard, Edmund Isidore Etienne): Medicine. See: Dorland; Stedman.

Prejevalsky, Nikolai Mikhailovich. See: Przhevalsky, Nikolai Mikhailovich.

PRENTICE, CHARLES F. 1854-1946. American optician. See: Amer. Men Sci., 6th ed. Prentice's rule.

PRENTICE, JOHN. fl. 1928. American metallurgical engineer. Cited in: Chem. Abstr., Decenn. Index, 1927-1936. Pehrson-Prentice process?

Prentice's rule (Prentice, Charles F.): Medicine. See: Stedman.

Preobrazhenskite (Preobrazhensky, Paul Ivanovich): Earth Sciences. See: Thrush.

PREOBRAZHENSKY, PAUL IVANOVICH. 1874-1944. Russian geologist. Cited in: Min. Mag., vol. 31 (1956-1958), p. 970. Preobrazhenskite.

PRESSENDA, JOHANNES FRANCISCUS. 1777-1854. Italian violin maker. See: Grove. Pressenda (violin).

Pressenda (violin) (Pressenda, Johannes Franciscus): Music. See: Partridge.

Pressey device (Pressey, Sidney L.): Education. See: Good.

PRESSEY, SIDNEY L. b. 1888. American educational psychologist. See: Biog. Direct. Amer. Psych. Assoc., 1973. Pressey device.

PRESTON, CHARLES. fl. 17th c. Scottish physician. See: Biog. Notes Upon Botanists. Prestonia.

PRESTON, GEORGE DAWSON. 1896- . English physicist. See: Who's Who Brit. Sci., 1953. Guinier-Preston zones.

PRESTON, JOSEPH HENRY. 1911- . English mechanical engineer. See: Who's Who, 1974-1975. Preston tube.

PRESTON, THOMAS. 1860-1900. Irish physicist. See: Encyc. Brit., 1973. Preston's rule.

Preston tube (Preston, Joseph Henry): Engineering and Industry. See: Auger.

Prestonia (Preston, Charles): Botany. See: Charnock.

Preston's rule (Preston, Thomas): Physics. See: Ballentyne.

Pretenderism (James Francis Edward Stuart, "Old Pretender" and Charles Edward Stuart, "Young Pretender"): History. See: Webster's 3d.

PREVOST, CHARLES PAUL. 1899- . French organic chemist. See: World Who's Who Sci. Prevost reaction.

PREVOST, FLORENT. fl. 1846-1899. French ornithologist. Cited in: Royal Soc. Cat. Sci. Pap., 1800-1863; 1884-1900. Prevost's ground sparrow?

PREVOST, PIERRE. 1751-1839. Swiss philosopher and physicist. See: Encyc. Brit., 1911. Prevost theory of heat exchange (or law of exchanges).

Prevost reaction (Prevost, Charles Paul): Chemistry. See: Van Nostrand Chem. Dict.

Prevost theory of heat exchange (or law of exchanges) (Prevost, Pierre): Physics. See: Ballentyne; Internat. Dict. Phys. Elec.

Prevost's ground sparrow (Prevost, Florent?): Zoology. See: Gray.

Preyevalsky, Nikolai Mikhailovich. See: Przhevalsky, Nikolai Mikhailovich.

Priapean (verse) (Priapus): Literature. See: Partridge; Preminger; Webster's 3d.

Priapic (or Priapean) (Priapus): Generic Word (phallic). See: Webster's 3d.

Priapism (1) (Priapus): Medicine. See: Dorland; New Encyc. Brit., 1974, Microp.; Stedman.

Priapism (2) (Priapus): Generic Word (lewdness). See: Hinsie; Webster's 3d.

PRIAPUS. Greco-Roman god of procreation and fertility. See: New Encyc. Brit., 1974, Microp. Priapean (verse), Priapic (or Priapean), Priapism (1), Priapism (2), Priapusian.

Priapusian (Priapus): Mythology. See: Webster's 3d.

Price-Anderson Act (Price, Charles Melvin and Anderson, Clinton Presba): Politics. Cited in: Encyc. Brit., 1973 under "Health and Safety Laws," p. 209 b.

PRICE, CHARLES MELVIN. 1905- . American legislator. See: Biog. Direct. Amer. Congress. Price-Anderson Act.

PRICE, E. A. fl. 1926. English biochemist. Cited in: Chem. Abstr., vol. 20, p. 3020. Carr-Price reagent, Carr-Price tests for vitamin A.

PRICE-JONES, CECIL. 1863-1943. English hematologist. See: Lancet, vol. 2 (Sept. 18, 1943), p. 370. Price-Jones curve.

Price-Jones curve (Price-Jones, Cecil): Medicine. See: Dorland; Stedman.

Price meter (Price, William Arthur?): Earth Sciences. See: Glazebrook, vol. 3; Huschke.

Price raid (Price, Sterling): History. See: Mathews, M. M.

PRICE, STERLING. 1809-1867. American politician and Confederate general. See: Dict. Amer. Biog. Price raid.

PRICE, THOMAS. fl. 1873. American chemist. Cited in: Hintze, vol. 1, pt. 4, half 1, p. 167. Priceite.

PRICE, WILLIAM ARTHUR. fl. 1892-1900. English electrical physicist. Cited in: Royal Soc. Cat. Sci. Pap., 1884-1900. Price meter?

Priceite (Price, Thomas): Earth Sciences. See: New Encyc. Brit., 1974, Microp.; Thrush.

PRICK, JOSEPH JULES GUILLAUME. 1909- . Dutch physician. See: Who's Who Netherl., 1962-1963. Godfried-Prick-Carol-Prakken syndrome.

PRIDE, THOMAS. d. 1658. English partliamentary general. See: Dict. Nat. Biog. Pride's purge.

PRIDER, REX TREGILGAS. 1910- . Australian geologist. See: Who's Who Brit. Sci., 1953. Priderite.

Priderite (Prider, Rex Tregilgas): Earth Sciences. See: Thrush.

Pride's purge (Pride, Thomas): History. See: Brewer; Latham; Phyfe; Steinberg.

Priessnitz bandage (or compress) (Priessnitz, Vincenz): Medicine. See: Dorland.

PRIESSNITZ, VINCENZ. 1799-1851. German hydrotherapist. See: World Who's Who Sci. Priessnitz bandage (or compress).

Priestman engine (Priestman, William Dent): Engineering and Industry. See: Auger.

PRIESTMAN, WILLIAM DENT. 1847-1936. English engineer. (Biography source unavailable.) Priestman engine.

PRIEUR, MAURICE. b. 1885. French dermatologist. Cited in: Index-Cat. Libr. Surg.-Gen. Off., 3d Ser., vol. 8, 1929. Prieur-Trenel syndrome.

Prieur-Trenel syndrome (Prieur, Maurice and Trenel, M.): Medicine. See: Jablonski.

PRILESCHAIEV, NIKOLAY ALEKSANDROVICH. 1872-1944. Russian chemist. See: Who Was Who USSR. Prileschaiev (Prileschajew) reaction, Prileschajew reagent.

Prileschaiev (Prileschajew) reaction (Prileschaiev, Nikolay Aleksandrovich): Chemistry. See: Ballentyne; Van Nostrand Chem. Dict.

Prileschajew, Nikolay Aleksandrovich. See: Prileschaiev, Nikolay Aleksandrovich.

Prileschajew reagent (Prileschaiev, Nikolay Aleksandrovich): Chemistry. See: Van Nostrand Chem. Dict.

Prilezhayev, Nikolay Aleksandrovich. See: Prileschaiev, Nikolay Aleksandrovich.

PRIM, OBADIAH. Character in Susannah Centlivre's comedy, "A Bold Stroke for a Wife," (1718). (Biography source unavailable.) Obadiah.

Primatt, John. See: Redcliffe-Maud, John Primatt, Baron.

Primianists (Primianus): Religion. See: Canney.

PRIMIANUS. fl. 392. Donatist bishop of Carthage. See: Dict. Christian Biog. Primianists.

PRIMOT, CH. fl. 1913. French chemist. Cited in: Chem. Abstr., vol. 5, p. 759; vol. 7, p. 1069. Primot reagent for antipyrine and cryogenine, Primot reagent for nitrite.

Primot reagent for antipyrine and cryogenine (Primot, Ch.): Chemistry. See: Van Nostrand Chem. Dict.

Primot reagent for nitrite (Primot, Ch.): Chemistry. See: Van Nostrand Chem. Dict.

Prince Ahmed's apple (Ahmed, Prince): (cure) Generic Word. See: Brewer.

Prince Albert frock-coat (Albert): Fashion. See: Clapin; Hendrickson; Partridge.

Prince Albert slipper (Albert): Fashion. See: Picken.

Prince Albert's lyrebird (Albert): Zoology. Cited in: Gray.

Prince Charles' men (Charles I?): Theater. See: Hartnoll.

PRINCE CHARMING. Hero of Charles Perrault's fairy tale, "Cendrillon," 1697). See: Jobes. Prince Charming.

Prince Charming (Prince Charming): Generic Word (ideal suitor). See: Webster's 3d.

Prince of Wales Trophy (Windsor, Edward, Duke of Windsor): Recreation and Sports. See: Encyc. Brit., 1973 under "Ice Hockey," pp. 1033-1034.

Prince Rupert('s) drops (Rupert, Prince): Engineering and Industry. See: Hackh; Hendrickson; Phyfe.

Prince Rupert's metal (Rupert, Prince): Engineering and Industry. See: Brewer; Hendrickson; Webster's 3d.

Prince's metal (Rupert, Prince). See: Prince Rupert's metal.

PRINCETEAU, L. R. b. 1884. French physician. Cited in: Index-Cat. Libr. Surg.-Gen. Off., 2d Ser., vol. 13, 1908. Princeteau's tubercle.

Princeteau's tubercle (Princeteau, L. R.): Medicine. See: Stedman.

principle of Le Chatelier (Le Chatelier, Henry Louis). See: Le Chatelier('s) law.

principle of Pascal (Pascal, Blaise). See: Pascal law.

PRINGLE, JOHN JAMES. 1855-1922. English dermatologist. See: World Who's Who Sci. Pringle's disease (or adenoma).

Pringle's disease (or adenoma) (Pringle, John James). See: Bourneville's syndrome.

PRINGSHEIM, ALFRED. 1850-1941. German mathematician. See: World Who's Who Sci. Pringsheim's theorem.

Pringsheim's theorem (Pringsheim, Alfred): Mathematics. See: Ballentyne; James.

PRINS, GIJSBARTUS. 1923- . Dutch mechanical engineer. See: Who's Who Sci. Europe, 1972. Zernike-Prins formula?

PRINS, HENDRIK JACOBUS. 1889-1958. Dutch chemist. See: Pogg., vol. 6. Prins reaction.

PRINS, KLAAS. fl. 1936-1952. American mining engineer. Cited in: Chem. Abstr., vol. 30, p. 6; Decenn. Index, 1947-1956. Prins process, Prins washer.

Prins process (Prins, Klaas): Engineering and Industry. See: Thrush.

Prins reaction (Prins, Hendrik Jacobus): Chemistry. See: Ballentyne; Krauch and Kunz; Van Nostrand Chem. Dict. Also known as: Kriewitz-Prins reaction.

Prins washer (Prins, Klaas): Engineering and Industry. See: Thrush.

PRINSEP, JAMES. 1799-1840. English meteorologist. See: Pogg., vol. 2. Prinsepia.

Prinsepia (Prinsep, James): Botany. See: Taylor, N.

Prinzmetal-Massumi syndrome (Prinzmetal, Myron and Massumi, Rashid A.): Medicine. See: Jablonski.

PRINZMETAL, MYRON. 1908- . American internist. See: Direct. Med. Specialists., 1965-1966. Prinzmetal-Massumi syndrome.

PRIOR, GEORGE THURLAND. 1862-1936. English mineralogist. See: Who Was Who, 1929-1940. Priorite, Prior's rules.

PRIOR, J. fl. 1884. German bacteriologist. Cited in: Kelly. Finkler-Prior spirillum.

Priorite (Prior, George Thurland): Earth Sciences. See: Webster's 3d.

Prior's rules (Prior, George Thurland): Earth Sciences. See: New Encyc. Brit., 1974, Microp.

PRISCIAN (PRISCIANUS CAESARIENSIS). fl. 500. Roman grammarian at Constantinople. See: Encyc. Brit., 1973. Priscian's head.

Priscian's head (Priscian): Generic Word (rules of grammar). See: Brewer; Harvey; Partridge.

PRISCILLA (OR PRISCA). fl. late 2d. c. Montanist prophetess. See: Dict. Christian Biog. Priscillianists (1).

PRISCILLIAN. d. 385. Spanish religious reformer. See: Encyc. Brit., 1973. Priscillianists (2) (or Priscillianism).

Priscillianists (1) (Priscilla): Religion. See: Canney.

Priscillianists (2) (or Priscillianism) (Priscillian): Religion. See: Attwater; Mathews, S.; Webster's 3d.

PRITCHARD, WILLIAM T. fl. 1860. English diplomat. Cited in: Royal Soc. Cat. Sci. Pap., 1864-1873. Pritchardia.

Pritchardia (Pritchard, William T.): Botany. See: Taylor, N.; Webster's 3d.

PRIVEY, PAUL. fl. 1910. French physician. (Biography source unavailable.) Lesieur-Privey sign.

Prix Goncourt (Goncourt, Edmond Louis Antoine de and Goncourt, Jules Alfred Huot de): Literature. See: Harvey.

PROBERT, FRANK HOLMAN. 1876-1940. English-born American mining engineer. See: Who Was Who Amer., vol. 1. Probertite.

Probertite (Probert, Frank Holman): Earth Sciences. See: Thrush; Webster's 3d.

problem of Apollonius (Apollonius of Perga): Mathematics. See: James.

problem of Bolza (Bolza, Oskar): Mathematics. See: Ballentyne; James.

problem of Boussinesq (Boussinesq, Joseph Valentin). See: problem of Boussinesq and Cerruti.

problem of Boussinesq and Cerruti (Boussinesq, Joseph Valentin and Cerruti, Valentino?): Physics. See: Internat. Dict. Ap. Math. Also known as: problem of Boussinesq.

PROCA, ALEXANDRE. 1897-1955. French physicist. See: Pogg., vol. 6. Proca equation(s).

Proca equation(s) (Proca, Alexandre): Physics. See: Ballentyne; Internat. Dict. Phys. Elec.

PROCHOWNICK, LUDWIG. 1851-1923. German obstetrician. See: Biog. Lex. hervorr. Aerzte. Prochownick's diet, Prochowinick's method.

Prochownick's diet (Prochownick. Ludwig): Medicine. See: Stedman.

Prochownick's method (Prochownick, Ludwig): Medicine. See: Stedman.

PROCKE, OTTO. fl. 1938. Czechoslovakian chemist. See: Chemicke Listy, vol. 30 (1939), p. 345 ff. Procke-Uzel solution.

Procke-Uzel solution (Procke, Otto and Uzel, Radim): Chemistry. See: Van Nostrand Chem. Dict.

Procopiu effect (Procopiu, Stefan): Physics. See: Ballentyne.

Procopiu phenomenon (Procopiu, Stefan): Physics. Cited in: World Who's Who Sci.

PROCOPIU, STEFAN. b. 1890. Rumanian physicist. See: World Who's Who Sci. Procopiu effect, Procopiu phenomenon.

Procopius Legend (Procopius, Saint): Religion. See: Attwater.

PROCOPIUS, SAINT. fl. before 283. Christian martyr. See: Holweck. Procopius Legend.

Procrustean (or Procrustean bed) (Procrustes): Generic Word (forced conformity). See: Partridge; Scott; Webster's 3d.

PROCRUSTES. Legendary Greek robber. See: Jobes. Procrustean (or Procrustean bed).

PROCTER, HENRY RICHARDSON. 1848-1927. English leather chemist. See: Who Was Who, 1916-1928. Proctor test reaction for tannic acid.

Proctor curve (Proctor, Ralph R.): Engineering and Industry. See: Thrush.

Proctor order (Proctor, Robert George Collier): Library Science. See: Avis.

Proctor penetration needle (Proctor, Ralph R.): Engineering and Industry. See: Thrush.

Proctor penetration resistance (and curve) (Proctor, Ralph R.): Engineering and Industry. See: Thrush.

Proctor plasticity needle (Proctor, Ralph R.): Engineering and Industry. See: Thrush.

PROCTOR, RALPH R. fl. 1938-1941. American engineer. Cited in: Chem. Abstr., Decenn. Index, 1937-1946. Proctor curve, Proctor penetration needle, Proctor penetration resistance (and curve), Proctor plasticity needle.

PROCTOR, ROBERT GEORGE COLLIER. 1868-1903. English bibliographer. See: Dict. Nat. Biog., 2d. suppl. Proctor order.

Proctor test reaction for tannic acid (Procter, Henry Richardson): Chemistry. See: Van Nostrand Chem. Dict.

Proell governor (Proell, Wilhelm Rudolph): Engineering and Industry. See: Auger.

PROELL, WILHELM RUDOLPH. fl. 1881. German engineer. Cited in: Royal Soc. Cat. Sci. Pap., 1864-1873; 1884-1900. Proell governor.

Profaci gang (Profaci, Joseph): Sociology. Cited in: Laughlin.

PROFACI, JOSEPH. fl. 1960. American cirminal. Cited in: New York Times Index, 1960. Profaci gang.

PROFETA, GIUSEPPE. 1840-1910. Italian dermatologist. See: Biog. Lex. hervorr. Aerzte. Profeta's law.

Profeta's law (Profeta, Giuseppe): Medicine. See: Stedman.

PROFICHET, GEORGES CHARLES. b. 1873. French physician. Cited in: Index-Cat. Libr. Surg.-Gen. Off., 2d Ser., 1908. Profichet's disease.

Profichet's disease (Profichet, Georges Charles): Medicine. See: Jablonski; Stedman.

Profumo affair (Profumo, John Dennis): Politics. See: Morris and Irwin; New Encyc. Brit., 1973, Microp.

PROFUMO, JOHN DENNIS. 1915- . English diplomat. See: Who's Who, 1974-1975. Profumo affair.

PROKIN, S. S. fl. 1937. Russian chemist. Cited in: Chem. Abstr., Decenn. Index, 1937-1946. Makarov-Zemlianski-Prokin method.

Promethea (Prometheus) moth (Prometheus): Zoology. See: Webster's 3d.

Promethean (or Prometheus) (Prometheus): Generic Word (daring rebel or victim of the gods). See: Partridge; Webster's 3d.

Promethean fire (Prometheus): Generic Word (divine spark). See: Brewer; Harvey; Jobes.

Promethean (safety matches or glass tube) (Prometheus): Engineering and Industry. See: Brewer; Harvey; Jobes; Partridge.

Promethean unguent (Prometheus): Mythology. See: Jobes.

Promethean will (Prometheus): Psychology. See: Chaplin.

PROMETHEUS. Titan in Greek mythology. See: Jobes. Promethea (Prometheus) moth, Promethean (or Prometheus), Promethean fire, Promethean (safety matches or glass tube), Promethean unguent, Promethean will, Promethium.

Promethium (Prometheus): Chemistry. See: Markus; New Encyc. Brit., 1974, Microp.; Thrush; Van Nostrand Sci. Encyc.

Prony(s) brake (or dynamometer) (De Prony, Baron Gaspard-Clair-Francois-Marie Riche): Engineering and Industry. See: Auger; Thrush; Webster's 3d.

Prony, Gaspard-Clair-Francois-Marie Riche, Baron de. See: De Prony, Baron Gaspard-Clair-Francois-Marie Riche.

property of Baire (Baire, Rene Louis): Mathematics. See: James.

Prophecies of St. Malachy (Malachy, Saint): Religion. See: Attwater.

Proserpinaca (Persephone): Botany. See: Charnock; Webster's 3d.

Proserpine. See: Persephone.

PROSKAUER, BERNHARD. 1851-1915. German bacteriologist. See: Biog. Lex. hervorr. Aerzte. Voges-Proskauer reaction.

Prosopium Williamsoni (Williamson, Henry Charles): Zoology. See: Pennak.

Prosser engine (Prosser, J. G.): Engineering and Industry. See: Auger.

PROSSER, GABRIEL. ca. 1777-1800. American slave insurrectionist. See: Afro-Amer. Encyc., vol. 7. Gabriel's insurrection.

PROSSER, J. G. fl. 20th c. American? engineer. (Biography source unavailable.) Prosser engine.

PROT, MARCEL (In full: E. MARCEL). fl. 1930. French engineer. Cited in: Chem. Abstr., Decenn. Index, 1927-1936. Prot test.

Prot test (Prot, Marcel): Engineering and Industry. See: Auger.

Protea (Proteus): Botany. See: Charnock; Webster's 3d.

Protean (Proteus): Generic Word (ever-changing). See: Charnock; Partridge; Webster's 3d.

Protean stone (Proteus): Engineering and Industry. See: Charnock.

Proteomyxa (Proteus): Botany. See: Webster's 3d.

PROTEUS. Old man of the sea in Greek mythology. See: Jobes. haemoproteus, Protea, Protean, Protean stone, Proteomyxa, Proteus (bacteria genus), Proteus (salamander genus).

Proteus (bacteria genus) (Proteus): Zoology. See: Pennak; Stedman; Webster's 3d.

Proteus (salamander genus) (Proteus): Zoology. See: Webster's 3d.

PROUST, JOSEPH LOUIS. 1754-1826. French chemist. See: World Who's Who Sci. Proustite, Proust's law.

PROUST, MARCEL. 1871-1922. French novelist. See: Encyc. Brit., 1973. Proustian.

PROUST, P. T. fl. 1822. French physician. Cited in: Index-Cat. Libr. Surg.-Gen. Off., 1st Ser., vol. 11, 1890. Proust's space.

Proustian (Proust, Marcel): Literature. See: Webster's 3d.

Proustite (Proust, Joseph Louis): Earth Sciences. See: Thrush; Van Nostrand Sci. Encyc.; Webster's 3d.

Proust's law (Proust, Joseph Louis): Chemistry. See: Asimov; Hackh; Webster's 3d.

Proust's space (Proust, P. T.): Anatomy. See: Stedman.

Prout (Prout, William?): Physics. See: Dresner.

Prout('s) hypothesis (Prout, William): Chemistry. See: Asimov; Ballentyne; Van Nostrand Chem. Dict.; Webster's 3d.

PROUT, SAMUEL. 1783-1852. English artist. See: Dict. Nat. Biog. Prout's brown.

PROUT, WILLIAM. 1785-1850. English physiologist and chemist. See: World Who's Who Sci. Prout?, Prout('s) hypothesis

Prout's brown (Prout, Samuel): Fine Arts. See: Webster's 3d.

Prouty kiln (Prouty, Theodore C. and Prouty, Willis O.): Engineering and Industry. See: Thrush.

PROUTY, THEODORE C. fl. 1932. American engineer. Cited in: Chem. Abstr., Decenn. Index, 1927-1936. Prouty kiln.

PROUTY, WILLIS O. fl. 1932. American engineer. Cited in: Chem. Abstr., Decenn. Index, 1927-1936. Prouty kiln.

Prowazek bodies (Prowazek, Stanislas Josef Mathias Edler von Lanow): Medicine. See: Dorland; Stedman. Also known as: Paschen bodies.

Prowazek-Greeff bodies (Prowazek, Stanislas Josef Mathias Edler von Lanow and Greeff, Carl Richard): Medicine. See: Dorland; Stedman. Also known as: Halberstaedter-Prowazek bodies.

ROWAZEK, STANISLAS JOSEF MATHIAS EDLER VON LANOW. 1875-1915. German protozoologist. See: Biog. Lex. hervorr. Aerzte. Prowazek bodies, rowazek-Greeff bodies, Prowazekia.

rowazekella (Prowazek, Stanislas Josef Mathias Edler von Lanow). See: rowazekia.

rowazekia (Prowazek, Stanislas Josef Mathias Edler von Lanow): Zoology. ee: Dorland; Stedman.

ROWER. fl. 20th c. American? hospital patient. (Biography source unavail-ble.) Stuart-Prower factor.

RUDHOMME, JOSEPH. Character in Henri Monnier's novel, "Memoires de 1. Joseph Prudhomme," (1857). See: Harvey and Heseltine. Prudhommerie.

RUD'HOMME, MAURICE. d. 1927. French chemist. See: Pogg., vols. , 6. Prud'homme reagent for aldehydes.

rud'homme reagent for aldehydes (Prud'homme, Maurice): Chemistry. See: an Nostrand Chem. Dict.

rudhommerie (Prudhomme, Joseph): Generic Word (pomposity). See: Brewer.

RUSSAK, ALEXANDER. 1839-1897. Russian otologist. See: Biog. Lex. ervorr. Aerzte. Prussak's fibers, Prussak's space (or pouch).

russak's fibers (Prussak, Alexander): Anatomy. See: Donath; Stedman.

russak's space (or pouch) (Prussak, Alexander): Anatomy. See: Donath; tedman.

RY, PAUL. Meddlesome hero of John Poole's comedy, "Paul Pry", (1853). ee: Harvey. Paul Pry.

RYM, FRIEDRICH. 1841-1915. German mathematician. See: World Who's Vho Sci. Prym's functions.

rym's functions (Prym, Friedrich): Mathematics. See: Ballentyne.

RZHEVALSKY, NIKOLAI MIKHAILOVICH. 1839-1888. Russian explorer. ee: Encyc. Brit., 1973. Przhevalsky's (Prejevalski's) horse.

rzhevalsky's (Prejevalski's) horse (Przhevalsky, Nikolai Mikhailovich): Zoology. ee: New Encyc. Brit., 1974, Microp.; Pennak; Van Nostrand Sci. Encyc. nder "Horse."

sathyrians (Psathyropola, Theoctistus): Religion. See: Canney.

SATHYROPOLA, THEOCTISTUS. fl. 390. Syrian confectioner. See: Dict. Christian Biog. Psathyrians.

SAUME, JEAN. fl. 1954. French stomatologist. (Biography source unavail-ble.) Papillon-Leage and Psaume syndrome.

PSCHORR, ROBERT FRANZ. 1868-1930. German organic chemist. See: ogg., vols. 4, 5. Pschorr synthesis (or reaction).

schorr synthesis (or reaction) (Pschorr, Robert Franz): Chemistry. See: Bal-entyne; Krauch and Kunz; Van Nostrand Chem. Dict.

oseudo-Isidore (decretals) (Mercator, Isidore): Religion. See: Attwater.

PSYCHE. Greek personification of the human soul. See: Jobes. Psyche-glass, Psyche knot, Psychean, Psyche's task.

Psyche-glass (Psyche): Generic Word (long mirror). See: Partridge; Webster's 3d.

Psyche knot (Psyche): Fashion. See: Webster's 3d.

Psychean (Psyche): Mythology. See: Webster's 3d.

Psyche's task (Psyche): Generic Word (impossible task). See: Jobes; Partridge.

Ptolemaic (or Ptolemaean) (Ptolemy I, Soter): History. See: Webster's 3d.

Ptolemaic system (Ptolemy): Astronomy. See: Asimov; Brewer; Webster's 3d.

PTOLEMY (CLAUDIUS PTOLEMAEUS). fl. 140. Alexandrian astronomer, geographer and mathematician. See: New Encyc. Brit., 1974. Ptolemaic system, Ptolemy's canon, Ptolemy's theorem.

PTOLEMY I, SOTER. 367?-283 B.C. King of Egypt. See: New Encyc. Brit., 1974. Ptolemaic (or Ptolemaean).

PTOLEMY II, PHILADELPHUS. 309-246 B.C. King of Egypt. See: Encyc. Brit., 1911. Philadelphian, Philadelphus?

tolemy's canon (Ptolemy): History. See: New Encyc. Brit., 1974, Microp.

Ptolemy's theorem (Ptolemy): Mathematics. See: Ballentyne; James; New Encyc. Brit., 1974, Microp.

PUCCINI, TOMMASO. d. 1735. Italian anatomist. (Biography source un-available.) Puccinia.

Puccinia (Puccini, Tommaso): Botany. See: Van Nostrand Sci. Encyc. under "Rust fungi;" Webster's 3d.

PUCH, STEYR DAIMLER. fl. 20th c. Austrian weapons designer. (Biography source unavailable.) Steyr 9mm parabellum submachine gun.

PUCK. Mischievous goblin in medieval English folklore. See: Jobes. Puck (or Puckish).

Puck (or Puckish) (Puck): Generic Word (mischievous sprite). See: New Encyc. Brit., 1974, Microp.; Partridge.

PUCKLE, OWEN STANDIGE. fl. 1943. English electrical engineer. Cited in: Sci. Abstr. (Elec. Engin.), vol. 45 B, no. 1238. Puckle time base.

Puckle time base (Puckle, Owen Standige): Electronics. See: Hughes.

PUDLAK, P. fl. 1959. Czech internist. (Biography source unavailable.) Hermansky-Pudlak syndrome.

PUERARI, MARC-NICOLAS. 1766-1845. Swiss botanist in Copenhagen. See: Dict. Hist. Biog. Suisse. Pueraria.

Pueraria (Puerari, Marc-Nicolas): Botany. See: Taylor, N.; Webster's 3d.

PUGACHEV, EMELYAN IVANOVICH. 1726-1775. Russian soldier and rebel. See: Encyc. Brit., 1973. Pugachev's rebellion.

Pugachev's rebellion (Pugachev, Emelyan Ivanovich): History. See: Morris and Irwin.

Pugin (Pugin, Augustus Welby Northmore): Architecture. See: Attwater.

PUGIN, AUGUSTUS WELBY NORTHMORE. 1812-1852. English architect. See: Encyc. Brit., 1973. Pugin.

PUJO, ARSENE PAULIN. 1861-1939. American legislator. See: Who Was Who Amer., vol. 1. Pujo Committee Report.

Pujo Committee Report (Pujo, Arsene Paulin): History. See: Morris.

PULASKI, EDWARD C. fl. 20th c. American forest ranger. (Biography source unavailable.) Pulaski tool.

PULASKI, KAZIMIERZ. 1747-1779. Polish nobleman and patriot. See: New Encyc. Brit., 1974, Microp. Pulaski's legion.

Pulaski tool (Pulaski, Edward C.): Earth Sciences. See: Webster's 3d.; Win-burne.

Pulaski's legion (Pulaski, Kazimierz): History. See: Jameson.

PULFRICH, CARL. 1858-1927. German physicist. See: World Who's Who Sci. Pulfrich (Pulfric) effect (or phenomenon), Pulfrich refractometer, Pulfrich stereocomparer.

Pulfrich (Pulfric) effect (or phenomenon) (Pulfrich, Carl): Physiology. See: Chaplin; English.

Pulfrich refractometer (Pulfrich, Carl): Physics. See: Hackh; Internat. Dict. Phys. Elec.; Van Nostrand Sci. Encyc. under "Refractometers."

Pulfrich stereocomparer (Pulfrich, Carl): Physics. Cited in: World Who's Who Sci.

PULITZER, JOSEPH. 1847-1911. Hungarian-born American journalist. See: Dict. Amer. Biog. Pulitzer prize(s).

Pulitzer prize(s) (Pulitzer, Joseph): Literature. See: Harvey; Hendrickson; New Encyc. Brit., 1974, Microp.; Webster's 3d.

pull a Houdini (or do a Houdini) (Houdini, Harry): Generic Word (perform disappearing act or escape). See: Hendrickson; Partridge.

PULLMAN, GEORGE MORTIMER. 1831-1897. American inventor. See: Dict. Amer. Biog. Pullman (railroad car).

Pullman (railroad car) (Pullman, George Mortimer): Engineering and Industry. See: Hendrickson; Mathews, M. M.; Partridge; Webster's 3d.

PUMPELLY, RAPHAEL. 1837-1923. American geologist. See: Dict. Amer. Biog. Pumpellyite, Pumpelly's rule?

Pumpellyite (Pumpelly, Raphael): Earth Sciences. See: Thrush; Webster's 3d.

Pumpelly's rule (Pumpelly, Raphael?): Earth Sciences. See: Thrush.

PUMPHREY, ROBERT E. 1933- . American otolaryngologist. See: Direct. Med. Specialists, 14th ed. Bart-Pumphrey syndrome.

PUNCH (OR PUNCHINELLA). Puppet character traceable to the Roman clown and Pulcinella, a character in the Italian commedia dell'arte in the 17th c. See: New Encyc. Brit., 1974, Microp. pleased as Punch, Punch and Judy (show).

Punch and Judy (show) (Punch and Judy, the puppet characters): Theater. See: Charnock.

Puncheon (Pilate, Pontius): Generic Word (cask). See: Partridge.

Pungernite (Derivation undetermined): Earth Sciences. See: Thrush.

Pupin coil (Pupin, Michael Idvorsky): Electronics. See: Markus.

PUPIN, MICHAEL IDVORSKY. 1858-1935. Yugoslavian-born American physicist. See: World Who's Who Sci. Pupin coil, Pupin system.

Pupin system (Pupin, Michael Idvorsky): Physics. See: Webster's 3d.

PURCELL, EDWARD MILLS. 1912- . American physicist. See: World Who's Who Sci. Smith-Purcell effect.

PURCELL, HENRY. 1659-1695. English composer. See: Dict. Nat. Biog. Purcell Society.

PURCELL-LLEWELLIN. fl. 19th c. English dog breeder. (Biography source unavailable.) Llewellin setter.

Purcell Society (Purcell, Henry): Music. See: Scholes.

Purdie method of alkylation (or methylation) (Purdie, Thomas): Chemistry. See: Ballentyne; Van Nostrand Chem. Dict.

PURDIE, THOMAS. 1843-1916. Scottish chemist. See: Pogg., vol. 4. Purdie method of alkylation (or methylation).

PURDON. fl. before 1851. English inventor. (Biography source unavailable.) Purdonion (or Purdonium).

Purdonion (or Purdonium) (Purdon): Engineering and Industry. See: Partridge.

PURDY, CHARLES WESLEY. 1846-1901. American physician. See: Chicago Med. Recorder, vol. 20 (1901), pp. 212, 247. Purdy's method, Purdy's solution, Purdy's test.

PURDY, L. H. fl. 1926. American chemist. Cited in: Chem. Abstr., vol. 14, p. 703. Krauskopf-Purdy reagent.

Purdy's method (Purdy, Charles Wesley): Medicine. See: Dorland; Stedman.

Purdy's solution (Purdy, Charles Wesley): Medicine. See: Dorland; Stedman.

Purdy's test (Purdy, Charles Wesley): Medicine. See: Dorland.

PURGOTTI, ATTILIO. 1863-1929. Italian chemist. See: Pogg., vols. 4, 5. Purgotti molybdate reagent.

Purgotti molybdate reagent (Purgotti, Attilio): Chemistry. See: Van Nostrand Chem. Dict.

Purkinje('s) afterimage (Purkinje, Jan Evangelista): Physiology. See: Chaplin; Drever; Webster's 3d. Also known as: Bidwell's ghost.

Purkinje('s) cells (or corpuscles) (Purkinje, Jan Evangelista): Anatomy. See: Dorland; Henderson; Stedman; Webster's 3d.

Purkinje conduction (Purkinje, Jan Evangelista): Physiology. See: Stedman.

Purkinje effect (phenomenon or shift) (Purkinje, Jan Evangelista): Physiology. See: Ballentyne; Chaplin; Drever.

Purkinje('s) fiber(s) (fibres) (Purkinje, Jan Evangelista): Anatomy. See: Dorland; Henderson; Stedman; Webster's 3d.

Purkinje('s) figure(s) (Purkinje, Jan Evangelista): Anatomy. See: Chaplin; Dorland; Stedman; Webster's 3d.

PURKINJE, JAN EVANGELISTA. 1787-1869. Czech physiologist. See: World Who's Who Sci. Purkinje('s) afterimage, Purkinje('s) cells (or corpuscles), Purkinje conduction, Purkinje effect (phenomenon or shift), Purkinje('s) fiber(s) (fibres), Purkinje('s) figure(s), Purkinje system, Purkinje-Sanson images, Purkinje's layer, Purkinje's network (or tissue), Purkinje's vesicle.

Purkinje-Sanson images (Purkinje, Jan Evangelista and Sanson, Louis Joseph): Physiology. See: Dorland; Drever; Stedman; Wolman. Also known as: Prkinje's images, Sanson's images.

Purkinje system (Purkinje, Jan Evangelista): Anatomy. See: Stedman.

Purkinje's layer (Purkinje, Jan Evangelista): Anatomy. See: Stedman.

Purkinje's network (or tissue) (Purkinje, Jan Evangelista): Anatomy. See: Dorland; Stedman; Webster's 3d.

Purkinje's vesicle (Purkinje, Jan Evangelista): Anatomy. See: Donath.

PURMANN, MATTHAEUS GOTTFRIED. 1648-1721. German surgeon. See: World Who's Who Sci. Purmann's method.

Purmann's method (Purmann, Matthaeus Gottfried): Medicine. See: Dorland; Stedman.

purple of Cassius (or Cassius purple) (Cassius, Andreas): Chemistry. See: Charnock; Thrush; Wagner (Names).

PURSH, FREDERICK TRAUGOTT. 1774-1820. German botanist in America. See: Dict. Amer. Biog. Purshia, Pursh's plaintain.

Purshia (Pursh, Frederick Traugott): Botany. See: Taylor, N.: Webster's 3d.

Pursh's plaintain (Pursh, Frederick Traugott): Botany. See: Webster's 3d.

PURTSCHER, OTMAR. 1852-1927. German ophthalmologist. See: Biog. Lex. hervorr. Aerzte. Purtscher's disease.

Purtscher's disease (Purtscher, Otmar): Medicine. See: Jablonski; Stedman.

PURVES. fl. 19th c. English engineer. (Biography source unavailable.) Purves flue (or tube).

Purves flue (or tube) (Purves): Engineering and Industry. See: Webster's 3d.

PURVIS, EDWARD "UKULELE." fl. 19th c. English army officer. (Biography source unavailable.) Ukulele.

Puschkin, Apollo A. M. Mussin-. See: Mussin-Puschkin, Apollo A. M.

Puschkinia (Mussin-Puschkin, Apollo A. M.): Botany. See: Taylor, N.; Webster's 3d.

PUSEY, EDWARD BOUVERIE. 1800-1882. English Anglican theologian. See: Dict. Nat. Biog. Puseyism (or Puseyites).

PUSEY, WILLIAM ALLEN. 1865-1940. American dermatologist. See: Who Was Who Amer., vol. 1. Pusey's emulsion.

Puseyism (or Puseyites) (Pusey, Edward Bouverie): Religion. See: Canney; Charnock; Phyfe; Webster's 3d. Also known as: Pussey-cats.

Pusey's emulsion (Pusey, William Allen): Medicine. See: Dorland.

Pussey-cats (Pusey, Edward Bouverie): See: Puseyism (or Puseyites).

Pussyfoot (Johnson, William Eugene "Pussyfoot"): Generic Word (cunning and cautious). See: Hendrickson.

Putnam-Dana syndrome (Putnam, James Jackson and Dana, Charles Loomis). See: Dana's syndrome.

PUTNAM, JAMES JACKSON. 1846-1918. American neurologist. See: World Who's Who Sci. Putnam-Dana syndrome, Putnam's acroparesthesia, Putnam's disease.

Putnam's acroparesthesia (Putnam, James Jackson): Medicine. See: Jablonski.

Putnam's disease (Putnam, James Jackson). See: Dana's syndrome.

Putti-Chavany syndrome (Putti, Vittorio and Chavany, Jean Alfred Emile): Medicine. See: Jablonski.

Putti-Platt operation (or procedure) (Putti, Vittorio? and Platt, John Edward?): Medicine. See: Stedman.

PUTTI, VITTORIO. 1880-1940. Italian physician. See: Biog. Lex. hervorr. Aerzte. Putti-Chavany syndrome, Putti-Platt operation (or procedure)? Putti's syndrome, Putti's treatment.

Putti's syndrome (Putti, Vittorio): Medicine. See: Jablonski.

Putti's treatment (Putti, Vittorio): Medicine. See: Kelly.

JUSSEPP, LYUDVIG MARTINOVICH. 1875-1942. Estonian neurosurgeon. See: Folia Neuropath. Eston., vols. iii/iv, (1925), pp. 9-16. Puussepp's operation, Puussepp's reflex.

Puussepp's operation (Puussepp, Lyudvig Martinovich): Medicine. See: Dorland.

Puussepp's reflex (Puussepp, Lyudvig Martinovich): Medicine. See: Dorland.

Puzos' method (Puzos, Nicholas): Medicine. See: Dorland.

PUZOS, NICHOLAS. 1686-1753. French surgeon. See: Nouv. Biog. Univ. Puzos' method.

PYE, JOSEPH. No dates. American Indian medicine man. (Biography source unavailable.) Joe-Pye weed.

PYGMALION. In Greek mythology, Cyprian King who fell in love with his own statue of Aphrodite. See: Jobes. not Pygmalion likely!, Pygmalion (brown color), Pygmalion effect, Pygmalionism.

Pygmalion (brown color) (Pygmalion): Chemistry. See: Webster's 3d.

Pygmalion effect (Pygmalion): Psychology. See: Good.

Pygmalionism (Pygmalion): Psychology. See: Hinsie; Webster's 3d.

PYLADES. Husband of Electra and faithful friend of Orestes in Greek mythology. See: Jobes. Pylades and Orestes.

Pylades and Orestes (Pylades, the nephew and Orestes, the son of Agamemnon): Generic Word (friendship). See: Brewer.

Pyle-Cohn disease (Pyle, Edwin and Cohn, Max). See: Pyle's disease.

PYLE, EDWIN. b. 1892. American orthopedic surgeon. See: Direct. Med. Specialists, 8th ed. Pyle's disease.

PYLE, JOHN. fl. 1781. American loyalist in Revolutionary war. See: Wicklire. Pyle massacre (or hacking match).

Pyle massacre (or hacking match) (Pyle, John): History. See: Jameson.

Pyle's disease (Pyle, Edwin): Medicine. See: Jablonski. Also known as: Bakwin-Krida syndrome, Pyle-Cohn disease.

PYM, SIR WILLIAM. 1772-1861. English military surgeon. See: World Who's Who Sci. Pym's fever.

Pym's fever (Pym, Sir William): Medicine. See: Stedman.

Pyrrhic dance (Pyrrichos): Dance. See: Brewer; Harvey; Wagner (Names).

Pyrrhic (metrical foot) (Pyrrichos): Literature. See: Preminger; Scott.

Pyrrhic victory (Pyrrhus): Generic Word (costly victory). See: Harvey; Henrickson; Partridge; Webster's 3d.

PYRRHO OF ELIS. ca. 365-275 B.C. Greek sceptic philosopher. See: Encyc. Brit., 1973. Pyrrhonism (or Pyrrhonists).

Pyrrhonism (or Pyrrhonists) (Pyrrho of Elis): Philosophy. See: Brewer; Canney; Webster's 3d.

PYRRHUS. 318?-272 B.C. King of Epirus. See: New Encyc. Brit., 1974, Microp. Pyrrhic victory.

PYRRICHOS. Legendary Greek flutist. See: Dict. Grk. Rom. Antiq. Pyrrhic dance, Pyrrhic (metrical foot).

PYTHAGORAS OF SAMOS. ca. 580-500 B.C. Greek philosopher and mathematician. See: New Encyc. Brit., 1974, Microp. pentagram of Pythagoras, Pythagorean brotherhood, Pythagorean comma, Pythagorean identity (identities), Pythagorean letter, Pythagorean numbers, Pythagorean relation between direction cosines, Pythagorean scale, Pythagorean semitone, The Pythagorean system, Pythagorean theorem (or proposition, Pythagoreanism (or Pythagoreans), table of Pythagoras.

Pythagorean brotherhood (Pythagoras of Samos): Religion. See: New Encyc. Brit., 1974, Microp.

Pythagorean comma (Pythagoras of Samos): Music. See: New Encyc. Brit., 1974, Microp.; Webster's 3d.

Pythagorean identity (identities) (Pythagoras of Samos): Mathematics. See: Ballentyne; James.

Pythagorean letter (Pythagoras of Samos): Philosophy. See: Harvey.

Pythagorean numbers (Pythagoras of Samos): Mathematics. See: Ballentyne; James.

Pythagorean relation between direction cosines (Pythagoras of Samos): Mathematics. See: James.

Pythagorean scale (Pythagorus of Samos): Music. See: Apel; Van Nostrand Sci. Encyc.; Webster's 3d.

Pythagorean semitone (Pythagoras of Samos): Music. See: Webster's 3d.

Pythagorean system (Pythagoras of Samos): Astronomy. See: Brewer.

Pythagorean theorem (or proposition) (Pythagoras of Samos): Mathematics. See: James; New Encyc. Brit., 1974, Microp.

Pythagoreanism (or Pythagoreans) (Pythagoras of Samos): Philosophy. See: Canney; New Encyc. Brit., 1974, Microp.; Partridge; Webster's 3d.

PYTHIA. Priestess of the Pythian Apollo at Delphi. See: Jobes. Pythian.

Pythian (Pythia): Mythology. See: Charnock.

Pythian Apollo. See: Apollo.

PYTHIAS. fl. 4th c. B.C. Syracusan philosopher. See: Dict. Grk. Rom. Biog. Myth. Damon and Pythias, Knight of Pythias.

Q

Qadiriyeh (Abd al-Qadir al Jilani): Religion. See: Canney.

Qarmat. See: Hamdan Qarmat.

Qarmatians (Hamdan Karmat). See: Karmatians (or Karmatis).

quadratrix of Dinostratus (Dinostratus): Mathematics. See: Van Nostrand Sci. Encyc.

QUAIN, SIR RICHARD. 1816-1898. English chest physician. See: Dict. Nat. Biog., 3d suppl. Quain's fatty heart.

Quain's fatty heart (Quain, Sir Richard): Medicine. See: Dorland.

Quant's sign (Derivation undetermined): Medicine. See: Stedman.

QUARELLI, GUSTAVO. fl. 1930. Italian physician. Cited in: Quart. Cum. Index Medicus, vol. 8, 1930. Quarelli's syndrome.

Quarelli's syndrome (Quarelli, Gustavo): Medicine. See: Jablonski.

QUASIMODO. Bellringer in Victor Hugo's novel, "The Hunchback of Notre Dame," (1831). See: Magill. Quasimodo complex.

Quasimodo complex (Quasimodo): Psychology. See: Hinsie.

QUASSI, GRAMAN. fl. 18th c. Surinam negro slave. See: Webster's Biog. Dict. Quassia, Quassin (or Quassite).

Quassia (Quassi, Graman): Botany. See: Charnock; Hendrickson; Partridge; Webster's 3d.

Quassin (or Quassite) (Quassi, Graman): Botany. See: Charnock; Hendrickson.

Quatrefage's angle (De Quatrefages de Breau, Jean Louis Armand): Anatomy. See: Donath; Dorland; Stedman.

Quatrefages de Breau, Jean Louis Armand. See: De Quatrefages de Breau, Jean Louis Armand.

QUECKENSTEDT, HANS HEINRICH GEORG. 1876-1918. German physician. Cited in: Index-Cat. Libr. Surg.-Gen. Off., 2d Ser., vol. 14, 1909. Queckenstedt's sign (test, maneuver or phenomenon).

Queckenstedt-Stookey test (Queckenstedt, Hans Heinrich Georg and Stookey, Byron Polk). See: Queckenstedt's sign (maneuver, phenomenon or test).

Queckenstedt's sign (test, maneuver or phenomenon) (Queckenstedt, Hans Heinrich Georg): Medicine. See: Dorland. Also known as: Queckenstedt-Stookey test.

Queen Anne style (Anne): Architecture. See: Brewer; Briggs; Osborne.

Queen Anne's bounty (Anne): History. See: Harbottle; Montgomery; Steinberg.

Queen Anne's dead! (Anne): Generic Word. See: Hendrickson; Partridge.

Queen Anne's fan (Anne): Generic Word. See: Brewer; Hendrickson.

Queen Anne's farthings (Anne): Numismatics. See: Phyfe.

Queen Anne's lace (Anne of Bohemia): Botany. See: Hendrickson.

Queen Anne's men (Anne): Theater. See: Hartnoll.

Queen Anne's War (Anne): History. See: Jameson; Latham; Morris.

Queen Elizabeth's men (Elizabeth I): Theater. See: Hartnoll.

Queen Elizabeth's pocket-pistol (Elizabeth I): Weapons. See: Latham.

Queen Henrietta's Men (Henrietta Maria of England): Theater. See: Hartnoll.

Queen Margaret (plant) (Derivation undetermined): Botany. See: Charnock.

Queen Mary's thistle (Mary Stuart): Botany. See: Blumberg.

Queensberry, 2nd Duke of. See: Douglas, James, 2nd Duke of Queensberry.

Queensberry, 8th Marquis of. See: Douglas, John Sholto, 8th Marquis of Queensberry.

Queensberry plot (Douglas, James, 2nd Duke of Queensberry): History. See: Harbottle.

Queensberry rules (Douglas, John Sholto, 8th Marquis of Queensberry): Recreation and Sports. See: Barnhart (Eng. Lit.); Hendrickson.

QUENOUILLE, MAURICE HENRY. 1924-   . English statistician. See: Who's Who Sci. Europe, 1972. Quenouille's test.

Quenouille's test (Quenouille, Maurice Henry): Statistics. See: Kendall.

QUENSEL, PERCY DUDGEON. b. 1881. Swedish mineralogist, geologist and petrographer. See: Svenska Maen Och Kvinnor. Quenselite.

Quensel-Posner cadmium-methylene blue stain (Quensel, Ulrik and Posner, Carl?): Medicine. Cited in: Biog. Lex. hervorr. Aerzte, 1880-1930.

QUENSEL, ULRIK. b. 1863. Swedish physician. See: Biog. Lex. hervorr. Aerzte, 1880-1930. Quensel-Posner cadmium-methylene blue stain.

Quenselite (Quensel, Percy Dudgeon): Earth Sciences. See: Thrush; Webster's 3d.

QUENSTEDT, FRIEDRICH AUGUST. 1809-1889. German mineralogist, geologist and paleontologist. See: Encyc. Brit., 1911. Quenstedtite.

Quenstedtite (Quenstedt, Friedrich August): Earth Sciences. See: Thrush; Webster's 3d.

QUENU, EDOUARD ANDRE VICTOR ALFRED. 1852-1933. French surgeon and anatomist. See: Biog. Lex. hervorr. Aerzte. Quenu-Mayo operation, Quenu-Muret sign, Quenu's hemorrhoidal plexus, Quenu's thoracoplasty.

Quenu-Mayo operation (Quenu, Edouard Andre Victor Alfred and Mayo, William James): Medicine. See: Dorland; Stedman.

Quenu-Muret sign (Quenu, Edouard Andre Victor Alfred and Muret, Paul-Louis): Medicine. See: Stedman.

Quenu's hemorrhoidal plexus (Quenu, Edouard Andre Victor Alfred): Medicine. See: Stedman.

Quenu's thoracoplasty (Quenu, Edouard Andre Victor Alfred): Medicine. See: Stedman.

QUERVAIN, FRITZ DE. 1868-1940. Swiss physician. See: Biog. Lex. hervorr. Aerzte. Quervain's disease (1), Quervain's disease (2), Quervain's fracture.

Quervain's disease (1) (Quervain, Fritz de): Medicine. See: Dorland; Jablonski; Stedman.

Quervain's disease (2) (Quervain, Fritz de): Medicine. See: Jablonski; Stedman. Also known as: De Quervain's thyroiditis.

Quervain's fracture (Quervain, Fritz de): Medicine. See: Stedman.

QUESNAY, FRANCOIS. 1694-1774. French economist and physician. See: Internat. Encyc. Soc. Sci. Quesnay's classification of economic classes.

Quesnay's classification of economic classes (Quesnay, Francois): Economics. See: Zadrozny.

QUESNEL, MAURICE. fl. 1920. French physician. Cited in: Index-Cat. Libr. Surg.-Gen. Off., 3d Ser., vol. 9, 1931. Lhermitte-Cornil-Quesnel syndrome?

QUEST, ROBERT. b. 1874. German physician. See: Biog. Lex. hervorr. Aerzte. Quest's rule.

Quest's rule (Quest, Robert): Medicine. See: Dorland.

QUETELET, LAMBERT ADOLPH JACQUES. 1796-1874. Belgian statistician and astronomer. See: World Who's Who Sci. binomial law of Quetelet-Gauss, Quetelet's rule.

Quetelet's rule (Quetelet, Lambert Adolph Jacques): Statistics. See: Dorland.

QUEVENNE, THEODORE. 1805-1855. French pharmacist. See: Biog. Lex. hervorr. Aerzte. Quevenne's iron.

Quevenne's iron (Quevenne, Theodore): Chemistry. See: Webster's 3d.

QUEYRAT, LOUIS. 1856-1933. French dermatologist. See: Bull. Soc. Fr. Derm. Syph., vol. 40 (Nov. 1933), pp. 1375-1376. Queyrat's erythroplasia.

Queyrat's erythroplasia (Queyrat, Louis): Medicine. See: Dorland; Jablonski; Stedman.

QUICK, ARMAND JAMES. b. 1894. American hematologist. See: World Who's Who Sci. Quick's hippuric acid test, Quick's method (of preparation of thromboplastin, Quick's test for prothrombin.

Quick's hippuric acid test (Quick, Armand James): Medicine. See: Dorland; Kelly; Stedman.

Quick's method (of preparation of thromboplastin) (Quick, Armand James): Medicine. See: Kelly.

Quick's test for prothrombin (Quick, Armand James): Medicine. See: Dorland; Stedman.

Quignon Breviary (Quinonez, Francisco de): Religion. See: Attwater.

QUIMBY, PHINEAS PARKHURST. 1802-1866. American mental healer. See: Encyc. Brit., 1973. Quimbyism.

Quimby pump (Derivation undetermined): Engineering and Industry. See: Auger.

Quimbyism (Quimby, Phineas Parkhurst): Religion. See: Canney.

QUIN, WINDHAM THOMAS WYNDHAM, 4TH EARL OF DUNRAVEN. 1841-1926. Irish politician. See: Dict. Nat. Biog., 4th suppl. Dunraven Conference, Dunraven scheme.

Quinby hive (Derivation undetermined): Agriculture. See: Winburne.

Quincke balance (Quincke, Georg Hermann): Physics. See: Thewlis.

Quincke effect (Quincke, Georg Hermann): Physics. See: Ballentyne.

QUINCKE, GEORG HERMANN. 1834-1924. German physicist. See: World Who's Who Sci. Quincke balance, Quincke effect, Quincke('s) (Quinke) tube(s) (1), Quincke tube (2), Quincke's method.

QUINCKE, HEINRICH IRENAEUS. 1842-1922. German physician. See: World Who's Who Sci. Quincke's edema (or disease), Quincke's meningitis, Quincke's pulse (or sign), Quincke's puncture.

Quincke('s) (Quinke) tube(s) (1) (Quincke, Georg Hermann): Physics. See: Chaplin; Drever; English; Webster's 3d.

Quincke tube (2) (Quincke, Georg Hermann): Physics. See: English; Hughes; Internat. Dict. Phys. Elec.

Quincke's edema (or disease) (Quincke, Heinrich Irenaeus): Medicine. See: Dorland; Jablonski; Stedman. Also known as: Bannister's disease, Milton's disease (or urticaria).

Quincke's meningitis (Quincke, Heinrich Irenaeus): Medicine. See: Jablonski. Also known as: Symonds' syndrome.

Quincke's method (Quincke, Georg Hermann): Physics. See: Hughes.

Quincke's pulse (or sign) (Quincke, Heinrich Irenaeus): Medicine. See: Dorland; Stedman.

Quincke's puncture (Quincke, Heinrich Irenaeus): Medicine. See: Dorland; Stedman.

Quinina (Quinia or Quinine) (Chinchon, Dona Francisca Henriquez de Ribera, Countess of?): Botany. See: Charnock.

Quinlan's test (Derivation undetermined): Medicine. See: Stedman.

QUINN, JOSEPH PATRICK. b. 1889. American poultry geneticist. See: Amer. Men Sci., 6th ed. Burrows and Quinn method.

QUINONEZ, FRANCISCO DE. 1480-1540. Spanish cardinal and reformer. See: New Catholic Encyc. Quignon Breviary.

QUINQUAUD, CHARLES-EUGENE. 1843-1894. French physician. See: World Who's Who Sci. Quinquaud's disease, Quinquaud's sign (or phenomenon).

Quinquaud's disease (Quinquaud, Charles-Eugene): Medicine. See: Dorland; Jablonski; Stedman.

Quinquaud's sign (or phenomenon) (Quinquaud, Charles-Eugene): Medicine. See: Dorland.

Quintilians (or Quintillianists) (Quintilla): Religion. See: Brewer; Canney.

QUINTILLA. fl. 2d c. Supposed Montanist prophetess. See: Dict. Christian Biog. Quintilians (or Quintillianists).

Quintinia (Quintinie, Jean de la): Botany. See: Webster's 3d.

QUINTINIE, JEAN DE LA. 1626-1688. French botanist. See: Michaud. Quintinia.

Quirinalia (Quirinus): Mythology. See: Barnhart (Eng. Lit.).

QUIRINUS. Roman Sabine god of agriculture and war. See: Jobes. Quirinalia.

Quisling (or Quisle) (Quisling, Vidkun Abraham Lauritz Jonsson): Generic Word (traitor). See: Brewer; Hendrickson; Partridge; Webster's 3d.

QUISLING, VIDKUN ABRAHAM LAURITZ JONSSON. 1887-1945. Norwegian politician. See: Encyc. Brit., 1973. Quisling (or Quisle).

Quixote, Don. See: Don Quixote.

Quixotic (Don Quixote, the country gentleman): Generic Word (romantic idealist). See: Brewer; Partridge; Webster's 3d.

R

RAABE, GUSTAV. b. 1875. German physician. Cited in: Index-Cat. Libr. Surg.-Gen. Off., 2nd Ser., vol. 14, 1909. Raabe's test.

RAABE, JOSEF LUDWIG. 1801-1859. Mathematician. Cited in: Royal Soc. Cat. Sci. Pap., 1800-1863. Raabe's ratio test (or test for convergence).

Raabe's ratio test (or test for convergence) (Raabe, Josef Ludwig): Mathematics. See: Ballentyne; James; Van Nostrand Sci. Encyc.

Raabe's test (Raabe, Gustav): Medicine. See: Dorland; Stedman.

RABAUT, CHARLES. fl. 1908-1915. French chemist. Cited in: Chem. Abstr., vol. 2, p. 1838. Aloy-Rabaut test.

RABBITT, JOHN CHARLES. 1907-1957. American mineralogist. See: Amer. Min., vol. 43 (1958), pp. 307-309. Rabbittite.

Rabbittite (Rabbitt, John Charles): Earth Sciences. See: Thrush.

RABE, FRITZ. b. 1884. German physician. See: Biog. Lex. hervorr. Aerzte. Rabe-Salomon syndrome.

Rabe-Salomon syndrome (Rabe, Fritz and Salomon, E.): Medicine. See: Jablonski.

RABEL, ARSENE-PIERRE-CLEMENT. fl. 1865. French physician. Cited in: Index-Cat. Libr. Surg.-Gen. Off., 1st Ser., vol. 11, 1890. Rabel water?

Rabel water (Rabel, Arsene-Pierre-Clement?): Medicine. See: Charnock.

RABELAIS, FRANCOIS. 1494?-1553. French humorist and satirist. See: Encyc. Brit., 1973. Rabelaisian.

Rabelaisian (Rabelais, Francois): Generic Word (robust humor). See: Brewer; Hendrickson; Partridge; Webster's 3d.

RABI, ISIDOR ISAAC. 1898- . Austrian-born American physicist. See: Encyc. Brit., 1973. Rabi method for determining nuclear moments by "radio-frequency spectrometry."

Rabi method for determining nuclear moments by "radio-frequency spectrometry" (Rabi, Isidor Isaac): Physics. See: Internat. Dict. Phys. Elec.

RABINOVICH, L. M. fl. 1936. Russian chemist. Cited in: Chem. Abstr. vol. 30, p. 5524. Tananaev-Rabinovich test for antimony (antimonius).

RABINOWITCH, EUGENE. 1901- . Russian-born American biophysicist. See: World Who's Who Sci. Franck-Rabinowitch hypothesis.

RABINOWITZ, SOLOMON (Pseud., SHOLEM ALEICHEM). 1859-1916. Russian-born American Yiddish humorist. See: Encyc. Brit., 1973. Sholem Aleichem school.

RABL, CARL. 1853-1917. Austrian anatomist. See: Biog. Lex. hervorr. Aerzte. Rabl chromo-formic acid, Rabl fluid?

Rabl chromo-formic acid (Rabl, Carl): Chemistry. See: Van Nostrand Chem. Dict.

Rabl fluid (Rabl, Carl?): Chemistry. See: Van Nostrand Chem. Dict.

Racah coefficient (Racah, Giulio): Physics. See: Internat. Dict. Ap. Math.; Internat. Dict. Phys. Elec.

RACAH, GIULIO. 1909-1965. Italian-born Israeli physicist. See: Encyc. Judaica. Racah coefficient.

Rachel (face powder) (Felix, Elisa): Cosmetics. See: Hendrickson; Partridge; Webster's 3d.

Rachel, Mademoiselle. See: Felix, Elisa.

RACHMAN, PETER. 1920-1962. Polish-born English realtor. See: Time, vol. 82 (July 26, 1963), p. 28. Rachmanism.

Rachmanism (Rachman, Peter): Generic Word (tenant exploitation). See: Brewer; Hendrickson.

RACINE, WILLY. 1898-1946. Swiss otorhinolaryngologist. See: Revue Medic. Suisse Rom., vol. 66 (1946), pp. 383-385. Racine's syndrome.

Racine's syndrome (Racine, Willy): Medicine. See: Jablonski.

RACOUCHOT, JEAN. 1908- . French dermatologist. Cited in: Index-Cat. Libr. Surg.-Gen. Off., 5th Ser., vol. 1, 1959. Favre-Racouchot disease.

RADCLIFFE-CROCKER, HENRY. 1845-1909. English dermatologist and medical writer. See: Dict. Nat. Biog., 2d suppl. Crocker's disease.

RADCLIFFE, LIONEL GUY. fl. 1893-1928. English chemist. Cited in: Chem. Abstr., Decenn. Indexes, 1907-1916; 1917-1926. Radcliffe tests for carbon tetrachloride.

Radcliffe tests for carbon tetrachloride (Radcliffe, Lionel Guy): Chemistry. See: Van Nostrand Chem. Dict.

RADCLIFFE, SIR THOMAS (3RD EARL OF SUSSEX). 1526?-1583. English nobleman. See: Dict. Nat. Biog. Sussex's men?

RADEMACHER. fl. 1962. American hospital patient. (Biography source unavailable.) Rademacher's disease.

RADEMACHER, JOHANN GOTTFRIED. 1772-1850. German physician. See: Biog. Lex. hervorr. Aerzte. Rademacher's system (or Rademacherism).

Rademacher's disease (Rademacher): Medicine. See: Jablonski.

Rademacher's system (or Rademacherism) (Rademacher, Johann Gottfried): Medicine. See: Dorland.

RADFORD, EDWARD PARISH, JR. 1922- . American physiologist. See: Amer. Men and Women Sci., 12th ed. Radford nomogram?

Radford nomogram (Radford, Edward Parish, Jr.?): Medicine. See: Stedman.

radial compression test of Allen (Allen, Frederick Madison): Medicine. See: Stedman.

Raeder-Harbitz syndrome (Raeder, Johan Georg and Harbitz, Francis Gottfred). See: Takayasu's syndrome (or disease).

RAEDER, JOHAN GEORG. 1889-1956. Norwegian? physician. (Biography source unavailable.) Raeder-Harbitz syndrome, Raeder's syndrome.

Raeder's syndrome (Raeder, Johan Georg): Medicine. See: Jablonski; Stedman. Also known as: incomplete Horner's syndrome.

Raffaelesque (Raphael). See: Raphaelesque.

Raffles (Raffles, A. J.): Generic Word (gentleman burglar). See: Partridge; Webster's 3d.

RAFFLES, A. J. Hero of Ernest William Hornung's story "The Amateur Cracksman," (1899). See: Barnhart (Eng. Lit.) Raffles.

Raffles' malkoha (bird) (Raffles, Sir Thomas Stamford Bingley?): Zoology. See: Gray.

RAFFLES, SIR THOMAS STAMFORD BINGLEY. 1781-1826. English administrator. See: Dict. Nat. Biog. Raffles' malkoha (bird)?, Rafflesia.

Rafflesia (Raffles, Sir Thomas Stamford Bingley): Botany. See: Hendrickson; Partridge; Webster's 3d.

flesia Arnoldi (Arnold, Joseph): Botany. Cited in: Chambers' Biog. Dict.

FINESQUE, CONSTANTINE SAMUEL. 1783-1840. Constantinople-born nch naturalist. See: Encyc. Brit., 1973. Rafinesquina.

nesquina (Rafinesque, Constantine Samuel): Zoology. See: Pennak.

GAMUFFIN. Demon in "Piers Plowman," (1393), attributed to William gley. See: Jobes. Ragamuffin.

amuffin (Ragamuffin, the demon): Generic Word. See: Webster's 3d.

GGEDY ANN. Child's story book character. (Biography source unavailable.) gedy Ann costume.

gedy Ann costume (Raggedy Ann): Fashion. See: Picken.

GIMUND. No dates. Scottish legate. (Biography source unavailable.) man's roll.

imund's roll (Ragimund, the legate). See: Ragman's roll.

lan, 1st Baron. See: Somerset, Fitzroy James Henry (1st Baron Raglan).

lan (overcoat) (Somerset, Fitzroy James Henry, 1st Baron Raglan): Fashion. : Hendrickson; Partridge; Picken.

lan sleeve (Somerset, Fitzroy James Henry, 1st Baron Raglan): Fashion. : Picken.

man's roll (Ragimund): History. See: Black; Harbottle; Webster's 3d. o known as: Ragimund's roll.

GSKY, FRANZ. fl. 1847. Austrian chemist. Cited in: Royal Soc. Cat. . Pap., 1800-1863. Ragsky test.

sky test (Ragsky, Franz): Chemistry. See: Hackh.

HBEK, KNUD. b. 1891. Danish engineer. See: Kraks Blaa Bog., 1935. nsen (Johnson)-Rahbek effect.

gh test for magnesium (Derivation undetermined): Chemistry. See: Van strand Chem. Dict.

KOV, D. A. fl. 1937-1939. Russian mathematician. Cited in: Kendall Doig. Raikov's theorem.

kov, Pentscho N. See: Raikow, Pentscho N.

kov's theorem (Raikov, D. A.): Statistics. See: Kendall.

KOW, PENTSCHO N. b. 1864. Bulgarian chemist. See: Pogg., vol. 6. kow reagent for sulfur, Raikow test for calcium, Raikow test for methanol.

kow reagent for sulfur (Raikow, Pentscho N.): Chemistry. See: Van strand Chem. Dict.

kow test for calcium (Raikow, Pentscho N.): Chemistry. See: Van strand Chem. Dict.

kow test for methanol (Raikow, Pentscho N.): Chemistry. See: Van strand Chem. Dict.

ILLIET, ALCIDE (In full: LOUIS-JOSEPH ALCIDE). 1852-1930. French ologist. See: Bull. Acad. Vet. Fr., vol. 7 (1934), pp. 403-429. llietina.

llietina (Railliet, Alcide): Zoology. See: Stedman; Webster's 3d.

INES, JOHN. 1840-1909. American legislator. See: Dict. Amer. Biog. ines Law.

ines Law (Raines, John): Politics. See: Mathews, M. M.

INEY, GEORGE. 1801-1884. English anatomist. See: Dict. Nat. Biog. iney's corpuscles, Rainey's tubes.

iney's corpuscles (Rainey, George): Medicine. See: Dorland; Henderson; edman; Webster's 3d.

iney's tubes (Rainey, George): Medicine. See: Henderson. Also known as: escher's tubes.

is, Baron de. See: Retz, Baron de.

jania (Ray, John): Botany. See: Charnock.

AJMANN, E. fl. 1931. German chemist. Cited in: Chem. Abstr., vol. 25, . 2387, 4197. Krumholz-Feigl-Rajmann reagent for palladium and platinum, umholz-Feigl-Rajmann reagent for zirconium.

koczi March (Rakoczy, Ferencz II): Music. See: Apel.

RAKOCZY, FERENCZ II. 1676-1735. Hungarian rebel. See: New Encyc. Brit., 1974, Microp. Rakoczi March, Rakoczy's rebellion.

Rakoczy's rebellion (Rakoczy, Ferencz II): History. See: Harbottle.

RAKY, ANTON. 1868-1943. German engineer. Cited in: Singer, vol. 5. Raky boring method.

Raky boring method (Raky, Anton): Engineering and Industry. See: Thrush.

RALFE, CHARLES HENRY. 1842-1896. English physician. See: Lancet, vol. 2 (1896), p. 135. Ralfe's tests.

Ralfe's tests (Ralfe, Charles Henry): Medicine. See: Dorland; Stedman.

RALSTON, J. GRIER. fl. 19th c. American clergyman. Cited in: Hintze, vol. 1, pt. 2, p. 2529. Ralstonite.

RALSTON, OLIVER CALDWELL. b. 1887. American metallurgist. See: Pogg., vol. 6. Ralston's classification of coal.

Ralstonite (Ralston, J. Grier): Earth Sciences. See: Thrush; Webster's 3d.

Ralston's classification of coal (Ralston, Oliver Caldwell): Earth Sciences. See: Thrush.

RAMA. Hindu deity. See: New Encyc. Brit., 1974, Microp. Ramadan, Ramaites (or Ramaism), Ramayana.

Ramadan (Rama): Religion. See: Brewer.

RAMAGE, ADAM. 1770-1850. American printer. See: Hamilton. Ramage press.

Ramage press (Ramage, Adam): Printing. See: Lockwood; Mathews, M. M.

Ramaites (or Ramaism) (Rama): Religion. See: Canney; Webster's 3d.

Ramakrishna (Ramakrishna, Sri): Religion. See: Webster's 3d.

RAMAKRISHNA, SRI. 1836-1886. Indian mystic and religious leader. See: New Encyc. Brit., 1974, Microp. Ramakrishna.

RAMAN, SIR CHANDRA-SEKHARA VENKATA. 1888-1970. Indian physicist. See: World Who's Who Sci. Raman effect, Raman lines, Raman scattering, Raman spectra, Raman spectrometer, Raman spectrometry (or spectroscopy), Raman spectrophotometers.

Raman effect (Raman, Sir Chandra-Sekhara Venkata): Physics. See: Internat. Dict. Phys. Elec.; Thewlis; Van Nostrand Sci. Encyc.; Webster's 3d. Also known as: Smekal-Raman effect.

Raman lines (Raman, Sir Chandra-Sekhara Venkata): Physics. See: Hackh.

Raman scattering (Raman, Sir Chandra-Sekhara Venkata): Physics. See: Ballentyne; Hughes; Markus.

Raman spectra (Raman, Sir Chandra-Sekhara Venkata): Physics. See: Asimov; Hackh; Van Nostrand Sci. Encyc. under "Spectrum"; Webster's 3d.

Raman spectrometer (Raman, Sir Chandra-Sekhara Venkata): Physics. See: Markus.

Raman spectrometry (or spectroscopy) (Raman, Sir Chandra-Sekhara Venkata): Physics. See: Thewlis; Van Nostrand Sci. Encyc.

Raman spectrophotometers (Raman, Sir Chandra-Sekhara Venkata): Physics. See: Van Nostrand Sci. Encyc.

RAMANANDA. fl. 13th or 15th c. Hindu religious and social reformer. See: New Encyc. Brit., 1974, Microp. Ramanandis.

Ramanandis (Ramananda): Religion. See: Canney; Mathews, S.

Ramayana (Rama): Literature. See: Brewer; Mathews, S.

Ramberg-Osgood parameters (Ramberg, Walter and Osgood, William R.): Engineering and Industry. See: Internat. Dict. Ap. Math.

RAMBERG, WALTER. 1904- . Italian-born American physicist. See: Amer. Men and Women Sci., 12th ed. Ramberg-Osgood parameters.

RAMDOHR, CAESAR A. VON. 1855-1912. American surgeon. See: New York Times, Nov. 20, 1912, p. 15, col. 6. Ramdohr's suture.

RAMDOHR, PAUL GEORG KARL FREIDRICH. b. 1890. German mineralogist. See: Who's Who Sci. Europe, 1972. Ramdohrite.

Ramdohrite (Ramdohr, Paul Georg Karl Freidrich): Earth Sciences. See: Webster's 3d.

Ramdohr's suture (Ramdohr, Caesar A. von): Medicine. See: Dorland.

RAMELLI, AGOSTINO. ca. 1531-1600. Italian engineer. See: Encic. Ital. Ramelli pump.

Ramelli pump (Ramelli, Agostino): Engineering and Industry. See: Auger.

Rameseum (Ramses II, the Great): History. See: Webster's 3d.

Ramesside dynasty (Ramses III): History. See: Webster's 3d.

Ramism (or Ramist) (Ramus, Petrus): Philosophy. See: Charnock; Webster's 3d.

RAMMELSBERG, KARL FRIEDRICH. 1813-1899. German mineralogist. See: World Who's Who Sci. Rammelsbergite.

Rammelsbergite (Rammelsberg, Karl Friedrich): Earth Sciences. See: Thrush; Webster's 3d.

RAMMLER, ERICH (In full: HELMUTH ERICH). 1901- . German engineer. See: Pogg., vol. 7a. Rosin-Rammler equation.

RAMNULF I, COUNT OF POITOU. fl. 840. French nobleman. Cited in: Encyc. Brit., 1973. Poitevins.

RAMON, GASTON. 1886-1963. French bacteriologist. See: World Who's Who Sci. Ramon's flocculation test.

RAMON Y CAJAL, SANTIAGO. 1852-1934. Spanish histologist. See: Encyc. Brit., 1973. Cajal's astrocyte stain, Cajal's cell, Cajal's nucleus, horizontal cell of Cajal.

Ramon y Cajal's cells (Ramon y Cajal, Santiago). See: Cajal's cells.

Ramon y Cajal's nucleus (Ramon y Cajal, Santiago). See: Cajal's nucleus.

RAMONA. Heroine of a novel of the same name, (1884) by Helen Hunt Jackson. See: Hart. Ramona.

Ramona (Ramona, the heroine): Botany. See: Webster's 3d. Also known as: Audibertia.

Ramond agar (Ramond, Felix): Medicine. Cited in: Kelly.

RAMOND DE CARBONNIERES, LOUIS-FRANCOIS-ELISABETH. 1755-1827. French geologist. See: World Who's Who Sci. Ramonda.

RAMOND, FELIX. b. 1871. French physician. Cited in: Index Medicus, 2d Ser., vol. 14, 1909. Chauffard-Ramond syndrome, Ramond agar.

RAMOND, LOUIS. b. 1879. French internist. See: Biog. Lex. hervorr. Aerzte. Ramond's sign.

Ramonda (Ramond de Carbonnieres, Louis-Francois-Elisabeth): Botany. See: Taylor, N.

Ramond's sign (Ramond, Louis): Medicine. See: Dorland.

Ramon's flocculation test (Ramon, Gaston): Medicine. See: Dorland.

Ramos gin fizz (Ramos, Henry Charles): Food and Drink. See: Webster's 3d.

RAMOS, HENRY CHARLES. fl. early 20th c. American bartender. (Biography source unavailable.) Ramos gin fizz.

RAMSAUER, CARL. 1879-1955. German physicist. See: World Who's Who Sci. Ramsauer effect, Ramsauer well.

Ramsauer effect (Ramsauer, Carl): Physics. See: Ballentyne; Hughes; Internat. Dict. Phys. Elec.; Thewlis. Also known as: Ramsauer-Townsend effect.

Ramsauer-Townsend effect (Ramsauer, Carl and Townsend, John Sealy Edward). See: Ramsauer effect.

Ramsauer well (Ramsauer, Carl): Physics. See: Thewlis.

RAMSAY, SIR ANDREW CROMBIE. 1814-1891. English geologist. See: World Who's Who Sci. Ramsayite.

Ramsay Hunt. See: Hunt, James Ramsay.

Ramsay Hunt's paralysis (Hunt, James Ramsay). See: Hunt's paralysis (or syndrome (3)).

Ramsay Hunt's syndrome (Hunt, James Ramsay). See: Hunt's syndrome (1) and Hunt's syndrome (2).

RAMSAY, SIR WILLIAM. 1852-1916. English chemist. See: Dict. Nat. Biog., 3d suppl. Eotvos-Ramsay-Shields law, Ramsay-Young rule (law or equation).

Ramsay-Young rule (law or equation) (Ramsay, Sir William and Young, Sydney): Chemistry. See: Ballentyne; Hackh; Van Nostrand Sci. Encyc.

Ramsayite (Ramsay, Sir Andrew Crombie): Earth Sciences. See: Webster's 3d.

RAMSBOTTOM, JOHN. 1814-1897. English engineer. See: Royal Soc. Cat. Sci. Pap., 1884-1900. Ramsbottom piston ring, Ramsbottom safety valve.

Ramsbottom piston ring (Ramsbottom, John): Engineering and Industry. See: Auger.

Ramsbottom safety valve (Ramsbottom, John): Engineering and Industry. See: Auger; Webster's 3d.

RAMSDELL, LEWIS STEPHEN. 1895- . American mineralogist. See: Amer. Men Sci., 10th ed. Ramsdellite.

Ramsdellite (Ramsdell, Lewis Stephen): Earth Sciences. See: Webster's 3d.

Ramsden circle (Ramsden, Jesse): Astronomy. See: Van Nostrand Sci. Encyc.

Ramsden eyepiece (Ramsden, Jesse): Astronomy. See: Internat. Dict. Phys. Elec.; Satterthwaite; Thewlis; Van Nostrand Sci. Encyc. under "Eyepiece."

RAMSDEN, JESSE. 1735-1800. English astronomical instrument maker. See: Dict. Nat. Biog. Ramsden circle, Ramsden eyepiece.

RAMSES II, THE GREAT. fl. 1288 B.C. King of Egypt. See: New Encyc. Brit., 1974. Rameseum.

RAMSES III. fl. ca. 1200 B.C. King of Egypt. See: New Encyc. Brit., 1974, Microp. Ramesside dynasty.

RAMSPECK, ROBERT C. WORD. b. 1890. American legislator. See: Biog. Direct. Amer. Congress. O'Mahoney-Ramspeck Act.

Ramstead. See: Ranstead.

RAMSTEDT, CONRAD. b. 1867. German surgeon. See: Biog. Lex. hervorr. Aerzte. Fredet-Ramstedt operation.

Ramstedt operation (Ramstedt, Conrad). See: Fredet-Ramstedt operation.

RAMUS, PETRUS (PIERRE DE LA RAMEE). 1515-1572. French philosopher and mathematician. See: Encyc. Brit., 1973. Ramism (or Ramist).

RAND, MICHAEL JOHN. 1927- . English-born Australian pharmacologist. See: World Who's Who Sci. Burn and Rand theory.

RANDACIO, FRANCESCO. 1821-1903. Italian anatomist. See: Biog. Lex. hervorr. Aerzte. Randacio's nerves.

Randacio's nerves (Randacio, Francesco): Anatomy. See: Stedman.

RANDAL, JACK. fl. 19th c.? English prize fighter. (Biography source unavailable.) Randal's-man.

RANDALL, BENJAMIN. 1749-1808. American religious leader. See: Dict. Amer. Biog. Randallites.

RANDALL, JOHN W. fl. 1838-1839. American zoologist. Cited in: Royal Soc. Cat. Sci. Pap., 1800-1863. Randallia?

RANDALL, MERLE. b. 1888. American chemist. See: Pogg., vol. 6. Lewis-Randall rule.

RANDALL, SAMUEL JACKSON. 1828-1890. American legislator. See: Dict. Amer. Biog. Randallite.

Randallia (Randall, John W.?): Zoology. See: Pennak.

Randallite (Randall, Samuel Jackson): Politics. See: Mathews, M. M.

Randallites (Randall, Benjamin): Religion. See: Canney; Webster's 3d.

Randal's-man (Randal, Jack): Fashion. See: Charnock.

RANDOLPH, EDMUND JENNINGS. 1753-1813. American statesman. See: Dict. Amer. Biog. Randolph Plan.

RANDOLPH, NATHANIEL ARCHER. 1858-1887. American physician. See: Proc. Amer. Phil. Soc., Phila., vol. 26 (1889, pp. 359-365. Randolph's test.

Randolph Plan (Randolph, Edmund Jennings): History. See: Jameson; Smith.

Randolph plow (Randolph, Thomas Mann): Agriculture. See: Winburne.

Randolph process (Derivation undetermined): Engineering and Industry. See: Thrush.

RNDOLPH, THOMAS MANN. 1768-1828. American political leader. See: ct. Amer. Biog. Randolph plow.

ndolph's test (Randolph, Nathaniel Archer): Medicine. See: Dorland; dman.

ndupson process (Derivation undetermined): Engineering and Industry. See: rush.

NEY, MURRAY. 1885-1966. American engineer and manufacturer. See: t. Cycl. Amer. Biog., vol. 51, p. 443. Raney nickel catalyst, Raney's oy.

ney nickel catalyst (Raney, Murray): Chemistry. See: Hackh; Webster's .

ney's alloy (Raney, Murray): Chemistry. See: Hackh.

NFURLY, HERMIONE KNOX, COUNTESS OF. fl. 1960's -1970's. glish noblewoman. See: Who's Who, 1974-1975 under "Ranfurly, 6th Earl ." Ranfurly libraries.

nfurly libraries (Ranfurly, Hermione Knox, Countess of): Library Science. e: Harrod.

ANGER, RICHARD HOWLAND. 1889-1962. American electronics nufacturer. See: Who Was Who Amer., vol. 4. Rangertone.

ngertone (Ranger, Richard Howland): Music. See: Scholes.

NGNEKAR, SHARU S. fl. 1970. Indian student at University of Michigan. iography source unavailable.) Rangnekar's law of committee size, Rangnekar's les for decision avoidance, Rangnekar's techniques for decision avoidance.

ngnekar's law of committee size (Rangnekar, Sharu S.): Sociology. See: artin.

ngnekar's rules for decision avoidance (Rangnekar, Sharu S.): Sociology. e: Martin.

ngnekar's techniques for decision avoidance (Rangnekar, Sharu S.): ociology. See: Martin.

NK, OTTO. 1884-1939. Austrian psychoanalyst in America. See: ternat. Encyc. Soc. Sci. Rankian psychoanalysis.

NKE, HANS (In full: JOHANNES FRIEDRICH KARL RUDOLF). 1849-1887. utch surgeon. See: Nieuw Nederl. Biog. Woordenb. Ranke's angle.

NKE, KARL ERNST VON. 1870-1926. German chemist. See: Biog. ex. hervorr. Aerzte. Ranke's formula, Ranke's stages.

nke's angle (Ranke, Hans): Medicine. See: Dorland; Stedman.

nke's formula (Ranke, Karl Ernst von): Medicine. See: Dorland; Stedman.

nke's stages (Ranke, Karl Ernst von): Medicine. See: Dorland.

nkian psychoanalysis (Rank, Otto): Psychiatry. See: English.

NKIN, FRED WHARTON. 1886-1954. American surgeon. See: Who Was ho Amer., vol. 3. Rankin's clamp.

NKIN, GEORGE ATWATER. 1884-1963. American chemist. See: Amer. Men Sci., 10th ed. Rankinite.

nkin process (Derivation undetermined): Engineering and Industry. See: hrush.

nkine apparatus for gas viscosity (Rankine, William John Macquorn): Physics. ee: Internat. Dict. Phys. Elec.

nkine balance (Rankine, William John Macquorn): Physics. See: Thewlis.

nkine cycle (Rankine, William John Macquorn): Engineering and Industry. ee: Ballentyne; Internat. Dict. Ap. Math.; Thewlis; Van Nostrand Sci. ncyc. Also known as: Clausius-Rankine cycle.

nkine degree (Rankine, William John Macquorn): Physics. See: Dresner.

Rankine efficiency (Rankine, William John Macquorn): Engineering and ndustry. See: Ballentyne; Internat. Dict. Ap. Math.

nkine-Hugoniot relations (Rankine, William John Macquorn and Hugoniot, Henri): Physics. See: Ballentyne; Internat. Dict. Ap. Math.

nkine temperature scale (Rankine, William John Macquorn): Physics. See: uschke; Internat. Dict. Phys. Elec.; Thewlis; Van Nostrand Sci. Encyc. under 'Temperature."

nkine vortex (Rankine, William John Macquorn): Physics. See: Huschke; nternat. Dict. Phys. Elec.; Van Nostrand Sci. Encyc.

RANKINE, WILLIAM JOHN MACQUORN. 1820-1872. Scottish civil engineer and physicist. See: World Who's Who Sci. degrees Rankine, Gordon-Rankine formula (column formula or equation), Rankine apparatus for gas viscosity, Rankine balance, Rankine cycle, Rankine degree, Rankine efficiency, Rankine-Hugoniot relations, Rankine temperature scale, Rankine vortex, Rankine's formula, Rankine's theory.

Rankine's formula (Rankine, William John Macquorn): Engineering and Industry. See: Ballentyne.

Rankine's theory (Rankine, William John Macquorn): Engineering and Industry. See: Thrush.

Rankinite (Rankin, George Atwater): Earth Sciences. See: Thrush; Webster's 3d.

Rankin's clamp (Rankin, Fred Wharton): Medicine. See: Stedman.

RANQUE, GEORGES. fl. 1921-1938. French metallurgical engineer. Cited in: Chem. Abstr., Decenn. Indexes, 1917-1926; 1927-1936. Ranque tube?

Ranque tube (Ranque, Georges ?): Engineering and Industry. See: Auger.

Ranschburg inhibition (Ranschburg, Paul): Psychology. See: Drever.

RANSCHBURG, PAUL. 1870-1945. Hungarian psychiatrist and neurologist. See: Magyar Eletr. Lex. Ranschburg inhibition.

RANSOHOFF, JOSEPH. 1853-1921. American surgeon. See: Who Was Who Amer., vol. 1. Ransohoff's operation, Ransohoff's sign.

Ransohoff's operation (Ransohoff, Joseph): Medicine. See: Dorland; Stedman.

Ransohoff's sign (Ransohoff, Joseph): Medicine. See: Stedman.

RANSOME, FREDERICK LESLIE. 1868-1935. English-born American mining geologist. See: World Who's Who Sci. Ransomite.

Ransomite (Ransome, Frederick Leslie): Earth Sciences. See: Thrush; Webster's 3d.

RANSTEAD. fl. 18th c. Welsh-born American botanist. (Biography source unavailable.) Ranstead (toadflax).

Ranstead (toadflax) (Ranstead): Botany. See: Webster's 3d.

RANVIER, LOUIS ANTOINE. 1835-1922. French pathologist. See: Encyc. Brit., 1973. Merkel-Ranvier corpuscle, Ranvier's crosses, Ranvier's disks, Ranvier's membrane, Ranvier's motor points, Ranvier's nodes (or constrictions), Ranvier's plexus, Ranvier's segments.

Ranvier's crosses (Ranvier, Louis Antoine): Anatomy. See: Donath; Dorland; Stedman.

Ranvier's disks (Ranvier, Louis Antoine): Anatomy. See: Dorland; Stedman.

Ranvier's membrane (Ranvier, Louis Antoine): Anatomy. See: Dorland. Also known as: Renaut's layer.

Ranvier's motor points (Ranvier, Louis Antoine): Anatomy. See: Donath.

Ranvier's nodes (or constrictions) (Ranvier, Louis Antoine): Anatomy. See: Donath; Dorland; Pennak; Stedman.

Ranvier's plexus (Ranvier, Louis Antoine): Anatomy. See: Stedman.

Ranvier's segments (Ranvier, Louis Antoine): Anatomy. See: Donath; Stedman.

RANZANI, CAMILLO A. 1775-1841. Italian naturalist. See: Encic. Ital. Ranzania.

Ranzania (Ranzani, Camillo A.): Zoology. See: Webster's 3d.

RAO, CALYAMPUDI RADHAKRISHNA. 1920- . Indian statistician. See: Who's Who, 1974-1975. Cramer-Rao efficiency, Cramer-Rao inequality, Rao's scoring test.

RAO, R. V. G. 1927- . Indian chemist and physicist. See: World Who's Who Sci. Rao's law.

Rao's law (Rao, R. V. G.): Chemistry. See: Van Nostrand Sci. Encyc.

Rao's scoring test (Rao, Calyampudi Radhakrishna): Statistics. See: Kendall.

RAOUL, ETIENNE FIACRE LOUIS. 1815-1852. French surgeon. See: Biog. Lex. hervorr. Aerzte. Raoulia.

Raoulia (Raoul, Etienne Fiacre Louis): Botany. See: Webster's 3d.

RAOULT, FRANCOIS MARIE. 1830-1901. French physicist and chemist. See: World Who's Who Sci. Raoult's law, Raoult's method.

Raoult's law (Raoult, Francois Marie): Chemistry. See: Ballentyne; Hackh; Huschke; Thrush.

Raoult's method (Raoult, Francois Marie): Chemistry. See: Thrush; Webster's 3d; Winburne.

RAPHAEL (RAFFAELLO SANTI OR SANZIO). 1483-1520. Italian painter. See: Bryan. Pre-Raphaelite Brotherhood, Raphael cartoons, Raphaelesque, Raphaelism (or Raphaelite).

Raphael bridge (Raphael, Francis Charles): Electronics. See: Internat. Dict. Phys. Elec.; Markus.

Raphael cartoons (Raphael): Fine Arts. Cited in: Focal Encyc. Photog. under "Camera History."

RAPHAEL, FRANCIS CHARLES. 1871-1945. English electrical engineer. See: Who Was Who, 1941-1950. Raphael bridge.

Raphaelesque (Raphael): Fine Arts. See: Brewer; Partridge; Webster's 3d.

Raphaelism (or Raphaelite) (Raphael): Fine Arts. See: Webster's 3d.

RAPHSON, JOSEPH. d. ca. 1716. English mathematician. See: Pogg., vol. 2. Newton-Raphson method.

RAPP, GEORGE (In full: JOHANN GEORG). 1757-1847. German-born American religious leader. See: Dict. Amer. Biog. Rappists.

Rappists (Rapp, George): Religion. See: Canney; Mathews, M. M.; Morris.

RAQUET, D. fl. 1919. French chemist. Cited in: Chem. Abstr., vol. 13, p. 1435. Caron-Raquet test for manganese.

Ras Tafari. See: Haile Selassie.

Ras Tafarian (Haile Selassie): Religion. See: Barnhart (New Eng.).

RASCH, HERMANN. b. 1873. German obstetrician. Cited in: Index-Cat. Libr. Surg.-Gen. Off., 2d Ser., vol. 14, 1909. Rasch's sign.

Raschel knitting (Felix, Elisa): Applied Arts. See: Webster's 3d.

Raschette furnace (Derivation undetermined): Engineering and Industry. See: Thrush.

RASCHIG, FRITZ (In full: FRIEDRICH AUGUST). 1863-1928. German chemist and industrialist. See: Pogg., vols. 4, 5, 6. Raschig process, Raschig rings.

Raschig process (Raschig, Fritz): Chemistry. See: Ballentyne; Van Nostrand Chem. Dict.

Raschig rings (Raschig, Fritz): Engineering and Industry. See: Thrush; Van Nostrand Chem. Dict.; Van Nostrand Sci. Encyc.

Rasch's sign (Rasch, Hermann): Medicine. See: Dorland; Stedman.

RASHI (SOLOMON BEN ISAAC). 1040-1105. French-Jewish commentator on the Bible and Talmud. See: Encyc. Brit., 1973. Rashi's commentaries.

RASHID, MOHAMMED IBN 'ABD ALLAH. fl. 1889. Arabian political leader. (Biography source unavailable.) Rashidis.

Rashidis (Rashid, Mohammed ibn 'Abd Allah): History. See: Morris and Irwin.

Rashi's commentaries (Rashi): Religion. See: Mathews, S.

RASMUSSEN, VALDEMAR (In full: FRITZ VALDEMAR). 1834-1887. Danish physician. See: Biog. Lex. hervorr. Aerzte. Rasmussen's aneurysm.

Rasmussen's aneurysm (Rasmussen, Valdemar): Medicine. See: Dorland; Jablonski; Stedman.

RASO, MARIO. 1906- . Italian anatomist and pathologist. See: Who's Who Italy, 1958. Mattioli-Foggia and Raso syndrome.

RASOR, CLARENCE M. fl. 1927. American engineer. Cited in: Min. Mag., vol. 22 (Mar. 1929-Sept. 1931), p. 627. Rasorite.

Rasorite (Rasor, Clarence M.): Earth Sciences. See: Webster's 3d.

RASOUMOVSKY, COUNT ANDREAS KYRILLOVITCH. 1752-1836. Russian admiral, ambassador and musician. See: Grove; Thompson, O. Rasoumovsky Quartets.

Rasoumovsky Quartets (Rasoumovsky, Count Andreas Kyrillovitch): Music. See: Apel; Scholes.

RASP, CHARLES. fl. 19th c. Australian prospector. Cited in: Hintze, vol. 1, pt. 3, half 2, pp. 4031, 4096. Raspite.

RASPAIL, FRANCOIS VINCENT. 1794-1878. French chemist and politician. See: World Who's Who Sci. Raspail test reaction.

Raspail test reaction (Raspail, Francois Vincent): Chemistry. See: Van Nostrand Chem. Dict.

Raspite (Rasp, Charles): Earth Sciences. See: Webster's 3d.

Rasputin (or Rasputinism) (Rasputin, Grigori Efimovich): Generic Word (malevolent advisor). See: Hendrickson; Weekley.

RASPUTIN, GRIGORI EFIMOVICH. 1871?-1916. Russian holy man and court intriguer. See: Encyc. Brit., 1973. Rasputin (or Rasputinism).

RAST, KARL. fl. 1922. German chemist. Cited in: Chem. Abstr., vol. 16, pp. 519, 2060; Partington, vol. 4. Rast molecular weight method.

Rast molecular weight method (Rast, Karl): Chemistry. See: Van Nostrand Chem. Dict.; Van Nostrand Sci. Encyc.

Rastall measurement (Rastall, Samuel): Printing. See: Lockwood.

RASTALL, SAMUEL. fl. 19th c. American inventor. (Biography source unavailable.) Rastall measurement.

Rasumovsky, Count Andreas Kyrillovitch. See: Rasoumovsky, Count Andreas Kyrillovitch.

RATEAU, AUGUSTE (In full: CAMILLE EDMOND AUGUSTE). 1863-1930. French engineer. See: World Who's Who Sci. Rateau stage, Rateau steam turbine.

Rateau stage (Rateau, Auguste): Engineering and Industry. See: Van Nostrand Sci. Encyc. under "Steam Turbine."

Rateau steam turbine (Rateau, Auguste): Engineering and Industry. See: Auger.

RATH, GERHARD VON. 1830-1888. German mineralogist. See: Allg. Deut. Biog.; Encyc. Brit., 1911. Rathite.

RATH, MARIE VON. fl. 1860. Wife of the German mineralogist, Gerhard von Rath, 1830-1888. See: Allg. Deut. Biog. under "Rath, Gerhard von." Marialite.

RATHBUN, JOHN CAMPBELL. 1915- . Canadian pediatrician. See: Amer. Men and Women Sci., 12th ed. Rathbun's syndrome.

RATHBUN, RICHARD. 1852-1918. American zoologist. See: Dict. Amer. Biog. Rathbunula.

Rathbun's syndrome (Rathbun, John Campbell): Medicine. See: Jablonski.

Rathbunula (Rathbun, Richard): Zoology. See: Pennak.

RATHGEN, FRIEDRICH. fl. 1914. German chemist. Cited in: Chem. Abstr., vol. 8, p. 1070. Rathgen micro-chemical test for alumina.

Rathgen micro-chemical test for alumina (Rathgen, Friedrich): Chemistry. See: Van Nostrand Chem. Dict.

Rathite (Rath, Gerhard von): Earth Sciences. See: Thrush; Webster's 3d.

RATHKE, HEINRICH (In full: MARTIN HEINRICH). 1793-1860. German anatomist. See: World Who's Who Sci. Rathkea?, Rathke's bundles, Rathke's pouch (pocket or diverticulum), Rathke's pouch tumor, Rathke's trabeculae.

Rathkea (Rathke, Heinrich?): Anatomy. See: Pennak.

Rathke's bundles (Rathke, Heinrich): Anatomy. See: Donath.

Rathke's pouch (pocket or diverticulum) (Rathke, Heinrich): Anatomy. See: Donath; Dorland; Pennak; Stedman.

Rathke's pouch tumor (Rathke, Heinrich). See: Erdheim tumor.

Rathke's trabeculae (Rathke, Heinrich): Anatomy. See: Donath.

RATISH, HERMAN D. fl. 1930. American chemist. Cited in: Chem. Abstr., vol. 32, p. 7946[4]. Scudi-Ratish test.

RATNER, SARAH. 1903- . American biochemist. See: World Who's Who Sci. Kurzrok-Ratner test?

RATZEL, FRIEDRICH. 1844-1904. German anthropogeographer. See: Internat. Encyc. Soc. Sci. Ratzel's theory of race and culture.

Ratzel's theory of race and culture (Ratzel, Friedrich): Anthropology. See: Zadrozny.

RATZENHOFER, GUSTAV. 1842-1904. Austrian general, philosopher and sociologist. See: Internat. Encyc. Soc. Sci. Ratzenhofer's interests, Ratzenhofer's principle of conquest and assimilation.

Ratzenhofer's interests (Ratzenhofer, Gustav): Sociology. See: Zadrozny.

Ratzenhofer's principle of conquest and assimilation (Ratzenhofer, Gustav): Sociology. See: Zadrozny.

RAU, JOHANN JACOB (RAVIUS). 1668-1719. Dutch anatomist. See: Biog. Lex. hervorr. Aerzte. Rau's process.

RAUBER, AUGUST ANTINOUS. 1841-1917. Estonian anatomist. See: Biog. Lex. hervorr. Aerzte. Rauber's layer.

Rauber's layer (Rauber, August Antinous): Anatomy. See: Dorland; Henderson; Stedman.

RAUCHFUSS, KARL ANDREYEVICH. 1835-1916. Russian physician. See: Biog. Lex. hervorr. Aerzte. Rauchfuss' sling, Rauchfuss' triangle.

Rauchfuss' sling (Rauchfuss, Karl Andreyevich): Medicine. See: Dorland.

Rauchfuss' triangle (Rauchfuss, Karl Andreyevich). See: Grocco's triangle (or sign (3)).

Rau's process (Rau, Johann Jacob): Anatomy. See: Donath; Dorland; Stedman. Also known as: Folli's process.

RAUSCHER, FRANK JOSEPH. 1931- . American virologist. See: Amer. Men and Women Sci., 12th ed. Rauscher leukemia (or virus).

Rauscher leukemia (or virus) (Rauscher, Frank Joseph): Medicine. See: Jablonski; Stedman.

RAUSCHKOLB, J. E. fl. 1930. American dermatologist. (Biography source unavailable.) Cole-Rauschkolb-Toomey syndrome.

RAUWOLF, LEONHARD. d. 1596. German physician and botanist. See: Allg. Deut. Biog. Rauwolfia.

Rauwolfia (Rauwolf, Leonhard): Botany. See: Stedman; Webster's 3d.

RAUZIER, GEORGES. 1862-1920. French physician. See: Biog. Lex. hervorr. Aerzte. Rauzier's disease.

Rauzier's disease (Rauzier, Georges): Medicine. See: Dorland.

RAVEN, J. C. fl. 1944. English psychologist. Cited in: Cum. Auth. Index to Psych. Index, 1894-1935, and Psych. Abstr., 1927-1958. Raven's controlled projection test.

RAVENEL, HENRY WILLIAM. 1814-1887. American botanist. See: World Who's Who Sci. Ravenelia.

Ravenelia (Ravenel, Henry William): Botany. See: Webster's 3d.

Raven's controlled projection test (Raven, J. C.): Psychology. See: Wolman.

RAVENSTEIN, ERNST GEORG. 1834-1913. German cartographer. See: Biog. Jahrb. Deut. Nekr., 1913. Ravenstein's law of migration.

Ravenstein's law of migration (Ravenstein, Ernst Georg): Sociology. See: Zadrozny.

Ravian process (Rau, Johann Jacob). See: Rau's process.

Ravius. See: Rau, Johann Jacob.

RAWSON, ARTHUR JOY. 1896- . American medical physicist. See: Amer. Men Sci., 7th ed. Abbott-Rawson tube.

Rawson, Sir William Adams. See: Adams, Sir William.

RAY, B. J. fl. 1911. American chemist. Cited in: Chem. Abstr., vol. 5, 2045. Withers and Ray solution.

Ray-Gupta reagent for metals (Ray, Priyada Ranjan and Gupta, Jagannath): Chemistry. See: Van Nostrand Chem. Dict.

RAY, ISAAC. 1807-1881. American physician. See: Dict. Amer. Biog. Ray's mania.

RAY, JOHN. 1627?-1705. English naturalist. See: Dict. Nat. Biog. Rajania.

RAY, MAN. b. 1890. American painter and photographer. See: Webster's Biog. Dict. Rayographs.

RAY, PRIYADA RANJAN. b. 1888. Indian chemist. See: Pogg., vol. 6. Ray-Gupta reagent for metals, Ray-Ray reagent for copper.

RAY, R. M. fl. 1926-1930. Indian chemist. Cited in: Pogg., vol. 6 under "Ray, Priyada Ranjan." Ray-Ray reagent for copper.

Ray-Ray reagent for copper (Ray, Priyada Ranjan and Ray, R. M.): Chemistry. See: Van Nostrand Chem. Dict.

RAY, SURENDRA N. fl. 1930. English? chemist. Cited in: Chem. Abstr., Decenn. Index, 1927-1936. Harris and Ray test.

RAYBIN, HARRY W. fl. 1933-1938. American chemist. Cited in: Kelly. Raybin sucrose reaction, Raybin test reaction for vitamin B$_1$ (thiamine).

Raybin sucrose reaction (Raybin, Harry W.): Medicine. See: Kelly.

Raybin test reaction for vitamin B$_1$ (thiamine) (Raybin, Harry W.): Chemistry. See: Kelly; Van Nostrand Chem. Dict.

RAYBURN, SAM. 1882-1961. American legislator. See: Biog. Direct. Amer. Congress. Rayburn's rule, Wheeler-Rayburn Act.

Rayburn's rule (Rayburn, Sam): Sociology. See: Martin.

RAYER, PIERRE FRANCOIS OLIVE. 1793-1867. French physician. See: World Who's Who Sci. Rayer's disease.

Rayer's disease (Rayer, Pierre Francois Olive). See: Addison-Gull disease.

RAYET, GEORGES ANTOINE PONS. 1839-1906. French astronomer. See: World Who's Who Sci. Wolf-Rayet stars.

RAYGER, KAROLY. 1641-1707. Hungarian physician. See: Biog. Lex. hervorr. Aerzte. Rayger's test?

Rayger's test (Rayger, Karoly?): Medicine. See: Stedman.

Rayleigh, 3rd Baron. See: Strutt, John William (3rd Baron Rayleigh).

Raymond-Cestan syndrome (Raymond, Fulgence and Cestan, Raymond): Medicine. See: Jablonski.

RAYMOND, FULGENCE. 1844-1910. French neurologist. See: World Who's Who Sci. Raymond-Cestan syndrome, Raymond type of apoplexy.

RAYMOND, JOHN H. 1911- . American mathematician. See: Amer. Men Sci., 9th ed. Birnbaum-Raymond-Zuckerman inequality.

Raymond type of apoplexy (Raymond, Fulgence): Medicine. See: Dorland; Stedman.

RAYNAUD, MAURICE. 1834-1881. French physician. See: World Who's Who Sci. Raynaud's disease (or gangrene), Raynaud's phenomenon.

Raynaud's disease (or gangrene) (Raynaud, Maurice): Medicine. See: Dorland; Jablonski; Stedman; Van Nostrand Sci. Encyc.

Raynaud's phenomenon (Raynaud, Maurice): Medicine. See: Dorland; Jablonski; Stedman.

Rayner refractometer (Derivation undetermined): Physics. See: Thrush.

Raynier's white mycetoma (Derivation undetermined): Medicine. See: Stedman.

Rayographs (Ray, Man): Photography. See: Focal Encyc. Photog.

Ray's mania (Ray, Isaac): Medicine. See: Jablonski.

rays of Sagnac (Sagnac, Georges Marc Marie). See: Sagnac rays.

RAZUMOVSKY, GREGOR VON. d. 1837. Russian-born German and French mineralogist. See: Pogg., vol. 2. Razumovskyn?

Razumovskyn (Razumovsky, Gregor von?): Earth Sciences. See: Thrush.

Read boiler (Read, Nathan): Engineering and Industry. See: Auger.

READ, JAY MARION. b. 1889. American physician. See: Amer. Men Sci., 10th ed. Read's formula.

READ, NATHAN. 1759-1849. American inventor and industrialist. See: Dict. Amer. Biog. Read boiler.

READ, WILLIAM THORNTON JR. 1921- . American physicist. See: Amer. Men Sci., 9th ed. Frank-Read source.

Read's formula (Read, Jay Marion): Medicine. See: Dorland; Kelly.

Reagan Bill (Reagan, John Henninger): Politics. See: Jameson.

REAGAN, JOHN HENNINGER. 1818-1905. American legislator. See: Biog. Direct. Amer. Congress. Reagan Bill.

real McCoy (McCoy, Kid? McCoy, Elijah? or MacKay, A.M.?): Generic Word (the genuine article). See: Det. Free Press, May 5, 1975; Hendrickson; Partridge.

Reaumur degree (Reaumur, Rene Antoine Ferchault de): Physics. See: Dresner; Hackh.

Reaumur porcelain (Reaumur, Rene Antoine Ferchault de): Engineering and Industry. See: Thrush.

REAUMUR, RENE ANTOINE FERCHAULT DE. 1683-1757. French naturalist and physicist. See: World Who's Who Sci. degree Reaumur, Reaumur degree, Reaumur porcelain, Reaumur scale, Reaumuria.

Reaumur scale (Reaumur, Rene Antoine Ferchault de): Physics. See: Ballentyne; Huschke; Stedman; Thrush.

Reaumuria (Reaumur, Rene Antoine Ferchault de): Botany. See: Charnock.

REBECCA. Biblical wife of Isaac and mother of Esau and Jacob. See: Hastings (Dict. Bible). Rebecca riots (and Rebeccaites).

Rebecca riots (and Rebeccaites) (Rebecca): History. See: Brewer; Harbottle; Steinberg.

Rebello-Alves reaction for copper (Rebello-Alves, S.): Chemistry. See: Van Nostrand Chem. Dict.

REBELLO-ALVES, S. fl. 1918. Italian chemist. Cited in: Chem. Abstr., vol. 12, p. 375. Rebello-Alves reaction for copper.

REBER, KARL. fl. 1928-1943. Swiss chemist. Cited in: Chem. Abstr., vol. 22, p. 2526. Reber test reaction for beta naphthol.

Reber test reaction for beta naphthol (Reber, Karl): Chemistry. See: Van Nostrand Chem. Dict.

Rebinder, Petr Aleksandrovich. See: Rehbinder, Petr Aleksandrovich.

Reboul effect (Reboul, Georges Scipion Antoine): Physics. See: Hughes.

REBOUL, GEORGES SCIPION ANTOINE. b. 1879. French physicist. See: Pogg., vols. 5, 6. Reboul effect.

REBOUL, HENRI PAUL IRENEE. 1763-1839. French naturalist and administrator. See: Nouv. Biog. Univ. Reboulia.

Reboulia (Reboul, Henri Paul Irenee): Botany. See: Webster's 3d.

rebound phenomenon of Gordon Holmes (Holmes, Gordon Morgan). See: Holmes's phenomenon.

RECAMIER, JEANNE FRANCOISE JULIE ADELAIDE. 1777-1849. French society beauty and wit. See: Encyc. Brit., 1973. Recamier (pink color).

RECAMIER, JOSEPH CLAUDE ANTHELME. 1774-1852. French gynecologist. See: World Who's Who Sci. Recamier's operation.

Recamier (pink color) (Recamier, Jeanne Francoise Julie Adelaide): Fashion. See: Webster's 3d.

Recamier's operation (Recamier, Joseph Claude Anthelme): Medicine. See: Stedman.

RECHAB. Biblical personage. Cited in: New Encyc. Brit., 1974, Microp. Rechabites.

Rechabites (Rechab): Sociology. See: Brewer; Harvey; Phyfe.

RECHCIGL, MILOSLAV, JR. 1930- . Czechoslovakian-born American biochemist. See: Amer. Men and Women Sci., 12th ed. Rechcigl-Sidransky hepatoma.

Rechcigl-Sidransky hepatoma (Rechcigl, Miloslav, Jr. and Sidransky, Herschel): Medicine. See: Jablonski.

reciprocal Ohm (Ohm, George Simon): Physics. See: Dresner.

reciprocity theorem of Maxwell and Betti (Maxwell, James Clerk and Betti, Enrico). See: Betti's reciprocal theorem.

Recklinghausen-Appelbaum disease (Recklinghausen, Friedrich Daniel von and Appelbaum, L.?): Medicine. See: Jablonski.

RECKLINGHAUSEN, FRIEDRICH DANIEL VON. 1833-1910. German pathologist. See: Encyc. Brit., 1973. Recklinghausen-Appelbaum disease, Recklinghausen's canals, Recklinghausen's disease (1) (multiple neurofibromatosis), Recklinghausen's disease (2) (osteitis fibrosa cystica), Recklinghausen's disease (3) (neoplastic arthritis deformans), Recklinghausen's tumor.

Recklinghausen's canals (Recklinghausen, Friedrich Daniel von): Anatomy. See: Donath; Dorland.

Recklinghausen's disease (1) (multiple neurofibromatosis) (Recklinghausen, Friedrich Daniel von): Medicine. See: Dorland; Jablonski; Stedman. Also known as: Von Recklinghausen's disease.

Recklinghausen's disease (2) (osteitis fibrosa cystica) (Recklinghausen, Freidrich Daniel von): Medicine. See: Dorland; Jablonski; Stedman. Also known as: Engel-Von Recklinghausen syndrome, Von Recklinghausen's disease.

Recklinghausen's disease (3) (neoplastic arthritis deformans) (Recklinghausen, Friedrich Daniel von): Medicine. See: Dorland.

Recklinghausen's tumor (Recklinghausen, Friedrich Daniel von): Medicine. See: Stedman.

Reckna clay beams (Derivation undetermined): Engineering and Industry. See: Thrush.

RECKNAGEL, KARL. fl. 1939-1944. German biochemist. Cited in: Chem. Abstr., Decenn. Indexes, 1927-1936; 1937-1946. Recknagel phenomenon?

Recknagel phenomenon (Recknagel, Karl?): Chemistry. See: Winburne.

Reclus' disease (Reclus, Paul): Medicine. See: Jablonski. Also known as: Cooper's disease.

Reclus' operation (Reclus, Paul): Medicine. See: Stedman.

RECLUS, PAUL. 1847-1914. French surgeon. See: Biog. Lex. hervorr. Aerzte. Reclus' disease, Reclus' operation, Reclus' syndrome.

Reclus' syndrome (Reclus, Paul). See: Cheatle's disease.

Red Riding-hood (and costume) (Red Ridinghood): Fashion. See: Picken.

RED RIDINGHOOD. Fairy tale heroine. See: Jobes. Red Riding-hood (and costume).

REDCLIFFE-MAUD, JOHN PRIMATT, BARON. 1906- . English administrator. See: Who's Who, 1974-1975. Redcliffe-Maud report.

Redcliffe-Maud report (Redcliffe-Maud, John Primatt, Baron): Library Science. See: Harrod. Also known as: Maud report.

REDDELIEN, GUSTAV. 1882-1938. German chemist. See: Pogg., vols, 5, 6. Reddelien test reaction.

Reddelien test reaction (Reddelien, Gustav): Chemistry. See: Van Nostrand Chem. Dict.

REDI, FRANCESCO. 1626?-1697. Italian physician, naturalist and poet. See: Biog. Lex. hervorr. Aerzte. Redia.

Redia (Redi, Francesco): Zoology. See: Pennak; Stedman; Webster's 3d.

REDLICH, EMIL. 1866-1930. Austrian neurologist. See: Biog. Lex. hervorr. Aerzte. Obersteiner-Redlich area, Redlich phenomenon, Redlich's encephalitis.

Redlich-Flatau syndrome (Redlich, Emil and Flatau, Eduard?). See: Redlich's encephalitis.

REDLICH, OTTO. 1896- . Austrian-born American physical chemist. See: Amer. Men and Women Sci., 12th ed. Teller-Redlich product rule.

Redlich phenomenon (Redlich, Emil): Medicine. See: Dorland.

Redlich's encephalitis (Redlich, Emil): Medicine. See: Jablonski. Also known as: Munch-Petersen's encephalomyelitis, Redlich-Flatau syndrome.

REDSTON, GERALD D. fl. 1943-1967. English glass technologist. See: Direct. Brit. Scientists, 1966-1967. Redston-Stanworth annealing schedule.

Redston-Stanworth annealing schedule (Redston, Gerald D. and Stanworth, John Edwin): Engineering and Industry. See: Thrush.

Redwood-Baringer water finder (Redwood, Sir Boverton and Baringer): Engineering and Industry. See: Thrush.

REDWOOD, SIR BOVERTON. 1846-1919. English chemist. See: Who Was Who, 1916-1928. Dewar-Redwood process, Redwood-Baringer water finder, Redwood viscometer.

Redwood viscometer (Redwood, Sir Boverton): Chemistry. See: Thrush; Van Nostrand Chem. Dict.

REECH, FREDERIC. 1805-1874. French marine engineer and physicist. See: Pogg., vol. 3. Reech number, Reech's theorem.

Reech number (Reech, Frederic): Physics. See: Huschke.

Reech's theorem (Reech, Frederic): Chemistry. See: Hackh.

Reed cells (Reed, Dorothy). See: Reed-Sternberg cells.

REED, CHARLES ALFRED LEE. 1856-1928. American gynecologist. See: Who Was Who Amer., vol. 1. Reed's operation.

REED, CORTES F. fl. 1936. American chemist. Cited in: Chem. Abstr., vol. 30, p. 5593. Reed reaction.

REED, DOROTHY MENDENHALL. 1874-1964. American pathologist. Cited in: Kelly. Reed-Sternberg cells.

REED, FRANK S. fl. 1955. American mineralogist. Cited in: Amer. Min., vol. 40 (1955), pp. 326-327. Reedmergnerite.

REED, LOWELL JACOB. 1886-1966. American statistician. See: Who Was Who Amer., vol. 4. Pearl-Reed curve, Reed-Muench method.

Reed-Muench method (Reed, Lowell Jacob and Muench, Hugo, Jr.): Statistics. See: Kendall.

Reed reaction (Reed, Cortes F.): Chemistry. See: Van Nostrand Chem. Dict.

REED, RUFUS DANIEL. b. 1894. American chemist. See: Amer. Men Sci., 9th ed. Reed test for cerium?, Reed-Withrow test for potassium.

Reed-Sternberg cells (Reed, Dorothy and Sternberg, George Miller): Medicine. See: Stedman. Also known as: Reed cells, Sternberg cells.

Reed test for cerium (Reed, Rufus Daniel?): Chemistry. See: Van Nostrand Chem. Dict.

Reed-Withrow test for potassium (Reed, Rufus Daniel and Withrow, James Renwick): Chemistry. See: Van Nostrand Chem. Dict.

Reedmergnerite (Reed, Frank S. and Mergner, John L.): Earth Sciences. See: Thrush.

Reed's operation (Reed, Charles Alfred Lee): Medicine. See: Stedman.

REENSTIERNA, JOHN LIBERT. b. 1882. Swedish dermatologist. See: Svenska Maen Och Kvinnor. Ito-Reenstierna test.

Rees-Ecker fluid (Rees, H. Maynard and Ecker, Enrique Eduardo): Medicine. See: Stedman.

REES, GEORGE OWEN. 1813-1899. English physician. See: Dict. Nat. Biog. Rees' test.

REES, H. MAYNARD. fl. 1922. American physician. Cited in: Chem. Abstr., Decenn. Index, 1917-1926. Rees-Ecker fluid.

Rees-Hugill flask (Rees, Walter James and Hugill, W.): Engineering and Industry. See: Thrush.

Rees' test (Rees, George Owen): Medicine. See: Dorland; Stedman.

Ree's torsion anemometer (Derivation undetermined): Engineering and Industry. See: Thrush.

REES, WALTER JAMES. b. 1879. English ceramics and glass chemist. See: Who's Who Brit. Science, 1953. Rees-Hugill flask.

REESE, ALGERON BEVERLY. 1896- . American ophthalmologist. See: Amer. Men and Women Sci., 12th ed. Krause-Reese syndrome, Reese's syndrome (or dysplasia).

Reese-Blodi syndrome (Reese, Algeron Beverly and Blodi, Frederick D.). See: Reese's syndrome (or dysplasia).

Reese's syndrome (or dysplasia) (Reese, Algeron Beverly): Medicine. See: Jablonski. Also known as: Reese-Blodi syndrome.

REEVE, JOHN. 1608-1658. English religious leader. See: Dict. Nat. Biog. Reevites.

Reevites (Reeve, John): Religion. See: Canney.

Refa'iyeh (Ahmed er-Refa'i): Religion. See: Canney.

REFORMATSKY, ALEXANDR NIKOLAYVICH. 1860-1934. Russian chemist. See: Pogg., vol. 4. Reformatsky reaction.

Reformatsky reaction (Reformatsky, Alexandr Nikolayvich): Chemistry. See: Ballentyne; Hackh; Van Nostrand Chem. Dict.

REFSDAL, ANDREAS (In full: IVAR ANDREAS). 1866-1939. Norwegian cartographer. See: Norsk Biog. Lek. Refsdal diagram.

Refsdal diagram (Refsdal, Andreas): Earth Sciences. See: Huschke.

REFSUM, SIGVALD BERNHARD. 1907- . Norwegian physician. See: Hvem er Hvem?, 1973. Refsum's disease (or syndrome).

Refsum-Thiebaut disease (Refsum, Sigvald and Thiebaut, Francois). See: Refsum's disease (or syndrome).

Refsum's disease (or syndrome) (Refsum, Sigvald Bernhard): Medicine. See: Hinsie; Jablonski; Stedman.

REGALA, ARSENIO C. fl. 1946. Phillipine pediatrician. (Biography source unavailable.) Stransky-Regala syndrome.

REGEL, EDWARD AUGUST VON. 1815-1892. German botanist in Russia. See: Allg. Deut. Biog. Regel's privet.

Regel's privet (Regel, Edward August von): Botany. See: Webster's 3d.

Regge trajectory (Regge, Tullio Eugenio): Physics. See: Hughes; Van Nostrand Sci. Encyc. under "Particle Physics."

REGGE, TULLIO EUGENIO. 1931- . Italian-born American physicist. See: World Who's Who Sci. Regge trajectory.

Regina Medal (Mary, Virgin-Mother): Library Science. See: Harrod.

REGNAULD, JULES ANTOINE. fl. 1884-1895. French pharmaceutical chemist. See: J. Pharm, vol. 1 (1895), pp 271-273. Regnauld test for chloroform.

Regnauld test for chloroform (Regnauld, Jules Antoine): Chemistry. See: Van Nostrand Chem. Dict.

Regnault cell (Regnault, Henri Victor): Chemistry. See: Hackh.

REGNAULT, HENRI VICTOR. 1810-1878. French chemist and physicist. See: World Who's Who Sci. Regnault cell, Regnault value, Regnault's formula, Regnault's law.

Regnault value (Regnault, Henri Victor): Chemistry. See: Hackh.

Regnault's formula (Regnault, Henri Victor): Physics. See: Webster's 3d.

Regnault's law (Regnault, Henri Victor): Physics. See: Webster's 3d.

Reguir cell (Derivation undetermined): Chemistry. See: Hackh.

Regular Clark of Saint Paul (Paul the Apostle, Saint): Religion. See: Webster's 3d.

Rehbinder effect (Rehbinder, Petr Aleksandrovich): Chemistry. See: Thewlis.

REHBINDER, PETR ALEKSANDROVICH. 1898- . Russian physical chemist. See: World Who's Who Sci. Rehbinder effect.

REHFUSS, MARTIN E. 1887-1964. American physician. See: New York Times, July 30, 1964, p. 27, col. 3. Rehfuss method, Rehfuss stomach tube.

Rehfuss method (Rehfuss, Martin E.): Medicine. See: Dorland; Stedman.

Rehfuss stomach tube (Rehfuss, Martin E.): Medicine. See: Dorland; Stedman; Webster's 3d.

REHMANN, JOSEPH. d. 1831. Russian physician. See: Biog. Lex. hervorr. Aerzte. Rehmannia.

Rehmannia (Rehmann, Joseph): Botany. See: Taylor, N.

REHOBOAM. ca. 933-917 B.C. King of Judah and son of Solomon. See: New Encyc. Brit., 1974, Microp. Rehoboam.

Rehoboam (Rehoboam, the King): Generic Word (oversize wine bottle). See: Hendrickson; Partridge; Webster's 3d.

REICH, CHARLES ALAN. 1928- . American educator. See: Who's Who Amer., 1974-1975. Reich's law of hierarchical reality, Reich's laws of administration.

REICH, RICHARD. fl. 1909. German chemist. Cited in: Chem. Abstr., vol. 3, pp. 354-355. Reich test reaction for oils.

Reich test reaction for oils (Reich, Richard): Chemistry. See: Van Nostrand Chem. Dict.

REICHARD, C. fl. 1912. German chemist. Cited in: Chem. Abstr., Decenn. Index, 1907-1916. Reichard test reaction for nickel?, Reichard test reaction for stannic ion?, Reichard test reactions for lactic acid.

Reichard test reaction for nickel (Reichard, C.?): Chemistry. See: Van Nostrand Chem. Dict.

Reichard test reaction for stannic ion (Reichard, C.?): Chemistry. See: Van Nostrand Chem. Dict.

Reichard test reactions for lactic acid (Reichard, C.): Chemistry. See: Van Nostrand Chem. Dict.

REICHE, FRITZ. b. 1883. German physicist. See: Pogg., vols. 5, 6. Kuhn-Thomas-Reiche f-sum rule.

Reichel-Jones-Henderson syndrome (Reichel, Paul; Jones, Hugh T.; and Henderson, Melvin S.). See: Reichel's syndrome.

REICHEL, PAUL (In full: FRIEDRICH PAUL). 1858-1934. German physician. See: Biog. Lex. hervorr. Aerzte. Reichel-Polya stomach resection, Reichel's chondromatosis, Reichel's duct, Reichel's syndrome.

Reichel-Polya stomach resection (Reichel, Paul and Polya, Jeno): Medicine. See: Stedman.

Reichel's chondromatosis (Reichel, Paul): Medicine. See: Dorland.

Reichel's duct (Reichel, Paul): Medicine. See: Dorland.

Reichel's syndrome (Reichel, Paul): Medicine. See: Dorland; Jablonski. Also known as: Henderson-Jones syndrome (or disease), Reichel-Jones-Henderson syndrome.

REICHERT, FREDERICK LEET. b. 1894. American surgeon. See: Direct. Med. Specialists, 1965-1966. Reichert's syndrome.

REICHERT, KARL BOGISLAUS. 1811-1883. German anatomist. See: Biog. Lex. hervorr. Aerzte. Reichert-Meissl number (or value), Reichert number (or value), Reichert-Wollny number?, Reichert's cartilage, Reichert's membrane, Reichert's recess, Reichert's scar, Reichert's substance.

Reichert-Meissl number (or value) (Reichert, Karl Bogislaus and Meissl, Emerich): Chemistry. See: Ballentyne; Stedman; Van Nostrand Sci. Encyc. under "Oil, Fat and Wax."

Reichert number (or value) (Reichert, Karl Bogislaus): Chemistry. See: Hackh; Van Nostrand Chem. Dict.; Webster's 3d.

Reichert-Wollny number (Reichert, Karl Bogislaus and Wollny, Ewald?): Chemistry. See: Hackh.

Reichert's cartilage (Reichert, Karl Bogislaus): Anatomy. See: Donath; Dorland; Stedman.

Reichert's membrane (Reichert, Karl Bogislaus): Anatomy. See: Donath.

Reichert's recess (Reichert, Karl Bogislaus): Anatomy. See: Donath; Dorland; Stedman.

Reichert's scar (Reichert, Karl Bogislaus): Anatomy. See: Dorland; Stedman.

Reichert's substance (Reichert, Karl Bogislaus): Anatomy. See: Donath.

Reichert's syndrome (Reichert, Frederick Leet): Medicine. See: Jablonski.

REICHL, DRAGO. fl. 1955. Czechoslovakian chemist. Cited in: Chem. Abstr., Decenn. Index, 1947-1956. Reichl test reaction for albumin?, Reichl test reaction for glycerin?

Reichl test reaction for albumin (Reichl, Drago?): Chemistry. See: Van Nostrand Chem. Dict.

Reichl test reaction for glycerin (Reichl, Drago?): Chemistry. See: Van Nostrand Chem. Dict.

REICHMANN, FRIEDA. fl. 1916. German neurologist. Cited in: Index Medicus, 2d Ser., vol. 17, 1919. Goldstein-Reichmann syndrome.

Reichmann, Nicolas. See: Rejchman, Mikolaj.

Reichmann's disease (and sign) (Rejchman, Mikolaj). See: Rejchman's disease (and sign).

Reich's law of hierarchical reality (Reich, Charles Alan): Sociology. See: Martin.

Reich's laws of administration (Reich, Charles Alan): Sociology. See: Martin.

Reichstein reagents (Reichstein, Tadeus): Chemistry. See: Van Nostrand Chem. Dict.

REICHSTEIN, TADEUS. 1897- . Polish-born Swiss chemist. See: Who's Who Sci. Europe, 1972. Reichstein reagents, Reichstein's substances (or cortis).

Reichstein's substances (or cortis) (Reichstein, Tadeus): Medicine. See: Stedman.

REID, EUGENE H. fl. 1935. American chemist. Cited in: Chem. Abstr., Decenn. Index, 1937-1946. Reid vapor pressure?

REID, ROBERT WILLIAM. 1851-1939. Scottish anatomist. See: Who Was Who, 1929-1940. Reid's base line.

Reid vapor pressure (Reid, Eugene H.?): Engineering and Industry. See: Thrush.

Reid's base line (Reid, Robert William): Anatomy. See: Donath; Dorland; Stedman.

REIF, WILHELM. fl. 1933. German chemist. Cited in: Chem. Abstr., vol. 27, p. 2108. Holzer-Reif test reaction.

REIFENSTEIN, EDWARD CONRAD, JR. 1908- . American endocrinologist. See: Amer. Men and Women Sci., 12th ed. Klinefelter-Reifenstein-Albright syndrome, Reifenstein's syndrome.

Reifenstein's syndrome (Reifenstein, Edward Conrad, Jr.): Medicine. See: Jablonski.

REIGHARD, JACOB ELLSWORTH. b. 1861. American zoologist. See: Amer. Men Sci., 5th ed. Reighardia?

Reighardia (Reighard, Jacob Ellsworth?): Zoology. See: Pennak.

REIL, JOHANN CHRISTIAN. 1759-1813. German physician. See: Biog. Lex. hervorr. Aerzte. Reil's ansa, Reil's band, Reil's circular sulcus, Reil's island (or insula), Reil's ribbon, Reil's triangle.

Reilly bodies (Reilly, William Anthony): Medicine. See: Wolman.

REILLY, CHARLES HERBERT. 1874-1948. English architect, teacher and writer. See: Who Was Who, 1941-1950. Reilly plan.

REILLY, J. fl. 1942. French neuropathologist. Cited in: Index-Cat. Libr. Surg.-Gen. Off., 5th Ser., vol. 1, 1959. Reilly's syndrome (or phenomenon)?

Reilly plan (Reilly, Charles Herbert): Architecture. See: Briggs.

REILLY, WILLIAM ANTHONY. 1901- . American pediatrician. See: Direct. Med. Specialists, 1974-1975. Alder-Reilly anomaly, Reilly bodies.

Reilly's syndrome (or phenomenon) (Reilly, J.?): Medicine. See: Jablonski.

Reil's ansa (Reil, Johann Christian): Anatomy. See: Donath; Dorland; Stedman.

Reil's band (Reil, Johann Christian): Anatomy. See: Donath; Dorland; Stedman.

Reil's circular sulcus (Reil, Johann Christian): Anatomy. See: Donath; Dorland; Stedman.

Reil's island (or insula) (Reil, Johann Christian): Anatomy. See: Donath; Dorland; Stedman.

Reil's ribbon (Reil, Johann Christian): Anatomy. See: Donath; Stedman.

Reil's triangle (Reil, Johann Christian): Anatomy. See: Donath; Stedman.

REIMANN, HOBART ANSTETH. 1897- . American physician. See: Amer. Men and Women Sci., 12th ed. Reimann's diarrhea, Reimann's periodic disease.

Reimann's diarrhea (Reimann, Hobart Ansteth): Medicine. See: Dorland.

Reimann's periodic disease (Reimann, Hobart Ansteth): Medicine. See: Dorland; Jablonski. Also known as: Siegal-Cattan-Mamou disease.

REIMER, CARL LUDWIG. 1856-1921. German chemist. See: Pogg., vols. 3, 4, 6. Reimer-Tiemann reaction.

Reimer-Tiemann reaction (Reimer, Carl Ludwig and Tiemann, Ferdinand): Chemistry. See: Ballentyne; Hackh; Van Nostrand Chem. Dict.; Webster's 3d.

Reimer's reflex (Derivation undetermined): Medicine. See: Stedman. Also known as: Guillain-Barre reflex, Weingrow's reflex.

REIN, CHARLES. fl. 1936. American dermatologist. (Biography source unavailable.) Wise-Rein disease.

Reinartz crystal oscillator (Derivation undetermined): Electronics. See: Markus.

REINCKE, JOHANN JULIUS. fl. 1868. German physician. Cited in: Index-Cat. Libr. Surg.-Gen. Off., 1st Ser., vol. 12, 1891. Mills-Reincke phenomenon.

Reine-Claude (plums) (Claude): Food and Drink. See: Hendrickson.

REINECKE, A. fl. 1863-1867. German chemist. Cited in: Royal Soc. Cat. Sci. Pap., 1864-1873. Reinecke salt, Reinecke's acid.

REINECKE, JOHANN HEINRICH JULIUS. 1799-1871. German gardener. See: Ascherson and Graebner, vol. 3, p. 315. Reineckia.

einecke salt (Reinecke, A.): Chemistry. See: Hackh; Webster's 3d.

einecke's acid (Reinecke, A.): Chemistry. See: Hackh; Webster's 3d.

eineckia (Reinecke, Johann Heinrich Julius): Botany. See: Taylor, N.

EINER, WILLY. fl. 1958. German chemist in Africa. Cited in: Hintze, d suppl., pp. 827-828. Reinerite.

einerite (Reiner, Willy): Earth Sciences. See: Thrush.

EINHARDT, CARL. fl. 1884. German chemist. Cited in: Treadwell, vol. . Zimmermann-Reinhardt solution.

EINKE, FRIEDRICH BERTHOLD. 1862-1919. German anatomist. See: entralb. Allg. Path. path. Anat., vol. 30 (1919), pp. 401-403. Reinke's rystalloids, Reinke's edema.

einke's crystalloids (Reinke, Friedrich Berthold): Anatomy. See: Stedman.

einke's edema (Reine, Friedrich Berthold): Medicine. See: Jablonski.

EINSCH, ADOLF. 1862-1916. German physician. See: Deut. Biog. ahrb., 1914-1916. Reinsch test, Reinsch's medium.

einsch test (Reinsch, Adolf): Chemistry. See: Hackh; Stedman; Thrush; an Nostrand Chem. Dict.

einsch's medium (Reinsch, Adolf): Medicine. See: Kelly.

EINWARDT, CASPAR GEORG KARL. 1773-1854. Dutch botanist. See: Nieuw Nederl. Biog. Woordenb. Reinwardtia.

einwardtia (Reinwardt, Caspar Georg Karl): Botany. See: Taylor, N.; Webster's 3d.

eis-Buecklers disease (Reis, Wilhelm and Buecklers, Max Hermann Eduard): Medicine. See: Jablonski. Also known as: Buecklers' dystrophy.

EIS, WILHELM (In full: HEINRICH MARIA WILHELM). b. 1872. German phthalmologist. See: Biog. Lex. hervorr. Aerzte. Reis-Buecklers disease.

EISING, EUGENE G. d. 1967. American gun designer. See: New York imes, Feb. 22, 1967, p. 29, col. 4. Reising submachine gun.

eising submachine gun (Reising, Eugene G.): Weapons. See: Quick.

EISNER. fl. 17th c. German cabinetmaker. (Biography source unavailable.) eisner work.

eisner work (Reisner): Applied Arts. See: Webster's 3d.

EISSEISEN, FRANZ DANIEL. 1773-1828. Strasbourg anatomist. See: iog. Lex. hervorr. Aerzte. Reisseisen's muscles.

eisseisen's muscles (Reisseisen, Franz Daniel): Anatomy. See: Donath; Dorland; Stedman.

EISSERT, ARNOLD (In full: CARL ARNOLD). 1860-1945. German chemist. ee: Pogg., vols. 4 to 7a. Reissert compounds, Reissert reaction.

eissert compounds (Reissert, Arnold): Chemistry. See: Van Nostrand Chem. Dict.

eissert reaction (Reissert, Arnold): Chemistry. See: Van Nostrand Chem. Dict.

EISSNER, ERNST. 1824-1878. German anatomist. See: Biog. Lex. hervorr. Aerzte. Reissner's canal, Reissner's corpuscles, Reissner's fibers, Reissner's membrane.

eissner's canal (Reissner, Ernst): Anatomy. See: Donath; Dorland.

eissner's corpuscles (Reissner, Ernst): Anatomy. See: Dorland.

eissner's fibers (Reissner, Ernst): Anatomy. See: Stedman.

eissner's membrane (Reissner, Ernst): Anatomy. See: Donath; Dorland; Stedman.

EISZ, E. fl. 1929. German electrical engineer. Cited in: Sci. Abstr. (Elec. Engin.), vol. 33B (1930), p. 143. Reisz microphone.

eisz microphone (Reisz, E.): Electronics. See: Hughes.

EITER, HANS CONRAD JULIUS. b. 1881. German physician. See: Biog. Lex. hervorr. Aerzte. Reiter's disease (syndrome or triad).

Reiter test (Derivation undetermined): Medicine. See: Stedman.

Reiter's disease (syndrome or triad) (Reiter, Hans Conrad Julius): Medicine. See: Dorland; Jablonski; Stedman. Also known as: Fiessinger-Leroy syndrome, Fiessinger-Leroy-Reiter syndrome, Waelsch's urethritis.

Reitz, Friedrich Wolfgang. See: Reiz, Friedrich Wolfgang.

REIZ, FRIEDRICH WOLFGANG. 1733-1790. German metrist and philologist. See: Allg. Deut. Biog. Reizianum.

Reizianum (Reiz, Friedrich Wolfgang): Literature. See: Preminger; Webster's 3d.

REJANE, GABRIELLE CHARLOTTE (Real name: REJU). 1856-1920. French actress. See: Encyc. Brit., 1911. Rejane green.

Rejane green (Rejane, Gabrielle Charlotte): Fashion. See: Webster's 3d.

REJCHMAN, MIKOLAJ. 1851-1918. Polish physician. See: Biog. Lex. hervorr. Aerzte. Rejchman's disease (and sign).

Rejchman's disease (and sign) (Rejchman, Mikolaj): Medicine. See: Dorland; Jablonski.

Reju, Gabrielle Charlotte. See: Rejane, Gabrielle Charlotte.

Rekoss disk (Derivation undetermined): Medicine. See: Stedman.

Religious of St. Andrew (Andrew, Saint): Religion. See: Attwater.

RELLY, JAMES. 1722?-1778. English religious leader. See: Dict. Nat. Biog. Rellyanists.

Rellyanists (Relly, James): Religion. See: Canney; Webster's 3d.

RELPH, HARRY "LITTLE TICH". 1868-1928. English comedian. See: Hartnoll. Tich.

REMAK, ERNST JULIUS. 1849-1911. German physician. See: Biog. Lex. hervorr. Aerzte. Remak's paralysis, Remak's reflex, Remak's sign.

REMAK, ROBERT. 1815-1865. German anatomist and histologist. See: World Who's Who Sci. Remak's band, Remak's fibers, Remak's ganglia, Remak's nuclear division, Remak's plexus.

Remak's band (Remak, Robert): Anatomy. See: Donath; Dorland; Stedman.

Remak's fibers (Remak, Robert): Anatomy. See: Donath; Dorland; Stedman; Webster's 3d.

Remak's ganglia (Remak, Robert): Anatomy. See: Donath; Dorland; Stedman.

Remak's nuclear division (Remak, Robert): Anatomy. See: Donath; Stedman.

Remak's paralysis (Remak, Ernst Julius): Medicine. See: Jablonski; Stedman.

Remak's plexus (Remak, Robert). See: Meissner's plexus.

Remak's reflex (Remak, Ernst Julius): Medicine. See: Dorland; Stedman.

Remak's sign (Remak, Ernst Julius): Medicine. See: Dorland; Stedman.

REMAZZANO, A. L. fl. 1937. Spanish chemist. Cited in: Chem. Abstr., vol. 31, p. 4449. Del Boca-Remazzano test.

REMBRANDT (In full: REMBRANDT HARMENSZ VAN RIJN). 1606-1669. Dutch painter. See: Bryan. Rembrandt (brown color), Rembrandt hat, Rembrandt lighting, Rembrandt tulip, Rembrandtesque, Rembrandt's madder.

Rembrandt (brown color) (Rembrandt): Fine Arts. See: Webster's 3d.

Rembrandt hat (Rembrandt): Fashion. See: Picken.

Rembrandt lighting (Rembrandt): Fine Arts. See: Focal Encyc. Photog.

Rembrandt tulip (Rembrandt): Botany. See: Webster's 3d; Winburne.

Rembrandtesque (Rembrandt): Fine Arts. See: Partridge; Webster's 3d.

Rembrandt's madder (Rembrandt): Fine Arts. See: Webster's 3d.

Remington breechloader rifle (Remington, Philo): Weapons. See: Dict. Amer. Biog.; Cited in: Mathews, M. M.; Cited in: Partridge.

REMINGTON, ELIPHALET. 1793-1861. American firearms manufacturer. See: Dict. Amer. Biog. Remington pistol (or revolver), Remington rifle (or shotgun).

REMINGTON, PHILO. 1816-1889. American inventor and firearms manufacturer. See: Dict. Amer. Biog. Remington breechloader rifle, Remington pistols, Remington sewing-machine, Remington typewriter.

Remington pistol (or revolver) (Remington, Eliphalet): Weapons. See: Dict. Amer. Biog.; Cited in: Partridge.

Remington pistols (Remington, Philo): Weapons. See: Dict. Amer. Biog.; Cited in: Mathews, M. M.; Cited in: Partridge.

Remington rifle (or shotgun) (Remington, Eliphalet): Weapons. See: Dict. Amer. Biog. Cited in: Partridge.

Remington sewing-machine (Remington, Philo): Engineering and Industry. See: Dict. Amer. Biog.; Cited in: Partridge.

Remington typewriter (Remington, Philo): Engineering and Industry. See: Dict. Amer. Biog.; Cited in: Partridge.

REMLINGER, PAUL AMBROISE. b. 1871. French physician. See: World Who's Who Sci. Remlinger's sign.

Remlinger's sign (Remlinger, Paul Ambroise): Medicine. See: Dorland.

REMON, JOSE. d. 1955. Panamanian president. See: Hist. Dict. Panama. Eisenhower-Remon treaty.

REMSEN, IRA. 1846-1927. American chemist and educator. See: Dict. Amer. Biog. Remsen's law.

Remsen's law (Remsen, Ira): Chemistry. See: Morris and Irwin.

REMY, HEINRICH. b. 1890. German chemist. See: Pogg., vols. 6, 7a. Remy test.

Remy test (Remy, Heinrich): Chemistry. See: Van Nostrand Chem. Dict.

RENAN, JOSEPH ERNEST. 1823-1892. French philologist and historian. See: Encyc. Brit., 1911. Renanian.

Renanian (Renan, Joseph Ernest): History. See: Webster's 3d.

RENARD, ALPHONSE FRANCOIS. 1842-1903. Belgian geologist and mineralogist. See: World Who's Who Sci. Renardite.

Renard number (Renard, T.?): Chemistry. See: Hackh.

RENARD, T. fl. 1917. French chemist. Cited in: Chem. Abstr., Decenn. Index, 1907-1916; 1917-1926. Renard number?

Renardite (Renard, Alphonse Francois): Earth Sciences. See: Thrush; Webster's 3d.

RENAUT, JOSEPH LOUIS. 1844-1917. French physician. See: World Who's Who Sci. Renaut's bodies, Renaut's layer.

Renaut's bodies (Renaut, Joseph Louis): Anatomy. See: Dorland.

Renaut's layer (Renaut, Joseph Louis): Anatomy. See: Dorland. Also known as: Ranvier's membrane.

RENDU, HENRY JULES LOUIS MARIE. 1844-1902. French physician. See: World Who's Who Sci. Fiessinger-Rendu syndrome, Rendu-Weber-Osler syndrome (or disease), Rendu's tremor.

Rendu-Osler syndrome (Rendu, Henry Jules Louis Marie and Osler, Sir William). See: Osler's syndrome (2).

Rendu-Weber-Osler syndrome (or disease) (Rendu, Henry Jules Louis Marie; Weber, Frederick Parkes; and Osler, Sir William). See: Osler's syndrome (2).

Rendu's tremor (Rendu, Henry Jules Louis Marie): Medicine. See: Dorland; Stedman.

Renealmia (Reneaulme, Paul de): Botany. See: Webster's 3d.

RENEAULME, PAUL DE. 1560-1624. French botanist and physician. See: Nouv. Biog. Univ. Renealmia.

RENIER, ARMAND-MARIE-VINCENT-JOSEPH. 1876-1951. Belgian geologist. See: Biog. Nat. de Belgique. Renierite.

Renierite (Renier, Armand-Marie-Vincent-Joseph): Earth Sciences. See: Thrush.

RENN, CHARLES EASTERDAY. 1905- . American sanitary engineer. See: World Who's Who Sci. Krupp-Renn process, Renn-Walz process.

Renn-Walz process (Renn, Charles Easterday and Walz): Engineering and Industry. See: Thrush.

RENNIE, JOHN. 1761-1821. Scottish civil engineer. See: World Who's Who Sci. Rennie's hatch.

Rennie's hatch (Rennie, John): Engineering and Industry. See: Auger.

Renold chain (Renold, Hans): Engineering and Industry. See: Auger.

RENOLD, HANS. 1852-1943. Swiss inventor. (Biography source unavailable.) Renold chain.

Renon-Delille syndrome (Renon, Louis and Delille, Arthur): Medicine. See: Dorland; Jablonski.

RENON, LOUIS. 1863-1922. French physician. See: Biog. Lex. hervorr. Aerzte. Renon-Delille syndrome.

RENSCH, BERNHARD CARL EMMANUEL. 1900- . German zoologist. See: World Who's Who Sci. Rensch's desert rule, Rensch's hair rule, Rensch's laws.

Rensch's desert rule (Rensch, Bernhard Carl Emmanuel): Zoology. See: Winick.

Rensch's hair rule (Rensch, Bernhard Carl Emmanuel): Zoology. See: Winick.

Rensch's laws (Rensch, Bernhard Carl Emmanuel): Zoology. See: Gray.

Renshaw cells (Derivation undetermined): Medicine. See: Stedman.

Rensselaer, Stephen van. See: Van Rensselaer, Stephen.

Rensselaerite (Van Rensselaer, Stephen): Earth Sciences. See: Mathews, M. M.; Thrush.

Renteln solution (Derivation undetermined): Chemistry. See: Van Nostrand Chem. Dict.

RENWICK, JAMES. 1662-1688. Scottish clergyman. See: Dict. Nat. Biog. Renwickites.

RENWICK, T. K. fl. 1956. English physician. (Biography source unavailable.) Fisch-Renwick syndrome.

Renwickites (Renwick, James): Religion. See: Encyc. Brit. 1973.

RENZ, CARL. fl. 1920. Swiss? chemist. Cited in: Chem. Abstr., Decenn. Index, 1917-1926. Renz test reaction?

Renz test reaction (Renz, Carl?): Chemistry. See: Van Nostrand Chem. Dict.

Reppe chemistry (Reppe, Walter): Chemistry. See: Van Nostrand Sci. Encyc.; Webster's 3d.

REPPE, WALTER. b. 1892. German chemist. See: World Who's Who Sci. Reppe chemistry.

Reppmann test (Reppmann, W.): Chemistry. See: Van Nostrand Chem. Dict.

REPPMANN, W. fl. 1934. German chemist. Cited in: Chem. Abstr., vol. 29, p. 5037. Reppmann test.

RESCIA, RICHARD R. fl. 1953. American statistician. Cited in: Kendall and Doig. Beall-Rescias generalization.

reservoir of Pecquet (Pecquet, Jean). See: Pecquet's cistern (receptaculum or reservoir).

RESSY, MARCELLE. fl. 1923. French chemist. Cited in: Chem. Abstr., vol. 17, p. 3145. Ortodoscu-Ressy micro-test for antimony and tin.

RESTORFF, HEDWIG VON. fl. 1933-1935. German psychologist. Cited in: Internat. Encyc. Soc. under "Koehler, Wolfgang." Koehler-Restorff phenomenon.

RESUGGAN, JOHN CHARLES LOVELL. 1907- . English chemist. See: Who's Who Brit. Sci., 1953. Stevenson-Resuggan reagent.

rete Malpighii (Malpighi, Marcello). See: Malpighian layer.

Retger liquid (Retgers, Jan Willem): Chemistry. See: Van Nostrand Chem. Dict.

RETGERS, JAN WILLEM. 1856-1896. Dutch chemical crystallographer. Cited in: Min. Mag., vol. 28 (1949), p. 737. Retger liquid, Retger's law (or law of Retger's), Retgers' salt, Retgersite.

Retgers' law (or law of Retger's) (Retgers, Jan Willem): Chemistry. See: Hackh; Internat. Dict. Phys. Elec.

Retgers' salt (Retgers, Jan Willem): Chemistry. See: Thrush.

Retgersite (Retgers, Jan Willem): Earth Sciences. See: Thrush.

RETHERFORD, ROBERT C. fl. 1950. American physicist. Cited in: Chem. Abstr., Decenn. Index, 1947-1956. Lamb-Retherford shift.

RETIF, NICOLAS EDME (RETIF DE LA BRETONNE). 1734-1806. French novelist. See: Encyc. Brit., 1973. Retifism.

Retifism (Retif, Nicolas Edme): Psychology. See: Hinsie.

RETZ, BARON DE. 1404-1440. French marshal. See: Barnhart (Cycl. Names). Gilles de Retz.

Retzian (Retzius, Anders Johan): Earth Sciences. See: Webster's 3d.

RETZIUS, ANDERS ADOLF. 1796-1860. Swedish anatomist. See: Encyc. Brit., 1973. Retzius' fibers, Retzius' ligament (or band), Retzius' space (or cavity), Retzius' veins.

RETZIUS, ANDERS JOHAN. 1742-1821. Swedish botanist. See: Nouv. Biog. Univ. Retzian.

Retzius' fibers (Retzius, Anders Adolf): Anatomy. See: Dorland; Stedman.

Retzius' foramina (Retzius, Gustav Magnus): Anatomy. See: Dorland; Stedman. Also known as: Key-Retzius foramina (or foramina of Key-Retzius), Luschka's foramina (or foramen).

RETZIUS, GUSTAV MAGNUS. 1842-1919. Swedish anatomist and anthropologist. See: World Who's Who Sci. Key-Retzius corpuscles, Retzius' foramina, Retzius' gyrus, Retzius' lines, Retzius' striae, sheath of Key and Retzius.

Retzius' gyrus (Retzius, Gustav Magnus): Anatomy. See: Donath; Stedman.

Retzius' ligament (or band) (Retzius, Anders Adolf): Anatomy. See: Donath; Dorland; Stedman.

Retzius' lines (Retzius, Gustav Magnus): Anatomy. See: Gray; Stedman. Also known as: Owen's lines.

Retzius' space (or cavity) (Retzius, Anders Adolf): Anatomy. See: Donath; Dorland; Stedman.

Retzius' striae (Retzius, Gustav Magnus): Anatomy. See: Donath; Dorland; Stedman.

Retzius' veins (Retzius, Anders Adolf): Anatomy. See: Donath; Dorland; Stedman. Also known as: Ruysch's vein.

Retz's red-billed shrike (Derivation undetermined): Zoology. See: Gray.

REUBEN. Biblical son of Jacob in the Old Testament. See: Hastings (Dict. Bible). Reubenite.

Reuben-Mallory cell (Reuben, S.? and P.R. Mallory and Co., Inc.): Electronics. See: Hughes.

REUBEN, S. fl. 1929. English? engineer. Cited in: Chem. Abstr., Decenn. Index, 1927-1936. Reuben-Mallory cell?

Reubenite (Reuben): Religion. See: Webster's 3d.

REUBER, MELVIN D. 1930- . American pathologist. See: Amer. Men and Women Sci., 12th ed. Reuber's hepatoma.

Reuber's hepatoma (Reuber, Melvin D.): Medicine. See: Jablonski.

Reuleaux diagram (Reuleaux, Franz): Engineering and Industry. See: Auger.

REULEAUX, FRANZ. 1829-1905. German engineer. See: Pogg., vols. 3, 4. Reuleaux diagram.

REUSS, AUGUST EMANUEL VON. 1811-1873. Austrian mineralogist and paleontologist. See: Pogg., vols. 2, 3. Reussinite.

REUSS, AUGUST RITTER VON. 1841-1924. Austrian ophthalmologist. See: Biog. Lex. hervorr. Aerzte. Reuss' color tables, Reuss' formula, Reuss' test.

Reuss' color tables (Reuss, August Ritter von): Medicine. See: Dorland; Stedman.

Reuss' formula (Reuss, August Ritter von): Medicine. See: Stedman.

REUSS, FRANZ AMBROSIUS. 1761-1830. Czechoslovakian physician and mineralogist. See: Pogg., vol. 2. Reussine.

Reuss' test (Reuss, August Ritter von): Medicine. See: Stedman.

Reussine (Reuss, Franz Ambrosius): Earth Sciences. See: Charnock; Thrush.

Reussinite (Reuss, August Emanuel von): Earth Sciences. See: Thrush.

REUTER, BARON PAUL JULIUS VON. 1816-1899. German founder of news agency. See: Encyc. Brit., 1911. Reuter's (telegraph news agency).

Reuter's (telegraph news agency) (Reuter, Baron Paul Julius von): Mass Media. See: Latham; Stenhouse.

REVERDIN, AUGUSTE. 1848-1908. Swiss surgeon. See: Biog. Lex. hervorr. Aerzte. Reverdin's needle?

REVERDIN, FREDERIC. 1849-1931. Swiss chemist. See: World Who's Who Sci. Reverdin rearrangement.

REVERDIN, JACQUES-LOUIS. 1842-1929. Swiss surgeon. See: World Who's Who Sci. Reverdin's disease, Reverdin's graft (method or operation).

Reverdin rearrangement (Reverdin, Frederic): Chemistry. Van Nostrand Chem. Dict.

Reverdin's disease (Reverdin, Jacques-Louis): Medicine. Cited in: World Who's Who Sci.

Reverdin's graft (method or operation) (Reverdin, Jacques-Louis): Medicine. See: Dorland; Stedman.

Reverdin's needle (Reverdin, Auguste?): Medicine. See: Dorland; World Who's Who Sci.

reverse Gougerot-Sjoegren syndrome (Gougerot, Henri and Sjoegren, Henrik Samuel Conrad). See: Creyx-Levy syndrome.

REVILLIOD, LEON. 1835-1919. See: Biog. Lex. hervorr. Aerzte. Revilliod's sign.

Revilliod's sign (Revilliod, Leon): Medicine. See: Dorland; Stedman.

REVILLION. fl. 1830. ? Engineer. (Biography source unavailable.) Revillion pump.

Revillion pump (Revillion): Engineering and Industry. See: Auger.

REVOL, L. fl. 1950. French hematologist. (Biography source unavailable.) Revol's disease, Revol's syndrome.

Revol's disease (Revol, L.). See: Mortensen's disease.

Revol's syndrome (Revol, L.). See: Glanzmann's syndrome.

revolt of Masaniello (Masaniello): History. See: Harbottle.

REY, JEAN-ALEXANDRE. 1861-1935. Swiss-born engineer. See: World Who's Who Sci. Blondel-Rey law.

REYE, E. fl. 1928. German physician. (Biography source unavailable.) Reye-Sheehan syndrome.

REYE, R. D. K. fl. 1963. Australian physician. (Biography source unavailable.) Reye's syndrome.

Reye-Sheehan syndrome (Reye, E. and Sheehan, Harold Leeming). See: Simmonds' syndrome.

Reye's syndrome (Reye, R. D. K.): Medicine. See: Jablonski; Stedman.

Reyn (Reynolds, Osborne): Physics. See: Dresner.

Reynals' factor (Reynals, Francesc Duran): Medicine. See: Dorland; Stedman.

REYNALS, FRANCESC DURAN. fl. 1928. French-born American physician. Cited in: Kelly. Reynals' factor.

Reynier, Jean Pierre de. See: De Reynier, Jean Pierre.

REYNOLDS. fl. 18th c.? English physician. (Biography source unavailable.) Reynolds' specific.

Reynolds analogy (Reynolds, Osborne): Physics. See: Internat. Dict. Ap. Math.; Van Nostrand Sci. Encyc.

Reynolds and Moorby method for mechanical equivalent of heat (Reynolds, Osborne and Moorby, William Henry): Physics. See: Internat. Dict. Phys. Elec.

Reynolds criterion (Reynolds, Osborne): Physics. See: Internat. Dict. Phys. Elec.; Thrush; Van Nostrand Sci. Encyc.

Reynolds effect (Reynolds, Osborne): Physics. See: Huschke.

Reynolds equation (Reynolds, Osborne): Physics. See: Internat. Dict. Ap. Math.; Van Nostrand Sci. Encyc.

Reynolds group (Reynolds, Osborne): Physics. See: Van Nostrand Sci. Encyc.

REYNOLDS, JAMES EMERSON. 1844-1920. English chemist. See: World Who's Who Sci. Reynolds' test.

Reynolds number (Reynolds, Osborne): Physics. See: Auger; Ballentyne; Internat. Dict. Ap. Math.; Thewlis; Thrush.

REYNOLDS, OSBORNE. 1842-1912. Irish engineer and physicist. See: Dict. Nat. Biog., 3d. suppl. Reyn, Reynolds analogy, Reynolds and Moorby method for mechanical equivalent of heat, Reynolds criterion, Reynolds effect, Reynolds equation, Reynolds group, Reynolds number, Reynolds pump, Reynolds stresses.

Reynolds pump (Reynolds, Osborne): Engineering and Industry. See: Auger.

Reynolds' specific (Reynolds): Medicine. See: Charnock.

REYNOLDS, STEPHEN EDWARD. 1916- . American mechanical engineer. See: Amer. Men and Women Sci., 12th ed. Workman-Reynolds effect.

Reynolds stresses (Reynolds, Osborne): Physics. See: Huschke; Internat. Dict. Ap. Math.

Reynolds' test (Reynolds, James Emerson): Chemistry. See: Stedman.

REYS, L. fl. 1926. French physician. (Biography source unavailable.) Weill-Reys-Adie syndrome.

REZA SHAH PAHLAVI. 1878-1944. Shah of Iran. See: New Encyc. Brit., 1974, Microp. Pahlavi (or Pahlevi).

REZZONICO, GIULIO. fl. 1881. Italian physician. Cited in: Royal Soc. Cat. Sci. Pap., 1800-1883. Rezzonico-Golgi threads (or spirals).

Rezzonico-Golgi threads (or spirals) (Rezzonico, Giulio and Golgi, Camillo): Anatomy. See: Dorland.

Rhadamanthine (or Rhadamanthus) (Rhadamanthus): Generic Word (stern judge). See: Partridge; Webster's 3d.

RHADAMANTHUS. Judge of the dead in Greek mythology. See: Jobes. Rhadamanthine (or Rhadamanthus).

RHEA. Daughter of Uranus and Gaea in Greek mythology. See: Jobes. Rhea (ostrich).

RHEA, JOHN. 1753-1832. Irish-born American politician. See: Dict. Amer. Biog. Rhea letter.

Rhea letter (Rhea, John): History. See: Jameson; Morris.

Rhea (ostrich) (Rhea): Zoology. See: Partridge.

RHEDEN, JOSEF. 1873-1946. Austrian astronomer. See: Pogg., vols. 5, 6, 7a. Rheden's exposure tables.

Rheden's exposure tables (Rheden, Josef): Astronomy. See: Focal Encyc. Photog. under "Austria," p. 74.

RHEINBERG, JULIUS. fl. 1912. English optics manufacturer. Cited in: Chem. Abstr., Decenn. Indexes, 1907-1916; 1917-1926. Rheinberg microscope.

Rheinberg microscope (Rheinberg, Julius): Biology. See: Stedman.

RHEINBOLDT, HEINRICH. 1891-1955. German chemist in Brazil. See: Pogg., vols. 6, 7a. Rheinboldt test for mercaptans, Rheinboldt test reaction for oximes.

Rheinboldt test for mercaptans (Rheinboldt, Heinrich): Chemistry. See: Van Nostrand Chem. Dict.

Rheinboldt test reaction for oximes (Rheinboldt, Heinrich): Chemistry. See: Van Nostrand Chem. Dict.

Rheinhard's myocarditis (Derivation undetermined): Medicine. See: Jablonski.

RHESUS. Mythical King of Thrace. See: Dict. Grk. Rom. Biog. Myth. Rhesus (monkey).

Rhesus (monkey) (Rhesus): Zoology. See: Partridge.

Rhetorians (Rhetorius): Religion. See: Canney.

RHETORIUS. fl. 4th c. Egyptian heretic. See: Dict. Christian Biog. Rhetorians.

RHOADS, CORNELIUS PACKARD. 1898-1959. American pathologist. See: World Who's Who Sci. Bomford-Rhoads anemia, Rhoads' method.

Rhoads' method (Rhoads, Cornelius Packard): Medicine. See: Kelly.

RHODE, C. MARTIN. fl. 1949. American physiologist. Cited in: Chem. Abstr., Decenn. Index, 1947-1956. Rhode test?

Rhode test (Rhode, C. Martin?): Chemistry. See: Hackh.

RHODES, CECIL JOHN. 1853-1902. English statesman and financier in South Africa. See: Dict. Nat. Biog., 2d suppl. Rhodes' grass, Rhodes scholar (and scholarship), Rhodesite.

Rhode's giant cell (Derivation undetermined): Zoology. See: Gray.

Rhodes' grass (Rhodes, Cecil John): Botany. See: Gray; Webster's 3d.

RHODES, O. S. fl. 1929. English textile chemist. Cited in: Chem. Abstr., vol. 23, p. 3349. Rhodes reagent.

Rhodes reagent (Rhodes, O. S.): Chemistry. See: Van Nostrand Sci. Encyc.

Rhodes scholar (and scholarship) (Rhodes, Cecil John): Education. See: Barnhart (Eng. Lit.); Hendrickson; Webster's 3d.

Rhodesite (Rhodes, Cecil John): Earth Sciences. See: Thrush.

Rhodomontade (Rodomonte, the braggart). See: Rodomontade.

Rhondda, Viscount. See: Thomas, David Alfred (Viscount Rhondda).

Rhonddaed (Thomas, David Alfred, Viscount Rhondda): Generic Word (lost). See: Partridge; Weekley.

rhythm of St. Bernard (Bernard of Clairvaux, Saint): Religion. See: Attwater.

RIBAGA, CONSTANTINO. fl. 1897-1929. Italian zoologist. Cited in: Royal Soc. Cat. Sci. Pap., 1884-1900. Ribaga's organ.

Ribaga's organ (Ribaga, Constantino): Zoology. See: Henderson.

RIBBERT, HUGO (In full: MORITZ W. HUGO). 1855-1920. German pathologist. See: World Who's Who Sci. Ribbert's theory.

Ribbert's theory (Ribbert, Hugo): Medicine. See: Dorland; Stedman.

RIBBING, SEVED. 1902- . Swedish radiologist. See: Vem Ar Det?, 1975. Ribbing's syndrome.

Ribbing's syndrome (Ribbing, Seved): Medicine. See: Jablonski. Also known as: Lehmann-Ribbing-Mueller syndrome, Mueller-Ribbing-Clement syndrome.

RIBERA Y SANS, JOSE. 1853-1912. Spanish surgeon. Cited in: Index Medicus, 2d Ser., vol. 10, 1912. Ribera's method.

Ribera's method (Ribera y Sans, Jose): Medicine. See: Dorland; Stedman.

RIBES, FRANCOIS. 1765-1845. French surgeon. See: Nouv. Biog. Univ. Ribes' ganglion.

Ribes' ganglion (Ribes, Francois): Anatomy. See: Donath; Dorland; Stedman.

RICARD, ALFRED LOUIS. b. 1858. French surgeon. Cited in: Index-Cat. Libr. Surg.-Gen. Off., 1st Ser., vol. 12, 1891. Ricard's amputation.

Ricardian (Ricardo, David): Economics. See: Webster's 3d.

RICARDO, DAVID. 1772-1823. English economist. See: Internat. Encyc. Soc. Sci. Ricardian.

Ricardo engine (Ricardo, Sir Harry Ralph): Engineering and Industry. See: Auger.

RICARDO, SIR HARRY RALPH. b. 1885. English mechanical engineer. See: World Who's Who Sci. Ricardo engine.

Ricard's amputation (Ricard, Alfred Louis): Medicine. See: Stedman.

Riccati-Bessel functions (Riccati, Count Jacopo Francesco and Bessel, Friedrich Wilhelm): Mathematics. See: Ballentyne.

Riccati equation (Riccati, Count Jacopo Francesco): Mathematics. See: Internat. Dict. Ap. Math.; James.

RICCATI, COUNT JACOPO FRANCESCO. 1676-1754. Italian mathematician. See: World Who's Who Sci. Riccati-Bessel functions, Riccati equation.

Ricci calculus (Ricci, Curbastro Gregorio): Mathematics. See: Internat. Dict. Ap. Math.

RICCI, CURBASTRO GREGORIO. 1853-1925. Italian mathematician. See: World Who's Who Sci. Ricci calculus, Ricci identity, Ricci tensor, Ricci theorem (or lemma).

Ricci identity (Ricci, Curbastro Gregorio): Mathematics. See: Internat. Dict. Ap. Math.

RICCI, PIETRO FRANCESCO. fl. 18th c. Italian botanist. See: Biog. Notes Upon Botanists. Riccia.

Ricci tensor (Ricci, Curbastro Gregorio): Mathematics. See: Internat. Dict. Ap. Math.; James. Also known as: Einstein tensor.

Ricci theorem (or lemma) (Ricci, Curbastro Gregorio): Mathematics. See: Internat. Dict. Ap. Math.

RICCI, VINCENZO. fl. 1949. Italian physician in France. (Biography source unavailable.) Cacchi-Ricci syndrome.

Riccia (Ricci, Pietro Francesco): Botany. See: Van Nostrand Sci. Encyc. under "Bryophytes"; Webster's 3d.

RICCO, ANNIBALE. 1844-1911. Italian astronomer. See: World Who's Who Sci. Ricco's law?

Ricco's law (Ricco, Annibale?): Physiology. See: Stedman; Webster's 3d.

RICE, ANDREW CARL. 1900- . American chemist. See: Amer. Men Sci., 6th ed. Rice-Fogg-James reagent.

Rice bromine solution (Derivation undetermined): Chemistry. See: Van Nostrand Chem. Dict.

RICE, C. G. fl. 1947. American? electronics engineer. Cited in: Sci. Abstr. (Elec. Engin.), vol. 50 B (1947), p. 333. Rice neutralization (or neutralizing circuit)?

Rice-Fogg-James reagent (Rice, Andrew Carl; Fogg, Heman Charles; and James, Charles): Chemistry. See: Van Nostrand Chem. Dict.

Rice neutralization (or neutralizing circuit) (Rice, C. G.?): Electronics. See: Hughes; Markus.

Rice test for phenol (Derivation undetermined): Chemistry. See: Van Nostrand Chem. Dict.

RICH, ARNOLD RICE. b. 1893. American pathologist. See: World Who's Who Sci. Hamman-Rich syndrome.

rich as Plutus (Plutus): Generic Word (wealthy). See: Brewer.

RICHARD (DUKE OF YORK). 1411-1460. English leader of Yorkists. See: Dict. Nat. Biog. Yorkist.

RICHARD (EARL OF CAMBRIDGE). d. 1415. English conspirator. See: Dict. Nat. Biog. Cambridge conspiracy.

RICHARD I, THE LION-HEARTED. 1157-1199. King of England. See: Dict. Nat. Biog. King Richard's ransom.

RICHARD, FELIX-ADOLPHE. 1822-1872. French surgeon. See: Biog. Lex. hervorr. Aerzte. Richard's fringe.

RICHARD, LOUIS CLAUDE MARIE. 1754-1821. French botanist. See: Nouv. Biog. Univ. Richardia.

Richard test for mercury oxycyanide (Derivation undetermined): Chemistry. See: Van Nostrand Chem. Dict.

Richardia (Richard, Louis Claude Marie): Botany. See: Webster's 3d.

Richardia (Richardson, Richard): Botany. See: Webster's 3d.

RICHARDS, CHARLES BRINKERHOFF. 1833-1909. American mechanical engineer. See: Dict. Amer. Biog. Richards indicator.

RICHARDS, CHARLES RUSS. 1871-1941. American engineer and educator. See: Who Was Who Amer., vol. 1. Richards' formula.

Richards' formula (Richards, Charles Russ): Education. See: Good.

Richard's fringe (Richard, Felix-Adolphe): Medicine. See: Stedman.

Richards indicator (Richards, Charles Brinkerhoff): Engineering and Industry. See: Auger; Webster's 3d.

Richards' pulsator classifier (Richards, Robert Hallowell?): Engineering and Industry. See: Thrush.

Richards' pulsator jig (Richards, Robert Hallowell?): Engineering and Industry. See: Thrush.

RICHARDS, ROBERT HALLOWELL. 1884-1945. American mining engineer. See: Who Was Who Amer., vol. 2. Richards' pulsator classifier?, Richards' pulsator jig?, Richards' shallow-pocket hindered-settling classifier?

Richards' rule (Richards, Theodore William): Chemistry. See: Ballentyne.

Richards' shallow-pocket hindered-settling classifier (Richards, Robert Hallowell?): Engineering and Industry. See: Thrush.

RICHARDS, THEODORE WILLIAM. 1868-1928. American chemist. See: World Who's Who Sci. Richards' rule.

Richard's weed (Richardson, Richard): Botany. See: Webster's 3d.

RICHARDSON, SIR BENJAMIN WARD. 1828-1896. English physician. See: World Who's Who Sci. Richardson's sign.

Richardson-Dushman equation (Richardson, Sir Owen Williams and Dushman, Saul): Physics. See: Ballentyne; Hughes; Internat. Dict. Phys. Elec.; Thewlis. Also known as: Edison equation, Richardson equation.

Richardson effect (Richardson, Sir Owen Williams). See: Einstein-De Haas effect.

Richardson equation (Richardson, Sir Owen Williams). See: Richardson-Dushman equation.

RICHARDSON, FREDERIC WILLIAM. fl. 1892. English chemist. Cited in: Royal Soc. Cat. Sci. Pap., 1884-1900. Richardson test for naphthols.

Richardson ground squirrel (Richardson, Sir John): Zoology. See: Mathews, M. M.; Pennak.

RICHARDSON, SIR JOHN. 1787-1865. Scottish naturalist. See: World Who's Who Sci. Richardson ground squirrel, Richardsonius?, Richardson's falcon, Richardson's grouse, Richardson's hawk gull, Richardson's jaeger, Richardson's owl.

RICHARDSON, JOHN CLIFFORD. 1909- . Canadian neurologist. See: Canadian Who's Who, 1964-1966. Steele-Richardson-Olszewski syndrome.

RICHARDSON, LEWIS FRY. b. 1881. English physicist and psychologist. See: New Encyc. Brit., 1974, Microp. Richardson number.

RICHARDSON, MARION WEBSTER. b. 1891. American psychologist. See: Amer. Men Sci., 8th ed. Kuder-Richardson coefficients of equivalence (or formulas).

Richardson number (Richardson, Lewis Fry): Physics. See: Huschke; Internat. Dict. Phys. Elec.

RICHARDSON, SIR OWEN WILLIAMS. 1879-1959. English physicist. See: World Who's Who Sci. Richardson-Dushman equation, Richardson effect, Richardson plot.

Richardson plot (Richardson, Sir Owen Williams): Physics. See: Internat. Dict. Phys. Elec.

RICHARDSON, RICHARD. 1663-1741. English physician and botanist. See: Dict. Nat. Biog. Richardia, Richard's weed.

RICHARDSON, SAMUEL. 1689-1761. English novelist. See: Dict. Nat. Biog. Richardsonian.

Richardson test for naphthols (Richardson, Frederic William): Chemistry. See: Van Nostrand Chem. Dict.

Richardsonia (Richardson, Richard). See: Richardia.

Richardsonian (Richardson, Samuel): Literature. See: Webster's 3d.

Richardsonius (Richardson, Sir John?): Zoology. See: Pennak.

Richardson's falcon (Richardson, Sir John): Zoology. Cited in: Partridge.

Richardson's grouse (Richardson, Sir John): Zoology. See: Webster's 3d.

Richardson's hawk gull (Richardson, Sir John): Zoology. Cited in: Partridge.

Richardson's jaeger (Richardson, Sir John): Zoology. See: Webster's 3d.

Richardson's owl (Richardson, Sir John): Zoology. See: Pennak; Webster's 3d.

Richardson's sign (Richardson, Sir Benjamin Ward): Medicine. See: Dorland.

RICHAUD, ALBERT. fl. 1909. French chemist. Cited in: Chem. Abstr., vol. 7, p. 1746. Richaud-Bidot solution.

Richaud-Bidot solution (Richaud, Albert and Bidot, Emile?): Chemistry. See: Van Nostrand Chem. Dict.

RICHE, CLAUDE ANTOINE GASPAR. 1762-1797. French naturalist. See: Biog. Notes Upon Botanists. Richea?

Richea (Riche, Claude Antoine Gaspar?): Botany. See: Webster's 3d.

RICHELIEU, ARMAND JEAN DU PLESSIS, CARDINAL AND DUC DE. 1585-1642. French statesman and prelate. See: New Encyc. Brit., 1974. a la Richelieu, Richelieu embroidery, Richelieu (shoes).

Richelieu embroidery (Richelieu, Armand Jean du Plessis, Cardinal and Duc de): Fashion. See: Picken.

Richelieu (shoes) (Richelieu, Armand Jean du Plessis, Cardinal and Duc de): Fashion. See: Stenhouse.

RICHET, CHARLES ROBERT. 1850-1935. French physiologist. See: World Who's Who Sci. Richet's bandage, Richet's fascia.

RICHET, DIDIER DOMINIQUE ALFRED. 1816-1891. French physician. See: Biog. Lex. hervorr. Aerzte. Demarquay-Richet syndrome, Richet's aneurysm.

RICHET, EMILE. fl. 1948. Belgian geologist in Belgian Congo. Cited in: Hintze, 2d suppl., p. 329. Richetite.

Richetite (Richet, Emile): Earth Sciences. See: Thrush.

Richet's aneurysm (Richet, Didier Dominique Alfred): Medicine. See: Dorland.

Richet's bandage (Richet, Charles Robert): Medicine. See: Dorland.

Richet's fascia (Richet, Charles Robert): Medicine. See: Dorland.

RICHMAN, EUDICE. fl. 1930. American biochemist. Cited in: Chem. Abstr. Levine-Richman reagent for turpines, Levine-Richman test to differentiate irradiated from non-irradiated sterols.

Richmond-Boseley test for formaldehyde in milk (Richmond, Henry Droop and Boseley, Leonard Kidgell): Chemistry. See: Van Nostrand Chem. Dict.

Richmond-Boseley test reaction for formaldehyde (Richmond, Henry Droop and Boseley, Leonard Kidgell): Chemistry. See: Van Nostrand Chem. Dict.

RICHMOND, C. M. 1835-1902. American dentist. (Biography source unavailable.) Richmond crown.

RICHMOND, CHARLES WALLACE. 1868-1932. American ornithologist. See: Dict. Amer. Biog. Richmondena.

Richmond crown (Richmond, C. M.): Dentistry. See: Stedman.

Richmond, Earl of. See: Henry VII of England.

RICHMOND, HENRY DROOP. fl. 1889-1930. American dairy chemist. Cited in: Chem. Abstr., Decenn. Indexes, 1907-1916; 1917-1926. Richmond-Boseley test for formaldehyde in milk, Richmond-Boseley test reaction for formaldehyde, Richmond's formula.

Richmondena (Richmond, Charles Wallace): Zoology. See: Webster's 3d.

Richmond's formula (Richmond, Henry Droop): Chemistry. See: Winburne.

Richner-Hanhart syndrome (Richner, Hermann and Hanhart, Ernst): Medicine. See: Jablonski. Also known as: Hanhart's syndrome, Richner's syndrome.

RICHNER, HERMANN. 1908- . Swiss ophthalmologist. Cited in: Index-Cat. Libr. Surg.-Gen. Off., 5th Ser., vol. 1, 1959. Richner-Hanhart syndrome.

Richner's syndrome (Richner, Hermann). See: Richner-Hanhart syndrome.

RICHTER, AUGUST GOTTLIEB. 1742-1812. German surgeon. See: World Who's Who Sci. Monro-Richter line, Richter's hernia, Richter's suture.

RICHTER, CHARLES FRANCIS. 1900- . American seismologist. See: Amer. Men and Women Sci., 12th ed. Gutenberg-Richter scale, Richter scale.

Richter cinnoline synthesis (Von Richter, Viktor): Chemistry. See: Van Nostrand Chem. Dict.

RICHTER, ERWIN. fl. 1911. German chemist. Cited in: Chem. Abstr., vol. 5, p. 3549. Lenz-Richter test reactions for per-salts.

RICHTER, INA M. fl. 1918. American physician. (Biography source unavailable.) Clough-Richter syndrome.

RICHTER, JEREMIAS BENJAMIN. 1762-1807. German chemist. See: World Who's Who Sci. Richter's law.

RICHTER, JOHANN PAUL FRIEDRICH (Pseud., JEAN PAUL). 1763-1825. German author. See: Encyc. Brit., 1911. Jeanpaulia.

Richter-Monro line (Richter, August Gottlieb and Monro, Alexander Secundus): See: Monro-Richter line.

Richter scale (Richter, Charles Francis): Earth Sciences. See: Barnhart (New Eng.); Monkhouse; Thewlis.

RICHTER, THEODORE (In full: HIERONYMOUS THEODORE). 1824-1898. German metallurgical chemist. See: Biog. Jahrb. Deut. Nekr., 1900. Richterite.

Richter, Viktor von. See: Von Richter, Viktor.

Richterite (Richter, Theodore): Earth Sciences. See: Thrush; Webster's 3d.

Richter's hernia (Richter, August Gottlieb): Medicine. See: Dorland; Jablonski; Stedman. Also known as: Littre's hernia (2) (parietal).

Richter's law (Richter, Jeremias Benjamin): Chemistry. See: Hackh; Van Nostrand Chem. Dict. Also known as: Wenzel's law.

Richter's suture (Richter, August Gottlieb): Medicine. See: Stedman.

RICKARD, THOMAS ARTHUR. 1864-1953. American mining engineer. See: Amer. Men Sci., 1st ed. Rickardite.

Rickardite (Rickard, Thomas Arthur): Earth Sciences. See: Thrush; Webster's 3d.

RICKETTS, HOWARD TAYLOR. 1871-1910. American pathologist. See: Dict. Amer. Biog., 1st suppl. Rickettsia (and Rickettsial).

Rickettsia (and Rickettsial) (Ricketts, Howard Taylor): Medicine. See: Dorland; Pennak; Stedman; Webster's 3d.

RICKEY, COLONEL. fl. 1895. American military officer. (Biography source unavailable.) gin Rickey.

RIDDOCH, GEORGE. 1888-1947. English neurologist. See: Lancet, vol. 2 (Nov. 1, 1947), p. 672. Riddoch's syndrome.

Riddoch's syndrome (Riddoch, George): Medicine. See: Jablonski.

RIDEAL, SIR ERIC KEIGHTLEY. b. 1890. English physical chemist. See: World Who's Who Sci. Blackett and Rideal method.

Rideal reagent for formaldehyde (Rideal, Samuel): Chemistry. See: Van Nostrand Chem. Dict.

RIDEAL, SAMUEL. 1863-1929. English chemist and bacteriologist. See: Who Was Who, 1929-1940. Rideal reagent for formaldehyde, Rideal-Walker coefficient, Rideal-Walker test.

Rideal-Walker coefficient (Rideal, Samuel and Walker, J. T. Ainslie): Medicine. See: Dorland; Hackh; Stedman.

Rideal-Walker test (Rideal, Samuel and Walker, J. T. Ainslie): Medicine. See: Hackh; Webster's 3d.

RIDELL, A. R. fl. 1947. American physician. (Biography source unavailable.) Shaver-Ridell syndrome.

Ridell's operation (Derivation undetermined): Medicine. See: Stedman.

Ridenour test reaction for salicylic acid (Ridenour, William E.): Chemistry. See: Van Nostrand Chem. Dict.

RIDENOUR, WILLIAM E. fl. 1895-1910. American pharmaceutical chemist. Cited in: Chem. Abstr., Decenn. Index, 1907-1916. Ridenour test reaction for salicylic acid.

RIDER, A. K. fl. 19th c. Engineer. (Biography source unavailable.) Rider engine, Rider valve.

Rider engine (Rider, A. K.): Engineering and Industry. See: Auger.

Rider valve (Rider, A. K.): Engineering and Industry. See: Auger.

Ridgeway filter (Derivation undetermined): Engineering and Industry. See: Thrush.

Ridgway color system (Ridgway, Robert): Zoology. See: Drever; English.

Ridgway osteogenic sarcoma (Derivation undetermined): Medicine. See: Jablonski.

RIDGWAY, RAYMOND RONALD. 1897- . American electrochemist. See: Amer. Men Sci., 7th ed. Ridgway's extension of Mohs' scale.

RIDGWAY, ROBERT. 1850-1929. American ornithologist. See: Dict. Amer. Biog. Ridgway color system.

Ridgway's extension of Mohs' scale (Ridgway, Raymond Ronald): Earth Sciences. See: Van Nostrand Sci. Encyc. under "Hardness."

RIDLEY, FRANK F. fl. 1946. English engineer. Cited In: Chem. Abstr., vol. 40, p. 2702. Ridley-Scholes bath.

RIDLEY, HUMPHREY. 1653-1708. English anatomist. See: Dict. Nat. Biog. Ridley's sinus (or circle).

RIDLEY, JOSEPH. fl. 1795. English printer. Cited in: Dict. Cat. Hist. Print. Ridley press.

Ridley press (Ridley, Joseph): Printing. See: Lockwood.

Ridley-Scholes bath (Ridley, Frank F. and Scholes, William): Engineering and Industry. See: Thrush.

Ridley's sinus (or circle) (Ridley, Humphrey): Anatomy. See: Donath; Dorland; Stedman.

Ridolfi plot (Ridolfi, Roberto di): History. See: Harbottle; Harvey; Steinberg.

RIDOLFI, ROBERTO DI. 1531-1612. Italian conspirator in England. See: Dict. Nat. Biog. Ridolfi plot.

Ridolfo, Roberto di. See: Ridolfi, Roberto di.

RIEBECK, EMIL. d. 1885. German explorer. Cited in: Hintze, vol. 2, pp. 1263-1264. Riebeckite.

Riebeckite (Riebeck, Emil): Earth Sciences. See: Thrush; Van Nostrand Sci. Encyc.; Webster's 3d.

RIECKE, CARL VIKTOR EDUARD. 1845-1915. German physicist. See: World Who's Who Sci. Riecke's principle (or law).

RIECKENBERG, HEINRICH. b. 1885. German physician. Cited in: Index-Cat. Libr. Surg. - Gen. Off., 3d Ser., vol. 9, 1931. Rieckenberg's phenomenon (or reaction).

Rieckenberg's phenomenon (or reaction) (Rieckenberg, Heinrich): Medicine. See: Dorland.

Riecke's principle (or law) (Riecke, Carl Viktor Eduard): Physics. See: Thrush; Van Nostrand Sci. Encyc.

RIEDEL, BERNHARD MORITZ KARL LUDWIG. 1846-1916. German surgeon. See: World Who's Who Sci. Riedel's disease (struma or thyroiditis), Riedel's lobe.

Riedel's disease (struma or thyroiditis) (Riedel, Bernhard Moritz Karl Ludwig): Medicine. See: Dorland; Jablonski; Stedman.

Riedel's lobe (Riedel, Bernhard Moritz Karl Ludwig): Anatomy. See: Donath; Dorland; Stedman.

Rieder cell leukemia (Rieder, Hermann): Medicine. See: Stedman.

Rieder cells (Rieder, Hermann): Medicine. See: Dorland; Stedman.

RIEDER, HERMANN. 1858-1932. German pathologist. See: World Who's Who Sci. Rieder cell leukemia, Rieder cells, Rieder's lymphocyte, Rieder's paralysis.

Rieder's lymphocyte (Rieder, Hermann): Medicine. See: Stedman.

Rieder's paralysis (Rieder, Hermann): Medicine. See: Jablonski.

RIEDLER, ALOIS. 1850-1936. German engineer. See: Pogg., vol. 7a. Riedler pump, Riedler-Stumpf turbine.

Riedler pump (Riedler, Alois): Engineering and Industry. See: Auger.

Riedler-Stumpf turbine (Riedler, Alois and Stumpf, J.): Engineering and Industry. See: Auger.

Rieffer's hummingbird (Derivation undetermined): Zoology. See: Gray.

Riefler clock (Riefler, Siegmund): Horology. See: Thewlis; Webster's 3d.

RIEFLER, SIEGMUND. 1847-1912. German engineer. See: Biog. Jahrb. Deut. Nekr., 1913. Riefler clock.

RIEGEL, FRANZ. 1843-1904. German physician. See: Biog. Lex. hervorr. Aerzte. Riegel's pulse, Riegel's test.

RIEGEL, WILHELM. fl. 1900. German physician. (Biography source unavailable.) Riegel's symptom.

Riegel's pulse (Riegel, Franz): Medicine. See: Stedman.

Riegel's symptom (Riegel, Wilhelm): Medicine. See: Dorland; Jablonski; Kelly.

Riegel's test (Riegel, Franz): Medicine. See: Dorland; Stedman.

RIEGER, HERWIGH. 1898- . German ophthalmologist. See: World Who's Who Sci. Rieger's syndrome (anomaly or malformation).

Rieger's syndrome (anomaly or malformation) (Rieger, Herwigh): Medicine. See: Jablonski; Stedman.

RIEGLER, EMANUEL. 1854-1929. Rumanian pharmacologist. See: Biog. Lex. hervorr. Aerzte. Riegler reagent for ammonia, Riegler reagent for bile pigments, Riegler reagent for blood pigments, Riegler reagent for nitrites, Riegler reagent for saccharin, Riegler reagent for uric acid, Riegler reagents for albumin, albumoses, and peptones, Riegler test for acetic acid in urine, Riegler test for albumin, Riegler test for dextrose, Riegler test for formaldehyde in milk, Riegler test for hydrochloric acid in gastric juice, Riegler test for indican in urine, Riegler test for glucose in urine, Riegler test for iodine in urine, Riegler test for lactose in milk, Riegler test for urea.

Riegler reagent for ammonia (Riegler, Emanuel): Chemistry. See: Van Nostrand Chem. Dict.

Riegler reagent for bile pigments (Riegler, Emanuel): Medicine. See: Kelly; Van Nostrand Chem. Dict.

Riegler reagent for blood pigments (Riegler, Emanuel): Medicine. See: Kelly; Van Nostrand Chem. Dict.

Riegler reagent for nitrites (Riegler, Emanuel): Chemistry. See: Van Nostrand Chem. Dict.

Riegler reagent for saccharin (Riegler, Emanuel): Chemistry. See: Van Nostrand Chem. Dict.

Riegler reagent for uric acid (Riegler, Emanuel): Medicine. See: Kelly; Van Nostrand Chem. Dict.

Riegler reagents for albumin, albumoses, and peptones (Riegler, Emanuel): Medicine. See: Dorland; Van Nostrand Chem. Dict.

Riegler test for acetic acid in urine (Riegler, Emanuel): Medicine. See: Kelly.

Riegler test for albumin (Riegler, Emanuel): Medicine. See: Dorland.

Riegler test for dextrose (Riegler, Emanuel): Medicine. See: Dorland.

Riegler test for formaldehyde in milk (Riegler, Emanuel): Chemistry. See: Van Nostrand Chem. Dict.

Riegler test for glucose in urine (Riegler, Emanuel): Medicine. See: Kelly.

Riegler test for hydrochloric acid in gastric juice (Riegler, Emanuel): Medicine. See: Dorland.

Riegler test for indican in urine (Riegler, Emanuel): Medicine. See: Kelly.

Riegler test for iodine in urine (Riegler, Emanuel): Medicine. See: Kelly.

Riegler test for lactose in milk (Riegler, Emanuel): Chemistry. See: Van Nostrand Chem. Dict.

Riegler test for urea (Riegler, Emanuel): Medicine. See: Kelly.

RIEHL, GUSTAV. 1855-1943. Austrian dermatologist. See: Biog. Lex. hervorr. Aerzte. Riehl's melanosis.

Riehl's melanosis (Riehl, Gustav): Medicine. See: Dorland; Jablonski; Stedman.

RIEHM, PAUL. fl. 1885. German chemist. Cited in: Krauch and Kunz. Riehm quinoline synthesis.

Riehm quinoline synthesis (Riehm, Paul): Chemistry. See: Van Nostrand Chem. Dict.

Rieke diagram (Rieke, Foster Frederick?): Electronics. See: Ballentyne; Markus; Thewlis; Van Nostrand Sci. Encyc.

RIEKE, FOSTER FREDERICK. 1905- . American physicist. See: Amer. Men Sci., 10th ed. Rieke diagram?

RIEL, LOUIS. 1844-1885. Canadian insurgent leader. See: Encyc. Brit., 1973. Riel's rebellion.

Riel's rebellion (Riel, Louis): History. See: Harbottle.

RIEMANN. fl. 1809. German scientist. Cited in: Bailey. Riemannite.

RIEMANN, BERNHARD (In full: GEORG FRIEDRICH BERNHARD). 1826-1866. German mathematician. See: New Encyc. Brit., 1974. Cauchy-Riemann equation(s), Riemann-Cristoffel tensor (or curvature tensor), Riemann function, Riemann hypothesis about the zeros of the zeta function, Riemann integral, Riemann-Lebesgue lemma, Riemann mapping theorem, Riemann method, Riemann-Papperitz equation, Riemann-Roch theorem, Riemann sphere, Riemann-Stielties integral, Riemann('s) surface(s), Riemann zeta function, Riemannian curvature, Riemannian geometry, Riemannian space, Riemann's symbol.

Riemann-Cristoffel tensor (or curvature tensor) (Riemann, Bernhard and Christoffel, Elwin Bruno): Mathematics. See: Internat. Dict. Ap. Math.; Internat. Dict. Phys. Elec.; James.

Riemann function (Riemann, Bernhard): Mathematics. See: Internat. Dict. Ap. Math.

Riemann hypothesis about the zeros of the zeta function (Riemann, Bernhard): Mathematics. See: James.

Riemann integral (Riemann, Bernhard): Mathematics. See: Internat. Dict. Ap. Math.; Internat. Dict. Phys. Elec.; James. Also known as: Riemann sum.

Riemann–Lebesgue lemma (Riemann, Bernhard and Lebesgue, Henri Leon): Mathematics. See: James. Also known as: Riemann's lemma.

Riemann mapping theorem (Riemann, Bernhard): Mathematics. See: Internat. Dict. Ap. Math.; James.

Riemann method (Riemann, Bernhard): Mathematics. See: Internat. Dict. Ap. Math.

Riemann P-function (Riemann, Bernhard). See: Riemann–Papperitz equation.

Riemann–Papperitz equation (Riemann, Bernhard and Papperitz, Erwin): Mathematics. See: Van Nostrand Sci. Encyc. Also known as: Papperitz's equation, Riemann P-function.

Riemann–Roch theorem (Riemann, Bernhard and Roch, Gustav): Mathematics. Cited in: Encyc. Brit., 1974, Microp.

Riemann sphere (Riemann, Bernhard): Mathematics. See: Internat. Dict. Ap. Math.; James.

Riemann–Stieltjes integral (Riemann, Bernhard and Stieltjes, Thomas Jean): Mathematics. See: Internat. Dict. Ap. Math.; Van Nostrand Sci. Encyc.

Riemann sum (Riemann, Bernhard). See: Riemann integral.

Riemann('s) surface(s) (Riemann, Bernhard): Mathematics. See: Ballentyne; James; Van Nostrand Sci. Encyc.

Riemann zeta function (Riemann, Bernhard): Mathematics. See: Ballentyne; Internat. Dict. Ap. Math.; James; Van Nostrand Sci. Encyc.

Riemannian curvature (Riemann, Bernhard): Mathematics. See: James.

Riemannian geometry (Riemann, Bernhard): Mathematics. See: Van Nostrand Sci. Encyc. under "Geometry;" Webster's 3d.

Riemannian space (Riemann, Bernhard): Mathematics. See: Internat. Dict. Phys. Elec.; James; Thewlis.

Riemannite (Riemann): Earth Sciences. See: Thrush.

Riemann's lemma (Riemann, Bernhard). See: Riemann–Lebesgue lemma.

Riemann's symbol (Riemann, Bernhard): Mathematics. See: Ballentyne.

Riemer formula (Derivation undetermined): Engineering and Industry. See: Thrush.

RIEMSDIJK, M. VAN. fl. 1922. Dutch chemist. Cited in: Chem. Abstr., vol. 16, p. 3920. Rienisdijk reagent.

Rienisdijk reagent (Riemsdijk, M. van): Chemistry. See: Van Nostrand Chem. Dict.

RIESELER. fl. 20th c. German engineer. (Biography source unavailable.) Rieseler transmission.

Rieseler transmission (Rieseler): Engineering and Industry. See: Auger.

RIESMAN, DAVID. 1867-1940. American physician. See: World Who's Who Sci. Riesman's myocardosis, Riesman's pneumonia, Riesman's sign.

Riesman's myocardosis (Riesman, David): Medicine. See: Dorland.

Riesman's pneumonia (Riesman, David): Medicine. See: Dorland.

Riesman's sign (Riesman, David): Medicine. See: Dorland.

Riesz–Fischer theorem (Riesz, Frigyes and Fischer, Ernst Sigismund): Mathematics. See: James.

RIESZ, FRIGYES. 1880-1956. Hungarian mathematician. See: New Encyc. Brit., 1974, Microp. Riesz–Fischer theorem.

RIETTI, FERNANDO. fl. 1929. Italian physician. Cited in: Index-Cat. Libr. Surg.-Gen. Off., 5th Ser., vol. 1, 1959. Rietti–Greppi–Micheli syndrome.

Rietti–Greppi–Micheli syndrome (Rietti, Fernando; Greppi, Enrico; and Micheli, Ferdinando?): Medicine. See: Jablonski. Also known as: Micheli–Rietti syndrome, Rietti's disease.

Rietti's disease (Rietti, Fernando). See: Rietti–Greppi–Micheli syndrome.

RIEUX, LEON. fl. 1853. French surgeon. Cited in: Garrison and Morton. Rieux's hernia.

Rieux's hernia (Rieux, Leon): Medicine. See: Dorland; Jablonski.

RIFKIND, BASIL MAIR. fl. 1957-1972. Scottish physician. See: Med. Direct., 1972. Rifkind's sign?

Rifkind's sign (Rifkind, Basil Mair?): Medicine. See: Jablonski.

RIGA, ANTONIO. 1832-1919. Italian physician. Cited in: Index-Cat. Libr. Surg.-Gen. Off., 5th Ser., vol. 1, 1959. Riga-Fede syndrome (or disease).

Riga–Fede syndrome (or disease) (Riga, Antonio and Fede, Francesco): Medicine. See: Dorland; Jablonski; Stedman. Also known as: Cardarelli's aphthae (or disease), Fede's syndrome, Riga's aphthae (disease or papilloma).

Rigadoon (Rigaud): Dance. See: Hendrickson; Partridge.

RIGAL, JOSEPH JEAN ANTOINE. 1797-1865. French surgeon. See: Biog. Lex. hervorr. Aerzte. Rigal's suture.

Rigal's suture (Rigal, Joseph Jean Antoine): Medicine. See: Dorland.

Riga's aphthae (disease or papilloma) (Riga, Antonio). See: Riga–Fede syndrome (or disease).

RIGAUD. fl. ca. 1630. French dancing master. Cited in: New Encyc. Brit., 1974, Microp. Rigadoon.

RIGDEN, P. J. fl. 1943. English engineer. Cited in: Chem. Abstr., Decenn. Index, 1937-1946. Rigden's apparatus.

Rigden's apparatus (Rigden, P. J.): Engineering and Industry. See: Thrush.

RIGG, ARTHUR. fl. 1885. English engineer. Cited in: Royal Soc. Cat. Sci. Pap., 1884-1900. Rigg hydraulic engine.

Rigg hydraulic engine (Rigg, Arthur): Engineering and Industry. See: Auger.

Riggs' disease (Riggs, John Mankey). See: Fauchard's disease.

RIGGS, JOHN MANKEY. 1810-1885. American dentist. See: Dict. Amer. Biog. Riggs' disease.

RIGHI, AUGUSTO. 1850-1921. Italian physicist. See: World Who's Who Sci. Righi experiment, Righi–Leduc effect.

Righi experiment (Righi, Augusto): Physics. See: Internat. Dict. Phys. Elec.

Righi–Leduc effect (Righi, Augusto and Leduc, Sylvestre Anatole): Physics. See: Ballentyne; Hackh; Markus; Thewlis; Van Nostrand Sci. Encyc. Also known as: Leduc effect, Maggi–Righi–Leduc effect.

RIJKE, PETR LEON. fl. 1859. Dutch engineer. Cited in: Royal Soc. Cat. Sci. Pap., 1800-1863. Rijke tube.

Rijke tube (Rijke, Petr Leon): Engineering and Industry. See: Auger.

RIJKEBOER, A. fl. 1963. Dutch metallurgist. Cited in: Hintze, suppl. 3, p. 270. Rijkeboerite.

Rijkeboerite (Rijkeboer, A.): Earth Sciences. See: Thrush.

Rijn, Rembrandt Harmenz van. See: Rembrandt.

RIKER, ALBERT JOYCE. b. 1894. American botanist. See: World Who's Who Sci. Riker mount.

Riker mount (Riker, Albert Joyce): Botany. See: Webster's 3d.

RILEY, CONRAD MILTON. 1913- . American pediatrician. See: Amer. Men and Women Sci., 12th ed. Riley–Day syndrome, Riley–Shwachman syndrome.

Riley–Day syndrome (Riley, Conrad Milton and Day, Richard Lawrence): Medicine. See: Jablonski; Stedman.

RILEY, DENNIS PARKER. 1916- . English physicist. See: Who's Who Brit. Sci., 1953. Nelson–Riley function.

RILEY, HARRY LISTER. 1899- . English chemist. See: Pogg., vol. 6. Riley oxidation reaction.

RILEY, JAMES WHITCOMB. 1849-1916. American poet. See: Dict. Amer. Biog. life of Riley.

Riley oxidation reaction (Riley, Harry Lister): Chemistry. See: Van Nostrand Chem. Dict.

Riley–Shwachman syndrome (Riley, Conrad Milton and Shwachman, Harry): Medicine. See: Jablonski.

RILEY, VERNON TODD. 1914- . American microbiologist and virologist. See: Amer. Men and Women Sci., 12th ed. Riley virus.

Riley virus (Riley, Vernon Todd): Medicine. See: Stedman.

Riley's indispensable (Derivation undetermined): Printing. See: Lockwood.

RIMBAUD, LOUIS. b. 1877. French physician. Cited in: Index-Cat. Libr. Surg.-Gen. Off., 5th Ser., vol. 1, 1959. Rimbaud–Passouant–Vallat syndrome.

Rimbaud–Passouant–Vallat syndrome (Rimbaud, Louis; Passouant, P.; and Vallat, Georges): Medicine. See: Jablonski. Also known as: Rimbaud–Jusse syndrome.

RIMINGTON, A. WALLACE. 1854-1918. English artist. See: Who Was Who, 1916-1928. Rimington colour organ.

Rimington colour organ (Rimington, A. Wallace): Music. See: Scholes.

RIMINI, ENRICO. fl. 1895-1907. Italian chemist. See: Pogg., vol. 5. Angeli–Rimini reaction, Rimini's test.

Rimini's test (Rimini, Enrico): Medicine. See: Stedman.

RINDFLEISCH, GEORG EDUARD. 1836-1908. German physician. See: Biog. Lex. hervorr. Aerzte. Rindfleisch's cells, Rindfleisch's fold.

Rindfleisch's cells (Rindfleisch, Georg Eduard): Anatomy. See: Donath; Dorland; Stedman.

Rindfleisch's fold (Rindfleisch, Georg Eduard): Anatomy. See: Donath; Dorland; Stedman.

ring of Saturn (Saturn): Parapsychology. See: Webster's 3d.

ring of Solomon (Solomon): Parapsychology. See: Hendrickson; Webster's 3d.

RINGELMANN. fl. 1903. French scientist. (Biography source unavailable.) Ringelmann chart (or smoke chart).

Ringelmann chart (or smoke chart) (Ringelmann): Engineering and Industry. See: Auger; Hackh; Huschke; Thrush.

RINGER, SIDNEY. 1835-1910. English physiologist. See: World Who's Who Sci. Krebs–Ringer solution, Locke–Ringer solution, Ringer('s) solution (or fluid), Ringer's injection.

Ringer('s) solution (or fluid) (Ringer, Sidney): Medicine. See: Dorland; Hackh; Pennak; Stedman.

Ringer's injection (Ringer, Sidney): Medicine. See: Stedman.

RINGGOLD, MAJOR SAMUEL. 1800-1846. American soldier. See: Nat. Cycl. Amer. Biog., vol. 7. Gringo?

Ringite (Derivation undetermined): Earth Sciences. See: Thrush.

Ringrose firedamp alarm (Ringrose, Henry T.): Engineering and Industry. See: Thrush.

RINGROSE, HENRY T. fl. 1921-1954. English engineer. Cited in: Chem. Abstr., Decenn. Indexes, 1917-26 to 1947-1956. Ringrose firedamp alarm, Ringrose methane recorder, Ringrose pocket methanometer.

Ringrose methane recorder (Ringrose, Henry T.): Engineering and Industry. See: Thrush.

Ringrose pocket methanometer (Ringrose, Henry T.): Engineering and Industry. See: Thrush.

RINGSTED, AXEL CARL PEDER. 1904- . Danish physician. See: Kraks Bla Bog, 1971. Ringsted's syndrome.

Ringsted's syndrome (Ringsted, Axel Carl Peder): Medicine. See: Jablonski.

RINGWOOD, ALFRED EDWARD. 1930- . Australian geochemist. See: World Who's Who Sci. Ringwoodite.

Ringwoodite (Ringwood, Alfred Edward): Earth Sciences. See: New Encyc. Brit., 1974, Microp.

RINIKER, PAUL. fl. 1950. Swiss pathologist. (Biography source unavailable.) Glanzmann–Riniker syndrome.

RINK, HEINRICH JOHANNES. 1819-1893. Danish explorer. See: Dansk Biog. Lek. Rinkite.

Rinkite (Rink, Heinrich Johannes): Engineering and Industry. See: Thrush; Webster's 3d.

Rinman scale (Derivation undetermined): Engineering and Industry. See: Thrush.

RINMAN, SVEN. 1720-1792. Swedish mineralogist. See: Svenska Maen Och Kvinnor. Rinman's (Rinmann's) green (reaction).

Rinmann, Sven. See: Rinman, Sven.

Rinman's (Rinmann's) green (reaction) (Rinman, Sven): Chemistry. See: Ballentyne; Hackh; Webster's 3d.

RINNE, FRIEDRICH or FRITZ WILHELM BERTHOLD. 1863-1933. German mineralogist. See: Min. Mag., vol. 23 (Mar. 1932-Sept. 1934), pp. 358-359. Rinneite.

RINNE, HEINRICH ADOLF. 1819-1868. German otologist. See: Biog. Lex. hervorr. Aerzte. Rinne's tests.

Rinneite (Rinne, Friedrich): Earth Sciences. See: Thrush; Webster's 3d.

Rinnemann, Sven. See: Rinman, Sven.

Rinne's tests (Rinne, Heinrich Adolf): Medicine. See: Dorland; Stedman.

RIO-HORTEGA, PIO DEL. 1882-1945. Spanish anatomist in Argentina. See: Arch. Neurocir. Buenos Aires, vol. 2. (1945) pp. 1-6. Hortega('s) cell(s).

Rio-Hortega's glia (Rio-Hortega, Pio del). See: Hortega('s) cell(s).

RIOLAN, JEAN. 1577-1657. French anatomist and botanist. See: World Who's Who Sci. Riolan's arch (arcade or anastomosis), Riolan's bones, Riolan's bouquet (or nosegay), Riolan's muscle.

Riolan's arch (arcade or anastomosis) (Riolan, Jean): Anatomy. See: Donath; Dorland; Stedman.

Riolan's bones (Riolan, Jean): Anatomy. See: Donath; Dorland; Stedman.

Riolan's bouquet (or nosegay) (Riolan, Jean): Anatomy. See: Donath; Dorland.

Riolan's muscle (Riolan, Jean): Anatomy. See: Donath; Dorland; Stedman. Also known as: Bowman's muscle.

Riolite (Del Rio, Andres Manuel): Earth Sciences. See: Charnock.

RIP VAN WINKLE. Character in Washington Irving's "The Sketch Book," (1819-20). See: Benet. Rip Van Winkle.

Rip Van Winkle (Rip Van Winkle, the character): Generic Word (backward). See: Mathews, M. M.; Partridge; Webster's 3d.

RIPAN, RALUCA. b. 1894. Rumanian chemist. See: Pogg., vol. 6. Ripan reactions for cyanate, Ripan reagent for phthalic and terephthalic acids, Ripan test for cobalt, Ripan test for zinc.

Ripan reactions for cyanate (Ripan, Raluca): Chemistry. See: Van Nostrand Chem. Dict.

Ripan reagent for phthalic and terephthalic acids (Ripan, Raluca): Chemistry. See: Van Nostrand Chem. Dict.

Ripan test for cobalt (Ripan, Raluca): Chemistry. See: Van Nostrand Chem. Dict.

Ripan test for zinc (Ripan, Raluca): Chemistry. See: Van Nostrand Chem. Dict.

RIPAULT, LOUIS H. ANTOINE. 1807-1856. French physician. See: Biog. Lex. hervorr. Aerzte. Ripault's sign.

Ripault's sign (Ripault, Louis H. Antoine): Medicine. See: Dorland; Stedman.

RIPLEY, ROBERT LEROY. 1893-1949. American cartoonist. See: Who Was Who Amer., vol. 2. one for Ripley.

RISLER, E. fl. 1881. German chemist. Cited in: Pogg., vol. 3 under "Claus, Adolph." Claus–Risler benzidine tests for chlorine and bromine.

Risley & Lake machine (Derivation undetermined): Printing. See: Lockwood.

Risley act (Carlisle, Richard Risley): Recreation and Sports. See: Webster's 3d.

Risley('s) prism (or rotary prism) (Risley, Samuel Doty): Medicine. See: Dorland; Internat. Dict. Phys. Elec.; Stedman.

RISLEY, SAMUEL DOTY. 1845-1920. American ophthalmologist. See: Who Was Who Amer., vol. 1. Risley('s) prism (or rotary prism).

RISQUEZ, FRANCISCO ANTONIO. 1856-1941. Venezuelan pathologist. See: Dicc. Biog. Venezuela. Risquez's sign.

Risquez's sign (Risquez, Francisco Antonio): Medicine. See: Dorland.

RISSO, GIOVANNI ANTONIO. 1777-1845. Italian naturalist. See: World Who's Who Sci. Rissoa, Risso's dolphin.

Rissoa (Risso, Giovanni Antonio): Zoology. See: Pennak; Webster's 3d.

Risso's dolphin (Risso, Giovanni Antonio): Zoology. See: Gray; Pennak.

Ritchey–Chretien telescope (Ritchey, George Willis and Chretien, Henry): Astronomy. See: Satterthwaite; Van Nostrand Sci. Encyc. Also known as: Chretien telescope.

RITCHEY, GEORGE WILLIS. 1864–1945. American astronomer. See: World Who's Who Sci. Ritchey–Chretien telescope.

Ritchie wedge (Ritchie, William): Physics. See: Internat. Dict. Phys. Elec.

RITCHIE, WILLIAM. d. 1837. Scottish physicist. See: Pogg., vol. 2. Ritchie wedge.

RITGEN, FERDINAND AUGUST MARIE FRANZ VON. 1787–1867. German obstetrician. See: Biog. Lex. hervorr. Aerzte. Ritgen's maneuver.

Ritgen's maneuver (Ritgen, Ferdinand August Marie Franz von): Medicine. See: Dorland; Stedman.

Rith diagram (Rith, L.): Engineering and Industry. See: Auger.

RITH, L. fl. 1905. (Biography source unavailable.) Rith diagram.

RITSCHL, ALBRECHT. 1822–1889. German Protestant theologian. See: Encyc. Brit., 1973. Ritschlian (or Ritschlianism).

Ritschlian (or Ritschlianism) (Ritschl, Albrecht): Religion. See: Mathews, S.; Webster's 3d.

Ritter, Gottfried. See: Ritter von Rittershain, Gottfried.

RITTER, JOHANN JACOB. 1714–1784. Swiss physician. See: Biog. Lex. hervorr. Aerzte. Rittera.

RITTER, JOHANN WILHELM. 1776–1810. German physicist and physician. See: New Encyc. Brit., 1974, Microp. Ritter–Rollet phenomenon, Ritter–Valli law, Ritter's law, Ritter's opening tetanus.

RITTER, JOHN JOSEPH. 1895– . American organic chemist. See: Amer. Men Sci., 10th ed. Ritter reaction.

Ritter method (Ritter, Wilhelm): Engineering and Industry. See: Internat. Dict. Ap. Math.

Ritter reaction (Ritter, John Joseph): Chemistry. See: Ballentyne; Van Nostrand Chem. Dict.

Ritter–Rollet phenomenon (Ritter, Johann Wilhelm and Rollett, Alexander): Physiology. See: Dorland; Stedman.

Ritter–Valli law (Ritter, Johann Wilhelm and Valli, Eusebio): Physiology. See: World Who's Who Sci.

RITTER VON RITTERSHAIN, GOTTFRIED. 1820–1883. German physician. See: Biog. Lex. hervorr. Aerzte. Ritter's disease (1) (or dermatitis), Ritter's disease (2).

Ritter von Zumbusch, Leo. See: Zumbusch, Leo von.

RITTER, WILHELM. 1847–1906. Swiss engineer. See: Pogg., vol. 6. Ritter method.

Rittera (Ritter, Johann Jacob): Botany. See: Charnock.

Ritter's disease (1) (or dermatitis) (Ritter von Rittershain, Gottfried): Medicine. See: Dorland; Jablonski; Stedman.

Ritter's disease (2) (Ritter von Rittershain, Gottfried). See: Winckel's disease.

Ritter's law (Ritter, Johann Wilhelm): Physiology. See: Dorland; Stedman.

Ritter's opening tetanus (Ritter, Johann Wilhelm): Physiology. See: Dorland; Stedman.

RITTINGER, PETER VON. 1811–1872. German engineer and geologist. See: Pogg., vol. 2. Rittinger pump, Rittinger ratio?, Rittinger table?, Rittinger's law?

Rittinger pump (Rittinger, Peter von): Engineering and Industry. See: Auger.

Rittinger ratio (Rittinger, Peter von?): Engineering and Industry. See: Thrush.

Rittinger table (Rittinger, Peter von?): Engineering and Industry. See: Thrush.

Rittinger's law (Rittinger, Peter von?): Engineering and Industry. See: Thrush.

RITZ, CESAR. 1850–1918. Swiss-born restaurateur. See: Webster's Biog. Dict. Ritzy.

Ritz combination principle (Ritz, Walter): Physics. See: Ballentyne; Internat. Dict. Ap. Math.; Thewlis; Van Nostrand Chem. Dict. Also known as: Rydberg–Ritz combination principle.

Ritz formula (or series formula) (Ritz, Walter): Physics. See: Hackh; Internat. Dict. Ap. Math.; Thewlis.

Ritz method (Ritz, Walter): Physics. See: Internat. Dict. Ap. Math.

Ritz–Paschen series (Ritz, Walther and Paschen, Friedrich). See: Paschen series.

RITZ, WALTHER. 1878–1909. Swiss physicist. See: World Who's Who Sci. Rayleigh–Ritz method, Ritz combination principle, Ritz formula (or series formula), Ritz method, Ritz–Paschen series.

Ritzy (Ritz, Cesar): Generic Word (lavish). See: Hendrickson; Mathews, M. M.

RIVA, CARLO. d. 1902. Italian mineralogist. See: Zentralb. f. Mineralogie, 1902, p. 674 f. Rivaite.

RIVA-ROCCI, SCIPIONE. 1863–1937. Italian physician. See: Biog. Lex. hervorr. Aerzte. Riva-Rocci sphygmomanometer.

Riva-Rocci sphygmomanometer (Riva-Rocci, Scipione): Medicine. See: Dorland.

Rivaite (Riva, Carlo): Earth Sciences. See: Hintze.

Rivalta's disease (Rivolta, Sebastiano): Medicine. See: Dorland; Jablonski.

Rivalta's reaction (or test) (Rivolta, Sebastiano?): Medicine. See: Dorland; Stedman.

Riverius' potion (Riviere, Lazare): Medicine. See: Dorland.

Rivers' cocktail (Rivers, William Halse): Medicine. See: Stedman.

RIVERS, WILLIAM HALSE. 1864–1922. English physician and anthropologist. See: Internat. Encyc. Soc. Sci. Rivers' cocktail.

RIVIERE, CLIVE. 1873–1929. English physician. See: Who Was Who, 1929–1940. Riviere's sign.

RIVIERE, LAZARE (RIVERIUS). 1589–1655. French physician. See: Nouv. Biog. Univ. Riverius' potion, Riviere's salt.

Riviere's salt (Riviere, Lazare): Medicine. See: Dorland; Stedman.

Riviere's sign (Riviere, Clive): Medicine. See: Dorland.

Rivina (Rivinus, August Quirinus): Botany. See: Taylor, N.; Webster's 3d.

RIVINGTON, JAMES. 1724–1803. English publisher in American colonies. See: Dict. Amer. Biog. Rivington's New York Gazetteer.

Rivington's New York Gazetteer (Rivington, James): Printing. See: Jameson.

RIVINUS, AUGUST QUIRINUS (AUGUST BACHMANN). 1652–1723. German anatomist and botanist. See: Allg. Deut. Biog. Rivina, Rivinus' ducts (or canals), Rivinus' foramen, Rivinus' gland, Rivinus' membrane.

Rivinus' ducts (or canals) (Rivinus, August Quirinus): Anatomy. See: Donath; Dorland; Stedman.

Rivinus' foramen (Rivinus, August Quirinus): Anatomy. See: Donath; Dorland; Stedman. Also known as: Bochdalek's foramen (or canal).

Rivinus' gland (Rivinus, August Quirinus): Anatomy. See: Donath; Dorland; Stedman.

Rivinus' membrane (Rivinus, August Quirinus): Anatomy. See: Donath; Dorland; Stedman. Also known as: Shrapnell's membrane.

RIVOLI, ANDRE MASSENA, DUC DE. 1758–1817. French marshall under Napoleon. See: New Encyc. Brit., 1974, Microp. a la Massena, Massena partridge (or quail), Rivoli(s) hummingbird.

Rivoli(s) hummingbird (Rivoli, Andre Massena, Duc de): Zoology. See: Gray; Mathews, M. M.

RIVOLTA, SEBASTIANO. 1832–1893. Italian veterinary surgeon. See: Biog. Lex. hervorr. Aerzte. Rivalta's disease, Rivalta's reaction (or test)?

Rizal Day (Rizal, Jose): History. See: Webster's 3d.

RIZAL, JOSE. 1861–1896. Philippine patriot. See: New Encyc. Brit., 1974, Microp. Rizal Day.

RIZO-PATRON, ANTENOR. fl. ca. 1906. Peruvian engineer. Cited in: Hintze, 1st suppl., p. 434. Patronite.

Roach clasp (Roach, F. Ewing): Dentistry. See: Stedman.

ROACH, F. EWING. fl. 1907. American dentist. Cited in: Chem. Abstr., Decenn. Index, 1907-1916. Roach clasp.

rob Peter to pay Paul (Peter the Apostle, Saint and Paul the Apostle, Saint): Generic Word (mock exchange). See: Jobes.

Rob Roy. See: Campbell, Robert Macgregor.

Rob Roy (canoe) (MacGregor, John): Transportation. See: Partridge.

Rob Roy (cocktail) (Macgregor, Robert): Food and Drink. See: Hendrickson.

ROBBIA, LUCA DELLA. 1400?-1482. Florentine sculptor. See: New Encyc. Brit., 1974, Microp. Della Robbia colors (or blue), Della Robbia ware, Della Robbia work.

ROBBINS, HERBERT ELLIS. 1915- . American mathematical statistician. See: Amer. Men and Women Sci., 12th ed. Robbins-Munro process.

Robbins-Munro process (Robbins, Herbert Ellis and Munro, William Delmar): Statistics. See: Kendall.

Roberd's (Robert's) man (Robin Hood): Generic Word (thief). See: Charnock.

Robert (Peel, Sir Robert). See: Bobby.

ROBERT, CESARE-ALPHONSE. 1801-1862. French surgeon. See: Biog. Lex. hervorr. Aerzte. Robert's ligament.

ROBERT, HEINRICH LUDWIG FERDINAND. 1814-1878. German gynecologist. See: Biog. Lex. hervorr. Aerzte. Robert's pelvis.

ROBERT, HENRY MARTYN. 1837-1923. American military engineer and parliamentarian. See: Encyc. Brit., 1973. Robert's Rules.

Robert Joffrey Ballet (or Joffrey Ballet) (Joffrey, Robert): Dance. See: Chujoy; New Encyc. Brit., 1974, Microp.

Robert Macaire (Macaire, Robert): Generic Word (Frenchman). See: Latham; New Encyc. Brit., 1974, Microp.; Phyfe.

Robert of Geneva. See: Clement VII.

ROBERT, SAINT. d. 1067. French ecclesiastic. See: Holweck. herb Robert.

Robert sauce (Derivation undetermined): Food and Drink. See: Charnock.

ROBERTS, A. fl. 1915. English? engineer. Cited in: Chem. Abstr., Decenn. Indexes, 1907-1916; 1917-1926. Roberts coke oven.

ROBERTS-AUSTEN, WILLIAM CHANDLER. 1843-1902. English metallurgist. See: Dict. Nat. Biog., 2d suppl. Austemper (or Austempering), Austenite, Austenitic (stainless steels), Austenitizing.

ROBERTS, BRIGHAM HENRY. 1857-1933. American Mormon leader. See: Dict. Amer. Biog. Roberts case.

Roberts case (Roberts, Brigham Henry): History. See: Jameson under "Mormons."

Roberts coke oven (Roberts, A.): Engineering and Industry. See: Van Nostrand Chem. Dict.

ROBERTS, FREDERICK SLEIGH. 1832-1914. English soldier. See: Dict. Nat. Biog., 3d suppl. Bob's own (or Bobs), Robert's march.

ROBERTS, JOHN. fl. 1886. English politician. (Biography source unavailable.) John Roberts.

ROBERTS, KENNETH. 1885-1957. American novelist. See: Who Was Who Amer., vol. 3. Kenneth Roberts Memorial Award.

Robert's law (Roberts, Samuel Oliver?): Engineering and Industry. See: Ballentyne.

Robert's ligament (Robert, Cesare-Alphonse): Anatomy. See: Donath; Dorland; Stedman.

Roberts' march (Roberts, Frederick Sleigh): History. See: Harbottle.

Roberts movement (Roberts, Richard): Engineering and Industry. See: Auger.

Roberts parallel motion (Roberts, Samuel Oliver): Engineering and Industry. See: Auger.

Robert's pelvis (Robert, Heinrich Ludwig Ferdinand): Medicine. See: Dorland; Jablonski; Stedman.

Roberts report (Roberts, Sir Sydney Castle): Library Science. See: Harrod.

ROBERTS, RICHARD. 1789-1864. English civil engineer. See: Dict. Nat. Biog. Roberts movement.

Robert's Rules (Robert, Henry Martyn): Generic Word (parliamentary procedure). See: Hendrickson.

ROBERTS, SAMUEL OLIVER. 1827-1899. English mathematician. See: Pogg., vol. 3. Robert's law?, Roberts parallel motion.

ROBERTS, SIR SYDNEY CASTLE. 1887-1966. English educator. See: Who Was Who, 1961-1970. Roberts report.

Roberts' test (or reagent) (Roberts, Sir William): Medicine. See: Dorland; Stedman; Van Nostrand Chem. Dict. Also known as: Worm-Mueller's formula.

ROBERTS, SIR WILLIAM. 1830-1899. English physician. See: World Who's Who Sci. Roberts' test (or reagent).

ROBERTSON, A. WILLIS. b. 1887. American legislator. See: Biog. Direct. Amer. Congress. Pitman-Robertson Act.

Robertson, Douglas Moray Cooper Lamb Argyll. See: Argyll Robertson.

ROBERTSON, HARRY M. fl. 1924-1937. American engineer. Cited in: Chem. Abstr., Decenn. Indexes, 1917-1926 to 1937-1946. Robertson kiln.

ROBERTSON, HOWARD PERCY. 1903-1961. American physicist. See: Who Was Who Amer., vol. 4. Poynting-Robertson effect.

Robertson kiln (Robertson, Harry M.): Engineering and Industry. See: Thrush.

Robertson's syndrome (Argyll Robertson, Douglas Moray Cooper Lamb). See: Argyll-Robertson pupil.

Roberval('s) balance(s) (Roberval, Gilles Personne de): Engineering and Industry. See: Auger; Webster's 3d.

ROBERVAL, GILLES PERSONNE DE. 1602-1675. French mathematician. See: Encyc. Brit., 1973. Roberval('s) balance(s).

Robespierre collar (Robespierre, Maximilien Francois Marie Isidore de): Fashion. See: Picken.

ROBESPIERRE, MAXIMILIEN FRANCOIS MARIE ISIDORE DE. 1758-1794. French revolutionist. See: Encyc. Brit., 1973. Robespierre collar, Robespierre's knitters (or weavers), Robespierrist.

Robespierre's knitters (or weavers) (Robespierre, Maximilien Francois Marie Isidore de): History. See: Harbottle; Phyfe.

Robespierrist (Robespierre, Maximilien Francois Marie Isidore de): History. See: Webster's 3d.

Robey oven (Derivation undetermined): Engineering and Industry. See: Thrush.

ROBIETTE, A. G. E. fl. 1930-1955. English engineer. Cited in: Chem. Abstr., Decenn. Indexes, 1927-1936 to 1947-1956. Robiette process.

Robiette process (Robiette, A. G. E.): Engineering and Industry. See: Thrush.

Robigalia (Robigus): Mythology. See: Webster's 3d.

ROBIGUS. Roman god associated with wheat blight. See: Jobes. Robigalia.

ROBIN, ALBERT. 1847-1928. French physician. See: World Who's Who Sci. Gubler-Robin syndrome.

ROBIN, CHARLES PHILIPPE. 1821-1885. French anatomist. See: World Who's Who Sci. Charcot-Robin crystals, Robin's myeloplax, Virchow-Robin spaces.

Robin('s) function (Robin, G.?): Mathematics. See: Internat. Dict. Ap. Math.; James.

ROBIN, G. fl. 1879-1880. French scientist. Cited in: Royal Soc. Cat. Sci. Pap., 1874-1883; Partington, vol. 4. Robin('s) function? Robin's law.

Robin Goodfellow. See: Puck.

ROBIN HOOD. Hero of English folk ballads. See: New Encyc. Brit., 1974, Microp. Roberd's (Robert's) man, Robin Hood, Robin Hood costume, Robin Hood hat, Robin Hood legend, Robin Hood('s) wind, Robin Hood's barn, Robin Hood's larder.

Robin Hood (Robin Hood): Generic Word (redresser of wrong). See: Hendrickson; Partridge; Webster's 3d.

Robin Hood costume (Robin Hood): Fashion. See: Picken.

Robin Hood hat (Robin Hood): Fashion. See: Picken.

Robin Hood legend (Robin Hood): History. See: Steinberg.

Robin Hood('s) wind (Robin Hood): Earth Sciences. See: Brewer; Huschke.

Robin Hood's barn (Robin Hood): Generic Word (wander circuitously). See: Hendrickson; Webster's 3d.

Robin Hood's larder (Robin Hood): History. See: Brewer.

ROBIN, JEAN. 1550-1629. French botanist. See: Nouv. Biog. Univ. Robinia.

ROBIN, PIERRE. 1867-1950. French physician. (Biography source unavailable.) Pierre Robin syndrome.

Robin triad (Robin, Pierre). See: Pierre Robin syndrome.

Robinia (Robin, Jean): Botany. See: Webster's 3d.

ROBINS, BENJAMIN. 1707-1751. English mathematician and military engineer. See: Dict. Nat. Biog. Robins' rotating arm.

Robin's law (Robin, G.): Chemistry. See: Van Nostrand Sci. Encyc.

Robins-Messiter system (Derivation undetermined): Engineering and Industry. See: Thrush.

Robin's myeloplax (Robin, Charles Philippe): Medicine. See: Dorland; Stedman.

Robin's pincushion (Derivation undetermined): Zoology. See: Gray.

Robins' rotating arm (Robins, Benjamin): Engineering and Industry. See: Auger.

Robin's space (Robin, Charles P.). See: Virchow-Robin spaces.

Robin's syndrome (Robin, Pierre). See: Pierre Robin syndrome.

ROBINSON. Character in story by Richard Doyle (1870's). See: Benet under "Brown, Jones, and Robinson." Brown, Jones, and Robinson.

Robinson (Robinson Crusoe): Generic Word (umbrella). See: Wagner (More Names).

Robinson and Rodger system (Derivation undetermined): Engineering and Industry. See: Thrush.

ROBINSON, ANDREW ROSE. 1845-1924. American dermatologist. See: New York Times, July 10, 1924, p. 21, col. 6. Robinson's disease.

Robinson axioms (Robinson, Gilbert de Beauregard?): Mathematics. See: Van Nostrand Sci. Encyc. under "Geometry."

Robinson bridge (Robinson, James?): Electronics. See: Hughes. Also known as: Robinson-Wien bridge.

ROBINSON CRUSOE. Hero of the novel, "Robinson Crusoe" (1719) by Daniel Defoe. See: Benet. Crusoe, Robinson, Robinsonade.

Robinson direction-finder (Robinson, James): Electronics. See: Hughes.

ROBINSON, EDWARD STEVENS. fl. 1919-1937. American psychologist. See: Psych. Register, 1932, p. 416 f. Kjersted-Robinson law, Skaggs-Robinson hypothesis (or phenomenon).

ROBINSON, F. J. fl. 20th c. American physician. (Biography source unavailable.) Robinson-Kepler-Power test.

ROBINSON, FRANCIS PLEASANT. 1906- . American psychologist. See: World Who's Who Sci. Robinson's formula for efficient learning.

ROBINSON, FREDERICK. fl. 20th c. English librarian. (Biography source unavailable.) Robinson medal.

ROBINSON, FREDERICK BYRON. 1857-1910. American anatomist. See: Dict. Amer. Biog. Robinson's circle.

ROBINSON, GERTRUD MAUD. fl. 1918. English chemist. See: Pogg., vol. 6. Piloty-Robinson pyrrole synthesis.

ROBINSON, GILBERT DE BEAUREGARD. 1906- . Canadian mathematician. See: World Who's Who Sci. Robinson axioms?

ROBINSON, HEATH (In full: WILLIAM HEATH). 1872-1944. English illustrator and cartoonist. See: New Encyc. Brit., 1974, Microp. Heath Robinson (or Heath Robinsonian).

ROBINSON, JACK. Legendary eccentric. See: Jobes. before you can say Jack Robinson.

ROBINSON, JAMES. 1884-1956. English physicist. See: Pogg., vols. 5, 6. Robinson bridge?, Robinson direction-finder.

ROBINSON, JOSEPH TAYLOR. 1872-1937. American legislator. See: New Encyc. Brit., 1974, Microp. Robinson-Patman Act.

Robinson-Kepler-Power test (Robinson, F. J.; Kepler, Edwin J.; and Power, Marschelle Harnly): Medicine. See: Stedman.

Robinson medal (Robinson, Frederick): Library Science. See: Harrod.

Robinson-Patman Act (Robinson, Joseph Taylor and Patman, Wright): Politics. See: Clark; Greenwald; Smith.

ROBINSON SIR ROBERT. b. 1886. English chemist. See: World Who's Who Sci. Kostanecki-Robinson reaction, Piloty-Robinson pyrrole synthesis.

ROBINSON, ROBERT ALEXANDER. 1914- . American orthopedic surgeon. See: Amer. Men and Women Sci., 12th ed. Smith-Robinson operation.

ROBINSON, STEPHEN CLIVE. 1911- . Candian geologist. See: Amer. Men and Women Sci., 12th ed. Robinsonite.

ROBINSON, THOMAS ROMNEY. 1792-1882. Irish astronomer. See: World Who's Who Sci. Romneya?

Robinson-Wien bridge (Robinson, James? and Wien, Max). See: Robinson bridge.

Robinsonade (Robinson Crusoe): Literature. See: Webster's 3d.

Robinsonite (Robinson, Stephen Clive): Earth Sciences. See: Thrush; Webster's 3d.

Robinson's circle (Robinson, Frederick Byron): Anatomy. See: Donath; Dorland.

Robinson's disease (Robinson, Andrew Rose): Medicine. See: Dorland; Jablonski; Stedman.

Robinson's formula for efficient learning (Robinson, Francis Pleasant): Psychology. See: Chaplin.

ROBIQUET, PIERRE JEAN. 1780-1840. French physician and chemist. See: World Who's Who Sci. Robiquet's paste.

Robiquet's paste (Robiquet, Pierre Jean): Medicine. See: Dorland.

Robison-Embden ester (Robison, Robert and Embden, Gustav). See: Robison ester.

Robison ester (Robison, Robert): Chemistry. See: Dorland; Hackh; Stedman; Webster's 3d. Also known as: Robison-Embden ester.

ROBISON, ROBERT. 1884-1941. English chemist. See: World Who's Who Sci. Robison ester.

ROBITZCH, MAX. b. 1887. German meteorologist. See: Pogg., vol. 6. Robitzsch actinograph.

Robitzsch actinograph (Robitzch, Max): Earth Sciences. See: Huschke.

Robles' (Roble's) disease (Robles, Rudolfo): Medicine. See: Jablonski; Stedman.

ROBLES, RUDOLFO. fl. 1915. Central American physician. (Biography source unavailable.) Robles' (Roble's) disease.

Robson and Crowder process (Derivation undetermined): Engineering and Industry. See: Thrush.

Robson engine (Robson, J.): Engineering and Industry. See: Auger.

ROBSON, J. 1833-1913. English engineer. (Biography source unavailable.) Robson engine.

ROCCO, ALFREDO. 1875-1935. Italian jurist and statesman. See: Encic. Ital. Rocco law on corporations.

Rocco law on corporations (Rocco, Alfredo): Politics. See: Morris and Irwin.

ROCH, GUSTAV. 1839-1866. German mathematician. See: Pogg., vol. 3. Riemann-Roch theorem.

ROCH, SAINT. 1295?-1327. French monk. See: Encyc. Brit., 1911. Saint Roch's disease.

ROCHAIX, A. fl. 1909. French chemist. Cited in: Chem. Abstr., vol. 3, p. 1133. Rochaix test for nitrite in water.

Rochaix test for nitrite in water (Rochaix, A.): Chemistry. See: Van Nostrand Chem. Dict.

ROCHE, EDOUARD ALBERT. 1820-1883. French mathematician and astronomer. See: Pogg., vols. 2, 3. Roche('s) limit.

Roche('s) limit (Roche, Edouard Albert): Astronomy. See: Satterthwaite; Webster's 3d.

Rochea (Delaroche, Francois): Botany. See: Taylor, N.; Webster's 3d.

ROCHER, HENRI GASTON LOUIS. b. 1876. French surgeon. Cited in: Kelly. Rocher-Sheldon syndrome, Rocher's sign.

Rocher-Sheldon syndrome (Rocher, Henri Gaston Louis and Sheldon, W. T.). See: Guerin-Stern syndrome.

Rocher's sign (Rocher, Henri Gaston Louis): Medicine. See: Stedman.

Rochon, Alexis Marie de. See: De Rochon, Alexis Marie.

Rochon prism (De Rochon, Alexis Marie): Physics. See: Internat. Dict. Phys. Elec.; Thewlis; Webster's 3d.

Roch's lipomatosis (Derivation undetermined): Medicine. See: Jablonski.

Rockefeller (Rockefeller, John Davison): Generic Word (wealthy). See: Hendrickson; Partridge.

Rockefeller Foundation (Rockefeller, John Davison): Philanthropy. See: Harvey; Hendrickson.

Rockefeller Institute for Medical Research (Rockefeller, John Davison): Medicine. See: Harvey; Hendrickson.

ROCKEFELLER, JOHN DAVISON. 1839-1937. American oil magnate and philanthropist. See: New Encyc. Brit., 1974, Microp. oysters Rockefeller, Rockefeller, Rockefeller Foundation, Rockefeller Institute for Medical Research.

Rockingham, 2d Marquis of. See: Watson-Wentworth, Charles, 2d Marquis of Rockingham.

Rockingham ware (porcelain) (Watson-Wentworth, Charles, 2d Marquis of Rockingham): Applied Arts. See: Thrush; Webster's 3d.

Rockinghamites (Watson-Wentworth, Charles, 2d Marquis of Rockingham): History. See: Morris and Irwin.

Rockwell hardness (Rockwell, Stanley P.): Engineering and Industry. See: Clark; Internat. Dict. Phys. Elec.; Thrush; Webster's 3d.

Rockwell hardness number (Rockwell, Stanley P.): Engineering and Industry. See: Dresner.

Rockwell hardness test (Rockwell, Stanley P.): Engineering and Industry. See: Auger; Thrush; Van Nostrand Sci. Encyc. under "Hardness."

ROCKWELL, STANLEY P. fl. 1922. American metallurgist. Cited in: Chem. Abstr., vol. 16, p. 3296. Rockwell hardness, Rockwell hardness number, Rockwell hardness test, Rockwell (unit).

Rockwell (unit) (Rockwell, Stanley P.): Engineering and Industry. See: Thrush.

ROCQUELAURE, ANTOINE GASTON JEAN BAPTISTE, DUC DE. 1656-1738. French marshal. See: Nouv. Biog. Univ. Roquelaure (cloak).

RODANO, A. G. fl. 1913. Italian chemist. Cited in: Chem. Abstr., vol. 7, p. 1604. Armani-Rodano test.

RODGERS, JOHN. 1812-1882. American admiral. See: Dict. Amer. Biog. Rodgersia.

Rodgersia (Rodgers, John): Botany. See: Taylor, N.

RODILLON, GEORGES. fl. 1913. French pharmaceutical chemist. Cited in: Chem. Abstr., Decenn. Index, 1907-1916. Rodillon reagent for nitrite?

Rodillon reagent for nitrite (Rodillon, Georges?): Chemistry. See: Van Nostrand Chem. Dict.

Rodio-Dehottay process (Rodio, Giovanni? and Dehottay, Henri?): Engineering and Industry. See: Thrush.

RODIO, GIOVANNI. fl. 1934-1939. Italian? engineer. Cited in: Chem. Abstr., Decenn. Indexes, 1927-1936; 1937-1946. Rodio-Dehottay process?

Rodman gun (Rodman, Thomas Jackson): Weapons. See: Mathews, M. M.; Partridge; Phyfe.

RODMAN, THOMAS JACKSON. 1815-1871. American soldier. See: Dict. Amer. Biog. Rodman gun.

RODMAN, WILLIAM LOUIS. 1858-1916. American surgeon. See: Who Was Who Amer., vol. 1. Rodman's operation.

Rodman's operation (Rodman, William Louis): Medicine. See: Dorland; Stedman.

Rodomontade (Rodomonte): Generic Word (boasting speech). See: Barnhart (Eng. Lit.); Partridge; Webster's 3d.

RODOMONTE. Character in Matteo Boiardo's epic poem "Orlando Innamorato," (1487). See: Magill. Rodomontade.

Rodriques formula (Rodrigues, Olinde): Mathematics. See: Ballentyne; Internat. Dict. Ap. Math.; James.

RODRIGUES, OLINDE (In full: BENJAMIN-OLINDE). 1794-1851. French mathematician, economist and social reformer. See: Michaud. equations of Rodrigues, Euler-Rodrigues parameter, Rodrigues formula.

ROE, JOSEPH HYRAM. b. 1892. American biochemist. See: World Who's Who Sci. Roe reaction for vitamin C (ascorbic acid).

Roe reaction for vitamin C (ascorbic acid) (Roe, Joseph Hyram): Chemistry. See: Van Nostrand Chem. Dict.

ROEBLING, WASHINGTON AUGUSTUS. 1837-1926. American civil engineer. See: Dict. Amer. Biog. Roeblingite.

Roeblingite (Roebling, Washington Augustus): Earth Sciences. See: Mathews, M. M.; Thrush; Webster's 3d.

ROEDER, KARL. b. 1881. German engineer. See: Handb. der Deut. Wissensch. Thyssen-Roeder turbine?

ROEDERER, JOHANN GEORGE. 1727-1763. German obstetrician. See: Biog. Lex. hervorr. Aerzte. Roederer's ecchymoses, Roederer's obliquity.

Roederer's ecchymoses (Roederer, Johann George): Medicine. See: Stedman.

Roederer's obliquity (Roederer, Johann George): Medicine. See: Dorland; Stedman.

ROEHL, WILHELM. 1881-1929. German physician. See: Biog. Lex. hervorr. Aerzte. Roehl's marginal corpuscles.

Roehl's marginal corpuscles (Roehl, Wilhelm): Medicine. See: Dorland.

Roehrer's index (Derivation undetermined): Medicine. See: Stedman.

ROEHRIG, A. fl. 1911. German chemist. Cited in: Chem. Abstr., vol. 5, p. 799. Roehrig tube.

Roehrig tube (Roehrig, A.): Chemistry. See: Hackh; Van Nostrand Chem. Dict.

Roella (Roelle, Wilhelmus): Botany. See: Charnock.

ROELLE, WILHELMUS. 1700-1775. Dutch anatomist. See: Biog. Woordenb. der Nederl. (Aa). Roella.

ROEMER, FRIEDRICH ADOLF. 1809-1869. German geologist. See: Encyc. Brit., 1911. Roemerite.

ROEMER, PAUL HEINRICH. 1876-1916. German bacteriologist. See: Biog. Lex. hervorr. Aerzte. Roemer's experiment, Roemer's test.

Roemerite (Roemer, Friedrich Adolf): Earth Sciences. See: Thrush; Webster's 3d.

Roemer's experiment (Roemer, Paul Heinrich): Medicine. See: Dorland; Stedman.

Roemer's test (Roemer, Paul Heinrich): Medicine. See: Dorland; Stedman.

ROEMHELD, LUDWIG. 1871-1938. German physician. See: Deut. Med. Wchnschr., vol. 64 (April 1, 1938), pp. 512-513. Roemheld's syndrome.

Roemheld's syndrome (Roemheld, Ludwig): Medicine. See: Jablonski.

ROENNE, HENNING KRISTIAN TRAPPAUD. 1878-1947. Danish ophthalmologist. See: Brit. J. Ophth., vol. 32 (Jan. 1948), not paged. Roenne's nasal step.

Roenne's nasal step (Roenne, Henning Kristian Trappaud): Medicine. See: Dorland; Stedman.

Roentgen meter (Roentgen, Wilhelm Konrad): Physics. See: Markus.

Roentgen ray (Roentgen, Wilhelm Konrad): Physics. See: Markus; Thrush; Van Nostrand Chem. Dict.; Van Nostrand Sci. Encyc.

Roentgen (unit) (Roentgen, Wilhelm Konrad): Physics. See: Dresner; Internat. Dict. Phys. Elec.; Thewlis; Van Nostrand Sci. Encyc.

ROENTGEN, WILHELM KONRAD. 1845-1923. German physicist. See: World Who's Who Sci. gram (or gramme) roentgen, kiloroentgen, megaroentgen, micro-roentgen, milliroentgen, Roentgen meter, Roentgen ray, Roentgen (unit), Roentgenite, Roentgenkymograph, Roentgenography, Roentgenogram, Roentgenology, Roentgenoscope (and Roentgenoscopy), Roentgenotherapy, Tyndall-Roentgen effect.

Roentgenite (Roentgen, Wilhelm Konrad): Earth Sciences. See: Thrush.

Roentgenkymograph (Roentgen, Wilhelm Konrad): Medicine. See: Dorland; Stedman.

Roentgenogram (Roentgen, Wilhelm Konrad): Medicine. See: Dorland; Stedman; Webster's 3d.

Roentgenography (Roentgen, Wilhelm Konrad): Medicine. See: Dorland; Stedman.

Roentgenology (Roentgen, Wilhelm Konrad): Medicine. See: Dorland; Markus; Stedman.

Roentgenoscope (and Roentgenoscopy) (Roentgen, Wilhelm Konrad): Medicine. See: Dorland; Stedman.

Roentgenotherapy (Roentgen, Wilhelm Konrad): Medicine. See: Dorland; Stedman.

Roeschen method (Derivation undetermined): Engineering and Industry. See: Thrush.

Roese-Gottlieb method (Derivation undetermined): Chemistry. See: Hackh.

ROESING, B. fl. 1911. German metallurgist. Cited in: Chem. Abstr., vol. 5, p. 452. Roesing wires.

Roesing lead pump (Derivation undetermined): Engineering and Industry. See: Thrush.

Roesing wires (Roesing, B.): Engineering and Industry. See: Thrush.

Roesler('s) process (Derivation undetermined): Engineering and Industry. See: Hackh; Thrush; Van Nostrand Chem. Dict.

ROESSLE, ROBERT. 1876-1956. German pathologist. See: Biog. Lex. hervorr. Aerzte. Hanot-Roessle syndrome, Roessle-Urbach-Wiethe lipoproteinosis.

Roessle-Urbach-Wiethe lipoproteinosis (Roessle, Robert; Urbach, Erich; and Wiethe, Camillo). See: Urbach-Wiethe syndrome.

ROESSLER, KARL. fl. 19th c. German scientist. Cited in: Dana, p. 556. Roesslerite.

Roesslerite (Roessler, Karl): Earth Sciences. See: Webster's 3d.

ROESTEL. fl. ca. 1800. German pharmacist. See: Biog. Notes Upon Botanists. Roestelia.

Roestelia (Roestel): Botany. See: Webster's 3d.

ROFFO, ANGEL H. 1882-1947. Argentinian pathologist. See: Gran. Encic. Argentina. Roffo's test.

Roffo's test (Roffo, Angel H.): Medicine. See: Dorland.

ROGAI, A. fl. 1915. Italian chemist. Cited in: Chem. Abstr., vol. 9, p. 772. Rogai test.

Rogai test (Rogai, A.): Chemistry. See: Van Nostrand Chem. Dict.

Rogatiani (Rogatus): Religion. See: Canney.

ROGATUS. fl. 372-73. Donatist. See: Dict. Christian Biog. Rogatiani.

Roger-Anderson pin fixation appliance (Derivation undetermined): Medicine. See: Stedman.

Roger de Coverley (or Sir Roger de Coverley) (Coverley, Sir Roger de): Dance. See: Chujoy; Webster's 3d.

ROGER, GEORGES HENRI. 1860-1946. French physiologist. See: Biog. Lex. hervorr. Aerzte. Roger's reflex.

ROGER, HENRI LOUIS. 1809-1891. French physician. See: Biog. Lex. hervorr. Aerzte. Roger-Josue test, Roger's disease, Roger's murmur, Roger's reaction.

Roger-Josue test (Roger, Henri Louis and Josue, Otto): Medicine. See: Dorland; Stedman.

Rogerene (Rogers, John): Religion. See: Mathews, M. M.

Rogerians (Rogers, John): Religion. See: Canney.

Rogers act (Rogers, John Jacob?): Politics. See: Smith.

ROGERS, AUSTIN FLINT. 1877-1957. American mineralogist. See: Who Was Who Amer., vol. 3. Austinite.

Rogers-Bond comparator (Rogers, William Augustus and Bond, George M.): Engineering and Industry. See: Auger.

Rogers-Calamari test for rotenone (Rogers, H. D. and Calamari, Joseph A.): Chemistry. See: Van Nostrand Chem. Dict.

ROGERS, CARL RANSOM. 1902- . American psychologist. See: World Who's Who Sci. Rogers' self theory of personality.

Roger's disease (Roger, Henri Louis): Medicine. See: Dorland; Jablonski; Stedman.

Rogers group (Rogers, John): Fine Arts. See: Mathews, M. M.

ROGERS, H. D. fl. 1936. American chemist. Cited in: Chem. Abstr., vol. 30, p. 3577. Rogers-Calamari test for rotenone.

ROGERS, JOHN (Pseud.: THOMAS MATTHEW). ca. 1500-1555. English Protestant martyr. See: Dict. Nat. Biog. Matthew's Bible.

ROGERS, JOHN. 1648-1721. American religious sect founder. See: Dict. Amer. Biog. Rogerene.

ROGERS, JOHN. fl. 1677. American religious sect founder. (Biography source unavailable.) Rogerians.

ROGERS, JOHN. 1829-1904. American sculptor. See: Dict. Amer. Biog. Rogers group.

ROGERS, JOHN JACOB. 1881-1925. American legislator. See: Biog. Direct. Amer. Congress. Rogers act?

Roger's murmur (Roger, Henri Louis): Medicine. See: Jablonski; Stedman.

ROGERS, OSCAR H. 1857-1941. American physician. See: Who Was Who Amer., vol. 1. Rogers' sphygmomanometer.

Rogers' Rangers (Rogers, Robert): History. See: Brewer.

Roger's reaction (Roger, Henri Louis): Medicine. See: Dorland; Stedman.

Roger's reflex (Roger, Georges Henri): Medicine. See: Stedman.

ROGERS, ROBERT. 1731-1795. American frontier soldier. See: Dict. Amer. Biog. Rogers' Rangers.

Rogers' self theory of personality (Rogers, Carl Ransom): Psychology. See: Chaplin.

Rogers' sphygmomanometer (Rogers, Oscar H.): Medicine. See: Dorland; Stedman.

Rogers test reaction for aldehydes (Derivation undetermined): Chemistry. See: Van Nostrand Chem. Dict.

Rogers typesetting machine (Derivation undetermined): Printing. See: Lockwood, p. 563.

ROGERS, WILLIAM AUGUSTUS. 1832-1898. American astronomer and physicist. See: Dict. Amer. Biog. Rogers-Bond comparator.

Roget (Roget, Peter Mark): Generic Word (thesaurus). Cited in: Hendrickson.

ROGET, PETER MARK. 1779-1869. English physician and philologist. See: World Who's Who Sci. Roget, Roget(s) spiral.

Roget(s) spiral (Roget, Peter Mark): Physics. See: Markus; Webster's 3d.

Roha salt (Derivation undetermined): Chemistry. See: Hackh.

ROHDE, MICHAEL. 1782-1812. German physician and botanist. See: Allg. Deut. Biog. Rohdea.

Rohdea (Rohde, Michael): Botany. See: Taylor, N.

Rohn mill (Rohn, Wilhelm Julius Paul?): Engineering and Industry. See: Auger.

ROHN, WILHELM JULIUS PAUL. b. 1887. German engineer. See: Pogg., vol. 6. Rohn mill?

ROHR, JULIUS BERNHARD VON. 1688-1742. German economist and scientist. See: Allg. Deut. Biog. Rohria.

ROHR, KARL. b. 1863. German anatomist. See: Biog. Lex. hervorr. erzte. Rohr's agranulocytosis, Rohr's stria.

ROHRBACH, CARL ERNST MARTIN GUSTAV. 1861-1932. German mineralo-st and mathematician. See: Pogg., vols. 4, 6. Rohrbach('s) solution?

hrbach('s) solution (Rohrbach, Carl Ernst Martin Gustav?): Chemistry. See: ackh; Thrush; Van Nostrand Chem. Dict.

hria (Rohr, Julius Bernhard von): Botany. See: Charnock.

hr's agranulocytosis (Rohr, Karl): Medicine. See: Jablonski.

hr's stria (Rohr, Karl): Anatomy. See: Stedman.

kitansky-Aschoff sinuses (Rokitansky, Karl Freiherr von and Aschoff, Ludwig): edicine. See: Stedman.

kitansky-Cushing ulcer (Rokitansky, Karl Freiherr von and Cushing, Harvey illiams): Medicine. See: Jablonski.

ROKITANSKY, KARL FREIHERR VON. 1804-1878. German pathologist. See: orld Who's Who Sci. Mayer-Rokitansky-Kuester syndrome, Rokitansky-Aschoff uses, Rokitansky-Cushing ulcer, Rokitansky's disease, Rokitansky's diverticulum, kitansky's hernia, Rokitansky's kidney, Rokitansky's pelvis, Rokitansky's tumor.

kitansky's disease (Rokitansky, Karl Freiherr von). See: Budd-Chiari syn-rome.

rokitansky's diverticulum (Rokitansky, Karl Freiherr von): Medicine. See: edman.

kitansky's hernia (Rokitansky, Karl Freiherr von): Medicine. See: Stedman.

kitansky's kidney (Rokitansky, Karl Freiherr von): Medicine. See: Stedman.

kitansky's pelvis (Rokitansky, Karl Freiherr von): Medicine. See: Stedman.

kitansky's tumor (Rokitansky, Karl Freiherr von): Medicine. See: Dorland; edman.

OLAND. French legendary hero. See: Jobes. Roland for an Oliver.

land for an Oliver (Roland): Generic Word (even match). See: Hendrickson; artridge; Phyfe.

ROLANDO, LUIGI. 1773-1831. Italian anatomist. See: World Who's Who ci. Rolandometer, Rolando's angle, Rolando's (Rolandic) area (or zone), olando's cells, Rolando's column, Rolando's (Rolandic) fissure (or sulcus), olando's lobe, Rolando's points, Rolando's substance, Rolando's tubercle.

olandometer (Rolando, Luigi): Medicine. See: Stedman.

olando's angle (Rolando, Luigi): Anatomy. See: Stedman.

olando's (Rolandic) area (or zone) (Rolando, Luigi): Anatomy. See: Stedman; ebster's 3d.

olando's cells (Rolando, Luigi): Anatomy. See: Stedman.

olando's column (Rolando, Luigi): Anatomy. See: Stedman.

olando's (Rolandic) fissure (or sulcus) (Rolando, Luigi): Anatomy. See: onath; Stedman; Webster's 3d.

olando's lobe (Rolando, Luigi): Anatomy. See: Donath; Stedman.

olando's points (Rolando, Luigi): Anatomy. See: Donath; Stedman.

olando's substance (Rolando, Luigi): Anatomy. See: Donath; Stedman.

olando's tubercle (Rolando, Luigi): Anatomy. See: Stedman.

OLF, IDA. fl. 20th c. Scientist. (Biography source unavailable.) olfing.

olfing (Rolf, Ida): Physiology. See: Psycho Sources.

OLFS, FREDERICK MAAS. 1875-1956. American botanist. See: Amer. Men ci., 7th ed. Rolfs' oak.

olfs' oak (Rolfs, Frederick Maas): Botany. See: Webster's 3d.

olin Madonna (Rolin, Nicolas): Fine Arts. See: Osborne under "Flemish rt."

ROLIN, NICOLAS. 1380-1462. French Chancellor of Burgundy. See: Nouv. Biog. Univ. Rolin Madonna.

ROLLE, LORD JOHN. 1750-1842. English politician. See: Dict. Nat. Biog. Rolliad.

ROLLE, MICHEL. 1652-1719. French mathematician. See: World Who's Who Sci. Rolle('s) theorem.

Rolle('s) theorem (Rolle, Michel): Mathematics. See: Ballentyne; James; Van Nostrand Sci. Encyc.

ROLLER, CHRISTIAN FRIEDRICH WILHELM. 1802-1878. German psychiatrist and alienist. See: Allg. Deut. Biog. Roller's nucleus.

ROLLER, PAUL S. 1902- . American chemical engineer. See: Amer. Men Sci., 9th ed. Roller's equation, Roller's plasticity test.

Roller's equation (Roller, Paul S.): Engineering and Industry. See: Thrush.

Roller's nucleus (Roller, Christian Friedrich Wilhelm): Anatomy. See: Donath; Dorland; Stedman.

Roller's plasticity test (Roller, Paul S.): Engineering and Industry. See: Thrush.

ROLLESTON, SIR HUMPHREY DAVY. 1862-1944. English physician. See: World Who's Who Sci. Rolleston's rule.

Rolleston's rule (Rolleston, Sir Humphrey Davy): Medicine. See: Dorland; Stedman.

ROLLET, JOSEPH PIERRE MARTIN. 1824-1894. French surgeon and syphi-lologist. See: World Who's Who Sci. Rollet's chancre, Rollet's syndrome.

Rollet's chancre (Rollet, Joseph Pierre Martin): Medicine. See: Dorland; Jablonski.

Rollet's syndrome (Rollet, Joseph Pierre Martin): Medicine. See: Jablonski.

ROLLETT, ALEXANDER. 1834-1903. Austrian physiologist. See: Biog. Lex. hervorr. Aerzte. Ritter-Rollett phenomenon, Rollett's stroma.

Rollett's stroma (Rollett, Alexander): Medicine. See: Dorland; Stedman.

Rolliad (Rolle, Lord John): Politics. See: Stenhouse.

ROLLIER, AUGUSTE. b. 1874. Swiss physician. See: Biog. Lex. hervorr. Aerzte. Rollier's treatment.

Rollier's treatment (Rollier, Auguste): Medicine. See: Dorland.

ROMAN, WADIM. fl. 1935. German chemist. Cited in: Chem. Abstr., vol. 29, p. 1742. Pietsch-Roman reagent.

ROMANA, CECILIO FENIX. 1899- . Argentinian physician in Brazil. See: Gran Encic. Argentina. Romana's sign.

Romana's sign (Romana, Cecilio Fenix): Medicine. See: Dorland; Jablonski.

ROMANES, GEORGE JOHN. 1848-1894. Canadian-born English biologist. See: Dict. Nat. Biog. Romanes lectures.

Romanes lectures (Romanes, George John): Education. See: Harvey.

ROMANI, BRUNO. fl. 1931. Italian chemist. Cited in: Chem. Abstr., vol. 26, p. 1878. Romani test for sucrose.

Romani test for sucrose (Romani, Bruno): Chemistry. See: Van Nostrand Chem. Dict.

ROMANINK, A. N. fl. 1937. Russian chemist. Cited in: Chem. Abstr. vol. 31, p. 2962. Tananaev-Romanink test for osmium.

ROMANOFF, FEDORA. Character in Victorien Sardou's play "Fedora," (1822). (Biography source unavailable.) Fedora (hat).

Romanov (breed of sheep) (Yuriyev, Roman): Zoology. See: Webster's 3d.

Romanov dynasty (Yuriyev, Roman): History. See: New Encyc. Brit., 1974, Microp.

ROMANOVSKY, DIMITRI LEONIDOVITCH. 1861-1921. Russian physician. See: Biog. Lex. hervorr. Aerzte. Romanovsky's (Romanowsky) stain.

Romanovsky's (Romanowsky) stain (Romanovsky, Dimitri Leonidovitch): Medicine. See: Dorland; Stedman; Webster's 3d.

ROMANZOFF, COUNT NICHOLAS. fl. 1820. Russian nobleman. Cited in: Dana. Romanzoffia, Romanzovite.

Romanzoffia (Romanzoff, Count Nicholas): Botany. See: Taylor, N.

Romanzovite (Romanzoff, Count Nicholas): Earth Sciences. See: Charnock.

ROMBERG, ARNOLD. b. 1882. American geophysicist. See: Amer. Men Sci., 9th ed. McComb-Romberg seismograph?

ROMBERG, FREDERICK ERNST. 1910- . American geophysicist. See: Amer. Men Sci., 10th ed. LaCoste-Romberg gravimeter.

Romberg-Howship sign (Romberg, Moritz Heinrich von and Howship, John). See: Howship-Romberg syndrome (or sign).

ROMBERG, MORITZ HEINRICH VON. 1795-1873. German neurologist. See: World Who's Who Sci. Cavare-Romberg-Westphal syndrome, Howship-Romberg syndrome (or sign), Romberg-Paessler syndrome, Romberg's sign (or symptom) (1), Romberg's spasm, Romberg's syndrome (disease or trophoneurosis).

Romberg-Paessler syndrome (Romberg, Moritz Heinrich von and Paessler, H.): Medicine. See: Dorland.

Rombergism (Romberg, Moritz Heinrich von). See: Romberg's sign (or symptom).

Romberg's sign (or symptom) (1) (Romberg, Moritz Heinrich von): Medicine. See: Dorland; English; Jablonski; Stedman.

Romberg's sign (or symptom) (2) (Romberg, Moritz Heinrich von). See: Howship-Romberg syndrome (or sign).

Romberg's spasm (Romberg, Moritz Heinrich von): Medicine. See: Jablonski.

Romberg's syndrome (disease or trophoneurosis) (Romberg, Moritz Heinrich von): Medicine. See: Dorland; Jablonski; Stedman. Also known as: Parry-Romberg syndrome.

ROME DE LISLE, JEAN BAPTISTE LOUIS. 1736-1790. French mineralogist. See: Encyc. Brit., 1911. Romeite.

Romeite (Rome de Lisle, Jean Baptiste Louis): Earth Sciences. See: Thrush; Webster's 3d.

ROMEO. Ill-fated lover in William Shakespeare's play "Romeo and Juliet." (1597). See: Harvey. Romeo, Romeo and Juliet, Romeo (slipper).

Romeo (Romeo): Generic Word (lover). See: Hendrickson; Webster's 3d.

Romeo and Juliet (Romeo): Generic Word (romantic love). See: Brewer; Hendrickson; Partridge.

Romeo (slipper) (Romeo): Fashion. See: Picken; Webster's 3d.

ROMIEU, MARC. fl. 1925. French histologist. Cited in: Kelly. Romieu test for protein material.

Romieu test for protein material (Romieu, Marc): Chemistry. See: Van Nostrand Chem. Dict.

ROMIJN, GYSBERT. fl. 1897. Dutch chemist. Cited in: Kelly; Royal Soc. Cat. Sci. Pap., 1884-1900. Romijn reagent for glucose.

Romijn reagent for glucose (Romijn, Gysbert): Chemistry. See: Van Nostrand Chem. Dict.

ROMMELAERE, GUILLAUME. 1836-1916. See: Biog. Lex. hervorr. Aerzte. Rommelaere's sign.

Rommelaere's sign (Rommelaere, Guillaume): Medicine. See: Dorland; Stedman.

Romneya (Robinson, Thomas Romney?): Botany. See: Taylor, N.

RONDELET, GUILLAUME. 1507-1566. French naturalist and physician. See: Nouv. Biog. Univ. Rondeletia.

Rondeletia (Rondelet, Guillaume): Botany. See: Taylor, N.; Webster's 3d.

RONSARD, PIERRE DE. 1524-1585. French poet. See: Encyc. Brit., 1973. Ronsardian pessimism.

Ronsardian pessimism (Ronsard, Pierre de): Literature. See: Preminger under "Science and Poetry."

ROOD, MICAH. fl. 1693. American farmer. (Biography source unavailable.) Micah Rood's apples.

ROOD, OGDEN NICHOLAS. 1831-1902. American physicist. See: Dict. Amer. Biog. Rood's hue circle.

Rood's hue circle (Rood, Ogden Nicholas): Physics. See: Focal Encyc. Photog.

ROOKER, THOMAS N. fl. 1859. American printer. (Biography source unavailable.) Rooker type case.

Rooker type case (Rooker, Thomas N.): Printing. See: Lockwood under "Case" and "Lay of the Case."

ROOM, THOMAS GERALD. 1902- . English mathematician. See: Who's Who Brit. Sci., 1953. Room's squares?

Room's squares (Room, Thomas Gerald?): Statistics. See: Kendall.

ROONEY, HANDY ANDY. Hero of the novel "Handy Andy," (1842) by Samuel Lover. See: Magill. Handy-Andy.

ROONEY, WILLIAM JOSEPH. b. 1890. American physicist. See: Amer. Men Sci., 4th ed. Gish-Rooney method.

Roorback (Roorback, Baron von): Generic Word (false political allegation). See: Clapin; Mathews, M. M.; Webster's 3d.

ROORBACK, BARON VON. Fictional author of the imaginary book "Roorback's Tour through the Western and Southern States," (1844). See: Dict. Amer. Hist., vol. IV. Roorback.

Roosa pump (Roosa, Vernon): Engineering and Industry. See: Auger.

ROOSA, VERNON. fl. 1939. American engineer. (Biography source unavailable.) Roosa pump.

Roosevelt corollary (Roosevelt, Theodore): Politics. See: Morris.

Roosevelt doctrine (Roosevelt, Theodore): Politics. See: Smith.

ROOSEVELT, ELEANOR (In full: ANNA ELEANOR). 1884-1962. American first lady and author. See: New Encyc. Brit., 1974, Microp. Eleanor blue.

Roosevelt elk (Roosevelt, Theodore): Zoology. See: Webster's 3d.

ROOSEVELT, FRANKLIN DELANO. 1882-1945. American president. See: New Encyc. Brit., 1974. Rooseveltian (or Rooseveltism) (1), Rooseveltiana (1), Rooseveltite.

ROOSEVELT, THEODORE. 1858-1919. American president. See: Dict. Amer. Biog. Roosevelt corollary, Roosevelt doctrine, Roosevelt elk, Roosevelt trout, Roosevelt trust policy, Rooseveltian (or Rooseveltism) (2), Rooseveltiana (2), Teddy bear.

Roosevelt trout (Roosevelt, Theodore): Zoology. See: Webster's 3d.

Roosevelt trust policy (Roosevelt, Theodore): Politics. See: Morris and Irwin.

Rooseveltian (or Rooseveltism) (1) (Roosevelt, Franklin Delano): Politics. See: Webster's 3d.

Rooseveltian (or Rooseveltism) (2) (Roosevelt, Theodore): Politics. See: Mathews, M. M.; Webster's 3d.

Rooseveltiana (1) (Roosevelt, Franklin Delano): History. See: Mathews, M. M.; Webster's 3d.

Rooseveltiana (2) (Roosevelt, Theodore): History. See: Webster's 3d.

Rooseveltite (Roosevelt, Franklin Delano): Earth Sciences. See: Thrush; Webster's 3d.

ROOT, ELIHU. 1845-1937. American statesman. See: New Encyc. Brit., 1974, Microp. Root-Takahira agreement.

Root-Takahira agreement (Root, Elihu and Takahira, Kogoro): Politics. See: Morris; Smith.

Roots (Rootes) blower (Roots, J. D.): Engineering and Industry. See: Auger; Thrush.

ROOTS, J. D. fl. 1866. American engineer. (Biography source unavailable.) Roots (Rootes) blower.

rope (or cord) of Ocnus (Ocnus): Generic Word (profitless labor). See: Harvey; Phyfe.

Ropp furnace (Derivation undetermined): Engineering and Industry. See: Thrush.

Roquelaure (cloak) (Rocquelaure, Antoine Gaston Jean Baptiste, Duc de): Fashion. See: Brewer; Partridge; Picken.

Roques benzidine reagent (Roques, Joseph?): Chemistry. See: Van Nostrand Chem. Dict.

ROQUES, JOSEPH. 1772-1850. French scientist. Cited in: Index-Cat. Libr. Surg.-Gen. Off., 5th Ser., vol. 1, 1959. Roques benzidine reagent?

ROQUES, MAURICE. 1911- . French mineralogist. See: Who's Who Sci. Europe, 1967. Roquesite.

ROQUES, R. fl. 1949. French cardiologist. (Biography source unavailable.) Roques' syndrome.

Roques' syndrome (Roques, R.): Medicine. See: Jablonski.

Roquesite (Roques, Maurice): Earth Sciences. See: Thrush.

Rorschach category (and protocol) (Rorschach, Hermann): Psychology. See: Chaplin; English; Webster's 3d.

Rorschach determinant (Rorschach, Hermann): Psychology. See: Chaplin; Wolman.

Rorschach experience balance (Rorschach, Hermann): Psychology. See: Good.

RORSCHACH, HERMANN. 1884-1922. Swiss psychiatrist. See: Internat. Encyc. Soc. Sci. Behn-Rorschach test, Rorschach category (and protocol), Rorschach determinant, Rorschach experience balance, Rorschach ranking test, Rorschach test (or inkblots test).

Rorschach ranking test (Rorschach, Hermann): Psychology. See: Chaplin; English.

Rorschach test (or inkblots test) (Rorschach, Hermann): Psychology. See: Chaplin; English; Hinsie; Wolman.

Rosa and Dorsey method (Rosa, Edward Bennett and Dorsey, Noah Ernest): Physics. See: Internat. Dict. Phys. Elec.

ROSA, EDWARD BENNETT. 1861-1921. American physicist. See: Dict. Amer. Biog. Atwater-Rosa calorimeter, Rosa and Dorsey method.

ROSANOFF, AARON JOSHUA. 1878-1943. American psychologist. See: New York Times, Jan. 20, 1943, p. 20, col. 3. Kent-Rosanoff test (series or list).

Rosback automatic wire-stitcher (Rosback, Frederick P.): Printing. See: Lockwood.

ROSBACK, FREDERICK P. fl. 1890. American inventor. (Biography source unavailable.) Rosback automatic wire-stitcher.

ROSCHER, WALTER. fl. 1914. German mineral collector and apothecary. Cited in: Min. Mag., vol. 17 (1913-1916), p. 356. Roscherite.

Roscherite (Roscher, Walter): Earth Sciences. See: Thrush; Webster's 3d.

Roscius (or Roscian) (Roscius, Quintus Gallus): Generic Word (fine actor). See: Brewer; Hendrickson; Partridge.

ROSCIUS, QUINTUS GALLUS. ca. 126-62 B.C. Roman actor. See: Encyc. Brit., 1973. Roscius (or Roscian).

ROSCOE. fl. 19th c.? American inventor or manufacturer. (Biography source unavailable.) Roscoe.

Roscoe (Roscoe): Generic Word (gun). See: Partridge.

Roscoe-Bunsen law (Roscoe, Henry Enfield and Bunsen, Robert). See: Bunsen-Roscoe law.

ROSCOE, HENRY ENFIELD. 1833-1915. English chemist. See: World Who's Who Sci. Bunsen-Roscoe law, Roscoelite.

ROSCOE, WILLIAM. 1753-1831. English historian. See: Dict. Nat. Biog. Roscoe's yellowthroat (bird).

Roscoelite (Roscoe, Henry Enfield): Earth Sciences. See: Thrush; Webster's 3d.

Roscoe's yellowthroat (bird) (Roscoe, William): Zoology. See: Mathews, M. M.

ROSE, ANTON R. 1877-1948. American biochemist. See: New York Times, Sept. 24, 1948, p. 25, col. 4. Exton-Rose test.

Rose case (Rose, Fred): Politics. See: Morris and Irwin.

rose du Barry (Du Barry, Marie Jeanne Becu): Botany. See: Webster's 3d. Also known as: rose Pompadour.

ROSE, EDMUND. 1836-1914. German physician. See: Biog. Lex. hervorr. Aerzte. Rose's tetanus (or cephalic tetanus).

ROSE, FRANK ATCHERLY. fl. 20th c.? English surgeon. (Biography source unavailable.) Rose's position.

ROSE, FRED. 1907?- . Polish-born Canadian politician. See: Time, vol. 47 (March 25, 1946), p. 40. Rose case.

ROSE, GEORGE GIBSON. 1922- . American tissue culture scientist. See: World Who's Who Sci. Rose-Waaler test?

ROSE, GUSTAV. 1798-1873. German mineralogist. See: World Who's Who Sci. Roselite.

rose Hortensia (Nassau, Hortense van): Fashion. See: Webster's 3d.

ROSE, JOSEPH CONSTANTIN. 1826-1893. German physician. See: Biog. Lex. hervorr. Aerzte. Rose's test (or blood test).

ROSE OF LIMA, SAINT. 1586-1617. Peruvian ascetic. See: Holweck. Saint Rose's disease.

rose Pompadour (Pompadour, Jeanne Antoinette Poisson, Marquise de): Applied Arts. See: Webster's 3d. Also known as: rose du Barry.

Rose process (Rose, Thomas K.?): Chemistry. See: Van Nostrand Chem. Dict.

ROSE, THOMAS K. fl. 1915. English metallurgist. Cited in: Chem. Abstr., Decenn. Index, 1907-1916. Rose process?

ROSE, VALENTIN. 1736-1771. German apothecary. See: New Encyc. Brit., 1974, Microp. Rose's metal.

Rose-Waaler test (Rose, George Gibson? and Waaler, Erik?): Medicine. See: Stedman.

Roselite (Rose, Gustav): Earth Sciences. See: Charnock.

ROSELLINI, FERDINANDO P. 1817-1873. Italian botanist. See: Ascherson and Graebner, vol. 2, p. 320. Rosellinia.

Rosellinia (Rosellini, Ferdinando P.): Botany. See: Webster's 3d.

Rosen-Castleman-Liebow syndrome (Rosen, Samuel Harry; Castleman, Benjamin; and Liebow, Averill Abraham): Medicine. See: Jablonski.

ROSEN, SAMUEL HARRY. 1903- . American pathologist. See: Amer. Men and Woman Sci., 12th ed. Rosen-Castleman-Liebow syndrome, Rosen's neuralgia.

ROSENBACH, ANTON JULIUS FRIEDRICH. 1842-1923. German surgeon. See: World Who's Who Sci. Rosenbach's disease, Rosenbach's tuberculin.

Rosenbach-Gmelin test (Rosenbach, Ottomar and Gmelin, Leopold). See: Gmelin's test (for bile pigments).

ROSENBACH, OTTOMAR. 1851-1907. German physician. See: Biog. Lex. hervorr. Aerzte. Rosenbach-Gmelin test, Rosenbach's disease, Rosenbach's law, Rosenbach's sign (1), Rosenbach's sign (2) (or digestive reflex), Rosenbach's syndrome, Rosenbach's test.

Rosenbach's disease (Rosenbach, Anton Julius Friedrich): Medicine. See: Dorland; Jablonski. Also known as: Klauder's disease.

Rosenbach's disease (Rosenbach, Ottomar). See: Heberden's nodes.

Rosenbach's law (Rosenbach, Ottomar): Medicine. See: Dorland; Stedman.

Rosenbach's sign (1) (Rosenbach, Ottomar): Medicine. See: Dorland; Hinsie; Stedman.

Rosenbach's sign (2) (or digestive reflex) (Rosenbach, Ottomar): Medicine. See: Dorland; Stedman.

Rosenbach's syndrome (Rosenbach, Ottomar): Medicine. See: Jablonski.

Rosenbach's test (Rosenbach, Ottomar): Medicine. See: Dorland; Stedman.

Rosenbach's tuberculin (Rosenbach, Anton Julius Friedrich): Medicine. See: Dorland.

ROSENBAUM, S. fl. 1951-1954. English statistician. Cited in: Kendall and Doig. Wilks-Rosenbaum tests?

ROSENBERG, CAROLINE FRIDERIKE. 1810-1902. Danish amateur botanist. See: Biog. Notes Upon Botanists. Rosenbergia.

Rosenberg cross-field generator (Rosenberg, Emanuel): Physics. See: Internat. Dict. Phys. Elec.

ROSENBERG, EDWARD FRANK. 1908- . American physician. See: Amer. Men and Woman Sci., 12th ed. Hench-Rosenberg syndrome.

ROSENBERG, EMANUEL. b. 1872. Austrian physicist. See: Pogg., vol. 6. Rosenberg cross-field generator.

ROSENBERG, LEON EMANUEL. 1933- . American geneticist. See: Amer. Men and Woman Sci., 12th ed. Rowley-Rosenberg syndrome.

Rosenbergia (Rosenberg, Caroline Friderike): Botany. See: Webster's 3d.

ROSENBLADT, TH. fl. 1887. German chemist. Cited in: Royal Soc. Cat. Sci. Pap., 1884-1900. Rosenblat test for boric acid?

Rosenblat test for boric acid (Rosenbladt, Th.?): Chemistry. See: Van Nostrand Chem. Dict.

Rosenblueth and Cannon test (Rosenbleuth, Arturo Stearns and Cannon, Walter Bradford): Medicine. See: Stedman.

ROSENBLUETH, ARTURO STEARNS. 1900- . Mexican neurophysiologist. See: World Who's Who Sci. Rosenblueth and Cannon test.

ROSENBUSCH, HARRY (In full: KARL HEINRICH FERDINAND). 1836-1914. German geologist. See: World Who's Who Sci. Rosenbuschite, Rosenbusch's law (or rule).

Rosenbusch vaccine (Derivation undetermined): Medicine. See: Stedman.

Rosenbuschite (Rosenbusch, Harry): Earth Sciences. See: Thrush; Webster's 3d.

Rosenbusch's law (or rule) (Rosenbusch, Harry): Earth Sciences. See: Thrush.

ROSENFELD, HANS. fl. ca. 1763. German religious fanatic. (Biography source unavailable.) Rosenfelders.

Rosenfelders (Rosenfeld, Hans): Religion. See: Canney.

Rosenhain–Haughton reagent (Rosenhain, Walter and Haughton, John L.): Chemistry. See: Van Nostrand Chem. Dict.

ROSENHAIN, WALTER. 1876-1934. Australian metallurgist. See: Pogg., vol. 6. Rosenhain-Haughton reagent.

Rosenheim–Callow test reactions for sterols (Rosenheim, Otto and Callow, Robert K.): Chemistry. See: Van Nostrand Chem. Dict.

Rosenheim–Drummond test for vitamin A (Rosenheim, Otto and Drummond, Sir Jack Cecil): Chemistry. See: Van Nostrand Chem. Dict.

ROSENHEIM, OTTO (In full: SIGMUND OTTO). 1871-1955. German-born English biochemist. See: Pogg., vol. 6; World Who's Who Sci. Acree-Rosenheim test (or reaction), Rosenheim-Callow test reactions for sterols, Rosenheim-Drummond test for vitamin A, Rosenheim reagent for choline.

Rosenheim reagent for choline (Rosenheim, Otto): Chemistry. See: Van Nostrand Chem. Dict.

Rosenheim test (Rosenheim, Otto). See: Acree-Rosenheim test (or reaction).

ROSENKREUTZ, CHRISTIAN (FRATER ROSAE CRUCIS). fl. 15th c.? Reputed Austrian founder of secret society. See: Hastings (Encyc. Rel. Ethics). Rosicrucians (or Rosicrucianism).

ROSENMUELLER, JOHANN CHRISTIAN. 1771-1820. German anatomist. See: World Who's Who Sci. Rosenmueller's gland (or node), Rosenmueller's organ, Rosenmueller's recess (or fossa), Rosenmueller's valve.

Rosenmueller's gland (or node) (Rosenmueller, Johann Christian): Anatomy. See: Donath; Stedman.

Rosenmueller's organ (Rosenmueller, Johann Christian): Anatomy. See: Donath; Stedman.

Rosenmueller's recess (or fossa) (Rosenmueller, Johann Christian): Anatomy. See: Donath; Stedman.

Rosenmueller's valve (Rosenmueller, Johann Christian): Anatomy. See: Donath; Stedman. Also known as: Hasner's valve (fold or valve of Hasner), Huschke's valve.

Rosenmund arsonic acid reaction (Rosenmund, Karl Wilhelm): Chemistry. See: Van Nostrand Chem. Dict.

ROSENMUND, KARL WILHELM. b. 1884. German chemist. See: Pogg., vols. 5, 6, 7a. Rosenmund arsonic acid reaction, Rosenmund reduction (or reduction reaction), Rosenmund-Von Braun synthesis.

Rosenmund reduction (or reduction reaction) (Rosenmund, Karl Wilhelm): Chemistry. See: Ballentyne; Van Nostrand Chem. Dict.

Rosenmund–Von Braun synthesis (Rosenmund, Karl Wilhelm and Von Braun, Julius): Chemistry. See: Van Nostrand Chem. Dict.

ROSENOW, EDWARD CARL. b. 1875. American bacteriologist. See: World Who's Who Sci. Rosenow's stain.

Rosenow's stain (Rosenow, Edward Carl): Medicine. See: Stedman.

Rosen's neuralgia (Rosen, Samuel Harry): Medicine. See: Jablonski.

ROSENSTEIN, LUDWIG. b. 1886. American chemist. See: Amer. Men Sci., 4th ed. Rosenstein process.

Rosenstein process (Rosenstein, Ludwig): Chemistry. See: Hackh; Van Nostrand Chem. Dict.

ROSENSTHIEL, AUGUSTE (In full: DANIEL AUGUSTE). 1839-1916. French chemist. See: Pogg., vols. 3, 4, 5. Rosensthiel's (Rosentiehl's) green?

Rosensthiel's (Rosenstiehl's) green (Rosensthiel, Auguste?): Chemistry. See: Hackh; Thrush.

ROSENTHAL, CURT. fl. 1927. German psychiatrist. See: Kuerschner's Deut. Gel. Kal., vol. IV, 1931. Melkersson-Rosenthal syndrome, Muenzer-Rosenthal syndrome, Rosenthal's disease.

Rosenthal–Erdelyi reagent (Rosenthal, Jeno and Erdelyi, Janos): Chemistry. See: Van Nostrand Chem. Dict.

ROSENTHAL, FRIEDRICH CHRISTIAN. 1780-1829. German anatomist. See: Allg. Deut. Biog. Rosenthal's vein.

ROSENTHAL, ISIDOR. 1836-1915. German physiologist. See: Biog. Lex. hervorr. Aerzte. Rosenthal's canal.

ROSENTHAL, JENO. fl. 1933. Hungarian chemist. Cited in: Chem. Abstr., Decenn. Index, 1927-1936. Rosenthal-Erdelyi reagent.

ROSENTHAL, NATHAN. fl. 1925. American physician. (Biography source unavailable.) Brill-Baehr-Rosenthal disease.

ROSENTHAL, ROBERT LOUIS. 1923- . American hematologist. See: Amer. Men and Women Sci., 12th ed. Rosenthal's disease.

ROSENTHAL, SANFORD MORRIS. 1897- . American pharmacologist. See: Amer. Men and Women Sci., 12th ed. Rosenthal's test.

Rosenthaler–Goerner test reagents for alkaloids (Rosenthaler, Leopold and Goerner, Paul): Chemistry. See: Van Nostrand Chem. Dict.

ROSENTHALER, LEOPOLD. b. 1875. German pharmacological chemist. See: Pogg., vols., 5, 6. Rosenthaler-Goerner test reagents for alkaloids, Rosenthaler test for nitrogen in organic compounds, Rosenthaler test for sulfur in organic compounds, Rosenthaler test reaction for ascorbic acid (vitamin C), Rosenthaler test reaction for differentiating alcohols, Rosenthaler test reaction for hydroxyl group, Rosenthaler test reaction for lactic acid, Rosenthaler-Tuerk reagent.

Rosenthaler test for nitrogen in organic compounds (Rosenthaler, Leopold): Chemistry. See: Van Nostrand Chem. Dict.

Rosenthaler test for sulfur in organic compounds (Rosenthaler, Leopold): Chemistry. See: Van Nostrand Chem. Dict.

Rosenthaler test reaction for ascorbic acid (vitamin C) (Rosenthaler, Leopold): Chemistry. See: Van Nostrand Chem. Dict.

Rosenthaler test reaction for differentiating alcohols (Rosenthaler, Leopold): Chemistry. See: Van Nostrand Chem. Dict.

Rosenthaler test reaction for hydroxyl group (Rosenthaler, Leopold): Chemistry. See: Van Nostrand Chem. Dict.

Rosenthaler test reaction for lactic acid (Rosenthaler, Leopold): Chemistry. See: Van Nostrand Chem. Dict.

Rosenthaler–Tuerk reagent (Rosenthaler, Leopold and Tuerk, F.): Chemistry. See: Stedman; Van Nostrand Chem. Dict.

Rosenthal's canal (Rosenthal, Isidor): Anatomy. See: Dorland; Stedman.

Rosenthal's disease (Rosenthal, Curt): Medicine. See: Jablonski.

Rosenthal's disease (Rosenthal, Robert Louis): Medicine. See: Jablonski.

Rosenthal's test (Rosenthal, Sanford Morris): Medicine. See: Dorland; Stedman.

Rosenthal's vein (Rosenthal, Friedrich Christian): Anatomy. See: Donath; Dorland; Stedman.

Rosenzweig picture frustration study (or test) (Rosenzweig, Saul): Psychology. See: Chaplin; English; Wolman.

ROSENZWEIG, ROBERT MYRON. 1931- . American political analyst and academic administrator. See: Amer. Men and Women Sci., 12th ed. (Soc. Behav. Sci.). Rosenzweig's rubric.

ROSENZWEIG, SAUL. 1907- . American psychologist. See: American Men and Women Sci., 12th ed. Rosenzweig picture frustration study (or test).

Rosenzweig's rubric (Rosenzweig, Robert Myron): Education. See: Martin

Roser–Braun sign (Roser, Wilhelm and Braun, Heinrich?). See: Roser's sign.

Roser–Nelaton's line (Roser, Wilhelm and Nelaton, Auguste). See: Nelaton's line.

ROSER, WILHELM. 1817-1888. German surgeon. See: Allg. Deut. Biog. Roser–Nelaton's line, Roser's sign.

Roser's sign (Roser, Wilhelm): Medicine. See: Dorland; Stedman. Also known as: Roser–Braun sign.

Rose's metal (Rose, Valentin): Earth Sciences. See: Partridge; Stedman.

Rose's position (Rose, Frank Atcherly): Medicine. See: Dorland; Stedman.

Rose's test (or blood test) (Rose, Joseph Constantin): Medicine. See: Dorland; Stedman.

Rose's tetanus (or cephalic tetanus) (Rose, Edmund): Medicine. See: Dorland; Jablonski; Stedman. Also known as: Janin's tetanus, Klemm's tetanus.

ROSICKY, VOJTECH. 1880-1942. Czech mineralogist. See: Min. Mag., vol. 28 (Mar. 1947-Sept. 1949), pp. 217-218. Rosickyite.

Rosickyite (Rosicky, Vojtech): Earth Sciences. See: Webster's 3d.

Rosicrucians (or Rosicrucianism) (Rosenkreutz, Christian): Religion. See: Barnhart (Eng. Lit.); Brewer; Canney.

ROSIN, HEINRICH. b. 1863. German physician. See: Biog. Lex. hervorr. Aerzte. Rosin's test.

ROSIN, PAUL. 1890- . German engineer. See: Pogg., vol. 6. Rosin–Rammler equation.

Rosin–Rammler equation (Rosin, Paul and Rammler, Erich): Engineering and Industry. See: Thrush.

Rosin's test (Rosin, Heinrich): Medicine. See: Dorland.

ROSIWAL, AUGUSTE KARL. 1860-1923. Austrian geologist. See: Pogg., vol. 6. Rosiwal method.

Rosiwal method (Rosiwal, Auguste Karl): Earth Sciences. See: Thrush.

Roske–De Toni–Caffey–Smyth disease (Roske, Georg; De Toni, Giovanni; Caffey, John; and Smyth, Francis Scott). See: Caffey–Silverman syndrome.

ROSKE, GEORG. fl. 1930. German pediatrician. (Biography source unavailable.) Roske–De Toni–Caffey–Smyth disease.

ROSKOPF, GEORGES–FREDERIC. 1812-1889. Swiss watchmaker. See: Dict. Hist. Biog. Suisse. Roskopf (watch).

Roskopf (watch) (Roskopf, Georges–Frederic): Horology. See: Webster's 3d.

ROSMINI–SERBATI, ANTONIO. 1797-1855. Italian philosopher. See: Encyc. Brit., 1973. Rosminian(s) (or Rosminianism).

Rosminian(s) (or Rosminianism) (Rosmini–Serbati, Antonio): Philosophy. See: Attwater; Canney; Webster's 3d.

Rosolimo, Grigoriy Ivanovich. See: Rossolimo, Grigoriy Ivanovich.

Ross .303 rifle (Ross, Sir Charles): Weapons. See: Quick.

Ross and Welter furnace (Derivation undetermined): Engineering and Industry. See: Thrush.

ROSS, ANDREW. 1798-1859. English physicist. See: Pogg., vol. 6. Ross concentric lens, Ross homocentric lens.

ROSS, ART (ARTHUR H.). d. 1964. American sportsclub owner. See: New York Times, Aug. 6, 1924, p. 29, col. 3. Art Ross Trophy.

ROSS, BERNARD ROGAN. 1827-1874. Irish fur-trader. See: Who Was Who Amer., Hist. vol. Ross's goose.

ROSS, SIR CHARLES. fl. 1905-1910. Canadian weapons designer. (Biography source unavailable.) Ross .303 rifle.

ROSS, CLARENCE SAMUEL. 1880-1953. American geologist. See: Pogg., vol. 6. Rossite.

Ross concentric lens (Ross, Andrew): Photography. See: Focal Encyc. Photog. under "Lens History."

Ross' desires (Ross, Edward Allsworth): Sociology. See: Zadrozny.

ROSS, EDWARD ALLSWORTH. 1866-1951. American sociologist. See: Internat. Encyc. Soc. Sci. Ross' desires.

ROSS, EDWARD HALFORD. 1875-1928. English pathologist. Cited in: Index-Cat. Libr. Surg.-Gen. Off., 3rd Ser., vol. 9, 1931. Ross's bodies.

Ross effect (Ross, Frank Elmore): Astronomy. See: Van Nostrand Sci. Encyc.

Ross feeder (Ross, W.?): Engineering and Industry. See: Thrush.

ROSS, FRANK ELMORE. 1874-1966. American astronomer. See: World Who's Who Sci. Ross effect.

ROSS, SIR GEORGE WILLIAM. 1841-1931. Canadian physician. Cited in: Kelly. Ross–Jones test.

Ross homocentric lens (Ross, Andrew): Photography. See: Focal Encyc. Photog. under "Lens History."

ROSS, HUGH CAMPBELL. 1875-1926. English pathologist. See: Who Was Who, 1916-1928. Ross's test (for syphilis).

ROSS, SIR JAMES CLARK. 1800-1862. Scottish polar explorer. See: World Who's Who Sci. Ross's gull, Ross's seal.

Ross–Jones test (Ross, Sir George William and Jones, Ernst): Medicine. See: Dorland; Kelly; Stedman.

ROSS, SIR RONALD. 1857-1932. English protozoologist. See: World Who's Who Sci. Ross's black spores, Ross's cycle.

Ross test (Derivation undetermined): Zoology. See: Winburne.

ROSS, W. fl. 1918-1920. Candian? chemist. Cited in: Chem. Abstr., Decenn. Index, 1917-1926. Ross feeder?

ROSSBACH, MICHAEL JOSEF. 1842-1899. German physician. See: Biog. Lex. hervorr. Aerzte. Rossbach's disease.

Rossbach's disease (Rossbach, Michael Josef): Medicine. See: Dorland; Jablonski.

ROSSBY, CARL–GUSTAF ARVID. 1898-1957. Swedish meteorologist. See: World Who's Who Sci. Rossby diagram, Rossby formula, Rossby number, Rossby parameter (or term), Rossby regime, Rossby wave(s).

Rossby diagram (Rossby, Carl–Gustaf Arvid): Earth Sciences. See: Huschke; Van Nostrand Sci. Encyc.

Rossby formula (Rossby, Carl–Gustaf Arvid): Earth Sciences. See: Huschke; Internat. Dict. Ap. Math.

Rossby number (Rossby, Carl–Gustaf Arvid): Earth Sciences. See: Huschke; Internat. Dict. Ap. Math.; Van Nostrand Sci. Encyc.

Rossby parameter (or term) (Rossby, Carl–Gustaf Arvid): Earth Sciences. See: Huschke.

Rossby regime (Rossby, Carl–Gustaf Arvid): Earth Sciences. See: Huschke.

Rossby wave(s) (Rossby, Carl–Gustaf Arvid): Earth Sciences. See: Huschke; Internat. Dict. Ap. Math.; Van Nostrand Sci. Encyc.

ROSSEL, OTTO. 1875-1911. Swiss physician. Cited in: Kelly. Rossel's test.

Rossel's test (Rossel, Otto): Medicine. See: Dorland; Stedman.

ROSSER, JOHN BARKLEY. 1900- . American mathematician. See: Amer. Men and Women Sci., 12th ed. Church–Rosser theorem.

Rossi–Celsi microreagent (Rossi, Luis and Celsi, Santiago A.): Chemistry. See: Van Nostrand Chem. Dict.

Rossi chloral hydrate reagent (Rossi, Luis): Chemistry. See: Van Nostrand Chem. Dict.

Rossi counter (Rossi, Harald H.?): Physics. See: Hughes.

ROSSI, ETTORE. fl. 1947. Swiss pediatrician. (Biography source unavailable.) Rossi's syndrome.

Rossi–Forel scale (or intensity scale) (De Rossi, Michele Stefano and Forel, Francois–Alphonse): Earth Sciences. See: Monkhouse; Thrush; Webster's 3d.

ROSSI, HARALD H. 1917- . Austrian-born American radiophysicist. See: World Who's Who Sci. Rossi counter?

ROSSI, LUIS. b. 1884. Argentine chemist. See: Pogg., vol. 6. Rossi–Celsi microreagent, Rossi chloral hydrate reagent.

Rossi test reaction for phosphates (Derivation undetermined): Chemistry. See: Van Nostrand Chem. Dict.

Rossie furnace (Derivation undetermined): Engineering and Industry. See: Thrush.

ROSSINI, GIOACHINNO ANTONIO. 1792-1868. Italian operatic composer. See: Encyc. Brit., 1973. a la Rossini, potage Rossini.

Rossi's crowd classifications (Rossi, Pasquale): Sociology. See: Zadrozny.

Rossi's syndrome (Rossi, Ettore). See: Guerin-Stern syndrome.

Rossite (Ross, Clarence Samuel): Earth Sciences. See: Thrush; Webster's 3d.

ROSSOLIMO, GRIGORIY IVANOVICH. 1860-1928. Russian neurologist. See: Who Was Who USSR. Rossolimo's reflex (or sign), Rossolino method?

Rossolimo's reflex (or sign) (Rossolimo, Grigoriy Ivanovich): Medicine. See: Dorland; Hinsie; Stedman.

Rossolino method (Rossolimo, Grigoriy Ivanovich?): Psychology. See: Drever.

Ross's black spores (Ross, Sir Ronald): Zoology. See: Dorland.

Ross's bodies (Ross, Edward Halford): Medicine. See: Dorland.

Ross's cycle (Ross, Sir Ronald): Zoology. See: Dorland.

Ross's goose (Ross, Bernard Rogan): Zoology. See: Mathews, M. M.; Pennak; Webster's 3d.

Ross's gull (Ross, Sir James Clark): Zoology. See: Gray; Pennak; Webster's 3d.

Ross's seal (Ross, Sir James Clark): Zoology. See: Pennak; Webster's 3d.

Ross's test (for syphilis) (Ross, Hugh Campbell): Medicine. See: Dorland.

ROSTAN, LEON LOUIS. 1790-1866. French physician. See: World Who's Who Sci. Rostan's asthma.

Rostan's asthma (Rostan, Leon Louis): Medicine. See: Dorland; Jablonski.

ROSTER, GIORGIO. fl. 1880. Italian mineralogist. Cited in: Royal Soc. Cat. Sci. Pap., 1874-1883. Rosterite.

Rosterite (Roster, Giorgio): Earth Sciences. See: Thrush.

ROSTHORN, FRANZ VON. fl. 1871. Carinthian geologist. Cited in: Hintze, vol. 1, pt. 4, half 2, p. 1417. Rosthornite.

Rosthornite (Rosthorn, Franz von): Engineering and Industry. See: Thrush.

Roswitha. See: Hrosvitha.

Rot-Bernhardt disease (Rot, Vladimir Karlovich and Bernhardt, Martin): Medicine. See: Jablonski. Also known as: Bernhardt's disease (or paralysis), Rot's meralgia.

Rot-Bielschowsky syndrome (Rot, Vladimir Karlovich and Bielschowsky, Alfred): Medicine. See: Jablonski.

ROT, VLADIMIR KARLOVICH. 1848-1916. Russian physician. See: Biog. Lex. hervorr. Aerzte. Rot-Bernhardt disease, Rot-Bielschowsky syndrome.

ROTCH, THOMAS MORGAN. 1848-1914. American physician. See: World Who's Who Sci. Rotch's sign.

Rotch's sign (Rotch, Thomas Morgan): Medicine. See: Dorland; Stedman.

ROTES-QUEROL, J. fl. 1950. French? physician. (Biography source unavailable.) Forestier and Rotes-Querol syndrome.

ROTH. fl. 1955-1958. Mathematician. (Biography source unavailable.) Roth's theorem.

ROTH, ALBRECHT WILHELM. 1757-1834. German physician and botanist. See: Biog. Lex. hervorr. Aerzte. Rothia.

ROTH, HUBERT. fl. 1930. German chemist. Cited in: Chem. Abstr., Decenn. Index, 1927-1936. Kuhn-Roth method.

ROTH, MORITZ. 1839-1914. Swiss pathologist. See: Biog. Lex. hervorr. Aerzte. Roth's spot, Roth's vas aberrans.

ROTH, PAUL. b. 1871. American physiologist. Cited in: Chem. Abstr., vol. 16, p. 2703. Benedict-Roth apparatus (or calorimeter)?

Roth solution (Derivation undetermined): Chemistry. See: Van Nostrand Chem. Dict.

Roth, Wladimir Karlowicz. See: Rot, Vladimir Karlovich.

ROTHENFUSSER, S. fl. 1910-1931. German food chemist. Cited in: Chem. Abstr., Decenn. Indexes, 1907-1916; 1927-1936. Hilger-Rothenfusser reagent, Rothenfusser test, Rothenfusser test for formaldehyde?

Rothenfusser test (Rothenfusser, S.): Chemistry. See: Winburne.

Rothenfusser test for formaldehyde (Rothenfusser, S.?): Chemistry. See: Van Nostrand Chem. Dict.

ROTHERA, ARTHUR CECIL HAMEL. 1880-1915. English biochemist. See: Bio-Chem. J. London, vol. 10 (1916-1917), pp. 11-13. Rothera solution, Rothera's test for acetone and acetoacetic acid in urine (or nitroprusside test).

Rothera solution (Rothera, Arthur Cecil Hamel): Chemistry. See: Van Nostrand Chem. Dict.

Rothera's test for acetone and acetoacetic acid in urine (or nitroprusside test) (Rothera, Arthur Cecil Hamel): Chemistry. See: Ballentyne; Stedman.

Rothia (Roth, Albrecht Wilhelm): Botany. See: Charnock.

Rothmann-Makai syndrome (Rothmann, Max and Makai, Endre): Medicine. See: Jablonski.

ROTHMANN, MAX. 1868-1915. German pathologist. See: Biog. Lex. hervorr. Aerzte. Rothmann-Makai syndrome.

ROTHMUND, AUGUST VON, JR. 1830-1906. German physician. See: Biog. Lex. hervorr. Aerzte. Rothmund's syndrome (or dystrophy).

Rothmund-Thomson syndrome (Rothmund, August von, Jr. and Thomson, M. Sidney). See: Rothmund's syndrome.

Rothmund's syndrome (or dystrophy) (Rothmund, August von, Jr.): Medicine. See: Jablonski; Stedman. Also known as: Bloch-Stauffer dyshormonal dermatosis, Rothmund-Thomson syndrome.

ROTHOFF, E. fl. 19th c. German? scientist. Cited in: Bailey. Rothoffite.

Rothoffite (Rothoff, E.): Earth Sciences. See: Thrush.

Rothrock grama (Rothrock, Joseph Trimble): Botany. See: Webster's 3d; Winburne.

ROTHROCK, JOSEPH TRIMBLE. 1839-1922. American physician and botanist. See: Dict. Amer. Biog. Rothrock grama.

Roth's spot (Roth, Moritz): Medicine. See: Dorland; Jablonski; Stedman.

Roth's theorem (Roth): Mathematics. See: Ballentyne.

Roth's vas aberrans (Roth, Moritz): Medicine. See: Donath; Dorland.

Rothschild (Rothschild, Meyer Amschel): Generic Word (millionaire). See: Brewer.

ROTHSCHILD, MEYER AMSCHEL. 1743-1812. German financier. See: Encyc. Brit., 1911. Rothschild.

ROTOR, ARTURO B. fl. 1949. Philippine internist. (Biography source unavailable.) Rotor's syndrome.

Rotor's syndrome (Rotor, Arturo B.): Medicine. See: Jablonski.

Rot's meralgia (Rot, Vladimir Karlovich). See: Rot-Bernhardt disease.

ROTTBOELL, CHRISTIAN FRIIS. 1727-1797. German anatomist and botanist. See: Biog. Lex. hervorr. Aerzte. Rottboella (or Rottbollia.)

Rottboella (or Rottbollia) (Rottboell, Christian Frues): Botany. See: Charnock.

Rotter board (Rotter, Julian Bernard): Psychology. See: English.

Rotter-Erb syndrome (Rotter, Wolfgang and Erb, Werner): Medicine. See: Jablonski.

ROTTER, HEINRICH. fl. 1937. German? physician in Hungary. Cited in: Chem. Abstr., vol. 31, p. 8577. Rotter's test.

Rotter incomplete sentence blank (Rotter, Julian Bernard): Psychology. See: Wolman.

ROTTER, JULIAN BERNARD. 1916- . American psychologist. See: Amer. Men and Women Sci., 12th ed. (Soc. Behav. Sci.). Rotter board, Rotter incomplete sentence blank.

ROTTER, WOLFGANG. 1910- . German pathologist. See: World Who's Who Sci., 1972. Rotter-Erb syndrome.

Rotter's test (Rotter, Heinrich): Medicine. See: Dorland.

ROUCHE, EUGENE. 1832-1910. French mathematician. See: World Who's Who Sci. Rouche's theorem.

Rouche's theorem (Rouche, Eugene): Mathematics. See: James.

Rouget cell (Rouget, Charles Marie Benjamin): Anatomy. See: Donath; Dorland; Stedman.

ROUGET, CHARLES MARIE BENJAMIN. 1824-1904. French physiologist. Cited in: Royal Soc. Cat. Sci. Pap., 1884-1900. Rouget cell, Rouget-Neumann sheath, Rouget's bulb (or veins), Rouget's muscle.

Rouget-Neumann sheath (Rouget, Charles Marie Benjamin and Neumann, Ernst F. C.): Anatomy. See: Stedman.

Rouget's bulb (or veins) (Rouget, Charles Marie Benjamin): Anatomy. See: Donath; Dorland; Stedman.

Rouget's muscle (Rouget, Charles Marie Benjamin). See: Mueller's muscle (2).

ROUGNON DE MAGNY, NICOLAS FRANCOIS. 1727-1799. French physician. See: World Who's Who Sci. Rougnon de Magny's disease.

Rougnon-Heberden disease (Rougnon de Magny, Nicolas Francois and Heberden, William). See: Heberden's asthma.

ROUND, H. J. fl. 20th c. English engineer. Cited in: Glazebrook. Round valve?

Round valve (Round, H. J.?): Engineering and Industry. See: Hughes.

ROUS, FRANCIS PEYTON. 1879-1970. American physician. See: Who Was Who Amer., vol. 5. Rous sarcoma (or tumor).

Rous sarcoma (or tumor) (Rous, Francis Peyton): Medicine. See: Dorland; Jablonski; Stedman.

Rouse-Shearer (or R & S) plastometer (Rouse and Shearer, W. L.?): Engineering and Industry. See: Thrush. Also known as: Shearer plastometer.

Roussea (Rousseau, Jean Jacques): Botany. See: Charnock.

ROUSSEAU. fl. early 20th c. French physicist. (Biography source unavailable.) Rousseau diagram.

Rousseau diagram (Rousseau): Physics. See: Internat. Dict. Phys. Elec.

ROUSSEAU, JEAN JACQUES. 1712-1778. French philosopher and author. See: Internat. Encyc. Soc. Sci. Roussea, Rousseauism (or Rousseauian).

Rousseauism (or Rousseauian) (Rousseau, Jean Jacques): Philosophy. See: Partridge; Webster's 3d.

ROUSSEL, G. fl. 1936. French chemist. Cited in: Chem. Abstr., vol. 30, 2216. Gruzewska-Roussel test.

ROUSSEL, THEOPHILE VICTOR JEAN BAPTISTE. 1816-1903. French physician. See: Biog. Lex. hervorr. Aerzte. Roussel's sign.

Roussel's sign (Roussel, Theophile Victor Jean Baptiste): Medicine. See: Dorland.

ROUSSIN, FRANCOIS-ZACHARIE. 1817-1894. French chemist. See: World Who's Who Sci. Roussin's salt.

Roussin's salt (Roussin, Francois-Zacharie): Chemistry. See: Hackh; Webster's 3d.

Roussy-Cornil syndrome (Roussy, Gustave and Cornil, Lucien): Medicine. See: Jablonski.

Roussy-Dejerine syndrome (Roussy, Gustave and Dejerine, Joseph Jules). See: Dejerine-Roussy syndrome.

ROUSSY, GUSTAVE. 1874-1948. French pathologist and neurologist. See: World Who's Who Sci. Darier-Roussy sarcoid, Dejerine-Roussy syndrome, Roussy-Cornil syndrome, Roussy-Levy syndrome (or disease).

Roussy-Levy syndrome (or disease) (Roussy, Gustave and Levy, Gabrielle): Medicine. See: Dorland; Jablonski; Stedman.

ROUTH, EDWARD JOHN. 1831-1907. English mathematician. See: Dict. Nat. Biog., 2d suppl. Routh('s) rule of inertia.

Routh('s) rule of inertia (Routh, Edward John): Mathematics. See: Ballentyne; Internat. Dict. Ap. Math.

ROUVIERE, HENRI. b. 1875. French anatomist and embryologist. See: Biog. Lex. hervorr. Aerzte. node of Rouviere.

ROUX, CESAR. 1857-1926. Swiss surgeon. See: Biog. Lex. hervorr. Aerzte. Roux-en-Y operation, Roux's sign.

Roux-en-Y operation (Roux, Cesar): Medicine. See: Stedman.

ROUX, PHILIBERT JOSEPH. 1780-1854. French surgeon. See: World Who's Who Sci. Roux's method.

ROUX, PIERRE PAUL EMILE. 1853-1933. French bacteriologist. See: World Who's Who Sci. Roux serum, Roux's stain.

Roux serum (Roux, Pierre Paul Emile): Medicine. See: Dorland; Stedman.

Roux's method (Roux, Philibert Joseph): Medicine. See: Dorland; Stedman.

Roux's sign (Roux, Cesar): Medicine. See: Dorland.

Roux's stain (Roux, Pierre Paul Emile): Medicine. See: Stedman.

Rover effect (Derivation undetermined): Engineering and Industry. See: Auger.

ROVIGHI, ALBERTO. 1856-1919. Italian physician. See: Biog. Lex. hervorr. Aerzte. Rovighi's sign.

Rovighi's sign (Rovighi, Alberto): Medicine. See: Dorland.

ROVSING, NIELS THORKILD. 1862-1927. Danish surgeon. See: World Who's Who Sci. Rovsing's sign.

Rovsing's sign (Rovsing, Niels Thorkild): Medicine. See: Dorland; Stedman.

Rowan boiler (Rowan, J. M.): Engineering and Industry. See: Auger.

ROWAN, J. M. fl. 1858. English? engineer. (Biography source unavailable.) Rowan boiler.

ROWE, GEORGE. fl. 1937. American mineralogist. Cited in: Amer. Min., vol. 22 (1937), pp. 301-303. Roweite.

Roweite (Rowe, George): Earth Sciences. See: Thrush; Webster's 3d.

Rowites (Campbell, John McLeod). See: Campbellite(s).

Rowland (or Rowland's value) (Rowland, Henry Augustus): Physics. See: Dresner; Hackh.

Rowland circle (Rowland, Henry Augustus): Physics. See: Ballentyne; Internat. Dict. Phys. Elec.; Thewlis.

Rowland ghosts (Rowland, Henry Augustus): Physics. See: Internat. Dict. Phys. Elec.; Thewlis.

Rowland grating (Rowland, Henry Augustus): Physics. See: Thewlis.

ROWLAND, HENRY AGUSTUS. 1848-1901. American physicist. See: World Who's Who Sci. Joule-Rowland method for mechanical equivalent of heat, Rowland (or Rowland's value), Rowland circle, Rowland ghosts, Rowland grating, Rowland mounting (or mount), Rowlandite.

Rowland mounting (or mount): Physics. See: Internat. Dict. Phys. Elec.; Thewlis; Van Nostrand Sci. Encyc. under "Reflection Grating."

ROWLAND, RUSSELL STURGIS. 1874-1938. American physician. See: Amer. J. Dis. Child., vol. 57 (Jan. 1939), p. 170. Hand-Rowland disease.

Rowlandite (Rowland, Henry Augustus): Earth Sciences. See: Thrush; Webster's 3d.

Rowlatt Act(s) (Rowlatt, Sir Sidney Arthur Taylor): Politics. See: Morris and Irwin; Steinberg.

ROWLATT, SIR SIDNEY ARTHUR TAYLOR. 1862-1945. English judge. See: Ann. Register. Rowlatt Act(s).

ROWLEY, PETER TEMPLETON. 1929- . American geneticist. See: Amer. Men and Women Sci., 12th ed. Rowley-Rosenberg syndrome.

The Rowley poems (Rowley, Thomas): Literature. See: Barnhart(Eng. Lit.); Brewer; Phyfe.

Rowley-Rosenberg syndrome (Rowley, Peter Templeton and Rosenberg, Leon Emanuel): Medicine. See: Jablonski.

ROWLEY, THOMAS. fl. 15th c. Mythical English priest. See: Dict. Nat. Biog. under "Chatterton, Thomas." The Rowley poems.

Rowntree and Geraghty test (Rowntree, Leonard George and Geraghty, John Timothy): Medicine. See: Dorland; Stedman.

ROWNTREE, LEONARD GEORGE. b. 1883. American physician. See: World Who's Who Sci. Rowntree and Geraghty test.

ROXBURGH, WILLIAM. 1751-1815. Scottish botanist. See: Dict. Nat. Biog. Roxburghia.

Roxburghe, 3d Duke of. See: Ker, John (3d Duke of Roxburghe).

Roxburghe binding (Ker, John): Library Science. See: Harrod; Partridge.

Roxburghe Club (Ker, John): Literature. See: Brewer; Harvey; Latham.

Roxburghia (Roxburgh, William): Botany. See: Charnock.

ROY, CLAUDE CHARLES. 1928- . Canadian pediatrician and gastroenterologist. See: Amer. Men and Women Sci., 12th ed. Scriver-Goldbloom-Roy syndrome.

ROY, J. N. fl. 1936. Canadian physician. (Biography source unavailable.) Roy-Jutras syndrome.

ROY, JAMES EVANS. 1914- . American psychiatrist. See: Direct. Med. Specialists, 1965-1966. Friedman-Roy syndrome.

Roy-Jutras syndrome (Roy, J. N. and Jutras, Albert). See: Uehlinger's syndrome.

ROY, S. N. fl. 1937. Indian chemist. Cited in: Chem. Abstr., vol. 31, p. 7192. Chakravarti-Roy test reaction.

Royal Order of Victoria and Albert (Victoria, Queen and Albert, King): History. Cited in: Encyc. Brit., 1973 under "Knighthood."

ROYCE, JOSIAH. 1855-1916. American philosopher. See: Dict. Amer. Biog. Roycean.

Roycean (Royce, Josiah): Philosophy. See: Webster's 3d.

ROYEN, ADRIAN VAN. 1704-1779. Dutch botanist. See: Nieuw Nederl. Biog. Woordenb. Royena.

Royena (Royen, Adrian van): Botany. See: Webster's 3d.

ROYER-COLLARD, PIERRE PAUL "DOCTRINAIRE." 1763-1845. French philosopher and politician. See: Encyc. Brit., 1973. Doctrinaire.

ROYER, PIERRE. 1917- . French pediatrician. See: Who's Who Sci. Europe, 1972. Royer's syndrome.

Royer's syndrome (Royer, Pierre): Medicine. See: Jablonski.

Roy's syndrome (Roy, J. N.). See: Uehlinger's syndrome.

Roystonea (Stone, Roy): Botany. See: Hendrickson; Taylor, N.; Webster's 3d.

Rozan process (Rozan). See: Luce and Rozan process.

ROZIN, SAMUEL. fl. 1930. Swiss? physician. (Biography source unavailable.) Zondek-Bromberg-Rozin syndrome?

RUBARTH, SVEN (In full: CARL SVEN). 1905- . Swedish veterinarian. See: Who's Who Sci. Europe, 1972. Rubarth's disease.

Rubarth's disease (Rubarth, Sven): Medicine. See: Jablonski; Stedman; Webster's 3d.

Rube Goldberg (Goldberg, Reuben Lucius): Generic Word (impractical invention). See: Hendrickson; Webster's 3d.

Rubel test for nitrite (Rubel, W. M.): Chemistry. See: Van Nostrand Chem. Dict.

RUBEL, W. M. fl. 1930. German? chemist. Cited in: Chem. Abstr., vol. 25, p. 3928. Rubel test for nitrite.

Rubenesque (Rubens, Peter Paul): Fine Arts. See: Webster's 3d.

Ruben's brown (Rubens, Peter Paul): Fine Arts. See: Thrush.

RUBENS, HEINRICH. 1865-1922. German physicist. See: World Who's Who Sci. Hagen-Rubens relation.

Rubens' madder (Rubens, Peter Paul): Fine Arts. See: Webster's 3d.

RUBENS, PETER PAUL. 1577-1640. Flemish painter. See: Bryan. Rubenesque, Ruben's brown, Rubens' madder.

Rubicon micro-volt potentiometer (Derivation undetermined): Physics. See: Internat. Dict. Phys. Elec.

RUBIN, EDGAR J. 1886-1951. Danish phenomenologist. See: Kraks Bla Bog., 1949. Rubin's figure (or goblet figure).

RUBIN, ISIDOR CLINTON. 1883-1958. American physician. See: New York Times, July 11, 1958, p. 23, col. 1. Rubin test.

RUBIN, LOUIS CARL. 1905- . American chemical engineer. See: Amer. Men Sci., 9th ed. Benedict-Webb-Rubin equation.

Rubin test (Rubin, Isidor Clinton): Medicine. See: Dorland; Stedman; Webster's 3d.

Rubino's reaction (Derivation undetermined): Medicine. See: Stedman.

Rubin's figure (or goblet figure) (Rubin, Edgar J.): Psychology. See: Drever; English; Wolman.

RUBINSTEIN, HELENA. d. 1965. Polish-born American business executive. See: Who Was Who Amer., vol. 4. Helena Rubinstein prize.

RUBINSTEIN, JACK HERBERT. 1925- . American child psychiatrist and pediatrician. See: Direct. Med. Specialists, 1974-1975. Rubinstein (Rubenstein)-Taybi syndrome.

Rubinstein (Rubenstein)-Taybi syndrome (Rubinstein, Jack Herbert and Taybi, Hooshang): Medicine. See: Hinsie; Jablonski; Stedman.

Ruble hydraulic elevator (Derivation undetermined): Engineering and Industry. See: Thrush.

RUBNER, MAX. 1854-1932. German hygienist and biochemist. See: World Who's Who Sci. Rubner's laws of growth, Rubner's test for dextrose and lactose.

Rubner's laws of growth (Rubner, Max): Medicine. See: Dorland; Stedman.

Rubner's test for dextrose and lactose (Rubner, Max): Medicine. See: Dorland; Stedman; Van Nostrand Chem. Dict.

RUCK, KARL VON. 1849-1922. American physician. See: Biog. Lex. hervorr. Aerzte. Ruck's tuberculin.

RUCKER, E. fl. 1836. American politician. (Biography source unavailable.) Ruckerize.

Ruckerize (Rucker, E.): Politics. See: Mathews, M. M.

Ruck's tuberculin (Ruck, Karl von): Medicine. See: Dorland; Stedman.

RUD, EINAR. b. 1892. Danish physician. See: Kraks Bla Bog, 1949. Rud's syndrome.

RUD, M. I. fl. 1938. Russian chemist. Cited in: Chem. Abstr., vol. 32, p. 4459. Shapiro-Rud test.

RUDBECK, OLOF. 1630-1702. Swedish scientist. See: World Who's Who Sci. Rudbeckia.

Rudbeckia (Rudbeck, Olof): Botany. See: Hendrickson; Taylor, N.; Webster's 3d.

RUDD. fl. 1888. English adventurer. Cited in: Dict. Nat. Biog., 2d suppl. under "Rhodes, Cecil John," p. 185. Rudd concession.

Rudd concession (Rudd): History. See: Morris and Irwin.

Rudin's law (Derivation undetermined): Sociology. See: Martin.

Rudisch-Boroschek reagent (Rudisch, Julius and Boroschek, L.): Chemistry. See: Van Nostrand Chem. Dict.

RUDISCH, JULIUS. b. 1847. American physician. Cited in: Index-Cat. Libr. Surg.-Gen. Off., 1st Ser., vol. 12, 1891. Rudisch-Boroschek reagent.

Rudolf II (Holy Roman emperor). See: Rudolph II.

RUDOLF, ALEXANDER J. fl. 1895. American librarian. See: Ranz, p. 89-91. Rudolf continuous indexer.

Rudolf continuous indexer (Rudolf, Alexander J.): Library Science. See: Thompson.

Rudolfi, Max. See: Rudolphi, Max.

Rudolfi's equation (Rudolphi, Max): Chemistry. See: Hackh.

RUDOLPH II. 1552-1612. Holy Roman emperor. See: Encyc. Brit., 1911. Rudolphine tables.

RUDOLPH, O. fl. 1921. German chemist. Cited in: Chem. Abstr., vol. 15, p. 3798. Rudolph test reaction.

RUDOLPH OF HAPSBURG. 1858-1889. Archduke of Austria. See: Neue Osterr. Biog. Archduke trio.

Rudolph test reaction (Rudolph, O.): Chemistry. See: Van Nostrand Chem. Dict.

RUDOLPHI, MAX. fl. 1895. German chemist. Cited in: Partington, vol. 4; Royal Soc. Cat. Sci. Pap., 1884-1900. Rudolfi's equation.

Rudolphine tables (Rudolph II): Astronomy. See: Phyfe; Webster's 3d.

Rudorff mirrors (Derivation undetermined): Physics. See: Thewlis.

ud's syndrome (Rud, Einar): Medicine. See: Jablonski.

uecking algorithm (Ruecking, Frederick Henry, Jr.): Library Science. See: . Libr. Automation, vol. 1, no. 4 (Dec., 1968), pp. 227-238.

UECKING, FREDERICK HENRY, JR. 1926- . American data processor. ee: Who's Who Libr. Serv., 1966. Ruecking algorithm.

UEGHEIMER, LEOPOLD. 1850-1917. German pharmaceutical chemist. See: ogg., vols. 3, 4, 5. Staedel-Ruegheimer pyrazine synthesis.

UEL, JEAN (RUELLIUS). 1479-1539. French physician and botanist. See: ouv. Biog. Univ. Ruellia.

UELF, J. fl. 1913-1914. German psychiatrist. Cited in: Index-Med. 2d er., vol. 11, 1914. Rulf's convulsions?

uellia (Ruel, Jean): Botany. See: Taylor, N.; Webster's 3d.

UEPING, MAX. fl. 1912. German timber engineer. Cited in: Chem. bstr., Decenn. Indexes, 1907-1916; 1917-1926. Rueping process.

ueping process (Rueping, Max): Engineering and Industry. See: Thrush; Vebster's 3d.

UEPPELL, EDUARD (In full: WILHELM PETER EDUARD SIMON). 1794-1884. German naturalist and explorer in Africa. See: New Encyc. Brit., 1974, Microp. Ruppell's griffon, Ruppell's robin-chat, Ruppell's warbler.

UFA, ACHMET. fl. 12th c. Religious leader. (Biography source available- ble.) Rufa'i.

ufa'i (Rufa, Achmet): Religion. See: Canney.

uff degradation (Ruff, Otto): Chemistry. See: Ballentyne.

uff-Fenton degradation (Ruff, Otto and Fenton, Henry John Horstman): hemistry. See: Van Nostrand Chem. Dict.

UFF, OTTO (In full: KARL OTTO). 1871-1939. German chemist. See: ogg., vols. 4, 5, 6. Ruff degradation, Ruff-Fenton degradation.

UFFINI, ANGELO. 1864-1929. Italian anatomist. See: Biog. Lex. hervorr. erzte. Ruffini('s) corpuscles (nerve endings, organs, cylinder or brushes), Ruffini apillary endings (or plumes).

uffini('s) corpuscles (nerve endings, organs, cylinder or brushes) (Ruffini, Angelo): natomy. See: Donath; Dorland; Henderson; Stedman; Wolman.

uffini papillary endings (or plumes) (Ruffini, Angelo): Anatomy. See: nglish; Wolman.

uffmann test (Derivation undetermined): Medicine. See: Stedman.

uge-Phillipp test (Ruge, Reinhold and Philipp, Ernst): Medicine. See: orland.

RUGE, REINHOLD. 1862-1936. German physician. See: Biog. Lex. hervorr. Aerzte. Ruge-Phillipp test.

RUGEL, FERDINAND. 1806-1879? German botanist. See: Biog. Notes Upon Botanists. Rugel's plantain.

Rugel's plantain (Rugel, Ferdinand): Botany. See: Webster's 3d.

RUGGERI, RUGGERO. fl. 1898. Italian chemist. Cited in: Royal Soc. Cat. Sci. Pap., 1884-1900. Tortelli-Ruggeri test for peanut oil.

Ruggles-Coles dryer (Ruggles, W. B. and Coles, W. J.): Engineering and ndustry. See: Thrush.

Ruggles press (Derivation undetermined): Printing. See: Lockwood, under "Press," p. 446.

RUGGLES, W. B. fl. 1910. English engineer. Cited in: Chem. Abstr., Decenn. Index, 1907-1916. Ruggles-Coles dryer.

RUGGLI, PAUL (In full: EMIL PAUL). b. 1884. Swiss chemist. See: Pogg., vols. 5, 6. Ruggli principle.

Ruggli principle (Ruggli, Paul): Chemistry. See: Ballentyne.

Ruhmkorff coil (Ruhmkorff, Heinrich Daniel): Electronics. See: Hackh; Hughes; Webster's 3d.

RUHMKORFF, HEINRICH DANIEL. 1803-1877. German electrician. See: World Who's Who Sci. Ruhmkorff coil.

RUITER, M. fl. 1948-1953. Dutch physician. (Biography source unavailable.) Gougerot-Ruiter syndrome, Ruiter-Pompen-Wyers syndrome.

Ruiter-Pompen syndrome (Ruiter, M. and Pompen, Arnold Willem Maria). See: Fabry's syndrome.

Ruiter-Pompen-Wyers syndrome (Ruiter, M.; Pompen, Arnold Willem Maria; and Wyers, Herman Joseph Gerard). See: Fabry's syndrome.

RUIZ, HIPPOLITO. fl. 1813. Spanish botanist. Cited in: Royal Soc. Cat. Sci. Pap., 1800-1863. Ruizia.

Ruizia (Ruiz, Hippolito): Botany. See: Charnock.

the Rule in Shelley's Case (Derivation undetermined): Law. See: Black.

Rule of Saint Anthony (Anthony, Saint): Religion. See: Attwater.

Rule of St. Basil. See: Basilian rule.

Rule of St. Benedict (Benedict of Nursia, Saint): Religion. See: Attwater; Good.

Rule of Saint Columbanus (Columbanus, Saint): Religion. See: Attwater; Canney.

Rule of St. Dominic (Dominic, Saint): Religion. See: Attwater.

Rule of St. Francis (Francis of Assisi, Saint): Religion. See: Attwater.

Rule of Saint Pachomius (Pachomius, Saint): Religion. See: Attwater.

Rulf's convulsions (Ruelf, J.): Medicine. See: Jablonski.

Rulon formula for reliability (Rulon, Phillip Justin): Education. See: Good.

RULON, PHILLIP JUSTIN. 1900- . American educational psychologist. See: Amer. Men Sci., 10th ed. Rulon formula for reliability.

Rumbold (and Rumble) (carriage) (Derivation undetermined): Generic Word. See: Charnock.

Rumford, Count. See: Thompson, Sir Benjamin (Count Rumford).

Rumford Medal (Thompson, Sir Benjamin, Count Rumford): Physics. See: Hendrickson; Phyfe.

Rumford professorship (Thompson, Sir Benjamin, Count Rumford): Physics. Cited in: World Who's Who Sci.

Rumford stove (Thompson, Sir Benjamin, Count Rumford): Engineering and Industry. See: Charnock; Hendrickson; Mathews, M. M.

Rumford's photometer (Thompson, Sir Benjamin, Count Rumford): Physics. See: Thrush.

Rumi. See: Jalal-Ud-Din Rumi.

RUMMO, GAETANO. 1853-1917. Italian physician. See: Biog. Lex. hervorr. Aerzte. Rummo's disease.

Rummo's disease (Rummo, Gaetano): Medicine. See: Dorland; Jablonski.

Rumpel-Leede test (sign or phenomenon) (Rumpel, Theodor and Leede, Carl Stockbridge): Medicine. See: Stedman.

Rumpel operation (Rumpel, Theodor): Medicine. See: Kelly.

RUMPEL, THEODOR. 1862-1923. German physician. See: Biog. Lex. hervorr. Aerzte. Rumpel-Leede test (sign or phenomenon), Rumpel operation.

Rumpf('s) sign (or symptom) (Rumpf, Theodor): Medicine. See: Dorland; Hinsie; Stedman.

RUMPF, THEODOR. 1851-1923. German physician. See: Biog. Lex. hervorr. Aerzte. Rumpf('s) sign (or symptom).

RUMPH, ELBERTA. fl. ca. 1870. Wife of American cultivator. (Biography source unavailable.) Elberta peach.

Rundles-Falls syndrome (Rundles, Ralph Wayne and Falls, Harold Francis): Medicine. See: Jablonski.

RUNDLES, RALPH WAYNE. 1911- . American internist. See: Amer. Men and Women Sci., 12th ed. Rundles-Falls syndrome.

RUNEBERG, JOHAN WILHELM. 1843-1918. Finnish physician. See: Biog. Lex. hervorr. Aerzte. Runeberg's anemia, Runeberg's formula.

Runeberg's anemia (Runeberg, Johan Wilhelm): Medicine. See: Jablonski; Stedman.

Runeberg's formula (Runeberg, Johan Wilhelm): Medicine. See: Dorland; Stedman.

RUNGE, CARL DAVID TOLME. 1856-1927. German mathematician. See: World Who's Who Sci. Paschen-Runge mounting, Runge-Kutta method, Runge's law, Runge's rule, Schumann-Runge bands, Schumann-Runge continuum.

RUNGE, HANS. 1892-1964. German obstetrician. Cited in: Index-Cat. Libr. Surg.-Gen. Off., 5th Ser., vol. 1, 1959. Ballantyne-Runge syndrome.

Runge-Kutta method (Runge, Carl David Tolme and Kutta, Martin Wilhelm): Mathematics. See: Ballentyne; Internat. Dict. Ap. Math.; James.

RUNGE, MAX. 1849-1909. German gynecologist. See: Biog. Lex. hervorr. Aerzte. Runge's method.

Runge's law (Runge, Carl David Tolme): Physics. See: Ballentyne.

Runge's method (Runge, Max): Medicine. See: Dorland.

Runge's rule (Runge, Carl David Tolme): Physics. See: Ballentyne.

Runge's syndrome (Runge, Hans). See: Ballantyne-Runge syndrome.

Ruoss jig (Ruoss, Walter): Engineering and Industry. See: Thrush.

RUOSS, WALTER. fl. 1936. German? engineer. Cited in: Chem. Abstr., Decenn. Index, 1937-1946. Ruoss jig.

RUOTTE, PAUL. b. 1862. French surgeon. Cited in: Index-Cat. Libr. Surg.-Gen. Off., 1st Ser., vol. 21, 1891. Ruotte's operation.

Ruotte's operation (Ruotte, Paul): Medicine. See: Stedman.

Rupe-Becherer reagent (Rupe, Hans and Becherer, Fritz): Chemistry. See: Van Nostrand Chem. Dict.

RUPE, HANS. 1866-1951. Swiss chemist. See: World Who's Who Sci. Rupe-Becherer reagent.

RUPERT OF BAVARIA. 1869-1955. German military commander. See: Webster's Biog. Dict. Rupert (stationary balloon).

RUPERT, PRINCE. 1619-1682. German-English military leader and scientist. See: Dict. Nat. Biog. Prince Rupert('s) drops, Prince Rupert's metal.

Rupert (stationary balloon) (Rupert of Bavaria): Engineering and Industry. See: Partridge.

Rupert's drops (Rupert, Prince). See: Prince Rupert('s) drops.

RUPP, ERWIN TH. b. 1872. German pharmaceutical chemist. See: Pogg., vols. 5, 6. Rupp-Poggendorf reagent.

RUPP, HEINRICH B. (RUPPIUS). d. 1719. German botanist. (Biography source unavailable.) Ruppia.

RUPP, PHILIP. b. 1862. American chemist. See: Amer. Men Sci., 4th ed. Rupp's test.

Rupp-Poggendorf reagent (Rupp, Erwin Th. and Poggendorf, Adolf): Chemistry. See: Van Nostrand Chem. Dict.

Ruppell's griffon (Rueppell, Eduard): Zoology. See: Gray.

Ruppell's robin-chat (Rueppell, Eduard): Zoology. See: Gray.

Ruppell's warbler (Rueppell, Eduard): Zoology. See: Gray.

Ruppia (Rupp, Heinrich B.): Botany. See: Webster's 3d.

Rupp's test (Rupp, Philip): Chemistry. See: Hackh.

RUSCONI, MAURO. 1776-1849. Italian biologist. See: Biog. Lex. hervorr. Aerzte. Rusconi's anus.

Rusconi's anus (Rusconi, Mauro): Medicine. See: Dorland.

Rush-Bagot agreement (Rush, Richard and Bagot, Sir Charles): History. See: Morris.

RUSH, RICHARD. 1780-1859. American statesman and diplomat. See: Dict. Amer. Biog. Rush-Bagot agreement.

RUSHTON, STANLEY. 1920- . English mathematical statistician. See: Who's Who Brit. Sci., 1953. WAGR test.

RUSKIN, JOHN. 1819-1900. English art critic and sociological writer. See: Dict. Nat. Biog. Ruskin School, Ruskinian.

Ruskin School (Ruskin, John): Fine Arts. See: Osborne.

Ruskinian (Ruskin, John): Literature. See: Partridge; Webster's 3d.

Russel Haden. See: Haden, Russel L.

Russel press (Derivation undetermined): Printing. See: Lockwood.

Russelia (Russell, Alexander): Botany. See: Charnock; Taylor, N.; Webster's 3d.

RUSSELL. No dates. English? manufacturer. (Biography source unavailable.) Russell (cord).

RUSSELL, ALEXANDER. ca. 1715-1768. Scottish physician at Aleppo. See: Dict. Nat. Biog. Russelia.

RUSSELL, ALEXANDER. fl. 1935-1964. English pediatrician. See: Med. Direct., 1964. Russell's syndrome (1) (or dwarf), Russell's syndrome (2).

Russell angles (Russell, Henry Norris?): Mathematics. See: Internat. Dict. Ap. Math.

RUSSELL, ARTHUR EDWARD IAN MONTAGU. 1878-1964. English mineralogist. See: Who Was Who, 1961-1970. Arthurite, Russellite.

RUSSELL, BERTRAND ARTHUR WILLIAM. 1872-1970. English mathematician and philosopher. See: New Encyc. Brit., 1974. Russellian, Russell's paradox.

Russell (Russel's) bodies (Russell, William): Anatomy. See: Donath; Dorland; Stedman.

RUSSELL, CHARLES TAZE. 1852-1916. American religious leader. See: Dict. Amer. Biog. Russellite.

Russell (cord) (Russell): Generic Word. See: Partridge.

Russell diagram (Russell, Henry Norris). See: Hertzsprung-Russell (or H-N) diagram.

Russell effect (Russell, William James): Photography. See: Van Nostrand Sci. Encyc. Also known as: Vogel-Colson-Russell effect.

RUSSELL, FRANCIS, 4TH EARL OF BEDFORD. 1593-1641. English nobleman. See: Dict. Nat. Biog. Bedford level.

RUSSELL, HENRY NORRIS. 1877-1957. American astronomer and astrophysicist. See: World Who's Who Sci. Hertzsprung-Russell (or H-N) diagram, Russell angles?, Russell mixture, Russell-Saunders coupling, Russell-Saunders notation.

RUSSELL, JAMES THOMAS. 1902- . American psychologist. See: Amer. Psych. Assoc. Direct., 1948. Taylor-Russell tables.

RUSSELL, JOHN, 4TH DUKE OF BEDFORD. 1710-1771. English statesman and diplomat. See: Dict. Nat. Biog. Bedford protest.

RUSSELL, LILLIAN (Real name: HELEN LOUISE LEONARD). 1861-1922. American singer and actress. See: New Encyc. Brit., 1974, Microp. Lillian Russell costume, Lillian Russell (dessert).

Russell mixture (Russell, Henry Norris): Astronomy. See: Satterthwaite.

RUSSELL, PATRICK. 1727-1805. English physician at Aleppo. See: Dict. Nat. Biog. Russell's viper.

RUSSELL, R. HAMILTON. fl. 1924. Australian surgeon. Cited in: Kelly. Russell traction.

Russell-Saunders coupling (Russell, Henry Norris and Saunders, Frederick Albert): Physics. See: Ballentyne; Internat. Dict. Ap. Math.; Internat. Dict. Phys. Elec.

Russell-Saunders notation (Russell, Henry Norris and Saunders, Frederick Albert): Physics. See: Hackh.

RUSSELL, SIR THOMAS WALLACE. 1841-1920. Scottish-Irish politician. See: Who Was Who, 1916-1928. Russellites.

Russell traction (Russell, R. Hamilton): Medicine. See: Stedman.

RUSSELL, WILLIAM. 1852-1940. Scottish physician. See: Who Was Who, 1929-1940. Russell (Russel's) bodies.

RUSSELL, WILLIAM JAMES. 1830-1909. English photographic chemist. See: Pogg., vols. 3, 4, 5. Russell effect.

Russellian (Russell, Bertrand Arthur William): Philosophy. See: Webster's 3d.

Russellite (Russell, Arthur Edward Ian Montagu): Earth Sciences. See: Thrush.

Russellite (Russell, Charles Taze): Religion. See: Webster's 3d.

Russellites (Russell, Sir Thomas Wallace): Politics. See: Montgomery.

Russell's paradox (Russell, Bertrand Arthur William): Mathematics. See: James; Webster's 3d.

ussell's syndrome (1) (or dwarf) (Russell, Alexander): Medicine. See: ablonski.

ussell's syndrome (2) (Russell, Alexander): Medicine. See: Jablonski.

ussell's viper (Russell, Patrick): Zoology. See: Stedman; Webster's 3d.

USSO, MARIO. b. 1866. Italian physician. Cited in: Kelly. Russo's eaction.

usso's reaction (Russo, Mario): Medicine. See: Dorland; Stedman.

ust cotton picker (Rust, John Daniel and Rust, Mack Donald): Engineering nd Industry. Cited in: Webster's Biog. Dict.

UST, JOHANN NEPOMUK. 1775-1840. Austrian surgeon. See: Biog. ex. hervorr. Aerzte. Rust's disease, Rust's phenomenon.

UST, JOHN DANIEL. 1892-1954. American inventor. See: Who Was Who Amer., vol. 3. Rust cotton picker.

UST, MACK DONALD. 1900-1966. American inventor. See: Who Was Who Amer., vol. 4. Rust cotton picker.

ustig test reaction for cobalt (Derivation undetermined): Chemistry. See: an Nostrand Chem. Dict.

USTITSKII, J. VON. fl. 1873. German surgeon. Cited in: Royal Soc. at. Sci. Pap., 1800-1883; 1874-1883. Rustitskii's disease.

ustitskii's disease (Rustitskii, J. von). See: Kahler's syndrome.

ust's disease (Rust, Johann Nepomuk): Medicine. See: Dorland; Jablonski; tedman.

ust's phenomenon (Rust, Johann Nepomuk): Medicine. See: Dorland; tedman.

utger(s) equation (Rutgers, Arend Joan): Physics. See: Ballentyne; Thewlis.

UTGERS, AREND JOAN. 1903- . Dutch physical chemist. See: Who's Who Sci. Europe, 1972. Rutger(s) equation.

UTH, GEORGE HERMAN "BABE." 1895-1948. American professional base-all player. See: New Encyc. Brit., 1974, Microp. Babe Ruth, Ruthian blast.

utherford (Rutherford, Lord Ernest): Physics. See: Dresner; Internat. Dict. hys. Elec.; Van Nostrand Sci. Encyc.

utherford atom (atomic theory or nuclear atom) (Rutherford, Lord Ernest): hysics. See: Hackh; Hughes; Internat. Dict. Phys. Elec.

UTHERFORD, LORD ERNEST, 1ST BARON RUTHERFORD. 1871-1937. New ealand-born English physicist. See: World Who's Who Sci. Rutherford, utherford atom (atomic theory or nuclear atom), Rutherford scattering (or cross-ection), Rutherfordine, Rutherfordium.

UTHERFORD, FOREST. b. 1871. American metallurgical engineer. See: Who's Who Engin., 1922-1923. Rutherford solution?

RUTHERFORD, R. S. G. fl. 1954. English statistician. Cited in: Kendall nd Doig. Rutherford's contagious distribution.

utherford scattering (or cross-section) (Rutherford, Lord Ernest): Physics. See: allentyne; Internat. Dict. Ap. Math.; Internat. Dict. Phys. Elec.

utherford solution (Rutherford, Forest?): Chemistry. See: Van Nostrand hem. Dict.

utherfordine (Rutherford, Lord Ernest): Earth Sciences. See: Thrush; Webster's 3d.

utherfordium (Rutherford, Lord Ernest): Chemistry. See: Barnhart, (New ng.)

utherford's contagious distribution (Rutherford, R. S. G.): Statistics. See: Kendall.

RUTHERFURD, MARGARET ELIZABETH. fl. 1910-1964. English surgeon. See: Med. Direct., 1964. Rutherfurd's syndrome.

Rutherfurd's syndrome (Rutherfurd, Margaret Elizabeth): Medicine. See: Jablonski.

Ruthian blast (Ruth, George Herman): Recreation and Sports. See: Hendrick-son.

Ruths accumulator (Ruths, Johannes Carl): Engineering and Industry. See: Auger.

RUTHS, JOHANNES CARL. 1879-1935. Swedish engineer. See: Svenska Maen Och Kvinnor. Ruths accumulator.

RUTHVEN, JOHN. fl. 1813. Scottish printer. (Biography source unavail-able.) Ruthven press.

RUTHVEN, JOHN, 3RD EARL OF GOWRIE. 1578?-1600. Scottish conspirator. See: Dict. Nat. Biog. Gowrie conspiracy.

Ruthven press (Ruthven, John): Printing. See: Harrod; Lockwood.

RUTISHAUSER, E. fl. 1945. Swiss physician. (Biography source unavailable.) Martin du Pan-Rutishauser disease.

Ruymbeke, J. van. See: Van Ruymbeke, J.

RUYSCH, FREDERIK. 1638-1731. Dutch anatomist. See: Nieuw Nederl. Biog. Woordenb. Ruysch's membrane, Ruysch's muscle, Ruysch's tube (or duct), Ruysch's vein.

Ruysch's membrane (Ruysch, Frederik): Anatomy. See: Donath; Dorland; Stedman.

Ruysch's muscle (Ruysch, Frederik): Anatomy. See: Donath; Dorland; Stedman.

Ruysch's tube (or duct) (Ruysch, Frederik): Anatomy. See: Donath; Dorland; Stedman.

Ruysch's vein (Ruysch, Frederik). See: Retzius' vein.

Ruzicka large ring synthesis (Ruzicka, Leopold Stephen): Chemistry. See: Van Nostrand Chem. Dict.

RUZICKA, LEOPOLD STEPHEN. b. 1887. Yugoslovakian-born Swiss chemist. See: World Who's Who Sci. Ruzicka large ring synthesis, Ruzicka test re-actions for aromatic amines.

Ruzicka test reactions for aromatic amines (Ruzicka, Leopold Stephen): Chemistry. See: Van Nostrand Chem. Dict.

RYAN, A. H. No dates. American physician. (Biography source unavail-able.) Ryan's skin test.

RYAN, JAMES JAY, JR. 1903- . American mechanical engineer. See: Amer. Men and Women Sci., 12th ed. Ryan monoplane?

RYAN, JOHN. fl. 18th c. English physician. (Biography source unavail-able.) Ryania (1), Ryania (2).

Ryan monoplane (Ryan, James Jay, Jr.?): Engineering and Industry. See: Van Nostrand Sci. Encyc. under "Flight (Artificial)."

Ryania (1) (Ryan, John): Botany. See: Webster's 3d.

Ryania (2) (Ryan, John): Chemistry. See: Webster's 3d.

Ryan's skin test (Ryan, A. H.): Medicine. See: Dorland.

RYAZONOV, I. P. fl. 1950-1960. Russian chemist. Cited in: Chem. Abstr., Decenn. Index, 1947-1956; 1957-1961. Ryazonov test reaction for cobalt?

Ryazonov test reaction for cobalt (Ryazonov, I. P.?): Chemistry. See: Van Nostrand Chem. Dict.

Rydberg (1) (Rydberg, Johannes Robert): Physics. See: Dresner.

Rydberg (2) (Rydberg, Johannes Robert): Physics. See: Dresner.

Rydberg constant (Rydberg, Johannes Robert): Physics. See: Hackh; Internat. Dict. Ap. Math.; Internat. Dict. Phys. Elec.

Rydberg correction (Rydberg, Johannes Robert): Physics. See: Internat. Dict. Phys. Elec.

Rydberg equation (Rydberg, Johannes Robert): Physics. See: Internat. Dict. Ap. Math.

Rydberg formula (or series formula) (Rydberg, Johannes Robert): Physics. See: Hackh; Internat. Dict. Ap. Math.; Internat. Dict. Phys. Elec.

RYDBERG, JOHANNES ROBERT. 1854-1919. Swedish physicist. See: Pogg., vols. 4, 5, 6. Rydberg (1), Rydberg (2), Rydberg constant, Rydberg correction, Rydberg equation, Rydberg formula (or series formula), Rydberg number, Rydberg relation, Rydberg-Ritz combination principle, Rydberg-Schuster law, Rydberg series.

Rydberg number (Rydberg, Johannes Robert): Physics. See: Hackh.

RYDBERG, RAGNAR. fl. 1933. Swedish? physicist. Cited in: Chem. Abstr. Klein-Rydberg method (or construction).

Rydberg relation (Rydberg, Johannes Robert): Physics. See: Hackh.

Rydberg–Ritz combination principle (Rydberg, Johannes Robert and Ritz, Walter): Physics. See: Ritz combination principle.

Rydberg–Schuster law (Rydberg, Johannes Robert and Schuster, Arthur): Physics. See: Ballentyne.

Rydberg series (Rydberg, Johannes Robert): Physics. See: Internat. Dict. Ap. Math.; Thewlis.

Ryder Cup (Ryder, Samuel): Recreation and Sports. Cited in: Laughlin.

RYDER, DUDLEY FRANCIS STUART, 3RD EARL OF HARROWBY AND VISCOUNT OF SANDON. 1831–1900. English social reformer. See: Dict. Nat. Biog., 1st suppl. Sandon Act.

RYDER, SAMUEL. fl. 1927. English seed merchant. Cited in: New Encyc. Brit., 1974, Microp. Ryder Cup.

RYDYGIER, ANTONI. No dates. Polish surgeon in South America. (Biography source unavailable.) Rydygier's operation.

Rydygier's operation (Rydygier, Antoni): Medicine. See: Dorland.

RYKEN, THEODORE JACQUES (FRANCIS XAVIER). 1797–1871. Dutch monk. See: Nieuw Nederl. Biog. Woordenb. Xaverian Brothers.

RYLE, JOHN ALFRED. 1889–1950. English physician. See: Who Was Who, 1941–1950. Ryle's tube.

Ryle's tube (Ryle, John Alfred): Medicine. See: Dorland; Stedman.

Rymsza test reaction for picric acid (Derivation undetermined): Chemistry. See: Van Nostrand Chem. Dict.

RZEPPA, A. H. fl. 20th c. European engineer. (Biography source unavailable.) Rzeppa joint.

Rzeppa joint (Rzeppa, A. H.): Engineering and Industry. See: Auger.

RZIHA, FRANZ VON. 1831–1897. Austrian engineer. Cited in: Singer. Rziha's theory.

Rziha's theory (Rziha, Franz von): Engineering and Industry. See: Thrush.

S

SA'AD AL-DIN AL-JABANI. d. 1335. Muslim religious sect founder. Cited in: Hastings (Dict. Rel. Ethics), vol. 10, p. 724a. Sa'adi'yeh (or Jebawiyeh).

Saadian dynasty (Sa'id I): History. See: Webster's 3d.

Sa'adi'yeh (or Jebawiyeh) (Sa'ad al-Din al-Jabani): Religion. See: Canney.

SABANIN, A. fl. 1878. German chemist. Cited in: Royal Soc. Cat. Sci. Pap., 1874-1883. Sabanin-Laskowsky test reaction.

Sabanin-Laskowsky test reaction (Sabanin, A. and Laskowsky, N.): Chemistry. See: Van Nostrand Chem. Dict.

SABATHE. fl. 19th c.? French engineer. (Biography source unavailable.) Sabathe cycle.

Sabathe cycle (Sabathe): Engineering and Industry. See: Auger.

SABATIER, ARMAND. 1834-1910. French physician and scientist. See: World Who's Who Sci. Sabatier (Sabattier) effect.

Sabatier (Sabattier) effect (Sabatier, Armand): Photography. See: Focal Encyc. Photog.; Van Nostrand Sci. Encyc.

SABATIER, PAUL. 1854-1941. French chemist. See: Pogg., vols. 3 to 6. Sabatier-Senderens reduction (or reaction), Sabatier-Senderens test.

SABATIER, RAPHAEL BIENVENU. 1732-1811. French surgeon. See: Nouv. Biog. Univ. Sabatier's suture.

Sabatier-Senderens reduction (or reaction) (Sabatier, Paul and Senderens, Jean-Baptiste): Chemistry. See: Ballentyne; Van Nostrand Chem. Dict.

Sabatier-Senderens test (Sabatier, Paul and Senderens, Jean-Baptiste): Chemistry. See: Van Nostrand Chem. Dict.

Sabatier's suture (Sabatier, Raphael Bienvenu): Medicine. See: Dorland.

SABBATAI-ZEBI. 1626-1676. Hebrew mystic. See: Encyc. Brit., 1911. Sabbatians.

SABBATI, LIBERATUS. fl. 1745-1778. Italian botanist. See: Michaud. Sabbatia (Sabatia).

Sabbatia (Sabatia) (Sabbati, Liberatus): Botany. See: Mathews, M. M.; Taylor, N.; Webster's 3d.

Sabbatian(s) (Sabbatius): Religion. See: Canney; Latham; Webster's 3d.

Sabbatians (Sabbatai-Zebi): Religion. See: Brewer; Canney; Webster's 3d.

SABBATIUS. fl. 380. Christian heretic. See: Dict. Christian Biog. Sabbatian(s).

Sabellianism (or Sabellians) (Sabellius): Religion. See: Attwater; Canney; Phyfe.

SABELLIUS. fl. 230. African presbyter and heretic in Rome. See: Encyc. Brit., 1911. Sabellianism (or Sabellians).

Sabetay reagent for detecting unsaturation (Sabetay, Sebastien): Chemistry. See: Van Nostrand Chem. Dict.

SABETAY, SEBASTIEN. 1897- . Rumanian-born French chemist. See: Pogg., vol. 6. Sabetay reagent for detecting unsaturation.

Sabin (Sabine, Wallace Clement Ware): Physics. See: Ballentyne; Dresner; Van Nostrand Sci. Encyc.

SABIN, ALBERT BRUCE. 1906- . Russian-born American microbiologist. See: World Who's Who Sci. Sabin-Feldman dye test, Sabin-Feldman syndrome, Sabin vaccine.

Sabin-Feldman dye test (Sabin, Albert Bruce and Feldman, Harry Alfred): Medicine. See: Stedman.

Sabin-Feldman syndrome (Sabin, Albert Bruce and Feldman, Harry Alfred): Medicine. See: Jablonski.

SABIN, FLORENCE RENA. 1871-1953. American anatomist. See: World Who's Who Sci. megaloblast of Sabin.

Sabin vaccine (Sabin, Albert Bruce): Medicine. See: Asimov; Stedman.

Sabine absorption (Sabine, Wallace Clement Ware): Physics. See: Markus.

Sabine coefficient (Sabine, Wallace Clement Ware): Physics. See: Markus.

SABINE, SIR EDWARD. 1788-1883. English physicist, explorer and soldier. See: World Who's Who Sci. Sabine's gull.

Sabine formula (reverberation formula or law) (Sabine, Wallace Clement Ware): Physics. See: Ballentyne; Hughes; Internat. Dict. Phys. Elec.

SABINE, JOSEPH. 1770-1837. English horticulturist. See: World Who's Who Sci. Sabine pine, Sabinea.

Sabine pine (Sabine, Joseph): Botany. See: Webster's 3d.

SABINE, WALLACE CLEMENT WARE. 1868-1919. American physicist. See: World Who's Who Sci. Sabin, Sabine absorption, Sabine coefficient, Sabine formula (reverberation formula or law).

Sabinea (Sabine, Joseph): Botany. See: Charnock. Cited in: World Who's Who Sci.

Sabine's gull (Sabine, Sir Edward): Zoology. See: Gray; Pennak; Webster's 3d.

Sabouraud meter (Sabouraud, Raymond Jacques Adrian): Medicine. See: Stedman.

Sabouraud-Noire instrument (Sabouraud, Raymond Jacques Adrian and Noire, Henri): Medicine. See: Stedman.

SABOURAUD, RAYMOND JACQUES ADRIAN. 1864-1938. French dermatologist. See: World Who's Who Sci. Sabouraud meter, Sabouraud-Noire instrument, Sabouraud's agar, Sabouraud's pastilles, Sabouraud's syndrome.

Sabouraud's agar (Sabouraud, Raymond Jacques Adrian): Medicine. See: Stedman.

Sabouraud's pastilles (Sabouraud, Raymond Jacques Adrian): Medicine. See: Stedman.

Sabouraud's syndrome (Sabouraud, Raymond Jacques Adrian): Medicine. See: Jablonski.

SABRAZES, JEAN. 1867-1943. French physician. See: Biog. Lex. hervorr. Aerzte. Sabrazes test.

Sabrazes test (Sabrazes, Jean): Medicine. See: Dorland.

SACCARDI, PIETRO. b. 1889. Italian pharmaceutical chemist. See: Pogg., vol. 6. Saccardi test reagent.

Saccardi test reagent (Saccardi, Pietro): Chemistry. See: Van Nostrand Chem. Dict.

saccharomyces Busse (Busse, Otto Emil Franz Ulrich): Medicine. See: Stedman.

SACCO, NICOLA. 1891-1927. Italian-born American political radical and convicted murderer. See: Webster's Biog. Dict. Sacco-Vanzetti case, Sacco-Vanzetti pencils.

Sacco-Vanzetti case (Sacco, Nicola and Vanzetti, Bartolomeo): Law. See: Jameson; Morris; Smith.

Sacco-Vanzetti pencils (Sacco, Nicola and Vanzetti, Bartolomeo): Generic Word. See: Hendrickson.

SACHER. Family of 19th and 20th c. Austrian hotel and restaurant owners. (Biography source unavailable.) Sachertorte.

SACHER-MASOCH, LEOPOLD VON. 1836-1895. Austrian novelist. See: Allg. Deut. Biog. Masochism.

Sachertorte (Sacher): Food and Drink. See: De Sola; Webster's 3d.

Sacheverell affair (Sacheverell, Henry): History. See: Brewer; Steinberg.

Sacheverell (chamber pot) (Sacheverell, Henry): Generic Word. See: Hendrickson; Partridge.

SACHEVERELL, HENRY. 1674?-1724. English political preacher. See: Dict. Nat. Biog. Sacheverell affair, Sacheverell (chamber pot), Sacheverell iron door (or blower).

Sacheverell iron door (or blower) (Sacheverell, Henry): Generic Word. See: Hendrickson.

SACHS, ANTON. fl. 19th c. Czechoslovakian? physician. (Biography source unavailable.) Ghon and Sachs' bacillus.

Sachs' bacillus (Sachs, Anton). See: Ghon and Sachs' bacillus.

SACHS, BERNARD PARNEY. 1858-1944. American neurologist. See: Who Was Who Amer., vol. 2. Tay-Sachs disease.

Sach's curvature (Sachs, Julius von): Botany. See: Gray.

SACHS, FRANZ. 1875-1919. German chemist. See: Pogg., vols. 4, 5. Ehrlich-Sachs reaction.

Sachs-Georgi reaction (Sachs, Hans and Georgi, Walter): Medicine. See: Dorland; Stedman.

SACHS, HANS. 1877-1945. German bacteriologist. See: Biog. Lex. hervorr. Aerzte; Pogg., vol. 6. Sachs-Georgi reaction.

SACHS, HEINRICH B. 1898- . American physician. (Biography source unavailable.) Sachs's test.

SACHS, JULIUS VON. 1832-1897. German botanist. See: World Who's Who Sci. Sach's curvature, Sachs's law.

SACHS, ROBERT GREEN. 1916- . American physicist. See: Amer. Men and Women Sci., 12th ed. Eisner-Lachs theorem.

SACHSE, HERMANN. fl. 1888-1892. German chemist. Cited in: Partington, vol. 4; Royal Soc. Cat. Sci. Pap., 1884-1900. Sachse-Mohr theory.

Sachse-Mohr theory (Sachse, Hermann and Mohr, Ernst W. M.): Chemistry. See: Ballentyne.

Sachs's law (Sachs, Julius von): Botany. See: Gray.

Sachs's test (Sachs, Heinrich B.): Medicine. See: Dorland.

SACHSSE, GEORG ROBERT. 1840-1895. German chemist. Cited in: Index-Cat. Libr. Surg.-Gen. Off., 1st Ser., vol. 12, 1891. Sachsse('s) solution, Sachsse's tests.

Sachsse('s) solution (Sachsse, Georg Robert): Chemistry. See: Dorland; Van Nostrand Chem. Dict.

Sachsse's tests (Sachsse, Georg Robert): Chemistry. See: Dorland.

SACKS, BENJAMIN. 1896- . American physician. (Biography source unavailable.) Libman-Sacks syndrome (or disease).

SACKS, JEROME. 1931- . American mathematical statistician. See: Amer. Men Sci., 10th ed. Sack's theorem.

Sack's theorem (Sacks, Jerome): Statistics. See: Kendall.

SACKUR, OTTO. 1880-1914. German physical chemist. See: Pogg., vols. 4, 5. Sackur-Tetrode equation.

Sackur-Tetrode equation (Sackur, Otto and Tetrode, H.): Physics. See: Ballentyne; Van Nostrand Sci. Encyc.

Sacred Congregation of the Venerable Fabric of St. Peter's (Peter the Apostle, Saint): Religion. See: Attwater.

Sacred Constantinian Order (Constantine I): Religion. See: Attwater.

Sacred Heart of Jesus (Jesus Christ): Religion. See: Mathews, S.

SACY, ISAAC-LOUIS LE MAISTRE, DE. 1613-1684. French theologian and Jansenist. See: Nouv. Biog. Univ. Sacy's Bible.

Sacy's Bible (Sacy, Isaac-Louis le Maistre, de): Religion. See: Brewer.

SADE, COMTE DONATIEN ALPHONSE FRANCOIS, MARQUIS DE. 1740-1814. French soldier and writer. See: Encyc. Brit., 1911. Sadism.

Sadism (Sade, Comte Donatien Alphonse Francois, Marquis de): Generic Word. See: English; Hendrickson; Hinsie.

SADLER, LADY. fl. before 1710. English benefactor. (Biography source unavailable.) Sadlerian lectures.

SADLER, MICHAEL T. 1834-1923. English obstetrician. See: Lancet, vol. II (1923), p. 908. Hofacker and Sadler law(s).

SADLER, MICHAEL THOMAS. 1780-1835. English social reformer and economist. See: Encyc. Brit., 1911. Sadler's hypothesis on human fertility.

Sadlerian lectures (Sadler, Lady): Education. See: Wagner (More Names).

Sadler's hypothesis on human fertility (Sadler, Michael Thomas): Sociology. See: Zadrozny.

SAEFFTIGEN, ARM. ALEX. fl. 1885. German? zoologist. Cited in: Royal Soc. Cat. Sci. Pap., 1884-1900. Saefftigen's pouch.

Saefftigen's pouch (Saefftigen, Arm. Alex.): Zoology. See: Gray.

SAEMISCH, EDWIN THEODOR. 1833-1909. German ophthalmologist. See: Biog. Lex. hervorr. Aerzte. Saemisch's operation, Saemisch's section, Saemisch's ulcer.

Saemisch's operation (Saemisch, Edwin Theodor): Medicine. See: Dorland; Stedman.

Saemisch's section (Saemisch, Edwin Theodor): Medicine. See: Stedman.

Saemisch's ulcer (Saemisch, Edwin Theodor): Medicine. See: Dorland; Jablonski; Stedman.

SAENGER, ALFRED. 1860-1921. German neurologist. See: Biog. Lex. hervorr. Aerzte. Saenger's sign, Saenger's syndrome.

SAENGER, MAX. 1853-1903. German obstetrician in Prague. See: Biog. Lex. hervorr. Aerzte. Saenger's macula, Saenger's operation.

Saenger's macula (Saenger, Max): Medicine. See: Dorland; Stedman.

Saenger's operation (Saenger, Max): Medicine. See: Dorland; Stedman.

Saenger's sign (Saenger, Alfred): Medicine. See: Dorland; Stedman.

Saenger's syndrome (Saenger, Alfred). See: Adie's syndrome.

Saenz Pena law (Saenz Pena, Roque): Politics. See: Encyc. Brit., 1973.

SAENZ PENA, ROQUE. 1851-1914. Argentinian president. See: New Encyc. Brit., 1974, Microp. Saenz Pena law.

Safavid dynasty (Safi, od-Din): History. See: New Encyc. Brit., 1974, Microp.; Weekley.

SAFI OD-DIN. 1253-1334. Persian sheik. See: New Encyc. Brit., 1974, Microp. Safavid dynasty.

Sage Foundation (Sage, Russell): Philanthropy. See: Jameson.

SAGE, RUSSELL. 1816-1906. American financier. See: Dict. Amer. Biog. Sage Foundation.

SAGERET, AUGUSTIN. 1763-1852. French agronomist. See: Michaud. Sageretia.

ageretia (Sageret, Augustin): Botany. See: Charnock; Webster's 3d.

AGNAC, GEORGES MARC MARIE. 1869-1928. French physicist. See: Ogg., vols. 4, 5, 6. Sagnac rays.

agnac rays (Sagnac, Georges Marc Marie): Physics. See: Stedman.

ah-Chang-Lei test reagent (Sah, Peter P. T.; Chang, Shih-Hsu; and Lei, sing-Han): Chemistry. See: Van Nostrand Chem. Dict.

ah-Lei reagents (Sah, Peter P. T. and Lei, Hsing-Han): Chemistry. See: an Nostrand Chem. Dict.

ah-Ma reagent for alcohols (Sah, Peter P. T. and Ma, Tsu-Sheng): Chemistry. ee: Van Nostrand Chem. Dict.

ah-Ma reagent for organic halogens (Sah, Peter P. T. and Ma, Tsu-Sheng): hemistry. See: Van Nostrand Chem. Dict.

ah-Ma reagent for phenols (Sah, Peter P. T. and Ma, Tsu-Sheng): Chemistry. ee: Van Nostrand Chem. Dict.

AH, PETER PEN TIEH. 1900- . Chinese chemist in America. See: Amer. en Sci., 9th ed., Biol. Sci. Chen-Sak reagent, Kao-Fang-Sah reagent, ao-Tao-Sah reagent, Sah-Chang-Lei test reagent, Sah-Lei reagents, Sah-Ma agent for alcohols, Sah-Ma reagent for organic halogens, Sah-Ma reagent for henols, Tung-Kao-Sah reagent, Wang-Kao-Sak reagent.

aha('s) equation (Saha, Meghnad Nad): Physics. See: Ballentyne; Thewlis; an Nostrand Sci. Encyc.

AHA, MEGHNAD NAD. 1893-1956. Indian astrophysicist. See: World ho's Who Sci. Saha('s) equation.

AHAJANAND SWAMI. b. 1780. Indian religious sect leader. Cited in: New ncyc. Brit., 1974, Microp. Swami-Narayan sect.

AHAMA, THURE GEORG. fl. 1957. Finnish geologist. Cited in: Hintze, ppl. 2. Sahamalite.

ahamalite (Sahama, Thure Georg): Earth Sciences. See: Thrush.

AHLI, HERMANN. 1856-1933. Swiss physician. See: World Who's Who ci. Sahli reagent, Sahli's stain, Sahli's test.

ahli reagent (Sahli, Hermann): Chemistry. See: Van Nostrand Chem. Dict.

AHLIN, CARL ANDREAS. 1861-1943. Swedish scientist. See: Svenska aen Och Kvinnor. Sahlinite.

ahlin respirator (Derivation undetermined): Medicine. See: Stedman.

ahlinite (Sahlin, Carl Andreas): Earth Sciences. See: Thrush; Webster's 3d.

ahli's stain (Sahli, Hermann): Chemistry. See: Hackh.

ahli's test (Sahli, Hermann): Medicine. See: Dorland; Stedman.

aid (or Seyd) (slave of Mohammed). See: Zaid.

A'ID I. fl. 1358. Eponymous ancestor of the Saadian dynasty. See: Encyc. it., 1911 under "Morocco." Saadian dynasty.

int Agatha's disease (Agatha, Saint): Medicine. See: Stedman.

int Agnes' Eve (Agnes, Saint): Religion. See: Barnhart, (New Eng.).

. Agnes' flower (Agnes, Saint): Botany. See: Gray.

int Aignan's disease (Aignan, Saint): Medicine. See: Stedman.

int Andrew (Andrew, Saint): Numismatics. See: Webster's 3d.

int Andrew's cross (Andrew, Saint): Botany. See: Gray; Mathews, M. M.; ebster's 3d.

int Andrew's Day (Andrew, Saint): Generic Word. See: Webster's 3d.

int Anne marble (Anna, Saint?): Earth Sciences. See: Thrush.

int Ann's bark (Anna, Saint): Botany. See: Webster's 3d.

int Anthony (Anthony, Saint): Religion. See: Partridge.

int Anthony variations (Anthony, Saint): Music. See: Apel.

int Anthony's cross (Anthony, Saint): Religion. See: Brewer; Webster's 3d.

Saint Anthony's dance (Anthony, Saint): Medicine. Cited in: Stedman.

Saint Anthony's fire (Anthony, Saint): Medicine. See: Attwater; Hendrickson; Partridge.

St. Audrey's lace. See: Tawdrey lace.

St. Augustine grass (Augustine of Hippo, Saint): Botany. See: Partridge; Webster's 3d.

Saint Austin pear (Austin, Saint): Botany. See: Charnock.

Saint Austin's summer (Austin, Saint): Generic Word. See: Webster's 3d.

Saint Avertin's disease (Avertin, Saint): Medicine. See: Stedman.

Saint Barnabas Day (Barnabas, Saint). See: Barnaby bright (or day).

Saint Barnaby's thistle (Barnabas, Saint): Botany. See: Brewer; Gray; Webster's 3d.

St. Bartholomew's Day (Bartholomew, Saint): Generic Word. See: Harbottle.

Saint Benoit (Benoit, Saint): Generic Word (Negro). See: Webster's 3d.

St. Bernard (dog) (Bernard of Clairvaux, Saint): Animals. See: Hendrickson.

St. Bernard's lily (Bernard of Clairvaux, Saint): Botany. See: Gray; Webster's 3d.

Saint Blaise's disease (Blaise, Saint): Medicine. See: Stedman.

St. Boniface's cup (Boniface VI): Generic Word (extra drink). See: Brewer; Hendrickson.

St. (Saint) Bruno's lily (Bruno of Querfurt, Saint): Botany. See: Gray; Webster's 3d.

Saint Catherine's flower (Catherine, Saint): Botany. See: Webster's 3d.

St. Cecelia Society (Cecilia, Saint): Religion. See: Jameson.

SAINT, CHARLES FREDERICK MORRIS. b. 1886- . South-African roent-genologist. See: Med. Direct., 1972. Saint's triad.

Saint Clair-Blue process (Deville, Henri Etienne Sainte-Claire): Chemistry. See: Van Nostrand Chem. Dict.

Saint Claire's disease (Clare of Assisi, Saint): Medicine. See: Stedman.

Saint (St.) Crispin's Day (Crispin, Saint): Generic Word. See: Blumberg; Brewer.

St. Crispin's holiday (Crispin, Saint): Generic Word (Monday). See: Brewer.

St. Crispin's lance (Crispin, Saint): Generic Word (awl). See: Brewer; Charnock.

Saint (St.) Cuthbert's beads (Cuthbert, Saint): Zoology. See: Brewer; Harvey; Webster's 3d.

Saint Cuthbert's duck (Cuthbert, Saint). See: Cuthbert duck.

Saint Daboec's heath (Beoc, Saint). See: Daboecia.

St. David's Day (David, Saint): History. See: Wagner (Names).

Saint Dymphna's disease (Dympna, Saint): Psychiatry. See: Hinsie; Stedman.

Saint Edward's crown (Edward the Confessor, Saint): Generic Word (royal crown). See: Webster's 3d.

Saint Elmo's fire (Erasmus, Saint): Earth Sciences. See: Attwater; Blumberg; Hendrickson.

Saint Erasmus' disease (Erasmus, Saint): Medicine. See: Stedman.

Saint Fiacre's disease (Fiacre, Saint): Medicine. See: Stedman.

St. Francis' fire (Derivation undetermined): Medicine. See: Stedman.

Saint George's Day (George, Saint): Generic Word. See: Webster's 3d.

Saint George's duck (George, Saint): Zoology. See: Webster's 3d.

St. George's herb (Gerorge, Saint): Botany. See: Gray.

Saint George's mushroom (George, Saint): Botany. See: Webster's 3d.

Saint George's round (George, Saint): Recreation and Sports. See: Webster's 3d.

Saint Gervasius' disease (Gervasius, Saint): Medicine. See: Stedman.

Saint Gete's disease (Derivation undetermined): Medicine. See: Stedman.

Saint Giles' disease (Giles, Saint?): Medicine. See: Stedman.

Saint Guy's disease (Vitus, Saint). See: Saint Vitus's dance.

SAINT-HILAIRE, AUGUSTE (In full: AUGUSTIN FRANCOIS CESAR PROUVENCAL), DE. 1799-1853. French botanist. See: Webster's Biog. Dict. Hilaria.

SAINT-HILAIRE, MARCQ. fl. 1875. French navigator. Cited in: Royal Soc. Cat. Sci. Pap., 1874-1883. Saint Hilaire tables.

Saint Hilaire tables (Saint-Hilaire, Marcq): Navigation. See: Van Nostrand Sci. Encyc. under "Celestial Navigation."

Saint Hubert's disease (Hubert, Saint): Medicine. See: Stedman.

Saint Ignatius('s) bean (Ignatius Azevedo, Saint): Botany. See: Blumberg; Charnock; Webster's 3d.

Saint Ignatius' itch (Ignatius of Antioch, Saint): Botany. See: Stedman.

St. Jacob's dipper (Jacob): Botany. See: Mathews, M. M.; Webster's 3d.

St. James wort (James the Greater, Saint). See: Jacobaea.

Saint James's lily (James the Greater, Saint). See: Jacobean lily.

Saint John the Baptist's Day (John the Baptist, Saint): Generic Word. See: Webster's 3d.

Saint John's bread (John the Baptist, Saint): Botany. See: De Sola; Gray; Webster's 3d.

Saint John's Christians (John the Baptist, Saint). See: Christians (or Disciples) of St. John.

Saint John's dance (John the Baptist, Saint?): Medicine. See: Stedman.

Saint John's eve (John the Baptist, Saint): Generic Word. See: Webster's 3d.

St. John's evil (or disease) (John the Baptist, Saint?): Medicine. See: Hinsie; Stedman.

Saint John's fire (John the Baptist, Saint): Mythology. See: Webster's 3d.

Saint John's wort (John the Baptist, Saint): Botany. See: Blumberg; Gray; Stedman; Webster's 3d. Also known as: Aaron's beard, St. Andrew's cross, St. Peter's wort.

St. Jonathan's Day (Trumbull, Jonathan?): History. See: Mathews, M. M.

Saint Joseph's lily (Joseph, Saint): Botany. See: Gray; Webster's 3d.

St. Joseph's rod (Joseph, Saint): Botany. See: Mathews, M. M.

Saint Joseph's Society of the Sacred Heart (Joseph, Saint). See: Josephites (2).

St. Lambert's Day (Lambert, Saint): Generic Word. See: Brewer.

St. Lawrence's tears (Lawrence, Saint): Astronomy. See: Hendrickson

ST. LEGER, SIR ANTHONY. ca. 1496-1559. Lord deputy of Ireland. See: Dict. Nat. Biog. St. Leger (or St. Leger sweepstakes) (horse race), Sellinger's (Sellenger's) round?
St. Leger (or St. Leger sweepstakes) (horse race) (St. Leger, Sir Anthony): Recreation and Sports. See: Latham.

St. Lucas Guild (Luke, Saint): Fine Arts. See: Osborne.

St. Lucas thrush (Luke, Saint): Zoology. See: Mathews, M. M.

Saint Lucy's Day (Lucy, Saint). See: Lucy light.

St. Luke's summer (Luke, Saint): Generic Word. See: Huschke; Partridge; Webster's 3d.

Saint Main's (or St. Meen's) evil (Mevan, Saint): Medicine. See: Butler's Lives of the Saints; Stedman.

St. Mark's Eve (Mark, Saint): Folklore. See: Brewer.

Saint Mark's fly (Mark, Saint): Zoology. See: Webster's 3d.

SAINT-MARTIN, LOUIS CLAUDE DE. 1743-1803. French mystic philosopher. See: Encyc. Brit., 1973. Martinists.

St. Martin's beads (Martin of Tours, Saint): Generic Word (counterfeit jewelry). See: Hendrickson.

Saint Martin's bird (Martin of Tours, Saint): Zoology. See: Hendrickson; Webster's 3d.; Weekley.

Saint Martin's evil (Martin of Tours, Saint): Medicine. See: Stedman.

St. Martin's goose (Martin of Tours, Saint): Folklore. See: Hendrickson.

Saint Martin's summer (Martin of Tours, Saint): Generic Word. See: Blumberg; Hendrickson; Huschke; Webster's 3d.

St. (Saint) Mary's thistle (Mary, Virgin-Mother): Botany. See: Gray; Webster's 3d.

Saint Mathurin's disease (Mathurin, Saint): Medicine. See: Hinsie; Stedman.

St. Matthew Passion (Matthew, Saint): Music. See: Apel.

St. Michael's pear (Michael the Archangel, Saint): Botany. See: Mathews, M. M.

Saint Modestus disease (Modestus, Saint): Medicine. See: Stedman.

Saint Nicholas bishop (Nicholas of Myra, Saint): History. See: Oxford Eng. Dict.

Saint Nicholas's clerk (1) (Nicholas of Myra, Saint): Generic Word (thief). See: Webster's 3d.

Saint Nicholas's clerk (2) (Nicholas of Myra, Saint): Generic Word (scholar). See: Oxford Eng. Dict.

Saint Patrick's cabbage (Patrick, Saint): Botany. See: Blumberg; Gray; Webster's 3d.

Saint Patrick's cross (Patrick, Saint): Religion. See: Brewer.

Saint Patrick's Day (Patrick, Saint): Generic Word. See: Barnhart (Eng. Lit.); Blumberg; Webster's 3d.

Saint Paul (oratorio) (Paul the Apostle, Saint): Music. See: Apel.

SAINT PAUL, BARON WALTER VON. d. 1910. German soldier and colonial administrator in East Africa. (Biography source unavailable.) Saintpaulia (or St. Paulia).

Saint Paul's speedwell (Paul the Apostle, Saint?): Botany. See: Gray.

Saint Peter's chains (Peter the Apostle, Saint): Religion. See: Attwater.

Saint Peter's chair (Peter the Apostle, Saint): Religion. See: Attwater; Brewer.

Saint Peter's fingers (Peter the Apostle, Saint): Generic Word (thief's fingers). See: Brewer.

Saint Peter's fish (or cock) (Peter the Apostle, Saint): Zoology. See: Hendrickson; Partridge; Webster's 3d.

Saint Peter's keys (Peter the Apostle, Saint): Religion. See: Brewer.

Saint Peter's men (Peter the Apostle, Saint). See: Sampietrini.

Saint Peter's sandstone (Peter the Apostle, Saint?): Earth Sciences. See: Thrush.

Saint Peter's wort (Peter the Apostle, Saint): Botany. See: Charnock; Gray; Webster's 3d.

Saint Peter's wreath (Peter the Apostle, Saint): Botany. See: Webster's 3d.

Saint Pfau-Plattner azulene synthesis (Pfau, Alexandre Stanislas and Plattner, Placidus Andreas): Chemistry. See: Van Nostrand Chem. Dict.

Saint Roch's disease (Roch, Saint): Medicine. See: Stedman.

Saint Rose's disease (Rose of Lima, Saint): Medicine. See: Stedman.

SAINT-SIMON, CLAUDE HENRI DE ROUVRAY, COUNT DE. 1760-1825. French philosopher and social scientist. See: Internat. Encyc. Soc. Sci. Saint-Simonism (or Saint-Simonianism).

Saint-Simonism (or Saint-Simonianism) (Saint-Simon, Claude Henri de Rouvray Count de): Politics. See: Brewer; Canney; Phyfe.

Saint Stephen's Day (Stephen, Saint): Religion. See: Charnock; Thrush.

Saint Stephen's stone (Stephen, Saint): Earth Sciences. See: Charnock; Thrush.

St. Swithin's Day (Swithin, Saint): Religion. See: Hendrickson; Huschke; Phyfe.

Saint Tammany (Tammany): History. See: Mathews, M. M.

Saint Thomas Christians (Thomas the Apostle, Saint): Religion. See: Attwater; Mathews, S.; Webster's 3d. Also known as: Christians of St. Thomas.

Saint Thomas tree (Thomas the Apostle, Saint): Botany. See: Webster's 3d.

Saint Valentine's Day. See: Valentine's Day.

Saint Valentine's disease (Valentine, Saint): Medicine. See: Hinsie; Stedman.

Saint-Venant, Adhemar-Jean-Claude Barre. See: De Saint-Venant, Adhemar-Jean-Claude Barre.

Saint-Venant-Mises material (De Saint-Venant, Adhemar-Jean-Claude Barre and Mises, Richard von): Physics. See: Internat. Dict. Ap. Math.

Saint Venant plasticity (De Saint-Venant, Adhemar-Jean-Claude Barre): Physics. See: Ballentyne.

Saint-Venant('s) principle (De Saint-Venant, Adhemar-Jean-Claude Barre): Physics. See: Ballentyne; Internat. Dict. Ap. Math.; James.

Saint-Venant's compatibility equations (De Saint-Venant, Adhemar-Jean-Claude Barre): Mathematics. See: James.

Saint-Venant's problem (De Saint-Venant, Adhemar-Jean-Claude Barre): Mathematics. See: World Who's Who Sci.

Saint Vincent de Paul Society (Vincent de Paul, Saint): Religion. See: Attwater.

Saint-Vincent, Gregoire de. See: De Saint-Vincent, Gregoire.

Saint Vitus's dance (Vitus, Saint: Medicine. See: Barnhart (Eng. Lit.); Charnock; Harvey. Also known as: chorea St. Viti, Saint Guy's disease, Sydenham's chorea.

Saint With's dance (Vitus, Saint). See: Saint Vitus dance.

Saint Zachary's disease (Zachary, Saint): Medicine. See: Stedman.

Sainte-Claire Deville. See: Deville, Henri Etienne Sainte-Claire.

SAINTON, RAYMOND. fl. 1897. French physician. (Biography source unavailable.) Scheuthauer-Marie-Sainton syndrome.

Saintpaulia (or St. Paulia) (Saint Paul, Baron Walter von): Botany. See: Partridge; Taylor, N.; Webster's 3d.

Saint's triad (Saint, Charles Frederick Morris): Medicine. See: Jablonski; Stedman.

Saivism (Siva, the god). See: Sivaism.

Sakaguchi('s) reaction (or arginine reaction) (Sakaguchi, Schoyo): Chemistry. See: Ballentyne; Stedman.

SAKAGUCHI, SCHOYO. fl. 1925. Japanese chemist. Cited in: Chem. Abstr., vol. 19, p. 3506. Sakaguchi('s) reaction (or arginine reaction).

SAKAIDA KAKIEMON. 1596-1666. Japanese potter. See: New Encyc. Brit., 1974, Microp. Kakiemon (porcelain style).

SAKAMOTO, A. fl. 1961. Japanese? physician. (Biography source unavailable.) Sakamoto's disease.

Sakamoto's disease (Sakamoto, A.): Medicine. See: Jablonski.

SAKATA, SHOICHI. 1911-   . Japanese chemist. See: World Who's Who Sci. Sakata-Taketani equation.

Sakata-Taketani equation (Sakata, Shoichi and Taketani, Mitsuo): Physics. See: Internat. Dict. Phys. Elec.

SAKURAI, JOJI. 1858-1939. Japanese chemist. See: Pogg., vols. 4 to 6. Sakurai-Landsberger apparatus.

Sakurai-Landsberger apparatus (Sakurai, Joji and Landsberger, Willy?). See: Landsberger method and apparatus.

SALA, LUIGI. 1863-1930. Italian zoologist. See: Monitore Zool. Ital., vol. 41 (1930), pp. 184-194. Sala's cells.

SALADIN. 1138-1193. Sultan of Egypt and Syria. See: Encyc. Brit., 1911. Saladin (Saladine) tenth (or tithe).

Saladin (Saladine) tenth (or tithe) (Saladin): History. See: Black; Steinberg.

Salah's sternal puncture needle (Derivation undetermined): Medicine. See: Stedman.

SALAND, S. fl. 1935. Swiss physician. (Biography source unavailable.) Glanzmann-Saland syndrome.

Sala's cells (Sala, Luigi): Zoology. See: Dorland.

SALATI-MONGELLAZ, ARCHDUCHESSE MARIE IMMACULATE. No dates. European noblewoman. (Biography source unavailable.) Souvenir de Madame Salati-Mongellaz, Archduchesse Marie Immaculate (rose).

SALEE, ACHILLE. d. 1932. Belgian paleontologist. See: Bibliographie Academique Louvain, 1911/13, p. 68; 1914/34, p. 267 f. Saleeite.

Saleeite (Salee, Achille): Earth Sciences. See: Thrush.

SALERNI, PIERO GIRI DE TERAMALA. fl. 20th c. Italian engineer. (Biography source unavailable.) Ferguson-Teramala transmission, Salerni transmission.

Salerni transmission (Salerni, Piero Giri de Teramala): Engineering and Industry. See: Auger. Also known as: Teramala transmission.

SALES, RENO HABER. b. 1876. American geologist. See: Amer. Men Sci., 4th ed. Salesite.

Salesian(s) (Francis of Sales, St.): Religion. See: Attwater; Webster's 3d.

Salesite (Sales, Reno Haber): Earth Sciences. See: Thrush; Webster's 3d.

Salisbury, 3rd Marquis of. See: Cecil, Robert Arthur Talbot Gascoyne (3rd Marquis of Salisbury).

Salisbury circular (Cecil, Robert Arthur Talbot Gascoyne): History. See: Dict. Nat. Biog.; Montgomery.

SALISBURY, JAMES HENRY. 1823-1905. American physician. See: Dict. Amer. Biog. Salisbury steak.

Salisbury steak (Salisbury, James Henry): Food and Drink. See: De Sola; Hendrickson; Webster's 3d.

SALK, JONAS EDWARD. 1914-   . American microbiologist. See: World Who's Who Sci. Salk vaccine.

Salk vaccine (Salk, Jonas Edward): Medicine. See: Asimov; Dorland; Stedman.

SALKOWSKI, ERNST LEOPOLD. 1844-1923. German physician. See: Biog. Lex. hervorr. Aerzte. Salkowski's solution, Salkowski's test (for cholesterol), Salkowski's tests.

Salkowski's solution (Salkowski, Ernst Leopold): Medicine. See: Hackh.

Salkowski's test (for cholesterol) (Salkowski, Ernst Leopold): Medicine. See: Ballentyne; Dorland; Stedman.

Salkowski's tests (Salkowski, Ernst Leopold): Medicine. See: Dorland; Stedman.

Sallmann, Ludwig von. See: Von Sallmann, Ludwig.

Sally Bee (Bernhardt, Sarah). Generic Word (tall woman). See: Hendrickson.

Sally Lunn (tea cake) (Lunn, Sally): Food and Drink. See: Brewer; Charnock; Hendrickson; Partridge; Webster's 3d.

SALM-REIFFERSCHEID-DYCK, JOSEPH FRANZ MARIA ANTON HUBERT IGNATZ ZU. 1773-1861. German botanist. See: Biog. Notes Upon Botanists. Dyckia.

Salmagundi (Salmagundi, Mme.): Food and Drink. See: Brewer; Hendrickson.

SALMAGUNDI, MME. fl. 17th c. French lady-in-waiting to Marie de Medici, wife of Henri IV. (Biography source unavailable.) Salmagundi.

SALMON, DANIEL ELMER. 1850-1914. American pathologist. See: World Who's Who Sci. Salmonella, Salmonellosis.

SALMON, UDALL J. 1904- . American obstetrician. See: Who Was Who Amer., vol. 4. Salmon's sign.

Salmonella (Salmon, Daniel Elmer): Zoology. See: Dorland; Hendrickson; Stedman.

Salmonellosis (Salmon, Daniel Elmer): Medicine. See: Hendrickson.

SALMONS, FRANK A. fl. 20th c. American mineralogist. Cited in: Min. Mag., vol. 16 (July 1913), p. 371. Salmonsite.

Salmon's sign (Salmon, Udall J.): Medicine. See: Dorland.

Salmonsite (Salmons, Frank A.): Earth Sciences. See: Thrush; Webster's 3d.

SALOMON, E. fl. 1920. German physician. (Biography source unavailable.) Rabe-Salomon syndrome.

SALOMON, EUGEN. b. 1883. German physician. Cited in: Index-Cat. Libr. Surg.-Gen. Off., 3rd ser., vol. 9, 1931. Rabe-Salomon syndrome?

SALOMON, HUGO. 1872-1954. Austrian physician. See: Biog. Lex. hervorr. Aerzte. Porges-Salomon test, Salomon's test.

SALOMON, JOHANN PETER. 1745-1815. German violinist and composer in England. See: Dict. Nat. Biog. Salomon symphonies.

Salomon symphonies (Salomon, Johann Peter): Music. See: Apel; Scholes.

Salomon's test (Salomon, Hugo): Medicine. See: Dorland; Stedman.

SALPETER, EDWIN ERNEST. 1924- . Austrian-born American physicist. See: World Who's Who Sci. Bethe-Salpeter equation.

SALTER, SAMUEL JAMES A. 1825-1897. English dentist. Cited in: Index-Cat. Libr. Surg.-Gen. Off., 1st Ser., vol. 12, 1891. Salter's incremental lines.

Salter's incremental lines (Salter, Samuel James A.): Dentistry. See: Dorland; Stedman.

SALUS, ROBERT. b. 1877. Austrian ophthalmologist in Prague. See: Biog. Lex. hervorr. Aerzte. Koerber-Salus-Elschnig syndrome.

SALVADOR Y BOSCA, JUAN. 1598-1681. Spanish botanist. See: Michaud. Salvadora.

Salvadora (Salvador y Bosca, Juan): Botany. See: Webster's 3d.

SALVADORI, ROBERTO. fl. 1915. Italian chemist. Cited in: Chem. Abstr., vol. 10, p. 1483. Salvadori solution.

Salvadori solution (Salvadori, Roberto): Chemistry. See: Van Nostrand Chem. Dict.

SALVIATI, ANTONIO. 1816-1900. Italian mosaicist. See: Encic. Italiana. Salviati glass.

Salviati glass (Salviati, Antonio): Fine Arts. See: Partridge.

SALVINI, ANTONIO MARIA. 1653-1729. Italian linguist. See: Nouv. Biog. Univ. Salvinia.

Salvinia (Salvini, Antonio Maria): Botany. See: Taylor, N.; Webster's 3d.

SALVIOLI, GAETANO. b. 1894. Italian pediatrician. See: Chie?, 1961. Salvioli's syndrome.

Salvioli's syndrome (Salvioli, Gaetano): Medicine. See: Jablonski.

SALZER, FRITZ ADALBERT. 1858-1892. Austrian surgeon in the Netherlands. See: Nieuw Nederl. Biog. Woordenb. Salzer's operation.

Salzer test for paraffin (Salzer, Theodore?): Chemistry. See: Van Nostrand Chem. Dict.

SALZER, THEODORE. d. 1900. German pharmaceutical chemist. Cited in: Royal Soc. Cat. Sci. Pap., 1884-1900. Salzer test for paraffin?

Salzer's operation (Salzer, Fritz Adalbert): Medicine. See: Dorland; Stedman.

Salzmann differential lock (Salzmann, W.): Engineering and Industry. See: Auger.

SALZMANN, MAXIMILIAN. 1862-1954. Austrian ophthalmologist. See: Biog. Lex. hervorr. Aerzte. Salzmann's dystrophy (or nodular corneal dystrophy).

SALZMANN, W. fl. 20th c. Swiss engineer. (Biography source unavailable.) Salzmann differential lock.

Salzmann's dystrophy (or nodular corneal dystrophy) (Salzmann, Maximilian): Medicine. See: Dorland; Jablonski; Stedman.

Sam (or stand Sam) (Wilson, Samuel): Generic Word (pay for anything). See: Charnock.

Sam Browne belt (Browne, Sir Samuel James): Fashion. See: Brewer; Hendrickson; Partridge.

Sam (political party) (Wilson, Samuel?): History. See: Jameson.

SAMAN, ISMAIL AL. fl. early 9th c. Persian ruler. See: Webster's Biog. Dict. Samanid dynasty (or Samanids).

Samanid dynasty (or Samanids) (Saman, Ismail al): History. See: Brewer; New Encyc. Brit., 1974, Microp.

Samarium (Samarski, Col. M. von): Chemistry. See: Hendrickson; Partridge; Stedman.

SAMARSKI, COL. M. VON. fl. 19th c. Russian mine official. Cited in: Bailey. Samarium, Samarskite.

Samarskite (Samarski, Col. M. von): Earth Sciences. See: Hendrickson; Thrush; Webster's 3d.

Samphire (or Sampire) (Peter the Apostle, Saint): Botany. See: Charnock; Partridge.

Sampietrini (Peter the Apostle, Saint): Religion. See: Attwater.

SAMPLE, MAT. fl. 20th c. American mine superintendent in Chile. Cited in: Min. Mag., vol. 26 (June 1943), p. 341. Sampleite.

Sampleite (Sample, Mat): Earth Sciences. See: Webster's 3d.

Sampson fox (Samson, Biblical judge). See: Samson fox.

SAMPSON, JOHN ALBERTSON. 1873-1946. American gynecologist. See: Who Was Who Amer., vol. 2. Sampson's cyst.

Sampson-Schley controversy (Sampson, William Thomas and Schley, Winfield S.). See: Schley controversy.

SAMPSON, WILLIAM THOMAS. 1840-1902. American naval officer. See: Dict. Amer. Biog. Sampson-Schley controversy.

Sampson's cyst (Sampson, John Albertson): Medicine. See: Dorland; Stedman.

Sampson's snake-root (Derivation undetermined): Botany. See: Gray.

SAMSON, Hebrew judge in the Old Testament. See: New Encyc. Brit., 1974, Microp. Samson (or Samsonian), Samson fox, Samson (gin), Samson loader, Samson('s) post, Samson stripper.

Samson (or Samsonian) (Samson): Generic Word (heroic strength). See: Brewer; Hendrickson; Partridge.

Samson fox (Samson): Zoology. See: Webster's 3d.

Samson (gin) (Samson): Food and Drink. See: Charnock.

Samson loader (Samson): Engineering and Industry. See: Thrush.

Samson('s) post (Samson): Engineering and Industry. See: Charnock; Partridge; Thrush.

Samson stripper (Samson): Engineering and Industry. See: Thrush.

Samuel A. Levine professorship of medicine (Levine, Samuel Albert): Medicine. Cited in: World Who's Who Sci.

SAMUEL, SIR HERBERT LOUIS SAMUEL, 1ST VISCOUNT. 1870-1963. English statesman and philosopher. See: New Encyc. Brit., 1974. Samuel report, Samuelized.

Samuel L. Warner Memorial Award (Warner, Samuel L.): Photography. See: Focal Encyc. Photog.

Samuel Levine Cardiac Center (Levine, Samuel Albert): Medicine. Cited in: World Who's Who Sci.

Samuel report (Samuel, Sir Herbert Louis Samuel): Politics. See: Steinberg.

Samuela (Trelease, Sam F.): Botany. See: Taylor, N.

Samuelized (Samuel, Sir Herbert Louis Samuel): Politics. See: Stenhouse.

SAN SEVERO, RAIMONDO DI SANGRO, PRINCE OF. d. 1774. Italian scholar. (Biography source unavailable.) Sansevieria.

SANARELLI, GIUSEPPE. 1864-1940. Italian physician. See: Biog. Lex. hervorr. Aerzte. Sanarelli-Shwartzman phenomenon (or reaction).

Sanarelli-Shwartzman phenomenon (or reaction) (Sanarelli, Giuseppe and Shwartzmann, Gregory): Medicine. See: Jablonski; Stedman. Also known as: Shwartzmann phenomenon.

Sanbenito (or Sanbenite) (Benedict of Nursia, Saint): Fashion. See: Attwater; Harvey; Picken.

SANBORN, FRANK. d. 1945. American mineralogist. Cited in: Hintze, suppl. 1. Sanbornite.

Sanborn, Kate Emery. See: Jones, Kate Emery Sanborn.

Sanbornite (Sanborn, Frank): Earth Sciences. See: Thrush; Webster's 3d.

SANCHEZ, JOSEF. No dates. Spanish professor. (Biographical source unavailable.) Sanchezia.

SANCHEZ, JUAN A. No dates. Argentinian pharmacologist. See: Pogg., vol. 6. Sanchez reagent for iron, Sanchez test for differentiating ammonium salts, amines, and amides, Sanchez test reaction for aldehydes, Sanchez test reaction for primary cyclic amines, Sanchez test reactions for alkaloids derived from morphine and for eucodal.

SANCHEZ, MANUEL R. "MANOLETE." d. 1947. Spanish matador. (Biography source unavailable.) Manoletina.

Sanchez reagent for iron (Sanchez, Juan A.): Chemistry. See: Van Nostrand Chem. Dict.

Sanchez test for differentiating ammonium salts, amines, and amides (Sanchez, Juan A.): Chemistry. See: Van Nostrand Chem. Dict.

Sanchez test reaction for aldehydes (Sanchez, Juan A.): Chemistry. See: Van Nostrand Chem. Dict.

Sanchez test reaction for primary cyclic amines (Sanchez, Juan A.): Chemistry. See: Van Nostrand Chem. Dict.

Sanchez test reactions for alkaloids derived from morphine and for eucodal (Sanchez, Juan A.): Chemistry. See: Van Nostrand Chem. Dict.

SANCHEZ-VELLO, LEOPOLDO. fl. 20th c. Spanish inventor. (Biography source unavailable.) Vello process.

Sanchezia (Sanchez, Josef): Botany. See: Taylor, N.

SANCHO PANZA. Don Quixote's squire in Cervantes novel, "Don Quixote de la Mancha," (1605, 1615). See: New Encyc. Brit., 1974, Microp. Sancho Panza, Sancho Pedro (card-game).

Sancho Panza (Sancho Panza, the squire): Generic Word (realist). See: Brewer; Webster's 3d.

Sancho Pedro (card-game) (Sancho Panza): Recreation and Sports. See: Partridge.

Sancy diamond (Sancy, Nicholas de Harlay, Sieur de): History. See: Brewer; Phyfe.

SANCY, NICHOLAS DE HARLAY, SIEUR DE. 1546-1629. French statesman and soldier. See: Encyc. Brit., 1911. Sancy diamond.

Sand (chrysanthemum) (Sand, Georges): Botany. See: Charnock. Also known as: Georges Sand (chrysanthemum).

SAND, GEORGES (Pseud. of: AMANDINE AURORE LUCIE DUDEVANT). 1804-1876. French writer. See: New Encyc. Brit., 1974. Sand (chrysanthemum).

SAND, JULIUS. fl. 1899. German chemist. Cited in: Pogg., vol. 4 under "Hofmann, Karl Andreas." Hofmann-Sand reaction.

Sandberg bluegrass (Sandberg, John Herman): Botany. See: Webster's 3d.

SANDBERG, JOHN HERMAN. 1848-1917. Swedish-born American botanist. See: Biog. Notes Upon Botanists. Sandberg bluegrass.

SANDELL, ERNEST BIRGER. 1906- . American chemist. See: Amer. Men and Women Sci., 12th ed. Sandell-Wishnick reagent.

Sandell-Wishnick reagent (Sandell, Ernest Birger; Wishnick, Dorothy M.; and Wishnick, Ethel C.): Chemistry. See: Van Nostrand Chem. Dict.

SANDEMAN, ROBERT. 1718-1771. Scottish-born religious sectarian in America. See: Dict. Amer. Biog. Sandemanians.

Sandemania (Sandemann, Sir Robert Groves): History. See: Montgomery.

Sandemanians (Sandeman, Robert): Religion. See: Brewer; Canney; Matthews, S. Also known as: Glassites.

SANDEMANN, SIR ROBERT GROVES. 1835-1892. English administrator in India. See: Dict. Nat. Biog. Sandemania.

SANDER, BRUNO HERMANN MAX. b. 1884. Austrian mineralogist and petrographer. See: Pogg., vol. 7a. Sanderite.

SANDER, WILHELM. 1838-1922. German physician. See: Biog. Lex. hervorr. Aerzte. Sander's disease.

SANDER, WILHELM. fl. 1923. German engineer. Cited in: Chem. Abstr., Decenn. Index, 1917-1926. Sander's process?

Sanderite (Sander, Bruno Hermann Max): Earth Sciences. See: Thrush.

Sander's disease (Sander, Wilhelm): Psychiatry. See: Dorland; Jablonski.

Sanders' disease (or syndrome) (Sanders, Murray): Medicine. See: Dorland; Jablonski.

SANDERS, JAMES. 1777-1843. Scottish physician. See: Biog. Lex. hervorr. Aerzte. Sanders' sign.

SANDERS, MURRAY. 1910- . American bacteriologist. See: Amer. Men and Women Sci., 12th ed. Sanders' disease (or syndrome).

Sander's process (Sander, Wilhelm?): Engineering and Industry. See: Thrush.

Sanders' sign (Sanders, James): Medicine. See: Dorland.

SANDISON, CALVIN (In full: JAMES CALVIN). 1899- . American surgeon. See: Amer. Men Sci., 7th ed. Sandison-Clark chamber.

Sandison-Clark chamber (Sandison, Calvin and Clark, Eliot): Medicine. See: Stedman.

SANDLER, SAMUEL ABRAHAM. b. 1894. American psychiatrist. See: Direct. Med. Specialists, 1963-1964. Sandler's triad.

Sandler's triad (Sandler, Samuel Abraham): Psychology. See: Hinsie.

Sandmeyer isatin synthesis (Sandmeyer, Traugott): Chemistry. See: Van Nostrand Chem. Dict.

Sandmeyer('s) reaction (or diazo reaction) (Sandmeyer, Traugott): Chemistry. See: Ballentyne; Hackh; Van Nostrand Chem. Dict.

SANDMEYER, TRAUGOTT. 1854-1922. Swiss chemist. See: Dict. Hist. Biog. Suisse. Sandmeyer isatin synthesis, Sandmeyer('s) reaction (or diazo reaction).

Sandon Act (Ryder, Dudley Francis Stuart, 3rd Earl of Harrowby and Viscount of Sandon): Education. See: Montgomery.

Sandon, Viscount of. See: Ryder, Dudley Francis Stuart, 3rd Earl of Harrowby and Viscount of Sandon.

SANDSTROEM, IVAR VICTOR. 1852-1889. Swedish anatomist. See: World Who's Who Sci. Sandstroem's bodies.

Sandstroem's bodies (Sandstroem, Ivar Victor): Anatomy. See: Donath; Dorland; Stedman.

Sandwich (Montagu, John, 4th Earl of Sandwich): Food and Drink. See: Funk; Hendrickson; Partridge.

Sandwich, 4th Earl of. See: Montagu, John (4th Earl of Sandwich).

SANDWITH, FLEMING MANT. 1853-1918. English physician. See: Who Was Who, 1916-1928. Sandwith's bald tongue.

Sandwith's bald tongue (Sandwith, Fleming Mant): Medicine. See: Dorland.

SANFILIPPO, SYLVESTER J. fl. 1963. American pediatrician. (Biography source unavailable.) SanFilippo's (San Filippo) syndrome.

Sanfilippo's (San Filippo) syndrome (Sanfilippo, Sylvester J.): Medicine. See: Jablonski; Stedman; Wolman.

SANFORD, EDMUND CLARK. d. 1924. American psychologist. See: Amer. J. Psych., vol. 36 (1925), pp. 167-170. Sanford envelopes, Sanford's pendulum chronoscope.

Sanford envelopes (Sanford, Edmund Clark): Psychology. See: Drever.

Sanford's pendulum chronoscope (Sanford, Edmund Clark): Psychology. See: Drever.

Sanforize (Cluett, Sanford Lockwood): Engineering and Industry. See: Mathews, M. M.

Sanger-Brown. See: Brown, Sanger.

Sanger-Brown ataxia (Brown, Sanger): Medicine. See: Stedman.

SANGER, FREDERICK. 1918- . English biochemist. See: World Who's Who Sci. Sanger's reagent.

SANGER, GEORGE. 1825-1911. English circus owner. See: Dict. Nat. Biog. Sanger's circus.

SANGER, JOHN. 1816-1889. English circus owner. See: Dict. Nat. Biog. Sanger's circus.

Sanger's circus (Sanger, John and George): Recreation and Sports. See: Brewer.

Sanger's reagent (Sanger, Frederick): Chemistry. See: Asimov; Stedman.

Sangrado (Sangrado, Dr.): Generic Word (quack physician). See: Brewer; Partridge; Webster's 3d.

SANGRADO, DR. Character in the novel "Gil Blas," (1715) by Rene Lesage. See: Magill. Sangrado.

Sanin reagent (Derivation undetermined): Chemistry. See: Van Nostrand Chem. Dict.

SANIO, KARL GUSTAV. 1832-1891. German botanist. See: Allg. Deut. Biog. bar of Sanio, Sanio's bean, Sanio's rim.

Sanio's bean (Sanio, Karl Gustav): Botany. See: Webster's 3d.

Sanio's rim (Sanio, Karl Gustav): Botany. See: Gray.

SANKEY. fl. 1910. English engineer. Cited in: Glazebrook. Sankey diagram?

Sankey (Sankey, John, 1st Viscount Sankey): Generic Word (wage deduction). See: Stenhouse.

SANKEY, COLONEL. fl. 1708-1711. English soldier. (Biography source unavailable.) Sankey's Horse.

Sankey commission (Sankey, John, 1st Viscount Sankey): History. See: Steinberg.

Sankey diagram (Sankey): Engineering and Industry. See: Hackh; Thrush.

SANKEY, JOHN, 1ST VISCOUNT SANKEY. 1866-1948. English jurist. See: Who Was Who, 1941-1950. Sankey, Sankey commission.

Sankey's Horse (Sankey, Colonel): Military Science. See: Brewer; Wagner (More Names).

Sansevieria (San Severo, Raimondo di Sangro, Prince of): Botany. See: Webster's 3d.

SANSOM, ARTHUR ERNST. 1838-1907. English physician. See: Who Was Who, 1897-1916. Sansom's sign.

Sansom's sign (Sansom, Arthur Ernst): Medicine. See: Dorland; Stedman.

SANSON, ADRIEN. d. 1708. French geographer. See: Nouv. Biog. Univ. Sanson-Flamsteed projection (or sinusoidal projection).

Sanson-Flamsteed projection (or sinusoidal projection) (Sanson, Adrien and Flamsteed, John): Geography. See: Monkhouse; Moore.

SANSON, LOUIS JOSEPH. 1790-1841. French surgeon. See: World Who's Who Sci. Purkinje-Sanson images.

Santa Claus (Nicholas of Myra, Saint): Generic Word. See: Attwater; Hendrickson; Webster's 3d.

Santa Claus suit (Nicholas of Myra, Saint): Fashion. See: Picken.

Santa Maria tree (Mary, Virgin-Mother?): Botany. See: Webster's 3d.

SANTAYANA, GEORGE. 1863-1952. American poet and philosopher. See: New Encyc. Brit., 1974. Santayanian.

Santayanian (Santayana, George): Philosophy. See: Webster's 3d.

Santi, Raffaello. See: Raphael.

Santini's booming sound (Derivation undetermined): Medicine. See: Dorland; Stedman.

Santorin cement (Derivation undetermined): Engineering and Industry. See: Thrush.

SANTORINI, GIOVANNI DOMENICO. 1681-1737. Italian anatomist. See: World Who's Who Sci. Santorini's cartilage, Santorini's concha, Santorini's duct (or canal), Santorini's incisures (sulcus or fissures), Santorini's labyrinth, Santorini's major caruncle (or papilla), Santorini's muscle, Santorini's tubercle, Santorini's veins.

Santorini's cartilage (Santorini, Giovanni Domenico): Anatomy. See: Donath; Dorland; Stedman.

Santorini's concha (Santorini, Giovanni Domenico): Anatomy. See: Donath; Stedman.

Santorini's duct (or canal) (Santorini, Giovanni Domenico): Anatomy. See: Donath; Dorland; Stedman. Also known as: Bernard's canal.

Santorini's incisures (sulcus or fissures) (Santorini, Giovanni Domenico): Anatomy. See: Dorland; Stedman.

Santorini's labyrinth (Santorini, Giovanni Domenico): Anatomy. See: Stedman.

Santorini's major caruncle (or papilla) (Santorini, Giovanni Domenico): Anatomy. See: Donath; Stedman.

Santorini's muscle (Santorini, Giovanni Domenico): Anatomy. See: Donath; Dorland; Stedman.

Santorini's tubercle (Santorini, Giovanni Domenico): Anatomy. See: Donath; Stedman.

Santorini's veins (Santorini, Giovanni Domenico): Anatomy. See: Donath; Stedman.

Sanusi (Senussi, Sanusiya or Brotherhood of As-Sanus) (Sanusi, Muhammad ibn Ali as-): Religion. See: Canney; Harbottle; New Encyc. Brit., 1974, Microp.; Webster's 3d.

SANUSI, MUHAMMAD IBN ALI AS-. 1787-1859. Algerian religious leader. See: New Encyc. Brit., 1974, Microp. Sanusi (Senussi, Sanusiya or Brotherhood of As-Sanus).

SANVITALI. d. 1761. Italian mathematician. (Biography source unavailable.) Sanvitalia.

Sanvitalia (Sanvitali): Botany. See: Taylor, N.; Webster's 3d.

SANYAL, S. fl. 1929. Indian physician. (Biography source unavailable.) Sanyal's conjunctivitis.

Sanyal's conjunctivitis (Sanyal, S.): Medicine. See: Jablonski.

Sanzio, Raffaello. See: Raphael.

SAPOLINI, GIUSEPPE. 1812-1893. Italian anatomist. Cited in: Index-Cat. Libr. Surg.-Gen. Off., 1st Ser., vol. 12, 1891. Sapolini's nerve.

Sapolini's nerve (Sapolini, Giuseppe): Anatomy. See: Stedman.

SAPPEY, MARIE PHILIBERT CONSTANT. 1810-1896. French anatomist. See: World Who's Who Sci. Sappey's fibers, Sappey's ligament, Sappey's nerve, Sappey's plexus, Sappey's vein.

Sappey's fibers (Sappey, Marie Philibert Constant): Anatomy. See: Donath; Dorland; Stedman.

Sappey's ligament (Sappey, Marie Philibert Constant): Anatomy. See: Donath; Dorland; Stedman.

Sappey's nerve (Sappey, Marie Philibert Constant): Anatomy. See: Donath.

Sappey's plexus (Sappey, Marie Philibert Constant): Anatomy. See: Stedman.

Sappey's vein (Sappey, Marie Philibert Constant): Anatomy. See: Donath; Dorland; Stedman.

Sapphic (verse or stanza) (Sappho): Literature. See: Brewer; Preminger; Scott.

Sapphism (Sappho): Generic Word (lesbianism). See: Fairchild; Hinsie; Partridge.

SAPPHO. fl. ca. 600 B.C. Greek lyric poet of Lesbos. See: Encyc. Brit., 1911. Sapphic (verse or stanza), Sapphism, Sappho.

Sappho (Sappho, the poet): Zoology. See: Webster's 3d.

Saraband (Zarabanda): Dance. See: Wagner (Names).

Sarada (Sarada Nandan): Linguistics. See: Webster's 3d.

SARADA NANDAN. No dates. Kashmirian? linguist. (Biography source unavailable.) Sarada.

Sarah Bernhardt (Bernhardt, Sarah). Generic Word (great actress). See: Hendrickson.

Sarah Josepha Hale Award (Hale, Sarah Josepha): Literature. See: Harrod.

Sarata test reaction (Sarata, Uichiro): Chemistry. See: Van Nostrand Chem. Dict.

SARATA, UICHIRO. fl. 1933. Japanese chemist. Cited in: Chem. Abstr., vol. 28, p. 1372. Sarata test reaction.

SARDANAPALUS. fl. ca. 822 B.C. Legendary ruler of Assyria. See: New Encyc. Brit., 1974, Microp. Sardanapalus (or Sardanapalian).

Sardanapalus (or Sardanapalian) (Sardanapalus, the Assyrian): Generic Word (luxury-loving). See: Brewer; Hendrickson; Partridge.

Sardoodledum (Sardou, Victorien): Literature. See: Webster's 3d.

SARDOU, VICTORIEN. 1831-1908. French playwright. See: New Encyc. Brit., 1974, Microp. Sardoodledum.

SARGENT, B.W. 1906- . Canadian physicist. See: Nature, vol. 167 (April 21, 1951), pp. 630-631; vol. 168 July 14, 1951), p. 60. Sargent curve(s) (or diagram), Sargent rule.

Sargent burner (Sargent, James?): Chemistry. See: Van Nostrand Chem. Dict.

SARGENT, CHARLES SPRAGUE. 1841-1927. American dendrologist. See: World Who's Who Sci. Sargent cypress, Sargent juniper.

Sargent curve(s) (or diagram) (Sargent, B. W.): Physics. See: Markus; Thewlis; Van Nostrand Sci. Encyc.

Sargent cycle (Sargent, James?): Physics. See: Van Nostrand Sci. Encyc.

Sargent cypress (Sargent, Charles Sprague): Botany. See: Webster's 3d.

SARGENT, HELEN DURHAM. 1904- . American psychologist. See: Amer. Psych. Assoc. Direct., 1948. Sargent insight test.

Sargent insight test (Sargent, Helen Durham): Psychology. See: Wolman.

SARGENT, JAMES. 1824-1910. American inventor. See: World Who's Who Sci. Sargent burner?, Sargent cycle?, Sargent timelocks.

SARGENT, SIR JOHN. fl. 1944. English educator. Cited in: Encyc. Brit., 1973 under "Education, History of," p. 1012. Sargent report.

Sargent juniper (Sargent, Charles Sprague): Botany. See: Webster's 3d.

Sargent report (Sargent, Sir John): Education. See: Morris and Irwin.

Sargent rule (Sargent, B. W.): Physics. See: Van Nostrand Chem. Dict.

Sargent timelocks (Sargent, James): Engineering and Industry. Cited in: World Who's Who Sci.

SARNOFF, DAVID. 1891-1971. American radio and television executive. See: Webster's Biog. Dict. David Sarnoff Medal.

Sarracenia (Sarrazin, Michel): Botany. See: Mathews, M. M.; Partridge; Webster's 3d.

SARRAZIN, MICHEL. 1659-1734. French-Canadian physician and naturalist. See: World Who's Who Sci. Sarracenia.

SARROUY, C. fl. 1954. Algerian physician. (Biography source unavailable.) Sarrouy's disease.

Sarrouy's disease (Sarrouy, C.): Medicine. See: Jablonski.

SARRUS, PIERRE FREDERIC. 1823-1861. French mathematician. See: World Who's Who Sci. Sarrus' rule.

Sarrus' rule (Sarrus, Pierre Frederic): Mathematics. See: Ballentyne.

SARRUS, W. fl. 1856. French bandmaster. Cited in: Riemann. Sarrusophone.

Sarrusophone (Sarrus, W.): Music. See: Scholes.

Sarsaparilla (Parillo?): Botany. See: Charnock.

Sartorite (Sartorius von Waltershausen, Baron Wolfgang): Earth Sciences. See: Thrush; Webster's 3d.

SARTORIUS VON WALTERSHAUSEN, BARON WOLFGANG. 1809-1876. German geologist. See: Allg. Deut. Biog. Sartorite.

SARTRE, JEAN PAUL. 1905- . French author, playwright and philosopher. See: New Encyc. Brit., 1974. Sartrian.

Sartrian (Sartre, Jean Paul): Philosophy. See: Webster's 3d.

SARVER, LANDON ARNDALE. 1896- . American chemist. See: Amer. Men Sci., 5th ed. Sarver reagent.

Sarver reagent (Sarver, Landon Arndale): Chemistry. See: Van Nostrand Chem. Dict.

Saryarkite (Derivation undetermined): Earth Sciences. See: Thrush.

SASAN. fl. before 225. Persian ruler. Cited in: New Encyc. Brit., 1974, Microp. Sassanides (or Sasanian) dynasty.

Sassanides (or Sasanian) dynasty (Sasan): History. See: Brewer.

SATAN. In the Old Testament, author of sin and man's accuser. See: Jobes. Satanic school, Satanism (or Satanic) (1), Satanism (or Satanic) (2).

Satanic school (Satan): Literature. See: Preminger; Scott.

Satanism (or Satanic) (1) (Satan): Religion. See: Attwater.

Satanism (or Satanic) (2) (Satan): Generic Word (cruel). See: Partridge.

SATPAEV, KANYSH IMANTAEVICH. 1899- . Russian geologist. See: World Who's Who Sci. Satpaevite.

Satpaevite (Satpaev, Kanysh Imantaevich): Earth Sciences. See: Thrush.

SATTERTHWAITE, THOMAS EDWARD. 1843-1934. American physician. See: World Who's Who Sci. Satterthwaite's method.

Satterthwaite's method (Satterthwaite, Thomas Edward): Medicine. See: Dorland; Stedman.

SATTLER, HUBERT. 1844-1928. Austrian ophthalmologist. See: Biog. Lex. hervorr. Aerzte. Sattler's elastic layer, Sattler's veil.

Sattler's elastic layer (Sattler, Hubert): Medicine. See: Dorland; Stedman.

Sattler's veil (Sattler, Hubert): Medicine. See: Jablonski; Stedman.

Saturday (Saturn): Generic Word. See: Brewer; Funk; Webster's 3d.

Saturday Office of the Blessed Virgin Mary (Mary, Virgin-Mother): Religion. See: Attwater.

Satureia (Satyr): Botany. See: Charnock.

SATURN. Roman god of sowing. See: Jobes. geocronite, line of Saturn, mount of Saturn, ring of Saturn, Saturday, Saturnalia, Saturnalian, Saturnian (days), Saturnian (verse(s)), Saturnine, Saturnismus.

Saturnalia (Saturn): Religion. See: Brewer; Canney; Webster's 3d.

Saturnalian (Saturn): Generic Word (dissolute). See: Charnock; Webster's 3d.

Saturnia (Juno): Zoology. See: Webster's 3d.

Saturnian (days) (Saturn): Generic Word (golden age). See: Charnock; Phyfe; Stenhouse.

Saturnian (verse(s)) (Saturn): Literature. See: Brewer; Preminger; Webster's 3d.

Saturnine (Saturn): Generic Word (gloomy). See: Charnock; Funk; Webster's 3d.

Saturninians (Saturninus): Religion. See: Canney.

SATURNINUS. fl. early 2d c. Gnostic teacher in Antioch, Syria. See: Dict. Christian Biog. under "Saturninus (1)." Saturninians.

Saturnismus (Saturn, the god). See: Remak's paralysis.

SATYR. Race of woodland spirits. See: Jobes. Satureia, Satyriasis, Satyrus.

Satyriasis (Satyr, a wood nymph). See: Hansen's disease.

Satyrus (Satyr): Zoology. See: Pennak.

sauce Caruso (Caruso, Enrico): Food and Drink. See: Hendrickson.

sauce Mornay (Mornay, Philippe de, Seigneur du Plessis-Marly): Food and Drink. See: Hendrickson.

sauce Robert (Vinot, Robert): Food and Drink. See: Hendrickson.

SAUCI. fl. 1835. French gentleman. (Biography source unavailable.) Sauci (diamond).

Sauci (diamond) (Sauci): Applied Arts. See: Wagner (Names).

SAUD, MOHAMMED IBN. fl. 1742. Arabian ruler. Cited in: Encyc. Brit., 1911 under "Arabia," p. 268. Saudi Empires.

Saudi Empires (Saud, Mohammed ibn): History. See: Morris and Irwin.

SAUER, LOUIS WENDLIN. b. 1885. American pediatrician and immunologist. See: Amer. Men Sci., 10th ed. Sauer's vaccine.

SAUERBRUCH, FERDINAND (In full: ERNST FERDINAND). 1875-1951. German surgeon. See: World Who's Who Sci. Sauerbruch's cabinet, Sauerbruch's prosthesis.

Sauerbruch's cabinet (Sauerbruch, Ferdinand): Medicine. See: Dorland; Stedman.

Sauerbruch's prosthesis (Sauerbruch, Ferdinand): Medicine. See: Dorland; Stedman.

Sauer's vaccine (Sauer, Louis Wendlin): Medicine. See: Dorland.

Saul-Crawford test (Saul, J. E. and Crawford, D.): Chemistry. See: Van Nostrand Chem. Dict.

SAUL, J. E. fl. 1918. English chemist. Cited in: Chem. Abstr., Decenn. Index, 1907-1916. Saul-Crawford test, Saul test reaction for gold.

Saul of Tarsus. See: Paul the Apostle, Saint.

Saul test reaction for gold (Saul, J. E.): Chemistry. See: Van Nostrand Chem. Dict.

SAUNDBY, ROBERT. 1849-1918. English physician. See: Who Was Who, 1916-1928. Saundby's test.

Saundby's test (Saundby, Robert): Medicine. See: Dorland; Stedman.

Saunders' disease (Saunders, Edward Watts): Medicine. See: Dorland.

SAUNDERS, EDWARD WATTS. 1854-1927. American physician. See: Who Was Who Amer., vol. 1. Saunders' disease, Saunders' sign.

SAUNDERS, FREDERICK ALBERT. b. 1875. American physicist. See: Amer. Men Sci., 9th ed; Pogg., vols. 5, 6. Russell-Saunders coupling.

SAUNDERS, JOHN WARREN, JR. 1919- . American embryologist. See: Amer. Men and Women Sci., 12th ed. Saunder's ridge.

Saunders' laws of educational innovation (Saunders, Robert Mallough): Sociology. See: Martin.

Saunders, Richard, pseud. See: Franklin, Benjamin.

Saunder's ridge (Saunders, John Warren, Jr.): Zoology. See: Gray.

SAUNDERS, ROBERT MALLOUGH. 1915- . American electrical engineer. See: Amer. Men and Women Sci., 12th ed. Saunders' laws of educational innovation.

Saunders' sign (Saunders, Edward Watts): Medicine. See: Dorland.

Saunders-Sutton syndrome (Saunders, William and Sutton, Thomas): Medicine. See: Jablonski.

SAUNDERS, WILLIAM. 1743-1817. Scottish physician. See: Dict. Nat. Biog. Saunders-Sutton syndrome.

SAURAU, COUNT FRANZ JOSEPH. 1760-1832. Austrian statesman. See: Wurzbach. Saurauia.

Saurauia (Saurau, Count Franz Joseph): Botany. See: Webster's 3d.

SAUREL, PAUL LOUIS. 1871-1934. American mathematician. See: Pogg., vols. 5, 6. Saurel theorem.

Saurel theorem (Saurel, Paul Louis): Mathematics. See: Internat. Dict. Ap. Math.; Van Nostrand Sci. Encyc.

SAUSSURE, FERDINAND DE. 1857-1913. Swiss linguist. See: Internat. Encyc. Soc. Sci. Saussurean linguistics.

SAUSSURE, HORACE BENEDICT DE. 1740-1799. Swiss naturalist. See: Encyc. Brit., 1911. Saussuria, Saussurite, Saussuritization.

SAUSSURE, NICHOLAS THEODORE DE. 1767-1845. Swiss naturalist. See: Encyc. Brit., 1911. Saussuria.

Saussurean linguistics (Saussure, Ferdinand de): Linguistics. See: Hartmann.

Saussuria (Saussure, Horace Benedict de and Nicholas Theodore de): Botany. See: Webster's 3d.

Saussurite (Saussure, Horace Benedict de): Earth Sciences. See: Thrush; Webster's 3d.

Saussuritization (Saussure, Horace Benedict de): Earth Sciences. See: Thrush.

SAUVAGES, PIERRE-AUGUSTIN BOISSIER DE LA CROIX DE. 1710-1795. French botanist. See: Michaud. Sauvagesia.

Sauvagesia (Sauvages, Pierre-Augustin Boissier de la Croix de): Botany. See: Webster's 3d.

SAUVEUR, ALBERT. 1863-1939. Belgian metallurgist. See: World Who's Who Sci. Sauveur reagent.

Sauveur reagent (Sauveur, Albert): Chemistry. See: Van Nostrand Chem. Dict.

SAVAGE, HENRY. 1810-1900. English anatomist and gynecologist. See: Brit. Med. J., vol. II (1900), p. 1058. Savage's perineal body.

Savage's perineal body (Savage, Henry): Anatomy. See: Stedman.

Savalle test (Derivation undetermined): Chemistry. See: Van Nostrand Chem. Dict.

Savarin (egg bread) (Brillat-Savarin, Jean Anthelme): Food and Drink. See: De Sola; Hendrickson; Webster's 3d.

SAVART, FELIX. 1791-1841. French physicist. See: World Who's Who Sci. Biot-Savart law, Savart plate (or polariscope), Savart (unit), Savart wheel.

Savart plate (or polariscope) (Savart, Felix): Physics. See: Huschke; Internat. Dict. Phys. Elec.

Savart (unit) (Savart, Felix): Physics. See: Dresner.

Savart wheel (Savart, Felix): Physics. See: Drever.

Savelsberg process (Savelsberg, Walter): Engineering and Industry. See: Thrush.

SAVELSBERG, WALTER. fl. 1930. Swedish engineer. Cited in: Chem. Abstr., Decenn. Index, 1927-1936. Savelsberg process.

Savery fire engine (Savery, Thomas): Engineering and Industry. See: Auger.

SAVERY, THOMAS. 1650?-1715. English engineer. See: New Encyc. Brit., 1974. Savery fire engine.

SAVI, PAOLO. 1798-1871. Italian zoologist and geologist. See: Encyc. Brit., 1911. Savi's ampulla, Savi's warbler, Savite.

SAVILE, SIR HENRY. 1549-1622. English classical scholar. See: Dict. Nat. Biog. Savilian professor (or professorships).

Savilian professor (or professorships) (Savile, Sir Henry): Mathematics. See: Harvey; Wagner (More Names).

SAVILL, THOMAS DIXON. 1856-1910. English physician. See: Dict. Nat. Biog. Savill's disease.

Savill's disease (Savill, Thomas Dixon): Medicine. See: Dorland; Jablonski; Stedman.

Savi's ampulla (Savi, Paolo): Zoology. See: Gray.

Savi's warbler (Savi, Paolo): Zoology. See: Gray.

Savite (Savi, Paolo): Earth Sciences. See: Charnock.

Savonarola chair (Savonarola, Cirolamo Maria Francesco Matteo): Applied Arts. See: Webster's 3d.

SAVONAROLA, CIROLAMO MARIA FRANCESCO MATTEO. 1452-1498. Italian religious reformer. See: Encyc. Brit., 1911. Savonarola chair, Savonarolists.

Savonarolists (Savonarola, Cirolamo Maria Francesco Matteo): Religion. Cited in: Laughlin.

Sawarizkij, Aleksandr Nikolaevic. See: Zavarickij, Aleksandr Nikolaevic.

SAWYER, CHARLES BALDWIN. b. 1894. American metallurgist. See: Amer. Men Sci., 8th ed. Sawyer-Kjellgren process.

Sawyer-Kjellgren process (Sawyer, Charles Baldwin and Kjellgren, Bengt Ragnar Fritiof): Engineering and Industry. See: Thrush.

SAX, ADOLPHE (ANTOINE JOSEPH). 1814-1894. Belgian maker of musical instruments. See: Encyc. Brit., 1911. Sax tuba, Saxhorn(s), Saxophone, Saxotromba.

Sax tuba (Sax, Adolphe): Music. See: Apel; Webster's 3d.

SAXA, Q. VOCONIUS. fl. 169 B. C. Roman tribune. See: Dict. Grk. Rom. Biog. Myth. Voconian law.

Saxhorn(s) (Sax, Adolphe): Music. See: Scholes; Webster's 3d.

Saxophone (Sax, Adolphe): Music. See: Apel; Funk; Hendrickson.

Saxotromba (Sax, Adolphe): Music. See: Partridge.

SAXTON, JOSEPH. 1799-1873. American inventor. See: Dict. Amer. Biog. Saxton's pulley.

Saxton's pulley (Saxton, Joseph): Engineering and Industry. See: Auger.

Saxtorph maneuver (Saxtorph, Matthias): Medicine. See: Stedman. Also known as: Osiander's maneuver, Pajot's maneuver.

SAXTORPH, MATTHIAS. 1740-1800. Danish obstetrician and gynecologist. See: Biog. Lex. hervorr. Aerzte. Saxtorph maneuver.

Say blister beetle (Say, Thomas): Zoology. See: Webster's 3d.

SAY, JEAN BAPTISTE. 1767-1832. French economist. See: Internat. Encyc. Soc. Sci. Say's law (of markets).

SAY, LORD. fl. 1631. English colonialist. Cited in: Dict. Nat. Biog. under "Rich, Robert, 2d Earl of Warwick." Saybrook patent.

Say stinkbug (Say, Thomas): Zoology. See: Webster's 3d.

SAY, THOMAS. 1787-1834. American entomologist. See: World Who's Who Sci. Say blister beetle, Say stinkbug, Say's flycatcher, Say's phoebe (or pewee).

Saybolt colorimeter (Saybolt, George M.?): Engineering and Industry. See: Thrush.

SAYBOLT, GEORGE M. d. 1924. American chemist. Cited in: Chem. Abstr., Decenn. Index, 1907-1916. Saybolt colorimeter?, Saybolt seconds, Saybolt viscosimeter, Saybolt viscosity.

Saybolt seconds (Saybolt, George M.): Chemistry. See: Thrush.

Saybolt viscosimeter (Saybolt, George M.): Chemistry. See: Internat. Dict. Phys. Elec.; Van Nostrand Sci. Encyc. under "Viscosity;" Webster's 3d.

Saybolt viscosity (Saybolt, George M.): Chemistry. See: Webster's 3d.

Saybrook patent (Say, Lord and Brook, Lord): History. Cited in: Encyc. Brit., 1973 under "Warwick, Robert Rich, 2d Earl of."

Sayers Memorial Prize (Sayers, William Charles Berwick): Library Science. See: Harrod.

SAYERS, WILLIAM CHARLES BERWICK. 1881-1960. English librarian. See: Who Was Who, 1951-1960. Sayers Memorial Prize.

SAYRE, LEWIS ALBERT. 1820-1900. American surgeon. See: World Who's Who Sci. Sayre's jacket, Sayre's suspension apparatus.

Sayre's jacket (Sayre, Lewis Albert): Medicine. See: Dorland; Stedman.

Sayre's suspension apparatus (Sayre, Lewis Albert): Medicine. See: Dorland; Stedman.

Say's flycatcher (Say, Thomas): Zoology. See: Mathews, M. M.

Say's law (of markets) (Say, Jean Baptiste): Economics. See: Greenwald; Seldon; Webster's 3d.

Say's phoebe (or pewee) (Say, Thomas): Zoology. See: Gray; Mathews, M. M.; Webster's 3d.

SAYTZEFF, MICHAIL MICHAJLOVICH. b. 1845. Russian chemist. See: Pogg., vol. 3. Saytzeff rule.

Saytzeff rule (Saytzeff, Michail Michajlovich): Chemistry. See: Van Nostrand Chem. Dict.

Sazerac-Pouzergues tests (Sazerac, Robert and Pouzergues, J.): Chemistry. See: Van Nostrand Chem. Dict.

SAZERAC, ROBERT. fl. 1930. French pharmaceutical chemist. Cited in: Chem. Abstr., vol. 26, pp. 2391, 3202. Sazerac-Pouzergues tests.

SBORGI, UMBERTO. 1883-1955. Italian chemist. See: Pogg., vols. 5, 6. Sborgite.

Sborgite (Sborgi, Umberto): Earth Sciences. See: Thrush.

SCACCHI, ARCANGELO. 1810-1894. Italian mineralogist. See: Pogg., vols. 2, 3. Scacchite.

Scacchite (Scacchi, Arcangelo): Earth Sciences. See: Thrush; Webster's 3d.

Scaevola (Scaevola, Gaius Mucius): Botany. See: Webster's 3d.

SCAEVOLA, GAIUS MUCIUS. fl. 6th c. B. C. Roman hero. See: New Encyc. Brit., 1974, Microp. Scaevola.

Scaglietti-Dagnini syndrome (Scaglietti, Oscar and Dagnini, Guido). See: Erdheim's syndrome.

SCAGLIETTI, OSCAR. fl. 1935. Italian orthopedic surgeon. See: Who's Who Sci. Europe, 1972. Scaglietti-Dagnini syndrome.

Scaife process (Derivation undetermined): Engineering and Industry. See: Thrush.

SCALIGER, JULIUS CAESAR. 1484-1558. Italian philologist and scholar. See: Encyc. Brit., 1911. Julian Day.

SCALLAN, HUGH (FATHER HUGO). fl. 1889. Catholic missionary. (Biography source unavailable.) Father Hugo's rose.

Scammozzi's rule (Scamozzi, Vincenzo): Architecture. See: Brewer.

Scamozzi (Scamozzi, Vincenzo): Architecture. See: Webster's 3d.

SCAMOZZI, VINCENZO. 1552-1616. Italian architect. See: New Encyc. Brit., 1974, Microp. Scamozzi's rule, Scamozzi.

SCANLON, JOSEPH NORBERT. 1899?-1956. American labor leader. See: New York Times, Feb. 11, 1956, p. 17. Scanlon plan.

Scanlon plan (Scanlon, Joseph Norbert): Engineering and Industry. See: Greenwald.

SCANZONI, FRIEDRICH WILHELM. 1821-1891. German obstetrician. See: Biog. Lex. hervorr. Aerzte. Scanzoni's maneuver, Scanzoni's second os.

Scanzoni's maneuver (Scanzoni, Friedrich Wilhelm): Medicine. See: Dorland; Stedman.

Scanzoni's second os (Scanzoni, Friedrich Wilhelm): Medicine. See: Stedman. Also known as: Bandl's ring.

SCARAMOUCH. Stock character in the Italian Commedia dell'Arte. See: New Encyc. Brit., 1974, Microp. Scaramouch.

Scaramouch (Scaramouch, the character): Generic Word (boastful coward). See: Hargrave; Partridge; Webster's 3d.

SCARFF, FREDERICK W. d. 1931. English soldier. (Biography source unavailable.) Scarff mount.

SCARFF, JOHN EDWIN. 1898- . American neurosurgeon. See: Amer. Men and Women Sci., 12th ed. Stookey-Scarff operation.

Scarff mount (Scarff, Frederick W.): Weapons. See: Quick.

SCARPA, ANTONIO. 1747-1832. Italian anatomist, orthopedist and ophthalmologist. See: Biog. Lex. hervorr. Aerzte. Scarpa's fascia, Scarpa's fluid (or liquid), Scarpa's foramina, Scarpa's ganglion, Scarpa's habenula, Scarpa's hiatus (or orifice), Scarpa's membrane, Scarpa's method, Scarpa's nerve, Scarpa's sheath, Scarpa's shoe, Scarpa's triangle.

Scarpa's fascia (Scarpa, Antonio): Anatomy. See: Donath; Dorland; Stedman.

Scarpa's fluid (or liquid) (Scarpa, Antonio): Anatomy. See: Donath; Stedman.

Scarpa's foramina (Scarpa, Antonio): Anatomy. See: Donath; Dorland; Stedman.

Scarpa's ganglion (Scarpa, Antonio): Anatomy. See: Donath; Hinsie; Stedman.

Scarpa's habenula (Scarpa, Antonio). See: Haller's habenula.

Scarpa's hiatus (or orifice) (Scarpa, Antonio): Anatomy. See: Donath; Stedman.

Scarpa's membrane (Scarpa, Antonio): Anatomy. See: Donath; Dorland; Stedman.

Scarpa's method (Scarpa, Antonio): Medicine. See: Stedman.

Scarpa's nerve (Scarpa, Antonio): Anatomy. See: Donath; Stedman.

Scarpa's sheath (Scarpa, Antonio): Anatomy. See: Stedman. Also known as: Cooper's fascia.

Scarpa's shoe (Scarpa, Antonio): Medicine. See: Dorland; Stedman.

Scarpa's triangle (Scarpa, Antonio): Anatomy. See: Donath; Dorland; Stedman.

SCELETH, CHARLES EDWARD. 1873-1942. American physician. See: Proc. Inst. Med. Chicago, vol. 14 (June 15, 1942), pp. 198-199. Sceleth treatment.

Sceleth treatment (Sceleth, Charles Edward): Medicine. See: Dorland.

SCHACHER, POLYCARP GOTTLIEB. 1674-1737. German physician. See: Biog. Lex. hervorr. Aerzte. Schacher's ganglion.

Schacher's ganglion (Schacher, Polycarp Gottlieb): Medicine. See: Dorland; Stedman.

SCHACHOWA, SERAPHINA. fl. 1873. Russian histologist in Switzerland. Cited in: Royal Soc. Cat. Sci. Pap., 1800-1883. Schachowa's tube(s).

Schachowa's tube(s) (Schachowa, Seraphina): Anatomy. See: Donath; Dorland; Stedman. Also known as: Ferrein's tube.

SCHACK, ADOLPH. fl. 1881. German pharmaceutical chemist. Cited in: Royal Soc. Cat. Sci. Pap., 1800-1883. Schack test reaction.

Schack test reaction (Schack, Adolph): Chemistry. See: Van Nostrand Chem. Dict.

SCHACT, HJALMAR (In full: HORACE GREELEY HJALMAR). 1877-1970. German financier. See: New Encyc. Brit., 1974, Microp. Schactism (or Schachtianism).

Schactism (or Schachtianism) (Schact, Hjalmar): Economics. See: Webster's 3d.

SCHAD, CHRISTIAN. fl. 1918. German photographic chemist. (Biography source unavailable.) Schadographs.

Schadographs (Schad, Christian): Photography. See: Focal Encyc. Photog. under "Abstract Photography."

SCHAEFER. fl. 20th c. German engineer. (Biography source unavailable.) Schaefer petrol injection system.

SCHAEFER, ERICH. 1897- . German dermatologist. Cited in: Index-Cat. Libr. Surg.-Gen. Off., 5th Ser., vol. 1, 1959. Schaefer's syndrome.

SCHAEFER, GEORGE L. fl. 1898. American pharmaceutical chemist. Cited in: Royal Soc. Cat. Sci. Pap., 1884-1900. Schaeffer test for other coca alkaloids in cocaine.

SCHAEFER, LOUIS. fl. 1887. German pharmaceutical chemist. Cited in: Royal Soc. Cat. Sci. Pap., 1884-1900. Schaefer test for other cinchona alkaloids in quinine sulfate.

Schaefer petrol injection system (Schaefer): Engineering and Industry. See: Auger.

Schaefer-Siemens syndrome (Schaefer, Erich and Siemens, Hermann Werner). See: Schaefer's syndrome.

Schaefer test for other cinchona alkaloids in quinine sulfate (Schaefer, Louis): Chemistry. See: Van Nostrand Chem. Dict.

Schaefer's syndrome (Schaefer, Erich): Medicine. See: Jablonski. Also known as: Schaefer-Siemens syndrome.

SCHAEFFER, GEORGE C. fl. 1850-1863. American chemist. Cited in: Royal Soc. Cat. Sci. Pap., 1800-1863. Schaffer's test?

SCHAEFFER, JACOB CHRISTIAN. 1718-1790. German naturalist. See: World Who's Who Sci. Schaeffera (Schaefferia).

SCHAEFFER, LOUIS. fl. 1869. German chemist. Cited in: Royal Soc. Cat. Sci. Pap., 1864-1873. Schaeffer's acid, Schaeffer's salt.

SCHAEFFER, MAX. 1852-1923. German neurologist. (Biography source unavailable.) Schaeffer(s) reflex.

Schaeffer(s) reflex (Schaeffer, Max): Medicine. See: Dorland; Hinsie; Stedman.

Schaeffer test for other coca alkaloids in cocaine (Schaefer, George L.): Chemistry. See: Van Nostrand Chem. Dict.

Schaeffera (Schaefferia) (Schaeffer, Jacob Christian): Botany. See: Charnock; Webster's 3d.

Schaeffer's acid (Schaeffer, Louis): Chemistry. See: Hackh; Webster's 3d.

Schaeffer's salt (Schaeffer, Louis): Chemistry. See: Webster's 3d.

SCHAER, EDUARD. 1842-1913. Swiss pharmaceutical chemist. See: Pogg., vols. 3, 4, 5. Schaer('s) reagent, Schaer test for blood.

Schaer('s) reagent (Schaer, Eduard): Chemistry. See: Stedman; Van Nostrand Chem. Dict.

Schaer test for blood (Schaer, Eduard): Chemistry. See: Van Nostrand Chem. Dict.

SCHAERGES, K. F. M. fl. 1913. German? chemist. Cited in: Chem. Abstr., Decenn. Index, 1907-1916. Schaerges test reaction?

Schaerges test reaction (Schaerges, K. F. M.?): Chemistry. See: Van Nostrand Chem. Dict.

SCHAFARZIK, FERENC. 1854-1927. Hungarian mineralogist. See: Min. Mag., vol. 22 (Sept. 1930), p. 405. Schafarzikite.

Schafarzikite (Schafarzik, Ferenc): Earth Sciences. See: Thrush; Webster's 3d.

Schafer, Sir Edward Albert Sharpey-. See: Sharpey-Schafer, Sir Edward Albert.

Schafer (Schaefer's) method (Sharpey-Schafer, Sir Edward Albert): Medicine. See: Dorland; Stedman; Thrush.

Schafer (Schaefer)-Nielsen-Drinker method (Sharpey-Schafer, Sir Edward Albert; Nielsen, Holger; and Drinker, Cecil Kent): Medicine. See: Stedman; Thrush.

Schaffer's test (Schaeffer, George C.?): Chemistry. See: Stedman.

SCHAIRER, JOHN FRANK. 1904- . American physical chemist and geologist. See: World Who's Who Sci. Schairerite.

Schairerite (Schairer, John Frank): Earth Sciences. See: Thrush; Webster's 3d.

SCHALLER, WALDEMAR THEODORE. b. 1882. American mineralogist. See: Amer. Men Sci., 10th ed. Schallerite.

Schallerite (Schaller, Waldemar Theodore): Earth Sciences. See: Thrush; Webster's 3d.

SCHAMBERG, JAY FRANK. 1870-1934. American dermatologist. See: World Who's Who Sci. Schamberg's disease (or dermatosis).

Schamberg's disease (or dermatosis) (Schamberg, Jay Frank): Medicine. See: Dorland; Jablonski; Stedman.

SCHANZ, ALFRED. 1868-1931. German orthopedic surgeon. See: Biog. Lex. hervorr. Aerzte. Schanz's disease, Schanz's syndrome.

Schanz's disease (Schanz, Alfred): Medicine. See: Jablonski.

Schanz's syndrome (Schanz, Alfred): Medicine. See: Dorland; Jablonski; Stedman.

SCHAPIRO, HEINRICH. 1852-1901. Russian physician. See: Biog. Lex. hervorr. Aerzte. Schapiro's sign.

Schapiro's sign (Schapiro, Heinrich): Medicine. See: Dorland; Stedman.

Schapringer test for lignin in paper (Derivation undetermined): Chemistry. See: Van Nostrand Chem. Dict.

Schapringer test for shellac in varnish (Derivation undetermined): Chemistry. See: Van Nostrand Chem. Dict.

Schardinger dextrin (Schardinger, Franz): Chemistry. See: Webster's 3d.

Schardinger enzyme (Schardinger, Franz): Chemistry. See: Stedman; Webster's 3d.

SCHARDINGER, FRANZ. fl. 1902. Austrian chemist. Cited in: Royal Soc. Cat. Sci. Pap., 1884-1900. Schardinger dextrin, Schardinger enzyme, Schardinger reaction.

Schardinger reaction (Schardinger, Franz): Chemistry. See: Ballentyne; Stedman.

SCHATZKI, RICHARD. 1901-   . American roentgenologist. See: Direct. Med. Specialists, 1974-1975. Schatzki's ring.

Schatzki's ring (Schatzki, Richard): Medicine. See: Jablonski.

SCHAUDINN, FRITZ RICHARD. 1871-1906. German zoologist. See: World Who's Who Sci. Schaudinn's fluid (or fixation).

Schaudinn's fluid (or fixation) (Schaudinn, Fritz Richard): Zoology. See: Dorland; Pennak; Stedman.

SCHAUER, JOHANN KONRAD. 1813-1848. German botanist. See: Allg. Deut. Biog. Schaueria.

Schaueria (Schauer, Johann Konrad): Botany. See: Taylor, N.

Schaumann bodies (Schaumann, Joergen): Medicine. See: Dorland; Stedman.

SCHAUMANN, JOERGEN. 1879-1953. Swedish dermatologist. See: Nord. Med., vol. 51 (January 7, 1954), pp. 71-76. Besnier-Boeck-Schaumann syndrome, Schaumann bodies, Schaumann's lymphogranuloma.

Schaumann's disease (Schaumann, Joergen). See: Besnier-Boeck-Schaumann syndrome.

Schaumann's lymphogranuloma (Schaumann, Joergen). See: Boeck's sarcoid.

SCHAUTA, FRIEDRICH. 1849-1910. Austrian gynecologist. See: Biog. Lex. hervorr. Aerzte. Schauta's operation.

Schauta's operation (Schauta, Friedrich): Medicine. See: Dorland.

SCHEDE, MAX. 1844-1902. German surgeon. See: Biog. Lex. hervorr. Aerzte. Schede's method (or clot).

Schede's method (or clot) (Schede, Max): Medicine. See: Dorland; Stedman.

SCHEELE, KARL WILHELM. 1742-1786. Swedish chemist. See: World Who's Who Sci. Scheelite, Scheele's green.

Scheele's green (Scheele, Karl Wilhelm): Chemistry. See: Dorland; Hackh; Webster's 3d.

Scheelite (Scheele, Karl Wilhelm): Earth Sciences. See: Thrush; Van Nostrand Sci. Encyc.; Webster's 3d.

SCHEERER, CAPT. fl. 1822. Swiss? traveler. Cited in: Dana. Scheererite.

SCHEERER, MARTIN. 1900-1961. German-born American psychologist. See: Amer. Psych. Assoc. Direct., 1962. Gelb-Goldstein-Weigl-Scheerer object sorting test, Goldstein-Scheerer cube test, Goldstein-Scheerer stick test, Weigl-Goldstein-Scheerer test.

Scheererite (Scheerer, Capt.): Earth Sciences. See: Thrush.

SCHEFFE, HENRY. 1907-   . American mathematician. See: Amer. Men and Women Sci., 12th ed. Scheffe's test.

SCHEFFER, HENRIC THEOPHIL. 1710-1759. Swedish chemist. See: World Who's Who Sci. Schefferite.

Schefferite (Scheffer, Henric Theophil): Earth Sciences. See: Thrush; Webster's 3d.

Scheffe's test (Scheffe, Henry): Statistics. See: Kendall.

SCHEFFLER, J. C. fl. 18th c. German botanist. (Biographical source unavailable.) Schefflera.

Schefflera (Scheffler, J. C.): Botany. See: Taylor, N.; Webster's 3d.

SCHEHEREZADE. Fictitious queen and narrator of the stories in the "Arabian Nights Entertainment." See: Magill. Scheherezade (or Scheherazadian).

Scheherezade (or Scheherazadian) (Scheherezade, Queen): Generic Word (storyteller). See: Partridge; Webster's 3d.

Scheibeite (Derivation undetermined): Earth Sciences. See: Thrush.

SCHEIBLER, CARL. 1827-1899. German chemist. See: World Who's Who Sci. Scheibler('s) reagent (or test).

Scheibler('s) reagent (or test) (Scheibler, Carl): Chemistry. See: Hackh; Stedman; Van Nostrand Chem. Dict.

SCHEIE, HAROLD GLENDON. 1909-   . American ophthalmologist. See: Amer. Men and Women Sci., 12th ed. Scheie's syndrome.

Scheie's syndrome (Scheie, Harold Glendon): Medicine. See: Jablonski; Stedman; Wolman. Also known as: Forme fruste of Harler's syndrome, late Hurler's syndrome.

SCHEINER, CHRISTOPH. ca. 1575-1650. German astronomer. See: World Who's Who Sci. Scheiner's experiment.

SCHEINER, JULIUS. 1858-1913. German astrophysicist. See: World Who's Who Sci. Scheiner speed.

Scheiner speed (Scheiner, Julius): Photography. See: Focal Encyc. Photog.; Van Nostrand Sci. Encyc. under "Sensitivity Determination of Photographic Material;" Webster's 3d.

Scheiner's experiment (Scheiner, Christoph): Physiology. See: Dorland; Drever; Stedman.

Schellbach tubing (Derivation undetermined): Engineering and Industry. See: Thrush.

SCHELLING, FRIEDRICH WILHELM JOSEPH VON. 1775-1854. German philosopher. See: New Encyc. Brit., 1974, Microp. Schellingian.

Schellingian (Schelling, Friedrich Wilhelm Joseph von): Philosophy. See: Webster's 3d.

SCHELLONG, FRITZ. 1891-1953. German physician. See: Deut. Med. Wchnschr., vol. 78 (April 10, 1953), p. 576. Schellong-Strisower phenomenon, Schellong test.

Schellong-Strisower phenomenon (Schellong, Fritz and Strisower, Rudolf): Medicine. See: Stedman.

Schellong test (Schellong, Fritz): Medicine. See: Stedman.

SCHEMELLI, GEORG CHRISTIAN. ca. 1676-1762. German cantor. Cited in: Grove under "Bach, Johann Sebastien." Schemelli Hymn-Book.

Schemelli Hymn-Book (Schemelli, Georg Christian): Music. See: Scholes.

Schemjakin, F. M. See: Shemyakin, F. M.

SCHENCK, A. T. fl. 1927. German? engineer. Cited in: Chem. Abstr., Decenn. Index, 1927-1936. Schenck porosimeter?

SCHENCK, BENJAMIN ROBINSON. 1872-1920. American surgeon. See: World Who's Who Sci. Schenck's (Schenk's) disease.

Schenk-Burmeister test (Schenk, Daniel Johannes and Burmeister, Hermann Carl Gustav): Chemistry. See: Van Nostrand Chem. Dict.

Schenck porosimeter (Schenck, A. T.?): Engineering and Industry. See: Thrush.

Schenck's (Schenk's) disease (Schenck, Benjamin Robinson): Medicine. See: Dorland; Jablonski; Stedman. Also known as: Beurmann-Gougerot disease, Beurmann's disease.

SCHENK, DANIEL JOHANNES. b. 1880. German chemist. See: Pogg., vols. 6, 7a. Schenk-Burmeister test, Schenk test for copper?

Schenk test for copper (Schenk, Daniel Johannes?): Chemistry. See: Van Nostrand Chem. Dict.

SCHENKER, HEINRICH. 1868-1935. Polish-born Austrian music theorist. See: New Encyc. Brit., 1974, Microp. Schenker system.

Schenker system (Schenker, Heinrich): Music. See: Apel.

SCHENKER, VICTOR JOSEPH. 1908- . Canadian-born American neurochemist. See: World Who's Who Sci. Selye and Schenker test.

Scherbatschew, D. See: Sherbatschev, D.

SCHERER, HANS JOACHIM. 1906- . Austrian physician. Cited in: Index-Cat. Libr. Surg.-Gen. Off., 5th Ser., vol. 1, 1959. Van Bogaert-Scherer-Epstein syndrome.

SCHERER, JOHANN JOSEPH VON. 1814-1869. German physician and chemist. See: Allg. Deut. Biog. Scherer's test.

SCHERER, OTTO. fl. 1927. German chemist. Cited in: Chem. Abstr., vol. 21, p. 1774. Manchot-Scherer reagent.

Scherer's test (Scherer, Johann Joseph von): Medicine. See: Dorland; Stedman.

Schering bridge (Schering, Harald Ernst Malmsten): Electronics. See: Hughes; Internat. Dict. Phys. Elec.; Markus.

SCHERING, HARALD ERNST MALMSTEN. b. 1880. German engineer. See: Pogg., vols. 6, 7a. Schering bridge.

SCHERINGA, KLAAS. 1886-1936. Dutch pharmaceutical chemist. See: Pogg., vol. 6. Scheringa test reaction for neoarsphenamine.

Scheringa test reaction for neoarsphenamine (Scheringa, Klaas): Chemistry. See: Van Nostrand Chem. Dict.

SCHERK, HEINRICH FERDINAND. 1798-1885. German mathematician and astronomer. See: Allg. Deut. Biog. surface of Scherk.

SCHERLING, GABRIEL. fl. 16th c. German religious sect founder. (Biography source unavailable.) Gabrielites.

SCHERRER, PAUL HERMAN. 1890-1969. Swiss physicist. See: New Encyc. Brit., 1974, Microp. Debye-Scherrer-Hull method.

SCHETELIG, JACOB GRUBBE COCK. 1875-1935. Norwegian mineralogist. See: Min. Mag., vol. 24 (June 1936), pp. 300-301. Scheteligite.

Scheteligite (Schetelig, Jacob Grubbe Cock): Earth Sciences. See: Thrush; Webster's 3d.

SCHEUCHZER, JOHANN. 1684-1738. Swiss botanist and physician. See: Allg. Deut. Biog. Scheuchzeria.

SCHEUCHZER, JOHANN JACOB. 1672-1733. Swiss botanist and geologist. See: World Who's Who Sci. Scheuchzeria.

Scheuchzeria (Scheuchzer, Johann Jacob and Johann): Botany. See: Charnock; Webster's 3d.

SCHEUERMANN, HOLGER WERFEL. 1877-1960. Danish orthopedist. See: World Who's Who Sci. Scheuermann's disease.

Scheuermann's disease (Scheuermann, Holger Werfel): Medicine. See: Dorland; Jablonski; Stedman.

SCHEUSTER. fl. mid-19th c. American lawyer. (Biography source unavailable.) Shyster.

SCHEUTHAUER, GUSTAV. 1832-1894. German physician. See: Biog. Lex. hervorr. Aerzte. Scheuthauer-Marie-Sainton syndrome.

Scheuthauer-Marie-Sainton syndrome (Scheuthauer, Gustav; Marie, Pierre; and Sainton, Raymond): Medicine. See: Jablonski. Also known as: Hulkrantz's syndrome, Marie-Sainton disease, Scheuthauer-Marie syndrome.

Scheuthauer-Marie syndrome (Scheuthauer, Gustav and Marie, Pierre). See: Scheuthauer-Marie-Sainton syndrome.

SCHEVKET, OMER. fl. 1914. German chemist. Cited in: Chem. Abstr., Decenn. Index, 1907-1916. Schewket test for gallic and tannic acids in plant powders, Schewket test reaction for di- and tri-phenols, Schewket test reaction for lead.

Schewket test for gallic and tannic acids in plant powders (Schevket, Omer): Chemistry. See: Van Nostrand Chem. Dict.

Schewket test reaction for di- and tri-phenols (Schevket, Omer): Chemistry. See: Van Nostrand Chem. Dict.

Schewket test reaction for lead (Schevket, Omer): Chemistry. See: Van Nostrand Chem. Dict.

SCHIASSI, BENEDETTO. fl. 1903. Italian surgeon. Cited in: Kelly. Schiassi's operation.

Schiassi's operation (Schiassi, Benedetto): Medicine. See: Dorland.

Schicht mixed-flow fan (Derivation undetermined): Engineering and Industry. See: Thrush.

SCHICK, BELA. 1877-1967. Hungarian-born American pediatrician. See: World Who's Who Sci. Schick control, Schick('s) test, Schick's method.

Schick control (Schick, Bela): Medicine. See: Stedman.

Schick('s) test (Schick, Bela): Medicine. See: Dorland; Stedman; Van Nostrand Sci. Encyc.

Schick's method (Schick, Bela): Medicine. See: Stedman.

Schicksal analysis (Derivation undetermined): Psychiatry. See: Hinsie.

SCHIEFFERDECKER, PAUL. 1849-1931. German anatomist. See: Biog. Lex. hervorr. Aerzte. Schiefferdecker's disk, Schiefferdecker's theory.

Schiefferdecker's disk (Schiefferdecker, Paul): Medicine. See: Dorland.

Schiefferdecker's theory (Schiefferdecker, Paul): Medicine. See: Dorland.

SCHIELE, CHRISTIAN. fl. 1856. English engineer. Cited in: Singer. Schiele's pivot.

Schiele's pivot (Schiele, Christian): Engineering and Industry. See: Webster's 3d.

SCHIEMANN, GUENTHER. 1899- . Polish-born German chemist. See: World Who's Who Sci. Balz-Schiemann reaction.

Schiemann reaction (Schiemann, Guenther). See: Balz-Schiemann reaction.

Schiff base(s) (Schiff, Hugo): Chemistry. See: Ballentyne; Hackh; Stedman.

SCHIFF, HUGO. 1834-1915. German organic chemist. See: Pogg., vols. 2 to 6. periodic acid-Schiff stain, Schiff base(s), Schiff test (or test reagents) for aldehydes, Schiff test reaction for carbohydrates, Schiff test reaction for chromate?, Schiff test reactions for cholesterol, Schiff test solution for allantoin or urea, Schiff test solution for hydrogen peroxide?

SCHIFF, MORITZ. 1823-1896. German physiologist. See: World Who's Who Sci. Schiff-Sherrington phenomenon.

Schiff-Sherrington phenomenon (Schiff, Moritz and Sherrington, Charles Scott): Medicine. See: Stedman.

Schiff test (or test reagents) for aldehydes (Schiff, Hugo): Chemistry. See: Ballentyne; Van Nostrand Chem. Dict.

Schiff test reaction for carbohydrates (Schiff, Hugo): Chemistry. See: Van Nostrand Chem. Dict.

Schiff test reaction for chromate (Schiff, Hugo?): Chemistry. See: Van Nostrand Chem. Dict.

Schiff test reactions for cholesterol (Schiff, Hugo): Chemistry. See: Van Nostrand Chem. Dict.

Schiff test solution for allantoin or urea (Schiff, Hugo): Chemistry. See: Dorland; Stedman; Van Nostrand Chem. Dict.

Schiff test solution for hydrogen peroxide (Schiff, Hugo?): Chemistry. See: Van Nostrand Chem. Dict.

SCHIFRIN, ARTHUR. 1904- . American pathologist. See: Direct. Med. Specialists, 1965-1966. Baehr-Schifrin disease.

SCHILD, HEINZ OTTO. 1906- . English pharmacologist. See: World Who's Who Sci. Gaddum and Schild test.

Schilder-Foix disease (Schilder, Paul Ferdinand and Foix, Charles): Medicine. See: Jablonski.

SCHILDER, PAUL FERDINAND. 1886-1940. American neurologist and psychiatrist. See: World Who's Who Sci. Schilder-Foix disease, Schilder's disease.

Schilder's disease (Schilder, Paul Ferdinand): Medicine. See: Dorland; Hinsie; Jablonski; Stedman. Also known as: Flatau-Schilder disease, Heubner-Schilder syndrome.

SCHILLER, JOHANN CHRISTOPH FRIEDRICH VON. 1759-1805. German poet. See: New Encyc. Brit., 1974. Schillerlocken.

SCHILLER, WALTER. 1887-1960. Austrian-born American pathologist. See: World Who's Who Sci. Schiller's test.

Schillerlocken (Schiller, Johann Christoph Friedrich von): Food and Drink. See: Hendrickson.

Schiller's test (Schiller, Walter): Medicine. See: Dorland; Stedman.

Schilling('s) leukemia (or type of monocytic leukemia) (Shilling, Victor Theodore Adolf Georg): Medicine. See: Jablonski; Stedman.

Schilling test (Shilling, Victor Theodore Adolf Georg): Medicine. See: Stedman.

Schilling's band cell (Shilling, Victor Theodore Adolf Georg): Medicine. See: Stedman.

Schilling's blood count (or index) (Shilling, Victor Theodore Adolf Georg): Medicine. See: Dorland; Stedman; Webster's 3d.

SCHIMMELBUSCH, CURT. 1860-1895. German surgeon. See: Biog. Lex. hervorr. Aerzte. Schimmelbusch mask, Schimmelbusch's bacillus, Schimmelbusch's disease.

Schimmelbusch mask (Schimmelbusch, Curt): Medicine. See: Stedman.

Schimmelbusch's bacillus (Schimmelbusch, Curt): Medicine. See: Stedman.

Schimmelbusch's disease (Schimmelbusch, Curt). See: Cheatle's disease.

Schimper-Braun theory (Schimper, Carl Friedrich and Braun, Alexander Carl Heinrich): Botany. Cited in: Dict. Sci. Biog. under "Braun, Alexander."

SCHIMPER, CARL FRIEDRICH. 1803-1867. German plant morphologist. See: World Who's Who Sci. Schimper-Braun theory.

SCHINDELMEISER, J. fl. 1910-1935. German? chemist. Cited in: Chem. Abstr., Decenn. Indexes, 1907 to 1936. Schindelmeiser test reaction?

Schindelmeiser test reaction (Schindelmeiser, J.?): Chemistry. See: Van Nostrand Chem. Dict.

SCHIOETZ, HJALMAR. 1850-1927. Norwegian physician. See: Biog. Lex. hervorr. Aerzte. Schioetz tonometer.

Schioetz tonometer (Schioetz, Hjalmar): Medicine. See: Dorland; Stedman.

SCHIRM, E. fl. 1912. German chemist. Cited in: Chem. Abstr., Decenn. Index, 1907-1916. Schirm reagent.

Schirm reagent (Schirm, E.): Chemistry. See: Van Nostrand Chem. Dict.

SCHIRMER, J. F. L. fl. 1874. American mint superintendent. Cited in: Dana. Schirmerite.

SCHIRMER, RUDOLPH. 1831-1896. German ophthalmologist. See: Biog. Lex. hervorr. Aerzte. Schirmer test, Schirmer's syndrome.

Schirmer test (Schirmer, Rudolph): Medicine. See: Stedman.

Schirmerite (Schirmer, J. F. L.): Earth Sciences. See: Webster's 3d.

Schirmer's syndrome (Schirmer, Rudolph). See: Sturge-Weber syndrome.

Schism of Cerularius (Cerularius, Michael): Religion. See: Attwater.

Schism of Photius (Photius): Religion. See: Attwater; New Encyc. Brit. 1974, Microp.

SCHITTLER, EMIL. 1906- . Swiss pharmaceutical chemist. See: Pogg., vol. 7a. Schittler-Mueller reaction.

Schittler-Mueller reaction (Schittler, Emil and Mueller, Johann M.): Chemistry. See: Van Nostrand Chem. Dict.

Schlaefli('s) integral (or formula) (Schlaefli, Ludwig): Mathematics. See: Ballentyne; Internat. Dict. Phys. Elec.; James.

SCHLAEFLI, LUDWIG. 1814-1895. Swiss mathematician. See: World Who's Who Sci. Schlaefli('s) integral (or formula).

SCHLAGDENHAUFFEN, FREDERIC (In full: CHARLES FREDERIC). 1830-1907. French pharmaceutical chemist. See: Pogg., vols. 2, 3, 4. Schlagdenhauffen solution for alkaloids, Schlagdenhauffen test.

Schlagdenhauffen solution for alkaloids (Schlagdenhauffen, Frederic): Chemistry. See: Van Nostrand Chem. Dict.

Schlagdenhauffen test (Schlagdenhauffen, Frederic): Chemistry. See: Van Nostrand Chem. Dict.

SCHLAGENHAUFER, FRIEDRICH. 1866-1930. German pathologist. See: Biog. Lex. hervorr. Aerzte. Gaucher-Schlagenhaufer syndrome.

SCHLAMANN. fl. 1963. German? engineer. (Biography source unavailable.) Schlamann engine.

Schlamann engine (Schlamann): Engineering and Industry. See: Auger.

SCHLAPP, ROBERT. fl. 1926-1937. English? physicist. Cited in: Chem. Abstr., Decenn. Indexes, 1917-1926; 1927-1936; 1937-1946. Schlapp's formula.

Schlapp's formula (Schlapp, Robert): Physics. See: Internat. Dict. Ap. Math.

SCHLATTER, CARL. 1864-1934. Swiss surgeon. See: World Who's Who Sci. Osgood-Schlatter syndrome (or disease), Schlatter's operation.

Schlatter-Osgood disease (Schlatter, Carl and Osgood, Robert Bayley). See: Osgood-Schlatter syndrome (or disease).

Schlatter's disease (Schlatter, Carl). See: Osgood-Schlatter syndrome (or disease).

Schlatter's operation (Schlatter, Carl): Medicine. See: Dorland; Stedman.

SCHLEICH, KARL LUDWIG. 1859-1922. German surgeon. See: World Who's Who Sci. Schleich's anesthesia, Schleich's solution.

SCHLEICHER, HENRY M. fl. 1922. American metallurgist. Cited in: Chem. Abstr., vol. 16, p. 2392. Hayward-Schleicher process.

Schleich's anesthesia (Schleich, Karl Ludwig): Medicine. See: Dorland.

Schleich's solution (Schleich, Karl Ludwig): Medicine. See: Dorland.

Schlemiehl (or Shelumiel) (Shelumiel or Salamiel): Generic Word. See: Brewer; Hendrickson.

SCHLEMM, FRIEDRICH S. 1795-1858. German anatomist. See: Biog. Lex. hervorr. Aerzte. Schlemm's canal, Schlemm's ligament.

Schlemm's canal (Schlemm, Friedrich S.): Anatomy. See: Donath; Dorland; Stedman. Also known as: Lauth's canal (or canal of Lauth).

Schlemm's ligament (Schlemm, Friedrich S.): Anatomy. See: Donath.

Schlenke loudspeaker (Derivation undetermined): Electronics. See: Hughes.

Schlenkermann's stone (Derivation undetermined): Earth Sciences. See: Thrush.

SCHLESINGER, BERNARD EDWARD. fl. 1930-1964. English pediatrician. See: Med. Direct., 1964. Fanconi-Schlesinger syndrome?

SCHLESINGER, HERMANN. 1868-1934. Austrian physician. See: Wien Med. Wchnschr., vol. 84 (April 14, 1934), pp. 450-51. Schlesinger's sign.

Schlesinger's sign (Schlesinger, Hermann): Medicine. See: Dorland; Stedman. Also known as: Pool-Schlesinger sign.

Schley controversy (Schley, Winfield Scott): History. See: Jameson. Also known as: Sampson-Schley controversy.

SCHLEY, WINFIELD SCOTT. 1839-1911. American naval officer. See: Dict. Amer. Biog. Schley controversy.

SCHLICHTING, HANS. fl. 1941. German ophthalmologist. (Biography source unavailable.) Schlichting's dystrophy.

Schlichting's dystrophy (Schlichting, Hans): Medicine. See: Jablonski.

SCHLICKUM, OSKAR. fl. 1887-1909. German pharmaceutical chemist. Cited in: Royal Soc. Cat. Sci. Pap., 1884-1900. Schlickum test for arsenic?, Schlickum test for other cinchona alkaloids in quinine sulfate?

Schlickum test for arsenic (Schlickum, Oskar?): Chemistry. See: Van Nostrand Chem. Dict.

Schlickum test for other cinchona alkaloids in quinine sulfate (Schlickum, Oskar?): Chemistry. See: Van Nostrand Chem. Dict.

SCHLIEFFEN, COUNT ALFRED VON. 1833-1913. German military officer. See: Encyc. Brit., 1973. Schlieffen plan.

Schlieffen plan (Schlieffen, Count Alfred von): History. See: Morris and Irwin.

SCHLIPPE, KARL FRIEDRICH VON. 1799-1874. German-born Russian chemist. See: Pogg., vol. 2. Schlippe's salt.

Schlippe's salt (Schlippe, Karl Friedrich von): Chemistry. See: Dorland; Hackh; Webster's 3d.

SCHLOEMILCH, OSKAR XAVER. 1823-1901. German mathematician. See: Pogg., vols. 2, 3, 4. Schlomilch's expansion, Schloemilch's form of the remainder for Taylor's theorem.

Schloemilch's form of the remainder for Taylor's theorem (Schloemilch, Oskar Xaver): Mathematics. See: James.

SCHLOESING, JEAN JACQUES THEOPHILE. 1824-1919. French chemist. See: Pogg., vols. 3, 4. Schlosing test.

SCHLOESSER, KARL. 1857-1925. German ocultist. See: Biog. Lex. hervorr. Aerzte. Schloesser's method.

Schloesser's method (Schloesser, Karl): Medicine. See: Dorland; Stedman.

SCHLOFFER, HERMANN. 1868-1937. German surgeon in Prague. See: Biog. Lex. hervorr. Aerzte. Schloffer's tumor.

Schloffer's tumor (Schloffer, Hermann): Medicine. See: Dorland; Jablonski.

Schlomilch's expansion (Schloemilch, Oskar Xaver): Mathematics. See: Ballentyne.

Schlosing test (Schloesing, Jean Jacques Theophile): Chemistry. See: Van Nostrand Chem. Dict.

SCHLOSS, ERNST. b. 1882. German pharmaceutical chemist. Cited in: Kelly. Schloss reagent.

Schloss reagent (Schloss, Ernst): Chemistry. See: Van Nostrand Chem. Dict.

Schlossberger test (Derivation undetermined): Chemistry. See: Van Nostrand Chem. Dict.

SCHLOSSMAN, ABRAHAM. 1918- . American ophthalmologist. See: Amer. Men and Women Sci., 12th ed. Posner-Schlossman syndrome.

SCHLOTTERBECK, FRITZ. fl. 1907. German chemist. Cited in: Chem. Abstr. Decenn. Index, 1907-16. Buchner-Curtius-Schlotterbeck reaction, Schlotterbeck reaction.

Schlotterbeck reaction (Schlotterbeck, Fritz): Chemistry. See: Hackh; Van Nostrand Chem. Dict.

SCHLUMBERGER, FREDERICK. No dates. Belgian horticulturist. (Biographical source unavailable.) Schlumbergera.

Schlumbergera (Schlumberger, Frederick): Botany. See: Taylor, N.

SCHMATOLLA, OTTO. fl. 1913. German chemist. See: Pogg., vol. 6. Schmatolla reaction for tin, Schmatolla test for benzoic acid, Schmatolla test for hydrogen peroxide in water.

Schmatolla reaction for tin (Schmatolla, Otto): Chemistry. See: Van Nostrand Chem. Dict.

Schmatolla test for benzoic acid (Schmatolla, Otto): Chemistry. See: Van Nostrand Chem. Dict.

Schmatolla test for hydrogen peroxide in water (Schmatolla, Otto): Chemistry. See: Van Nostrand Chem. Dict.

Schmeiderite (Derivation undetermined): Earth Sciences. See: Thrush.

SCHMID, RUDI. 1922- . Swiss-born American biochemist. See: Amer. Men and Women Sci., 12th ed. McArdle-Schmid-Pearson syndrome.

SCHMIDEL, CASIMIR CHRISTOPHER. 1718-1792. German anatomist and botanist. See: Biog. Lex. hervorr. Aerzte. Schmidelia, Schmidel's anastomosis.

Schmidelia (Schmidel, Casimir Christopher): Botany. See: Charnock.

Schmidel's anastomosis (Schmidel, Casimir Christopher): Anatomy. See: Donath; Dorland; Stedman.

SCHMIDLIN, JULIUS. fl. 1903-1910. Swoss chemist. See: Pogg., vol. 5. Schmidlin ketene synthesis, Schmidlin-Massini test reaction.

Schmidlin ketene synthesis (Schmidlin, Julius): Chemistry. See: Van Nostrand Chem. Dict.

Schmidlin-Massini test reaction (Schmidlin, Julius and Massini, Paul): Chemistry. See: Van Nostrand Chem. Dict.

Schmid's law of critical stress shear (Derivation undetermined): Chemistry. See: Ballentyne.

SCHMIDT. fl. 1910. German engineer. (Biography source unavailable.) Schmidt valve.

SCHMIDT, ADOLF. 1865-1918. German physician. See: Deut. Biog. Jahrb., 1917-1920. Schmidt's syndrome, Schmidt's test.

Schmidt apparatus (Derivation undetermined): Engineering and Industry. See: Thrush.

SCHMIDT, BERNHARD VOLDEMAR. 1879-1955. Russian-born German optician. See: New Encyc. Brit., 1974, Microp. Meniscus-Schmidt camera, Meniscus-Schmidt telescope, Schmidt camera, Schmidt-Cassegrain telescope, Schmidt lens (mirror lens or correction plate), Schmidt objective, Schmidt system (or optical system), Schmidt telescope.

Schmidt camera (Schmidt, Bernhard Voldemar): Astronomy. See: Focal Encyc. Photog.; Thewlis; Webster's 3d.

SCHMIDT, CARL FREDERICK. b. 1893. American physician and pharmacologist. See: World Who's Who Sci. Schmidt test for ephedrine.

Schmidt-Cassegrain telescope (Schmidt, Bernhard Voldemar and Cassegrain, Giovanni D.): Astronomy. See: Satterthwaite.

Schmidt cherry (Derivation undetermined): Botany. See: Hendrickson under "Bing."

Schmidt cycle (Schmidt, Gustav Johann Leopold): Engineering and Industry. See: Auger.

SCHMIDT, EDUARD OSKAR. 1823-1886. German anatomist. See: World Who's Who Sci. Schmidt's fibrinoplastin.

SCHMIDT, ERHARD. 1876-1959. German mathematician. See: Pogg., vol. 6. Gram-Schmidt process, Hilbert-Schmidt theory of integral equations with symmetric kernels.

SCHMIDT, ERNST HEINRICH WILHELM. b. 1892. German engineer. See: Pogg., vol. 6. Schmidt graphical method?, Schmidt number.

SCHMIDT, EUGEN. fl. 1911. German chemist. Cited in: Chem. Abstr., vol. 5, p. 803. Schmidt test.

SCHMIDT, GERHARD. 1901- . German-born American biochemist. See: Amer. Men Sci., 10th ed. Schmidt-Thannhauser method.

Schmidt graphical method (Schmidt, Ernst Heinrich Wilhelm?): Engineering and Industry. See: Thewlis.

SCHMIDT, GUSTAV JOHANN LEOPOLD. 1826-1883. Austrian engineer. See: Pogg., vols. 2, 3. Schmidt cycle.

Schmidt hammer (Derivation undetermined): Engineering and Industry. See: Thrush.

Schmidt-Hartmann boiler (Schmidtsche Heissdampf Company and Hartmann, Otto H.): Engineering and Industry. See: Auger. Also known as: Hartmann boiler.

SCHMIDT, HENRY D. 1823-1888. American anatomist and pathologist. Cited in: Royal Soc. Cat. Sci. Pap., 1874-1883. Schmidt-Lanterman incisures (or clefts).

Schmidt-Hilbert method (Schmidt, Erhard and Hilbert, David). See: Hilbert-Schmidt theory of integral equations with symmetric kernels.

Schmidt-Hinderer test for metals (Schmidt, Julius and Hinderer, Walter): Chemistry. See: Van Nostrand Chem. Dict.

SCHMIDT, HUBERT. fl. 1911. German chemist. Cited in: Chem. Abstr., vol. 5, p. 3081. Abderhalden-Schmidt reagent.

SCHMIDT, J. GUSTAV. fl. 1881. German organic chemist. Cited in: Royal Soc. Cat. Sci. Pap., 1874-1883. Claisen-Schmidt condensation.

SCHMIDT, JOHANN FRIEDRICH MORITZ. 1838-1907. German laryngologist. See: Biog. Jahrb. Deut. Nekr., 1907. Schmidt's syndrome.

SCHMIDT, JULIUS. 1872-1933. German chemist. See: Pogg., vols. 4 to 6. Schmidt-Hinderer test for metals, Schmidt-Lumpp reagent.

SCHMIDT, KARL FRIEDRICH. b. 1887. German organic chemist. See: Pogg., vol. 7a. Schmidt reaction.

Schmidt-Lanterman incisures (or clefts) (Schmidt, Henry D. and Lanterman, A. J.): Anatomy. See: Donath; Dorland; Stedman. Also known as: Lanterman's clefts (or incisures).

Schmidt lens (mirror lens or correction plate) (Schmidt, Bernhard Voldemar): Astronomy. See: Focal Encyc. Photog.; Internat. Dict. Phys. Elec.; Satterthwaite.

Schmidt line(s) (or limits) (Schmidt, Theodor): Physics. See: Hughes; Internat. Dict. Phys. Elec.; Markus.

Schmidt–Lumpp reagent (Schmidt Julius and Lumpp, Hermann): Chemistry. See: Van Nostrand Chem. Dict.

Schmidt–Maksutov telescope (Schmidt, Bernhard Voldemar and Maksutov, Dmitriy Dmitrievich). See: Meniscus-Schmidt telescope.

SCHMIDT, MARTIN BENNO. 1863-1949. German pathologist. See: Biog. Lex. hervorr. Aerzte. Schmidt's syndrome.

Schmidt model of nuclei (Schmidt, Theodor): Physics. See: Internat. Dict. Ap. Math.

Schmidt number (Schmidt, Ernst Heinrich Wilhelm): Physics. See: Ballentyne; Thewlis.

Schmidt objective (Schmidt, Bernhard Voldemar): Astronomy. See: Van Nostrand Sci. Encyc.

SCHMIDT, P. fl. 1931. German engineer? (Biography source unavailable.) Schmidt tube.

SCHMIDT, PAUL. fl. 1927. German physician. Cited in: Chem. Abstr., vol. 21, p. 1284. Necke-Schmidt-Klostermann reagent for lead.

Schmidt process (Schmidt, Erhard). See: Gram-Schmidt process.

SCHMIDT, R. fl. 1914. German chemist. Cited in Chem. Abstr., vol. 9, p. 251. Appelius-Schmidt reagent.

Schmidt reaction (Schmidt, Karl Friedrich): Chemistry. See: Ballentyne; Van Nostrand Chem. Dict.

SCHMIDT, ROLF. 1906- . German ophthalmologist. Cited in: Kelly. Schmidt's keratitis.

Schmidt system (or optical system) (Schmidt, Bernhard Voldemar): Engineering and Industry. See: Hughes; Markus; Webster's 3d.

Schmidt telescope (Schmidt, Bernhard Voldemar): Astronomy. See: Satterthwaite; Thewlis; Webster's 3d.

Schmidt test (Schmidt, Eugen): Chemistry. See: Hackh.

Schmidt test for ephedrine (Schmidt, Carl Frederick): Chemistry. See: Van Nostrand Chem. Dict.

Schmidt test reactions for gelatin (Derivation undetermined): Chemistry. See: Van Nostrand Chem. Dict.

Schmidt–Thannhauser method (Schmidt, Gerhard and Thannhauser, Siegfried Josef): Medicine. See: Stedman.

SCHMIDT, THEODOR. 1908- . German physicist. See: Pogg., vol. 7a. Schmidt line(s) (or limits), Schmidt model of nuclei.

Schmidt tube (Schmidt, P.): Engineering and Industry. See: Auger.

Schmidt–type magnetic field balance (Derivation undetermined): Earth Sciences. See: Thrush.

Schmidt valve (Schmidt): Engineering and Industry. See: Auger.

Schmidt–Waldmann vaccine (Derivation undetermined): Medicine. See: Stedman.

Schmidt's conjugate-power laws (Derivation undetermined): Earth Sciences. See: Huschke.

Schmidt's fibrinoplastin (Schmidt, Eduard Oskar): Medicine. See: Dorland; Stedman.

Schmidt's keratitis (Schmidt, Rolf): Medicine. See: Jablonski.

Schmidt's syndrome (Schmidt, Adolf): Medicine. See: Jablonski.

Schmidt's syndrome (Schmidt, Johann Friedrich Moritz): Medicine. See: Dorland; Hinsie; Stedman.

Schmidt's syndrome (Schmidt, Martin Benno): Medicine. See: Jablonski.

Schmidt's test (Schmidt, Adolf): Medicine. See: Dorland; Stedman.

SCHMIEDEBERG, OSTWALD (In full: JOHANN ERNST OSTWALD). 1838-1921. German pharmacologist. See: World Who's Who Sci. Schmiedeberg's digitalin.

Schmiedeberg's digitalin (Schmiedeberg, Ostwald): Medicine. See: Stedman.

Schmiedel process (Schmiedel, Theodor): Chemistry. See: Van Nostrand Chem. Dict.

SCHMIEDEL, ROLAND. b. 1888. German pharmaceutical chemist. See: Pogg., vol. 7a. Schmiedel test?

Schmiedel test (Schmiedel, Roland?): Chemistry. See: Van Nostrand Chem. Dict.

SCHMIEDEL, THEODOR. fl. 1920. German chemist. Cited in: Chem. Abstr., vol. 15, p. P404. Schmiedel process.

SCHMIEDEN, VICTOR. b. 1874. German surgeon. See: Biog. Lex. hervorr. Aerzte. Schmieden's disease.

Schmieden's disease (Schmieden, Victor): Medicine. See: Jablonski.

SCHMINCKE, ALEXANDER. 1877-1953. German pathologist. See: Biog. Lex. hervorr. Aerzte. Schmincke('s) tumor, Schmincke's tumor–unilateral cranial paralysis syndrome.

Schmincke('s) tumor (Schmincke, Alexander): Medicine. See: Dorland; Jablonski; Stedman.

Schmincke's tumor–unilateral cranial paralysis syndrome (Schmincke, Alexander). See: Garcin's syndrome.

Schmitt box (Schmitt, P. Jerome): Zoology. See: Webster's 3d.

SCHMITT, H. G. fl. 1951. German physician. (Biography source unavailable.) Schmitt's disease.

SCHMITT, OTTO HERBERT. 1913- . American biophysicist and electronics engineer. See: Amer. Men and Women Sci., 12th ed. Schmitt trigger (or limiter).

SCHMITT, P. JEROME. d. 1904. American priest. Cited in: Royal Soc. Cat. Sci. Pap., 1884-1900. Schmitt box.

SCHMITT, RUDOLF WILHELM. 1830-1898. German chemist. See: Biog. Jahrb. Deut. Nekr., 1900, "Totenliste 1898," p. 56. Kolbe-Schmitt reaction (or synthesis).

Schmitt trigger (or limiter) (Schmitt, Otto Herbert): Engineering and Industry. See: Hughes; Markus; Van Nostrand Sci. Encyc.

Schmitt's disease (Schmitt, H. G.): Medicine. See: Jablonski.

Schmitz bacillus (Schmitz, Karl Eitel Friedrich): Medicine. See: Dorland.

Schmitz dysentery (Schmitz, Karl Eitel Friedrich): Medicine. Cited in: Van Nostrand Sci. Encyc. under "Dysentery."

SCHMITZ, H. fl. 1934. German chemist. Cited in: Chem. Abstr., vol. 29, p. 4285. Ammer-Schmitz test reaction.

SCHMITZ, KARL EITEL FRIEDRICH. b. 1889. German physician. Cited in: Kelly. Schmitz bacillus, Schmitz dysentery.

SCHMIZ, EDUARD. fl. 1927. German chemist. Cited in: Chem. Abstr., vol. 21, p. 1774. Schmiz test.

Schmiz test (Schmiz, Eduard): Chemistry. See: Van Nostrand Chem. Dict.

Schmoluchowski, Maryan. See: Smoluchowski, Maryan.

Schmoluchowski's equation (Smoluchowski, Maryan Ritter von Smolan): Physics. See: Hackh.

SCHMORL, CHRISTIAN GEORG. 1861-1932. German pathologist. See: Biog. Lex. hervorr. Aerzte. Schmorl's bacillus, Schmorl's disease, Schmorl's furrow, Schmorl's nodes (or nodules).

Schmorl's bacillus (Schmorl, Christian Georg): Medicine. See: Dorland; Stedman.

Schmorl's disease (Schmorl, Christian Georg): Medicine. See: Dorland; Jablonski.

Schmorl's furrow (Schmorl, Christian Georg): Medicine. See: Dorland.

Schmorl's nodes (or nodules) (Schmorl, Christian Georg): Medicine. See: Dorland; Jablonski; Stedman.

SCHNABEL, ISIDOR. 1842-1908. Austrian ophthalmologist. See: Biog. Lex. hervorr. Aerzte. Schnabel's atrophy (or caverns).

Schnabel's atrophy (or caverns) (Schnabel, Isidor): Medicine. See: Dorland; Jablonski.

SCHNEERSOHN, JOSEPH ISAAC (LUBAVITCHER RABBI). 1880-1950. Russian Jewish rabbi in Poland and America. See: Encyc. Judaica under "Schneersohn family." Lubavitcher school.

SCHNEIDER. fl. 19th c. German? mine director in Italy. Cited in: Dana. Schneiderite.

Schneider aceto-carmine solution (Derivation undetermined): Chemistry. See: Van Nostrand Chem. Dict.

SCHNEIDER, CONRAD VIKTOR. 1610-1680. German anatomist. See: World Who's Who Sci. Schneiderian membrane.

Schneider converter (Schneider, H.): Engineering and Industry. See: Auger.

SCHNEIDER, EDWARD CHRISTIAN. 1874-1954. American biologist. See: World Who's Who Sci. Schneider index.

SCHNEIDER, FRANZ C. 1813-1897. German chemist. See: Biog. Jahrb. Deut. Nekr., 1899, Toten liste, p. 22. Schneider's carmine.

Schneider('s) furnace (Derivation undetermined): Engineering and Industry. See: Hackh; Thrush.

SCHNEIDER, H. fl. 1924. German engineer. (Biography source unavailable.) Schneider converter.

SCHNEIDER, HANS. fl. 1915. German chemist. Cited in: Chem. Abstr., vol. 9, p. 1188. Schneider test for lignified plant tissue.

SCHNEIDER, HANS. fl. 1931. German physician. (Biography source unavailable.) Schneider's disease.

Schneider index (Schneider, Edward Christian): Physiology. See: Webster's 3d.

Schneider test for lignified plant tissue (Schneider, Hans): Chemistry. See: Van Nostrand Chem. Dict.

Schneider test reaction for alkaloids (Derivation undetermined): Chemistry. See: Van Nostrand Chem. Dict.

SCHNEIDER, THEODOR. 1911- . German mathematician. See: Handb. der Deut. Wissensch. Gelfond-Schneider theorem.

Schneiderian membrane (Schneider, Conrad Viktor): Anatomy. See: Donath; Dorland; Stedman.

Schneiderite (Schneider): Earth Sciences. See: Charnock.

Schneider's carmine (Schneider, Franz C.): Medicine. See: Dorland; Stedman.

Schneider's disease (Schneider, Hans): Medicine. See: Jablonski.

Schnitter-Kurashige method (Derivation undetermined): Medicine. See: Stedman.

Schnitzler's gold purple (Derivation undetermined): Engineering and Industry. See: Thrush.

SCHNYDER, WALTER. fl. 1929. Swiss ophthalmologist. (Biography source unavailable.) Schnyder's dystrophy.

Schnyder's dystrophy (Schnyder, Walter): Medicine. See: Jablonski.

SCHODER, WILLIAM PAUL. 1900- . American research chemist. See: Amer. Men Sci., 9th ed. Schoderite.

Schoderite (Schoder, William Paul): Earth Sciences. See: Thrush.

SCHOEBL, JOSEF. 1837-1902. Czechoslovakian physician. See: Biog. Lex. hervorr. Aerzte. Schoebl's scleritis.

Schoebl's scleritis (Schoebl, Josef): Medicine. See: Jablonski.

SCHOELER, HEINRICH LEOPOLD. 1844-1918. German ophthalmologist. See: Biog. Lex. hervorr. Aerzte. Schoeler's method.

Schoeler's method (Schoeler, Heinrich Leopold): Medicine. See: Dorland; Stedman.

SCHOEMAKER, JAN. 1871-1940. Dutch surgeon. See: Biog. Lex. hervorr. Aerzte. Schoemaker's line.

Schoemaker's line (Schoemaker, Jan): Medicine. See: Dorland.

SCHOENAICH-CAROLATH, EMIL RUDOLF OSMAN, PRINZ VON. 1852-1908. Silesian prince. Cited in: Bailey. Carolathine.

SCHOENBEIN, CHRISTIAN FRIEDRICH. 1799-1868. German chemist. See: World Who's Who Sci. Almen-Schoenbein solution, Pagenstecher-Schoenbein cyanide paper, Schoenbein pyrogallol test for nitrite and nitrate, Schoenbein reagents and test for hydrogen peroxide, Schoenbein test for nitrite in nitric acid, Schoenbein test for nitrite in the presence of nitrate, Schoenbein test reaction for copper, Schoenbein test reaction for ozone, Schoenbein test reagent for nitrite, ozone, and hydrogen peroxide, Schoenbein's test for blood.

Schoenbein pyrogallol test for nitrite and nitrate (Schoenbein, Christian Friedrich): Chemistry. See: Van Nostrand Chem. Dict.

Schoenbein reagents and test for hydrogen peroxide (Schoenbein, Christian Friedrich): Chemistry. See: Van Nostrand Chem. Dict.

Schoenbein test for nitrite in nitric acid (Schoenbein, Christian Friedrich): Chemistry. See: Van Nostrand Chem. Dict.

Schoenbein test for nitrite in the presence of nitrate (Schoenbein, Christian Friedrich): Chemistry. See: Van Nostrand Chem. Dict.

Schoenbein test reaction for copper (Schoenbein, Christian Friedrich): Chemistry. See: Van Nostrand Chem. Dict.

Schoenbein test reaction for ozone (Schoenbein, Christian Friedrich): Chemistry. See: Van Nostrand Chem. Dict.

Schoenbein test reagent for nitrite, ozone, and hydrogen peroxide (Schoenbein, Christian Friedrich): Chemistry. See: Van Nostrand Chem. Dict.

Schoenbein's test for blood (Schoenbein, Christian Friedrich). See: Almen's solution (or test) for blood.

SCHOENBERG, ALEXANDER JULIUS WILHELM. b. 1892. German chemist. See: Pogg., vols. 6, 7a. Schoenberg-Urban test.

Schoenberg-Urban test (Schoenberg, Alexander Julius Wilhelm and Urban, Wilhelm): Chemistry. See: Van Nostrand Chem. Dict.

SCHOENE. fl. 19th c. German mining officer. Cited in: Bailey. Schoenite.

SCHOENENBERG, HANS. 1915- . German pediatrician. See: Wer Ist's Wer?, 1971-1973. Schoenenberg's syndrome.

Schoenenberg's syndrome (Schoenenberg, Hans): Medicine. See: Jablonski.

SCHOENER, W. fl. 1941. German physician. (Biography source unavailable.) Heilmeyer-Schoener erythoblastosis.

SCHOENFLIES, ARTHUR MORITZ. 1853-1928. German mathematician. See: Pogg., vols. 3 to 6. Schoenflies notation (or crystal symbols).

Schoenflies notation (or crystal symbols) (Schoenflies, Arthur Moritz): Physics. See: Van Nostrand Sci. Encyc.

SCHOENHERR, OTTO WILHELM. b. 1861. German applied chemist. See: Pogg., vol. 6. Schoenherr (Schonherr) process.

Schoenherr (Schonherr) process (Schoenherr, Otto Wilhelm): Chemistry. See: Ballentyne; Hackh; Van Nostrand Chem. Dict.

SCHOENHOEFER, FRITZ. b. 1892. German chemist. See: Pogg., vol. 7a. Schulemann-Schoenhoefer-Wingler test.

Schoenite (Schoene): Earth Sciences. See: Thrush.

Schoenlein-Henoch purpura (disease or syndrome) (Schoenlein, Johann Lukas and Henoch, Heinrich): Medicine. See: Jablonski; Stedman. Also known as: Henoch-Schoenlein purpura, Henoch's disease, Schoenlein's disease (or purpura).

SCHOENLEIN, JOHANN LUKAS. 1793-1864. German physician. See: Allg. Deut. Biog. Schoenlein-Henoch purpura (disease or syndrome).

Schoenlein's disease (or purpura) (Schoenlein, Johann Lukas). See: Schoenlein-Henoch purpura (disease or syndrome).

SCHOENN, JOHANN LUDWIG. 1836-1894. German chemist and physicist. See: Pogg., vol. 3. Schoenn test reaction for hydrogen peroxide, Schoenn test reaction for molybdenum.

Schoenn test reaction for hydrogen peroxide (Schoenn, Johann Ludwig): Chemistry. See: Van Nostrand Chem. Dict.

Schoenn test reaction for molybdenum (Schoenn, Johann Ludwig): Chemistry. See: Van Nostrand Chem. Dict.

Schoental micro-test (Schoental, R.): Chemistry. See: Van Nostrand Chem. Dict.

SCHOENTAL, R. fl. 1938. German chemist. Cited in: Chem. Abstr., vol. 32, p. 4464. Schoental micro-test.

Schoenvogel test (Derivation undetermined): Chemistry. See: Van Nostrand Chem. Dict.

SCHOEP, ALFRED FERNAND MARIE GHISLAIN. b. 1881. Belgian mineralogist. See: Pogg., vol. 6. Schoepite.

SCHOEPF, JOHANN DAVID. 1752-1800. German physician in America. See: Biog. Lex. hervorr. Aerzte. Schoepfia.

Schoepfia (Schoepf, Johann David): Botany. See: Charnock.

Schoepite (Schoep, Alfred Fernand Marie Ghislain): Earth Sciences. See: Thrush; Webster's 3d.

Scholander apparatus (Scholander, Per Fredrik): Medicine. See: Stedman.

SCHOLANDER, PER FREDRIK. 1905- . Swedish-born American physiologist. See: Amer. Men and Women Sci., 12th ed. Scholander apparatus.

SCHOLES, WILLIAM. fl. 1946. English engineer. Cited in: Chem. Abstr., vol. 40, p. 2702. Ridley-Scholes bath.

SCHOLL, CLARENCE E. fl. 1919. American chemist. Cited in: Chem. Abstr., Decenn. Index, 1917-1926. Scholl's method?

Scholl reaction (Scholl, Roland): Chemistry. See: Van Nostrand Chem. Dict.

SCHOLL, ROLAND. 1865-1945. German organic chemist. See: Pogg., vols. 4 to 7a. Scholl reaction.

SCHOLLER, HEINRICH. fl. 1923-1959. German chemist. Cited in: Krauch and Kunz. Scholler saccharification process.

Scholler saccharification process (Scholler, Heinrich): Chemistry. See: Van Nostrand Chem. Dict.

Scholl's method (Scholl, Clarence E.?): Engineering and Industry. See: Thrush.

SCHOLTE, A. J. fl. 1930. Austrian physician. (Biography source unavailable.) Scholte's syndrome.

Scholte's syndrome (Scholte, A. J.). See: Cassidy's syndrome.

Scholvein test (Derivation undetermined): Chemistry. See: Van Nostrand Chem. Dict.

SCHOLZ, A. fl. 1948? German chemist and mineral collector. Cited in: Amer. Min., vol. 36 (1951), p. 382. Scholzite.

Scholz-Bielschowsky-Henneberg syndrome (Scholz, Willibald Oscar; Bielschowsky, Max; and Henneberg, Richard). See: Greenfield's disease.

SCHOLZ, WILLIBALD OSCAR. b. 1889. German neurologist and psychiatrist. See: World Who's Who Sci. Scholz's syndrome (or disease), Scholz's theory.

Scholzite (Scholz, A.): Earth Sciences. See: Thrush.

Scholz's syndrome (or disease) (Scholz, Willibald Oscar). See: Greenfield's disease.

Scholz's theory (Scholz, Willibald Oscar): Medicine. See: Stedman.

Schomburgk Line (Schomburgk, Sir Robert Herman): History. See: Harbottle; Latham.

SCHOMBURGK, SIR ROBERT HERMAN. 1804-1865. German-born English traveler and surveyor. See: Dict. Nat. Biog. Schomburgk Line, Schomburgkia.

Schomburgkia (Schomburgk, Sir Robert Herman): Botany. See: Webster's 3d.

Schone's apparatus (Derivation undetermined): Engineering and Industry. See: Thrush.

School of Spenser (Spenser, Edmund): Literature. See: Preminger.

Schoop metallizing (or process) (Schoop, Ulrich): Engineering and Industry. See: Thrush; Webster's 3d.

SCHOOP, ULRICH (In full: MAX ULRICH). 1870-1956. Swiss engineer. See: Pogg., vols. 6, 7a. Schoop metallizing (or process).

SCHOORL, NICOLAAS. 1872-1942. Dutch chemist. See: Pogg., vols. 5, 6. Lenz-Schoorl test, Schoorl test for differentiating chloroform and carbon tetrachloride, Schoorl test for water in glacial acetic acid, Schoorl test reaction for naphthalene.

Schoorl test for differentiating chloroform and carbon tetrachloride (Schoorl, Nicolaas): Chemistry. See: Van Nostrand Chem. Dict.

Schoorl test for water in glacial acetic acid (Schoorl, Nicolaas): Chemistry. See: Van Nostrand Chem. Dict.

Schoorl test reaction for naphthalene (Schoorl, Nicolaas): Chemistry. See: Van Nostrand Chem. Dict.

SCHOPENHAUER, ARTHUR. 1788-1860. German philosopher. See: Encyc. Brit., 1911. Schopenhauerean (or Schopenhauereanism).

Schopenhauerean (or Schopenhauereanism) (Schopenhauer, Arthur): Philosophy. See: Webster's 3d.

SCHORIGIN, PAUL. fl. 1907-1931. German chemist. See: Pogg., vol. 6. Schorigin reaction.

Schorigin reaction (Schorigin, Paul): Chemistry. See: Van Nostrand Chem. Dict.

SCHORN, E. J. fl. 1925-1930. American chemist. Cited in: Chem. Abstr., vol. 24, p. 4586. Schorn reagent for aloe, Schorn reagent for eucalyptol.

Schorn reagent for aloe (Schorn, E. J.): Chemistry. See: Van Nostrand Chem. Dict.

Schorn reagent for eucalyptol (Schorn, E. J.): Chemistry. See: Van Nostrand Chem. Dict.

SCHOSSBERGER, F. 1905- . German-born chemist in America. See: Amer. Men Sci., 9th ed. Schossberger test reaction?

Schossberger test reaction (Schossberger F.?): Chemistry. See: Van Nostrand Chem. Dict.

SCHOT, RICHARD. fl. 18th c.? Explorer. (Biography source unavailable.) Schotia.

Schotia (Schot, Richard): Botany. See: Taylor, N.

SCHOTT, AUGUST. 1839-1886. German physician. See: Biog. Lex. hervorr. Aerzte. Schott treatment.

SCHOTT, F. fl. 1912. Swiss chemist. Cited in: Chem. Abstr., vol. 6, p. 725. Schott test reaction.

SCHOTT, OTTO (In full: FRIEDRICH OTTO). 1851-1935. German glass technologist. See: Pogg., vols. 3 to 7a. Winkelmann and Scott equation.

Schott test reaction (Schott, F.): Chemistry. See: Van Nostrand Chem. Dict.

SCHOTT, THEODOR. 1852-1921. German physician. See: Deut. Biog. Jahrb., 1921. Schott treatment.

Schott treatment (Schott, August and Schott, Theodor): Medicine. See: Dorland; Stedman.

Schotten-Baumann reaction (Schotten, Carl Ludwig and Baumann, Eugen): Chemistry. See: Ballentyne; Van Nostrand Chem. Dict.; Webster's 3d.

SCHOTTEN, CARL LUDWIG. 1853-1910. German chemist. See: World Who's Who Sci. Schotten-Baumann reaction.

Schottky anomaly (Schottky, Walter): Physics. See: Ballentyne.

Schottky defect (or disorder) (Schottky, Walter): Physics. See: Ballentyne; Thewlis; Van Nostrand Sci. Encyc.

Schottky (Shottky) effect (or noise) (Schottky, Walter): Physics. See: Markus; Thewlis; Van Nostrand Sci. Encyc.

Schottky emission (Schottky, Walter): Physics. See: Internat. Dict. Phys. Elec.

Schottky line (Schottky, Walter): Physics. See: Internat. Dict. Phys. Elec.

Schottky theory (Schottky, Walter): Physics. See: Van Nostrand Sci. Encyc.

SCHOTTKY, WALTER. b. 1886. German physicist. See: World Who's Who Sci. Child-Langmuir-Schottky equation, Schottky anomaly, Schottky defect (or disorder), Schottky (Shottky) effect (or noise), Schottky emission, Schottky line, Schottky theory.

SCHOTTMUELLER, HUGO A. G. 1867-1936. German physician. See: World Who's Who Sci. Schottmueller's bacillus, Schottmueller's disease.

Schottmueller's bacillus (Schottmueller, Hugo A. G.): Medicine. See: Stedman.

Schottmueller's disease (Schottmueller, Hugo A. G.): Medicine. See: Dorland; Jablonski; Stedman. Also known as: Brion-Kayser disease.

Schouvaloff, Count Petr Andreivich. See: Shuvalov, Count Petr Andreivich.

Schouvaloff Treaty (Shuvalov, Count Petr Andreivich): History. See: Montgomery.

Schradan (Schrader, Gerhard): Chemistry. See: Webster's 3d.

SCHRADER, GERHARD. 1903- . German chemist. See: Pogg., vol. 7a. Schradan.

SCHRADER, HEINRICH ADOLF. 1767-1836. German botanist. See: Allg. Deut. Biog. Schradera.

Schradera (Schrader, Heinrich Adolf): Botany. See: Charnock.

SCHRAMM, HILARY. b. 1857. Polish physician. See: Biog. Lex. hervorr. Aerzte. Schramm's phenomenon?

SCHRAMM, W. H. fl. 1917. German chemist. Cited in: Chem. Abstr., vol. 11, p. 2870. Mayer-Schramm test for copper.

SCHRAMMEL, JOHANN. 1850-1893. Austrian violinist. See: Riemann. Schrammel quartet.

Schrammel quartet (Schrammel, Johann): Music. See: Scholes.

Schramm's phenomenon (Schramm, Hilary?): Medicine. See: Stedman.

SCHRAUF, ALBRECHT. 1837-1897. Austrian mineralogist. See: Pogg., vols. 2, 3, 4. Schraufite.

Schraufite (Schrauf, Albrecht): Earth Sciences. See: Thrush.

Schreber case (Schreiber, Daniel Paul): Psychology. See: Wolman.

SCHREBER, JOHANN CHRISTIAN DANIEL VON. 1739-1810. German botanist. See: Allg. Deut. Biog. Schrebera.

Schrebera (Schreber, Johann Christian Daniel von): Botany. See: Charnock; Webster's 3d.

SCHREGER, CHRISTIAN H. T. 1768-1833. Danish anatomist. See: Biog. Lex. Hervorr. Aerzte. Schreger's line(s).

Schreger's line(s) (Schreger, Christian H. T.): Anatomy. See: Dorland; Gray; Stedman.

SCHREIBER, DANIEL PAUL. fl. 1903. Austrian judge. Cited in: Cum. Auth. Index to Psych. Index, 1894-1935, and Psych. Abstr., 1927-1958. Schreber case.

SCHREIBER, ERNST. 1896- ? German physician and pharmacognosist. See: Pogg., vol. 7a. Schreiber reagent?

SCHREIBER, JULIUS. 1848-1932. German physician. See: Biog. Lex. hervorr. Aerzte. Schreiber's maneuver.

SCHREIBER, KARL FRANZ ANTON VON. 1775-1852. Austrian zoologist and museum director. See: Allg. Deut. Biog. Schreibersite.

Schreiber reagent (Schreiber, Ernst?): Chemistry. See: Van Nostrand Chem. Dict.

Schreiber's maneuver (Schreiber, Julius): Medicine. See: Stedman.

Schreibersite (Schreiber, Karl Franz Anton von): Earth Sciences. See: Thrush; Webster's 3d.

SCHREINEMAKERS, FRANCISCUS ANTONIUS HUBERTUS. b. 1864. Dutch chemist. See: Pogg., vols. 4, 5, 6. Schreinemakers residue method.

Schreinemakers residue method (Schreinemakers, Franciscus Antonius Hubertus): Chemistry. See: Van Nostrand Chem. Dict.

SCHREINER, WERNER EMIL. 1921- . Swiss physician. See: World Who's Who Sci. Schreiner's base?

Schreiner's base (Schreiner, Werner Emil?): Medicine. See: Stedman.

Schridde cancer hairs (Schridde, Hermann August): Medicine. See: Dorland; Stedman.

SCHRIDDE, HERMANN AUGUST. b. 1875. German pathologist. See: Biog. Lex. hervorr. Aerzte. Schridde cancer hairs, Schridde's syndrome.

Schridde's syndrome (Schridde, Hermann August): Medicine. See: Jablonski.

SCHRIEFFER, JOHN ROBERT. 1931- . American physicist. See: Amer. Men Sci., 10th ed. Bardeen-Cooper-Schrieffer theory of superconductivity.

SCHROECKINGER, J. VON. fl. 19th c. Austrian mineralogist. Cited in: Hintze. Schroeckingerite.

Schroeckingerite (Schroeckinger, J. von): Earth Sciences. See: Thrush; Webster's 3d.

Schroeder-Bernstein theorem (Schroeder, Ernst and Bernstein): Mathematics. See: James.

SCHROEDER, ERNST. 1841-1902. German logician and mathematician. See: New Encyc. Brit., 1974, Microp. Schroeder-Bernstein theorem.

SCHROEDER, HENRY ALFRED. 1906- . American physician. See: Amer. Men and Women Sci., 12th ed. Schroeder's syndrome.

SCHROEDER, KARL LUDWIG ERNST. 1838-1887. German gynecologist. Cited in: Kelly. Schroeder's method?, Schroeder's operation.

SCHROEDER, ROBERT. 1884-1959. German physician. See: Biog. Lex. hervorr. Aerzte. Schroeder's disease.

SCHROEDER VAN DER KOLK, JACOB L. C. 1797-1862. Dutch physiologist. See: World Who's Who Sci. Schroeder's fibers.

SCHROEDER, WALDEMAR VON. 1850-1898. German physician. See: Biog. Lex. hervorr. Aerzte. Schroeder's portion of urea, Schroeder's test for urea.

SCHROEDER, WESLEY DEAN. 1910- ? American organic chemist. See: Amer. Men and Women Sci., 12th ed. Schroeder's paradox?

Schroeder's disease (Schroeder, Robert): Medicine. See: Dorland; Stedman.

Schroeder's fibers (Schroeder van der Kolk, Jacob L. C.): Anatomy. See: Stedman.

Schroeder's method (Schroeder, Karl Ludwig Ernst): Medicine. See: Stedman.

Schroeder's operation (Schroeder, Karl Ludwig Ernst): Medicine. See: Stedman.

Schroeder's paradox (Schroeder, Wesley Dean?): Chemistry. See: Hackh.

Schroeder's portion of urea (Schroeder, Waldemar von): Medicine. See: Stedman.

Schroeder's syndrome (Schroeder, Henry Alfred): Medicine. See: Dorland; Jablonski.

Schroeder's test for urea (Schroeder, Waldemar von): Medicine. See: Dorland; Stedman.

Schroedinger atom (Schroedinger, Erwin): Physics. See: Hackh; Webster's 3d.

Schroedinger equation (1) (Schroedinger, Erwin): Physics. See: Thewlis.

Schroedinger equation (2) (or wave equation) (Schroedinger, Erwin): Physics. See: Ballentyne; Internat. Dict. Phys. Elec.; Thewlis.

SCHROEDINGER, ERWIN. 1887-1961. Austrian physicist. See: Pogg., vols. 5, 6, 7a; World Who's Who Sci. Rayleigh-Schroedinger perturbation formula, Schroedinger atom, Schroedinger equation (1), Schroedinger equation (2) (or wave equation), Schroedinger-Gordon equation, Schroedinger picture, Schroedinger representation, Schroedinger wave function, Tomonaga-Schroedinger equation.

Schroedinger-Gordon equation (Schroedinger, Erwin and Gordon, Walter). See: Klein-Gordon equation.

Schroedinger picture (Schroedinger, Erwin): Physics. See: Internat. Dict. Ap. Math.

Schroedinger representation (Schroedinger, Erwin): Physics. See: Internat. Dict. Phys. Elec.

Schroedinger wave function (Schroedinger, Erwin): Physics. See: Markus.

CHROEN, OTTO VON. 1837-1913. German pathologist in Naples. See: Biog. Lex. hervorr. Aerzte. Schroen's granule.

Schroen's granule (Schroen, Otto von): Medicine. See: Dorland.

CHROETTER, ANTON RITTER VON KRISTELLI. 1802-1875. German chemist and mineralogist. See: Pogg., vols. 2, 3. Schroetter apparatus, Schroetterite (Schrotterite).

Schroetter apparatus (Schroetter, Anton Ritter von Kristelli): Chemistry. See: Hackh.

CHROETTER VON KRISTELLI, LEOPOLD. 1837-1908. Austrian laryngologist. See: Biog. Lex. hervorr. Aerzte. Paget-Schroetter syndrome, Schroetter's chorea.

Schroetterite (Schrotterite) (Schroetter, Anton Ritter von Kristelli): Earth Sciences. See: Charnock; Thrush.

Schroetter's chorea (Schroetter von Kristelli, Leopold): Medicine. See: Dorland; Jablonski; Stedman.

CHRYVER, SAMUEL BARNETT. fl. 19th c. English? chemist. Cited in: Royal Soc. Cat. Sci. Pap., 1884-1900. Schryver test?

Schryver test (Schryver, Samuel Barnett?): Chemistry. See: Van Nostrand Chem. Dict.

CHUBERT, JACK. 1917- . American chemist. See: Amer. Men Sci., 8th ed. Boyd, Schubert and Adamson equation.

CHUCHARDT, KARL AUGUST. 1856-1901. German surgeon. See: Biog. Lex. hervorr. Aerzte. Schuchardt's operation.

Schuchardt's operation (Schuchardt, Karl August): Medicine. See: Dorland; Stedman.

SCHUEBLER. fl. 1747. Austrian music publisher. Cited in: Thompson, O. under "Bach, Johann Sebastian." Schuebler Chorales.

Schuebler Chorales (Schuebler): Music. See: Apel.

CHUECK, BERNHARD. fl. 1907. German chemist. Cited in: Chem. Abstr., vol. 1, pp. 150, 644. Grossmann-Schueck reagent for metallic salts, Grossmann-Schueck reagent for nickel.

CHUEFFNER, WILHELM AUGUST PAUL. 1867-1949. German pathologist in Sumatra. See: World Who's Who Sci. Schueffner's granules (or dots).

Schueffner's granules (or dots) (Schueffner, Wilhelm August Paul): Medicine. See: Dorland; Pennak; Stedman.

CHUEFFTAN, EUGEN. 1893- . German photographer. See: Sadoul. Schuefftan process.

Schuefftan process (Schuefftan, Eugen): Photography. See: Focal Encyc. Film.

Schuegner's granules (Derivation undetermined). See: Plehn's karyochromatophil granules.

SCHUELE, HEINRICH. 1840-1916. German psychiatrist. See: Biog. Lex. hervorr. Aerzte. Schuele's sign.

Schuele's sign (Schuele, Heinrich): Medicine. See: Dorland; Hinsie; Stedman.

CHUELLER, ARTUR. b. 1874. Austrian neurologist. See: Biog. Lex. hervorr. Aerzte. Hand-Schueller-Christian syndrome, Schueller's phenomenon.

Schueller-Christian disease (Schueller, Artur and Christian, Henry A.). See: Hand-Schueller-Christian syndrome.

SCHUELLER, KARL HEINRICH ANTON LUDWIG MAX. 1843-1907. German surgeon. See: Biog. Lex. hervorr. Aerzte. Schueller's ducts, Schueller's method.

Schueller's disease (or syndrome) (Schueller, Artur). See: Hand-Schueller-Christian syndrome.

Schueller's ducts (Schueller, Karl Heinrich Anton Ludwig Max): Anatomy. See: Stedman.

Schueller's method (Schueller, Karl Heinrich Anton Ludwig Max): Medicine. See: Dorland.

Schueller's phenomenon (Schueller, Artur): Medicine. See: Dorland; Stedman.

Schueltze solution for alkaloids (Derivation undetermined): Chemistry. See: Van Nostrand Chem. Dict.

SCHUERENBERG. fl. 20th c. German? physician. (Biography source unavailable.) Axenfeld-Schuerenberg syndrome.

SCHUERMANN, ERNST. fl. 1888. German metal chemist. Cited in: Royal Soc. Cat. Sci. Pap., 1884-1900. Schuermann series?

Schuermann series (Schuermann, Ernst?): Chemistry. See: Thrush.

SCHUERMANN, WALTER (In full: JOHANN WILHELM WALTER). b. 1880. German bacteriologist. See: World Who's Who Sci. Schuermann's test.

Schuermann's test (Schuermann, Walter): Medicine. See: Dorland.

SCHUETTE, CURT NICOLAUS. fl. 1930. American mineralogist. Cited in: Min. Mag., vol. 32 (1959-1961, pt. 2), p. 979. Schuetteite.

Schuetteite (Schuette, Curt Nicolaus): Earth Sciences. See: Thrush.

Schuetz-Borrisow (Bourison) rule (Derivation undetermined): Chemistry. See: Hackh; Van Nostrand Chem. Dict.

Schuetz' bundle (or tract) (Schuetz, H.): Anatomy. See: Stedman.

SCHUETZ, FRANZ. fl. 1928. German chemist. Cited in: Chem. Abstr., vol. 22, p. 3716. Hahn-Schutze-Pavlides reagent.

SCHUETZ, H. No dates. German anatomist. (Biography source unavailable). Schuetz' bundle (or tract).

SCHUETZENBERGER, PAUL. 1829-1897. French chemist. See: Pogg., vols. 3, 4. Schuetzenberger test reaction.

Schuetzenberger test reaction (Schuetzenberger, Paul): Chemistry. See: Van Nostrand Chem. Dict.

Schuftan, Eugene. See: Schuefftan, Eugene.

SCHUILING, H. J. fl. 20th c. German? geologist. Cited in: Amer. Min., vol. 33 (1948), pp. 385-386. Schuilingite.

Schuilingite (Schuiling, H. J.): Earth Sciences. See: Thrush.

SCHUKOWSKI, NIKOLAI EGOROVIC. 1847-1921. Russian engineer. See: Pogg., vols. 3, 4, 6. Joukowski airfoils (or airfoil profile), Joukowski condition, Joukowski transformation, Joukowski's proof, Kutta-Joukowski law (or hypothesis).

Schuleman-Schoenhoefer-Wingler test (Schulemann, Werner; Schoenhoefer, Fritz; and Wingler, August): Chemistry. See: Van Nostrand Chem. Dict.

SCHULEMANN, WERNER. b. 1888. German chemist. See: Pogg., vols. 6, 7a. Schuleman-Schoenhoefer-Wingler test.

Schuler (Schuler, Max): Physics. See: Hughes.

Schuler clock (Schuler, Max): Physics. See: Thewlis.

SCHULER, MAX. b. 1882. German physicist. See: World Who's Who Sci. Schuler, Schuler clock, Schuler pendulum.

Schuler pendulum (Schuler, Max): Physics. See: Hughes; Thewlis.

Schuller process (Schuller, Werner?): Engineering and Industry. See: Thrush.

SCHULLER, WERNER. fl. 1944-1954. German glass technologist. Cited in: Chem. Abstr., Decenn. Indexes, 1937-1946; 1947-1956. Schuller process?

SCHULTE-TIGGES, HUGO. b. 1885. German bacteriologist. Cited in: Kelly. Schulte-Tigges stain.

Schulte-Tigges stain (Schulte-Tigges, Hugo): Medicine. See: Stedman.

SCHULTEN, BARON AUGUST BENJAMIN DE. 1856-1912. German chemist. See: Pogg., vols. 3, 4, 5. Schultenite.

Schultenite (Schulten, Baron August Benjamin de): Earth Sciences. See: Thrush; Webster's 3d.

Schultz-Charlton reaction (or phenomenon) (Schultz, Werner and Charlton, Willy): Medicine. See: Dorland; Stedman.

Schultz-Dale reaction (Schultz, Werner and Dale, Sir Henry Hallett): Medicine. See: Stedman; Webster's 3d.

SCHULTZ, GUSTAV THEODOR AUGUST OTTO. 1851-1928. German chemist. See: World Who's Who Sci. Schultz number.

Schultz number (Schultz, Gustav Theodor August Otto): Chemistry. See: Hackh.

SCHULTZ, WERNER. 1878-1947. German internist. See: Biog. Lex. hervorr. Aerzte. Schultz-Charlton reaction (or phenomenon), Schultz-Dale reaction, Schultz's disease, Schultz's syndrome (or angina).

SCHULTZE, BERNHARD SIGMUND. 1827-1919. German obstetrician. See: Biog. Lex. hervorr. Aerzte. Schultze's method, Schultze's phantom.

SCHULTZE, EDWARD. fl. 1865. German chemist. Cited in: Encyc. Brit., 1911. Schultze powder.

SCHULTZE, FRIEDRICH. 1848-1934. German physician. See: Biog. Lex. hervorr. Aerzte. Schultze's acroparesthesia.

SCHULTZE, KARL. b. 1887. German chemist. See: Pogg., vols. 6, 7a. Schultze solution for cellulose?

SCHULTZE, MAX JOHANN SIGISMUND. 1825-1874. German histologist and zoologist. See: Biog. Lex. hervorr. Aerzte. Schultze's cell(s), Schultze's fascicle (or comma tract), Schultze's membrane, Schultze's sign.

Schultze powder (Schultze, Edward): Weapons. See: Quick; Webster's 3d.

Schultze solution for cellulose (Schultze, Karl?): Chemistry. See: Van Nostrand Chem. Dict.

Schultze's acroparesthesia (Schultze, Friedrich): Medicine. See: Jablonski.

Schultze's cell(s) (Schultze, Max Johann Sigismund): Anatomy. See: Donath; Dorland; Stedman.

Schultze's fascicle (or comma tract) (Schultze, Max Johann Sigismund): Anatomy. See: Donath; Stedman.

Schultze's membrane (Schultze, Max Johann Sigismund): Anatomy. See: Stedman.

Schultze's method (Schultze, Bernhard Sigmund): Medicine. See: Dorland; Stedman.

Schultze's phantom (Schultze, Bernhard Sigmund): Medicine. See: Stedman.

Schultze's sign (Schultze, Max Johann Sigismund): Medicine. See: Stedman.

Schultze's test (Schulze, Ernst A.): Medicine. See: Dorland; Stedman.

Schultz's disease (Schultz, Werner): Medicine. See: Dorland; Jablonski.

Schultz's syndrome (or angina) (Schultz, Werner): Medicine. See: Jablonski.

SCHULZ. fl. 1908. German engineer. (Biography source unavailable.) Schulz turbine.

SCHULZ, A. No dates. German engineer. (Biography source unavailable.) Schulz's theory.

Schulz and Sing formula (Schulz, Guenter Victor and Sing, Gertrud): Chemistry. See: Ballentyne.

SCHULZ, GUENTER VICTOR. 1905- . German chemist. See: Pogg., vol. 7a. Schulz and Sing formula.

SCHULZ, HUGO. 1853-1932. German pharmacologist. See: Biog. Lex. hervorr Aerzte. Arndt-Schulz law, Schulz test reaction for salicylic acid?

Schulz test reaction for salicylic acid (Schulz, Hugo?): Chemistry. See: Van Nostrand Chem. Dict.

Schulz turbine (Schulz): Engineering and Industry. See: Auger.

SCHULZ, WILHELM. fl. 1920. German chemist. Cited in: Chem. Abstr., vol. 14, p. 2611. Meyer-Schulz solution.

Schulze elutriator (Derivation undetermined): Engineering and Industry. See: Thrush.

SCHULZE, ERNST A. 1840-1912. German-Swiss physiological chemist. Cited in: Royal Soc. Cat. Sci. Pap., 1884-1900. Schultze's test.

SCHULZE, HANS. fl. 1853-1892. German chemist. Cited in: Partington, vol. 4. Schulze-Hardy rule.

Schulze-Hardy rule (Schulze, Hans and Hardy, Sir William Bate): Chemistry. See: Ballentyne; Thrush; Van Nostrand Sci. Encyc. Also known as: Hardy-Schulze rule.

Schulz's theory (Schulz, A.): Earth Sciences. See: Thrush.

Schumacher hand-press (Derivation undetermined): Printing. Cited in: Lockwood under Hand-Press, p. 256.

SCHUMACHER-KOPP, EMIL. d. 1927. Swiss chemist. Cited in: Royal Soc. Cat. Sci. Pap., 1884-1900. Schumacher-Kopp test reactions for methyl violet and tropeolin.

Schumacher-Kopp test reactions for methyl violet and tropeolin (Schumacher-Kopp, Emil): Chemistry. See: Van Nostrand Chem. Dict.

Schuman plan (Schuman, Robert): Politics. See: Seldon; Smith.

SCHUMAN, ROBERT. 1886-1963. French politician. See: New Encyc. Brit., 1974, Microp. Schuman plan.

SCHUMANN, FRIEDRICH. fl. 1887-1932. German psychologist. See: Psych. Register, 1932, p. 872. Mueller-Schumann law (or paradigm of associative inhibition).

SCHUMANN, G. fl. 1920. German engineer. Cited in: Chem. Abstr., Decenn. Index, 1917-1926. Schumann plot?

Schumann plate(s) (Schumann, Viktor): Physics. See: Focal Encyc. Photog.; Hughes; Thewlis.

Schumann plot (Schumann, G.?): Engineering and Industry. See: Thrush.

Schumann region (or rays) (Schumann, Viktor): Physics. See: Hackh; Webster's 3d.

Schumann-Runge bands (Schumann, Viktor and Runge, Carl David Tolme?): Physics. See: Huschke

Schumann-Runge continuum (Schumann, Viktor and Runge, Carl David Tolme?): Physics. See: Huschke; Van Nostrand Sci. Encyc.

SCHUMANN, VIKTOR. 1841-1913. German physicist. See: World Who's Who Sci. Schumann plate(s), Schumann region (or rays), Schumann-Runge bands?, Schumann-Runge continuum.

SCHUPPHAUS, ROBERT C. fl. 1890. American inventor. Cited in: Nat. Cycl. Amer. Biog., vol. 13, p. 520 under "Maxim, Hudson." Maxim-Schupphaus smokeless powder.

SCHUR, FRIEDRICH HEINRICH. 1856-1932. German mathematician. See: World Who's Who Sci. Schur's theorem.

SCHUR, ISSAI. 1875-1941. Israeli mathematician. See: Pogg., vols. 5, 6. Schur('s) lemma.

Schur('s) lemma (Schur, Issai): Mathematics. See: Ballentyne; Internat. Dict. Ap. Math.; James.

SCHURECHT, H. G. fl. 1928-1935. American chemist. Cited in: Chem. Abstr., Decenn. Index, 1927-1936. Schurecht's ratio.

Schurecht's ratio (Schurecht, H. G.): Engineering and Industry. See: Thrush.

Schurman commission (Schurman, Jacob Gould): History. See: Morris and Irwin.

SCHURMAN, JACOB GOULD. 1854-1942. American educator and diplomat. See: Who Was Who Amer. Schurman commission.

Schur's theorem (Schur, Friedrich Heinrich): Mathematics. See: James.

SCHUSTER, SIR ARTHUR. 1851-1934. English mathematician and physicist. See: Pogg., vols. 3 to 6. Rydberg-Schuster law, Schuster-Gannon method for mechanical equivalent of heat, Schuster method, Schuster periodogram.

Schuster-Gannon method for mechanical equivalent of heat (Schuster, Sir Arthur and Gannon, William): Physics. See: Internat. Dict. Phys. Elec.

SCHUSTER, KURT. fl. 1922. German chemist. Cited in: Krauch and Kunz. Meyer-Schuster rearrangement.

Schuster method (Schuster, Sir Arthur): Physics. See: Internat. Dict. Phys. Elec.

Schuster periodogram (Schuster, Sir Arthur): Statistics. See: Kendall.

Schuster test reaction for urethane (Derivation undetermined): Chemistry. See: Van Nostrand Chem. Dict.

SCHUTTLER, PETER. 1812-1865. German-born American wagon builder. See: Dict. Amer. Biog. Schuttler (wagon).

chuttler (wagon) (Schuttler, Peter): Engineering and Industry. See: Mathews, M. M.

CHUTZ, ERICH. 1902- . German biochemist and physician. (Biography source unavailable.) Schutz' rule.

chutz' rule (Schutz, Erich): Medicine. See: Stedman.

CHWABACH, DAGOBERT. 1846-1920. German otologist. See: Biog. Lex. hervorr. Aerzte. Schwabach test.

chwabach test (Schwabach, Dagobert): Medicine. See: Dorland; Stedman.

CHWALBE. No dates. Physician. (Biography source unavailable.) Schwalbea.

CHWALBE, CARL GUSTAV. 1871-1938. German chemist. See: Pogg., ols. 4 to 6, 7a. Schwalbe test.

CHWALBE, GUSTAV A. 1844-1917. German anatomist and anthropologist. ee: World Who's Who Sci. Schwalbe's corpuscle(s), Schwalbe's nucleus, chwalbe's rings, Schwalbe's space(s).

chwalbe test (Schwalbe, Carl Gustav): Chemistry. See: Van Nostrand hem. Dict.

chwalbea (Schwalbe): Botany. See: Charnock.

chwalbe's corpuscle(s) (Schwalbe, Gustav A.): Anatomy. See: Donath; orland; Stedman.

chwalbe's nucleus (Schwalbe, Gustav A.): Anatomy. See: Donath; Stedman.

chwalbe's rings (Schwalbe, Gustav A.): Anatomy. See: Stedman.

chwalbe's space(s) (Schwalbe, Gustav A.): Anatomy. See: Donath; Dorland; tedman.

chwann('s) cell (Schwann, Theodor): Anatomy. See: Henderson; Stedman; Webster's 3d.

chwann('s) sheath (or tube) (Schwann, Theodor): Anatomy. See: Dorland; Henderson; Pennak.

CHWANN, THEODOR. 1810-1882. German anatomist and physiologist. ee: World Who's Who Sci. Schwann('s) cell, Schwann('s) sheath (or tube), chwannian, Schwannoma, Schwannosis, Schwann's substance (or white substance), chwann's tumor, Von Schwann's law.

chwannian (Schwann, Theodor): Anatomy. See: Webster's 3d.

chwannoma (Schwann, Theodor): Medicine. See: Stedman; Webster's 3d.

chwannosis (Schwann, Theodor). See: Guillain-Barre syndrome.

chwann's substance (or white substance) (Schwann, Theodor): Anatomy. See: onath; Dorland; Stedman.

chwann's tumor (Schwann, Theodor): Medicine. See: Stedman.

chwartz-Bartter syndrome (Schwartz, William Benjamin and Bartter, Frederic C.): Medicine. See: Jablonski.

CHWARTZ, C. fl. 1932. American physician. Cited in: Kelly. Hamilton-wartz test.

CHWARTZ, CHARLES EDOUARD. b. 1852. French surgeon. Cited in: ndex-Cat. Libr. Surg.-Gen. Off., 1st Ser., vol. 12, 1891. Schwartz' method.

CHWARTZ, HENRY GERARD. 1909- . American neurosurgeon. See: mer. Men and Women Sci., 12th ed. Schwartz tractotomy.

chwartz-Jampel syndrome (Schwartz, Oscar and Jampel, Robert). See: chwartz's syndrome.

chwartz' method (Schwartz, Charles Edouard): Medicine. See: Dorland; tedman.

CHWARTZ, OSCAR. 1919- . American pediatrician. See: Direct. Med. pecialists, 1974-75. Schwartz's syndrome.

CHWARTZ, STEVEN OTTO. 1911- . Hungarian-born American hematolo-ist. See: Amer. Men and Women Sci., 12th ed. Schwartz's leukemia.

chwartz tractotomy (Schwartz, Henry Gerard): Medicine. See: Stedman.

SCHWARTZ, WILLIAM BENJAMIN. 1922- . American physician. See: mer. Men and Women Sci., 12th ed. Schwartz-Bartter syndrome.

SCHWARTZE, HERMANN. 1837-1910. German otologist. See: Biog. Lex. hervorr. Aerzte. Schwartze operation, Schwartze-Stacke operation.

Schwartze operation (Schwartze, Hermann): Medicine. See: Dorland; Stedman.

Schwartze-Stacke operation (Schwartze, Hermann and Stacke, Ludwig): Medicine. See: Stedman.

SCHWARTZEMBERG. fl. 19th c. Chilean mineral assayer. Cited in: Dana. Schwartzembergite.

Schwartzembergite (Schwartzemberg): Earth Sciences. See: Webster's 3d.

Schwartz's leukemia (Schwartz, Steven Otto): Medicine. See: Jablonski.

Schwartz's syndrome (Schwartz, Oscar): Medicine. See: Jablonski. Also known as: Schwartz-Jampel syndrome.

Schwartzschild antenna (Schwarzschild, Martin?): Physics. See: Hughes.

Schwarz-Christoffel transformation (Schwarz, Hermann Amandus and Christoffel, Elwin Bruno): Mathematics. See: Internat. Dict. Ap. Math.

SCHWARZ, FRITZ. fl. 1928. Swiss physician. Cited in: Kelly. Schwarz reagent for blood.

SCHWARZ, HELMUT JULIUS. 1915- . German-born American physicist. See: World Who's Who Sci. Schwarz principle of reflection?

SCHWARZ, HERMANN AMANDUS. 1843-1921. German mathematician. See: World Who's Who Sci. Cauchy-Schwarz inequality, Schwarz-Christoffel transformation, Schwarz's lemma.

SCHWARZ, KARL L. H. 1824-1890. German chemist. Cited in: Partington, vol. 4. Schwarz's test.

Schwarz principle of reflection (Schwarz, Helmut Julius?): Physics. See: Ballentyne.

Schwarz reaction for naphthalene (Derivation undetermined): Chemistry. See: Van Nostrand Chem. Dict.

Schwarz reagent for blood (Schwarz, Fritz): Chemistry. See: Van Nostrand Chem. Dict.

Schwarz strain (Derivation undetermined): Medicine. See: Stedman, App. 1A under measles virus vaccine..., p. 1439.

Schwarz test for lime in magnesite (Derivation undetermined): Chemistry. See: Van Nostrand Chem. Dict.

SCHWARZLOSE, ANDREA. fl. 1898. Austrian engineer. (Biography source unavailable.) Schwarzlose automatic pistol.

Schwarzlose automatic pistol (Schwarzlose, Andrea): Weapons. See: Quick.

Schwarz's inequality (Schwarz, Hermann Amandus). See: Cauchy-Schwarz inequality.

Schwarz's lemma (Schwarz, Hermann Amandus): Mathematics. See: James.

Schwarz's test (Schwarz, Karl L. H.): Medicine. See: Dorland; Stedman.

Schwarzschild anastigmat (Schwarzschild, Karl): Astronomy. See: Internat. Dict. Phys. Elec.

Schwarzschild effect (Schwarzschild, Karl): Photography. See: Focal Encyc. Photog.; Van Nostrand Sci. Encyc.

SCHWARZSCHILD, KARL. 1873-1916. German astronomer. See: World Who's Who Sci. Schwarzschild anastigmat, Schwarzschild effect. Schwarzschild-Kohlschuetter formulas, Schwarzschild reflector, Schwarzschild (Schwartzschild) telescope, Schwarzschild's law.

Schwarzschild-Kohlschuetter formulas (Schwarzschild, Karl and Kohlschuetter, Arnold): Physics. See: Internat. Dict. Ap. Math.

SCHWARZSCHILD, MARTIN. 1912- . German-born American astrophysicist. See: World Who's Who Sci. Schwartzschild antenna?, Schwarzschild radius, Schwarzschild solution?

Schwarzschild radius (Schwarzschild, Martin): Physics. See: Barnhart (New Eng.).

Schwarzschild reflector (Schwarzschild, Karl): Astronomy. See: Van Nostrand Sci. Encyc. under "Telescopes (Astronomical)."

Schwarzschild solution (Schwarzschild, Martin?): Physics. See: Internat. Dict. Phys. Elec.

Schwarzschild (Schwartzschild) telescope (Schwarzschild, Karl): Astronomy. See: Satterthwaite; Van Nostrand Sci. Encyc.

Schwarzschild's law (Schwarzschild, Karl): Photography. See: Focal Encyc. Photog.

Schwediauer, Francois X. See: Swediauer, Francois X.

Schweiger–Seidel sheath (Schweigger–Seidel, Franz). See: sheath of Schweigger–Seidel.

SCHWEIGGER-SEIDEL, FRANZ. 1834-1871. German physiologist. See: Biog. Lex. hervorr. Aerzte. sheath of Schweigger–Seidel.

SCHWEISSINGER, OTTO. fl. 1884. German pharmaceutical chemist. Cited in: Royal Soc. Cat. Sci. Pap., 1884-1900. Schweissinger test for alkalies, Schweissinger test for pyridine.

Schweissinger test for alkalies (Schweissinger, Otto): Chemistry. See: Van Nostrand Chem. Dict.

Schweissinger test for pyridine (Schweissinger, Otto): Chemistry. See: Van Nostrand Chem. Dict.

SCHWEITZER, MATTHIAS EDUARD. 1818-1860. German chemist. Cited in: Royal Soc. Cat. Sci. Pap., 1800-1863. Schweitzer('s) reagent (for wool, cotton, and silk).

Schweitzer('s) reagent (for wool, cotton, and silk) (Schweitzer, Matthias Eduard): Chemistry. See: Hackh; Van Nostrand Chem. Dict.; Van Nostrand Sci. Encyc.

Schweitzer test reaction for quinine (Derivation undetermined): Chemistry. See: Van Nostrand Chem. Dict.

SCHWEIZER, G. fl. 1926. German chemist. Cited in: Chem. Abstr., vol. 20, p. 2965. Schweizer test reaction.

Schweizer test reaction (Schweizer, G.): Chemistry. See: Van Nostrand Chem. Dict.

SCHWENCKE, MARTIN WILHELM. 1707-1785. Dutch physician. See: Biog. Lex. hervorr. Aerzte. Schwenkia.

SCHWENCKFELD VON OSSIG, KASPAR. 1490-1561. German theologian, mystic, and religious reformer. See: New Encyc. Brit., 1974, Microp. Schwenckfeldians (Schwenkfeldians or Schwenkenfelder).

Schwenckfeldians (Schwenkfeldians or Schwenkenfelder) (Schwenckfeld von Ossig, Kaspar): Religion. See: Canney; Mathews, S.; Webster's 3d.

SCHWENINGER, ERNST. 1850-1924. German physician. See: Biog. Lex. hervorr. Aerzte. Schweninger's method.

Schweninger's method (Schweninger, Ernst): Medicine. See: Dorland.

Schwenkia (Schwencke, Martin Wilhelm): Botany. See: Charnock.

Schwinger coupler (or coupling) (Schwinger, Julian Seymour?): Electronics. See: Hughes; Van Nostrand Sci. Encyc.

SCHWINGER, JULIAN SEYMOUR. 1918- . American physicist. See: Amer. Men and Women Sci., 12th ed. Schwinger coupler (or coupling)?

SCLAVO, ACHILLE. 1861-1930. Italian physician. See: Biog. Lex hervorr. Aerzte. Sclavo's serum.

Sclavo's serum (Sclavo, Achille): Medicine. See: Dorland.

Scoggin (Scoggin, John): Generic Word (coarse jester). See: Webster's 3d.

SCOGGIN, JOHN. fl. 1480-1500. English jester. See: Dict. Nat. Biog. under "Scogan, Henry." Scoggin.

SCOGGIN, MARGARET CLARA. 1905-1968. American librarian. Cited in: Amer. Libr. Assoc. Membership Direct., 1967. Margaret Scoggin Scholarship.

SCOPES, JOHN T. fl. 1925. American biology teacher. Cited in: New Encyc. Brit., 1974, Microp. Scopes trial.

Scopes trial (Scopes, John T.): Law. See: Pennak; Smith.

SCORTECCI, ANTONIO. fl. 20th c. Italian metallurgist. See: Who's Who Sci. Europe, 1972. Scortecci process.

Scortecci process (Scortecci, Antonio): Engineering and Industry. See: Thrush.

SCORZA, EVARISTO PENA. fl. 1948. Brazilian mineralogist. Cited in: Min. Mag., vol. 28 (March 1947-September 1949), p. 738. Scorzalite.

Scorzalite (Scorza, Evaristo Pena): Earth Sciences. See: Thrush; Webster's 3d.

Scotists (Duns Scotus, John): Religion. See: Barnhart (Eng. Lit.); Brewer; Phyfe.

Scott-Adams reagent and test (Scott, Alfred Witherspoon and Adams, Eleanor G.): Chemistry. See: Van Nostrand Chem. Dict.

SCOTT, ALFRED WITHERSPOON. 1896- . American chemist. See: Amer. Men Sci., 6th ed. Scott-Adams reagent and test.

SCOTT, CHARLES FELTON. b. 1864. American electrical engineer. See: Amer. Men Sci., 1st ed. Scott transformer?

SCOTT, DRED. ca. 1795-1858. American slave. See: Dict. Amer. Biog. Dred Scott Decision, Dred Scott dictum, Dred-Scottite.

SCOTT, DUKINFIELD HENRY. 1854-1934. English botanist. See: Who Was Who. Scott's spleenwort.

SCOTT, F. H. fl. 1909. English chemist. Cited in: Chem. Abstr., Decenn. Index, 1907-1916. Scott-Plimmer reagent.

Scott furnace (Derivation undetermined): Engineering and Industry. See: Thrush; Van Nostrand Chem. Dict.

SCOTT, SIR HENRY HAROLD. 1874-1956. English physician. See: World Who's Who Sci. Strachan-Scott syndrome.

SCOTT, JAMES, DUKE OF MONMOUTH. 1649-1685. English claimant to throne. See: Dict. Nat. Biog. Monmouth's rebellion.

SCOTT, JOHN. 1798-1846. English surgeon. See: Dict. Nat. Biog. Scott's dressing.

SCOTT, M. fl. 1937. Canadian? chemist. Cited in: Chem. Abstr., Decenn. Index, 1939-1946. Thompson-Beamish-Scott test reactions for platinum, Thompson-Beamish-Scott tests for osmium.

Scott-Plimmer reagent (Scott, F. H. and Plimmer, Robert Henry Aders): Chemistry. See: Van Nostrand Chem. Dict.

Scott presses (Scott, Walter): Printing. See: Lockwood.

SCOTT-RUSSELL, J. 1802-1882. English engineer. (Biography source unavailable.) Scott-Russell straight-line motion.

Scott-Russell straight-line motion (Scott-Russell, J.): Engineering and Industry. See: Auger.

SCOTT, S. F. fl. 1908. American chemist. Cited in: Chem. Abstr., vol. 2, p. 2971. Dehn-Scott test reaction for alkaloids, Dehn-Scott test reaction for aromatic amines, Dehn-Scott test reaction for phenolic compounds.

SCOTT-SMITH, GEORGE EGERTON. fl. 1911. English chemist. Cited in: Chem. Abstr., vol. 5, p. 3121. Allen and Scott-Smith test reaction.

Scott transformer (Scott, Charles Felton?): Electronics. See: Van Nostrand Sci. Encyc.

SCOTT, WALTER. b. 1844. Scottish-born American press builder. (Biography source unavailable.) Scott presses.

SCOTT-WILSON, H. fl. 1911. English scientist. Cited in: Chem. Abstr., Decenn. Index, 1907-1916. Scott-Wilson reagent.

Scott-Wilson reagent (Scott-Wilson, H.): Medicine. See: Stedman; Van Nostrand Chem. Dict.

SCOTT, WINFIELD. 1786-1866. American military hero. See: Dict. Amer. Biog. Great Scott!?, Scott's oriole.

Scottish Chaucerians (Chaucer, Geoffrey): Literature. See: Harvey; Preminger; Scott.

Scott's dressing (Scott, John): Medicine. See: Carter.

Scott's oriole (Scott, Winfield): Zoology. See: Gray; Mathews, M. M.

Scott's spleenwort (Scott, Dukinfield Henry): Botany. See: Webster's 3d.

Scotus, John Duns. See: Duns Scotus, John.

Scoville test (Scoville, Wilbur Lincoln): Chemistry. See: Van Nostrand Chem. Dict.

SCOVILLE, WILBUR LINCOLN. b. 1865. American chemist. See: Amer. Men Sci., 4th ed. Scoville test.

SCRIBA, KARL. 1907- . German pathologist. See: Kuerschner's Deut. Gel. Kal, vol. 9, 1961. Scriba test?

Scriba test (Scriba, Karl?): Chemistry. See: Van Nostrand Chem. Dict.

Scriblerus Club (Scriblerus, Martinus): Literature. See: Scott.

SCRIBLERUS, MARTINUS. Fictional character created by Alexander Pope, Jonathan Swift, John Gay, Thomas Parnell, and John Arbuthnot. Cited in: New Encyc. Brit., 1974, Microp. Scriblerus Club.

Scribner decimal rule (Derivation undetermined): Forestry. See: Winburne.

Scribner rule (Derivation undetermined): Forestry. See: Winburne.

SCRIPTURE, EDWARD WHEELER. b. 1864. American psychologist. See: Amer. Men Sci., 1st ed. Scripture weights, Scripture's blocks.

Scripture weights (Scripture, Edward Wheeler): Psychology. See: Drever.

Scripture's blocks (Scripture, Edward Wheeler): Psychology. See: Drever.

SCRIVER, CHARLES ROBERT. 1930- . Canadian pediatrician and geneticist. See: Amer. Men and Women Sci., 12th ed. Scriver-Goldbloom-Roy syndrome.

Scriver-Goldbloom-Roy syndrome (Scriver, Charles Robert; Goldbloom, Richard B.; and Roy, Claude C.): Medicine. See: Jablonski.

Scrooge (Scrooge, Ebenezer): Generic Word (curmudgeon). See: Partridge.

SCROOGE, EBENEZER. Character in Charles Dickens' novel "A Christmas Carol," (1843). See: Magill. Scrooge.

SCUDDER, HEYWARD. fl. 1899. American chemist. Cited in: Royal Soc. Cat. Sci. Pap., 1884-1900. Mullikan-Scudder test for methanol.

SCUDI, JOHN VINCENT. 1908- . American pharmacologist and biochemist. See: Amer. Men and Women Sci., 12th ed. Scudi-Ratish test.

Scudi-Ratish test (Scudi, John Vincent and Ratish, Herman D.): Chemistry. See: Van Nostrand Chem. Dict.

SCULLY, ROBERT EDWARD. 1921- . American pathologist. See: Amer. Men and Women Sci., 12th ed. Scully's tumor.

Scully's tumor (Scully, Robert Edward): Medicine. See: Jablonski.

Scultetus' bandage (Scultetus, Jan): Medicine. See: Stedman.

SCULTETUS, JAN (JAN SCHULTZ). 1595-1645. German surgeon. See: Allg. Deut. Biog. Scultetus' bandage, Scultetus' position.

Scultetus' position (Scultetus, Jan): Medicine. See: Stedman.

SCYLLA. In Greco-Roman mythology, a female monster. See: Jobes. Between Scylla and Charybdis, Scyllaea.

Scyllaea (Scylla): Zoology. See: Webster's 3d.

Seabright bantam syndrome (Derivation undetermined): Medicine. See: Stedman.

Seabury Commission (Seabury, Samuel): Politics. See: Smith.

SEABURY, SAMUEL. b. 1873. American lawyer. See: Nat. Cycl. Amer. Biog., vol. D, p. 76. Seabury Commission.

Seailles-Dyckerhoff process (Seailles, Jean C.; Seailles, Speranza; and Dyckerhoff, Walter). See: Seailles process.

SEAILLES, JEAN C. fl. 1925-1932. French chemist. Cited in: Chem. Abstr., vol. 19, p. 3579; vol. 20, p. 3551. Seailles process.

Seailles process (Seailles, Jean C. and Speranza): Engineering and Industry. See: Thrush. Also known as: Seailles-Dyckerhoff process.

SEAILLES, SPERANZA. fl. 1925-1932. French chemist. Cited in: Chem. Abstr., vol. 19, p. 3579; vol. 20, p. 3551. Seailles process.

Seale construction (Derivation undetermined): Engineering and Industry. See: Thrush.

Seale rope (Derivation undetermined): Engineering and Industry. See: Thrush.

Seale's lay (Derivation undetermined): Engineering and Industry. See: Auger; Thrush.

SEAMAN, ELIZABETH COCHRANE (Pseud.: NELLY BLY). 1867-1922. American journalist. See: Dict. Amer. Biog. Nelly Bly.

SEARLES, JOHN W. fl. 19th c. American settler in California. Cited in: Hintze. Searlesite.

Searlesia (Derivation undetermined): Zoology. See: Pennak.

Searlesite (Searles, John W.): Earth Sciences. See: Webster's 3d.

SEARS, FRANCIS WESTON. 1898- . American physicist. See: World Who's Who Sci. Debye-Sears cell, Debye-Sears effect.

SEASHORE, CARL EMIL. 1866-1949. American psychologist. See: Internat. Encyc. Soc. Sci. Seashore test(s) (of musical ability or talent), Seashore's audiometer.

Seashore test(s) (of musical ability or talent) (Seashore, Carl Emil); Psychology. See: Drever; English; Wolman.

Seashore's audiometer (Seashore, Carl Emil): Psychology. See: Drever.

SEATON, THOMAS. 1684-1741. English divine. See: Dict. Nat. Biog. Seatonian Prize.

Seatonian Prize (Seaton, Thomas): Literature. See: Harvey; Latham.

Sebastianite (Derivation undetermined): Earth Sciences. See: Thrush.

SEBELIEN, JOHN ROBERT FRANCIS. 1858-1932. Danish chemist. See: Pogg., vols. 5, 6. Sebelien reagent.

Sebelien reagent (Sebelien, John Robert Francis): Chemistry. See: Van Nostrand Chem. Dict.

SEBILEAU, PIERRE. 1860-1953. French anatomist. See: Biog. Lex. hervorr. Aerzte. Sebileau's hollow, Sebileau's muscle.

Sebileau's hollow (Sebileau, Pierre): Anatomy. See: Dorland; Stedman.

Sebileau's muscle (Sebileau, Pierre): Anatomy. See: Stedman.

SECCHI, ANGELO (In full: PIETRO ANGELO). 1818-1878. Italian astronomer. See: World Who's Who Sci. Secchi('s) classification (or spectral classification), Secchi disk?

Secchi('s) classification (or spectral classification) (Secchi, Angelo): Astronomy. See: Ballentyne; Satterthwaite.

Secchi disk (Secchi, Angelo?): Earth Sciences. See: Huschke; Thrush.

Secenov, Ivan Mikhailovich. See: Siechenoff, Ivan Mikhailovich.

SECKEL. fl. 18th c. American farmer. (Biography source unavailable.) Seckel (pear).

SECKEL, HELMUT PAUL GEORGE. 1900- . German physician. See: Corsten. Seckel's syndrome.

Seckel (pear) (Seckel): Botany. See: De Sola; Hendrickson; Mathews, M. M.

Seckel's syndrome (Seckel, Helmut Paul George): Medicine. See: Jablonski. Also known as: Virchow-Seckel dwarfism.

secohm (Ohm, Georg Simon): Physics. See: Dresner.

second law of Laplace (Laplace, Pierre-Simon, Marquis de): Statistics. See: Kendall under "Normal Distribution."

SECRETAN, HENRI FRANCOIS. 1856-1916. Swiss physician. See: Revue Medic. Suisse Rom., vol. 36 (1916), p. 201. Secretan's disease.

Secretan's disease (Secretan, Henri Francois): Medicine. See: Dorland; Jablonski.

Sedgwick feeding-machine (Derivation undetermined): Printing. See: Lockwood under "Feeding-Machine."

Sedgwick-Rafter counting chamber (Derivation undetermined): Biology. See: Pennak.

SEDGWICK, ROBERT POST. 1918- . American neurologist. See: Amer. Med. Direct., 1950. Boder-Sedgwick syndrome.

SEDILLOT. fl. 1931. French physician. (Biography source unavailable.) Sedillot syndrome.

SEDILLOT, CHARLES E. 1804-1883. French surgeon. See: World Who's Who Sci. Sedillot's operation.

Sedillot syndrome (Sedillot): Medicine. See: Jablonski.

Sedillot's operation (Sedillot, Charles E.): Medicine. See: Dorland.

SEE, GEORGES. 1904- . French pediatrician. Cited in: Index-Cat. Libr. Surg.–Gen. Off., 5th Ser., vol. 1, 1959. Marie-See syndrome.

Seebeck effect (Seebeck, Thomas Johann): Physics. See: Ballentyne; Thewlis; Van Nostrand Chem. Dict.

SEEBECK, THOMAS JOHANN. 1770-1831. Russian-born German physicist. See: Pogg., vol. 2; World Who's Who Sci. Seebeck effect.

SEEBERGER, LUDWIG. fl. 1891-1893. German chemist. Cited in: Pogg., vol. 4 under "Bamberger, Eugen." Bamberger-Seeberger test reaction.

Seeboard process (or purification process) (Derivation undetermined): Engineering and Industry. See: Thrush; Van Nostrand Chem. Dict.

SEELEY, STUART WILLIAM. 1901- . American engineer. See: Amer. Men Sci., 9th ed. Foster-Seeley discriminator.

Seeliger reagent (Seeliger, Rudolf?): Chemistry. See: Van Nostrand Chem. Dict.

SEELIGER, RUDOLF. fl. 20th c. German botanist. See: Kuerschner's Deut. Gel. Kal., 1940-1941. Seeliger reagent?

SEELIGMANN, E. fl. 1841. German physician. (Biography source unavailable.) Seeligmann's disease.

Seeligmann's disease (Seeligmann, E.). See: Carini's syndrome.

SEELIGMUELLER, OTTO LUDWIG GUSTAV ADOLF. 1837-1912. German neurologist. See: Biog. Lex. hervorr. Aerzte. Seeligmueller's neuralgia, Seeligmueller's sign.

Seeligmueller's neuralgia (Seeligmueller, Otto Ludwig Gustav Adolf): Medicine. See: Jablonski.

Seeligmueller's sign (Seeligmueller, Otto Ludwig Gustav Adolf); Medicine. See: Dorland; Stedman.

SEESSEL, ALBERT. 1850-1910. American embryologist. See: Biog. Lex. hervorr. Aerzte. Seessel's (Sessel's) pocket (or pouch).

Seessel's (Sessel's) pocket (or pouch) (Seessel, Albert): Medicine. See: Dorland; Gray; Stedman.

Seewer aerofoil vane (Seewer, P. W.): Engineering and Industry. See: Auger.

SEEWER, P. W. fl. 1920? German engineer. (Biography source unavailable.) Seewer aerofoil vane.

Seger cone(s) (Seger, Hermann August): Engineering and Industry. See: Hackh; Thrush; Van Nostrand Sci. Encyc.

SEGER, E. fl. 20th c. Swedish engineer. (Biography source unavailable.) Seger turbine.

Seger formula (Seger, Hermann August): Engineering and Industry. See: Thrush.

SEGER, HERMANN AUGUST. 1839-1893. German ceramics technologist. See: Chem. Ztg., vol. 17 (1893), p. 1633. Seger cone(s), Seger formula, Seger's porcelain, Seger's rules.

Seger turbine (Seger, E.): Engineering and Industry. See: Auger.

Seger's porcelain (Seger, Hermann August): Engineering and Industry. See: Thrush.

Seger's rules (Seger, Hermann August): Engineering and Industry. See: Thrush.

SEGLAS, JULES. 1856-1939. French physician. See: Presse Med., vol. 48 (Feb. 7-10, 1940), pp. 173-174. Seglas type (paranoia).

Seglas type (paranoia) (Seglas, Jules): Medicine. See: Dorland; Hinsie.

SEGNER. fl. 19th c. German? engineer. (Biography source unavailable.) Segner's wheel.

SEGNER, JOHANN ANDRES VON. 1704-1777. German naturalist and mathematician. See: World Who's Who Sci. Segner's cycle.

Segner's cycle (Segner, Johann Andres von): Mathematics? Cited in: World Who's Who Sci.

Segner's wheel (Segner): Engineering and Industry. See: Auger.

Segre chart (Segre, Emilio Gino): Physics. See: Hughes.

SEGRE, EMILIO GINO. 1905- . Italian-born American physicist. See: Amer. Men and Women Sci., 12th ed. Segre chart.

SEGUIN, EDOUARD. 1812-1880. French physician. See: Biog. Lex. hervorr. Aerzte. Seguin's symptom.

SEGUIN, MARC. 1786-1875. French engineer. See: Pogg., vol. 3. Seguin's boiler.

Seguin's boiler (Seguin, Marc): Engineering and Industry. See: Auger.

Seguin's symptom (Seguin, Edouard): Medicine. See: Dorland.

SEHRT, ERNST. b. 1879. German surgeon. See: Deut. Chirurgen Verzeichnis (1938) p. 621. Sehrt's clamp (or compressor).

Sehrt's clamp (or compressor) (Sehrt, Ernst): Medicine. See: Dorland.

Seidel (Seidal) aberrations (Seidel, Ludwig Philipp von): Physics. See: Ballentyne; Internat. Dict. Ap. Math.; Thewlis.

SEIDEL, ERICH. 1882-1946. German ophthalmologist. See: Biog. Lex. hervorr. Aerzte. Seidel's sign (or scotoma).

SEIDEL, LUDWIG PHILIPP VON. 1821-1896. German scientist. See: New Encyc. Brit., 1974, Microp. Gauss-Seidel method, Seidel (Seidal) aberrations, Seidel method, Seidel theory of aberrations of lenses.

Seidel method (Seidel, Ludwig Philipp von): Mathematics. See: Internat. Dict. Ap. Math.

Seidel theory of aberrations of lenses (Seidel, Ludwig Philipp von): Physics. See: Internat. Dict. Phys. Elec.

Seidelin bodies (Seidelin, Harold): Medicine. See: Dorland.

SEIDELIN, HAROLD. No dates. English physician. (Biography source unavailable.) Seidelin bodies.

Seidel's sign (or scotoma) (Seidel, Erich): Medicine. See: Dorland; Stedman.

SEIDLMAYER, HUBERT. 1910- . German physician. Cited in: Index-Cat. Libr. Surg.–Gen. Off., 5th Ser., vol. 1, 1959. Seidlmayer's syndrome.

Seidlmayer's syndrome (Seidlmayer, Hubert): Medicine. See: Jablonski.

Seiffert's spherical spiral (Derivation undetermined): Mathematics. See: Ballentyne.

Seignette electric (or electricity) (Seignette, Pierre): Physics. See: Ballentyne; Thrush.

SEIGNETTE, PIERRE. 1660-1719. French apothecary. See: World Who's Who Sci. Seignette electric (or electricity), Seignette's salt.

Seignette's salt (Seignette, Pierre): Medicine. See: Dorland; Stedman; Webster's 3d.

SEILER, CARL. 1849-1905. Swiss laryngologist and anatomist in America. Cited in: Royal Soc. Cat. Sci. Pap., 1884-1900. Seiler's cartilage.

Seiler's cartilage (Seiler, Carl): Anatomy. See: Stedman.

Seip-Berardinelli syndrome (Seip, Martin Fredrik and Berardinelli, Waldemar). See: Berardinelli's syndrome.

SEIP, MARTIN FREDRIK. 1921- . Norwegian pediatrician. See: Who's Who Sci. Europe, 1972. Seip's syndrome.

Seip's syndrome (Seip, Martin Fredrik). See: Berardinelli's syndrome.

SEITELBERGER, FRANZ. 1916- . Austrian neuropathologist. See: World Who's Who Sci. Seitelberger's disease (1), Seitelberger's disease (2).

Seitelberger's disease (1) (Seitelberger, Franz): Medicine. See: Jablonski.

Seitelberger's disease (2) (Seitelberger, Franz): Medicine. See: Jablonski.

SEITZ, FREDERICK. 1911- . American physicist. See: World Who's Who Sci. Wigner-Seitz cell, Wigner-Seitz method.

seive of Eratosthenes (Erastosthenes): Mathematics. See: Asimov; Ballentyne; Good.

SEJOURNET, JEAN. fl. 1923. French metallurgical engineer. Cited in: Chem. Abstr., Decenn. Index, 1917-1926. Ugine-Sejournet process?

journet process (Sejournet, Jean?). See: Ugine-Sejournet process.

...ladon. See: Celadon.

...lbourne, 1st Earl of. See: Palmer, Roundell, 1st Earl of Selbourne.

...LENGUT, DAVID S. 1927- . American physicist. See: Amer. Men ...d Women Sci., 12th ed. Goertzel-Selengut method.

...leucidae (or Seleucids) (Seleucus I): History. See: Brewer; Harvey; Phyfe.

...LEUCUS I (NICATOR). ca. 356-281 B.C. Macedonian general and founder ...dynasty. See: New Encyc. Brit., 1974, Microp. Seleucidae (or Seleu-...ds).

...LIGMANN, GUSTAV. 1849-1920. German banker and mineral collector. ...e: Pogg., vols. 4, 6. Seligmannite.

...ligmannite (Seligmann, Gustav): Earth Sciences. See: Thrush; Webster's 3d.

...LIWANOFF, FEODOR FEDOROVIC. b. 1859. Russian chemist. See: ...gg., vols. 4, 5. Seliwanoff('s) (Selivanoff's) test (or reagent).

...liwanoff('s) (Selivanoff's) test (or reagent) (Seliwanoff, Feodor Fedorovic): ...hemistry. See: Ballentyne; Dorland; Van Nostrand Chem. Dict.

...LJUK. fl. early 11th c.? Turkish chieftain. Cited in: Encyc. Brit., ...1. Seljuks.

...juks (Seljuk): History. See: Brewer.

...LLARDS, ANDREW WATSON. b. 1884. American physician. See: Amer. ...en Sci., 5th ed. Sellards' test.

...llards' test (Sellards, Andrew Watson): Medicine. See: Dorland; Stedman.

...llers hob (Sellers, William): Engineering and Industry. See: Webster's 3d.

...llers' injector (Sellers, William): Engineering and Industry. See: Auger.

...llers' screw thread (Sellers, William): Engineering and Industry. See: ...ger; Webster's 3d.

...LLERS, WILLIAM. 1824-1905. American engineer and inventor. See: Who ...as Who Amer., vol. 1. Sellers hob, Sellers' injector, Sellers' screw thread.

...llick's maneuver (Derivation undetermined): Medicine. See: Stedman.

...llinger's (Sellenger's) round (Sellynger, Sir Thomas or St. Leger, Sir Anthony): ...ance. See: Brewer; Webster's 3d.

...llmeier equation (or dispersion formula) (Sellmeier, W.): Physics. See: ...ewlis; Van Nostrand Chem. Dict.; Van Nostrand Sci. Encyc. Also known as: ...tteler-Helmholtz formula.

...LLMEIER, W. fl. 1871. German? physicist. (Biography source unavailable.) ...llmeier equation (or dispersion formula).

...LLYNGER, SIR THOMAS. d. ca. 1470. English gentleman. (Biography ...urce unavailable.) Sellinger's (Sellenger's) round?

...LMI, FRANCESCO. fl. 1841-1888. Italian chemist. Cited in: Royal Soc. ...t. Sci. Pap., 1800-1863; 1874-1883; 1884-1900. Selmi reaction for strych-...ne, Selmi reagents.

...lmi reaction for strychnine (Selmi, Francesco): Chemistry. See: Van ...ostrand Chem. Dict.

...lmi reagents (Selmi, Francesco): Chemistry. See: Van Nostrand Chem. ...ct.

...LTER, PAUL. b. 1866. German pediatrician. See: Biog. Lex. hervorr. ...erzte. Selter's disease.

...lter-Swift-Feer syndrome (Selter, Paul; Swift, H.; and Feer, Emil). See: ...er's disease.

...lter's disease (Selter, Paul). See: Feer's disease.

...lye and Schenker test (Selye, Hans and Schenker, Victor Joseph): Medicine. ...ee: Stedman.

...LYE, HANS. 1907- . Austrian-born Canadian endocrinologist. See: ...orld Who's Who Sci. Selye and Schenker test, Selye's syndrome.

...lye's syndrome (Selye, Hans): Medicine. See: Jablonski.

Sem. See: Shem.

Semayne's case (Derivation undetermined): Law. See: Black.

SEMELAIGNE, GEORGES. fl. 1934. French pediatrician. (Biography source unavailable.) Debre-Semelaigne syndrome.

SEMO. Roman deity. See: Jobes. Semolina.

Semolina (Semo): Food and Drink. See: Charnock.

SEMON, SIR FELIX. 1849-1921. English laryngologist. See: World Who's Who Sci. Gerhardt-Semon law, Semon's law, Semon's sign.

Semon-Hering theory (Semon, Richard Wolfgang and Hering, Ewald): Biology. See: Dorland; Stedman.

SEMON, RICHARD WOLFGANG. 1859-1908. German biologist. See: Biog. Lex. hervorr. Aerzte. Semon-Hering theory.

Semon's law (Semon, Sir Felix): Medicine. See: Dorland; Stedman.

Semon's sign (Semon, Sir Felix): Medicine. See: Dorland; Stedman.

SEMPER, KARL GOTTFRIED. 1832-1893. German zoologist and anatomist. See: Allg. Deut. Biog. Semper's cell, Semper's larva, Semper's rib, Semper's warbler.

Semper's cell (Semper, Karl Gottfried): Zoology. See: Gray.

Semper's larva (Semper, Karl Gottfried): Zoology. See: Gray.

Semper's rib (Semper, Karl Gottfried): Zoology. See: Gray.

Semper's warbler (Semper, Karl Gottfried): Zoology. See: Gray.

SEMPLE, SIR DAVID. 1856-1937. English bacteriologist. See: Dict. Nat. Biog. Semple type vaccine.

Semple type vaccine (Semple, Sir David): Medicine. See: Dorland; Stedman.

SEMSEY, ANDOR VON. 1833-1923. Hungarian nobleman and mineralogist. See: Jasznigi. Andorite, Semseyite.

Semseyite (Semsey, Andor von): Earth Sciences. See: Van Nostrand Sci. Encyc.; Webster's 3d.

SEN, PRAFULLA KUMAR. 1915- . Indian surgeon. See: World Who's Who Sci. Sen's syndrome.

SENA, JOACHIM DA COSTA. fl. 19th c. Brazilian mineralogist. Cited in: Hintze. Senaite.

Senaite (Sena, Joachim da Costa): Earth Sciences. See: Webster's 3d.

Senarmont, Henri Hureau de. See: De Senarmont, Henri Hureau.

Senarmontite (De Senarmont, Henri Hureau): Earth Sciences. See: Webster's 3d.

SENATOR, HERMANN. 1834-1911. German physician. See: Biog. Lex. hervorr. Aerzte. Senator's angina.

Senator's angina (Senator, Hermann): Medicine. See: Jablonski.

SENDERENS, JEAN-BAPTISTE. 1856-1939. French organic chemist. See: Pogg., vols. 4, 5, 6. Sabatier-Senderens reduction (or reaction), Sabatier-Senderens test.

Sendzimir mill (Sendzimir, Thaddeus K.): Engineering and Industry. See: Auger.

SENDZIMIR, THADDEUS K. fl. 1932. English engineer. Cited in: Chem. Abstr., Decenn. Index, 1927-1936. Sendzimir mill.

SENEAR, FRANCIS EUGENE. 1888-1958. American dermatologist. See: Who Was Who Amer. Senear-Usher disease (or syndrome).

Senear-Usher disease (or syndrome) (Senear, Francis Eugene and Usher, Barney, D.): Medicine. See: Dorland; Jablonski; Stedman.

SENEBIER, JEAN. 1742-1809. Swiss naturalist and historian. See: Pogg., vol. 2. Senebiera.

Senebiera (Senebier, Jean): Botany. See: Charnock.

SENECA (LUCIUS ANNAEUS SENECA). ca. 3 B.C.-65 A.D. Roman philosopher and playwright. See: Encyc. Brit., 1911. Senecan, Senecan sentence, Senecan tragedy.

Senecan (Seneca): Philosophy. See: Webster's 3d.

Senecan sentence (Seneca): Literature. See: Barnet.

Senecan tragedy (Seneca): Literature. See: Barnet; Barnhart (Eng. Lit.).

SENEFELDER, ALOIS. 1771-1834. Austrian-German engraver and inventor of lithography. See: Encyc. Brit., 1911. Senefelder's press, Senefelder's process.

Senefelder's press (Senefelder, Alois): Printing. See: Lockwood.

Senefelder's process (Senefelder, Alois): Printing. See: Focal Encyc. Photog.

SENFT, EMANUEL. 1870-1922. Czechoslovakian pharmacognosist. See: Pogg., vol. 6. Senft reaction for coumarin?, Senft reagent?

Senft reaction for coumarin (Senft, Emanuel?): Chemistry. See: Van Nostrand Chem. Dict.

Senft reagent (Senft, Emanuel?): Chemistry. See: Van Nostrand Chem. Dict.

SENGIER, EDGARD. fl. 1949. Belgian mine director. Cited in: Hintze. Sengierite.

Sengierite (Sengier, Edgard): Earth Sciences. See: Thrush; Webster's 3d.

Sengstaken-Blakemore tube (Sengstaken, Robert William and Blakemore, William Stephen): Medicine. See: Stedman.

SENGSTAKEN, ROBERT WILLIAM. 1923- . American surgeon. See: Direct. Med. Specialists, 1964-1965. Sengstaken-Blakemore tube.

SENGUPTA, SURESH C. fl. 1932. Indian chemist. Cited in: Chem. Abstr., vol. 27, pp. 84, 502. Bardhan-Sengupta synthesis.

SENN, NICHOLAS. 1844-1908. American surgeon. See: World Who's Who Sci. Kader-Senn operation, Senn's bone plates, Senn's test.

Senn's bone plates (Senn, Nicholas): Medicine. See: Dorland.

Senn's test (Senn, Nicholas): Medicine. See: Dorland.

Sen's syndrome (Sen, Prafulla Kumar): Medicine. See: Jablonski.

Senusi (or Senussi), al. See: Sanusi, Muhammad ibn Ali as-.

Senussi (Sanusi, Muhammad ibn Ali as-): See: Sanusi.

Sequoia (tree) (Sequoyah): Botany. See: Hendrickson; Mathews, M. M.; Partridge.

SEQUOYAH. ca. 1770-1843. American Indian chief. See: Dict. Amer. Biog. Sequoia (tree), Sequoyan (syllabary).

Sequoyan (syllabary) (Sequoyah): Linguistics. See: Mathews, M. M.

SERAND, J. M. fl. 20th c. West African mineral collector. Cited in: Hintze. Serandite.

Serandite (Serand, J. M.): Earth Sciences. See: Webster's 3d.

Serber potential (or force) (Serber, Robert): Physics. See: Ballentyne; Hughes.

SERBER, ROBERT. 1909- . American physicist. See: World Who's Who Sci. Serber potential (or force), Serber-Wilson method.

Serber-Wilson method (Serber, Robert and Wilson, Robert Rathbun?): Physics. See: Internat. Dict. Ap. Math.

Serenoa (Watson, Sereno): Botany. See: Taylor, N.

Sergeant Baker (fish) (Derivation undetermined): Zoology. See: Gray.

SERGENT, EMILE. 1867-1943. French physician. See: Biog. Lex. hervorr. Aerzte. Bernard-Sergent syndrome, Sergent's white line.

Sergent's white line (Sergent, Emile): Medicine. See: Dorland; Stedman.

SERGER, HERMANN. fl. 1911-1952. German chemist. Cited in: Chem. Abstr., Decenn. Indexes, 1907-16; 1947-56. Serger solution.

Serger solution (Serger, Hermann): Chemistry. See: Van Nostrand Chem. Dict.

SERINI, ARTHUR. fl. 1939. German? chemist. Cited in: Chem. Abstr., Decenn. Index, 1937-1946. Serini reaction.

Serini reaction (Serini, Arthur): Chemistry. See: Van Nostrand Chem. Dict.

Serjania (Serjeant, Philippe): Botany. See: Webster's 3d.

SERJEANT, PHILIPPE. fl. 17th c. French botanist. (Biography source unavailable.) Serjania.

SERKE, KURT. fl. 1929. German chemist. Cited in: Chem. Abstr., vol. 23, p. 5129. Serke test.

Serke test (Serke, Kurt): Chemistry. See: Van Nostrand Chem. Dict.

SERNANDER, JOHAN RUTGER. b. 1866. Swedish botanist. See: Krok. Blytt-Sernander system.

SERPIERI, J. B. fl. 19th c. Italian engineer. Cited in: Bailey. Serpierite.

Serpierite (Serpieri, J. B.): Earth Sciences. See: Thrush; Webster's 3d.

Serpollet boiler (Serpollet, Leon): Engineering and Industry. See: Auger.

SERPOLLET, LEON. 1859-1907. French engineer. Cited in: Singer. Gardner-Serpollet steam car, Serpollet boiler.

SERRATI, SERAFINO. fl. 18th c. Italian physicist. (Biography source unavailable.) Serratia.

Serratia (Serrati, Serafino): Zoology. See: Stedman.

SERRES, ANTOINE ETIENNE REYNAUD AUGUSTIN. 1786-1868. French physician. See: World Who's Who Sci. Serres' glands, Serres' metafacial angle.

Serres' glands (Serres, Antoine Etienne Reynaud Augustin): Anatomy. See: Stedman.

Serres' metafacial angle (Serres, Antoine Etienne Reynaud Augustin): Anatomy. See: Donath; Dorland; Stedman.

Serret-Frenet formulae (Serret, Joseph Alfred and Frenet, Jean-Frederic): Mathematics. See: Ballentyne; Internat. Dict. Ap. Math. Also known as: Frenet formulae, Frenet-Serret formulas.

SERRET, JOSEPH ALFRED. 1819-1885. French mathematician. See: World Who's Who Sci. Serret-Frenet formulae.

Sertoli-cell syndrome (Sertoli, Enrico). See: Del Castillo's syndrome.

Sertoli cell tumor (Sertoli, Enrico): Medicine. See: Stedman.

Sertoli(s) cells (Sertoli, Enrico): Anatomy. See: Donath; Dorland; Pennak.

SERTOLI, ENRICO. 1842-1910. Italian histologist. See: World Who's Who Sci. Sertoli-cell syndrome, Sertoli cell tumor, Sertoli(s) cells, Sertoli's columns.

Sertoli's columns (Sertoli, Enrico): Anatomy. See: Dorland; Stedman.

SERULLAS, GEORGES SIMON. 1774-1832. French chemist. See: Pogg., vol. 2; World Who's Who Sci. Serullas reagents for alkaloids and morphine, Serullas test for differentiating formic and acetic acids.

Serullas reagents for alkaloids and morphine (Serullas, Georges Simon): Chemistry. See: Van Nostrand Chem. Dict.

Serullas test for differentiating formic and acetic acids (Serullas, Georges Simon): Chemistry. See: Van Nostrand Chem. Dict.

Servants of Mary (Mary, Virgin-Mother): Religion. See: Attwater; Encyc. Brit., 1973.

Servetian (Servetus, Miguel): Religion. See: Webster's 3d.

Servetus' circulation (Servetus, Miguel): Medicine. See: Stedman.

SERVETUS, MIGUEL. ca. 1509-1553. Spanish theologian and physician. See: Encyc. Brit., 1911. Servetian, Servetus' circulation.

SESLER, LEONARD. No dates. Botanist. (Biography source unavailable.) Sesleria.

Sesleria (Sesler, Leonard): Botany. See: Charnock.

SETCHENOV, IVAN MICHAILOVICH. 1829-1905. Russian neurologist. See: World Who's Who Sci. Setschenow's center (or nucleus).

SETH. 3rd son of Adam in the Old Testament. See: Hastings (Dict. Bible). Sethite.

ethite (Seth): Religion. See: Webster's 3d.

etschenow, Ivan Michailovich. See: Setchenov, Ivan Michailovich.

etschenow's center (or nucleus) (Setchenov, Ivan Michailovich): Medicine. ee: Dorland.

EUTIN, LOUIS JOSEPH. 1793-1862. Belgian surgeon. See: Biog. Nat. e Belgique. Seutin's bandage.

eutin's bandage (Seutin, Louis Joseph): Medicine. See: Dorland.

EVAREID, ERIC (In full: ARNOLD ERIC). 1912- . American broadcaster nd author. See: Who's Who Amer., 1974-1975. Sevareid's law.

evareid's law (Sevareid, Eric): Sociology. See: Martin.

evensma prize (Sevensma, Tietse Pieter): Library Science. See: Harrod.

VENSMA, TIETSE PIETER. b. 1879. Dutch librarian. See: Wie Is Dat?, *31. Sevensma prize.

EVER, JAMES WARREN. b. 1878. American orthopedic surgeon. Cited in: elly. Sever's disease.

everian(s) (Severus): Religion. See: Canney; Latham; Webster's 3d.

everian (spirit) (Severus, Lucius Septimius): History. See: Stenhouse.

everinia (Severino, Marcus Aurelius): Botany. See: Taylor, N.

EVERINO, MARCUS AURELIUS. 1580-1656. Italian physician. See: Nouv. og. Univ. Severinia.

ever's disease (Sever, James Warren): Medicine. See: Dorland.

EVERUS. fl. 2d c. Gnostic from Antioch. See: Dict. Christian Biog., ol. 4, pp. 632-633. Severian(s).

EVERUS, LUCIUS SEPTIMIUS. 146-211. Roman emperor. See: Encyc. Brit., 911. Severian (spirit).

ewall Wright effect (or law) (Wright, Sewall): Genetics. See: Gray; ennak; Winick.

EWARD, WILLIAM HENRY. 1801-1872. American statesman. See: Dict. mer. Biog. Sewardism (or Sewardite), Seward's folly (or icebox).

ewardism (or Sewardite) (Seward, William Henry): Politics. See: athews, M. M.

eward's folly (or icebox) (Seward, William Henry): History. See: Hendrick-on; Mathews, M. M.

exton Blake (Blake, Sexton): Generic Word. See: Partridge.

EYBERT, HENRY. 1801-1883. American mineralogist and philanthropist. ee: Dict. Amer. Biog. Seybertite.

eybertite (Seybert, Henry): Earth Sciences. See: Thrush; Webster's 3d.

eyd (or Said). See: Zaid.

EYDA, ANTON. fl. 1883. German? chemist. Cited in: Royal Soc. Cat. ci. Pap. Seyda test?

eyda test (Seyda, Anton?): Chemistry. See: Van Nostrand Chem. Dict.

EYLER, CLARENCE A. fl. 1884-1928. American coal chemist. Cited in: hem. Abstr., Decenn. Indexes to 1936. Seyler's classification.

eyler's classification (Seyler, Clarence A.): Earth Sciences. See: Thrush.

EYMER. HENRY. fl. 19th c. English naturalist. (Biography source unavail-ble.) Seymeria.

eymeria (Seymer, Henry): Botany. See: Webster's 3d.

EYMOUR-CONWAY, FRANCIS, 1ST MARQUIS OF HERTFORD. 1719-1794. nglish art collector and statesman. See: Dict. Nat. Biog. Hertford ambu-ance, Hertford-Wallace collection.

eymourite (Derivation undetermined): Engineering and Industry. See: Thrush.

EZARY, ALBERT. 1880-1956. French physician. See: Biog. Lex. hervorr. erzte. Sezary cell, Sezary('s) syndrome (or reticulosis).

ezary-Baccaredda syndrome (Sezary, Albert and Baccaredda, Aldo). See: ezary('s) syndrome (or reticulosis).

Sezary-Bouvrain disease (Sezary, Albert and Bouvrain, Yves Robert). See: Sezary('s) syndrome (or reticulosis).

Sezary cell (Sezary, Albert): Medicine. See: Stedman.

Sezary('s) syndrome (or reticulosis) (Sezary, Albert): Medicine. See: Jab-lonski; Stedman. Also known as: Sezary-Baccaredda syndrome, Sezary-Bouvrain disease.

Sforza dynasty (Sforza, Francesco): History. See: Osborne.

SFORZA, FRANCESCO. 1409-1466. Duke of Milan. See: Encyc. Brit., 1911. Sforza dynasty.

SFORZINI, PAOLO. fl. 1948-1955. Italian physician. Cited in: Chem. Abstr., Decenn. Index, 1947-1956. Sforzini's syndrome.

Sforzini's syndrome (Sforzini, Paolo): Medicine. See: Jablonski.

SGAMBATI, O. fl. 20th c. Italian physician. (Biography source unavail-able.) Sgambati's test.

Sgambati's test (Sgambati, O): Medicine. See: Dorland; Stedman.

Shabbathians (Sabbatai-Zebi). See: Sabbatians.

Shaddock (Shaddock, Captain): Botany. See: Hendrickson; Partridge; Webster's 3d.

SHADDOCK, CAPTAIN. fl. 17th c. English ship commander. Cited in: New Encyc. Brit., 1974, Microp. Shaddock, Shaddock tree.

Shaddock tree (Shaddock, Captain): Botany. See: Webster's 3d.

SHADRACH. One of the three Hebrews unharmed by the fiery furnace. See: Hastings (Dict. Bible). Shadrach.

Shadrach (Shadrach, the Hebrew): Engineering and Industry. See: Charnock; Mathews, M. M.

Shaefer's syndrome (Schaefer, Erich). See: Schaefer's syndrome.

Shaffer-Hartman method (Shaffer, Philip Anderson and Hartman, Alexis Frank): Medicine. See: Stedman. Also known as: Somogyi-Shaffer-Hartman method (or test).

SHAFFER, PHILIP ANDERSON. 1881-1960. American biochemist. See: World Who's Who Sci. Coleman-Shaffer diet, Shaffer-Hartman method.

SHAF'I, ABU 'ABD ALLAH ASH-. 767-820. Muslim theologian and jurist. See: New Encyc. Brit., 1974, Microp. Shafiites.

Shafiites (Shaf'i, Abu 'Abd Allah ash-): Religion. See: Latham.

SHAIKH AHMAD AL-AHSA'I. d. 1826. Shi'ite religious teacher. Cited in: New Encyc. Brit., 1974, Microp. Shaikhi.

Shaikhi (Shaikh Ahmad al-Ahasa'i): Religion. See: Webster's 3d.

Shaivism (Siva, the god). See: Sivaism.

Shakespeare-Bacon controversy (Shakespeare, William and Bacon, Sir Francis): Literature. See: Phyfe.

Shakespeare collar (Shakespeare, William): Fashion. See: Picken.

SHAKESPEARE, WILLIAM. 1564-1616. English dramatist and poet. See: Dict. Nat. Biog. Shakespeare-Bacon controversy, Shakespeare collar, Shakespearean (Shakespearian), Shakespearean sonnet, Shakespeariana.

Shakespearean (Shakespearian) (Shakespeare, William): Literature. See: Hendrickson; Partridge; Webster's 3d.

Shakespearean sonnet (Shakespeare, William): Literature. See: Barnet; Scott; Webster's 3d.

Shakespeariana (Shakespeare, William): Literature. See: Webster's 3d.

SHAKHKELDIAN, A. B. fl. 1929. Russian chemist. Cited in: Chem. Abstr., vol. 24, p. 4236. Shakhkeldian test.

Shakhkeldian test (Shakhkeldian, A. B.): Chemistry. See: Van Nostrand Chem. Dict.

SHAMMAI. fl. 1st c. B. C. Jewish teacher. See: Jewish Encyc., 1925. Shammaite.

Shammaite (Shammai): Religion. See: Webster's 3d.

SHAND, SAMUEL JAMES. 1882-1957. English geologist. See: Who Was Who. Shandite, Shand's classification.

Shandean (Shandy, Tristram): Literature. See: Brewer; Harvey; Webster's 3d.

Shandite (Shand, Samuel James): Earth Sciences. See: Webster's 3d.

Shand's classification (Shand, Samuel James): Earth Sciences. See: Thrush.

SHANDY, TRISTRAM. Character in the novel of the same name, (1760-67) by Laurence Sterne. See: Magill. Shandean.

SHANER, RALPH FAUST. 1893- . American embryologist. See: World Who's Who Sci. Shaner-Willard reactions.

Shaner-Willard reactions (Shaner, Ralph Faust and Willard, Hobart Hurd): Chemistry. See: Van Nostrand Chem. Dict.

Shank system (Derivation undetermined): Engineering and Industry. See: Van Nostrand Chem. Dict.

SHANNON, CLAUDE ELWOOD. 1916- . American applied mathematician. See: World Who's Who Sci. Nyquist-Shannon theorem, Shannon formula (or equation), Shannon's sampling theorem.

Shannon formula (or equation) (Shannon, Claude Elwood): Mathematics. See: Hughes; Van Nostrand Sci. Encyc.

SHANNON, WILLIAM VINCENT. 1927- . American journalist. See: Who's Who Amer., 1974-1975. Shannon's law of administration.

Shannon's law of administration (Shannon, William Vincent): Sociology. See: Martin.

Shannon's sampling theorem (Shannon, Claude Elwood): Mathematics. See: Ballentyne.

SHAPIRO, JESSE MARSHALL. 1929- . American statistician. See: Amer. Men Sci., 10th ed. Shapiro-Wilk test.

SHAPIRO, M. YA. fl. 1938. Russian chemist. Cited in: Chem. Abstr., vol. 32, pp. 4459, 5329, 5722. Komarovskii-Shapiro reagent for niobium and tantalum, Shapiro-Rud test, Shapiro test.

Shapiro-Rud test (Shapiro, M. Ya and Rud, M. I.): Chemistry. See: Van Nostrand Chem. Dict.

Shapiro test (Shapiro, M. Ya): Chemistry. See: Van Nostrand Chem. Dict.

Shapiro-Wilk test (Shapiro, Jesse Marshall and Wilk, Martin Bradbury): Statistics. See: Kendall.

SHAPLEY, LLOYD STOWELL. 1923- . American mathematician and economist. See: Amer. Men and Woman Sci., 12th ed. Shapley value.

Shapley value (Shapley, Lloyd Stowell): Mathematics. See: Van Nostrand Sci. Encyc.

SHARP, BECKY. Principal character in Thackeray's "Vanity Fair," (1848). See: Benet; Magill. Becky Sharp.

SHARP, R. R. fl. 1915. English army officer. Cited in: Hintze. Sharpite.

SHARPE, JACK. fl. 1952-1960. English physicist. Cited in: Chem. Abstr., Decenn. Indexes, 1947-1956; 1957-1961. Chambers-Imrie-Sharpe curve?

SHARPE, MONTROYD. fl. 20th c. American mine owner. Cited in: Hintze. Montroydite.

SHARPE, RICHARD BOWDLER. 1847-1909. English ornithologist. See: World Who's Who Sci. Sharpe's starling.

Sharpe's starling (Sharpe, Richard Bowdler): Zoology. See: Gray .

SHARPEY-SCHAFER, SIR EDWARD ALBERT. 1850-1935. English physiologist. See: World Who's Who Sci. Schafer (Schaefer's) method, Schafer (Schaefer)-Nielsen-Drinker method.

SHARPEY, WILLIAM. 1802-1880. Scottish anatomist. See: World Who's Who Sci. Sharpey's fibers.

Sharpey's fibers (Sharpey, William): Anatomy. See: Dorland; Gray; Stedman.

Sharpite (Sharp, R. R.): Earth Sciences. See: Webster's 3d.

SHARPS, CHRISTIAN. 1811-1874. American inventor. See: Nat. Cycl. Amer. Biog. Sharps rifle.

Sharps rifle (Sharps, Christian): Weapons. See: Mathews, M. M.; Quick.

SHATTOCK, SAMUEL GEORGE. 1852-1924. English pathologist. See: World Who's Who Sci. Shattock's disease.

Shattock's disease (Shattock, Samuel George): Medicine. See: Jablonski.

SHAUGHNESSY, FRANK J. "SHAG." fl. 20th c. Canadian baseball official. Cited in: Menke, p. 440. Shaughnessy playoff.

Shaughnessy playoff (Shaughnessy, Frank J.): Recreation and Sports. See: Webster's 3d.

SHAVER, CECIL GORDON. fl. 1947-1968. Canadian physician. See: Canadian Med. Direct., 1968. Shaver's syndrome.

Shaver's syndrome (Shaver, Cecil Gordon): Medicine. See: Jablonski. Also known as: Shaver-Ridell syndrome.

Shavian (wit) (Shaw, George Bernard): Literature. See: Barnhart (Eng. Lit.); Hendrickson; Partridge.

Shaviana (Shaw, George Bernard): Literature. See: Webster's 3d.

Shaw contorograph (Shaw, H.): Engineering and Industry. See: Auger.

SHAW, GEORGE BERNARD. 1856-1950. English dramatist, critic and novelist. See: New Encyc. Brit., 1974, Microp. Shavian (wit), Shaviana.

SHAW, H. fl. 20th c. English engineer. (Biography source unavailable.) Shaw contorograph.

SHAW, HENRY WHEELER (Pseud.: JOSH BILLINGS). 1818-1885. American humorist. See: Dict. Amer. Biog. Josh.

SHAW, J. J. fl. 1915. English seismologist. Cited in: Richter. Milne-Shaw seismograph.

Shaw kiln (Derivation undetermined): Engineering and Industry. See: Thrush.

Shaw process (Derivation undetermined): Engineering and Industry. See: Thrush. Also known as: Osborn-Shaw process.

Shaw test (Derivation undetermined): Chemistry. See: Van Nostrand Chem. Dict.

SHAY, HARRY. 1898- . American physician. See: Direct. Med. Specialists, 1964-1965. Shay's leukemia, Shay's ulcer.

Shaykhi (Shaikh Ahmad al-Ahsa'i). See: Shaikhi.

SHAYS, DANIEL. 1747-1825. American insurgent. See: Dict. Amer. Biog. Shays'(s) Rebellion, Shaysite.

Shay's leukemia (Shay, Harry): Medicine. See: Jablonski.

Shays'(s) Rebellion (Shays, Daniel): History. See: Jameson; Morris; Phyfe.

Shay's ulcer (Shay, Harry): Medicine. See: Jablonski.

Shaysite (Shays, Daniel): History. See: Mathews, M. M.; Webster's 3d.

SHCHIGOL, M. fl. 1934. Russian chemist. Cited in: Chem. Abstr., vol. 28, p. 3688. Shchigol test.

Shchigol test (Shchigol, M.): Chemistry. See: Van Nostrand Chem. Dict.

Shea-Anthony antral baloon (Derivation undetermined): Medicine. See: Stedman.

SHEAR, MURRAY JACOB. 1899- . American biological chemist. See: Amer. Men Sci., 4th ed. Shear reagent.

Shear reagent (Shear, Murray Jacob): Chemistry. See: Van Nostrand Chem. Dict.

Shearer plastometer (Shearer, W. L.?): See: Rouse and Shearer plastometer.

SHEARER, W. L. fl. 1924. American ceramics chemist. Cited in: Chem. Abstr., Decenn. Index, 1917-1926. Rouse-Shearer plastometer?

sheath of Henle (Henle, Friedrich Gustav Jacob). See: Henle's sheath.

sheath of Key and Retzius (Key, Ernst Axel Henrik and Retzius Magnus G.): Anatomy. See: Stedman. Also known as: Henle's sheath.

sheath of Schwann (Schwann, Theodor). See: Schwann('s) sheath (or tube).

sheath of Schweigger-Seidel (Schweigger-Seidel, Franz): Medicine. See: Dorland; Gray; Stedman.

heba (Sheba, Queen of): Generic Word (attractive woman). See: Partridge.

HEBA, QUEEN OF. fl. 10th c. B.C. Ruler of Arabian Kingdom. See: New Encyc. Brit., 1974, Microp. Sheba.

HEDD, OLIVER MARCH. b. 1880. American chemist. See: Amer. Men ci., 9th ed. Kastle-Shedd reagent.

HEEHAN, HAROLD LEEMING. fl. 1937-1964. English pathologist. See: Med. Direct., 1964. Sheehan's syndrome.

heehan's syndrome (Sheehan, Harold Leeming). See: Simmonds' syndrome.

HEEHY, WILLIAM ROBERT. 1919- . American child psychiatrist. See: mer. Men and Women Sci., 12th ed. Sheehy's syndrome?

heehy's syndrome (Sheehy, William Robert?): Medicine. See: Jablonski.

HEFFER, HENRY MAURICE. 1883-1964. American philosopher. See: Who Vas Who Amer., vol. 4. Sheffer's stroke.

heffer's stroke (Sheffer, Henry Maurice): Philosophy. See: Webster's 3d.

HEINKMAN, A. I. fl. 1932. Russian chemist. Cited in: Chem. Abstr., ol. 27, p. 244. Sheinkman test.

heinkman test (Sheinkman, A. I.): Chemistry. See: Van Nostrand Chem. ict.

HEINTZIS, O. G. fl. 1935. Russian chemist. Cited in: Chem. Abstr., ol. 30, p. 984. Gapchenko-Sheintzis micro-test for bismuth, Gapchenko-heintzis micro-test for magnesium, Gapchenko-Sheintzis test for bismuth, Gapchenko-Sheintzis test for titanium.

helby tube (or Shelby-tube sampler) (Derivation undetermined): Earth Sciences. ee: Thrush.

heldon-Ellis syndrome (Sheldon, Joseph Harold and Ellis, Richard White ernard). See: Hurler's syndrome.

HELDON, JOSEPH HAROLD. fl. 1920-1964. English pediatrician. See: Med. Direct., 1964. Freeman-Sheldon syndrome, Sheldon-Ellis syndrome, heldon's necrotic purpura.

heldon('s) type (or constitutional theory of personality) (Sheldon, William H.): sychology. See: Chaplin; English.

HELDON, W. T. fl. 1932. English physician. (Biography source unavailble.) Rocher-Sheldon syndrome.

HELDON, SIR WILFRID S. 1901- . English pediatrician. See: Who's Vho Sci. Europe, 1972. Luder-Sheldon syndrome.

HELDON, WILLIAM H. 1899- . American psychologist. See: Wolman. heldon('s) type (or constitutional theory of personality).

heldon's necrotic purpura (Sheldon, Joseph Harold). See: De Gimard's yndrome.

HELLEY, PERCY BYSSHE. 1792-1822. English poet. See: Dict. Nat. Biog. helleyan (or Shelleyesque).

helleyan (or Shelleyesque) (Shelley, Percy Bysshe): Literature. See: Vebster's 3d.

HELTON, CARL, JR. 1925- . American mining engineer. See: Amer. Aen and Women Sci., 12th ed. Shelton loader?

helton loader (Shelton, Carl, Jr.?): Engineering and Industry. See: Thrush.

HELUMIEL OR SALAMIEL. Leader of tribe of Simeon in the Old Testament. ee: Buttrick. Schlemiehl.

helumiel (foolish bargainer). See: Schlemiehl.

HEM. Son of Noah in the Old Testament. See: Hastings (Dict. Bible). hemitic (Semitic or Semite).

hemitic (Semitic or Semite) (Shem): Generic Word. See: Charnock; Vebster's 3d.

hemyakin-Belokon micro-reactions (Shemyakin, F. M. and Belokon, A. N.): Chemistry. See: Van Nostrand Chem. Dict.

HEMYAKIN, F. M. fl. 1938. Russian chemist. Cited in: Chem. Abstr., Decenn. Index, 1937-1946. Shemyakin-Belokon micro-reactions, Shemyakin eactions, Shemyakin test reactions.

hemyakin reactions (Shemyakin, F. M.): Chemistry. See: Van Nostrand Chem. Dict.

Shemyakin test reactions (Shemyakin, F. M.): Chemistry. See: Van Nostrand Chem. Dict.

SHENTON, EDWARD WARREN HINE. 1872-1955. English radiologist. See: Who Was Who. Shenton's line (or arch).

Shenton's line (or arch) (Shenton, Edward Warren Hine): Medicine. See: Donath; Dorland; Stedman.

Shepardite (Shephard, Charles Upham): Earth Sciences. See: Charnock.

SHEPHARD, CHARLES UPHAM. 1804-1886. American mineralogist. See: Dict. Amer. Biog. Shepardite.

SHEPHERD, FRANCIS JOHN. 1851-1929. Canadian surgeon. See: Who Was Who, 1929-1940. Shepherd's fracture.

SHEPHERD, JOHN. d. 1836. English botanist. (Biography source unavailable.) Shepherdia.

Shepherd tube (Shepherd, William Gerald?): Electronics. See: Hughes.

SHEPHERD, WILLIAM GERALD. 1911- . American electronics engineer. See: Amer. Men and Women Sci., 12th ed. Shepherd tube?

Shepherdia (Shepherd, John): Botany. See: Taylor, N.; Webster's 3d.

Shepherd's fracture (Shepherd, Francis John): Medicine. See: Dorland; Jablonski; Stedman.

SHEPPARD, MORRIS. 1875-1941. American legislator. See: Biog. Direct. Amer. Congress. Sheppard-Towner Act.

SHEPPARD, MAJOR R. V. fl. 1941. English army officer. (Biography source unavailable.) Sten gun.

Sheppard-Towner Act (Sheppard, Morris and Towner, Horace Mann): Politics. See: Morris; Smith.

SHEPPARD, WILLIAM FLEETWOOD. 1863-1936. Australian mathematician. See: Pogg., vols, 4 to 6. Sheppard's correction.

Sheppard's correction (Sheppard, William Fleetwood): Statistics. See: Ballentyne; James; Kendall.

SHERARD, WILLIAM. 1659-1728. English botanist. See: Dict. Nat. Biog. Sherardia, Sherardian Professor.

Sherardia (Sherard, William): Botany. See: Charnock.

Sherardian Professor (Sherard, William): Botany. See: Wagner (More Names).

Sherardizing (or Sherardize) (Cowper-Coles, Sherard Osborn): Chemistry. See: Thewlis; Thrush; Van Nostrand Chem. Dict.

Sheraton (style) (Sheraton, Thomas): Applied Arts. See: Hendrickson; Partridge; Webster's 3d.

SHERATON, THOMAS. 1751-1806. English furniture maker and designer. See: Dict. Nat. Biog. Sheraton (style).

SHERBATSCHEV, D. fl. 1910. Russian chemist. Cited in: Chem. Abstr., Decenn. Index, 1907-1916. Sherbatschew test.

Sherbatschew test (Sherbatschev, D.): Chemistry. See: Van Nostrand Chem. Dict.

SHERESHEVSKII, NIKOLAY ADOL'FOVICH. 1885-1961. Russian physician. See: Who Was Who USSR. Shereshevskii-Turner syndrome.

Shereshevskii-Turner syndrome (Shereshevskii, Nikolay Adol'fovich and Turner, Henry Herbert). See: Turner's syndrome.

SHERIDAN, PHILIP HENRY. 1831-1888. Irish-born American general. See: Dict. Amer. Biog. General Sheridan (airborne assault vehicle)?, Sheridan's raids in Virginia.

Sheridan's raids in Virginia (Sheridan, Philip Henry): History. See: Jameson.

Sherlock (Holmes, Sherlock): Generic Word (act as a detective). See: Webster's 3d.

Sherlock Holmes (Holmes, Sherlock, the detective): Generic Word. See: Partridge; Webster's 3d.

Sherlockian (Holmes, Sherlock): Generic Word. See: Webster's 3d.

SHERMAN. fl. 1800-1836. American printer. Cited in: Dict. Cat. Hist. Print. Sherman case?

Sherman Antitrust Act (Sherman, John): Politics. See: Greenwald; Morris; Smith.

SHERMAN, BERNARD. 1919- . American statistician. See: Amer. Men Sci., 10th ed. Sherman's test statistic?

Sherman-Bourquin unit (Sherman, Henry Clapp and Bourquin, Ann): Medicine. See: Dorland; Stedman.

Sherman case (Sherman): Printing. See: Lockwood, p. 330.

SHERMAN, HARRY MITCHELL. 1854-1921. American orthopedic surgeon. See: J. A. M. A., vol. 76 (1921), p. 1591. Sherman plate.

SHERMAN, HENRY CLAPP. 1875-1955. American biochemist. See: World Who's Who Sci. Kendall-Sherman test, Sherman-Bourquin unit, Sherman-Munsell unit, Sherman unit.

SHERMAN, JOHN. 1823-1900. American legislator. See: Dict. Amer. Biog. Sherman Antitrust Act, Sherman note, Sherman Silver Purchase Act.

Sherman-Munsell unit (Sherman, Henry Clapp and Munsell, Hazel Edith): Medicine. See: Dorland; Stedman.

Sherman note (Sherman, John): Politics. See: Mathews, M. M.

Sherman plate (Sherman, Harry Mitchell): Medicine. See: Stedman.

Sherman settler (Derivation undetermined): Engineering and Industry. See: Thrush.

Sherman Silver Purchase Act (Sherman, John): Politics. See: Jameson; Morris.

Sherman unit (Sherman, Henry Clapp): Medicine. See: Dorland; Stedman.

SHERMAN, WILLIAM TECUMSEH. 1820-1891. American general. See: Dict. Amer. Biog. General Sherman sequoia, General Sherman (tank), Sherman's bummers, Sherman's hairpin, Sherman's March, Sherman's monuments.

Sherman's bummers (Sherman, William Tecumseh): History. See: Mathews, M. M.

Sherman's hairpin (Sherman, William Tecumseh): History. See: Mathews, M. M.

Sherman's March (Sherman, William Tecumseh): History. See: Harbottle; Phyfe.

Sherman's monuments (Sherman, William Tecumseh): History. See: Mathews, M. M.

Sherman's test statistic (Sherman, Bernard?): Statistics. See: Kendall.

SHERRINGTON, CHARLES SCOTT. 1856-1952. English physiologist. See: Internat. Encyc. Soc. Sci. Liddell-Sherrington reflex, Schiff-Sherrington phenomenon, Sherrington phenomenon, Sherrington's law.

Sherrington phenomenon (Sherrington, Charles Scott): Physiology. See: Stedman.

Sherrington's law (Sherrington, Charles Scott): Physiology. See: Dorland; Stedman.

Sherwen shaker (Derivation undetermined): Engineering and Industry. See: Thrush.

Sherwin and Cope's press (Sherwin and Cope, Richard Whittaker): Printing. See: Lockwood.

SHERWOOD, ALEXANDER M. fl. 1958? American scientist. Cited in: Min. Mag., vol. 32 (1959-1961, pt. 2), p. 980. Sherwoodite.

Sherwoodite (Sherwood, Alexander M.): Earth Sciences. See: Thrush.

Shewhart control chart (Shewhart, Walter Andrew): Statistics. See: Kendall.

SHEWHART, WALTER ANDREW. 1891- . American physicist. See: Pogg., vol. 6. Shewhart control chart.

shield of David (David, the king). See: magen (or mogen) David.

SHIELDS, JOHN. fl. 1893. English chemist. Cited in: Royal Soc. Cat. Sci. Pap., 1884-1900. Eotvos-Ramsay-Shields law.

Shield's method (Derivation undetermined): Education. See: Good.

SHIGA, KIYOSHI. 1870-1957. Japanese bacteriologist. See: New Encyc. Brit., 1974, Microp. Shiga-Kruse bacillus, Shiga-Kruse disease, Shigella.

Shiga-Kruse bacillus (Shiga, Kiyoshi and Kruse, Walter): Medicine. See: Stedman.

Shiga-Kruse disease (Shiga, Kiyoshi and Kruse, Walter): Medicine. See: Jablonski; Stedman. Also known as: Shigellosis.

Shigella (Shiga, Kiyoshi): Zoology. See: Pennak; Stedman; Webster's 3d.

Shigella flexneri (Shiga, Kiyoshi and Flexner, Simon). See: Flexner's bacillus.

Shigellosis (Shiga, Kiyoshi). See: Shiga-Kruse disease.

SHIH, CHIA-CHUNG. fl. 1932. Chinese chemist. Cited in: Chem. Abstr., vol. 26, p. 49. Chen-Shik reagent.

SHIH, TSAI-MIN. fl. 1937. Chinese chemist. Cited in: Chem. Abstr., vol. 31, p. 6130. Chien-Shih solution.

Shillaber (Shillaber, Benjamin Penhallow?): Generic Word (circus employee). See: Partridge.

SHILLABER, BENJAMIN PENHALLOW. 1814-1890. American humorist. See: Dict. Amer. Biog. Shillaber?

Shillibeer (Shillibeer, George): Generic Word (hearse). See: Hendrickson; Partridge; Webster's 3d.

SHILLIBEER, GEORGE. 1797-1866. English coach proprietor. See: Dict. Nat. Biog. Shillibeer.

SHILLING, VICTOR THEODORE ADOLF GEORG. 1883-1960. German hematologist. See: World Who's Who Sco. Schilling('s) leukemia (or type of monocytic leukemia), Schilling test, Schilling's band cell, Schilling's blood count (or index).

SHIMKIN, MICHAEL BORIS. 1912- . Russian-born American cancer researcher. See: Amer. Men and Women Sci., 12th ed. Shimkin's principles of administration, Shimkin's rule.

Shimkin's principles of administration (Shimkin, Michael Boris): Sociology. See: Martin.

Shimkin's rule (Shimkin, Michael Boris): Sociology. See: Martin.

Shimose (or Shimose powder) (Kogakubachi, Masashika Shimonose): Chemistry. See: Hendrickson; Partridge; Webster's 3d.

Shimose, Masashika. See: Kogakubachi, Masashika Shimonose.

Shin sect (Shinran Shonin): Religion. See: Canney.

SHINRAN SHONIN. 1173-1262. Japanese Buddhist theologian. See: New Encyc. Brit., 1974. Shin sect.

Shipley-Hartford scale (Shipley, Walter C. and Hartford, Conn.?): Psychology. See: Stedman.

Shipley polariscope (Shipley, Robert Morrill): Engineering and Industry. See: Thrush.

SHIPLEY, ROBERT MORRILL. fl. 1945. American gemmologist. Cited in: Thrush. Shipley polariscope.

SHIPLEY, WALTER C. 1903- . American psychiatrist. Cited in: Kelly. Shipley-Hartford scale.

SHIPTON, URSULA "MOTHER." fl. 1525. English reputed prophet. See: Dict. Nat. Biog. Mother Shipton (1), Mother Shipton (2).

Shirodkar operation (Derivation undetermined): Medicine. See: Stedman.

Shivaism (Shiva, the god). See: Sivaism.

Shlikh method (Derivation undetermined): Earth Sciences. See: Thrush.

Shockley diode (Shockley, William Bradford): Electronics. See: Internat. Dict. Phys. Elec.; Markus.

Shockley partial dislocation (Shockley, William Bradford?): Physics. See: Ballentyne.

SHOCKLEY, WILLIAM BRADFORD. 1910- . English-born American physicist. See: World Who's Who Sci. Haynes-Shockley experiment, Shockley diode, Shockley partial dislocation?

SHOHL, ALFRED THEODORE. b. 1889. American pediatrician. Cited in: Kelly. Shohl's solution.

hohl's solution (Shohl, Alfred Theodore): Medicine. See: Stedman.

holem Aleichem, pseud. See: Rabinowitz, Solomon.

holem Aleichem school (Rabinowitz, Solomon): Education. See: Good.

HONE, I. fl. 1877. English engineer. (Biography source unavailable.) hone sewage ejector.

HONE, JOHN DESMOND. fl. 1953-1964. English cardiologist. See: Med. Direct., 1964. Shone's syndrome (or anomaly).

hone sewage ejector (Shone, I.): Engineering and Industry. See: Auger.

hone's syndrome (or anomaly) (Shone, John Desmond): Medicine. See: ablonski; Stedman.

hope fibroma virus (Shope, Richard Edwin): Medicine. See: Stedman.

hope papilloma (Shope, Richard Edwin): Medicine. See: Dorland; ablonski; Stedman.

HOPE, RICHARD EDWIN. 1902-1966. American physician. See: Who Vas Who Amer. Shope fibroma virus, Shope papilloma.

HORE, ALBERT F. fl. 1906-1918. American manufacturer. Cited in: Chem. Abstr., Decenn. Index, 1907-1916. Shore hardness (test or scale), Shore cleroscope (or hardness tester).

hore hardness (test or scale) (Shore, Albert F.): Engineering and Industry. See: Auger; Hackh; Internat. Dict. Phys. Elec.

HORE, JOHN (LORD TEIGNMOUTH). 1751-1834. Governor-general of India. See: Dict. Nat. Biog. Shorea.

hore scleroscope (or hardness tester) (Shore, Albert F.): Engineering and ndustry. See: Thrush; Webster's 3d.

horea (Shore, John): Botany. See: Webster's 3d.

SHORT, CHARLES WILKINS. 1794-1863. American physician and botanist. See: Dict. Amer. Biog. Shortia.

SHORT, MAXWELL NAYLOR. 1889-1952. American mineralogist. See: Amer. Min., vol. 38 (1953), pp. 309-312. Shortite.

hortia (Short, Charles Wilkins): Botany. See: Hendrickson; Mathews, M. M.; Taylor, N.

hortite (Short, Maxwell Naylor): Earth Sciences. See: Webster's 3d.

hortt clock (Shortt, William H.): Horology. See: Webster's 3d.

SHORTT, WILLIAM H. fl. 20th c. English inventor. (Biography source unavailable.) Shortt clock.

SHOWALTER, ALBERT KENNETH. 1908- . American meteorologist. See: Amer. Men and Women Sci., 12th ed. Showalter stability index.

Showalter stability index (Showalter, Albert Kenneth): Earth Sciences. See: Huschke.

SHRADY, GEORGE FREDERICK. 1837-1907. American surgeon. See: Dict. Amer. Biog. Shrady's subcutaneous saw.

Shrady's subcutaneous saw (Shrady, George Frederick): Medicine. See: Dorland; Stedman.

SHRAPNEL, HENRY. 1761-1842. English artillery officer. See: World Who's Who Sci. Shrapnel (shell).

Shrapnel (shell) (Shrapnel, Henry): Weapons. See: Charnock; Hendrickson; Webster's 3d.

SHRAPNELL, HENRY JONES. 1761-1841. English anatomist. Cited in: Royal Soc. Cat. Sci. Pap., 1800-1863. Shrapnell's membrane.

Shrapnell's membrane (Shrapnell, Henry Jones): Anatomy. See: Donath; Dorland; Stedman. Also known as: Rivinus' membrane.

SHUBNIKOV, ALEKSEI VASILEVICH. 1887- . Russian crystallographer. See: World Who's Who Sci. Shubnikov-de Haas effect, Shubnikov groups.

Shubnikov-de Haas effect (Shubnikov, Aleksei Vasilevich and Haas, Wander Johannes de): Physics. See: Ballentyne.

Shubnikov groups (Shubnikov, Aleksei Vasilevich): Physics. See: Ballentyne; Van Nostrand Sci. Encyc. under "Symmetry Classes."

Shuckers typesetting machine (Derivation undetermined): Printing. See: Lockwood, p. 563.

SHUMARD, BENJAMIN FRANKLIN. d. 1869. American geologist. See: Bull. U.S. Geol. Survey, no. 746 (1923), p. 946f. Shumard oak.

Shumard oak (Shumard, Benjamin Franklin): Botany. See: Webster's 3d.

Shuster mission (Shuster, William Morgan): Politics. See: Morris and Irwin.

SHUSTER, WILLIAM MORGAN. 1877-1960. American lawyer, diplomat, financial expert and publisher. See: New Encyc. Brit., 1974, Microp. Shuster mission.

SHUTTLEWORTH, ROY. fl. 1948-1967. English metallurgical chemist. See: Direct. Brit. Sci., 1966-1967. Mackenzie-Shuttleworth equation.

SHUVALOV, COUNT PETR ANDREIVICH. 1827-1889. Russian diplomat. See: Encyc. Brit., 1911. Schouvaloff Treaty.

SHWACHMAN, HARRY. 1910- . American pediatrician. See: Amer. Men and Women Sci., 12th ed. Riley-Shwachman syndrome.

SHWARTZMAN, GREGORY. 1896-1965. American physician. See: New York Times, July 24, 1965, p. 21, col. 4. Sanarelli-Schwartzman phenomenon (or reaction).

Shwartzman phenomenon (Shwartzman, Gregory). See: Sanarelli-Shwartzman phenomenon.

Shy-Drager syndrome (Shy, George Milton and Drager, Glenn A.): Medicine. See: Jablonski; Stedman.

SHY, GEORGE MILTON. 1919-1967. American physician. See: World Who's Who Sci. Shy-Drager syndrome, Shy-Magee disease.

Shy-Magee disease (Shy, George Milton and Magee, Kenneth Raymond): Medicine. See: Jablonski.

Shylock (Shylock, the usurer): Generic Word (moneylender). See: Brewer; Partridge; Webster's 3d.

SHYLOCK, THE USURER. Character in William Shakespeare's play "The Merchant of Venice", (1596). See: Magill. Shylock.

Shyster (Scheuster): Generic Word (disreputable lawyer). See: Hendrickson.

SIBBALD, SIR ROBERT. 1641-1722. Scottish physician, antiquarian and geographer. See: Dict. Nat. Biog. Sibbaldia, Sibbald's rorqual, Sibbaldus.

Sibbaldia (Sibbald, Sir Robert): Botany. See: Charnock.

Sibbald's rorqual (Sibbald, Sir Robert): Zoology. See: Webster's 3d.

Sibbaldus (Sibbald, Sir Robert): Zoology. See: Webster's 3d.

SIBLEY, HENRY HASINGS. 1811-1891. American army officer. See: Dict. Amer. Biog. Sibley stove, Sibley tent.

Sibley stove (Sibley, Henry Hastings): Engineering and Industry. See: Mathews, M. M.; Partridge; Webster's 3d.

Sibley tent (Sibley, Henry Hastings): Generic Word. See: Mathews, M. M.; Partridge; Webster's 3d.

SIBSON, FRANCIS. 1814-1876. English anatomist. See: World Who's Who Sci. Sibson's aortic vestibule, Sibson's aponeurosis, Sibson's fascia, Sibson's groove, Sibson's muscle.

Sibson's aortic vestibule (Sibson, Francis): Anatomy. See: Dorland; Stedman.

Sibson's aponeurosis (Sibson, Francis): Anatomy. See: Dorland; Stedman.

Sibson's fascia (Sibson, Francis): Anatomy. See: Donath; Stedman.

Sibson's groove (Sibson, Francis): Anatomy. See: Donath; Dorland; Stedman.

Sibson's muscle (Sibson, Francis): Anatomy. See: Stedman.

SICARD, JEAN ATHANASE. 1872-1929. French physician. See: World Who's Who Sci. Brissaud-Sicard syndrome, Collet-Sicard syndrome.

Sicard's syndrome (Sicard, Jean Athanase). See: Collet-Sicard syndrome.

SICCARDI, GIUSEPPE. 1802-1857. Italian statesman. See: Encic. Ital. Siccardi laws.

Siccardi laws (Siccardi, Giuseppe): History. See: Morris and Irwin.

SICHEL, JULES. 1802-1868. French ophthalmologist. Cited in: Garrison and Morton. Sichel's disease (or ptosis).

Sichel's disease (or ptosis) (Sichel, Jules): Medicine. See: Jablonski.

SICKELS, FRED ELLSWORTH. 1819-1895. American inventor. See: Dict. Amer. Biog. Sickels' steering gear.

Sickels' steering gear (Sickels, Fred Ellsworth): Engineering and Industry. See: Auger.

SICKINGEN, FRANZ VON. 1481-1523. German knight. See: Encyc. Brit., 1911. Sickingia.

Sickingia (Sickingen, Franz von): Botany. See: Webster's 3d.

SICKLER FAMILY. fl. ca. 1920. American mine owners? Cited in: Bailey. Sicklerite.

Sicklerite (Sickler family): Earth Sciences. See: Thrush; Webster's 3d.

Sidcott suit (Cotton, Sidney): Fashion. See: Partridge.

Sideburns (or Burnsides) (Burnside, Ambrose Everett): Fashion. See: Brewer; Hendrickson; Picken.

SIDLER-HUGUENIN, ERNST. 1869-1922. German ophthalmologist. See: Biog. Lex. hervorr. Aerzte. Sidler-Huguenin's endothelioma.

Sidler-Huguenin's endothelioma (Sidler-Huguenin, Ernst): Medicine. See: Jablonski.

SIDNEY, EDWIN. d. ca. 1872. English naturalist. Cited in: Royal Soc. Cat. Sci. Pap., 1800-1863. Sidneyia?

SIDNEY, SIR PHILIP. 1554-1586. English statesman, poet and soldier. See: Dict. Nat. Biog. Sir Philip Sidney's oak.

Sidneyia (Sidney, Edwin?): Zoology. See: Pennak.

SIDOT, TH. fl. 1875. French chemist. Cited in: Royal Soc. Cat. Sci. Pap., 1874-1883. Sidot's blende.

Sidot's blende (Sidot, Th.): Chemistry. See: Hackh.

SIDRANSKY, HERSCHEL. 1925- . American pathologist. See: Amer. Men and Women Sci., 12th ed. Rechcigl-Sidransky hepatoma.

Siebe-Gorman self-rescuer (Siebe, Paul? and Gorman): Engineering and Industry. See: Thrush.

SIEBE, PAUL. 1892-1933. German metallurgist. See: Pogg., vols. 6, 7a. Siebe-Gorman self-rescuer?

SIEBER, HENRY. No dates. Botanical collector. (Biography source unavailable.) Siebera.

Siebera (Sieber, Henry): Botany. See: Charnock.

SIEBOLD, CARL CASPAR VON. 1736-1807. German surgeon. See: Biog. Lex. hervorr. Aerzte. Siebold's operation, Siebold's organ.

Siebold's operation (Siebold, Carl Caspar von): Medicine. See: Dorland; Stedman. Also known as: Gigli's operation.

Siebold's organ (Siebold, Carl Caspar von): Zoology. See: Gray.

SIECHENOFF, IVAN MEKHAILOVICH. 1829-1905. Russian neurologist. Cited in: Royal Soc. Cat. Sci. Pap., 1884-1900. Siechenoff's center.

Siechenoff's center (Siechenoff, Ivan Mekhailovich): Medicine. See: Dorland; Stedman.

Siegal-Cattan-Mamou disease (Siegal, Sheppard; Cattan, Roger; and Mamou, Henry). See: Reimann's periodic disease.

SIEGAL, SHEPPARD. 1909- . American physician. See: Direct. Med. Specialists, 1964-1965. Siegal-Cattan-Mamou disease.

SIEGBAHN, KARL MANNE GEORG. 1886- . Swedish physicist. See: Pogg., vols. 5, 6. Siegbahn notation, Siegbahn unit.

Siegbahn notation (Siegbahn, Karl Manne Georg): Physics. See: Hackh.

Siegbahn unit (Siegbahn, Karl Manne Georg): Physics. See: Ballentyne; Dresner; Webster's 3d.

SIEGERT, FERDINAND. 1865-1946. German pediatrician. See: Biog. Lex. hervorr. Aerzte. Siegert's sign.

Siegert's sign (Siegert, Ferdinand): Medicine. See: Dorland; Stedman.

SIEGLE, EMIL. 1833-1900. German otologist. See: Biog. Lex. hervorr. Aerzte. Siegle's otoscope.

Siegle's otoscope (Siegle, Emil): Medicine. See: Dorland; Stedman.

SIEGRIST, AUGUST. b. 1865. Swiss physican. See: Biog. Lex. hervorr. Aerzte. Siegrist-Hutchinson syndrome, Siegrist's spots (or streaks).

Siegrist-Hutchinson syndrome (Siegrist August and Hutchinson, Johathan, Jr.): Medicine. See: Jablonski. Also known as: Siegrist's syndrome.

Siegrist's spots (or streaks) (Siegrist, August): Medicine. See: Jablonski.

Siegrist's syndrome (Siegrist, August). See: Siegrist-Hutchinson syndrome.

SIEKERT, ROBERT GEORGE. 1924- . American neurologist. See: World Who's Who Sci. Millikan-Siekert syndrome.

SIELISCH, JOHANNES. fl. 1912. German chemist. Cited in: Chem. Abstr., vol. 7, p. 345. Sielisch test.

Sielisch test (Sielisch, Johannes): Chemistry. See: Van Nostrand Chem. Dict.

Siemens (Siemens, Werner): Physics. See: Dresner; Markus. Also known as: mho.

Siemens and Halske process (Siemens Werner and Halske, Johann Georg): Engineering and Industry. See: Hackh; Thrush; Van Nostrand Chem. Dict.

Siemens-Bloch pigmented dermatosis (Siemens, Hermann Werner and Bloch, Bruno). See: Bloch-Sulzberger syndrome.

SIEMENS, SIR CHARLES WILLIAM. 1822-1883. German-born English engineer. See: Pogg., vols. 2, 3, 6, 7a suppl. Cowper-Siemens stove, Siemens countercurrent heat exchanger, Siemens direct process, Siemens furnace, Siemens-Martin process, Siemens-Martin steel, Siemens ozonizer, Siemens producer, Siemens-Silesian furnace, Siemensite?

Siemens countercurrent heat exchanger (Siemens, Sir Charles William): Engineering and Industry. See: Internat. Dict. Phys. Elec.

Siemens direct process (Siemens, Sir Charles William): Engineering and Industry. See: Hackh; Thrush.

Siemens furnace (Siemens, Sir Charles William): Engineering and Industry. See: Hackh; Thrush; Van Nostrand Chem. Dict.

SIEMENS, HERMANN WERNER. 1891- . German dermatologist. See: Biog. Lex. hervorr. Aerzte. Bloch-Siemens syndrome, Christ-Siemens-Touraine syndrome, Siemens-Schaefer syndrome, Siemens' syndrome (1).

Siemens law (Siemens, Werner): Physics. See: Webster's 3d.

Siemens-Martin process (Siemens, Sir Charles William and Martin, Pierre Blaise Emile): Engineering and Industry. See: Hackh; Thrush; Van Nostrand Chem. Dict.

Siemens-Martin steel (Siemens, Sir Charles William and Martin, Pierre Blaise Emile): Engineering and Industry. See: Thrush.

Siemens ozonizer (Siemens, Sir Charles William): Engineering and Industry. See: Hackh.

Siemens producer (Siemens, Sir Charles William): Engineering and Industry. See: Hackh; Thrush.

Siemens-Schaefer syndrome (Siemens, Hermann Werner and Schaefer, Erich). See: Schaefer's syndrome.

Siemens-Silesian furnace (Siemens, Sir Charles William): Engineering and Industry. See: Thrush.

Siemens' syndrome (1) (Siemens, Hermann Werner): Medicine. See: Jablonski.

Siemens' syndrome (2) (or dermatosis) (Siemens, Hermann Werner). See: Christ-Siemens-Touraine syndrome.

SIEMENS, WERNER (In full: ERNST WERNER). 1816-1892. German electrical engineer. See: Pogg., vols. 2 to 6, 7a suppl. Siemens, Siemens and Halske process, Siemens law.

Siemensite (Siemens, Sir Charles William?): Engineering and Industry. See: Thrush.

SIEMERLING, ERNST. 1857-1931. German neurologist and psychiatrist. See: Biog. Lex. hervorr. Aerzte. Siemerling's nucleus.

iemerling's nucleus (Siemerling, Ernst): Medicine. See: Dorland.

IEMSSEN, J. A. fl. 1912. German chemist. Cited in: Chem. Abstr., ol. 5, p. 1886; vol. 6, pp. 1408, 3241. Siemssen test reaction for gold, iemssen test reactions for uranium and mercury.

iemssen test reaction for gold (Siemssen, J. A.): Chemistry. See: Van Nostrand Chem. Dict.

iemssen test reactions for uranium and mercury (Siemssen, J. A.): Chemistry. ee: Van Nostrand Chem. Dict.

ierpinski set (Sierpinski, Waclaw): Mathematics. See: James.

IERPINSKI, WACLAW. b. 1882. Polish mathematician. See: Pogg., vols. , 6. Sierpinski set.

IEUR, CELESTIN. b. 1860. French surgeon. See: Biog. Lex. hervorr. erzte. Sieur's test.

ieurin process (Sieurin, Sven E.): Engineering and Industry. See: Thrush.

IEURIN, SVEN E. fl. 1925. English? chemist. Cited in: Chem. Abstr., ecenn. Index, 1917-1926. Sieurin process.

ieur's test (Sieur, Celestin): Medicine. See: Dorland.

IEVERS, J. fl. 18th c. German botanist. (Biography source unavailable.) ieversia.

ieversia (Sievers, J.): Botany. See: Webster's 3d.

IEVERTS, ADOLF FERDINAND. 1874-1947. German chemist. See: Pogg., ols. 5, 6, 7a. Hagen-Sieverts test reaction.

IGAULT, JEAN RENE. b. 1740. French obstetrician. See: Biog. Lex. ervorr. Aerzte. Sigault's operation.

igault's operation (Sigault, Jean Rene): Medicine. See: Stedman.

iggaard-Andersen nomogram (Siggaard-Andersen, Ole): Medicine. See: tedman.

IGGAARD-ANDERSEN, OLE. 1932- . Danish physician and biochemist. ee: Who's Who Sci. Europe, 1972. Siggaard-Andersen nomogram.

IGNORELLI, ANGELO. 1876-1952. Italian physician. See: Chir. Torac., ol. 5 (1952), pp. 523-525. Signorelli's sign.

ignorelli's sign (Signorelli, Angelo): Medicine. See: Dorland; Stedman.

IGUIER, FRED. 1909- . French physician. See: Who's Who Sci. urope, 1972. Lian-Siguier-Welti syndrome.

IKES, BARTHOLOMEW. fl. 1816. English official. Cited in: Glazebrook. ikes' hydrometer (or scale).

IKES, BILL. Character in Charles Dickens novel, "Oliver Twist", (1837-38). ee: Magill. Bill Sikes.

ikes' hydrometer (or scale) (Sikes, Bartholomew): Chemistry. See: Hackh; artridge.

ikorsky helicopter (Sikorsky, Igor Ivan): Engineering and Industry. See: Van ostrand Sci. Encyc. under "Helicopter".

IKORSKY, IGOR IVAN. 1889- . Russian-born American aeronautical ngineer. See: Amer. Men and Women Sci., 12th ed. Sikorsky helicopter.

ILBER, ROBERT HOWARD. 1915- . American biochemist. See: World ho's Who Sci. Porter-Silber chromogens.

ilene (Silenus, the god): Botany. See: Partridge.

ilenus (Silenus, the god): Generic Word. See: Partridge.

ILENUS, THE GOD. Son of Hermes or Pan. See: Jobes. Silene, Silenus.

ILEX, PAUL. 1858-1929. German ophthalmologist. See: Biog. Lex. hervorr. erzte. Silex's sign.

ilex's sign (Silex, Paul): Medicine. See: Dorland.

ILFVERSKIOLD, NILS OTTO. 1888- . Swedish physician. See: Svenska aen Och Kvinnor. Silfverskiold's syndrome.

ilfverskiold's syndrome (Silfverskiold, Nils Otto): Medicine. See: Jablonski; tedman. Also known as: Grudzinski's osteochondropathy, Morquio-Silfverskiold yndrome.

Silhouette (Silhouette, Etienne de): Generic Word (profile). See: Harvey; Hendrickson; Osborne.

SILHOUETTE, ETIENNE DE. 1709-1767. French finance minister and political writer. See: Encyc. Brit., 1911. Silhouette.

SILLEBAWBY, ALEXANDER ORROK, LAIRD OF. fl. 1548. Scottish mint-master. (Biography source unavailable.) Bawbee.

Sillery (champaigne) (Sillery, Marquis de): Food and Drink. See: Wagner (Names).

SILLERY, MARQUIS DE. No dates. French vineyard owner. (Biography source unavailable.) Sillery (champaigne).

SILLIMAN, BENJAMIN. 1779-1864. American chemist. See: World Who's Who Sci. Sillimanite.

Sillimanite (Silliman, Banjamin): Earth Sciences. See: Thrush; Van Nostrand Sci. Encyc.; Webster's 3d.

Silsbee effect (rule or hypothesis) (Silsbee, Francis Briggs): Physics. See: Ballentyne; Internat. Dict. Phys. Elec.; Markus.

SILSBEE, FRANCIS BRIGGS. 1889- . American physicist. See: Pogg., vol. 6. Silsbee effect (rule or hypothesis).

SILVER, HENRY K. 1918- . American pediatrician. See: Direct. Med. Specialists, 1965-1966. Silver's syndrome.

SILVERMAN, FREDERIC NOAH. 1914- . American pediatrician. See: Amer. Men and Women Sci., 12th ed. Silverman's disease.

SILVERMAN, IRVING. 1904- . American surgeon. Cited in: Kelly. Silverman needle.

Silverman needle (Silverman, Irving): Medicine. See: Kelly. Also known as: Vim-Silverman needle.

SILVERMAN, WILLIAM AARON. 1917- . American physician. See: World Who's Who Sci. Caffey-Silverman syndrome.

Silverman's disease (Silverman, Frederic Noah): Medicine. See: Jablonski.

Silver's syndrome (Silver, Henry K.): Medicine. See: Jablonski.

SILVESTER I, SAINT. d. 335. Pope. See: Holweck. Order of St. Silvester.

SILVESTER, HENRY ROBERT. 1829-1908. English physician. See: Biog. Lex. hervorr. Aerzte. Silvester's method.

Silvester's method (Silvester, Henry Robert): Medicine. See: Dorland; Stedman; Thrush.

Silvestroni-Bianco syndrome (Silvestroni, E. and Bianco, I.): Medicine. See: Jablonski. Also known as: Cooley's trait.

SILVESTRONI, E. fl. 1948. Italian physician. (Biography source unavailable.) Silvestroni-Bianco syndrome.

Silvio Negri's syndrome (Negri, Silvio). See: Jacod's syndrome.

Simbal breathing apparatus (Derivation undetermined): Engineering and Industry. See: Thrush.

Simenon (Simenon, Georges Joseph Christian): Literature. See: Hendrickson.

SIMENON, GEORGES JOSEPH CHRISTIAN. 1903- . Belgian-French novelist. See: New Encyc. Brit., 1974, Microp. Simenon.

SIMEON. Priest in the New Testament. Cited in: Hastings (Dict. Bible). Song of Simeon.

SIMEON. Second son of the patriarch Jacob in the Bible. See: Hastings (Dict. Bible). Simeonite (1).

SIMEON, CHARLES. 1759-1836. English evangelical preacher. See: Dict. Nat. Biog. Simeonite (2) (Simeonism or Sim).

SIMEON STYLITES, SAINT. 390? - 459. Syrian ascetic and theologian. See: Encyc. Brit., 1973. Stylites.

Simeonite (1) (Simeon): Religion. See: Webster's 3d.

Simeonite (2) (Simeonism or Sim) (Simeon, Charles): Religion. See: Charnock; Webster's 3d.

SIMMONDS, MORRIS. 1855-1925. German physician. See: Biog. Lex. hervorr. Aerzte. Simmonds' syndrome (disease or cachexia).

Simmonds' syndrome (disease or cachexia) (Simmonds, Morris): Medicine. See: Dorland; Jablonski; Stedman. Also known as: Glinski-Simmonds syndrome, Reye-Sheehan syndrome, Sheehan's syndrome.

SIMMONS, FURNIFOLD McLENDELL. 1854-1940. American lawyer and legislator. See: Who Was Who Amer., vol. 1. Underwood-Simmons Tariff Act.

Simmons jar block (or collar) (Derivation undetermined): Engineering and Industry. See: Thrush.

SIMON, ALFRED WALTER. 1897- . American physicist. See: Amer. Men Sci., 4th ed. Compton-Simon experiment.

Simon and Lange vacuum calorimeter (Simon, Sir Francis Eugene and Lange, Fritz): Chemistry. See: Van Nostrand Sci. Encyc.

SIMON, CHARLES EDMUND. 1866-1927. American physician. See: Who Was Who Amer. Simon's sign.

Simon-Chavaune test reactions (Simon, Louis Jacques and Chavanne, Georges): Chemistry. See: Van Nostrand Chem. Dict.

Simon Commission (Simon, Sir John Allsebrook Simon, 1st Viscount Simon): Politics. See: Morris and Irwin.

SIMON, SIR FRANCIS EUGENE (FRANZ EUGEN). 1893-1956. German-born English physicist. See: World Who's Who Sci. Nernst-Simon statement (of the third law of thermodynamics), Simon and Lange vacuum calorimeter, Simon liquefier, Simon melting equation.

SIMON, GUSTAV (In full: KARL GUSTAV THEODORE). 1810-1857. German physician. See: Biog. Lex. hervorr. Aerzte. Simonea folliculorum.

SIMON, GUSTAV. 1824-1876. German surgeon. See: World Who's Who Sci. Simon's operation, Simon's position.

SIMON, SIR JOHN. 1816-1904. English surgeon. See: World Who's Who Sci. Simon's operation.

SIMON, SIR JOHN ALLSEBROOK SIMON, 1st VISCOUNT SIMON. 1873-1954. English politician. See: Who Was Who. Simon Commission.

Simon Legree (Legree, Simon): Generic Word (slave-driver). See: Mathews, M. M.; Partridge; Webster's 3d.

Simon liquefier (Simon, Sir Francis Eugene): Chemistry. See: Thewlis.

SIMON, LOUIS JACQUES. 1867-1925. French chemist. See: Pogg., vols. 4, 5, 6. Simon-Chavaune test reactions, Simon reaction for phenylhydrazine, Simon test for aldehydes, Simon test for amines, Simon test reaction for pyruvic acid.

SIMON MAGUS. fl. 1st c. Samaritan sorcerer. See: New Encyc. Brit., 1974, Microp. Simonians (or Simoniani), Simony (Simoniac, Simonical and Simonious).

Simon melting equation (Simon, Sir Francis Eugene): Chemistry. See: Thewlis.

Simon Pure (Simon Pure, the Quaker): Generic Word (authentic). See: Barnhart (Eng. Lit.); Funk; Mathews, M. M.

SIMON PURE, THE QUAKER. Character in Susanna Centlivre's play "A Bold Stroke for a Wife", (1718). See: Harvey. Simon Pure, Simon Pures.

Simon Pures (Simon Pure, the Quaker): Politics. See: Mathews, M. M.

Simon reaction for phenylhydrazine (Simon, Louis Jacques): Chemistry. See: Van Nostrand Chem. Dict.

Simon test for aldehydes (Simon, Louis Jacques): Chemistry. See: Hackh; Van Nostrand Chem. Dict.

Simon test for amines (Simon, Louis Jacques): Chemistry. See: Van Nostrand Chem. Dict.

Simon test reaction for pyruvic acid (Simon, Louis Jacques): Chemistry. See: Van Nostrand Chem. Dict.

SIMON, THEODORE. 1873-1961. French psychologist. See: World Who's Who Sci. Binet-Simon scale, Binet-Simon tests.

SIMONART, PIERRE JOSEPH CECILIEN. 1817-1847. Belgian obstetrician. See: Biog. Lex. hervorr. Aerzte. Simonart's bands (ligaments, or threads).

Simonart's bands (ligaments, or threads) (Simonart, Pierre Joseph Cecilien): Medicine. See: Dorland; Stedman.

Simonea folliculorum (Simon, Gustav): Medicine. See: Stedman.

SIMONELLI, F. No dates. Italian physician. (Biography source unavailable.) Simonelli's test.

Simonelli's test (Simonelli, F.): Medicine. See: Dorland.

Simonians (or Simoniani) (Simon Magus): Religion. See: Dict. Christian Biog.; Harvey; Hendrickson.

SIMONIS, HUGO GERHARD CORNELIUS. b. 1874. German chemist. See: Pogg., vols. 4, 5, 6. Simonis reaction.

Simonis reaction (Simonis, Hugo Gerhard Cornelius): Chemistry. See: Van Nostrand Chem. Dict.

SIMONS, ARTHUR. b. 1879. German physician. See: Biog. Lex. hervorr. Aerzte. Simons' disease (or syndrome).

Simons' disease (or syndrome) (Simons, Arthur): Medicine. See: Dorland; Jablonski; Stedman. Also known as: Barraquer-Simons syndrome, Barraquer's syndrome, Hollaender-Simons syndrome.

SIMONS, JOSEPH H. 1897- . American chemist and physicist. See: Amer. Men Sci., 9th ed. Fryberg and Simons gauge.

Simon's operation (Simon, Gustav): Medicine. See: Dorland; Stedman. Also known as: Marckwald's operation.

Simon's operation (Simon, Sir John): Medicine. See: Dorland.

Simon's position (Simon, Gustav): Medicine. See: Dorland; Stedman.

Simon's sign (Simon, Charles Edmund): Medicine. See: Dorland, Stedman.

Simon's theory (Derivation undetermined): Engineering and Industry. See: Thrush.

Simony (Simoniac, Simonical and Simonious) (Simon Magus): Generic Word (commercializing sacred things). See: Attwater; Charnock; Hendrickson; Partridge; Steinberg; Webster's 3d.

SIMONY, FRIEDRICH. fl. 1846-1873. German geographer. Cited in: Royal Soc. Cat. Sci. Pap., 1800-1863; 1864-1873. Simonyite.

Simonyite (Simony, Friedrich): Earth Sciences. See: Thrush. Also known as: Bloedite.

SIMPLE SIMON. Character in anonymous nursery rhyme. Cited in: Jobes under "Simon." Simple Simon.

Simple Simon (Simple Simon): Generic Word (gullible person). See: Brewer; Phyfe.

SIMPLOT, J. R. fl. 20th c. American mine owner. Cited in: Min. Mag., vol. 31 (1956-1958), p. 972. Simplotite.

Simplotite (Simplot, J. R.): Earth Sciences. See: Thrush.

SIMPSON, ADELE (Orig. surname: Smithline). 1903- . American fashion designer. See: Cur. Biog., 1970. Simpson style.

SIMPSON, EDWARD S. 1875-1939. Australian mineralogist. See: Who Was Who. Simpsonite.

SIMPSON, SIR GEORGE. 1792-1860. Scottish-born Canadian explorer. See: Dict. Nat. Biog.

SIMPSON, SIR JAMES YOUNG. 1811-1870. Scottish obstetrician. See: Dict. Nat. Biog. Simpson's forceps.

Simpson light (Simpson, William S.): Engineering and Industry. See: Dorland; Stedman.

SIMPSON, SAMUEL LEONARD. fl. 1930-1964. English physician. See: Med. Direct., 1964. Simpson's syndrome.

Simpson style (Simpson, Adele): Fashion. See: Picken.

SIMPSON, THOMAS. 1710-1761. English mathematician. See: World Who's Who Sci. Simpson's rule.

Simpson, Wallis Warfield. See: Windsor, Wallis Warfield Simpson.

SIMPSON, WILLIAM K. 1855-1914. American laryngologist. See: Dict. Amer. Biog. Simpson's plug.

SIMPSON, WILLIAM S. fl. 1917? English civil engineer. (Biography source unavailable.) Simpson light.

Simpsonite (Simpson, Edward S.): Earth Sciences. See: Thrush; Webster's 3d.

Simpson's forceps (Simpson, Sir James Young): Medicine. See: Dorland; Stedman.

Simpson's honey plant (Simpson, Sir George): Botany. See: Webster's 3d.

Simpson's plug (Simpson, William K.): Medicine. See: Dorland; Stedman.

Simpson's rule (Simpson, Thomas): Mathematics. See: Ballentyne; Internat. Dict. Phys. Elec.; James.

Simpson's syndrome (Simpson, Samuel Leonard): Medicine. See: Jablonski.

SIMROTH, HEINRICH RUDOLF. d. 1917. German zoologist. Cited in: Royal Soc. Cat. Sci. Pap., 1800-1883; 1884-1900. Simroth's appendages.

Simroth's appendages (Simroth, Heinrich Rudolf): Zoology. See: Gray.

Sims engine (Sims, James): Engineering and Industry. See: Auger.

SIMS, J. MARION. 1813-1883. American gynecologist. See: World Who's Who Sci. Sims' position, Sims' speculum.

SIMS, JAMES. fl. 1840. English engineer. Cited in: Royal Soc. Cat. Sci. Pap., 1800-1863. Sims engine.

Sims' law of town and country relations (Sims, Newell Leroy): Sociology. See: Zadrozny.

SIMS, NEWELL LEROY. 1878-1965. American sociologist. See: Who Was Who Amer. Sims' law of town and country relations.

SIMS, PHILIP HAL. d. 1949. American bridge expert. See: New York Times, Feb. 28, 1949, p. 19, col. 1. Sims system.

Sims' position (Sims, J. Marion): Medicine. See: Dorland; Stedman.

Sims' speculum (Sims, J. Marion): Medicine. See: Dorland; Stedman.

Sims system (Sims, Philip Hal): Recreation and Sports. See: Webster's 3d.

SIMSON, ROBERT. 1687-1768. Scottish mathematician. See: World Who's Who Sci. Simson's line.

Simson's line (Simson, Robert): Mathematics. See: Ballentyne; Webster's 3d.

sin to Davy Crockett (Crockett, David): Generic Word (exceptional). See: Mathews, M. M.

Sinclair coupling (Sinclair, H.): Engineering and Industry. See: Auger.

SINCLAIR, H. fl. 1935. English engineer. (Biography source unavailable.) Sinclair coupling.

SINDING-LARSEN, CHRISTIAN MAGNUS FALSEN. 1866-1930. Norwegian physician. See: Hygiea, vol. 92 (Feb. 28, 1930), pp. 113-116. Larsen-Johansson syndrome (or disease).

Sinding Larsen-Johansson syndrome (or disease) (Sinding-Larsen, Christian Magnus Falsen and Johansson, Sven Christian). See: Larsen-Johansson syndrome (or disease).

SING, GERTRUD. fl. 1947. German chemist. Cited in: Chem. Abstr., Decenn. Index, 1947-1956. Schulz and Sing formula.

SINGER, FELIX GUSTAV. b. 1888. German technologist. See: Pogg., vol. 6. Singer's test.

SINGER, HAROLD DOUGLAS. b. 1875. English-born American physician. See: Who's Who Amer. Med., 1925. Moschowitz-Singer-Symmers syndrome?

SINGER, ISAAC MERRIT. 1811-1875. American inventor. See: Dict. Amer. Biog. Singer sewing machine.

Singer sewing machine (Singer, Isaac Merrit): Engineering and Industry. See: Partridge.

Singer's test (Singer, Felix Gustav): Engineering and Industry. See: Thrush.

Singleton test reactions (Singleton, W.): Chemistry. See: Van Nostrand Chem. Dict.

SINGLETON, W. fl. 1927. English chemist. Cited in: Chem. Abstr., vol. 21, pp. 1605-1606. Singleton test reactions.

SINNING, WILHELM d. 1874. German horticulturist. (Biography source unavailable.) Sinningia.

Sinningia (Sinning, Wilhelm): Botany. See: Taylor, N.; Webster's 3d.

Sinon (Sinon, the Greek): Generic Word (deceiver). See: Brewer.

SINON, THE GREEK. Hero in Trojan War. See: Jobes. Sinon.

sinus of Morgagni syndrome (Morgagni, Giovanni Battista). See: Trotter's syndrome.

sinus of Valsalva (Valsalva, Antonio Maria) See: Valsalva's sinus.

SIPPLE, JOHN H. 1930- . American physician. See: Direct Med. Specialists, 1974-1975. Sipple's syndrome.

Sipple's syndrome (Sipple, John H.): Medicine. See: Jablonski; Stedman.

SIPPY, BERTRAM WELTON. 1866-1924. American physician. See: Who Was Who Amer. Sippy's method.

Sippy's method (Sippy, Bertram Welton): Medicine. See: Stedman.

Sir Philip Sidney's oak (Sidney, Sir Philip): History. See: Brewer.

Siren (Siren, the monster): Generic Word (whistle). See: Brewer.

SIREN, THE MONSTER. In Greek mythology, a witch of the shoals. See: Jobes. Siren.

Sisley-Frehse reagent (Sisley, Paul Edouard Louis and Frehse): Chemistry. See: Van Nostrand Chem. Dict.

SISLEY, PAUL EDOUARD LOUIS. 1866-1933. French chemist. See: Pogg., vol. 6. Sisley-Frehse reagent.

Sister of the Immaculate Heart of Mary (Mary, Virgin-Mother): Religion. See: Webster's 3d.

Sisters of Marie Auxiliatrice (Mary, Virgin-Mother): Religion. See: Attwater.

Sisters of Marie Reparatrice (Mary, Virgin-Mother): Religion. See: Attwater.

Sisters of St. Joseph (Joseph, Saint): Religion. See: Attwater; Webster's 3d.

Sisters of St. Mary (Mary, Virgin-Mother): Religion. See: Attwater.

Sisters of Saint Vincent (Vincent de Paul, Saint): Religion. See: Webster's 3d.

Sisters of the Holy Child Jesus (Jesus Christ): Religion. See: Attwater.

Sisters of the Holy Names of Jesus and Mary (Jesus Christ and Mary, the Virgin-Mother): Religion. See: Webster's 3d.

Sisters of the Poor Child Jesus (Jesus Christ): Religion. See: Attwater.

Sisters of the Sacred Hearts of Jesus and Mary (Jesus Christ and Mary, the Virgin-Mother): Religion. See: Attwater.

SISTO, GENARO. 1870-1923. Argentinian pediatrician. See: Gran Encic. Argentina. Sisto's sign.

Sisto's sign (Sisto, Genaro): Medicine. See: Dorland; Stedman.

Sisyphean (toil) (Sisyphus): Generic Word (endless job). See: Brewer; Partridge; Webster's 3d.

SISYPHUS. Mythical king of Corinth. See: Jobes. Sisyphean (toil).

SITA. Hindu fertility goddess. See: Jobes. Sita's lizard?

Sita's lizard (Sita, the goddess?): Zoology. See: Gray.

SITTER, WILLEM DE. 1872-1934. Dutch astronomer. See: World Who's Who Sci. De Sitter universe.

SIVA. Supreme god of many Hindu sects. See: Jobes. Sivaism, Sivatherium.

SIVADJIAN, JOSEPH. 1898- . Turkish-born French pharmacologist. See: World Who's Who Sci. Sivadjian test for carbon tetrachloride in chloroform, Sivadjian test reaction for alkaloids of ephedra, Sivadjian test reaction for amines.

Sivadjian test for carbon tetrachloride in chloroform (Sivadjian, Joseph): Chemistry. See: Van Nostrand Chem. Dict.

Sivadjian test reaction for alkaloids of ephedra (Sivadjian, Joseph): Chemistry. See: Van Nostrand Chem. Dict.

Sivadjian test reaction for amines (Sivadjian, Joseph): Chemistry. See: Van Nostrand Chem. Dict.

Sivaism (Siva): Religion. See: Mathews, S.; Webster's 3d.

Sivatherium (Siva): Zoology. See: Charnock.

SIWE, STURE AUGUST. b. 1897. Swedish pediatrician. See: Vem Ar Det?, 1949. Abt-Letterer-Siwe syndrome.

SIX, ACHILLE. fl. 1885. French geologist. Cited in: Royal Soc. Cat. Sci. Pap., 1800-1883; 1884-1900. Six's thermometer?

Six's thermometer (Six, Achille?): Earth Sciences. See: Van Nostrand Sci. Encyc.

SJOEGREN, HENRIK SAMUEL CONRAD. 1899- . Swedish physician. See: Vem Ar Det?, 1973. Sjoegren's syndrome (or disease).

Sjoegren-Larsson syndrome (Sjoegren, Torsten and Larsson, Tage): Medicine. See: Jablonski; Stedman.

Sjoegren-Mikulicz syndrome (Sjoegren, Henrik Samuel Conrad and Von Mikulicz-Radecki, Johann). See: Sjoegren's syndrome (or disease).

SJOEGREN, TORSTEN (In full: KARL GUSTAF TORSTEN). 1896- . Swedish physician. See: Vem ar Det?, 1973. Graefe-Sjoegren syndrome, Marinesco-Sjoegren syndrome, Sjoegren-Larsson syndrome.

Sjoegren's syndrome (Sjoegren, Torsten). See: Graefe-Sjoegren syndrome.

Sjoegren's syndrome (or disease) (Sjoegren, Henrik Samuel Conrad): Medicine. See: Jablonski; Stedman. Also known as: Gougerot-Houwer-Sjoegren syndrome, Gougerot-Sjoegren syndrome (or disease), Sjoegren-Mikulicz syndrome.

SJOEQVIST, JOHN AUGUST. 1863-1934. Swedish physician and biochemist. See: Svenska Maen Och Kvinnor. Sjoeqvist's method.

SJOEQVIST, OLOF (In full: CARL OLOF). 1901- . Swedish neurosurgeon. See: World Who's Who Sci. Sjoeqvist's tractotomy.

Sjoeqvist's method (Sjoeqvist, John August): Medicine. See: Stedman. Also known as: Moerner-Sjoeqvist method.

Sjoeqvist's tractotomy (Sjoeqvist, Olof): Medicine. See: Stedman.

SJOGREN, HJALMAR (In full: STEN ANDERS HJALMAR). 1856-1922. Swedish mineralogist and geologist. See: Svenska Maen Och Kvinnor. Sjogrenite.

Sjogrenite (Sjogren, Hjalmar): Earth Sciences. See: Thrush; Webster's 3d.

SKAGGS, ERNEST BURTON. fl. 1923-1947. American psychologist. See: Psych. Register, 1932, p. 448f. Skaggs-Robinson hypothesis (or phenomenon).

Skaggs-Robinson hypothesis (or phenomenon) (Skaggs, Ernest Burton and Robinson, Edward Stevens): Psychology. See: Chaplin; English; Wolman.

SKEFFINGTON, LEONARD. fl. mid 16th c. English Lieutenant of the Tower of London. See: Dict. Nat. Biog. under "Skeffington, Sir William." Skeffington's daughter.

Skeffington's daughter (Skeffington, Leonard): Weapons. See: Harvey; Partridge; Webster's 3d.

SKELTON, JOHN. 1460? - 1529. English poet. See: Dict. Nat. Biog. Skeltonic verse.

Skeltonic verse (Skelton, John): Literature. See: Harvey; Preminger; Webster's 3d.

SKENE, ALEXANDER JOHNSTON CHALMERS. 1838-1900. Scottish-born American gynecologist. See: Dict. Amer. Biog. Skeneitis; Skeneoscope; Skene's glands.

SKENE, JAMES. fl. 1825. Scottish zoologist. Cited in: Royal Soc. Cat. Sci. Pap., 1800-1863. Skenea?

Skenea (Skene, James?): Zoology. See: Pennak.

Skeneitis (Skene, Alexander Johnston Chalmers): Medicine. See: Stedman.

Skeneoscope (Skene, Alexander Johnston Chalmers): Medicine. See: Stedman.

Skene's glands (Skene, Alexander Johnston Chalmers): Anatomy. See: Donath; Stedman. Also known as: Guerin's glands.

Skey reagent (Skey, William?): Chemistry. See: Van Nostrand Chem. Dict.

Skey test reaction for cobalt (Skey, William?): Chemistry. See: Van Nostrand Chem. Dict.

SKEY, WILLIAM. fl. 1866-1900. New Zealander chemist. Cited in: Royal Soc. Cat. Sci. Pap., 1874-1883. 1884-1900. Skey reagent?, Skey test reaction for cobalt?.

Skidmore crucible (Derivation undetermined): Engineering and Industry. See: Van Nostrand Chem. Dict.

SKILLERN, PENN GASKELL, JR. b. 1882. American surgeon. (Biography source unavailable.) Skillern's fracture?

Skillern's fracture (Skillern, Penn Gaskell?): Medicine. See: Dorland; Stedman.

Skinner box (Skinner, Burrhus Frederic): Psychology. See: Chaplin; English; Wolman.

SKINNER, BURRHUS FREDERIC. 1904- . American psychologist. See: World Who's Who Sci. Skinner box, Skinner device, Skinnerian, Skinner's operant conditioning.

Skinner device (Skinner, Burrhus Frederic): Psychology. See: Harrod.

Skinnerian (Skinner, Burrhus Frederic): Psychology. See: Barnhart (New Eng.).

Skinner's operant conditioning (Skinner, Burrhus Frederic): Psychology. See: Chaplin.

SKITA, ALADAR. 1876-1953. German chemist. See: Pogg., vols. 5, 6, 7a. Auwers-Skita rule, Gattermann-Skita synthesis.

SKITOVICH, V. P. fl. 1954. Russian statistician. Cited in: Kendall and Doig, vol. 3. Darmois-Skitovich theorem.

Sklenar engine (Sklenar, M.): Engineering and Industry. See: Auger.

SKLENAR, M. fl. 1938. Hungarian engineer. (Biography source unavailable.) Sklenar engine.

Sklodowskite (Curie, Marie): Earth Sciences. See: Thrush; Webster's 3d.

SKLOWSKY, E. L. fl. 20th c. German physician. (Biography source unavailable.) Sklowsky's symptom.

Sklowsky's symptom (Sklowsky, E.L.): Medicine. See: Dorland; Stedman.

SKODA, JOSEPH. 1805-1881. Bohemian clinician in Austria. See: World Who's Who Sci. Skodaic resonance (or tympany), Skoda's rale.

Skodaic resonance (or tympany) (Skoda, Joseph): Medicine. See: Stedman. Also known as: Skoda's sign.

Skoda's rale (Skoda, Joseph): Medicine. See: Dorland; Stedman.

Skoda's sign (Skoda, Joseph). See: Skodaic resonance (or tympany).

SKOOG, TORSTEN OLOF. b. 1894. Swedish otolaryngologist. See: Vem Ar Det?, 1949. Forssman-Skoog syndrome.

Skraup synthesis (or reaction) (Skraup, Zdenko/Hans): Chemistry. See: Ballentyne; Van Nostrand Chem. Dict.; Webster's 3d.

Skraup test reaction (for thalline solutions) (Skraup, Zdenko/Hans): Chemistry. See: Van Nostrand Chem. Dict.

SKRAUP, ZDENKO/HANS. 1850-1910. Czechoslovakian chemist. See: World Who's Who Sci. Skraup synthesis (or reaction), Skraup test reaction (for thalline solutions).

Slater determinant (Slater, John Clarke): Physics. See: Internat. Dict. Ap. Math.

Slater factor (Derivation undetermined): Medicine. See: Stedman.

SLATER, J. W. fl. 1851-1855. English chemist. Cited in: Royal Soc. Cat. Sci. Pap., 1864-1873. Slater test.

SLATER, JOHN CLARKE. 1900- . American physicist. See: World Who's Who Sci. Bethe-Slater curve, Heitler-London-Slater-Pauling method (or HLSP method), Slater determinant, Slater method, Slater sum.

Slater method (Slater, John Clarke): Physics. See: Internat. Dict. Phys. Elec.

SLATER, ROBERT JAMES. 1923- . Canadian-born pediatrician in America. See: Amer. Men and Women Sci., 12th ed. Bearn-Kunkel-Slater syndrome.

Slater sum (Slater, John Clarke): Physics. See: Internat. Dict. Ap. Math.

Slater test (Slater, J. W.): Chemistry. See: Van Nostrand Chem. Dict.

SMITH, GEORGE W. fl. 1922. American engineer. Cited in: Chem. Abstr., vol. 17, p. 229. Greenburg-Smith impinger.

SMITH, GIDEON B. fl. 19th c. American physician. Cited in: Index-Cat. Libr. Surg.-Gen. Off., Ser. 1, vol. 13, 1892. Smith's longspur.

Smith-Helmholtz equation (Smith, Robert and Helmholtz, Hermann Ludwig Ferdinand von). See: Helmholtz's equation (2).

Smith-Helmholtz law (Smith, Robert and Helmholtz, Hermann Ludwig Ferdinand von). See: Lagrange theorem.

SMITH, HENRY. 1862-1948. Irish-born English military surgeon in India. See: Who Was Who. Smith's operation.

SMITH, HENRY LEE. d. 1957. American? mathematician. (Biography source unavailable.) Moore-Smith convergence.

SMITH, HENRY LEE JR. 1913- . American educator. See: Who's Who Amer., 1964-1965. Trager-Smith metrics.

SMITH, HERMAN LYLE. b. 1892. American mathematician. See: Pogg., vol. 6. Moore-Smith convergence (or set), Moore-Smith sequence.

SMITH, HOKE. 1855-1931. American legislator. See: Biog. Direct. Amer. Congress. Smith-Hughes Act, Smith-Lever Act.

SMITH, HORACE. 1808-1893. American inventor. See: Dict. Amer. Biog. Smith and Wesson pistol.

SMITH, HOWARD ALEXANDER. 1880-1966. American legislator. See: Biog. Direct. Amer. Congress. Smith-Mundt Act.

SMITH, HOWARD WORTH. b. 1883. American legislator. See: Biog. Direct. Amer. Congress. Smith Act.

Smith-Hughes Act (Smith, Hoke and Hughes, Dudley Mays): Politics. See: Good; Morris; Smith.

SMITH, J. KENT. fl. ca. 1914. American discoverer of mineral. Cited in: Min. Mag., vol. 20 (Mar. 1923-Dec. 1925), p. 457. Kentsmithite.

SMITH, SIR JAMES EDWARD. 1759-1828. Scottish botanist and physician. See: Dict. Nat. Biog. Smithia.

SMITH, JAN. fl. 1930. English? engineer. (Biography source unavailable.) Lysholm-Smith converter.

SMITH, JEAN. fl. 1932. English physician. (Biography source unavailable.) Smith's syndrome.

SMITH, JOHN BLACKBURN. 1865-1928. Irish pathologist. See: Who Was Who. Smith-Pitfield stain.

SMITH, JOHN "BUCKHORSE". fl. mid-18th c. English prize fighter. (Biography source unavailable.) Buckhorse.

SMITH, JOHN FERGUSON. fl. 1934. English dermatologist. (Biography source unavailable.) Ferguson Smith's epithelioma (or keratoacanthoma).

SMITH, JOHN LAWRENCE. 1818-1883. American chemist and mineralogist. See: World Who's Who Sci. Lawrencite.

SMITH, JOSEPH, THE YOUNGER. 1832-1914. American Mormon religious reformer. See: Dict. Amer. Biog. Josephite.

SMITH, LEIGHTON BRUERTON. 1896- . American physical chemist. See: Amer. Men Sci., 9th ed. Keyes-Smith-Gerry equation.

Smith-Lemli-Opitz syndrome (Smith, David W.; Lemli, Luc; and Opitz, John M.): Medicine. See: Jablonski.

Smith-Lever Act (Smith, Hoke and Lever, Asbury Francis): Politics. See: Good; Morris; Smith.

SMITH, LUCIAN ANDERSON. 1910- . American physician. See: Amer. Men and Women Sci., 12th ed. Achor-Smith syndrome.

Smith-McIntyre mud sampler (Derivation undetermined): Engineering and Industry. See: Thrush.

SMITH, MARIA ANN. fl. 19th c.? Australian apple cultivator. (Biography source unavailable.) Granny Smith (apple).

Smith-Mundt Act (Smith, Howard Alexander and Mundt, Karl Earl): Politics. See: Good.

SMITH, P. H. fl. 1939. American? electronics engineer. Cited in: Electronics, vol. 12 (Jan. 1939), p. 29. Smith chart (or diagram).

SMITH, PETER. fl. 1821. American? printer. (Biography source unavailable.) Smith press.

SMITH-PETERSON, MARIUS NYGAARD. 1886-1953. Norwegian-born American orthopedic surgeon. See: World Who's Who Sci. Smith-Peterson nail.

Smith-Peterson nail (Smith-Peterson, Marius Nygaard): Medicine. See: Dorland; Stedman. Webster's 3d.

Smith-Pitfield stain (Smith, John Blackburn, and Pitfield, Robert L.): Medicine. See: Stedman.

Smith press (Smith, Peter): Printing. See: Lockwood under "Hand-Press."

Smith process (copper refining) (Smith, Elias A. Cappelen): Engineering and Industry. See: Thrush.

Smith process (for sponge iron) (Derivation undetermined): Engineering and Industry. See: Thrush.

Smith propeller (Smith, Sir Francis Pettit): Engineering and Industry. See: Auger.

Smith-Purcell effect (Smith, Stephen Judson and Purcell, Edward Mills): Physics. See: Thewlis.

Smith reagent for free acids (Derivation undetermined): Chemistry. See: Van Nostrand Chem. Dict.

Smith refractometer (Smith, George Frederick Herbert): Earth Sciences. See: Thrush.

SMITH, ROBERT. 1689-1768. English mathematician and astronomer. See: Dict. Nat. Biog. Smith-Helmholtz equation, Smith-Helmholtz law, Smith's prizes.

SMITH, ROBERT ANGUS. 1817-1884. English chemist. See: Dict. Nat. Biog. Angus-Smith compound, Angus-Smith process.

SMITH, ROBERT WILLIAM. 1807-1873. Irish surgeon. See: Boase. Smith's fracture.

Smith-Robinson operation (Smith, Gardner Watkins and Robinson, Robert A.): Medicine. See: Stedman.

SMITH, SIDNEY. 1912- . American surgeon. See: Direct. Med. Specialists, 1965-1966. Potts-Smith-Gibson operation.

Smith-Smith test (Derivation undetermined): Medicine. See: Stedman.

SMITH, STEPHEN JUDSON. 1924- . American physicist. See: Amer. Men Sci., 9th ed. Smith-Purcell effect.

Smith test for formic acid (Derivation undetermined): Chemistry. See: Van Nostrand Chem. Dict.

Smith test reaction for alkaloids (Derivation undetermined): Chemistry. See: Van Nostrand Chem. Dict.

Smith test reaction for fluoride (Derivation undetermined): Chemistry. See: Van Nostrand Chem. Dict.

Smith test reactions for carbazides (Derivation undetermined): Chemistry. See: Van Nostrand Chem. Dict.

SMITH, THEOBALD. 1859-1934. American pathologist. See: World Who's Who Sci. Theobald Smith's phenomenon.

SMITH, WALTER G. 1844-1932. Irish physician. See: Lancet, vol. I (Feb. 27, 1932), p. 488-490. Smith's test.

Smith welding (Derivation undetermined): Engineering and Industry. See: Thrush.

SMITH, WILLIAM. fl. 1847. English con artist. (Biography source unavailable.) Billies and Charlies.

SMITH, WILLIAM HENRY. fl. late 19th c. American bacteriologist. Cited in: Royal Soc. Cat. Sci. Pap., 1884-1900. Smith's stain.

Smithia (Smith, Sir James Edward): Botany. See: Charnock.

Smithian (Smith, Adam): Economics. See: Webster's 3d.

Smithite (Smith, George Frederick Herbert): Earth Sciences. See: Thrush; Webster's 3d.

Smith's disease (Smith, Carl Henry): Medicine. See: Jablonski. Also known as: Carl Smith's disease.

Smith's disease (Smith, Eustace): Medicine. See: Dorland.

Smith's fracture (Smith, Robert William): Medicine. See: Dorland; Jablonski; Stedman. Also known as: reverse Colles' fracture.

Smith's longspur (Smith, Gideon B.): Zoology. See: Gray; Webster's 3d.

Smith's operation (Smith, Henry): Medicine. See: Dorland; Stedman.

Smith's prizes (Smith, Robert): Mathematics. See: Barnhart (Eng. Lit.); Harvey.

Smith's sign (Smith, Eustace): Medicine. See: Dorland.

Smith's stain (Smith, William Henry): Medicine. See: Stedman.

Smith's syndrome (Smith, Jean). See: Hutchinson's disease.

Smith's test (Smith, Walter G.). See: Kathrein's test.

SMITHSON, JAMES. 1765-1829. English chemist and mineralogist. See: World Who's Who Sci. Smithsonite.

Smithsonite (Smithson, James): Earth Sciences. See: Thrush; Van Nostrand Sci. Encyc.; Webster's 3d.

SMITT, FREDRIK ADAM. d. 1904. Swedish zoologist. See: Svenska Vetensk. Akad. Arsbok, 1905, pp. 237-240. Smittina.

Smittina (Smitt, Fredrik Adam): Zoology. See: Pennak.

SMOLUCHOWSKI, MARYAN RITTER VON SMOLAN. 1872-1917. Polish physicist. See: Pogg., vols. 4 to 6. Schmoluchowski's equation.

Smoot-Burton bill (Smoot, Reed and Burton, Theodore Elijah): Politics. See: Jameson.

Smoot-Hawley Tariff Act (Smoot, Reed and Hawley, Willis Chatman). See: Hawley-Smoot Tariff Act.

SMOOT, REED. 1862-1941. American legislator and Mormon leader. See: Who Was Who Amer. Hawley-Smoot Tariff Act, Smoot-Burton bill.

SMYTH, CHARLES HENRY, JR. 1866-1937. American geologist. See: Who Was Who Amer. Smythite.

SMYTH, CHARLES PIAZZI. 1819-1900. Italian-born Scottish astronomer. See: World Who's Who Sci. Charles Piazzi Smyth's camera.

SMYTH, DAVID McCONNELL. 1833-1907. American inventor. See: Nat. Cycl. Amer. Biog. Smyth sewing.

SMYTH, FRANCIS SCOTT. b. 1895. American pediatrician. See: Direct. Med. Specialists, 1965-1966. Caffey-Smyth disease.

Smyth sewing (Smyth, David McConnell): Engineering and Industry. See: Webster's 3d.

Smythite (Smyth, Charles Henry, Jr.): Earth Sciences. See: Thrush.

SNEDDON, IAN BRUCE. 1915- . English dermatologist. See: Who's Who Sci. Europe, 1972. Sneddon-Wilkinson syndrome (or disease).

Sneddon-Wilkinson syndrome (or disease) (Sneddon, Ian Bruce and Wilkinson, Darrell Sheldon): Medicine. See: Jablonski; Stedman. Also known as: Duhring-Sneddon-Wilkinson syndrome.

SNEDECOR, GEORGE WADDEL. b. 1881. American statistician. See: Amer. Men Sci., 11th ed. Brandt-Snedecor method, Snedecor's F-distribution.

Snedecor's F-distribution (Snedecor, George Waddel): Statistics. See: Kendall.

SNELL, GEORGE DAVIS. 1903- . American geneticist. See: Amer. Men and Women Sci., 12th ed. Snell's waltzer.

SNELL, HANNAH. 1723-1792. English soldier. See: Dict. Nat. Biog. Hannah.

SNELL, WILLEBRORD VAN ROIJEN. 1591-1626. Dutch astronomer and mathematician. See: New Encyc. Brit., 1974, Microp. Snell's law(s).

Snellen chart (or test) (Snellen, Hermann): Physiology. See: English; Good; Wolman.

SNELLEN, HERMAN ADRIANUS. 1905- . Dutch cardiologist. See: Wie Is Dat?, 1948. Taussig-Snellen-Albers syndrome.

SNELLEN, HERMANN. 1834-1908. Dutch ophthalmologist. See: World Who's Who Sci. Snellen chart (or test), Snellen notation, Snellen scale, Snellen's reform eye.

Snellen notation (Snellen, Hermann): Physiology. See: Good.

Snellen scale (Snellen, Hermann): Physiology. See: Good.

Snellen's reform eye (Snellen, Hermann): Medicine. See: Dorland; Stedman.

Snell's law(s) (Snell, Willebrord van Roijen): Physics. See: Huschke; Internat. Dict. Phys. Elec.; James.

Snell's waltzer (Snell, George Davis): Genetics. See: Gray.

SNIDER, JACOB. d. 1866. American inventor. (Biography source unavailable.) Snider rifle.

Snider rifle (Snider, Jacob): Weapons. See: Partridge; Quick.

Snoek effect (Snoek, Jacob Louis): Physics. See: Thewlis.

SNOEK, JACOB LOUIS. 1902- . Dutch physicist. See: Pogg., vol. 6. Snoek effect, Snoek's law.

Snoek's law (Snoek, Jacob Louis): Physics. See: Ballentyne.

SNOW WHITE. German folklore heroine. See: Jobes. Snow White costume.

Snow White costume (Snow White): Fashion. See: Picken.

SNYDER, C. J. fl. 1932. American chemist. Cited in: Chem. Abstr., Decen. Index, 1927-1936. Bassett-Snyder reagent.

SNYDER, JOHN BUELL. 1877-1946. American legislator. See: Biog. Direct. Amer. Congress. Guffey-Snyder Coal Act (or bituminous coal stabilization Act).

Snyder reagent (Derivation undetermined): Chemistry. See: Hackh.

Snyder sampler (Derivation undetermined): Engineering and Industry. See: Thrush.

Soapy Sam (Wilberforce, Samuel): Generic Word (unctuous speaker). See: Hendrickson.

SOBOLEWA, W. fl. 1910. Polish chemist. Cited in: Pogg., vol. 6 under "Zaleski, Jan." Sobolewa-Zaleski test.

Sobolewa-Zaleski test (Sobolewa, W. and Zaleski, Jan): Chemistry. See: Van Nostrand Chem. Dict.

SOBRAL, FRANCISCO M. fl. 18th c. Spanish physician and botanist. (Biography source unavailable.) Sobralia

Sobralia (Sobral, Francisco M.): Botany. See: Taylor, N.; Webster's 3d.

SOBRERO, ASCANIO. 1812-1888. Italian chemist. See: World Who's Who Sci. Sobrerol.

Sobrerol (Sobrero, Ascanio): Chemistry. See: Webster's 3d.

Society of Jesus (Jesus Christ). See: Jesuits.

Society of the Cincinnati (Cincinnatus, Lucius Quinctius): History. See: Encyc. Assoc.; Jameson; Latham.

Socinians (or Socinianism) (Socinus, Faustus and Laelius): Religion. See: Canney; Mathews, S.; Phyfe.

SOCINUS, FAUSTUS (FAUSTO SOZZINI). 1539-1604. Italian theologian. See: New Encyc. Brit., 1974, Microp. Socinians (or Socinianism).

SOCINUS, LAELIUS (LELIO SOZZINI). 1525-1562. Italian theologian. See: New Encyc. Brit., 1974, Microp. Socinians (or Socinianism).

SOCRATES. ca. 470-399 B.C. Greek philosopher. See: New Encyc. Brit., 1974, Microp. Socratic irony, Socratic method, Socratism.

Socratic irony (Socrates): Literature. See: Hendrickson; Scott; Webster's 3d.

Socratic method (Socrates): Philosophy. See: Partridge; Phyfe; Webster's 3d.

Socratism (Socrates): Philosophy. See: Webster's 3d.

Soddy-Fajans displacement law (Soddy, Frederick and Fajans, Kashmir). See: Fajans-Soddy law.

SODDY, FREDERICK. 1877-1956. English chemist and physicist. See: World Who's Who Sci. Fajans-Soddy law, Soddyite.

Soddyite (Soddy, Frederick): Earth Sciences. See: Thrush; Webster's 3d.

SODERBERG, C. W. fl. 1922. American? metallurgical chemist. Cited in: Chem. Abstr., vol. 16, p. 3443. Soderberg cell? Soderberg electrode.

Soderberg cell (Soderberg, C. W.?): Chemistry. See: Van Nostrand Chem. Dict.

Soderberg electrode (Soderberg, C. W.): Engineering and Industry. See: Thrush.

SOEDERSTROEM, A. L. fl. 1868. Scandinavian? engineer. (Biography source unavailable.) Soederstroem engine.

Soederstroem engine (Soederstroem, A. L.): Engineering and Industry. See: Auger.

SOEMMERING, SAMUEL TH. VON. 1755-1830. German anatomist. See: Biog. Lex. hervorr. Aerzte. Soemmering's foramen, Soemmering ganglion (or substance), Soemmering's ligament, Soemmering's muscle, Soemmering's nerve, Soemmering's spot.

Soemmering's foramen (Soemmering, Samuel Th. von): Anatomy. See: Donath; Stedman.

Soemmering's ganglion (or substance) (Soemmering, Samuel Th. von): Anatomy. See: Donath; Stedman.

Soemmering's ligament (Soemmering, Samuel Th. von): Anatomy. See: Donath; Stedman.

Soemmering's muscle (Soemmering, Samuel Th. von): Anatomy. See: Stedman.

Soemmering's nerve (Soemmering, Samuel Th. von): Anatomy. See: Stedman.

Soemmering's spot (Soemmering, Samuel Th. von): Anatomy. See: Stedman.

SOEMMERRING, WILHELM (In full: DETMAR WILHELM). 1793-1885. German physician. See: Biog. Lex. hervorr. Aerzte. Soemmerring's ring.

Soemmerring's ring (Soemmerring, Wilhelm): Medicine. See: Jablonski.

Soerensen indicators (Soerensen, Soeren/Peer Lauritz): Chemistry. See: Hackh.

Soerensen pH scale (value or symbols) (Soerensen, Soeren/Peer Lauritz): Chemistry. See: Ballentyne; Hackh.

SOERENSEN, SOEREN/PEER LAURITZ. 1868-1939. Danish biochemist. See: Pogg., vols. 4, 5, 6; World Who's Who Sci. Soerensen indicators, Soerensen pH scale (value or symbols), Soerensen standard phosphate solutions, Soerensen titration (or formol method).

Soerensen standard phosphate solutions (Soerensen, Soeren/Peer Lauritz): Chemistry. See: Hackh; Van Nostrand Chem. Dict.

Soerensen titration (or formol method) (Soerensen, Soeren/Peer Lauritz): Chemistry. See: Ballentyne; Van Nostrand Sci. Encyc.

Soerkedalite (Derivation undetermined): Earth Sciences. See: Thrush.

SOISSON, CAMILLE. fl. 1950-1955. French metallurgical engineer. Cited in: Chem. Abstr., vol. 48, p. P 6949h. Soisson Rodange process.

Soisson Rodange process (Soisson, Camille and Rodange): Engineering and Industry. See: Thrush.

Sokolskii-Bouillaud disease (Sokolskii, Grigorii Ivanovich and Bouillaud, Jean Baptiste). See: Bouillaud's disease.

SOKOLSKII, GRIGORII IVANOVICH. 1807-1886. Russian physician. See: Biog. Lex. hervorr. Aerzte. Bouillaud-Sokolskii disease.

Solander case (box or cover) (Solander, Daniel Charles): Library Science. See: Harrod; Partridge; Webster's 3d.

SOLANDER, DANIEL CHARLES. 1736-1782. Swedish botanist in England. See: Dict. Nat. Biog. Solander case (box or cover), Solandra.

Solandra (Solander, Daniel Charles): Botany. See: Charnock; Taylor, N.; Webster's 3d.

SOLDAINI, ARTURO. fl. 1897. Italian chemist. Cited in: Royal Soc. Cat. Sci. Pap., 1884-1900. Soldaini's reagent (or solution).

Soldaini's reagent (or solution) (Soldaini, Arturo): Medicine. See: Dorland; Stedman; Van Nostrand Chem. Dict.

Soldier's syndrome (Derivation undetermined): Medicine. See: Stedman.

SOLEIL, JEAN BAPTISTE FRANCOIS. 1798-1878. French optician. See: World Who's Who Sci. Soleil plate?

Soleil plate (Soleil, Jean Baptiste Francois?): Engineering and Industry. See: Internat. Dict. Phys. Elec.

SOLENTE, G. fl. 1935. French? physician. (Biography source unavailable.) Touraine-Solente-Gole syndrome.

Soller slits (Soller, Theodore): Physics. See: Thewlis.

SOLLER, THEODORE. 1927- . American physicist. See: Amer. Men and Women Sci., 12th ed. Soller slits.

SOLLY, RICHARD HORSEMAN. 1774-1858. English botanist. See: Boase. Sollya.

Sollya (Solly, Richard Horsman): Botany. See: Webster's 3d.

SOLOMON. d. ca 933 B.C. King of Israel. See: New Encyc. Brit., 1974, Macrop. ring of Solomon, Solomon (or Solomonic), Salomonica, Solomon's leaf, Solomon's lily, Solomon's plume, Solomon's seal (1), Solomon's seal (2), Solomon's zigzag.

Solomon (or Solomonic) (Solomon): Generic Word (wise man). See: Partridge; Webster's 3d.

Solomon R. Guggenheim Foundation (Guggenheim, Solomon R.): Philanthropy. Cited in: New Encyc. Brit., 1974, Microp under "Guggenheim, Meyer and Daniel."

Salomonica (Solomon): Architecture. See: Webster's 3d.

Solomon's leaf (Solomon): Botany. Cited in: Charnock.

Solomon's lily (Solomon): Botany. See: Gray; Webster's 3d.

Solomon's plume (Solomon): Botany. See: Webster's 3d.

Solomon's seal (1) (Solomon): Mythology. See: Webster's 3d.

Solomon's seal (2) (Solomon): Botany. See: Charnock; Partridge; Webster's 3d.

Solomon's zigzag (Solomon): Botany. See: Gray.

SOLON. ca 630-560 B.C. Greek statesman and poet. See: Encyc. Brit., 1974, Macrop. Solon, Solon's happiness, Solon's laws.

Solon (Solon, the lawgiver): Generic Word (lawmaker). See: Hendrickson; Partridge.

SOLONINA, R. fl. 1903. Russian chemist. (Biography source unavailable.) Solonina test reaction?

Solonina test reaction (Solonina, R.?): Chemistry. See: Van Nostrand Chem. Dict.

Solon's happiness (Solon): Generic Word (death). See: Phyfe.

Solon's laws (Solon): Law. See: Phyfe.

SOLVAY, ERNST. 1838-1922. Belgian chemist. See: World Who's Who Sci. Solvay process.

Solvay process (Solvay, Ernst): Chemistry. See: Ballentyne; Hackh; Thrush.

Somerset (Somerset, Fitzroy James Henry, 1st Baron Raglan): Generic Word (padded saddle). See: Partridge.

SOMERSET, EDWARD, MARQUESS OF WORCESTER AND EARL OF GLAMORGAN. 1601-1667. English general and scientist. See: Dict. Nat. Biog. Glamorgan Treaty.

SOMERSET, FITZROY JAMES HENRY, 1ST BARON RAGLAN. 1788-1855. English soldier. See: Dict. Nat. Biog. Raglan (overcoat), Raglan sleeve, Somerset.

SOMERSET, HENRY (1ST DUKE OF BEAUFORT OR BADMINTON). 1629-1700. English statesman. See: Dict. Nat. Biog. Badminton (cup).

SOMERSETT, JAMES. fl. 1772. Negro slave. Cited in: New Encyc. Brit., 1974, Microp. Somersett's case.

Somersett's case (Somersett, James): Law. See: Black.

SOMERVILLE. fl. early 19th c. English? scientist. Cited in: Bailey. Somervillite.

Somervillite (Somerville): Earth Sciences. See: Charnock.

SOMMELET, MARCEL. fl. 1906-1927. French chemist. See: Pogg., vols. 5, 6. Sommelet reaction, Sommelet rearrangement.

Sommelet reaction (Sommelet, Marcel): Chemistry. See: Ballentyne; Hackh; Van Nostrand Chem. Dict.

Sommelet rearrangement (Sommelet, Marcel): Chemistry. See: Van Nostrand Chem. Dict.

SOMMER, ROBERT (In full: KARL ROBERT). d. 1937. German psychologist. See: Psych. Register, 1932, p. 873 f. Sommer tridimensional analyser.

Sommer tridimensional analyser (Sommer, Robert): Psychology. See: Drever.

SOMMERFELD, ARNOLD JOHANNES. 1868-1951. German physicist. See: Pogg., vols. 4, 5, 6. Bohr-Sommerfeld atom, Bohr-Sommerfeld (old) quantum theory, Fermi-Dirac-Sommerfeld velocity-distribution law, Kossel-Sommerfeld displacement law (or law), Sommerfeld fine structure constant, Sommerfeld law of regular or relativistic doublets, Sommerfeld notation, Sommerfeld number, Sommerfeld orbits, Sommerfeld waves, Sommerfeld's equation (or formula), Sommerfeld's theory (of the thermal conductivity of metals).

Sommerfeld atom (Sommerfeld, Arnold Johannes). See: Bohr-Sommerfeld atom.

Sommerfeld fine structure constant (Sommerfeld, Arnold Johannes): Physics. See: Ballentyne; Internat. Dict. Ap. Math.

Sommerfeld-Kossel displacement law (or law) (Sommerfeld, Arnold Johannes and Kossel, Walther). See: Kossel-Sommerfeld displacement law (or law).

Sommerfeld law of regular or relativistic doublets (Sommerfeld, Arnold Johannes): Physics. See: Internat. Dict. Phys. Elec.

Sommerfeld notation (Sommerfeld, Arnold Johannes): Physics. See: Hackh.

Sommerfeld number (Summerfeld, Arnold Johannes): Engineering and Industry. See: Auger.

Sommerfeld orbits (Sommerfeld, Arnold Johannes): Physics. See: Thewlis.

Sommerfeld waves (Sommerfeld, Arnold Johannes): Physics. See: Thewlis.

Sommerfeld's equation (or formula) (Sommerfeld, Arnold Johannes): Physics. See: Markus; Internat. Dict. Phys. Elec.

Sommerfeld's theory (of the thermal conductivity of metals) (Sommerfeld, Arnold Johannes): Physics. See: Ballentyne.

SOMOGYI, MICHAEL. 1883-1971. Austrian-born American biochemist. See: Amer. Men Sci., 9th ed. Somogyi-Shaffer-Hartman method (or test), Somogyi unit.

Somogyi-Shaffer-Hartmann method (or test) (Somogyi, Michael; Shaffer, Philip Anderson; and Hartmann, Alexis Frank). See: Shaffer-Hartmann method.

Somogyi unit (Somogyi, Michael): Medicine. See: Stedman.

Song of Simeon (Simeon): Religion. See: Mathews, S.

SONN, ADOLF. b. 1882. German chemist. See: Pogg., vol. 6. Sonn-Mueller method.

Sonn-Mueller method (Sonn, Adolf and Mueller, Ernst): Chemistry. See: Van Nostrand Chem. Dict.

Sonne bacillus (Sonne, Carl Olaf): Medicine. See: Stedman.

Sonne camera (Sonne, Fred Theodore): Photography. See: Webster's 3d.

SONNE, CARL OLAF. 1882-1948. Danish bacteriologist. See: Dansk Biog. Lex. Sonne bacillus, Sonne dysentery.

Sonne dysentery (Sonne, Carl Olaf): Medicine. See: Dorland; Stedman.

SONNE, FRED THEODORE. 1899-1965. American engineer. See: Who Was Who Amer. Sonne camera.

SONNENBURG, EDUARD. 1848-1915. German surgeon. See: Deut. Biog. Jahrb., 1914-1916. Sonnenburg's test.

Sonnenburg's test (Sonnenburg, Eduard): Medicine. See: Dorland.

SONNENSCHEIN, FRANZ LEOPOLD. 1819-1879. German chemist. See: Pogg., vols. 2, 3, 7a suppl. Sonnenschein reagents for alkaloids.

Sonnenschein reagents for alkaloids (Sonnenschein, Franz Leopold): Chemistry. See: Hackh; Van Nostrand Chem. Dict.

SONNERAT, PIERRE. 1749-1814. French naturalist and traveler. See: Nouv. Biog. Univ. Sonneratia.

Sonneratia (Sonnerat, Pierre): Botany. See: Webster's 3d.

SONSTADT, EDWARD. fl. 1864-1899. English chemist. Cited in: Royal Soc. Cat. Sci. Pap., 1864-1873; 1884-1900. Sonstadt solution.

Sonstadt solution (Sonstadt, Edward). See: Thoulet solution.

SONTAG, HENRIETTE GERTRUDE WALPURGIS, COUNTESS ROSSI. 1803-1854. German singer and actress. See: Grove. Sontag (jacket).

Sontag (jacket) (Sontag, Henriette Gertrude Walpurgis, Countess Rossi): Fashion. See: Partridge.

SOPHIA CAROLINE. No dates. Margravine of Baden. (Biography source unavailable.) Carolinea.

Sophia-Jacoba process (Derivation undetermined). See: Vooys process.

Sophoclean irony (Sophocles): Literature. See: Barnet.

SOPHOCLES. ca. 496-406 B.C. Greek playwright. See: New Encyc. Brit., 1974. Sophoclean irony.

Sophy dynasty (Safi od-Din). See: Safavid dynasty.

Sorbite (Sorby, Henry Clifton): Chemistry. See: Webster's 3d.

SORBON, ROBERT DE. 1201-1274. French founder of University. See: Nouv. Biog. Univ. Sorbonist.

Sorbonist (Sorbon, Robert de): Religion. See: Charnock.

SORBY, HENRY CLIFTON. 1826-1908. English geologist and chemist. See: New Encyc. Brit., 1974, Microp. Sorbite.

SOREL. fl. 1867. French scientist. Cited in: Royal Soc. Cat. Sci. Pap., 1864-1873. Sorel cement, Sorel dental cement, Sorel floor cement.

Sorel cement (Sorel): Chemistry. See: Hackh; Thrush.

Sorel dental cement (Sorel): Chemistry. See: Hackh.

Sorel floor cement (Sorel): Chemistry. See: Hackh.

Sorel slag (Derivation undetermined): Engineering and Industry. See: Thrush.

SORET, C. d. 1931. French radiologist. (Biography source unavailable.) Soret's band.

SORET, CHARLES. 1854-1904. French physicist. See: Pogg., vols. 3, 4. Soret effect (or principle).

Soret effect (or principle) (Soret, Charles): Physics. See: Ballentyne; Hackh; Hughes. Also known as: Ludwig phenomenon.

Soret's band (Soret, C.): Medicine. See: Dorland; Stedman.

SORIANO, M. fl. 1952. Italian? physician. (Biography source unavailable.) Soriano's syndrome.

Soriano's syndrome (Soriano, M.): Medicine. See: Jablonski.

SORSBY, ARNOLD. fl. 1948-1967. English physician. See: Direct. Brit. Sci., 1966-1967. Sorsby's disease, Sorsby's macular degeneration, Sorsby's syndrome.

Sorsby's disease (Sorsby, Arnold): Medicine. See: Jablonski.

Sorsby's macular degeneration (Sorsby, Arnold): Medicine. See: Jablonski.

Sorsby's syndrome (Sorsby, Arnold): Medicine. See: Jablonski.

Sotadean (or Sotadic) verse (Sotades of Maroneia): Literature. See: Harvey; Partridge; Preminger.

SOTADES OF MARONEIA. fl. 276 B.C. Greek satiric poet. See: Harper. Sotadean (or Sotadic) verse.

SOTOS, JUAN FERNANDEZ. 1927- . Spanish-born American pediatrician. See: Amer. Men and Women Sci., 12th ed. Sotos' syndrome.

Sotos' syndrome (Sotos, Juan Fernandez): Medicine. See: Jablonski.

SOTTAS, JULES. b. 1866. French neurologist. See: Biog. Lex. hervorr. Aerzte. Dejerine-Sottas syndrome.

SOTTERY, CONSTANTINE THEODORE. 1896- . American chemist. See: Amer. Men Sci., 9th ed. Hammett-Sottery test for aluminum.

SOUBISE, CHARLES DE ROHAN, PRINCE DE. 1715-1787. French military leader. See: Nouv. Biog. Univ. Soubise (cravat), Soubise (sauce).

Soubise (cravat) (Soubise, Charles de Rohan, Prince de): Fashion. See: Partridge.

Soubise (sauce) (Soubise, Charles de Rohan, Prince de): Food and Drink. See: Hendrickson; Partridge; Webster's 3d.

SOULE, BYRON AVERY. b. 1891. American chemist. See: Amer. Men Sci., 5th ed. Soule test reaction.

Soule test reaction (Soule, Byron Avery): Chemistry. See: Van Nostrand Chem. Dict.

SOULIER, JEAN PIERRE. 1915- . French hematologist. See: Who's Who Sci. Europe, 1972. Bernard-Soulier syndrome.

SOUQUES, ALEXANDER ACHILLE. 1860-1944. French physician. See: Biog. Lex. hervorr. Aerzte. Souques-Charcot geroderma.

Souques-Charcot geroderma (Souques, Alexander Achille and Charcot, Jean Martin): Medicine. See: Jablonski.

SOUSA, JOHN PHILIP. 1854-1932. American bandmaster. See: Dict. Amer. Biog. Sousaphone.

Sousaphone (Sousa, John Philip): Music. See: Apel; Partridge.

SOUTHCOTT, JOANNA. 1750-1814. English visionary and founder of religious sect. See: Dict. Nat. Biog. Joanna Southcotts' box, Joannas, Southcottians.

Southcottians (Southcott, Joanna): Religion. See: Brewer; Canney; Latham. Also known as: Joannes.

SOUTHERN, JOHN. 1758-1815. English engineer. Cited in: Royal Soc. Cat. Sci. Pap., 1800-1863. Southern steam indicator.

Southern steam indicator (Southern, John): Engineering and Industry. See: Auger.

SOUTHEY, REGINALD S. 1835-1899. English physician. See: Who Was Who, 1897-1916. Southey's tubes.

Southey's tubes (Southey, Reginald S.): Medicine. See: Dorland; Stedman.

SOUTHWORTH, HAMILTON. 1907- . American physican. See: World Who's Who Sci. Southworth's sympton complex.

Southworth's symptom complex (Southworth, Hamilton): Medicine. See: Jablonski.

Souvenir de Madame Salati-Mongellaz, Archduchesse Marie Immaculate (rose) (Salati-Mongellaz, Archduchesse Marie Immaculate): Botany. See: Hendrickson.

SOUZA, ANTONIO JOSE ALVES DE. fl. 20th c. Brazilian mineralogist. Cited in: Min. Mag., vol. 28 (March 1947- Sept. 1949), p. 739. Souzalite.

Souzalite (Souza, Antonio Jose Alves de): Earth Sciences. See: Thrush; Webster's 3d.

Soxhlet apparatus (or extractor) (Soxhlet, Franz Ritter von): Chemistry. See: Hackh; Van Nostrand Chem. Dict.; Webster's 3d.

SOXHLET, FRANZ RITTER VON. 1848-1926. German agricultural chemist. See: Pogg., vols. 3, 4. Soxhlet apparatus (or extractor), Soxhlet thimble?

Soxhlet thimble (Soxhlet, Franz Ritter von?): Engineering and Industry. See: Thrush.

SOYER, J. fl. 1919. French chemist. Cited in: Chem. Abstr., vol. 13, p. 294. Soyer test.

Soyer test (Soyer, J.): Chemistry. See: Van Nostrand Chem. Dict.

SOYKA, ISIDOR. 1850-1889. Czechoslovakian pathologist. See: Biog. Lex. hervorr. Aerzte. Soyka's plates.

Soyka's plates (Soyka, Isidor): Medicine. See: Dorland.

space of Retzius (Retzius, Anders Adolf). See: Retzius' space.

Spackman system (Spackman, William, Jr.): Engineering and Industry. See: Thrush.

SPACKMAN, WILLIAM, JR. 1919- . American geologist. See: Amer. Men Sci., 10th ed. Spackman system.

SPACU, GHEORGHE. 1883-1955. Rumanian chemist. See: Pogg., vol. 6. Spacu-Kuras reagent, Spacu-Spacu test for iodate, Spacu-Spacu test for thiosulfate, Spacu test reaction for cadmium, Spacu test reaction for zinc, Spacu test reactions for copper.

Spacu-Kuras reagent (Spacu, Gheorghe and Kuras, M.): Chemistry. See: Van Nostrand Chem. Dict.

SPACU, P. fl. 1927-1956. Rumanian chemist. Cited in: Chem. Abstr., Decen. Index, 1927-1936; 1937-1946; 1947-1956. Spacu-Spacu test for iodate, Spacu-Spacu test for thiosulfate.

Spacu-Spacu test for iodate (Spacu, Gheorghe and Spacu, P.): Chemistry. See: Van Nostrand Chem. Dict.

Spacu-Spacu test for thiosulfate (Spacu, Gheorghe and Spacu, P.): Chemistry. See: Van Nostrand Chem. Dict.

Spacu test reaction for cadmium (Spacu, Gheorghe): Chemistry. See: Van Nostrand Chem. Dict.

Spacu test reaction for zinc (Spacu, Gheorghe): Chemistry. See: Van Nostrand Chem. Dict.

Spacu test reactions for copper (Spacu, Gheorghe): Chemistry. See: Van Nostrand Chem. Dict.

SPADA DE' MEDICI, LAVINIO. 1801-1863. Italian writer, politician, and mineralogist. See: Diz. Encic. Ital. Spadaite.

Spadaite (Spada de' Medici, Lavinio): Earth Sciences. See: Webster's 3d.

SPAHLINGER, HENRY. 1882- . Swiss bacteriologist. See: World Who's Who Sci. Spahlinger's treatment.

Spahlinger's treatment (Spahlinger, Henry): Medicine. See: Dorland.

Spahr report (Spahr, Robert Hoover): Engineering and Industry. See: Good.

SPAHR, ROBERT HOOVER. 1883- . American engineer and educator. See: Who's Who Engin., 1941. Spahr report.

Spaldeen (ball) (Spalding, Albert Goodwill): Recreation and Sports. See: Hendrickson.

SPALDING, ALBERT GOODWILL. 1850-1915. American sportsman. See: Dict. Amer. Biog. Spaldeen (ball), Spalding (baseball).

Spalding (baseball) (Spalding, Albert Goodwill): Recreation and Sports. See: Hendrickson.

SPALLANZANI, LAZARO. 1722-1799. Italian priest and biologist. See: World Who's Who Sci. Spallanzani's law.

Spallanzani's law (Spallanzani, Lazaro): Medicine. See: Dorland; Stedman.

SPANG, NORMAN. fl. 19thc. American mineralogist. Cited in: Bailey. Spangolite.

Spangolite (Spang, Norman): Earth Sciences. See: Thrush; Webster's 3d.

SPANLANG, HERBERT. fl. 1937. Austrian ophthalmologist. (Biography source unavailable.) Spanlang-Tappeiner syndrome.

Spanlang-Tappeiner syndrome (Spanlang, Herbert and Tappeiner, Sepp): Medicine. See: Jablonski.

SPARMANN, ANDREAS. 1747-1820. Swedish botanist. See: World Who's Who Sci. Sparmannia.

Sparmannia (Sparmann, Andreas): Botany. See: Taylor, N.; Webster's 3d.

Spartacists (Spartacus): History. See: Brewer; Partridge.

SPARTACUS. ca. 113-71 B.C. Thracian gladiator and rebel. See: Encyc. Brit., 1911. Spartacists, Spartacus' Insurrection.

Spartacus' Insurrection (Spartacus): History. See: Phyfe.

SPATZ, HUGO. fl. 1922. German neuropathologist. (Biography source unavailable.) Hallervorden-Spatz syndrome.

Spaulding rule (Derivation undetermined): Engineering and Industry. See: Winburne.

Spearman-Brown formula (Spearman, Charles Edward and Brown, W.): Psychology. See: English; Hoult; Kendall. Also known as: Brown-Spearman prophecy formula, Brown's formula, Spearman's prophecy formula.

SPEARMAN, CHARLES EDWARD. 1863-1945. English psychologist. See: Internat. Encyc. Soc. Sci. Spearman-Brown formula, Spearman estimator, Spearman-Kaerber method, Spearman two factor theorem, Spearman's footrule method of gains, Spearman's rho.

Spearman estimator (Spearman, Charles Edward): Statistics. See: Kendall.

Spearman-Kaerber method (Spearman, Charles Edward and Kaerber, Gerhard Hermann): Statistics. See: Kendall.

Spearman two factor theorem (Spearman, Charles Edward): Statistics. See: Kendall.

Spearman's footrule method of gains (Spearman, Charles Edward): Statistics. See: Good; Kendall; Wolman.

Spearman's rho (Spearman, Charles Edward): Statistics. See: Kendall.

specific acoustical Ohm (Ohm, Georg Simon): Physics. See: Dresner.

SPEDDING, CHARLES. fl. ca. 1740-1750. English inventor. Cited in: Singer. Spedding's flint mill.

Spedding's flint mill (Spedding, Charles): Engineering and Industry. See: Thrush.

SPEE, FERDINAND GRAF VON. 1855-1937. German embryologist. See: Wer ist's?, 1906. curve of Spee.

SPEERS, BILLY. fl. 1820. American mineworker. (Biography source unavailable.) Billy cups.

SPEHL, PAUL EMILE. b. 1887. Belgian physician and pharmacologist. See: Who's Who Sci. Europe, 1972. Spehl solution.

Spehl solution (Spehl, Paul Emile): Chemistry. See: Van Nostrand Chem. Dict.

SPEKE, JOHN HANNING. 1827-1864. English explorer in Africa. See: Dict. Nat. Biog. Speke's antelope.

Speke's antelope (Speke, John Hanning): Zoology. See: Webster's 3d.

SPEMANN, HANS. 1869-1941. German zoologist. See: World Who's Who Sci. Spemann's induction, Spemann's organiser.

Spemann's induction (Spemann, Hans): Physiology. See: Dorland.

Spemann's organiser (Spemann, Hans): Zoology. See: Gray.

Spence automatic desulfurizer (Derivation undetermined): Engineering and Industry. See: Thrush.

Spence furnace (Derivation undetermined): Engineering and Industry. See: Thrush.

SPENCE, HUGH S. fl. 1925. Canadian geologist and mineralogist. Cited in: Min. Mag., vol. 32, pt. 2 (1959-1961), p. 981. Spence shale?, Spencite.

Spence shale (Spence, Hugh S.?): Earth Sciences. See: Thrush.

SPENCE, THOMAS. 1750-1814. English bookseller and socialist. See: Dict. Nat. Biog. Spencean philanthropists (or system).

Spencean philanthropists (or system) (Spence, Thomas): Politics. See: Brewer.

Spencer carbine (or rifle) (Spencer, Christopher Miner): Weapons. See: Hendrickson under "Spencer, Spencer Rifle...", Mathews, M. M., Quick.

SPENCER, CHARLES, 3RD EARL OF SUTHERLAND. 1644-1722. English statesman and bibliophile. See: Dict. Nat. Biog. Spencer (wig).

SPENCER, CHRISTOPHER MINER. 1833-1922. American inventor and manufacturer. See: Dict. Amer. Biog. Spencer carbine (or rifle).

Spencer-Fano method (Spencer, Roy Clarence and Fano, Ugo): Physics. See: Internat. Dict. Ap. Math.

Spencer formula (Spencer, J.): Statistics. See: Kendall.

SPENCER, GEORGE (4TH DUKE OF MARLBOROUGH). 1739-1817. English politician. See: Dict. Nat. Biog. Marlborough foot, Marlborough leg.

SPENCER, GEORGE JOHN. 1758-1834. English statesman. See: Dict. Nat. Biog. Spencer (men's jacket).

SPENCER, HERBERT. 1820-1903. English philosopher. See: Internat. Encyc. Soc. Sci. Spencerian (or Spencerianism), Spencer's stages of society, Spencer's theory of change.

SPENCER, J. fl. 1904. English statistician. Cited in: Kendall and Doig, vol. 1. Spencer formula.

SPENCER, JOHN CHARLES (VISCOUNT ALTHORP). 1782-1845. English statesman. See: Dict. Nat. Biog. Althorp's Irish Church Act.

SPENCER, KNIGHT. fl. 1803. English garment designer. (Biography source unavailable.) Spencer (women's jacket).

SPENCER, LEONARD JAMES. 1870-1959. English mineralogist. See: World Who's Who. Sci. Spencerite.

Spencer (men's jacket) (Spencer, George John): Fashion. See: Charnock; Hendrickson; Partridge.

Spencer-Parker vaccine (Spencer, Roscoe Ray and Parker, Ralph Robinson): Medicine. See: Dorland.

SPENCER, PLATT ROGERS. 1800-1864. American calligraphist. See: Dict. Amer. Biog. Spencerian handwriting (penmanship or script).

SPENCER, ROSCOE ROY. b. 1880. American physician. See: Amer. Men Sci., 10th ed. Spencer-Parker vaccine.

SPENCER, ROY CLARENCE. 1901- . American physicist. See: World Who's Who Sci. Spencer-Fano method.

SPENCER, WALTER. No dates. English? physician. (Biography source unavailable.) Spencer's disease.

Spencer (wig) (Spencer, Charles, 3rd Earl of Sutherland): Fashion. See: Stenhouse.

Spencer (women's jacket) (Spencer, Knight): Fashion. See: Partridge; Picken.

Spencerian (or Spencerianism) (Spencer, Herbert): Philosophy. See: Hendrickson under "Spencerian..."; Partridge; Webster's 3d.

Spencerian handwriting (penmanship or script) (Spencer, Platt Rogers): Applied Arts. See: Brewer; Hendrickson; Webster's 3d.

Spencerite (Spencer, Leonard James): Earth Sciences. See: Thrush; Webster's 3d.

Spencer's disease (Spencer, Walter): Medicine. See: Jablonski. Also known as: Bradley's disease, Goodall's disease.

Spencer's stages of society (Spencer, Herbert): Sociology. See: Zadrozny.

Spencer's theory of change (Spencer, Herbert): Sociology. See: Zadrozny.

Spencite (Spence, Hugh S.): Earth Sciences. See: Thrush.

SPENER, PHILIPP JACOB. 1635-1705. German Protestant theologian. See: Encyc. Brit., 1911. Spenerism.

Spenerism (Spener, Philipp Jacob): Religion. See: Webster's 3d.

SPENGLER, CARL. 1860-1937. Swiss physician. See: Biog. Lex. hervorr. Aerzte. Spengler's fragments, Spengler's method, Spengler's tuberculin.

SPENGLER, OSWALD. 1880-1936. German writer on philosophy of history. See: New Encyc. Brit., 1974, Microp. Spenglerian.

SPENGLER, THEODORE. fl. 1911. Swiss chemist. Cited in: Chem. Abstr., vol. 5, p. 3423. Pictet-Spengler isoquinoline synthesis.

Spenglerian (Spengler, Oswald): History. See: Webster's 3d.

Spengler's fragments (Spengler, Carl): Medicine. See: Dorland; Stedman.

Spengler's method (Spengler, Carl): Medicine. See: Stedman.

Spengler's tuberculin (Spengler, Carl): Medicine. See: Dorland; Stedman.

SPENLOW. Character from Charles Dickens' novel, "David Copperfield", (1849-50). See: Harvey. Spenlow and Jorkins.

Spenlow and Jorkins (Spenlow and Jorkins): Generic Word. See: Partridge.

Spens report (Spens, Sir Will): Education. See: Good.

Spens' syndrome (Spens, Thomas). See: Morgagni-Adams-Stokes syndrome.

SPENS, THOMAS. 1769-1842. Scottish physician. See: Biog. Lex. hervorr. Aerzte. Spens' syndrome.

SPENS, SIR WILL. 1882-1962. English educator. See: Who Was Who. Spens report.

SPENSER, EDMUND. ca. 1552-1559. English poet. See: Dict. Nat. Biog. School of Spenser, Spenserian, Spenserian sonnet, Spenserian stanza (or Spenserians).

Spenserian (Spenser, Edmund): Literature. See: Barnhart (Eng. Lit.); Partridge; Webster's 3d.

Spenserian sonnet (Spenser, Edmund): Literature. See: Scott; Webster's 3d.

Spenserian stanza (or Spenserians) (Spenser, Edmund): Literature. See: Brewer; Partridge; Scott.

SPERRY, ELMER AMBROSE. 1860-1930. American electrical engineer. See: Dict. Amer. Biog. Sperry process.

SPERRY, FRANCIS L. fl. 19th c. Canadian chemist. Cited in: Royal Soc. Cat. Sci. Pap., 1884-1900. Sperrylite.

Sperry process (Sperry, Elmer Ambrose): Engineering and Industry. See: Thrush; Van Nostrand Chem. Dict.

Sperrylite (Sperry, Francis L.): Earth Sciences. See: Thrush; Van Nostrand Sci. Encyc.; Webster's 3d.

sphincter of Oddi (Oddi, Ruggero). See: Oddi's sphincter.

SPIEGEL, LEOPOLD JULIUS. 1865-1927. German chemist. See: Pogg., vols. 4, 5, 6. Spiegel-Maass test.

Spiegel-Maas test (Spiegel, Leopold Julius and Maass, Theodor A.): Chemistry. See: Van Nostrand Chem. Dict.

Spieghel, Adrian van der. See: Spigelius, Adrian.

SPIEGLER, EDUARD. 1860-1908. Austrian dermatologist. See: Biog. Lex. hervorr. Aerzte. Spiegler-Fendt sarcoid (or sarcomatosis), Spiegler's reagent (or test) for albumin in urine, Spiegler's tumor.

Spiegler-Fendt sarcoid (or sarcomatosis) (Spiegler, Eduard and Fendt, Heinrich). See: Baefverstedt's syndrome.

Spiegler's reagent (or test) for albumin in urine (Spiegler, Eduard): Medicine. See: Ballentyne; Stedman; Van Nostrand Chem. Dict.

Spiegler's tumor (Spiegler, Eduard): Medicine. See: Jablonski. Also known as: Ancell-Spiegler cylindroma.

Spiel engine (Spiel, Johannes): Engineering and Industry. See: Auger.

SPIEL, JOHANNES. fl. 1884. German? engineer. (Biography source unavailable.) Spiel engine.

SPIELMANN, JACOB REINBOLD. 1722-1783. French chemist. See: World Who's Who Sci. Spielmannia.

Spielmannia (Spielmann, Jacob Reinbold): Botany. See: Charnock.

Spielmeyer-Vogt disease (Spielmeyer Walter and Vogt, Oskar). See: Stock-Spielmeyer-Vogt syndrome.

SPIELMEYER, WALTER. b. 1879. German physician. See: Biog. Lex hervorr. Aerzte. Spielmeyer's acute swelling, Stock-Spielmeyer-Vogt syndrome.

Spielmeyer's acute swelling (Spielmeyer, Walter): Medicine. See: Stedman.

SPIES, TOM DOUGLAS. 1902- . American physician. See: World Who's Who Sci. Vilter-Spies-Mathews test reaction.

Spigelia (Spigelius, Adrian): Botany. See: Taylor, N.

Spigelian hernia (Spigelius, Adrian): Medicine. See: Stedman.

SPIGELIUS, ADRIAN (VAN DER SPIEGHEL). 1578-1625. Flemish botanist and anatomist. See: Biog. Nat. de Belgique. Spigelia, Spigelian hernia, Spigelius' line, Spigelius' lobe.

Spigelius' line (Spigelius, Adrian): Anatomy. See: Donath; Stedman.

Spigelius' lobe (Spigelius, Adrian): Anatomy. See: Donath; Henderson; Stedman.

SPILHAUS, ATHELSTAN FREDERICK. 1911- . South African born American meteorologist and oceanographer. See: Amer. Men Sci., 11th ed. Spilhaus-Miller sea samples, Spilhaus space clock.

Spilhaus-Miller sea sampler (Spilhaus, Athelstan Frederick and Miller, Arthur R.): Engineering and Industry. See: Thrush.

Spilhaus space clock (Spilhaus, Athelstan Frederick): Engineering and Industry. Cited in: Amer. Men Sci., 11th ed.

SPILLER, WILLIAM GIBSON. 1863-1940. American neurologist. See: Who Was Who Amer. Frazier-Spiller operation, Spiller's syndrome.

Spiller's syndrome (Spiller, William Gibson): Medicine. See: Jablonski.

Spinelli operation (Spinelli, Pier Giuseppe): Medicine. See: Dorland; Stedman.

SPINELLI, PIER GIUSEPPE. 1862-1929. Italian gynecologist. See: Biog. Lex. hervorr. Aerzte. Spinelli operation.

Spinet (Spinetti, Giovanni): Music. See: Hendrickson; Partridge.

SPINETTI, GIOVANNI. fl. 1500. Italian manufacturer of musical instruments. See: Webster's Biog. Dict. Spinet.

SPINOZA, BENEDICT (OR BARUCH) DE. 1632-1677. Dutch philosopher. See: Internat. Encyc. Soc. Sci. Spinozism.

Spinozism (Spinoza, Benedict de): Philosophy. See: Canney; Webster's 3d.

SPIRA, LEO. fl. 1930. English? biochemist. (Biography source unavailable.) Spira's disease.

Spira's disease (Spira, Leo): Medicine. See: Jablonski.

Spirelmo smoke helmet (Derivation undetermined): Engineering and Industry. See: Thrush.

spirit of Mindererus (Minderer, Raymond): Chemistry. See: Dorland.

SPIRO, KARL. 1867-1932. German physiological chemist. See: Pogg., vol. 6. Moffatt-Spiro test?, Spiro test reaction for hydrogen peroxide, Spiro's test (for ammonia and urea).

Spiro test reaction for hydrogen peroxide (Spiro, Karl): Chemistry. See: Van Nostrand Chem. Dict.

SPIROFF, KIRIL. 1901- . Bulgarian-born American geologist and mineralogist. See: Amer. Men Sci., 11th ed. Spiroffite.

Spiroffite (Spiroff, Kiril): Earth Sciences. See: Thrush.

Spiro's test (for ammonia and urea) (Spiro, Karl): Medicine. See: Dorland; Stedman.

Spisula (Spix, Johann Baptist von): Zoology. See: Webster's 3d.

Spitz-Holter valve (Derivation undetermined): Medicine. See: Van Nostrand Sci. Encyc. under "Artificial Organs."

SPITZER, ALEXANDER. fl. 1923. Austrian anatomist. Cited in: Kelly. Spitzer's theory.

SPITZER, FRANK L. 1926- . Austrian-born American mathematician. See: Amer. Men Sci., 11th ed. Spitzer's identity.

Spitzer's identity (Spitzer, Frank L.): Statistics. See: Kendall.

Spitzer's theory (Spitzer, Alexander): Anatomy. See: Stedman.

SPITZKA, EDWARD CHARLES. 1852-1914. American neurologist and psychiatrist. See: Amer. Men Sci., 11th ed. Spitzka's bundle, Spitzka's nucleus, Spitzka's marginal tract (or zone).

Spitzka's bundle (Spitzka, Edward Charles): Anatomy. See: Donath; Dorland; Stedman.

Spitzka's marginal tract (or zone) (Spitzka, Edward Charles): Anatomy. See: Dorland; Stedman. Also known as: Lissauer's tract (column, fasciculus, zone or column of Lissauer).

Spitzka's nucleus (Spitzka, Edward Charles). See: Perlia's nucleus.

SPIX, JOHANN BAPTIST VON. 1781-1826. German zoologist and anatomist. See: Allg. Deut. Biog. Spisula, Spix's spine.

Spix's spine (Spix, Johann Baptist von): Anatomy. See: Dorland; Stedman.

SPLENDORE, ALPHONSO. fl. 1912. Italian physician in Brazil. See: Ann. Univers. Roma, 1913/1914, pp. 191-193. Lutz-Splendore-de Almeida syndrome.

SPODE, JOSIAH. 1754-1827. English potter. See: Dict. Nat. Biog. Spode (porcelain ware).

Spode (porcelain ware) (Spode, Josiah): Applied Arts. See: Hendrickson; Partridge.

SPOERER, GUSTAV-FRIEDRICH WILHELM. 1822-1896. German astronomer. See: World Who's Who Sci. Spoerer's law.

Spoerer's law (Spoerer, Gustav-Friedrich Wilhelm): Astronomy. See: Satterthwaite.

Sponer-Franck, Hertha. See: Sponer, Hertha.

SPONER, HERTHA DOROTHEA ELISABETH. b. 1895. German physicist. See: Pogg., vols. 6, 7a. Birge-Sponer extrapolation.

spongiform pustule of Kogoj (Kogoj, Franjo): Medicine. See: Stedman.

SPOONER, WILLIAM ARCHIBALD. 1844-1930. English clergyman and educator. See: Dict. Nat. Biog. Spoonerism.

Spoonerism (Spooner, William Archibald): Generic Word. See: Brewer; Hendrickson; Partridge.

SPOTTISWOODE, ANDREW. 1787-1866. English printer. See: Boase. Spottiswoode press.

Spottiswoode press (Spottiswoode, Andrew): Printing. See: Lockwood.

SPRAGUE, ISAAC. 1811-1895. American illustrator of botanical works. (Biography source unavailable.) Sprague's grass, Sprague's lark, Sprague's pipit.

SPRAGUE, JOSEPH A. No dates. American photographer. (Biography source unavailable.) Joseph A. Sprague Memorial Award.

Sprague's grass (Sprague, Isaac): Botany. See: Webster's 3d.

Sprague's lark (Sprague, Isaac): Zoology. See: Mathews, M. M.

Sprague's pipit (Sprague, Isaac): Zoology. See: Mathews, M.M.; Webster's 3d.

Sprekelia (Sprekelson, J. H. von): Botany. See: Taylor, N.

SPREKELSON, J. H. VON. No dates. German botanist. (Biography source unavailable.) Sprekelia.

Sprengel explosive (Sprengel, Herman Johannes Philip): Engineering and Industry. See: Webster's 3d.

SPRENGEL, HERMAN JOHANNES PHILIP. 1834-1906. German-born English chemist. See: Dict. Nat. Biog. Sprengel explosive, Sprengel mercury pump, Sprengel tube.

Sprengel mercury pump (Sprengel, Herman Johannes Philip): Engineering and Industry. See: Hackh; Van Nostrand Sci. Encyc. under "Air Pumps"; Webster's 3d.

SPRENGEL, OTTO GERHARD KARL. 1852-1915. German surgeon. See: Biog. Lex. hervorr. Aerzte. Sprengel's deformity.

Sprengel tube (Sprengel, Herman Johannes Philip): Engineering and Industry. See: Webster's 3d; Winburne.

Sprengel's deformity (Sprengel, Otto Gerhard Karl): Medicine. See: Dorland; Jablonski; Stedman.

Sprenger asparagus (Derivation undetermined): Botany. See: Winburne.

Springfield type of amortization (Derivation undetermined): Business. See: Winburne.

SPRINZ, HELMUTH. 1911- . German-born American pathologist. See: Amer. Men and Women Sci., 12th ed. Dubin-Sprinz syndrome.

Sproat (fishhook) (Sproat, W. H.): Recreation and Sports. See: Hendrickson.

SPROAT, W. H. fl. 19th c. English angler. (Biography source unavailable.) Sproat (fishhook).

SPURR, JOSIAH EDWARD. 1870-1950. American geologist. See: World Who's Who Sci. Spurrite.

Spurrite (Spurr, Josiah Edward): Earth Sciences. See: Webster's 3d

SPURSTOWE, WILLIAM. 1605?-1666. English Nonconformist divine. See: Dict. Nat. Biog. Smectymnians.

Spurway-Eddowes syndrome (Spurway, John and Eddowes, Alfred). See: Lobstein's syndrome (or disease).

SPURWAY, JOHN. fl. 1896. English physician. (Biography source unavailable.) Spurway-Eddowes syndrome.

Squeers (Squeers, the headmaster): Generic Word (shady headmaster). See: Partridge.

SQUEERS, THE HEADMASTER. Character from Charles Dickens' novel "Nicholas Nickleby", (1839). See: Harvey. Squeers.

SQUIRE, TRUMANN HOFFMAN. 1823-1889. American surgeon. Cited in: Index-Cat. Libr. Surg.-Gen. Off., 1st Ser., vol. 13, 1892. Squire's catheter.

Squire's catheter (Squire, Trumann Hoffman): Medicine. See: Dorland.

SRB, J. fl. 1865. Austrian? physician. (Biography source unavailable.) Srb's syndrome.

Srb's syndrome (Srb, J.): Medicine. See: Jablonski.

Ssabanejew-Frank operation (Ssabanejew, J. and Frank, Rudolf): Medicine. See: Dorland.

SSABANEJEW, J. fl. 19th c.? Russian surgeon. (Biography source unavailable.) Ssabanejew-Frank operation.

STACKE, LUDWIG. 1859-1918. German otologist. See: Biog. Lex. hervorr. Aerzte. Schwartze-Stacke operation, Stacke operation.

Stacke operation (Stacke, Ludwig): Medicine. See: Dorland; Stedman.

STACKHOUSE, JOHN. 1742-1819. English botanist. See: Dict. Nat. Biog. Stackhousia.

Stackhousia (Stackhouse, John): Botany. See: Webster's 3d.

STACY, EDNEY WEBB. 1919- . American mathematical statistician. See: Amer. Men Sci., 11th ed. Stacy's distribution?

Stacy's distribution (Stacy, Edney Webb?): Statistics. See: Kendall.

STADDON, D. E. fl. 1913. English chemist. Cited in: Chem. Abstr., vol. 7, p. 1149. Staddon test.

Staddon test (Staddon, D. E.): Chemistry. See: Van Nostrand Chem. Dict.

STADER, OTTO. b. 1894. American veterinary surgeon. (Biography source unavailable.) Stader splint.

Stader splint (Stader, Otto): Medicine. See: Dorland; Stedman; Webster's 3d.

STADERINI, RUTILIO. fl. 1892-1900. Italian neuroanatomist. Cited in: Royal Soc. Cat. Sci. Pap., 1884-1900. Staderini's nucleus.

Staderini's nucleus (Staderini, Rutilio): Anatomy. See: Dorland; Stedman.

STADLER, ANTON. 1753-1812. Austrian clarinet player. See: Baker. Stadler Quintet.

Stadler Quintet (Stadler, Anton): Music. See: Scholes.

Stadlin test (Stadlin, W.): Chemistry. See: Van Nostrand Chem. Dict.

STADLIN, W. fl. 1917. German chemist. Cited in: Chem. Abstr., vol. 11, p. 1695. Stadlin test.

STADLINGER, HERMANN FRIEDRICH AUGUST. 1875-1961. German chemist. See: Pogg., vols. 6, 7a. Stadlinger test reactions.

Stadlinger test reactions (Stadlinger, Hermann Friedrich August): Chemistry. See: Van Nostrand Chem. Dict.

STAEBLE, FRANZ. 1876-1950. German optician. See: Pogg., vol. 7a. Staeble-Lihotzky condition.

Staeble-Lihotzky condition (Staeble, Franz and Lihotzky): Physics. See: Internat. Dict. Ap. Math.

Staedel-Ruegheimer pyrazine synthesis (Staedel, Wilhelm and Ruegheimer, Leopold): Chemistry. See: Van Nostrand Chem. Dict.

STAEDEL, WILHELM. 1843-1919. German chemist. See: Pogg., vols. 3, 4, 5. Staedel-Ruegheimer pyrazine synthesis.

STAEHLER, ARTHUR (In full: FRIEDRICH ARTHUR). b. 1877. German chemist. See: Pogg., vols. 5, 6. Staehler test reaction?

Staehler test reaction (Staehler, Arthur?): Chemistry. See: Van Nostrand Chem. Dict.

STAEHLI, JEAN. b. 1890. Swiss ophthalmologist. (Biography source unavailable.) Hudson-Staehli line.

Staehli's line (Staehli, Jean). See: Hudson-Staehli line.

staff of Mercury (Mercury): Medicine. See: Stedman.

Stafford Press (Stafford, Simon): Printing. See: Lockwood.

STAFFORD, SIMON. fl. 1596-1626. English printer. Cited in: Dict. Cat. Hist. Print. Stafford Press.

STAFNE, EDWARD CHRISTIAN. b. 1894. American oral pathologist. See: Amer. Men Sci., 9th ed. Stafne's mandibular defect (or cyst).

Stafne's mandibular defect (or cyst) (Stafne, Edward Christian): Dentistry. See: Jablonski.

STAHL, FRIEDRICH KARL. 1811-1873. German physician. See: Biog. Lex. hervorr. Aerzte. Stahl's ear.

STAHL, GEORGE ERNST. 1660-1734. German physician and chemist. See: Encyc. Brit., 1973. Stahl's phlogiston theory (or Stahlian).

Stahl reaction for orientation of hydroxyl group (Derivation undetermined): Chemistry. See: Van Nostrand Chem. Dict.

STAHL, RUDOLF. b. 1889. German physician. See: Wer Ist's? 1962. Stahl's original applicator?

Stahl test for moisture (Derivation undetermined): Chemistry. See: Van Nostrand Chem. Dict.

Stahl test for pyrogallol (Derivation undetermined): Chemistry. See: Van Nostrand Chem. Dict.

Stahl's ear (Stahl, Friedrich Karl): Medicine. See: Dorland; Stedman.

Stahl's original applicator (Stahl, Rudolf?): Chemistry. See: Van Nostrand Sci. Encyc. under "Electrophoresis."

Stahl's phlogiston theory (or Stahlian): Chemistry. See: Ballentyne; Stedman; Webster's 3d.

STAHR, HERMANN. b. 1868. German anatomist and pathologist. See: Biog. Lex. hervorr. Aerzte. Stahr's gland.

Stahr's gland (Stahr, Hermann): Anatomy. See: Dorland.

STAINIER, XAVIER. b. 1865. Belgian geologist. See: Seyn. Stainierite.

Stainierite (Stainier, Xavier): Earth Sciences. See: Thrush; Webster's 3d.

STAINTON, C. W. fl. 1892. American dentist. (Biography source unavailable.) Stainton's syndrome.

Stainton-Capdepont syndrome (Stainton, C. W. and Capdepont, Charles). See: Capdepont's syndrome.

Stainton's syndrome (Stainton, C. W.). See: Capdepont's syndrome.

STAJANO, CARLOS. fl. 1946. Spanish physician. Cited in: Index-Cat. Libr. Surg.-Gen. Off., 5th Ser., vol. 1, 1959. Stajano's subcostal syndrome.

Stajano's subcostal syndrome (Stajano, Carlos). See: Fitzhugh's syndrome.

STAKHANOV, ALEKSEI GRIGORIEVICH. 1905-   . Russian miner. See: Webster's Biog. Dict. Stakhanovite (or Stakhanovism).

Stakhanovite (or Stakhanovism) (Stakhanov, Aleksei Grigorievich): Engineering and Industry. See: Brewer; Hendrickson; Partridge.

STALIN, JOSEPH (Real name: IOSIF VISSARIONOVICH DZHUGASHVILI). 1879-1953. Russian political leader. See: Encyc. Brit., 1973. de-Stalinization; Stalin tank; Stalinism.

Stalin tank (Stalin, Joseph): Weapons. See: Quick.

Stalinism (Stalin, Joseph): Politics. See: Hendrickson; Webster's 3d.

STAMM, JOHANNES. b. 1881. German pharmaceutical chemist and pharmacognosist. See: Pogg., vol. 7a. Stamm reaction for boric acid, Stamm reagent for cyanide? Stamm test for decomposition in oils and fats.

Stamm reaction for boric acid (Stamm, Johannes): Chemistry. See: Van Nostrand Chem. Dict.

Stamm reagent for cyanide (Stamm, Johannes?): Chemistry. See: Van Nostrand Chem. Dict.

Stamm test for decomposition in oils and fats (Stamm, Johannes): Chemistry. See: Van Nostrand Chem. Dict.

Stanbury-Hedge defect (Stanbury, John Bruton, and Hedge, Alice N.): Medicine. See: Jablonski.

STANBURY, JOHN BRUTON. 1915-   . American physician. See: Amer. Men and Women Sci., 12th ed. Stanbury-Hedge defect.

stand Sam (Wilson, Samuel). See: Sam (or stand Sam).

Standt's theorem (Derivation undetermined): Mathematics. See: Ballentyne.

STANEK, J. fl. 1850. Czechoslovakian scientist. Cited in: Đana. Stanekite.

Stanekite (Stanek, J.): Earth Sciences. See: Thrush.

Stanford-Binet test (or scale) (Stanford University and Binet, Alfred): Psychology. See: Chaplin; English; Hinsie; Webster's 3d.

Stanford joint (Stanford, Leland?): Engineering and Industry. See: Thrush.

STANFORD, LELAND (In full: AMASA LELAND). 1824-1893. American capitalist and politician. See: Encyc. Brit., 1973. Stanford joint?

STANGER, WILLIAM. 1812-1854. English surveyor-general in Natal. See: Ann. Register. Stangeria.

Stangeria (Stanger, William): Botany. See: Webster's 3d.

Stanhope (carriage) (Stanhope, Fitzroy Henry Richard): Generic Word. See: Partridge; Phyfe; Webster's 3d.

STANHOPE, CHARLES STANHOPE, 3D EARL. 1753-1816. English politician and scientist. See: Dict. Nat. Biog. Stanhope lens, Stanhope press, Stanhope stereotyping process, Stanhope type case.

STANHOPE, CHARLES STANHOPE, 3D EARL HARRINGTON AND LORD PETERSHAM. 1780-1851. English officer. See: Dict. Nat. Biog. Petersham (cloth), Petersham great-coat (or jacket), Petersham (ribbon).

STANHOPE, EDWARD. 1840-1893. English statesman. See: Dict. Nat. Biog. Stanhope memorandum.

STANHOPE, FITZROY HENRY RICHARD. 1787-1864. English clergyman. See: Boase. Stanhope (carriage).

Stanhope lens (Stanhope, Charles, 3rd Earl): Engineering and Industry. See: Brewer; Charnock.

Stanhope memorandum (Stanhope, Edward): Politics. See: Montgomery.

STANHOPE, PHILIP DORMER (4TH EARL OF CHESTERFIELD). 1694-1773. English statesman and writer. See: Dict. Nat. Biog. Chesterfield (couch), Chesterfield (overcoat), Chesterfieldian.

STANHOPE, PHILIP HENRY, 4TH EARL. 1781-1855. English botanist and author. See: Nouv. Biog. Univ. Stanhopea.

Stanhope press (Stanhope, Charles, 3rd Earl): Printing. See: Lockwood; Webster's 3d.

Stanhope stereotyping process (Stanhope, Charles, 3rd Earl): Printing. See: Webster's 3d.

Stanhope type case (Stanhope, Charles, 3rd Earl): Printing. See: Lockwood, p. 330.

Stanhopea (Stanhope, Philip Henry, 4th Earl): Botany. See: Taylor, N.; Webster's 3d.

STANISLAUS, SAINT. 1030-1079. Polish bishop. See: Encyc. Brit., 1973. Order of St. Stanislaus.

Stanislavsky and Nemirovich Danchenko Lyric Theatre Ballet Company (Stanislavsky, Konstantin and Nemirovich-Danchenko, Vladimir Ivanovich): Dance. See: Chujoy.

STANISLAVSKY, KONSTANTIN (Professional name of: KONSTANTIN SERGEEVICH ALEKSEYEV). 1863-1938. Russian actor and producer. See: Encyc. Brit., 1973. Stanislavsky and Nemirovich-Danchenko Lyric Theatre Ballet Company, Stanislavsky method.

Stanislavsky method (Stanislavsky, Konstantin): Theatre. See: Hendrickson.

Stanley compensating diaphragm (Stanley, William Ford Robinson): Engineering and Industry. See: Thrush.

Stanley cup (Stanley, Sir Frederick Arthur): Recreation and Sports. See: Hendrickson.

STANLEY, EDWARD. 1793-1862. English surgeon. See: Dict. Nat. Biog. Stanley's cervical ligaments.

STANLEY, EDWARD, 13TH EARL OF DERBY. 1775-1851. English zoologist. See: Dict. Nat. Biog. Derby flycatcher, Stanleya.

STANLEY, EDWARD GEORGE VILLIERS, 17TH EARL OF DERBY. 1865-1948. See: Dict. Nat. Biog., 1941-1950. Derbyite (and Derby Scheme).

STANLEY, EDWARD SMITH, 12TH EARL OF DERBY. 1752-1834. English aristocrat. (Biography source unavailable.) Derby Day, Derby dog, Derby hat, Derby (stakes).

Stanley expedition (Stanley, Henry Morton): History. See: Morris and Irwin.

STANLEY, FERDINANDO, 5TH EARL OF DERBY ("LORD STRANGE"). ca. 1559-1594. See: Dict. Nat. Biog. Strange's men.

STANLEY, SIR FREDERICK ARTHUR. 1841-1908. English-born Canadian statesman. See: Dict. Nat. Biog. Stanley cup.

STANLEY, G. H. fl. 1908. South African? chemist. Cited in: Chem. Abstr., vol. 2, p. 1405. Stanley test.

STANLEY, HENRY MORTON. 1841-1904. Welsh journalist and explorer. See: Dict. Nat. Biog. Stanley expedition.

STANLEY, J. No dates. English? physician. (Biography source unavailable.) Stanley's syndrome.

STANLEY, J. fl. 1822. English engineer. (Biography source unavailable.) Stanley stoker.

Stanley Miller's apparatus (Miller, Stanley Lloyd): Biology. See: Van Nostrand Sci. Encyc. under "Abiogenesis."

Stanley "shell-type" transformer (Stanley, William): Engineering and Industry. Cited in: World Who's Who Sci.

Stanley stoker (Stanley, J.): Engineering and Industry. See: Auger.

Stanley test (Stanley, G. H.): Chemistry. See: Van Nostrand Chem. Dict.

STANLEY, WILLIAM. 1858-1916. American electrical engineer and inventor. See: Dict. Amer. Biog. Stanley "shell-type" transformer.

STANLEY, WILLIAM FORD ROBINSON. 1829-1909. English scientific instrument maker and author. See: Dict. Nat. Biog. Stanley compensating diaphragm.

Stanleya (Stanley, Edward, 13th Earl of Derby): Botany. See: Taylor, N.

Stanley's cervical ligaments (Stanley, Edward): Medicine. See: Stedman.

Stanley's syndrome (Stanley, J.): Medicine. See: Jablonski.

Stanley's wash tub (Derivation undetermined): Botany. See: Gray.

Stannius' corpuscle (Stannius, Friedrich Hermann): Zoology. See: Gray.

STANNIUS, FRIEDRICH HERMANN. 1808-1883. German physician and physiologist. See: Allg. Deut. Biog. Stannius' corpuscle, Stannius' ligature.

Stannius' ligature (Stannius, Friedrich Hermann): Zoology. See: Dorland; Stedman.

Stansbury press (Stansbury, Samuel): Printing. See: Lockwood under "Handpress."

STANSBURY, SAMUEL. fl. 1804. American printer. Cited in: Dict. Cat. Hist. Print. Stansbury press.

STANSBY, MAURICE EARL. 1908-   . American chemist. See: Amer. Men Sci., 9th ed. Kolthoff-Stansby reagent for fluorine.

Stanton diagram (Stanton, Sir Thomas Edward): Engineering and Industry. See: Thrush.

Stanton number (Stanton, Sir Thomas Edward): Physics. See: Ballentyne; Thewlis.

STANTON, SIR THOMAS EDWARD. 1865-1931. English engineer. See: Pogg., vol. 6. Stanton diagram, Stanton number.

STANWORTH, JOHN EDWIN. fl. 1936-1967. English glass technologist. See: Direct. Brit. Scientists, 1966-1967. Redston-Stanworth annealing schedule.

STAPEL, JOHN BODAEUS. d. 1636. Dutch physician and botanist. See: Nieuw Nederl. Biog. Woordenb. Stapelia.

Stapelia (Stapel, John Bodaeus): Botany. See: Taylor, N.; Webster's 3d.

star of David (David, the king). See: magen (or mogen) David.

STARGARDT, KARL. 1875-1927. German ophthalmologist. See: Biog. Lex. hervorr. Aerzte. Stargardt's syndrome (or disease).

Stargardt's syndrome (or disease) (Stargardt, Karl): Medicine. See: Jablonski; Stedman.

Stark broadening (Stark, Johannes): Physics. See: Markus; Thewlis.

Stark effect (Stark, Johannes): Physics. See: Ballentyne; Internat. Dict. Ap. Math.; Thewlis.

Stark-Einstein equation (Stark, Johannes and Einstein, Albert): Physics. See: Van Nostrand Sci. Encyc.

Stark-Einstein law (Stark, Johannes and Einstein, Albert): Physics. See: Ballentyne; Van Nostrand Sci. Encyc. Also known as: Einstein law of photochemical equivalence.

STARK, JOHANNES. 1874-1957. German physicist. See: Encyc. Brit., 1973; Pogg., vols. 4 to 6, 7a. Stark broadening, Stark effect, Stark-Einstein equation, Stark-Einstein law, Stark-Lunelund effect.

Stark-Lunelund effect (Stark, Johannes and Lunelund, Harald): Physics. See: Van Nostrand Sci. Encyc.

STARK, OTTO. b. 1877. German chemist. See: Pogg., vol. 5. Stark test reaction?

Stark test reaction (Stark, Otto?): Chemistry. See: Van Nostrand Chem. Dict.

STARLING, ERNEST HENRY. 1866-1927. English physiologist. See: Who Was Who, 1916-1928. Starling's curve, Starling's law, Starling's reflex.

Starling's curve (Starling, Ernest Henry): Physiology. See: Stedman.

Starling's law (Starling, Ernest Henry): Physiology. See: Stedman; Webster's 3d.

Starling's reflex (Starling, Ernest Henry): Physiology. See: Stedman.

STARR, ALBERT. 1926-   . American surgeon. See: Amer. Men of Sci., 11th ed. Starr-Edwards ball valve prosthesis.

Starr (apple) (Derivation undetermined): Botany. See: De Sola.

Starr-Edwards ball valve prosthesis (Starr, Albert and Edwards, M. L.): Medicine. See: Stedman.

STARRY, ALLEN C. b. 1890. American pathologist. See: Amer. Med. Direct., 1958. Warthin-Starry silver stain.

STAS, JEAN-SERVAIS. 1813-1891. Belgian chemist. See: Biog. Nat. de Belgique. Stas-Otto method, Stas pipet.

Stas-Otto method (Stas, Jean-Servais and Otto, Friedrich Julius?): Medicine. See: Stedman.

Stas pipet (Stas, Jean-Servais): Chemistry. See: Hackh.

Stassano furnace (Derivation undetermined): Engineering and Industry. See: Thrush.

STATHIS, E. C. fl. 1948. Greek chemist. Cited in: Chem. Abstr., Decenn. Index, 1937-1946. Stathis test.

Stathis test (Stathis, E. C.): Chemistry. See: Van Nostrand Chem. Dict.

statue of Condillac (Condillac, Etienne Bonnet de): Psychology. See: Chaplin; Drever; English.

STAUB, HANS. b. 1890. Swiss internist. See: Kuerschner's Deut. Gel. Kal., vol. 4, 1931. Staub-Traugott effect.

Staub-Traugott effect (Staub, Hans and Traugott, Carl): Medicine. See: Dorland; Stedman.

Stauber gas turbine (Stauber, Georg): Engineering and Industry. See: Auger.

STAUBER, GEORG. b. 1875. German engineer. See: Wer Ist's?, 1922. Stauber gas turbine.

Staudinger equation (Staudinger, Hermann): Chemistry. See: Webster's 3d.

STAUDINGER, HERMANN. 1881-1965. German chemist. See: World Who's Who Sci. Staudinger equation.

STAUFFER, H. No dates. German? physician. (Biography source unavailable.) Bloch-Stauffer dyshormonal dermatosis.

STAUNTON, SIR GEORGE LEONARD. 1737-1801. English diplomat. See: Dict. Nat. Biog. Stauntonia.

Stauntonia (Staunton, Sir George Leonard): Botany. See: Taylor, N.

Stavisky affair (Stavisky, Serge Alexandre): Politics. See: Morris and Irwin.

STAVISKY, SERGE ALEXANDRE. 1886? - 1934. French swindler. See: Webster's Biog. Dict. Stavisky affair.

Stayman convention (Stayman, Samuel M.): Recreation and Sports. See: Webster's 3d.

STAYMAN, J. No dates. American cultivator. (Biography source unavailable.) Stayman winesap (apple).

STAYMAN, SAMUEL M. 1909- . American bridge expert. (Biography source unavailable.) Stayman convention.

Stayman winesap (apple) (Stayman, J.): Botany. See: De Sola.

STEAD, JOHN EDWARD. 1851-1923. English metallurgist. See: Who Was Who, 1916-1928. Steadite, Stead's brittleness, Stead's reagent.

Steadite (Stead, John Edward): Earth Sciences. See: Van Nostrand Sci. Encyc.; Webster's 3d.

Stead's brittleness (Stead, John Edward): Chemistry. See: Thrush.

Stead's reagent (Stead, John Edward): Chemistry. See: Thrush; Van Nostrand Chem. Dict.

STEAGALL, HENRY BASCOM. 1873-1943. American legislator. See: Biog. Direct. Amer. Congress. Glass-Steagall Act, Steagall National Housing Act, Wagner-Steagall Act.

Steagall National Housing Act (Steagall, Henry Bascom): Politics. See: Smith.

STEARNS, ALBERT WARREN. 1885-1959. American physician. See: Who Was Who Amer., vol. 3. Stearns' alcoholic amentia.

Stearns' alcoholic amentia (Stearns, Albert Warren): Medicine. See: Dorland; Stedman.

STEARNS, GENEVIEVE. b. 1892. American chemist. See: World Who's Who Sci. Boyd-Stearns syndrome.

Steart fan (Derivation undetermined): Engineering and Industry. See: Thrush.

Stebinger drum (Stebinger, Eugen?): Earth Sciences. See: Thrush.

STEBINGER, EUGEN. 1883-1951. American geologist. See: Proc. Vol. Geol. Soc. Amer., 1953, p. 154. Stebinger drum?

STECKEL, ABRAM P. fl. 1930. American engineer. Cited in: Chem. Abstr., Decenn. Index, 1927-1936. Steckel mill.

Steckel mill (Steckel, Abram P.): Engineering and Industry. See: Thrush.

Stedman (Stedman, Fabian): Printing. See: Webster's 3d.

STEDMAN, FABIAN. fl. 17th c. English printer. (Biography source unavailable.) Stedman.

STEDMAN, JOHN CLOES. fl. 1970. American law professor. See: Nat. Faculty Direct., 1970. Stedman's killer phrases?

Stedman's killer phrases (Stedman, John Cloes?): Sociology. See: Martin.

Steele acid (Steele, L. L.): Chemistry. See: Hackh.

Steele and Steele dry table (Steele, Edwin G. and Steele, Walter L.). See: Sutton, Steele and Steele dry table.

STEELE, BERTRAM DILLON. 1876-1934. English chemist in Australia. See: Pogg., vol. 5. Steele microbalance.

STEELE, EDWIN G. fl. 1909. American engineer. Cited in: Chem. Abstr., vol. 3, p. P306. Sutton, Steele, and Steele dry table.

STEELE, JOHN C. fl. 1951-1968. Canadian physician. See: Canadian Med. Direct., 1968. Steele-Richardson-Olszewski syndrome.

STEELE, L. L. fl. 1922. American chemist. Cited in: Chem. Abstr., vol. 16, p. 2324. Steele acid.

Steele microbalance (Steele, Bertram Dillon): Chemistry. See: Hackh.

Steele-Richardson-Olszewski syndrome (Steele, John C.; Richardson, John Clifford; and Olszewski, Jerzy): Medicine. See: Jablonski; Stedman.

STEELE, WALTER L. fl. 1909. American engineer. Cited in: Chem. Abstr., vol. 3, p. P306. Sutton, Steele, and Steele dry table.

STEELL, GRAHAM. 1851-1942. English physician. See: Who Was Who, 1941-1950. Steell's murmur.

Steell's murmur (Steell, Graham): Medicine. See: Dorland; Jablonski; Stedman. Also known as: Graham Steell's murmur.

STEEN, JAN HAVICKSZOON. 1626-1679. Dutch painter. See: Bryan. Jan Steen household.

STEENBOCK, HARRY. 1886-1967. American physiologist and chemist. See: Who Was Who Amer., vol. 4. Steenbock unit.

Steenbock unit (Steenbock, Harry): Medicine. See: Dorland; Stedman.

STEENHAUER, A. J. fl. 1925. Dutch chemist. Cited in: Chem. Abstr., vol. 29, p. 5385. Steenhauer microtest, Van Itallie-Steenhauer test reaction for alkaloids.

Steenhauer microtest (Steenhauer, A. J.): Chemistry. See: Van Nostrand Chem. Dict.

STEENLAND, MARTINUS JAN. 1918- . Dutch physicist. See: Who's Who Netherl., 1962-1963. Vacquier-Steenland method.

STEENSMA, F. A. fl. 1908. Dutch chemist. Cited in: Chem. Abstr., vol. 2, pp. 1600; 2573. Steensma reagent, Steensma test reaction for antipyrine.

Steensma reagent (Steensma, F. A.): Chemistry. See: Van Nostrand Chem. Dict.

Steensma test reaction for antipyrine (Steensma, F. A.): Chemistry. See: Van Nostrand Chem. Dict.

STEENSTRUP, KNUD JOHANNES VOGELINS. 1842-1913. Danish geologist. See: Meddelelser Dansk Geolog. Foren., vol. 4 (1912/1915), pp. 211-214. Steenstrupine.

Steenstrupine (Steenstrup, Knud Johannes Vogelins): Earth Sciences. See: Webster's 3d.

Stefan-Boltzmann constant (Stefan, Josef and Boltzmann, Ludwig Eduard): Physics. See: Dresner; Huschke; Satterthwaite. Also known as: Boltzmann factor, Stefan's constant.

Stefan-Boltzmann equation (Stefan, Josef and Boltzmann, Ludwig Eduard): Physics. See: Hackh; Van Nostrand Chem. Dict.

Stefan-Boltzmann law (Stefan, Josef and Boltzmann, Ludwig Eduard): Physics. See: Internat. Dict. Ap. Math.; Internat. Dict. Phys. Elec.; Thewlis. Also known as: Boltzmann law of radiation, Stefan's law.

STEFAN, JOSEF. 1835-1893. Austrian physicist. See: Encyc. Brit., 1973; World Who's Who Sci. Stefan-Boltzmann constant, Stefan-Boltzmann equation, Stefan-Boltzmann law.

Stefanelli test (Derivation undetermined): Chemistry. See: Van Nostrand Chem. Dict.

Stefan's constant (Stefan, Josef). See: Stefan-Boltzmann constant.

Stefan's law (Stefan, Josef). See: Stefan-Boltzmann law.

STEFFEN, CARL. fl. 1910. Austrian chemist. Cited in: Chem. Abstr., vol. 4, p. 1557. Steffen's process, Steffen's waste.

Steffen's process (Steffen, Carl): Chemistry. See: Ballentyne; Van Nostrand Chem. Dict.; Webster's 3d.

Steffen's waste (Steffen, Carl): Chemistry. See: Hackh; Webster's 3d.

STEGER, WALTER FRIEDRICH. b. 1889. German ceramics chemist. See: Pogg., vols. 6, 7a. Steger's crazing test.

Steger's crazing test (Steger, Walter Friedrich): Engineering and Industry. See: Thrush.

STEIDELE, RAPHAEL JOHANN. 1737-1823. Austrian obstetrician. See: Biog. Lex. hervorr. Aerzte. Steidele's complex.

Steidele's complex (Steidele, Raphael Johann): Medicine. See: Stedman.

STEIGER, GEORGE. 1869-1944. American chemist. See: World Who's Who Sci. Steiger test?, Steigerite.

Steiger test (Steiger, George?): Chemistry. See: Van Nostrand Chem. Dict.

Steigerite (Steiger, George): Earth Sciences. See: Thrush; Webster's 3d.

STEIGMANN, ALBERT (In full: ERNST ALBERT). 1897- . German chemist. See: Pogg., vols. 6, 7a. Steigmann test reactions.

Steigmann test reactions (Steigmann, Albert): Chemistry. See: Van Nostrand Chem. Dict.

STEIN, ARTHUR. 1918- . American mathematical statistician. See: Amer. Men and Women Sci., 12th ed. Stein's two sample procedure?

STEIN, IRVING FREILER. b. 1887. American gynecologist. See: Who's Who Among Physicians and Surg., 1938. Stein-Leventhal syndrome.

Stein-Leventhal syndrome (Stein, Irving Freiler and Leventhal, Michael L.) Medicine. See: Jablonski; Stedman. Also known as: Stein's syndrome.

STEIN, MAX. fl. 1949. German chemist. (Biography source unavailable.) Stein test for free alkali in soaps?

STEIN, STANISLAV ALEKSANDR FYODOROVICH VON. b. 1855. Russian otologist. (Biography source unavailable.) Stein's test.

Stein test for free alkali in soaps (Stein, Max?): Chemistry. See: Van Nostrand Chem. Dict.

Stein test for iodine in nitric acid or nitrates (Derivation undetermined): Chemistry. See: Van Nostrand Chem. Dict.

STEINACH, EUGEN. 1861-1944. Austrian surgeon. See: World Who's Who Sci. Steinach's method (or operation).

Steinach's method (or operation) (Steinach, Eugen): Medicine. See: Dorland. Stedman.

STEINBRINCK, W. fl. 1948. German physician. (Biography source unavailable.) Beguez Cesar-Steinbrinck-Chediak-Higashi syndrome, Chediak-Steinbrinck anomaly.

STEINBROCKER, OTTO. b. 1898. German? physician. (Biography source unavailable.) Steinbrocker's syndrome.

Steinbrocker's syndrome (Steinbrocker, Otto): Medicine. See: Jablonski.

STEINDLER, ARTHUR. 1878-1959. American orthopaedic surgeon. See: Who Was Who Amer. Steindler's posterior syndrome.

Steindler's posterior syndrome (Steindler, Arthur): Medicine. See: Jablonski.

STEINER, GABRIEL. b. 1883. German neurologist. See: Biog. Lex. hervorr. Aerzte. Steiner's syndrome.

STEINER, JAKOB. 1796-1863. Swiss mathematician. See: World Who's Who Sci. Steinerian, Steiner's theorem, Steiner's triple systems.

STEINER, LUDWIG. fl. 1909. German physician. (Biography source unavailable.) Steiner-Voerner syndrome, Steiner's tumor.

Steiner-Voerner syndrome (Steiner, Ludwig and Voerner, Hans): Medicine. See: Jablonski.

Steinerian (Steiner, Jakob): Mathematics. See: Webster's 2d.

Steiner's syndrome (Steiner, Gabriel). See: Curtius' syndrome.

Steiner's theorem (Steiner, Jakob): Mathematics. See: Ballentyne.

Steiner's triple systems (Steiner, Jakob): Mathematics. See: Kendall.

Steiner's tumor (Steiner, Ludwig). See: Jeanselme's nodule.

STEINERT, HANS GUSTAV WILHELM. b. 1875. German physician. See: Wer Ist's, 1906. Curschmann-Batten-Steinert syndrome.

STEINHAUS, H. fl. 1926. German? mathematician. Cited in: Pogg., vol. 6 under "Banach, Stefan." Banach-Steinhaus theorem.

STEINHEIL. fl. ca. 1815? Governor of Finland. Cited in: Hintze. Steinheilite.

STEINHEIL, ADOLPH (In full: HUGO ADOLPH). 1832-1893. German designer of optical instruments. See: Pogg., vols. 3,4. Porro-Steinheil lens, Steinheil's Aplanat lens.

Steinheilite (Steinheil): Earth Sciences. See: Thrush.

Steinheil's Aplanat lens (Steinheil, Adolph): Photography. See: Focal Encyc. Photog. under "Steinheil, Hugo Adolph."

STEINLE, JOHN VERNON. b. 1898. American chemist. See: Amer. Men Sci., 4th ed. Steinle-Kahlenberg test reaction.

Steinle-Kahlenberg test reaction (Steinle, John Vernon and Kahlenberg, Louis Albert Berthold): Chemistry. See: Van Nostrand Chem. Dict.

STEINMANN. fl. 19th c. German scientist. Cited in: Hintze. Steinmannite.

STEINMANN, FRITZ. 1872-1932. Swiss surgeon. See: World Who's Who Sci. Steinmann's extension (pin or nail).

Steinmannite (Steinmann): Earth Sciences. See: Charnock; Thrush.

Steinmann's extension (pin, or nail) (Steinmann, Fritz): Medicine. See: Dorland; Webster's 3d.

STEINMETZ, CHARLES PORTEUS. 1865-1923. German-born American electrical engineer. See: World Who's Who Sci. Steinmetz coefficient, Steinmetz law (or formula).

Steinmetz coefficient (Steinmetz, Charles Porteus): Engineering and Industry. See: Hughes; Internat. Dict. Phys. Elec.; Webster's 3d.

Steinmetz law (or formula) (Steinmetz, Charles Porteus): Engineering and Industry. See: Ballentyne; Markus; Thewlis.

Stein's syndrome (Stein, Irving Freiler). See: Stein-Leventhal syndrome.

Stein's test (Stein, Stanislav Aleksandr Fyodorovich von): Medicine. See: Dorland; Stedman.

Stein's two sample procedure (Stein, Arthur?): Statistics. See: Kendall.

STEINWAY HENRY ENGELHARD (Orig.: HEINRICH ENGELHARD STEINWEG). 1797-1871. German-born American piano manufacturer. See: Dict. Amer. Biog. Steinway piano.

Steinway piano (Steinway, Henry Engelhard): Music. See: Partridge.

STEINWEHR, HELLMUTH VON. 1874-1951. German physicist. See: Pogg., vols. 4, 5, 6, 7a. Jaeger-Steinwehr method for mechanical equivalent of heat.

Steiver pulses (Derivation undetermined): Physics. See: Hughes.

STELLER, GEORG WILHELM. 1709-1746. German zoologist. See: World Who's Who Sci. Steller's eider (or duck), Steller's jay, Steller's sea cow, Steller's sea eagle, Steller's sea-lion.

Steller's eider (or duck) (Steller, Georg Wilhelm): Zoology. See: Gray; Webster's 3d.

Steller's jay (Steller, Georg Wilhelm): Zoology. See: Gray; Pennak; Webster's 3d

Steller's sea cow (Steller, Georg Wilhelm): Zoology. See: Pennak; Webster's 3d.

Steller's sea eagle (Steller, Georg Wilhelm): Zoology. See: Gray; Webster's 3d.

Steller's sea-lion (Steller, Georg Wilhelm): Zoology. See: Gray; Pennak; Webster's 3d.

STELLWAG, CARL VON CARION. 1823-1904. Austrian ophthalmologist. See: Biog. Lex. hervorr. Aerzte. Stellwag's brawny edema, Stellwag's sign.

Stellwag's brawny edema (Stellwag, Carl von Carion): Medicine. See: Jablonski.

Stellwag's sign (Stellwag, Carl von Carion): Medicine. See: Dorland; Stedman.

Sten gun (Sheppard, Major R. V.; Turpin, H. J.; and Enfield, England): Weapons. See: Hendrickson; Partridge; Quick.

STENBERG. fl. 1877. Swedish engineer. (Biography source unavailable.) Stenberg engine.

Stenberg engine (Stenberg): Engineering and Industry. See: Auger.

Stender dish (Stender, Wilhelm P.): Medicine. See: Dorland; Stedman.

STENDER, WILHELM P. fl. 19th c. German manufacturer of scientific apparatus. Cited in: Index-Cat. Libr. Surg. Gen. Off., 1st ser., v. 13, 1892. Stender dish.

Stenger's test (Derivation undetermined): Medicine. See: Stedman.

Steno, Nicolaus. See: Stensen, Niels.

STENSEN, NIELS (NICOLAUS STENO). 1638-1686. Danish anatomist. See: Encyc. Brit., 1911. Stensen's canal, Stensen's duct, Stensen's gland, Stensen's experiment, Stensen's foramen, Stensen's law, Stensen's plexus, Stensen's veins.

Stensen's canal (Stensen, Niels): Anatomy. See: Donath.

Stensen's duct (Stensen, Niels): Anatomy. See: Donath; Dorland; Stedman. Also known as: Blasius' duct.

Stensen's experiment (Stensen, Niels): Anatomy. See: Dorland; Stedman.

Stensen's foramen (Stensen, Niels): Anatomy. See: Donath; Dorland; Stedman.

Stensen's gland (Stensen, Niels): Anatomy. See: Gray.

Stensen's law (Stensen, Niels): Earth Sciences. See: New Encyc. Brit., 1974, Microp.

Stensen's plexus (Stensen, Niels): Anatomy. See: Stedman.

Stensen's veins (Stensen, Niels): Anatomy. See: Stedman.

Stent (Stent, Charles R.): Dentistry. See: Dorland; Stedman.

STENT, CHARLES R. d. 1901. English dentist. (Biography source unavailable.) Stent.

STENTOR. Greek herald of the Trojan War. See: Harper. Stentor (monkey), Stentor (protozoans), Stentorian, Stentorophonic horn, Stentorphone.

Stentor (monkey) (Stentor): Zoology. See: Hendrickson.

Stentor (protozoans) (Stentor): Zoology. See: Webster's 3d.

Stentorian (Stentor): Generic Word (loud). See: Charnock; Hendrickson; Stenhouse.

Stentorophonic horn (Stentor): Generic Word. See: Stenhouse.

Stentorphone (Stentor): Engineering and Industry. See: Hendrickson.

STEPHAN, ARCHDUKE. d. 1867. Austrian mining director. Cited in: Dana. Stephanite.

STEPHAN, FREDERICK FRANKLIN. 1903- . American statistician. See: Amer. Men. Sci., 7th ed. Stephan's iterative process.

Stephanite (Stephan, Archduke): Earth Sciences. See: Charnock; Van Nostrand Sci. Encyc.; Webster's 3d.

Stephan's iterative process (Stephan, Frederick Franklin): Statistics. See: Kendall.

Stephen aldehyde reaction (Stephen, Henry): Chemistry. See: Ballentyne; Van Nostrand Chem. Dict.

STEPHEN, HENRY. fl. 1911-1926. English-born South African chemist. See: Pogg., vol. 6. Stephen aldehyde reaction.

STEPHEN, SAINT. d. 33? Christian protomartyr. See: Encyc. Brit., 1911. Saint Stephen's Day, Saint Stephen's stone.

STEPHENS, ADRIAN. 1795-1876. English inventor. (Biography source unavailable.) Stephens whistle.

Stephens whistle (Stephens, Adrian): Engineering and Industry. See: Auger.

STEPHENSON, GEORGE. 1781-1848. English engineer and inventor. See: Dict. Nat. Biog. Stephenson lamp, Stephenson link motion valve gear.

Stephenson lamp (Stephenson, George): Engineering and Industry. See: Hendrickson; Thrush. Also known as: Geordie (miners' safety lamp).

Stephenson link motion valve gear (Stephenson, George): Engineering and Industry. See: Auger; Van Nostrand Sci. Encyc.

STEPHENSON, WILLIAM. 1837-1908. Scottish obstetrician. (Biography source unavailable.) Stephenson's wave.

Stephenson's wave (Stephenson, William): Medicine. See: Dorland; Stedman.

Sterba-curtain array (Derivation undetermined): Electronics. See: Internat. Dict. Phys. Elec.; Markus.

Sterculia (Sterculius): Botany. See: Webster's 3d.

Sterculia tree (Sterculius): Mythology. See: Jobes.

STERCULIUS. Ancient Latin god of cultivation and manuring. See: Jobes. Sterculia, Sterculia tree.

STERKIN, E. I. fl. 1929. German? chemist. Cited in: Chem. Abstr., vol. 23, p. 3050. Sterkin-Helfgat solution.

Sterkin-Helfgat solution (Sterkin, E. I. and Helfgat, I. I.): Chemistry. See: Van Nostrand Chem. Dict.

Stern-Gerlach experiment (or effect) (Stern, Otto and Gerlach, Walther): Physics. See: Ballentyne; Hughes; Thewlis.

STERN, HEINRICH. 1862-1918. American physician. See: New York Times, Feb. 2, 1918, p. 11, col. 4. Stern's position.

STERN, JULIUS. 1820-1883. German music teacher. See: Baker. Stern variator?

STERN, L. fl. 1909. German? chemist. Cited in: Chem. Abstr., vol. 3, p. 1415. Battelli-Stern solution.

STERN, LINA. fl. 1909. Swiss chemist. Cited in: Chem. Abstr., vol. 3, p. 1415. Battelli-Stern solution.

STERN, OTTO. b. 1888. German-born American physicist. See: Amer. Men. Sci., 11th ed.; Pogg., vols. 5,6,7a. Stern-Gerlach experiment (or effect), Stern-Zartman experiment.

STERN, SUZANNE. fl. 1908. American scientist. Cited in: Kelly. Goodman-Suzanne reagent.

Stern variator (Stern, Julius?): Music. See: Chaplin; Drever.

STERN, WALTER G. fl. 1923. American surgeon. (Biography source unavailable.) Guerin-Stern syndrome.

Stern-Zartman experiment (Stern, Otto and Zartman, Ira Forry): Physics. See: Internat. Dict. Phys. Elec. Also known as: Zartman experiment.

STERNBERG, CARL VON. 1872-1935. Austrian pathologist. See: Biog. Lex. hervorr. Aerzte. Albright-McCune-Sternberg syndrome, Hodgkin-Paltauf-Sternberg disease, Paltauf-Sternberg disease, Reed-Sternberg cell, Sternberg's disease.

Sternberg cell (Sternberg, Carl von). See: Reed-Sternberg cell.

STERNBERG, COUNT KASPAR MARIA VON. 1761-1838. German paleontologist and geologist. See: Allg. Deut. Biog. Sternbergia, Sternbergite.

Sternberg-Reed cell (Sternberg, Carl von and Reed, Dorothy). See: Reed-Sternberg cell.

Sternbergia (Sternberg, Count Kaspar Maria von): Botany. See: Taylor, N.; Webster's 3d.

Sternbergite (Sternberg, Count Kaspar Maria von): Earth Sciences. See: Thrush; Webster's 3d.

Sternberg's disease (Sternberg, Carl von). See: Hodgkin's disease.

Sterneck, Robert Daublesky von. See: Von Sterneck, Robert Doublesky.

Stern's position (Stern, Heinrich): Medicine. See: Dorland.

STERRETT, DOUGLAS B. 1883- . American geologist. Cited in: Hintze. Sterrettite.

Sterrettite (Sterrett, Douglas B.): Earth Sciences. See: Thrush; Webster's 3d.

STERRY, J. fl. 1912. English photographic chemist. (Biography source unavailable.) Sterry process?

Sterry process (Sterry, J.?): Photography. See: Focal Encyc. Photog.

Stesichorean (Stesichorus): Literature. See: Webster's 3d.

STESICHORUS. d. 550 B.C.? Greek poet. See: Encyc. Brit., 1911. Stesichorean.

Stetefeldite (Stetefeldt, Carl August): Earth Sciences. See: Thrush.

STETEFELDT, CARL AUGUST. 1838-1896. German-born American mining engineer. See: World Who's Who Sci. Stetefeldt furnace, Stetefeldite.

Stetefeldt furnace (Stetefeldt, Carl August): Engineering and Industry. See: Thrush; Webster's 3d.

tetson hat (Stetson, John Batterson): Fashion. See: Hendrickson; Mathews, . M.; Partridge. Also known as: John B. hat.

ETSON, JOHN BATTERSON. 1830-1906. American manufacturer. See: ct. Amer. Biog. Stetson hat.

EUDEL, HERMANN (In full: FRIEDRICH PETER HERMANN) b. 1871. erman physiological chemist. See: Pogg., vol. 7a. Steudel reaction for cleic acid.

eudel reaction for nucleic acid (Steudel, Hermann): Chemistry. See: Van ostrand Chem. Dict.

EVEN. Character in Jonathan Swift's "Journal to Stella" (1713). (Biography urce unavailable). even Steven.

evengraph (Stevens, Thomas): Applied Arts. See: Barnhart (New Eng.)

TEVENS, ALBERT MASON. 1884-1945. American pediatrician. See: New ork Times, Aug. 12, 1945, p.39, col. 3. Stevens-Johnson syndrome.

evens alpha-methoxyketone synthesis (Stevens, Philip Greeley): Chemistry. e: Van Nostrand Chem. Dict.

evens boiler (Stevens, John): Engineering and Industry. See: Auger.

evens-Craig distribution (Stevens, W. L. and Craig, Cecil Calvert): atistics. See: Kendall.

TEVENS, E. A. fl. 19th c. American founder of the Stevens Institute of chnology in Hoboken, N.J. Cited in: Amer. Min. vol. 38 (Nov.-Dec. 953), p. 973. Stevensite.

TEVENS, FRANCIS B. fl. 1840. American engineer. (Biography source navailable.) Stevens valve gear.

TEVENS, JOHN. 1749-1838. American engineer. See: World Who's Who i. Stevens boiler.

evens-Johnson syndrome (Stevens, Albert Mason and Johnson, Frank Chambliss): edicine. See: Dorland; Jablonski; Stedman. Also known as: Baader's ermatostomatitis, Baader's syndrome, Fiessinger-Rendu syndrome, Klauder's ndrome, Neumann's aphthosis.

TEVENS, PHILIP GREELEY. 1902- . American chemist. See: Amer. en. Sci., 6th ed. Stevens alpha-methoxyketone synthesis.

evens' power law (Stevens, Stanley Smith): Psychology. See: Wolman.

evens rearrangement (Stevens, Thomas Stevens): Chemistry. See: Van ostrand Chem. Dict.

TEVENS, STANLEY SMITH. 1906- . American psychophysicist. See: orld Who's Who Sci. Stevens' power law.

TEVENS, THOMAS. fl. 1879. English inventor. (Biography source navailable.) Stevengraph.

TEVENS, THOMAS STEVENS. 1900- . Scottish chemist. See: Pogg., ol. 6; World Who's Who Sci. McFadyen-Stevens aldehyde synthesis, Stevens earrangement.

evens valve gear (Stevens, Francis B.): Engineering and Industry. See: uger.

TEVENS, W. L. fl. 1939-1950. English? statistician. (Biography source navailable.) Ising-Stevens distribution, Stevens-Craig distribution.

tevensite (Stevens, E. A.): Earth Sciences. See: Thrush.

tevenson-Resuggan reagent (Stevenson, S. G. and Resuggan, John Charles ovell): Chemistry. See: Van Nostrand Chem. Dict.

TEVENSON, ROBERT LOUIS BALFOUR. 1850-1894. Scottish essayist, ovelist, and poet. See: Dict. Nat. Biog. Stevensonian, Stevensoniana.

TEVENSON, S. G. fl. 1938. English chemist. Cited in: Chem. Abstr., ol. 32, p. 3298⁹. Stevenson-Resuggan reagent.

tevenson screen (Stevenson, Thomas): Earth Sciences. See: Huschke; Monkhouse.

TEVENSON, THOMAS. 1818-1887. Scottish engineer and meteorologist. See: World Who's Who Sci. Stevenson screen, Stevenson's formula.

tevensonian (Stevenson, Robert Louis Balfour): Literature. See: Webster's 3d.

tevensoniana (Stevenson, Robert Louis Balfour): Literature. See: Webster's 3d.

Stevenson's formula (Stevenson, Thomas): Earth Sciences. See: Thrush.

Stevia (Esteve, Pedro Jacob): Botany. See: Webster's 3d.

STEWART, BALFOUR. 1828-1887. Scottish physicist and meteorologist. See: World Who's Who Sci. Stewart-Kirchhoff law.

STEWART, CHARLES. fl. 1880. English zoologist. Cited in: Royal Soc. Cat. Sci. Pap., 1874-1883. Stewart's organs?

STEWART, DOUGLAS HUNT. 1860-1933. American surgeon. See: Who Was Who Amer. Morgagni-Stewart-Morel syndrome, Stewart-Morel syndrome, Stewart's purple, Stewart's solution.

STEWART, FRED CARLTON. 1868-1946. American plant pathologist. See: Who Was Who Amer. Stewart's disease of sweet corn.

STEWART, FRED WALDORF. b. 1894. American pathologist. See: Direct. Med. Specialists, 1965-1966. Stewart-Treves syndrome.

STEWART, GEORGE WALTER. 1876-1956. American physicist. See: Pogg., vols. 4,5,6. Stewart-Hovda relationship.

Stewart-Holmes sign (Stewart, Purves and Holmes, Eric Gordon): Medicine. See: Stedman.

Stewart-Hovda relationship (Stewart, George Walter and Hovda, Olaf): Physics. See: Internat. Dict. Phys. Elec.

Stewart, John (Earl of Carrick). See: Robert III.

STEWART, KENNETH C. 1917- . American audiologist. See: Amer. Men and Women Sci., 12th ed. Doerfler-Stewart test?

Stewart-Kirchhoff law (Stewart, Balfour and Kirchhoff, Gustave-Robert): Physics. See: Ballentyne; Hackh.

Stewart-Morel syndrome (Stewart, Douglas Hunt and Morel, Ferdinand). See: Morgagni's syndrome.

STEWART, PURVES (In full: JAMES PURVES). 1869-1949. English physician. See: Who Was Who. Stewart-Holmes sign.

Stewart-Treves syndrome (Stewart, Fred Waldorf and Treves, Norman): Medicine. See: Jablonski.

STEWART, ULMONT P. fl. 1918. American army physician. Cited in: Chem. Abstr., vol. 12, p. 2582. Stewart's solution.

Stewart White. See: White, Stewart Edward.

Stewart White trout (White, Stewart Edward): Zoology. See: Webster's 3d.

Stewartia (or Stuartia) (Stuart, John, 3rd Earl of Bute): Botany. See: Mathews, M. M.; Taylor, N.; Webster's 3d.

Stewart's disease of sweet corn (Stewart, Fred Carlton): Botany. See: Webster's 3d.

Stewart's organs (Stewart, Charles?): Zoology. See: Henderson; Pennak.

Stewart's purple (Stewart, Douglas Hunt): Medicine. See: Dorland.

Stewart's solution (Stewart, Douglas Hunt): Medicine. See: Dorland.

Stewart's solution (Stewart, Ulmont P.): Chemistry. See: Van Nostrand Chem. Dict.

Stewart's test (Derivation undetermined): Medicine. See: Stedman.

Steyr 9mm parabellum submachine gun (Puch, Steyr Daimler): Weapons. See: Quick.

STICH, CONRAD. 1864-1953. German pharmacist. See: Pogg., vol. 7a. Stich test.

Stich test (Stich, Conrad): Chemistry. See: Van Nostrand Chem. Dict.

STICHT, ROBERT CARL. 1856-1922. American-born Australian metallurgist. See: Australian Encyc. Stichtite.

Stichtite (Sticht, Robert Carl): Earth Sciences. See: Webster's 3d.

STICKER, ANTON. b. 1861. German physician. See: Biog. Lex. hervorr. Aerzte. Sticker's sarcoma.

STICKER, GEORG. 1860-1960. German physician. See: World Who's Who Sci. Sticker's disease.

Sticker's disease (Sticker, Georg): Medicine. See: Dorland; Jablonski; Stedman.

Sticker's sarcoma (Sticker, Anton): Medicine. See: Jablonski.

STIEDA, ALFRED. b. 1869. German surgeon. See: Biog. Lex. hervorr. Aerzte. Laurer-Stieda canal?, Stieda-Pellegrini syndrome.

STIEDA, LUDWIG. 1837-1918. German anatomist. See: Deut. Biog. Jahrb., 1917-1920. Stieda's process.

Stieda-Pellegrini syndrome (Stieda, Alfred and Pellegrini, Augusto): Medicine. See: Jablonski. Also known as: Koehler-Stieda-Pellegrini syndrome, Pellegrini-Stieda disease, Pellegrini's disease, Stieda's disease (or fracture).

Stieda's disease (or fracture) (Stieda, Alfred). See: Stieda-Pellegrini syndrome.

Stieda's process (Stieda, Ludwig): Anatomy. See: Donath; Dorland; Stedman.

Stiegel glass (Stiegel, Henry William): Engineering and Industry. See: Webster's 3d.

STIEGEL, HENRY WILLIAM. 1729-1785. American glassmaker, industrialist and eccentric. See: Dict. Amer. Biog. Stiegel glass.

STIEGLITZ, JULIUS OSCAR. 1867-1937. American chemist. See: World Who's Who Sci. Stieglitz rearrangement.

Stieglitz rearrangement (Stieglitz, Julius Oscar): Chemistry. See: Van Nostrand Chem. Dict.

Stieltjes integral (Stieltjes, Thomas Jean). See: Lebesque-Stieltjes integral.

STIELTJES, THOMAS JEAN. 1856-1894. Dutch-born French mathematician. See: World Who's Who Sci. Laplace-Stieltjes transform, Lebesque-Stieltjes integral, Riemann-Stieltjes integral.

STIERLIN, EDUARD. 1878-1919. German surgeon. See: Biog. Lex. hervorr. Aerzte. Stierlin's sign.

Stierlin's sign (Stierlin, Eduard): Medicine. See: Dorland; Stedman.

Stifel's figure (Derivation undetermined): Medicine. See: Stedman.

Stiggins (Stiggins, the hypocrite): Generic Word. See: Partridge.

STIGGINS, THE HYPOCRITE. Character in Charles Dickens's novel "The Pickwick Papers" (1836-1837). See: Harvey. Stiggins.

Stiles-Crawford effect (Stiles, Walter Stanley and Crawford, Brian Hewson): Physiology. See: Ballentyne; English; Thewlis.

STILES, WALTER STANLEY. 1901-   . English physiologist. See: Who's Who, 1974-1975. Stiles-Crawford effect.

Still engine (Still, W.J.): Engineering and Industry. See: Auger.

STILL, SIR GEORGE FREDERICK. 1868-1941. English physician. See: World Who's Who Sci. Still's murmur, Still's syndrome.

STILL, W. J. fl. 1912. English engineer. (Biography source unavailable.) Still engine.

STILLER, BERTHOLD. 1837-1922. Hungarian physician. See: Magyar Eletr. Lex. Stiller's asthenia (disease, habitus, or theory), Stiller's sign (or rib).

Stiller's asthenia (disease, habitus, or theory) (Stiller, Berthold): Medicine. See: Jablonski.

Stiller's sign (or rib) (Stiller, Berthold): Medicine. See: Dorland; Hinsie; Stedman.

STILLING, BENEDIKT. 1810-1879. German anatomist. See: World Who's Who Sci. fleece of Stilling, Stilling's canal, Stilling's fibers, Stilling's gelatinous substance, Stilling's nucleus (or column).

STILLING, JAKOB. 1842-1915. German ophthalmologist. See: Deut. Biog. Jahrb., 1914-1916. Stilling test, Stilling-Tuerk-Duane syndrome, Stilling's root.

Stilling test (Stilling, Jakob): Physiology. See: English.

Stilling-Tuerk-Duane syndrome (Stilling, Jakob; Tuerk, Sigmund; and Duane, Alexander): Medicine. See: Jablonski. Also known as: Duane's syndrome, Stilling's syndrome, Tuerk-Stilling syndrome, Tuerk's syndrome.

STILLINGFLEET, BENJAMIN. 1702-1771. English botanist and poet. See: Dict. Nat. Biog. Stillingia.

Stillingia (Stillingfleet, Benjamin): Botany. See: Webster's 3d.

Stilling's canal (Stilling, Benedikt): Anatomy. See: Dorland; Stedman.

Stilling's fibers (Stilling, Benedikt): Anatomy. See: Stedman.

Stilling's gelatinous substance (Stilling, Benedikt): Anatomy. See: Stedman.

Stilling's nucleus (or column) (Stilling, Benedikt): Anatomy. See: Dorland; Stedman.

Stilling's root (Stilling, Jakob): Medicine. See: Stedman.

Stilling's syndrome (Stilling, Jakob). See: Stilling-Tuerk-Duane syndrome.

STILLMAN, BESSIE WHITMORE. b. 1871. American educator. Cited in: Mansell, under "Gillingham, Anna." Gillingham-Stillman method.

Still's murmur (Still, Sir George Frederick): Medicine. See: Stedman.

Still's syndrome (Still, Sir George Frederick): Medicine. See: Dorland; Jablonski; Stedman. Also known as: Chauffard-Ramon syndrome, Chauffard-Still syndrome.

STILLSON, DANIEL C. fl. 1869. American inventor. (Biography source unavailable.) Stillson pipe wrench.

Stillson pipe wrench (Stillson, Daniel C.): Engineering and Industry. See: Mathews, M. M.; Van Nostrand Sci. Encyc.

STILLWELL, FRANK LESLIE. fl. 20th c. Australian scientist. Cited in: Min. Mag., vol. 31 (1956-1958), p. 973. Stillwellite.

Stillwellite (Stillwell, Frank Leslie): Earth Sciences. See: Thrush.

Stimson Doctrine (Stimson, Henry Lewis): Politics. See: Morris; Smith.

STIMSON, HAROLD FREDERIC. b. 1890. American physicist. See: Amer. Men Sci., 4th ed. Osborne, Stimson and Ginnings method for mechanical equivalent of heat.

STIMSON, HENRY LEWIS. 1867-1950. American statesman. See: Who Was Who Amer. Stimson Doctrine.

STINTZING, RODERICH. 1854-1933. German internist. See: Biog. Lex. hervorr. Aerzte. Stintzing's tables.

Stintzing's tables (Stintzing, Roderich): Physiology. See: Dorland.

STIRLING, ALLAN. fl. 1885. American engineer. Cited in: Royal Soc. Cat. Sci. Pap., 1884-1900. Stirling boiler.

Stirling boiler (Stirling, Allan): Engineering and Industry. See: Auger.

Stirling cycle (Stirling, Robert): Engineering and Industry. See: Thewlis; Webster's 3d.

Stirling distribution (Stirling, James): Statistics. See: Kendall.

Stirling engine (Stirling, Robert): Engineering and Industry. See: Auger; Webster's 3d.

Stirling formula for interpolation (Stirling, James): Mathematics. See: Ballentyne; Internat. Dict. Ap. Math.; Van Nostrand Sci. Encyc. Also known as: Newton-Stirling interpolation formula.

STIRLING, JAMES. 1692-1770. Scottish mathematician. See: Dict. Nat. Biog. Stirling distribution, Stirling formula for interpolation, Stirling numbers, Stirling's formula (or approximation), Stirling's series (for the gamma function).

Stirling numbers (Stirling, James): Mathematics. See: Internat. Dict. Ap. Math.; Van Nostrand Sci. Encyc.

STIRLING, ROBERT. 1790-1878. Scottish engineer. See: Dict. Nat. Biog. Stirling cycle, Stirling engine.

STIRLING, WILLIAM. 1851-1932. English histologist and physiologist. See: World Who's Who Sci. Stirling's modification of Gram's stain.

Stirling's formula (or approximation) (Stirling, James): Mathematics. See: Internat. Dict. Ap. Math.; James; Thewlis.

Stirling's modification of Gram's stain (Stirling, William): Medicine. See: Stedman.

Stirling's series (for the gamma function) (Stirling, James): Mathematics. See: Ballentyne.

TISHOV, S. M. fl. 1961. Russian professor. Cited in: Amer. Min. vol. 7, no. 5-6 (May-June 1962), p. 807. Stishovite.

tishovite (Stishov, S. M.): Earth Sciences. See: Thrush.

tobbe condensation (Stobbe, Hans): Chemistry. See: Ballentyne; Van Nostrand Chem. Dict.

TOBBE, HANS (In full: JOHANN HERMANN AUGUST ADOLPH). 1860-1938. German chemist. See: Pogg., vols. 5,6. Stobbe condensation.

TOCK, ALFRED E. 1876-1946. German chemist. See: World Who's Who ci. Stock system.

tock-Spielmeyer-Vogt syndrome (Stock, Wolfgang; Spielmeyer, Walter; and ogt, Oskar): Medicine. See: Jablonski. Also known as: Batten-Mayou yndrome, Batten's disease, Spielmeyer-Vogt syndrome.

tock system (Stock, Alfred E.): Chemistry. See: Webster's 3d.

TOCK, WOLFGANG. b. 1874. German physician. See: Biog. Lex. ervorr. Aerzte. Stock-Spielmeyer-Vogt syndrome.

TOCKBARGER, DONALD CHARLES. 1895-1952. American physicist. See: ogg., vol. 6. Bridgman-Stockbarger method.

TOCKER, FREDERICK WILLIAM. b. 1893. Swiss-born American ophthalmolo-ist. See: Direct. Med. Specialists, 1965-1966. Stocker's line.

tocker's line (Stocker, Frederick William): Medicine. See: Jablonski; tedman.

tockmayer potential (Stockmayer, Walter Hugo): Chemistry. See: Ballentyne; nternat. Dict. Ap. Math.

TOCKMAYER, WALTER HUGO. 1914- . American chemist. See: World Vho's Who Sci. Stockmayer potential.

TODDARD, J. W. "Dixie". fl. 1925. Canadian? chemist. Cited in: Chem. Abstr., vol. 19, p. 2750. Stoddard's solvent.

toddard's solvent (Stoddard, J. W.): Chemistry. See: Webster's 3d.

toeltzner test (Stoeltzner, Wilhelm): Chemistry. See: Van Nostrand Chem. Dict.

TOELTZNER, WILHELM. b. 1872. German pediatrician. See: Handb. der Deut. Wissensch. Stoeltzner test.

TOERCK, KARL. 1832-1899. Austrian laryngologist. See: Biog. Lex. ervorr. Aerzte. Stoerck's blennorrhea.

toerck's blennorrhea (Stoerck, Karl): Medicine. See: Dorland; Stedman.

toermer cone (Stoermer, Fredrik Carl): Physics. See: Thewlis.

TOERMER, FREDRIK CARL. 1874-1957. Norwegian mathematician and eophysicist. See: World Who's Who Sci. Stoermer cone, Stoermer method for the numerical solution of an ordinary differential equation of second order), toermer unit.

toermer method (for the numerical solution of an ordinary differential equation f second order) (Stoermer, Fredrik Carl): Mathematics. See: Internat. Dict. Ap. Math.

TOERMER, RICHARD (In full: HEINRICH FRIEDRICH RICHARD). 1870-1940. German organic chemist. See: Pogg., vols. 4 to 6, 7a. Stoermer test eaction?, Widman-Stoermer synthesis.

toermer test reaction (Stoermer, Richard?): Chemistry. See: Van Nostrand Chem. Dict.

toermer unit (Stoermer, Fredrik Carl): Physics. See: Ballentyne.

TOFFEL, ADOLF. 1880-1937. German orthopedic surgeon. See: Biog. Lex. ervorr. Aerzte. Stoffel's operation.

toffel's operation (Stoffel, Adolf): Medicine. See: Dorland; Stedman.

TOKES, ADRIAN. 1887-1927. Irish pathologist. See: Dict. Nat. Biog. tokesiella?

tokes' amputation (Stokes, Sir William): Medicine. See: Dorland; Stedman.

tokes' aster (Stokes, Jonathan): Botany. See: Mathews, M. M.; Webster's 3d.

STOKES, CHARLES F. 1863-1931. American naval officer. See: Who Was Who Amer. Stokes stretcher (or litter).

Stokes diameter (Stokes, Sir George Gabriel): Physics. See: Thrush.

Stokes drift (of gravity waves) (Stokes, Sir George Gabriel): Physics. See: Internat. Dict. Phys. Elec.

Stokes-Einstein equation (Stokes, Sir George Gabriel and Einstein, Albert): Physics. See: Thewlis.

Stokes' expectorant mixture (Stokes, William): Medicine. See: Dorland; Stedman.

Stokes flow (Stokes, Sir George Gabriel): Physics. See: Internat. Dict. Ap. Math.; Van Nostrand Sci. Encyc.

STOKES, SIR FREDERIC WILFRID SCOTT. 1860-1927. English engineer and inventor. See: Dict. Nat. Biog. Stokes trench mortar.

STOKES, SIR GEORGE GABRIEL. 1819-1903. Irish mathematician and physi-cist. See: Dict. Nat. Biog. Clairaut and Stokes theorems, Navier-Stokes equation(s), Stokes diameter, Stokes drift (of gravity waves), Stokes-Einstein equation, Stokes flow, Stokes' law for viscosity, Stokes' law of fluorescence (luminescence, or radiation), Stokes' lens, Stokes lines, Stokes' phenomenon, Stokes polarization theorem, Stokes' stream function, Stokes' theorem, Stokes (unit), Stokesite.

STOKES, JOHN S. fl. 1932. American chemist. (Biography source unavail-able.) Stokes reagent for gums?

STOKES, JONATHAN. 1755-1831. English botanist. (Biography source unavailable.) Stokes' aster, Stokesia.

Stokes' law (Stokes, William): Medicine. See: Dorland; Stedman.

Stokes' law for viscosity (Stokes, Sir George Gabriel): Physics. See: Huschke; Internat. Dict. Phys. Elec.; Thewlis.

Stokes' law of fluorescence (luminescence, or radiation) (Stokes, Sir George Gabriel): Physics. See: Ballentyne; Thewlis; Van Nostrand Sci. Encyc.

Stokes' lens (Stokes, Sir George Gabriel): Physics. See: Dorland.

Stokes lines (Stokes, Sir George Gabriel): Physics. See: Internat. Dict. Ap. Math.; Internat. Dict. Phys. Elec.; Thewlis.

Stokes' phenomenon (Stokes, Sir George Gabriel): Physics. See: Ballentyne.

Stokes polarization theorem (Stokes, Sir George Gabriel): Physics. See: Internat. Dict. Ap. Math.

Stokes' reagent (Stokes, William Royal): Medicine. See: Dorland; Stedman; Van Nostrand Chem. Dict.

Stokes reagent for gums (Stokes, John S.?): Chemistry. See: Van Nostrand Chem. Dict.

Stokes' stream function (Stokes, Sir George Gabriel): Physics. See: Huschke; Van Nostrand Sci. Encyc.

Stokes stretcher (or litter) (Stokes, Charles F.): Medicine. See: Thrush; Webster's 3d.

Stokes' syndrome (Stokes, William). See: Morgagni-Adams-Stokes syndrome.

Stokes' theorem (Stokes, Sir George Gabriel): Physics. See: Huschke; James; Thewlis.

Stokes trench mortar (Stokes, Sir Frederic Wilfrid Scott): Weapons. See: Partridge; Quick.

Stokes (unit) (Stokes, Sir George Gabriel): Physics. See: Ballentyne; Dresner.

STOKES, WILLIAM. 1804-1878. Irish physician. See: World Who's Who Sci. Cheyne-Stokes asthma, Cheyne-Stokes psychosis, Cheyne-Stokes respira-tion, Morgagni-Adams-Stokes syndrome, Stokes' amputation, Stokes' expectorant mixture, Stokes' law.

STOKES, WILLIAM ROYAL. 1870-1930. American pathologist. See: Biog. Lex hervorr. Aerzte. Stokes' reagent.

Stokesia (Stokes, Jonathan): Botany. See: Taylor, N.; Webster's 3d.

Stokesiella (Stokes, Adrian?): Zoology. See: Pennak.

Stokesite (Stokes, Sir George Gabriel): Earth Sciences. See: Thrush; Webster's 3d.

STOKVIS, BAREND JOSEPH E. 1834-1902. Dutch physician. See: World Who's Who Sci. Stokvis-Talma syndrome, Stokvis' test.

Stokvis–Talma syndrome (Stokvis, Barend Joseph and Talma, Sape): Medicine. See: Jablonski. Also known as: Van den Bergh's disease.

Stokvis' test (Stokvis, Barend Joseph E.): Medicine. See: Dorland; Stedman.

STOLBA, FRANZ. fl. 1870. Czechoslovakian chemist. Cited in: Royal Soc. Cat. Sci. Pap. Stolba test reaction for cesium, Stolba test reaction for potassium, Stolba test reaction for tellurites and selenites.

Stolba test reaction for cesium (Stolba, Franz): Chemistry. See: Van Nostrand Chem. Dict.

Stolba test reaction for potassium (Stolba, Franz): Chemistry. See: Van Nostrand Chem. Dict.

Stolba test reaction for tellurites and selenites (Stolba, Franz): Chemistry. See: Van Nostrand Chem. Dict.

STOLL, L. fl. 1921. German chemist. Cited in: Chem. Abstr., vol. 15 p. 780. Thiel–Stoll solution.

STOLLE, ROBERT. 1869–1938. German chemist. See: Pogg., vols. 4,5,6, 7a. Stolle synthesis, Stolle test reaction.

Stolle synthesis (Stolle, Robert): Chemistry. See: Van Nostrand Chem. Dict.

Stolle test reaction (Stolle, Robert): Chemistry. See: Van Nostrand Chem. Dict.

STOLOFF, E. GORDON. fl. 1933. American physician. (Biography source unavailable.) Kugel–Stoloff syndrome.

STOLTZ, JOSEPH ALEXIS. 1803–1896. French gynecologist. See: World Who's Who Sci. Stoltz' operation.

Stoltz' operation (Stoltz, Joseph Alexis). See: Gigli's operation.

STOLZ. fl. 19th c. Bohemian scientist. Cited in: Dana. Stolzite.

STOLZE, F. fl. 1872. German engineer. (Biography source unavailable.) Stolze gas turbine.

Stolze gas turbine (Stolze, F.): Engineering and Industry. See: Auger.

Stolzite (Stolz): Earth Sciences. See: Thrush; Webster's 3d.

STONE, BARTON WARREN. 1772–1844. American evangelist. See: Dict. Amer. Biog. Stoneite.

STONE, BENTLEY. fl. 1929–1961. American dancer, teacher and choreographer. (Biography source unavailable.) Page–Stone Ballet Company.

Stone–Cech compactification (Stone, Marshall Harvey and Cech, Eduard): Mathematics. See: James.

STONE, IRWIN. fl. 1930. American chemist. (Biography source unavailable.) Stone test for magnesium, Stone test for mercury in organic compounds.

STONE, LUCY. 1818–1893. American suffragette. See: Dict. Amer. Biog. Lucy Stoner.

STONE, MARSHALL HARVEY. 1903– . American mathematician. See: World Who's Who Sci. Stone–Cech compactification.

STONE, ROY. d. 1905. American engineer. (Biography source unavailable.) Roystonea.

Stone test for magnesium (Stone, Irwin): Chemistry. See: Van Nostrand Chem. Dict.

Stone test for mercury in organic compounds (Stone, Irwin): Chemistry. See: Van Nostrand Chem. Dict.

Stoneite (Stone, Barton Warren): Religion. See: Mathews, M. M.; Morris; Webster's 3d.

STONER, EDMUND CLIFTON. 1899– . English physicist. See: World Who's Who Sci. Stoner quanta (or energy levels).

Stoner quanta (or energy levels) (Stoner, Edmund Clifton): Physics. See: Hackh.

Stonewall (Jackson, Thomas "Stonewall"): Generic Word (block opponent). See: Stenhouse.

Stonewall brigade (Jackson, Thomas "Stonewall"): History. See: Mathews, M. M.

Stonewall Guard (Jackson, Thomas "Stonewall"): History. See: Mathews, M. M.

STONEY, BINDON BLOOD. 1828–1909. Irish engineer. See: Dict. Nat. Biog. Stoney gate.

Stoney gate (Stoney, Bindon Blood): Engineering and Industry. See: Webster's 3d.

STONOR, JOHN DE. d. 1354. English judge and landowner. See: Dict. Nat. Biog. Stonor papers.

Stonor papers (Stonor, John de): History. See: Steinberg.

STOOKEY, BYRON POLK. 1887–1966. American neurosurgeon. See: Who Was Who Amer. Queckenstedt–Stookey test, Stookey–Scarff operation, Stookey's reflex.

Stookey–Scarff operation (Stookey, Byron Polk and Scarff, John Edwin): Medicine. See: Stedman.

Stookey's reflex (Stookey, Byron Polk): Medicine. See: Dorland.

Stopes–Heerlen system (Stopes, Marie Charlotte Carmichael and Heerlen): Earth Sciences. Cited in: Thrush under "coal constituent classification; Spackman System."

STOPES, MARIE CHARLOTTE CARMICHAEL. 1880–1958. English paleobotanist and family planning expert. See: World Who's Who Sci. Stopes–Heerlen system.

Storch–Morawski test (Derivation undetermined): Chemistry. See: Van Nostrand Chem. Dict.

STORER, DAVID HUMPHREYS. 1804–1891. American obstetrician and naturalist. See: Dict. Amer. Biog. Storeria.

Storeria (Storer, David Humphreys): Zoology. See: Webster's 3d.

STORFER, ERNST. fl. 1935. German chemist. Cited in: Chem. Abstr., vol. 29, p. 5379. Storfer reagent.

Storfer reagent (Storfer, Ernst): Chemistry. See: Van Nostrand Chem. Dict.

STORM, DOUGLAS. fl. 1911. German? chemist. Cited in: Pogg., vol. 5 under "Hofmann, Karl Andreas." Hofmann–Storm reagent.

Stormer viscometer (Derivation undetermined): Engineering and Industry. See: Thrush under "Viscometer".

STORROW, CHARLES STORER. 1809–1904. American engineer. See: Dict. Amer. Biog. Storrow whirling hygrometer?

Storrow whirling hygrometer (Storrow, Charles Storer?): Engineering and Industry. See: Thrush.

STORY–MASKELYNE, NEVIL (In full: MERVYN HERBERT NEVIL). 1823–1911. English mineralogist. See: World Who's Who Sci. Maskelynite.

STOTT, CHARLES E. fl. 20th c. South-African director of mine. Cited in: Amer. Min. vol. 43, no. 9-10 (Sept.-Oct. 1958), p. 1006. Stottite.

Stottite (Stott, Charles E.): Earth Sciences. See: Thrush.

STOUT, WALTER CLAY. 1908– . American dentist. See: Amer. Men and Women Sci., 12th ed. Stout's wiring?

Stout's wiring (Stout, Walter Clay?): Dentistry. See: Stedman.

stovaine (Fourneau, Ernest Francois Auguste): Medicine. See: Partridge.

stovepipe Leary (hat) (Leary): Fashion. See: Mathews, M. M.

STOVIN, PETER GEORGE INGLE. fl. 1950-1964. English pathologist. See: Med. Direct., 1964. Hughes–Stovin syndrome.

STRACHAN, JAMES. fl. 1910-1926. English paper chemist. Cited in: Chem. Abstr., vol. 5, p. 2945. Strachan test.

Strachan–Scott syndrome (Strachan, William Henry and Scott, Henry Harold): Medicine. See: Jablonski. Also known as: Hawes–Pallister–Landor syndrome.

Strachan test (Strachan, James): Chemistry. See: Van Nostrand Chem. Dict.

STRACHAN, WILLIAM HENRY WILLIAMS. 1857–1921. English physician. See: Who Was Who. Strachan–Scott syndrome.

STRADIVARI, ANTONIO (ANTONIUS STRADIVARIUS). ca. 1644-1737. Italian stringed instrument maker. See: Grove. Stradivarius (violin).

Stradivarius (violin) (Stradivari, Antonio): Music. See: Harvey; Hendrickson; Partridge.

trafford, 1st Earl of. See: Wentworth, Thomas (1st Earl of Strafford).

traffordian (Wentworth, Thomas, 1st Earl of Strafford): Politics. See: ebster's 3d.

TRANDBERG, JAMES VICTOR. b. 1883. Swedish physician. See: Biog. ex. hervorr. Aerzte. Groenblad-Strandberg syndrome.

TRANG, JAMES JESSE. 1813-1856. American Mormon leader. See: Dict. mer. Biog. Strangite.

range, Lord. See: Stanley, Ferdinando, 5th Earl of Derby.

range's men (Stanley, Ferdinando): Theatre. See: Hartnoll.

rangite (Strang, James Jesse): Religion. See: Mathews, M. M.; Webster's .

TRANSKI, IWAN N. b. 1897. Bulgarian-born German physicist and chemist. ee: Pogg., vol. 7a; World Who's Who Sci. Stranskiite.

ranskiite (Stranski, Iwan N.): Earth Sciences. See: Thrush.

TRANSKY, EUGENE. b. 1871. German pediatrician. See: Biog. Lex. ervorr. Aerzte. Stransky-Regala syndrome.

ransky-Regala syndrome (Stransky, Eugene and Regala, Arsenio C.): Medicine. ee: Jablonski.

ranvaesia (Fox-Strangways, William Thomas Horner): Botany. See: Taylor, N.

TRASBURGER, EDUARD ADOLF. 1844-1912. Polish-born German histologist nd botanist. See: World Who's Who Sci. Strasburger's cell-plate.

rasburger's cell-plate (Strasburger, Eduard Adolf): Medicine. See: Dorland.

rass (lead-glass) (Strasser, Joseph): Applied Arts. See: Partridge.

TRASSBURG, GUSTAV A. b. 1848. German physiologist. Cited in: Royal oc. Cat. Sci. Pap., 1874-1883. Strassburg's test.

rassburg's test (Strassburg, Gustav A.): Medicine. See: Dorland; Stedman.

TRASSER, JOSEPH. fl. 18th c. German jeweller. See: Wurzbach. Strass ead-glass).

TRASSMAN, PAUL F. 1866-1938. German gynecologist. See: Biog. Lex. ervorr. Aerzte. Strassman's phenomenon.

rassman's phenomenon (Strassman, Paul F.): Medicine. See: Dorland; tedman.

TRATTON, GEORGE MALCOLM. 1865-1957. American psychologist. See: World Who's Who Sci. Stratton's experiment.

tratton's experiment (Stratton, George Malcolm): Physiology. See: English; Volman.

traub hardening (Straub, Wolf Deter?): Engineering and Industry. See: Van Nostrand Sci. Encyc.

traub test for phosphorous (Straub, Walther?): Chemistry. See: Van Nostrand hem. Dict.

TRAUB, WALTHER. 1874-1944. German pharmacologist. See: Pogg., ols. 6, 7a. Straub test for phosphorous?

TRAUB, WOLF DETER. 1927- . American physicist. See: World Who's Vho Sci. Straub hardening?

TRAUS, ISIDORE. 1845-1896. French physician. See: Biog. Lex. hervorr. erzte. Straus reaction, Straus' sign.

traus reaction (Straus, Isidore): Medicine. See: Dorland; Stedman.

traus' sign (Straus, Isidore): Medicine. See: Dorland; Stedman.

TRAUSS, ALFRED A. fl. 1940. American? psychiatrist. Cited in: Cum. Auth. Index to Psych. Index, 1894-1935, and Psych. Abstr., 1927-1958. trauss syndrome, Werner-Strauss theory.

TRAUSS, HERMANN. 1868-1944. German physician. See: Biog. Lex. ervorr. Aerzte. Strauss' test.

TRAUSS, JEROME. b. 1893. American metallurgist. See: Amer. Men ci., 6th ed. Strauss solution.

STRAUSS, LEVI. fl. 19th c. American overall manufacturer. (Biography source unavailable.) Levis.

STRAUSS, RICHARD. 1864-1949. German conductor and composer. See: New Encyc. Brit., 1974, Microp. Straussian.

Strauss solution (Strauss, Jerome): Chemistry. See: Van Nostrand Chem. Dict.

Strauss syndrome (Strauss, Alfred A.): Medicine. See: Good.

Strauss' test (Strauss, Hermann): Medicine. See: Dorland; Stedman.

Straussian (Strauss, Richard): Music. See: Webster's 3d.

STRAW, JACK. fl. 1381. English peasant revolutionary leader. See: Webster's Biog. Dict. Jackstraw.

STRECKER, ADOLF FRIEDRICH LUDWIG. 1822-1871. German chemist. See: Pogg., vols. 2,3,7a suppl. Strecker degradation, Strecker's alkyl sulfonate synthesis (or reaction), Strecker's amino acid synthesis (method, or reaction).

Strecker degradation (Strecker, Adolf Friedrich Ludwig): Chemistry. See: Ballentyne; Van Nostrand Chem. Dict.

Strecker's alkyl sulfonate synthesis (or reaction) (Strecker, Adolf Friedrich Ludwig): Chemistry. See: Ballentyne; Van Nostrand Chem. Dict.

Strecker's amino acid synthesis (method, or reaction) (Strecker, Adolf Friedrich Ludwig): Chemistry. See: Hackh; Van Nostrand Chem. Dict.; Van Nostrand Soc. Encyc. under "Amino Acids."

Street engine (Street, Robert): Engineering and Industry. See: Auger.

STREET, ROBERT. fl. 1794. English engineer. (Biography source unavailable.) Street engine.

STREETER, GEORGE LINIUS. 1873-1948. American embryologist. See: Who Was Who Amer. Streeter horizons.

Streeter horizons (Streeter, George Linius): Medicine. See: Stedman.

Strehl definition (Strehl, Karl Wilhelm): Physics. See: Internat. Dict. Ap. Math.

STREHL, KARL WILHELM. 1864-1940. German optics physicist. See: Pogg., vols. 4,5,6,7a. Strehl definition.

STREIFF, ENRICO BERNARD. 1908- . Italian-born Swiss ophthalmologist. See: World Who's Who Sci. Hallerman-Streiff syndrome.

Strelitzia (Charlotte Sophia, Princess of Mecklenburg-Strelitz): Botany. See: Taylor, N.; Webster's 3d.

STRENG, JOHANN A. 1830-1897. German mineralogist. See: Pogg., vols. 2,3,4. Streng test reactions, Strengite.

Streng test reactions (Streng, Johann A.): Chemistry. See: Van Nostrand Chem. Dict.

Strengite (Streng, Johann A.): Earth Sciences. See: Webster's 3d.

Strephon (Strephon, the lover): Generic Word (rustic lover). See: Brewer.

STREPHON, THE LOVER. Character in Sir Philip Sidney's prose romance, "Arcadia" (1590). See: Harvey. Strephon.

STRICKLER, ALBERT. b. 1886. American dermatologist. (Biography source unavailable.) Strickler's solution.

Strickler's solution (Strickler, Albert): Medicine. See: Dorland.

strip area of Hines (Hines, Marion): Anatomy. See: Stedman.

STRIPPELMANN, LEO. fl. 19th c. German director of salt works. Cited in: Hintze, vol. 1, part 3, half 2, p. 4471. Leonite.

STRISOWER, RUDOLF. fl. 1921. German scientist. Cited in: Chem. Abstr., Decenn. Index, 1917-1926. Schellong-Strisower phenomenon.

STRNAD, M. fl. 1937. Czechoslovakian chemist. Cited in: Pogg., vol. 7b under "Dubsky, Jan Vaclav." Dubsky-Langer-Stonad reagents.

STROGANOFF, COUNT PAUL. fl. 19th c. Russian diplomat. (Biography source unavailable.) beef Stroganoff.

STROGANOFF, VASILI VASILOVICH. 1857-1938. Russian obstetrician. See: Biog. Lex. hervorr. Aerzte. Stroganoff's method.

Stroganoff's method (Stroganoff, Vasili Vasilovich): Medicine. See: Stedman.

STROGANOV. fl. 1845. President of Moscow natural history society. Cited in: Hintze. Stroganovite.

STROGANOV, ANIKA. fl. early 16th c. Russian merchant and manufacturer. See: Encyc. Brit., 1973. Stroganov school of icon painting.

Stroganov school of icon painting (Stroganov, Anika): Fine Arts. See: Encyc. Brit., 1973.

Stroganovite (Stroganov): Earth Sciences. See: Charnock.

STROHL, ANDRE. b. 1887. French physician. See: Pogg., vol. 6. Guillain-Barre-Strohl syndrome.

STROHMEYER, FRIEDRICH. 1776-1835. German chemist. See: World Who's Who Sci. Strohmeyer test reaction? Stromeyerite.

Strohmeyer test reaction (Strohmeyer, Friedrich?): Chemistry. See: Van Nostrand Chem. Dict.

STROM, ROAR. fl. 1953. Scandinavian physician. (Biography source unavailable.) Strom-Zollinger-Ellison syndrome.

Strom-Zollinger-Ellison syndrome (Strom, Roar; Zollinger, Robert Milton; and Ellison, Edwin H.). See: Zollinger-Ellison syndrome.

STROMEYER, GEORG FRIEDRICH LOUIS. 1804-1876. German surgeon. See: Allg. Deut. Biog. Stromeyer-Little operation, Stromeyer's splint.

Stromeyer-Little operation (Stromeyer, Georg Friedrich Louis and Little, William John): Medicine. See: Stedman.

Stromeyerite (Strohmeyer, Friedrich): Earth Sciences. See: Thrush; Webster's 3d.

Stromeyer's splint (Stromeyer, Georg Friedrich Louis): Medicine. See: Dorland; Stedman.

STRONG, EDWARD KELLOGG, JR. 1884-1963. American psychologist. See: Nat. Cyc. Amer. Biog., vol. 51, p. 254. Strong vocational interest blank.

Strong equality (Strong, Theodore?): Mathematics. See: Internat. Dict. Phys. Elec.

STRONG, RICHARD PEARSON. 1872-1948. American physician. See: World Who's Who Sci. Strong's bacillus.

STRONG, THEODORE. 1790-1869. American mathematician. See: World Who's Who Sci. Strong equality?

Strong vocational interest blank (Strong, Edward Kellogg, Jr.): Psychology. See: Chaplin.

STRONG, WILLIAM WALKER. b. 1883. American physicist and chemist. See: Pogg., vols. 5,6. Ficklen-Strong thermal precipitator?

STRONGIN, EDWARD I. fl. 1941-1973. American psychologist. See: Biog. Direct. Amer. Psych. Assoc., 1973. Strongin-Hinsie-Peck test.

Strongin-Hinsie-Peck test (Strongin, Edward I.; Hinsie, Leland E.; and Peck, Robert E.): Psychology. See: Hinsie.

Strong's bacillus (Strong, Richard Pearson): Medicine. See: Dorland.

STROOP, J. R. fl. 1935. American? psychologist. Cited in: Cum. Auth. Index to Psych. Index, 1894-1935, and Psych. Abstr., 1927-1958. Stroop test.

Stroop test (Stroop, J. R.): Psychology. See: Wolman.

Stroud and Oates bridge (Derivation undetermined): Physics. See: Internat. Dict. Phys. Elec.

STROUD, BERT BRENETTE. b. 1865. American physiologist, anatomist, and zoologist. See: Amer. Men Sci., 1st ed. Stroud's pectinated area.

Stroud's pectinated area (Stroud, Bert Brenette): Medicine. See: Stedman.

Strouhal formula (Strouhal, Vincent?): Physics. See: Internat. Dict. Phys. Elec.

Strouhal number (Strouhal, Vincent?): Physics. See: Ballentyne; Hushke; Internat. Dict. Ap. Math.

STROUHAL, VINCENT. fl. 1878-1900. Czechoslovakian physicist. Cited in: Royal Soc. Cat. Sci. Pap., 1874-1883; 1884-1900. Strouhal formula? Strouhal number?

STROUP, FREEMAN P. fl. 1920. American pharmaceutical chemist. Cited in: Chem. Abstr., vol. 13, p. 2834. Stroup test.

Stroup test (Stroup, Freeman P.): Chemistry. See: Van Nostrand Chem. Dict.

STROWGER, ALMON B. fl. 1889. American? engineer. (Biography source unavailable.) Strowger system.

Strowger system (Strowger, Almon B.): Engineering and Industry. See: Markus.

Struebing-Marchiafava syndrome (Struebing, Paul and Marchiafava, Ettore). See: Marchiafava-Micheli syndrome (or anemia).

STRUEBING, PAUL. b. 1852. German physician. See: Kukula. Struebing-Marchiafava syndrome.

STRUEMPELL, ADOLPH (In full: ERNST ADOLPH GUSTAV GOTTFRIED VON). 1853-1925. German neurologist. See: Biog. Lex. hervorr. Aerzte. Bekhterev-Struempell-Marie syndrome, Struempell-Leichtenstern encephalitis, Struempell-Lorrain disease, Struempell's disease (1), Struempell's disease (2), Struempell's phenomenon, Struempell's reflex, Struempell's sign, Westphal-Struempell syndrome (or disease).

Struempell-Leichtenstern encephalitis (Struempell, Adolph and Leichtenstern, Otto): Medicine. See: Jablonski.

Struempell-Lorrain disease (Struempell, Adolph and Lorrain, Maurice): Medicine. See: Jablonski.

Struempell's disease (1) (Struempell, Adolph): Medicine. See: Jablonski; Stedman.

Struempell's disease (2) (Struempell, Adolph). See: Erb-Charcot syndrome.

Struempell's phenomenon (Struempell, Adolph): Medicine. See: Dorland; Stedman.

Struempell's reflex (Struempell, Adolph): Medicine. See: Stedman.

Struempell's sign (Struempell, Adolph): Medicine. See: Hinsie.

STRUMPFF, CHRISTOPHER CAR. fl. 1752. German botanist and chemist. (Biography source unavailable.) Strumpfia.

Strumpfia (Strumpff, Christopher Car): Botany. See: Charnock.

STRUNSKY, MAX. 1873-1957. American orthopedic surgeon. See: New York Times, Dec. 2, 1957, p. 27, col. 5. Strunsky's sign.

Strunsky's sign (Strunsky, Max): Medicine. See: Dorland.

STRUNZ, HUGO. 1910- . German mineralogist. See: Pogg., vol. 7a. Strunzite.

Strunzite (Strunz, Hugo): Earth Sciences. See: Thrush.

Struve functions (Struve, Jacob?): Mathematics. See: Ballentyne.

STRUVE, HEINRICH. 1751-1826. French mineralogist. See: Pogg., vol. 2. Struve ventilator.

STRUVE, HEINRICH. fl. 1880. German physician. See: Royal Soc. Cat. Sci. Pap., 1874-1883. Struve test reaction for morphine?, Struve's test.

STRUVE, HEINRICH CHRISTIAN GOTTFRIED VON. 1772-1851. German-born Russian diplomat and mineralogist. See: Pogg., vol. 2. Struvite, Svanberg-Struve test reaction?

STRUVE, JACOB. 1755-1841. German mathematician. See: Pogg., vol. 2. Struve functions?

Struve test reaction for morphine (Struve, Heinrich?): Chemistry. See: Van Nostrand Chem. Dict.

Struve ventilator (Struve, Heinrich): Engineering and Industry. See: Thrush.

Struve's test (Struve, Heinrich): Medicine. See: Dorland; Stedman.

Struvite (Struve, Heinrich Christian Gottfried von): Earth Sciences. See: Thrush; Webster's 3d.

STRUYCKEN, HUBERT JOHANN LEONARD. b. 1869. Dutch physician. See: Lijst geschr. ver. Kath. Nederl., 1922, p. 54f. Gradenigo-Struyken triangle?

Stryker frame (Stryker, Garold V.?): Medicine. See: Stedman.

STRYKER, GAROLD V. b. 1896. American pathologist. See: Amer. Men Sci., 8th ed. Stryker frame?, Stryker-Halbeisen syndrome.

Stryker-Halbeisen syndrome (Stryker, Garold V. and Halbeisen, William A.): Medicine. See: Jablonski; Stedman.

TUART. fl. 20th c. American? hospital patient. (Biography source available.) Stuart factor.

uart–Bras disease (Stuart, Kenneth Lamont and Bras, Gerrit?): Medicine. e: Jablonski.

uart–Briegleb molecular models (Stuart, Herbert Arthur and Briegleb, Guenther): ysics. See: Van Nostrand Sci. Encyc.

uart, Charles Edward. See: Charles Edward Stuart.

uart factor (Stuart): Medicine. See: Stedman. Also known as: Stuart– ower factor.

UART, HERBERT ARTHUR. b. 1899. Swiss-born German physicist. See: gg., vol. 6; World Who's Who Sci. Stuart–Briegleb molecular models.

UART, JAMES EWELL BROWN "JEB". 1833-1864. American soldier. See: ct. Amer. Biog. General Stuart tank?

uart, James Francis Edward. See: James Francis Edward Stuart.

TUART, JOHN (3RD EARL OF BUTE). 1713-1792. English prime minister. e: Dict. Nat. Biog. Butea (Butia), Stewartia (or Stuartia).

UART, KENNETH LAMONT. fl. 1952-1964. English physician in the West dies. See: Med. Direct., 1964. Stuart–Bras disease.

uart–Prower factor (Stuart and Prower). See: Stuart factor.

ubenrauch test reaction (Derivation undetermined): Chemistry. See: Van ostrand Chem. Dict.

ubs' iron gauge (Stubs, Peter): Engineering and Industry. See: Auger; Thrush. so known as: Peter Stubs' gauge.

UBS, PETER. fl. 1881. English? engineer. (Biography source unavailable.) ubs' iron gauge.

udent. See: Gossett, William Sealy.

udentisation (Gossett, William Sealy): Statistics. See: Kendall.

udentised maximum absolute deviate (Gossett, William Sealy): Statistics. e: Kendall.

udentised range (Gossett, William Sealy): Statistics. See: Kendall.

udent's hypothesis (Gossett, William Sealy): Statistics. See: Kendall.

udent's t–distribution (or test) (Gossett, William Sealy): Statistics. See: uschke; James; Kendall; Van Nostrand Sci. Encyc.

UDINGER, JOSEF. fl. 1927. German chemist. Cited in: Chem. Abstr., l. 22, pp. 1432, 1823. Kreis-Studinger reagent.

udite (Studius): Religion. See: Webster's 3d.

UDIUS. fl. 5th c. Roman official. See: Dict. Christian Biog. Studite.

uetz's test (Derivation undetermined). See: Fuerbringer's test.

ueve diagram (Stueve, Georg Heinrich Friedrich): Earth Sciences. See: uschke; Van Nostrand Sci. Encyc. under "Thermodynamic Diagram."

UEVE, GEORG HEINRICH FRIEDRICH. 1885-1935. German meteorologist. e: Pogg., vols. 6,7a. Stueve diagram.

uffer law (or rule) (Derivation undetermined): Chemistry. See: Hackh; an Nostrand Chem. Dict.

UHL, L. fl. 1954. French? physician. (Biography source unavailable). eismann-Netter and Stuhl syndrome.

UMPF, J. fl. 1890. German engineer. Cited in: Royal Soc. Cat. Sci. p., 1884-1900. Riedler-Stumpf turbine.

urge–Weber–Dimitri syndrome (Sturge, William Allen; Weber, Frederick Parkes, d Dimitri, Vicente). See: Sturge–Weber syndrome (or disease).

urge–Weber syndrome (or disease) (Sturge, William Allen and Weber, Frederick rkes): Medicine. See: Jablonski; Stedman. Also known as: Jahnke's ndrome, Kalischer's syndrome, Krabbe's syndrome, Lawford's syndrome, Milles' ndrome, Parkes Weber syndrome, Parkes–Weber and Dimitri syndrome, chirmer's syndrome, Sturge–Weber–Dimitri syndrome, Sturge's disease, Weber– imitri syndrome.

TURGE, WILLIAM ALLEN. 1850-1919. English physician. See: Who Was ho. Sturge–Weber syndrome (or disease).

Sturgeon (unit) (Sturgeon, William): Physics. See: Dresner.

STURGEON, WILLIAM. 1783-1850. English electrician and inventor. See: Dict. Nat. Biog. Sturgeon (unit).

Sturge's disease (Sturge, William Allen). See: Sturge–Weber syndrome (or disease).

STURGES, H. A. fl. 1926. American statistician. (Biography source unavailable.) Sturges' rule.

Sturges' rule (Sturges, H. A.): Statistics. See: Kendall.

Sturm comparison theorem (Sturm, Jacques Charles Francois): Mathematics. See: James.

STURM, ERNST. fl. 1941. American physician. (Biography source unavailable.) Murphy-Sturm lymphosarcoma.

STURM, JACQUES CHARLES FRANCOIS. 1803-1855. Swiss-French mathematician. See: Encyc. Brit., 1973. Sturm comparison theorem, Sturm–Liouville differential equation, Sturm–Liouville problem, Sturm separation theorem, Sturm's functions (or sequence), Sturm's theorem.

STURM, JOHANN CHRISTOPHER. 1635-1703. German mathematician, physician and philosopher. See: Nouv. Biog. Univ. Sturm's conoid, Sturm's interval.

Sturm–Liouville differential equation (Sturm, Jacques Charles Francois and Liouville, Joseph): Mathematics. See: Internat. Dict. Ap. Math.; James; Van Nostrand Sci. Encyc.

Sturm–Liouville problem (Sturm, Jacques Charles Francois and Liouville, Joseph): Mathematics. See: Internat. Dict. Ap. Math.

Sturm separation theorem (Sturm, Jacques Charles Francois): Mathematics. See: James.

Sturmey–Archer gear (Sturmey, Henry and Archer, James): Engineering and Industry. See: Auger.

STURMEY, HENRY. fl. 1902. English engineer. (Biography source unavailable.) Sturmey–Archer gear.

Sturm's conoid (Sturm, Johann Christopher): Medicine. See: Stedman.

Sturm's functions (or sequence) (Sturm, Jacques Charles Francois): Mathematics. See: Ballentyne; Internat. Dict. Ap. Math.; James.

Sturm's interval (Sturm, Johann Christopher): Medicine. See: Stedman.

Sturm's theorem (Sturm, Jacques Charles Francois): Mathematics. See: Ballentyne; James; Van Nostrand Sci. Encyc.

STURT, CHARLES. 1795-1869. English-born Australian explorer. See: Dict. Nat. Biog. Sturtite.

Sturtevant ring roll crusher (Derivation undetermined): Engineering and Industry. See: Thrush.

Sturtevant roll jaw crusher (Derivation undetermined): Engineering and Industry. See: Thrush.

Sturtite (Sturt, Charles): Earth Sciences. See: Webster's 3d.

Sturzelberger iron reduction process (Derivation undetermined): Engineering and Industry. See: Thrush.

STUTZER, ALBERT. fl. 1881. German chemist. Cited in: Royal Soc. Cat. Sci. Pap., 1800-1883. Stutzer's reagent.

Stutzer's reagent (Stutzer, Albert): Chemistry. See: Hackh; Van Nostrand Chem. Dict.

Stylites (Simeon Stylites, Saint): Religion. See: Brewer; Mathews, S.; Webster's 3d.

Stylites, Saint Simeon. See: Simeon Stylites, Saint.

SUAREZ, FRANCISCO. 1548-1617. Spanish theologian and philosopher. See: Encyc. Brit., 1911. Suarezianism.

Suarezianism (Suarez, Francisco): Philosophy. See: Webster's 3d.

SUCHIER, A. fl. 1929. German? chemist. Cited in: Chem. Abstr. vol. 24, p. 1056. Suchier reagent.

Suchier reagent (Suchier, A.): Chemistry. See: Van Nostrand Chem. Dict.

SUCKLEY, GEORGE. 1830-1869. American surgeon and naturalist. Cited in: Royal Soc. Cat. Sci. Pap., 1800-1863, 1874-1883. Suckley's gull, Suckley's salmontrout.

Suckley's gull (Suckley, George): Zoology. See: Mathews, M. M.

Suckley's salmontrout (Suckley, George): Zoology. See: Mathews, M. M.

SUCKOW, EARL E. 1924- . American pathologist. See: Direct. Med. Specialists, 1974-1975. Brock–Suckow polyposis.

Sucksmith ring balance (Sucksmith, Willie): Physics. See: Thewlis.

SUCKSMITH, WILLIE. b. 1896. English physicist. See: Who's Who Brit. Sci., 1971-1972. Sucksmith ring balance.

SUCQUET, J. P. 1840-1870. French anatomist. (Biography source unavailable.) Sucquet's canals.

Sucquet's canals (Sucquet, J. P.): Medicine. See: Stedman.

Sudborough–Hibbert test reaction (Sudborough, John Joseph and Hibbert, Harold): Chemistry. See: Van Nostrand Chem. Dict.

SUDBOROUGH, JOHN JOSEPH. b. 1869. English chemist. See: Pogg., vols. 4,5,6. Sudborough–Hibbert test reaction.

Sudeck–Leriche syndrome (Sudeck, Paul Hermann Martin and Leriche, Rene). See: Sudeck's atrophy (porosis, or syndrome).

SUDECK, PAUL HERMANN MARTIN. 1866-1938. German surgeon. See: Biog. Lex. hervorr. Aerzte. Sudeck's atrophy (porosis, or syndrome), Sudeck's critical point.

Sudeck's atrophy (porosis, or syndrome) (Sudeck, Paul Hermann Martin): Medicine. See: Jablonski; Stedman. Also known as: Kienboeck's atrophy, Leriche's syndrome, Sudeck–Leriche syndrome.

Sudeck's critical point (Sudeck, Paul Hermann Martin): Medicine. See: Stedman.

Suess test for salicylic acid in milk (Derivation undetermined): Chemistry. See: Van Nostrand Chem. Dict.

Suess test for sodium carbonate in milk (Derivation undetermined): Chemistry. See: Van Nostrand Chem. Dict.

Sugarman counter (Derivation undetermined): Physics. See: Hughes.

SUGARMAN, EDWARD J. No dates. American chemist. (Biography source unavailable). Dorn and Sugarman test.

Suhl effect (Suhl, Harry): Physics. See: Hughes; Internat. Dict. Phys. Elec.; Markus.

SUHL, HARRY. 1922- . German-born American physicist. See: World Who's Who Sci. Suhl effect.

SUIDA, HERMANN. b. 1887. German chemical technologist. See: Pogg., vols, 5,6,7a. Suida process.

Suida process (Suida, Hermann): Chemistry. See: Ballentyne; Van Nostrand Chem. Dict.

Suida test reaction (Suida, Wilhelm): Chemistry. See: Van Nostrand Chem. Dict.

SUIDA, WILHELM. 1853-1922. German chemist. See: Pogg., vol. 6. Suida test reaction.

SUITSU, KANOICHIRO. fl. 1926. Japanese chemist. Cited in: Chem. Abstr., vol. 20, p. 3000. Suitsu–Okuma test reaction.

Suitsu–Okuma test reaction (Suitsu, Kanoichiro and Okuma, Kiyoshi): Chemistry. See: Van Nostrand Chem. Dict.

Sukhatme d-statistic (Sukhatme, P. V.): Statistics. See: Kendall.

SUKHATME, P. V. fl. 1951. Indian statistician. Cited in: Kendall and Doig. Sukhatme d-statistic.

SULKOWITCH, HIRSH WOLF. 1906- . American physician. (Biography source unavailable.) Sulkowitch's reagent.

Sulkowitch's reagent (Sulkowitch, Hirsh Wolf): Medicine. See: Stedman.

SULLA, LUCIUS CORNELIUS. 138-78 B.C. Roman dictator. See: Encyc. Brit., 1973. Cornelian law (or Lex Cornelia).

SULLIVAN, ARTHUR SEYMOUR. 1842-1900. English musical composer. See: Dict. Nat. Biog., 1st suppl. Gilbert and Sullivan.

SULLIVAN, JOHN DANIEL. 1900- . American chemist. See: World Who's Who Sci. Healy–Sullivan process, Sullivan process.

SULLIVAN, MICHAEL XAVIER. 1875-1963. American biochemist. See: Who Was Who Amer. Sullivan's test (for cystine).

Sullivan process (Sullivan, John Daniel?): Engineering and Industry. See: Thrush.

Sullivan's test (for cystine) (Sullivan, Michael Xavier): Chemistry. See: Ballentyne.

Sulman and Picard processes (Sulman, Henry Livingstone and Picard, Hugh F. K.): Engineering and Industry. See: Thrush.

SULMAN, HENRY LIVINGSTONE. 1861-1940. English metallurgist. See: Encyc. Brit., 1973. Sulman and Picard processes, Sulman–Teed process of gold extraction.

Sulman–Teed process of gold extraction (Sulman, Henry Livingstone and Teed, Frank L.): Engineering and Industry. Cited in: Royal Soc. Cat. Sci. Pap., 1884-1900.

SULPICE II, SAINT. d. ca. 647. French bishop. See: Holweck. method of Saint Sulpice.

Sulzberger–Garbe syndrome (or disease) (Sulzberger, Marion Baldur and Garbe, William): Medicine. See: Jablonski; Stedman.

SULZBERGER, MARION BALDUR. 1895- . American dermatologist. See: World Who's Who Sci. Bloch–Sulzberger syndrome (incontinentia pigmenti or melanoblastosis), Sulzberger–Garbe syndrome (or disease).

SULZER BROTHERS. fl. 1948. Swiss engineers. (Biography source unavailable.) Sulzer gas turbine, Sulzer monotube steam generator.

Sulzer gas turbine (Sulzer brothers): Engineering and Industry. See: Auger.

Sulzer monotube steam generator (Sulzer brothers): Engineering and Industry. See: Van Nostrand Sci. Encyc. under "Boiler."

SUMNER, F. W. fl. 20th c. English surgeon. (Biography source unavailable.) Sumner's sign.

Sumner line (or method) (Sumner, Thomas H.): Earth Sciences. See: Van Nostrand Sci. Encyc.; Webster's 3d.

SUMNER, THOMAS H. fl. 19th c. American sea captain. (Biography source unavailable.) Sumner line (or method).

SUMNERS, JOHN WILLIAM. 1870-1937. American legislator. See: Biog. Direct. Amer. Congress. Ashurst–Sumners Act.

Sumner's sign (Sumner, F. W.): Medicine. See: Stedman.

Sumptner principle (Sumptner, William E.): Engineering and Industry. See: Internat. Dict. Ap. Math.

SUMPTNER, WILLIAM E. fl. 1892. English electrical scientist. Cited in: Royal Soc. Cat. Sci. Pap., 1884-1900. Sumptner principle.

SUN YAT-SEN. 1866-1925. Chinese statesman. See: New Encyc. Brit., 1974, Microp. Sun Yat-senism.

Sun Yat-senism (Sun Yat-sen): History. See: Webster's 3d.

SUNDBERG, HJALMAR E. fl. 1926. Scandinavian? electrical chemist. (Biography source unavailable). Sundberg method?

Sundberg method (Sundberg, Hjalmar E.?): Engineering and Industry. See: Thrush.

Sundiusite (Derivation undetermined): Earth Sciences. See: Thrush.

sup with Sir Thomas Gresham (Gresham, Sir Thomas): Generic Word (go dinnerless). See: Hendrickson.

SUPAN, ALEXANDER GEORG. 1847-1920. Austrian geographer. See: Pogg., vols. 3, 4. Koeppen–Supan line.

Supplication of William of Orange (William I of Orange): History. See: Harbottle.

Supreme Order of Christ (Jesus Christ): Religion. See: Attwater.

urface of Henneberg (Henneberg, Lebrecht): Mathematics. See: James.

urface of Joachimsthal (Joachimsthal, Ferdinand): Mathematics. See: James.

urface of Monge (Monge, Gaspard): Mathematics. See: James.

urface of Scherk (Scherk, Heinrich Ferdinand): Mathematics. See: James.

urface of Voss (Voss, Aurel Edmund): Mathematics. See: James.

URIAN, DONAT. fl. early 18th c. French botanist. See: World Who's Who Sci. Suriania.

uriania (Surian, Donat): Botany. See: Charnock; Webster's 3d.

URTEES, ROBERT. 1779-1834. English antiquary, topographer and poet. See: ict. Nat. Biog. Surtees Society.

urtees Society (Surtees, Robert): History. See: Latham.

urwell clinograph (Derivation undetermined): Engineering and Industry. See: hrush.

ussex, 3rd Earl of. See: Radcliffe, Sir Thomas (3rd Earl of Sussex).

ussex's men (Radcliffe, Sir Thomas, 3d Earl of Sussex?): Theater. See: artnoll.

utherland, 3d Earl of. See: Spencer, Charles, 3d Earl of Sutherland.

utherland constant (Sutherland, William): Chemistry. See: Van Nostrand hem. Dict.

utherland-Einstein equation (Sutherland, William and Einstein, Albert): hemistry. See: Hackh.

utherland equation (or formula) (Sutherland, William): Chemistry. See: allentyne; Hackh; Van Nostrand Chem. Dict.

UTHERLAND, GEORGE FRASER. 1900-   . American neurophysiologist. ee: Amer. Men Sci., 8th ed. James-Lange-Sutherland theory?

utherland model (or potential) (Sutherland, William): Physics. See: Internat. ict. Ap. Math.

UTHERLAND, WILLIAM. 1859-1912. Scottish-born Australian physicist. ee: Pogg., vols. 4,5. Sutherland constant, Sutherland-Einstein equation, utherland equation (or formula), Sutherland model (or potential).

UTTER. fl. ca. 1958. American? hospital patient. (Biography source navailable.) Sutter blood group.

utter blood group (Sutter): Medicine. See: Stedman.

UTTON, GEORGE MIKSCH. b. 1898. American ornithologist. See: World Who's Who Sci. Sutton's warbler?

UTTON, HENRY GAWEN. 1837-1891. English physician. See: Biog. Lex. ervorr. Aerzte. Gull-Sutton disease.

UTTON, HENRY M. fl. 1909. American engineer. Cited in: Chem. Abstr., ol. 3, p. 306. Sutton Steele, and Steele dry table.

UTTON, RICHARD LIGHTBURN. 1878-1952. American dermatologist. See: Who Was Who Amer. Sutton's halo nevus (or disease).

utton, Steel, and Steele dry table (Sutton, Henry M; Steele, Edwin G; nd Steele, Walter L.): Engineering and Industry. See: Thrush.

UTTON, THOMAS. 1767-1835. English physician. See: World Who's Who ci. Saunders-Sutton syndrome.

utton's halo nevus (or disease) (Sutton, Richard Lightburn): Medicine. See: Dorland; Jablonski; Stedman.

utton's warbler (Sutton, George Miksch?): Zoology. See: Gray.

uvarov, Aleksandr Vasilievich. See: Suwarrow, Aleksandr Vasilievich.

UWARROW, ALEKSANDR VASILIEVICH. 1729-1800. Russian field marshal. ee: Encyc. Brit., 1973. Suwarrow boot.

uwarrow boot (Suwarrow, Aleksandr Vasilievich): Fashion. See: Mathews, M. M.

UZANNE, JEAN GEORGES. b. 1859. French physician. (Biography source navailable.) Suzanne's gland.

uzanne's gland (Suzanne, Jean Georges): Anatomy. See: Donath; Dorland; tedman.

SVAB, ANTON. 1702-1768. Swedish mining official. See: Svenska Maen Och Kvinnor. Svabite.

Svabite (Svab, Anton): Earth Sciences. See: Thrush; Webster's 3d.

SVANBERG, LARS FREDRIK. 1805-1878. Swedish chemist. See: Svenska Maen Och Kvinnor. Svanberg-Struve test reaction, Svanbergite.

Svanberg-Struve test reaction (Svanberg, Lars Fredrik and Struve, Heinrich Christian Gottfried?): Chemistry. See: Van Nostrand Chem. Dict.

Svanbergite (Svanberg, Lars Fredrik): Earth Sciences. See: Thrush; Webster's 3d.

SVEC, FRANTISEK. fl. 1957. Czechoslovakian pharmacologist. See: Who's Who Sci. Europe, 1972. Svec's leukemia.

Svec's leukemia (Svec, Frantisek): Medicine. See: Jablonski.

Sveda pump (Sveda, Vladimir): Engineering and Industry. See: Auger.

SVEDA, VLADIMIR. fl. 1963. Czechoslovakian engineer. (Biography source unavailable.) Sveda pump.

Svedberg of flotation (Svedberg, Theodor): Medicine. See: Stedman.

SVEDBERG, THEODOR. 1884-1971. Swedish chemist. See: World Who's Who Sci. Svedberg of flotation, Svedberg (unit), Svedberg's equation.

Svedberg (unit) (Svedberg, Theodor): Chemistry. See: Ballentyne; Dresner; Webster's 3d.

Svedberg's equation (Svedberg, Theodor): Chemistry. See: Hackh; Van Nostrand Chem. Dict.

SVEJDA, JAROSLAV. fl. 1941-1972. Czechoslovakian anatomist. See: Who's Who Sci. Europe, 1972. Brada-Svejda tumor.

Svengali (Svengali, the hypnotist): Generic Word. See: Webster's 3d.

SVENGALI, THE HYPNOTIST. Character in George du Maurier's novel "Trilby" (1894). See: Harvey. Svengali.

SWABIA, FRIEDRICH VON HOHENSTAUFEN, DUKE OF. 1090-1146. German emperor. See: Nouv. Biog. Univ. Swabian emperors.

Swabian emperors (Swabia, Friedrich von Hohenstaufen, Duke of): History. See: Latham.

SWAINSON, ISAAC. d. 1806. English gardener. (Biography source unavailable.) Swainson pea, Swainsona.

Swainson pea (Swainson, Isaac): Botany. See: Webster's 3d.

SWAINSON, WILLIAM. 1789-1855. English-born New Zealand naturalist. See: Dict. Nat. Biog. Swainson's cliff swallow, Swainson's hawk, Swainson's thrush, Swainson's warbler, Swainson's warbling vireo.

Swainsona (Swainson, Isaac): Botany. See: Taylor, N.; Webster's 3d.

Swainson's cliff swallow (Swainson, William): Zoology. See: Mathews, M. M.

Swainson's hawk (Swainson, William): Zoology. See: Mathews, M. M.; Webster's 3d.

Swainson's thrush (Swainson, William): Zoology. See: Gray; Mathews, M. M.

Swainson's warbler (Swainson, William): Zoology. See: Gray; Mathews, M. M.; Pennak.

Swainson's warbling vireo (Swainson, William): Zoology. See: Mathews, M. M.

Swami-Narayan sect (Sahajanand Swami and Narayana): Religion. See: Canney; New Encyc. Brit., 1974, Microp.

SWAMINATHAN, M. 1912-   . Indian nutritionist. See: World Who's Who Sci. Swaminathan test.

Swaminathan test (Swaminathan, M.): Chemistry. See: Van Nostrand Chem. Dict.

SWAMMERDAM, JAN. 1637-1680. Dutch naturalist and anatomist. See: Encyc. Brit., 1973. Swammerdam's glands, Swammerdam's vesicle.

Swammerdam's glands (Swammerdam, Jan): Zoology. See: Henderson.

Swammerdam's vesicle (Swammerdam, Jan): Zoology. See: Henderson.

SWAN, SIR JOSEPH WILSON. 1828-1914. English physicist and chemist. See: World Who's Who Sci. Edison-Swan lamp.

SWAN, KENNETH CARL. 1912- . American ophthalmologist. See: World Who's Who Sci. Swan's syndrome.

Swan spectrum (or bands) (Swan, William): Physics. See: Thewlis; Webster's 3d.

SWAN, WILLIAM. 1818-1894. English physicist. See: Dict. Nat. Biog. Swan spectrum (or bands).

Swan's syndrome (Swan, Kenneth Carl): Medicine. See: Jablonski.

Sward hardness (Derivation undetermined): Engineering and Industry. See: Thrush.

Swartout (Swartout, Samuel): Generic Word (embezzler). See: Partridge.

SWARTOUT, SAMUEL. 1793-1856. American soldier and speculator. See: Dict. Amer. Biog. Swartout.

SWARTS, FREDERIC JEAN EDMOND. b. 1866. Belgian chemist. See: Pogg., vols. 5, 6. Swarts' reaction.

Swarts' reaction (Swarts, Frederic Jean Edmond): Chemistry. See: Ballentyne; Van Nostrand Chem. Dict.

SWARTZ, CARL ERRETT. 1900- . American metallurgist. See: Amer. Men Sci., 9th ed. Krauskopf-Swartz test for molybdenum.

SWARTZ, GEORGE KEPHART. 1861-1949. American geologist. See: Proc. Vol. of Geol. Soc. Amer. 1950 (1951), p. 134. Swartzite.

SWARTZ, OLAUS. 1760-1818. Swedish botanist. See: Encyc. Brit., 1911. Swartzia.

Swartzia (Swartz, Olaus): Botany. See: Partridge; Webster's 3d.

Swartzite (Swartz, George Kephart): Earth Sciences. See: Thrush; Webster's 3d.

SWEDENBORG, EMANUEL. 1688-1772. Swedish scientist, philosopher and theologian. See: Encyc. Brit., 1973. Swedenborgians (or Swedenborgianism), Swedenborgite.

Swedenborgians (or Swedenborgianism) (Swedenborg, Emanuel): Religion. See: Attwater; Canney; Partridge.

Swedenborgite (Swedenborg, Emanuel): Earth Sciences. See: Thrush; Webster's 3d.

SWEDIAUER, FRANCOIS X. 1748-1824. Austrian physician. See: Biog. Lex. hervorr. Aerzte. Swediauer's disease.

Swediauer's disease (Swediauer, Francois X.). See: Albert's disease.

SWEELEY, CHARLES CRAWFORD. 1930- . American biochemist and organic chemist. See: Amer. Men and Women Sci., 12th ed. Sweeley-Klionsky disease.

Sweeley-Klionsky disease (Sweeley, Charles Crawford, and Klionsky, Bernard Leon). See: Fabry's syndrome.

SWEENEY, ORLAND RUSSEL. b. 1883. American chemical engineer. See: Amer. Men Sci., 7th ed. Gilman-Sweeney-Heck reaction.

Sweert, Emanuel. See: Swert, Emanuel.

sweet Maudlin (Mary Magdalene, Saint?): Botany. See: Charnock.

SWEET, ROBERT. 1783-1835. English horticulturist. See: Dict. Nat. Biog. Sweetia.

SWEET, ROBERT DOUGLAS. fl. 1942-1964. English dermatologist. See: Med. Direct., 1964. Sweet's syndrome.

Sweetia (Sweet, Robert): Botany. See: Charnock.

Sweet's syndrome (Sweet, Robert Douglas): Medicine. See: Jablonski.

SWERT, EMANUEL. b. 1572. Dutch botanist. See: Biog. Woordenb. der Nederl. (Aa). Swertia.

Swertia (Swert, Emanuel): Botany. See: Charnock; Webster's 3d.

SWIETEN, GERARD VAN. 1700-1772. Dutch physician in Austria. See: Nouv. Biog. Univ. Swietenia.

Swietenia (Swieten, Gerard van): Botany. See: Charnock; Taylor, N.; Webster's 3d.

Swift cupping test (Swift, H. W.): Engineering and Industry. See: Auger.

Swift-Ellis treatment (Swift, Homer Fordyce and Ellis, Arthur W. M.): Medicine. Cited in: World Who's Who Sci.

Swift-Feer syndrome (Swift, H. and Feer, Emil). See: Feer's disease.

SWIFT, H. fl. 1918. Austrian physician. Cited in: Lancet, vol. II (1918), p. 611. Selter-Swift-Feer syndrome, Swift-Feer syndrome, Swift's disease.

SWIFT, H. W. fl. 1940. American engineer. Cited in: Chem. Abstr., vol. 34 (1940), p. 7811[4]. Swift cupping test.

SWIFT, HOMER FORDYCE. 1881-1953. American physician. See: World Who's Who Sci. Swift-Ellis treatment.

SWIFT, JONATHAN (Pseud.: M. B. DRAPIER). 1667-1745. English satirist. See: Dict. Nat. Biog. Drapier's letters, Swiftian (or Swiftean).

Swiftian (or Swiftean) (Swift, Jonathan): Literature. See: Partridge; Webster's 3d.

Swift's disease (Swift, H.). See: Feer's disease.

SWINBURNE, ALGERNON CHARLES. 1837-1909. English poet and critic. See: Dict. Nat. Biog. Swinburnian.

Swinburnian (Swinburne, Algernon Charles): Literature. See: Partridge; Webster's 3d.

Swindell-Dressler kiln (Swindell, William? and Dressler, Conrad). See: Dressler kiln.

Swindell producer (Swindell, William?): Engineering and Industry. See: Thrush.

SWINDELL, WILLIAM. fl. 1930. American engineer. Cited in: Chem. Abstr., Decennial Index, 1927-1936. Swindell-Dressler kiln?, Swindell producer?

SWINDLE, PERCY FORD. 1889-1916. American physiologist. See: World Who's Who Sci. Swindle's ghost.

Swindle's ghost (Swindle, Percy Ford): Physiology. See: Drever; English.

Swineburne-Ashcroft process (Derivation undetermined): Engineering and Industry. See: Thrush.

SWING, CAPTAIN. Imaginary name assumed by distressed agricultural workers in southern England in early 1830's. See: Harvey. Swing riots.

Swing riots (Swing, Captain): History. See: Brewer.

SWINHOE, ROBERT. d. 1877. English ornithologist. Cited in: Royal Soc. Cat. Sci. Pap., 1874-1883. Swinhoe's snipe?

Swinhoe's snipe (Swinhoe, Robert?): Zoology. See: Gray.

SWITHIN, SAINT. d. 862. English bishop. See: Dict. Nat. Biog. St. Swithin's Day.

sword of Damocles (Damocles): Generic Word (impending evil). See: Brewer; Hendrickson; Partridge.

Swyer-James syndrome (Swyer, Paul Robert and James, G. C. W.): Medicine. See: Jablonski.

SWYER, PAUL ROBERT. 1921- . English-born Canadian physician. See: Amer. Men and Women Sci., 12th ed. Swyer-James syndrome.

Sydenham, 1st Lord. See: Clarke, George Sydenham (1st Lord Sydenham).

Sydenham, Baron. See: Thomson, Charles Edward Poulett, Baron Sydenham.

Sydenham-Harrison Resolutions (Thomson, Charles Edward Poulett, Baron Sydenham and Harrison, Samuel Bealey): History. See: Morris and Irwin.

SYDENHAM, THOMAS. 1624-1689. English physician. See: Dict. Nat. Biog. Sydenham's chorea, Sydenham's laudanum.

Sydenham's chorea (Sydenham, Thomas): Medicine. See: Hinsie; Jablonski; Stedman. Also known as: chorea St. Viti, Saint Guy's disease, St. Vitus' dance.

Sydenham's laudanum (Sydenham, Thomas): Medicine. See: Webster's 3d.

...ee's striated swallow (Derivation undetermined): Zoology. See: Gray.

...KES, ALAN O'NEIL. 1899- . American acoustics physicist. See: Amer. ...n and Women Sci., 12th ed. Sykes microphone?

...KES, SIR MARK. 1879-1919. English traveller, soldier and politician. ...: Dict. Nat. Biog. Sykes-Picot Agreement.

...es microphone (Sykes, Alan O'Neil?): Engineering and Industry. See: ...ghes.

...es-Picot Agreement (Sykes, Sir Mark and Picot, Georges): History. See: ...cyc. Brit., 1973.

...KORA, VACLAV. fl. 1938-1952. Czechoslovakian chemist. Cited in: ...em. Abstr., vol. 32, p. 4460. Hovorka-Sykora reagent.

...LOW, LUDWIG (In full: PETER LUDWIG). 1832-1918. Norwegian ...thematician. See: World Who's Who Sci. Sylow's theorem.

...ow's theorem (Sylow, Ludwig): Mathematics. See: James.

...LVEST, EJNAR. 1880-1931. Danish physician. (Biography source unavail- ...e.) Sylvest's syndrome (or disease).

...vester (Sylvester, George R.?): Engineering and Industry. See: Thrush.

...LVESTER, GEORGE R. fl. 1951. American metallurgical engineer. Cited ...Chem. Abstr., vol. 46, p. 390e. Sylvester?, Sylvester process.

...LVESTER GOZZOLINI, SAINT. 1177-1267. Italian abbott. See: Holweck. ...vestrines.

...LVESTER, JAMES JOSEPH. 1814-1897. English mathematician. See: Dict. ...t. Biog. Sylvester's dialytic method, Sylvester's law of inertia, Sylvester's ...orem.

...lvester process (Sylvester, George R.): Engineering and Industry. See: ...rush.

...lvester's dialytic method (Sylvester, James Joseph): Mathematics. See: ...ernat. Dict. Ap. Math.; James.

...lvester's law of inertia (Sylvester, James Joseph): Mathematics. See: James.

...lvester's theorem (Sylvester, James Joseph): Mathematics. See: Ballentyne.

...lvestrines (Sylvester Gozzolini, Saint): Religion. See: Attwater.

...lvest's syndrome (or disease) (Sylvest, Ejnar): Medicine. See: Jablonski; ...edman. Also known as: Balme's disease, Bornholm disease, Dabney's grippe.

...lvian angle (Sylvius, Franciscus): Anatomy. See: Stedman.

...lvian aqueduct (Sylvius, Franciscus): Anatomy. See: Donath; Stedman.

...lvian artery (Sylvius, Franciscus): Anatomy. See: Donath.

...lvian fissure (Sylvius, Franciscus): Anatomy. See: Donath; Stedman; Webster's ...

...lvian fossa (Sylvius, Franciscus): Anatomy. See: Stedman.

...lvian line (Sylvius, Franciscus): Anatomy. See: Stedman.

...lvian point (Sylvius, Franciscus): Anatomy. See: Stedman.

...lvian tract (Sylvius, Franciscus): Anatomy. See: Stedman.

...lvian valve (Sylvius, Franciscus): Anatomy. See: Donath; Stedman. Also ...own as: Eustachian valve.

...lvian vein (Sylvius, Franciscus): Anatomy. See: Donath.

...lvian ventricle (Sylvius, Franciscus): Anatomy. See: Stedman. Also known ...Duncan's ventricle.

...lvite (Sylvius, Franciscus): Earth Sciences. See: Thrush; Webster's 3d.

...lvius' bone (Sylvius, Jacobus): Anatomy. See: Gray; Stedman.

...LVIUS, FRANCISCUS. 1614-1672. Dutch physician and chemist. See: ...cyc. Brit., 1973. Sylvian angle, Sylvian aqueduct, Sylvian artery, Sylvian ...sure, Sylvian fossa, Sylvian line, Sylvian point, Sylvian tract, Sylvian valve, ...lvian vein, Sylvian ventricle, Sylvite, Sylvius' substance.

...LVIUS, JACOBUS. 1478-1555. French physician. See: Encyc. Brit., ...11. Sylvius' bone.

Sylvius' substance (Sylvius, Franciscus): Anatomy. See: Donath.

SYME, JAMES. 1799-1870. Scottish surgeon. See: Dict. Nat. Biog. Syme's amputation, Syme's operation.

Syme's amputation (Syme, James): Medicine. See: Stedman.

SYMES, MICHAEL. ca. 1753-1809. English soldier and envoy. See: Dict. Nat. Biog. Symes mission.

Symes mission (Symes, Michael): History. See: Morris and Irwin.

Syme's operation (Syme, James): Medicine. See: Stedman.

Symington engine (Symington, William): Engineering and Industry. See: Auger.

SYMINGTON, JOHNSON. 1851-1924. Scottish anatomist. See: Who Was Who. Symington's anococcygeal body.

SYMINGTON, WILLIAM. 1763-1831. Scottish civil engineer and inventor. See: Dict. Nat. Biog. Symington engine.

Symington's anococcygeal body (Symington, Johnson): Anatomy. See: Stedman.

Symmachians (Symmachus): Religion. See: Canney.

SYMMACHUS. fl. late 2nd c. A.D. Samarian Bible translator of the Old Testament into Greek. See: Hastings (Dict. Bible). Symmachians, Symmachus' version.

Symmachus' version (Symmachus): Religion. See: Encyc. Brit., 1911 under "Bible, pp. 856-57.

SYMMERS, DOUGLAS. 1879-1952. American pathologist. See: Who Was Who Amer. Brill-Symmers disease (or syndrome), Brown-Symmers disease, Moschcowitz-Singer-Symmers syndrome.

Symmers' syndrome (Symmers, Douglas). See: Brill-Symmers disease (or syndrome).

SYMMES, JOHN CLEVES. 1742-1814. American pioneer. See: Dict. Amer. Biog. Symmes' purchase.

Symmes' purchase (Symmes, John Cleves): History. See: Jameson.

Symon fault (Derivation undetermined): Engineering and Industry. See: Thrush.

SYMONDS, SIR CHARLES PUTNAM. fl. 1919-1966. English physician. See: Med. Direct., 1964. Symonds' syndrome.

SYMONDS, PERCIVAL MALLON. 1893-1960. American psychologist. See: Who Was Who Amer. Symonds' picture study test.

Symonds' picture study test (Symonds, Percival Mallon): Psychology. See: Chaplin; Wolman.

Symonds' syndrome (Symonds, Sir Charles Putnam). See: Quincke's meningitis.

Symon's cone crusher (Derivation undetermined): Engineering and Industry. See: Thrush.

Symon's disk crusher (Derivation undetermined): Engineering and Industry. See: Thrush.

SYMS, PARKER. 1860-1933. American surgeon. (Biography source unavail- able.) Syms' tractor.

Syms' tractor (Syms, Parker): Medicine. See: Stedman.

Syphilis (Syphilis, the shepherd): Medicine. See: Charnock; Hendrickson; Webster's 3d.

SYPHILIS, THE SHEPHERD. Hero of Girolamo Fracastoro's poem "Syphilis sive Morbus Gallicus" (1530). See: Encyc. Brit., 1973. Syphilis.

SYRINX. Greek nymph. See: Jobes. Syrinx.

Syrinx (Syrinx, the nymph). See: Pan pipes.

SZABO, DIONYS (or DENES). 1856-1918. Hungarian physician. See: Magyar Eletr. Lex. Szabo's test.

Szabo's test (Szabo, Dionys): Medicine. See: Stedman.

SZAILBELY, STEPHAN. d. 1855. Hungarian mine surveyor. Cited in: Dana. Szaibelyite.

Szaibelyite (Szailbely, Stephan): Earth Sciences. See: Thrush; Webster's 3d.

Szebelledy–Ajtai test (Szebelledy, Lazlo Franz Ferdinand and Ajtai, Miklos): Chemistry. See: Van Nostrand Chem. Dict.

Szebelledy–Bartfay test (Szebelledy, Lazlo Franz Ferdinand and Bartfay, M.): Chemistry. See: Van Nostrand Chem. Dict.

Szebelledy–Jonas test (Szebelledy, Lazlo Franz Ferdinand and Jonas, Janos): Chemistry. See Van Nostrand Chem. Dict.

SZEBELLEDY, LAZLO FRANZ FERDINAND. 1901-1944. Hungarian chemist. See: Magyar Eletr. Lex. Szebelledy–Ajtai test, Szebelledy–Bartfay test, Szebelledy–Jonas test, Szebelledy–Tanay test.

Szebelledy–Tanay test (Szebelledy, Lazlo Franz Ferdinand and Tanay, St.): Chemistry. See: Van Nostrand Chem. Dict.

Szell formula (Szell, Kalman von): History. See: Harbottle.

SZELL, KALMAN VON. 1843-1915. Hungarian statesman. See: Magyar Eletr. Lex. Szell formula.

Szent-Gyorgyi cycle (Szent-Gyorgyi von Nagyrapolt, Albert): Chemistry. See: Dorland; Ballentyne.

Szent-Gyorgyi hypothesis (Szent-Gyorgyi von Nagyrapolt, Albert): Chemistry. See: Hackh.

Szent-Gyorgyi test reaction (Szent-Gyorgyi von Nagyrapolt, Albert): Chemistry. See: Van Nostrand Chem. Dict.

SZENT-GYORGYI VON NAGYRAPOLT, ALBERT. 1893- . Hungarian chemist. See: World Who's Who Sci. Szent-Gyorgyi cycle, Szent-Gyorgyi hypothesis, Szent-Gyorgyi test reaction.

Szilard–Chalmers method (reaction or process) (Szilard, Leo and Chalmers, T. A.): Physics. See: Hughes; Markus; Thewlis.

SZILARD, LEO. 1898-1964. Hungarian-born American physicist. See: World Who's Who Sci. Einstein-Szillard pump, Szilard–Chalmers method (reaction or process).

SZMIK, IGNAZ. fl. 19th c. Hungarian mining official. Cited in: Hintze. Szmikite.

Szmikite (Szmik, Ignaz): Earth Sciences. See: Webster's 3d.

SZONDI, LIPOT (or LEOPOLD). b. 1893. Hungarian-born Swiss psychotherapist. See: Internat. Direct. Psych., 1966. Szondi test.

Szondi test (Szondi, Lipot): Psychology. See: Hinsie; Wolman.

T

Duckett Jones Memorial Award (Jones, Thomas Duckett): Medicine. Cited Laughlin.

AFFE, COUNT EDWARD CHARLES RICHARD b. 1898. Bohemian-born Irish immologist. Cited in: Min. Mag. vol. 29 (1950-1952), p. 994. Taaffeite.

affeite (Taaffe, Count Edward Charles Richard): Earth Sciences. See: rush; Webster's 3d.

ber abraser (Taber, Edmund Rhett, Jr.?): Engineering and Industry. See: rush.

ABER, EDMUND RHETT, JR. b. 1883. American mining engineer. See: no's Who Engin., 1922-1923. Taber abraser?

bernaemontana (Tabernaemontanus, James Theodore): Botany. See: Hendrick-n, Taylor, N.; Webster's 3d.

BERNAEMONTANUS, JAMES THEODORE. 1520?-1590. German physician d botanist. See: Nouv. Biog. Univ. Tabernamontanain, Tabernaemontana.

bernamontanain (Tabernaemontanus, James Theodore): Medicine. See: edman.

ble of Cebes (Cebes): Philosophy. See: Brewer.

ble of Pythagoras (Pythagoras of Samos): Mathematics. See: Brewer; Phyfe.

CHARD, GUI. 1650?-1712. French Jesuit missionary in East Indies and am. See: Nouv. Biog. Univ. Tachardia.

chardia (Tachard, Gui): Zoology. See: Pennak.

citean (Tacitus, Gaius Cornelius): History. See: Webster's 3d.

citean prose (Tacitus, Gaius Cornelius): Literature. See: Harvey.

CITUS, GAIUS CORNELIUS. fl. ca. 55-120. Roman statesman and historian. e: Encyc. Brit., 1911. Tacitean, Tacitean prose.

ADPOLE. Character from Benjamin Disraeli's novels "Coningsby", (1844), d "Sybil", (1845). See: Harvey. Tadpoleonic.

dpoleonic (Tadpole): Generic Word (political nonentity). See: Partridge.

AENZER, PAUL R. 1858-1919. German dermatologist. See: Biog. Lex. rvorr. Aerzte. Taenzer's disease, Taenzer's stain.

aenzer's disease (Taenzer, Paul R.): Medicine. See: Dorland; Jablonski. lso known as: Unna-Taenzer disease.

aenzer's stain (Taenzer, Paul R.): Medicine. See: Stedman. Also known : Unna-Taenzer stain.

afari, Ras. See: Haile Selassie.

afel equation (Tafel, Julius?): Chemistry. See: Ballentyne.

AFEL, JULIUS. 1862-1915. German chemist. See: Pogg. vol. 4,5. Tafel quation?, Tafel line?, Tafel reaction for anilides, Tafel reaction for rychnine, Tafel rearrangement.

afel line (Tafel, Julius?): Chemistry. See: Ballentyne.

afel reaction for anilides (Tafel, Julius): Chemistry. See: Van Nostrand hem. Dict.

afel reaction for strychnine (Tafel, Julius): Chemistry. See: Van Nostrand hem. Dict.

afel rearrangement (Tafel, Julius): Chemistry. See: Van Nostrand Chem. ict.

Taft Commission (Taft, William Howard): Politics. See: Jameson; Morris.

Taft-Hartley Act (Taft, Robert Alphonso and Hartley, Fred Allan, Jr.): Politics. See: Greenwald; Morris; Smith.

TAFT, ROBERT ALPHONSO. 1889-1953. American legislator. See: Encyc. Brit., 1973. Taft-Hartley Act.

TAFT, WILLIAM HOWARD. 1857-1930. American president. See: Dict. Amer. Biog. Taft commission, Taftian.

Taftian (Taft, William Howard): Politics. See: Mathews, M. M.

TAGES. Etruscan divinity who took human form. See: Jobes. Tagetes.

Tagetes (Tages): Botany. See: Partridge; Webster's 3d.

Tagg's method (Derivation undetermined): Engineering and Industry. See: Thrush.

Tagliacotian operation (Tagliacozzi, Gasparo): Medicine. See: Partridge; Stedman; Stenhouse.

TAGLIACOZZI, GASPARO. 1546-1599. Italian surgeon. See: Encyc. Brit., 1911. Tagliacotian operation.

TAGLIAVINI, ACHILLE. fl. 1915. Italian chemist. (Biography source unavailable.) Tagliavini test reaction?

Tagliavini test reaction (Tagliavini, Achille?): Chemistry. See: Van Nostrand Chem. Dict.

Taglioni great-coat (Taglioni, Maria Sophie): Fashion. See: Harvey; Partridge.

TAGLIONI, MARIA SOPHIE. 1809-1884. Swedish-born Italian ballet dancer. See: Dict. Nat. Biog. Taglioni great-coat.

T'ai P'ing. See: Hung Hsiu-ch'uan.

Tainton process (Tainton, Urlyn Clifton): Engineering and Industry. See: Thrush.

TAINTON, URLYN CLIFTON. fl. 1935. American engineer. See: Who's Who Engin., 1937. Tainton process.

Taiping rebellion (Hung Hsiu-ch'uan): History. See: Weekley.

TAIT, ROBERT LAWSON. 1845-1899. English gynecologist and surgeon. See: Dict. Nat. Biog. Tait's knot, Tait's law, Tait's operation.

Tait's knot (Tait, Robert Lawson): Medicine. See: Dorland; Stedman.

Tait's law (Tait, Robert Lawson): Medicine. See: Dorland; Stedman.

Tait's operation (Tait, Robert Lawson): Medicine. See: Dorland; Stedman.

TAKACS, LAJOS FERENC. 1924- . Hungarian-born American mathematician. See: Amer. Men and Women Sci., 12th ed. Takacs process.

Takacs process (Takacs, Lajos Ferenc): Statistics. See: Kendall.

Takadiastase (Takamine, Jokichi): Chemistry. See: Asimov.

TAKAHARA, SHIGEO. fl. 1952. Japanese physician. (Biography source unavailable.) Takahara's syndrome.

Takahara's syndrome (Takahara, Shigeo): Medicine. See: Jablonski.

TAKAHASHI, M. fl. 1908. Japanese chemist. Cited in: Chem. Abstr. vol. 2, p. 1477. Takahashi test reaction for methyl lactate.

TAKAHASHI, MATARO. fl. 1951. Japanese physician. (Biography source unavailable.) Tamura-Takahashi disease.

Takahashi reagent for aliphatic alcohols and ethers (Takahashi, Teizo): Chemistry. See: Van Nostrand Chem. Dict.

TAKAHASHI, TEIZO. fl. 1911-1931. Japanese chemist. See: Pogg., vol. 6. Takahashi reagent for aliphatic alcohols and ethers.

Takahashi test reaction for methyl lactate (Takahashi, M.): Chemistry. See: Van Nostrand Chem. Dict.

TAKAHIRA, KOGORO. 1854-1926. Japanese diplomat. See: Webster's Biog. Dict. Root-Takahira agreement.

TAKAMINE, JOKICHI. 1854-1922. Japanese-born American chemist. See: Dict. Amer. Biog. Takadiastase.

Takata-Ara reaction (Takata, Maki and Ara, Kiyoshi): Medicine. See: Stedman.

Takata-Ara test (Takata, Maki and Ara, Kiyoshi): Medicine. See: Dorland; Stedman.

TAKATA, MAKI. b. 1892. Japanese physician. (Biography source unavailable.) Takata-Ara reaction, Takata-Ara test, Takata's reagent.

Takata's reagent (Takata, Maki): Medicine. See: Dorland; Stedman.

TAKAYAMA, MASAO. b. 1871. Japanese physician. See: Biog. Lex. hervorr. Aerzte. Takayama reagents for blood, Takayama's solution.

Takayama reagents for blood (Takayama, Masao): Medicine. See: Van Nostrand Chem. Dict.

Takayama's solution (Takayama, Masao): Medicine. See: Dorland; Stedman.

TAKAYASU, MICHISHIGE. b. 1872. Japanese physician. (Biography source unavailable.) Takayasu's syndrome (or disease).

Takayasu-Onishi syndrome (Takayasu, Michishige, and Onishi, Yoshikira). See: Takayasu's syndrome (or disease).

Takayasu's syndrome (or disease) (Takayasu, Michishige): Medicine. See: Jablonski; Stedman. Also known as: Martorell-Fabre syndrome, Martorell's syndrome, Raeder-Harbitz syndrome, Takayasu-Onishi syndrome.

TAKETANI, MITSUO. fl. 20th c. Japanese physicist. Cited in: World Who's Who Sci. under "Sakata, Shoichi." Sakata-Taketani equation.

TAKEUCHI, K. fl. 1919. Japanese chemist. Cited in: Chem. Abstr. vol. 13, p. 456. Takeuchi solution for indican.

Takeuchi solution for indican (Takeuchi, K.): Chemistry. See: Van Nostrand Chem. Dict.

TAKOS. fl. 20th c. ? physician. (Biography source unavailable.) Petzetakis-Takos syndrome.

Talbor's powder (Talbot-Talbor, Sir Robert): Medicine. See: Charnock.

Talbot (Talbot, William Henry Fox): Physics. See: Ballentyne; Dresner; Van Nostrand Sci. Encyc.

TALBOT, BENJAMIN. fl. 1899. American engineer. (Biography source unavailable.) Talbot process.

Talbot boiler (Talbot, P.A.): Engineering and Industry. See: Auger.

Talbot dog (or hound) (Talbot, Gilbert de, 1st Baron Talbot): Generic Word. See: Partridge; Wagner (More Names); Webster's 3d.

TALBOT, GILBERT DE, IST BARON TALBOT. 1277?-1346. English nobleman. See: Dict. Nat. Biog. Talbot dog (or hound).

TALBOT, P. A. fl. 1916. American engineer. (Biography source unavailable.) Talbot boiler.)

Talbot-Plateau disc (Talbot, William Henry Fox and Plateau, Jean Antoine Francois): Physics. See: Drever.

Talbot-Plateau law (Talbot, William Henry Fox and Plateau, Joseph Antoine Ferdinand): Physics. See: Chaplin; Drever; English.

Talbot process (Talbot, Benjamin): Engineering and Industry. See: Thrush.

TALBOT-TALBOR, SIR ROBERT. 1642-1681. English physician. See: Biog. Lex. hervorr. Aerzte. Talbor's powder.

TALBOT, WILLIAM HENRY FOX. 1800-1877. English pioneer photographer, physicist and mathematician. Talbot, Talbot-Plateau disc, Talbot-Platueau law, Talbot's bands, Talbot's law, Talbotype.

Talbot's bands (Talbot, William Henry Fox): Physics. See: Ballentyne; Internat. Dict. Phys. Elec.; Thewlis.

Talbot's law (Talbot, William Henry Fox): Physics. See: Ballentyne; Hackh; Van Nostrand Sci. Encyc.

Talbotype (Talbot, William Henry Fox): Photography. See: Focal Encyc. Photog.; Harrod; Webster's 3d.

Taliacotian operation (Tagliacozzi, Gasparo). See: Tagliacotian operation.

Taliacotius, Gaspar. See: Tagliacozzi, Gasparo.

Tallerman apparatus (Tallerman, Lewis A.): Medicine. See: Dorland; Stedman.

TALLERMAN, LEWIS A. fl. 19th c. English inventor. (Biography source unavailable.) Tallerman apparatus.

Tallerman reagent (Derivation undetermined): Chemistry. See: Van Nostrand Chem. Dict.

Talleyrand collar (Talleyrand-Perigord, Charles Maurice de): Fashion. See: Picken.

TALLEYRAND-PERIGORD, CHARLES MAURICE DE. 1754-1838. French bishop, diplomat and statesman. See: Nouv. Biog. Univ. Talleyrand collar.

Tallis' Canon (Tallis, Thomas): Music. See: Scholes.

TALLIS, THOMAS. 1510?-1585. English musician and composer. See: Dict. Nat. Biog. Tallis' Canon.

Tallmadge Amendment (Tallmadge, James): Politics. See: Morris.

TALLMADGE, JAMES. 1778-1853. American lawyer and statesman. See: Dict. Amer. Biog. Tallmadge Amendment.

TALLQVIST, THEODOR WALDEMAR. 1871-1927. Finnish physician. See: Biog. Lex. hervorr. Aerzte. Tallqvist's hemoglobin scale.

Tallqvist's hemoglobin scale (Tallqvist, Theodor Waldemar): Medicine. See: Dorland; Hackh; Stedman.

Talma (Talma, Francois Joseph): Fashion. See: Partridge; Picken.

TALMA, FRANCOIS JOSEPH. 1763-1826. French actor. See: Nouv. Biog. Univ. Talma.

TALMA, SAPE. 1847-1918. Dutch physician. See: Biog. Lex. hervorr. Aerzte. Stokvis-Talma syndrome, Talma's disease, Talma's operation.

Talma's disease (Talma, Sape): Medicine. See: Dorland; Jablonski; Stedman.

Talma's operation (Talma, Sape): Medicine. See: Stedman.

TALOS. Greek demigod and guardian of Crete. See: Jobes. Talos (missile).

Talos (missile): Military science. See: Markus; Van Nostrand Sci. Encyc.

Talwalkar-Parmelee plasticity index (Talwalkar, T. W. and Parmelee, Cullen Warner): Engineering and Industry. See: Thrush.

TALWALKAR, T. W. fl. 1927. American engineer. Cited in: Chem. Abstr. vol. 21, p. 3436. Talwalkar-Parmelee plasticity index.

Tam (or Tammy) (Tam o'shanter). See: Tam o'shanter bonnet (or cap).

TAM O'SHANTER. Character from Robert Burns poem of the same name (1791). Tam o'Shanter bonnet (or cap), Tam o'Shanter (stone).

Tam o'Shanter bonnet (or cap) (Tam o'Shanter): Fashion. See: Partridge; Picken; Webster's 3d.

Tam o'Shanter (stone): Earth Sciences. See: Thrush.

Tamerlane. See: Timur.

TAMM. fl. 1872. English? scientist. Cited In: Dana, Appendix II. Tammite.

Tamm-Dancoff method (Tamm, Igor Yevgenevich and Dancoff, Sidney M.?) Physics. See: Internat. Dict. Phys. Elec.

Tamm, Hugo, pseud. See: Guyard, Anthony.

AMM, IGOR YEVGENEVICH. 1895-1971. Russian physicist. See: Pogg., ol. 6; World Who's Who Sci. Tamm-Dancoff method, Tamm levels.

amm levels (Tamm, Igor Yevgenevich): Physics. See: Internat. Dict. Phys. ec.

amm test reaction (Guyard, Anthony?): Chemistry. See: Van Nostrand hem. Dict.

AMMANN, GUSTAV HEINRICH JOHANN APPOLLON. 1861-1938. German hysical chemist. See: World Who's Who Sci. Tammann temperature.

ammann temperature (Tammann, Gustav Heinrich Johann Apollon): Chemistry. e: Ballentyne; Thewlis; Webster's 3d.

AMMANY. fl. 1682-1698. American Indian chief. See: Dict. Amer. og. Saint Tammany, Tammanyism (or Tammanyite).

ammanyism (or Tammanyite) (Tammany): Politics. See: Mathews, M. M.; artridge; Webster's 3d.

ammite (Tamm): Earth Sciences. See: Thrush.

AMURA, AKIRA. fl. 1951. Japanese physician. (Biography source unavail-le.) Tamura-Takahashi disease.

amura-Takahashi disease (Tamura, Akira and Takahashi, Mataro): Medicine. e: Jablonski.

ANAKA, YOSHIO. fl. 1897. Japanese botanist. Cited in: Royal Soc. at. Sci. Pap., 1884-1900. Tanakaea.

nakaea (Tanaka, Yoshio): Botany. See: Taylor, N.

nanaev-Dolgov tests for gold, palladium, and platinum (Tananaev, Nikolaj eksandrovic): Chemistry. See: Van Nostrand Chem. Dict.

ANANAEV, IVAN VLADIMIRIVICH. 1904- . Russian chemist. See: orld Who's Who Sci. Tananaev-Tananaev micro-tests for chromium and manga-se.

ANANAEV, NIKOLAJ ALEKSANDROVIC. fl. 1930. Russian chemist. See: gg., vol. 6. Tananaev-Dolgov tests for gold, palladium, and platinum, nanaev-Panchenko test for tungstate, Tananaev-Panchenko test for vanadium, nanaev-Panchenko tests for titanium and uranium, Tananaev-Rabinovich test antimony (antimonous), Tananaev reaction for mercurous salts, Tananaev agent for bismuth, Tananaev-Romanink test for osmium, Tananaev spot reaction magnesium, Tananaev spot test for lead, Tananaev spot reactions for cesium, bidium, and thallium, Tananaev-Tananaev micro-tests for chromium and manga-se, Tananaev test for cadmium and zinc, Tananaev tests for tin and mercury, nanaev-Yunitzkaya test for mercury.

nanaev-Rabinovich test for antimony (antimonous) (Tananaev, Nikolaj eksandrovic and Rabinovich, L. M.): Chemistry. See: Van Nostrand Chem. ct.

nanaev reaction for mercurous salts (Tananaev, Nikolaj Aleksandrovic): emistry. See: Van Nostrand Chem. Dict.

nanaev reagent for bismuth (Tananaev, Nikolaj Aleksandrovic): Chemistry. e: Van Nostrand Chem. Dict.

nanaev spot reaction for magnesium (Tananev, Nikolaj Aleksandrovic): emistry. See: Van Nostrand Chem. Dict.

nanaev spot reactions for cesium, rubidium, and thallium (Tananaev, Nikolaj eksandrovic): Chemistry. See: Van Nostrand Chem. Dict.

nanaev spot test for lead (Tananaev, Nikolaj Aleksandrovic): Chemistry. e: Van Nostrand Chem. Dict.

nanaev-Tananaev micro-tests for chromium and manganese (Tananaev, Nikolaj eksandrovic, and Tananaev, Ivan Vladimirivich): Chemistry. See: Van ostrand Chem. Dict.

nanaev test for cadmium and zinc (Tananaev, Nikolaj Aleksandrovic): emistry. See: Van Nostrand Chem. Dict.

nanaev tests for tin and mercury (Tananaev, Nikolaj Aleksandrovic): emistry. See: Van Nostrand Chem. Dict.

nanaev-Yunitzkaya test for mercury (Tananaev, Nikolaj Aleksandrovic and nitzkaya, N. V.): Chemistry. See: Van Nostrand Chem. Dict.

natar-Petroff test reaction (Tanatar, Sebastien Moisseevic and Petrov, S.): emistry. See: Van Nostrand Chem. Dict.

NATAR, SEBASTIEN MOISSEEVIC. b. 1849. Ukrainian chemist. See: gg., vols. 3 to 5. Tanatar-Petroff test reaction.

TANAY, ST. fl. 1936. Hungarian chemist. Cited in: Chem. Abstr. vol. 31, p. 67. Szebelledy-Tanay test.

TANCHELM. d. ca. 1115. Flemish heretic. See: Nouv. Biog. Univ. Tanchelmian.

Tanchelmian (Tanchelm): Religion. See: Webster's 3d.

TANNER, J. C. fl. 1951-1958. English? mathematician. (Biography source unavailable.) Borel-Tanner distribution.

TANNHAEUSER. fl. ca. 1200-ca. 1270. German poet. See: Encyc. Brit., 1911. Tannhaeuser.

Tannhaeuser (Tannhaeuser the poet): Music. See: Hendrickson.

TANRET, CHARLES. 1847-1917. French physician. See: World Who's Who Sci. Mayer-Tanret test, Tanret reagent for albumin, Tanret reagent for alka-loids.

Tanret reagent for albumin (Tanret, Charles): Medicine. See: Dorland; Stedman; Van Nostrand Chem. Dict.

Tanret reagent for alkaloids (Tanret, Charles): Chemistry. See: Van Nostrand Chem. Dict.

TANSINI, IGINIO. 1855-1943. Italian surgeon. See: Biog. Lex. hervorr. Aerzte. Tansini's operation.

Tansini's operation (Tansini, Iginio): Medicine. See: Dorland; Stedman.

Tantalean (Tantalus): Mythology. See: Webster's 3d.

Tantalize (Tantalus): Generic Word (tease). See: Brewer; Charnock; Partridge.

Tantalum (Tantalus): Earth Sciences. See: Stedman; Thrush; Van Nostrand Sci. Encyc.

TANTALUS. Greek god and king. See: Jobes. Cup of Tantalus, Tantalean, Tantalize, Tantalum, Tantalus (case), Tantalus (stork).

Tantalus (case) (Tantalus): Generic Word. See: Partridge; Webster's 3d.

Tantalus (stork) (Tantalus): Zoology. See: Webster's 3d.

Tantony bell (Anthony, Saint): Religion. See: Harvey.

Tantony (pig) (Anthony, Saint): Zoology. See: Hendrickson; Partridge; Weekley.

TAO, TUAN-KO. fl. 1936. Chinese chemist. Cited in: Chem. Abstr., vol. 30, p. 8074. Kao-Tao-Sah reagent.

TAPIA, ANTONIO GARCIA. 1875-1950. Spansih otolaryngologist. See: Biog. Lex. hervorr. Aerzte. Tapia's syndrome.

Tapia's syndrome (Tapia, Antonio Garcia): Medicine. See: Dorland; Jablonski; Stedman.

TAPLEY, MARK. Character in Charles Dickens's novel "Martin Chuzzlewit" (1843-1844). See: Magill. Mark Tapley.

TAPPEINER, SEPP. 1909- . Austrian dermatologist. See: Kuerschner's Deut. Gel. Kal., 1961. Spannlang-Tappeiner syndrome.

TAR, ALOYS. b. 1886. Hungarian physician. (Biography source unavailable.) Tar's symptom.

TARAMELLI, TORQUATO. 1845-1922. Italian geologist. See: Pogg., vol. 3, 4. Taramellite.

Taramellite (Taramelli, Torquato): Earth Sciences. See: Thrush; Webster's 3d.

TARAS, M. H. fl. 1937. American pharmaceutical chemist. Cited in: Chem. Abstr., vol. 31, p. 8630. Pacini-Taras test for vitamin A in oils.

TARBUTT, PERCY COVENTRY. fl. 20th c. Australian mine director. Cited in: Hintze. Tarbuttite.

Tarbuttite (Tarbutt, Percy Coventry): Earth Sciences. See: Thrush; Webster's 3d.

TARCHANOFF, IVAN ROMANOVICH. 1846-1908. Russian physiologist. See: Biog. Lex. hervorr. Aerzte. Tarchanoff phenomenon.

Tarchanoff phenomenon (Tarchanoff, Ivan Romanovich): Physiology. See: Drever; Wolman.

TARDE, GABRIEL. 1843-1904. French sociologist. See: Internat. Encyc. Soc. Sci. Tarde's law of imitation.

Tarde's law of imitation (Tarde, Gabriel): Sociology. See: Zadrozny.

TARDIEU, AUGUSTE AMBROISE. 1818-1879. French physician. See: World Who's Who Sci. Tardieu's ecchymoses (or spots).

Tardieu's ecchymoses (or spots) (Tardieu, Auguste Ambroise): Medicine. See: Dorland; Stedman.

TARIN, PIERRE. 1725-1761. French anatomist and medical writer. See: Nouv. Biog. Univ. Tarin's fascia, Tarin's foramen, Tarin's fossa, Tarin's hole, Tarin's space, Tarin's tenia, Tarin's valve (or plate).

Tarin's fascia (Tarin, Pierre): Anatomy. See: Dorland; Stedman.

Tarin's foramen (Tarin, Pierre): Anatomy. See: Stedman. Also known as: Fallopian aqueduct.

Tarin's fossa (Tarin, Pierre): Anatomy. See: Donath; Stedman.

Tarin's hole (Tarin, Pierre): Anatomy. See: Donath.

Tarin's space (Tarin, Pierre): Anatomy. See: Donath; Stedman.

Tarin's tenia (Tarin, Pierre): Anatomy. See: Stedman. Also known as: Foville's fasciculus.

Tarin's valve (or plate) (Tarin, Pierre): Anatomy. See: Donath; Dorland; Stedman.

TARLOV, ISIDORE MAX. 1905- . American physician. See: Direct. Med. Specialists, 1965-1966. Tarlov's cyst.

Tarlov's cyst (Tarlov, Isidore Max): Medicine. See: Jablonski.

TARNIER, ETIENNE STEPHANE. 1828-1897. French obstetrician. See: World Who's Who Sci. Tarnier's forceps, Tarnier's sign of coming abortion.

Tarnier's forceps (Tarnier, Etienne Stephane): Medicine. See: Dorland; Stedman.

Tarnier's sign of coming abortion (Tarnier, Etienne Stephane): Medicine. See: Dorland; Stedman.

TARNOW, G. fl. 1956. German physician. (Biography source unavailable.) Kulenkampff-Tarnow syndrome.

TARQUIN (LUCIUS TARQUINIUS SUPERBUS). 534-510 B.C. Legendary King of early Rome. See: Harper. Tarquinian (or Tarquinish).

Tarquinian (or Tarquinish) (Tarquin): Generic Word (proud). See: Charnock; Webster's 3d.

Tarral-Besnier disease (Tarral, Claudius and Besnier, Ernst). See: Kaposi's disease (2).

TARRAL, CLAUDIUS. fl. 19th c. French physician. (Briography source unavailable.) Tarral-Besnier disease.

Tar's symptom (Tar, Aloys): Medicine. See: Dorland.

TARSKI, ALFRED. 1902- . Polish-born American mathematician. See: World Who's Who Sci. Banach-Tarski paradox.

TARTARINI, M. fl. 1926. Italian chemist. Cited in: Pogg., vol 6 under "Bernardi, Alessandro." Bernardi-Tartarini test for vanillin and piperonal in sugar solutions.

TARTINI, GIUSEPPE. 1692-1770. Italian violinist. See: Encyc. Brit., 1973. Tartini's tone.

Tartini's tone (Tartini, Giuseppe): Music. See: Apel; Drever; English.

TARTUFFE. Character from Moliere's comedy of the same name, (1664). See: Harvey. Tartuffe (or Tartuffism).

Tartuffe (or Tartuffism) (Tartuffe the fictional character): Generic Word (hypocrite). See: Charnock; Partridge; Webster's 3d.

Tarugi-Lenci reaction for amino and imino groups (Tarugi, Nazzareno and Lenci, Francesco): Chemistry. See: Van Nostrand Chem. Dict.

Tarugi-Lenci reaction for benzoquinone and 2,6-dibromoquinone (Tarugi, Nazzareno and Lenci, Francesco): Chemistry. See: Van Nostrand Chem. Dict.

TARUGI, NAZZARENO. b. 1867. Italian chemist. See: Pogg., vols. 4 to 6. Tarugi-Lenci reaction for amino and imino groups, Tarugi-Lenci reaction for benzoquinone and 2,6-dibromoquinone.

TARZAN. Character from Edgar Rice Burroughs's story "Tarzan of the Apes", (1914). See: Benet. Tarzan.

Tarzan (Tarzan the fictional character): Generic Word (strong person). See: Mathews, M. M.; Webster's 3d.

Taschen's test (Derivation undetermined): Medicine. See: Hinsie.

Tashunca-Uitco. See: Crazy Horse.

TASKER, H. S. fl. 1910. English chemist. Cited in: Chem. Abstr., vol. 4, p. 746. Jones-Tasker test reaction.

TASMAN, ABEL JANSSEN. 1603-1659. Dutch navigator and explorer. See: Encyc. Brit., 1911. Tasmanite.

Tasmanite (Tasman, Abel Janssen): Earth Sciences. Cited in: Partridge.

TASSIE, JAMES. 1735-1799. Scottish gem engraver and modeller. See: Dict. Nat. Biog. Tassie paste.

Tassie paste (Tassie, James): Applied Arts. See: Thrush.

TASSINARI, PAOLO. fl. 1855. Italian chemist. Cited in: Royal Soc. Cat. Sci. Pap., 1800-1863. Tassinari-Piazza test.

Tassinari-Piazza test (Tassinari, Paolo and Piazza, Pietro): Chemistry. See: Van Nostrand Chem. Dict.

Tatarskite (Tatarsky, V. B.): Earth Sciences. See: Thrush.

TATARSKY, V. B. fl. 20th c. Russian scientist. Cited in: Min. Mag. vol. 33, pt. 2 (1963-1964), p. 1152. Tatarskite.

Tate double-piston air pump (Tate, Thomas Turner): Engineering and Industry. Cited in: World Who's Who Sci.

TATE, HARRY. fl. early 20th c.? Englishman? (Biography source unavailable.) Harry Tate (airplane).

TATE, THOMAS TURNER. 1807-1888. English engineer and mathematician. See: World Who's Who Sci. Fairbairn and Tate method for vapor pressure, Tate double-piston air pump, Tate's law.

Tate's law (Tate, Thomas Turner): Engineering and Industry. See: Ballentyne.

Tatham furnace (Derivation undetermined): Engineering and Industry. See: Thrush.

TATIAN. b. ca. 120. Christian writer and heretic. See: Nouv. Biog. Univ. Tatianist.

Tatianist (Tatian): Religion. See: Webster's 3d.

Tattersall (fabric) (Tattersall, Richard): Generic Word. See: Webster's 3d.

Tattersall reaction for cobalt (Derivation undetermined): Chemistry. See: Van Nostrand Chem. Dict.

Tattersall reaction for delphinine (Derivation undetermined): Chemistry. See: Van Nostrand Chem. Dict.

Tattersall reaction for morphine (Derivation undetermined): Chemistry. See: Van Nostrand Chem. Dict.

Tattersall reaction for papaverine and codeine (Derivation undetermined): Chemistry. See: Van Nostrand Chem. Dict.

TATTERSALL, RICHARD. 1724-1795. English horseman. See: Dict. Nat. Biog. Tattersall (fabric).

TAUBER, ALFRED. b. 1866. Austrian mathematician. See: Pogg., vols. 4, 5, 6. Tauberian theorem.

Tauber benzidine reagent (Tauber, Henry): Chemistry. See: Van Nostrand Chem. Dict.

TAUBER, HENRY. b. 1897. Hungarian-born American biochemist. See: Amer. Men Sci., 1st ed. Tauber benzidine reagent, Tauber reagent for vitamin C, Tauber reagents for monose sugars, Tauber test reaction for vitamin B1.

TAUBER, MAURICE FALCOLM. 1908- . American librarian. See: Who's Who Libr. Service, 1966. Tauber report.

Tauber reagent for vitamin C (Tauber, Henry): Chemistry. See: Van Nostrand Chem. Dict.

Tauber reagents for monose sugars (Tauber, Henry): Chemistry. See: Van Nostrand Chem. Dict.

Tauber report (Tauber, Maurice Falcolm): Library Science. See: Harrod.

Tauber test reaction for vitamin B_1 (Tauber, Henry): Chemistry. See: Van Nostrand Chem. Dict.

Tauberian theorem (Tauber, Alfred): Mathematics. See: James.

TAUCHNITZ, KARL CHRISTOPHER TRAUGOTT. 1761-1836. German printer and bookseller. See: Allg. Deut. Biog. Tauchnitz (reprint).

Tauchnitz (reprint) (Tauchnitz, Karl Christopher Traugott): Printing. See: Partridge.

TAUFEL, KURT (In full: Albert Kurt). b. 1892. German chemist. See: Wer Ist's?, 1935. Taufel-Thaler test reaction.

Taufel-Thaler test reaction (Taufel, Kurt and Thaler, Helmut): Chemistry. See: Van Nostrand Chem. Dict.

Taupenot dry plates (Taupenot, J. M.): Photography. See: Focal Encyc. Photog.

TAUPENOT, J. M. 1824-1856. French chemist and physicist. (Biography source unavailable.) Taupenot dry plates.

Taussig-Bing syndrome (disease, complex or heart) (Taussig, Helen Brooke and Bing, Richard J.): Medicine. See: Dorland; Jablonski; Stedman.

TAUSSIG, HELEN BROOKE. 1898- . American pediatrician. See: World Who's Who Sci. Blalock-Taussig operation, Taussig-Bing syndrome (disease, complex or heart), Taussig-Snellen-Albers syndrome.

Taussig-Snellen-Albers syndrome (Taussig, Helen Brooke; Snellen, Herman Adrianus; and Albers, F. H.): Medicine. See: Jablonski.

TAVERNER, RICHARD. 1505?-1575. English religious writer and reformer. See: Dict. Nat. Biog. Taverner's Bible.

Taverner's Bible (Taverner, Richard): Religion. See: Brewer; Mathews, S.

TAWARA, K. SUNAO. 1873-1938. Japanese physician. See: Biog. Lex. Hervorr. Aerzte. Aschoff-Tawara's node, His-Tawara system, Tawara's stalk.

Tawara's node (Tawara, K. Sunao). See: Aschoff-Tawara's node.

Tawara's stalk (Tawara, K. Sunao): Anatomy. See: Donath.

Tawdry (Audrey, Saint): Generic Word (gaudy). See: Brewer; Charnock; Funk.

Tawdry lace (Audrey, Saint): Fashion. See: Picken; Webster's 3d.

Tay-Sachs disease (Tay, Warren and Sachs, Bernard): Medicine. See: Dorland; Jablonski; Stedman.

TAY, WARREN. 1843-1927. English physician. See: Who Was Who. Tay-Sachs disease, Tay's cherry red spot, Tay's choroiditis.

TAYBI, HOOSHANG. 1919- . Iranian-born American radiologist. See: Amer. Men and Women Sci., 12th ed. Rubinstein-Taybi syndrome, Taybi's syndrome.

Taybi's syndrome (Taybi, Hooshang): Medicine. See: Jablonski.

TAYLOR, ALBERT HOYT. 1879-1961. American physicist, radio technician and radar engineer. See: Pogg., vol. 6,; World Who's Who Sci. Taylor connection?

TAYLOR, ALFRED MILLS. b. 1865. English engineer. See: Who's Who Engin., 1922-1923. Taylor producer?

TAYLOR, ALVA B. fl. ca. 1840. American printer. See: Lockwood. A. B. Taylor cylinder press.

Taylor Amendment (Taylor, John W.): Politics. See: Morris.

TAYLOR, BROOK. 1685-1731. English mathematician. See: Dict. Nat. Biog. Taylor series, Taylor's formula, Taylor's theorem.

TAYLOR, CHARLES FAYETTE. 1827-1899. American orthopaedic surgeon. See: Dict. Amer. Biog. Taylor's apparatus (or splint).

Taylor connection (Taylor, Albert Hoyt?): Engineering and Industry. See: Markus.

TAYLOR, DAVID WATSON. 1864-1940. American engineer. See: World Who's Who Sci. Taylor quotient.

Taylor effect (Taylor, Sir Geoffrey Ingram): Earth Sciences. See: Huschke.

TAYLOR, FREDERICK WINSLOW. 1865-1915. American inventor and efficiency engineer. See: Dict. Amer. Biog. Taylor-White process, Taylorism (or Taylor system).

TAYLOR, SIR GEOFFREY INGRAM. b. 1886. British meteorologist and physicist. See: World Who's Who Sci. Rayleigh-Taylor instability, Taylor effect, Taylor interference experiment, Taylor number, Taylor spiral, Taylor's fog prediction diagram.

Taylor grazing act (Taylor, John Clarence): Politics. See: Smith.

TAYLOR, HAROLD CLAIRE. 1905- . American psychologist and statistician. See: Amer. Psych. Assoc. Direct., 1948. Taylor-Russell tables.

TAYLOR, HOWARD CANNING, JR. 1900- . American physician. See: World Who's Who Sci. Taylor's syndrome.

TAYLOR, HUGH STOTT. b. 1890. English-born American chemist. See: Pogg., vol. 6. Taylor-Orowan dislocation.

Taylor interference experiment (Taylor, Sir Geoffrey Ingram): Physics. See: Internat. Dict. Phys. Elec.

TAYLOR, JANET ALLISON. 1923- . American psychologist. See: Amer. Psych. Assoc. Direct., 1960. Taylor manifest anxiety scale.

TAYLOR, JOHN CLARENCE. b. 1890. American legislator. See: Biog. Direct. Amer. Congress. Taylor grazing act.

TAYLOR, JOHN W. 1784-1854. American legislator. See: Dict. Amer. Biog. Taylor Amendment.

Taylor manifest anxiety scale (Taylor, Janet Allison): Psychology. See: Wolman.

TAYLOR, NATHANIEL WILLIAM. 1786-1858. American theologian. See: Dict. Amer. Biog. Taylorism (or Taylorites).

Taylor number (Taylor, Sir Geoffrey Ingram): Earth Sciences. See: Huschke.

Taylor-Orowan dislocation (Taylor, Hugh Stott and Orowan, Egon?): Physics. See: Ballentyne; Internat. Dict. Phys. Elec.

Taylor principle (Taylor, William): Engineering and Industry. See: Auger.

Taylor process (Taylor, William Chittenden?): Engineering and Industry. See: Thrush.

Taylor producer (Taylor, Alfred Mills?): Engineering and Industry. See: Thrush.

Taylor quotient (Taylor, David Watson): Engineering and Industry. See: Encyc. Brit., 1973 under "Naval Architecture", p. 127.

TAYLOR, ROBERT WILLIAM. 1842-1908. American dermatologist. See: World Who's Who Sci. Taylor's disease.

Taylor-Russell tables (Taylor, Harold Claire and Russell, James Thomas): Statistics. See: English.

TAYLOR, S. E. fl. 1960. American educator. (Biography source unavailable.) Taylor slate.

TAYLOR, SAMUEL ALFRED. b. 1863. American engineer. See: Who's Who Engin., 1922-1923. Taylor stoker?

Taylor series (Taylor, Brook): Mathematics. See: James; Van Nostrand Sci. Encyc.

Taylor slate (Taylor, S. E.): Education. See: Good.

Taylor slide comparator (Derivation undetermined): Physics. See: Van Nostrand Sci. Encyc. under "Color Comparators (Visual)".

Taylor spiral (Taylor, Sir Geoffrey Ingram): Earth Sciences. See: Internat. Dict. Ap. Math.

Taylor stoker (Taylor, Samuel Alfred?): Engineering and Industry. See: Auger.

TAYLOR, W. J. d. 1864. American mineral chemist. Cited in: Dana. Taylorite.

Taylor-White process (Taylor, Frederick Winslow, and White, Maunsel): Engineering and Industry. See: Encyc. Brit., 1973 under "High-Speed Steel;" Hackh, Webster's 3d.

TAYLOR, WILLIAM. 1865-1937. English designer of scientific instruments. See: Dict. Nat. Biog. Taylor principle.

TAYLOR, WILLIAM CHITTENDEN. b. 1886. American glass and ceramics chemist. See: Amer. Men Sci., 6th ed. Taylor process?

TAYLOR, ZACHARY. 1784-1850. American general and president. See: Dict. Amer. Biog. Taylorism (or Taylorite).

Taylorism (or Taylor system) (Taylor, Frederick Winslow): Engineering and Industry. See: Drever; Webster's 3d.

Taylorism (or Taylorites) (Taylor, Nathaniel William): Religion. See: Encyc. Brit., 1911.

Taylorism (or Taylorite) (Taylor, Zachary): Politics. See: Mathews, M. M.

Taylorite (Taylor, W. J.): Earth Sciences. See: Thrush; Webster's 3d.

Taylor's apparatus (or splint) (Taylor, Charles Fayette): Medicine. See: Dorland; Stedman.

Taylor's disease (Taylor, Robert William). See: Herxheimer's disease.

Taylor's fog prediction diagram (Taylor, Sir Geoffrey Ingram): Earth Sciences. See: Encyc. Brit., 1973 under "Fog", p. 510.

Taylor's formula (Taylor, Brook): Mathematics. See: James.

Taylor's syndrome (Taylor, Howard Canning, Jr.): Medicine. See: Jablonski.

Taylor's theorem (Taylor, Brook): Mathematics. See: Ballentyne; James.

Tay's cherry red spot (Tay, Warren): Medicine. See: Stedman.

Tay's choroiditis (Tay, Warren). See: Hutchinson's disease.

Tchaikovsky, Peter Ilich. See: Tschaikovsky, Peter Ilich.

Tchebischeff's parallel motion (Chebyshev, Pafnuty Lvovich): Engineering and Industry. See: Auger.

Tchebychev-Hermite polynomials (Chebyshev, Pafnuty Lvovich and Hermite, Charles): Statistics. See: Kendall.

Tchebychev (or Tchebischeff), Pafnuti L. See: Chebyshev, Pafnuti L.

Tchekhov, Anton Pavlovich. See: Chekhov, Anton Pavlovich.

TEACHER, JOHN HAMMOND. 1869-1930. Scottish embryologist. See: World Who's Who Sci. Bryce Teacher ovum.

TEALE, THOMAS PRIDGIN, SR. 1801-1868. English surgeon. See: Biog. Lex. hervorr. Aerzte. Teale's amputation.

Teale's amputation (Teale, Thomas Pridgin, Sr.): Medicine. See: Dorland; Stedman.

TEALL, JETHRO JUSTINIAN HARRIS. 1849-1924. English geologist. See: World Who's Who Sci. Teallite.

Teallite (Teall, Jethro Justinian Harris): Earth Sciences. See: Webster's 3d.

Teclu burner (Teclu, Nicolae): Chemistry. See: Hackh.

TECLU, NICOLAE. 1839-1916. Rumanian chemist. See: World Who's Who Sci. Teclu burner.

Teddy bear (Roosevelt, Theodore): Generic Word (cloth-stuffed toy bear). See: Hendrickson; Mathews, M. M.; Partridge.

TEED, FRANK LITHERLAND. 1858-1937. English metallurgist. See: Who Was Who, 1929-1940. Sulman-Teed process of gold extraction.

TEED, KORESH R. d. 1908. American physicain. (Biography source unavailable.) Koreshan (or Koreshanity).

TEICHMANN-STAWIARSKI, LUDWIG CARL. 1823-1895. German histologist. See: Biog. Lex. hervorr. Aerzte. Teichmann's crystals, Teichmann's plexus, Teichmann's test.

Teichmann's crystals (Teichmann-Stawiarski, Ludwig Carl): Medicine. See: Dorland; Hackh; Stedman.

Teichmann's plexus (Teichmann-Stawiarski, Ludwig Carl): Anatomy. See: Donath.

Teichmann's test (Teichmann-Stawiarski, Ludwig Carl): Medicine. See: Dorland; Stedman.

Teignmouth, Lord. See: Shore, John (Lord Teignmouth).

TEILHARD DE CHARDIN, PIERRE. 1881-1955. French theologian, paleontologist and explorer. See: World Who's Who Sci. Teilhardian.

Teilhardian (Teilhard de Chardin, Pierre): Religion. See: Barnhart (Eng. Lit.).

TEITELBAUM, M. fl. 1928. German chemist. Cited in: Chem. Abstr., Decenn. Index, 1927-1936. Berg-Teitelbaum test reaction for selenite.

TELAMON. Greek legendary hero. See: Harper. Telamones.

Telamones (Telamon): Architecture. See: Brewer; Charnock.

Telephium (Telephus): Medicine. See: Charnock.

TELEPHUS. In Greek mythology, son of Heracles and Augea, King of Mysia. See: Oxford Clas. Dict. Telephium.

TELESILLA. fl. 510 B.C.? Greek poetess. See: Harper. Telesilleum.

Telesilleum (Telesilla): Literature. See: Preminger.

TELFAIR, CHARLES. ca. 1777?-1833. Irish naturalist. See: Dict. Nat. Biog. Telfairia.

Telfairia (Telfair, Charles): Botany. See: Webster's 3d.

Telford (or Telfordize) (Telford, Thomas): Engineering and Industry. See: Partridge; Thrush; Webster's 3d.

TELFORD, THOMAS. 1757-1834. Scottish engineer, poet and writer. See: Dict. Nat. Biog. Telford (or Telfordize).

Teller amendment (or resolution) (Teller, Henry Moore): Politics. See: Morris; Smith.

TELLER, EDWARD. 1908- . Hungarian-born American physicist. See: World Who's Who Sci. Brunauer, Emmett and Teller adsorption equation (method or theory), Gamow-Teller interaction, Gamow-Teller matrix element, Gamow-Teller selection rules, Jahn-Teller rule (or effect), Lyddane-Sachs-Teller relation, Teller-Redlich product rule.

TELLER, HENRY MOORE. 1830-1914. American senator and general. See: Dict. Amer. Biog. Teller amendment (or resolution).

Teller-Redlich product rule (Teller, Edward and Redlich, Otto): Physics. See: Internat. Dict. Phys. Elec.

TELLERA, GIACOMO. 1870-1934. Italian chemist. See: Pogg., vol. 6. Tellera test.

Tellera test (Tellera, Giacomo): Chemistry. See: Van Nostrand Chem. Dict.

Tellurium (Tellus): Chemistry. See: Partridge.

TELLUS. Roman goddess of the earth. See: Jobes. Tellurium.

TELLYESNICZKY, KALMAR. 1868-1932. Hungarian anatomist. See: Anat. Anz. vol. 76 (1933), p. 235. Tellyesniczky's fluid.

Tellyesniczky's fluid (Tellyesniczky, Kalmar): Medicine. See: Dorland.

Telsmith breaker (Derivation undetermined): Engineering and Industry. See: Thrush.

Telsmith gyrasphere (Derivation undetermined): Engineering and Industry. See: Thrush.

Temin enzyme (Temin, Howard M.): Genetics. See: Barnhart (New Eng.).

TEMIN, HOWARD M. 1934- . American virologist. See: Amer. Men Sci., 11th ed. Temin enzyme, Teminism.

Teminism (Temin, Howard M.): Genetics. See: Barnhart (New Eng.).

TEMMINCK, CONRAD JACOBUS. 1778-1858. Dutch naturalist. See: World Who's Who Sci. Temminck's stint.

Temminck's stint (Temminck, Conrad Jacobus): Zoology. See: Gray.

Temple-Darley test (Temple, Mildred C. and Darley, Frederic L.): Psychology. See: Wolman.

Temple, Earl of. See: Grenville, Richard Temple, Earl Temple.

TEMPLE, HENRY JOHN (3RD VISCOUNT PALMERSTON). 1784-1865. English statesman. See: Dict. Nat. Biog. Palmerstonism, Palmerston's follies.

TEMPLE, MILDRED C. 1913- . American psychologist. See: Biog. Direct. Amer. Psych. Assoc., 1973. Temple-Darley test.

Temple orange (Temple, William Chase): Botany. See: Hendrickson.

TEMPLE, WILLIAM CHASE. 1862-1917. American businessman and fruit-grower. See: Who Was Who Amer. Temple orange.

TEMPLETON, JOHN. 1766-1825. Irish botanist. See: World Who's Who Sci. Templetonia.

mpletonia (Templeton, John): Botany. See: Webster's 3d.

mplewood, Viscount. See: Hoare, Sir Samuel John Gurney, 2d Baronet Hoare nd Viscount Templewood.

n Hove, David. See: Hoven, David.

ndinous ring of Zinn (Zinn, Johann Gottfried). See: Zinn's ligament nnulus, ring or tendon).

ENNANT, SMITHSON. 1761-1815. English chemist. See: Dict. Nat. og. Tennantite.

ennantite (Tennant, Smithson): Earth Sciences. See: Thrush; Webster's 3d.

ENNESON, HENRI. 1836-1913. French dermatologist. See: Biog. Lex. ervorr. Aerzte. Besnier-Tenneson syndrome.

ENNYSON, ALFRED LORD. 1809-1892. English poet. See: Dict. Nat. og. Tennysonian.

ennysonian (Tennyson, Alfred Lord): Literature. See: Partridge; Webster's d.

.NON, JACQUES RENE. 1724-1816. French anatomist and oculist. See: orld Who's Who Sci. Tenon's capsule, Tenon's space.

enon's capsule (Tenon, Jacques Rene): Anatomy. See: Donath; Dorland; edman.

non's space (Tenon, Jacques Rene): See: Donath; Stedman; Webster's 3d.

NORE, MICHELO. 1781-1861. Italian botanist. See: World Who's Who i. Tenorite.

norio, Don Juan. See: Don Juan (Tenorio).

norite (Tenore, Michelo): Earth Sciences. See: Thrush; Van Nostrand Sci. ncyc., Webster's 3d.

entelew process (Derivation undetermined): Chemistry. See: Van Nostrand hem. Dict.

enterden, 1st Baron. See: Abbott, Charles (1st Baron Tenterden).

enterden's Act (Abbott, Charles, 1st Baron Tenterden): Law. See: Black.

eramala transmission (Salerni, Piero Giri de Teramala). See: Salerni transmis- on.

rawatt (Watt, James): Physics. See: Markus.

eremin, Lev. See: Theremin, Lev.

ERENCE (PUBLIUS TERENTIUS AFER). d. 161 B.C. Roman playwright. See: xford Clas. Dict. Terentian.

erentian (Terence): Literature. See: Charnock; Webster's 3d.

ERESA OF AVILA, SAINT. 1515-1582. Spanish saint. See: Holweck. eresians.

eresians (Teresa of Avila, Saint): Religion. See: Attwater; Webster's 3d.

ermagant (Termagant, the Idol): Generic Word (brawling person). See: harnock; Partridge; Stenhouse.

ERMAGANT, THE IDOL. Mohammedan deity. See: Jobes. Termagant.

ERMAN, FREDERICK EMMONS. 1900- . American electronics engineer. ee: Amer. Men and Women Sci., 12th ed. Terman's law, Terman's law of nnovation.

erman group test of mental ability (Terman, Lewis Madison): Psychology. See: rever.

ERMAN, LEWIS MADISON. 1877-1956. American psychologist. See: ternat. Encyc. Soc. Sci. Terman group test of mental ability, Terman- McNemar test of mental ability, Terman-Merrill tests, Terman-Miles attitude- nterest blank.

erman-McNemar test of mental ability (Terman, Lewis Madison and Mc Nemar, Quinn): Psychology. See: Wolman.

erman-Merrill tests (Terman, Lewis Madison and Merrill, Maud A.): Psycholo- y. See: Drever.

erman-Miles attitude-interest blank (Terman, Lewis Madison and Miles, atherine Cox): Psychology. See: English.

Terman's law (Terman, Frederick Emmons): Sociology. See: Martin.

Terman's law of innovation (Terman, Frederick Emmons): Sociology. See: Martin.

Terminalia (Terminus): Mythology. See: Charnock.

TERMINUS. Roman field deity. See: Oxford Clas. Dict. Terminalia.

TERNSTROEM, CHRISTOPHER. d. 1746. Swedish botanist. (Biography source unavailable.) Ternstroemia.

Ternstroemia (Ternstroem, Christopher): Botany. See: Webster's 3d.

TERPSICHORE. Greek muse of dance. See: Jobes. Terpsichore.

Terpsichore (Terpsichore, the Muse): Generic Word (dancing). See: Partridge.

Terrail, Pierre. See: Bayard, Pierre Terrail, Seigneur de.

TERREY, MARY. f. 1952. American physician. (Biography source unavaila- ble.) Lowe-Terrey-MacLachlan syndrome.

TERRIEN, FELIX. 1872-1940. French ophthalmologist. See: Arch. d' Ophth. vol. 3 (1940), pp. 961-66. Terrien-Viel syndrome.

Terrien-Viel syndrome (Terrien, Felix and Viel, Prosper). See: Posner- Schlossman syndrome.

TERRIER, LOUIS-FELIX. 1837-1908. French surgeon. See: World Who's Who Sci. Courvoisier-Terrier syndrome, Terrier's valve.

Terrier's valve (Terrrier, Louis-Felix): Medicine. See: Stedman.

TERRILLON, OCTAVE R. S. 1844-1895. French surgeon. See: World Who's Who Sci. Terrillon's operation.

Terrillon's operation (Terrillon, Octave R. S.): Medicine. See: Dorland; Stedman.

TERRY, B. F. fl. 1860's American soldier. Cited in: Boatner under "Texas Rangers." Terry's Texas rangers.

Terry clock (Terry, Eli): Horology. See: Webster's 3d.

TERRY, ELI. 1772-1852. American clock manufacturer. See: Dict. Amer. Biog. Terry clock.

TERRY, MILTON EVERETT. 1916- . American mathematical statistician. See: Amer. Men Sci., 10th ed. Terry's test.

TERRY, THEODORE LASATER. 1899-1946. American ophthalmologist. See: World Who's Who Sci. Terry's syndrome (1), Terry's syndrome (2).

Terry's syndrome (1) (Terry, Theodore Lasater): Medicine. See: Jablonski.

Terry's syndrome (2) (Terry, Theodore Lasater): Medicine. See: Jablonski; Stedman.

Terry's test (Terry, Milton Everett): Statistics. See: Kendall.

Terry's Texas rangers (Terry, B. F.): History. Cited in: Encyc. Brit., 1973 under "Ranger."

TERSON, ALBERT. 1867-1935. French ophthalmologist. See: Biog. Lex. hervorr. Aerzte. Terson's disease?, Terson's glands.

Terson's disease (Terson, Albert?): Medicine. See: Jablonski.

Terson's glands (Terson, Albert): Anatomy. See: Stedman.

TERTSCH, HERMANN. b. 1880. Austrian mineralogist. See: Pogg., vols. 5, 6, 7a. Tertschite.

Tertschite (Tertsch, Hermann): Earth Sciences. See: Thrush.

TERTULLIAN (TERTULLIANUS, QUINTUS SEPTIMIUS FLORENS). 160?-222? Latin Church father of Carthage. See: Encyc. Brit., 1973. Tertullianists.

Tertullianists (Tertullian): Religion. See: Canney; Webster's 3d.

TERZIAN, H. fl. 1955. American neurologist. (Biography source unavaila- ble.) Kluever-Bucy-Terzian syndrome.

TESCHEMACHER, FREDERICK E. dl. 1863. English chemist. Cited in: Dana. Teschemacherite.

Teschemacherite (Teschemacher, Frederick E.): Earth Sciences. See: Webster's 3d.

TESCHENDORF, WERNER. b. 1895. German roentgenologist. (Biography source unavailable.) Barsony-Teschendorf syndrome.

Tesla (Tesla, Nikola): Physics. See: Dresner; Thewlis.

Tesla coil (or transformer) (Tesla, Nikola): Engineering and Industry. See: Hughes; Internat. Dict. Phys. Elec., Markus.

Tesla current (Tesla, Nikola): Engineering and Industry. See: Stedman; Webster's 3d.

TESLA, NIKOLA. 1857-1943. Croatian-born American electrical engineer and inventor. See: Dict. Amer. Biog. Tesla, Tesla coil (or transformer), Tesla current, Tesla tube.

Tesla tube (Tesla, Nikola): Engineering and Industry. Cited in : Partridge.

Testivin's sign (Derivation undetermined): Medicine. See: Stedman.

TETRAZZINI, LUISA. 1871-1940. Italian operatic vocalist. See: Who Was Who Amer. chicken tetrazzini.

TETTAMANZI, ANGELO. fl. 1935. Italian analytical chemist. See: Who's Who Sci. Europe, 1972. Garelli-Tettamanzi test reaction, Tettamanzi reagent.

Tettamanzi reagent (Tettamanzi, Angelo): Chemistry. See: Van Nostrand Chem. Dict.

TEUCER. In Greek mythology the first ancestor of the Trojan kings. See: Oxford Clas. Dict. Teucrium.

Teucrium (Teucer): Botany. See: Charnock.

TEUTLEBEN, FRIEDRICH ERNST KARL VON. b. 1842. German physician. Cited in: Royal Soc. Cat. Sci. Pap., 1874-1883. Teutleben's ligament.

Teutleben's ligament (Teutleben, Friedrich Ernst Karl von): Anatomy. See: Stedman.

TEUTSCHLAENDER, OTTO RICHARD. 1874-1950. German pathologist. See: Kuerschner's Deut. Gel.-Kal., 1931. Teutschlaender's syndrome.

Teutschlaender's syndrome (Teutschlaender, Otto Richard): Medicine. See: Jablonski.

THACKERAY, WILLIAM MAKEPEACE. 1811-1863. English novelist. See: Dict. Nat. Biog. Thackerayan.

Thackerayan (Thackeray, William Makepeace): Literature. See: Webster's 3d.

THAL, JOHANN. 1542?-1583. German physician and naturalist. See: Allg. Deut. Biog. Thalia.

THALEN, TOBIAS ROBERT. 1827-1905. Swedish physicist. See: Svenska Maen Ock Kvinnor. Thalenite.

Thalenite (Thalen, Tobias Robert): Earth Sciences. See: Webster's 3d.

THALER, HELMUT. 1904- . German chemist. See: Pogg., vol. 7a. Taufel-Thaler test reaction.

THALES OF MILETUS. d. 546 B.C. Greek philosopher and scientist. See: World Who's Who Sci. Thalesian.

Thalesian (Thales of Miletus): Philosophy. See: Webster's 3d.

THALIA. Greek muse of comedy. See: Jobes. Thalian.

Thalia (Thal, Johann): Botany. See: Taylor, N.

Thalian (Thalia): Literature. See: Partridge.

Thalleioquin test reaction (Derivation undetermined): Chemistry. See: Van Nostrand Chem. Dict.

THALMANN, ARTHUR ARNO. fl. 1906. German physician. Cited in: Index-Cat. Libr. Surg.-Gen. Off., 2nd ser., vol. 18., 1913. Thalmann's agar?

Thalmann's agar (Thalmann, Arthur Arno?): Medicine. See: Stedman.

Thamm's tuberculin (Derivation undetermined): Medicine. See: Stedman.

THANATOS. Greek mythical personification of death. See: Oxford Clas. Dict. Thanatos.

Thanatos (Thanatos, the mythical person): Psychology (death instinct). See: Chaplin.

THANE, SIR GEORGE DANCER. 1850-1930. English anatomist. See: Who Was Who, 1929-40. Thane's method.

Thane's method (Thane, Sir George Dancer): Medicine. See: Dorland; Stedman.

Thannhauser-Magendantz syndrome (Thannhauser, Siegfried J. and Magendantz, Heinz). See: Hanot-MacMahon-Thannhauser syndrome.

THANNHAUSER, SIEGFRIED JOSEF. b. 1885. German-born American physiologist. See: Pogg., vol. 6, 7a. Hanot-MacMahon-Thannhauser syndrome, Schmidt-Thannhauser method.

Thaumaturgus (Gregory Thaumaturgus, Saint): Generic Word (miracle-worker). See: Brewer.

Thaumaturgus, Gregory. See: Gregory Thaumaturgus.

THAYSEN, THORNWALD EINAR HESS. 1883-1936. Danish physician. See: Hospitalstidende vol. 74 (1936), pp. 431-434. Gee-Thaysen disease, Thaysen's disease, Thaysen's syndrome.

Thaysen's disease (Thaysen, Thornwald Einar Hess): Medicine. See: Dorland.

Thaysen's syndrome (Thaysen, Thornwald Einar Hess): Medicine. See: Jablonski. Also known as: MacLennan's syndrome.

THEARLE, ERNEST LATHROP. 1895- . American mechanical engineer. See: Who's Who Engin., 1937. Leblanc-Thearle balancing machine.

Theatines (Paul IV, Giovanni Pietro Caraffa, bishop of Theate): Religion. See: Attwater; Canney. Also known as: Cajetani, Chietini.

Thebesian foramen (Thebesius, Adam Christian): Anatomy. See: Donath; Stedman.

Thebesian valve (Thebesius, Adam Christian): Anatomy. See: Donath; Stedman; Webster's 3d.

Thebesian vein (vessel, or channel) (Thebesius, Adam Christian): Anatomy. See: Donath; Stedman; Webster's 3d.

THEBESIUS, ADAM CHRISTIAN. 1686-1732. German physician. See: Biog. Lex. hervorr. Aerzte. Thebesian foramen, Thebesian valve, Thebesian vein (vessel, or channel).

THEDEN, JOHANN CHRISTIAN ANTON. 1714-1797. German surgeon. See: Allg. Deut. Biog. Theden's method.

Theden's method (Theden, Johann Christian Anton): Medicine. See: Dorland; Stedman.

Thedford crown bit (Derivation undetermined): Engineering and Industry. See: Thrush.

THEILE, FRIEDRICH WILHELM. 1801-1879. German anatomist. See: Allg. Deut. Biog. Theile's canal, Theile's glands, Theile's muscle.

THEILER, SIR ARNOLD. 1867-1936. Swiss-born South-African veterinary bacteriologist. See: Ann. Register. Theileria, Theileriosis.

THEILER, MAX. 1899-1972. South African microbiologist. See: World Who's Who Sci. Theiler's disease, Theiler's virus.

Theileria (Theiler, Sir Arnold): Zoology. See: Dorland; Stedman; Webster's 3d.

Theileriosis (Theiler, Sir Arnold): Zoology. See: Stedman.

Theiler's disease (Theiler, Max): Medicine. See: Dorland; Jablonski; Stedman.

Theiler's virus (Theiler, Max): Medicine. See: Stedman.

Theile's canal (Theile, Friedrich Wilhelm): Anatomy. See: Donath; Dorland; Stedman.

Theile's glands (Theile, Friedrich Wilhelm): Anatomy. See: Donath; Dorland; Stedman.

Theile's muscle (Theile, Friedrich Wilhelm): Anatomy. See: Stedman.

THELLUSSON (or THELUSSON), PETER ISAAC. 1737-1797. French-English banker and eccentric. See: Dict. Nat. Biog. Thellusson's Act.

Thellusson's Act (Thellusson (or Thelusson) Peter Isaac): Law. See: Brewer; Harbottle; Harvey.

THEMIS. Greek goddess of the earth and a prophetess. See: Oxford Clas. Dict. Themis.

Themis (Themis, the goddess): Generic Word (justice). See: Harvey; Partridge.

Themistian (Themistius): Religion. See: Webster's 3d.

HEMISTIUS. fl. 6th c. Deacon of Alexandria. See: Dict. Christian Biog. Themistian.

HENARD, BARON LOUIS-JACQUES. 1777-1857. French chemist. See: World Who's Who Sci. Thenardia, Thenardite, Thenard's blue.

Thenardia (Thenard, Baron Louis-Jacques): Botany. See: Charnock.

Thenardite (Thenard, Baron Louis-Jacques): Earth Sciences. See: Thrush; Webster's 3d.

Thenard's blue (Thenard, Baron Louis-Jacques): Chemistry. See: Hackh; Thrush; Van Nostrand Chem. Dict.

HEOBALD, FREDERIC VINCENT. 1868-1930. British zoologist. See: Who Was Who. Theobaldia.

Theobald Smith's phenomenon (Smith, Theobald): Medicine. See: Dorland; Stedman.

Theobaldia (Theobald, Frederic Vincent): Zology. See: Dorland; Van Nostrand Sci. Encyc. under "Black Fly."

Theodolite (Theodolum, D. Carolum): Physics. See: Charnock; Huschke; Hewlis.

HEODOLUM, D. CAROLUM. fl. 1865. Italian scientist. Cited in: Charnock. Theodolite.

HEODORE TIRO "THE GENERAL," SAINT. d. 306. Syrian or Armenian-born soldier in the Roman army. See: Holweck. Columns of St. Mark and St. Theodore.

Theodosian (Theodosius I): History. See: Webster's 3d.

Theodosian (Theodosius II): History. See: Webster's 3d.

Theodosian Code (Theodosius II): Law. See: Charnock.

HEODOSIUS I. fl. ca. 346-395. Roman emperor. See: Encyc. Brit., 1911. Theodosian.

HEODOSIUS II. d. 450. Eastern Roman emperor. See: Encyc. Brit., 1911. Theodosian, Theodosian Code.

Theodotians (Theodotus): Religion. See: Canney; Webster's 3d.

HEODOTION. fl. 2nd c. Ephesian translator of the Old Testament into Greek. See: Encyc. Brit., 1973. Theodotion version.

Theodotion version (Theodotion): Religion. See: Encyc. Brit., 1911 under "Bible," p. 856.

HEODOTUS. fl. late 2nd c. Byzantine tanner and heresiarch. See: Dict. Grk. Rom. Biog. Myth. Theodotians.

THEON. Ancient Roman poet. See: Benet. Theon's tooth.

Theon's tooth (Theon): Generic Word (carping critic). Brewer.

HEOPHILUS. d. ca. 536. Jurist of Constantinople. See: Nouv. Biog. Univ. Theophilus' Institutes.

Theophilus' Institutes (Theophilus): Law. See: Black.

Theophrasta (Theophrastus): Botany. See: Charnock.

HEOPHRASTUS. fl. ca. 374-287 B.C. Greek philosopher and naturalist. See: Nouv. Biog. Univ. Theophrasta.

HEOPHRONIUS OF CAPPADOCIA. fl. ca. 370. Asia Minor heretic. (Biography source unavailable.) Eunomio-Theophronians.

Theorem of Weierstrass (Weierstrass, Karl Theodor Wilhelm). See: equations of Weierstrass.

Theorems of Pappus (Pappus of Alexandria). See: Pappus' theorems.

Therblig (Gilbreth, Frank Bunker): Business. See: Hendrickson; Webster's 3d.

Theremin (Theremin, Lev): Music. See: Apel; Scholes; Webster's 3d.

THEREMIN, LEV. b. 1896. Russian engineer and instrument inventor. See: Baker. Theremin.

Theresienmesse (or Theresa Mass) (Maria Theresa): Music. See: Scholes.

THERICLES. fl. 5th c. B.C. Greek potter. See: Harper. Thericlia.

Thericlia (Thericles). Applied Arts. See: Stenhouse.

thermal Ohm (Ohm, Georg Simon): Physics. See: Dresner.

THERSITES. Legendary Greek who besieged Troy. See: Oxford Clas. Dict. Thersitical (or Thersitean).

Thersitical (or Thersitean) (Thersites): Generic Word (loudmouthed). See: Hendrickson; Partridge.

Theseis (Theseus): Fashion. See: Stenhouse.

THESEUS. Attic legendary hero. See: Dict. Grk. Rom. Biog. Myth. Theseis.

THESIGER, FREDERIC JOHN NAPIER (1ST VISCOUNT CHELMSFORD). 1868-1933. English viceroy of India. See: Dict. Nat. Biog., 5th suppl. Montagu-Chelmsford Report.

Thespian (Thespis): Theater (actor). See: Hendrickson; Partridge; Webster's 3d.

THESPIS. fl. 535 B.C. Greek tragic poet. See: Harper. Thespian.

THETIS. Greek ocean nymph or Nereid. See: Jobes. Thetis hairstone.

Thetis hairstone (Thetis): Earth Sciences. See: Thrush.

THEVENARD, ANDRE. b. 1898. French physician. (Biography source unavailable). Thevenard's disease.

Thevenard's disease (Thevenard, Andre). See: Hick's syndrome.

Thevenin acoustical theorem (Thevenin, M. L.): Engineering and Industry. See: Internat. Dict. Ap. Math.

Thevenin-Helmholtz theorem (Thevenin, M. L. and Helmholtz, Hermann Ludwig Ferdinand von). See: Thevenin's theorem.

THEVENIN, M. L. fl. 1883. French engineer. (Biography source unavailable.) Thevenin acoustical theorem, Thevenin mechanical rectilineal theorem, Thevenin mechanical rotational theorem, Thevenin's theorem.

Thevenin mechanical rectilineal theorem (Thevenin, M. L.): Engineering and Industry. See: Internat. Dict. Ap. Math.

Thevenin mechanical rotational theorem (Thevenin, M. L.): Engineering and Industry. See: Internat. Dict. Ap. Math.

Thevenin's theorem (Thevenin, M. L.): Engineering and Industry. See: Ballentyne; Hughes; Huschke; Internat. Dict. Ap. Math.; Van Nostrand Sci. Encyc. Also known as: Helmholtz's theorem, Thevenin-Helmholtz theorem.

THEVENON, L. fl. 1920. French chemist. Cited in: Chem. Abstr. vol. 15, p. 997, 1050. Thevenon test for nitrite in water, Thevenon test reaction for saccharin.

Thevenon test for nitrite in water (Thevenon, L.): Chemistry. See: Van Nostrand Chem. Dict.

Thevenon test reaction for saccharin (Thevenon, L.): Chemistry. See: Van Nostrand Chem. Dict.

THEVET, ANDRE. 1502-1590. French traveler and author. See: Michaud. Thevetia.

Thevetia (Thevet, Andre): Botany. See: Stedman; Taylor, N.; Webster's 3d.

THIBIERGE, GEORGES. 1856-1926. French physician. See: Biog. Lex. hervorr Aerzte. Thibierge-Weissenbach syndrome.

Thibierge-Weissenbach syndrome (Thibierge, Georges and Weissenbach, Raymond Joseph Emil): Medicine. See: Jablonski.

THIEBAUT, F. fl. 1945-1972. French physician. See: Who's Who Sci. Europe, 1972. Refsum-Thiebaut disease.

THIEL, ALFRED. 1879-1942. German physical chemist. See: Pogg., vols. 4 to 6, 7a. Thiel-Stoll solution.

Thiel-Stoll solution (Thiel, Alfred and Stoll, L.): Chemistry. See: Hackh; Van Nostrand Chem. Dict.

Thielavia (Thielaw, F. von): Botany. See: Webster's 3d.

THIELAW, F. von. fl. 19th c. German botanist. (Biography source unavailable. Thielavia.

Thiele-Bailey test reaction (Thiele, Johannes and Bailey, James): Chemistry. See: Van Nostrand Chem. Dict.

Thiele-Dralle reagent (Thiele, Johannes and Dralle, Edward): Chemistry. See: Van Nostrand Chem. Dict.

THIELE, GEORGE HENRY. 1896- . American proctologist. See: Who's Who Amer., 1972-1973. Thiele's syndrome.

THIELE, JOHANNES (In full: FRIEDRICH KARL JOHANNES). b. 1865. German chemist. See: Pogg., vols. 4, 5. Thiele-Bailey test reaction, Thiele-Dralle reagent, Thiele reaction?, Thiele theory of partial valencies, Thiele tube.

Thiele reaction (Thiele, Johannes?): Chemistry. See: Van Nostrand Chem. Dict.

Thiele theory of partial valencies (Thiele, Johannes): Chemistry. See: Ballentyne.

Thiele tube (Thiele, Johannes): Chemistry. See: Hackh; Van Nostrand Chem. Dict.

Thiele's syndrome (Thiele, George Henry): Medicine. See: Dorland.

THIELMANN, KARL HEINRICH. 1802-1872. German internist. See: Allg. Deut. Biog. Thielmann's diarrhea drops (or mixture).

Thielmann's diarrhea drops (or mixture) (Thielmann, Karl Heinrich): Medicine. See: Dorland.

Thiemann-Fleischner disease (Thiemann, H., and Fleischner, Felix). See: Thiemann's disease.

THIEMANN, H. fl. 1909. Dutch? surgeon. (Biography source unavailable). Thiemann's disease.

Thiemann's disease (Thiemann, H.): Medicine. See: Jablonski.

THIER, CARL JOERG. fl. 1958. Dutch ophthalmologist. (Biography source unavailable). Weyers-Thier syndrome.

THIERRY, BARON CHARLES PHILIPPE HIPPOLYTUS DE. 1793-1864. French-English colonist in New Zealand. See: Dict. Nat. Biog. Thierry land claim.

Thierry land claim (Thierry, Baron Charles Philippe Hippolytus de): History. See: Morris and Irwin.

THIERS, JOSEPH. b. 1885. French physician. See: Who's Who France, 1957-1958. Archard-Thiers syndrome.

THIERSCH, F. VON. fl. 1853. German scientist. Cited in: Dana. Thierschite.

THIERSCH, KARL. 1822-1895. German surgeon and embryologist. See: Allg. Deut. Biog. Thiersch's canaliculi, Thiersch's knife, Thiersch's method (or graft).

Thierschite (Thiersch, F. von): Earth Sciences. See: Thrush.

Thiersch's canaliculi (Thiersch, Karl): Medicine. See: Stedman.

Thiersch's knife (Thiersch, Karl): Medicine. See: Stedman.

Thiersch's method (or graft) (Thiersch, Karl): Medicine. See: Dorland; Stedman. Also known as: Ollier's method (or graft).

THIERY. fl. 1921. French chemist. (Biography source unavailable.) Thiery test for cyanide?

Thiery test for cyanide (Thiery?): Chemistry. See: Van Nostrand Chem. Dict.

Thiess (or Thies) process (Derivation undetermined): Engineering and Industry. See: Hackh; Thrush.

Thiessen polygon method (Derivation undetermined): Earth Sciences. See: Huschke.

Thiron, Saint Bernard of. See: Bernard of Tiron, Saint.

THIRY, LUDWIG. 1817-1897. Austrian physiologist. (Biography source unavailable). Thiry-Vella fistula, Thiry's fistula.

Thiry-Vella fistula (Thiry, Ludwig and Vella, Luigi): Medicine. See: Stedman.

Thiry's fistula (Thiry, Ludwig): Medicine. See: Dorland; Stedman.

THIVOLLE, LUCIEN. fl. 1925-1935. French chemist. (Biography source unavailable.) Thivolle reagent.

Thivolle reagent (Thivolle, Lucien): Chemistry. See: Van Nostrand Chem. Dict.

THOBURN, WILBUR WILSON. fl. 1995. American naturalist. Cited in: Royal Soc. Cat. Sci. Pap., 1884-1900. Thoburnia?

Thoburnia (Thoburn, Wilbur Wilson?): Zoology. See: Pennak.

Thokoly, Count Imre. See: Tokoly, Count Imre.

THOLLON, LOUIS. 1829-1887. French astrophysicist. See: Pogg., vols. 3, 4. Thollon prism.

Thollon prism (Thollon, Louis): Physics. See: Internat. Dict. Phys. Elec.

THOMA, HANS. b. 1887. German engineer. See: Pogg., vols. 6, 7a. Thoma pump.

Thoma pump (Thoma, Hans): Engineering and Industry. See: Auger.

THOMA, RICHARD. 1847-1923. German histologist. See: Biog. Lex. hervorr. Aerzte. Thoma-Zeiss hemocytometer, Thoma's ampulla, Thoma's fluid, Thoma's laws.

Thoma-Zeiss hemocytometer (Thoma, Richard and Zeiss, Carl): Medicine. See: Dorland; Stedman.

Thomas Acquinas, Saint. See: Acquinas, Saint Thomas.

Thomas Amendment (Thomas, Jesse Burgess): Politics. See: Morris.

Thoma's ampulla (Thoma, Richard): Medicine. See: Dorland; Stedman.

THOMAS, ANDRE. b. 1867. French physician. Cited in: Index-Cat. Libr. Surg.-Gen. Off., 3rd ser., vol. 10, 1932. Dejerine-Thomas syndrome, Thomas' syndrome.

Thomas-Carpentier reagent (Thomas, Pierre and Carpentier, G.): Chemistry. See: Van Nostrand Chem. Dict.

Thomas converter (Thomas, Sidney Gilchrist): Engineering and Industry. See: Thrush.

Thoma's counting chamber (Thoma, Richard) See: Thoma-Zeiss hemocytometer.

Thomas cyclotron (Thomas, Llewellyn Hilleth): Physics. See: Van Nostrand Sci. Encyc.

THOMAS, DAVID. 1762-1831. American soldier and politician. See: Dict. Amer. Biog. Thomas elm.

THOMAS, DAVID ALFRED (VISCOUNT RHONDDA). 1856-1918. English administrator and politician. See: Dict. Nat. Biog., 3d suppl. Rhonddaed.

Thomas distribution (Thomas, M.): Statistics. See: Kendall.

Thomas elm (Thomas, David): Botany. See: Mathews, M. M.

Thomas-Fermi differential equation (Thomas, Llewellyn Hilleth and Fermi, Enrico): Physics. See: Van Nostrand Sci. Encyc.

Thomas-Fermi model (Thomas, Llewellyn Hilleth and Fermi, Enrico): Physics. See: Internat. Dict. Phys. Elec.

Thoma's fluid (Thoma, Richard): Medicine. See Dorland; Stedman.

Thomas-Gilchrist process (Thomas, Sidney Gilchrist and Gilchrist, Percy Carlyle): Engineering and Industry. See: Thrush; Van Nostrand Chem. Dict.; Webster's 3d. Also known as: Thomas process.

Thomas-Gilchrist steel (Thomas, Sidney Gilchrist and Gilchrist, Percy Carlyle). See: Thomas steel.

Thomas heel (Thomas, Hugh Owen): Medicine. See: Picken.

THOMAS, HENRY M., JR. b. 1891. American physician. See: Direct. Med. Specialists, 1965-1966. Thomas' syndrome.

THOMAS, HUGH OWEN. 1834-1891. English surgeon. See: World Who's Who Sci. Thomas heel, Thomas splint.

THOMAS, J. S. G. fl. 1920-1925. English engineer. See: Pogg., vol. 6. Thomas meter.

THOMAS, JESSE BURGESS. 1777-1853. American legislator. See: Dict. Amer. Biog. Thomas Amendment.

THOMAS, JOHN. 1805-1871. American physician and religious leader. See: Webster's Biog. Dict. Thomasites.

Thoma's laws (Thoma, Richard): Medicine. See: Stedman.

THOMAS, LLEWELLYN HILLETH. 1903- . English-born American physicist. See: World Who's Who Sci. Thomas cyclotron, Thomas-Fermi differential equation, Thomas-Fermi model, Thomas precession.

THOMAS, M. fl. 1949. English statistician. (Biography source unavailable.) Thomas distribution.

Thomas meal (slag or phosphate): Engineering and Industry. See: Hackh; Thrush; Webster's 3d.

Thomas meter (Thomas, J. S. G.) Engineering and Industry. See: Van Nostrand Sci. Encyc.

Thomas-Micsa test (Derivation undetermined): Chemistry. See: Van Nostrand Chem. Dict.

Thomas More, Saint. See: More, Sir Thomas.

Thomas' personality typology (Thomas, William Isaac): Sociology. See: Zadrozny.

Thomas' pessary (Thomas, Theodore Gaillard): Medicine. See: Dorland.

THOMAS, PIERRE. fl. 1920. French chemist. See: Pogg., vol. 6. Thomas-Carpentier reagent.

Thomas precession (Thomas, Llewellyn Hilleth): Physics. See: Internat. Dict. Ap. Math.; Webster's 3d.

Thomas process (Thomas, Sidney Gilchrist). See: Thomas-Gilchrist process.

Thomas-Reiche-Kuhn f-sum rule (Thomas, W.?; Reiche, Fritz; and Kuhn, Werner). See: Kuhn-Thomas-Reiche f-sum rule.

Thomas (or Thomas type) resistor (Derivation undetermined): Electronics. See: Hughes; Internat. Dict. Phys. Elec.

THOMAS, RICHARD GARLAND. 1923- . American physicist. See: Amer. Men and Women Sci., 12th ed. Porter-Thomas distribution.

THOMAS, ROBERT. 1782-1860. Welsh-Australian newspaper proprietor. See: Australian Biog. Dict. Thomasia?.

THOMAS, SIDNEY GILCHRIST. 1850-1885. English metallurgist and inventor. See: Dict. Nat. Biog. Thomas converter, Thomas-Gilchrist process, Thomas meal (slag or phosphate), Thomas steel.

Thomas splint (Thomas, Hugh Owen): Medicine. See: Dorland; Stedman; Webster's 3d.

Thomas steel (Thomas, Sidney Gilchrist): Engineering and Industry. See: Thrush. Also known as: Thomas-Gilchrist steel.

Thomas' syndrome (Thomas, Andre): Medicine. See: Jablonski.

Thomas' syndrome (Thomas, Henry M., Jr.): Medicine. See: Jablonski.

THOMAS THE APOSTLE, SAINT. One of the twelve apostles of Jesus Christ. See: Holweck. doubting Thomas, Saint Thomas Christians, Saint Thomas tree, Thomasing.

THOMAS, THEODORE GAILLARD. 1831-1903. American physician. See: World Who's Who Sci. Thomas' pessary.

THOMAS, W. fl. 1925. German physicist. (Biography source unavailable.) Kuhn-Thomas-Reiche f-sum rule?

THOMAS, WILLIAM ISAAC. 1863-1947. American sociologist. See: Internat. Encyc. Soc. Sci. Thomas' personality typology.

Thomasia (Thomas, Robert?): Botany. See: Taylor, N.

Thomasing (Thomas the Apostle, Saint): Generic Word (begging). See: Webster's 3d.

Thomasites (Thomas, John): Religion. See: Brewer; Canney; Mathews, M. M. Also known as: Christadelphians.

THOMAYER, JOSEF. 1853-1925. Czechoslovakian physician. See: Biog. Lex. hervorr. Aerzte. Thomayer's sign.

Thomayer's sign (Thomayer, Josef): Medicine. See: Dorland.

Thomism (or Thomists) (Aquinas, Saint Thomas): Philosophy. See: Attwater; Barnhart, (Eng. Lit.); Good.

THOMPSON, ALBERT HUGH. fl. 1926-1968. English physician. See: Med. Direct., 1964. Thompson's syndrome?

THOMPSON, ASHBURTON. (In full: JOHN ASHBURTON). 1846-1915). English-born Australian physician. See: Who Was Who. Thompson's solution.

Thompson-Beamish-Scott test reactions for platinum (Thompson, S. O.; Beamish, Fred Earl; and Scott, M.): Chemistry. See: Van Nostrand Chem. Dict.

Thompson-Beamish-Scott tests for osmium (Thompson, S. O.; Beamish, Fred Earl; and Scott, M.): Chemistry. See: Van Nostrand Chem. Dict.

THOMPSON, SIR BENJAMIN (COUNT RUMFORD). 1753-1814. American-born English physicist. See: Dict. Nat. Biog. Rumford Medal, Rumford professorship, Rumford stove, Rumford's photometer.

THOMPSON, CHARLES EUGENE. 1913- . American psychologist. See: Amer. Psych. Assoc. Direct., 1948. Thompson thematic apperception test.

Thompson clinometer (Derivation undetermined): Engineering and Industry. See: Thrush.

THOMPSON, DONAVAN JEROME. 1919- . American biostatistician. See: Amer. Men Sci., 9th ed., Biol. Sci. Horvitz and Thompson estimator.

Thompson, Elihu. See: Thomson, Elihu.

THOMPSON, FRANCIS. fl. 1791. English engineer. (Biography source unavailable. Thompson's engine.

THOMPSON, G. R. fl. 1910. English chemist. Cited in: Chem. Abstr. vol. 4, p. 1389. Thompson-Hurst test.

Thompson (grape) (Derivation undetermined): Botany. See: De Sola.

THOMPSON, SIR HENRY. 1820-1904. English surgeon and novelist. See: Dict. Nat. Biog. Thompson's test.

Thompson-Hurst test (Thompson, G. R. and Hurst, H.): Chemistry. See: Van Nostrand Chem. Dict.

THOMPSON, JOHN TALIAFERRO. 1860-1940. American soldier and inventor. See: Who Was Who Amer. Thompson submachine gun.

THOMPSON, JOHN VAUGHAN. 1779-1847. English zoologist. See: Dict. Nat. Biog. Thompsonia.

Thompson limestone (Derivation undetermined): Earth Sciences. See: Thrush.

Thompson pilot shoulder reamer (Derivation undetermined): Engineering and Industry. See: Thrush.

Thompson Pink (grapefruit) (Derivation undetermined): Botany. See: De Sola.

THOMPSON, S. O. fl. 1937. Canadian? chemist. Cited in: Chem. Abstr., Decenn. Index, 1937-1946. Thompson-Beamish-Scott test reactions for platinum, Thompson-Beamish-Scott tests for osmium.

Thompson-Stewart process (Thompson, William P. and Stewart): Chemistry. See: Van Nostrand Chem. Dict.

Thompson submachine gun (Thompson, John Taliaferro): Weapons. See: Hendrickson; Partridge; Quick. Also known as: Tommygun.

Thompson thematic apperception test (Thompson, Charles Eugene): Psychology. See: Wolman.

THOMPSON, WILLIAM "BENDIGO". 1811-1880. English prize fighter. See: Internat. Encyc. Soc. Sci. Bendigo (fur cap).

THOMPSON, WILLIAM P. fl. 1919. English chemist. Cited in: Chem. Abstr., vol. 13, p. 1645. Thompson-Stewart process.

THOMPSON, WILLIAM RAE. b. 1896. American mathematician and biochemist. See: Amer. Men. Sci., 6th ed. Thompson's rule.

Thompsonia (Thompson, John Vaughan): Zoology. See: Pennak.

Thompson's engine (Thompson, Francis): Engineering and Industry. See: Auger.

Thompson's rule (Thompson, William Rae): Statistics. See: Kendall.

Thompson's solution (Thompson, Ashburton): Medicine. See: Dorland.

Thompson's syndrome (congenital optic atrophy) (Thompson, Albert Hugh?): Medicine. See: Jablonski.

Thompson's syndrome (mucopolysaccharidosis I) (Derivation undetermined). See: Hurler's syndrome (disease or polydystrophy).

Thompson's test (Thompson, Sir Henry): Medicine. See: Dorland; Stedman.

THOMS, HERMANN. 1859-1931. German pharmaceutical chemist. See: Pogg., vols. 4, 5, 6. Thoms reaction for g-strophanthin, Thoms reagent for copper, Thoms test for diethylphthalate in essential oils.

Thoms reaction for g-strophanthin (Thoms, Hermann): Chemistry. See: Van Nostrand Chem. Dict.

Thoms reagent for cooper (Thoms, Hermann): Chemistry. See: Van Nostrand Chem. Dict.

Thoms test for diethylphthalate in essential oils (Thoms, Hermann): Chemistry. See: Van Nostrand Chem. Dict.

THOMSEN, ASMUS JULIUS THOMAS. 1815-1896. Danish physician. See: Biog. Lex. hervorr. Aerzte. Thomsen's disease.

Thomsen-Berthelot principle (Thomsen, Julius and Berthelot, Pierre Eugene Marcellin). See: Berthelot-Thomsen principle.

THOMSEN, JULIUS (In full: HANS PETER JOERGEN JULIUS). 1826-1909. Danish chemist. See: World Who's Who Sci., Berthelot-Thomsen principle, Thomsen process, Thomsenolite.

THOMSEN, OLUF. 1878-1940. Danish physician. See: Acta Path. Microbiol. Scand., vol. 17 (1940), pp. 257-259. Thomsen's phenomenon.

Thomsen process (Thomsen, Julius): Chemistry. See: Hackh; Van Nostrand Chem. Dict.

Thomsenolite (Thomsen, Julius): Earth Sciences. See: Thrush; Webster's 3d.

Thomsen's disease (Thomsen, Asmus Julius Thomas): Medicine. See: Dorland; Jablonski; Stedman.

Thomsen's phenomenon (Thomsen, Oluf): Medicine. See: Dorland.

THOMSON, ALLEN. 1809-1884. Scottish anatomist and biologist. See: Dict. Nat. Biog. Thomson's fascia.

Thomson arc cutter (Thomson, Elihu): Engineering and Industry. See: Thrush.

Thomson atom (Thomson, Sir Joseph John): Physics. See: Internat. Dict. Phys. Elec.

Thomson bridge (Thomson, William, Lord Kelvin). See: Kelvin double bridge (or bridge).

THOMSON, CHARLES EDWARD POULETT, BARON SYDENHAM. 1799-1841. English economist and statesman. See: Dict. Nat. Biog. Sydenham-Harrison Resolutions.

Thomson coefficient (Thomson, William, Lord Kelvin): Electronics. See: Markus; Webster's 3d.

Thomson cross-section (Thomson, Sir Joseph John): Physics. See: Ballentyne; Markus.

Thomson effect (or heat) (Thomson, William, Lord Kelvin): Physics. See: Ballentyne; Internat. Dict. Phys. Elec.; Markus; Thewlis; Webster's 3d. Also known as: Kelvin effect (2).

Thomson electromotive force (or E.M.F.) (Thomson, William, Lord Kelvin): Physics. See: Van Nostrand Sci. Encyc.; Webster's 3d.

THOMSON, ELIHU. 1853-1957. English-born American electrical engineer. See: Dict. Amer. Biog. Thomson arc cutter, Thomson integrating wattmeter, Thomson process.

THOMSON, FREDERICK HOLLAND. 1867-1938. English physician. See: Lancet, vol. 2 (Oct. 15, 1938) p. 921. Thomson's sign.

Thomson-Freundlich equation (Thomson, Sir Joseph John? and Freundlich, Herbert Max Findlay): Physics. See: Ballentyne.

THOMSON, SIR GEORGE PAGET. 1892-   . English physicist. See: World Who's Who Sci. Thomson's hypothesis.

Thomson integrating wattmeter (Thomson, Elihu): Engineering and Industry. See: Dict. Amer. Biog.

Thomson isotherm (Thomson, Sir Joseph John): Physics. See: Internat. Dict. Phys. Elec.

THOMSON, JAMES. 1700-1748. Scottish poet. See: Dict. Nat. Biog. Thomsonian.

THOMSON, JAMES. 1822-1892. Irish physician, engineer and inventor. See: Dict. Nat. Biog. Thomson vortex wheel.

THOMSON, JOSEPH. 1858-1895. Scottish explorer, geologist and botanist in Africa. See: Dict. Nat. Biog. Thomson's gazelle.

THOMSON, SIR JOSEPH JOHN. 1856-1940. English physicist. See: Pogg., vols. 3 to 6; World Who's Who Sci. Nernst-Thomson rule, Thomson atom, Thomson cross-section, Thomson-Freundlich equation, Thomson isotherm, Thomson parabola method, Thomson scattering, Thomson's theoretical gas/liquid curve.

THOMSON, MATTHEW SIDNEY. 1894-1969. English dermatologist. See: Who Was Who. Rothmund-Thomson syndrome.

Thomson parabola method (Thomson, Sir Joseph John): Physics. See: Ballentyne; Van Nostrand Sci. Encyc.

THOMSON, PETER. No dates. American tailor. (Biography source unavailable. Peter Thomson dress.

Thomson principle (Thomson, William, Lord Kelvin): Physics. See: Van Nostrand Sci. Encyc.

Thomson process (Thomson, Elihu): Engineering and Industry. See: Hackh; Thrush; Webster's 3d.

Thomson relations (or thermocouple relations) (Thomson, William, Lord Kelvin): Physics. See: Ballentyne; Internat. Dict. Phys. Elec.

THOMSON, SAMUEL. 1796-1843. American physician. See: Dict. Amer. Biog. Thomsonianism.

Thomson scattering (Thomson, Sir Joseph John): Physics. See: Ballentyne; Internat. Dict. Ap. Math.; Thewlis.

THOMSON, THOMAS. 1773-1852. Scottish chemist and scientific writer. See: Dict. Nat. Biog. Thomsonite.

Thomson voltage (Thomson, William, Lord Kelvin): Electronics. See: Markus.

Thomson vortex wheel (Thomson, James): Engineering and Industry. See: Auger.

THOMSON, WILLIAM, LORD KELVIN. 1824-1907. English physicist. See: Dict. Nat. Biog. Joule-Thomson inversion temperature, Joule-Thomson coefficient, Joule-Thomson (or Joule-Kelvin) effect, Joule-Thomson valve, Kelvin (1) (unit), Kelvin (2) (unit), Kelvin (3) (unit), Kelvin balance (or ampere-Balance), Kelvin('s) circulation theorem, Kelvin clamp, Kelvin compass, Kelvin double bridge (or bridge), Kelvin electrometer, Kelvin equation for surface tension, Kelvin galvanometer (or astatic galvanometer), Kelvin-Hughes projector?, Kelvin-Hughes system of rapid processing?, Kelvin('s) law, Kelvin material, Kelvin method of measuring galvanometer resistance, Kelvin model, Kelvin skin effect (or effect (1)), Kelvin temperature scale (temperature or Kelvin), Kelvin('s) theorem, Kelvin tide predictor, Kelvin-Varley slide, Kelvin wave, Kelvin-White sounding machine, Kelvinator, Kelvin's coupling, Kelvin's equation, Kelvin's problem, Kelvin's statement (of the second law of thermodynamics), Kelvin's warming engine, law of Thomson (or Thomson's rule), Planck-Kelvin formulation of the second law of thermodynamics, Thomson coefficient, Thomson effect (or heat), Thomson electromotive force (or E.M.F.), Thomson principle, Thomson relations (or thermocouple relations), Thomson voltage, Thomson's formula.

Thomsonian (Thomson, James): Literature. See: Webster's 3d.

Thomsonianism (Thomson, Samuel): Medicine. See: Dorland; Mathews, M. M.

Thomsonite (Thomson, Thomas): Earth Sciences. See: Thrush; Webster's 3d.

Thomson's fascia (Thomson, Allen): Anatomy. See: Donath.

Thomson's formula (Thomson, William, Lord Kelvin): Physics. See: Ballentyne.

Thomson's gazelle (Thomson, Joseph): Zoology. See: Webster's 3d.

Thomson's hypothesis (Thomson, Sir George Paget): Physics. See: Webster's 3d.

Thomson's law (or rule) (Thomson, William, Lord Kelvin). See: law of Thomson (or Thomson's rule).

Thomson's sign (Thomson, Frederick Holland). See: Pastia's sign.

Thomson's theoretical gas/liquid curve (Thomson, Sir Joseph John): Physics. See: Ballentyne.

THOR. Norse god of thunder. See: Jobes. Thor (rocket), Thorite, Thorium, Thursday.

Thor (rocket) (Thor): Engineering and Industry. See: Markus; Van Nostrand Sci. Encyc. under "Rockets and Launch Vehicles".

Thoraeus filter (Thoraeus, Robert): Engineering and Industry. See: Markus; Thewlis.

THORAEUS, ROBERT. fl. 1932. Swedish physicist. See: Pogg., vol. 6. Thoraeus filter.

THOREAU, HENRY DAVID. 1817-1862. American writer, philosopher and naturalist. See: Dict. Amer. Biog. Thoreau's Law, Thoreauvian.

THOREAU, JACQUES. b. 1886. Belgian mineralogist. See: Bibliographie Academique Louvain VI, 1914/1934, p. 275. Thoreaulite.

Thoreaulite (Thoreau, Jacques): Earth Sciences. See: Thrush; Webster's 3d.

oreau's Law (Thoreau, Henry David): Sociology. See: Martin.

oreauvian (Thoreau, Henry David): Literature. See: Webster's 3d.

OREL, CHARLES. 1868-1935. German pathologist. See: Verh. Deutsch. thol. Ges., vol. 28 (1935), p. 378ff. Thorel's bundle.

orel's bundle (Thorel, Charles): Anatomy. See: Dorland; Donath.

orite (Thor): Earth Sciences. See: Thrush; Van Nostrand Sci. Encyc.

orium (Thor): Chemistry. See: Markus; Thrush; Van Nostrand Sci. Encyc.

ORMAEHLEN, JOHANN. fl. 1885. German physician. (Biography source available.) Thormaehlen's test.

ormaehlen's test (Thormaehlen, Johann): Medicine. See: Dorland; Stedman.

ORN, GEORGE WIDMER. 1906- . American physician. See: Amer. en and Women Sci., 12th ed. Thorn test, Thorn's syndrome.

orn test (Thorn, George Widmer): Medicine. See: Stedman.

ORNDIKE, EDWARD LEE. 1874-1949. American psychologist. See: ternat. Encyc. Soc. Sci. Thorndike handwriting scale, Thorndike-Lorge list, orndike's law of transfer, Thorndike's trial and error learning.

ORNDIKE, EDWARD MOULTON. 1905- . American physicist. See: mer. Men Sci., 5th ed. Kennedy-Thorndike experiment.

orndike handwriting scale (Thorndike, Edward Lee): Psychology. See: glish; Wolman.

orndike-Lorge list (Thorndike, Edward Lee and Lorge, Irving): Psychology. e: Wolman.

orndike's law of transfer (Thorndike, Edward Lee): Psychology. See: aplin.

orndike's trial and error learning (Thorndike, Edward Lee): Psychology: See: aplin; Wolman.

ORNE. fl. 1880. American? printer. (Biography source unavailable.) orne typesetting-machine.

orne typesetting-machine (Thorne): Printing. See: Lockwood.

orn's syndrome (Thorn, George Widmer): Medicine. See: Jablonski; Stedman.

ORNTHWAITE, CHARLES WAREN. 1899-1963. American climatologist. ee: Who Was Who Amer. Thornthwaite's bioclimatological system.

ornthwaite's bioclimatological system (Thornthwaite, Charles Waren): Earth ciences. See: Van Nostrand Sci Encyc. under "Climatic Classification".

ornton Pickard focal plane shutter (Derivation undetermined): Photography. ee: Focal Encyc. Photog.

ORNWALDT, GUSTAV LUDWIG. 1843-1910. German physician. See: iog. Lex. hervorr. Aerzte. Thornwaldt's syndrome (bursa or cyst).

ornwaldt's syndrome (bursa or cyst) (Thornwaldt, Gustav Ludwig): Medicine. ee: Dorland; Jablonski; Stedman.

orold's deer (Derivation undetermined): Zoology. See: Gray.

ORPE, SIR EDWARD (In full: THOMAS EDWARD). 1845-1925. English hemist. See: Dict. Nat. Biog. Thorpe's ratio.

ORPE, SIR JOCELYN FIELD. 1872-1940. English chemist. See: World ho's Who Sci. Thorpe reaction.

orpe reaction (Thorpe, Sir Jocelyn Field): Chemistry. See: Van Nostrand hem. Dict.

orpe's ratio (Thorpe, Sir Edward): Chemistry. See: Thrush.

ORSON, AKE. fl. 1952. Swedish physician. (Biography source unavailble.) Bioerk-Thorson syndrome.

ORTVEIT, OLAUS. fl. early 20th c. Norwegian mineralogist. Cited in: intze. Thortveitite.

ortveitite (Thortveit, Olaus): Earth Sciences. See: Thrush; Webster's 3d.

OST, ARTHUR. b. 1854. German physician. See: Biog. Lex. hervorr. erzte. Unna-Thost syndrome.

OULET, JULIEN (In full: MARIE JULIEN OLIVER). 1843-1936. French ineralogist. See: Pogg., vols. 3, 4, 5. Thoulet solution, Thoulet's law.

Thoulet solution (Thoulet, Julien): Chemistry. See: Hackh; Thrush; Van Nostrand Chem. Dict.

Thoulet's law (Thoulet, Julien): Earth Sciences. See: Thrush.

Thounelier hand-press (Derivation undetermined): Printing. See: Lockwood under "Hand-Press," p. 256b.

THRASO. Bragging character in Terence's play "Eunuchus". See: Harvey. Thrasonical.

Thrasonical (Thraso): Generic Word. See: Partridge; Stenhouse; Webster's 3d.

threads of Rezzonico-Golgi (Rezzonico, Giulio and Golgi, Camillo). See: Rezzonico-Golgi threads (or spirals).

THRESH, JOHN COUGH. 1850-1932. English chemist. See: Who Was Who, 1929-1940. Thresh reagent, Thresh test reaction.

Thresh reagent (Thresh, John Clough): Chemistry. See: Van Nostrand Chem. Dict.

Thresh test reaction (Thresh, John Clough): Chemistry. See: Van Nostrand Chem. Dict.

THROCKMORTON, FRANCIS. 1554-1584. English conspirator. See: Dict. Nat. Biog. Throckmorton plot (or conspiracy).

Throckmorton plot (or conspiracy) (Throckmorton, Francis): History. See: Harbottle; Steinberg.

THROCKMORTON, THOMAS BENTLEY. 1885-1961. American neurologist. See: Who Was Who Amer., vol. 4. Throckmorton's reflex.

Throckmorton's reflex (Throckmorton, Thomas Bentley). Medicine. See: Dorland.

Throgmorton, Francis. See: Throckmorton, Francis.

Thrun test reaction (Thrun, Walter Eugene): Chemistry. See: Van Nostrand Chem. Dict.

THRUN, WALTER EUGENE. b. 1892. American chemist. See: Amer. Men Sci., 5th ed. Thrun test reaction.

Thucydidean (Thucydides): History. See: Stenhouse; Webster's 3d.

THUCYDIDES. 471?-400? B.C. Greek historian. See: Harper. Thucydidean.

THUDICHUM, JOHANN L. W. 1829-1901. German physician in London. See: Biog. Jahrb. Deut. Nekr., 1901. Thudichum's test.

Thudichum's test (Thudichum, Johann L. W.): Medicine. See: Dorland; Stedman.

THUE, AXEL. 1863-1922. Norwegian mathematician. See: New Encyc. Brit., 1974, Microp. Thue's theorem.

THUENEN, JOHANNES HEINRICH VON. 1783-1850. German economist. See: Internat. Encyc. Soc. Sci. Thuenen's rings.

Thuenen's rings (Thuenen, Johannes Heinrich von): Economics. See: Monkhouse.

Thue's theorem (Thue, Axel): Mathematics. See: Ballentyne.

Thum-Balbach process (Thum, William? and Balbach, Edward): Engineering and Industry. See: Thrush.

Thum furnace (Thum, William?): Engineering and Industry. See: Thrush.

THUM, WILLIAM. fl. 1910. American engineer. (Biography source unavailable.) Thum-Balbach process?, Thum furnace?

THUNBERG, KARL PETER. 1743-1828. Swedish botanist. See: World Who's Who Sci. Thunberg lespedeza, Thunbergia.

Thunberg lespedeza (Thunberg, Karl Peter): Botany. See: Webster's 3d.

THUNBERG, TORSTEN LUDWIG. 1873-1952. Swedish physiologist. See: Svenska Maen Och Kvinnor. Thunberg's respirator.

Thunbergia (Thunberg, Karl Peter): Botany. See: Taylor, N.; Webster's 3d.

Thunberg's respirator (Thunberg, Torsten Ludwig): Medicine. See: Stedman.

THURBER, GEORGE. 1821-1890. American botanist. See: Dict. Amer. Biog. Thurberia.

Thurberia (Thurber, George): Botany. See: Webster's 3d.

Thurlow's weeping willow (Derivation undetermined): Botany. See: Gray.

Thurman Act (Thurman, Allen Granberry): Politics. See: Jameson.

THURMAN, ALLEN GRANBERRY. 1813-1895. American legislator. See: Biog. Direct. Amer. Congress. Thurman Act.

THURN, SIR EVERARD F. d. 1932. English botanist. (Biography source unavailable.) Thurnia.

Thurnia (Thurn, Sir Everard F.): Botany. See: Webster's 3d.

Thursday (Thor): Generic Word. See: Barnhart (Eng. Lit.); Funk; Harvey.

Thurstone attitude scale (Thurstone, Louis Leon): Psychology. See: Chaplin; English; Wolman.

THURSTONE, LOUIS LEON. 1887-1955. American psychologist. See: Internat. Encyc. Soc. Sci. Thurstone attitude scale, Thurstone's theory of primary mental abilities.

Thurstone's theory of primary mental abilities (Thurstone, Louis Leon): Psychology. See: Chaplin; Wolman.

THURY, MARC (In full: JEAN MARC ANTOINE). 1822-1905. Swiss natural scientist and botanist. See: Dict. Hist. Biog. Suisse. Thury thread, Thury's compass.

Thury thread (Thury, Marc): Engineering and Industry. See: Auger.

Thury's compass (Thury, Marc): Engineering and Industry. Cited in: Dict. Hist. Biog. Suisse.

THWAITE, BENJAMIN HOWARTH. fl. 1890. English engineer. Cited in: Royal Soc. Cat. Sci. Pap., 1884-1900. Thwaite gas engine.

Thwaite gas engine (Thwaite, Benjamin Howarth): Engineering and Industry. See: Auger.

THWENG, ROBERT DE. ca. 1205-ca. 1268. English divine and crusader. See: Dict. Nat. Biog. Thweng's riots.

Thweng's riots (Thweng, Robert de): History. See: Harbottle.

Thyestean banquet (or revenge) (Thyestes): Mythology. See: Brewer; Partridge; Phyfe.

THYESTES. Son of Pelops in Greek mythology who seduced his brother's wife. See: Harper. Thyestean banquet (or revenge).

THYGESON, PHILLIPS. 1903-   . American opthalmologist. See: Amer. Men and Women Sci., 12th ed. Thygeson's keratitis.

Thygeson's keratitis (Thygeson, Phillips): Medicine. See: Jablonski.

Thynne, Thomas, 1st Viscount Weymouth. See: Weymouth, Thomas Thynne, 1st Viscount of.

THYSSEN, AUGUST. 1842-1926. German industrialist. See: Ann. Register. Thyssen collection, Thyssen-Roder turbine.

Thyssen collection (Thyssen, August): Fine Arts. Cited in: Osborne under "Memling, Hans."

THYSSEN, FRITZ. 1873-1951. German industrialist. See: Webster's Biog. Dict. Thyssen gravimeter?

Thyssen gravimeter (Thyssen, Fritz?): Engineering and Industry. See: Thrush.

Thyssen-Roder turbine (Thyssen, August and Roeder, Karl?): Engineering and Industry. See: Auger.

Tiberian (Tiberius): History. See: Webster's 3d.

TIBERIUS. 42 B.C.-37 A.D. Second emperor of Rome. See: Encyc. Brit., 1911. Tiberian.

Tich (Relph, Harry "Little Tich"): Generic Word (diminutive person). See: Brewer.

Tichborne claimant (and case) (Tichborne, Sir Roger Charles): Law. See: Brewer; Latham; Phyfe.

Tichborne dole (Tichborne, Lady Mabel): History. See: Brewer.

TICHBORNE, LADY MABEL. fl. 1150. English noblewoman. (Biography source unavailable.) Tichborne dole.

TICHBORNE, SIR ROGER CHARLES. 1829-1854. English nobleman. See: Encyc. Brit., 1973. Tichborne claimant (and case).

TICKELL, FREDERICK GEORGE. b. 1886. American geologist. See: Amer. Men Sci., 5th ed. Tickell roundness number.

Tickell roundness number (Tickell, Frederick George): Earth Sciences. See: Thrush.

TICKELL, SAMUEL RICHARD. fl. 1833-1862. English ornithologist. See: Royal Soc. Cat. Sci. Pap., 1800-1863. Tickell's ousel.

Tickell's ousel (Tickell, Samuel Richard): Zoology. See: Gray.

TIDY, CHARLES MEYMOTT. 1843-1892. English physician, chemist and writer. See: Dict. Nat. Biog. Tidy's test.

Tidy's test (Tidy, Charles Meymott): Medicine. See: Dorland; Stedman.

TIECHE, MAX. 1878-1938. Swiss physician. See: Schweiz. Med. Wchenschr. vol. 68 (May 28, 1938), p. 657. Jadassohn-Tieche nevus.

TIEDEMANN, FRIEDRICH. 1781-1861. German anatomist and physiologist. See: World Who's Who. Tiedemann-Gmelin test reaction for acetate, Tiedemann-Gmelin test reaction for tryptophane, Tiedemann's bodies (or vesicles), Tiedemann's gland, Tiedemann's nerve.

Tiedemann-Gmelin test reaction for acetate (Tiedemann, Friedrich, and Gmelin, Leopold): Chemistry. See: Van Nostrand Chem. Dict.

Tiedemann-Gmelin test reaction for tryptophane (Tidemann, Friedrich and Gmelin, Leopold): Chemistry. See: Van Nostrand Chem. Dict.

Tiedemann's bodies (or vesicles) (Tiedmann, Friedrich): Anatomy. See: Henderson; Pennak; Van Nostrand Sci. Encyc.

Tiedemann's gland (Tiedemann, Friedrich): Anatomy. See: Donath; Dorland; Stedman. Also known as: Bartholin's gland.

Tiedemann's nerve (Tiedemann, Friedrich): Anatomy. See: Donath; Dorland; Stedman.

TIEGS, OSCAR WERNER. 1897-1956. Australian zoologist. See: Who Was Who. Tiegs reagent and test.

Tiegs reagent and test (Tiegs, Oscar Werner): Chemistry. See: Van Nostrand Chem. Dict.

TIEMANN, FERDINAND (In full: JOHANN KARL WILHELM FERDINAND): Chemistry. See: Van Nostrand Chem. Dict. Reimer-Tiemann reaction, Tiemann reaction.

Tiemann reaction (Tiemann, Ferdinand): Chemistry. See: Van Nostrand Chem. Dict.

TIEMANN, W. fl. 19th c. German scientist. Cited in: Dana, p. 56. Tiemannite.

Tiemannite (Tiemann, W.): Earth Sciences. See: Thrush; Webster's 3d.

TIETZE, ALEXANDER. 1864-1927. German surgeon. See: Biog. Lex. hervorr. Aerzte. Tietze's syndrome (or disease).

Tietze's syndrome (or disease) (Tietze, Alexander): Medicine. See: Dorland; Jablonski; Stedman.

TIFFANY, CHARLES LEWIS. 1812-1902. American jeweler. See: Dict. Amer. Biog. Tiffany setting, Tiffanyite.

Tiffany (effect) (Tiffany, Louis Comfort): Applied Arts. See: Webster's 3d.

Tiffany glass (Tiffany, Louis Comfort): Applied Arts. See: Hendrickson; Webster's 3d.

Tiffany lamp shade (Tiffany, Louis Comfort): Applied Arts. Cited in: Hendrickson.

TIFFANY, LOUIS COMFORT. 1848-1933. American artist. See: Webster's Biog. Dict. Tiffany (effect), Tiffany glass, Tiffany lamp shade.

Tiffany setting (Tiffany, Charles Lewis): Applied Arts. See: Hendrickson; Webster's 3d.

Tiffanyite (Tiffany, Charles Lewis): Earth Sciences. See: Thrush.

TIFFENAU, MARC EMILE PIERRE ADOLPHE. 1873-1945. French chemist and pharmacologist. See: World Who's Who Sci. Tiffenau reaction.

Tiffenau reaction (Tiffenau, Marc Emile Pierre Adolphe): Chemistry. See: Van Nostrand Chem. Dict.

TIKHONENKOV, I. P. fl. 20th c. Russian mineralogist. Cited in: Min. Mag. vol. 33, pt. 2 (1963-1964), p. 1152. Tikhonenkovite.

Tikhonenkovite (Tikhonenkov, I. P.): Earth Sciences. See: Thrush.

Tikhonov, Andrei Nikolaevich. See: Tychonoff, Andrei Nikolaevich.

TILAS, DANIEL. 1712-1772. Swedish mining engineer. See: Svenska Maen Och Kvinnor. Tilasite.

Tilasite (Tilas, Daniel): Earth Sciences. See: Webster's 3d.

TILBURY. fl. early 19th c. English coachmaker. (Biography source unavailable.) Tilbury (carriage).

Tilbury (carriage) (Tilbury): Generic Word. See: Partridge; Phyfe; Webster's 3d.

Tilbury Fox. See: Fox, William Tilbury.

TILLANDS, ELIAS. 1640-1693. Swedish botanist and physician. See: Finsk Biog. Handb. Tillandsia.

Tillandsia (Tillands, Elias): Botany. See: Partridge; Taylor, N.; Webster's 3d.

TILLAUX, PAUL JULES. 1834-1904. French surgeon. See: Biog. Lex. hervorr. Aerzte. Tillaux-Phocas disease.

Tillaux-Phocas disease (Tillaux, Paul Jules, and Phocas, B. Gerasime). See: Cheatle's disease.

Tillmans-Alt test reaction for tryptophane (Tillmans, Josef and Alt, A.): Chemistry. See: Van Nostrand Chem. Dict.

Tillmans-Hirsch test reactions for ascorbic acid (Tillmans, Josef and Hirsch, Paul): Chemistry. See: Van Nostrand Chem. Dict.

TILLMANS, JOSEF. 1876-1935. German biochemist. See: Pogg., vol. 6. Tillmans-Alt test reaction for tryptophane, Tillmans-Hirsch test reactions for ascorbic acid, Tillmans' reagent.

Tillmans' reagent (Tillmans, Josef): Chemistry. See: Hackh.

TIMME, WALTER. 1874-1956. American physician. See: Who Was Who Amer., vol. 3. Timme's syndrome.

Timme's syndrome (Timme, Walter): Medicine. See: Dorland; Jablonski.

TIMOFEEV, DMITRI ALEKSANDROVICH. b. 1859. Russian anatomist. Cited in: Index-Cat. Libr. Surg.-Gen. Off., 2nd Ser., vol. 18, 1913. Timofeev's corpuscles.

Timofeev's corpuscles (Timofeev, Dmitri Aleksandrovich): Anatomy. See: Henderson.

TIMON. fl. ca. 430 B.C. Athenian misanthrope. See: Encyc. Brit., 1911. Timon (or Timonism).

Timon (or Timonism) (Timon): Generic Word (misanthrope). See: Partridge; Webster's 3d.

Timothy (or Timothy grass and hay) (Hanson, Timothy): Botany. See: Hendrickson; Mathews, M. M.; Partridge; Wagner (More Names); Weekley.

Timothy trimmer (Hanson, Timothy): Recreation and Sports. See: Mathews, M. M.

TIMUR. 1336-1405. Turkic conqueror. See: Encyc. Brit., 1973. Timurid dynasty.

Timurid dynasty (Timur): History. Cited in: Osborne under "Islamic Art."

TINEL, JULES. 1879-1952. French neurologist. See: Bull. Mem. Soc. Med. Hop. Paris vol. 68 (Mar. 21-Apr. 4, 1952), pp. 389-91. Tinel's sign.

Tinel's sign (Tinel, Jules): Medicine. See: Dorland; Stedman.

TINKER, JOSEPH. d. 1948. American baseball player. See: New York Times, July 28, 1948, p. 23, col. 1. Tinker to Evers to Chance.

Tinker to Evers to Chance (Tinker, Joseph; Evers, Johnny; and Chance, Frank): Recreation and Sports. See: Hendrickson.

Tinsley-Gall ac polar potentiometer (Tinsley, H., and Gall, D. C.): Engineering and Industry. Cited in: McGraw-Hill Encyc. Sci. Tech. under "Potentiometer (variable resistor)."

TINSLEY, H. fl. early 20th c. English electrical engineer. (Biography source unavailable.) Tinsley-Gall ac polar potentiometer, Tinsley Vernier potentiometer.

Tinsley Vernier potentiometer (Tinsley, H. and Vernier, Pierre): Engineering and Industry. See: Internat. Dict. Phys. Elec.

TINY TIM. Character in the story "A Christmas Carol", (1843) by Charles Dickens. See: Harvey. Tiny Tim.

Tiny Tim (Tiny Tim, the fictional character): Botany. See: Webster's 3d.

Tippecanoe(s) (Harrison, William Henry "Tippecanoe"): History. See: Mathews, M. M.

Tippecanoe and Tyler Too (Harrison, William Henry "Tippecanoe" and Tyler, John): History. See: Mathews, M. M.

TIRO, MARCUS TULLIUS. fl. 1st c. B.C. Roman secretary to Cicero. See: Harper. Tironian notes, Tironian sign.

Tironian notes (Tiro, Marcus Tullius): Dictation. See: Brewer; Charnock; Hendrickson.

Tironian sign (Tiro, Marcus Tullius): Dictation. See: Brewer; Hendrickson.

Tischenko reaction (Tischenko, Vyacheslav Yevgen'yevich): Chemistry. See: Ballentyne; Van Nostrand Chem. Dict.; Webster's 3d.

TISCHENKO, VYACHESLAV YEVGEN'YEVICH. 1861-1941. Russian chemist. See: Who Was Who USSR. Tischenko reaction.

TISCHLER, RICHARD J. fl. 1941. American chemist. (Biography source unavailable.) Tischler test?

Tischler test (Tischler, Richard J.?): Chemistry. See: Van Nostrand Chem. Dict.

Tiselius apparatus (tube or cell) (Tiselius, Arne Wilhelm Kaurin): Chemistry. See: Asimov; Stedman; Webster's 3d.

TISELIUS, ARNE WILHELM KAURIN. 1902-1971. Swedish chemist. See: Encyc. Brit., 1973. Tiselius apparatus (tube or cell), Tiselius method.

Tiselius method (Tiselius, Arne Wilhelm Kaurin): Chemistry. See: Internat. Dict. Phys. Elec.

TISSOT, NICOLAS AUGUSTE. fl. 1881. French geographer. Cited in: Royal Soc. Cat. Sci. Pap., 1874-1883, 1884-1900. Tissot's indicatrix.

Tissot's indicatrix (Tissot, Nicolas Auguste): Geography. See: Monkhouse.

Tite Barnacle (Barnacle, Tite): Generic Word (incompetent bureaucrat). See: Partridge.

Tithonia (Tithonus): Botany. See: Taylor, N.; Webster's 3d.

Tithonic (Tithonus): Chemistry. See: Charnock.

TITHONUS. Son of Laomedon and brother of Priam of Troy in Greek mythology. See: Harper. Tithonia, Tithonic, Tithonus.

Tithonus (Tithonus the mythological figure): Generic Word (old man). See: Harper.

TITIAN (TIZIANO VECELLI). 1477-1576. Italian painter. See: Encyc. Brit., 1973. Titian hair, Titian (red), Titianesque.

Titian hair (Titian): Fine Arts. See: Hendrickson; Partridge.

Titian (red) (Titian): Fine Arts. See: Picken; Webster's 3d.

Titianesque (Titian): Fine Arts. See: Partridge; Webster's 3d.

Titius-Bode law (or series) (Titius, Johann Daniel and Bode, Johann Elert). See: Bode's law (or relation).

TITIUS, JOHANN DANIEL. 1729-1796. German mathematician and physicist. See: Allg. Deut. Biog. Titius-Bode law (or series).

TITO (Real name: BROZ OR BROZOVICH, JOSIP). b. 1892. Yugoslavian premier. See: Encyc. Brit., 1973. Titoism.

Titoism (Tito): Politics. See: Hendrickson.

TITUS (In full: TITUS FLAVIUS SABINUS VESPASIANUS). 40?-81 A.D. Roman emperor. See: Encyc. Brit., 1973. Titus hair cut.

Titus hair cut (Titus): Fashion. See: Picken.

TITYOS. Greek mythical giant. See: Jobes. Tityus (scorpion).

Tityus (scorpion) (Tityos): Zoology. See: Webster's 3d.

TIW or TYR. Teutonic god of the day sky and of war. See: Jobes. Tuesday.

TIZZONI, GUIDO. 1853-1932. Italian bacteriologist. See: Biochim. Terap. Sper., vol. 19 (Nov. 30, 1932), pp. 353-61. Tizzoni's antitoxin, Tizzoni's test.

Tizzoni's antitoxin (Tizzoni, Guido): Medicine. See: Stedman.

Tizzoni's test (Tizzoni, Guido): Medicine. See: Dorland; Stedman.

to Bishop (Bishop): Generic Word (murder). See: Hendrickson; Partridge.

to raise Cain (Cain): Generic Word (noisy disturbance). See: Brewer; Clapin; Partridge.

Tobe formula (Davis, Tobe Coller): Fashion. See: Picken.

Tobe-wise store (Davis, Tobe Coller): Fashion. See: Picken.

Tobey-Ayer test (Tobey, George Loring and Ayer, James Bourne): Medicine. See: Dorland.

TOBEY, GEORGE LORING. 1881-1947. American otolaryngologist. See: Who's Who Among Physicians and Surg. Tobey-Ayer test.

Tobiad (Tobias): History. See: Webster's 3d.

TOBIAS. fl. ca. 210 B.C. Father of Joseph. See: Encyc. Brit., 1973. Tobiad, Tobias nights.

Tobias acid (Tobias, Georg): Chemistry. See: Webster's 3d.

TOBIAS, GEORG. fl. 1882. German chemist. Cited in: Royal Soc. Cat. Sci. Pap., 1874-1883, 1884-1900. Tobias acid.

TOBIAS, JOSE WENCESLAV. b. 1893. Argentinian physician. See: Gran Encic. Argentina. Pancoast-Tobias syndrome, Tobias' syndrome.

Tobias nights (Tobias): Anthropology. See: Winick.

Tobias' syndrome (Tobias, Jose Wenceslav). See: Pancoast's syndrome (apex syndrome or tumor).

Tobin bronze (Tobin, John A.): Engineering and Industry. See: Mathews, M. M.; Partridge; Thrush.

TOBIN, JOHN A. fl. 1882. American inventor and naval officer. (Biography source unavailable.) Tobin bronze.

TOBIN, MARTIN. fl. 1872. English inventor. (Biography source unavailable.) Tobin's tube.

Tobin's tube (Tobin, Martin): Engineering and Industry. See: Partridge.

TOBOLD, ADELBERT AUGUST. 1827-1907. German laryngologist. See: Biog. Lex. hervorr. Aerzte. Tobold's apparatus.

Tobold's apparatus (Tobold, Adelbert August): Medicine. See: Dorland.

TOCHER, JAMES FOWLER. 1864-1942. English chemist and statistician. See: Who Was Who. Tocher test reactions.

Tocher test reactions (Tocher, James Fowler): Chemistry. See: Van Nostrand Chem. Dict.

TOD, HUNTER FINLAY. 1871-1923. English otologist. See: Biog. Lex. hervorr. Aerzte. Tod's muscle?

TODARO, FRANCESCO. 1839-1918. Italian anatomist. See: Biog. Lex hervorr. Aerzte. Todaro's tendon.

Todaro's tendon (Todaro, Francesco): Anatomy. See: Stedman.

TODD, ALEXANDER ROBERTUS. 1907- . English biochemist. See: World Who's Who Sci. Barger-Bergel-Todd test reaction.

Todd-AO process (Todd, Michael): Photography. See: Focal Encyc. Photog. under "Cine History."

Todd atomizer (Todd, George William?): Engineering and Industry. See: Auger.

TODD, GEORGE WILLIAM. b. 1886. English experimental physicist. See: Pogg., vol. 6. Todd atomizer?

TODD, MICHAEL. 1907-1958. American theatrical producer. See: Who Was Who Amer. Todd-AO process.

TODD, ROBERT BENTLEY. 1809-1860. English physician and anatomist. See: Dict. Nat. Biog. Todd's paralysis.

Todd's paralysis (Todd, Robert Bentley): Medicine. See: Hinsie; Jablonski; Stedman.

TODE, HEINRICH JULIUS. 1733-1797. German botanist. See: Michaud. Todea.

Todea (Tode, Heinrich Julius): Botany. See: Partridge; Webster's 3d.

Tod's muscle (Tod, Hunter Finlay?): Anatomy. See: Stedman.

TOEPFER, ALFRED EDUARD FRANZ. b. 1858. German physician. (Biography source unavailable.) Toepfer's test (or reagent).

Toepfer's test (or reagent) (Toepfer, Alfred Eduard Franz): Medicine. See: Dorland; Stedman; Van Nostrand Chem. Dict.

TOEPLER, AUGUST JOSEPH IGNAZ. 1836-1912. German physicist. See: Encyc. Brit., 1973. Toepler-Holtz machine, Toepler pump.

Toepler-Holtz machine (Toepler, August and Holtz, Wilhelm): Engineering and Industry. See: Internat. Dict. Phys. Elec. Also known as: Holtz machine.

Toepler pump (Toepler, August): Engineering and Industry. See: Auger; Thewlis; Webster's 3d.

TOERNEBOHM, ALFRED ELIS. 1838-1911. Swedish geologist. See: Encyc. Brit., 1973. Toernebohmite.

Toernebohmite (Toernebohm, Alfred Elis): Earth Sciences. See: Thrush; Webster's 3d.

TOFANA. d. 1730. Greek or Italian inventor of poison. See: Gerwig. aqua Tofana (Toffana).

TOFFLER, ALVIN. 1928- . American author. See: Who's Who Amer. 1974-1975. Toffler's definition of management.

Toffler's definition of management (Toffler, Alvin): Sociology. See: Martin.

TOFIELD, THOMAS. d. 1779. English botanist. (Biography source unavailable.) Tofieldia.

Tofieldia (Tofield, Thomas): Botany. See: Webster's 3d.

TOFT, THOMAS. fl. 1660-1680. English potter. See: New Encyc. Brit., 1974, Microp. Toft ware.

Toft ware (Toft, Thomas): Applied Arts. See: Webster's 3d.

TOISON, J. 1858-1950. French histologist. (Biography source unavailable.) Toison solution (or fluid).

Toison solution (or fluid) (Toison, J.): Medicine. See: Dorland; Hackh; Van Nostrand Chem. Dict.

TOKOLY, COUNT IMRE. 1657-1705. Hungarian patriot. See: Encyc. Brit., 1973. Tokoly's rebellion.

Tokoly's rebellion (Tokoly, Count Imre): History. See: Harbottle.

TOLDT, KARL. 1840-1920. Austrian anatomist. See: Biog. Lex. hervorr. Aerzte. Toldt's fascia, Toldt's membrane.

Toldt's fascia (Toldt, Karl): Anatomy. See: Stedman.

Toldt's membrane (Toldt, Karl): Anatomy. See: Stedman.

Tolle governor (Tolle, M.): Engineering and Industry. See: Auger.

TOLLE, M. fl. 1895. German engineer. (Biography source unavailable.) Tolle governor.

TOLLENS, BERNHARD CHRISTIAN GOTTFRIED. 1841-1918. German chemist. See: World Who's Who Sci. Oshima-Tollens method for detection of methyl pentose or methyl pentosan, Tollens-Oshima test, Tollens reagent (or test) for aldehydes, Tollens solution, Tollens test for galactose, Tollens test for glycuronic acid, Tollens test (or reaction) for pentoses in urine, Weber-Tollens test reaction.

Tollens-Oshima test (Tollens, Bernhard Christian Gottfried and Oshima, Kintaro): Chemistry. See: Van Nostrand Chem. Dict.

Tollens reagent (or test) for aldehydes (Tollens, Bernard Christian Gottfried): Chemistry. See: Ballentyne; Hackh; Van Nostrand Chem. Dict.

Tollens solution (Tollens, Bernhard Christian Gottfried): Chemistry. Cited in: Van Nostrand Sci. Encyc. under "Carbohydrate Metabolism."

Tollens test for galactose (Tollens, Bernhard Christian Gottfried): Chemistry. See: Van Nostrand Chem. Dict.

Tollens test for glycuronic acid (Tollens, Bernard Christian Gottfried): Chemistry. See: Ballentyne; Van Nostrand Chem. Dict.

Tollens test (or reaction) for pentoses in urine (Tollens, Bernhard Christian Gottfried): Chemistry. See: Ballentyne.

Tolles eyepiece (Derivation undetermined): Astronomy. See: Satterthwaite.

TOLMAN. No dates. American fruit grower. (Biography source unavailable.) Tolman sweet (apple).

TOLMAN, EDWARD CHASE. 1886-1959. American psychologist. See: Internat. Encyc. Soc. Sci. Tolman's purposive behaviorism.

Tolman sweet (apple) (Tolman): Botany. See: Partridge.

Tolman's purposive behaviorism (Tolman, Edward Chase): Psychology. See: Chaplin; Wolman.

TOLMIE, WILLIAM FRASER. 1812-1886. Scottish-born Canadian surgeon, fur-trader and politician. See: Dict. Canad. Biog. Tolmiea.

Tolmiea (Tolmie, William Fraser): Botany. See: Taylor, N.

TOLOSA, EDUARDO. fl. 1954. Spanish cardiologist. (Biography source unavailable.) Tolosa-Hunt syndrome.

Tolosa-Hunt syndrome (Tolosa, Eduardo and Hunt, William Edward): Medicine. See: Jablonski.

TOLSTOY, COUNT LEO NIKOLAEVICH. 1828-1910. Russian novelist and religious philosopher. See: Encyc. Brit., 1973. Tolstoyan, Tolstoyans (or Tolstoyism).

Tolstoyan (Tolstoy, Count Leo Nikolaevich): Literature. See: Webster's 3d.

Tolstoyans (or Tolstoyism) (Tolstoy, Count Leo Nikolaevich): Religion. See: Canney; Mathews, S.; Partridge.

TOM AND JERRY. Characters from Pierce Egan's "Life in London" (1821). See: Harvey. Tom and Jerry.

Tom and Jerry (Tom and Jerry, the fictional characters): Food and Drink. See: De Sola; Partridge; Webster's 3d.

Tom Bowling (Bowling, Tom): Generic Word (model sailor). See: Brewer.

Tom Collins (Collins, Tom): Food and Drink. See: Partridge. Also known as: John Collins.

Tom Jones' first law (Jones, Thomas Franklin, Jr.): Sociology. See: Martin.

TOM OF COVENTRY. Legendary 11th c. English tailor. See: Jobes. Peeping Tom.

Tom show (Uncle Tom): Theatre. See: Bowman; Webster's 3d.

TOM THUMB. Dwarf hero of an old nursery tale of the 16th c. See: Harvey. Tom Thumb, Tom Thumb (geranium), Tom Thumb (lily).

Tom Thumb (Tom Thumb): Generic Word (insignificant person). See: Brewer; Partridge; Webster's 3d.

Tom Thumb (geranium) (Tom Thumb): Botany. See: Charnock.

Tom Thumb (lily) (Tom Thumb): Botany. See: Gray.

TOM TIDDLER. Imaginary name for the player in a children's game. See: Harvey. Tom Tiddler's ground.

Tom Tiddler's ground (Tom Tiddler): Generic Word. See: Brewer.

Tom Tram (Tram, Tom): Generic Word (jester). See: Webster's 3d.

Toma's sign (Derivation undetermined): Medicine. See: Stedman.

Tomaselli, Salvatore. See: Tommaselli, Salvatore.

Tomassi process (Tomassi, Witold?): Engineering and Industry. See: Thrush.

TOMASSI, WITOLD. fl. 1950. Polish chemist. (Biography source unavailable.) Tomassi process?

Tome of St. Leo (or Leo's Tome) (Leo I the Great, Saint): Religion. See: Attwater; New Encyc. Brit., 1974, Microp. under "Leo I the Great, Saint."

TOMES, CHARLES SISSMORE. 1846-1928. English dentist and anatomist. See: Who Was Who. Tomes' processes.

Tomes' fibers (or fibrils) (Tomes, Sir John): Dentistry. See: Donath; Dorland; Stedman.

Tomes' granular layer (Tomes, Sir John): Dentistry. See: Donath; Dorland; Stedman.

TOMES, SIR JOHN. 1815-1895. English dentist and anatomist. See: Dict. Nat. Biog. Tomes' fibers (or fibrils), Tomes' granular layer.

Tomes' processes (Tomes, Charles Sissmore): Dentistry. See: Donath; Dorland; Stedman.

TOMICEK, OLDRICH. b. 1891. Czechoslovakian chemist. See: Pogg., vol. 6. Tomicek test reaction.

Tomicek test reaction (Tomicek, Oldrich): Chemistry. See: Van Nostrand Chem. Dict.

Tomkin's damper (Derivation undetermined): Engineering and Industry. See: Auger.

Tomkins-Horn picture arrangement test (Tomkins, Silvan S. and Horn, C. A.): Psychology. See: Hoult.

TOMKINS, SILVAN S. 1911- . American psychologist. See: Biog. Direct. Amer. Psych. Assoc., 1973. Tomkins-Horn picture arrangement test.

TOMLINSON, G. A. fl. 1927. English engineer. See: Pogg., vol. 6. Tomlinson machine?

Tomlinson machine (Tomlinson, G. A.?): Engineering and Industry. See: Auger.

TOMLINSON, NORMAN. fl. 1952-1972. English librarian. See: Who's Who Librarianship and Info. Sci., 1972. Norman Tomlinson Award.

TOMMASELLI, SALVATORE. 1834-1906. Italian physician. See: Biog. Lex. hervorr. Aerzte. Tommaselli's disease.

Tommaselli's disease (Tommaselli, Salvatore): Medicine. See: Dorland; Stedman.

TOMMASI, L. No dates. Italian physician. (Biography source unavailable.) Tommasi's sign (or test).

Tommasi's sign (or test) (Tommasi, L.): Medicine. See: Dorland.

TOMMILA, EERO AKSELI. 1900- . Finnish chemist. See: World Who's Who Sci. Tommila reaction for aldehydes, Tommila test for bismuth.

Tommila reaction for aldehydes (Tommila, Eero Akseli): Chemistry. See: Van Nostrand Chem. Dict.

Tommila test for bismuth (Tommila, Eero Akseli): Chemistry. See: Van Nostrand Chem. Dict.

Tommy (Atkins, Tommy): Food and Drink. See: De Sola.

Tommy Atkins (Atkins, Tommy): Generic Words. See: Wagner (Names); Webster's 3d.

Tommygun (Thompson, John T.) See: Thompson submachine gun.

Tomonaga-Schroedinger equation (Tomonaga, Sin-itiro and Schroedinger, Erwin): Physics. See: Internat. Dict. Phys. Elec.

TOMONAGA, SIN-ITIRO. 1906- . Japanese physicist. See: World Who's Who Sci. Tomonaga-Schroedinger equation.

TOMOSVARY, ODON. fl. 1880. Hungarian zoologist. Cited in: Royal Soc. Cat. Sci. Pap., 1800-1883, suppl. vol. Tomosvary's organ?

Tomosvary's organ (Tomosvary, Odon?): Zoology. See: Gray; Webster's 3d.

Tompion clock (Tompion, Thomas): Horology. See: Partridge; Weekley.

TOMPION, THOMAS. 1639-1713. English watchmaker. See: Dict. Nat. Biog. Tompion clock.

TONEGUTTI, M. fl. 1911. Italian chemist. Cited in: Chem. Abstr. vol. 5, p. 2721. Tonegutti test.

Tonegutti test (Tonegutti, M.): Chemistry. See: Van Nostrand Chem. Dict.

TONTI, LORENZO. 1635-1690. Italian banker. See: Michaud. Tontine.

Tontine (Tonti, Lorenzo): Business. See: Brewer; Harvey; Phyfe.

Tony (award) (Perry, Antoinette): Theater. See: Hendrickson.

TOOMEY, JAMES JOSEPH. b. 1895. American physician. See: Direct. Med. Specialists, 1974-1975. Cole-Rauschkolb-Toomey syndrome?

TOOTH, HOWARD HENRY. 1856-1925. English physician. See: World Who's Who Sci. Charcot-Marie-Tooth-Hoffmann syndrome, Charcot-Marie-Tooth's disease, Tooth's muscular atrophy.

Tooth's muscular atrophy (Tooth, Howard Henry). See: Charcot-Marie-Tooth-Hoffmann syndrome.

TOPALANSKI, ALFRED. b. 1861. Austrian ophthalmologist. See: Biog. Lex. hervorr. Aerzte. Topalanski's sign.

Topalanski's sign (Topalanski, Alfred): Medicine. See: Stedman.

Topcliffe (Topcliffe, Richard): Generic Word (torture). See: Stenhouse.

TOPCLIFFE, RICHARD. 1532-1604. English politician and persecutor of Catholics. See: Dict. Nat. Biog. Topcliffe.

TOPINARD, PAUL. 1830-1912. French physical anthropologist. See: Webster's Biog. Dict. Topinard's angle, Topinard's line.

Topinard's angle (Topinard, Paul): Anatomy. See: Donath; Dorland; Stedman. Also known as: Jacquart's facial angle.

Topinard's line (Topinard, Paul): Anatomy. See: Dorland; Stedman.

Tor (Torricelli, Evangelista): Physics. See: Dresner.

Torbernite (Bergman, Torbern Olof): Earth Sciences. See: Thrush; Webster's 3d.

torcular Herophili (or Herophilus' wine press) (Herophilus): Anatomy. See: Stedman.

TOREK, FRANZ J. A. 1861-1938. American surgeon. See: World Who's Who Sci. Torek operation.

Torek operation (Torek, Franz J. A.): Medicine. See: Dorland; Stedman.

Torelli, Ludovica, Countess of Guastalla. See: Guastalla, Ludovica Torelli, Countess of.

TOREN, OLAF. 1718-1753. Swedish clergyman and botanist. See: Svenska Maen Och Kvinnor. Torenia.

Torenia (Toren, Olaf): Botany. See: Taylor, N.; Webster's 3d.

TORI, KURATSUKURI-NO. fl. ca. 600-630. Japanese sculptor. Cited in: New Encyc. Brit., 1974, Microp. under "Tori style." Tori style.

Tori style (Tori, Kuratsukuri-no): Fine Arts. Cited in: Osborne under "Japanese Art."

TORKILDSEN, ARNE. b. 1899. Norwegian neurosurgeon. See: Hvem er Hvem?, 1950. Torkildsen shunt.

Torkildsen shunt (Torkildsen, Arne): Medicine. See: Stedman.

TORNANI, E. fl. 1904. Italian chemist. (Biography source unavailable.) Bruni-Tomani test.

Tornwaldt, Gustav Ludwig. See: Thornwaldt, Gustav Ludwig.

Torquemada (Torquemada, Tomas de): Generic Word (persecutor). See: Harvey; Hendrickson.

TORQUEMADA, TOMAS DE. 1420-1498. Spanish monk and Grand Inquisitor. See: Encyc. Brit., 1973. Torquemada.

Torr (Torricelli, Evangelista): Physics. See: Ballentyne; Dresner; Markus.

TORRANCE, JOHN R. fl. 1933. English engineering manufacturer. (Biography source unavailable.) Torrance mixer?

Torrance mixer (Torrance, John R.?): Engineering and Industry. See: Van Nostrand Chem. Dict.

TORRE, DOUGLAS P. 1919-   . American dermatologist. See: Amer. Men and Women Sci., 12th ed. Bloom-Torre-Machacek syndrome.

TORRENS, SIR ROBERT RICHARD. 1814-1884. Irish politician and Premier of South Australia. See: Internat. Encyc. Soc. Sci. Torrens system.

Torrens system (Torrens, Sir Robert Richard): Business. See: Clark; Smith; Webster's 3d.

TORREY, JOHN. 1796-1873. American botanist and chemist. See: World Who's Who Sci. Torrey pine, Torrey tree, Torreya, Torreyite, Torrey's pycnanthemum.

Torrey pine (Torrey, John): Botany. See: Mathews, M. M.; Webster's 3d.

Torrey tree (Torrey, John): Botany. See: Webster's 3d.

Torreya (Torrey, John): Botany. See: Partridge; Taylor, N.; Webster's 3d.

Torreyite (Torrey, John): Earth Sciences. See: Thrush; Webster's 3d.

Torrey's pycnanthemum (Torrey, John): Botany. See: Mathews, M. M.

TORRICELLI, EVANGELISTA. 1608-1647. Italian physician, mathematician and physicist. See: World Who's Who Sci. Tor, Torr, Torricellian experiment, Torricellian tube, Torricellian vacuum, Torricelli's law (or theorem).

Torricellian experiment (Torricelli, Evangelista): Physics. See: Asimov; Harvey.

Torricellian tube (Torricelli, Evangelista): Physics. See: Charnock; Harvey; Webster's 3d.

Torricellian vacuum (Torricelli, Evangelista): Physics. See: Asimov; Ballentyne; Webster's 3d.

Torricelli's law (or theorem) (Torricelli, Evangelista): Physics. See: Ballentyne; Van Nostrand Sci. Encyc.; Webster's 3d.

Torrubia (Torrubia, Jose): Botany. See: Webster's 3d.

TORRUBIA, JOSE. d. 1768. Spanish naturalist. See: Michaud. Torrubia.

Torsten Sjoegren. See: Sjoegren, Torsten.

Torsten Sjoegren's syndrome (Sjoegren, Torsten). See: Marinesco-Sjoegren syndrome.

Tortelli-Gaffe test (Tortelli, Massimo and Jaffe, E.): Chemistry. See: Van Nostrand Chem. Dict.

TORTELLI, MASSIMO. fl. 1914. Italian chemist. Cited in: Chem. Abstr. vol. 8, p. 3723; vol. 9, p. 1255. Tortelli-Gaffe test, Tortelli-Ruggeri test for peanut oil.

Tortelli-Ruggeri test for peanut oil (Tortelli, Massimo and Ruggeri, Ruggero): Chemistry. See: Van Nostrand Chem. Dict.

TORTONI. fl. 19th c. Italian caterer in Paris. (Biography source unavailable.) Tortoni (ice cream).

Tortoni (ice cream) (Tortoni): Food and Drink. See: Hendrickson.

TORY, GEOFFROY. 1480?-1533. French printer, engraver and miniaturist. See: Bryan. Tory style.

Tory style (Tory, Geoffroy): Printing. See: Harrod.

Tosa School (Mitsunobu, Tosa): Fine Arts. See: Osborne.

Toschi-Angiolani reagent (Toschi, B. and Angiolani, A.): Chemistry. See: Van Nostrand Chem. Dict.

TOSCHI, B. fl. 1915. Italian chemist. Cited in: Chem. Abstr. vol. 9, p. .2388. Toschi-Angiolani reagent.

TOTI, ADDEO. b. 1861. Italian ophthalmologist and laryngologist. See: Biog. Lex. hervorr. Aerzte. Toti's operation.

Toti's operation (Toti, Addeo): Medicine. See: Dorland; Stedman.

TOTTEL, RICHARD. d. 1594. English printer and publisher. See: Dict. Nat. Biog. Tottel's Miscellany.

Tottel's Miscellany (Tottel, Richard): Literature. See: Barnhart (Eng. Lit.).

touch of Caruso (Caruso, Enrico): Generic Word. See: Hendrickson.

TOUMEY, JAMES WILLIAM. 1865-1932. American forester. See: Dict. Amer. Biog. Toumey oak.

Toumey oak (Toumey, James William): Botany. See: Webster's 3d.

TOURAINE, ALBERT. b. 1883. French dermatologist. See: Who's Who France, 1959-1960. Christ-Siemens-Touraine syndrome, Touraine-Solente-Gole syndrome, Touraine's aphthosis, Touraine's syndrome.

TOURAINE, HENRI. 1883-1961. French dermatologist. (Biography source unavailable.) Peutz-Touraine syndrome.

TOURAINE, M. A. fl. 1940. French physician. (Biography source unavailable.) Touraine's syndrome.

Touraine's aphthosis (Touraine, Albert). See: Behcet's syndrome.

Touraine's syndrome (Touraine, Albert). See: Osterreicher-Turner syndrome.

Touraine's syndrome (Touraine, M. A.): Medicine. See: Jablonski.

Tourette, Georges Edmound Albert Brutus. See: Gilles De La Tourette, Georges Edmound Albert Brutus.

ourette's syndrome (Gilles de la Tourette, Georges Edouard Albert Brutus). ee: Gilles de la Tourette's syndrome.

OURNAY, AUGUSTE. b. 1878. French ophthalmologist. (Biography source navailable.) Tournay sign.

ournay sign (Tournay, Auguste): Medicine. See: Stedman.

OURNEFORT, JOSEPH PITTON DE. 1656-1708. French botanist. See: ncyc. Brit., 1911. Tournefortia.

ournefortia (Tournefort, Joseph Pitton de): Botany. See: Webster's 3d.

ourte bow (Tourte, Francois): Music. See: Apel.

OURTE, FRANCOIS. 1747-1835. French violin bow maker. See: Grove. ourte bow.

OURTUAL, CASPAR THEOBALD. 1802-1865. German anatomist. See: Allg. Deut. Biog. Tourtual's membrane, Tourtual's sinus.

ourtual's membrane (Tourtual, Caspar Theobald): Anatomy. See: Stedman.

ourtual's sinus (Tourtual, Caspar Theobald): Anatomy. See: Stedman.

OUSSAINT, ALBERT. fl. 1937. French aerodynamics engineer. Cited in: ibr. Congress Cat. Printed Cards. Toussaint's formula?

oussaint-Heintzmann arch (Toussaint and Heintzmann, H. F.?): Engineering nd Industry. See: Thrush.

oussaint's formula (Toussaint, Albert?): Science. See: Huschke.

outon giant cell (Touton, Karl): Medicine. See: Dorland; Stedman.

OUTON, KARL. 1858-1934. German dermatologist. See: Biog. Lex. ervorr. Aerzte. Touton giant cell.

OVAR, SIMON E. fl. 1586. Spanish physician and botanist. See: Biog. ex. hervorr. Aerzte. Tovaria.

ovaria (Tovar, Simon e): Botany. See: Webster's 3d.

OWER, OLIN FREEMAN. b. 1872. American chemist. See: Pogg., vols. to 6. Tower's magnetic stirrer?

ower's magnetic stirrer (Tower, Olin Freeman?): Engineering and Industry. ee: Thrush.

OWLER, F. H. and J.M. fl. 1937. English engineers. (Biography source navailable.) Towler pump.

owler pump (Towler, F. H. and J. M.): Engineering and Industry. See: uger.

OWNE, EDWARD BANCROFT. 1883-1957. American physician. See: .A.M.A., vol. 163, no. 14 (April 6, 1957), p. 1279. Towne projection oentgenogram.

owne projection roentgenogram (Towne, Edward Bancroft): Medicine. See: tedman.

OWNER, HORACE MANN. 1855-1937. American legislator. See: Biog. Direct. Amer. Congress. Sheppard-Towner Act.

OWNLEY, CHARLES. 1737-1805. English scholar and antiquary. See: Dict. Nat. Biog. Townley Marbles, Townley Mysteries.

ownley Marbles (Townley, Charles): Fine Arts. Cited in: Dict. Nat. Biog.

ownley Mysteries (Townley, Charles): Literature. See: Wagner (More Names).

ownsend avalanche (Townsend, John Sealy Edward): Engineering and Industry. ee: Hughes; Markus; Van Nostrand Chem. Dict.; Van Nostrand Sci. Encyc.

ownsend characteristic (Townsend, John Sealy Edward): Engineering and ndustry. See: Markus.

ownsend coefficient (Townsend, John Sealy Edward): Engineering and Industry. ee: Ballentyne; Internat. Dict. Phys. Elec.; Markus.

OWNSEND, DAVID. 1787-1858. American botanist. (Biography source navailable.) Townsendia.

ownsend discharge (Townsend, John Sealy Edward): Engineering and Industry. ee: Ballentyne; Internat. Dict. Phys. Elec.; Markus.

OWNSEND, FRANCIS EVERETT. 1867-1960. American physician. See: Vho Was Who Amer. Townsend plan, Townsendism (or Townsendite).

TOWNSEND, JOHN KIRK. 1809-1851. American ornithologist. See: Dict. Amer. Biog. Townsend's bunting, Townsend's cormorant, Townsend's flycatcher, Townsend's flycathing thrush, Townsend's fox sparrow, Townsend's mocking thrush, Townsend's shearwater, Townsend's solitaire, Townsend's sparrow, Townsend's warbler.

TOWNSEND, JOHN SEALY EDWARD. 1868-1957. Irish physicist. See: Dict. Nat. Biog. Ramsauer-Townsend effect, Townsend avalanche, Townsend characteristic, Townsend coefficient, Townsend discharge, Townsend support?, Townsend theory.

TOWNSEND, JOSEPH. 1739-1816. English divine and geologist. See: Dict. Nat. Biog. Townsend's mixture.

Townsend plan (Townsend, Francis Everett): Politics. See: Mathews, M. M.; Smith.

Townsend support (Townsend, John Sealy Edward?): Engineering and Industry. See: Huschke.

Townsend theory (Townsend, John Sealy Edward): Engineering and Industry. See: Internat. Dict. Phys. Elec.

Townsendia (Townsend, David): Botany. See: Mathews, M. M.; Partridge; Taylor, N.

Townsendism (or Townsendite) (Townsend, Francis Everett): History. See: Mathews, M. M.

Townsend's bunting (Townsend, John Kirk): Zoology. See: Mathews, M. M.

Townsend's cormorant (Townsend, John Kirk): Zoology. See: Mathews, M. M.

Townsend's flycatcher (Townsend, John Kirk): Zoology. See: Mathews, M. M.

Townsend's flycatching thrush (Townsend, John Kirk): Zoology. See: Mathews, M. M.

Townsend's fox sparrow (Townsend, John Kirk): Zoology. See: Mathews, M. M.

Townsend's mixture (Townsend, Joseph): Medicine. See: Dorland.

Townsend's mocking thrush (Townsend, John Kirk): Zoology. See: Mathews, M. M.

Townsend's shearwater (Townsend, John Kirk): Zoology. See: Gray.

Townsend's solitaire (Townsend, John Kirk): Zoology. See: Gray, Pennak; Webster's 3d.

Townsend's sparrow (Townsend, John Kirk): Zoology. See: Mathews, M. M.

Townsend's warbler (Townsend, John Kirk): Zoology. See: Gray; Mathews, M. M.

Townshend Acts (Townshend, Charles): History. See: Jameson; Morris; Smith.

TOWNSHEND, CHARLES. 1725-1767. English statesman and orator. See: Dict. Nat. Biog. Townshend Acts.

TOYAMA, IKUZO. b. 1877. Japanese physician. See: Biog. Lex. hervorr. Aerzte. Toyama's disease.

Toyama's disease (Toyama, Ikuzo): Medicine. See: Jablonski.

TOYNBEE, JOSEPH. 1815-1866. English otologist. See: Dict. Nat. Biog. Toynbee's corpuscles, Toynbee's experiment, Toynbee's law, Toynbee's muscle, Toynbee's otoscope.

Toynbee's corpuscles (Toynbee, Joseph): Anatomy. See: Dorland; Stedman. Also known as: Virchow's cells (or corpuscles).

Toynbee's experiment (Toynbee, Joseph): Medicine. See: Dorland; Stedman.

Toynbee's law (Toynbee, Joseph): Medicine. See: Dorland; Stedman.

Toynbee's muscle (Toynbee, Joseph): Anatomy. See: Stedman.

Toynbee's otoscope (Toynbee, Joseph): Medicine. See: Stedman.

TOYOKUNI, UTAGAWA, 1769-1825. Japanese painter and printmaker. See: Webster's Biog. Dict. Utagawa School.

TRACHTENBERG, JAKOW. b. 1888. Ukrainian inventor. (Biography source unavailable.) Trachtenberg system (or method).

Trachtenberg system (or method) (Trachtenberg, Jakow): Mathematics. See: Brewer; Good.

tract of Schuetz (Schuetz, H.). See: Schuetz' bundle (or tract).

tractrix of Huygens (Huygens, Christiaan): Mathematics. See: Van Nostrand Sci. Encyc.

TRAGER, GEORGE LEONARD. 1906- . American educator and linguist. See: Who's Who Amer., 1964-1965. Trager-Smith metrics.

Trager-Smith metrics (Trager, George Leonard and Smith, Henry Lee, Jr.): Literature. See: Preminger.

TRAILL, THOMAS STEWART. 1781-1862. Scottish professor of medical jurisprudence, scientific writer, and encyclopedist. See: Dict. Nat. Biog. Traill's flycatcher.

Traill's flycatcher (Traill, Thomas Stewart): Zoology. See: Mathews, M. M.; Webster's 3d.

TRAJAN. 53-117. Roman emperor. See: Encyc. Brit., 1911. Trajan's column, Trajan's column (cactus).

Trajan's column (Trajan): Fine Arts. See: Latham; Osborne.

Trajan's column (cactus) (Trajan): Botany. See: Gray.

TRAM, TOM. Legendary English buffoon. (Biography source unavailable.) Tom Tram.

TRAMBUSTI, ARNALDO. b. 1863. Italian pathologist. See: Biog. Lex. hervorr. Aerzte. Trambusti's reaction (or test).

Trambusti's reaction (or test) (Trambusti, Arnaldo): Medicine. See: Dorland.

TRAMMELL, PARK. 1876-1936. American legislator. See: Biog. Direct. Amer. Congress. Vinson-Trammell Naval Parity Act.

TRANTAS, ALEXIOS. b. 1867. Greek ophthalmologist. See: Biog. Lex. hervorr. Aerzte. Horner-Trantas dots.

Trantas' dots (Trantas, Alexios). See: Horner-Trantas spots.

TRANTENROTH, ADOLPH ARTHUR. b. 1867. German physician. (Biography source unavailable.) Bunge-Trantenroth stain.

TRAPANI, DOMENICO. fl. 1935. Italian pharmaceutical chemist. Trapani reagent?

Trapani reagent (Trapani, Domenico?): Chemistry. See: Van Nostrand Chem. Dict.

Trapp-Haeser formula (Trapp, Julius and Haeser, Heinrich). See: Haeser's formula (or coefficient).

TRAPP, JULIUS. 1815-1908. Russian pharmaceutist. See: Farm. Vestnik Mosk. vol 3 (1899), pp. 235-37. Trapp-Haeser formula.

TRAQUAIR, HARRY MOSS. 1875-1954. English ophthalmic surgeon. See: Who Was Who. Traquair's scotoma.

Traquair's scotoma (Traquair, Harry Moss): Medicine. See: Jablonski.

TRASK, JOHN. b. ca. 1617? English preacher. (Biography source unavailable.) Traskites.

Traskites (Trask, John): Religion. See: Brewer; Canney.

TRATTINICK, LEOPOLD. 1764-1849. Austrian botanist, entomologist and mineralogist. See: Allg. Deut. Biog. Trattinickia.

Trattinickia (Trattinick, Leopold): Botany. See: Charnock.

Traube-Hering waves (or curves) (Traube, Ludwig and Hering, Ewald): Physiology. See: Drever; English; Stedman.

TRAUBE, ISIDOR. 1860-1943. German physical chemist. See: World Who's Who Sci. Traube stalagmometer, Traube test for hydrogen peroxide?, Traube's rule.

TRAUBE, LUDWIG. 1818-1876. German physician. See: World Who's Who Sci. Traube-Hering waves (or curves), Traube's bruit, Traube's corpuscles, Traube's double tone, Traube's dyspnea, Traube's heart, Traube's plugs, Traube's space.

Traube purine synthesis (Traube, Wilhelm): Chemistry. See: Van Nostrand Chem. Dict.

Traube stalagmometer (Traube, Isidor): Chemistry. See: Hackh.

Traube test for hydrogen peroxide (Traube, Isidor?): Chemistry. See: Van Nostrand Chem. Dict.

TRAUBE, WILHELM. 1866-1942. German chemist. See: Pogg., vols. 4-6, 7a. Traube purine synthesis.

Traube's bruit (Traube, Ludwig): Physiology. See: Stedman.

Traube's corpuscles (Traube, Ludwig): Medicine. See: Stedman. Also known as: Ponfick's shadow.

Traube's double tone (Traube, Ludwig): Medicine. See: Stedman.

Traube's dyspnea (Traube, Ludwig): Medicine. See: Jablonski; Stedman.

Traube's heart (Traube, Ludwig): Medicine. See: Jablonski.

Traube's plugs (Traube, Ludwig). See: Dittrich's plugs.

Traube's rule (Traube, Isidor): Chemistry. See: Ballentyne; Hackh; Van Nostrand Sci. Encyc.

Traube's space (Traube, Ludwig): Medicine. See: Dorland; Stedman.

TRAUGOTT, CARL. b. 1885. German physician. See: Biog. Lex. hervorr. Aerzte. Staub-Traugott effect.

TRAUTMANN, MORITZ FERDINAND. 1832-1902. German surgeon. See: Biog. Lex. hervorr. Aerzte. Trautmann's triangular space.

Trautmann's triangular space (Trautmann, Moritz Ferdinand): Medicine. See: Stedman.

Trautonium (Trautwein, Friedrich): Music. See: Scholes.

TRAUTVETTER, ERNST RUDOLF VON. d. 1889. German botanist. See: Ann. Bot. vol. 3 (1889-1890), pp. 489-93. Trautvetteria.

Trautvetteria (Trautvetter, Ernst Rudolf von): Botany. See: Charnock; Taylor, N.

TRAUTWEIN, FRIEDRICH. 1888-1956. German acoustical music technologist. See: Pogg., vol. 7a. Trautonium.

TRAUZL, ISIDOR. fl. 1883. German technologist. Cited in: Royal Soc. Cat. Sci. Pap., 1874-1883. Trauzl test.

Trauzl test (Trauzl, Isidor): Chemistry. See: Hackh; Van Nostrand Chem. Dict.

TRAVERS, ALEXANDRE. 1883-1949. French chemist. See: Pogg., vol. 6; World Who's Who Sci. Travers test reaction.

Travers test reaction (Travers, Alexandre): Chemistry. See: Van Nostrand Chem. Dict.

TRAVIS, PIERCE MASON. b. 1887. American chemical engineer. See: Amer. Men. Sci., 7th ed. Palo-Travis analyser.

Treacher Collins. See: Collins, Edward Treacher.

Treacher Collins' syndrome (Collins, Edward Treacher): Medicine. See: Jablonski; Stedman.

TREACY, PETER B. fl. 1949-1970. Australian physicist. Cited in: Internat. Physics Astr. Direct., 1969-1970. Makinson and Treacy gauge.

TREADWELL, DANIEL. 1791-1872. American inventor. See: Dict. Amer. Biog. Treadwell press.

Treadwell press (Treadwell, Daniel): Printing. See: Lockwood.

Treaty of Ferdinand (Ferdinand I): History. See: Harbottle.

Treaty with Adam Kok (Kok III, Adam): History. See: Harbottle.

Trebellianick (Trebellius): Law. See: Charnock.

TREBELLIUS. fl. 47 B.C. Roman tribune. See: Dict. Grk. Rom. Biog. Myth. Trebellianick.

TRECHMANN, CHARLES OTTO. 1851-1917. English mineralogist. See: Min. Mag. vol. 18, no. 87 (Nov. 1919), p. 398. Trechmannite.

Trechmannite (Trechmann, Charles Otto): Earth Sciences. See: Webster's 3d.

Trecuhon-Kieffer annealing schedule (Derivation undetermined): Engineering and Industry. See: Thrush.

TRECUL, AUGUSTE ADOLPHE LUCIEN. 1818-1896. French botanist. See: World Who's Who Sci. Treculia.

Treculia (Trecul, Auguste): Botany. See: Webster's 3d.

...e of Porphyry (Porphyry, the scholar). See: Porphyrian tree.

...eitz-Broesicke hernia (Treitz, Wenzel and Broesicke, Gustav). See: Treitz's ...rnia.

...EITZ, WENZEL. 1819-1872. German anatomist. See: Allg. Deut. Biog. ...itz's arch, Treitz's fascia, Treitz's fossa, Treitz's hernia, Treitz's muscle (ligament).

...itz's arch (Treitz, Wenzel): Anatomy. See: Dorland; Stedman.

...itz's fascia (Treitz, Wenzel): Anatomy. See: Donath; Dorland; Stedman.

...itz's fossa (Treitz, Wenzel): Anatomy. See: Donath; Dorland; Stedman.

...itz's hernia (Treitz, Wenzel): Medicine. See: Dorland; Jablonski; Stedman. ...so known as: Treitz-Broesicke hernia.

...itz's muscle (or ligament) (Treitz, Wenzel): Anatomy. See: Donath; Dor- ...nd; Stedman.

...ELAT, ULYSSE, JR. 1828-1890. French surgeon. See: Biog. Lex. hervorr. ...rzte. Leser-Trelat sign, Trelat's sign (1), Trelat's speculum, Trelat's stools.

...elat's sign (1) (Trelat, Ulysse, Jr.): Medicine. See: Dorland; Stedman.

...elat's sign (2) (Trelat, Ulysse, Jr.). See: Leser-Trelat sign.

...elat's speculum (Trelat, Ulysse, Jr.): Medicine. See: Stedman.

...elat's stools (Trelat, Ulysse, Jr.): Medicine. See: Stedman.

...ELEASE, SAM F. 1892-1958. American botanist. See: Who Was Who ...mer., vol. 3. Samuela.

...ELLES, JULIO OSCAR. 1904- . French? physician. (Biography source ...available.) Lhermitte-Trelles syndrome?

...EMAIN, H. EARL. fl. 1931. American chemist. Cited in: Chem. Abstr. ...l. 25, p. 2664. Tremain test.

...emain test (Tremain, H. Earl): Chemistry. See: Van Nostrand Chem. Dict.

...EMENHEERE VON TENASSERIM, CAPT. fl. 1852? German officer. Cited ...: Hintze. Tremenheerite.

...emenheerite (Tremenheere von Tenasserim, Capt.): Earth Sciences. See: ...rush.

...EML, H. fl. 1911. German chemist. Cited in: Chem. Abstr., Decenn. ...uthor Index, 1907-1916. Buchwald-Treml test?

...EMOILLE, ANNA MARIA DE LA. d. 1722. Princess of Nerole. (Biography ...urce unavailable.) Neroli oil.

...ENAUNAY, PAUL. b. 1875. French physician. (Biography source ...available.) Klippel-Trenaunay syndrome, Klippel-Trenaunay-Weber syndrome, ...llier-Klippel-Trenaunay syndrome.

...RENDELENBURG, FREIDRICH. 1844-1924. German surgeon. See: World ...ho's Who Sci. Trendelenburg's cannula (or tampon), Trendelenburg's operation, ...endelenburg's position, Trendelenburg's sign, Trendelenburg's symptom, ...endelenburg's test.

...endelenburg's cannula (or tampon) (Trendelenburg, Freidrich): Medicine. ...ee: Stedman.

...endelenburg's operation (Trendelenburg, Freidrich): Medicine. See: Stedman.

...endelenburg's position (Trendelenburg, Freidrich): Medicine. See: Stedman; ...ebster's 3d.

...endelenburg's sign (Trendelenburg, Freidrich): Medicine. See: Stedman.

...endelenburg's symptom (Trendelenburg, Freidrich): Medicine. See: Jablon- ...ki; Stedman.

...endelenburg's test (Trendelenburg, Freidrich): Medicine. See: Stedman.

...RENEL, M. fl. 1930. French ophthalmologist. (Biography source unavail- ...ble.) Prieur-Trenel syndrome.

...rent process (Trent, W. E.?): Engineering and Industry. See: Thrush.

...RENT, W. E. fl. 1922. American engineer. (Biography source unavailable.) ...rent process?

...RENTEPOHL, JOHANN FRIEDRICH. 1748-1806. German botanist and ...heologian. See: Allg. Deut. Biog. Trentepohlia.

...rentepohlia (Trentepohl, Johann Friedrich): Botany. See: Webster's 3d.

TRESILIAN, FREDERICK J. 1862-1926. English physician. (Biography source unavailable.) Tresilian's sign.

Tresilian's sign (Tresilian, Frederick J.): Medicine. See: Dorland; Stedman.

TREVELYAN, SIR HUMPHREY. fl. 20th c. English scientist and administrator. See: Who's Who Sci. Europe, 1972. Trevelyan rocker?

Trevelyan rocker (Trevelyan, Sir Humphrey?): Engineering and Industry. See: Thewlis.

Treves' fold (Treves, Sir Frederick): Anatomy. See: Donath; Dorland; Stedman.

TREVES, SIR FREDERICK. 1853-1923. English surgeon. See: Dict. Nat. Biog. Treves' fold.

TREVES, NORMAN. 1894-1964. American surgeon. See: Who Was Who Amer. Stewart-Treves syndrome.

TREVOR, TUDOR GRUFFYD. 1865-1958. Welsh-born South African geologist and mining official. See: Rosenthal. Trevorite.

Trevorite (Trevor, Tudor Gruffyd): Earth Sciences. See: Thrush; Webster's 3d.

triads of Doebereiner (Doebereiner, Johann Wolfgang): Chemistry. See: Van Nostrand Chem. Dict.

triangle of Hesselbach (Hesselbach, Franz Kaspar). See: Hesselbach's triangle.

triangle of Mars (Mars): Parapsychology. See: Webster's 3d.

tribe of Ben (Jonson, Ben): Literature. See: Preminger.

TRICK. fl. 19th c. German inventor. (Biography source unavailable.) Trick valve.

Trick valve (Trick): Engineering and Industry. See: Auger.

TRICOT, ROBERT. 1915- . French physician. See: Who's Who Sci. Europe, 1972. Degos-Delort-Tricot syndrome.

tricoteuses de Robespierre (Robespierre, Maximilien Francois Marie Isidore de). See: Robespierre's knitters.

trident of Newton (Newton, Isaac): Mathematics. See: Ballentyne; James.

TRIER, GEORG. 1884-1944. Czechoslovakian-born Swiss chemist. See: Pogg., vol. 6. Trier test reaction.

Trier test reaction (Trier, Georg): Chemistry. See: Van Nostrand Chem. Dict.

Triffin plan (Triffin, Robert): Economics. See: Greenwald.

TRIFFIN, ROBERT. 1911- . American economist and educator. See: Who's Who Amer., 1964-1965. Triffin Plan.

TRIGER, M. fl. 19th c. French engineer. (Biography source unavailable.) Triger process.

Triger process (Triger, M.): Engineering and Industry. See: Thrush; Webster's 3d.

trigone of Lieutaud (Lieutaud, Joseph). See: Lieutaud's triangle (or trigone).

Trilbies (Trilby): Generic Word (feet). See: Partridge; Webster's 3d.

TRILBY. Character from George du Maurier's novel of the same name, (1894). See: Benet. Trilby hat, Trilbies.

Trilby hat (Trilby): Fashion. See: Partridge; Stenhouse; Webster's 3d.

TRILLAT, AUGUSTE (In full: JEAN AUGUSTE). 1861-1944. French chemist. See: Pogg., vol. 5. Trillat test for lead and manganese dioxides?, Trillat tests for formaldehyde, Trillat-Turchet test.

Trillat test for lead and manganese dioxides (Trillat, Auguste?): Chemistry. See: Van Nostrand Chem. Dict.

Trillat tests for formaldehyde (Trillat, Auguste): Chemistry. See: Van Nostrand Chem. Dict.

Trillat-Turchet test (Trillat, Auguste and Turchet): Chemistry. See: Van Nostrand Chem. Dict.

trilogy of Fallot (Fallot, Etienne Louis Arthur): Medicine. See: Stedman.

TRINKER, I. fl. before 1870. Austrian geologist. Cited in: Hintze. Trinkerite.

Trinkerite (Trinker, I.): Earth Sciences. See: Thrush.

TRIONFETTI, GIOVANNI BATTISTA. 1656-1722. Italian botanist. See: Michaud. Triumfetta.

TRIPIER, LEON. 1842-1891. French surgeon. (Biography source unavailable.) Tripier's amputation.

TRIPIER, V. fl. 19th c. French engineer. (Biography source unavailable.) Tripier valve gear.

Tripier valve gear (Tripier, V.): Engineering and Industry. See: Auger.

Tripier's amputation (Tripier, Leon): Medicine. See: Dorland; Stedman.

TRIPPKE, PAUL. d. 1880. Polish mineralogist. Cited in: Hintze. Trippketite.

Trippketite (Trippke, Paul): Earth Sciences. Webster's 3d.

trisectrix of Maclaurin (Maclaurin, Colin): Mathematics. See: James; Van Nostrand Sci. Encyc.

TRISTAN, JULES M. C. d. 1861. French botanist. (Biography source unavailable.) Tristania.

Tristania (Tristan, Jules M. C.): Botany. See: Taylor, N.; Webster's 3d.

TRITON. Greek demigod of the sea. See: Harper. Triton among the minnows, Triton (mollusc).

Triton among the minnows (Triton): Generic Word. See: Partridge.

Triton (mollusc) (Triton): Zoology. See: Charnock.

Triumfetta (Trionfetti, Giovanni Battista): Botany. See: Webster's 3d.

TROEGER, R. fl. 19th c. German mining official. Cited in: Hintze. Troegerite, Troeger's classification.

Troegerite (Troeger, R.): Earth Sciences. See: Thrush; Webster's 3d.

Troeger's classification (Troeger, R.): Earth Sciences. See: Thrush.

TROELL, ABRAHAM (In full: NIELS ABRAHAM). 1881-1954. Swedish surgeon. See: Svenska Maen Och Kvinnor. Troell-Junet syndrome.

Troell-Junet syndrome (Troell, Abraham and Junet, Robert Maurice): Medicine. See: Jablonski.

TROELTSCH, ANTON FRIEDRICH VON. 1829-1890. German otologist. See: World Who's Who Sci. Troeltsch's corpuscles, Troeltsch's fold, Troeltsch's recess (or pocket).

Troeltsch's corpuscles (Troeltsch, Anton Friedrich von): Anatomy. See: Dorland; Stedman.

Troeltsch's fold (Troeltsch, Anton Friedrich von): Anatomy. See: Stedman.

Troeltsch's recess (or pocket) (Troeltsch, Anton Friedrich von): Anatomy. See: Donath; Dorland; Stedman.

TROEMNER, ERNEST L. O. b. 1868. German neurologist. (Biography source unavailable.) Troemner's (or Troemmer's) reflex (or sign).

Troemner's (or Troemmer's) reflex (or sign) (Troemner, Ernest L. O.): Medicine. See: Dorland; Stedman. Also known as: Hoffmann's sign (2) (or reflex).

TROILI, DOMINICO. fl. 1766. Italian scientist. Cited in: Dana. Troilite.

Troilite (Troili, Dominico): Earth Sciences. See: Thrush; Webster's 3d.

TROILUS. Son of Priam, King of Troy. See: New Encyc. Brit., 1974., Microp. Troilus butterfly.

TROILUS. Character in the poem "Troilus and Criseyde" (ca. 1385) by Chaucer. See: New Encyc. Brit., 1974, Microp. Troilus verse (or stanza).

Troilus butterfly (Troilus): Zoology. See: Webster's 3d.

Troilus verse (or stanza) (Troilus): Literature. See: Webster's 3d.

TROISIER, CHARLES EMILE. 1844-1919. French physician. See: World Who's Who Sci. Troisier-Hanot-Chauffard syndrome, Troisier's node (or ganglion.)

Troisier-Hanot-Chauffard syndrome (Troisier, Charles Emile; Hanot, Victor Charles; and Chauffard, Anatole Marie Emile): Medicine. See: Jablonski. Also known as: Hanot-Chauffard syndrome.

Troisier's node (or ganglion) (Troisier, Charles Emile): Medicine. See: Stedman. Also known as: Virchow-Troisier node.

Troland (Troland, Leonard Thompson): Physics. See: Dresner; Van Nostrand Sci. Encyc.; Webster's 3d.

Troland and Fletcher theories (Troland, Leonard Thompson and Fletcher, Harvey): Physiology. See: Internat. Dict. Phys. Elec.

TROLAND, LEONARD THOMPSON. 1889-1932. American psychologist and physicist. See: Dict. Amer. Biog. Troland, Troland and Fletcher theories.

TROLARD, PAULIN. 1842-1910. French anatomist. See: Biog. Lex. hervorr. Aerzte. Trolard's net (or plexus), Trolard's vein.

Trolard's net (or plexus) (Trolard, Paulin): Anatomy. See: Donath; Dorland; Stedman.

Trolard's vein (Trolard, Paulin): Anatomy. See: Donath; Dorland; Stedman.

TROLLE, B. fl. 1930. Danish physicist. Cited in: Pogg., vol. 6 under "Hartmann, Julius Fredrik Georg." Hartmann-Trolle modification of the Galton whistle.

TROLLOPE, ANTHONY. 1815-1882. English novelist. See: Dict. Nat. Biog. Trollopian.

TROLLOPE, FRANCES MILTON. 1780-1863. English writer. See: Dict. Nat. Biog. Trollopize.

Trollopian (Trollope, Anthony): Literature. See: Webster's 3d.

Trollopize (Trollope, Frances Milton): Generic Word (criticize). See: Mathews, M. M.; Partridge.

TROMMER, KARL AUGUST. 1806-1879. German chemist. See: Biog. Lex. hervorr Aerzte. Trommer's test.

Trommer's test (Trommer, Karl August): Medicine. See: Dorland; Hackh; Stedman. Also known as: Warren's test.

TROMP, KLAAS F. fl. 1938. Dutch engineer. (Biography source unavailable.) Tromp process?

Tromp process (Tromp, Klaas F.?): Engineering and Industry. See: Thrush.

TROOST, GERARD. 1776-1850. Dutch-born American geologist. See: Dict. Amer. Biog. Troostite (1).

TROOST, LOUIS JOSEPH. 1825-1911. French chemist. See: World Who's Who Sci. Troostite (2).

Troostite (1) (Troost, Gerard): Earth Sciences. See: Thrush; Webster's 3d.

Troostite (2) (Troost, Louis Joseph): Chemistry. See: Thrush; Webster's 3d.

Trophonian (Trophonius): Generic Word (gloomy): See: Partridge.

TROPHONIUS. Greek legendary builders of Temple of Apollo. See: Harper. Trophonian.

trophotropic zone of Hess (Hess, Walter Rudolf): Physiology. See: Stedman.

TROPSCH, HANS. d. 1935. Czech-born German chemist. Cited in: Chem. Abstr., Decenn. Index, 1917-1926. Fisher-Tropsch process.

Trot (Trote, Dame): Generic Word (old woman). See: Weekley.

TROTARELLI, GIACOMO. fl. 1879. Italian chemist. Cited in: Royal Soc. Cat. Sci. Pap., 1874-1883. Trotarelli test.

Trotarelli test (Trotarelli, Giacomo): Chemistry. See: Van Nostrand Chem. Dict.

TROTE, DAME. fl. 11th c. Italian doctoress and witch (Biography source unavailable.) Trot.

TROTSKY, LEON (Real name: LEIB DAVYDOVICH BRONSTEIN). 1879-1940. Russian Communist leader. See: Internat. Encyc. Soc. Sci. Trotskyism.

Trotskyism (Trotsky, Leon): Politics. See: Hendrickson; Webster's 3d.

TROTTER, JOHN. fl. 1805. English engineer. (Biography source unavailable.) Trotter pump.

Trotter pump (Trotter, John): Engineering and Industry. See: Auger.

TROTTER, WILFRED BATTEN LEWIS. 1872-1939. English surgeon and physiologist. See: World Who's Who Sci. Trotter's syndrome.

Trotter's syndrome (Trotter, Wilfred Batten Lewis): Medicine. See: Jablonski. Also known as: sinus of Morgagni syndrome.

TROUGHTON, EDWARD. 1753-1835. English instrument maker. See: World Who's Who Sci. Troughton level.

Troughton level (Troughton, Edward): Engineering and Industry. See: Webster's 3d.

ROUSSEAU, ARMAND. 1801-1867. French physician. See: Nouv. Biog. Univ. Trousseau's point, Trousseau's sign, Trousseau's spot, Trousseau's syndrome.

Trousseau's point (Trousseau, Armand): Medicine. See: Stedman.

Trousseau's sign (Trousseau, Armand): Medicine. See: Dorland; Stedman.

Trousseau's spot (Trousseau, Armand): Medicine. See: Dorland; Stedman.

Trousseau's syndrome (Trousseau, Armand): Medicine. See: Jablonski; Stedman.

Trouton constant (Trouton, Frederick Thomas): Chemistry. Cited in: Van Nostrand Sci. Encyc. under "Hydrogen fluoride, Hydrofluoric acid, and fluorides."

TROUTON, FREDERICK THOMAS. 1863-1922. English physical chemist. See: Who Was Who. Trouton constant, Trouton-Noble experiment, Trouton's law (or rule).

Trouton-Nobel experiment (Trouton, Frederick Thomas and Noble, Sir Andrew): Chemistry. See: Van Nostrand Sci. Encyc.

Trouton's law (or rule) (Trouton, Frederick Thomas): Chemistry. See: Ballenne; Hackh; Internat. Dict. Phys. Elec.

TRUBETZKOI, NIKOLAI. d. 1938. Russian linguist. See: Arch. f. es. Phonetik I, 3 (1939), pp. 55-61. Trubetzkoyan.

Trubetzkoyan (Trubetzkoi, Nikolai): Linguistics. See: Webster's 3d.

TRUCHOT, P. fl. 1922. French chemist. (Biography source unavailable.) Truchot reagent?

Truchot reagent (Truchot, P.?): Chemistry. See: Van Nostrand Chem. Dict.

TRUDEAU, JEAN BAPTISTE. 1748-1827. French explorer and trader. (Biography source unavailable.) Trudeau's tern.

Trudeau's tern (Trudeau, Jean Baptiste): Zoology. See: Mathews, M. M.

TRUDELL, HARRY W. 1884-1964. American mineralogist. See: New York Times, Jan 8, 1964, p. 31, col 1. Trudellite.

Trudellite (Trudell, Harry W.): Earth Sciences. See: Thrush; Webster's 3d.

TRUDGEN, JOHN ARTHUR. 1852-1902. English amateur swimmer. See: Menke. Trudgen stroke.

Trudgen stroke (Trudgen, John Arthur): Recreation and Sports. See: Hendrickson; Partridge; Webster's 3d.

TRUETA, JOSE. 1897- . Spanish surgeon in England. See: Who's Who, 1973-1974. Trueta method (or treatment).

Trueta method (or treatment) (Trueta, Jose): Medicine. See: Dorland.

TRUHAUT, RENE. 1909- . French chemist. See: World Who's Who Sci. Peronnet-Truhaut reaction for aldehydes, Peronnet-Truhaut reaction for amino acids and uric acid.

TRULLIBER. Character in Henry Fielding's novel "Joseph Andrews" (1742). See: Benet. Trulliberian.

Trulliberian (Trulliber): Generic Word (boorishness): See: Partridge; Weekley.

Truman Doctrine (Truman, Harry S.): Politics. See: Morris; Morris and Irwin; Smith.

Truman gravimeter (Truman, Orley Hosmer): Earth Sciences. See: Thrush under "Humble (Truman) gravimeter".

TRUMAN, HARRY S. 1884-1972. American president. See: Who Was Who Amer. Truman Doctrine, Truman's Law.

TRUMAN, ORLEY HOSMER. b. 1888. American astronomer and geophysicist. See: Amer. Men Sci., 9th ed. Truman gravimeter.

Truman's Law (Truman, Harry S.): Sociology. See: Martin.

TRUMBULL, JONATHAN. 1710-1785. American governor and jurist. See: Dict. Amer. Biog. Brother Jonathan, St. Jonathan's Day?

TRUNECEK, KAREL. b. 1865. Czechoslovakian physician. See: Biog. Lex. hervorr. Aerzte. Trunecek's symptom.

Trunecek's symptom (Trunecek, Karel): Medicine. See: Dorland; Stedman.

TRUOG, EMIL. b. 1884. American agricultural chemist. See: Amer. Men Sci., 5th ed. Barker-Truog process.

TRUSCOTT, SAMUEL JOHN. 1870-1950. English mineralogist. See: Who Was Who. Truscottite.

Truscottite (Truscott, Samuel John): Earth Sciences. See: Thrush.

Tryllite (Tyrrell, Joseph Burr): Earth Sciences. See: Thrush.

TRYON, GEORGE WASHINGTON. 1838-1888. American conchologist. See: Dict. Amer. Biog. Tryonia.

TRYON, HENRY. 1857-1943. Australian naturalist and scientist. See: Australian Encyc. Tryon's scab.

Tryonia (Tryon, George Washington): Zoology. See: Pennak.

Tryon's scab (Tryon, Henry): Botany. See: Winburne.

TSALAPATANI, LUCAS. fl. 1915. Argentine chemist. Cited in: Chem. Abstr., Decenn. Index, 1907-1916. Tsalapatani reaction for quinine, Tsalapatani test for acrolein, Tsalapatani test for amyl alcohol and methylamines.

Tsalapatani reaction for quinine (Tsalapatani, Lucas): Chemistry. See: Van Nostrand Chem. Dict.

Tsalapatani test for acrolein (Tsalapatani, Lucas): Chemistry. See: Van Nostrand Chem. Dict.

Tsalapatani test for amyl alcohol and methylamines (Tsalapatani, Lucas): Chemistry. See: Van Nostrand Chem. Dict.

Tsar (Caesar, Gaius Julius). See: Czar.

Tschebycheff, Pafnuti Lvovich. See: Chebyshev, Pafnuti Lvovich.

TSCHEFFKIN, KONSTANTIN V. dl. 1875. Russian general and mining director. Cited in: Dana. Tscheffkinite (Chevkinite).

Tscheffkinite (Chevkinite) (Tscheffkin, Konstantin V.): Earth Sciences. See: Thrush; Webster's 3d.

TSCHERMAK VON SEYSENEGG, GUSTAV. 1836-1927. Austrian mineralogist. See: World Who's Who Sci. Tschermakite.

Tschermakite (Tschermak von Seysenegg, Gustav): Earth Sciences. See: Thrush.

TSCHIRCH, ALEXANDER (In full: WILHELM OSWALD ALEXANDER). 1856-1939. German pharmacologist and botanist. See: World Who's Who Sci. Tschirch-Edner reagent, Tschirch reaction for ergot, Tschirch test for shellac and its substitutes.

Tschirch-Edner reagent (Tschirch, Alexander and Edner, J.): Chemistry. See: Van Nostrand Chem. Dict.

Tschirch reaction for ergot (Tschirch, Alexander): Chemistry. See: Van Nostrand Chem. Dict.

Tschirch test for shellac and its substitutes (Tschirch, Alexander): Chemistry. See: Van Nostrand Chem. Dict.

TSCHIRWINSKY, KOLOVRAT. fl. 1925. Russian mineralogist. Cited in: Hintze, vol. 1, part 4, half 2, p. 1088. Kolovratite.

Tschugaev, Lev Aleksandrovich. See: Chugaev, Lev Aleksandrovich.

Tschugaev-Orelkin test for ferrous iron (Chugaev, Lev Aleksandrovich and Orelkin, B.): Chemistry. See: Van Nostrand Chem. Dict.

Tschugaev reagent and test for nickel (Chugaev, Lev Aleksandrovich): Chemistry. See: Van Nostrand Chem. Dict.

Tschugaev tests for differentiating borneol and isoborneol (Chugaev, Lev Aleksandrovich): Chemistry. See: Van Nostrand Chem. Dict.

Tschugaev's ring rule (Chugaev, Lev Aleksandrovich): Chemistry. Cited in: Who's Who USSR.

Tseou-Chow test reaction (Tseou, Heou-Feo and Chow, Tse-Shui): Chemistry. See: Van Nostrand Chem. Dict.

TSEOU, HEOU-FEO. fl. 1937. Chinese chemist. Cited in: Chem. Abstr. vol. 31, p. 8442[7]. Tseou-Chow test reaction.

TSIEN, HSUE-SHEN. 1910- . Chinese physicist in America. See: Amer. Men Sci., 7th ed. Karman-Tsien relation.

Tswett column (Tswett, Mikhail Semenovitch): Botany. See: Webster's 3d.

TSWETT, MIKHAIL SEMENOVITCH. 1872-1919. Russian botanist. See: World Who's Who Sci. Tswett column.

TUBAKAIEV, V. A. fl. 1937. Russian? chemist. Cited in: Chem. Abstr., vol. 24, p. 3966. Malitzkii-Tubakaiev micro-test for sodium.

Tubbs' dilator (Tubbs, O. S.): Medicine. See: Stedman.

TUBBS, O. S. fl. 1938. American surgeon. Cited in: Kelly. Tubbs' dilator.

tube of Bellini (Bellini, Lorenzo). See: Bellini's tube.

tubercle of Lower (Lower, Richard). See: Lower's tubercle.

tubercle of Morgagni (Morgagni, Giovanni Battista). See: Morgagni's tubercle.

tubercle of Rolando (Rolando, Luigi). See: Rolando's tubercle.

tubercle of Zuckerkandl (Zuckerkandl, Emil): Medicine. See: Stedman. Also known as: Morgagni's tubercle.

tubules of Henle (Henle, Friedrich Gustav Jacob). See: Henle's tubules.

TUCHMAN, BARBARA WERTHEIM. 1912- . American writer. See: Who's Who Amer., 1974-1975. Tuchman's Law.

Tuchman's Law (Tuchman, Barbara Wertheim): Sociology. See: Martin.

Tucker circles (Tucker, Robert): Mathematics. See: Webster's 2d.

TUCKER, EDWARD. fl. 1845. English gardener. (Biography source unavailable.) Tucker's vine disease.

Tucker–McLean forceps (Derivation undetermined): Medicine. See: Stedman.

Tucker porcelain (Tucker, William Ellis): Applied Arts. See: New Encyc. Brit., 1974, Microp.

TUCKER, ROBERT. fl. 1885. English mathematician. Cited in: Royal Sci. Cat. Sci. Pap., 1884-1900. Tucker circles, Tucker's triangle?

TUCKER, SAMUEL AUCHMATY. b. 1869. American chemist. See: Amer. Men Sci., 1st ed. Tucker solution?

Tucker solution (Tucker, Samuel Auchmaty?): Chemistry. See: Van Nostrand Chem. Dict.

TUCKER, WILLIAM ELLIS. 1801-1857. American pottery manufacturer and engraver. See: Fielding. Tucker porcelain.

TUCKERMAN, HENRY THEODORE. 1813-1871. American critic, essayist and poet. See: Dict. Amer. Biog. Tuckermanity.

Tuckermanity (Tuckerman, Henry Theodore): Literature. See: Hendrickson; Partridge.

Tucker's triangle (Tucker, Robert?): Navigation. Noted in exhibit at: Dossin Great Lakes Museum.

Tucker's vine disease (Tucker, Edward): Botany. See: Charnock.

Tudor arch (Tudor, Owen): Architecture. See: Webster's 3d.

Tudor (dynasty) (Tudor, Owen): History. See: Steinberg; Webster's 3d.

Tudor flower (Tudor, Owen): Applied Arts. See: Webster's 3d.

TUDOR, OWEN. d. 1461. Welsh chieftain. See: Dict. Nat. Biog. Tudor arch, Tudor (dynasty), Tudor flower, Tudor (or Tudoresque) style, Tudor rose, Tudor type.

Tudor rose (Tudor, Owen): History. See: Brewer.

Tudor (or Tudoresque) style (Tudor, Owen): Architecture. See: Webster's 3d.

Tudor type (Tudor, Owen): Printing. See: Partridge.

TUERCK, LUDWIG. 1810-1868. Austrian neurologist and laryngologist. See: Biog. Lex. hervorr. Aerzte. Tuerck's column, Tuerck's degeneration, Tuerck's tract (or bundle), Tuerck's zone.

Tuerck's column (Tuerck, Ludwig): Anatomy. See: Dorland; Stedman.

Tuerck's degeneration (Tuerck, Ludwig): Medicine. See: Dorland; Stedman.

Tuerck's tract (or bundle) (Tuerck, Ludwig): Anatomy. See: Donath; Stedman.

Tuerck's zone (Tuerck, Ludwig): Medicine. See: Dorland.

TUERK, F. fl. 1907. Strasbourg chemist. Cited in: Chem. Abstr., Decenn. Index, 1907-1916. Rosenthaler-Tuerk reagent.

TUERK, SIEGMUND. fl. early 20th c. Swiss ophthalmologist. (Biography source unavailable.) Ehrlich-Tuerk line, Stilling-Tuerk-Duane syndrome, Tuerk-Stilling syndrome, Tuerk's syndrome.

Tuerk-Stilling syndrome (Tuerk, Siegmund and Stilling, Jakob). See: Stilling-Tuerk-Duane syndrome.

TUERK, WILHELM. 1871-1916. Austrian hematologist. See: Biog. Lex. hervorr. Aerzte. Tuerk's cell (or leukocyte), Tuerk's stain.

Tuerk's cell (or leukocyte) (Tuerk, Wilhelm): Medicine. See: Dorland; Stedman; Webster's 3d.

Tuerk's stain (Tuerk, Wilhelm): Medicine. See: Stedman.

Tuerk's syndrome (Tuerk, Siegmund). See: Stilling-Tuerk-Duane syndrome.

TUERLER, U. fl. 1951. Swiss physician. (Biography source unavailable.) Fanconi-Tuerler syndrome.

Tuesday (Tiw or Tyr): Generic Word. See: Charnock; Funk; Webster's 3d.

TUFFIER, THEODORE (In full: MARIN THEODORE). 1857-1929. French surgeon. See: World Who's Who Sci. Tuffier's test.

Tuffier's test (Tuffier, Theodore). See: Hallion's test.

TUFFNELL, THOMAS JOLLIFFE. 1818-1885. English military surgeon. See: Dict. Nat. Biog. Tufnell's bandage, Tuffnell's diet, Tuffnell's treatment.

Tuffnell's bandage (Tuffnell, Thomas Jolliffe): Medicine. See: Stedman.

Tuffnell's diet (Tuffnell, Thomas Jolliffe): Medicine. See: Dorland.

Tuffnell's treatment (Tuffnell, Thomas Jolliffe): Medicine. See: Dorland.

TUKEY, JOHN WILDER. 1915- . American mathematician. See: World Who's Who Sci. Tukey statistic, Tukey's gap test, Tukey's q-test, Tukey's quick test.

Tukey statistic (Tukey, John Wilder): Statistics. See: Kendall.

Tukey's gap test (Tukey, John Wilder): Statistics. See: Kendall.

Tukey's q-test (Tukey, John Wilder): Statistics. See: Kendall.

Tukey's quick test (Tukey, John Wilder): Statistics. See: Kendall.

Tukon hardness test (and tester) (Derivation undetermined): Engineering and Industry. See: Thrush; Van Nostrand Sci. Encyc. under "Hardness."

TULBAGH, RYK. 1699-1771. Dutch governor of Cape Colony. See: Rosenthal. Tulbaghia.

Tulbaghia (Tulbagh, Ryk): Botany. See: Charnock; Taylor N.

Tulipan radiometer (Derivation undetermined): Physics. See: Huschke.

Tully limestone (Derivation undetermined): Earth Sciences. See: Thrush.

Tully refractometer (Derivation undetermined): Engineering and Industry. See: Thrush.

TULLY, WILLIAM. 1785-1859. American physician. See: Dict. Amer. Biog. Tully's powder.

Tully's powder (Tully, William): Medicine. See: Webster's 3d.

TULP, NICHOLAS. 1593-1674. Dutch anatomist. See: Nieuw Nederl. Biog. Woordenb. Tulp's valve.

Tulp's valve (Tulp, Nicholas): Anatomy. See: Donath; Stedman. Also known as: valve of Varolius.

Tulunids (Ahmed ibn-Tulun): History. Cited in: Webster's Biog. Dict.

Tung-Kao-Sah reagent (Tung, Wen-Li; Kao, Chen-Heng; Kao, Chung-Hsi; and Sah, Peter P. T.): Chemistry. See: Van Nostrand Chem. Dict.

TUNG, TA-CHENG. fl. 1952. American? chemist. (Biography source unavailable.) Tung-Kao-Sah reagent?

TUNMANN, OTTO. d. 1919. German botanist. See: Ber. Deutsch. Botan. Ges. vol. 37 (1919), Nekr. pp. 80-84. Tunmann test reaction for nicotine.

Tunmann test reaction for nicotine (Tunmann, Otto): Chemistry. See: Van Nostrand Chem. Dict.

tunnel of Corti (Corti, Alfonso Giacomo Gaspare). See: Corti's tunnel (or canal).

TUNNICLIFF, RUTH. 1876-1946. American bacteriologist and immunologist. See: Who's Who Among Physicians and Surg., 1938. Tunnicliff's toxin.

Tunnicliff's toxin (Tunnicliff, Ruth): Medicine. See: Stedman.

Tweedledum and Tweedledee (Handel, George Frederick and Bononcini, Giovanni Battista): Generic Word. See: Hendrickson.

Tweedmouth, Baron of. See: Marjoribanks, Edward (Baron of Tweedmouth).

Tweedmouth committee (Marjoribanks, Edward): Politics. See: Montgomery.

Tweng, Twenge or Thwinge, Robert de. See: Thweng, Robert de.

Twiss (Twiss, Richard): Generic Word (chamber pot). See: Hendrickson; Partridge.

TWISS, RICHARD. 1747-1821. English traveler and writer. See: Dict. Nat. Biog. Twiss.

Twitchell-Allen three dimensional personality test (Allen, Doris Twitchell): Psychology. See: Wolman.

TWITCHELL, ERNST. d. 1929. American chemist. Cited in: Royal Soc. Cat. Sci. Pap., 1884-1900. Twitchell process, Twitchell reagent.

Twitchell process (Twitchell, Ernst): Chemistry. See: Webster's 3d.

Twitchell reagent (Twitchell, Ernst): Chemistry. See: Hackh; Van Nostrand Chem. Dict.; Webster's 3d.

Twort-d'Herelle phenonomen (Twort, Frederick William and d'Herelle, Felix): Medicine. See: Stedman. Also known as: Twort phenomenon, d'Herelle phenomenon.

TWORT, FREDERICK WILLIAM. 1877-1950. English bacteriologist. See: World Who's Who Sci. Twort-d'Herelle phenomenon.

Twort phenomenon (Twort, Frederick William). See: Twort d'Herelle phenomenon.

TWYMAN, FRANK. fl. 1904-1932. English physicist. See: Pogg., vol. 6. Twyman-Green interferometer.

Twyman-Green interferometer (Twyman, Frank and Green, George): Physics. See: Internat. Dict. Phys. Elec.

TYCHE. Greek goddess of chance. See: Oxford Clas. Dict. Tychism.

TYCHIOS. A maker of shields in Homer's "Iliad:" See: Dict. Grk. Rom. Biog. Myth. Tychius.

Tychism (Tyche): Generic Word. See: Mathews, S.

Tychius (Tychios): Zoology. See: Webster's 3d.

Tychonic system (Brahe, Tycho): Astronomy. See: Carter; Charnock; Webster's 3d.

TYCHONOFF, ANDREI NIKOLAEVICH. 1906- . Russian mathematician. See: World Who's Who Sci. Tychonoff space, Tychonoff theorem.

Tychonoff space (Tychonoff, Andrei Nikolaevich): Mathematics. See: James.

Tychonoff theorem (Tychonoff, Andrei Nikolaevich): Mathematics. See: James.

Tydings-McDuffie Act (Tydings, Millard Evelyn and McDuffie, John): Politics. See: Morris; Morris and Irwin.

TYDINGS, MILLARD EVELYN. 1890-1961. American legislator. See: Biog. Direct. Amer. Congress. Miller-Tydings Act (or Enabling Act), Tydings-McDuffie Act.

TYLER, BENNET, 1783-1858. American theologian and educator. See: Dict. Amer. Biog. Tylerism.

Tyler grippe (Tyler, John): Medicine. See: Brewer; Mathews, M. M.

TYLER, JOHN. 1790-1862. American president. See: Dict. Amer. Biog. Tippecanoe and Tyler too, Tyler grippe, Tylerism (or Tylerite), Tylerize.

Tyler sieve (Tyler, W.S.?): Engineering and Industry. See: Thrush.

Tyler standard scale (Tyler, W.S.?): Engineering and Industry. See: Thrush.

Tyler standard series (Tyler, W.S.?): Engineering and Industry. See: Thrush.

TYLER, W. S. fl. 1940. American manufacturer. (Biography source unavailable.) Tyler sieve?, Tyler standard scale?, Tyler standard series?.

TYLER, WAT. d. 1381. English rebel. See: Dict. Nat. Biog. Wat Tyler's rebellion.

Tylerism (Tyler, Bennet): Religion. Cited in: Webster's Biog. Dict.

Tylerism (or Tylerite) (Tyler, John): Politics. See: Mathews, M. M.

Tylerize (Tyler, John): Politics. See: Mathews, M. M.

Tyler's insurrection (Tyler, Wat). See: Wat Tyler's rebellion.

TYLOR, SIR EDWARD BURNETT. 1832-1917. English anthropologist. See: World Who's Who Sci. Tylorian.

Tylorian (Tylor, Sir Edward Burnett): Anthropology. See: Webster's 3d.

TYNDALE, WILLIAM. 1492?-1536. English Bible translator, religious reformer and martyr. See: Dict. Nat. Biog. Tyndale's Bible.

Tyndale's Bible (Tyndale, William): See: Brewer; Phyfe.

Tyndall beam (or cone) (Tyndall, John): Physics. See: Webster's 3d.

Tyndall blue (Tyndall, John): Physics. See: Webster's 3d.

Tyndall effect (or phenomenon) (Tyndall, John): Physics. See: Asimov; Ballentyne; Thewlis.

Tyndall flowers (Tyndall, John): Earth Sciences. See: Huschke.

TYNDALL, JOHN. 1820-1893. Irish physicist. See: Dict. Nat. Biog. Tyndall beam (or cone), Tyndall blue, Tyndall effect (or phenomenon), Tyndall flowers, Tyndall-Roentgen effect, Tyndallimetry, Tyndallization, Tyndallometer or Tyndalloscope).

Tyndall-Roentgen effect (Tyndall, John and Roentgen, Wilhelm Conrad): Physics. See: Thewlis.

Tyndallimetry (Tyndall, John): Physics. See: Thewlis.

Tyndallization (Tyndall, John): Medicine. See: Stedman.

Tyndallometer or Tyndalloscope (Tyndall, John): Physics. See: Thrush; Webster's 3d.

Typhoean (Typhoeus): Mythology. See: Webster's 3d.

TYPHOEUS. Giant of Greek mythology buried under Mt. Edna. See: Jobes. Typhoean.

typhoid Mary (Mallon, Mary): Generic Word (disease-carrier). See: Webster's 3d.

TYPHON. Monster of Greek mythology identified with the Egyptian god Set. See: Jobes. Typhonian (or Typhonic).

Typhonian (or Typhonic) (Typhon): Mythology. See: Webster's 3d.

Tyr, Teutonic god of war. See: Tiw.

TYRER, DANIEL. fl. 1912. English chemist. See: Pogg., vol 5. Tyrer process.

Tyrer process (Tyrer, Daniel): Chemistry. See: Van Nostrand Chem. Dict.

TYRODE, MAURICE VEJUX. 1878-1930. American pharmacologist. See: Biog. Lex. hervorr. Aerzte. Tyrode's solution.

Tyrode's solution (Tyrode, Maurice Vejux): Medicine. See: Dorland; Stedman.

Tyrone, 2nd Earl of. See: O'Neill, Hugh (2nd Earl of Tyrone).

Tyrone's revolt (O'Neill, Hugh): History. See: Steinberg. Also known as: O'Neill's revolt.

TYRRELL, FREDERICK. ca. 1793-1843. English physician and surgeon. See: Dict. Nat. Biog. Tyrrell's fascia, Tyrrell's hook.

TYRRELL, JOSEPH BURR. 1858-1957. Canadian geologist. See: World Who's Who Sci. Tryllite.

Tyrrell's fascia (Tyrrell, Frederick): Anatomy. See: Donath; Dorland; Stedman.

Tyrrell's hook (Tyrell, Frederick): Medicine. See: Dorland; Stedman.

TYRTAEUS. fl. mid-7th c. B.C. Greek poet. See: Oxford Clas. Dict. Tyrtaeus or Tyrtaean.

Tyrtaeus (or Tyrtaean) (Tyrtaeus): Literature. See: Brewer; Webster's 3d.

TYSON, EDWARD. 1649-1708. English anatomist and naturalist. See: Dict. Nat. Biog. Tyson's gland.

TYSON, S. T. fl. 1880. American naturalist. Cited in: Hintze. Tysonite.

Tysonite (Tyson, S. T.): Earth Sciences. See: Webster's 3d.

son's gland (Tyson, Edward): Anatomy. See: Donath; Dorland; Stedman.

ZANK, ARNAULT. 1886-1954. Russian dermatologist. See: Press Med. l. 62 (Apr. 17, 1954), pp. 595-96. Tzank cells, Tzank test.

ank cells (Tzank, Arnault): Medicine. See: Dorland; Stedman.

ank test (Tzank, Arnault): Medicine. See: Dorland; Stedman.

Tzerevitinov, Th. See: Zerevitinov, Th.

TZONI, HARIKLIA. fl. 1936. German? chemist. Cited in: Chem. Abstr. vol. 30, p. 8280[7]. Tzoni reagent.

Tzoni reagent (Tzoni, Hariklia): Chemistry. See: Van Nostrand Chem. Dict.

U

U-coefficient of John (John, Walter, Jr.?): Physics. See: Internat. Dict. Phys. Elec.

Ubbonites (or Obbenite) (Philipsz, Obbe): Religion. See: Canney; Webster's 3d.

Uchatius bronze (or metal) (Uchatius, Baron Franz): Engineering and Industry. See: Webster's 3d.

UCHATIUS, BARON FRANZ. 1811-1881. Austrian general and inventor. See: Allg. Deut. Biog. Uchatius bronze (or metal).

UCKO, H. No dates. French physician. (Biography source unavailable.) Ucko's test.

Ucko's test (Ucko, H.): Medicine. See: Dorland.

UDA, SHINTARO. 1896- . Japanese radio engineer. See: Japanese Biog. Encyc. and Who's Who, 1964-1965. Yagi-Uda antenna.

UDDEN, JOHANNES AUGUST. 1859-1932. Swedish-born American geologist. See: Dict. Amer. Biog. Udden scale.

Udden scale (Udden, Johannes August): Earth Sciences. See: Thrush.

UDEN, KONRAD FRIEDRICH. b. 1776. German-born physician in Russia. See: Biog. Lex. hervorr. Aerzte. Uden's syndrome?

Uden's syndrome (Uden, Konrad Friedrich?): Medicine. See: Jablonski.

UDRANSZKY, LASZLO. 1862-1914. Hungarian physiologist. See: Biog. Lex. hervorr. Aerzte. Udranszky's test for bile, Udranszky test reaction for cholesterol?.

Udranszky test reaction for cholesterol (Udranszky, Laszlo?): Medicine. See: Van Nostrand Chem. Dict.

Udranszky's test for bile (Udranszky, Laszlo): Medicine. See: Dorland; Stedman.

UEHER, EDMUND. fl. 1928. Hungarian printer. (Biography source unavailable.) Uehertype.

Uehertype (Ueher, Edmund): Printing. See: Harrod.

UEHLING, EDWARD A. 1849-1952. American mechanical engineer. See: Who Was Who Amer., 1951-1960. Uehling pig iron casting machine.

UEHLING, EDWARD ALBRECHT. 1901- . American physicist. See: World Who's Who Sci. Uehling force (or effect), Uehling terms.

Uehling force (or effect) (Uehling, Edward Albrecht): Physics. See: Hughes; Internat. Dict. Ap. Math.

Uehling pig iron casting machine (Uehling, Edward A.): Engineering and Industry. Cited in: Who Was Who Amer., 1951-1960.

Uehling terms (Uehling, Edward Albrecht): Physics. See: Internat. Dict. Phys. Elec.

UEHLINGER, ERWIN. b. 1899. Swiss pathologist. See: Who's Who Switz., 1970-1971. Jaffe-Lichtenstein-Uehlinger syndrome, Meyenberg-Altherr-Uehlinger syndrome, Uehlinger's syndrome.

Uehlinger's syndrome (Uehlinger, Erwin): Medicine. See: Jablonski; Stedman. Also known as: Audry's syndrome, Friedrich-Erb-Arnold syndrome, Marie-Bamberger syndrome (idiopathic), Pierre Marie-Bamberger syndrome (idiopathic), Roy's syndrome, Roy-Jutras syndrome, Touraine-Solente-Gole syndrome.

UFFELMANN, JULIUS AUGUST CHRISTIAN. 1837-1894. German hygienist. See: Allg. Deut. Biog. Uffelmann reagent for lactic acid, Uffelmann test for corn meal in flour, Uffelmann tests for fusel oil in alcohol and in alcoholic liquors.

Uffelmann reaction for lactic acid (Uffelmann, Julius August Christian): Chemistry. See: Ballentyne; Stedman; Van Nostrand Chem. Dict.

Uffelmann test for corn meal in flour (Uffelmann, Julius August Christian): Chemistry. See: Van Nostrand Chem. Dict.

Uffelmann tests for fusel oil in alcohol and in alcoholic liquors (Uffelmann, Julius August Christian): Chemistry. See: Van Nostrand Chem. Dict.

UHL, HENRY STEPHEN MAGRAW. 1921- . American internist. See: Amer. Men and Women Sci., 12th ed. Uhl's anomaly.

UHLENBECK, GEORGE EUGENE. 1900- . Dutch East Indian-born American physicist. See: World Who's Who Sci. Goudsmit and Uhlenbeck assumption, Ornstein-Uhlenbeck process.

Uhlenhut test (Derivation undetermined): Chemistry. See: Van Nostrand Chem. Dict.

UHLENHUTH, PAUL THEODORE. 1870-1957. German bacteriologist and hygienist. See: World Who's Who Sci. Uhlenhuth's method.

Uhlenhuth's method (Uhlenhuth, Paul Theodore): Medicine. See: Dorland; Stedman.

UHLIG, HERBERT HENRY. 1907- . American chemist. See: World Who's Who Sci. Uhligite?

Uhligite (Uhlig, Herbert Henry?): Earth Sciences. See: Thrush.

Uhl's anomaly (Uhl, Henry Stephen Magraw): Medicine. See: Jablonski.

UHTHOFF, WILHELM. 1853-1927. German ophthalmologist. See: Biog. Lex. hervorr. Aerzte. Uhtoff's sign.

Uhtoff's sign (Uhthoff, Wilhelm): Medicine. See: Dorland; Stedman.

Ukewallists (Walles, Uke): Religion. See: Canney.

Ukulele (Purvis, Edward "Ukulele"): Music. See: Webster's 3d.

ULBRICHT, RICHARD. 1849-1923. German electrical engineer. See: Pogg., vol. 6. Ulbricht sphere.

Ulbricht sphere (Ulbricht, Richard): Engineering and Industry. See: Hughes; Internat. Dict. Phys. Elec.

ULEX, GEORGE LUDWIG. d. 1883. German chemist. See: Repert. Anal. Chem. vol. 3 (1883), pp. 113-114. Ulexite.

Ulexite (Ulex, George Ludwig): Earth Sciences. See: Thrush; Webster's 3d.

ULFSSON, GUNNBJOERN. fl. ca. 900. Discoverer of Greenland. Cited in: Hintze, 2d suppl., p. 142. Gunnbjarnite.

ULLMANN, EMERICH. 1861-1937. Hungarian surgeon. See: Biog. Lex. hervorr. Aerzte. Ullmann's line.

ULLMANN, FRITZ. 1875-1939. German chemist. See: Pogg., vols. 4 to 6, 7a. Graebe-Ullmann synthesis, Jourdan-Ullmann-Goldberg synthesis (or acridone synthesis), Ullmann reaction.

ULLMANN, JOHANN CHRISTOPHER. 1771-1821. German mineralogist. See: Allg. Deut. Biog. Ullmannite.

Ullmann reaction (Ullmann, Fritz): Chemistry. See: Ballentyne; Van Nostrand Chem. Dict.

Ullmannia (Derivation undetermined): Botany. See: Encyc. Brit., 1973. vol. 7, p. 105d.

Ullmannite (Ullmann, Johann Christopher): Earth Sciences. See: Thrush; Webster's 3d.

Ullmann's line (Ullmann, Emerich): Medicine. See: Dorland; Stedman.

ULLOA, ANTONIO DE. 1716-1795. Spanish naval officer and governor of Louisiana. See: Dict. Amer. Biog. Ulloa's ring (bow or circle).

Ulloa's ring (bow or circle) (Ulloa, Antonio de): Earth Sciences. See: Brewer; Huschke; Webster's 3d. Also known as: Bouguer's halo.

Ullrich and Fremerey-Dohna syndrome (Ullrich, Otto and Fremerey-Dohna, H.). See: Hallermann-Streiff syndrome.

Ullrich-Feichtiger syndrome (Ullrich, Otto and Feichtiger, H): Medicine. See: Jablonski.

ULLRICH, G. fl. 1911. German engineer. Cited in: Chem. Abstr. vol. 6, p. 2827; vol 7, p. 2039. Ullrich magnetic separators.

Ullrich magnetic separators (Ullrich, G.): Engineering and Industry. See: Thrush.

ULLRICH, OTTO. 1894-1957. German pediatrician. See: Wer Ist Wer?, 1951. Bonnevie-Ullrich syndrome, Morquio-Ullrich syndrome (or disease), Ullrich and Fremerey-Dohna syndrome, Ullrich-Feichtiger syndrome, Ullrich-Turner syndrome, Ullrich's syndrome.

Ullrich-Turner syndrome (Ullrich, Otto and Turner, Henry Hubert): Medicine. See: Jablonski.

Ullrich's syndrome (Ullrich, Otto): Medicine. See: Jablonski.

Ulmo, Saint. See: Elmo, Saint.

Ulrichite (Derivation undetermined): Earth Sciences. See: Thrush.

ULTEE, ARNOLDUS JOHANNUS, JR. 1921- . Dutch-born American organic chemist. See: Amer. Men and Women Sci., 12th ed. Ultee cyanhydrin method.

Ultee cyanhydrin method (Ultee, Arnoldus Johannus, Jr.): Chemistry. See: Van Nostrand Chem. Dict.

ULTZMANN, ROBERT. 1842-1889. German chemist. See: Biog. Lex. hervorr. Aerzte. Ultzmann's test.

Ultzmann's test (Ultzmann, Robert): Medicine. See: Dorland; Stedman.

Ulyanov, Vladimir Ilich. See: Lenin.

Ulyssean (Ulysses or Odysseus): Literature. See: Webster's 3d.

ULYSSES OR ODYSSEUS. Greek hero of Homer's "Odyssey." See: Jobes. Ulyssean.

Umayyad dynasty (or period) (Umayyah): History. See: Osborne under "Islamic Art.", Webster's 3d.

Umayyad verse (Umayyah): Literature. See: Preminger under "Arabic Poetry."

UMAYYAH. Islamic ancestor of Muawiyah I (d. 680) and founder of the dynasty. Cited in: Encyc. Brit., 1884 under "Mohammedanism." Umayyad dynasty (or period), Umayyad verse.

UMBER, FRIEDRICH. b. 1871. German physician. See: Biog. Lex. hervorr. Aerzte. Umber's test.

Umber's test (Umber, Friedrich): Medicine. See: Dorland.

Umpleby engine (Umpleby, F.): Engineering and Industry. See: Auger.

UMPLEBY, F. fl. 1909. English engineer. (Biography source unavailable.) Umpleby engine.

un cri de Melusine (Melusine): Generic Word (sudden scream). See: Brewer.

Uncle Sam (Wilson, Samuel): Generic Word (U.S. government). See: Clapin; Hendrickson; Mathews, M. M.; Webster's 3d.

Uncle Sam bird (Wilson, Samuel): Zoology. See: Gray.

Uncle Sam's men (Wilson, Samuel): History. See: Mathews, M. M.

UNCLE TOM. Negro hero of Harriet Beecher Stowe's novel, "Uncle Tom's Cabin", (1851-52). See: Benet. Tom show, Uncle Tom (or Uncle Tomism).

Uncle Tom (or Uncle Tomism) (Uncle Tom): Generic Word. See: Frey; Mathews, M. M.; Smith.

UNDERWOOD, MICHAEL. 1736-1820. English pediatrician. See: Dict. Nat. Biog. Underwood's disease.

UNDERWOOD, OSCAR WILDER. 1862-1929. American legislator. See: Biog. Direct. Amer. Congress. Underwood Tariff Act.

Underwood Tariff Act (Underwood, Oscar Wilder): Politics. See: Jameson; Morris; Smith.

Underwood's disease (Underwood, Michael): Medicine. See: Dorland; Jablonski; Stedman.

UNDINE (ONDINE). Female water sprite in medieval legend. See: Jobes. Ondine's (or Undine's) curse.

Unna-Golodetz test reaction (Unna, Paul Gerson and Golodetz, L.): Chemistry. See: Van Nostrand Chem. Dict.

UNNA, MARIE. fl. 1925. German physician. (Biography source unavailable.) Unna's syndrome.

Unna-Pappenheim stain (Unna, Paul Gerson and Pappenheim, Artur): Medicine. See: Stedman.

UNNA, PAUL GERSON. 1850-1929. German dermatologist. See: World Who's Who Sci. Unna-Golodetz test reaction, Unna-Pappenheim stain, Unna-Taenzer disease, Unna-Taenzer stain, Unna-Thost syndrome, Unna's disease, Unna's mark, Unna's paste, Unna's stain (or solution).

Unna-Taenzer disease (Unna, Paul Gerson and Taenzer, Paul): See: Taenzer's disease.

Unna-Taenzer stain (Unna, Paul Gerson and Taenzer, Paul). See: Taenzer's stain.

Unna-Thost syndrome (Unna, Paul Gerson and Thost, Arthur): Medicine. See: Jablonski. Also known as: Brauer's syndrome, Bruenauer's syndrome.

Unna's disease (Unna, Paul Gerson): Medicine. See: Dorland; Jablonski; Stedman.

Unna's mark (Unna, Paul Gerson): Medicine. See: Stedman.

Unna's paste (Unna, Paul Gerson): Medicine. See: Dorland; Stedman.

Unna's stain (or solution) (Unna, Paul Gerson): Medicine. See: Dorland; Stedman; Van Nostrand Chem. Dict.

Unna's syndrome (Unna, Marie): Medicine. See: Jablonski.

UNSCHULD, PAUL. b. 1835. German internist. (Biography source unavailable.) Unschuld's sign.

Unschuld's sign (Unschuld, Paul): Medicine. See: Dorland.

Unterberger's test (Derivation undetermined): Medicine. See: Stedman.

Unverhau test reactions (Derivation undetermined): Chemistry. See: Van Nostrand Chem. Dict.

UNVERRICHT, HEINRICH. 1853-1912. German physician. See: Biog. Lex. hervorr. Aerzte. Unverricht's disease, Wagner-Unverricht syndrome.

Unverricht-Lafora disease (Unverricht, Heinrich and Lafora, Gonzalo R.). See: Unverricht's disease.

Unverricht's disease (Unverricht, Heinrich): Medicine. See: Dorland; Jablonski; Stedman. Also known as: Lundborg-Unverricht syndrome; Unverricht-Lafora disease.

UNWIN, WILLIAM CAWTHORNE. 1838-1933. English engineer. See: Dict. Nat. Biog. Unwin's extensometer.

Unwin's extensometer (Unwin, William Cawthorne): Engineering and Industry. See: Auger.

Upcher's warbler (Derivation undetermined): Zoology. See: Gray.

URANIA (Or OURANIA). Greek muse of astronomy. See: Jobes. Urania, Uranian.

Urania (Urania, the Muse): Botany. See: Charnock.

Uranian (Urania or (Ourania)): Astronomy. See: Webster's 3d.

Uranism (Uranus): Generic Word (homosexuality). Stedman; Webster's 3d.

URANUS. Greek god of the sky. See: Harper. Uranism.

URBACH, ERICH. 1893-1946. American dermatologist. See: New York Times, Dec. 18, 1946, p. 29, col. 1. Oppenheim-Urbach syndrome, Urbach-Wiethe disease (or syndrome).

URBACH, FRANZ. 1902- . Austrian-born American physicist. See: World Who's Who Sci. Urbach's rule

Urbach–Oppenheim disease (Urbach, Erich and Oppenheim, Maurice). See: Oppenheim–Urbach syndrome.

Urbach–Wiethe disease (or syndrome) (Urbach, Erich and Wiethe, Camille): Medicine. See: Jablonski; Stedman. Also known as: Roessle–Urbach–Wiethe lipoproteinosis, Urbach's lipoproteinosis.

Urbach's lipoproteinosis (Urbach, Erich): See: Urbach–Wiethe syndrome.

Urbach's rule (Urbach, Franz): Physics. See: Ballentyne.

URBAIN, WALTER MATHIAS. 1910– . American chemist. See: Amer. Men Sci., 10th ed. Jensen–Urbain reagent.

URBAN VIII (Real name: MAFFEO BARBERINI). 1568–1644. Italian pope. See: Encyc. Brit., 1911. Pre-Urbanite hymns.

URBAN, F. M. fl. 1927. American? psychophysicist. Cited in: Cum. Auth. Index to Psych. Index, 1894–1935, and Psych. Abstr., 1927–1958. Mueller–Urban method, Mueller–Urban weights (or weighting), Urban's constant process, Urban's tables.

URBAN, WILHELM. fl. 1934. German chemist. Cited in: Chem. Abstr., vol. 29, p. 1032. Schoenberg–Urban test.

Urban's constant process (Urban, F. M.): Psychology. See: Chaplin; English.

Urban's tables (Urban, F. M.): Psychology. See: Drever; English.

Urban's weights (Urban, F. M.). See: Mueller–Urban weights (or weighting).

URE, ANDREW. 1778–1857. Scottish chemist. See: Pogg., vol. 2; World Who's Who Sci. Ure eudiometer, Ure thermostat, Ure's process.

Ure eudiometer (Ure, Andrew): Chemistry. See: Hackh.

Ure thermostat (Ure, Andrew): Engineering and Industry. See: Auger.

Urech cyanhydrin method (Urech, Friedrich Wilhelm Karl): Chemistry. See: Van Nostrand Chem. Dict.

URECH, FRIEDRICH WILHELM KARL. b. 1844. German chemist. See: Pogg., vol 4. Urech cyanhydrin method, Urech hydantoin synthesis?

Urech hydantoin synthesis (Urech, Friedrich Wilhelm Karl?): Chemistry. See: Van Nostrand Chem. Dict.

Ure's process (Ure, Andrew): Engineering and Industry. See: Thrush.

Uriah Heep (Heep, Uriah, the fictional character): Generic Word (hypocrite). See: Barnhart (Eng. Lit.); Partridge.

Urk, Hendrik Willem Van. See: Van Urk, Hendrik Willem.

Ursinia (Ursinus, Johann Heinrich): Botany. See: Taylor, N.; Webster's 3d.

URSINUS, JOHANN HEINRICH (G. BAER). 1608–1667. German theologian and botanist. See: Allg. Deut. Biog. Ursinia.

URSULA OF COLOGNE, SAINT. d. 238 or 283 or 451. English virgin and Christian martyr in Germany. See: Dict. Nat. Biog. Ursulines.

Ursulines (Ursula of Cologne, Saint): Religion. See: Attwater; Brewer; Canney.

Usami reagent (Usami, Shunichi): Chemistry. See: Van Nostrand Chem. Dict.

USAMI, SHUNICHI. 1924– . Japanese-born American physiologist. See: Amer. Men and Women Sci., 12th ed. Usami reagent.

USHER, BARNEY DAVID. 1899– . Canadian dermatologist. See: Direct. Med. Specialist, 1974–1975. Senear–Usher syndrome.

USHER, CHARLES HOWARD. 1865–1942. English physician. See: Ann. Eugen. vol. 11 (Dec. 1942) pp. 309–313. Usher's syndrome.

Usher's syndrome (Usher, Charles Howard): Medicine. See: Jablonski.

USPENSKY, JAMES VICTOR. fl. 20th c. Russian-born American mathematician. See: Pogg., vol. 6. Uspensky's inequality?

Uspensky's inequality (Uspensky, James Victor?): Statistics. See: Kendall.

USSHER, JAMES. 1581–1656. Irish archbishop. See: Dict. Nat. Biog. Bishop Usher's model, Ussherian.

Ussherian (Ussher, James): Religion. See: Webster's 3d.

USSING, NIELS VIGGO. 1864–1911. Danish mineralogist. See: Dansk Biog. Lek. Ussingite.

Ussingite (Ussing, Niels Viggo): Earth Sciences. See: Webster's 3d.

Utagawa School (Toyokuni, Utagawa): Fine Arts. See: Osborne.

UTHER PENDRAGON. Brythonic sky deity. See: Jobes. Pendragon.

UTZ, F. fl. 1910–1925. Austrian chemist. Cited in: Chem. Abstr., Decen. Index 1907–16; 1917–26. Utz reagent for cottonseed oil, Utz test for differentiating arsphenamine and neoarsphenamine, Utz test for formaldehyde in milk, Utz test for mineral acids in vinegar.

Utz reagent for cottonseed oil (Utz, F.): Chemistry. See: Van Nostrand Chem. Dict.

Utz test for differentiating arsphenamine and neoarsphenamine (Utz, F.): Chemistry. See: Van Nostrand Chem. Dict.

Utz test for formaldehyde in milk (Utz, F.): Chemistry. See: Van Nostrand Chem. Dict.

Utz test for mineral acids in vinegar (Utz, F.): Chemistry. See: Van Nostrand Chem. Dict.

UVAROV, COUNT SERGEI SEMENOVITCH. 1785–1855. Russian statesman. See: Michaud. Uvarovite.

Uvarovite (Uvarov, Count Sergei Semenovitch): Earth Sciences. See: Thrush; Van Nostrand Sci. Encyc; Webster's 3d.

UYEMURA, MISAO. fl. 1928. Japanese ophthalmologist. (Biography source unavailable.) Uyemura's syndrome.

Uyemura's syndrome (Uyemura, Misao): Medicine. See: Jablonski.

UZEL, RADIM. fl. 1938. Czechoslovakian chemist. See: Who's Who Central East. Europe, 1937. Procke–Uzel solution.

Uzi 9mm submachine gun (Gal, Uziel): Weapons. See: Quick.

UZMAN, L. LAHUT. fl. 1952. American? physician. (Biography source unavailable.) Farber–Uzman syndrome.

V

B. rifle grenade (Viven and Bessiere): Weapons. See: Quick.

ACHELL. No dates. English missionary in China. (Biography source unailable.) Vachellia.

chellia (Vachell): Botany. See: Charnock.

cquier magnetometer (Vacquier, Victor): Engineering and Industry. See: rush under "Gulf-type (Vacquier) magnetometer."

cquier-Steenland method (Vacquier, Victor and Steenland, Martinus Jan): rth Sciences. See: Thrush.

ACQUIER, VICTOR. 1907- . Russian-born American geophysicist. See: her. Men and Women Sci., 12th ed. Vacquier magnetometer, Vacquier- eenland method.

AES, JOHANNES. fl. 1943. Belgian mineralogist. Cited in: Amer. Min. 30 (1945) pp. 483-497. Vaesite.

esite (Vaes, Johannes): Earth Sciences. See: Thrush; Webster's 3d.

ageler equation (Vageler, P. W. E.?): Chemistry. See: Van Nostrand em. Dict.

AGELER, P. W. E. fl. 1913. German chemist. (Biography source unavail- le.) Vageler equation?

AHL, MARTIN. 1749-1804. Norwegian botanist. See: Nouv. Biog. Univ. hlia.

hlia (Vahl, Martin): Botany. See: Charnock.

AHLQUIST, BO CONRADSSON. 1909- . Swedish pediatrician. See: m Ar Det?, 1959. Vahlquist-Gasser syndrome.

hlquist-Gasser syndrome (Vahlquist, Bo Conradsson and Gasser, Konrad Johann): dicine. See: Jablonski.

AIL, CHARLES ROWE. 1915- . American electrical engineer and university ministrator. See: Amer. Men and Women Sci., 12th ed. Vail's axioms, il's proposition.

AIL, HARRIS HOLMES. 1892-1939. American otolaryngologist. See: n. Otol. Rhinol. Lar. vol. 48 (1939), pp. 560-561. Vail's syndrome.

AILLANT, SEBASTIEN. 1669-1722. French botanist. See: World Who's ho Sci. Valantia.

il's axioms (Vail, Charles Rowe): Sociology. See: Martin.

ail's proposition (Vail, Charles Rowe): Sociology. See: Martin.

ail's syndrome (Vail, Harris Holmes): Medicine. See: Jablonski.

aisala comparator (Vaisala, Vilho): Astronomy. See: Thewlis.

AISALA, VILHO. b. 1889. Finnish astronomer. See: New Encyc. Brit., 74. Vaisala comparator.

l separator (Derivation undetermined): Engineering and Industry. See: Thrush.

ALANGIN, FRANCIS JOSEPH PAHUD DE. 1725-1805. English physician. ography source unavailable.) Valangin's solution.

alangin's solution (Valangin, Francis Joseph Pahud de): Medicine. See: rland.

lantia (Vaillant, Sebastien): Botany. See: Charnock.

VALDIGUIE, A. fl. 1923. French chemist. Cited in: Chem. Abstr. Aloy-Valdiguie morphine reagent, Aloy-Valdiguie strychnine reagent, Aloy-Valdiguie test for copper and hydroquinone, Aloy-Valdiguie test reaction for formaldehyde, trioxymethylene and methenamine, Valdiguie test reaction.

Valdiguie test reaction (Valdiguie, A.): Chemistry. See: Van Nostrand Chem. Dict.

Valdo, Pierre. See: Waldo, Pierre.

Valenta reagent for differentiating aliphatic and aromatic hydrocarbons (Valenta, Zdenek): Chemistry. See: Van Nostrand Chem. Dict.

Valenta reagent for fats (Valenta, Zdenek): Chemistry. See: Van Nostrand Chem. Dict.

Valenta test for pine oil in turpentine oil (Valenta, Zdenek): Chemistry. See: Van Nostrand Chem. Dict.

VALENTA, ZDENEK. 1927- . Czechoslovakian-born Canadian organic chemist. See: Amer. Men and Women Sci., 12th ed. Valenta reagent for differentiating aliphatic and aromatic hydrocarbons, Valenta reagent for fats, Valenta test for pine oil in turpentine oil.

VALENTIN, GABRIEL GUSTAV. 1810-1883. German physiologist. See: Allg. Deut. Biog.; World Who's Who Sci. Valentin's corpuscles, Valentin's ganglion, Valentin's knife, Valentin's nerve.

Valentine (Valentine, Saint): Generic Word. See: Charnock; Hargrave; Partridge.

VALENTINE, BASIL. fl. 15th c. German alchemist. See: Michaud. Valentinite.

Valentine bun (Valentine, Saint): Food and Drink. See: Hendrickson.

VALENTINE, FERDINAND C. 1851-1909. American surgeon. See: New York Times, Dec. 14, 1909, p. 11, col. 4. Valentine's position, Valentine's test.

VALENTINE, JAN. d. 1897. German? geologist. See: Ber. Senckenberg. Naturf. Ges. 1898, LXIVff. Valentine scale?

VALENTINE, JIMMY. Character in O. Henry's story "A Retrieved Reformation," (before 1909). See: Hart. Jimmy Valentine.

VALENTINE, SAINT. fl. ca. 270. Christian priest and martyr in Rome. See: Encyc. Brit., 1973. Saint Valentine's disease, Valentine, Valentine bun, Valentine's Day, Valentining.

Valentine scale (Valentine, Jan?): Earth Sciences. See: Thrush.

Valentine's Day (Valentine, Saint): Generic Word. See: Attwater; Wager (Names); Webster's 3d.

Valentine's position (Valentine, Ferdinand C.): Medicine. See: Stedman.

Valentine's test (Valentine, Ferdinand C.): Medicine. See: Stedman.

VALENTINI, MICHAEL BERNHARD. 1657-1729. German physician and naturalist. See: World Who's Who Sci. Valentinia (herb), Valentinia (moth).

Valentinia (herb) (Valentini, Michael Bernhard): Botany. See: Charnock.

Valentinia (moth) (Valentini, Michael Bernhard): Zoology. See: Pennak.

Valentinians (or Valentinianism) (Valentinus): Religion. See: Attwater; Canney.

Valentining (Valentine, Saint): History. See: Hendrickson.

Valentinite (Valentine, Basil): Earth Sciences. See: Thrush; Webster's 3d.

Valentino (Valentino, Rudolph): Generic Word (handsome lover). See: Hendrickson.

VALENTINO, RUDOLPH (Real name: RODOLPHO D'ANTONGUOLLA). 1895-1926. Italian-born American film actor. See: Who Was Who Amer. Valentino.

Valentin's corpuscles (Valentin, Gabriel Gustav): Medicine. See: Donath; Dorland; Stedman.

Valentin's ganglion (Valentin, Gabriel Gustav): Medicine. See: Dorland; Stedman.

Valentin's knife (Valentin, Gabriel Gustav): Medicine. See: Webster's 3d.

Valentin's nerve (Valentin, Gabriel Gustav): Medicine. See: Stedman.

VALENTINUS. fl. 2nd c. Egyptian leader of the Gnostic movement. See: Encyc. Brit., 1911. Valentinians (or Valentinianism).

VALERIAN (PUBLIUS LICINIUS VALERIANUS). d. 269. Roman emperor. See: Encyc. Brit., 1911. Valeriana.

Valeriana (Valerian): Botany. See: Charnock; Taylor, N.

Valkeria (Derivation undetermined): Zoology. See: Pennak.

VALLABHA. 1479-1530. Indian religious teacher and founder of sect. See: Encyc. Brit., 1973. Vallabhacharya sect.

Vallabhacharya sect (Vallabha): Religion. See: Canney.

VALLANDIGHAM, CLEMENT LAIRD. 1820-1871. American politician. See: Dict. Amer. Biog. Vallandigham's case, Vallandinghamer.

Vallandighamer (Vallandigham, Clement Laird): History. See: Jameson; Mathews, M. M.

Vallandigham's case (Vallandigham, Clement Laird): History. See: Jameson; Mathews, M. M.

VALLAT, GEORGES. 1918- . French physician. See: Who's Who France, 1973-1974. Rimbaud-Pasouant-Vallat syndrome.

Vallee's elastic roller gum (Derivation undetermined): Printing. See: Lockwood.

VALLEIX, FRANCOIS L. I. 1807-1855. French physician. See: Biog. Lex. hervorr. Aerzte. Valleix's points.

Valleix's points (Valleix, Francois L. I.): Medicine. See: Dorland; Stedman.

VALLENTIN, RUPERT. fl. 1888. English? scientist. (Biography source unavailable.) Vallentinia?

Vallentinia (Vallentin, Rupert?): Zoology. See: Pennak.

Valleriite (Vallerius, Goeran): Earth Sciences. See: Webster's 3d.

VALLERIUS, GOERAN. 1683-1742. Swedish mineralogist. See: Pogg., vol. 2. Valleriite.

Vallery-Radot and Blamoutier lipomatosis (Vallery-Radot, Pasteur and Blamoutier, Pierre): Medicine. See: Jablonski.

VALLERY-RADOT, PASTEUR (In full: JOSEPH LOUIS PASTEUR). 1886-1970. French physician. See: Who Was Who. Vallery-Radot and Blamoutier lipomatosis.

VALLI, EUSEBIO. 1755-1816. Italian physiologist. See: World Who's Who Sci. Ritter-Valli law.

Valli-Ritter law (Valli, Eusebio and Ritter, Johann Wilhelm): See: Ritter-Valli law.

Vallisneria (Vallisnieri, Antonio): Botany. See: Charnock; Webster's 3d.

VALLISNIERI, ANTONIO. 1661-1730. Italian naturalist and physician. See: Nouv. Biog. Univ. Vallisneria.

Vallonia (Derivation undetermined): Zoology. See: Pennak.

VALLOT, ANTOINE. 1594-1671. French physician and botanist. See: Nouv. Biog. Univ. Vallota.

Vallota (Vallot, Antoine): Botany. See: Partridge; Taylor, N. Webster's 3d.

VALMONT DE BOMARE, JACQUES CHRISTOPHE. 1731-1807. French naturalist. See: Biog. Notes Upon Botanists. Bomarea.

VALSALVA, ANTONIO MARIA. 1666-1723. Italian anatomist and physician. See: Nouv. Biog. Univ. Valsalva maneuver, Valsalva test, Valsalva's antrum, Valsalva's experiment, Valsalva's ligaments, Valsalva's muscle, Valsalva's sinus.

Valsalva maneuver (Valsalva, Antonio Maria): Medicine. See: Dorland; Stedman; Webster's 3d.

Valsalva test (Valsalva, Antonio Maria): Medicine. See: Stedman.

Valsalva's antrum (Valsalva, Antonio Maria): Anatomy. See: Donath; Stedman.

Valsalva's experiment (Valsalva, Antonio Maria): Medicine. See: Dorland; Stedman.

Valsalva's ligaments (Valsalva, Antonio Maria): Anatomy. See: Stedman.

Valsalva's muscle (Valsalva, Antonio Maria): Anatomy. See: Stedman.

Valsalva's sinus (Valsalva, Antonio Maria): Anatomy. See: Donath; Dorland; Stedman. Also known as: Petit's sinus.

Valser solution (Derivation undetermined): Chemistry. See: Van Nostrand Chem. Dict.

VALSON, CLAUDE ALPHONS. 1826-1901. French chemist and mathematician. Cited in: Royal Soc. Cat. Sci. Pap., 1864-1873. Valson law of moduli.

Valson law of moduli (Valson, Claude Alphons): Chemistry. See: Van Nostrand Chem. Dict.

VALSUANI, EMILIO. fl. 1870. Italian physician. (Biography source unavailable.) Valsuani's disease.

Valsuani's disease (Valsuani, Emilio): Medicine. See: Jablonski.

VALTON, P. A. fl. 1924. English? chemist. Cited in: Chem. Abstr. vol. 19, p. 1237. Valton test.

Valton test (Valton, P. A.): Chemistry. See: Van Nostrand Chem. Dict.

valve of Bauhin (Bauhin, Gaspard). See: Bauhin's valve.

valve of Gerlach (Gerlach, Joseph). See: Gerlach's valve.

valve of Hasner (Hasner, Joseph Ritter von Artha). See: Hasner's valve.

valve of Heister (Heister, Lorenz). See: Heister's valve(s) (or valve of Heister).

valve of Houston (Houston, John). See: Houston's valve (or fold).

valve(s) of Kerckring (Kerckring, Theodor). See: Kerckring's valves.

valve of Thebesius (Thebesius, Adam Christian). See: Thebesian valve.

valve of Variolus (Varolius, Constantius): Anatomy. See: Stedman. Also known as: Tulpius' valve.

valve of Vieussens (Vieussens, Raymond de). See: Vieussens' valve.

VAMVAKAS, J. fl. 1911. Cretan? chemist. (Biography source unavailable.) Vamvakas test.

Vamvakas test (Vamvakas, J.): Chemistry. See: Van Nostrand Chem. Dict.

VANADIS. Latinized name of Freya, Scandinavian goddess of love and beauty. See: Funk & Wagnalls. Vanadium.

Vanadium (Vanadis): Chemistry. See: Partridge; Thrush; Van Nostrand Sci. Encyc.

VAN ALLEN, JAMES ALFRED. 1914- . American physicist. See: Amer. Men Sci., 11th ed. Van Allen radiation belts.

Van Allen radiation belts (Van Allen, James Alfred): Physics. See: Ballentyne; Markus; Satterthwaite.

VAN ALPHEN, PIETER MARTINUS. fl. 20th c. Dutch chemist. Cited in: Mansell. DeHaas-Van Alphen effect.

Van Arkel and De Boer process (Van Arkel, Anton Eduard, and De Boer, Jan Hendrik): Engineering and Industry. See: Ballentyne; Thewlis; Thrush.

AN ARKEL, ANTON EDUARD. 1893- . Dutch chemist. World Who's ho Sci. Van Arkel and De Boer process.

an Atta array (Van Atta, Lester Clare): Engineering and Industry. See: arkus.

AN ATTA, LESTER CLARE. 1905- . American physicist. See: World ho's Who Sci. Van Atta array.

an Bogaert-Bertrand syndrome (Van Bogaert, Ludo, and Bertrand, Ivan eorges). See: Canavan's disease.

an Bogaert-Divry syndrome (Van Bogaert, Ludo and Divry, Paul): Medicine. e: Jablonski.

an Bogaert-Hozay syndrome (Van Bogaert, Ludo and Hozay, Jean): Medicine. e: Jablonski.

AN BOGAERT, LUDO. fl. 1923-1952. Belgian neurologist. See: Internat. Neur., vol. 1, no. 1 (1967) p. 94. Van Bogaert-Bertrand syndrome, Van gaert-Divry syndrome, Van Bogaert-Hozay syndrome, Van Bogaert-Nyssen sease, Van Nogaert-Nyssen-Peiffer disease, Van Bogaert-Scherer-Epstein syn- ome, Van Bogaert's encephalitis.

an Bogaert-Nyssen disease (Van Bogaert, Ludo and Nyssen, Rene): See: reenfield's disease.

an Bogaert-Nyssen-Peiffer disease (Van Bogaert, Ludo; Nyssen, Rene; and iffer, Jurgen). See: Greenfield's disease.

an Bogaert-Scherer-Epstein syndrome (Van Bogaert, Ludo; Scherer, Hans J.; d Epstein, Emil): Medicine. See: Jablonski.

an Bogaert's encephalitis (Van Bogaert, Ludo): Medicine. See: Jablonski. so known as: Bodechtel-Guttmann disease, Dawson's encephalitis.

an Buchem, Francis Steven Peter. See: Buchem. Francis Steven Peter van.

an Buchem's syndrome (Buchem, Francis Steven Peter van): Medicine. See: ablonski.

an Buren convention (Van Buren, Martin): History. See: Mathews, M. M.

an Buren Democrat (Van Buren, Martin): History. See: Mathews, M. M.

AN BUREN, MARTIN. 1782-1862. American president. See: Dict. Amer. og. O. K., Van Buren convention, Van Buren Democrat, Van Burenism (or an Burenite), Vanite (Vanjack or Vanocrat).

AN BUREN, WILLIAM HOLME. 1819-1883. American surgeon and physician. e: Dict. Amer. Biog. Van Buren's disease.

an Burenism (or Van Burenite) (Van Buren, Martin): Politics. See: Mathews, . M.

an Buren's disease (Van Buren, William Holme): Medicine. See: Dorland; edman.

AN CAULAERT, CAMILLE. 1900- . French physician. (Biography source available.) Blum-Van Caulaert syndrome.

ANCOUVER, GEORGE. 1758-1798. English navigator. See: Dict. Nat. og. Vancouveria.

ancouveria (Vancouver, George): Botany. See: Hendrickson, Taylor, N.

AN CREVELD, SIMON. 1894- . Dutch pediatrician. See: World Who's ho Sci. Ellis-Van Creveld syndrome, Von Gierke-Van Creveld syndrome.

AN DEEN, IZAAK ABRAHAMSZOON. 1804-1869. Dutch physiologist. ee: Biog. Lex. hervorr. Aerzte. Van Deen test reaction.

an Deen test reaction (Van Deen, Izaak Abrahamszoon): Medicine. See: an Nostrand Chem. Dict. Also known as: Almen's test for blood, Deen's st.

an de Graaff generator (or accelerator) (Van de Graaff, Robert Jemison): ngineering and Industry. See: Hughes; Markus; Thewlis.

AN DE GRAAFF, ROBERT JEMISON. 1901-1967. American physicist. See: ho Was Who Amer. Van de Graaff generator (or accelerator).

ANDELLI, DOMINGOS. 1730?-1816. Italian-born Portuguese naturalist. ee: Serrao. Vandellia.

andellia (Vandelli, Domingos): Botany. See: Charnock.

ANDENBERG, GENERAL O. fl. 1860's. American army officer. (Biography ource unavailable.) Vandenberg volley gun.

Vandenberg volley gun (Vandenberg, General O.): Weapons. See: Quick.

Van den Bergh, A. A. Hymans. See: Bergh, A. A. Hymans van der.

Van den Bergh's disease (Bergh, A. A. Hymans van der). See: Stokvis-Talma syndrome.

Van den Bergh's test (Bergh, A. A. Hymans van der): Medicine. See: Dorland; Stedman.

VAN DEN BRANDE, PIERRE. 1896-1957. Belgian geologist. See: Bull. Soc. Belge Geolog. vol. 67 (1958 (1959)), pp. 296-99. Vandenbrandite.

Vandenbrandite (Van den Brande, Pierre): Earth Sciences. See: Thrush.

VANDENDRIESSCHE, ADRIAAN. 1914-1940. Belgian mineralogist and geologist. See: Natuurwetensch. Tijdschr. vol. 22 (1940), p. 236. Vandendriesscheite.

Vandendriesscheite (Vandendriessche, Adriaan): Earth Sciences. See: Thrush.

Van der Hoeve-de Kleyn syndrome (Hoeve, Jan van der and Kleijn, Adrianus Paulus Huibertus Antonie de). See: Van der Hoeve's syndrome.

Van der Hoeve-Halbertsma-Waardenburg syndrome (Hoeve, Jan van der; Halbertsma, Ir. Nicolaas Adolf; and Waardenburg P. Johannes). See: Klein-Waardenburg syndrome.

Van der Hoeve, Jan. See: Hoeve, Jan van der.

Van der Hoeve-Waardenburg-Gualdi syndrome (Hoeve, Jan van der; Waardenburg, P. Johannes; and Gualdi, Augusto). See: Klein-Waardenburg syndrome.

Van der Hoeve's syndrome (or triad) (Hoeve, Jan van der): Medicine. See: Jablonski. Also known as: Adair Dighton's syndrome, van der Hoeve-de Kleyn syndrome.

VAN DER KOLK, JACOB LUDWIG CONRAD SCHROEDER. 1797-1862. Dutch physician. See: Biog. Lex. hervorr. Aerzte. Van der Kolk's law.

VAN DER KOLK, JACOB LUDWIG CONRAD SCHROEDER. 1865-1906. Dutch geologist and mineralogist. See: Nieuw Nederl. Biog. Woordenb. Van der Kolk method.

Van der Kolk method (Van der Kolk, Jacob Ludwig Conrad Schroeder): Earth Sciences. See: Thrush.

Van der Kolk's law (Van der Kolk, Jacob Ludwig Conrad Schroeder): Physiology. See: Stedman.

VAN DER LUHE, CHARLES. No dates. German botanist. (Biography source unavailable.) Luhea.

VANDERMONDE, ALEXANDRE THEOPHILE. 1735-1796. French mathematician and philosopher. See: Nouv. Biog. Univ. Vandermonde determinant, Vandermonde's theorem.

Vandermonde determinant (Vandermonde, Alexandre Theophile): Mathematics. See: Ballentyne; James.

Vandermonde's theorem (Vandermonde, Alexandre Theophile): Mathematics. See: Ballentyne.

VAN DER PAELE, CANON. fl. ca. 1440. Dutch prelate and art patron. Cited in: Upjohn, pp. 168-169. Van der Paele madonna.

Van der Paele madonna (Van der Paele, Canon): Fine Arts. See: Osborne.

VAN DER POL, BALTHASAR. b. 1889. Dutch electrotechnician. See: Pogg., vol. 6. Van der Pol oscillator.

Van der Pol oscillator (Van der Pol, Balthasar): Engineering and Industry. See: Hughes.

van der Spieghel, Adrian. See: Spiegelius.

VAN DER VELDEN, REINHARDT. 1851-1903. German physician. See: Biog. Lex. hervorr. Aerzte. Van der Velden's test.

Van der Velden's test (Van der Velden, Reinhardt): Medicine. See: Dorland; Stedman.

Van der Velden's test for free hydrochloric acid (Velden, Reinhard von den): Medicine. See: Dorland. Also known as: Maly's test.

Van der Waals adsorption (Van der Waals, Johannes Diderik): Chemistry. See: Ballentyne; Thewlis; Thrush.

Van der Waals constant (Van der Waals, Johannes Diderik): Chemistry. See: Hackh.

Van der Waals equation of state (Van der Waals, Johannes Diderik): Chemistry. See: Ballentyne; Huschke; Thewlis.

Van der Waals forces (Van der Waals, Johannes Diderik): Chemistry. See: Internat. Dict. Ap. Math.; Thewlis; Thrush.

VAN DER WAALS, JOHANNES DIDERIK. 1837-1923. Dutch physical chemist. See: World Who's Who Sci. Van der Waals adsorption, Van der Waals constant, Van der Waals equation of state, Van der Waals forces, Van der Waals-London interaction, Van der Waals radius, Van der Waals surface tension relationship.

Van der Waals-London interaction (Van der Waals, Johannes Diderik and London, Fritz Wolfgang): Physics. See: Ballentyne.

Van der Waals radius (Van der Waals, Johannes Diderik): Physics. See: Thewlis; Van Nostrand Sci. Encyc. under "Atomic Radius."

Van der Waals surface tension relationship (Van der Waals, Johannes Diderik): Physics. See: Internat. Dict. Phys. Elec.

VAN DER WAERDEN, BARTEL LEENDERT. 1903- . Dutch mathematician. See: World Who's Who Sci. Van der Waerden's test.

Van der Waerden's test (Van der Waerden, Bartel Leendert): Statistics. See: Kendall.

Van Diemen, Antonio. See: Diemen, Antonio van.

Van Doran sampler (Derivation undetermined): Engineering and Industry. See: Thrush.

VANDYKE, SIR ANTHONY. 1599-1641. Flemish-born English painter and etcher. See: Dict. Nat. Biog. Vandyke beard, Vandyke brown, Vandyke collar (or cape), Vandyke fashion style, Vandyke paper, Vandyke process, Vandyke red, Vandykes (or Vandyked).

Vandyke beard (Vandyke, Sir Anthony): Fashion. See: Brewer; Hendrickson.

Vandyke brown (Vandyke, Sir Anthony): Fine Arts. See: Thrush; Wagner (Names).

Vandyke collar (or cape) (Vandyke, Sir Anthony): Fashion. See: Charnock; Picken; Wagner (More Names).

Vandyke fashion style (Vandyke, Sir Anthony): Fashion. See: Picken.

Vandyke paper (Vandyke, Sir Anthony): Photography. See: Van Nostrand Sci. Encyc.

Vandyke process (Vandyke, Sir Anthony): Photography. See: Van Nostrand Sci. Encyc. under "Photographic Printing Processes."

Vandyke red (Vandyke, Sir Anthony): Fine Arts. See: Thrush.

Vandykes (or Vandyked) (Vandyke, Sir Anthony): Generic Word. See: Brewer; Partridge; Weekley.

VANE, SIR HENRY. 1613-1662. English Puritan and statesman. See: Dict. Nat. Biog. Vanists.

VAN ECK, C. L. VON PANTHALEON. fl. 20th c. Dutch physical chemist. See: Who's Who Sci. Europe, 1972. Van Eck reagent, Van Eck test reaction.

Van Eck reagent (Van Eck, C.L. von Panthaleon): Chemistry. See: Van Nostrand Chem. Dict.

Van Eck test reaction (Van Eck, C. L. von Panthaleon): Chemistry. See: Van Nostrand Chem. Dict.

Van Ekenstein-Blanksma test reaction (Van Ekenstein, Willem Alberda and Blanksma, Jan Johannes): Chemistry. See: Van Nostrand Chem. Dict.

VAN EKENSTEIN, WILLEM ALBERDA. 1858-1937. Dutch chemist. See: Pogg., vol. 6. Lobry de Bruyn-Van Ekenstein rearrangement (transformation or conversion), Van Ekenstein-Blanksma test reaction.

VAN ERMENGEN, EMILE PIERRE MARIE. 1851-1932. Belgian bacteriologist. See: World Who's Who Sci. Van Ermengen's method.

Van Ermengen's method (Van Ermengen, Emile Pierre Marie): Medicine. See: Stedman.

VAN GEHUCHTEN, ARTHUR. 1861-1915. Belgian anatomist. See: Seyn. Van Gehuchten's fixation.

Van Gehuchten's fixation (Van Gehuchten, Arthur): Medicine. See: Dorland; Stedman.

VANGHETTI, GIULIANO. 1861-1940. Italian surgeon. See: World Who's Who Sci. Vanghetti's prosthesis.

Vanghetti's prosthesis (Vanghetti, Giuliano): Medicine. See: Dorland; Stedman.

VAN GIESON, IRA THOMPSON. 1865-1913. American histologist and bacteriologist. See: New York Times, March 25, 1913, p. 13, col. 5. Van Gieson's stain.

Van Gieson's stain (Van Gieson, Ira Thompson): Medicine. See: Dorland; Stedman.

Van Goergoe, Rolf. See: Goergey, Rolf.

VAN HALBAN, JOSEF. 1870-1937. Austrian gynecologist. See: World Who's Who Sci. Halban's sign.

VAN HASSELT. No dates. Dutch botanist. (Biography source unavailable.) Hasseltia.

VAN HELMONT, JEAN BAPTISTE. 1577-1644. Flemish physician and chemist. See: Encyc. Brit., 1911. Van Helmont's mirror.

Van Helmont's mirror (Van Helmont, Jean Baptiste): Anatomy. See: Donath; Dorland; Stedman.

VAN HOOK, WELLER. 1862-1933. American surgeon. See: World Who's Who Sci. Van Hook's operation.

Van Hooks' operation (Van Hook, Weller): Medicine. See: Dorland.

VAN HOORNE, JAN. 1621-1670. Dutch anatomist. See: Nouv. Biog. Univ. Van Hoorne's canal.

Van Hoorne's canal (Van Hoorne, Jan): Anatomy. See: Donath; Dorland; Stedman.

VANIER, G. P. fl. 1912. American chemist. Cited in: Chem. Abstr. vol. 6, p. 2021. Vanier's tube.

Vanier's tube (Vanier, G. P.): Chemistry. See: Hackh.

Vanino-Guyot reagent (Vanino, Ludwig and Guyot, O.): Chemistry. See: Van Nostrand Chem. Dict.

Vanino-Hartl test reaction (Vanino, Ludwig and Hartl, F.): Chemistry. See: Van Nostrand Chem. Dict.

VANINO, LUDWIG. 1861-1944. German chemist. See: Pogg., vol. 4 to 7a. Vanino-Guyot reagent, Vanino-Hartl test reaction, Vanino test.

Vanino test (Vanino, Ludwig): Chemistry. See: Van Nostrand Chem. Dict.

Vanists (Vane, Sir Henry): Religion. See: Canney.

VAN ITALLIE, LEOPOLD. b. 1886. Dutch chemist. See: Pogg., vol. 6. Van Itallie-Steenhauer test reaction for alkaloids, Van Itallie test for differentiating phenol and resorcinol from salicylic acid, Van Itallie test for hydrogen sulfide, Van Itallie test reaction for antipyrine, Van Itallie test reaction for thymol.

Van Itallie-Steenhauer test reaction for alkaloids (Van Itallie, Leopold, and Steenhauer, A. J.): Chemistry. See: Van Nostrand Chem. Dict.

Van Itallie test for differentiating phenol and resorcinol from salicylic acid (Van Itallie, Leopold): Chemistry. See: Van Nostrand Chem. Dict.

Van Itallie test for hydrogen sulfide (Van Itallie, Leopold): Chemistry. See: Van Nostrand Chem. Dict.

Van Itallie test reaction for antipyrine (Van Itallie, Leopold): Chemistry. See: Van Nostrand Chem. Dict.

Van Itallie test reaction for thymol (Van Itallie, Leopold): Chemistry. See: Van Nostrand Chem. Dict.

Vanite (Vanjack or Vanocrat) (Van Buren, Martin): History. See: Mathews, M. M.

VAN KLOOSTER, HENDRIK SJOERD. fl. 1910. Dutch chemist. See: Chem. Weekblad vol. 32 (1935), p. 562. Van Klooster test.

Van Klooster test (Van Klooster, Hendrik Sjoerd): Chemistry. See: Van Nostrand Chem. Dict.

Van Laer, Pieter. See: Laar, Pieter van.

VAN LEEUWEN, JOHANNA (In full: HENDRIKA JOHANNA). b. 1887. Dutch physicist. See: Pogg., vol. 6. Bohr-Van Leeuwen theorem.

an Lohuizen, Cato H. J. See: Lohuizen, Cato H. J. van.

an Lohuizen's disease (Lohuizen, Cato H. J. van): Medicine. See:
ablonski.

AN NECK, M. fl. 1920's. Franco-Belgian surgeon. (Biography source un-
vailable.) Van Neck's disease.

an Neck-Odelberg syndrome (Van Neck, M. and Odelberg, Axel Axelsson).
ee: Van Neck's disease.

an Neck's disease (Van Neck, M.): Medicine. See: Jablonski. Also
nown as: Odelberg's disease, Van Neck-Odelberg syndrome.

AN NORDSTRAND, ROBERT ALEXANDER. 1917- . American chemist.
ee: Amer. Men Sci., 9th ed. Nordstrandite.

AN PREHN, COL. fl. 1783. Dutch governor of South Africa. Cited in:
ana, p. 411. Prehnite.

AN RENSSELAER, STEPHEN. 1764-1839. American soldier and politician.
ee: Dict. Amer. Biog. Rensselaerite.

an Rijn, Rembrandt Harmenz. See: Rembrandt.

AN RUYMBEKE, J. fl. 1921. Dutch? chemist. (Biography source unavail-
ble.) Van Ruymbeke process.

an Ruymbeke process (Van Ruymbeke, J.): Chemistry. See: Van Nostrand
hem. Dict.

ANSITTART, SIR ROBERT GILBERT, 1ST BARON. 1881-1957. English
atesman. See: Dict. Nat. Biog. Vansittartism.

ansittartism (Vansittart, Sir Robert Gilbert, 1st Baron): History. See:
endrickson; Partridge.

an Slyke apparatus (Van Slyke, Donald Dexter): Chemistry. See: Hackh;
ennak; Stedman.

an Slyke carbon monoxide reagent (Van Slyke, Donald Dexter): Chemistry.
ee: Van Nostrand Chem. Dict.

AN SLYKE, DONALD DEXTER. 1883-1971. American physician and
emist. See: World Who's Who Sci. Van Slyke apparatus, Van Slyke car-
n monoxide reagent, Van Slyke method, Van Slyke's formula.

an Slyke method (Van Slyke, Donald Dexter): Chemistry. See: Ballentyne;
ackh; Van Nostrand Chem. Dict.

an Slyke's formula (Van Slyke, Donald Dexter): Medicine. See: Dorland;
edman.

an Stone pipe joint (Derivation undetermined): Engineering and Industry. See:
an Nostrand Sci. Encyc.

an't Hoff equation (or formula) for osmotic pressure (Van't Hoff, Jacobus
endricus): Chemistry. See: Ballentyne; Internat. Dict. Ap. Math.

an't Hoff factor (Van't Hoff, Jacobus Hendricus): Chemistry. See: Ballenne; Hackh; Van Nostrand Chem. Dict.

an't Hoff isotherm (Van't Hoff, Jacobus Hendricus): Chemistry. See:
llentyne.

AN'T HOFF, JACOBUS HENDRICUS. 1852-1911. Dutch chemist and
ysician. See: World Who's Who Sci. Van't Hoff equation (of formula)
r osmotic pressure, Van't Hoff factor, Van't Hoff isotherm, Van't Hoff-Le
l theory, Van't Hoff principle (or theorem), Van't Hoff principle of super-
sition, Van't Hoff reaction isochore (or equation), Van't Hoff solution,
anthoffite, Van't Hoff's law (or theory).

an't Hoff-Le Bel theory (Van't Hoff, Jacobus Hendricus and Le Bel, Joseph
chille): Chemistry. See: Ballentyne. Also known as: Le Be-Van't Hoff
le.

an't Hoff principle (or theorem) (Van't Hoff, Jacobus Hendricus): Chemistry.
e: Ballentyne; Internat. Dict. Ap. Math.; Van Nostrand Sci. Encyc. under
quilibrium (Chemical)."

an't Hoff principle of superposition (Van't Hoff, Jacobus Hendricus):
emistry. See: Ballentyne.

an't Hoff reaction isochore (or equation) (Van't Hoff, Jacobus Hendricus):
emistry. See: Ballentyne; Thewlis; Van Nostrand Sci. Encyc.

an't Hoff solution (Van't Hoff, Jacobus Hendricus): Chemistry. See: Hackh.

anthoffite (Van't Hoff, Jacobus Hendricus): Earth Sciences. See: Thrush.

Van't Hoff's law (or theory) (Van't Hoff, Jacobus Hendricus): Chemistry.
See: Hackh; Stedman; Van Nostrand Sci. Encyc.

VAN URK, HENDRIK WILLEM. fl. 1924. Dutch chemist. See: Pogg., vol.
6. Van Urk reactions for arsphenamine and neoarsphenamine, Van Urk reaction
for ergotamine, ergotoxine, and ergotonine, Van Urk test for organic drugs,
Van Urk tests for differentiating chloramine-T from hypochlorites.

Van Urk reaction for ergotamine, ergotoxine, and ergotonine (Van Urk, Hendrik
Willem): Chemistry. See: Van Nostrand Chem. Dict.

Van Urk reactions for arsphenamine and neoarsphenamine (Van Urk, Hendrik
Willem): Chemistry. See: Van Nostrand Chem. Dict.

Van Urk test for organic drugs (Van Urk, Hendrik Willem): Chemistry. See:
Van Nostrand Chem. Dict.

Van Urk tests for differentiating chloramine-T from hypochlorites (Van Urk,
Hendrik Willem): Chemistry. See: Van Nostrand Chem. Dict.

VAN VLECK, JOHN HASBROUCK. 1899- . American physicist. See:
World Who's Who Sci. Van Vleck paramagnetism.

Van Vleck paramagnetism (Van Vleck, John Hasbrouck): Physics. See:
Ballentyne; Internat. Dict. Phys. Elec.

Van Winkle, Rip. See: Rip van Winkle.

VANZETTI, BARTOLOMEO. 1888-1927. Italian-American political radical.
See: Dict. Amer. Biog. Sacco-Vanzetti case.

VANZETTI, TITO. 1809-1888. Italian surgeon. See: Biog. Lex. hervorr.
Aerzte. Vanzetti's sign.

Vanzetti's sign (Vanzetti, Tito): Medicine. See: Dorland; Stedman.

VAN ZIJP, C. fl. 1922. Dutch chemist. (Biography source unavailable.)
Van Zijp test for cholesterol.

Van Zijp test for cholesterol (Van Zijp, C.): Chemistry. See: Van Nostrand
Chem. Dict.

VAQUEZ, LOUIS HENRI. 1860-1936. French physician. See: World Who's
Who Sci. Babinski-Vaquez syndrome, Vaquez-Osler disease.

Vaquez-Osler disease (Vaquez, Louis Henri and Osler, Sir William): Medicine.
See: Jablonski. Also known as: Osler-Vaquez disease, Osler's disease,
Vaquez's disease.

Vaquez's disease (Vaquez, Louis Henri). See: Vaquez-Osler disease.

VARAS, ANTONIO. 1817-1886. Chilean statesman. See: Dicc. Biog.
General de Chile, 1550-1887 vol. Montt-Varistas (political party).

VARDEN, DOLLY. Coquette in the novel "Barnaby Rudge" by Charles Dickens.
See: Harvey. Dolly Varden crab, Dolly Varden (dress), Dolly Varden
pattern, Dolly Varden spotted horse, Dolly Varden trout (or char).

Vardhamana Jnatiputra, Mahavira. See: Mahavira, Vardhamana Jnatiputra.

VARGAS, MANOLO. fl. 1945-1955. Mexican dancer. (Biography source
unavailable.) Ximenez-Vargas Ballet Espanol.

Varian nuclear magnetometer (Varian, Russell Harrison): Physics. See:
Thrush.

VARIAN, RUSSELL HARRISON. 1898-1959. American physicist. See:
World Who's Who Sci. Varian nuclear magnetometer.

VARIGNON, PIERRE. 1654-1722. French mathematician. See: Nouv.
Biog. Univ. Varignon theorem?

Varignon theorem (Varignon, Pierre?): Mathematics. See: Internat. Dict.
Ap. Math.

VARLEY, CROMWELL FLEETWOOD. 1828-1883. English electrical engineer.
See: World Who's Who Sci. Kelvin-Varley slide, Varley effect, Varley loop
test.

Varley effect (Varley, Cromwell Fleetwood): Physics. See: Ballentyne.

Varley loop test (Varley, Cromwell Fleetwood): Engineering and Industry.
See: Hughes; Markus; Van Nostrand Sci. Encyc.

VAROLIUS, CONSTANTIUS. 1543-1575. Italian anatomist and surgeon.
See: World Who's Who Sci. pons Varolii, valve of Variolus, Varolius'
sphincter.

Varolius' pons (or bridge) (Varolius, Constantius). See: pons Varolii.

Varolius' sphincter (Varolius, Constantius): Anatomy. See: Stedman.

VARRO, MARCUS TERENTIUS. 116?-27? B.C. Roman man of letters. See: Harper. Varronia.

Varronia (Varro, Marcus Terentius): Botany. See: Charnock.

Vasey acetaldehyde solution (Vasey, George?): Chemistry. See: Van Nostrand Chem. Dict.

VASEY, GEORGE. 1822-1893. American physician and botanist. See: Dict. Amer. Biog. Vasey acetaldehyde solution?, Vasey grass.

Vasey grass (Vasey, George): Botany. See: Webster's 3d.

Vasil'ev test reaction (Derivation undetermined): Chemistry. See: Van Nostrand Chem. Dict.

VASILIEV, NIKOLAI PORFIRYEVICH. b. 1861. Russian physician. (Biography source unavailable.) Vasiliev's disease.

Vasiliev's disease (Vasiliev, Nikolai Porfiryevich): Medicine. See: Dorland.

Vasmer test reaction (Derivation undetermined): Chemistry. See: Van Nostrand Chem. Dict.

vasovagal attack of Gowers (Gowers, Sir William Richard). See: Gowers' syndrome (3).

VASQUEZ, S. fl. 1935. Spanish? chemist. Cited in: Chem. Abstr. vol. 29, p. 5385. Feigl-Zappert-Vasquez test for acetic acid, Feigl-Zappert-Vasquez test for methyl ketones.

VASQUEZ SANCHEZ, J. fl. 1934. Spanish chemist in Germany? Cited in: Chem. Abstr., vol. 28, p. 6388. Krumholz-Sanchez reagent.

VASSALLO, ETTORE. fl. 1912. Italian chemist. Cited in: Chem. Abstr. vol. 6, p. 49. Vassallo test reaction.

Vassallo test reaction (Vassallo, Ettore): Chemistry. See: Van Nostrand Chem. Dict.

VATER, ABRAHAM. 1684-1751. German anatomist and botanist. See: World Who's Who Sci. Vater-Pacini corpuscles, Vateria, Vater's ampulla, Vater's fold (or papilla).

VATER, HEINRICH, AUGUST. 1859-1930. German mineralogist and geologist. See: Pogg., vol. 4,5,6. Vaterite.

Vater-Pacini corpuscles (Vater, Abraham and Pacini, Filippo): Anatomy. See: Donath; Dorland; Stedman. Also known as: Pacinian (or Pacini's) corpuscles (or bodies), Vater's corpuscles.

Vateria (Vater, Abraham): Botany. See: Webster's 3d.

Vaterite (Vater, Heinrich August): Earth Sciences. See: Thrush; Webster's 3d.

Vater's ampulla (Vater, Abraham): Anatomy. See: Donath; Dorland; Stedman.

Vater's corpuscles (Vater, Abraham). See: Vater-Pacini corpuscles.

Vater's fold (or papilla) (Vater, Abraham): Anatomy. See: Donath; Dorland; Stedman.

VAUCHER, JEAN PIERRE ETIENNE. 1763-1841. Swiss botanist. See: World Who's Who Sci. Vaucheria.

Vaucheria (Vaucher, Jean Pierre Etienne): Botany. See: Van Nostrand Sci. Encyc. under "Algae," Webster's 3d.

VAUCLAIN, ANDREW C. d. 1938. American engineer and industrialist. See: New York Times, Aug. 20, 1938, p. 15, col. 5. Vauclain drill.

Vauclain drill (Vauclain, Andrew C.): Engineering and Industry. See: Auger.

VAUCLAIN, SAMUEL M. 1856-1940. American manufacturer. See: Who Was Who Amer. Vauclain system.

Vauclain system (Vauclain, Samuel M.): Engineering and Industry. See: Webster's 2d.

VAUGHAN, DAME JANET MARIA. fl. 1931-1972. English physician. See: Med. Direct., 1972. Vaughan's disease.

VAUGHAN, JOHN THOMAS. 1932- . American veterinarian. See: Amer. Men Sci., 11th ed. Vaughan's cage?

Vaughan-Novy test (Vaughan, Victor Clarence and Novy, Frederick George): Medicine. See: Dorland; Stedman.

VAUGHAN, THOMAS WAYLAND. 1870-1952. American geologist. See: Nat. Acad. Sci. Biog. Mem. vol. 32 (1958), pp. 410-37. Vaughanite?

VAUGHAN, VICTOR CLARENCE. 1851-1929. American chemist and physician. See: Who Was Who Aerm. Vaughan-Novy test.

Vaughanite (Vaughan, Thomas Wayland?): Earth Sciences. See: Thrush.

Vaughan's cage (Vaughan, John Thomas?): Zoology. See: Hackh.

Vaughan's disease (Vaughan, Dame Janet Maria): Medicine. See: Jablonski. Also known as: Harrison-Vaughan disease.

VAUQUELIN, LOUIS NICOLAS. 1763-1829. French chemist. See: Nouv. Biog. Univ. Vauquelinite.

Vauquelinite (Vauquelin, Louis Nicolas): Earth Sciences. See: Thrush; Webster's 3d. Also known as: Laxmannite.

VAUX, GEORGE. 1863-1927. American lawyer and industrialist. See: Who Was Who Amer. Vauxite.

VAUX, W. S. 1811-1882. American friend of John Kirk Townsend. (Biography source unavailable.) Vaux's swift.

Vauxite (Vaux, George): Earth Sciences. See: Thrush; Webster's 3d.

Vaux's swift (Vaux, W. S.): Zoology. See: Mathews, M. M.

VAVILOV. N. V. fl. 1938. Russian chemist. Cited in: Chem. Abstr. vol. 32, p. 5725. Vavilov test reaction.

Vavilov test reaction (Vavilov, N. V.): Chemistry. See: Van Nostrand Chem Dict.

VEATCH, JOHN A. fl. 1856. American mineralogist. Cited in: Amer. Min. vol. 23 (July, 1938), pp. 490-11. Veatchite.

Veatchite (Veatch, John A.): Earth Sciences. See: Thrush; Webster's 3d.

Veblen axiom(s) (Veblen, Oswald): Mathematics. See: Van Nostrand Sci. Encyc. under "Geometry."

VEBLEN, OSWALD. 1880-1960. American mathematician. See: World Who's Who Sci. Veblen axiom(s).

VEBLEN, THORSTEIN BUNDE. 1857-1929. American social scientist. See: Internat. Encyc. Soc. Sci. Veblenian (or Veblenism).

Veblenian (or Veblenism) (Veblen, Thorstein Bunde): Sociology. See: Webster's 3d.

VECCHI, V. fl. 1956. Italian physician. (Biography source unavailable.) Zanoli-Vecchi syndrome.

VEDDER, EDWARD BRIGHT. 1878-1952. American army surgeon. See: World Who's Who Sci. Vedder's medium, Vedder's sign.

Vedder's medium (Vedder, Edward Bright): Medicine. See: Dorland.

Vedder's sign (Vedder, Edward Bright): Medicine. See: Dorland.

VEENEKLAAS, G. M. H. fl. 1952. Dutch pediatrician. See: Who's Who Sci. Europe, 1972. Veeneklaas' syndrome.

Veeneklaas' syndrome (Veeneklaas, G. M. H.): Medicine. See: Jablonski.

VEGARD, LARS. b. 1880. Norwegian physicist. See: Pogg., vol. 5, 6. Vegard's law.

Vegard's law (Vegard, Lars): Physics. See: Ballentyne; Thewlis; Thrush.

VEIL, PROSPER. 1892-1941. French ophthalmologist. (Biography source unavailable.) Terrien-Veil syndrome.

VEILLON, ADRIEN. 1864-1931. French bacteriologist. See: Biog. Lex. hervorr. Aerzte. Veillonella.

Veillonella (Veillon, Adrien): Zoology. See: Dorland; Stedman.

vein(s) of Galen (or Galen's vein) (Galen): Medicine. See: Henderson; Stedman; Webster's 3d.

vein of Latarjet (Latarjet, Andre). See: Latarjet's vein.

vein of Mayo (Mayo, William J.). See: Mayo's vein.

Veitch diagram (Veitch, John?): Engineering and Industry. See: Hughes; Markus.

VEITCH, JOHN. 1829-1894. Scottish logician, philosopher and man of letters. See: Dict. Nat. Biog. Veitch diagram?

VELARDI, GIUSEPPE. fl. 1920. Italian chemist. (Biography source unavailable.) Velardi test,

Velardi test (Velardi, Giuseppe): Chemistry. See: Van Nostrand Chem. Dict.

VELASQUEZ, DIEGO RODRIGUEZ DA SILVA Y. 1599-1660. Spanish portrait painter. See: Bryan. Velasquez silhouette.

Velasquez silhouette (Velasquez, Diego Rodriguez da Silva y): Fashion. See: Picken.

VELDEN, REINHARD VON DEN. 1851-1903. German physician. See: Biog. Lex. hervorr. Aerzte, 1880-1930. van der Velden's test for free hydrochloric acid.

VELLA, LUIGI. 1825-1886. Italian physiologist. See: Biog. Lex. hervorr. Aerzte. Thiry-Vella fistula.

Vella's fistula (Vella, Luigi). See: Thiry-Vella fistula.

VELLEDA. fl. 1st c. A.D. Legendary German prophetess. See: Hastings Encyc. Rel. Ethics) under "Teutonic Religion," vol. 12, p. 254b. Velleda moth.

Velleda moth (Velleda): Zoology. See: Webster's 3d.

Vello process (Sanchez-Vello, Leopoldo): Engineering and Industry. See: Thrush; Webster's 3d.

VELLOSO-XAVIER, JOSE. d. 1811. Brazilian botanist. (Biography source unavailable.) Vellozia.

Vellozia (Velloso-Xavier, Jose): Botany. See: Webster's 3d.

VELPEAU, ALFRED LOUIS ARMAND MARIE. 1795-1867. French surgeon. See: World Who's Who Sci. Velpeau's bandage, Velpeau's canal, Velpeau's deformity, Velpeau's fossa, Velpeau's hernia.

Velpeau's bandage (Velpeau, Alfred Louis Armand Marie): Medicine. See: Dorland; Stedman.

Velpeau's canal (Velpeau, Alfred Louis Armand Marie): Anatomy. See: Stedman.

Velpeau's deformity (Velpeau, Alfred Louis Armand Marie): Medicine. See: Dorland; Stedman.

Velpeau's fossa (Velpeau, Alfred Louis Armand Marie): Anatomy. See: Stedman.

Velpeau's hernia (Velpeau, Alfred Louis Armand Marie): Medicine. See: Dorland; Stedman.

VELTHEIM, AUGUST FERDINAND VON. 1741-1801. German jurist and historian. See: Allg. Deut. Biog. Veltheimia.

Veltheimia (Veltheim, August Ferdinand von): Botany. See: Taylor, N.

VENABLE, FRANCIS PRESTON. 1856-1934. American chemist. See: Pogg., vols. 4 to 6. Venable test reaction?

Venable test reaction (Venable, Francis Preston?): Chemistry. See: Van Nostrand Chem. Dict.

VENEGAS, PERE MICHEL. fl. 18th c. Spanish Jesuit missionary in California. See: Michaud. Venegasia.

Venegasia (Venegas, Pere Michel): Botany. See: Charnock.

Venereal disease (Venus): Medicine. See: Funk; Partridge; Webster's 3d.

Venerean (Venus): Mythology. See: Webster's 3d.

Venery (Venus): Generic Word (love). See: Partridge; Webster's 3d.

VENING-MEINESZ, FELIX ANDRIES. b. 1887. Dutch geodesist. See: Pogg., vol. 6. Meinesz zone.

Venn diagram (Venn, John): Mathematics. See: Ballentyne; Good; Monkhouse. Also known as: Euler diagram.

VENN, JOHN. 1834-1923. English logician and man of letters. See: Dict. Nat. Biog. Venn diagram.

VENNER, THOMAS. d. 1661. English conspirator. See: Dict. Nat. Biog. Venner's rising (or plot).

Venner's rising (or plot) (Venner, Thomas): History. See: Brewer; Harbottle.

VENNING, ELEANOR HILL. 1900- . Canadian physian and biochemist. See: World Who's Who Sci. Browne-Venning test.

VENTRE, JULES. fl. 1914. French chemist. (Biography source unavailable.) Ventre test reaction.

Ventre test reaction (Ventre, Jules): Chemistry. See: Van Nostrand Chem. Dict.

VENTURI, A. fl. 19th c. Italian botanist. (Biography source unavailable.) Venturia.

Venturi blower (Venturi, Giovanni Battista): Engineering and Industry. See: Thrush.

Venturi carburetor (Venturi, Giovanni Battista): Engineering and Industry. Cited in: Van Nostrand Sci. Encyc. under "Carburetion" and "Carburetor Types."

Venturi flume (Venturi, Giovanni Battista): Engineering and Industry. See: Thrush.

VENTURI, GIOVANNI BATTISTA. 1746-1822. Italian physicist. See: World Who's Who Sci. Venturi blower, Venturi carburetor, Venturi flume, Venturi meter, Venturi principle, Venturi pump, Venturi throat, Venturi tube.

Venturi meter (Venturi, Giovanni Battista): Engineering and Industry. See: Auger; Thewlis; Thrush.

Venturi principle (Venturi, Giovanni Battista): Engineering and Industry. Cited in: Encyc. Brit., 1973 under "Venturi tube."

Venturi pump (Venturi, Giovanni Battista): Engineering and Industry. Cited in: Encyc. Brit., 1973 under "Venturi tube."

Venturi throat (Venturi, Giovanni Battista): Engineering and Industry. Cited in: Encyc. Brit., 1973 under "Venturi tube."

Venturi tube (Venturi, Giovanni Battista): Engineering and Industry. See: Huschke; Thrush; Winburne.

Venturia (Venturi, A.): Botany. See: Webster's 3d.

VENTUROLI, GIUSEPPE. fl. 1911. Italian pharmaceutical chemist. (Biography source unavailable.) Venturoli tests.

Venturoli tests (Venturoli, Giuseppe): Chemistry. See: Van Nostrand Chem. Dict.

Venulite (shell) (Venus): Earth Sciences. See: Charnock.

VENUS (epithet, CYTHEREA). Roman goddess of love, growth and beauty. See: Harper. crocus of Venus, Cytherea, Cytherean, Cytherella, girdle of Venus, mount of Venus, Venereal disease, Venerean, Venery, Venulite (shell), Venus and Adonis stanza, Venus' basin, Venus' chariot, Venus' (clam), Venus' collar, Venus' comb, Venus (copper), Venus' cup, Venus' ear, Venus' fan, Venus' flower basket, Venus' fly-trap, Venus' girdle, Venus' golden apple, Venus' hair fern, Venus' hairstone, Venus' looking-glass, Venus' navelwort, Venus' pride, Venus' purse, Venus' shell, Venus' shoe (or slipper), Venus' sumac, Venusberg, Venusian, Venust.

Venus and Adonis stanza (Venus and Adonis): Literature. See: Preminger; Webster's 3d.

Venus' basin (Venus): Botany. Cited in : Partridge.

Venus' chariot (Venus): Botany. See: Webster's 3d.

Venus (clam) (Venus): Zoology. See: Pennak; Webster's 3d.

Venus' collar (Venus): Medicine. See: Stedman.

Venus' comb (Venus): Botany. See: Gray; Webster's 3d.

Venus (copper) (Venus): Chemistry. See: Charnock.

Venus' cup (Venus): Botany. See: Webster's 3d.

Venus' ear (Venus): Zoology. See: Gray; Webster's 3d.

Venus' fan (Venus): Zoology. See: Webster's 3d.

Venus' flower basket (Venus): Zoology. See: Gray; Pennak; Webster's 3d.

Venus' fly-trap (Venus): Botany. See: Gray; Mathews, M. M.; Pennak; Van Nostrand Sci. Encyc.

Venus' girdle (Venus): Zoology. See: Gray; Pennak; Van Nostrand Sci. Encyc.

Venus' golden apple (Venus): Botany. Cited in: Partridge.

Venus' hair fern (Venus): Botany. See: Webster's 3d.

Venus' hairstone (Venus): Earth Sciences. See: Thrush; Webster's 3d.

Venus' looking-glass (Venus): Botany. See: Gray; Webster's 3d.

Venus' navelwort (Venus): Botany. See: Webster's 3d.

Venus' pride (Venus): Botany. See: Mathews, M. M.; Webster's 3d.

Venus' purse (Venus): Botany. Cited in: Partridge.

Venus' shell (Venus): Zoology. See: Webster's 3d.

Venus' shoe (or slipper) (Venus): Botany. See: Webster's 3d.

Venus' sumac (Venus): Botany. Cited in: Partridge.

Venusberg (Venus): Mythology. See: Partridge.

Venusian (Venus): Parapsychology. See: Webster's 3d.

Venust (Venus): Generic Word (beautiful). See: Charnock.

VERAGUTH, OTTO. 1870-1940. German neurologist. See: Biog. Lex. hervorr. Aerzte. fold of Veraguth.

VERBIEST, HENK. 1909-   . Dutch neurosurgeon. See: Who's Who Sci. Europe, 1972. Verbiest's syndome.

Verbiest's syndrome (Verbiest, Henk): Medicine. See: Jablonski.

VERBRYCKE, J. RUSSEL, JR. fl. 1940. American physician. (Biography source unavailable.) Verbrycke's syndrome.

Verbrycke's syndrome (Verbrycke, J. Russel, Jr.): Medicine. See: Jablonski.

VERCO, SIR JOSEPH COOKE. 1851-1933. Australian physician. See: Who Was Who. Verco's sign.

Verco's sign (Verco, Sir Joseph Cooke): Medicine. See: Dorland.

VERDA, ANTONIO FRANCESCO ALESSANDRO. b. 1876. Italian chemist. See: Pogg., vol. 6. Verda reagent for saffron.

Verda reagent for saffron (Verda, Antonio Francesco Alessandro): Chemistry. See: Van Nostrand Chem. Dict.

VERDAN, CLAUDE EDOUARD. 1909-   . Swiss surgeon. See: Who's Who Sci. Europe, 1972. Verdan's syndrome.

Verdan's syndrome (Verdan, Claude Edouard): Medicine. See: Jablonski.

VERDE, MARIO. 1920-   . Italian physicist. See: Who's Who Sci. Europe, 1972. method of Verde and Wick.

Verdet constant (Verdet, Marcel E.): Physics. See: Ballentyne; Hackh; Internat. Dict. Phys. Elec.

VERDET, MARCEL E. 1824-1866. French physicist. See: World Who's Who Sci. Verdet constant, Verdet's equation

Verdet's equation (Verdet, Marcel E.): Physics. See: Hackh.

VERDI, GIUSEPPE FORTUNINO FRANCESCO. 1813-1901. Italian composer. See: Grove. Verdi's Requiem.

Verdi's Requiem (Verdi, Giuseppe Fortunino Francesco): Music. Cited in: Apel under "Manzoni Requiem." Also known as: Manzoni Requiem.

VERE, AUBREY DE (20TH EARL OF OXFORD). 1626-1703. English royalist and soldier. See: Dict. Nat. Biog. The Oxford Blues.

VERE DE VERE, LADY CLARA. Heroine of poem by Alfred, Lord Tennyson (1842). See: Gerwig. Lady Clara Vere de Vere.

VERE, EDWARD DE (17TH EARL OF OXFORD). 1550-1604. English courtier and lyric poet. See: Dict. Nat. Biog. Oxfordian.

VERE, JOHN DE (16TH EARL OF OXFORD). ca. 1512-1562. English nobleman. See: Dict. Nat. Biog. Oxford's men.

VERGA, ANDREA. 1811-1895. Italian neurologist. See: Biog. Lex. hervorr. Aerzte. Verga's ventricle.

Verga's ventricle (Verga, Andrea): Anatomy. See: Donath; Dorland; Stedman.

Verhassel test reactions (Derivation undetermined): Chemistry. See: Van Nostrand Chem. Dict.

VERHEYEN, PHILIPPE. 1648-1710. Flemish anatomist. See: Biog. Nat. de Belgique. Verheyen's stars.

Verheyen's stars (Verheyen, Philippe): Anatomy. See: Donath; Dorland; Stedman.

VERHOEFF, FREDERICK, HERMAN. 1874-1968. American ophthalmologist. See: Who Was Who Amer. Agnew-Verhoeff incision, Verhoeff's operation.

Verhoeff's operation (Verhoeff, Frederick Herman): Medicine. See: Dorland; Stedman.

VERLEY, ALBERT. fl. 1908-1926. French chemist. Cited in: Chem. Abstr., Decenn. Indexes, 1907-1916; 1917-1926. Meerwein-Ponndorf-Verley reduction (or reaction).

VERMALE, RAYMOND DE. fl. 1751. French surgeon. See: Biog. Lex. hervorr. Aerzte. Vermale's operation.

Vermale's operation (Vermale, Raymond de.): Medicine. See: Stedman.

VERMANDE, JAN. fl. 1918. Dutch pharmaceutical chemist. Cited in: Chem. Abstr. vol. 12, p. 2294. Vermande microchemical reagents.

Vermande microchemical reagents (Vermande, Jan): Chemistry. See: Van Nostrand Chem. Dict.

Vermorel (Vermorel, Victor B.): Engineering and Industry. See: Webster's 3d.

VERMOREL, VICTOR B. d. 1927. French industrialist and author. (Biography source unavailable.) Vermorel.

VERNADSKI, VLADIMIR IVANOVICH. 1863-1945. Russian geologist. See: World Who's Who Sci. Vernadskite.

Vernadskite (Vernadski, Vladimir Ivanovich): Earth Sciences. See: Thrush; Webster's 3d.

VERNE, JULES. 1828-1905. French writer. See: Encyc. Brit., 1911. Jules Verne garnish.

VERNER, JOHN VICTOR. 1927-   . American physician. See: Amer. Med. Direct., 1973. Verner-Morrison syndrome.

VERNER, KARL ADLOPH. 1846-1896. Danish philologist. See: Allg. Deut. Biog. Verner's law.

Verner-Morrison syndrome (Verner, John Victor, and Morrison, Ashton Byrom): Medicine. See: Jablonski.

Verner's law (Verner, Karl Adolph): Linguistics. See: Hartmann; Webster's 3d.

VERNES, ARTHUR THEODORE. b. 1879. French physician. See: Who's Who France, 1973-1974. Vernes' resorcin test, Vernes' test for syphilis.

Vernes' resorcin test (Vernes, Arthur Theodore): Medicine. See: Stedman.

Vernes' test for syphilis (Vernes, Arthur Theodore): Medicine. See: Dorland; Stedman.

VERNET, MAURICE ALBIN. b. 1887. French physician. See: Who's Who France, 1973-1974. Vernet's paralysis.

Vernet's paralysis (Vernet, Maurice Albin): Medicine. See: Jablonski.

VERNEUIL, ARISTIDE AUGUSTE STANISLAS. 1823-1895. French surgeon. See: World Who's Who Sci. hidradenitis of Verneuil, Kuemmell-Verneuil disease, Verneuil's bursitis.

VERNEUIL, AUGUST VICTOR LEWIS. d. 1913. French chemist and mineralogist. See: Bull. Soc. Chim. France, vol. 4, Ser. XIII (1913), Nr. 15, pp. VII-X. Verneuil process or method.

Verneuil process (or method) (Verneuil, August Victor Lewis): Earth Sciences. See: Ballentyne; Thrush; Webster's 3d.

Verneuil's bursitis (Verneuil, Aristide Auguste Stanislas): Medicine. Cited in: World Who's Who Sci.

Vernicle (Veronica, Saint): Religion. See: Attwater; Osborne; Webster's 3d.

Vernier (Vernier, Pierre): Engineering and Industry. See: Internat. Dict. Phys. Elec.; Satterthwaite.

Vernier acuity (Vernier, Pierre?): Physics. See: Thewlis.

Vernier caliper (or micrometer) (Vernier, Pierre): Engineering and Industry. See: Thrush; Van Nostrand Sci. Encyc. under "Measurement"; Webster's 3d.

Vernier closure meter (Vernier, Pierre): Engineering and Industry. See: Thrush.

Vernier compass (Vernier, Pierre): Engineering and Industry. See: Thrush; Webster's 3d.

Vernier engine (Vernier, Pierre): Engineering and Industry. See: Hendrickson.

Vernier gage (Vernier, Pierre): Engineering and Industry. See: Webster's 3d.

VERNIER, PIERRE. 1580-1637. French mathematician. See: Encyc. Brit., 1911. Tinsley-Vernier potentiometer, Vernier, Vernier acuity?, Vernier caliper (or micrometer), Vernier closure meter, Vernier compass, Vernier engine, Vernier gage, Vernier potentiometer.

Vernier potentiometer (Vernier, Pierre): Engineering and Industry. See: Hughes.

Vernis Martin (or Martin varnish) (Martin brothers): Applied Arts. See: Hendrickson under "Berenice's Hair..;" Webster's 3d.

VERNON, ADMIRAL EDWARD "OLD GROG". 1684-1757. English naval officer. See: Dict. Nat. Biog. Grog, Groggy.

VERNON-HARCOURT, AUGUSTUS GEORGE. 1834-1919. English chemist. See: World Who's Who Sci. Vernon-Harcourt lamp.

Vernon-Harcourt lamp (Vernon-Harcourt, Augustus George): Engineering and Industry. See: Hughes; Thewlis.

VERNON, PHILIP EWART. 1905- . English psychologist. See: Internat. Direct. Psych., 1966. Allport-Vernon-Lindzey study of values, Watts-Vernon test.

VERNON, WILLIAM. d. 1711. English botanist (Biography source unavailable.) Vernonia.

Vernonia (Vernon, William): Botany. See: Stedman; Taylor, N.; Webster's 3d.

Verocay bodies (Verocay, Jose): Medicine. See: Dorland; Stedman.

VEROCAY, JOSE. 1876-1927. Czechoslovakian pathologist. See: Biog. Lex. hervorr. Aerzte. Verocay bodies.

VERONESE, PAUL (Real name: PAOLA CAGLIARI or CALLIARI). 1528-1588. Italian painter. See: Nouv. Biog. Univ. Paul Veronese green.

Verongia (Derivation undetermined): Zoology. See: Pennak.

Veronica (Veronica, Saint): Botany. See: Partridge; Stedman; Taylor, N.

VERONICA, SAINT. Legendary woman who wiped Christ's face. See: Holweck. Vernicle, Veronica.

VERPLANCK, GULIAN CROMMELIN (Pseud., ABIMELECK COODY). 1786-1870. American writer. See: Dict. Amer. Biog. Coodies (political party).

VERSCHOOR, JACOB. 1648-1700. Dutch theologian. See: Biog. Woordenb. der Nederl. (Aa). Verschoorists.

Verschoorists (Verschoor, Jacob): Religion. See: Canney.

VERSON, SAVERIO. fl. 1913. Italian scientist. (Biography source unavailable.) Verson's glands?

Verson's glands (Verson, Saverio?): Zoology. See: Gray; Henderson.

Verulam (Bacon, Francis, 1st Baron of Verulam): Botany. See: Charnock.

Verulam, Francis Bacon, 1st Baron of. See: Bacon, Francis, 1st Baron of Verulam.

Verulamian (Bacon, Francis, 1st Baron of Verulam): Philosophy. See: Webster's 3d.

Verven solution (Derivation undetermined): Chemistry. See: Van Nostrand Chem. Dict.

VERY, EDWARD WILSON. 1847-1910. American inventor and naval officer. See: New York Times, Mar. 2, 1910, p. 9., col. 4. Very lights, Very night signal system, Very pistol.

Very lights (Very, Edward Wilson): Engineering and Industry. See: Hendrickson; Webster's 3d.

Very night signal system (Very, Edward Wilson): Engineering and Industry. See: Webster's 3d.

Very pistol (Very, Edward Wilson): Engineering and Industry. See: Quick.

VESALIUS, ANDREAS. 1514-1564. Flemish anatomist. See: Encyc. Brit., 1973. Vesalius' bones, Vesalius' foramen, Vesalius' ligament, Vesalius' vein.

Vesalius' bones (Vesalius, Andreas): Anatomy. See: Donath; Stedman.

Vesalius' foramen (Vesalius, Andreas): Anatomy. See: Donath.

Vesalius' ligament (Vesalius, Andreas): Anatomy. See: Donath; Stedman. Also known as: Fallopian arch and Poupart's ligament.

Vesalius' vein (Vesalius, Andreas): Anatomy. See: Donath; Stedman.

VESEY, DENMARK. 1767?-1822. American conspirator. See: Dict. Amer. Biog. Vesey slave plot.

Vesey slave plot (Vesey, Denmark): History. See: Morris.

VESIGNIE, COLONEL LOUIS. 1870-1954. French mineralogist. Cited in: Amer. Min. vol. 40 (1955), pp. 942-3. Vesignieite.

Vesignieite (Vesignei, Colonel Louis): Earth Sciences. See: Thrush.

VESLINGIUS, JOHANNES. 1598-1649. German anatomist and botanist. See: Allg. Deut. Biog. Veslingius' line.

Veslingius' line (Veslingius, Johannes): Anatomy. See: Stedman.

VESTA. Roman goddess of the hearth. See: Harper. Vesta, Vestal, Vestal virgins, Vestalia.

Vesta (Vesta, the goddess): Generic Word (wax match). See: Hargrave; Partridge; Webster's 3d.

Vestal (Vesta): Generic Word (chaste). See: Charnock, Partridge; Webster's 3d.

Vestal virgins (Vesta): Mythology. See: Mathews, S.; Partridge; Webster's 3d.

Vestalia (Vesta): Mythology. See: Canney.

Vestorian blue (Vestorius): Chemistry. See: Thrush; Webster's 3d.

VESTORIUS. fl. 44 B.C. Roman banker. See: Dict. Grk. Rom. Biog. Myth. Vestorian blue.

VESZELY, A. fl. 19th c. Hungarian mining engineer. Cited in: Hintze vol. 1, p. 4. vol. 2, p. 981. Veszelyite.

Veszelyite (Veszely, A.): Earth Sciences. See: Thrush; Webster's 3d.

VETTERLI, FRIEDRICH. 1822-1882. Swiss engineer. See: Dict. Hist. Biog. de la Suisse. Vetterli rifle.

Vetterli rifle (Vetterli, Friedrich): Weapons. See: Quick.

Vezin's sampler (Derivation undetermined): Engineering and Industry. See: Thrush.

VIATOR, SAINT. 360?-390. French confessor and lector of Lyons Cathedral. See: Holweck. Clerks of Saint Viator.

Vicar of Bray (Bray, Vicar of): Generic Word (opportunist). See: Webster's 3d.

Vicar of Jesus Christ (Jesus Christ): Religion. See: Attwater.

Vicario test (Derivation undetermined): Chemistry. See: Van Nostrand Chem. Dict.

VICAT, LOUIS JOSEPH. 1786-1861. French engineer. See: Michaud. Vicat needle.

Vicat needle (Vicat, Louis Joseph): Engineering and Industry. See: Stedman; Thrush.

VICKERS, EDWARD. 1804-1897. English steel manufacturer. See: Webster's Biog. Dict. Vickers gun, Vickers hardness number, Vickers hardness test (or tester), Vickers-Maxim gun.

Vickers gun (Vickers, Edward). See: Maxim gun (or machine gun).

Vickers hardness number (Vickers, Edward): Engineering and Industry. See: Dresner; Van Nostrand Sci. Encyc.

Vickers hardness test (or tester) (Vickers, Edward): Engineering and Industry. See: Thrush; Van Nostrand Sci. Encyc.; Webster's 3d.

Vickers-Maxim gun (Vickers, Edward and Maxim, Sir Hiram Stevens). See: Maxim gun (or machine gun).

VICQ D'AZYR, FELIX. 1748-1894. French anatomist. See: Nouv. Biog. Univ. Vicq-d'Azyr's band (or line), Vicq d'Azyr's bundle, Vicq d'Azyr's caecum foramen, Vicq d'Azyr's centrum.

Vicq-d'Azyr's band (or line) (Vicq d'Azyr, Felix): Anatomy. See: Donath; Gray.

Vicq d'Azyr's bundle (Vicq d'Azyr, Felix): Antomy. See: Donath; Stedman.

Vicq d' Azyr's caecum foramen (Vicq d'Azyr, Felix): Anatomy. See: Donath; Stedman.

Vicq d'Azyr's centrum (Vicq d'Azyr, Felix): Anatomy. See: Donath; Stedman.

Victor Meyer method for vapor pressure (Meyer, Victor): Chemistry. See: Internat. Dict. Phys. Elec.

Victor Meyer synthesis (Meyer, Victor): Chemistry. See: Van Nostrand Chem. Dict.

Victoria blight (Victoria, Queen): Botany. See: Webster's 3d.

Victoria blue dyes (Victoria, Queen): Chemistry. See: Stedman; Webster's 3d.

Victoria cage (Victoria, Queen): Fashion. See: Picken.

Victoria (carriage) (Victoria, Queen): Generic Word. See: Partridge; Phyfe; Webster's 3d.

Victoria Cross (Victoria, Queen): Military Science. See: Brewer; Steinberg; Weekley.

Victoria Day (Victoria, Queen): Generic Word. See: Hendrickson; Webster's 3d.

Victoria green (Victoria, Queen): Chemistry. See: Thrush; Webster's 3d.

Victoria lawn (Victoria, Queen): Fashion. See: Picken.

Victoria orange (Victoria, Queen): Chemistry. See: Stedman.

Victoria (plant) (Victoria, Queen): Botany. See: Taylor, N.; Webster's 3d.

Victoria plum (Victoria, Queen): Botany. See: Partridge.

VICTORIA, QUEEN (In full: ALEXANDRINA VICTORIA). 1819-1901. Queen of England and Ireland and Empress of India. See: Dict. Nat. Biog. Royal Order of Victoria and Albert, Victora blight, Victoria blue dyes, Victoria cage, Victoria (carriage), Victoria Cross, Victoria Day, Victoria green, Victoria lawn, Victoria orange, Victoria (plant), Victoria plum, Victoria red, Victoria regia water lily, Victoria violet dyes, Victorian (or Victorianism), Victorine.

Victoria red (Victoria, Queen): Chemistry. See: Webster's 3d.

Victoria regia water lily (Victoria, Queen): Botany. See: Phyfe; Van Nostrand Sci. Encyc. under "Water lilies", Webster's 3d.

Victoria violet dyes (Victoria, Queen): Chemistry. See: Webster's 3d.

Victorian (or Victorianism) (Victoria, Queen): Generic Word. See: Barnet; Harvey; Partridge.

Victorine (Victoria, Queen): Fashion. See: Partridge.

VIDAL DE CASSIS, AUGUSTE THEODORE. 1803-1856. French surgeon. See: Biog. Lex. hervorr. Aerzte. Vidal's operation.

VIDAL, EMILE (In full: JEAN BAPTISTE EMILE). 1825-1893. French dermatologist. See: Biog. Lex. hervorr. Aerzte. Vidal's disease.

Vidal's disease (Vidal, Emile). See: Brocq's disease (1).

Vidal's operation (Vidal de Cassis, Auguste Theodore): Medicine. See: Dorland; Stedman.

Vidian artery (Vidius): Anatomy. See: Donath; Stedman; Webster's 3d.

Vidian canal (Vidius): Anatomy. See: Donath; Stedman; Webster's 3d. Also known as: Guidi's canal.

Vidian nerve (Vidius): Anatomy. See: Donath; Stedman; Webster's 3d.

Vidian vein (Vidius): Anatomy. See: Donath; Stedman.

Vidie barometer (Vidie, Lucien): Engineering and Industry. See: Auger.

VIDIE, LUCIEN. 1805-1866. French scientist. See: Webster's Biog. Dict. Vidie barometer.

VIDIUS (GUIDO GUIDI). 1500?-1569. Italian anatomist in France. See: Nouv. Biog. Univ. Vidian artery, Vidian canal, Vidian nerve, Vidian vein.

VIEHOVER, ARNO. fl. 1916. American pharmaceutical chemist. See: Amer. J. Pharm. vol. XCV (1923), pp. 761-63. Viehover test.

Viehover test (Viehover, Arno): Chemistry. See: Van Nostrand Sci. Encyc.

VIEL, E. fl. 1923. French chemist. Cited in: Chem. Abstr., vol. 17, p. 3518. Caille-Viel solution.

VIEL, GUY. fl. 20th c. French phytopharmacologist. See: Who's Who Sci. Europe, 1972. Viel reagent?

Viel reagent (Viel, Guy?): Chemistry. See: Van Nostrand Chem. Dict.

Vielle-Montagne furnace (Derivation undetermined): Engineering and Industry. See: Thrush.

VIERENDEEL, ARTHUR. b. 1852. Belgian engineer. See: Seyn. Vierendeel truss (or girder).

Vierendeel truss (or girder) (Vierendeel, Arthur): Engineering and Industry. See: Internat. Dict. Ap. Math.; Van Nostrand Sci. Encyc.; Webster's 3d.

VIERORDT, KARL VON. 1818-1884. German physiologist. See: Allg. Deut. Biog. Vierordt's hemotachometer, Vierordt's law.

Vierordt's hemotachometer (Vierordt, Karl von): Medicine. See: Dorland.

Vierordt's law (Vierordt, Karl von): Physiology. See: Drever; English; Wolman.

VIETH, GERHARD ULRICH ANTON. 1763-1836. German mathematician. See: Pogg., vol. 2. Vieth-Mueller circle?, Vieth-Mueller torus?

Vieth-Mueller circle (Vieth, Gerhard Ulrich Anton? and Mueller, Johannes Peter): Mathematics. See: Chaplin; Internat. Dict. Ap. Math. Also known as: horopter circle of Johannes Mueller.

Vieth-Mueller torus (Vieth, Gerhard Ulrich Anton? and Meuller, Johannes Peter): Mathematics. See: Internat. Dict. Ap. Math.

VIETH, PAUL. d. 1918. German chemist. See: Milchwirtschaftliche Forschung. vol. I (1924) Origin., pp. 232-44. Vieth's ratio.

Vieth's ratio (Vieth, Paul): Chemistry. See: Hackh; Winburne.

VIETORIS, LEOPOLD. b. 1891. Austrian mathematician. See: Pogg., vol. 6. Mayer-Vietoris sequence.

Vieussens' ansa (or loop) (Vieussens, Raymond de): Anatomy. See: Donath; Dorland; Stedman.

Vieussens' centrum (Vieussens, Raymond de): Anatomy. See: Stedman.

Vieussens' ganglion (Vieussens, Raymond de): Anatomy. See: Stedman.

Vieussens' limbus (isthmus, ring, or anulus) (Vieussens, Raymond de): Anatomy. See: Donath; Stedman.

VIEUSSENS, RAYMOND DE. 1641-1715. French anatomist. See: World Who's Who Sci. Vieussens' ansa (or loop), Vieussens' centrum, Vieussens' ganglion, Vieussens' limbus (isthmus, ring, or anulus), Vieussens' scyphus, Vieussens' valve, Vieussens' veins, Vieussens' ventricle.

Vieussens' scyphus (Vieussens, Raymond de): Anatomy. See: Donath.

Vieussens' valve (Vieussens, Raymond de): Anatomy. See: Dorland; Henderson; Stedman; Webster's 3d.

Vieussens' veins (Vieussens, Raymond de): Anatomy. See: Donath; Stedman.

Vieussens' ventricle (Vieussens, Raymond de): Anatomy. See: Stedman.

VIGANI, JOHN FRANCIS. 1650?-1712. Italian-born English chemist. See: Dict. Nat. Biog. Vigani's elixir.

Vigani's elixir (Vigani, John Francis): Chemistry. See: Charnock.

Vigenere cipher (De Vigenere, Blaise): Linguistics. See: Webster's 3d.

Vigenere tableau (or square) (De Vigenere, Blaise): Linguistics. See: Webster's 3d.

Vigna (Vigna, Domenico): Botany. See: Webster's 3d.

VIGNA, DOMENICO. d. 1647. Italian botanist. (Biography source unavailable.) Vigna.

VIGNAL, GUILLAUME. 1852-1893. French physiologist. See: Paris, Soc. Biol. Mem. vol. XL (1894), pp. 845-55. Vignal's cells.

Vignal's cells (Vignal, Guillaume): Medicine. See: Dorland.

VIGNOLES, CHARLES BLACKER. 1793-1875. English engineer. See: World Who's Who Sci. Vignoles rail.

Vignoles rail (Vignoles, Charles Blacker): Engineering and Industry. See: Webster's 3d.

VIGNON, LEO. 1850-1923. French chemist. See: Pogg., vols. 4, 5, 6. Vignon test.

Vignon test (Vignon, Leo): Chemistry. See: Van Nostrand Chem. Dict.

VIGORS, NICHOLAS AYLWARD. 1785-1840. Irish zoologist. See: Dict. Nat. Biog. Vigors' vireo (or warbler), Vigors' wren.

Vigors' vireo (or warbler) (Vigors, Nicholas Aylward): Zoology. See: Mathews, M.M.

Vigors' wren (Vigors, Nicholas Aylward): Zoology. See: Mathews, M.M.

Vigotsky, Lev Semionovitch. See: Vygotsky, Lev Semionovitch.

VIGOUROUX, AUGUSTE. fl. 1858. French neurologist. (Biography source unavailable.) Vigouroux's sign?

Vigouroux's sign (Vigouroux, Auguste?): Medicine. See: Dorland. Also known as: Charcot-Vigouroux sign.

Vigreux column (Vigreux, Leon): Engineering and Industry. See: Webster's 3d.

VIGREUX, LEON. d. 1891. French hydraulic engineer. See: Genie Civil vol 20 (1891-92), p. 82. Vigreux column.

VIK, KNUT. b. 1885. Norwegian engineer. See: Hvem er Hvem?, 1934. Knut-Vik square?

Vilanova-Canadell syndrome (Vilanova, Xavier and Canadell-Vidal, Jose Maria): Medicine. See: Jablonski.

Vilanova-Pinol Aguade syndrome (Vilanova, Xavier and Pinol Aguade, Joaquin): Medicine. See: Jablonski.

VILANOVA, XAVIER. fl. 1949. Spanish dermatologist. (Biography source unavailable.) Vilanova-Canadell syndrome, Vilanova-Pinol Aguade syndrome.

Vilella etch for aluminum (Vilella, J. R.): Chemistry. See: Van Nostrand Chem. Dict.

Vilella etch for lead (Vilella, J. R.): Chemistry. See: Van Nostrand Chem. Dict.

VILELLA, J. R. fl. 1926. American chemist. (Biography source unavailable.) Vilella etch for aluminum, Vilella etch for lead, Vilella's reagent.

Vilella's reagent (Vilella, J. R.): Chemistry. See: Thrush.

VILGERDARSON, FLOKI. fl. 9th c. Viking. Cited in: Hintze, suppl. I, p. 175. Flokite.

VILLA, FRANCISCO "PANCHO" (Real name: Doroteo Arango). 1877-1923. Mexican bandit and revolutionary leader. See: Encyc. Brit., 1973. Villa's raid.

Villard circuit (Villard, Paul-Ulrich): Engineering and Industry. See: Thewlis.

Villard effect (Villard, Paul-Ulrich): Physics. See: Van Nostrand Sci. Encyc.

VILLARD, EUGENE. b. 1868. French surgeon. See: Biog. Lex hervorr. Aerzte. Villard's button.

VILLARD, PAUL-ULRICH. 1860-1934. French physicist. See: World Who's Who Sci. Villard circuit, Villard effect, Villard's valve.

Villard's button (Villard, Eugene): Medicine. See: Dorland; Stedman.

Villard's valve (Villard, Paul-Ulrich): Physics. Cited in: World Who's Who Sci.

VILLARET, MAURICE. 1877-1946. French neurologist. See: Biog. Lex. hervorr. Aerzte. Villaret's syndrome.

Villaret's syndrome (Villaret, Maurice): Medicine. See: Dorland; Jablonski.

Villari effect (Villari, Emilio): Engineering and Industry. See: Ballentyne; Thewlis; Van Nostrand Sci. Encyc. under "Magneto-Striction."

VILLARI, EMILIO. 1836-1904. Italian physicist. See: Pogg., vol. 3,4,5. Villari effect.

VILLARS, DOMINIC. 1745-1814. French botanist. See: World Who's Who Sci. Villarsia.

Villarsia (Villars, Dominic): Botany. See: Dorland.

Villa's raid (Villa, Francisco "Pancho"): History. See: Smith.

Villavecchia reagent (or test) (Villavecchia, V.): Chemistry. See: Hackh; Van Nostrand Chem. Dict.

VILLAVECCHIA, V. fl. 1912. Italian chemist. (Biography source unavailable.) Villavecchia reagent (or test).

Villebois hand-press (Villebois, L. de): Printing. See: Lockwood.

VILLEBOIS, L. DE. fl. 1829. French royal printer. (Biography source unavailable.) Villebois hand-press.

VILLEMIN, JEAN ANTOINE. 1827-1892. French surgeon. See: World Who's Who Sci. Villemin's theory.

Villemin's theory (Villemin, Jean Antoine): Medicine. See: Dorland.

VILLIAUME. fl. 20th c. French explorer in Africa. Cited in: Min. Mag. vol. 15, no. 72 (1908-1910), p. 433. Villiaumite.

Villiaumite (Villiaume): Earth Sciences. See: Thrush; Webster's 3d.

VILLIERS, A. fl. 1911. French? chemist. (Biography source unavailable.) Villiers-Fayolle reagent for free chlorine.

Villiers-Fayolle reagent for free chlorine (Villiers, A. and Fayolle, M.): Chemistry. See: Van Nostrand Chem. Dict.

VILLIERS, GEORGE WILLIAM FREDERICK (4TH EARL OF CLARENDON). 1800-1870. English statesman and diplomat. See: Dict. Nat. Biog. Clarendon Note, Dallas-Clarendon Treaty.

VILLIGER, VIKTOR. fl. 1900-1910. German chemist. Cited in: Chem. Abstr., Decenn. Index, 1907-1916. Baeyer-Villiger reaction, Baeyer-Villiger test reaction for acetone.

VILTER, S. P. fl. 1938. American chemist. Cited in: Chem. Abstr., vol. 33, p. 5426^8. Vilter-Spies-Mathews test reaction.

Vilter-Spies-Mathews test reaction (Vilter, S. P.; Spies, Tom and Mathews, Albert Prescott): Chemistry. See: Van Nostrand Chem. Dict.

Vim-Silverman needle (Vim and Silverman, Irving). See: Silverman needle.

VINCENT DE PAUL, SAINT. 1576-1660. French priest. See: Encyc. Brit., 1911. Saint Vincent de Paul Society, Sisters of Saint Vincent, Vincentians.

VINCENT, JEAN HYACINTHE. 1862-1950. French bacteriologist. See: World Who's Who Sci. Vincent's angina, Vincent's bacillus, Vincent's infection (disease or stomatitis), Vincent's spirillum, Vincent's tonsilitis, Vincent's white mycetoma.

Vincent learning curve (Vincent, Stella Burnham?): Psychology. See: Chaplin; English; Wolman.

VINCENT OF LERINS, SAINT. d. ca. 450? French priest and theologian. See: Encyc. Brit., 1911. Vincentian Canon.

VINCENT, STELLA BURNHAM. b. 1862. American psychologist. See: Amer. Men Sci., 5th ed. Vincent learning curve?

Vincent test reaction for alpha-and beta-naphthol (Derivation undetermined): Chemistry. See: Van Nostrand Chem. Dict.

Vincentian Canon (Vincent of Lerins, Saint): Religion. See: Attwater.

Vincentians (Vincent de Paul, Saint): Religion. See: Attwater; Brewer; Webster's 3d. Also known as: Lazarists.

Vincent's angina (Vincent, Jean Hyacinthe): Medicine. See: Jablonski; Webster's 3d.

Vincent's bacillus (Vincent, Jean Hyacinthe): Medicine. See: Dorland; Stedman. Also known as: Plaut's bacillus.

Vincent's infection (disease or stomatitis) (Vincent, Jean Hyacinthe): Medicine. See: Jablonski; Stedman; Webster's 3d. Also known as: Plaut-Vincent stomatitis, Plaut's ulcer.

Vincent's spirillum (Vincent, Jean Hyacinthe): Medicine. See: Stedman.

Vincent's tonsillitis (Vincent, Jean Hyacinthe): Medicine. See: Stedman.

Vincent's white mycetoma (Vincent, Jean Hyacinthe): Medicine. See: Stedman.

VINEBERG, ARTHUR. 1903- . Canadian heart surgeon. See: Canadian Who's Who, 1964-1966. Vineberg procedure (or operation).

Vineberg procedure (or operation) (Vineberg, Arthur): Medicine. See: Stedman.

VINER, CHARLES. 1678-1756. English jurist and author. See: Dict. Nat. Biog. Vinerian professorship.

Vinerian professorship (Viner, Charles): Law. See: Harvey; Wagner (More Names).

VINOT, ROBERT. fl. early 17th c. French gourmet. (Biography source unavailable.) sauce Robert.

VINSON, CARL. b. 1883. American legislator. See: Biog. Direct. Amer. Congress. Vinson Naval Act, Vinson-Trammell Naval Parity Act.

VINSON, FREDERICK MOORE. 1890-1953. American legislator. See: Biog. Direct. Amer. Congress. Guffey-Vinson Act (or bituminous coal Act).

Vinson Naval Act (Vinson, Carl): Politics. See: Morris.

VINSON, PORTER PAISLEY. 1890-1959. American surgeon. See: World Who's Who Sci. Plummer-Vinson syndrome.

Vinson-Trammell Naval Parity Act (Vinson, Carl and Trammell, Park): Politics. See: Morris.

VINTILESCU, J. fl. 1915. Rumanian pharmaceutical chemist. Cited in: Chem. Abstr. vol. 10, p. 646. Vintilescu-Popescu test.

Vintilescu-Popescu test (Vintelescu, J. and Popescu, Alin): Chemistry. See: Van Nostrand Chem. Dict.

Violle (Violle, Jules): Physics. See: Dresner; Webster's 3d.

VIOLLE, JULES (In full: LOUIS JULES GABRIEL). 1841-1923. French physicist. See: World Who's Who Sci. Violle.

Vipond's sign (Derivation undetermined): Medicine. See: Stedman.

Virchow-Hassall bodies (Virchow, Rudolf and Hassall, Arthur Hill). See: Hassall's (or Hassal's) corpuscles (concentric corpuscles, bodies or corpuscle(s) of Hassall).

Virchow-Holder angle (Virchow, Rudolf and Hoelder, Hermann Friedrich?). See: Virchow's angle.

Virchow-Robin spaces (Virchow, Rudolf Ludwig Karl and Robin, Charles P.): Anatomy. See: Donath; Stedman.

VIRCHOW, RUDOLF LUDWIG KARL. 1821-1902. German pathologist and politician. See: World Who's Who Sci. Virchow-Hassall bodies, Virchow-Robin spaces, Virchow-Seckel dwarfism, Virchow's angle, Virchow's cells (or corpuscles), Virchow's crystals, Virchow's disease, Virchow's granulations, Virchow's law, Virchow's node, Virchow's psammoma.

Virchow-Seckel dwarfism (Virchow, Rudolf and Seckel, Helmuth Paul Georg). See: Seckel's syndrome.

Virchow-Troisier node (Virchow, Rudolf and Troisier, Emile). See: Virchow's node.

Virchow's angle (Virchow, Rudolf Ludwig Karl): Anatomy. See: Dorland; Stedman. Also known as: Virchow-Holder angle.

Virchow's cells (or corpuscles) (Virchow, Rudolf Ludwig Karl): Anatomy. See: Stedman. Also known as: Toynbee's corpuscles.

Virchow's crystals (Virchow, Rudolf Ludwig Karl): Medicine. See: Stedman.

Virchow's disease (Virchow, Rudolf Ludwig Karl): Medicine. See: Dorland; Stedman.

Virchow's granulations (Virchow, Rudolf Ludwig Karl): Medicine. See: Stedman.

Virchow's law (Virchow, Rudolf Ludwig Karl): Medicine. See: Stedman.

Virchow's node (Virchow, Rudolf Ludwig Karl): Medicine. See: Stedman. Also known as: Virchow-Troisier node, Troisier's node, Troisier's ganglion.

Virchow's psammoma (Virchow, Rudolf Ludwig Karl): Medicine. See: Stedman.

VIRGIL (PUBLIUS VERGILIUS MARO). 70-19 B.C. Roman poet. See: Oxford Clas. Dict. Virgilia, Virgilian.

VIRGIL, ALMON KINCAID. b. 1842. American music teacher. See: Who Was Who Amer. Virgil practice clavier.

Virgil practice clavier (Virgil, Almon Kincaid): Music. See: Scholes.

Virgilia (Virgil): Botany. See: Charnock; Mathews, M. M.; Webster's 3d.

Virgilian (Virgil): Literature. See: Partridge; Webster's 3d. Weekley.

Virgin Mary's Bodyguard (Maria Theresa): History. See: Brewer; Wagner (More Names).

Virgin Mary's honeysuckle (Mary, Virgin-Mother): Botany. See: Encyc. Brit., 1973 under "Honeysuckle."

Virginal (Mary, Virgin-Mother): Religion. See: Webster's 3d.

Virginia's warbler (Anderson, Virginia): Zoology. Cited in: Gray; Mathews, M. M.

virtual parabolas of St. Vincent (De Saint-Vincent, Gregoire): Mathematics. Cited in: World Who's Who Sci.

VISHNIAC, WOLF. 1922- . German-born American microbiologist. See: World Who's Who Sci. Wolf trap.

VISHNU. Hindu deity. See: Funk & Wagnalls. Vishnuism.

Vishnuism (Vishnu): Religion. See: Weekley.

VISME. fl. 18th c. Portuguese botanist. (Biography source unavailable.) Vismia.

Vismia (Visme): Botany. See: Webster's 3d.

VISSAC GUSTAVE ANDRE. fl. 1935. French engineer. Cited in: Chem. Abstr., Decenn. Index, 1927-1936. McNally-Vissac dryer, Vissac jig.

Vissac jig (Vissac, Gustave Andre): Engineering and Industry. See: Thrush.

VITALI. fl. 1887. Italian engineer. (Biography source unavailable.) Vetterli-Vitali rifle.

Vitali covering (Vitali, Giuseppe): Mathematics. See: James.

VITALI, DIOSCORIDE. 1832-1917. Italian physician and chemist. See: Biog. Lex. hervorr. Aerzte. Vitali test for differentiating atropine and strychnine, Vitali test for ethyl alcohol, Vitali test for morphine and codeine, Vitali test reaction for bromide, Vitali test reaction for formaldehyde, Vitali test reaction for iodoform, Vitali test reaction for phenol, Vitali test reaction for quinine, Vitali test reactions for acetanilid, Vitali test reactions for atropine and daturine, Vitali tests for alkaloids, Vitali's test for bile in the urine, Vitali's test for pus in the urine.

VITALI, GIUSEPPE. 1875-1932. Italian mathematician. See: Pogg., vol. 5,6. Vitali covering, Vitali set.

Vitali set (Vitali, Giuseppe): Mathematics. See: James.

Vitali test for differentiating atropine and strychnine (Vitali, Dioscoride): Chemistry. See: Van Nostrand Chem. Dict.

Vitali test for ethyl alcohol (Vitali, Dioscoride): Chemistry. See: Van Nostrand Chem. Dict.

Vitali test for morphine and codeine (Vitali, Dioscoride): Chemistry. See: Van Nostrand Chem. Dict.

Vitali test reaction for bromide (Vitali, Dioscoride): Chemistry. See: Van Nostrand Chem. Dict.

Vitali test reaction for formaldehyde (Vitali, Dioscoride): Chemistry. See: Van Nostrand Chem. Dict.

Vitali test reaction for iodoform (Vitali, Dioscoride): Chemistry. See: Van Nostrand Chem. Dict.

Vitali test reaction for phenol (Vitali, Dioscoride): Chemistry. See: Van Nostrand Chem. Dict.

Vitali test reaction for quinine (Vitali, Dioscoride): Chemistry. See: Van Nostrand Chem. Dict.

Vitali test reactions for acetanilid (Vitali, Dioscoride): Chemistry. See: Van Nostrand Chem. Dict.

Vitali test reactions for atropine and daturine (Vitali, Dioscoride): Chemistry. See: Van Nostrand Chem. Dict.

Vitali tests for alkaloids (Vitali, Dioscoride): Chemistry. See: Van Nostrand Chem. Dict.

Vitalians (Vitalis of Meletius): Religion. See: Canney.

VITALIS OF MELETIUS. fl. 4th c. Apollinarian bishop. See: Hastings (Encyc. Rel. Ethics) under "Apollinarism," vol. 1, pp. 606-607. Vitalians.

Vitali's test for bile in the urine (Vitali, Dioscoride): Chemistry. See: Stedman.

Vitali's test for pus in the urine (Vitali, Dioscoride): Chemistry. See: Stedman.

Vitruvian scroll (Vitruvius): Architecture. See: Partridge.

VITRUVIUS (MARCUS VITRUVIUS POLLIO). fl. 1st c. B.C. Roman architect and engineer. See: Encyc. Brit., 1973. Vitruvian scroll.

ITTADINI, CARLO. d. 1865. Italian physician and botanist. See: Milani, t. Lomb. Rendiconti, vol. IV (1867), pp. 40–67. Vittadinia.

ittadinia (Vittadini, Carlo): Botany. See: Taylor, N.

ITTE, G. fl. 1930–1972. French pharmacodynamist. See: Who's Who Sci. urope, 1972. Vitte microchemical test for barbital and phenobarbital in brain ssue.

itte microchemical test for barbital and phenobarbital in brain tissue (Vitte, .): Chemistry. See: Van Nostrand Chem. Dict.

ITUS, SAINT. fl. late 3d c. Christian child martyr under Diocletian or egendary person. See: Holweck. Saint Vitus's dance.

IVEN. No dates. French engineer. (Biography source unavailable.) .B. rifle grenade.

IVIAN, J. G. fl. 1817. English mineralogist. Cited in: Dana, p. 558. ivianite.

ivianite (Vivian, J. G.): Earth Sciences. See: Thrush; Van Nostrand Sci. ncyc.; Webster's 3d.

ladimiroff, Alexander Alex. See: Wladimiroff, Alexander Alex.

ladimiroff–Mikulicz amputation (or operation) (Wladimiroff, Alexander Alex nd Mikulicz–Radecki, Johann von). See: Mikulicz–Vladimiroff amputation or operation).

LASOV, ALEXKSEJ KONSTANTINOVIC. 1868–1922. Russian mathematician. ee: Matematika v. SSSR 1917–1957, vol. 2, 1959. Boltzmann–Vlasov equations.

LASOV, KUZMA ALEKSEIVICH. 1905– . Russian geochemist. See: World Who's Who Sci. Vlasovite.

lasovite (Vlasov, Kuzma Alekseivich): Earth Sciences. See: Thrush.

leck, John Hasbrouck van. See: Van Vleck, John Hasbrouck.

LEMINCKX, JEAN FRANCOIS. 1800–1876. Belgian physician. See: Biog. ex. hervorr. Aerzte. Vleminckx's solution (or lotion).

leminckx's solution (or lotion) (Vleminckx, Jean Francois): Medicine. See: orland; Stedman; Webster's 3d.

oconian law (Saxa, Q. Voconius): Law. See: Charnock.

OEGTLIN, CARL. b. 1879. Swiss-born American pharmacologist. See: World Who's Who Sci. Voegtlin unit.

oegtlin unit (Voegtlin, Carl): Medicine. See: Dorland.

OERNER, HANS. d. 1938. German dermatologist. See: Deutsch. Dermatologenkal., 1929. Steiner–Voerner syndrome, Voerner's heloderma.

oerner's heloderma (Voerner, Hans): Medicine. See: Jablonski.

OET, GISBERT. 1589–1676. Dutch Calvanist theologian. See: Encyc. Brit., 1911. Voetian.

oetian (Voet, Gisbert): Religion. See: Webster's 3d.

OGE, C. I. B. No dates. English physician. (Biography source unavailable.) oge's test.

ogel–Colson–Russell effect (Vogel, Hermann Wilhelm; Colson, Rene; and Russell, William James). See: Russell effect.

VOGEL, HERMANN WILHELM. 1834–1898. German photochemist. See: World Who's Who Sci. Vogel–Colson–Russell effect, Vogel–Obernetter silver eosin plate.

OGEL, J. F. fl. 1853. German mineralogist. Cited in: Hintze I. 3,1, 3508; I 3,2, 4444. Voglianite, Voglite.

OGEL, MABEL. fl. 1932. American educator. (Biography source unavailable.) Washburne–Vogel readability formula.

Vogel micro-test for spoiled flour (Derivation undetermined): Chemistry. See: Van Nostrand Chem. Dict.

ogel–Obernetter silver eosin plate (Vogel, Hermann Wilhelm and Obernetter, Johann Baptist): Photography. See: Focal Encyc. Photog.

OGEL, RUDOLF. b. 1882. German physical chemist. See: Pogg., vols. 5, 6. Vogel's red?

OGEL, RUDOLPH AUGUSTUS. 1724–1774. German physical chemist. See: Allg. Deut. Biog. Vogel test for alcohol in chloroform?

Vogel test for alcohol in chloroform (Vogel, Rudolph Augustus?): Chemistry. See: Van Nostrand Chem. Dict.

Vogel test for nitrate in water (Derivation undetermined): Chemistry. See: Van Nostrand Chem. Dict.

Vogel test reaction for narceine (Derivation undetermined): Chemistry. See: Van Nostrand Chem. Dict.

Vogel's red (Vogel, Rudolf?): Engineering and Industry. See: Thrush.

VOGES, OTTO (In full: DANIEL WILHELM OTTO). b. 1867. German physician. (Biography source unavailable.) Voges–Proskauer reaction (or test).

Voges–Proskauer reaction (or test) (Voges, Otto and Proskauer, Bernard): Medicine. See: Dorland; Stedman; Webster's 3d.

Voge's test (Voge, C. I. B.): Medicine. See: Dorland.

VOGET, ALBERT RULEMANN LUDWIG. fl. 1836–49. French? pharmacist and editor. (Biography source unavailable.) Voget test reactions?

Voget test reactions (Voget, Albert Rulemann Ludwig?): Chemistry. See: Van Nostrand Chem. Dict.

Voglianite (Vogel, J.F.): Earth Sciences. See: Thrush.

Voglite (Vogel, J.F.): Earth Sciences. See: Thrush; Webster's 3d.

VOGT, ALFRED. 1879–1943. Swiss ophthalmologist. See: Biog. Lex. hervorr. Aerzte. Vogt–Koyanagi syndrome, Vogt's cataract, Vogt's cornea, Vogt's degeneration, Vogt's disease, Vogt's syndrome.

VOGT, CECILE. 1875–1962. German neurologist. See: Kuerschner's Deut. Gel. Kal., 1961. Vogt's syndrome.

Vogt–Hueter point (Vogt, Paul Frederick Emmanuel and Hueter, Karl): Medicine. See: Dorland; Stedman. Also known as: Vogt's point.

VOGT, KARL. 1817–1895. German physiologist and naturalist. See: Encyc. Brit., 1911. Vogt's angle.

Vogt–Koyanagi syndrome (Vogt, Alfred and Koyanagi, Yoshizo): Medicine. See: Jablonski; Stedman.

VOGT, OSKAR. 1870–1959. German neurologist. See: World Who's Who Sci. Spielmeyer–Vogt disease, Stock–Spielmeyer–Vogt syndrome.

VOGT, PAUL FREDERICK EMMANUEL. 1844–1885. German surgeon. See: Allg. Deut. Biog. Vogt–Hueter point.

VOGT, W. fl. 1911. German chemist. Cited in: Chem. Abstr., vol. 5, p. 1913. Fries–Vogt test reaction.

Vogt's angle (Vogt, Karl): Medicine. See: Dorland; Stedman.

Vogt's cataract (Vogt, Alfred): Medicine. See: Jablonski.

Vogt's cornea (Vogt, Alfred): Medicine. See: Jablonski.

Vogt's degeneration (Vogt, Alfred): Medicine. See: Jablonski.

Vogt's disease (Vogt, Alfred): Medicine. See: Jablonski.

Vogt's point (Vogt, Paul Frederick Emmanuel). See: Vogt–Hueter point.

Vogt's syndrome (Vogt, Alfred). See: Waardenburg's syndrome.

Vogt's syndrome (Vogt, Cecile): Medicine. See: Dorland; Jablonski; Stedman.

VOHWINKEL, KARL HERMANN. fl. 1929. German dermatologist. See: Derm.-Verseich. Vohwinkel's syndrome.

Vohwinkel's syndrome (Vohwinkel, Karl Hermann): Medicine. See: Jablonski.

VOIGHT, CHRISTIAN AUGUST. 1809–1890. Austrian anatomist. See: Biog. Lex. hervorr. Aerzte. Voight's lines.

VOIGHT, KARL. fl. 1886. German chemist. (Biography source unavailable.) Voigt reaction.

Voightlaender camera (Voightlaender, Peter Wilhelm Friedrich): Photography. See: Focal Encyc. Photog. under "Camera History."

Voightlaender heliar lens (Voightlaender, Peter Wilhelm Friedrich): Photography. See: Focal Encyc. Photog. under "Lens History."

Voightlaender medals (Voightlaender, Peter Wilhelm Friedrich): Photography. See: Focal Encyc. Photog. under "Awards (Austria)."

VOIGHTLAENDER, PETER WILHELM FRIEDRICH. 1812–1878. Austrian optical manufacturer. See: Allg. Deut. Biog. Petzval–Voightlaender lens, Voightlaender camera, Voightlaender heliar lens, Voightlaender medals.

Voight's lines (Voight, Christian August): Anatomy. See: Dorland.

Voigt effect (Voigt, Woldemar): Physics. See: Ballentyne; Thewlis; Van Nostrand Sci. Encyc.

Voigt notation (Voigt, Woldemar): Physics. See: Hughes; Internat. Dict. Phys. Elec.

Voigt reaction (Voight, Karl): Chemistry. See: Van Nostrand Chem. Dict.

VOIGT, WOLDEMAR. 1850-1919. German physicist. See: World Who's Who Sci. Voigt effect, Voigt notation.

VOILLEMIER, LEON CLEMONT. 1809-1878. French urologist. See: Biog. Lex. hervorr. Aerzte. Voillemier's point.

Voillemier's point (Voillemier, Leon Clemont): Medicine. See: Dorland; Stedman.

VOISENET, E. fl. 1910. French chemist. (Biography source unavailable.) Voisenet test reaction.

Voisenet test reaction (Voisenet, E.): Chemistry. See: Van Nostrand Chem. Dict.

VOIT, KARL VON. 1831-1908. German physiologist. See: Encyc. Brit., 1973. Voit's nerve, Voit's nucleus.

Voit's nerve (Voit, Karl von): Medicine. See: Stedman.

Voit's nucleus (Voit, Karl von): Medicine. See: Dorland; Stedman.

VOLAVSEK, W. fl. 1941. Austrian dermatologist. (Biography source unavailable.) Volavsek's syndrome.

Volavsek's syndrome (Volavsek, W.): Medicine. See: Jablonski.

VOLBORTH, ALEXANDER VON. d. 1876. Russian paleontologist. Cited in: Dana, pp. 611-612. Volborthite.

Volborthite (Volborth, Alexander von): Earth Sciences. See: Thrush; Webster's 3d.

Volcanism (Vulcan, the god). See: Vulcanism.

Volcano (Vulcan): Earth Sciences. See: Moore; Van Nostrand Sci. Encyc.; Webster's 3d.

VOLCY-BOUCHER. fl. 1910. French chemist. Cited in: Chem. Abstr. vol. 3, p. 228; vol. 4, p. 950. Volcy-Boucher-Girard test, Volcy-Boucher test reaction for alpha and beta naphthol.

Volcy-Boucher-Girard test (Volcy-Boucher, and Girard, J.): Chemistry. See: Van Nostrand Chem. Dict.

Volcy-Boucher test reaction for alpha and beta naphthol (Volcy-Boucher): Chemistry. See: Van Nostrand Chem. Dict.

VOLGER, OTTO (In full: GEORG HEINRICH OTTO). 1822-1897. German geologist. See: Pogg., vol. 2,3. Volgerite?

Volgerite (Volger, Otto?): Earth Sciences. See: Thrush.

Volhard-Erdmann thiophene synthesis (Volhard, Jakob, and Erdmann, Hugo Wilhelm Traugott): Chemistry. See: Van Nostrand Chem. Dict.

VOLHARD, FRANZ. 1872-1950. German physician. See: Biog. Lex. hervorr. Aerzte. Volhard's nephritis, Volhard's test.

VOLHARD, JAKOB. 1834-1910. German chemist. See: World Who's Who Sci. Hell-Volhard-Zelinsky reaction, Volhard-Erdmann thiophene synthesis, Volhard's solution, Volhard's volumetric method (or titration).

Volhard's nephritis (Volhard, Franz): Medicine. See: Jablonski.

Volhard's solution (Volhard, Jakob): Chemistry. See: Dorland; Hackh.

Volhard's test (Volhard, Franz): Medicine. See: Dorland; Stedman.

Volhard's volumetric method (or titration) (Volhard, Jakob): Chemistry. See: Hackh; Webster's 3d.

VOLKMANN, ALFRED WILHELM. 1800-1877. German physiologist. See: World Who's Who Sci. Volkmann's canals.

VOLKMANN, RICHARD VON. 1830-1899. German surgeon. See: Allg. Deut. Biog. Volkmann's cheilitis, Volkmann's contracture, Volkmann's disease (or deformity), Volkmann's ischemic paralysis, Volkmann's splint, Volkmann's spoon, Volkmann's subluxation.

Volkmann's canals (Volkmann, Alfred Wilhelm): Anatomy. See: Donath; Dorland; Stedman.

Volkmann's cheilitis (Volkmann, Richard von). See: Baelz's syndrome.

Volkmann's contracture (Volkmann, Richard von): Medicine. See: Jablonski; Stedman.

Volkmann's disease (or deformity) (Volkmann, Richard von): Medicine. See: Dorland; Jablonski; Stedman.

Volkmann's ischemic paralysis (Volkmann, Richard von): Medicine. See: Jablonski.

Volkmann's splint (Volkmann, Richard von): Medicine. See: Dorland; Stedman.

Volkmann's spoon (Volkmann, Richard von): Medicine. See: Dorland; Stedman.

Volkmann's subluxation (Volkmann, Richard von): Medicine. See: Stedman.

Volkov, Michail Matveeic. See: Wolkow, Michail Matveeic.

Volland test (Volland, Walter?): Chemistry. See: Van Nostrand Chem. Dict.

VOLLAND, WALTER, 1908-1961. German pathologist. See: Kuerschner's Deut. Gel. Kal., 1961. Volland test?

VOLLMER, HERMAN. b. 1896. American pediatrician. (Biography source unavailable.) Vollmer test.

Vollmer test (Vollmer, Herman): Medicine. See: Stedman.

Volmar-Leber reagent (Volmar, Y., and Leber, M.): Chemistry. See: Van Nostrand Chem. Dict.

VOLMAR, Y. fl. 1930's. French chemist. See: Pogg., vol. 6. Volmar-Leber reagent.

Volstead Act (Volstead, Andrew Joseph): Politics. See: Jameson; Matthews, M.M.; Morris.

VOLSTEAD, ANDREW JOSEPH. 1860-1947. American legislator. See: Biog. Direct. Amer. Congress. Capper-Volstead Act, Volstead Act, Volstead-Jones Act, Volsteadian (or Volsteadism).

Volsteadian (or Volsteadism) (Volstead, Andrew Joseph): Generic Word. See: Hendrickson; Webster's 3d.

Volt (Volta, Alessandro): Physics. See: Ballentyne; Dresner; Van Nostrand Sci. Encyc.

Volt-Ampere (Volta, Alessandro and Ampere, Andre Marie): Physics. See: Dresner; Internat. Dict. Phys. Elec.; Van Nostrand Sci. Encyc.

Volt-Ampere reactive (Volta, Alessandro and Ampere, Andre Marie): Physics. See: Dresner; Markus.

Volt-Ohm-milliammeter (Volta, Alessandro and Ohm, Georg Simon): Physics. See: Markus.

VOLTA, ALLESSANDRO (In full: ALESSANDRO GIUSEPPE ANTONIO ANASTASIO). 1745-1827. Italian physicist. See: World Who's Who Sci. Volt, Volt-Ampere, Volt-Ampere reactive, Volt-Ohm-milliammeter, Volta effect, Voltage, Voltaic cell (or pile), Voltaism, Voltaite, Voltameter, Voltmeter, Volta's law, Volta's series.

Volta couple (Volta, Alessandro). See: Voltaic cell (or pile).

Volta effect (Volta, Alessandro): Physics. See: Hackh; Markus; Webster's 3d.

Voltage (Volta, Alessandro): Physics. See: Markus; Van Nostrand Sci. Encyc.

Voltaic cell (or pile) (Volta, Alessandro): Physics. See: Internat. Dict. Phys. Elec.; Markus; Phyfe.

VOLTAIRE (Real name: JEAN FRANCOIS AROUET). 1694-1778. French philosopher, historian, and dramatist. See: Internat. Encyc. Soc. Sci.; Nouv. Biog. Univ. Voltaire chair, Voltairean (or Voltaireanism).

Voltaire chair (Voltaire): Applied Arts. See: Webster's 3d.

Voltairean (or Voltaireanism) (Voltaire): Philosophy. See: Partridge; Webster's 3d.

Voltaism (Volta, Alessandro). See: Galvanism.

Voltaite (Volta, Alessandro): Earth Sciences. See: Thrush; Webster's 3d.

Voltameter (Volta, Alessandro). See: Coulometer.

Volta's law (Volta, Alessandro): Physics. See: Markus.

Volta's series (Volta, Alessandro): Physics. See: Hackh.

Volterra dislocation (Volterra, Vito): Mathematics. See: Ballentyne; Internat. Dict. Phys. Elec.

Volterra integral equations (Volterra, Vito): Mathematics. See: Ballentyne; Internat. Dict. Ap. Math.; Internat. Dict. Phys. Elec.; James.

VOLTERRA, VITO. 1860-1940. Italian physicist and mathematician. See: World Who's Who Sci. Volterra dislocation, Volterra integral equations, Volterra's reciprocal functions, Volterra's solution.

Volterra's reciprocal functions (Volterra, Vito): Mathematics. See: James.

Volterra's solution (Volterra, Vito): Mathematics. See: James.

Voltmeter (Volta, Alessandro): Physics. See: Markus.

VOLTOLINI, FRIEDRICH EDWARD RUDOLPH. 1819-1889. German laryngologist. See: Allg. Deut. Biog.; World Who's Who Sci. Voltolini-Heryng sign, Voltolini's disease.

Voltolini-Heryng sign (Voltolini, Friedrich Edward Rudolph and Heryng, Theodor). See: Heryng's sign.

Voltolini's disease (Voltolini, Friedrich Edward Rudolph): Medicine. See: Dorland; Jablonski; Stedman.

Voltolini's sign (Voltolini, Friedrich). See: Heryng's sign.

VOLTZ, PHILIPPE LOUIS. d. 1840. French mining engineer and geologist. See: Bull. Soc. Geolog. France vol. 12 (1840), pp. 24-32. Voltzite.

Voltzite (Voltz, Philippe Louis): Earth Sciences. See: Thrush; Webster's 3d.

VON ABICH, OTTO WILHELM HERMANN. 1806-1886. German geologist. See: World Who's Who Sci. Abichite.

Von Alberti, Friedrich August. See: Alberti, Friedrich August von.

VON AMMON, FRIEDRICH AUGUST. 1799-1861. German ophthalmologist and pathologist. See: World Who's Who Sci. Ammon's fissure, Ammon's operation.

Von Arlt, Carl Ferdinand Ritter. See: Arlt, Carl Ferdinand Ritter von.

VON ARNIM. German family owning a mine near Planitz, Germany. Cited in: Bailey. Arnimite.

Von Auwers, Karl Friedrich. See: Auwers, Karl Friedrich von.

Von Bach, Julius Carl. See: Bach, Julius Carl von.

Von Baelz, Erwin. See: Baelz, Erwin von.

Von Baer, Karl Ernst. See: Baer, Karl Ernst von.

Von Baer's law (Baer, Karl Ernst von): Zoology. See: Drever; Henderson; Webster's 3d.

Von Baeyer, Adolf Johann Friedrich Wilhelm. See: Baeyer, Adolf Johann Friedrich Wilhelm von.

Von Bamberger, Heinrich. See: Bamberger, Heinrich von.

VON BANDROWSKY, ERNST TITUS. 1853-1891. Polish chemist. See: World Who's Who Sci. Bandrowski's base.

VAN BARDELEBEN, HEINRICH ADOLF. 1819-1895. German surgeon. See: World Who's Who Sci. Bardeleben's bandage.

Von Basedow, Karl Adolph. See: Basedow, Karl Adolph von.

Von Baumgarten, Paul Clemens. See: Baumgarten, Paul Clemens von.

Von Bechterew, Wladimir Michailowich. See: Bekhterev, Vladimir Mikhailovich von.

Von Behring, Emil Adolf. See: Behring, Emil Adolf von.

VON BERGEN, KARL AUGUST. 1704-1759. German anatomist. See: World Who's Who Sci. Bergenia (herbs).

Von Bergmann, Ernst. See: Bergmann, Ernst von.

Von Bergmann, Gustav. See: Bergmann, Gustav von.

Von Bernuth, Fritz. See: Bernuth, Fritz von.

Von Bezold, Albert. See: Bezold, Albert von.

Von Bezold assimilation (Derivation undetermined): Psychology. See: Wolman.

Von Bezold, Friedrich. See: Bezold, Friedrich von.

Von Biela, Wilhelm. See: Biela, Wilhelm von.

VON BITTO, BELA. b. 1865. Hungarian chemist. See: Magyar Eletr. Lex. Von Bitto test for monohydric alcohols, Von Bitto test reaction for creatinine, Von Bitto test reactions for aldehydes and ketones.

Von Bitto test for monohydric alcohols (Von Bitto, Bela): Chemistry. See: Van Nostrand Chem. Dict.

Von Bitto test reaction for creatinine (Von Bitto, Bela): Chemistry. See: Van Nostrand Chem. Dict.

Von Bitto test reactions for aldehydes and ketones (Von Bitto, Bela): Chemistry. See: Van Nostrand Chem. Dict.

Von Bohnenberger, Johann Gottlieb. See: Bohnenberger, Johann Gottlieb Friedrich von.

Von Born, Ignaz. See: Born, Ignaz von.

Von Braun benzamide reaction (Von Braun, Julius): Chemistry. See: Van Nostrand Chem. Dict.

Von Braun degradation reactions (Von Braun, Julius): Chemistry. See: Van Nostrand Chem. Dict.

VON BRAUN, JULIUS. 1875-1939. Polish-born German chemist. See: Pogg., vol. 7a. Rosenmund-Von Braun synthesis, Von Braun benzamide reaction, Von Braun degradation reactions, Von Braun reaction, Von Braun reagent for carbonyl compounds.

Von Braun reaction (Von Braun, Julius): Chemistry. See: Ballentyne.

Von Braun reagent for carbonyl compounds (Von Braun, Julius): Chemistry. See: Van Nostrand Chem. Dict.

Von Bruecke, Ernst Wilhelm. See: Bruecke, Ernst Wilhelm von.

VON BRUNNER, JOHANN CONRAD. 1653-1727. Swiss anatomist. See: World Who's Who Sci. Brunneroma, Brunnerosis, Brunner's glands.

Von Buch, Baron Christian Leopold. See: Buch, Baron Christian Leopold von.

VON BUHL, LUDWIG. 1816-1880. German pathologist. See: World Who's Who Sci. Buhl's disease.

Von Dechen, Heinrich von. See: Dechen, Heinrich von.

VON DITTEL, LEOPOLD RITTER. 1815-1898. Austrian urologist. See: World Who's Who Sci. Dittel's operation.

VON DREYSE, JOHANN NIKOLAUS. 1787-1867. German inventor. See: World Who's Who Sci. Dreyse rifle.

VON DRIGALSKI, WILHELM (In full: KARL RUDOLF ARNOLD ARTUR WILHELM). 1871-1950. German bacteriologist. See: World Who's Who in Sci. Conradi-Drigalski agar.

VON ECONOMO, CONSTANTIN ALEXANDER. 1876-1931. Austrian neurologist. See: World Who's Who Sci. Economo's disease.

Von Economo's disease (Von Economo, Constantin). See: Economo's disease.

VON ESMARCH, JOHANN FRIEDRICH AUGUST. 1823-1908. German surgeon. See: World's Who Who Sci. Esmarch mask, Esmarch's bandage, Heiberg-Esmarch maneuver.

VON FABER DU FAUR, ADOLF FRIEDRICH. 1826-1918. German-born engineer and metallurgist. See: World Who's Who Sci. Faber du Faur furnace.

VON FEHLING, HERMANN CHRISTIAN. 1812-1885. German chemist. See: World Who's Who Sci. Fehling('s) solution (or reagent).

VON FLEISCHL MARXOW, ERNST. 1846-1891. Austrian physiologist. See: Sci., vol. 8 (1898), p. 744. Fleischl('s) hemometer, Fleischl's test.

VON FRERICH, FRIEDRICH THEODOR. 1819-1885. German pathologist and clinician. See: World Who's Who Sci. Frerich's theory.

VON FREY, MAX (In full: RUPPERT FRANZ MAX). 1852-1932. Austrian physiologist. See: Pogg., vol. 3,4,5,6; World Who's Who Sci. Von Frey's aesthesiometer.

Von Frey's aesthesiometer (Von Frey, Max): Physiology. See: Drever.

VON FRORIEP, AUGUST FRIEDRICH. 1849-1917. German anatomist. See: World Who's Who Sci. Froriep's ganglion, Froriep's induration.

VON FUERTH, OTTO. 1867-1938. Austrian chemist. See: World Who's Who Sci. Czyhlarz-Furth test, Fuerth-Hermann test reaction, Fuerth's myosin.

VON GIERKE, EDGAR OTTO KONRAD. 1877-1945. German pathologist. See: World Who's Who Sci. Fibiger-Debre-von Gierke syndrome, Von Gierke's syndrome.

Von Gierke–Van Creveld syndrome (Von Gierke, Edgar Otto Conrad and Van Creveld, Simon). See: Von Gierke's syndrome.

Von Gierke's syndrome (Von Gierke, Edgar Otto Konrad): Medicine. See: Jablonski. Also known as: Von Gierke–Van Creveld syndrome.

VON GRAEFE, ALBRECHT FRIEDRICH WILHELM ERNST. 1828–1870. German ophthalmologist. See: World Who's Who Sci. Graefe-Sjoegren syndrome, Graefe's disease (or syndrome), Graefe's knife, Graefe's operation, Graefe's spots, Graefe's test, Von Graefe's (or Graefe's) sign.

Von Graefe's (or Graefe's) sign (Von Graefe, Albrecht Friedrich Wilhelm Ernst): Medicine. See: Dorland; Hinsie; Stedman; Webster's 3d.

VON GROTH, PAUL HEINRICH. 1843–1927. German crystallographer and mineralogist. See: World Who's Who Sci. Grothit.

VON GRUBER, MAXIMILIAN FRANZ MARIA. 1853–1927. Austrian bacteriologist. See: World Who's Who Sci. Gruber–Widal reaction.

VON GUEDDEN, JOHANN BERNHARD ALOYS. 1824–1886. German psychiatrist. See: World Who's Who Sci. Gudden's atrophy, Gudden's commissure, Gudden's ganglion, Gudden's tract.

Von Guericke, Otto. See: Guericke, Otto von.

Von Guericke pump (Guericke, Otto von): Engineering and Industry. See: Auger.

Von Haberer, Hans. See: Haberer, Hans von.

Von Haidinger, Wilhelm Karl von. See: Haidinger, Wilhelm Karl von.

VON HALLER, ALBRECHT. 1708–1777. Swiss anatomist. See: World Who's Who Sci. Haller's ansa, Haller's arch(es), Haller's circle (1) (circulus arteriosus nervi optici), Haller's circle (2) (plexus venosus areolaris), Haller's circle (3) (circulosus callosus), Haller's cone(s), Haller's habenula, Haller's insula (or anulus), Haller's layer, Haller's line, Haller's plexus, Haller's rete (or network), Haller's tripod, Haller's tunica vasculosa, Haller's unguis, Haller's vas aberrans, Haller's vascular tissue.

VON HAMMER, ERNST HERMANN HEINRICH. 1858–1925. German geodesist and mathematician. See: World Who's Who Sci. Hammer projection.

VON HAUER, FRANZ. 1822–1899. Austrian geologist. See: World Who's Who Sci. Hauerite.

VON HEBRA, FERDINAND RITTER. 1816–1880. Austrian dermatologist. See: World Who's Who Sci. Hebra's disease (or pityriasis), Hebra's syndrome.

VON HEFNER–ALTENECK, FRIEDRICH. 1845–1904. German electrical engineer. See: World Who's Who Sci. Hefner (Hefner candle or Hefnerkerze) (unit), Hefner lamp.

VON HEINE, JAKOB. 1800–1879. German orthopedist. See: World Who's Who Sci. Heine–Medin disease.

Von Herrenschwand, F. See: Herrenschwand, F. von.

VON HERTWIG, RICHARD CARL WILHELM THEODOR. 1850–1937. German zoologist. See: World Who's Who Sci. Hertwig–Magendie syndrome (phenomenon or sign), Hertwigia.

Von Hevesy, George Charles. See: Hevesy, Gyorgy.

Von Hevesy–Loegstrup test reaction (Hevesy, Gyorgy and Loegstrup, Marie): Chemistry. See: Van Nostrand Chem. Dict.

Von Hildenbrand, Johann Valentin. See: Hildenbrand, Johann Valentin von.

Von Hippel, Eugen. See: Hippel, Eugen von.

Von Hippel–Lindau disease (Hippel, Eugen von and Lindau, Arvid). See: Hippel–Lindau syndrome (or disease).

VON HOCHENEGG, JULIUS. 1859–1940. Austrian surgeon. See: World Who's Who Sci. Hochenegg's operation, Hochenegg's symptom, Hochenegg's ulcer.

Von Hofmann, August Wilhelm. See: Hofmann, August Wilhelm von.

Von Hontheim, Johann Nicholas. See: Hontheim, Johann Nicholas von.

VON HUEFNER, CARL GUSTAV. 1840–1908. German physiologist. See: World Who's Who Sci. Huefner spectrophotometer.

Von Jaksch, Rudolf. See: Jaksch, Rudolf von.

Von Jaksch's anemia (Jaksch–Wartenhorst, Rudolf von). See: Jaksch's syndrome (anemia or disease).

VON JOLLY, PHILIPP JOHANN GUSTAV. 1809–1884. German physicist. See: World Who's Who Sci. Jolly balance.

VON KARMAN, THEODORE. 1881–1963. Hungarian aeronautical engineer. See: World Who's Who Sci. Born (and) Von Karman theory (of specific heat), Born–Von Karman boundary conditions, Karman boundary layer theorem, Karmán-Friedrich equations, Karman (or von Karman's) constant, Karman similarity theory, Karman–Tsien relation, Karman vortex street (street of vortices, street of eddies or vortices).

Von Karman's constant (Von Karman, Theodore). See: Karman constant.

VON KLEIST, EWALD GEORG. d. 1748. German scientist and dean of the cathedral of Kamin. See: World Who's Who Sci. Kleistian jar.

VON KOBELL, FRANZ (In full: WOLFGANG XAVER FRANZ). 1803–1882. German mineralogist. See: World Who's Who Sci. Kobellite, Von Kobell scale.

Von Kobell scale (Von Kobell, Franz): Earth Sciences. See: Van Nostrand Chem. Dict.

VON KOELLIKER, RUDOLF ALBERT. 1817–1905. Swiss-born anatomist and physiologist. See: World Who's Who Sci. Koelliker's canal, Koelliker's cells, Koelliker's dental crest, Koelliker's gland, Koelliker's layer, Koelliker's nucleus, Koelliker's pit, Koelliker's reticulum.

VON KOSSA, JULIUS. 1865– . Hungarian pharmacologist. See: Biog. Lex. hervorr. Aerzte. Von Kossa stain.

Von Kossa stain (Von Kossa, Julius): Medicine. See: Stedman.

VON KRIES, JOHANNES ADOLF. 1853–1928. German physiologist. See: World Who's Who Sci. Von Kries theory.

Von Kries theory (Von Kries, Johannes Adolf): Physiology. See: Drever.

Von Leyden, Ernst Victor. See: Leyden, Ernst Victor von.

Von Linne, Carl. See: Linnaeus.

Von Ludwig, Wilhelm Friedrich. See: Ludwig, Wilhelm Friedrich von.

Von Luschka, Hubert. See: Luschka, Hubert von.

Von Meyenburg, Hans. See: Meyenburg, Hans von.

VON MIDDELDORPF, ALBRECHT THEODOR. 1824–1868. German surgeon. See: World Who's Who Sci. Middeldorpf's splint, Middeldorpf's triangle.

VON MIKULICZ–RADECKI, JOHANN. 1850–1905. Romanian-born surgeon in Germany. See: World Who's Who Sci. Heineke–Mikulicz pyloroplasty, Mikulicz' cells, Mikulicz' clamp, Mikulicz' dictum, Mikulicz's disease (or syndrome), Mikulicz' drain, Mikulicz' kentotribe, Mikulicz' line, Mikulicz mask, Mikulicz' method, Mikulicz' operation (1) (exsection of sternocleidomastoid muscles), Mikulicz' operation (2) (colectomy), Mikulicz' pad, Mikulicz's resection of the intestine, Mikulicz–Vladimiroff amputation (or operation).

Von Mises distribution (Mises, Richard von): Statistics. See: Kendall.

Von Mises, Richard. See: Mises, Richard von.

VON MONAKOW, CONSTANTIN. 1853–1930. Russian-born Swiss neurologist. See: World Who's Who Sci. Monakow's tract (bundle or fibers), Monakow's fasciculus, Monakow's nucleus, Monakow's syndrome.

Von Monakow's tract (bundle or fibers) (Von Monakow, Constantin). See: Monakow's tract (bundle or fibers).

Von Munchausen, Baron Karl Friedrich Hieronymous. See: Munchausen, Baron Karl Friedrich Hieronymous von.

Von Neumann algebras (Neumann, John von): Mathematics. Cited in: Encyc. Brit., 1973 under "Neumann, John (Janos) von."

Von Neumann, John. See: Neumann, John von.

Von Neumann matrix (Neumann, John von): Mathematics. See: Internat. Dict. Phys. Elec.

Von Neumann spike (Neumann, John von?): Engineering and Industry. See: Thrush.

Von Neumann–Wigner rule (Neumann, John von and Wigner, Paul Eugene): Physics. See: Internat. Dict. Phys. Elec.

Von Neumann's ratio (Neumann, John von): Statistics. See: Kendall.

VON NEUREITHER, F. fl. 1923. German chemist. Cited in: Chem. Abstr. vol. 18, p. 1627. Von Neureither micro-test for cyanide.

Von Neureither micro-test for cyanide (Von Neureither, F.): Chemistry. See: Van Nostrand Chem. Dict.

VON NEUSSER, EDMUND. 1852-1912. Austrian physician. See: World Who's Who Sci. Neusser's granules.

VON NOORDEN, CARL HARKO. 1858-1944. German physician. See: World Who's Who Sci. Noorden treatment.

VON OLSHAUSEN, ROBERT. 1835-1915. German obstetrician. See: World Who's Who Sci. Olshausen's method.

Von Passow, Arnold. See: Passow, Arnold von.

VON PECHMANN, HANS. 1850-1902. German chemist. See: World Who's Who Sci. Pechmann condensation, Pechmann pyrazole synthesis.

Von Pettenkofer, Max Josef. See: Pettenkofer, Max Josef von.

Von Pfaundler, Meinhard. See: Pfaundler, Meinhard von.

Von Pirquet, Clemens Freiherr. See: Pirquet, Clemens Freiherr von.

Von Pirquet's test (or reaction) (Pirquet, Clemens Freiherr von). See: Pirquet's test (or reaction).

Von Plenck, Josef Jakob Edler. See: Plenck, Josef Jakob Edler von.

Von Prowazek, Stanislas Josef Mathias Edler. See: Prowazek, Stanislas Josef Mathias Edler von.

Von Rath, Marie or Gerhard. See: Rath, Marie or Gerhard von.

Von Recklinghausen, Friedrich Daniel. See: Recklinghausen, Friedrich Daniel von.

Von Recklinghausen's disease (Recklinghausen, Friedrich Daniel von). See: Recklinghausen's diseases (1), (2), (3), and (4).

Von Reuter, Baron Paul Julius. See: Reuter, Baron Paul Julius von.

Von Richter reaction (Von Richter, Viktor?): Chemistry. See: Van Nostrand Chem. Dict.

VON RICHTER, VIKTOR. 1841-1891. German chemist. See: Pogg., vol. 3, 4, 5, 6. Richter cinnoline synthesis, Von Richter reaction?

Von Rokitansky, Karl Freiherr. See: Rokitansky, Karl Freiherr von.

Von Rokitansky's disease (Rokitansky, Karl Freiherr von). See: Budd-Chiari syndrome.

Von Romberg, Moritz Heinrich. See: Romberg, Moritz Heinrich von.

VON SALLMANN, LUDWIG. 1892- . Austrian-born American ophthalmologist. See: Direct. Med. Specialists, vol. 14. Witkop-Von Sallmann syndrome.

Von Schroetter, Leopold. See: Schroetter von Kristelli, Leopold.

Von Schroetter's syndrome (Schroetter von Kristelli, Leopold). See: Paget-Schroetter syndrome.

Von Schwann's law (Schwann, Theodor): Physiology. See: Winick.

Von Seidel, Ludwig Philipp. See: Seidel, Ludwig Philipp von.

Von Semsey, Andor. See: Semsey, Andor von.

VONSEN. fl. early 20th c. American scientist. Cited in: Min. Mag. vol. 19 (1920-1922), p. 353. Vonsenite.

Vonsenite (Vonsen): Earth Sciences. See: Thrush.

Von Seysenegg, Gustav Tschermak. See: Tschermak von Seysenegg, Gustav.

Von Spee, Ferdinand Graf. See: Spee, Ferdinand Graf von.

Von Spee's curve (Spee, Ferdinand Graf von). See: curve of Spee.

Von Sternberg, Carl. See: Sternberg, Carl von.

Von Sterneck-Askania pendulum (Daublesky von Sterneck, Robert and Askania-Werke): Physics. See: Thrush.

Von Sterneck, Robert Daublebsky. See: Daublebsky von Sterneck, Robert.

Von Struempell, Adolf. See: Struempell, Adolf von.

Von Thuenen, Johannes Heinrich. See: Thuenen, Johannes Heinrich von.

Von Trautvetter, Ernst Rudolf. See: Trautvetter, Ernst Rudolf von.

Von Troeltsch, Anton Friedrich. See: Troeltsch, Anton Friedrich von.

Von Vierordt, Karl. See: Vierordt, Karl von.

Von Voit, Karl. See: Voit, Karl von.

Von Volborth, Alexander. See: Volborth, Alexander von.

Von Volkmann, Richard. See: Volkmann, Richard von.

Von Wagner, Franz Michael. See: Wagner, Franz Michael von.

Von Wahl, Eduard Georg. See: Wahl, Eduard Georg von.

Von Waldheim, G. F. See: Waldheim, G. F. von.

Von Wassermann, August Paul. See: Wassermann, August Paul von.

Von Weigel, Christian Ehrenfried. See: Weigel, Christian Ehrenfried von.

Von Weimarn equation (Von Weimarn, Peter Petrovic): Chemistry. See: Van Nostrand Sci. Encyc.

VON WEIMARN, PETER PETROVIC. 1879-1935. Russian chemist. See: Pogg., vol. 5,6. Von Weimarn equation.

VON WIESE, LEOPOLD MAX WALTER. b. 1876. German sociologist and economist. See: Internat. Encyc. Soc. Sci. Becker-Von Wiese personality types.

Von Wild, Heinrich. See: Wild, Heinrich von.

Von Willebrand syndrome (Willebrand, Erik Adolf von). See: Willebrand-Juergens syndrome.

Von Winckel, Franz Karl Ludwig Wilhelm. See: Winckel, Franz Karl Ludwig Wilhelm von.

Von Winiwarter, Felix. See: Winiwarter, Felix von.

VON WOLFF, FERDINAND (In full: LUDWIG FERDINAND). 1874-1952. German petrographer, mineralogist and geologist. See: Pogg., vol. 6,7a. Von Wolff's classification.

Von Wolff's classification (Von Wolff, Ferdinand): Earth Sciences. See: Thrush.

Von Zeppelin, Count Ferdinand Graf. See: Zeppelin, Count Ferdinand Graf von.

Von Ziemssen, Hugo Wilhelm. See: Ziemssen, Hugo Wilhelm von.

Von Zumbusch's disease (Zumbusch, Leo von). See: Hallopeau's disease (1).

Voorhees bag (Voorhees, James D.): Medicine. See: Dorland; Stedman.

VOORHEES, JAMES D. 1869-1929. American obstetrician. See: Who Was Who Amer. Voorhees bag.

Voorhis Act (Voorhis, Horace Jerry): Politics. See: Smith.

VOORHIS, HORACE JERRY. 1901- . American legislator. See: Biog. Direct. Amer. Congress. Voorhis Act.

VOORHOEVE, NICOLAAS. 1879-1927. Dutch physician. See: Biog. Lex. hervorr. Aerzte. Voorhoeve's dyschondroplasia (or disease).

Voorhoeve's dyschondroplasia (or disease) (Voorhoeve, Nicolaas): Medicine. See: Jablonski.

VOOYS, GERARD JAN DE. fl. 1934. Dutch mining engineer. Cited in: Chem. Abstr., Decenn. Index 1927-36. Vooys process.

Vooys process (Vooys, Gerard Jan de): Engineering and Industry. See: Thrush. Also known as: Barvoys process, De Vooys process, Sophia-Jacoba process.

Vorce cell (Vorce, Lafayette Denton): Engineering and Industry. See: Webster's 3d.

VORCE, LAFAYETTE DENTON. d.1953. American chemical engineer. See: New York Times, Feb. 4, 1953, p. 27, col. 1. Vorce cell.

VORLAENDER, DANIEL. 1867-1941. German chemist. See: Pogg., vol. 4,5,6,7a. Vorlaender reagent for aldehydes, Vorlaender test for differentiating allyl- and propenylphenol ethers, Vorlaender test for hydrochloric acid in chloroform, Vorlaender's rule.

Vorlaender reagent for aldehydes (Vorlaender, Daniel): Chemistry. See: Van Nostrand Chem. Dict.

Vorlaender test for diferentiating allyl- and propenylphenol ethers (Vorlaender, Daniel): Chemistry. See: Van Nostrand Chem. Dict.

Vorlaender test for hydrochloric acid in chloroform (Vorlaender, Daniel): Chemistry. See: Van Nostrand Chem. Dict.

Vorlaender's rule (Vorlaender, Daniel): Chemistry. See: Ballentyne.

VOROB'EV, VIKTOR IVANOVIC. d. 1906. Russian mineralogist. See: Annuaire Geolog. Mineralog., Russie vol. IX (1907), p. 49. Vorobyevite.

Vorobyevite (Vorob'ev, Viktor Ivanovic): Earth Sciences. See: Thrush. Also known as: Morganite.

Voronin, Michajl Stepahovic. See: Woronin, Michajl Stepanovic.

VORONOFF, SERGE. 1866-1951. Russian-born French physiologist. See: World Who's Who Sci. Voronoff's method (or operation).

Voronoff's method (or operation) (Voronoff, Serge): Medicine. See: Dorland; Stedman.

Vortmann-Binder solution (Vortmann, Georg and Binder, F.): Chemistry. See: Van Nostrand Chem. Dict.

VORTMANN, GEORG. 1854-1932. Austrian chemist. See: Pogg., vol. 3,4,6. Vortmann-Binder solution, Vortmann test for cyanide, Vortmann test reaction for phenol.

Vortmann test for cyanide (Vortmann, George): Chemistry. See: Van Nostrand Chem. Dict.

Vortmann test reaction for phenol (Vortmann, Georg): Chemistry. See: Van Nostrand Chem. Dict.

VOSS, AUREL EDMUND. 1845-1931. German mathematician. See: Pogg., vol. 3-6. surface of Voss, Voss polariscope.

Voss polariscope (Voss, Aurel Edmund): Physics. See: Huschke.

VOSSIUS, ADOLF. 1855-1925. German ophthalmologist. See: Biog. Lex. hervorr. Aerzte. Vossius' lenticular ring (or karatitis).

Vossius' lenticular ring (or keratitis) (Vossius, Adolf): Medicine. See: Dorland; Jablonski; Stedman.

VOTOCEK, EMIL. b.1872. Czechoslovakian chemist. See: Pogg., vol. 5,6. Votocek test for ketoses, Votocek test for sulfite in the presence of thiosulfate, Votocek test for wood pulp in paper, Votocek test reaction for methylfurfural.

Votocek test for ketoses (Votocek, Emil): Chemistry. See: Van Nostrand Chem. Dict.

Votocek test for sulfite in the presence of thiosulfate (Votocek, Emil): Chemistry. See: Van Nostrand Chem. Dict.

Votocek test for wood pulp in paper (Votocek, Emil): Chemistry. See: Van Nostrand Chem. Dict.

Votocek test reaction for methylfurfural (Votocek, Emil): Chemistry. See: Van Nostrand Chem. Dict.

VOURNASOS, ALEXANDER CHRIST. b.1877. Greek chemist. See: Pogg., vol. 5,6. Vournasos reagent, Vournasos test for arsenic and phosphorus.

Vournasos reagent (Vournasos, Alexander Christ): Chemistry. See: Van Nostrand Chem. Dict.

Vournasos test for arsenic and phosphorus (Vournasos, Alexander Christ): Chemistry. See: Van Nostrand Chem. Dict.

VOWEL, PETER. fl. 1654. English schoolteacher and conspirator. See: Lomas.

Vowel's plot (Vowel, Peter): History. See: Harbottle.

VRBA, KAREL. d. 1922. Bohemian mineralogist. See: Zeitschr. f. Kristallogr. vol. LIX (1924), p. 433f. Vrbaite.

Vrbaite (Vrba, Karel): Earth Sciences. See: Thrush, Webster's 3d.

Vreden, Robert Robertovich. See: Wreden, Robert Robertovich.

VREELAND, EDWARD BUTTERFIELD. 1856-1936. American legislator. See: Biog. Direct. Amer. Congress. Aldrich-Vreeland Act.

VREVEN, S. fl. 1911. Belgian chemist. (Biography source unavailable.) Vreven test for cod liver oil, Vreven test for differentiating creosote and guaiacol, Vreven test reaction for fats.

Vreven test for cod liver oil (Vreven, S.): Chemistry. See: Van Nostrand Chem. Dict.

Vreven test for differentiating creosote and guaiacol (Vreven, S.): Chemistry. See: Van Nostrand Chem. Dict.

Vreven test reaction for fats (Vreven, S.): Chemistry. See: Van Nostrand Chem. Dict.

VRIESE, WILLEM HENDRIK DE. 1806-1862. Dutch botanist. See: Biog. Woordenb. der Nederl. (Aa). Vriesia.

Vriesia (Vriese, Willem Hendrik): Botany. See: Taylor, N.; Webster's 3d.

VROLIK, WILLEM. 1801-1863. Dutch physician. See: Nieuw Nederl. Biog. Woordenb. Vrolik's syndrome (or disease).

Vrolik's syndrome (or disease) (Vrolik, Willem): Medicine. See: Jablonski. Also known as: Porak-Durante syndrome.

VUCETICH, JUAN. 1858-1925. Argentinian functionary. See: Gran. Encic. Argentina. Vecetich method.

Vucetich method (Vucetich, Juan): Sociology. See: Fairchild.

VULCAN. Roman god of fire. See: Harper. Volcano, Vulcan, Vulcan powder, Vulcanian (or Vulcanean), Vulcanism (or Volcanism), Vulcanist (or Volcanist), Vulcanite, Vulcanites, Vulcanization.

Vulcan (Vulcan): Generic Word. See: Webster's 3d.

Vulcan powder (Vulcan): Engineering and Industry. See: Partridge; Thrush.

Vulcanian (or Vulcanean) (Vulcan): Generic Word. See: Webster's 3d.

Vulcanism (or Volcanism) (Vulcan): Earth Sciences. See: Moore; Thewlis; Thrush.

Vulcanist (or Volcanist) (Vulcan): Earth Sciences. See: Thrush.

Vulcanite (Vulcan): Engineering and Industry. See: Focal Encyc. Photog.; Thrush.

Vulcanites (Vulcan): Earth Sciences. See: Thrush.

Vulcanization (Vulcan): Engineering and Industry. See: Thrush; Van Nostrand Sci. Encyc. under "Rubbers and Elastomers."; Webster's 3d.

VULPIAN, EDME-FELIX-ALFRED. 1826-1887. French physician. See: World Who's Who Sci. Vulpian's atrophy, Vulpian's conjugate deviation, Vulpian's effect (or phenomenon), Vulpian's test (1), Vulpian's test (2).

Vulpian's atrophy (Vulpian, Edme-Felix-Alfred): Medicine. See: Dorland; Stedman.

Vulpian's conjugate deviation (Vulpian, Edme-Felix-Alfred): Medicine. See: Stedman.

Vulpian's effect (or phenomenon) (Vulpian, Edme-Felix-Alfred): Medicine. See: Stedman.

Vulpian's test (1) Vulpian, Edme-Felix-Alfred): Medicine. See: Dorland; Stedman.

Vulpian's test (2) (Vulpian, Edme-Felix-Alfred): Medicine. See: Dorland; Stedman.

VULPIUS, G. fl. 1880. German pharmaceutical chemist. (Biography source unavailable.) Vulpius test for acetanilid, Vulpius test for tartaric acid in citric acid, Vulpius test reaction for morphine, Vulpius test reaction for sulfonal.

Vulpius test for acetanilid (Vulpius, G.): Chemistry. See: Van Nostrand Chem. Dict.

Vulpius test for tartaric acid in citric acid (Vulpius, G.): Chemistry. See: Van Nostrand Chem. Dict.

Vulpius test reaction for morphine (Vulpius, G.): Chemistry. See: Van Nostrand Chem. Dict.

Vulpius test reaction for sulfonal (Vulpius, G.): Chemistry. See: Van Nostrand Chem. Dict.

Vvedenskiy, Nikolay Yevgen'yevich. See: Wedensky, Nikolay Yevgen'yevich.

VYGOTSKY, LEV SEMIONOVICH. 1896-1934. Russian psychologist. See: Wolman. Vygotsky (or Vigotsky) test.

Vygotsky (or Vigotsky) test (Vygotsky, Lev Semionovich): Psychology. See: English; Wolman.

VYSOTSKII, N. K. fl. 1963. Soviet geologist. Cited in: Amer. Min. vol. 48 (1963), p. 708. Vysotskite.

Vysotskite (Vysotskii, N. K.): Earth Sciences. See: Thrush.

W

AGR test (Wald, Abraham; Arnold, Kenneth James; Goldberg, Samuel; and Rushton, Stanley): Statistics. See: Kendall.

. K. B. J. method (or approximation) (Wentzel, Gregor; Kramers, Henrik Anthony; Brillouin, Louis Marcel; and Jeffreys, Sir Harold). See: Wentzel-Kramers-Brillouin-Jeffreys approximation (or method).

. K. Kellogg Foundation (Kellogg, Will Keith): Philanthropy. See: New Encyc. Brit., 1974, Microp.

AAGE, PETER. 1833-1900. Norwegian chemist. See: World Who's Who Sci. Guildberg and Waage's law (or law of Guldberg and Waage).

AALER, ERIK. fl. 1956. Norwegian biologist. Cited in: Biolog. Abstr., vol. 31, 1957. Rose-Waaler test?

aals, Johannes Diderik van der. See: Van der Waals, Johannes Diderik.

aardenburg-Jonkers disease (Waardenburg, Petrus Johannes and Jonkers, Garrit Hendrik?): Medicine. See: Jablonski.

AARDENBURG, PETRUS JOHANNES. b. 1886. Dutch ophthalmologist. See: Wie is dat?, 1956. Klein-Waardenburg syndrome, Waardenburg-Jonkers disease, Waardenburg's syndrome (1), Wildervanck-Waardenburg-Franceschetti-Klein syndrome.

aardenburg's syndrome (1) (Waardenburg, Petrus Johannes): Medicine. See: Jablonski.

aardenburg's syndrome (2) (Waardenburg, Petrus Johannes). See: Klein-Waardenburg syndrome.

ACH, HUGO. b.1872. German engineer. See: Wer Ist?, 1935. Bauer-Wach turbine?

ACHENDORFF, EBERHARD JACOB. 1703-1758. Dutch physician, botanist and chemist. See: Nieuw Nederl. Biog Woordenb. Wachendorff's membrane, Wachendorfia.

achendorff's membrane (Wachendorff, Eberhard Jacob): Medicine. See: Donath; Dorland; Stedman.

achendorfia (Wachendorff, Eberhard Jacob): Botany. See: Taylor, N.

ACHSMUTH, H. fl. 1935. Belgian pharmaceutical chemist. Cited in: Chem. Abstr. vol 30, p. 1696. Wachsmuth test.

ACHSMUTH, HANS. 1872-1931. German neurologist. See: Psychiatr.-Neurolog. Wochenschr. vol. XXXIV (1932), p. 62f. Wachsmuth's mixture.

achsmuth test (Wachsmuth, H.): Chemistry. See: Van Nostrand Chem. Dict.

achsmuth's mixture (Wachsmuth, Hans): Medicine. See: Dorland.

ACKENRODER, HEINRICH WILHELM FERDINAND. 1798-1854. German pharmacist. See: Allg. Deut. Biog. Wackenroder reaction (or solution).

ackenroder reaction (or solution) (Wackenroder, Heinrich Wilhelm Ferdinand): Chemistry. See: Hackh; Van Nostrand Chem. Dict.; Webster's 3d.

ACKER, LEONHARD. 1864-1936. German chemist. See: Pogg., vols. 6,7a. Wacker reagent for alcohols, aldehydes, or carbohydrates?

acker reagent for alcohols, aldehydes, or carbohydrates (Wacker, Leonhard?): Chemistry. See: Van Nostrand Chem. Dict.

ada-Cutter hingeless heart valve (Wada, Juro and Cutter, Ephraim?): Medicine. Cited in: World Who's Who Sci.

Wada dominance test (Wada, Juhn Atsushi): Physiology. See: Good; Hinsie.

WADA, ISABURO. fl. 1920's. Japanese chemist. Cited in: Chem. Abstr, Decenn. Indexes 1917-26, 1927-36. Wada-Nakazono reagent, Wada test.

WADA, JUHN ATSUSHI. 1924-   . Japanese-born Canadian neurologist. See: World Who's Who Sci. Wada dominance test.

WADA, JURO. 1922-   . Japanese-born Canadian surgeon. See: World Who's Who Sci. Wada-Cutter hingeless heart valve.

Wada-Nakazono reagent (Wada, Isaburo and Nakazono, T.): Chemistry. See: Van Nostrand Chem. Dict.

Wada test (Wada, Isaburo): Chemistry. See: Van Nostrand Chem. Dict.

WADE, ARTHUR. d. 1951. English geologist. See: London Times, May 18, 1951, p. 4f. Wadeite.

WADE, BENJAMIN FRANKLIN. 1800-1878. American lawyer and politician. See: Dict. Amer. Biog. Wade-Davis Bill, Wade-Davis Manifesto.

Wade-Davis Bill (Wade, Benjamin Franklin and Davis, Henry Winter): History. See: Morris.

Wade-Davis Manifesto (Wade, Benjamin Franklin and Davis, Henry Winter): History. See: Webster's Biog. Dict.

WADE, DEWITT CLINTON. 1838-1904. American physician. See: Albany Med. Ann. vol. XXVI (1905), p. 45. Wade's balsam.

Wadeite (Wade, Arthur): Earth Sciences. See: Thrush.

Wade's balsam (Wade, Dewitt Clinton): Medicine. See: Stedman.

WADSWORTH, AUGUSTUS B. 1872-1954. American bacteriologist. See: Who Was Who Amer. Wadsworth's stain.

WADSWORTH, FRANK LAWTON OLCOTT. 1867-1936. American engineer and inventor. See: World Who's Who Sci. Wadsworth mounting for spectrometers.

WADSWORTH, GUY WOODBRIDGE, JR. 1901-   . American psychologist. See: Amer. Psych. Assoc., Direct., 1948. Humm-Wadsworth temperament scale.

WADSWORTH, JAMES WOLCOTT, JR. 1877-1952. American businessman and political leader. See: Biog. Direct. Amer. Congress. Burke-Wadsworth Bill.

Wadsworth mounting for spectrometers (Wadsworth, Frank Lawton Olcott): Physics. See: Thewlis; Van Nostrand Sci. Encyc.

Wadsworth's stain (Wadsworth, Augustus B.): Medicine. See: Stedman.

WAECHTER, ALEXANDER. fl. 1849. German chemist. (Biography source unavailable.) Waechter's gold purple?

WAECHTER, HERMANN JULIUS GUSTAV. b.1878. German physician. (Biography source unavailable.) Bracht-Waechter lesion.

Waechter's gold purple (Waechter, Alexander?): Applied Arts. See: Thrush.

Waegner reagent (Derivation undetermined): Chemistry. See: Van Nostrand Chem. Dict.

WAELSCH, LUDWIG. 1867-1924. Czechoslovakian physician. See: Biog. Lex. hervorr. Aerzte. Waelsch's urethritis.

Waelsch's urethritis (Waelsch, Ludwig). See: Reiter's disease (syndrome or triad).

Waelz process (Derivation undetermined): Engineering and Industry. See: Hackh; Thrush.

Waerden, Bartel Leendert van der. See: Van der Waerden, Bartel Leendert.

Waffle's law (Derivation undetermined): Sociology. See: Martin.

WAGENAAR, M. fl. 1914-1924. Dutch pharmaceutical chemist. Cited in: Chem. Abstr., Cecenn. Indexes 1907-16, 1917-26. Wagenaar test for citric acid, Wagenaar test for distinguishing citric, oxalic and tartaric acids, Wagenaar test for nickel in hardened fats, Wagenaar test reaction for caffeine.

Wagenaar test for citric acid (Wagenaar, M.): Chemistry. See: Van Nostrand Chem. Dict.

Wagenaar test for distinguishing citric, oxalic and tartaric acids (Wagenaar, M.): Chemistry. See: Van Nostrand Chem. Dict.

Wagenaar test for nickel in hardened fats (Wagenaar, M.): Chemistry. See: Van Nostrand Chem. Dict.

Wagenaar test reaction for caffeine (Wagenaar, M.): Chemistry. See: Van Nostrand Chem. Dict.

WAGENER, GUIDO RICHARD. 1822-1896. German anatomist. See: Allg. Deut. Biog. Wagener's larva.

WAGENER, HENRY PATRICK. b. 1890. American ophthalmologist. See: Amer. J. Ophth. vol. 52 (Aug., 1961), p. 281. Wagener's retinitis.

Wagener's larva (Wagener, Guido Richard): Zoology. See: Gray.

Wagener's retinitis (Wagener, Henry Patrick): Medicine. See: Jablonski.

WAGGONER, C. STANLEY. fl. 1926-1930. American pharmaceutical chemist. (Biography source unavailable.) Waggoner solution?

Waggoner solution (Waggoner, C. Stanley?): Chemistry. See: Van Nostrand Chem. Dict.

Wagner Act (Wagner, Robert Ferdinand): Politics. See: Clark; Smith.

Wagner beam (Wagner, Herbert): Engineering and Industry. See: Van Nostrand Sci. Encyc.

WAGNER, CARL ERNST ALBRECHT. 1827-1871. German surgeon. See: Arch. f. Klin. Chir., Berlin vol. XII (1871), pp. 1091-2003. Wagner's line?

Wagner-Connery Act (Wagner, Robert Ferdinand and Connery, William Patrick, Jr.): Politics. See: Morris.

Wagner-Crosser Railroad Retirement Act (Wagner, Robert Ferdinand and Crosser, Robert): Politics. See: Morris.

WAGNER, E. fl. 1935. German chemist. Cited in: Chem. Abstr. vol. 29, p. 53759. Dubsky-Wagner test for aluminum, Dubsky-Wagner tests for magnesium.

Wagner earth (or ground) (Wagner, Karl Willy): Engineering and Industry. See: Hughes; Internat. Dict. Phys. Elec.; Markus.

Wagner effect (Wagner, Herbert): Engineering and Industry. See: Internat. Dict. Ap. Math.

WAGNER, ERNST LEBERECHT. 1829-1888. German pathologist. See: World Who's Who Sci. Wagner-Unverricht syndrome, Wagner's disease.

WAGNER, FRANZ MICHAEL VON. d. 1851. German mining engineer. Cited in: Dana. Wagnerite.

Wagner-Garner Bill (Wagner, Robert Ferdinand and Garner, John Nance): Politics. See: Morris.

WAGNER, GEORG (In full: JEGOR JEGOROWITSCH). 1849-1903. Russian chemist. See: Pobb., vol. 4. Wagner-Meerwein rearrangement, Wagner rearrangement.

WAGNER, GEORG. b. 1869. German physician. (Biography source unavailable.) Wagner's osteogenic sarcoma?

WAGNER, H. fl. 1938. Swiss ophthalmologist. (Biography source unavailable.) Wagner's disease.

WAGNER, HERBERT. 1900- . German aerodynamics engineer. See: Pogg., vol. 7a. Wagner effect, Wagner beam.

WAGNER, HILDEBERT. 1929- . German phytochemist. See: World Who's Who Sci. Wagner('s) reagent (or reagent for alkaloids)?

WAGNER-JAUREGG, JULIUS. 1857-1940. Austrian neuropsychiatrist. See: World Who's Who Sci. Wagner-Jauregg treatment.

Wagner-Jauregg reaction (Wagner-Jauregg, Theodor): Chemistry. See: Van Nostrand Chem. Dict.

WAGNER-JAUREGG, THEODOR. 1903- . Austrian chemist. See: Pogg., vol. 7a. Wagner-Jauregg reaction.

Wagner-Jauregg treatment (Wagner-Jauregg, Julius): Medicine. See: Dorland.

WAGNER, JOHANN PHILIP. 1799-1879. German physicist. See: Allg. Deut. Biog. Wagner's hammer.

WAGNER, KARL WILLY. 1883-1953. German electrical engineer. See: Pogg., vols. 5, 6, 7a. Maxwell-Wagner effect, Maxwell-Wagner mechanism, Wagner earth (or ground).

Wagner-Meerwein rearrangement (Wagner, Georg and Meerwein, Hans Lebrecht): Chemistry. Cited in: Van Nostrand Chem. Dict.

WAGNER, MORITZ FRIEDRICH. 1813-1887. German naturalist. See: World Who's Who Sci. Wagner's separation theory.

WAGNER, PAUL. 1943-1930. German agricultural chemist. See: Pogg., vol. 6. Wagner solution for phosphate analysis?

Wagner-Peyser Act (Wagner, Robert Ferdinand and Peyser, Theodore Albert): Politics. See: Smith.

Wagner('s) reagent (or reagent for alkaloids) (Wagner, Hildebert?): Chemistry. See: Hackh; Van Nostrand Chem. Dict.

Wagner reagent for differentiating textile fibers (Wagner, Walter): Chemistry. See: Van Nostrand Chem. Dict.

Wagner rearrangement (Wagner, Georg): Chemistry. See: Ballentyne; Van Nostrand Chem. Dict.; Webster's 3d.

WAGNER, RICHARD (In full: WILHELM RICHARD). 1813-1883. German musical composer. See: Allg. Deut. Biog.; Grove. Wagner tuba, Wagnerian (or Wagneresque), Wagnerian opera.

WAGNER, ROBERT FERDINAND. 1877-1953. American lawyer and legislator. See: Biog. Direct. Amer. Congress. Lea-Wagner Act, Wagner Act, Wagner-Connery Act, Wagner-Crosser Railroad Retirement Act, Wagner-Garner Bill, Wagner-Peyser Act, Wagner-Steagall Act.

WAGNER, RUDOLF. 1805-1864. German anatomist and zoologist. See: Allg. Deut. Biog.; World Who's Who Sci. Wagner's corpuscles, Wagner's spot.

Wagner solution for phospate analysis (Wagner, Paul?): Chemistry. See: Van Nostrand Chem. Dict.

Wagner-Steagall Act (Wagner, Robert Ferdinand and Steagall, Henry Bascom): Politics. See: Morris; Smith.

Wagner tuba (Wagner, Richard): Music. See: Apel; Scholes; Webster's 3d.

Wagner turbidimeter (Wagner, Walter?): Engineering and Industry. See: Thrush.

Wagner-Unverricht syndrome (Wagner, Ernst Leberecht and Unverricht, Heinrich): Medicine. See: Jablonski. Also known as: Wagner's polymyositis, Wagner's syndrome.

WAGNER, WALTER. fl. 1925. American? engineer. (Biography source unavailable.) Wagner turbidimeter?

WAGNER, WALTER. fl. 1927. German textile chemist. Cited in: Chem. Abstr. vol. 21, p. 2068. Wagner reagent for differentiating textile fibers.

WAGNER, WILHELM. 1848-1900. German surgeon. See: Biog. Lex. hervorr. Aerzte. 1848-1900. Wagner's operation.

Wagnerian (or Wagneresque) (Wagner, Richard): (grandiose) Generic Word. See: Partridge; Webster's 3d.

Wagnerian opera (Wagner, Richard): Music. See: Morris and Irwin.

Wagnerite (Wagner, Franz Michael von): Earth Sciences. See: Thrush; Webster's 3d.

Wagner's corpuscles (Wagner, Rudolf): Medicine. See: Donath; Dorland; Henderson.

Wagner's disease (Wagner, Ernst Leberecht): Medicine. See: Dorland.

Wagner's disease (Wagner, H.): Medicine. See: Jablonski.

Wagner's hammer (Wagner, Johann Philip): Medicine. See: Dorland.

Wagner's line (Wagner, Carl Ernst Albrecht?): Medicine. See: Stedman.

Wagner's operation (Wagner, Wilhelm): Medicine. See: Dorland; Stedman.

Wagner's osteogenic sarcoma (Wagner, Georg): Medicine. See: Jablonski.

Wagner's polymyositis (or syndrome) (Wagner, Ernst Leberecht). See: Wagner-Unverricht syndrome.

Wagner's separation theory (Wagner, Moritz Friedrich): Zoology. See: Dorland.

Wagner's spot (Wagner, Rudolf): Medicine. See: Donath.

WAGSTAFFE, WILLIAM WARWICK. 1843-1910. English surgeon. See: Biog. Lex. hervorr. Aerzte. Wagstaffe's fracture.

Wagstaffe's fracture (Wagstaffe, William Warwick): Medicine. See: Dorland; Stedman.

Wahabis (Abdul-Wahhab): Religion. See: Canney; Harbottle; Phyfe.

WAHL, ARTHUR MUNZENMAIER. 1901- . American mechanical engineer. See: Amer. Men. Sci., 11th ed. Wahl formula.

WAHL, EDUARD GEORG VON. 1833-1890. German surgeon. See: Biog. Lex. hervorr. Aerzte. Wahl's sign.

Wahl formula (Wahl, Arthur Munzenmaier): Engineering and Industry. See: Auger.

WAHLENBERG, GOERAN. 1780-1851. Swedish botanist and biologist. See: Svenska Maen Och Kvinnor. Wahlenbergia.

Wahlenbergia (Wahlenberg, Goeran): Botany. See: Taylor, N.; Webster's 3d.

Wahl's sign (Wahl, Eduard Georg von): Medicine. See: Dorland.

WAIBLINGEN (GHIBELLINES). fl. 12th c. German princely family. See: Webster's Biog. Dict. Guelfs and Ghibellines.

Waidner-Burgess standard (Waidner, Charles and Burgess, George Kimball): Physics. See: Internat. Dict. Phys. Elec.; Webster's 3d.

WAIDNER, CHARLES WILLIAM. 1873-1922. American physicist. See: Dict. Amer. Biog. Waidner-Burgess standard.

WAIT, RUDOLF. fl. 1937. German chemist. Cited in: Chem. Abstr. vol. 31, p. 53983. Wait test reaction.

Wait test reaction (Wait, Rudolf): Chemistry. See: Van Nostrand Chem. Dict.

WAKEFIELD, FELIX. 1807-1875. New Zealander engineer. See: Dict. Nat. Biog. Wakefield sheet pile?

Wakefield sheet pile (Wakefield, Felix?): Engineering and Industry. See: Thrush.

WAKEMAN, RHODA. fl. 1855. American prophetess. (Biography source unavailable.) Wakemanites.

Wakemanites (Wakeman, Rhoda): Religion. See: Canney.

WALCH, JOHANN ERNST IMMANUEL. 1725-1778. German mineralogist, philologist and divine. See: Allg. Deut. Biog.; Encyc. Brit., 1911. Walchia.

WALCHER, GUSTAV A. 1865-1935. German obstetrician. See: Biog. Lex. hervorr. Aerzte. Walcher position.

Walcher position (Walcher, Gustav A.): Medicine. See: Dorland; Stedman.

Walchia (Walch, Johann Ernst Immanuel): Botany. See: Webster's 3d.

WALD, ABRAHAM. 1902-1950. American statistician. See: Internat. Encyc. Soc. Sci. WAGR test, Wald's classification statistic, Wald-Wolfowitz runs test.

Wald-Wolfowitz runs test (Wald, Abraham and Wolfowitz, Jacob): Statistics. See: Hoult; Kendall.

Waldegg. See: Heusinger von Waldegg, Edmund.

Waldegg gear (Heusinger von Waldegg, Edmund). See: Heusinger valve gear.

Walden inversion (Walden, Paul): Chemistry. See: Ballentyne; Hackh; Van Nostrand Chem. Dict.

WALDEN, PAUL. 1863-1957. Latvian-born German chemist. See: World Who's Who Sci. Walden inversion, Walden rule (or empirical equation).

Walden rule (or empirical equation) (Walden, Paul): Chemistry. See: Ballentyne; Internat. Dict. Phys. Elec.; Van Nostrand Chem. Dict.

Waldenses (Waldo, Pierre): Religion. See: Canney; Harvey; Mathews, S.

WALDENSTROEM, HENNING (In full: JOHANN HENNING). b. 1877. Swedish physician. See: Svenska Maen Och Kvinnor. Perthes-Calve-Legg-Waldenstroem syndrome .

WALDENSTROEM, JAN GOESTA. 1906- . Swedish physician. See: World Who's Who Sci. Waldenstroem's disease, Waldenstroem's hepatitis, Waldenstroem's macroglobulinemia (or purpura), Waldenstroem's syndrome, Waldenstroem's test, Waldenstroem's uveoparotitis.

Waldenstroem's disease (Waldenstroem, Jan Goesta): Medicine. See: Jablonski.

Waldenstroem's hepatitis (Waldenstroem, Jan Goesta): Medicine. See: Jablonski.

Waldenstroem's macroglobulinemia (or purpura) (Waldenstroem, Jan Goesta): Medicine. See: Jablonski; Stedman.

Waldenstroem's syndrome (Waldenstroem, Henning). See: Calve-Legg-Perthes syndrome.

Waldenstroem's syndrome (Waldenstroem, Jan Goesta): Medicine. See: Jablonski.

Waldenstroem's test (Waldenstroem, Jan Goesta): Medicine. See: Stedman.

Waldenstroem's uveoparotitis (Waldenstroem, Jan Goesta): Medicine. See: Jablonski.

WALDEYER, HEINRICH WILHELM GOTTFRIED. 1836-1921. German anatomist. See: World Who's Who Sci. Waldeyer's epithelium, Waldeyer's fossae, Waldeyer's glands, Waldeyer's neuron, Waldeyer's plasma cell, Waldeyer's tonsillar ring, Waldeyer's vascular layer, Waldeyer's zonal layer (or tract).

Waldeyer's epithelium (Waldeyer, Heinrich Wilhelm Gottfried): Anatomy. See: Donath.

Waldeyer's fossae (Waldeyer, Heinrich Wilhelm Gottfried): Anatomy. See: Donath; Dorland; Stedman.

Waldeyer's glands (Waldeyer, Heinrich Wilhelm Gottfried): Anatomy. See: Dorland; Stedman.

Waldeyer's neuron (Waldeyer, Heinrich Wilhelm Gottfried): Anatomy. See: Stedman.

Waldeyer's plasma cell (Waldeyer, Heinrich Wilhelm Gottfried): Anatomy. See: Webster's 3d.

Waldeyer's tonsillar ring (Waldeyer, Heinrich Wilhelm Gottfried): Anatomy. See: Donath; Dorland; Stedman.

Waldeyer's vascular layer (Waldeyer, Heinrich Wilhelm Gottfried): Anatomy. See: Donath.

Waldeyer's zonal layer (or tract) (Waldeyer, Heinrich Wilhelm Gottfried): Anatomy. See: Dorland; Stedman; Webster's 3d.

WALDHEIM, G. F. VON. d. 1853. German paleontologist. (Biography source unavailable.) Waldheimia.

Waldheimia (Waldheim, G. F. von): Zoology. See: Webster's 3d.

Waldo patent (Waldo, Samuel): History. See: Jameson.

WALDO, PIERRE. fl. late 12th c. French religious reformer. See: Nouv. Biog. Univ. Waldenses.

WALDO, SAMUEL. 1695-1729. American merchant, capitalist and politician. See: Dict. Amer. Biog. Waldo patent.

Wald's classification statistic (Wald, Abraham): Statistics. See: Kendall.

WALDSTEIN, FERDINAND ERNST GABRIEL. 1762-1823. German nobleman and friend of Beethoven. See: Grove. Waldstein sonata.

WALDSTEIN, FRANZ ADAM GRAF VON. 1759-1823. Austrian botanist. See: Wurzbach. Waldsteinia.

Waldstein sonata (Waldstein, Ferdinand Ernst Gabriel): Music. See: Apel; Scholes.

Waldsteinia (Waldstein, Franz Adam Graf von): Botany. See: Taylor, N.; Webster's 3d.

walk like Agag (Agag): Generic Word (walk softly). See: Hendrickson; Partridge.

WALKER, ARTHUR EARL. 1907- . American neurologist. See: World Who's Who Sci. Dandy-Walker syndrome, Walker tractotomy.

Walker cup (Walker, George Herbert): Recreation and Sports. See: Hendrickson.

Walker disk machine (Walker, J. S.): Engineering and Industry. See: Thrush.

WALKER, E. R. fl. 1887. English mining engineer. (Biography source unavailable.) Walker fan.

Walker/Eastman roller-slide camera (Walker, W. H. and Eastman, George): Photography. See: Focal Encyc. Photog.

WALKER, F. W., JR. fl 1916. American ceramics engineer. (Biography source unavailable.) Walker vacuum mixer?

Walker fan (Walker, E. R.; J. S.; and T. A.): Engineering and Industry. See: Auger.

WALKER, GEORGE. 1869- . American surgeon. See: Who's Who Among Physicians and Surg., 1938. Walker rat tumor (carcinosarcoma or sarcoma).

WALKER, GEORGE HERBERT. fl. 1920's. American sportsman. (Biography source unavailable.) Walker cup.

WALKER, SIR GILBERT THOMAS. 1868-1958. English applied mathematician and meteorologist. See: Dict. Nat. Biog. Walker probability function.

Walker hound (Walker, John W.): Sports and Recreation. See: Webster's 3d.

WALKER, J. S. fl. 1868. English mining engineer. (Biography source unavailable.) Walker disk machine.

WALKER, J. T. AINSLIE. 1868-1930. English chemist. (Biography source unavailable.) Rideal-Walker coefficient, Rideal-Walker test.

WALKER, SIR JAMES. 1863-1935. Scottish chemist. See: World Who's Who Sci. Crum-Brown and Walker synthesis (or reaction).

WALKER, JOHN. 1768-1833. Irish religious sect founder, classical scholar and mathematician. See: Dict. Nat. Biog. Walkerites.

WALKER, JOHN W. 1774-1809. American sportsman and legislator. See: Who Was Who Amer. Walker hound.

WALKER, MARY EDWARDS. 1832-1919. American physician and feminist. See: Dict. Amer. Biog. Mary Walkers.

Walker probability function (Walker, Sir Gilbert Thomas): Statistics. See: Kendall.

Walker rat tumor (carcinosarcoma or sarcoma) (Walker, George): Medicine. See: Jablonski; Stedman.

WALKER, RICHARD. 1679-1764. English philosophy professor. See: Dict. Nat. Biog. Walkeria.

WALKER, ROBERT JAMES OR JOHN. 1801-1869. American statesman and economist. See: Dict. Amer. Biog. Walker tariff.

WALKER, T. A. fl. 1887. English mining engineer. (Biography source unavailable.) Walker fan.

Walker tariff (Walker, Robert James or John): Politics. See: Morris; Smith.

Walker tractotomy (Walker, Arthur Earl): Medicine. See: Stedman.

Walker vacuum mixer (Walker, F. W., Jr?): Engineering and Industry. See: Thrush.

WALKER, W. H. fl. 1885. American photographer. (Biography source unavailable.) Walker/Eastman roller-slide camera.

Walkeria (Walker, Richard): Botany. See: Charnock.

Walkerites (Walker, John): Religion. See: Canney.

Wallace agitator (Wallace, Harry V.): Engineering and Industry. See: Thrush.

WALLACE, ALFRED RUSSEL. 1823-1913. English naturalist. See: Dict. Nat. Biog. Wallace's line, Wallace's standard-wing.

WALLACE, GEORGE CORLEY. 1919- . American politician. See: Who's Who Amer., 1972-1973. Wallaceism.

WALLACE, HARRY V. fl. 1937. American engineer. Cited in: Chem. Abstr. vol. 31, p. 37495. Wallace agitator.

WALLACE, SIR WILLIAM. ca. 1272-1305. Scottish patriot and defender. See: Dict. Nat. Biog. Wallace's larder, Wallace's trench.

Wallaceism (Wallace, George Corley): Politics. See: Barnhart, (New Eng.)

Wallace's larder (Wallace, Sir William): History. See: Brewer; Harbottle.

Wallace's line (Wallace, Alfred Russel): Zoology. See: Gray; Monkhouse; Winick.

Wallace's standard-wing (Wallace, Alfred Russel): Zoology. See: Encyc. Brit., 1973 under "Bird of Paradise."

Wallace's trench (Wallace, Sir William): History. See: Encyc. Brit., 1973 under "Selkirk."

Wallach degradation reaction (Wallach, Otto): Chemistry. See: Van Nostrand Chem. Dict.

WALLACH, OTTO. 1847-1931. German organic chemist. See: World Who's Who Sci. Wallach degradation reaction, Wallach rearrangement (or transformation).

Wallach rearrangement (or transformation) (Wallach, Otto): Chemistry. See: Ballentyne; Van Nostrand Chem. Dict.

WALLEN, MATTHEW. fl. before 1893. Jamaican botanist. See: Britten and Boulger. Wallenia.

WALLENBERG, ADOLF. 1862-1949. German physician. See: Biog. Lex. hervorr. Aerzte. Wallenberg's syndrome.

Wallenberg's syndrome (Wallenberg, Adolf): Medicine. See: Dorland; Hinsie; Jablonski.

Wallenia (Wallen, Matthew): Botany. See: Charnock.

WALLER, AUGUSTUS VOLNEY. 1816-1870. English physiologist. See: Dict. Nat. Biog. Wallerian degeneration, Wallerian (or Waller's) law.

WALLER, EDMUND. 1606-1687. English poet, conspirator and turncoat. See: Dict. Nat. Biog. Waller's plot.

WALLER, HORACE. 1833-1896. English traveler and writer on Africa. See: Dict. Nat. Biog. Waller's gazelle.

WALLER, IVAR. 1898- . Swedish physicist. See: World Who's Who Sci. Debye-Waller factor (or temperature factor).

Wallerian degeneration (Waller, Augustus Volney): Medicine. See: Drever; Jablonski; Stedman.

Wallerian (or Waller's) law (Waller, Augustus Volney): Physiology. See: Dorland; Gray; Stedman.

Wallerius, Goeran. See: Vallerius, Goeran.

Waller's gazelle (Waller, Horace): Zoology. See: Van Nostrand Sci. Encyc. under "Gerenuk."

Waller's plot (Waller, Edmund): History. See: Harbottle; Harvey.

WALLES, UKE. 1593-1653. Dutch theological writer. See: Nieuw Nederl. Biog. Woordenb. Ukewallists.

WALLGREN, ARVID J. b. 1898. Swedish physician. See: World Who's Who Sci. Wallgren's disease.

Wallgren's disease (Wallgren, Arvid J.): Medicine. See: Jablonski.

Wallhauser and Whitehead's method (Wallhauser, Andrew and Whitehead, J. M.): Medicine. See: Dorland.

WALLHAUSER, ANDREW. 1892- . American pathologist. See: Who's Who Among Physicians and Surg., 1938. Wallhauser and Whitehead's method.

WALLICH, NATHANIEL. 1786-1854. Danish-born English explorer and botanist. See: Dict. Nat. Biog. Wallichia.

Wallichia (Wallich, Nathaniel): Botany. See: Charnock.

Wallis formulas (Wallis, John): Mathematics. See: Internat. Dict. Ap. Math; James.

WALLIS, JOHN. 1616-1703. English divine and mathematician. See: Dict. Nat. Biog. Wallis formulas, Wallis product (or theorem) for pi.

Wallis product (or theorem) for pi (Wallis, John): Mathematics. See: Ballentyne; Internat. Dict. Ap. Math.; James.

ALLIS, WILSON ALLEN. 1912- . American statistician and economist. See: Amer. Men Sci., 10th ed., Soc. and Behav. Kruskal-Wallis test.

allman amplifier (Wallman, Henry): Engineering and Industry. See: Hughes; Van Nostrand Sci. Encyc.

ALLMAN, HENRY. 1915- . American mathematical and electrical engineer. See: Amer. Men and Women Sci., 12th ed. Wallman amplifier.

allop (Wallop, Sir John): Generic Word. See: Charnock.

ALLOP, SIR JOHN. 1490?-1551. English soldier and diplomat. See: Dict. Nat. Biog. Wallop.

ALLROTH, KARL FRIEDRICH WILHELM. 1792-1857. German physician and botanist. See: Allg. Deut. Biog. Wallrothia.

allrothia (Wallroth, Karl Friedrich Wilhelm): Botany. See: Charnock.

ally blue (Windsor, Wallis Warfield Simpson): Fashion. See: Picken.

ALPERS, WILHELM GERHARD. 1816-1853. German botanist. See: Allg. Deut. Biog. Walpersia.

alpersia (Walpers, Wilhelm Gerhard): Botany. See: Charnock.

alpole group (Walpole, Thomas): History. See: Morris.

ALPOLE, HORACE, 4TH EARL OF ORFORD. 1717-1797. English politician and man of letters. See: Dict. Nat. Biog. Walpolian.

ALPOLE, SIR ROBERT, 1ST EARL OF ORFORD. 1676-1745. English statesman. See: Dict. Nat. Biog. Bob, Walpolian.

ALPOLE, THOMAS. 1727-1803. English merchant-banker. See: Valentine. Walpole group.

alpolian (Walpole, Horace, 4th Earl of Orford): History. See: Webster's 3d.

alpolian (Walpole, Sir Robert, 1st Earl of Orford): History. See: Webster's 3d.

alpurgis night (Walpurgis, Saint): Mythology. See: Brewer; Canney; Harvey.

alpurgis oil (Walpurgis, Saint): Religion. See: Brewer.

ALPURGIS, SAINT. d. 779? English abbess. See: Dict. Nat. Biog. Walpurgis night, Walpurgis oil.

ALSCHAERTS, EGIDE. 1820-1901. Swiss engineer. See: Wood. Walschaerts' valve gear.

alschaerts' valve gear (Walschaerts, Egide): Engineering and Industry. See: Wood.

ALSH, DAVID IGNATIUS. 1872-1947. American legislator. See: Biog. Direct. Amer. Congress. Walsh-Healey Act.

alsh-Healey Act (Walsh, David Ignatius and Healey, Arthur Daniel): Politics. See: Clark; Morris; Smith.

alsham forceps (Walsham, William Johnson): Medicine. See: Stedman.

ALSHAM, WILLIAM JOHNSON. 1847-1903. English surgeon. See: Dict. Nat. Biog. Walsham forceps.

alter-Bohmann syndrome (Derivation undetermined): Medicine. See: Jablonski.

ALTER, FRANCIS EUGENE. 1894-1963. American legislator. See: Biog. Direct. Amer. Congress. McCarran-Walter Act, Walter-Logan Act.

ALTER, FRIEDRICH KARL. 1881-1935. German neurologist. See: Biog. Lex. hervorr. Aerzte. Walter's test.

ALTER, JOHANN GOTTLIEB. 1734-1818. German anatomist. See: Allg. Deut. Biog. Walter's nerve.

ALTER, JOHN. 1818-1894. English proprietor of the Times. See: Dict. Nat. Biog. Walter press.

alter-Logan Act (Walter, Francis Eugene and Logan): Politics. See: Smith.

alter Mitty (Mitty, Walter): Generic Word. See: Webster's 3d.

alter press (Walter, John): Printing. See: Harrod; Lockwood.

ALTER, THOMAS. 1704-1789. English-born American botanist. See: Dict. Nat. Biog. Walter's pine.

Walter's nerve (Walter, Johann Gottlieb): Anatomy. See: Stedman.

Walter's pine (Walter, Thomas): Botany. See: Webster's 3d.

Walter's test (Walter, Friedrich Karl): Medicine. See: Dorland.

WALTHALL, JOHN HENRY. 1900- . American chemical engineer. See: Amer. Men Sci., 9th ed. Copson, Walthall, and Hignett process.

WALTHARD, MAX. 1867-1933. Swiss gynecologist. See: Biog. Lex. hervorr. Aerzte. Walthard's cell nest.

Walthard's cell nest (Walthard, Max): Anatomy. See: Stedman.

WALTHER, AUGUSTINE FRIEDRICH. 1688-1746. German anatomist and botanist. See: Allg. Deut. Biog. Waltheria, Walther's ducts (or canals), Walther's ganglion, Walther's plexus.

WALTHER, MR. fl. 19th c. Austrian mining official. (Biography source unavailable.) Waltherite.

Waltheria (Walther, Augustine Friedrich): Botany. See: Charnock.

Waltherite (Walther, Mr.): Earth Sciences. See: Thrush; Webster's 3d.

Walther's ducts (or canals) (Walther, Augustine Friedrich): Anatomy. See: Donath; Dorland; Stedman.

Walther's ganglion (Walther, Augustine Friedrich): Anatomy. See: Donath; Dorland; Stedman.

Walther's plexus (Walther, Augustine Friedrich): Anatomy. See: Stedman.

WALTON, ERNEST THOMAS SINTON. 1903- . Irish physicist. See: World Who's Who Sci. Cockcroft-Walton accelerator, Cockcroft-Walton experiment.

Walton filter (Walton, James Henri?): Earth Sciences. See: Thrush.

WALTON, IZAAK. 1593-1683. English biographer and author. See: Dict. Nat. Biog. Waltonian.

WALTON, JAMES HENRI. b. 1878. American chemist. See: Pogg., vol. 5,6. Walton filter?, Walton's law.

Waltonian (Walton, Izaak): Literature. See: Webster's 3d.

Walton's law (Walton, James Henri): Chemistry. See: Stedman.

WANG, CHUNG TIK. 1888-1930. Chinese pathologist. See: Lancet (Jan. 24, 1931), p. 220. Wang's test.

Wang dynasty (Wang Kon): History. See: Osborne under "Korean Art."

Wang-Kao-Sak reagent (Wang, Si-Min; Kao, Chen-Heng; Kao, Chung-Hsi; and Sah, Peter P. T.): Chemistry. See: Van Nostrand Chem. Dict.

WANG KON. fl. 935. Korean soldier and ruler. See: Encyc. Brit., 1973 under "Korea," p. 458B. Wang dynasty.

WANG, S. fl. 1938. Chinese? chemist. Cited in: Chem. Abstr., vol. 32, p. 3295. Anger-Wang test.

WANG, SI-MIN. fl. 1936. Chinese chemist. Cited in: Chem. Abstr., vol. 30, p. 2875. Wang-Kao-Sak reagent.

WANGENSTEEN, OWEN HARDING. 1898- . American surgeon. See: World Who's Who Sci. Braun-Wangensteen graft, Wangensteen suction, (tube or apparatus).

Wangensteen suction, (tube or apparatus) (Wangensteen, Owen Harding): Medicine. See: Dorland; Stedman; Webster's 3d.

WANGER, J. O. fl. 1933. American physician. (Biography source unavailable.) Blackberg and Wanger's test.

Wang's test (Wang, Chung Tik): Medicine. See: Dorland; Stedman.

Wankel engine (Wankel, Felix): Engineering and Industry. See: Auger; Barnhart, (New Eng.); Hendrickson.

WANKEL, FELIX. 1902- . German engineer. See: Who's Who Sci. Europe, 1972. Wankel engine.

WANKLYN, JAMES ALFRED. 1834-1906. English analytical chemist. See: Dict. Nat. Biog. Wanklyn reaction.

Wanklyn reaction (Wanklyn, James Alfred): Chemistry. See: Van Nostrand Chem. Dict.

WANNER, FRIEDRICH CHRIST. b. 1870. German otologist. See: Biog. Lex. hervorr. Aerzte. Wanner's symptom.

Wanner's symptom (Wanner, Friedrich Christ): Medicine. See: Dorland.

Wannier function (Wannier, Gregory Hugh): Physics. See Internat. Dict. Phys. Elec.

WANNIER, GREGORY HUGH. 1911- . Swiss-born American physicist. See: World Who's Who Sci. Mott-Wannier exciton, Wannier function.

WANSCHER, OSCAR. 1846-1906. Danish physician. See: Biog. Lex. hervorr. Aerzte. Wanscher's mask.

Wanscher's mask (Wanscher, Oscar): Medicine. See: Dorland.

War of Jenkins'('s) ear (or Jenkins'('s) ear (incident)) (Jenkins, Robert): History. See: Barnhart (Eng. Lit.); Brewer; Harvey; Hendrickson; Morris; Steinberg.

War of William and Mary (William III of Orange and Mary II). See: King William's War.

Warburg apparatus (or flasks) (Warburg, Otto Heinrich): Medicine. See: Pennak; Stedman; Webster's 3d. Also known as: Warburg respirometer or manometer.

WARBURG, CARL. fl. 1840. Austrian physician. Cited in: Index-Cat. Libr. Surg.-Gen. Off., ser. 1, vol. 16, (1895). Warburg's tincture.

WARBURG, EMIL GABRIEL. 1846-1931. German physicist. See: Pogg., vol. 3,4,5,6. Warburg's law.

WARBURG, OTTO HEINRICH. 1883-1970. German biochemist and physiologist. See: Asimov. Warburg apparatus (or flasks), Warburg's factor, Warburg's theory, Warburg's yellow enzyme.

Warburg respirometer (or manometer) (Warburg, Otto Heinrich). See: Warburg apparatus (or flasks).

Warburg's factor (Warburg, Otto Heinrich): Medicine. See: Dorland; Henderson.

Warburg's law (Warburg, Emil Gabriel): Physics. See: Ballentyne.

Warburg's theory (Warburg, Otto Heinrich): Medicine. See: Stedman.

Warburg's tincture (Warburg, Carl): Medicine. See: Webster's 3d.

Warburg's yellow enzyme (Warburg, Otto Heinrich): Medicine. See: Dorland; Henderson; Stedman.

Ward drill (Ward, James Clifton?): Engineering and Industry. See: Thrush.

WARD, HENRY AUGUSTUS. 1834-1906. American naturalist. See: Dict. Amer. Biog. Wardite, Ward's cabinets.

WARD, HENRY BALDWIN. 1865-1945. American zoologist. See: Who Was Who Amer. Wardius.

WARD, JAMES CLIFTON. 1843-1880. English geologist. See: Dict. Nat. Biog. Ward drill?

Ward Leonard double-arm circuit breaker (Leonard, Ward): Electronics. See: Nat. Cycl. Amer. Biog. under "Leonard, (Harry) Ward," vol. 15, p. 4.

Ward Leonard system (or control) (Leonard, Ward): Engineering and Industry. See: Thrush; Webster's 3d.

WARD, LESTER FRANK. 1841-1913. American sociologist and geologist. See: Internat. Encyc. Soc. Sci. Ward's willow.

WARD, NATHANIEL BAGSHAW. 1791-1868. English botanist. See: Dict. Nat. Biog. Wardian case.

WARD, WILLIAM. 1534-1604. English physician. See: Dict. Nat. Biog. Ward's triangle?

WARD, WILLIAM HERBERT. fl. 1959-1970. Australian physician. See: Med. Direct. Australia, 1970. Ward's syndrome.

Wardian case (Ward, Nathaniel Bagshaw): Botany. See: Webster's 3d.

Wardite (Ward, Henry Augustus): Earth Sciences. See: Thrush; Webster's 3d.

Wardius (Ward, Henry Baldwin): Zoology. See: Pennak.

WARDROP, JAMES. 1782-1869. English surgeon. See: Dict. Nat. Biog. Wardrop's disease, Wardrop's method.

Wardrop's disease (Wardrop, James): Medicine. See: Dorland; Jablonski; Stedman.

Wardrop's method (Wardrop, James): Medicine. See: Dorland; Stedman.

Ward's cabinets (Ward, Henry Augustus): Earth Sciences. See: Webster's Biog. Dict.

Ward's syndrome (Ward, William Herbert): Medicine. See: Jablonski.

Ward's triangle (Ward, William?): Anatomy. See: Stedman.

Ward's willow (Ward, Lester Frank): Zoology. See: Mathews, M. M.

WARE, ALAN H. fl. 1929. American pharmaceutical chemist. Cited in: Chem. Abstr., Decenn. Indexes 1917-26, 1927-36. Ware test for nitrate, Ware test for phenol, cresol, naphthol, and thymol.

WARE, NORMAN JOSEPH. 1886-1949. Canadian-born American economist and sociologist. See: Who Was Who Amer. Ware plan?

Ware plan (Ware, Norman Joseph?): Politics. See: Smith.

Ware test for nitrate (Ware, Alan H.): Chemistry. See: Van Nostrand Chem. Dict.

Ware test for phenol, cresol, naphthol, and thymol (Ware, Alan H.): Chemistry. See: Van Nostrand Chem. Dict.

Waring distribution (Waring, Edward): Mathematics. See: Kendall.

WARING, EDWARD. 1734-1798. English mathematician. See: Dict. Nat. Biog. Waring distribution, Waring's formula, Waring's problem.

WARING, GEORGE EDWARD. 1833-1898. American agricultural and sanitary engineer. See: Dict. Amer. Biog. Waring's method (or system).

Waring's formula (Waring, Edward): Mathematics. See: Ballentyne.

Waring's method (or system) (Waring, George Edward): Engineering and Industry. See: Dorland.

Waring's problem (Waring, Edward): Mathematics. See: James.

WARLOP. fl. before 1937. German? inventor. (Biography source unavailable.) Warlop bearing.

Warlop bearing (Warlop): Engineering and Industry. See: Auger.

Warner method of determining class status (Warner, W. Lloyd): Sociology. See: Zadrozny.

WARNER, SAMUEL L. 1888-1927. American filmmaker. See: Sadoul. Samuel L. Warner Memorial Award.

WARNER, W. LLOYD. 1898- . American anthropologist and sociologist. See: World Who's Who Sci. Warner method of determining class status.

WARNERKE, LEON (Real name: VLADISLAV MALAKHOVSKII). 1837-1900. Russian civil engineer. See: Focal Encyc. Photog. Warnerke's folding roll-film camera.

Warnerke's folding roll-film camera (Warnerke, Leon): Photography. See: Focal Encyc. Photog.

Warren Act (Warren, Francis Emory): Politics. See: Smith.

WARREN, CHARLES HYDE. 1876-1950. American mineralogist. See: Who Was Who Amer. Warrenite.

Warren Commission (Warren, Earl): History. See: Encyc. Brit., 1973.

WARREN, CYRUS MOORS. 1824-1891. American chemist. See: Pogg., vol. 3,4,7. Warren test reaction for oils?

WARREN, E. R. fl. 1888. American scientist. Cited in: Dana. Warrenite.

WARREN, EARL. 1891-1974. American chief justice. See: Encyc. Brit., 1973. Warren Commission.

WARREN, FRANCIS EMORY. 1844-1929. American legislator. See: Dict. Amer. Biog. Warren Act.

WARREN, GEORGE FREDERICK. 1874-1938. American agricultural economist and presidential advisor on money policy. See: Dict. Amer. Biog. Warren monetary plan.

WARREN, JOHN COLLINS. 1778-1856. American surgeon. See: World Who's Who Sci. Warren's fat columns.

WARREN, MRS. Character in George Bernard Shaw's play, "Mrs. Warren's Profession," (1898). See: Barnhart, (Eng. Lit.) under "Mrs. Warren's Profession." Mrs. Warren's profession.

arren monetary plan (Warren, George Frederick): Economics. See: Dict. mer. Biog. under "Warren, George Frederick."

ARREN, RUSSELL. 1783-1860. American architect and engineer. See: ct. Amer. Biog. Warren truss (or girder).

ARREN, SAMUEL. 1781-1862. English divine. See: Dict. Nat. Biog. arrenites.

arren test reaction for oils (Warren, Cyrus Moors?): Chemistry. See: Van ostrand Chem. Dict.

arren truss (or girder) (Warren, Russell): Engineering and Industry. See: rush; Van Nostrand Sci. Encyc.; Webster's 3d.

arrenite (Warren, Charles Hyde): Earth Sciences. See: Thrush.

arrenite (Warren, E. R.): Earth Sciences. See: Thrush.

arrenites (Warren, Samuel): Religion. See: Canney.

arren's fat columns (Warren, John Collins): Medicine. See: Dorland.

arren's test (Derivation undetermined): See: Trommer's test.

ARSOP, G. fl. before 1870. English engineer. (Biography source un-ailable.) Warsop's engine.

arsop's engine (Warsop, G.): Engineering and Industry. See: Auger.

artegg drawing completion form (Wartegg, Ehrig): Psychology. See: Wolman.

ARTEGG, EHRIG. 1897- . German psychologist. See: Internat. Direct. ych., 1966. Wartegg drawing completion form.

ARTENBERG, ROBERT. 1887-1956. German neurologist. See: Kuerschner's eut. Gel. Kal., 1931. Wartenberg's disease (1), Wartenberg's disease (2).

artenberg's disease (1) (Wartenberg, Robert): Medicine. See: Dorland; blonski; Stedman.

artenberg's disease (2) (Wartenberg, Robert): Medicine. See: Jablonski.

ARTHIN, ALDRED SCOTT. 1866-1931. American pathologist. See: Dict. mer. Biog. Warthin-Finkeldey cells, Warthin-Starry silver stain, Warthin's mor.

arthin-Finkeldey cells (Warthin, Aldred Scott and Finkeldey, W.): Medicine. e: Stedman.

arthin-Starry silver stain (Warthin, Aldred Scott and Starry, Allen C.): Med-ine. See: Stedman.

arthin's tumor (Warthin, Aldred Scott): Medicine. See: Dorland; Jablonski; edman.

arwick, 2nd Earl of. See: Rich, Robert (2nd Earl of Warwick).

arwick grant (Warwick, Robert Rich, 2nd Earl of): History. See: Jameson.

arwick's powder (Derivation undetermined): See: Count Warwick's powder.

ashburn and Moen gauge (Washburn, Ichabod and Moen, Philip L.): Engin-ring and Industry. See: Van Nostrand Sci. Encyc. under "Gauge Number."

ashburn cell (Washburn, Edward Wight): Chemistry. See: Hackh.

ashburn corrections (Washburn, Edward Wight): Physics. See: Thewlis.

ASHBURN, EDWARD WIGHT. 1881-1934. American chemist. See: Dict. mer. Biog. Washburn cell, Washburn corrections.

ASHBURN, ICHABOD. 1798-1868. American manufacturer. See: Dict. mer. Biog. Washburn and Moen gauge.

ASHBURN, JACK. 1921- . American metallurgist. See: World Who's ho Sci. Parker-Washburn boundary.

ASHBURNE, CARLETON WOLSEY. b.1889. American educator. See: ho's Who Amer. Educ., 1929-30. Washburne-Vogel readability formula.

ashburne-Vogel readability formula (Washburne, Carleton Wolsey and Vogel, abel): Education. See: Good.

ashington and Adams federalist (Washington, George and Adams, John): olitics. See: Mathews, M. M.

ashington cake (or pie) (Washington, George): Food and Drink. See: athews, M. M.; Webster's 3d.

Washington canvasback (Washington, George): Zoology. See: Mathews, M. M.

Washington cedar (Washington, George): Botany. See: Mathews, M. M.

Washington elm (Washington, George): History. See: Jameson; Mathews, M. M.

Washington fan palm (or Washingtonia) (Washington, George): Botany. See: Mathews, M. M.; Taylor, N.; Webster's 3d.

WASHINGTON, GEORGE. 1732-1799. American general and president. See: Dict. Amer. Biog. by Washington, George Washington, George Washington submarine, Washington and Adams federalist, Washington cake (or pie), Washington canvasback, Washington cedar, Washington elm, Washington fan palm (or Washingtonia), Washington gun, Washington handpress, Washington influenza, Washington lily, Washington lottery wheel, Washington navel orange, Washington penny, Washington plum, Washington thorn, Washingtonia, Washingtonian (1), Washingtonian (2), Washingtoniana, Washingtonianism, Washington's birthday.

Washington gun (Washington, George): Weapons. See: Mathews, M. M.

Washington handpress (Washington, George): Printing. See: Mathews, M. M.; Webster's 3d.

Washington influenza (Washington, George): History. See: Mathews, M. M.

Washington lily (Washington, George): Botany. See: Mathews, M. M.

Washington lottery wheel (Washington, George): Recreation and Sports. See: Mathews, M. M.

WASHINGTON, MARTHA. 1732-1802. American First Lady. See: Encyc. Brit., 1973. Martha Washington armchair, Martha Washington geranium, Martha Washington table (or sewing cabinet).

Washington navel orange (Washington, George): Botany. See: Mathews, M. M.

Washington penny (Washington, George): Numismatics. See: Mathews, M. M.

Washington plum (Washington, George): Botany. See: Mathews, M. M.

Washington thorn (Washington, George): Botany. See: Mathews, M. M.

Washingtonia (Washington, George): History. See: Mathews, M. M.

Washingtonian (1) (Washington, George): Politics. See: Mathews, M. M.; Webster's 3d.

Washingtonian (2) (Washington, George): History. See: Mathews, M. M.; Webster's 3d.

Washingtoniana (Washington, George): History. See: Webster's 3d.

Washingtonianism (Washington, George): History. See: Mathews, M. M.

Washington's birthday (Washington, George): Generic Word. See: Mathews, M. M.

Wasicky reagent (Wasicky, Richard Balthasar): Chemistry. See: Van Nostrand Chem. Dict.

WASICKY, RICHARD BALTHASAR. b. 1884. German-born Brazilian pharma-cologist. See: World Who's Who Sci. Wasicky reagent.

WASMANN, ADOLPHUS. fl. 19th c. German anatomist. (Biography source unavailable.) Wasmann's glands.

Wasmann's glands (Wasmann, Adolphus): Anatomy. See: Stedman.

WASSEN, ERIK (In full: KNUT ERIK). 1901- . Danish physician. (Biogra-phy source unavailable.) Wassen test.

Wassen test (Wassen, Erik): Medicine. See: Stedman.

Wassermann antibody (Wassermann, August Paul von): Medicine. See: Sted-man.

WASSERMANN, AUGUST PAUL VON. 1866-1925. German bacteriologist. See: Encyc. Brit., 1973. Wassermann antibody, Wassermann-fast, Wassermann test (or reaction).

Wassermann-fast (Wassermann, August Paul von): Medicine. See: Dorland; Stedman.

Wassermann-positive pneumonia (or pulmonary infiltration) (Wassermann, August Paul von). See: Fanconi-Heggelin syndrome.

Wassermann test (or reaction) (Wassermann, August Paul von): Medicine. See: Hinsie; Stedman; Van Nostrand Sci. Encyc.

Wassilieff, Nikolai Porfiryevich. See: Vasiliev, Nikolai Porfirievich.

WASTLE, WILLIE. fl. 1650. English governor of Hume Castle. See: Lomas, vol. 2, pp. 165-166. Willie-Wastle (child's game).

Wat (or Watt's) dyke (Wat (or Watt)): History. See: Columbia Encyc.

Wat Tyler's rebellion (Tyler, Wat): History. See: Barnhart (Eng. Lit.); Phyfe.

WATASE, SHOZABURO. fl. 1920's. Japanese biologist. See: Hirsch. Watasenia.

Watasenia (Watase, Shozaburo): Zoology. See: Pennak.

water Leyner (Leyner, J(ohn) George): Engineering and Industry. See: Thrush. Also known as: Leyner-Ingersoll drill.

Waterhouse-Friderichsen syndrome (Waterhouse, Rupert and Friderichsen, Carl): Medicine. See: Dorland; Jablonski; Stedman. Also known as: Marchand-Waterhouse-Friderichsen syndrome.

WATERHOUSE, JAMES. 1842-1922. English soldier and photochemist. See: Who Was Who. Waterhouse stop.

WATERHOUSE, RUPERT. 1873-1958. English physician. See: World Who's Who Sci. Waterhouse-Friderichsen syndrome.

Waterhouse stop (Waterhouse, James): Photography. See: Focal Encyc. Photog.; Webster's 3d.

WATERS, CHARLES ALEXANDER. 1888-1961. American radiologist. See: Amer. Med. Direct., 1958. Waters' view roentgenogram (or projection).

Waters' view roentgenogram (or projection) (Waters, Charles Alexander): Medicine. See: Stedman.

WATKIN, F. fl. 1913. English ceramics engineer. (Biography source unavailable.) Watkin heat recorder?

Watkin heat recorder (Watkin, F.?): Engineering and Industry. See: Thrush.

WATKINS, ALFRED. fl. early 20th c. American photochemist. (Biography source unavailable.) Watkins factor.

Watkins factor (Watkins, Alfred): Photography. See: Focal Encyc. Photog.

Watkins' operation (Watkins, Thomas James): Medicine. See: Dorland.

WATKINS, THOMAS JAMES. 1863-1925. American gynecologist. See: Who Was Who Amer. Watkins' operation.

Watson (Watson, Dr.): Generic Word (uncomprehending, dull assistant). See: Partridge.

Watson-Crick helix (or model) (Watson, James Dewey and Crick, Francis Harry Compton): Genetics. See: Barnhart (New Eng.); Pennak; Stedman.

WATSON, DR. Character of the dull assistant in the Sherlock Holmes detective stories created by Sir Arthur Conan Doyle from 1891 to 1904. See: Gerwig. Watson.

WATSON, GEOFFREY STUART. 1921- . Australian-born American mathematical statistician. See: Amer. Men and Women Sci., 12th ed. Durbin-Watson statistic, Watson's 'U' statistic.

WATSON, HENRY WILLIAM. 1827-1903. English scientist. See: Who Was Who, 1897-1915. Galton-Watson process.

WATSON, HENRY WINFIELD. 1856-1933. American legislator. See: Biog. Direct. Amer. Congress. Watson-Parker Act.

WATSON, JAMES DEWEY. 1928- . American molecular biologist. See: World Who's Who Sci. Watson-Crick helix (or model).

WATSON, JOHN BROADUS. 1878-1958. American psychologist. See: Internat. Encyc. Soc. Sci. Watson's behaviorism.

WATSON, SIR MALCOLM. 1873-1955. English physician. See: Who Was Who. Watsonius.

Watson-Parker Act (Watson, Henry W. and Parker, James S.): Politics. Cited in: Encyc. Brit., 1973, Index.

WATSON, SERENO. 1826-1892. American botanist. See: Dict. Amer. Biog. Serenoa.

WATSON-WENTWORTH, CHARLES, 2D MARQUIS OF ROCKINGHAM. 1730-1782. English statesman. See: New Encyc. Brit., 1974, Microp. Rockingham ware (porcelain), Rockinghamites.

WATSON, WILLIAM 1559?-1603. English secular priest and conspirator. See: Dict. Nat. Biog. Watson's plot.

WATSON, SIR WILLIAM. 1715-1787. English physician and naturalist. See: Dict. Nat. Biog. Watsonia.

Watsonia (Waton, Sir William): Botany. See: Partridge; Taylor, N.

Watsonius (Watson, Sir Malcolm): Zoology. See: Dorland; Stedman; Webster's 3d.

Watson's behaviorism (Watson, John Broadus): Psychology. See: Chaplin; Wolman.

Watson's plot (Watson, William): History. See: Brewer; Steinberg.

Watson's 'U' statistic (Watson, Geoffrey Stuart); Statistics. See: Kendall.

Watt (Watt, James): Physics. See: Ballentyne; Dresner; Markus; Thewlis.

WATT, BOB E. 1917- . American physicist. See: Amer. Men and Women Sci., 12th ed. Watt spectrum.

Watt current (Watt, James): Physics. See: Webster's 3d.

Watt governor (Watt, James): Engineering and Industry. See: Auger.

Watt-hour (Watt, James): Physics. See: Hughes; Markus; Thrush.

WATT, JAMES. 1736-1819. Scottish engineer and inventor. See: Dict. Nat. Biog. abwatt, Boulton-Watt steam engine, gigawatt, international Watt, kilowatt, light-Watt, megawatt, microwatt, milliwatt, nanowatt, picowatt, terawatt, Watt, Watt current, Watt governor, Watt-hour, Watt parallel (or straight-line motion), Watt-second, Watt steam engine, Wattage, Watter, Watt-full loss, Wattmeter, Watt's curve, Watt's law.

Watt parallel (or straight-line motion) (Watt, James): Engineering and Industry. See: Auger; Van Nostrand Sci. Encyc.

Watt-second (Watt, James): Physics. See: Focal Encyc. Photog.; Markus; Thrush.

Watt spectrum (Watt, Bob E.): Physics. See: Internat. Dict. Ap. Math.

Watt steam engine (Watt, James): Engineering and Industry. See: Harvey.

Wattage (Watt, James): Physics. See: Webster's 3d.

Watteau (or Watteauesque) (Watteau, Jean Antoine): Fine Arts. See: Partridge; Picken; Webster's 3d.

Watteau back (Watteau, Jean Antoine): Fashion. See: Picken.

Watteau bodice (Watteau, Jean Antoine): Fashion. See: Picken.

Watteau gown (or dress) (Watteau, Jean Antoine): Fashion. See: Picken; Webster's 3d.

Watteau hat (Watteau, Jean Antoine): Fashion. See: Picken; Webster's 3d.

WATTEAU, JEAN ANTOINE. 1684-1721. French painter. See: Encyc. Brit., 1911. Watteau (or Watteauesque), Watteau back, Watteau bodice, Watteau gown (or dress), Watteau hat, Watteau mantle, Watteau pleat, Watteau sacque.

Watteau mantle (Watteau, Jean Antoine): Fashion. See: Picken.

Watteau pleat (Watteau, Jean Antoine): Fashion. See: Picken.

Watteau sacque (Watteau, Jean Antoine): Fashion. See: Picken.

Watter (Watt, James): Physics. See: Webster's 3d.

WATTEVILLE, BARON OSCAR DE. fl. 19th c. French nobleman. (Biography source unavailable.) Wattevillite.

Wattevillite (Watteville, Baron Oscar de): Earth Sciences. See: Thrush; Webster's 3d.

Wattfull loss (Watt, James). See: Ohmic loss.

Wattmeter (Watt, James): Physics. See: Thrush, Van Nostrand Sci. Encyc.

WATTS, ARTHUR FREDERICK. 1897-1970. Australian statesman and educator. See: Who Was Who. Watts-Vernon test.

Watts' bath (Watts, Oliver Patterson?): Engineering and Industry. See: Encyc. Brit. 1973 under "Electroplating."

Watt's curve (Watt, James?): Engineering and Industry. See: Encyc. Brit., 1973 under "Curves, Special."

WATTS, HUGH. 1582?-1643. English bell-founder. See: Dict. Nat. Biog. Watts's nazarenes.

WATTS, JOHN. fl. 1820. English-born American printer. (Biography source unavailable.) Watts press.

Watt's law (Watt, James): Engineering and Industry. See: Ballentyne.

Watts' nazarenes (Watts, Hugh): Religion. See: Canney.

WATTS, OLIVER PATTERSON. fl. 1927-33. American electrochemist. See: Amer. Men Sci., 5th ed. Watts' bath?

Watts press (Watts, John): Printing. See: Lockwood.

Watts-Vernon test (Watts, Arthur Frederick and Vernon, Philip Ewart): Education. See: Harrod.

WAUGH, SIR ANDREW SCOTT. 1810-1878. English general and engineer. See: Dict. Nat. Biog. Waugh drill?

Waugh drill (Waugh, Sir Andrew Scott?): Engineering and Industry. See: Thrush.

WAVELL, WILLIAM. d. 1829. English physician. (Biography source unavailable.) Wavellite.

Wavellite (Wavell, William): Earth Sciences. See: Thrush; Van Nostrand Sci. Encyc.; Webster's 3d.

way of Martha (Martha, Saint): Generic Word (active life). See: Partridge.

WAYLAND. Legendary smith and wizard. See: Jobes. Waylands' geweroc, Wayland's smithy (or stocc).

Wayland's geweroc (Wayland): Mythology. See: Jobes.

Wayland's smithy (or stocc) (Wayland): Mythology. See: Encyc. Brit., 1973 under "Wayland the Smith."; Jobes.

Wayne solution (Wayne, Winston Joe): Chemistry. See: Van Nostrand Chem. Dict.

WAYNE, WINSTON JOE. 1914- . American chemist. See: Amer. Men and Women Sci., 12th ed. Wayne solution.

WEAVER, ELMER RUPEL. b. 1887. American chemist. See: Pogg., vol. 6. Weaver test.

WEAVER, JAMES BAIRD. 1833-1912. American soldier and politician. See: Dict. Amer. Biog. Weaverite.

WEAVER, JOHN ERNST. b. 1884. American botanist. See: Columbia Encyc. Weaver plum?

Weaver plum (Weaver, John Ernst?): Botany. See: Encyc. Brit. 1973 under "Plum."

Weaver test (Weaver, Elmer Rupel): Chemistry. See: Van Nostrand Chem. Dict.

Weaverite (Weaver, James Baird): Politics. See: Mathews, M. M.

web of Penelope (Penelope). See: Penelope's web (or Penelopize).

WEBB, EDWIN YATES. 1872-1955. American lawyer and legislator. See: Who Was Who Amer. Webb-Kenyon Act, Webb-Pomerene Act.

Webb effect (Webb, J. T.?): Engineering and Industry. See: Thrush.

WEBB, GEORGE BARLOW. 1914- . American chemical engineer. See: Amer. Men Sci., 9th ed. Benedict-Webb-Rubin equation.

WEBB, J. T. fl. 1915. American ceramics engineer. (Biography source unavailable.) Webb effect?

Webb-Kenyon Act (Webb, Edwin Yates and Kenyon, William Squire): Politics. See: Morris; Smith.

Webb-Pomerene Act (Webb, Edwin Yates and Pomerene, Atlee): Politics. See: Clark; Greenwald; Morris.

Webber dynamometer (Webber, Samuel): Engineering and Industry. See: Auger.

WEBBER, MORTON. fl. 1911. American mining engineer. Cited in: Chem. Abstr. vol. 5, p. 3781. Webber's method.

WEBBER, SAMUEL. fl. 1889. American engineer. (Biography source unavailable.) Webber dynamometer.

Webber's method (Webber, Morton): Engineering and Industry. See: Thrush.

Weber (Weber, Wilhelm Eduard): Physics. See: Ballentyne; Dresner; Van Nostrand Sci. Encyc.

Weber-Christian disease (or syndrome) (Weber, Frederick Parkes and Christian, Henry Asbury): Medicine. See: Dorland; Jablonski; Stedman. Also known as: Pfeifer-Weber-Christian syndrome.

Weber-Cockayne syndrome (Weber, Frederick Parkes and Cockayne, Edward Alfred). See: Fox's disease.

Weber differential equation (Weber, Heinrich): Mathematics. See: Internat. Dict. Ap. Math.

Weber-Dimitri syndrome (Weber, Frederick Parkes and Dimitri, Vincente). See: Sturge-Weber syndrome.

WEBER, ERNST HEINRICH. 1795-1878. German anatomist. See: Internat. Encyc. Soc. Sci. Weber-Fechner law, Weber fraction, Weberian apparatus (or organ), Weberian ossicles, Weber's experiment, Weber's paradox, Weber's test for hearing, Weber's test for indican.

Weber-Fechner law (Weber, Ernst Heinrich and Fechner, Gustav Theodor). See: Fechner's law.

Weber fraction (Weber, Ernst Heinrich): Physiology. See: English.

WEBER, FREDERICK PARKES. 1863?-1962. English physician. See: World Who's Who Sci. Hutchinson-Weber-Peutz syndrome, Rendu-Weber-Osler syndrome, Sturge-Weber syndrome, Weber-Christian disease (or syndrome), Weber-Cockayne syndrome, Weber's syndrome.

WEBER, FRIEDRICH EUGEN. 1832-1891. German otologist. See: Biog. Lex. hervorr. Aerzte. Weber's test.

WEBER, G. fl. 1948. German physician. (Biography source unavailable.) Hoerlein-Weber disease.

WEBER, HEINRICH. 1842-1913. German mathematician. See: World Who's Who Sci. Bessel functions of Weber, Weber differential equation.

WEBER, SIR HERMANN DAVID. 1823-1918. English physician. See: Who Was Who, 1917-1928. Weber's syndrome (sign, symptom or paralysis).

WEBER, K. fl. 1897. German chemist. (Biography source unavailable.) Weber-Koch test, Weber-Tollens test reaction.

Weber-Koch test (Weber, K. and Koch, G.?): Chemistry. See: Van Nostrand Chem. Dict.

Weber-Leyden syndrome (Weber, Sir Hermann David, and Leyden, Ernst Victor von). See: Leyden's paralysis (1) (or syndrome).

WEBER, MAX. 1864-1920. German economist. See: Internat. Encyc. Soc. Sci. Weberian theory, Weber's law of religious determinism.

WEBER, MAX WILHELM KARL. d. 1937. German zoologist. See: Royal Soc. Obit. Not. of Fellows vol. II (1938), pp. 347-355. Weber's line.

WEBER, MORITZ. b. 1871. German mechanician. See: Kuerschner's Deut. Gel.-Kal., 1931. Weber number?

WEBER, MORITZ IGNAZ. 1795-1875. German anatomist. See: Allg. Deut. Biog. Weber's corpuscle (or pouch), Weber's glands, Weber's organ.

Weber number (Weber, Moritz?): Engineering and Industry. See: Ballentyne; Internat. Dict. Ap. Math.; Huschke.

Weber process (Weber, Wilhelm?): Engineering and Industry. See: Thrush.

WEBER, RUDOLF H. G. 1874-1920. Swiss physical chemist. See: Pogg., vol. 4,5. Weber theory of ferromagnetism?

WEBER, THEOBALD. 1823-1886. Danish industrialist. See: Dansk Biog. Lek. Weberite.

WEBER, THEODOR. 1829-1914. German physician. See: Biog. Lex. hervorr. Aerzte. Weber's douceh, Weber's maneuver?

Weber theory of ferromagnetism (Weber, Rudolf H. G.?): Physics. See: Thewlis.

Weber-Tollens test reaction (Weber, K. and Tollens, Bernard): Chemistry. See: Van Nostrand Chem. Dict.

WEBER, WILHELM. fl. 1915. German engineer. (Biography source unavailable.) Weber process?

WEBER, WILHELM EDUARD. 1804-1891. German physicist and physiologist. See: Allg. Deut. Biog. Weber, Weber's point, Weber's triangle.

Weberian apparatus (or organ) (Weber, Ernst Heinrich): Zoology. See: Gray; Henderson; Pennak.

Weberian ossicles (Weber, Ernst Heinrich): Zoology. See: Pennak; Webster's 3d.

Weberian theory (Weber, Max): Sociology. See: Webster's 3d.

Weberite (Weber, Theobald): Earth Sciences. See: Thrush; Webster's 3d.

Weber's corpuscle (or pouch) (Weber, Moritz Ignaz): Anatomy. See: Dorland; Webster's 3d.

Weber's douche (Weber, Theodor): Medicine. See: Dorland.

Weber's experiment (Weber, Ernst Heinrich): Physiology. See: Stedman.

Weber's glands (Weber, Moritz Ignaz): Anatomy. See: Dorland; Stedman.

Weber's law of religious determinism (Weber, Max): Sociology. See: Zadrozny.

Weber's line (Weber, Max Wilhelm Karl): Zoology. See: Henderson; Pennak.

Weber's maneuver (Weber, Theodor?). See: Valsalva's maneuver.

Weber's organ (Weber, Moritz Ignaz): Anatomy. See: Donath; Dorland; Gray; Stedman.

Weber's paradox (Weber, Ernst Heinrich): Physiology. See: Stedman.

Weber's point (Weber, Wilhelm Eduard): Anatomy. See: Stedman.

Weber's syndrome (Weber, Frederick Parkes). See: Klippel-Trenaunay syndrome.

Weber's syndrome (sign, symptom or paralysis) (Weber, Sir Hermann David): Medicine. See: Dorland; Hinsie; Jablonski; Stedman. Also known as: Leyden's paralysis (1) (or syndrome), Weber-Leyden syndrome.

Weber's test (Weber, Friedrich Eugen): Medicine. See: Dorland.

Weber's test for hearing (Weber, Ernst Heinrich): Physiology. See: Stedman.

Weber's test for indican (Weber, Ernst Heinrich): Medicine. See: Dorland; Stedman.

Weber's triangle (Weber, Wilhelm Eduard): Anatomy. See: Stedman.

WEBLEY, F. fl. early 20th c. English gun manufacturer. (Biography source unavailable.) Webley revolver.

Webley revolver (Webley, F.): Weapons. See: Partridge.

Webster (1) (Webster, Noah): Generic Word (lexicographer). See: Partridge.

Webster (2) (or Webster's) (Webster, Noah): Generic Word (dictionary). See: Hendrickson; Mathews, M. M.; Partridge.

Webster-Ashburton Treaty (Webster, Daniel and Ashburton, Alexander Baring, 1st Lord): History. See: Morris; Morris and Irwin.

Webster-Baldy operation (Webster, John Clarence and Baldy, John Montgomery): See: Webster's operation.

Webster blue back speller (Webster, Noah): Education. See: Matthews, M. M.

WEBSTER, DANIEL. 1782-1852. American statesman. See: Dict. Amer. Biog. Webster-Ashburton Treaty. Webster fly, Webster-Hayne debate, Webster ticket, Websterian.

Webster fly (Webster, Daniel): Zoology. See: Mathews, M. M.

Webster-Hayne debate (Webster, Daniel and Hayne, Robert Young): History. See: Morris and Irwin.

WEBSTER, JOHN. 1878-1927. English chemist. See: Biochem. J. vol. 21 (1927), pp. 265-66. Webster's test.

WEBSTER, JOHN CLARENCE. 1863-1950. Canadian-born American gynecologist. See: Who Was Who Amer. Webster's operation.

WEBSTER, NOAH. 1758-1843. American philologist, lexicographer and journalist. See: Dict. Amer. Biog. Webster (1), Webster (2) (or Webster's), Webster blue back speller.

WEBSTER, THOMAS. 1773-1844. English geologist. See: Dict. Nat. Biog. Websterite.

Webster ticket (Webster, Daniel): Political Science. See: Mathews, M. M.

Websterian (Webster, Daniel): Generic Word. See: Mathews, M. M.

Websterite (Webster, Thomas): Earth Sciences. See: Charnock.

Webster's operation (Webster, John Clarence): Medicine. See: Dorland; Stedman. Also know as: Webster-Baldy operation.

Webster's test (Webster, John): Chemistry. See: Dorland; Stedman.

WECHSBERG, FRIEDRICH. 1873-1929. German physician. See: Biog. Lex. hervorr. Aerzte, 1880-1930. Neisser-Wechsburg phenomenon.

Wechsler adult intelligence scale (Wechsler, David): Psychology. See: Chaplin; Wolman.

Wechsler-Bellevue scale (or test) (Wechsler, David): Psychology. See: English; Good; Hinsie; Wolman.

WECHSLER, DAVID. 1896- . Rumanian-born American psychologist. See: World Who's Who Sci. Wechsler adult intelligence scale, Wechsler-Bellevue scale (or test), Wechsler intelligence scale for children, Wechsler preschool and primary scale of intelligence.

Wechsler intelligence scale for children (Wechsler, David): Psychology. See: Chaplin; Wolman.

Wechsler preschool and primary scale of intelligence (Wechsler, David): See: Good; Wolman.

WEDDELL, GRAHAM (In full: ALEXANDER GRAHAM McDONNELL). 1908- . English anatomist and physiologist. See: Med. Direct. 1972. Falconer-Weddell syndrome.

WEDDELL, JAMES. 1787-1834. English antarctic explorer, sealer and navigator. See: Dict. Nat. Biog. Weddellite, Weddell's seal.

Weddellite (Weddell, James): Earth Sciences. See: Thrush.

Weddell's seal (Weddell, James): Zoology. See: Pennak; Webster's 3d.

WEDDERBURN, JOSEPH HENRY MACLAGAN. 1882-1948. Scottish mathematician. See: World Who's Who Sci. Wedderburn theorem on finite division rings, Wedderburn's structure theorems.

Wedderburn theorem on finite division rings (Wedderburn, Joseph Henry Maclagan): Mathematics. See: James.

Wedderburn's structure theorems (Wedderburn, Joseph Henry Maclagan): Mathematics. See: James.

WEDDLE, THOMAS. 1818-1853. English mathematician. See: Boase, suppl. Weddle's rule.

Weddle's rule (Weddle, Thomas): Mathematics: See. Ballentyne; Internat. Dict. Ap. Math.; James.

Wedensky effect (or inhibition) (Wedensky, Nikolay Yevgen'yevich): Psychology. See: Drever; English; Stedman.

WEDENSKY, NIKOLAY YEVGEN'YEVICH. 1852-1922. Russian physiologist. See: Who Was Who USSR. phenomenon of Wedensky, Wedensky effect (or inhibition).

Wedgwood-arbeit (Wedgwood, Josiah): Applied Arts. See: Encyc. Brit., 1973 under "Pottery and Porcelain."

WEDGWOOD, HENSLEIGH. 1803-1891. English philologist. See: Dict. Nat. Biog. Wooden wedge.

WEDGWOOD, JOSIAH. 1730-1795. English potter. See: Dict. Nat. Biog. Wedgwood-arbeit, Wedgwood print, Wedgwood pyrometer (or scale), Wedgwood ware.

Wedgwood print (Wedgwood, Josiah): Fashion. See: Picken.

Wedgwood pyrometer (or scale) (Wedgwood, Josiah): Engineering and Industry. See: Hendrickson; Thrush.

Wedgwood ware (Wedgwood, Josiah): Applied Arts. See: Hendrickson; Partridge; Thrush.

Wednesday (Odin): Generic Word. See: Funk.

WEECH, A. ASHLEY. 1895- . American pediatrician. See: Amer. Med. Direct., 1973. Weech's syndrome.

Weech's syndrome (Weech, A. Ashley). See: Christ-Siemens-Touraine syndrome.

WEEHUIZEN, F. fl. 1905. Dutch? chemist. Cited in: Chem. Zentralblatt, 1905, p. 1191. Weehuizen test for cyanide.

Weehuizen test for cyanide (Weehuizen, F.): Chemistry. See: Van Nostrand Chem. Dict.

Weeks' bacillus (Weeks, John). See: Koch-Weeks bacillus.

WEEKS, JOHN. 1853-1949. American ophthalmologist. See: World Who's Who Sci. Koch-Weeks bacillus, Koch-Weeks conjunctivitis.

WEEKS, JOHN WINGATE. 1860-1926. American broker and politician. See: Dict. Amer. Biog. Weeks Law.

Weeks Law (Weeks, John Wingate): Law. See: Smith.

WEEMS, PHILIP VAN HORN. b. 1889. American air navigator. (Biography source unavailable.) Weems system of navigation.

Weems system of navigation (Weems, Philip Van Horn): Engineering and Industry. See: Van Nostrand Sci. Encyc. under "Celestial Navigation."

Weerman degradation (Weerman, Rudolf Adriaan): Chemistry. See: Ballentyne; Van Nostrand Chem. Dict.

WEERMAN, RUDOLF ADRIAAN. fl. 1931. Dutch chemist. See: Chem. Weekblad vol. xxviii (1931), p. 326. Weerman degradation.

Weg rescue apparatus (Weg, Ruth Bass?): Engineering and Industry. See: Thrush.

WEG, RUTH BASS. 1920- . American biologist and biochemist. (Biography source unavailable.) Weg rescue apparatus?

WEGENER, ALFRED LOTHAR. 1880-1930. German geophysicist and meteorologist. See: World Who's Who Sci. Wegener-Bergeron process, Wegener hypothesis.

Wegener-Bergeron process (Wegener, Alfred Lothar and Bergeron, Jules). See: Bergeron-Findeisen theory.

WEGENER, F. fl. 1939. German pathologist. (Biography source unavailable.) Wegener's granulomatosis.

Wegener hypothesis (Wegener, Alfred Lothar): Earth Sciences. See: Webster's 3d.

Wegener's granulomatosis (Wegener, F.): Medicine. See: Jablonski; Stedman.

Weger aspirator (Weger, Nikolaus?): Earth Sciences. See: Huschke.

WEGER, NIKOLAUS. 1891- . German agricultural meteorologist. See: Auerschner's Deutsch. Gel. Kal., 1940-1941. Weger aspirator?

WEGIERKO, JAKUB. 1889-1960. Polish physician. See: Wiadomosci Lekarskie vol. 23, no. 13 (1970), p. 1157. Wegierko's coma.

Wegierko's coma (Wegierko, Jakub): Medicine. See: Jablonski.

WEGNER, FRIEDRICH RUDOLF GEORG. 1843-189?. German pathologist. (Biography source unavailable.) Wegner's disease (or osteochondritis), Wegner's sign.

Wegner's disease (or osteochondritis) (Wegner, Friedrich Rudolf Georg): Medicine. See: Dorland; Stedman. Also known as: Parrot's disease (1) (paralysis, pseudo-paralysis or Parrot disease).

Wegner's sign (Wegner, Friedrich Rudolf Georg): Medicine. See: Dorland; Stedman.

WEGSCHEIDER, RUDOLF FRANZ. 1859-1935. Austrian electrochemist. See: Pogg. vols. 4-7a. Wegscheider test for side reactions?, Wegscheiderite.

Wegscheider test for side reactions (Wegscheider, Rudolf Franz?): Chemistry. See: Van Nostrand Chem. Dict.

Wegscheiderite (Wegscheider, Rudolf Franz): Earth Sciences. See: Thrush.

WEHNELT, ARTUR RUDOLPH BERTHOLD. 1871-1944. German physicist. See: World Who's Who Sci. Wehnelt cathode, Wehnelt cylinder, Wehnelt's interrupter (or breaker).

Wehnelt cathode (Wehnelt, Artur Rudolph Berthold): Engineering and Industry. See: Markus.

Wehnelt cylinder (Wehnelt, Artur Rudolph Berthold): Engineering and Industry. See: Markus.

Wehnelt's interrupter (or breaker) (Wehnelt, Artur Rudolph Berthold): Engineering and Industry. See: Dorland.

WEHRLE, ALOIS. 1791-1835. Austrian mining commissioner. See: Allg. Deut. Biog. Wehrlite.

Wehrlite (Wehrle, Alois): Earth Sciences. See: Charnock; Thrush; Webster's 3d.

WEIBEL, RAYMOND. fl. 1935. Swiss chemist. Cited in: Chem. Abstr., vol. 29, p. 2471. Gutzeit-Wiebel spot test for antimony.

WEIBKE, FRIEDRICH. d. 1941. German chemist. Cited in: Chem. Abstr., vol. 27, p. 42. Geilmann-Wrigge-Weibke test for rhenium.

Weibull distribution (Weibull, Ernst Hjalmar Waloddi): Statistics. See: Kendall.

WEIBULL, ERNST HJALMAR WALODDI. 1887- . Swedish applied physicist. See: World Who's Who Sci. Weibull distribution, Weibull's theory.

WEIBULL, MATS (In full: KRIST. OSKAR MATS). d. 1923. Swedish mineralogist. See: Geolog. Foren. Forhandlingar vol. XLVI (1924), pp. 692-95. Weibullite.

Weibullite (Weibull, Mats): Earth Sciences. See: Thrush; Webster's 3d.

Weibull's theory (Weibull, Ernst Hjalmar Waloddi): Statistics. See: Thrush.

WEICHARDT, WOLFGANG (In full: JULIUS WOLFGANG). 1875-1945. German pathologist. See: Biog. Lex hervorr. Aerzte. Weichardt's antikenotoxin.

Weichardt's antikenotoxin (Weichardt, Wolfgang): Medicine. See: Dorland.

WEICHBRODT, RAPHAEL. b. 1886. German neurologist. See: Biog. Lex. hervorr. Aerzte. Weichbrodt's reaction.

Weichbrodt's reaction (Weichbrodt, Raphael): Medicine. See: Dorland.

WEICHERT, EMIL (In full: JOHANN EMIL). 1861-1928. German geophysicist. See: Pogg., vols. 4,5,6. Wiechert seismograph.

WEICHSELBAUM, ANTON. 1845-1920. Austrian pathologist. See: World Who's Who Sci. Fraenkel-Weichselbaum pneumococcus, Weichselbaum's coccus.

Weichselbaum's coccus (Weichselbaum, Anton): Medicine. See: Dorland; Stedman.

WEIDEL, HUGO. 1849-1899. Austrian chemist. See: Pogg., vol. 4. Weidel's reaction, Weidel's test.

Weidel's reaction (Weidel, Hugo): Medicine. See: Dorland; Stedman.

Weidel's test (Weidel, Hugo): Medicine. See: Stedman.

Weid's lana-head (Derivation undetermined): Zoology. Cited in: Stedman under "Snakebite antivenins, app. 1B".

Weierstrass' approximation theorem (Weierstrass, Karl Theodor): Mathematics. See: Ballentyne; Internat. Dict. Ap. Math.; James.

Weierstrass elliptic (or P) function (Weierstrass, Karl Theodor Wilhelm): Mathematics. See: Ballentyne; Internat. Dict. Ap. Math; Internat. Dict. Phys. Elec.

Weierstrass inequalities (Weierstrass, Karl Theodor Wilhelm): Mathematics. See: Ballentyne.

Weierstrass' infinite product (Weierstrass, Karl Theodor Wilhelm): Mathematics. See: Ballentyne.

WEIERSTRASS, KARL THEODOR WILHELM. 1815-1897. German mathematician. See: Allg. Deut. Biog. Pogg., vols. 2-5. World Who's Who Sci. Bolzano-Weierstrass theorem; equations of Weierstrass, Weierstrass' approximation theorem, Weierstrass elliptic or P function, Weierstrass inequalities, Weierstrass' infinite product, Weierstrass' M-test for uniform convergence, Weierstrass' necessary condition, Weierstrass' preparation theorem, Weierstrass' zeta function.

Weierstrass' M-test for uniform convergence (Weierstrass, Karl Theodor Wilhelm): Mathematics. See: Ballentyne; Internat. Dict. Ap. Math.; James.

Weierstrass' necessary condition (Weierstrass, Karl Theodor Wilhelm): Mathematics. See: James.

Weierstrass' preparation theorem (Weierstrass, Karl Theodor Wilhelm): Mathematics. See: James.

Weierstrass' zeta function (Weierstrass, Karl Theodor Wilhelm): Mathematics. See: Internat. Dict. Ap. Math.

WEIGEL, CHRISTIAN EHRENFRIED VON. 1748-1831. German physician and botanist. See: Allg. Deut. Biog. Weigela (or Weigelia) (honeysuckle), Weigelia (red).

WEIGEL, VALENTINE. 1533-1588. German theologian and mystic philosopher. See: Allg. Deut. Biog., Nouv Biog. Univ. Weigelians.

Weigela (or Weigelia) (honeysuckle) (Weigel, Christian Ehrenfried von): Botany. See: Hendrickson; Partridge; Taylor, N.

Weigelia (red) (Weigel, Christian Ehrenfried von): Botany. See: Webster's 3d.

Weigelians (Weigel, Valentine): Religion. See: Canney.

WEIGERT, CARL. 1845-1904. German histologist and pathologist. See: World Who's Who Sci. Weigert-Gram stain for bacteria in tissues, Weigert's iodine solution, Weigert's law, Weigert's methods, Weigert's stains.

Weigert effect (Weigert, Fritz): Chemistry. See: Hackh.

WEIGERT, FRITZ. b. 1876. German photochemist. See: Pogg., vols. 5, 6. Weigert effect.

Weigert-Gram stain for bacteria in tissues (Weigert, Carl, and Gram, Hans Christian Joachim): Medicine. See: Stedman.

Weigert's iodine solution (Weigert, Carl): Medicine. See: Stedman.

Weigert's law (Weigert, Carl): Medicine. See: Dorland; Stedman.

Weigert's method (Weigert, Carl): Medicine. See: Webster's 3d.

Weigert's stains (Weigert, Carl): Medicine. See: Dorland; Stedman.

weighted mean of Cooke and Ponder (Cooke, William Edmond and Ponder, Eric). See: Cooke-Ponder method.

WEIGL, EGON. fl. 1929-1968. Rumanian-born German? psychologist. (Biography source unavailable.) Gelb-Goldstein-Weigl-Scheerer object sorting test, Weigl-Goldstein-Scheerer test.

Weigl-Goldstein-Scheerer test (Weigl, Egon; Goldstein, Kurt; and Scheerer, Martin): Psychology. See: Chaplin; English; Wolman.

WEIL, ARTHUR. b. 1887. German-born American neuropathologist. See: Who's Who Among Physicians and Surg., 1938. Abderhalden-Weil test reaction, Weil's stain.

WEIL, EDMUND. 1879-1922. Austrian bacteriologist. See: Biog. Lex. hervorr. Aerzte. Weil-Felix reaction (or agglutination test).

Weil-Felix reaction (or agglutination test) (Weil, Edmund and Felix, Arthur): Medicine. See: Dorland; Hackh; Stedman.

WEIL, H. ADOLF. 1848-1916. German physician. See: Biog. Lex. hervorr. Aerzte; World Who's Who in Sci. Weil's disease (or icterus), Weil's syndrome.

WEIL, HUGO. b. 1863. German chemist. See: Pogg., vol. 5. Weil test reaction.

WEIL, L. A. fl. 19th c. German dentist. (Biography souce unavailable.) Weil's basal layer (or zone).

Weil-Marchesani syndrome (Weil, Georges and Marchesani, Oswald). See: Marchesani's syndrome.

WEIL, RICHARD. 1876-1917. American physician. See: World Who's Who Sci. Weil's test.

Weil test reaction (Weil, Hugo): Chemistry. See: Van Nostrand Chem. Dict.

Weiler's law (Derivation undetermined): Sociology. See: Martin.

WEILL, EDMOND. 1858-1924. French pediatrician. See: Biog. Lex. hervorr. Aerzte. Weill's sign.

WEILL, GEORGES. 1866-1952. French ophthalmologist. See: Bull. et Mem. Soc. Franc. Opht., vol. 65 (1952 F). Weill-Marchesani syndrome, Weill's syndrome.

WEILL, JEAN. 1903- . French physician. See: Who's Who France, 1971-72. Leri-Weill syndrome.

Weill-Reys-Adie syndrome (Weill, Georges; Reys, L.; and Adie, William John). See: Adie's syndrome.

Weill-Reys syndrome (Weill, Georges and Reys, L.). See: Adie's syndrome.

Weiller disc (Weiller, Lazare): Engineering and Industry. See: Focal Encyc. Film.

WEILLER, LAZARE. fl. 1889. German scientist. (Biography source unavailable.) Weiller disc.

Weill's sign (Weill, Edmond): Medicine. See: Dorland.

Weill's syndrome (Weill, Georges). See: Adie's syndrome.

Weil's basal layer (or zone) (Weil, L. A.): Dentistry. See: Dorland.

Weil's disease (or icterus) (Weil, H. Adolf): Medicine. See: Dorland; Jablonski; Stedman. Also known as: Fiedler's disease, Landouzy's disease, Larrey-Weil disease, Mathieu's disease, Vasilev's disease.

Weil's stain (Weil, Arthur): Medicine. See: Dorland.

Weil's syndrome (Weil, H. Adolf): Medicine. See: Dorland; Stedman.

Weil's test (Weil, Richard): Medicine. See: Dorland; Stedman.

Weimarn, Peter Petrovic von. See: Von Weimarn, Peter Petrovic.

Weinberg-Himelfarb syndrome (Weinberg, Tobias Bernard and Himelfarb, Albert J.): Medicine. See: Jablonski.

WEINBERG, MICHEL. 1868-1940. French pathologist. See: Rev. Stiint. Med. vol. 29 (1933), pp. 440-44. Weinberg's reaction.

WEINBERG, TOBIAS BERNARD. 1887- . American radiologist. See: Amer. Med. Direct., 1973. Weinberg-Himelfarb syndrome.

WEINBERG, WILHELM. b. 1862. German physician. See: Biog. Lex. hervorr Aerzte, 1880-1930. Hardy-Weinberg law (or formula).

Weinberg's reaction (Weinberg, Michel): Medicine. See: Dorland: Stedman.

WEINGAERTNER, ERNST. fl. 1952. German chemist. (Biography source unavailable.) Weingaertner solution?

Weingaertner solution (Weingaertner, Ernst?): Chemistry. See: Van Nostrand Chem. Dict.

Weingarten formulas (Weingarten, Julius?): Mathematics. See: Internat. Dict. Ap. Math.

WEINGARTEN, JULIUS (In full: JOHANNES LEONHARD GOTTFRIED JULIUS). 1836-1910. German mathematician. See: Pogg. vols. 3-5. Weingarten formulas?, Weingarten surface.

WEINGARTEN, R. J. fl. 1943. German physician. (Biography source unavailable.) Weingarten's syndrome.

Weingarten surface (Weingarten, Julius): Mathematics. See: James.

Weingarten's syndrome (Weingarten, R. J.): Medicine. See: Jablonski.

Weingrow's heel reflex (Derivation undetermined): Medicine. See: Stedman. Also known as: Guillain-Barre reflex, Reimer's reflex.

WEINIG, ARTHUR JOHN. b. 1883. American mining engineer. See: Who's Who Engin., 1937. Weinig flotation cell.

Weinig flotation cell (Weinig, Arthur John): Engineering and Industry. See: Thrush.

Weinland-Doettinger test reaction (Weinland, Rudolf Heinrich Friedrich and Doettinger, Anna): Chemistry. See: Van Nostrand Chem. Dict.

Weinland-Heinzler reagent (Weinland, Rudolf and Heinzler, J.): Chemistry. See: Van Nostrand Chem. Dict.

WEINLAND, RUDOLF HEINRICH FRIEDRICH. 1865-1936. German chemist. See: Pogg., vols. 4, 5, 6. Binder-Weinland reagent, Weinland-Doettinger test reaction, Weinland-Heinzler reagent.

WEINMANN, J. W. 18th c. German apothecary (Biography source unavailable.) Weinmannia.

Weinmannia (Weinmann, J. W.): Botany. See: Webster's 3d.

WEINSCHENK, ERNST H. O. K. 1865-1921. German petrographer. See: Deut. Biog. Jahrb., 1921; Pogg., vols. 4, 5. Weinschenkite.

Weinschenkite (Weinschenk, Ernst H. O. K.): Earth Sciences. See: Thrush; Webster's 3d.

WEINSTEIN, JULIUS WILLIAM. 1873-1923. American physician. See: Amer. Med. Direct., 1923. Weinstein's test.

Weinstein's test (Weinstein, Julius William): Medicine. See: Dorland; Stedman.

Weir Mitchell, Silas. See: Mitchell, Silas Weir.

Weir Mitchell treatment (Mitchell, Silas Weir). See: Mitchell's treatment (or rest cure).

Weir Mitchell's disease (Mitchell, Silas Weir). See: Mitchell's syndrome (1).

WEIR, ROBERT FULTON. 1838-1927. American surgeon. See: Dict. Amer. Biog. Weir's operation, Weir's technique.

Weir's operation (Weir, Robert Fulton): Medicine. See: Dorland; Stedman.

Weir's technique (Weir, Robert Fulton): Medicine. See: Stedman.

WEISBACH, ALBIN (In full: JULIUS ALBIN). 1833-1901. German mineralogist. See: Biog. Jahrb. Deut. Nekr., 1901; Pogg., vols. 3, 4. Weisbachite.

WEISBACH, AUGUSTIN or ALBIN W. 1837-1914. Bohemian-born Austrian anatomist and anthropologist. See: Biog. Lex. hervorr. Aerzte. Weisbach's angle.

WEISBACH, JULIUS (In full: LUDWIG ALBIN JULIUS). 1806-1871. German mineralogist. See: Allg. Deut. Biog., Pogg., vols. 2, 3, 7a suppl. Weisbach triangle?

Weisbach triangle (Weisbach, Julius?): Earth Sciences. See: Thrush.

Weisbachite (Weisbach, Albin): Earth Sciences. See: Webster's 3d.

Weisbach's angle (Weisbach, Augustin): Anatomy. See: Dorland; Stedman.

WEISMAN, ABNER I. 1907-   . American obstetrician and gynecologist. See: Amer. Men Sci., 10th ed. Weisman's test.

WEISMANN, AUGUST FRIEDRICH LEOPOLD. 1834-1914. German biologist. See: Encyc. Brit., 1911; World Who's Who Sci. Weismannism (or Weismann's theory), Weismann's bundle, Weismann's gland.

WEISMANN-NETTER, R. fl. 1954. French? physician. (Biography source unavailable.) Weismann-Netter's syndrome.

Weismann-Netter's syndrome (Weismann-Netter, R.): Medicine. See: Jablonski. Also known as: Weismann-Netter and Stuhl syndrome, Weismann-Netter's dysostosis.

Weismannism (or Weismann's theory) (Weismann, August Friedrich Leopold): Genetics. See: Drever; Henderson; Stedman; Wolman.

Weismann's bundle (Weismann, August Friedrich Leopold): Anatomy. See: Stedman.

Weismann's gland (Weismann, August Friedrich Leopold): Anatomy. See: Henderson.

Weisman's test (Weisman, Abner I): Medicine. See: Dorland.

WEISS, CHRISTIAN ERNST. d. 1890. German mineralogist. See: Pogg., vol. 3. Weiss quadrilateral?

WEISS, CHRISTIAN SAMUEL. 1780-1856. German physicist and mineralogist. See: Pogg., vols. 2, 7a. Weiss zone law.

Weiss, Erich. See: Houdini, Harry.

WEISS, HERBERT KLEMM. 1917-   . American aeronautical engineer. See: Amer. Men and Women Sci., 12th ed. Weiss integrator.

Weiss integrator (Weiss, Herbert Klemm): Mathematics. See: Encyc. Brit., 1973 under "Mathematical Instruments."

WEISS, KONRAD. 1891-   . Austrian radiologist. See: Kuerschner's Deut. Gel. Kal., 1961. Mueller-Weiss disease.

WEISS, LEONHARD. b. 1881. German physician. See: Derm. Verzeich., 1939. Weiss' stain.

WEISS, LEOPOLD. 1849-1901. German oculist. See: Biog. Lex. hervorr. Aerzte. Weiss' reflex.

WEISS, LOUIS. fl. early 20th c. American mine owner. (Biography source unavailable.) Weissite.

Weiss magneton (Weiss, Pierre Ernst): Physics. See: Internat. Dict. Phys. Elec.

WEISS, NATHAN. 1851-1883. Austrian physician. See: Biog. Lex. hervorr. Aerzte. Weiss' sign.

WEISS, PIERRE ERNST. 1865-1940. French physicist. See: World Who's Who Sci. Curie-Weiss law, Weiss magneton, Weiss theory of ferromagnetism.

Weiss quadrilateral (Weiss, Christian Ernst?): Engineering and Industry. See: Thrush.

Weiss' reflex (Weiss, Leopold): Medicine. See: Dorland; Stedman.

Weiss' sign (Weiss, Nathan). See: Chvostek's sign.

WEISS, SOMA. 1898-1942. Hungarian-born American physician. See: Ann. Int. Med. vol. 16 (April, 1942), pp. 804-06. Charcot-Weiss-Baker syndrome, Mallory-Weiss syndrome.

Weiss' stain (Weiss, Leonhard): Medicine. See: Stedman. Also known as: Much-Weiss stain.

Weiss theory of ferromagnetism (Weiss, Pierre Ernst): Physics. See: Internat. Dict. Phys. Elec.; McGraw-Hill Encyc. Sci. Tech. under "Ferromagnetism."

Weiss zone law (Weiss, Christian Samuel): Earth Sciences. See: Ballentyne.

WEISSENBACH, RAYMOND JOSEPH EMIL. 1885-1963. French physician. See: Who's Who France, 1953-54. Thibierge-Weissenbach syndrome.

Weissenberg effect (Weissenberg, Karl): Chemistry. See: Ballentyne; Hackh; Internat. Dict. Ap. Math.

Weissenberg geometry (Weissenberg, Karl): Physics. Cited in: Van Nostrand Sci. Encyc. under "Crystal Structure Determination."

WEISSENBERG, KARL. 1893-   . Austrian physical chemist. See: Pogg., vols. 6, 7a. Weissenberg effect, Weissenberg geometry, Weissenberg method.

Weissenberg method (Weissenberg, Karl): Physics. See: Hughes; Internat. Dict. Phys. Elec.

Weissite (Weiss, Louis): Earth Sciences. See: Thrush; Webster's 3d.

Weisskopf (unit) (Weisskopf, Victor Frederick): Physics. See: Ballentyne.

WEISSKOPF, VICTOR FREDERICK. 1908-   . Austrian-born American physicist. See: Amer. Men and Women Sci., 12th ed. Conwell-Weisskopf equation (or formula), Pauli-Weisskopf equation, Weisskopf (unit).

WEISZ, MORIZ. b. 1877. Slovak-born Austrian physician. See: Biog. Lex. hervorr. Aerzte. Weisz's test.

Weisz's test (Weisz, Moriz): Medicine. See: Dorland; Stedman.

WEITBRECHT, JOSIAS W. 1702-1747. German anatomist in Russia. See: Allg. Deut. Biog. Weitbrecht's cartilage, Weitbrecht's cord (or ligament), Weitbrecht's fibers, Weitbrecht's foramen.

Weitbrecht reagent (Weitbrecht, W.): Chemistry. See: Van Nostrand Chem. Dict.

WEITBRECHT, W. fl. 1909. Swiss chemist. Cited in: Chem. Abstr. vol. 3 p. 820. Weitbrecht reagent.

Weitbrecht's cartilage (Weitbrecht, Josias W.): Anatomy. See: Donath; Dorland; Stedman.

Weitbrecht's cord (or ligament) (Weitbrecht, Josias W.): Anatomy. See: Dorland; Stedman.

Weitbrecht's fibers (Weitbrecht, Josias W.): Anatomy. See: Stedman.

Weitbrecht's foramen (Weitbrecht, Josias W.): Anatomy. See: Donath; Stedman.

WEIZMANN, CHAIM. 1874-1952. Russian-born Israeli chemist, scholar and Zionist leader. See: Encyc. Brit., 1973, World Who's Who Sci. Weizmann process.

Weizmann process (Weizmann, Chaim): Chemistry. See: Ballentyne.

WEIZSAECKER, CARL FRIEDRICH FREIHERR VON. 1912-   . German physicist and philosopher. See: World Who's Who Sci. Bethe-Weizsaecker cycle, Weizsaecker-Williams method, Weizsaecker's formula.

Weizsaecker-Williams method (Weizsaecker, Carl Friedrich Freiherr and Williams, Evan James): Physics. See: Internat. Dict. Phys. Elec.

Weizsaecker's formula (Weizsaecker, Carl Friedrich Freiherr): Physics. See: Ballentyne.

Weland the Smith. See: Wayland.

WELANDER, EDUARD. 1846-1917. Swedish dermatologist. See: Biog. Lex. hervorr. Aerzte. Welander's ulcer.

WELANDER, LISA. 1909-   . Swedish neurologist. See: Vem ar det, 1973. Wohlfart-Kugelberg-Welander disease.

Welander's ulcer (Welander, Eduard): Medicine. See: Dorland.

WELCH, WILLIAM HENRY. 1850-1934. American pathologist. See: Dict. Amer. Biog. Welch's bacillus, Welch's stain.

Welch's bacillus (Welch, William Henry): Medicine. See: Dorland; Stedman.

Welch's stain (Welch, William Henry): Medicine. See: Stedman. Also known as: Nuttall's stain for capsules.

WELCKER, HERMANN. 1822-1899. German anatomist. See: Allg. Deut. Biog., World Who's Who Sci. Welcker's angle.

Welcker's angle (Welcker, Hermann): Anatomy. See: Stedman.

WELD-BLUNDELL, CHARLES JOSEPH. 1845-1927. English traveler, art collector and naturalist. See: Who Was Who. Weld-Blundell prism?

Weld-Blundell's prism (Weld-Blundell, Charles Joseph?): Fine Arts. See: Winick.

Weldon process (Weldon, Walter): Chemistry. See: Ballentyne; Thrush; Van Nostrand Chem. Dict.

WELDON, WALTER. 1832-1885. English industrial chemist. See: Dict. Nat. Biog. Weldon process.

WELF (GUELF). fl. 12th-15th c. German princely family. See: New Encyc. Brit., 1974, Microp. Guelfs and Ghibellines.

WELLER, SAM. Character in Charles Dickens's "Pickwick Papers" (1836-1837). See: Benet, Harvey. Wellerism (or Welleresque).

Wellerism (or Welleresque) (Weller, Sam): Generic Word. See: Partridge; Scott.

Wellesley, Arthur, 1st Duke of Wellington. See: Wellington, Arthur Wellesley, 1st Duke of.

Wellington (Wellington, Arthur Wellesley): Recreation and Sports. See: Brewer; Hendrickson.

WELLINGTON, ARTHUR MELLEN. 1847-1895. American engineer and editor. See: Dict. Amer. Biog. Wellington formula.

WELLINGTON, ARTHUR WELLESLEY, 1st DUKE OF. 1769-1852. English fieldmarshall and statesman. See: Dict. Nat. Biog. beef Wellington, Wellington, Wellington boots, Wellingtonia, Wellingtonian.

Wellington boots (Wellington, Arthur Wellesley): Fashion. See: Hendrickson; Picken.

Wellington formula (Wellington, Arthur Mellen): Engineering and Industry. See: Thrush.

Wellington intensifier (Wellington, J. B. B.): Photography. See: Focal Encyc. Photog.

WELLINGTON, J. B. B. fl. 1889. English? photographer. (Biography source unavailable.) Wellington intensifier.

Wellingtonia (Wellington, Arthur Wellesley): Botany. See: Brewer; Hendrickson; Partridge.

Wellingtonian (Wellington, Arthur Wellesley): History. See: Webster's 3d.

Wellman producer (Wellman, Samuel Thomas): Engineering and Industry. See: Thrush.

WELLMAN, SAMUEL THOMAS. 1847-1919. American engineer and inventor. See: Dict. Amer. Biog. Wellman producer.

WELLS, BILLY. fl. around World War I. English boxer. (Biography source unavailable.) Billy Wells (gun or shell).

Wells' facies (Wells, Sir Thomas Spencer): Medicine. See: Dorland; Stedman.

Wells' forceps (Wells, Sir Thomas Spencer): Medicine. See: Stedman.

WELLS, JOHN I. fl. 1819. American printer. (Biography source unavailable.) Wells press.

WELLS, MICHAEL VERNON. fl. 1955-1972. English physician. See: Med. Direct., 1972. Muckle-Wells syndrome.

Wells press (Wells, John I.): Printing. See: Lockwood.

WELLS, SIR THOMAS SPENCER. 1818-1897. English surgeon. See: Dict. Nat. Biog. Wells' facies, Wells' forceps.

Wellsian (Wells, Herbert George): Literature. See: Partridge.

Welman's solution (Derivation undetermined): Chemistry. See: Van Nostrand Chem. Dict.

Welsbach mantle (Auer von Welsbach, Baron Karl): Physics. See: Hackh; Thrush; Van Nostrand Sci. Encyc.

WELTER, JEAN JOSEPH. ca. 1763-1852. French chemist. See: Pogg., vol. 2. Welter's rule?, Welter's tube.

Welter's rule (Welter, Jean Joseph?): Chemistry. See: Hackh; Van Nostrand Chem. Dict.

Welter's tube (Welter, Jean Joseph): Chemistry. See: Charnock.

WELTI, JEAN JACQUES. 1913- . French physician. See: Who's Who France, 1953-54. Lian-Siguier-Welti syndrome.

WELTMANN, OSKAR. 1885-1934. Austrian physician. See: Biog. Lex. hervorr. Aerzte. Weltmann's coagulation band.

Weltmann's coagulation band (Weltmann, Oskar): Medicine. See: Dorland; Stedman.

WELTMER, SIDNEY ABRAM. 1858-1930. American mental scientist. See: Who Was Who Amer., vol. I. Weltmerism.

Weltmerism (Weltmer, Sidney Abram): Psychology. See: Hinsie.

WELWITSCH, FRIEDRICH MARTIN JOSEPH. 1807-1872. Austrian botanist and traveler. See: Allg. Deut. Biog. Welwitschia.

Welwitschia (Welwitsch, Friedrich Martin Joseph): Botany. Cited in: Van Nostrand Sci. Encyc. under "Gymnosperms"; Webster's 3d.

WENCESLAS I, SAINT. ca. 908-935. Duke of Bohemia and patron saint of Czechoslovakia. See: Holweck, Nouv. Biog. Univ. Wenzel.

WENCKEBACH, KAREL FREDERIK. 1864-1940. Dutch internist. See: Biog. Lex. hervorr. Aerzte. Wenckebach period, Wenckebach phenomenon.

Wenckebach period (Wenckebach, Karel Frederik): Medicine. See: Dorland; Stedman.

Wenckebach phenomenon (Wenckebach, Karel Frederik): Medicine. See: Dorland; Stedman.

WENDER, NEUMANN. fl. 19th c. Austrian pharmaceutical chemist. (Biography source unavailable.) Wender's test.

Wender's test (Wender, Neumann): Medicine. See: Dorland; Stedman.

Wendy house (Darling, Wendy): Generic Word (playhouse). See: Barnhart (New Eng.).

Wenger-Duckert-Blancpain reagent (Wenger, Paul Eugene Etienne; Duckert, Roger; and Blancpain, Claude-Paul): Chemistry. See: Van Nostrand Chem. Dict.

WENGER, PAUL EUGENE ETIENNE. 1888- . Swiss chemist. See: Pogg., vols. 6, 7a. Wenger-Duckert-Blancpain reagent.

WENHAM, FRANCIS HERBERT. 1824-1908. English engineer. (Biography source unavailable.) Wenham's engine.

Wenham's engine (Wenham, Francis Herbert): Engineering and Industry. See: Auger.

WENK, EDUARD. 1907- . Swiss mineralogist and petrographer. See: Pogg., vol. 7a; Who's Who Sci. Europe, 1972. Wenkite.

Wenkite (Wenk, Eduard): Earth Sciences. See: Thrush.

Wenner configuration (Wenner, Frank): Engineering and Industry. See: Thrush.

Wenner difference potentiometer (Wenner, Frank): Engineering and Industry. See: Internat. Dict. Phys. Elec.

WENNER, FRANK. 1873-1954. American physicist. See: Pogg., vols. 5, 6.; Who Was Who Amer. Wenner configuration, Wenner difference potentiometer, Wenner winding, Wenner seismograph (or seismometer).

Wenner seismograph (or seismometer) (Wenner, Frank): Earth Sciences. Cited in: Van Nostrand Sci. Encyc. under "Earthquake."

Wenner winding (Wenner, Frank): Engineering and Industry. See: Hughes.

Wensleydale, Baron. See: Parke, James (Baron Wensleydale).

Wensleydale case (Parke, James, Baron Wensleydale): Law. See: Montgomery.

WENSTROM, OLAF. b. 1864. Swedish-born American mining engineer. See: Who's Who Engin., 1937. Wenstrom rolling mill?

Wenstrom rolling mill (Wenstrom, Olaf?): Engineering and Industry. See: Thrush.

Wentworth, Charles Watson, 2d Marquis of Rockingham. See: Watson-Wentworth, Charles, 2d Marquis of Rockingham.

WENTWORTH, CHESTER KEELER. 1891- . American geologist. See: Amer. Men Sci., 10th ed. Wentworth scale.

Wentworth scale (Wentworth, Chester Keeler): Earth Sciences. Monkhouse; Thrush.

WENTWORTH, THOMAS (1ST EARL OF STRAFFORD). 1593-1641. English statesman. See: Dict. Nat. Biog. Straffordian.

WENTZEL, GREGOR. 1898- . German-born American theoretical physicist. See: Amer. Men and Women Sci., 12th ed.; Pogg., vols. 6, 7a. Wentzel-Kramers-Brillouin-Jeffreys approximation (or method).

Wentzel-Kramers-Brillouin-Jeffreys approximation (or method) (Wentzel, Gregor; Kramers, Henrik Anthony; Brillouin, Louis Marcel and Jeffreys, Sir Harold): Physics. See: Ballentyne; Internat. Dict. Phys. Elec.

Wenzel (Wenceslas I, Saint): Recreation and Sports. See: Webster's 3d.

WENZEL, JOSEPH. 1768-1808. German anatomist and physiologist. See: Allg. Deut. Biog., Biog Lex. hervorr. Aerzte. Wenzel's ventricle.

WENZEL, KARL FRIEDRICH. 1740-1793. German chemist and metallurgist. See: Allg. Deut. Biog., World Who's Who Sci. Wenzel's law.

WENZELL, WILLIAM THEODORE. 1829-1913. American physician. See: Amer. Men Sci., 1st. ed. Wenzell's test.

Wenzell's test (Wenzell, William Theodore): Medicine. See: Dorland.

Wenzel's law (Wenzel, Karl Friedrich): Chemistry. See: Hackh; Thrush. Also known as: Richter's law.

Wenzel's ventricle (Wenzel, Joseph): Anatomy. See: Stedman. Also known as: Duncan's ventricle.

WEPFER, JOHANN JAKOB. 1620-1695. Swiss physician. See: Biog. Lex. hervorr. Aerzte., World Who's Who Sci. Wepfer's gland.

Wepfer's gland (Wepfer, Johann Jakob): Anatomy. See: Stedman.

Wepman test of auditory discrimination (Derivation undetermined): Physiology. See: Wolman.

WERDNIG, GUIDO. 1844-1919. Austrian neurologist. See: Wien. Klin. Wchnschr., vol. 77, no. 18 (June, 1965) p. 47. Werdnig-Hoffmann syndrome (or disease).

Werdnig-Hoffmann syndrome (or disease) (Werdnig, Guido and Hoffmann, Johann): Medicine. See: Dorland; Jablonski; Stedman. Also known as: Hoffman's atrophy (or muscular atrophy), Werdnig's disease.

Werdnig's disease (Werdnig, Guido): See: Werdnig-Hoffmann syndrome.

WERLHOF, PAUL GOTTLIEB. 1699-1767. German physician. See: Allg. Deut. Biog.; Biog. Lex. hervorr. Aerzte. Werlhof's disease (or purpura).

Werlhof-Wichmann syndrome (Werlhof, Paul Gottlieb and Wichmann, Johann Ernst). See: Werlhof's disease (or purpura).

Werlhof's disease (or purpura) (Werlhof, Paul Gottlieb): Medicine. See: Dorland; Jablonski; Stedman. Also known as: Werlhof-Wichmann syndrome.

WERMER, PAUL. fl. 1954-1974. American physician. See: Direct. Med. Specialists, 1974-1975. Wermer's syndrome.

Wermer's syndrome (Wermer, Paul): Medicine. See: Jablonski.

WERNEKINCK, FRIEDRICH CHRISTIAN GREGOR. 1798-1835. German anatomist. See: Allg. Deut. Biog.; Biog. Lex. hervorr. Aerzte. Wernekinck's commissure.

Wernekinck's commissure (Wernekinck, Friedrich Christian Gregor): Anatomy. See: Donath; Stedman.

WERNER, ABRAHAM GOTTLOB. 1750-1817. German geologist and mineralogist. See: Encyc. Brit., 1911.; World Who's Who Sci. Werneria, Wernerian system (or theory), Wernerite, Werneritite.

WERNER, ALFRED. 1866-1919. Swiss chemist. See: World Who's Who Sci. Werner's coordination theory.

WERNER, DANIEL PAUL. 1938- . American mechanical engineer. See: Amer. Men and Women Sci., 12th ed. Werner leaf gauge?

WERNER, F. F. fl. 1912. German chemist. Cited in: Chem. Abstr. vol. 6 p. 2586. Werner test reaction.

WERNER, HEINRICH. b. 1874. German physician. See: Biog. Lex. hervorr. Aerzte. Werner-His disease.

WERNER, HEINZ. 1890-1964. German-born American psychologist. See: Amer. Men Sci., 9th ed., Soc. & Behav. Werner-Strauss theory.

Werner-His disease (Werner, Heinrich and His, Wilhelm, Jr.): Medicine. See: Dorland; Jablonski; Stedman.

Werner leaf guage (Werner, Daniel Paul?): Engineering and Industry. See: Internat. Dict. Phys. Elec.

WERNER, OTTO. b. 1879. German physician. (Biography source unavailable.) Werner's disease (or syndrome).

Werner-Strauss theory (Werner, Heinz and Strauss, Alfred A.?): Psychology. See: Wolman.

Werner test reaction (Werner, F. F.): Chemistry. See: Van Nostrand Chem. Dict.

Werneria (Werner, Abraham Gottlob): Botany. See: Charnock.

Wernerian system (or theory) (Werner, Abraham Gottlob): Earth Sciences. See: Charnock; Webster's 3d.

Wernerite (Werner, Abraham Gottlob): Earth Sciences. See: Thrush; Van Nostrand Sci. Encyc.; Webster's 3d.

Werneritite (Werner, Abraham Gottlob): Earth Sciences. See: Thrush.

Werner's coordination theory (Werner, Alfred): Chemistry. See: Ballentyne; Hackh; Van Nostrand Chem. Dict.

Werner's disease (or syndrome) (Werner, Otto): Medicine. See: Jablonski; Stedman.

WERNICKE, F. ALEXANDER. 1857-1915. German mathematician and physicist. See: Deut. Biog. Jahrb., 1914-1916. Wernicke's prism.

WERNICKE, KARL. 1848-1905. German neuropsychiatrist. See: Biog. Lex. hervorr. Aerzte.; World Who's Who Sci. hypermetamorphosis of Wernicke, Wernicke area (or center), Wernicke-Mann hemiplegia (or type), Wernicke's agnosia?, Wernicke's aphasia, Wernicke's convolution (or gyrus), Wernicke's cramp, Wernicke's dementia, Wernicke's encephalopathy (or disease), Wernicke's fibers, Wernicke's reaction (or sign), Wernicke's syndrome.

Wernicke-Mann hemiplegia (or type) (Wernicke, Karl and Mann, Ludwig): Medicine. See: Dorland; Jablonski.

WERNICKE, ROBERT. 1854-1922. Argentine pathologist. See: Gran Encic. Argentina. Posadas-Wernicke disease.

Wernicke's agnosia (Wernicke, Karl?): Medicine. See: Wolman.

Wernicke's aphasia (Wernicke, Karl): Medicine. See: Dorland; Jablonski; Stedman. Also known as: Bastian's aphasia.

Wernicke's area (or center) (Wernicke, Karl): Anatomy. See: Donath; English; Stedman; Wolman.

Wernicke's convolution (or gyrus) (Wernicke, Karl): Anatomy. See: Webster's 3d.

Wernicke's cramp (Wernicke, Karl): Medicine. See: Jablonski.

Wernicke's dementia (Wernicke, Karl): Medicine. See: Jablonski.

Wernicke's encephalopathy (or disease) (Wernicke, Karl): Medicine. See: Hinsie; Jablonski; Stedman. Also known as: Gayet's disease, Gayet-Wernicke's syndrome.

Wernicke's fibers (Wernicke, Karl): Anatomy. See: Stedman.

Wernicke's prism (Wernicke, F. Alexander): Physics. See: Webster's 3d.

Wernicke's radiation (Wernicke, Karl). See: Gratiolet's radiation.

Wernicke's reaction (or sign) (Wernicke, Karl): Medicine. See: Stedman.

Wernicke's syndrome (Wernicke, Karl): Medicine. See: Stedman.

Wertheim effect (Wertheim, Gunther Klaus): Engineering and Industry. See: Markus.

WERTHEIM, ERNST. 1864-1920. German gynecologist. See: Deut. Biogr. Jahrb., 1917-1920. Wertheim's operation.

WERTHEIM, GUNTHER KLAUS. 1927- . German-born American physicist. See: World Who's Who Sci. Wertheim effect.

WERTHEIM, GUSTAV. 1822-1888. German physician. See: Allg. Deut. Biog.; Biog. Lex. hervorr. Aerzte. Wertheim's ointment.

Wertheim's ointment (Wertheim, Gustav): Medicine. See: Dorland.

Wertheim's operation (Wertheim, Ernst): Medicine. See: Dorland; Stedman.

WERTHER. Hero of Johann Goethe's novel "The Sorrows of Werther." See: Benet. Wertherism (or Wertherian).

Wertherism (or Wertherian) (Werther): Generic Word. See: Partridge.

WESLEY, JOHN. 1703-1791. English founder of Methodism. See: Dict. Nat. Biog. Wesleyan Methodist (or Wesleyanism).

Wesleyan Methodist (or Wesleyanism) (Wesley, John): Religion. See: Attwater; Canney.

WESSON, DANIEL BAIRD. 1825-1906. American inventor and manufacturer. See: Who Was Who Amer., 1897-1942. Smith and Wesson pistol.

WESSON, EDWARD. fl. 1921. American industrial chemist. See: J. Ind. Eng. Chem. vol. 13 (1921), pp. 355-57. Wesson tube?

Wesson tube (Wesson Edward?): Chemistry. See: Hackh.

WEST, BENJAMIN. 1730-1813. American astronomer. See: Dict. Amer. Biog. West's solution?

WEST, JOHN. fl. 1911. English chemist. Cited in: Chem. Abstr., vol. 5, p. 2546. Glover and West coking retort.

WEST, MAE. 1892?- . American film actress. See: Chambers Biog. Dict. Mae West (lifejacket), Mae West silhouette.

WEST, RANDOLPH. b. 1890. American physician. See: Amer. Men Sci., 8th ed. Dakin-West reaction.

WEST, W. J. fl. 1840. English physician. (Biography source unavailable.) West's syndrome.

WEST, WILLIAM. 1801-1879. English engineer. See: Boase. Harvey and West valve.

WESTBERG, FRIEDRICH. fl. 1892. German physician. (Biography source unavailable.) Westberg's space.

WESTBERG, JOHN EDWIN. 1922- . American chemical engineer. See: Amer. Men and Women, Sci., 12th ed. Westberg test reactions?

Westberg test reactions (Westberg, John Edwin?): Chemistry. See: Van Nostrand Chem. Dict.

Westberg's space (Westberg, Friedrich): Anatomy. See: Dorland; Stedman.

WESTCOTT, CHARLES H. fl. 1876. American printer. (Biography source unavailable.) Westcott type-casting machine.

Westcott type-casting machine (Westcott, Charles H.): Printing. See: Lockwood.

WESTERGREN, ALF. 1891- . Swedish physician. See: Vem Ar Det?, 1951. Westergren method.

Westergren method (Westergren, Alf): Medicine. See: Stedman.

WESTGREN, ARNE FREDRIK. 1889- . Swedish metallurgist. See: Pogg., vols. 5, 6. Westgrenite.

Westgrenite (Westgren, Arne Fredrik): Earth Sciences. See: Thrush.

Westinghouse brake (Westinghouse, George): Engineering and Industry. See: Auger; Partridge.

WESTINGHOUSE, GEORGE. 1846-1914. American engineer and inventor. See: Dict. Amer. Biog. Westinghouse brake, Westinghouse retarder, Westinghouse skotch.

Westinghouse retarder (Westinghouse, George): Engineering and Industry. See: Thrush.

Westinghouse skotch (Westinghouse, George): Engineering and Industry. See: Thrush.

WESTLAKE, HARRY EDWARD. 1915- . American patent chemist. See: Chem. Who's Who, 4th ed. Westlake process?

Westlake process (Westlake, Harry Edward?): Engineering and Industry. See: Thrush.

Westley-Richards (rifle) (Derivation undetermined): Weapons. See: Partridge.

Weston brake (Weston, Thomas A.): Engineering and Industry. See: Auger.

WESTON, EDWARD. 1850-1936. English-born American electrical engineer. See: Dict. Nat. Biog. Weston photronic cell, Weston standard cadmium cell.

WESTON, EDWARD. 1886-1957. American photographer. See: Who Was Who Amer., vol. 3. Weston meter, Weston speed.

WESTON, FRANK EDWIN. fl. 1918. English chemist. Cited in: Chem. Abstr., vol. 12, p. 770. Fryer-Weston reagent for fats.

Weston meter (Weston, Edward): Photography. See: Encyc. Brit., 1973 under "Photography."

Weston photronic cell (Weston, Edward): Engineering and Industry. See: Thrush.

Weston speed (Weston, Edward): Photography. See: Focal Encyc. Photog.

Weston standard cadmium cell (Weston, Edward): Engineering and Industry. See: Hughes; Markus; Thewlis.

WESTON, THOMAS A. fl. 1868. English engineer. (Biography source unavailable.) Weston brake.

WESTPHAL, ALEXANDER KARL OTTO. 1863-1941. German neurologist. See: Biog. Lex. hervorr. Aerzte. Westphal-Leyden syndrome, Westphal-Piltz phenomenon, Westphal-Piltz reflex.

Westphal balance (Westphal, Wilhelm Heinrich): Chemistry. See: Internat. Dict. Phys. Elec.; Thrush; Van Nostrand Chem. Dict. Also known as: Mohr balance, Mohr-Westphal balance.

WESTPHAL, KARL FRIEDRICH OTTO. 1833-1890. German neurologist and psychiatrist. See: Allg. Deut. Biog. Edinger-Westphal('s) nucleus, Westphal-Struempell syndrome, Westphal's nucleus, Westphal's sign (or phenomenon), Westphal's syndrome (or neurosis), Westphal's syndrome with hyperkalemia.

Westphal-Leyden syndrome (Westphal, Alexander Karl Otto and Leyden, Ernst Victor von): Medicine. See: Jablonski. Also known as: Leyden's ataxia, Westphal's ataxia.

Westphal-Piltz phenomenon (Westphal, Alexander Karl Otto and Piltz, Jan): Medicine. See: Dorland; Stedman. Also known as: Piltz-Westphal phenomenon, Piltz's sign.

Westphal-Piltz reflex (Westphal, Alexander Karl Otto and Piltz, Jan): Medicine. See: Dorland.

Westphal-Struempell syndrome (Westphal, Karl Friedrich Otto and Struempell, Adolf von). See: Wilson's disease.

WESTPHAL, WILHELM HEINRICH. b. 1882. German physicist. See: Pogg. vols. 5, 7a. Westphal balance.

Westphal's ataxia (Westphal, Alexander Karl Otto). See: Westphal-Leyden syndrome.

Westphal's nucleus (Westphal, Karl Friedrich Otto): Anatomy. See: Dorland; Stedman.

Westphal's sign (or phenomenon) (Westpahl, Karl Friedrich Otto): Medicine. See: Dorland; Hinsie; Stedman.

Westphal's syndrome (or neurosis) (Westphal, Karl Friedrich Otto): Medicine. See: Jablonski. Also known as: Cavare-Romberg syndrome, Cavare-Romberg-Westphal syndrome, Cavare-Westphal syndrome.

Westphal's syndrome with hyperkalemia (Westphal, Karl Friedrich Otto). See: Gamstorp's syndrome.

WESTRING, JOHANN PETER. 1753-1833. Swedish physician. See: Pogg., vol. 2. Westringia.

Westringia (Westring, Johann Peter): Botany. See: Charnock.

West's solution (West, Benjamin?): Chemistry. See: Thrush.

West's syndrome (West, W.J.): Medicine. See: Jablonski.

WETHERILL, JOHN PRICE. 1844-1906. American industrialist. See: Dict. Amer. Biog. under "Samuel Wetherill." Wetherill vacuum casting process, Wetherill's furnace, Weterill's magnetic separator.

Wetherill process (Wetherill, Samuel): Engineering and Industry. See: Thrush.

WETHERILL, SAMUEL. 1821-1890. American inventor and industrialist. See: Dict. Amer. Biog. Wetherill process.

Wetherill vacuum casting process (Wetherill, John Price): Engineering and Industry. See: Thrush.

Wetherill's furnace (Wetherill, John Price): Engineering and Industry. See: Thrush.

Wetherill's magnetic separator (Wetherill, John Price): Engineering and Industry. See: Thrush.

WETHEY, A. H. fl. 1910. American metallurgical engineer. Cited in: Chem. Abstr. vol. 4. p. 740. Wethey furnace.

Wethey furnace (Wethey, A.H.): Engineering and Industry. See: Thrush.

WETTER, JOSEPH. fl. 19th c. American manufacturer. (Biography source unavailable.) Wetter numbering-machine.

Wetter numbering-machine (Wetter, Joseph): Printing. See: Lockwood.

WETZEL, GEORG. 1871-1951. German anatomist. See: Biog. Lex. hervorr. Aerzte. Wetzel's test.

Wetzel grid (Wetzel, Norman Carl): Medicine. See: Chaplin; English; Stedman.

WETZEL, NORMAN CARL. 1897- . American pediatrician. See: Amer. Men Sci., 9th ed. Wetzel grid.

Wetzel's test (Wetzel, Georg): Medicine. See: Dorland.

Wever-Bray phenomenon (or effect) (Wever, Ernest Glen and Bray, Charles William): Psychology. See: Chaplin; English; Stedman; Wolman.

WEVER, ERNEST GLEN. 1902- . American psychologist. See: World Who's Who Sci. Wever-Bray phenomenon (or effect).

Weyers-Fuelling syndrome (Weyers, Helmut and Fuelling, Georg): Medicine. See: Jablonski.

WEYERS, HELMUT. fl. 1960. German pediatrician. (Biography source unavailable.) Weyers-Fuelling syndrome, Weyers' syndrome (1), Weyers' syndrome (2), Weyers' syndrome (3), Weyers-Thier syndrome.

Weyers' syndrome (1) (Weyers, Helmut): Medicine. See: Jablonski.

Weyers' syndrome (2) (Weyers, Helmut): Medicine. See: Jablonski; Stedman.

Weyers' syndrome (3) (Weyers, Helmut): Medicine. See: Jablonski.

Weyers-Thier syndrome (Weyers, Helmut and Thier, Carl Joerg): Medicine. See: Jablonski.

Weyl equation (Weyl, Hermann): Physics. See: Internat. Dict. Ap. Math.

WEYL, HERMANN. 1885-1955. German-born American mathematician. See: World Who's Who Sci. Weyl equation, Weyl unified field theory.

WEYL, THEODOR. 1851-1913. German chemist. See: Biog. Lex. hervorr. Aerzte. Weyl's test.

Weyl unified field theory (Weyl, Hermann): Physics. See: Internat. Dict. Phys. Elec.

Weyl's test (Weyl, Theodor): Chemistry. See: Ballentyne; Dorland; Stedman.

Weymouth pine (Weymouth, Thomas Thynne): Botany. See: Webster's 3d.

WEYMOUTH, THOMAS THYNNE, 1ST VISCOUNT OF. 1640-1714. English ambassador and statesman. See: Dict. Nat. Biog. Weymouth pine.

WHARNCLIFFE, EDWARD MONTAGU STUART GRANVILLE, 1ST EARL OF. English railway chairman. See: Boase. Wharncliffe meeting.

Wharncliffe meeting (Wharncliffe, Edward Montagu Stuart Granville): History. See: Webster's 3d.

WHARTON, THOMAS. 1614-1673. English anatomist. See: Dict. Nat. Biog. Whartonitis, Wharton's duct (or duct of Wharton), Wharton's jelly.

Whartonitis (Wharton, Thomas): Medicine. See: Dorland; Stedman.

Wharton's duct (or duct of Wharton) (Wharton, Thomas): Anatomy. See: Dorland; Henderson; Stedman; Webster's 3d.

Wharton's jelly (Wharton, Thomas): Anatomy. See: Donath; Dorland; Stedman.

WHATMAN, JAMES. 1741-1798. English paper manufacturer. See: Glaister. Whatman paper.

Whatman paper (Whatman, James): Printing. See: Harrod; Partridge.

WHEATLEY, HENRY BENJAMIN. 1838-1917. English scholar and bibliographer. See: Who Was Who. Wheatley medal.

Wheatley medal (Wheatley, Henry Benjamin): Library Science. See: Harrod.

Wheatstone bridge (Wheatstone, Sir Charles): Engineering and Industry. See: Hackh; Hughes; Internat. Dict. Phys. Elec.

WHEATSTONE, SIR CHARLES. 1802-1875. English physicist. See: Dict. Nat. Biog. Wheatstone bridge, Wheatstone cipher, Wheatstone-Hipp chronoscope, Wheatstone transmitter, Wheatstone stereoscope.

Wheatstone cipher (Wheatstone, Sir Charles): Linguistics. See: Webster's 3d.

Wheatstone-Hipp chronoscope (Wheatstone, Sir Charles and Hipp, Matthaus). See: Hipp chronoscope.

Wheatstone stereoscope (Wheatstone, Sir Charles): Physics. See: Focal Encyc. Photog.; Stedman.

Wheatstone transmitter (Wheatstone, Sir Charles): Engineering and Industry. See: Webster's 3d.

WHEELER, BURTON KENDALL. 1882- . American lawyer and politician. See: Biog. Direct. Amer. Congress. Lea-Wheeler Act (1940), Wheeler-Howard Act, Wheeler-Lea Act (1938), Wheeler-Rayburn Act.

WHEELER, C. W. fl. before 1924. American scientist. (Biography source unavailable.) C. W. Wheeler radial-flow condenser.

Wheeler-Feynman theory (Wheeler, John Archibald and Feynman, Richard Phillips): Physics. See: Internat. Dict. Phys. Elec.

WHEELER, GEORGE MONTAGUE. 1842-1905. American topographical engineer. See: Dict. Amer. Biog. Wheelerite.

WHEELER, HENRY LORD. 1867-1914. American chemist. See: Pogg., vols. 4, 5.; Who Was Who Amer. Wheeler-Johnson test, Wheeler-Tollens test.

Wheeler-Howard Act (Wheeler, Burton Kendall and Howard, Edgar). See: Bursum Bill.

WHEELER, JOHN ARCHIBALD. 1911- . American physicist. See: Amer. Men and Women Sci., 12th ed. Bohr-Wheeler empirical mass formula, Bohr-Wheeler theory of fission, Wheeler-Feynman theory.

WHEELER, JOHN M. 1879-1938. American ophthalmologist. See: Who Was Who Amer. Wheeler method.

Wheeler-Johnson test (Wheeler, Henry Lord and Johnson, Treat Baldwin): Chemistry. See: Stedman.

Wheeler-Lea Act (1938) (Wheeler, Burton Kendall and Lea, Clarence Frederick): Politics. See: Clark; Morris; Smith.

Wheeler method (Wheeler, John M.): Medicine. See: Stedman.

Wheeler pan (Wheeler, Zenas): Earth Sciences. See: Mathews, M. M.

Wheeler-Rayburn Act (Wheeler, Burton Kendall and Rayburn, Sam Taliaferro): Politics. See: Morris and Irwin.

Wheeler-Tollens test (Wheeler, Henry Lord and Tollens, Bernhard Christian Gottfried): Chemistry. See: Van Nostrand Chem. Dict.

WHEELER, ZENAS. No dates. American miner. (Biography source unavailable.) Wheeler pan.

Wheelerite (Wheeler, George Montague): Earth Sciences. See: Mathews, M. M.; Thrush.

WHEELHOUSE, CLAUDIUS GALEN. 1826-1909. English surgeon. See: Dict. Amer. Biog. 2d. suppl. Wheelhouse's operation.

Wheelhouse's operation (Wheelhouse, Claudius Galen): Medicine. See: Dorland; Stedman.

WHEELOCK, FRANK CAWTHORNE, JR. 1918- . American surgeon. See: Direct. Med Specialists, 1974-1975. McKittrick-Wheelock syndrome.

Wherry–Doolittle method (or technique) (Wherry, Robert James and Doolittle, M. H.): Psychology. See: Chaplin; English; Good; Wolman.

WHERRY, EDGAR THEODORE. 1885- . American mineralogist and geologist. See: Pogg., vol. 6. Wherryite.

WHERRY, ROBERT JAMES. 1904- . American psychologist. See: Amer. Psych. Assoc., Direct., 1948. Wherry–Doolittle method (or technique).

Wherryite (Wherry, Edgar Theodore): Earth Sciences. See: Thrush.

WHEWELL, WILLIAM. 1794-1866. English philosopher, scientist and scholar. See: Dict. Nat. Biog., Internat. Encyc. Soc. Sci. Whewellite.

Whewellite (Whewell, William): Earth Sciences. See: Thrush; Webster's 3d.

WHIDDINGTON, RICHARD. 1885- . English experimental physicist. See: Pogg., vols. 5, 6. Whiddington's law.

Whiddington's law (Whiddington, Richard): Physics. See: Ballentyne.

WHIELDON, THOMAS. 1719-1795. English potter. See: New Encyc. Brit. Whieldon ware.

Whieldon ware (Whieldon, Thomas): Applied Arts. See: Webster's 3d.

Whippany effect (Derivation undetermined): Electronics. See: Markus.

WHIPPLE, ALLEN OLDFATHER. 1881-1963. American surgeon. See: Who Was Who Amer. Whipple's operation.

WHIPPLE, GEORGE HOYT. 1878- . American pathologist. See: World Who's Who Sci. Whipple's disease (or syndrome).

Whipple's disease (or syndrome) (Whipple, George Hoyt): Medicine. See: Dorland; Jablonski; Stedman. Also known as: Whipple's intestinal lipodystrophy.

Whipple's intestinal lipodystrophy (Whipple, George Hoyt). See: Whipple's disease (or syndrome).

Whipple's operation (Whipple, Allen Oldfather): Medicine. See: Dorland; Stedman.

WHITBY, GEORGE STAFFORD. b. 1887. English-born American chemist. See: Pogg., vol. 6. Whitby test?

Whitby test (Whitby, George Stafford?): Chemistry. See: Van Nostrand Chem. Dict.

WHITE, ALFRED HOLMES. 1873-1953. American chemist. See: Pogg., vol. 6. White's micro-test.

WHITE, CLEVELAND JAMES. 1893- . American dermatologist. See: Amer. Men and Women Sci., 12th ed. Marshall–White syndrome.

White combination potentiometer (White, Walter Porter): Engineering and Industry. See: Internat. Dict. Phys. Elec.

WHITE, FRANCIS. d. 1711. English coffee and clubhouse owner. See: Dict. Nat. Biog. White's chocolate house (or club).

WHITE, GILBERT. 1720-1793. English clergyman and naturalist. See: Dict. Nat. Biog. White's thrush.

WHITE, HENRY LUKE. 1860-1927. Australian ornithologist and philatelist. See: Australian Encyc. White's treefrog.

White–Howell furnace (White, J. Maunsel and Howell, J. T.?): Engineering and Industry. See: Thrush.

WHITE, J. MAUNSEL. 1856-1912. American inventor and metallurgist. See: Webster's Biog. Dict. Taylor–White process (or treatment), White–Howell furnace.

WHITE, JAMES. fl. 1858. Scottish instruments designer. Cited in: Thompson, S. P. Kelvin–White sounding machine.

WHITE, JAMES (Pseud. JAMES JERSHOM JEZREEL). 1840-1885. English founder of religious sect. See: Dict. Nat. Biog. Jezreelites.

WHITE, JAMES CLARKE. 1833-1916. American dermatologist. See: Dict. Amer. Biog. White's disease.

WHITE, JAMES WILLIAM. 1850-1916. American surgeon. See: World Who's Who Sci. White's operation.

WHITE, PAUL DUDLEY. 1886-1973. American cardiologist. See: World Who's Who Sci. Bland–White–Garland syndrome, Lee–White method, Wolff–Parkinson–White syndrome.

White scout car (Derivation undetermined): Engineering and Industry. See: Quick.

WHITE, STEWART EDWARD. 1873-1946. American fiction writer. See: Who Was Who Amer., 1943-1950. Stewart White trout.

WHITE, THOMAS. 1550?-1624. English philosopher. See: Dict. Nat. Biog. White's professor.

WHITE, WALLACE HUMPHREY, JR. 1877-1952. American legislator. See: Biog. Direct. Amer. Congress. Jones–White Act.

WHITE, WALTER PORTER. 1867-1946. American physicist. See: Amer. Men Sci., 7th ed; Pogg., vols. 5, 6. White combination potentiometer.

WHITEFIELD, GEORGE. 1714-1770. English Methodist leader and writer in America. See: Dict. Nat. Biog. Whitefieldites (or Whitefieldians).

Whitefieldites (or Whitefieldians) (Whitefield, George): Religion. See: Canney; Webster's 3d.

WHITEHEAD, ALFRED NORTH. 1861-1947. English mathematician and philosopher. See: Internat. Encyc. Soc. Sci. Whitehead theory of gravitation, Whiteheadian.

WHITEHEAD, J. M. fl. 20th c. American physician. (Biography source unavailable.) Wallhauser and Whitehead's method.

WHITEHEAD, ROBERT. fl. 1866. Inventor. (Biography source unavailable.) Whitehead torpedo.

Whitehead theory of gravitation (Whitehead, Alfred North): Physics. See: Internat. Dict. Phys. Elec.

Whitehead torpedo (Whitehead, Robert): Weapons. See: Quick.

WHITEHEAD, WALTER. 1840-1913. English surgeon. See: Biog. Lex. hervorr. Aerzte. Whitehead's operation.

Whiteheadian (Whitehead, Alfred North): Philosophy. See: Webster's 3d.

Whitehead's operation (Whitehead, Walter): Medicine. See: Dorland; Stedman.

WHITEHORN, JOHN CLARE. 1894- . American psychiatrist and chemist. See: Amer. Men and Women Sci., 12th ed. Whitehorn reagent.

Whitehorn reagent (Whitehorn, John Clare): Chemistry. See: Van Nostrand Chem. Dict.

WHITEHURST, JOHN. 1713-1788. English horologer. See: Dict. Nat. Biog. Whitehurst machine.

Whitehurst machine (Whitehurst, John): Engineering and Industry. See: Auger.

White's chocolate house (or club) (White, Francis): History. See: Dict. Nat. Biog. under "White, Francis."

White's disease (White, James Clarke): See: Darier's disease.

White's micro-test (White, Alfred Holmes): Chemistry. See: Thrush; Van Nostrand Chem. Dict.

White's operation (White, James William): Medicine. See: Dorland.

White's professor (White, Thomas): Philosophy. See: Wagner (More Names).

White's thrush (White, Gilbert): Zoology. Cited in: Gray; Webster's 3d.

White's treefrog (White, Henry Luke): Zoology. Cited in: Gray.

WHITESIDE, CHARLES HUGH. 1932- . American agricultural chemist. See: Amer. Men and Women Sci., 12th ed. Whiteside test?

Whiteside test (Whiteside, Charles Hugh?): Chemistry. See: Winburne.

WHITFIELD, ARTHUR. 1868-1947. English dermatologist. See: Who Was Who. Whitfield's ointment.

Whitfield's ointment (Whitfield, Arthur): Medicine. See: Dorland; Hackh; Stedman.

Whiting cell (Whiting, Jasper): Chemistry. See: Van Nostrand Chem. Dict.

WHITING, DONALD A. 1937- . English organic chemist. See: Internat. Chem. Direct., 1970. Whiting's pycnometer?

WHITING, JASPER. 1868-1941. American chemist and inventor. See: New York Times, Aug. 19, 1941, p. 21, col. 2. Whiting cell.

WHITING, PHILIP E. b. 1886. American materials handling engineer. See: Who's Who Engin. 1948. Whiting system?

Whiting system (Whiting, Philip E.?): Engineering and Industry. See: Thrush.

Whiting's pycnometer (Whiting, Donald A.?): Chemistry. Cited in: Encyc. Brit., 1973 under "Density," vol. 7, p. 255d.

Whitley councils (Whitley, John Henry): Sociology. See: Partridge.

WHITLEY, JOHN HENRY. 1866-1935. English social reformer. See: Dict. Nat. Biog. Whitley councils, Whitleyism.

Whitleyism (Whitley, John Henry): Sociology. See: Partridge; Stedman; Webster's 3d.

WHITLOCK, HERBERT P. 1868-1948. American mineralogist. See: Who Was Who Amer. Whitlockite.

Whitlockite (Whitlock, Herbert P.): Earth Sciences. See: Thrush; Webster's 3d.

WHITMAN, ROYAL. 1857-1946. American surgeon. See: Who Was Who Amer. Whitman's frame.

WHITMAN, COLONEL ROYAL EMERSON. fl. 1862. American military officer. See: Heitman, vol. I. Whitman saddle.

Whitman saddle (Whitman, Colonel Royal Emerson): Generic Word. See: Mathews, M. M.

WHITMAN, WALT. 1819-1892. American poet. See: Dict. Amer. Biog. Whitmanese, Whitmanesque (or Whitmanian), Whitmanite (or Whitmaniac).

Whitmanese (Whitman, Walt): Literature. See: Webster's 3d.

Whitmanesque (or Whitmanian) (Whitman, Walt): Literature. See: Mathews, M. M.; Webster's 3d.

Whitmanite (or Whitmaniac) (Whitman, Walt): Literature. See: Mathews, M. M.; Webster's 3d.

Whitman's frame (Whitman, Royal): Medicine. See: Dorland; Stedman.

WHITMORE, ALFRED. 1876-1946. English surgeon. See: Med. Direct., 1930. Whitmore's bacillus, Whitmore's disease (or fever).

WHITMORE, FRANK CLIFFORD. 1887- . American chemist. See: Amer. Men Sci., 7th ed. Whitmore mechanism.

Whitmore mechanism (Whitmore, Frank Clifford): Chemistry. See: Ballentyne.

Whitmore's bacillus (Whitmore, Alfred): Medicine. See: Dorland; Stedman.

Whitmore's disease (or fever) (Whitmore, Alfred): Medicine. See: Jablonski.

WHITNALL, SAMUEL ERNEST. 1876-1952. English anatomist. See: Biog. Lex. hervorr. Aerzte. Whitnall's tubercle.

Whitnall's tubercle (Whitnall, Samuel Ernest): Anatomy. See: Stedman.

WHITNEY, AMOS. fl. 1865. American manufacturer. Cited in: Webster's Biog. Dict. under "Pratt, Francis Ashbury." Pratt and Whitney key.

WHITNEY, CHARLES SMITH. b. 1892. American consulting civil engineer. See: Amer. Men Sci., 9th ed. Whitney stress diagram?

WHITNEY, DONALD RANSOM. 1915- . American mathematical statistician. See: Amer. Men Sci., 10th ed. Mann-Whitney test.

WHITNEY, ELI. 1765-1825. American inventor. See: Dict. Amer. Biog. Whitney's rifle.

WHITNEY, JOSIAH DWIGHT. 1819-1896. American geologist. See: Dict. Amer. Biog. Whitneyite.

Whitney stress diagram (Whitney, Charles Smith?): Engineering and Industry. See: Thrush.

Whitneyite (Whitney, Josiah Dwight): Earth Sciences. See: Mathews, M. M.

Whitney's rifle (Whitney, Eli): Weapons. See: Mathews, M. M.

Whittaker differential equation (Whittaker, Sir Edmund Taylor): Mathematics. See: Internat. Dict. Ap. Math.

WHITTAKER, SIR EDMUND TAYLOR. 1873-1956. English mathematician, physicist and astronomer. See: Dict. Nat. Biog. Whittaker differential equation, Whittaker functions, Whittaker integral, Whittaker periodogram.

Whittaker functions (Whittaker, Sir Edmund Taylor): Mathematics. See: Internat. Dict. Ap. Math.

Whittaker integral (Whittaker, Sir Edmund Taylor): Mathematics. Cited in: Dict. Nat. Biog. under "Whittaker, Sir Edmund Taylor."

Whittaker periodogram (Whittaker, Sir Edmund Taylor): Mathematics. See: Kendall.

WHITTLE, SIR FRANK. 1907- . English inventor. See: Who's Who Brit. Scientists, 1971-1972. Whittle gas turbine.

Whittle gas turbine (Whittle, Sir Frank): Engineering and Industry. See: Auger.

WHITWELL, GEORGE E. fl. 1923. American engineer. (Biography source unavailable.) Whitwell stove, Young-Whitwell backrun gas process.

Whitwell stove (Whitwell, George E.): Engineering and Industry. See: Thrush.

Whitworth cannon (Whitworth, William Allen): Religion. See: Wagner (More Names).

WHITWORTH, SIR JOSEPH. 1803-1887. English mechanical engineer and inventor. See: Dict. Nat. Biog. Whitworth rifle, Whitworth scholarships, Whitworth steel, Whitworth thread, Whitworth's quick return motion.

Whitworth rifle (Whitworth, Sir Joseph): Weapons. Cited in: Dict. Nat. Biog.

Whitworth scholarships (Whitworth, Sir Joseph): Engineering and Industry. Cited in: Chambers Biog. Dict.

Whitworth steel (Whitworth, Sir Joseph): Engineering and Industry. Cited in: World Who's Who Sci.

Whitworth thread (Whitworth, Sir Joseph): Engineering and Industry. See: Auger; Partridge; Van Nostrand Sci. Encyc.

WHITWORTH, WILLIAM ALLEN. 1840-1905. English mathematician and religious writer. See: Dict. Nat. Biog. Whitworth cannon, Whitworth's theorem?

Whitworth's quick return motion (Whitworth, Sir Joseph): Engineering and Industry. See: Auger.

Whitworth's theorem (Whitworth, William Allen?): Mathematics. See: Ballentyne.

WHORF, BENJAMIN LEE. 1897-1941. American anthropological linguist and chemical engineer. See: Internat. Encyc. Soc. Sci. Whorfian hypothesis.

Whorfian hypothesis (Whorf, Benjamin Lee): Linguistics. See: Chaplin; Hartmann, Hoult; Wolman. Also known as: Humboldtism.

WHYTE, WILLIAM HOLLINGSWORTH. 1917- . American writer. See: Who's Who Amer., 1974-1975. Whyte's laws of committee operation.

Whyte's laws of committee operation (Whyte, William Hollingsworth): Sociology. See: Martin.

WHYTT, ROBERT. 1714-1766. Scottish physician and medical writer. See: Dict. Nat. Biog. Whytt's disease.

Whytt's disease (Whytt, Robert): Medicine. See: Dorland; Jablonski; Stedman.

Wiancko pressure-measuring system (Derivation undetermined): Engineering and Industry. See: Thrush.

WIART, PIERRE. 1870-1946. French anatomist. See: Mem. Acad. de Chir. vol. 72 (June 5-12, 1946), pp. 323-24. Wiart's duodenal notch.

Wiart's duodenal notch (Wiart, Pierre): Anatomy. See: Stedman.

WICHERT, E. M. fl. 1941. American engineer. (Biography source unavailable.) Wichert truss.

Wichert truss (Wichert, E. M.): Engineering and Industry. See: Van Nostrand Sci. Encyc.

WICHMANN, JOHAN ERNST. 1740-1802. German physician. See: Allg. Deut. Biog. Werlhof-Wichmann syndrome, Wichmann's asthma.

Wichmann's asthma (Wichmann, Johann Ernst): Medicine. See: Dorland; Stedman.

WICHURA, MAX ERNST. 1817-1866. German lawyer, botanist and traveler. See: Allg. Deut. Biog. Wichuraiana.

Wichuraiana (Wichura, Max Ernst): Botany. See: Webster's 3d.

Wick-Chandrasekhar method (Wick, Gian Carlo and Chandrasekhar, Subrahmanyan): Mathematics. See: Internat. Dict. Ap. Math.

WICK, GIAN CARLO. 1909-   . Italian-born American physicist. See: World Who's Who Sci. method of Verde and Wick, Wick-Chandrasekhar method, Wick method.

Wick method (Wick, Gian Carlo): Mathematics. See: Internat. Dict. Ap. Math.

WICKERSHEIMER, J. 1832-1896. Conservator of Berlin anatomical museum. (Biography source unavailable.) Wickersheimer's fluid.

Wickersheimer's fluid (Wickersheimer, J.): Anatomy. See: Dorland; Stedman.

WICKHAM, LOUIS FREDERIC. 1861-1913. French dermatologist. See: Brit. Med. J. vol. ii (1913), p. 1265. Wickham's striae.

Wickham's striae (Wickham, Louis Frederic): Medicine. See: Dorland; Stedman.

Widal-Abrami syndrome (Widal, Fernand and Abrami, Pierre). See: Hayem-Widal syndrome.

WIDAL, FERNAND (In full: GEORGES FERNAND ISIDORE). 1862-1929. French physician. See: World Who's Who Sci. Hayem-Widal syndrome, Widal('s) reaction.

Widal('s) reaction (Widal, Fernand): Medicine. See: Dorland; Stedman; Van Nostrand Sci. Encyc. Also known as: Gruber-Widal reaction, Gruber's reaction.

Widal's disease (Widal, Fernand). See: Hayem-Widal syndrome.

Wideroe linear accelerator (Wideroe, Rolf): Physics. See: New Encyc. Brit.; Van Nostrand Sci. Encyc.

WIDEROE, ROLF. 1902-   . Norwegian-born Swiss nuclear physcist. See: Pogg., vol. 7a. Wideroe linear accelerator.

WIDMAN, OSCAR (In full: KARL OSCAR). 1852-1930. Swedish chemist. See: Pogg., vols. 3,4,5. Hantzch-Widman name, Widman-Stoermer synthesis.

Widman-Stoermer synthesis (Widman, Oscar and Stoermer, Richard): Chemistry. See: Van Nostrand Chem. Dict.

WIDMANSTAETTEN, ALOIS JOSEP. 1754-1849. Austrian mineralogist. See: New Encyc. Brit. Widmanstaetten structure.

Widmanstaetten structure (Widmanstaetten, Alois Josep): Earth Sciences. See: Thewlis; Thrush; Van Nostrand Sci. Encyc.

WIDMARK, JOHAN (In full: ERIK JOHAN). 1850-1909. Swedish ophthalmologist. See: Biog. Lex. hervorr. Aerzte. Widmark's conjunctivitis.

Widmark's conjunctivitis (Widmark, Johan): Medicine. See: Jablonski.

Widowitz sign (Derivation undetermined): Medicine. See: Stedman.

WIECHERT, EMIL. 1861-1928. German geophysicist. See: Pogg., vols. 4-6. Lienard-Wiechert potential?, Wiechert seismograph.

Wiechert seismograph (Wiechert, Emil): Earth Sciences. See: Van Nostrand Sci. Encyc. under "Earthquake."

Wiedemann effect (Wiedemann, Gustav Heinrich): Engineering and Industry. See: Ballentyne; Hughes; Markus.

Wiedemann-Franz law (Wiedemann, Gustav Heinrich and Franz, Rudolf): Engineering and Industry. See: Internat. Dict. Phys. Elec.; Thewlis; Van Nostrand Sci. Encyc. Also known as: Wiedemann-Franz-Lorenz law.

Wiedemann-Franz-Lorenz law (Wiedmann, Gustav Heinrich; Franz, Rudolf; and Lorenz, Ludwig Valentin. See: Wiedemann-Franz law.

WIEDEMANN, GUSTAV HEINRICH. 1826-1899. German physicist and chemist. See: Pogg., vols. 2,3,4; World Who's Who Sci. Wiedemann effect, Wiedemann-Franz law, Wiedemann store, Wiedemann's additivity law (or rule).

WIEDMANN, HANS RUDOLF. 1915-   . German pediatrician. See: World Who's Who Sci. Wiedemann's syndrome.

Wiedemann store (Wiedemann, Gustav Heinrich): Engineering and Industry. See: Hughes.

Wiedemann's additivity law (or rule) (Wiedemann, Gustav Heinrich): Physics. See: Ballentyne; New Encyc. Brit.; Van Nostrand Sci. Encyc.

Wiedemann's syndrome (Wiedemann, Hans Rudolf): Medicine. See: Jablonski. Also known as: Lenz's syndrome.

WIEGNER, BRUNO GEORG. 1883-1936. German agricultural chemist. See: Pogg., vols. 5,6,7a. Wiegner sedimentation tube?

Wiegner sedimentation tube (Wiegner, Bruno Georg?): Engineering and Industry. See: Thrush.

WIELAND, HEINRICH. 1877-1957. German chemist. See: Surrey. Barbier-Wieland degradation.

Wieland, Melchior. See: Guilandini, Melchior.

Wien bridge (Wien, Max Carl): Engineering and Industry. See: Markus; Thewlis.

Wien effect (Wien, Max Carl): Engineering and Industry. See: Ballentyne; Internat. Dict. Phys. Elec.

Wien equation (Wien, Wilhelm): Physics. See: Hackh; Van Nostrand Chem. Dict.

WIEN, MAX CARL. 1866-1938. German physicist. See: World Who's Who Sci. Maxwell-Wien bridge, Wien bridge, Wien effect, Robinson-Wien bridge.

WIEN, WILHELM. 1864-1928. German physicist. See: World Who's Who Sci. Wien equation, Wien's constant, Wien's displacement law, Wien's distribution (or radiation) law.

Wiener and Hopf equation (Wiener, Norbert and Hopf, Eberhard): Mathematics. See: Ballentyne.

Wiener experiment (Wiener, Otto): Physics. See: Internat. Dict. Phys. Elec.

Wiener-Hopf technique (Wiener, Norbert and Hopf, Eberhard): Statistics. See: Kendall.

Wiener-Khintchine theorem (Wiener, Norbert and Khintchine, Aleksandr Y.): Statistics. See: Ballentyne; Kendall.

WIENER, NORBERT. 1894-1964. American mathematician. See: Internat. Encyc. Soc. Sci. Wiener and Hopf equation, Wiener-Hopf technique, Wiener-Khintchine theorem, Wiener process.

WIENER, OTTO. 1862-1927. German physicist. See: World Who's Who Sci. Wiener experiment, Wiener spectrum?

Wiener process (Wiener, Norbert). See: Brownian motion process.

Wiener spectrum (Wiener, Otto?): Physics. See: Focal Encyc. Photog.

Wien's constant (Wien, Wilhelm): Physics. See: Ballentyne.

Wien's displacement law (Wien, Wilhelm): Physics. See: Asimov; Huschke; Internat. Dict. Phys. Elec.

Wien's distribution (or radiation) law (Wien, Wilhelm): Physics. See: Huschke; Internat. Dict. Phys. Elec.; Thewlis.

Wierl equation (Wierl, Raimund Franz Josef): Physics. See: Internat. Dict. Phys. Elec.

WIERL, RAIMUND FRANZ JOSEF. 1903-1932. German physicist. See: Pogg., vol. 6. Wierl equation.

Wiese, Leopold Max Walter von. See: Von Wiese, Leopold Max Walter.

WIESER, FRIEDRICH VON. 1851-1926. Austrian economist and sociologist. See: Neue Oesterr. Biog. Wieser's law of costs.

Wieser's law of costs (Wieser, Friedrich von): Economics. See: Seldon.

WIESNER, KAREL. 1919-   . Czechoslovakian-born Canadian chemist. See: Amer. Men and Women Sci., 12th ed. Wiesner solution for lignin?

Wiesner solution for lignin (Wiesner, Karel?): Chemistry. See: Van Nostrand Chem. Dict.

WIETHE, CAMILLO. 1888-1949. Austrian otologist. See: Wien. Klin. Wchnschr., vol. 61 (July 29, 1949), pp. 465-466. Urbach-Wiethe syndrome.

Wigan von Theben. See: Calembour, Abbe de.

WIGAND, JOHANNES. 1523-1587. German bishop. See: Allg. Deut. Biog. Wigandia.

WIGAND, JUSTUS HEINRICH. 1769-1817. German gynecologist in Russia. See: Allg. Deut. Biog.; Biog. Lex hervorr. Aerzte. Wigand maneuver.

Wigand maneuver (Wigand, Justus Heinrich): Medicine. See: Dorland; Stedman.

Wigandia (Wigand, Johannes): Botany. See: Taylor, N.

Wigham burner (Wigham, John Richardson): Engineering and Industry. Cited in: Focal Encyc. Photog. under "Artificial Light History-Gas Light."

WIGHAM, JOHN RICHARDSON. 1829-1906. Scottish inventor and engineer. See: Dict. Nat. Biog. Wigham burner.

WIGHTMAN, ARTHUR STRONG. 1922- . American physicist. See: Amer. Men and Women Sci., 12th ed.; World Who's Who Sci. Wightman functions.

Wightman Cup (Wightman, Hazel Hotchkiss): Recreation and Sports. See: New Encyc. Brit.; Hendrickson under "Davis Cup."

Wightman functions (Wightman, Arthur Strong): Mathematics. See: Internat. Dict. Ap. Math.

WIGHTMAN, HAZEL HOTCHKISS. b. 1887. American tennis player. See: New Yorker (Aug. 30, 1952), p. 31. Wightman Cup.

WIGHTMAN, RANDALL H. 1902- . American mining engineer. See: Who's Who Engin., 1959. Wightmanite.

Wightmanite (Wightman, Randall H.): Earth Sciences. See: Thrush.

Wigner coefficient (Wigner, Eugene Paul): Mathematics. See: Internat. Dict. Ap. Math.; Internat. Dict. Phys. Elec.

Wigner effect (Wigner, Eugene Paul): Physics. See: Ballentyne; Hughes; Thewlis.

Wigner energy (Wigner, Eugene Paul): Physics. See: Hughes; Thewlis.

WIGNER, EUGENE PAUL. 1902- . Hungarian-born American mathematical physicist. See: Amer. Men Sci., 11th ed.; World Who's Who Sci. Bohr-Breit-Wigner theory, Breit-Wigner cross section, Breit-Wigner formula, Jordan-Wigner commutation rules, Von Neumann-Wigner rule, Wigner coefficient, Wigner effect, Wigner energy, Wigner force, Wigner nuclides, Wigner-Seitz cell, Wigner-Seitz method, Wigner theorem, Wigner-Wilkins model.

Wigner force (Wigner, Eugene Paul): Physics. See: Ballentyne; Internat. Dict. Ap. Math.; Van Nostrand Sci. Encyc.

Wigner nuclides (Wigner, Eugene Paul): Physics. See: Markus; Thewlis; Van Nostrand Sci. Encyc.

Wigner-Seitz cell (Wigner, Eugene Paul and Seitz, Frederick): Physics. See: Ballentyne.

Wigner-Seitz method (Wigner, Eugene Paul and Seitz, Frederick): Physics. See: Internat. Dict. Phys. Elec.; Thewlis.

Wigner theorem (Wigner, Eugene Paul): Physics. See: Ballentyne; Internat. Dict. Phys. Elec.; Markus.

Wigner-Wilkins model (Wigner, Eugene Paul and Wilkins, Thomas Russell): Physics. See: Internat. Dict. Ap. Math.

WIIK, FREDRIK JOHAN. 1839-1909. Finnish mineralogist. See: Finsk Biog. Handb. Wiikite.

Wiikite (Wiik, Fredrik Johan): Earth Sciences. See: Webster's 3d.

Wijers, Herman Joseph Gerard. See: Wyers, Herman Joseph Gerard.

Wijs iodine monochloride solution (or method) (Wijs, Jacob Jan Alexander): Chemistry. See: Ballentyne; Hackh; Van Nostrand Chem. Dict.

WIJS, JACOB JAN ALEXANDER. 1864-1942. Dutch analytical chemist. See: Chem. Weekblad vol. 40 (1943), pp. 140-141. Wijs iodine monochloride solution (or method), Wijs special iodine solution, Wijs value.

Wijs special iodide solution (Wijs, Jacob Jan Alexander): Chemistry. See: Van Nostrand Chem. Dict.

Wijs value (Wijs, Jacob Jan Alexander): Chemistry. See: Hackh.

WIKSTROEM, JOHANN EMANUEL. 1789-1856. Swedish botanist. See: Svenska Maen Och Kvinnor. Wikstroemia.

Wikstroemia (Wikstroem, Johann Emanuel): Botany. See: Webster's 3d.

WILBERFORCE, SAMUEL "SOAPY SAM." 1805-1873. English bishop and religious writer. See: Dict. Nat. Biog. Soapy Sam.

Wilbert vaultmaker (Wilbert, William L.?): Engineering and Industry. See: Thrush.

WILBERT, WILLIAM L. fl. 1952. American? engineer. (Biography source unavailable.) Wilbert vaultmaker?

WILBUR, JOHN. 1774-1856. American Quaker preacher. See: Dict. Amer. Biog. Wilburites.

Wilburites (Wilbur, John): Religion. See: Canney; Mathews, M. M.

Wilcox boiler (Wilcox, Stephen). See: Babcock and Wilcox boiler.

WILCOX, STEPHEN. 1830-1893. American inventor. See: Dict. Amer. Biog. Babcock and Wilcox boiler, Babcock and Wilcox mill.

WILCOX, TIMOTHY ERASTUS. 1840-1932. American surgeon and general. See: Who Was Who Amer., vol. I. Wilcoxia.

Wilcoxia (Wilcox, Timothy Erastus): Botany. See: Taylor, N.

WILCOXON, FRANK. 1892- . Irish-born American chemist and statistician. See: Amer. Men. Sci., 10th ed. Wilcoxon signed rank test, Wilcoxon's test.

Wilcoxon signed rank test (Wilcoxon, Frank): Statistics. See: Kendall.

Wilcoxon's test (Wilcoxon, Frank): Statistics. See: Hoult; Internat. Dict. Ap. Math.; Kendall. Also known as: Mann-Whitney test.

Wild fence (Wild, Heinrich von): Earth Sciences. See: Huschke.

WILD, HEINRICH VON. 1883-1902. Swiss physicist and meteorologist. See: Pogg., vols. 2, 3, 4; World Who's Who Sci. Wild fence.

WILD, WILHELM. fl. 1896. German chemist. Cited in: Royal Soc. Cat. Sci. Pap., 1884-1900. Engler-Wild test.

WILDBOLZ, HANS. 1873-1940. Swiss urologist. See: Biog. Lex. hervorr. Aerzte. Wildbolz reaction.

Wildbolz reaction (Wildbolz, Hans): Medicine. See: Dorland; Stedman.

WILDE, OSCAR O'FLAHERTIE WILLS. 1854-1900. Irish poet and dramatist. See: Dict. Nat. Biog., 1st suppl. Oscar (Oscarizing or Oscar-Wilding), Oscar (award), Wildean (wit).

WILDE, SIR WILLIAM ROBERT WILLS. 1815-1876. Irish oculist, otologist and antiquarian. See: Dict. Nat. Biog. Wilde's cords, Wilde's incision, Wilde's triangle.

Wildean (wit) (Wilde, Oscar): Generic Word. See: Hendrickson under "Oscar..."

WILDENSTEIN, RAOUL. fl. 1856. French chemist. (Biography source unavailable.) Wildenstein reagent.

Wildenstein reagent (Wildenstein, Raoul): Chemistry. See: Van Nostrand Chem. Dict.

WILDER, BURT GREEN. 1841-1925. American anatomist, neurologist and zoologist. See: Who Was Who Amer. Wilder's quadrant.

WILDER, JOSEPH. 1895- . American neuropsychiatrist. See: Amer. Med. Direct., 1973. Wilder's law of initial value.

WILDER, LAURA INGALLS. 1867-1957. American writer of children's stories. See: Who Was Who Amer., vol. 3. Laura Ingalls Wilder medal.

WILDER, RUSSELL MORSE. 1885-1959. American internist. See: World Who's Who Sci. Cutler-Power-Wilder test, Wilder's diet.

WILDER, WILLIAM HAMLIN. 1860-1935. American ophthalmologist. See: Who Was Who Amer. Wilder's sign.

WILDERMUTH, HERMANN A. 1852-1907. German psychiatrist and neurologist. See: Biog. Lex. hervorr. Aerzte. Wildermuth's ear.

Wildermuth's ear (Wildermuth, Hermann A.): Anatomy. See: Dorland; Stedman.

Wilder's diet (Wilder, Russell Morse): Medicine. See: Dorland.

Wilder's law of initial value (Wilder, Joseph): Medicine. See: Dorland; Stedman.

Wilder's quadrant (Wilder, Burt Green): Anatomy. See: Stedman.

Wilder's sign (Wilder, William Hamlin): Medicine. See: Dorland; Stedman.

WILDERVANCK, L. S. fl. 1960. Dutch physician. (Biography source unavailable.) Wildervanck's syndrome.

Wildervanck-Waardenburg-Franceschetti-Klein syndrome (Wildervanck, L. S.; Waardenburg, Petrus Johannes; Franceschetti, Adolphe; and Klein, David). See: Wildervanck's syndrome.

Wildervanck's syndrome (Wildervanck, L. S.): Medicine. See: Jablonski. Also known as: Franceschetti-Klein-Wildervanck syndrome, Wildervanck-Waardenburg-Franceschetti-Klein syndrome.

Wilde's cords (Wilde, Sir William Robert Wills): Anatomy. See: Donath; Dorland; Stedman.

Wilde's incision (Wilde, Sir William Robert Wills): Anatomy. See: Dorland; Stedman.

Wilde's triangle (Wilde, Sir William Robert Wills): Anatomy. See: Stedman. Also known as: Politzer's luminous cone, Woelde's triangle.

WILDHABER, ERNEST. 1892- . Swiss-born American engineer. See: Who's Who Engin. 1964. Wildhaber-Novikov gear.

Wildhaber-Novikov gear (Wildhaber, Ernest and Novikov, M. L.). See: Novikov gear.

WILDI, ERWIN. fl. 20th c. Swiss pathologist. See: Who's Who Sci. Europe, 2nd ed. Morel-Wildi syndrome.

WILE, R. S. fl. 1914. American? or German? metallurgical engineer. Cited in: Chem. Abstr. vol. 8 p. 3536. Wile's process.

Wile's process (Wile, R. S.): Engineering and Industry. See: Thrush.

Wiley Act (Wiley, Harvey Washington): Politics. See: Smith.

WILEY, HARVEY WASHINGTON. 1844-1930. American chemist and pure food reformer. See: Dict. Amer. Biog. Wiley Act.

WILFLEY, ARTHUR REDMAN. 1860-1927. American mining engineer and inventor. See: Nat. Cyc. Amer. Biog. Wilfley table, Wilfley slimer.

Wilfley slimer (Wilfley, Arthur Redman): Engineering and Industry. See: Thrush.

Wilfley table (Wilfley, Arthur Redman): Engineering and Industry. See: Thrush.

Wilgefortis legend (Wilgefortis, Saint): Religion. See: Attwater.

WILGEFORTIS, SAINT. Fabulous saint of the Middle Ages. See: Holweck. Wilgefortis legend.

Wilhelmians (Wilhelmina): Religion. See: Canney.

WILHELMINA. d. 1281. Italian religious enthusiast. Cited in: Hastings under "Religious Enthusiasts." Wilhelmians.

WILK, MARTIN BRADBURY. 1922- . Canadian-born American statistician. See: Amer. Men Sci., 10th ed., Soc. and Behav. Sci. Shapiro-Wilk test.

WILKE, FR. fl. 1939. German physician. (Biography source unavailable.) Meesmann-Wilke disease.

WILKE, R. M. fl. 1914. American mineral collector. (Biography source unavailable.) Wilkeite.

Wilkeite (Wilke, R. M.): Earth Sciences. See: Thrush; Webster's 3d.

WILKERSON, WILLIAM. fl. 1970. American writer. (Biography source unavailable.) Wilkerson's law.

Wilkerson's law (Wilkerson, William): Sociology. See: Martin.

WILKIE, SIR DAVID PERCIVAL DALBRECK. 1882-1938. Scottish surgeon. See: Dict. Nat. Biog. Wilkie's artery, Wilkie's disease.

Wilkie's artery (Wilkie, Sir David Percival Dalbreck): Medicine. See: Stedman.

Wilkie's disease (Wilkie, Sir David Percival Dalbreck): Medicine. See: Jablonski; Stedman.

Wilkins' disease (Wilkins, Lawson): Medicine. See: Jablonski.

WILKINS, LAWSON. 1894-1963. American physician. See: Who Was Who Amer. Wilkins' disease.

WILKINS, THOMAS RUSSELL. 1891-1940. Canadian physicist in America. See: World Who's Who Sci. Wigner-Wilkins model.

WILKINSON, DARRELL SHELDON. fl. 1947-1972. English dermatologist. See: Med. Direct., 1972. Sneddon-Wilkinson syndrome.

WILKINSON, DAVID. 1771-1852. American inventor and manufacturer. See: World Who's Who Sci. Wilkinson lathe.

WILKINSON, JEMIMA. 1752-1819. American religious leader. See: Dict. Amer. Biog. Jemimaite, Wilkinsonians.

WILKINSON, JOHN. 1728-1808. English ironmaster. See: Dict. Nat. Biog. four Wilkinson blast-furnace, Wilkinson's boring engine.

WILKINSON, JOHN ANDERSON. b. 1880. American chemist. See: Amer. Men Sci., 9th ed. Kelm-Wilkinson test.

WILKINSON, JOHN FREDERICK. 1897- . English physician. See: Who's Who, 1973-74. Wilkinson's anemia.

Wilkinson lathe (Wilkinson, David): Engineering and Industry. See: Auger.

Wilkinson oven (Derivation undetermined): Engineering and Industry. See: Thrush.

WILKINSON, ROBERT H. 1926- . American radiologist in pediatrics. See: Amer. Med. Direct., 1973. Moncrieff-Wilkinson syndrome.

Wilkinsonians (Wilkinson, Jemima): Religion. See: Canney.

Wilkinson's anemia (Wilkinson, John Frederick): Medicine. See: Jablonski. Also known as: Israels-Wilkinson anemia.

Wilkinson's boring engine (Wilkinson, John): Engineering and Industry. See: Auger.

Wilks criterion (Wilks, Samuel Stanley): Statistics. See: Internat. Dict. Ap. Math.; Kendall.

Wilks' disease (Wilks, Sir Samuel Baronet): Medicine. See: Dorland; Jablonski.

Wilks internal scatter (Wilks, Samuel Stanley): Statistics. See: Kendall.

Wilks-Lawley U statistic (Wilks, Samuel Stanley and Lawley, D. N.): Statistics. See: Kendall.

Wilks-Rosenbaum tests (Wilks, Samuel Stanley, and Rosenbaum, S.): Statistics. See: Kendall.

WILKS, SIR SAMUEL BARONET. 1824-1911. English physician. See: Biog. Lex. hervorr. Aerzte. Wilks' disease.

WILKS, SAMUEL STANLEY. 1906-1964. American mathematical statistician. See: Internat. Encyc. Soc. Sci. Wilks criterion, Wilks internal scatter, Wilks-Lawley U statistic, Wilks-Rosenbaum tests.

Willan-Plumbe syndrome (Willan, Robert and Plumbe, Samuel). See: Willan's lepra.

WILLAN, ROBERT. 1757-1812. English dermatologist. See: Dict. Nat. Biog. Willan's lepra, Willan's lupus.

Willan's lepra (Willan, Robert): Medicine. See: Dorland; Jablonski, Stedman. Also known as: Willan-Plumbe syndrome.

Willans line (Willans, Peter William): Engineering and Industry. See: Auger; Van Nostrand Sci. Encyc.

Willan's lupus (Willan, Robert): Medicine. See: Stedman.

WILLANS, PETER WILLIAM. 1851-1892. English engineer. See: Boase. Willans line, Willans steam engine.

Willans steam engine (Willans, Peter William): Engineering and Industry. See: Auger.

Willard-Hall reagent (Willard, Hobart Hurd and Hall, Dorothy): Chemistry. See: Van Nostrand Chem. Dict.

WILLARD, HOBART HURD. 1881- . American chemist. See: Pogg., vol. 6. Shaner-Willard test reactions, Willard-Hall reagent.

Willatts collapsible camera (Willatts, Richard): Photography. See: Focal Encyc. Photog.

WILLATTS, RICHARD. fl. 1851. English photographer. Cited in: Singer. Willatts collapsible camera.

WILLEBRAND, ERIK ADOLF VON. 1870-1949. Finnish physician. See: Biog. Lex. hervorr. Aerzte. Willebrand-Juergens syndrome.

Willebrand-Juergens syndrome (Willebrand, Erik Adolf von and Juergens, Rudolf): Medicine. See: Jablonski. Also known as: Minot-von Willebrand syndrome, von Willebrand's syndrome, Willebrand's syndrome.

Willebrand's syndrome (Willebrand, Erik Adolf von). See: Willebrand-Juergens syndrome.

WILLEM I. 1772-1843. King of the Netherlands and Grand-Duke of Luxemburg. See: Encyc. Brit., 1911; Nouv. Biog. Univ. Willemite.

WILLEME, FRANCOIS. 1830-1905. French painter and sculptor. (Biography source unavailable.) Willeme's method.

Willeme's method (Willeme, Francois): Photography. See: Focal Encyc. Photog.

Willemite (Willem I): Earth Sciences. See: Markus; Thrush; Van Nostrand Sci. Encyc.

WILLEMS, CHARLES. b. 1859. Belgian surgeon. See: Bull. de l'Acad. Royale de Med. de Belgique vol. 13 (1933), pp. 488-498. Willem's method.

Willems' method (Willems, Charles): Medicine. See: Dorland; Stedman.

WILLETT, JOHN ABERNETHY. 1872-1932. English obstetrician. See: Brit. Med. J. vol. 2 (July 23, 1932), p. 176. Willett's forceps (or clamp).

Willett's forceps (or clamp) (Willett, John Abernethy): Medicine. See: Dorland; Stedman.

WILLGERODT, KONRAD HEINRICH CHRISTOPH. 1841-1930. German chemist. See: Pogg., vols. 3-5. Willgerodt reaction.

Willgerodt reaction (Willgerodt, Konrad Heinrich Christoph): Chemistry. See: Ballentyne; Van Nostrand Chem. Dict.

WILLI, HEINRICH. fl. 1956. Swiss pediatrician. See: Kuerschner's Deut. Gel. Kal., 1970. Prader-Willi syndrome.

WILLIAM I. 1027-1087. King of England and Duke of Normandy. See: Dict. Nat. Biog. William the Conqueror's oak.

WILLIAM I OF ORANGE. 1533-1584. Prince of Orange and first Dutch stadtholder. See: Encyc. Brit., 1911; Nouv. Biog. Univ. Apologie of William of Orange, Supplication of William of Orange.

WILLIAM III OF ORANGE. 1650-1702. Stadtholder of Holland and King of England. See: Dict. Nat. Biog. King William's War, Orangeism (or Orangemen), William and Mary furniture style, Williamite.

WILLIAM IV (DUKE OF CLARENCE). 1765-1837. King of England. See: Dict. Nat. Biog. Clarence (carriage), King William pine.

William and Mary furniture style (William III of Orange, and Mary II): Applied Arts. See: Webster's 3d.

William of Ockham (Occam). See: Ockham, William of.

William pear (Williams): Botany. See: Brewer; Partridge; Weekley.

William Randolph Hearst Foundation (Hearst, William Randolph): Philanthropy. See: Nat. Cycl. Amer. Biog., vol. 39, p. 9.

William the Conqueror's oak (William I): History. See: Brewer.

Williamite (William III of Orange): History. See: Webster's 3d.

WILLIAMS. fl. 1814. English fruit importer. (Biography source unavailable.) William pear.

WILLIAMS, ALPHEUS FULLER. 1874-1953. American mining engineer. See: Encyc. Southern Africa, 6th ed. Afwillite.

Williams and Janney gear (Williams, H. D. and Janney, R.): Engineering and Industry. See: Auger. Also known as: Janney-Williams transmission.

WILLIAMS, ANNA WESSELS. 1863-1955. American bacteriologist. See: Who Was Who Amer., vol. 5. Park-Williams bacillus, Park-Williams fixative, Williams' stain.

Williams-Campbell syndrome (Williams, Howard Owen, and Campbell, Peter): Medicine. See: Jablonski.

WILLIAMS, CHARLES JAMES BLASIUS. 1805-1889. English physician. See: Dict. Nat. Biog. Williams' sign (or tracheal tone).

WILLIAMS, D. R. or R. S. fl. 1860. American Confederate army captain. (Biography source unavailable.) Williams machine gun.

WILLIAMS, DUDLEY. 1912- . American physicist. See: Amer. Men and Women Sci., 12th ed. Williams' plastometer?

WILLIAMS, EVAN JAMES. 1903-1945. English physicist. See: Royal Soc. Obit. Notices of Fellows. Weizaecker-Williams method.

WILLIAMS, FREDERICK CALLARD. 1911- . English electrical engineer. See: Who's Who, 1973-1974. Williams tube.

WILLIAMS, GARDNER STEWART. 1866-1931. American hydraulic engineer. See: Nat. Cycl. Amer. Biog., vol. 54, p. 105. Hazen and Williams formula.

Williams gauge (Williams, Robley Cook): Physics. See: Internat. Dict. Phys. Elec.

WILLIAMS, GEORGE KAY. b. 1872. American construction and designing engineer. See: Who's Who Engin., 1922-23. Williams' hinged-hammer crusher?

WILLIAMS, H. D. fl. early 20th c. English engineer. (Biography source unavailable.) Williams and Janney gear.

Williams' hinged-hammer crusher (Williams, George Kay?): Engineering and Industry. See: Thrush.

WILLIAMS, HOWARD OWEN. fl. 1941-1972. English physician. See: Med. Direct., 1972. Williams-Campbell syndrome.

WILLIAMS, JOHN F. fl. 1928. American chemist. Cited in: Chem. Abstr., vol. 22, p. 3633. Phillips-Williams test for nickel.

WILLIAMS, L. WHITE. fl. 19th c. American mineral collector. (Biography source unavailable.) Williamsite.

Williams machine gun (Williams, D. R. or R. S.): Weapons. See: Quick.

WILLIAMS, MERLIN CHARLES. 1931- . American meteorologist and engineer. See: Amer. Men and Women Sci., 12th ed. Williams riser?

WILLIAMS, NEIL HOOKER. b. 1870. American physicist. See: Amer. Men Sci., 6th ed. Cleeton and Williams magnetron.

Williams' plastometer (Williams, Dudley?): Engineering and Industry. See: Thrush.

Williams refractometer (Williams, Samuel Robinson?): Physics. See: Internat. Dict. Phys. Elec.

Williams riser (Williams, Merlin Charles?): Engineering and Industry. See: Thrush.

WILLIAMS, ROBLEY COOK. 1908- . American biophysicist. See: Amer. Men and Women Sci., 12th ed. Williams gauge.

WILLIAMS, S. H. fl. 1947. American chemist. (Biography source unavailable.) Williams unit.

WILLIAMS, SAMUEL ROBINSON. b. 1879. American physicist. See: Pogg., vols. 5, 6. Williams refractometer?

Williams' sign (or tracheal tone) (Williams, Charles James Blasius): Medicine. See: Dorland.

Williams' stain (Williams, Anna Wessels): Medicine. See: Stedman.

Williams tube (Williams, Frederick Callard): Engineering and Industry. See: Hughes; Markus.

Williams unit (Williams, S. H.): Chemistry. See: Chem. Abstr., vol. 41, p. 4926e.

Williamsite (Williams, L. White): Earth Sciences. See: Mathews, M. M.; Thrush; Webster's 3d.

Williamson (Williamson, Robert Logan): Generic Word (itinerant hustler). See: Hendrickson.

Williamson Act (Williamson, William): Politics. See: Jameson.

WILLIAMSON, ALEXANDER EDWARD. 1824-1904. English chemist. See: Dict. Nat. Biog. Williamson reaction (or synthesis), Williamson's blue (or violet).

Williamson amplifier (Williamson, David Theodore Nelson): Engineering and Industry. See: Markus.

WILLIAMSON, CARL SNEED. 1896-1952. American surgeon. See: JAMA vol. 149 (Aug. 16, 1952), p. 1481. Mann-Williamson operation (or ulcer).

WILLIAMSON, DAVID THEODORE NELSON. 1923- . English electrical engineer. See: Who's Who, 1973-1974. Williamson amplifier.

WILLIAMSON, EDWARD BRUCE. b. 1877. American zoologist. See: Hirsch. Williamsonia.

WILLIAMSON, ERSKINE DOUGLAS. b. 1886. Scottish-born American physical chemist. See: Amer. Men Sci., 3d ed. Adams-Williamson annealing schedule.

WILLIAMSON, HENRY CHARLES. b. 1871. Canadian zoologist. See: Hirsch. Gomphoides Williamsoni, Prosopium Williamsoni.

WILLIAMSON, JOHN. fl. 1928. English ceramics engineer. Cited in: Chem. Abstr. vol. 22 p. 2251. Williamson kiln.

Williamson kiln (Williamson, John): Engineering and Industry. See: Thrush.

WILLIAMSON, OLIVER KEY. 1866-1941. English physician. See: Who Was Who. Williamson's sign.

Williamson reaction (or synthesis) (Williamson, Alexander Edward): Chemistry. See: Ballentyne; Hackh; Van Nostrand Chem. Encyc.

WILLIAMSON, RICHARD T. 1862-1937. English physician. See: Who Was Who. Williamson's test.

WILLIAMSON, ROBERT LOGAN. fl. 1890. Scottish-born American hustler. (Biography source unavailable.) Williamson.

WILLIAMSON, ROBERT STOCKTON. 1824-1882. American topographical engineer. See: Heitman, vol. I. Williamson's sapsucker, Williamson's woodpecker.

WILLIAMSON, WILLIAM. 1875-1972. American legislator. See: Biog. Direct. Amer. Congress. Williamson Act.

WILLIAMSON, WILLIAM CRAWFORD. 1816-1895. English naturalist. See: Dict. Nat. Biog. Williamsonia, Williamsoniella, Williamson's canal.

Williamsonia (Williamson, Edward Bruce): Zoology. See: Pennak.

Williamsonia (Williamson, William Crawford): Botany. See: Webster's 3d.

Williamson's blue (or violet) (Williamson, Alexander Edward): Chemistry. See: Hackh; Webster's 3d.

Williamson's canal (Williamson, William Crawford): Zoology. See: Gray.

Williamson's sapsucker (Williamson, Robert Stockton): Zoology. See: Mathews, M. M.

Williamson's sign (Williamson, Oliver Key): Medicine. See: Dorland.

Williamson's test (Williamson, Richard T.): Medicine. See: Dorland; Stedman.

Williamson's woodpecker (Williamson, Robert Stockton): Zoology. See: Mathews, M. M.

Willie-Wastle (child's game) (Wastle, Willie): History. See: Brewer.

Willis arteries (or vessels) (Willis, Thomas): Anatomy. See: Donath; Stedman.

Willis' centrum nervosum (Willis, Thomas): Anatomy. See: Stedman.

Willis' circle (or circle of Willis) (Willis, Thomas): Anatomy. See: Dorland; Henderson; Stedman; Webster's 3d.

Willis' cords (Willis, Thomas): Anatomy. See: Dorland; Stedman; Webster's 3d.

Willis' nerve (Willis, Thomas): Anatomy. See: Donath; Stedman.

Willis' pancreas (Willis, Thomas): Anatomy. See: Stedman.

Willis paracusis (Willis, Thomas): Anatomy. See: Stedman.

Willis' pouch (Willis, Thomas): Anatomy. See: Stedman.

WILLIS, ROBERT. 1800-1875. English mechanician and archaeologist. See: Dict. Nat. Biog. Willis system.

Willis system (Willis, Robert): Engineering and Industry. See: Webster's 3d.

Willis' theory (Willis, Thomas): Zoology. See: Gray.

WILLIS, THOMAS. 1621-1675. English physician. See: Dict. Nat. Biog. Willis' arteries (or vessels), Willis' centrum nervosum, Willis' circle (or circle of Willis), Willis' cords, Willis' nerve, Willis' pancreas, Willis' paracusis, Willis' pouch, Willis' theory.

Willison coupler (Derivation undetermined): Engineering and Industry. See: Thrush.

WILLISTON, SAMUEL WENDELL. 1852-1918. American paleontologist. See: Dict. Amer. Biog. Williston's law.

Williston's law (Williston, Samuel Wendell): Zoology. See: Winick.

WILLITS, CHARLES OLIVER. 1901- . American chemist. See: Amer. Men Sci., 6th ed. Clark-Willit test.

Wills' anemia (Wills, Lucy): Medicine. See: Jablonski.

WILLS, LUCY. fl. 1931. English scientist. (Biography source unavailable.) Wills' anemia.

WILLSTAEDT, HARRY. fl. 1935. German? biochemist. Cited in: Chem. Abstr. vol. 32 p. 2968[6]. Willstaedt test reaction.

Willstaedt test reaction (Willstaedt, Harry): Chemistry. See: Van Nostrand Chem. Dict.

Willstaetter lignin (Willstaetter, Richard): Chemistry. See: Hackh.

WILLSTAETTER, RICHARD. 1872-1942. German chemist. See: Pogg., vols. 4, 5, 6, 7a; World Who's Who Sci. Bergius-Willstaetter saccharification process, Willstaetter lignin.

Willughbeia (Willughby, Francis): Botany. See: Webster's 3d.

WILLUGHBY, FRANCIS. 1635-1672. English naturalist. See: Dict. Nat. Biog. Willughbeia.

WILMOT, DAVID. 1814-1868. American politician. See: Dict. Amer. Biog. Wilmot district, Wilmot Proviso.

Wilmot district (Wilmot, David): History. See: Jameson.

WILMOT, GEORGE. fl. 1931. American mining engineer. (Biography source unavailable.) Wilmot jig?

Wilmot jig (Wilmot, George?): Engineering and Industry. See: Thrush.

Wilmot Proviso (Wilmot, David): History. See: Jameson; Morris; Phyfe.

WILMS, MAX. 1867-1918. German surgeon. See: Biog. Lex. hervorr. Aerzte. Wilms' method, Wilms' operation, Wilms' tumor (or nephroblastoma).

Wilms' method (Wilms, Max): Medicine. See: Stedman.

Wilms' operation (Wilms, Max): Medicine. See: Stedman.

Wilms' tumor (or nephroblastoma) (Wilms, Max): Medicine. See: Dorland; Jablonski; Stedman. Also known as: Birch-Hirschfeld's tumor.

Wilputte coke oven (Wilputte, Louis): Engineering and Industry. See: Thrush; Van Nostrand Chem. Dict.

WILPUTTE, LOUIS. fl. 1911. American metallurgical engineer. (Biography source unavailable.) Wilputte coke oven.

WILSON, A. fl. 1911. English? metallurgical engineer. Cited in: Chem. Abstr. vol. 6 p. 2836. Wilson producer.

Wilson Act (or Law) (Wilson, James Falconer): Politics. See: Webster's Biog. Dict.

WILSON, ALEXANDER. 1714-1786. Scottish astronomer. See: World Who's Who Sci. Wilson effect.

WILSON, ALEXANDER. 1766-1813. Scottish-born American ornithologist. See: Dict. Amer. Biog. Wilsonia, Wilson's bluebird, Wilson's owl, Wilson's petrel, Wilson's phalarope, Wilson's plover, Wilson's sandpiper, Wilson's snipe, Wilson's tern, Wilson's thrush (or veery), Wilson's warbler.

Wilson Bill (Wilson, William Lyne): Politics. Cited in: Jameson.

Wilson block (Wilson, George?): Medicine. See: Stedman.

WILSON, CECIL. L. 1912- . English analytical chemist. See: Internat. Chem. Direct., 1969-1970. Wilson test for nitrite?

WILSON, CHARLES BRANCH. 1861-1941. American parasitologist. See: Who Was Who Amer. Wilson's method?

WILSON, CHARLES THOMSON REES. 1869-1959. Scottish physicist. See: Asimov; Dict. Nat. Biog. Wilson cloud-chamber, Wilson electroscope, Wilson line.

WILSON, CLIFFORD. 1906- . English physician. See: Who's Who, 1973-1974. Kimmelstiel-Wilson syndrome.

Wilson cloud-chamber (Wilson, Charles Thomson Rees): Physics. See: Huschke; Internat. Dict. Phys. Elec.; Markus.

WILSON, EDMUND BEECHER. 1856-1939. American zoologist. See: Nat. Acad. Sci. Biog. Mem., vol. 21. Wilson type xx-xo sex chromesome, Wilsonema?

WILSON, EDWIN BIDWELL. 1879-1964. American mathematical statistician. See: Pogg., vols. 4, 5, 6. Wilson-Hilferty transformation.

Wilson effect (Wilson, Alexander): Astronomy. See: Satterthwaite.

Wilson effect (or experiment) (Wilson, Harold Albert); Physics. See: Hughes; Van Nostrand Sci. Encyc.

Wilson electroscope (Wilson, Charles Thomson Rees): Engineering and Industry. See: Hughes; Van Nostrand Sci. Encyc.

Wilson elevator (Derivation undetermined): Engineering and Industry. See: Thrush.

WILSON, F. B. fl. 1918. American chemist. Cited in: Chem. Abstr. vol. 12 p. 1954. Wilson test for fluorine.

WILSON, FLIP. 1933- . American comedian. See: Who's Who Amer., 1974-1975. Flip Wilson's law.

Wilson gear box (Wilson, Walter Gordon): Engineering and Industry. See: Auger.

WILSON, GEORGE. b. 1888. American neurologist. See: Amer. Neurolog. Assoc., Anniv. vol., 1924, p. 647. Wilson block?

Wilson-Gorman Tariff (Wilson, William Lyne and Gorman, Arthur P.): Politics. See: Jameson; Montgomery; Morris. Also known as: Wilson Tariff Act.

WILSON, HAROLD ALBERT. 1874-1964. English-born physicist in America. See: Amer. Men Sci., 10th ed. Wilson effect (or experiment).

Wilson-Hilferty transformation (Wilson, Edwin Bidwell and Hilferty, M. M.): Statistics. See: Kendall.

WILSON, JAMES. 1765-1821. English surgeon. See: Edinburgh Med. Surg. J. vol. 18 (1822), pp. 313-314. Wilson's muscle.

WILSON, JAMES FALCONER. 1828-1895. American lawyer and politician. See: Dict. Amer. Biog. Wilson Act (or Law).

WILSON, JAMES HARRISON. 1837-1925. American topographical engineer and soldier. See: Dict. Amer. Biog. Wilson's raid.

WILSON, JAMES LEROY. 1898- . American pediatrician. See: Direct. Med. Specialists, 1974-1975. Jirasek-Zuelzer-Wilson syndrome.

WILSON, SIR JAMES MILNE. 1812-1880. Scottish premier of Tasmania. See: Dict. Australian Biog. Wilsonite?

WILSON, SIR JOHN. 1741-1793. English mathematician and jurist. See: Dict. Nat. Biog. Wilson's theorem.

WILSON, JOHN. fl. 1852. English engineer. (Biography source unavailable.) Wilson water calorimeter.

WILSON, JOHN LEWIS. 1898- . American chemist. See: Amer. Men Sci., 7th ed. Wilson reagents for determining the hardness of water?

WILSON, KARL MILLER. b. 1885. American gynecologist. See: Amer. Men Sci., 10th ed. Wilson's test for pregnancy.

Wilson line (Wilson, Charles Thomson Rees): Engineering and Industry. See: Auger.

Wilson-Mikity syndrome (Wilson, Miriam Geisendorfer and Mikity, Victor G.): Medicine. See: Jablonski; Stedman.

WILSON, MIRIAM GEISENDORFER. 1922- . American pediatrician. See: Amer. Men and Women Sci., 12th ed. Wilson-Mikity syndrome.

Wilson producer (Wilson, A.): Engineering and Industry. See: Thrush.

Wilson reagents for determining the hardness of water (Wilson, John Lewis?): Chemistry. See: Van Nostrand Chem. Dict.

WILSON, ROBERT RATHBUN. 1914- . American physicist. See: World Who's Who Sci. Serber-Wilson force?

WILSON, SAMUEL. 1766-1854. American meat packer. See: Dict. Amer. Biog. Sam (or stand Sam), Sam (political party)?, Uncle Sam, Uncle Sam bird, Uncle Sam's men.

WILSON, SAMUEL ALEXANDER KINNIER. ca. 1877-1937. English neurologist. See: Dict. Nat. Biog.; World Who's Who Sci. Foville-Wilson syndrome, Wilson's disease (or syndrome).

Wilson Tariff Act (Wilson, William Lyne). See: Wilson-Gorman Tariff.

Wilson test for fluorine (Wilson, F. B.): Chemistry. See: Van Nostrand Chem. Dict.

Wilson test for nitrite (Wilson, Cecil L.?): Chemistry. See: Van Nostrand Chem. Dict.

Wilson type xx-xo sex chromosome (Wilson, Edmund Beecher): Zoology. See: Nat. Acad. Sci. Biog. Mem., vol. 21.

WILSON, WALTER GORDON. 1874-1957. English engineer. See: Dict. Nat. Biog. Wilson gear box.

Wilson water calorimeter (Wilson, John): Engineering and Industry. See: Auger.

WILSON, SIR WILLIAM JAMES ERASMUS. 1809-1884. English dermatologist, surgeon and philanthropist. See: Dict. Nat. Biog. Wilson's disease (1), Wilson's disease (2).

WILSON, WILLIAM LYNE. 1843-1900. American educator and legislator. See: Dict. Amer. Biog. Wilson bill, Wilson-Gorman Tariff.

WILSON, WOODROW. 1856-1924. American president. See: Internat. Encyc. Soc. Sci. Wilsonian (or Wilsonism), Wilson's fourteen points.

Wilsonema (Wilson, Edmund Beecher?): Zoology. See: Pennak.

Wilsonia (Wilson, Alexander): Zoology. See: Pennak.

Wilsonian (or Wilsonism) (Wilson, Woodrow): Politics. See: Mathews, M. M.; Webster's 3d.

Wilsonite (Wilson, Sir James Milne?): Earth Sciences. See: Thrush.

Wilson's bluebird (Wilson, Alexander): Zoology. See: Mathews, M. M.

Wilson's disease (or syndrome) (Wilson, Samuel Alexander Kinnier): Medicine. See: Dorland; Jablonski; Stedman. Also known as: Kinnier Wilson's disease, Westphal-Struempell syndrome.

Wilson's disease (1) (Wilson, Sir William James Erasmus): Medicine. See: Jablonski.

Wilson's disease (2) (Wilson, Sir William James Erasmus): Medicine. See: Jablonski.

Wilson's fourteen points (Wilson, Woodrow): History. See: Jameson.

Wilson's method (Wilson Charles Branch?). See: Hung's method.

Wilson's muscle (Wilson, James): Anatomy. See: Donath; Dorland; Stedman.

Wilson's owl (Wilson, Alexander): Zoology. See: Mathews, M. M.

Wilson's petrel (Wilson, Alexander): Zoology. See: Gray; Hendrickson under "Petrel..."; Mathews, M. M.

Wilson's phalarope (Wilson, Alexander): Zoology. See: Gray; Pennak.

Wilson's plover (Wilson, Alexander): Zoology. See: Gray.

Wilson's raid (Wilson, James Harrison): History. See: Jameson.

Wilson's sandpiper (Wilson, Alexander): Zoology. See: Mathews, M. M.

Wilson's snipe (Wilson, Alexander): Zoology. See: Gray.

Wilson's tern (Wilson, Alexander): Zoology. See: Mathews, M. M.

Wilson's test for pregnancy (Wilson, Karl Miller): Medicine. See: Dorland.

Wilson's theorem (Wilson, Sir John): Mathematics. See: Ballentyne; James.

Wilson's thrush (or veery) (Wilson, Alexander): Zoology. See: Mathews, M. M.

Wilson's warbler (Wilson, Alexander): Zoology. See: Mathews, M. M.

WIMSHURST, JAMES. 1832-1903. English engineer. See: Dict. Nat. Biog. Wimshurst machine.

Wimshurst machine (Wimshurst, James): Engineering and Industry. See: Markus; Thewlis; Webster's 3d.

WINCHELL, NEWTON HORACE. 1839-1914. American geologist and archaeologist. See: Dict. Amer. Biog. Winchelite.

Winchellite (Winchell, Newton Horace): Earth Sciences. See: Thrush.

WINCHESTER, OLIVER FISHER. 1810-1880. American rifle manufacturer. See: Dict. Amer. Biog. Winchester repeating rifle.

Winchester repeating rifle (Winchester, Oliver Fisher): Weapons. See: Hendrickson; Matthews, M. M.; Partridge.

WINCKEL, FRANZ KARL LUDWIG WILHELM VON. 1837-1911. German gynecologist and obstetrician. See: Biog. Jahr. Deut. Nekr., 1911. Winckel's disease.

Winckel's disease (Winckel, Franz Karl Ludwig Wilhelm von): Medicine. See: Dorland; Jablonski; Stedman. Also known as: Charrin-Winckel disease, Ritter's disease.

WINCKLER, GEORGES MARIE. 1901- . French anatomist. See: World Who's Who Sci. Winckler's reaction?

Winckler's reaction (Winckler, Georges Marie?): Medicine. See: Stedman.

WINDAUS, ADOLF OTTO REINHOLD. 1876-1959. German chemist. See: World Who's Who Sci. Windaus test reaction for cholesterol.

Windaus test reaction for cholesterol (Windaus, Adolf Otto Reinhold): Chemistry. See: Van Nostrand Chem. Dict.

Windisch test for lactic acid (Windisch, Wilhelm?): Chemistry. See: Van Nostrand Chem. Dict.

WINDISCH, WILHELM. 1860-1944. German chemist. See: Pogg., vols. 6, 7a. Windisch test for lactic acid?

WINDOM. fl. 20th c. American? amateur radio operator. (Biography source unavailable.) Windom antenna.

Windom antenna (Windom): Engineering and Industry. See: Markus.

WINDSCHEID, FRANZ. 1862-1910. German physician. See: Biog. Jahr. Deut. Nekr., 1910. Windscheid's disease.

Windscheid's disease (Windscheid, Franz): Medicine. See: Stedman.

WINDSOR, EDWARD, DUKE OF WINDSOR (EDWARD VIII). 1894-1972. English king and nobleman. See: New York Times, May 29, 1972, p. 1. Prince of Wales Trophy.

WINDSOR, WALLIS WARFIELD SIMPSON. b. 1896. American-born English duchess. See: Ewart. Wally blue.

WINEBRENNER, JOHN. 1797-1860. American religious leader. See: Dict. Amer. Biog. Winebrennerians.

Winebrennerians (Winebrenner, John): Religion. See: Canney; Jameson; Mathews, M.M.

WINGLER, AUGUST. 1898-1960. German chemist. See: Pogg., vol. 7a. Schulemann-Schoenhoefer-Wingler test.

WINIWARTER, ALEXANDER (Also: ALEXANDRE-JOSEPH). 1848-1917. Austrian-born Belgian surgeon. See: Biog. Nat. de Belgique. Winiwarter's operation.

Winiwarter-Buerger syndrome (Winiwarter, Felix von and Buerger, Leo). See: Buerger's disease.

WINIWARTER, FELIX VON. 1852-1931. Austrian surgeon. See: Biog. Lex. hervorr. Aerzte. Winiwarter-Buerger syndrome.

Winiwarter's operation (Winiwarter, Alexander): Medicine. See: Dorland.

WINKEL, OSWALD. 1874-1953. German cartographer. Cited in: Westermann Lexikon der Geographie. Winkel's tripel projection.

WINKELMAN, NATHANIEL WILLIAM. 1891-1956. American neurologist. See: Who Was Who Amer. Winkelman's disease.

WINKELMANN, ADOLPH AUGUST. 1848-1910. German physicist. See: Pogg., vol. 3, 4, 5, 7a suppl. Winkelmann and Schott equation.

Winkelmann and Schott equation (Winkelmann, Adolph August and Schott, Otto): Engineering and Industry. See: Thrush.

Winkelman's disease (Winkelman, Nathaniel William): Medicine. See: Dorland; Stedman.

Winkel's tripel projection (Winkel, Oswald): Geography. See: Monkhouse.

Winkle, Rip van. See: Rip van Winkle.

WINKLER, ANTON. d. 1892. German mathematician. See: Pogg., vols. 2, 3, 4. Gauss-Winckler inequality?

Winkler-Bach formula (Winkler, E. and Bach, Julius): Engineering and Industry. See: Internat. Dict. Ap. Math.

WINKLER, CLEMENS. 1838-1904. German chemist. See: World Who's Who Sci. Bettendorff-Winkler reagent, Winkler reagent for ammonia, Winkler reagent for carbon monoxide, Winkler reagent for nitric oxide gas, Winkler reagent for oxygen, Winkler test reaction for germanium.

WINKLER, E. 1855-1888. German engineer. (Biography source unavailable.) Winkler-Bach forumula.

WINKLER, FRITZ. 1888-1950. German chemical technologist. See: Pogg., vol. 7a. Winkler system (or process).

Winkler generator (Winkler, Fritz). See: Winkler system (or process).

WINKLER, L. W. fl. 1920. German chemist. Cited in: Chem. Abst., Decenn. Index, 1917-1926. Winkler method.

WINKLER, MAX. 1875-1952. Swiss physician. See: Hautzart 3 (June 1952 G), 287. Winkler's disease.

Winkler method (Winkler, L. W.): Chemistry. See: Pennak.

Winkler reagent for ammonia (Winkler, Clemens): Chemistry. See: Van Nostrand Chem. Dict.

Winkler reagent for arsenic, antimony, and phosphorus hydrides (Winkler, L. W.): Chemistry. See: Van Nostrand Chem. Dict.

Winkler reagent for carbon monoxide (Winkler, Clemens): Chemistry. See: Van Nostrand Chem. Dict.

Winkler reagent for iodine (Winkler, L. W.): Chemistry. See: Van Nostrand Chem. Dict.

Winkler reagent for nitric oxide gas (Winkler, Clemens): Chemistry. See: Van Nostrand Chem. Dict.

Winkler reagent for oxygen (Winkler, Clemens): Chemistry. See: Van Nostrand Chem. Dict.

Winkler reagents for determining hardness in water (Winkler, L. W.): Chemistry. See: Van Nostrand Chem. Dict.

Winkler system (or process) (Winkler, Fritz): Engineering and Industry. See: Thrush. Also known as: Winkler generator.

Winkler test for dissolved oxygen in water (Winkler, L. W.): Chemistry. See: Van Nostrand Chem. Dict.

Winkler test for hypochlorite in drinking water (Winkler, L. W.): Chemistry. See: Van Nostrand Chem. Dict.

Winkler test reaction for germanium (Winkler, Clemens): Chemistry. See: Van Nostrand Chem. Dict.

Winkler's disease (Winkler, Max): Medicine. See: Dorland; Jablonski; Stedman.

Winsloev, Jacques Benigne. See: Winslow, Jakob Benignus.

WINSLOW, JAKOB BENIGNUS. 1669-1760. Danish-born French anatomist. See: Nouv. Biog. Univ. Winslow's foramen, Winslow's ligament, Winslow's pancreas, Winslow's stars.

Winslow point system (Winslow, Thomas Newby): Recreation and Sports. See: Webster's 3d.

WINSLOW, THOMAS NEWBY. 1861-1942. American lawyer, mathematician, and bridge expert. See: New York Times, Dec. 12, 1942, p. 17, col. 2. Winslow point system.

Winslow's foramen (Winslow, Jakob Benignus): Medicine. See: Donath; Dorland; Stedman.

Winslow's ligament (Winslow, Jakob Benignus): Medicine. See: Donath; Dorland; Stedman.

Winslow's pancreas (Winslow, Jakob Benignus): Medicine. See: Donath; Stedman. Also known as: Willis' pancreas.

Winslow's stars (Winslow, Jakob Benignus): Medicine. See: Donath; Dorland; Stedman.

WINSOR, CHARLES P. 1896-1951. American biostatistician. See: New York Times, April 7, 1951, p. 15, col. 4. Winsorised estimation.

WINSOR, FREDERICK. 1900- . American author of children's stories. Cited in: Nat. Union Cat., 1958-1962. Winsor's wisdom.

Winsorised estimation (Winsor, Charles P.): Statistics. See: Kendall.

Winsor's wisdom (Winsor, Frederick): Sociology. See: Martin.

WINTER, JOHN. fl. 16th c. English naval officer. (Biography source unavailable.) Wintera, Winter's bark.

Wintera (Winter, John): Botany. See: Webster's 3d.

WINTERBOTTOM, THOMAS MASTERMAN. 1765-1859. English physician. See: Dict. Nat. Biog. Winterbottom's sign (or symptom).

Winterbottom's sign (or symptom) (Winterbottom, Thomas Masterman): Medicine. See: Dorland; Jablonski; Stedman.

Winterhalter costume (Winterhalter, Franz Xavier): Fashion. See: Picken.

WINTERHALTER, FRANZ XAVIER. 1806-1873. German portrait painter. See: Allg. Deut. Biog. Winterhalter costume.

WINTERNITZ, WILHELM. 1835-1917. German-born physician in Austria. See: Deut. Biog. Jahr., 1917-1920. Winternitz's sound, Winternitz's test.

Winternitz's sound (Winternitz, Wilhelm): Medicine. Dorland; Stedman.

Winternitz's test (Winternitz, Wilhelm): Medicine. Stedman.

Winter's bark (Winter, John): Botany. See: Charnock.

WINTERSTEINER, HUGO. 1865-1918. Austrian ophthalmologist. See: Biog. Lex hervorr. Aerzte. Wintersteiner rosettes.

WINTERSTEINER, OSKAR PAUL. 1898-1971. Austrian-born American bio-chemist. See: Amer. Men Sci., 10th ed. Wintersteiner's compound F. Also known as: Kendall's compound E.

Wintersteiner rosettes (Wintersteiner, Hugo): Medicine. See: Stedman.

Wintersteiner's compound F (Wintersteiner, Oskar Paul): Medicine. See: Stedman. Also known as: Kendall's compound E.

WINTHER, ADOLF. fl. 1880. German chemist. Cited in: Royal Soc. Cat. Sci. Pap., 1874-1883. Nevile and Winther's acid.

WINTHROP, JOHN. 1588-1649. English-born governor of Massachusetts and founder of Boston. See: Dict. Nat. Biog. Governor Winthrop desk.

WINWICK. No dates. English bargainer. (Biography source unavailable.) Winwicked.

Winwicked (Winwick): Generic Word (overreached). See: Charnock.

WIRSUNG, JOHANN GEORG. 1600-1643. German-born anatomist in Italy. See: Allg. Deut. Biog. Wirsung's canal (or duct).

Wirsung's canal (or duct) (Wirsung, Johann Georg.): Medicine. See: Donath; Dorland; Stedman. Also known as: Hoffman's duct.

WIRTEL, A. F. fl. 1926. American chemist. Cited in: Chem. Abstr., vol. 20, p. 2319. French-Wittel reagent.

WIRTH, FRITZ. b. 1883. German chemist. See: Pogg., vol. 7a. Wirth's method?

WIRTH, PIERRE CHARLES. 1910- . French pharmaceutical chemist. See: Who's Who in France, 1967-1968. Wirth test?

Wirth test (Wirth, Pierre Charles?): Chemistry. See: Van Nostrand Chem. Dict.

Wirth's method (Wirth, Fritz?): Chemistry. See: Van Nostrand's Sci. Encyc. under "Chromatography."

WISCHO, FRITZ. fl. 1926. German pharmaceutical chemist. Cited in: Chem. Abstr. Decennial Index, 1927-1936. Wischo reagent for aloin, Wischo reagents for phenols, Wischo test for differentiating hypochlorite and chlorate.

Wischo reagent for aloin (Wischo, Fritz): Chemistry. See: Van Nostrand Chem. Dict.

Wischo reagents for phenols (Wischo, Fritz): Chemistry. See: Van Nostrand Chem. Dict.

Wischo test for differentiating hypochlorite and chlorate (Wischo, Fritz): Chemistry. See: Van Nostrand Chem. Dict.

WISE, FRED. 1881-1950. American dermatologist. See: A.M.A. Arch. Derm. Syph. 62:5, Nov., 1950. Wise-Rein disease, Wise's disease.

Wise-Rein disease (Wise, Fred and Rein, Charles R.). See: Kaposi's disease.

WISEMAN, BRUCE KENNETH. 1898-1960. American physician. See: Who Was Who Amer. Wiseman-Doan syndrome.

Wiseman-Doan syndrome (Wiseman, Bruce Kenneth and Doan, Charles A.): Medicine. See: Jablonski.

Wise's disease (Wise, Fred). See: Mucha-Habermann syndrome.

Wishart distribution (Wishart, John): Statistics. See: Internat. Dict. Ap. Math.; Kendall.

WISHART, JOHN. 1898-1956. English statistician. See: Who Was Who. Wishart distribution.

WISHART, JOHN HENRY. 1782-1834. Scottish surgeon. (Biography source unavailable.) Wishart's disease.

WISHART, MARY B. No dates. English? physician. (Biography source unavailable.) Wishart's test.

Wishart's disease (Wishart, John Henry): Medicine. See: Jablonski.

Wishart's test (Wishart, Mary B.): Medicine. See: Dorland.

WISHNICK, DOROTHY M. and WISHNICK ETHEL C. fl. 1938. American chemists. Cited in: Chem. Abstr., vol. 32, p. 6973. Sandell-Wishnick reagent.

Wiskott-Aldrich-Huntley syndrome (Wiskott, Alfred; Aldrich, Robert A.; and Huntley, Carolyn Coker). See: Wiskott-Aldrich syndrome.

Wiskott-Aldrich syndrome (Wiskott, Alfred and Aldrich, Robert A.): Medicine. See: Jablonski. Also known as Aldrich's syndrome; Wiskott-Aldrich-Huntley syndrome.

WISKOTT, ALFRED. 1898- German pediatrician. See Wer Ist Wer? 1971-1973. Wiskott-Aldrich syndrome.

WISLICENUS, HANS (In full: JOHANNES ADOLPH). 1867-1951. German chemist. See: Pogg. v. 4 - 7a. Wislicenus-Kaufmann test reaction. Wislicenus reagent for tannins.

Wislicenus-Kaufmann test reaction (Wislicenus, Hans and Kaufmann, Ludwig): Chemistry. See: Van Nostrand Chem. Dict.

Wislicenus reagent for tannins (Wislicenus, Hans): Chemistry. See: Van Nostrand Chem. Dict.

Wislizenus cottonwood (Wislizenus, Frederick Adolphe): Botany. See: Webster's 3d.

WISLIZENUS, FREDERICK ADOLPHE. 1810-1889. German-born American physician and explorer. See: Dict. Nat. Biog. Wislizenus cottonwood, Wislizenus oak.

Wislizenus oak (Wislizenus, Frederick Adolphe): Botany. See: Webster's 3d.

Wissler-Fanconi syndrome (Wissler, Hans and Fanconi, Guido): Medicine. See: Jablonski. Also known as Wissler's syndrome.

WISSLER, HANS. 1906- . Swiss pediatrician. See: Who's Who in Switzerland, 1970-1971. Wissler-Fanconi syndrome.

Wissler's syndrome (Wissler, Hans). See: Wissler-Fanconi syndrome.

WISTAR, CASPAR. 1696-1752. German-born American glass manufacturer. See: Dict. Amer. Biog. Wistar glass.

WISTAR, CASPAR. 1761-1818. American anatomist. See: Dict. Nat. Biog. Wistaria.

Wistar glass (Wistar, Caspar): Applied Arts. See: Webster's 3d.

Wistaria (Wistar, Caspar): Botany. See: Hendrickson; Matthews, M.M.; Taylor, N.

witch of Agnesi (Agnesi, Maria Gaetana): Mathematics. See: Ballentyne; Van Nostrand Sci. Encyc.

WITHAM, HENRY F.M. fl. 1833. Scottish geologist. Cited in: Edinburgh J. of Sci., vol. 11, (1825) p. 218. Withamite.

Withamite (Witham, Henry F. M.): Earth Sciences. See: Charnock; Thrush.

WITHERING, WILLIAM. 1741-1799. English physician, botanist and mineralogist. See: Dict. Nat. Biog. Witheringia, Witherite.

Witheringia (Withering, William) Botany. See: Charnock.

Witherite (Withering, William): Earth Sciences. See: Van Nostrand Sci. Encyc.

Withers and Ray solution (Withers, William Alphonso and Ray, B. J.): Chemistry. See: Van Nostrand Chem. Dict.

WITHERS, WILLIAM ALPHONSO. 1864-1924. American chemist. See: Who Was Who Amer. Withers and Ray solution.

WITHROW, JAMES RENWICK. b. 1878. American chemist. See: Amer. Men Sci., 4th ed. Reed-Withrow test for potassium.

Witka circuit (Derivation undetermined): Engineering and Industry. See: Thewlis.

WITKOP, CARL JACOB. 1920- . American oral pathologist. See: Amer. Men Sci., 10th ed. Witkop-Von Sallmann syndrome.

Witkop-Von Sallmann syndrome (Witkop, Carl Jacob and Von Sallmann, Ludwig): Medicine. See: Jablonski.

WITSEN, NICHOLAS. 1641-1717. Dutch traveler and diplomat. See: Nieuw Nederlandsch biografisch Woordenbock. Witsenia.

Witsenia (Witsen, Nicholas): Botany. See: Charnock

Witt colour theory (Witt, Otto Nikolaus): Chemistry. See: Ballentyne; Hackh; Van Nostrand Chem. Dict.

WITT, OTTO NIKOLAUS. 1853-1915. Russian chemist. See: World Who's Who Sci. Witt colour theory, Witt test reactions for para-diamines.

Witt test reactions for para-diamines (Witt, Otto Nikolaus): Chemistry. See: Van Nostrand Chem. Dict.

WITT, THOMAS. fl. ca. 1924. Swedish mining engineer. Cited in: Hintze (Neue Mineralien). Wittite.

WITTGENSTEIN, LUDWIG JOSEF JOHANN. 1889-1951. Austrian philosopher. See: Dict. Nat. Biog. Wittgensteinian.

Wittgensteinian (Wittgenstein, Ludwig Josef Johann): Philosophy. See: Webster's 3d.

Wittite (Witt, Thomas): Earth Sciences. See: Thrush.

Wittmaack-Ekbom syndrome (Wittmaack, Theodor and Ekbom, Karl Axel): Medicine. See: Jablonski. Also known as: Ekbom's syndrome.

WITTMAACK, THEODOR. fl. 1861. German physician. (Biography source unavailable.) Wittmaack-Ekbom syndrome.

WITTMACK, LUDWIG (In full: MAX KARL LUDWIG). 1839-1929. German botanist. See: Ber. Deut. Bot. Ges. (1931 Nekr), pp. 200-219. Wittmack test?

Wittmack test (Wittmack, Ludwig?): Chemistry. See: Van Nostrand Chem. Dict.

Witton-Kramer magnet (Derivation undetermined): Engineering and Industry. See: Thrush.

Witts' anemia (Witts, Leslie John). See: Faber's anemia.

WITTS, LESLIE JOHN. 1898- . English physician. See: Med. Direct., 1967-1968. Witt's anemia.

WITZ, WILFRED MILLER. 1922- . American nutritionist. See: Amer. Men Sci., 10th ed. Witz's test?

WITZEL, OSKAR (In full: FRIEDRICH OSKAR). 1856-1925. German physician. See: Biog. Lex. hervorr. Aerzte. Witzel's operation.

Witzel's operation (Witzel, Oskar): Medicine. See: Dorland.

Witzky injection system (Witzky, Julius E.): Engineering and Industry. See: Auger.

WITZKY, JULIUS E. 1903- . German-born American engineer. See: Amer. Men Sci., 10th ed. Witzky injection system.

Witz's test (Witz, Wilfred Miller?): Medicine. See: Stedman.

WLADIMIROFF, ALEXANDER ALEX. 1837-1903. Russian surgeon. (Biography source unavailable.) Mikulicz-Vladimiroff amputation (or operation), Wladimiroff's operation.

Wladimiroff's operation (Wladimiroff, Alexander Alex.): Medicine. See: Dorland.

WLADYSLAW II JAGIELLO. 1350-1434. Grand duke of Lithuania and king of Poland. See: Encyc. Brit., 1973. Jagiellon (Jagellon or Jagellonian) (dynasty).

WODEHOUSE, JOHN, 1ST EARL OF KIMBERLEY. 1826-1902. English statesman. See: Dict. Nat. Biog. 2d suppl. Aoki-Kimberley Treaty.

Wodin (or Woden). See: Odin.

WOEHLER, AUGUST. 1819-1914. German engineer. See: Deut. Biog. Jahr., 1914-1916. Woehler machine, Woehler test.

WOEHLER, FRIEDRICH. 1800-1882. German chemist. See: Allg. Deut. Biog.; Encyc. Brit., 1911. Woehler reaction for cyanuric acid, Woehler synthesis, Wohlerite, Woehler's law.

WOEHLER, LOTHAR. b. 1870. German chemist. See: Wer Ist's? (1935). Woehler-Metz test reactions, Woehler reaction for platinum.

Woehler machine (Woehler, August): Engineering and Industry. See: Auger.

Woehler-Metz test reactions (Woehler, Lothar and Metz, Ludwig): Chemistry. See: Van Nostrand Chem. Dict.

Woehler reaction for cyanuric acid (Woehler, Friedrich): Chemistry. See: Van Nostrand Chem. Dict.

Woehler reaction for platinum (Woehler, Lothar): Chemistry. See: Van Nostrand Chem. Dict.

Woehler synthesis (Woehler, Friedrich): Chemistry. See: Van Nostrand Chem. Dict.

Woehler test (Woehler, August): Engineering and Industry. See: Thrush.

Woehlerite (Woehler, Friedrich): Earth Sciences. See: Thrush.

Woehler's law (Woehler, Friedrich): Chemistry. See: Hackh; Webster's 3d.

Woelde's triangle (Derivation undetermined): Medicine. See: Stedman. Also known as: Politzer's luminous cone, Wilde's triangle (or cone of light).

Woelffenstein-Boeters reaction (Woelffenstein, Richard and Boeters, Oskar): Chemistry. See: Ballentyne; Van Nostrand Chem. Dict.

WOELFFENSTEIN, RICHARD. 1864-1929. German chemist. See: Pogg., vol. 4, 5, 6. Woelffenstein-Boeters reaction.

WOELFLER, ANTON. 1850-1917. Austrian surgeon. See: Deut. Biog. Jahr. 1917-1920. Woelfler's gland, Woelfler's operation, Woelfler's suture.

Woelfler's gland (Woelfler, Anton): Medicine. See: Stedman.

Woelfler's operation (Woelfler, Anton): Medicine. See: Stedman; Dorland.

Woelfler's suture (Woelfler, Anton): Medicine. See: Dorland; Stedman.

WOERNER, RUBY KATHRYN. 1900- . American chemist. See: Amer. Men and Women Sci. Woerner test reaction?

Woerner test reaction (Woerner, Ruby Kathryn?): Chemistry. See: Van Nostrand Chem. Dict.

WOESTYN, A. C. fl. 1848. Flemish? chemist. Cited in: Mellor, vol. 1, p. 806. Woestyn's law (or rule).

Woestyn's law (or rule) (Woestyn, A.C.). See: Joule('s) law (3) (molecular heat), Kopp('s) law.

WOHL, ALFRED. 1863-1939. German chemist. See: Pogg., vol. 5, 6. Wohl degradation (or reaction), Wohl-Ziegler reaction.

Wohl block (Derivation undetermined): Engineering and Industry. See: Thrush.

Wohl degradation (or reaction) (Wohl, Alfred): Chemistry. See: Ballentyne; Hackh; Van Nostrand Chem. Dict.

Wohl-Ziegler reaction (Wohl, Alfred and Ziegler, Karl): Chemistry. See: Van Nostrand Chem. Dict.

WOHLFART, GUNNAR (In full: KARL GUNNAR VILHELM). 1910-1961. Swedish neurologist. See: Vem ar det?, 1959. Wohlfart-Kugelberg-Welander disease.

Wohlfart-Kugelberg-Welander disease (Wohlfart, Gunnar; Kugelberg, Eric Klas Henrik and Welander, Lisa): Medicine. See: Jablonski; Stedman. Also known as: Kugelberg-Welander disease.

WOHLGEMUTH, JULIUS. 1874-1948. German physician. See: Pogg., vol. 6 6, 7a. Wohlgemuth unit, Wohlgemuth's method (or test).

Wohlgemuth unit (Wohlgemuth, Julius): Medicine. See: Stedman.

Wohlgemuth's method (or test) (Wohlgemuth, Julius): Medicine. See: Ballentyne; Dorland; Stedman.

Wohlwill-Corino Andrade syndrome (Wohlwill, Joachim Friedrich and Andrade, Corino M.). See: Andrade's syndrome.

WOHLWILL, EMIL. 1835-1912. German inventor. See: Pogg., vol. 4, 5. Wohlwill process.

WOHLWILL, JOACHIM FRIEDRICH. b. 1881. German physician in Portugal. See: Gazeta Medica Portugesa 4 (1951), 492-493. Wohlwill-Corino Andrade syndrome.

Wohlwill process (Wohlwill, Emil): Chemistry. See: Hackh; Thrush; Webster's 3d.

WOILLEZ, EUGENE JOSEPH. 1811-1882. French physician. See: Biog. Lex. hervorr. Aerzte. Woillez's disease.

Woillez's disease (Woillez, Eugene Joseph): Medicine. See: Dorland; Jablonski.

Wolchonskoite (Wolchonsky, Ehren von Prinz A.): Earth Sciences. See: Thrush.

WOLCHONSKY, EHREN VON PRINZ A. No. dates. Russian nobleman. Cited in: Dana, 1889. Wolchonskoite.

WOLCOTT, ALEXANDER S. 1804-1844. American instrument maker and daguerrotypist. (Biography source unavailable.) Wolcott's mirror camera.

Wolcott's mirror camera (Wolcott, Alexander S.): Photography. See: Focal Encyc. Photog. under "Camera History."

WOLD, HERMAN OSKAR ANDERSON. 1887-1960. Swedish statistician. See: Ann. Math. Stat., vol. 32: 3 (Sept. 1961), pp. 651-660. Wold's decomposition theorem, Wold's Markov process of intervals.

WOLDMAN, EDWARD ELBERT. 1897- . American physician. See: Amer. Med. Direct., 1965. Woldman's test.

Woldman's test (Woldman, Edward Elbert): Medicine. See: Dorland.

Wold's decomposition theorem (Wold, Herman Oskar Anderson): Statistics. See: Kendall.

Wold's Markov process of intervals (Wold, Herman Oskar Anderson): Statistics. See: Kendall.

WOLESKY, F. and R. fl. 1912. German chemists. (Biography source unavailable.) Wolesky solution?

Wolesky solution (Wolesky, F. and R.?): Chemistry. See: Van Nostrand Chem. Dict.

WOLF, CHARLES JOSEPH ETIENNE. 1827-1918. French astronomer. See: World Who's Who Sci. Wolf-Rayet stars.

WOLF, FRIEDRICH AUGUST. 1759-1824. German classical philologist, Homeric critic and archaeologist. See: Allg. Deut. Biog.; Encyc. Brit., 1911. Wolfian.

WOLF, HANS. 1898- . German chemist. Cited in: Chem. Abstr., vol. 19, p. 797. Hahn-Wolf-Jaeger reagent.

WOLF, HANS. fl. 1924. German chemist. Cited in: Chem. Abstr. 18:2661. Wolf-Heymann test.

WOLF, HARRY JOHN. 1908- . American mining engineer. See: Amer. Men Sci., 10th ed. Wolf nickel-cadmium battery?

Wolf-Heymann test (Wolf, Hans and Heymann, Erich): Chemistry. See: Van Nostrand Chem. Dict.

WOLF, JACOB D. fl. 1903. English? metallurgist. (Biography source unavailable.) Wolf process.

WOLF, LUDWIG. fl. 1912. German chemist. Cited in: Chem. Abstr., vol. 7, p. 3332. Hilpert-Wolf reagent.

Wolf nickel-cadmium battery (Wolf, Harry John?): Engineering and Industry. See: Thrush.

Wolf number (or equation) (Wolf, Rudolf): Astronomy. See: Hughes; Huschke; Webster's 3d. Also known as: Wolf-Wolfer number.

Wolf process (Wolf, Jacob D.): Chemistry. See: Hackh; Thrush.

Wolf-Rayet stars (Wolf, Charles Joseph Etienne and Rayet, Georges Antoine Pons): Astronomy. See: Thewlis.

WOLF, RUDOLF (In full: JOHANN RUDOLF). 1816-1893. Swiss astronomer. See: Pogg., vol. 3, 4, World Who's Who Sci. Wolf number (or equation).

Wolf trap (Vishniac, Wolf): Engineering and Industry. See: Hackh; Markus.

WOLF, U. fl. 1965. German physician. (Biography source unavailable.) Wolf's syndrome.

Wolf-Wolfer number (Wolf, Rudolf and Wolfer, Alfred): See: Wolf number (or equation).

Wolfahrtia (Wolfart, Peter): Zoology. See: Pennak; Stedman; Webster's 3d.

WOLFART, PETER. 1675-1726. German physician. See: Pogg., vol. 2. Wolfhartia.

WOLFE, CALEB WROE. 1908- . American crystallographer. See: Amer. Men Sci., 11th ed. Wolfeite.

WOLFE, JAMES. 1727-1759. English general. See: Dict. Nat. Biog. Wolfe's own.

WOLFE, JOHN REISSBERG. 1824-1904. Scottish ophthalmologist. See: Biog. Lex. hervorr. Aerzte. Wolfe's graft, Wolfe's method.

Wolfeite (Wolfe, Caleb Wroe): Earth Sciences. See: Thrush.

WOLFENDEN, RICHARD NORRIS. fl. 1887. English laryngologist. Cited in: Index Cat. Libr. Surg. - Gen Off., 1st ser., vol. 16. Wolfenden's position.

Wolfenden's position (Wolfenden, Richard Norris): Medicine. See: Dorland.

WOLFER, ALFRED. 1854-1931. Swiss astronomer. See: Pogg., vol. 4, 5, 6. Wolf-Wolfer number.

Wolfe's graft (Wolfe, John Reissberg): Medicine. See: Dorland; Stedman.

Wolfe's method (Wolfe, John Reissberg): Medicine. See: Stedman.

Wolfe's own (Wolfe, James): History. See: Brewer.

WOLFF, CHRISTIAN VON. 1679-1754. German philosopher and mathematician. See: Allg. Deut. Biog. Leibnizo-Wolffian philosophy (or philosophical system), Wolffian.

WOLFF, HAROLD GEORGE. 1898-1962. American physician. See: Who Was Who Amer., 1961-1968. Wolff-Junghans test.

WOLFF, SIR HENRY DRUMMOND CHARLES. 1830-1908. English politician and diplomat. See: Dict. Nat. Biog., 2nd. suppl. Drummond-Wolff Mission.

WOLFF, JOHANN FRIEDRICH. 1778-1806. German physician and botanist. Cited in: Biog. Notes Upon Botanists. Wolffia.

WOLFF, JULIUS. 1836-1902. German anatomist. See: Biog. Lex. hervorr. Aerzte. Wolff's law.

Wolff-Junghans test (Wolff, Harold George and Junghans, Paul): Medicine. See: Stedman.

WOLFF, KASPAR FRIEDRICH. 1733-1794. German embryologist, physician and botanist in Russia. See: Allg. Deut. Biog. Wolffian bodies, Wolffian cyst, Wolffian duct, Wolffian ridge, Wolffian tubule.

Wolff-Kishner reduction (or reaction) (Wolff, Ludwig and Kizhner, Nikolay Matveyevich): Chemistry. See: Ballentyne; Van Nostrand Chem. Dict.

WOLFF, LOUIS. 1898- . American physician. See: Direct. Med. Specialists, 1965-66. Wolff-Parkinson-White syndrome.

WOLFF, LUDWIG. 1859-1919. German chemist. See: Pogg., vol. 4, 5, 6. Wolff-Kishner reduction (or reaction), Wolff reaction for benzidine and tolidine, Wolff reaction for thiocyanate, Wolff rearrangement, Wolff test for methanol.

Wolff-Parkinson-White syndrome (Wolff, Louis; Parkinson, Sir John and White, Paul Dudley): Medicine. See: Jablonski; Stedman.

Wolff reaction for benzidine and tolidine (Wolff, Ludwig): Chemistry. See: Van Nostrand Chem. Dict.

Wolff reaction for thiocyanate (Wolff, Ludwig): Chemistry. See: Van Nostrand Chem. Dict.

Wolff rearrangement (Wolff, Ludwig): Chemistry. See: Van Nostrand Chem. Dict.

Wolff test for methanol (Wolff, Ludwig): Chemistry. See: Van Nostrand Chem. Dict.

Wolffia (Wolff, Johann Friedrich): Botany. See: Partridge.

Wolffian (Wolff, Christian von): Philosophy. See: Webster's 3d.

Wolffian bodies (Wolff, Kaspar Friedrich): Anatomy. See: Charnock; Gray; Henderson.

Wolffian cyst (Wolff, Kaspar Friedrich): Anatomy. See: Stedman.

Wolffian duct (Wolff, Kaspar Friedrich): Anatomy. See: Donath; Pennak; Stedman. Also known as: Leydig's duct.

Wolffian ridge (Wolff, Kaspar Friedrich): Anatomy. See: Henderson; Stedman;

Wolffian tubule (Wolff, Kaspar Friedrich): Anatomy. See: Webster's 3d.

WOLFFRAM, H. fl. 1924. German chemist. Cited in: Mellor, 16:271. Wolffram's salt.

Wolffram's salt (Wolffram, H.): Chemistry. See: Hackh.

Wolff's law (Wolff, Julius): Anatomy. See: Stedman; Winick.

Wolfian (Wolf, Friedrich August): Linguistics. See: Webster's 3d.

WOLFOWITZ, JACOB. 1910- . Polish-born American mathematical statistician. See: Amer. Men Sci., 11th ed. Kiefer-Wolfowitz process, Wald-Wolfowitz test.

WOLFRING, EMILIJ F. VON. 1832-1906. Polish ophthalmologist. See: Kosminski: Slownik lekarzow polskich 1888 S. 558 w. 630. Wolfring's glands.

Wolfring's glands (Wolfring, Emilij F. von.): Medicine. See: Dorland; Henderson; Stedman.

Wolf's syndrome (Wolf, U.): Medicine. See: Jablonski.

Wolgidite (Derivation undetermined): Earth Sciences. See: Thrush.

Wolkow-Baumann test reaction (Wolkow, Michajl Matveeic and Baumann, Eugen Albert Georg): Chemistry. See: Van Nostrand Chem. Dict.

WOLKOW, MICHAJL MATVEEIC. fl. 1891. Russian? physical chemist. Cited in: Royal Soc. Cat. Sci. Pap., 1884-1900. Wolkow-Baumann test reaction.

Wollaston medal (Wollaston, William Hyde): Earth Sciences. See: Asimov.

Wollaston meniscus lens (Wollaston, William Hyde): Photography. See: Focal Encyc. Photog. under "Lens History."

Wollaston prism (Wollaston, William Hyde): Physics. See: Internat. Dict. Phys. Elec.; Thewlis; Webster's 3d.

WOLLASTON, WILLIAM HYDE. 1766-1828. English chemist, physicist and physician. See: Dict. Nat. Biog. Wollaston medal, Wollaston meniscus lens, Wollaston prism, Wollaston wire, Wollastonite, Wollaston's doublet, Wollaston's theory.

Wollaston wire (Wollaston, William Hyde): Physics. See: Hackh; Thewlis; Webster's 3d.

Wollastonite (Wollaston, William Hyde): Earth Science. See: Charnock; Thrush; Van Nostrand Sci. Encyc.

Wollaston's doublet (Wollaston, William Hyde): Physics. See: Dorland; Stedman; Webster's 3d.

Wollaston's theory (Wollaston, William Hyde): Medicine. See: Stedman.

WOLLNY, EWALD (In full: MARTIN EWALD). fl. 1873-1900. Cited in: Royal Soc. Cat. Sci. Pap., 1800-1883; 1884-1900. Reichert-Wollny number?

WOLMAN, MOSHE. 1914- Polish-born Israeli pathologist. See: World Who's Who Sci. Wolman's disease.

Wolman's disease (Wolman, Moshe): Medicine. See: Jablonski; Stedman.

WOLPERT, HEINRICH. fl. 1896. German chemical engineer. Cited in: Royal Soc. Cat. Sci. Pap., 1884-1900. Wolpert's air tester?

Wolpert's air tester (Wolpert, Heinrich?): Chemistry. See: Hackh.

WOLSELEY, GARNET JOSEPH, 1st Viscount. 1833-1913. British field marshal. See: Dict. Nat. Biog. All Sir Garnet.

WOLTERING, H.W.F.C. fl. 1895. Dutch? physiological chemist. Cited in: Royal Soc. Cat. Sci. Pap., 1884-1900. Woltering reagent?

Woltering reagent (Woltering, H.W.F.C.?): Chemistry. See: Van Nostrand Chem. Dict.

WOLTERS, MAX (In full: MAXIMILIAN). 1861-1914. German dermatologist. See: Biog. Lex. hervorr. Aerzte. Wolters' nevus.

Wolters' nevus (Wolters, Max): Medicine. See: Jablonski

WOLTMANN, HENRY WILLIAM. 1889-1964. American neurologist. See: Who Was Who Amer. Moersch-Woltmann syndrome.

WONDERLIC, ELDON F. 1909- . American psychologist. See: Biog. Direct. Amer. Psych. Assoc., 1966. Wonderlic personnel test.

Wonderlic personnel test (Wonderlic, Eldon F.): Psychology. See: English.

WONNESCH, M. fl. 1925. Rumanian? chemist. Cited in: Chem. Abstr., vol. 19, p. 22. Pamfil-Wonnesch reagent.

Wood-Anderson seismograph (Wood, Harry Oscar and Anderson, John August): Earth Sciences. See: Van Nostrand Sci. Encyc. under "Earthquake".

WOOD, B. fl. 20th c. American metallurgist. (Biography source unavailable.) Wood's metal (or alloy).

WOOD, EDWARD FREDERICK LINDLEY, 1ST EARL OF HALIFAX AND BARON IRWIN. 1881-1959. English statesman. See: Dict. Nat. Biog., 7th suppl. Irwin-Gandhi pact.

Wood effect (Wood, Robert Williams): Physics. See: Internat. Dict. Ap. Math.

WOOD, GOVERNOR. No dates. American administrator. (Biography source unavailable.) Governor Wood cherry.

WOOD, HARRY OSCAR. 1879-1958. American seismologist. See: Proc. vol. of Geol. Soc. Amer., vol. 59 (1958) pp. 219-224. Wood-Anderson seismograph, Wood-Neumann scale.

WOOD, HENRY E. fl. 1913. American mining engineer. Cited in: Chem. Abstr. vol. 7, p. 52. Wood process.

WOOD, IAN JEFFREYS. 1903- . Australian physician. See: Who's Who Australia, 1968. Wood's biopsy instrument.

WOOD, JOHN T. fl. 1941. English chemist. (Biography source unavailable.) Wood's process?

WOOD, MARIA. fl. 1816- English daughter of the mayor of London, Matthew Wood. Cited in: Dict. Nat. Biog., under "Matthew Wood." Maria Wood, the pleasure barge.

Wood-Neumann scale (Wood, Harry Oscar and Neumann, Franz): Physics. See: Van Nostrand Sci. Encyc. under "Intensity scales."

WOOD, NORMAN. fl. 1903-1973. English physician. See: Med. Direct., 1950. Norman-Wood syndrome.

Wood process (Wood, Henry E.): Engineering and Industry. See: Thrush.

WOOD, ROBERT WILLIAMS. 1868-1955. American physicist. See: World Who's Who Sci. Loomis-Wood diagram, Wood effect, Wood's glass (or filter), Wood's lamp (or light).

WOOD, WILLIAM. 1671-1730. English ironmaster. See: Dict. Nat. Biog. Wood's coins, Wood's halfpence.

Woodall-Duckham coking retort (Woodall, Harold Whiteman and Duckham, Sir Arthur MacDougall): Engineering and Industry. See: Van Nostrand Chem. Dict.

Woodall-Duckham kiln (Woodall, Harold Whiteman and Duckham, Sir Arthur MacDougall): Engineering and Industry. See: Thrush.

WOODALL, HAROLD WHITEMAN. 1872-1951. English industrialist. See: Who Was Who, 1951-1960. Woodall-Duckham coking retort, Woodall-Duckham kiln.

WOODBRIDGE, JOHN ELIOT. 1845-1901. American physician. See: JAMA vol. xxxviii (1901), p. 789. Woodbridge treatment.

Woodbridge treatment (Woodbridge, John Eliot): Medicine. See: Dorland.

WOODBURY, J. C. fl. 1909. American scientist. (Biography source unavailable.) Woodbury jig?, Woodbury table?

Woodbury jig (Woodbury, J.C.?): Engineering and Industry. See: Thrush.

Woodbury table (Woodbury, J.C.?): Engineering and Industry. See: Thrush.

WOODBURY, WALTER BENTLEY. 1834-1885. English traveler, photographer and inventor. See: Dict. Nat. Biog. Woodburytype.

Woodburytype (Woodbury, Walter Bentley): Printing. See: Focal Encyc. Photog.; Partridge.

WOODCROFT, BENNET. 1803-1879. English inventor, and writer on inventions. See: Dict. Nat. Biog. Woodcroft propeller.

Woodcroft propeller (Woodcroft, Bennet): Engineering and Industry. See: Auger.

WOODELL, CHARLES E. fl. 1944. American scientist. Cited in: Chem. Abstr. P38: 6064. Woodell scale.

Woodell scale (Woodell, Charles E.): Earth Sciences. See: Thrush.

Wooden wedge (Wedgwood, Hensleigh): Education. See: Charnock.

WOODHOUSE, CHARLES DOUGLAS. b. 1888. American mineralogist. See: Amer. Men Sci., 11th ed. Woodhouseite.

Woodhouse jay (Woodhouse, Samuel W.): Zoology. See: Pennak.

WOODHOUSE, SAMUEL W. No dates given. American physician and ornithologist. See: Who Was Who Amer., hist. vol. Woodhouse jay, Woodhouse toad?

Woodhouse toad (Woodhouse, Samuel W.?): Zoology. See: Pennak.

Woodhouseite (Woodhouse, Charles Douglas): Earth Sciences. See: Thrush; Webster's 3d.

Woodruff key (Woodruff, William N.): Engineering and industry. See: Auger; Van Nostrand Sci. Encyc. under "Key."

WOODRUFF, SAMUEL. d. ca. 1952. American industry worker. Cited in: Amer. Min. 38 (1953), 761-769. Woodruffite.

WOODRUFF, WILLIAM N. fl. 1890. American mechanical engineer. (Biography source unavailable.) Woodruff key.

Woodruffite (Woodruff, Samuel): Earth Sciences. See: Thrush.

Wood's biopsy instrument (Wood, Ian Jeffreys): Medicine. See: Stedman.

Wood's coins (Wood, William): Numismatics. See: Jameson.

Wood's glass (or filter) (Wood, Robert Williams): Physics. See: Dorland; Stedman; Thrush.

Wood's halfpence (Wood, William): Numismatics. See: Brewer; Harbottle; Steinberg.

WOODS, JOSEPH. 1776-1864. English botanist and architect. See: Dict. Nat. Biog. Woodsia.

Wood's lamp (or light) (Wood, Robert Williams): Physics. See: Focal Encyc. Photog; Webster's 3d.

Wood's metal (or alloy) (Wood, B.): Chemistry. See: Hackh; Partridge; Van Nostrand Sci. Encyc.

Wood's process (Wood, John T.?): Engineering and Industry. See: Thrush. Also known as: Schuller process.

Woodsia (Woods, Joseph): Botany. See: Charnock; Taylor, N.; Webster's 3d.

WOODWARD, SAMUEL PICKWORTH. 1821-1865. English naturalist. See: Dict. Nat. Biog. Woodwardite.

WOODWARD, THOMAS JENKINSON. ca. 1745-1820. English botanist. See: Dict. Nat. Biog. Woodwardia.

Woodwardia (Woodward, Thomas Jenkinson): Botany. See: Charnock; Taylor, N.; Webster's 3d.

Woodwardite (Woodward, Samuel Pickworth): Earth Sciences. See: Thrush; Webster's 3d.

Woodworth-Mathews personal data sheet (Woodworth, Robert Sessions and Mathews, Chester Ora): Psychology. See: Chaplin; English.

WOODWORTH, ROBERT SESSIONS. 1869-1962. American psychologist. See: Internat. Encyc. Soc. Sci., 1968. Woodworth-Mathews personal data sheet.

WOODYATT, ROLLIN TURNER. 1878-1953. American physician. See: Who Was Who Amer. Woodyatt's pump.

Woodyatt's pump (Woodyatt, Rollin Turner): Medicine. See: Dorland.

WOOLF, ARTHUR. 1766-1837. English mining engineer. See: Dict. Nat. Biog. Woolf engine.

Woolf engine (Woolf, Arthur): Engineering and Industry. See: Auger; Dict. Nat. Biog; Webster's 3d.

Woolfe's apparatus (Derivation undetermined): Medicine. See: Charnock.

WOOLNER, THOMAS. 1825-1892. English sculptor, painter and poet. See: Dict. Nat. Biog. Woolner's tubercle (point or tip).

Woolner's tubercle (point or tip) (Woolner, Thomas): Anatomy. See: Henderson; Webster's 3d.

WOOLTON, FREDERICK JAMES MARQUIS. 1883-1964. English businessman. See: Who Was Who, 1961-1970. Woolton pie.

Woolton pie (Woolton, Frederick James Marquis): Food and Drink. See: Webster's 3d.

Woolworth (civilization) (Woolworth, Frank Winfield): Generic Word (mass production). See: Hendrickson; Partridge.

WOOLWORTH, FRANK WINFIELD. 1852-1919. American merchant. See: Dict. Amer. Biog. Woolworth civilization.

Worden gravimeter (Worden, Sam Paul): Physics. See: Thrush.

WORDEN, SAM PAUL. 1909- . American geophysicist. See: Amer. Men Sci., 11th ed. Worden gravimeter.

WORDSWORTH, WILLIAM. 1770-1850. English poet. See: Dict. Nat. Biog. Wordsworthian.

Wordsworthian (Wordsworth, William): Literature. See: Webster's 3d.

WORINGER, FREDERIC. 1903-1964. French dermatologist. See: Ann. de Derm. Syph., vol. 91, (Oct.-Dec., 1964), p. 483. Pautrier-Woringer syndrome.

WORINGER, PIERRE. 1890-1964. French pediatrician. See: Ann. Nestle vol. 43, p. 54. Woringer's disease.

Woringer's disease (Woringer, Pierre): Medicine. See: Jablonski.

WORKMAN, EVERLY JOHN. 1899- . American physicist. See: World Who's Who Sci. Workman-Reynolds effect.

Workman-Reynolds effect (Workman, Everly John and Reynolds, Stephen Edward): Earth Sciences. See: Huschke.

WORM-MUELLER, JACOB W. 1834-1889. Norwegian physician. See: Biog. Lex. hervorr. Aerzte. Worm-Mueller's formula.

Worm-Mueller's formula (Worm-Mueller, Jacob W.): Medicine. See: Dorland; Stedman.

WORM, OLE (OLAUS WORMIUS). 1588-1654. Danish physician. See: Nouv. Biog. Univ. Wormian bone.

WORMALD, THOMAS. 1802-1873. English surgeon and medical writer. See: Dict. Nat. Biog. Wormaldia?

Wormaldia (Wormald, Thomas?): Zoology. See: Pennak.

Wormian bone (Worm, Ole): Medicine. See: Donath; Henderson; Stedman.

WORMLEY, THEODORE GEORGE. 1826-1897. American chemist, physician and toxicologist. See: Dict. Amer. Biog. Wormley's test.

Wormley's test (Wormley, Theodore George): Medicine. See: Dorland; Stedman.

Woronin bodies (Woronin, Michajl Stepanovic): Zoology. See: Henderson.

Woronin hypha (Woronin, Michajl Stepanovic): Zoology. See: Henderson.

WORONIN, MICHAJL STEPANOVIC. d. 1903. Russian botanist. See: Materialy Biograf. Slovar Imp. Akad. Nauk, vol. 1 (1915), pp. 182-187. Woronin bodies, Woronin hypha.

Worsley, Charles Anderson, 2d Earl of Yarborough. See: Yarborough, Charles Anderson Worsley, 2nd Earl of.

WORTH, CLAUD. 1869-1936. British ophtalmologist. See: Who Was Who, 1929-1940. Worth's amblyoscope.

WORTHINGTON, HENRY ROSSITER. 1817-1880. American engineer and inventor. See: Dict. Amer. Biog. Worthington pump.

Worthington pump (Worthington, Henry Rossiter): Engineering and Industry. See: Auger.

Worth's amblyoscope (Worth, Claud): Medicine. See: Stedman.

WOTHLY, J. fl. 1864. German inventor. (Biography source unavailable.) Wothlytype.

Wothlytype (Wothly, J.): Photography. See: Charnock; Focal Encyc. Photog.

Woulfe bottle (Woulfe, Peter): Chemistry. See: Hackh; Stedman; Van Nostrand Chem. Dict.

WOULFE, PETER. 1727-1803. English chemist and mineralogist. See: Dict. Nat. Biog. Woulfe bottle.

WOUTHUYSEN, S. A. fl. 1950-1967. Dutch physicist. See: Who's Who Sci. Europe, 1967. Foldy-Wouthuysen representation.

WOYNOFF, K. fl. 1932. German? chemist. Cited in: Brit. Chem. Abstr. 1932, 1934. Woynoff test for cobalt, Woynoff test reactions for vanadium chloride.

Woynoff test for cobalt (Woynoff, K.): Chemistry. See: Van Nostrand Chem. Dict.

Woynoff test reactions for vanadium chloride (Woynoff, K.): See: Van Nostrand Chem. Dict.

WOZENCRAFT, FRANK McREYNOLDS. 1923- . American lawyer. See: Who's Who South Southwest, 1973-1974. Wozencraft's law.

Wozencraft's law (Wozencraft, Frank McReynolds): Sociology. See: Martin.

WRAMBY, G. O. fl. 1946. Swedish veterinarian. (Biography source unavailable.) Hjarre-Wramby disease.

Wratten filter (Wratten, S.H.): Photography. See: Markus.

WRATTEN, S. H. b. 1871. English photographic manufacturer. See: Webster's Biog. Dict. Wratten filter.

Wray, John. See: Ray, John.

WREDEN, ROBERT ROBERTOVICH. 1837-1893. Russian otologist. See: Voyenno-Med. J. vol. clxxviii (1893), pp. 1-5. Wreden's sign.

Wreden's sign (Wreden, Robert Robertovich): Medicine. See: Dorland; Stedman.

WREN, SIR CHRISTOPHER. 1632-1723. English architect. See: Dict. Nat. Biog. Wrennean (or Wrennian), Wren's flower.

Wrennean (or Wrennian) (Wren, Sir Christopher): Architecture. See: Webster's 3d.

Wren's flower (Wren, Sir Christopher). See: herb Robert.

WRIGGE, F. W. fl. 1932. German chemist. Cited in: Chem. Abstr., vol. 27, p. 42. Geilmann-Wrigge-Weibke test for rhenium.

WRIGHT. fl. 20th c. American? metallurgist. (Biography source unavailable.) Hayward-Wright process.

WRIGHT, SIR ALMROTH EDWARD. 1861-1947. English bacteriologist. See: World Who's Who Sci. Wright's solution.

WRIGHT, BARBARA EVELYN. 1926- . American biochemist. See: World Who's Who Sci. Wright respirator.

Wright buckwheat (Wright, Charles): Botany. See: Webster's 3d.

WRIGHT, C. F. fl. 1885. American engineer. (Biography source unavailable.) Wright's tube.

WRIGHT CHARLES. 1811-1885. American explorer and botanist. See: Dict. Amer. Biog. Wright buckwheat, Wright lippia.

WRIGHT, F. B. No dates. Astronomer. (Biography source unavailable.) Wright telescope.

WRIGHT, FRANCES ("FANNY"). 1795-1852. Scottish-American reformer. See: Dict. Amer. Biog. Fanny Wright (or Wrightism).

WRIGHT, IRVING SHERWOOD. 1901- . American physician. See: World Who's Who Sci. Wright's syndrome.

WRIGHT, JAMES HOMER. 1871-1928. American pathologist. See: Who Was Who Amer. Wright's stain.

Wright lippia (Wright, Charles): Botany. See: Webster's 3d.

WRIGHT, MARMADUKE BURR. 1803-1879. American obstetrician. See: Cincin. Lancet and Clinic iii (1879, n.s.), 311-317. Wright's version.

Wright respirator (Wright, Barbara Evelyn): Medicine. See: Stedman.

WRIGHT, SEWALL. 1889- . American geneticist. See: Amer. Men Sci., 9th ed. Sewell Wright effect (or law).

Wright telescope (Wright, F. B.): Astronomy. See: Satterthwaite.

WRIGHT, WILLIAM. 1735-1819. Scottish physician and botanist. See: World Who's Who Sci. Wrightine.

WRIGHT, WILLIAM HAMMOND. 1871-1959. American astronomer. See: World Who's Who Sci. Wright's phenomenon.

Wrightine (Wright, William): Medicine. See: Stedman.

Wright's phenomenon (Wright, William Hammond): Astronomy. See: Satterthwaite.

Wright's solution (Wright, Sir Almroth Edward): Medicine. See: Dorland.

Wright's stain (Wright, James Homer): Medicine. See: Hackh; Pennak; Stedman.

Wright's syndrome (Wright, Irving Sherwood): Medicine. See: Dorland; Jablonski.

Wright's tube (Wright, C. F.): Engineering and Industry. See: Auger.

Wright's version (Wright, Marmaduke Burr): Medicine. See: Stedman.

WRISBERG, HEINRICH AUGUST. 1739-1808. German anatomist. See: Allg. Deut. Biog. Wrisberg's anastomosis, Wrisberg's cartilage, Wrisberg's ganglion, Wrisberg's ligament, Wrisberg's loop, Wrisberg's nerve, Wrisberg's tubercle.

Wrisberg's anastomosis (Wrisberg, Heinrich August): Anatomy. See: Donath.

Wrisberg's cartilage (Wrisberg, Heinrich August): Medicine. See: Donath; Dorland; Stedman. Also known as: Morgagni's cartilage (or tubercle (2)) (cartilago cuneiformis).

Wrisberg's ganglion (Wrisberg, Heinrich August): Anatomy. See: Donath; Stedman.

Wrisberg's ligament (Wrisberg, Heinrich August): Anatomy. See: Stedman.

Wrisberg's loop (Wrisberg, Heinrich August): Anatomy. See: Donath.

Wrisberg's nerve (Wrisberg, Heinrich August): Anatomy. See: Donath; Dorland Stedman.

Wrisberg's tubercle (Wrisberg, Heinrich August): Anatomy. See: Donath; Stedman.

WROE, JOHN. 1782-1863. English religious sect founder. See: Dict. Nat. Biog. Wroeites.

Wroeites (Wroe, John): Religion. See: Canney.

WRONSKI, JOZEF MARIA. 1778-1853. Polish mathematician. See: Nouv. Biog. Univ. Wronskian.

Wronskian (Wronski, Jozef Maria): Mathematics. See: Internat. Dict. Ap. Math; James; Van Nostrand Sci. Encyc.

WUCHERER, OTTO EDUARD HEINRICH. 1820-1874. German physician in Brazil. See: World Who's Who Sci. Wuchereria.

Wuchereria (Wucherer, Otto Eduard Heinrich): Zoology. Pennak; Stedman; Webster's 3d.

WUELLNER, FRIEDRICH HUGO ANTON ADOLF. 1835-1908. German physicist. See: World Who's Who Sci. Wuellner's law.

Wuellner's law (Wuellner, Friedrich Hugo Anton Adolf): Chemistry. See: Hackh; Internat. Dict. Phys. Elec.; Van Nostrand Chem. Dict.

WUENSCH, CHARLES ERB. 1892- . American mining engineer. See: Who's Who Engin., 1922-1923. Wuensch process.

Wuensch process (Wuensch, Charles Erb): Earth Science. See: Thrush.

WUERTZ, ADOLPHE (In full: CHARLES ADOLPHE). 1817-1884. French chemist. See: Encyc. Brit., 1911. Wuertz column, Wuertz-Fittig-Frankland reaction, Wuertz-Fittig reaction, Wuertz flask, Wuertz reaction, Wurtzite.

Wuertz column (Wuertz, Adolphe): Chemistry. See: Webster's 3d.

Wuertz-Fittig-Frankland reaction (Wuertz, Adolphe; Fittig, Rudolph; and Frankland, Sir Edward): Chemistry. See: Van Nostrand Sci. Encyc.

Wuertz–Fittig reaction (Wuertz, Adolphe and Fittig, Rudolph): Chemistry. See: Ballentyne; Van Nostrand Chem. Dict.

Wuertz flask (Wuertz, Adolphe): Chemistry. See: Hackh.

Wuertz reaction (Wuertz, Adolphe): Chemistry. See: Ballentyne; Hackh; Van Nostrand Chem. Dict.

WUEST, EWALD. 1875–1934. German geologist. See: Pogg. vol. 4, 6, 7a. Wuestite.

Wuestite (Wuest, Ewald): Earth Science. See: Thrush; Webster's 3d.

WUHRMANN, FERDINAND. 1906– . Swiss physician. See: Who's Who Switz., 1950–1951. Wuhrmann's disease.

Wuhrmann's disease (Wuhrmann, Ferdinand): Medicine. See: Jablonski.

WUJEK, JAKUB. 1540–1597. Polish Jesuit and translator. See: New Catholic Encyc. under "Bible" and "Poland"; Webster's Biog. Dict. Wujek's Bible.

Wujek's Bible (Wujek, Jakub): Religion. See: Brewer.

Wulf electrometer (Wulf, Theodor): Engineering and Industry. See: Hughes; Internat. Dict. Phys. Elec.

Wulf potentiometer (Wulf, Theodor): Engineering and Industry. See: Internat. Dict. Phys. Elec.

WULF, THEODOR. b. 1868. German physicist. See: Pogg., vol. 5, 6. Wulf electrometer, Wulf potentiometer.

WULFEN, FRANZ XAVER VON. 1728–1805. Austrian naturalist, mineralogist and mathematician. See: Allg. Deut. Biog. Wulfenia, Wulfenite.

Wulfenia (Wulfen, Franz Xaver Von): Botany. See: Taylor, N.

Wulfenite (Wulfen, Franz Xaver von): Earth Sciences. See: Thrush; Van Nostrand Sci. Encyc.; Webster's 3d.

WULFF, GEORGY VIKTOROWICZ. 1862–1925. Russian crystallographer. See: Pogg., vol. 5, 6. Wulff net, Wulff surface, Wulff theorem.

Wulff net (Wulff, Georgy Viktorowicz): Physics. See: Hackh; Thewlis.

Wulff surface (Wulff, Georgy Viktorowicz): Physics. See: Ballentyne.

Wulff theorem (Wulff, Georgy Viktorowicz): Physics. See: Ballentyne; Thewlis.

Wullenweber antenna (Derivation undetermined): Electronics. See: Markus.

WULZEN, ROSALIND. b. 1886. American physiologist. See: Amer. Men Sci., 6th ed. cone of Wulzen.

WUNDERLICH, CARL REINHOLD AUGUST. 1815–1877. German physician. See: World Who's Who Sci. Wunderlich's curve, Wunderlich's syndrome.

Wunderlich's curve (Wunderlich, Carl Reinhold August): Medicine. See: Dorland.

Wunderlich's syndrome (Wunderlich, Carl Reinhold August): Medicine. See: Jablonski.

Wundt illusion (Wundt, Wilhelm Max): Psychology. See: Drever.

Wundt sound pendulum (Wundt, Wilhelm Max): Psychology. See: Drever.

WUNDT, WILHELM MAX. 1832–1920. German physiologist and psychologist. See: Internat. Encyc. Soc. Sci., 1968. Wundt illusion, Wundt sound pendulum, Wundt's fall or gravity phonometer, Wundt's principles of emotional expression, Wundt's tetanus.

Wundt's fall (or gravity) phonometer (Wundt, Wilhelm Max): Psychology. See: Drever.

Wundt's principles of emotional expression (Wundt, Wilhelm Max): Psychology. See: Drever.

Wundt's tetanus (Wundt, Wilhelm Max): Medicine. See: Dorland.

WURSTER, CASIMIR. 1854–1913. German chemist. See: Pogg. vol. 4, 5. Wurster's blue (salt), Wurster's reagent, Wurster's red (salt), Wurster's test.

Wurster's blue (salt) (Wurster, Casimir): Chemistry. See: Hackh; Webster's 3d.

Wurster's reagent (Wurster, Casimir): Chemistry. See: Stedman.

Wurster's red (salt) (Wurster, Casimir): Chemistry. See: Hackh; Webster's 3d.

Wurster's test (Wurster, Casimir): Chemistry. See: Dorland; Stedman.

WURTZ, HENRY. 1828–1910. American chemist and mineralogist. See: Dict. Amer. Biog. Wurtzilite.

Wurtzilite (Wurtz, Henry): Earth Sciences. See: Mathews, M.M.; Thrush.

Wurtzite (Wuertz, Adolphe): Earth Sciences. See: Thrush; Van Nostrand Sci. Encyc.; Webster's 3d.

WYART, JEAN. 1902– . French chemist and physicist. See: Who's Who Sci. Europe, 1st ed. Wyartite.

Wyartite (Wyart, Jean): Earth Sciences. See: Thrush.

WYATT, JOHN POYNER. fl. 1950–1974. Canadian pathologist. See: Direct. Med. Specialists, 1974–75. Wyatt's disease.

WYATT, SIR THOMAS THE YOUNGER. 1521?–1554. See: Dict. Nat. Biog. Wyatt's rebellion.

WYATT, WALTER. fl. 1927–1972. Australian? pediatrician. See: Med. Direct., 1972. Brushfield–Wyatt disease?

Wyatt's disease (Wyatt, John Poyner): Medicine. See: Jablonski.

Wyatt's rebellion (Wyatt, Sir Thomas the Younger): History. See: Steinberg.

WYBURN–MASON, ROGER. fl. 1943–1972. English physician. See: Med. Direct., 1972. Wyburn–Mason's syndrome.

Wyburn–Mason's syndrome (Wyburn–Mason, Roger): Medicine. See: Jablonski.

WYCLIFFE, JOHN. 1324?–1384. English religious reformer and theologian. See: Dict. Nat. Biog. Wycliffites, Wycliffe's Bible.

Wycliffe's Bible (Wycliffe, John): Religion. See: Brewer; Hargrave; Mathews, S.

Wycliffites (Wycliffe, John) Religion. See: Attwater; Phyfe; Steinberg.

WYERS, HERMAN JOSEPH GERARD. b. 1894. Dutch physician. See: Wie is dat?, 1956. Ruiter–Pompen–Wyers syndrome.

WYETH, JOHN ALLAN. 1845–1922. American surgeon. See: Dict. Amer. Biog. Wyeth's operation.

WYETH, NATHANIEL JARVIS. 1802–1856. American trader and explorer. See: Dict. Amer. Biog. Wyethia.

Wyethia (Wyeth, Nathaniel Jarvis): Botany. See: Taylor, N.; Webster's 3d.

Wyeth's operation (Wyeth, John Allan): Medicine. See: Dorland; Stedman.

Wykeham professor (Wykeham, William of): Philosophy. See: Wagner, (More Names).

WYKEHAM, WILLIAM of. 1324–1404. English bishop, Chancellor of England and founder of New College, Oxford. See: Dict. Nat. Biog. Wykeham professor, Wykehamist.

Wykehamist (Wykeham, William of): Education. See: Brewer; Weekley.

WYLE, C. J. fl. 1947. American scientist. (Biography source unavailable.) Wyle's test?

Wyle's test (Wyle, C. J.?): Medicine. See: Stedman.

WYLIE, WALKER GILL. 1848–1923. American gynecologist. See: Who Was Who Amer. Wylie's drain, Wylie's operation.

Wylie's drain (Wylie, Walker Gill): Medicine. See: Dorland; Stedman.

Wylie's operation (Wylie, Walker Gill): Medicine. See: Dorland; Stedman.

Wyndham Act (Wyndham, George): History. See: Montgomery.

WYNDHAM, GEORGE. 1863–1913. English statesman and man of letters. See: Dict. Nat. Biog. Wyndham Act.

WYSLER, F. No dates. German surgeon. (Biography source unavailable.) Wysler's suture.

Wysler's suture (Wysler, F.): Medicine. See: Dorland.

WYSOR, HENRY. b. 1880. American chemist and metallurgist. See: Amer. Men Sci., 3rd ed. Wysor machine?

Wysor machine (Wysor, Henry?): Earth Sciences. See: Hackh.

WYSS, FERNAND. fl. 1925. French? chemist. Cited in: Chem. Abstr. vol. 19, p. 3507. Wyss test for insulin.

WYSS, H. VON. fl. 1911. German chemist. Cited in: Chem. Abstr. vol. 5, p.1459. Wyss test for amyl alcohol.

Wyss test for amyl alcohol (Wyss, H. von): Chemistry. See: Van Nostrand Chem. Dict.

Wyss test for insulin (Wyss, Fernand): Chemistry. See: Van Nostrand Chem. Dict.

Wyulda (Derivation undetermined): Zoology. See: Pennak.

XYZ

-ray cap of Zinn (Zinn, Johann Gottfried): Anatomy. See: Stedman.

XANTHIPPE. fl. 5th c. B.C. Wife of Socrates. See: Harper. Xanthippe.

Xanthippe (Xanthippe): Generic Word (quarrelsome wife). See: Brewer; Hendrickson; Partridge.

XANTUS, JANOS. 1825-1894. Hungarian-born American ornithologist. See: Dict. Amer. Biog. Xantus' murrelet, Xantusiidae.

Xantus' murrelet (Xantus, Janos): Zoology. See: Gray; Stedman.

Xantusiidae (Xantus, Janos): Zoology. See: Webster's 3d.

Xaverian Brothers (Ryken, Theodore Jacques): Religion. See: Attwater; Brewer; Canney.

XAVIER, SAINT FRANCIS. 1506-1552. Spanish Jesuit missionary. See: Nouv. Biog. Univ. Francis Xavier's hymn, Xaverian.

Xaverian (Xavier, Saint Francis): Religion. See: Hendrickson.

XENOCRATES. 396-314 B.C. Greek philosopher. See: Encyc. Brit., 1911. Xenocratic.

Xenocratic (Xenocrates): Philosophy. See: Brewer; Webster's 3d.

Xenophanean (Xenophanes of Colophon): Philosophy. See: Webster's 3d.

XENOPHANES OF COLOPHON. 619?-520? B.C. Greek Eleatic philosopher and poet. See: Encyc. Brit., 1911; Nouv. Biog. Univ. Xenophanean.

XENOPHON. 430?-355? B.C. Greek historian, philosopher and essayist. See: Encyc. Brit., 1911; Nouv. Biog. Univ. Xenophontean (or Xenophontine).

Xenophontean (or Xenophontine) (Xenophon): Philosophy. See: Webster's 3d.

XIMENES, FRANCISCO. d. ca. 1620. Spanish missionary in Guatemala. See: Michaud. Ximenia.

XIMENES, PEDRO. No dates. Spanish wine grower. (Biography source unavailable.) Peter-see-me (Peter or Pedro Ximenes) (wine).

Ximenia (Ximenes, Francisco): Botany. See: Charnock; Webster's 3d.

Yagi antenna (or aerial) (Yagi, Hidetsuga): Engineering and Industry. See: Focal Encyc. Film; Internat. Dict. Phys. Elec.; Markus. Also known as Yagi-Uda antenna.

YAGI, HIDETSUGA. b. 1886. Japanese electrical engineer. See: Who's Who, 1964-65. Yagi antenna (or aerial.)

Yagi-Uda antenna (Yagi, Hidetsuga and Uda, Shintaro). See: Yagi antenna.

YAGODA, HERMAN. 1908-1964. American chemist. See: Amer. Men Sci., 9th ed. Yagoda test.

Yagoda test (Yagoda, Herman): Chemistry. See: Van Nostrand Chem. Dict.

YALE, ELIHU. 1648-1721. American administrator in England and India. See: Dict. Amer. Biog. Eli.

YALE, LINUS. 1821-1868. American inventor. See: Dict. Amer. Biog. Yale lock.

Yale lock (Yale, Linus): Engineering and Industry. See: Hendrickson; Mathews, M.M.; Partridge.

YANG, CHEN NING. 1922- . Chinese-born American physicist. See: World Who's Who Sci. Yang-Feldman formalism and the S-matrix, Yang theorem on angular distributions.

Yang-Feldman formalism and the S-matrix (Yang, Chen Ning and Feldman, David): Physics. See: Internat. Dict. Ap. Math.

Yang theorem on angular distrubutions (Yang, Chen Ning): Physics. See: Internat. Dict. Ap. Math.

Yanowski-Hynes microreagent (Yanowski, Leo Kasimir and Hynes, Walter Aloysius): Chemistry. See: Van Nostrand Chem. Dict.

YANOWSKI, LEO KASIMIR. 1901- . American chemist. See: World Who's Who Sci. Hynes-Yanowski micro reagent, Yanowski-Hynes microreagent.

Yarborough (Yarborough, Charles Anderson Worsley): Recreation and Sports. See: Brewer; Partridge.

YARBOROUGH, CHARLES ANDERSON WORSLEY, 2d. EARL OF. 1809-1862. English nobleman. See: Boase. Yarbourgh.

Yarkovsky effect (Derivation undetermined): Astronomy. See: Internat. Dict. Phys. Elec.

YASUDA, MORIO. fl. 1937. Japanese biochemist. Cited in: Chem. Abstr. vol. 31, p. 8581. Yasuda's method.

Yasuda's method (Yasuda, Morio): Medicine. See: Stedman.

Yates correction (Yates, Frank): Statistics. See: Internat. Dict. Ap. Math.; James; Kendall.

YATES, FRANK. 1902- . English research statistician. See: World Who's Who Sci. Fisher-Yates test, Yates correction.

YEATMAN, POPE. 1861-1953. American mining engineer. See: Who Was Who Amer., vol 3. Yeatmanite.

Yeatmanite (Yeatman, Pope): Earth Science. See: Thrush; Webster's 3d.

YEATS, WILLIAM BUTLER. 1865-1939. Irish poet and dramatist. See: Dict. Nat. Biog., 5th suppl. Yeatsian.

Yeatsian (Yeats, William Butler): Literature. See: Webster's 3d.

Yegg (Yegg, John): Generic Word (safecracker). See: Hendrickson; Mathews, M.M.

YEGG, JOHN. fl. late 19th c. American safeblower. (Biography source unavailable.) Yegg.

YELLOTT, JOHN I. fl. 1947. English engineer. (Biography source unavailable.) Yellott turbine.

Yellott turbine (Yellott, John I.): Engineering. See: Auger.

yellow Hercules (Hercules, the mythological character). See: Hercules club.

YEO, ISAAC BURNEY. 1835-1914. English physician. See: Who Was Who, 1897-1916. Yeo's treatment.

Yeo's treatment (Yeo, Isaac Burney): Medicine. See: Dorland.

Yerkes-Bridges point scale (Yerkes, Robert Mearns and Bridges, James Winfred): Psychology. See: Chaplin; Drever; English.

YERKES, ROBERT MEARNS. 1876-1956. American psychobiologist. See: Internat. Encyc. Soc. Sci., 1968. Yerkes-Bridges point scale.

YERSIN, ALEXANDRE JOHN EMILE. 1863-1943. Swiss bacteriologist in France. See: World Who's Who Sci. Yersinia, Yersin's serum.

Yersinia (Yersin, Alexandre John Emile): Zoology. See: Stedman.

Yersin's serum (Yersin, Alexandre John Emile): Medicine. See: Dorland; Stedman.

Yi dynasty (Yi Songye): History. See: Encyc. Brit., 1973 under "Korea"; Osborne under "Korean Art"; Preminger under "Korean poetry."

YI SONGYE. fl. 1392. Korean general and ruler. See: Encyc. Brit., 1973 under "Korea." Yi dynasty.

YOAKAM, GERALD A. fl. 1937-1949. American educator. (Biography source unavailable.) Yoakam readability formula.

Yoakam readability formula (Yoakam, Gerald A.): Education. See: Good; Nat. Soc. Stud. Educ. Yearbook 36 (1937), 419-438.

YOE, JOHN HOWE. b. 1892. American chemist. See: World Who's Who Sci. Yoe reagent.

Yoe reagent (Yoe, John Howe): Chemistry. See: Van Nostrand Chem. Dict.

YOKOGAWA, SADAMU. fl. 1939. Japanese microbiologist. Cited in: Chem. Abstr. 34:17504. Yokogawa's fluke.

Yokogawa's fluke (Yokogawa, Sadamu): Zoology. See: Stedman.

YOLDI, COUNT. 1764-1852. Spanish nobleman. See: Dansk Biog. Lek. Yoldia.

Yoldia (Yoldi, Count): Zoology. See: Pennak; Webster's 3d.

YONGJO. fl. 1724-1776. King of Korea. (Biography source unavailable.) Yongjong era.

Yongjong era (Chongjo and Yongjo): History. See: Morris and Irwin.

York, 3rd Duke of. See: Richard (Duke of York).

York, James Stuart, Duke of. See: James II.

YORKE, CHARLES. 1722-1770. English political leader. See: Dict. Nat. Biog. Camden-Yorke opinion.

YORKE, PHILIP, 1ST EARL OF HARDWICKE. 1690-1764. English jurist. See: Dict. Nat. Biog. Lord Hardwicke's Act.

YORKE, WARRINGTON. 1883-1943. English physician. See: Dict. Nat. Biog. Yorke's autolytic reaction.

Yorke's autolytic reaction (Yorke, Warrington): Medicine. See: Stedman.

Yorkist (Richard, Duke of York): History. See: Brewer.

Yorkists (Edward IV, Duke of York): History. See: Steinberg.

YOSHIDA, TOMIZO. 1903- . Japanese pathologist. See: Japanese Biog. Encyc. and Who's Who, 1961. Yoshida tumor (or sarcoma).

Yoshida tumor (or sarcoma) (Yoshida, Tomizo): Medicine. See: Jablonski.

Youden square (Youden, William John): Statistics. See: Hackh; Kendall; Van Nostrand Sci. Encyc.

YOUDEN, WILLIAM JOHN. 1900-1971. Australian-born American mathematical statistician. See: Amer. Men Sci., 10th ed. Youden square.

YOUNG, ANNA M. 1898- . American physician. (Biography source unavailable.) Kline-Young test.

YOUNG, B. M. fl. 1900. American fruit grower. (Biography source unavailable.) Youngberry.

YOUNG, BRIGHAM. 1801-1877. American Mormon leader. See: Dict. Amer. Biog. Brigham tea, Brighamite.

Young construction (Young, Thomas): Physics. See: Internat. Dict. Phys. Elec.

YOUNG, DANIEL J. fl. 1923. American? engineer. (Biography source unavailable.) Young-Whitwell backrun gas process.

YOUNG, ERNEST CHARLES. 1892-1968. American agricultural economist. See: Amer. Men Sci., 10th ed. Young's migration hypothesis.

YOUNG, FRANK GEORGE. 1908- . English biochemist. See: Who's Who, 1973-1974. Young's syndrome.

YOUNG, FREIDA. fl. 1938-1972. English physician. See: Med. Direct., 1972. Dyke-Young syndrome.

Young-Helmholtz theory (Young, Thomas and Helmholtz, Hermann Ludwig Ferdinand von): Physics. See: Stedman; Van Nostrand Sci. Encyc.; Wolman.

YOUNG, HUGH HAMPTON. 1870-1945. American urologist. See: World Who's Who Sci. Young's operation.

Young interference experiment (Young, Thomas): Physics. See: Internat. Dict. Phys. Elec.; Van Nostrand Sci. Encyc.

YOUNG, OWEN D. 1874-1962. American lawyer and corporation executive. See: Who Was Who Amer. Young plan.

Young plan (Young, Owen D): History. Jameson; Morris; Smith.

YOUNG, STEWART WOODFORD. 1869-1930. American chemist. See: Who Was Who Amer. Young test for cocaine in the presence of novocain?

YOUNG, SYDNEY. 1857-1937. English chemist. See: World Who's Who Sci. Ramsay and Young equation; Young test for gallic acid in tannin.

Young test for cocaine in the presence of novocain (Young, Stewart Woodford?): Chemistry. See: Van Nostrand Chem. Dict.

Young test for gallic acid in tannin (Young, Sydney): Chemistry. See: Van Nostrand Chem. Dict.

YOUNG, THOMAS. 1587-1655. Scottish clergyman. See: Dict. Nat. Biog. Smectymnians.

YOUNG, THOMAS. 1773-1829. English physician, physicist and Egyptologist. See: Dict. Nat. Biog. Young construction, Young-Helmholtz theory, Young interference experiment, Young's modulus, Young's rule.

Young-Whitwell backrun gas process (Young, Daniel J. and Whitwell, George E.): Engineering and Industry. Cited in: Chem. Abstr., vol. 17, p. 3914.

YOUNG, WILLIAM HENRY. 1863-1942. English mathematician. See: Dict. Nat. Biog. Young's inequality.

YOUNG, WILLIAM JOHN. fl. 1940. Australian biochemist. Cited in: Dict. Sci. Biog. under "Hardy, Sir Arthur." Harden-Young ester.

Youngberry (Young, B. M.): Botany. See: Hendrickson; Webster's 3d.

Young's inequality (Young, William Henry): Mathematics. See: James.

Young's migration hypothesis (Young, Ernest Charles): Sociology. See: Zadrozny.

Young's modulus (Young, Thomas): Physics. See: Hackh; Internat. Dict. Ap. Math.; James.

Young's operation (Young, Hugh Hampton): Medicine. See: Dorland.

Young's rule (Young, Thomas): Medicine. See: Dorland; Stedman.

Young's syndrome (Young, Frank George): Medicine. See: Jablonski.

YOUSSEF, MOHAMMED ABDEL FATTAH. 1934- . Egyptian-born American obstetrician and gynecologist. See: Direct. Med. Specialists, 1974-1975. Youssef's syndrome.

Youssef's syndrome (Youssef, Mohammed Abdel Fattah): Medicine. See: Jablonski.

yrneh (Henry, Joseph): Physics. See: Hughes.

YUKAWA, HIDEKI. 1907- . Japanese physicist. See: World Who's Who Sci. Yukawa interaction, Yukawa kernel, Yukawa particle, Yukawa potential.

Yukawa interaction (Yukawa, Hideki): Physics. See: Internat. Dict. Phys. Elec.

Yukawa kernel (Yukawa, Hideki): Physics. See: Markus.

Yukawa particle (Yukawa, Hideki): Physics. See: Hackh; Thewlis.

Yukawa potential (Yukawa, Hideki): Physics. See: Ballentyne; Hughes; Van Nostrand Sci. Encyc.

Yule distribution (Yule, George Udny): Statistics. See: Kendall.

YULE, GEORGE UDNY. 1871-1951. English statistician. See: Dict. Nat. Biog.; World Who's Who Sci. Yule distribution, Yule process, Yule's equation, Yule's Q, Slutzky-Yule effect.

Yule process (Yule, George Udny): Statistics. See: Kendall.

Yule's equation (Yule, George Udny): Statistics. See: Kendall.

Yule's Q (Yule, George Udny): Statistics. See: Hoult.

YUNITZKAYA, N.V. fl. 1935. Russian chemist. Cited in: Chem. Abstr., vo. 29, p. 77. Tananaev-Yunitzkaya test for mercury.

YURIYEV, ROMAN. d. 1543. Russian ancestor of Romanov dynasty. Cited in: New Encyc. Brit., 1974, Microp. Romanov (breed of sheep), Romanov dynasty.

Yvon method (Yvon-Villarceau, Antoine Joseph Francois): Mathematics. See: Internat. Dict. Ap. Math.

YVON, PAUL. 1848-1913. French physician and chemist. See: Biog. Lex. hervorr. Aerzte. Yvon reagent for water in alcohol, Yvon reagents for alpha and beta naphthol, Yvon test for acetanilid in the urine, Yvon test for alcohol in chloroform, Yvon test for alkaloids.

Yvon reagent for water in alcohol (Yvon, Paul): Chemistry. See: Van Nostrand Chem. Dict.

Yvon reagents for alpha and beta naphthol (Yvon, Paul): Chemistry. See: Van Nostrand Chem. Dict.

Yvon test for acetanilid in the urine (Yvon, Paul): Medicine. See: Dorland; Stedman.

Yvon test for alcohol in chloroform (Yvon, Paul): Chemistry. See: Van Nostrand Chem. Dict.

Yvon test for alkaloids (Yvon, Paul): Medicine. See: Dorland; Stedman.

YVON-VILLARCEAU, ANTOINE JOSEPH FRANCOIS. 1813-1883. French astronomer and mathematician. See: Pogg., vol. 2, 3; World Who's Who Sci. Yvon method.

YZQUIERDO, VICENTE. No dates. Histologist in Chile. (Biography source unavailable.) Yzquierdo's bacillus.

Yzquierdo's bacillus (Yzquierdo, Vicente): Medicine. See: Dorland.

ZACHARY, SAINT. fl. 1 B.C. Father of John the Baptist. See: Holweck. Saint Zachary's disease.

Zadkiel (Morrison, Richard James): Generic Word (astrological almanac). See: Partridge.

Zadkiel, pseud. See: Morrison, Richard James.

ZAFFUTO, GIUSEPPE. fl. 1931. Italian chemist. See: Who's Who Sci. Europe. Zaffuto test reaction.

Zaffuto test reaction (Zaffuto, Giuseppe): Chemistry. See: Van Nostrand Chem. Dict.

ZAGARI, GIUSEPPE. 1863-1946. Italian physician. See: Biog. Lex. hervorr. Aerzte. Zagari's disease.

Zagari's disease (Zagari, Giuseppe): Medicine. See: Dorland.

Zaglas' band (or ligament) (Zaglas, J.): Medicine. See: Donath; Stedman.

ZAGLAS, J. fl. 19th c. American surgeon. (Biography source unavailable.) Zaglas' band (or ligament).

ZAGORSKIKH, A. fl. 1932. Russian chemist. Cited in: Chem. Abstr. 27: 1593. Zagorskikh solution.

Zagorskikh solution (Zagorskikh, A.): Chemistry. See: Van Nostrand Chem. Dict.

Zahn cup (Zahn, Erwin A.): Chemistry. See: Thrush.

ZAHN, ERWIN A. fl. 1939. American scientist. Cited in: Chem. Abstr. vol. 33, p. 2373. Zahn cup.

ZAHN, FRIEDRICH WILHELM. 1845-1904. German pathologist. See: Biog. Jahr. Deut. Nekr., 1904. Zahn's infarct (lines or ribs).

Zahn's infarct (lines or ribs) (Zahn, Friedrich Wilhelm): Medicine. See: Dorland; Jablonski; Stedman.

ZAHORSKY, JOHN. 1871-1963. Hungarian-born American pediatrician. See: Who Was Who Amer. Zahorsky's disease, Zahorsky's syndrome.

Zahorsky's disease (Zahorsky, John): Medicine. See: Jablonski.

Zahorsky's syndrome (Zahorsky, John): Medicine. See: Jablonski.

ZAID. Slave of Mohammed. See: Hastings (Dict. Rel. Ethics), vol. 12, p. 844. Zaid (or Zeid), Zaidites.

Zaid (or Zeid) (Zaid, slave of Mohammed): Generic Word (blind devotion to another). See: Charnock. Also known as: Seyd (or Said).

Zaidites (Zaid, slave of Mohammed): Religion. See: Encyc. Brit., 1973.

ZAITZEV, PHILIPPE. b. 1877. Russian zoologist. See: Hirsch. Zaitzevia.

Zaitzevia (Zaitzev, Philippe): Zoology. See: Pennak.

Zajdela ascites hepatoma (Zajdela, Francois Engelbert): Medicine. See: Jablonski.

ZAJDELA, FRANCOIS ENGELBERT. 1920- . Yugoslavian biologist. See: World Who's Who Sci. Zajdela ascites hepatoma.

ZALESKI, JAN. 1868-1932. Polish chemist. See: Pogg., vol. 6. Sobolewa-Zaleski test.

Zaluzania (Zaluziansky von Zaluzian, Adam): Botany. See: Hendrickson.

ZALUZIANSKY VON ZALUZIAN, ADAM. 1558-1613. Polish physician. See: Biog. Notes Upon Botanists. Zaluzania, Zaluzianskya.

Zaluzianskya (Zaluziansky von Zaluzian, Adam): Botany. See: Hendrickson; Taylor, N.

ZAMBELLI, PIA. fl. 1929. Italian chemist. (Biography source unavailable.) Zambelli test?

Zambelli test (Zambelli, Pia?): Chemistry. See: Van Nostrand Chem. Dict.

ZAMBONI, GIUSEPPE. 1776-1846. Italian physicist. See: World Who's Who Sci., Pogg., vol. 2. Zamboni pile.

Zamboni pile (Zamboni, Giuseppe): Engineering and Industry. See: Hughes.

ZAMBONINI, FERRUCCI. 1880-1932. Italian mineralogist. See: Pogg., vol. 6. Ferruccite.

ZAMBRINI, ANTONIO R. b. 1883. Argentinian otorhinolaryngologist. See: Gran Encic. Argentina. Zambrini's ptyaloreaction.

Zambrini's ptyaloreaction (Zambrini, Antonio R.): Medicine. See: Dorland.

ZAMENHOF, LAZARUS LUDWIG (Pseud., DR. ESPERANTO). 1859-1917. Polish oculist and philologist. See: Jewish Encyc. 1925. Esperanto.

ZAMPARO, A. fl. 1929. Italian pharmacist. Cited in: Brit. Chem. Abstr., Collective Index, 1923-1932. Zamparo reaction for resorcinol and phloroglucinol, Zamparo tests for the differentiation of the naphthols.

Zamparo reaction for resorcinol and phloroglucinol (Zamparo, A.): Chemistry. See: Van Nostrand Chem. Dict.

Zamparo tests for the differentiation of the naphthols (Zamparo, A.): Chemistry. See: Van Nostrand Chem. Dict.

Zander apparatus (Zander, Jonas Gustav Wilhelm): Medicine. See: Dorland.

ZANDER, JONAS GUSTAV WILHELM. 1835-1920. Swedish physician. See: Biog. Lex. hervorr. Aerzte. Zander apparatus.

Zanella (cloth) (Zanelli, Antonio); Fashion. See: Partridge.

ZANELLI, ANTONIO. fl. 1878. Italian author of a work on fabrics. (Biography source unavailable.) Zenella (cloth).

Zaner-Bloser handwriting system (Zaner, C. P. and Bloser, Elmer, W.): Education. See: Good.

ZANER, C. P. fl. 1906. American educator. Cited in: Cum. Auth. Index to Psych. Index, 1894-1935 and Psych. Abstr., 1927-1958. Zaner-Bloser handwriting system.

ZANFROGNINI, A. fl. 1910. Italian pathologist. (Biography source unavailable.) Zanfrognini reagent.

Zanfrognini reagent (Zanfrognini, A.): Chemistry. See: Van Nostrand Chem. Dict.

ZANG, CHRISTOPH BONIFACIUS. 1772-1835. German surgeon. See: Allg. Deut. Biog. Zang's space.

ZANGE, JOHANNES. 1880-1969. German otorhinolaryngologist. See: Biog. Lex. hervorr. Aerzte. Zange-Kindler syndrome.

Zange-Kindler syndrome (Zange, Johannes and Kindler, Werner): Medicine. See: Jablonski.

ZANGEMEISTER, WILHELM. 1871-1930. German gynecologist. See: Biog. Lex. hervorr. Aerzte. Zangemeister's test.

Zangemeister's test (Zangemeister, Wilhelm): Medicine. See: Dorland.

Zang's space (Zang, Christoph Bonifacius): Medicine. See: Donath; Dorland.

ZANNICHELLI, GIOVANNI GIROLAMO. 1662-1729. Italian botanist. See: Biog. Notes Upon Botanists. Zannichellia.

Zannichellia (Zannichelli, Giovanni Girolamo): Botany. See: Charnock; Webster's 3d.

ZANOLI, RAFFAELE. 1897-1971. Italian physician. See: Chi e?, 1961. Zanoli-Vecchi syndrome.

Zanoli-Vecchi syndrome (Zanoli, Raffaele and Vecchi, V.): Medicine. See: Jablonski.

ZANONI, ALONZO. fl. 1798. Colombian official. (Biography source unavailable.) Alonsoa.

ZANONI, GIACOMO. 1615-1682. Italian physician and botanist. See: Nouv. Biog. Univ. Zanonia.

Zanonia (Zanoni, Giacomo): Botany. See: Charnock; Webster's 3d.

ZANTEDESCHI, FRANCESCO. 1773-1846. Italian botanist. See: Biog. Notes Upon Botanists. Zantedeschia.

Zantedeschia (Zantedeschi, Francesco): Botany. See: Partridge.

Zanzalians (Jacob of Edessa): Religion. See: Canney; Latham.

ZAP, EDWARD F. d. 1952. American aeronautical engineer. See: New York Times, 1952, 25:2. Zap flap.

Zap flap (Zap, Edward F.): Engineering and Industry. See: Webster's 3d.

Zapania (Zappa, P.A.): Botany. See: Charnock.

ZAPARANICK, JOSEPH. fl. 1932. American chemist. Cited in: Chem. Abstr. vol. 27, p. 3898. Zaparanick test.

Zaparanick test (Zaparanick, Joseph): Chemistry. See: Van Nostrand Chem. Dict.

ZAPATA, EMILIANO. 1877?-1919. Mexican revolutionist. See: Webster's Biog. Dict. Zapatismo (or Zapatista).

Zapatismo (or Zapatista) (Zapata, Emiliano): History. See: Barnhart (New Eng.).

ZAPPA, P. A. No dates. Italian botanist. (Biography source unavailable.) Zapania.

Zappert counting chamber (Zappert, Julius): Medicine. See: Dorland; Stedman.

ZAPPERT, JULIUS. 1867-1942. Czech-born physician. See: Biog. Lex. hervorr. Aerzte. Heller-Zappert syndrome, Zappert counting chamber, Zappert's syndrome.

ZAPPERT, R. fl. 1935. German chemist. Cited in: Chem. Abstr., vol. 29, p. 5385. Feigl-Zappert-Vasquez test for acetic acid, Feigl-Zappert-Vasquez test for methyl ketones.

Zappert's syndrome (Zappert, Julius): Medicine. See: Jablonski.

ZARABANDA. fl. 16th c. Spanish dancer. (Biography source unavailable.) Saraband.

ZARATE, SENOR. fl. 19th c. Spanish national. Cited in: Dana, 1889. Zaratite.

Zarathustra. See: Zoroaster.

Zaratite (Zarate, Senor): Earth Sciences. See: Webster's 3d.

ZAREMBA, E. fl. 1909. American? chemist. Cited in: Chem. Abstr. 3:1916. Zaremba horizontal tube evaporator.

Zaremba horizontal tube evaporator (Zaremba, E.): Engineering and Industry. See: Van Nostrand Sci. Encyc.

ZARISKI, OSCAR. 1899- . Russian-born American mathematician. See: World Who's Who Sci. Zariski topology.

Zariski topology (Zariski, Oscar): Mathematics. See: Encyc. Brit., 1973 under "Algebraic Geometry."

Zartmann experiment (Zartmann, Ira Forry). See: Stern-Zartmann experiments.

ZARTMANN, IRA FORRY. 1899- . American physicist. See: Amer. Men Sci., 11th ed. Stern-Zartmann experiments.

ZAUFAL, EMANUAL. 1837-1910. Czechoslovakian rhinologist. See: Wer ist's? 1906. Zaufal's sign.

Zaufal's sign (Zaufal, Emanuel): Medicine. See: Dorland; Stedman.

ZAUSCHNER, JOHANN BAPTISTA JOSEF. 1737-1799. Bohemian naturalist. See: Biog. Notes Upon Botanists. Zauschneria.

Zauschneria (Zauschner, Johann Baptista Josef): Botany. See: Charnock; Taylor N.; Webster's 3d.

ZAVARICKIJ, ALEKSANDR NIKOLAEVIC. 1884-1952. Russian mineralogist. See: Materialy k Biobibliografii ucenych SSSR, vol. 35, (1946), p. 40 S. Zavaritskite.

Zavaritskite (Zavarickij, Aleksandr Nikolaevic): Earth Sciences. See: Thrush.

ZAVREL, JAN. fl. 1939. Czechoslovakian entomologist. See: Casopis Ceske Spolecnost Entomol, vol. xxxvi (1939), pp. 1-4. Zavreliella?

Zavreliella (Zavrel, Jan?): Zoology. See: Pennak.

ZDANSKY, O. fl. 1927. German anthropologist. (Biography source unavailable.) Sinanthropus pekinensis Black and Zdansky.

ZDARSKY, MATHIAS. d. 1940. Austrian skiing expert. (Biography source unavailable.) Zdarsky tent.

Zdarsky tent (Zdarsky, Mathias): Recreation and Sports. See: Webster's 3d.

ZEBULUN. In the Bible, tenth son of Jacob (Gen. 30:20) and ancestor of the tribe. See: Hastings. Zebulunite.

Zebulunite (Zebulun): Religion. See: Webster's 3d.

Zeeman displacement (or splitting constant) (Zeeman, Pieter): Physics. See: Ballentyne; Markus.

Zeeman effect (or separation) (Zeeman, Pieter): Physics. See: Ballentyne; Internat. Dict. Ap. Math; Van Nostrand Sci. Encyc.

ZEEMAN, PIETER. 1865-1943. Dutch physicist. See: World Who's Who Sci. Zeeman displacement (or splitting constant), Zeeman effect (or separation).

ZEIGARNIK, BLUMA. 1900- . Russian psychologist. See: Internat. Direct. of Psych., 2. Zeigarnik effect (or phenomenon), Zeigarnik quotient.

Zeigamik effect (or phenomenon) (Zeigarnik, Bluma): Psychology. See: Chaplin; English; Good.

Zeigamik quotient (Zeigarnik, Bluma): Psychology. Cited in: Internat. Encyc. Soc. Sci., 1968 under "Field Theory."

ZEIS, EDUARD. 1807-1868. German ophthalmologist. See: Allg. Deut. Biog. Zeis' gland, Zeisian sty.

Zeis' gland (Zeis, Eduard): Medicine. See: Donath; Dorland; Stedman.

Zeisberg concentrator (Zeisberg, Frederick Clemens): Chemistry. See: Van Nostrand Chem. Dict.

ZEISBERG, FREDERICK CLEMENS. 1888-1938. American chemist. See: Amer. Men. Sci., 5th ed.; Who Was Who Amer. Zeisberg concentrator.

Zeisel method (Zeisel, Simon Josef Maria): Chemistry. See: Van Nostrand Chem. Dict.

Zeisel reaction (Zeisel, Simon Josef Maria): Chemistry. See: Hackh; Van Nostrand Chem. Dict.

ZEISEL, SIMON JOSEF MARIA. 1854-1933. Austrian chemist. See: Pogg., vol. 3, 4, 5. Zeisel method, Zeisel reaction.

Zeisian sty (Zeis, Eduard): Medicine. See: Stedman.

ZEISING, ADOLF. 1810-1876. German poet. See: Allg. Deut. Biog. Zeising's principle?

Zeising's principle (Zeising, Adolf?): Psychology. See: Drever.

Zeiss anastigmat (lens) (Zeiss, Carl): Photography. Cited in: Focal Encyc. Photog. under "Camera History".

ZEISS, CARL. 1816-1888. German optician and industrialist. See: Allg. Deut. Biog. Abbe-Zeiss apparatus, Abbe-Zeiss counting cell, Thoma-Zeiss hemocytometer, Zeiss anastigmat (lens), Zeiss Double Protar lens, Zeiss Ikon camera, Zeiss konimeter?, Zeiss microscope, Zeiss photoelectric polarimeters, Zeiss Protar lens, Zeiss telescope, Zeiss Tessar lens.

Zeiss Double Protar lens (Zeiss, Carl): Photography. Cited in: Focal Encyc. Photog. under "Lens History".

Zeiss Ikon camera (Zeiss, Carl and Ika): Photography. Cited in: Focal Encyc. Photog. under "Germany".

Zeiss konimeter (Zeiss, Carl?): Engineering and Industry. See: Thrush.

Zeiss microscope (Zeiss, Carl): Engineering and Industry. Cited in: Partridge.

Zeiss photoelectric polarimeters (Zeiss, Carl): Engineering and Industry. See: Van Nostrand Sci. Encyc.

Zervanism (Zervan Akarcina): Religion. See: Webster's 3d.

ZERVAS, LEONIDAS. fl. 1926. German? chemist. (Biography source unavailable.) Bergmann–Zervas carbobenzoxy method.

Zespedez. See: Lespedez.

Zetsche–Nachmann reagent (Zetzsche, Fritz and Nachmann, Marcel): Chemistry. See: Van Nostrand Chem. Dict.

ZETTERHOLM, STEN G. 1907- . Swedish physician. See: Svensk Laekarmatrikel, 1970. Myhrman–Zetterholm disease.

ZETTERSTROEM, ROLF OLAF FREDRIK. 1920- . Swedish pediatrician. See: Vem ar det, 1965. Broberger–Zetterstroem syndrome.

ZETTNOW, EMIL. fl. 1900. Austrian chemist. Cited in: Royal Soc. Cat. Sci. Pap., 1884-1889. Zettnow test reactions.

Zettnow test reactions (Zettnow, Emil): Chemistry. See: Van Nostrand Chem. Dict.

ZETZSCHE, FRITZ. 1892-1945. German chemist. See: Pogg., vol. 6, 7a. Zetsche–Nachmann reagent.

ZEUNER, GUSTAV A. 1828-1907. German physicist and engineer. See: World Who's Who Sci. Zeuner valve diagram, Zeunerite.

Zeuner valve diagram (Zeuner, Gustav A.): Engineering and Industry. See: Auger.

Zeunerite (Zeuner, Gustav A.): Earth Sciences. See: Thrush; Webster's 3d.

ZEUS. Greek King of gods. See: Harper. Zeus.

Zeus (Zeus): Generic Words. See: Partridge.

Zeuxian art (Zeuxis): Fine Arts. See: Stenhouse.

ZEUXIS. fl. 420-380 B.C. Greek painter. See: Bryan. Zeuxian art, Zeuxite.

Zeuxite (Zeuxis): Earth Sciences. See: Charnock.

ZHDANOV, ANDREI ALEXSANDROVICH. 1896-1948. Russian politician. See: Webster's Biog. Dict. Zhdanovism (or Zhdanovite).

Zhdanovism (or Zhdanovite) (Zhdanov, Andrei Alexsandrovich): History. See: Barnhart, (New Eng.).

ZHEMCHUZHNIKOV, YURI APPOLLONOWITSCH. 1885-1957. Russian coal geologist. Cited in: Min. Abstr., vol. 16, 1963-1964, p. 551-552. Zhemchuzhnikovite.

Zhemchuzhnikovite (Zhemchuzhnikov, Yuri Appollonowitsch): Earth Sciences. See: Thrush.

Ziegfeld (Ziegfeld, Florenz): Generic Word (showman). See: Hendrickson.

ZIEGFELD, FLORENZ. 1869-1932. American theatrical producer. See: Dict. Amer. Biog. Ziegfeld.

Ziegler catalyst (Ziegler, Karl): Chemistry. See: Hackh; Webster's 3d.

ZIEGLER, HEINRICH ERNST. 1858-1925. German zoologist. See: Biog. Lex. hervorr. Aerzte. Ziegler's theory?

ZIEGLER, KARL. 1898- . German chemist. See: Pogg., vol. 6; World Who's Who Sci. Wohl–Ziegler reaction, Ziegler catalyst, Ziegler method, Ziegler process.

Ziegler method (Ziegler, Karl): Chemistry. See: Van Nostrand Chem. Dict.

Ziegler process (Ziegler, Karl): Chemistry. See: Hackh.

ZIEGLER, SAMUEL LEWIS. 1861-1926. American opthalmologist. See: Who Was Who Amer. Ziegler's operation.

ZIEGLER, WILLIAM. 1843-1905. American baking-powder manufacturer and patron of polar exploration. See: Dict. Amer. Biog. Baldwin–Ziegler polar expedition.

Ziegler's operation (Ziegler, Samuel Lewis): Medicine. See: Dorland; Stedman.

Ziegler's theory (Ziegler, Heinrich Ernst?): Zoology. See: Gray.

ZIEHEN, GEORG THEODOR. 1862-1950. German philosopher and psychiatrist. See: Wer Ist's?, 1935. Ziehen–Oppenheim syndrome (or disease), Ziehen test.

Ziehen–Oppenheim syndrome (or disease) (Ziehen, Georg Theodor and Oppenheim, Hermann): Medicine. See: Jablonski. Also known as: Oppenheim's dystonia musculorum deformans.

Ziehen test (Ziehen, Georg Theodor): Medicine. See: Dorland; Stedman.

ZIEHL, FRANZ. 1857-1926. German bacteriologist. See: Biog. Lex. hervorr. Aerzte. Ziehl–Neelsen stain, Ziehl's solution.

Ziehl–Neelsen stain (Ziehl, Franz and Neelsen, Friedrich Carl Adolf): Medicine. See: Dorland; Stedman. Also known as: Ziehl's stain.

Ziehl's solution (Ziehl, Franz): Medicine. See: Stedman.

Ziehl's stain (Ziehl, Franz): See: Ziehl–Neelsen stain.

ZIEMANN, HANS RICHARD PAUL. 1865-1939. German pathologist. See: Biog. Lex. hervorr. Aerzte. Ziemann's stippling.

Ziemann's stippling (Ziemann, Hans Richard Paul): Medicine. See: Stedman.

ZIEMSSEN, HUGO WILHELM VON. 1829-1902. German physician. See: Biog. Jahrb. Deut. Nekr., 1902; World Who's Who Sci. Ziemssen's motor points, Ziemssen's treatment.

Ziemssen's motor points (Ziemssen, Hugo Wilhelm von): Medicine. See: Dorland.

Ziemssen's treatment (Ziemssen, Hugo Wilhelm von): Medicine. See: Dorland.

ZIER, JOHN. d. 1796. Polish-born botanist in England. See: Biog. Notes Upon Botanists. Zieria.

Zieria (Zier, John): Botany. See: Charnock.

ZIERVOGEL. fl. 19th c. German metallurgist. (Biography source unavailable.) Ziervogel process.

Ziervogel process (Ziervogel): Earth Sciences. See: Thrush; Van Nostrand Chem. Dict.; Webster's 3d.

ZIEVE, LESLIE. 1915- . American physician. See: Amer. Men and Women Sci., 12th ed. Zieve's syndrome.

Zieve's syndrome (Zieve, Leslie): Medicine. See: Jablonski; Stedman.

Zijp, C. van. See: Van Zijp, C.

ZIMMERLIN, FRANZ. 1858-1932. Swiss physician. See: Schweiz. Med. Wchnschr., vol. 62 (July 30, 1932), p. 715. Zimmerlin's atrophy.

Zimmerlin's atrophy (Zimmerlin, Franz): Medicine. See: Dorland; Stedman.

Zimmerman (revolver) (Derivation undetermined): Weapons. See: Partridge.

ZIMMERMAN, WAYNE S. 1916- . American psychologist. See: Biog. Direct. Amer. Psych. Assoc., 1975. Guilford–Zimmerman temperament survey.

ZIMMERMANN, ARTHUR. 1864-1940. German statesman. See: Encyc. Brit., 1973; Webster's Biog. Dict. Zimmermann note.

ZIMMERMANN, C. fl. 1881. German chemist. Cited in: Treadwell, vol. 2. Zimmermann–Reinhardt solution.

ZIMMERMANN, CL. fl. 1880. German chemist. Cited in: Jahresbericht der Chemie (1880), p. 1184. Zimmermann reaction for uranium.

ZIMMERMANN, KARL GOTTFRIED. 1796-1876. German physician and geologist. See: Allg. Deut. Biog. Zimmermann's rule?

ZIMMERMANN, KARL WILHELM. 1861-1935. German histologist. See: Anat. Anz., vol. 82 (June 23, 1936), pp. 300-313. polkissen of Zimmermann, Zimmermann's corpusele (particle, granule, or arch).

Zimmermann note (Zimmermann, Arthur): History. See: Jameson; Morris; Morris and Irwin.

Zimmermann reaction for uranium (Zimmermann, Cl.): Chemistry. See: Van Nostrand Chem. Dict.

Zimmermann reagent for bases (Zimmermann, Walther): Chemistry. See: Van Nostrand Chem. Dict.

Zimmermann–Reinhardt solution (Zimmermann, C. and Reinhardt, Carl): Chemistry. See: Van Nostrand Chem. Dict.

Zimmermann test (or reaction) (Zimmermann, Wilhelm): Medicine. See: Stedman.

Zimmermann test for arsenic, antimony, and phosphorus (as the hydrides) (Zimmermann, Walther): Chemistry. See: Van Nostrand Chem. Dict.